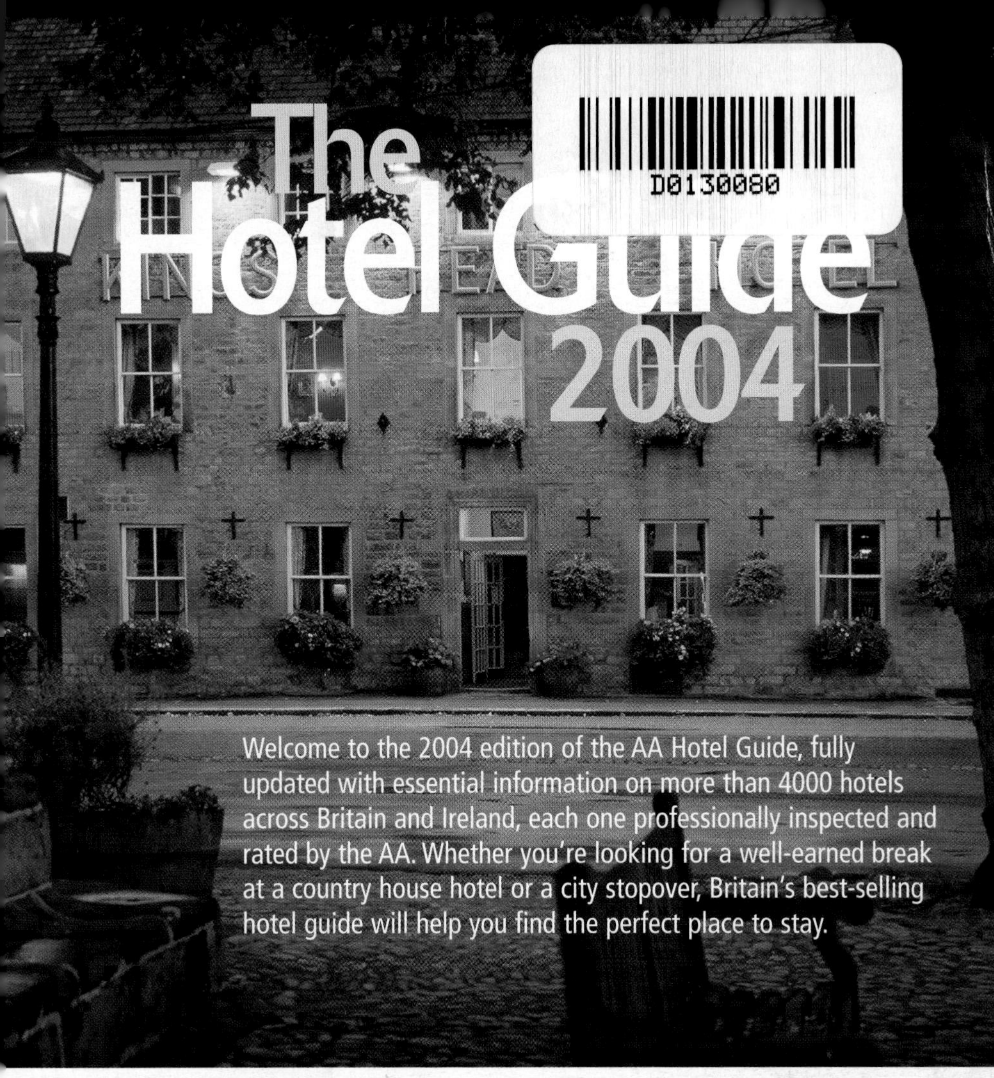

Welcome to the 2004 edition of the AA Hotel Guide, fully updated with essential information on more than 4000 hotels across Britain and Ireland, each one professionally inspected and rated by the AA. Whether you're looking for a well-earned break at a country house hotel or a city stopover, Britain's best-selling hotel guide will help you find the perfect place to stay.

37th edition September 2003

First published by the Automobile Association as the Hotel and Restaurant Guide, 1967

Maps prepared by the Cartography Department of The Automobile Association.

Maps © Automobile Association Developments Limited

Feature: Who's Been Sleeping in My Bed? by Julia Hynard

The main cover photograph shows Fawsley Hall, Fawsley, Northamptonshire. Image courtesy of the General Manager.

Preliminary pages designed by Kingswood Graphics, Burghfield, Berkshire

Typesetting and colour repro by Microset Graphics Ltd, Basingstoke, Hampshire

Printed and bound in Spain
by Printer Industria Grafica S.A., Barcelona

Directory compiled by the AA Hotel Services Department and generated from the AA establishment database.

www.theAA.com

To contact us:
Advertising Sales Department: advertisingsales@theAA.com
Editorial Department: lifestyleguides@theAA.com
AA Hotel Scheme Enquiries: 01256 844455

The contents of this publication are believed correct at the time of printing. Nevertheless, the publishers cannot be held responsible for any errors or omissions or for any changes in the details given in this guide or for the consequences of any reliance on the information provided by the same. This does not affect your statutory rights. Assessments of AA inspected establishments are based on the experience of the Hotel and Restaurant Inspectors on the occasion(s) of their visit(s) and therefore descriptions given in this guide necessarily contain an element of subjective opinion which may not reflect or dictate a reader's own opinion on another occasion. We have tried to ensure accuracy in this guide but things do change and we would be grateful if readers would advise us of any inaccuracies they may encounter.

A CIP catalogue record for this book is available from the British Library

ISBN 0 7495 33754 X

Published by AA Publishing, a trading name of Automobile Association Developments Limited, whose registered office is Millstream, Maidenhead Road, Windsor, Berkshire SL4 5GD. Registered number 1878835

A01593

Contents

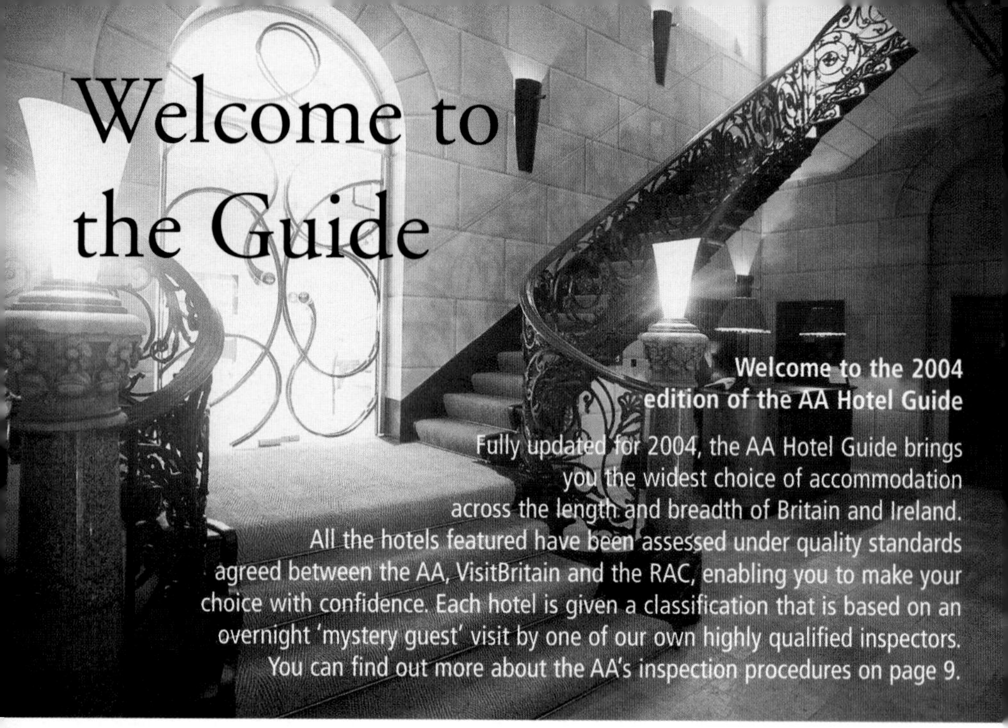

Welcome to the Guide

Welcome to the 2004 edition of the AA Hotel Guide

Fully updated for 2004, the AA Hotel Guide brings you the widest choice of accommodation across the length and breadth of Britain and Ireland. All the hotels featured have been assessed under quality standards agreed between the AA, VisitBritain and the RAC, enabling you to make your choice with confidence. Each hotel is given a classification that is based on an overnight 'mystery guest' visit by one of our own highly qualified inspectors. You can find out more about the AA's inspection procedures on page 9.

We know that people use the AA Hotel Guide for finding many different types of accommodation for many varied reasons, and as the AA inspects such a wide range of establishments it's no wonder that this guide proves an invaluable asset in finding just the right place.

Leisure...
The sporting and leisure facilities at many of the hotels featured is comprehensive and to find exactly what's on offer consult the FACILITIES section for each entry. Some hotels offer special leisure breaks too, indicated by LB in the guide.

Somewhere special...
If you're searching for somewhere really special take a look at the AA Top 200 Hotels in Britain & Ireland on pages 19-26. These hotels stand out as the very best in the country, regardless of size or type of operation. They range from large, luxury destination hotels to small country inns. Top 200 hotels are easily identified by their special highlighted entry and red star symbols.

Restaurants with Rooms
Food lovers will welcome the addition of the AA Restaurants with Rooms category. These are local or national dining destinations that also provide AA-rated accommodation. So now you can try a restaurant that's perhaps a little further afield without the hassle of a long drive home after your meal. For more information on Restaurants with Rooms and other categories of accommodation, turn to page 13.

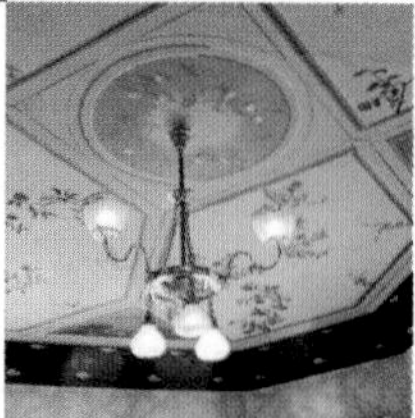

AA Awards 2003-2004
Every year we present a range of awards to the finest AA-inspected and rated hotels from England, Scotland, Ireland and Wales. The Hotel of the Year Award is our ultimate accolade and is awarded to those hotels that are recognised as outstanding examples in their field. Often innovative, the winning hotels always set high standards in hotel-keeping. The Courtesy and Care Award recognises establishments that offer exceptional standards of guest care, service and hospitality. Find out who this year's winners are on page 31.

AA Accessible Awards
The AA Accessible Hotel of the Year Award is presented to the hotel which has made the greatest effort in their accommodation for the independent disabled traveller. This year's winner and runners-up are listed on page 27.

Action for Blind People Hotels
Four hotels owned and managed by the charity Action for Blind People are included in our guide. They are run more in a normal hotel style than in an institutional manner. Most guests are unsighted or partially sighted, but sometimes sighted guests are welcome (as friends of guests or last minute bookers). These hotels are inspected annually by the AA in conjunction with the owning charity. Additionally they are working towards a national classification. The AA feels information about these hotels would be useful to many of its readers.

Hints on booking your stay
It's always worth booking as early as possible, particularly for the peak holiday period from the beginning of June to the end of September. Bear in mind that Easter and other public holidays may be busy too and in some parts of Scotland, the ski season is a peak holiday period. Some hotels will ask for a deposit or full payment in advance, especially for one-night bookings, and not all hotels will take advance bookings for bed and breakfast, overnight or short stays. Some will not make reservations from mid week. Some hotels charge half-board (bed, breakfast and dinner) whether you eat the meals or not, while others may only accept full-board bookings.

Once a booking is confirmed, let the hotel know at once if you are unable to keep your reservation. If the hotel cannot re-let your room you may be liable to pay about two-thirds of the room price (a deposit will count towards this payment). In Britain a legally binding contract is made when you accept an offer of accommodation, either in writing or by telephone, and illness is not accepted as a release from this contract. You are advised to take out insurance against possible cancellation, for example AA Single Trip Insurance (0870 606 1612) or consult the AA website www.theAA.com for details.

AA Hotel Booking Service
Booking a place to stay can be a time-consuming process. Why not ask the AA Hotel Booking Service to find the hotel or B&B that best suits your needs? You can speak to a reservations consultant about your accommodation requirements on 0870 50 50 505 or e-mail the AA Hotel Booking Service at accommodation@AAbooking.com. Alternatively, search and book online at www.theAA.com, receiving an instant online confirmation. No booking fee is payable.

Latebeds
If you need a last-minute place to stay, visit Latebeds at www.theAA.com, the AA's late availability booking service. Latebeds offers last-minute deals at AA-approved hotels and B&Bs. Find the deal that meets your needs and then book it online in an instant. No booking fee is payable.

Feedback
We welcome your feedback about the hotels included and about the guide itself. You can write to us at AA Lifestyle Guides, Fanum House, Basingstoke RG21 4EA or e-mail us at: lifestyleguides@theAA.com. Please note, however, that if you have a complaint to make during a visit, we strongly recommend that you discuss the matter with the hotel management there and then so that they have a chance to put things right before your visit is spoilt. The AA does not undertake to arbitrate between you and the hotel management, or to obtain compensation or engage in correspondence.

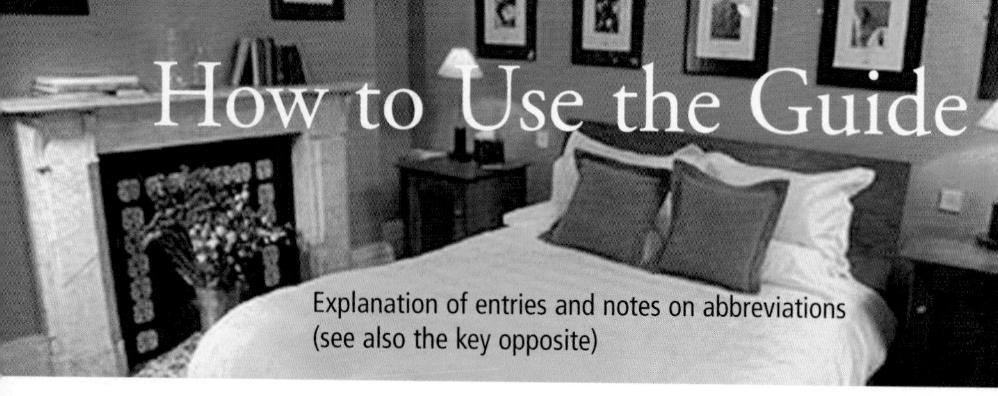

How to Use the Guide

Explanation of entries and notes on abbreviations (see also the key opposite)

1 — ANYTOWN, Anyshire Map 4 SU46

2 — ★★★★ 71% ® **The Example Hotel**
Any Road XX1 11XX
☎ 0022 001122 0022 001122
e-mail: sendto@isp.co.uk

3 — ***Dir:*** *2m north of Any Town - Any Road signed turn left at Business Park.*

— 9

A purpose-built hotel with a well equipped leisure and conference centre in a separate, linked building. Bedrooms are generously planned to give working space and adequate power points and lighting. Reception rooms consist of a bar lounge and carvery-style dining room.

4 — **ROOMS:** 50 en suite (6 fmly) s fr £68; d fr £125 (incl. bkfst) (5GF) **LB**

5 — **FACILITIES: Spa** STV air con. Indoor swimming(H) Squash Snooker Gym Sauna
CONF: BC Thtr 80 Class 30 Board 40 **PARKING:** 30 — 6

7 — **NOTES:** No dogs No children 14 yrs No smoking in restaurant Civ Wed 80

8 — **CARDS:**

1 Towns
These are listed alphabetically within each country section: England, Channel Islands, Isle of Man, Scotland, Wales, Ireland. The administrative county or region follows the town name. Towns on islands are listed under the island (e.g. Wight, Isle of). The map reference gives the map page number, then the National Grid Reference. Read the first figure horizontally and the second figure vertically within the lettered square.

2 Hotel name
This is preceded by the star rating, Quality Assessment Score (see page 9) and Rosette Award, followed by the address, phone/fax numbers and e-mail address where applicable. Please note that e-mail addresses are believed correct at the time of printing but may change during the currency of the guide. Hotels are listed in star and Quality Assessment Score order within each location. If the hotel name is in italic type the information that follows has not been confirmed by the hotel management. A company or consortium name or logo may appear (hotel groups are listed on pages 33-39); for those with a central reservation number, specify the name and location of your chosen hotel when booking.

Country House Hotels offer a relaxed, informal atmosphere, with an emphasis on personal welcome. They are usually, but not always, in a secluded or rural setting and should offer peace and quiet regardless of location.

3 Dir
Directions to the hotel.

4 Rooms
The first figure shows the number of en suite letting bedrooms, or total number of bedrooms, then the number with en suite or family facilities. Bedrooms in an annexe or extension are only noted if they are at least equivalent to those in the main building, but facilities and prices may differ. In some hotels all bedrooms are in an annexe/extension. **Prices** (per room per night) are provided by hoteliers in good faith and are indications not firm quotations. Some hotels only accept cheques if notice is given and a cheque card produced. Not all hotels take travellers cheques. **LB** indicates that the hotel offers special leisure breaks; these may be activity-based breaks or 'two nights for the price of one' type offers.

5 Facilities
Colour TV is provided in all bedrooms unless otherwise

indicated. Where **entertainment** appears, weekly live entertainment should be available at least once a week all year. Some other hotels provide entertainment only in summer or on special occasions; check when booking. **Leisure facilities** are as stated. **Child facilities** may include: baby intercom, babysitting service, playroom, playground, laundry, drying/ironing facilities, cots, high chairs, special meals. In some hotels children can sleep in parents' rooms at no extra cost; check all details when booking.

6 **Parking**
Shows number of spaces available for guests' use. May include covered, charged spaces.

7 **Notes**
No dogs Although many hotels allow dogs, some breeds may be forbidden and dogs may be excluded from areas of the hotel, especially the dining room. It is essential to check when booking. **No children** A minimum age may be given, e.g. 'No children 4 y'rs'. If neither 'ch fac' (see FACILITIES) nor 'no children' appears, the hotel accepts children but may not offer special facilities such as high chairs; check before booking if you have very young children. **RS** Some hotels have a restricted service during quieter months, when some of the listed facilities are not available; ask when booking. **Civ Wed 50** indicates that the hotel is licensed for civil weddings and can accommodate up to 50 guests for the ceremony

N.B. All hotels in Scotland are licensed for civil weddings; check details with the hotel.

8 **Cards**
Credit cards may be subject to a surcharge; check when booking if this is how you intend to pay.

9 **Photograph**
Establishments may choose to include a photograph with their entry.

Symbols and Abbreviations

AA Rating & Awards

★ Star Classification (see page 11)

% Quality Assessment Score (see p9)

★ Red Stars indicate the AA's Top 200 Hotels in Britain & Ireland (see p9 and 19-26)

Rosette Award for quality of food (see p15)

Country House Hotel

Different accommodation categories
(see p13 for explanation)

Town House Accommodation

Restaurant with Rooms

Travel Accommodation

○ Hotel due to open during the currency of the guide (see p13)

U Star rating not yet confirmed (see p13)

A Associate Entries (see p13)

Rooms

fmly – Family rooms (and number)

GF – Ground floor room (and number)

s – Single room

d – Double room

incl. bkfst – Breakfast included

LB – Special leisure breaks available

Bedroom restrictions are stated, e.g. no smoking in 15 bedrooms

Facilities

STV – Satellite television

air con – Air conditioning

Indoor swimming (H) – Heated indoor swimming pool

Outdoor swimming (H) – Heated outdoor swimming pool

ch fac – Special facilities for children

Xmas – Special programme for Christmas/New Year

Leisure facilities are as stated, e.g. Squash, Snooker, Spa

CONF – Conference facilities available

BC – Business centre available

Thtr – Seats theatre style (and number)

Class – Seats classroom style (and number)

Board – Seats boardroom style (and number)

Del – Typical overnight delegate rate

Notes

No dogs – No dogs allowed in bedrooms (guide dogs for the blind may be accepted)

No children – Indicates that children cannot be accommodated

RS – Restricted opening, e.g. RS Jan-Mar, Closed Xmas/New Year

Civ Wed – Licensed for civil weddings (and maximum number of guests for ceremony)

Other restrictions as stated, e.g. No smoking in restaurant

Cards

Cards accepted where symbols are shown

How Does the AA Assess a Hotel?

Hotels applying for AA recognition are visited on a 'mystery guest' basis by one of the AA's team of qualified hotel and restaurant inspectors. The inspector stays overnight to make a thorough test of the accommodation, food and hospitality offered and as many of the hotel's facilities as possible. After settling the bill the following morning they declare their identity and ask to be shown round the entire premises. The inspector completes a full report, making a recommendation for the appropriate star classification and Quality Assessment Score.

Any hotel applying for AA recognition receives an annual unannounced visit to check standards. If the hotel changes hands, the new owners must reapply for classification as AA recognition is not transferable.

Hotels featured pay an annual fee for AA inspection, recognition and rating. The annual fee varies according to the star classification and the number of rooms. AA inspectors pay as a guest for their inspection visit. One of the benefits of such recognition is a text entry in the AA Hotel Guide. In addition to the text entry, hotels may purchase additional advertising such as a photograph or display advertisement.

Quality Assessment Score – making hotel choice easier

In addition to establishing the star classification, AA inspectors supplement their general report with an additional quality assessment of everything the hotel offers, including hospitality, based on what they experience as the 'mystery guest'. This enables them to award an overall Quality Assessment Score.

The Quality Assessment Score offers a comparison of quality within each star classification. So when using the guide, guests can see at a glance, for example, that a two star hotel with a percentage score of 69 offers a higher quality experience within its star classification than a two star hotel with a percentage score of 59. To gain AA recognition in the first place, a hotel must achieve a minimum quality score of 50 per cent.

AA Top 200 Hotels in Britain and Ireland

The AA's Top 200 Awards recognise the very best hotels in Britain and Ireland in each Star, Townhouse and Restaurant with Rooms category. A Top 200 hotel will offer outstanding levels of quality, comfort, cleanliness and customer care and (with the possible exception of town house properties) will serve food of at least one AA Rosette standard. Top 200 hotels can be easily identified in the guide by their Red Stars and highlighted 'Top 200' entry. The AA's Top 200 are assessed and announced annually.

The AA's Top 200 hotels are listed on pages 19-26

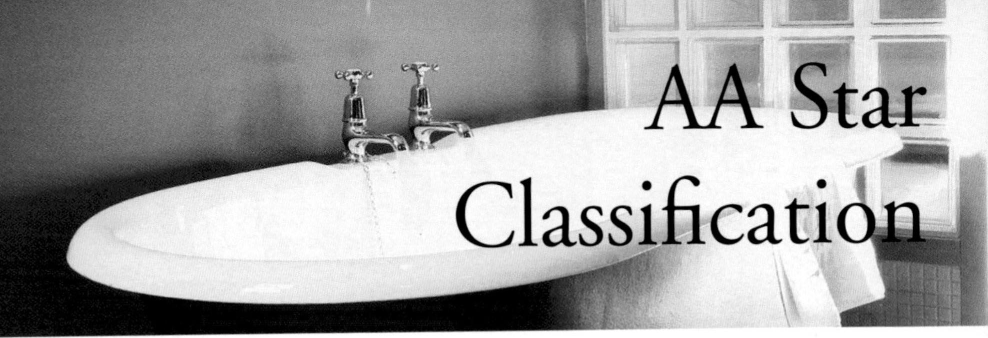

AA Star Classification

Quality standards you can expect from an AA recognised hotel
All hotels recognised by the AA should have the highest standards of cleanliness, proper records of booking, give prompt and professional service to guests, assist with luggage on request, accept and deliver messages, provide a designated area for breakfast and dinner with drinks available in a bar or lounge, provide an early morning call on request, good quality furniture and fittings, adequate heating and lighting and proper maintenance.
A guide to some of the general expectations for each star classification is as follows:

What you can expect from a one star hotel ★
Polite, courteous staff providing a relatively informal yet competent style of service, available during the day and evening to receive guests. At least one designated eating area open to residents for breakfast. Dinner does not have to be offered. However if an establishment does offer dinner it should be on at least 5 days a week, last order should be no later than 6.30pm, there should be a reasonable choice of hot and cold dishes and a short range of wines should be available. Television in lounge or bedroom. Majority of rooms en suite, bath or shower room available at all times.

What you can expect from a two star hotel ★★
Smartly and professionally presented management and staff providing competent, often informal service, available throughout the day and evening to greet guests. At least one restaurant or dining room open to residents for breakfast (and for dinner at least five days a week). Last orders for dinner no earlier than 7pm, a choice of substantial hot and cold dishes and a short range of wines available. Television in bedroom. En suite or private bath or shower and WC.

What you can expect from a three star hotel ★★★
Management and staff smartly and professionally presented and usually uniformed. Technical and social skills of a good standard in responding to requests. A dedicated receptionist on duty at peak times, clear direction to rooms and some explanation of hotel facilities. At least one restaurant or dining room open to residents and non-residents for breakfast and dinner whenever the hotel is open. A wide selection of drinks served in a bar or lounge, available to residents and their guest throughout the day and evening. Last orders for dinner no earlier than 8pm, full dinner service provided. Remote-control television, direct-dial telephone. En suite bath or shower and WC.

What you can expect from a four star hotel ★★★★
A formal, professional staffing structure with smartly presented, uniformed staff, anticipating and responding to your needs or requests. Usually spacious, well-appointed public areas. Bedrooms offering superior quality and comfort than at three star. A strong emphasis on food and beverages and a serious approach to cuisine. Reception staffed 24 hours per day by well-trained staff. Express checkout facilities where appropriate. Porterage available on request and readily provided by uniformed staff. Night porter available. Newspapers can be ordered and delivered to your room, additional services and concierge as appropriate to the style and location of the hotel. At least one restaurant open to residents and non-residents for breakfast and dinner seven days per week, and lunch to be available in a designated eating area. Drinks available to residents and their guests throughout the day and evening, table service available. Last orders for dinner no earlier than 9pm, an extensive choice of hot and cold dishes and a comprehensive list of wines. Remote-control television, direct-dial telephone, a range of high-quality toiletries. En suite bath with fixed overhead shower, WC.

What you can expect from a five star hotel ★★★★★
Flawless guest services, professional, attentive staff, technical and social skills of the highest order. Spacious and luxurious accommodation and public areas with a range of extra facilities. As a minimum, first-time guests shown to their bedroom. Multilingual service consistent with the needs of the hotel's normal clientele. Guest accounts well explained and presented. Porterage offered and provided by uniformed staff. Luggage handling on arrival and departure. Doorman or means of greeting guests at the hotel entrance, full concierge service provided. At least one restaurant open to residents and non-residents for all meals seven days per week. Staff showing excellent knowledge of food and wine. A wide selection of drinks, including cocktails, available in a bar or lounge, table service provided. Last orders for dinner no earlier than 10pm. High-quality menu and wine list properly reflecting and complementing the style of cooking and providing exceptional quality. Evening turn-down service. Remote-control television, direct-dial telephone at bedside and desk, a range of luxury toiletries, bath sheets and robes. En suite bath with fixed overhead shower, WC.

Other Categories of Accommodation

Town House Accommodation
These individual, city or town-centre properties provide a high degree of personal service and privacy. They concentrate on luxuriously furnished bedrooms and suites, rather than the public rooms or formal dining rooms normally associated with hotels. Town house accommodation may have some restaurant provision but if not, a high standard of room service will be offered - in any case, they are usually in areas well served by restaurants. All fall within the four or five star classification, though no Quality Assessment Score is shown in the guide. Town house hotels have a special highlighted entry.

Restaurants with Rooms
A Restaurant with Rooms is usually a local (or national) destination for eating out which also offers accommodation, albeit on a smaller scale. Most have 12 bedrooms or less, and public areas may be limited to the restaurant itself. No star rating is shown in the guide but bedrooms reflect at least the level of quality normally associated with a two star hotel.

Travel Accommodation
This classification indicates budget or lodge accommodation, usually in purpose-built units close to main roads and motorways, (often forming part of motorway service areas) and in town and city centres. They provide consistent levels of accommodation and service.

U Hotels with an unconfirmed star classification
A small number of hotels in the guide have a U symbol instead of a star rating. These had not had their star classification confirmed at the time of going to print. Check the AA website **www.theAA.com** for current information.

○ Hotels with no star classification
Hotels preceded by a ○ symbol were not open at the time of going to print but are due to open during the year. Check the AA website **www.theAA.com** for current information.

A Associate Entries
These are establishments that have been inspected and rated by the RAC, VisitBritain, VisitScotland, Welsh Tourist Board or Northern Ireland Tourist Board. They are rated with stars ★ although VisitScotland, WTB and Northern Ireland Tourist Board use a slightly different set of criteria. The Associate Hotels shown have paid to belong to the AA Associate Hotels Scheme and therefore receive a limited entry in this guide. Descriptions of these establishments can be found on our website **www. theAA.com**.

AA Rosette Awards

Out of around 40,000 UK restaurants, the AA awards around 1,800 with Rosettes. The following is an outline of what to expect from restaurants with AA Rosette Awards.

Excellent local restaurants serving food prepared with care, understanding and skill, using good quality ingredients. These restaurants stand out in their local area. The same expectations apply to hotel restaurants where guests should be able to eat in with confidence and a sense of anticipation. of the total number of establishments with rosettes around 50% have one rosette.

The best local restaurants, which aim for and achieve higher standards, better consistency and where a greater precision is apparent in the cooking. There will be obvious attention to the selection of quality ingredients.

Outstanding restaurants that demand recognition well beyond their local area. The cooking will be underpinned by the selection and sympathetic treatment of the highest quality ingredients. Timing, seasoning and the judgement of flavour combinations will be consistently excellent, supported by other elements such as intelligent service and a well-chosen wine list. Around 10% of restaurants with rosettes have been awarded three.

Amongst the very best restaurants in the British Isles where the cooking demands national recognition. These restaurants will exhibit intense ambition, a passion for excellence, superb technical skills and remarkable consistency. They will combine appreciation of culinary traditions with a passionate desire for further exploration and improvement. Around a dozen restaurants have four rosettes.

The finest restaurants in the British Isles, where the cooking stands comparison with the best in the world. These restaurants will have highly individual voices, exhibit breathtaking culinary skills and set the standards to which others aspire. Less than half a dozen restaurants have five rosettes.

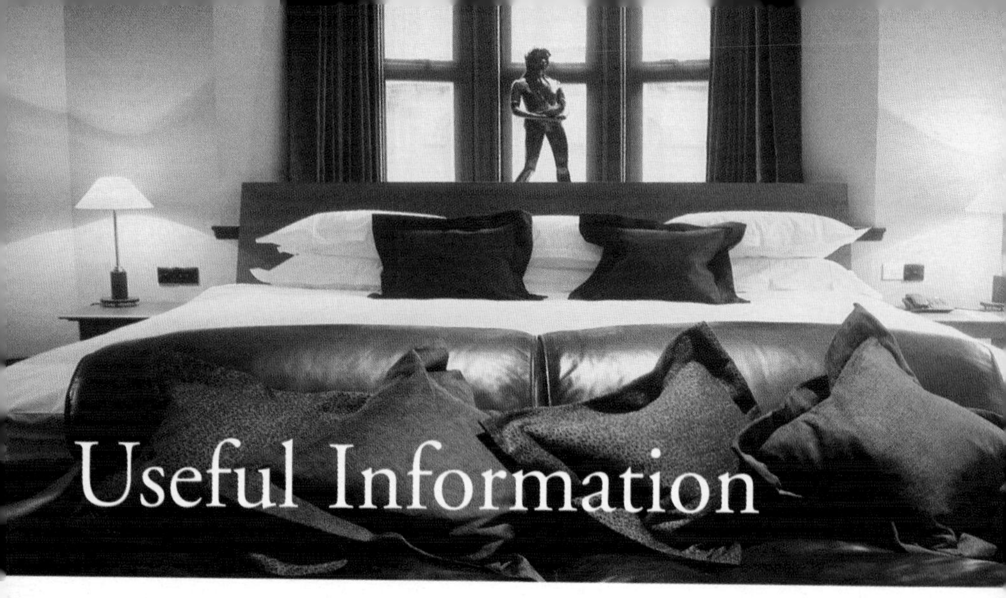

Useful Information

BRITAIN

The Fire Precautions Act does not apply to the Channel Islands, Republic of Ireland, or the Isle of Man, which have their own rules. As far as we are aware, all hotels listed in Great Britain have applied for and not been refused a fire certificate.

Licensing laws differ in England, Wales, Scotland, the Republic of Ireland, the Isle of Man, the Isles of Scilly and the Channel Islands. Public houses are generally open from mid morning to early afternoon, and from about 6 or 7pm until 11pm, although closing times may be earlier or later and some pubs are open all afternoon. Unless otherwise stated, establishments listed are licensed. Hotel residents can obtain alcoholic drinks at all times, if the licensee is prepared to serve them. Non-residents eating at the hotel restaurant can have drinks with meals. Children under 14 (or 18 in Scotland) may be excluded from bars where no food is served. Those under 18 may not purchase or consume alcoholic drinks. Club licence means that drinks are served to club members only, 48 hours must elapse between joining and ordering.

Prices The AA encourages the use of the Hotel Industry Voluntary Code of Booking Practice, which aims to ensure that guests know how much they will have to pay and what services and facilities that includes, before entering a financially binding agreement. If the price has not previously been confirmed in writing, guests should be given a card stipulating the total obligatory charge when they register at reception.

The Tourism (Sleeping Accommodation Price Display) **Order of 1977** compels hotels, travel accommodation, guest houses, farmhouses, inns and self-catering accommodation with four or more letting bedrooms, to display in entrance halls the minimum and maximum prices charged for each category of room. Tariffs shown are the minimum and maximum for one or two persons but they may vary without warning.

London Congestion Charging Scheme From 17th Feb 2003 The Transport for London introduced a congestion charging scheme for most vehicles being used in a designated zone in Central London (roughly all the roads inside the Inner Ring Road – as marked on the London Street Plans in this guide).

The charge is an area licence – vehicles used in the central London area must be registered. You pay £5 for the day (zone operates 7am-6.30pm weekdays) and can cross into and out of the zone as much as you want within the day. If your journey takes you into the charging zone you must either pre-pay the £5 charge or pay it before 10pm that day. Between 10pm and midnight the charge increases to £10 to encourage prompt payment. The system is controlled using a database of registered car registration numbers and a network of numberplate-reading cameras. At midnight each day all paid accounts are deleted from the system. Any vehicle recorded as having been in the zone during charging hours but with an unpaid account must pay a penalty charge. Payment can be made at any time, via the call centre - 0845 900 1234; via the congestion charging website www.cclondon.com or at paystations, selected petrol stations & retailers displaying the PayPoint logo.

For further details on London Congestion Charges see the AA website **www.TheAA.com**. The AA produces a Central Congestion Charging Zone Map obtainable from bookshops or from the AA Travel Bookshop on 01256 491524.

NORTHERN IRELAND & REPUBLIC OF IRELAND

The Euro In 2002, Euro banknotes and coins came into circulation throughout the Republic of Ireland. Prices in the guide for hotels in the Republic of Ireland are therefore shown in Euros.

The Fire Services (NI) Order 1984 covers establishments accommodating more than six people, which must have a certificate from the Northern Ireland Fire Authority. Places accommodating fewer than six persons need adequate exits. AA officials inspect emergency notices, fire-fighting equipment and fire exits here. Republic of Ireland safety regulations are a matter for local authority regulations. For your own and others' safety, read the emergency notices and be sure you understand them.

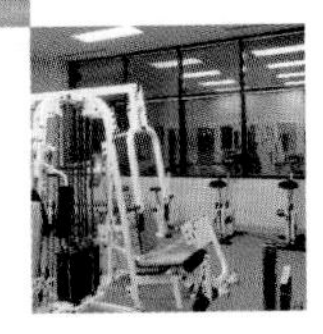

Licensing Regulations

Northern Ireland: Public houses open Mon-Sat 11.30-23.00 and Sun 12.30-14.30 and 19.00-22.00. Hotels can serve residents without restriction. Non-residents can be served from 12.30-22.00 on Christmas Day. Children under 18 are not allowed in the bar area and may neither buy nor consume liquor in hotels.

Republic of Ireland: General licensing hours are Mon-Sat 10.30-23.00 (23.30 in summer). Sun and St Patrick's Day (17 March), 12.30-14.00 and 16.00-23.00. Hotels can serve residents without restriction. There is no service on Christmas Day (except for hotel residents) or Good Friday.

Telephone numbers Area codes for numbers in the Republic of Ireland apply only within the Republic. If dialling from outside check the telephone directory. Area codes for numbers in Britain and Northern Ireland cannot be used directly from the Republic.

For the latest travel information on Ireland, visit AA Ireland's website www.aaireland.ie

Bank and public holidays 2004

New Year's Day	1 January
Bank Holiday	2 January (SCOTLAND ONLY)
St Patrick's Day	17 March (N.I. & R.O.I. ONLY)
Good Friday	9 April
Easter Monday	12 April
May Day Bank Holiday	3 May
Spring Bank Holiday	31 May (EXCLUDING R.O.I.)
June Bank Holiday	7 June (R.O.I. ONLY)
Battle of the Boyne	12 July (N.I. ONLY)
Summer Bank Holiday	2 August (SCOTLAND & R.O.I. ONLY)
Summer Bank Holiday	30 August (EXCLUDING R.O.I.)
Bank Holiday	25 October (R.O.I. ONLY)
Christmas Day	25 December
Boxing Day	26 December (ST STEPHEN'S DAY IN R.O.I.)

Top 200 Hotels in Britain & Ireland 2003-2004

Assessed and announced annually, the AA's Top 200 Awards recognise the very best hotels in Britain and Ireland. A Top 200 hotel will offer consistently outstanding levels of quality, comfort, cleanliness and customer care.

Central London
Regent's Park
BLOOMSBURY
MARYLEBONE
STRAND
MAYFAIR
Hyde Park
KNIGHTSBRIDGE
WESTMINSTER
LAMBETH
Thames
Inverness
Aberdeen
Fort William
Perth
Glasgow
Edinburgh
Stranraer
Newcastle
Carlisle
Belfast
Middlesbrough
Kendal
York
Leeds
Kingston upon Hull
Galway
Dublin
Liverpool
Manchester
Sheffield
Holyhead
Lincoln
Limerick
Nottingham
Rosslare
Norwich
Birmingham
Cork
Aberystwyth
Cambridge
Carmarthen
Gloucester
Oxford
Colchester
LONDON
Cardiff
Bristol
Guildford
Maidstone
Barnstaple
Southampton
Dover
Brighton
Exeter
Weymouth
Plymouth
Penzance
Isles of Scilly
The Channel Islands

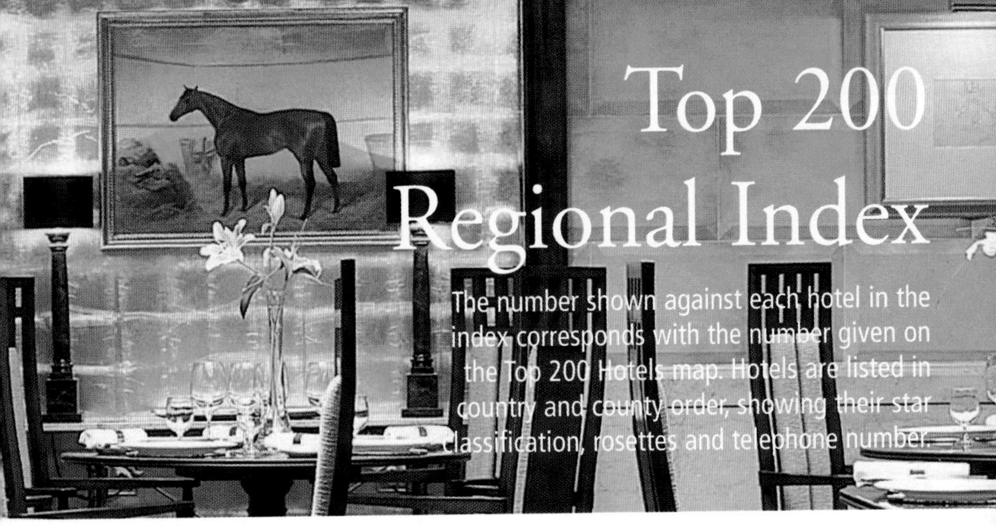

Top 200 Regional Index

The number shown against each hotel in the index corresponds with the number given on the Top 200 Hotels map. Hotels are listed in country and county order, showing their star classification, rosettes and telephone number.

England

BEDFORDSHIRE

No.	Stars	Rosettes	Location	Hotel	Telephone
1	★★★	◉◉	FLITWICK	Menzies Flitwick Manor	☎ 01525 712242

BERKSHIRE

No.	Stars	Rosettes	Location	Hotel	Telephone
2	★★★★	◉◉◉	MAIDENHEAD	Fredrick's Hotel	☎ 01628 581000
3	★★★★★	◉◉◉◉	NEWBURY	The Vineyard at Stockcross	☎ 01635 528770

BUCKINGHAMSHIRE

No.	Stars	Rosettes	Location	Hotel	Telephone
4	★★★★	◉◉◉	AYLESBURY	Hartwell House	☎ 01296 747444
5	★★★★★	◉◉◉	TAPLOW	Cliveden	☎ 01628 668561

CHESHIRE

No.	Stars	Rosettes	Location	Hotel	Telephone
6	★★★★★	◉◉◉	CHESTER	The Chester Grosvenor	☎ 01244 324024
7	★★★★	◉◉	CHESTER	The Chester Crabwall Manor Hotel	☎ 01244 851666
8	★★★	◉◉	NANTWICH	Rookery Hall	☎ 01270 610016

CORNWALL & ISLES OF SCILLY

No.	Stars	Rosettes	Location	Hotel	Telephone
9	★★	◉◉	FOWEY	Marina Hotel	☎ 01726 833315
10	★★	◉	GILLAN	Tregildry Hotel	☎ 01326 231378
11	★★	◉◉◉	LISKEARD	Well House Hotel	☎ 01579 342001
12	★★★	◉◉	PORTSCATHO	Rosevine Hotel	☎ 01872 580206
13	★★★	◉◉◉	ST MARTIN'S	St Martin's on the Isle	☎ 01720 422090
14	★★★	◉◉	TRESCO	The Island	☎ 01720 422883

CUMBRIA

No.	Stars	Rosettes	Location	Hotel	Telephone
15	★★★	◉◉	BRAMPTON	Farlam Hall Hotel	☎ 016977 46234
16	★	◉	GRASMERE	White Moss House	☎ 015394 35295
17	★★★	◉◉◉	HOWTOWN	Sharrow Bay Country House Hotel	☎ 017684 86301
18	★	◉◉	KESWICK	Swinside Lodge	☎ 017687 72948
19	★	◉	KIRKBY LONSDALE	Hipping Hall	☎ 015242 71187
20	★★★	◉◉◉	WATERMILLOCK	Rampsbeck Country House Hotel	☎ 017684 86442
21	★★★	◉◉◉	WINDERMERE	Gilpin Lodge Country House Hotel & Restaurant	☎ 015394 88818
22	★★★	◉◉◉	WINDERMERE	Holbeck Ghyll Country House Hotel	☎ 015394 32375
23	★★	◉	WINDERMERE	Lindeth Fell Country House Hotel	☎ 015394 43286
24	★★★	◉◉	WINDERMERE	Linthwaite House Hotel & Restaurant	☎ 015394 88600
25	★★	◉◉	WINDERMERE	Miller Howe Hotel	☎ 015394 42536
26	★★★	◉◉◉	WINDERMERE	The Samling	☎ 015394 31922

DERBYSHIRE

No.	Stars	Rosettes	Location	Hotel	Telephone
27	★★	◉◉◉	BASLOW	Fischer's Baslow Hall	☎ 01246 583259

*(Hotels marked with an asterisk * had not had their Rosette rating confirmed at the time of going to press. See the AA website www.theAA.com for current information.)*

DEVON

28 ★★ ⊛⊛ ASHWATER – Blagdon Manor Hotel & Restaurant ☎ 01409 211224

29 ★★★ ⊛⊛ BURRINGTON – Northcote Manor ☎ 01769 560501

30 ★★★ ⊛⊛⊛⊛ CHAGFORD – Gidleigh Park ☎ 01647 432367

31 ★★★ ⊛⊛ HONITON – Combe House Hotel ☎ 01404 540400

32 ★★★ ⊛⊛ KINGSBRIDGE – Buckland-Tout-Saints ☎ 01548 853055

33 ★★★ ⊛⊛ LEWDOWN – Lewtrenchard Manor ☎ 01566 783256

34 ★★ ⊛ TWO BRIDGES – Prince Hall Hotel ☎ 01822 890403

DORSET

35 ★★★ ⊛⊛⊛ EVERSHOT – Summer Lodge ☎ 01935 83424

36 ★★★ ⊛⊛⊛ GILLINGHAM – Stock Hill Country House Hotel ☎ 01747 823626

37 ★★★ ⊛⊛ POOLE – Mansion House Hotel ☎ 01202 685666

CO DURHAM

38 ★★ ⊛⊛ ROMALDKIRK – Rose & Crown Hotel ☎ 01833 650213

39 ★★★★ ⊛⊛⊛ SEAHAM – Seaham Hall Hotel ☎ 0191 516 1400

ESSEX

40 ★★★ ⊛⊛ DEDHAM – Maison Talbooth ☎ 01206 322367

GLOUCESTERSHIRE

41 ★★★ ⊛⊛⊛ BUCKLAND – Buckland Manor ☎ 01386 852626

42 ★★★ ⊛⊛⊛ CHELTENHAM – The Greenway ☎ 01242 862352

43 ★★★ ⊛⊛ CHELTENHAM – Hotel on the Park ☎ 01242 518898

44 ★★★ ⊛⊛ CHIPPING CAMPDEN – Cotswold House ☎ 01386 840330

45 ★★ ⊛⊛ COLN ST ALDWYNS – The New Inn At Coln ☎ 01285 750651

46 ★★★ ⊛⊛ LOWER SLAUGHTER – Lower Slaughter Manor ☎ 01451 820456

47 ★★★ ⊛ TETBURY – Calcot Manor ☎ 01666 890391

48 ★★★ ⊛⊛⊛ TETBURY – The Close Hotel ☎ 01666 502272

49 ★★★ ⊛⊛ THORNBURY – Thornbury Castle ☎ 01454 281182

50 ★★★ ⊛⊛⊛ UPPER SLAUGHTER – Lords of the Manor ☎ 01451 820243

HAMPSHIRE

51 ★★★ ⊛⊛ BEAULIEU – Montagu Arms ☎ 01590 612324

52 ★★★ ⊛⊛⊛ LYNDHURST – Le Poussin at Parkhill ☎ 023 8028 2944

53 ★★★ ⊛⊛ MILFORD ON SEA – Westover Hall Hotel ☎ 01590 643044

54 ★★★★★ ⊛⊛⊛ NEW MILTON – Chewton Glen Hotel ☎ 01425 275341

55 ★★★★ ⊛⊛ ROTHERWICK – Tylney Hall Hotel ☎ 01256 764881

56 ★★★★ ⊛⊛ WINCHESTER – Lainston House Hotel ☎ 01962 863588

HEREFORDSHIRE

57 ★★★ ⊛⊛⊛⊛ HEREFORD – Castle House Hotel ☎ 01432 356321

ISLE OF WIGHT

58 ★★★ ⊛⊛⊛ YARMOUTH – George Hotel ☎ 01983 760331

KENT

59 ★★★★ ⊛⊛ ASHFORD – Eastwell Manor ☎ 01233 213000

60 ★★★★ ⊛⊛ LENHAM – Chilston Park ☎ 01622 859803

LEICESTERSHIRE

61 ★★★★ ⊛ MELTON MOWBRAY – Stapleford Park ☎ 01572 787522

LINCOLNSHIRE

62 ⊛⊛⊛⊛⊛ WINTERINGHAM – Winteringham Fields ☎ 01724 733096

LONDON POSTAL DISTRICTS

63	★★★★★ ◎ LONDON E14	Four Seasons Hotel Canary Wharf ☎ 020 7510 1999
64	★★★★★ ◎◎◎ LONDON EC2	Great Eastern Hotel ☎ 020 7618 5000
65	★★★★★ ◎ LONDON NW1	Landmark London Hotel ☎ 020 7631 8000
66	★★★★★ LONDON SW1	The Berkeley * ☎ 020 7235 6000
67	★★★★★ ◎◎ LONDON SW1	The Goring ☎ 020 7396 9000
68	★★★★ ◎◎◎ LONDON SW1	The Halkin Hotel ☎ 020 7333 1000
69	★★★★★ ◎◎ LONDON SW1	The Lanesborough ☎ 020 7259 5599
70	★★★★★ ◎◎◎◎ LONDON SW1	Mandarin Oriental Hyde Park ☎ 020 7235 2000
71	★★★★★ 🏠 LONDON SW1	No 41 ☎ 020 7300 0041
72	★★★★ ◎◎ LONDON SW1	The Stafford ☎ 020 7493 0111
73	★★★★★ 🏠 ◎◎◎◎ LONDON SW3	The Capital ☎ 020 7589 5171
74	★★★★★ 🏠 ◎ LONDON W1	Athenaeum Hotel & Apartments ☎ 020 7499 3464
75	★★★★★ ◎◎◎ LONDON W1	Claridge's ☎ 020 7629 8860
76	★★★★★ ◎◎◎ LONDON W1	The Connaught ☎ 020 7499 7070
77	★★★★★ ◎◎◎ LONDON W1	The Dorchester ☎ 020 7629 8888
78	★★★★★ ◎◎ LONDON W1	Four Seasons Hotel London ☎ 020 7499 0888
79	★★★★★ ◎◎ LONDON W1	The Ritz ☎ 020 7493 8181
80	★★★★★ ◎◎◎ LONDON W8	Royal Garden Hotel ☎ 020 7937 8000
81	★★★★★ 🏠 LONDON W8	Milestone Hotel & Apartments ☎ 020 7917 1000
82	★★★★★ ◎◎ LONDON WC2	One Aldwych ☎ 020 7300 1000
83	★★★★★ ◎◎ LONDON WC2	The Savoy ☎ 020 7836 4343

NORFOLK

84	★★ ◎◎◎ BLAKENEY	Morston Hall ☎ 01263 741041
85	★★★ ◎◎ GRIMSTON	Congham Hall Country House Hotel ☎ 01485 600250
86	★★ ◎◎ NORTH WALSHAM	Beechwood Hotel ☎ 01692 403231
87	★★ ◎ NORWICH	The Old Rectory ☎ 01603 700772

NORTHAMPTONSHIRE

88	★★★★ ◎◎ DAVENTRY	Fawsley Hall ☎ 01327 892000

NOTTINGHAMSHIRE

89	🏨 ◎◎◎ NOTTINGHAM	Restaurant Sat Bains at Hotel des Clos ☎ 0115 986 6566

OXFORDSHIRE

90	★★★★ ◎◎◎◎◎ GREAT MILTON	Le Manoir Aux Quat' Saisons ☎ 01844 278881

RUTLAND

91	★★★ ◎◎◎◎ OAKHAM	Hambleton Hall ☎ 01572 756991

SHROPSHIRE

92	★★★ ◎◎◎ WORFIELD	Old Vicarage Hotel ☎ 01746 716497

SOMERSET

93	★★★★ ◎◎◎ BATH	Bath Priory ☎ 01225 331922
94	★★★ ◎◎ BATH	The Queensberry Hotel ☎ 01225 447928
95	★★ ◎ DULVERTON	Ashwick House Hotel ☎ 01398 323868
96	★★ ◎ PORLOCK	The Oaks Hotel ☎ 01643 862265
97	★★★ ◎◎◎ SHEPTON MALLET	Charlton House & Mulberry Restaurant ☎ 01749 342008
98	★★★★ ◎◎ STON EASTON	Ston Easton Park ☎ 01761 241631
99	★★★ ◎◎◎ TAUNTON	Castle Hotel ☎ 01823 272671
100	★★★ ◎◎ WELLINGTON	Bindon Country House Hotel & Restaurant ☎ 01823 400070
101	★ ◎◎◎ YEOVIL	Little Barwick House ☎ 01935 423902

SUFFOLK

102 ★★★★ ◎◎◎
HINTLESHAM
Hintlesham Hall Hotel
☎ 01473 652334

SURREY

103 ★★★★★ ◎◎◎
BAGSHOT
Pennyhill Park Hotel & Country Club
☎ 01276 471774

104 ★★★ ◎◎
HORLEY
Langshott Manor
☎ 01293 786680

SUSSEX EAST

105 ★★★★ ◎◎
FOREST ROW
Ashdown Park Hotel and Country Club
☎ 01342 824988

106 ★★★ ◎◎
NEWICK
Newick Park Hotel & Country Estate
☎ 01825 723633

107 ★★★ ◎◎
UCKFIELD
Horsted Place
☎ 01825 750581

SUSSEX WEST

108 ★★★ ◎◎
AMBERLEY
Amberley Castle
☎ 01798 831992

109 ★★★ ◎◎◎
EAST GRINSTEAD
Gravetye Manor Hotel
☎ 01342 810567

110 ★★★★ ◎◎◎
LOWER BEEDING
South Lodge Hotel
☎ 01403 891711

111 ★★★ ◎◎
TURNERS HILL
Alexander House Hotel
☎ 01342 714914

WARWICKSHIRE

112 ★★★ ◎◎◎
ROYAL LEAMINGTON SPA
Mallory Court Hotel
☎ 01926 330214

WEST MIDLANDS

113 ★★★★ ⌂ ◎
BIRMINGHAM
Hotel Du Vin & Bistro
☎ 0121 200 0600

114 ★★★ ◎◎◎
HOCKLEY HEATH
Nuthurst Grange Country House Hotel
☎ 01564 783972

WILTSHIRE

115 ★★★★ ◎◎◎
CASTLE COMBE
Manor House Hotel
☎ 01249 782206

116 ★★★★ ◎◎◎
COLERNE
Lucknam Park
☎ 01225 742777

WORCESTERSHIRE

117 ★★★ ◎◎
CHADDESLEY CORBETT
Brockencote Hall Country House Hotel
☎ 01562 777876

YORKSHIRE NORTH

118 ★★★ ◎◎◎
BOLTON ABBEY
The Devonshire Arms Country House Hotel
☎ 01756 710441

119 ★★★★ ◎◎
CRATHORNE
Crathorne Hall Hotel
☎ 01642 700398

120 ★★★★ ◎◎
HARROGATE
Rudding Park Hotel & Golf
☎ 01423 871350

121 ★★★★ ◎◎
MASHAM
Swinton Park
☎ 01765 680900

122 ⌂ ◎◎◎
RAMSGILL
Yorke Arms
☎ 01423 755243

123 ★★★ ◎◎◎
YARM
Judges Country House Hotel
☎ 01642 789000

124 ★★★ ◎◎
YORK
The Grange Hotel
☎ 01904 644744

125 ★★★ ◎◎◎
YORK
Middlethorpe Hall Hotel
☎ 01904 641241

CHANNEL ISLANDS

JERSEY

126 ★★★ ◎◎
ROZEL BAY
Château La Chaire
☎ 01534 863354

127 ★★★★ ◎◎
ST BRELADE
The Atlantic Hotel
☎ 01534 744101

128 ★★★★ ◎◎◎
ST SAVIOUR
Longueville Manor Hotel
☎ 01534 725501

SCOTLAND

ABERDEENSHIRE

129 ★★ ◎◎ BALLATER — Balgonie Country House Hotel ☎ 013397 55482

130 ★★★ ◎◎◎ BALLATER — Darroch Learg Hotel ☎ 013397 55443

ANGUS

131 ★★★ ◎◎ GLAMIS — Castleton House Hotel ☎ 01307 840340

ARGYLL & BUTE

132 ★★★★ ◎◎◎ ERISKA — Isle of Eriska ☎ 01631 720371

133 ★★★ ◎◎◎ PORT APPIN — Airds Hotel ☎ 01631 730236

134 ★★ ◎◎ TOBERMORY — Highland Cottage ☎ 01688 302030

CITY OF EDINBURGH

135 ★★★★ 🏠 ◎◎ EDINBURGH — The Bonham Hotel ☎ 0131 623 6060

136 ★★★★ 🏠 EDINBURGH — The Howard Hotel ☎ 0131 315 2220

137 ★★★★★ 🏠 ◎◎ EDINBURGH — The Scotsman ☎ 0131 556 5565

DUMFRIES & GALLOWAY

138 ★ ◎◎ MOFFAT — Well View Hotel ☎ 01683 220184

139 ★★★ ◎◎ NEWTON STEWART — Kirroughtree House ☎ 01671 402141

EAST LOTHIAN

140 ★★★ ◎◎ GULLANE — Greywalls Hotel ☎ 01620 842144

FIFE

141 ★★★★ ◎◎ MARKINCH — Balbirnie House ☎ 01592 610066

142 ★★ ◎◎◎ PEAT INN — The Peat Inn ☎ 01334 840206

143 ★★★★★ ◎◎ ST ANDREWS — The Old Course Hotel ☎ 01334 474371

144 ★★★ ◎◎ ST ANDREWS — Rufflets Country House & Garden Restaurant ☎ 01334 472594

145 ★★★ ◎◎ ST ANDREWS — St Andrews Golf Hotel ☎ 01334 472611

CITY OF GLASGOW

146 ★★★★ 🏠 ◎◎◎ GLASGOW — One Devonshire Gardens ☎ 0141 339 2001

HIGHLAND

147 🏛 ◎◎◎ COLBOST — The Three Chimneys & House Over-By ☎ 01470 511258

148 ★★★★ ◎◎◎ FORT WILLIAM — Inverlochy Castle Hotel ☎ 01397 702177

149 🏛 ◎◎ KINGUSSIE — The Cross ☎ 01540 661166

150 ★★★ ◎ LOCHINVER — Inver Lodge Hotel ☎ 01571 844496

151 ★ ◎◎ MUIR OF ORD — The Dower House ☎ 01463 870090

152 ★★ ◎◎◎ NAIRN — Boath House ☎ 01667 454896

153 ★★★ ◎◎ POOLEWE — Pool House Hotel ☎ 01445 781272

154 ★★ ◎◎ STRONTIAN — Kilcamb Lodge Hotel ☎ 01967 402257

155 ★★ ◎◎ TAIN — The Glenmorangie Highland Home ☎ 01862 871671

156 ★★★ ◎◎ TORRIDON — Loch Torridon Country House Hotel ☎ 01445 791242

NORTH AYRSHIRE

157 ★★ ◎◎ BRODICK — Kilmichael Country House Hotel ☎ 01770 302219

PERTH & KINROSS

158 ★★★★★ ◎◎◎ AUCHTERARDER — The Gleneagles Hotel ☎ 01764 662231

159 ★★★ ◎◎ BLAIRGOWRIE — Kinloch House Hotel ☎ 01250 884237

160 ★★★ ◎◎◎ DUNKELD — Kinnaird ☎ 01796 482440

161 ★★★ ◎◎ KINCLAVEN — Ballathie House Hotel ☎ 01250 883268

162 ★★★ ◎◎ PERTH — Kinfauns Castle ☎ 01738 620777

SOUTH AYRSHIRE

163 ★★★ ◎◎ BALLANTRAE — Glenapp Castle ☎ 01465 831212

164 ★★ ◎ MAYBOLE — Ladyburn ☎ 01655 740585

165 ★★★ ◎◎◎ TROON — Lochgreen House ☎ 01292 313343

166 ★★★★★ ◎ TURNBERRY — The Westin Turnberry Resort ☎ 01655 331000

STIRLING

167 ★★★ ◎◎◎ CALLANDER — Roman Camp Country House Hotel ☎ 01877 330003

168 ★★★ ◎◎ DUNBLANE — Cromlix House Hotel ☎ 01786 822125

169 ★ ◎◎ STRATHYRE — Creagan House ☎ 01877 384638

WALES

CEREDIGION

170	★★★ ❁❁❁ EGLWYSFACH	Ynyshir Hall ☎ 01654 781209

CONWY

171	★★ ❁❁❁ BETWS-Y-COED	Tan-y-Foel Country House ☎ 01690 710507
172	★★ ❁❁❁ CONWY	The Old Rectory Country House ☎ 01492 580611
173	★★★★ ❁❁ LLANDUDNO	Bodysgallen Hall Hotel ☎ 01492 584466
174	★★★★ ⌂ LLANDUDNO	Osborne House ☎ 01492 860330
175	★★ ❁❁❁ LLANDUDNO	St Tudno Hotel and Restaurant ☎ 01492 874411

DENBIGHSHIRE

176	⌂ ❁❁ LLANDRILLO	Tyddyn Llan Restaurant with Rooms ☎ 01490 440264

GWYNEDD

177	★★★ ❁❁ CAERNARFON	Seiont Manor ☎ 01286 673366
178	★★★ ❁ PORTMEIRION	Castell Deudraeth ☎ 01766 772400
179	★★ ❁❁ TALSARNAU	Maes y Neuadd Country House Hotel ☎ 01766 780200

POWYS

180	★★★ ❁❁ LLANGAMMARCH WELLS	Lake Country House Hotel ☎ 01591 620202

SWANSEA

181	★★ ❁❁❁ REYNOLDSTON	Fairyhill ☎ 01792 390139
182	★★★★ ❁❁ SWANSEA	Morgans Hotel ☎ 01792 484848

IRELAND

CLARE

183	★★★ ❁❁ BALLYVAUGHAN	Gregans Castle ☎ 065 7077005
184	★★★★★ ❁❁ NEWMARKET-ON-FERGUS	Dromoland Castle Hotel ☎ 061 368144

CORK

185	★★★ ❁❁ BALLYLICKEY	Sea View House Hotel ☎ 027 50073
186	★★★★ ❁❁ CORK	Hayfield Manor ☎ 021 4845900
187	★★★ ❁❁❁ MALLOW	Longueville House Hotel ☎ 022 47156

DUBLIN

188	★★★★ ❁❁ DUBLIN	The Clarence ☎ 01 4070800
189	★★★★★ ❁❁❁❁ DUBLIN	The Merrion Hotel ☎ 01 6030600
190	★★★★ ❁❁❁ PORTMARNOCK	Portmarnock Hotel & Golf Links ☎ 01 8460611

GALWAY

191	★★★ ❁❁ CASHEL	Cashel House Hotel ☎ 095 31001

KERRY

192	★★★★ ❁❁❁ KENMARE	Park Hotel Kenmare ☎ 064 41200
193	★★★★ ❁❁ KENMARE	Sheen Falls Lodge ☎ 064 41600
194	★★★★ ❁❁❁ KILLARNEY	Aghadoe Heights Hotel ☎ 064 31766
195	★★★★ ❁❁ KILLARNEY	Killarney Park Hotel ☎ 064 35555

KILDARE

196	★★★★★ ❁❁❁ STRAFFAN	The Kildare Hotel & Golf Club ☎ 01 6017200

KILKENNY

197	★★★★ ❁❁ THOMASTOWN	Mount Juliet Conrad Hotel ☎ 056 73000

WATERFORD

198	★★★★ ❁❁ WATERFORD	Waterford Castle Hotel ☎ 051 878203

WEXFORD

199	★★★ ❁❁❁ GOREY	Marlfield House Hotel ☎ 055 21124
200	★★★★ ❁❁ ROSSLARE	Kelly's Resort Hotel ☎ 053 32114

AA Accessible Hotel of the Year Award 2003-2004

These awards highlight establishments which are making particular progress in their welcome to disabled guests in the lead-up to the introduction of part 3 of the Disability Discrimination Act from 2004. From nearly 8000 establishments in the AA accommodation schemes, two Highly Commended and an outright Winner were chosen. The selection process involves assessment of accessible facilities against an 80 point checklist, mystery telephone enquiry, and an overnight visit by an independent judge.

Winner

Castle House Hotel

Hereford, Herefordshire

Castle House is very serious about its attention to disabled guests, with two specially designed bedrooms for mobility impaired guests. Additionally our visually impaired independent judge praised the real service ethos, "what they did for me, they regarded as part of their service to everyone, and did it without creating the impression they were doing something special".

Highly Commended

Huntingdon Marriott Hotel

Huntingdon, Cambridgeshire

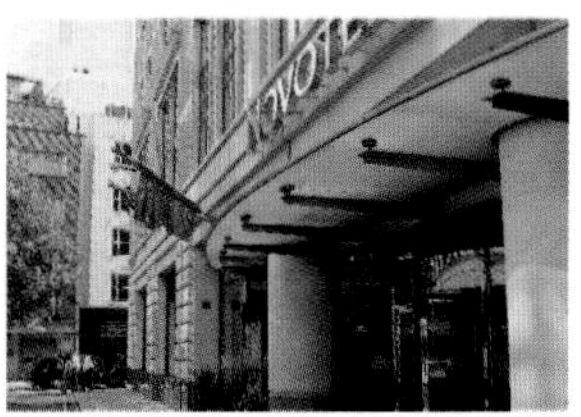

Highly Commended

Novotel London Tower Bridge

London EC3

AA Awards 2003-2004

Hotel of the Year Award

Hotel of the Year is the AA's most prestigious award. Winning hotels receive a specially commissioned, framed watercolour of the hotel by artist Duncan Palmar. National awards are made for England, Scotland, Wales and Ireland; a photograph of the winning hotel opens each country section in the guide. Awards for 2003-2004 are as follows:

England

★★★★ ❀❀❀

Seaham Hall Hotel

Seaham, Co. Durham

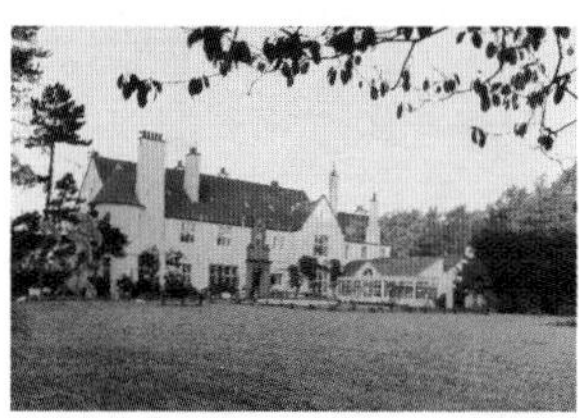

Scotland

★★★ ❀❀❀

Lochgreen House

Troon, South Ayrshire

Wales

★★★★ ❀❀

Morgans Hotel

Swansea

Republic of Ireland

★★★★ ❀❀

Hayfield Manor Hotel

Cork, Co. Cork

Hotel Group of the Year Award

This award reflects the hotel group which has demonstrated an outstanding commitment to improving and developing their portfolio of hotels, whilst maintaining a high level of consistency throughout the group.

AA Awards 2003-2004

Courtesy and Care Award

This award is made to hotels where staff offer exceptionally high standards of courtesy and care. National awards are made for England, Scotland & Northern Ireland, Wales and the Republic of Ireland. Members of staff receive a specially designed lapel badge to wear on duty. In addition, a large framed certificate is commissioned for display by the hotels and they have a highlighted entry in the guide. Awards for 2003-2004 are as follows:

England

★★★

The Montagu Arms

Beaulieu, Hampshire

Scotland & Northern Ireland

★★★ 79%

Glenmoriston Town House Hotel

Inverness, Highland

Wales

★★ 74%

West Arms Hotel

Llanarmon Dyffryn Ceiriog, Wrexham

Republic of Ireland

★★★

Cashel House Hotel

Cashel, Co. Galway

Hotel Groups Information

The following hotel groups have at least four hotels and 400 rooms or are part of an internationally significant brand with a central reservations number.

	Company Statement	Central Reservations Contact Number
	Britain's largest group has around 350 independently owned and managed hotels, modern and traditional, in the two, three and four star markets. Many have leisure facilities and many have rosette awards	**Best Western** **08457 73 73 73**
	A privately owned group of 11 three and four star hotels in Devon and Cornwall	**Brend** **01271 34 44 96**
CRERAR HOTELS	A division of North British Trust Group, comprising of a selection of three star hotels, providing accommodation throughout Scotland and the north of England	**Crerar** **08700 507 711**
	Campanile offers modern accommodation for the budget market	**Campanile** **0208 572 3663**
     CHOICE HOTELS EUROPE	Choice offers mainly three brands in the UK: Quality Hotels in the three star market, Comfort Inns at two star and Sleep Inns in the travel accommodation market	**Choice** **0800 44 44 44**
	A consortium of independent hotels at the four star and high-quality three star level, categorised by quality and style, and marketed under the Classic British Hotels hallmark	**Classic British** **0845 0 70 70 90**
	Part of the Millennium and Copthorne group, comprising 11 four star hotels in primary provincial locations	**Copthorne** **0800 414741**
	A large group of three star hotels ranging from rural to city centre locations across the UK	**Corus** **0845 300 2000**
	There are 11 hotels in the UK, part of the international brand of modern three star hotels	**Courtyard by Marriott** **0800 221 222 or 0800 699 996**
	A small group of three star hotels all located in the Cotswolds, each individual in style and character	**Cotswold Inns and Hotels** **0800 975 1629**
	Good quality modern budget accommodation at motorway services	**Days Inn** **0800 02 80 400**
DE VERE HOTELS	De Vere comprises 21 four and five star hotels, which specialise in leisure, golf and conferences	**De Vere** **0870 606 3606**
	A small privately owned group of luxury five nd four star hotels all located in the South of England	**Exclusive** **01276 471774**

	Company Statement	Central Reservations Contact Number
	Express by Holiday Inn offers superior budget accommodation with complimentary breakfast at over 70 modern hotels in the UK	**Express by Holiday Inn** **0800 43 40 40**
	A privately owned group of 18 three star hotels across the south of England	**Forestdale** **0808 1449494**
	Half a dozen three and four star hotels based in the Oxfordshire area	**Four Pillars** **01993 700100**
	A small group of personally managed three and four star hotels in leisure locations, with business facilities	**Furlong** **01225 867123** **(Head Office)**
	A collection of privately owned hotels, six located in central London and one in Bracknell, Berkshire	**Grange Hotels** **020 7233 7888**
	Part of the Ryan Hotels group, Gresham is a collection of four star properties, conveniently located in city centre locations in the Republic of Ireland.	**Gresham Hotels** **00 353 1 878 7966** **(Head Office)**
HandPICKED	A group of 15 three and four star, high quality country house hotels, with a real emphasis on quality food	**Handpicked** **0800 9 177 877**
	A group of three and four star hotels located mainly in the central counties of England	**Hanover International** **08457 444 123**
	This internationally known group offers a wide range of hotels throughout the UK	**Holiday Inn** **0800 40 50 60**
	Ibis is a growing chain of modern travel accommodation with properties across the UK	**Ibis** **020 8283 4550**
	A consortium of independently owned, mainly two and three star hotels across Britain	**Independents** **0800 88 55 44**
	Travel accommodation from Bass Leisure Retail, featuring comfortable rooms and complimentary breakfast	**Innkeepers Lodges** **0870 243 0500**
	This internationally renowned group is primarily represented in the UK with three five star hotels in central London	**Inter-Continental** **0800 0289 387**
	An association of owner-managed establishments across Ireland	**Ireland's Blue Book** **00 353 1 676 9914**
	Friendly and informal in style, Irish Country Hotels is a collection of 30 individual family owned and run hotels, located throughout the country	**Irish Country Hotels** **00 353 1 295 8900**
JURYS DOYLE HOTELS	This Irish company has a range of three and four star hotels in the UK and the Republic of Ireland	**Jury's Doyle** **00 353 1 607 0070** **(Group Information)**
	A group of 14 two star hotels located in the 'Best of British' seaside resorts	**Leisureplex** **08451 305888 (Head Office)**

Part

	Company Statement	Central Reservations Contact Number
	A large group of predominately four star hotels, traditional and modern in style, located across the UK	**Macdonald** **0870 400 90 90**
	A growing brand of three star city centre hotels, all rated over 70%	**Malmaison** **0207 479 9512 (Head Office)**
	Located throughout Northern and Southern Ireland, Manor House Hotels is an independent group comprising Georgian manors, country houses, shooting lodges, castles and four star guest houses	**Manor House** **00 353 1 295 8900**
	This international brand offers four star hotels in primary locations. Most are modern and have leisure facilities; some have a focus on golf	**Marriott** **0800 221 222** **0800 699 996**
	A quality independent group of mainly four star hotels with leisure facilities in primary locations across England	**Marston** **0845 1300 700**
	Menzies hotels owns a portfolio of predominantly four star hotels located throughout the UK	**Menzies** **0870 600 3013**
	An international brand of four and five star hotels, with good representation in and around London	**Le Meridien** **08000 28 28 40**
	Part of the Millennium and Copthorne group, comprising six high-quality four star hotels, mainly in central London	**Millennium** **0800 41 47 41**
	Part of French group Accor, Novotel provides modern three star hotels in key locations throughout the UK	**Novotel** **020 8283 4500**
	A large collection of former coaching inns, mainly in the two and three star markets	**Old English Inns & Hotels** **0800 917 3085**
	A group of predominately four star hotels, many with leisure facilities	**Paramount** **0500 342 543**
	A Europe based group increasing its presence within the UK through quality four star hotels in primary locations	**Park Plaza Hotels** **0800 1696128**
	A Europe based group increasing its presence within the UK through quality four star hotels in primary locations	**Peel** **0845 6017 335**
	Modern travel accommodation across the UK. Every lodge features an adjacent licensed popular restaurant, such as Millers Kitchen, Outside Inn or Chef & Brewer	**Premier Lodge** **08702 01 02 03**
	A consortium of privately owned British hotels, often in the country house style	**Pride of Britain** **01666 824666 (Head Office)**
	This high-quality London-based group offers mainly four star hotels in key locations throughout the capital	**Radisson Edwardian** **0800 374411**

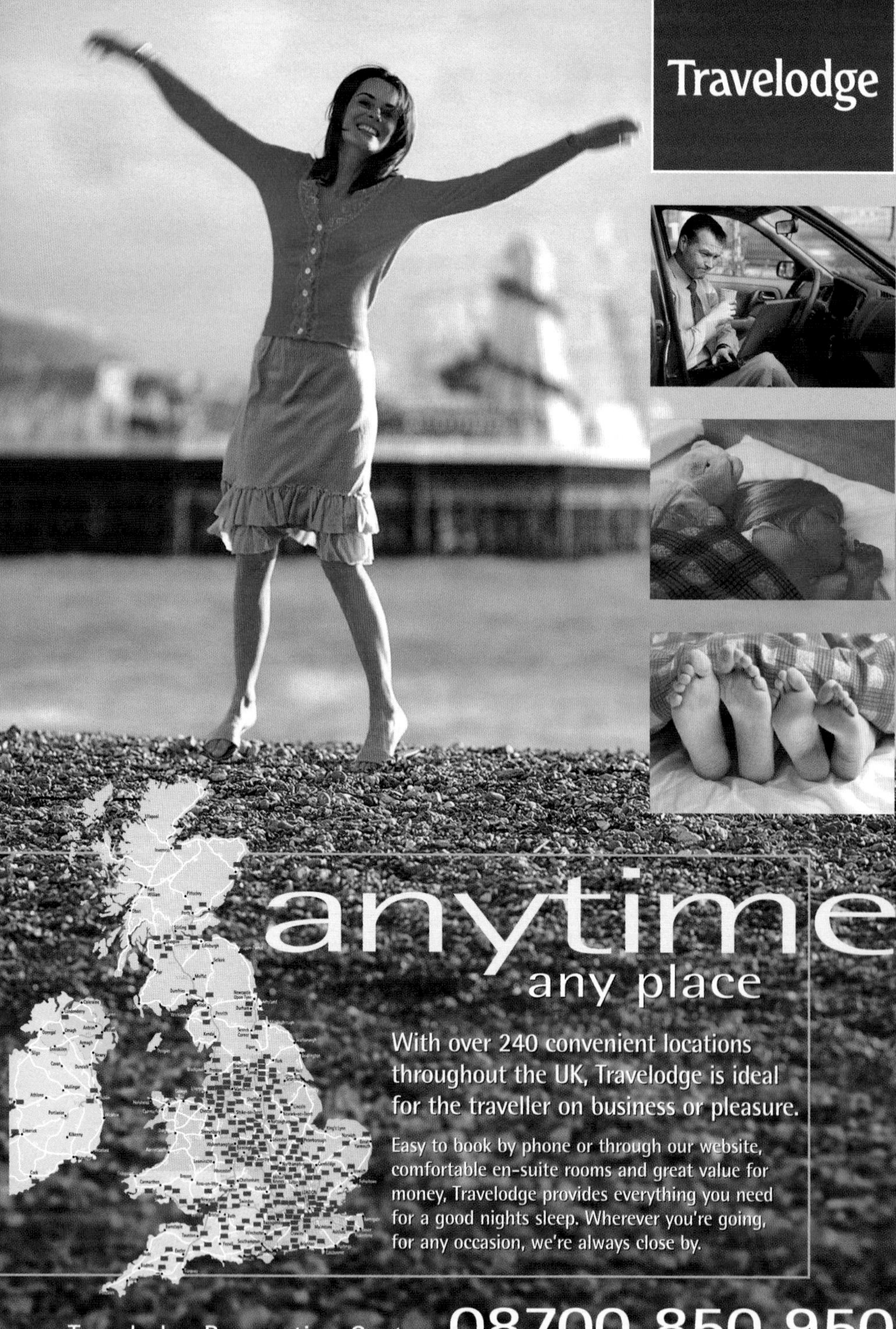

Travelodge
anytime
any place
With over 240 convenient locations throughout the UK, Travelodge is ideal for the traveller on business or pleasure.
Easy to book by phone or through our website, comfortable en-suite rooms and great value for money, Travelodge provides everything you need for a good nights sleep. Wherever you're going, for any occasion, we're always close by.
Travelodge Reservation Centre: 08700 850 950
or visit: www.travelodge.co.uk

	Company Statement	Central Reservations Contact Number
	A recognised international brand increasing its presence in the UK, offering high-quality four star hotels in key locations	**Radisson SAS** **0800 37 44 11**
	A unique collection of prestigious four and five star central London hotels, providing luxurious surroundings and attentive service	**Red Carnation** **020 7514 5633** **(Head Office)**
	An international consortium of rural, privately owned hotels, mainly in the country house style	**Relais et Chateaux** **00 33 1 457 296 50**
	One of the Marriott brands, Renaissance is a collection of individual hotels offering comfortable guest rooms, quality cuisine and good levels of service	**Renaissance** **0800 221 222** **0800 699 996**
	A prestigious group of four five star hotels in central London and a four star hotel in the Cotswolds	**Savoy Group** **00800 7671 7671** **020 7950 5494** **(General Enquiries)**
	A consortium of independent Scottish hotels, in the three and four star market	**Scotland's Hotels of Distinction** **01333 360 888**
	Sheraton is represented in the UK by a small number of four and five star hotels in London and Scotland	**Sheraton** **0800 35 35 35**
	A small group of mostly four star hotels many of which many feature spa facilities	**Shire** **01282 414141 (Head Office)**
	Part of an international consortium of mainly privately owned hotels, often in the country house style	**Small Luxury Hotels of the World** **00800 525 48000** **00 49 69 664 19601**
	A consortium of independently owned mainly two and three star hotels across Britain	**The Circle** **0845 345 1965**
	A large group of mainly four star hotels across the UK, with many in London and some country house properties	**Thistle** **0800 18 17 16**
	Good-quality, modern, budget accommodation across the UK. Almost every lodge has an adjacent family restaurant, often a Little Chef, Harry Ramsden's or Burger King	**Travelodge** **08700 850950**
	Good-quality, modern, budget accommodation. Every Travel Inn has an adjacent licensed family restaurant, often a Beefeater, Brewer's Fayre or TGI Fridays	**Travel Inn** **0870 242 8000**
	A privately owned collection of country house hotels, all individual in style and based predominately in the south of England	**Von Essen** **01761 241631**
	Good-quality, modern, budget accommodation at motorway services	**Welcome Break** **0800 731 4466**
	A small group of individual character hotels, located in countryside settings and in the historic towns of Windsor and Eton	**Wrens Hotels** **01753 838 854** **(Head Office)**

King Charles I

Who's Been Sleeping in My Bed

By Julia Hynard

Have you ever wondered whether someone famous has stayed in the same room you have booked? Many of the hotels in this guide have had famous visitors, past and present…

By Royal Appointment

Many of our finest hotels have been developed from stately country homes and townhouses on the grand scale, so associations with the aristocracy are abundant. We also have several reports of royal visits over the centuries. Henry VIII enjoyed staying with Bishop Vesey at **Moor Hall**, Sutton Coldfield. The bishop kept his house in a state of some splendour, all his 140 staff wore scarlet caps and gowns and his weekly household expenses amounted to £1,500 - pretty lavish by 16th-century standards. Queen Elizabeth I stayed at **Bodidris Hall**, Llandegla (there are suites named in her honour), and Mary Queen of Scots visited **Dalmahoy House** during her lifetime (now a Marriot hotel near Edinburgh), though it has only been in the Douglas family since 1760. A Douglas of Loch Leven was a Custodian of Queen Mary when she was imprisoned in Loch Leven Castle, but it was a Douglas son who freed her, casting the keys of the castle into the loch, from where they were recovered in the 19th century when the loch was drained.

Some hotels were originally royal properties, such as **Dromoland Castle**, Newmarket-on-Fergus, the seat of the O'Brien clan, descended from Brian Boru, High King of Ireland in the 11th century. **The Speech House**, Coleford, began as a royal hunting lodge for King Charles II, and the **Carlton Mitre Hotel** at Hampton Court was built in 1665 as additional accommodation for courtiers. In the same way, the site of the **Crowne Plaza London St James** was developed at Queen Victoria's command as elegant apartment blocks to accommodate overflow guests from neighbouring Buckingham Palace.

Queen Elizabeth I

The Mandarin Oriental (formerly Hyde Park Hotel) has an entrance from the park for the exclusive use of the Royal Family. **The Goring** is another royal favourite, but **The Ritz** is the only hotel in the world to hold a royal warrant.

King Charles I stopped at the **Red Lion**, Henley-on-Thames in 1632 (his crest can still be seen in one of the bedrooms). Napoleon Bonaparte III stayed at **Abington Hotel** in 1839 (they still have his chair). The Russian Royal Family holidayed at **Tor-na-Coille**, Banchory, and the Emperor of Ethiopia, Haile Selassie, was a regular visitor to the **White Hart**, Okehampton.

Queen Victoria got about a fair bit during her long reign, putting up at the **Quality Hotel**, Hull, the **Royal Station Hotel**, Carnforth, and the **Royal Hotel**, Comrie among many. Edward VII put it about a bit - two hotels bear blue plaques in the name of his mistress, Lillie Langtry: the **Cadogan Hotel**, which incorporates her former home at 21 Pont Street, and the couple's celebrated love nest at **Langtry Manor**, Bournemouth.

Blue Plaque Hotels

Twenty-five hotels have been awarded official blue plaques by the heritage scheme designed to commemorate famous figures and events. **Waterton Park Hotel**, Wakefield, was home to Charles Waterton, the pioneering naturalist, traveller and explorer, while **Grim's Dyke Hotel**, at Old Redding, 10 miles from London, was W S Gilbert's country house. **Sir Christopher Wren's House Hotel**, Windsor, is self-explanatory, and coming right up to date is the **Longview Hotel**, Knutsford, its plaque naming Martin Bell, war correspondent and MP Charles Kingsley - clergyman, naturalist and author of The Waterbabies - lived at what is now **Livermead House Hotel**, Torquay, while another hotel in the town, **The Regina**, is the former home of poet Elizabeth Barratt Browning. Further along the coast at Brixham is the **Berryhead Hotel**, where the Rev Henry Cyte wrote 'Abide With Me'.

Word Association

Another famous hymnist, the Rev Sabine Baring-Gould ('Onward Christian Soldiers') hails from **Lewtrenchard Manor**, West Devon. His inspiration was clearly divine, but physical surroundings also play their part: Sir Arthur Conan Doyle stayed at **Prince Hall**, Two Bridges, one of the ancient tenements of Dartmoor, and was inspired by the wildness of the landscape to write The Hound of the Baskervilles. R D Blackmore wrote parts of Lorna Doone while staying at the **Crown Hotel**, Exford and the **Rising Sun** at Lynmouth; and it was while visiting his brother at **Chewton Glen**, New Milton, that Captain Frederick Marryat wrote Children of the New Forest.

George Farquhar wrote and set his famous restoration comedy The Beaux' Stratagem at the **George Hotel**, Lichfield, basing his characters on real people working and staying at the George, which was at that time a prominent coaching inn.

Robert Burns

Alfred Lord Tennyson stayed at the **Falcon Hotel**, Bude in 1848 while researching material for Idylls of the King. **Farringford**, at Freshwater on the Isle of Wight, was his home from 1853 until his death in 1892 and remained in the family for some years afterwards before it became a hotel.

In 1793 Robert Burns penned the unofficial Scottish National Anthem Scots wha hae at the **Murray Arms Hotel**, Gatehouse of Fleet, recalling the Battle of Bannockburn in 1314 'that glorious struggle for freedom' led by Robert Bruce and associating it with political struggles of his own day.

P G Wodehouse lived in Emsworth and many local place names appear in his works, including **Brookfield House** - now a hotel. The character of Jeeves is based on a gardener at **Stone House**, Hawes. Wodehouse was a great pal of the original owner of the property, which is also now a hotel.

Several more hotels appear in works of literature, such as **Bodkin House**, Badminton, mentioned by Jane Austen in Northanger Abbey, and **Kinfauns Castle** in Walter Scott's The Fair Maid of Perth. Charlotte Brontë reputedly stayed at the **George at Hathersage** when writing Jane Eyre, and she mentions the inn anonymously using the landlord's name of Morton.

Stories From The Stars

Top hotels attract celebrities from across the spectrum. London's **Cadogan Hotel** was a great favourite with the Queen Mother, who celebrated her 99th and 100th birthdays there, and with Princess

continued on page 45

Diana who would meet her best friend Lucia Flecha de Lima for tea in the Drawing Room. Oscar Wilde's association with the hotel was ultimately less happy, as he was arrested in room 118 on April 5, 1895 and charged with gross indecency. A little over a hundred years later, however, the hotel was the venue for Britain's first gay wedding on September 7, 2001. Oscar Wilde is also reputed to have stayed at the **Old Parsonage**, Oxford, when he was rusticated from Magdalen College for being late at the start of a new term.

The **Radisson Edwardian Hampshire Hotel** (London WC2) regularly entertains royalty and does all the premieres for the Odeon Leicester Square, attracting many an A-list celeb. Vintage film star Clark Gable stayed at the **Headland Hotel**, Newquay in the 1930s, while Richard Burton and Elizabeth Taylor liked the **Aberavon Beach Hotel**, Port Talbot, though they also used the **Bear Hotel** in Woodstock as a romantic hideaway during the course of their passionate affair. **Jurys Cork Hotel** has put up both Michael Jackson and Kylie Minogue, and the ancient **Witchery by the Castle** in Edinburgh boasts a self-portrait by Jack Nicholson and cartoons by Simpsons' creator Matt Groening in its celebrity-studded visitors' book. Gail Porter's wedding do was at the Witchery, and David Beckham and Victoria Adams got engaged at **Rookery Hall**, near Stoke-on-Trent.

For a total celebrity experience, at the **Marine Hotel** in Aberystwyth you can sleep in Robert Maxwell's bed - a huge one as you might imagine. But lest you should think that celebrities are entirely feather-bedded, Dannii Minogue, while ensconced at **Bath Priory**, reported a spider in her bath late one night. The night porter, thinking it inappropriate to enter a lady's room, woke the duty manager who was able to save the situation.

On the other side of the counter, comedian Tony Hancock was raised at the **Quality Hotel Bournemouth**; David Niven worked as a barman at the **Prince's House** in Glenfinnan during World War II, and the **Clarence Hotel** in Dublin is owned by Bono and The Edge from U2.

Queen Victoria

Colourful Characters

Many notable characters from the pages of history are associated with hotels. Thomas Paine, who wrote The Rights of Man and helped instigate the American Revolution, was born on the site of the **Thomas Paine Hotel**, Thetford, and drafted the basis for the US constitution in the **White Hart Hotel**, Lewes.

In 1695, from an upper window of **The Crown** at Wells, William Penn, a Quaker who later gave his name to Pennsylvannia USA, preached to a crowd of some 2-3,000 in the Market Place below. A local constable interrupted him with a warrant from the mayor to arrest him for unlawful assembly. London's **22 Jermyn Street**, now owned by Henry Togna, has been in the Togna family since 1915. When Henry's mother was a child, one of the residents was the Marchese Gugliemo Marconi. She was fascinated by the cobweb of wires strung across Marchese Marconi's suite and was intrigued to learn that he was developing a 'wireless'. Subsequently, Marconi made one of his first test transmissions from the garden at the **Cliff Hotel**, Harwich.

Whitworth Hall & Country Park Hotel, Spennymoor, was once the home of Robert Shafto, man of fashion and MP for County Durham. He died in 1797 but his name was made famous by the ballad of Bonny Bobbie Shafto.

Randolph Caldecott, the Victorian artist, painted his first published work at the **Queen Hotel Chester**. The subject? The Queen Hotel on fire! Another 19th-century artist, John Dawson, lived at **Castle Hotel**, Conwy and 'paid' for his stay with oil paintings.

Be you ever so humble - there's no place like a hotel

There's scarcely an AA-registered hotel in the land that's unaccustomed to accommodating celebrities. The good news is that the celebrity experience, with all its grace, opulence and ease, is open to all in these egalitarian days for the price of a decent hotel room.

Location, Location, Location

Hotels play an important role in the world of film - TV and cinema - and many have provided accommodation for cast and crew and sometimes even the location for a shoot. The film credits are really too numerous to mention, but here are our top 10 hotels appearing on film (in alphabetical order).

Crown Hotel, Stamford	Middlemarch
Danum Hotel, Doncaster	Brassed Off
Grim's Dyke Hotel, Old Redding	Sliding Doors
Headland Hotel, Newquay	The Witches
Inter Continental, London	Bulls Eye
London Marriott	Friends
Renaissance Chancery Court, London	Howards End & Wilde
Summer Lodge, Evershot	Pride and Prejudice & Emma
The Ritz, London	Notting Hill
Tufton Arms Hotel, Appleby-in-Westmoreland	The Monocled Mutineer

Hotel of the Year, England

Seaham Hall Hotel
Seaham, County Durham

A

ABBERLEY, Worcestershire Map 10 SO76

★★★73% The Elms
Stockton Rd WR6 6AT
☎ 01299 896666 01299 896804
e-mail: elmshotel@ukonline.co.uk
Dir: *on A443 2m beyond Great Witley*

Surrounded by its own well manicured grounds, this imposing Queen Anne mansion dates back to 1710 and offers a sophisticated and relaxed ambience throughout. The spacious public rooms and generously proportioned bedrooms exude elegance and charm, and the restaurant overlooks the gardens and serves imaginative and memorable dishes.
ROOMS: 16 en suite 5 annexe en suite (1 fmly) s £90-£110; d £120-£210 (incl. bkfst) **LB** **FACILITIES:** Tennis (grass) Croquet lawn Xmas **CONF:** Thtr 70 Class 30 Board 30 **PARKING:** 100 **NOTES:** No dogs (ex guide dogs) No smoking in restaurant Civ Wed 90
CARDS:

ABBOT'S SALFORD, Warwickshire Map 10 SP05

★★★74% Salford Hall
WR11 8UT
☎ 01386 871300 01386 871301
e-mail: reception@salfordhall.co.uk

Dir: *A46 take road signed Salford Priors, Abbot's Salford & Harvington. Hotel 1.5m on left*

Built in 1470 as a retreat for the Abbot of Evesham, this impressive building retains many original features. Bedrooms have their own individual character and most offer a view of the attractive gardens. Oak-panelling, period tapestries, open fires and fresh flowers grace the public areas, while leisure facilities include a snooker room, tennis court, solarium and sauna.
ROOMS: 14 en suite 19 annexe en suite (4 GF) No smoking in 4 bedrooms s £70-£85; d £118-£150 (incl. bkfst) **LB** **FACILITIES:** STV Tennis (hard) Snooker Sauna Solarium **CONF:** Thtr 50 Class 35 Board 25 Del from £120 **PARKING:** 51 **NOTES:** No dogs (ex guide dogs) No smoking in restaurant Closed 24-30 Dec Civ Wed 50
CARDS:

See advert under STRATFORD-UPON-AVON

ABINGDON, Oxfordshire Map 05 SU49

★★★68% Upper Reaches
Thames St OX14 3JA
☎ 0870 400 8101 01235 555182
e-mail: upperreaches@macdonald-hotels.co.uk
Dir: *on A415 in Abingdon follow signs for Dorchester, turn left just before bridge over Thames*

MACDONALD HOTELS

This former 17th-century watermill enjoys a tranquil setting on the banks of the River Thames and is within walking distance of the town centre. The spacious bedrooms are furnished and equipped to a high standard, and public areas include an atmospheric restaurant which features one of the oldest working millwheels in the country.
ROOMS: 31 en suite (4 fmly) No smoking in 15 bedrooms s £89-£161; d £118-£172 (incl. bkfst) **LB** **FACILITIES:** STV Fishing Free use of nearby leisure centre Xmas **CONF:** Thtr 25 Class 15 Board 16 Del from £120 **PARKING:** 60 **NOTES:** No smoking in restaurant
CARDS:

★★★66% Abingdon Four Pillars Hotel
Marcham Rd OX14 1TZ
☎ 0800 374 692 01235 554117
e-mail: abingdon@four-pillars.co.uk
Dir: *A34 at junct with A415, in Abingdon, turn right at rdbt, hotel on right*

FOUR PILLARS HOTELS

This is a busy hotel, close to the major road links, offering a good base for business or conference guests. It has well-equipped, comfortable bedrooms each with satellite TV and a trouser press. Food and drink services are available all day in the lounge and the conservatory.
ROOMS: 62 en suite (7 fmly) (31 GF) No smoking in 40 bedrooms s £73-£92; d £83-£105 **LB** **FACILITIES:** STV entertainment Xmas **CONF:** Thtr 140 Class 80 Board 48 Del £130 **PARKING:** 85 **NOTES:** No dogs (ex guide dogs) No smoking in restaurant Civ Wed 100
CARDS:

Travel Inn
Marcham Rd OX14 1AD
☎ 08701 977014 01235 554149
Dir: *on A415 0.5m from Abingdon town centre. Approx. 0.5 m from A34 at Abingdon South junction.*

travel inn

Travel Inn offers good-quality, value-for-money accommodation. Spacious, en suite rooms with bath and shower comfortably accommodate a family of up to two adults and two children (to age 15). The restaurant and bar offers a varied menu. For further details and the Travel Inn phone number, consult the Hotel Groups page.
ROOMS: 25 en suite s £44.95; d £44.95

ACCRINGTON, Lancashire Map 18 SD72

★★★★65% Dunkenhalgh
Blackburn Rd, Clayton-le-Moors BB5 5JP
☎ 01254 398021 01254 872230
e-mail: dunkenhalgh@macdonald-hotels.co.uk
Dir: *adjacent to M65 junct 7*

MACDONALD HOTELS

Set in 17 acres of parkland, yet only minutes from the motorway network, the original building, around which the hotel has developed, dates back around 700 years and features turrets and porticos. Modern features include a fully equipped indoor leisure centre and a brand new state-of-the-art conference centre.
ROOMS: 53 en suite 69 annexe en suite (33 fmly) No smoking in 56 bedrooms **FACILITIES: Spa** STV Indoor swimming (H) Sauna Solarium Gym Jacuzzi Health & beauty spa, Dance studio entertainment **CONF:** Thtr 400 Class 200 Board 100 Del from £100 **SERVICES:** Lift **PARKING:** 400 **NOTES:** No smoking in restaurant Civ Wed 400
CARDS:

★★★64% Sparth House Hotel

Whalley Rd, Clayton Le Moors BB5 5RP
☎ 01254 872263 01254 872263
e-mail: mail.sparth@btinternet.com
Dir: *A6185 to Clitheroe along Dunkenhalgh Way, right at lights onto A678, left at next lights, A680 to Whalley. Hotel on left after 2 sets of lights*

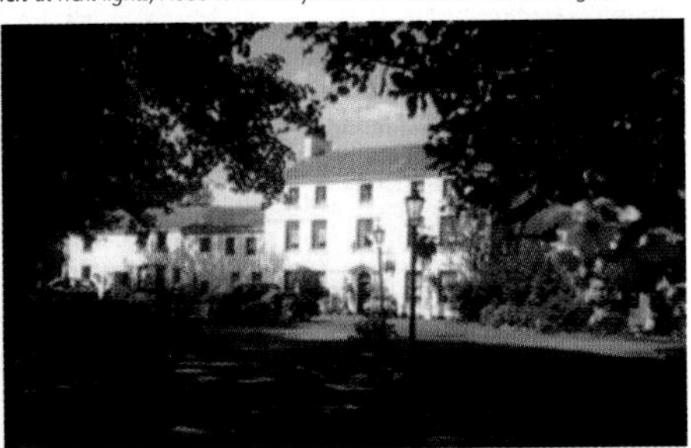

This 18th-century listed building nestles in three acres of well-tended gardens close to the motorway. Bedrooms are individually styled and those in the original house are particularly spacious, including one with original furnishings from one of the great liners. The panelled restaurant is a peaceful setting in which to enjoy a wide range of dishes.
ROOMS: 16 en suite (3 fmly) No smoking in 2 bedrooms s £55-£85; d £66-£99 (incl. bkfst) **LB** **FACILITIES:** ch fac **CONF:** Thtr 160 Class 50 Board 40 Del from £85 **PARKING:** 50 **NOTES:** No smoking in restaurant Civ Wed 100 **CARDS:**

ACLE, Norfolk — Map 13 TG41

Travelodge Great Yarmouth

Travelodge

NR13 3BE
☎ 08700 850 950 01493 751970
Dir: *junct of A47 & Acle by-pass*
Travelodge offers good quality, good value, modern accommodation. Ideal for families, the spacious, en suite bedrooms include remote-control TV, tea and coffee-making facilities, luxury beds and free morning newspaper. Meals can be taken at the nearby family restaurant. For further details and the Travelodge phone number, consult the Hotel Groups page.
ROOMS: 40 en suite s fr £42.95; d fr £42.95

ALBRIGHTON, Shropshire

★★★62% *Lea Manor Hotel & Restaurant*

Holyhead Rd WV7 3BX
☎ 01902 373266 01902 372853
e-mail: hotel@leamanor.co.uk
Dir: *M54 junct 3/A41 towards Wolverhampton then A464 towards Shifnal for approx 2m, hotel on left*
This privately owned hotel provides well-equipped bedrooms, half of which are located in a separate, single storey, purpose-built block. There is also a large function room and three conference rooms. The owners plan to make many changes and improvements to the hotel.
ROOMS: 8 en suite 8 annexe en suite No smoking in 10 bedrooms **CONF:** Thtr 200 Class 50 Board 50 **PARKING:** 200 **NOTES:** No dogs (ex guide dogs) No smoking in restaurant Civ Wed 100
CARDS:

ALCESTER, Warwickshire — Map 10 SP05

★★★67% *Kings Court*

Kings Coughton B49 5QQ
☎ 01789 763111 01789 400242
e-mail: info@kingscourthotel.co.uk
Dir: *1m N on A435*
This privately-owned hotel dates back to Tudor times and the bedrooms in the original house have oak beams. Most guests are accommodated in the well-appointed modern wings. The bar and restaurant have undergone complete refurbishment and offer a range of menus. The hotel is licensed to hold civil ceremonies and the pretty garden is ideal for summer weddings.
ROOMS: 4 en suite 38 annexe en suite (3 fmly) No smoking in 15 bedrooms **CONF:** Thtr 120 Class 40 Board 30 **PARKING:** 120
NOTES: Closed 24-26 Dec Civ Wed 60
CARDS:

Travelodge Stratford Alcester

Travelodge

Oversley Mill Roundabout B49 6AA
☎ 08700 850 950
Dir: *at junct A46/A435*
Travelodge offers good quality, good value, modern accommodation. Ideal for families, the spacious, en suite bedrooms include remote-control TV, tea and coffee-making facilities, luxury beds and free morning newspaper. Meals can be taken at the nearby family restaurant. For further details and the Travelodge phone number, consult the Hotel Groups page.
ROOMS: 66 en suite s fr £42.95; d fr £42.95

ALDEBURGH, Suffolk — Map 13 TM45

★★★77% The Brudenell

The Parade IP15 5BU
☎ 01728 452071 01728 454082
e-mail: info@brudenellhotel.co.uk
Dir: *A12/A1094, on reaching town, turn right at junct into High St. Hotel on seafront adjoining Fort Green car park*

Situated at the far end of the town centre just a step away from the beach. The hotel is newly reopened after a total refurbishment and all areas now have a contemporary appearance, enhanced by subtle lighting and quality soft furnishings; many of the bedrooms have superb sea views. Deluxe rooms, with king-sized beds, and superior rooms suitable for families are available. Local seafood and grills are a speciality in the restaurant.
ROOMS: 42 en suite (21 fmly) No smoking in all bedrooms s £61-£91; d £96-£186 (incl. bkfst) **LB** **FACILITIES:** STV Xmas **SERVICES:** Lift
PARKING: 22 **NOTES:** No smoking in restaurant
CARDS:

ALDEBURGH, continued

A

★★★76% ◎ **Wentworth**
Wentworth Rd IP15 5BD
☎ 01728 452312 🖹 01728 454343
e-mail: stay@wentworth-aldeburgh.co.uk
Dir: *off A12 onto A1094, 6m to Aldeburgh, with church on left & left at bottom of hill*

A delightful privately owned hotel overlooking the beach and sea beyond. The attractive, well-maintained public rooms include three stylish lounges as well as a bar and elegant restaurant. Bedrooms are smartly decorated with co-ordinated fabrics and have many thoughtful touches; some rooms have superb sea views. Several very spacious Mediterranean-style rooms are located across the road.
ROOMS: 30 rms (28 en suite) 7 annexe en suite No smoking in all bedrooms s £69-£82; d £133-£157 (incl. bkfst) **LB FACILITIES:** STV Xmas **CONF:** Thtr 15 Class 12 Board 12 Del from £100 **PARKING:** 30 **NOTES:** No smoking in restaurant Closed 28 Dec-9 Jan
CARDS:

See advert on opposite page

★★★76% **White Lion**
Market Cross Place IP15 5BJ
☎ 01728 452720 🖹 01728 452986
e-mail: whitelionaldeburgh@btinternet.com
Dir: *Follow signs to Aldeburgh and town centre. At crossroads turn left, hotel in Market Cross Place*

Best Western

A popular 15th-century hotel situated at the quiet end of town overlooking the sea. Public areas include two lounges and an elegant restaurant where locally caught fish and seafood are served. There is also a modern brasserie. Bedrooms are pleasantly decorated and thoughtfully equipped, many rooms have lovely sea views.
ROOMS: 38 en suite (1 fmly) No smoking in 19 bedrooms s £61-£86; d £96-£160 (incl. bkfst) **LB FACILITIES:** STV Xmas **CONF:** Thtr 120 Class 50 Board 50 Del from £85 **PARKING:** 15 **NOTES:** No smoking in restaurant **CARDS:**

ALDERLEY EDGE, Cheshire Map 16 SJ87

★★★76% ◎◎ **Alderley Edge**
Macclesfield Rd SK9 7BJ
☎ 01625 583033 🖹 01625 586343
e-mail: sales@alderleyedgehotel.com
Dir: *off A34 in Alderley Edge onto B5087 towards Macclesfield. Hotel 200yds on right*

This well-furnished hotel with its charming grounds was originally a country house built for one of the region's cotton kings. The bedrooms and suites are attractively furnished, offering excellent quality and comfort. The welcoming bar and adjacent lounge lead into the split-level conservatory restaurant, which offers well cooked and very imaginative dishes.
ROOMS: 52 en suite (6 GF) No smoking in 19 bedrooms s £120-£400; d £140-£400 **LB FACILITIES:** STV entertainment Xmas **CONF:** Thtr 120 Class 80 Board 40 Del £165 **SERVICES:** Lift **PARKING:** 90 **NOTES:** No dogs (ex guide dogs) Civ Wed 100 **CARDS:**

⌂ **Innkeeper's Lodge Alderley Edge**
5-9 Wilmslow Rd SK9 7NZ
☎ 01625 599959 🖹 01625 599432
Dir: *M56 junct 6, S on A538. Right at traffic lights towards Alderley Edge. Lodge on left, after 2nd rdbt*

Innkeeper's Lodge

A new concept in the travel accommodation market. Smart rooms meet essential business requirements but also have home comforts. Dining options include all-day menus plus the added advantage of breakfast, which is included in the room price. For further details, consult the Hotel Groups page.
ROOMS: 10 en suite s £45-£57.50; d £45-£57.50

⌂ **Premier Lodge (Alderley Edge)**
Congleton Rd, Alderley Edge SK9 7AA
☎ 0870 9906498 🖹 0870 9906499

PREMIER LODGE

Premier Lodge offers modern, well-equipped, en suite accommodation suitable for both business and leisure travellers. Meals can be taken at the adjacent popular restaurant and bar, which is fully licensed. For further details, consult the Hotel Groups page.
ROOMS: 37 en suite s £44; d £44

ALDERMINSTER, Warwickshire Map 10 SP24

★★★★77% ◎◎ **Ettington Park**
CV37 8BU
☎ 01789 450123 🖹 01789 450472
e-mail: ettington@arcadianhotels.co.uk
Dir: *off A3400, 5m S of Stratford just outside village of Alderminster*

HandPICKED

Ettington Park offers the peaceful calm of Shakespeare country within easy access of the road network. Bedrooms have views over the manicured parkland or the formal gardens and chapel. All are spacious and individually designed with comfort in mind.

continued

A

Public rooms include a period drawing room, oak-panelled dining room and contemporary meeting rooms and leisure centre.

ROOMS: 28 en suite 20 annexe en suite (5 fmly) s £195-£385; d £195-£385 (incl. bkfst) **FACILITIES: Spa** STV Indoor swimming (H) Tennis (hard) Fishing Sauna Croquet lawn Jacuzzi Clay pigeon shooting, Archery, Health & Beauty salon entertainment Xmas **CONF:** Thtr 75 Class 40 Board 48 Del from £150 **SERVICES:** Lift **PARKING:** 150 **NOTES:** No dogs (ex guide dogs) No smoking in restaurant Civ Wed 60
CARDS:

ALDERSHOT, Hampshire — Map 05 SU85

★★★68% Potters International
1 Fleet Rd GU11 2ET
☎ 01252 344000 📠 01252 311611
Dir: *access via A325 & A321 towards Fleet*
This modern hotel is located within easy reach of Aldershot. Extensive air-conditioned public areas include ample lounge areas, a pub and a more formal restaurant; there are also conference rooms and a very good leisure club. Bedrooms are mostly spacious, well equipped and have been attractively decorated and furnished.
ROOMS: 100 en suite (6 fmly) (8 GF) No smoking in 10 bedrooms s £105-£120; d £120-£140 (incl. bkfst) **FACILITIES:** STV Indoor swimming (H) Sauna Solarium Gym Jacuzzi Swimming pool supervised **CONF:** Thtr 400 Del £165 **SERVICES:** Lift **PARKING:** 120 **NOTES:** No dogs (ex guide dogs) No smoking in restaurant
CARDS:

⌂ Travel Inn
travel inn
Wellington Av GU11 1SQ
☎ 08701 977015 📠 01252 344073
Dir: *Exit M3 (J4), join A331. Take second of four lanes - A324 through Farnborough, past airfield and over roundabout. Travel Inn is ahead, 8 miles from M3*
Travel Inn offers good-quality, value-for-money accommodation. Spacious, en suite rooms with bath and shower comfortably accommodate a family of up to two adults and two children (to age 15). The restaurant and bar offers a varied menu. For further details and the Travel Inn phone number, consult the Hotel Groups page.
ROOMS: 60 en suite s £44.95; d £44.95

ALDWARK, North Yorkshire — Map 19 SE46

★★★★75% ®® Aldwark Manor
MARSTON HOTELS
YO61 1UF
☎ 01347 838146 📠 01347 838867
e-mail: aldwark@marstonhotels.com
Dir: *A1/A59 towards Green Hammerton, then B6265 Little Ouseburn. Follow signs for Aldwark Bridge/Manor. A19 through Linton on Ouse*

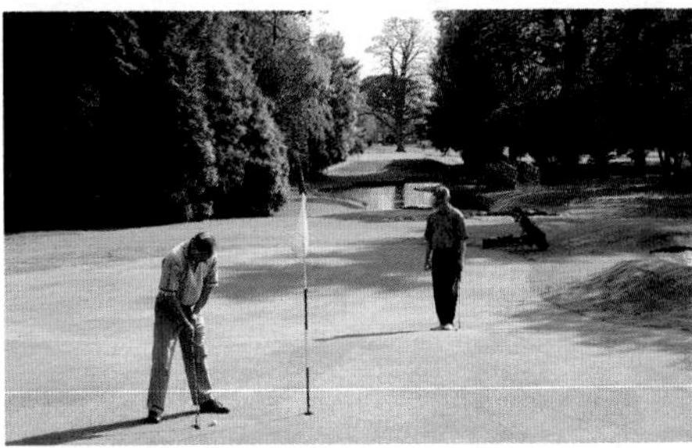

The mature parkland setting, with the River Ure running slowly through the 18-hole golf course, forms an impressive backdrop for this rambling 19th-century mansion. Bedrooms vary – traditional in the house and more modern in the extension. Public areas are a mix of period style and modern.
ROOMS: 60 en suite (2 fmly) s fr £75; d fr £125 **LB FACILITIES: Spa** STV Indoor swimming (H) Golf 18 Fishing Sauna Solarium Gym Putting green Jacuzzi Health & beauty Xmas **CONF:** Thtr 250 Class 100 Board 80 Del from £150 **PARKING:** 150 **NOTES:** No dogs (ex guide dogs) No smoking in restaurant Civ Wed 100
CARDS:

See advert under YORK

ALFRETON, Derbyshire
Map 16 SK45

Travelodge
Old Swanwick Colliery Rd DE55 1HJ
☎ 08700 850 950 📠 01773 520040
Dir: *3m from M1 junct 28 at A38/A61 junct*
Travelodge offers good quality, good value, modern accommodation. Ideal for families, the spacious, en suite bedrooms include remote-control TV, tea and coffee-making facilities, luxury beds and free morning newspaper. Meals can be taken at the nearby family restaurant. For further details and the Travelodge phone number, consult the Hotel Groups page.
ROOMS: 60 en suite s fr £42.95; d fr £42.95

ALFRISTON, East Sussex
Map 06 TQ50

★★★70% Deans Place
Seaford Rd BN26 5TW
☎ 01323 870248 📠 01323 870918
e-mail: mail@deansplacehotel.co.uk
Dir: *off A27 signed Alfriston & Drusillas Zoo Park. Continue S through village*
Situated on the southern fringe of the village, this friendly hotel is set in attractive gardens. Bedrooms vary in size and are well appointed with good facilities. A wide range of food is offered including an extensive bar menu, and both fine dining and less formal menus in Harcourt's Restaurant.
ROOMS: 36 en suite (2 fmly) (8 GF) No smoking in 16 bedrooms s £53-£95; d £74-£132 (incl. bkfst) **LB FACILITIES:** STV Outdoor swimming (H) Croquet lawn Putting green ch fac Xmas **CONF:** Thtr 200 Class 70 Board 45 Del £130 **PARKING:** 100 **NOTES:** No smoking in restaurant Civ Wed 150 **CARDS:**

★★★69% *The Star Inn*
BN26 5TA
☎ 0870 400 8102 📠 01323 870922
e-mail: reservations@star-inn-alfriston.com
Dir: *2m off A27 at Drusillas rdbt*
A warm, friendly atmosphere prevails inside this 14th-century inn. On the edge of the South Downs, its feature rooms offer the useful additions of sofa beds. There are two beamed lounges with open fires and a bar with a flag-stoned floor, while the restaurant offers good quality cuisine to suit all tastes.
ROOMS: 37 en suite (1 fmly) No smoking in 10 bedrooms **CONF:** Thtr 30 Class 15 Board 25 **PARKING:** 27 **NOTES:** No smoking in restaurant **CARDS:**

★★★69% White Lodge Country House
Sloe Ln BN26 5UR
☎ 01323 870265 📠 01323 870284
e-mail: sales@whitelodge-hotel.com
Dir: *on B2108 between A27 and A259*

An ideal retreat in peaceful surroundings, with views over the Cuckmere River Valley. Bedrooms are individually decorated.
continued

Weekend breaks are well-planned and special events are very popular. Public areas include a choice of elegant lounges and two restaurants.
ROOMS: 19 en suite (1 fmly) (4 GF) No smoking in 2 bedrooms s £45-£150; d £90-£150 (incl. bkfst) **LB FACILITIES:** STV Croquet lawn Putting green entertainment Xmas **CONF:** Thtr 24 Class 16 Board 16 Del from £65 **SERVICES:** Lift **PARKING:** 40 **NOTES:** No smoking in restaurant **CARDS:**

ALMONDSBURY, Gloucestershire
Map 04 ST68

★★★★71% Aztec

Aztec West Business Park BS32 4TS
☎ 01454 201090 📠 01454 201593
e-mail: aztec@shirehotels.co.uk
(For full entry see Bristol)

See advert on opposite page

ALNWICK, Northumberland
Map 21 NU11

See also Embleton

★★★58% White Swan
Bondgate Within NE66 1TD
☎ 01665 602109 📠 01665 510400
Dir: *A1 town centre signs. Hotel situated in town centre nr Bondgate Tower*

Located in the centre of Alnwick, this historic former coaching inn is a popular base for touring Northumberland. Public areas include the Atlantic Suite, featuring original wooden panelling and fittings from the sister ship of the SS Titanic.
ROOMS: 56 en suite (5 fmly) (11 GF) No smoking in 23 bedrooms s £79; d £112 (incl. bkfst) **LB FACILITIES:** Xmas **CONF:** Thtr 150 Class 50 Board 40 Del from £79 **PARKING:** 25 **NOTES:** No smoking in restaurant Civ Wed 150 **CARDS:**

ALSAGER, Cheshire
Map 15 SJ75

★★★69% Manor House
Audley Rd ST7 2QQ
☎ 01270 884000 📠 01270 882483
e-mail: mhres@compasshotels.co.uk
Dir: *M6 junct 16/A500 toward Stoke. After 0.5m take 1st slip road to Alsager. Left at top & continue, hotel on left approaching village*
Developed around an old farmhouse, the original oak beams are still very much a feature in the hotel bars and restaurant. Modernised and extended over the years, the hotel today is well geared towards the needs of the modern traveller. Some of the main features include a range of conference rooms, a lovely patio garden and an indoor swimming pool.
ROOMS: 57 en suite (4 fmly) No smoking in 20 bedrooms s £82-£91; d £91-£112 (incl. bkfst) **LB FACILITIES:** STV Indoor swimming (H) Jacuzzi Xmas **CONF:** Thtr 200 Class 108 Board 82 Del from £110 **PARKING:** 150 **NOTES:** No dogs (ex guide dogs) No smoking in restaurant RS Sat & Sun Civ Wed 100
CARDS:

ALSTON, Cumbria

Map 18 NY74

★★75% ®® Lovelady Shield Country House

CA9 3LF
☎ 01434 381203 & 381305 ▤ 01434 381515
e-mail: enquiries@lovelady.co.uk
Dir: *2m E, signed off A689 at junct with B6294*

Located in the heart of the Pennines close to England's highest market town, this delightful country house is set in three acres of landscaped gardens. Accommodation is provided in thoughtfully equipped bedrooms with classical décor. Carefully prepared meals are served in the elegant dining room and there is a choice of appealing lounges.
ROOMS: 10 en suite (1 fmly) **CONF:** Class 12 Board 12 **PARKING:** 20
NOTES: No smoking in restaurant Civ Wed 100
CARDS:

★★71% Nent Hall Country House Hotel

CA9 3LQ
☎ 01434 381584 ▤ 01434 382668
e-mail: info@nenthallhotel.com
Dir: *2m SE of Alston, on A689 towards Nenthend, Stanhope & Durham*
Family owned and personally run, this delightful old house has a wealth of charm and stands in extensive gardens. It provides warm and friendly hospitality and well-equipped accommodation, with ground floor and family bedded rooms available. There is a choice of bars and lounge areas, including one for non-smokers.
ROOMS: 7 en suite 9 annexe en suite (2 fmly) (9 GF) No smoking in all bedrooms s £45; d £65 (incl. bkfst) **LB** **PARKING:** 35 **NOTES:** No smoking in restaurant Closed 24-30 Dec Civ Wed 60
CARDS:

★★70% Lowbyer Manor Country House

CA9 3JX
☎ 01434 381230 ▤ 01434 381425
e-mail: stay@lowbyer.com
Dir: *on A686 edge of town towards Hexham*
This interesting 18th-century manor house is set in mature gardens on the edge of town and provides friendly and attentive service. There is an inviting lounge and an adjoining library, and imaginative meals are served in an attractive dining room.
ROOMS: 9 en suite 2 annexe en suite No smoking in all bedrooms s £60-£70; d £120-£140 (incl. bkfst & dinner) **LB** **FACILITIES:** Xmas **CONF:** Board 10 Del £90 **PARKING:** 12 **NOTES:** No dogs No smoking in restaurant **CARDS:**

ALTON, Hampshire

Map 05 SU73

★★★70% ®® Alton Grange

London Rd GU34 4EG
☎ 01420 86565 ▤ 01420 541346
e-mail: info@altongrange.co.uk
Dir: *from A31 right at rdbt signed Alton/Holybourne/Bordon B3004. Hotel 300yds on left*
A friendly and family owned hotel conveniently located on the outskirts of this market town and set in its own well manicured grounds. The individually styled bedrooms include three suites and are thoughtfully equipped, and diners can choose between the more formal Truffles Restaurant or relaxed Muffins Brasserie. The attractive public areas also include a function suite.
ROOMS: 26 en suite 4 annexe en suite (4 fmly) (7 GF) No smoking in 4 bedrooms s £81-£99; d £99-£115 (incl. bkfst) **FACILITIES:** STV Hot air ballooning **CONF:** BC Thtr 80 Class 30 Board 40 Del from £142
PARKING: 48 **NOTES:** No children 3yrs No smoking in restaurant Closed 24 Dec-2 Jan Civ Wed 100
CARDS:

★★★67% Alton House

Normandy St GU34 1LD
☎ 01420 80033 ▤ 01420 89222
e-mail: mail@altonhouse.com
Dir: *off A31, close to railway station*
Conveniently located on the edge of the town, this popular hotel offers comfortably furnished and well-equipped bedrooms. The

continued on p56

ALTON, continued

restaurant serves both carte and daily set menus, and informal meals are also served within the bar. Attractive rear gardens are a plus, along with an outdoor pool and tennis courts.
ROOMS: 39 en suite (3 fmly) (3 GF) No smoking in 2 bedrooms s fr £79; d fr £84 **LB** **FACILITIES:** STV Outdoor swimming (H) Tennis (hard) Snooker **CONF:** Thtr 170 Class 80 Board 50 Del from £120 **PARKING:** 94 **NOTES:** No dogs (ex guide dogs) Closed 25-26 Dec RS 27-29 Dec Civ Wed 70 **CARDS:**

ALTRINCHAM, Greater Manchester — Map 15 SJ78

★★★67% Cresta Court

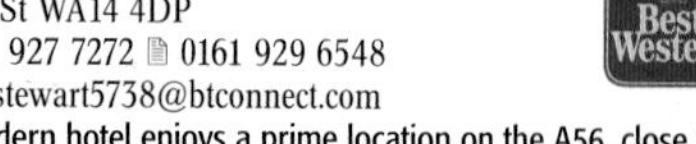

Church St WA14 4DP
☎ 0161 927 7272 📠 0161 929 6548
e-mail: stewart5738@btconnect.com
This modern hotel enjoys a prime location on the A56, close to the station and town centre shops and amenities. Bedrooms vary in style from spacious four-posters to smaller, traditionally furnished rooms. Public areas include a choice of bars, a small gym, hair and beauty salon and extensive function and conference facilities.
ROOMS: 136 en suite (2 fmly) No smoking in 80 bedrooms s £49.50-£64.50; d £59.50-£74.50 (incl. bkfst) **LB** **FACILITIES:** STV Tennis (hard & grass) Solarium Gym Putting green Beauty salon/fitness & cardiovascular training room ch fac Xmas **CONF:** BC Thtr 350 Class 200 Board 150 Del from £75 **SERVICES:** Lift **PARKING:** 200 **NOTES:** No smoking in restaurant Civ Wed 350
CARDS:

★★★67% Quality Hotel Altrincham

Langham Rd, Bowdon WA14 2HT
☎ 0161 928 7121 📠 0161 927 7560
e-mail: admin@gb064.u-net.com
Dir: *M6 junct 19 to airport, join A556, over M56 rdbt onto A56, right at traffic lights onto B5161. Hotel 1m on right*
This popular hotel is located within easy reach of the motorways and airport. It provides comfortable and well-equipped bedrooms. The public areas consist of the modern Cafe Continental, the main restaurant which offers modern cuisine, and a leisure club. A range of conference rooms are also available.
ROOMS: 91 en suite (6 fmly) No smoking in 19 bedrooms s fr £99; d fr £104 **LB** **FACILITIES:** STV Indoor swimming (H) Sauna Solarium Gym Jacuzzi Beauty treatments, Swimming pool supervised Xmas **CONF:** Thtr 165 Class 60 Board 48 Del from £120 **PARKING:** 160 **NOTES:** Civ Wed 165 **CARDS:**

⇧ Premier Lodge (Altrincham North)

Manchester Rd, West Timperley WA14 5NH
☎ 0870 9906330 📠 0870 9906631
Premier Lodge offers modern, well-equipped, en suite accommodation suitable for both business and leisure travellers. Meals can be taken at the adjacent popular restaurant and bar, which is fully licensed. For further details, consult the Hotel Groups page.
ROOMS: 48 en suite s £48; d £48

⇧ Premier Lodge (Altrincham South)

Manchester Rd WA14 4PH
☎ 0870 9906580 📠 0870 9906581
Premier Lodge offers modern, well-equipped, en suite accommodation suitable for both business and leisure travellers. Meals can be taken at the adjacent popular restaurant and bar, which is fully licensed. For further details, consult the Hotel Groups page.
ROOMS: 46 en suite s £48; d £48

ALVELEY, Shropshire — Map 10 SO78

★★★★66% Mill Hotel & Restaurant

WV15 6HL
☎ 01746 780437 📠 01746 780850
Dir: *Midway between Kidderminster & Bridgnorth, turn off A442 signposted Enville & Turley Green*
Built around a 17th-century flour mill, with the original water wheel still on display, this modern hotel is set in eight acres of landscaped grounds. Bedrooms are pleasant and include some superior rooms, which have sitting areas, and some rooms with four-poster beds. The restaurant provides carefully prepared dishes.
ROOMS: 21 en suite (3 fmly) No smoking in 18 bedrooms s £75-£110; d £88-£125 (incl. cont bkfst) **LB** **FACILITIES:** STV Small gymnasium **CONF:** Thtr 220 Class 150 Board 80 Del £120 **SERVICES:** Lift **PARKING:** 200 **NOTES:** No dogs No smoking in restaurant Civ Wed 200
CARDS:

ALVESTON, Gloucestershire — Map 04 ST68

★★★75% Alveston House

Davids Ln BS35 2LA
☎ 01454 415050 📠 01454 415425
e-mail: info@alvestonhousehotel.co.uk
Dir: *M5 junct 14 from N or junct 16 from S, on A38*
Conveniently located in a quiet area with easy access to the city and a short drive from both the M4 and M5, this smartly presented hotel provides an impressive combination of good service, friendly hospitality and a relaxed atmosphere. Bedrooms are well equipped and comfortable for either business or leisure use. The restaurant offers carefully prepared fresh food, and a pleasant bar and conservatory are the newest additions.
ROOMS: 30 en suite (1 fmly) (6 GF) No smoking in 18 bedrooms s £89.50-£99.50; d £99.50-£109.50 (incl. bkfst) **LB** **FACILITIES:** STV **CONF:** Thtr 85 Class 48 Board 50 Del from £135 **PARKING:** 75 **NOTES:** No smoking in restaurant Civ Wed 75
CARDS:

See advert under BRISTOL

⇧ Premier Lodge (Bristol North)

Thornbury Rd BS35 3LL
☎ 0870 9906496 📠 0870 9906497
Dir: *on A38 outskirts of Thornbury, approx 10m N of Bristol*
Premier Lodge offers modern, well-equipped, en suite accommodation suitable for both business and leisure travellers. Meals can be taken at the adjacent popular restaurant and bar, which is fully licensed. For further details, consult the Hotel Groups page.
ROOMS: 74 en suite s £50; d £50 **CONF:** Thtr 70 Class 40 Board 40

AMBERLEY, Gloucestershire — Map 04 SO80

★★69% ® The Amberley Inn

Culver Hill GL5 5AF
☎ 01453 872565 📠 01453 872738
e-mail: theamberley@zoom.co.uk
Dir: *on A46*
Situated on a hillside, on the edge of the common, this traditional Cotswold inn provides an equally warm welcome to both visitors and locals alike. Most bedrooms have now been upgraded and offer high standards of comfort and quality, with front facing rooms boasting wonderful panoramic views over the Woodchester Valley. Public areas include a choice of bars and the attractive

continued

restaurant where excellent local produce is used in the creation of impressive and innovative dishes.
ROOMS: 14 rms (9 en suite) (1 fmly) s £55-£65; d £75-£125 (incl. bkfst) **LB** **FACILITIES:** Xmas **CONF:** Thtr 20 Class 14 Board 14 Del from £109.50 **PARKING:** 14 **NOTES:** No smoking in restaurant
CARDS:

AMBERLEY, West Sussex Map 06 TQ01

Top 200 - Hotel

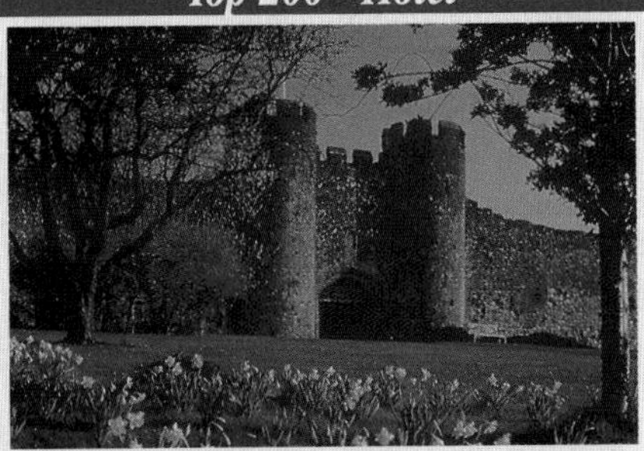

★★★ Amberley Castle

BN18 9ND
☎ 01798 831992 01798 831998
e-mail: info@amberleycastle.co.uk
Dir: *SW of village, off B2139 between Storrington and Bury Hill*
The castle has a varied and well documented history. Now a luxury hotel, guests can learn about the many past owners during a stay here. It is a treasure trove of historical interest, featuring an impressive gatehouse, portcullis and immaculate gardens. Bedrooms are charming and individually decorated, some with direct access to the battlements and ramparts. The antique-filled day rooms are the ideal place to relax with a book or take tea. Dining is a treat with accomplished cooking served in such elegant surroundings.
ROOMS: 14 en suite 5 annexe en suite (7 GF) s £145-£345; d £145-£345 **LB** **FACILITIES:** Golf 18 Tennis (hard) Croquet lawn Putting green Jacuzzi Xmas **CONF:** Thtr 50 Class 24 Board 24 Del from £250 **PARKING:** 50 **NOTES:** No dogs (ex guide dogs) No children 12yrs No smoking in restaurant Civ Wed 48
CARDS:

Late for dinner?
Quality Standards mean that last orders for dinner vary according to star rating and should be no earlier than:
★★ 7.00pm ★★★ 8.00pm ★★★★ 9.00pm
★★★★★ 10.00pm

AMBLESIDE, Cumbria Map 18 NY30
See also Elterwater

★★★77% Rothay Manor

Rothay Bridge LA22 0EH
☎ 015394 33605 015394 33607
e-mail: hotel@rothaymanor.co.uk
Dir: *In Ambleside follow signs for Coniston (A593). Hotel 0.25 mile SW of Ambleside opposite rugby pitch*
The former home of a Liverpool merchant, this attractive listed building, built in Regency style, is a short walk from both the town centre and Lake Windermere. Spacious bedrooms, including suites, family rooms and rooms with balconies, have been

continued

refurbished to a high standard. Public areas include a choice of lounges, a spacious restaurant and conference facilities.

Rothay Manor

ROOMS: 14 en suite 3 annexe en suite (7 fmly) (3 GF) No smoking in all bedrooms s £72-£90; d £120-£150 (incl. bkfst) **LB**
FACILITIES: Nearby leisure centre free to guests Xmas **CONF:** Thtr 22 Board 18 Del from £135 **PARKING:** 45 **NOTES:** No dogs (ex guide dogs) No smoking in restaurant Closed 3 Jan-6 Feb
CARDS:

See advert on this page

★★★75% Regent

Waterhead Bay LA22 0ES
☎ 015394 32254 015394 31474
e-mail: info@regentlakes.co.uk
Dir: *1m S on A591*
This attractive holiday hotel, situated close to Waterhead Bay, offers a warm welcome. Bedrooms come in a variety of styles,

continued on p58

AMBLESIDE, continued

including three suites and five bedrooms in the garden wing. There is a modern swimming pool and the restaurant offers a fine dining experience in a contemporary setting.

Regent, Ambleside

ROOMS: 30 en suite (7 fmly) No smoking in 4 bedrooms **FACILITIES:** Indoor swimming (H) **PARKING:** 39 **NOTES:** No smoking in restaurant **CARDS:**

★★★71% Ambleside Salutation Hotel

Best Western

Lake Rd LA22 9BX
☎ 015394 32244 015394 34157
e-mail: enquiries@hotelambleside.uk.com
Dir: *A591 to Ambleside, onto one-way system down Wansfell Rd into Compston Rd. Right at lights back into village*

A former coaching inn, this hotel has been welcoming guests since the 1600s. Bedrooms vary in size, and all are tastefully appointed and thoughtfully equipped; many boast balconies and delightful views. Bright public areas include an attractive restaurant and there is also a choice of spacious lounges.
ROOMS: 38 en suite 4 annexe en suite (4 fmly) No smoking in 9 bedrooms s £45-£56; d £90-£112 (incl. bkfst) **LB FACILITIES: Spa** STV Sauna Gym Jacuzzi Free membership of nearby leisure club Xmas **CONF:** Thtr 150 Class 40 Board 16 Del from £90 **PARKING:** 50 **NOTES:** No smoking in restaurant **CARDS:**

See advert on opposite page

★★★67% Skelwith Bridge

Skelwith Bridge LA22 9NJ
☎ 015394 32115 015394 34254
e-mail: skelwithbr@aol.com
Dir: *2.5m W on A593 at junct with B5343 to Langdale*
This delightful 17th-century inn is peacefully located at the heart of the Lake District National Park. It offers high standards of comfort and friendly service. Bedrooms include rooms with four-poster beds, and are tastefully appointed and thoughtfully equipped.

continued

Spacious public areas include a choice of lounges and bars and the elegant Bridge restaurant overlooks the stunning Lakeland fells.
ROOMS: 22 en suite 6 annexe en suite (2 fmly) No smoking in 22 bedrooms s £38-£58; d £66-£106 (incl. bkfst) **LB FACILITIES:** Xmas **CONF:** Thtr 45 Class 25 Board 25 Del from £75 **PARKING:** 60 **NOTES:** No smoking in restaurant **CARDS:**

★★76% ®® *Fisherbeck*

Lake Rd LA22 0DH
☎ 015394 33215 015394 33600
e-mail: email@fisherbeck.com
Dir: *S of Ambleside on A591*

This friendly, family-owned and run hotel offers a high standard of service and memorable hospitality. Bedrooms, many of which offer modern décor, vary in size and include rooms with balconies affording lovely mountain views. Carefully prepared, creative food is served in the elegant split-level restaurant, and impressive bar meals are also available.
ROOMS: 18 en suite (2 fmly) No smoking in 6 bedrooms **FACILITIES:** Free use of nearby Leisure Complex **PARKING:** 24 **NOTES:** No dogs No smoking in restaurant Closed 26 Dec-15 Jan **CARDS:**

★★70% *Waterhead*

Lake Rd LA22 0ER
☎ 015394 32566 015394 31255
e-mail: waterhead@elhmail.co.uk
Dir: *A591 into Ambleside, hotel opposite Waterhead Pier*
With an enviable location opposite the bay, this well established hotel offers fine views across the lake from many bedrooms. In addition to the main restaurant there is also an informal Mediterranean-style café bar and a lively Irish theme bar. Extensive alterations will close the hotel during the winter of 2003/2004, reopening at Easter in a new superior style.
ROOMS: 27 en suite (3 fmly) No smoking in 14 bedrooms **FACILITIES:** STV Use of sister hotel's leisure facilities entertainment **CONF:** Thtr 40 Class 30 Board 25 **PARKING:** 50 **NOTES:** No smoking in restaurant **CARDS:**

AMERSHAM, Buckinghamshire Map 06 SU99

★★★69% The Crown

MACDONALD HOTELS

High St HP7 0DH
☎ 0870 400 8103 01494 431283
e-mail: crown@macdonald-hotels.co.uk
Combining the charm of a bygone era with the modern conveniences expected by today's traveller, this 16th-century coaching inn is a great base for antique shopping and walks in the Chilterns. One claim to fame is that the hotel was featured in the film 'Four Weddings and a Funeral'. Bedrooms are a strength, all

continued

A

are individually styled and some feature original hand-painted murals.
ROOMS: 19 en suite 18 annexe en suite (3 fmly) No smoking in 21 bedrooms **FACILITIES:** STV **CONF:** Board 15 Del from £150 **PARKING:** 30 **NOTES:** No smoking in restaurant
CARDS:

AMESBURY, Wiltshire Map 05 SU14

★★61% *Antrobus Arms*

15 Church St SP4 7EU
☎ 01980 623163 01980 622112
e-mail: reception@antrobushotel.co.uk
Dir: *A303 rdbt through one way system. Turn left at t-junct & hotel on left*
Claiming to be the nearest hotel to Stonehenge, The Antrobus Arms offers individually furnished bedrooms, some of which overlook the walled Victorian garden at the rear of the property. With a history dating back to the 17th century, there is much character here, with public rooms reflecting the elegance of the past. Bar meals are available as an alternative to the main restaurant.
ROOMS: 16 en suite (2 fmly) **FACILITIES:** STV Tennis (hard) **CONF:** Thtr 40 Class 40 Board 20 **PARKING:** 15 **NOTES:** No smoking in restaurant **CARDS:**

Travelodge

Countess Services SP4 7AS
☎ 08700 850 950 01980 624966
Dir: *junct A345 & A303 eastbound*
Travelodge offers good quality, good value, modern accommodation. Ideal for families, the spacious, en suite bedrooms include remote-control TV, tea and coffee-making facilities, luxury beds and free morning newspaper. Meals can be taken at the nearby family restaurant. For further details and the Travelodge phone number, consult the Hotel Groups page.
ROOMS: 48 en suite s fr £42.95; d fr £42.95

ANDOVER, Hampshire Map 05 SU34

★★★72% Esseborne Manor

SP11 0ER
☎ 01264 736444 01264 736725
e-mail: esseborne@aol.com
Dir: *halfway between Andover & Newbury on A343, just N of Hurstbourne Tarrant*

Set in two acres of well-tended gardens, this attractive manor house is surrounded by the open countryside of the North Wessex Downs. Bedrooms are delightfully individual and are split between the main house, an adjoining courtyard and separate garden

continued on p60

ANDOVER, continued

cottage. A wonderfully relaxed atmosphere pervades throughout, with public rooms combining elegance with comfort.
ROOMS: 6 en suite 8 annexe en suite (6 GF) s £95-£130; d £100-£180 (incl. bkfst) **LB** **FACILITIES:** STV Tennis (hard) Croquet lawn
CONF: Thtr 40 Class 35 Board 20 Del £140 **PARKING:** 50 **NOTES:** No smoking in restaurant Civ Wed 120
CARDS:

See advert on opposite page

★★★62% Quality Hotel Andover

Micheldever Rd SP11 6LA
☎ 01264 369111 🖷 01264 369000
e-mail: andover@quality-hotels.co.uk
Dir: *off A303 at A3093. 1st rdbt take 1st exit, 2nd rdbt take 1st exit. Turn left immediately before BP petrol station, then left*
Located on the outskirts of the town, this hotel is popular with business guests. Bedrooms offer some smart new rooms, and public areas consist of a cosy lounge, a hotel bar and a traditional style restaurant serving a range of meals. There is also a large conference suite available.
ROOMS: 13 en suite 36 annexe en suite (13 GF) No smoking in 21 bedrooms s £55-£79; d £65-£89 (incl. bkfst) **LB** **FACILITIES:** STV Xmas
CONF: BC Thtr 180 Class 40 Board 60 Del from £85 **PARKING:** 100
NOTES: No dogs (ex guide dogs) No smoking in restaurant Civ Wed 85
CARDS:

ANSTY, Warwickshire — Map 11 SP48

★★★★70% Ansty Hall

Main Rd CV7 9HZ
☎ 024 7661 2222 🖷 024 7660 2155
e-mail: ansty@macdonald-hotels.co.uk
Dir: *M6 junct 2 onto B4065 signed 'Ansty'. Hotel 1.5m on left*
At 300ft above sea level, this lovely Georgian house, set in an acre of beautiful gardens and woodland, is literally one of the high spots in the county. The hotel's central location makes this an ideal base from which to explore the many attractions in the area. Bedrooms are traditional in style, richly furnished and well equipped; rooms in the main house are particularly spacious.
ROOMS: 23 en suite 39 annexe en suite (4 fmly) (22 GF) No smoking in 24 bedrooms s £90-£160; d £90-£160 **LB** **FACILITIES:** Xmas
CONF: Thtr 200 Class 60 Board 60 Del from £135 **SERVICES:** Lift
PARKING: 150 **NOTES:** No smoking in restaurant Civ Wed 100
CARDS:

APPLEBY-IN-WESTMORLAND, Cumbria — Map 18 NY62

★★★77% ® Appleby Manor Country House

Roman Rd CA16 6JB
☎ 017683 51571 🖷 017683 52888
e-mail: reception@applebymanor.co.uk
Dir: *M6 junct 40/A66 towards Brough. Take Appleby turn, then immediately right. Continue 0.5m*
This imposing country mansion is set in extensive grounds amid fabulous Cumbrian scenery. The Dunbobbin family and their experienced staff ensure a warm welcome and attentive service. Bedrooms, including a number with patios, vary in style, with the garden rooms having been refurbished. The bar offers a wide range of malt whiskies and the restaurant serves carefully prepared meals.

ROOMS: 23 en suite 7 annexe en suite (9 fmly) No smoking in 12 bedrooms s £75-£93; d £110-£146 (incl. bkfst) **LB** **FACILITIES:** STV Indoor swimming (H) Sauna Solarium Putting green Jacuzzi Steam room, Table tennis, Pool table **CONF:** Thtr 38 Class 25 Board 28 Del from £119.50 **PARKING:** 53 **NOTES:** No smoking in restaurant Closed 24-26 Dec **CARDS:**

See advert on opposite page

★★★69% Tufton Arms

Market Square CA16 6XA
☎ 017683 51593 🖷 017683 52761
e-mail: info@tuftonarmshotel.co.uk
Dir: *in centre of Appleby, by-passed by A66, on B6260*
Located in the centre of the medieval Cumbrian market town, this former coaching inn has been stylishly refurbished to retain much of its Victorian character. Bedrooms, which vary in size and style, include some fine period suites, studio rooms and mews rooms. Meals are served in the conservatory restaurant and the bar boasts an impressive range of wines served by the glass.
ROOMS: 21 en suite (4 fmly) (2 GF) s £57.50-£95; d £95-£150 (incl. bkfst) **LB** **FACILITIES:** STV Fishing Shooting Xmas **CONF:** BC Thtr 100 Class 60 Board 50 Del from £99 **PARKING:** 16 **NOTES:** Civ Wed 100
CARDS:

★★67% Royal Oak Inn

Bongate CA16 6UN
☎ 017683 51463 🖷 017683 52300
e-mail: RoyalOakInn@mortalmaninns.fsnet.co.uk
Dir: *M6 junct 38 follow B6260, hotel 0.5m from Appleby centre on A66 towards Scotch Corner*

This traditional 17th-century coaching inn, with exposed beams and open fires, offers a choice of bars where locals mingle with visitors. Meals can be taken in the lounge bar, and the wide-ranging menu is also served in the atmospheric restaurant.

continued

Bedrooms vary in size and style, the superior rooms offering greater comfort.
ROOMS: 9 rms (7 en suite) (1 fmly) d £69 (incl. bkfst) **LB** **FACILITIES:** Xmas **CONF:** Class 20 Board 15 **PARKING:** 13 **NOTES:** No smoking in restaurant **CARDS:**

ARNCLIFFE, North Yorkshire Map 18 SD97

★★76% **Amerdale House**
BD23 5QE
☎ 01756 770250 01756 770266
Dir: *left at Threshfield-Kettlewell road 0.5m past Kilnsey Crag*

This former manor house enjoys a peaceful, idyllic location with wonderful views of the dale and fells from every room. Spacious, inviting public areas are tastefully furnished and have real fires in winter. A daily-changing imaginative menu and impressive wine list are offered in the elegant dining room. Bedrooms are beautifully decorated and elegantly furnished.
ROOMS: 10 en suite 1 annexe en suite (3 fmly) d £156-£161 (incl. bkfst & dinner) **LB** **PARKING:** 30 **NOTES:** No dogs (ex guide dogs) No smoking in restaurant Closed mid Nov-mid Mar
CARDS:

ARUNDEL, West Sussex Map 06 TQ00

★★★71% **Burpham Country House & Restaurant**
Old Down, Burpham BN18 9RJ
☎ 01903 882160 01903 884627
e-mail: burphamchh@ukonline.co.uk
Dir: *3m NE off A27 turn by Arundel railway station signed to hotel, Warningcamp & Burpham, continue for 2.5m along lane, hotel on right*

Dating back to the 18th century, this charming hotel is quietly located in a fold of the Sussex Downs. Bedrooms are attractively presented and public rooms include a cosy bar and lounge. The smart restaurant, which is part conservatory, serves good quality food and a warm welcome awaits all.
ROOMS: 10 en suite No smoking in all bedrooms **FACILITIES:** Croquet lawn **CONF:** Board 12 **NOTES:** No dogs No children 12yrs No smoking in restaurant **CARDS:**

ARUNDEL, continued

A

★★★66% Norfolk Arms
High St BN18 9AD
☎ 01903 882101 🖷 01903 884275
e-mail: norfolk.arms@forestdale.com

Forestdale Hotels

Built by the 10th Duke of Norfolk, this Georgian coaching inn enjoys a superb setting beneath the battlements of Arundel Castle. Bedrooms come in a variety of sizes and styles, all are well equipped. Public areas include two bars, a comfortable lounge, a traditional English restaurant and a range of meeting rooms.
ROOMS: 21 en suite 13 annexe en suite (4 fmly) (8 GF) No smoking in 6 bedrooms s fr £75; d fr £115 (incl. bkfst) **LB** **FACILITIES:** Xmas **CONF:** Thtr 100 Class 40 Board 40 Del from £110 **PARKING:** 34 **NOTES:** No smoking in restaurant Civ Wed 60
CARDS:

★★66% Comfort Inn
Crossbush BN17 7QQ
☎ 01903 840840 🖷 01903 849849
e-mail: admin@gb642.u-net.com
Dir: *A27/A284, 1st right into services*

Comfort Inn BY CHOICE HOTELS

This modern, purpose-built hotel provides a good base for exploring the nearby historic town of Arundel and the ancient walled city of Chichester. Good access to local road networks and a range of meeting rooms, all air conditioned, also make this an ideal venue for business guests. Bedrooms are spacious, smartly decorated and well-equipped.
ROOMS: 53 en suite (25 GF) No smoking in 39 bedrooms **FACILITIES:** STV **CONF:** Thtr 30 Class 30 Board 30 Del from £50 **PARKING:** 53 **NOTES:** No smoking in restaurant
CARDS:

⌂ Travel Inn
Crossbush Ln BN18 9PQ
☎ 08701 977016 🖷 01903 884381
Dir: *1m E of Arundel at intersection of A27/A284*

travel inn

Travel Inn offers good-quality, value-for-money accommodation. Spacious, en suite rooms with bath and shower comfortably accommodate a family of up to two adults and two children (to age 15). The restaurant and bar offers a varied menu. For further details and the Travel Inn phone number, consult the Hotel Groups page.
ROOMS: 30 en suite s £44.95; d £44.95 **CONF:** Thtr 50 Board 26

ASCOT, Berkshire Map 06 SU96

★★★★70% ◎ The Royal Berkshire Ramada Plaza
London Rd, Sunninghill SL5 0PP
☎ 01344 623322 🖷 01344 627100
e-mail: royalberkshireRS@jarvis.co.uk
Dir: *A30 towards Bagshot, right opp Wentworth Club onto A329, continue for 2m, hotel entrance on right*

Once occupied by the Churchill family, this delightful Queen Anne house is set in 14 acres of attractive gardens on the edge of Ascot. Public areas include a comfortable lounge bar, an attractive restaurant which overlooks the rear gardens and extensive conference facilities. The main house has been skilfully extended to offer smart, well-equipped bedrooms.
ROOMS: 63 en suite (1 fmly) No smoking in 34 bedrooms s £79-£215; d £99-£240 **LB** **FACILITIES:** STV Indoor swimming (H) Tennis (hard) Sauna Gym Croquet lawn Putting green Jacuzzi **CONF:** BC Thtr 90 Class 60 Board 35 Del from £175 **PARKING:** 250 **NOTES:** No smoking in restaurant Civ Wed 93 **CARDS:**

★★★★64% The Berystede
Bagshot Rd, Sunninghill SL5 9JH
☎ 0870 400 8111 🖷 01344 872301
e-mail: berystede@macdonald-hotels.co.uk
Dir: *A30/B3020 (Windmill Pub). Continue 1.25m to hotel on left just before junct with A330*

MACDONALD HOTELS

This impressive Victorian mansion, close to Ascot Racecourse, is set in nine acres of wooded grounds. Spacious bedrooms have comfortable armchairs and internet facilities for guest use. There is a cosy bar and fine traditional restaurant which overlooks the heated outdoor swimming pool and gardens. An excellent range of modern meeting rooms is available.
ROOMS: 90 en suite (26 fmly) No smoking in 58 bedrooms s £49-£200; d £98-£200 (incl. bkfst) **LB** **FACILITIES:** STV Outdoor swimming (H) Croquet lawn Putting green Xmas **CONF:** BC Thtr 150 Class 90 Board 70 Del from £160 **SERVICES:** Lift **PARKING:** 240 **NOTES:** No smoking in restaurant Civ Wed 60 **CARDS:**

★★69% Highclere
19 Kings Rd, Sunninghill SL5 9AD
☎ 01344 625220 🖷 01344 872528
e-mail: info@highclerehotel.com
Dir: *opp Sunninghill Post Office*
This privately owned establishment is situated in a quiet residential area, not far from local attractions and road networks. Modest bedrooms are attractively decorated and well equipped. A cosy bar is available adjacent to the comfortable conservatory lounge. A range of home cooked meals is on offer in the restaurant.
ROOMS: 11 en suite (1 fmly) (2 GF) No smoking in 5 bedrooms s £85-£100; d £95-£110 (incl. bkfst) **FACILITIES:** Xmas **CONF:** Board 20 Del from £120 **PARKING:** 11 **NOTES:** No dogs (ex guide dogs) No smoking in restaurant **CARDS:**

★★65% Brockenhurst
Brockenhurst Rd SL5 9HA
☎ 01344 621912 🖷 01344 873252
Dir: *on A330*
This attractive Edwardian house is situated south of the town and offers easy access to the racecourse, the historic town of Windsor and several local golf courses. Relaxed, informal service is provided in a friendly manner throughout including the small bar, lounge and restaurant. Bedrooms are mostly spacious and feature a range of thoughtful extras.
ROOMS: 12 en suite 5 annexe en suite (2 fmly) (2 GF) s £89-£100; d £100-£200 (incl. cont bkfst) **FACILITIES:** STV **CONF:** Thtr 50 Class 25 Board 30 **PARKING:** 32 **NOTES:** No dogs (ex guide dogs) No smoking in restaurant **CARDS:**

⌂ Innkeeper's Lodge Ascot
London Rd SL5 7SB
☎ 01344 870931 🖷 01344 870932
Dir: *M25 junct 13, at rdbt take A30 towards Sunningdale. Turn right onto A329 towards Ascot, continue for 1m and Lodge on right*

Innkeeper's Lodge

A new concept in the travel accommodation market. Smart rooms meet essential business requirements but also have home

continued

comforts. Dining options include all-day menus plus the added advantage of breakfast, which is included in the room price. For further details, consult the Hotel Groups page.
ROOMS: 10 en suite

ASHBOURNE, Derbyshire Map 10 SK14

★★★74% Callow Hall
Mappleton Rd DE6 2AA
01335 300900 01335 300512
e-mail: reservations@callowhall.demon.co.uk
Dir: *A515 through Ashbourne towards Buxton, left at Bowling Green pub, then 1st right*
This delightful, creeper-clad, early Victorian house, set on a 44-acre estate, enjoys views over Bentley Brook and the Dove Valley. The atmosphere is relaxed and welcoming and some spacious bedrooms in the main house have comfortable sitting areas. Public rooms feature high ceilings, ornate plasterwork and antique furniture. There is a good range of dishes available on both the fixed price and carte menus.
ROOMS: 16 en suite (2 fmly) No smoking in 8 bedrooms s £90-£110; d £130-£195 (incl. bkfst) **LB FACILITIES:** Fishing **CONF:** Thtr 30 Board 16 Del from £144 **PARKING:** 21 **NOTES:** No dogs (ex guide dogs) No smoking in restaurant Closed 25-26 Dec RS Sunday
CARDS:

See advert on this page

★★★66% Hanover International Hotel & Club
Derby Rd DE6 1XH
01335 346666 01335 346549
e-mail: hanoversales@ashbourneh.freeserve.co.uk
Dir: *A52 to Ashbourne, at rdbt turn right to Airfield Ind Est, hotel 400yds on right*

This modern, purpose-built hotel is just a short drive from the town on the Derby Road. It offers comfortable, well-equipped bedrooms, some of which are especially designed for visitors with disabilities. The indoor leisure facilities, which include a good-sized swimming pool and sauna, are an added attraction.
ROOMS: 50 en suite (5 fmly) No smoking in 10 bedrooms **FACILITIES:** STV Indoor swimming (H) Sauna Gym Steam room Fitness room **CONF:** Thtr 200 Class 100 Board 80 Del £130 **SERVICES:** Lift **PARKING:** 130 **NOTES:** No dogs (ex guide dogs) No smoking in restaurant Civ Wed 200 **CARDS:**

★★64% The Dog & Partridge Country Inn
THE INDEPENDENTS
Swinscoe DE6 2HS
01335 343183 01335 342742
e-mail: info@dogandpartridge.co.uk
Dir: *A52 towards Leek, hotel 4m on left*
This 17th-century inn sits in the hamlet of Swinscoe, within easy

continued

reach of Alton Towers. Accommodation styles vary; most are separate weather-boarded rooms within the grounds. Well-presented self-catering units are sometimes used during quieter periods. Meals are available every evening until late and can be enjoyed either in the bar or the newly added conservatory.
ROOMS: 25 en suite (15 fmly) s £40-£65; d £70-£95 (incl. bkfst) **LB FACILITIES:** Fishing ch fac Xmas **CONF:** Thtr 20 Class 15 Board 18 Del from £75 **PARKING:** 115 **NOTES:** No smoking in restaurant
CARDS:

ASHBURTON, Devon Map 03 SX77

★★★74% Holne Chase
Two Bridges Rd TQ13 7NS
01364 631471 01364 631453
e-mail: info@holne-chase.co.uk
Dir: *3m N on unclass Two Bridges/Tavistock road*

This former hunting lodge is peacefully situated in a secluded

continued on p64

ASHBURTON, continued

position, with sweeping lawns leading to the river and panoramic views of the moor. Bedrooms are attractively and individually furnished, and there are a number of split-level suites available. Good quality local produce features on the daily-changing menu.
ROOMS: 10 en suite 7 annexe en suite (9 fmly) (1 GF) s £95-£105; d £140-£230 (incl. bkfst) **LB** **FACILITIES:** Fishing Riding Croquet lawn Putting green Fly fishing, Riding, Beauty treatments for people and dogs Xmas **CONF:** Thtr 40 Class 60 Board 60 Del from £150 **PARKING:** 40 **NOTES:** No smoking in restaurant **CARDS:**

ASHBY-DE-LA-ZOUCH, Leicestershire Map 11 SK31

Travel Inn

Flagstaff Island LE65 1DS
☎ 08701 977281 🖷 01530 561211
Dir: *at junction of A66 & A67 turn left by Morrisons towards Darlington. The Travel Inn 100mtrs ahead*
Travel Inn offers good-quality, value-for-money accommodation. Spacious, en suite rooms with bath and shower comfortably accommodate a family of up to two adults and two children (to age 15). The restaurant and bar offers a varied menu. For further details and the Travel Inn phone number, consult the Hotel Groups page.
ROOMS: 40 en suite s £44.95; d £44.95

ASHFORD, Kent Map 07 TR04

Top 200 - Hotel

★★★★ Eastwell Manor

Eastwell Park, Boughton Lees TN25 4HR
☎ 01233 213000 🖷 01233 635530
e-mail: eastwell@marstonhotels.com
Dir: *on A251, 200yds on left when entering Boughton Aluph*
Set in 62 acres of beautifully kept grounds, this lovely hotel dates back to the Norman conquest and boasts a number of interesting features, including carved wood-panelled rooms and huge baronial stone fireplaces. Accommodation is divided between the manor house bedrooms and the courtyard apartments in the mews cottages.
ROOMS: 23 en suite 39 annexe en suite (2 fmly) No smoking in 4 bedrooms s fr £159; d fr £178 **LB** **FACILITIES:** **Spa** STV Indoor swimming (H) Outdoor swimming (H) Tennis (hard) Sauna Solarium Gym Croquet lawn Putting green Jacuzzi Boules, Hairdressing salon & Beauty spa Xmas **CONF:** Thtr 200 Class 60 Board 48 Del from £185 **SERVICES:** Lift **PARKING:** 200 **NOTES:** No smoking in restaurant Civ Wed 250
CARDS:

★★★★66% Ashford International

Simone Weil Av TN24 8UX
☎ 01233 219988 🖷 01233 647743
e-mail: info@ashfordinthotel.com
Dir: *off M20 junct 9*

Ideally situated just off the M20, with its links to the channel tunnel and ferry terminal. Public areas feature a superb mall which houses a range of boutiques and eating places, including a popular brasserie, the Alhambra Restaurant and Florentine Bar. The spacious bedrooms are pleasantly furnished and equipped with modern facilities.
ROOMS: 200 en suite (4 fmly) No smoking in 57 bedrooms s £70-£110; d £90-£110 **LB** **FACILITIES:** STV Indoor swimming (H) Sauna Solarium Gym Jacuzzi **CONF:** BC Thtr 400 Class 160 Del from £145 **SERVICES:** Lift **PARKING:** 400 **NOTES:** No smoking in restaurant Closed 24-28 Dec Civ Wed 200 **CARDS:**

U *Holiday Inn Ashford-Central*

Canterbury Rd TN24 8QQ
☎ 0870 400 9001 🖷 01233 643176
e-mail: ashford@ichotelsgroup.com
Dir: *off A28*
At the time of going to press, the star classification for this hotel was not confirmed. Please refer to the AA internet site www.theAA.com for current information.
ROOMS: 103 en suite (47 fmly) No smoking in 60 bedrooms **FACILITIES:** ch fac **CONF:** Thtr 120 Class 65 Board 40 **PARKING:** 110 **NOTES:** No dogs (ex guide dogs) **CARDS:**

Travel Inn

Maidstone Rd, Hothfield Common TN26 1AP
☎ 08701 977018 🖷 01233 713945
Dir: *on A20, between Ashford & Charing, close to M20 junct 8/9*
Travel Inn offers good-quality, value-for-money accommodation. Spacious, en suite rooms with bath and shower comfortably accommodate a family of up to two adults and two children (to age 15). The restaurant and bar offers a varied menu. For further details and the Travel Inn phone number, consult the Hotel Groups page.
ROOMS: 60 en suite s £44.95; d £44.95

Travel Inn (Ashford Central)

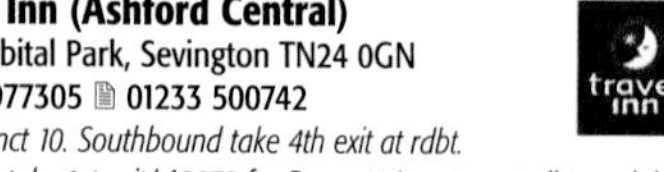

Hall Av, Orbital Park, Sevington TN24 0GN
☎ 08701 977305 🖷 01233 500742
Dir: *M20 junct 10. Southbound take 4th exit at rdbt. Northbound take 1st exit/ A2070 for Brenzett. Inn at next rdbt on right*
Travel Inn offers good-quality, value-for-money accommodation. Spacious, en suite rooms with bath and shower comfortably

continued

accommodate a family of up to two adults and two children (to age 15). The restaurant and bar offers a varied menu. For further details and the Travel Inn phone number, consult the Hotel Groups page.
ROOMS: 60 en suite s £44.95; d £44.95

Travelodge
Eureka Leisure Park TN25 4BN
☎ 08700 850 950
Dir: *M20 junct 9, take 1st exit on left*
Travelodge offers good quality, good value, modern accommodation. Ideal for families, the spacious, en suite bedrooms include remote-control TV, tea and coffee-making facilities, luxury beds and free morning newspaper. Meals can be taken at the nearby family restaurant. For further details and the Travelodge phone number, consult the Hotel Groups page.
ROOMS: 67 en suite s fr £42.95; d fr £42.95

ASHFORD-IN-THE-WATER, Derbyshire — Map 16 SK16

★★★79% Riverside House
Fennel St DE45 1QF
☎ 01629 814275 01629 812873
e-mail: riversidehouse@enta.net
Dir: *turn right off A6 Bakewell/Buxton road 2m from Bakewell, hotel at end of main street*
Partly dating back to 1630, this delightful hotel in the centre of the village is surrounded by gardens beside the River Wye. It offers individually decorated bedrooms, and public rooms include a conservatory, an oak-panelled lounge with inglenook fireplace, a drawing room and two dining rooms. Good quality cuisine is served and service is very attentive.
ROOMS: 15 en suite No smoking in all bedrooms s £85-£120; d £125-£140 (incl. bkfst) **LB FACILITIES:** STV Croquet lawn Xmas **CONF:** BC Thtr 15 Class 15 Board 15 Del from £170 **PARKING:** 40 **NOTES:** No dogs (ex guide dogs) No children 10yrs No smoking in restaurant Civ Wed 30 **CARDS:**

ASHTON-UNDER-LYNE, Greater Manchester — Map 16 SJ99

★★71% York House
York Place, Richmond St OL6 7TT
☎ 0161 330 9000 0161 343 1613
e-mail: enquiries@yorkhouse-hotel.co.uk
Dir: *Take A635 to Ashton-under-Lyne, 2nd left at the police station, then take left.*
This elegant Victorian style hotel, offering friendly and attentive service, is conveniently located for Manchester Airport and the city centre. Set around a central courtyard, the bedrooms, some housed in delightful cottages, are comfortable and thoughtfully equipped. Seasons Restaurant offers a classical carte menu as well as more imaginative dishes on a seasonal theme.
ROOMS: 24 en suite 10 annexe en suite (2 fmly) (6 GF) s £52-£65; d £60-£80 (incl. bkfst) **LB FACILITIES:** STV Reduced cost at local gym/pool ch fac **CONF:** Thtr 70 Class 30 Board 24 Del from £80 **PARKING:** 34 **NOTES:** Closed 26 Dec RS Sun Civ Wed 60
CARDS:

ASHWATER, Devon — Map 03 SX39

Top 200 - Hotel

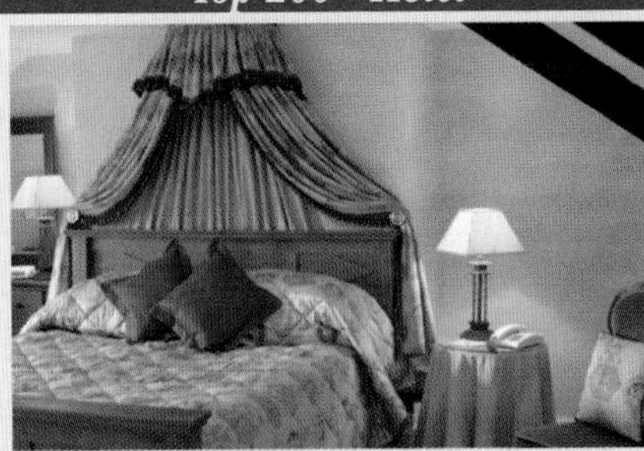

★★ Blagdon Manor Hotel & Restaurant
EX21 5DF
☎ 01409 211224 01409 211634
e-mail: stay@blagdon.com
Dir: *Take A388 N of Launceston towards Holsworthy. Approx 2m N of Chapman's Well take 2nd right for Ashwater. Next right beside Blagdon Lodge, hotel 0.25m*
Located on the Devon and Cornwall border, this small and friendly hotel offers a charming 'home-from-home' atmosphere. From the moment you arrive the tranquillity of the secluded setting, the character and charm of the house and its unhurried pace ensures calm and relaxation. High levels of service, personal touches and thoughtful extras are all part of a stay here. Stephen Morey cooks with passion and his dependence on only the finest of local ingredients speaks volumes.
ROOMS: 7 en suite No smoking in all bedrooms s £72; d £90 (incl. bkfst) **FACILITIES:** Croquet lawn Boules, giant chess/draughts **CONF:** Board 14 Del £110 **PARKING:** 10 **NOTES:** No children 12yrs No smoking in restaurant Closed 2wks Jan/Feb & 2wks Oct/Nov
CARDS:

ASPLEY GUISE, Bedfordshire — Map 11 SP93

★★★68% Moore Place
The Square MK17 8DW
☎ 01908 282000 01908 281888
e-mail: manager@mooreplace.com
Dir: *M1 junct 13, take A507 signed Aspley Guise & Woburn Sands. Hotel on left side of village square*
This impressive Georgian house, set in delightful gardens in the village centre, is very conveniently located for the M1. Bedrooms do vary in size, but consideration has been given to guest comfort, with many thoughtful extras provided. There is a wide range of meeting rooms and private dining options.
ROOMS: 39 en suite 25 annexe en suite (10 GF) No smoking in 45 bedrooms s £55-£100; d £75-£210 (incl. bkfst) **LB FACILITIES:** Xmas **CONF:** Thtr 40 Class 24 Board 20 Del £160 **PARKING:** 70 **NOTES:** No smoking in restaurant Civ Wed 80
CARDS:

ASTON CLINTON, Buckinghamshire Map 05 SP81

Innkeeper's Lodge Aylesbury East

London Rd HP22 5HP
☎ 01296 632777 📠 01296 632685
Dir: *on A41 in Aston Clinton, between Aylesbury & Tring*
A new concept in the travel accommodation market. Smart rooms meet essential business requirements but also have home comforts. Dining options include all-day menus plus the added advantage of breakfast, which is included in the room price. For further details, consult the Hotel Groups page.
ROOMS: 11 en suite

AXMINSTER, Devon Map 04 SY29
See also Colyford

★★★73% Fairwater Head

Hawkchurch EX13 5TX
☎ 01297 678349 📠 01297 678459
e-mail: reception@fairwater.demon.co.uk
Dir: *off B3165, Crewkerne to Lyme Regis road. Hotel sign to Hawkchurch*
This longstanding and well-managed hotel is peacefully located in the countryside in well-tended gardens. The proprietors and staff provide a friendly and attentive service in a relaxing environment. Bedrooms are individually decorated, spacious and comfortable, and guests can enjoy well-cooked dishes in the dining room.
ROOMS: 14 en suite 7 annexe en suite No smoking in 17 bedrooms s £80-£95; d £160-£170 (incl. bkfst) **LB FACILITIES:** Croquet lawn entertainment Xmas **CONF:** Thtr 10 Class 10 Board 10 **PARKING:** 30 **NOTES:** No smoking in restaurant Closed mid Dec- Feb (ex Xmas packages) **CARDS:**

AYLESBURY, Buckinghamshire Map 11 SP81

Top 200 - Hotel

★★★★ Hartwell House

Oxford Rd HP17 8NL
☎ 01296 747444 📠 01296 747450
e-mail: info@hartwell-house.com
Dir: *from S - M40 junct 7, follow A329 to Thame, then A418 towards Aylesbury. After 6m, through Stone, hotel on left. From N - M40 junct 9 for Bicester. Follow A41 to Aylesbury, then A418 to Oxford for 2m. Hotel on right*
This beautiful, historic house is set in 90 acres of unspoilt parkland. The grand public rooms are truly magnificent, and feature many fine artworks. Bedrooms are spacious and very comfortable, with high ceilings and sumptuous fabrics, and provide many thoughtful extras. The elegant restaurant serves an imaginative selection of seasonal dishes, created from quality local produce. Service is of a high standard.
ROOMS: 30 en suite 16 annexe en suite (10 GF) No smoking in 12 bedrooms s fr £145; d fr £240 **LB FACILITIES: Spa** STV Indoor swimming (H) Tennis (hard) Fishing Sauna Solarium Gym Croquet lawn Jacuzzi Treatment rooms & Steam rooms Supervised indoor pool entertainment Xmas **CONF:** BC Thtr 100 Class 40 Board 40 Del from £265 **SERVICES:** Lift **PARKING:** 91 **NOTES:** No children 8yrs No smoking in restaurant Civ Wed 60
CARDS:

continued

Holiday Inn Aylesbury

Aston Clinton Rd HP22 5AA
☎ 0870 400 9002 📠 01296 392211
e-mail: reservations-aylesbury@ichotelsgroup.com
Dir: *M25 junct 20, follow A41. Holiday Inn on left entering Aylesbury*
At the time of going to press, the classification for this hotel was not confirmed. Please refer to the AA internet site www.theAA.com for current information.
ROOMS: 140 en suite (46 fmly) No smoking in 46 bedrooms
FACILITIES: Indoor swimming (H) Sauna Solarium Gym Jacuzzi
CONF: Thtr 110 Class 80 Board 40 **PARKING:** 164 **NOTES:** Civ Wed 90
CARDS:

Innkeeper's Lodge Aylesbury South

40 Main St, Weston Turville HP22 5RW
☎ 01296 613131 & 0870 243 0500 📠 01296 616902
Dir: *M25 junct 20, onto A41(Hemel Hempstead). Continue for 12m to Aston Clinton. Left onto B4544 to Weston Turville, Lodge on left*
A new concept in the travel accommodation market. Smart rooms meet essential business requirements but also have home comforts. Dining options include all-day menus plus the added advantage of breakfast, which is included in the room price. For further details, consult the Hotel Groups page.
ROOMS: 16 en suite

Travel Inn

Buckingham Rd HP19 9QL
☎ 08701 977019 📠 01206 330432
Dir: *N from Aylesbury centre on A413, Travel Inn 1m on left, adjacent to rdbt*

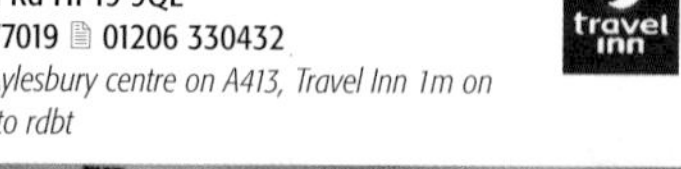

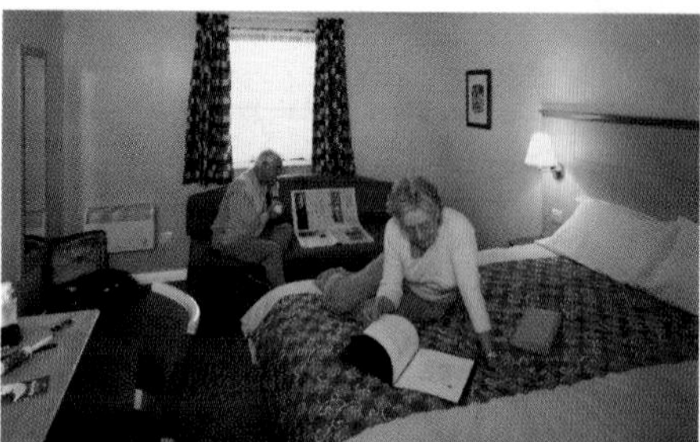

Travel Inn offers good-quality, value-for-money accommodation. Spacious, en suite rooms with bath and shower comfortably accommodate a family of up to two adults and two children (to age 15). The restaurant and bar offers a varied menu. For further details and the Travel Inn phone number, consult the Hotel Groups page.
ROOMS: 64 en suite s £44.95; d £44.95

B

AYSGARTH, North Yorkshire Map 19 SE08

★★67% **George & Dragon Inn**
DL8 3AD
☎ 01969 663358 📠 01969 663773
Dir: *A684 from Leyburn, on left entering village*
This 17th-century coaching inn offers spacious, comfortably appointed rooms, many with original wooden beams. Popular with walkers, the cosy bar has a real fire and a good selection of local beers. The restaurant serves fresh local produce and hearty breakfasts.
ROOMS: 7 en suite (2 fmly) s £31-£49.50; d £62-£69 (incl. bkfst) **LB**
FACILITIES: Xmas **PARKING:** 35 **NOTES:** No smoking in restaurant
CARDS:

BABBACOMBE See Torquay

BADMINTON, Gloucestershire Map 04 ST88

★★68% **Bodkin House Hotel & Restaurant**
Petty France GL9 1AF
☎ 01454 238310 📠 01454 238422
e-mail: info@bodkin-house-hotel.co.uk
Dir: *4.8m N of M4 junct 18 on A46*
Charming 17th-century inn situated just a short drive from the M4. The property has a wealth of historic character such as open fires, flagstone floors and oak panelling. Bedrooms are pleasantly decorated, furnished with pine pieces and have a good range of useful extras. Public rooms include an intimate restaurant, a sunny conservatory and a popular lounge bar.
ROOMS: 11 en suite (3 fmly) (2 GF) No smoking in 6 bedrooms s £65; d £80-£95 (incl. bkfst) **LB** **FACILITIES:** Children's play area ch fac Xmas **CONF:** BC Thtr 50 Class 50 Board 20 Del from £100 **PARKING:** 40 **NOTES:** No smoking in restaurant **CARDS:**

BAGINTON, Warwickshire Map 11 SP37

★★70% ***Old Mill***
Mill Hill CV8 3AH
☎ 024 7630 2241 📠 024 7630 7070
Dir: *in village 0.25m from junct A45 & A46*

Enjoying a peaceful riverside location, yet within easy reach of the motorway networks, the Old Mill has been completely refurbished to a high standard. Public areas include the popular Chef & Brewer bar and restaurant, with a pleasant patio for summer evenings. Spacious bedrooms are smartly appointed and well equipped.
ROOMS: 28 en suite (6 fmly) **CONF:** Class 16 Board 20 **PARKING:** 200
NOTES: No dogs (ex guide dogs) No smoking in restaurant
CARDS:

BAGSHOT, Surrey Map 06 SU96

Top 200 - Hotel

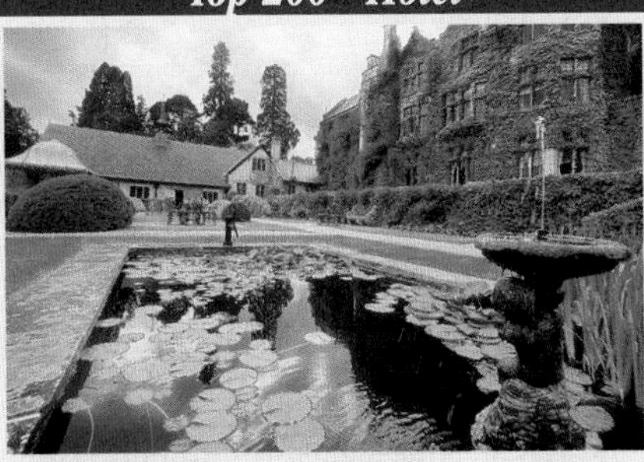

★★★★★ ⊛⊛⊛ **Pennyhill Park**
London Rd GU19 5EU
☎ 01276 471774 📠 01276 473217
e-mail: enquiries@pennyhillpark.co.uk
Dir: *on A30 between Bagshot & Camberley opposite Texaco garage*
EXCLUSIVE HOTELS & GOLF CLUBS
This well-loved country house hotel, set in 120 acres of grounds, has a jogging trail and golf course and provides every modern comfort. Bedrooms are individually decorated and very stylish. There are two dining options, a number of bars and lounges, and extensive lounge and room service. Phase one of 'The Spa at Pennyhill' is now open and boasts state-of-the-art leisure facilities, the second phase due to open towards the end of 2003.
ROOMS: 26 en suite 97 annexe en suite (6 fmly) (26 GF) No smoking in 20 bedrooms s £175-£500; d £180-£500 **LB**
FACILITIES: STV Golf 9 Tennis (hard) Fishing Snooker Gym Croquet lawn Archery, Clay pigeon shooting, Volleyball, spa treatment rooms entertainment Xmas **CONF:** BC Thtr 160 Class 80 Board 60 Del from £230 **SERVICES:** Lift **PARKING:** 500 **NOTES:** No smoking in restaurant Civ Wed 160 **CARDS:**

⌂ **Travel Inn**
1 London Rd GU19 5HR
☎ 08701 977021 📠 01276 451357
Dir: *on A30, 0.25m from Bagshot*
travel inn
Travel Inn offers good-quality, value-for-money accommodation. Spacious, en suite rooms with bath and shower comfortably accommodate a family of up to two adults and two children (to age 15). The restaurant and bar offers a varied menu. For further details and the Travel Inn phone number, consult the Hotel Groups page.
ROOMS: 40 en suite s £44.95; d £44.95

BAINBRIDGE, North Yorkshire Map 18 SD99

★★67% ***Rose & Crown***
DL8 3EE
☎ 01969 650225 📠 01969 650735
e-mail: stay@rose-and-crown.freeserve.co.uk
Dir: *on A684 between Hawes & Leyburn*
This old traditional coaching Inn overlooking the village green is full of character. Bedrooms are tastefully furnished and comfortably equipped. There are two well-stocked bars, one very popular with locals, both offering an interesting range of dishes.
continued on p68

BAINBRIDGE, continued

Finer dining is offered in the restaurant and a residents' lounge is also provided.

Rose & Crown, Bainbridge

ROOMS: 12 rms (11 en suite) (1 fmly) No smoking in 2 bedrooms **CONF:** Class 30 Board 30 **PARKING:** 65 **NOTES:** No smoking in restaurant **CARDS:**

BAKEWELL, Derbyshire Map 16 SK26

★★★67% Rutland Arms

The Square DE45 1BT
☎ 01629 812812 01629 812309
e-mail: rutland@bakewell.demon.co.uk
Dir: *M1 junct 28 to Matlock, A6 to Bakewell. Hotel in town centre*

This 19th-century hotel lies at the very centre of Bakewell and offers a wide range of quality accommodation. The friendly staff are attentive and welcoming, both in the adjacent Tavern bar and in the main hotel. The Four Seasons candlelit restaurant offers an interesting fine dining menu with dishes cooked to order.
ROOMS: 18 en suite 17 annexe en suite (2 fmly) No smoking in 10 bedrooms s £53-£69; d £85-£99 (incl. bkfst) **LB** **FACILITIES:** STV Xmas **CONF:** Thtr 100 Class 60 Board 40 Del from £99 **PARKING:** 25 **NOTES:** No smoking in restaurant **CARDS:**

★★73% Croft Country House

Great Longstone DE45 1TF
☎ 01629 640278 01629 640369
e-mail: jthursby@ukonline.co.uk
Dir: *3m N of Bakewell via A619 or A6 & A6020, follow A6020 for 1 mile from Ashford- in-the-Water, left to Great Longstone, hotel on right*
Set in mature gardens and grounds, this delightful Victorian house exudes charm. Public rooms leading off from the central galleried lounge include a cosy bar and a restaurant with an interesting four-course set menu. Bedrooms have modern comforts and some fine period pieces. The proprietor is an accomplished magician and there is usually an after-dinner performance on a Saturday night.

ROOMS: 9 en suite No smoking in all bedrooms s £63-£85; d £88.50-£104 (incl. bkfst) **LB** **FACILITIES:** entertainment Xmas **SERVICES:** Lift **PARKING:** 30 **NOTES:** No dogs (ex guide dogs) No children 10yrs No smoking in restaurant Closed Jan-mid Feb **CARDS:**

See advert on opposite page

★★69% Monsal Head Hotel

Monsal Head DE45 1NL
☎ 01629 640250 01629 640815
e-mail: christine@monsalhead.com
Dir: *A6 from Bakewell to Buxton. After 2m turn into Ashford-in-the-Water, take B6465 for 1m*
Popular with walkers, this friendly hotel commands one of the most splendid views in the Peak Park, overlooking Monsal Dale and the walking path along the disused railway line. Bedrooms are well equipped, and four have superb views down the valley. There is a comfortable lounge with an open fire and a wide selection of games. The hotel specialises in local foods and an extensive selection of real ales and rarer wines.
ROOMS: 7 en suite (1 fmly) s £45-£70; d £50-£100 (incl. bkfst) **LB** **CONF:** Thtr 60 Class 30 Board 30 **PARKING:** 20 **NOTES:** No smoking in restaurant Closed 25 Dec RS Nov-Mar **CARDS:**

BALDOCK, Hertfordshire Map 12 TL23

⌂ *Sleep Inn*

Baldock Services (A1M/A507), Radwell SG7 5TR
☎ 01462 832900 01462 832901
e-mail: admin@gb100.u-net.com
Dir: *400yds E of A1(M) junct 10 & A507*
This modern, purpose built accommodation offers smartly appointed, well-equipped bedrooms, with good power showers. There is a choice of adjacent food outlets where guests may enjoy breakfast, snacks and meals.
ROOMS: 62 en suite

⌂ Travelodge

Travelodge

Great North Rd, Hinxworth SG7 5EX
☎ 08700 850 950 01462 835329
Dir: *on A1, southbound*
Travelodge offers good quality, good value, modern accommodation. Ideal for families, the spacious, en suite bedrooms include remote-control TV, tea and coffee-making facilities, luxury beds and free morning newspaper. Meals can be taken at the nearby family restaurant. For further details and the Travelodge phone number, consult the Hotel Groups page.
ROOMS: 40 en suite s fr £42.95; d fr £42.95

BALSALL COMMON, West Midlands Map 10 SP27

★★★★66% Nailcote Hall

Nailcote Ln, Berkswell CV7 7DE
☎ 024 7646 6174 024 7647 0720
e-mail: info@nailcotehall.co.uk
Dir: *on B4101*

This 17th-century house, set in 15 acres of grounds, boasts a 9-hole championship golf course and Roman bath style swimming pool amongst its many facilities. Rooms are spacious and elegantly furnished. Dinner may be taken in the fine dining restaurant (elegant dress required) or the less formal Rick's Cafe & Bar.
ROOMS: 21 en suite 19 annexe en suite (2 fmly) (4 GF) s £165-£275; d £175-£275 (incl. bkfst) **LB FACILITIES: Spa** Indoor swimming (H) Golf 9 Tennis (hard) Snooker Solarium Gym Croquet lawn Putting green Jacuzzi Swimming pool supervised entertainment Xmas
CONF: Thtr 100 Class 80 Board 44 Del from £140 **SERVICES:** Lift
PARKING: 200 **NOTES:** No dogs (ex guide dogs) No smoking in restaurant Civ Wed 120 **CARDS:**

See advert under SOLIHULL

★★78% Haigs

Kenilworth Rd CV7 7EL
☎ 01676 533004 01676 535132
Dir: *on A452 4m N of Kenilworth & 6m S of M6 junct 4. 5m S of M42 junct 6. 8m N of M40 junct 15*
This family-run hotel, set in residential surroundings, offers a warm welcome, highly attentive service and very good food. The comfortable bedrooms are decorated in an attractive, homely style, and facilities include a lounge bar (offering very decent wines by the glass) and a meeting room.
ROOMS: 23 en suite No smoking in 8 bedrooms s £75-£107; d £107-£120 (incl. bkfst) **CONF:** Thtr 35 Class 20 Board 20 Del £140
PARKING: 22 **NOTES:** No dogs (ex guide dogs) No smoking in restaurant Closed 26 Dec-3 Jan & Etr RS Mon-Sat & Sun Lunch
CARDS:

Travel Inn (Balsall Common Nr NEC)

Kenilworth Rd CV7 7EX
☎ 08701 977022 01676 535929
Dir: *M42 junct 6, A45 towards Coventry for 0.5m, then A452 towards Leamington, Travel Inn 3m on right*
Travel Inn offers good-quality, value-for-money accommodation. Spacious, en suite rooms with bath and shower comfortably accommodate a family of up to two adults and two children (to age 15). The restaurant and bar offers a varied menu. For further details and the Travel Inn phone number, consult the Hotel Groups page.
ROOMS: 42 en suite s £44.95; d £44.95

B

BAMBURGH, Northumberland
Map 21 NU13

★★★71% Waren House
Waren Mill NE70 7EE
☎ 01668 214581 01668 214484
e-mail: enquiries@warenhousehotel.co.uk
Dir: *2m E of A1 turn onto B1342 to Waren Mill, at t-junct turn right, hotel 100yds on right.*

This delightful Georgian mansion is set in six acres of woodlands and offers views of the coastline. The individually designed bedrooms, including suites, are differently themed, and many have large bathrooms. Good, home-cooked food is served in the atmospheric dining room. A comfortable lounge and library are also available.
ROOMS: 11 en suite (4 fmly) No smoking in 9 bedrooms s £54-£90; d £84-£195 (incl. bkfst) **LB** **FACILITIES:** Croquet lawn Xmas **CONF:** Class 24 Board 24 Del from £98 **PARKING:** 20 **NOTES:** No children 14yrs No smoking in restaurant
CARDS:

★★73% *Victoria*
Front St NE69 7BP
☎ 01668 214431 01668 214404
e-mail: enquiries@victoriahotel.net
Dir: *off A1 N of Alnwick onto B1342, near Belford & follow signs to Bamburgh. Hotel in centre of Bamburgh opposite village green*

Overlooking the village green, this hotel has been sympathetically upgraded and offers an interesting blend of tradition and modernity. Bedrooms, some with views to Bamburgh Castle and Holy Island, are elegantly furnished. The bar is popular with locals and has a children's play area.
ROOMS: 29 en suite (2 fmly) No smoking in 18 bedrooms **FACILITIES:** Games room Childrens play den ch fac **CONF:** Thtr 50 Class 30 Board 20 **PARKING:** 12 **NOTES:** No smoking in restaurant
CARDS:

★★69% The Lord Crewe
Front St NE69 7BL
☎ 01668 214243 01668 214273
e-mail: lca@tinyonline.co.uk
Dir: *just below the castle*
Located in the heart of the village and in the shadows of the imposing Bamburgh Castle, this hotel has been developed from an old country inn. Bedrooms are generally spacious and offer good levels of comfort and facilities. Public areas include a choice of lounges, and meals are served in both the bar and the traditionally styled restaurant.
ROOMS: 18 rms (17 en suite) s £45-£75; d £86-£96 (incl. bkfst) **PARKING:** 20 **NOTES:** No dogs (ex guide dogs) No children 5yrs No smoking in restaurant Closed 7 Jan-Feb RS Dec-6 Jan
CARDS:

★★65% *The Mizen Head*
Lucker Rd NE69 7BS
☎ 01668 214254 01668 214104
Dir: *off A1 onto B1341 for Bamburgh. Hotel 1st building on left entering village*

A friendly atmosphere prevails at this family run hotel, on the western edge of the village. A wide range of meals are served in both the bar and the restaurant. Ample car parking is provided and the hotel's location makes it an ideal base for exploring the beautiful Northumbrian coastline.
ROOMS: 13 rms (12 en suite) (2 fmly) **FACILITIES:** Darts ch fac **CONF:** Class 45 **PARKING:** 30 **NOTES:** No smoking in restaurant
CARDS:

BAMFORD, Derbyshire
Map 16 SK28

★★72% Yorkshire Bridge Inn
Ashopton Rd, Hope Valley S33 0AZ
☎ 01433 651361 01433 651361
e-mail: mr@ybridge.force9.co.uk
Dir: *A57 Sheffield/Glossop road, at Ladybower Reservoir take A6013 Bamford road, inn 1m on right*

A well-established country inn, ideally located beside Ladybower

continued

Dam and within reach of the Peak District's many beauty spots. The hotel offers a wide range of excellent dishes in both the bar and dining area, along with a good selection of real ales. Bedrooms are attractively furnished, comfortable and well equipped.
ROOMS: 14 en suite (3 fmly) No smoking in 10 bedrooms s £45; d £64-£80 (incl. bkfst) **LB** **FACILITIES:** Xmas **CONF:** Class 12 **PARKING:** 40 **NOTES:** No smoking in restaurant
CARDS:

BANBURY, Oxfordshire — Map 11 SP44

★★★70% Banbury House

Oxford Rd OX16 9AH
☎ 01295 259361 🖹 01295 270954
e-mail: sales@banburyhouse.co.uk
Dir: *approx 200yds from Banbury Cross on A423 towards Oxford*
Within easy reach of the Banbury Cross, this attractive Georgian property is smartly presented and offers comfortable accommodation in individually decorated and furnished bedrooms. The public areas include a spacious foyer lounge, contemporary bar and a restaurant, which serves both fixed price and carte menus. The attentive, friendly staff provide a welcoming atmoshpere.
ROOMS: 63 en suite (4 fmly) (8 GF) No smoking in 24 bedrooms **FACILITIES:** STV **CONF:** Thtr 70 Class 35 Board 28 Del £130 **PARKING:** 60 **NOTES:** No dogs (ex guide dogs) Closed 24 Dec-1 Jan
CARDS:

★★★70% Whately Hall

Banbury Cross OX16 0AN
☎ 0870 400 8104 🖹 01295 271736
e-mail: whatelyhall@macdonald-hotels.co.uk
Dir: *M40 junct 11, straight over 2 rdbts, left at 3rd, 0.25m to Banbury Cross, hotel on right*
Dating back to 1677, this ancient inn boasts many original features such as stone passages, priests' holes and a fine wooden staircase. The spacious public areas include the oak-panelled restaurant, which overlooks the attractive, well-tended gardens. Bedrooms vary in size and style; all have now been upgraded and have good facilities.
ROOMS: 69 en suite (3 fmly) No smoking in 41 bedrooms s £55-£110; d £110-£125 (incl. bkfst) **LB** **FACILITIES:** STV Croquet lawn Xmas **CONF:** Thtr 150 Class 80 Board 40 Del from £135 **SERVICES:** Lift **PARKING:** 80 **NOTES:** No smoking in restaurant Civ Wed 100
CARDS:

★★★69% Wroxton House

Wroxton St Mary OX15 6QB
☎ 01295 730777 🖹 01295 730800
e-mail: reservations@wroxtonhouse.com
Dir: *A422 from Banbury, 2.5m to Wroxton, hotel on right entering village*
Dating in parts from 1647, this partially thatched hotel is set just off the main road. Bedrooms, which have either been created out of converted cottages or situated in a tastefully built wing, are well equipped. The public areas are open plan and consist of a reception lounge and a bar, and the Inglenook Restaurant offers a peaceful atmosphere.
ROOMS: 29 en suite 3 annexe en suite (1 fmly) (7 GF) No smoking in 14 bedrooms s fr £70; d fr £85 (incl. bkfst) **LB** **FACILITIES:** Xmas **CONF:** Thtr 45 Class 20 Board 28 Del £145 **PARKING:** 100 **NOTES:** No dogs (ex guide dogs) No smoking in restaurant RS 31 Dec & 1 Jan Civ Wed 60 **CARDS:**

★★63% *Cromwell Lodge Hotel*

North Bar OX16 0TB
☎ 01295 259781 🖹 (0295) 276619
Dir: *M40 junct 11, B4662 to Banbury, left at 3rd rdbt. Follow road to traffic lights, straight over, hotel on left.*
Within walking distance of the town centre this characterful hotel dates back to the 17th century. Bedrooms are well equipped and sympathetically decorated. There is a delightful walled garden complete with ancient beech trees. Diners can choose between eating in the pleasant bar or the popular restaurant.
ROOMS: 29 en suite (2 fmly) No smoking in 21 bedrooms **FACILITIES:** STV **CONF:** Thtr 30 Class 20 Board 25 **PARKING:** 30 **NOTES:** No dogs (ex guide dogs) No smoking in restaurant
CARDS:

⌂ Premier Lodge (Banbury)

Warwick Rd, Warmington OX17 1JJ
☎ 0870 9906512 🖹 0870 9906513
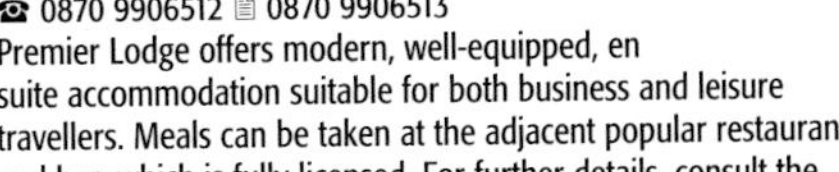
Premier Lodge offers modern, well-equipped, en suite accommodation suitable for both business and leisure travellers. Meals can be taken at the adjacent popular restaurant and bar, which is fully licensed. For further details, consult the Hotel Groups page.
ROOMS: 15 en suite s £48; d £48

BARFORD, Warwickshire — Map 10 SP26

★★★68% *The Glebe at Barford*

Church St CV35 8BS
☎ 01926 624218 🖹 01926 624625
e-mail: sales@glebehotel.co.uk
Dir: *M40 junct 15/A429 Barford/Wellesbourne. At mini island turn left, hotel 500mtrs on right*
The giant Lebanese cedar tree in front of this hotel was ancient even in 1820, when the original rectory was built. Public rooms within the house include a lounge bar and the aptly named Cedars Conservatory Restaurant which offers interesting cuisine. Individually appointed bedrooms are tastefully decorated in soft pastel fabrics, with coronet, tented ceiling or four-poster style beds.
ROOMS: 39 en suite (3 fmly) **FACILITIES:** STV Indoor swimming (H) Sauna Solarium Gym Croquet lawn Jacuzzi Beauty salon **CONF:** Thtr 120 Class 60 Board 60 **SERVICES:** Lift **PARKING:** 60
CARDS:

BARKING, Greater London — Map 06 TQ48

⌂ Hotel Ibis

Highbridge Rd IG11 7BA
☎ 020 8477 4100 🖹 020 8477 4101
e-mail: H2042@accor-hotels.com
Dir: *exit Barking on A406*
Modern, budget hotel offering comfortable accommodation in bright and practical bedrooms. Breakfast is self-service and dinner is available in the restaurant. For further details, consult the Hotel Groups page.
ROOMS: 86 en suite s £49.95-£54.95; d £49.95-£54.95

⌂ Premier Lodge (Barking)

Highbridge Rd IG11 7BA
☎ 0870 9906318 🖹 0870 9906319
Dir: *1.5m W of Barking & 0.75m from junct of A13/A406*
Premier Lodge offers modern, well-equipped, en suite accommodation suitable for both business and leisure travellers. Meals can be taken at the adjacent popular restaurant and bar, which is fully licensed. For further details, consult the Hotel Groups page.
ROOMS: 88 en suite s £56; d £56

BARLBOROUGH, Derbyshire Map 16 SK47

⌂ Hotel Ibis Sheffield South

Tallys End, Chesterfield Rd S43 4TX
☎ 01246 813222 ▯ 01246 813444
e-mail: H3157@accor-hotels.com
Dir: *M1 junct 30. Towards A619, right at rdbt towards Chesterfield. Hotel immediately left*

Modern, budget hotel offering comfortable accommodation in bright and practical bedrooms. Breakfast is self-service and dinner is available in the restaurant. For further details, consult the Hotel Groups page.
ROOMS: 86 en suite s £29.95-£39.95; d £29.95-£39.95 **CONF:**

BARNBY MOOR, Nottinghamshire Map 16 SK68

★★★66% Ye Olde Bell Hotel

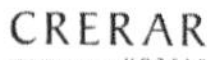

DN22 8QS
☎ 01777 705121 ▯ 01777 860424
e-mail: yeoldebell@crerarhotels.com
Dir: *on A638 midway between Retford and Bawtry*

Formerly a posting house on the London to York mail coach route, this charming inn has been welcoming guests for more than three centuries. Public rooms include the very smart, oak-panelled 1650 restaurant, a choice of lounges and an informal bar. Bedrooms vary in size and some overlook the attractive and well-kept gardens.
ROOMS: 51 en suite (12 fmly) No smoking in 21 bedrooms s £45-£75; d £80-£125 (incl. bkfst) **LB FACILITIES:** Croquet lawn Xmas
CONF: Thtr 250 Class 50 Board 40 Del from £85 **PARKING:** 100
NOTES: No smoking in restaurant Civ Wed 250
CARDS:

BARNHAM BROOM, Norfolk Map 13 TG00

★★★75% Barnham Broom Hotel, Golf & Country Club

CLASSIC BRITISH

NR9 4DD
☎ 01603 759393 759522 ▯ 01603 758224
e-mail: enquiry@barnhambroomhotel.co.uk

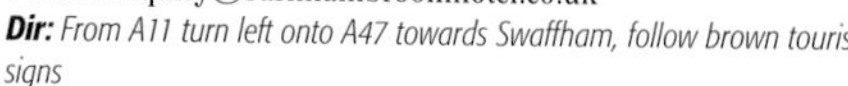

Dir: *From A11 turn left onto A47 towards Swaffham, follow brown tourist signs*

Situated in a peaceful rural location just a short drive from Norwich. Bedrooms are tastefully furnished in a contemporary style and equipped with a range of useful extras. The informal bar serves a range of snacks and meals throughout the day, or guests may choose from the carte menu in the more formal Flints *continued*

Restaurant. The hotel also has extensive leisure, conference and banqueting facilities.
ROOMS: 52 en suite (8 fmly) (6 GF) No smoking in 37 bedrooms s £95-£155; d £120-£180 (incl. bkfst) **LB FACILITIES: Spa** STV Indoor swimming (H) Golf 36 Tennis (hard) Squash Sauna Solarium Gym Putting green Aerobics & Tai chi tuition, Swimming pool supervised ch fac Xmas **CONF:** Thtr 150 Class 90 Board 70 Del from £127.50
PARKING: 200 **NOTES:** No dogs (ex guide dogs) No smoking in restaurant Civ Wed 120 **CARDS:**

BARNSDALE BAR SERVICE AREA (A1), North Yorkshire Map 16 SE51

⌂ Travelodge Pontefract Barnsdale

Travelodge

Wentbridge WF8 3QQ
☎ 08700 850 950 ▯ 01977 620711
Dir: *on A1, southbound*

Travelodge offers good quality, good value, modern accommodation. Ideal for families, the spacious, en suite bedrooms include remote-control TV, tea and coffee-making facilities, luxury beds and free morning newspaper. Meals can be taken at the nearby family restaurant. For further details and the Travelodge phone number, consult the Hotel Groups page.
ROOMS: 56 en suite s fr £42.95; d fr £42.95

BARNSLEY, South Yorkshire Map 16 SE30
See also Tankersley

★★★★71% Tankersley Manor

Church Ln S75 3DQ
☎ 01226 744700 ▯ 01226 745405
e-mail: tankersley@marstonhotels.com
(For full entry see Tankersley)

★★★72% Ardsley House

Forestdale Hotels

Doncaster Rd, Ardsley S71 5EH
☎ 01226 309955 ▯ 01226 205374
e-mail: ardsley.house@forestdale.com
Dir: *on A635, 0.75m from Stairfoot rdbt*

Quietly situated on the Barnsley to Doncaster Road, the hotel has many regulars. Comfortable and well-equipped bedrooms, very good leisure facilities including gym and pool, and good conference facilities are just some of the attractions. Public rooms include a choice of bars and a busy restaurant. Parking is plentiful.
ROOMS: 75 en suite (12 fmly) (14 GF) No smoking in 50 bedrooms s fr £95; d fr £110 (incl. bkfst) **LB FACILITIES:** STV Indoor swimming (H) Sauna Solarium Gym Jacuzzi Beauty Spa, Swimming pool supervised entertainment Xmas **CONF:** Thtr 350 Class 250 Board 40 Del from £125 **PARKING:** 200 **CARDS:**

⌂ Travel Inn Barnsley

travel inn

Meadow Gate, Dearne Valley, Wombwell S73 0UN
☎ 08701 977024 ▯ 01226 273810
Dir: *M1 junct 36, eastbound. Take A6195 (A635) to Doncaster for 5 miles. Travel Inn is adjacent to rdbt*

Travel Inn offers good-quality, value-for-money accommodation. Spacious, en suite rooms with bath and shower comfortably accommodate a family of up to two adults and two children (to age 15). The restaurant and bar offers a varied menu. For further details and the Travel Inn phone number, consult the Hotel Groups page.
ROOMS: 41 en suite s £44.95; d £44.95

⌂ Travelodge
School St S70 3PE
☎ 08700 850 950 🖷 01226 298799
Dir: *at Stairfoot rdbt A633/A635*
Travelodge offers good quality, good value, modern accommodation. Ideal for families, the spacious, en suite bedrooms include remote-control TV, tea and coffee-making facilities, luxury beds and free morning newspaper. Meals can be taken at the nearby family restaurant. For further details and the Travelodge phone number, consult the Hotel Groups page.
ROOMS: 32 en suite s fr £42.95; d fr £42.95

BARNSTAPLE, Devon Map 03 SS53

★★★★71% The Imperial
Taw Vale Pde EX32 8NB
☎ 01271 345861 🖷 01271 324448
e-mail: info@brend-imperial.co.uk
Dir: *M5 junct 27/A361 to Barnstaple. Follow town centre signs, passing Tesco. Straight on at next 2 rdbts. Hotel on right*

This smart and attractive hotel is pleasantly located at the centre of Barnstaple and overlooks the river. The staff are friendly and offer attentive service and comfortable bedrooms are in a range of sizes, some with balconies and many overlooking the river. Afternoon tea is available in the refurbished lounge. Cuisine is appetising and freshly prepared.
ROOMS: 63 en suite (7 fmly) (4 GF) s £75-£125; d £80-£145 **LB**
FACILITIES: STV leisure facilities at sister hotel entertainment Xmas
CONF: Thtr 60 Class 40 Board 30 **SERVICES:** Lift **PARKING:** 80
NOTES: No dogs (ex guide dogs) No smoking in restaurant
CARDS:

See advert on this page

★★★71% Royal & Fortescue
Boutport St EX31 1HG
☎ 01271 342289 🖷 01271 340102
e-mail: info@royalfortescue.co.uk
Dir: *A361 along Barbican Rd signed town centre, turn right into Queen St & left onto Boutport St, hotel on left*
Formerly a coaching inn, this friendly and convivial hotel is conveniently located in the centre of town. Bedrooms vary in size and all are decorated and furnished to a consistently high standard. In addition to the formal restaurant, guests can take snacks in the popular coffee shop or dine more informally in 'The Bank', a bistro and cafe bar.
ROOMS: 50 en suite (5 fmly) (3 GF) s £47-£72; d £47-£72 **LB**
FACILITIES: STV entertainment Xmas **CONF:** Thtr 25 Class 25 Board 25
SERVICES: Lift **PARKING:** 40 **CARDS:**

★★★70% Barnstaple Hotel
Braunton Rd EX31 1LE
☎ 01271 376221 🖷 01271 324101
e-mail: info@barnstaplehotel.co.uk
Dir: *outskirts of Barnstaple on A361*
This well-established hotel enjoys a convenient location on the edge of town. Bedrooms are spacious and well equipped, many with balconies overlooking the outdoor pool. An excellent choice is offered in the restaurant with freshly prepared and interesting dishes, and there is an excellent range of leisure and conference facilities.
ROOMS: 60 en suite (3 fmly) (17 GF) s £45-£75; d £55-£85 **LB**
FACILITIES: Spa STV Indoor swimming (H) Outdoor swimming (H) Snooker Sauna Solarium Gym Swimming pools supervised ch fac Xmas
CONF: BC Thtr 250 **PARKING:** 250 **NOTES:** No dogs (ex guide dogs) Civ Wed 100 **CARDS:**

★★★67% Park
Taw Vale EX32 9AE
☎ 01271 372166 🖷 01271 323157
e-mail: info@parkhotel.co.uk
Dir: *opposite Rock Park, 0.5m from town centre*
Enjoying views across the park and in easy walking distance of the town centre, this modern hotel offers a choice of bedrooms in both the main building and the Garden Court, just across the car park. Public rooms are open-plan in style and the friendly staff offer attentive service in a relaxed atmosphere.
ROOMS: 25 en suite 17 annexe en suite (7 fmly) (5 GF) s £47-£72; d £47-£72 **LB** **FACILITIES:** STV entertainment Xmas **PARKING:** 80
NOTES: Civ Wed 100 **CARDS:**

BARNSTAPLE, continued

⌂ Travel Inn

Eastern Av, Whiddon Valley EX32 8RY
☎ 08701 977025 📠 01271 377710
Dir: *adjacent to North Devon Link Rd at junct with A39*
Travel Inn offers good-quality, value-for-money accommodation. Spacious, en suite rooms with bath and shower comfortably accommodate a family of up to two adults and two children (to age 15). The restaurant and bar offers a varied menu. For further details and the Travel Inn phone number, consult the Hotel Groups page.
ROOMS: 40 en suite s £44.95; d £44.95

BARROW-IN-FURNESS, Cumbria — Map 18 SD26

★★★69% Clarke's Hotel & Brasserie

Rampside LA13 0PX
☎ 01229 820303 📠 01229 430594
e-mail: clarkeshotel@lineone.net
Dir: *A590 to Ulverston then A5087, take coastal route for 8m, turn left at rdbt into Rampside*

This smart, well-maintained hotel enjoys a peaceful location on the south Cumbrian coastline, overlooking Morecambe Bay. The tastefully appointed bedrooms come in a variety of sizes and are thoughtfully equipped for the business guest. Inviting public areas include an open plan bar and brasserie offering freshly prepared food throughout the day.
ROOMS: 14 en suite (1 fmly) No smoking in 3 bedrooms **FACILITIES:** STV entertainment **PARKING:** 50 **NOTES:** No smoking in restaurant **CARDS:**

★★65% Lisdoonie

307/309 Abbey Rd LA14 5LF
☎ 01229 827312 📠 01229 820944
Dir: *on A590, at 1st set of lights in town (Strawberry pub on left) continue for 100yds, hotel on right*
This friendly hotel is conveniently located for access to the centre of the town and is popular with commercial visitors. The comfortable bedrooms are well equipped, and vary in size and style. There are two comfortable lounges, one with a bar and restaurant adjacent. There is also a large function suite.
ROOMS: 12 en suite (2 fmly) **CONF:** Class 255 **PARKING:** 30 **NOTES:** Closed Xmas & New Year Civ Wed **CARDS:**

BARTON, Lancashire — Map 18 SD53

★★★72% Barton Grange

Garstang Rd PR3 5AA
☎ 01772 862551 📠 01772 861267
e-mail: stay@bartongrangehotel.com
Dir: *M6 junct 32, follow signs to Garstang (A6) for 2.5 miles. Hotel on right*

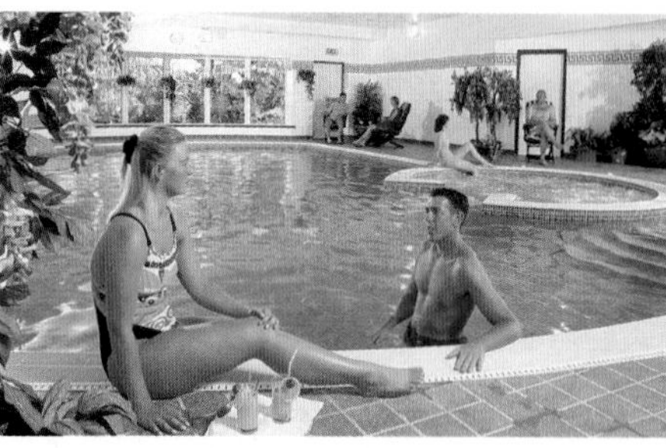

Situated close to the M6, this modern, stylish hotel benefits from extensive public areas that include an award-winning garden centre, spa and leisure facilities. Comfortable, well-appointed bedrooms include four-poster and family rooms, as well as attractive rooms in an adjacent cottage. The unique Walled Garden restaurant offers all day dining and refreshments.
ROOMS: 42 en suite 8 annexe en suite (4 fmly) (4 GF) No smoking in 28 bedrooms s £50-£93; d £50-£93 **LB FACILITIES:** STV Indoor swimming (H) Sauna Gym Jacuzzi Garden Centre within the grounds Xmas **CONF:** BC Thtr 300 Class 100 Board 80 Del from £125 **SERVICES:** Lift **PARKING:** 250 **NOTES:** No dogs (ex guide dogs) No smoking in restaurant Civ Wed 120
CARDS:

BARTON MILLS, Suffolk — Map 12 TL77

⌂ Travelodge

Fiveways IP28 6AE
☎ 08700 850 950 📠 01638 717675
Dir: *on A11*
Travelodge offers good quality, good value, modern accommodation. Ideal for families, the spacious, en suite bedrooms include remote-control TV, tea and coffee-making facilities, luxury beds and free morning newspaper. Meals can be taken at the nearby family restaurant. For further details and the Travelodge phone number, consult the Hotel Groups page.
ROOMS: 40 en suite s fr £42.95; d fr £42.95

BARTON STACEY, Hampshire — Map 05 SU44

⌂ Travelodge

SO21 3NP
☎ 08700 850 950 📠 01264 720260
Dir: *on A303*
Travelodge offers good quality, good value, modern accommodation. Ideal for families, the spacious, en suite bedrooms include remote-control TV, tea and coffee-making facilities, luxury beds and free morning newspaper. Meals can be taken at the nearby family restaurant. For further details and the Travelodge phone number, consult the Hotel Groups page.
ROOMS: 20 en suite s fr £42.95; d fr £42.95

BARTON-UNDER-NEEDWOOD, Staffordshire Map 10 SK11

Travelodge Burton-upon-Trent

DE13 8EG
☎ 08700 850 950 🖷 01283 716343
Dir: *on A38, northbound*
Travelodge offers good quality, good value, modern accommodation. Ideal for families, the spacious, en suite bedrooms include remote-control TV, tea and coffee-making facilities, luxury beds and free morning newspaper. Meals can be taken at the nearby family restaurant. For further details and the Travelodge phone number, consult the Hotel Groups page.
ROOMS: 20 en suite s fr £42.95; d fr £42.95

Travelodge Burton (South)

Rykneld St DE13 8EH
☎ 08700 850 950 🖷 01283 716784
Dir: *on A38, southbound*
Travelodge offers good quality, good value, modern accommodation. Ideal for families, the spacious, en suite bedrooms include remote-control TV, tea and coffee-making facilities, luxury beds and free morning newspaper. Meals can be taken at the nearby family restaurant. For further details and the Travelodge phone number, consult the Hotel Groups page.
ROOMS: 40 en suite s fr £42.95; d fr £42.95

BARTON-UPON-HUMBER, Lincolnshire Map 17 TA02

★★★70% Reeds Hotel

Westfield Lakes, Far Ings Rd DN18 5RG
☎ 01652 632313 🖷 01652 636361
e-mail: info@reedshotel.co.uk
Dir: *A15 rdbt take 2nd exit (Humber Bridge) & leave road at Barton-upon-Humber, turn left at rdbt. In 200yds turn right at sign for hotel, down hill & hotel at junct*

Situated in a quiet wildlife sanctuary, this hotel enjoys splendid views of the Humber Bridge. Public rooms include an attractive restaurant and foyer lounge with panoramic views. Bedroom sizes vary; all are well equipped and well presented, and service from the small team is both friendly and helpful.
ROOMS: 31 en suite (3 fmly) No smoking in all bedrooms s £70; d £85 (incl. bkfst) **LB** **FACILITIES:** STV Alternative therapy centre Xmas **CONF:** Thtr 300 Class 200 Board 70 Del £105 **SERVICES:** Lift **PARKING:** 100 **NOTES:** No dogs (ex guide dogs) No smoking in restaurant Civ Wed 340 **CARDS:**

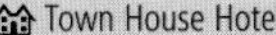

Town House Hotel
Country House Hotel
Travel Accommodation

BASILDON, Essex Map 06 TQ78

★★★69% Chichester

Old London Rd, Wickford SS11 8UE
☎ 01268 560555 🖷 01268 560580
Dir: *off A129*
This friendly hotel has been owned and run by the same family for over 25 years. The property is set in its own landscaped grounds and surrounded by open farmland. The spacious bedrooms are located around an attractive courtyard; each room is pleasantly decorated and equipped with many useful extras. Carte and daily changing menus are offered in the smart restaurant whereas more informal fare is served in the bar area.
ROOMS: 2 en suite 32 annexe en suite (16 GF) s fr £60; d fr £70 **LB** **FACILITIES:** STV **PARKING:** 150 **NOTES:** No dogs (ex guide dogs) No children 5yrs No smoking in restaurant
CARDS:

Holiday Inn Basildon - Rayleigh

Cranes Farm Rd SS14 3DG
☎ 0870 400 9003 🖷 01268 530119
Dir: *off A1235, via A127*
At the time of going to press, the classification for this hotel was not confirmed. Please refer to the AA internet site www.theAA.com for current information.
ROOMS: 149 en suite (30 fmly) No smoking in 70 bedrooms **FACILITIES:** Use of nearby Leisure Club (David Lloyd) **CONF:** Thtr 300 Class 80 Board 80 **SERVICES:** Lift **PARKING:** 200 **NOTES:** No dogs (ex guide dogs) Civ Wed 180 **CARDS:**

Campanile

Pipps Hill, Southend Arterial Rd SS14 3AE
☎ 01268 530810 🖷 01268 286710
Dir: *M25 junct 29 Basildon exit., back under A127, then left at rdbt*

This modern building offers accommodation in smart, well-equipped bedrooms, all with en suite bathrooms. Refreshments may be taken at the informal Bistro. For further details and the Campanile phone number, consult the Hotel Groups page.
ROOMS: 97 annexe en suite **CONF:** Thtr 35 Class 18 Board 20

Premier Lodge (Basildon)

Festival Leisure Park, Pipps Hill Rd South, off Cranes Farm Rd SS14 3WB
☎ 0870 9906598 🖷 0870 9906599
Dir: *M25 junct 29/A127 towards Basildon then E*
Premier Lodge offers modern, well-equipped, en suite accommodation suitable for both business and leisure travellers. Meals can be taken at the adjacent popular restaurant and bar, which is fully licensed. For further details, consult the Hotel Groups page.
ROOMS: 64 en suite s £50; d £50 **CONF:** Thtr 20 Class 20 Board 12

B

BASILDON, continued

Travel Inn
Felmores, East Mayne SS13 1BW
☎ 08701 977026 📠 01268 530092
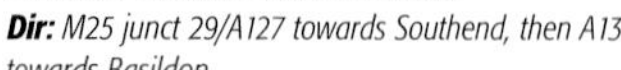
Dir: *M25 junct 29/A127 towards Southend, then A132 towards Basildon*
Travel Inn offers good-quality, value-for-money accommodation. Spacious, en suite rooms with bath and shower comfortably accommodate a family of up to two adults and two children (to age 15). The restaurant and bar offers a varied menu. For further details and Travel Inn phone number, consult Hotel Groups page.
ROOMS: 32 en suite s £44.95; d £44.95

Travel Inn (Basildon South)
High Rd, Fobbing, Stanford le Hope SS17 9NR
☎ 08701 977027 📠 01268 581752
Dir: *From M25 junct 30/31 take A13, Southend. Take A176, follow signs for Fobbing (Five Bells rdbout junction)*
Travel Inn offers good-quality, value-for-money accommodation. Spacious, en suite rooms with bath and shower comfortably accommodate a family of up to two adults and two children (to age 15). The restaurant and bar offers a varied menu. For further details and Travel Inn phone number, consult Hotel Groups page.
ROOMS: 60 en suite s £44.95; d £44.95 **CONF:** Thtr 40

Travelodge Basildon
Festival Leisure Park, Festival Way SS14 3WB
☎ 08700 850 950 📠 01268 186559
Dir: *M25 junct 29/A127, follow signs for Basildon centre to A176, follow signs for Festival Park, lodge next to bowling alley*
Travelodge offers good quality, good value, modern accommodation. Ideal for families, the spacious, en suite bedrooms include remote-control TV, tea and coffee-making facilities, luxury beds and free morning newspaper. Meals can be taken at the nearby family restaurant. For further details and the Travelodge phone number, consult the Hotel Groups page.
ROOMS: 60 en suite (incl. bkfst) s fr £42.95; d fr £42.95

BASINGSTOKE, Hampshire Map 05 SU65
See also North Waltham, Odiham & Stratfield Turgis

★★★★ Tylney Hall Hotel

RG27 9AZ
☎ 01256 764881 📠 01256 768141
e-mail: sales@tylneyhall.com
(For full entry see Rotherwick)

★★★★69% Hanover International Hotel & Club
Scures Hill, Nately Scures, Hook RG27 9JS
☎ 01256 764161 📠 01256 768341
e-mail: reception.basingstoke@hanover-international.com
Dir: *M3 junct 5, at rdbt towards Hook. Left at lights. Hotel 200mtrs on right*
This modern hotel is popular with both business and leisure guests. Comfortable bedrooms are well equipped and include a number of spacious executive rooms. Guests have a choice of dining in the formal restaurant, or for lighter meals and snacks there is a relaxing café or a smart bar. Extensive conference and leisure facilities complete the picture.
ROOMS: 100 en suite (2 fmly) (26 GF) No smoking in 45 bedrooms s £45-£148; d £90-£158 **FACILITIES:** STV Indoor swimming (H) Sauna Solarium Gym Jacuzzi Swimming pool supervised Xmas **CONF:** Thtr 240 Class 100 Board 80 Del from £85 **SERVICES:** Lift air con **PARKING:** 200 **NOTES:** No smoking in restaurant Civ Wed 160
CARDS:

See advert on opposite page

★★★★67% Apollo
Aldermaston Roundabout RG24 9NU
☎ 01256 796700 📠 01256 796701
e-mail: admin@apollo-hotels.co.uk
Dir: *M3 junct 6. Follow ringroad N, exit A340 (Aldermaston). Hotel on rdbt, 5th exit into Popley Way for access*
This modern hotel provides well equipped accommodation and spacious public areas, appealing to both the leisure and business guest. Facilities include a smartly appointed leisure club, a business centre, along with a good choice of formal and informal dining within two restaurants; 'Vespers' is the fine dining option.
ROOMS: 125 en suite No smoking in 100 bedrooms s £140-£240; d £180-£240 **LB FACILITIES: Spa** STV Indoor swimming (H) Sauna Solarium Gym Jacuzzi Swimming pool supervised Xmas **CONF:** Thtr 255 Class 196 Board 30 **SERVICES:** Lift air con **PARKING:** 200 **NOTES:** No dogs (ex guide dogs) Civ Wed 180
CARDS:

★★★★67% Audleys Wood
Alton Rd RG25 2JT
☎ 01256 817555 📠 01256 817500
e-mail: audleyswood@thistle.co.uk
Dir: *1.5m S of Basingstoke on A339*
Set in its own grounds, this hotel is within easy reach of the town centre. The spacious bedrooms have a good range of facilities and are comfortably appointed. Characterful public areas retain many original features; and include an oak-panelled lounge, cosy cocktail bar and pleasant airy restaurant.
ROOMS: 72 en suite (6 fmly) (34 GF) No smoking in 35 bedrooms s £100-£207; d £100-£207 (incl. bkfst) **LB FACILITIES:** STV Croquet lawn Putting green Archery Xmas **CONF:** Thtr 50 Class 20 Board 26 Del from £87.50 **PARKING:** 100 **NOTES:** No smoking in restaurant Civ Wed 100 **CARDS:**

★★★73% Romans
Little London Rd RG7 2PN
☎ 0118 970 0421 📠 0118 970 0691
e-mail: romanhotel@hotmail.com
(For full entry see Silchester)

See advert on opposite page

★★★71% The Hampshire Centrecourt Hotel
Centre Dr, Chineham RG24 8FY
☎ 01256 816664 📠 01256 816727
e-mail: hampshirec@marstonhotels.com
Dir: *off A33 Reading road behind the Chineham Shopping Centre via Great Binfields Rd*
This modern hotel enjoys a convenient location on the outskirts of Basingstoke within easy reach of the M3 and the M4. The hotel boasts impressive leisure and tennis facilities including indoor and outdoor courts. There is a choice of bars and an airy restaurant. Bedrooms are spacious, well equipped and some have balconies.
ROOMS: 90 en suite (6 fmly) No smoking in 25 bedrooms s fr £120; d fr £130 **LB FACILITIES: Spa** STV Indoor swimming (H) Tennis (hard) Sauna Solarium Gym Jacuzzi Steam room Beauty salon **CONF:** Thtr 220 Del from £155 **SERVICES:** Lift **PARKING:** 120 **NOTES:** No dogs (ex guide dogs) No smoking in restaurant
CARDS:

B

BASINGSTOKE, continued

★★★61% **Red Lion**
24 London St RG21 7NY
☎ 01256 328525 📠 01256 844056
e-mail: redlion.enquiries@zolahotels.com
Dir: *M3 junct 6 to Black Dam rdbt. 2nd exit onto Ringway East (A339). Take slip road signed town centre onto Churchill Way East (A3010). At rdbt take 1st exit onto Timberlake Rd, leading into New Rd. After pedestrian traffic lights, right into Red Lion Ln*
Centrally located in Basingstoke, the Red Lion is an ideal choice for business guests. Bedrooms are mostly spacious and include no-smoking rooms, interconnecting rooms and rooms with four-poster beds. Public areas comprise an attractive lounge and restaurant, and a popular bar. Other facilities include a selection of function and conference rooms.
ROOMS: 59 en suite (2 fmly) No smoking in 16 bedrooms s £45-£120; d £65-£140 (incl. bkfst) **LB FACILITIES:** STV Xmas **CONF:** Thtr 80 Class 40 Board 20 Del from £110 **SERVICES:** Lift **PARKING:** 62
NOTES: No smoking in restaurant **CARDS:**

Holiday Inn Basingstoke
Grove Rd RG21 3EE
☎ 0870 400 9004 📠 01256 840081
e-mail: reservations-basingstoke@ichotelsgroup.com
Dir: *on A339 Alton road S of Basingstoke*
At the time of going to press, the classification for this hotel was not confirmed. Please refer to the AA internet site www.theAA.com for current information.
ROOMS: 86 en suite (5 fmly) No smoking in 42 bedrooms **CONF:** Thtr 150 Class 80 Board 80 **PARKING:** 150
CARDS:

Travel Inn
Basingstoke Leisure Park, Worting Rd RG22 6PG
☎ 08701 977028 📠 01256 819329
Dir: *M3 junct 6 follow signs for Leisure Park*
Travel Inn offers good-quality, value-for-money accommodation. Spacious, en suite rooms with bath and shower comfortably accommodate a family of up to two adults and two children (to age 15). The restaurant and bar offers a varied menu. For further details and the Travel Inn phone number, consult the Hotel Groups page.
ROOMS: 71 en suite s £44.95; d £44.95

Travelodge
Stag and Hounds, Winchester Rd RG22 6HN
☎ 08700 850 950 📠 01256 843566
Dir: *off A30, S of town centre*
Travelodge offers good quality, good value, modern accommodation. Ideal for families, the spacious, en suite bedrooms include remote-control TV, tea and coffee-making facilities, luxury beds and free morning newspaper. Meals can be taken at the nearby family restaurant. For further details and the Travelodge phone number, consult the Hotel Groups page.
ROOMS: 44 en suite s fr £42.95; d fr £42.95

BASLOW, Derbyshire — Map 16 SK27

★★★76% **Cavendish**
DE45 1SP
☎ 01246 582311 📠 01246 582312
e-mail: info@cavendish-hotel.net
Dir: *M1 junct 29/A617 W to Chesterfield & A619 to Baslow. Hotel in village centre, off main road*
This stylish property, dating back to the 18th century, is delightfully situated on the edge of the Chatsworth Estate. Elegantly appointed bedrooms offer a host of thoughtful amenities, while comfortable public areas are furnished with period pieces and paintings. Guests have a choice of dining in the informal conservatory Garden Room or the elegant Gallery Restaurant.
ROOMS: 24 en suite (3 fmly) (2 GF) No smoking in 2 bedrooms s £100-£110; d £130-£140 **LB FACILITIES:** STV Fishing Putting green ch fac Xmas **CONF:** Thtr 25 Board 18 Del from £174 **PARKING:** 50
NOTES: No dogs (ex guide dogs) No smoking in restaurant
CARDS:

Top 200 - Hotel

★★ ®®® **Fischer's Baslow Hall**
Calver Rd DE45 1RR
☎ 01246 583259 📠 01246 583818
e-mail: m.s@fischers-baslowhall.co.uk
Dir: *on A623 between Baslow & Calver*
Located at the end of a chestnut tree-lined drive on the edge of the Chatsworth Estate, this beautiful Derbyshire manor house offers sumptuous accommodation and facilities. Staff provide very friendly and personally attentive hospitality and service. Two styles of bedrooms include traditional, individually-themed rooms in the main house and spacious, more contemporary-styled rooms with Italian marble bathrooms in the Garden House. The cuisine is extremely memorable and a highlight of any stay.
ROOMS: 6 en suite 5 annexe en suite (4 GF) No smoking in all bedrooms d £100-£180 (incl. cont bkfst) **LB CONF:** Thtr 40 Board 18 Del from £155 **PARKING:** 40 **NOTES:** No dogs (ex guide dogs) No smoking in restaurant Closed 25-26 Dec Civ Wed 40
CARDS:

BASSENTHWAITE, Cumbria — Map 18 NY23

★★★★71% ® **Armathwaite Hall**
CA12 4RE
☎ 017687 76551 📠 017687 76220
e-mail: reservations@armathwaite-hall.com
Dir: *M6 junct 40/A66 to Keswick rdbt then A591 signed Carlisle. 8m to Castle Inn junct, turn left. Hotel 300yds*
Enjoying fine views over Bassenthwaite Lake, this impressive mansion, dating from the 17th century in parts, is peacefully situated amid 400 acres of deer park. Comfortably furnished bedrooms are complemented by a choice of lounges featuring

continued

splendid wood panelling and roaring log fires. The indoor and outdoor leisure facilities are an added attraction.

ROOMS: 43 en suite (4 fmly) (8 GF) s £70-£150; d £140-£280 (incl. bkfst) **LB** **FACILITIES: Spa** STV Indoor swimming (H) Tennis (hard) Fishing Snooker Sauna Solarium Gym Croquet lawn Putting green Jacuzzi Archery, Beauty salon, Clayshooting, Quad bikes, Falconry, Mountain Bikes ch fac Xmas **CONF:** Thtr 80 Class 50 Board 60 Del from £105 **SERVICES:** Lift **PARKING:** 100 **NOTES:** No smoking in restaurant Civ Wed 80 **CARDS:**

See advert on this page

★★★75% The Pheasant

CA13 9YE

☎ 01768 776234 01768 76002

e-mail: info@the-pheasant.co.uk

Dir: *Midway between Keswick & Cockermouth, signed from A66*

Enjoying a rural setting on the western side of Bassenthwaite Lake, this 500-year-old, friendly inn is steeped in tradition. The attractive oak-panelled bar has seen few changes in recent years and features log fires and a great selection of malt whisky. The individually decorated bedrooms are stylish and thoughtfully equipped.

ROOMS: 13 en suite s £70-£90; d £130-£160 (incl. bkfst) **LB** **PARKING:** 40 **NOTES:** No dogs (ex guide dogs) No children 8yrs No smoking in restaurant Closed 25 Dec **CARDS:**

★★★65% The Castle Inn Hotel

CA12 4RG

☎ 0870 609 6178 017687 76604

e-mail: accounts.castleinn@corushotels.com

Dir: *leave A66 at Keswick, onto A591 towards Carlisle, pass Bassenthwaite village on right & hotel 6m on left*

Located to the north of the lake and enjoying distant views of the hills, this hotel stands in extensive grounds and gardens. It has a wide range of indoor and outdoor leisure facilities, spacious public areas and a selection of rooms for conferences and functions.

continued

Bedrooms are well equipped and come in a variety of styles and sizes.

ROOMS: 48 en suite (6 fmly) (8 GF) No smoking in 14 bedrooms s £57-£80; d £84-£130 (incl. bkfst & dinner) **LB** **FACILITIES:** STV Indoor swimming (H) Tennis (grass) Sauna Solarium Gym Putting green Jacuzzi Badminton, Table tennis, Health/Beauty spa, Swimming pool supervised Xmas **CONF:** Thtr 90 Class 35 Board 40 Del from £95 **PARKING:** 100 **NOTES:** No smoking in restaurant Civ Wed 120 **CARDS:**

★★70% Ravenstone

CA12 4QG

☎ 017687 76240 017687 76733

e-mail: info@ravenstone-hotel.co.uk

Dir: *4.5m N of Keswick on A591 Carlisle road*

Set in terraced gardens and enjoying fine panoramic views across the valley, this delightful country house retains its original character and features oak panelling and artefacts. This is a

continued on p80

BASSENTHWAITE, continued

relaxing and friendly hotel, run by a young family who make families most welcome. The set menu features good freshly prepared dishes.
ROOMS: 20 en suite (2 fmly) No smoking in all bedrooms s fr £40; d £80-£90 (incl. bkfst) **LB** **FACILITIES:** Snooker Table tennis Xmas **PARKING:** 25 **NOTES:** No dogs No smoking in restaurant
CARDS:

BATH, Somerset Map 04 ST76
See also Colerne & Hinton Charterhouse

★★★★★69% The Royal Crescent
16 Royal Crescent BA1 2LS
☎ 01225 823333 01225 339401
e-mail: reservations@royalcrescent.co.uk
Dir: *on A4, right at traffic lights. 2nd left onto Bennett St. Continue into the Circus, 2nd exit onto Brock St, No.16 on cobbled street*

In the centre of the world famous Royal Crescent, John Wood's masterpiece of fine Georgian architecture provides the setting for this elegant hotel. Spacious, air-conditioned bedrooms are individually designed and furnished with antiques. Delightful central grounds lead to a second house which is home to further rooms, Pimpernells restaurant and the Bath House, offering complementary therapies and treatments.
ROOMS: 45 en suite (8 fmly) No smoking in 8 bedrooms
FACILITIES: Indoor swimming (H) Sauna Gym Croquet lawn Hot air ballooning, 1920s river launch, Outdoor heated plunge pool **CONF:** Thtr 30 Class 30 **SERVICES:** Lift air con **PARKING:** 27 **NOTES:** No smoking in restaurant Civ Wed 40 **CARDS:**

★★★★★62% The Bath Spa
Sydney Rd BA2 6JF
☎ 0870 400 8222 01225 444006
e-mail: fivestar@bathspa.u-net.com
MACDONALD HOTELS
Dir: *M4 junct 18/A46 for Bath/A4 city centre. Left onto A36 at 1st traffic lights. Right at mini rdbt then left into Sydney Place. Hotel 200yds on right*
Delightful Georgian mansion set amidst seven acres of pretty landscaped grounds, just a short walk from the many and varied delights of the city centre. A timeless elegance pervades the gracious public areas and bedrooms. Facilities include a popular leisure club, a choice of dining options and a number of meeting rooms.
ROOMS: 102 en suite No smoking in 31 bedrooms s £190-£220; d £190-£220 **LB** **FACILITIES:** STV Indoor swimming (H) Tennis (hard) Sauna Gym Croquet lawn Jacuzzi Beauty treatment, Hair salon, Swimming pool supervised entertainment Xmas **CONF:** Thtr 120 Class 100 Board 50 Del from £159 **SERVICES:** Lift **PARKING:** 156 **NOTES:** No smoking in restaurant Civ Wed 120
CARDS:

Top 200 - Hotel

★★★★ Bath Priory
Weston Rd BA1 2XT
☎ 01225 331922 01225 448276
e-mail: 106076.1265@compuserve.com
Set in delightful walled gardens, this attractive Georgian house provides peace and tranquillity overlooking the city. In the sumptuously furnished public rooms an extensive display of pictures and fine art create a charming style. Cuisine is accomplished with excellently sourced ingredients and flavours and an impressive wine list. Bedrooms, some of which are suites in an adjacent building, are well proportioned and offer the many thoughtful touches expected in an establishment of this quality and standing
ROOMS: 28 en suite (6 fmly) s £145-£260; d fr £260 (incl. bkfst) **LB** **FACILITIES:** STV Indoor swimming (H) Outdoor swimming (H) Sauna Solarium Gym Croquet lawn Jacuzzi Steam room, swimming pool supervised Xmas **CONF:** BC Thtr 60 Class 30 Board 30 Del from £190 **PARKING:** 28 **NOTES:** No dogs (ex guide dogs) No smoking in restaurant Civ Wed 64
CARDS:

Town House

★★★★ The Windsor Hotel
69 Great Pulteney St BA2 4DL
☎ 01225 422100 01225 422550
e-mail: sales@bathwindsorhotel.com
Dir: *M4 junct 18/A4. Turn left onto A36, after 500yds turn right at mini rdbt. 2nd left into Great Pulteney St*
This delightful Grade I listed terraced Georgian town house is a short walk from the town centre. It has been refurbished to the highest standard and sumptuously furnished with antique pieces. The restaurant has Japanese décor and offers a choice of either sukiyaki or shabu shabu; fresh ingredients are cooked at the table. The Windsor is a non-smoking establishment.
ROOMS: 14 en suite (3 fmly) No smoking in all bedrooms s £85-£115; d £135-£275 (incl. bkfst) **LB** **FACILITIES:** STV **CONF:** Thtr 16 Class 14 Board 18 Del from £155 **PARKING:** 12 **NOTES:** No dogs (ex guide dogs) No children 12yrs No smoking in restaurant **CARDS:**

Late for dinner?
Quality Standards mean that last orders for dinner vary according to star rating and should be no earlier than:
★★ 7.00pm ★★★ 8.00pm ★★★★ 9.00pm
★★★★★ 10.00pm

★★★★65% Menzies Waterside

Rossiter Rd, Widcombe Basin BA2 4JP

☎ 01225 338855 ▤ 01225 428941

e-mail: waterside@menzies-hotels.co.uk

Dir: *A36, hotel situated on Rossiter Rd*

In a quiet location within walking distance of the main town and train station, this hotel is a popular leisure break destination. Now refurbished, the bedrooms are compact but well designed with comfortable seating and duvets on beds. The brasserie serves contemporary cuisine in air-conditioned surroundings overlooking the water.

ROOMS: 107 en suite 6 annexe en suite No smoking in 67 bedrooms **CONF:** Thtr 120 Class 70 Board 60 Del from £135 **SERVICES:** Lift **PARKING:** 80 **NOTES:** No smoking in restaurant

CARDS:

★★★★63% ◎ Combe Grove Manor Hotel & Country Club

FURLONG

Brassknocker Hill, Monkton Combe BA2 7HS

☎ 01225 834644 ▤ 01225 834961

e-mail: julian.ebbutt@combegrovemanor.com

Dir: *M4 junct 18/A46 to city centre, then signs for University & American Museum. Hotel 2m past University on left*

Set in over 80 acres of gardens, this Georgian mansion commands stunning views over Limpley Stoke Valley. Most bedrooms are in the Garden Lodge, a short walk from the main house. The superb range of indoor and outdoor leisure facilities include a beauty clinic with holistic therapies, golf, tennis and two pools.

ROOMS: 9 en suite 31 annexe en suite (11 fmly) (9 GF) s £110-£320; d £110-£320 (incl. bkfst) **LB** **FACILITIES: Spa** STV Indoor swimming (H) Outdoor swimming (H) Golf 5 Tennis (hard) Sauna Solarium Gym Croquet lawn Putting green Jacuzzi Aerobics, Beauty salon, Jogging trail, Swimming pools supervised, Indoor tennis **CONF:** Thtr 120 Class 50 Board 40 Del from £135 **PARKING:** 150 **NOTES:** No dogs (ex guide dogs) No smoking in restaurant Civ Wed 50

CARDS:

See advert on this page

Want to get away without the hassle
of finding a place to stay?
Let the AA Hotel Booking Service find the place that best suits your needs. No fuss, no worries and no booking fee.
Call 0870 50 50 505
or visit www.theAA.com

Popped the question?
Hotels with Civ Wed in their entry are licensed for civil wedding ceremonies. Maximum numbers for the ceremony only are shown, e.g. Civ Wed 120

Top 200 - Hotel

★★★ ◎◎ Queensberry

Russel St BA1 2QF

☎ 01225 447928 ▤ 01225 446065

e-mail: enquiries@bathqueenberry.com

Dir: *100mtrs from the Assembly Rooms*

Four developed townhouses make this delightful hotel, nestling in a quiet residential street near the city centre. Spacious bedrooms are tastefully furnished, and deep armchairs, fresh flowers and marble bathrooms add to their appeal. There are comfortable lounges, a small bar and a courtyard garden. The Olive Tree is an informal restaurant, which offers carefully cooked food in a modern style. Valet parking is a useful additional service.

ROOMS: 29 en suite s £95-£300; d £95-£300 (incl. cont bkfst) **LB** **FACILITIES:** Xmas **CONF:** Thtr 35 Board 25 Del from £145.50 **SERVICES:** Lift **PARKING:** 6 **NOTES:** No dogs (ex guide dogs) No smoking in restaurant **CARDS:**

B

BATH, continued

★★★74% The Lansdown Grove

Lansdown Rd BA1 5EH
☎ 01225 483888 01225 483838
e-mail: lansdown@marstonhotels.com
Dir: follow signs to Lansdown Park & Ride & continue towards town centre. Hotel on left

MARSTON HOTELS

A short uphill walk from the city centre, this hotel offers a relaxed atmosphere and comfortable accommodation. Well-equipped, tastefully decorated bedrooms include a number of stylish executive rooms. There is a reception lounge, bar and peaceful drawing room. Innovative, award-winning cuisine using fresh ingredients is served in the elegant restaurant.

ROOMS: 60 en suite (3 fmly) No smoking in 9 bedrooms s fr £80; d fr £100 **LB FACILITIES:** STV Xmas **CONF:** Thtr 100 Class 45 Board 40 Del from £127.50 **SERVICES:** Lift **PARKING:** 35 **NOTES:** No dogs (ex guide dogs) No smoking in restaurant
CARDS:

★★★72% Cliffe

Cliffe Dr, Crowe Hill, Limpley Stoke BA2 7FY
☎ 01225 723226 01225 723871
e-mail: cliffe@bestwestern.co.uk
Dir: A36 S from Bath, at A36/B3108 lights turn left toward Bradford on Avon, 0.5m. Turn right before bridge, through village, hotel on right

Best Western

With stunning views over the surrounding countryside, this attractive country house is just a short drive from the City of Bath. Bedrooms vary in size and style and are well equipped; several are particularly spacious and a number of rooms are on the ground floor. The restaurant overlooks the well-tended garden and offers a tempting selection of carefully prepared dishes.

ROOMS: 8 en suite 3 annexe en suite (2 fmly) No smoking in 4 bedrooms s £60-£80; d £100-£120 (incl. bkfst) **LB FACILITIES:** STV Outdoor swimming (H) Xmas **CONF:** Thtr 20 Class 15 Board 15 Del from £136 **PARKING:** 20 **NOTES:** No smoking in restaurant
CARDS:

See advert on opposite page

★★★72% The Francis

Queen Square BA1 2HH
☎ 0870 400 8223 01225 319715
e-mail: francis@macdonald-hotels.co.uk
Dir: M4 junct 18/A46 to Bath junct. Take 3rd exit onto A4. Right fork into George St, sharp left into Gay St onto Queen Sq, hotel on left

MACDONALD HOTELS

Overlooking Queen Square in the city centre, The Francis is a long established hotel. Various eating options include a traditional lounge, a café-bar and a more formal restaurant. Bedrooms, which are on three floors, are comfortable and attractively decorated.

ROOMS: 95 en suite (16 fmly) No smoking in 38 bedrooms s fr £35; d fr £70 (incl. bkfst) **LB FACILITIES:** Xmas **CONF:** BC Thtr 80 Class 40 Board 30 Del from £110 **SERVICES:** Lift **PARKING:** 42 **NOTES:** No smoking in restaurant **CARDS:**

★★★69% Pratts

South Pde BA2 4AB
☎ 01225 460441 01225 448807
e-mail: pratts@forestdale.com
Dir: take A46 into city centre. Left at 1st lights (Curfew Pub), right at next rdbt. 2nd exit at next rdbt, right at lights & left at next rdbt, then 1st left into South Pde

Part of a Georgian terrace, this long-established and popular hotel stands close to the city centre. Public rooms and bedrooms have undergone a refurbishment programme and all décor has been chosen to complement the Georgian surroundings. The ground floor day rooms include two lounges, a writing room and a very comfortable restaurant.

ROOMS: 46 en suite (2 fmly) No smoking in 8 bedrooms s fr £90; d fr £125 (incl. bkfst) **LB FACILITIES:** Xmas **CONF:** Thtr 50 Class 12 Board 30 Del from £90 **SERVICES:** Lift **NOTES:** No smoking in restaurant **CARDS:**

★★★66% The Abbey Hotel

North Pde BA1 1LF
☎ 01225 461603 01225 447758
e-mail: ahres@compasshotels.co.uk
Dir: close to the Abbey in city centre

Best Western

Originally built for a wealthy merchant in the 1740s and forming part of a handsome Georgian terrace, this welcoming hotel is situated in the heart of the city. The thoughtfully equipped bedrooms vary in size and style. Public areas include a smart lounge bar and a refurbished restaurant offering a regularly changing menu.

ROOMS: 60 en suite (4 fmly) No smoking in 22 bedrooms s £80-£95; d £125-£155 (incl. bkfst) **LB FACILITIES:** STV Xmas **SERVICES:** Lift **NOTES:** No smoking in restaurant **CARDS:**

★★75% Haringtons

Queen St BA1 1HE
☎ 01225 461728 01225 444804
e-mail: post@haringtonshotel.co.uk
Dir: A4 to George St & turn into Milsom St. 1st right into Quiet St & 1st left into Queen St

Dating back to the 18th century, this hotel has been completely refurbished to accommodate all modern facilities and comforts. The cafe-bar is open throughout the day for light meals and refreshments. A warm welcome is assured from the proprietors and their staff who create a delightful place to stay.

ROOMS: 13 en suite (3 fmly) No smoking in all bedrooms s £68-£98; d £88-£128 (incl. bkfst) **LB FACILITIES:** STV **NOTES:** No dogs (ex guide dogs) No smoking in restaurant Closed 24-26 Dec
CARDS:

★★69% Avondale Hotel & Waterside Restaurant
London Rd East, Bathford BA1 7RB
☎ 01225 859847 & 852207 Fax 01225 859847
Dir: *A46/A4 junct follow signs Chippenham/Batheaston/Bathford. Continue through Batheaston, hotel on right just before large rdbt*
The peaceful riverside location of this hotel is convenient for the city, and easily accessible from all major transport links. Bedrooms are well equipped, comfortable and some have balconies that overlook the extensive gardens. The restaurant is memorable for its many interesting architectural features as well as its varied menu, which includes vegetarian options.
ROOMS: 15 rms (13 en suite) (3 fmly) s £49-£55; d £69-£130 (incl. bkfst) **LB** **FACILITIES:** Fishing Boating, Fishing **CONF:** Thtr 50 Class 50 Board 40 **PARKING:** 60 **CARDS:**

★★68% Old Malt House
Radford, Timsbury BA2 0QF
☎ 01761 470106 Fax 01761 472726
e-mail: hotel@oldmalthouse.co.uk
Dir: *A367 towards Radstock for 1m pass Park & Ride, turn right onto B3115 towards Tunley/Timsbury. At sharp bend continue straight ahead & hotel is 2nd left*
An ideal base for exploring the many attractions the area has to offer, this former brewery malt house is peacefully located within easy striking distance of Bath. Bedrooms, including several on the ground floor, are well equipped and include some thoughtful touches. A varied choice of home-cooked meals is served in the pleasant restaurant.
ROOMS: 10 en suite (2 fmly) No smoking in all bedrooms s £55-£60; d £64-£78 (incl. bkfst) **LB** **PARKING:** 25 **NOTES:** No smoking in restaurant **CARDS:**

★★68% Wentworth House Hotel
106 Bloomfield Rd BA2 2AP
☎ 01225 339193 Fax 01225 310460
e-mail: stay@wentworthhouse.co.uk
Dir: *A367 Radstock/Shepton Mallet signs to small shopping area, 'The Bear' pub on right. Take 2nd turning past pub. Hotel on right*

Built in 1887, this imposing Victorian mansion enjoys a peaceful location overlooking the City of Bath, just 15 minutes' walk from the centre. Bedrooms are individually furnished, some with fine four-poster beds and include many thoughtful extras. Enjoyable home-cooked dinners are served in the conservatory restaurant. Outdoor attractions include a swimming pool and a hot tub.
ROOMS: 18 en suite (2 fmly) (9 GF) No smoking in 5 bedrooms s £55-£75; d £70-£105 (incl. bkfst) **LB** **FACILITIES: Spa** Outdoor swimming (H) Jacuzzi **PARKING:** 18 **NOTES:** No dogs No children 7yrs No smoking in restaurant Closed Xmas & New Year
CARDS:

See advert on this page

BATH, continued

⌂ Express By Holiday Inn Bath

Lower Bristol Rd, Brougham Hayes BA2 3QU
☎ 0870 444 2792 📠 0870 444 2793
e-mail: bath@ebhi.fsnet.co.uk

Dir: *from A4, right into Bathwick St, over rdbt onto Pultney Rd. Into Claverton St, straight over at next rdbt (Lower Bristol Rd). Hotel opposite Sainsburys*

A modern hotel ideal for families and business travellers. Fresh and uncomplicated, the spacious bedrooms include Sky TV, power shower and tea and coffee-making facilities. Continental buffet breakfast is included in the room rate; other meals may be taken at the nearby family pub or restaurant. For further details and the Express by Holiday Inn phone number, consult the Hotel Groups pages.
ROOMS: 126 en suite s £50-£89; d £50-£89 (incl. cont bkfst)
CONF: Thtr 30 Class 10 Board 18

⌂ Travelodge Bath (Royal Oak)

York Buildings, George St BA1 2EB
☎ 08700 850 950

Travelodge offers good quality, good value, modern accommodation. Ideal for families, the spacious, en suite bedrooms include remote-control TV, tea and coffee-making facilities, luxury beds and free morning newspaper. Meals can be taken at the nearby family restaurant. For further details and the Travelodge phone number, consult the Hotel Groups page.
ROOMS: 66 en suite (incl. bkfst) s fr £42.95; d fr £42.95

BATLEY, West Yorkshire — Map 19 SE22

★★70% Alder House

Towngate Rd, Healey Ln WF17 7HR
☎ 01924 444777 📠 01924 442644
e-mail: info@alderhousehotel.co.uk

Dir: *M62 junct 27/A62. After 2m turn left into Whitelee Rd, left at next junct. Left into Healey Ln & after 0.25m hotel on left down Towngate Rd*

An attractive Georgian house tucked away in leafy grounds. Bedrooms are pleasantly furnished and contain many comfortable extras. There is an intimate dining room offering a selection of interesting dishes, as well as a bar with a separate lounge area. The service and hospitality are both very good.
ROOMS: 20 en suite (1 fmly) (2 GF) No smoking in 3 bedrooms s £36-£50; d £55-£65 (incl. bkfst) **LB FACILITIES:** STV **CONF:** BC Thtr 80 Class 40 Board 35 Del from £80 **PARKING:** 52 **NOTES:** No smoking in restaurant Civ Wed 100
CARDS:

BATTLE, East Sussex — Map 07 TQ71

★★★73% Powder Mills

Powdermill Ln TN33 0SP
☎ 01424 775511 📠 01424 774540
e-mail: powdc@aol.com

Dir: *pass Abbey on A2100. 1st right, hotel 1m on right*

A delightful 18th-century country house hotel set amidst 150 acres of landscaped grounds with lakes and woodland. The individually decorated bedrooms are tastefully furnished and thoughtfully equipped, some rooms have sun terraces with lovely views over the lake. Public rooms include a cosy lounge bar, music room, drawing room, library, restaurant and conservatory.
ROOMS: 30 en suite 10 annexe en suite s £85-£90; d £110 (incl. bkfst) **LB FACILITIES:** STV Outdoor swimming Fishing Xmas **CONF:** Thtr 250 Class 50 Board 16 Del £45 **PARKING:** 101 **NOTES:** No smoking in restaurant Civ Wed 100 **CARDS:**

See advert on opposite page

BAWTRY, South Yorkshire — Map 16 SK69

★★★61% The Crown

High St DN10 6JW
☎ 0870 609 6147 📠 01302 711798
e-mail: crownbawtry@corushotels.com

Dir: *leave A1 at Blyth Service Station/A614 to Bawtry. Hotel on left in town centre*

A 12th-century port and a starting point for the Pilgrim Fathers, this market town coaching inn now caters for race-goers and shoppers visiting the Yorkshire Retail Outlet. The various public areas include an oak-panelled bar and a relaxed dining restaurant. Bedrooms are well equipped and come in a variety of styles and sizes.
ROOMS: 57 en suite (4 fmly) (20 GF) No smoking in 18 bedrooms s £32-£75; d £64-£85 (incl. bkfst) **LB CONF:** Thtr 150 Class 80 Board 60 Del from £85 **PARKING:** 50 **NOTES:** No smoking in restaurant Civ Wed 100 **CARDS:**

> Early start?
> Hotels at all star levels should provide in-room alarm clocks and/or alarm calls

BEACONSFIELD, Buckinghamshire Map 06 SU99

★★★★67% De Vere Bellhouse

Oxford Rd HP9 2XE
☎ 01753 887211 📠 01753 888231
e-mail: bellhouse@devere-hotels.com
Dir: *M40 junct 2, exit signed Gerrards Cross/Beaconsfield. At rdbt take A40 to Gerrards Cross. Hotel 1m on right*

DE VERE HOTELS

Surrounded by beautiful countryside, this distinctive, Mediterranean-style hotel is nevertheless conveniently located for access to major motorway networks. There is a range of conference and banqueting rooms, a smart restaurant and intimate cocktail bar. Guests also have the use of the indoor leisure club with its own bar and informal poolside brasserie.
ROOMS: 136 en suite (11 fmly) No smoking in 86 bedrooms s £155; d £175 (incl. bkfst) **LB FACILITIES: Spa** STV Indoor swimming (H) Squash Snooker Sauna Solarium Gym Jacuzzi Beauty therapy room Xmas **CONF:** BC Thtr 350 Class 200 Board 80 Del from £199 **SERVICES:** Lift **PARKING:** 405 **NOTES:** No smoking in restaurant Civ Wed 200 **CARDS:**

Innkeeper's Lodge

Aylesbury End HP9 1LW
☎ 01494 671211 📠 01494 685042
Dir: *M40 junct 2 turn left at next two rdbts. Pub on rdbt*
A new concept in the travel accommodation market. Smart rooms meet essential business requirements but also have home comforts. Dining options include all-day menus plus the added advantage of breakfast, which is included in the room price. For further details, consult the Hotel Groups page.
ROOMS: 32 en suite

BEAMINSTER, Dorset Map 04 ST40

★★★71% Bridge House

3 Prout Bridge DT8 3AY
☎ 01308 862200 📠 01308 863700
e-mail: enquiries@bridge-house.co.uk
Dir: *off A3066, 100yds from Town Square*
Dating back to the 13th century, this family-owned property offers friendly and attentive service. Bedrooms are tastefully furnished and decorated; those in the main house are generally more spacious than those in the adjacent coach house. Smartly presented public areas include the Georgian dining room, cosy bar and adjacent sitting room, together with a breakfast room overlooking the attractive garden.
ROOMS: 9 en suite 5 annexe en suite (1 fmly) (4 GF) No smoking in all bedrooms s £55-£99; d £104-£138 (incl. bkfst) **LB FACILITIES:** Tennis (hard) Xmas **CONF:** Thtr 20 Class 16 Board 16 Del from £132 **PARKING:** 22 **NOTES:** No smoking in restaurant Closed 27-30 Dec **CARDS:**

BEAMISH, Co Durham Map 19 NZ25

★★★69% Beamish Park

Beamish Burn Rd NE16 5EG
☎ 01207 230666 01207 281260
e-mail: reception@beamish-park-hotel.co.uk
Dir: *A1(M)/A692 towards Consett, then A6076 towards Stanley. Hotel on left behind Causey Arch Inn*
The Metro Centre, Beamish Museum and south Tyneside are all within striking distance of this modern hotel, set in open countryside alongside its own golf course and floodlit range. Bedrooms, some with their own patios, provide a diverse mix of styles and sizes. The conservatory bistro offers a modern menu.
ROOMS: 47 en suite (7 fmly) No smoking in 20 bedrooms **FACILITIES:** STV Golf 9 Putting green 20 bay floodlit golf driving range. Golf tuition by PGA professional **CONF:** Thtr 50 Class 20 Board 30 **PARKING:** 100 **CARDS:**

BEAULIEU, Hampshire Map 05 SU30

Courtesy & Care Award Top 200 - Hotel

★★★ Montagu Arms

Palace Ln SO42 7ZL
☎ 01590 612324 01590 612188
e-mail: reservations@montaguarmshotel.co.uk
Dir: *M27 junct 2, turn left at rdbt, follow signs for Beaulieu. Continue towards Dibden Purlieu, then right at rdbt. Hotel on left*
Old World charm is combined with modern cuisine and genuine hospitality at this well-known hotel. All of the bedrooms are individually decorated and thoughtfully equipped. The lounge, with its log burning fires, and the adjoining conservatory are an ideal place to enjoy an afternoon tea. Guests may choose to dine at either the stylish restaurant or the more informal Monty's. The Montagu Arms has been awarded The AA Courtesy & Care Award for England 2003-4
ROOMS: 23 en suite s £100-£160; d £145-£210 (incl. bkfst) **LB** **FACILITIES:** Croquet lawn Use of health club in Brockenhurst Xmas **CONF:** Thtr 50 Class 16 Board 26 Del £165 **PARKING:** 86 **NOTES:** No dogs (ex guide dogs) Civ Wed 60 **CARDS:**

See advert on page 83

★★★76% Master Builders House Hotel

SO42 7XB
☎ 01590 616253 01590 616297
e-mail: res@themasterbuilders.co.uk
Dir: *M27 junct 2, follow Beaulieu signs. At T-junct left onto B3056, 1st left to Bucklers Hard. Hotel 2m on left before village entrance*
The name of the hotel is a testament to the master shipbuilder Henry Adams whose house this once was. A full list of the famous ships built within the village may be found in the Yachtsman's Bar. The Riverside Restaurant and many of the individually styled bedrooms enjoy views over the Beaulieu River. For guests wishing to travel to the Isle of Wight, the hotel has its own boat.
ROOMS: 8 en suite 17 annexe en suite (2 fmly) (8 GF) No smoking in 19 bedrooms s £125-£215; d £165-£215 (incl. bkfst) **LB** **FACILITIES:** STV Fishing can sail from hotel on Beaulieu river Xmas **CONF:** Thtr 50 Board 25 Del from £155 **PARKING:** 70 **NOTES:** No dogs (ex guide dogs) Civ Wed 60 **CARDS:**

★★★63% Beaulieu

Beaulieu Rd SO42 7YQ
☎ 023 8029 3344 023 8029 2729
e-mail: reservations@newforesthotels.co.uk
Dir: *M27 junct 1/A337 towards Lyndhurst. Left at lights in Lyndhurst, through village, turn right onto B3056, continue for 3m.*
Conveniently located in the heart of the New Forest and close to Beaulieu Road railway station, this popular, small hotel provides an ideal base for exploring the surrounding area. Facilities include an indoor swimming pool, an outdoor children's play area and an adjoining pub. A daily changing menu is offered in the restaurant.
ROOMS: 15 en suite 3 annexe en suite (2 fmly) s £72.50-£80; d £115-£130 (incl. bkfst) **LB** **FACILITIES:** Indoor swimming (H) Steam room Xmas **CONF:** Thtr 60 Class 40 Board 30 Del from £90 **PARKING:** 60 **NOTES:** No smoking in restaurant Civ Wed 80 **CARDS:**

BEBINGTON, Merseyside Map 15 SJ38

Travelodge Wirral

New Chester Rd CH62 9AQ
☎ 08700 850 950 0151 327 2489
Dir: *on A41, northbound off M53 junct 5*
Travelodge offers good quality, good value, modern accommodation. Ideal for families, the spacious, en suite bedrooms include remote-control TV, tea and coffee-making facilities, luxury beds and free morning newspaper. Meals can be taken at the nearby family restaurant. For further details and the Travelodge phone number, consult the Hotel Groups page.
ROOMS: 31 en suite s fr £42.95; d fr £42.95

BECKENHAM, Greater London
See LONDON SECTION plan 1 G1

Innkeeper's Lodge

422 Upper Elmers End Rd BR3 3HQ
☎ 020 8650 2233
Dir: *From M25 junct 6 Croydon, A232 for Shirley. At West Wickham take A214 opposite Eden Park Station*
A new concept in the travel accommodation market. Smart rooms meet essential business requirements but also have home comforts. Dining options include all-day menus plus the added advantage of breakfast, which is included in the room price. For further details, consult the Hotel Groups page.
ROOMS: 24 en suite

BECKINGTON, Somerset Map 04 ST85

★★68% Woolpack Inn

BA3 6SP
☎ 01373 831244 01373 831223
Dir: *on A36*
This charming coaching inn dates back to the 16th century and retains many original features including flagstone floors, open fireplaces and exposed beams. There is a cosy lounge and a choice of places to eat: the bar for light snacks and for more

continued

substantial meals the Oak Room or the Garden Room, which leads onto a pleasant inner courtyard.
ROOMS: 12 en suite No smoking in 1 bedroom **FACILITIES:** STV **CONF:** Thtr 30 Class 20 Board 20 **PARKING:** 16 **NOTES:** No children 5yrs **CARDS:**

⇧ Travelodge

BA3 6SF
☎ 08700 850 950 🖷 01373 830251
Dir: *on A36*
Travelodge offers good quality, good value, modern accommodation. Ideal for families, the spacious, en suite bedrooms include remote-control TV, tea and coffee-making facilities, luxury beds and free morning newspaper. Meals can be taken at the nearby family restaurant. For further details and the Travelodge phone number, consult the Hotel Groups page.
ROOMS: 40 en suite s fr £42.95; d fr £42.95

BEDFORD, Bedfordshire — Map 12 TL04

★★★74% ⊛⊛ Woodlands Manor

Green Ln, Clapham MK41 6EP
☎ 0871 871 3248 🖷 0871 871 3249
e-mail: woodlands.manor@pageant.co.uk
Dir: *A6 towards Kettering. Clapham 1st village N of town centre. On entering village 1st right into Green Lane, Manor 200mtrs on right*

Sitting in acres of well-tended grounds, this Victorian manor offers a warm welcome. Bedrooms are spacious and well appointed providing a variety of thoughtful extras. Traditional public areas include a cosy bar and restaurant where award-winning food is served.
ROOMS: 30 en suite 3 annexe en suite (4 fmly) (10 GF) No smoking in 6 bedrooms s £45-£65; d £75-£135 (incl. bkfst) **LB** **FACILITIES:** STV Full leisure facilities nearby at no extra cost. Xmas **CONF:** Thtr 80 Class 40 Board 40 Del from £105 **PARKING:** 100 **NOTES:** No smoking in restaurant Civ Wed 80 **CARDS:**

★★★67% The Barns

Cardington Rd MK44 3SA
☎ 0870 609 6108 🖷 01234 273102
e-mail: barns@corushotels.com
Dir: *From M1 J13 follow A421 for approx 10m until A603 Sandy / Bedford exit, hotel on right at 2nd rdbt*
A tranquil location on the outskirts of Bedford, friendly staff and well-equipped bedrooms are the main attractions here. Cosy day rooms and two informal bars add to the appeal, while large windows in the restaurant make the most of the view over the

continued

river. The original barn now houses the conference and function suite.

ROOMS: 48 en suite (20 GF) No smoking in 16 bedrooms s £75-£112; d £85-£133 (incl. bkfst) **LB** **FACILITIES:** STV Free use of local leisure centre (1mile) Xmas **CONF:** Thtr 120 Class 40 Board 40 Del from £110 **PARKING:** 90 **NOTES:** No smoking in restaurant Civ Wed 90 **CARDS:**

⇧ Innkeeper's Lodge Bedford

403 Goldington Rd MK41 0DS
☎ 0870 243 0500 & 01234 272707
🖷 01234 343926
Dir: *on A428*
A new concept in the travel accommodation market. Smart rooms meet essential business requirements but also have home comforts. Dining options include all-day menus plus the added advantage of breakfast, which is included in the room price. For further details, consult the Hotel Groups page.
ROOMS: 47 en suite **CONF:** Thtr 25 Class 25 Board 20

⇧ Travel Inn

Priory Country Park, Barkers Ln MK41 9DJ
☎ 08701 977030 🖷 01234 352883
Dir: *M1 junct 13/A421/A6 towards Bedford then A428 signed Cambridge. Cross River Ouse & right at next rdbt, follow signs for Priory Country Park*
Travel Inn offers good-quality, value-for-money accommodation. Spacious, en suite rooms with bath and shower comfortably accommodate a family of up to two adults and two children (to age 15). The restaurant and bar offers a varied menu. For further details and the Travel Inn phone number, consult the Hotel Groups page.
ROOMS: 32 en suite s £44.95; d £44.95

⇧ Travelodge Bedford East

Black Cat Roundabout MK44 3OT
☎ 08700 850 950
Dir: *A1 North*
Travelodge offers good quality, good value, modern accommodation. Ideal for families, the spacious, en suite bedrooms include remote-control TV, tea and coffee-making facilities, luxury beds and free morning newspaper. Meals can be taken at the nearby family restaurant. For further details and the Travelodge phone number, consult the Hotel Groups page.
ROOMS: 40 en suite (incl. bkfst) s fr £42.95; d fr £42.95

BELFORD, Northumberland Map 21 NU13

Purdy Lodge

Adderstone Services NE70 7JU
☎ 01668 213000 📠 01668 213131
e-mail: james@purdylodge.co.uk
Dir: *turn off A1 onto B1341 then immediate left*

Situated on the A1, this family-owned lodge provides convenient practical accommodation. All the bedrooms look out over fields towards Bamburgh Castle, and are quiet. Food is readily available in the attractive restaurant, the smart 24-hour café, or the cosy lounge bar.

ROOMS: 20 en suite s £45; d £45 **CONF:** Thtr 40 Class 30 Board 20

BELLINGHAM, Northumberland Map 21 NY88

★★69% *Riverdale Hall*

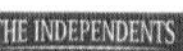

NE48 2JT
☎ 01434 220254 📠 01434 220457
e-mail: iben@riverdalehall.demon.co.uk
Dir: *turn off B6320, after bridge, hotel on left*

Dating from 1866 this hotel is the former home of Lord Strafford. Public areas are decorated with sporting memorabilia and the hotel boasts its own cricket square, football pitch and fishing on the Tyne. Bedrooms, some with balconies, are spacious and offer modern décor. Local produce and Thai specialities feature on the interesting menus.

ROOMS: 20 en suite (11 fmly) **FACILITIES:** Indoor swimming (H) Fishing Sauna Croquet lawn Putting green Cricket field ch fac **CONF:** Thtr 60 Class 40 Board 40 **PARKING:** 60 **CARDS:**

BELPER, Derbyshire Map 11 SK34

★★★71% Makeney Hall Hotel

Makeney, Milford DE56 0RS
☎ 0870 609 6136 📠 01332 842777
e-mail: makeneyhall@corushotels.com
Dir: *off A6 at Milford, signed Makeney. Hotel 0.25m on left*

This restored Victorian mansion stands in six acres of landscaped gardens and grounds above the River Derwent. Bedrooms vary in style and are generally very spacious. They are divided between the main house and the ground floor courtyard. Comfortable

continued

public rooms include a lounge, bar and spacious restaurant with views of the gardens.

ROOMS: 27 en suite 18 annexe en suite (8 fmly) No smoking in 15 bedrooms s £94-£150; d £104-£150 **LB FACILITIES:** STV Xmas **CONF:** Thtr 180 Class 80 Board 50 Del from £125 **SERVICES:** Lift **PARKING:** 150 **NOTES:** No smoking in restaurant Civ Wed 150 **CARDS:**

★★70% The Lion Hotel & Restaurant

Bridge St DE56 1AX
☎ 01773 824033 📠 01773 828393
e-mail: enquiries@lionhotel.uk.com
Dir: *8m NW of Derby, hotel on A6*

Situated in the centre of town and on the border of the Peak District, this 18th-century hotel provides an ideal base for exploring local attractions. The tasteful bedrooms are well equipped and the public rooms include an attractive restaurant and two cosy bars; a modern function suite also proves popular.

ROOMS: 22 en suite (2 fmly) No smoking in 7 bedrooms s fr £67.50; d fr £80 (incl. bkfst) **FACILITIES:** STV Xmas **CONF:** Thtr 130 Class 60 Board 50 Del from £85 **PARKING:** 30 **NOTES:** No dogs (ex guide dogs) No smoking in restaurant Civ Wed 60 **CARDS:**

BELTON, Lincolnshire Map 11 SK93

★★★★75% De Vere Belton Woods

NG32 2LN
☎ 01476 593200 📠 01476 574547
e-mail: belton.woods@devere-hotels.com
Dir: *A1/B1174, signed to Belton House. Turn left towards Great Gonerby, then left onto A607. Hotel 0.5m on left*

Beautifully located amidst 475 acres of picturesque countryside, this is a destination venue for lovers of golf and sports, as well as

continued

a relaxing executive retreat for seminars. Comfortable and well-equipped accommodation complements the elegant and spacious public areas, which provide a good choice of drinking and dining options.

ROOMS: 136 en suite (20 fmly) (68 GF) No smoking in 115 bedrooms s £135-£215; d £155-£235 (incl. bkfst) **LB** **FACILITIES:** STV Indoor swimming (H) Golf 18 Tennis (hard) Squash Snooker Sauna Solarium Gym Croquet lawn Putting green Jacuzzi On-site outdoor activity company Swimming pool supervised entertainment ch fac Xmas **CONF:** BC Thtr 245 Class 180 Board 80 Del from £150 **SERVICES:** Lift **PARKING:** 500 **NOTES:** No smoking in restaurant Civ Wed 80 **CARDS:**

BEMBRIDGE See Wight, Isle of

BERKELEY, Gloucestershire

Map 04 ST69

★★66% *The Old Schoolhouse Hotel & Restaurant*

34 Canonbury St GL13 9BG

☎ 01453 811711 📠 01453 511761

Dir: *0.5m off A38 next to Berkeley Castle. Follow tourist signs*

Situated just 10 minutes from the M5, this unique hotel is a conversion of a chapel and schoolhouse. Many original features have been retained. Bedrooms, all of a generous size, have extensive modern facilities, and public areas include a drawing room and dining room, both with crackling log fires in winter. Cooking is accomplished.

ROOMS: 8 en suite (1 fmly) No smoking in all bedrooms **CONF:** Class 12 Board 12 **PARKING:** 12 **NOTES:** No dogs (ex guide dogs) No smoking in restaurant **CARDS:**

BERKELEY ROAD, Gloucestershire

Map 04 SO70

★★★66% Prince of Wales

Berkeley Rd GL13 9HD

☎ 01453 810474 📠 01453 511370

e-mail: PrinceofWaleshotel@Berkeleyglos.fsnet.co.uk

Dir: *on A38, 6m S of M5 junct 13/6m N of junct 14*

Handily situated by the A38, this smartly presented hotel is convenient for major road networks. Bedrooms are generally a good size with a range of facilities. The public bar is popular with both residents and the local trade, whilst the restaurant menu features a selection of Italian dishes.

ROOMS: 43 en suite (2 fmly) No smoking in 10 bedrooms s £63-£69; d £73-£79 **LB** **FACILITIES:** STV **CONF:** Thtr 200 Class 60 Board 60 Del from £90 **PARKING:** 150 **CARDS:**

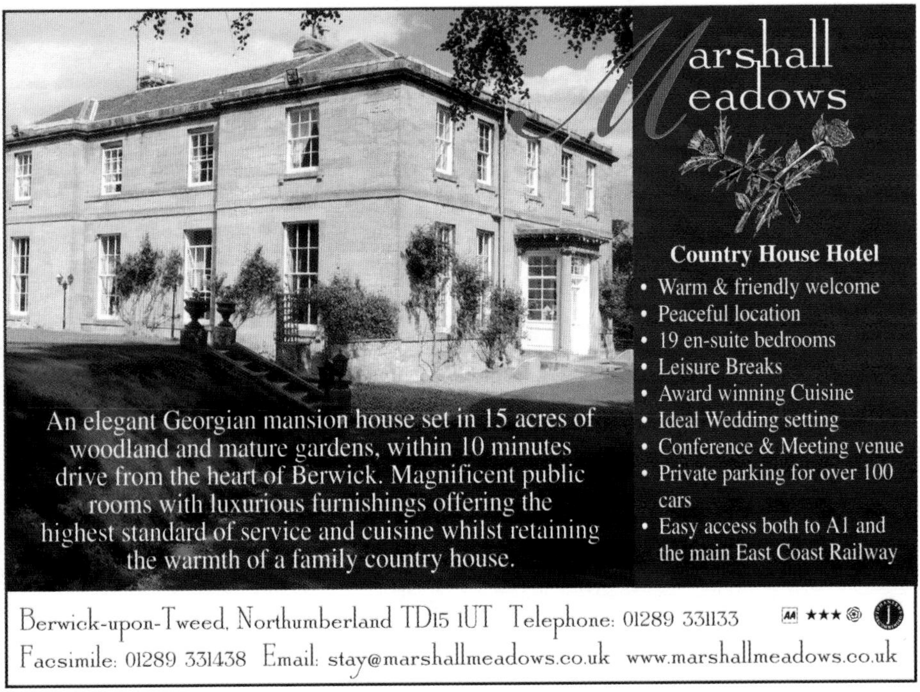

B

BERWICK-UPON-TWEED, Northumberland Map 21 NT95

★★★70% Marshall Meadows Country House

TD15 1UT
☎ 01289 331133 01289 331438
e-mail: stay@marshallmeadows.co.uk
Dir: *signed directly off A1, 300yds from Scottish Border*

This stylish Georgian mansion is set in wooded grounds flanked by farmland and has convenient access from the A1. A popular venue for weddings and conferences, it offers comfortable and well-equipped bedrooms. Public rooms include a cosy bar, a relaxing lounge and a two-tier restaurant, which serves imaginative dishes.

ROOMS: 19 en suite (2 fmly) No smoking in 10 bedrooms s £80-£90; d £105-£120 (incl. bkfst) **LB FACILITIES:** Croquet lawn Petanque **CONF:** Thtr 180 Class 120 Board 60 Del from £105 **PARKING:** 87 **NOTES:** No smoking in restaurant Closed 15-27 Dec Civ Wed 180 **CARDS:**

See advert on page 89

★★★63% King's Arms

43 Hide Hill TD15 1EJ
☎ 01289 307454 01289 308867
e-mail: king's_arms.hotel@virgin.net
Dir: *follow town centre signs from A1. Hotel behind Guild Hall, on left of Hide Hill*

Now a hotel of contrasting styles, the Kings Arms was built in the 17th century. The bar, restaurant and adjoining café are modern and trendy. A walled garden is perfect for a relaxing drink in summer months. Though bedrooms are being upgraded, most are set on traditional lines but have the benefit of being of good size.

ROOMS: 35 en suite (3 fmly) No smoking in 20 bedrooms s £69-£84; d £109-£139 (incl. bkfst & dinner) **LB FACILITIES:** Xmas **CONF:** Thtr 200 Class 100 Board 50 Del from £95 **NOTES:** No smoking in restaurant Civ Wed 50 **CARDS:**

★★64% Queens Head

Sandgate TD15 1EP
☎ 01289 307852 01289 307858
e-mail: queensheadhotel@berwickontweed.fsbusiness.co.uk
Dir: *A1 towards centre & Town Hall, along High St. Turn right at bottom to Hide Hill, located next to cinema*

A small hotel situated close to the old walls of this former garrison town that continues to undergo a makeover. The cosy bar remains, but the reception lounge and restaurant have been transformed into modern stylish areas. Both provide an impressive choice of tasty freshly prepared dishes from a daily-changing blackboard menu. Bedrooms are being upgraded with pine furnishings.

ROOMS: 6 en suite (5 fmly) No smoking in all bedrooms s £40; d £60 (incl. bkfst) **LB NOTES:** No smoking in restaurant
CARDS:

BEVERLEY, East Riding of Yorkshire Map 17 TA03

★★★68% Tickton Grange

Tickton HU17 9SH
☎ 01964 543666 01964 542556
e-mail: maggy@tickton-grange.demon.co.uk
Dir: *3m NE on A1035*

A charming Georgian country house situated in four acres of private grounds and attractive gardens. Bedrooms are individual, and redecorated to a high specification. Pre-dinner drinks may be enjoyed in the comfortable library lounge, prior to enjoying fine, modern British cooking in the restaurant. The hotel has excellent facilities for both weddings and business conferences.

ROOMS: 17 en suite (2 fmly) (4 GF) No smoking in all bedrooms s £70; d £80 **LB CONF:** Thtr 200 Class 100 Board 80 Del from £101 **PARKING:** 65 **NOTES:** No dogs (ex guide dogs) No smoking in restaurant RS 25-29 Dec Civ Wed 150
CARDS:

★★★67% The Beverley Arms Hotel

corus hotels

North Bar Within HU17 8DD
☎ 01482 869241 01482 870907
e-mail: 113566,1542@compuserve.com
Dir: *opp St Marys Church. Left lane at lights just before North Bar. Hotel 100yds on left. Car park at rear*

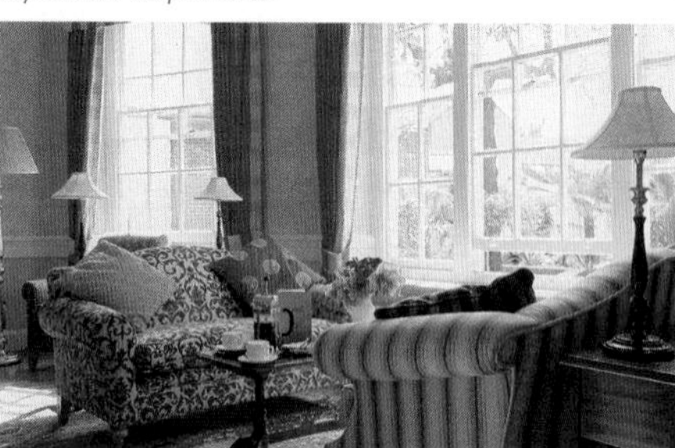

This hotel has historic links to the highwayman Dick Turpin, and today it features the spacious, flagstoned, Shires Lounge, which includes the bar and several cosy sitting areas with a lounge menu. The attractively appointed restaurant also offers careful and friendly service. Bedrooms are all equipped with modern comforts and there are good parking facilities.

ROOMS: 56 en suite (4 fmly) No smoking in 41 bedrooms
FACILITIES: Complimentary use of David Lloyd Racquet & Health Club
CONF: Thtr 80 Class 40 Board 30 Del £112 **SERVICES:** Lift
PARKING: 50 **NOTES:** No smoking in restaurant
CARDS:

★★★67% Lairgate Hotel

30/32 Lairgate HU17 8EP
☎ 01482 882141 01482 861067
e-mail: beverleylairgate@aol.com
Dir: *A63 towards town centre. Hotel 220yds on left (follow one-way system)*

Located just off the market square, this pleasing Georgian hotel has now been refurbished to offer comfortable accommodation and public areas. Bedroom styles vary and each room is suitably equipped and fully en suite. Public rooms include a comfortable lounge, a lounge bar, restaurant and popular sun terrace.

ROOMS: 16 en suite (1 fmly) (2 GF) No smoking in 12 bedrooms s fr £60; d fr £85 (incl. bkfst) **LB CONF:** Board 20 Del from £27.15 **PARKING:** 16 **NOTES:** No dogs (ex guide dogs) No smoking in restaurant Civ Wed 40 **CARDS:**

★★73% ❀❀ The Manor House

Northlands, Walkington HU17 8RT
☎ 01482 881645 ▤ 01482 866501
e-mail: the-manor-house@fsbusiness.co.uk
Dir: *4m SW off B1230. Follow 'Walkington' signs from M62 junct 38*

This delightful country-house hotel is set in open country amid well-tended gardens. The spacious bedrooms have been attractively decorated and thoughtfully equipped. Public rooms include a conservatory restaurant and a very inviting lounge. A good range of dishes is available from two menus, with an emphasis on local produce.

ROOMS: 6 en suite 1 annexe en suite (1 fmly) (1 GF) s £75-£80; d £85-£110 **LB** **CONF:** Thtr 20 Class 20 Board 20 **PARKING:** 40 **NOTES:** No smoking in restaurant Closed 24 Dec-4 Jan RS Sun Civ Wed 100 **CARDS:**

BEWDLEY, Worcestershire — Map 10 SO77

★★65% The George

Load St DY12 2AW
☎ 01299 402117 ▤ 01299 401269
e-mail: enquiries@georgehotelbewdley.co.uk
Dir: *in town centre opposite town hall*

Situated in the heart of Bewdley, this friendly 16th-century inn features large oak beams, panelling, slate tiles and traditional fireplaces. Bedrooms are individually decorated and furnished to a good standard. Public areas include a coffee shop, function rooms, bars and a restaurant serving a wide-ranging menu.

ROOMS: 11 en suite s £50-£58; d £72-£85 (incl. bkfst) **LB** **CONF:** Thtr 50 Class 50 Board 40 **PARKING:** 50 **NOTES:** No dogs (ex guide dogs) No smoking in restaurant **CARDS:**

★★63% Black Boy

Kidderminster Rd DY12 1AG
☎ 01299 402119 ▤ 01299 402119
e-mail: rc@midnet.co.uk
Dir: *follow town centre signs*

This privately-owned and personally-run 18th-century inn stands close to both the River Severn and the centre of this lovely old town. The Severn Valley steam railway is also nearby. A good range of food is served in both the cosy restaurant and bar. The accommodation includes a two-bedroom unit, which is located in a separate house and is ideal for families.

ROOMS: 8 en suite (2 fmly) d £60-£80 (incl. bkfst) **LB** **CONF:** Thtr 20 Class 20 Board 20 **PARKING:** 28 **NOTES:** No dogs (ex guide dogs) No smoking in restaurant **CARDS:**

> Late for dinner?
> Quality Standards mean that last orders for dinner vary according to star rating and should be no earlier than:
> ★★ 7.00pm ★★★ 8.00pm ★★★★ 9.00pm
> ★★★★★ 10.00pm

> Town House Hotel
> Country House Hotel
> Travel Accommodation

BEXLEY, Greater London — Map 06 TQ47

★★★★65% Bexleyheath Marriott Hotel

1 Broadway DA6 7JZ
☎ 020 8298 1000 ▤ 020 8298 1234
e-mail: bexleyheath@marriotthotels.co.uk
Dir: *M25 junct 2/A2 towards London. Exit at Black Prince junct onto A220, signed Bexleyheath. Turn left at 2nd set of lights into hotel*

Well-positioned for access to major road networks, this large, modern hotel offers spacious, air-conditioned bedrooms with a comprehensive range of extra facilities. Planters Bar is a popular venue for pre-dinner drinks and traditional English fare is served in the Copper Restaurant. The hotel also boasts a well-equipped leisure centre.

ROOMS: 142 en suite (16 fmly) No smoking in 53 bedrooms s £64-£70; d £78-£90 (incl. bkfst) **LB** **FACILITIES: Spa** STV Indoor swimming (H) Solarium Gym Steam room Xmas **CONF:** Thtr 250 Class 120 Board 34 Del from £135 **SERVICES:** Lift air con **PARKING:** 77 **NOTES:** Civ Wed 40 **CARDS:**

U *Holiday Inn Bexley*

Black Prince Interchange, Southwold Rd DA5 1ND
☎ 0870 400 9006 ▤ 01322 526113
Dir: *A2 to exit for A220/A223 Black Prince interchange Bexley, Bexleyheath & Crayford*

At the time of going to press, the classification for this hotel was not confirmed. Please refer to the AA internet site www.theAA.com for current information.

ROOMS: 108 en suite (18 fmly) No smoking in 50 bedrooms **CONF:** Thtr 130 Class 41 Board 50 **SERVICES:** Lift **PARKING:** 200 **NOTES:** Civ Wed 80 **CARDS:**

BIBURY, Gloucestershire — Map 05 SP10

★★★77% ❀❀ *Swan*

GL7 5NW
☎ 01285 740695 ▤ 01285 740473
e-mail: info@swanhotel.co.uk
Dir: *off B4425, by bridge over the River Coln*

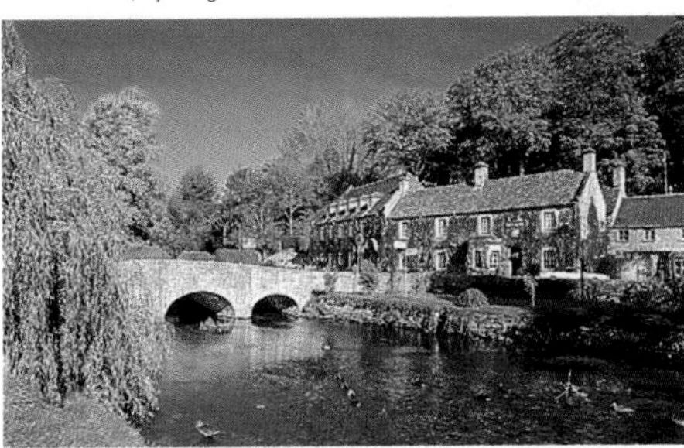

The Swan hotel, originally built as a 17th-century coaching inn, is set in peaceful, picturesque and beautiful surroundings. It now provides well-equipped and smartly presented accommodation, and public areas that are comfortable and elegant. There is a choice of dining options to suit all tastes.

ROOMS: 20 en suite (1 fmly) **FACILITIES:** Fishing Jacuzzi **CONF:** Thtr 80 Board 35 **SERVICES:** Lift **PARKING:** 27 **NOTES:** No dogs (ex guide dogs) No smoking in restaurant Civ Wed **CARDS:**

See advert on page 93

BIBURY, continued

★★★74% Bibury Court
GL7 5NT
☎ 01285 740337 01285 740660
e-mail: info@biburycourt.co.uk
Dir: *on B4425 beside the River Coln, behind St Marys Church*
Dating back to Tudor times, this elegant manor is the perfect antidote to the hustle and bustle of the modern world. Spacious public areas have abundant charm and character, while bedrooms offer solid quality and contemporary comfort. Seasonal produce is used to good effect in carefully prepared dishes served by a friendly team of helpful staff.
ROOMS: 18 en suite (3 fmly) (1 GF) s £115; d £130-£200 (incl. cont bkfst) **LB** **FACILITIES:** Fishing Croquet lawn **CONF:** Board 12 Del £190 **PARKING:** 100 **NOTES:** No smoking in restaurant Civ Wed 32
CARDS:

See advert on opposite page

BICESTER, Oxfordshire Map 11 SP52

★★★71% Bignell Park Hotel & Restaurant
THE INDEPENDENTS
Chesterton OX26 1UE
☎ 01869 326550 01869 322729
e-mail: enq@bignellparkhotel.co.uk
Dir: *M40 junct 9/A41 to Bicester, over 1st & 2nd rdbt, left at mini rdbt & follow signs to Witney A4095. Hotel 0.5m from Witney turn off*
Situated in the pretty village of Chesterton, this friendly and charming hotel offers a beamed and characterful restaurant complete with gallery in which an imaginative and varied menu is served. All bedrooms are spacious and furnishings are of a high standard throughout.
ROOMS: 23 en suite s £80-£135; d £80-£145 (incl. bkfst) **LB** **FACILITIES:** Xmas **CONF:** Thtr 20 Class 8 Board 14 Del from £130 **PARKING:** 40 **NOTES:** No dogs (ex guide dogs) No smoking in restaurant Civ Wed 60 **CARDS:**

Travelodge (Cherwell Valley)
Travelodge
Moto Service Area, Northampton Rd, Ardley OX6 9RD
☎ 08700 850 950 01869 345030
Dir: *M40 junct 10*
Travelodge offers good quality, good value, modern accommodation. Ideal for families, the spacious, en suite bedrooms include remote-control TV, tea and coffee-making facilities, luxury beds and free morning newspaper. Meals can be taken at the nearby family restaurant. For further details and the Travelodge phone number, consult the Hotel Groups page.
ROOMS: 98 en suite s fr £42.95; d fr £42.95 **CONF:** Thtr 40 Class 20 Board 20

BIDEFORD, Devon Map 03 SS42

★★★69% Royal
Brend Hotels
Barnstaple St EX39 4AE
☎ 01237 472005 01237 478957
e-mail: info@royalbideford.co.uk
Dir: *at eastern end of Bideford Bridge*
A quiet and relaxing hotel, the Royal is set on the river bank within five minutes' walk of the busy town centre and quay. Well-maintained public areas are bright and retain much of the charm and style of its 16th-century origins, particularly in the wood-panelled Kingsley Suite. Bedrooms are well equipped and comfortable. Dinner and lounge snacks are appetising and well cooked.
ROOMS: 32 en suite (3 fmly) (2 GF) s £47-£72; d £47-£72 **LB** **FACILITIES:** STV entertainment Xmas **CONF:** Thtr 100 Class 100 Board 100 **SERVICES:** Lift **PARKING:** 70 **NOTES:** Civ Wed 100
CARDS:

★★74% Yeoldon Country House
Durrant Ln, Northam EX39 2RL
☎ 01237 474400 01237 476618
e-mail: yeoldonhouse@aol.com
Dir: *A39 from Barnstaple over River Torridge Bridge. At rdbt turn right onto A386 towards Northam, then 3rd right into Durrant Ln*

In a tranquil location with superb views over the River Torridge and attractive grounds, the Yeoldon is a charming Victorian house. Bedrooms are individually decorated, some have balconies with breathtaking views and all are well equipped. The public rooms are full of character with many interesting features and artefacts. Dinner offers a daily changing menu with fresh local produce and imaginative dishes.
ROOMS: 10 en suite No smoking in all bedrooms s £55-£65; d £90-£105 (incl. bkfst) **LB** **PARKING:** 20 **NOTES:** No smoking in restaurant Closed 24-27 Dec **CARDS:**

See advert on opposite page

BIGBURY-ON-SEA, Devon Map 03 SX64

★★72% Henley
TQ7 4AR
☎ 01548 810240 01548 810240
Dir: *through Bigbury, past Golf Centre into Bigbury-on-Sea. Hotel on left as road slopes towards shore*
Built in Edwardian times and complete with its own private cliff path to a sandy beach, this small hotel boasts stunning views from an elevated position. The Henley has an unhurried atmosphere which, when combined with its understated style, makes it a peaceful retreat and perfect for relaxing. The menu offers innovative dishes cooked with care from local produce.
ROOMS: 6 en suite (1 fmly) No smoking in all bedrooms **PARKING:** 9 **NOTES:** No smoking in restaurant Closed Dec-Feb
CARDS:

BILBROUGH, North Yorkshire Map 16 SE54

Travel Inn (York South West)
travel inn
Bilborough Top, Colton YO23 3PP
☎ 0870 238 3317 01937 835934
Dir: *on A64 between Tadcaster & York*
Travel Inn offers good-quality, value-for-money accommodation. Spacious, en suite rooms with bath and shower comfortably

continued

accommodate a family of up to two adults and two children (to age 15). The restaurant and bar offers a varied menu. For further details and the Travel Inn phone number, consult the Hotel Groups page.
ROOMS: 59 en suite s £44.95; d £44.95 **CONF:** Thtr 20 Board 12

⌂ Travelodge York

Travelodge

Tadcaster LS24 8EG
☎ 08700 850 950 📠 01937 531823
Dir: *A64 eastbound*
Travelodge offers good quality, good value, modern accommodation. Ideal for families, the spacious, en suite bedrooms include remote-control TV, tea and coffee-making facilities, luxury beds and free morning newspaper. Meals can be taken at the nearby family restaurant. For further details and the Travelodge phone number, consult the Hotel Groups page.
ROOMS: 62 en suite s fr £42.95; d fr £42.95

BILLINGHAM See Stockton-on-Tees

BILSBORROW, Lancashire

Map 18 SD53

⌂ Premier Lodge (Preston North)

PREMIER LODGE

Garstang Rd PR3 0RN
☎ 0870 9906410 📠 0870 9906411
Dir: *M6 junct 32 on A6 towards Garstang*
Premier Lodge offers modern, well-equipped, en suite accommodation suitable for both business and leisure travellers. Meals can be taken at the adjacent popular restaurant and bar, which is fully licensed. For further details, consult the Hotel Groups page.
ROOMS: 40 en suite s £48; d £48

B

BINFIELD, Berkshire
Map 05 SU87

Travelodge Bracknell
London Rd RG12 4AA
☎ 08700 850 950
Dir: *M4 junct 10 (Bracknell) take 1st exit towards Binfield*
Travelodge offers good quality, good value, modern accommodation. Ideal for families, the spacious, en suite bedrooms include remote-control TV, tea and coffee-making facilities, luxury beds and free morning newspaper. Meals can be taken at the nearby family restaurant. For further details and the Travelodge phone number, consult the Hotel Groups page.
ROOMS: 35 en suite s fr £42.95; d fr £42.95

BINGLEY, West Yorkshire
Map 19 SE13

Travel Inn (Bradford North)
Off Bradford Rd BD20 5NH
☎ 08701 977038 📠 01274 551692
Dir: *M62 (J27) follow signs for A650, then to Bingley Main Street. At next rndbt straight on 50mtrs on left. (15 minutes drive from Leeds/Bradford Airport)*
Travel Inn offers good-quality, value-for-money accommodation. Spacious, en suite rooms with bath and shower comfortably accommodate a family of up to two adults and two children (to age 15). The restaurant and bar offers a varied menu. For further details and the Travel Inn phone number, consult the Hotel Groups page.
ROOMS: 40 en suite s £44.95; d £44.95

BIRCHANGER GREEN MOTORWAY SERVICE AREA (M11), Essex
Map 06 TL52

Welcome Lodge
Birchanger Green, Bishop Stortford CM23 5QZ
☎ 01279 656477 📠 01279 656590
e-mail: birchanger.hotel@welcomebreak.co.uk
Dir: *M11 junct 8*
This modern building offers accommodation in smart, spacious and well-equipped bedrooms, suitable for families and business travellers, and all with en suite bathrooms. Refreshments may be taken at the nearby family restaurant. For further details and the Welcome Break phone number, consult the Hotel Groups page.
ROOMS: 60 en suite s £69; d £69

BIRCH MOTORWAY SERVICE AREA (M62), Greater Manchester
Map 16 SD80

Travelodge Manchester North (Eastbound)
M62 Service Area East Bound OL10 2HQ
☎ 08700 850 950
Travelodge offers good quality, good value, modern accommodation. Ideal for families, the spacious, en suite bedrooms include remote-control TV, tea and coffee-making facilities, luxury beds and free morning newspaper. Meals can be taken at the nearby family restaurant. For further details and the Travelodge phone number, consult the Hotel Groups page.
ROOMS: 55 en suite s fr £42.95; d fr £42.95

Travelodge Manchester North (Westbound)
M62 Service Area West Bound OL10 2HQ
☎ 08700 850 950
Travelodge offers good quality, good value, modern accommodation. Ideal for families, the spacious, en suite bedrooms include remote-control TV, tea and coffee-making facilities, luxury beds and free morning newspaper. Meals can be taken at the nearby family restaurant. For further details and the Travelodge phone number, consult the Hotel Groups page.
ROOMS: 35 en suite (incl. bkfst) s fr £42.95; d fr £42.95

BIRKENHEAD, Merseyside
Map 15 SJ38

★★★69% The Bowler Hat Hotel
2 Talbot Rd, Prenton CH43 2HH
☎ 0151 652 4931 📠 0151 653 8127
e-mail: bowlerhathotel@corushotels.com
Dir: *M53 junct 3, follow Birkenhead signs, left at lights before Swan pub into Holm Ln, continue to t-junct, left into Talbot Rd. Hotel 200yds on left*

This friendly hotel is situated in a quiet, leafy area on the edge of town. Extensive function facilities are provided and the hotel is popular for wedding receptions. Bedrooms are well equipped with modern facilities. There is a popular restaurant and a selection of lighter meals is available in the bar.
ROOMS: 32 en suite No smoking in 18 bedrooms s £55-£85; d £65-£95 (incl. bkfst) **LB FACILITIES:** Xmas **CONF:** Thtr 150 Class 80 Board 40 Del £100 **PARKING:** 85 **NOTES:** No smoking in restaurant RS Saturdays Civ Wed 90 **CARDS:**

★★★67% *Riverhill*
Talbot Rd, Prenton CH43 2HJ
☎ 0151 653 3773 📠 0151 653 7162
e-mail: reception@theriverhill.co.uk
Dir: *1m from M53 junct 3, along A552. Turn left onto B5151 at lights, hotel 0.5m on right*
Pretty lawns and gardens provide the setting for this friendly hotel, conveniently situated about a mile from the M53. Attractively furnished, well-equipped bedrooms include ground floor, family, and four-poster rooms. Business meetings and weddings can be catered for. A wide choice of dishes is available in the restaurant, overlooking the garden.
ROOMS: 14 en suite (1 fmly) **FACILITIES:** STV Free use of local leisure facilities **CONF:** Thtr 50 Class 30 Board 52 **PARKING:** 32 **NOTES:** No dogs (ex guide dogs) Civ Wed 40 **CARDS:**

Premier Lodge (Wirral)
1 Greasby Rd CH49 2PP
☎ 0870 9906588 📠 0870 9906589
Dir: *2m from M53 junct 2, just off B5139*
Premier Lodge offers modern, well-equipped, en suite accommodation suitable for both business and leisure travellers. Meals can be taken at the adjacent popular restaurant and bar, which is fully licensed. For further details, consult the Hotel Groups page.
ROOMS: 30 en suite s £48; d £48

BIRMINGHAM, West Midlands Map 10 SP08
See also Bromsgrove, Lea Marston, Oldbury & Sutton Coldfield

Top 200 - Town House

★★★★ Hotel Du Vin & Bistro
25 Church St B3 2NR
☎ 0121 200 0600 0121 236 0889
e-mail: info@birmingham.hotelduvin.com
Dir: *M6 junct 6/A38(M) to city centre, over flyover. Keep left & exit at St Chads Circus signed Jewellery Quarter. At traffic lights & rdbt take 1st exit, follow signs for Colmore Row, opposite Cathedral. Right into Church St, across Berwick St. Hotel on right).*
The former Birmingham Eye Hospital has undergone a dramatic transformation, with the Victorian structure now housing a chic, sophisticated hotel. Stylish, high-ceilinged rooms, with a wine theme, are luxuriously appointed and feature stunning bathrooms, sumptuous duvets and Egyptian cotton sheets. The Bistro offers relaxed dining and a top-notch wine list, while other attractions include a champagne bar, a cigar and wine boutique and a health club.
ROOMS: 66 en suite s £115-£395; d £115-£395 **FACILITIES:** STV Snooker Sauna Solarium Gym Pool table Treatment rooms Xmas **CONF:** Thtr 80 Class 40 Board 40 Del £185 **SERVICES:** Lift **NOTES:** No dogs (ex guide dogs) Civ Wed 50 **CARDS:**

★★★★70%
Birmingham Marriott Hotel
Marriott HOTELS·RESORTS·SUITES
12 Hagley Rd, Five Ways B16 8SJ
☎ 0121 452 1144 0121 456 3442
e-mail: claire.lawson@whitbread.com
Situated in the suburb of Edgbaston, this Edwardian hotel is a prominent landmark on the outskirts of the city centre. Air-conditioned bedrooms are decorated in a comfortable modern style and provide a comprehensive range of extra facilities. Public rooms include the contemporary, brasserie style West 12 Bar and Restaurant.
ROOMS: 98 en suite No smoking in 60 bedrooms **FACILITIES: Spa** STV Indoor swimming (H) Solarium Gym Jacuzzi Beauty salon, Steam room entertainment **CONF:** Thtr 30 Board 20 **SERVICES:** Lift air con **PARKING:** 50 **CARDS:**

Destination dining!
This symbol indicates a Restaurant with Rooms

★★★★70% **The Burlington**
Burlington Arcade, 126 New St B2 4JQ
☎ 0121 643 9191 0121 628 5005
e-mail: mail@burlingtonhotel.com
Dir: *M6 junct 6, follow signs for city centre, then onto A38*
The Burlington's original Victorian grandeur - marble and iron staircases, high ceilings - has been blended together with modern facilities. Bedrooms are equipped to a good standard and public areas include a stylish bar and coffee lounge. The Berlioz Restaurant specialises in innovative dishes using fresh produce.
ROOMS: 112 en suite (6 fmly) No smoking in 49 bedrooms s £75-£125; d £99-£155 **LB FACILITIES: Spa** STV Sauna Gym Jacuzzi Xmas **CONF:** Thtr 400 Class 175 **SERVICES:** Lift **NOTES:** Closed 25 Dec - 26 Dec Civ Wed 200 **CARDS:**

★★★★66% **Copthorne Hotel Birmingham**
COPTHORNE
Paradise Circus B3 3HJ
☎ 0121 200 2727 0121 200 1197
e-mail: sales.birmingham@mill-cop.com
Dir: *follow 'International Convention Centre' signs then bear right for hotel*

This hotel is one of the few establishments in the city that benefits from its own car park. Bedrooms are spacious and come in a choice of styles, all with excellent facilities. Guests can enjoy a variety of dining options, including the contemporary menu in Goldies Brasserie.
ROOMS: 212 en suite No smoking in 108 bedrooms s £75-£175; d £85-£190 **LB FACILITIES:** STV Indoor swimming (H) Sauna Solarium Gym Jacuzzi Swimming pool supervised Xmas **CONF:** Thtr 200 Class 120 Board 30 Del from £99 **SERVICES:** Lift **PARKING:** 88 **NOTES:** No dogs (ex guide dogs) **CARDS:**

★★★78% **Malmaison Birmingham**
Malmaison
Royal Mail St, The Mailbox B1 1XL
☎ 0121 246 5000 0121 246 5002
e-mail: birmingham@malmaison.com
Dir: *M6 J6, follow A38 towards B'ham, hotel located within The Mailbox, signed from A38*
This is the sixth and newest hotel in this stylish boutique group. Situated in a classy new shopping mall, the hotel has an excellent location within the city and there is parking nearby. Bedrooms are stylish, comfortable and air-conditioned. The popular brasserie has already become a focal point in the city; booking is recommended.
ROOMS: 189 en suite No smoking in 68 bedrooms s £99-£125; d £99-£125 **FACILITIES:** STV Sauna Solarium Gym Jacuzzi **CONF:** Thtr 40 Class 24 Board 24 Del £160 **SERVICES:** Lift air con **NOTES:** No dogs (ex guide dogs) **CARDS:**

BIRMINGHAM, continued

★★★70% The Westley
80-90 Westley Rd, Acocks Green B27 7UJ
☎ 0121 706 4312 ▯ 0121 706 2824
e-mail: reservations@westley-hotel.co.uk
Dir: *A41 signed Birmingham on Solihull by-pass, continue to Acocks Green. At rdbt, 2nd exit B4146 Westley Rd. Hotel 200yds on left*

Set in the city suburbs and conveniently located for the N.E.C and airport, this friendly hotel provides well-equipped, smartly presented bedrooms. In addition to the main restaurant, there is also a lively bar and brasserie together with a large function room.
ROOMS: 27 en suite 11 annexe en suite (1 fmly) No smoking in 10 bedrooms s £65-£78; d fr £88 (incl. bkfst) **LB FACILITIES:** STV entertainment **CONF:** Thtr 200 Class 80 Board 50 Del from £108 **PARKING:** 150 **NOTES:** No smoking in restaurant Civ Wed 170
CARDS:

★★★67% Novotel Birmingham Centre
70 Broad St B1 2HT
☎ 0121 643 2000 ▯ 0121 643 9796
e-mail: h1077@accor-hotels.com
This large, modern, purpose built hotel benefits from an excellent city centre location, with the bonus of secure car parking. Bedrooms are spacious, modern and well-equipped for business users. Four rooms have facilities for disabled guests. Public areas include the Garden Brasserie, function rooms and a fitness room.
ROOMS: 148 en suite (148 fmly) No smoking in 98 bedrooms s £60-£145; d £85-£155 (incl. bkfst) **LB FACILITIES:** STV Sauna Gym Jacuzzi **CONF:** Thtr 300 Class 120 Board 90 Del £145 **SERVICES:** Lift air con **PARKING:** 50 **CARDS:**

★★★66% Westmead Hotel
Redditch Rd, Hopwood B48 7AL
☎ 0870 609 6119 ▯ 0121 445 6163
e-mail: westmead@corushotels.com
Dir: *M42 junct 2 towards Birmingham on A441. At rdbt turn right and follow A441 for 1m. Hotel on right*

In a quiet location on the outskirts of the city, yet close to the M42, this hotel offers a number of meeting and conference rooms. The bedrooms are generally spacious, well equipped and comfortable. A spacious bar offers carvery lunches and dinner is served in the adjacent restaurant.

ROOMS: 58 en suite (2 fmly) No smoking in 28 bedrooms s £65-£105; d £75-£115 **LB FACILITIES:** STV Sauna Solarium **CONF:** BC Thtr 220 Class 120 Board 80 Del from £105 **PARKING:** 155 **NOTES:** No smoking in restaurant Civ Wed 120 **CARDS:**

★★★64% Jurys Inn Birmingham
245 Broad St B1 2HQ
JURYS DOYLE HOTELS
☎ 0121 626 0626 ▯ 0121 626 0627
e-mail: jurysinn_birmingham@jurysdoyle.com
This large hotel is ideally located in the centre of the city offers extensive conference facilities and is well equipped to cater for both leisure and business guests. Bedrooms are spacious and modern and the restaurant is designed for efficiency and offers a buffet style operation.
ROOMS: 445 en suite (336 fmly) No smoking in 325 bedrooms s £71-£125; d £71-£125 **FACILITIES:** STV **CONF:** Thtr 280 Class 148 Board 44 Del from £115 **SERVICES:** Lift **PARKING:** 230 **NOTES:** No dogs (ex guide dogs) No smoking in restaurant Closed 24-26 Dec
CARDS:

★★★64% The Plough & Harrow Hotel
135 Hagley Rd B16 8LS
☎ 0870 609 6118 ▯ 0121 454 1868
e-mail: reservations@plough.co.uk
Dir: *from the city, A456 (Hagley Road). Hotel on right after rdbt*

corus hotels

This well-established hotel is approximately a mile west of the city centre, with a relaxed and friendly atmosphere. Bedrooms come in a variety of styles and sizes and the attractive garden restaurant offers a good selection of freshly prepared dishes. Free parking for residents is an added bonus.
ROOMS: 44 en suite No smoking in 20 bedrooms s £90-£115; d £110-£135 (incl. bkfst) **LB FACILITIES:** STV Xmas **CONF:** Thtr 80 Class 40 Board 40 Del from £100 **SERVICES:** Lift **PARKING:** 90 **NOTES:** No smoking in restaurant Civ Wed 55
CARDS:

continued

★★★61% **Great Barr Hotel & Conference Centre**

Pear Tree Dr, Newton Rd, Great Barr B43 6HS
☎ 0121 357 1141 🖷 0121 357 7557
e-mail: sales@thegreatbarrhotel.co.uk
Dir: *M6 junct 7, at Scott Arms x-rds turn right towards West Bromwich (A4010) Newton Rd. Hotel 1m from Scotts Arms, on right*
This busy hotel, situated in a residential area, is particularly popular with business people. Bedrooms are well equipped and modern in style. There is a wide range of meeting rooms, a traditional oak-panelled bar and formal restaurant.
ROOMS: 105 en suite (6 fmly) No smoking in 50 bedrooms s £35-£75; d £55-£115 **LB** **FACILITIES:** STV Xmas **CONF:** Thtr 200 Class 90 Board 60 Del from £79 **PARKING:** 200 **NOTES:** No dogs (ex guide dogs) RS BH (restaurant may be closed) Civ Wed 200
CARDS:

★★72% **Copperfield House**

60 Upland Rd, Selly Park B29 7JS
☎ 0121 472 8344 🖷 0121 415 5655
e-mail: info@copperfieldhousehotel.fsnet.co.uk
Dir: *M6 junct 6/A38 through city centre. After tunnels, right at lights into Belgrave Middleway. Right at rdbt onto A441. At Selly Park Tavern, right into Upland Rd*
A delightful Victorian hotel, situated in a leafy suburb, close to the BBC's Pebble Mill Studios and within easy reach of the centre. Accommodation is smartly presented and well-equipped; the executive rooms are particularly spacious. A tasteful lounge with honesty bar, carefully prepared, seasonally-inspired food and a well-chosen wine list add to the attractions.
ROOMS: 17 en suite (1 fmly) (2 GF) s £62.50-£72.50; d £75-£85 (incl. bkfst) **LB** **PARKING:** 11 **NOTES:** No smoking in restaurant Closed 24 Dec - 2 Jan **CARDS:**

★★68% ***Norwood***

87-89 Bunbury Rd, Northfield B31 2ET
☎ 0121 411 2202 🖷 0121 477 7447
e-mail: norwoodhotel@aol.com
Dir: *left on A38 at Grosvenor shopping centre, 5m S of city centre*
This comfortable hotel provides well equipped accommodation with several executive rooms. Pleasant public rooms enjoy an outlook over the pretty garden. Carefully prepared home-cooking is served in the attractive dining room.
ROOMS: 18 en suite **FACILITIES:** STV **CONF:** Thtr 40 Class 24 Board 20 **PARKING:** 11 **NOTES:** No dogs (ex guide dogs) Closed 23 Dec-2 Jan
CARDS:

★★66% **Fountain Court**

THE INDEPENDENTS

339-343 Fountain Court Hotel B17 8NH
☎ 0121 429 1754 🖷 0121 429 1209
e-mail: info@fountain-court.net
Dir: *on A456, towards Birmingham, 3 miles from M5 junct 3*
This family-owned hotel is on the A456, near to the M5 and a short drive from the city centre. Hospitality is excellent, the accommodation simple, and imaginative, home-cooked food is usually available.
ROOMS: 23 en suite (4 fmly) s £45; d £65 (incl. bkfst) **PARKING:** 20
CARDS:

★★64% **Comfort Inn Norfolk**

Comfort Inn BY CHOICE HOTELS

257/267 Hagley Rd, Edgbaston B16 9NA
☎ 0121 454 8071 🖷 0121 455 6149
e-mail: admin@gb606.u-net.com
Dir: *M6 junct 8/A38 onto ringroad towards Kidderminster. After 4m right at rdbt, hotel on right*

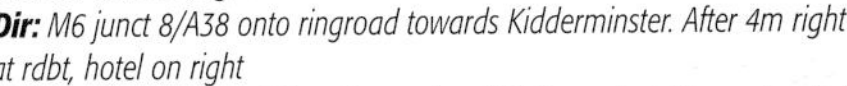

Within easy access of the city centre, this large hotel is particularly

continued on p98

BIRMINGHAM, continued

popular with business travellers. The bedrooms vary both in size and style. Guests may use the leisure facilities at a nearby sister hotel. Evening meals are provided in the Headingley Restaurant.
ROOMS: 169 en suite (2 fmly) (30 GF) No smoking in 45 bedrooms s fr £59.50; d £69.50-£89.50 **LB** **FACILITIES:** STV **CONF:** Thtr 80 Class 50 Board 30 **SERVICES:** Lift **PARKING:** 90 **NOTES:** No dogs (ex guide dogs) No smoking in restaurant Civ Wed 80
CARDS:

★★63% Astoria
311 Hagley Rd B16 9LQ
☎ 0121 454 0795 📠 0121 456 3537
e-mail: anne@astoriahotel.uk.com
Dir: *on A456 2m from city centre*

This Victorian property stands between the city centre and the M5 motorway. Personally run, it provides simple yet spacious accommodation that includes some family and ground floor rooms. There is a choice of lounges and a homely bar. The traditionally furnished dining room serves a selection of grill-orientated dishes.
ROOMS: 26 en suite (6 fmly) (5 GF) No smoking in 2 bedrooms s £45-£50; d £55-£63 (incl. bkfst) **FACILITIES:** STV **CONF:** BC **PARKING:** 27 **NOTES:** No dogs (ex guide dogs) No smoking in restaurant **CARDS:**

U *Holiday Inn Birmingham*
Chapel Ln, Great Barr B43 7BG
☎ 0870 400 9009 📠 0121 357 7503
Dir: *M6 junct 7/A34 signed Walsall. Hotel 200yds on right across the carriageway in Chapel Lane*

At the time of going to press, the classification for this hotel was not confirmed. Please refer to the AA internet site www.theAA.com for current information.
ROOMS: 192 en suite (36 fmly) No smoking in 108 bedrooms **FACILITIES:** Indoor swimming (H) Sauna Solarium Gym Jacuzzi Aerobics studio Beauty treatments **CONF:** Thtr 120 Class 70 Board 50 **PARKING:** 400 **CARDS:**

U *Holiday Inn Birmingham City*
Smallbrook Queensway B5 4EW
☎ 0870 400 9008 📠 0121 631 2528
e-mail: birminghamcity@ichotelsgroup.com
Dir: *M6 junct 6/A38 follow city centre signs through two tunnels. Take 2nd slip road, then 1st left to hotel*

At the time of going to press, the classification for this hotel was not confirmed. Please refer to the AA internet site www.theAA.com for current information.
ROOMS: 280 en suite (3 fmly) No smoking in 205 bedrooms **CONF:** Thtr 630 Class 380 Board 50 **SERVICES:** Lift
CARDS:

> Popped the question?
> Hotels with Civ Wed in their entry are licensed for civil wedding ceremonies. Maximum numbers for the ceremony only are shown, e.g. Civ Wed 120

⌂ *Campanile*
Aston Locks, Chester St B6 4BE
☎ 0121 359 3330 📠 0121 359 1223
Dir: *next to rdbt at junct of A4540/A38*

This modern building offers accommodation in smart, well-equipped bedrooms, all with en suite bathrooms. Refreshments may be taken at the informal Bistro. For further details and the Campanile phone number, consult the Hotel Groups page.

ROOMS: 111 en suite **CONF:** Thtr 245 Class 105 Board 122

⌂ Express by Holiday Inn Birmingham City Centre

Lionel St
☎ 0121 200 1900 📠 0121 200 1910
e-mail: ebhi-bhamcity@btconnect.com

A modern hotel ideal for families and business travellers. Fresh and uncomplicated, the spacious bedrooms include Sky TV, power shower and tea and coffee-making facilities. Continental buffet breakfast is included in the room rate; other meals may be taken at the nearby family pub or restaurant. For further details and the Express by Holiday Inn phone number, consult the Hotel Groups pages.
ROOMS: 120 en suite

⌂ Express by Holiday Inn Birmingham North

Birmingham Rd, Great Barr B43 7AG
☎ 0121 358 4044 📠 0121 358 4644
e-mail: ebhi-walsall@btconnect.com
Dir: *M6 junct 7, onto A34 towards Walsall*

A modern hotel ideal for families and business travellers. Fresh

continued

and uncomplicated, the spacious bedrooms include Sky TV, power shower and tea and coffee-making facilities. Continental buffet breakfast is included in the room rate; other meals may be taken at the nearby family pub or restaurant. For further details and the Express by Holiday Inn phone number, consult the Hotel Groups pages.
ROOMS: 32 en suite **CONF:** Thtr 30 Class 24 Board 16

⇧ Express by Holiday Inn Birmingham South

Stratford Rd, Hall Green B28 9ES
☎ 0121 744 4414 🖷 0121 744 4700
e-mail: ebhi-hallgreen@btconnect.com
Dir: *M42 junct 4, follow city centre signs (A34) for 7km, hotel on rdbt at junct with A4040*

A modern hotel ideal for families and business travellers. Fresh and uncomplicated, the spacious bedrooms include Sky TV, power shower and tea and coffee-making facilities. Continental buffet breakfast is included in the room rate; other meals may be taken at the nearby family pub or restaurant. For further details and the Express by Holiday Inn phone number, consult the Hotel Groups pages.
ROOMS: 51 en suite **CONF:** Thtr 30 Class 24 Board 16

⇧ *Express by Holiday Inn Castle Bromwich*

1200 Chester Rd, Castle Bromwich B35 7AF
☎ 0121 747 6633 🖷 0121 747 6644
e-mail: castlebromwich@holidayinnexpress.co.uk
Dir: *M6 junct 5/6/A38 for Tyburn, right into Chester Rd, follow Park signs*

A modern hotel ideal for families and business travellers. Fresh and uncomplicated, the spacious bedrooms include Sky TV, power shower and tea and coffee-making facilities. Continental buffet breakfast is included in the room rate; other meals may be taken at the nearby family pub or restaurant. For further details and the Express by Holiday Inn phone number, consult the Hotel Groups pages.
ROOMS: 110 en suite **CONF:** Thtr 30 Class 10 Board 18

⇧ Hotel Ibis Birmingham Holloway

55 Irving St B1 1DH
☎ 0121 622 4925 🖷 0121 622 4195
e-mail: h2092@accor-hotels.com
Dir: *150yds from Dome Night Club, just off Bristol Street*
Modern, budget hotel offering comfortable accommodation in bright and practical bedrooms. Breakfast is self-service and dinner is available in the restaurant. For further details, consult the Hotel Groups page.
ROOMS: 51 en suite s £36.95-£40.95; d £36.95-£40.95

⇧ Hotel Ibis

Arcadian Centre, Ladywell Walk B5 4ST
☎ 0121 622 6010 🖷 0121 622 6020
e-mail: h1459@accor-hotels.com
Dir: *M6 junct 7/A34 to city centre & follow signs to Market areas. M5 junct 3 take A456 to centre then Market areas*
Modern, budget hotel offering comfortable accommodation in bright and practical bedrooms. Breakfast is self-service and dinner is available in the restaurant. For further details, consult the Hotel Groups page.
ROOMS: 159 en suite s £38.95-£48.95; d £38.95-£48.95

⇧ Hotel Ibis Birmingham Bordesley

1 Bordesley Park Rd, Bordesley B10 0PD
☎ 0121 506 2600 🖷 0121 506 2610
e-mail: H2178@accor-hotels.com
Modern, budget hotel offering comfortable accommodation in bright and practical bedrooms. Breakfast is self-service and dinner is available in the restaurant. For further details, consult the Hotel Groups page.
ROOMS: 87 en suite s £37.95-£46.95; d £37.95-£46.95

⇧ Innkeeper's Lodge Birmingham West

563 Hagley Rd West, Quinton B32 1HP
☎ 0870 243 0500 & 0121 423 3895
Dir: *M5 junct 3/A456 westbound. On opposite side of dual carriageway, accessed a short distance from rdbt*
A new concept in the travel accommodation market. Smart rooms meet essential business requirements but also have home comforts. Dining options include all-day menus plus the added advantage of breakfast, which is included in the room price. For further details, consult the Hotel Groups page.
ROOMS: 24 en suite

⇧ Premier Lodge (Birmingham City Centre)

80 Broad St B15 1AU
☎ 0870 9906404 🖷 0870 9906405
Premier Lodge offers modern, well-equipped, en suite accommodation suitable for both business and leisure travellers. Meals can be taken at the adjacent popular restaurant and bar, which is fully licensed. For further details, consult the Hotel Groups page.
ROOMS: 60 en suite s £54; d £54

⇧ Premier Lodge (Birmingham South)

Birmingham Great Park, Ashbrook Drive, Parkway, Rubery B45 9PA
☎ 0870 9906538 🖷 0870 9906539
Dir: *M5 junct 4/A38, follow for 0.5m. Lodge behind Safeway on left*
Premier Lodge offers modern, well-equipped, en suite accommodation suitable for both business and leisure travellers. Meals can be taken at the adjacent popular restaurant and bar, which is fully licensed. For further details, consult the Hotel Groups page.
ROOMS: 62 en suite s £48; d £48 **CONF:** Board 12

BIRMINGHAM, continued

⌂ Travel Inn (Birmingham Central East)
Richard St, Aston, Waterlinks B7 4AA
☎ 0870 238 3312 🖷 0121 333 6490
Dir: *on ring road A4540 at A38(M). From M6 (J6) take 2nd exit off A38M, ring road, left at island, 1st left*
Travel Inn offers good-quality, value-for-money accommodation. Spacious, en suite rooms with bath and shower comfortably accommodate a family of up to two adults and two children (to age 15). The restaurant and bar offers a varied menu. For further details and the Travel Inn phone number, consult the Hotel Groups page.
ROOMS: 60 en suite s £44.95; d £44.95 **CONF:** Thtr 14

⌂ Travel Inn (Birmingham City Centre)
20 Bridge St B1 2JH
☎ 08701 977031 🖷 0121 633 4779
Dir: *From M6/M5/M42 follow signs for city centre. Bridge St off A456 (Broad Street). Turn left in front of Hyatt Hotel for Travel Inn on right*

Travel Inn offers good-quality, value-for-money accommodation. Spacious, en suite rooms with bath and shower comfortably accommodate a family of up to two adults and two children (to age 15). The restaurant and bar offers a varied menu. For further details and the Travel Inn phone number, consult the Hotel Groups page.
ROOMS: 53 en suite s £52.95-£54.95; d £52.95-£54.95

⌂ Travelodge (Birmingham Central)
230 Broad St B15 1AY
☎ 08700 850 950
Travelodge offers good quality, good value, modern accommodation. Ideal for families, the spacious, en suite bedrooms include remote-control TV, tea and coffee-making facilities, luxury beds and free morning newspaper. Meals can be taken at the nearby family restaurant. For further details and the Travelodge phone number, consult the Hotel Groups page.
ROOMS: 136 en suite s fr £42.95; d fr £42.95

⌂ Travelodge (Birmingham East)
A45 Coventry Rd, Acocks Green, Yardley B26 1DS
☎ 08700 850 950
Travelodge offers good quality, good value, modern accommodation. Ideal for families, the spacious, en suite bedrooms include remote-control TV, tea and coffee-making facilities, luxury beds and free morning newspaper. Meals can be taken at the nearby family restaurant. For further details and the Travelodge phone number, consult the Hotel Groups page.
ROOMS: 40 en suite s fr £42.95; d fr £42.95

BIRMINGHAM AIRPORT, West Midlands Map 10 SP08

★★★67% Novotel Birmingham Airport
B26 3QL
☎ 0121 782 7000 🖷 0121 782 0445
e-mail: H1158@accor-hotels.com
Dir: *M42 junct 6/A45 to Birmingham, signed to airport. Hotel opposite main terminal*
This large, purpose-built hotel is located opposite the main passenger terminal. Bedrooms are spacious, modern in style and well equipped, including Playstations to keep the children busy. Two rooms have facilities for disabled guests. The Garden Brasserie is open from noon until midnight and room service is extensive.
ROOMS: 195 en suite (20 fmly) No smoking in 150 bedrooms s £65-£131; d £65-£131 **FACILITIES:** STV **CONF:** BC Thtr 35 Class 20 Board 22 Del from £137 **SERVICES:** Lift air con
CARDS:

U Holiday Inn Birmingham Airport
Coventry Rd B26 3QW
☎ 0870 400 9007 🖷 0121 782 2476
Dir: *M6 junct 7/M42 junct 6 take A45 towards Birmingham for 1.5m*
At the time of going to press, the classification for this hotel was not confirmed. Please refer to the AA internet site www.theAA.com for current information.
ROOMS: 141 en suite

BIRMINGHAM (NATIONAL EXHIBITION CENTRE), West Midlands Map 10 SP08
See also Sutton Coldfield

★★★★73% ⊛ Crowne Plaza Birmingham NEC
National Exhibition Centre, Pendigo Way B40 1PS
☎ 0121 781 4000 🖷 0121 781 4321
e-mail: sales@cpbirminghamnec.com
Dir: *M42 J6, follow signs for NEC, take 2nd exit on left, South Way for hotel entrance 50mtrs on right*
Within walking distance of the NEC, this hotel has many attributes among which are the bar and restaurant facilities. The restaurant is run by celebrity chef Brian Turner and the bar is affiliated to the 606 jazz club in Chelsea. Bedrooms are air conditioned with duvet covered beds and well designed workstations. Leisure facilities include gym and sauna.
ROOMS: 242 en suite No smoking in 190 bedrooms s £100-£225; d £110-£225 **LB FACILITIES:** STV Sauna Solarium Gym entertainment **CONF:** BC Thtr 192 Class 114 Board 52 Del from £140 **SERVICES:** Lift air con **PARKING:** 180 **NOTES:** No dogs (ex guide dogs) Civ Wed 70
CARDS:

★★★★68% Moor Hall
Moor Hall Dr, Four Oaks B75 6LN
☎ 0121 308 3751 🖷 0121 308 8974
e-mail: mail@moorhallhotel.co.uk
(For full entry see Sutton Coldfield)

★★★★66% ⊛⊛ Nailcote Hall
Nailcote Ln, Berkswell CV7 7DE
☎ 024 7646 6174 🖷 024 7647 0720
e-mail: info@nailcotehall.co.uk
(For full entry see Balsall Common)

★★★68% Arden Hotel & Leisure Club
Coventry Rd, Bickenhill B92 0EH

☎ 01675 443221 🖹 01675 445604
e-mail: enquiries@ardenhotel.co.uk
Dir: *M42 junct 6/A45 towards Birmingham. Hotel 0.25m on right, just off Birmingham International railway island*
This smart hotel neighbouring the NEC offers modern rooms and well-equipped leisure facilities. After dinner in the formal restaurant, the place to relax is the spacious lounge area. A buffet breakfast is served in the bright and airy Meeting Place.
ROOMS: 216 en suite (6 fmly) (6 GF) s £65-£105; d £75-£135 **FACILITIES:** STV Indoor swimming (H) Snooker Sauna Solarium Gym Jacuzzi Steamroom, Swimming pool supervised Xmas **CONF:** Thtr 200 Class 40 Board 60 Del £145 **SERVICES:** Lift **PARKING:** 300 **NOTES:** No smoking in restaurant Civ Wed 120
CARDS:

See advert on this page

★★★66% Sutton Court
60-66 Lichfield Rd B74 2NA
☎ 0121 354 4991 🖹 0121 355 0083
e-mail: res@schotel.co.uk
(For full entry see Sutton Coldfield)

★★78% Haigs
Kenilworth Rd CV7 7EL
☎ 01676 533004 🖹 01676 535132
(For full entry see Balsall Common)

★★67% Heath Lodge
117 Coleshill Rd, Marston Green B37 7HT
☎ 0121 779 2218 🖹 0121 779 2218
e-mail: reception@heathlodgehotel.freeserve.co.uk
Dir: *M6 junct 4/A446 towards N Coleshill. After 0.5m turn left into Coleshill Heath Rd, signed to Marston Green. Hotel on right*
This privately-owned and personally-run hotel is ideally located for visitors to the NEC and Birmingham Airport. Hospitality and service standards are high and while some bedrooms are compact, all are well equipped and suitably comfortable. Public areas include a bar, a lounge and a dining room which overlooks the garden.
ROOMS: 17 rms (16 en suite) (1 fmly) s £49-£59; d £59-£77 (incl. bkfst) **CONF:** Thtr 20 Class 16 Board 14 **PARKING:** 22 **NOTES:** No smoking in restaurant **CARDS:**

Express by Holiday Inn
Bickenhill Parkway B40 1QA

☎ 0121 782 3222 🖹 0121 780 4224
e-mail: sales_nec@ingramhotels.co.uk
Dir: *follow signs for NEC from M42 junct 6*

A modern hotel ideal for families and business travellers. Fresh and uncomplicated, the spacious bedrooms include Sky TV, power

continued on p102

BIRMINGHAM (NATIONAL EXHIBITION CENTRE), continued

shower and tea and coffee-making facilities. Continental buffet breakfast is included in the room rate; other meals may be taken at the nearby family pub or restaurant. For further details and the Express by Holiday Inn phone number, consult the Hotel Groups pages.
ROOMS: 179 en suite **CONF:** Thtr 100

⌂ Premier Lodge (Birmingham NEC/Airport)

Northway, National Exhibition Centre B40 3QE
☎ 0870 9906326 🖷 0870 9906327
Dir: *2m NE of Birmingham International Airport & 1.5m from M42 junct 6*
Premier Lodge offers modern, well-equipped, en suite accommodation suitable for both business and leisure travellers. Meals can be taken at the adjacent popular restaurant and bar, which is fully licensed. For further details, consult the Hotel Groups page.
ROOMS: 199 en suite s £54; d £54

BISHOP'S STORTFORD, Hertfordshire — Map 06 TL42

★★★★71% ⊛⊛ Down Hall Country House

Hatfield Heath CM22 7AS
☎ 01279 731441 🖷 01279 730416
e-mail: reservations@downhall.co.uk
Dir: *A1060, at Hatfield Heath keep left. Turn right into lane opposite Hunters Meet restaurant & left at end, follow sign*

This imposing Victorian country house hotel is set amidst 100 acres of mature grounds yet ideally situated for Stansted Airport. Bedrooms are generally quite spacious; each one is pleasantly decorated, tastefully furnished and equipped with modern facilities. Public rooms include a choice of restaurants, a cocktail bar, two lounges and leisure facilities.
ROOMS: 100 en suite No smoking in 18 bedrooms s £130-£260; d £150-£260 **LB** **FACILITIES:** STV Indoor swimming (H) Tennis (hard) Snooker Sauna Croquet lawn Putting green Jacuzzi Giant chess, Whirlpool Xmas **CONF:** Thtr 200 Class 140 Board 68 Del £180 **SERVICES:** Lift **PARKING:** 150 **NOTES:** No dogs (ex guide dogs) No smoking in restaurant Civ Wed 120
CARDS:

BISHOPSTEIGNTON, Devon — Map 03 SX97

★★65% Cockhaven Manor Hotel

THE INDEPENDENTS

Cockhaven Rd TQ14 9RF
☎ 01626 775252 🖷 01626 775572
e-mail: cockhaven.manor@virgin.net
Dir: *M5/A380 towards Torquay, then A381 towards Teignmouth. Turn left at Metro Motors. Hotel 500yds on left*
A friendly, family run inn, the Cockhaven Manor dates back to the

continued

16th century. Bedrooms are well equipped and many enjoy views across the beautiful Teign estuary. A choice of dining options is offered, and traditional and interesting dishes along with locally caught fish are popular with visitors and locals alike.
ROOMS: 12 en suite (2 fmly) No smoking in 10 bedrooms s £35-£40; d £55-£65 (incl. bkfst) **LB** **FACILITIES:** Petanque **CONF:** BC Thtr 50 Class 50 Board 30 Del from £60 **PARKING:** 50 **NOTES:** No smoking in restaurant RS 26 Dec **CARDS:**

BLACKBURN, Lancashire — Map 18 SD62

See also Langho

★★★★65% ⊛ Clarion Hotel & Suites Foxfields

Whalley Rd, Billington BB7 9HY
☎ 01254 822556 🖷 01254 824613
e-mail: admin@gb065.u-net.com
Dir: *off A59 at signpost for Billington/Whalley & hotel 0.5m on right*
This modern, stylish hotel is easily accessible from major road networks. Bedrooms are comfortable and spacious, and include some suites and others with separate dressing areas. Facilities include a good-sized swimming pool, a small gym and conference suites. The traditional restaurant has a regular trade and serves creative cuisine.
ROOMS: 44 en suite (27 fmly) (21 GF) No smoking in 17 bedrooms s £99-£115; d £115-£130 **LB** **FACILITIES:** STV Indoor swimming (H) Sauna Gym Steam room entertainment Xmas **CONF:** Thtr 180 Class 60 Board 60 Del from £100 **PARKING:** 170 **NOTES:** No dogs (ex guide dogs) No smoking in restaurant Civ Wed 100
CARDS:

★★75% ⊛ Millstone

Church Ln, Mellor BB2 7JR
☎ 01254 813333 🖷 01254 812628
e-mail: millstone@shirehotels.co.uk
Dir: *3m NW off A59*

Once a coaching inn, the Millstone is situated in a village just outside the town. The hotel provides a very high standard of accommodation, professional and friendly service and good food. Bedrooms, some in an adjacent house, are comfortable and generally spacious. All are very well equipped. Rooms on the ground floor and a room for disabled guests are also available.
Shire Hotels – AA Hotel Group of the Year 2003-2004.
ROOMS: 18 en suite 6 annexe en suite (5 fmly) (8 GF) No smoking in 10 bedrooms s £64-£98; d £78-£125 (incl. bkfst) **LB** **FACILITIES:** STV Xmas **CONF:** Thtr 25 Class 15 Board 16 Del from £95 **PARKING:** 40 **NOTES:** No dogs (ex guide dogs) No smoking in restaurant Civ Wed 50
CARDS:

See advert on opposite page

Premier Lodge (Blackburn)

Myerscough Rd, Balderstone BB2 7LE
☎ 0870 9906388 📠 0870 9906389
Premier Lodge offers modern, well-equipped, en suite accommodation suitable for both business and leisure travellers. Meals can be taken at the adjacent popular restaurant and bar, which is fully licensed. For further details, consult the Hotel Groups page.
ROOMS: 20 en suite s £48; d £48 **CONF:** Board 12

BLACKPOOL, Lancashire — Map 18 SD33

★★★★67% De Vere Heron's Reach

DE VERE HOTELS

East Park Dr FY3 8LL
☎ 01253 838866 📠 01253 798800
e-mail: reservations.herons@devere-hotels.com
Dir: *M6 junct 32/M55 junct 4/A583. At 4th set of traffic lights turn right into South Park Drive for 0.25 mile, right at mini-rdbt onto East Park Drive, hotel 0.25 mile on right*

Set in over 200 acres of grounds, this hotel is popular with both business and leisure guests. The pleasure beach is a few minutes walk from the hotel, while the Lake District and Trough of Bowland are an hour away. There are extensive indoor and outdoor leisure facilities within the hotel complex, including an 18-hole championship golf course.
ROOMS: 172 en suite No smoking in 70 bedrooms s £95-£125; d £95-£125 (incl. bkfst) **LB FACILITIES:** STV Indoor swimming (H) Golf 18 Tennis (hard) Squash Snooker Sauna Solarium Gym Putting green Jacuzzi Aerobic studio, Beautyroom, Spinning Studio, Swimming pool supervised Xmas **CONF:** BC Thtr 650 Class 250 Board 50 **SERVICES:** Lift **PARKING:** 500 **NOTES:** No dogs (ex guide dogs) No smoking in restaurant Civ Wed 600
CARDS:

★★★★64% Imperial

North Promenade FY1 2HB
☎ 01253 623971 📠 01253 751784
e-mail: imperialblackpool@paramount-hotels.co.uk
Enjoying a prime seafront location, this grand Victorian hotel offers smartly appointed, well-equipped bedrooms and spacious, elegant public areas. Facilities include a smart leisure club; a comfortable lounge, the No.10 bar and an attractive split level restaurant that overlooks the seafront. Conferences and functions are extremely well catered for.
ROOMS: 180 en suite (9 fmly) No smoking in 80 bedrooms s £57-£125; d £114-£195 (incl. bkfst) **LB FACILITIES:** STV Indoor swimming (H) Sauna Solarium Gym Jacuzzi Swimming pool supervised Xmas **CONF:** Thtr 600 Class 240 Board 128 Del from £140 **SERVICES:** Lift **PARKING:** 150 **NOTES:** No smoking in restaurant Civ Wed 336
CARDS:

BLACKPOOL, continued

★★★66% Carlton
282-286 North Promenade FY1 2EZ
☎ 01253 628966 🖹 01253 752587
e-mail: reservations@carltonhotelblackpool.co.uk
Dir: *M6 junct 32/M55 follow signs for North Shore situated between Blackpool tower and Gynn Sq*

Enjoying a prime seafront location, this hotel has been extensively refurbished throughout. Bedrooms are brightly appointed and modern in style. Public areas include an open plan dining room and bar, and a spacious additional bar where lunches are served. Ample parking is available.
ROOMS: 58 en suite No smoking in 20 bedrooms s £60-£70; d £90-£105 (incl. bkfst) **LB** **FACILITIES:** STV Xmas **CONF:** Thtr 80 Class 40 Board 40 **SERVICES:** Lift **PARKING:** 43 **NOTES:** No dogs (ex guide dogs) No smoking in restaurant **CARDS:**

See advert on page 103

★★★63% Savoy
Queens Promenade, North Shore FY2 9SJ
☎ 01253 352561 🖹 01253 595549
e-mail: events.savoy@macdonald-hotels.co.uk
Dir: *M6 J32, onto M55, cross rdbt on Yeadon Way follow signs to promenade, turn right, 2 miles to Gynn Sq, hotel on right*
This imposing hotel enjoys a prime seafront location on the North Promenade. Public areas are spacious and include a large, wood pannelled, split-level dining room and open-plan lounge and bar area. The bedrooms vary in size and style between those more recently refurbished bedrooms and slightly more dated rooms.
ROOMS: 131 en suite (17 fmly) No smoking in 60 bedrooms s £68.50-£88; d £97-£137 (incl. bkfst) **LB** **FACILITIES:** Xmas **CONF:** Thtr 400 Class 100 Board 50 Del from £95 **SERVICES:** Lift **PARKING:** 46 **NOTES:** No smoking in restaurant Civ Wed 250 **CARDS:**

★★70% Hotel Sheraton
54-62 Queens Promenade FY2 9RP
☎ 01253 352723 🖹 01253 595499
e-mail: email@hotelsheraton.co.uk
Dir: *1m N from Blackpool Tower on promenade towards Fleetwood*
This family owned and run hotel is situated at the quieter, northern end of the promenade. Public areas include a choice of spacious lounges with sea views, a large function suite where popular dancing and cabaret evenings are held, and a heated indoor swimming pool. Bedrooms vary in size and style, with the newly refurbished bedrooms offering good value for money.
ROOMS: 104 en suite (44 fmly) s £30-£70; d £60-£120 (incl. bkfst & dinner) **LB** **FACILITIES:** Indoor swimming (H) Sauna Table tennis Darts entertainment Xmas **CONF:** Thtr 200 Class 100 Board 150 Del from £35 **SERVICES:** Lift **PARKING:** 20 **NOTES:** No dogs (ex guide dogs) No smoking in restaurant **CARDS:**

See advert on opposite page

★★65% Belgrave Madison
270-274 Queens Promenade FY2 9HD
☎ 01253 351570 🖹 01253 500698
This friendly family-run hotel enjoys a seafront location at the quieter end of town. Thoughtfully equipped bedrooms vary in size and include family and four poster rooms. Spacious public areas include a choice of lounges with views over the promenade, a bar lounge where guests can enjoy live entertainment and a bright restaurant.
ROOMS: 43 en suite (10 fmly) **FACILITIES:** **SERVICES:** Lift **PARKING:** 32 **NOTES:** No dogs No smoking in restaurant **CARDS:**

★★60% Warwick
603-609 New South Promenade FY4 1NG
☎ 01253 342192 🖹 01253 405776
Dir: *M55 junct 4/A5230 for South Shore then right on A584, Promenade South*
This friendly hotel enjoys a seafront position close to Pleasure Beach, making it particularly attractive to families. Spacious public areas include a choice of lounges, an attractive bar and restaurant and an indoor swimming pool.
ROOMS: 51 en suite (11 fmly) s £43-£55; d £86-£110 (incl. bkfst & dinner) **LB** **FACILITIES:** Indoor swimming (H) Solarium Pool entertainment Xmas **CONF:** Thtr 50 Class 24 Board 30 **SERVICES:** Lift **PARKING:** 32 **NOTES:** No dogs (ex guide dogs) No smoking in restaurant Closed Jan **CARDS:**

⌂ Premier Lodge (Blackpool)
Whitehills Park, Preston New Rd FY4 5NZ
☎ 0870 9906608 🖹 0870 9906609
Dir: *M55 junct 4 1st left off rdbt, lodge on right*
Premier Lodge offers modern, well-equipped, en suite accommodation suitable for both business and leisure travellers. Meals can be taken at the adjacent popular restaurant and bar, which is fully licensed. For further details, consult the Hotel Groups page.
ROOMS: 81 en suite s £48; d £48

⌂ Travel Inn

Yeadon Way, South Shore FY1 6BF
☎ 08701 977032 🖹 01253 343805
Dir: *M55, follow signs for central car park/coach area. Located next to Total garage*
Travel Inn offers good-quality, value-for-money accommodation. Spacious, en suite rooms with bath and shower comfortably accommodate a family of up to two adults and two children (to age 15). The restaurant and bar offers a varied menu. For further details and the Travel Inn phone number, consult the Hotel Groups page.
ROOMS: 79 en suite s £44.95; d £44.95 **CONF:** Thtr 40

⌂ Travel Inn (Blackpool Airport)
Squires Gare Ln FY4 2QS
☎ 08701 977034 🖹 01253 362413
Dir: *M55 junct 4/A5230 & turn left at 1st rdbt towards airport. Travel Inn is just before Squires Gate railway station*
Travel Inn offers good-quality, value-for-money accommodation. Spacious, en suite rooms with bath and shower comfortably accommodate a family of up to two adults and two children (to age 15). The restaurant and bar offers a varied menu. For further details and the Travel Inn phone number, consult the Hotel Groups page.
ROOMS: 39 en suite s £44.95; d £44.95 **CONF:** Thtr 15 Board 8

⌂ Travel Inn (Blackpool Bispham)
Devonshire Rd, Bispham FY2 0AR
☎ 08701 977033 🖷 01253 590498
Dir: *At M55 junct 4 turn right onto A583. At 5th set of lights turn right (Whitegate Drive) for approx. 4-5 miles onto Devonshire Road (A587)*
Travel Inn offers good-quality, value-for-money accommodation. Spacious, en suite rooms with bath and shower comfortably accommodate a family of up to two adults and two children (to age 15). The restaurant and bar offers a varied menu. For further details and the Travel Inn phone number, consult the Hotel Groups page.
ROOMS: 39 en suite s £44.95; d £44.95 **CONF:** Thtr 50 Board 20

BLAKENEY, Norfolk

Map 13 TG04

★★★74% The Blakeney
The Quay NR25 7NE
☎ 01263 740797 🖷 01263 740795
e-mail: reception@blakeney-hotel.co.uk
Dir: *off A149 coast road, 8m W of Sheringham*
A traditional privately owned hotel situated on the quayside with superb views across the estuary and the salt marshes to Blakeney Point. Public rooms feature an elegant restaurant, ground floor lounge, bar and a further first floor sun lounge overlooking the harbour. Bedrooms vary in size and style but all are smartly decorated and equipped with modern facilities, some have lovely sea views.
ROOMS: 49 en suite 10 annexe en suite (11 fmly) (10 GF) No smoking in all bedrooms s £74-£124; d £148-£248 (incl. bkfst & dinner) **LB** **FACILITIES: Spa** Indoor swimming (H) Snooker Sauna Gym Jacuzzi Table tennis Xmas **CONF:** Thtr 100 Class 54 Board 32 Del from £99 **SERVICES:** Lift **PARKING:** 60 **NOTES:** No smoking in restaurant
CARDS:

Top 200 - Hotel

★★ ◎◎◎ Morston Hall
Morston, Holt NR25 7AA
☎ 01263 741041 🖷 01263 740419
e-mail: reception@morstonhall.com
Dir: *1m W of Blakeney on A149 Kings Lynn/Cromer Rd coastal road*
Travelling west from Blakeney on the north Norfolk coastline that is a haven for wildlife, this delightful 17th-century country house hotel enjoys a tranquil setting amid well-tended gardens. The comfortable public rooms offer a choice of attractive lounges and a sunny conservatory, while the elegant dining room is a perfect setting to enjoy Galton Blackiston's award winning cuisine. The spacious bedrooms are individually decorated and stylishly furnished with modern opulence.
ROOMS: 7 en suite (1 GF) s £140-£150; d £220-£230 (incl. bkfst & dinner) **LB** **PARKING:** 40 **NOTES:** No smoking in restaurant Closed 25-26 Dec & Jan **CARDS:**

★★72% The Pheasant
Coast Rd, Kelling NR25 7EG
☎ 01263 588382 🖷 01263 588101
e-mail: enquiries@pheasanthotelnorfolk.co.uk
Dir: *on A419 coast road, mid-way between Sheringham & Blakeney*
This popular hotel is situated on the main cost road amidst landscaped grounds. Bedrooms are split between the main house and a modern wing of spacious rooms to the rear of the property. Public rooms include a busy lounge bar; a residents' lounge and a large restaurant where a wide-ranging selection of appetising dishes are served.
ROOMS: 30 rms (27 en suite) No smoking in all bedrooms s fr £51; d fr £82 (incl. bkfst) **LB** **FACILITIES:** Xmas **CONF:** Thtr 80 Class 50 Board 50 Del from £78.95 **PARKING:** 80 **NOTES:** No smoking in restaurant **CARDS:**

★★68% Blakeney Manor
The Quay, Blakeney NR25 7ND
☎ 01263 740376 🖷 01263 741116
e-mail: reception@blakeneymanor.co.uk
Dir: *turn off A149 at Blakeney towards Blakeney Quay. Hotel at end of quay between Mariner's Hill & Friary Hills*
An attractive Norfolk flint building overlooking Blakeney Marshes and within easy walking distance of the quayside. The bedrooms have been sympathetically converted from flint-faced barns and are located in courtyards adjacent to the main building. The spacious public rooms include a choice of lounges, a conservatory, popular bar and a large restaurant offering an interesting choice of dishes.
ROOMS: 8 en suite 29 annexe en suite (26 GF) s £34-£51; d £68-£106 (incl. bkfst) **LB** **FACILITIES:** Xmas **PARKING:** 40 **NOTES:** No children 14yrs No smoking in restaurant Closed 4-25 Jan
CARDS:

BLANCHLAND, Northumberland

Map 18 NY95

★★69% Lord Crewe Arms

DH8 9SP
☎ 01434 675251 📠 01434 675337
e-mail: lord@crewearms.freeserve.co.uk
Dir: *10m S of Hexham via B6306*

Adjacent to Blanchland Abbey, many rooms in this historic, monastic hotel date from medieval times. Public areas feature flagstone floors, vaulted ceilings and original inglenook fireplace. Bedrooms, some of which are housed in what was the village's second hotel, are well equipped, and retain a period style. Bar meals are popular and there is an elegant restaurant.

ROOMS: 9 en suite 10 annexe en suite (2 fmly) s fr £80; d fr £110 (incl. bkfst) **LB** **FACILITIES:** Xmas **CONF:** Thtr 20 Class 16 Board 16 Del from £79 **NOTES:** Civ Wed 65 **CARDS:**

BLANDFORD FORUM, Dorset

Map 04 ST80

★★★67% Crown

West St DT11 7AJ
☎ 01258 456626 📠 01258 451084
Dir: *100mtrs from town bridge*

Efficient and friendly service is provided at this attractive, former coaching inn. A choice of menus is offered in the panelled dining room, while in the bar an extensive range of meals is served in a less formal atmosphere. The well-equipped bedrooms were undergoing a refurbishment programme at the time of our last inspection.

ROOMS: 32 en suite (2 fmly) No smoking in 11 bedrooms s fr £75; d fr £96 (incl. bkfst) **LB** **FACILITIES:** STV **CONF:** BC Thtr 250 Class 200 Board 60 Del from £100 **SERVICES:** Lift **PARKING:** 144 **NOTES:** Closed 25-28 Dec Civ Wed 180 **CARDS:**

> Popped the question?
> Hotels with Civ Wed in their entry are licensed for civil wedding ceremonies. Maximum numbers for the ceremony only are shown, e.g. Civ Wed 120

BLYTH, Nottinghamshire

Map 16 SK68

★★★70% Charnwood

Best Western

Sheffield Rd S81 8HF
☎ 01909 591610 📠 01909 591429
e-mail: reception@charnwood-hotel.com
Dir: *A614 into Blyth village, right past church onto A634 Sheffield road. Hotel 0.5m on right past humpback bridge*

This hotel enjoys a rural setting, surrounded by attractive gardens complete with a pond. Bedrooms are comfortably furnished and attractively decorated. A range of carefully prepared meals and snacks is offered in the restaurant, or in the comfortable lounge bar overlooking the gardens. Service is both friendly and attentive.

ROOMS: 34 en suite (1 fmly) No smoking in 10 bedrooms s £55-£65; d £65-£75 (incl. bkfst) **LB** **FACILITIES:** STV Mini-gym **CONF:** Thtr 135 Class 60 Board 45 Del from £100 **PARKING:** 70 **NOTES:** No dogs (ex guide dogs) No smoking in restaurant Civ Wed 120
CARDS:

⌂ Travelodge

Travelodge

Hilltop Roundabout S81 8HG
☎ 08700 850 950
Dir: *at junct of A1M/A614*

Travelodge offers good quality, good value, modern accommodation. Ideal for families, the spacious, en suite bedrooms include remote-control TV, tea and coffee-making facilities, luxury beds and free morning newspaper. Meals can be taken at the nearby family restaurant. For further details and the Travelodge phone number, consult the Hotel Groups page.

ROOMS: 38 en suite s fr £42.95; d fr £42.95

BODMIN, Cornwall & Isles of Scilly

Map 02 SX06

★★75% Trehellas House Hotel & Restaurant

Washaway PL30 3AD
☎ 01208 72700 & 74499 📠 01208 73336
e-mail: trehellashouse@aol.com
Dir: *A30/A389. Through Bodmin towards Wadebridge into Washaway. 0.25m after layby with phone box take slip road to right. Hotel on right*

This early 18th-century former posting inn retains many original features, with contemporary additions, and offers appealing and stylish accommodation. Bedrooms are located in the main house and adjacent coach houses, all of which reflect the same high standards. An interesting choice of dishes is offered in the impressive slate-floored restaurant, with an emphasis on locally sourced produce.

ROOMS: 5 en suite 7 annexe en suite (5 GF) No smoking in all bedrooms s £40-£80; d £83-£135 (incl. bkfst) **LB** **FACILITIES:** Outdoor swimming (H) **CONF:** Thtr 6 Class 6 Board 6 Del from £77 **PARKING:** 30 **NOTES:** No dogs (ex guide dogs) No children 12yrs No smoking in restaurant Closed 21 Dec - 5 Jan RS Sun
CARDS:

★★66% Westberry

Rhind St PL31 2EL
☎ 01208 72772 📠 01208 72212
e-mail: westberry@btconnect.com
Dir: *on ring road off A30 & A38. St Petroc's Church on right, at mini rdbt turn right. Hotel on right*

This popular hotel is convenient for Bodmin town centre and the A30. Bedrooms are comfortably furnished and equipped with a range of facilities. A spacious bar lounge and a billiard room are

continued

also provided. The restaurant serves both fixed-price and carte menus, and an extensive bar menu is available for lunch.

ROOMS: 12 en suite 8 annexe en suite (1 fmly) (6 GF) No smoking in 4 bedrooms s £48-£68; d £68-£88 (incl. bkfst) **LB** **FACILITIES:** STV Snooker Gym **CONF:** Thtr 60 Class 20 Board 30 **PARKING:** 30 **NOTES:** No smoking in restaurant **CARDS:**

BOGNOR REGIS, West Sussex Map 06 SZ99

★★★62% The Inglenook

255 Pagham Rd, Nyetimber PO21 3QB
☎ 01243 262495 & 265411 01243 262668
e-mail: reception@the-inglenook.com
Dir: *A27 to Vinnetrow Rd left at Walnut Tree 2.5m on right*

This 16th-century inn retains much of its original character, including exposed beams throughout. Bedrooms are individually decorated and vary in size. There is a cosy lounge, a well-kept garden and a busy, traditional pub-style bar (complete with a parrot and a couple of cats). The restaurant offers a wide range of home-made dishes.
ROOMS: 18 en suite (1 fmly) No smoking in all bedrooms s £50-£70; d £90-£200 (incl. bkfst) **LB** **FACILITIES:** Xmas **CONF:** BC Thtr 100 Class 50 Board 50 Del from £95 **PARKING:** 35 **NOTES:** Civ Wed 120 **CARDS:**

★★71% Beachcroft

Clyde Rd, Felpham Village PO22 7AH
☎ 01243 827142 01243 863500
e-mail: reservations@beachcroft-hotel.co.uk
Dir: *off A259 at Butlins rdbt into Felpham Village. In 800mtrs right into Sea Rd then 2nd left into Clyde Rd*

This popular family-run hotel overlooks a secluded part of the sea front. Bedrooms are bright and spacious with a good range of facilities, and leisure facilities include a heated indoor swimming pool. Diners may choose from the varied choice of the traditional restaurant menus or the more informal cosy bar.
ROOMS: 34 en suite (4 fmly) No smoking in 6 bedrooms **FACILITIES:** STV Indoor swimming (H) **CONF:** Thtr 50 Class 30 Board 30 Del from £80.25 **PARKING:** 27 **NOTES:** No dogs **CARDS:**

Action for Blind People Hotel

U *The Russell*

King's Pde PO21 2QP
☎ 01243 871300
e-mail: russell_h@afbp.org
Dir: *A27 follow signs for town centre, Hotel located on the seafront*

Close to the seafront, the Russell has been rebuilt to provide large, luxury bedrooms, a heated indoor swimming pool and a small gym, together with a choice of bars and restaurants. The hotel caters for the specific needs of blind and partially sighted people, their friends, relatives, carers and guide dogs.
ROOMS: 41 rms (40 en suite) (4 fmly) No smoking in all bedrooms **FACILITIES:** Indoor swimming (H) Gym Putting green entertainment **SERVICES:** Lift **PARKING:** 12 **NOTES:** No dogs (ex guide dogs) No smoking in restaurant **CARDS:**

⌂ Premier Lodge (Bognor Regis)

PREMIER LODGE

Shripney Rd PO22 9PA
☎ 0870 9906434 0870 9906435
Dir: *on A29*

Premier Lodge offers modern, well-equipped, en suite accommodation suitable for both business and leisure travellers. Meals can be taken at the adjacent popular restaurant and bar, which is fully licensed. For further details, consult the Hotel Groups page.
ROOMS: 24 en suite s £48; d £48 **CONF:** Thtr 80 Class 40 Board 30

BOLTON, Greater Manchester Map 15 SD70

★★★★69% Last Drop Hotel

MACDONALD HOTELS

The Last Drop Village & Hotel, Bromley Cross BL7 9PZ
☎ 01204 591131 01204 304122
e-mail: lastdrop@macdonald-hotels.co.uk
Dir: *3m N of Bolton off B5472*

Built along the lines of a self contained little village, the hotel complex includes a variety of shops, a pub and a tearoom. A collection of stylish photographs chronicles the hotel's evolution from working farm to stylish, modern hotel. Bedrooms are varied, some smaller rooms are located around a delightful courtyard, others have been developed from former cottages and outbuildings and there are a number of executive rooms located in the more recently built extension.
ROOMS: 118 en suite 10 annexe en suite (72 fmly) (36 GF) No smoking in 60 bedrooms s £75-£93; d £85-£103 (incl. bkfst) **LB** **FACILITIES:** STV Snooker Craft shops, Leisure facilities re-open Feb 2004 entertainment Xmas **CONF:** Thtr 700 Class 350 Board 95 Del from £115 **SERVICES:** Lift **PARKING:** 400 **NOTES:** No smoking in restaurant Civ Wed 500 **CARDS:**

BOLTON, continued

★★★70% Egerton House

Blackburn Rd, Egerton BL7 9PL
☎ 01204 307171 🖷 01204 593030
e-mail: egerton@macdonald-hotels.co.uk
Dir: *M61 junct 3/A666. Hotel 3m N of town centre*

Peace and relaxation come as standard at this popular hotel, nestling in acres of well-tended woodland gardens. The location offers the best of both worlds, close to the City of Manchester and the natural beauty of the West Pennine Moors. Public rooms and many guest bedrooms enjoy garden views.

ROOMS: 32 en suite (8 fmly) No smoking in 21 bedrooms
FACILITIES: STV Complimentary use of nearby leisure club **CONF:** Thtr 160 Class 90 Board 60 Del from £110 **PARKING:** 70 **NOTES:** No smoking in restaurant Civ Wed 160
CARDS:

U *Holiday Inn Bolton*

Beaumont Rd BL3 4TA
☎ 0870 400 9011 🖷 01204 61064
Dir: *M61 junct 5, follow A58, W of town*

At the time of going to press, the classification for this hotel was not confirmed. Please refer to the AA internet site www.theAA.com for current information.

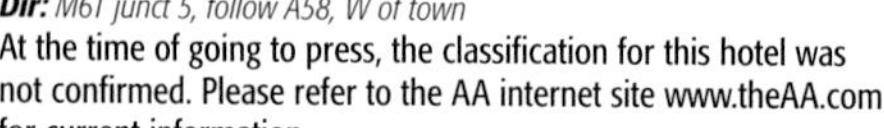

ROOMS: 96 en suite No smoking in 50 bedrooms **CONF:** Thtr 120 Class 80 Board 80 **PARKING:** 150 **NOTES:** Civ Wed 50
CARDS:

⌂ Express by Holiday Inn Bolton

Arena Approach 3, Horwich BL6 6LB
☎ 01204 469111 🖷 469222
e-mail: ebhi-bolton@btconnect.com
Dir: *off M61 junct 6 onto slip road, right at rdbt & left at 2nd*

A modern hotel ideal for families and business travellers. Fresh and uncomplicated, the spacious bedrooms include Sky TV, power shower and tea and coffee-making facilities. Continental buffet breakfast is included in the room rate; other meals may be taken at the nearby family pub or restaurant. For further details and the Express by Holiday Inn phone number, consult the Hotel Groups pages.

ROOMS: 74 en suite **CONF:** Thtr 30 Class 24 Board 16

> Late for dinner?
> Quality Standards mean that last orders for dinner vary according to star rating and should be no earlier than:
> ★★ 7.00pm ★★★ 8.00pm ★★★★ 9.00pm
> ★★★★★ 10.00pm

⌂ Travel Inn

991 Chorley New Rd, Horwich BL6 4BA
☎ 08701 977282 🖷 01204 692585
Dir: *M61(J6) follow dual carriageway to Bolton/Horwich with Reebok Stadium on left . Continue and Travel Inn on 2nd roundabout*

Travel Inn offers good-quality, value-for-money accommodation. Spacious, en suite rooms with bath and shower comfortably accommodate a family of up to two adults and two children (to age 15). The restaurant and bar offers a varied menu. For further details and the Travel Inn phone number, consult the Hotel Groups page.

ROOMS: 40 en suite s £44.95; d £44.95

⌂ Travelodge Bolton West

Bolton West Service Area, Horwich BL6 5UZ
☎ 08700 850 950

Travelodge offers good quality, good value, modern accommodation. Ideal for families, the spacious, en suite bedrooms include remote-control TV, tea and coffee-making facilities, luxury beds and free morning newspaper. Meals can be taken at the nearby family restaurant. For further details and the Travelodge phone number, consult the Hotel Groups page.

ROOMS: 32 en suite s fr £42.95; d fr £42.95 **CONF:** Thtr 60 Class 60 Board 30

BOLTON ABBEY, North Yorkshire

Map 19 SE05

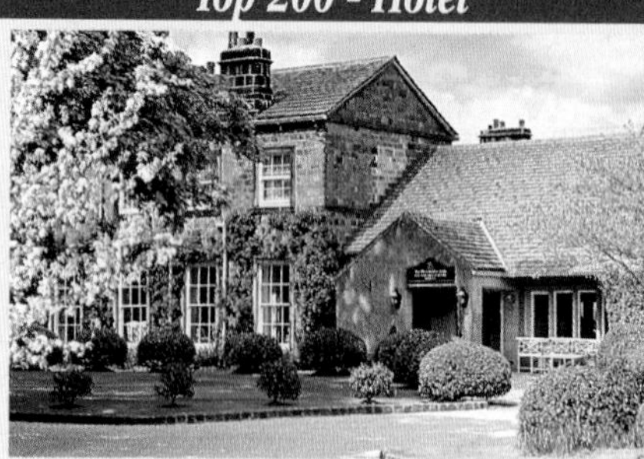

★★★ ⊛⊛⊛ The Devonshire Arms Country House

BD23 6AJ
☎ 01756 710441 🖷 01756 710564
e-mail: reservations@thedevonshirearms.co.uk
Dir: *on B6160, 250yds N of junct with A59*

With stunning views of the Wharfedale countryside, this beautiful hotel, owned by the Duke and Duchess of Devonshire, dates back to the 17th century. Bedrooms are elegantly furnished; those in the old part of the house are particularly spacious, complete with four-posters and fine antiques. The sitting rooms are delightfully cosy with log fires and dedicated staff deliver service with a blend of friendliness and professionalism. The Burlington Restaurant offers highly accomplished dishes, while the Brasserie provides a lighter alternative.

ROOMS: 41 en suite (18 GF) No smoking in 12 bedrooms s £145-£300; d £200-£300 (incl. bkfst) **LB** **FACILITIES:** Indoor swimming (H) Tennis (hard) Fishing Sauna Solarium Gym Croquet lawn Putting green Jacuzzi Laser pigeon shooting, Falconry, Swimming pool supervised Xmas **CONF:** Thtr 120 Class 80 Board 30 Del from £217.35 **PARKING:** 150 **NOTES:** No smoking in restaurant Civ Wed 90 **CARDS:**

B

BONCHURCH See Wight, Isle of

BOOTLE, Merseyside Map 15 SJ39

⌂ Travel Inn (Liverpool North)

Northern Perimiter Rd, Bootle L30 7PT
☎ 08701 977158 📠 0151 520 1842
Dir: *on A5207, off A5036, 0.25m from end of M58/M57*

travel inn

Travel Inn offers good-quality, value-for-money accommodation. Spacious, en suite rooms with bath and shower comfortably accommodate a family of up to two adults and two children (to age 15). The restaurant and bar offers a varied menu. For further details and the Travel Inn phone number, consult the Hotel Groups page.

ROOMS: 63 en suite s £44.95; d £44.95 **CONF:** Thtr 50

BOREHAMWOOD, Hertfordshire Map 06 TQ19

⌂ Innkeeper's Lodge Borehamwood

Studio Way WD6 5JY
☎ 020 8905 1455 📠 020 8236 9822
Dir: *M25 junct 23/A1(M) signed to London. Follow signs to Borehamwood after double rdbt turn into Studio Way*

Innkeeper's Lodge

A new concept in the travel accommodation market. Smart rooms meet essential business requirements but also have home comforts. Dining options include all-day menus plus the added advantage of breakfast, which is included in the room price. For further details, consult the Hotel Groups page.

ROOMS: 55 en suite **CONF:** Thtr 38 Class 20 Board 20

BOROUGHBRIDGE, North Yorkshire Map 19 SE36

★★★71% Crown

Horsefair YO51 9LB
☎ 01423 322328 📠 01423 324512
e-mail: sales@crownboroughbridge.co.uk
Dir: *A1(M) junct 48. Hotel 1m towards town centre at t-junct*

Best Western

Situated in the centre of town but only a minute from the A1, The Crown provides modern well-appointed bedrooms and a range of comfortable public rooms, including a delightful restaurant, which serves a wide range of well-prepared food. Service is both relaxed and friendly. Several modern conference rooms are available, as well as a full leisure complex.

ROOMS: 37 en suite (3 fmly) No smoking in all bedrooms s £71-£92; d £92-£110 (incl. bkfst) **LB** **FACILITIES:** STV Indoor swimming (H) Sauna Solarium Gym Jacuzzi Beauty therapist, Swimming pool supervised Xmas **CONF:** Thtr 150 Class 80 Board 80 Del from £130 **SERVICES:** Lift **PARKING:** 60 **NOTES:** No dogs (ex guide dogs) No smoking in restaurant Civ Wed 70

CARDS:

BORROWDALE, Cumbria Map 18 NY21

See also Keswick & Rosthwaite

★★★77% Borrowdale Gates Country House

CA12 5UQ
☎ 017687 77204 📠 017687 77254
e-mail: hotel@borrowdale-gates.com
Dir: *follow Borrowdale signs on B5289, after 4m right at sign for Grange. Hotel on right 0.25m through village*

This attractive, well-maintained and friendly hotel enjoys an idyllic, peaceful, woodland location in the middle of the Borrowdale Valley. Inviting public rooms include a choice of lounges and a smart restaurant enjoying stunning views. Bedrooms come in a variety of styles and sizes and include superior rooms that are particularly thoughtfully equipped.

ROOMS: 31 en suite (1 fmly) s £80-£89; d £157-£180 (incl. bkfst & dinner) **LB** **FACILITIES:** STV ch fac Xmas **PARKING:** 40 **NOTES:** No dogs (ex guide dogs) No smoking in restaurant Closed Jan

CARDS:

★★★70% Borrowdale

CA12 5UY
☎ 017687 77224 📠 017687 77338
e-mail: theborrowdalehotel@yahoo.com
Dir: *on B5289 at S end of Lake Derwentwater*

Situated in the beautiful Borrowdale Valley overlooking Derwentwater, this traditional hotel has been family run for over 25 years. Extensive public areas include a choice of lounges, a stylish dining room, and a lounge bar, plus a conservatory. There are a wide variety of bedroom sizes and styles, some rather spacious.

ROOMS: 33 en suite (9 fmly) s £62-£73; d £124-£168 (incl. bkfst & dinner) **LB** **FACILITIES:** Free use of nearby Health Club ch fac Xmas **PARKING:** 100 **NOTES:** No smoking in restaurant

CARDS:

★69% Royal Oak

CA12 5XB
☎ 017687 77214 📠 017687 77214
e-mail: info@royaloakhotel.co.uk
Dir: *6m S of Keswick on B5289 in centre of Rosthwaite*

Set in a village in one of Lakeland's most picturesque valleys, this family-run hotel offers friendly and obliging service. There is a variety of accommodation styles, with particularly impressive rooms located on the ground and first floors of a converted barn across the courtyard and backed by a stream. Family rooms are available. The cosy bar is for residents and diners only. A set home-cooked dinner is served at 7pm.

ROOMS: 11 rms (8 en suite) 4 annexe en suite (6 fmly) s £26-£43; d £56-£80 (incl. bkfst) **LB** **FACILITIES:** no TV in bdrms **PARKING:** 15 **NOTES:** No smoking in restaurant Closed 5-19 Jan & 7-27 Dec

CARDS:

BOSCASTLE, Cornwall & Isles of Scilly Map 02 SX09

★★71% The Bottreaux Hotel and Restaurant
PL35 0BG
☎ 01840 250231 🖷 01840 250170
e-mail: info@boscastlecornwall.co.uk
Built some 200 years ago, this hotel is just a short walk from the picturesque harbour. Refurbishment has resulted in a stylish establishment where guests are genuinely welcomed. Bedrooms are light and airy, the doubles featuring wonderful 6ft teak beds. The bar is a convivial venue for a drink and perusal of the imaginative menu, which makes good use of local produce.
ROOMS: 8 en suite No smoking in all bedrooms **PARKING:** 10
NOTES: No dogs No children 10yrs No smoking in restaurant
CARDS:

★★66% The Wellington Hotel
The Harbour PL35 0AQ
☎ 01840 250202 🖷 01840 250621
Dir: *A30/A395, right at Davidstow, signed to Boscastle*
Affectionately known as 'The Welly', this 16th century coaching inn, in extensive grounds, has an abundance of charm and character. The 'Long Bar' is a popular watering hole for both visitors and locals alike. Bedrooms come in varying sizes, including the spacious 'Tower' rooms; all are comfy and suitably equipped. There is a bar menu and a daily changing carte offered in the restaurant.
ROOMS: 15 en suite (1 fmly) s £29-£38; d £58-£116 (incl. bkfst) **LB**
FACILITIES: entertainment Xmas **CONF:** Thtr 20 Class 4 Board 20 Del from £49 **PARKING:** 20 **NOTES:** No smoking in restaurant
CARDS:

BOSHAM, West Sussex Map 05 SU80

★★★75% ❀ The Millstream
Bosham Ln PO18 8HL
☎ 01243 573234 🖷 01243 573459
e-mail: info@millstream-hotel.co.uk
Dir: *4m W of Chichester on A259, left at Bosham rdbt. After 1m right at t-junct signed to church & quay. Hotel 0.5m on right*

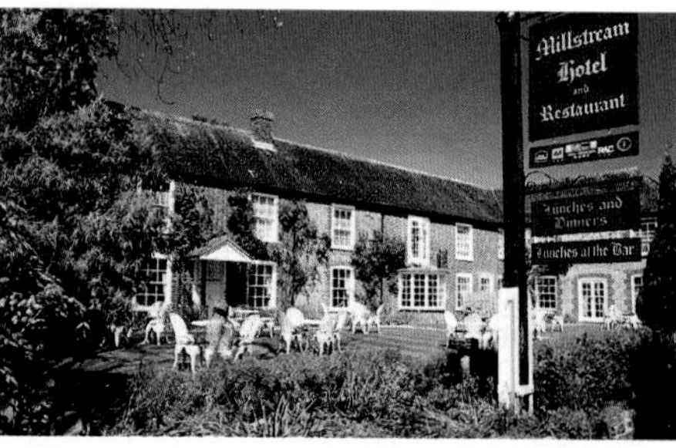

Lying in the idyllic village of Bosham, this attractive hotel provides comfortable, well-equipped and tastefully decorated bedrooms. Many guests regularly return here for the relaxed ambience created by the notably efficient and friendly staff. Public rooms include a cocktail bar opening out onto the garden and a pleasant restaurant offers varied and freshly prepared cuisine.
ROOMS: 33 en suite 2 annexe en suite (2 fmly) (9 GF) No smoking in all bedrooms s £79-£89; d £129-£139 (incl. bkfst) **LB**
FACILITIES: Bridge breaks entertainment Xmas **CONF:** Thtr 45 Class 20 Board 20 Del from £99 **PARKING:** 44 **NOTES:** No smoking in restaurant Civ Wed 90 **CARDS:**
See advert under CHICHESTER

BOSTON, Lincolnshire Map 12 TF34

★★★62% New England
49 Wide Bargate PE21 6SH
THE INDEPENDENTS
☎ 01205 365255 🖷 01205 310597
e-mail: newengland@fsmail.net
Dir: *Boston (S) A16, follow Skegness signs to end of dual carriageway, at rdbt turn left, hotel left*

Enjoying a prime town centre location, this busy hotel is being upgraded and improved. The refurbished bedrooms are smartly appointed and well equipped. Morning coffee and afternoon tea is served in the open plan bar lounge which is equipped with a well stocked bar offering a large range of beers and spirits.
ROOMS: 27 en suite (2 fmly) No smoking in 7 bedrooms s £59-£65; d £79-£85 (incl. bkfst) **LB** **FACILITIES:** STV entertainment Xmas
CONF: Thtr 120 Class 40 Board 40 Del from £70 **PARKING:** 40
NOTES: No smoking in restaurant **CARDS:**

★★65% *Comfort Inn*
Donnington Rd, Bicker Bar Roundabout
PE20 3AN
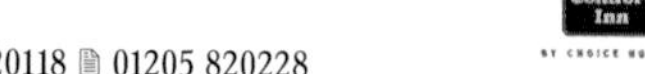
☎ 01205 820118 🖷 01205 820228
e-mail: admin@gb607.u-net.com
Dir: *towards A16 Spaking, situated on A17/A52 rdbt, 11m from Boston*
Public areas within this purpose-built hotel include an open plan lounge bar and adjacent restaurant; reasonably priced meals are available all day. Well-equipped bedrooms offering good levels of comfort and value for money. Several meeting rooms are also available.
ROOMS: 55 en suite (15 fmly) No smoking in 25 bedrooms
FACILITIES: STV **CONF:** Thtr 70 Class 30 Board 35 **PARKING:** 60
NOTES: No smoking in restaurant **CARDS:**

⌂ Travel Inn

Wainfleet Rd PE21 9RW
☎ 08701 977035 🖷 01205 366494
Dir: *A52, 300yds E of junct with A16 Boston/Grimsby road. (Nearest landmark is Pilgrim Hospital)*
Travel Inn offers good-quality, value-for-money accommodation. Spacious, en suite rooms with bath and shower comfortably
continued

accommodate a family of up to two adults and two children (to age 15). The restaurant and bar offers a varied menu. For further details and the Travel Inn phone number, consult the Hotel Groups page.
ROOMS: 34 en suite s £44.95; d £44.95 **CONF:** Thtr 12 Board 8

BOTLEY, Hampshire
Map 05 SU51

★★★★68% Botley Park Hotel Golf & Country Club
MACDONALD HOTELS

Winchester Rd, Boorley Green SO32 2UA
☎ 01489 780888 🖹 01489 789242
e-mail: botleypark@macdonald-hotels.co.uk
Dir: *A334 towards Botley, left at 1st rdbt past M&S, continue over next 4 mini-rdbts, at 3rd rdbt follow hotel signs*

This modern and spacious hotel sits peacefully in the midst of its own 176 acres parkland golf course. Bedrooms are comfortably appointed with a good range of extras and an extensive range of leisure facilities is on offer. Attractive public areas include a relaxing restaurant and the more informal Swing and Divot Bar.
ROOMS: 100 en suite (34 GF) No smoking in 52 bedrooms s £75-£125; d £85-£135 (incl. bkfst) **LB FACILITIES:** STV Indoor swimming (H) Golf 18 Tennis (hard) Squash Sauna Solarium Gym Jacuzzi Aerobics studio, Beauty salon, Golf driving range Xmas **CONF:** Thtr 240 Class 100 Board 60 Del from £130 **PARKING:** 250 **NOTES:** No smoking in restaurant Civ Wed 200 **CARDS:**

BOURNEMOUTH, Dorset
Map 05 SZ09
See also Christchurch & Ferndown

★★★★75% Bournemouth Highcliff Marriott
Marriott HOTELS · RESORTS · SUITES

St Michaels Rd, West Cliff BH2 5DU
☎ 01202 557702 🖹 01202 292734
e-mail: reservations.bournemouth@marriotthotels.co.uk
Dir: *A338 through Bournemouth. Follow BIC signs to West Cliff Rd. 2nd right into St Michaels Rd. Hotel at end of road on left*

Originally built as a row of coastguard cottages, the hotel has expanded over the years into a most elegant and charming hotel. Impeccably maintained throughout, many of the bedrooms have sea views. An excellent range of leisure, business and conference facilities are offered, as well as private dining and banqueting rooms. The hotel also has direct access to the BIC.
ROOMS: 138 en suite 19 annexe en suite (26 fmly) No smoking in 65 bedrooms **FACILITIES:** STV Indoor swimming (H) Outdoor swimming (H) Tennis (hard) Sauna Solarium Gym Croquet lawn Putting green Jacuzzi Beautician Volleyball Childs play area **CONF:** Thtr 350 Class 180 Board 90 Del from £95 **SERVICES:** Lift **PARKING:** 100 **NOTES:** No dogs (ex guide dogs) No smoking in restaurant Civ Wed 100
CARDS:

★★★★75% Menzies East Cliff Court
MENZIES HOTELS

East Overcliff Dr BH1 3AN
☎ 01202 554545 🖹 01202 557456
e-mail: info@menzies-hotels.co.uk
Dir: *From M3/M27 approach Bournemouth on A338, follow signs to the East Cliff, hotel on sea front*

Enjoying panoramic views across the bay, extensive refurbishment at this popular hotel has had impressive results. Bedrooms, modern and contemporary in style, have been appointed to a very high standard, with many benefiting from balconies and sea views.

continued

Stylish public areas include a range of inviting lounges, a spacious restaurant and a selection of conference rooms.
ROOMS: 67 en suite (10 fmly) **FACILITIES:** STV Outdoor swimming (H) Leisure facilities at nearby hotel **CONF:** Thtr 150 Class 40 Board 45 Del from £130 **SERVICES:** Lift **PARKING:** 70 **NOTES:** No smoking in restaurant Civ Wed 100 **CARDS:**

★★★★70% De Vere Royal Bath
DE VERE HOTELS

Bath Rd BH1 2EW
☎ 01202 555555 🖹 01202 554158
e-mail: royalbath@devere-hotels.com
Dir: *A338 follow signs for pier & beaches. Hotel on Bath Rd just before Lansdowne rdbt and Pier*

Overlooking the bay, this well-established seafront hotel is surrounded by beautifully kept gardens. Public rooms, which include lounges, a choice of restaurants and indoor leisure facilities, are of a scale and style befitting the golden era in which the hotel was built. Local attractions include the motor museum at Beaulieu and the Oceanarium. Valet parking is provided for a small charge.
ROOMS: 140 en suite (16 fmly) (5 GF) s fr £135; d fr £165 (incl. bkfst) **LB FACILITIES: Spa** STV Indoor swimming (H) Sauna Solarium Gym Jacuzzi Beauty salon, Hairdressing, Swimming pool supervised Xmas **CONF:** Thtr 400 Class 220 Board 100 Del from £180 **SERVICES:** Lift **PARKING:** 70 **NOTES:** No dogs (ex guide dogs) No smoking in restaurant Civ Wed 200 **CARDS:**

★★★★70% Menzies Carlton

East Overcliff BH1 3DN
☎ 01202 552011 🖹 01202 299573
e-mail: info@menzies-hotels.co.uk
Dir: *From M3/M27, approach Bournemouth on A338, follow signs to East Cliff, hotel on seafront*

Enjoying a prime location on the East Cliff, and with views of the Isle of Wight and Dorset coastline, the Carlton has attractive gardens and pool area. Conference and banqueting facilities are varied. Most of the spacious bedrooms enjoy sea views and all are well-equipped. Guests can enjoy an interesting range of carefully prepared dishes in Fredericks restaurant.
ROOMS: 73 en suite No smoking in 20 bedrooms **FACILITIES:** STV Indoor swimming (H) Outdoor swimming (H) Sauna Solarium Gym Jacuzzi Spa pool **CONF:** Thtr 140 Class 90 Board 45 Del from £130 **SERVICES:** Lift **PARKING:** 70 **NOTES:** No smoking in restaurant Civ Wed 80 **CARDS:**

B

BOURNEMOUTH, continued

★★★77% ⊛ Chine

Best Western

Boscombe Spa Rd BH5 1AX
☎ 01202 396234 🖷 01202 391737
e-mail: reservations@chinehotel.co.uk
Dir: *follow BIC signs, A338/Wessex Way to St Pauls rdbt. 1st exit - St Pauls Rd to next rdbt, 2nd exit signed Eastcliff/Boscombe/Southbourne. Next rdbt, 1st exit into Christchurch Rd. After 2nd lights, right into Boscombe Spa Rd*

Set in delightful gardens with private access to the seafront and beach, this popular hotel benefits from superb views. An excellent range of facilities includes an indoor and outdoor pool, a small leisure centre and a selection of meeting rooms. The spacious bedrooms, some of which have balconies, are well appointed and thoughtfully equipped.
ROOMS: 65 en suite 22 annexe en suite (13 fmly) No smoking in 14 bedrooms s £50-£70; d £100-£140 (incl. bkfst) **LB FACILITIES: Spa** STV Indoor swimming (H) Outdoor swimming (H) Sauna Solarium Gym Croquet lawn Putting green Games room, Outdoor & indoor childrens play area, Swimming pools supervised ch fac Xmas **CONF:** Thtr 140 Class 70 Board 40 Del from £75 **SERVICES:** Lift **PARKING:** 50 **NOTES:** No dogs (ex guide dogs) No smoking in restaurant Civ Wed 120 **CARDS:**

See advert under POOLE and on opposite page

★★★76% ⊛ Langtry Manor - Lovenest of a King

Derby Rd, East Cliff BH1 3QB
☎ 01202 553887 🖷 01202 290115
e-mail: lillie@langtrymanor.com
Dir: *A31/A338, 1st rdbt by rail station turn left. Over next rdbt, 1st left into Knyveton Rd. Hotel opposite*

Retaining a stately air, this property was originally built in 1877 by Edward VII for his mistress Lillie Langtry. The individually furnished and decorated bedrooms include several feature four-poster beds. Enjoyable cuisine is served in the magnificent dining hall, complete with several large Tudor tapestries. There is an Edwardian banquet on Saturday evenings.
ROOMS: 12 en suite 8 annexe en suite (2 fmly) (3 GF) No smoking in 4 bedrooms s £90-£130; d £140-£220 (incl. bkfst) **LB FACILITIES:** STV Free use of local health club entertainment Xmas **CONF:** Thtr 100 Class 60 Board 40 Del from £100 **PARKING:** 30 **NOTES:** No smoking in restaurant Civ Wed 100 **CARDS:**

★★★75% Elstead

Knyveton Rd BH1 3QP
☎ 01202 293071 🖷 01202 293827
e-mail: info@the-elstead.co.uk

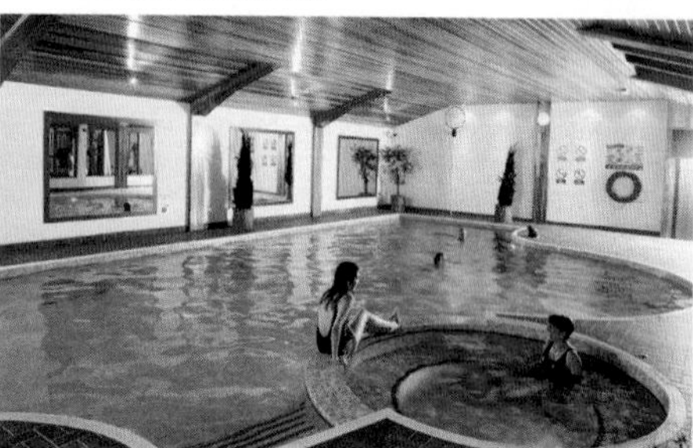

Most rooms have now been refurbished to a high standard at this quietly located and comfortable hotel, which is situated close to both the seafront, town centre attractions and the BIC. Ideal as a base for either the business or touring guest, the Elstead offers an impressively wide range of leisure and business facilities.
ROOMS: 50 en suite (15 fmly) No smoking in 30 bedrooms s £56-£72; d £91-£101 (incl. bkfst) **LB FACILITIES: Spa** STV Indoor swimming (H) Snooker Sauna Gym Steam room, Pool Table, Swimming pool supervised Xmas **CONF:** Thtr 80 Class 60 Board 40 Del from £85 **SERVICES:** Lift **PARKING:** 40 **NOTES:** No smoking in restaurant Closed 23 Dec-28 Dec **CARDS:**

★★★74% Durley Hall

Durley Chine Rd, West Cliff BH2 5JS
☎ 01202 751000 🖷 01202 757585
e-mail: Sales@durleyhall.co.uk
Dir: *A338 follow signs to West Cliff & BIC*
This attractive hotel, conveniently situated, provides guests with friendly and attentive service and offers extensive leisure, beauty and therapy treatments along with a diverse range of business and conference facilities. The smart bedrooms are well designed, comfortable and well equipped. A candlelight dinner dance is normally held every Saturday.
ROOMS: 67 en suite 11 annexe en suite (27 fmly) **FACILITIES: Spa** STV Indoor swimming (H) Outdoor swimming (H) Sauna Solarium Gym Jacuzzi Beauty therapist Table tennis Hydro Therapy entertainment **CONF:** Thtr 200 Class 80 Board 35 **SERVICES:** Lift **PARKING:** 150 **NOTES:** No dogs (ex guide dogs) No smoking in restaurant Civ Wed 85 **CARDS:**

★★★71% East Anglia

Best Western

6 Poole Rd BH2 5QX
☎ 01202 765163 🖷 01202 752949
e-mail: info@eastangliahotel.com
Dir: *A338 at Bournemouth West rdbt. Follow signs for BIC & West Cliff. At next rdbt right into Poole Rd. Hotel on right*
This privately owned and well-managed hotel provides modern

continued

accommodation, including ground floor bedrooms. This is complemented by the friendly team of staff, who ensure a warm welcome and attentive service throughout. Public areas include a number of function and conference rooms, ample lounges and an air-conditioned restaurant. There is also an outdoor swimming pool.
ROOMS: 45 en suite 25 annexe en suite (18 fmly) No smoking in 23 bedrooms s fr £54; d fr £100 (incl. bkfst) **LB** **FACILITIES: Spa** STV Outdoor swimming (H) Sauna American Pool Room Xmas **CONF:** Thtr 150 Class 75 Board 60 Del from £90 **SERVICES:** Lift **PARKING:** 70 **NOTES:** No dogs (ex guide dogs) No smoking in restaurant
CARDS:

★★★71% *Hermitage*

Exeter Rd BH2 5AH
☎ 01202 557363 🖹 01202 559173
e-mail: info@hermitage-hotel.co.uk
Dir: *Hotel opposite BIC and pier.*

Occupying an impressive position overlooking the seafront, at the heart of Bournemouth's town centre, the Hermitage offers friendly and attentive service. The smart bedrooms are comfortable and very well equipped, and many rooms have sea views. The wood-panelled lounge provides an elegant and tranquil area as does the restaurant where well-cooked and interesting dishes are served.
ROOMS: 63 en suite 12 annexe en suite (10 fmly) No smoking in 52 bedrooms **FACILITIES:** Free swimming at Bournemouth International Centre **CONF:** Thtr 180 Class 60 Board 60 **SERVICES:** Lift **PARKING:** 58 **NOTES:** No dogs (ex guide dogs) No smoking in restaurant **CARDS:**

★★★71% *Hotel Miramar*

East Overcliff Dr, East Cliff BH1 3AL
☎ 01202 556581 🖹 01202 291242
e-mail: sales@miramar-bournemouth.com
Dir: *Wessex Way rdbt turn into St Pauls Rd. Right at next rdbt. 3rd exit at next rdbt. 2nd exit at next rdbt into Grove Rd. Hotel car park 50mtrs on right*

Conveniently located on the East Cliff and surrounded by well-tended gardens, this Edwardian hotel overlooks the sea. Friendly staff provide a relaxing environment, and bedrooms are spacious, comfortable and well equipped. The versatile public areas offer a choice of lounges and there are a number of meeting and function rooms.
ROOMS: 43 en suite (6 fmly) No smoking in 10 bedrooms **FACILITIES:** STV Croquet lawn entertainment **CONF:** Thtr 200 Class 50 Board 50 **SERVICES:** Lift **PARKING:** 80 **NOTES:** No smoking in restaurant Civ Wed 130 **CARDS:**

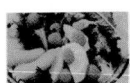

B

BOURNEMOUTH, continued

★★★71% *Montague*
Durley Rd South, West Cliff BH2 5JH
☎ 01202 551074 📠 01202 553948
e-mail: enquiries@montaguehotel.co.uk
Dir: *A31/A338 to Bournemouth turn left into Cambridge Rd at Bournemouth West rdbt, take 2nd exit at next rdbt into Durley Chine Rd. Next rdbt take 2nd exit. Hotel on right*
This splendid hotel enjoys a convenient location close to the BIC, just a short walk from the attractions of the town centre. Friendly and attentive staff provide a relaxing environment and comfort is assured. Bedrooms are most attractive and very well equipped. Guests can unwind on the terrace or in the relaxing bar. Dinner provides appetising dishes featuring fresh local produce.
ROOMS: 37 rms (34 en suite) (9 fmly) No smoking in 6 bedrooms **FACILITIES:** STV Outdoor swimming (H) **CONF:** Thtr 20 Class 12 Board 12 **SERVICES:** Lift **PARKING:** 50 **NOTES:** No smoking in restaurant Civ Wed 40 **CARDS:**

★★★71% Piccadilly
Bath Rd BH1 2NN
☎ 01202 298024 📠 01202 298235
Dir: *follow signs for Lansdowne*
This hotel offers a friendly welcome to guests, many of whom return on a regular basis, particularly for the superb ballroom dancing facilities and short breaks which are a feature here. Bedrooms are smartly decorated, well maintained and offer comfortable. Dining in the attractive restaurant is always popular and dishes are freshly prepared and appetising.
ROOMS: 45 en suite (2 fmly) s £65; d £95 (incl. bkfst) **LB** **FACILITIES:** Ballroom dancing Xmas **SERVICES:** Lift **PARKING:** 30 **NOTES:** No dogs (ex guide dogs) No smoking in restaurant **CARDS:**

★★★70% The Connaught
West Hill Rd, West Cliff BH2 5PH
☎ 01202 298020 📠 01202 298028
e-mail: sales@theconnaught.co.uk
Dir: *follow Town Centre West & BIC signs*
Best Western
Conveniently located on the West Cliff, close to the BIC, beaches and town centre, this attractive hotel offers well equipped, neatly decorated rooms, some with balconies. The hotel boasts a very well equipped leisure complex, with large pool, snooker table and comprehensive gym facilities. Breakfast and dinner offer imaginative dishes made with quality local ingredients.
ROOMS: 56 en suite (15 fmly) No smoking in 18 bedrooms s £49-£68; d £98-£136 (incl. bkfst & dinner) **LB** **FACILITIES: Spa** STV Indoor swimming (H) Snooker Sauna Solarium Gym Jacuzzi Cardio-vascular suite, Table tennis, Pool table Xmas **CONF:** Thtr 200 Class 70 Board 70 Del from £85 **SERVICES:** Lift **PARKING:** 45 **NOTES:** No smoking in restaurant **CARDS:**

★★★69% Hotel Collingwood
11 Priory Rd, West Cliff BH2 5DF
☎ 01202 557575 📠 01202 293219
e-mail: info@hotel-collingwood.co.uk
Dir: *A338 left at West Cliff sign, over 1st rdbt and left at 2nd rdbt. Hotel 500yds on left*
This friendly hotel is privately owned and managed, situated close to the BIC. Bedrooms are airy, with the emphasis on comfort. An excellent range of leisure facilities is available and the public areas are spacious and comfortable. Dining in Pinks Restaurant offers carefully prepared cuisine and a 5-course, fixed-price dinner.
ROOMS: 53 en suite (16 fmly) (6 GF) No smoking in 6 bedrooms s £57-£64; d £114-£128 (incl. bkfst & dinner) **LB** **FACILITIES:** STV Indoor swimming (H) Snooker Sauna Solarium Jacuzzi Mini gym, Steam room, Games room entertainment Xmas **SERVICES:** Lift **PARKING:** 55 **NOTES:** No smoking in restaurant Closed First 2 weeks of Jan.
CARDS:

See advert on opposite page

★★★69% Cumberland
East Overcliff Dr BH1 3AF
☎ 01202 290722 📠 01202 311394
e-mail: reservations@cumberlandhotel.uk.com
Many of the well-equipped and attractively decorated bedrooms benefit from sea views and balconies here. The public areas are spacious and comfortable. The restaurant offers a daily changing fixed price menu. Guests have use of the leisure club at the sister hotel, The Queens.
ROOMS: 102 en suite (12 fmly) s £50-£69; d £99-£138 (incl. bkfst) **LB** **FACILITIES:** Outdoor swimming (H) Free membership of nearby Leisure Club Xmas **CONF:** Thtr 120 Class 70 Board 45 Del from £79 **SERVICES:** Lift **PARKING:** 51 **NOTES:** No smoking in restaurant **CARDS:**

★★★69% Menzies Anglo-Swiss
16 Gervis Rd, East Cliff BH1 3EQ
☎ 01202 554794 📠 01202 299615
e-mail: info@menzies-hotels.co.uk
MENZIES HOTELS
Dir: *On A338 to Bournemouth follow signs for East Cliff and seafront*
Well located near the East Cliff and town centre, this is a popular, friendly hotel. Bedrooms vary in style; many offer balconies, and some family suites are available. An exciting new and stylish brasserie has now been completed. The indoor pool is reputed to be one of the largest in the area.
ROOMS: 57 en suite 8 annexe en suite (19 fmly) No smoking in 16 bedrooms **FACILITIES:** STV Indoor swimming (H) Sauna Solarium Gym Jacuzzi **CONF:** Thtr 75 Class 30 Board 30 Del from £105 **SERVICES:** Lift **PARKING:** 70 **NOTES:** No smoking in restaurant Civ Wed 150 **CARDS:**

★★★69% Trouville
Priory Rd BH2 5DH
☎ 01202 552262 📠 01202 293324
e-mail: mail@trouvillehotel.uk.com
Dir: *A338 onto A35, follow signs for BIC*
With a location near Bournemouth's International Centre and the seafront, this family owned hotel is conveniently situated whether staying for business or pleasure. The attractive bedrooms are modern and tastefully furnished and the inviting public areas include a comfortable bar, a separate lounge and a smart restaurant.
ROOMS: 77 en suite (21 fmly) s £53-£61; d £130-£149 (incl. bkfst) **LB** **FACILITIES:** Indoor swimming (H) Sauna Solarium Gym Jacuzzi entertainment Xmas **CONF:** Thtr 100 Class 45 Board 50 **SERVICES:** Lift **PARKING:** 55 **NOTES:** No smoking in restaurant **CARDS:**

B

★★★69% Wessex

West Cliff Rd BH2 5EU

Forestdale Hotels

☎ 01202 551911 📠 01202 297354

e-mail: wessex@forestdale.com

Dir: *Follow M27/A35 or A338 from Dorchester & A347 N. Hotel on West Cliff side of town*

Centrally located for the town centre and beach, the Wessex is a popular, relaxing hotel. Bedrooms vary in size and include premier rooms; all are comfortable, and equipped with a range of modern amenities. There are excellent leisure facilities, ample function rooms and an open-plan bar and lounge.

ROOMS: 109 en suite (22 fmly) No smoking in 3 bedrooms s fr £70; d fr £115 (incl. bkfst) **LB FACILITIES:** STV Indoor swimming (H) Outdoor swimming (H) Snooker Sauna Solarium Gym Table tennis Xmas **CONF:** Thtr 400 Class 160 Board 160 **SERVICES:** Lift **PARKING:** 160 **NOTES:** No smoking in restaurant Civ Wed **CARDS:**

★★★68% Cliffeside

East Overcliff Dr BH1 3AQ

☎ 01202 555724 📠 01202 314534

e-mail: hotels@arthuryoung.co.uk

Dir: *M27/A338 approx 7m, then 1st rdbt left into East Cliff*

A traditionally run and friendly hotel benefiting from an elevated position on the seafront. Bedrooms and public areas are attractively appointed and many have sea views; the appealing Atlantic Restaurant offers guests a fixed-price menu and a relaxing ambience.

ROOMS: 62 en suite (10 fmly) **FACILITIES:** Outdoor swimming (H) Table tennis **CONF:** Thtr 180 Class 140 Board 60 **SERVICES:** Lift **PARKING:** 45 **CARDS:**

★★★68% Hinton Firs

Manor Rd, East Cliff BH1 3ET

☎ 01202 555409 📠 01202 299607

e-mail: reservations@hintonfirshotel.co.uk

Dir: *A338 turn W at St Paul's rdbt, over next 2 rdbts then fork left to side of church. Hotel on next corner*

This efficient and friendly hotel is conveniently located on East Cliff. Guests are offered leisure facilities including indoor and outdoor pools and a games room, and there is also a spacious lounge, bar and restaurant in which to relax. Bedrooms are light and airy, and six are situated in a separate wing.

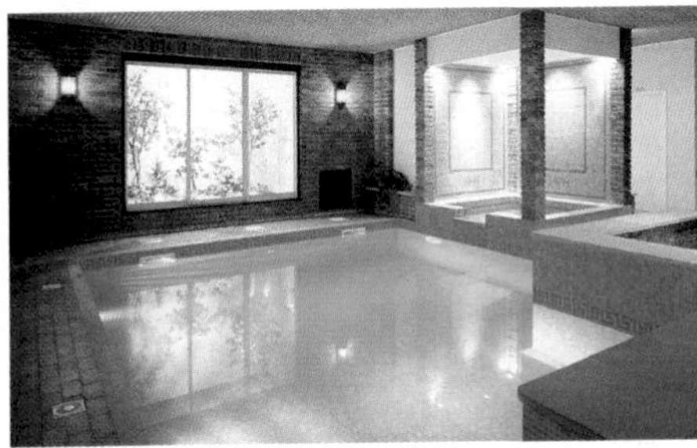

ROOMS: 46 en suite 6 annexe en suite (12 fmly) (6 GF) s £45-£65; d £90-£120 (incl. bkfst & dinner) **LB FACILITIES: Spa** Indoor swimming (H) Outdoor swimming (H) Sauna Games room entertainment Xmas **CONF:** Thtr 60 Class 40 Board 30 Del from £55 **SERVICES:** Lift **PARKING:** 40 **NOTES:** No dogs No smoking in restaurant **CARDS:**

BOURNEMOUTH, continued

★★★68% Quality Hotel, Bournemouth (Durlston Court)

47 Gervis Rd, East Cliff BH1 3DD
☎ 01202 316316 🖷 01202 316999
e-mail: durlston@excelsior-leisure.com

Dir: *A338 left at rdbt, right at next rdbt. Take 2nd exit at next rdbt into Meyrick Rd. Then at next rdbt right into Gervis Rd. Hotel on left*

Formerly the home of comedian Tony Hancock, and previously called Durlston Court, this hotel has undergone some refurbishment. Bedrooms are pleasantly appointed, comfortable and well equipped. In the spacious restaurant, both fixed-price and carte menus are available, and in the new patio and garden area, drinks and light lunches are served.

ROOMS: 57 en suite (11 fmly) (2 GF) No smoking in 8 bedrooms s £37-£64.50; d £74-£94 (incl. bkfst & dinner) **LB** **FACILITIES:** Indoor swimming (H) Sauna Gym Pool table Gym privately run prebooking necessary Xmas **CONF:** Thtr 120 Class 60 Board 35 Del from £65 **SERVICES:** Lift **PARKING:** 36 **NOTES:** No smoking in restaurant **CARDS:**

★★★68% Queens

Meyrick Rd, East Cliff BH1 3DL
☎ 01202 554415 🖷 01202 294810
e-mail: hotels@arthuryoung.co.uk

Dir: *A338 St Paul's rdbt take Holdenhurst Rd. 2nd exit at Lansdown rdbt onto Meyrick Rd*

This attractive hotel enjoys a good location on the seafront and is popular for conferences and functions. The public areas include a bar, lounge and a stunning restaurant. The Queensbury Leisure Club has much to offer guests. Bedrooms vary in size and style, and all are well equipped and comfortable.

ROOMS: 109 en suite (15 fmly) s £50-£70; d £90-£120 (incl. bkfst) **LB** **FACILITIES: Spa** Indoor swimming (H) Snooker Sauna Solarium Gym Jacuzzi Beauty salon, Games Room entertainment ch fac Xmas **CONF:** Thtr 220 Class 120 Board 50 Del from £89 **SERVICES:** Lift **PARKING:** 80 **NOTES:** No smoking in restaurant **CARDS:**

★★★67% Belvedere

Bath Rd BH1 2EU
☎ 01202 297556 & 293336 🖷 01202 294699
e-mail: enquiries@belvedere-hotel.co.uk

Dir: *from A338 with railway station and Asda on left. At rdbt 1st left then 3rd exit at next 2 rdbts. Hotel on Bath Hill after 4th rdbt*

Close to the town centre and the seafront, this friendly, family-run hotel offers spacious public areas and comfortable bedrooms. The lively bar and attractive restaurant are both popular with locals, and there are meeting rooms which provide an ideal location for both conferences and functions.

ROOMS: 61 en suite (12 fmly) s £49-£59; d £98-£108 (incl. bkfst) **LB** **FACILITIES:** STV Beauty breaks with local natural spa entertainment Xmas **CONF:** Thtr 80 Class 30 Board 30 **SERVICES:** Lift **PARKING:** 55 **NOTES:** No dogs (ex guide dogs) No smoking in restaurant **CARDS:**

★★★67% Marsham Court

Russell Cotes Rd, East Cliff BH1 3AB
☎ 01202 552111 🖷 01202 294744
e-mail: reservations@marshamcourt.co.uk

Dir: *From Wessex Way take Bournemouth East exit at St Pauls rdbt. Over station rdbt. Follow ringroad, over St Swithuns rdbt. Left with church on left over Meyrick rdbt. Left at St Peters rdbt. Hotel on left*

This hotel is set in attractive gardens with splendid views over the sea and town, and is very accessible and convenient for the town and BIC. Bedrooms vary in size, are comfortably appointed and some have sea views. There is a well-stocked bar, lounge areas, terrace and pool, as well as impressive conference rooms.

ROOMS: 86 en suite (15 fmly) No smoking in all bedrooms s £57-£66; d £94-£112 (incl. bkfst) **LB** **FACILITIES:** STV Outdoor swimming (H) Free swimming at BIC, Pool table Xmas **CONF:** Thtr 200 Class 100 Board 80 Del from £78 **SERVICES:** Lift **PARKING:** 100 **NOTES:** No dogs (ex guide dogs) No smoking in restaurant Civ Wed 200 **CARDS:**

★★★67% The Riviera

Burnaby Rd, Alum Chine BH4 8JF
☎ 01202 763653 🖷 01202 768422
e-mail: reservations@rivierabournemouth.co.uk

Dir: *A338, follow signs to Alum Chine*

Part of the Calotels group, this refurbished hotel offers a range of comfortable, well-furnished bedrooms and bathrooms. Welcoming staff provide a pleasant combination of efficient service delivered in a friendly manner. In addition to a spacious lounge with regular entertainment, there is an indoor and outdoor pool.

ROOMS: 69 en suite 4 annexe en suite (25 fmly) (11 GF) s £40-£60; d £80-£140 (incl. bkfst) **LB** **FACILITIES:** Indoor swimming (H) Outdoor swimming (H) Sauna Jacuzzi Games room entertainment Xmas **CONF:** Thtr 180 Class 120 Board 50 Del from £59.95 **SERVICES:** Lift **PARKING:** 70 **NOTES:** No smoking in restaurant **CARDS:**

★★★67% Suncliff

29 East Overcliff Dr BH1 3AG
☎ 01202 291711 🖷 01202 293788
e-mail: reservations@suncliffbournemouth.co.uk

Dir: *A338 to B'mouth. 1st left at rdbt, follow signs East Cliff*

Enjoying splendid views from the East Cliff, this friendly hotel provides a range of facilities and services. Catering mainly for leisure guests, bedrooms are well equipped and comfortable and many have sea views. Public areas include a large conservatory, attractive bar and pleasant lounges.

ROOMS: 94 en suite (29 fmly) s £35-£95; d £70-£130 (incl. bkfst) **LB** **FACILITIES:** Indoor swimming (H) Squash Snooker Sauna Solarium Gym Jacuzzi Table tennis Pool table entertainment Xmas **CONF:** Thtr 100 Class 70 Board 60 Del from £69.50 **SERVICES:** Lift **PARKING:** 60 **NOTES:** No smoking in restaurant **CARDS:**

★★★66% Bay View Court

35 East Overcliff Dr BH1 3AH
☎ 01202 294449 🖹 01202 292883
e-mail: enquiry@bayviewcourt.co.uk
Dir: *on A338 left at St Pauls rdbt. Over St Swithuns rdbt. Bear left onto Manor Rd, 1st right, next right*

This relaxed and friendly hotel enjoys far reaching sea views from many of the public areas and bedrooms. Bedrooms vary in size and are attractively furnished; there is a choice of south facing lounges and, for the more energetic, an indoor swimming pool. Live entertainment is provided during the evenings.
ROOMS: 64 en suite (11 fmly) (5 GF) s £52-£58; d £104-£116 (incl. bkfst & dinner) **LB FACILITIES: Spa** STV Indoor swimming (H) Snooker Gym Jacuzzi Steam room entertainment Xmas **CONF:** Thtr 170 Class 85 Board 50 Del from £65 **SERVICES:** Lift **PARKING:** 58 **NOTES:** No smoking in restaurant **CARDS:**

★★★66% Carrington House

Forestdale Hotels

31 Knyveton Rd BH1 3QQ
☎ 01202 369988 🖹 01202 292221
e-mail: carrington.house@forestdale.com
Dir: *A338 at St Paul's rdbt, continue 200mtrs & turn left into Knyveton Rd. Hotel 400mtrs on right*
Carrington House occupies a prominent position on a tree-lined avenue, set slightly back from the seafront. Bedrooms are generally spacious and comfortable. In addition to the hotel's bar and restaurant there are extensive conference facilities. Staff are friendly and welcoming.
ROOMS: 145 en suite (42 fmly) No smoking in 40 bedrooms s fr £65; d fr £100 (incl. bkfst) **FACILITIES:** STV Indoor swimming (H) Snooker Gym Purpose built children's play area Xmas **CONF:** Thtr 500 Class 260 Board 80 **SERVICES:** Lift **PARKING:** 100 **NOTES:** No smoking in restaurant Civ Wed 250 **CARDS:**

★★★66% Heathlands Hotel

12 Grove Rd, East Cliff BH1 3AY
☎ 01202 553336 🖹 01202 555937
e-mail: info@heathlandshotel.com
Dir: *A338 St Pauls rdbt 1st exit to East Cliff, 3rd exit at next rdbt to Holdenhurst Rd, 2nd exit off Lansdowne rdbt into Meyrick Rd. Left into Gervis Rd. Hotel on right*
This is a large hotel on the East Cliff. The Heathlands is popular with many groups and conferences and the public areas are bright and spacious. There is a coffee shop that is open all day and there is regular live entertainment provided for the guests.
ROOMS: 115 en suite (16 fmly) (11 GF) No smoking in 15 bedrooms s £47-£77; d £94-£154 (incl. bkfst) **LB FACILITIES:** STV Outdoor swimming (H) Sauna Gym Jacuzzi Health suite entertainment ch fac Xmas **CONF:** Thtr 270 Class 102 Board 54 Del from £69.50 **SERVICES:** Lift **PARKING:** 100 **NOTES:** No smoking in restaurant Civ Wed 150 **CARDS:**

★★★65% Burley Court

Bath Rd BH1 2NP
☎ 01202 552824 & 556704 🖹 01202 298514
e-mail: info@burleycourthotel.co.uk
Dir: *leave A338 at St Pauls rdbt, take 3rd exit at next rdbt into Holdenhurst Rd. 3rd exit at next rdbt into Bath Rd, over crossing, 1st left*
Located on Bournemouth's West Cliff, this well established hotel is easily located and convenient for the town and beaches. Bedrooms, many now refurbished, are pleasantly furnished and decorated in bright colours. A daily changing menu is served in the spacious dining room.
ROOMS: 38 en suite (8 fmly) No smoking in 20 bedrooms s £32-£46; d £64-£88 (incl. bkfst) **LB FACILITIES:** Outdoor swimming (H) Solarium Xmas **CONF:** Thtr 30 Class 15 Board 15 **SERVICES:** Lift **PARKING:** 35 **NOTES:** No smoking in restaurant Closed 30 Dec-14 Jan
CARDS:

★★★65% Grosvenor

Bath Rd, East Cliff BH1 2EX
☎ 01202 558858 🖹 01202 298332
e-mail: enquiries@grosvenor-bournemouth.co.uk
This friendly hotel is conveniently located and an ideal base for either the business or leisure guest. Bedrooms are comfortable and spacious and service is attentive. Public areas offer business, function and leisure facilities. At both lunch and dinner attractive and freshly prepared dishes provide enjoyable dining.
ROOMS: 39 en suite (12 fmly) s £39-£56; d £78-£112 (incl. bkfst) **LB FACILITIES:** Indoor swimming (H) Sauna Gym Jacuzzi entertainment Xmas **CONF:** Thtr 30 Class 50 Board 20 Del from £60 **SERVICES:** Lift **PARKING:** 40 **NOTES:** No smoking in restaurant
CARDS:

B

BOURNEMOUTH, continued

★★★63% Chesterwood
East Overcliff Dr BH1 3AR
☎ 01202 558057 🖷 01202 556285
e-mail: enquiry@chesterwoodhotel.co.uk
Splendid sea views can be enjoyed from all of the public rooms at this popular East Cliff hotel. Bedrooms vary in size, and all are light, airy and well equipped. A comfortable bar/lounge offers an informal alternative to the drawing room, whilst the spacious restaurant offers a fixed-price menu every evening.
ROOMS: 52 rms (51 en suite) (13 fmly) **FACILITIES:** Outdoor swimming (H) Indoor leisure suite at Bayview Court Hotel (sister hotel) entertainment **CONF:** Thtr 120 Class 100 Board 30 Del £58 **SERVICES:** Lift **PARKING:** 39 **NOTES:** No smoking in restaurant Civ Wed 100 **CARDS:**

See advert on page 117

★★★63% New Durley Dean
West Cliff Rd BH2 5HE
☎ 01202 557711 🖷 01202 292815
e-mail: enquiries@newdurleydeanhotel.co.uk
Dir: *From A338 or A35 turn off at West Cliff and BIC exit. Hotel on West Cliff rdbt*
Conveniently situated close to the BIC and attractions, this impressive period building has undergone major refurbishment in recent years. Bedrooms are well equipped and spacious. Public areas include comfortable lounges, a lively night-club and quieter areas. Appetising cuisine is served in the bright and spacious dining room.
ROOMS: 123 en suite (27 fmly) s £30-£65; d £60-£130 (incl. bkfst) **LB** **FACILITIES: Spa** Indoor swimming (H) Sauna Solarium Gym Table tennis Steam room entertainment Xmas **CONF:** Thtr 120 Class 30 Board 30 Del from £80 **SERVICES:** Lift **PARKING:** 35 **NOTES:** No dogs No smoking in restaurant **CARDS:**

★★★63% Pavilion
22 Bath Rd BH1 2NS
☎ 01202 291266 🖷 01202 559264
e-mail: info@pavilion-hotel.com
Dir: *A388 left at St Paul's rdbt. 3rd exit at Bournemouth Station rdbt. Straight on at Lansdowne rdbt onto Bath Road. Hotel 150yds on left*
Close to the town centre and within easy access of the seafront and other attractions, this popular hotel offers comfortable accommodation. A number of meeting and function rooms are available and guests may relax in the refurbished bar or lounge. The friendly staff provide a warm welcome.
ROOMS: 43 en suite (6 fmly) s £37-£40; d £74-£80 (incl. bkfst) **LB** **FACILITIES:** Special rates for International Centre Xmas **CONF:** Thtr 100 Class 50 Board 50 Del from £65 **SERVICES:** Lift **PARKING:** 40 **NOTES:** No dogs (ex guide dogs) No smoking in restaurant **CARDS:**

★★★63% Royal Exeter
Exeter Rd BH2 5AG
☎ 01202 438000 🖷 01202 297963
e-mail: royalexeterhotel@aol.com
Dir: *opposite Bournemouth International Centre*
Ideally located opposite the Bournemouth International Centre, and convenient for the beach and town centre, this busy hotel caters for business and leisure guests. A versatile range of public areas is available from the cosy lounge to the choice of the Lighthouse Bar and also a relaxing patio; in addition secure car parking is available for guests. Bedrooms are spacious and comfortable and well equipped.

ROOMS: 54 en suite (13 fmly) s £55-£70; d £80-£120 (incl. bkfst) **FACILITIES:** STV Xmas **CONF:** Thtr 40 Class 20 Board 35 Del from £35 **SERVICES:** Lift **PARKING:** 50 **NOTES:** No dogs (ex guide dogs) **CARDS:**

★★★61% Cadogan
8 Poole Rd BH2 5QU
☎ 01202 757758 🖷 01202 757756
e-mail: cadogan@future3000plc.com
Conveniently accessible from the ringroad and town centre, this modern hotel is also a good base for visiting the local attractions and beach. Bedrooms vary in size and are attractively decorated whilst public areas include a cosy bar and a bright basement dining room.
ROOMS: 54 en suite (7 fmly) No smoking in 10 bedrooms s £19-£49; d £38-£98 (incl. bkfst) **FACILITIES:** STV Xmas **CONF:** Thtr 60 Class 50 Board 30 Del from £55 **SERVICES:** Lift **NOTES:** No smoking in restaurant **CARDS:**

★★71% Arlington
Exeter Park Rd BH2 5BD
☎ 01202 552879 & 553012 🖷 01202 298317
e-mail: enquiries@arlingtonbournemouth.co.uk
Dir: *follow BIC signs through Priory Rd, onto rdbt and exit at Royal Exeter Hotel sign. Hotel along Exeter Park Rd*
Well-equipped bedrooms and comfortable accommodation along with friendly hospitality are offered at this privately owned and run hotel. Conveniently located, midway between the square and the pier and ideally situated for the BIC, the Arlington has direct access to the flower gardens, which are overlooked from the hotel's lounge and terrace bar.
ROOMS: 27 en suite 1 annexe en suite (6 fmly) s £39-£47; d £77-£93 (incl. bkfst & dinner) **LB** **FACILITIES:** STV Xmas **SERVICES:** Lift **PARKING:** 21 **NOTES:** No dogs No children 2yrs No smoking in restaurant Closed 4-15 Jan **CARDS:**

★★71% Sun Court
West Hill Rd BH2 5PH
☎ 01202 551343 🖷 01202 316747
e-mail: info@suncourthotel.co.uk
Located on the West Cliff, this privately owned hotel is well placed to offer convenient access to the town centre and seafront attractions. Bedrooms come in a range of sizes, some have sun lounges and there are also some family rooms. Public areas include an airy restaurant, a residents' lounge and a friendly bar where live entertainment is laid on for guests' enjoyment.
ROOMS: 32 en suite (5 fmly) s £33-£44; d £66-£88 (incl. bkfst) **LB** **FACILITIES:** STV Outdoor swimming (H) entertainment Xmas **SERVICES:** Lift **PARKING:** 35 **NOTES:** No dogs (ex guide dogs) No children 5yrs No smoking in restaurant **CARDS:**

★★70% Whitehall
Exeter Park Rd BH2 5AX
☎ 01202 554682 📠 01202 554682
e-mail: whitehallhotel@lineone.net
Dir: *follow BIC signs then turn into Exeter Park Rd off Exeter Rd*
The warmest of welcomes awaits guests at this comfortable hotel, with bright bedrooms attractively decorated in co-ordinating fabrics. Enjoyable home-cooked meals are served in the large dining room, before which guests can enjoy a drink in the small, well-stocked bar. Two attractive lounges are available, and in the summer months a programme of entertainment is also provided.
ROOMS: 45 en suite (5 fmly) No smoking in 18 bedrooms s £33-£38; d £66-£76 (incl. bkfst) **LB SERVICES:** Lift **PARKING:** 25 **NOTES:** No smoking in restaurant Closed Nov-Feb **CARDS:**

★★69% Chinehurst
Alum Chine, 18-20 Studland Rd, Westbourne BH4 8JA
☎ 01202 764583 📠 01202 762854
e-mail: chinehurst@aol.com
Dir: *off A338, 2nd junct off Frizzel rdbt, signed for Alum Chine*
A warm welcome is assured at this family run hotel, peacefully situated on the west side of town. Bedrooms are bright and attractive; some have sea views, including the honeymoon suite. There is a path leading to the beach and regular buses run to the town centre. Entertainment is provided on most evenings in season.
ROOMS: 30 en suite (4 fmly) (3 GF) No smoking in 4 bedrooms s £35-£48; d £70-£96 (incl. bkfst) **LB FACILITIES:** Games room entertainment Xmas **PARKING:** 14 **NOTES:** No children 3yrs No smoking in restaurant Closed 3 months pre-Easter
CARDS:

★★69% Durley Grange
6 Durley Rd, West Cliff BH2 5JL
☎ 01202 554473 & 290743 📠 01202 293774
e-mail: durleygrangehotel@btopenworld.com
Dir: *A338/St Michaels rdbt. Over next rdbt, 1st left into Sommerville Rd & right into Durley Rd*
This friendly hotel is located in a quiet area, within easy walking distance of the pier and town centre. Bedrooms are simply decorated, comfortable and well-equipped. Home-cooked meals are served in the dining room and there is a relaxing lounge bar, and a swimming pool available for guests' use.
ROOMS: 51 en suite (6 fmly) (4 GF) No smoking in 2 bedrooms s £38-£50; d £76-£100 (incl. bkfst & dinner) **LB FACILITIES: Spa** STV Indoor swimming (H) Sauna Solarium entertainment Xmas **SERVICES:** Lift **PARKING:** 35 **NOTES:** No children 5yrs No smoking in restaurant Closed 2 Jan-1 Feb **CARDS:**

★★68% Mansfield
West Cliff Gardens BH2 5HL
☎ 01202 552659
e-mail: mail@bournemouthhotel.net
Dir: *from A338 follow signs for West Cliff, over 2 rdbts via Cambridge & Durley Chine Rd*
The Mansfield Hotel is located in a quiet crescent on the West Cliff. It is convenient for access to the seafront and to the town centre. All of the bedrooms are comfortably furnished, and the staff make every effort to ensure that guests have an enjoyable stay.
ROOMS: 30 en suite (7 fmly) (3 GF) s £32-£40; d £64-£80 (incl. bkfst & dinner) **LB FACILITIES:** Xmas **PARKING:** 12 **NOTES:** No dogs No smoking in restaurant Closed 29 Dec-17 Jan
CARDS:

★★66% Cliff Court
15 Westcliff Rd BH2 5EX
☎ 01202 555994 📠 01202 780954
e-mail: info@cliffcourthotel.com
Dir: *A338 Wessex Way into Cambridge Rd. Follow Durley Chine Rd into West Cliff Rd*
This hotel is located on the West Cliff within easy reach of the town centre, beach and the many attractions of the area. In addition to the spacious dining room, the public rooms include a bar and small lounge. In the comfortable bedrooms, the best use has been made of the available space.
ROOMS: 40 en suite (4 fmly) **FACILITIES:** STV entertainment **SERVICES:** Lift **PARKING:** 31 **NOTES:** No smoking in restaurant
CARDS:

★★66% New Westcliff
27-29 Chine Crescent, West Cliff BH2 5LB
☎ 01202 551926 & 551062 📠 01202 315377
e-mail: reservations@newwestcliffhotel.co.uk
Dir: *off Wessex Way at signs for Westcliff and BIC. Over Poole Road rdbt, continue along Durley Chine Rd, hotel 0.5m right*
A warm welcome awaits guests at this family-run hotel, ideally located for the town and beach. The bedrooms are of varying sizes and are attractively decorated and well equipped. There is a lovely garden, a bowling green and three comfortable lounges. All-weather leisure facilities, including a small cinema, are a definite plus.
ROOMS: 55 en suite (16 fmly) (3 GF) No smoking in 45 bedrooms s £32-£52; d £64-£104 (incl. bkfst) **LB FACILITIES:** Indoor swimming (H) Sauna Solarium Jacuzzi Cinema, Bowling Green, Ballroom entertainment Xmas **SERVICES:** Lift **PARKING:** 70 **NOTES:** No dogs (ex guide dogs) No smoking in restaurant **CARDS:**

★★66% Ullswater
West Cliff Gardens BH2 5HW
☎ 01202 555181 📠 01202 317896
e-mail: enq@ullswater.uk.com
Dir: *In Bournemouth follow signs to West Cliff. Hotel just off Westcliff Rd*
This pleasant and friendly hotel offers comfortable accommodation. Attracting a loyal following, the Ullswater is conveniently situated close to Bournemouth's city centre and seafront. Bedrooms, many now refurbished, are pleasantly appointed and come in a range of sizes. The lounge and dining room are spacious and there is a good choice of dishes on the daily changing menu.
ROOMS: 42 en suite (8 fmly) (2 GF) s £29-£36; d £58-£72 (incl. bkfst) **LB FACILITIES:** Snooker Table tennis entertainment Xmas **CONF:** Thtr 40 Class 30 Board 24 **SERVICES:** Lift **PARKING:** 10 **NOTES:** No smoking in restaurant **CARDS:**

★★65% Aaron Croham Hurst
9 Durley Rd South, West Cliff BH2 5JH
☎ 01202 552353 📠 01202 311484
e-mail: enquiries@crohamhurst.co.uk
This friendly hotel is popular with individuals and coach parties alike and is conveniently located for the beach and town centre. Bedrooms come in a variety of sizes and styles and all are well equipped. The lounge is also the venue for regular evening entertainment and the restaurant offers traditional home-cooked meals.
ROOMS: 41 en suite (11 fmly) (8 GF) s £22.50-£48; d £45-£96 (incl. bkfst & dinner) **LB FACILITIES:** STV entertainment Xmas
SERVICES: Lift **PARKING:** 28 **NOTES:** No dogs No smoking in restaurant **CARDS:**

B

BOURNEMOUTH, continued

★★65% Bourne Hall Hotel
14 Priory Rd, West Cliff BH2 5DN
☎ 01202 299715 01202 552669
e-mail: info@bournehall.co.uk
Dir: *M27/A31 from Ringwood into Bournemouth on A338, Wessex Way. Follow signs to BIC, onto West Cliff. Hotel on right*
A friendly, comfortable hotel conveniently located close to the BIC and seafront. Bedrooms are well equipped; some rooms are located on the ground floor and some have sea views. There is a spacious lounge, two bars and a meeting area provided.
ROOMS: 48 en suite (9 fmly) (5 GF) No smoking in all bedrooms s £30-£55; d £55-£75 (incl. bkfst) **LB FACILITIES:** STV entertainment Xmas **CONF:** Thtr 130 Class 60 Board 40 Del from £55 **SERVICES:** Lift **PARKING:** 35 **NOTES:** No smoking in restaurant
CARDS:

★★65% Fircroft
4 Owls Rd BH5 1AE
☎ 01202 309771 01202 395644
e-mail: info@fircrofthotel.co.uk
Dir: *off A338 signed Boscombe Pier. Hotel 400yds from pier close to Christchurch Rd*
This friendly hotel is pleasantly located close to Boscombe Pier. Offering a range of comfortable lounges and meeting facilities, the hotel is popular with tour and dance groups. In addition, entertainment is provided most nights throughout the year. All of the bedrooms are comfortable and well equipped.
ROOMS: 51 en suite (20 fmly) s £26-£34; d £52-£68 (incl. bkfst) **LB FACILITIES:** Indoor swimming (H) Squash Sauna Solarium Gym Jacuzzi Sports at health club owned by hotel Xmas **CONF:** Thtr 200 Class 100 Board 40 **SERVICES:** Lift **PARKING:** 50 **NOTES:** No smoking in restaurant **CARDS:**

★★63% *Bournemouth Sands*
2 West Cliff Gardens BH2 5HR
☎ 01202 312314 01202 312315
e-mail: hotels@excelsior-leisure.com
Conveniently located for the Bournemouth International Centre, beaches and other attractions, this friendly hotel offers a relaxed and informal atmosphere to guests. Bedrooms are simply furnished and comfortable. A choice of bars and lounges are available and entertainment is provided most evenings throughout the year.
ROOMS: 65 en suite (17 fmly) **FACILITIES:** Guests have use of leisure facilities at sister hotel **CONF:** Thtr 120 Class 60 Board 30 **SERVICES:** Lift **PARKING:** 65 **NOTES:** No smoking in restaurant
CARDS:

★★62% Devon Towers
Leisureplex
58-62 St Michael's Rd, West Cliff BH2 5ED
☎ 01202 553863 01202 315265
e-mail: devontowers.bournemouth@alfatravel.co.uk
Dir: *A338 into Bournemouth, follow signs for BIC. Left into St. Michaels Rd at top of hill. Hotel 100mtrs on left*
Located in a quiet road within walking distance of the West Cliff and central shops, this hotel appeals to the budget leisure market. The 4-course menus offer plenty of choice and entertainment is featured on most evenings. The bar and lobby area offer plenty of space for relaxing.
ROOMS: 54 en suite (6 GF) s £27-£33; d £46-£58 (incl. bkfst) **LB FACILITIES:** entertainment Xmas **SERVICES:** Lift **PARKING:** 6 **NOTES:** No dogs (ex guide dogs) No smoking in restaurant Closed Jan-mid Feb ex Xmas RS Nov, Feb & Mar **CARDS:**

★★57% Russell Court
Bath Rd BH1 2EP
☎ 01202 295819 01202 293457
e-mail: russellcrt@aol.com
Bright, well-maintained bedrooms are provided at this popular coaching hotel, several of which benefit from sea views. Live entertainment features on some evenings in the spacious and comfortable public rooms. Informal and friendly service is provided by the young staff.
ROOMS: 62 rms (58 en suite) (6 fmly) s £35-£70; d £59-£110 (incl. bkfst) **LB FACILITIES:** entertainment Xmas **CONF:** Thtr 20 **SERVICES:** Lift **PARKING:** 60 **NOTES:** No dogs (ex guide dogs) No smoking in restaurant **CARDS:**

Innkeeper's Lodge Bournemouth
Innkeeper's Lodge
Cooper Dean Roundabout, Castle Ln East BH7 7DP
☎ 01202 390837 01202 390378
Dir: *A338 Bournemouth spur road, follow until exit signed Bournemouth Hospital. Hotel on corner next to hospital*
A new concept in the travel accommodation market. Smart rooms meet essential business requirements but also have home comforts. Dining options include all-day menus plus the added advantage of breakfast, which is included in the room price. For further details, consult the Hotel Groups page.
ROOMS: 28 en suite **CONF:** Thtr 30 Class 22 Board 18

BOURTON-ON-THE-WATER, Gloucestershire Map 10 SP12

★★74% Dial House
The Chestnuts, High St GL54 2AN
☎ 01451 822244 01451 810126
e-mail: info@dialhousehotel.com
Dir: *off A429, 0.5m to village centre*
Tucked away in the centre of a beguiling village, this mellow Cotswold-stone hotel dates back to 1698. In summer, guests can enjoy the delightful gardens, and in winter log fires and comfy sofas ensure relaxation. Two intimate dining rooms provide the settings for quality cuisine; and comfortably furnished bedrooms are well equipped and include some four-posters.
ROOMS: 14 en suite (1 fmly) (7 GF) No smoking in all bedrooms s £57-£89; d £110-£150 (incl. bkfst) **LB FACILITIES:** Croquet lawn Putting green Xmas **CONF:** Class 15 Board 15 Del from £35 **PARKING:** 20 **NOTES:** No smoking in restaurant
CARDS:

> Late for dinner?
> Quality Standards mean that last orders for dinner vary according to star rating and should be no earlier than:
> ★★ 7.00pm ★★★ 8.00pm ★★★★ 9.00pm
> ★★★★★ 10.00pm

BOVEY TRACEY, Devon Map 03 SX87

★★69% Coombe Cross
Coombe Cross TQ13 9EY
☎ 01626 832476 01626 835298
e-mail: info@coombecross.co.uk
Dir: *A38 signed Bovey Tracey & town centre, along High St, up hill 400yds beyond Parish Church. Hotel on left*
With delightful views over Dartmoor and the surrounding countryside, this peaceful hotel is set in well-tended gardens on the edge of the town. In addition to the comfortable public areas and bedrooms, a range of leisure and fitness facilities is available.

continued

At dinner, carefully prepared dishes are served in the spacious dining room.

ROOMS: 22 en suite (1 fmly) No smoking in all bedrooms **FACILITIES: Spa** Indoor swimming (H) Sauna Solarium Gym Table tennis **CONF:** Thtr 80 Class 30 Board 30 Del from £50 **PARKING:** 26 **NOTES:** No smoking in restaurant Closed 24 Dec-31 Jan **CARDS:**

BOWNESS ON WINDERMERE See Windermere

BOXWORTH, Cambridgeshire Map 12 TL36

⇧ *Sleep Inn Cambridge*

Cambridge Services A14 CB3 8WG
☎ 01954 268400 🖷 01954 268419
e-mail: admin@gbo98.u-net.com
Dir: *A14 junct 28 6m N of Cambridge. 8m S of Huntington*

This modern, purpose built accommodation offers smartly appointed, well-equipped bedrooms, with good power showers. There is a choice of adjacent food outlets where guests may enjoy breakfast, snacks and meals.

ROOMS: 82 en suite

BRACKNELL, Berkshire Map 05 SU86

See also Crowthorne & Wokingham

Early start?
Hotels at all star levels should provide in-room alarm clocks and/or alarm calls

★★★★72% Coppid Beech

John Nike Way RG12 8TF
☎ 01344 303333 🖷 01344 301200
e-mail: welcome@coppid-beech-hotel.co.uk
Dir: *M4 junct 10 take Wokingham/Bracknell onto A329. In 2m take B3408 to Binfield at rdbt. Hotel 200yds on right*

This chalet-style complex offers extensive facilities and includes a ski-slope, ice rink, nightclub, health club and Bier Keller. Bedrooms offer a range of suites and standard rooms, all of which are impressively equipped. A choice of dining is offered and a full bistro menu is available in the Keller. For more formal dining Rowan's restaurant provides award-winning cuisine.

ROOMS: 205 en suite (6 fmly) No smoking in 138 bedrooms s £165; d £185-£295 (incl. bkfst) **LB FACILITIES: Spa** STV Indoor swimming (H) Sauna Solarium Gym Jacuzzi Dry ski slope, Ice rink, Swimming pool supervised entertainment Xmas **CONF:** BC Thtr 400 Class 240 Board 24 Del from £165 **SERVICES:** Lift **PARKING:** 350 **NOTES:** Civ Wed 150 **CARDS:**

See advert on this page

BRACKNELL, continued

★★★★67% Grange Bracknell

Charles Square RG12 1DF
☎ 01344 474000 🖷 01344 474125
e-mail: bracknell@grangehotels.co.uk

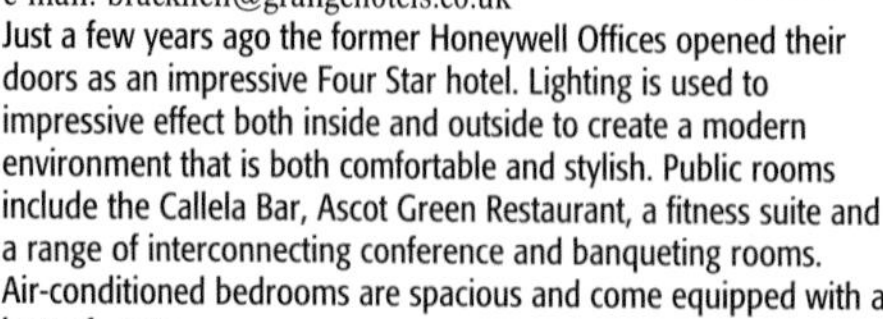

Just a few years ago the former Honeywell Offices opened their doors as an impressive Four Star hotel. Lighting is used to impressive effect both inside and outside to create a modern environment that is both comfortable and stylish. Public rooms include the Callela Bar, Ascot Green Restaurant, a fitness suite and a range of interconnecting conference and banqueting rooms. Air-conditioned bedrooms are spacious and come equipped with a host of extras.

ROOMS: 120 en suite (6 fmly) No smoking in 60 bedrooms s £160-£265; d £160-£265 **LB** **FACILITIES:** STV Gym Xmas **CONF:** Thtr 200 Class 120 Board 70 Del from £220 **SERVICES:** Lift air con **PARKING:** 111 **NOTES:** No dogs (ex guide dogs)
CARDS:

★★★70% Stirrups Country House

Maidens Green RG42 6LD
☎ 01344 882284 🖷 01344 882300
e-mail: reception@stirrupshotel.co.uk
Dir: *3m N on B3022 towards Windsor*

Situated in a peaceful location between Maidenhead, Bracknell and Windsor, this hotel has high standards of comfort in the bedrooms, with newer rooms boasting a small sitting room area. There is a popular bar, a refurbished restaurant, function rooms and the grounds are delightful.

ROOMS: 29 en suite (4 fmly) (2 GF) No smoking in 20 bedrooms s £90-£150; d £90-£150 (incl. bkfst) **LB** **FACILITIES:** STV **CONF:** Thtr 100 Class 50 Board 40 Del from £140 **SERVICES:** Lift **PARKING:** 100 **NOTES:** No dogs (ex guide dogs) No smoking in restaurant Civ Wed 100
CARDS:

⇧ Travel Inn

Arlington Square, Wokingham Rd RG42 1NA
☎ 08701 977036 🖷 01344 319526
Dir: *M4 (J10) A329(M) Bracknell to lights. 1st left, 3rd exit rdbt by Safeway to town centre. Left at rdbt, left at next rdbt. Travel Inn on left.*

Travel Inn offers good-quality, value-for-money accommodation. Spacious, en suite rooms with bath and shower comfortably accommodate a family of up to two adults and two children (to age 15). The restaurant and bar offers a varied menu. For further details and the Travel Inn phone number, consult the Hotel Groups page.

ROOMS: 60 en suite s £49.95-£52.95; d £49.95-£52.95

BRADFORD, West Yorkshire — Map 19 SE13
See also Gomersal & Shipley

★★★★63% Hanover International Hotel & Club

Mayo Av, Off Rooley Ln BD5 8HZ
☎ 01274 406606 & 406601 🖷 01274 406600
e-mail: enquiries.bradford@hanover-international.com
Dir: *M62 junct 26/M606. At end take 3rd exit off rdbt onto A6177 towards Bradford. Take 1st sharp right at lights*

This modern attractive hotel is conveniently located just off the motorway and within easy access of the city centre and the airport. The hotel boasts extensive function and conference facilities, a well-equipped leisure club and an elegant restaurant. Bedrooms are comfortably appointed for both business and leisure guests.

ROOMS: 131 en suite (7 fmly) No smoking in 75 bedrooms s £35-£110; d £70-£120 **LB** **FACILITIES:** STV Indoor swimming (H) Sauna Solarium Gym Jacuzzi Pool table **CONF:** BC Thtr 800 Class 300 Board 100 Del from £99 **SERVICES:** Lift **PARKING:** 300 **NOTES:** Civ Wed 600
CARDS:

★★★69% *Midland Hotel*

Forster Square BD1 4HU
☎ 01274 735735 🖷 01274 720003
e-mail: info@midland-hotel-bradford.com
Dir: *A6177/ A641/A6181. Past St Georges Hall to Eastbrook Well rdbt. Take 1st exit along Petergate to Forster Sq, left to Cheapside. Hotel on right*

Ideally situated in the heart of the city, this grand Victorian hotel provides modern, well-equipped accommodation and comfortable, spacious day rooms. Ample, parking is available in what used to be the city's railway station, and a preserved Victorian passage linking the hotel to the old platform can still be used today.

ROOMS: 90 en suite (4 fmly) No smoking in 18 bedrooms **FACILITIES:** STV Free use of local health club entertainment **CONF:** Thtr 450 Class 150 Board 100 **SERVICES:** Lift **PARKING:** 50 **NOTES:** No dogs (ex guide dogs) Civ Wed 400 **CARDS:**

★★★68% Courtyard by Marriott Leeds/Bradford

The Pastures, Tong Ln BD4 0RP
☎ 0870 400 7218 🖷 0870 400 7318
Dir: *M62 junct 27/A650 towards Bradford. 3rd rdbt, take 3rd exit to Tong Village & Pudsey. Left into Tong Lane. Hotel 0.5m on right*

Built onto an elegant, 19th-century former vicarage, this modern, stylish hotel has been sympathetically designed to complement its Victorian heritage. The hotel is particularly well located for both Leeds and Bradford as well as local motorway networks. The well-equipped bedrooms are furnished and decorated to a high standard.

ROOMS: 53 en suite (8 fmly) (11 GF) No smoking in 31 bedrooms s £91-£101; d £91-£101 **FACILITIES:** STV Gym **CONF:** Thtr 200 Class 150 Board 100 Del from £125 **SERVICES:** Lift **PARKING:** 230 **NOTES:** No dogs (ex guide dogs) Civ Wed 100
CARDS:

Town House Hotel
Country House Hotel
⇧ Travel Accommodation

★★★68% **Guide Post Hotel**
Common Rd, Low Moor BD12 0ST
☎ 01274 607866 🖷 01274 671085
e-mail: sales@guideposthotel.net
Dir: *A638 towards Oakenshaw/Low Moor, pass CIBA factory & petrol station on left. Take 2nd left into Common Rd*

Situated south of the city, this hotel offers attractively furnished, comfortable bedrooms. The restaurant offers an extensive range of food using fresh, local produce; lighter snack meals are served in the bar. There is a choice of well-equipped meeting and function rooms.
ROOMS: 43 en suite (3 fmly) (14 GF) No smoking in 9 bedrooms s £45-£90; d £55-£110 (incl. bkfst) **LB** **FACILITIES:** STV **CONF:** Thtr 120 Class 80 Board 60 Del from £92.50 **PARKING:** 100
NOTES: Civ Wed 100 **CARDS:**

★★★63% **Novotel Bradford**
6 Roydsdale Way BD4 6SA
☎ 01274 683683 🖷 01274 651342
e-mail: h0510@accor-hotels.com
Dir: *M606 junct 2, exit to Euroway Trading Estate turn right at traffic lights at bottom of slip road, take 2nd right onto Roydsdale Way*
This purpose built hotel stands in an ideal location for access to the motorway. It provides spacious bedrooms that have now benefited from refurbishment. Open plan day rooms include a stylish bar, and a lounge that leads into the Garden Brasserie. Several function rooms are also available, and an outside swimming pool proves popular in the summer.
ROOMS: 127 en suite (37 fmly) (12 GF) s £60; d £60 **LB**
FACILITIES: STV Outdoor swimming (H) Xmas **CONF:** Thtr 200 Class 100 Board 100 Del £95 **SERVICES:** Lift **PARKING:** 200
NOTES: Civ Wed 200 **CARDS:**

★★★62% **Victoria**
Bridge St BD1 1JX
☎ 01274 728706 🖷 01274 736358
e-mail: thevictoriahotel@brook-hotels.co.uk
Dir: *M606/A641, right to Hall Ings; right at next lights. Hotel on left*
This grand Victorian hotel enjoys a central position close to the railway station. It benefits from wide ranging conference facilities and a choice of dining and drinking options in the form of a popular Brasserie and a lively bar. Many of the bedrooms have been thoughtfully refurbished to provide contemporary, modern facilities.
ROOMS: 60 en suite (4 fmly) No smoking in 40 bedrooms s £50-£85; d £60-£95 (incl. bkfst) **FACILITIES:** STV Sauna Gym Xmas **CONF:** Thtr 200 Class 50 Board 50 Del from £110 **SERVICES:** Lift **PARKING:** 70
NOTES: No smoking in restaurant Civ Wed 200
CARDS:

★★65% **Park Drive**
12 Park Dr BD9 4DR
☎ 01274 480194 🖷 01274 484869
e-mail: info@parkdrivehotel.co.uk
Dir: *off A650 Keighley Rd into Emm Ln at Lister Park, turn 2nd right*
Personally run by the owners, this hotel stands in a quiet leafy residential area overlooking open country north of the city centre. Both bedrooms and public areas are comfortable, the latter offering a cosy lounge bar (residents only) and dining room.
ROOMS: 11 en suite (1 fmly) (1 GF) s £49-£54; d £59-£64 (incl. bkfst) **LB** **CONF:** Thtr 20 Class 8 Board 12 Del from £75 **PARKING:** 10
NOTES: No smoking in restaurant **CARDS:**

⌂ **Express by Holiday Inn Bradford**
The Leisure Exchange, Vicar Ln BD1 5LD
☎ 0870 787 2064 🖷 0870 787 2066
e-mail: bradford@exbhi.fsnet.co.uk
Dir: *M62 junct 26/M606 last exit at rdbt onto A6177 take 2nd left onto A650 & follow signs for The Leisure Exchange*

A modern hotel ideal for families and business travellers. Fresh and uncomplicated, the spacious bedrooms include Sky TV, power shower and tea and coffee-making facilities. Continental buffet breakfast is included in the room rate; other meals may be taken at the nearby family pub or restaurant. For further details and the Express by Holiday Inn phone number, consult the Hotel Groups pages.
ROOMS: 120 en suite (incl. cont bkfst) s £45-£59; d £45-£59
CONF: Thtr 40 Class 30 Board 30 Del from £81

BRADFORD, continued

Travel Inn (Leeds Bradford South)

Wakefield Rd, Drighlington BD11 1EA
☎ 08701 977152 🖷 0113 287 9115
Dir: *on Drighlington Bypass, adjacent to M62(J27). Follow signs for Drighlington, turn right and Inn on left - (landmark – Old Brickworks chimney)*
Travel Inn offers good-quality, value-for-money accommodation. Spacious, en suite rooms with bath and shower comfortably accommodate a family of up to two adults and two children (to age 15). The restaurant and bar offers a varied menu. For further details and the Travel Inn phone number, consult the Hotel Groups page.
ROOMS: 42 en suite s £44.95; d £44.95

BRADFORD-ON-AVON, Wiltshire — Map 04 ST86

★★★72% Woolley Grange

Woolley Green BA15 1TX
☎ 01225 864705 🖷 01225 864059
e-mail: info@woolleygrange.com
Dir: *Turn off A4 onto B3109. Bradford Leigh, left at crossroads, hotel 0.5m on right at Woolley Green*

A splendid Cotswold manor house set in beautiful countryside. Children are made especially welcome; there is a trained nanny on duty in the nursery. Bedrooms and public areas are charmingly furnished and decorated in true country-house style with many thoughtful touches and luxurious extras. The hotel offers a varied and well-balanced menu selection, including ingredients from the hotel's own garden.
ROOMS: 14 en suite 12 annexe en suite (8 fmly) (6 GF) s £86-£135; d £95-£250 (incl. bkfst) **LB** **FACILITIES:** STV Outdoor swimming (H) Croquet lawn Putting green Badminton, Games room ch fac Xmas **CONF:** Thtr 35 Class 12 Board 22 Del from £150 **PARKING:** 40 **NOTES:** No smoking in restaurant **CARDS:**

See advert on opposite page

Packed in a hurry?
Ironing facilities should be available at all star levels, either in rooms or on request

★★★69% Leigh Park Hotel

Leigh Park West BA15 2RA
☎ 01225 864885 🖷 01225 862315
e-mail: leighparkhotel@lineone.net
Dir: *A363 Bath/Frome road. Take B3105 signed Holt/Woolley Green. Hotel 0.25m on right on x-roads of B3105/B3109. N side of Bradford-on-Avon*
Enjoying splendid views over the surrounding countryside, this relaxing Georgian hotel is set in five acres of well-tended grounds, complete with a vineyard. Combining charm and character with modern facilities, the hotel is equally suited to both business and leisure travellers. The restaurant serves dishes cooked to order, using home-grown fruit and vegetables, and wine from the vineyard.
ROOMS: 22 en suite (4 fmly) (7 GF) No smoking in 14 bedrooms s £65-£75; d £98-£115 (incl. bkfst) **LB** **FACILITIES:** Xmas **CONF:** Thtr 120 Class 60 Board 60 Del from £95 **PARKING:** 80 **NOTES:** No smoking in restaurant Civ Wed 120 **CARDS:**

BRAINTREE, Essex — Map 07 TL72

★★★63% *White Hart*

Bocking End CM7 9AB
☎ 01376 321401 🖷 01376 552628
e-mail: reservations@thewhiteharthotel.freeserve.co.uk
Dir: *off A120 towards town centre. Hotel at junct B1256 & Bocking Causeway*
This popular inn is ideally placed in the heart of the bustling town centre and dates back to the 18th century when it was a coaching inn. Public rooms include a large lounge bar, restaurant and meeting rooms. The pleasantly decorated, well-equipped bedrooms provide a good level of comfort throughout.
ROOMS: 31 en suite (8 fmly) No smoking in 9 bedrooms **FACILITIES:** STV Sauna Solarium Gym **CONF:** Thtr 40 Class 16 Board 24 **PARKING:** 52 **NOTES:** No dogs (ex guide dogs) Civ Wed 60 **CARDS:**

Express by Holiday Inn Braintree

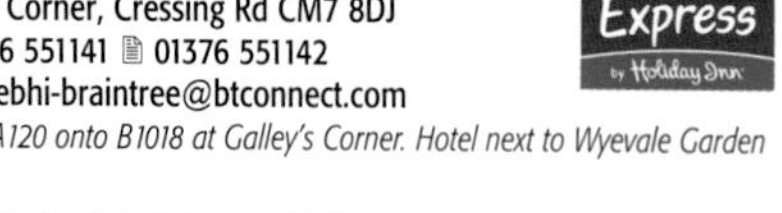

Galley's Corner, Cressing Rd CM7 8DJ
☎ 01376 551141 🖷 01376 551142
e-mail: ebhi-braintree@btconnect.com
Dir: *off A120 onto B1018 at Galley's Corner. Hotel next to Wyevale Garden Centre*

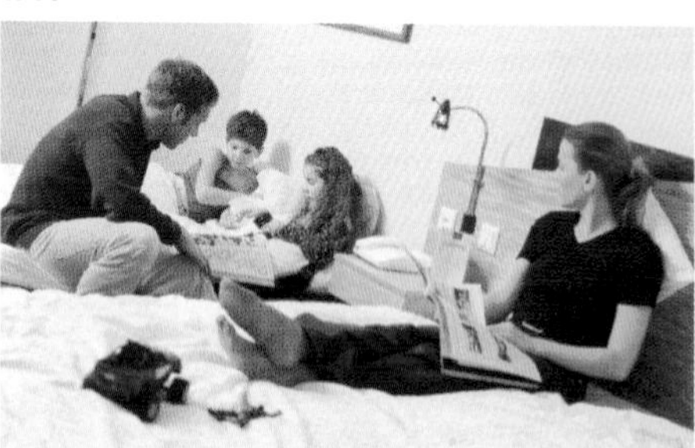

A modern hotel ideal for families and business travellers. Fresh and uncomplicated, the spacious bedrooms include Sky TV, power shower and tea and coffee-making facilities. Continental buffet breakfast is included in the room rate; other meals may be taken at the nearby family pub or restaurant. For further details and the Express by Holiday Inn phone number, consult the Hotel Groups pages.
ROOMS: 47 en suite **CONF:** Thtr 30 Class 24 Board 16

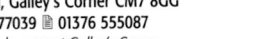

Travel Inn

Cressing Rd, Galley's Corner CM7 8GG
☎ 08701 977039 🖷 01376 555087
Dir: *on A120 by-pass at Galley's Corner*
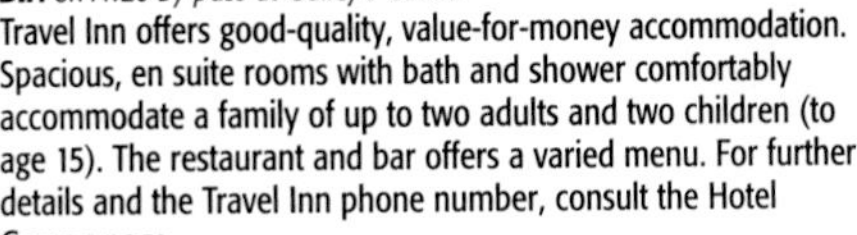
Travel Inn offers good-quality, value-for-money accommodation. Spacious, en suite rooms with bath and shower comfortably accommodate a family of up to two adults and two children (to age 15). The restaurant and bar offers a varied menu. For further details and the Travel Inn phone number, consult the Hotel Groups page.
ROOMS: 40 en suite s £44.95; d £44.95

BRAITHWAITE, Cumbria — Map 18 NY22

★★69% The Cottage in the Wood
Whinlatter Pass CA12 5TW
☎ 017687 78409 🖷 017687 78064
e-mail: info@thecottageinthewood.co.uk
Dir: *A66 for Cockermouth & Keswick. After Keswick, turn off for Braithwaite & Lorton via Whinlatter Pass. Hotel at top of Whinlatter Pass*
Aptly named, this charming little hotel sits amid wooded hillsides with striking views of distant peaks, and is convenient for Keswick. Enthusiastic owners provide excellent hospitality in a friendly relaxed manner. Dinner is freshly prepared from a set menu offering a vegetarian choice, and there is a small residents' bar.
ROOMS: 10 en suite (1 fmly) (1 GF) No smoking in all bedrooms s £35-£50; d £70-£80 (incl. bkfst) **LB FACILITIES:** Xmas **PARKING:** 15 **NOTES:** No children 6yrs No smoking in restaurant Closed Jan-mid Feb **CARDS:**

BRAMHALL, Greater Manchester — Map 16 SJ88

★★★61% The County Hotel
Bramhall Ln South SK7 2EB
☎ 0870 609 6148 🖷 0161 440 8071
Dir: *A34 by-pass to Bramhall. In Bramhall village at rdbt right under bridge. Hotel 100yds on right.*

This hotel is situated in a quiet residential area on the edge of Bramhall, within easy reach of the airport and Cheadle shopping centre. Bedrooms are well equipped and include a number of ground floor rooms. Public areas include an open plan lounge restaurant and the traditional Shires Pub.
ROOMS: 65 en suite (3 fmly) (20 GF) No smoking in 20 bedrooms **CONF:** Thtr 200 Class 80 Board 60 Del from £85 **PARKING:** 120 **NOTES:** No smoking in restaurant Civ Wed 150 **CARDS:**

Town House Hotel
Country House Hotel
Travel Accommodation

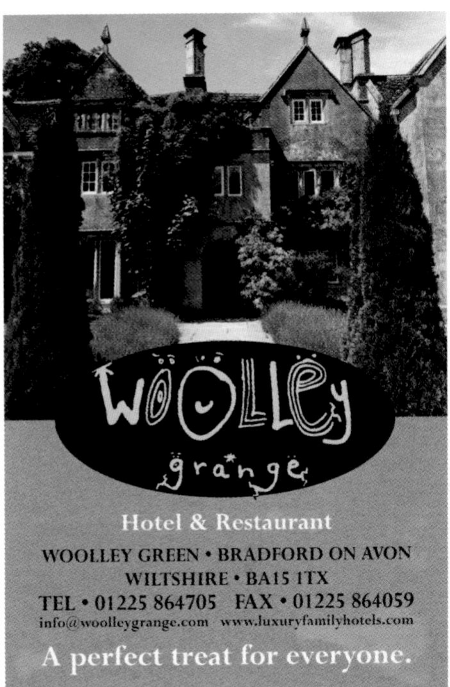

Woolley grange
Hotel & Restaurant
WOOLLEY GREEN • BRADFORD ON AVON
WILTSHIRE • BA15 1TX
TEL • 01225 864705 FAX • 01225 864059
info@woolleygrange.com www.luxuryfamilyhotels.com
A perfect treat for everyone.

BRAMHOPE, West Yorkshire — Map 19 SE24

Holiday Inn Leeds Bradford Airport
Leeds Rd LS16 9JJ
☎ 0113 284 2911 🖷 0113 284 3451
Dir: *on A660, 6m N of Leeds city centre. Follow Leeds/Bradford Airport signs*
At the time of going to press, the classification for this hotel was not confirmed. Please refer to the AA internet site www.theAA.com for current information.
ROOMS: 124 en suite No smoking in 40 bedrooms **FACILITIES:** STV Indoor swimming (H) Sauna Solarium Gym Jacuzzi **CONF:** Thtr 160 Class 80 Board 40 **SERVICES:** Lift air con **PARKING:** 126 **NOTES:** No smoking in restaurant **CARDS:**

BRAMPTON, Cambridgeshire — Map 12 TL27

★★68% The Grange
115 High St PE28 4RA
☎ 01480 459516 🖷 01480 459391
e-mail: nsteiger@grangehotelbrampton.com
Dir: *A1(M)/A14 towards Cambridge. After 0.5m take B1514 (racecourse) towards Huntingdon. After mini rdbt turn right into Grove Ln, hotel opp t-junct at bottom of road*
Located on the high street in the quiet village of Brampton, this historic building offers smartly appointed bedrooms; some have now been refurbished are most attractively decorated. Imaginative cuisine is served in both the light and airy restaurant or more informally within the inviting bar area; service is both friendly and attentive.
ROOMS: 7 en suite No smoking in all bedrooms s £60-£75; d £75-£90 (incl. bkfst) **CONF:** Thtr 30 Class 15 Board 36 **PARKING:** 20 **NOTES:** No dogs (ex guide dogs) No smoking in restaurant RS 29 Dec-5 Jan **CARDS:**

BRAMPTON, continued

Travel Inn (Huntingdon)
Brampton Hut PE28 4NQ
☎ 08701 977139 ▯ 01480 811298
Dir: *junct of A1/A14. (From north do not use junct 14 but take next main exit for Huntingdon & Brampton). Access via services*
Travel Inn offers good-quality, value-for-money accommodation. Spacious, en suite rooms with bath and shower comfortably accommodate a family of up to two adults and two children (to age 15). The restaurant and bar offers a varied menu. For further details and the Travel Inn phone number, consult the Hotel Groups page.
ROOMS: 80 en suite s £44.95; d £44.95 **CONF:** Thtr 25

BRAMPTON, Cumbria Map 21 NY56

Top 200 - Hotel

★★★ **Farlam Hall**
CA8 2NG
☎ 016977 46234 ▯ 016977 46683
e-mail: farlamhall@dial.pipex.com
Dir: *On A689 from Brampton to Alston. Hotel 2m on left, not in Farlam village*
This delightful family-run country house dates back to 1428. Steeped in history, the hotel is set in beautifully landscaped Victorian gardens complete with an ornamental lake and stream. Lovingly restored over many years, it now provides the highest standards of comfort and hospitality. Carefully prepared English country-house cooking can be enjoyed in the elegant dining room, which has lovely rural views across the garden.
ROOMS: 11 en suite 1 annexe en suite (2 GF) s £130; d £240-£270 (incl. bkfst & dinner) **LB** **FACILITIES:** Croquet lawn **CONF:** Thtr 12 Class 12 Board 12 **PARKING:** 35 **NOTES:** No children 5yrs No smoking in restaurant Closed 25-30 Dec **CARDS:**

★★69% **Kirkby Moor Country House Hotel**
Longtown Rd CA8 2AB
☎ 016977 3893 ▯ 016977 41847
e-mail: info@kirbymoor-hotel.com
Dir: *M6 junct 46/A69 to Brampton, then A6071 to Longtown, hotel just past school*
Situated on the edge of town, this Victorian house offers fine views over unspoilt open countryside. Well-equipped bedrooms come with many thoughtful extras. Hearty, homemade meals are a feature of the Bella Vista restaurant and warm hospitality is guaranteed. There is a cosy bar with an excellent selection of drinks and a coal fire in the cooler months.
ROOMS: 7 en suite (2 fmly) No smoking in 5 bedrooms **CONF:** Board 15 **PARKING:** 24 **NOTES:** No smoking in restaurant

★★67% **Tarn End House**
Talkin Tarn CA8 1LS
☎ 016977 2340 ▯ 016977 2089
Dir: *A69/B6413 for 2m & turn off to Talkin*

This former estate farmhouse enjoys an idyllic, peaceful position overlooking Talkin Tarn. The hotel is family run and a friendly, informal atmosphere prevails. Bedrooms are thoughtfully equipped and attractively decorated. Public rooms, all enjoying stunning views of the tarn, include an inviting lounge, a well-stocked bar and a smart restaurant offering good home cooking.
ROOMS: 7 en suite (1 fmly) (1 GF) No smoking in all bedrooms s £40-£58; d £65-£85 (incl. bkfst) **LB** **FACILITIES:** Xmas **CONF:** Board 20 Del £75 **PARKING:** 40 **NOTES:** No smoking in restaurant Closed 27-29 Dec & 3-25 Jan **CARDS:**

See advert on opposite page

BRANCASTER STAITHE, Norfolk Map 13 TF74

★★75% **White Horse**
PE31 8BY
☎ 01485 210262 ▯ 01485 210930
e-mail: reception@whitehorsebrancaster.co.uk
Dir: *A149/A1067 to Fakenham then B1355*

A charming hotel on the north Norfolk coast with stunning views over the tidal marsh to Scolt Head Island. The contemporary bedrooms are in two wings with some featuring an interesting cobbled fascia. Each room is attractively decorated and thoughtfully equipped. There is a large bar and a lounge area leading through to the conservatory restaurant, which overlooks the marshes.
ROOMS: 15 en suite (5 fmly) (8 GF) s £38-£58; d £96 (incl. bkfst) **LB** **FACILITIES:** Xmas **PARKING:** 60 **NOTES:** No smoking in restaurant **CARDS:**

BRANDESBURTON, East Riding of Yorkshire Map 17 TA14

★★68% Burton Lodge
YO25 8RU
☎ 01964 542847 ▯ 01964 544771
e-mail: email@burtonlodge.fsnet.co.uk
Dir: *7m from Beverley off A165, adjoining Hainsworth Park Golf Club*
A tennis court, sports play area and extensive lawn are features of this friendly hotel, which is situated on a golf course. Rooms are modern and there is a comfortable lounge, while the spacious restaurant serves excellent home cooking.
ROOMS: 7 en suite 2 annexe en suite (3 fmly) (2 GF) No smoking in 5 bedrooms s £38-£40; d £54-£57 (incl. bkfst) **LB FACILITIES:** Golf 18 Tennis (grass) Putting green Pitch and putt **CONF:** Class 20 Del from £55 **PARKING:** 15 **NOTES:** No smoking in restaurant
CARDS:

BRANDON, Suffolk Map 13 TL78

★★68% Brandon House
High St IP27 0AX
☎ 01842 810171 ▯ 01842 814859
e-mail: reservations@brandonhouse.co.uk
Dir: *In town centre left at traffic lights into High St. Hotel 400yds on right after small bridge over River Ouse*
An 18th-century red brick manor house set in landscaped gardens just a short walk from the town centre. The pleasantly decorated, well-maintained bedrooms are thoughtfully equipped and come in a variety of styles. Public rooms include a comfortable lounge bar, the Conifers English Restaurant and a more relaxed bistro.
ROOMS: 15 en suite (3 fmly) s £55-£60; d £75-£95 (incl. bkfst) **LB FACILITIES:** STV **CONF:** Thtr 70 Class 25 Board 20 Del from £120 **PARKING:** 40 **NOTES:** No smoking in restaurant Closed 25-26 Dec & 1 Jan **CARDS:**

BRANDON, Warwickshire Map 11 SP47

★★★66% Brandon Hall
Main St CV8 3FW
☎ 0870 400 8105 ▯ 024 7654 4909
e-mail: general.brandonhall@macdonald-hotels.co.uk

Dir: *A45 towards Coventry S. After Peugeot-Citroen garage on left, at island take 5th exit to M1 South/London (back onto A45). After 200yds, immediately after Texaco garage, left into Brandon Ln, hotel after 2.5m*
Formerly a shooting lodge, the hotel is set in 17 acres of well-kept lawns and woodland and is located within easy reach of Coventry and Rugby. Public rooms are stylish and modern, while bedrooms are more traditional in style. Leisure facilities include squash courts and a pitch-and-putt course on site.
ROOMS: 60 en suite (7 fmly) (20 GF) No smoking in 35 bedrooms s £105-£145; d £125-£190 **LB FACILITIES:** STV Squash Croquet lawn Putting green Xmas **CONF:** Thtr 120 Class 40 Board 36 Del from £130 **PARKING:** 100 **NOTES:** No smoking in restaurant Civ Wed 80
CARDS:

BRANDS HATCH, Kent Map 06 TQ56

★★★72% Brandshatch Place
Brands Hatch Rd, Fawkham DA3 8NQ
HandPICKED
☎ 01474 875000 ▯ 01474 879652
e-mail: brandshatch@arcadianhotels.co.uk
Dir: *M25 junct 3/A20 West Kingsdown. Left at paddock entrance/Fawkham Green sign. 3rd left signed Fawkham Rd. Hotel 500mtrs on right*
This charming 18th-century Georgian country house close to the famous racing circuit has undergone an extensive refurbishment

continued

programme. Public areas have been completely transformed and include a range of stylish and elegant rooms. Bedrooms have also been upgraded to a very high standard offering impressive levels of comfort, quality and facilities. The hotel also features a comprehensive leisure club including substantial creche facilities.

Brandshatch Place

ROOMS: 26 en suite 12 annexe en suite (1 fmly) No smoking in 10 bedrooms s £100-£150; d £100-£150 **LB FACILITIES: Spa** STV Indoor swimming (H) Tennis (hard) Squash Snooker Sauna Solarium Gym Jacuzzi Use of health/leisure club Xmas **CONF:** Thtr 120 Class 60 Board 50 Del from £165 **PARKING:** 100 **NOTES:** No smoking in restaurant Civ Wed 80 **CARDS:**

BRANKSOME See Poole

For central reservation numbers and more information on Hotel Groups, turn to pages 33-39

B

BRANSCOMBE, Devon Map 04 SY18

★★67% The Masons Arms

EX12 3DJ
☎ 01297 680300 01297 680500
e-mail: reception@masonsarms.co.uk
Dir: *off A3052 towards Branscombe, hotel in valley at bottom of hill*

This delightful 14th-century village inn is just half a mile from the sea. Bedrooms in the thatched annexed cottages tend to be more spacious and most have their own patio area with seating. Those in the inn enjoy the characters and charm of the period as do the bars and public areas. An extensive selection of dishes, which includes many local specialities, is offered.

ROOMS: 6 rms (4 en suite) 16 annexe rms (15 en suite) (2 fmly) s £30-£130; d £50-£150 (incl. bkfst) **LB FACILITIES:** Xmas **PARKING:** 43 **NOTES:** No smoking in restaurant
CARDS:

BRANSTON, Lincolnshire Map 17 TF06

★★★70% Branston Hall

Branston Park LN4 1PD
☎ 01522 793305 01522 790734
e-mail: info@branstonhall.com
Dir: *5 min drive from Lincoln on B1188*

Many original features have been retained in this attractive property, which sits in beautiful grounds complete with a lake. There is an elegant restaurant, a spacious bar and a beautiful lounge in addition to impressive conference and leisure facilities. Individually styled bedrooms vary in size and include several with four-poster beds.

ROOMS: 40 en suite 7 annexe en suite (3 fmly) No smoking in 6 bedrooms s £69-£90; d £90-£150 (incl. bkfst) **LB FACILITIES: Spa** STV Indoor swimming (H) Sauna Gym Jacuzzi Xmas **CONF:** Thtr 200 Class 54 Board 40 Del from £95 **SERVICES:** Lift **PARKING:** 200 **NOTES:** No dogs (ex guide dogs) No smoking in restaurant Civ Wed 120
CARDS:

BRAY, Berkshire Map 06 SU97

★★★★65% Monkey Island

Old Mill Ln SL6 2EE
☎ 01628 623400 01628 784732
e-mail: info@monkeyisland.co.uk
Dir: *M4 junct 8/9/A308 signed Windsor. 1st left into Bray, 1st right into Old Mill Lane, opp Crown pub*

This riverside hotel is charmingly set on an island in the Thames, within easy reach of major routes. Access is by footbridge or boat, but there is a large car park nearby. The hotel comprises two buildings, one for accommodation and the other for dining and

continued

drinking. Ample grounds are beautifully maintained and provide a peaceful haven for wildlife.

ROOMS: 26 en suite (1 fmly) (12 GF) s £130-£170; d £190-£295 (incl. bkfst) **LB FACILITIES:** STV Fishing Croquet lawn Boating entertainment Xmas **CONF:** Thtr 120 Class 70 Board 50 Del from £230 **PARKING:** 100 **NOTES:** No dogs (ex guide dogs) No smoking in restaurant Civ Wed 120
CARDS:

BREADSALL, Derbyshire Map 11 SK33

★★★★65% Marriott Breadsall Priory Hotel, Country Club

Marriott HOTELS · RESORTS · SUITES

Moor Rd DE7 6DL
☎ 01332 832235 01332 833509
Dir: *A52 to Derby, then signs to Chesterfield. Right at 1st rdbt, left at next. Follow A608 to Heanor Rd, after 3m left then left again*

This extended mansion house is set in 400 acres of parkland and well-tended gardens. The smart bedrooms are mostly contained in the modern wing. There is a vibrant café-bar, a more formal restaurant and a large room service menu. The extensive leisure facilities, golf course and swimming pool are an asset. Dinner in the Priory Restaurant is a highlight of a stay here.

ROOMS: 12 en suite 100 annexe en suite (35 fmly) No smoking in 69 bedrooms s fr £95; d fr £118 (incl. bkfst) **LB FACILITIES:** STV Indoor swimming (H) Golf 18 Tennis (hard) Sauna Solarium Gym Croquet lawn Putting green Jacuzzi Health, beauty & hair salon, dance studio Xmas **CONF:** Thtr 120 Class 50 Board 36 Del from £150 **SERVICES:** Lift **PARKING:** 300 **NOTES:** No smoking in restaurant Civ Wed 100
CARDS:

Town House Hotel
Country House Hotel
Travel Accommodation

BRENTFORD, Greater London
See LONDON plan 1 C3

Travelodge (London Kew Bridge)

North Rd, High St TW8 0BO
☎ 08700 850 950 🖹 0208 758 1190
Dir: *M4 junct 2, Chiswick Roundabout turn right towards Kew, at traffic lights turn right in to Kew Bridge Road*

Travelodge offers good quality, good value, modern accommodation. Ideal for families, the spacious, en suite bedrooms include remote-control TV, tea and coffee-making facilities, luxury beds and free morning newspaper. Meals can be taken at the nearby family restaurant. For further details and the Travelodge phone number, consult the Hotel Groups page.
ROOMS: 111 en suite (incl. bkfst) s fr £42.95; d fr £42.95

○ Premier Lodge (London Brentford)

PREMIER LODGE

Ferry Ln TW8 0AW
☎ 0870 9906304 🖹 0870 9906305
ROOMS: 141 en suite **NOTES:** Due to open Oct 2003

BRENT KNOLL, Somerset Map 04 ST35

★★72% Woodlands Country House

Hill Ln TA9 4DF
☎ 01278 760232 🖹 01278 769090
e-mail: info@woodlands-hotel.co.uk
Dir: *A38 take 1st left into village, then 5th right & 1st left, follow brown tourist information signs*

With glorious views over the surrounding countryside, this family-run hotel is set in four acres of gardens and grounds and offers a relaxed and peaceful environment. The attractively co-ordinated bedrooms are comfortable and well equipped.
continued

Imaginative dishes make up the daily-changing dinner menu and guests can relax by a log fire in the lounge bar.
ROOMS: 9 en suite (2 fmly) (2 GF) No smoking in all bedrooms s £55-£80; d £79-£115 (incl. bkfst) **LB FACILITIES:** Outdoor swimming Xmas **CONF:** Thtr 40 Class 25 Board 36 Del from £75 **PARKING:** 16
NOTES: No smoking in restaurant RS Sun Civ Wed 65
CARDS:

See advert under WESTON-SUPER-MARE

★★68% Battleborough Grange Hotel

Bristol Rd TA9 4HJ
☎ 01278 760208 🖹 01278 761950
e-mail: info@battleboroughgrangehotel.co.uk
Dir: *M5 J22, right at rndbt onto A38 past garden centre on right, hotel 500yds on left*

Conveniently located, this popular hotel is surrounded by mellow Somerset countryside. Bedrooms are well equipped and some have superb views of the Iron Age fort of Brent Knoll. In the conservatory restaurant, both fixed-price and carte menus are offered. Relax in the convivial bar after a busy day either working or exploring the area's many attractions. Extensive function facilities are also provided.
ROOMS: 15 en suite (1 fmly) s £54-£109; d £69-£139 (incl. bkfst)
FACILITIES: Spa ch fac **CONF:** Thtr 85 Class 40 Board 40 Del £80
PARKING: 50 **NOTES:** No dogs (ex guide dogs) No smoking in restaurant Closed 26 Dec - 1 Jan Civ Wed 85
CARDS:

BRENTWOOD, Essex Map 06 TQ59

★★★★72% ❁ Marygreen Manor

London Rd CM14 4NR
☎ 01277 225252 🖹 01277 262809
e-mail: info@marygreenmanor.co.uk
Dir: *M25 J28, onto A1023 over 2 sets of lights, hotel on left*

An impressive 16th-century house situated just a short drive from the M25. In 1535, Robert Wright named the house his 'Manor of Mary Green' after his young bride. Public rooms have a wealth of
continued on p130

BRENTWOOD, continued

original features such as beamed ceilings and carved panelling, and the baronial restaurant is particularly impressive. The spacious bedrooms are housed in courtyard-style buildings; each one is tastefully decorated and thoughtfully equipped.
ROOMS: 4 en suite 40 annexe en suite (35 GF) No smoking in 8 bedrooms s £130-£192; d £145-£228 **FACILITIES:** STV **CONF:** Thtr 60 Class 20 Board 25 Del £199 **PARKING:** 100 **NOTES:** No dogs (ex guide dogs) No smoking in restaurant Civ Wed 60
CARDS:

See advert on opposite page

Holiday Inn Brentwood
Brook St CM14 5NF
☎ 0870 400 9012 📠 01277 264264
Dir: *close to M25/A12 interchange*
At the time of going to press, the classification for this hotel was not confirmed. Please refer to the AA internet site www.theAA.com for current information.
ROOMS: 150 en suite (30 fmly) No smoking in 80 bedrooms **FACILITIES:** STV Indoor swimming (H) Sauna Solarium Gym Health & fitness club **CONF:** Thtr 120 Class 60 Board 50 **SERVICES:** Lift **PARKING:** 190 **CARDS:**

BRIDGNORTH, Shropshire
Map 10 SO79
See also Alveley

★★★★66% **Mill Hotel & Restaurant**
WV15 6HL
☎ 01746 780437 📠 01746 780850
(For full entry see Alveley)

★★★ **Old Vicarage Hotel**
Worfield WV15 5JZ
☎ 01746 716497 📠 01746 716552
e-mail: admin@the-old-vicarage.demon.co.uk
(For full entry see Worfield)

★★65% **Parlors Hall**
Mill St WV15 5AL
☎ 01746 761931 📠 01746 767058
e-mail: info@parlorshallhotel.co.uk
Dir: *left off A454, right & right again in 200yds*
Parlors Hall has been a hotel since 1929 and retains many original features, such as oak panelling and magnificent fireplaces. Named after the family who lived here between 1419 and 1539, the property now features well-equipped bedrooms, some with four-poster beds, a restaurant and charming bar.
ROOMS: 15 en suite (2 fmly) s fr £45; d £60-£66 (incl. bkfst) **FACILITIES:** Xmas **CONF:** Thtr 50 Class 25 Board 25 **PARKING:** 24 **NOTES:** No dogs (ex guide dogs) **CARDS:**

See advert on opposite page

★★64% **Falcon Hotel**
Saint John St, Lowtown WV15 6AG
☎ 01746 763134 📠 01746 765401
e-mail: enquiries@thefalconhotel.co.uk
Dir: *A442 Telford to Kidderminster road. Follow Bridgnorth town centre signs. Hotel 100yds on left before bridge over River Severn*
This 17th-century former coaching inn stands near the River Severn in the Lowtown area of Bridgnorth, and offers comfortable bedrooms which are equipped to modern standards. A good

continued

selection of dishes is served in the open-plan bar with its beamed restaurant.

ROOMS: 12 en suite (4 fmly) No smoking in 5 bedrooms s £42-£47; d £59-£65 (incl. bkfst) **LB** **CONF:** Thtr 40 Class 20 Board 25 Del from £75 **PARKING:** 100 **CARDS:**

BRIDGWATER, Somerset
Map 04 ST23
See also Holford

★★★72% **Walnut Tree Hotel**

North Petherton TA6 6QA
☎ 01278 662255 📠 01278 663946
e-mail: sales@walnut-tree-hotel.co.uk
Dir: *on A38, 1m S of M5 junct 24*

Popular with business and leisure guests, this 18th-century former coaching inn is located within easy reach of the M5. Smartly decorated bedrooms are well furnished and are equipped with a range of facilities. An extensive selection of meals is offered and guests can eat in the restaurant, bistro area or bar.
ROOMS: 33 en suite (5 fmly) No smoking in 7 bedrooms s £70-£80; d £80-£95 (incl. bkfst) **LB** **FACILITIES:** STV Xmas **CONF:** Thtr 120 Class 76 Board 70 Del £149 **PARKING:** 70 **NOTES:** No dogs (ex guide dogs) Civ Wed 72 **CARDS:**

★★70% **Apple Tree**
Keenthorne TA5 1HZ
☎ 01278 733238 📠 01278 732693
e-mail: appletreehotel@hotmail.com
(For full entry see Nether Stowey)

Travel Inn
Express Park, Bristol Rd
☎ 0870 242 3344 📠 0870 241 9000
Travel Inn offers good-quality, value-for-money accommodation. Spacious, en suite rooms with bath and shower comfortably accommodate a family of up to two adults and two children (to age 15). The restaurant and bar offers a varied menu. For further details and the Travel Inn phone number, consult the Hotel Groups page.
ROOMS: 40 en suite

B

Parlors Hall Hotel ★★

Mill Street, Bridgnorth
Shropshire WV15 5AL
Tel: (01746) 761931 Fax: (01746) 767058

The original Parlors Hall which dates back to the 12th century became an hotel in 1929. Since then it has been carefully refurbished but keeping many of the ancient features, including the fireplaces and oak panelling. Today the hotel offers fifteen luxury en suite bedrooms, each individually decorated in keeping with the character of the building. The attractive restaurant offers an à la carte and carvery menus. Ideally located for business visitors or visiting the many tourist attractions of the area.

Marygreen Manor Hotel

Pantheon Hotels & Leisure Ltd

AA ★★★★

In the warm and friendly atmosphere of this genuine Tudor House, you can enjoy the traditional comfort of open log fires in oak panelled lounges. Accommodation consists of 30 garden suites facing onto an olde-worlde garden – four authentic period ensuite rooms with four-posters – and seven rooms and three Suites in luxurious 'Country House style' incorporating every modern hi-tech facility for the busy executive.
The elegant restaurant offers imaginative fresh-produce menus. Twenty-four hour room service, afternoon teas and all day snack menu. You will find us just half a mile from the M25 Junction 28.

London Road, Brentwood, Essex CM14 4NR
Tel: 01277-225252 Fax: 01277-262809
www.marygreenmanor.co.uk

The Expanse Hotel

A haven of peace and comfort overlooking the Beach and Flamborough Head Heritage Coast, where the beach and cliff walks beckon. The Expanse is a place to relax, with a feel all of its own – built to capture those unique views, where friendly old world courtesy and modern facilities combine for a special break.

North Marine Drive · Bridlington · YO15 2LS
Tel 01262 675347
Fax 01262 604928

B

BRIDLINGTON, East Riding of Yorkshire Map 17 TA16

★★★70% Revelstoke
1-3 Flamborough Rd YO15 2HU
☎ 01262 672362 📠 01262 672362
e-mail: info@revelstokehotel.co.uk
Dir: *B1255 Flamborough Head Rd, 0.5m right at mini rdbt to junct of Promenade & Flamborough Rd. Hotel opp Holy Trinity Church*
Family owned and run this friendly hotel is close to both the town centre and the North Bay seafront. A popular place to stay, the bedrooms are well equipped, and very comfortable. Lounges are well furnished, and in addition to the restaurant where a wide range of well-produced dishes is served, there is an extensive informal menu available in the bar.
ROOMS: 26 en suite (6 fmly) s fr £42; d £66-£95 **LB** **FACILITIES:** STV entertainment Xmas **CONF:** BC Thtr 250 Class 200 Board 100 **PARKING:** 14 **NOTES:** No dogs (ex guide dogs) RS 25-28 Dec Civ Wed 200 **CARDS:**

★★★67% Expanse
North Marine Dr YO15 2LS
☎ 01262 675347 📠 01262 604928
e-mail: expanse@brid.demon.co.uk
Dir: *follow North Beach signs, pass under railway arch for North Marine Drive. Hotel at bottom of hill*

This traditional seaside hotel overlooks the bay and has been in the same family ownership for many years. Service is relaxed and friendly and the modern bedrooms are well equipped. Comfortable public areas include a conference suite, a large bar and an inviting lounge.
ROOMS: 48 en suite (4 fmly) s £38-£49; d £72-£92 (incl. bkfst) **LB** **FACILITIES:** STV entertainment Xmas **CONF:** Thtr 180 Class 50 Board 50 **SERVICES:** Lift **PARKING:** 23 **NOTES:** No dogs (ex guide dogs) No smoking in restaurant Civ Wed 75 **CARDS:**

See advert on page 131

BRIDPORT, Dorset Map 04 SY49

★★★64% Haddon House
West Bay DT6 4EL
☎ 01308 423626 & 425323 📠 01308 427348
Dir: *At Crown Inn rdbt take B3157 West Bay Road, hotel on right at mini-rdbt*
This attractive, creeper-clad hotel offers good standards of accommodation and is situated a few minutes' walk from the sea front and the quay. A friendly and relaxed style of service is provided. An extensive range of dishes from lighter bar snacks to main meals is on offer in the Tudor-style restaurant.

ROOMS: 12 en suite (2 fmly) **FACILITIES:** STV Solarium ch fac **CONF:** Thtr 40 Class 20 Board 26 **PARKING:** 44 **NOTES:** No dogs (ex guide dogs) No smoking in restaurant **CARDS:**

★★71% Roundham House
Roundham Gardens, West Bay Rd DT6 4BD
☎ 01308 422753 📠 01308 421500
e-mail: cyprencom@compuserve.com
Dir: *A35 Bridport road to Crown Inn rdbt (do not take road to Bridport). Follow signs to West Bay along West Bay Rd. Hotel signed*

Many guests regularly return to this welcoming hotel, now refurbished, located on the edge of town. Several rooms have wonderful views across the well-tended gardens to the countryside beyond. There is a comfortable and relaxing lounge and guests can enjoy home-cooked dinners in the pleasant dining room.
ROOMS: 8 en suite (2 fmly) No smoking in all bedrooms s £35-£40; d £60-£84 (incl. bkfst) **LB** **CONF:** Thtr 20 Class 20 Board 15 **PARKING:** 12 **NOTES:** No children 7yrs No smoking in restaurant Closed Jan-Feb **CARDS:**

★65% Bridge House
THE INDEPENDENTS
115 East St DT6 3LB
☎ 01308 423371 📠 01308 459573
e-mail: info@bridgehousebridport.co.uk
Dir: *follow signs to town centre from A35 rdbt, hotel 200mtrs on right*
A short stroll from the town centre, this 18th-century Grade II listed property is undergoing a major refurbishment. The well-equipped bedrooms vary in size. In addition to the main lounge, there is a small bar-lounge and a separate breakfast room. An interesting range of home-cooked meals are provided in the restaurant.
ROOMS: 10 en suite (3 fmly) No smoking in 5 bedrooms s fr £39; d fr £59 (incl. bkfst) **PARKING:** 13 **CARDS:**

BRIGG, Lincolnshire
Map 17 TA00

★★64% The Red Lion Hotel
Main Rd, Redbourne DN21 4QR
☎ 01652 648302 📠 01652 648302
e-mail: enquiries@redlion.org
Dir: *from M180 junct 4 take A15. After 4m left at mini-rdbt, take signs left to Redbourne. Hotel 1st building on left in village*
Dating back to the 17th century, this former coaching inn overlooks the village green and holds a key to the old fire station which is just next door. It offers pleasantly furnished bedrooms and a good range of food is available either in the bar or dining room. There is a friendly atmosphere and staff are very helpful.
ROOMS: 11 en suite (2 fmly) No smoking in 2 bedrooms s fr £40; d fr £55 (incl. bkfst) **LB** **CONF:** Thtr 35 Class 35 Board 35 Del from £50 **PARKING:** 30 **NOTES:** No smoking in restaurant
CARDS:

BRIGHOUSE, West Yorkshire
Map 16 SE12

Holiday Inn Leeds/Brighouse
Clifton Village HD6 4HW
☎ 0870 400 9013 📠 01484 400068
e-mail: brighouse@ichotelsgroup.com
Dir: *M62 junct 25/A644 Spur Rd to Brighouse. Hotel on right*
At the time of going to press, the classification for this hotel was not confirmed. Please refer to the AA internet site www.theAA.com for current information.
ROOMS: 94 en suite (12 fmly) No smoking in 59 bedrooms
FACILITIES: Spa Indoor swimming (H) Sauna Gym Croquet lawn Jacuzzi steam room **CONF:** Thtr 200 Class 120 Board 60
PARKING: 210 **NOTES:** No dogs (ex guide dogs) Civ Wed 120
CARDS:

Premier Lodge (Huddersfield North)
Wakefield Rd HD6 4HA
☎ 0870 9906360 📠 0870 9906361
Premier Lodge offers modern, well-equipped, en suite accommodation suitable for both business and leisure travellers. Meals can be taken at the adjacent popular restaurant and bar, which is fully licensed. For further details, consult the Hotel Groups page.
ROOMS: 71 en suite s £48; d £48

BRIGHTON & HOVE, East Sussex
Map 06 TQ30

★★★★★67% De Vere Grand Brighton
King's Rd BN1 2FW
☎ 01273 224300 📠 01273 224321
e-mail: reservations@grandbrighton.co.uk
Dir: *on seafront between piers, next to Brighton Centre*
Dating back to the mid 19th century, this landmark seafront hotel, with its eye-catching white façade and intricate balconies, is as grand as the name suggests. Bedrooms include a number of deluxe sea view rooms, some with balconies, and suites, also with sea views. The hotel is perhaps best known for its extensive conference and banqueting facilities; there is also a well-equipped leisure centre and an impressive conservatory adjoining the bar.
ROOMS: 200 en suite (60 fmly) s £165; d £245-£400 (incl. bkfst) **LB**
FACILITIES: Spa STV Indoor swimming (H) Sauna Solarium Gym Hairdresser, Tropicorium, Swimming pool supervised entertainment Xmas
CONF: Thtr 800 Class 420 Board 50 Del from £225 **SERVICES:** Lift
PARKING: 70 **NOTES:** Civ Wed 800
CARDS:

Town House

★★★★ Alias Hotel Seattle
The Strand, Brighton Marina BN2 5WA
☎ 01273 679799 📠 01273 679899
e-mail: info@aliasseattle.com
This smart and modern hotel enjoys a prime position overlooking Brighton Marina and has much to offer guests whether on business or leisure. The chic saloon lounge and trendy Black and White bar both have balconies with sea views whilst the spacious and atmospheric Café Paradis offers cuisine with a Mediterranean theme and comes complete with a wood-fired pizza oven.
ROOMS: 71 en suite s £95-£135; d £95-£135 **FACILITIES:** STV Special rates for hotel guests at nearby David Lloyd Leisure Centre **CONF:** Thtr 150 Class 80 Board 70 **SERVICES:** Lift **NOTES:** No smoking in restaurant **CARDS:**

Town House

★★★★ Hotel Du Vin Brighton
2-6 Ship St BN1 1AD
☎ 01273 718588 📠 01273 718599
e-mail: info@brighton.hotelduvin.com
This tastefully converted mock Tudor building occupies a convenient location in a quiet side street close to the sea front. The individual bedrooms all have a wine theme, are comprehensively equipped and include some suites. Public areas offer a spacious split-level bar, an atmospheric and locally popular restaurant and some useful private dining and meeting facilities.
ROOMS: 37 en suite **FACILITIES:** STV Snooker **CONF:** Thtr 36 Class 36 Board 24 **SERVICES:** air con **PARKING:** 5 **NOTES:** No dogs (ex guide dogs) **CARDS:**

Town House

★★★★ The Royal Pavilion Townhouse
12A Regency Square BN1 2FG
☎ 01273 722123 📠 01273 722293
e-mail: info@rpthotel.co.uk
An elegant Regency townhouse on four floors enjoying close proximity to the West Pier and seafront. The spacious and individually themed bedrooms are comprehensively equipped and those on the front of the building offer views over the square. There is also a comfortable bar, a lounge and parking is available in the NCP car park opposite.
ROOMS: 8 en suite No smoking in 4 bedrooms s £120-£150; d £150-£220 (incl. bkfst) **LB** **FACILITIES:** STV Xmas **NOTES:** No children 21yrs **CARDS:**

★★★★65% Old Ship
King's Rd BN1 1NR
☎ 01273 329001 📠 01273 820718
e-mail: oldship@paramount-hotels.co.uk
Dir: *A23 to seafront, right at rdbt along Kings Rd. Hotel 200yds on right*
The Old Ship enjoys a stunning seafront location and offers guests elegant surroundings in which to relax. Bedrooms are well designed, with modern facilities ensuring guest comfort. Many original features have been retained, including the oak-panelled bar. Facilities include a variety of conference rooms.
ROOMS: 152 en suite (10 fmly) No smoking in 15 bedrooms s £99-£135; d £158-£175 **LB** **FACILITIES:** STV Xmas **CONF:** Thtr 300 Class 100 Board 60 Del from £100 **SERVICES:** Lift **PARKING:** 40 **NOTES:** No dogs (ex guide dogs) Civ Wed 70 **CARDS:**

BRIGHTON & HOVE, continued

★★★68% Imperial
First Av BN3 2GU
☎ 01273 777320 🖷 01273 777310
e-mail: info@imperial-hove.com
Dir: *M23 to seafront, right at rdbt to Hove, 1.5m to First Avenue turn right*

Located within minutes of the seafront, this Regency hotel is constantly being improved and upgraded. A good range of conference suites complement the comfortable public rooms, which include a lounge, a smart bar area and an attractive restaurant. Bedrooms are generally of comfortable proportions, well appointed and with a good range of facilities.
ROOMS: 76 en suite (4 fmly) No smoking in 10 bedrooms s £45-£75; d £75-£105 (incl. bkfst) **LB FACILITIES:** Xmas **CONF:** BC Thtr 110 Class 30 Board 34 Del from £85 **SERVICES:** Lift **NOTES:** No dogs (ex guide dogs) No smoking in restaurant **CARDS:**

See advert on opposite page

★★★67% The Courtlands
15-27 The Drive BN3 3JE
☎ 01273 731055 🖷 01273 328295
e-mail: courtlands@pavilion.co.uk
Dir: *A23/A27 junct. 1st exit to Hove, 2nd exit at rdbt, right at 1st junct and left at shops. Straight on at junct. Hotel on left*
This hotel is within walking distance of the seafront and has its own small car park. The majority of bedrooms are newly decorated and have smart bathrooms. Guests have the use of a comfortable lounge, a light and spacious restaurant; service is both friendly and attentive.
ROOMS: 60 en suite 7 annexe en suite (8 fmly) No smoking in 20 bedrooms s £51-£68; d £78-£105 (incl. bkfst) **LB FACILITIES:** Indoor swimming (H) Xmas **CONF:** Thtr 60 Class 20 Board 30 Del from £75 **SERVICES:** Lift **PARKING:** 24 **NOTES:** No dogs (ex guide dogs) No smoking in restaurant **CARDS:**

★★★66% Brighton Hotel
Best Western
143/145 King's Rd BN1 2PQ
☎ 01273 820555 🖷 01273 821555
e-mail: b-thotel@pavilion.co.uk
Dir: *signs to Brighton Pier, turn right & hotel 100yds past West Pier*
This friendly family-run hotel is well placed and enjoys a prime seafront location, close to the historic West Pier. All of the bedrooms are bright, comfortably appointed and well equipped and public rooms have been fully refurbished. The car parking facilities are a real bonus in Brighton.
ROOMS: 52 en suite s £40-£74; d £65-£94 (incl. bkfst) **LB FACILITIES:** STV **CONF:** Thtr 130 Class 35 Board 35 Del from £87.50 **SERVICES:** Lift **PARKING:** 18 **NOTES:** No dogs (ex guide dogs) No smoking in restaurant **CARDS:**

★★★66% Princes Marine
Best Western
153 Kingsway BN3 4GR
☎ 01273 207660 🖷 01273 325913
e-mail: princesmarine@bestwestern.co.uk
Dir: *right at Brighton Pier, follow seafront for 2m. Hotel 200yds from King Alfred leisure centre*

This friendly hotel enjoys a seafront location and offers spacious, comfortable bedrooms equipped with a good range of facilities. There is a cosy restaurant, bar and useful meeting room and limited parking at the rear.
ROOMS: 48 en suite (4 fmly) No smoking in 12 bedrooms s £45-£65; d £80-£120 (incl. bkfst) **LB FACILITIES:** Xmas **CONF:** BC Thtr 80 Class 40 Board 40 Del from £95 **SERVICES:** Lift **PARKING:** 30 **CARDS:**

★★★66% Queens Hotel
1 King's Rd BN1 1NS
☎ 01273 321222 🖷 01273 203059
e-mail: res@queenshotelbrighton.com
Dir: *A23 to Brighton town centre - follow signs for seafront. At Brighton Pier right onto seafront, hotel 500mtrs*
Located on the seafront, this hotel has been refurbished to a high standard. All the bedrooms are richly decorated with warm colours, offer good facilities and many have wonderful sea views. A modern leisure centre and Atrium bar are great places to relax and the restaurant serves contemporary meals.
ROOMS: 97 en suite (12 fmly) No smoking in 23 bedrooms s £50-£120; d £60-£250 (incl. bkfst) **LB FACILITIES:** Indoor swimming (H) Sauna Solarium Gym Swimming pool supervised entertainment **CONF:** BC Thtr 150 Class 50 Board 50 Del from £140 **SERVICES:** Lift **NOTES:** No dogs (ex guide dogs) No smoking in restaurant Civ Wed 80
CARDS:

★★★64% The Granville
124 King's Rd BN1 2FA
☎ 01273 326302 🖷 01273 728294
e-mail: granville@brighton.co.uk
Dir: *opposite West Pier*
This stylish hotel is located on Brighton's busy seafront. Bedrooms are carefully furnished and decorated with great style. An informal service and atmosphere is provided in Trogs vegetarian restaurant and the adjoining bar; great care is taken to source quality organic foods. Tasty traditional breakfasts are also available.
ROOMS: 24 en suite (2 fmly) No smoking in all bedrooms s £55-£105; d £85-£185 (incl. bkfst) **LB FACILITIES:** Jacuzzi **CONF:** Thtr 50 Class 30 Board 30 Del from £100 **SERVICES:** Lift **PARKING:** 3
CARDS:

★★★64% Quality Hotel Brighton

West St BN1 2RQ
☎ 01273 220033 📠 01273 778000
e-mail: admin@gb057.u-net.com

Dir: *A23 into Brighton, then town centre/seafront signs. A259 to Hove & Worthing. Hotel next to Brighton Centre*

Conveniently located for the seafront and close to the town centre, this purpose built hotel offers refurbished, modern and well-equipped bedrooms. Public areas include a spacious, open plan lounge bar area with a feature staircase. A choice of restaurants serves a wide selection of dishes.

ROOMS: 138 en suite No smoking in 60 bedrooms s £49-£99; d £69-£115 **LB FACILITIES:** STV **CONF:** Thtr 200 Class 80 Board 60 Del £115 **SERVICES:** Lift **NOTES:** No dogs (ex guide dogs) No smoking in restaurant **CARDS:**

★★★63% The Dudley

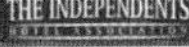

Lansdowne Place BN3 1HQ
☎ 01273 736266 📠 01273 729802
e-mail: admin@thedudleyhotel.co.uk

Dir: *M23 & A23 into Brighton. Right at seafront heading W, in Hove Lansdowne Place, 1st turn after Brunswick Sq*

This Regency-fronted hotel is located just a few metres from the seafront and dates from Victorian times. The Dudley offers traditional well-appointed public areas, including Marty's Bar and Restaurant, and an extensive range of function rooms. Bedroom refurbishment is restoring the accommodation to its former glory.

ROOMS: 71 en suite (3 fmly) No smoking in 40 bedrooms s £40-£84; d £80-£138 (incl. bkfst) **LB FACILITIES:** Xmas **CONF:** Thtr 150 Class 100 Board 90 Del from £80 **SERVICES:** Lift **PARKING:** 20 **NOTES:** No dogs (ex guide dogs) No smoking in restaurant
CARDS:

See advert on this page

⌂ Premier Lodge (Brighton City Centre)

144 North St BN1 1RE
☎ 0870 9906340 📠 0870 9906341

Premier Lodge offers modern, well-equipped, en suite accommodation suitable for both business and leisure travellers. Meals can be taken at the adjacent popular restaurant and bar, which is fully licensed. For further details, consult the Hotel Groups page.

ROOMS: 160 en suite s £52; d £52

⌂ Travelodge Brighton Central

Preston Rd BN1 6AU
☎ 08700 850 950

Travelodge offers good quality, good value, modern accommodation. Ideal for families, the spacious, en suite bedrooms include remote-control TV, tea and coffee-making facilities, luxury beds and free morning newspaper. Meals can be taken at the nearby family restaurant. For further details and the Travelodge phone number, consult the Hotel Groups page.

ROOMS: 94 en suite s fr £42.95; d fr £42.95

BRISTOL, Bristol Map 04 ST57

Town House

★★★★ Hotel du Vin & Bistro

The Sugar House, Narrow Lewins Mead BS1 2NU
☎ 0117 925 5577 0117 925 1199
e-mail: info@bristol.hotelduvin.com
Dir: *A4 follow city centre signs. After 400yds pass Rupert St NCP on right. Hotel on opp*

The third property in one of Britain's most innovative and now expanding hotel groups extends the high standards for which the chain is renowned. The hotel is housed in a Grade II listed, converted 18th-century sugar refinery. Bedrooms are exceptionally well-designed and the hotel provides great facilities with a modern minimalist feel. The bistro offers an excellent menu.

ROOMS: 40 en suite s £120-£395; d £120-£395 **FACILITIES:** STV Snooker Xmas **CONF:** Thtr 50 Class 25 Board 26 Del £195 **SERVICES:** Lift **PARKING:** 33 **NOTES:** No dogs (ex guide dogs) **CARDS:**

★★★★73% *Bristol Marriott Royal Hotel*

Marriott HOTELS · RESORTS · SUITES

College Green BS1 5TA
☎ 0117 925 5100 0117 925 1515
e-mail: bristol.royal@marriotthotels.co.uk
Dir: *next to cathedral*

A truly stunning hotel located in the centre of the city, next to the cathedral. Public areas are particularly impressive with luxurious lounges and a leisure club. Dining options include the more informal terrace restaurant and Palm Court (closed Sunday and Monday). The spacious bedrooms have the benefit of air conditioning, comfortable armchairs and marbled bathrooms.

ROOMS: 242 en suite (14 fmly) No smoking in 163 bedrooms **FACILITIES:** STV Indoor swimming (H) Sauna Solarium Gym Jacuzzi **CONF:** Thtr 300 Class 140 Board 30 **SERVICES:** Lift air con **PARKING:** 200 **NOTES:** No dogs (ex guide dogs) No smoking in restaurant Civ Wed 220 **CARDS:**

★★★★71% Aztec

Aztec West Business Park BS32 4TS
☎ 01454 201090 01454 201593
e-mail: aztec@shirehotels.co.uk
Dir: *access via M5 junct 16 & M4*

Situated close to Cribbs Causeway shopping centre and major motorway links, this stylish hotel offers very well-equipped comfortable bedrooms. Built in a Nordic style, public rooms boast log fires and vaulted ceilings. Leisure facilities include a very well equipped gym and good sized pool. The new-look Quarterjacks restaurant offers relaxed informal dining with a focus on regional foods. *Shire Hotels – AA Hotel Group of the Year 2003-4.*

ROOMS: 128 en suite (6 fmly) (29 GF) No smoking in 84 bedrooms s £140-£220; d £160-£245 (incl. bkfst) **LB FACILITIES: Spa** STV Indoor swimming (H) Squash Sauna Solarium Gym Jacuzzi Indoor pool supervised Steam room, Health & beauty, Childrens splash pool, Xmas **CONF:** BC Thtr 200 Class 120 Board 36 Del £175 **SERVICES:** Lift air con **PARKING:** 240 **NOTES:** No dogs (ex guide dogs) No smoking in restaurant Civ Wed 250 **CARDS:**

★★★★67% Bristol Marriott City Centre

Marriott HOTELS · RESORTS · SUITES

Lower Castle St BS1 3AD
☎ 0870 400 7210 0870 400 7310
Dir: *M32 follow signs to Broadmead, take slip road to large rdbt, take 3rd exit. Hotel on right*

Situated at the foot of the picturesque Castle Park, this mainly business-orientated hotel is well-located for the city centre. Free parking is available for residents along with complimentary; temporary membership of the hotel's leisure club. In addition to a coffee bar and lounge menu, the Mediterrano restaurant offers an interesting selection of well-prepared dishes.

ROOMS: 289 en suite (138 fmly) No smoking in 221 bedrooms s £129; d £129 **LB FACILITIES: Spa** STV Indoor swimming (H) Sauna Solarium Gym Jacuzzi Steam room **CONF:** Thtr 600 Class 280 Board 40 Del from £145 **SERVICES:** Lift air con **NOTES:** No dogs (ex guide dogs) No smoking in restaurant Civ Wed 500 **CARDS:**

★★★★66% The Brigstow

5-7 Welsh Back BS1 4SP
☎ 0117 929 1030 0117 929 2030
e-mail: brigstow@fullers.co.uk
Dir: *Follow signs to City Centre. Turn left into Baldwin St, 2nd right into Queen Charlotte St. NCP on left*

In a prime position, with its own riverside frontage, this handsome purpose-built structure is designed and finished with care in every detail. The shopping centre is within easy walking distance, as are the city's theatres. Bedrooms are stylish and extremely well equipped, even down to plasma television screens in bathrooms.

continued

There is an integrated state-of-the-art conference and meeting centre, and a smart restaurant and bar overlooking the quay.

ROOMS: 116 en suite No smoking in 78 bedrooms s £89-£140; d £89-£140 **LB** **FACILITIES:** STV **CONF:** BC Thtr 60 Class 40 Board 36 Del from £170 **SERVICES:** Lift air con **NOTES:** No dogs (ex guide dogs) RS 24 Dec - 5 Jan Civ Wed 40 **CARDS:**

★★★★64% Jurys Bristol Hotel

JURYS DOYLE HOTELS

Prince St BS1 4QF
☎ 0117 923 0333 Fax 0117 923 0300
e-mail: bristol_hotel@jurysdoyle.com
Dir: *from Temple Meads right at 1st rdbt into Victoria St. At Bristol Bridge lights left into Baldwin St, 2nd left into Marsh St, right at rdbt*

This modern hotel enjoys an excellent location near Bristol's Millennium project. Bedrooms vary in size and are well appointed with a range of facilities. There is a choice of eating options, including a Quayside restaurant and adjoining inn. Extensive conference facilities are also available.

ROOMS: 191 en suite (22 fmly) No smoking in 53 bedrooms s £49-£140; d £59-£150 **LB** **FACILITIES:** STV Complimentary use of local gym entertainment Xmas **CONF:** Thtr 400 Class 160 Board 80 Del from £125 **SERVICES:** Lift **NOTES:** No dogs (ex guide dogs) **CARDS:**

★★★72% @@ *City Inn Bristol*

Temple Way BS1 6BF
☎ 0117 925 1001 Fax 0117 907 4116
e-mail: bristol.reservations@cityinn.co.uk

The City Inn offers spacious, contemporary public areas and bedrooms, and is situated within walking distance of the city centre and railway station. The young staff are well motivated and friendly. The City Café offers an interesting selection of carefully prepared quality ingredients and the adjacent bar serves coffee and tea throughout the day.

ROOMS: 167 en suite No smoking in 134 bedrooms **FACILITIES:** STV Gym **CONF:** Thtr 45 Class 22 Board 24 **SERVICES:** Lift air con **NOTES:** No dogs (ex guide dogs) **CARDS:**

★★★69% Arno's Manor

Forestdale Hotels

470 Bath Rd, Arno's Vale BS4 3HQ
☎ 0117 971 1461 Fax 0117 971 5507
e-mail: arnos.manor@forestdale.com

Once the home of a wealthy merchant, this historic 18th-century building is now a comfortable hotel and has now been fully refurbished to a high standard. The lounge was once the chapel and has many original features. Bedrooms are spacious and very well equipped with good working areas.

ROOMS: 73 en suite (1 fmly) (7 GF) s fr £90; d fr £115 (incl. bkfst) **LB** **FACILITIES:** STV Xmas **CONF:** Thtr 150 Class 60 Board 40 Del from £130 **SERVICES:** Lift **PARKING:** 200 **NOTES:** No dogs (ex guide dogs) No smoking in restaurant Civ Wed 100 **CARDS:**

★★★69% Berkeley Square

Best Western

15 Berkeley Square, Clifton BS8 1HB
☎ 0117 925 4000 Fax 0117 925 2970
e-mail: berkeleysquare@bestwestern.co.uk
Dir: *M32 follow Clifton signs. 1st left at traffic lights by Nills Memorial Tower (University) into Berkeley Sq*

Set in a peaceful square close to the university, art gallery and Clifton village, this smart, elegant Georgian hotel has tastefully decorated bedrooms that include many welcome extras. There is a busy bar in the basement, and the restaurant features interesting dishes from a choice of menus.

ROOMS: 42 en suite No smoking in 12 bedrooms s £54-£106; d £85-£127 (incl. bkfst) **LB** **FACILITIES:** STV complimentry use of local gym and swimming pool **CONF:** Thtr 40 Class 12 Board 12 **SERVICES:** Lift **PARKING:** 20 **CARDS:**

★★★67% Henbury Lodge

Station Rd, Henbury BS10 7QQ
☎ 0117 950 2615 Fax 0117 950 9532
e-mail: enquiries@henburylodge.com
Dir: *M5 junct 17/A4018 towards city centre, 3rd rdbt right into Crow Ln. At end turn right & hotel 200mtrs on right*

This comfortable 18th-century country house has a relaxed and welcoming atmosphere and is conveniently situated within easy access of the M5. Bedrooms are available both within the main house and in the adjoining stable conversion; all are attractively decorated and well equipped. The pleasant dining room offers a selection of carefully prepared dishes using fresh ingredients.

ROOMS: 12 en suite 9 annexe en suite (4 fmly) (3 GF) No smoking in 8 bedrooms s £57-£102; d £94-£112 (incl. bkfst) **LB** **FACILITIES:** STV Sauna Solarium Xmas **CONF:** Thtr 32 Class 20 Board 20 Del from £125 **PARKING:** 24 **NOTES:** No smoking in restaurant **CARDS:**

BRISTOL, continued

★★★67% Redwood Lodge Hotel & Country Club
Beggar Bush Ln, Failand BS8 3TG
☎ 0870 609 6144 🖷 01275 392104
e-mail: reservations.redwoodlodge@corushotels.com
Dir: *M5 junct 19, A369 for 3m then right at traffic lights. Hotel 1m on left*

Situated close to the suspension bridge, this popular hotel offers guests a peaceful location combined with excellent leisure facilities including a cinema, gym, squash, badminton and tennis facilities, plus indoor and outdoor pools. Bedrooms have plenty of amenities and are well suited for the business guest.
ROOMS: 112 en suite (1 fmly) (52 GF) No smoking in 81 bedrooms s £42-£105; d £84-£120 (incl. bkfst) **LB FACILITIES:** STV Indoor swimming (H) Outdoor swimming Tennis (hard) Squash Sauna Solarium Gym 175 seater Cinema, Aerobics/Dance studios, Badminton courts entertainment Xmas **CONF:** Thtr 175 Class 80 Board 40 Del from £99 **PARKING:** 1000 **NOTES:** No smoking in restaurant Civ Wed 200 **CARDS:**

★★★65% The Avon Gorge
Sion Hill, Clifton BS8 4LD
☎ 0117 973 8955 🖷 0117 923 8125
e-mail: info@avongorge-hotel-bristol.com
Dir: *M5 junct 19, follow signs for Clifton Toll, over suspension bridge, 1st right into Sion Hill*
Overlooking Avon Gorge and Brunel's famous suspension bridge, this popular hotel offers rooms with some glorious views. Bedrooms are very well equipped and include welcome extras such as additional telephone points and ceiling fans. The hotel offers a choice of bars (one with a pleasant outdoor terrace area) and an attractive restaurant.
ROOMS: 76 en suite (6 fmly) No smoking in 30 bedrooms s £65-£120; d £95-£130 (incl. bkfst) **LB FACILITIES:** STV Childrens activity play area entertainment Xmas **CONF:** Thtr 100 Class 50 Board 26 Del from £130 **SERVICES:** Lift **PARKING:** 23 **NOTES:** No smoking in restaurant Civ Wed 100 **CARDS:**

★★71% Best Western Victoria Square
Victoria Square, Clifton BS8 4EW
☎ 0117 973 9058 🖷 0117 970 6929
e-mail: victoriasquare@btopenworld.com
Dir: *M5 junct 19, follow Clifton signs. Over suspension bridge, right into Clifton Down Rd. Left at mini rdbt into Merchants Rd then into Victoria Sq*
This Victorian property has undergone a refurbishment programme throughout. Location is convenient for the city and Clifton village. Bedrooms are generally spacious; all are well equipped including a range of useful extras such as modem points for Internet access. A pleasant conference room and small rear car park are also on hand.

ROOMS: 21 en suite 19 annexe en suite (6 fmly) (2 GF) No smoking in 22 bedrooms s £65-£85; d £85-£95 (incl. bkfst) **FACILITIES:** STV **CONF:** Thtr 30 Class 25 Board 20 Del from £100 **PARKING:** 16 **NOTES:** Closed 20 Dec-2 Jan **CARDS:**

★★71% *Clifton*
St Pauls Rd, Clifton BS8 1LX
☎ 0117 973 6882 🖷 0117 974 1082
e-mail: clifton@cliftonhotels.com
Dir: *M32 follow Bristol/Clifton signs, along Park St. Left at lights into St Pauls Rd*
This popular hotel offers very well-equipped bedrooms and relaxed, friendly service. There is a smart lounge at reception and during summer months drinks and meals can be taken on the terrace. Racks Bar and Restaurant offers an interesting selection of modern dishes from an imaginative menu. Some street parking is possible although for a small charge, secure garage parking is available.
ROOMS: 59 en suite (2 fmly) No smoking in 28 bedrooms **FACILITIES:** STV **SERVICES:** Lift **PARKING:** 20 **CARDS:**

★★70% Seeley's
17-27 St Paul's Rd, Clifton BS8 1LX
☎ 0117 973 8544 🖷 0117 973 2406
e-mail: admin@seeleys.demon.co.uk
Dir: *M5 junct 17/A4018 for 4.5m to BBC studios. Right at lights, hotel on left*

Within walking distance of Clifton village, the suspension bridge and the picturesque Durdham Downs, this family-run hotel benefits from its own car park. Bedrooms are equipped with modern comforts and eating options range from snacks in the informal bar to the carte menu in Le Chasseur Restaurant.
ROOMS: 37 en suite 18 annexe en suite (10 fmly) (9 GF) s £50-£65; d £65-£82 (incl. bkfst) **LB FACILITIES:** STV Garden **CONF:** Thtr 70 Class 30 Board 25 Del from £92.50 **PARKING:** 25 **NOTES:** No dogs (ex guide dogs) Closed 24 Dec-2 Jan **CARDS:**

★★68% The Bowl Inn
16 Church Rd, Lower Almondsbury BS32 4DT
☎ 01454 612757 📠 01454 619910
e-mail: reception@thebowlinn.co.uk
Dir: *M5 junct 16 onto Gloucester road, N for 500yds. Turn left into Over Lane, turn right by Garden Centre. Hotel next to church on right*

With easy access to the motorway network, this village inn offers all the comforts of modern life in a charming 16th-century hostelry. Each bedroom has been individually furnished to complement the many original features. Dining options include an extensive bar menu, with cask ales, or a more intimate restaurant.
ROOMS: 11 en suite 2 annexe en suite (1 GF) No smoking in 5 bedrooms s £45-£106; d £71-£128 (incl. bkfst) **LB** **FACILITIES:** STV **CONF:** Thtr 30 Class 20 Board 24 **PARKING:** 30 **NOTES:** RS 25 Dec
CARDS:

★★67% Rodney Hotel
4 Rodney Place, Clifton BS8 4HY
☎ 0117 973 5422 📠 0117 946 7092
e-mail: rodney@cliftonhotels.com
Dir: *off Clifton Down Rd*
With easy access from the M5, this attractive, listed building in Clifton is conveniently close to the city centre. The individually decorated bedrooms provide a useful range of extra facilities for the business traveller. Snacks are served in the bar-lounge or by way of room service, and the more formal restaurant offers an appealing selection of dishes.
ROOMS: 31 en suite (2 GF) No smoking in 10 bedrooms s £40-£64; d £65-£79 (incl. bkfst) **FACILITIES:** STV **CONF:** Thtr 30 Class 20 Board 15 **NOTES:** Closed 22 Dec-3 Jan RS Sun
CARDS:

★★63% Westbourne

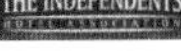

40-44 St Pauls Rd, Clifton BS8 1LR
☎ 0117 973 4214 📠 0117 974 3552
e-mail: westbournehotel@bristol8.fsworld.co.uk
Dir: *M32/A4018 along Park St to Triangle, then Whiteladies Rd. Turn left at 1st lights opp the BBC onto St Pauls Rd. Hotel 200yds on right*

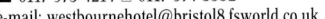

This privately owned hotel is centrally situated in the heart of Clifton and is popular with business guests during the week. It offers comfortable, well-equipped bedrooms. Freddie's Bar and Restaurant provides a range of eating options and during the summer months guests can enjoy a drink on the rear terrace.
ROOMS: 29 en suite (7 fmly) (1 GF) No smoking in 1 bedroom s £50-£70; d £75-£80 (incl. bkfst) **PARKING:** 9 **NOTES:** No dogs (ex guide dogs) **CARDS:**

U Holiday Inn Bristol Filton
Filton Rd, Hambrook BS16 1QX
☎ 0870 400 9014 📠 0117 956 9735
Dir: *M4 junct 19/M32 junct 1/A4174 towards Filton & Bristol. Hotel 800yds on left*
At the time of going to press, the classification for this hotel was not confirmed. Please refer to the AA internet site www.theAA.com for current information.
ROOMS: 198 en suite (36 fmly) No smoking in 131 bedrooms **FACILITIES:** STV Indoor swimming (H) Fishing Sauna Solarium Gym childrens play area ch fac **CONF:** Thtr 250 Class 130 Board 60 **SERVICES:** Lift **PARKING:** 400 **NOTES:** Civ Wed 80
CARDS:

⇧ Express by Holiday Inn Bristol
Temple Gate BS1 6PL
☎ 0117 930 4800 📠 0117 930 4900
e-mail: bristol@expressbyholidayinn.co.uk
Dir: *M4 junct 19/M32 into Bristol. Keep left & follow signs to Temple Meads train station. Hotel opp station*

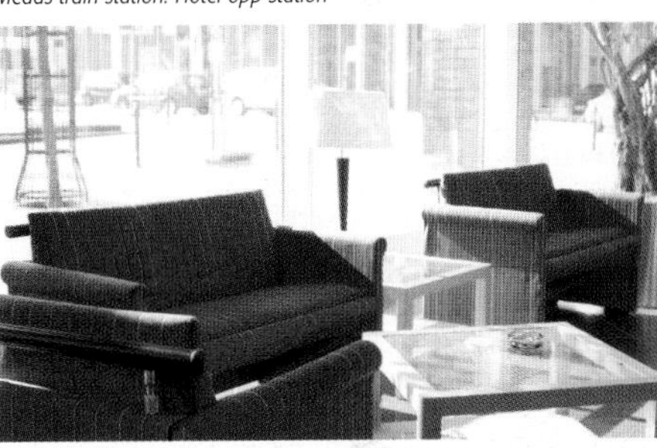

A modern hotel ideal for families and business travellers. Fresh and uncomplicated, the spacious bedrooms include Sky TV, power shower and tea and coffee-making facilities. Continental buffet breakfast is included in the room rate; other meals may be taken at the nearby family pub or restaurant. For further details and the Express by Holiday Inn phone number, consult the Hotel Groups pages.
ROOMS: 96 en suite (incl. cont bkfst) s £60-£73; d £60-£73

⇧ Express By Holiday Inn - Bristol North
New Rd, Bristol Parkway Business Park BS34 8SJ
☎ 0870 443 0036 📠 0870 443 0037
e-mail: managerbristolnorth@expressholidayinn.co.uk
Dir: *M4 junct 19/M32 junct 1. Follow signs for Bristol Parkway Station, right at main rdbt, hotel on left. For access, left at next 2 rdbts onto New Road, hotel entrance 100yds past Bristol & West building*
A modern hotel ideal for families and business travellers. Fresh and uncomplicated, the spacious bedrooms include Sky TV, power shower and tea and coffee-making facilities. Continental buffet breakfast is included in the room rate; other meals may be taken

continued on p140

BRISTOL, continued

at the nearby family pub or restaurant. For further details and the Express by Holiday Inn phone number, consult the Hotel Groups pages.

Express by Holiday Inn – Bristol North

ROOMS: 133 en suite (incl. cont bkfst) s £55-£73; d £55-£73
CONF: Thtr 30 Class 22 Board 22

⌂ Premier Lodge (Bristol City East)

Shield Retail Park, Gloucester Rd North, Filton BS34 7BR
☎ 0870 9906456 🖷 0870 9906457

Premier Lodge offers modern, well-equipped, en suite accommodation suitable for both business and leisure travellers. Meals can be taken at the adjacent popular restaurant and bar, which is fully licensed. For further details, consult the Hotel Groups page.

ROOMS: 60 en suite s £50; d £50 **CONF:** Board 12

⌂ Premier Lodge (Bristol North West)

Cribbs Causeway, Catbrain Ln BS10 7TQ
☎ 0870 9906570 🖷 0870 9906571

Premier Lodge offers modern, well-equipped, en suite accommodation suitable for both business and leisure travellers. Meals can be taken at the adjacent popular restaurant and bar, which is fully licensed. For further details, consult the Hotel Groups page.

ROOMS: (incl. bkfst) s £50; d £50

⌂ Premier Lodge (Bristol City Centre)

Landoger Trow, Kings St BS1 4ER
☎ 0870 9906424 🖷 0870 9906425

Premier Lodge offers modern, well-equipped, en suite accommodation suitable for both business and leisure travellers. Meals can be taken at the adjacent popular restaurant and bar, which is fully licensed. For further details, consult the Hotel Groups page.

ROOMS: 60 en suite (incl. bkfst) s £52; d £52

⌂ Travel Inn (Bristol City Centre)

Haymarket BS1 3LR
☎ 0870 238 3307 🖷 0117 9100619
Dir: *M4 junct 19/M32 towards city centre. Through 2 sets of lights, at 3rd set, turn right. To rdbt, take 2nd exit. Travel Inn on left.*

Travel Inn offers good-quality, value-for-money accommodation. Spacious, en suite rooms with bath and shower comfortably accommodate a family of up to two adults and two children (to age 15). The restaurant and bar offers a varied menu. For further details and the Travel Inn phone number, consult the Hotel Groups page.

ROOMS: 224 en suite s £49.95-£54.95; d £49.95-£54.95

⌂ Travel Inn (Bristol City East)

200/202 Westerleigh Rd, Emersons Green
BS16 7AN
☎ 08701 977042 🖷 0117 956 4644
Dir: *follow A4174 (Avon Ring Rd), E from M32 junct 1*

Travel Inn offers good-quality, value-for-money accommodation. Spacious, en suite rooms with bath and shower comfortably accommodate a family of up to two adults and two children (to age 15). The restaurant and bar offers a varied menu. For further details and the Travel Inn phone number, consult the Hotel Groups page.

ROOMS: 40 en suite s £44.95; d £44.95 **CONF:** Thtr 26 Board 17

⌂ Travel Inn (Bristol South)

Hengrove Leisure Park, Hengrove Way BS14 0HR
☎ 08701 977043 🖷 01275 834721
Dir: *From city centre take A37 to Wells and Shepton Mallet. Turn right onto A4174. Travel Inn at 2nd set of lights*

Travel Inn offers good-quality, value-for-money accommodation. Spacious, en suite rooms with bath and shower comfortably accommodate a family of up to two adults and two children (to age 15). The restaurant and bar offers a varied menu. For further details and the Travel Inn phone number, consult the Hotel Groups page.

ROOMS: 40 en suite s £44.95; d £44.95

⌂ Travelodge (Bristol Central)

Anchor Rd, Harbourside BS1 5TT
☎ 08700 850 950

Travelodge offers good quality, good value, modern accommodation. Ideal for families, the spacious, en suite bedrooms include remote-control TV, tea and coffee-making facilities, luxury beds and free morning newspaper. Meals can be taken at the nearby family restaurant. For further details and the Travelodge phone number, consult the Hotel Groups page.

ROOMS: 119 en suite s fr £42.95; d fr £42.95

⌂ Travelodge (Bristol Cribbs Causeway)

Cribbs Causeway BS10 7TL
☎ 08700 850 950 🖷 0117 950 1530
Dir: *A4018, off M5 junct 17*

Travelodge offers good quality, good value, modern accommodation. Ideal for families, the spacious, en suite bedrooms include remote-control TV, tea and coffee-making facilities, luxury beds and free morning newspaper. Meals can be taken at the nearby family restaurant. For further details and the Travelodge phone number, consult the Hotel Groups page.

ROOMS: 56 en suite s fr £42.95; d fr £42.95

TV dinner?
Room service at three stars and above

BRIXHAM, Devon
Map 03 SX95

★★★70% Quayside
41-49 King St TQ5 9TJ
☎ 01803 855751 Fax 01803 882733
e-mail: reservations@quaysidehotel.co.uk
Dir: *A380, at 2nd rdbt at Kinkerswell towards Brixham on A3022. Hotel overlooks harbour*

Formerly six cottages, the Quayside Hotel enjoys panoramic views over the harbour and bay. The owners and their team of local staff provide friendly and attentive service. The public rooms retain a cosiness and intimacy, and include the lounge, residents' bar and Ernie Lister's public bar. Freshly landed fish features on the menu in the well-appointed restaurant.
ROOMS: 29 en suite (2 fmly) No smoking in 6 bedrooms s £54-£83; d £76-£110 (incl. bkfst) **LB** **FACILITIES:** entertainment Xmas **CONF:** Thtr 25 Class 18 Board 18 **PARKING:** 30 **NOTES:** No smoking in restaurant **CARDS:**

★★★66% Berryhead

Berryhead Rd TQ5 9AJ
☎ 01803 853225 Fax 01803 882084
e-mail: stay@berryheadhotel.com
Dir: *Turn left at town hall to harbour. Right past statue, sharp left - leave Marina, 1m, hotel on left*
From its stunning cliff-top location, this imposing property dating back to 1809 has spectacular views across Torbay. Public areas include two comfortable lounges, an outdoor terrace, a swimming pool, together with a bar serving a range of popular dishes. Many of the bedrooms have the benefit of the splendid sea views.
ROOMS: 32 en suite (7 fmly) s £55-£110; d £110-£172 (incl. bkfst & dinner) **LB** **FACILITIES: Spa** Indoor swimming (H) Croquet lawn Jacuzzi Petanque Sailing Deep sea fishing entertainment Xmas **CONF:** BC Thtr 300 Class 250 Board 40 Del from £65 **PARKING:** 200 **NOTES:** No smoking in restaurant Civ Wed 200 **CARDS:**

See advert on this page

★62% Smuggler's Haunt
Church Hill East TQ5 8HH
☎ 01803 853050 & 859416 Fax 01803 858738
e-mail: enquiries@smugglershaunt-hotel-devon.co.uk
Dir: *end of A3022 turn left, hotel 200yds*
Situated in the centre of this historic fishing village and close to the public car park, this 300-year-old hotel offers straightforward accommodation. In both the beamed bar and restaurant, a wide range of carefully cooked dishes is available.
ROOMS: 14 en suite (4 fmly) s £31-£34; d £52-£58 (incl. bkfst) **LB** **FACILITIES:** Xmas **CARDS:**

BROADSTAIRS, Kent
Map 07 TR36

★★★65% Royal Albion
Albion St CT10 1AN
☎ 01843 868071 Fax 01843 861509
e-mail: enquiries@albionbroadstairs.co.uk
Dir: *follow signs for seafront and town centre*
This traditional seafront hotel enjoys delightful views from most bedrooms, and the newly refurbished bar and lounge. The restaurant is two doors down the street in Marchesi's. Staff are friendly and the atmosphere is relaxed and informal.
ROOMS: 19 en suite (3 fmly) No smoking in 4 bedrooms s £59-£79; d £77-£112 (incl. bkfst) **LB** **FACILITIES:** STV entertainment Xmas **CONF:** Thtr 30 Class 20 Board 20 Del from £60 **PARKING:** 21 **NOTES:** No dogs (ex guide dogs) **CARDS:**

Late for dinner?
Quality Standards mean that last orders for dinner vary according to star rating and should be no earlier than:
★★ 7.00pm ★★★ 8.00pm ★★★★ 9.00pm
★★★★★ 10.00pm

Popped the question?
Hotels with Civ Wed in their entry are licensed for civil wedding ceremonies. Maximum numbers for the ceremony only are shown, e.g. Civ Wed 120

BROADWAY, Worcestershire Map 10 SP03
See also Buckland

★★★★73% The Lygon Arms
High St WR12 7DU
☎ 01386 852255 01386 858611
e-mail: info@the-lygon-arms.co.uk
Dir: *Turn off A44, signed Broadway, hotel on High Street*
A hotel with a wealth of historical charm and character, situated in the heart of Broadway. The Lygon Arms dates back to the 16th century, and offers comfortable bedrooms with modern facilities and some fine antique furniture. Public rooms include a variety of lounge areas, some with open fires, and a choice of dining options - the Great Hall or the more informal Oliver's Brasserie.
ROOMS: 69 rms (66 en suite) (3 fmly) (8 GF) s £143-£179; d £215-£239 (incl. bkfst) **LB** **FACILITIES: Spa** STV Indoor swimming (H) Tennis (hard) Snooker Sauna Gym Croquet lawn Beauty treatments, Steam Room, Bike Hire, Horse riding nearby, Walking Xmas **CONF:** BC Thtr 80 Class 48 Board 30 Del from £185 **PARKING:** 152 **NOTES:** No smoking in restaurant Civ Wed 80 **CARDS:**

★★★78% Dormy House
Willersey Hill WR12 7LF
☎ 01386 852711 01386 858636
e-mail: reservations@dormyhouse.co.uk.
Dir: *2m E off A44, top of Fish Hill, turn for Saintbury/Picnic area. After 0.5m fork left and hotel on left*
A converted 17th-century farmhouse set in extensive grounds and with stunning views over Broadway. Some rooms are in a collection of honey-coloured stone cottages; some have four-poster beds. Furnishings are tasteful throughout, with some stylish contemporary touches. The best traditions have been retained - real fires, comfortable sofas and afternoon teas.
ROOMS: 25 en suite 23 annexe en suite (3 fmly) s £80-£110; d £155-£165 (incl. bkfst) **LB** **FACILITIES:** Sauna Gym Croquet lawn Putting green Games room, nature & jogging trail **CONF:** Thtr 200 Class 100 Board 25 **PARKING:** 80 **NOTES:** Closed 25 & 26 Dec Civ Wed 170
CARDS:

See advert on opposite page

★★★68% Broadway
The Green, High St WR12 7AA
☎ 01386 852401 01386 853879
e-mail: bookings@cotswold-inns-hotels.co.uk
A half-timbered Cotswold stone property, built in the 15th century as a retreat for the Abbots of Pershore. Following refurbishment the hotel now combines modern, attractive decor with original charm and character. Bedrooms are tastefully furnished and well equipped while public rooms include a relaxing lounge, cosy bar and charming restaurant.
ROOMS: 20 en suite (1 fmly) No smoking in 4 bedrooms s £75-£85; d £125-£145 (incl. bkfst) **LB** **FACILITIES:** Xmas **CONF:** Thtr 20 Board 16 Del from £125 **PARKING:** 20 **NOTES:** No smoking in restaurant Civ Wed 50 **CARDS:**

BROCKENHURST, Hampshire Map 05 SU30

★★★77% Rhinefield House
Rhinefield Rd SO42 7QB
☎ 01590 622922 01590 622800
e-mail: info@rhinefieldhousehotel.co.uk
Dir: *A35 towards Chistchurch. 3m from Lyndhurst turn left to Rhinefield, 1.5m to hotel*
This splendid 19th-century, mock-Elizabethan mansion is set in 40 acres of beautifully landscaped gardens. Bedrooms are spacious and great consideration is given to guest comfort. The open-plan lounge and bar overlook an ornamental pond and the elegant restaurant is impressive with antique features.

ROOMS: 34 en suite No smoking in 12 bedrooms s £100-£175; d £120-£220 (incl. bkfst) **LB** **FACILITIES:** STV Indoor swimming (H) Outdoor swimming (H) Tennis (hard) Sauna Solarium Gym Croquet lawn Putting green Jacuzzi Swimming pool supervised, new leisure facilities available from 2004 Xmas **CONF:** Thtr 120 Class 50 Board 35 Del from £140 **PARKING:** 100 **NOTES:** No dogs (ex guide dogs) No smoking in restaurant Civ Wed 125
CARDS:

★★★75% Balmer Lawn
Lyndhurst Rd SO42 7ZB
☎ 01590 623116 01590 623864
e-mail: info@balmerlawnhotel.co.uk
Dir: *A337 towards Lymington, hotel on left behind village cricket green*

Situated in the heart of the New Forest, this historic house provides comfortable public rooms and a good range of bedrooms. The terrace is ideal for watching the world go by. A selection of varied and enjoyable dishes is offered in the pleasant restaurant. This hotel is a popular conference venue.
ROOMS: 55 en suite (9 fmly) No smoking in 45 bedrooms s £70-£80; d £120-£140 (incl. bkfst) **LB** **FACILITIES: Spa** Indoor swimming (H) Outdoor swimming (H) Tennis (hard) Squash Sauna Gym Jacuzzi Xmas **CONF:** Thtr 150 Class 50 Board 50 Del from £120 **SERVICES:** Lift **PARKING:** 100 **NOTES:** No smoking in restaurant Civ Wed 120
CARDS:

See advert on opposite page

★★★75% Whitley Ridge Country House
Beaulieu Rd SO42 7QL
☎ 01590 622354 01590 622856
e-mail: whitleyridge@brockenhurst.co.uk
Dir: *via B3055 towards Beaulieu*
This charming hotel enjoys a picturesque setting in the heart of the New Forest. Day rooms include two relaxing lounges and large dining room, all with lovely views of the forest. Each bedroom has

continued

an individual style and bathrooms have been refurbished to a high standard. Enjoyable dining is another strong feature of this hotel, with fresh local ingredients playing a key role.

ROOMS: 14 rms (13 en suite) (1 GF) No smoking in all bedrooms s £65-£70; d £110-£112 (incl. bkfst) **LB FACILITIES:** STV Tennis (hard) Xmas **CONF:** Thtr 40 Class 40 Board 20 Del from £110 **PARKING:** 32 **NOTES:** No smoking in restaurant **CARDS:**

★★★74% ◎◎ *New Park Manor*

Lyndhurst Rd SO42 7QH
☎ 01590 623467 Y 🖷 01590 622268
e-mail: enquiries@newparkmanor.co.uk
Dir: *M21 junct 1, A337 to Lyndhurst & Brockenhurst. Hotel 1.5m on right*

Once the favoured hunting lodge of King Charles II, this well presented hotel enjoys a peaceful setting in extensive acreage of the New Forest and comes complete with an equestrian centre. Bedrooms have now been refurbished and are divided between the old house and a purpose-built wing, and the smart public areas include a new mezzanine lounge.

ROOMS: 24 en suite **FACILITIES:** Outdoor swimming (H) Tennis (hard) Riding Mountain biking **CONF:** Thtr 120 Class 52 Board 60 **PARKING:** 70 **NOTES:** No smoking in restaurant Civ Wed 120 **CARDS:**

★★★72% ◎ Careys Manor

New Forest SO42 7RH
☎ 01590 623551 🖷 01590 622799
e-mail: info@careysmanor.co.uk
Dir: *A337 towards Lyndhurst. Approaching Brockenhurst, hotel on left after 30mph sign*

An imposing building set back from the road on the outskirts of this New Forest town. The well-proportioned public areas include a spacious lounge, complete with inglenook fireplace, and an airy restaurant. Bedrooms are well equipped and of a generous size.

continued on p144

BROCKENHURST, continued

Le Blaireau Café within the grounds offers an alternative dining option with a French flavour.
ROOMS: 15 en suite 64 annexe en suite (32 GF) No smoking in 28 bedrooms s £89-£109; d £129-£199 (incl. bkfst) **LB** **FACILITIES:** STV Indoor swimming (H) Sauna Gym Croquet lawn Jacuzzi Steam room, Beauty therapists, Swimming pool supervised Xmas **CONF:** Thtr 120 Class 70 Board 40 Del from £155 **PARKING:** 180 **NOTES:** No dogs (ex guide dogs) No children 10yrs No smoking in restaurant Civ Wed 100
CARDS:

★★★67% Forest Park

Rhinefield Rd SO42 7ZG
☎ 01590 622844 01590 623948
e-mail: forest.park@forestdale.com
Forestdale Hotels
Dir: *A337 to Brockenhurst turn into Meerut Rd, follow road through Waters Green. Right at t-junct into Rhinefield Rd*
A friendly hotel offering good facilities for both adults and children. A heated pool, riding, children's meal times and a quiet location in the forest are a few of the advantages here. The well-equipped, comfortable bedrooms vary in size and style, and a choice of lounge and bar areas is available.
ROOMS: 38 en suite (2 fmly) (7 GF) No smoking in 2 bedrooms s fr £85; d fr £115 (incl. bkfst) **LB** **FACILITIES:** Outdoor swimming (H) Tennis (hard) Riding Sauna Xmas **CONF:** Thtr 50 Class 20 Board 24 Del from £115 **PARKING:** 80 **NOTES:** No smoking in restaurant Civ Wed 50 **CARDS:**

★★75% Cloud

Meerut Rd SO42 7TD
☎ 01590 622165 01590 622818
e-mail: enquiries@cloudhotel.co.uk
Dir: *1st right off A337, follow tourist signs*
This charming hotel enjoys a peaceful location on the edge of the village. The bedrooms are bright and comfortable with pine furnishings and smart en suite facilities. Public rooms include a selection of cosy lounges, a delightful rear garden with outdoor seating and a restaurant specialising in home-cooked wholesome English food.
ROOMS: 18 en suite (3 fmly) s £65; d £100-£130 (incl. bkfst) **LB** **FACILITIES:** Croquet lawn Xmas **CONF:** Thtr 40 Class 12 Board 12 Del £95 **PARKING:** 20 **NOTES:** No smoking in restaurant
CARDS:

★★66% Watersplash

The Rise SO42 7ZP
☎ 01590 622344 01590 624047
e-mail: bookings@watersplash.co.uk
Dir: *M3 junct 13/M27 junct 1/A337 S through Lyndhurst to Brockenhurst. Through Brockenhurst, The Rise on left, hotel on left*
This popular, welcoming Victorian hotel has been in the same family for 40 years. Upgraded bedrooms have co-ordinated decor and good facilities. The restaurant overlooks the neatly tended garden and there is also a comfortably furnished lounge, separate bar and an outdoor pool.
ROOMS: 23 en suite (6 fmly) s £49-£79; d £78-£174 (incl. bkfst) **LB** **FACILITIES:** Outdoor swimming (H) Xmas **CONF:** Thtr 80 Class 20 Board 20 **PARKING:** 29 **NOTES:** No smoking in restaurant
CARDS:

BROMBOROUGH, Merseyside — Map 15 SJ38

Travel Inn (Wirral Bromborough)

High St, Bromborough Cross CH62 7EZ
☎ 08701 977273 0151 344 0443
travel inn
Dir: *on A41 New Chester Road, 2m from M53 junct 5*
Travel Inn offers good-quality, value-for-money accommodation. Spacious, en suite rooms with bath and shower comfortably accommodate a family of up to two adults and two children (to age 15). The restaurant and bar offers a varied menu. For further details and the Travel Inn phone number, consult the Hotel Groups page.
ROOMS: 32 en suite s £44.95; d £44.95 **CONF:** Thtr 80 Board 35

BROME, Suffolk — Map 13 TM17

★★★76% Cornwallis Country Hotel & Restaurant

IP23 8AJ
☎ 01379 870326 01379 870051
e-mail: info@thecornwallis.com
Dir: *off B1077, at junct with A140, 50yds towards Eye*

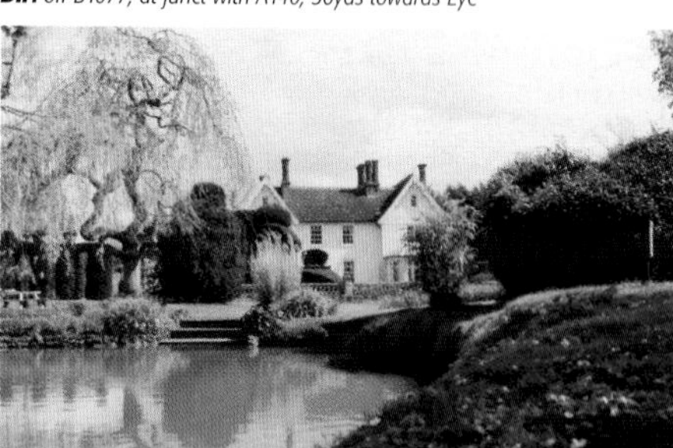

This attractive former manor house sits at the end of a tree-lined drive amid a topiary garden. Bedrooms, which are comfortable and tastefully furnished with period pieces, are divided between the main house and the former coach house. The popular bar serves a wide range of brasserie dishes and the main restaurant provides a more formal option.
ROOMS: 11 en suite 5 annexe en suite (2 fmly) (2 GF) No smoking in 4 bedrooms s £91-£96; d £113-£165 (incl. bkfst) **LB** **FACILITIES:** STV Archery Hot air ballooning Xmas **CONF:** Thtr 120 Class 60 Board 48 Del £129.95 **PARKING:** 200 **NOTES:** No smoking in restaurant Civ Wed 120
CARDS:

BROMLEY, Greater London
See LONDON SECTION plan 1 G1

★★★73% Bromley Court

Bromley Hill BR1 4JD
☎ 020 8461 8600 020 8460 0899
e-mail: bromleyhotel@btinternet.com
Best Western
Dir: *N, signed off A21. Opposite Mercedes Benz garage on Bromley Hill*
This grand mansion is set in three acres of grounds. The refurbished restaurant offers good choice of meals in comfortable surroundings. Bedrooms are appointed to a good modern standard, each well designed and thoughtfully equipped. Extensive facilities include a leisure club and a good range of meeting rooms.
ROOMS: 116 en suite (4 fmly) No smoking in 35 bedrooms s £95-£107; d £105-£120 (incl. bkfst) **LB** **FACILITIES:** **Spa** STV Sauna Gym Jacuzzi entertainment **CONF:** Thtr 150 Class 80 Board 45 Del from £140 **SERVICES:** Lift **PARKING:** 100 **NOTES:** Civ Wed 50
CARDS:

BROMSGROVE, Worcestershire — Map 10 SO97

★★★★66% ֍ Hanover International Hotel & Club

Kidderminster Rd B61 9AB
☎ 01527 576600 📠 01527 878981
e-mail: jason.thorley@hanover-international.com
Dir: *on A448, 1m W of Bromsgrove town centre*

Public areas in this striking building have a Mediterranean theme with white-washed walls, a courtyard garden and plenty of natural light. Bedrooms are in a variety of styles; some are more compact than others and all offer an excellent working environment for the business guest. Leisure facilities include a steam room, pool and gym.
ROOMS: 114 en suite (17 fmly) (34 GF) No smoking in 77 bedrooms s £135; d £150 **LB FACILITIES: Spa** STV Indoor swimming (H) Snooker Sauna Solarium Gym Jacuzzi Childrens play area Xmas **CONF:** BC Thtr 200 Class 140 Board 30 Del from £99 **SERVICES:** Lift **PARKING:** 250 **NOTES:** No smoking in restaurant RS Xmas wk Civ Wed 200 **CARDS:**

⌂ Innkeeper's Lodge Bromsgrove

462 Birmingham Rd, Marlbrook B61 0HR
☎ 01527 878060
Dir: *on A38 0.5m between M5 & M42*
A new concept in the travel accommodation market. Smart rooms meet essential business requirements but also have home comforts. Dining options include all-day menus plus the added advantage of breakfast, which is included in the room price. For further details, consult the Hotel Groups page.
ROOMS: 29 en suite

⌂ Premier Lodge (Bromsgrove)

Worcester Rd, Upton Warren B61 7ET
☎ 0870 9906408 📠 0870 9906409
Premier Lodge offers modern, well-equipped, en suite accommodation suitable for both business and leisure travellers. Meals can be taken at the adjacent popular restaurant and bar, which is fully licensed. For further details, consult the Hotel Groups page.
ROOMS: 27 en suite s £48; d £48 **CONF:** Board 10

⌂ Travel Inn Bromsgrove

Birmingham Rd B61 0BA
☎ 08701 977 044 📠 01527 - 834719
Travel Inn offers good-quality, value-for-money accommodation. Spacious, en suite rooms with bath and shower comfortably accommodate a family of up to two adults and two children (to age 15). The restaurant and bar offers a varied menu. For further details and the Travel Inn phone number, consult the Hotel Groups page.
ROOMS: 74 en suite

⌂ Travel Inn Bromsgrove

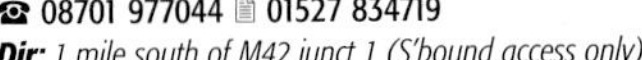

Birmingham Rd B61 0BA
☎ 08701 977044 📠 01527 834719
Dir: *1 mile south of M42 junct 1 (S'bound access only). M5 junct 4 (S'bound). Follow A38 to Bromsgrove. M5 junct 5 (N'bound). Follow A38 through Bromsgrove. Inn 0.5 N of town centre*
Travel Inn offers good-quality, value-for-money accommodation. Spacious, en suite rooms with bath and shower comfortably accommodate a family of up to two adults and two children (to age 15). The restaurant and bar offers a varied menu. For further details and the Travel Inn phone number, consult the Hotel Groups page.
ROOMS: 74 en suite s £44.95; d £44.95

BROOK (NEAR CADNAM), Hampshire — Map 05 SU21

★★★67% ֍ Bell Inn

SO43 7HE
☎ 023 8081 2214 📠 023 8081 3958
e-mail: bell@bramshaw.co.uk
Dir: *M27 junct 1 onto B3079, hotel 1.5m on right*

The Inn is part of the Bramshaw Golf Club and has tailored its style to suit this market, but it is also an ideal base from which to visit the New Forest. Bedrooms are comfortable and attractively furnished, and the public areas, particularly the welcoming bar, have a cosy and friendly atmosphere.
ROOMS: 25 en suite (8 GF) No smoking in 11 bedrooms s £65-£75; d £90-£110 (incl. bkfst) **LB FACILITIES:** Golf 18 Putting green Xmas **CONF:** Thtr 50 Class 20 Board 30 Del from £92 **PARKING:** 150 **NOTES:** No dogs (ex guide dogs) No smoking in restaurant
CARDS:

BROXTON, Cheshire — Map 15 SJ45

★★★★74% De Vere Carden Park

Carden Park CH3 9DQ
☎ 01829 731000 📠 01829 731599
e-mail: reservations.carden@devere-hotels.com
Dir: *M56 junct 15/M53 Chester. Take A41 for Whitchurch for approx 8m. At Broxton rdbt right onto A534 Wrexham. Hotel 1.5m on left*
This impressive 17th-century Cheshire estate is set amid 750 acres of mature parkland. The hotel offers superb leisure facilities including challenging golf courses, a fully equipped gym, a swimming pool and popular spa. Traditionally furnished and decorated bedrooms are spacious and equipped with a

continued on p146

BROXTON, continued

comprehensive range of extras. Staff throughout are keen to please.

De Vere Carden Park, Broxton

ROOMS: 115 en suite 77 annexe en suite (24 fmly) No smoking in 134 bedrooms s £130-£150; d £150-£170 (incl. bkfst) **LB** **FACILITIES: Spa** STV Indoor swimming (H) Golf 27 Tennis (hard) Snooker Sauna Solarium Gym Croquet lawn Putting green Jacuzzi Archery, Quadbikes, Off road driving, Mountain biking, Walking trails Xmas **CONF:** BC Thtr 400 Class 240 Board 125 Del from £145 **SERVICES:** Lift **PARKING:** 500 **NOTES:** No dogs (ex guide dogs) No smoking in restaurant Civ Wed 100 **CARDS:**

★★71% Broxton Hall

Whitchurch Rd CH3 9JS
☎ 01829 782321 01829 782330
e-mail: reservations@broxtonhall.co.uk
Dir: *On A41 S of Chester at Broxton rdbt (on Whitchurch side) A534, between Whitchurch & Chester*

Set in beautiful grounds, this impressive half-timbered Tudor hall offers elegant public areas with antique and period furnishings. The bedrooms are individually furnished to a high standard, some with beautiful antique four-poster beds. The hotel boasts a popular restaurant, which overlooks the well-tended gardens. There is a spacious and comfortable bar and a choice of comfortable sitting rooms.

ROOMS: 10 en suite **FACILITIES:** Croquet lawn **CONF:** Thtr 25 Class 25 Board 25 **PARKING:** 30 **NOTES:** No smoking in restaurant Civ Wed 55 **CARDS:**

BRUTON, Somerset — Map 04 ST63

Restaurant with Rooms

The Claire de Lune Restaurant with Rooms

2-4 HIgh St BA10 0AA
☎ 01749 813395 01749 813395
e-mail: enquiries@claredelune.co.uk
Dir: *in centre of Bruton at eastern end of High Street*

This pleasant restaurant with rooms offers comfortable bedrooms and a delightful lounge and terrace. Fine dining in the restaurant presents interesting, well-prepared dishes, which use the freshest local produce and provide a memorable aspect to your stay. The welcoming proprietors make every effort to ensure guests' comfort.

ROOMS: 3 en suite s £35; d £55 (incl. bkfst) **LB** **FACILITIES:** Xmas **NOTES:** No dogs (ex guide dogs) No children 8yrs No smoking in restaurant Closed 1st 2 weeks Jan RS Oct-Nov & Feb-Mar
CARDS:

BRYHER See Scilly, Isles of

BUCKDEN, North Yorkshire — Map 18 SD97

★★70% Buck Inn

BD23 5JA
☎ 01756 760228 & 760416 01756 760227
e-mail: thebuckinn@buckden.yorks.net
Dir: *A59/B6265 to Threshfield, then B6160 to Buckden through Kettlewell & Starbotton*

This traditional Georgian inn is privately owned, personally run and provides warm and friendly hospitality. Fine views can be enjoyed from many of the well-equipped bedrooms, which are smartly presented. There is a cosy lounge area for visitors and a wide range of interesting snacks and meals is served in the lounge bar. The Courtyard restaurant provides a more formal menu using fresh, local, quality produce.

ROOMS: 14 en suite (2 fmly) **CONF:** Class 30 **PARKING:** 30 **NOTES:** No smoking in restaurant Closed 2 wks early Jan **CARDS:**

BUCKHURST HILL, Essex — Map 06 TQ49

★★★62% The Roebuck Hotel

corus hotels

North End IG9 5QY
☎ 020 8505 4636 020 8504 7826
e-mail: theroebuck@corushotels.com
Dir: *M25 junct 26 to B1393 Epping, then take A104 for Woodford, turn left directly after Fiat garage & at top of hill left again. Hotel 200yds on right*

An 18th-century former alehouse situated in a peaceful residential area, yet only ten minutes drive from the M25. Public areas feature the smart Addendum Brasserie with its bold colour scheme, which also extends to the bar and adjacent lounge. Bedrooms are generally quite spacious; each one is pleasantly furnished and thoughtfully equipped.

ROOMS: 28 en suite No smoking in 10 bedrooms **FACILITIES:** STV **CONF:** Thtr 200 Class 60 Board 14 **PARKING:** 40 **NOTES:** Civ Wed 120 **CARDS:**

Express by Holiday Inn

Express by Holiday Inn

High Rd IG9 5HT
☎ 020 8504 4450 020 8498 0011

A modern hotel ideal for families and business travellers. Fresh and uncomplicated, the spacious bedrooms include Sky TV, power shower and tea and coffee-making facilities. Continental buffet breakfast is included in the room rate; other meals may be taken at the nearby family pub or restaurant. For

continued

further details and the Express by Holiday Inn phone number, consult the Hotel Groups pages.

ROOMS: 49 en suite **CONF:** Thtr 30 Class 24 Board 16

BUCKINGHAM, Buckinghamshire Map 11 SP63

★★★★69% Villiers

3 Castle St MK18 1BS
☎ 01280 822444 01280 822113
e-mail: villiers@villiers-hotels.demon.co.uk

Guests can enjoy a town centre location with a high degree of comfort at this 400-year-old former coaching inn. Relaxing public areas feature flagstone floors, oak panelling and real fires whilst bedrooms are modern, spacious and equipped to a high level. Diners can unwind in the atmospheric Swan and Castle bar before taking dinner in the award-winning Henry's restaurant.

ROOMS: 46 en suite (43 fmly) **FACILITIES:** STV Free membership of nearby private leisure club entertainment **CONF:** Thtr 250 Class 120 Board 80 **SERVICES:** Lift **PARKING:** 53 **NOTES:** No dogs (ex guide dogs) Civ Wed 150 **CARDS:**

See advert on this page

★★★66% Buckingham Beales

Buckingham Ring Rd MK18 1RY
☎ 01280 822622 01280 823074
e-mail: buckingham@bealeshotels.co.uk

Dir: *M1 junct 13/14 follow signs to Buckingham-A422/A421. M40 exit junct 9/10 follow signs Buckingham. Hotel on ring road*

A purpose built hotel which offers spacious rooms with well-designed working spaces for business travellers. There are also extensive conference facilities. The open-plan restaurant and bar offers a good range of dishes, and the well-equipped leisure suite is popular with guests.

ROOMS: 70 en suite (6 fmly) No smoking in 24 bedrooms s £75-£80; d £85-£90 **LB FACILITIES:** STV Indoor swimming (H) Sauna Solarium Gym Jacuzzi Xmas **CONF:** Thtr 160 Class 90 Board 30 Del from £125 **PARKING:** 120 **NOTES:** No smoking in restaurant Civ Wed 160 **CARDS:**

Late for dinner?
Quality Standards mean that last orders for dinner vary according to star rating and should be no earlier than:
★★ 7.00pm ★★★ 8.00pm ★★★★ 9.00pm
★★★★★ 10.00pm

Need a break without breaking the bank?
Latebeds offers last-minute deals with no nasty surprises at AA-approved hotels and B&Bs. Visit www.theAA.com to find out more

BUCKLAND (NEAR BROADWAY), Gloucestershire Map 10 SP03

Top 200 - Hotel

★★★ Buckland Manor

WR12 7LY ***Dir:*** *off B4632*
☎ 01386 852626 01386 853557
e-mail: buckland-manor-uk@msn.com

A grand 13th-century manor house in extensive grounds with beautiful gardens. Crackling log fires warm the wonderful lounges; everything is geared to encourage rest and relaxation. Bedrooms and public areas are furnished with high quality pieces and decorated in keeping with the style of the manor. The cuisine continues to impress, with high quality produce skilfully used.

ROOMS: 13 en suite (2 fmly) (4 GF) s £225-£360; d £235-£370 (incl. bkfst) **FACILITIES:** STV Outdoor swimming Tennis (hard) Croquet lawn Putting green Xmas **PARKING:** 30 **NOTES:** No dogs No children 12yrs No smoking in restaurant **CARDS:**

B

BUDE, Cornwall & Isles of Scilly

Map 02 SS20

★★★70% Falcon

Breakwater Rd EX23 8SD
☎ 01288 352005 📠 01288 356359
e-mail: reception@falconhotel.com
Dir: *off A39 into Bude, follow road to Widemouth Bay. Hotel on right over canal bridge*

Dating back to 1798, this long-established hotel boasts delightful walled gardens, ideal for afternoon teas. Bedrooms all offer high standards of comfort and quality, with a four-poster room available complete with spa bath. A choice of menus is offered in the elegant restaurant or the friendly bar, and there is an impressive function room.
ROOMS: 29 en suite (7 fmly) s £48-£51; d £96-£102 (incl. bkfst) **LB** **FACILITIES:** STV Croquet lawn Mini gym **CONF:** BC Thtr 200 Class 50 Board 50 Del from £70 **PARKING:** 40 **NOTES:** No smoking in restaurant RS 25 Dec Civ Wed 150 **CARDS:**

★★★68% Camelot

Downs View EX23 8RE
☎ 01288 352361 📠 01288 355470
e-mail: stay@camelot-hotel.co.uk
Dir: *off A39 into Bude town centre, join one-way system, left lane, bottom of hill on left*

This friendly and welcoming Edwardian property offers a range of facilities including a smart and comfortable conservatory bar and lounge, a games room and Hawkers restaurant, which offers skilful cooking using much local produce. Bedrooms are light and airy, with high standards of housekeeping and maintenance.
ROOMS: 24 en suite (2 fmly) (7 GF) No smoking in 21 bedrooms s £39-£53; d £78-£86 (incl. bkfst) **LB** **FACILITIES:** Darts Pool table Table tennis ch fac **PARKING:** 21 **NOTES:** No dogs (ex guide dogs) No smoking in restaurant Closed Xmas & New Year
CARDS:

★★★68% *Hartland*

Hartland Ter EX23 8JY
☎ 01288 355661 📠 01288 355664
e-mail: hartlandhotel@aol.com
Dir: *off A39 to Bude, follow town centre signs. Left into Hartland Terrace opp Boots chemist. Hotel at seaward end of road*

Enjoying a pleasantly quiet, yet convenient location, the Hartland has excellent sea views. A popular stay for those wishing to tour the area and also with families, this hotel offers entertainment on many evenings throughout the year. Bedrooms are comfortable and offer a range of sizes. The public areas are smart, and in the dining room, a pleasant fixed price menu is available.
ROOMS: 28 en suite (2 fmly) No smoking in 8 bedrooms **FACILITIES:** Outdoor swimming (H) entertainment **SERVICES:** Lift **PARKING:** 30 **NOTES:** No smoking in restaurant Closed mid Nov-Etr (ex Xmas & New Year)

★★69% ◎ Atlantic House

17-18 Summerleaze Crescent EX23 8HJ
☎ 01288 352451 📠 01288 356666
e-mail: enq@atlantichousehotel.co.uk
Dir: *M5 junct 31, follow A30 to by-pass in Okehampton. Follow signs to Bude via Halwill & Holsworthy*

Facing south overlooking the beach, this relaxed and personally run hotel is set in a quiet area. Bedrooms vary in size and style, all are comfortable and well maintained. The sunsets are memorable, ask for a room on the front. An important component of a stay here is the impressive cuisine, which features an imaginative, well-balanced fixed-price menu.
ROOMS: 16 en suite (2 fmly) No smoking in all bedrooms s £26-£28; d £52-£56 (incl. bkfst) **LB** **FACILITIES:** Games room Multi-activity outdoor sports **PARKING:** 10 **NOTES:** No dogs (ex guide dogs) No smoking in restaurant Closed mid-Nov - mid-Feb
CARDS:

★★67% Penarvor

Crooklets Beach EX23 8NE
☎ 01288 352036 📠 01288 355027
e-mail: hotel.penarvor@mcmail.com
Dir: *From A39 towards Bude for 1.5m. At 2nd rdbt right, pass shops. Top of hill left signed Crooklets Beach*

Adjacent to the golf course and overlooking Crooklets Beach, this family owned hotel benefits from a relaxed and friendly atmosphere. Bedrooms vary in size and are all equipped to a similar standard. An interesting selection of dishes, using fresh local produce, is available in the restaurant; bar meals are also provided.
ROOMS: 16 en suite (6 fmly) No smoking in all bedrooms s £30-£40; d £54-£68 (incl. bkfst) **LB** **PARKING:** 20 **NOTES:** No smoking in restaurant **CARDS:**

B

★★66% ***Maer Lodge***
Maer Down Rd, Crooklets Beach EX23 8NG

☎ 01288 353306 🖷 01288 354005
e-mail: maerlodgehotel@btinternet.com
Dir: *exit A39 at Stratton. Right at mini rdbt into The Strand, up Belle Vue past shops. Left at Somerfield to Crooklets Beach, hotel on right*
With views over the Downs and surrounding countryside, this long established, family-run hotel is quietly located. Traditionally furnished public areas are comfortable and include a convivial bar and spacious lounge. A short fixed-price menu is offered in the dining room. Bedrooms are soundly furnished and well appointed, and some have lovely views.
ROOMS: 19 en suite (4 fmly) No smoking in all bedrooms
FACILITIES: STV Putting green **CONF:** Thtr 60 Class 40 Board 15
PARKING: 15 **NOTES:** No smoking in restaurant
CARDS:

A ★★ **Barrel Rock**
41-43 Killerton Rd EX23 8EN
☎ 01288 352252 🖷 01288 353122
e-mail: peter@barrelrockhotel.co.uk
ROOMS: 9 en suite (1 GF) No smoking in all bedrooms s £32-£36; d £50-£65 (incl. bkfst) **PARKING:** 6 **NOTES:** No smoking in restaurant Closed 24 Dec-16 Jan **CARDS:**

BUNGAY, Suffolk Map 13 TM38

★★64% **Kings Head**
2 Market Place NR35 1AW
☎ 01986 893583 🖷 01986 893583
Dir: *Off A143 to town centre. Hotel located in town centre opposite The Three Tuns*
This 18th-century coaching inn is situated in the heart of town, amid a range of antique shops. The spacious bedrooms are furnished in pine pieces and equipped with a good range of useful extras; one room has a superb four-poster bed. Public rooms include the Oddfellows bar, Luciano's restaurant and the Duke of Wellington lounge bar.
ROOMS: 12 en suite (1 fmly) No smoking in 4 bedrooms s £35; d £59.50 (incl. bkfst) **LB** **CONF:** Thtr 80 Class 50 Board 30
PARKING: 29 **NOTES:** No dogs (ex guide dogs) No smoking in restaurant **CARDS:**

BURFORD, Oxfordshire Map 05 SP21

★★★74% 🏵🏵 **The Lamb Inn**
Sheep St OX18 4LR
☎ 01993 823155 🖷 01993 822228
e-mail: info@lambinn-burford.co.uk
Dir: *Turn off A40 into Burford, downhill, take 1st left into Sheep St, hotel last on right*

A stone's throw from the centre of this quintessential Cotswold town, this delightful old inn possesses an abundance of character and charm. The bedrooms retain many original features and there is a selection of comfortable lounges with flagstone floors and log fires together with an atmospheric bar in which to relax. In the elegant restaurant carefully cooked meals are served, using the best of ingredients.
ROOMS: 15 en suite (3 GF) No smoking in all bedrooms s £100; d fr £130 (incl. bkfst) **LB** **FACILITIES:** Xmas **NOTES:** No smoking in restaurant **CARDS:**

★★★73% 🏵 **The Bay Tree**
12-14 Sheep St OX18 4LW
☎ 01993 822791 🖷 01993 823008
e-mail: bookings@cotswold-inns-hotels.co.uk
Dir: *off A40, down hill onto A361 towards Burford, Sheep St 1st left*
History and modern flair sit happily side by side at this delightful old inn, situated near to the town centre. Bedrooms are tastefully furnished using the original features to good effect and some have four-poster and half tester beds. Public areas consist of a characterful bar, a sophisticated, airy restaurant, a selection of meeting rooms and an attractive walled garden.
ROOMS: 7 en suite 14 annexe en suite (2 fmly) s £119-£230; d £155-£230 (incl. bkfst) **LB** **FACILITIES:** Croquet lawn Xmas
CONF: Thtr 40 Class 12 Board 25 Del from £145 **PARKING:** 50
NOTES: No smoking in restaurant Civ Wed 70
CARDS:

★★★68% **Cotswold Gateway**
Cheltenham Rd OX18 4HX
☎ 01993 822695 🖷 01993 823600
e-mail: cotswold.gateway@dial.pipex.com
Dir: *Hotel on rdbt at A40 Oxford/Cheltenham at junct with A361*
Ideally suited for both business and pleasure guests, The Cotswold Gateway Hotel is prominently situated on the A40 and yet only a short walk away from Burford. The tastefully decorated bedrooms include two, four-poster rooms. Diners have an extensive choice of popular dishes and the option of eating in the character bar or in the more formal atmosphere of the restaurant. A small coffee shop is also available.
ROOMS: 13 en suite 8 annexe en suite (2 fmly) No smoking in all bedrooms **CONF:** Thtr 40 Class 20 Board 24 **PARKING:** 60
NOTES: No dogs (ex guide dogs) No smoking in restaurant
CARDS:

★★★61% 🏵 **The Inn For All Seasons**
The Barringtons OX18 4TN
THE INDEPENDENTS
☎ 01451 844324 🖷 01451 844375
e-mail: sharp@innforallseasons.com
Dir: *3m W of Burford on A40 towards Cheltenham*

This 16th-century coaching inn is conveniently near to Burford. Bedrooms are steadily being upgraded with bright and attractive décor and public areas retain a feeling of period charm with

continued on p150

B

BURFORD, continued

original fireplaces and oak beams. A good selection of bar meals is available at lunchtime whilst the evening menu includes an appetising selection of fresh fish.
ROOMS: 9 en suite 1 annexe en suite (2 fmly) (1 GF) s £52-£55; d £89-£93 (incl. bkfst) **LB** **FACILITIES:** STV Clay pigeon shooting Xmas **CONF:** Thtr 25 Class 30 Board 30 Del from £115 **PARKING:** 62 **CARDS:**

★★65% Golden Pheasant
91 High St OX18 4QA
☎ 01993 823223 📠 01993 822621
e-mail: goldenpheasant.burford@oldenglishinns.co.uk
Dir: *M40 junct 8, follow signs A40 Cheltenham into Burford*
This attractive old inn is set on Burford's main street and dates, in part, back to the 16th century. Bedrooms can be compact and are well furnished with attractive fabrics, period furniture and many useful extras. The bar boasts a fine selection of wines, and meals are available here and in the restaurant.
ROOMS: 12 rms (11 en suite) (1 fmly) (2 GF) s £65-£75; d £85-£110 (incl. bkfst) **LB** **FACILITIES:** Xmas **PARKING:** 12 **NOTES:** No smoking in restaurant **CARDS:**

Travelodge (Cotswolds)
Bury Barn OX8 4JF
☎ 08700 850 950 📠 01993 822699
Dir: *A40*
Travelodge offers good quality, good value, modern accommodation. Ideal for families, the spacious, en suite bedrooms include remote-control TV, tea and coffee-making facilities, luxury beds and free morning newspaper. Meals can be taken at the nearby family restaurant. For further details and the Travelodge phone number, consult the Hotel Groups page.
ROOMS: 40 en suite s fr £42.95; d fr £42.95

BURLEY, Hampshire — Map 05 SU20

★★★68% Burley Manor
Ringwood Rd BH24 4BS
☎ 01425 403522 📠 01425 403227
e-mail: burley.manor@forestdale.com
Dir: *leave A31 at Burley sign, hotel 3m on left*
Set in extensive grounds, this 18th-century hotel enjoys a relaxed ambience and a peaceful setting. Half of the well-equipped, comfortable bedrooms, including several with four-posters, are located in the main house and the remainder, many of which have balconies, in the adjacent converted stable block. Cosy public rooms benefit from log fires in winter months.
ROOMS: 21 en suite 17 annexe en suite (3 fmly) (17 GF) No smoking in 4 bedrooms s fr £105; d fr £125 (incl. bkfst) **LB** **FACILITIES:** Outdoor swimming (H) Fishing Riding Croquet lawn Xmas **CONF:** Thtr 60 Class 40 Board 40 Del from £121 **PARKING:** 60 **NOTES:** No smoking in restaurant Civ Wed **CARDS:**

★★★66% Moorhill House
BH24 4AH
☎ 01425 403285 📠 01425 403715
e-mail: moorhill@newforesthotels.co.uk
Dir: *M27, A31, follow signs to Burley village, through village, up hill, turn right opposite school and cricket grounds*
Situated deep in the heart of the New Forest and formerly a grand gentleman's residence, this charming hotel offers a relaxed and friendly environment. Bedrooms are of varying size and smartly decorated. A range of facilities is provided and guests can relax by walking around the extensive grounds. Both dinner and breakfast offer a choice of interesting and freshly prepared dishes.
ROOMS: 31 en suite (13 fmly) (3 GF) s £68-£80; d £120-£130 (incl. bkfst) **LB** **FACILITIES:** Indoor swimming (H) Sauna Gym Croquet lawn Putting green badminton (Apr-Sep) Xmas **CONF:** Thtr 120 Class 60 Board 65 Del from £90 **PARKING:** 50 **NOTES:** No smoking in restaurant Civ Wed **CARDS:**

BURNHAM, Buckinghamshire — Map 06 SU98

★★★72% Grovefield
Taplow Common Rd SL1 8LP
☎ 01628 603131 📠 01628 668078
e-mail: grovefield@macdonald-hotels.co.uk
Dir: *From M4 left on A4 towards Maidenhead. Next rdbt turn right under railway bridge. Straight over mini rdbt, garage on right. Continue for 1.5m, hotel on right*

Set in its own spacious grounds, the Grovefield is conveniently located for Heathrow Airport as well as the industrial centres of Slough and Maidenhead. Accommodation is spacious and well presented and most have views over the attractive gardens. Public areas include a range of meeting rooms, comfortable bar/lounge area and Hamilton's restaurant.
ROOMS: 40 en suite (5 fmly) (7 GF) No smoking in 24 bedrooms s £90-£145; d £120-£195 (incl. bkfst) **LB** **FACILITIES:** STV Fishing Croquet lawn Putting green Xmas **CONF:** Thtr 180 Class 80 Board 80 Del from £140 **SERVICES:** Lift **PARKING:** 155 **NOTES:** No smoking in restaurant Civ Wed 200 **CARDS:**

★★★67% *Burnham Beeches Hotel*
Grove Rd SL1 8DP
☎ 01628 429955 📠 01628 603994
Dir: *A355 towards Slough. Over 1st rbt, right at 2nd and right at 3rd, follow hotel signs*

Set in attractive mature grounds on the fringes of woodland, this extended Georgian manor house has spacious and comfortable bedrooms which are well equipped. Public rooms include a cosy lounge-bar offering all-day snacks, an elegant wood-panelled

continued

B

restaurant providing interesting cuisine, conference facilities, a fitness centre and pool.
ROOMS: 82 en suite (19 fmly) No smoking in 18 bedrooms **FACILITIES:** STV Indoor swimming (H) Tennis (hard) Sauna Gym Croquet lawn Jacuzzi **CONF:** Thtr 180 Class 100 Board 60 **SERVICES:** Lift **PARKING:** 200 **NOTES:** No dogs (ex guide dogs) Civ Wed 120 **CARDS:**

BURNHAM MARKET, Norfolk Map 13 TF84

★★77% Hoste Arms

The Green PE31 8HD
☎ 01328 738777 01328 730103
e-mail: reception@hostearms.co.uk
Dir: *signed on B1155, 5m W of Wells-next-the-Sea*

Stylish, privately owned inn situated in the heart of this bustling village close to the North Norfolk coastline. The extensive public rooms feature a range of dining areas that include a conservatory with plush furniture, a sunny patio and a traditional pub. The tastefully furnished, thoughtfully equipped bedrooms are generally very spacious and offer a high degree of comfort.
ROOMS: 36 en suite (1 fmly) (7 GF) s £74-£156; d £102-£172 (incl. bkfst) **LB FACILITIES:** Xmas **CONF:** BC Thtr 43 Class 22 Board 26 Del from £115 **PARKING:** 45 **CARDS:**

BURNLEY, Lancashire Map 18 SD83

★★★74% Oaks

Colne Rd, Reedley BB10 2LF
☎ 01282 414141 01282 433401
e-mail: oaks@shirehotels.co.uk
Dir: *M65 junct 12. Follow signs to Burnley. At B&Q mini rdbt left, right at rdbt, right onto A682. Hotel 1m on left*

SHIRE HOTELS

The friendly team here provide super hospitality in this former Victorian coffee merchant's house. The hotel offers traditional

continued on p152

BURNLEY, continued

public areas and modern, well-equipped bedrooms. Gym, pool, sauna and steam rooms are all available in the leisure club on site. *Shire Hotels – AA Hotel Group of the Year 2003-2004.*
ROOMS: 50 en suite (10 fmly) No smoking in 31 bedrooms s £73-£114; d £96-£134 (incl. bkfst) **LB** **FACILITIES: Spa** STV Indoor swimming (H) Sauna Solarium Gym Steam room, Swimming pool supervised Xmas **CONF:** Thtr 120 Class 48 Board 60 Del from £85 **PARKING:** 110 **NOTES:** No dogs (ex guide dogs) No smoking in restaurant Civ Wed 100 **CARDS:**

See advert on page 151

★★★71% Sparrow Hawk
Church St BB11 2DN
☎ 01282 421551 01282 456506
e-mail: enquiries@sparrowhawkhotel.co.uk
Dir: *M65 junct 10, 5th exit at traffic island (Cavalry Way), left at next island right lane along Westway, right at lights. Take 2nd exit from rdbt, 2nd exit at next rdbt. Hotel 300yds on right*
This grand Victorian hotel is centrally located and is handy for key local attractions. Bedrooms vary in size and style but all are modern, well equipped and have a host of thoughtful extras. Stylish public areas include the bright Mediterranean-style Smithies Café Bar, Farriers Restaurant and a traditional bar serving speciality ale. Staff throughout are particularly friendly.
ROOMS: 35 en suite (1 fmly) No smoking in 9 bedrooms s £47-£55; d £53-£75 (incl. bkfst) **LB** **FACILITIES:** STV entertainment Xmas **CONF:** BC Thtr 80 Class 50 Board 40 Del from £49.50 **PARKING:** 20 **NOTES:** No dogs (ex guide dogs) **CARDS:**

★★★68% Rosehill House
Rosehill Av BB11 2PW
☎ 01282 453931 01282 455628
e-mail: rhhotel@provider.co.uk
Dir: *0.5m S of Burnley town centre, off A682*
This fine Grade II listed building stands its own leafy grounds in a quiet area of town. There are two restaurants (one a tapas bar) and a comfortable lounge bar. In addition to the standard accommodation, two loft conversions and a former coach house offer a range of stylish individual bedrooms.
ROOMS: 30 en suite (3 fmly) No smoking in 1 bedroom s £50-£65; d £56-£75 (incl. bkfst) **LB** **FACILITIES:** STV Snooker Gym **CONF:** BC Thtr 50 Class 30 Board 30 **PARKING:** 52 **NOTES:** No dogs (ex guide dogs) Civ Wed 100 **CARDS:**

Travel Inn

Queen Victoria Rd BB10 3EF
☎ 08701 977045 01282 448431
Dir: *M65 junct 12 take 5th exit at rdbt, 1st exit at rdbt, keep in right lane at lights, at next rdbt, 2nd exit then 3rd at next rdbt, under bridge turn left before football ground*
Travel Inn offers good-quality, value-for-money accommodation. Spacious, en suite rooms with bath and shower comfortably accommodate a family of up to two adults and two children (to age 15). The restaurant and bar offers a varied menu. For further details and Travel Inn phone number, consult Hotel Groups page.
ROOMS: 40 en suite s £44.95; d £44.95

Travelodge

Cavalry Barracks, Barracks Rd BB11 4AS
☎ 08700 850 950 01282 416039
Dir: *junct A671/A679*
Travelodge offers good quality, good value, modern accommodation. Ideal for families, the spacious, en suite bedrooms include remote-control TV, tea and coffee-making facilities, luxury beds and free morning newspaper. Meals can be taken at the nearby family restaurant. For further details and the Travelodge phone number, consult the Hotel Groups page.
ROOMS: 32 en suite s fr £42.95; d fr £42.95

BURNSALL, North Yorkshire Map 19 SE06

★★70% Red Lion Hotel
By the Bridge BD23 6BU
☎ 01756 720204 01756 720292
e-mail: redlion@daelnet.co.uk
Dir: *on B6160 between Grassington and Bolton Abbey*
This delightful 16th-century Dales inn stands adjacent to a five-arch bridge over the idyllic River Wharfe. Attractive, comfortable bedrooms are well equipped and public areas include a homely lounge and a traditional oak-panelled bar. The elegant restaurant makes excellent use of fresh local ingredients and breakfasts are memorable. Guests are free to fish in the hotel's own stretch of water.
ROOMS: 7 en suite 4 annexe en suite (2 fmly) (2 GF) s £58-£65; d £115-£140 (incl. bkfst) **LB** **FACILITIES:** Fishing Xmas **CONF:** Thtr 30 Class 10 Board 20 Del from £100 **PARKING:** 80 **NOTES:** No smoking in restaurant Civ Wed 50 **CARDS:**

BURRINGTON (NEAR PORTSMOUTH ARMS STATION), Devon Map 03 SS61

Top 200 - Hotel

★★★ Northcote Manor
EX37 9LZ
☎ 01769 560501 01769 560770
e-mail: rest@northcotemanor.co.uk
Dir: *off A377 opp Portsmouth Arms, into hotel drive. Do not enter Burrington village*
A warm and friendly welcome is assured at this beautiful country house hotel. Built in 1716, the house sits in 20 acres of grounds and woodlands. Guests can enjoy wonderful views over the Taw River Valley whilst relaxing in the environment created by the attentive staff. An elegant restaurant is a highlight with the finest of local produce used in well-prepared dishes. Bedrooms, including some suites, are individually styled, spacious and well appointed.
ROOMS: 11 en suite s £99-£165; d £140-£235 (incl. bkfst) **LB** **FACILITIES:** STV Tennis (hard) Croquet lawn Xmas **CONF:** Thtr 20 Class 20 Board 20 Del from £120 **PARKING:** 30 **NOTES:** No smoking in restaurant Civ Wed 80
CARDS:

BURTON MOTORWAY SERVICE AREA (M6), Cumbria — Map 18 SD57

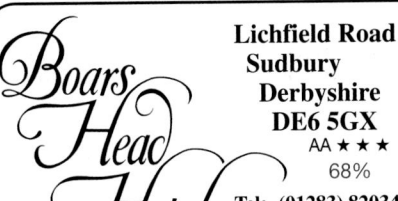

Travelodge
Burton in Kendal LA6 1JF
☎ 08700 850 950
Dir: *between M6 junct 35/36 southbound*

Travelodge offers good quality, good value, modern accommodation. Ideal for families, the spacious, en suite bedrooms include remote-control TV, tea and coffee-making facilities, luxury beds and free morning newspaper. Meals can be taken at the nearby family restaurant. For further details and the Travelodge phone number, consult the Hotel Groups page.

ROOMS: 47 en suite s fr £42.95; d fr £42.95

BURTON UPON TRENT, Staffordshire — Map 10 SK22

Riverside
Riverside Dr, Branston DE14 3EP
☎ 01283 511234 01283 511441
e-mail: riverside.branston@oldenglishinns.co.uk
Dir: *follow signs for Branston on A5121 until small humped bridge, over bridge and right turn into Warren Lane. Second left into Riverside Drive*

At the time of going to press, the star classification for this hotel was not confirmed. Please refer to the AA internet site www.theAA.com for current information.

ROOMS: 22 en suite (10 GF) No smoking in all bedrooms s £55-£75; d £75-£90 (incl. bkfst) **LB FACILITIES:** STV Fishing Xmas **CONF:** Thtr 120 Class 60 Board 30 Del £120 **PARKING:** 200 **NOTES:** No smoking in restaurant Civ Wed 120 **CARDS:**

Express by Holiday Inn
2nd Av, Centrum 100 DE14 2WF
☎ 01283 504300 01283 504301
e-mail: Jeannette@firstinn.co.uk
Dir: *From A38 Branston exit take A5121 Town Centre. At McDonalds rdbt, turn left into 2nd Avenue. Hotel on left*

A modern hotel ideal for families and business travellers. Fresh and uncomplicated, the spacious bedrooms include Sky TV, power shower and tea and coffee-making facilities. Continental buffet breakfast is included in the room rate; other meals may be taken at the nearby family pub or restaurant. For further details and the Express by Holiday Inn phone number, consult the Hotel Groups pages.

ROOMS: 82 en suite s £55-£70; d £55-£70 (incl. cont bkfst) **CONF:** Thtr 70 Class 30 Board 30 Del £125

> Popped the question?
> Hotels with Civ Wed in their entry are licensed for civil wedding ceremonies. Maximum numbers for the ceremony only are shown, e.g. Civ Wed 120

BURTONWOOD MOTORWAY SERVICE AREA (M62), Cheshire — Map 15 SJ59

Welome Lodge
Burtonwood Services (M62), Great Sankey WA5 3AX
☎ 01925 710376 01925 710378
e-mail: burtonwood.hotel@welcomebreak.co.uk
Dir: *between M62 junct 7-9*

This modern building offers accommodation in smart, spacious and well-equipped bedrooms, suitable for families and business travellers, and all with en suite bathrooms. Refreshments may be taken at the nearby family restaurant. For further details and the Welcome Break phone number, consult the Hotel Groups page.

ROOMS: 39 en suite s £35-£45; d £35-£45 **CONF:** Board 8

BURWARDSLEY, Cheshire — Map 15 SJ55

★★72% Pheasant Inn
Higher Burwardsley CH3 9PF
☎ 01829 770434 01829 771097
e-mail: reception@thepheasant-burwardsley.com
Dir: *from A41, left to Tattenhall, right at 1st junct left at 2nd to Higher Burwardsley. At post office left, hotel signed*

This delightful 300-year-old inn sits high in the Peckforton Hills and enjoys spectacular views over the Cheshire plain. Well equipped, comfortable bedrooms are housed in an adjacent converted barn. Creative dishes are served either in the stylish restaurant or in the traditional beamed bar. Real fires are lit in the winter months.

ROOMS: 2 en suite 8 annexe en suite (2 fmly) (3 GF) No smoking in all bedrooms s £55; d £70-£80 (incl. bkfst) **LB FACILITIES:** STV Xmas **CONF:** Thtr 16 **PARKING:** 35 **NOTES:** No dogs No smoking in restaurant **CARDS:**

BURY, Greater Manchester Map 15 SD81

★★★66% Bolholt Country Park

Walshaw Rd BL8 1PU
☎ 0161 762 4000 🖷 0161 762 4100
e-mail: enquiries@bolholt.co.uk

Dir: *M60 junct 17 for Whitefield, A56 to Bury for 4m. Follow signs for A58 to Bolton. Take 3rd lane at car showroom signed Tottington. Left at pub, left again*

This former mill owner's house is located in attractive parkland and secluded gardens just a short walk from the town centre. Bolholt Country Park Hotel provides comfortable yet modern bedrooms. The newly extended leisure club includes a fashionable café-bar. Wide ranging conference and banqueting facilities are available and the setting is ideal for weddings.

ROOMS: 65 en suite (13 fmly) No smoking in 14 bedrooms **FACILITIES:** STV Indoor swimming (H) Fishing Squash Sauna Solarium Gym Jacuzzi Fitness & leisure centre, Swimming pool supervised **CONF:** Thtr 300 Class 120 Board 40 Del from £89 **PARKING:** 300 **NOTES:** No dogs (ex guide dogs) No smoking in restaurant Civ Wed 140 **CARDS:**

BURY ST EDMUNDS, Suffolk Map 13 TL86

★★★77% Angel

Angel Hill IP33 1LT
☎ 01284 714000 🖷 01284 714001
e-mail: sales@theangel.co.uk

Dir: *from A134, left at rdbt into Northgate St. Continue to t-junct with traffic lights, right into Mustow St, left into Angel Hill, hotel on right*

Impressive building situated just a short walk from the town centre. One of the Angel's more notable guests over the last 400 years was Charles Dickens who is reputed to have written part of the *Pickwick Papers* whilst in residence. The hotel offers a range of individually designed bedrooms that include a selection of four-poster rooms and a suite.

ROOMS: 64 en suite (4 fmly) No smoking in 6 bedrooms s £85-£100; d £119-£139 (incl. bkfst) **LB** **FACILITIES:** STV entertainment Xmas **CONF:** Thtr 80 Class 20 Board 30 Del from £120 **SERVICES:** Lift **PARKING:** 54 **NOTES:** No smoking in restaurant Civ Wed 100 **CARDS:**

★★★74% Ravenwood Hall

Rougham IP30 9JA
☎ 01359 270345 🖷 01359 270788
e-mail: enquiries@ravenwoodhall.co.uk

Dir: *3m E off A14*

Delightful 15th-century property set in seven acres of woodland and landscaped gardens. The building has many original features including carved timbers and inglenook fireplaces. The spacious bedrooms are attractively decorated, tastefully furnished with well-chosen pieces and equipped with many thoughtful touches. Public rooms include an elegant restaurant and a smart lounge bar with an open fire.

ROOMS: 7 en suite 7 annexe en suite (5 GF) No smoking in all bedrooms s £73-£98; d £96-£133 (incl. bkfst) **LB** **FACILITIES:** Outdoor swimming (H) Riding Croquet lawn Shooting & fishing Xmas **CONF:** Thtr 200 Class 80 Board 40 Del from £125 **PARKING:** 150 **NOTES:** No smoking in restaurant Civ Wed 200 **CARDS:**

Town House Hotel
Country House Hotel
Travel Accommodation

★★★73% The Priory

Tollgate IP32 6EH
☎ 01284 766181 🖷 01284 767604
e-mail: reservations@prioryhotel.co.uk

Dir: *from A14 Bury St. Edmunds W sliproad. Follow signs to Brandon. At mini rdbt turn right. Hotel 0.5 m on left.*

Delightful Grade II listed building dating back to the 18th century that set in its own landscaped grounds on the outskirts of the town centre. Public rooms feature a smart restaurant, two further conservatory-style dining areas and a lounge bar. Bedrooms are split between the main house and garden wings, which have their own patios. All rooms are attractively decorated, tastefully furnished and equipped with modern facilities.

ROOMS: 9 en suite 30 annexe en suite (1 fmly) No smoking in 15 bedrooms s £75-£84; d £99-£115 (incl. bkfst) **LB** **FACILITIES:** Xmas **CONF:** Thtr 40 Class 20 Board 20 Del from £126 **PARKING:** 60 **NOTES:** No smoking in restaurant **CARDS:**

BUTTERMERE, Cumbria Map 18 NY11

★★74% Bridge

CA13 9UZ
☎ 017687 70252 🖷 017687 70215
e-mail: enquiries@bridge-hotel.com

Dir: *A66 around town centre, off at Braithwaite. Over Newlands Pass. Follow Buttermere signs. Hotel in village*

This delightful hotel enjoys a tranquil setting between Buttermere and Crummock Water. Accommodation is of a high standard and individually styled bedrooms offer a mix of traditional and more contemporary fittings. Afternoon tea is served in the inviting lounge and the cosy bar, popular with walkers, serves a range of meals all day.

ROOMS: 21 en suite No smoking in 10 bedrooms s £60-£76; d £120-£152 (incl. bkfst & dinner) **LB** **FACILITIES:** no TV in bdrms Xmas **CONF:** Board 10 **PARKING:** 40 **NOTES:** No smoking in restaurant **CARDS:**

BUXTON, Derbyshire Map 16 SK07

★★★★65% Palace Hotel

Palace Rd SK17 6AG
☎ 01298 22001 🖷 01298 72131
e-mail: palace@paramount-hotels.co.uk

Dir: *Exit M6 junct 20, follow M56/M60 signs to Stockport then follow A6 to Buxton, hotel adjacent to railway station*

This impressive Victorian hotel is located on the hill overlooking the town. Public areas are traditional and elegant, with chandeliers and decorative ceilings setting the style. The bedrooms are spacious and equipped with modern facilities and The Dovedale restaurant provides modern British cuisine.

ROOMS: 122 en suite (20 fmly) No smoking in 80 bedrooms s fr £110; d fr £125 (incl. bkfst) **LB** **FACILITIES:** STV Indoor swimming (H) Sauna Solarium Gym Beauty and hairdressing facilities, Swimming pool supervised Xmas **CONF:** Thtr 300 Class 125 Board 80 Del from £148 **SERVICES:** Lift **PARKING:** 200 **NOTES:** No smoking in restaurant Civ Wed 300 **CARDS:**

★★★77% Best Western Lee Wood

The Park SK17 6TQ
☎ 01298 23002 🖷 01298 23228
e-mail: leewoodhotel@btinternet.com

Dir: *NE on A5004, 300mtrs beyond Devonshire Royal Hospital*

This elegant Georgian hotel offers high standards of comfort and hospitality. Individually furnished bedrooms are generally spacious, with all of the expected modern conveniences. There is a choice of two comfortable lounges and a conservatory restaurant.

continued

Quality cooking is a feature of the hotel, as is good service and fine hospitality.
ROOMS: 35 en suite 5 annexe en suite (4 fmly) No smoking in 14 bedrooms s £65-£95; d £85-£125 (incl. bkfst) **LB FACILITIES:** STV Xmas **CONF:** Thtr 120 Class 65 Board 40 Del from £110 **SERVICES:** Lift **PARKING:** 50 **NOTES:** No smoking in restaurant Civ Wed 160
CARDS:

★★★66% Buckingham Hotel

THE INDEPENDENTS

1 Burlington Rd SK17 9AS
☎ 01298 70481 📠 01298 72186
e-mail: frontdesk@buckinghamhotel.co.uk
Dir: *follow tourist signs for Pavilion Gardens Car Park. Hotel opposite car park at junct of St Johns (A53) & Burlington Rd*

The Buckingham is close to the Pavilion Gardens and offers pleasant, modern public areas. These include Ramsay's Bar, serving bar meals and real ales, and the popular carvery, serving grills and other dishes. Bedrooms are spacious and comfortable; many overlook the Pavilion Gardens. Walls throughout the hotel are adorned with photographs of film stars.
ROOMS: 37 en suite (13 fmly) No smoking in 27 bedrooms s £75-£85; d £115-£125 (incl. bkfst & dinner) **LB FACILITIES:** STV Xmas **CONF:** Thtr 75 Class 20 Board 16 Del from £75 **SERVICES:** Lift **PARKING:** 35 **NOTES:** No smoking in restaurant Civ Wed 75
CARDS:

★★63% Portland Hotel & Park Restaurant

32 St John's Rd SK17 6XQ
☎ 01298 22462 📠 01298 27464
e-mail: robert@portland-hotel.freeserve.co.uk
Dir: *on A53 opposite the Pavilion & Gardens*

This privately owned and personally run hotel is situated near the famous opera house and the Pavilion Gardens. Facilities include a comfortable lounge and an open plan bar & restaurant area with an adjacent conservatory. An extensive refurbishment is planned.
ROOMS: 22 en suite (3 fmly) No smoking in 3 bedrooms s £45-£55; d £65-£100 (incl. bkfst) **LB CONF:** Thtr 50 Class 30 Board 25 **PARKING:** 18 **NOTES:** No smoking in restaurant
CARDS:

CADNAM, Hampshire — Map 05 SU31

★★★71% Bartley Lodge

Lyndhurst Rd SO40 7DU
☎ 023 8081 2248 📠 023 8081 2075
e-mail: bartley@newforesthotels.co.uk
Dir: *M27 junct 1 at 1st rdbt 1st exit, at 2nd rdbt 3rd exit onto A337. Hotel sign on left*

This 18th-century former hunting lodge is very quietly situated, yet just minutes from the M27/A35 junction. Bedrooms vary in size and all are well-equipped. There is a grand entrance hall, a selection of small lounge areas, a cosy bar and an indoor pool

continued

together with a small fitness suite. The Crystal dining room offers a tempting selection of carefully prepared dishes.
ROOMS: 31 en suite (14 fmly) s £68-£80; d £120-£130 (incl. bkfst) **LB FACILITIES:** Indoor swimming (H) Tennis (hard) Sauna Gym Croquet lawn Xmas **CONF:** Thtr 120 Class 60 Board 60 Del from £90 **PARKING:** 60 **NOTES:** No smoking in restaurant Civ Wed 100
CARDS:

See advert on this page

CALNE, Wiltshire — Map 04 ST97

★★★67% Lansdowne Strand

Best Western

The Strand SN11 0EH
☎ 01249 812488 📠 01249 815323
e-mail: reservations@lansdownestrand.co.uk
Dir: *on A4*

In the centre of the market town, this former 16th-century coaching inn still retains many period features. Individually decorated bedrooms vary in size. There are two friendly bars; one offers a wide selection of ales and a cosy fireplace. An interesting menu and choice of wines is available in the brasserie-style restaurant.
ROOMS: 20 en suite 5 annexe en suite (3 fmly) No smoking in 9 bedrooms s £69; d £92 (incl. bkfst & dinner) **LB FACILITIES:** STV Complimentary use of nearby leisure centre Xmas **CONF:** Thtr 90 Class 28 Board 30 **PARKING:** 21 **CARDS:**

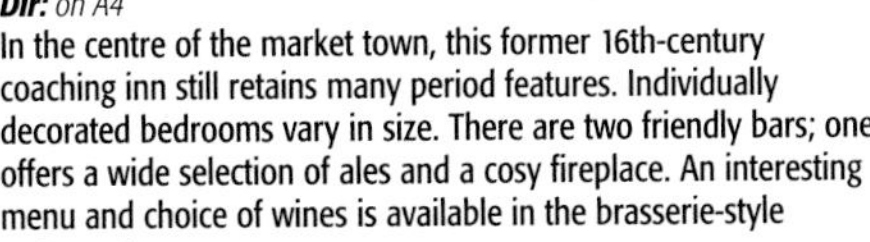

CAMBERLEY, Surrey — Map 06 SU86

★★★74% Frimley Hall

Lime Av GU15 2BG
☎ 0870 400 8224 📠 01276 691253
e-mail: general.frimleyhall@macdonald-hotels.co.uk

MACDONALD HOTELS

***Dir:** M3 junct 3 follow Bagshot signs on A321. Over traffic lights, left onto A30 signed Camberley/Basingstoke. Follow road on to 2nd exit onto Portsmouth Rd (A325), take 5th right turn*

Classic English elegance in the heart of rural Surrey, this ivy-clad Victorian manor house is set in two acres of immaculate grounds. With continued investment in the hotel, both bedrooms and public areas are looking particularly smart and feature a modern yet timeless decorative theme.

ROOMS: 86 en suite (2 fmly) No smoking in 33 bedrooms s £162-£212; d £172-£222 (incl. bkfst) **LB** **FACILITIES:** Croquet lawn Putting green entertainment **CONF:** Thtr 60 Class 25 Board 25 Del from £150 **PARKING:** 100 **NOTES:** Civ Wed 100
CARDS:

★★★66% Lakeside International

Wharf Rd, Frimley Green GU16 6JR
☎ 01252 838000 📠 01252 837857

***Dir:** off A321, at mini rdbt turn into Wharf Rd, Lakeside on right*

This hotel, geared towards the business market, enjoys a lakeside location with noteworthy views. Bedrooms are modern, comfortable and with a range of facilities. Public areas are spacious and include a residents' lounge, bar and games room, a smart restaurant and an established health and leisure club.

ROOMS: 98 en suite (1 fmly) No smoking in 18 bedrooms s £50-£120; d £70-£140 (incl. bkfst) **FACILITIES:** STV Indoor swimming (H) Squash Snooker Sauna Solarium Gym Jacuzzi **CONF:** Thtr 120 Class 100 Board 40 Del from £165 **SERVICES:** Lift **PARKING:** 250 **NOTES:** No dogs (ex guide dogs) No smoking in restaurant Civ Wed 100
CARDS:

Travel Inn

221 Yorktown Rd, College Town LU6 3QP
☎ 08701 977047 📠 01582 842811

travel inn

***Dir:** M3 junct 4 follow A331 to Camberley. At large rdbt, exit to A321 towards Bracknell. At 3rd set of traffic lights, Travel Inn on left*

Travel Inn offers good-quality, value-for-money accommodation. Spacious, en suite rooms with bath and shower comfortably accommodate a family of up to two adults and two children (to age 15). The restaurant and bar offers a varied menu. For further details and the Travel Inn phone number, consult the Hotel Groups page.

ROOMS: 40 en suite s £44.95; d £44.95

CAMBORNE, Cornwall & Isles of Scilly — Map 02 SW64

★★★62% Tyacks

27 Commercial St TR14 8LD
☎ 01209 612424 📠 01209 612435
e-mail: tyacks@westcountryhotelrooms.co.uk

***Dir:** W on A30 past A3047 junct & turn off at Camborne West junct. Left & left again at rdbt, follow town centre signs. Hotel on left*

This 18th-century former coaching inn has spacious, well-furnished public areas which include a smart lounge and bar, a popular public bar and a restaurant serving fixed-price and carte menus. The comfortable bedrooms are attractively decorated and well equipped; two have separate sitting areas.

ROOMS: 15 en suite (2 fmly) No smoking in 4 bedrooms s fr £47.50; d fr £70 (incl. bkfst) **LB** **FACILITIES:** STV entertainment Xmas **PARKING:** 27 **CARDS:**

CAMBOURNE, Cambridgeshire

○ The Cambridge Belfry

Back St
☎ 0845 1300 700

MARSTON HOTELS

ROOMS: 120 en suite
NOTES: Due to open Summer 2004

CAMBRIDGE, Cambridgeshire — Map 12 TL45

★★★★76% Hotel Felix

Whitehouse Ln CB3 0LX
☎ 01223 277977 📠 01223 277973
e-mail: help@hotelfelix.co.uk

Beautiful Victorian mansion set amidst three acres of landscaped gardens. The property was originally built in 1852 for a surgeon from the famous Addenbrookes Hospital. The contemporary style bedrooms have carefully chosen furniture and many thoughtful touches. Public rooms feature a large open plan bar and the adjacent Graffiti restaurant.

ROOMS: 52 en suite (5 fmly) (26 GF) No smoking in 11 bedrooms s £125-£175; d £155-£260 (incl. cont bkfst) **FACILITIES:** STV Xmas **CONF:** Thtr 50 Class 36 Board 34 Del £170 **SERVICES:** Lift **PARKING:** 90 **NOTES:** No smoking in restaurant Civ Wed 75
CARDS:

See advert on opposite page

★★★★66% De Vere University Arms

Regent St CB2 1AD
☎ 01223 351241 📠 01223 273037
e-mail: dua.sales@devere-hotels.com

DE VERE HOTELS

***Dir:** M11 junct 11, follow city centre signs for 3m. Right at 2nd mini rdbt, left at lights into Regent St. Hotel 600yds on right*

This historic, Victorian-style hotel enjoys an enviable position in the heart of the city, on the edge of Parker's Piece. Elegant public areas include the central domed lounge, a smart restaurant with its own cocktail bar, a separate bar lounge and extensive conference facilities. Bedrooms vary in size, and are well equipped and stylishly appointed.

ROOMS: 118 en suite (4 fmly) No smoking in 81 bedrooms s £200; d £200 **LB** **FACILITIES:** STV Reduced rate at local fitness centre Xmas **CONF:** Thtr 308 Class 150 Board 90 Del £195 **SERVICES:** Lift **PARKING:** 88 **NOTES:** No smoking in restaurant Civ Wed 308
CARDS:

★★★72% Cambridge Quy Mill Hotel

Newmarket Rd CB5 9AG
☎ 01223 293383 📠 01223 293770
e-mail: cambridgequy@bestwestern.co.uk

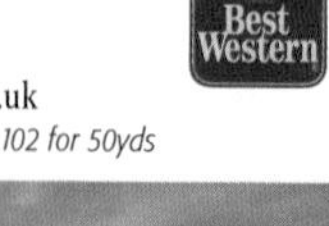

***Dir:** off A14 at junct E of Cambridge onto B1102 for 50yds*

Convenient for Cambridge city centre, this 19th-century former watermill is set in an expanse of water meadows. Well-designed

continued

public areas include several spacious bar and lounge areas, with options of casual and formal eating areas; service is both friendly and helpful. Bedrooms styles differ, yet each room is smartly appointed and brightly decorated.
ROOMS: 24 en suite 18 annexe en suite (3 fmly) (18 GF) No smoking in 18 bedrooms s £80-£120; d £95-£180 **LB** **FACILITIES:** Indoor heated pool, gym and sauna open Aug 2003 Clay pigeon shooting **CONF:** Thtr 80 Class 30 Board 24 Del from £135 **PARKING:** 100 **NOTES:** No dogs (ex guide dogs) Closed 24-30 Dec RS 31 Dec Civ Wed 80
CARDS:

★★★70% Gonville

Gonville Place CB1 1LY
☎ 01223 366611 & 221111 🖹 01223 315470
e-mail: all@gonvillehotel.co.uk
Dir: *M11 junct 11, on A1309 follow city centre signs. At 2nd mini rdbt right into Lensfield Rd, over junct with traffic lights. Hotel 25yds on right*

This hotel is situated on the inner ring road, just a short walk across the green from the city centre. Well-established, with regular guests and very experienced staff, the Gonville is popular for its relaxing, informal atmosphere. The air-conditioned public areas are cheerfully furnished, and bedrooms are well appointed and appealing.
ROOMS: 78 en suite (1 fmly) (5 GF) No smoking in 38 bedrooms s fr £99; d fr £120 **LB** **FACILITIES:** Arrangement with gym/swimming pool Xmas **CONF:** BC Thtr 200 Class 100 Board 50 Del from £145 **SERVICES:** Lift **PARKING:** 80 **NOTES:** No smoking in restaurant
CARDS:

★★★68% Royal Cambridge

Trumpington St CB2 1PY
☎ 01223 351631 🖹 01223 352972
e-mail: royal.cambridge@forestdale.com
Dir: *M11 junct 11, signed city centre. 1st mini rdbt left into Fen Causeway. Hotel 1st right*

This an impressive Georgian hotel enjoys a central location. The public areas are traditionally decorated to a good standard: the elegant restaurant is a popular choice and the lounge bar serves evening bar snacks. Bedrooms are well equipped and comfortable and include new superior bedrooms/apartments. Parking and conferencing are added benefits.
ROOMS: 57 en suite (9 fmly) No smoking in 28 bedrooms s fr £120; d fr £155 (incl. bkfst) **LB** **FACILITIES:** STV Xmas **CONF:** Thtr 120 Class 40 Board 40 Del from £147 **SERVICES:** Lift **PARKING:** 80 **NOTES:** No smoking in restaurant Civ Wed 100 **CARDS:**

★★★66% Sorrento

190-196 Cherry Hinton Rd CB1 7AN
☎ 01223 243533 🖹 01223 213463
e-mail: info@sorrentohotel.com

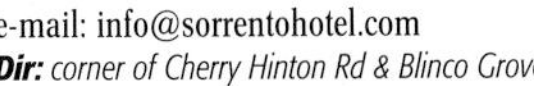

Dir: *corner of Cherry Hinton Rd & Blinco Grove*

Friendly, family run hotel situated within easy striking distance of the city centre. Although the bedrooms vary in size and style they

continued

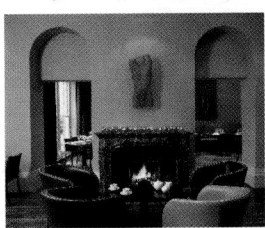

are all are pleasantly decorated and equipped with many thoughtful extras. Public rooms have an Italian feel with superb marble flooring throughout; they include a smart lounge bar, attractive restaurant and a huge conservatory.
ROOMS: 30 en suite (4 fmly) (8 GF) No smoking in 20 bedrooms s £70-£95; d £99-£140 (incl. bkfst) **LB** **FACILITIES: Spa** STV Sauna Jacuzzi Xmas **CONF:** Thtr 60 Class 35 Board 35 **PARKING:** 40 **NOTES:** No smoking in restaurant **CARDS:**

★★71% Arundel House

Chesterton Rd CB4 3AN
☎ 01223 367701 🖹 01223 367721
e-mail: info@arundelhousehotels.co.uk
Dir: *city centre on A1303*

Overlooking the Cam and enjoying views over open parkland, this popular hotel was originally a row of Victorian townhouses. The smart public areas feature a conservatory for informal snacks, a spacious bar and an elegant restaurant for serious dining;

continued on p158

CAMBRIDGE, continued

restaurant is being redesigned in warm colour schemes to offer a modern dining experience. Bedrooms are attractive and have a special character.
ROOMS: 81 en suite 22 annexe en suite (7 fmly) No smoking in all bedrooms s £75-£95; d £89-£120 (incl. cont bkfst) **LB** **CONF:** Thtr 50 Class 34 Board 32 Del from £107.50 **PARKING:** 70 **NOTES:** No dogs No smoking in restaurant Closed 25-26 Dec
CARDS:

★★70% Centennial
63-71 Hills Rd CB2 1PG
☎ 01223 314652 🖹 01223 315443
e-mail: reception@centennialhotel.co.uk
Dir: *M11 junct 11 take A1309 to Cambridge. Right onto Brooklands Ave to end. Left, hotel 100yds on right*
This friendly hotel is conveniently situated for the railway station and town centre. Well presented public areas include a welcoming quiet lounge and a relaxing bar and restaurant. Bedrooms are generally quite spacious, well maintained and thoughtfully equipped with a good range of facilities; several rooms are available on the ground floor.
ROOMS: 39 en suite (1 fmly) (7 GF) No smoking in 26 bedrooms s £70-£80; d £88-£96 (incl. bkfst) **LB** **CONF:** Thtr 25 Class 25 Board 25 **PARKING:** 30 **NOTES:** No dogs No smoking in restaurant Closed 23 Dec-1 Jan **CARDS:**

See advert on opposite page

U *Holiday Inn Cambridge*
Lakeview, Bridge Rd, Impington CB4 9PH
☎ 0870 400 9015 🖹 01223 233426
Dir: *2.5m N, on N side of rdbt junct A14/B1049*
At the time of going to press, the classification for this hotel was not confirmed. Please refer to the AA internet site www.theAA.com for current information.
ROOMS: 165 en suite (14 fmly) No smoking in 105 bedrooms **FACILITIES:** Indoor swimming (H) Sauna Gym Jacuzzi **CONF:** Thtr 60 Class 30 Board 30 **PARKING:** 200 **NOTES:** RS 24-27 Dec & 31 Dec
CARDS:

Travelodge (Cambridge South)
Fourwentways CB8 6AP
☎ 08700 850 950
Dir: *adjacent to Little Chef at junct A11/A1307, 5m S of Cambridge*
Travelodge offers good quality, good value, modern accommodation. Ideal for families, the spacious, en suite bedrooms include remote-control TV, tea and coffee-making facilities, luxury beds and free morning newspaper. Meals can be taken at the nearby family restaurant. For further details and the Travelodge phone number, consult the Hotel Groups page.
ROOMS: 40 en suite s fr £42.95; d fr £42.95

CAMELFORD, Cornwall & Isles of Scilly — Map 02 SX18

★★★65% Bowood Park Hotel & Golf Course
Lanteglos PL32 9RF
☎ 01840 213017 🖹 01840 212622
e-mail: golf@bowoodpark.com
Dir: *A39 W through Camelford, 0.5m, turn right for Tintagel/Boscastle, 1st left after garage*
Nestling in wonderfully picturesque rolling countryside, this relatively new hotel is constantly improving and provides much for golfers and non-golfers alike. Spacious bedrooms are comfortable and contemporary and some have private patio areas and wonderful views over the course. Salmon and trout fishing is available on the River Camel and the hotel's treatment room is just the place for a relaxing massage or beauty treatment.
ROOMS: 31 en suite (3 fmly) No smoking in 12 bedrooms s £45-£85; d £60-£70 (incl. bkfst & dinner) **LB** **FACILITIES:** Golf 18 Fishing Putting green Massage, Sports therapy Xmas **CONF:** BC Thtr 160 Class 100 Board 100 **PARKING:** 100 **NOTES:** No dogs (ex guide dogs) No smoking in restaurant **CARDS:**

CANNOCK, Staffordshire — Map 10 SJ91

★★★67% The Whitehouse Hotel & Restaurant
Marquis Dr, Penkridge Bank Rd WS12 4PR
☎ 01543 422712 🖹 01543 422639
e-mail: info@thewhitehouse-hotel.co.uk
Dir: *Turn off A34 at rdbt with wooden wigwam, towards Rugeley through Forest. Hotel approx 2m on right*
This privately owned and personally run hotel is quietly situated in the heart of Cannock Chase, only a short drive from Stafford and the motorway network. Bedrooms are modern and well equipped. There is an attractive lounge bar and a pleasant restaurant where a good selection of grill type dishes is available. The hotel also has a large function suite.
ROOMS: 6 en suite No smoking in 1 bedroom d £65-£125 (incl. bkfst) **LB** **CONF:** Thtr 180 Class 140 Board 50 **PARKING:** 80 **NOTES:** No dogs (ex guide dogs) Closed 26-30 Dec
CARDS:

★★★63% The Roman Way Hotel
Watling St, Hatherton WS11 1SH
☎ 0870 609 6125 🖹 01543 502749
Dir: *M6 junct 11 towards Cannock on A460. At rdbt take A5 to Telford. Hotel 100yds on left. Or M6 junct 12, then A5 towards Cannock. Hotel 2m on right*

Named after the Roman road on which it stands, this modern hotel provides a good standard of accommodation. Doric columns and marble floors feature in the reception area and Nero's Restaurant and Gilpin's Lounge provide formal or informal eating.
ROOMS: 56 en suite (17 fmly) (23 GF) No smoking in 23 bedrooms s £65-£85; d £85-£105 **LB** **FACILITIES:** STV Xmas **CONF:** BC Thtr 150 Class 100 Board 50 Del £110 **PARKING:** 150 **NOTES:** No smoking in restaurant Civ Wed 150 **CARDS:**

Travel Inn
Watling St WS11 1SJ
☎ 08701 977048 🖹 01543 466130
Dir: *on junct of A5/A460, 2m from M6 junct 11/12*
Travel Inn offers good-quality, value-for-money accommodation. Spacious, en suite rooms with bath and shower comfortably accommodate a family of up to two adults and two children (to age 15). The restaurant and bar offers a varied menu. For further details and the Travel Inn phone number, consult the Hotel Groups page.
ROOMS: 60 en suite s £44.95; d £44.95 **CONF:** Thtr 80 Board 40

CANTERBURY, Kent Map 07 TR15

★★★★66% The County

High St CT1 2RX
☎ 01227 766266 📠 01227 451512
MACDONALD HOTELS
e-mail: county@macdonald-hotels.co.uk
Dir: *M2, junct 7. Follow Canterbury signs onto ringroad. At Wincheap rdbt turn into city. Left into Rosemary Ln, into Stour St. Hotel at end*

This historic hotel has cellars which date back to the 12th century. It offers warm hospitality and comfortable accommodation in the heart of the city. Bedrooms are individually decorated and tastefully furnished, while public areas include the tea rooms, offering traditional cream teas and Sully's Restaurant, where the emphasis is on fine dining.

ROOMS: 74 en suite (3 fmly) No smoking in 33 bedrooms s £45-£110; d £55-£120 **LB** **FACILITIES:** STV Xmas **CONF:** BC Thtr 120 Class 80 Board 60 Del from £95 **SERVICES:** Lift **PARKING:** 62 **NOTES:** No smoking in restaurant Civ Wed 100
CARDS:

★★★67% The Falstaff Hotel

8-10 St Dunstan's St CT2 8AF
☎ 0870 609 6102 📠 01227 463525
e-mail: thefalstaff@corushotels.com
Dir: *In city take 2nd rndbt into St Peters Place, hotel is opposite Westgate, turn right then immediately left for car park*

Located next to the Westgate Tower, the hotel offers easy access to the city centre and motorway network. Many original 16th-century features are still present in this historic coaching inn, especially in the cosy lounge and bar. Bedrooms are split between the newer annexe and the main building.

ROOMS: 25 en suite 22 annexe en suite (1 fmly) (14 GF) No smoking in 27 bedrooms s £100; d £110 **LB** **FACILITIES:** STV Xmas **PARKING:** 34 **NOTES:** No smoking in restaurant
CARDS:

★★★67% Howfield Manor

Chartham Hatch CT4 7HQ
☎ 01227 738294 📠 01227 731535
e-mail: enquiries@howfieldmanor.co.uk
Dir: *from A2, follow Canterbury on slip rd. 1st R signed Chartham Hatch, R at T-junct, follow winding rd 3m. L at T-Junct, hotel 2m on left*

This pleasant family run hotel is set in several acres of well-manicured grounds, offering a peaceful setting even though the hotel is conveniently situated for the city. Bedrooms are divided between those in the main house and a purpose-built wing.

ROOMS: 15 en suite (2 GF) s £79.50; d £99.50 (incl. bkfst) **LB** **FACILITIES:** STV Xmas **CONF:** Thtr 80 Class 45 Board 60 Del £105 **PARKING:** 80 **NOTES:** No dogs (ex guide dogs) No children 10yrs Civ Wed 100 **CARDS:**

★★★64% The Chaucer

Ivy Ln CT1 1TU
☎ 0870 400 8106 📠 01227 450397
MACDONALD HOTELS

e-mail: chaucer@macdonald-hotels.co.uk
Dir: *towards city on A2, follow Dover signs. Right at 5th rdbt, then 1st left*

Once a private house, the red brick exterior and traditional tiled roof of The Chaucer is reminiscent of the rustic Georgian style once favoured by the landed gentry. Located just outside the ancient city walls, the hotel is within easy walking distance of the centre and all its attractions. Named for the famous author Chaucer, many of the hotel rooms are named after characters from his Canterbury Tales.

ROOMS: 42 en suite (5 fmly) No smoking in 29 bedrooms s £95; d £110 **LB** **FACILITIES:** Xmas **CONF:** Thtr 120 Class 45 Board 45 Del from £95 **PARKING:** 45 **NOTES:** No smoking in restaurant Civ Wed 100
CARDS:

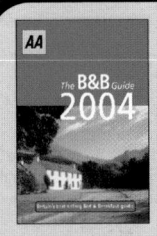

CANTERBURY, continued

★★75% **Ebury**
65/67 New Dover Rd CT1 3DX
☎ 01227 768433 🖹 01227 459187
e-mail: info@ebury-hotel.co.uk
Dir: *A2 Canterbury take ring road. Follow Dover signs, after 5th rdbt hotel 1m on left*
This former Victorian residence is set in two acres of attractive gardens and is only a short walk from the city centre. The elegant and spacious public rooms include a restaurant and lounge where the proprietor's collection of rare and unusual clocks tick away peacefully. Bedrooms are maintained to a high standard and contain a good range of useful facilities.
ROOMS: 15 en suite (2 fmly) s £55-£65; d £75-£95 (incl. bkfst) **LB** **FACILITIES:** Indoor swimming (H) Jacuzzi **PARKING:** 30 **NOTES:** No smoking in restaurant Closed 21 Dec-13 Jan
CARDS:

★★70% **Bow Window Inn**
50 High St, Littlebourne CT3 1ST
☎ 01227 721264 🖹 01227 721250
e-mail: bow@windowhotel.freeserve.co.uk
A country cottage offering friendly hospitality and comfortable accommodation. Bedrooms are furnished to suit the style of the house and are all well-equipped. Public areas are cosy with exposed beams providing character, especially within the restaurant, which provides an interesting menu.
ROOMS: 10 en suite (1 fmly) No smoking in 3 bedrooms s £40-£50; d £55-£78 (incl. bkfst) **LB** **PARKING:** 16 **NOTES:** No smoking in restaurant **CARDS:**

★★69% ⊛ **Canterbury**
71 New Dover Rd CT1 3DZ
☎ 01227 450551 🖹 01227 780145
e-mail: canterbury.hotel@btinternet.com
Dir: *on A2, Dover road*
This smart Georgian-style hotel is conveniently located ten minutes' walk from the city centre. Bedrooms are all well equipped and come in two styles: standard and superior. The attractive bright restaurant serves classical French food and there is a small bar adjacent. Drinks and light snacks are served in the lounge or on the patio.
ROOMS: 23 en suite (1 fmly) s £52-£75; d £71-£110 **LB** **FACILITIES:** STV **SERVICES:** Lift **PARKING:** 50
CARDS:

Town House Hotel
Country House Hotel
Travel Accommodation

★★63% ***Victoria***
59 London Rd CT2 8JY
☎ 01227 459333 🖹 01227 781552
e-mail: manager@vichotel.fsnet.co.uk
Dir: *M2/A2 onto A2052, hotel on left off 1st rdbt*
Just 15 minutes' walk from the city, the hotel is away from the hustle and bustle of the centre, yet within sight of the cathedral. Bedrooms vary in size and shape, and all are attractively decorated with an excellent range of facilities. Public areas include a busy bar and carvery restaurant.

ROOMS: 34 en suite (12 fmly) No smoking in 4 bedrooms **CONF:** Thtr 20 Class 20 Board 20 **PARKING:** 70 **NOTES:** No dogs (ex guide dogs)
CARDS:

⌂ **Express by Holiday Inn Canterbury**
Upper Harbledown CT2 9HX
☎ 01227 865 000 🖹 01227 865 100
e-mail: canterbury@oriel-leisure.co.uk
Dir: *On A2, 4m from city centre. Hotel accessed via Texaco petrol station at Upper Harbledown*

Express by Holiday Inn

A modern hotel ideal for families and business travellers. Fresh and uncomplicated, the spacious bedrooms include Sky TV, power shower and tea and coffee-making facilities. Continental buffet breakfast is included in the room rate; other meals may be taken at the nearby family pub or restaurant. For further details and the Express by Holiday Inn phone number, consult the Hotel Groups pages.
ROOMS: 89 en suite (incl. cont bkfst) s £49-£65; d £49-£65 **CONF:** Thtr 30 Class 30 Board 20

⌂ **Innkeeper's Lodge**
162 New Dover Rd CT1 3EL
☎ 01227 829951 🖹 01227 829952
Dir: *M2 junct 7, A2 left at junct for Rough Common onto A2050. At 2nd rdbt follow signs for Dover (A2), lodge on right*

Innkeeper's Lodge

A new concept in the travel accommodation market. Smart rooms meet essential business requirements but also have home comforts. Dining options include all-day menus plus the added advantage of breakfast, which is included in the room price. For further details, consult the Hotel Groups page.
ROOMS: 9 en suite s £50; d £50

⌂ Travelodge (Canterbury West)

A2 Gate Services, Dunkirk ME13 9LN
☎ 08700 850 950 🖷 01227 752781
Dir: *5m W on A2 northbound*

Travelodge offers good quality, good value, modern accommodation. Ideal for families, the spacious, en suite bedrooms include remote-control TV, tea and coffee-making facilities, luxury beds and free morning newspaper. Meals can be taken at the nearby family restaurant. For further details and the Travelodge phone number, consult the Hotel Groups page.

ROOMS: 40 en suite s fr £42.95; d fr £42.95

CARBIS BAY See St Ives

CARCROFT, South Yorkshire Map 16 SE50

⌂ Travelodge Doncaster

Great North Rd DN6 9LF
☎ 08700 850 950 🖷 01302 330841
Dir: *on A1 northbound*

Travelodge offers good quality, good value, modern accommodation. Ideal for families, the spacious, en suite bedrooms include remote-control TV, tea and coffee-making facilities, luxury beds and free morning newspaper. Meals can be taken at the nearby family restaurant. For further details and the Travelodge phone number, consult the Hotel Groups page.

ROOMS: 40 en suite s fr £42.95; d fr £42.95

CARLISLE, Cumbria Map 18 NY35

See also Brampton

★★★71% Crown

Wetheral CA4 8ES
☎ 01228 561888 🖷 01228 561637
e-mail: info@crownhotelwetheral.co.uk
Dir: *M6 junct 42 take B6263 to Wetheral, right at village shop, car park at rear of hotel*

Set in the attractive village of Wetheral and with landscaped gardens to the rear, this hotel is well suited to both business and leisure guests. Rooms vary in size and style and include two apartments in an adjacent house ideal for long stays. A choice of dining options is available, with the popular Waltons Bar an informal alternative to the main restaurant.

ROOMS: 49 en suite 2 annexe en suite (10 fmly) (3 GF) No smoking in 30 bedrooms s £70-£102; d £80-£126 (incl. bkfst) **LB** **FACILITIES: Spa** STV Indoor swimming (H) Squash Sauna Solarium Gym Jacuzzi Children's splash pool Steam room Xmas **CONF:** BC Thtr 175 Class 90 Board 50 Del from £110 **PARKING:** 80 **NOTES:** No smoking in restaurant Civ Wed 120 **CARDS:**

★★★69% Cumbria Park

32 Scotland Rd, Stanwix CA3 9DG
☎ 01228 522887 🖷 01228 514796
e-mail: enquiries@cumbriaparkhotel.co.uk
Dir: *M6 junct 44, 1.5 miles on main road into Carlisle on left*

Just minutes from the M6, this privately owned hotel, with its own feature garden, is also convenient for the city centre.
Well-equipped bedrooms are a variety of sizes, and several have four-poster or tester beds and whirlpool baths. Conferences and functions are well catered for, with a wide choice of meeting rooms and suites.

ROOMS: 47 en suite (3 fmly) (7 GF) No smoking in 13 bedrooms s £74-£90; d £95-£125 (incl. bkfst) **LB** **FACILITIES:** STV Sauna Solarium Gym Jacuzzi Steam room **CONF:** Thtr 120 Class 50 Board 35 Del £105 **SERVICES:** Lift **PARKING:** 51 **NOTES:** No dogs (ex guide dogs) Closed 25-26 Dec **CARDS:**

★★★64% Lakes Court

Court Square CA1 1QY
☎ 01228 531951 🖷 01228 547799
e-mail: reservations@lakescourthotel.co.uk
Dir: *M6 junct 43, to city centre, then follow road to left & railway station*

This Victorian building is located in the heart of the city centre, adjacent to the railway station. Bedrooms, including a four poster room, are modern in style and most are spacious. Extensive conference facilities and a secure car park are ideal for guests on business. A comfortable bar serves light meals and a wide range of drinks.

ROOMS: 70 en suite (3 fmly) No smoking in 19 bedrooms s £60-£70; d £70-£90 (incl. bkfst) **LB** **CONF:** Thtr 175 Class 60 Board 60 Del from £95 **SERVICES:** Lift **PARKING:** 20 **NOTES:** No smoking in restaurant Civ Wed 80 **CARDS:**

★★★62% Central Plaza

Victoria Viaduct CA3 8AL
☎ 01228 520256 🖷 01228 514657
e-mail: info@centralplazahotel.co.uk
Dir: *In city centre, just N of railway station on A6*

With a convenient city centre location close to the station this hotel offers accommodation in a variety of styles. Service is obliging and the dinner menu offers an interesting range of dishes. Meeting rooms have now been added in what was formerly the basement bar.

ROOMS: 84 en suite (3 fmly) No smoking in 7 bedrooms **FACILITIES:** entertainment **CONF:** Thtr 100 Class 54 Board 40 Del from £95 **SERVICES:** Lift **PARKING:** 17 **NOTES:** No smoking in restaurant **CARDS:**

★★★61% The Crown & Mitre

4 English St CA3 8HZ
☎ 01228 525491 🖷 01228 514553
e-mail: info@crownandmitre-hotel-carlisle.com
Dir: *A6 to city centre, pass station & Woolworths on left. Right into Blackfriars St. Rear entrance at end*

Located in the heart of the city, this Edwardian hotel is close to the cathedral and a few minutes' walk from the castle. Hotel bedrooms vary in size and style from smart executive rooms to more functional standard rooms. Public rooms include the lovely bar with its feature stained glass windows and a comfortable lounge area.

ROOMS: 74 en suite 20 annexe en suite (4 fmly) No smoking in 10 bedrooms s fr £90; d fr £115 (incl. bkfst) **LB** **FACILITIES:** STV Indoor swimming (H) Jacuzzi Xmas **CONF:** Thtr 400 Class 250 Board 50 Del from £95 **SERVICES:** Lift **PARKING:** 42
CARDS:

> Destination dining!
> This symbol indicates a Restaurant with Rooms

CARLISLE, continued

★★66% Pinegrove

262 London Rd CA1 2QS
☎ 01228 524828 📠 01228 810941
e-mail: londonrd262@msn.com
Dir: *on A6, 1.5 miles from M6 junct 42*

The Pinegrove is a privately-owned, friendly hotel located to the south of the city, within easy reach of the M6. Public rooms include a comfortable bar, spacious restaurant and a room for pool and darts. There is also a large function room and the hotel has a licence for civil wedding ceremonies. Bedrooms are well equipped and include rooms on ground floor level.

ROOMS: 27 rms (25 en suite) 4 annexe en suite (8 fmly) s £40-£48; d £50-£60 (incl. bkfst) **LB FACILITIES:** STV Xmas **CONF:** Thtr 120 Class 100 Board 100 **PARKING:** 50 **NOTES:** No smoking in restaurant Closed 25 Dec Civ Wed 200 **CARDS:**

Holiday Inn Carlisle

Parkhouse Rd CA3 0HR
☎ 0870 400 9018 📠 01228 543178
e-mail: reservations-carlisle@6c.com
Dir: *M6 junct 44, take A7 signed Carlisle. Hotel on right at 1st set of lights*

At the time of going to press, the star classification for this hotel was not confirmed. Please refer to the AA internet site www.theAA.com for current information.

ROOMS: 127 en suite (34 fmly) No smoking in 85 bedrooms **FACILITIES:** Indoor swimming (H) Sauna Gym Jacuzzi **CONF:** Thtr 120 Class 64 Board 60 **PARKING:** 150 **NOTES:** No dogs (ex guide dogs) **CARDS:**

Premier Lodge (Carlisle)

Kingstown Rd CA3 0AT
☎ 0870 9906502 📠 0870 9906503

Premier Lodge offers modern, well-equipped, en suite accommodation suitable for both business and leisure travellers. Meals can be taken at the adjacent popular restaurant and bar, which is fully licensed. For further details, consult the Hotel Groups page.

ROOMS: 49 en suite s £48; d £48 **CONF:** Board 12

Travel Inn Carlisle (South)

Carleton CA4 0AD
☎ 08701 977054 📠 01228 633313
Dir: *just off J42 on M6 south of Carlisle*

Travel Inn offers good-quality, value-for-money accommodation. Spacious, en suite rooms with bath and shower comfortably accommodate a family of up to two adults and two children (to age 15). The restaurant and bar offers a varied menu. For further details and the Travel Inn phone number, consult the Hotel Groups page.

ROOMS: 40 en suite s £44.95; d £44.95 **CONF:** Thtr 50 Class 50

Travel Inn (Carlisle Southwaite)

Warwick Rd CA1 2WF
☎ 08701 977053 📠 01228 534096
Dir: *M6 junct 43, on A69*

Travel Inn offers good-quality, value-for-money accommodation. Spacious, en suite rooms with bath and shower comfortably accommodate a family of up to two adults and two children (to age 15). The restaurant and bar offers a varied menu. For further details and the Travel Inn phone number, consult the Hotel Groups page.

ROOMS: 44 en suite s £44.95; d £44.95

Travelodge (Carlisle North)

A74 Southbound, Todhills CA6 4HA
☎ 08700 850 950

Travelodge offers good quality, good value, modern accommodation. Ideal for families, the spacious, en suite bedrooms include remote-control TV, tea and coffee-making facilities, luxury beds and free morning newspaper. Meals can be taken at the nearby family restaurant. For further details and the Travelodge phone number, consult the Hotel Groups page.

ROOMS: 40 en suite s fr £42.95; d fr £42.95

CARNFORTH, Lancashire — Map 18 SD47

★★65% Royal Station

Market St LA5 9BT
☎ 01524 732033 & 733636 📠 01524 720267
e-mail: royalstation@mitchellshotels.co.uk
Dir: *M6 junct 35 onto A6 signed Carnforth. After 1m at x-rds in town centre right into Market St. Hotel opposite railway station*

This commercial hotel enjoys a town centre location close to the railway station. Bedrooms are well equipped and comfortably furnished. A good range of tasty, good value meals can be taken in either the bright attractive lounge bar or the restaurant.

ROOMS: 13 en suite (1 fmly) s £38-£47; d £50-£70 (incl. bkfst) **LB FACILITIES:** Xmas **CONF:** Thtr 150 Class 100 Board 100 **PARKING:** 4 **NOTES:** No smoking in restaurant **CARDS:**

CARSHALTON, Greater London — Map 06 TQ26

★★★64% Greyhound

2 High St SM5 3PE
☎ 020 8647 1511 📠 020 8647 4687
e-mail: greyhound@youngs.co.uk
Dir: *on A232 where Carshalton High St becomes Pound St*

Overlooking the charming ponds this 18th-century coaching inn offers contemporary facilities. Smartly presented bedrooms are comfortable and well appointed, and the more traditional public areas include an informal popular bar. A wide range of freshly prepared dishes are served in the adjoining dining area.

ROOMS: 21 en suite (2 fmly) (6 GF) No smoking in 11 bedrooms s £65-£99; d £75-£109 (incl. bkfst) **LB FACILITIES:** STV **PARKING:** 40 **NOTES:** No dogs (ex guide dogs) **CARDS:**

CARTMEL, Cumbria — Map 18 SD37

★★76% Aynsome Manor

LA11 6HH
☎ 015395 36653 📠 015395 36016
e-mail: info@aynsomemanorhotel.co.uk
Dir: *M6 junct 36, follow A590 signed Barrow-in-Furness towards Cartmel. Left at end of road, hotel before village*

Dating back to the early 16th century in parts, this manor house

continued

overlooks rolling fells and the nearby Priory. Spacious bedrooms, including some courtyard rooms, are comfortably furnished. There is a choice of lounges to relax in after taking dinner, which features local produce whenever possible and is served in the elegant restaurant.
ROOMS: 10 en suite 2 annexe en suite (2 fmly) s £68-£85; d £110-£150 (incl. bkfst & dinner) **LB** **FACILITIES:** Xmas **PARKING:** 20 **NOTES:** No smoking in restaurant Closed 2-31 Jan **CARDS:**

CASTLE ASHBY, Northamptonshire Map 11 SP85

★★73% Falcon
NN7 1LF
☎ 01604 696200 01604 696673
e-mail: falcon@castleashby.co.uk
Dir: *off A428*
Set in the heart of a peaceful village, this family-run hotel consists of a main house and two neighbouring cottages. Bedrooms are all individually decorated and feature a wealth of extras. Public rooms, in the main house, include a first-floor sitting area, a choice of bars and a pretty restaurant.
ROOMS: 5 en suite 11 annexe en suite (1 fmly) No smoking in 3 bedrooms **FACILITIES:** STV **CONF:** Thtr 50 Class 30 Board 25 **PARKING:** 75 **NOTES:** Civ Wed 60 **CARDS:**

CASTLE CARY, Somerset Map 04 ST63

★★64% The George
Market Place BA7 7AH
☎ 01963 350761 01963 350035
e-mail: rob@georgehotel-castlecary.co.uk
Dir: *Turn off A303 onto A361. Signed Castle Cary, 2m on left*
A 15th-century coaching inn with a distinctive thatched roof and bay windows. Rooms are generally spacious, offering a good standard of accommodation and comfort. Most rooms are at the back of the house, enjoying a quiet aspect. Guests can choose to eat in the more formal dining room, or in one of the two cosy bars.
ROOMS: 12 en suite 5 annexe en suite (1 fmly) (5 GF) s £55-£75; d £75-£95 (incl. bkfst) **LB** **FACILITIES:** Xmas **CONF:** Thtr 50 Class 40 Del from £90 **PARKING:** 7 **NOTES:** No smoking in restaurant **CARDS:**

CASTLE COMBE, Wiltshire Map 04 ST87

Top 200 - Hotel

★★★★ Manor House
SN14 7HR
☎ 01249 782206 01249 782159
e-mail: enquiries@manor-housecc.co.uk
Dir: *M4 junct 17 follow Chippenham signs onto A420 Bristol, then right onto B4039. Through village, right after crossing bridge*
This hotel is situated in a secluded valley near the village, where there have been no new buildings for 300 years. There are 26 acres of grounds to enjoy, complete with an Italian garden and 18-hole golf course. Bedrooms, some of which are in a row of stone cottages, have been superbly furnished, and public rooms include a number of cosy lounges with roaring fires. Service is a pleasing blend of professionalism and friendliness, while food focuses on top quality local produce.

ROOMS: 21 en suite 26 annexe en suite (8 fmly) (12 GF) s £145-£500; d £145-£500 **LB** **FACILITIES:** STV Outdoor swimming (H) Golf 18 Tennis (hard) Fishing Snooker Sauna Gym Croquet lawn Putting green Jogging track Xmas **CONF:** BC Thtr 60 Class 36 Board 30 Del from £160 **PARKING:** 100 **NOTES:** No dogs (ex guide dogs) No smoking in restaurant Civ Wed 100
CARDS:

CASTLE DONINGTON See East Midlands Airport

CASTLEFORD, West Yorkshire Map 16 SE42

Premier Lodge (Castleford)
Pioneer Way WF10 5TG
☎ 0870 9906592 0870 9906593
Dir: *M62 junct 31 onto A655 to Castleford. At traffic lights right onto Commerce park. Lodge 2nd on left*
Premier Lodge offers modern, well-equipped, en suite accommodation suitable for both business and leisure travellers. Meals can be taken at the adjacent popular restaurant and bar, which is fully licensed. For further details, consult the Hotel Groups page.
ROOMS: 62 en suite s £48; d £48 **CONF:** Thtr 20 Class 8 Board 10

CASTLETON, Derbyshire Map 16 SK18

Innkeeper's Lodge Castleton
Castle St S33 8WG ☎ 01433 620578
Dir: *on A6187 in village centre*
A new concept in the travel accommodation market. Smart rooms meet essential business requirements but also have home comforts. Dining options include all-day menus plus the added advantage of breakfast, which is included in the room price. For further details, consult the Hotel Groups page.
ROOMS: 6 en suite 6 annexe en suite

CHADDESLEY CORBETT, Worcestershire Map 10 SO87

Top 200 - Hotel

★★★ Brockencote Hall Country House
DY10 4PY
☎ 01562 777876 01562 777872
e-mail: info@brockencotehall.com
Dir: 0.5m W, off A448, opposite St Cassians Church
Glorious countryside extends in all directions around this magnificent mansion, including grazing sheep outside the conservatory. Unsurprisingly, relaxation comes high on the list of priorities here. However, despite the Worcestershire location, the owner hails from Alsace and the feel is very much that of a provincial French château. The chef too is French (from Brittany) and the chandeliered dining room is a popular venue for accomplished modern French cuisine.
ROOMS: 17 en suite (2 fmly) (5 GF) s £96-£140; d £116-£180 (incl. bkfst) **LB** **FACILITIES:** STV Tennis (hard) Croquet lawn Jacuzzi Reflexology /aromatherapy Xmas **CONF:** Thtr 30 Class 20 Board 20 Del from £155 **SERVICES:** Lift **PARKING:** 45 **NOTES:** No dogs (ex guide dogs) No smoking in restaurant
CARDS:

CHAGFORD, Devon Map 03 SX78

Top 200 - Hotel

★★★ Gidleigh Park
TQ13 8HH
☎ 01647 432367 01647 432574
e-mail: gidleighpark@gidleigh.co.uk
Dir: from Chagford, right at Lloyds Bank into Mill St. After 150yds fork right, follow lane 2m to end
2003 saw the hotel celebrating the 25th anniversary of its opening. This hotel has won accolades from across the globe and is set in 45 acres of lovingly tended grounds and gardens.
continued

Bedrooms are lovingly furnished, many with views across the valley. Oak-panelled lounges have comfortable sofas, log fires and plenty of space. Dinner features the finest fare and is a major part of any visit to the hotel, accompanied by a wine list which displays the proprietors' enthusiasm for the subject.
ROOMS: 12 en suite 3 annexe en suite s £270-£475; d £420-£550 (incl. bkfst & dinner) **LB** **FACILITIES:** STV Tennis (hard) Fishing Croquet lawn Putting green Bowls **CONF:** Board 22 **PARKING:** 25 **NOTES:** No smoking in restaurant
CARDS:

★★★76% Mill End
Dartmoor National Park, Sandy Park TQ13 8JN
☎ 01647 432282 01647 433106
e-mail: millendhotel@talk21.com
Dir: from A30 at Whiddon Down follow A382 to Moretonhampstead. After 3.5m hump back bridge at Sandy Park, hotel on right by river

In a peaceful and attractive location, Mill End is set on the riverside and offers six miles of angling on the River Teign. Bedrooms are available in a range of sizes and all are stylishly decorated and thoughtfully equipped. Cuisine is a feature here and menus offer exciting dishes featuring local produce.
ROOMS: 15 en suite (3 GF) s £60-£120; d £80-£160 (incl. bkfst) **LB** **FACILITIES:** Fishing Croquet lawn Xmas **CONF:** Thtr 40 Class 20 Board 30 **PARKING:** 21 **NOTES:** No smoking in restaurant
CARDS:

★★68% *Three Crowns Hotel*
High St TQ13 8AJ
☎ 01647 433444 01647 433117
e-mail: threecrowns@msn.com
Dir: left off A30 at Whiddon Down, in Chagford town centre opposite church

This 13th-century inn is located in the heart of the village. Exposed beams, mullioned windows and open fires are part of the charm, which is well maintained here. There is a range of rooms, several with four-poster beds, all are comfortable and now upgraded.
continued

A choice of bars is available along with a pleasant lounge and separate dining room.
ROOMS: 17 en suite (1 fmly) No smoking in 8 bedrooms
FACILITIES: STV **CONF:** Board 90 **PARKING:** 20 **NOTES:** No smoking in restaurant **CARDS:**

CHARD, Somerset — Map 04 ST30

★★★70% Lordleaze
Henderson Dr, Forton Rd TA20 2HW
☎ 01460 61066 01460 66468
e-mail: lordleaze@fsbdial.co.uk
Dir: *from Chard take A358, at St Mary's Church turn left to Forton & Winsham on B3162. Follow signs to hotel*

The Lordleaze is an excellent base from which to explore the West Country. The comfortable bedrooms, some on the ground floor, are well equipped. A focal point is the relaxed and friendly lounge bar where a wood burning stove adds to the character and atmosphere. In addition to the carte menu offered in the restaurant, a tempting selection of bar meals is also available.
ROOMS: 16 en suite (1 fmly) No smoking in 4 bedrooms **CONF:** Thtr 180 Class 60 Board 40 **PARKING:** 55 **NOTES:** No smoking in restaurant Civ Wed 110 **CARDS:**

CHARINGWORTH, Gloucestershire — Map 10 SP13

★★★79% Charingworth Manor
GL55 6NS
☎ 01386 593555 01386 593353
e-mail: charingworthmanor@englishrosehotels.co.uk
Dir: *on B4035 3m E of Chipping Campden*
This 14th-century manor house retains many original features including flagstone floors, exposed beams and open fireplaces. The house has a beautiful setting in 50 acres of grounds and has been carefully extended to provide high quality accommodation and a delightful small leisure spa. Spacious bedrooms are furnished with period pieces and modern amenities.
ROOMS: 26 en suite s £115-£150; d £150-£275 (incl. bkfst) **LB**
FACILITIES: STV Indoor swimming (H) Tennis (hard) Sauna Solarium Gym Croquet lawn Steam room Xmas **CONF:** Thtr 60 Class 40 Board 40 Del from £150 **PARKING:** 50 **NOTES:** No dogs (ex guide dogs) No smoking in restaurant Civ Wed 50
CARDS:

See advert under CHIPPING CAMPDEN

GF Indicates the number of bedrooms at ground floor level.

CHARLBURY, Oxfordshire — Map 11 SP31

★★65% The Bell
Church St OX7 3PP
☎ 01608 810278 01608 811447
e-mail: llequitour@aol.com
Dir: *from Oxford take A34 towards Woodstock, 2nd turn off B4437 towards Charlbury. In village, 2nd left, hotel opposite St Mary's Church*
A mellow Cotswold Stone inn dating back to the 16th century when it was home to customs and excise and sitting close to the centre of this ancient town. Popular with locals the enjoyable and relaxed atmosphere of the bar comes complete with flagstone floors and log fires. The well-equipped bedrooms are situated in the main building and the converted adjacent barn.
ROOMS: 7 en suite 4 annexe en suite (3 fmly) No smoking in all bedrooms s fr £69; d fr £85 (incl. bkfst) **LB** **CONF:** Thtr 60 Class 60 Board 30 Del from £120 **PARKING:** 40 **NOTES:** No smoking in restaurant **CARDS:**

CHARMOUTH, Dorset — Map 04 SY39

★★72% White House
2 Hillside, The Street DT6 6PJ
☎ 01297 560411 01297 560702
e-mail: ian@whitehousehotel.com
Dir: *off A35 signed Charmouth. Hotel opposite church halfway up hill*

Famed for its fossils and cliff-top walks, the interesting beach is within walking distance of this charming Regency property. Comfortable accommodation is provided at this friendly, small hotel where individually styled bedrooms are equipped with modern facilities. In the evening, imaginative cuisine is served in the attractive restaurant, cooked using fresh, local produce.
ROOMS: 7 rms (6 en suite) 2 annexe en suite (2 GF) No smoking in all bedrooms s £40-£55; d £80-£120 (incl. bkfst) **LB** **FACILITIES:** Xmas **PARKING:** 9 **NOTES:** No children 14yrs No smoking in restaurant Closed Jan **CARDS:**

CHARNOCK RICHARD MOTORWAY SERVICE AREA (M6), Lancashire — Map 15 SD51

Welcome Lodge
Welcome Break Service Area PR7 5LR
☎ 01257 791746 01257 793596
e-mail: charnockhotel@welcomebreak.co.uk
Dir: *on northbound side between junct 27 & 28 of M6. 500yds from Camelot Theme Park via Mill Lane*
This modern building offers accommodation in smart, spacious and well-equipped bedrooms, suitable for families and business

Welcome Break

continued on p166

CHARNOCK RICHARD SERVICE AREA (M6), continued

travellers, and all with en suite bathrooms. Refreshments may be taken at the nearby family restaurant. For further details and the Welcome Break phone number, consult the Hotel Groups page.
ROOMS: 100 en suite s £35-£50; d £35-£50 **CONF:** Thtr 40 Class 16 Board 24

CHATHAM, Kent Map 07 TQ76

★★★★75% @@
Bridgewood Manor Hotel
Bridgewood Roundabout, Walderslade Woods ME5 9AX
☎ 01634 201333 📠 01634 201330
e-mail: bridgewoodmanor@marstonhotels.co.uk
Dir: *adjacent to Bridgewood rdbt on A229. Take 3rd exit signed Walderslade and Lordswood. Hotel 50mtrs on left*
A modern, purpose-built hotel situated on the outskirts of Rochester. Bedrooms are pleasantly decorated, comfortably furnished and equipped with many thoughtful touches. The hotel has an excellent range of leisure and conference facilities. Guests can dine in the informal Terrace Bistro or experience fine dining in the more formal Squires restaurant, where the service is both attentive and friendly.
ROOMS: 100 en suite (12 fmly) No smoking in 63 bedrooms s fr £108; d fr £130 **LB** **FACILITIES:** STV Indoor swimming (H) Tennis (hard) Snooker Sauna Solarium Gym Putting green Jacuzzi Beauty treatments Xmas **CONF:** Thtr 200 Class 110 Board 80 Del from £145
SERVICES: Lift **PARKING:** 178 **NOTES:** No smoking in restaurant Civ Wed 120 **CARDS:**

CHEADLE, Greater Manchester Map 16 SJ88

Travel Inn (Manchester Cheadle)
Royal Crescent SK8 3FE
☎ 08701 977172 📠 0161 491 5886
Dir: *off Cheadle Royal rdbt off A34 behind TGI Friday's*
Travel Inn offers good-quality, value-for-money accommodation. Spacious, en suite rooms with bath and shower comfortably accommodate a family of up to two adults and two children (to age 15). The restaurant and bar offers a varied menu. For further details and the Travel Inn phone number, consult the Hotel Groups page.
ROOMS: 40 en suite s £44.95; d £44.95 **CONF:** Thtr 30

CHELMSFORD, Essex Map 06 TL70

★★★72% **Pontlands Park Country**
West Hanningfield Rd, Great Baddow CM2 8HR
☎ 01245 476444 📠 01245 478393
e-mail: sales@pontlandsparkhotel.co.uk
Dir: *A12 junct A130. Take A1114 to Chelmsford. 1st available exit at rdbt, 1st slip road on left. Left towards Gt Baddow, 1st left into West Hanningfield Rd. Hotel 400yds on left*
A Victorian country house hotel in a peaceful rural setting amidst attractive landscaped grounds. The stylishly furnished bedrooms are generally quite spacious; each is individually decorated and equipped with modern facilities. The elegant public rooms include a tastefully furnished sitting room, a cosy lounge bar, smart conservatory restaurant and an intimate dining room.
ROOMS: 36 en suite (10 fmly) (12 GF) No smoking in 7 bedrooms s £105-£125; d £125-£165 **LB** **FACILITIES:** STV Indoor swimming (H) Outdoor swimming (H) Sauna Gym Jacuzzi Beauty salon **CONF:** Thtr 100 Class 20 Board 22 Del from £145 **PARKING:** 100 **NOTES:** No dogs (ex guide dogs) Closed 24 Dec-3Jan (ex 31 Dec) Civ Wed 100
CARDS:

★★★71% ***County***
Rainsford Rd CM1 2PZ
☎ 01245 455700 📠 01245 492762
e-mail: sales@countyhotel-essex.co.uk
Dir: *from town centre, past rail and bus station. Hotel 300yds left beyond lights*
Expect a friendly welcome from the young and enthusiastic team of staff at this popular hotel, which is ideally situated within easy walking distance of the railway station, bus depot and town centre. The property has been extended and includes a new wing of smartly appointed, well-equipped bedrooms. Public areas include the Artista Brasserie and the plushly furnished wine bar.
ROOMS: 53 en suite 8 annexe en suite **CONF:** Thtr 150 Class 60 Board 40 **SERVICES:** Lift **PARKING:** 80 **NOTES:** No dogs (ex guide dogs) Closed 27-30 Dec Civ Wed 80 **CARDS:**

★★★70% **Atlantic**
New St CM1 1PP
☎ 01245 268168 📠 01245 268169
e-mail: info@atlantichotel.co.uk
Ideally situated just a short walk from the railway station with its quick links to London, this modern, purpose built hotel has contemporary style bedrooms equipped with modern facilities. The open plan public areas include the popular New Street Brasserie, a lounge bar and a conservatory.
ROOMS: 59 en suite (24 fmly) No smoking in 28 bedrooms s fr £85; d fr £95 **FACILITIES:** STV Sauna Solarium Gym entertainment **CONF:** Thtr 15 Board 10 **SERVICES:** air con **PARKING:** 60 **NOTES:** No dogs (ex guide dogs) Closed 21 Dec-1 Jan
CARDS:

Premier Lodge Chelmsford
Main Rd, Borham CM3 3HJ
☎ 0870 9906394 📠 0870 9906395
Dir: *M25 junct 28, A12 to Colchester, then B1137 to Borham*
Premier Lodge offers modern, well-equipped, en suite accommodation suitable for both business and leisure travellers. Meals can be taken at the adjacent popular restaurant and bar, which is fully licensed. For further details, consult the Hotel Groups page.
ROOMS: 78 en suite s £48; d £48

Travel Inn
Chelmsford Service Area, Colchester Rd, Springfield CM2 5PY

☎ 0870 238 3310 📠 01245 464010
Dir: *at A12 and A138 junct, 2nd service area from A12*
Travel Inn offers good-quality, value-for-money accommodation. Spacious, en suite rooms with bath and shower comfortably accommodate a family of up to two adults and two children (to age 15). The restaurant and bar offers a varied menu. For further details and the Travel Inn phone number, consult the Hotel Groups page.
ROOMS: 61 en suite s £44.95; d £44.95

CHELTENHAM, Gloucestershire Map 10 SO92

Town House

★★★★ ⊛ 🏠 **Kandinsky**
Bayshill Rd, Montpellier GL50 3AS
☎ 01242 527788 📠 01242 226412
e-mail: info@hotelkandinsky.com
Dir: *M5 junct 11, A40 to town centre. Right at 2nd rdbt. 2nd exit at 3rd rdbt into Bayshill Rd. Hotel on corner of Bayshill/Parabola Rds*
A large white Regency villa which blends modern comfort with quirky eclectic decoration. Stylish bedrooms vary in size and have additional facilities such as CD/video players. There are various lounges, a conservatory, and the bright Café Paradiso restaurant. Hidden in the cellars is 'U-bahn', a wonderful 1950's style cocktail bar.
ROOMS: 48 en suite (3 fmly) (5 GF) No smoking in 4 bedrooms s £65-£115; d £89-£115 **LB** **FACILITIES:** STV Access to local pool & gym entertainment Xmas **CONF:** Thtr 20 Class 16 Board 16 Del from £140 **SERVICES:** Lift **PARKING:** 32 **NOTES:** No dogs (ex guide dogs) No smoking in restaurant
CARDS:

See advert on this page

★★★★69% **The Queen's**
The Promenade GL50 1NN
☎ 0870 400 8107 📠 01242 224145
e-mail: general.queens@macdonald-hotels.co.uk
MACDONALD HOTELS
Dir: *follow town centre signs. Left at Montpellier Walk rdbt. Entrance 500mtrs right*
With its spectacular position at the top of the main promenade, this landmark hotel is an ideal base from which to explore the charms of this Regency Spa town and the surrounding Cotswolds. An extensive bedroom refurbishment was due for completion in 2003; early results were most impressive. Smart public rooms include the popular Gold Cup bar and a choice of dining options.
ROOMS: 79 en suite No smoking in 26 bedrooms s £145; d £149 (incl. bkfst) **LB** **FACILITIES:** STV Xmas **CONF:** Thtr 100 Class 60 Board 40 Del from £160 **SERVICES:** Lift **PARKING:** 80 **NOTES:** No smoking in restaurant Civ Wed 100 **CARDS:**

🏠 Town House Hotel
Country House Hotel
Travel Accommodation

★★★★65% **Cheltenham Park**
Cirencester Rd, Charlton Kings GL53 8EA
☎ 01242 222021 📠 01242 254880
e-mail: cheltenhamparkreservations@paramount-hotels.co.uk

Dir: *on A435, 2m SE of Cheltenham near Lilley Brook Golf Course*
Conveniently located south of Cheltenham, this attractive Georgian hotel is set in its own landscaped gardens, adjacent to Lilley Brook Golf Course. All of the bedrooms are spacious and well equipped and the hotel has an impressive leisure club and extensive meeting facilities. The Lakeside restaurant serves carefully prepared cuisine.
ROOMS: 33 en suite 110 annexe en suite (2 fmly) No smoking in 67 bedrooms s £105-£125; d £140-£160 **LB** **FACILITIES:** STV Indoor swimming (H) Sauna Solarium Gym Jacuzzi Beauty treatment rooms, Swimming pool supervised Xmas **CONF:** BC Thtr 350 Class 180 Board 110 Del from £100 **SERVICES:** Lift **PARKING:** 170 **NOTES:** No smoking in restaurant Civ Wed 300 **CARDS:**

Late for dinner?
Quality Standards mean that last orders for dinner vary according to star rating and should be no earlier than:
★★ 7.00pm ★★★ 8.00pm ★★★★ 9.00pm
★★★★★ 10.00pm

CHELTENHAM, continued

Top 200 - Hotel

★★★ ⓐⓐⓐ The Greenway
Shurdington GL51 4UG
☎ 01242 862352 📠 01242 862780
e-mail: greenway@btconnect.com
Dir: *2.5m SW on A46*

This hotel, with a wealth of history, is peacefully located in a delightful setting close to the A46 and the M5. Within easy reach of the many attractions of the Cotswolds as well as the interesting City of Cheltenham, The Greenway certainly offers something special in terms of environment. The attractive dining room overlooks the sunken garden and is the venue for exciting food, proudly served by dedicated and attentive staff.

ROOMS: 11 en suite 10 annexe en suite (1 fmly) (4 GF) No smoking in 8 bedrooms s £99-£159; d £150-£280 (incl. bkfst) **LB** **FACILITIES:** STV Croquet lawn Clay pigeon shooting, Horse riding, Mountain biking, Beauty treatment Xmas **CONF:** Thtr 45 Class 25 Board 18 Del £205 **PARKING:** 50 **NOTES:** No smoking in restaurant Civ Wed 45 **CARDS:**

Top 200 - Hotel

★★★ ⓐⓐ Hotel on the Park
38 Evesham Rd GL52 2AH
☎ 01242 518898 📠 01242 511526
e-mail: stay@hotelonthepark.co.uk
Dir: *opposite Pittville Park. Join one-way system, off A435 towards Evesham*

The Hotel on the Park is a wonderfully different hotel with style, originality and flair throughout. Bedrooms have tremendous character, comfort and above all personality. Similar comments apply to public areas, comprising the elegant drawing room, library and the Bacchanalian Restaurant, the venue for accomplished and enjoyable cuisine.
continued

Look out for the two huge bears who sit dressed for dinner at one of the dining room tables.

ROOMS: 12 en suite No smoking in 4 bedrooms s £85-£143; d £108-£158 **LB** **FACILITIES:** STV **CONF:** Board 18 **PARKING:** 8 **NOTES:** No children 8yrs No smoking in restaurant
CARDS:

★★★69% Charlton Kings
London Rd, Charlton Kings GL52 6UU
THE INDEPENDENTS
☎ 01242 231061 📠 01242 241900
e-mail: enquires@charltonkingshotel.co.uk
Dir: *entering Cheltenham from Oxford on A40, 1st on left*

Conveniently located on the outskirts of Cheltenham, the Charlton Kings is an attractive and friendly hotel providing comfortable, modern accommodation. Neatly presented bedrooms are both comfortable and well-equipped with tasteful furnishings. The popular and stylish restaurant serves a variety of dishes for all tastes from a menu based on quality ingredients.

ROOMS: 14 en suite (1 fmly) (4 GF) No smoking in 12 bedrooms s £65-£85; d £95-£120 (incl. bkfst) **LB** **CONF:** Thtr 20 Class 20 Board 20 **PARKING:** 26 **NOTES:** No smoking in restaurant
CARDS:

★★★68% George Hotel
St Georges Rd GL50 3DZ
☎ 01242 235751 📠 01242 224359
e-mail: hotel@stayatthegeorge.co.uk
Dir: *M5 junct 11 town centre signs. At 1st lights left into Gloucester Rd, past rail station over mini rdbt. At lights right into St Georges Rd. Hotel 0.75m on left*

Just a short stroll from the town centre, this genuinely friendly hotel is privately owned and occupies part of an elegant Regency terrace. Bedrooms are well-equipped and tastefully furnished with additional facilities such as satellite TV and trouser presses. An
continued

interesting menu is offered in the comfort of Seasons Restaurant with attentive staff ensuring a relaxed and enjoyable meal.
ROOMS: 38 en suite (1 GF) No smoking in 30 bedrooms s £60-£75; d £85-£105 (incl. bkfst) **LB FACILITIES:** STV **CONF:** Thtr 40 Board 24 Del from £123 **PARKING:** 30 **NOTES:** No dogs (ex guide dogs) No smoking in restaurant RS 24-26 Dec
CARDS:

★★★67% Carlton

Parabola Rd GL50 3AQ
☎ 01242 514453 📠 01242 226487
e-mail: enquiries@thecarltonhotel.co.uk
Dir: *Follow signs to town centre, at Town Hall straight on at 2 sets of lights, turn left, then first right.*
This well-presented Regency property is conveniently situated within a short walk of the town centre. Family owned and run, it provides comfortable accommodation with a relaxed and friendly atmosphere. Bedrooms are located both in the main hotel and also within an annexe building, where rooms are larger and more luxurious. Other features include a choice of bars, lounge and conference facilities.
ROOMS: 62 en suite 13 annexe en suite (2 fmly) (4 GF) No smoking in 15 bedrooms s £40-£73; d £79-£94 (incl. bkfst) **LB FACILITIES:** STV Xmas **CONF:** Thtr 200 Class 150 Board 100 Del from £90 **SERVICES:** Lift **PARKING:** 85 **NOTES:** No smoking in restaurant Civ Wed 170 **CARDS:**

★★★65% *Royal George*

Birdlip GL4 8JH
☎ 01452 862506 📠 01452 862277
e-mail: royalgeorgehotel@birdlip.freeserve.co.uk
Dir: *on B4070, off A417*
Situated in a pretty village, this attractive 18th-century, Cotswold building has been sympathetically converted and extended into a pleasant hotel. Bedrooms are spacious and comfortably furnished with modern facilities. The public areas have been designed around a traditional English pub with the bar leading onto a terrace overlooking extensive lawns. A path links the hotel to the Cotswold Way.
ROOMS: 34 en suite (1 fmly) No smoking in 12 bedrooms **FACILITIES:** STV **CONF:** Thtr 100 Class 60 Board 60 **PARKING:** 120 **NOTES:** No smoking in restaurant **CARDS:**

★★★65% *White House*

Gloucester Rd GL51 0ST
☎ 01452 713226 📠 01452 857590
e-mail: stay@white-house-hotel.co.uk
Dir: *M5 junct 11 onto A40 to Cheltenham. Left at rdbt, hotel 0.5m on left*
The White House Hotel is situated on the edge of town, and provides comfortable and modern accommodation. The lounge bar and the restaurant are attractively presented with a number of function rooms also available. Friendly service and helpful staff ensure a pleasant stay.
ROOMS: 49 en suite (4 fmly) No smoking in 13 bedrooms **FACILITIES:** STV pool table bar games entertainment **CONF:** Thtr 180 Class 80 Board 45 **PARKING:** 150 **NOTES:** No smoking in restaurant RS 12-16 Mar & 10-12 Nov Civ Wed 180
CARDS:

★★★64% The Prestbury House Hotel & Oaks Restaurant

The Burgage, Prestbury GL52 3DN
☎ 01242 529533 📠 01242 227076
e-mail: sandjw@freenetname.co.uk
Dir: *1m NE of Cheltenham. Follow all signs for racecourse. From racecourse follow Prestbury signs. Hotel 2nd left, 500mtrs from racecourse*
This hotel retains much of its historical charm and is well situated for the town centre and racecourse. Well-equipped, spacious accommodation is offered in the main house and converted coach house. An interesting range of dishes is offered in 'Oaks', the hotel's elegant, oak-panelled restaurant. The owners also run a management training company, and team-building activities are sometimes held here.
ROOMS: 7 en suite 8 annexe en suite (3 GF) No smoking in 16 bedrooms s £55-£97; d £60-£104 (incl. bkfst) **LB FACILITIES:** STV Riding Gym Croquet lawn Putting green Clay pigeons, Archery, Bike hire, Trim Trail Hill Walking, Target golf, Petanque Xmas **CONF:** BC Thtr 65 Class 30 Board 25 Del from £115 **PARKING:** 40 **NOTES:** No dogs (ex guide dogs) No smoking in restaurant Civ Wed 60
CARDS:

★★68% *Cotswold Grange*

Pittville Circus Rd GL52 2QH
☎ 01242 515119 📠 01242 241537
e-mail: paul@cotswold-grange.fsnet.co.uk
Dir: *from town centre, follow Prestbury signs. Right at 1st rdbt, hotel 200yds on left*
Built from mellow Cotswold limestone, this attractive Georgian property retains many impressive architectural features. Situated conveniently close to the centre of Cheltenham, this long established, family-run hotel offers well-equipped and comfortable accommodation. The convivial bar is a popular venue, and additional facilities include a spacious restaurant, cosy lounge and ample parking.
ROOMS: 25 en suite (4 fmly) **CONF:** Thtr 20 Class 15 Board 15 **PARKING:** 20 **NOTES:** No smoking in restaurant Closed 24 Dec-1 Jan RS Sat & Sun evening (food by arrangement)
CARDS:

★★64% North Hall

Pittville Circus Rd GL52 2PZ
☎ 01242 520589 📠 01242 261953
e-mail: northhallhotel@btinternet.com
Dir: *from Cheltenham town centre, follow Pittville signs. At Pittville Circus take 1st left into Pittville Circus Rd. Hotel on right*

This three storey Victorian house is within easy reach of the town
continued on p170

CHELTENHAM, continued

centre. Well-equipped bedrooms come in various sizes and a number have been refurbished. There is a comfortable bar-lounge, which offers light meals all day.
ROOMS: 20 en suite (2 fmly) No smoking in 8 bedrooms s £45-£65; d £65-£90 (incl. bkfst) **LB** **FACILITIES:** Xmas **CONF:** Thtr 40 Class 25 Board 15 **PARKING:** 25 **NOTES:** No smoking in restaurant
CARDS:

Travel Inn

Tewkesbury Rd, Uckington GL51 9SL
☎ 08701 977055 🖷 01242 244887
Dir: *opposite Sainsbury's & Homebase on A4019, 2 miles from J10 (southbound exit only) and 3 miles from J11 (both exits) of the M5*
Travel Inn offers good-quality, value-for-money accommodation. Spacious, en suite rooms with bath and shower comfortably accommodate a family of up to two adults and two children (to age 15). The restaurant and bar offers a varied menu. For further details and the Travel Inn phone number, consult the Hotel Groups page.
ROOMS: 40 en suite s £44.95; d £44.95 **CONF:** Thtr 30 Class 30

Travel Inn (Cheltenham Central)

374 Gloucester Rd GL51 7AY
☎ 08701 977056 🖷 01242 260042

Dir: *M5 junct 11 onto A40 (Cheltenham). Follow dual carriageway to end, straight at 1st rdbt, turn right at 2nd*

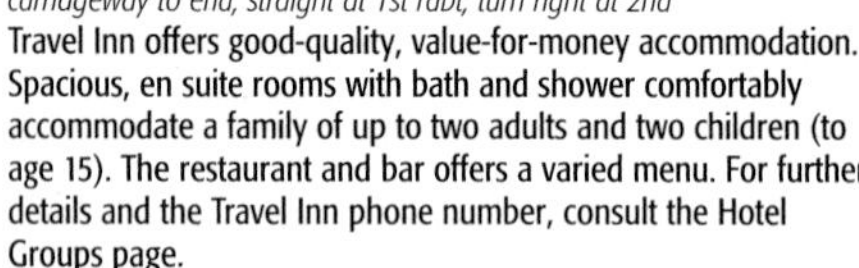

Travel Inn offers good-quality, value-for-money accommodation. Spacious, en suite rooms with bath and shower comfortably accommodate a family of up to two adults and two children (to age 15). The restaurant and bar offers a varied menu. For further details and the Travel Inn phone number, consult the Hotel Groups page.
ROOMS: 40 en suite s £44.95; d £44.95

○ Travelodge

Golden Valley Roundabout, Hatherley Ln GL51 6PN
☎ 0870 191 1701
ROOMS: 106 en suite **NOTES:** Due to open Jan 2004

CHENIES, Buckinghamshire Map 06 TQ09

★★★72% The Bedford Arms

WD3 6EQ
☎ 01923 283301 🖷 01923 284825
e-mail: contact@bedfordarms.co.uk
Dir: *M25 J18, follow signs for Amersham, approx 2.5m*
This attractive, 19th-century country inn enjoys a peaceful rural setting. Comfortable bedrooms are decorated in traditional style and feature a range of thoughtful extras. Each room is named after a relation of the Duke of Bedford, whose family has an historic association with the hotel. There are two bars, a lounge and a cosy, wood-panelled restaurant.
ROOMS: 10 en suite No smoking in 3 bedrooms s £60-£90; d £120-£130 (incl. bkfst) **FACILITIES:** STV **CONF:** Thtr 25 Class 10 Board 15 Del from £177 **PARKING:** 60 **NOTES:** No dogs (ex guide dogs) No smoking in restaurant **CARDS:**

CHERTSEY, Surrey Map 06 TQ06

★★★64% The Crown

7 London St KT16 8AP
☎ 01932 564657 🖷 01932 570839
e-mail: crownhotel@youngs.co.uk
Dir: *adjacent to Old Town Hall, located in town centre*
Once a Victorian coaching inn, this hotel is located in the heart of the town centre. Modern spacious, well-equipped bedrooms are situated in a purpose built annexe. Traditional public areas feature a busy bar and popular restaurant.
ROOMS: 30 annexe en suite (4 fmly) (14 GF) No smoking in 13 bedrooms s £50-£105; d £65-£115 (incl. bkfst) **LB** **FACILITIES:** STV Xmas **CONF:** Thtr 100 Class 40 Board 35 **SERVICES:** air con **PARKING:** 50 **CARDS:**

CHESSINGTON, Greater London Map 06 TQ16

Travel Inn

Leatherhead Rd KT9 2NE
☎ 08701 977057 🖷 01372 720889
Dir: *on A423, 2m from M25 junct 9, towards Kingston*
Travel Inn offers good-quality, value-for-money accommodation. Spacious, en suite rooms with bath and shower comfortably accommodate a family of up to two adults and two children (to age 15). The restaurant and bar offers a varied menu. For further details and the Travel Inn phone number, consult the Hotel Groups page.
ROOMS: 42 en suite s £54.95; d £54.95

CHESTER, Cheshire Map 15 SJ46
See also Puddington

Top 200 - Hotel

★★★★★ ◎◎◎ The Chester Grosvenor & Grosvenor Spa

Eastgate CH1 1LT
☎ 01244 324024 🖷 01244 313246
e-mail: chesgrov@chestergrosvenor.co.uk
Dir: *off M56 for M53, then A56. Follow city centre hotels signs*
Located within the Roman walls of the city, this Grade II listed, half-timbered building is the essence of Englishness. The brasserie is bustling, whilst the Library has a discreet club-like feel. In the Arkle Restaurant, guests are offered creative cuisine of flair and style. Furnished with fine fabrics and queen or king-size beds, the suites and bedrooms are of the

continued

highest standard, each designed with guest comfort as a priority. A new luxury spa & fitness centre has now opened.
ROOMS: 80 en suite No smoking in all bedrooms s £200-£617; d £247-£617 **LB FACILITIES: Spa** STV Sauna Solarium Gym Jacuzzi Membership of nearby Country Club entertainment **CONF:** BC Thtr 250 Class 120 Board 48 Del from £185 **SERVICES:** Lift air con **NOTES:** No dogs (ex guide dogs) No smoking in restaurant Closed 25-26 Dec RS 27-30 Dec & 1-20 Jan Civ Wed 150 **CARDS:**

Top 200 - Hotel

★★★★ The Chester Crabwall Manor Hotel

Parkgate Rd, Mollington CH1 6NE
☎ 01244 851666 01244 851400
e-mail: crabwall@marstonhotels.com
Dir: *NW off A540*

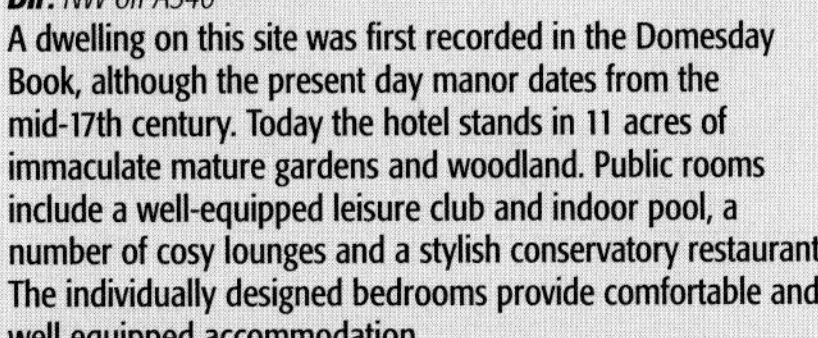

A dwelling on this site was first recorded in the Domesday Book, although the present day manor dates from the mid-17th century. Today the hotel stands in 11 acres of immaculate mature gardens and woodland. Public rooms include a well-equipped leisure club and indoor pool, a number of cosy lounges and a stylish conservatory restaurant. The individually designed bedrooms provide comfortable and well equipped accommodation.
ROOMS: 48 en suite No smoking in 2 bedrooms s fr £135; d fr £153 **LB FACILITIES:** STV Indoor swimming (H) Snooker Sauna Solarium Gym Croquet lawn Jacuzzi Heli pad Xmas **CONF:** Thtr 100 Class 60 Board 40 Del from £170 **PARKING:** 120 **NOTES:** No dogs (ex guide dogs) No smoking in restaurant Civ Wed 90 **CARDS:**

★★★★74% De Vere Carden Park

Carden Park CH3 9DQ
☎ 01829 731000 01829 731599
e-mail: reservations.carden@devere-hotels.com
(For full entry see Broxton)

★★★★68% The Queen Hotel

City Rd CH1 3AH
☎ 01244 305000 01244 318483
Dir: *follow signs for railway station, hotel opposite*
This former railway hotel has been offering accommodation to visitors to this historic city since the 19th century. The friendly staff and the attentive service lead many guests to return regularly. Bedrooms tend to be spacious and many have views over the garden. Public rooms include an impressive central gallery staircase, two lounges, two bars and a popular restaurant.
ROOMS: 128 en suite (6 fmly) (10 GF) No smoking in 66 bedrooms s £55-£109; d £75-£145 (incl. bkfst) **LB FACILITIES:** Croquet lawn entertainment Xmas **CONF:** BC Thtr 280 Class 100 Board 50 Del from £85 **SERVICES:** Lift **PARKING:** 100 **NOTES:** No smoking in restaurant Civ Wed 250 **CARDS:**

★★★★66% Mollington Banastre

Parkgate Rd CH1 6NN
☎ 01244 851471 01244 851165
e-mail: events.mollington@arcadianhotels.co.uk
Dir: *M56 junct 16 at rdbt left for Chester on A540. Hotel 2m on right*

Set in its own attractive grounds, this hotel remains popular with both the business and the leisure markets. The bedrooms, which come in various shapes and sizes, are well equipped. Stylish, open-plan public areas include a comfortable bar and lounge, the Garden Room restaurant and a large leisure club.
ROOMS: 63 en suite (7 fmly) No smoking in 40 bedrooms s £85-£90; d £105-£110 (incl. bkfst) **LB FACILITIES:** STV Indoor swimming (H) Squash Sauna Solarium Gym Jacuzzi Hairdressing Health & beauty salon entertainment Xmas **CONF:** BC Thtr 260 Class 60 Board 50 Del from £120 **SERVICES:** Lift **PARKING:** 200 **NOTES:** No smoking in restaurant Civ Wed 150 **CARDS:**

★★★72% Rowton Hall Country House Hotel

Whitchurch Rd, Rowton CH3 6AD
☎ 01244 335262 01244 335464
e-mail: rowtonhall@rowtonhall.co.uk
Dir: *2m SE of Chester at Rowton off A41 towards Whitchurch*

This refurbished Georgian manor house lies in several acres of mature grounds. Original features include a superb carved staircase and several eye-catching fireplaces. The modern extensions house a leisure centre and extensive function facilities.

continued on p172

CHESTER, continued

The rooms in the manor house are luxuriously spacious and well-equipped. Modern rooms are available in the courtyard.
ROOMS: 38 en suite (4 fmly) (8 GF) s £90-£200; d £90-£200 **LB** **FACILITIES:** STV Indoor swimming (H) Tennis (hard) Sauna Solarium Gym Croquet lawn Jacuzzi Xmas **CONF:** Thtr 170 Class 48 Board 50 Del from £155 **PARKING:** 120 **NOTES:** No dogs (ex guide dogs) No smoking in restaurant Civ Wed 120 **CARDS:**

C

★★★69% Westminster

City Rd CH1 3AF
☎ 01244 317341 📠 01244 325369

Best Western

Dir: *A56 3m to Chester city centre, left signed rail station. Hotel opp station, on right*
Situated close to the railway station and city centre, the Westminster is an old-established hotel which has been extensively upgraded. It has an attractive Tudor-style exterior while bedrooms are brightly decorated with a modern theme. No smoking bedrooms and family rooms are both available. There is a choice of bars and lounges, and the large dining room serves a good range of dishes.
ROOMS: 75 en suite (5 fmly) (6 GF) No smoking in 20 bedrooms s £55-£65; d £85-£120 (incl. bkfst) **LB** **FACILITIES:** STV entertainment Xmas **CONF:** Thtr 150 Class 60 Board 40 Del from £90 **SERVICES:** Lift **PARKING:** 50 **NOTES:** No dogs (ex guide dogs) No smoking in restaurant Civ Wed 100 **CARDS:**

★★★68% Grosvenor Pulford

Wrexham Rd, Pulford CH4 9DG
☎ 01244 570560 📠 01244 570809
e-mail: enquiries@grosvenorpulfordhotel.co.uk
Dir: *M53/A55 exit for A483 signed Chester, Wrexham & North Wales. Take B5445, hotel 2m on right*
Set in rural surroundings, this hotel features a magnificent leisure club with a large Roman-style swimming pool. A choice of rooms includes several executive suites and others contain spiral staircases leading to the bedroom sections. A Victorian-style, beamed restaurant and bar provide a wide range of imaginative dishes in a relaxed atmosphere.
ROOMS: 73 en suite (6 fmly) (21 GF) No smoking in 10 bedrooms s £75-£95; d £100-£150 (incl. bkfst) **LB** **FACILITIES:** STV Indoor swimming (H) Snooker Sauna Solarium Gym Jacuzzi Hairdressing & Beauty salon Xmas **CONF:** Thtr 200 Class 100 Board 50 Del from £108 **SERVICES:** Lift **PARKING:** 200 **NOTES:** Civ Wed 250
CARDS:

See advert on opposite page

★★★66% Blossoms

St John St CH1 1HL
☎ 0870 400 8108 📠 01244 346433
e-mail: general.blossoms@macdonald-hotels.co.uk
Dir: *in city centre, follow signs for Eastgate and City Centre Hotels, continue through pedestrianised zone, hotel on the left*
For those seeking to explore this charming, medieval walled city, the central location of this elegant hotel is ideal. The public areas retain much of their Victorian charm and on occasion at dinner, piano music adds to the intimate atmosphere.
ROOMS: 64 en suite (3 fmly) No smoking in 43 bedrooms s £98-£118; d £118-£148 **LB** **FACILITIES:** STV Discount at local health club Xmas **CONF:** Thtr 80 Class 60 Board 60 Del from £105 **SERVICES:** Lift **NOTES:** No smoking in restaurant Civ Wed 100
CARDS:

★★★66% The Gateway To Wales

Welsh Rd, Sealand, Deeside CH5 2HX
☎ 01244 830332 📠 01244 836190
e-mail: mikesudbury@gatewaytowaleshotel.co.uk
Dir: *4m NW via A548 towards Sealand and Queensferry*
A modern hotel well located for exploring the area, with easy access to Chester. Public areas include The Louis XVI lounge bar, Regency Room restaurant and well-equipped leisure facilities. Bedrooms are a good size and well designed, and the Imperial Suite can cater for conferences, wedding and exhibitions.
ROOMS: 39 en suite (18 GF) No smoking in 20 bedrooms s £49-£62; d £60-£75 (incl. bkfst) **LB** **FACILITIES:** Indoor swimming (H) Sauna Solarium Gym Jacuzzi Use of Indoor Bowls & Snooker Club Xmas **CONF:** Thtr 150 Class 50 Board 50 Del from £80 **SERVICES:** Lift **PARKING:** 60 **NOTES:** No dogs (ex guide dogs) No smoking in restaurant **CARDS:**

★★★66% Mill

Milton St CH1 3NF
☎ 01244 350035 📠 01244 345635
e-mail: reservations@millhotel.com
Dir: *M53 Junct 12, turn right A56 straight ahead A56 & at 2nd roundabout left A5268 then 1st left, 2nd left*
This hotel is a stylish conversion of an old corn mill and enjoys an idyllic canal side location close to the city. The bedrooms offer varying styles and public rooms are spacious and comfortable. Dinner is often served on a canal boat that cruises Chesters locks between courses. A well-equipped leisure centre is also provided.
ROOMS: 80 en suite 49 annexe en suite (57 fmly) No smoking in 51 bedrooms s £62-£80; d £78-£95 (incl. bkfst) **FACILITIES:** STV Indoor swimming (H) Sauna Solarium Gym Jacuzzi Steam room, Swimming pool supervised entertainment Xmas **CONF:** Thtr 40 Class 15 Board 20 Del from £95 **SERVICES:** Lift **PARKING:** 120 **NOTES:** No dogs (ex guide dogs) **CARDS:**

★★★61% *Hoole Hall Hotel*

Warrington Rd, Hoole Village CH2 3PD
☎ 01244 408800 📠 01244 320251
e-mail: hoolehall@corushotels.com

corus hotels

Dir: *M53 junct 12, A56 for 0.5m towards city centre, hotel 500yds on left*

Nestling in extensive gardens on the outskirts of the city, parts of this hotel dates back to the 18th century. It is now much extended and modernised, with smart, well-equipped bedrooms. Meetings, banquets and conferences are well catered for and ample car parking space is available.
ROOMS: 97 en suite (4 fmly) No smoking in 48 bedrooms **FACILITIES:** STV **CONF:** Thtr 150 Class 40 Board 50 **SERVICES:** Lift **PARKING:** 200 **NOTES:** No smoking in restaurant Civ Wed 140
CARDS:

★★72% Dene
95 Hoole Rd CH2 3ND
☎ 01244 321165 Fax 01244 350277
e-mail: info@denehotel.com
Dir: *M53 junct 12 take A56 towards Chester. Hotel 1m from M53 next to Alexander Park*
Located close to the city centre and motorway network, The Dene provides stylish, well equipped accommodation. Bedrooms, split between the main house and adjacent garden rooms, vary in size and all are very well equipped. As well as bar meals, an interesting choice of dishes is offered in the welcoming Franc's Brasserie which is also very popular with locals.
ROOMS: 44 en suite 8 annexe en suite (5 fmly) No smoking in 16 bedrooms s fr £50; d fr £68 (incl. bkfst) **LB FACILITIES:** STV Pool table **CONF:** Thtr 30 Class 12 Board 16 Del from £80 **PARKING:** 55 **NOTES:** No smoking in restaurant **CARDS:**

★★71% *Broxton Hall*
Whitchurch Rd CH3 9JS
☎ 01829 782321 Fax 01829 782330
e-mail: reservations@broxtonhall.co.uk
(For full entry see Broxton)

★★68% Chester Court
48 Hoole Rd CH2 3NL
☎ 01244 320779 or 317809 Fax 01244 344795
e-mail: info@chestercourthotel.com
Dir: *M53 junct 12. At large rdbt onto A56. Hotel on right opp All Saints Church*
This privately owned hotel is conveniently located for access to both the city centre and M53 motorway. Bedrooms are well equipped with modern facilities and many are located in a

continued on p174

CHESTER, continued

purpose built single storey building in a peaceful courtyard. Some rooms have four-poster beds, and family accommodation is available. The hotel has a no smoking lounge plus a bar, and a well-appointed restaurant with a conservatory extension.
ROOMS: 8 en suite 12 annexe en suite (4 fmly) (12 GF) No smoking in 8 bedrooms s £45; d £65-£70 (incl. bkfst) **LB** **FACILITIES:** STV **CONF:** Thtr 20 Class 9 Board 12 **PARKING:** 30 **NOTES:** No dogs (ex guide dogs) No smoking in restaurant Closed 2 wks Xmas
CARDS:

★★68% Curzon
52/54 Hough Green CH4 8JQ
☎ 01244 678581 01244 680866
e-mail: curzon.chester@virgin.net
Dir: *on A5104*

A smart detached period property in a predominantly residential suburb, close to the racecourse. The spacious bedrooms are comfortable, some have four-poster beds, and all are well equipped. The atmosphere is very friendly and the dinner menu offers a creative choice of freshly prepared dishes.
ROOMS: 16 en suite (7 fmly) (1 GF) No smoking in 9 bedrooms s £50-£65; d £70-£95 (incl. bkfst) **LB** **PARKING:** 20 **NOTES:** No dogs (ex guide dogs) No smoking in restaurant Closed 20-29 Dec
CARDS:

See advert on page 173

★★66% Brookside
Brook Ln CH2 2AN
☎ 01244 381943 01244 651910
e-mail: info@brookside-hotel.co.uk
Dir: *From city centre, take A5116 towards of Birkenhead/Ellesmere Port. Right at mini-rdbt into Brook Ln, hotel 200yds on left. From M53, take A56 then A41, left into Plas Newton Ln, right into Brook Ln, hotel on right*
This friendly hotel is conveniently located in a residential area just north of the city centre. The attractive public areas consist of a foyer lounge, a small bar and a split-level restaurant. Bedrooms are modern and well equipped. Facilities include a meeting room for up to 20.
ROOMS: 26 en suite (9 fmly) (4 GF) s £40-£45; d £55-£60 (incl. bkfst) **LB** **FACILITIES:** Xmas **CONF:** Class 20 Board 12 **PARKING:** 20 **NOTES:** No smoking in restaurant **CARDS:**

★★66% Eaton
29/31 City Rd CH1 3AE
☎ 01244 320840 01244 320850
e-mail: welcome@eatonhotelchester.co.uk
Dir: *400mtrs from station, towards city centre, adjacent to canal*
This privately-owned hotel is situated just a short walk from the city centre and conveniently placed for the railway station. There is an attractive cane-furnished bar and a wood-panelled dining room with a small, fixed-price menu. Guests will find enclosed car parking available.
ROOMS: 16 en suite (3 fmly) **PARKING:** 10 **NOTES:** No smoking in restaurant **CARDS:**

U Holiday Inn Chester South

Wrexham Rd CH4 9DL
☎ 0870 400 9019 01244 674100
e-mail: chestersouth@ichotelsgroup.com
Dir: *near Wrexham junct on A483, off A55*
At the time of going to press, the classification for this hotel was not confirmed. Please refer to the AA internet site www.theAA.com for current information.
ROOMS: 143 en suite (44 fmly) No smoking in 99 bedrooms **FACILITIES: Spa** STV Indoor swimming (H) Sauna Gym Jacuzzi **CONF:** Thtr 100 Class 50 Board 40 **PARKING:** 220 **NOTES:** No smoking in restaurant **CARDS:**

Innkeeper's Lodge Chester
Whitchurch Rd CH3 6AE
☎ 01244 332200 01244 336415
Dir: *on A41. 1m outside Chester towards Whitchurch*
A new concept in the travel accommodation market. Smart rooms meet essential business requirements but also have home comforts. Dining options include all-day menus plus the added advantage of breakfast, which is included in the room price. For further details, consult the Hotel Groups page.
ROOMS: 5 en suite 9 annexe en suite

Innkeeper's Lodge Chester Northeast
Warrington Rd, Mickle Trafford CH2 4EX
☎ 01244 301391 01244 302002
Dir: *M53 junct 12, onto A56 signed Helsby, hotel 0.25m on right*
A new concept in the travel accommodation market. Smart rooms meet essential business requirements but also have home comforts. Dining options include all-day menus plus the added advantage of breakfast, which is included in the room price. For further details, consult the Hotel Groups page.
ROOMS: 36 en suite **CONF:** Thtr 20 Class 12 Board 20

Premier Lodge (Chester)
76 Liverpool Rd CH2 1AU
☎ 0870 9906470 0870 9906471
Premier Lodge offers modern, well-equipped, en suite accommodation suitable for both business and leisure travellers. Meals can be taken at the adjacent popular restaurant and bar, which is fully licensed. For further details, consult the Hotel Groups page.
ROOMS: 31 en suite s £48; d £48 **CONF:** Class 17

Travel Inn (Chester South East)
Caldy Valley Rd CH3 5QJ
☎ 08701 977058 01244 403687
Dir: *off A41, 3rd exit off Boughton Heath rdbt signed Huntingdon. Opposite Sainsburys*
Travel Inn offers good-quality, value-for-money accommodation. Spacious, en suite rooms with bath and shower comfortably accommodate a family of up to two adults and two children (to age 15). The restaurant and bar offers a varied menu. For further details and the Travel Inn phone number, consult the Hotel Groups page.
ROOMS: 70 en suite s £44.95; d £44.95 **CONF:** Class 20

CHESTERFIELD, Derbyshire

Map 16 SK37

See also Renishaw

★★★64% Sandpiper

Sheffield Rd, Sheepbridge S41 9EH
☎ 01246 450550 📠 01246 452805
e-mail: sales.sandpiper@virgin.net

Dir: *M1 junct 29, A617 to Chesterfield then A61 to Sheffield. 1st exit take Dronfield Rd. Hotel 0.5m on left*

Conveniently situated for the A61 and M1, and provides a good touring centre being just three miles from Chesterfield. This modern hotel offers comfortable and well-furnished bedrooms. Public areas are situated in a separate building across the car park, and include a cosy bar and open plan restaurant, serving a range of interesting and popular dishes.

ROOMS: 46 en suite (8 fmly) (18 GF) No smoking in 32 bedrooms s £43-£50; d £43-£50 **LB FACILITIES:** STV Xmas **CONF:** Thtr 100 Class 35 Board 35 Del from £90 **SERVICES:** Lift **PARKING:** 120 **NOTES:** No smoking in restaurant Civ Wed 90

CARDS:

See advert on this page

★★70% Abbeydale

Cross St S40 4TD
☎ 01246 277849 📠 01246 558223
e-mail: abbeydale1ef@aol.com

Dir: *M1 junct 29 onto A619 towards Buxton. At B&Q island turn by KFC into Flojambe Rd. Over lights into West St, right into Cross St*

Conveniently situated in a quiet residential area of the town, this friendly hotel is run personally by the proprietors and offers excellent service and warm hospitality. Bedrooms are bright, fresh and well equipped. A short selection of skilfully prepared dishes is served in the dining room, adjacent to the cosy lounge and bar.

ROOMS: 11 en suite (1 fmly) No smoking in all bedrooms s £43-£48; d £55-£65 (incl. bkfst) **LB PARKING:** 14 **NOTES:** No smoking in restaurant RS 23-25 & 31 Dec, 1 Jan **CARDS:**

⌂ Hotel Ibis Chesterfield

Lordsmill St S41 7RW
☎ 01246 221333 📠 01246 221444
e-mail: H3160@accor-hotels.com

Dir: *M1 junct 29, take A617 to Chesterfield. Over main rdbt. Hotel on next rdbt*

Modern, budget hotel offering comfortable accommodation in bright and practical bedrooms. Breakfast is self-service and dinner is available in the restaurant. For further details, consult the Hotel Groups page.

ROOMS: 86 en suite s £39.95-£45.95; d £39.95-£45.95

⌂ Travel Inn

Tapton Lock Hill, Off Rotherway S41 7NJ
☎ 08701 977060 📠 01246 560707

Dir: *adjacent to Tesco, A61 and A619 rdbt, 1m N of city centre*

Travel Inn offers good-quality, value-for-money accommodation. Spacious, en suite rooms with bath and shower comfortably accommodate a family of up to two adults and two children (to age 15). The restaurant and bar offers a varied menu. For further details and the Travel Inn phone number, consult the Hotel Groups page.

ROOMS: 60 en suite s £44.95; d £44.95 **CONF:** Thtr 25

⌂ Travelodge

Brimmington Rd, Inner Ring Rd, Wittington Moor S41 9BE
☎ 08700 850 950 📠 01246 455411

Dir: *on A61, N of town centre*

Travelodge offers good quality, good value, modern accommodation. Ideal for families, the spacious, en suite bedrooms include remote-control TV, tea and coffee-making facilities, luxury beds and free morning newspaper. Meals can be taken at the nearby family restaurant. For further details and the Travelodge phone number, consult the Hotel Groups page.

ROOMS: 20 en suite s fr £42.95; d fr £42.95

CHESTER-LE-STREET, Co Durham

Map 19 NZ25

⌂ Innkeeper's Lodge Durham North

Church Mouse, Great North Rd, Chester Moor DH2 3RJ
☎ 0191 389 2628

Dir: *A1(M) J63, take A167 S Durham/Chester-Le-Street on at 3 rdbts, Inn on left*

A new concept in the travel accommodation market. Smart rooms meet essential business requirements but also have home comforts. Dining options include all-day menus plus the added advantage of breakfast, which is included in the room price. For further details, consult the Hotel Groups page.

ROOMS: 21 en suite s fr £53; d fr £53

CHESTER MOTORWAY SERVICE AREA (M56), Cheshire
Map 15 SJ47

⇧ Travel Inn (Chester East)

Junction 14 M56, Chester East Service Area, Elton CH2 4QZ
☎ 08701 977059 ⎙ 01928 726721
Dir: *M56 junct 14/A5117 interchange*
Travel Inn offers good-quality, value-for-money accommodation. Spacious, en suite rooms with bath and shower comfortably accommodate a family of up to two adults and two children (to age 15). The restaurant and bar offers a varied menu. For further details and the Travel Inn phone number, consult the Hotel Groups page.
ROOMS: 40 en suite s £44.95; d £44.95 **CONF:** Thtr 20

CHICHESTER, West Sussex
Map 05 SU80

★★★★72% ®® *Marriott Goodwood Park Hotel & Country Club*

PO18 0QB
☎ 01243 775537 ⎙ 01243 520120
e-mail: reservations.goodwood@marriotthotels.co.uk
(For full entry see Goodwood)

★★★75% ® The Millstream
Bosham Ln PO18 8HL
☎ 01243 573234 ⎙ 01243 573459
e-mail: info@millstream-hotel.co.uk
(For full entry see Bosham)

★★★70% ® Crouchers Country Hotel & Restaurant
Birdham Rd PO20 7EH
☎ 01243 784995 ⎙ 01243 539797
e-mail: crouchers_bottom@btconnect.com
Dir: *off A27 to A286, 1.5m from Chichester centre opposite Black Horse pub*
This friendly, family run hotel is situated in open countryside and within a short drive from the harbour. The comfortable and well-equipped rooms include some in a separate barn and coachhouse and the open-plan public areas enjoy a spacious and attractive aspect.
ROOMS: 18 en suite (1 fmly) (12 GF) No smoking in 9 bedrooms s £58-£85; d £85-£115 (incl. bkfst) **LB** **FACILITIES:** Xmas **CONF:** BC Thtr 80 Class 80 Board 50 Del from £85 **PARKING:** 50 **NOTES:** No smoking in restaurant **CARDS:**

See advert on opposite page

★★★70% The Ship Hotel
North St PO19 1NH
☎ 01243 778000 ⎙ 01243 788000
e-mail: bookings@shiphotel.com
Dir: *from A27, onto inner ring road to Northgate. At large Northgate rdbt left into North St, hotel on left*
This well-presented former Georgian hotel has a prime position at the top of North Street. The bar and restaurant offer a comfortable venue for refreshments and meals. Bedrooms have been refurbished to a high standard, and the restyled bar and restaurant offers a lively and exciting venue.
ROOMS: 36 en suite (2 fmly) No smoking in all bedrooms s £79; d £99 (incl. bkfst) **FACILITIES:** STV Xmas **CONF:** Thtr 70 Class 35 Board 30 **SERVICES:** Lift **PARKING:** 35 **CARDS:**

★★62% Suffolk House
3 East Row PO19 1PD
☎ 01243 778899 ⎙ 01243 787282
e-mail: admin@suffolkhousehotel.co.uk
Dir: *right off East St into Little London, follow into East Row, hotel on left*
This former Georgian residence is situated in a quiet side street and yet only a few minutes' walk from the town centre. Bedrooms vary in shape and size and offer a good level of comfort and facilities. There is also a small bar area, a pleasant patio and a peaceful dining room. Telephone beforehand for advice on parking.
ROOMS: 11 en suite (2 fmly) (4 GF) No smoking in 3 bedrooms s £59-£74; d £95-£125 (incl. bkfst) **LB** **CONF:** Thtr 25 Class 12 Board 16 **NOTES:** No dogs (ex guide dogs) No smoking in restaurant
CARDS:

⇧ Premier Lodge (Chichester)

Chichester Gate Leisure Park, Terminus Rd PO19 8EL
☎ 0870 9906578 ⎙ 0870 9906579
Premier Lodge offers modern, well-equipped, en suite accommodation suitable for both business and leisure travellers. Meals can be taken at the adjacent popular restaurant and bar, which is fully licensed. For further details, consult the Hotel Groups page.
ROOMS: 83 en suite s £48; d £48

CHIDEOCK, Dorset
Map 04 SY49

★★71% ® Chideock House
Main St DT6 6JN
☎ 01297 489242 ⎙ 01297 489184
e-mail: aa@chideockhousehotel.com
Dir: *on A35 between Lyme Regis and Bridport*
Partly thatched, this delightful house dates back to the 15th century and retains many original features, such as beams and fireplaces. Relaxed and quietly attentive the service is genuinely friendly and welcoming. Lots of thoughtful extras are provided in the bedrooms. An interesting and innovative menu featuring local produce is served in the comfortable restaurant.
ROOMS: 9 rms (8 en suite) s £75-£95; d £75-£95 (incl. bkfst) **LB** **FACILITIES:** Xmas **PARKING:** 20 **NOTES:** No children 12yrs No smoking in restaurant **CARDS:**

CHILDER THORNTON, Cheshire
Map 15 SJ37

⇧ Travel Inn (Wirral South)
New Chester Rd CH66 1QW
☎ 08701 977275 ⎙ 0151 347 1401
Dir: *on A41, near M53 junct 5, heading towards Chester*
Travel Inn offers good-quality, value-for-money accommodation. Spacious, en suite rooms with bath and shower comfortably accommodate a family of up to two adults and two children (to age 15). The restaurant and bar offers a varied menu. For further details and the Travel Inn phone number, consult the Hotel Groups page.
ROOMS: 31 en suite s £44.95; d £44.95 **CONF:** Thtr 20

CHILWORTH, Hampshire
Map 05 SU41

★★★65% Chilworth Manor
SO16 7PT
☎ 023 8076 7333 ⎙ 023 8076 6979
e-mail: general@chilworth-manor.co.uk
Dir: *1m from M3/M27 junct on A27 Romsey Rd N from Southampton. Pass Clump Inn on left, 200mtrs turn left at Chilworth Science Park sign. Hotel immediately right*
This attractive Edwardian manor house is set in 12 acres of

continued

landscaped grounds; the rhododendrons in spring are spectacular. Bedrooms are located in the main house and an adjoining modern wing; rooms are peaceful, well equipped and well presented. This is a popular venue for conferences and wedding parties.
ROOMS: 95 en suite (6 fmly) No smoking in 45 bedrooms s £105-£120; d £120-£135 **LB** **FACILITIES:** Tennis (hard) Croquet lawn Trim trail walking, Giant chess, Petanque **CONF:** Thtr 160 Class 50 Board 50 Del from £157.50 **SERVICES:** Lift **PARKING:** 200 **NOTES:** No smoking in restaurant Civ Wed 130 **CARDS:**

CHIPPENHAM, Wiltshire — Map 04 ST97

★★★72% Angel Hotel

Market Place SN15 3HD
☎ 01249 652615 📠 01249 443210
e-mail: reception@angelhotelchippenham.co.uk
Dir: *follow tourist signs for Bowood House. Under railway arch, follow 'Borough Parade Parking' signs. Hotel next to car park*
These impressive buildings are home to a smart, comfortable hotel. The well-equipped bedrooms vary from the main house, where character is the key, to the smart executive-style, courtyard rooms. The lounge and restaurant are bright and modern where in addition to the imaginative carte, an all day menu is served.
ROOMS: 15 en suite 35 annexe en suite (3 fmly) (12 GF) No smoking in 29 bedrooms s £63-£103; d £80-£144 (incl. bkfst) **LB** **FACILITIES:** STV Indoor swimming (H) Gym **CONF:** Thtr 100 Class 50 Board 50 Del from £130 **PARKING:** 50 **NOTES:** No smoking in restaurant **CARDS:**

★★★72% Stanton Manor Country House Hotel

SN14 6DQ
☎ 01666 837552 📠 01666 837022
e-mail: reception@stantonmanor.co.uk
(For full entry see Stanton St Quintin)

⌂ Travel Inn

West Cepen Park SN14 6UZ
☎ 08701 977061 📠 01249 461359
Dir: *M4 junct 17, take A350 towards Chippenham. Travel Inn at 1st main rdbt at gateway to Chippenham*
Travel Inn offers good-quality, value-for-money accommodation. Spacious, en suite rooms with bath and shower comfortably accommodate a family of up to two adults and two children (to age 15). The restaurant and bar offers a varied menu. For further details and the Travel Inn phone number, consult the Hotel Groups page.
ROOMS: 79 en suite s £44.95; d £44.95

CHIPPERFIELD, Hertfordshire — Map 06 TL00

★★72% *The Two Brewers*

The Common WD4 9BS
☎ 01923 265266 📠 01923 261884
Dir: *left in centre of village overlooking common*
This 16th-century inn retains much of its old-world charm while providing modern comforts and amenities. The spacious bedrooms are tastefully furnished and decorated, offering a comprehensive range of in-room facilities. The bar, popular with

continued on p178

CHIPPERFIELD, continued

locals, is the focal point of the hotel, which serves enjoyable pub-style meals.

The Two Brewers, Chipperfield

ROOMS: 20 en suite No smoking in 10 bedrooms **FACILITIES:** STV **CONF:** Board 16 **PARKING:** 25 **NOTES:** No dogs (ex guide dogs) **CARDS:**

CHIPPING CAMPDEN, Gloucestershire Map 10 SP13

Top 200 - Hotel

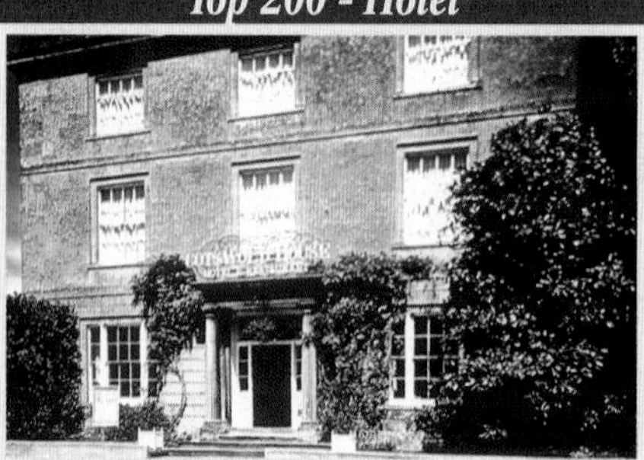

★★★ Cotswold House

The Square GL55 6AN
☎ 01386 840330 01386 840310
e-mail: reception@cotswoldhouse.com
Dir: *A44 take B4081 to Chipping Campden. Right at T-junct into High St. House in The Square*

Guests are encouraged to relax at this mellow Cotswold stone house, set in the centre of the town, overlooking the main square. Bedrooms, including spacious suites in the courtyard, have been refurbished to a high standard, combining style and quality with true comfort and practicality. There is a choice of dining options, with the Garden restaurant using local ingredients wherever possible in imaginative combinations, complemented by the more informal Hicks Brasserie and Bar.

ROOMS: 20 en suite No smoking in 18 bedrooms s £115-£120; d £175-£395 (incl. bkfst) **LB** **FACILITIES:** STV Gym Croquet lawn Access to local Sports Centre Xmas **CONF:** Thtr 50 Class 30 Board 30 Del from £175 **PARKING:** 15 **NOTES:** No smoking in restaurant Civ Wed 55 **CARDS:**

For central reservation numbers and more information on Hotel Groups, turn to pages 33-39

★★★73% Three Ways House

Mickleton GL55 6SB
☎ 01386 438429 01386 438118
e-mail: threeways@puddingclub.com
Dir: *in centre of Mickleton, on B4632 Stratford-upon-Avon to Broadway Rd*

Built in 1870, this charming hotel has welcomed guests for over 100 years and is home to the world famous Pudding Club, formed in 1985 to promote traditional English puddings. Individuality is a hallmark here, as reflected in a number of speciality bedrooms which have been styled according to a pudding theme. Public areas are stylish and include the air-conditioned restaurant, lounges and meeting rooms.

ROOMS: 41 en suite (5 fmly) s £72-£80; d £110-£135 (incl. bkfst) **LB** **FACILITIES:** entertainment Xmas **CONF:** Thtr 100 Class 40 Board 35 Del from £130 **PARKING:** 37 **NOTES:** No smoking in restaurant Civ Wed 80 **CARDS:**

See advert on opposite page

★★★72% Seymour House

High St GL55 6AH
☎ 01386 840429 01386 840369
e-mail: enquiry@seymourhousehotel.com
Dir: *Hotel in middle of High St opposite Lloyds Bank*

Centrally located in one of the most idyllic villages in England, this lovely Cotswold property dates back to the early 18th century. Bedrooms vary in size and style, and all offer good levels of comfort and individuality. Public rooms, including the elegant drawing room, the Vinery restaurant and separate bar, reflect the originality, charm and character that features throughout.

ROOMS: 11 en suite 5 annexe en suite s £80-£140; d £100-£180 (incl. bkfst) **LB** **FACILITIES:** STV entertainment Xmas **CONF:** Thtr 65 Class 26 Board 30 Del from £145 **PARKING:** 28 **NOTES:** No dogs (ex guide dogs) No smoking in restaurant Civ Wed 65 **CARDS:**

★★★70% Noel Arms

High St GL55 6AT
☎ 01386 840317 01386 841136
e-mail: bookings@cotswold-inns-hotels.co.uk
Dir: *off A44 onto B4081 to Chipping Campden, 1st right down hill into town. Hotel on right opposite Market Hall*

This historic 14th-century hotel has a wealth of character and charm, and retains some original features. Bedrooms are very individual in style, and all share high levels of comfort and interesting interior design. Such distinctiveness is also evident throughout public areas which include the popular bar, conservatory lounge and attractive restaurant.

ROOMS: 26 en suite (1 fmly) s £115-£120; d £120-£140 (incl. bkfst) **LB** **FACILITIES:** Xmas **CONF:** Thtr 50 Class 16 Board 25 Del from £135 **PARKING:** 30 **NOTES:** No smoking in restaurant Civ Wed 70 **CARDS:**

CHITTLEHAMHOLT, Devon

Map 03 SS62

★★★66% Highbullen

EX37 9HD
☎ 01769 540561 01769 540492
e-mail: highbullen@sosi.net

Dir: *M5 junct 27 onto A361 to South Molton, then B3226 Crediton Rd. After 5.2m turn right to Chittlehamholt. Hotel 0.5m beyond village*

Set in magnificent parkland with extensive views and an 18-hole golf course, Highbullen also offers leisure and therapy treatments. The range of bedrooms, situated in the main house and in converted out buildings, are all spacious and comfortable. Dinner is served in the restaurant, which looks out over the impressive country views.

ROOMS: 12 en suite 25 annexe en suite **FACILITIES:** Indoor swimming (H) Outdoor swimming (H) Golf 18 Tennis (hard) Fishing Squash Snooker Sauna Solarium Gym Croquet lawn Putting green Hairdressing Beauty Massage **CONF:** Board 20 **PARKING:** 60 **NOTES:** No dogs (ex guide dogs) No children 8yrs No smoking in restaurant
CARDS:

CHORLEY, Lancashire

Map 15 SD51

★★★71% Shaw Hill Hotel Golf & Country Club

Preston Rd, Whittle-le-Woods PR6 7PP
☎ 01257 269221 01257 261223
e-mail: info@shaw-hill.co.uk

Dir: *off A6, S of junct with B5248 at Whittle-le-Woods*

Complete with its own 18-hole championship golf course, this former Georgian mansion has been carefully restored whilst still retaining many original features. Spacious bedrooms are thoughtfully equipped and comfortably furnished. Extensive public areas include smart leisure and impressive conference facilities, a choice of inviting lounges and an elegant restaurant.

ROOMS: 26 en suite 4 annexe en suite (1 fmly) **FACILITIES:** STV Indoor swimming (H) Golf 18 Snooker Sauna Solarium Gym Putting green Jacuzzi Beauty salon Hairdresser **CONF:** Thtr 350 Class 100 Board 150 **PARKING:** 200 **NOTES:** No dogs (ex guide dogs) Closed 24-27 Dec Civ Wed 200 **CARDS:**

★★★69% Park Hall

Park Hall Rd, Charnock Richard PR7 5LP
☎ 01257 452090 455000 01257 451838
e-mail: conference@parkhall-hotel.co.uk

Dir: *off A49 W of village. Follow tourist signs from M6/M61*

The popular Camelot Theme Park is just a short stroll across the grounds from this hotel, which provides a choice of well-equipped bedrooms ranging from contemporary rooms to themed cottage-style accommodation. The Park View Restaurant has light modern décor; less formal eating is available in the lounge bar. Packages including entrance to the theme park are available.

ROOMS: 54 en suite 84 annexe en suite (59 fmly) No smoking in 11 bedrooms **FACILITIES:** STV Indoor swimming (H) Sauna Solarium Gym Jacuzzi Steam room Weights room ch fac **CONF:** Thtr 700 Class 240 Board 40 **SERVICES:** Lift **PARKING:** 2600 **NOTES:** No dogs (ex guide dogs) No smoking in restaurant Civ Wed 200
CARDS:

See advert under PRESTON

Late for dinner?
Quality Standards mean that last orders for dinner vary according to star rating and should be no earlier than:
★★ 7.00pm ★★★ 8.00pm ★★★★ 9.00pm
★★★★★ 10.00pm

CHORLEY, continued

🏠 Premier Lodge (Chorley)

Malthouse Farm, Moss Ln, Whittle le Woods PR6 8AB
☎ 0870 9906376 📠 0870 9906377
e-mail: malthousefarm20@hotmail.com
Dir: *M61 junct 8 onto A647 towards Wheelton. 1st left onto Moss Lane signed Whittle-Le-Woods/Whittle springs*

Premier Lodge offers modern, well-equipped, en suite accommodation suitable for both business and leisure travellers. Meals can be taken at the adjacent popular restaurant and bar, which is fully licensed. For further details, consult the Hotel Groups page.
ROOMS: 81 en suite s £44; d £44 **CONF:** Board 15

🏠 Premier Lodge (Chorley South)

Bolton Rd PR7 4AB
☎ 0870 9906604 📠 0870 9906605

Dir: *On A6 1m from Chorley. M61 junct 8 from N/M6 junct 27 from S*

Premier Lodge offers modern, well-equipped, en suite accommodation suitable for both business and leisure travellers. Meals can be taken at the adjacent popular restaurant and bar, which is fully licensed. For further details, consult the Hotel Groups page.
ROOMS: 29 en suite s £44; d £44 **CONF:** Board 12

🏠 Travelodge Preston Chorley

Preston Rd, Clayton-le-Woods PR6 7JB
☎ 08700 850 950

Dir: *from M6 junct 28 take B5256 for 2m, next to Halfway House pub*

Travelodge offers good quality, good value, modern accommodation. Ideal for families, the spacious, en suite bedrooms include remote-control TV, tea and coffee-making facilities, luxury beds and free morning newspaper. Meals can be taken at the nearby family restaurant. For further details and the Travelodge phone number, consult the Hotel Groups page.
ROOMS: 40 en suite s fr £42.95; d fr £42.95

CHRISTCHURCH, Dorset Map 05 SZ19

★★★75% ◎◎ Waterford Lodge

87 Bure Ln, Friars Cliff BH23 4DN
☎ 01425 272948 & 278801 📠 01425 279130
e-mail: waterford@bestwestern.co.uk
Dir: *from A35 take A337 towards Highcliffe. Take right turn from rdbt signed Mudeford. Hotel 0.5m on left*

Peacefully located within easy reach of Christchurch, this welcoming hotel is popular with business guests as well as holidaymakers. It offers attractive, spacious and well-equipped bedrooms, a comfortable bar lounge overlooking the gardens and a pleasant restaurant serving carefully prepared, award-winning cuisine.
ROOMS: 18 en suite (2 fmly) (3 GF) No smoking in 3 bedrooms s £79; d £108 (incl. bkfst) **LB FACILITIES:** STV Xmas **CONF:** Thtr 100 Class 48 Board 36 Del from £105.75 **PARKING:** 38 **NOTES:** No dogs (ex guide dogs) No children 7yrs No smoking in restaurant
CARDS:

★★★68% *The Avonmouth*

95 Mudeford BH23 3NT
☎ 01202 483434 📠 01202 479004
e-mail: info@avonmouth-hotel.co.uk
Dir: *A35 to Christchurch from Lyndhurst. Left at rdbt on A337 to Highcliffe. Right at rdbt, hotel 1.5m on left*

In a superb location alongside Mudeford Quay, this friendly hotel offers a variety of bedrooms including smart garden rooms with their own small patios. Several bedrooms in the main house overlook the quay and have private balconies. Modern facilities and decor enhance the overall comfort. Enjoyable cuisine is served in the pleasant restaurant.
ROOMS: 26 en suite 14 annexe en suite (7 fmly) (14 GF) No smoking in 20 bedrooms **FACILITIES:** STV Outdoor swimming (H) Croquet lawn **CONF:** Thtr 70 Class 20 Board 24 Del from £110 **PARKING:** 80 **NOTES:** No dogs (ex guide dogs) No smoking in restaurant Civ Wed 70
CARDS:

🏠 Travel Inn (Christchurch East)

Somerford Rd BH23 3QG
☎ 08701 977062 📠 01202 474939
Dir: *from M27 take A337 to Lyndhurst, then A35 to Christchurch. On B3059 rdbt towards Somerford*

Travel Inn offers good-quality, value-for-money accommodation. Spacious, en suite rooms with bath and shower comfortably accommodate a family of up to two adults and two children (to age 15). The restaurant and bar offers a varied menu. For further details and the Travel Inn phone number, consult the Hotel Groups page.
ROOMS: 70 en suite s £44.95; d £44.95

🏠 Travel Inn (Christchurch West)

Barrack Rd BH23 2BN
☎ 08701 977063 📠 01202 483453
Dir: *from A338 take A3060 towards Christchurch. Turn left onto A35, Travel Inn on right*

Travel Inn offers good-quality, value-for-money accommodation. Spacious, en suite rooms with bath and shower comfortably accommodate a family of up to two adults and two children (to age 15). The restaurant and bar offers a varied menu. For further details and the Travel Inn phone number, consult the Hotel Groups page.
ROOMS: 42 en suite s £44.95; d £44.95

CHURCHILL, Somerset Map 04 ST45

★★63% *Winston Manor*

Bristol Rd BS25 5NL
☎ 01934 852348 📠 01934 852033
Dir: *On A38 100yds N of junct with A368 Bath to Weston-Super-Mare*

A friendly small hotel, run in a relaxed manner by the resident proprietors. It is conveniently located for Bristol International Airport and the many local attractions. Bedrooms, including several on the ground floor, are neatly decorated and well-equipped. The dinner menu includes an interesting selection of home cooking.
ROOMS: 14 en suite (1 fmly) No smoking in 4 bedrooms **CONF:** Thtr 40 Class 30 Board 30 **PARKING:** 24 **NOTES:** No smoking in restaurant
CARDS:

CHURCH STRETTON, Shropshire Map 15 SO49

★★★68% Stretton Hall Hotel

All Stretton SY6 6HG
☎ 01694 723224 01694 724365
e-mail: aa@strettonhall.co.uk
Dir: *from Shrewsbury, on A49, right onto B4370 signed All Stretton. Hotel 1m on left opposite The Yew Tree pub*

This fine 18th-century country house stands in spacious gardens. Original oak panelling features throughout the lounge bar, lounge and halls. Bedrooms are traditionally furnished and have modern facilities. Family and four-poster rooms are available and the restaurant has been tastefully refurbished.

ROOMS: 12 en suite (1 fmly) s fr £50; d £80-£110 (incl. bkfst) **LB** **FACILITIES:** Xmas **CONF:** BC Thtr 70 Class 24 Board 18 Del from £90 **PARKING:** 70 **NOTES:** No smoking in restaurant Civ Wed 60 **CARDS:**

★★70% Mynd House

Ludlow Rd, Little Stretton SY6 6RB
☎ 01694 722212
e-mail: info@myndhouse.co.uk
Dir: *A49 onto B4370, signed Little Stretton. Hotel 0.75m on left beyond Ragleth Inn*

This large Edwardian house is situated in the sleepy hamlet of Little Stretton, and is reached via a steep driveway. The bedrooms have many thoughtful extras and are well-equipped. Public areas include a comfortable lounge, a pleasant bar and a traditional style dining room.

ROOMS: 7 en suite (2 fmly) No smoking in all bedrooms s £40-£50; d £60-£120 (incl. bkfst) **LB** **PARKING:** 8 **NOTES:** No smoking in restaurant RS mid Nov-mid Feb **CARDS:**

★★65% Longmynd Hotel

Cunnery Rd SY6 6AG
☎ 01694 722244 01694 722718
e-mail: info@longmynd.co.uk
Dir: *A49 into Church Stretton town centre along Sandford Ave, left at Lloyds TSB, over mini rdbt, 1st right into Cunnery Rd, up hill, at top on left.*

This family-run hotel overlooks the country town of Church Stretton and the views from many of the rooms are breathtaking. Bedrooms are generally spacious and comfortable, and guest facilities include two restaurants, the Pavilion and the Alpine, as well as a range of comfortable lounges. There is also an outdoor swimming pool, and the hotel is set in attractive gardens.

ROOMS: 50 en suite (9 fmly) No smoking in all bedrooms s £65-£75; d £130-£150 (incl. bkfst) **LB** **FACILITIES:** Outdoor swimming (H) Sauna Croquet lawn Putting green Pitch and putt course Xmas **CONF:** Thtr 100 Class 50 Board 40 Del £105 **SERVICES:** Lift **PARKING:** 100 **NOTES:** No smoking in restaurant Civ Wed 100 **CARDS:**

CHURT, Surrey Map 05 SU83

★★★70% Frensham Pond Hotel

Bacon Ln GU10 2QB
☎ 01252 795161 01252 792631
e-mail: frenshampondhotel@bestwestern.co.uk
Dir: *A3 onto A287. 4m left at 'Beware Horses' sign. Hotel 0.25m*

This 15th-century house occupies a superb location on the edge of Frensham Pond. Bedrooms are mostly spacious and there are also some pleasant garden suites available. Public areas are light and well-appointed and a good range of leisure facilities is offered, including a squash court.

ROOMS: 39 en suite 12 annexe en suite No smoking in 15 bedrooms s £75-£125; d £85-£150 (incl. cont bkfst) **LB** **FACILITIES:** STV Indoor swimming (H) Squash Sauna Solarium Gym Jacuzzi Steam room Xmas **CONF:** Thtr 120 Class 45 Board 40 Del from £125 **PARKING:** 120 **NOTES:** No dogs (ex guide dogs) No smoking in restaurant **CARDS:**

See advert under FARNHAM

★★69% Pride of the Valley

Jumps Rd GU10 2LE
☎ 01428 605799 01428 605875
e-mail: rpov@aol.com
Dir: *off A3 at Hindhead traffic lights for Farnham. Follow Tilford signs and in 0.5m turn right. Hotel 2m on left*

This hotel enjoys a peaceful location in the Surrey countryside. Following refurbishment, it now has a modern feel and this is particularly evident in the Dragon Bar. Bedrooms are all individually decorated, some with Mediterranean or Art Deco themes. Both the bar and the restaurant offer good menus and high levels of comfort.

ROOMS: 13 en suite 3 annexe en suite (1 fmly) No smoking in all bedrooms s fr £95; d fr £125 (incl. bkfst) **LB** **FACILITIES:** **Spa** Jacuzzi entertainment Xmas **PARKING:** 85 **NOTES:** No dogs (ex guide dogs) No smoking in restaurant **CARDS:**

CIRENCESTER, Gloucestershire Map 05 SP00

★★★69% Stratton House

Gloucester Rd GL7 2LE
☎ 01285 651761 01285 640024
e-mail: stratton.house@forestdale.com
Dir: *M4 junct 15, A419 to Cirencester. Hotel on left on A417 or M5 junct 11 to Cheltenham onto B4070 to A417. Hotel on right*

This attractive 17th-century manor house is quietly situated half a mile or so from the town centre. Bedrooms are well presented, and spacious premier rooms are available. The comfortable drawing rooms and restaurant have views over well-tended gardens: the perfect place to enjoy pre-dinner drinks on a summer evening.

ROOMS: 41 en suite (10 GF) No smoking in 19 bedrooms s fr £95; d fr £120 (incl. bkfst) **LB** **FACILITIES:** Xmas **CONF:** Thtr 150 Class 50 Board 40 Del from £110 **PARKING:** 100 **NOTES:** No smoking in restaurant Civ Wed **CARDS:**

CIRENCESTER, continued

★★★68% ◎ The Crown of Crucis

Ampney Crucis GL7 5RS
☎ 01285 851806 📠 01285 851735
e-mail: info@thecrownofcrucis.co.uk
Dir: *A417 to Fairford, hotel 2.5m on left*

This delightful hotel consists of two buildings, one a 16th-century coaching inn, which now houses the bar and restaurant, and a more modern bedroom block which surrounds a courtyard. Rooms are attractively appointed and offer modern facilities; the restaurant serves a range of imaginative dishes.

ROOMS: 25 en suite (2 fmly) (13 GF) No smoking in 10 bedrooms s fr £67; d fr £95 (incl. bkfst) **LB FACILITIES:** Free membership of local leisure centre **CONF:** Thtr 80 Class 40 Board 25 Del from £120 **PARKING:** 82 **NOTES:** No smoking in restaurant Closed 25 Dec **CARDS:**

★★★65% *Fleece Hotel*

Market Place GL7 2NZ
THE INDEPENDENTS
☎ 01285 658507 📠 01285 651017
e-mail: relax@fleecehotel.co.uk
Dir: *A417/A419 Burford Rd junct, follow signs for town centre. Right at lights into "The Waterloo", hotel car park 250yds on left*

This old town-centre coaching inn, which dates back to the Tudor period, retains many original features such as flagstone floors and oak beams. Well-equipped bedrooms vary in size and shape, all offering good levels of comfort and plenty of character. The bar lounge is a popular venue for morning coffee, and the stylish restaurant offers a range of dishes in an informal and convivial atmosphere.

ROOMS: 26 en suite (3 fmly) No smoking in 3 bedrooms **PARKING:** 10 **CARDS:**

★★ ◎◎ The New Inn At Coln

GL7 5AN
☎ 01285 750651 📠 01285 750657
e-mail: stay@new-inn.co.uk
(For full entry see Coln St Aldwyns)

⌂ Travelodge

Hare Bushes, Burford Rd GL7 5DS
Travelodge
☎ 08700 850 950 📠 01285 655290

Travelodge offers good quality, good value, modern accommodation. Ideal for families, the spacious, en suite bedrooms include remote-control TV, tea and coffee-making facilities, luxury beds and free morning newspaper. Meals can be taken at the nearby family restaurant. For further details and the Travelodge phone number, consult the Hotel Groups page.

ROOMS: 43 en suite s fr £42.95; d fr £42.95

CLACKET LANE MOTORWAY SERVICE AREA (M25), Surrey — Map 06 TQ45

⌂ Travel Inn (Westerham)

TN16 2ER
travel inn
☎ 08701 977265 📠 01959 561311
Dir: *M25 between junct 5 & 6*

Travel Inn offers good-quality, value-for-money accommodation. Spacious, en suite rooms with bath and shower comfortably accommodate a family of up to two adults and two children (to age 15). The restaurant and bar offers a varied menu. For further details and the Travel Inn phone number, consult the Hotel Groups page.

ROOMS: 58 en suite s £46.95-£52.95; d £46.95-£52.95 **CONF:** Thtr 50 Board 30

CLACTON-ON-SEA, Essex — Map 07 TM11
See also Weeley

★★67% Esplanade Hotel

27-29 Marine Pde East CO15 1UU
☎ 01255 220450 📠 01255 221800
e-mail: mjs@esplanadehoteluk.com
Dir: *from A133 to Clacton-on-Sea, follow seafront signs. At seafront turn right and hotel on right in 50yds*

Situated in a prominent position on the seafront overlooking the pier and just a short walk from the town centre. Bedrooms vary in size and style and are pleasantly decorated and well equipped; some rooms have lovely sea views. Public rooms include a comfortable lounge bar and Coasters Restaurant.

ROOMS: 29 en suite (2 fmly) s £35-£50; d £60-£70 (incl. bkfst) **LB FACILITIES:** Xmas **CONF:** BC Thtr 80 Class 50 Board 50 Del from £35 **PARKING:** 13 **NOTES:** No dogs (ex guide dogs) No smoking in restaurant Civ Wed 80 **CARDS:**

★73% Chudleigh

13 Agate Rd, Marine Pde West CO15 1RA
☎ 01255 425407 📠 01255 470280
e-mail: reception@chudleighhotel.com
Dir: *follow town centre, seafront and pier signs. Right at seafront, right into Agate Rd after traffic lights at the pier*

Expect a warm welcome from the caring hosts, now celebrating their 40th year at this small, privately owned hotel. It is situated just off the seafront and within easy walking distance of the town centre and pier. Bedrooms are generally quite spacious; each is attractively decorated and equipped with many thoughtful touches. Public rooms include a cosy lounge and a smart restaurant serving freshly prepared meals.

ROOMS: 10 en suite (2 fmly) (2 GF) No smoking in 2 bedrooms s £40-£43; d £50-£55 (incl. bkfst) **PARKING:** 7 **NOTES:** No smoking in restaurant RS Oct-Mar **CARDS:**

CLANFIELD, Oxfordshire — Map 05 SP20

★★★69% Plough at Clanfield

Bourton Rd OX18 2RB
☎ 01367 810222 📠 01367 810596
e-mail: ploughatclanfield@hotmail.com
Dir: *on edge of village at junct of A4095/B4020*

Improvements continue at this delightful wisteria-clad village centre Cotswold hotel. The main public area is a spacious lounge with an attractive Elizabethan fireplace. The hotel has original bedrooms, which have period character, and some contemporary rooms that are spacious and well designed.

ROOMS: 12 en suite (3 GF) No smoking in all bedrooms s £90; d £120 (incl. bkfst) **LB FACILITIES:** STV **CONF:** Board 10 Del £152.75 **PARKING:** 30 **NOTES:** No dogs (ex guide dogs) No children 12yrs No smoking in restaurant Closed 24-26 Dec **CARDS:**

CLAVERDON, Warwickshire — Map 10 SP16

★★★★74% ◎ Ardencote Manor Hotel & Country Club

Lye Green Rd CV35 8LS
☎ 01926 843111 📠 01926 842646
e-mail: hotel@ardencote.com
Dir: *in centre of Claverdon, follow Shrewley signs off A4189. Hotel 0.5m on right*

Originally built as a gentleman's residence around 1860 this hotel is set in 45 acres of landscaped grounds. Public rooms include a choice of lounge areas, cocktail bar and conservatory breakfast

continued

room. Main meals are served within the Lodge, a separate building which sits on the lake. An extensive range of leisure and conference facilities are provided and bedrooms are smartly decorated and tastefully furnished.

ROOMS: 75 en suite (3 fmly) No smoking in 49 bedrooms s £105; d £95-£145 (incl. bkfst) **LB** **FACILITIES: Spa** STV Indoor swimming (H) Golf 9 Tennis (hard) Squash Sauna Solarium Gym Croquet lawn Putting green Jacuzzi Ardencote Spa Xmas **CONF:** Thtr 250 Class 100 Board 50 Del from £100 **SERVICES:** Lift air con **PARKING:** 150 **NOTES:** No dogs No smoking in restaurant Civ Wed 150 **CARDS:**

See advert under WARWICK

CLEARWELL, Gloucestershire — Map 04 SO50

★★★64% The Wyndham Arms

GL16 8JT
☎ 01594 833666 📠 01594 836450
e-mail: nigel@thewyndhamarmshotel.co.uk
Dir: *in centre of village on B4231*

The history of this charming village inn can be traced back over 600 years. It has exposed stone walls, original beams and an impressive inglenook fireplace in the friendly bar. Most bedrooms are in a modern extension, while rooms in the main house are more traditional in style. A range of dishes is offered in the bar or restaurant.

ROOMS: 6 en suite 12 annexe en suite (3 fmly) (6 GF) s £55-£65; d £65-£110 (incl. bkfst) **LB** **FACILITIES:** Xmas **CONF:** Thtr 56 Class 30 Board 22 Del from £109.50 **PARKING:** 54 **NOTES:** No smoking in restaurant **CARDS:**

★★72% ❀ *Tudor Farmhouse Hotel & Restaurant*

GL16 8JS
☎ 01594 833046 📠 01594 837093
e-mail: reservations@tudorfarmhse.u-net.com
Dir: *At Lydney, left on A48 to Bream. Through Bream and right at junct, left to Clearwell, pass Castle and Church. Right at x-roads, hotel on left*

Dating back to the 13th-century, this idyllic former farmhouse

continued

retains a host of original features including exposed stonework, oak beams, wall panelling and inglenook fireplaces. Bedrooms have great individuality and style and are located in the main house and in converted buildings within the grounds. Creative, quality cuisine is served in the intimate restaurant.

ROOMS: 6 en suite 15 annexe en suite (6 fmly) No smoking in 13 bedrooms **FACILITIES:** STV Riding ch fac **CONF:** Thtr 30 Class 20 Board 20 **PARKING:** 30 **NOTES:** No smoking in restaurant Closed 24-27 Dec **CARDS:**

CLEATOR, Cumbria — Map 18 NY01

★★★76% Ennerdale Country House

Best Western

CA23 3DT
☎ 01946 813907 📠 01946 815260
e-mail: ennerdale@bestwestern.co.uk
Dir: *A5086 to Egremont, approx 12m to Cleator Moor. A5086 for 1m to Cleator*

This fine Grade II listed building lies on edge of the village and is backed by landscaped gardens. Impressive bedrooms, including split-level suites and four-poster rooms, are richly furnished, smartly decorated and offer an amazing array of facilities. Attractive public areas include an elegant restaurant, an inviting lounge and an American theme bar which offers a good range of bar meals.

ROOMS: 30 en suite (4 fmly) No smoking in 4 bedrooms **FACILITIES:** STV **CONF:** Thtr 150 Class 100 Board 40 **PARKING:** 65 **NOTES:** No dogs (ex guide dogs) No smoking in restaurant Civ Wed 150 **CARDS:**

 AA Rosette Award for culinary excellence

C

CLECKHEATON, West Yorkshire
Map 19 SE12

★★★64% The Whitcliffe
Prospect Rd BD19 3HD
☎ 01274 873022 🖷 01274 870376
e-mail: info@thewhitcliffehotel.co.uk
Dir: *M62 junct 26, follow A638 to Dewsbury, over 1st lights, right into Mount St, to T-junct, right then 1st left*
This popular commercial hotel offers modern, well-equipped accommodation. Spacious public areas provide a variety of amenities, including several meeting rooms, two attractive bars, and a traditionally styled restaurant. Hospitality is a major strength here.
ROOMS: 34 en suite 6 annexe en suite (1 fmly) (6 GF) No smoking in 17 bedrooms s £39-£50; d £55-£65 (incl. bkfst) **LB FACILITIES:** STV Xmas **CONF:** Thtr 100 Class 60 Board 30 Del from £49.95 **PARKING:** 150 **NOTES:** No dogs (ex guide dogs) **CARDS:**

⌂ Travel Inn (Bradford South)
Whitehall Rd BD19 6HG
☎ 08701 977037 🖷 01274 855901
Dir: *on A58 at intersection with M62 & M606*
Travel Inn offers good-quality, value-for-money accommodation. Spacious, en suite rooms with bath and shower comfortably accommodate a family of up to two adults and two children (to age 15). The restaurant and bar offers a varied menu. For further details and the Travel Inn phone number, consult the Hotel Groups page.
ROOMS: 40 en suite s £44.95; d £44.95

CLEETHORPES, Lincolnshire
Map 17 TA30

★★★69% Kingsway
Kingsway DN35 0AE
☎ 01472 601122 🖷 01472 601381
e-mail: reception@kingsway-hotel.com
Dir: *leave A180 at Grimsby, to Cleethorpes seafront. Hotel at Kingsway and Queen Parade junct (A1098)*
This seafront hotel has been in the same family for four generations and continues to provide traditional comfort and professional, friendly service. The lounges are comfortable and good food is served in the pleasant dining room. Most of the bedrooms are of good, comfortable proportions, and all are bright and pleasantly furnished.
ROOMS: 49 en suite s £49-£75; d £84-£90 (incl. bkfst) **LB FACILITIES:** STV **CONF:** Thtr 22 Board 18 Del £94 **SERVICES:** Lift **PARKING:** 50 **NOTES:** No dogs (ex guide dogs) No children 5yrs Closed 25-26 Dec **CARDS:**

CLEVEDON, Somerset
Map 04 ST47

★★★66% Walton Park
Wellington Ter BS21 7BL
☎ 01275 874253 🖷 01275 343577
e-mail: latona@aol.com
Dir: *M5 junct 20, signs for seafront. Stay on coast road, past pier into Wellington Terrace, hotel on left*
Quietly located and enjoying spectacular views across the Bristol Channel to Wales, this popular Victorian hotel offers a friendly welcome and relaxed atmosphere. Bedrooms are well-decorated and equipped to meet the demands of both business and leisure guests. In the comfortable restaurant, a high standard of

continued

home-cooked food is served, alternatively, meals are available in the convivial bar.
ROOMS: 40 en suite (4 fmly) No smoking in 12 bedrooms s £48-£77; d £81-£96 (incl. bkfst) **LB FACILITIES:** STV **CONF:** Thtr 150 Class 80 Board 80 Del from £95 **SERVICES:** Lift **PARKING:** 50 **NOTES:** Civ Wed 120 **CARDS:**

CLITHEROE, Lancashire
Map 18 SD74

★★★60% Stirk House
BB7 4LJ
☎ 01200 445581 🖷 01200 455744
e-mail: stirkhousehotel@ukhotels.com
Dir: *W of village, on A59. Hotel 0.5m on left*
This delightful historic hotel enjoys a peaceful location in its own grounds, set back from the A59. Extensive public areas include excellent conference and banqueting facilities, an elegant restaurant and inviting lounges. Bedrooms vary in size and style and include some particularly attractive, individually designed rooms. Hospitality is warm and friendly, and service is attentive.
ROOMS: 37 en suite 14 annexe en suite (1 fmly) No smoking in 10 bedrooms **FACILITIES:** STV Indoor swimming (H) Squash Sauna Solarium Gym Xmas **CONF:** Thtr 500 Class 300 **PARKING:** 300 **NOTES:** No smoking in restaurant Civ Wed 300 **CARDS:**

★★69% Shireburn Arms
Whalley Rd, Hurst Green BB7 9QJ
☎ 01254 826518 🖷 01254 826208
e-mail: sales@shireburnarmshotel.com
Dir: *A59 to Clitheroe, left at lights to Ribchester, follow Hurst Green signs. Hotel on B6243 at entrance to Hurst Green village*
This long established, family-owned hotel dates back to the 17th century and enjoys panoramic views over the Ribble Valley. Rooms are individually designed and thoughtfully equipped. The lounge bar offers a selection of real ales, and the spacious restaurant, opening onto an attractive patio and garden, offers home-cooked food.
ROOMS: 18 en suite (3 fmly) No smoking in 3 bedrooms s £45-£55; d £70-£90 (incl. bkfst) **LB FACILITIES:** ch fac Xmas **CONF:** Thtr 100 Class 50 Board 50 Del £75 **PARKING:** 71 **NOTES:** No smoking in restaurant Civ Wed 100 **CARDS:**

CLOVELLY, Devon
Map 03 SS32

★★72% Red Lion Hotel
The Quay EX39 5TF
☎ 01237 431237 🖷 01237 431044
e-mail: redlion@clovelly.co.uk
Dir: *turn off A39 at Clovelly Cross onto B3237. To bottom of hill and take 1st left by white rails to harbour*
A charming 18th-century inn, enjoying an idyllic location in this historic fishing village. Bedrooms are spacious and stylish with spectacular views. Fresh local fish, landed alongside the hotel, features on the daily-changing menu. The friendly and attentive service contributes to make a relaxing and memorable stay.
ROOMS: 11 en suite (2 fmly) s £44-£69; d £87-£108 (incl. bkfst) **LB FACILITIES:** Tennis can be arranged Xmas **PARKING:** 11 **NOTES:** No dogs (ex guide dogs) No smoking in restaurant
CARDS:

★★70% New Inn
High St EX39 5TQ
☎ 01237 431303 📠 01237 431636
e-mail: newinn@clovelly.co.uk
Dir: *at Clovelly Cross, off A39 onto B3237. Follow road down hill for 1.5m. Right at sign "All vehicles for Clovelly"*
Famed for its cobbled descent to the harbour, this fascinating fishing village is a traffic-free zone. Consequently, luggage is conveyed by sledge or donkey to this much-photographed hotel. Carefully renovated bedrooms and public areas are smartly presented with quality, locally-made furnishings. Meals may be taken in the elegant restaurant or the popular Upalongs bar.
ROOMS: 8 en suite (2 fmly) s £37-£59; d £74-£88 (incl. bkfst) **LB** **FACILITIES:** Xmas **NOTES:** No dogs (ex guide dogs) No smoking in restaurant **CARDS:**

COALVILLE, Leicestershire — Map 11 SK41

★★59% *Charnwood Arms*
Beveridge Ln, Bardon Hill LE67 1TB
☎ 01530 813644 📠 01530 815425
e-mail: charnwoodarms@work.gb.com
Dir: *1m W of M1 junct 22, on A511*
This popular inn is conveniently located minutes' drive from the M1. Public areas include a spacious open-plan lounge bar and restaurant offering a selection of cask ales and serving food throughout the day. The extremely well equipped bedrooms are situated around a courtyard.
ROOMS: 34 en suite (1 fmly) No smoking in 6 bedrooms **CONF:** Thtr 200 Class 100 Board 60 **PARKING:** 150 **NOTES:** No dogs (ex guide dogs) Civ Wed 80 **CARDS:**

COBHAM, Surrey — Map 06 TQ16

⌂ Premier Lodge (Cobham)

Portsmouth Rd, Fairmile KT11 1BW
☎ 0870 9906358 📠 0870 9906359
Premier Lodge offers modern, well-equipped, en suite accommodation suitable for both business and leisure travellers. Meals can be taken at the adjacent popular restaurant and bar, which is fully licensed. For further details, consult the Hotel Groups page.
ROOMS: 48 en suite s £56; d £56 **CONF:** Board 12

COCKERMOUTH, Cumbria — Map 18 NY13

★★★74% ❀ The Trout
Crown St CA13 0EJ
☎ 01900 823591 📠 01900 827514
e-mail: enquiries@trouthotel.co.uk
Dir: *next to Wordsworth House*
Dating back to 1670, this privately owned hotel has an enviable setting on the banks of the River Derwent. The well-equipped bedrooms vary in style and there is a well-stocked bar, a choice of comfortable lounges and an attractive, traditional style dining room offering a good choice of table d'hôte and carte dishes.
ROOMS: 29 en suite (4 fmly) No smoking in 12 bedrooms s £90-£129; d £109-£149 (incl. bkfst) **LB** **FACILITIES:** STV Fishing Xmas **CONF:** Thtr 50 Class 30 Board 25 Del from £105 **PARKING:** 60 **NOTES:** No smoking in restaurant Civ Wed 60 **CARDS:**

★★★61% The Manor House Hotel
Crown St CA13 0EH
☎ 01900 828663 📠 01900 828679
Dir: *off A66 at Cockermouth junct, continue 0.75m to T- junct. Hotel 700yds on left*
This impressive looking house was built in 1847 and has had a variety of uses before being converted to a hotel. Now under private family ownership, guests can be assured of friendly and attentive service with especially good meals being served in the formal dining room. Bedrooms, on the first and second floors, come in a variety of sizes and are attractively decorated.
ROOMS: 12 en suite (1 fmly) No smoking in all bedrooms s £55; d £69 (incl. bkfst) **LB** **PARKING:** 20 **NOTES:** No smoking in restaurant **CARDS:**

⌂ Shepherds Hotel
Lakeland Sheep & Wool Centre, Egremont Rd CA13 0QX
☎ 01900 822673 📠 01900 822673
e-mail: reception@shepherdshotel.co.uk
Dir: *At junct of A66 and A5086 S of Cockermouth, entrance off A5086 200mtrs off rdbt*
This hotel is modern in style and offers thoughtfully equipped accommodation. The property also houses the Lakeland Sheep and Wool Centre, with live sheep shows from Easter to mid November. A restaurant serving a wide variety of meals and snacks is open all day.
ROOMS: 13 en suite s £42-£50; d £42-£50 **CONF:** BC Thtr 200 Class 10 Board 10 Del from £60

COGGESHALL, Essex — Map 07 TL82

★★★68% *White Hart*
Market End CO6 1NH
☎ 01376 561654 📠 01376 561789
e-mail: wharthotel@ndirect.co.uk
Dir: *from A12 through Kelvedon & onto B1024 to Coggeshall*
This small cosy hotel in the centre of the town has been completely refurbished. Bedrooms vary in size and all offer good quality and comfort with touches such as CD players, filter machines, fruit and mineral water. Public areas are heavily beamed with a popular bar serving a varied menu, a large restaurant with an Italian menu and a cosy residents' lounge.
ROOMS: 18 en suite (1 fmly) **FACILITIES:** STV **CONF:** Thtr 30 Class 10 Board 22 **PARKING:** 47 **NOTES:** No dogs **CARDS:**

COLCHESTER, Essex — Map 13 TL92

★★★★73% ❀❀ Five Lakes Country House, Golf & Country Club
Colchester Rd CM9 8HX
☎ 01621 868888 📠 01621 869696
e-mail: enquiries@fivelakes.co.uk
(For full entry see Tolleshunt Knights)

★★★ ❀❀ Maison Talbooth
Stratford Rd CO7 6HN
☎ 01206 322367 📠 01206 322752
e-mail: maison@talbooth.co.uk
(For full entry see Dedham)

★★★73% George
116 High St CO1 1TD
☎ 01206 578494 📠 01206 761732
e-mail: colcgeorge@aol.com
Dir: *200yds beyond Town Hall on High St*
A 15th-century coaching inn situated in the centre of this bustling

continued on p186

COLCHESTER, continued

town. Bedrooms are pleasantly decorated, have co-ordinated fabrics and offer a good level of comfort; many of the rooms have original features such as exposed beams. An interesting choice of dishes and daily-changing specials is served in the smart restaurant, and bar snacks are available in the lounge.
ROOMS: 47 en suite No smoking in 32 bedrooms s £56-£95; d £77-£105 **FACILITIES:** STV **CONF:** Thtr 70 Class 30 Board 30 **PARKING:** 40
CARDS:

★★★69% The Stoke by Nayland Club Hotel

Keepers Ln, Leavenheath CO6 4PZ
☎ 01206 262836 📠 01206 263356
e-mail: info@golf-club.co.uk
Dir: *off A134 at Leavenheath onto B1068, hotel 0.75m on right*

This hotel is ideally situated on the edge of the Dedham Vale, amidst 300 acres of undulating countryside, two golf courses and lakes. The spacious bedrooms are attractively decorated and thoughtfully equipped with modern facilities including ISDN lines. Public rooms include the Spikes bar, a conservatory, a lounge, a smart restaurant and a superb leisure complex as well as conference and banqueting suites.
ROOMS: 30 en suite (4 fmly) (15 GF) No smoking in 22 bedrooms s £75-£86; d £97-£108 (incl. bkfst) **LB** **FACILITIES: Spa** STV Indoor swimming (H) Golf 36 Fishing Squash Snooker Sauna Solarium Gym Putting green Jacuzzi Health/beauty salon, Driving range, Swimming pool supervised Xmas **CONF:** BC Thtr 500 Class 200 Board 36 Del £130 **SERVICES:** Lift **PARKING:** 300 **NOTES:** No dogs (ex guide dogs) No smoking in restaurant Civ Wed 500
CARDS:

★★★68% Milsom's

Stratford Rd, Dedham CO7 6HW
☎ 01206 322795 📠 01206 323689
e-mail: milsoms@talbooth.co.uk
(For full entry see Dedham)

Early start?
Hotels at all star levels should provide in-room alarm clocks and/or alarm calls

★★★68% The Rose & Crown

East St CO1 2TZ
☎ 01206 866677 📠 01206 866616
e-mail: info@rose-and-crown.com
Dir: *From A12 follow signs for "Rollerworld", hotel by level crossing*
This delightful coaching inn is situated close to the shops and is full of original charm. The public areas feature a wealth of exposed beams and timbered walls and include a Tudor Bar and a fusion restaurant serving Indian and French cuisine. Bedrooms vary in size and style, are pleasantly decorated and equipped with many thoughtful extras.
ROOMS: 30 en suite (3 fmly) (6 GF) No smoking in 5 bedrooms s £64-£79; d £74-£120 (incl. bkfst) **FACILITIES:** STV **CONF:** Thtr 100 Class 50 Board 45 Del from £120 **PARKING:** 50 **NOTES:** No dogs (ex guide dogs) No smoking in restaurant Civ Wed 150
CARDS:

U *Holiday Inn Colchester*

Abbotts Ln, Eight Ash Green CO6 3QL
☎ 0870 400 9020 📠 01206 766577
e-mail: colchester@ichotelsgroup.com
Dir: *at junct of A1124 & A12 signposted to Halstead*
At the time of going to press, the classification for this hotel was not confirmed. Please refer to the AA internet site www.theAA.com for current information.
ROOMS: 110 en suite (30 fmly) No smoking in 58 bedrooms **FACILITIES:** Indoor swimming (H) Sauna Solarium Gym Jacuzzi Steam room Treatment rooms **CONF:** Thtr 150 Class 70 Board 60 **PARKING:** 150 **CARDS:**

Travel Inn

Ipswich Rd CO4 4WP
☎ 08701 977065 📠 01206 751327
Dir: *take A120 (A1232) junct off A12, follow A1232 towards Colchester, Travel Inn on right*
Travel Inn offers good-quality, value-for-money accommodation. Spacious, en suite rooms with bath and shower comfortably accommodate a family of up to two adults and two children (to age 15). The restaurant and bar offers a varied menu. For further details and the Travel Inn phone number, consult the Hotel Groups page.
ROOMS: 40 en suite s £44.95; d £44.95

COLEFORD, Gloucestershire — Map 04 SO51

★★★67% The Speech House

GL16 7EL
☎ 01594 822607 📠 01594 823658
e-mail: relax@thespeechhouse.co.uk
Dir: *on B4226 between Cinderford and Coleford*

Dating back to 1676, this former hunting lodge is tucked away in the Forest of Dean. Bedrooms, some with impressive four-poster beds, combine modern amenities with period charm. The beamed restaurant serves good, imaginative food, while additional features include a mini gym, aqua spa and conference facilities.
ROOMS: 16 en suite 17 annexe rms (16 en suite) (4 fmly) (12 GF) No smoking in 6 bedrooms s £50-£90; d £70-£120 (incl. bkfst) **LB** **FACILITIES:** Golf 18 Sauna Solarium Gym Jacuzzi Beauty Salon Xmas **CONF:** BC Thtr 70 Class 40 Board 40 Del from £100 **PARKING:** 70 **NOTES:** No smoking in restaurant Civ Wed 60
CARDS:

See advert on opposite page

★★65% **The Angel Hotel**
Market Place GL16 8AE
☎ 01594 833113 ▤ 01594 832413
Dir: *access to hotel via A48 or A40*
This friendly 17th-century coaching inn is centrally located and provides an excellent base for exploring the area. All bedrooms are spacious, well equipped and suitable for both business and leisure guests. Additional features include a choice of bars, all with a relaxing atmosphere, a good range of real ales and wholesome cuisine.
ROOMS: 9 en suite (1 fmly) s £45-£50; d £65-£85 (incl. bkfst)
FACILITIES: STV entertainment **PARKING:** 9
CARDS:

COLERNE, Wiltshire — Map 04 ST87

Top 200 - Hotel

★★★★ ◎◎◎ **Lucknam Park**
SN14 8AZ
☎ 01225 742777 ▤ 01225 743536
e-mail: reservations@lucknampark.co.uk
RELAIS & CHATEAUX
Dir: *M4 junct 17, A350 to Chippenham, then A420 to Bristol for 3m. At Ford village, left to Colerne, after 3m right at x-rds. Entrance on right*
There is a fantastic sense of 'arrival' on approaching this Palladian Mansion along a magnificent mile-long avenue of beech and lime trees. Surrounded by 500 acres of parkland and beautiful gardens, this fine hotel offers a wealth of activities ranging from pampering treatments to more vigorous exercise. Elegant bedrooms and suites are split between the main building and adjacent courtyard. Dining options range from the informal Pavilion Restaurant, to the more formal, but very accomplished main restaurant.
ROOMS: 23 en suite 18 annexe en suite (16 GF) s £215; d £215-£350 **LB** **FACILITIES:** STV Indoor swimming (H) Tennis (hard) Riding Snooker Sauna Solarium Gym Croquet lawn Jacuzzi Whirlpool, Beauty & hair salon, Steam room, Cross country course, Mountain bikes entertainment Xmas **CONF:** Thtr 60 Class 24 Board 24 Del from £250 **PARKING:** 70 **NOTES:** No dogs (ex guide dogs) No smoking in restaurant Civ Wed 60
CARDS:

COLESHILL, Warwickshire — Map 10 SP28

★★★65% **Grimstock Country House**
Gilson Rd, Gilson B46 1LJ
☎ 01675 462121 & 462161 ▤ 01675 467646
e-mail: enquiries@grimstockhotel.co.uk
Dir: *off A446 onto B4117 to Gilson, hotel 100yds on right*
Although convenient for Birmingham International Airport and the NEC, this privately owned hotel is in a peaceful rural setting. Bedrooms are spacious and comfortable. Public rooms include a choice of restaurants, a wood-panelled bar, good conference facilities and a gym featuring the latest cardiovascular equipment.
ROOMS: 44 en suite (1 fmly) s £65-£89; d £75-£99 (incl. bkfst) **LB** **FACILITIES:** STV Solarium Gym Xmas **CONF:** Thtr 100 Class 60 Board 50 Del from £125 **PARKING:** 100 **NOTES:** No smoking in restaurant Civ Wed 90 **CARDS:**

> Popped the question?
> Hotels with Civ Wed in their entry are licensed for civil wedding ceremonies. Maximum numbers for the ceremony only are shown, e.g. Civ Wed 120

COLN ST ALDWYNS, Gloucestershire Map 05 SP10

Top 200 - Hotel

★★ ◎◎ **The New Inn At Coln**
GL7 5AN
☎ 01285 750651 🖹 01285 750657
e-mail: stay@new-inn.co.uk
Dir: *8m E of Cirencester, between Bibury and Fairford*
It would be hard to find a more delightful location than this inn, set in the heart of the beautiful Coln Valley. Dating back to the reign of Elizabeth I, this peaceful inn offers engaging hospitality and enchantingly individual bedrooms. Flagstone floors, wooden beams and inglenook fireplaces all contribute to the charming atmosphere. Cuisine is a central focus here and both the popular bar and restaurant serve enjoyable food prepared to a high standard.
ROOMS: 8 en suite 6 annexe en suite (1 GF) s £99-£126; d £115-£148 (incl. bkfst) **LB** **FACILITIES:** Fishing **CONF:** Thtr 20 Board 12 Del from £148 **PARKING:** 22 **NOTES:** No children 10 yrs No smoking in restaurant **CARDS:**

COLSTERWORTH, Lincolnshire Map 11 SK92

⌂ **Travelodge Grantham Colsterworth**
NG35 5JR
☎ 08700 850 950 🖹 01476 861078
Dir: *on A1/A151 southbound at junct with B151/B676*
Travelodge

Travelodge offers good quality, good value, modern accommodation. Ideal for families, the spacious, en suite bedrooms include remote-control TV, tea and coffee-making facilities, luxury beds and free morning newspaper. Meals can be taken at the nearby family restaurant. For further details and the Travelodge phone number, consult the Hotel Groups page.
ROOMS: 31 en suite s fr £42.95; d fr £42.95

COLYFORD, Devon Map 04 SY29

★★77% ◎ **Swallows Eaves**
EX24 6QJ
☎ 01297 553184 🖹 01297 553574
e-mail: swallows.eaves@talk21.com
Dir: *on A3052 between Lyme Regis and Sidmouth, in village centre, opp post office store*
This delightful hotel has gained a well deserved reputation for excellent standards of service, food and hospitality; many guests returning year after year. Bedrooms combine comfort with quality, each individually styled and equipped with many thoughtful extras. The restaurant serves a daily menu of carefully prepared dishes, making good use of fresh local ingredients.
ROOMS: 8 en suite (1 GF) No smoking in all bedrooms s £49-£54; d £78-£98 (incl. bkfst) **LB** **FACILITIES:** Free use of nearby Swimming Club **PARKING:** 10 **NOTES:** No dogs (ex guide dogs) No children 14yrs No smoking in restaurant RS Nov-Feb **CARDS:**

CONSETT, Co Durham Map 19 NZ1

★★★67% **Derwent Manor**
Allensford DH8 9BB
☎ 01207 592000 🖹 01207 502472
e-mail: info@royal-derwent-hotel.com
Dir: *A69/A68 S, hotel 11m on left*
Best Western

This hotel built in the style of a manor house is set in open grounds overlooking the River Derwent. The spacious bedrooms are comfortably equipped and include a number of suites. A popular wedding venue, there are also extensive conference facilities. The Grouse & Claret bar serves a wide range of drinks and light meals, and Guinevere's restaurant offers fine dining.
ROOMS: 45 en suite (3 fmly) No smoking in 10 bedrooms s fr £95; d fr £105 (incl. bkfst) **LB** **FACILITIES:** STV Indoor swimming Sauna Solarium Gym Jacuzzi Xmas **CONF:** BC Thtr 300 Class 200 Board 80 Del from £90 **SERVICES:** Lift **PARKING:** 150 **NOTES:** No smoking in restaurant Civ Wed 200 **CARDS:**

★★★64% **The Raven Hotel**
Broomhill, Ebchester DH8 6RY
☎ 01207 562562 🖹 01207 560262
e-mail: enquiries@ravenhotel.co.uk
Dir: *on B6309*
This modern hotel stands on a hillside overlooking the village and surrounding countryside. Bedrooms, including some four-poster rooms, are spacious and many have stunning views.
Well-prepared meals are served in the attractive conservatory restaurant and a range of popular bar dishes and excellent selection of cask ales are available in the refurbished bar.
ROOMS: 28 en suite 1 annexe en suite (7 fmly) s £44-£55; d £56-£70 (incl. bkfst) **LB** **FACILITIES: Spa** STV Xmas **CONF:** Thtr 150 Class 80 Board 40 Del £79.95 **PARKING:** 75 **NOTES:** No dogs (ex guide dogs) No smoking in restaurant Civ Wed 150
CARDS:

CONSTANTINE, Cornwall & Isles of Scilly Map 02 SW72

★★69% ◎ **Trengilly Wartha Inn**
Nancenoy TR11 5RP
☎ 01326 340332 🖹 01326 340332
e-mail: reception@trengilly.co.uk
Dir: *A39 to Falmouth. At rdbt by Asda in Penryn, signed to Constantine then Gweek. Hotel signed on left in 1m*
THE CIRCLE
Selected Individual Hotels

The charm and tranquillity of this character Inn, which is located close to the Helford River, provides a welcoming environment. Interesting cuisine using local produce, fine wine, hand pulled ales and an impressive selection of malts are offered along with comfortable bedrooms and pleasant public rooms.
ROOMS: 6 en suite 2 annexe en suite (2 fmly) No smoking in 2 bedrooms s £49; d £72-£78 (incl. bkfst) **LB** **PARKING:** 50 **NOTES:** RS 25 Dec (b'fast only) 31 Dec **CARDS:**

ONSTANTINE BAY, Cornwall & Isles of Scilly Map 02 SW87

★★79% Treglos
L28 8JH
01841 520727 01841 521163
-mail: stay@tregloshotel.com
ir: right at Constantine Bay stores, hotel 50yds on left

wned by the same family for over 30 years, this hotel has a radition of high standards of service and hospitality. The genuine velcome, a choice of comfortable lounges, an indoor pool and hildren's play facilities, entices guests back year after year. edrooms vary in size; those with sea views are always popular. he restaurant continues to provide imaginative menus ncorporating seasonal, local produce.
OOMS: 42 en suite (12 fmly) (1 GF) No smoking in all bedrooms £66-£89; d £132-£178 (incl. bkfst & dinner) **LB** **FACILITIES:** Indoor wimming (H) Snooker Croquet lawn Jacuzzi Converted 'boat house' for ble tennis ch fac **CONF:** Board 20 **SERVICES:** Lift **PARKING:** 58
OTES: No smoking in restaurant Closed 17 Nov-5 Mar
ARDS:

See advert on this page

OOKHAM DEAN, Berkshire Map 05 SU88

Restaurant with Rooms

The Inn on the Green Garry Holihead
he Old Cricket Common SL6 9NZ
01628 482638 01628 487474
-mail: reception@theinnonthegreen.com
ir: A404 towards Marlow High St. Cross suspension bridge towards isham. 1st left into Quarry Wood Rd, right Hills Lane, right at Memorial ross

traditional English country inn set in rural Berkshire. Bedrooms re individually decorated, spacious and comfortable. Now efurbished and modernised, the building retains many traditional features including a wood-panelled dining room and Old English bar with log fire. Food is imaginative and noteworthy.
ROOMS: 9 en suite s £110-£150; d £120-£160 (incl. bkfst) **LB**
FACILITIES: Spa STV Croquet lawn Jacuzzi Xmas **CONF:** BC Thtr 30 Class 30 Board 30 Del from £150 **PARKING:** 50 **NOTES:** Civ Wed 40
CARDS:

COPTHORNE See Gatwick Airport

CORBRIDGE, Northumberland Map 21 NY96

★★66% Angel of Corbridge
Main St NE45 5LA
01434 632119 01434 633496
e-mail: info@theangelofcorbridge.co.uk
***Dir:** From A1 onto A69 (Hexham) for approx 10m, Corbridge exit, 2m to Corbridge, hotel 1st large building*
Corbridge's oldest inn provides well-equipped, modern accommodation and yet retains much of its original character. Guests can relax in the traditional lounge or enjoy light meals and drinks in the modernised, trendy bar. The stylishly refurbished restaurant opens for dinner and Sunday lunch, and offers carefully cooked, contemporary menus. Staff are efficient throughout.
ROOMS: 5 en suite (1 fmly) No smoking in all bedrooms s £49; d £74 (incl. bkfst) **FACILITIES:** entertainment Xmas **PARKING:** 25
NOTES: No dogs (ex guide dogs) No smoking in restaurant
CARDS:

CORFE CASTLE, Dorset

Map 04 SY98

★★★76% Mortons House

49 East St BH20 5EE
☎ 01929 480988 01929 480820
e-mail: stay@mortonshouse.co.uk
Dir: *on A351 between Wareham/Swanage*

Set in delightful gardens and grounds with excellent views of Corfe Castle, this impressive building dates back to Tudor times. The oak-panelled drawing room has a roaring log fire and an interesting range of enjoyable cuisine is available in the well-appointed dining room. Bedrooms, many with views of the castle, are comfortable and well equipped with a range of thoughtful extras.

ROOMS: 14 en suite 3 annexe en suite (2 fmly) (3 GF) No smoking in all bedrooms s £75-£150; d £124-£138 (incl. bkfst) **LB** **FACILITIES:** Jacuzzi Xmas **CONF:** BC Thtr 45 Class 45 Board 20 Del from £115 **PARKING:** 40 **NOTES:** No dogs (ex guide dogs) No smoking in restaurant Civ Wed 60 **CARDS:**

CORNHILL-ON-TWEED, Northumberland

Map 21 NT83

★★★74% Tillmouth Park Country House

TD12 4UU
☎ 01890 882255 01890 882540
e-mail: reception@tillmouthpark.force9.co.uk
Dir: *off A1(M) at East Ord rdbt at Berwick-upon-Tweed. Take A698 to Cornhill and Coldstream. Hotel 9m on left*

Built in 1882, this imposing mansion is set in mature grounds by the banks of the River Till. The house has gracious public rooms including a choice of relaxing lounges. The quietly elegant dining room offers a range of imaginative dishes, and lunches and early dinners are available in the bistro. Bedrooms retain a traditional character and include several magnificent master rooms.

ROOMS: 12 en suite 2 annexe en suite (1 fmly) s £90-£140; d £135-£180 (incl. bkfst) **LB** **FACILITIES:** STV Fishing Croquet lawn Clay pigeon, 3/4 snooker table, Game shooting Xmas **CONF:** Thtr 50 Class 20 Board 20 Del from £125 **PARKING:** 50 **NOTES:** No smoking in restaurant Civ Wed 30 **CARDS:**

CORSE LAWN, Gloucestershire

Map 10 SO83

★★★77% Corse Lawn House

GL19 4LZ
☎ 01452 780479 780771 01452 780840
e-mail: hotel@corselawn.com
Dir: *on B4211 5m SW of Tewkesbury*

This gracious Grade II Queen Anne house has been home to the Hine family since 1978. Augmented by an enthusiastic and committed team, the family still preside over all aspects and have created a relaxed, wonderfully comforting environment. Bedrooms

continued

offer a reassuring mix of comfort and quality. Impressive cuisine is based upon excellent produce, much being locally sourced.

ROOMS: 19 en suite (2 fmly) (5 GF) s £80-£100; d £130-£165 (incl. bkfst) **LB** **FACILITIES:** STV Indoor swimming (H) Tennis (hard) Croquet lawn Badminton Croquet Table tennis **CONF:** Thtr 50 Class 30 Board 25 Del £135 **PARKING:** 62 **NOTES:** No smoking in restaurant Closed 24-26 Dec Civ Wed 120 **CARDS:**

See advert on opposite page

COVENTRY, West Midlands

Map 10 SP37

See also Brandon, Meriden & Nuneaton

★★★72% Brooklands Grange Hotel & Restaurant

Holyhead Rd CV5 8HX
☎ 024 7660 1601 024 7660 1277
e-mail: brooklands.grange@virgin.net
Dir: *leave A45 at city centre rdbt. At next rdbt take A4114. Hotel 100yds on left*

Behind the Jacobean façade of Brooklands Grange is a well run modern and comfortable business hotel. Well-appointed bedrooms are thoughtfully equipped for corporate guests and a smartly appointed four-poster bedroom has now been created. The food continues to be worthy of note, with the emphasis on contemporary, well-flavoured dishes.

ROOMS: 31 en suite (3 fmly) (11 GF) No smoking in 25 bedrooms s £50-£90; d £70-£90 (incl. bkfst) **LB** **CONF:** BC Thtr 16 Class 16 Board 16 Del from £110 **PARKING:** 52 **NOTES:** No smoking in restaurant Closed 26-28 Dec & 1-2 Jan **CARDS:**

★★★71% Menzies Leofric

Broadgate CV1 1LZ
☎ 024 7622 1371 024 7655 1352
e-mail: info@menzies-hotels.co.uk
Dir: *junct 9 off Coventry ring road, follow signs to West Orchards Car Park, situated to rear of hotel*

Right in the centre of the city, this refurbished hotel has the advantage of preferred parking rates in the nearby multi-storey car park, and most rooms having a quiet outlook. Bedrooms are well-lit and comfortable with good business facilities. Contemporary public areas include two bars, a brasserie, plus a hairdresser.

ROOMS: 94 en suite (5 fmly) No smoking in 20 bedrooms **FACILITIES:** STV **CONF:** Thtr 500 Class 200 Board 80 Del from £130 **SERVICES:** Lift **NOTES:** No dogs (ex guide dogs) No smoking in restaurant Civ Wed 500 **CARDS:**

★★★70%
Courtyard by Marriott Coventry

London Rd, Ryton on Dunsmore CV8 3DY
☎ 0870 400 7216 0870 400 7316
e-mail: meetings.coventry@courtyardhotels.co.uk
Dir: *M6 junct 2, take A46 towards Warwick, then A45 London at Coventry Airport*

Located on the outskirts of the city, this modern hotel is popular with both business and leisure guests. A range of meeting rooms along with convenient access to the road networks makes this an ideal business venue, while the hotel's proximity to a number of attractions also makes it an ideal base for a weekend of sightseeing.

ROOMS: 51 en suite (2 fmly) (22 GF) No smoking in 25 bedrooms s £45-£125; d £70-£132 (incl. bkfst) **LB** **FACILITIES:** STV Gym Xmas **CONF:** Thtr 300 Class 100 Board 24 Del from £99 **PARKING:** 120 **NOTES:** No dogs (ex guide dogs) No smoking in restaurant Civ Wed 112 **CARDS:**

★★★67% Hylands

Warwick Rd CV3 6AU
☎ 024 7650 1600 024 7650 1027
-mail: hylands@bestwestern.co.uk
Dir: *on A429, 500yds from junct 6 of town centre ring road, opposite Memorial Park*

This hotel is convenient for the station and the city centre and overlooks an attractive park. Restaurant 153 offers good standards of food and service. Bedroom styles vary and each room is well-equipped and fully en suite; the most recent additions are smartly decorated with bold colour schemes.

ROOMS: 61 en suite No smoking in 54 bedrooms s £45-£92; d £60-£102 **LB** **FACILITIES:** STV Xmas **CONF:** Thtr 60 Class 40 Board 30 Del from £100 **PARKING:** 60 **NOTES:** No dogs (ex guide dogs) **CARDS:**

★★★66% The Chace

London Rd, Toll Bar End CV3 4EQ
☎ 0870 609 6130 024 7630 1816
e-mail: chacehotel@corushotels.com
Dir: *A45 or A46 follow to Toll Bar Roundabout / Coventry Airport, take B4116 to Willenhall, over mini-rdbt, hotel on left*

A former doctor's mansion, the main building retains many of its original Victorian features including public rooms with high ceilings, stained glass windows, oak panelling and an impressive staircase. Attractive bedrooms are situated in this part of the hotel and an extension, and there is a patio and well-kept gardens.

ROOMS: 66 en suite (23 fmly) (24 GF) No smoking in 34 bedrooms s £95; d £110 **LB** **FACILITIES:** STV Croquet lawn Pool Table, Free use of nearby leisure centre Xmas **CONF:** Thtr 65 Class 40 Board 36 Del from £90 **PARKING:** 120 **NOTES:** No dogs (ex guide dogs) No smoking in restaurant Civ Wed 60 **CARDS:**

★★★64% Allesley

Birmingham Rd, Allesley Village CV5 9GP
☎ 024 7640 3272 024 7640 5190
e-mail: stay@allesley-hotel.co.uk
Dir: *from A45 onto A4114 Brownshill Green and city centre road. 4th exit at rdbt, 1st exit next rdbt into Allesley Village. Hotel 150yds on left*

This purpose built hotel provides well-equipped bedrooms suited to the corporate guest. Public rooms are split over two levels and include a spacious reception foyer, a large restaurant and a lounge bar. Extensive conference and function facilities are also available and prove popular.

ROOMS: 75 en suite 15 annexe en suite (2 fmly) No smoking in 45 bedrooms s £35-£100; d £70-£125 (incl. bkfst) **LB** **CONF:** BC Thtr 450 Class 150 Board 80 Del from £120 **SERVICES:** Lift **PARKING:** 500 **NOTES:** No smoking in restaurant Civ Wed 350 **CARDS:**

★★★64% Novotel Coventry

Wilsons Ln CV6 6HL
☎ 024 7636 5000 024 7636 2422
e-mail: h0506@accor-hotels.com
Dir: *M6 junct 3. Follow signs for B4113 towards Longford and Bedworth. 3rd exit on large rdbt*

A modern hotel, convenient for Birmingham, Coventry and the motorway network, offering spacious, well-equipped accommodation. The bright brasserie offers extended dining hours, or alternatively there is an extensive room service menu. Family rooms and a play area make this a child-friendly hotel, and there is also a selection of meeting rooms.

ROOMS: 98 en suite (15 fmly) No smoking in 70 bedrooms s £69; d £69 **LB** **FACILITIES:** Outdoor swimming (H) Petanque, Pool table **CONF:** Thtr 200 Class 100 Board 40 Del from £99 **SERVICES:** Lift air con **PARKING:** 120 **CARDS:**

★★69% Toffs Country House

Wall Hill Rd, Corley CV7 8AD
☎ 024 7633 2030 024 7633 2102
e-mail: stay@toffs-hotel.co.uk
Dir: *from N leave A45 at Oak Lane (signed Corley), 2m to T-junct & turn right. Hotel on left. From S A45 onto A4114. Follow city centre signs on dual carriageway. Left onto Coundon Wedge Rd, then left & right at White Lion pub. Hotel on right*

Toffs Country House, as the name suggests, is set in an attractive rural setting yet with close road links to the city. Bedrooms

continued on p192

COVENTRY, continued

afford country views, and are furnished with much thought to guest comfort. Guests have a wide choice of lounges, a bar and even a games room.
ROOMS: 10 en suite (1 fmly) (1 GF) No smoking in 8 bedrooms s £50-£60; d £65-£75 (incl. bkfst) **FACILITIES:** Croquet lawn Snooker, Pool, Amusement machine **CONF:** BC **PARKING:** 14 **NOTES:** No smoking in restaurant **CARDS:**

U *Holiday Inn Coventry*
Hinckley Rd, Walsgrave CV2 2HP
☎ 0870 400 9021 📠 024 7662 1736
e-mail: reservations-coventry@ichotelsgroup.com
Dir: *M6 junct 2/on A4600*
At the time of going to press, the classification for this hotel was not confirmed. Please refer to the AA internet site www.theAA.com for current information.
ROOMS: 160 en suite (15 fmly) No smoking in 112 bedrooms **FACILITIES:** Indoor swimming (H) Sauna Gym Jacuzzi Steam room Childrens play areas entertainment ch fac **CONF:** Thtr 250 Class 150 Board 50 **SERVICES:** Lift **PARKING:** 300 **NOTES:** No smoking in restaurant **CARDS:**

Express by Holiday Inn Coventry -A45
Kenpas Highway CV3 6PB
☎ 024 7641 7555 📠 024 7641 3388
e-mail: ebhi-coventry@btconnect.com
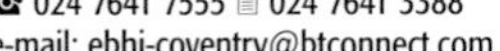
Dir: *M6 junct 2 onto A46. Follow A45 towards Birmingham. Hotel off rdbt, behind the Harvester*

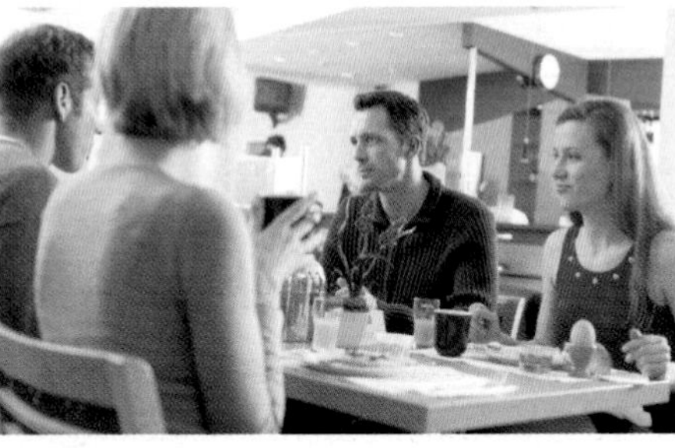

A modern hotel ideal for families and business travellers. Fresh and uncomplicated, the spacious bedrooms include Sky TV, power shower and tea and coffee-making facilities. Continental buffet breakfast is included in the room rate; other meals may be taken at the nearby family pub or restaurant. For further details and the Express by Holiday Inn phone number, consult the Hotel Groups pages.
ROOMS: 37 en suite **CONF:** Thtr 30 Class 24 Board 16

Hotel Campanile

4 Wigston Rd, Walsgrave CV2 2SD
☎ 024 7662 2311 📠 024 7660 2362
Dir: *M6 exit 2, 2nd rdbt turn right*
This modern building offers accommodation in smart, well-equipped bedrooms, all with en suite bathrooms. Refreshments may be taken at the informal Bistro. For further details and the Campanile phone number, consult the Hotel Groups page.

ROOMS: 50 en suite **CONF:** Thtr 35 Class 18 Board 20

Hotel Ibis Coventry Centre

Mill Ln, St John's Ringway CV1 2LN
☎ 024 7625 0500 📠 024 7655 3548
e-mail: H2793@accor.hotels.com
Dir: *From M45 junct 17 to Coventry. Follow City Centre ring road signs for Birmingham. A45 to Coventry, then A4114 signed to Jaguar Assembly Plant. At inner ring road towards ring road S. Off exit 5 for Mill Lane*
Modern, budget hotel offering comfortable accommodation in bright and practical bedrooms. Breakfast is self-service and dinner is available in the restaurant. For further details, consult the Hotel Groups page.
ROOMS: 88 en suite s £35.95-£45.95; d £35.95-£45.95

Hotel Ibis Coventry South
Abbey Rd, Whitley CV3 4BJ
☎ 024 7663 9922 📠 024 7630 6898
e-mail: H2094@accor-hotels.com
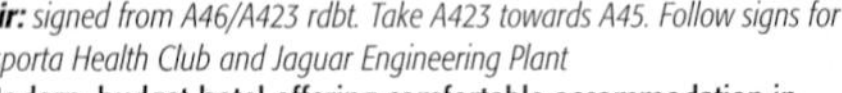
Dir: *signed from A46/A423 rdbt. Take A423 towards A45. Follow signs for Esporta Health Club and Jaguar Engineering Plant*
Modern, budget hotel offering comfortable accommodation in bright and practical bedrooms. Breakfast is self-service and dinner is available in the restaurant. For further details, consult the Hotel Groups page.
ROOMS: 51 en suite s £29.95-£42.95; d £29.95-£42.95

Innkeeper's Lodge Meriden
Main Rd, Meriden CV7 7NN
☎ 01676 523798 📠 01676 531922
Dir: *in village of Meriden, just off main A45 between Coventry & Birmingham on B4102. Lodge on left down hill from Meriden Village Green*
A new concept in the travel accommodation market. Smart rooms meet essential business requirements but also have home comforts. Dining options include all-day menus plus the added advantage of breakfast, which is included in the room price. For further details, consult the Hotel Groups page.
ROOMS: 13 rms (9 en suite)

Premier Lodge (Coventry)
Combe Fields Rd, Ansty CV7 9JP
☎ 0870 9906472 📠 0870 9906473
Dir: *M6 junct 2, follow B4065 through Ansty village, right onto B4029. Past golf club and right to lodge*
Premier Lodge offers modern, well-equipped, en suite accommodation suitable for both business and leisure travellers. Meals can be taken at the adjacent popular restaurant and bar, which is fully licensed. For further details, consult the Hotel Groups page.
ROOMS: 28 en suite s £48; d £48 **CONF:** Thtr 12 Class 14 Board 14

⌂ Travel Inn

Rugby Rd, Binley Woods CV3 2TA
☎ 08701 977066 📠 024 7643 1178
Dir: *M6 junct 2 on right of A46 Eastern by-pass at junct with Rugby Rd*
Travel Inn offers good-quality, value-for-money accommodation. Spacious, en suite rooms with bath and shower comfortably accommodate a family of up to two adults and two children (to age 15). The restaurant and bar offers a varied menu. For further details and the Travel Inn phone number, consult the Hotel Groups page.
ROOMS: 75 en suite s £44.95; d £44.95 **CONF:** Thtr 25 Board 18

COWES See Wight, Isle of

CRAMLINGTON, Northumberland — Map 21 NZ27

⌂ Innkeeper's Lodge Cramlington

Blagdon Ln NE23 8AU
☎ 01670 736111 📠 01670 715709
Dir: *from A1, exit for A19. At rdbt, left onto A1068, lodge at junct of Blagdon Lane and Fisher Lane.*
A new concept in the travel accommodation market. Smart rooms meet essential business requirements but also have home comforts. Dining options include all-day menus plus the added advantage of breakfast, which is included in the room price. For further details, consult the Hotel Groups page.
ROOMS: 18 en suite **CONF:** Board 24

⌂ Travel Inn (Newcastle-Upon-Tyne Cramlington)

Moor Farm Roundabout, off Front St NE23 7RG
☎ 08701 977188 📠 0191 2500783
Dir: *at rdbt on junction of A19/A189 S of Cramlington*
Travel Inn offers good-quality, value-for-money accommodation. Spacious, en suite rooms with bath and shower comfortably accommodate a family of up to two adults and two children (to age 15). The restaurant and bar offers a varied menu. For further details and the Travel Inn phone number, consult the Hotel Groups page.
ROOMS: 40 en suite s £44.95; d £44.95

CRANBROOK, Kent — Map 07 TQ73

★★68% *The George*

Stone St TN17 3HE
☎ 01580 713348 📠 01580 715532
Dir: *off A21 to Goudhurst & Cranbrook. At large rdbt, right into Cranbrook*
A delightful coaching inn situated in the heart of the town and dating back to the 13th century it is reputed that Edward I stayed here. The bedrooms have a wealth of original features such as exposed beams, and some rooms have lovely four-poster beds. Public rooms include a popular lounge bar, an informal wine bar and the elegant Brooks restaurant.
ROOMS: 8 en suite (1 fmly) No smoking in all bedrooms **FACILITIES:** STV Jacuzzi **CONF:** Thtr 75 Class 60 Board 50 **PARKING:** 10 **NOTES:** No smoking in restaurant
CARDS:

CRANTOCK, Cornwall & Isles of Scilly — Map 02 SW76

★★★71% Crantock Bay

West Pentire TR8 5SE
☎ 01637 830229 📠 01637 831111
e-mail: stay@crantockbayhotel.co.uk
Dir: *off A3075 at West Pentire Headland*
This family run hotel has spectacular sea views and continues its tradition of friendly and attentive service. With direct access to the beach from its four acres of grounds, and its extensive leisure facilities, the hotel is a great place for family guests. There are separate lounges and a spacious bar; in the dining room, enjoyable cuisine is served.
ROOMS: 33 en suite (3 fmly) (10 GF) s £49-£83; d £99-£167 (incl. bkfst & dinner) **LB FACILITIES:** Indoor swimming (H) Tennis (hard) Sauna Gym Croquet lawn Putting green Jacuzzi Hotel leads on to sandy beach Xmas **CONF:** Thtr 60 Class 30 Board 30 Del from £14.50 **PARKING:** 40 **NOTES:** No smoking in restaurant Closed 2 wks Nov & Jan RS Dec & Feb
CARDS:

CRATHORNE, North Yorkshire — Map 19 NZ40

Top 200 - Hotel

★★★★ Crathorne Hall

TS15 0AR — HandPICKED
☎ 01642 700398 📠 01642 700814
e-mail: crathorne@arcadianhotels.co.uk
Dir: *off A19, take slip road signed Teesside Airport and Kirklevington, then right signed Crathorne to hotel*
This splendid Edwardian hall sits in its own landscaped grounds and enjoys fine views of the Leven Valley and rolling Cleveland Hills. Both the impressively equipped bedrooms and the delightful public areas offer sumptuous levels of luxury and comfort, with elegant antique furnishings that complement the hotel's architectural style. Expertly crafted dishes in the restaurant make this a serious destination for dining out. Service is friendly and attentive.
ROOMS: 37 en suite (4 fmly) No smoking in 15 bedrooms s £93-£290; d £140-£290 (incl. bkfst) **LB FACILITIES:** STV Fishing Croquet lawn Jogging track, Clay pigeon shooting Xmas **CONF:** Thtr 120 Class 80 Board 60 Del from £140 **PARKING:** 120 **NOTES:** No smoking in restaurant Civ Wed 120
CARDS:

See advert on page 195

CRAWLEY See Gatwick Airport

CREWE, Cheshire

Map 15 SJ75

★★★★76% Crewe Hall
Weston Rd CW1 6UZ
☎ 01270 253333 📠 01270 253322
e-mail: reservations@crewehall.com
Dir: *M6 junct 16 follow A500 to Crewe. Last exit at rdbt onto A5020. 1st exit next rdbt to Crewe. Crewe Hall 150yds on right*

Proudly standing in 500 acres of mature grounds, this historic hall, converted into a very comfortable hotel, dates back to the 17th century. It retains a very elaborate interior, which reflects the Victorian style of its architecture. Bedrooms are spacious, well equipped and comfortable and are split between traditionally styled rooms in the main hall, with ultra modern suites housed in the west wing. Quality modern cooking is served in the elegant Ranulph restaurant.

ROOMS: 26 en suite 39 annexe en suite (5 fmly) (17 GF) No smoking in 40 bedrooms s £135-£320; d £160-£380 (incl. bkfst) **LB** **FACILITIES:** STV Tennis (hard) Croquet lawn Full size football pitch Xmas **CONF:** Thtr 220 Class 110 Board 100 Del from £205.62 **SERVICES:** Lift **PARKING:** 140 **NOTES:** No smoking in restaurant Civ Wed 200 **CARDS:**

★★★70% Hunters Lodge
Sydney Rd, Sydney CW1 5LU
☎ 01270 583440 📠 01270 500553
e-mail: info@hunterslodge.co.uk
Dir: *1m from Crewe station, off A534*

Dating back to the 18th century, this family-run hotel has been extended and modernised. Accommodation, mainly located in adjacent well-equipped bedroom wings, includes family and four-poster rooms. Imaginative dishes are served in the spacious restaurant, and the popular bar also offers a choice of tempting meals. Service throughout is friendly.

ROOMS: 47 en suite (2 fmly) No smoking in 21 bedrooms s £71-£87; d £95-£104 (incl. bkfst) **FACILITIES: Spa** STV Sauna Gym **CONF:** Thtr 160 Class 100 Board 80 Del from £108.50 **PARKING:** 240 **NOTES:** No dogs (ex guide dogs) No smoking in restaurant RS Sunday Civ Wed 130 **CARDS:**

★★★66% White Lion
Weston CW2 5NA
☎ 01270 587011 & 500303 📠 01270 500303
Dir: *M6 junct 16, A500 signed Crewe/Nantwich/Chester. 2nd rdbt right into Weston village. Hotel in centre on left*

Once a Tudor farmhouse, this privately owned hotel provides comfortable, modern accommodation, yet retains much of its old charm. In addition to The White Lion Restaurant and its adjoining cocktail lounge, a selection of bar snacks is available in the oak-beamed lounge bar.

ROOMS: 16 en suite (2 fmly) (7 GF) s £58; d £68-£75 (incl. bkfst) **LB** **FACILITIES:** Crown Green bowling **CONF:** Thtr 50 Class 28 Board 20 Del £90 **PARKING:** 100 **NOTES:** No smoking in restaurant Closed Xmas & New Year Civ Wed 65 **CARDS:**

⌂ Travel Inn
Coppenhall Ln, Woolstanwood CW2 8SD
☎ 08701 977068 📠 01270 256316
Dir: *at junct of A530 & A532, 9m from M6 junct 16 N'bound*

Travel Inn offers good-quality, value-for-money accommodation. Spacious, en suite rooms with bath and shower comfortably accommodate a family of up to two adults and two children (to age 15). The restaurant and bar offers a varied menu. For further details and the Travel Inn phone number, consult the Hotel Groups page.

ROOMS: 41 en suite s £44.95; d £44.95

⌂ Travelodge
Alsager Rd, Barthomley CW2 5PT
☎ 08700 850 950 📠 01270 883157
Dir: *5m E, at junct 16 M6/A500*

Travelodge offers good quality, good value, modern accommodation. Ideal for families, the spacious, en suite bedrooms include remote-control TV, tea and coffee-making facilities, luxury beds and free morning newspaper. Meals can be taken at the nearby family restaurant. For further details and the Travelodge phone number, consult the Hotel Groups page.

ROOMS: 42 en suite s fr £42.95; d fr £42.95

CRICK, Northamptonshire

Map 11 SP57

U *Holiday Inn Rugby/Northampton*
NN6 7XR
☎ 0870 400 9059 📠 01788 823955
e-mail: rugbyhi@ichotelsgroup.com
Dir: *M1 junct 18*

At the time of going to press, the classification for this hotel was not confirmed. Please refer to the AA internet site www.theAA.com for current information.

ROOMS: 88 en suite (17 fmly) No smoking in 51 bedrooms **FACILITIES:** Indoor swimming (H) Sauna Solarium Gym Jacuzzi ch fac **CONF:** Thtr 200 Class 100 Board 142 **PARKING:** 200 **CARDS:**

⌂ Hotel Ibis Rugby East
Parklands NN6 7EX
☎ 01788 824331 📠 01788 824332
e-mail: H3588@accor-hotels.com
Dir: *M1 junct 18/A428*

Modern, budget hotel offering comfortable accommodation in bright and practical bedrooms. Breakfast is self-service and dinner is available in the restaurant. For further details, consult the Hotel Groups page.

ROOMS: 111 en suite s £29.95-£49.95; d £29.95-£49.95

CRICKLADE, Wiltshire

Map 05 SU09

★★★70% Cricklade Hotel
Common Hill SN6 6HA
☎ 01793 750751 📠 01793 751767
e-mail: info@crickladehotel.co.uk
Dir: *off A419 onto B4040. Turn left at clock tower. Right at rdbt. Hotel 0.5m up hill on left*

Providing a haven for peace and tranquility, this hotel is surrounded by over 30 acres of Wiltshire countryside and enjoys spectacular views. Bedrooms vary in size and style; the rooms in the main building offering high levels of comfort and quality. In

continued

addition to the elegant lounge and dining room, a Victorian style conservatory runs the full length of the building.
ROOMS: 25 en suite 21 annexe en suite (1 fmly) No smoking in 26 bedrooms s £105-£120; d £140-£145 (incl. bkfst) **LB FACILITIES:** STV Indoor swimming (H) Golf 9 Tennis (hard) Snooker Sauna Solarium Gym Croquet lawn Jacuzzi Aromatherapy Beautician entertainment Xmas **CONF:** Thtr 120 Class 60 Board 30 Del £155 **PARKING:** 100 **NOTES:** No dogs (ex guide dogs) No children 14yrs No smoking in restaurant Closed 25-26 Dec Civ Wed 80
CARDS:

CROMER, Norfolk — Map 13 TG24

★★70% The Cliftonville

NR27 9AS
☎ 01263 512543 01263 515700
e-mail: reservations@cliftonvillehotel.co.uk

Imposing Edwardian Hotel situated on the main coast road with stunning views of the sea. Public rooms feature a magnificent staircase, Minstrels' gallery, coffee shop, lounge bar, a further residents' lounge, Boltons Bistro and an additional restaurant. The spacious bedrooms are pleasantly decorated and thoughtfully equipped, all rooms have lovely sea views.
ROOMS: 30 en suite (5 fmly) No smoking in 14 bedrooms s £40-£48; d £80-£96 (incl. bkfst) **LB FACILITIES:** Xmas **CONF:** Thtr 150 Class 100 Board 60 Del from £75 **SERVICES:** Lift **PARKING:** 20
CARDS:

★★70% Red Lion

Brook St NR27 9HD
☎ 01263 514964 01263 512834
e-mail: yeolderedlionhotel@uk2.net
Dir: *from town centre 1st left after church*

Well-maintained Victorian property situated in an elevated position overlooking the beach and sea beyond. The smartly appointed public areas include a billiard room, lounge bar, a popular restaurant, a sunny conservatory and a first floor residents' lounge with superb views of the sea. The spacious bedrooms are pleasantly decorated, with co-ordinated soft furnishings and many thoughtful touches.
ROOMS: 12 en suite (1 fmly) s £50-£52; d £84-£88 (incl. bkfst) **FACILITIES:** Snooker Sauna Solarium Discount for local leisure centre **CONF:** Thtr 60 Class 50 Board 40 **PARKING:** 12 **NOTES:** No dogs No smoking in restaurant Closed Xmas Day **CARDS:**

★★62% Hotel de Paris

High St NR27 9HG
☎ 01263 513141 01263 515217
Leisureplex
e-mail: deparis.cromer@alfatravel.co.uk
Dir: *enter Cromer on A140 Norwich Rd. Left at lights onto Mount St. 2nd traffic lights right into Prince of Wales Rd. 2nd right into New St leading into High St*

Imposing, traditional-style resort hotel, situated in a prominent position overlooking the pier and beach. The bedrooms are pleasantly decorated and equipped with a good range of useful extras; many rooms have lovely sea views. The spacious public areas include a large lounge bar, restaurant, games room and a further lounge.
ROOMS: 56 en suite (5 fmly) s £28-£37; d £42-£66 (incl. bkfst) **LB FACILITIES:** Games room entertainment Xmas **SERVICES:** Lift **PARKING:** 14 **NOTES:** No dogs (ex guide dogs) No smoking in restaurant Closed Dec-Feb RS Mar & Nov **CARDS:**

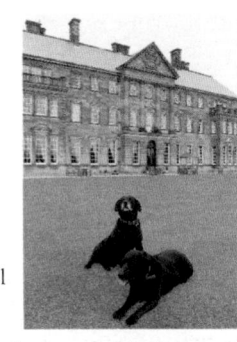

CROOKLANDS, Cumbria — Map 18 SD58

★★★63% Crooklands

LA7 7NW
☎ 015395 67432 015395 67525
Best Western
e-mail: reception@crooklands.com
Dir: *M6 junct 36 onto A65. Left at rdbt, Hotel 1.5m on right past garage*

Although only a short drive from the M6, this hotel enjoys a peaceful rural location. Housed in a converted 200-year-old farmhouse, the restaurant retains many original features such as beams and stone walls. Bedrooms are a mix of modern and traditional and vary in size.
ROOMS: 30 en suite No smoking in 15 bedrooms s £48-£60; d £48-£60 **LB CONF:** Thtr 80 Class 50 Board 40 **SERVICES:** air con **PARKING:** 80 **NOTES:** No dogs (ex guide dogs) No smoking in restaurant Closed 24-26 Dec **CARDS:**

CROSTHWAITE, Cumbria — Map 18 SD49

A ★★★ Damson Dene

LA8 8JE
☎ 015395 68676 015395 68227
e-mail: info@damsondene.co.uk
Dir: *M6, junct 36 follow A590, right onto A5074. Hotel 5m on right*
ROOMS: 37 en suite (4 fmly) (9 GF) s £59-£79; d £78-£118 (incl. bkfst) **LB FACILITIES: Spa** Indoor swimming (H) Squash Sauna Solarium Gym Jacuzzi Beauty salon, steam room Xmas **CONF:** Thtr 140 Class 60 Board 40 Del from £67 **PARKING:** 60 **NOTES:** No smoking in restaurant
CARDS:

C

CROWTHORNE, Berkshire Map 05 SU86

★★★68% Corus hotel Bracknell
Duke's Ride RG45 6DW
☎ 0870 609 6111 🖷 01344 778913
e-mail: reservations.bracknell@corushotels.com
Dir: *M3 J4, A331 to Camberley, follow signs to Sandhurst/Crowthorne A3095, left B3348, hotel past 2nd rdbt*

Situated in a quiet location but convenient for both the M3 and M4, this hotel attracts a high proportion of business guests. The modern bedrooms, which include interconnecting pairs of rooms, are attractively appointed and well maintained. Public areas include a pleasant brasserie-style restaurant and a choice of bar areas.
ROOMS: 79 en suite No smoking in 43 bedrooms s £115; d £140 **LB FACILITIES:** STV Discounts at local leisure facilities Xmas **CONF:** Thtr 50 Class 20 Board 24 Del from £120 **PARKING:** 96 **NOTES:** No smoking in restaurant Civ Wed 50 **CARDS:**

★★67% Dial House
62 Dukes Ride RG45 6DL
☎ 01344 776941 🖷 01344 777191
e-mail: dhh@fardellhotels.com
Dir: *A3095/B3348 towards Crowthorne*
Located close to the station, this friendly hotel would suit guests who require good connections into London. Bedrooms are comfortable; most have showers in bathrooms. The welcoming bar and restaurant attract residents with its home-from-home atmosphere and interesting, competent cooking.
ROOMS: 21 en suite (2 fmly) (5 GF) No smoking in all bedrooms s £45-£105; d £60-£115 (incl. bkfst) **FACILITIES:** STV **CONF:** Thtr 16 Class 10 Board 12 Del from £130 **PARKING:** 20 **NOTES:** No dogs (ex guide dogs) No smoking in restaurant Closed 22 Dec-3 Jan
CARDS:

CROYDON, Greater London Map 06 TQ36

★★★★77% Coulsdon Manor
Coulsdon Court Rd, Coulsdon CR5 2LL
☎ 020 8668 0414 🖷 020 8668 3118
e-mail: coulsdonmanor@marstonhotels.com
Dir: *A23 right into Stoats Nest Road. Hotel top of hill on left*
This delightful Victorian manor house is peacefully set amidst 140 acres of landscaped parkland, complete with its own professional 18-hole golf course. Bedrooms are spacious and comfortable, whilst public areas include a choice of lounges and an elegant restaurant serving carefully prepared, imaginative food. Excellent standards of hospitality and service are to be commended.
ROOMS: 35 en suite No smoking in 13 bedrooms s fr £108; d fr £130 **LB FACILITIES:** STV Golf 18 Tennis (hard) Squash Sauna Solarium Gym Putting green **CONF:** Thtr 180 Class 90 Board 70 Del £160 **SERVICES:** Lift **PARKING:** 200 **NOTES:** No dogs (ex guide dogs) No smoking in restaurant Civ Wed 60
CARDS:

★★★★70% Le Meridien Selsdon Park & Golf Course
Addington Rd, Sanderstead CR2 8YA
☎ 020 8657 8811 🖷 020 8651 6171
e-mail: selsdonpark@lemeridien.com
Dir: *3m SE off A2022*
Surrounded by 200 acres of mature parkland with its own 18-hole golf course, this imposing Jacobean mansion is less than 20 minutes, but a world away, from the hustle and bustle of central London. The hotel's impressive range of conference rooms, along with the spectacular North Downs countryside which the hotel overlooks, make this a popular venue for both weddings and meetings. Leisure facilities are impressive.
ROOMS: 204 en suite (12 fmly) **FACILITIES:** STV Indoor swimming (H) Outdoor swimming (H) Golf 18 Tennis (hard & grass) Squash Sauna Solarium Gym Croquet lawn Putting green Jacuzzi Boules Jogging track entertainment **CONF:** Thtr 350 Class 220 Board 60 **SERVICES:** Lift **PARKING:** 300 **NOTES:** No dogs (ex guide dogs) No smoking in restaurant Civ Wed 100 **CARDS:**

★★★68% Aerodrome
Purley Way CR9 4LT
☎ 020 8710 9000 🖷 020 8681 6438
e-mail: info@aerodrome-hotel.co.uk
Dir: *Follow A23 Central London. Hotel on left next to Airport House*
Conveniently located on the edge of Croydon, close to what was the first London airport site, this hotel has changed hands. The new owners provide well-equipped accommodation including good business facilities and soundproofing.
ROOMS: 84 en suite No smoking in 44 bedrooms s £55-£99; d £75-£140 (incl. bkfst) **LB FACILITIES:** Complimentary pass to nearby health club Xmas **CONF:** Thtr 100 Class 50 Board 40 Del £135 **PARKING:** 200 **NOTES:** No dogs (ex guide dogs) Civ Wed 100
CARDS:

★★★65% Jurys Inn
Wellesley Rd CR0 9XY
☎ 020 8448 6000 🖷 020 8448 6111
e-mail: jurysinncroydon@jurysdoyle.com
Dir: *From A232 bear left, at top of road take right lane at large set of traffic lights & turn right into George St. At top of this road at traffic lights go left, continue until mini rdbt & turn left. Hotel is at top of the road*
This newly built hotel is centrally located with good access to public transport. Bedrooms are spacious and modern and have air conditioning. Public areas are contemporary with a coffee bar, Barista, and a light and modern dining area. The state-of-the-art conference centre is very popular with local businesses having 14 dedicated meeting rooms with all modern amenities.
ROOMS: 240 en suite (168 fmly) No smoking in 140 bedrooms s £60-£85; d £60-£85 **FACILITIES:** STV **CONF:** BC Thtr 80 Class 50 Board 40 Del from £110 **SERVICES:** Lift air con **NOTES:** No dogs (ex guide dogs) Closed 24-28 Dec **CARDS:**

★★67% *South Park Hotel*
3-5 South Park Hill Rd, South Croydon CR2 7DY
☎ 020 8688 5644 🖷 020 8760 0861
e-mail: reception@southparkhotel.co.uk
Dir: *M25 junct 11 onto M23 towards Croydon. At Purley Cross follow A235 to Croydon town centre. At Coombe Rd lights turn right (A212) towards Addington 0.5m to rdbt take 3rd exit into South Park Hill Rd, hotel on left*
This small hotel is ideally located for road and rail links and there is some off-street parking for guests with cars. Bedrooms are attractively decorated and offer a good range of in-room facilities. Public areas consist of a cosy bar, a lounge with large sofas and a delightful back garden.
ROOMS: 21 en suite (2 fmly) No smoking in 8 bedrooms **PARKING:** 15 **NOTES:** No smoking in restaurant **CARDS:**

⇧ Innkeeper's Lodge Croydon South

415 Brighton Rd CR2 6EJ
☎ 020 8680 4559
Dir: *M23 junct 7/ A23 or M25 junct 6/A22. At Purley take A235 Brighton Rd, N towards South Croydon, for 1m. Lodge on right.*
A new concept in the travel accommodation market. Smart rooms meet essential business requirements but also have home comforts. Dining options include all-day menus plus the added advantage of breakfast, which is included in the room price. For further details, consult the Hotel Groups page.
ROOMS: 28 en suite

⇧ Premier Lodge (Croydon)

The Colonnades Leisure Park, 619 Purley Way CR0 4RQ
☎ 0870 9906554 📠 0870 9906555
Premier Lodge offers modern, well-equipped, en suite accommodation suitable for both business and leisure travellers. Meals can be taken at the adjacent popular restaurant and bar, which is fully licensed. For further details, consult the Hotel Groups page.
ROOMS: 81 en suite s £56; d £56 **CONF:** Thtr 120

⇧ Travel Inn

104 Coombe Rd CR0 5RB
☎ 08701 977069 📠 020 8686 6439
Dir: *M25 junct 7, A23 to Purley, then follow A235 to Croydon. Pass Tree House pub on left. Turn right at traffic lights, onto A212*
Travel Inn offers good-quality, value-for-money accommodation. Spacious, en suite rooms with bath and shower comfortably accommodate a family of up to two adults and two children (to age 15). The restaurant and bar offers a varied menu. For further details and the Travel Inn phone number, consult the Hotel Groups page.
ROOMS: 39 en suite s £52.95-£54.95; d £52.95-£54.95

CUCKFIELD, West Sussex — Map 06 TQ32

★★72% Hilton Park Hotel

Tylers Green RH17 5EG
☎ 01444 454555 📠 01444 457222
e-mail: hiltonpark@janus-systems.com
Dir: *halfway between Cuckfield and Haywards Heath on A272*
Situated between the delightful village of Cuckfield and Haywards Heath, this charming family-run, Victorian country house is set in three acres of landscaped grounds. The comfortable bedrooms are tastefully decorated and equipped with an excellent range of extra facilities. In addition to an elegant drawing room, the public rooms include a smartly presented dining room and a conservatory bar.
ROOMS: 11 en suite (2 fmly) s fr £80; d fr £115 (incl. bkfst) **LB** **FACILITIES:** STV **CONF:** Thtr 30 Board 12 **PARKING:** 50 **NOTES:** No dogs (ex guide dogs) No smoking in restaurant
CARDS:

DARLINGTON, Co Durham — Map 19 NZ21

See also Tees-Side Airport

★★★74% *Hall Garth Golf & Country Club*

Coatham Mundeville DL1 3LU
☎ 01325 300400 📠 01325 310083
e-mail: hallgarth@corushotels.com
Dir: *A1(M) junct 59, A167 towards Darlington. After 600yds left at top of hill, hotel on right*
This hotel, peacefully situated in its own grounds yet conveniently located for the motorway network, offers comfortable accommodation. Bedrooms are split between the original house, the converted water mill and the modern extension. Public areas display many original features, whilst the lounges and Hugo's restaurant provide views over the golf course.

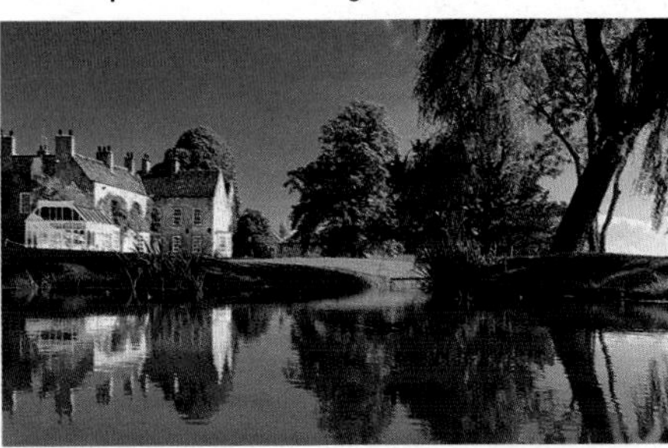

ROOMS: 40 en suite 11 annexe en suite (5 fmly) No smoking in 31 bedrooms **FACILITIES:** STV Indoor swimming (H) Golf 9 Sauna Solarium Gym Putting green Jacuzzi Steam room Beauty Salon **CONF:** Thtr 300 Class 120 Board 80 **PARKING:** 150 **NOTES:** No smoking in restaurant Civ Wed 170
CARDS:

★★★72% Headlam Hall

Headlam, Gainford DL2 3HA
☎ 01325 730238 📠 01325 730790
e-mail: admin@headlamhall.co.uk
Dir: *2m N of A67 between Piercebridge and Gainford*
This impressive Jacobean hall lies in farmland north east of Piercebridge. The main house retains many historical features including flagstone floors and a pillared hall. Bedrooms are well proportioned and traditionally styled. A converted coach house contains more modern rooms, as well as a conference and leisure centre.
ROOMS: 19 en suite 17 annexe en suite (4 fmly) (10 GF) No smoking in 25 bedrooms s £75-£115; d £90-£130 (incl. bkfst) **LB** **FACILITIES:** STV Indoor swimming (H) Tennis (hard) Fishing Sauna Gym Croquet lawn **CONF:** Thtr 150 Class 40 Board 40 Del £112 **PARKING:** 60 **NOTES:** No dogs (ex guide dogs) No smoking in restaurant Closed 24-25 Dec Civ Wed 150 **CARDS:**

★★★67% Walworth Castle Hotel

Walworth DL2 2LY
☎ 01325 485470 📠 01325 462257
e-mail: enquiries@walworthcastle.co.uk
Dir: *A1(M) junct 58 follow signs to Corbridge. Left at rdbt, left at The Dog pub. Hotel on left after 1m*

This 12th-century castle is privately owned and has been tastefully converted. Accommodation is offered in a range of styles, including an impressive suite and more compact rooms in an

continued on p198

D

DARLINGTON, continued

adjoining wing. Dinner can be taken in the fine dining Hansards Restaurant or the more relaxed Farmer's Bar. A popular venue also for conferences and weddings.
ROOMS: 20 en suite 14 annexe en suite (4 fmly) No smoking in 6 bedrooms s £60-£75; d £75-£175 (incl. bkfst) **LB** **FACILITIES:** Xmas **CONF:** BC Thtr 150 Class 100 Board 80 Del from £92 **PARKING:** 100 **NOTES:** No smoking in restaurant Civ Wed 120
CARDS:

D

★★★66% The Blackwell Grange Hotel

Blackwell Grange DL3 8QH
☎ 0870 609 6121 📠 01325 380899
e-mail: blackwellgrange@corushotels.com
Dir: *on A167, 1.5m from central ring road*

This hotel, peacefully situated in its own grounds yet conveniently located for the motorway network, offers comfortable accommodation. Rooms are split between the original house, modern extension and the courtyard. Public areas are spacious and display many original features, comfortable lounges and meeting rooms along with a stylish dining room.
ROOMS: 99 en suite 11 annexe en suite (3 fmly) (36 GF) No smoking in 30 bedrooms s £90-£110; d £110-£150 **LB** **FACILITIES:** **Spa** STV Indoor swimming (H) Tennis Sauna Solarium Gym Jacuzzi Swimming pool supervised Xmas **CONF:** Thtr 300 Class 110 Board 50 Del from £90 **SERVICES:** Lift **PARKING:** 250 **NOTES:** No smoking in restaurant Civ Wed 200 **CARDS:**

★★★65% Kings Head

9-12 Priestgate DL1 1NW
☎ 01325 380222 📠 01325 382006
e-mail: admin@kingsheadhotel50.fsnet.co.uk
Dir: *A1 northbound signed Darlington. 3rd exit off rdbt, 2nd off next rdbt. At 3rd rdbt 1st exit. 1st right, then 1st left. Hotel on right*
Adjacent to the Cornmill Shopping Centre, this town centre hotel provides a variety of bedroom styles. Public areas include an inviting foyer lounge and upstairs a comfortable bar and restaurant. The hotel has a secure basement car park.
ROOMS: 85 en suite (3 fmly) No smoking in 51 bedrooms s £55-£65; d £70-£85 (incl. bkfst) **LB** **FACILITIES:** Free use of nearby leisure complex Xmas **CONF:** Thtr 250 Class 100 Board 50 Del from £98 **SERVICES:** Lift **PARKING:** 28 **CARDS:**

★★★64% White Horse Hotel

Harrogate Hill DL1 3AD
☎ 01325 382121 📠 01325 355953
e-mail: reservations@whitehorsedarlington.co.uk
Dir: *A1(M) junct 59, follow A167 towards Darlington to Harrowgate Village (2m). Hotel on right after village sign*
Situated just north of the town and convenient for the A1, this hotel provides comfortable well-equipped bedrooms suited especially to its business clientele. There is a choice of bars and an upstairs restaurant.
ROOMS: 40 en suite (3 fmly) (10 GF) No smoking in 20 bedrooms s £49-£63; d £59-£73 (incl. bkfst) **LB** **CONF:** Thtr 100 Class 50 Board 45 Del £95 **SERVICES:** Lift **PARKING:** 120 **NOTES:** No smoking in restaurant **CARDS:**

⌂ Travel Inn

Morton Park Way, Morton Park DL1 4PJ
☎ 08701 977300 📠 01325 373341
Travel Inn offers good-quality, value-for-money accommodation. Spacious, en suite rooms with bath and shower comfortably accommodate a family of up to two adults and two children (to age 15). The restaurant and bar offers a varied menu. For further details and the Travel Inn phone number, consult the Hotel Groups page.
ROOMS: (incl. bkfst) s £44.95; d £44.95

DARRINGTON, West Yorkshire — Map 16 SE42

⌂ Premier Lodge (Pontefract)

Great North Rd WF8 3BL
☎ 0870 9906386 📠 0870 9906387
Dir: *off A1, 2m S of A1/M62, junct 33*
Premier Lodge offers modern, well-equipped, en suite accommodation suitable for both business and leisure travellers. Meals can be taken at the adjacent popular restaurant and bar, which is fully licensed. For further details, consult the Hotel Groups page.
ROOMS: 27 en suite s £48; d £48 **CONF:** Thtr 24 Class 12 Board 12 Del from £77.50

DARTFORD, Kent — Map 06 TQ57

★★★★79% Rowhill Grange Hotel & Spa

DA2 7QH
☎ 01322 615136 📠 01322 615137
e-mail: admin@rowhillgrange.co.uk
Dir: *M25 junct 3 take B2173 to Swanley, followed by B258 to Hextable*

A country house hotel surrounded by nine acres of mature woodland and landscaped grounds that feature a walled Victorian garden. The stylish individually decorated bedrooms offer a high degree of comfort. An imaginative menu is served in the conservatory restaurant and there is an informal brasserie.
ROOMS: 38 en suite (3 fmly) (3 GF) No smoking in all bedrooms s £150-£265; d £175-£325 **LB** **FACILITIES:** **Spa** STV Indoor swimming (H) Sauna Solarium Gym Croquet lawn Jacuzzi Beauty treatment, Hair salon, Aerobic studio, Therapy pool Xmas **CONF:** Thtr 160 Class 64 Board 34 Del from £145 **SERVICES:** Lift **PARKING:** 150 **NOTES:** No dogs (ex guide dogs) No smoking in restaurant Civ Wed 200
CARDS:

⇧ *Campanile*
Clipper Boulevard West, Business Park, Crossways DA2 6QN
☎ 01322 278925 01322 278948
e-mail: dartford@envergure.co.uk
Dir: *follow signs for Ferry Terminal from Dartford Bridge*

This modern building offers accommodation in smart, well-equipped bedrooms, all with en suite bathrooms. Refreshments may be taken at the informal Bistro. For further details and the Campanile phone number, consult the Hotel Groups page.
ROOMS: 125 en suite **CONF:** Thtr 50 Class 20 Board 25

⇧ Express by Holiday Inn Dartford Bridge
University Way DA1 5PA
☎ 01322 290333 01322 290444
e-mail: dartford@khl.uk.com
Dir: *follow A206 to Erith. Hotel off University Way via signposted sliproad*

A modern hotel ideal for families and business travellers. Fresh and uncomplicated, the spacious bedrooms include Sky TV, power shower and tea and coffee-making facilities. Continental buffet breakfast is included in the room rate; other meals may be taken at the nearby family pub or restaurant. For further details and the Express by Holiday Inn phone number, consult the Hotel Groups pages.
ROOMS: 126 en suite d £39-£68 (incl. cont bkfst)
CONF: Thtr 35 Board 20

⇧ Travelodge
Charles St, Greenhithe DA9 9AP
☎ 08700 850 950 01322 387854
Travelodge offers good quality, good value, modern accommodation. Ideal for families, the spacious, en suite bedrooms include remote-control TV, tea and coffee-making facilities, luxury beds and free morning newspaper. Meals can be

continued

taken at the nearby family restaurant. For further details and the Travelodge phone number, consult the Hotel Groups page.

ROOMS: 65 en suite (incl. bkfst) s fr £42.95; d fr £42.95

DARTMOUTH, Devon — Map 03 SX85

★★★74% Royal Castle
11 The Quay TQ6 9PS
☎ 01803 833033 01803 835445
e-mail: enquiry@royalcastle.co.uk
Dir: *in centre of town, overlooking Inner Harbour*

At the edge of the harbour, this imposing 17th-century former coaching inn is filled with interesting curios, charm and character. Bedrooms are well equipped and comfortable; many have harbour views. A choice of quiet seating areas is offered as well as the a traditional and contemporary bar. Cuisine in the Adams restaurant features local produce and seafood.
ROOMS: 25 en suite (4 fmly) No smoking in all bedrooms s £55-£75; d £100-£170 (incl. bkfst) **LB FACILITIES:** STV Xmas **CONF:** Thtr 70 Class 40 Board 40 Del from £75 **PARKING:** 17 **NOTES:** No smoking in restaurant Civ Wed 60 **CARDS:**

★★★73% The Dart Marina
Sandquay TQ6 9PH
☎ 01803 832 580 01803 835040
e-mail: gm.dartmarina@macdonald-hotels.co.uk
Dir: *A3122 from Totnes to Dartmouth. Follow road which becomes College Way, before Higher Ferry. Hotel sharp left in Sandquay Rd*

MACDONALD HOTELS

This hotel is situated in an idyllic position by the marina, with direct access to the water. Bedrooms, or cabins as they are referred to, have a nautical theme and are named after famous ships, sailors and shipbuilders. Stylish and comfortable public areas enable guests to take full advantage of the waterside position.
ROOMS: 45 en suite 4 annexe en suite No smoking in 39 bedrooms s £67-£77; d £134-£178 (incl. bkfst & dinner) **LB FACILITIES:** Use of hotel boat slipway, Sailing Canoeing Xmas **CONF:** Board 16 **SERVICES:** Lift **PARKING:** 50 **NOTES:** No smoking in restaurant Civ Wed 70 **CARDS:**

DARTMOUTH, continued

★★★68% Stoke Lodge

Stoke Fleming TQ6 0RA
☎ 01803 770523 📠 01803 770851
e-mail: mail@stokelodge.co.uk
Dir: *2m S A379*

This family-run hotel continues to attract returning guests, and is set in three acres of gardens and grounds. There are views across the sea and a range of leisure facilities, along with a choice of comfortable lounges. Bedrooms are pleasantly appointed. The restaurant offers a choice of menus and an impressive wine list.
ROOMS: 25 en suite (5 fmly) s £55-£61; d £85-£110 (incl. bkfst) **LB** **FACILITIES: Spa** Indoor swimming (H) Outdoor swimming (H) Tennis (hard) Snooker Sauna Putting green Table tennis, Pool table Xmas **CONF:** Thtr 80 Class 60 Board 30 **PARKING:** 50 **NOTES:** No smoking in restaurant **CARDS:**

DARWEN, Lancashire — Map 15 SD62

Travelodge Blackburn

Darwen Motorway services BB3 0AT
☎ 08700 850 950
Dir: *Off M65 junct 4 towards Blackburn*

Travelodge

Travelodge offers good quality, good value, modern accommodation. Ideal for families, the spacious, en suite bedrooms include remote-control TV, tea and coffee-making facilities, luxury beds and free morning newspaper. Meals can be taken at the nearby family restaurant. For further details and the Travelodge phone number, consult the Hotel Groups page.
ROOMS: s fr £42.95; d fr £42.95

DAVENTRY, Northamptonshire — Map 11 SP56

Top 200 - Hotel

★★★★ Fawsley Hall

Fawsley NN11 3BA
☎ 01327 892000 📠 01327 892001
e-mail: reservations@fawsleyhall.com
Dir: *From A361 turn at 'Fawsley Hall' sign. Follow single track for 1.5m until reaching iron gates*

Dating back to the 15th-century, this delightful hotel is peacefully located in beautiful gardens designed by 'Capability' Brown. Spacious individually designed bedrooms and stylish public areas are beautifully furnished with antique and period pieces. Afternoon tea is served in the impressive Great Hall with its sumptuous deep cushioned sofas and real fires.
ROOMS: 43 en suite (2 GF) s £130-£140; d £160-£190 (incl. cont bkfst) **LB** **FACILITIES: Spa** STV Tennis (hard) Sauna Gym Croquet lawn Putting green Jacuzzi Health & Beauty treatment rooms Xmas **CONF:** Thtr 100 Class 45 Board 45 Del from £190 **PARKING:** 100 **NOTES:** No smoking in restaurant Civ Wed 100 **CARDS:**

★★★★60% Hanover International Hotel & Club

Sedgemoor Way NN11 5SG
☎ 0870 241 7078 📠 01455 630030
e-mail: rso@hanover-international.com
Dir: *N of Daventry on A361 Ring Road*

This modern, striking hotel overlooking Drayton Water boasts spacious public areas that include a good range of banqueting, meeting and leisure facilities. It is a popular venue for conferences. Bedrooms all have double beds and excellent showers.
ROOMS: 138 en suite No smoking in 73 bedrooms s £65-£115; d £65-£115 **LB** **FACILITIES: Spa** STV Indoor swimming (H) Sauna Solarium Gym Steam room Health & beauty salon **CONF:** Thtr 600 Class 200 Board 30 **SERVICES:** Lift **PARKING:** 350 **NOTES:** No dogs (ex guide dogs) No smoking in restaurant RS 26-30 Dec Civ Wed 200
CARDS:

DAWLISH, Devon — Map 03 SX97

★★★70% Langstone Cliff

Dawlish Warren EX7 0NA
☎ 01626 868000 📠 01626 868006
e-mail: reception@langstone-hotel.co.uk
Dir: *1.5m NE off A379 Exeter road to Dawlish Warren*

THE INDEPENDENTS

A family owned and run hotel, the Langstone Cliff offers a range of leisure, conference and function facilities. Bedrooms, many with sea views and balconies, are spacious, comfortable and well equipped. There are a number of attractive lounges and a well stocked bar. Dinner is served, often carvery style, in the restaurant.
ROOMS: 61 en suite 4 annexe en suite (52 fmly) (10 GF) s £60-£69; d £110-£118 (incl. bkfst) **LB** **FACILITIES:** STV Indoor swimming (H) Outdoor swimming (H) Tennis (hard) Snooker Gym Table tennis, Golf practice area, Hair and beauty salon entertainment ch fac Xmas
CONF: Thtr 400 Class 200 Board 80 Del from £85 **SERVICES:** Lift
PARKING: 200 **NOTES:** Civ Wed 400
CARDS:

DEAL, Kent — Map 07 TR35

★★★71% Dunkerleys Hotel & Restaurant

19 Beach St CT14 7AH
☎ 01304 375016 📠 01304 380187
e-mail: dunkerleysofdeal@btinternet.com
Dir: *from M20 or M2 follow signs for A258 Deal. Hotel on seafront close to Pier*

This hotel enjoys views of the seafront and is centrally located. Bedrooms are furnished to a high standard with a good range of amenities. The restaurant and bar have been attractively refurbished and menus make the best use of local ingredients. Service throughout is friendly and attentive.
ROOMS: 16 en suite (2 fmly) s £60-£80; d £100-£130 (incl. bkfst) **LB** **FACILITIES:** STV Jacuzzi Xmas **NOTES:** No dogs (ex guide dogs) RS Mon **CARDS:**

D

DEDDINGTON, Oxfordshire
Map 11 SP43

★★★71% *Holcombe Hotel & Restaurant*

High St OX15 0SL
☎ 01869 338274 01869 337167
e-mail: reception@holcombehotel.freeserve.co.uk
Dir: *on A4260*

This hotel enjoys a convenient roadside location, within easy reach of the village centre. Public areas include the stylish Picasso bar and an eye catching restaurant, and in the warmer months the gardens offer a peaceful place in which to relax. Bedrooms are traditional in design with many thoughtful touches.
ROOMS: 17 en suite (3 fmly) (1 GF) **CONF:** Thtr 25 Class 15 Board 18
PARKING: 40 **CARDS:**

★★★70% Deddington Arms
Horsefair OX15 0SH
☎ 0800 3287031 01869 337010
e-mail: deddarms@aol.com
Dir: *From S M40 junct 10 signed Northampton onto A43. 1st rdbt left to Aynho and left to Deddington. From N M40 junct 11 to Banbury. Through Banbury to hospital and Adderbury on A4260, then to Deddington*

This charming and friendly old inn is conveniently located off the Market Square. The well-equipped bedrooms are comfortably appointed and either situated in the main building or a purpose built courtyard wing. The bar is full of character and the delightful restaurant enjoys well-deserved local popularity.
ROOMS: 27 en suite (4 fmly) (9 GF) s £75-£90; d £85-£120 (incl. bkfst)
LB FACILITIES: STV Many facilities avaliable locally Xmas **CONF:** Thtr 40 Class 35 Board 35 Del £120 **PARKING:** 36
CARDS:

> Popped the question?
> Hotels with Civ Wed in their entry are licensed for civil wedding ceremonies. Maximum numbers for the ceremony only are shown, e.g. Civ Wed 120

DEDHAM, Essex
Map 13 TM03

Top 200 - Hotel

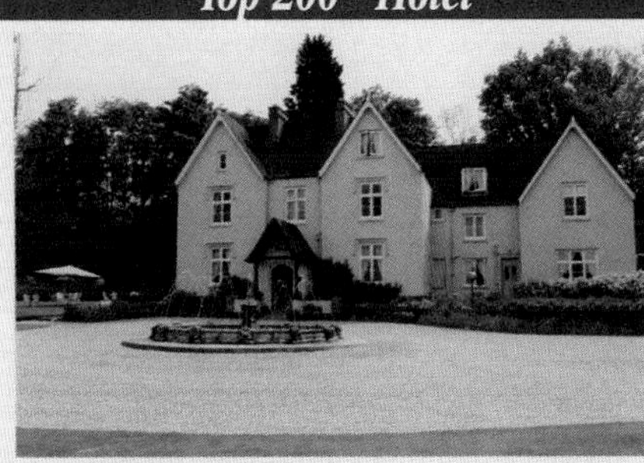

★★★ Maison Talbooth
Stratford Rd CO7 6HN
☎ 01206 322367 01206 322752
e-mail: maison@talbooth.co.uk
Dir: *A12 towards Ipswich, 1st turning signed Dedham, follow road until left bend, take right turn. Hotel 1m on right*
Victorian country house hotel situated in a peaceful rural location amidst pretty landscaped grounds overlooking the Stour River valley. Public areas include a comfortable drawing room where guests may take afternoon tea or snacks. Residents are chauffeured to the popular Le Talbooth Restaurant just a mile away for dinner. The spacious bedrooms are individually decorated, tastefully furnished, have lovely co-ordinated fabrics and many thoughtful touches. Hospitality is warm and friendly and quality service is to be expected.
ROOMS: 10 en suite (1 fmly) s £120-£150; d £160-£220 (incl. cont bkfst) **LB FACILITIES:** Croquet lawn Garden chess Xmas
CONF: Thtr 30 Class 20 Board 16 Del £150 **PARKING:** 20
NOTES: No dogs (ex guide dogs) Civ Wed 50
CARDS:

★★★68% Milsom's
Stratford Rd, Dedham CO7 6HW
☎ 01206 322795 01206 323689
e-mail: milsoms@talbooth.co.uk
Dir: *6m N of Colchester off A12*
Situated in the Dedham Vale, an Area of Outstanding Natural Beauty, this is the perfect base to explore the countryside on the Essex/Suffolk border. Milsom's is styled along the lines of a contemporary 'gastro bar' combining good food served in an informal atmosphere, with stylish bedrooms.
ROOMS: 14 en suite (3 fmly) (4 GF) s £73-£93; d fr £90
FACILITIES: STV **CONF:** Board 14 Del from £120 **PARKING:** 70
NOTES: No dogs (ex guide dogs) **CARDS:**

DERBY, Derbyshire
Map 11 SK33

★★★★73% Menzies Mickleover Court
Etwall Rd, Mickleover DE3 0XX
☎ 01332 521234 01332 521238
e-mail: info@menzies-hotels.co.uk
Dir: *Take A50 towards Derby, leave at junct 5 and follow A516 towards Derby, take exit signed Mickleover*
Located close to Derby, this large, modern hotel is well suited for conference and leisure guests. Bedrooms are spacious, with some traditional rooms and some more contemporary in style. A choice

continued on p202

DERBY, continued

of eating options, spacious seating and excellent conference and leisure facilities are all popular with residents and visitors.
ROOMS: 99 en suite (20 fmly) No smoking in 45 bedrooms **FACILITIES:** STV Indoor swimming (H) Sauna Solarium Gym Jacuzzi Beauty salon, Steam room **CONF:** Thtr 200 Class 80 Board 40 Del from £165 **SERVICES:** Lift air con **PARKING:** 270 **NOTES:** No dogs (ex guide dogs) No smoking in restaurant Civ Wed 200
CARDS:

★★★★65% Marriott Breadsall Priory Hotel, Country Club

Moor Rd DE7 6DL
☎ 01332 832235 01332 833509
(For full entry see Breadsall)

★★★75% Midland

Midland Rd DE1 2SQ
☎ 01332 345894 01332 293522
e-mail: sales@midland-derby.co.uk
Dir: *opposite Derby railway station*

This early Victorian hotel situated opposite Derby Midland Station provides very comfortable accommodation. The executive rooms are ideal for business travellers, equipped with writing desks and fax/computer points. Public rooms include a comfortable lounge and a popular restaurant. Service is skilled, attentive and friendly. There is also a walled garden and private car parking.
ROOMS: 100 en suite No smoking in 41 bedrooms s £88-£111; d £98-£121 **LB** **FACILITIES:** entertainment **CONF:** Thtr 150 Class 50 Board 40 Del £142 **SERVICES:** Lift **PARKING:** 120 **NOTES:** No dogs (ex guide dogs) No smoking in restaurant Closed 24-26 Dec & 1 Jan Civ Wed 100 **CARDS:**

See advert on opposite page

★★★65% Aston Court Hotel & Conference Centre

Midland Rd DE1 2SL
☎ 01332 342716 01332 293503
e-mail: astoncourtderby@hotelres.co.uk
Dir: *Midland Road opposite entrance of the Derby Railway Station*
Situated just a few minutes from the city centre, this hotel offers comfortable accommodation in refurbished and upgraded bedrooms. Public areas include a residents-only, open-plan bar, an air-conditioned restaurant and an attractive conservatory. Conference facilities and services for business guests are also available.
ROOMS: 55 en suite (5 fmly) (5 GF) No smoking in 25 bedrooms s £70; d £80 **LB** **FACILITIES: Spa** STV Jacuzzi More facilities available at a nearby health club Xmas **CONF:** BC Thtr 250 Class 80 Board 65 Del from £114.50 **SERVICES:** Lift **PARKING:** 70 **NOTES:** No smoking in restaurant Civ Wed 250 **CARDS:**

★★★65% *Littleover Lodge*

222 Rykneld Rd, Littleover DE23 7AN
☎ 01332 510161 01332 514010
e-mail: enquiries@littleoverlodge.co.uk
Dir: *A38 towards Derby approx 1m on left slip lane signed Littleover/Mickleover/Findon, take 2nd exit off island marked Littleover 0.25m on right*
Situated in a rural location off the A5250 beside the A38, this friendly hotel offers modern bedrooms with direct access from the car park. Two styles of dining, an informal carvery operation which enjoys a high local demand, and a more formal restaurant experience are available at both lunch and dinner every day.
ROOMS: 16 en suite (3 fmly) **FACILITIES:** STV entertainment **PARKING:** 75 **NOTES:** No smoking in restaurant
CARDS:

See advert on opposite page

★★★65% *Hotel Ristorante La Gondola*

220 Osmaston Rd DE23 8JX
☎ 01332 332895 01332 384512
e-mail: service@la-gondola.co.uk
Dir: *on A514 towards Melbourne*
Imaginatively designed and well-equipped bedrooms, including a spacious family suite, are offered at this elegant Georgian house, situated between the inner and outer ring roads. There are two small comfortable lounges and a well-established Italian restaurant. There are also extensive conference and banqueting rooms available.
ROOMS: 20 rms (19 en suite) (7 fmly) **FACILITIES:** STV entertainment **CONF:** Thtr 80 Class 50 Board 80 **PARKING:** 70 **NOTES:** No dogs (ex guide dogs) **CARDS:**

★★★63% International

288 Burton Rd DE23 6AD
☎ 01332 369321 01332 294430
e-mail: internationalhotel.derby@virgin.net
Dir: *0.5m from city centre on A5250*
Within easy reach of the city centre, this hotel offers comfortable, modern public rooms. An extensive range of dishes is served in the pleasant restaurant. There is a wide range of bedroom sizes and styles, and each room is very well equipped; some suites are also available, and parking is a bonus.
ROOMS: 41 en suite 21 annexe en suite (4 fmly) No smoking in 28 bedrooms s £46-£77; d £52-£85 (incl. bkfst) **LB** **FACILITIES:** STV entertainment Xmas **CONF:** Thtr 100 Class 40 Board 40 Del from £70 **SERVICES:** Lift **PARKING:** 100 **NOTES:** Civ Wed 100
CARDS:

European Inn

Midland Rd DE1 2SL
☎ 01332 292000 01332 293940
e-mail: admin@euro-derby.co.uk
Dir: *City centre, 200yds from railway station*
Excellent value accommodation is provided at this modern lodge. Bedrooms are well appointed and equipped with modern facilities. Shops form part of the complex and include an Italian pizza restaurant. A good choice of English breakfast is served buffet-style in the breakfast room; takeaway meals can also be eaten here.
ROOMS: 88 en suite s £53; d £53 **CONF:** Thtr 60 Class 30 Board 25 Del £96

> Destination dining!
> This symbol indicates a Restaurant with Rooms

⇧ Express by Holiday Inn Derby

Roundhouse Rd, Off Pride Parkway DE24 8HX
☎ 01332 388000 📠 01332 388038
e-mail: derby@expressholidayinn.co.uk
Dir: *A52 towards Derby, follow for 7m, exit signed Pride Park. Over 1st 3 rdbts. Right at 4th, left at next. Take 1st left & hotel on right*

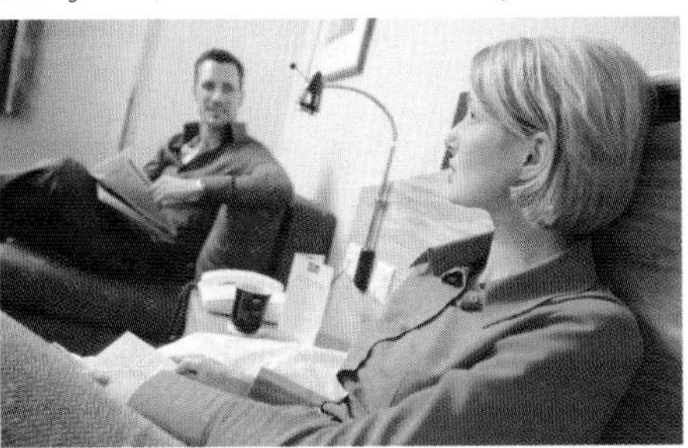

A modern hotel ideal for families and business travellers. Fresh and uncomplicated, the spacious bedrooms include Sky TV, power shower and tea and coffee-making facilities. Continental buffet breakfast is included in the room rate; other meals may be taken at the nearby family pub or restaurant. For further details and the Express by Holiday Inn phone number, consult the Hotel Groups pages.
ROOMS: 103 en suite s £64; d £64 (incl. cont bkfst) **CONF:** Thtr 20 Class 16 Board 16

⇧ Innkeeper's Lodge Derby

Nottingham Rd, Chaddesdon DE21 6LZ
☎ 0870 243 0500 & 01332 662504
📠 01332 673306
Dir: *from M1 junct 25 take A52 towards Derby, take exit signed Spondon & Chaddesden. At rdbt take exit signed Chaddesden pass Asda store, 1m at lights right into car park*
A new concept in the travel accommodation market. Smart rooms meet essential business requirements but also have home comforts. Dining options include all-day menus plus the added advantage of breakfast, which is included in the room price. For further details, consult the Hotel Groups page.
ROOMS: 29 en suite

⇧ Premier Lodge (Derby)

Foresters Leisure Park, Osmaston Park Rd DE23 8AG
☎ 0870 9906306 📠 0870 9906307
Premier Lodge offers modern, well-equipped, en suite accommodation suitable for both business and leisure travellers. Meals can be taken at the adjacent popular restaurant and bar, which is fully licensed. For further details, consult the Hotel Groups page.
ROOMS: 27 en suite s £48; d £48

⇧ Premier Lodge (Derby North)

Ashbourne Rd, Mackworth DE22 4LZ
☎ 0870 9906606 📠 0870 9906607
Premier Lodge offers modern, well-equipped, en suite accommodation suitable for both business and leisure travellers. Meals can be taken at the adjacent popular restaurant and bar, which is fully licensed. For further details, consult the Hotel Groups page.
ROOMS: 22 en suite s £48; d £48

DERBY, continued

⌂ Travel Inn (Derby East)
The Wyvern Business Park, Chaddesden Sidings
DE21 6BF
☎ 0870 238 3313 📠 01332 667827

***Dir:** From M1 junct 25 follow A52 to Derby. After 6.5m take exit for Wyvern/Pride Park. 1st exit at rdbt (A52 Nottingham), straight over next rdbt. Travel Inn on left*

Travel Inn offers good-quality, value-for-money accommodation. Spacious, en suite rooms with bath and shower comfortably accommodate a family of up to two adults and two children (to age 15). The restaurant and bar offers a varied menu. For further details and the Travel Inn phone number, consult the Hotel Groups page.
ROOMS: 82 en suite s £44.95; d £44.95

⌂ Travel Inn (Derby West)
Uttoxeter New Rd, Manor Park Way DE22 3HN
☎ 08701 977072 📠 01332 207506
***Dir:** From M1junct 24 follow A5111 (A38 Burton). Left at lights signed City Hospital. At rdbt take 3rd exit. Travel Inn is behind Aldi supermarket*
Travel Inn offers good-quality, value-for-money accommodation. Spacious, en suite rooms with bath and shower comfortably accommodate a family of up to two adults and two children (to age 15). The restaurant and bar offers a varied menu. For further details and the Travel Inn phone number, consult the Hotel Groups page.
ROOMS: 43 en suite s £44.95; d £44.95 **CONF:** Thtr 15

⌂ Travelodge
Kingsway, Rowditch DE22 3NN
☎ 08700 850 950 📠 01332 367255
Travelodge offers good quality, good value, modern accommodation. Ideal for families, the spacious, en suite bedrooms include remote-control TV, tea and coffee-making facilities, luxury beds and free morning newspaper. Meals can be taken at the nearby family restaurant. For further details and the Travelodge phone number, consult the Hotel Groups page.
ROOMS: 40 en suite s fr £42.95; d fr £42.95

DERBY SERVICE AREA (A50), Derbyshire — Map 11 SK42

⌂ Days Inn Donnington
Welcome Break Services DE72 2HA
☎ 01332 799666 📠 01332 794166
e-mail: derby.hotel@welcomebreak.co.uk
***Dir:** A50 Westbound*
This modern building offers accommodation in smart, spacious and well-equipped bedrooms, suitable for families and business travellers, and all with en suite bathrooms. Continental breakfast is available and other refreshments may be taken at the nearby family restaurant. For further details and the Days Inn phone number, consult the Hotel Groups page.
ROOMS: 48 en suite s £45-£60; d £45-£60 **CONF:** Board 10

DESBOROUGH, Northamptonshire — Map 11 SP88

⌂ Travelodge Market Harborough
Harborough Rd NN14 2UG
☎ 08700 850 950 📠 01536 762034
***Dir:** on A6, southbound*
Travelodge offers good quality, good value, modern accommodation. Ideal for families, the spacious, en suite bedrooms include remote-control TV, tea and coffee-making facilities, luxury beds and free morning newspaper. Meals can be taken at the nearby family restaurant. For further details and the Travelodge phone number, consult the Hotel Groups page.
ROOMS: 32 en suite s fr £42.95; d fr £42.95

DEVIZES, Wiltshire — Map 04 SU06

★★★64% *Bear*
Market Place SN10 1HS
☎ 01380 722444 📠 01380 722450
e-mail: beardevizes@aol.com
Set in the market place of this small Wiltshire town, this attractive hotel has a popular local following. The individually furnished and decorated bedrooms vary in size. The attractive lounge offers a quiet area for residents to enjoy afternoon tea. Homemade cakes are available throughout the day and the restaurant serves enjoyable meals.
ROOMS: 24 en suite (5 fmly) **FACILITIES:** Solarium **CONF:** Thtr 150 Board 50 **NOTES:** No smoking in restaurant Closed 25-26 Dec
CARDS:

DEWSBURY, West Yorkshire — Map 16 SE22

★★★66% *Heath Cottage Hotel & Restaurant*
Wakefield Rd WF12 8ET
☎ 01924 465399 📠 01924 459405
e-mail: info@heathcottage.co.uk
***Dir:** M1 junct 40 onto A638 for 2.5m towards Dewsbury. Hotel before traffic lights*

Standing in approximately an acre of grounds, Heath Cottage is two and a half miles from the M1. It has ample parking and the service is friendly and professional. The modern bedrooms are well appointed and some are in a converted stable building. The lounge bar and restaurant are both air conditioned.
ROOMS: 23 en suite 6 annexe en suite (3 fmly) No smoking in 18 bedrooms **CONF:** Thtr 90 Class 50 Board 30 **PARKING:** 70
NOTES: No dogs (ex guide dogs) No smoking in restaurant Civ Wed 90
CARDS:

★★72% ◎ **Healds Hall**
Leeds Rd, Liversedge WF15 6JA
☎ 01924 409112 ▯ 01924 401895
e-mail: enquire@healdshall.co.uk
Dir: *on A62 between Leeds and Huddersfield. 50yds on left after Swan Pub traffic lights*

This 18th-century house in the heart of West Yorkshire offers comfortable and well-equipped accommodation and excellent hospitality. The hotel has earned a good local reputation for the quality of its food and offers a choice of casual or more formal dining styles, with a wide range of dishes on the various menus.
ROOMS: 24 en suite (3 fmly) (3 GF) No smoking in 9 bedrooms s £45-£63; d £65-£75 (incl. bkfst) **LB CONF:** Thtr 100 Class 60 Board 80 Del from £95 **PARKING:** 90 **NOTES:** No dogs No smoking in restaurant Closed New Years Day and BH Mondays
CARDS:

DIDCOT, Oxfordshire — Map 05 SU59

⌂ **Travel Inn**
Milton Heights OX14 4DP
☎ 08701 977073 ▯ 01235 820465
Dir: *on A4130 at junct with A34*
Travel Inn offers good-quality, value-for-money accommodation. Spacious, en suite rooms with bath and shower comfortably accommodate a family of up to two adults and two children (to age 15). The restaurant and bar offers a varied menu. For further details and the Travel Inn phone number, consult the Hotel Groups page.
ROOMS: 60 en suite s £44.95; d £44.95

DIDSBURY, Greater Manchester — Map 16 SJ89

⌂ **Travelodge Manchester South**
Kingsway M20 5PG
☎ 08700 850 950 ▯ 0161 448 0393
Travelodge offers good quality, good value, modern accommodation. Ideal for families, the spacious, en suite bedrooms include remote-control TV, tea and coffee-making facilities, luxury beds and free morning newspaper. Meals can be taken at the nearby family restaurant. For further details and the Travelodge phone number, consult the Hotel Groups page.
ROOMS: 62 en suite s fr £42.95; d fr £42.95

 AA Rosette Award for culinary excellence

DISS, Norfolk — Map 13 TM18

Restaurant with Rooms

◎ **The Snailmakers**
65 Lower Denmark St, Fair Green IP22 4BE
☎ 01379 641300 ▯ 01379 643633
e-mail: thesnailmakers@aol.com
The Snailmakers is so called after a bronze statue of the same name created by the artist David Good. The intimate dining room has soft lighting and beamed walls, whilst the bar offers a specials blackboard and the ideal place for a pre-dinner drink. There are three individually designed bedrooms with stylish furniture, and one room features a four-poster bed.
ROOMS: 3 en suite (1 fmly) No smoking in all bedrooms
FACILITIES: Jacuzzi **NOTES:** No dogs (ex guide dogs) No smoking in restaurant Closed 25-26 Dec & 1-2 Jan
CARDS:

DONCASTER, South Yorkshire — Map 16 SE50

★★★73% **Mount Pleasant**
Great North Rd DN11 0HW
☎ 01302 868696 & 868219 ▯ 01302 865130
e-mail: reception@mountpleasant.co.uk
(For full entry see Rossington)

★★★67% **Danum**
High St DN1 1DN
☎ 01302 342261 ▯ 01302 329034
e-mail: admin@danumhotel.sagehost.co.uk
Dir: *M18 junct 3, A6182 to Doncaster. Over rdbt, right at next. Right at give way sign, left at mini rdbt, hotel ahead*
Situated in the centre of the town, this Edwardian hotel offers spacious public rooms together with soundly equipped accommodation. There has been major refurbishment to the popular ground floor lounge and bedrooms. A pleasant restaurant on the first floor serves quality dinners, and complimentary use of a local leisure centre is offered.
ROOMS: 66 en suite (5 fmly) No smoking in 12 bedrooms s £55-£75; d £75-£105 (incl. bkfst) **LB FACILITIES:** STV Jacuzzi special rates with Cannons health club entertainment Xmas **CONF:** Thtr 350 Class 160 Board 100 Del from £75 **SERVICES:** Lift **PARKING:** 36
NOTES: Civ Wed 250 **CARDS:**

★★★66% **Regent**
Regent Square DN1 2DS
☎ 01302 364180 ▯ 01302 322331
e-mail: admin@theregenthotel.co.uk
Dir: *on corner of A630 & A638, 1m from racecourse*
This town centre hotel overlooks a delightful small square. Public rooms include a choice of bars, and the restaurant, where an interesting range of dishes is offered; service is friendly and attentive. Most bedrooms have been furnished in a modern style with contemporary colour schemes; a rolling programme of refurbishment ensures that standards are maintained.
ROOMS: 52 en suite (6 fmly) (8 GF) s £50-£85; d £65-£90 (incl. bkfst)
LB FACILITIES: STV entertainment **CONF:** Thtr 80 Class 50 Board 40 Del £99.50 **SERVICES:** Lift **PARKING:** 20 **NOTES:** No smoking in restaurant Closed New Year's Day Xmas Day RS Bank Hols
CARDS:

DONCASTER, continued

★★★64% Grand St Leger
Bennetthorpe DN2 6AX
☎ 01302 364111 📠 01302 329865
e-mail: admin@grandstleger.com
Dir: *follow Doncaster Racecourse signs, at Racecourse rdbt hotel on corner*
This friendly hotel is located next to the racecourse and is only ten minutes' walk from the town centre. There is an extensive choice of dishes available in the elegant restaurant, a comfortable bar-lounge, and the bedrooms are thoughtfully equipped.
ROOMS: 20 en suite No smoking in all bedrooms s £60-£70; d £70-£120 (incl. bkfst) **LB** **CONF:** Thtr 65 Class 40 Board 40 Del £120 **PARKING:** 28 **NOTES:** No dogs (ex guide dogs) No smoking in restaurant Closed New Year's Day RS Xmas Day (open for lunch only) Civ Wed 60 **CARDS:**

Campanile
Doncaster Leisure Park, Bawtry Rd DN4 7PD
☎ 01302 370770 📠 01302 370813
e-mail: doncaster@envergure.co.uk
Dir: *follow signs to Doncaster Leisure Centre, left at rdbt before Dome complex*

This modern building offers accommodation in smart, well-equipped bedrooms, all with en suite bathrooms. Refreshments may be taken at the informal Bistro. For further details and the Campanile phone number, consult the Hotel Groups page.
ROOMS: 50 en suite **CONF:** Thtr 25 Class 18 Board 20

Travel Inn (Doncaster Central)
Wilmington Dr, Doncaster Carr DN4 5PJ
☎ 08701 977074 📠 01302 361134
Dir: *off A6182 near junct with access road to M18 junct 3*
Travel Inn offers good-quality, value-for-money accommodation. Spacious, en suite rooms with bath and shower comfortably accommodate a family of up to two adults and two children (to age 15). The restaurant and bar offers a varied menu. For further details and the Travel Inn phone number, consult the Hotel Groups page.
ROOMS: 42 en suite s £44.95; d £44.95 **CONF:** Class 32

Travelodge (Doncaster North)
DN8 5GS
☎ 08700 850 950 📠 01302 847711
Dir: *M18 junct 5*
Travelodge offers good quality, good value, modern accommodation. Ideal for families, the spacious, en suite bedrooms include remote-control TV, tea and coffee-making facilities, luxury beds and free morning newspaper. Meals can be taken at the nearby family restaurant. For further details and the Travelodge phone number, consult the Hotel Groups page.
ROOMS: 39 en suite s fr £42.95; d fr £42.95

DONNINGTON See Telford

DORCHESTER, Dorset Map 04 SY69

★★★65% The Wessex Royale
High West St DT1 1UP
☎ 01305 262660 📠 01305 251941
e-mail: info@wessex-royale-hotel.com
Close to the centre and many attractions of Dorchester, this hotel offers friendly service. Bedrooms are comfortable, well furnished and decorated to a good standard - some rooms have four-poster beds. Public areas are spacious and secure parking is available. The restaurant offers an interesting selection of French-themed dishes and at lunchtime a range of lighter meals is provided.
ROOMS: 25 en suite 2 annexe en suite (2 fmly) No smoking in 10 bedrooms s £65; d £85 (incl. bkfst) **FACILITIES:** STV Xmas **CONF:** Thtr 100 Class 40 Board 40 Del from £109 **PARKING:** 12 **NOTES:** No dogs (ex guide dogs) No smoking in restaurant
CARDS:

DORCHESTER (ON THAMES), Oxfordshire Map 05 SU59

★★★67% George
25 High St OX10 7HH
☎ 01865 340404 📠 01865 341620
e-mail: thegeorgehotel@fsmail.net
Dir: *M40 junct 6 onto B4009 through Watlington & Benson. Take A4074 at BP petrol station, follow signposts to Dorchester. Hotel on left*

Full of charactar and charm, this quintessential coaching inn stands beside Dorchester Abbey and dates back to the 15th century. The bedrooms are decorated in keeping with the style of the building, and are divided between the main house and the courtyard. Meals can be taken either in the lively, atmospheric bar or in the equally impressive restaurant which has an original beamed ceiling.
ROOMS: 9 en suite 8 annexe en suite (1 fmly) No smoking in 4 bedrooms s fr £75; d fr £85 (incl. cont bkfst) **LB** **CONF:** Thtr 40 Class 36 Board 24 Del from £110 **PARKING:** 75 **NOTES:** No smoking in restaurant **CARDS:**

★★★65% White Hart
High St OX10 7HN
☎ 01865 340074 📠 01865 341082
e-mail: whitehartdorch@aol.com
Dir: *M40 junct 6, take B4009 through Watlington & Benson to A4074. Follow signs to Dorchester. Hotel on right*
Period charm and character are plentiful throughout this 17th-century coaching inn set in the picturesque high street. Bedrooms are individually appointed and well equipped, and the

continued

bar and atmospheric restaurant, complete with vaulted timber ceiling, are situated in a separate building across the courtyard.

ROOMS: 22 en suite 4 annexe en suite (2 fmly) (9 GF) No smoking in 6 bedrooms s £75-£95; d £95-£120 (incl. bkfst) **LB** **FACILITIES:** STV Xmas **CONF:** Thtr 30 Class 20 Board 18 **PARKING:** 36 **CARDS:**

DORKING, Surrey — Map 06 TQ14

★★★★67% The Burford Bridge

Burford Bridge, Box Hill RH5 6BX
☎ 0870 400 8283 📠 01306 880386
e-mail: burfordbridge@macdonald-hotels.co.uk
Dir: *M25 junct 9 follow Dorking signs on A24. Hotel on left*

Full of history, this hotel was reputedly the site of the final meeting between Nelson and Lady Hamilton before the Battle of Trafalgar, and the landscape around the hotel has inspired poets. There are good transport links to major centres, including the capital, and local places of interest include Polesden Lacey and the RHS gardens at Wisley.

ROOMS: 57 en suite (14 fmly) (8 GF) No smoking in 37 bedrooms d £120-£160 (incl. bkfst) **LB** **FACILITIES:** Outdoor swimming (H) Croquet lawn Putting green entertainment Xmas **CONF:** Thtr 300 Class 100 Board 60 Del from £150 **PARKING:** 80 **NOTES:** No smoking in restaurant Civ Wed 120 **CARDS:**

★★★64% Gatton Manor Hotel Golf & Country Club

Standon Ln RH5 5PQ
☎ 01306 627555 📠 01306 627713
e-mail: gattonmanor@enterprise.net
(For full entry see Ockley)

★★★63% The White Horse

MACDONALD HOTELS

High St RH4 1BE
☎ 0870 400 8282 📠 01306 887241
e-mail: whitehorsedorking@macdonald-hotels.co.uk
Dir: *M25 junct 9 take A24 S towards Dorking. Hotel in centre of town*

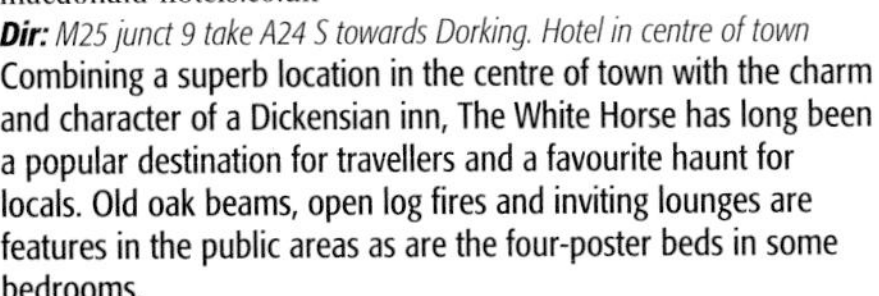

Combining a superb location in the centre of town with the charm and character of a Dickensian inn, The White Horse has long been a popular destination for travellers and a favourite haunt for locals. Old oak beams, open log fires and inviting lounges are features in the public areas as are the four-poster beds in some bedrooms.

ROOMS: 37 en suite 41 annexe en suite (2 fmly) (5 GF) No smoking in 59 bedrooms s £45-£90; d £138 (incl. bkfst) **LB** **FACILITIES:** STV Xmas **CONF:** Thtr 50 Class 30 Board 30 **PARKING:** 73 **NOTES:** No smoking in restaurant **CARDS:**

Travelodge

Travelodge

Reigate Rd RH4 1QB
☎ 08700 850 950 📠 01306 740361
Dir: *0.5m E, on A25*

Travelodge offers good quality, good value, modern accommodation. Ideal for families, the spacious, en suite bedrooms include remote-control TV, tea and coffee-making facilities, luxury beds and free morning newspaper. Meals can be taken at the nearby family restaurant. For further details and the Travelodge phone number, consult the Hotel Groups page.

ROOMS: 55 en suite s fr £42.95; d fr £42.95

DORRIDGE, West Midlands — Map 10 SP17

Restaurant with Rooms

The Forest

25 Station Approach B93 8JA
☎ 01564 772120 📠 01564 732680
e-mail: info@forest-hotel.com
Dir: *M42 junct 5, follow A4141 for 2m. After Knowle village turn right signed Dorridge in 1.5m. Left before rail bridge, hotel 200yds*

This well-established restaurant with rooms is situated in the heart of Dorridge village, 30 minutes from Stratford-upon-Avon and the Cotswolds. Rooms are very well equipped with modern facilities. Downstairs, a choice of bars serves meals; there is also a restaurant and a function room.

ROOMS: 10 en suite No smoking in 4 bedrooms s £63-£76; d £73-£98 (incl. bkfst) **CONF:** Thtr 100 Class 60 Board 24 Del from £126 **PARKING:** 50 **NOTES:** No dogs (ex guide dogs) No smoking in restaurant RS Sun evenings **CARDS:**

DOVER, Kent — Map 07 TR34

★★★75% Wallett's Court

West Cliffe, St Margarets-at-Cliffe CT15 6EW
☎ 01304 852424 & 0800 0351628 📠 01304 853430
e-mail: wc@wallettscourt.com
Dir: *from Dover take A258 towards Deal. 1st right to St Margarets-at-Cliffe & West Cliffe, 1m on right opposite West Cliffe church*

This country house hotel has at its core a lovely Jacobean manor. Bedrooms in the original house are traditionally furnished and rooms in the courtyard buildings are more modern; all are equipped to a high standard. The restaurant offers cuisine that fuses traditional and modern approaches to largely British dishes,

continued on p208

DOVER, continued

utilising local and some organic produce with great aplomb. A spa and gym are additional facilities.

Wallett's Court, Dover

ROOMS: 3 en suite 13 annexe en suite (2 fmly) (7 GF) s £75-£115; d £90-£150 (incl. bkfst) **LB** **FACILITIES: Spa** Indoor swimming (H) Tennis (hard) Sauna Solarium Gym Croquet lawn Putting green Jacuzzi Treatment suite, Aromatherapy Massage ch fac **CONF:** BC Thtr 25 Class 25 Board 16 Del from £127.50 **PARKING:** 30 **NOTES:** No dogs (ex guide dogs) No smoking in restaurant Closed 24-26 Dec
CARDS:

★★★71% The Churchill

Dover Waterfront CT17 9BP
☎ 01304 203633 01304 216320
e-mail: enquiries@churchill-hotel.com
Dir: *A20 follow signs for Hoverport, left onto seafront, hotel 800yds along*

Set in an enviable position overlooking Dover's harbour, this attractive waterfront terraced hotel is a popular venue. Offering a wide range of facilities including extensive meeting and leisure facilities, the hotel also has range beauty treatments to offer. Bedrooms, many of which enjoy the splendid views and some of which have balconies, are tastefully decorated. In the lounge and bar, an extensive Bistro menu is available throughout the day.
ROOMS: 66 en suite (5 fmly) No smoking in 12 bedrooms s £62; d £82 **LB** **FACILITIES:** STV Sauna Solarium Gym Henley Health Club Hair & Beauty Salons Xmas **CONF:** Thtr 110 Class 60 Board 50 Del £89 **SERVICES:** Lift **PARKING:** 32 **NOTES:** No dogs (ex guide dogs) No smoking in restaurant Civ Wed 100
CARDS:

> Late for dinner?
> Quality Standards mean that last orders for dinner vary according to star rating and should be no earlier than:
> ★★ 7.00pm ★★★ 8.00pm ★★★★ 9.00pm
> ★★★★★ 10.00pm

Premier Lodge (Dover)

Marine Court, Marine Pde CT16 1LW
☎ 0870 9906516 0870 9906517
Dir: *adjacent to ferry terminal*
Premier Lodge offers modern, well-equipped, en suite accommodation suitable for both business and leisure travellers. Meals can be taken at the adjacent popular restaurant and bar, which is fully licensed. For further details, consult the Hotel Groups page.
ROOMS: 100 en suite s £48; d £48

Travel Inn

Jubilee Way, Guston Wood CT15 5FD
☎ 08701 977075 01304 240614
Dir: *on rdbt of A2 & A258*
Travel Inn offers good-quality, value-for-money accommodation. Spacious, en suite rooms with bath and shower comfortably accommodate a family of up to two adults and two children (to age 15). The restaurant and bar offers a varied menu. For further details and the Travel Inn phone number, consult the Hotel Groups page.
ROOMS: 40 en suite s £44.95; d £44.95

Travel Inn (Dover West)

Folkestone Rd CT15 7AB
☎ 08701 977076 01304 214504
Dir: *At end of M20 continue through tunnel on A20 to Dover. Take 2nd exit onto B2011 signed "Local Services", West Hougham. Take 1st left at rndbt, Inn 1m on left.*
Travel Inn offers good-quality, value-for-money accommodation. Spacious, en suite rooms with bath and shower comfortably accommodate a family of up to two adults and two children (to age 15). The restaurant and bar offers a varied menu. For further details and the Travel Inn phone number, consult the Hotel Groups page.
ROOMS: 64 en suite s £44.95; d £44.95

DOWNHAM MARKET, Norfolk — Map 12 TF60

★★72% Castle

High St PE38 9HF
☎ 01366 384311 01366 384311
e-mail: howards@castle-hotel.com
Dir: *M11 take A10 for Ely into Downham Market, hotel opposite traffic lights, on corner of High St in town*
This popular coaching inn is situated close to the centre of town and has been welcoming guests for over 300 years. Well-maintained public areas include a cosy lounge bar and two smartly appointed restaurants. Inviting bedrooms, some with four-poster beds, are attractively decorated, thoughtfully equipped, and have bright modern décor.
ROOMS: 12 en suite s £59-£65; d £79-£99 (incl. bkfst) **LB** **FACILITIES:** Xmas **CONF:** Thtr 60 Class 30 Board 40 Del from £99 **PARKING:** 26 **NOTES:** No smoking in restaurant **CARDS:**

DRIFFIELD (GREAT), East Riding of Yorkshire — Map 17 TA05

★★★72% Bell

46 Market Place YO25 6AN
☎ 01377 256661 01377 253228
e-mail: bell@bestwestern.co.uk
Dir: *from A164, right at lights. Car park 50yds on left behind black railings*
This 250-year-old hotel now incorporates the old corn exchange and the old town hall. It is furnished with antique and period pieces, and contains many items of local historical interest. The bedrooms vary in size, but all offer modern facilities and some

continued

have their own sitting rooms. There is a good leisure club, and 300 whiskies on offer in the bar. The hotel has a relaxed and friendly atmosphere.
ROOMS: 16 en suite No smoking in 4 bedrooms s £90-£100; d £120-£135 (incl. bkfst) **LB** **FACILITIES: Spa** Indoor swimming (H) Squash Snooker Sauna Solarium Gym Jacuzzi Masseur, Hairdressing, Chiropody entertainment **CONF:** Thtr 150 Class 100 Board 40 **SERVICES:** Lift **PARKING:** 18 **NOTES:** No dogs (ex guide dogs) No children 16yrs No smoking in restaurant Civ Wed 100
CARDS:

DROITWICH, Worcestershire Map 10 SO86

★★★★67% Château Impney
WR9 0BN
☎ 01905 774411 01905 772371
e-mail: chateau@impney.demon.co.uk
Dir: *on A38, 1m from M5 junct 5 towards Droitwich/Worcester*
Overlooking 120 acres of beautiful parkland, this elegant and imposing French-style château dates back to the 1800s. All bedrooms are furnished and equipped to modern standards, and come in a variety of sizes. The hotel has excellent conference, function, exhibition and leisure facilities.
ROOMS: 67 en suite 53 annexe en suite (10 fmly) s £80-£120; d £90-£140 (incl. bkfst) **FACILITIES:** Tennis (hard) Sauna Solarium Gym 55 acres of parkland **CONF:** Thtr 1000 Class 550 Board 160 Del from £139.95 **SERVICES:** Lift **PARKING:** 1000 **NOTES:** No dogs (ex guide dogs) No smoking in restaurant Closed Xmas
CARDS:

★★★★65% Raven
Victoria Square WR9 8DQ
☎ 01905 772224 01905 797100
e-mail: sales@ravenhotel.demon.co.uk
Dir: *in town centre on A38, 1.5m from M5 junct 5 towards Droitwich/Worcester*
Situated in the heart of the spa town, close to the Brine Baths, this timber-framed property dates back to the early 16th century. Considerably extended over the years, it provides comfortable, well-equipped accommodation. Public areas have the atmosphere of a gentleman's club with leather sofas in the lounge and a relaxing bar, while the dessert trolley has pride of place in the restaurant.
ROOMS: 72 en suite (1 fmly) s £80-£120; d £90-£140 (incl. bkfst) **CONF:** Thtr 150 Class 70 Board 40 Del from £139.95 **SERVICES:** Lift **PARKING:** 250 **NOTES:** No dogs (ex guide dogs) No smoking in restaurant Closed Xmas **CARDS:**

★★64% *The Hadley Bowling Green Inn*
Hadley Heath WR9 0AR
☎ 01905 620294 01905 620771
e-mail: hbginn@backissues.freeserve.co.uk
Dir: *M5 junct 5 A38 towards Droitwich. Follow Ring Road (A38) towards Worcester. Take next left signed Ombersley/Tenbury and follow hotel signs*
Guy Fawkes and his confederates reputedly planned the Gunpowder Plot at this 16th-century inn, which also claims to have one of the country's oldest crown greens. The well-equipped accommodation includes two rooms with four-poster beds and family rooms. Food is served in the bar with a log fire in winter, or in the spacious restaurant.
ROOMS: 11 en suite 3 annexe en suite (2 fmly) **FACILITIES:** Clay pigeon shooting Crown bowling Craft weekends **PARKING:** 100 **NOTES:** Closed 26 Dec pm **CARDS:**

Travelodge
Travelodge

Rashwood Hill WR9 8DA
☎ 08700 850 950 01527 861545
Travelodge offers good quality, good value, modern accommodation. Ideal for families, the spacious, en suite bedrooms include remote-control TV, tea and coffee-making facilities, luxury beds and free morning newspaper. Meals can be taken at the nearby family restaurant. For further details and the Travelodge phone number, consult the Hotel Groups page.
ROOMS: 32 en suite s fr £42.95; d fr £42.95

D

DUDLEY, West Midlands Map 10 SO99
See also Himley

★★★★68% *Copthorne Hotel Merry Hill-Dudley*
COPTHORNE

The Waterfront, Level St, Brierley Hill DY5 1UR
☎ 01384 482882 01384 482773
e-mail: philip.bell@mill-cop.com
Dir: *follow signs for Merry Hill Centre*

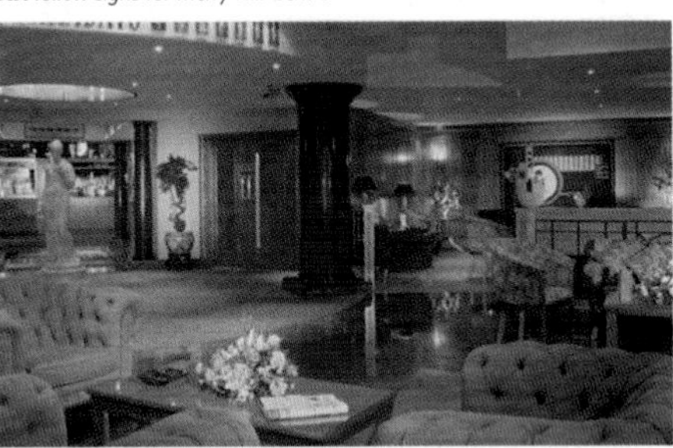

The hotel enjoys a waterfront aspect and is close to the Merry Hill shopping mall. Polished marble floors, rich fabrics and striking interior design are features of the stylish public areas. Bedrooms are spacious and some have Connoisseur status, which includes the use of a private lounge. A modern leisure centre with pool occupies the lower level.
ROOMS: 138 en suite (14 fmly) No smoking in 90 bedrooms **FACILITIES:** STV Indoor swimming (H) Sauna Solarium Gym Jacuzzi Aerobics Beauty/massage therapists **CONF:** Thtr 570 Class 240 Board 60 **SERVICES:** Lift **PARKING:** 100 **NOTES:** No dogs (ex guide dogs)
CARDS:

★★★63% The Ward Arms Hotel
corus hotels

Birmingham Rd DY1 4RN
☎ 0870 609 6113 01384 457502
e-mail: wardarms@corushotels.com
Dir: *on A461. M5 junct 2 1st left at rdbt, 3rd exit at next rdbt. After 1.5m 1st exit at 3rd rdbt, hotel 500yds on left*
This busy and popular modern hotel is within easy reach of the M5, in the heart of the Black Country. The bedrooms are well-equipped and rooms on ground floor level are available.
continued on p210

DUDLEY, continued

Public areas include the traditionally furnished conservatory restaurant and bar, where freshly prepared dishes are served.

The Ward Arms Hotel, Dudley

ROOMS: 72 en suite (36 GF) No smoking in 14 bedrooms s £70; d £70 **LB FACILITIES:** STV Xmas **CONF:** Thtr 140 Class 50 Board 60 Del £99 **PARKING:** 150 **CARDS:**

⇧ Travelodge Birmingham Dudley

Travelodge

Dudley Rd, Brierley Hill DY5 1LQ
☎ 08700 850 950 📠 01384 481579
Dir: *3m W, on A461*

Travelodge offers good quality, good value, modern accommodation. Ideal for families, the spacious, en suite bedrooms include remote-control TV, tea and coffee-making facilities, luxury beds and free morning newspaper. Meals can be taken at the nearby family restaurant. For further details and the Travelodge phone number, consult the Hotel Groups page.
ROOMS: 32 en suite s fr £42.95; d fr £42.95

DULVERTON, Somerset — Map 03 SS92

Top 200 - Hotel

★★ Ashwick House

TA22 9QD
☎ 01398 323868 📠 01398 323868
e-mail: ashwickhouse@talk21.com
Dir: *left at post office, 3m NW on B3223, over 2 cattlegrids, signed on left*

A small yet inviting Edwardian hotel, set in six beautiful acres above the breathtaking valley of the River Barle, on the edge of Exmoor. Exuding a quintessential country house ambience, the public areas include a galleried hall with welcoming log fire, whilst stylish lounges boast deep sofas. Bedrooms are spacious, comfortable and are equipped with a host of thoughtful touches. Each evening a set menu is served, with a choice of starter and pudding, using the finest local produce.
ROOMS: 6 en suite No smoking in 1 bedroom s £75-£86; d £130-£150 (incl. bkfst & dinner) **LB FACILITIES:** Solarium Croquet lawn Xmas **PARKING:** 27 **NOTES:** No dogs No children 8yrs No smoking in restaurant

★★64% Lion

Bank Square TA22 9BU
☎ 01398 323444 📠 01398 323980
e-mail: jeffeveritt@tiscali.co.uk
Dir: *from A361 at Tiverton rdbt onto A396. Left at Exbridge onto B3223. Over bridge in Dulverton, hotel in Bank Sq*

Good old-fashioned hospitality is always on offer at this charming, traditional inn in the centre of Dulverton. The bar is popular with locals and visitors alike, offering a variety of local real ales and quality meals. A pleasant dining room provides a quieter, non-smoking option. This is an ideal base from which to explore Exmoor National Park.
ROOMS: 13 en suite (2 fmly) No smoking in 2 bedrooms s fr £35; d fr £62 (incl. bkfst) **LB FACILITIES:** Xmas **PARKING:** 6 **NOTES:** No smoking in restaurant **CARDS:**

DUNCHURCH, Warwickshire — Map 11 SP47

⇧ Travelodge Rugby

Travelodge

London Rd, Thurlaston CV23 9LG
☎ 08700 850 950 📠 01788 521538
Dir: *A45, westbound*

Travelodge offers good quality, good value, modern accommodation. Ideal for families, the spacious, en suite bedrooms include remote-control TV, tea and coffee-making facilities, luxury beds and free morning newspaper. Meals can be taken at the nearby family restaurant. For further details and the Travelodge phone number, consult the Hotel Groups page.
ROOMS: 40 en suite s fr £42.95; d fr £42.95

DUNSTABLE, Bedfordshire — Map 11 TL02

★★★65% Hanover International Hotel

Church St LU5 4RT
☎ 01582 662201 📠 01582 696422
e-mail: gerard.vircombier@hanover-international.com
Dir: *M1 junct 11 and take A505. Hotel 2m on right opp Priory church*

Meeting the needs of a regular business trade, this hotel is ideally located close to the town centre and has ample private parking. Public areas include a comfortably furnished bar lounge and an

continued

attractive air-conditioned restaurant. Bedrooms are available in a variety of styles, club and executive rooms being the most plush.
ROOMS: 68 en suite (7 fmly) (21 GF) No smoking in 21 bedrooms s £109; d £119 (incl. bkfst) **LB** **FACILITIES:** STV **CONF:** Thtr 45 Class 18 Board 26 Del £135 **SERVICES:** Lift **PARKING:** 70 **NOTES:** No smoking in restaurant Civ Wed 120
CARDS:

Travel Inn (Dunstable/Luton)
350 Luton Rd LU5 4LL
☎ 08701 977083 📠 01582 664114
Dir: *on A505. From M1 junct 11 follow signs to Dunstable. At first rdbt turn right. The Travel Inn on left*
Travel Inn offers good-quality, value-for-money accommodation. Spacious, en suite rooms with bath and shower comfortably accommodate a family of up to two adults and two children (to age 15). The restaurant and bar offers a varied menu. For further details and the Travel Inn phone number, consult the Hotel Groups page.
ROOMS: 42 en suite s £44.95; d £44.95

Travel Inn (Dunstable South)
Watling St, Kensworth LU6 3QP
☎ 08701 977082 📠 01582 842811
Dir: *M1 junct 9 towards Dunstable on A5, Travel Inn on right past Packhorse pub*
Travel Inn offers good-quality, value-for-money accommodation. Spacious, en suite rooms with bath and shower comfortably accommodate a family of up to two adults and two children (to age 15). The restaurant and bar offers a varied menu. For further details and the Travel Inn phone number, consult the Hotel Groups page.
ROOMS: 40 en suite s £44.95; d £44.95

Travelodge
Watling St LU7 9LZ
☎ 08700 850 950 📠 01525 211177
Dir: *3m N, on A5*
Travelodge offers good quality, good value, modern accommodation. Ideal for families, the spacious, en suite bedrooms include remote-control TV, tea and coffee-making facilities, luxury beds and free morning newspaper. Meals can be taken at the nearby family restaurant. For further details and the Travelodge phone number, consult the Hotel Groups page.
ROOMS: 28 en suite s fr £42.95; d fr £42.95

DUNSTER, Somerset — Map 03 SS94

★★★75% **The Luttrell Arms Hotel**
High St TA24 6SG
☎ 01643 821555 📠 01643 821567
e-mail: info@luttrellarms.fsnet.co.uk
Dir: *A39/A396 S toward Tiverton. Hotel on left opposite Yarn Market*
Occupying an enviable position in the high street, this 15th-century hotel looks up to the town's famous castle. Beautifully renovated and decorated in a contemporary style, high levels of comfort can be found throughout. The warm and friendly staff deliver attentive service in a relaxed atmosphere.
ROOMS: 28 en suite (3 fmly) No smoking in all bedrooms s £65-£95; d £95-£140 (incl. bkfst) **LB** **FACILITIES:** Exmoor safaris, Historic tours, Walking tours Xmas **CONF:** Thtr 35 Class 20 Board 20 Del from £95 **PARKING:** 3 **NOTES:** No smoking in restaurant
CARDS:

DURHAM, Co Durham — Map 19 NZ24
See also Rushyford

★★★★72% **Durham Marriott Hotel, Royal County**
Old Elvet DH1 3JN
☎ 0191 386 6821 📠 0191 386 0704
e-mail: durhamroyal.marriott@whitbread.com
Dir: *from A1(M) junct 62 to Durham, over 1st rdbt, left at 2nd rdbt over bridge. Left at lights, hotel on left*
In a wonderful position on the banks of the River Wear, the hotel's central location makes it ideal for visiting the attractions of this historic city. The building was developed from a series of Jacobean town houses (once owned by the Bowes-Lyon family, ancestors of the late Queen Mother). Today the hotel offers up-to-date, air-conditioned bedrooms; a choice of restaurants; gymnasium and swimming pool.
ROOMS: 142 en suite 8 annexe en suite (4 fmly) No smoking in 99 bedrooms s fr £130; d fr £140 (incl. bkfst) **LB** **FACILITIES: Spa** STV Indoor swimming (H) Sauna Solarium Gym Jacuzzi Steamroom Plungepool Impulse showers Xmas **CONF:** Thtr 120 Class 50 Board 45 **SERVICES:** Lift **PARKING:** 80 **NOTES:** No smoking in restaurant Civ Wed 60 **CARDS:**

★★★71% **Ramside Hall**
Carrville DH1 1TD
☎ 0191 386 5282 📠 0191 386 0399
e-mail: mail@ramsidehall.co.uk
Dir: *from A1(M) junct 62 take A690 to Sunderland. 200mtrs after railway bridge turn right*
Close to the motorway, yet located in a delightful parkland setting with its own golf course, this is the largest privately owned hotel in the North East. Bedrooms, all furnished to a high specification, include two presidential suites. There are a number of comfortable lounges and a choice of three dining venues.
ROOMS: 80 en suite (10 fmly) (28 GF) No smoking in 36 bedrooms s £112-£175; d £132-£225 (incl. bkfst) **LB** **FACILITIES:** STV Golf 27 Snooker Sauna Putting green Steam room Golf academy Driving Range entertainment **CONF:** BC Thtr 400 Class 160 Board 40 Del from £140 **SERVICES:** Lift **PARKING:** 500 **NOTES:** Civ Wed 450
CARDS:

★★★67% ***Kings Lodge Hotel & Restaurant***
Flass Vale DH1 4BG
☎ 0191 370 9977 📠 0191 370 9988
Dir: *A1 junct 62, over 1st 3 rdbts, right at 4th. 1st left then 1st right. Hotel at end of road*
Benefiting from a city centre location, yet with the illusion of a secluded setting this stylish modern hotel is popular with both business and leisure guests. Accommodation is provided in compact, well designed rooms. Knights is a contemporary restaurant and champagne bar, there is also a less formal bar and beer terrace and a bright and comfortable lounge.
ROOMS: 21 en suite (1 fmly) No smoking in all bedrooms
FACILITIES: STV entertainment **CONF:** Thtr 25 Class 25 Board 18
SERVICES: air con **PARKING:** 35 **NOTES:** No smoking in restaurant
CARDS:

★★★60% **Bowburn Hall**
Bowburn DH6 5NH
☎ 0191 377 0311 📠 0191 377 3459
Dir: *towards Bowburn. Right at Cooperage Pub, then 0.5m to junct signed Durham. Hotel on left*
This hotel lies in five acres of grounds in a quiet residential area, and is within easy reach of the A1. The cosy bedrooms are attractively decorated, and the spacious lounge bar and

continued on p212

DURHAM, continued

conservatory overlook the gardens. Bar meals are popular with locals and visitors alike; more formal dining is available in the restaurant.
ROOMS: 19 en suite s £50-£60; d £65-£75 (incl. bkfst) **LB**
FACILITIES: STV **CONF:** Thtr 150 Class 80 Board 30 Del from £95
PARKING: 100 **NOTES:** RS 24-26 Dec & 1 Jan Civ Wed 120
CARDS:

Travel Inn Durham (East)

Broomside Park, Belmont Industrial Estate
DH1 1GG
☎ 08701 977084 🖹 0191 370 6501
Dir: *from A1(M) junct 62 take A690 west towards Durham. 1st exit, after 1m turn left. Travel Inn on left*
Travel Inn offers good-quality, value-for-money accommodation. Spacious, en suite rooms with bath and shower comfortably accommodate a family of up to two adults and two children (to age 15). The restaurant and bar offers a varied menu. For further details and the Travel Inn phone number, consult the Hotel Groups page.
ROOMS: 40 en suite s £44.95; d £44.95

Travel Inn Durham (North)

Adj Arnison Retail Centre, Pity Me DH1 5GB
☎ 08701 977086 🖹 0191 383 1166
Dir: *A1 junct 63 south onto A167 to Durham. Straight over 4 rdbts, at 5th rdbt turn left, Travel Inn on right after 200yds*
Travel Inn offers good-quality, value-for-money accommodation. Spacious, en suite rooms with bath and shower comfortably accommodate a family of up to two adults and two children (to age 15). The restaurant and bar offers a varied menu. For further details and the Travel Inn phone number, consult the Hotel Groups page.
ROOMS: 60 en suite s £44.95; d £44.95

Travelodge Durham

Station Rd, Gilesgate DH1 1LJ
☎ 08700 850 950 🖹 0191 383 2188
Travelodge offers good quality, good value, modern accommodation. Ideal for families, the spacious, en suite bedrooms include remote-control TV, tea and coffee-making facilities, luxury beds and free morning newspaper. Meals can be taken at the nearby family restaurant. For further details and the Travelodge phone number, consult the Hotel Groups page.
ROOMS: 57 en suite s fr £42.95; d fr £42.95

○ Premier Lodge (Durham City Centre)

Southfield Way, Aykley Heads DH1 5TR
☎ 0870 9906460 🖹 0870 9906461
ROOMS: 85 en suite **NOTES:** Due to open March 2004

DURHAM SERVICE AREA (A1(M)), Co Durham Map 19 NZ33

Travel Inn (Durham South)

Motorway Service Area, Tursdale Rd, Bowburn
DH6 5NP
☎ 08701 977087 🖹 0191 377 8722

Dir: *A1(M) junct 61& A177 Bowburn junction*
Travel Inn offers good-quality, value-for-money accommodation. Spacious, en suite rooms with bath and shower comfortably accommodate a family of up to two adults and two children (to age 15). The restaurant and bar offers a varied menu. For further details and the Travel Inn phone number, consult the Hotel Groups page.
ROOMS: 38 en suite s £44.95; d £44.95 **CONF:** Thtr 1 Board 10

DUXFORD, Cambridgeshire Map 12 TL4

★★★73% Duxford Lodge

Ickleton Rd CB2 4RU
☎ 01223 836444 🖹 01223 832271
e-mail: admin@duxfordlodgehotel.co.uk
Dir: *M11 junct 10, onto A505 to Duxford. 1st right at T-junct. Hotel on left*

A warm welcome is assured at this attractive red brick hotel in the heart of a delightful village. Public areas include a relaxing bar, separate lounge, and an attractive restaurant, where an excellent and imaginative menu is offered. The bedrooms are comfortable and smartly furnished.
ROOMS: 11 en suite 4 annexe en suite (2 fmly)
FACILITIES: entertainment **CONF:** Thtr 30 Class 20 Board 20
PARKING: 34 **NOTES:** No smoking in restaurant Closed 26-30 Dec
CARDS:

See advert on opposite page

EARLS COLNE, Essex Map 13 TL82

★★★80% De Vere Arms

53 High St CO6 2PB
☎ 01787 223353 🖹 01787 223365
e-mail: dining@deverearms.com

Situated in the heart of the Colne Valley in a delightful village. A unique blend of modern facilities enhanced by beautiful antiques, hand-painted murals and fine art create a relaxing atmosphere throughout. The stylish bedrooms are individually decorated and have attractive soft furnishings and public rooms include a smart bar, plush lounge and a large beamed restaurant.
ROOMS: 9 en suite (1 fmly) No smoking in all bedrooms s £85-£105; d £85-£105 (incl. bkfst) **FACILITIES:** Xmas **CONF:** Thtr 40 Board 20
PARKING: 12 **NOTES:** No dogs No smoking in restaurant
CARDS:

TV dinner?
Room service at three stars and above

EASINGWOLD, North Yorkshire
Map 19 SE56

★★72% George
THE CIRCLE
Selected Individual Hotels
GREAT BRITAIN

Market Place YO61 3AD
☎ 01347 821698 📠 01347 823448
e-mail: info@the-george-hotel.co.uk
Dir: *off A19 midway between York & Thirsk, in Market Place*
A former coaching inn facing the Georgian market square. Bedrooms are comfortably furnished and well equipped, and the mews rooms have external access. An extensive range of well-produced food is available both in the bar and restaurant. There are two comfortable lounges and complimentary use of a local fitness centre. Personal supervision by the proprietors ensures good hospitality.
ROOMS: 15 en suite (2 fmly) No smoking in all bedrooms s £55-£60; d £75-£80 (incl. bkfst) **LB FACILITIES:** Complimentry use of local fitness centre Xmas **CONF:** Board 12 Del from £80 **PARKING:** 10 **NOTES:** No dogs (ex guide dogs) No smoking in restaurant
CARDS:

EAST AYTON, North Yorkshire
Map 17 SE98

★★★60% East Ayton Lodge
Moor Ln, Forge Valley YO13 9EW
☎ 01723 864227 📠 01723 862680
e-mail: ealodge@cix.co.uk
Dir: *400yds off A170*
Set in three acres of grounds close to the River Derwent and discreetly situated in a quiet lane on the edge of the forest, this friendly, family operated hotel is constructed around what was originally two cottages. Bedrooms are well equipped and those in the courtyard are particularly spacious. A good range of food is available.
ROOMS: 10 en suite 20 annexe en suite (3 fmly) s £50-£70; d £65-£110 (incl. bkfst) **LB FACILITIES:** Xmas **CONF:** Thtr 46 Class 80 Board 32 **PARKING:** 50 **NOTES:** No smoking in restaurant
CARDS:

EASTBOURNE, East Sussex
Map 06 TV69

★★★★★71% 🏵🏵 Grand
King Edward's Pde BN21 4EQ
☎ 01323 412345 📠 01323 412233
e-mail: Reservations@Grandeastbourne.com
Dir: *on seafront W of Eastbourne, 1m from railway station*

This famous Victorian hotel offers high standards of service and hospitality. The property is situated on King Edwards Parade overlooking the beach and sea beyond. The extensive public rooms feature a magnificent Great Hall with marble columns and high ceilings where guests can relax and enjoy afternoon tea. The spacious bedrooms provide excellent levels of comfort and some
continued

rooms have balconies with stunning sea views. The hotel also has a choice of restaurants and bars as well as superb leisure facilities.
ROOMS: 152 en suite (20 fmly) s £135-£400; d £165-£430 (incl. bkfst) **LB FACILITIES: Spa** Indoor swimming (H) Outdoor swimming (H) Snooker Sauna Solarium Gym Putting green Jacuzzi Hairdressing, Beauty therapy, Swimming pools supervised entertainment ch fac Xmas **CONF:** BC Thtr 350 Class 200 Board 40 Del from £190 **SERVICES:** Lift **PARKING:** 60 **NOTES:** No smoking in restaurant Civ Wed 200
CARDS:

★★★72% Hydro
Mount Rd BN20 7HZ
☎ 01323 720643 📠 01323 641167
e-mail: Sales@hydrohotel.com
Dir: *from pier/seafront, right along Grand Parade. At Grand Hotel follow Hydro Hotel sign. Up South Cliff 200yds*

This well-managed and popular hotel enjoys an elevated position with views of attractive gardens and the sea beyond. The
continued on p214

EASTBOURNE, continued

refurbished, spacious bedrooms are attractive and well equipped. In addition to the comfortable lounges, guests also have access to fitness facilities and a hairdressing salon; service is both professional and efficient throughout.
ROOMS: 84 rms (82 en suite) (3 fmly) (3 GF) No smoking in 12 bedrooms s £38-£68; d £76-£130 (incl. bkfst) **LB FACILITIES:** STV Outdoor swimming (H) Sauna Gym Croquet lawn Putting green Beauty room Hairdressing Xmas **CONF:** Thtr 140 Class 90 Board 40 Del from £79.50 **SERVICES:** Lift **PARKING:** 50 **NOTES:** No smoking in restaurant RS 24-28 & 30-31 Dec Civ Wed 100 **CARDS:**

E

★★★72% Lansdowne

Best Western

King Edward's Pde BN21 4EE
☎ 01323 725174 📠 01323 739721
e-mail: reception@lansdowne-hotel.co.uk
Dir: *hotel at W end of seafront (B2103) facing Western Lawns*

Enjoying an enviable position at the quieter end of the parade, this hotel overlooks the Western Lawns and Wish Tower and is just a few minutes' walk from many of the city's attractions. Public rooms include a variety of lounges, a range of meeting rooms and games rooms. Bedrooms are attractively decorated and many offer sea views.
ROOMS: 110 en suite (9 fmly) No smoking in 25 bedrooms s £45-£72; d £80-£126 (incl. bkfst) **LB FACILITIES:** STV Snooker Darts,Table tennis & Pool table Xmas **CONF:** Thtr 100 Class 40 Board 40 Del from £85 **SERVICES:** Lift **PARKING:** 22 **NOTES:** No smoking in restaurant Closed 2-15 Jan Civ Wed 60 **CARDS:**

See advert on opposite page

★★★66% York House

Best Western

14/22 Royal Pde BN22 7AP
☎ 01323 412918 📠 01323 646238
e-mail: frontdesk@yorkhousehotel.co.uk
Dir: *A27 to Eastbourne. On seafront 0.25m E of pier*

Owned by the Williamson family since 1896, York House enjoys an enviable location on the seafront. Bedrooms and facilities continue

continued

to be upgraded. An open veranda makes the best of the location and sea views. Public areas include a spacious reception hall, cosy bar and separate lounge plus a games room and indoor swimming pool.
ROOMS: 87 en suite (14 fmly) No smoking in 30 bedrooms s £63; d £100 (incl. bkfst) **LB FACILITIES:** STV Indoor swimming (H) Games room, Table tennis, Swimming pool supervised **CONF:** Thtr 100 Class 30 Board 24 Del £115 **SERVICES:** Lift **NOTES:** No smoking in restaurant Civ Wed 40 **CARDS:**

See advert on opposite page

★★★65% Chatsworth

Grand Pde BN21 3YR
☎ 01323 411016 📠 01323 643270
e-mail: stay@chatsworth-hotel.com
Dir: *on seafront between pier and bandstand*

Within minutes of the town centre and pier, this attractive Edwardian hotel is located on the seafront. Service is friendly and helpful throughout. The public areas consist of the Dukes Bar, a cosy lounge and the Devonshire Restaurant. Bedrooms, many of which have sea views, are traditional in style and have a range of facilities.
ROOMS: 47 en suite (2 fmly) No smoking in 10 bedrooms s £50-£60; d £80-£120 (incl. bkfst) **LB FACILITIES:** STV entertainment Xmas **CONF:** Thtr 100 Class 60 Board 40 Del from £97.50 **SERVICES:** Lift **NOTES:** No smoking in restaurant Civ Wed 140 **CARDS:**

See advert on opposite page

★★70% New Wilmington

25 Compton St BN21 4DU
☎ 01323 721219 📠 01323 746255
e-mail: info@new-wilmington-hotel.co.uk
Dir: *A22 to Eastbourne along seafront. Right along promenade to Wish Tower. Right, then left at end of road, hotel 2nd on left*

This friendly, family-run hotel is conveniently located close to the town centre and the seafront, and adjacent to the Congress Theatre and Winter Gardens. Public rooms are well presented and include a cosy bar, a small comfortable no-smoking lounge and a spacious restaurant. Bedrooms are comfortably appointed and tastefully decorated; family and superior bedrooms are available.
ROOMS: 40 en suite (14 fmly) (3 GF) s £37-£43; d £64-£76 (incl. bkfst) **LB FACILITIES:** entertainment Xmas **SERVICES:** Lift **PARKING:** 2 **NOTES:** No dogs (ex guide dogs) No smoking in restaurant Closed 3 Jan - mid-Feb **CARDS:**

Popped the question?
Hotels with Civ Wed in their entry are licensed for civil wedding ceremonies. Maximum numbers for the ceremony only are shown, e.g. Civ Wed 120

★★70% West Rocks
Grand Pde BN21 4DL
☎ 01323 725217 🖹 01323 720421
e-mail: westrockshotel@tiscali.co.uk
Dir: *western end of seafront*
Located in a prime position on the Grand Parade, close to the pier and bandstand and a short walk from the town centre. Bedrooms vary in size, with many offering sea views; all are furnished and decorated to a good standard. Guests have the choice of two comfortable lounges and a bar in which to relax.
ROOMS: 47 rms (45 en suite) (8 fmly) (6 GF) s £48-£64; d £80-£148 (incl. bkfst & dinner) **LB** **FACILITIES:** entertainment Xmas **CONF:** BC Thtr 20 Class 12 Board 12 Del from £55 **SERVICES:** Lift **NOTES:** No dogs (ex guide dogs) No smoking in restaurant Closed 3 Jan -20 Feb **CARDS:**

★★69% The Downland Hotel & Restaurant
37 Lewes Rd BN21 2BU
☎ 01323 732689 🖹 01323 720321
e-mail: BestValuEastborn@aol.com
Dir: *on A22, take 1st exit at Willingdon rdbt, follow sign to seafront, past college and hospital over rdbt. Hotel in 0.5m*
Ideally situated within easy striking distance of the town centre, this friendly, family-run hotel offers high standards of hospitality and service. The spacious bedrooms are pleasantly decorated and thoughtfully equipped. Breakfast is served in the smart dining room and guests can choose from a daily-changing menu of home cooked dishes for dinner.
ROOMS: 12 en suite (2 fmly) No smoking in 4 bedrooms s £30-£35; d £50-£70 (incl. bkfst) **LB** **PARKING:** 10 **NOTES:** No dogs (ex guide dogs) No children 10yrs No smoking in restaurant **CARDS:**

EASTBOURNE, continued

★★68% Ashley Grange Hotel
Lewes Rd BN21 2BY
☎ 01323 721550 🖷 01323 721550
e-mail: ashleygrangehotel@hotmail.com
Dir: from A22 to Eastbourne, left at Willingdon rdbt signed hospital/seafront, pass hospital and school, hotel 100mtrs on left
Located on the edge of the town centre, this small, friendly hotel offers comfortably furnished, well-equipped bedrooms. Smartly appointed public areas include a cosy bar and attractive dining room with access to a large rear garden with a fun splasher pool.
ROOMS: 6 en suite s £35-£45; d £55-£70 (incl. bkfst) **LB** **FACILITIES:** Fun pool "Splasher" **PARKING:** 6 **NOTES:** No dogs No children 12yrs Closed 24-27 Dec **CARDS:**

THE CIRCLE Selected Individual Hotels GREAT BRITAIN

★★68% Farrar's Hotel
Wilmington Gardens BN21 4JN
☎ 01323 723737 🖷 01323 732902
Dir: off seafront by Wish Tower, hotel opposite Congress Theatre
Farrar's Hotel is situated just a short walk from the seafront, opposite Devonshire Park. The bedrooms are comfortably furnished, pleasantly decorated and equipped with a good range of useful extras. Public areas are smartly appointed and include a cosy bar, a separate lounge and an attractive downstairs dining room.
ROOMS: 45 en suite (4 fmly) **CONF:** Thtr 80 **SERVICES:** Lift **PARKING:** 35 **NOTES:** No smoking in restaurant Closed Jan **CARDS:**

★★68% Stanley House Hotel
9/10 Howard Square BN21 4BQ
☎ 01323 731393 🖷 01323 738823
Friendly, family-run hotel situated in a side road just off the seafront, within easy walking distance of the pier and bandstand. Bedrooms are generally quite spacious, pleasantly decorated and equipped with modern facilities. There is a cosy bar, a choice of lounges and a smart dining room.
ROOMS: 25 en suite (3 fmly) **FACILITIES:** entertainment **SERVICES:** Lift **NOTES:** No dogs No smoking in restaurant Closed Jan-Feb **CARDS:**

★★67% Quality Hotel Langham
Royal Pde BN22 7AH
☎ 01323 731451 🖷 01323 646623
e-mail: info@langhamhotel.co.uk
Dir: in Eastbourne, follow seafront signs. Hotel 0.5m E of pier
This popular hotel is situated in a prominent position with superb views of the sea and pier. Bedrooms, some of which have been refurbished, are pleasantly decorated and equipped with modern facilities. The spacious public rooms include a terrace restaurant, business lounge area and Grand Parade bar.
ROOMS: 87 en suite (5 fmly) s £40-£65; d £75-£119 (incl. bkfst) **LB** **FACILITIES:** Temporary membership of Sovereign Club Xmas **CONF:** Thtr 80 Class 40 Board 24 **SERVICES:** Lift **PARKING:** 4 **NOTES:** No smoking in restaurant Civ Wed 110 **CARDS:**

QUALITY HOTEL BY CHOICE HOTELS

★★65% Oban
King Edward's Pde BN21 4DS
☎ 01323 731581 🖷 01323 721994
Dir: opposite Wish Tower on seafront
Friendly, privately-owned hotel situated on the seafront overlooking the well-kept lawns and sea beyond. Bedrooms are pleasantly furnished and cheerfully decorated and public rooms include a large open-plan lounge/bar area overlooking the seafront, and a restaurant on the lower ground floor.
ROOMS: 31 en suite (2 fmly) (3 GF) s £25-£40; d £50-£80 (incl. bkfst) **LB** **FACILITIES:** Lounge bar activities entertainment Xmas **SERVICES:** Lift **NOTES:** No smoking in restaurant Closed Dec-Feb (ex Xmas) RS Nov **CARDS:**

★★61% Queens Hotel
Marine Pde BN21 3DY
☎ 01323 722822 🖷 01323 731056
e-mail: queens.eastbourne@alfatravel.co.uk
Dir: proceed to seafront, hotel opposite pier on left
Popular with tour groups, this long established hotel enjoys a central, prominent seafront location overlooking the pier. Spacious public areas include a choice of lounges and regular entertainment is also provided. Bedrooms are suitably appointed and equipped, many enjoying sea views.
ROOMS: 122 en suite (1 fmly) s £28-£37; d £48-£66 (incl. bkfst) **LB** **FACILITIES:** Snooker entertainment Xmas **CONF:** Thtr 100 Class 56 Board 40 **SERVICES:** Lift **PARKING:** 50 **NOTES:** No dogs (ex guide dogs) No smoking in restaurant Closed Jan RS Nov, Feb-Mar **CARDS:**

Leisureplex

Travel Inn
Willingdon Dr BN23 8AL
☎ 08701 977089 🖷 01323 767379
Dir: A22 towards Eastbourne. At next rbt left. Inn on left
Travel Inn offers good-quality, value-for-money accommodation. Spacious, en suite rooms with bath and shower comfortably accommodate a family of up to two adults and two children (to age 15). The restaurant and bar offers a varied menu. For further details and Travel Inn phone number, consult Hotel Groups page.
ROOMS: 47 en suite s £44.95; d £44.95

travel inn

EAST GRINSTEAD, West Sussex Map 06 TQ33

Top 200 - Hotel

★★★ *Gravetye Manor*
RH19 4LJ
☎ 01342 810567 🖷 01342 810080
e-mail: info@gravetyemanor.co.uk
Dir: B2028 to Haywards Heath. 1m after Turners Hill fork left towards Sharpthorne, immediate 1st left into Vowels Ln
This beautiful Elizabethan stone mansion was built in 1598 and enjoys a tranquil setting. It was one of the first country house hotels and remains a shining example in its class. The day rooms are comfortably furnished, and the bedrooms are decorated in traditional English style and furnished with antiques, with many thoughtful extras. The cuisine uses home-grown fruit and vegetables as well as local spring water.
ROOMS: 18 en suite **FACILITIES:** Fishing Croquet lawn **PARKING:** 35 **NOTES:** No dogs No children 7yrs No smoking in restaurant RS 25 Dec Civ Wed 45 **CARDS:**

RELAIS & CHATEAUX

Travel Inn
London Rd, Felbridge RH19 2QR
☎ 08701 977088 📠 01342 326187
Dir: *at junction of A22 & A264 south from M25 junct 6*
Travel Inn offers good-quality, value-for-money accommodation. Spacious, en suite rooms with bath and shower comfortably accommodate a family of up to two adults and two children (to age 15). The restaurant and bar offers a varied menu. For further details and the Travel Inn phone number, consult the Hotel Groups page.
ROOMS: 41 en suite s £44.95; d £44.95

EAST HORNDON, Essex — Map 06 TQ68

Travelodge Brentwood
CM13 3LL
☎ 08700 850 950 📠 01277 810819
Dir: *on A127, eastbound 4m off M25 junct 29*
Travelodge offers good quality, good value, modern accommodation. Ideal for families, the spacious, en suite bedrooms include remote-control TV, tea and coffee-making facilities, luxury beds and free morning newspaper. Meals can be taken at the nearby family restaurant. For further details and the Travelodge phone number, consult the Hotel Groups page.
ROOMS: 45 en suite s fr £42.95; d fr £42.95

EASTLEIGH, Hampshire — Map 05 SU41

Holiday Inn Eastleigh
Leigh Rd SO50 9PG
☎ 0870 400 9075 📠 023 8064 3945
e-mail: eastleigh@ichotelsgroup.com
Dir: *follow A335 to Eastleigh, hotel on right*
At the time of going to press, the classification for this hotel was not confirmed. Please refer to the AA internet site www.theAA.com for current information.
ROOMS: 120 en suite (3 fmly) No smoking in 89 bedrooms **FACILITIES:** STV Indoor swimming (H) Sauna Gym Jacuzzi Beauty treatment Leisure club **CONF:** Thtr 250 Class 90 Board 90 **SERVICES:** Lift **PARKING:** 160 **CARDS:**

Travel Inn
Leigh Rd SO50 9YX
☎ 08701 977090 📠 023 8062 9048
Dir: *adjacent to M3 junct 13, near Eastleigh on A335*
Travel Inn offers good-quality, value-for-money accommodation. Spacious, en suite rooms with bath and shower comfortably accommodate a family of up to two adults and two children (to age 15). The restaurant and bar offers a varied menu. For further details and the Travel Inn phone number, consult the Hotel Groups page.
ROOMS: 60 en suite s £44.95; d £44.95

Destination dining!
This symbol indicates a Restaurant with Rooms

Travelodge Southampton Eastleigh
Twyford Rd SO50 4LF
☎ 08700 850 950 📠 023 8061 6813
Dir: *M3 junct 12 on A335*
Travelodge offers good quality, good value, modern accommodation. Ideal for families, the spacious, en suite bedrooms include remote-control TV, tea and coffee-making facilities, luxury beds and free morning newspaper. Meals can be taken at the nearby family restaurant. For further details and the Travelodge phone number, consult the Hotel Groups page.
ROOMS: 32 en suite s fr £42.95; d fr £42.95

EAST MIDLANDS AIRPORT, Leicestershire — Map 11 SK42

★★★★74%
The Priest House on the River — HandPICKED
Kings Mills, Castle Donington DE74 2RR
☎ 01332 810649 📠 01332 811141
e-mail: priesthouse@arcadianhotels.co.uk
Dir: *M1 junct 24 on to A50, take 1st slip road signed Castle Donington. In Castle Donington go right at traffic lights, hotel within 2m*

An historic hotel nestling peacefully in a picturesque riverside setting. Public areas have been extensively refurbished and include new conference rooms, a fine dining restaurant and a brasserie. Bedrooms are situated in both the main building and converted cottages. Newly designed executive rooms feature state-of-the-art technology.
ROOMS: 24 en suite 19 annexe en suite (5 fmly) No smoking in 21 bedrooms **FACILITIES:** STV Fishing **CONF:** Thtr 130 Class 40 Board 40 **PARKING:** 150 **NOTES:** No smoking in restaurant Civ Wed 100
CARDS:

★★★73% **Best Western Yew Lodge Hotel**
Packington Hill, Kegworth DE74 2DF
☎ 01509 672518 📠 01509 674730
e-mail: info@yewlodgehotel.co.uk
Dir: *M1 junct 24. Follow signs to Loughborough & Kegworth on A6. At bottom of hill, 1st right, after 400yds lodge on right*
Significant investment has been made in this smart, family-owned hotel which is very conveniently and peacefully located. Bedrooms and public areas are well appointed and thoughtfully equipped.
continued on p218

EAST MIDLANDS AIRPORT, continued

The restaurant serves interesting award winning dishes from a choice of menus.

Yew Lodge Hotel, East Midlands Airport

ROOMS: 91 en suite (10 fmly) No smoking in 44 bedrooms s £50-£70; d £70-£90 **FACILITIES:** STV Xmas **CONF:** Thtr 280 Class 60 Board 70 Del from £99 **SERVICES:** Lift **PARKING:** 180 **NOTES:** No smoking in restaurant Civ Wed 150 **CARDS:**

★★★70% Donington Manor

High St, Castle Donington DE74 2PP
☎ 01332 810253 01332 850330
e-mail: enquiries@doningtonmanorhotel.co.uk
Dir: *1m into village on B5430, left at traffic lights*

Near the village centre, this refined Georgian building offers high standards of hospitality and a professional service. Many of the original architectural features have been preserved; the elegant dining room is particularly appealing. Bedrooms are individually designed, and the newer suites are especially comfortable and well equipped.
ROOMS: 26 en suite 6 annexe en suite (1 fmly) s £57-£70; d £85 (incl. bkfst) **LB** **FACILITIES:** STV **CONF:** Thtr 120 Class 60 Board 40 Del £98 **PARKING:** 40 **NOTES:** No dogs (ex guide dogs) Closed 24-30 Dec Civ Wed 120 **CARDS:**

★★66% Tudor Hotel & Restaurant

Bond Gate DE74 2NR
☎ 01332 810875 01332 850883
e-mail: tudorinn@commodoreinternational.co.uk
Dir: *M1 junct 24, A50 to Derby. Left to Long Eaton at rdbt, for Castle Donington*
This Tudor style hotel is close to Donington race track and the East Midlands airport. Bedrooms have been tastefully refurbished and are comfortable and very well equipped. Downstairs there is a large restaurant offering a wide range of dishes, a character bar and a beer garden.
ROOMS: 7 en suite (2 fmly) No smoking in all bedrooms s £43; d £58 (incl. bkfst) **LB** **FACILITIES:** STV Xmas **CONF:** BC Thtr 30 Class 30 Board 30 Del from £35 **PARKING:** 60 **NOTES:** No dogs (ex guide dogs) **CARDS:**

Express by Holiday Inn

Pegasus Business Park, Castle Donington DE74 2TQ
☎ 01509 678000 01509 670954
e-mail: ema@expressbyholidayinn.net
Dir: *signs for East Midlands Airport, right into Pegasus Business Park, hotel on left*

A modern hotel ideal for families and business travellers. Fresh and uncomplicated, the spacious bedrooms include Sky TV, power shower and tea and coffee-making facilities. Continental buffet breakfast is included in the room rate; other meals may be taken at the nearby family pub or restaurant. For further details and the Express by Holiday Inn phone number, consult the Hotel Groups pages.
ROOMS: 90 en suite **CONF:** Thtr 45 Class 30 Board 30

Travelodge Donnington Park

Travelodge

Castle Donington DE74 2TN
☎ 08700 850 950
Travelodge offers good quality, good value, modern accommodation. Ideal for families, the spacious, en suite bedrooms include remote-control TV, tea and coffee-making facilities, luxury beds and free morning newspaper. Meals can be taken at the nearby family restaurant. For further details and the Travelodge phone number, consult the Hotel Groups page.
ROOMS: 80 en suite s fr £42.95; d fr £42.95

EDGWARE, Greater London
See LONDON SECTION plan 1 C6

Premier Lodge (London Edgware)

PREMIER LODGE

435 Burnt Oak Broadway HA8 5AQ
☎ 0870 9906522 0870 9906523
Premier Lodge offers modern, well-equipped, en suite accommodation suitable for both business and leisure travellers. Meals can be taken at the adjacent popular restaurant and bar, which is fully licensed. For further details, consult the Hotel Groups page.
ROOMS: 111 en suite s £56; d £56

EGHAM, Surrey

Map 06 TQ07

★★★★73% *Runnymede Hotel & Spa*

Windsor Rd TW20 0AG
☎ 01784 436171 🖷 01784 436340
e-mail: info@runnymedehotel.com
Dir: *M25 junct 13, onto A308 towards Windsor*

Enjoying a peaceful location beside the River Thames, this large modern hotel attracts a largely business clientele during the week. Extensive function suites are available, together with spacious lounges and practically laid out bedrooms. At weekends, leisure visitors come to enjoy impressive spa facilities and regular dinner dances in the airy restaurant overlooking the river.

ROOMS: 180 en suite (19 fmly) No smoking in 116 bedrooms **FACILITIES:** STV Indoor swimming (H) Tennis (hard) Snooker Sauna Solarium Gym Croquet lawn Putting green Jacuzzi Beauty Salon Dance studio Hairdressers entertainment **CONF:** Thtr 300 Class 250 Board 76 **SERVICES:** Lift air con **PARKING:** 280 **NOTES:** No dogs (ex guide dogs) RS Restaurant closed Sat lunch/Sun dinner Civ Wed 150 **CARDS:**

See advert under WINDSOR

ELLESMERE PORT, Cheshire

Map 15 SJ47

★★★67% Quality Hotel Chester

Welsh Road/Berwick Rd, Little Sutton CH66 4PS
☎ 0151 339 5121 🖷 0151 339 3214
e-mail: admin@gb066.u-net.com
Dir: *M53 junct 5 left at rdbt. At 2nd lights right onto A550 over hump back bridge, left into Berwick Rd*

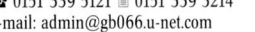

Conveniently located for the M53, this friendly hotel offers modern, well-equipped accommodation. There is a good range of facilities, including a leisure complex and versatile banqueting and conference suites. Staff are friendly and keen to please.

ROOMS: 53 en suite (8 fmly) (15 GF) No smoking in 18 bedrooms s £65-£110; d £75-£120 (incl. bkfst) **LB FACILITIES:** STV Indoor swimming (H) Sauna Steam room Exercise equipment entertainment Xmas **CONF:** Thtr 300 Class 150 Board 100 Del from £95 **PARKING:** 200 **NOTES:** No smoking in restaurant Civ Wed 200 **CARDS:**

★★62% Woodcote Hotel & Restaurant

3 Hooton Rd CH66 1QU
☎ 0151 327 1542 🖷 0151 328 1328
e-mail: thewoodcotehotel@lineone.net
Dir: *M53 junct 5, take A41 towards Chester, 1st lights right to Willaston. Hotel 300yds on left*

This popular commercial hotel offers generally spacious bedrooms, many of which are located in a separate building. There is a choice of attractive bars and a restaurant serving a range of popular, reasonably priced dishes. There is also a separate breakfast room.

ROOMS: 10 en suite 11 annexe en suite (1 fmly) s £28-£36; d £36-£42 **FACILITIES:** entertainment **CONF:** Thtr 90 Class 50 Board 48 **PARKING:** 35 **NOTES:** No dogs (ex guide dogs) RS Sun **CARDS:**

ELSTREE, Hertfordshire

Map 06 TQ19

★★★72% ® Edgwarebury

Barnet Ln WD6 3RE
☎ 0870 609 6151 🖷 020 8207 3668
e-mail: edgwarebury@corushotels.com
Dir: *M1 junct 5 follow A41 to Harrow, left onto A411 into Elstree. Through x-rds into Barnet Ln, hotel on right*

Sitting in 10 acres of landscaped gardens this hotel is full of charm and character, with a Tudor-style façade and interiors of a traditional design. The oak-panelled bar, with two large fireplaces and the Stately Cavendish restaurant enjoy wonderful views over the gardens and the city lights beyond.

ROOMS: 47 en suite (1 fmly) No smoking in 19 bedrooms s £125-£215; d £145-£215 **LB FACILITIES:** STV Xmas **CONF:** Thtr 80 Class 50 Board 10 Del from £140 **PARKING:** 100 **NOTES:** No smoking in restaurant Civ Wed 100 **CARDS:**

ELTERWATER, Cumbria

Map 18 NY30

★★★76% *Langdale Hotel & Country Club*

LA22 9JD
☎ 01539 437302 🖷 01539 437694
e-mail: itsgreat@langdale.co.uk
Dir: *into Langdale, hotel part of private estate on left*

Founded on the site of an abandoned 19th-century gunpowder works, this modern hotel is set in 35 acres of woodland and waterways. Comfortable bedrooms, many with spa baths, vary in size. Extensive public areas include a choice of stylish restaurants, conference and leisure facilities and an elegant bar with an interesting selection of snuff. There is also a traditional pub in the grounds.

ROOMS: 5 en suite 60 annexe en suite (8 fmly) **FACILITIES:** STV Indoor swimming (H) Tennis (hard) Fishing Squash Sauna Solarium Gym Jacuzzi Steam room Hair & beauty salon Cycle hire entertainment **CONF:** Thtr 80 Class 45 Board 45 **PARKING:** 65 **NOTES:** No dogs No smoking in restaurant **CARDS:**

ELTERWATER, continued

★★67% Britannia Inn
LA22 9HP
☎ 01539 437210 01539 437311
e-mail: info@britinn.co.uk
Dir: *from A593 at Skelwith Bridge Hotel turn right onto B5343, after cattle grid on main rd. Left into village of Elterwater*
This fine example of a traditional country inn is situated in the centre of the village overlooking the green. The well-maintained bedrooms are comfortable and well equipped. Welcoming real fires burn in cold weather in the oak-beamed public bar, which is popular with walkers. The inn provides an extensive choice of home-cooked dishes and a cosy lounge.
ROOMS: 9 rms (8 en suite) No smoking in all bedrooms s £60-£82; d £76-£92 (incl. bkfst) **LB** **FACILITIES:** entertainment **PARKING:** 10
NOTES: No smoking in restaurant Closed 25 & 26 Dec
CARDS:

★★66% New Dungeon Ghyll
Langdale LA22 9JX
☎ 015394 37213 015394 37666
e-mail: enquiries@dungeon-ghyll.com
Dir: *From Ambleside follow A593 towards Coniston for 3 miles, at Skelwith Bridge take right fork on B5343 towards "The Langdales".*

This friendly hotel enjoys a tranquil, idyllic position at the head of the valley. Bedrooms vary in size and style; refurbished rooms are brightly decorated and smartly furnished. Bar meals are served all day and dinner can be enjoyed in the restaurant overlooking landscaped gardens; there is also a cosy lounge bar.
ROOMS: 20 en suite s £50; d £78-£94 (incl. bkfst) **LB**
FACILITIES: Xmas **PARKING:** 30 **NOTES:** No smoking in restaurant
CARDS:

ELY, Cambridgeshire
Map 12 TL58

★★★65% Lamb
2 Lynn Rd CB7 4EJ
☎ 01353 663574 01353 662023
e-mail: lamb.ely@oldenglish.co.uk
Dir: *from A10 into Ely, hotel in town centre on corner of Lynn Road & High Street*
Centrally located, this 15th-century coaching inn is a focal point of this market town. Informal snacks are served either in the Fenman Bar or hotel bar, and traditional British cooking features on the menu in the Octagon Restaurant. Bedrooms offer good standards of comfort, with co-ordinated soft furnishings and modern, light wood furniture.
ROOMS: 32 en suite (6 fmly) s fr £70; d fr £95 (incl. bkfst) **LB**
FACILITIES: STV Xmas **CONF:** Thtr 45 Class 28 Board 30 Del from £95
PARKING: 20 **NOTES:** No smoking in restaurant
CARDS:

Travelodge
Witchford Rd CB6 3NN
☎ 08700 850 950 01353 668499
Dir: *at rdbt A10/A142*
Travelodge offers good quality, good value, modern accommodation. Ideal for families, the spacious, en suite bedrooms include remote-control TV, tea and coffee-making facilities, luxury beds and free morning newspaper. Meals can be taken at the nearby family restaurant. For further details and the Travelodge phone number, consult the Hotel Groups page.
ROOMS: 39 en suite s fr £42.95; d fr £42.95

EMBLETON, Northumberland
Map 21 NU22

★★70% Dunstanburgh Castle Hotel
NE66 3UN
☎ 01665 576111 01665 576203
e-mail: stay@dunstanburghcastlehotel.co.uk
Dir: *from A1, take B1340 to Denwick past Rennington & Masons Arms. Next right signed Embleton and into village*

This immaculately kept inn, a few minutes' walk from the sea, offers friendly hospitality and total guest care. Good food is served in both the restaurant and grill room, and two comfortable lounges include open fires in season. Accommodation is provided in comfortably appointed bedrooms.
ROOMS: 17 en suite (4 fmly) s £29-£39; d £58-£78 (incl. bkfst) **LB**
PARKING: 16 **NOTES:** No smoking in restaurant Closed Nov-Feb
CARDS:

EMPINGHAM, Rutland
Map 11 SK90

★★69% The White Horse Inn
Main St LE15 8PS
☎ 01780 460221 & 460521 01780 460521
e-mail: info@whitehorserutland.co.uk
Dir: *on A606, Oakham to Stamford road*
This attractive stone-built inn, offering bright, comfortable accommodation, is conveniently located just minutes from the A1. Bedrooms in the main building are spacious and include a number of family rooms. Public areas include a well-stocked bar, a bistro and restaurant where a wide range of meals are served.
ROOMS: 4 en suite 9 annexe en suite (3 fmly) (5 GF) No smoking in 1 bedroom s £45-£50; d £57-£65 (incl. bkfst) **LB** **FACILITIES:** Xmas
CONF: Thtr 60 Class 60 Board 34 Del from £65 **PARKING:** 60
NOTES: No smoking in restaurant **CARDS:**

Popped the question?
Hotels with Civ Wed in their entry are licensed for civil wedding ceremonies. Maximum numbers for the ceremony only are shown, e.g. Civ Wed 120

EMSWORTH, Hampshire Map 05 SU70

★★★66% Brookfield

Havant Rd PO10 7LF
☎ 01243 373363 📠 01243 376342
e-mail: bookings@brookfieldhotel.co.uk
Dir: *Emsworth junct off A27, onto A529. Hotel 0.5m on left*

This well-established family-run hotel has spacious public areas with popular conference and banqueting facilities. Bedrooms are in a modern style, and comfortably furnished. The popular Hermitage Restaurant offers a seasonally changing menu.

ROOMS: 40 en suite (4 fmly) (13 GF) No smoking in 20 bedrooms s £70-£75; d £90-£120 (incl. bkfst) **LB** **FACILITIES:** STV **CONF:** Thtr 100 Class 60 Board 40 Del from £125 **PARKING:** 80 **NOTES:** No dogs (ex guide dogs) Closed 25 Dec-1 Jan **CARDS:**

Restaurant with Rooms

36 on the Quay

47 South St PO10 7EG
☎ 01243 375592

Occupying a prime position on the Quay with far reaching views over the estuary, this 16th-century house is now home to the proprietor's accomplished and exciting cuisine. As would be expected the elegant restaurant occupies centre stage with peaceful pastel shades and crisp napery together with glimpses of the bustling harbour outside. The smart bedrooms offer style, comfort and thoughtful extras.

ROOMS: 4 en suite s £60-£80; d £80-£110 (incl. cont bkfst) **PARKING:** 6 **NOTES:** No smoking in restaurant Closed 1wk Jan **CARDS:**

Travelodge Chichester (West)

Travelodge

PO10 7RB
☎ 08700 850 950 📠 01243 370877
Dir: *on A27*

Travelodge offers good quality, good value, modern accommodation. Ideal for families, the spacious, en suite bedrooms include remote-control TV, tea and coffee-making facilities, luxury beds and free morning newspaper. Meals can be taken at the nearby family restaurant. For further details and the Travelodge phone number, consult the Hotel Groups page.

ROOMS: 36 en suite s fr £42.95; d fr £42.95

ENFIELD, Greater London Map 06 TQ39

★★★75% Royal Chace

The Ridgeway EN2 8AR
☎ 020 8884 8181 📠 020 8884 8150
e-mail: enquiries@royalchacehotel.co.uk
Dir: *M25 junct 24 take A1005 towards Enfield. Hotel 3m on right*

This professionally run, privately owned hotel enjoys a peaceful location with open fields to the rear. Refurbished public rooms are smartly appointed; the first floor Chace Brasserie is particularly appealing with its warm colour schemes, careful lighting, polished wood and friendly service. Bedrooms are well presented and thoughtfully equipped.

ROOMS: 92 en suite (2 fmly) (32 GF) No smoking in 34 bedrooms s £99-£195; d £115-£195 (incl. bkfst) **FACILITIES:** STV Outdoor swimming (H) Free access to local leisure centre **CONF:** Thtr 250 Class 100 Board 40 **PARKING:** 200 **NOTES:** No dogs (ex guide dogs) No smoking in restaurant Closed 24-30 Dec RS Restaurant closed lunchtime/Sun eve Civ Wed 220 **CARDS:**

★★74% Oak Lodge

80 Village Rd, Bush Hill Park EN1 2EU
☎ 020 8360 7082
e-mail: oaklodge@fsmail.net
Dir: *1 S of Enfield on A105*

This charming and privately-run hotel is located in a leafy, suburban area. Both the service and hospitality are particularly noteworthy and a warm welcome is offered to all guests. Bedrooms come in a variety of styles and sizes, each individually furnished; a ground floor 'Grade III' wheelchair friendly room is available. Public areas are inviting and comfortable, tastefully furnished.

ROOMS: 7 en suite (1 fmly) No smoking in 6 bedrooms s £70-£80; d £90-£110 (incl. bkfst) **FACILITIES:** Special arrangement with David Lloyd Sports Centre/Esporta entertainment Xmas **CONF:** Class 16 Board 16 **PARKING:** 4 **NOTES:** No smoking in restaurant **CARDS:**

★★65% Enfield

52 Rowantree Rd EN2 8PW
☎ 020 8366 3511 📠 020 8366 2432
e-mail: enfield@meridianleisure.com
Dir: *M25 junct 24, follow signs for A1005 towards Enfield, pass Hospital on left, down The Ridgeway, left into Bycullah Rd, 2nd left*

Situated in a quiet residential area on the edge of the town, this hotel offers well-equipped bedrooms. The public areas include a Grecian-style restaurant overlooking the attractive garden, a small bar and a cosy lounge. Meeting rooms and parking are also available.

ROOMS: 34 en suite (3 fmly) s £45-£65; d £65-£75 (incl. bkfst) **FACILITIES:** STV Sauna Xmas **CONF:** Thtr 75 Class 30 Board 25 Del from £115 **PARKING:** 18 **NOTES:** No dogs (ex guide dogs) No smoking in restaurant Civ Wed 75 **CARDS:**

Travel Inn

travel inn

Innova Park, Mollison Av EN3 7XY
☎ 0870 238 3306 📠 01992 707070
Dir: *M25 junct 25, take A10 towards London. Turn left at 1st lights onto Bullsmoor Ln, onto Mollison Av. Inn on right*

Travel Inn offers good-quality, value-for-money accommodation. Spacious, en suite rooms with bath and shower comfortably accommodate a family of up to two adults and two children (to age 15). The restaurant and bar offers a varied menu. For further details and the Travel Inn phone number, consult the Hotel Groups page.

ROOMS: 159 en suite s £49.95-£54.95; d £49.95-£54.95 **CONF:** Thtr 60 Board 26

E

EPSOM, Surrey

Map 06 TQ26

★★★72% Chalk Lane Hotel

Chalk Ln, Woodcote End KT18 7BB
☎ 01372 721179 01372 727878
e-mail: smcgregor@chalklanehotel.com
Dir: *from M25 junct 9 onto A24 to Epsom. Right at lights by BP garage. Left into Avenue Rd, right into Worple Rd. Left at T-junct & hotel on right*

This delightful, privately owned hotel is only a ten-minute walk from the racecourse. Staff are committed to providing a professional service and a warm and caring atmosphere. Bedrooms are mostly spacious, attractively furnished and thoughtfully equipped, while the smartly appointed restaurant offers an imaginative selection of dishes.
ROOMS: 22 en suite (1 fmly) s £85-£160; d £100-£160 (incl. bkfst) **FACILITIES:** STV Complimentary membership at local health club **CONF:** Thtr 140 Class 40 Board 30 Del £155 **PARKING:** 60 **NOTES:** No smoking in restaurant **CARDS:**

Premier Lodge (Epsom)

272 Kingston Rd, Ewell KT19 0SH
☎ 0870 9906466 0870 9906467
Dir: *on A240 between A3 & A24, 7m from M25 junct 8 & 9*
Premier Lodge offers modern, well-equipped, en suite accommodation suitable for both business and leisure travellers. Meals can be taken at the adjacent popular restaurant and bar, which is fully licensed. For further details, consult the Hotel Groups page.
ROOMS: 29 en suite s £56; d £56

Travel Inn

2-4 St Margarets Dr, Off Dorking Rd KT18 7LB
☎ 08701 977096 01372 739761
Dir: *M25 junct 9, A24 towards Epsom, Travel Inn on left*
Travel Inn offers good-quality, value-for-money accommodation. Spacious, en suite rooms with bath and shower comfortably accommodate a family of up to two adults and two children (to age 15). The restaurant and bar offers a varied menu. For further details and the Travel Inn phone number, consult the Hotel Groups page.
ROOMS: 40 en suite s £52.95-£54.95; d £52.95-£54.95 **CONF:** Thtr 40

ERMINGTON, Devon

Map 03 SX65

★★★66% Plantation House

Totnes Rd PL21 9NS
☎ 01548 831100 01548 831248
e-mail: enquiries@plantationhousehotel.com
Dir: *from A38 onto A3121 for 4.5m. Hotel on right past Ermington*
Transformed over recent years, this comfortable Georgian town house in the country offers a friendly atmosphere, comfortable accommodation and accomplished cooking. Dinner in the restaurant is a must for those who enjoy good food. The cities of Plymouth and Exeter are easily accessible as is all the beauty of the South Hams and Dartmoor.
ROOMS: 10 en suite (2 fmly) No smoking in all bedrooms **CONF:** Thtr 30 Class 20 Board 15 **PARKING:** 22 **NOTES:** No smoking in restaurant **CARDS:**

ESCRICK, North Yorkshire

Map 16 SE64

★★★72% Parsonage Country House

York Rd YO19 6LF
☎ 01904 728111 01904 728151
e-mail: reservations@parsonagehotel.co.uk
Dir: *next to St Helens Church on A19*

This former 19th-century parsonage has been lovingly restored and extended to provide delightful accommodation, set in well-tended gardens. Bedrooms are smartly appointed and well equipped for both business and leisure guests. Spacious public areas include an elegant restaurant, excellent meeting and conference facilities and a choice of attractive lounges.
ROOMS: 12 en suite 34 annexe en suite (4 fmly) (6 GF) No smoking in 30 bedrooms s fr £95; d fr £110 (incl. bkfst) **LB FACILITIES:** STV Xmas **CONF:** Thtr 160 Class 80 Board 50 Del from £120 **SERVICES:** Lift **PARKING:** 100 **NOTES:** No dogs (ex guide dogs) No smoking in restaurant Civ Wed 100 **CARDS:**

ESKDALE GREEN, Cumbria

Map 18 NY10

★★64% Bower House Inn

CA19 1TD
☎ 019467 23244 019467 23308
e-mail: Info@bowerhouseinn.freeserve.co.uk
Dir: *4m off A595 0.5m W of Eskdale Green*

This former farmhouse enjoys a countryside location with delightful mountain views and offers true peace and relaxation. The traditional bar and restaurant, where a good range of dishes

continued

are served, reflect the coaching inn origins of the house. Bedrooms are found in a smartly converted barn, in a secluded garden house and inside the original inn.
ROOMS: 5 en suite 19 annexe en suite (3 fmly) (9 GF) s £40-£53; d £68-£74 (incl. bkfst) **LB** **FACILITIES:** STV Xmas **CONF:** Thtr 40 Class 20 Board 30 Del £88 **PARKING:** 60 **NOTES:** No smoking in restaurant Civ Wed 60 **CARDS:**

EVERSHOT, Dorset

Map 04 ST50

Top 200 - Hotel

★★★ Summer Lodge

DT2 0JR
☎ 01935 83424 01935 83005
e-mail: enquiries@summerlodgehotel.com
Dir: *1m W of A37 halfway between Dorchester and Yeovil*

RELAIS & CHATEAUX

This picturesque hotel is situated in the heart of Dorset and is the ideal retreat for getting away from it all. A typical country house atmosphere prevails with a caring team of staff on hand to cater to guests' every need. Try to arrive for afternoon tea, which is a highlight of any visit. Bedrooms are individually decorated with excellent levels of comfort; most are spacious with views over the well-kept grounds.
ROOMS: 10 en suite 7 annexe en suite (2 fmly) (3 GF) s £95-£145; d £145-£305 (incl. bkfst) **LB** **FACILITIES:** Outdoor swimming (H) Tennis (hard & grass) Croquet lawn Xmas **CONF:** Thtr 20 Board 20 Del from £175 **PARKING:** 40 **NOTES:** No smoking in restaurant Civ Wed 60 **CARDS:**

EVESHAM, Worcestershire

Map 10 SP04

★★★★77% Wood Norton Hall

Wood Norton WR11 4YB
☎ 01386 425780 01386 425781
e-mail: info@wnhall.co.uk
Dir: *2m from Evesham on A44, after Chadbury*

Formerly owned and run by the BBC, this impressive Grade II listed Victorian house stands in a 170-acre estate and provides excellent accommodation along with fine cuisine. The bedrooms have all been thoughtfully furnished and include a wealth of extras. Bathrooms are particularly stylish. Oak-panelled public areas include a bar and a billiards room, while original photographs and sketches from the BBC archive grace the corridors (the hotel featured in an episode of Dr Who).
ROOMS: 15 en suite 30 annexe en suite (10 GF) No smoking in 40 bedrooms s £95-£160; d £130-£215 (incl. bkfst) **LB** **FACILITIES:** STV Tennis (hard) Fishing Squash Snooker Gym Croquet lawn Xmas **CONF:** BC Thtr 70 Class 35 Board 32 Del from £130 **PARKING:** 300 **NOTES:** No dogs (ex guide dogs) No smoking in restaurant Civ Wed 70 **CARDS:**

★★★75% The Evesham

Coopers Ln, Off Waterside WR11 1DA
☎ 01386 765566 & 0800 716969 (Res) 01386 765443
e-mail: reception@eveshamhotel.com
Dir: *Coopers Ln is off road alongside the River Avon*

Dating from 1540 and set in large grounds, this delightful hotel has well-equipped accommodation that includes a selection of quirkily themed rooms (Alice in Wonderland, Egyptian and Aquarium with a tropical fish tank in the bathroom). A reputation for food is well-deserved, with choice particularly strong for vegetarians, and children are welcome.
ROOMS: 39 en suite 1 annexe en suite (3 fmly) (11 GF) No smoking in 20 bedrooms s £74-£87; d £118 (incl. bkfst) **LB** **FACILITIES:** Indoor swimming (H) Croquet lawn Putting green ch fac **CONF:** Thtr 12 Class 12 Board 12 Del £128 **PARKING:** 50 **NOTES:** No smoking in restaurant Closed 25 & 26 Dec **CARDS:**

★★★69% Northwick Hotel

Best Western

Waterside WR11 6BT
☎ 01386 40322 01386 41070
Dir: *off A46 onto A44 over traffic lights and right at next set onto B4035. Past hospital, hotel on right opposite river*

Standing opposite the River Avon, this former coaching inn is within easy walking distance of the centre of Evesham. Bedrooms are tastefully decorated and well equipped, with one specially adapted for disabled guests. The refurbished public areas offer a choice of bars, meeting rooms and restaurant.
ROOMS: 31 en suite (4 fmly) No smoking in 15 bedrooms s £61-£71; d £85-£95 (incl. bkfst) **LB** **FACILITIES:** Hot air ballooning Clay pigeon shooting Archery Paint balling Xmas **CONF:** Thtr 240 Class 150 Board 80 Del from £110 **PARKING:** 200 **NOTES:** No smoking in restaurant Closed 23 Dec-3 Jan Civ Wed 70 **CARDS:**

★★73% Riverside

The Parks, Offenham Rd WR11 8JP
☎ 01386 446200 01386 40021
e-mail: info@theparksoffenham.freeserve.co.uk
Dir: *A46 follow signs for Offenham, right onto B4510(Offenham). Hotel, 0.5m on left along private drive The Parks*

This family owned and run hotel stands in three acres of gardens sloping down to the River Avon. The lounge, restaurant and many of the comfortable bedrooms overlook the river. Cooking remains one of the hotel's strong points, with a menu of imaginative dishes based on high-quality produce.
ROOMS: 7 en suite (5 GF) s £39-£49; d £78-£98 (incl. bkfst) **LB** **FACILITIES:** Fishing **PARKING:** 30 **NOTES:** No smoking in restaurant Closed 1-15 Jan **CARDS:**

EVESHAM, continued

⌂ Travel Inn

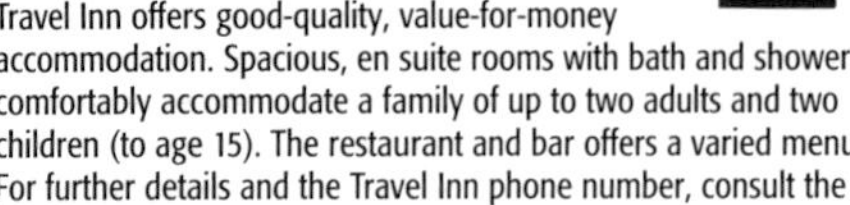

Evesham Country Park, A46 Trunk Rd
☎ 0870 238 3344 📠 0870 241 9000
Travel Inn offers good-quality, value-for-money accommodation. Spacious, en suite rooms with bath and shower comfortably accommodate a family of up to two adults and two children (to age 15). The restaurant and bar offers a varied menu. For further details and the Travel Inn phone number, consult the Hotel Groups page.
ROOMS: 40 en suite

EWEN, Gloucestershire — Map 04 SU09

★★66% ❀ Wild Duck Inn

Drakes Island GL7 6BY
☎ 01285 770310 📠 01285 770924
e-mail: wduckinn@aol.com
Dir: *from Cirencester take A429. At Kemble left to Ewen*

This bustling, ever-popular inn dates back to the early 16th century and is full of character. Open fires, old beams and rustic pine tables add to the charm in the bar and restaurant, where imaginative, robust cooking has earned a loyal following and well-deserved reputation. Bedrooms vary in style and are well equipped and tastefully furnished.
ROOMS: 11 en suite s fr £60; d fr £80 (incl. cont bkfst)
FACILITIES: Discounted leisure facilities within 3m **PARKING:** 50
NOTES: RS 25 Dec **CARDS:**

See advert under CIRENCESTER

EXETER, Devon — Map 03 SX99

Town House

★★★★ ❀ ⌂ Hotel Barcelona

Magdalen St EX2 4HY
☎ 01392 281000 📠 01392 281001
e-mail: info@aliasbarcelona.com
Dir: *from A30 Okehampton follow city centre signs. At Exe Bridges rdbt right for city centre, up hill, on at lights. Hotel on right*
Situated within walking distance of the city centre, Hotel Barcelona was formerly an eye hospital and has been totally transformed to provide stylish accommodation with a glamorous atmosphere. Public areas include Café Paradiso, an informal eatery with a varied menu, a night club, a range of meeting rooms and a delightful garden terrace ideal for al fresco dining.

ROOMS: 46 en suite No smoking in 3 bedrooms s £80; d £90-£110 **LB** **FACILITIES:** STV entertainment Xmas **CONF:** Thtr 65 Class 18 Board 22 Del from £130 **SERVICES:** Lift **PARKING:** 35 **NOTES:** No smoking in restaurant **CARDS:**

See advert on opposite page

★★★★69% The Southgate

MACDONALD HOTELS

Southernhay East EX1 1QF
☎ 0870 400 8333 📠 01392 413549
e-mail: southgate@macdonald-hotels.co.uk
Dir: *M5 J30, 3rd exit (Exeter), 2nd left towards city centre, 3rd exit at next rdbt, hotel 2m on right*
Centrally located and with excellent parking, The Southgate offers a diverse range of leisure and business facilities. Public areas are smart and spacious with comfortable seating in the bar and lounge; there is also a pleasant terrace. A range of bedroom sizes is available and all are well equipped with modern facilities.
ROOMS: 110 en suite (6 fmly) (13 GF) No smoking in 55 bedrooms s £83-£127; d £116-£146 (incl. bkfst) **LB** **FACILITIES: Spa** STV Indoor swimming (H) Sauna Solarium Gym Swimming pool supervised Xmas **CONF:** Thtr 150 Class 70 Board 50 **SERVICES:** Lift **PARKING:** 115 **NOTES:** No smoking in restaurant RS Sat (restaurant closed for lunch) Civ Wed 80 **CARDS:**

★★★73% ❀ Barton Cross Hotel & Restaurant

Huxham, Stoke Canon EX5 4EJ
☎ 01392 841245 📠 01392 841942
e-mail: bartonxhuxham@aol.com
Dir: *0.5m off A396 at Stoke Canon, 3m N of Exeter*
'17th-century charm combined with 21st-century luxury' perfectly sums up the appeal of this lovely countryside hotel. The eight bedrooms are spacious, tastefully decorated and well maintained. Public areas include the cosy first-floor lounge and the lounge/bar with its warming log fire. The restaurant offers a seasonally changing menu and consistently enjoyable cuisine.
ROOMS: 9 en suite (2 fmly) (2 GF) No smoking in 2 bedrooms s £69-£73; d £98-£108 (incl. bkfst) **LB** **FACILITIES:** STV ch fac Xmas **CONF:** Thtr 20 Class 20 Board 20 **PARKING:** 35 **NOTES:** No smoking in restaurant **CARDS:**

See advert on opposite page

★★★73% ❀❀ St Olaves Court Restaurant & Hotel

Mary Arches St EX4 3AZ
☎ 01392 217736 📠 01392 413054
e-mail: info@olaves.co.uk
Dir: *city centre, signed to Mary Arches Parking. Hotel entrance opposite car park entrance*
Only a short stroll from the cathedral and city centre and set in an attractive walled garden, St Olaves seems to be a country house in

continued

its almost hidden location. Bedrooms are comfortably furnished and full of character along with thoughtful extra touches. The daily changing menus offer imaginative cuisine and features West Country produce.

ROOMS: 15 en suite (2 fmly) (1 GF) No smoking in all bedrooms s £85-£105; d £95-£145 (incl. bkfst) **LB FACILITIES:** STV Xmas **CONF:** Thtr 45 Class 35 Board 35 Del from £100 **PARKING:** 15 **NOTES:** No smoking in restaurant Civ Wed 120 **CARDS:**

★★★72% **Lord Haldon Country House**

THE INDEPENDENTS

Dunchideock EX6 7YF

☎ 01392 832483 01392 833765

e-mail: enquiries@lordhaldonhotel.co.uk

Dir: *M5 junct 31or A30 signed to Ide, 2.5m through village. Left after phone box. 0.5m left after stone bridge*

Set amidst rural tranquility, this attractive country house goes from strength to strength. Guests are assured of a warm welcome from

continued on p226

EXETER, continued

the resident owners and the well-equipped bedrooms are comfortable, many with stunning views. Skilful cookery features on the daily changing menu, with most of the produce sourced locally.

Lord Haldon Country House, Exeter

ROOMS: 19 en suite (3 fmly) No smoking in 10 bedrooms s £55; d £85-£110 (incl. bkfst) **LB** **FACILITIES:** Xmas **CONF:** Thtr 300 Class 150 Board 60 Del £110 **PARKING:** 60 **NOTES:** No smoking in restaurant Civ Wed 120 **CARDS:**

See advert on page 225

★★★71% Devon

Exeter Bypass, Matford EX2 8XU

☎ 01392 259268 📠 01392 413142

e-mail: info@devonhotel.co.uk

Dir: *M5 junct 30, follow Marsh Barton Ind Est signs on A379, hotel on A38 rdbt*

Within easy access of the city centre, the M5 and the city's business parks, this smart Georgian hotel offers modern, comfortable accommodation. The 'Carriages' Bar and Brasserie is popular with guests and locals alike, offering a wide range of dishes as well as a carvery at both lunch and dinner. Service is friendly and attentive, and extensive meeting and business facilities are available.

ROOMS: 41 annexe en suite (3 fmly) (11 GF) s £52-£74; d £57-£74 **LB** **FACILITIES:** STV entertainment Xmas **CONF:** Thtr 150 Class 150 Board 150 **PARKING:** 250 **NOTES:** No smoking in restaurant Civ Wed 100 **CARDS:**

★★★69% ◎ Queens Court

Bystock Ter EX4 4HY

☎ 01392 272709 📠 01392 491390

e-mail: sales@queenscourt-hotel.co.uk

Dir: *M5 J30 to Middlemoor, follow sign for A377 Crediton. At clock tower rdbt exit to Crediton, 1st left, 1st left.*

Quietly located within walking distance of the city centre, this refurbished, privately owned hotel occupies early Victorian listed premises and provides friendly hospitality. The smart public areas and bedrooms are tastefully furnished in contemporary style. Rooms are available for conferences, meetings and other functions. The bright and attractive Olive Tree restaurant offers an interesting selection of Mediterranean influenced dishes.

ROOMS: 18 en suite (1 fmly) No smoking in 9 bedrooms s fr £59; d fr £64 **LB** **FACILITIES:** Xmas **CONF:** Thtr 80 Class 30 Board 40 Del from £120 **SERVICES:** Lift **NOTES:** No smoking in restaurant **CARDS:**

★★★67% Buckerell Lodge Hotel

Topsham Rd EX2 4SQ

☎ 01392 221111 📠 01392 491111

Dir: *M5 junct 30 follow city centre signs, hotel on Topsham Rd, 0.5m from Exeter*

Although situated outside the city centre, this hotel is easily accessed by car or public transport. Accommodation is comfortable, fairly spacious and generally quiet. Public areas include a variety of function rooms, a popular bar and restaurant and guests can also enjoy the attractive, extensive gardens.

ROOMS: 53 en suite (2 fmly) No smoking in 15 bedrooms s fr £99; d fr £125 **LB** **FACILITIES:** STV **CONF:** Thtr 80 Class 40 Board 40 **PARKING:** 60 **NOTES:** No smoking in restaurant Civ Wed 50 **CARDS:**

★★★67% ◎◎ *The Royal Clarence Hotel*

Cathedral Yard EX1 1HD

☎ 01392 319955 📠 01392 439423

Dir: *facing cathedral*

This historic, 14th-century building is a much-loved landmark in Exeter, situated opposite the magnificent cathedral. Bedrooms are full of character and range from compact to grand, some with views over the cathedral green. The hotel is known for its fine

continued

cuisine, in the Michael Caines' restaurant and more informal café bar or The Well House Tavern.
ROOMS: 56 en suite (6 fmly) No smoking in 16 bedrooms **CONF:** Thtr 120 Class 50 Board 50 **SERVICES:** Lift **PARKING:** 15 **NOTES:** No dogs (ex guide dogs) No smoking in restaurant Civ Wed 50
CARDS:

★★★64% Gipsy Hill

Gipsy Hill Ln, Pinn Ln, Monkerton EX1 3RN
☎ 01392 465252 🖹 01392 464302
e-mail: gipsyhill@bestwestern.co.uk
Dir: *3m E on B3181. From M5 junct 29, follow signs to Exeter to 1st rdbt, take 1st left into Pinn Ln. Hotel on right at brow of hill*
A popular hotel, just outside Exeter, and close to the M5 and the airport. Set in attractive, well-tended gardens with country views, the hotel offers a range of conference and function rooms, comfortable bedrooms and modern facilities. An intimate bar and lounge are next to the elegant restaurant.
ROOMS: 20 en suite 17 annexe en suite (5 fmly) No smoking in 6 bedrooms **FACILITIES:** STV **CONF:** Thtr 120 Class 55 Board 36 **PARKING:** 100 **NOTES:** No smoking in restaurant Closed 25-30 Dec Civ Wed 120 **CARDS:**

See advert on this page

★★64% Ebford House

Exmouth Rd EX3 0QH
☎ 01392 877658 🖹 01392 874424
e-mail: ebford@eclipse.co.uk
Dir: *1m E of Topsham on A376*
Set in pleasant, garden surroundings, this charming Georgian House is located halfway between Exeter and Exmouth and convenient for the motorway. Bedrooms vary in style and size and include many modern facilities. Home-cooked dishes are served in either the elegant dining room or the lower ground floor bistro.
ROOMS: 16 en suite (2 fmly) No smoking in 6 bedrooms **FACILITIES:** Sauna **CONF:** Thtr 40 Class 30 Board 25 **PARKING:** 45 **NOTES:** Closed 23 Dec-28 Dec **CARDS:**

★★62% *Red House*

2 Whipton Village Rd EX4 8AR
☎ 01392 256104 🖹 01392 666145
e-mail: red.house.hotel@eclipse.co.uk
Dir: *M5 junct 30. Left before Middlemoor services, right at rdbt towards Pinhoe & University. 0.75m left to Whipton/University, hotel 1m on right*

This hotel is located on the edge of the city, and offers an extensive menu, including a carvery, served either in the popular bar or in the adjacent dining room. The bedrooms are modern

continued

and well equipped, offering accommodation to suit all types of guest.
ROOMS: 12 en suite (2 fmly) No smoking in 8 bedrooms **FACILITIES:** STV **CONF:** Class 50 Board 20 **PARKING:** 28
CARDS:

⌂ Express by Holiday Inn Exeter

Guardian Rd EX1 3PE
☎ 01392 261000 🖹 01392 261061
e-mail: managerexeter@expressholidayinn.co.uk
Dir: *M5 junct 29, follow signs for Exeter city centre. Hotel on 1st rdbt*

A modern hotel ideal for families and business travellers. Fresh and uncomplicated, the spacious bedrooms include Sky TV, power shower and tea and coffee-making facilities. Continental buffet breakfast is included in the room rate; other meals may be taken at the nearby family pub or restaurant. For further details and the Express by Holiday Inn phone number, consult the Hotel Groups pages.
ROOMS: 122 en suite **CONF:** Thtr 32 Class 30 Board 24

EXETER, continued

⇧ Innkeeper's Lodge Exeter East

Clyst St George EX3 0QJ
☎ 01392 876121 📠 01392 872022
Dir: *M5 junct 30, A376 towards Exmouth. Right at 1st rdbt, straight over 2nd rdbt, at 3rd rdbt right into Bridge Hill, lodge on right*
A new concept in the travel accommodation market. Smart rooms meet essential business requirements but also have home comforts. Dining options include all-day menus plus the added advantage of breakfast, which is included in the room price. For further details, consult the Hotel Groups page.
ROOMS: 13 en suite **CONF:** Thtr 75 Class 45 Board 30

⇧ Travel Inn

398 Topsham Rd EX2 6HE
☎ 08701 977097 📠 01392 876174
Dir: *from M5 junct 30 and A30 junct 29. Follow signs for Exeter & Dawlish (A379). On dual carriageway take 2nd slip road on left at Countess Wear rdbt. Travel Inn next to Beefeater*
Travel Inn offers good-quality, value-for-money accommodation. Spacious, en suite rooms with bath and shower comfortably accommodate a family of up to two adults and two children (to age 15). The restaurant and bar offers a varied menu. For further details and the Travel Inn phone number, consult the Hotel Groups page.
ROOMS: 44 en suite s £44.95; d £44.95

⇧ Travelodge

Moor Ln, Sandygate EX2 7HF
☎ 08700 850 950 📠 01392 410406
Dir: *M5 junct 30*
Travelodge offers good quality, good value, modern accommodation. Ideal for families, the spacious, en suite bedrooms include remote-control TV, tea and coffee-making facilities, luxury beds and free morning newspaper. Meals can be taken at the nearby family restaurant. For further details and the Travelodge phone number, consult the Hotel Groups page.
ROOMS: 102 en suite s fr £42.95; d fr £42.95 **CONF:** Thtr 80 Class 18 Board 25

EXFORD, Somerset — Map 03 SS83

★★★71% ◎◎ Crown

TA24 7PP
☎ 01643 831554 📠 01643 831665
e-mail: info@crownhotelexmoor.co.uk
Dir: *M5 junct 25, follow Taunton signs. Take A358 out of Taunton, then B3224 via Wheddon Cross into Exford*

Guest comfort is certainly a hallmark at the Crown Hotel. Afternoon teas served in the lounge beside a roaring fire and

continued

tempting menus in the bar and restaurant are all part of the charm of this delightful old coaching inn which specialises in breaks for shooting and other country sports. Bedrooms retain a traditional style yet offer a range of modern comforts and facilities, many with views of the pretty moorland village.
ROOMS: 17 en suite No smoking in 3 bedrooms s fr £55; d fr £95 (incl. bkfst) **LB FACILITIES:** Fishing Riding Shooting, Riding Xmas **CONF:** BC Del from £120 **PARKING:** 30 **NOTES:** No smoking in restaurant
CARDS:

See advert on opposite page

EXMOUTH, Devon — Map 03 SY08

★★★68% Royal Beacon

The Beacon EX8 2AF
☎ 01395 264886 📠 01395 268890
e-mail: reception@royalbeaconhotel.co.uk
Dir: *From M5 take A376 and Marine Way. Follow seafront signs. On Imperial Rd turn left at T-junct then 1st right. Hotel 100yds on left*

This elegant Georgian property sits in an elevated position overlooking the town and has fine views of the estuary towards the sea. Bedrooms are individually styled and many have sea views. Public areas include a well stocked bar, cosy lounge, impressive function suite and restaurant, where freshly prepared and enjoyable cuisine is offered.
ROOMS: 30 en suite (2 fmly) No smoking in 10 bedrooms s £40-£60; d £80-£100 (incl. bkfst) **LB FACILITIES:** Xmas **CONF:** Thtr 150 Class 100 Board 40 Del from £79 **SERVICES:** Lift **PARKING:** 10 **NOTES:** No smoking in restaurant Civ Wed 150
CARDS:

See advert on opposite page

★★71% *Barn*

Foxholes Hill, Marine Dr EX8 2DF
☎ 01395 224411 📠 01395 225445
e-mail: Info@barnhotel.co.uk
Dir: *M5 junct 30 take A376 to Exmouth, then signs to seafront. At rdbt last exit into Foxholes Hill. Hotel on right*
This unique Grade II listed property is quietly situated just a couple of minutes' walk from the beach. Views across the bay from the elegant public areas and most of the bedrooms are breathtaking. Akin to that of a country house hotel, the atmosphere here is relaxed and hospitable.
ROOMS: 11 en suite (4 fmly) No smoking in all bedrooms
FACILITIES: Outdoor swimming Putting green **CONF:** Class 40 Board 20
PARKING: 24 **NOTES:** No dogs No smoking in restaurant Closed 23 Dec-10 Jan **CARDS:**

Packed in a hurry?
Ironing facilities should be available at all star levels, either in rooms or on request

★★65% ***Manor***
The Beacon EX8 2AG
☎ 01395 272549 & 274477 📠 01395 225519
e-mail: post@manorexmouth.co.uk
Dir: *M5 junct 30 take A376 to Exmouth. Hotel 300yds from seafront by Tourist Information Office*
Conveniently located for easy access to the town centre and with views overlooking the sea, this friendly, family-run hotel offers traditional values of hospitality and service, which draws guests back year after year. The well-equipped bedrooms vary in style and size; many have far-reaching views. The fixed price menu offers a varied selection of dishes.
ROOMS: 38 en suite (3 fmly) **CONF:** Thtr 100 Class 40 Board 40 **SERVICES:** Lift **PARKING:** 15 **NOTES:** No dogs (ex guide dogs) No smoking in restaurant **CARDS:**

★★63% **Cavendish Hotel**
11 Morton Crescent, The Esplanade EX8 1BE
☎ 01395 272528 📠 01395 269361
Leisureplex
e-mail: cavendish.exmouth@alfatravel.co.uk
Dir: *follow seafront signs, hotel in centre of large crescent*
Situated on the seafront, this terraced hotel attracts many groups from around the country. With fine views out to sea, the hotel is within walking distance of the town centre. The bedrooms are neatly presented; front facing rooms are always popular. Entertainment is provided on some evenings during the summer.
ROOMS: 72 en suite (3 fmly) (19 GF) s £27-£36; d £46-£64 (incl. bkfst) **LB FACILITIES:** Snooker entertainment Xmas **CONF:** Thtr 30 Board 12 **SERVICES:** Lift **PARKING:** 25 **NOTES:** No dogs (ex guide dogs) No smoking in restaurant Closed Dec-Jan ex Xmas RS Nov & Mar
CARDS:

FAIRFORD, Gloucestershire Map 05 SP10

★★66% Bull Hotel
The Market Place GL7 4AA
☎ 01285 712535 & 712217 ▯ 01285 713782
e-mail: info@thebullhotelfairford.co.uk
Dir: *on A417 in market square adjacent to post office*
Located in a picturesque Cotswold market town, this family-run inn can trace its history back to the 15th century and still retains much period character and charm. A wide range of meals can be enjoyed either within the popular bar or alternatively in the bistro restaurant. Bedrooms are all individual in style with a number overlooking the square.
ROOMS: 22 rms (20 en suite) 4 annexe en suite (4 fmly) s £49.50-£69.50; d £79.50-£99.50 (incl. bkfst) **LB FACILITIES:** Fishing Cycle hire **CONF:** Thtr 60 Class 40 Board 40 Del £82.50 **PARKING:** 10 **NOTES:** No smoking in restaurant **CARDS:**

See advert on page 229

FAKENHAM, Norfolk Map 13 TF92

★★71% *Crown*
6 Market Place NR21 9BP
☎ 01328 851418 ▯ 01328 862433
Dir: *A148, A1065 or A1065 to Fakenham town centre, follow signs to Market Place*

Once a 17th-century coaching inn, this friendly family run hotel is situated in the town centre. Bedrooms are attractively decorated with co-ordinated furnishings and many thoughtful touches. Public rooms include a comfortable lounge bar where an interesting choice of freshly made dishes is available, or guests can choose from the creative menu in the smart restaurant.
ROOMS: 12 en suite (2 fmly) No smoking in 1 bedroom **FACILITIES:** Garage lock up for bicycles **CONF:** Class 35 Board 22 **PARKING:** 25 **NOTES:** No dogs (ex guide dogs) Closed 25 Dec **CARDS:**

FALMOUTH, Cornwall & Isles of Scilly Map 02 SW83
See also Mawnan Smith

★★★★70% Royal Duchy
Cliff Rd TR11 4NX
☎ 01326 313042 ▯ 01326 319420
e-mail: info@royalduchy.com
Dir: *on Cliff Rd, along Falmouth seafront*
Looking out over the sea and towards Pendennis Castle, this hotel provides a friendly environment. The public rooms are well appointed and leisure facilities and meeting rooms are available as well as a comfortable lounge and cocktail bar. The restaurant serves carefully prepared dishes and bedrooms vary in size and aspect, with many rooms having sea views.

ROOMS: 43 en suite (6 fmly) (1 GF) s £67-£93; d £126-£216 (incl. bkfst) **LB FACILITIES: Spa** STV Indoor swimming (H) Sauna Table tennis entertainment ch fac Xmas **CONF:** Thtr 50 Class 50 Board 50 **SERVICES:** Lift **PARKING:** 50 **NOTES:** No dogs (ex guide dogs) Civ Wed 100 **CARDS:**

See advert on opposite page

★★★75% Penmere Manor
Mongleath Rd TR11 4PN
☎ 01326 211411 ▯ 01326 317588
e-mail: reservations@penmere.co.uk
Dir: *right off A39 at Hillhead rdbt, over double mini rdbt. After 0.75m left into Mongleath Rd*

Set in five acres of lovely grounds on the outskirts of Falmouth, this family-owned hotel offers friendly service and a range of facilities. Cuisine offers a choice of freshly prepared dishes served in either the bar, or in the more formal Bolitho's Restaurant. A wide range of bedrooms is available, and the spacious garden wing rooms are furnished and equipped to a particularly high standard.
ROOMS: 37 en suite (12 fmly) (13 GF) No smoking in all bedrooms s £58-£67; d £90-£108 (incl. bkfst) **LB FACILITIES: Spa** STV Indoor swimming (H) Outdoor swimming (H) Sauna Solarium Gym Croquet lawn Jacuzzi Beauty treatment room, Boules Xmas **CONF:** Thtr 60 Class 20 Board 30 Del from £107 **PARKING:** 50 **NOTES:** No smoking in restaurant Closed 24-27 Dec Civ Wed 80
CARDS:

See advert on opposite page

> Popped the question?
> Hotels with Civ Wed in their entry are licensed for civil wedding ceremonies. Maximum numbers for the ceremony only are shown, e.g. Civ Wed 120

A PLACE OF PEACE AND BEAUTY

...where the gardens sweep down to the sea

***Family run** Country House Hotel specialists in local seafood, traditional service, cosseted comforts, antiques, log fires and fresh flowers.*

Meudon

GOLF IS FREE

Please see full entry under Mawnan Smith

Tel 01 326 250541 • Fax 250543

www.meudon.co.uk

Falmouth's Only 4-star Hotel

Situated in a prime location on Falmouth's seafront, The Royal Duchy Hotel enjoys panoramic views across Falmouth's famous bay.
Renowned cuisine is matched by the hotel's lavish accommodation. Every bedroom enjoys private bathroom en-suite, colour television with satellite reception and direct dial telephone. A lift provides easy access to all floors.
Facilities include heated indoor swimming pool complex with sauna, solarium, spa bath and family games room.

AA ★★★★

FOR A FREE COLOUR BROCHURE & BREAKS TARIFFS, PLEASE CONTACT: Mr D. Reburn,
The Royal Duchy Hotel, Cliff Road, Falmouth, Cornwall TR11 4NX
Tel: (01326) 313042 Fax: (01326) 319420
www.royalduchy.co.uk
Email: info@royalduchy.co.uk

The Westcountry's Leading Hotel Group

An oasis of gracious living in 5 acres of gardens and woodland offering the last word in comfort, friendliness and attentive service, a real home away from home.

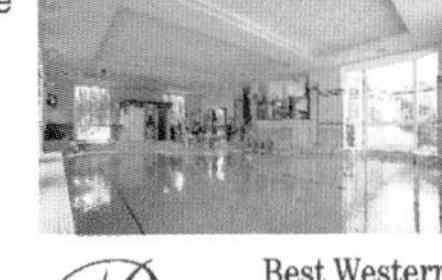

Best Western

Penmere MANOR

FALMOUTH, CORNWALL UK

Mongleath Road, Falmouth,
Cornwall TR11 4PN
FREEPHONE 0800 980 4611
Web: www.penmere.co.uk
Email: reservations@penmere.co.uk

FALMOUTH, continued

★★★72% Falmouth Beach Resort Hotel

Gyllyngvase Beach, Seafront TR11 4NA
☎ 01326 310500 📠 01326 319147
e-mail: info@falmouthbeachhotel.co.uk
Dir: *A39 to Falmouth, follow seafront signs.*

Enjoying wonderful views, this popular hotel is situated opposite the beach and within easy walking distance of Falmouth's attractions and port. A friendly atmosphere is maintained and guests have many choices, with leisure and fitness, entertainment and dining options. Bedrooms, many with balconies and sea views, are well equipped and comfortable.
ROOMS: 116 en suite 7 annexe en suite (20 fmly) (4 GF) No smoking in 94 bedrooms s £64-£94; d £98-£147 (incl. bkfst) **LB** **FACILITIES: Spa** STV Indoor swimming (H) Tennis (hard) Sauna Solarium Gym Jacuzzi Steam room, Swimming pool supervised entertainment Xmas **CONF:** Thtr 300 Class 200 Board 250 Del from £79.50 **SERVICES:** Lift **PARKING:** 88 **NOTES:** No smoking in restaurant Civ Wed 250 **CARDS:**

See advert on page 231

★★★72% ⊛ The Greenbank

Harbourside TR11 2SR
☎ 01326 312440 📠 01326 211362
e-mail: sales@greenbank-hotel.com
Dir: *500yds past Falmouth Marina on Penryn River*

Offering very much a maritime theme, this smart hotel is located close to the marina and has its own private 17th-century quay. Set at the water's edge, the lounge, restaurant and many bedrooms have harbour views. The restaurant offers a choice of interesting dishes featuring fresh local produce.
ROOMS: 60 en suite (4 fmly) No smoking in 30 bedrooms s £60-£85; d £95-£165 (incl. bkfst) **LB** **FACILITIES:** Private beach **CONF:** Thtr 60 Class 45 Board 20 **SERVICES:** Lift **PARKING:** 68 **NOTES:** No smoking in restaurant Civ Wed 80 **CARDS:**

★★★72% Green Lawns

Western Ter TR11 4QJ
☎ 01326 312734 📠 01326 211427
e-mail: info@greenlawnshotel.com
Dir: *on A39*

This attractive property enjoys a convenient location close to the town centre and within easy reach of the sea. Spacious, extensive public areas include inviting lounges, an elegant restaurant, conference and meeting facilities and a leisure centre. Bedrooms vary in size and style and all are well equipped and comfortable. Friendly service is a highlight.
ROOMS: 39 en suite (8 fmly) No smoking in 8 bedrooms s £60-£110; d £110-£170 (incl. bkfst) **LB** **FACILITIES:** Indoor swimming (H) Tennis (hard & grass) Squash Sauna Solarium Gym Jacuzzi Swimming pool cameras entertainment **CONF:** Thtr 200 Class 80 Board 100 **PARKING:** 69 **NOTES:** No smoking in restaurant Closed 24-30 Dec Civ Wed 60 **CARDS:**

See advert on opposite page

★★★68% Falmouth

Castle Beach TR11 4NZ
☎ 01326 312671 & 0800 0193121 📠 01326 319533
e-mail: info@falmouthhotel.com
Dir: *take A30 to Truro then A390 to Falmouth. Follow signs for beaches, hotel on seafront near Pendennis Castle*

This spectacular beachfront Victorian property affords wonderful sea views from many of its comfortable bedrooms, some which boast their own balconies. Spacious, public areas include a number of inviting lounges; beautiful leafy grounds, a choice of dining options and an impressive range of leisure facilities complete the picture.
ROOMS: 69 en suite 34 annexe en suite (13 fmly) No smoking in 18 bedrooms s £38-£44; d £60-£70 **LB** **FACILITIES:** STV Indoor swimming (H) Snooker Sauna Solarium Gym Putting green Jacuzzi Beauty Salon, Swimming pool supervised **CONF:** Thtr 250 Class 150 Board 100 **SERVICES:** Lift **PARKING:** 175 **NOTES:** No smoking in restaurant Closed 22 Dec-1 Jan Civ Wed 250 **CARDS:**

See advert on opposite page

★★★67% St Michaels of Falmouth
Gyllyngvase Beach, Seafront TR11 4NB
☎ 01326 312707 📠 01326 211772
e-mail: info@stmichaelshotel.com
Dir: *A39 into Falmouth, follow beach signs, at 2nd mini-rdbt into Pennance Rd. Take 2nd left & 2nd left again*

Currently refurbishing, St Michaels is in an excellent location, overlooking the sea and small bay. Spacious public areas include a lounge with super views, landscaped gardens and a leisure centre. Bedrooms vary in size and style and some benefit from sea views.
ROOMS: 57 en suite 8 annexe en suite (7 fmly) No smoking in 15 bedrooms s £35-£80; d £70-£150 (incl. bkfst) **LB FACILITIES:** Indoor swimming (H) Sauna Solarium Gym Croquet lawn Jacuzzi Concessionary golf rates Xmas **CONF:** Thtr 200 Class 150 Board 50 Del from £74 **PARKING:** 30 **NOTES:** No dogs (ex guide dogs) No smoking in restaurant Civ Wed 80 **CARDS:**

See advert on this page

FALMOUTH, continued

★★★66% Penmorvah Manor
Budock Water TR11 5ED
☎ 01326 250277 01326 250509
e-mail: reception@penmorvah.co.uk
Dir: *A39 to Hillhead rdbt, take 2nd exit. Right at Falmouth Football Club, through Budock and hotel opposite Penjerrick Gardens*

Situated within two miles of central Falmouth, this extended Victorian manor house is a peaceful hideaway, set in six acres of private woodland and gardens. Penmorvah is well positioned to visit the local gardens, and offers many garden-touring breaks. Dinner features locally sourced quality ingredients such as Cornish cheeses, meat fish and game.
ROOMS: 27 en suite (1 fmly) (10 GF) No smoking in all bedrooms s fr £60; d fr £90 (incl. bkfst) **LB** **FACILITIES:** Pool table Xmas **CONF:** Thtr 250 Class 100 Board 56 Del from £95 **PARKING:** 150 **NOTES:** No smoking in restaurant Closed 31 Dec - 31 Jan **CARDS:**

★★71% Crill Manor
Maen Valley, Budock Water TR11 5BL
☎ 01326 211880 01326 211229
e-mail: info@crillmanor.com
Dir: *A39 Truro towards Falmouth, then right for Mawnan Smith/Budock Water. Over double mini rdbt. Through village to 40mph sign then left*
Set in a secluded Area of Outstanding Natural Beauty, this delightful hotel offers friendly and attentive service. Bedrooms are well equipped and attractively decorated. An open plan lounge and bar area, overlooks the gardens. Dining offers a daily changing menu.
ROOMS: 12 en suite 2 annexe en suite (2 GF) No smoking in all bedrooms s £41-£57; d £82-£114 (incl. bkfst) **LB** **FACILITIES:** Xmas **PARKING:** 14 **NOTES:** No children 10yrs No smoking in restaurant **CARDS:**

★★68% *Broadmead*
66-68 Kimberley Park Rd TR11 2DD
☎ 01326 315704 & 318036 01326 311048
e-mail: broadmeadhotel@aol.com
Dir: *follow A39 into Falmouth and signs for town centre. At lights by Jaguar/Saab showroom left, hotel 100mtrs on left*
Conveniently located within easy walking distance of the beaches and town centre, this pleasant, family-run hotel offers smart and comfortable accommodation. Bedrooms are well equipped and attractively decorated. A choice of lounges is available and, fixed price and carte menus are offered.
ROOMS: 12 en suite (1 fmly) **PARKING:** 8 **NOTES:** No dogs No children 8yrs No smoking in restaurant Closed 13 Dec-13 Jan **CARDS:**

THE CIRCLE Selected Individual Hotels GREAT BRITAIN

★★67% Hotel Anacapri
Gyllyngvase Rd TR11 4DJ
☎ 01326 311454 01326 311454
e-mail: anacapri@btconnect.com
In an elevated position overlooking Gyllyngvase Beach and Falmouth Bay, this family run establishment extends a warm welcome. Bedrooms all share similar standards of comfort and quality, and the majority have sea views. There is a convivial bar, lounge and smart restaurant, where carefully prepared and enjoyable cuisine is offered.
ROOMS: 16 en suite (1 fmly) No smoking in 8 bedrooms s £35-£50; d £65-£80 (incl. bkfst) **LB** **PARKING:** 20 **NOTES:** No dogs No children 8yrs No smoking in restaurant **CARDS:**

★★67% Park Grove
Kimberley Park Rd TR11 2DD
☎ 01326 313276 01326 211926
e-mail: reception@parkgrovehotel.com
Dir: *off A39 at lights by Riders Garage towards harbour. Hotel 400yds on left opp park*
Within walking distance of the town centre, this friendly family-run hotel is situated in a pleasant residential area opposite Kimberly Park. Comfortable accommodation is provided and public areas include a relaxing and stylish lounge and well-spaced dining room and bar. Bedrooms, many now refurbished, are also comfortable and well equipped.
ROOMS: 17 en suite (6 fmly) s £33-£37; d £66-£74 (incl. bkfst) **LB** **PARKING:** 25 **NOTES:** No dogs (ex guide dogs) No smoking in restaurant Closed Dec-Feb **CARDS:**

THE INDEPENDENTS

★★64% Madeira Hotel
Cliff Rd TR11 4NY
☎ 01326 313531 01326 319143
e-mail: madeira.falmouth@alfatravel.co.uk
Dir: *A39 Truro to Falmouth, follow tourist signs "Hotels" to sea front*
This popular hotel offers splendid sea-views and a pleasantly convenient location, which is close to the town. Extensive sun lounges are popular haunts in which to enjoy the views, whilst additional facilities include an oak panelled cocktail bar. Bedrooms, many recently redecorated and with sea-views, are available in a range of sizes.
ROOMS: 50 en suite (8 fmly) (7 GF) s £28-£34; d £48-£66 (incl. bkfst) **LB** **FACILITIES:** entertainment Xmas **SERVICES:** Lift **PARKING:** 11 **NOTES:** No dogs (ex guide dogs) No smoking in restaurant Closed Dec-Feb RS Nov & Mar **CARDS:**

Leisureplex

★★64% Rosslyn
110 Kimberley Park Rd TR11 2JJ
☎ 01326 312699 01326 312699
e-mail: mail@rosslynhotel.co.uk
Dir: *on A39 towards Falmouth to Hillend rdbt, right and over next mini rdbt. At 2nd mini rdbt left into Trescobeas Rd. Hotel on left past hospital*
A relaxed and friendly atmosphere is maintained at this family run hotel. Situated on the northern edge of Falmouth, the Rosslynn is easily located and is suitable for either business or leisure guests. A comfortable lounge overlooks the well-tended garden, and in the spacious restaurant, freshly prepared dinners are enjoyable.
ROOMS: 27 rms (23 en suite) (2 fmly) (6 GF) No smoking in all bedrooms s £25-£35; d £50-£70 (incl. bkfst) **LB** **FACILITIES:** Putting green Table tennis Pool table Xmas **CONF:** Class 60 **PARKING:** 15 **NOTES:** No smoking in restaurant **CARDS:**

★★63% ***Membly Hall***
Sea Front, Cliff Rd TR11 4NT
☎ 01326 312869 & 311115 📠 01326 211751
e-mail: memblyhallhotel@btopenworld.com
Dir: *A39 to Falmouth. Follow seafront and beaches sign.*

Located conveniently on the seafront and enjoying sea views, this family run hotel offers friendly service. Bedrooms are pleasantly spacious and well equipped. Carefully prepared and enjoyable meals are served in the spacious dining room. Live entertainment is provided on some evenings in the attractive lounge bar area and there is also a sunroom.
ROOMS: 37 en suite (3 fmly) **FACILITIES:** STV Putting green Indoor short bowls Table tennis Pool table entertainment **CONF:** Thtr 150 Class 130 Board 60 **SERVICES:** Lift **PARKING:** 30 **NOTES:** No smoking in restaurant Closed Xmas week RS Dec-Jan

FAREHAM, Hampshire Map 05 SU50

★★★★72% ® **Solent**
Rookery Av, Whiteley PO15 7AJ
☎ 01489 880000 📠 01489 880007
e-mail: solent@shirehotels.co.uk
Dir: *M27 junct 9, hotel on Solent Business Park*

Although close to the M27, this smart, purpose-built hotel enjoys a peaceful location. Bedrooms are very spacious and well appointed. The well-equipped leisure centre and spa has a loyal following, as does the restaurant with an open log fire and beams. *Shire Hotels – AA Hotels Group of the Year 2003-2004.*
ROOMS: 111 en suite (9 fmly) (20 GF) No smoking in 80 bedrooms s £85-£135; d £120-£155 (incl. bkfst) **LB FACILITIES: Spa** STV Indoor swimming (H) Tennis (hard) Squash Sauna Solarium Gym Steam room, Childrens splash pool, Swimming pool supervised Xmas **CONF:** BC Thtr 250 Class 120 Board 80 Del from £105 **SERVICES:** Lift **PARKING:** 200 **NOTES:** No dogs (ex guide dogs) No smoking in restaurant Civ Wed **CARDS:**

See advert on this page

★★★66% ® **Lysses House**
51 High St PO16 7BQ
☎ 01329 822622 📠 01329 822762
e-mail: lysses@lysses.co.uk
Dir: *M27 junct 11 stay in left lane. At rdbt 3rd exit into East St and follow into High St. Hotel at top on right*
This attractive Georgian hotel is situated on the edge of the town in a quiet location and provides spacious and well-equipped accommodation. There are conference facilities and a lounge bar serving a range of snacks, whilst public areas have benefited from an extensive refurbishment. Cuisine in the Richmond Restaurant is both accomplished and imaginative.
ROOMS: 21 en suite (7 GF) s £50-£75; d £75-£95 (incl. bkfst) **CONF:** Thtr 95 Class 42 Board 28 Del from £112.50 **SERVICES:** Lift **PARKING:** 30 **NOTES:** No dogs (ex guide dogs) No smoking in restaurant Closed 25 Dec-1 Jan RS 24 Dec Civ Wed 95 **CARDS:**

U ***Holiday Inn Fareham***
Cartwright Dr, Titchfield PO15 5RJ
☎ 0870 400 9028 📠 01329 844666
e-mail: fareham@ichotelsgroup.com
Dir: *M27 junct 9, follow signs for A27. Over Segensworth rdbt 1.5m, left at next rdbt*

At the time of going to press, the classification for this hotel was not confirmed. Please refer to the AA internet site www.theAA.com for current information.
ROOMS: 125 en suite (25 fmly) No smoking in 78 bedrooms **FACILITIES:** Indoor swimming (H) Sauna Solarium Gym Jacuzzi Childrens play area **CONF:** Thtr 160 Class 80 Board 50 **PARKING:** 167 **NOTES:** No smoking in restaurant **CARDS:**

FAREHAM, continued

⌂ Travel Inn
Southampton Rd, Park Gate SO31 6AF
☎ 08701 977100 🖷 01489 577238
Dir: *on 2nd rdbt off M27 junct 9, signed A27 Fareham*
Travel Inn offers good-quality, value-for-money accommodation. Spacious, en suite rooms with bath and shower comfortably accommodate a family of up to two adults and two children (to age 15). The restaurant and bar offers a varied menu. For further details and the Travel Inn phone number, consult the Hotel Groups page.
ROOMS: 41 en suite s £44.95; d £44.95

FARINGDON, Oxfordshire
Map 05 SU29

★★★71% ⊛ Sudbury House Hotel & Conference Centre

London St SN7 8AA
☎ 01367 241272 🖷 01367 242346
e-mail: stay@sudburyhouse.co.uk
Dir: *off A420, signposted Folly Hill*

Sudbury House lies between Oxford and Swindon. Bedrooms are attractive, decorated in warm colour schemes, spacious and well equipped. Dining options include the restaurant, bar and a comprehensive room service menu. In addition to pleasant grounds, conference facilities, a small fitness room and private dining rooms are also available.
ROOMS: 49 en suite (2 fmly) (10 GF) No smoking in 22 bedrooms s £70-£110; d £80-£120 (incl. bkfst) **LB FACILITIES:** STV Gym Croquet lawn Putting green Pitch & Putt, Badminton, Boules Xmas **CONF:** Thtr 90 Class 90 Board 40 Del £142 **SERVICES:** Lift **PARKING:** 100 **NOTES:** No smoking in restaurant Civ Wed 150
CARDS:

See advert on opposite page

FARNBOROUGH, Hampshire
Map 05 SU85

★★★67% Falcon
68 Farnborough Rd GU14 6TH
☎ 01252 545378 🖷 01252 522539
e-mail: hotel@falconfarnborough.com
Dir: *on A325*
This well presented hotel is conveniently located for business guests. The modern bedrooms are practically furnished and equipped with a useful range of extras. Public areas include the conservatory restaurant and the bar and lounge, which are smartly decorated. Aircraft enthusiasts are well catered for with the adjacent aeronautical centre.
ROOMS: 30 en suite (1 fmly) (3 GF) s £55-£90; d £65-£105 (incl. bkfst) **FACILITIES:** STV Xmas **CONF:** Thtr 25 Class 8 Board 16 Del from £85 **PARKING:** 25 **NOTES:** No dogs (ex guide dogs) No smoking in restaurant RS 23 Dec - 4 Jan Civ Wed 50
CARDS:

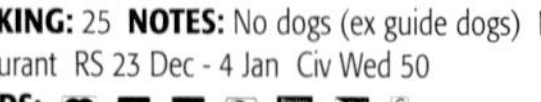

U *Holiday Inn Farnborough*
Lynchford Rd GU14 6AZ
☎ 0870 400 9029 🖷 01252 377210
Dir: *M3 junct 4, follow A325 through Farnborough towards Aldershot. Hotel on left at The Queen's rdbt*
At the time of going to press, the classification for this hotel was not confirmed. Please refer to the AA internet site www.theAA.com for current information.
ROOMS: 143 en suite (39 fmly) No smoking in 80 bedrooms **FACILITIES:** Indoor swimming (H) Sauna Solarium Gym Jacuzzi Health & fitness centre **CONF:** Thtr 180 Class 80 Board 60 **PARKING:** 175 **NOTES:** No dogs (ex guide dogs) **CARDS:**

⌂ Travel Inn
Ively Rd, Southwood GU14 0JP
☎ 08701 977101 🖷 01252 546427
Dir: *2m from M3 junct 4A towards Farnborough, next to Golf Club*
Travel Inn offers good-quality, value-for-money accommodation. Spacious, en suite rooms with bath and shower comfortably accommodate a family of up to two adults and two children (to age 15). The restaurant and bar offers a varied menu. For further details and the Travel Inn phone number, consult the Hotel Groups page.
ROOMS: 62 en suite s £44.95; d £44.95

FARNHAM, Surrey
Map 05 SU84
See also Churt

★★★74% ⊛⊛ Bishop's Table
27 West St GU9 7DR
☎ 01252 710222 🖷 01252 733494
e-mail: welcome@bishopstable.com
Dir: *from M3 junct 4 take A331 or from A3 take A31and follow town centre signs. Hotel next to library*
This family-run Georgian townhouse hotel is in the centre of town and offers comfortable accommodation, friendly and attentive service and good food. Bedrooms, some of which occupy a restored coach house, are all individual in style and tastefully appointed. Public areas include a cosy bar and an elegant restaurant offering an interesting range of quality well-executed dishes.
ROOMS: 9 en suite 8 annexe en suite (6 GF) No smoking in 5 bedrooms s £95-£105; d £95-£165 **LB FACILITIES:** free use of nearby gym **CONF:** BC Thtr 26 Class 10 Board 20 Del from £133 **NOTES:** No dogs (ex guide dogs) No children 16yrs No smoking in restaurant Closed 25 Dec-3 Jan RS Closed for lunch Mon **CARDS:**

See advert on opposite page

★★★70% Frensham Pond Hotel
Bacon Ln GU10 2QB
☎ 01252 795161 🖷 01252 792631
e-mail: frenshampond@bestwestern.co.uk
(For full entry see Churt & advert on opposite page)

★★★65% The Bush
The Borough GU9 7NN
☎ 0870 400 8225 🖷 01252 733530
e-mail: bush@macdonald-hotels.co.uk
Dir: *A31 and follow signs for town centre. At x-rds left, hotel on right*
Dating back to the 17th century, this coaching inn is attractively presented and has a courtyard and an extensive garden. The bedrooms are well appointed, with quality fabrics and good facilities. The public areas include the Oak Lounge and a smart

continued

cocktail bar; a new restaurant was planned at the time of our last inspection.
ROOMS: 83 en suite (20 GF) No smoking in 48 bedrooms s £50-£145; d £100-£165 (incl. bkfst) **LB** **FACILITIES:** Xmas **CONF:** Thtr 60 Class 30 Board 30 **PARKING:** 60 **NOTES:** No smoking in restaurant Civ Wed 90
CARDS:

★★★61% Farnham House

Alton Rd GU10 5ER
☎ 01252 716908 01252 722583
e-mail: mail@farnhamhousehotel.com
Dir: *1m from town, off A31 Alton road*

Popular for conferences and weddings, Farnham House is surrounded by five acres of grounds. The Victorian architecture is part Tudor, part baronial in style, and features an oak-panelled bar with an inglenook fireplace. Most bedrooms enjoy countryside views, and a tennis court and swimming pool are peacefully set in the tranquil gardens.
ROOMS: 25 en suite (1 fmly) No smoking in 7 bedrooms s £77-£95; d £87-£95 **LB** **FACILITIES:** STV Outdoor swimming (H) Tennis (hard) **CONF:** Thtr 55 Class 14 Board 25 Del £130 **PARKING:** 75 **NOTES:** No dogs (ex guide dogs) RS 25 & 26 Dec Civ Wed 75
CARDS:

FAVERSHAM, Kent — Map 07 TR06

Travelodge Canterbury North

Travelodge

Thanet Way ME13 9EL
☎ 08700 850 950
Dir: *from M2 junc 7, take A299*

Travelodge offers good quality, good value, modern accommodation. Ideal for families, the spacious, en suite

continued on p238

FAVERSHAM, continued

bedrooms include remote-control TV, tea and coffee-making facilities, luxury beds and free morning newspaper. Meals can be taken at the nearby family restaurant. For further details and the Travelodge phone number, consult the Hotel Groups page.
ROOMS: 40 en suite s fr £42.95; d fr £42.95

FEERING, Essex Map 07 TL82

⌂ Travelodge (Colchester)
A12 London Rd Northbound CO5 9EL
☎ 08700 850 950
Travelodge offers good quality, good value, modern accommodation. Ideal for families, the spacious, en suite bedrooms include remote-control TV, tea and coffee-making facilities, luxury beds and free morning newspaper. Meals can be taken at the nearby family restaurant. For further details and the Travelodge phone number, consult the Hotel Groups page.
ROOMS: 39 en suite s fr £42.95; d fr £42.95

FELIXSTOWE, Suffolk Map 13 TM33

★★★70% *Orwell*
Hamilton Rd IP11 7DX
☎ 01394 285511 📠 01394 670687
e-mail: office@orwellhotel.co.uk
Dir: *from A14 over Dock rdbt and next rdbt. At 3rd rdbt 4th exit to Peartrice Avenue. At end of road hotel over rdbt*

Imposing Victorian building situated just a short walk from the town centre. The pleasantly decorated, well-equipped bedrooms come in a variety of styles and feature several large 'superior' rooms. Elegant public rooms offer a wealth of charm and character, and include two bars, an informal buttery and a spacious restaurant.
ROOMS: 58 en suite (8 fmly) **FACILITIES:** STV entertainment **CONF:** Thtr 200 Class 100 Board 60 **SERVICES:** Lift **PARKING:** 70 **NOTES:** No dogs (ex guide dogs) No smoking in restaurant
CARDS:

★★64% Marlborough
Sea Front IP11 2BJ
☎ 01394 285621 📠 01394 670724
e-mail: hsm@marlborough-hotel-felix.com
Dir: *from A14 follow Docks signs. Over Dock rdbt, railway crossing and traffic lights. Left at T-junct and hotel 400mtrs on left*
Situated on the seafront, overlooking the beach and just a short stroll from the pier and town centre. This traditional resort hotel offers a good range of facilities including the smart Rattan Restaurant, Flying Boat Bar and L'Aperitif lounge. The pleasantly decorated bedrooms come in a variety of styles; some have lovely sea views.
ROOMS: 49 en suite No smoking in 3 bedrooms **FACILITIES:** STV Pool table **CONF:** Thtr 80 Class 60 Board 40 **SERVICES:** Lift **PARKING:** 16 **NOTES:** No dogs (ex guide dogs) No smoking in restaurant
CARDS:

FENNY BENTLEY, Derbyshire Map 16 SK14

★★67% The Bentley Brook Inn & Fenny's Restaurant
DE6 1LF
☎ 01335 350278 📠 01335 350422
e-mail: all@bentleybrookinn.co.uk
Dir: *2m N of Ashbourne at junct of A515 & B5056, entrance off B5056*

This busy, family owned and run inn lies within the Peak District National Park, just north of Ashbourne. It is a charming half-timbered building with an attractive terrace and sweeping lawns. A well-appointed restaurant dominates the ground floor and a wide range of dishes is available. The character bar is open throughout the day for informal dining. Bedrooms vary in styles and sizes, but all are well equipped.
ROOMS: 10 en suite 1 annexe en suite No smoking in 1 bedroom s £47.50; d £69.50 (incl. bkfst) **LB FACILITIES:** Fishing Boules Skittles Brewery tour Xmas **CONF:** Class 28 Board 18 **PARKING:** 100 **NOTES:** No smoking in restaurant **CARDS:**

FENSTANTON, Cambridgeshire Map 12 TL36

⌂ Travelodge Huntingdon
PE18 9LP
☎ 08700 850 950 📠 01954 230919
Dir: *4m SE of Huntingdon, on A14 eastbound*
Travelodge offers good quality, good value, modern accommodation. Ideal for families, the spacious, en suite bedrooms include remote-control TV, tea and coffee-making facilities, luxury beds and free morning newspaper. Meals can be taken at the nearby family restaurant. For further details and the Travelodge phone number, consult the Hotel Groups page.
ROOMS: 40 en suite s fr £42.95; d fr £42.95

FERNDOWN, Dorset Map 05 SU00

★★★★73% ®® De Vere Dormy
New Rd BH22 8ES
☎ 01202 872121 📠 01202 895388
e-mail: devere.dormy@devere-hotels.com
Dir: *town centre turn left at lights onto A347. Hotel 1 mile on left*
Set in attractive grounds, this popular, well-established hotel offers several dining options, including the new fine dining restaurant 'Hennessys', which provides a high standard of cuisine and service. Bedrooms are located both in the main building and in

continued

several nearby cottage wings. Public rooms feature traditional wood panelling and open fires.

ROOMS: 114 en suite s £95-£115; d £130-£160 (incl. bkfst) **LB** **FACILITIES:** STV Indoor swimming (H) Tennis (hard) Squash Snooker Sauna Solarium Gym Jacuzzi Beauty salon, Dance studio, Swimming pool supervised entertainment Xmas **CONF:** Thtr 300 Class 140 Board 50 Del from £120 **SERVICES:** Lift **PARKING:** 200 **NOTES:** No smoking in restaurant Civ Wed 150 **CARDS:**

Travel Inn Bournemouth/Ferndown

Ringwood Rd, Tricketts Cross BH22 9BB
☎ 08701 977102 01202 897794
Dir: *off A348 just before Tricketts Cross rdbt*
Travel Inn offers good-quality, value-for-money accommodation. Spacious, en suite rooms with bath and shower comfortably accommodate a family of up to two adults and two children (to age 15). The restaurant and bar offers a varied menu. For further details and the Travel Inn phone number, consult the Hotel Groups page.
ROOMS: 32 en suite s £44.95; d £44.95 **CONF:** Thtr 20

FERRYBRIDGE SERVICE AREA (M62/A1), West Yorkshire — Map 16 SE42

Travelodge Pontefract Ferrybridge

WF11 0AF
☎ 08700 850 950
Dir: *M62 junct 33*
Travelodge offers good quality, good value, modern accommodation. Ideal for families, the spacious, en suite bedrooms include remote-control TV, tea and coffee-making facilities, luxury beds and free morning newspaper. Meals can be taken at the nearby family restaurant. For further details and the Travelodge phone number, consult the Hotel Groups page.
ROOMS: 36 en suite s fr £42.95; d fr £42.95

FIR TREE, Co Durham — Map 19 NZ13

★★★66% Helme Park Hall Hotel

DL13 4NW
☎ 01388 730970 01388 731799
e-mail: johnwheeler@helmeparkhotel.co.uk
Dir: *1m N of A689/A68 rdbt between Darlington & Corbridge*
Dating back to the 13th century, this very friendly family-owned hotel commands superb panoramic views up the Wear Valley. The refurbished bedrooms are comfortably equipped and modern in style. The cosy lounge bar is extremely popular for its comprehensive selection of bar meals, and the restaurant offers both set and carte menus.
ROOMS: 13 en suite (1 fmly) s £52; d £82 (incl. bkfst) **LB** **FACILITIES:** STV Xmas **CONF:** BC Thtr 150 Class 80 Board 80 Del £89.95 **PARKING:** 70 **NOTES:** No smoking in restaurant Civ Wed 140 **CARDS:**

FIVE OAKS, West Sussex — Map 06 TQ02

Travelodge Billingshurst

Staines St RH14 9AE
☎ 08700 850 950 01403 782711
Dir: *on A29, northbound, 1m N of Billingshurst*
Travelodge offers good quality, good value, modern accommodation. Ideal for families, the spacious, en suite bedrooms include remote-control TV, tea and coffee-making facilities, luxury beds and free morning newspaper. Meals can be taken at the nearby family restaurant. For further details and the Travelodge phone number, consult the Hotel Groups page.
ROOMS: 26 en suite s fr £42.95; d fr £42.95

FLAMBOROUGH, East Riding of Yorkshire — Map 17 TA27

★★70% North Star

North Marine Dr YO15 1BL
☎ 01262 850379
Dir: *follow signs for North Landing. Hotel 100yds from sea*
Standing close to the North Landing of Flamborough Head, this family-run hotel overlooks delightful countryside. The hotel has been refurbished and provides excellent accommodation together with a very popular bar. A good range of well-produced food is available in both the bar and the spacious dining room.
ROOMS: 7 en suite s £45; d £65-£75 (incl. bkfst) **LB** **PARKING:** 30 **NOTES:** No dogs No smoking in restaurant Closed Xmas & 2wks Nov & Jan **CARDS:**

FLEET, Hampshire — Map 05 SU85

★★★63% *Lismoyne*

Church Rd GU51 4NE
☎ 01252 628555 01252 811761
e-mail: info@lismoynehotel.com
Dir: *on B3013, over railway bridge to town centre. Through lights, take 4th right. Hotel 0.25m on left*
Set in extensive grounds, this attractive hotel is located close to the town centre. Public rooms include a comfortable lounge and pleasant bar with a conservatory overlooking the garden, and a traditional restaurant. Accommodation is divided between bedrooms in the original building and those in the modern extension; styles vary and all rooms are well equipped.
ROOMS: 62 en suite (3 fmly) No smoking in 18 bedrooms **FACILITIES:** mini-gym **CONF:** Thtr 150 Class 95 Board 75 **PARKING:** 150 **NOTES:** No dogs (ex guide dogs) No smoking in restaurant Civ Wed 190 **CARDS:**

Innkeeper's Lodge

Cove Rd GU51 2SH
☎ 01252 774600
Dir: *M3, junct 4A*
A new concept in the travel accommodation market. Smart rooms meet essential business requirements but also have home comforts. Dining options include all-day menus plus the added advantage of breakfast, which is included in the room price. For further details, consult the Hotel Groups page.
ROOMS: 40 en suite

FLEET MOTORWAY SERVICE AREA (M3), Hampshire
Map 05 SU75

⌂ Days Inn
Fleet Services GU51 1AA
☎ 01252 815587 ▯ 01252 815587
e-mail: Fleet.hotel@welcomebreak.co.uk
Dir: *Welcome Break Fleet Motorway Service area between junct 4a & 5 southbound on M3*

This modern building offers accommodation in smart, spacious and well-equipped bedrooms, suitable for families and business travellers, and all with en suite bathrooms. Continental breakfast is available and other refreshments may be taken at the nearby family restaurant. For further details and the Days Inn phone number, consult the Hotel Groups page.
ROOMS: 58 en suite s £55-£65; d £55-£65 **CONF:** Board 10

FLITWICK, Bedfordshire
Map 11 TL03

Top 200 - Hotel

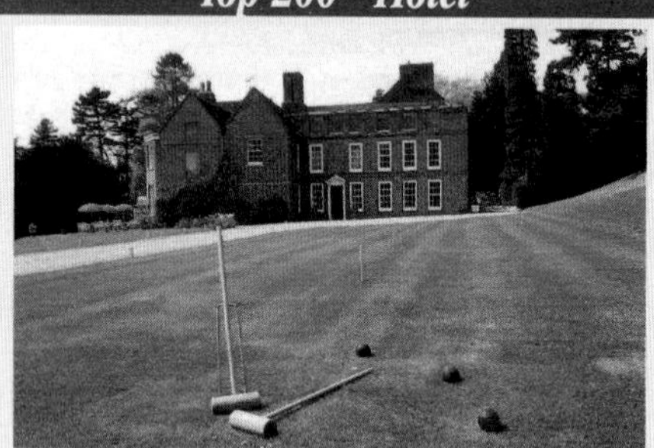

★★★ ◎◎ Menzies Flitwick Manor
Church Rd MK45 1AE
☎ 01525 712242 ▯ 01525 718753
e-mail: info@menzies-hotels.co.uk
Dir: *2m from M1 junct 12 towards Ampthill*

With its picturesque setting in acres of gardens and parkland, yet only minutes by car from the motorway, this lovely Georgian house combines the best of both worlds, accessible, yet peaceful. Bedrooms are individually decorated and furnished with period pieces; some are air-conditioned. Cosy and intimate, the lounge and restaurant help give the hotel a home-from-home feel, which makes it popular with many guests.
ROOMS: 17 en suite **FACILITIES:** Tennis (hard) Croquet lawn Putting green **CONF:** Thtr 40 Class 30 Board 24 Del from £215 **PARKING:** 50 **NOTES:** No smoking in restaurant Civ Wed 50
CARDS:

FLORE, Northamptonshire
Map 11 SP66

★★★72% Courtyard by Marriott Daventry
High St NN7 4LP
☎ 01327 349022 ▯ 01327 349017
e-mail: reservations.daventry@whitbread.com
Dir: *M1 junct 16 onto A45 towards Daventry. Hotel 1m on right between Upper Heyford and Flore*

Just off the M1 motorway in rural surroundings, this modern hotel is particularly suited to the business guest. Professional staff provide a warm welcome and helpful service throughout the public areas, which comprise a lounge bar and restaurant. Bedrooms provide smart décor, plenty of workspace and a good range of facilities.
ROOMS: 53 en suite (7 fmly) No smoking in 34 bedrooms s £44-£87; d £58-£94 (incl. bkfst) **LB** **FACILITIES:** STV Gym **CONF:** Thtr 80 Class 40 Board 48 Del from £105 **PARKING:** 120 **NOTES:** No dogs (ex guide dogs) No smoking in restaurant Civ Wed 100
CARDS:

FOLKESTONE, Kent
Map 07 TR23

★★★70% Clifton
The Leas CT20 2EB
☎ 01303 851231 ▯ 01303 223949
e-mail: reservations@thecliftonhotel.com
Dir: *M20 junct 13, 0.25m W of town centre on A259*

This privately-owned Victorian-style hotel occupies a prime location with views across the English Channel. The bedrooms are comfortably appointed and most have views of the sea. Public areas include a comfortable, traditionally furnished lounge, a popular bar serving a good range of beers and several well-appointed conference rooms.
ROOMS: 80 en suite (5 fmly) No smoking in 16 bedrooms s £59.50-£85; d £80-£101 (incl. bkfst) **LB** **FACILITIES:** STV Games room Xmas **CONF:** Thtr 80 Class 36 Board 32 Del from £97.50 **SERVICES:** Lift
CARDS:

See advert on opposite page

⌂ Travel Inn
Cherry Garden Ln CT19 4AP
☎ 08701 977103 ▯ 01303 273641
Dir: *M20 J13. At 1st rbt turn right, at 2nd rbt right signed Folkestone A20. At lights turn right, Travel Inn on the right.*

Travel Inn offers good-quality, value-for-money accommodation. Spacious, en suite rooms with bath and shower comfortably accommodate a family of up to two adults and two children (to age 15). The restaurant and bar offers a varied menu. For further details and the Travel Inn phone number, consult the Hotel Groups page.
ROOMS: 79 en suite s £44.95; d £44.95

FONTWELL, West Sussex
Map 06 SU90

⌂ Travelodge Bognor Regis
BN18 0SB
☎ 08700 850 950 ▯ 01243 543973
Dir: *on A27/A29 rdbt*

Travelodge offers good quality, good value, modern accommodation. Ideal for families, the spacious, en suite bedrooms include remote-control TV, tea and coffee-making facilities, luxury beds and free morning newspaper. Meals can be taken at the nearby family restaurant. For further details and the Travelodge phone number, consult the Hotel Groups page.
ROOMS: 63 en suite s fr £42.95; d fr £42.95

FORDINGBRIDGE, Hampshire
Map 05 SU11

★★72% ® Ashburn Hotel & Restaurant
Station Rd SP6 1JP
☎ 01425 652060 📠 01425 652150
e-mail: ashburn@mistral.co.uk
Dir: *from Fordingbridge High St, follow Damerham signs. Pass police and fire stations, hotel 400yds on left*

This friendly family-run hotel, situated in an elevated position on the edge of the village, is surrounded by beautiful countryside. Bedrooms, some in the original house and others in a purpose built extension, are comfortable and well equipped. There is a smart function room, a spacious bar, a cosy lounge and a wonderful garden. A good choice is offered at dinner and dishes are carefully prepared.

ROOMS: 20 en suite (3 fmly) No smoking in 10 bedrooms s £39.50-£80; d £80-£112 (incl. bkfst) **LB** **CONF:** Thtr 130 Class 80 Board 40 Del from £63 **PARKING:** 60 **NOTES:** No smoking in restaurant RS 24-29 Dec, 1-5 Jan Civ Wed 180 **CARDS:**

FOREST ROW, East Sussex
Map 06 TQ43

Top 200 - Hotel

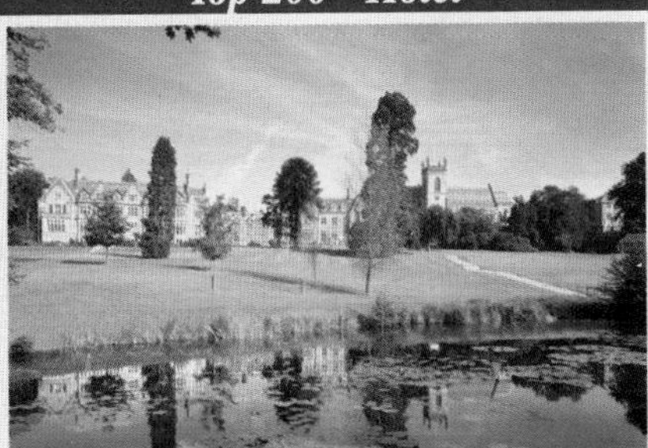

★★★★ ®® Ashdown Park Hotel and Country Club
Wych Cross RH18 5JR
☎ 01342 824988 📠 01342 826206
e-mail: reservations@ashdownpark.com
Dir: *A264 to East Grinstead, then A22 to Eastbourne, 2m S of Forest Row at Wych Cross traffic lights. Left to Hartfield, hotel on right 0.75m*

Magnificent country house hotel set amidst attractive landscaped grounds overlooking 186 acres of parkland in the heart of Ashdown Forest. The stylish bedrooms are full of character, each one is individually decorated and tastefully furnished to provide guests with an excellent degree of comfort. Public areas include a chapel, which has been converted into a conference room, a leisure club, a golf course and the Anderida Restaurant.

ROOMS: 107 en suite (15 GF) s £135-£325; d £165-£355 (incl. bkfst) **LB** **FACILITIES: Spa** STV Indoor swimming (H) Golf 18 Tennis (hard) Snooker Sauna Solarium Gym Croquet lawn Putting green Jacuzzi Beauty/Hair salon, Aerobics, Treatment room, Jogging trails, Mountain bike hire Xmas **CONF:** BC Thtr 170 Class 80 Board 60 Del from £200 **SERVICES:** Lift **PARKING:** 200 **NOTES:** No dogs (ex guide dogs) No smoking in restaurant Civ Wed 140 **CARDS:**

Packed in a hurry?
Ironing facilities should be available at all star levels, either in rooms or on request

FORMBY, Merseyside
Map 15 SD30

★★★66% *Tree Tops Country House Restaurant & Hotel*
Southport Old Rd L37 0AB
☎ 01704 572430 📠 01704 572430
Dir: *off A565 Southport to Liverpool road*

A country house residence with an attractive restaurant where good food is served by an attentive staff. Rooms are in delightful lodges situated in five acres of wooded grounds. The hotel is adjacent to a fabulous golf course, near to beaches and all local amenities.

ROOMS: 11 annexe en suite (3 fmly) **FACILITIES:** Outdoor swimming (H) (May-Sep) **CONF:** Thtr 200 Class 80 Board 40 **PARKING:** 100 **NOTES:** No dogs No smoking in restaurant Civ Wed 60 **CARDS:**

See advert under SOUTHPORT

FORTON MOTORWAY SERVICE AREA (M6), Lancashire
Map 18 SD55

⌂ Travelodge Lancaster Forton
White Carr Ln, Bay Horse LA2 9DU
☎ 08700 850 950 📠 01524 791703
Dir: *between junct 32 & 33 of M6*

Travelodge

Travelodge offers good quality, good value, modern accommodation. Ideal for families, the spacious, en suite bedrooms include remote-control TV, tea and coffee-making facilities, luxury beds and free morning newspaper. Meals can be taken at the nearby family restaurant. For further details and the Travelodge phone number, consult the Hotel Groups page.

ROOMS: 53 en suite s fr £42.95; d fr £42.95

FOUR MARKS, Hampshire Map 05 SU63

Travelodge Alton

156 Winchester Rd GU34 5HZ
☎ 08700 850 950 📠 01420 562659
***Dir:** 5m S of Alton on A31 northbound*

Travelodge

Travelodge offers good quality, good value, modern accommodation. Ideal for families, the spacious, en suite bedrooms include remote-control TV, tea and coffee-making facilities, luxury beds and free morning newspaper. Meals can be taken at the nearby family restaurant. For further details and the Travelodge phone number, consult the Hotel Groups page.
ROOMS: 31 en suite s fr £42.95; d fr £42.95

F

FOWEY, Cornwall & Isles of Scilly Map 02 SX15

★★★79% Fowey Hall

Hanson Dr PL23 1ET
☎ 01726 833866 📠 01726 834100
e-mail: info@foweyhall.com
***Dir:** in Fowey, cross mini rdbt into town centre. Pass school on right, after 400mtrs right into Hanson Dr*

Built in 1899, this listed mansion looks out onto the English Channel. The imaginatively designed bedrooms offer charm, individuality and sumptuous comfort, while beautifully appointed public rooms include the wood-panelled dining room where accomplished cuisine is served. Enjoying glorious views, the well-kept grounds have a covered pool and sunbathing area.
ROOMS: 16 en suite 8 annexe en suite (18 fmly) s £127.50-£335.75; d £150-£395 (incl. bkfst & dinner) **LB** **FACILITIES:** STV Indoor swimming (H) Croquet lawn Children's play area, Table tennis, Bicycle hire, Pool supervised Jul & Aug ch fac Xmas **CONF:** Thtr 30 Class 20 Board 20 Del from £130 **PARKING:** 40 **NOTES:** No smoking in restaurant Civ Wed 45 **CARDS:**

See advert on opposite page

★★★72% Fowey

The Esplanade PL23 1HX
☎ 01726 832551 📠 01726 832125
e-mail: fowey@richardsonhotels.co.uk
***Dir:** M5 take A30 to Okehampton, continue to Bodmin. Then B3269 to Fowey for 1m, on right bend left junct then right into Dagands Rd. Hotel 200mtrs on left*

Best Western

This attractive hotel stands proudly above the estuary, with marvellous views of the river from the public areas and the majority of the bedrooms. High standards are evident throughout, augmented by a relaxed and welcoming atmosphere. There is a spacious bar, elegant restaurant and smart drawing room. Imaginative dinners make good use of quality local ingredients.

ROOMS: 37 en suite (1 fmly) No smoking in 3 bedrooms
FACILITIES: Fishing **CONF:** Thtr 100 Class 60 Board 20 Del from £99
SERVICES: Lift **PARKING:** 13 **NOTES:** No smoking in restaurant
CARDS:

Top 200 - Hotel

★★ Marina

Esplanade PL23 1HY
☎ 01726 833315 📠 01726 832779
e-mail: marina.hotel@dial.pipex.com
***Dir:** into town down Lostwithiel St, near bottom of hill, right into Esplanade*

Built in 1815 as a seaside retreat, the Marina continues to serve its purpose with style and panache. From its setting on the water's edge, this relaxed, small hotel offers glorious views of the river to the sea. Bedrooms, some with balconies, are spacious and comfortable, not forgetting the host of thoughtful touches like fresh fruit and flowers provided to enhance the enjoyment of a stay here. Competent cooking with the freshest local produce, including fish landed near by, is the hallmark of dining in the waterside restaurant.
ROOMS: 13 en suite (1 fmly) No smoking in all bedrooms s £85-£105; d £154-£230 (incl. bkfst & dinner) **LB**
FACILITIES: Fishing Sailing Xmas **PARKING:** 13 **NOTES:** No smoking in restaurant Civ Wed **CARDS:**

FOWNHOPE, Herefordshire Map 10 SO53

★★68% Green Man Inn

HR1 4PE
☎ 01432 860243 📠 01432 860207
e-mail: greenman.hereford@nhguk.com
***Dir:** on B4224 midway between Ross-on-Wye and Hereford*

This charming, timber-framed inn is situated in the centre of this pleasant Herefordshire village. Bedrooms are thoughtfully and well

continued

equipped; some are located in separate cottage-style buildings. The public areas are full of character, with many period features, and include two lounges, a choice of bars and an attractive restaurant. The hotel also has a modern leisure and fitness centre.
ROOMS: 11 en suite 12 annexe en suite (6 fmly) s £38.50-£39.50; d £65-£67.50 (incl. bkfst) **LB** **FACILITIES: Spa** STV Indoor swimming (H) Fishing Sauna Solarium Gym Jacuzzi Swimming pool supervised Xmas **PARKING:** 80 **NOTES:** No smoking in restaurant
CARDS:

FRADDON, Cornwall & Isles of Scilly — Map 02 SW95

Travel Inn (Newquay)
Penhale TR9 6NA
☎ 08701 977194 📠 01726 860641
Dir: *on A30 2m S of Indian Queens*
Travel Inn offers good-quality, value-for-money accommodation. Spacious, en suite rooms with bath and shower comfortably accommodate a family of up to two adults and two children (to age 15). The restaurant and bar offers a varied menu. For further details and the Travel Inn phone number, consult the Hotel Groups page.
ROOMS: 40 en suite s £44.95; d £44.95

FRANKLEY MOTORWAY SERVICE AREA (M5), West Midlands — Map 10 SO98

Travelodge Birmingham South
Illey Ln, Frankley Motorway Service Area, Frankley B32 4AR
☎ 08700 850 950
Dir: *between junct 3 and 4 on southbound carriageway of M5*
Travelodge offers good quality, good value, modern accommodation. Ideal for families, the spacious, en suite bedrooms include remote-control TV, tea and coffee-making facilities, luxury beds and free morning newspaper. Meals can be taken at the nearby family restaurant. For further details and the Travelodge phone number, consult the Hotel Groups page.
ROOMS: 62 en suite s fr £42.95; d fr £42.95

FRESHWATER See Wight, Isle of

FRIMLEY, Surrey — Map 05 SU85

Innkeeper's Lodge Frimley
114 Portsmouth Rd GU15 1HS
☎ 01276 691939 📠 01276 605900
Dir: *M3 junct 4/ A321 for Frimley take A325 (towards A30 Bagshot), over 1st rdbt past Frimley Park Hospital, straight over 2nd rdbt into Portsmouth Rd. Lodge 500mtrs on left*
A new concept in the travel accommodation market. Smart rooms meet essential business requirements but also have home comforts. Dining options include all-day menus plus the added advantage of breakfast, which is included in the room price. For further details, consult the Hotel Groups page.
ROOMS: 43 en suite **CONF:** Thtr 40 Class 20 Board 20

FRITTON, Norfolk — Map 13 TG40

★★★72% Caldecott Hall Golf & Leisure
Caldecott Hall, Beccles Rd NR31 9EY
☎ 01493 488488 📠 01493 488561
e-mail: judithcollen@supanet.com
Dir: *On A143 Beccles to Great Yarmouth road, 4m from Gt Yarmouth*
This hotel is ideally situated amidst its own attractive landscaped grounds that include an 18-hole golf course, fishing lakes and the
continued

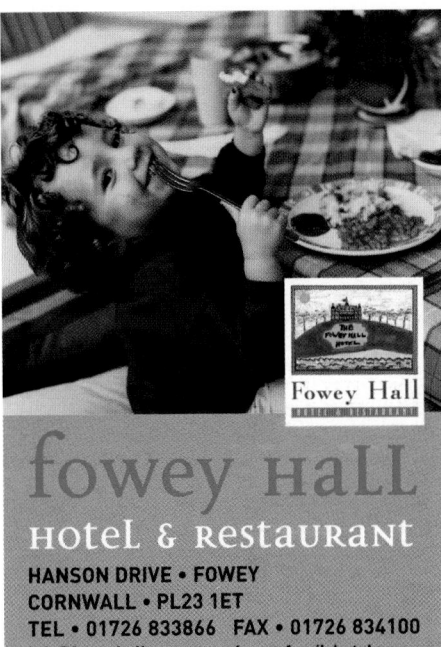

Redwings Horse sanctuary. The individually decorated bedrooms are spacious and equipped with many thoughtful extras. Public rooms include a smart sitting room, a lounge bar, restaurant, clubhouse and leisure facilities.
ROOMS: 8 en suite (6 fmly) No smoking in all bedrooms s £70; d £70-£95 **LB** **FACILITIES:** Golf 18 Fishing Putting green Driving range Pitch & Putt **CONF:** Thtr 100 Class 80 Board 20 Del from £70 **PARKING:** 100 **NOTES:** No dogs (ex guide dogs) No smoking in restaurant **CARDS:**

FRODSHAM, Cheshire — Map 15 SJ57

★★★69% Forest Hill Hotel & Leisure Complex
Overton Hill WA6 6HH
☎ 01928 735255 📠 01928 735517
e-mail: info@foresthillshotel.co.uk
Dir: *at Frodsham turn onto B5151. After 1m right into Manley Rd, right into Simons Ln after 0.5m. Hotel 0.5m past Frodsham golf course*
This modern, purpose built hotel is set high up on Overton Hill offering panoramic views. There is a range of spacious, well-equipped bedrooms, including executive rooms. Guests have a choice of bars and there is a tasteful split level restaurant, as well as conference facilities and a very well equipped leisure suite and gymnasium.
ROOMS: 58 en suite (4 fmly) No smoking in 5 bedrooms s £55-£78; d £78-£98 (incl. bkfst) **LB** **FACILITIES:** STV Indoor swimming (H) Snooker Sauna Solarium Gym Jacuzzi Nightclub entertainment Xmas **CONF:** Thtr 200 Class 80 Board 70 Del from £100 **PARKING:** 350 **NOTES:** No smoking in restaurant Civ Wed 150
CARDS:

FROME, Somerset

Map 04 ST74

★★65% *The George at Nunney*

11 Church St BA11 4LW
☎ 01373 836458 01373 836565
e-mail: georgenunneyhotel@barbox.net
(For full entry see Nunney)

Mendip Lodge

Bath Rd BA11 2HP
☎ 01373 463223 01373 463990
e-mail: latona@aol.com
Dir: *situated on the Bath side of Frome, on the B3090, opposite Frome College*
At the time of going to press, the star classification for this hotel was not confirmed. Please refer to the AA internet site www.theAA.com for current information.
ROOMS: 40 en suite (3 fmly) (20 GF) s fr £42.50; d fr £65 (incl. bkfst) **LB FACILITIES:** STV Xmas **CONF:** Thtr 80 Class 40 Board 40 Del from £100 **PARKING:** 80 **NOTES:** No smoking in restaurant Civ Wed 80
CARDS:

GARFORTH, West Yorkshire

Map 16 SE43

★★★73% Milford

Best Western

A1 Great North Rd, Peckfield LS25 5LQ
☎ 01977 681800 01977 681245
e-mail: enquiries@mlh.co.uk
Dir: *on southbound carriageway of A1, E of Leeds where A63 joins A1*

This modern, refurbished hotel provides comfortable bedrooms which are air conditioned, particularly spacious and have been superbly insulated against traffic noise. The contemporary styled Watermill Restaurant and Bar, which features a working waterwheel, provides a high standard of creative cuisine. Staff throughout are friendly and keen to please.
ROOMS: 47 en suite (10 fmly) (14 GF) No smoking in 19 bedrooms s £53-£63; d £53-£63 **LB FACILITIES:** STV Xmas **CONF:** Thtr 70 Class 35 Board 30 Del £105 **SERVICES:** air con **PARKING:** 80
CARDS:

See advert under LEEDS

GARSTANG, Lancashire

Map 18 SD44

★★★69% Pickerings

Garstang Rd, Catterall PR3 0HD
☎ 01995 600999 01995 602100
e-mail: pickerings@totalise.co.uk
Dir: *from S M6 junct 32 join the M55 exit junct 1& take A6 N, after Esso garage right onto B6430 then right after bus shelter*
This appealing and welcoming hotel dates back to the 17th century and nestles in carefully tended grounds that include a well-equipped children's play area. Bedrooms are spacious and include several smart four-poster rooms. Public areas include an inviting bar lounge, two elegant dining rooms and a purpose-built conference suite.
ROOMS: 12 en suite (1 fmly) s £50-£80; d £70-£115 (incl. bkfst) **LB FACILITIES:** Childrens play area Xmas **CONF:** BC Thtr 150 Class 80 Board 40 Del £75 **PARKING:** 50 **NOTES:** No dogs (ex guide dogs) No smoking in restaurant Civ Wed 150 **CARDS:**

★★★66% Garstang Country Hotel & Golf Club

Garstang Rd, Bowgreave PR3 1YE
☎ 01995 600100 01995 600950
e-mail: reception@garstanghotelandgolf.co.uk
Dir: *M6 junct 32 take 1st right after Rogers Esso garage on A6 onto B6430. Continue for 1m and hotel on left*

Conveniently situated for the M6, this smart, purpose-built hotel enjoys a peaceful location alongside its own 18-hole golf course. Modern, spacious bedrooms are well equipped for both business and leisure guests, while public areas include the informal Kingfisher Bar, a comfortable lounge bar and a choice of dining areas.
ROOMS: 32 en suite (16 GF) No smoking in 20 bedrooms s £60-£75; d £80-£95 (incl. bkfst) **LB FACILITIES:** STV Golf 18 Golf driving range **CONF:** Thtr 200 Class 100 Board 80 Del £85 **SERVICES:** Lift **PARKING:** 172 **NOTES:** No dogs (ex guide dogs) No smoking in restaurant Civ Wed 120 **CARDS:**

GATESHEAD, Tyne & Wear

Map 21 NZ26

See also Beamish & Whickham

★★★★68% Newcastle Marriott Hotel MetroCentre

Marriott HOTELS · RESORTS · SUITES

MetroCentre NE11 9XF
☎ 0191 493 2233 0191 493 2030
e-mail: reservations.newcastle@marriotthotels.co.uk
Dir: *from N leave A1 at MetroCentre exit, take 'Other Routes'. From S leave A1 at MetroCentre exit and turn right.*
Conveniently situated just off the A1, this modern hotel lies close to the MetroCentre. Bedrooms are comprehensively equipped, comfortable and spacious. The restaurant offers a choice of formal and informal dishes for dinner; lunch is served in the bar. There is a smart leisure centre and extensive conference and banqueting facilities.
ROOMS: 150 en suite (145 fmly) No smoking in 90 bedrooms s £115; d £115 **LB FACILITIES:** STV Indoor swimming (H) Sauna Solarium Gym Jacuzzi Health & beauty clinic Dance studio Xmas **CONF:** Thtr 450 Class 190 Board 40 Del £155 **SERVICES:** Lift air con **PARKING:** 300 **NOTES:** No dogs (ex guide dogs) Civ Wed 100
CARDS:

★★76% Eslington Villa
8 Station Rd, Low Fell NE9 6DR
☎ 0191 487 6017 & 420 0666 🖷 0191 420 0667
e-mail: admin@eslingtonvilla.fsnet.co.uk
Dir: *off A1 onto Team Valley Trading Est. Right at 2nd rdbt along Eastern Av then left past Belle Vue Motors, hotel on left*
Set in a residential area, this smart hotel marries a bright contemporary approach to the period style of a fine Victorian villa. The overall ambience is relaxed and inviting. Chunky sofas grace the cocktail lounge, while tempting dishes can be enjoyed in either the classical dining room or modern conservatory overlooking the Team Valley.
ROOMS: 17 en suite (2 fmly) (3 GF) s £65-£70; d £70-£80 (incl. bkfst) **CONF:** Thtr 36 Class 30 Board 25 **PARKING:** 15 **NOTES:** No dogs (ex guide dogs) No smoking in restaurant Closed 25-26 Dec RS Sun/BHs (restricted restaurant service) **CARDS:**

Express by Holiday Inn Newcastle Metro Centre
Express by Holiday Inn
Clasper Way, Riverside Way, Derwenthaugh NE16 3BE
☎ 01207 541100 🖷 01207 541136
e-mail: newcastle-metrocentre@oriel-leisure.co.uk
Dir: *Follow signs for Metro Centre, hotel on A1114 next to TGI Fridays and opp Shell/Honda garage*

A modern hotel ideal for families and business travellers. Fresh and uncomplicated, the spacious bedrooms include Sky TV, power shower and tea and coffee-making facilities. Continental buffet breakfast is included in the room rate; other meals may be taken at the nearby family pub or restaurant. For further details and the Express by Holiday Inn phone number, consult the Hotel Groups pages.
ROOMS: 100 en suite (incl. cont bkfst) s £65-£69; d £65-£69
CONF: Thtr 35 Class 30 Board 20

Premier Lodge (Newcastle South)
PREMIER LODGE
Lobley Hill Rd NE11 9NA
☎ 0870 9906590 🖷 0870 9906591
Premier Lodge offers modern, well-equipped, en suite accommodation suitable for both business and leisure travellers. Meals can be taken at the adjacent popular restaurant and bar, which is fully licensed. For further details, consult the Hotel Groups page.
ROOMS: 40 en suite s £48; d £48

Travel Inn
travel inn
Derwent Haugh Rd, Swalwell NE16 3BL
☎ 08701 977283 🖷 0191 414 5032
Dir: *Situated on Derwent Haugh Road leading from the A1/A694 intersection. One mile north of the Metro Centre*
Travel Inn offers good-quality, value-for-money accommodation. Spacious, en suite rooms with bath and shower comfortably accommodate a family of up to two adults and two children (to age 15). The restaurant and bar offers a varied menu. For further details and the Travel Inn phone number, consult the Hotel Groups page.
ROOMS: 40 en suite s £44.95; d £44.95

GATWICK AIRPORT (LONDON), West Sussex Map 06 TQ24
See also Dorking, East Grinstead & Reigate

★★★★70% Copthorne Hotel London Gatwick
COPTHORNE
Copthorne Way RH10 3PG
☎ 01342 348800 & 348888 🖷 01342 348833
e-mail: coplgw@mill-cop.com
Dir: *on A264, 2m E of A264/B2036 rdbt*

Situated in a tranquil position, the Copthorne is set in 100 acres of wooded, landscaped gardens which contain jogging tracks, a putting green and even a petanque pit. The sprawling building is built around a 16th-century farmhouse and has comfortable, well-maintained bedrooms. In addition to the brasserie there is a more formal restaurant.
ROOMS: 227 en suite (10 fmly) No smoking in 136 bedrooms s £99; d £99 **LB FACILITIES: Spa** STV Indoor swimming (H) Tennis (hard) Squash Sauna Solarium Gym Croquet lawn Putting green Jacuzzi Petanque pit Aerobic studio **CONF:** BC Thtr 135 Class 60 Board 40 Del from £129 **SERVICES:** Lift **PARKING:** 300 **NOTES:** Civ Wed 100
CARDS:

★★★★70% *Le Meridien London Gatwick*
Le MERIDIEN HOTELS & RESORTS
North Terminal RH6 0PH
☎ 01293 567070 🖷 01293 567739
e-mail: reservations.gatwick@lemeridien.com
Dir: *M23 junct 9, follow to 2nd rdbt. Hotel large white building straight ahead*
One of the closest hotels to the airport, this modern, purpose-built hotel is located only minutes from the terminals. Bedrooms are contemporary and all are air-conditioned. Guests have a choice of eating options including a French-style café, brasserie and oriental restaurant.
ROOMS: 494 en suite (18 fmly) No smoking in 283 bedrooms **FACILITIES:** STV Indoor swimming (H) Sauna Solarium Gym **CONF:** Thtr 300 Class 200 Board 120 **SERVICES:** Lift air con **PARKING:** 120 **NOTES:** No dogs (ex guide dogs) Civ Wed 220
CARDS:

Late for dinner?
Quality Standards mean that last orders for dinner vary according to star rating and should be no earlier than:
★★ 7.00pm ★★★ 8.00pm ★★★★ 9.00pm
★★★★★ 10.00pm

continued

GATWICK AIRPORT (LONDON), continued

★★★★66% Copthorne Hotel Effingham Park Gatwick
West Park Rd RH10 3EU
COPTHORNE
☎ 01342 714994 📠 01342 716039
e-mail: sales.effingham@mill-cop.com
Dir: *M23 junct 10, take A264 towards East Grinstead. Over rdbt and at 2nd rdbt left onto B2028. Effingham Park on right*

A former stately home, set in 40 acres of grounds, this hotel is popular for conference and weekend functions. The main restaurant is an open-plan, Mediterranean-themed brasserie, and snacks are also available in the bar. Bedrooms are spacious and well cared for. Facilities include an 18-hole golf course and a leisure club.
ROOMS: 122 en suite (6 fmly) No smoking in 48 bedrooms s £69-£135; d £69-£135 **LB FACILITIES:** STV Indoor swimming (H) Golf 9 Tennis (hard) Sauna Solarium Gym Croquet lawn Putting green Jacuzzi Aerobic studio Bowls Croquet **CONF:** BC Thtr 600 Class 250 Board 30 Del £169 **SERVICES:** Lift **PARKING:** 500 **NOTES:** No dogs (ex guide dogs) No smoking in restaurant Closed 26-30 Dec Civ Wed 140
CARDS:

Top 200 - Hotel

★★★ ◎◎ Langshott Manor
Langshott Ln RH6 9LN
☎ 01293 786680 📠 01293 783905
e-mail: admin@langshottmanor.com
Dir: *from A23 take Ladbroke Rd, off Chequers rdbt to Langshott, after 0.75m hotel on right*
Charming timber-framed Tudor house set amidst beautifully landscaped grounds on the outskirts of town. The stylish public areas feature a choice of plushly furnished lounges with polished oak panelling, exposed beams and log fires. The individually decorated bedrooms combine the most up-to-date modern comforts with flair, individuality and traditional elegance. The Mulberry restaurant overlooks a picturesque pond and offers an imaginative menu.
ROOMS: 14 en suite 8 annexe en suite No smoking in all bedrooms s £165-£200; d £185-£290 (incl. bkfst) **LB FACILITIES:** STV Croquet lawn Xmas **CONF:** Thtr 40 Class 20 Board 22 Del £215 **PARKING:** 25 **NOTES:** No dogs (ex guide dogs) No smoking in restaurant Civ Wed 60 **CARDS:**

★★★68% Stanhill Court
Stanhill Rd, Charlwood RH6 0EP
☎ 01293 862166 📠 01293 862773
e-mail: enquiries@stanhillcourthotel.co.uk
Dir: *N of Charlwood towards Newdigate*

Dating back to 1881, this hotel enjoys a secluded location in 35 acres of well-tended grounds with views over the Downs. Bedrooms are individually furnished and decorated, many having four-poster beds. Public areas include a library, a bright bar and a traditional wood-panelled restaurant.
ROOMS: 14 en suite (3 fmly) No smoking in 2 bedrooms s £95; d £125 **LB FACILITIES:** STV Fishing Croquet lawn Putting green **CONF:** Thtr 250 Class 100 Board 60 Del £159 **PARKING:** 100 **NOTES:** No dogs (ex guide dogs) No smoking in restaurant Civ Wed 180
CARDS:

★★★66% Gatwick Worth Hotel
Crabbet Park, Turners Hill Rd, Worth RH10 4ST
Best Western
☎ 01293 884806 📠 01293 882444
e-mail: reception@gatwickworthhotel.com
Dir: *M23 junct 10, left to A264. At 1st rdbt right signed to Maidenbower. 1st left into Old Hollow Rd, follow to end. At T junct right. Hotel 200yds right*
This purpose-built hotel is ideally placed for access to Gatwick Airport. The bedrooms are spacious and suitably appointed with good facilities. Public areas consist of a light and airy bar area and a brasserie-style restaurant offering good value meals. Guests have use of the superb leisure club next door.
ROOMS: 118 en suite (9 fmly) No smoking in 57 bedrooms s fr £60; d fr £75 (incl. bkfst) **FACILITIES: Spa** Indoor swimming (H) Riding Sauna Solarium Gym Jacuzzi Cannon's fitness centre adjacent to hotel. Swimming pool supervised ch fac **CONF:** Thtr 200 Class 100 Board 60 Del from £95 **NOTES:** No dogs (ex guide dogs) No smoking in restaurant Civ Wed 150 **CARDS:**

U Holiday Inn Gatwick Airport
Povey Cross Rd RH6 0BA
Holiday Inn HOTELS · RESORTS
☎ 0870 400 9030 📠 01293 771054
e-mail: gatwick@ichotelsgroup.com
Dir: *M23 junct 9, follow Gatwick, then Reigate signs. Hotel on left after 3rd rdbt*
At the time of going to press, the classification for this hotel was

continued

not confirmed. Please refer to the AA internet site www.theAA.com for current information.
ROOMS: 210 en suite (19 fmly) No smoking in 105 bedrooms
CONF: Thtr 160 Class 90 Board 60 **SERVICES:** Lift **PARKING:** 300
NOTES: No dogs (ex guide dogs) No smoking in restaurant
CARDS:

Holiday Inn Gatwick/Crawley

Langley Dr RH11 7SX
☎ 01293 529991 01293 515913
e-mail: reservations-gatwickcrawley@ichotelsgroup.com
Dir: *4m S of airport from M23 junct 10 take A264 following Horsham signs hotel at junct with A23*
At the time of going to press, the classification for this hotel was not confirmed. Please refer to the AA internet site www.theAA.com for current information.
ROOMS: 221 en suite **FACILITIES:** Outdoor swimming (H) Sauna Solarium Gym **CONF:** Thtr 300 Class 90 Board 50 **NOTES:** No dogs
CARDS:

Express by Holiday Inn Crawley

Haslett Av East RH10 1UA
☎ 01293 525523 01293 525529
e-mail: ebhi-crawley@btconnect.com

A modern hotel ideal for families and business travellers. Fresh and uncomplicated, the spacious bedrooms include Sky TV, power shower and tea and coffee-making facilities. Continental buffet breakfast is included in the room rate; other meals may be taken at the nearby family pub or restaurant. For further details and the Express by Holiday Inn phone number, consult the Hotel Groups pages.
ROOMS: 74 en suite **CONF:** Thtr 30 Class 24 Board 16

Hotel Ibis London Gatwick

London Rd, County Oak RH11 0PF
☎ 01293 590300 01293 590310
e-mail: H1889@accor-hotels.com
Dir: *M23 junct 10, take A2011 to Crawley. At rdbt 3rd exit, at next rdbt A23 London Rd towards Gatwick. Adjacent to Manor Industrial Est*
Modern, budget hotel offering comfortable accommodation in bright and practical bedrooms. Breakfast is self-service and dinner is available in the restaurant. For further details, consult the Hotel Groups page.
ROOMS: 141 en suite s £39.95-£46.95; d £39.95-£46.95

Premier Lodge (Gatwick Airport)

London Rd, Lowfield Heath RH10 9ST
☎ 0870 9906354 0870 9906355
Premier Lodge offers modern, well-equipped, en suite accommodation suitable for both business and leisure travellers. Meals can be taken at the adjacent popular restaurant and bar, which is fully licensed. For further details, consult the Hotel Groups page.
ROOMS: 102 en suite s £50; d £50 **CONF:** Thtr 200 Class 100 Board 80 Del from £105

Premier Lodge (Gatwick Crawley)

Goffs Park Rd RH11 8AX
☎ 0870 9906390 0870 9906391
Premier Lodge offers modern, well-equipped, en suite accommodation suitable for both business and leisure travellers. Meals can be taken at the adjacent popular restaurant and bar, which is fully licensed. For further details, consult the Hotel Groups page.
ROOMS: 56 en suite s £50; d £50 **CONF:** Thtr 120 Class 70 Board 40 Del from £12

Premier Lodge (Gatwick South)

Crawley Av, Gossops Green RH10 8BA
☎ 0870 9906546 0870 9906547
Premier Lodge offers modern, well-equipped, en suite accommodation suitable for both business and leisure travellers. Meals can be taken at the adjacent popular restaurant and bar, which is fully licensed. For further details, consult the Hotel Groups page.
ROOMS: 83 en suite s £50; d £50

Travel Inn

North Terminal, Longbridge Way RH6 0NX
☎ 0870 238 3305 01293 568278
Dir: *M23 junct 9/9A towards North Terminal, at rdbt take 3rd exit, hotel on right*
Travel Inn offers good-quality, value-for-money accommodation. Spacious, en suite rooms with bath and shower comfortably accommodate a family of up to two adults and two children (to age 15). The restaurant and bar offers a varied menu. For further

continued on p248

GATWICK AIRPORT (LONDON), continued

details and the Travel Inn phone number, consult the Hotel Groups page.

Travel Inn, Gatwick Airport

ROOMS: 219 en suite s £49.95; d £49.95

⇧ Travel Inn (Crawley)

Balcombe Rd RH10 3NL
☎ 08701 977067 📠 01293 873034
Dir: *On B2036 south towards Crawley from M23 junct 10*
Travel Inn offers good-quality, value-for-money accommodation. Spacious, en suite rooms with bath and shower comfortably accommodate a family of up to two adults and two children (to age 15). The restaurant and bar offers a varied menu. For further details and the Travel Inn phone number, consult the Hotel Groups page.
ROOMS: 41 en suite s £44.95; d £44.95

⇧ Travelodge Gatwick Airport

Church Rd, Lowfield Heath RH11 0PQ
☎ 08700 850 950 📠 01293 535369
Dir: *M23 junct 10, 1m S off A23*
Travelodge offers good quality, good value, modern accommodation. Ideal for families, the spacious, en suite bedrooms include remote-control TV, tea and coffee-making facilities, luxury beds and free morning newspaper. Meals can be taken at the nearby family restaurant. For further details and the Travelodge phone number, consult the Hotel Groups page.
ROOMS: 186 en suite s fr £42.95; d fr £42.95 **CONF:** Thtr 60 Class 25 Board 25

GERRARDS CROSS, Buckinghamshire — Map 06 TQ08

★★★69% Bull

Oxford Rd SL9 7PA
☎ 01753 885995 📠 01753 885504
e-mail: bull@sarova.co.uk
Dir: *M40 junct 2 follow Beaconsfield on A355. After 0.5m 2nd exit at rdbt signed A40 Gerrards Cross for 2m. The Bull on right*
This 17th-century inn, once the haunt of highwaymen, has been sympathetically refurbished. Guests have the use of the popular Jack Shrimpton bar or the attractive cocktail bar, and meals are served either in the comfortable restaurant or informally within the bar. Bedrooms are mostly spacious, tastefully furnished and provide an excellent range of facilities.
ROOMS: 123 en suite (3 fmly) No smoking in 74 bedrooms s fr £170; d fr £190 **LB** **FACILITIES:** STV Leisure facilities available nearby entertainment Xmas **CONF:** Thtr 150 Class 60 Board 50 Del £190 **SERVICES:** Lift **PARKING:** 200 **NOTES:** No dogs (ex guide dogs) No smoking in restaurant Civ Wed 150
CARDS:

★★70% *Ethorpe*

Packhorse Rd SL9 8HY
☎ 01753 882039 📠 01753 887012
Dir: *M40 junct 2 for Beaconsfield. At island right onto A40 to Gerrards Cross. At lights left into Packhouse Rd. Hotel at end on left*

This attractive hotel is located in the centre of town, within easy reach of the motorway network and Heathrow Airport. A complete programme of refurbishment and alterations has resulted in well-appointed and equipped, modern bedrooms. Meals are taken in the popular informal 'Chef and Brewer' restaurant and bar operation.
ROOMS: 34 rms (31 en suite) (2 fmly) **FACILITIES:** STV **CONF:** Thtr 30 Class 30 Board 18 **PARKING:** 80 **NOTES:** No dogs (ex guide dogs)
CARDS:

GILLAN, Cornwall & Isles of Scilly — Map 02 SW72

Top 200 - Hotel

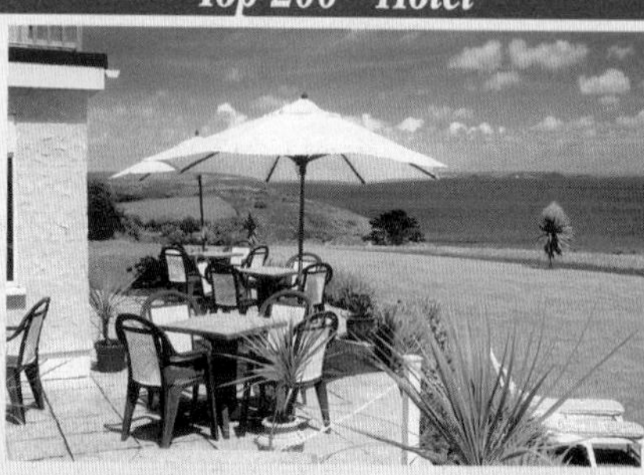

★★ ® Tregildry

TR12 6HG
☎ 01326 231378 📠 01326 231561
e-mail: trgildry@globalnet.co.uk
Dir: *From Helston take A3083 Lizard Rd. 1st left turn for St Keverne and follow signs for Manaccan & Gillan*
From its unspoilt and peaceful location Tregildry is blessed with both sea and river views. The tastefully furnished bedrooms and lounges are designed with comfort in mind and make the most of the wonderful views. Imaginative and innovative menus are served in the stylish dining room. There is direct access to the beach and adjacent coastal footpath.
ROOMS: 10 en suite No smoking in all bedrooms s £85-£100; d £140-£190 (incl. bkfst & dinner) **LB** **FACILITIES:** Boat hire Windsurfing **PARKING:** 15 **NOTES:** No children 8yrs No smoking in restaurant Closed Nov-Feb **CARDS:**

GF Indicates the number of bedrooms at ground floor level.

GILLINGHAM, Dorset Map 04 ST82

Top 200 - Hotel

★★★ ◎◎◎ **Stock Hill Country House**
Stock Hill SP8 5NR
☎ 01747 823626 🖹 01747 825628
e-mail: reception@stockhillhouse.co.uk
Dir: *3m E on B3081, off A303*

RELAIS & CHATEAUX

Set in eleven acres, this hotel has an impressive beech-lined driveway and beautiful gardens. The luxurious bedrooms are tastefully furnished with antiques, and provide high standards of comfort. Public rooms are sumptuously furnished and fine teas are served in front of the log fires. The accomplished cuisine uses top-quality local ingredients and has strong Austrian influences. Staff provide warm, attentive service.
ROOMS: 6 en suite 3 annexe en suite (3 GF) s £145-£165; d £240-£300 (incl. bkfst & dinner) **LB FACILITIES:** Tennis (hard) Sauna Croquet lawn Xmas **PARKING:** 20 **NOTES:** No dogs No children 7yrs No smoking in restaurant **CARDS:**

GILLINGHAM, Kent Map 07 TQ76

Travel Inn
Will Adams Way ME8 6BY
☎ 08701 977105 🖹 01634 261232
Dir: *From M2 (J4) turn left along A278 to A2. Turn left at Tesco and Travel Inn left at next rdbt*

Travel Inn offers good-quality, value-for-money accommodation. Spacious, en suite rooms with bath and shower comfortably accommodate a family of up to two adults and two children (to age 15). The restaurant and bar offers a varied menu. For further details and the Travel Inn phone number, consult the Hotel Groups page.
ROOMS: 45 en suite s £44.95; d £44.95 **CONF:** Thtr 20

Travelodge Medway
Medway Motorway Service Area, Rainham ME8 8PQ
☎ 08700 850 950 🖹 01634 360848
Dir: *between junct 4 & 5 of M2*

Travelodge

Travelodge offers good quality, good value, modern accommodation. Ideal for families, the spacious, en suite bedrooms include remote-control TV, tea and coffee-making facilities, luxury beds and free morning newspaper. Meals can be taken at the nearby family restaurant. For further details and the Travelodge phone number, consult the Hotel Groups page.
ROOMS: 58 en suite s fr £42.95; d fr £42.95

GLENRIDDING, Cumbria Map 18 NY31

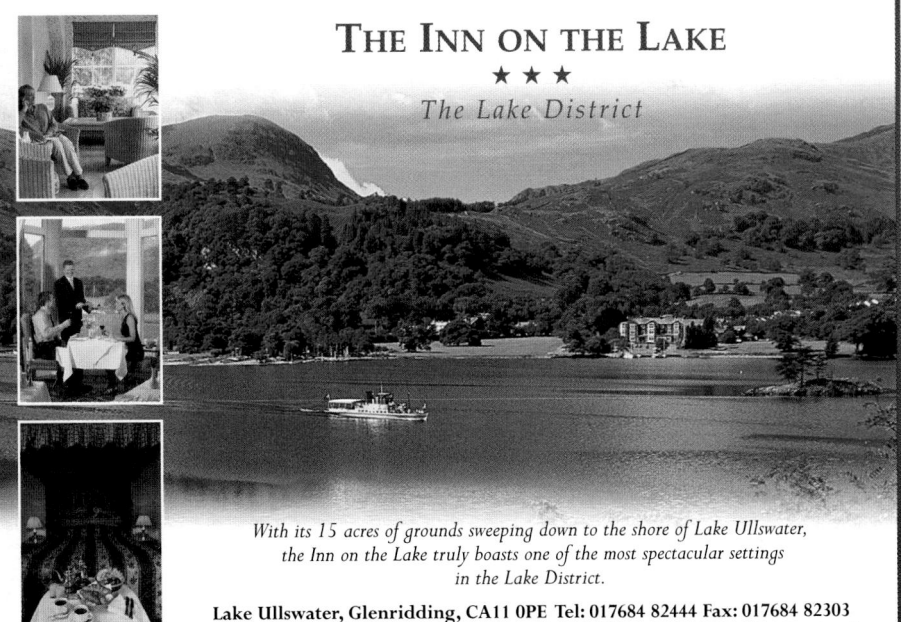

G

GLENRIDDING, Cumbria

Map 18 NY31

★★★72% The Inn on the Lake

Lake Ullswater, Glenridding CA11 0PE
☎ 017684 82444 017684 82303
e-mail: info@innonthelakeullswater.co.uk
Dir: *M6 junct 40, then A66 to Keswick. At rdbt take A592 to Ullswater Lake. Along lake to Glenridding. Hotel on left on entering village*

In a picturesque lakeside setting, this restored Victorian hotel is a popular destination for weddings and conferences. Superb Lakeland views may be enjoyed from the bedrooms which face the open lake or towering fells, and afternoon teas are served on the garden terrace during warmer months. Moorings for yachts are available to guests and sailing tuition can be provided.
ROOMS: 46 en suite (6 fmly) (2 GF) No smoking in 15 bedrooms s £59; d £96-£138 (incl. bkfst) **LB** **FACILITIES:** STV Tennis (grass) Fishing Sauna Solarium Gym Croquet lawn Putting green Jacuzzi Sailing, 9 hole pitch and putt, Bowls Xmas **CONF:** BC Thtr 120 Class 60 Board 40 Del from £110 **SERVICES:** Lift **PARKING:** 200 **NOTES:** No smoking in restaurant Civ Wed 100 **CARDS:**

See advert on page 249

★★★70% Glenridding

CA11 0PB
☎ 017684 82228 017684 82555
e-mail: glenridding@bestwestern.co.uk
Dir: *Northbound M6 exit 36, A591 Windermere then A592 14 miles. Southbound M6 exit 40, A592 for 13 miles*

Best Western

This friendly hotel benefits from a picturesque location in the centre of the village. Bedrooms, many with fine views of the surrounding fells and lake, include a number of recently upgraded rooms. Public areas are extensive and include a choice of restaurants and bars, a coffee shop and smart leisure facilities.
ROOMS: 36 en suite (9 fmly) No smoking in all bedrooms s £60-£108; d £77-£141 (incl. bkfst) **LB** **FACILITIES: Spa** STV Indoor swimming (H) Tennis (hard) Sauna Jacuzzi Billiards 3/4 Snooker table Table tennis Xmas **CONF:** Thtr 30 Class 30 Board 20 Del from £85 **SERVICES:** Lift **PARKING:** 38 **NOTES:** No smoking in restaurant Civ Wed 60
CARDS:

GLOSSOP, Derbyshire

Map 16 SK09

★★78% Wind in the Willows

Derbyshire Level SK13 7PT
☎ 01457 868001 01457 853354
e-mail: info@windinthewillows.co.uk
Dir: *1 mile E of Glossop on A57, turn right opp Royal Oak, hotel 400yds on right*

A warm and relaxed atmosphere prevails at this small and very comfortable hotel. The bedrooms are well furnished, each offering many thoughtful extras. Public areas include two comfortable

continued

lounges, a dining room, and a modern meeting room with views over the extensive grounds.
ROOMS: 12 en suite s £85-£95; d £105-£125 (incl. bkfst) **LB**
FACILITIES: Fishing **CONF:** Thtr 40 Class 12 Board 16 Del from £145
PARKING: 16 **NOTES:** No dogs No children 10yrs No smoking in restaurant **CARDS:**

GLOUCESTER, Gloucestershire

Map 10 SO81

★★★72% *Hatton Court*

Upton Hill, Upton St Leonards GL4 8DE
☎ 01452 617412 01452 612945
e-mail: res@hatton-court.co.uk
Dir: *leave Gloucester on B4073 Painswick Rd. Hotel at top of hill on right*

This beautifully preserved 17th-century Cotswold manor house is set in seven acres of well-kept gardens and is popular with both business and leisure guests. It stands at the top of Upton Hill and commands truly spectacular views of the Severn Valley. Bedrooms are comfortable and tastefully furnished with many extra facilities provided. The elegant Carringtons Restaurant offers a varied choice of menus, there is also a traditionally furnished bar and foyer lounge.
ROOMS: 17 en suite 28 annexe en suite No smoking in 11 bedrooms
FACILITIES: STV Sauna Gym Croquet lawn Jacuzzi **CONF:** Thtr 60 Class 30 Board 30 **PARKING:** 80 **NOTES:** No dogs (ex guide dogs) No smoking in restaurant Civ Wed 80
CARDS:

See advert on opposite page

★★★63% New County

44 Southgate St GL1 2DU
☎ 01452 307000 01452 500487
e-mail: mail@thenewcounty.com
Dir: *follow signs for City & Docks on A38. 2m, passing docks. At lights right lane onto one-way system, then left at Black Swan Inn into Southgate St. Hotel 100yds on left church*

Best Western

This traditional hotel in the heart of the city has been refurbished to offer modern comforts and well-equipped bedrooms. Public rooms include a bistro-style restaurant, a bar and a ballroom/function suite. Parking is available within close proximity of the hotel.
ROOMS: 39 en suite (3 fmly) No smoking in 8 bedrooms s £50-£62; d £60-£75 (incl. bkfst) **LB** **FACILITIES:** STV Xmas **CONF:** Thtr 160 Class 100 Board 60 Del from £80 **NOTES:** No smoking in restaurant
CARDS:

See advert on opposite page

> Popped the question?
> Hotels with Civ Wed in their entry are licensed for civil wedding ceremonies. Maximum numbers for the ceremony only are shown, e.g. Civ Wed 120

★★★62% ***Hatherley Manor***
Down Hatherley Ln GL2 9QA
☎ 01452 730217 🖷 01452 731032
e-mail: hatherleymanor@csmm.co.uk
Dir: *off A38 onto Down Hatherley Lane, signposted. Hotel 600yds on left*
Within easy striking distance of the M5, Gloucester, Cheltenham and the Cotswolds, this stylish 17th-century manor remains popular with both business and leisure guests. Some bedrooms are in the original building, and some are purpose-built; all offer contemporary comforts. A range of meeting and function rooms is available.
ROOMS: 52 en suite No smoking in 6 bedrooms **CONF:** Thtr 275 Class 90 Board 75 **PARKING:** 250 **NOTES:** No smoking in restaurant Civ Wed 300 **CARDS:** 

 ***Holiday Inn Gloucester***

Crest Way, Barnwood GL4 7RX
☎ 0870 400 9034 🖷 01452 371036
e-mail: reservations-gloucester@ichotelsgroup.com
Dir: *on A417 ring road to Barnwood, next to C & G building*
At the time of going to press, the classification for this hotel was not confirmed. Please refer to the AA internet site www.theAA.com for current information.
ROOMS: 122 en suite (25 fmly) No smoking in 60 bedrooms
FACILITIES: STV Indoor swimming (H) Sauna Solarium Gym Jacuzzi Spa pool Sauna Dance Studio **CONF:** Thtr 100 Class 45 Board 40
PARKING: 135 **NOTES:** No smoking in restaurant
CARDS: 

Destination dining!
This symbol indicates a Restaurant with Rooms

GLOUCESTER, continued

⌂ Express by Holiday Inn Gloucester South

Waterwells Business Park, Quedgeley GL2 4SA
☎ 01452 726400 📠 01452 722922
e-mail: gloucester@oriel-leisure.co.uk
Dir: *off M5 junct 12*

A modern hotel ideal for families and business travellers. Fresh and uncomplicated, the spacious bedrooms include Sky TV, power shower and tea and coffee-making facilities. Continental buffet breakfast is included in the room rate; other meals may be taken at the nearby family pub or restaurant. For further details and the Express by Holiday Inn phone number, consult the Hotel Groups pages.
ROOMS: 106 en suite s £49-£65; d £49-£65 (incl. cont bkfst)
CONF: Thtr 40 Class 30 Board 25

⌂ Premier Lodge (Gloucester East)

PREMIER LODGE

Barnwood GL4 3HR
☎ 0870 9906322 📠 0870 9906323
Dir: *M5 junct 11/A40 Gloucester, at 1st rdbt A417 Cirencester, next rdbt take 4th exit*
Premier Lodge offers modern, well-equipped, en suite accommodation suitable for both business and leisure travellers. Meals can be taken at the adjacent popular restaurant and bar, which is fully licensed. For further details, consult the Hotel Groups page.
ROOMS: 83 en suite s £48; d £48

⌂ Premier Lodge (Gloucester North)

Tewkesbury Rd, Twigworth GL2 9PG
☎ 0870 9906560 📠 0870 9906561
Premier Lodge offers modern, well-equipped, en suite accommodation suitable for both business and leisure travellers. Meals can be taken at the adjacent popular restaurant and bar, which is fully licensed. For further details, consult the Hotel Groups page.
ROOMS: 52 en suite s £48; d £48

⌂ Travel Inn (Gloucester Longford)

Tewkesbury Rd, Longford GL2 9BE
☎ 08701 977115 📠 01452 300924
Dir: *on A38 between Longford and Gloucester*
Travel Inn offers good-quality, value-for-money accommodation. Spacious, en suite rooms with bath and shower comfortably accommodate a family of up to two adults and two children (to age 15). The restaurant and bar offers a varied menu. For further details and the Travel Inn phone number, consult the Hotel Groups page.
ROOMS: 60 en suite s £44.95; d £44.95 **CONF:** Thtr 40

⌂ Travel Inn (Gloucester Witcombe)

travel inn

Witcombe GL3 4SS
☎ 08701 977116 📠 01452 864926
Dir: *M5 junct 11A follow A417 (Cirencester) at 1st exit turn right onto A46 towards Stroud/Witcombe. Left at next rdbt by Crosshands PH*
Travel Inn offers good-quality, value-for-money accommodation. Spacious, en suite rooms with bath and shower comfortably accommodate a family of up to two adults and two children (to age 15). The restaurant and bar offers a varied menu. For further details and the Travel Inn phone number, consult the Hotel Groups page.
ROOMS: 39 en suite s £44.95; d £44.95

GODALMING, Surrey Map 06 SU94

⌂ Innkeeper's Lodge

Innkeeper's Lodge

Ockford Rd GU7 1RH
☎ 01483 419997 📠 01483 410852
Dir: *Turn off A3/Milford at petrol station, turn left onto A3100, through Milford under railway bridge. Lodge on rdbt on right*
A new concept in the travel accommodation market. Smart rooms meet essential business requirements but also have home comforts. Dining options include all-day menus plus the added advantage of breakfast, which is included in the room price. For further details, consult the Hotel Groups page.
ROOMS: 20 en suite

GOMERSAL, West Yorkshire Map 19 SE22

★★★73% Gomersal Park

CLASSIC BRITISH

Moor Ln BD19 4LJ
☎ 01274 869386 📠 01274 861042
e-mail: gomersal@bestwestern.co.uk
Dir: *A62 to Huddersfield. At junct with A65, by Greyhound Pub right, after 1m take 1st right after Oakwell Hall*
Constructed around a 19th-century house, this stylish, modern hotel enjoys a peaceful location and pleasant grounds. Deep sofas ensure comfort in the open plan lounge while imaginative meals are served in the popular Restaurant 101. The well-equipped bedrooms have been recently refurbished to provide high quality and comfort. Extensive public areas include a well-equipped leisure complex and pool, and a wide variety of conference rooms.
ROOMS: 100 en suite (3 fmly) No smoking in 75 bedrooms s fr £95; d fr £95 (incl. bkfst) **LB FACILITIES:** STV Indoor swimming (H) Sauna Solarium Gym Jacuzzi Swimming pool supervised Xmas **CONF:** BC Thtr 250 Class 130 Board 60 Del from £115 **SERVICES:** Lift **PARKING:** 150 **NOTES:** No smoking in restaurant Civ Wed 150
CARDS:

★★65% *Gomersal Lodge*

Spen Ln BD19 4PJ
☎ 01274 861111 📠 01274 861111
e-mail: enquiries@gomersallodge.co.uk
Dir: *M62 junct 27, A62 towards Huddersfield. Right at Greyhound Pub, hotel 1m on right*
Gomersal Lodge Hotel nestles in five acres of landscaped grounds and attractive gardens. This 19th-century house offers well furnished bedrooms together with a cosy bar. The elegant restaurant is noted for its flexible, contemporary menu, and popularity as a venue for weddings.
ROOMS: 9 en suite (1 fmly) No smoking in 4 bedrooms **CONF:** Thtr 20 Class 12 Board 12 **PARKING:** 70 **NOTES:** No dogs (ex guide dogs) No smoking in restaurant **CARDS:**

GOODRICH, Herefordshire Map 10 SO51

★★71% **Ye Hostelrie**
HR9 6HX
☎ 01600 890241 Fax 01600 890838
e-mail: info@ye-hostelrie.co.uk
Dir: *1m off A40, between Ross-on-Wye and Monmouth, 100yds from Goodrich Castle*

Parts of this unusual building are reputed to date back to 1625. It is privately owned and personally run, and considerable improvements to both accommodation and public areas have been made in the last few years. Facilities include a function room, a pleasant garden and a patio area.
ROOMS: 7 en suite (1 fmly) s £33; d £55 (incl. bkfst) **CONF:** Thtr 80 Class 60 Board 20 **PARKING:** 25 **NOTES:** No smoking in restaurant
CARDS:

See advert under ROSS-ON-WYE

GOODRINGTON See Paignton

GOODWOOD, West Sussex Map 06 SU81

★★★★72% ◎◎ ***Marriott Goodwood Park Hotel & Country Club***
PO18 0QB
☎ 01243 775537 Fax 01243 520120
e-mail: reservations.goodwood@marriotthotels.co.uk
Dir: *off A285, 3m NE of Chichester*

This attractive and well-maintained hotel offers extensive indoor and outdoor leisure facilities. All bedrooms are furnished to a consistent high standard; some are upstairs in the original building. Quality cuisine is served in the Richmond restaurant and the smart cocktail bar has fascinating pictures of the Goodwood motor-racing heritage.
ROOMS: 94 en suite No smoking in 54 bedrooms **FACILITIES:** STV Indoor swimming (H) Golf 18 Tennis (hard) Sauna Solarium Gym Putting green Jacuzzi Beauty salons **CONF:** Thtr 150 Class 60 Board 60 **PARKING:** 350 **NOTES:** No dogs (ex guide dogs) No smoking in restaurant Civ Wed 120 **CARDS:**

GOOLE, East Riding of Yorkshire Map 17 SE72

Travel Inn
Rawcliffe Rd, Airmyn DN14 8JS
☎ 08701 977177 Fax 01405 722661
Dir: *Leave M62 at junct 36, onto A614 signed Rawcliffe. Travel Inn immediately on left.*
Travel Inn offers good-quality, value-for-money accommodation. Spacious, en suite rooms with bath and shower comfortably accommodate a family of up to two adults and two children (to age 15). The restaurant and bar offers a varied menu. For further details and the Travel Inn phone number, consult the Hotel Groups page.
ROOMS: 41 en suite s £44.95; d £44.95 **CONF:** Board 12

GORDANO SERVICE AREA (M5), Somerset Map 04 ST57

Days Inn
BS20 7XG
☎ 01275 373709 & 373624 Fax 01275 374104
e-mail: gordano.hotel@welcomebreak.co.uk
Dir: *M5 junct 19, follow signs for Gordano services*
This modern building offers accommodation in smart, spacious and well-equipped bedrooms, suitable for families and business travellers, and all with en suite bathrooms. Continental breakfast is available and other refreshments may be taken at the nearby family restaurant. For further details and the Days Inn phone number, consult the Hotel Groups page.
ROOMS: 60 en suite s £49-£60; d £49-£60 **CONF:** Board 10

GORLESTON-ON-SEA See Great Yarmouth

GOSFORTH, Cumbria Map 18 NY00

★★71% **Westlakes**
CA20 1HP
☎ 019467 25221 Fax 019467 25099
e-mail: wlhotel@aol.com
Dir: *at junct of A595 and B5344*
A Georgian country house set in tranquil, mature gardens; warm hospitality is a trademark of this characterful hotel. Public areas include a compact lounge bar and an attractive dining room comprising three rooms, one of which is ideal for private dining or meetings. Bedrooms vary in style and are all thoughtfully equipped.
ROOMS: 9 en suite (1 fmly) s £54-£60; d £61-£70 (incl. bkfst) **FACILITIES:** STV Croquet lawn **PARKING:** 25 **NOTES:** No dogs (ex guide dogs) No smoking in restaurant Closed 22 Dec-4 Jan
CARDS:

GRANGE-OVER-SANDS, Cumbria Map 18 SD47

★★★73% **Netherwood**
Lindale Rd LA11 6ET
☎ 015395 32552 Fax 015395 34121
e-mail: blawith@aol.com
Dir: *on B5277 before station*
This imposing hotel stands in terraced grounds and enjoys fine views of Morecambe Bay. Though a popular conference and wedding venue, good levels of hospitality and service ensure all guests are well looked after. Bedrooms vary in size but all are well furnished and decorated, and have smart modern bathrooms. Magnificent woodwork is a feature of public areas.
ROOMS: 28 en suite (5 fmly) No smoking in 14 bedrooms s £65-£75; d £130-£150 (incl. bkfst) **LB** **FACILITIES: Spa** Indoor swimming (H) Solarium Gym Croquet lawn Beauty salon, Steam room, Swimming pool supervised **CONF:** BC Thtr 150 Class 30 Board 40 Del from £115 **SERVICES:** Lift **PARKING:** 100 **NOTES:** No smoking in restaurant Civ Wed 150 **CARDS:**

GRANGE-OVER-SANDS, continued

★★★65% *Graythwaite Manor*

Fernhill Rd LA11 7JE
☎ 015395 32001 & 33755 015395 35549
e-mail: enquiries@graythwaitemanor.co.uk
Dir: *B5277 through Grange, Fernhill Rd opposite fire station behind small traffic island, hotel 1st left*

This well established hotel is set in extensive gardens, complete with sub-tropical plants, and offers a delightful outlook over Morecambe Bay. Public areas include an Orangery, a number of comfortable lounges and an elegant restaurant. Comfortable bedrooms, which vary in size, are traditional in style.

ROOMS: 21 en suite (2 fmly) **FACILITIES:** Tennis (hard) Putting green **CONF:** Thtr 50 Class 30 Board 20 **SERVICES:** Lift **PARKING:** 32 **NOTES:** No dogs (ex guide dogs) No smoking in restaurant
CARDS:

★★69% Hampsfell House

Hampsfell Rd LA11 6BG
☎ 015395 32567 015395 35995
e-mail: hampsfellhotel@msn.com
Dir: *M6 junct 36 take A590 signed Barrow-in-Furness. At junct with B5277, follow to Grange-over-Sands signs. Left at rdbt into Main St, 2nd rdbt right and right at x-rds. At Hampsfell Rd left*

Dating back to 1800, this family-run hotel is peacefully set in two acres of private grounds yet is only minutes' walk from the town centre. Bedrooms are smartly decorated and well maintained. The two cosy and comfortable lounges, where guests can enjoy pre-dinner drinks, share a central bar. Guests can enjoy very well-prepared meals in the refurbished formal dining room.

ROOMS: 9 en suite (1 fmly) No smoking in 4 bedrooms s £41-£47; d £82-£90 (incl. bkfst) **LB** **FACILITIES:** Xmas **PARKING:** 12 **NOTES:** No children 5yrs No smoking in restaurant
CARDS:

★78% Clare House

Park Rd LA11 7HQ
☎ 015395 33026 & 34253
e-mail: info@clarehousehotel.co.uk
Dir: *off A590 onto B5277, through Lindale into Grange, keep left, hotel 0.5m on left past Crown Hill and St Paul's Church*

A warm, genuine welcome awaits guests at this delightful, family-run hotel. Nestling in its own secluded gardens, it provides a relaxed haven in which to enjoy the panoramic views across Morecambe Bay. Bedrooms and public areas are comfortable and attractively furnished. Skilfully prepared dinners and hearty breakfasts are served in the elegant dining room.

ROOMS: 17 rms (16 en suite) (1 fmly) (2 GF) s £58-£60; d £116-£120 (incl. bkfst & dinner) **LB** **FACILITIES:** Croquet lawn Putting green **PARKING:** 18 **NOTES:** No dogs (ex guide dogs) No children 5yrs No smoking in restaurant Closed Dec-Mar RS 10-30 Nov
CARDS:

GRANTHAM, Lincolnshire

Map 11 SK93

★★★70% Grantham Marriott

Marriott HOTELS · RESORTS · SUITES

Swingbridge Rd NG31 7XT
☎ 01476 593000 01476 592592
e-mail: eckhard.oster@whitbread.com
Dir: *off A1 at junct Grantham/Melton Mowbray onto A607. From N 1st exit at mini rdbt, hotel on right. From S at T junct, right to Grantham under A1. Left to hotel*

This smart, modern hotel is a convenient base from which to explore the countryside. Hotel bedrooms are spacious, tastefully decorated and have a range of extras. Public rooms, which extend into a pretty courtyard in the summer, include function rooms and a small leisure club with swimming pool and fitness room.

ROOMS: 90 en suite No smoking in 68 bedrooms s £99; d £99 **LB** **FACILITIES:** **Spa** STV Indoor swimming (H) Sauna Gym Jacuzzi Steam room Xmas **CONF:** Thtr 200 Class 90 Board 50 Del £139 **PARKING:** 150 **NOTES:** No dogs (ex guide dogs) No smoking in restaurant Civ Wed 80 **CARDS:**

★★★70% Kings

Best Western

North Pde NG31 8AU
☎ 01476 590800 01476 577072
e-mail: kings@bestwestern.co.uk
Dir: *off A1 at rdbt N end of Grantham onto B1174, follow road for 2m. Hotel on left by bridge*

A friendly atmosphere exists within this extended Georgian house. Bedrooms are attractively decorated and furnished in modern light oak. Dining options include the formal Victorian restaurant and the popular Orangery, which also operates as a coffee shop and breakfast room; a lounge bar and a smart open-plan foyer lounge are also available.

ROOMS: 21 en suite (2 fmly) s £53-£63; d £63-£73 (incl. bkfst) **LB** **FACILITIES:** STV Tennis (hard) **CONF:** Thtr 100 Class 50 Board 40 Del from £82.50 **PARKING:** 36 **NOTES:** No smoking in restaurant
CARDS:

Travelodge Grantham North

Travelodge

Grantham Service Area, Grantham North, Gonerby Moor NG32 2AB
☎ 08700 850 950
Dir: *4m N on A1*

Travelodge offers good quality, good value, modern accommodation. Ideal for families, the spacious, en suite bedrooms include remote-control TV, tea and coffee-making facilities, luxury beds and free morning newspaper. Meals can be taken at the nearby family restaurant. For further details and the Travelodge phone number, consult the Hotel Groups page.

ROOMS: 39 en suite s fr £42.95; d fr £42.95

GRASMERE, Cumbria

Map 18 NY30

★★★★70% Wordsworth

LA22 9SW
☎ 015394 35592 015394 35765
e-mail: enquiry@wordsworth-grasmere.co.uk
Dir: *centre of village adjacent to St Oswald's Church*

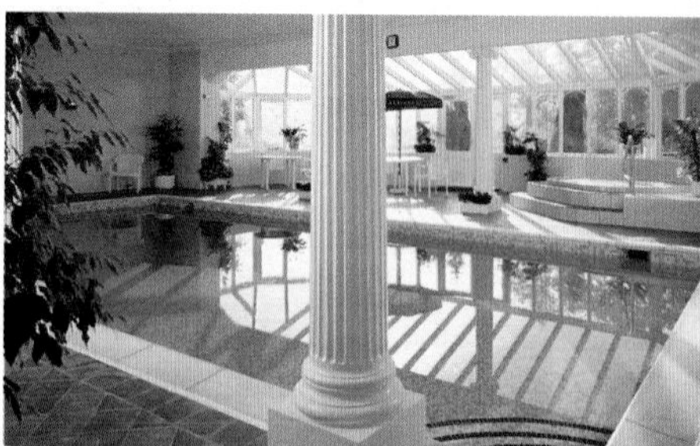

This traditional hotel, named after the poet buried in the adjacent churchyard, is set in well tended gardens with a backdrop of towering fells. Bedrooms, varying in size and style, are complemented by a choice of comfortable lounge areas. To complete the package there are comprehensive leisure facilities,

continued

whilst diners have a choice between the popular pub and the more formal Prelude restaurant.
ROOMS: 37 en suite (3 fmly) s £120-£200; d £190-£300 (incl. bkfst & dinner) **LB** **FACILITIES:** STV Indoor swimming (H) Sauna Solarium Gym Croquet lawn Jacuzzi entertainment Xmas **CONF:** BC Thtr 100 Class 50 Board 40 Del from £142.50 **SERVICES:** Lift **PARKING:** 60 **NOTES:** No dogs (ex guide dogs) No smoking in restaurant Civ Wed 120 **CARDS:**

See advert on this page

★★★73% Gold Rill Country House

Red Bank Rd LA22 9PU
☎ 015394 35486 🖷 015394 35486
e-mail: enquiries@gold-rill.com
Dir: *turn off A591 into village centre, turn into road opposite St Oswald's Church. Hotel 300yds on left*

This popular hotel enjoys a peaceful location on the edge of the village with spectacular views of the lake and surrounding fells. Spacious bedrooms, some with balconies, are tastefully decorated and many have separate, comfortable seating areas. The hotel boasts a private pier, an outdoor heated pool and a putting green. Public areas include a well-appointed restaurant and lounges complete with log fires.
ROOMS: 25 en suite 6 annexe en suite (2 fmly) s £48-£72; d £96-£144 (incl. bkfst & dinner) **LB** **FACILITIES:** STV Outdoor swimming (H) Croquet lawn Putting green Xmas **PARKING:** 35 **NOTES:** No dogs (ex guide dogs) No smoking in restaurant Closed mid Dec-mid Jan (open New Year) **CARDS:**

★★★72% Rothay Garden

Broadgate LA22 9RJ
☎ 015394 35334 🖷 015394 35723
e-mail: stay@rothay-garden.com
Dir: *off A591, opposite Swan Hotel, into Grasmere, 300yds on left*

Located on the northern approach to this unspoilt Cumbrian village, this hotel offers comfortable bedrooms, including some with four-posters and whirlpool baths. There is a choice of relaxing lounges and a cosy cocktail bar, as well as a conservatory restaurant, which enjoys magnificent views across the lawns up into the fells.
ROOMS: 25 en suite (2 fmly) (6 GF) No smoking in 6 bedrooms s £65-£73; d £129-£179 (incl. bkfst & dinner) **LB** **FACILITIES:** STV Fishing Jacuzzi use of local leisure club Xmas **PARKING:** 38 **NOTES:** No smoking in restaurant **CARDS:**

★★★72% Thistle Grasmere

THISTLE HOTELS

Keswick Rd LA22 9PR
☎ 0870 333 9135 🖷 0870 333 9235
e-mail: grasmere@thistle.co.uk
Dir: *A591 to Grasmere (don't go into village). Hotel opp Dove Cottage after 2nd turn for Grasmere*

This large hotel stands in its own gardens leading to the lake, and

continued on p256

G

GRASMERE, continued

many of the bedrooms have fine views over the surrounding fells. Bedrooms are comfortably furnished and include a stylish suite, complete with a four-poster bed. Service is friendly and the choice of meals, from a selection of restaurant and bar menus, should suit most tastes.
ROOMS: 72 en suite (8 fmly) No smoking in 58 bedrooms s £58-£100; d £75-£125 (incl. bkfst) **LB FACILITIES:** STV Fishing Xmas **CONF:** Thtr 110 Class 60 Board 40 **PARKING:** 60 **NOTES:** No smoking in restaurant Civ Wed 150 **CARDS:**

★★★71% Red Lion

Red Lion Square LA22 9SS
☎ 015394 35456 015394 35579
e-mail: enquires@hotelgrasmere.uk.com
Dir: *off A591, signed Grasmere Village, hotel in centre of village*

Best Western

This modernised and extended 18th-century coaching inn, located in the heart of the village, offers spacious well-equipped rooms and a number of meeting and conference facilities. The Lamb Inn offers a range of pub meals to complement the more formal Courtyard restaurant. The recently extended, comfortable lounge area is ideal for relaxing in with a drink after dinner.
ROOMS: 47 en suite (4 fmly) No smoking in 22 bedrooms s £45-£59; d £90-£128 (incl. bkfst) **FACILITIES:** STV Indoor swimming (H) Sauna Solarium Gym Jacuzzi Hairdressing Xmas **CONF:** Thtr 60 Class 30 Board 30 Del from £90 **SERVICES:** Lift **PARKING:** 38 **NOTES:** No smoking in restaurant **CARDS:**

See advert on page 255

★★★71% The Swan

LA22 9RF
☎ 0870 400 8132 015394 35741
e-mail: swangrasmere@macdonald-hotels.co.uk
Dir: *M6 junct 36, A591 towards Kendal, A590 to Keswick through Ambleside. The Swan on right on entering village*

MACDONALD HOTELS

Close to Dove Cottage and occupying a prominent position on the edge of the village, Wordsworth mentioned this 300-year-old inn in his poem *'The Waggoner'*. Attractive public areas are spacious and comfortable; bedrooms are equally stylish and have CD players. A good range of bar meals is available, while the elegant restaurant offers more formal dining.
ROOMS: 38 en suite (1 fmly) (28 GF) No smoking in 14 bedrooms s £40-£105; d £110-£150 (incl. bkfst & dinner) **LB FACILITIES:** Xmas **CONF:** Thtr 30 Class 24 Board 16 Del from £85 **PARKING:** 45 **NOTES:** No smoking in restaurant Civ Wed 60
CARDS:

Popped the question?
Hotels with Civ Wed in their entry are licensed for civil wedding ceremonies. Maximum numbers for the ceremony only are shown, e.g. Civ Wed 120

★★74% Grasmere

Broadgate LA22 9TA
☎ 015394 35277 015394 35277
e-mail: enquiries@grasmerehotel.co.uk
Dir: *A591 from Ambleside, 2nd left into town centre. Follow road over humpback bridge, past playing field. Hotel on left*
Attentive and hospitable service contribute to the atmosphere at this family-run hotel, set in secluded gardens bordered by the River Rothay. There are two inviting lounges (one with residents' bar) and an attractive dining room looking onto the garden. The thoughtfully prepared dinner menu makes careful use of fresh ingredients. Pine furniture is featured in most bedrooms, along with some welcome personal touches.
ROOMS: 13 en suite (2 GF) No smoking in all bedrooms s £50-£70; d £100-£140 (incl. bkfst & dinner) **LB FACILITIES:** Croquet lawn Putting green Xmas **PARKING:** 15 **NOTES:** No children 9yrs No smoking in restaurant Closed Jan-8 Feb **CARDS:**

★★71% Oak Bank

Broadgate LA22 9TA
☎ 015394 35217 015394 35685
e-mail: grasmereoakbank@btinternet.com
Dir: *on right in village centre*
This privately owned and personally run hotel provides well-equipped accommodation, including a bedroom on ground floor level and a four-poster room. Public areas include a choice of comfortable lounges with welcoming log fires when the weather is cold. There is a pleasant bar and an attractive restaurant with a conservatory extension overlooking the garden.
ROOMS: 15 en suite (1 fmly) No smoking in all bedrooms s £63-£65; d £106-£120 (incl. bkfst & dinner) **LB FACILITIES:** Jacuzzi Xmas **PARKING:** 11 **NOTES:** No smoking in restaurant Closed 6-20 Jan
CARDS:

Top 200 - Hotel

★ ® White Moss House

Rydal Water LA22 9SE
☎ 015394 35295 015394 35516
e-mail: sue@whitemoss.com
Dir: *on A591, 1m S of Grasmere*
This traditional Lakeland house was once bought by Wordsworth for his son. It benefits from a central location and has a loyal following. The individually styled bedrooms are comfortable and thoughtfully equipped. There is also a two-room suite in a cottage on the hillside above the hotel. The five-course set dinner makes good use of the quality local ingredients. Afternoon tea and pre-dinner drinks are served in the inviting lounge.
ROOMS: 5 en suite 2 annexe en suite s £85-£95; d £144-£190 (incl. bkfst & dinner) **LB FACILITIES:** Free use local leisure club, Free fishing at local waters **PARKING:** 10 **NOTES:** No dogs No smoking in restaurant Closed Dec-Jan RS Sun **CARDS:**

GRASSINGTON, North Yorkshire
Map 19 SE06

★★65% Grassington House
5 The Square BD23 5AQ
☎ 01756 752406 🖷 01756 752135
Dir: *B6265 from Skipton, on right side of village square*
A warm welcome awaits guests at this conveniently located, central hotel in the main square. Private parking is available. Comfortable accommodation is provided, with bedrooms of a good size. Public areas are spacious and pleasant to relax in. A good range of dishes is offered in both the informal bar and the modern well-appointed restaurant.
ROOMS: 9 en suite (2 fmly) No smoking in all bedrooms s fr £36; d fr £59 (incl. bkfst) **LB** **FACILITIES:** Xmas **PARKING:** 20 **NOTES:** No smoking in restaurant **CARDS:**

GRAVESEND, Kent
Map 06 TQ67

★★★72% Manor Hotel
Hever Court Rd DA12 5UQ
☎ 01474 353100 🖷 01474 354978
e-mail: manor@bestwestern.co.uk
Dir: *at junct of A2 Gravesend East turn off*
Conveniently located just off the A2, this hotel is ideal for local attractions, such as Bluewater shopping village. Attractively decorated bedrooms are spacious and fitted with numerous facilities. A refurbished bar and smart restaurant is available along with an impressive health club with swimming pool, sauna and gymnasium.
ROOMS: 52 en suite (3 fmly) No smoking in 37 bedrooms s fr £75; d £85-£175 (incl. bkfst) **FACILITIES:** STV Indoor swimming (H) Sauna Solarium Gym **CONF:** BC Thtr 200 Class 100 Board 25 Del from £115 **PARKING:** 100 **NOTES:** No dogs (ex guide dogs) No smoking in restaurant **CARDS:**

GRAVESEND, continued

Premier Lodge (Gravesend)

Hevercourt Rd, Singlewell DA12 5UQ
☎ 0870 9906352 📠 0870 9906353
Premier Lodge offers modern, well-equipped, en suite accommodation suitable for both business and leisure travellers. Meals can be taken at the adjacent popular restaurant and bar, which is fully licensed. For further details, consult the Hotel Groups page.
ROOMS: 31 en suite s £48; d £48

Travel Inn
Wrotham Rd DA11 7LF
☎ 08701 977118 📠 01474 323776

Dir: *1m from A2 on A227 towards Gravesend town centre*

Travel Inn offers good-quality, value-for-money accommodation. Spacious, en suite rooms with bath and shower comfortably accommodate a family of up to two adults and two children (to age 15). The restaurant and bar offers a varied menu. For further details and the Travel Inn phone number, consult the Hotel Groups page.
ROOMS: 36 en suite s £44.95; d £44.95 **CONF:** Thtr 40 Board 20

GREAT CHESTERFORD, Essex
Map 12 TL54

★★★66% **The Crown House**
CB10 1NY
☎ 01799 530515 📠 01799 530683
Dir: *From north leave M11 at J9, from south J10, follow signs for Saffron Walden and then Great Chesterford (B1383)*
Tudor coaching inn situated in a peaceful village location close to the M11. The property has been sympathetically restored and retains much of its original character. The well-equipped bedrooms are individually decorated; some rooms have four poster beds. Public rooms include an attractive lounge bar, an elegant restaurant and an airy conservatory.
ROOMS: 8 en suite 10 annexe en suite (1 fmly) (5 GF) s £55-£70; d £80-£95 (incl. bkfst) **LB CONF:** Thtr 38 Class 40 Board 30 **PARKING:** 30 **NOTES:** No smoking in restaurant Civ Wed 40
CARDS:

See advert on page 257

GREAT DUNMOW, Essex
Map 06 TL62

Restaurant with Rooms

Starr Restaurant with Rooms
Market Place CM6 1AX
☎ 01371 874321 📠 01371 876337
e-mail: starrrestaurant@btinternet.com
Dir: *M11 junct 8, onto A120. After 7m, left into Great Dunmow, then left into Market Place in town centre*
A 15th-century former coaching inn situated in the heart of this charming Essex village. It is well known locally for its quality food, which is served in the elegantly appointed beamed restaurant and conservatory. The spacious bedrooms are in a converted stable

continued

block adjacent to the main building and each is individually decorated and tastefully furnished.

ROOMS: 8 annexe en suite s £70; d £110-£130 (incl. bkfst) **CONF:** Thtr 36 Board 16 Del from £127.50 **PARKING:** 16 **NOTES:** No smoking in restaurant **CARDS:**

GREAT MILTON, Oxfordshire
Map 05 SP60

Top 200 - Hotel

★★★★
Le Manoir Aux Quat' Saisons

Church Rd OX44 7PD
☎ 01844 278881 📠 01844 278847
e-mail: lemanoir@blanc.co.uk
Dir: *from A329 2nd right to Great Milton Manor, hotel 200yds on right*
Luxury is the keyword at this renowned hotel, set in beautiful gardens which produce many of the organic ingredients for the kitchens. Individually styled bedrooms, some in the main house and others in the garden courtyard, offer the highest levels of comfort and quality, together with the many thoughtful touches which make a stay really memorable. Personally chosen pieces of artwork feature throughout the public rooms, which include the centrepiece of any visit to Le Manoir – the conservatory restaurant.
ROOMS: 9 en suite 23 annexe en suite s £265-£1200; d £265-£1200 (incl. bkfst) **LB FACILITIES:** STV Croquet lawn Cookery School, Water Gardens Xmas **CONF:** Thtr 24 Board 20 **PARKING:** 60 **NOTES:** No dogs (ex guide dogs) No smoking in restaurant Civ Wed 55 **CARDS:**

GREAT YARMOUTH, Norfolk Map 13 TG50

★★★75% ***Cliff***

Cliff Hill, Gorleston NR31 6DH
☎ 01493 662179 01493 653617
Dir: *M11 onto A11 to Norwich then A47 to Gt Yarmouth. At N end of Gorleston's Upper Marine Parade*

Overlooking the harbour just a short walk from the beach, promenade and Gorleston town centre. Public rooms include a choice of bars, an attractive lounge and a stylish restaurant where an interesting choice of dishes are served. Bedrooms are smartly decorated, with co-ordinated soft furnishings and feature many thoughtful touches; some rooms have lovely sea views.
ROOMS: 39 en suite (2 fmly) No smoking in 2 bedrooms **FACILITIES:** STV entertainment **CONF:** Thtr 170 Class 150 Board 80 **PARKING:** 70 **NOTES:** Civ Wed 120
CARDS:

★★★71% **Imperial**

THE INDEPENDENTS

North Dr NR30 1EQ
☎ 01493 842000 01493 852229
e-mail: imperial@scs-datacom.co.uk
Dir: *follow signs to seafront and turn left. Hotel opposite tennis courts*
A friendly, family-run hotel situated at the quieter end of the seafront within easy walking distance of the town. Bedrooms are attractively decorated with co-ordinated soft furnishings and equipped with modern facilities; many rooms have superb sea views. Public areas offer a good level of comfort and include the smart Savoie Lounge Bar and the Rambouillet Restaurant.
ROOMS: 39 en suite (4 fmly) No smoking in 21 bedrooms s £54-£74; d £64-£86 (incl. bkfst) **LB** **FACILITIES:** STV Xmas **CONF:** Thtr 140 Class 40 Board 30 Del from £75 **SERVICES:** Lift **PARKING:** 50 **NOTES:** Civ Wed 120 **CARDS:**

★★★68% **Regency Dolphin**
Albert Square NR30 3JH
☎ 01493 855070 01493 853798
e-mail: regencydolphin@countrytown-hotels.co.uk
Dir: *along seafront and right at Wellington Pier. Right into Kimberley Ter then left into Albert Sq, hotel on left*
Large privately owned hotel situated at the quieter end of town just off the seafront and within easy walking distance of the town centre. The pleasantly decorated bedrooms are generally quite spacious and well equipped. Public rooms include a comfortable lounge, a bar and intimate restaurant. The hotel also has an outdoor swimming pool.
ROOMS: 47 en suite (5 fmly) (2 GF) No smoking in 9 bedrooms s £50-£70; d £60-£78 **LB** **FACILITIES:** Outdoor swimming (H) Xmas **CONF:** Thtr 140 Class 50 Board 30 Del from £75 **PARKING:** 19 **NOTES:** No smoking in restaurant Civ Wed 120
CARDS:

★★★67% **Star**
Hall Quay NR30 1HG
☎ 01493 842294 01493 330215
e-mail: star.hotel@elizabethhotels.co.uk
Dir: *from Norwich on A47 over 1st rdbt. At 2nd rdbt 3rd exit. Hotel on left*
The black and white façade of this 17th-century property makes it one of the town's most striking buildings. The property overlooks the quayside and is situated just a short walk from the town centre. Public rooms are smartly appointed and include a choice of bars, a restaurant and a tastefully furnished lounge. Bedrooms are pleasantly decorated and equipped with modern facilities.
ROOMS: 40 en suite (1 fmly) No smoking in 13 bedrooms s £75-£100; d £90-£160 (incl. bkfst) **LB** **FACILITIES:** STV Discount for the marina leisure centre pool, gym Xmas **CONF:** Thtr 75 Class 30 Board 30 Del from £75 **SERVICES:** Lift **PARKING:** 20 **NOTES:** No smoking in restaurant **CARDS:**

★★74% **The Arden Court Hotel**
93-94 North Denes Rd NR30 4LW
☎ 01493 855310 01493 304913
e-mail: linda@ardencourt.fsnet.co.uk
Dir: *at seafront left along North Dr. At boating lake left. 2nd right at mini rdbt into North Denes Rd*
A warm welcome is offered at this friendly family-run hotel which is situated in a residential area just a short walk from the seafront. The individually decorated bedrooms are smartly furnished and equipped with a good range of useful extras. Public rooms are attractively presented and feature a smart lounge bar and a restaurant serving freshly prepared home-cooked dishes.
ROOMS: 14 en suite (4 fmly) No smoking in 8 bedrooms **PARKING:** 14 **NOTES:** No dogs (ex guide dogs) No smoking in restaurant
CARDS:

★★70% **Knights Court Hotel**
22 North Dr NR30 4EW
☎ 01493 843089 01493 850780
e-mail: davidandhazel@tinyworld.co.uk
Dir: *From A47 and A12, follow signs to seafront, turn left, hotel is opposite Venetian Waterways and Gardens*
Small, well-maintained and privately-owned hotel overlooking the Venetian waterways and the sea. The spacious bedrooms are pleasantly decorated and equipped with a good range of useful extras; many rooms have lovely sea views. Breakfast and dinner are served in the smart dining room and guests have the use of a cosy lounge bar.
ROOMS: 14 en suite 6 annexe en suite (4 fmly) (6 GF) No smoking in 13 bedrooms s £33-£44; d £46-£58 (incl. bkfst) **PARKING:** 20 **NOTES:** No dogs (ex guide dogs) No children 3yrs No smoking in restaurant Closed Nov-mid Mar **CARDS:**

★★69% **Furzedown**
19-20 North Dr NR30 4EW
☎ 01493 844138 01493 844138
e-mail: Paul@furzedownhotel.freeserve.co.uk
Dir: *at end of A47 or A12, head for seafront, left, hotel opposite Waterways*
This hotel is situated at the northern end of the seafront overlooking the beach and Venetian waterways. Bedrooms are pleasantly decorated and equipped with a good range of useful extras; many have superb sea views. The newly refurbished public

continued on p260

G

GREAT YARMOUTH, continued

areas include a comfortable lounge bar, a smartly appointed restaurant and a TV room.

Furzedown, Great Yarmouth

ROOMS: 24 rms (20 en suite) (11 fmly) s £43-£48; d £59-£69 (incl. bkfst) **LB** **FACILITIES:** STV **CONF:** Thtr 75 Class 80 Board 40 Del from £50.50 **PARKING:** 15 **NOTES:** No smoking in restaurant
CARDS:

★★68% ***Regency***
5 North Dr NR30 1ED
☎ 01493 843759 01493 330411
e-mail: regency35@hotmail.com
Dir: *on seafront*
The Barnett family has been welcoming guests to their privately-owned hotel for a number of years. The property is situated at the quieter end of the seafront overlooking the tennis courts, beach and sea beyond. The thoughtfully equipped, pleasantly decorated bedrooms come in a variety of sizes and styles; many have wonderful sea views. Public areas include a cosy lounge bar and a smart restaurant.
ROOMS: 14 en suite (2 fmly) **PARKING:** 10 **NOTES:** No dogs (ex guide dogs) No children 7yrs No smoking in restaurant Closed Jan
CARDS:

★★66% ***Burlington Palm Court***
11 North Dr NR30 1EG
☎ 01493 844568 & 842095 01493 331848
e-mail: enquiries@burlington-hotel.co.uk
Dir: *A12 to seafront, left at Britannia Pier. Hotel near tennis courts*

Privately-owned hotel situated at the quiet end of the resort, overlooking the sea. Bedrooms come in a variety of sizes and styles; they are pleasantly decorated and well-equipped, and many have lovely sea views. The spacious public rooms include a range of seating areas, a choice of dining rooms and two bars.
ROOMS: 71 en suite (9 fmly) No smoking in 14 bedrooms
FACILITIES: Spa STV Indoor swimming (H) Jacuzzi Turkish steam room entertainment **CONF:** Thtr 120 Class 60 Board 30 **SERVICES:** Lift **PARKING:** 70 **NOTES:** No dogs (ex guide dogs) No smoking in restaurant Closed Jan-Feb RS Dec-Feb (group bookings only)
CARDS:

★★63% **New Beach Hotel**
67 Marine Pde NR30 2EJ
☎ 01493 332300 01493 331880
Leisureplex
e-mail: newbeach.gtyarmouth@alfatravel.co.uk
Dir: *Follow signs to sea front, hotel facing Britannia Pier*
Impressive Victorian building centrally located on the seafront, overlooking Britannia Pier and the sandy beach. Bedrooms are pleasantly decorated and equipped with modern facilities; many have lovely sea views. Dinner is taken in the restaurant which doubles as the ballroom, and guests can also relax in the bar or sunny lounge.
ROOMS: 75 en suite (3 fmly) s £25-£30; d £42-£58 (incl. bkfst) **LB** **FACILITIES:** entertainment Xmas **SERVICES:** Lift **NOTES:** No dogs (ex guide dogs) No smoking in restaurant Closed Dec-Feb RS Nov & Mar
CARDS:

GREENFORD, Greater London
See LONDON SECTION plan 1 B4

★★★67% **The Bridge**
Western Av UB6 8ST
☎ 020 8566 6246 020 8566 6140
e-mail: bridgehotel@youngs.co.uk
Dir: *Turn off A40 before flyover onto A4127 towards Greenford, hotel on roundabout*
A popular venue for business guests this hotel on the A40, is ideally located for accessing central London. Spacious bedrooms offer good levels of comfort and a range of useful facilities. A popular public bar and bistro style restaurant are also on offer.
ROOMS: 68 en suite (4 fmly) No smoking in 44 bedrooms s £96; d £110 (incl. bkfst) **LB** **FACILITIES:** STV Arrangement with local leisure centre **CONF:** Thtr 130 Class 60 Board 60 Del from £130 **SERVICES:** Lift air con **PARKING:** 68 **NOTES:** No dogs (ex guide dogs) No smoking in restaurant Civ Wed 120 **CARDS:**

Travel Inn
Western Av UB6 8TR
☎ 08701 977119 020 8998 8823
travel inn
Dir: *opposite Hoover Building. Eastbound, take exit signposted Perivale, turn right, then turn left at 2nd set of traffic lights*
Travel Inn offers good-quality, value-for-money accommodation. Spacious, en suite rooms with bath and shower comfortably accommodate a family of up to two adults and two children (to age 15). The restaurant and bar offers a varied menu. For further details and the Travel Inn phone number, consult the Hotel Groups page.
ROOMS: 39 en suite s £56.95; d £56.95

GRIMSBY, Lincolnshire Map 17 TA21

★★★66% **Beeches**
42 Waltham Rd, Scartho DN33 2LX
☎ 01472 278830 01472 752880
e-mail: joeramsden@freeuk.com
Located in the suburb of Scartho, not far from the town centre, this contemporary hotel offers good modern accommodation and pleasing public rooms. Bedrooms are inviting and well equipped
continued

with a thoughtful range of facilities. There is a popular brasserie and a comfortable lounge bar; food choices offer interest and quality.
ROOMS: 10 en suite No smoking in all bedrooms s £49-£57; d £54-£74 (incl. bkfst) **LB CONF:** Class 40 **SERVICES:** Lift **PARKING:** 70 **NOTES:** No dogs (ex guide dogs) No smoking in restaurant Closed 25 Dec – 1st wk Jan **CARDS:**

★★★66% Elizabeth
Littlecoates Rd DN34 4LX
☎ 01472 240024 🖷 01472 241354
Dir: *A1136 signed Greatcoates, 1st rdbt left, 2nd rdbt right. Hotel on right in 200mtrs*
Bedrooms at this pleasantly situated hotel are equipped with modern comforts, and many have large windows and balconies overlooking the adjoining golf course. The popular restaurant shares the same tranquil view. There is a large banqueting suite, smaller meeting and conference rooms, and extensive parking which makes this an ideal business centre.
ROOMS: 52 en suite (4 fmly) No smoking in 27 bedrooms s fr £75; d fr £85 (incl. bkfst) **LB FACILITIES:** STV Xmas **CONF:** Thtr 300 Class 100 Board 60 **SERVICES:** Lift **PARKING:** 200 **NOTES:** No smoking in restaurant Civ Wed 60 **CARDS:**

Travel Inn
Europa Park, Appian Way, Off Gilbey Rd DN31 2UT
☎ 08701 977121 🖷 01472 241648
Dir: *M180 junct 5 take A180 towards Grimsby town centre, Travel Inn on 2nd exit from 1st rdbt on A180*
Travel Inn offers good-quality, value-for-money accommodation. Spacious, en suite rooms with bath and shower comfortably accommodate a family of up to two adults and two children (to age 15). The restaurant and bar offers a varied menu. For further details and the Travel Inn phone number, consult the Hotel Groups page.
ROOMS: 40 en suite s £44.95; d £44.95

GRIMSTON, Norfolk — Map 12 TF72

Top 200 - Hotel

★★★ Congham Hall Country House
Lynn Rd PE32 1AH
☎ 01485 600250 🖷 01485 601191
e-mail: info@conghamhallhotel.co.uk
Dir: *A149/A148 interchange NE of King's Lynn. Follow A148 to Sandringham, Fakenham and Cromer for 100yds. Right to Grimston, hotel 2.5m on left*
This elegant 18th-century Georgian manor is set amid 30 acres of mature landscaped grounds and surrounded by parkland. The elegant public rooms provide a range of tastefully furnished areas in which to sit and relax. Imaginative cuisine is served in the Orangery Restaurant, which has an intimate atmosphere and panoramic views of the gardens. The bedrooms are tastefully furnished with period pieces, and have modern facilities and many thoughtful touches. Service is attentive and extremely friendly.
ROOMS: 14 en suite No smoking in all bedrooms s £99-£140; d £155-£245 (incl. bkfst) **LB FACILITIES:** Outdoor swimming Tennis (hard) Croquet lawn Putting green Cricket Xmas **CONF:** Thtr 50 Class 20 Board 30 Del from £155 **PARKING:** 50 **NOTES:** No dogs (ex guide dogs) No smoking in restaurant Civ Wed 60 **CARDS:**

GRINDLEFORD, Derbyshire — Map 16 SK27

★★★70% Maynard Arms
Main Rd S32 2HE
☎ 01433 630321 🖷 01433 630445
e-mail: info@maynardarms.co.uk
Dir: *from Sheffield take A625 to Castleton. Left into Grindleford on B6521. After Fox House hotel on left*
A delightful country hotel set in attractive gardens with fine views. Bedrooms are very tastefully furnished and decorated; some have four-poster beds and two have separate sitting rooms. A residents' lounge is situated on the first floor, overlooking the garden, and the restaurant has similar views. Bar food is available at both lunch and dinner.
ROOMS: 10 en suite s £69-£89; d £79-£99 (incl. cont bkfst) **LB FACILITIES:** STV Xmas **CONF:** BC Thtr 140 Class 80 Board 40 Del from £99 **PARKING:** 80 **NOTES:** No smoking in restaurant Civ Wed 120 **CARDS:**

GUILDFORD, Surrey — Map 06 SU94

★★★68% The Manor
Newlands Corner GU4 8SE
☎ 01483 222624 🖷 01483 211389
e-mail: mail@hollybournehotels.com
Dir: *3.5m on A25 to Dorking*
Set peacefully in its own grounds, this conveniently located hotel is a popular choice for weddings and conferences. The well-appointed public areas include a selection of meeting rooms, a spacious lounge, a choice of bars and an attractive restaurant, while the bedrooms, which are mostly modern, are tastefully furnished and feature a good range of facilities.
ROOMS: 45 en suite (4 fmly) No smoking in 4 bedrooms s £79-£89; d £99 **LB FACILITIES:** Croquet lawn **CONF:** Thtr 150 Class 50 Board 50 Del from £150 **PARKING:** 100 **NOTES:** No smoking in restaurant Civ Wed 120 **CARDS:**

U *Holiday Inn Guildford*
Egerton Rd GU2 5XZ
☎ 0870 400 9036 🖷 01483 302960
e-mail: guildford@ichotelsgroup.com
Dir: *exit A3 for Hospital and Cathedral, 3rd exit at rdbt then 2nd exit at next*
At the time of going to press, the classification for this hotel was not confirmed. Please refer to the AA internet site www.theAA.com for current information.
ROOMS: 167 en suite (53 fmly) No smoking in 71 bedrooms **FACILITIES:** STV Indoor swimming (H) Sauna Gym **CONF:** Thtr 200 Class 100 Board 45 **PARKING:** 220 **CARDS:**

Bad hair day?
Hairdryers in all rooms three stars and above

GUILDFORD, continued

⌂ Travel Inn

Parkway GU1 1UP
☎ 08701 977122 🖷 01483 450678
Dir: *M25 junct 10 signed to Portsmouth (A3). Turn off to Guildford centre/Leisure Centre (A320/A25), turn left, hotel on left*
Travel Inn offers good-quality, value-for-money accommodation. Spacious, en suite rooms with bath and shower comfortably accommodate a family of up to two adults and two children (to age 15). The restaurant and bar offers a varied menu. For further details and the Travel Inn phone number, consult the Hotel Groups page.
ROOMS: 87 en suite s £52.95-£54.95; d £52.95-£54.95
CONF: Thtr 45 Board 25

GUISBOROUGH, North Yorkshire — Map 19 NZ61

★★★★71% Gisborough Hall

Whitby Ln TS14 6PT
☎ 0870 400 8191 🖷 01287 610844
e-mail: general.gisboroughhall@macdonald-hotels.co.uk
Dir: *A171, follow signs for Whitby until Waterfoil rdbt then into Whitby Lane, hotel 500yds on right*
Dating back to the mid 19th century, this elegant hall has been carefully refurbished and extended to provide a pleasing combination of original features and modern facilities. Bedrooms, including four poster and family rooms, are richly furnished, while there is a choice of welcoming lounges with log fires. Imaginative fare is served in Tockett's restaurant.
ROOMS: 71 en suite (2 fmly) (12 GF) No smoking in 37 bedrooms s £74-£89; d £108-£138 (incl. bkfst) **FACILITIES:** STV Sauna Xmas **CONF:** BC Thtr 400 Class 150 Board 32 Del from £145 **SERVICES:** Lift air con **PARKING:** 400 **NOTES:** No smoking in restaurant Civ Wed 400
CARDS:

⌂ Premier Lodge (Middlesbrough South)

Middlesbrough Rd, Upsall TS14 6RW
☎ 0870 9906540 🖷 0870 9906541
Dir: *A19 S onto A172/A19 N onto A174 follow Guisborough & Whitby signs*
Premier Lodge offers modern, well-equipped, en suite accommodation suitable for both business and leisure travellers. Meals can be taken at the adjacent popular restaurant and bar, which is fully licensed. For further details, consult the Hotel Groups page.
ROOMS: 20 en suite s £48; d £48

GULWORTHY, Devon — Map 03 SX47

★★★75% ®®® Horn of Plenty

PL19 8JD
☎ 01822 832528 🖷 01822 832528
e-mail: enquiries@thehornofplenty.co.uk
Dir: *from Tavistock take A390 W for 3m. Right at Gulworthy Cross. After 400yds turn left and after 400yds hotel on right*
With memorable and stunning views over the Tamar Valley, The Horn of Plenty maintains its reputation as one of Britain's impressive country houses. The bedrooms are well equipped and have many thoughtful extras; some, more simply decorated, are in adjacent converted cottages. Cuisine here is also impressive and local produce provides interesting and memorable dining.

ROOMS: 4 en suite 6 annexe en suite (3 fmly) (4 GF) No smoking in all bedrooms s £105-£190; d £115-£200 (incl. bkfst) **LB FACILITIES:** Xmas **CONF:** BC Thtr 20 Class 20 Board 12 Del from £120 **PARKING:** 25 **NOTES:** No smoking in restaurant Closed 24-26 Dec Civ Wed 120
CARDS:

GUNTHORPE, Nottinghamshire — Map 11 SK64

★★70% *Unicorn*

Gunthorpe Bridge NG14 7FB
☎ 0115 966 3612 🖷 0115 966 4801
Dir: *on A6097, between Lowdham and Bingham*
This popular riverside inn provides comfortable bedrooms, each thoughtfully equipped with many extra facilities. The spacious restaurant and bars feature exposed timbers and brickwork and the menus in each centre on good home-cooked food, with friendly, informal service.
ROOMS: 16 en suite (3 fmly) **FACILITIES:** STV Fishing **PARKING:** 200 **NOTES:** No dogs (ex guide dogs) **CARDS:**

HACKNESS, North Yorkshire — Map 17 SE99

★★★71% ®

Hackness Grange Country House

North York National Park YO13 0JW
☎ 01723 882345 🖷 01723 882391
e-mail: admin@englishrosehotels.co.uk
Dir: *A64 to Scarborough, then A171 to Whitby and Scalby. Follow Hackness and Forge Valley National Park signs, through Hackness village on left*
Close to Scarborough, and set in the North Yorkshire Moors National Park, Hackness Grange is surrounded by well-tended gardens. Comfortable bedrooms have views of the open countryside; those in the cottages are ideally suited to families, and the courtyard rooms include facilities for the less able. Lounges and the restaurant are spacious and relaxing.
ROOMS: 33 en suite (5 fmly) (8 GF) s £50-£78; d £90-£180 (incl. bkfst) **LB FACILITIES:** Indoor swimming (H) Tennis (hard) Putting green 9 hole pitch & putt Xmas **CONF:** Thtr 20 Board 14 Del from £75 **PARKING:** 60 **NOTES:** No dogs (ex guide dogs) No smoking in restaurant **CARDS:**

HADLEY WOOD, Greater London — Map 06 TQ29

★★★★72% ® West Lodge Park

Cockfosters Rd EN4 0PY
☎ 020 8216 3900 🖷 020 8216 3937
e-mail: westlodgepark@bealeshotels.co.uk
Dir: *on A111, 1m S of M25 junct 24*
An impressive country house hotel set in mature parkland and

continued

gardens, yet only 12 miles from London's West End. Bedrooms are individually furnished and decorated and offer comprehensive in-room facilities; four new superior rooms have air conditioning and exclusive access to an outdoor hot-tub and sauna. The Cedar Restaurant provides a choice of interesting dishes.
ROOMS: 46 en suite 13 annexe en suite (1 fmly) (11 GF) No smoking in 23 bedrooms s £128-£140; d £150-£170 **LB** **FACILITIES:** **Spa** STV Sauna Croquet lawn Putting green Massage, Manicure, Free use of nearby leisure club Xmas **CONF:** BC Thtr 70 Class 30 Board 30 Del from £192 **SERVICES:** Lift **PARKING:** 200 **NOTES:** No dogs (ex guide dogs) No smoking in restaurant RS Saturday Civ Wed 60
CARDS:

HAGLEY, Worcestershire — Map 10 SO98

Travel Inn

Birmingham Rd DY9 9JS
☎ 08701 977123 📠 01562 884416
Dir: *5m off M5 junct 3 on opposite side of A456 dual carriageway towards Kidderminster*
Travel Inn offers good-quality, value-for-money accommodation. Spacious, en suite rooms with bath and shower comfortably accommodate a family of up to two adults and two children (to age 15). The restaurant and bar offers a varied menu. For further details and the Travel Inn phone number, consult the Hotel Groups page.
ROOMS: 40 en suite s £44.95; d £44.95 **CONF:** Thtr 20 Board 18

HAILSHAM, East Sussex — Map 06 TQ50

★★★65% Boship Farm

Forestdale Hotels

Lower Dicker BN27 4AT
☎ 01323 844826 📠 01323 843945
e-mail: boship.farm@forestdale.com
Dir: *on A22 at Boship rdbt, junct of A22, A267 and A271*
Dating back to 1652, a lovely old farmhouse forms the hub of this hotel, which is set in 17 acres of well-tended grounds. Guests have the use of an all-weather tennis court, an outdoor pool and a croquet lawn. Bedrooms are smartly appointed and well equipped; most have views across open fields and countryside.
ROOMS: 47 annexe en suite (5 fmly) (21 GF) No smoking in 17 bedrooms s fr £75; d fr £110 (incl. bkfst) **LB** **FACILITIES:** Outdoor swimming (H) Tennis (hard) Sauna Croquet lawn Jacuzzi Xmas **CONF:** Thtr 175 Class 40 Board 46 Del from £95 **PARKING:** 100 **NOTES:** No smoking in restaurant Civ Wed 175
CARDS:

★★69% The Olde Forge Hotel & Restaurant

Magham Down BN27 1PN
☎ 01323 842893 📠 01323 842893
e-mail: theoldeforgehotelandrestaurant@tesco.net
Dir: *off Boship rdbt on A271 to Bexhill. 3m on left opposite Red Lion pub*
In the heart of the countryside, this family-run hotel offers a friendly welcome and an informal atmosphere. The bedrooms are attractively decorated with thoughtful extras. The restaurant, with its timbered beams and log fires, was once the site of a 16th-century forge, and it is gaining a growing reputation for its cuisine and service.
ROOMS: 7 en suite s fr £48; d fr £68 (incl. bkfst) **LB** **PARKING:** 11 **NOTES:** No smoking in restaurant **CARDS:**

Travelodge Hellingly Eastbourne

Travelodge

Boship Roundabout, Hellingly BN27 4DT
☎ 08700 850 950 📠 01323 844556
Dir: *on A22 at Boship rdbt*
Travelodge offers good quality, good value, modern accommodation. Ideal for families, the spacious, en suite bedrooms include remote-control TV, tea and coffee-making facilities, luxury beds and free morning newspaper. Meals can be taken at the nearby family restaurant. For further details and the Travelodge phone number, consult the Hotel Groups page.
ROOMS: 58 en suite s fr £42.95; d fr £42.95

HALIFAX, West Yorkshire — Map 19 SE02

★★★74% Holdsworth House

Holdsworth HX2 9TG
☎ 01422 240024 📠 01422 245174
e-mail: info@holdsworthhouse.co.uk
Dir: *from town centre take A629 Keighley Road. Right at garage up Shay Ln after 1.5m. Hotel on right after 1m*

This delightful 17th-century Jacobean manor house is set in well tended gardens and offers individually decorated, thoughtfully equipped bedrooms. Public rooms, adorned with beautiful paintings and antique pieces, include a choice of inviting lounges and superb conference and function facilities. Dinner provides the highlight of any stay and is served in the elegant restaurant, comprising three delightful interconnecting rooms, by friendly, attentive staff.
ROOMS: 40 en suite (2 fmly) No smoking in 15 bedrooms **FACILITIES:** STV **CONF:** Thtr 150 Class 75 Board 50 Del from £130 **PARKING:** 60 **NOTES:** No smoking in restaurant Civ Wed 118
CARDS:

★★★67% Rock Inn

Holywell Green HX4 9BS
☎ 01422 379721 📠 01422 379110
e-mail: reservations@rockinnhotel.com
Dir: *M62 junct 24, follow Blackley signs, left at x-rds 0.5m on left*
Situated in a quiet village between Huddersfield and Halifax, this hotel is popular with business guests and as a local dining venue. The newer bedrooms are particularly innovative with attractive design features, while the standard rooms – all with deep hip tubs – though more compact, are well laid out. A conservatory style brasserie adjoins the bar.
ROOMS: 30 en suite (5 fmly) No smoking in 15 bedrooms s £70-£130; d £70-£130 (incl. bkfst) **LB** **FACILITIES:** STV Xmas **CONF:** Thtr 200 Class 100 Board 100 Del from £99 **PARKING:** 122 **NOTES:** No smoking in restaurant Civ Wed 200 **CARDS:**

HALIFAX, continued

★★★63% Imperial Crown Hotel

42/46 Horton St HX1 1QE
☎ 0870 609 6114 📠 01422 349866
e-mail: imperialcrown@corushotels.com
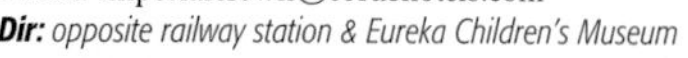
Dir: *opposite railway station & Eureka Children's Museum*

This friendly hotel is situated in the town centre opposite the railway station and the Eureka Children's Museum. Fifteen smart contemporary bedrooms are located above the hotel's American diner, which is next to the hotel's car park across the road. The Wallis Simpson Restaurant and Bar are in the main building, and complimentary use of a nearby gymnasium is also available.
ROOMS: 41 en suite 15 annexe en suite (3 fmly) No smoking in 22 bedrooms **FACILITIES:** STV **CONF:** Thtr 150 Class 120 Board 70 **PARKING:** 63 **NOTES:** No smoking in restaurant Civ Wed 200
CARDS:

Premier Lodge (Halifax)

Salterhebble Hill, Huddersfield Rd HX3 0QT
☎ 0870 9906308 📠 0870 9906309
Premier Lodge offers modern, well-equipped, en suite accommodation suitable for both business and leisure travellers. Meals can be taken at the adjacent popular restaurant and bar, which is fully licensed. For further details, consult the Hotel Groups page.
ROOMS: 31 en suite s £48; d £48

Travelodge (Halifax Central)

Dean Clough Park HX3 5AY
☎ 08700 850 950 📠 01422 362669
Travelodge offers good quality, good value, modern accommodation. Ideal for families, the spacious, en suite bedrooms include remote-control TV, tea and coffee-making facilities, luxury beds and free morning newspaper. Meals can be taken at the nearby family restaurant. For further details and the Travelodge phone number, consult the Hotel Groups page.
ROOMS: 52 en suite s fr £42.95; d fr £42.95

HAMPTON COURT, Greater London
See LONDON SECTION plan 1 B1

★★★★62% The Carlton Mitre

Hampton Court Rd KT8 9BN
☎ 020 8979 9988 📠 020 8979 9777
e-mail: mitre@carltonhotels.co.uk
Dir: *M3 junct 1 follow signs to Sunbury & Hampton Court Palace. At Hampton Court Palace rdbt right and hotel on right*
This hotel, dating back in parts to 1655, enjoys an enviable setting on the banks of the River Thames opposite Hampton Court Palace. The riverside restaurant and Edge bar/brasserie command wonderful views. Bedrooms are generally spacious with excellent facilities. Parking is limited.

ROOMS: 36 en suite (2 fmly) No smoking in 16 bedrooms s £110-£175; d £110-£175 (incl. bkfst) **LB** **FACILITIES:** STV Xmas **CONF:** Thtr 120 Class 60 Board 40 Del from £203.95 **SERVICES:** Lift **PARKING:** 13 **NOTES:** No smoking in restaurant Civ Wed 120
CARDS:

HANDFORTH See Manchester Airport

HARLOW, Essex Map 06 TL41

★★★65% The Green Man Hotel

Mulberry Green, Old Harlow CM17 0ET
☎ 0870 609 6146 📠 01279 626113
Dir: *M11 junct 7 onto A414. Right at 4th rdbt then left into Mulberry Green, hotel on left*

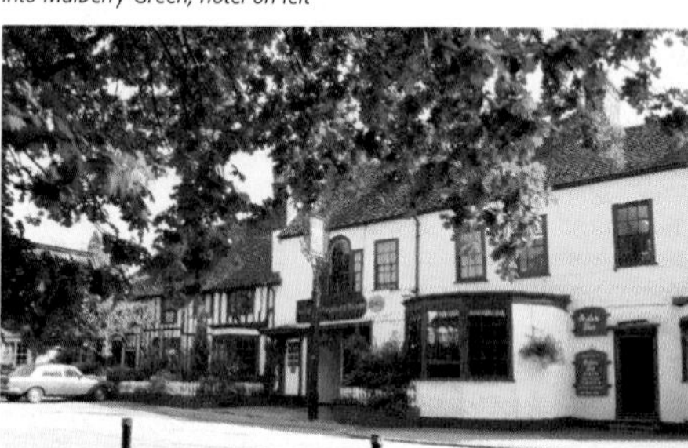

This popular coaching inn, dating back to the 14th century, is situated just a short drive from the town centre. The busy lounge bar is an enjoyable place for a drink, and there is also a trendy brasserie style restaurant offering both carte and daily changing menus. Modern, well-equipped bedrooms are located to the rear of the property.
ROOMS: 55 annexe en suite (14 GF) No smoking in 27 bedrooms s fr £96; d fr £105 **LB** **FACILITIES:** Xmas **CONF:** Thtr 60 Class 26 Board 30 **PARKING:** 75 **NOTES:** No smoking in restaurant
CARDS:

Travel Inn

Cambridge Rd CM20 2EP
☎ 08701 977125 📠 01279 452169
Dir: *off A414 on Sawbridgeworth and Bishop's Stortford Rd (A1184)*
Travel Inn offers good-quality, value-for-money accommodation. Spacious, en suite rooms with bath and shower comfortably accommodate a family of up to two adults and two children (to age 15). The restaurant and bar offers a varied menu. For further details and the Travel Inn phone number, consult the Hotel Groups page.
ROOMS: 61 en suite s £44.95; d £44.95

⌂ Travelodge Harlow East (Stansted)

A414 Eastbound, Tylers Green, North Weald CM16 6BJ
☎ 08700 850 950
Travelodge offers good quality, good value, modern accommodation. Ideal for families, the spacious, en suite bedrooms include remote-control TV, tea and coffee-making facilities, luxury beds and free morning newspaper. Meals can be taken at the nearby family restaurant. For further details and the Travelodge phone number, consult the Hotel Groups page.
ROOMS: 60 en suite s fr £42.95; d fr £42.95

HAROME See Helmsley

HARPENDEN, Hertfordshire Map 06 TL11

★★★69% Harpenden House
18 Southdown Rd AL5 1PE
☎ 01582 449955 📠 01582 769858
e-mail: harpendenhouse@corushotels.com

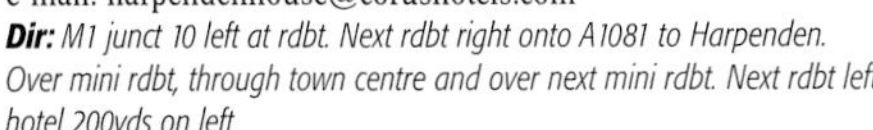

Dir: *M1 junct 10 left at rdbt. Next rdbt right onto A1081 to Harpenden. Over mini rdbt, through town centre and over next mini rdbt. Next rdbt left, hotel 200yds on left*

This attractive Grade II listed Georgian building overlooks East Common. The hotel gardens are particularly attractive while stylish public areas include a restaurant with an impressive decorative ceiling. Some bedrooms and a large suite are located in the original house, although most of the accommodation is in a more recent annexe.
ROOMS: 17 en suite 59 annexe en suite (13 fmly) (2 GF) No smoking in 49 bedrooms **FACILITIES:** STV Complimentary use of local leisure centre **CONF:** BC Thtr 150 Class 60 Board 60 **PARKING:** 80 **NOTES:** No dogs (ex guide dogs) No smoking in restaurant RS wknds & BH's Civ Wed 80 **CARDS:**

★★★68% Hanover International Hotel
1 Luton Rd AL5 2PX
☎ 01582 760271 📠 01582 460819
e-mail: reception.harpenden@hanover-international.com
Dir: *M1 junct 10 to Luton Airport. At rdbt right for Harpenden on A1081 for 5m. Hotel on right beyond Oggelsby's Vauxhall garage*
Located within easy reach of the M1, this hotel occupies a quiet location on the edge of town. Bedrooms are comfortable, providing guests with space and numerous facilities. A variety of well appointed function rooms are also available for corporate or private use.

continued

ROOMS: 60 en suite (12 fmly) (15 GF) No smoking in 25 bedrooms s £38-£170; d £76-£170 **LB FACILITIES:** STV Free membership of local leisure club **CONF:** Thtr 150 Class 60 Board 44 Del from £135 **SERVICES:** Lift **PARKING:** 85 **NOTES:** RS 25 Dec-4 Jan Civ Wed 120
CARDS:

HARROGATE, North Yorkshire Map 19 SE35
See also Knaresborough

Top 200 - Hotel

★★★★ @@ Rudding Park Hotel & Golf
Rudding Park, Follifoot HG3 1JH
☎ 01423 871350 📠 01423 872286
e-mail: sales@ruddingpark.com
Dir: *from A61 at rdbt with A658 take York exit and follow signs to Rudding Park*
In the heart of 200-year-old landscaped parkland, this modern hotel is elegant and stylish. Bedrooms, including two luxurious suites, are smartly presented and thoughtfully equipped. Carefully prepared meals are served in the Clocktower, with its striking, contemporary décor. A spacious bar and comfortable lounges are also available. The adjoining golf course has been recognised as the most environmentally friendly in Britain.
ROOMS: 50 en suite (10 GF) No smoking in 31 bedrooms s £128-£148; d £158-£178 (incl. bkfst) **LB FACILITIES:** STV Golf 18 Croquet lawn Driving range Jogging trail Membership of local gym Xmas **CONF:** BC Thtr 300 Class 150 Board 36 Del from £185 **SERVICES:** Lift **PARKING:** 150 **NOTES:** No dogs (ex guide dogs) No smoking in restaurant Civ Wed 300
CARDS:

See advert on page 267

HARROGATE, continued

★★★★68% The Majestic

Ripon Rd HG1 2HU
☎ 01423 700300 📠 01423 521332
e-mail: majestic@paramount-hotels.co.uk
Dir: *from M1 continue on A1(M) link road, leaving at Wetherby. Take A661 to Harrogate. Hotel in town centre adjacent to Royal Hall*

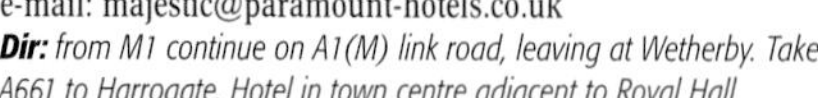

Popular for conferences and functions, this grand Victorian hotel is set in 12 acres of landscaped grounds and is centrally located and within walking distance of the town centre. The bedrooms, many of which have been recently refurbished, come in a variety of sizes and include several spacious suites.
ROOMS: 156 en suite (11 fmly) No smoking in 86 bedrooms s £55-£110; d fr £110 (incl. bkfst) **LB FACILITIES:** STV Indoor swimming (H) Tennis (hard) Squash Snooker Sauna Solarium Gym Jacuzzi Golf practice net entertainment Xmas **CONF:** BC Thtr 500 Class 250 Board 70 Del £183 **SERVICES:** Lift **PARKING:** 250 **NOTES:** No smoking in restaurant Civ Wed 300 **CARDS:**

★★★★65% Cedar Court

Queens Buildings, Park Pde HG1 5AH
☎ 01423 858585 & 858595(res) 📠 01423 504950
e-mail: cedarcourt@bestwestern.co.uk
Dir: *from A1(M) follow signs to Harrogate on A661 past Sainsburys. At rdbt left onto A6040. Hotel right after church*

This Grade II listed building was Harrogate's first hotel and enjoys a peaceful location in landscaped grounds, close to the town centre. It has been carefully refurbished to provide spacious, well-equipped accommodation. Public areas include an elegant restaurant, a gymnasium and an open plan lounge and bar. Functions and conferences are particularly well catered for.
ROOMS: 100 en suite (8 fmly) (7 GF) No smoking in 75 bedrooms s £70-£123; d £85-£138 (incl. bkfst) **LB FACILITIES:** STV Gym Xmas **CONF:** BC Thtr 323 Class 90 Board 80 Del from £110 **SERVICES:** Lift **PARKING:** 150 **NOTES:** No dogs (ex guide dogs) Civ Wed 171 **CARDS:**

★★★79% 🏵🏵 The Boar's Head Hotel

Ripley Castle Estate HG3 3AY
☎ 01423 771888 📠 01423 771509
e-mail: reservations@boarsheadripley.co.uk
Dir: *on A61 Harrogate to Ripon road. Hotel in centre of Ripley Village*
Situated in the private village of the Ripley Castle estate, this delightful and popular hotel is renowned for its warm hospitality and its restaurant, serving a mix of modern and traditional dishes. Bedrooms offer many comforts, and the luxurious day rooms feature works of art from the nearby castle.

ROOMS: 19 en suite 6 annexe en suite (2 fmly) No smoking in 15 bedrooms s £99-£120; d £120-£140 (incl. bkfst) **LB FACILITIES:** Tennis (hard) Fishing Clay pigeon shooting entertainment Xmas **CONF:** Thtr 60 Class 35 Board 30 Del from £145 **PARKING:** 50 **NOTES:** No smoking in restaurant Civ Wed 100 **CARDS:**

★★★74% 🏵 Cutlers on the Stray

19 West Park HG1 1BJ
☎ 01423 524471 📠 01423 506728
e-mail: info@cutlers-web.co.uk
Dir: *A59 or A61 to Harrogate to Prince of Wales rdbt, follow signs for town centre, hotel 100yds right*

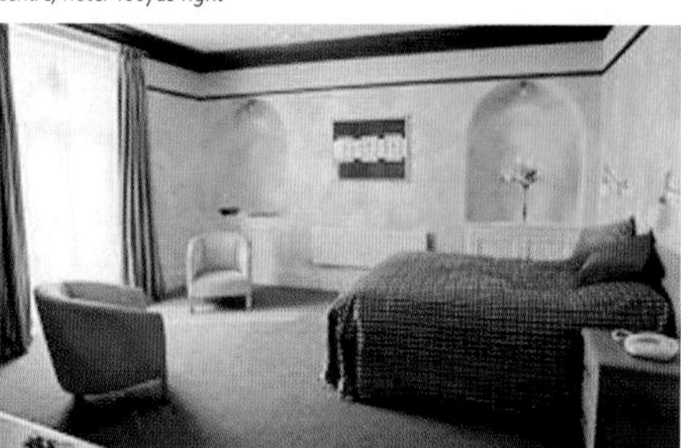

Enjoying a town centre location alongside one of the parks, this old coaching inn has been transformed into a trendy and stylish hotel and brasserie, offering contemporary styled accommodation. Taking its theme from its name, old cutlery adorns walls and reshaped spoons and forks become room key fobs and candle holders. Service is friendly and attentive and the versatile menus provide a great choice of dishes.
ROOMS: 19 en suite (1 fmly) No smoking in 16 bedrooms s £60-£90; d £80-£120 (incl. bkfst) **LB FACILITIES:** STV Complimentary day pass available for leisure & fitness centre entertainment Xmas **PARKING:** 12 **NOTES:** No dogs (ex guide dogs) Closed 26 Dec & 1 Jan **CARDS:**

★★★73% 🏵 Balmoral

Franklin Mount HG1 5EJ
☎ 01423 508208 📠 01423 530652
e-mail: info@balmoralhotel.co.uk
Dir: *from Conference Centre on to Kings Rd, turn left, hotel 200yds on right*
Situated close to the town centre, this hotel stands in gardens and offers comfortable bedrooms which vary between the elegant and the contemporary. Public rooms include a cosy bar dedicated to Harry Houdini, a lounge packed with cat curios and the modern Villu Toots restaurant which offers an exciting menu.
ROOMS: 20 en suite (2 fmly) (2 GF) s £85-£125; d £110-£130 (incl. bkfst) **LB FACILITIES:** Arrangement with leisure/fitness centre **PARKING:** 20 **CARDS:**

★★★72% **Grants**
3-13 Swan Rd HG1 2SS
☎ 01423 560666 🖹 01423 502550
e-mail: enquiries@grantshotel-harrogate.com
Dir: *off A61*

A long established, family-run hotel with an attractive flower bedecked patio. The smartly presented, well-equipped bedrooms include some with four-poster beds. A comfortable lounge bar with plenty of interesting old photographs, and imaginative food in the colourful Chimney Pots Bistro, are just some of the features of this friendly hotel.
ROOMS: 42 en suite (2 fmly) d £99-£174 (incl. bkfst) **LB** **FACILITIES:** STV Use of local Health & Leisure Club Xmas **CONF:** Thtr 70 Class 20 Board 30 Del from £90 **SERVICES:** Lift **PARKING:** 26 **NOTES:** No smoking in restaurant **CARDS:**

★★★69% **The Yorkshire**
CRERAR HOTELS
Prospect Place HG1 1LA
☎ 01423 565071 🖹 01423 500082
e-mail: theyorkshire@crerarhotels.com
Dir: *follow A61 into town centre. Hotel opposite Betty's Tea Rooms*

Having undergone a major refurbishment of public areas, this town centre hotel has transformed itself into a smart, contemporary venue for travellers. The hotel now has two lounges, the fifth-floor Upstairs Restaurant and the modern HG1 Bar and Brasserie. All bedrooms in the hotel are scheduled to benefit from a similar transformation.
ROOMS: 80 en suite (4 fmly) No smoking in 36 bedrooms s £85-£105; d £125-£175 (incl. bkfst) **LB** **FACILITIES:** Xmas **CONF:** Thtr 200 Class 80 Board 40 Del from £125 **SERVICES:** Lift **PARKING:** 35 **NOTES:** No dogs (ex guide dogs) No smoking in restaurant
CARDS:

★★★66% **Studley**
Swan Rd HG1 2SE
☎ 01423 560425 🖹 01423 530967
e-mail: info@studleyhotel.co.uk
Dir: *Swan Road is adjacent to the Valley Gardens and opposite the Mercer Gallery*
This friendly, well established hotel, close to the town centre and Valley Gardens, is renowned for its attentive service and cheery staff. The popular Orchid Restaurant provides a dynamic and authentic approach to Pacific Rim and Asian cuisine. Bedrooms are well-equipped and vary in size. Spacious day rooms are comfortably furnished.
ROOMS: 36 en suite (2 fmly) **FACILITIES:** STV Free use of local Health & Spa Club **CONF:** Thtr 15 Class 15 Board 12 **SERVICES:** Lift **PARKING:** 15 **NOTES:** No smoking in restaurant
CARDS:

★★★59% ***The Crown***
corus hotels
Crown Place HG1 2RZ
☎ 01423 567755 🖹 01423 502284
e-mail: thecrown@corushotels.com
Dir: *A61 to Harrogate down Parliament St to traffic lights by Royal Hall. Left to Valley Gardens and 1st left to rdbt. Hotel on right*
Centrally situated, this hotel has been welcoming guests for the past 250 years. Bedrooms are mixed in standard and size. All have good facilities such as a movie channel and modem links. Public

continued on p268

HARROGATE, continued

areas have all the hallmarks of a bygone era, tall ceilings with columns and plenty of space.

The Crown, Harrogate

ROOMS: 121 en suite (8 fmly) No smoking in 61 bedrooms **FACILITIES:** Free use of local sports club **CONF:** Thtr 400 Class 200 Board 80 **SERVICES:** Lift **PARKING:** 50 **NOTES:** No smoking in restaurant Civ Wed 400 **CARDS:**

★★74% Ascot House

53 Kings Rd HG1 5HJ
☎ 01423 531005 01423 503523
e-mail: admin@ascothouse.com
Dir: *on entering Harrogate follow signs to town centre, Conference and Exhibition Centre into Kings Rd, Centre for hotel on left after park*
This late Victorian house has been tastefully transformed into a friendly and meticulously maintained hotel. Situated a short distance from the International Conference and Exhibition Centre, it provides comfortable and extremely well-appointed bedrooms, an inviting lounge bar and a dining room offering a decent choice at dinner.
ROOMS: 19 en suite (2 fmly) (5 GF) s £57-£69; d £83-£93 (incl. bkfst) **LB FACILITIES:** Xmas **CONF:** Thtr 80 Class 36 Board 36 Del from £99 **PARKING:** 14 **NOTES:** No smoking in restaurant Closed 27 Dec-4 Jan & 23 Jan-8 Feb Civ Wed 90 **CARDS:**

Restaurant with Rooms

Harrogate Brasserie Hotel & Bar

THE INDEPENDENTS

28-30 Cheltenham Pde HG1 1DB
☎ 01423 505041 01423 722300
e-mail: info@brasserie.co.uk
Dir: *on A61 town centre behind theatre*
This town centre hotel is distinctly continental in style and provides individual, striking bedrooms. The popular brasserie features live jazz on Friday and Sunday nights, with a jazz pianist on Wednesday nights. The menu offers popular dishes with blackboard specials and makes good use of seasonal produce.
ROOMS: 13 en suite (3 fmly) s £53-£65; d £75-£85 (incl. bkfst) **LB FACILITIES:** entertainment Xmas **PARKING:** 12 **CARDS:**

Innkeeper's Lodge Harrogate West

Innkeeper's Lodge

Otley Rd, Beckwith Knowle HG3 1PR
☎ 01423 533091 01423 533092
Dir: *from A1(M) junct 47, take A59 for Harrogate. Over 2 rdbts, at 3rd rdbt straight over onto B6162. Hotel on left opposite church*
A new concept in the travel accommodation market. Smart rooms meet essential business requirements but also have home comforts. Dining options include all-day menus plus the added advantage of breakfast, which is included in the room price. For further details, consult the Hotel Groups page.
ROOMS: 11 en suite **CONF:** Thtr 30 Class 30 Board 30

Travel Inn

travel inn

Hornbeam Park Av, Hornbeam Park HG2 8RA
☎ 08701 977126 01423 878581
Dir: *A1(M) J46 west then A661 to Harrogate. After 2m turn left at The Woodlands lights. Hornbeam Park Avenue 1.5m on left*
Travel Inn offers good-quality, value-for-money accommodation. Spacious, en suite rooms with bath and shower comfortably accommodate a family of up to two adults and two children (to age 15). The restaurant and bar offers a varied menu. For further details and the Travel Inn phone number, consult the Hotel Groups page.
ROOMS: 50 en suite s £44.95; d £44.95 **CONF:** Class 20 Board 20

Travel Inn Harrogate

travel inn

Hornbeam Park Ave, Hornbeam Park HG2 8RA
☎ 08701 977 126 01423 878581
Travel Inn offers good-quality, value-for-money accommodation. Spacious, en suite rooms with bath and shower comfortably accommodate a family of up to two adults and two children (to age 15). The restaurant and bar offers a varied menu. For further details and the Travel Inn phone number, consult the Hotel Groups page.
ROOMS: 50 en suite

HARROW, Greater London
See LONDON SECTION plan 1 B5

★★★69% Best Western Cumberland

Best Western

1 St Johns Rd HA1 2EF
☎ 020 8863 4111 020 8861 5668
e-mail: sforsdyke@cumberlandhotel.co.uk
Dir: *from A404 or A409 into Gayton Rd, then into Lyon Rd. Hotel at end of road*

Situated within walking distance of the town centre, this hotel is ideally located for all local attractions and amenities. Bedrooms provide good levels of comfort and are practically equipped to meet the requirements of all travellers. Impressive public areas include a restaurant and recently refurbished bar, both serving a good variety of fresh food.
ROOMS: 31 en suite 53 annexe en suite (5 fmly) (15 GF) No smoking in 51 bedrooms s £60-£98; d £75-£110 (incl. bkfst) **LB FACILITIES:** STV Sauna Gym Xmas **CONF:** Thtr 130 Class 70 Board 62 Del from £99 **PARKING:** 57 **NOTES:** No dogs (ex guide dogs) **CARDS:**

See advert on opposite page

★★★68% **Quality Harrow Hotel**

12-22 Pinner Rd HA1 4HZ
☎ 020 8427 3435 📠 020 8861 1370
e-mail: info@harrowhotel.co.uk
Dir: *off rdbt on A404 at junct with A312*

This privately owned hotel offers a great variety of accommodation to suit all needs. At the top of the range are the new air-conditioned executive rooms and suites. These have hi-tech facilities including MD/CD, interactive TV and multiple phone lines. Public areas comprise a bar, conservatory lounge, meeting rooms and a smart restaurant.
ROOMS: 79 en suite 23 annexe en suite (2 fmly) No smoking in 48 bedrooms **FACILITIES:** STV **CONF:** Thtr 160 Class 60 Board 60 Del from £130 **SERVICES:** Lift **PARKING:** 70 **NOTES:** No smoking in restaurant RS Xmas (limited service) Civ Wed 120
CARDS:

See advert on this page

★★59% **The Lindal**
2 Hindes Rd HA1 1SJ
☎ 020 8863 3164 📠 020 8427 5435
Dir: *Turn off M40 or M1 towards Harrow, hotel is off A409, opposite Tesco*
This family-run hotel is conveniently located for the local shopping centre and provides good transport links to the centre of London. Bedrooms are modern and attractively furnished. Day rooms consist of a combined bar-lounge area and dining room.
ROOMS: 24 en suite (3 fmly) No smoking in 9 bedrooms s £40-£52; d £65-£69 (incl. bkfst) **LB** **PARKING:** 21 **NOTES:** No dogs (ex guide dogs) No children 6yrs No smoking in restaurant
CARDS:

HARROW WEALD, Greater London
LONDON SECTION plan 1 B6

★★★68% ® **Grim's Dyke**
Old Redding HA3 6SH
☎ 020 8385 3100 📠 020 8954 4560
e-mail: enquiries@grimsdyke.com
Dir: *Turn off A410 onto A409 North towards Bushey, at top of hill traffic lights turn left into Old Redding*
Once home to Sir William Gilbert, this Grade II mansion contains many references to well-known Gilbert and Sullivan productions. The house is set in over 40 acres of beautiful parkland and gardens. Rooms in the main house are elegant and traditional, while those in the adjacent lodge are aimed more at the business guest.
ROOMS: 9 en suite 35 annexe en suite (15 GF) No smoking in 20 bedrooms s £125-£300; d £155-£300 (incl. bkfst) **LB** **FACILITIES:** STV Croquet lawn Putting green entertainment **CONF:** BC Thtr 100 Class 80 Board 32 Del from £160 **PARKING:** 97 **NOTES:** No smoking in restaurant RS 24-26 Dec Civ Wed 90 **CARDS:**

HARTLEBURY, Worcestershire

Map 10 SO87

Travelodge

Shorthill Nurseries DY13 9SH
☎ 08700 850 950 📠 01299 250553
Dir: *A449 southbound*

Travelodge offers good quality, good value, modern accommodation. Ideal for families, the spacious, en suite bedrooms include remote-control TV, tea and coffee-making facilities, luxury beds and free morning newspaper. Meals can be taken at the nearby family restaurant. For further details and the Travelodge phone number, consult the Hotel Groups page.

ROOMS: 32 en suite s fr £42.95; d fr £42.95

HARTLEPOOL, Co Durham

Map 19 NZ53

Travel Inn

Maritme Av, Hartlepool Marina TS24 0XZ
☎ 08701 977127 📠 01429 890115
Dir: *approx 1m from A689/A179 link road on marina*

Travel Inn offers good-quality, value-for-money accommodation. Spacious, en suite rooms with bath and shower comfortably accommodate a family of up to two adults and two children (to age 15). The restaurant and bar offers a varied menu. For further details and the Travel Inn phone number, consult the Hotel Groups page.

ROOMS: 40 en suite s £44.95; d £44.95

HARTSHEAD MOOR MOTORWAY SERVICE AREA (M62), West Yorkshire

Map 19 SE12

Days Inn

Hartshead Moor Service Area, Clifton HD6 4JX
☎ 01274 851706 📠 01274 855169
e-mail: hartsheadmoor.hotel@welcomebreak.co.uk
Dir: *M62 between junct 25 and 26*

This modern building offers accommodation in smart, spacious and well-equipped bedrooms, suitable for families and business travellers, and all with en suite bathrooms. Continental breakfast is available and other refreshments may be taken at the nearby family restaurant. For further details and the Days Inn phone number, consult the Hotel Groups page.

ROOMS: 38 en suite s £45-£55; d £45-£55 **CONF:** Board 10

HARWICH, Essex

Map 13 TM23

★★★74% The Pier at Harwich

The Quay CO12 3HH
☎ 01255 241212 📠 01255 551922
e-mail: reception@thepieratharwich.co.uk
Dir: *from A12, take A120 to Quay. Hotel opposite lifeboat station*

This hotel is situated on the quay, overlooking the ports of Harwich and Felixstowe. The bedrooms are tastefully decorated, thoughtfully equipped, and furnished in contemporary style; many rooms have superb sea views. Public rooms include an informal bistro, the Harbour restaurant, a smart lounge bar and a plush residents' lounge.

ROOMS: 7 en suite 7 annexe en suite (5 fmly) (1 GF) s £68-£100; d £90-£160 (incl. cont bkfst) **LB FACILITIES:** STV entertainment Xmas **CONF:** Thtr 50 Class 50 Board 24 Del from £150 **PARKING:** 10 **NOTES:** No dogs (ex guide dogs) No smoking in restaurant Civ Wed 50 **CARDS:**

★★68% Cliff

Marine Pde, Dovercourt CO12 3RE
☎ 01255 503345 & 507373 📠 01255 240358
e-mail: reception@thecliffhotelharwich.fsnet.co.uk
Dir: *A120 to Parkeston rdbt, take road to Dovercourt, on seafront after Dovercourt town centre*

Conveniently situated on the seafront close to the railway station and ferry terminal. The newly refurbished public rooms are smartly appointed and include the Shade Bar, a comfortable lounge, a restaurant and the Marine Bar with views of Dovercourt Bay. The pleasantly decorated bedrooms have co-ordinated soft furnishings and modern facilities.

ROOMS: 26 en suite (3 fmly) No smoking in 1 bedroom s £55-£60; d £65-£70 (incl. bkfst) **LB FACILITIES:** STV Jacuzzi **CONF:** Thtr 200 Class 150 Board 40 Del from £66.50 **PARKING:** 50 **NOTES:** No dogs (ex guide dogs) RS Xmas & New Year **CARDS:**

★★67% Hotel Continental

28/29 Marine Pde, Dovercourt CO12 3RG
☎ 01255 551298 📠 01255 551698
e-mail: hotconti@aol.com
Dir: *off A120 at Ramsay rdbt onto B1352 to pedestrian crossing and Co-op store on right, turn right into Fronks Rd*

A privately owned hotel situated on the seafront within easy reach of the ferry terminals and town centre. Bedrooms are pleasantly decorated, well equipped and have many innovative features; some rooms also have lovely sea views. Public rooms include a popular lounge bar, a restaurant and a non-smoking lounge.

ROOMS: 14 en suite (2 fmly) No smoking in 1 bedroom s £35-£90; d £65-£90 (incl. bkfst) **LB FACILITIES: Spa** STV **CONF:** Thtr 10 Del from £56 **PARKING:** 4 **NOTES:** No dogs (ex guide dogs) No smoking in restaurant **CARDS:**

See advert on opposite page

continued

HASLEMERE, Surrey Map 06 SU93

★★★★70% Lythe Hill Hotel and Spa
Petworth Rd GU27 3BQ
☎ 01428 651251 📠 01428 644131
e-mail: lythe@lythehill.co.uk
Dir: *left from Haslemere High St onto B2131. Lythe Hill 1.25m on right*

This privately owned hotel sits in 30 acres of attractive parkland with lakes, and complete with roaming geese. The hotel has been described as a hamlet of character buildings, each furnished in a style that complements the age of the buildings, the oldest building dating back to 1475. Cuisine in the adjacent 'Auberge de France' offers interesting, quality dishes, whilst breakfast is served in the hotel dining room. The bedrooms are split between a number of 15th-century buildings and vary in size. The stylish, new Spa is a superb addition to the hotel, including a 16mtr swimming pool.
ROOMS: 41 en suite (8 fmly) (18 GF) s £98-£235; d £125-£235 **LB** **FACILITIES: Spa** STV Indoor swimming (H) Tennis (hard) Fishing Sauna Solarium Gym Croquet lawn Boules Games Room Xmas **CONF:** Thtr 60 Class 40 Board 30 Del from £118 **PARKING:** 200 **NOTES:** No smoking in restaurant Civ Wed 128
CARDS:

★★★65% Georgian House Hotel
High St GU27 2JY
☎ 01428 656644 📠 01428 645600
e-mail: mail@georgianhousehotel.com
Dir: *A3 follow signs to Milford then Haslemere*
An attractive and imposing Georgian building, situated on the high street. Bedrooms in the old wing offer the most character with oak beams and four-poster beds, and all rooms are are spacious and well furnished. Public areas include a bar and restaurant, while the newly-opened leisure centre boasts an indoor pool and jacuzzi.
ROOMS: 53 en suite (7 GF) s £75-£95; d £75-£95 **LB** **FACILITIES:** STV Indoor swimming (H) Sauna Solarium Gym Jacuzzi Flotation tank, Beauty treatments **CONF:** Thtr 150 Class 50 Board 30 Del from £135 **SERVICES:** Lift **PARKING:** 50 **NOTES:** No dogs (ex guide dogs) Civ Wed 60 **CARDS:**

HASTINGS & ST LEONARDS, East Sussex Map 07 TQ80

★★★69% Beauport Park
Battle Rd TN38 8EA
☎ 01424 851222 📠 01424 852465
e-mail: reservations@beauportprkhotel.co.uk
Dir: *3m N off A2100*
An elegant Georgian manor house nestling in 40 acres of mature gardens, just a short drive from Hastings. The individually decorated bedrooms are tastefully furnished and thoughtfully

continued on p272

HASTINGS & ST LEONARDS, continued

equipped with modern facilities. Public rooms convey much of the original character and feature a large conservatory, a lounge bar, a restaurant and a further lounge, as well as conference and banqueting rooms.

Beauport Park, Hastings & St Leonards

ROOMS: 25 en suite (2 fmly) No smoking in 11 bedrooms s £95; d £130 (incl. bkfst) **LB** **FACILITIES:** STV Outdoor swimming (H) Golf 18 Tennis (hard) Riding Croquet lawn Putting green entertainment ch fac Xmas **CONF:** Thtr 70 Class 25 Board 30 Del from £140 **PARKING:** 60 **NOTES:** No smoking in restaurant Civ Wed 65 **CARDS:**

See advert on page 271

★★★66% Royal Victoria

Marina, St Leonards-on-Sea TN38 0BD
☎ 01424 445544 01424 721995
e-mail: reception@royalvichotel.co.uk
Dir: *on A259 seafront road 1m W of Hastings pier*

This imposing 18th-century property is situated in a prominent position overlooking the sea. A superb marble staircase leads up from the lobby to the main public areas on the first floor, which have panoramic views of the sea. The spacious bedrooms are pleasantly decorated and well equipped, and include duplex and family suites.

ROOMS: 50 en suite (15 fmly) s £60-£90; d £70-£140 (incl. bkfst) **LB** **FACILITIES:** Xmas **CONF:** Thtr 100 Class 40 Board 40 Del from £85 **SERVICES:** Lift **PARKING:** 6 **NOTES:** No smoking in restaurant Civ Wed 50 **CARDS:**

★★★65% *Cinque Ports Hotel*

THE CIRCLE
Selected Individual Hotels
GREAT BRITAIN

Bohemia Rd TN34 1ET
☎ 01424 439222 01424 437277
e-mail: enquiries@cinqueports.co.uk
Dir: *A21 into Hastings. Police HQ and courts on left, hotel next left before ambulance HQ*

This modern hotel enjoys a central location and is close to the coast. Features of the public areas include old flagstone floors, oriental rugs, hanging tapestries, beams and open fireplaces. Bedrooms are well-equipped and offer a good degree of comfort throughout.

ROOMS: 40 en suite (8 fmly) No smoking in 6 bedrooms **FACILITIES:** STV free m/ship at next door leisure centre **CONF:** Thtr 200 Class 130 Board 60 **PARKING:** 80 **NOTES:** No smoking in restaurant **CARDS:**

★★69% Chatsworth

Carlisle Pde TN34 1JG
☎ 01424 720188 01424 445865
e-mail: mail@chatsworthhotel.com
Dir: *A21 to town centre. At seafront turn right before next set of lights.*

Enjoying a central position of the seafront, close to the pier, this much-improved hotel is a short walk from the old town and within easy reach of East Sussex's many attractions. Bedrooms are smartly decorated, equipped with a range of extras and many rooms enjoy splendid sea views.

ROOMS: 52 en suite (5 fmly) No smoking in 10 bedrooms s £35-£55; d £50-£80 (incl. bkfst) **LB** **FACILITIES:** Xmas **CONF:** Thtr 40 Class 20 Board 20 Del £65 **SERVICES:** Lift **PARKING:** 8 **NOTES:** No smoking in restaurant **CARDS:**

See advert on opposite page

U High Beech

Battle Rd TN37 7BS
☎ 01424 851383 01424 854265
e-mail: highbeech@barbox.net
Dir: *400yds from A2100 between Hastings and Battle*

At the time of going to press, the star classification for this hotel was not confirmed. Please refer to the AA internet site www.theAA.com for current information.

ROOMS: 17 en suite (4 fmly) s £65; d £95-£105 (incl. bkfst) **LB** **FACILITIES:** STV ch fac **CONF:** Thtr 200 Class 60 Board 50 Del from £77.50 **PARKING:** 60 **NOTES:** No dogs (ex guide dogs) No smoking in restaurant **CARDS:**

⌂ Travel Inn

1 John Macadam Way, St Leonards on Sea
TN37 7DB
☎ 08701 977128 🖹 01424 756911

Dir: *travelling into Hastings on A21 London Rd, Travel Inn on right after junct with A2100 Battle road*
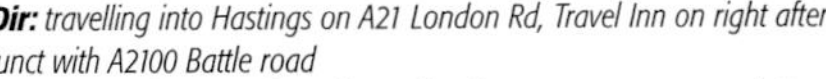
Travel Inn offers good-quality, value-for-money accommodation. Spacious, en suite rooms with bath and shower comfortably accommodate a family of up to two adults and two children (to age 15). The restaurant and bar offers a varied menu. For further details and the Travel Inn phone number, consult the Hotel Groups page.
ROOMS: 44 en suite s £44.95; d £44.95

HATFIELD, Hertfordshire — Map 06 TL20

★★★70% ❀❀ Bush Hall

Mill Green AL9 5NT
☎ 01707 271251 🖹 01707 272289
e-mail: enquiries@bush-hall.com
Dir: *From the A1(M) exit at junct 4. Take the 2nd left at rdbt onto A414 signed Hertford and Welwyn Garden City. Turn left at rdbt then take the A1000. Hotel is on the left.*

Standing in delightful grounds with a river running through it, this hotel boasts extensive facilities. Outdoor enthusiasts can enjoy a range of activities including go-karting and clay pigeon shooting. Bedrooms and public areas are comfortable and tastefully decorated. Kipling's restaurant offers a wide range freshly prepared dishes using quality produce.
ROOMS: 25 en suite (2 fmly) (8 GF) s £80-£100; d £85-£105 **FACILITIES:** Clay pigeon shooting, archery, quad bikes and karting - pre booked only **CONF:** Thtr 150 Class 70 Board 50 Del £155 **PARKING:** 100 **NOTES:** No dogs (ex guide dogs) Closed 26 Dec-3 Jan Civ Wed 150 **CARDS:**

★★★64% Quality Hotel Hatfield

Roehyde Way AL10 9AF
☎ 01707 275701 🖹 01707 266033
e-mail: admin@gb059.u-net.com
Dir: *M25 junct 23 take A1(M) northbound to junct 2. At rdbt take exit left, hotel 0.5m on right*
The well-equipped rooms at this hotel feature extras such as trouser presses and modem access. Executive rooms are very spacious. Room service is 24-hour, or guests may dine in the bar or main restaurant, where service is informal and friendly.
ROOMS: 76 en suite (14 fmly) (39 GF) No smoking in 39 bedrooms s £105; d £140 **LB FACILITIES:** STV Xmas **CONF:** Thtr 120 Class 60 Board 50 Del from £120 **PARKING:** 120 **NOTES:** No smoking in restaurant **CARDS:**

★★★62% Hatfield Lodge

Comet Way AL10 9NG
☎ 01707 288500 🖹 01707 256282
e-mail: hatfield@bealeshotels.co.uk
Dir: *From A1 junct 3, take A1001, Comet Way, towards Hatfield, over rdbt. Hotel on left (dual carriageway) opposite Galleria shopping centre*
With easy access to the M25, this modern hotel includes extensive conference facilities, a lounge, a small bar and a bright conservatory restaurant offering a short modern menu. Accommodation varies, and all rooms are smart and spacious.
ROOMS: 37 en suite (1 fmly) (25 GF) No smoking in 15 bedrooms s £50-£67; d £70-£89.50 **LB FACILITIES:** STV Swimming pass available for local pool **CONF:** Thtr 300 Class 100 Board 40 Del from £118 **PARKING:** 120 **NOTES:** No dogs (ex guide dogs) No smoking in restaurant Civ Wed 70 **CARDS:**

⌂ Travel Inn

Comet Way, Lemsford Rd AL10 0DA
☎ 08701 977129 🖹 01707 268293
Dir: *From A1(M) J4, follow A1001 towards Hatfield. At next rbt take 2nd exit and then 1st rd on right*
Travel Inn offers good-quality, value-for-money accommodation. Spacious, en suite rooms with bath and shower comfortably accommodate a family of up to two adults and two children (to age 15). The restaurant and bar offers a varied menu. For further details and the Travel Inn phone number, consult the Hotel Groups page.
ROOMS: 40 en suite s £44.95; d £44.95

HATHERSAGE, Derbyshire Map 16 SK28

★★★72% The George at Hathersage

Main Rd S32 1BB
☎ 01433 650436 01433 650099
e-mail: info@george-hotel.net
Dir: *in village centre on A6187 SW of Sheffield*

The George is a relaxing 500-year-old hostelry in the heart of this picturesque town. The beamed bar lounge has much character, and the restaurant is full of antique charm. Upstairs the decor is simpler with lots of light hues; the split-level and four-poster rooms are especially appealing.

ROOMS: 19 en suite (2 fmly) No smoking in 4 bedrooms s £68-£140; d £100-£162 (incl. bkfst) **LB FACILITIES:** Xmas **CONF:** Thtr 80 Class 20 Board 36 Del £140 **PARKING:** 40 **NOTES:** No dogs (ex guide dogs) No smoking in restaurant Civ Wed 45
CARDS:

HAVANT, Hampshire Map 05 SU70

Travel Inn (Havant Portsmouth)

65 Bedhampton Hill, Bedhampton PO9 3JN
☎ 08701 977130 023 9245 3471
Dir: *on rdbt just off A3(M) to Bedhampton*

Travel Inn offers good-quality, value-for-money accommodation. Spacious, en suite rooms with bath and shower comfortably accommodate a family of up to two adults and two children (to age 15). The restaurant and bar offers a varied menu. For further details and the Travel Inn phone number, consult the Hotel Groups page.

ROOMS: 36 en suite s £44.95; d £44.95

HAWES, North Yorkshire Map 18 SD88

★★72% Stone House

Sedbusk DL8 3PT
☎ 01969 667571 01969 667720
e-mail: daleshotel@aol.com
Dir: *from Hawes take road signed 'Muker & The Buttertubs' to T-junct then right to Sedbusk & Askrigg. Hotel 500yds on left*

Benefiting from a rural location with spectacular views of the unspoiled Wensleydale countryside, this elegant Edwardian hotel is bursting with character. Bedrooms are comfortably furnished; many have luxurious bathrooms and a number have their own private conservatories. Public rooms include a well-stocked library and various comfortable lounges.

ROOMS: 18 rms (17 en suite) 4 annexe en suite (1 fmly) No smoking in all bedrooms s £43.50-£100; d £77-£100 (incl. bkfst) **LB**
FACILITIES: Tennis (grass) Croquet lawn Billiards table Xmas
CONF: Thtr 35 Class 35 Board 35 **PARKING:** 30 **NOTES:** No smoking in restaurant Closed Jan RS mid Nov-Dec **CARDS:**

HAWKSHEAD (NEAR AMBLESIDE), Cumbria Map 18 SD39

★★70% Queen's Head

Main St LA22 0NS
☎ 015394 36271 015394 36722
e-mail: enquiries@queensheadhotel.co.uk
Dir: *M6 junct 36, then A590 to Newby Bridge. Over rdbt, 1st right for 8m into Hawkshead*

This 16th-century inn features a wood-panelled bar with low, oak-beamed ceilings and an open log fire. Substantial, carefully prepared meals are served in the bar and in the pretty dining room. The bedrooms, three of which are in an adjacent cottage, are attractively furnished and include some four-poster rooms.

ROOMS: 11 rms (9 en suite) 3 annexe en suite (2 fmly) (1 GF) No smoking in all bedrooms s £45-£55; d £60-£110 (incl. bkfst) **LB**
FACILITIES: Xmas **NOTES:** No dogs (ex guide dogs) No smoking in restaurant **CARDS:**

See advert on opposite page

HAWORTH, West Yorkshire Map 19 SE03

★★71% Old White Lion

Main St BD22 8DU
☎ 01535 642313 01535 646222
e-mail: enquiries@oldwhitelionhotel.com
Dir: *turn off A629 onto B6142, hotel 0.5m past Haworth Station. Hotel at top of cobbled main street next to Tourist Info Centre*

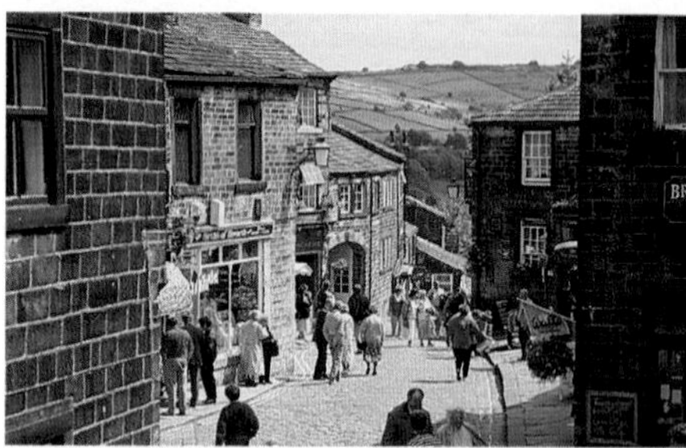

Prominently situated at the top of the old cobbled street in this popular village, this hotel is steeped in history. There is a small oak-panelled residents' lounge and a choice of cosy bars, serving a range of meals. Formal dining is available in the popular restaurant. Comfortably furnished bedrooms are well equipped and vary in size and style.

ROOMS: 15 en suite (3 fmly) s £47-£57; d £65-£75 (incl. bkfst) **LB**
FACILITIES: STV Xmas **CONF:** Thtr 90 Class 20 Board 38
PARKING: 10 **NOTES:** No dogs (ex guide dogs)
CARDS:

See advert under BRADFORD

Restaurant with Rooms

Weavers Bar Restaurant with Rooms

13-17 West Ln BD22 8DU
☎ 01535 643822 01535 644832
e-mail: weavers@amserve.net
Dir: *A629/B6142 towards Haworth, Stanbury and Colne. At top of village pass Brontë Weaving Shed on right. Left after 100yds to Parsonage car park*

Centrally located on the cobbled main street, this family-owned

continued

restaurant and bar provides well-equipped, stylish and comfortable bedrooms. All three rooms are en suite and boast many thoughtful extras. The kitchen serves modern and traditional dishes with flair and creativity.

ROOMS: 3 en suite s £55; d £80 (incl. bkfst) **NOTES:** No dogs (ex guide dogs) No smoking in restaurant RS Sun/Mon
CARDS:

HAYDOCK, Merseyside Map 15 SJ59

Holiday Inn Haydock

Lodge Ln WA12 0JG
☎ 0870 400 9039 01942 718419
e-mail: haydock@ichotelsgroup.com
Dir: *M6 junct 23, take A49 to Ashton in Nakerfield. Hotel 0.25m on right by racecourse*

At the time of going to press, the classification for this hotel was not confirmed. Please refer to the AA internet site www.theAA.com for current information.

ROOMS: 138 en suite (41 fmly) No smoking in 74 bedrooms **FACILITIES:** Indoor swimming (H) Snooker Sauna Solarium Gym Jacuzzi ch fac **CONF:** Thtr 180 Class 100 Board 60 **SERVICES:** Lift **PARKING:** 197 **NOTES:** Civ Wed 180
CARDS:

Travel Inn

Yew Tree Way, Golborne WA3 3JD
☎ 08701 977131 01942 296100
Dir: *M6 junct 23, take A580 towards Manchester. Proceed for approx 2m passing over one major rdbt. Travel Inn on your left*

Travel Inn offers good-quality, value-for-money accommodation. Spacious, en suite rooms with bath and shower comfortably accommodate a family of up to two adults and two children (to age 15). The restaurant and bar offers a varied menu. For further details and the Travel Inn phone number, consult the Hotel Groups page.

ROOMS: 60 en suite s £44.95; d £44.95

Travelodge

Piele Rd WA11 0JZ
☎ 08700 850 950 01942 272055
Dir: *2m W of junct 23 on M6, on A580 westbound*

Travelodge offers good quality, good value, modern accommodation. Ideal for families, the spacious, en suite bedrooms include remote-control TV, tea and coffee-making facilities, luxury beds and free morning newspaper. Meals can be taken at the nearby family restaurant. For further details and the Travelodge phone number, consult the Hotel Groups page.

ROOMS: 62 en suite s fr £42.95; d fr £42.95

HAYLE, Cornwall & Isles of Scilly Map 02 SW53

Travel Inn

Carwin Rise TR27 4PN
☎ 08701 977133 01736 759514
Dir: *on A30 at Loggans Moor rdbt, take 1st exit on left, Carwin Rise, Travel Inn on right*

Travel Inn offers good-quality, value-for-money accommodation. Spacious, en suite rooms with bath and shower comfortably accommodate a family of up to two adults and two children (to age 15). The restaurant and bar offers a varied menu. For further details and the Travel Inn phone number, consult the Hotel Groups page.

ROOMS: 40 en suite s £44.95; d £44.95

HAYTOR VALE, Devon Map 03 SX77

★★75% Rock Inn

TQ13 9XP
☎ 01364 661305 & 661465 01364 661242
e-mail: rockinn@eclipse.co.uk
Dir: *off A38 onto A382 to Bovey Tracey, after 0.5m turn left onto B3387 to Haytor*

Dating back to the 1750s, this former coaching inn is in a pretty hamlet on the edge of Dartmoor. Each named after a Grand National winner, the individually decorated bedrooms have good facilities and some nice extra touches. Bars are full of character, with flagstone floors and old beams and offer a wide range of dishes, cooked with imagination and flair.

ROOMS: 9 en suite (2 fmly) No smoking in 2 bedrooms s £66-£95.50; d £76-£95.50 (incl. bkfst) **LB FACILITIES:** STV **PARKING:** 20 **NOTES:** No dogs (ex guide dogs) **CARDS:**

HAYWARDS HEATH, West Sussex

Map 06 TQ32

★★★68% The Birch Hotel

Lewes Rd RH17 7SF
☎ 01444 451565 🖷 01444 440109
e-mail: info@birch-hotel.co.uk

***Dir:** on A272 opposite Princess Royal Hospital and behind Shell Garage*

Originally the home of an eminent Harley Street surgeon, this attractive Victorian property has been extended to combine modern facilities with the charm of its original period. Public rooms include the conservatory-style Pavilion Restaurant, along with an open-plan lounge and brasserie style bar serving a range of snacks.

ROOMS: 51 en suite (3 fmly) (12 GF) No smoking in 23 bedrooms s £62-£89; d £82-£99 (incl. bkfst) **FACILITIES:** STV **CONF:** Thtr 60 Class 30 Board 26 Del from £115 **PARKING:** 60 **NOTES:** No dogs (ex guide dogs) No smoking in restaurant Civ Wed 60
CARDS:

HEATHROW AIRPORT (LONDON), Greater London

See LONDON SECTION plan 1 A3
See also Slough & Staines

★★★★74% ◎ *London Marriott Hotel Heathrow*

Bath Rd UB3 5AN
☎ 020 8990 1100 🖷 020 8990 1110

***Dir:** M4 junct 4, follow Terminal 1 2 & 3 signs via M4 and Heathrow Airport. Left at rdbt signed A4/London. Hotel 0.5m left through 2 sets of traffic lights*

This smart modern hotel with its striking design meets all the expectations of a successful airport hotel. The light and airy atrium offers several eating and drinking options, each with a different theme. Spacious bedrooms are appointed to a good standard with an excellent range of facilities, and there are some indoor leisure facilities.

ROOMS: 390 en suite (140 fmly) No smoking in 327 bedrooms **FACILITIES: Spa** STV Indoor swimming (H) Sauna Solarium Gym Steam Room **CONF:** Thtr 540 Class 214 Board 62 **SERVICES:** Lift air con **PARKING:** 220 **NOTES:** No dogs (ex guide dogs) Civ Wed 112
CARDS:

★★★★72% Sheraton Skyline

Bath Rd UB3 5BP
☎ 020 8759 2535 🖷 020 8750 9150
e-mail: res268_skyline@sheraton.com

***Dir:** M4 junct 4 for Heathrow, follow Terminal 1,2 & 3 signs. Before airport entrance take slip road to left for 0.25m signed A4 Central London*

Within easy access of all terminals, this hotel offers spacious, well-equipped and air-conditioned bedrooms, some of which have been recently refurbished to a smart new standard. Refurbished public areas are light and modern, and guests can enjoy a varied

continued

range of food and drinks in various bars and food operations. Facilities include function rooms and a gym.

ROOMS: 350 en suite (12 fmly) No smoking in 212 bedrooms s £89-£216; d £89-£216 **LB** **FACILITIES:** STV Indoor swimming (H) Gym Pool table Xmas **CONF:** BC Thtr 500 Class 325 Board 100 Del from £170 **SERVICES:** Lift air con **PARKING:** 320 **NOTES:** RS Xmas Civ Wed 200 **CARDS:**

★★★★70% Slough/Windsor Marriott Hotel

Ditton Rd, Langley SL3 8PT
☎ 0870 400 7244 🖷 0870 400 7344
e-mail: reservations.sloughwindsor@marriotthotels.co.uk

***Dir:** M4 junct 5, follow 'Langley' signs and left at lights into Ditton Rd*

The hotel enjoys good access to the motorway and Heathrow. Guests can enjoy a range of food and drinks in the bars and restaurant. The recently refurbished leisure centre offers spa and beauty treatments together with the gym and pool. Bedrooms are spacious with excellent soundproofing and facilities to suit the needs of business travellers.

ROOMS: 382 en suite (120 fmly) (96 GF) No smoking in 267 bedrooms s £119-£169; d £119-£169 **FACILITIES:** STV Indoor swimming (H) Tennis (hard) Sauna Solarium Gym Swimming pool supervised Entertainment Xmas **CONF:** Thtr 400 Class 220 Board 42 Del from £140 **SERVICES:** Lift air con **PARKING:** 632 **NOTES:** No dogs (ex guide dogs) **CARDS:**

★★★★66% The Renaissance London Heathrow Hotel

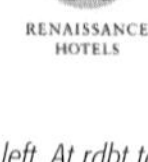

Bath Rd TW6 2AQ
☎ 020 8897 6363 🖷 020 8897 1113
e-mail: lhrrenaissance@aol.com

***Dir:** M4 junct 4 follow spur road towards airport, take 2nd left. At rdbt take 2nd exit signposted 'Renaissance Hotel'. Hotel next to Customs House*

Located right on the perimeter of the airport, this hotel commands superb views over the runways. Smartly refurbished bedrooms are fully soundproofed and equipped with air conditioning, each room is well suited to meet the needs of today's business travellers. The hotel boasts extensive conference facilities, and is a very popular venue for air travellers and conference organisers.

ROOMS: 649 en suite (59 GF) No smoking in 468 bedrooms s £84-£154; d £84-£169.95 (incl. bkfst) **LB** **FACILITIES:** STV Sauna Solarium Gym Steam Room Dance Studio Massage treatment Personal trainer Xmas **CONF:** BC Thtr 400 Class 300 Board 60 Del from £179 **SERVICES:** Lift air con **PARKING:** 700 **NOTES:** No dogs (ex guide dogs) Civ Wed 150 **CARDS:**

★★★★64% *Le Meridien Excelsior*

Bath Rd UB7 0DU
☎ 020 8759 6611 🖷 020 8759 3421
e-mail: reservations@lemeridien.com

***Dir:** adjacent to M4 spur at junct with A4*

This convenient, busy, large corporate hotel offers a wide range of facilities including a choice of bars and restaurants, modern conference rooms and a health club. Bedrooms vary from the standard type to the recently refurbished Executives and Crown Clubrooms.

ROOMS: 567 en suite (43 fmly) No smoking in 259 bedrooms **FACILITIES:** STV Indoor swimming (H) Sauna Solarium Gym Jacuzzi **CONF:** Thtr 250 Class 135 Board 60 **SERVICES:** Lift air con **PARKING:** 500 **NOTES:** No dogs (ex guide dogs) Civ Wed 200
CARDS:

TV dinner?
Room service at three stars and above

★★★70% Novotel London Heathrow

Junction 4 M4, Cherry Ln UB7 9HB
☎ 01895 431431 🖷 01895 431221
e-mail: H1551@accor-hotels.com
Dir: *M4 junct 4, follow Uxbridge signs on A408. Keep left and take 2nd exit off traffic island into Cherry Ln signed West Drayton. Hotel on left*
This modern hotel is conveniently located for the airport and motorway network. The huge indoor atrium is airy and stylish, creating a good sense of space in the public areas, which include a cocktail bar, meeting rooms, fitness centre and indoor swimming pool. Bedrooms are spacious and feature a good range of facilities.
ROOMS: 178 en suite (34 fmly) (10 GF) No smoking in 112 bedrooms s £70-£125; d £70-£135 **LB** **FACILITIES:** STV Indoor swimming (H) Gym **CONF:** Thtr 250 Class 100 Board 90 Del from £139 **SERVICES:** Lift **PARKING:** 100 **CARDS:**

★★★66% Master Robert

366 Great West Rd TW5 0BD
☎ 020 8570 6261 🖷 020 8569 4016
e-mail: stay@masterrobert.co.uk
Dir: *exit M4 junct 3. Take 3rd exit signed A312 to Heathrow Airport. At rdbt take 1st exit to A4 Central London. At 2nd rdbt straight on 100yds and left, Hotel on left by 2nd lights*
A well-known landmark on the Great West Road, this hotel is conveniently located near Heathrow and the area's business community. Bedrooms are set in motel-style buildings behind the main hotel; most are spacious with good facilities. There is residents' lounge bar, a restaurant and a popular pub.
ROOMS: 96 annexe en suite (22 fmly) (40 GF) No smoking in 50 bedrooms s £99; d £114 **FACILITIES:** STV Putting green **CONF:** Thtr 150 Class 60 Board 40 Del from £99 **PARKING:** 200 **NOTES:** No dogs (ex guide dogs) No smoking in restaurant Civ Wed 150
CARDS:

★★★65% Comfort Inn Heathrow

Shepiston Ln UB3 1LP
☎ 020 8573 6162 🖷 020 8848 1057
e-mail: info@comfortheathrow.com
Dir: *M4 junct 4, follow directions to Hayes & Shepiston Lane, hotel approx 1m, next to fire station*
This hotel is located a little way from the airport, and guests may prefer its quieter position. There is a frequent bus service, which runs to and from the hotel throughout the day. Bedrooms are well-equipped and many have the benefit of air conditioning.
ROOMS: 184 en suite (7 fmly) No smoking in 80 bedrooms **FACILITIES:** STV Gym **CONF:** Thtr 150 Class 72 Board 90 **SERVICES:** Lift **PARKING:** 120 **NOTES:** No dogs (ex guide dogs) No smoking in restaurant Civ Wed **CARDS:**

★★★62% Osterley Four Pillars Hotel

764 Great West Rd TW7 5NA
☎ 0800 374 692 🖷 020 8569 7819
e-mail: osterley@four-pillars.co.uk
(For full entry see Osterley)

U *Holiday Inn London Heathrow*

118 Bath Rd UB3 5AJ
☎ 0870 400 9040 🖷 020 8564 9265
Dir: *M4 junct 4, take Spur Rd to Heathrow Airport, 1st left onto A4 Bath Rd, through 3 sets of traffic lights. Hotel on left*
At the time of going to press, the classification for this hotel was not confirmed. Please refer to the AA internet site www.theAA.com for current information.
ROOMS: 186 en suite No smoking in 100 bedrooms **CONF:** Thtr 60 Class 10 Board 35 **SERVICES:** Lift **PARKING:** 105
CARDS:

U *Holiday Inn London Heathrow*

Sipson Rd UB7 0JU
☎ 020 8759 2323 🖷 020 8897 8659
Dir: *M4 junct 4, keep left, take 1st left into Holloway Lane, left at mini rdbt then left to hotel*
At the time of going to press, the classification for this hotel was not confirmed. Please refer to the AA internet site www.theAA.com for current information.
ROOMS: 610 en suite (284 fmly) No smoking in 359 bedrooms **FACILITIES:** STV **CONF:** Thtr 130 Class 60 Board 60 **SERVICES:** Lift **PARKING:** 478 **NOTES:** No dogs (ex guide dogs)
CARDS:

U ◎◎ The Radisson Edwardian

Bath Rd UB3 5AW
☎ 020 8759 6311 🖷 020 8759 4559
e-mail: resreh@radisson.com
At the time of going to press, the star classification for this hotel was not confirmed. Please refer to the AA internet site www.theAA.com for current information.
ROOMS: 459 en suite (83 GF) No smoking in 132 bedrooms s £88-£233; d £88-£257 **LB** **FACILITIES: Spa** STV Sauna Solarium Gym Jacuzzi Massage, Hairdressing Xmas **CONF:** BC Thtr 700 Class 300 Board 60 Del from £150 **SERVICES:** Lift air con **PARKING:** 550 **NOTES:** No dogs (ex guide dogs) **CARDS:**

⌂ Hotel Ibis Heathrow

112/114 Bath Rd UB3 5AL
☎ 020 8759 4888 🖷 020 8564 7894
e-mail: H0794@accor-hotels.com
Dir: *follow Heathrow Terminals 1,2 & 3 signs, then onto spur road, off at sign for A4 Central London. Hotel 0.5m on left*
Modern, budget hotel offering comfortable accommodation in bright and practical bedrooms. Breakfast is self-service and dinner is available in the restaurant. For further details, consult the Hotel Groups page.
ROOMS: 354 en suite s £49.95-£69.95; d £49.95-£69.95

⌂ Travel Inn

362 Uxbridge Rd UB4 0HF
☎ 08701 977132 🖷 020 8569 1204
Dir: *M4 junct 3 follow A312 north, straight across next rdbt onto dual carriageway, at A4020 junct turn left, Travel Inn 100yds on right*
Travel Inn offers good-quality, value-for-money accommodation. Spacious, en suite rooms with bath and shower comfortably accommodate a family of up to two adults and two children (to age 15). The restaurant and bar offers a varied menu. For further details and the Travel Inn phone number, consult the Hotel Groups page.
ROOMS: 62 en suite s £49.95-£54.95; d £49.95-£54.95

⌂ Travel Inn London Heathrow

362 Uxbridge Rd UB4 0HF
☎ 08701 242 8000977 132 🖷 02080-0569 1204
Travel Inn offers good-quality, value-for-money accommodation. Spacious, en suite rooms with bath and shower comfortably accommodate a family of up to two adults and two children (to age 15). The restaurant and bar offers a varied menu. For further details and the Travel Inn phone number, consult the Hotel Groups page.
ROOMS: 590 en suite

> Early start?
> Hotels at all star levels should provide in-room alarm clocks and/or alarm calls

HEATHROW AIRPORT (LONDON), continued

⌂ Travel Inn London Heathrow
11 Bath Rd TW3 3BQ
☎ 0870 6075 075 🖷 0870 241 9000
***Dir:** from M4 junct 4 follow signs for Heathrow Terminals 1, 2 & 3. Turn left onto Bath Rd signed A4/London. Travel Inn on right after 0.5 mile*
Travel Inn offers good-quality, value-for-money accommodation. Spacious, en suite rooms with bath and shower comfortably accommodate a family of up to two adults and two children (to age 15). The restaurant and bar offers a varied menu. For further details and the Travel Inn phone number, consult the Hotel Groups page.
ROOMS: 590 en suite s £49.95-£69.95; d £49.95-£69.95

○ Premier Lodge (Heathrow Airport junction 3)

9 Bath Rd, Heathrow TW6 2AA
☎ 0870 9906572 🖷 0870 9906573
ROOMS: 137 en suite **NOTES:** Due to open Dec 2003

○ Premier Lodge (Heathrow Airport junction 4)

Shepiston Ln, Heathrow Airport UB3 1RN
☎ 0870 9906612 🖷 0870 9906613
ROOMS: 133 en suite **NOTES:** Due to open Feb 2004

HECKFIELD, Hampshire
Map 05 SU76

★★66% New Inn
RG27 0LE
☎ 0118 932 6374 🖷 0118 932 6550
e-mail: newinn@heckfield.freeserve.co.uk
***Dir:** off A33 onto B3349, right at 1st island, over 2nd island. Hotel 0.5m on left*
Easily located, this characterful inn offers business focussed accommodation and early morning breakfast is available for an early start to the day. Bedrooms are well equipped and pleasantly spacious. Centred around the bar, the lounge, restaurant and a function suite are available. A friendly, informal service contributes towards the relaxed environment.
ROOMS: 16 en suite (1 fmly) s £50-£75; d £65-£85 (incl. bkfst) **LB**
CONF: Thtr 30 Class 25 Board 16 Del from £105 **PARKING:** 80
NOTES: No smoking in restaurant **CARDS:**

HELLIDON, Northamptonshire
Map 11 SP55

★★★★74% ◉ Hellidon Lakes Hotel & Country Club
NN11 6GG
☎ 01327 262550 🖷 01327 262559
e-mail: hellidon@marstonhotels.com
***Dir:** signed, off A361 between Daventry and Banbury*
Some 220 acres of beautiful countryside, which include 27 holes of golf and 12 lakes, combine to form a rather spectacular backdrop for this much improved and recently extended hotel. There is an extensive range of facilities available from meeting rooms to swimming pool, gymnasium and ten-pin bowling. Golfers of all levels can try some of the world's most challenging courses on the indoor golf simulator.
ROOMS: 110 en suite s fr £108; d fr £130 **LB FACILITIES: Spa** STV Indoor swimming (H) Golf 18 Tennis (hard) Fishing Solarium Gym Putting green Beauty therapist, Indoor smartgolf (simulator), 4 lane ten pin bowling Xmas **CONF:** Thtr 300 Class 150 Board 80 Del from £170
PARKING: 180 **NOTES:** No dogs (ex guide dogs) No smoking in restaurant Civ Wed 120 **CARDS:**

HELMSLEY, North Yorkshire
Map 19 SE68

★★★77% ◉ Feversham Arms
1 High St YO62 5AG
☎ 01439 770766 🖷 01439 770346
e-mail: fevershamarmshotel@msn.com
***Dir:** A168 'Thirsk' from A1 then A170 or A64 'York' from A1 to York North, then B1363 to Helmsley. Hotel 125mtrs from Market Place*
This comfortable hotel was substantially remodelled in 2000. Diners have a choice of formal or informal styles of eating and menus offer a wide selection. The bedrooms are comfortable and furnished to a high standard with many useful extras. There is a comprehensively equipped leisure centre and pleasant grounds with a pool and tennis court.
ROOMS: 17 en suite (3 fmly) (4 GF) No smoking in all bedrooms s £80-£120; d £100-£150 (incl. bkfst) **FACILITIES:** STV Outdoor swimming (H) Tennis (hard) Gym Xmas **CONF:** Thtr 20 Class 20 Board 24 Del £140 **PARKING:** 50 **NOTES:** No smoking in restaurant
CARDS:

★★★76% ◉ The Black Swan
Market Place YO62 5BJ
☎ 0870 400 8112 🖷 01439 770174
e-mail: blackswan@macdonald-hotels.co.uk
***Dir:** follow A170 towards Scarborough into Helmsley. Hotel at top of Market Sq*
The face of this former coaching inn is a blend of Elizabethan, Georgian and Tudor and inside are warm, welcoming interiors with candlelight, oak beams and open fireplaces. There are six guest lounges and plenty of cosy nooks for quiet conversation. The hotel also has comfortable, individually decorated bedrooms and a popular restaurant.
ROOMS: 45 en suite (4 fmly) No smoking in 13 bedrooms s £64-£69; d £128-£138 (incl. bkfst & dinner) **LB FACILITIES:** STV Xmas
CONF: Thtr 50 Class 16 Board 22 Del from £115 **PARKING:** 50
NOTES: No smoking in restaurant **CARDS:**

★★★71% Pheasant
Harome YO62 5JG
☎ 01439 771241 🖷 01439 771744
***Dir:** 2.5m SE, leave A170 after 0.25m. Right signed Harome for further 2m*
Guests can expect a family welcome at this hotel, which has spacious, comfortable bedrooms and enjoys a delightful setting next to the village pond. The beamed, flagstoned bar leads into the charming lounge and conservatory dining room, where very enjoyable English food is served. A separate building contains the swimming pool. The hotel offers dinner-inclusive tariffs, and has many regulars.
ROOMS: 12 en suite 2 annexe en suite s £67-£73; d £134-£146 (incl. bkfst & dinner) **LB FACILITIES:** STV Indoor swimming (H)
PARKING: 20 **NOTES:** No children 12yrs No smoking in restaurant Closed Xmas & Jan-Feb **CARDS:**

★★68% Crown
Market Square YO62 5BJ
☎ 01439 770297 🖷 01439 771595
***Dir:** on A170*
A 16th-century inn with plenty of character standing in the market square. It is noted for its colourful flower arrangements, excellent morning coffee and home-made scones. Bedrooms are individual and thoughtfully equipped. Public areas are pleasantly traditional and include cosy bars and a dining room serving wholesome dishes in generous portions.
ROOMS: 12 en suite (1 fmly) (1 GF) s £36-£37; d £72-£74 (incl. bkfst) **LB FACILITIES:** Xmas **PARKING:** 20 **CARDS:**

HELSTON, Cornwall & Isles of Scilly — Map 02 SW62

★★64% The Gwealdues

Falmouth Rd TR13 8JX
☎ 01326 572808 🖷 01326 561388
e-mail: gwealdueshotel@btinternet.com
Dir: *from Truro/Falmouth on A394. Hotel on approach into Helston*

A friendly, family-run establishment Gwealdues bedrooms are comfortable and well equipped. Attentive service is provided in the nautically themed bar and restaurant, where a choice of authentic Thai or European cuisine is offered. A 42' motor sailing yacht is available for hire.
ROOMS: 17 en suite (2 fmly) No smoking in 5 bedrooms s £38; d £55 (incl. bkfst) **LB** **FACILITIES:** Sailing on own yacht Xmas **CONF:** Thtr 70 Class 50 Board 50 **PARKING:** 50 **NOTES:** No smoking in restaurant
CARDS:

HEMEL HEMPSTEAD, Hertfordshire — Map 06 TL00

★★★66% The Bobsleigh Inn

Hempstead Rd, Bovingdon HP3 0DS
☎ 01442 833276 🖷 01442 832471
e-mail: bobsleigh@macdonald-hotels.co.uk
Dir: *turn left after Hemel Hempstead station onto B4505 towards Chesham and follow into Bovingdon, hotel on left*
Located just outside the town, the hotel enjoys a pleasant rural setting. There is an open-plan lobby and bar area and an attractive dining room with views over the garden. Bedrooms vary in size; all are modern in style.
ROOMS: 30 en suite 15 annexe en suite (8 fmly) (29 GF) No smoking in 39 bedrooms s £85-£123; d £95-£133 (incl. bkfst) **LB**
FACILITIES: Spa STV Jacuzzi Xmas **CONF:** Thtr 100 Class 50 Board 40 Del from £135 **PARKING:** 60 **NOTES:** No smoking in restaurant Civ Wed 97 **CARDS:**

U *Holiday Inn Hemel Hempstead*

Breakspear Way HP2 4UA
☎ 0870 400 9041 🖷 01442 211812
Dir: *M1 junct 8, over rdbt and 1st left after BP garage*
At the time of going to press, the classification for this hotel was not confirmed. Please refer to the AA internet site www.theAA.com for current information.
ROOMS: 145 en suite (33 fmly) No smoking in 76 bedrooms
FACILITIES: Indoor swimming (H) Sauna Solarium Gym Jacuzzi Kids playroom/play area at wknds **CONF:** Thtr 60 Class 22 Board 30
SERVICES: Lift **PARKING:** 195 **CARDS:**

Travel Inn

Stoney Ln, Bourne End Services HP1 2SB
☎ 0870 238 3309 🖷 01442 879149
Dir: *from M25 junct 20 (A41) exit at services. From M1 junct 8, follow A414, then A41, exit at services*
Travel Inn offers good-quality, value-for-money accommodation.
continued
Spacious, en suite rooms with bath and shower comfortably accommodate a family of up to two adults and two children (to age 15). The restaurant and bar offers a varied menu. For further details and the Travel Inn phone number, consult the Hotel Groups page.
ROOMS: 61 en suite s £44.95; d £44.95

Travelodge

Wolsey House, Wolsey Rd HP2 4SS
☎ 08700 850 950
Travelodge offers good quality, good value, modern accommodation. Ideal for families, the spacious, en suite bedrooms include remote-control TV, tea and coffee-making facilities, luxury beds and free morning newspaper. Meals can be taken at the nearby family restaurant. For further details and the Travelodge phone number, consult the Hotel Groups page.
ROOMS: 53 en suite s fr £42.95; d fr £42.95

HENLEY-IN-ARDEN, Warwickshire — Map 10 SP16

U Henley

Tanworth Ln B95 5RA
☎ 01564 794551 🖷 01564 795044
e-mail: reception@henleyhotel.co.uk
Dir: *Follow A3400 towards Henley-in-Arden*
At the time of going to press, the star classification for this hotel was not confirmed. Please refer to the AA internet site www.theAA.com for current information.
ROOMS: 32 en suite (2 fmly) (14 GF) No smoking in 19 bedrooms s £38-£48; d £48-£58 **LB** **CONF:** BC Thtr 80 Class 50 Board 24 Del from £80 **PARKING:** 40 **NOTES:** No smoking in restaurant Civ Wed 50
CARDS:

HENLEY-ON-THAMES, Oxfordshire — Map 05 SU78

See also Stonor

★★★70% Red Lion

Hart St RG9 2AR
☎ 01491 572161 🖷 01491 410039
e-mail: reservations@redlionhenley.co.uk
Dir: *adjacent to Henley Bridge*

The front rooms of this 16th-century Thames-side hotel offer fabulous river views. Bedrooms and public areas retain many original features, such as wood panelling, flagstone floors and beams. Bedrooms are comfortably appointed and decorated to a high standard; they feature period furniture and marble bathrooms.
ROOMS: 26 en suite (1 fmly) s £99-£135; d £145-£170 **FACILITIES:** STV **CONF:** Thtr 60 Class 20 Board 30 Del £185 **PARKING:** 25 **NOTES:** No dogs **CARDS:**

HENLEY-ON-THAMES, continued

Restaurant with Rooms

The White Hart Hotel

High St, Nettlebed RG9 5DD
☎ 01491 641245 01491 649018
e-mail: info@whitehartnettlebed.com
Dir: *on A4130 3.5m from Henley-on-Thames towards Oxford*

This pleasant Restaurant with Rooms is a popular venue. Its stylish and relaxed atmosphere and attentive and friendly staff provide an excellent environment. Chris Barber's innovative cuisine uses carefully sourced, organic ingredients to provide memorable dining. Guests can choose to eat in the Nettlebed Restaurant for fine dining or in the Bistro for classic pub dishes.

ROOMS: 6 en suite 6 annexe en suite (3 fmly) (3 GF) No smoking in all bedrooms s £105-£145; d £105-£145 (incl. cont bkfst) **LB**
FACILITIES: Xmas **CONF:** BC Thtr 30 Class 30 Board 20 Del from £165
PARKING: 50 **NOTES:** No dogs (ex guide dogs)
CARDS:

HEREFORD, Herefordshire

Map 10 SO53

See also Leominster & Much Birch

Accessible Hotel of the Year
Top 200 - Hotel

★★★ *Castle House*

Castle St HR1 2NW
☎ 01432 356321 01432 365909
e-mail: info@castlehse.co.uk
Dir: *follow city centre, near Cathedral*

Enjoying a prime city centre location and overlooking the castle moat, this delightful Victorian mansion is the epitome of elegance and sophistication. The characterful bedrooms are equipped with every luxury to ensure a memorable stay and are complemented perfectly by the well-proportioned and restful lounge and bar. The experience is completed by award winning cuisine in the topiary-themed restaurant. Castle House has been awarded AA Accessible Hotel of the Year 2003-2004.

ROOMS: 15 en suite **FACILITIES:** STV **SERVICES:** Lift
PARKING: 15 **NOTES:** No smoking in restaurant
CARDS:

See advert on opposite page

★★★69% Belmont Lodge & Golf Course

Belmont HR2 9SA
☎ 01432 352666 01432 358090
e-mail: info@belmont-hereford.co.uk
Dir: *off A465 into Ruckhall Ln. Hotel on right in 0.5m*

This impressive complex is based around Belmont House, a Grade II listed building that dates back to 1788. It is surrounded by its own golf course and commands delightful views over the surrounding countryside and River Wye. Bedrooms, in a modern lodge, are comfortable and well equipped and the modern restaurant and bar are situated in the main house.

ROOMS: 30 en suite (4 fmly) No smoking in 15 bedrooms s £52.95-£67.90; d £60.95-£75.85 (incl. bkfst) **LB** **FACILITIES:** Golf 18 Tennis (hard) Fishing Putting green Bowls Games room Xmas
CONF: Thtr 60 Class 14 Board 25 Del from £69 **PARKING:** 150
NOTES: No dogs (ex guide dogs) No smoking in restaurant
CARDS:

★★★67% Three Counties Hotel

Belmont Rd HR2 7BP
☎ 01432 299955 01432 275114
e-mail: enquiries@threecountieshotel.co.uk
Dir: *on A465 Abergavenny Rd*

A mile west of the city centre, this large, privately owned, modern complex has well-equipped, spacious bedrooms, many of which are located in separate single-storey buildings around the extensive car park. There is a spacious, comfortable lounge, a traditional bar and an attractive restaurant.

ROOMS: 28 en suite 32 annexe en suite (4 fmly) No smoking in 23 bedrooms s £50-£66; d £67-£86 (incl. bkfst) **LB** **FACILITIES:** STV
CONF: Thtr 300 Class 100 Board 60 Del from £83 **PARKING:** 250
NOTES: Civ Wed 200 **CARDS:**

See advert on opposite page

★★★61% The Green Dragon

Broad St HR4 9BG
☎ 0870 400 8113 01432 352139
e-mail: general.greendragon@countrytown-hotels.co.uk
Dir: *follow signs for Cathedral and Mappa Mundi to rdbt. 1st exit, then 2nd left into West St. 2nd right into Aubrey St and hotel garage*

Dating back to the 16th century, this inn was originally frequented by monks making pilgrimages to shrines of local saints. Gradually the inn was developed and the hotel now consists of four buildings, of which the Georgian front is the most recent addition.

ROOMS: 83 en suite (22 fmly) No smoking in 29 bedrooms **CONF:** Thtr 200 Class 60 Board 40 **SERVICES:** Lift **PARKING:** 110
NOTES: Civ Wed 100 **CARDS:**

★★70% Ancient Camp Inn

Ruckhall, Eaton Bishop HR2 9QX
☎ 01981 250449 01981 251581
e-mail: reservations@theancientcampinn.co.uk
Dir: *From A465 follow Ruckhall sign, after bridge follow Inn sign*

Situated in a superb location above the River Wye and enjoying stunning views, this inn is named after a nearby Iron Age fort. It features flagstone floors, exposed beams and fires in the bar and dining room. Bedrooms vary in style and are well equipped.

ROOMS: 5 en suite No smoking in all bedrooms s fr £50; d £60-£80 (incl. bkfst) **FACILITIES:** Fishing **PARKING:** 30 **NOTES:** No dogs (ex guide dogs) No children 16yrs No smoking in restaurant Closed last wk Jan-1st wk Feb RS Sun evening & Mon **CARDS:**

THE PILGRIM HOTEL

★★★

Ross Road, Much Birch, Hereford HR2 8HJ
Tel: 01981 540742 Fax: 01981 540620
Email: stay@pilgrimhotel.co.uk
Website: www.pilgrimhotel.co.uk

Set in 4 acres of parkland overlooking the Golden Valley, this peaceful Country House Hotel is midway between Hereford and Ross-on-Wye. Most of the spacious, well equipped bedrooms have superb views. The cosy beamed bar is open to residents and non-residents and guests can enjoy a delicious, candlelit meal in the Pilgrim Restaurant. We have a 3 hole pitch and putt course and croquet lawn to help you relax and unwind. For the business customer our conference room accommodates up to 40 delegates.

Three Counties Hotel

Belmont Road, Hereford
Herefordshire HR2 7BP
Tel: 01432 299955 Fax: 01432 275114
Web: www.threecountieshotel.co.uk
Email: enquiries@threecountieshotel.co.uk

A mile west of the city centre, this large, modern complex has well-equipped, spacious bedrooms, many of which are located in separate single-storey buildings around the extensive car park.

There is a spacious, comfortable lounge, traditional bar and an attractive restaurant.

THE 'HOTEL OF THE YEAR 2001' IS THE MOST ELEGANT HOTEL IN HEREFORD

Sited in Castle Street, formerly the historic cross roads of Norman Hereford, Castle House is a gracious and hospitable town house with just fifteen rooms where guests can enjoy unashamed luxury and unrivalled personal attention.

The award winning restaurant 'La Rive' promises to be an exquisite experience with impeccable service and outstanding cuisine. For guests staying on business, there is a fully equipped office for their exclusive use and Castle House is accessible for guests with walking difficulties.

With quiet garden views over the tranquil moat, and barely a hundred metres stroll from the Cathedral with its world famous Chained Library and Mappa Mundi, Castle House is centrally located in the heart of rural Herefordshire.

Castle House, Castle Street, Hereford, England, HR1 2NW.
Tel: +44(0)1432 356321 Fax: +44(0)1432 365909 Email: info@castlehse.co.uk www.castlehse.co.uk

HEREFORD, continued

⌂ Travel Inn
Holmer Rd, Holmer HR4 9RS
☎ 08701 977134 🖷 01432 343003
Dir: *from N M5 junct 7, follow A4103 to Worcester. M50 junct 4 take A49 Leominster road Travel Inn 800yds on left*
Travel Inn offers good-quality, value-for-money accommodation. Spacious, en suite rooms with bath and shower comfortably accommodate a family of up to two adults and two children (to age 15). The restaurant and bar offers a varied menu. For Travel Inn phone number, consult Hotel Groups page.
ROOMS: 60 en suite s £44.95; d £44.95 **CONF:** Thtr 20 Board 24

HERTFORD, Hertfordshire Map 06 TL31

★★★64% The White Horse
Hertingfordbury SG14 2LB
☎ 01992 586791 🖷 01992 550809
e-mail: whitehorsehertingfordbury@macdonald-hotels.co.uk
Dir: *from A10 follow signs for A414 from Hertford under rail bridge over rdbt, left at next rdbt, hotel 300yds on right*
The Georgian facade of this former coaching inn belies a much older interior with parts of the building dating back to the 17th century. Public rooms include a beamed bar with open fire and a spacious restaurant overlooking the rear gardens. Most of the tastefully decorated bedrooms are in a more modern extension.
ROOMS: 42 en suite (4 fmly) No smoking in 20 bedrooms s £65-£110; d £75-£130 (incl. bkfst) **FACILITIES:** Xmas **CONF:** Thtr 60 Class 30 Board 35 Del from £110 **PARKING:** 45 **NOTES:** No smoking in restaurant Civ Wed 90 **CARDS:**

HESTON MOTORWAY SERVICE AREA (M4), Greater London
See LONDON SECTION plan 1 B3

⌂ Travelodge (Eastbound)
Phoenix Way TW5 9NB
☎ 08700 850 950 🖷 01384 78578
Dir: *M4 junct 2 & 3*
Travelodge offers good quality, good value, modern accommodation. Ideal for families, the spacious, en suite bedrooms include remote-control TV, tea and coffee-making facilities, luxury beds and free morning newspaper. Meals can be taken at the nearby family restaurant. For further details and the Travelodge phone number, consult the Hotel Groups page.
ROOMS: 66 en suite s fr £42.95; d fr £42.95

⌂ Travelodge (Westbound)
Cranford Ln TW5 9NB
☎ 08700 850 950
Travelodge offers good quality, good value, modern accommodation. Ideal for families, the spacious, en suite bedrooms include remote-control TV, tea and coffee-making facilities, luxury beds and free morning newspaper. Meals can be taken at the nearby family restaurant. For further details and the Travelodge phone number, consult the Hotel Groups page.
ROOMS: 145 en suite s fr £42.95; d fr £42.95

HESWALL, Merseyside Map 15 SJ28

⌂ Travel Inn (Wirral North)
Chester Rd, Gayton, Heswall CH60 3FD
☎ 08701 977274 🖷 0151 342 1982
Dir: *M53 junct 4 follow A5137 signed Heswall for 3m & turn left at next rdbt, Travel Inn on left*
Travel Inn offers good-quality, value-for-money accommodation. Spacious, en suite rooms with bath and shower comfortably accommodate a family of up to two adults and two children (to age 15). The restaurant and bar offers a varied menu. For Travel Inn phone number, consult the Hotel Groups page.
ROOMS: 37 en suite s £44.95; d £44.95

HETHERSETT, Norfolk Map 13 TG10

★★★74% Park Farm
NR9 3DL
☎ 01603 810264 🖷 01603 812104
e-mail: enq@parkfarm-hotel.co.uk
Dir: *5m S of Norwich, off A11 on B1172*

Set amid landscaped grounds and surrounded by open countryside, this elegant Georgian farmhouse has been owned and run by the Gowing family since 1958. The pleasantly decorated bedrooms are tastefully furnished and decorated, and some rooms have patio doors with a sun terrace. The extensive public rooms include a smart conservatory, a lounge, a bar and an intimate restaurant.
ROOMS: 5 en suite 42 annexe en suite (20 fmly) (20 GF) s £88-£140; d £118-£180 (incl. bkfst) **LB** **FACILITIES:** Indoor swimming (H) Sauna Solarium Gym Jacuzzi Beauty salon, Hairdressing, Swimming pool supervised Xmas **CONF:** Thtr 120 Class 50 Board 50 Del from £130 **PARKING:** 150 **NOTES:** No dogs (ex guide dogs) No smoking in restaurant Civ Wed 100 **CARDS:**

See advert under NORWICH

HEXHAM, Northumberland Map 21 NY96

★★★★70% ◎ De Vere Slaley Hall
Slaley NE47 0BY
☎ 01434 673350 🖷 01434 673962
e-mail: slaley.hall@devere-hotels.com
Dir: *A1 from S to A68 link road follow signs for Slaley Hall*

One thousand acres of Northumbrian forest and parkland, two championship golf courses and indoor leisure facilities all add up to a range of possibilities for guests, whatever their reason for visiting. Spacious bedrooms are fully air-conditioned and equipped

continued

with a range of extras. Public rooms include a number of lounges, conference and banqueting rooms, the informal Golf Clubhouse restaurant and the refurbished main restaurant.
ROOMS: 139 en suite (22 fmly) No smoking in 101 bedrooms s £120-£140; d £170-£190 (incl. bkfst) **LB FACILITIES: Spa** STV Indoor swimming (H) Golf 18 Sauna Solarium Gym Jacuzzi Quad bikes, Archery, Clay pigeon shoot, 4x4 driving, Creche, Pool supervised Xmas **CONF:** Thtr 300 Class 220 Board 150 Del from £135 **SERVICES:** Lift air con **PARKING:** 500 **NOTES:** No smoking in restaurant Civ Wed 250
CARDS:

★★★★70% Langley Castle

Langley on Tyne NE47 5LU
☎ 01434 688888 🖹 01434 684019
e-mail: manager@langleycastle.com
Dir: *from A69 S on A686 for 2m. Castle on right*

Langley is a magnificent 14th-century fortified castle, set in ten acres of parkland. There is a restaurant, a comfortable drawing room and a cosy bar. Bedrooms are furnished with period pieces and most feature window seats, and restored buildings in the grounds have been converted into very comfortable 'Castle View' bedrooms.
ROOMS: 8 en suite 10 annexe en suite (4 fmly) (5 GF) s £94.50-£159.50; d £102.50-£209 (incl. bkfst) **LB FACILITIES:** STV Xmas **CONF:** Thtr 120 Class 60 Board 40 Del from £145 **PARKING:** 70 **NOTES:** No dogs (ex guide dogs) No smoking in restaurant Civ Wed 120
CARDS:

See advert on this page

★★★67% Beaumont

Beaumont St NE46 3LT
☎ 01434 602331 🖹 01434 606184
e-mail: beaumont.hotel@btinternet.com
Dir: *A69 towards Hexham town centre*

In a region of England steeped in history, this hotel is located in the centre of town, overlooking the park and 6th-century abbey. The hotel has two bars, a lobby seating area and a first floor restaurant with views of the park. Bedrooms vary in size and have a simple decorative style.
ROOMS: 25 en suite (3 fmly) No smoking in 18 bedrooms s £65-£75; d £85-£95 **LB FACILITIES:** STV Snooker Solarium **CONF:** Thtr 100 Class 60 Board 40 Del from £70 **SERVICES:** Lift **PARKING:** 16 **NOTES:** No dogs No smoking in restaurant Closed 25-26 Dec & 1 Jan
CARDS:

HICKSTEAD, West Sussex — Map 06 TQ22

★★★62% The Hickstead Hotel

Jobs Ln, Bolney RH17 5NZ
☎ 01444 248023 🖹 01444 245280
e-mail: gm.hickstead@macdonald-hotels.co.uk
Dir: *M23 South, take A2300 exit (Burgess Hill), left, next right, hotel 100yds on left*
In the heart of West Sussex, this hotel is located not far from the

continued

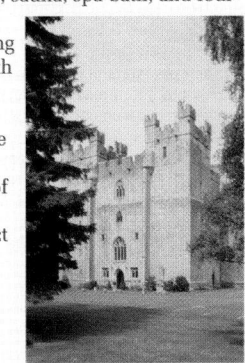

main London to Brighton road. The hotel's proximity to the local business park and its accessibility to a number of local attractions make it popular with both business and leisure guests who can make use of the indoor leisure centre.
ROOMS: 49 en suite (4 fmly) (24 GF) No smoking in 34 bedrooms s £50-£83; d £50-£83 **LB FACILITIES: Spa** STV Indoor swimming (H) Fishing Sauna Gym Jacuzzi Swimming pool supervised **CONF:** BC Thtr 80 Class 60 Board 50 Del from £85 **PARKING:** 100 **NOTES:** No smoking in restaurant Civ Wed 80 **CARDS:**

⌂ Travelodge

Jobs Ln RH17 5NX
☎ 08700 850 950 🖹 01444 881377
Dir: *A23 southbound*
Travelodge offers good quality, good value, modern accommodation. Ideal for families, the spacious, en suite bedrooms include remote-control TV, tea and coffee-making facilities, luxury beds and free morning newspaper. Meals can be taken at the nearby family restaurant. For further details and the Travelodge phone number, consult the Hotel Groups page.
ROOMS: 55 en suite s fr £42.95; d fr £42.95

HIGHBRIDGE, Somerset — Map 04 ST34

★★66% Sundowner

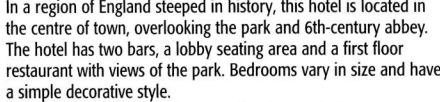

74 Main Rd, West Huntspill TA9 3QU
☎ 01278 784766 🖹 01278 794133
e-mail: runnalls@msn.com
Dir: *from M5 junct 22, 3m S on A38 or from M5 junct 23, 3m N on A38*
Friendly service and an informal atmosphere are just two of the highlights of this small hotel. The open-plan lounge/bar is a comfortable area in which to relax after a busy day exploring the

continued on p284

HIGHBRIDGE, continued

area or working in the locality. An extensive menu, featuring freshly cooked, imaginative dishes, is offered in the popular restaurant.
ROOMS: 8 en suite (1 fmly) s £40-£45; d £55-£60 (incl. bkfst)
CONF: Thtr 40 Board 24 Del £65 **PARKING:** 18 **NOTES:** No smoking in restaurant **CARDS:**

HIGH WYCOMBE, Buckinghamshire Map 05 SU89

See also Stokenchurch

U Ambassador Court

145 West Wycombe Rd HP12 3AB
☎ 01494 461818 🖷 01494 461919
e-mail: ach@fardellhotels.com
Dir: *M4 junct 4/A404 to A40*
At the time of going to press, the classification for this hotel was not confirmed. Please refer to the AA internet site www.theAA.com for current information.
ROOMS: 18 en suite (2 GF) No smoking in all bedrooms s £109; d £119 (incl. bkfst) **FACILITIES:** STV Xmas **CONF:** Thtr 20 Class 12 Board 16 Del from £110 **PARKING:** 18 **NOTES:** No dogs (ex guide dogs) No smoking in restaurant **CARDS:**

U *Holiday Inn High Wycombe*

Handy Cross HP11 1TL
☎ 0870 400 9042 🖷 01494 439071
Dir: *M40 junct 4, take A4010 towards Aylesbury*
At the time of going to press, the classification for this hotel was not confirmed. Please refer to the AA internet site www.theAA.com for current information.
ROOMS: 109 en suite (4 fmly) No smoking in 55 bedrooms
FACILITIES: STV **CONF:** Thtr 150 Class 80 Board 50 **PARKING:** 173
NOTES: No dogs (ex guide dogs) **CARDS:**

⌂ Travel Inn

Thanestead Farm, London Rd, Loudwater HP10 9YL
☎ 08701 977135 🖷 01494 446855
Dir: *on A40 near M40 junct 3, 3m from High Wycombe*
Travel Inn offers good-quality, value-for-money accommodation. Spacious, en suite rooms with bath and shower comfortably accommodate a family of up to two adults and two children (to age 15). The restaurant and bar offers a varied menu. For further details and the Travel Inn phone number, consult the Hotel Groups page.
ROOMS: 81 en suite s £44.95; d £44.95 **CONF:** Class 24 Board 24

HILLINGTON, Norfolk Map 12 TF72

★★67% Ffolkes Arms

Lynn Rd PE31 6BJ
☎ 01485 600210 🖷 01485 601196
e-mail: ffolkespub@aol.com
Dir: *on A149 at Knights Hill rdbt, right onto A148 towards Cromer. Hotel 6m along A148 at Hillington*
A popular 17th-century coaching inn, situated close to the Norfolk coastline and within easy reach of King's Lynn. Facilities include a bar, restaurant and lounge area. Bedrooms are housed in an annexe adjacent to the main building; each one is pleasantly appointed and well equipped. The hotel also has a function suite and social club.
ROOMS: 20 annexe en suite (2 fmly) No smoking in all bedrooms s £35-£43; d £50-£70 (incl. bkfst) **LB** **FACILITIES:** Xmas **CONF:** Thtr 200 Class 60 Board 50 Del from £66 **PARKING:** 200 **NOTES:** No dogs (ex guide dogs) No smoking in restaurant
CARDS:

HILTON PARK MOTORWAY SERVICE AREA (M6), West Midlands Map 10 SJ90

⌂ Travelodge Birmingham North

Hilton Park Services (M6), Essington WV11 2AT
☎ 08700 850 950 🖷 01922 701967
Dir: *M6 between junct 10a & 11*
Travelodge offers good quality, good value, modern accommodation. Ideal for families, the spacious, en suite bedrooms include remote-control TV, tea and coffee-making facilities, luxury beds and free morning newspaper. Meals can be taken at the nearby family restaurant. For further details and the Travelodge phone number, consult the Hotel Groups page.
ROOMS: 63 en suite s fr £42.95; d fr £42.95

HIMLEY, Staffordshire Map 10 SO89

★★★63% The Himley Country Hotel

School Rd DY3 4LG
☎ 0870 609 6112 🖷 01902 896668
e-mail: himleycountryhotel@corushotels.com
Dir: *leave A449 and turn into School Rd at lights by Dudley Arms*

This modern hotel has been tastefully built around a 19th-century village schoolhouse. Bedrooms are well equipped and many are quite spacious. Day rooms include a stylish conservatory restaurant in which wide-ranging menus are accompanied by traditional buffet roasts.
ROOMS: 73 en suite (1 fmly) No smoking in 38 bedrooms s £65; d £65 **LB** **FACILITIES:** STV Xmas **CONF:** Thtr 150 Class 80 Board 50 Del £99 **PARKING:** 100 **NOTES:** No smoking in restaurant Civ Wed 100
CARDS:

★★67% *Himley House Hotel*

Stourbridge Rd DY3 4LD
☎ 01902 892468 🖷 01902 892604
e-mail: himleyhouse@hotmail.com
Dir: *on A449 N of Stourbridge*

Dating back to the 17th century, and formerly the lodge for nearby

continued

Himley Hall, this hotel offers well-equipped and comfortable accommodation. The bedrooms of varying sizes are located both in the main house and separate buildings nearby, and the busy restaurant offers a wide selection of dishes.
ROOMS: 24 en suite (2 fmly) **FACILITIES:** ch fac **CONF:** Thtr 50 Class 30 Board 22 **PARKING:** 162 **NOTES:** No dogs (ex guide dogs)
CARDS:

HINCKLEY, Leicestershire — Map 11 SP49

★★★★71% ❀❀ Sketchley Grange

Best Western

Sketchley Ln, Burbage LE10 3HU
☎ 01455 251133 🖷 01455 631384
e-mail: reservations@sketchleygrange.co.uk
Dir: *SE of town, off A5/M69 junct 1, take B4109 to Hinckley. Left at 2nd rdbt. 1st right onto Sketchley Ln*

This smart hotel, peacefully set in its own grounds, enjoys a prime location near the Warwickshire and Leicestershire border. Excellent facilities include the stylish Roman's Health and Leisure Spa, complete with a 'Little Romans' crèche and a choice of bars and dining options. Thoughtfully equipped bedrooms include a range of spacious suites.
ROOMS: 52 en suite (9 fmly) (1 GF) No smoking in 15 bedrooms s £80-£110; d £100-£130 **LB** **FACILITIES: Spa** STV Indoor swimming (H) Sauna Solarium Gym Steam room, Hairdressing, Creche, Beauty therapy, Swimming pool supervised ch fac **CONF:** BC Thtr 300 Class 150 Board 50 Del from £120 **SERVICES:** Lift **PARKING:** 200 **NOTES:** No smoking in restaurant Civ Wed 250
CARDS:

See advert on this page

★★★★59% Hanover International Hotel & Club

Watling St (A5) LE10 3JA
☎ 01455 631122 🖷 01455 634536
e-mail: administration.crso@hanover-international.com
Dir: *on A5, S of junct 1 on M69*

A large hotel offering good facilities for conference and business guests. Bedrooms are spacious with the Club Floors providing high

continued

levels of comfort, such as leather seating at good-sized desks. The leisure centre has been refurbished, as have the new-look Brasserie and Conservatory restaurants.
ROOMS: 350 en suite (156 fmly) No smoking in 200 bedrooms s £118; d £128 **LB** **FACILITIES: Spa** STV Indoor swimming (H) Snooker Sauna Solarium Gym Putting green Jacuzzi Steam room, Swimming pool supervised **CONF:** Thtr 400 Class 180 Board 38 Del £150 **SERVICES:** Lift air con **PARKING:** 600 **NOTES:** No dogs (ex guide dogs) No smoking in restaurant Civ Wed 200
CARDS:

★★72% Kings Hotel & Restaurant

13/19 Mount Rd LE10 1AD
☎ 01455 637193 🖷 01455 636201
e-mail: kingshinck@aol.com
Dir: *follow A447 signed to Hinckley. Under railway bridge, right at rdbt. 1st road left opposite railway station, then 3rd right*

A friendly hotel situated in a quiet road, within easy walking

continued on p286

HINCKLEY, continued

distance of the town centre and station. Bedrooms are tastefully decorated and have attractive furnishings and tiled bathrooms. The public rooms include a residents' lounge, a lounge-bar with striking Chinese-style wallpaper and a large restaurant with a baby grand piano and attractive Victorian fireplace.
ROOMS: 7 en suite No smoking in all bedrooms s £64.90-£74.90; d £74.90-£84.90 (incl. bkfst) **LB FACILITIES: Spa** STV **CONF:** Thtr 30 Class 40 Board 20 Del from £90 **PARKING:** 20 **NOTES:** No dogs No children 10yrs No smoking in restaurant
CARDS:

HINDON, Wiltshire Map 04 ST93

★★69% The Angel Inn
High St SP3 6DJ
☎ 01747 820696 01747 820869
e-mail: eat@the-angel.co.uk
Dir: *village centre 1.5m from A303 & A350, through village on B3089 towards Salisbury*
A welcoming 18th-century inn, which attracts locals and visitors from farther afield for its interesting range of carefully prepared dishes, augmented by a selection of well chosen wines. Tastefully decorated bedrooms have been equipped with modern comforts, while public rooms include a character bar, complete with flag-stoned floors, inglenook fire-place and exposed beams, and a tree-lined patio area ideal for al fresco dining.
ROOMS: 7 en suite (2 fmly) No smoking in all bedrooms s £45-£55; d £65-£85 (incl. bkfst) **PARKING:** 18 **NOTES:** No smoking in restaurant Closed 26 Dec-2 Jan RS Jan **CARDS:**

HINTLESHAM, Suffolk Map 13 TM04

Top 200 - Hotel

★★★★ Hintlesham Hall
IP8 3NS
☎ 01473 652334 & 652268
01473 652463
e-mail: reservations@hintleshamhall.com
Dir: *4m W of Ipswich on A1071 to Sudbury*
Hospitality and service are key features at this imposing Grade I listed country house hotel, situated in 175 acres of grounds and landscaped gardens. Individually decorated bedrooms offer a high degree of comfort; each one is tastefully furnished and equipped with many thoughtful touches. The spacious public rooms include an elegant restaurant, which serves fine classical cuisine. The hotel also has an 18-hole golf course, club-house and leisure complex.
ROOMS: 33 en suite (1 fmly) (9 GF) s £98-£125; d £110-£295 (incl. cont bkfst) **LB FACILITIES: Spa** Outdoor swimming (H) Golf 18 Tennis (hard) Snooker Sauna Gym Croquet lawn Putting green Jacuzzi Health & beauty suite & treatments, Swimming pool supervised entertainment Xmas **CONF:** BC Thtr 80 Class 50 Board 32 Del from £175 **PARKING:** 100 **NOTES:** No smoking in restaurant RS Sat Civ Wed 120 **CARDS:**

HINTON CHARTERHOUSE, Somerset Map 04 ST75

★★★76% Homewood Park
BA2 7TB
☎ 01225 723731 01225 723820
e-mail: res@homewoodpark.com
Dir: *6m SE of Bath on A36, turn left at 2nd sign for Freshford*
Homewood Park, an unassuming yet stylish Georgian house set in delightful grounds, offers relaxed surroundings and maintains high standards of quality and comfort throughout. Bedrooms, all individually decorated, include thoughtful extras to ensure a comfortable stay. The hotel has a reputation for excellent cuisine – offering an imaginative interpretation of classical dishes.
ROOMS: 19 en suite (1 fmly) No smoking in 2 bedrooms s £115-£210; d £145-£265 (incl. bkfst) **LB FACILITIES:** STV Outdoor swimming (H) Tennis (hard) Croquet lawn Xmas **CONF:** Thtr 40 Class 30 Board 25 Del from £150 **PARKING:** 30 **NOTES:** No dogs (ex guide dogs) No smoking in restaurant Civ Wed 50
CARDS:

HITCHIN, Hertfordshire Map 12 TL12

★★67% Firs
83 Bedford Rd SG5 2TY
☎ 01462 422322 01462 432051
e-mail: info@firshotel.co.uk
Dir: *from M1 junct 10 take A505 or A1 junct 8 onto A602 to Hitchin. Then follow signs to Bedford on A600 for hotel 1m on left, next to Shell petrol station*
This family-run hotel is situated on the northern edge of town and caters for business as well as leisure guests. Well-equipped bedrooms vary in size and style, and most have been tastefully refurbished boasting smart bathrooms. The Italian-style restaurant complements the spacious public areas, which include a lounge, bar and conference room.
ROOMS: 29 en suite (3 fmly) No smoking in 15 bedrooms s £52-£57; d £62-£75 (incl. bkfst) **CONF:** Thtr 30 Class 24 Board 20 Del from £95 **PARKING:** 30 **NOTES:** No dogs (ex guide dogs) No smoking in restaurant **CARDS:**

HOCKLEY HEATH, West Midlands Map 10 SP17

Top 200 - Hotel

★★★
Nuthurst Grange Country House & Restaurant
Nuthurst Grange Ln B94 5NL
☎ 01564 783972 01564 783919
e-mail: info@nuthurst-grange.com
Dir: *0.5m S on A3400*
The approach to this period country house is a stunning avenue drive, and the hotel enjoys views over rolling countryside and several acres of well-tended gardens and mature grounds. Public areas include restful lounges, meeting rooms and a

continued

sunny restaurant. Spacious bedrooms offer considerable luxury and comfort. The kitchen brigade produces highly imaginative British and French cuisine, complemented by very attentive, professional restaurant service.

ROOMS: 15 en suite (2 GF) s £129-£139; d £165-£195 (incl. bkfst) **LB FACILITIES:** STV Croquet lawn Helipad **CONF:** BC Thtr 100 Class 50 Board 45 Del £179 **PARKING:** 86 **NOTES:** No smoking in restaurant Closed 1 wk Xmas Civ Wed 100 **CARDS:**

Travel Inn (Solihull Hockley Heath)

Stratford Rd, Hockley Heath B94 6NX
☎ 08701 977230 01564 783197
Dir: *on A3400 2m S of M42 junct 4*
Travel Inn offers good-quality, value-for-money accommodation. Spacious, en suite rooms with bath and shower comfortably accommodate a family of up to two adults and two children (to age 15). The restaurant and bar offers a varied menu. For further details and the Travel Inn phone number, consult the Hotel Groups page.
ROOMS: 55 en suite s £44.95; d £44.95 **CONF:** Thtr 25

HODNET, Shropshire
Map 15 SJ62

★★65% Bear

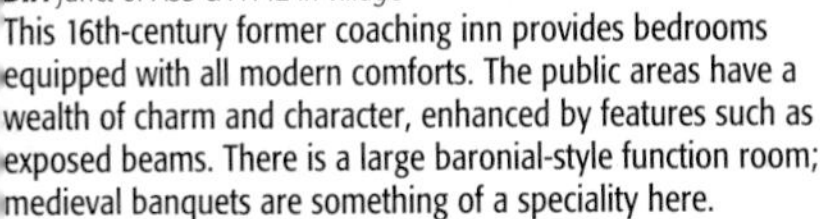

TF9 3NH
☎ 01630 685214 & 685788 01630 685787
e-mail: info@bearhotel.org
Dir: *junct of A53 & A442 in village*
This 16th-century former coaching inn provides bedrooms equipped with all modern comforts. The public areas have a wealth of charm and character, enhanced by features such as exposed beams. There is a large baronial-style function room; medieval banquets are something of a speciality here.
ROOMS: 6 en suite 2 annexe en suite (2 fmly) s £43-£45; d £60-£70 (incl. bkfst) **LB FACILITIES:** entertainment Xmas **CONF:** Thtr 100 Class 50 Board 40 **PARKING:** 70 **NOTES:** No dogs (ex guide dogs) Civ Wed 70 **CARDS:**

HOLCOMBE, Somerset
Map 04 ST64

★★69% The Ring O' Roses
Stratton Rd BA3 5EB
☎ 01761 232478 01761 233737
e-mail: ringorosesholcombe@tesco.net
Dir: *A367 to Stratton on The Fosse, look for hidden left turn opposite Downside Abbey, signposted Holcombe. Next right, hotel 1.5m on left*
Rurally located with views of Downside Abbey in the distance, the inn dates back to the 16th century. The attentive owners and pleasant staff create a friendly and relaxed atmosphere. The

continued

individually furnished and decorated bedrooms are comfortable and feature welcome extras. Real ales are served in the bar while in the restaurant, an imaginative and varied menu selection is offered, using local ingredients wherever possible.
ROOMS: 8 en suite No smoking in all bedrooms s £55-£65; d £75-£95 (incl. bkfst) **LB CONF:** Thtr 40 Class 40 Board 14 **PARKING:** 35 **NOTES:** No smoking in restaurant **CARDS:**

HOLFORD, Somerset
Map 04 ST14

★★72% Combe House
TA5 1RZ
☎ 01278 741382 01278 741322
e-mail: enquiries@combehouse.co.uk
Dir: *from A39 W turn left in Holford village then left at T junct. Left again at fork and continue 0.25m to Holford Combe*
Once a tannery, this 17th-century long house is peacefully situated in lovely grounds, and provides an ideal retreat for walking in the Quantock Hills. Bedrooms are traditional in style and the public rooms include a choice of sitting areas. There is a focus on home cooking in the dining room.
ROOMS: 16 en suite (2 fmly) No smoking in 10 bedrooms s £38; d £76-£117 (incl. bkfst) **LB FACILITIES:** Indoor swimming (H) Tennis (hard) Xmas **PARKING:** 17 **NOTES:** No smoking in restaurant Closed Jan RS Nov, Dec & Feb **CARDS:**

H

HOLKHAM, Norfolk
Map 13 TF84

★★73% The Victoria at Holkham
Park Rd NR23 1RG
☎ 01328 711008 01328 711009
e-mail: victoria@holkham.co.uk
Dir: *A149, 2m W of Wells-next-the-Sea*

A Grade II listed property built from local flintstone ideally situated on the North Norfolk coast road and forming part of the Holkham estate. Décor and furnishings are heavily influenced by the local landscape: the stylish bedrooms are individually decorated and tastefully furnished with pieces specially made for the hotel in India. The brasserie-style restaurant serves an interesting choice of dishes featuring local produce.
ROOMS: 10 en suite 1 annexe en suite (2 fmly) (1 GF) s £85-£125; d £110-£170 (incl. bkfst) **LB FACILITIES:** STV Fishing Shooting on Holkham Estate, Bird watching reserve nearby ch fac Xmas **CONF:** Thtr 12 Class 40 Board 30 Del from £70 **PARKING:** 30 **NOTES:** No dogs (ex guide dogs) No smoking in restaurant **CARDS:**

HOLMES CHAPEL, Cheshire Map 15 SJ76

★★★65% **Holly Lodge Hotel & "Truffles" Restaurant**
70 London Rd CW4 7AS
☎ 01477 537033 01477 535823
e-mail: sales@hollylodgehotel.co.uk
Dir: *A50/A54 x-rds, 1m from M6 junct 18*
Situated close to the centre of Holmes Chapel, this hotel caters for both business and leisure guests. Accommodation varies in style, with particularly comfortable, bright modern bedrooms located in an adjacent cottage. A carefully prepared menu is served in Truffles restaurant, and there are also several function rooms.
ROOMS: 17 en suite 25 annexe en suite (3 fmly) No smoking in 17 bedrooms s £69.50-£82; d £72-£93 (incl. bkfst) **LB FACILITIES:** STV Discounted rates with local gym Xmas **CONF:** Thtr 120 Class 60 Board 60 **PARKING:** 90 **NOTES:** No smoking in restaurant Civ Wed 120
CARDS:

HOLMFIRTH, West Yorkshire Map 16 SE10

★★65% **Old Bridge**
HD9 7DA
☎ 01484 681212 01484 687978
e-mail: oldbridgehotel@enterprise.net
Dir: *at traffic lights on A6024/A635 in centre of Holmfirth, turn into Victoria St, left after bank and shops to hotel*
Located centrally in the town famous for *The Last of the Summer Wine*, and with ample convenient parking, this stone built hotel offers well-equipped bedrooms and a variety of spacious public rooms. There is a wide range of food available in both the attractive restaurant and the cosy bars.
ROOMS: 20 en suite s £47.95; d £62.95 (incl. bkfst) **CONF:** Thtr 80 Class 50 Board 40 **PARKING:** 30 **NOTES:** No dogs (ex guide dogs)
CARDS:

HOLSWORTHY, Devon Map 03 SS30

★★72% **Court Barn Country House**
Clawton EX22 6PS
☎ 01409 271219 01409 271309
e-mail: courtbarnhotel@talk21.com
Dir: *2.5m S of Holsworthy off A388 Tamerton Rd next to Clawton Church*
This engaging, family-run Victorian country house is set in five acres of attractive grounds, including a 9-hole putting course and croquet. Comfortable bedrooms are individually furnished, and there are two comfortable lounges. A four-course dinner featuring fresh local produce is served in the spacious restaurant, and leisurely breakfasts are taken overlooking the garden.
ROOMS: 8 rms (7 en suite) (1 fmly) No smoking in all bedrooms s £40-£55; d £70-£90 (incl. bkfst) **LB FACILITIES:** Tennis (grass) Croquet lawn Putting green Badminton Xmas **CONF:** Thtr 25 Board 8 Del from £85 **PARKING:** 13 **NOTES:** No smoking in restaurant
CARDS:

HONILEY, Warwickshire Map 10 SP27

★★★66% **Honiley Court Hotel & Conference Centre**
corus hotels
Meer End Rd CV8 1NP
☎ 0870 609 6142 01926 484474
e-mail: honileycourt@corushotels.com
Dir: *M40 junct 15, take A46 then A4177 to Solihull. Right at 1st main rdbt, hotel 2m on left*
Incorporating an inn with 16-century origins, this busy hotel provides brightly decorated and open-plan public areas. The spacious bedrooms are comfortably appointed and well equipped for both business and leisure guests. A good choice of meals and snacks are readily available in the contemporary Boot Inn and Bistro.

ROOMS: 62 en suite (1 fmly) (14 GF) No smoking in 31 bedrooms s £43-£105; d £86-£120 **LB FACILITIES:** STV Xmas **CONF:** Thtr 200 Class 70 Board 30 Del from £97 **SERVICES:** Lift **PARKING:** 250 **NOTES:** No smoking in restaurant Civ Wed 160
CARDS:

HONITON, Devon Map 04 ST10

Top 200 - Hotel

★★★ ®® **Combe House Hotel & Restaurant**
Gittisham EX14 3AD
☎ 01404 540400 01404 46004
e-mail: stay@thishotel.com
Dir: *off A30 1m S of Honiton, follow Gittisham Heathpark signs*
This very special Elizabethan mansion enjoys memorable views over thousands of acres of woodland, meadow and pasture. Public areas and bedrooms are a blend of comfort and quality, with relaxation the ultimate objective. Dining is equally impressive; a skilled kitchen brigade maximises the best of local produce, augmented by excellent wines. Private dining is available in the magnificently restored old kitchen.
ROOMS: 15 en suite s £99-£125; d £138-£265 (incl. bkfst) **LB FACILITIES:** Fishing Croquet lawn Jacuzzi Xmas **CONF:** BC Thtr 60 Class 40 Board 26 Del from £142 **PARKING:** 51 **NOTES:** No smoking in restaurant Civ Wed 100
CARDS:

★★69% **Home Farm**
Wilmington EX14 9JR
☎ 01404 831278 01404 831411
e-mail: homefarmhotel@breathemail.net
Dir: *3m E on A35 in village of Wilmington*
Set in well-tended gardens, this thatched former farmhouse is now a comfortable hotel. Many of the original features have been

continued

retained, with the cobbled courtyard and farm implements attractively displayed. Appetising cuisine is offered either in the bar or in the more intimate restaurant. Bedrooms, some with private gardens, are well equipped and comfortably furnished.
ROOMS: 9 en suite 5 annexe en suite (2 fmly) (5 GF) No smoking in 9 bedrooms s £40-£65; d £65-£100 (incl. bkfst) **LB** **FACILITIES:** Xmas **PARKING:** 20 **NOTES:** No smoking in restaurant
CARDS:

★★68% Monkton Court

Monkton EX14 9QH
☎ 01404 42309 🖹 01404 46861
e-mail: yeotelsmonkton@aol.com
***Dir:** 2m E of Honiton on A30 towards Ilminster, opposite Monkton Church*
Set in five acres of grounds, this attractive 17th century manor house retains much of its historical character. Friendly staff provide attentive service, and many guests find the Monkton Court an ideal base for either business or leisure visits. A comfortable lounge and pleasant bar with crackling log fire are available. Cuisine offers a good choice of freshly cooked and imaginative dishes.
ROOMS: 6 en suite (1 fmly) s £45-£55; d £65-£75 (incl. bkfst) **LB** **CONF:** Thtr 50 Class 25 Board 25 **PARKING:** 40 **NOTES:** No dogs (ex guide dogs) No smoking in restaurant Closed Xmas & New Year
CARDS:

★★63% *Honiton Motel*

Turks Head Corner, Exeter Rd EX14 1BL
☎ 01404 43440 🖹 01404 47767
***Dir:** off A30*
The Honiton Motel offers well-maintained budget accommodation with modern facilities. All rooms have their own access and are set around the large car park. In the main building, additional features include bars, restaurant, a function suite and a fast-food bar.
ROOMS: 14 annexe en suite (3 fmly) **PARKING:** 50
CARDS:

HOOK, Hampshire — Map 05 SU75

★★73% Hook House

London Rd RG27 9EQ
☎ 01256 762630 🖹 01256 760232
e-mail: reception@hookhousehotel.co.uk
***Dir:** 1m E of Hook on A30*
Several acres of landscaped grounds and a relaxing environment are provided at this friendly, family-run small hotel. Bedrooms are well equipped, some located in an adjacent building. Public areas have a comfortable atmosphere and in the dining room guests can choose from an interesting menu. The hotel offers occasional jazz evenings.
ROOMS: 13 en suite 4 annexe en suite s £60-£90; d £70-£100 (incl. bkfst) **CONF:** Thtr 40 Class 20 Board 20 Del £120 **PARKING:** 20 **NOTES:** No dogs No smoking in restaurant Closed Xmas Civ Wed 50
CARDS:

HOPE COVE, Devon — Map 03 SX63

★★70% Cottage

TQ7 3HJ
☎ 01548 561555 🖹 01548 561455
e-mail: info@hopecove.com
***Dir:** from Kingsbridge on A381 to Salcombe. 2nd right at village of Marlborough, left for Inner Hope*
Glorious sunsets and moonlight can be seen over the attractive bay from this popular hotel. Friendly and attentive service from the staff and management mean many guests return here. Bedrooms, many with sea views and some with balconies, are well equipped. There are three lounges and particularly interesting is the cabin, built from shipwrecked timbers. The restaurant offers an enjoyable dining experience.
ROOMS: 35 rms (25 en suite) (5 fmly) (7 GF) s £49.75-£75.50; d £79.50-£131 (incl. bkfst & dinner) **LB** **FACILITIES:** Table Tennis Xmas **CONF:** Thtr 50 Class 20 Board 24 Del from £53.65 **PARKING:** 50 **NOTES:** No smoking in restaurant Closed Early Jan - Early Feb
CARDS:

★★70% Lantern Lodge

TQ7 3HE
☎ 01548 561280 🖹 01548 561736
***Dir:** right off A381 Kingsbridge to Salcombe road. 1st right after passing Hope Cove sign then 1st left along Grand View Rd*
This attractive, small hotel close to the South Devon coastal path benefits from a friendly team of loyal staff. Bedrooms are well-furnished, and some have the added bonus of balconies overlooking the rugged coastline. An imaginative range of home cooked meals is available. There is a choice of lounges and a pretty enclosed garden with putting green. The popular indoor pool has large doors opening directly on to the garden.
ROOMS: 14 en suite (1 fmly) (1 GF) s £62-£84; d £104-£140 (incl. bkfst & dinner) **LB** **FACILITIES:** Indoor swimming (H) Sauna Putting green Multi-gym **PARKING:** 15 **NOTES:** No dogs (ex guide dogs) No children 12yrs No smoking in restaurant Closed Dec-Feb
CARDS:

HORLEY — Map 06 TQ24

Hotels are listed under Gatwick Airport

HORNBY, Lancashire — Map 18 SD56

★★68% Castle Hotel

Main St LA2 8JT
☎ 015242 21204 🖹 015242 22258
e-mail: www.castlehotel@aol.com
***Dir:** M6 junct 34 onto A683, hotel just over bridge on left*

Dating back to the 17th century in parts, this traditional stone building is situated opposite the castle. Bedrooms vary in size and style, with family rooms and a split-level suite available. Extensive informal eating areas, including the atmospheric Stables, prove popular with locals and visitors alike, whilst the attractively furnished restaurant gives the opportunity to dine in style.
ROOMS: 8 en suite (2 fmly) No smoking in 6 bedrooms s £50-£70; d £60-£80 (incl. bkfst) **LB** **FACILITIES:** Pool table, Darts, Games room **CONF:** Del from £99 **PARKING:** 20 **NOTES:** No dogs (ex guide dogs) No smoking in restaurant RS 24-25 Dec **CARDS:**

H

HORNCASTLE, Lincolnshire
Map 17 TF26

★★71% Admiral Rodney

North St LN9 5DX
☎ 01507 523131 🖷 01507 523104
e-mail: reception@admiralrodney.com
Dir: *off A153 - Louth to Horncastle*

Enjoying a prime location in the centre of town, this smart hotel offers a high standard of accommodation. Bedrooms are well appointed and thoughtfully equipped for both business and leisure guests. Public areas include the Rodney public bar, a selection of meeting and conference rooms and an open-plan restaurant and lounge bar.

ROOMS: 31 en suite (3 fmly) (7 GF) No smoking in 10 bedrooms s £50-£55; d £70-£80 (incl. bkfst) **LB FACILITIES:** STV Xmas **CONF:** Thtr 140 Class 60 Board 50 Del £75 **SERVICES:** Lift **PARKING:** 60 **NOTES:** No dogs (ex guide dogs)
CARDS:

HORNING, Norfolk
Map 13 TG31

See also Wroxham

★★★66% Petersfield House
Lower St NR12 8PF
☎ 01692 630741 🖷 01692 630745
e-mail: reception@petersfieldhotel.co.uk
Dir: *from Wroxham take A1062 for 2.5m then right into Horning village. Hotel in centre of village on left*

Expect a warm welcome at this charming property which dates back to the 1920s. It is ideally situated amid pretty landscaped grounds in the heart of this delightful riverside village. Although the bedrooms vary in size and style, they are all comfortably furnished and thoughtfully equipped; many of the rooms have lovely views of the garden. Public areas include a large lounge, a bar and a restaurant.

ROOMS: 17 en suite (2 fmly) (3 GF) s £65-£70; d £90-£120 (incl. bkfst) **LB FACILITIES:** Fishing Putting green Private moorings Boating entertainment Xmas **CONF:** Thtr 50 Class 40 Board 30 **PARKING:** 70 **NOTES:** No smoking in restaurant Closed Jan Civ Wed 70
CARDS:

HORRINGER, Suffolk
Map 13 TL86

★★★★80% 🏵🏵 The Ickworth
IP29 5QE
☎ 01284 735350 🖷 01284 736300
e-mail: info@ickworthhotel.com
Dir: *Follow brown signs for Ickworth House; take 4th exit at rdbt, follow this road to staggered x-rds. Continue straight until t-junct, turn left into village & almost immediately turn right into Ickworth Estate*

This stunning property manages to combine a current National Trust property with clever retro design and yet still to be child friendly. The combination works as the staff here are friendly and easy going, with a children's den, horses and bikes to ride, yet the magic of 'Capability' Brown gardens to roam in as well. Quality produce and technical skill inspire food here.

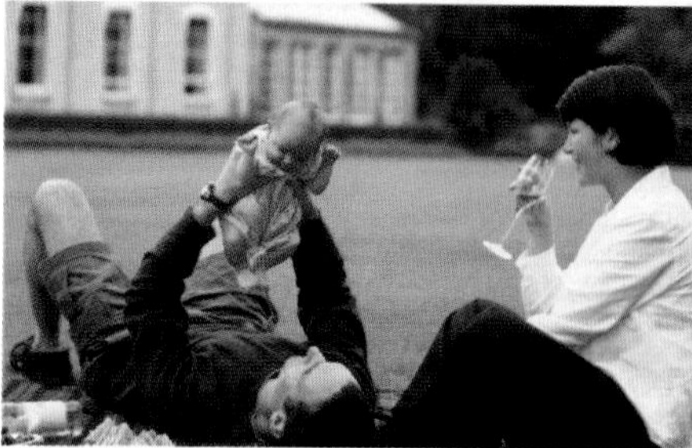

ROOMS: 27 en suite 11 annexe en suite (35 fmly) s £120-£297; d £195-£345 (incl. bkfst & dinner) **LB FACILITIES: Spa** STV Indoor swimming (H) Tennis (hard) Riding Croquet lawn Childrens creche ch fac Xmas **CONF:** Thtr 30 Board 18 **SERVICES:** Lift **PARKING:** 40 **NOTES:** No smoking in restaurant Civ Wed
CARDS:

See advert on opposite page

HORSHAM, West Sussex
Map 06 TQ13

★★★★ 🏵🏵🏵 South Lodge
Brighton Rd RH13 6PS
☎ 01403 891711 🖷 01403 891766
e-mail: enquiries@southlodgehotel.co.uk
(For full entry see Lower Beeding)

★★68% Ye Olde King's Head
Carfax RH12 1EG
☎ 01403 253126 🖷 01403 242291
Dir: *opposite old town hall, 0.5m from railway station, at junct of Carfax & East St*

A 14th-century former coaching inn situated in the heart of this busy town centre. Bedrooms are pleasantly decorated, well maintained and equipped with a good range of useful facilities. The spacious public rooms retain much of their original character; they include a lounge bar, a restaurant and a popular coffee shop serving quality homemade cakes.

ROOMS: 42 rms (41 en suite) (1 fmly) (7 GF) No smoking in 17 bedrooms s £85-£95; d £98-£125 (incl. bkfst) **LB FACILITIES:** STV Town leisure facilities nearby **CONF:** Thtr 40 Class 20 Board 20 **PARKING:** 30 **NOTES:** No dogs (ex guide dogs) No smoking in restaurant **CARDS:**

⌂ Travel Inn
57 North St RH12 1RB
☎ 08701 977136 🖷 01403 270797
Dir: *opposite railway station, 5m from M23 junct 11*

Travel Inn offers good-quality, value-for-money accommodation. Spacious, en suite rooms with bath and shower comfortably accommodate a family of up to two adults and two children (to age 15). The restaurant and bar offers a varied menu. For further details and the Travel Inn phone number, consult the Hotel Groups page.

ROOMS: 40 en suite s £44.95; d £44.95

HORTON-CUM-STUDLEY, Oxfordshire Map 05 SP51

★★★75% Studley Priory
OX33 1AZ
☎ 01865 351203 & 351254 01865 351613
e-mail: res@studley-priory.co.uk
Dir: *2.5m off B4027 between Wheatley & Islip*

Set in an elevated position deep in the countryside, this former 12th-century nunnery offers a warm welcome and attentive service. Bedrooms exude comfort and are filled with thoughtful extras. Afternoon tea can be enjoyed in either of the lounges overlooking the grounds and no stay would be complete without sampling the delightful cuisine of the talented kitchen team.

ROOMS: 18 en suite (4 GF) No smoking in 4 bedrooms s £120-£140; d £165-£175 (incl. bkfst) **LB FACILITIES:** STV Tennis (hard & grass) Croquet lawn Xmas **CONF:** Thtr 50 Board 25 Del from £195 **PARKING:** 100 **NOTES:** No dogs No smoking in restaurant Civ Wed 50 **CARDS:**

HORWICH, Greater Manchester Map 15 SD61

★★★★72% De Vere White's
De Havilland Way BL6 6SF
DE VERE HOTELS
☎ 01204 667788 01204 673721
e-mail: whites@devere-hotels.com
Dir: *M61 junct 6, 3rd right from slip road rdbt onto A6027 Mansell Way. Follow visitors carpark A for hotel*

Fully integrated within the Reebock Stadium, home of Bolton Wanderers Football Club, this modern hotel is a popular venue for business and conferences. Bedrooms are contemporary in style and equipped with a range of extras. The hotel has two eating options, a fine dining restaurant and informal brasserie, as well as fully equipped indoor leisure centre and spacious bar/lounge area.

ROOMS: 125 en suite (1 fmly) No smoking in 99 bedrooms s £55-£130; d £65-£205 **LB FACILITIES: Spa** STV Indoor swimming (H) Sauna Solarium Gym Jacuzzi Steam room, Beauty salon Xmas **CONF:** Thtr 1690 Class 1080 Board 72 Del from £120 **SERVICES:** Lift **PARKING:** 2750 **NOTES:** No dogs (ex guide dogs) No smoking in restaurant Civ Wed 550 **CARDS:**

HOUGHTON-LE-SPRING, Tyne & Wear Map 19 NZ34

★★66% Chilton Lodge
Black Boy Rd, Chilton Moor, Fencehouses DH4 6LX
☎ 0191 385 2694 0191 385 6762
Dir: *A1(M) junct 62, onto A690 to Sunderland. Left at Rainton Bridge and Fencehouses sign, cross rdbt and 1st left*

This country pub and hotel has been extended from the original farm cottages. Bedrooms are modern and comfortable and some rooms are particularly spacious. The hotel is popular for local

continued

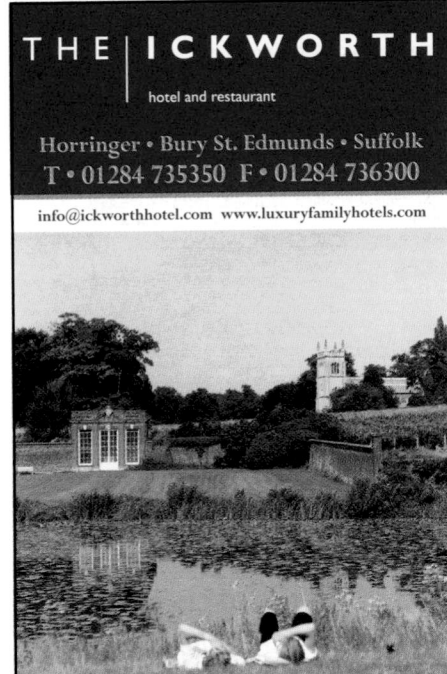

weddings and functions; there is also a well stocked bar and a wide range of dishes are served in the Orangery and restaurant.

Chilton Lodge

ROOMS: 25 en suite (7 fmly) No smoking in 7 bedrooms s £45-£48; d £55-£58 (incl. bkfst) **LB FACILITIES:** STV Horse riding entertainment Xmas **CONF:** Thtr 60 Class 50 Board 30 **PARKING:** 100 **NOTES:** No dogs (ex guide dogs) **CARDS:**

HOUNSLOW Hotels are listed under Heathrow Airport

HOVE See Brighton & Hove

HOVINGHAM, North Yorkshire Map 19 SE67

★★★67% ⊛⊛ **Worsley Arms**
High St YO62 4LA
☎ 01653 628234 🖷 01653 628130
e-mail: worsleyarms@aol.com
Dir: *from S take A64, signed York towards Malton. At dual carriageway left to Hovingham. At Slingsby left and Hovingham 2m ahead*
Overlooking the village green, this hotel has relaxing and attractive lounges with welcoming open fires. Bedrooms are also comfortable and several are contained in cottages across the green. The restaurant provides good quality cooking, with less formal dining in the Cricketers' Bar and Bistro to the rear.
ROOMS: 12 en suite 8 annexe en suite (2 fmly) (4 GF) No smoking in all bedrooms s £70-£85; d £95-£130 (incl. bkfst) **LB FACILITIES:** Tennis (hard) Squash Shooting Xmas **CONF:** BC Thtr 40 Class 40 Board 20 Del from £120 **PARKING:** 25 **NOTES:** No smoking in restaurant Civ Wed 90 **CARDS:**

HOWTOWN (NEAR POOLEY BRIDGE), Cumbria Map 18 NY41

Top 200 - Hotel

★★★ ⊛⊛⊛
Sharrow Bay Country House
Sharrow Bay CA10 2LZ
☎ 017684 86301 & 86483 🖷 017684 86349
e-mail: enquiries@sharrow-bay.com
Dir: *at Pooley Bridge right fork by church to Howtown. At x-rds right and follow Lakeside Rd for 2m*
Enjoying breathtaking views and an idyllic location on the shores of Lake Ullswater, Sharrow Bay is often described as the first country house hotel. Individually styled bedrooms, all with a host of thoughtful extras, are situated either in the main house, in delightful buildings in the hotel's grounds or at Bank House – an Elizabethan farmhouse complete with lounges and breakfast room. Opulently furnished public areas include a choice of inviting lounges and two elegant dining rooms.
ROOMS: 8 en suite 16 annexe en suite (5 GF) s £140-£145; d £150-£225 (incl. bkfst & dinner) **LB CONF:** BC Class 30 Board 20 Del from £160 **PARKING:** 35 **NOTES:** No dogs No children 13yrs No smoking in restaurant Closed 4 Dec-2 Mar Civ Wed 35
CARDS:

HOYLAKE, Merseyside Map 15 SJ28

★★★65% **Kings Gap Court**
CH47 1HE
☎ 0151 632 2073 🖷 0151 632 0247
e-mail: kingsgapcourt@aol.com
In the reign of William III 'Hoyle Lake' was an army staging post from where the invasion of Ireland was launched in 1690, and the 'Kings Gap' area commemorates this slice of history. The lake no longer exists but the hotel that has adopted the name enjoys a peaceful residential location just a short walk from glorious sandy beaches. Modern bedrooms are stylish and comfortable whilst the bright and spacious day rooms include a popular bar and a conservatory restaurant.
ROOMS: 30 en suite (4 fmly) (7 GF) No smoking in 15 bedrooms s £45-£50; d £50-£90 **LB CONF:** Thtr 150 Class 100 Board 32 Del from £85 **PARKING:** 60 **NOTES:** No smoking in restaurant
CARDS:

HUCKNALL, Nottinghamshire Map 16 SK54

⌂ **Premier Lodge (Nottingham North West)**
PREMIER LODGE
Nottingham Rd NG15 7PY
☎ 0870 9906518 🖷 0870 9906519
Premier Lodge offers modern, well-equipped, en suite accommodation suitable for both business and leisure travellers. Meals can be taken at the adjacent popular restaurant and bar, which is fully licensed. For further details, consult the Hotel Groups page.
ROOMS: 35 en suite s £48; d £48

HUDDERSFIELD, West Yorkshire Map 16 SE11

★★★★63% **Cedar Court**
Ainley Top HD3 3RH
☎ 01422 375431 🖷 01422 314050
e-mail: huddersfield@cedarcourthotels.co.uk
Dir: *500yds from M62 junct 24*
Conveniently close to the M62, this is an ideal location for business or touring West Yorkshire. Bedrooms are spacious and comfortable and there is a busy lounge with snacks available all day, a modern restaurant and a fully equipped leisure centre. There are extensive meeting and banqueting facilities.
ROOMS: 114 en suite (6 fmly) (10 GF) No smoking in 70 bedrooms **FACILITIES:** Indoor swimming (H) Sauna Solarium Gym Steam room **CONF:** Thtr 500 Class 150 Board 100 Del from £99 **SERVICES:** Lift **PARKING:** 250 **NOTES:** Civ Wed 400
CARDS:

★★★70% **The Old Golf House Hotel**
corus hotels
New Hey Rd, Outlane HD3 3YP
☎ 01422 379311 🖷 01422 372694
e-mail: oldgolfhouse@corushotels.com
Dir: *M62 junct 23 (eastbound only), or junct 24. Follow A640 to Rochdale. Hotel on A640*
Situated close to the M62, this traditionally styled hotel offers bedrooms which are well equipped to a good modern standard. A wide choice of dishes is served in the restaurant, and lighter meals

continued

are available in the comfortable lounge bar. The hotel is a popular venue for weddings.

ROOMS: 52 en suite (4 fmly) No smoking in 30 bedrooms s £45-£65; d £50-£65 **LB** **FACILITIES:** STV Putting green 5 Hole pitch & putt Xmas **CONF:** Thtr 70 Class 35 Board 30 Del from £99.50 **PARKING:** 100 **NOTES:** No smoking in restaurant Civ Wed 180 **CARDS:**

★★★67% Bagden Hall

Wakefield Rd, Scissett HD8 9LE
☎ 01484 865330 🖷 01484 861001
e-mail: info@bagdenhall.demon.co.uk
Dir: *on A636, between Scissett and Denby Dale*

Set in forty acres of well-tended grounds, with a par three nine-hole golf course, this elegant mansion house is close to the village of Scissett. The traditional public rooms include a bright conservatory where light meals are served, and a versatile conference/function room. Bedrooms vary in size, and all are well equipped and pleasantly furnished.
ROOMS: 17 en suite (3 fmly) s £60; d £80-£100 (incl. bkfst) **FACILITIES:** STV Golf 9 Putting green **CONF:** Thtr 80 Class 40 Board 30 Del from £105 **PARKING:** 96 **NOTES:** No dogs (ex guide dogs) No smoking in restaurant RS 24-25 Dec Civ Wed 86 **CARDS:**

★★★66% *George*

BROOK HOTELS

St George's Square HD1 1JA
☎ 01484 515444 🖷 01484 435056
e-mail: accounts@georgehotel.fsnet.co.uk
Dir: *adjacent to Huddersfield Railway Station in centre of town*

An impressive Georgian building, situated in the main square adjacent to the railway station, this hotel is noted as the birthplace of Rugby League football and there is a collection of related memorabilia in the hotel bar. Double/twin bedrooms are particularly spacious and comfortable. The restaurant serves a contemporary menu.
ROOMS: 60 en suite (1 fmly) No smoking in 15 bedrooms **FACILITIES:** STV Use of nearby sports centre **CONF:** Thtr 180 Board 50 **SERVICES:** Lift **PARKING:** 25 **NOTES:** No smoking in restaurant Civ Wed 100 **CARDS:**

★★★66% Huddersfield

33-47 Kirkgate HD1 1QT
☎ 01484 512111 🖷 01484 435262
e-mail: enquiries@huddersfieldhotel.com
Dir: *on A62 ring road, below parish church, opposite sports centre*

This modern, privately owned town centre hotel offers comfortable, smartly furnished bedrooms including family suites and rooms with four-poster beds. There is a good choice of bars and restaurants offering a wide variety of meals and snacks, a popular nightclub and a traditional pub. Friendly staff are helpful and attentive, and secure parking is a bonus.
ROOMS: 50 en suite (6 fmly) s £40-£59; d £50-£69 (incl. bkfst) **LB** **FACILITIES:** STV Pool tables entertainment Xmas **SERVICES:** Lift **PARKING:** 70 **CARDS:**

★★71% Lodge

48 Birkby Lodge Rd, Birkby HD2 2BG
☎ 01484 431001 🖷 01484 421590
e-mail: contact@birkbylodgehotel.com
Dir: *M62 junct 24, exit A629 for Birkby. Left at 1st lights, right after Nuffield Hospital(Birkby Lodge Rd) Hotel 100yds on left*

This family-run hotel is in a quiet residential area close to the city centre, and provides a relaxed ambience. Smart public areas include two comfortable lounges and an inviting restaurant where carefully prepared meals are served. Bedrooms vary in size and style and are well equipped; one has a grand four-poster bed. Service is friendly and efficient.
ROOMS: 13 en suite (2 fmly) (3 GF) No smoking in all bedrooms s £40-£55; d £40-£90 **CONF:** BC Thtr 40 Class 22 Board 22 Del from £105 **PARKING:** 41 **NOTES:** No smoking in restaurant Closed 26-27 Dec Civ Wed 50 **CARDS:**

★★69% Pennine Manor

Nettleton Hill Rd, Scapegoat Hill HD7 4NH
☎ 01484 642368 🖷 01484 642866
e-mail: penninemanor@bestwestern.co.uk
Dir: *M62 junct 24, signed for Rochdale (A640) – Outlane Village, left after Highlander pub, hotel signed from road*

Set high in the Pennines, this attractive stone hotel enjoys magnificent panoramic views. Bedrooms vary in size and all are thoughtfully equipped. There is a popular bar and restaurant offering a good selection of snacks and meals. The modern function facilities make this a popular venue for weddings and business meetings.
ROOMS: 31 en suite (4 fmly) (15 GF) No smoking in 23 bedrooms s £49-£58; d £60-£65 (incl. bkfst) **LB** **CONF:** BC Thtr 132 Class 56 Board 40 Del from £85 **PARKING:** 115 **NOTES:** No dogs (ex guide dogs) No smoking in restaurant Civ Wed 100 **CARDS:**

⌂ Premier Lodge (Huddersfield)

New Hey Rd, Ainley Top HD2 2EA
☎ 0870 9906488 🖷 0870 9906489
Premier Lodge offers modern, well-equipped, en suite accommodation suitable for both business and leisure travellers. Meals can be taken at the adjacent popular restaurant and bar, which is fully licensed. For further details, consult the Hotel Groups page.
ROOMS: 40 en suite s £48; d £48

HUDDERSFIELD, continued

⌂ Travelodge

Leeds Rd, Mirfield WF14 0BY
☎ 08700 850 950
Dir: *M62 junct 25, follow A62 across 2 rdbts. Lodge on right*

Travelodge

Travelodge offers good quality, good value, modern accommodation. Ideal for families, the spacious, en suite bedrooms include remote-control TV, tea and coffee-making facilities, luxury beds and free morning newspaper. Meals can be taken at the nearby family restaurant. For further details and the Travelodge phone number, consult the Hotel Groups page.
ROOMS: 27 en suite s fr £42.95; d fr £42.95

HUNMANBY, North Yorkshire Map 17 TA07

★★69% Wrangham House Hotel

10 Stonegate YO14 0NS
☎ 01723 891333 📠 01723 892973
e-mail: mervynpoulter@lineone.net
Dir: *A64 onto A1039 to Filey. Right onto Hunmanby Rd, hotel behind All Saints Church*

This former Georgian vicarage is only a few minutes' drive from lovely sandy beaches, and stands in beautiful wooded gardens next to the village church. The family owned and well-furnished hotel features individually styled bedrooms, a comfortable sitting room and cosy bar. The spacious dining room offers a good selection of well-produced dishes.
ROOMS: 8 en suite 4 annexe en suite (1 fmly) No smoking in all bedrooms s £42-£50; d £70-£90 (incl. bkfst) **LB** **FACILITIES:** Xmas **CONF:** Thtr 50 Class 20 Board 20 **PARKING:** 20 **NOTES:** No children 12yrs No smoking in restaurant **CARDS:**

HUNSTANTON, Norfolk Map 12 TF64

★★★68% Le Strange Arms

Golf Course Rd, Old Hunstanton PE36 6JJ
☎ 01485 534411 📠 01485 534724
e-mail: reception@lestrangearms.co.uk
Dir: *off A149 1m N of Hunstanton town. Left at sharp right bend by Pitch & Putt*

Best Western

Impressive hotel with superb views from the wide lawns down to the sandy beach and across The Wash. Public rooms include a comfortable lounge bar and an attractive restaurant, where an interesting choice of dishes is served. Bedrooms come in a variety

continued

of styles, from original rooms in the main house with period furnishings, to more contemporary rooms in the new wing.

ROOMS: 36 en suite (4 fmly) No smoking in 6 bedrooms s £59-£68; d £92-£117 (incl. bkfst) **LB** **FACILITIES:** STV Snooker Xmas **CONF:** Thtr 180 Class 150 Board 50 Del from £98 **PARKING:** 80 **NOTES:** No smoking in restaurant Civ Wed 70
CARDS:

★★74% Caley Hall

Old Hunstanton Rd PE36 6HH
☎ 01485 533486 📠 01485 533348
Dir: *1m from Hunstanton, on A149*

Charming 17th-century manor house situated in the older part of town. The smartly furnished bedrooms are in courtyard style blocks, tastefully converted from authentic farm buildings. The spacious public rooms include a cosy bar, an open-plan lounge, a billiard room and a large restaurant serving a daily-changing menu.
ROOMS: 33 annexe en suite (5 fmly) (28 GF) No smoking in 8 bedrooms s £42-£50; d £64-£74 (incl. bkfst) **LB** **FACILITIES:** STV Snooker Xmas **CONF:** Board 40 **PARKING:** 70 **NOTES:** No smoking in restaurant Closed Jan-Feb **CARDS:**

★★72% The Lodge Hotel & Restaurant

Old Hunstanton Rd PE36 6HX
☎ 01485 532896 📠 01485 535007
e-mail: reception@thelodge-hotel.co.uk
Dir: *1m E of Hunstanton on A149*

Expect a friendly welcome at this family run hotel, situated within easy reach of the beach and town centre. The spacious bedrooms are smartly decorated, well maintained and offer a good range of facilities. Public areas include a large lounge bar, an attractive restaurant with a cosy seating area and a large landscaped garden.
ROOMS: 16 en suite 6 annexe en suite (3 fmly) (4 GF) No smoking in 6 bedrooms s £35-£56; d £70-£108 (incl. bkfst) **LB** **FACILITIES:** STV Darts room Pool table Xmas **PARKING:** 70 **NOTES:** No smoking in restaurant **CARDS:**

See advert on opposite page

HUNSTRETE, Somerset Map 04 ST66

★★★80% ⊛⊛ Hunstrete House

BS39 4NS
☎ 01761 490490 📠 01761 490732
e-mail: user@hunstretehouse.co.uk
Dir: *from Bath take A4 to Bristol. At Globe Inn rdbt 2nd left onto A368 to Wells. 1m after Marksbury turn right for Hunstrete village. Hotel next left*

This delightful Georgian house enjoys a stunning setting in 92 acres of deer park and woodland on the edge of the Mendip Hills. Elegant bedrooms in the main building and coach house are both spacious and comfortable. Public areas feature antiques, paintings

continued

and fine china. The restaurant enjoys a well-deserved reputation for fine food and utilises much home-grown produce.
ROOMS: 25 en suite (2 fmly) No smoking in 14 bedrooms s £135-£145; d £170-£180 (incl. bkfst) **LB** **FACILITIES:** STV Outdoor swimming (H) Tennis (hard) Croquet lawn mini gym/fitness room Xmas **CONF:** Thtr 50 Class 40 Board 30 Del from £160 **PARKING:** 50 **NOTES:** No smoking in restaurant Civ Wed 50 **CARDS:**

HUNTINGDON, Cambridgeshire — Map 12 TL27

★★★★71% Huntingdon Marriott Hotel

Kingfisher Way, Hinchingbrooke Business Park PE29 6FL
☎ 01480 446000 🖷 01480 451111
e-mail: reservations.huntingdon@whitbread.com
Dir: *1m from Huntington centre on A14, close to Brampton racecourse*

With its excellent road links, this modern, purpose-built hotel is a popular venue for conferences and business meetings. Newmarket Races, Cambridge and the Cromwell Museum in Huntingdon are just some of the attractions which might appeal to leisure guests. Bedrooms are spacious and offer every modern comfort, including air conditioning. This hotel has been Highly Commended in AA Accessible Hotel of the Year Awards 2003-2004.
ROOMS: 150 en suite (45 GF) No smoking in 60 bedrooms s fr £65; d fr £90 (incl. bkfst) **LB** **FACILITIES: Spa** STV Indoor swimming (H) Sauna Solarium Gym Jacuzzi Swimming pool supervised entertainment Xmas **CONF:** Thtr 300 Class 150 Board 100 Del from £139 **SERVICES:** Lift air con **PARKING:** 250 **NOTES:** No smoking in restaurant Civ Wed 250 **CARDS:**

★★★77% 🏵🏵 The Old Bridge

1 High St PE29 3TQ
☎ 01480 424300 🖷 01480 411017
e-mail: oldbridge@huntsbridge.co.uk
Dir: *from A14 or A1 follow Huntingdon signs. Hotel visible from inner ring road*

An imposing 18th-century building situated on the ring road close to the shops and amenities. This charming hotel offers superb accommodation combined with classical architecture and modern facilities. Guests can choose from the same menu whether dining in the open-plan terrace or the more formal restaurant. The individually decorated bedrooms are designed with style and include many useful extras. The hotel also has a particularly good business centre with secretarial services.
ROOMS: 24 en suite (2 fmly) (2 GF) s £95-£140; d £120-£180 (incl. bkfst) **LB** **FACILITIES:** STV Fishing Private mooring for boats Xmas **CONF:** BC Thtr 50 Class 20 Board 24 Del £160 **SERVICES:** air con **PARKING:** 50 **NOTES:** No smoking in restaurant Civ Wed 80 **CARDS:**

★★65% The Stukeleys Country Hotel

Ermine St, Great Stukeley PE28 4AL
☎ 01480 456927 🖷 01480 450260
e-mail: janmick@stukeleys.freeservenet.co.uk
Dir: *on B1043, off A1/A14 junct*

A relaxed and friendly atmosphere prevails at this attractive 16th-century coaching inn, which features exposed beams and open fireplaces. The spacious and comfortable bedrooms are individually decorated and tastefully furnished in pine.
There is a popular cosy lounge bar and dining area, as well as a smart restaurant.
ROOMS: 8 en suite (1 fmly) s £69; d £80 (incl. cont bkfst) **LB** **FACILITIES:** Xmas **PARKING:** 30 **NOTES:** No dogs (ex guide dogs) RS 25 Dec & 1 Jan **CARDS:**

> Late for dinner?
> Quality Standards mean that last orders for dinner vary according to star rating and should be no earlier than:
> ★★ 7.00pm ★★★ 8.00pm ★★★★ 9.00pm
> ★★★★★ 10.00pm

HYDE, Cheshire
Map 16 SJ99

⇧ Premier Lodge (Manchester East)

Stockport Rd, Mottram SK14 3AU
☎ 0870 9906334 📠 0870 9906335
Dir: *3rd exit off rdbt at end of M67 behind McDonalds*
Premier Lodge offers modern, well-equipped, en suite accommodation suitable for both business and leisure travellers. Meals can be taken at the adjacent popular restaurant and bar, which is fully licensed. For further details, consult the Hotel Groups page.
ROOMS: 83 en suite s £44; d £44

HYTHE, Kent
Map 07 TR13

★★★★77% ® The Hythe Imperial
Princes Pde CT21 6AE
☎ 01303 267441 📠 01303 264610
e-mail: hytheimperial@marstonhotels.com
Dir: *M20, junct 11 onto A261. In Hythe follow Folkestone signs. Right into Twiss Rd to hotel*
Enjoying a seafront setting in the historic town, this lovely hotel is surrounded by 50 acres of golf course and beautiful gardens. Well-kept bedrooms are spacious and many enjoy views of the grounds or sea. Guests have a whole host of facilities on hand during their stay including indoor and outdoor leisure facilities, beauty salon and a choice of informal and more formal dining.
ROOMS: 100 en suite (5 fmly) No smoking in 38 bedrooms s fr £93; d fr £130 **LB FACILITIES:** STV Indoor swimming (H) Golf 9 Tennis (hard & grass) Squash Snooker Sauna Solarium Gym Croquet lawn Putting green Jacuzzi Beauty salon Fitness assessments Xmas **CONF:** Thtr 250 Class 100 Board 60 Del from £155 **SERVICES:** Lift **PARKING:** 201 **NOTES:** No dogs (ex guide dogs) No smoking in restaurant Civ Wed 200
CARDS:

★★★73% Stade Court
West Pde CT21 6DT
☎ 01303 268263 📠 01303 261803
e-mail: stadecourt@marstonhotels.com
Dir: *M20 junct 11 onto A261*
Built on the site of a landing place, or 'stade', the hotel is located right on the seafront in this historic Cinque Port. Many of the well-maintained bedrooms enjoy splendid sea views and some of these have additional seating areas. Guests also benefit from the excellent leisure facilities at the hotel's sister property, The Hythe Imperial.
ROOMS: 42 en suite (5 fmly) No smoking in 7 bedrooms s fr £63; d fr £83 **LB FACILITIES:** STV Indoor swimming (H) Golf 9 Tennis (hard & grass) Squash Snooker Sauna Solarium Gym Croquet lawn Putting green Jacuzzi All leisure facilities at sister hotel 600 mtrs away Xmas **CONF:** Thtr 40 Class 20 Board 30 Del £110 **SERVICES:** Lift **PARKING:** 11 **NOTES:** No smoking in restaurant
CARDS:

ILFORD, Greater London
See LONDON SECTION plan 1 H5

⇧ Travel Inn
Redbridge Ln East IG4 5BG
☎ 08701 977140 📠 020 8550 6214
Dir: *M11 (signed London East/A12 Chelmsford) follow A12 Chelmsford signs, Travel Inn on left at bottom of slip road*
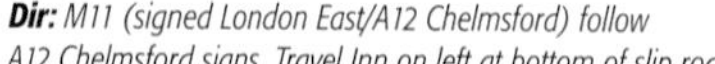
Travel Inn offers good-quality, value-for-money accommodation. Spacious, en suite rooms with bath and shower comfortably accommodate a family of up to two adults and two children (to age 15). The restaurant and bar offers a varied menu. For further details and the Travel Inn phone number, consult the Hotel Groups page.
ROOMS: 44 en suite s £54.95; d £54.95 **CONF:** Thtr 30

⇧ Travelodge London (Ilford Central)
Clements Rd IG1 1BA
☎ 08700 850 950
Travelodge offers good quality, good value, modern accommodation. Ideal for families, the spacious, en suite bedrooms include remote-control TV, tea and coffee-making facilities, luxury beds and free morning newspaper. Meals can be taken at the nearby family restaurant. For further details and the Travelodge phone number, consult the Hotel Groups page.
ROOMS: 91 en suite s fr £42.95; d fr £42.95

⇧ Travelodge London (Ilford North)
Beehive Ln, Gants Hill IG4 5DR
☎ 08700 850 950 📠 020 8550 4248
Travelodge offers good quality, good value, modern accommodation. Ideal for families, the spacious, en suite bedrooms include remote-control TV, tea and coffee-making facilities, luxury beds and free morning newspaper. Meals can be taken at the nearby family restaurant. For further details and the Travelodge phone number, consult the Hotel Groups page.
ROOMS: 32 en suite s fr £42.95; d fr £42.95

ILFRACOMBE, Devon
Map 03 SS54

★★71% Elmfield
Torrs Park EX34 8AZ
☎ 01271 863377 📠 01271 866828
e-mail: ann@elmfieldhotelilfracombe.co.uk
Dir: *A361 to Ilfracombe. Left at 1st lights, left at 2nd lights. After 10yds left, hotel near top of hill on left*
Set in attractive grounds and with good parking, this Victorian property maintains much of its charm and enjoys views over the town towards the sea. Bedrooms are well equipped and spacious. The friendly proprietor and staff provide attentive service and carefully prepared, home-cooked cuisine. Public areas include a cosy bar, a small games room and comfortable lounge.
ROOMS: 11 en suite 2 annexe en suite (3 GF) No smoking in 5 bedrooms s £35-£45; d £70-£90 (incl. bkfst) **LB FACILITIES:** Indoor swimming (H) Sauna Solarium Gym Jacuzzi Pool table Xmas **PARKING:** 14 **NOTES:** No dogs No children 8yrs No smoking in restaurant Closed Nov-Mar (ex Xmas) **CARDS:**
See advert on opposite page

★★68% Ilfracombe Carlton
Runnacleave Rd EX34 8AR
☎ 01271 862446 & 863711 📠 01271 865379
e-mail: enquiries@ilfracombecarlton.co.uk
Dir: *A361 to Ilfracombe, left at traffic lights, left at lights. Follow signs 'Tunnels, Beaches'*

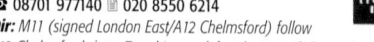

Situated in the town and just a short walk from the theatre and harbour, this well-maintained hotel has a loyal following. The public areas include two lounges and a bar with an entertainment
continued

area. The comfortable bedrooms are attractively decorated and well equipped. A short set-price menu is offered in the bright and airy dining room.
ROOMS: 48 en suite (8 fmly) No smoking in 24 bedrooms s £29.50-£32.50; d £59-£65 (incl. bkfst) **LB** **FACILITIES:** entertainment Xmas **CONF:** Thtr 50 Class 50 Board 50 **SERVICES:** Lift **PARKING:** 25 **NOTES:** No dogs (ex guide dogs) No smoking in restaurant Closed Jan RS Feb **CARDS:**

See advert on this page

★★66% *St Helier*

Hillsborough Rd EX34 9QQ
☎ 01271 864906 Fax 01271 864906
e-mail: st_helier_hotel@yahoo.co.uk
Dir: *M5 junct 27 onto A361 into Ilfracombe, take Combe Martin road through High St. Hotel opposite 'Old Thatched Inn'*

Within walking distance of the town centre and the harbour, this small hotel has been in the same family ownership for over 60 years. Some of the bedrooms have distant views of the sea. Public rooms include a comfortable lounge, a cellar bar and a separate dining room where the short fixed price menu offers both imaginative and popular dishes.
ROOMS: 10 en suite (2 fmly) **PARKING:** 18 **NOTES:** No smoking in restaurant Closed Nov-Mar **CARDS:**

★★64% Imperial Hotel

Wilder Rd EX34 9AL
☎ 01271 862536 Fax 01271 862571
e-mail: imperial.ilfracombe@alfatravel.co.uk
Dir: *hotel opposite Landmark Theatre*

This popular hotel is just a short walk from the shops and harbour, overlooking gardens and the sea. Public areas include the spacious sun lounge, where guests can relax and enjoy the excellent views. Comfortable bedrooms are well equipped with many having the added bonus of sea views.
ROOMS: 104 en suite (6 fmly) s £25-£33; d £42-£58 (incl. bkfst) **LB** **FACILITIES:** entertainment Xmas **SERVICES:** Lift **PARKING:** 10 **NOTES:** No dogs (ex guide dogs) No smoking in restaurant Closed Dec-Feb RS Mar & Nov **CARDS:**

★★58% Palm Court

Wilder Rd EX34 9AS
☎ 01271 866644 Fax 01271 863581
e-mail: contact@palmcourthotel.net
Dir: *A361 to Ilfracombe, then follow signs to seafront*

Within level walking distance of the harbour, the Palm Court Hotel is very popular with groups. Bedrooms are neatly presented and are all to a similar standard. While entertainment is provided in the bar/ballroom on certain evenings during the season, short mat bowls can be played in another large area.
ROOMS: 50 en suite (20 fmly) (3 GF) No smoking in 25 bedrooms s £35-£38; d £64-£70 (incl. bkfst & dinner) **LB** **FACILITIES:** Pool table, Short mat bowls, Skittles entertainment Xmas **CONF:** Del from £30 **SERVICES:** Lift **PARKING:** 16 **NOTES:** No dogs (ex guide dogs) No smoking in restaurant Closed 3-26 Jan **CARDS:**

A ★★ Beechwood

Torrs Park EX34 8AZ
☎ 01271 863800 Fax 01271 863800
e-mail: info@beechwoodhotel.co.uk
Dir: *A361 from Barnstaple into Ilfracombe, turn left at lights into Wilder Rd, left at next lights then left again into Torrs Park. Hotel at far end on right*
ROOMS: 7 en suite No smoking in all bedrooms s £28-£37.50; d £50-£55 (incl. bkfst) **LB** **PARKING:** 9 **NOTES:** No dogs (ex guide dogs) No children 16yrs No smoking in restaurant Closed Oct-Mar
CARDS:

ILFRACOMBE, continued

A ★★ Westwell Hall Hotel

Torrs Park EX34 8AZ
☎ 01271 862792 📠 01271 862792
e-mail: westwellh@llhotel.fsnet.co.uk
Dir: *along Ilfracombe high street onto Northfield Rd at lights. Left up Torrs Park. Right into Upper Torrs. Hotel 3rd drive on left*
ROOMS: 10 en suite s £25; d £50-£54 (incl. bkfst) **PARKING:** 10
NOTES: No smoking in restaurant Closed Nov-Etr
CARDS:

★64% Torrs

Torrs Park EX34 8AY
☎ 01271 862334
e-mail: torrshotel@aol.com
Dir: *A361 from Barnstaple, at 1st lights in Ilfracombe left into Wilder Rd. At next lights left and left again into Torrs Park. Hotel on right after 320yds*
The friendly proprietors provide attentive service and a relaxing environment at this quietly located hotel, which stands in its own grounds. Bedrooms are brightly decorated and many rooms offer family accommodation. Wonderful views of the surrounding countryside and over the town can be enjoyed from the lounge, dining room and most of the bedrooms.
ROOMS: 11 en suite (4 fmly) s £25-£28; d £45-£55 (incl. bkfst) **LB**
FACILITIES: Xmas **PARKING:** 10 **NOTES:** No smoking in restaurant
CARDS:

ILKLEY, West Yorkshire — Map 19 SE14

★★★75% ® Rombalds

11 West View, Wells Rd LS29 9JG
☎ 01943 603201 📠 01943 816586
e-mail: reception@rombalds.demon.co.uk
Dir: *on A65. Left at 2nd main lights, follow Ilkley Moor signs. Right at HSBC Bank onto Wells Rd. Hotel 600yds on left*

Best Western

This elegantly furnished Georgian town house is located on a peaceful terrace between the town and the moors. Delightful day rooms include a choice of comfortable lounges and an attractive restaurant which provides a relaxed, elegant venue in which to sample the skilfully prepared, imaginative meals. The bedrooms are well equipped and include several spacious suites.
ROOMS: 15 en suite (2 fmly) No smoking in 9 bedrooms s £55-£99; d £80-£119 (incl. bkfst) **LB** **FACILITIES:** STV Xmas **CONF:** Thtr 70 Class 40 Board 25 Del from £112.50 **PARKING:** 28 **NOTES:** No smoking in restaurant Closed 28 Dec-2 Jan Civ Wed 70
CARDS:

★★★66% The Crescent

Brook St LS29 8DG
☎ 01943 600012 📠 01943 601513
e-mail: creschot@dialstart.net
Dir: *at junct of Leeds Rd (A65) & Brook St*
This modern hotel is located in the heart of Ilkley, yet is convenient for major travel networks and the stunning surrounding countryside. Spacious bedrooms, including a honeymoon suite with fabulous bathroom, offer pleasing décor and facilities. The restaurant serves a variety of interesting dishes.
ROOMS: 21 en suite (3 fmly) No smoking in all bedrooms s £49.50-£62.50; d £74.25-£84.50 (incl. bkfst) **LB** **FACILITIES:** STV entertainment **CONF:** Thtr 100 Class 60 Board 40 Del from £60 **SERVICES:** Lift **PARKING:** 10 **NOTES:** No smoking in restaurant
CARDS:

★★★63% The Craiglands

Cowpasture Rd LS29 8RQ
☎ 01943 430001 📠 01943 430002
e-mail: reservations@craiglands.co.uk
Dir: *off A65 into Ilkley. At T-junct left. Past railway station and fork right into Cowpasture Rd. Hotel opposite school*

This grand Victorian hotel is ideally situated close to the town centre. Spacious public areas and a good range of services are ideal for business or leisure. Extensive conference facilities are available along with an elegant restaurant and traditionally styled bar and lounge. Bedrooms vary in size and style and are comfortably furnished and well equipped.
ROOMS: 60 en suite (6 fmly) No smoking in 19 bedrooms s £75-£85; d £90-£120 (incl. bkfst) **LB** **FACILITIES:** Complimentary use of local fitness centre Xmas **CONF:** Thtr 500 Class 200 Board 100 Del from £110 **SERVICES:** Lift **PARKING:** 200 **NOTES:** No dogs (ex guide dogs) Civ Wed 500 **CARDS:**

⌂ Innkeeper's Lodge Ilkley

Hangingstone Rd LS29 8BT
☎ 01943 607335 📠 01943 604712
Dir: *from A65 turn towards Ilkley town centre and then at the station turn right into Cowpasture Rd. The Cow & Calf is approx 0.75m on left*

Innkeeper's Lodge

A new concept in the travel accommodation market. Smart rooms meet essential business requirements but also have home comforts. Dining options include all-day menus plus the added advantage of breakfast, which is included in the room price. For further details, consult the Hotel Groups page.
ROOMS: 14 en suite

ILMINSTER, Somerset
Map 04 ST31

★★★64% Shrubbery
TA19 9AR
☎ 01460 52108 🖷 01460 53660
e-mail: stuart@shrubberyhotel.demon.co.uk
Dir: *0.5m from A303 towards Ilminster town centre*
Set in attractive terraced gardens, this Victorian hotel offers well-equipped bedrooms of various sizes, including three on the ground floor. A choice of menus is offered at dinner, along with a selection of market-fresh fish dishes. Less formal bar meals are also available. Additional facilities include a range of function rooms and a heated outdoor pool for those warmer summer days.
ROOMS: 17 en suite (3 fmly) s £65-£78; d £80-£97 (incl. bkfst) **LB** **FACILITIES:** STV Outdoor swimming (H) Tennis (grass) **CONF:** BC Thtr 250 Class 120 Board 80 Del from £120 **PARKING:** 100 **NOTES:** Civ Wed 200 **CARDS:**

Travelodge
Southfields Roundabout, Horton Cross TA19 9PT
☎ 08700 850 950 🖷 01460 53748
Dir: *on A303*
Travelodge offers good quality, good value, modern accommodation. Ideal for families, the spacious, en suite bedrooms include remote-control TV, tea and coffee-making facilities, luxury beds and free morning newspaper. Meals can be taken at the nearby family restaurant. For further details and the Travelodge phone number, consult the Hotel Groups page.
ROOMS: 32 en suite s fr £42.95; d fr £42.95

ILSINGTON, Devon
Map 03 SX77

★★★72% The Ilsington Country House
Ilsington Village TQ13 9RR
☎ 01364 661452 🖷 01364 661307
e-mail: hotel@ilsington.co.uk
Dir: *M5 onto A38 to Plymouth. Exit at Bovey Tracey. 3rd exit from rdbt to 'Ilsington', then 1st right. Hotel 5m by Post Office*

Peacefully situated with far-reaching views, this friendly hotel occupies an elevated position on the southern slopes of Dartmoor. Bedrooms, some of which are on the ground floor, are individually furnished. Local fish, meat and game feature on the daily-changing, innovative menus. On-site leisure facilities are available for hotel residents.
ROOMS: 25 en suite (2 fmly) (8 GF) No smoking in 5 bedrooms s £77-£90; d £122-£146 (incl. bkfst & dinner) **LB** **FACILITIES: Spa** Indoor swimming (H) Tennis (hard) Sauna Gym Jacuzzi Xmas **CONF:** Thtr 40 Class 30 Board 20 Del from £110 **SERVICES:** Lift **PARKING:** 100 **NOTES:** No smoking in restaurant **CARDS:**

INSTOW, Devon
Map 03 SS43

★★★74% Commodore
Marine Pde EX39 4JN
☎ 01271 860347 🖷 01271 861233
e-mail: admin@the-commodore.co.uk
Dir: *M5 junct 27 follow N Devon link road to Bideford. Right before bridge, hotel 3m from bridge*

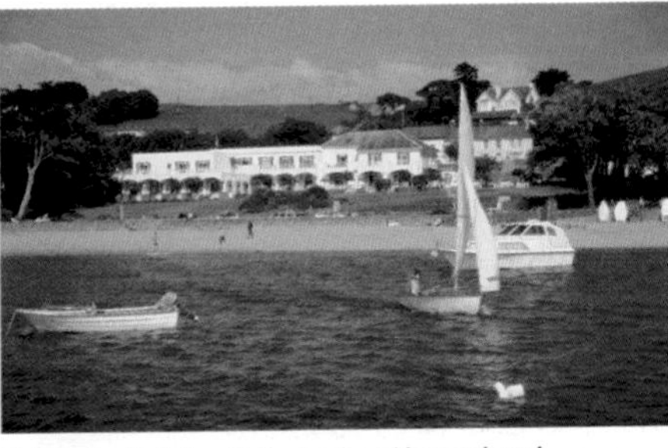

Maintaining its links with the local maritime and rural communities, The Commodore provides a comfortable and interesting place to stay. Situated at the mouth of the Tor and Torridge estuaries and overlooking the sandy beach, the hotel offers well-equipped bedrooms, many with balconies. Guests have the option of eating in the restaurant, less formally in the Quarterdeck bar or on the terrace in the warmer months.
ROOMS: 20 en suite (2 fmly) s £65-£75; d £110-£144 (incl. bkfst & dinner) **LB** **FACILITIES:** Xmas **CONF:** Thtr 250 Class 250 Board 80 Del from £79.50 **PARKING:** 200 **NOTES:** No dogs (ex guide dogs) No smoking in restaurant **CARDS:**

IPSWICH, Suffolk
Map 13 TM14

★★★★ Hintlesham Hall
IP8 3NS
☎ 01473 652334 & 652268 🖷 01473 652463
e-mail: reservations@hintleshamhall.com
(For full entry see Hintlesham)

★★★71% Courtyard by Marriott Ipswich
The Havens, Ransomes Europark IP3 9SJ
☎ 01473 272244 🖷 01473 272484
e-mail: reservations.ipswich@whitbread.com
Dir: *off A14 Ipswich bypass at 1st junct after Orwell Bridge, signed Ransomes Europark. Hotel faces slip road*
Conveniently situated within easy striking distance of the town centre and major road networks, this modern well-maintained hotel offers stylish accommodation with attractive, spacious bedrooms. The open plan public rooms include a restaurant, bar and a suite of conference rooms. Guests also have the use of a small fitness studio.
ROOMS: 60 en suite (28 fmly) (30 GF) No smoking in 44 bedrooms s £45-£94; d £64-£102 (incl. bkfst) **LB** **FACILITIES:** STV Gym Guests may use nearby leisure club at special rate **CONF:** Thtr 160 Class 70 Board 55 Del from £125 **SERVICES:** Lift **PARKING:** 150 **NOTES:** No dogs (ex guide dogs) Civ Wed 70 **CARDS:**

> Popped the question?
> Hotels with Civ Wed in their entry are licensed for civil wedding ceremonies. Maximum numbers for the ceremony only are shown, e.g. Civ Wed 120

IPSWICH, continued

★★★67% Claydon Country House
16-18 Ipswich Rd, Claydon IP6 0AR
☎ 01473 830382 📠 01473 832476
e-mail: kayshotels@aol.com
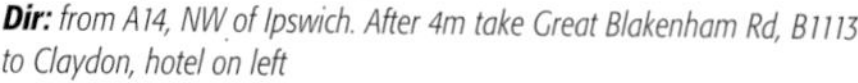
Dir: *from A14, NW of Ipswich. After 4m take Great Blakenham Rd, B1113 to Claydon, hotel on left*

This delightful hotel is within easy driving distance of Ipswich town centre. The pleasantly decorated bedrooms are thoughtfully equipped; one room has a lovely four-poster bed. An interesting choice of freshly prepared dishes is available in the smart restaurant, and guests also have the use of a relaxing lounge bar.
ROOMS: 19 en suite (2 fmly) No smoking in 10 bedrooms s £59-£69; d £69-£79 (incl. bkfst) **LB FACILITIES:** STV Xmas **CONF:** Thtr 120 Class 60 Board 55 Del from £99 **PARKING:** 60 **NOTES:** No dogs (ex guide dogs) No smoking in restaurant Civ Wed 70
CARDS:

★★★65% County Hotel Ipswich
London Rd, Copdock IP8 3JD
☎ 0870 609 6171 📠 01473 730801
e-mail: countyipswich@corushotels.com
Dir: *close to A12/A14 junct S of Ipswich. Exit A12 at sign Washbrook and Copdock. Hotel on A12 1m on left*

This purpose-built hotel is situated on the outskirts of the town centre, close to major road networks. The hotel is ideally suited to both business and leisure guests, and offers spacious bedrooms equipped with modern facilities and pleasantly decorated. The open-plan public areas include a smart restaurant, a bar and a comfortable lounge.
ROOMS: 76 en suite (51 fmly) (23 GF) No smoking in 50 bedrooms s £45-£79; d £45-£89 **LB FACILITIES:** Indoor swimming (H) Sauna Solarium Gym Jacuzzi Xmas **CONF:** Thtr 500 Class 200 Board 35 **SERVICES:** Lift **PARKING:** 360 **NOTES:** No dogs (ex guide dogs) No smoking in restaurant Civ Wed 120
CARDS:

★★★65% Novotel Ipswich
Greyfriars Rd IP1 1UP
☎ 01473 232400 📠 01473 232414
e-mail: h0995@accor-hotels.com
Dir: *from A14 towards Felixstowe. Left onto A137, follow for 2m into town centre. Hotel on double rdbt by Stoke Bridge*

Situated in the centre of town this modern redbrick hotel is close to shops, bars and restaurants. The open plan public areas include a Mediterranean style restaurant and a bar with a small games area. Bedrooms are well designed for most needs and simply decorated; three are suitable for the less able.
ROOMS: 100 en suite (6 fmly) No smoking in 76 bedrooms s £85; d £85 **LB FACILITIES:** STV Pool table, Complimentary use of gym, sauna, jacuzzi **CONF:** Thtr 180 Class 75 Board 45 Del from £80 **SERVICES:** Lift air con **PARKING:** 50 **CARDS:**

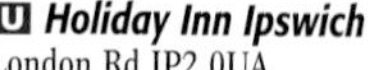

U *Holiday Inn Ipswich*
London Rd IP2 0UA
☎ 0870 400 9045 📠 01473 680412
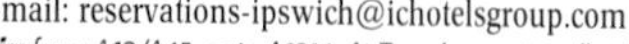
e-mail: reservations-ipswich@ichotelsgroup.com
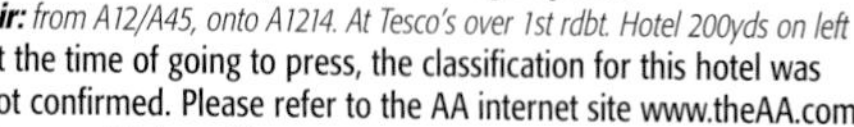
Dir: *from A12/A45, onto A1214. At Tesco's over 1st rdbt. Hotel 200yds on left*

At the time of going to press, the classification for this hotel was not confirmed. Please refer to the AA internet site www.theAA.com for current information.
ROOMS: 110 en suite (14 fmly) No smoking in 74 bedrooms **FACILITIES: Spa** Indoor swimming (H) Sauna Solarium Gym Jacuzzi ch fac **CONF:** Thtr 120 Class 50 Board 40 **PARKING:** 200 **NOTES:** No dogs (ex guide dogs) **CARDS:**

U Salthouse Harbour
No 1 Neptune Quay IP4 1AS
☎ 01473 226789 📠 01473 226927
e-mail: staying@salthouseharbour.co.uk

At the time of going to press, the star classification for this hotel was not confirmed. Please refer to the AA internet site www.theAA.com for current information.
ROOMS: 43 en suite (4 fmly) No smoking in 8 bedrooms s £90-£115; d £100-£125 (incl. bkfst) **LB FACILITIES:** STV Xmas **SERVICES:** Lift **PARKING:** 30 **NOTES:** No smoking in restaurant Civ Wed
CARDS:

⌂ Express by Holiday Inn Ipswich
Old Hadleigh Rd, Sproughton IP8 3AR
☎ 01473 222279 📠 01473 222297
e-mail: ebhi-ipswich@btconnect.com
Dir: *from A12/A14 junct follow town centre signs on A1214. At lights at hotel, turn left onto A1071. Mini rdbt right onto B113. Hotel on right*

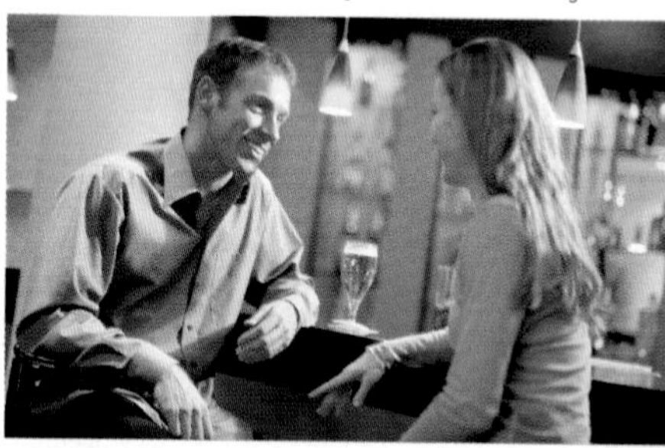

A modern hotel ideal for families and business travellers. Fresh and uncomplicated, the spacious bedrooms include Sky TV, power shower and tea and coffee-making facilities. Continental buffet breakfast is included in the room rate; other meals may be taken at the nearby family pub or restaurant. For further details and the Express by Holiday Inn phone number, consult the Hotel Groups pages.
ROOMS: 49 en suite **CONF:** Thtr 30 Class 24 Board 16

⌂ Travel Inn (Ipswich Bourne Hill)
Bourne Hill, Wherstead IP2 8ND
☎ 08701 977143 📠 01473 692283
Dir: *From A14 follow signs for Ipswich Central A137 and then Ipswich Central & Docks. At bottom of hill take 2nd exit off rndbt. Travel Inn on right*

Travel Inn offers good-quality, value-for-money accommodation. Spacious, en suite rooms with bath and shower comfortably accommodate a family of up to two adults and two children (to age 15). The restaurant and bar offers a varied menu. For further details and the Travel Inn phone number, consult the Hotel Groups page.
ROOMS: 40 en suite s £44.95; d £44.95 **CONF:** Thtr 30 Board 20

⌂ Travel Inn (Ipswich North)

Paper Mill Ln, Claydon IP6 0BE
☎ 0870 238 3311 🖷 01473 833127
e-mail: ipswich.mti@whitbread.com

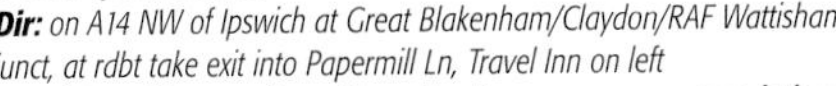

Dir: *on A14 NW of Ipswich at Great Blakenham/Claydon/RAF Wattisham junct, at rdbt take exit into Papermill Ln, Travel Inn on left*

Travel Inn offers good-quality, value-for-money accommodation. Spacious, en suite rooms with bath and shower comfortably accommodate a family of up to two adults and two children (to age 15). The restaurant and bar offers a varied menu. For further details and the Travel Inn phone number, consult the Hotel Groups page.

ROOMS: 59 en suite s £44.95; d £44.95

⌂ Travelodge (Ipswich Capel)

Capel St Mary IP9 2JP
☎ 08700 850 950 🖷 01473 312157
Dir: *5m S on A12*

Travelodge offers good quality, good value, modern accommodation. Ideal for families, the spacious, en suite bedrooms include remote-control TV, tea and coffee-making facilities, luxury beds and free morning newspaper. Meals can be taken at the nearby family restaurant. For further details and the Travelodge phone number, consult the Hotel Groups page.

ROOMS: 32 en suite s fr £42.95; d fr £42.95

ISLE OF Places incorporating the words 'Isle of' or 'Isle' will be found under the actual name - eg Isle of Wight is listed under Wight, Isle of.

IVYBRIDGE, Devon — Map 03 SX65

★★73% *Glazebrook House Hotel & Restaurant*

TQ10 9JE
☎ 01364 73322 🖷 01364 72350
e-mail: enquiries@glazebrookhouse.com
Dir: *off A38 at Avonwick/South Brent from Plymouth. Take 2nd exit after London Inn*

A tranquil and convenient location next to the Dartmoor National Park and set within four acres of gardens, this 18th-century former gentleman's residence offers comfortable and friendly accommodation. Bedrooms are well appointed and public areas are spacious. Cuisine offers interesting combinations and features fresh local produce.

ROOMS: 10 en suite No smoking in all bedrooms **CONF:** BC Thtr 100 Class 60 Board 40 Del from £79.70 **PARKING:** 40 **NOTES:** No dogs (ex guide dogs) No smoking in restaurant Civ Wed 60
CARDS:

★★66% *Sportsmans Inn Hotel & Restaurant*

Exeter Rd PL21 0BQ
☎ 01752 892280 🖷 01752 690714
e-mail: info@thesportsmaninn.co.uk
Dir: *off A38 Devon expressway at Ivybridge. Through town, hotel on main road*

This deservedly popular and friendly inn continues to enjoy a healthy trade from both locals and visitors alike, attracted to the wide choice of good value meals and snacks available in its open-plan bar and restaurant. Bedrooms are well-equipped and include both a ground floor room and an impressive four-poster.

ROOMS: 14 en suite **FACILITIES:** entertainment **PARKING:** 50 **NOTES:** No dogs (ex guide dogs) RS 25 Dec
CARDS:

KEGWORTH See East Midlands Airport

KEIGHLEY, West Yorkshire — Map 19 SE04

★★65% Dalesgate

406 Skipton Rd, Utley BD20 6HP
☎ 01535 664930 🖷 01535 611253
e-mail: stephen.e.atha@btinternet.com
Dir: *In town centre follow A629 over rdbt. Right after 0.75m into St. John's Rd. 1st right into hotel car park*

Originally the residence of a local chapel minister, this modern, well-established hotel has been expanded with the addition of a new wing to provide well-equipped, comfortable bedrooms. The hotel also boasts a cosy bar and pleasant restaurant, serving an imaginative range of well-produced dishes. A large car park is provided to the rear.

ROOMS: 20 en suite (2 fmly) (3 GF) s £35-£40; d £50-£60 (incl. bkfst) **LB PARKING:** 25 **NOTES:** No smoking in restaurant RS 22 Dec-4 Jan
CARDS:

⌂ Innkeeper's Lodge

Bradford Rd BD21 4BB
☎ 01535 610611
Dir: *From M606 rndbt take A6177, at next rndbt A641 and A650 towards Keighley. Lodge on 2nd rndbt*

A new concept in the travel accommodation market. Smart rooms meet essential business requirements but also have home comforts. Dining options include all-day menus plus the added advantage of breakfast, which is included in the room price. For further details, consult the Hotel Groups page.

ROOMS: 43 en suite

KENDAL, Cumbria — Map 18 SD59

See also Crooklands

★★★75% The Castle Green Hotel in Kendal

LA9 6BH
☎ 01539 734000 🖷 01539 735522
e-mail: reception@castlegreen.co.uk
Dir: *M6 junct 36, towards Kendal. Right at 1st lights, left at rdbt to 'K' Village then right for 0.75m to hotel at T- junct*

This smart, modern hotel enjoys a peaceful location and is conveniently situated for access to both the town centre and the M6. Stylish bedrooms are thoughtfully equipped for both the business and leisure guest. The Greenhouse Restaurant provides imaginative dishes, alternatively Alexander's pub serves food all day. The hotel has a fully equipped business centre.

ROOMS: 100 en suite (3 fmly) (25 GF) No smoking in 20 bedrooms s £69-£89; d £78-£118 (incl. bkfst) **LB FACILITIES:** STV Indoor swimming (H) Solarium Gym Steam Room, Aerobics, Yoga, Beauty Salon, Swimming pool supervised entertainment **CONF:** Thtr 350 Class 200 Board 120 **SERVICES:** Lift **PARKING:** 200 **NOTES:** No dogs (ex guide dogs) No smoking in restaurant Civ Wed 130
CARDS:

★★★68% Riverside Hotel

Stramongate Bridge LA9 4BZ
☎ 01539 734861 🖷 01539 734863
e-mail: info@riverside.macdonald-hotels.co.uk
Dir: *M6 junct 37 Sedburgh, Kendal 7m, left at end of Ann St, 1st right onto Beelow Rd, hotel on left*

Centrally located in this market town, and enjoying a peaceful riverside location, this 17th-century tannery provides an ideal base for both business people and tourists. The comfortable bedrooms

continued on p302

KENDAL, continued

are well equipped while open plan day rooms include the attractive restaurant and bar. Conference and leisure facilities are also available. Staff throughout are friendly and professional.
ROOMS: 47 en suite (11 fmly) No smoking in 20 bedrooms s £40-£70; d £70-£120 (incl. bkfst) **LB** **FACILITIES:** STV Games room Xmas **CONF:** Thtr 140 Class 70 Board 50 Del from £78 **SERVICES:** Lift **PARKING:** 35 **NOTES:** No smoking in restaurant Civ Wed 140
CARDS:

★★66% Garden House
Fowl-Ing Ln LA9 6PH
☎ 01539 731131 01539 740064
e-mail: gardenhouse.hotel@virgin.net
Dir: *M6 junct 36, follow signs for A685 to Brough. Right at Duke of Cumberland, 2nd right after 200yds, next to car showroom*
This early 19th-century country house is situated in wooded grounds and formal gardens close to the town centre. Privately-owned and personally-run, it provides a variety of well-equipped, traditionally styled bedrooms, one of which is on the ground floor. Public rooms include a choice of lounges and an elegant restaurant with conservatory extension overlooking the garden.
ROOMS: 11 en suite (2 fmly) No smoking in 4 bedrooms s £49.50-£59; d £79-£85 (incl. bkfst) **LB** **FACILITIES:** Croquet lawn Putting green **CONF:** Thtr 60 Class 40 Board 30 **PARKING:** 30 **NOTES:** No smoking in restaurant Closed 26-30 Dec **CARDS:**

K

KENILWORTH, Warwickshire
Map 10 SP27

★★★★67% *Chesford Grange*
Chesford Bridge CV8 2LD
☎ 01926 859331 01926 859075
e-mail: chesfordgrange@paramount-hotels.co.uk
Dir: *0.5m SE of junct A46/A452. At rdbt right signed Leamington Spa. After 250yds at x-rds right. Hotel on left*
This much-extended hotel set in 17 acres of private grounds is well located for Birmingham International Airport, the NEC and major routes. Bedrooms range from traditional style to brand new, contemporary 'Art + Tech' rooms featuring state-of-the-art technology. Public areas include a leisure club and extensive conference and banqueting facilities.
ROOMS: 210 en suite 9 annexe en suite (12 fmly) No smoking in 80 bedrooms **FACILITIES: Spa** STV Indoor swimming (H) Fishing Sauna Solarium Gym Jacuzzi entertainment **CONF:** Thtr 860 Class 350 Board 60 **SERVICES:** Lift **PARKING:** 700 **NOTES:** No smoking in restaurant Civ Wed 200 **CARDS:**

★★★★62% De Montfort
Abbey End CV8 1ED
☎ 01926 855944 01926 857830
e-mail: demontfort@macdonald-hotels.co.uk
Dir: *from A46 take A452 towards Leamington. At rdbt left to Kenilworth town centre, along high street. Hotel at top opposite clock tower*
Situated in the centre of the town, in the heart of Shakespeare country, this popular business hotel is well-located for the major commercial centres of the Midlands. Public areas include a range of meeting and function rooms, comfortable lounge/bar area and traditional restaurant.
ROOMS: 108 en suite (15 fmly) No smoking in 55 bedrooms s £35-£145; d £70-£160 (incl. bkfst) **LB** **FACILITIES:** STV Free use of nearby pool and gym, Hotel leisure facilities open Autumn 2003 Xmas **CONF:** Thtr 300 Class 100 Board 40 Del from £110 **SERVICES:** Lift **PARKING:** 65 **NOTES:** No smoking in restaurant Civ Wed 116
CARDS:

★★★75% Peacock
149 Warwick Rd CV8 1HY
☎ 01926 851156 & 864500 01926 864644
e-mail: reservations@peacockhotel.com
Dir: *A46/A452 signed to Kenilworth. Hotel in 0.25m on right after St John's Church*
Conveniently located for the town centre, the Peacock offers a peaceful retreat and service is delivered in a most professional manner by friendly staff. Vibrant colour schemes through pleasing public rooms and attractive accommodation are complemented by two dining options: the Malabar room, offering modern European dining, and the award-winning Coconut Lagoon serving Southern Indian dishes.
ROOMS: 27 en suite (5 fmly) No smoking in 18 bedrooms s £39-£100; d £49-£120 (incl. bkfst) **FACILITIES:** STV Xmas **CONF:** Thtr 80 Class 50 Board 50 Del from £90 **PARKING:** 30 **NOTES:** No dogs
CARDS:

★★72% Clarendon House
Old High St CV8 1LZ
☎ 01926 857668 01926 850669
e-mail: info@claredonhousehotel.com
Dir: *from A452 pass castle, then left into Castle Hill. Continue into High Street*
Incorporating the original 15th-century Castle Tavern, this comfortable hotel has plenty of old-world charm, including a wealth of beams and an indoor well. Bedrooms have character and are thoughtfully equipped with useful extras. Meals can be taken in the spacious, atmospheric brasserie or alternatively an extensive menu is available in the bar.
ROOMS: 22 en suite (2 fmly) (2 GF) No smoking in 6 bedrooms s £57.50-£69.50; d £79.50-£125 (incl. bkfst) **LB** **FACILITIES:** STV **CONF:** Thtr 150 Class 100 Board 70 Del £99 **PARKING:** 30 **NOTES:** No smoking in restaurant Civ Wed 150
CARDS:

KENTON, Greater London
See LONDON SECTION plan 1 C5

⌂ Travel Inn Harrow
Kenton Rd HA3 8AT
☎ 08701 977146 020 8909 1604
Dir: *M1 junct 5 follow signs to Harrow & Kenton. Between Harrow & Wembley on A4006 opposite Kenton Railway Station*
Travel Inn offers good-quality, value-for-money accommodation. Spacious, en suite rooms with bath and shower comfortably accommodate a family of up to two adults and two children (to age 15). The restaurant and bar offers a varied menu. For further details and the Travel Inn phone number, consult the Hotel Groups page.
ROOMS: 70 en suite s £54.95; d £54.95 **CONF:** Class 50

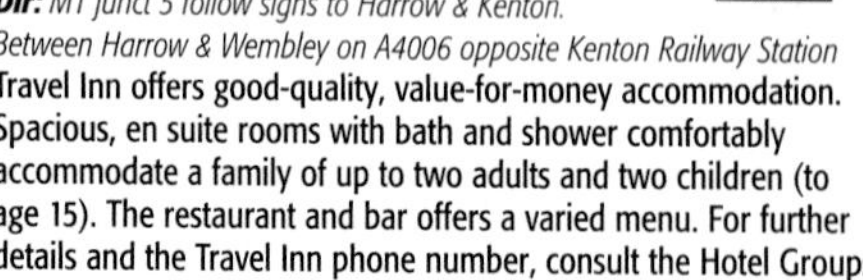

Late for dinner?
Quality Standards mean that last orders for dinner vary according to star rating and should be no earlier than:
★★ 7.00pm ★★★ 8.00pm ★★★★ 9.00pm
★★★★★ 10.00pm

Town House Hotel
Country House Hotel
⌂ Travel Accommodation

KESWICK, Cumbria Map 18 NY22

★★★75% ◎◎ Dale Head Hall Lakeside
Lake Thirlmere CA12 4TN
☎ 017687 72478 🖷 017687 71070
e-mail: onthelakeside@daleheadhall.info
Dir: *between Keswick and Grasmere. Off A591 onto private drive*

Formerly the summer residence of the mayor of Manchester, the main house dates from the mid 16th-century and has a spectacular lakeside location. Dinner is served in the atmospheric, beamed restaurant and features the best local produce. Bedrooms, many now upgraded, are spacious and feature high quality furniture made by the proprietor.
ROOMS: 12 en suite (1 fmly) No smoking in all bedrooms s £70-£80; d £90-£110 (incl. bkfst) **LB** **FACILITIES:** no TV in bdrms Fishing Xmas **PARKING:** 31 **NOTES:** No dogs (ex guide dogs) No smoking in restaurant Closed 31 Dec-31 Jan **CARDS:**

See advert on this page

KESWICK, continued

★★★75% Derwentwater

Portinscale CA12 5RE
☎ 017687 72538 🖷 017687 71002
e-mail: info@derwentwater-hotel.co.uk
Dir: *off A66 turn into Portinscale and through village then as road turns right take left turn as signed*

This is a popular and friendly holiday hotel with gardens that stretch down to the shores of Derwentwater. It offers a wide range of bedrooms, all thoughtfully equipped and some with good views of the lake. Inviting public areas include a conservatory lounge and shop.
ROOMS: 48 en suite (1 fmly) (2 GF) s £80-£85; d £130-£190 (incl. bkfst) **LB** **FACILITIES:** Fishing Croquet lawn Putting green Access to local leisure facilities entertainment Xmas **CONF:** Thtr 20 Class 10 Board 14 Del from £55 **SERVICES:** Lift **PARKING:** 100 **NOTES:** No smoking in restaurant **CARDS:**

See advert on opposite page

★★★68% Keswick Country House

Station Rd CA12 4NQ
☎ 0845 458 4333 🖷 01253 754222
e-mail: reservations@choice-hotels.co.uk
Dir: *M6 junct 40/A66, 1st slip road into Keswick, then follow signs for leisure pool*

This impressive Victorian hotel is set amid landscaped gardens. Eight superior bedrooms have been created in the Station Wing, which is accessed through the Victorian conservatory. Main house rooms are comfortably modern in style and offer a good range of amenities. Public areas include a well-stocked bar, a spacious and relaxing lounge, and an attractive restaurant.
ROOMS: 74 en suite (6 fmly) s £41-£54; d £82-£128 (incl. bkfst) **FACILITIES:** STV Snooker Croquet lawn Putting green Leisure facilities close by. Xmas **CONF:** Thtr 70 Class 40 Board 40 Del from £85 **SERVICES:** Lift **PARKING:** 70 **NOTES:** No dogs (ex guide dogs) No smoking in restaurant Civ Wed 100
CARDS:

> Early start?
> Hotels at all star levels should provide in-room alarm clocks and/or alarm calls

★★★68% Kings Head Hotel & Inn

Thirlspot, Thirlmere CA12 4TN
☎ 017687 72393 🖷 017687 72309
e-mail: stay@lakedistrictinns.co.uk
Dir: *M6 junct 40 onto A66 to Keswick, then A591 to Grasmere. Hotel in 4m*

This tastefully modernised 17th century coaching inn enjoys a fabulous setting in a picturesque valley. Attractive bedrooms, some of which have outstanding views, vary in size. A smart lounge provides an alternative to the busy public bar, which serves a range of meals and snacks all day.

ROOMS: 17 en suite (2 fmly) No smoking in all bedrooms s £35-£45; d £70-£90 (incl. bkfst) **FACILITIES:** STV Free use of local Leisure Centre Xmas **CONF:** Thtr 100 Class 40 Board 20 Del from £65 **PARKING:** 60 **NOTES:** No smoking in restaurant Civ Wed 50
CARDS:

See advert on opposite page

★★★66% Skiddaw

Main St CA12 5BN
☎ 017687 72071 🖷 017687 74850
e-mail: info@skiddawhotel.co.uk
Dir: *A66 to Keswick, follow signs for town centre. Hotel in Market Sq*

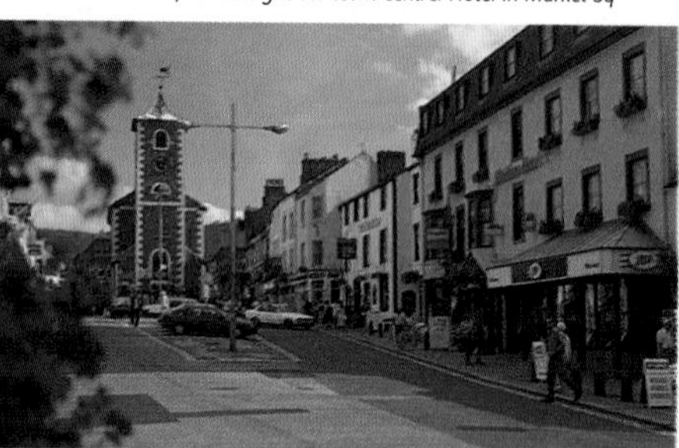

This privately owned hotel is centrally located overlooking Market Square. The smartly furnished bedrooms include some family suites and a room with a four-poster bed. Facilities include an attractive and spacious restaurant, a lounge bar, a quiet lounge for residents and two conference/function rooms.
ROOMS: 40 en suite (7 fmly) No smoking in 10 bedrooms **FACILITIES:** STV Sauna Free use of out of town leisure fac **CONF:** Thtr 70 Class 60 Board 40 Del from £90 **SERVICES:** Lift **PARKING:** 22 **NOTES:** No dogs (ex guide dogs) No smoking in restaurant Civ Wed 90
CARDS:

See advert on page 307

★★75% *Lyzzick Hall Country House*

Under Skiddaw CA12 4PY
☎ 017687 72277 🖷 017687 72278
e-mail: lyzzickhall@netscapeonline.co.uk
Dir: *M6 junct 40 onto A66 to Keswick. Do not enter town, keep on Keswick by pass. At rdbt 3rd exit onto A591 to Carlisle. Hotel 1.5m on right*

This privately-owned and personally run, delightful hotel stands in lovely landscaped gardens among the foothills of Skiddaw and enjoys fabulous views across the valley. Bedrooms are smartly appointed and thoughtfully equipped. Public areas include two spacious lounges, a small bar and an attractive restaurant offering a wide range of international cuisine.
ROOMS: 28 en suite 1 annexe en suite (3 fmly) **FACILITIES:** Indoor swimming (H) Sauna Jacuzzi ch fac **CONF:** Board 15 **PARKING:** 40 **NOTES:** No dogs No smoking in restaurant Closed 24-26 Dec & mid Jan-mid Feb **CARDS:**

The Derwentwater Hotel

Privately owned, on the shore of Derwentwater one mile from Keswick.

48 bedrooms many with Lake and Borrowdale Valley view. 16 acres of conservation gardens and grounds down to the Lake.

Magnificent Garden Room/Conservatory with views over putting green to the Lake.

Excellent 'Deer's Leap' restaurant with friendly staff, serving a wide variety of locally produced fare, all prepared with care by our Head Chef.

Guests have temporary membership of luxury health club and spa (no children under 16) at nearby Oxley's Health Club.

Well mannered dogs welcome, and full disabled facilities in two ground floor rooms.

Telephone 017687 72538
www.derwentwater-hotel.co.uk

The King's Head from the 17th century, an original, old world coaching inn offering guests all the best Lakeland traditions. Gloriously situated in the heart of the Lake District near Keswick, the inn gives you a wonderfully warm atmosphere, oak beams, real fires and real ales, along with award-winning archetypal English cooking, using the freshest local produce. Beautifully decorated, en suite bedrooms provide stunning views of the surrounding fells. Free membership of the nearby leisure club is included. Enjoy a traditional Lakeland break, whatever the season. Send now for our free brochure and prove that you can have too much of a good inn.

FOR RESERVATIONS CALL
0870 011 2152

Thirlspot
Near Keswick
Cumbria CA12 4TN
Tel (017687) 72393
Fax (017687) 72309
Email:
kings@lakelandinns.com
www.lakelandinns.com

KESWICK, continued

★★74% ⚘ Highfield

The Heads CA12 5ER
☎ 017687 72508 📠 017687 80634
e-mail: info@highfieldkeswick.co.uk
Dir: *M6 junct 40, take A66 2nd exit at rdbt. Left following road to T- junct. Left again and right at mini rdbt. Then turn 4th right*

This family run attractive hotel enjoys a peaceful setting with stunning views of both Skiddaw and Derwentwater. Bedrooms are individually and elegantly styled, smartly furnished and thoughtfully equipped. Guests can relax in a choice of inviting lounges that overlook the well-tended gardens. An innovative menu is offered in the smartly appointed dining room.

ROOMS: 20 en suite (2 GF) No smoking in all bedrooms s £122; d £102-£122 (incl. bkfst & dinner) **LB** **PARKING:** 20 **NOTES:** No dogs No children 8yrs No smoking in restaurant Closed Dec-Jan excl. Xmas & New Year **CARDS:**

★★74% Lairbeck

Vicarage Hill CA12 5QB
☎ 017687 73373 📠 017687 73144
e-mail: aa@lairbeckhotel-keswick.co.uk
Dir: *A66 to rdbt with A591. Left then right onto Vicarage Hill, hotel 150yds on right*

This impeccably maintained, fine Victorian country house is situated close to the town in peacefully secluded, attractive gardens. There is a welcoming residents' bar and a comfortable dining room in which a range of freshly prepared dishes are served each day. Bedrooms, which include rooms on ground floor level, are individually styled and well equipped.

ROOMS: 14 en suite (1 fmly) (1 GF) No smoking in all bedrooms s £38-£44; d £76-£88 (incl. bkfst) **LB** **PARKING:** 15 **NOTES:** No dogs No children 5yrs No smoking in restaurant Closed 1st 2 wks Dec, Jan & Feb **CARDS:**

★★67% Crow Park

The Heads CA12 5ER
☎ 017687 72208 📠 017687 74776
e-mail: crowpark@marsh1.fsnet

Guests are warmly welcomed at this smartly presented hotel enjoying lovely views towards the lake and the Borrowdale Valley. Attractive day rooms include a lounge, a residents' bar and a dining room featuring photos of historic Lakeland scenes. Bedrooms come in a variety of sizes and offer a good range of amenities.

ROOMS: 26 en suite (1 fmly) No smoking in 1 bedroom s £27.50-£35.50; d £55-£71 (incl. bkfst) **LB** **FACILITIES:** Xmas **PARKING:** 27 **NOTES:** No smoking in restaurant **CARDS:**

★★67% Edwardene

26 Southey St CA12 4EF
☎ 017687 73586 📠 017687 73824
e-mail: info@edwardenehotel.com
Dir: *take A591 towards Keswick town centre. Just before pedestrian lights turn left into Southey St*

Just a stone's throw from the town centre and forming part of a grand Victorian terrace, this hotel provides well-equipped accommodation. The stylish bedrooms vary in size and style and are all comfortably furnished. There is a spacious lounge, and a delightfully decorated dining room.

ROOMS: 11 en suite (1 fmly) No smoking in all bedrooms s £30-£32; d £56-£62 (incl. bkfst) **LB** **FACILITIES:** Xmas **CONF:** BC **PARKING:** 2 **NOTES:** No smoking in restaurant **CARDS:**

Top 200 - Hotel

★ ⚘⚘ Swinside Lodge

Grange Rd, Newlands CA12 5UE
☎ 017687 72948 📠 017687 72948
e-mail: info@swinsidelodge-hotel.co.uk
Dir: *off A66 left at Portinscale. Follow road to Grange for 2m ignoring signs to Swinside & Newlands Valley*

No visit to the Lake District is complete without a stay at this delightful country house. Superb hospitality and astute service means that not only are new guests received like old friends, but the house party atmosphere that prevails makes booking for dinner a growing necessity. Bedrooms are elegantly furnished and thoughtfully equipped whilst cosy comfortable lounges provide an ideal pre-dinner venue. The four course set dinner menu is creative and skilfully prepared and provides super value for money.

ROOMS: 7 en suite No smoking in all bedrooms s £88-£98; d £134-£190 (incl. bkfst & dinner) **LB** **FACILITIES:** Boules Xmas **CONF:** BC **PARKING:** 12 **NOTES:** No dogs (ex guide dogs) No children 5yrs No smoking in restaurant **CARDS:**

KETTERING, Northamptonshire Map 11 SP87

★★★★74% Kettering Park

Kettering Parkway NN15 6XT
☎ 01536 416666 01536 416171
e-mail: kpark@shirehotels.co.uk
Dir: *off junct 9 A14, M1 to A1 link road, on Kettering Venture Park*

A modern, stylish hotel providing a warm welcome and spacious, meticulously maintained bedrooms. Classical and contemporary dishes are served in the restaurant, light meals in the bar. The leisure facilities have been extended and refurbished. *Shire Hotels – AA Hotel Group of the Year 2003-2004.*

ROOMS: 119 en suite (28 fmly) (20 GF) No smoking in 80 bedrooms s £90-£135; d £130-£160 (incl. bkfst) **LB FACILITIES: Spa** STV Indoor swimming (H) Snooker Sauna Solarium Gym Steam rooms, Childrens splash pool, Activity studio Xmas **CONF:** BC Thtr 260 Class 120 Board 40 Del from £135 **SERVICES:** Lift air con **PARKING:** 200 **NOTES:** No dogs (ex guide dogs) No smoking in restaurant Civ Wed 120
CARDS:

See advert on this page

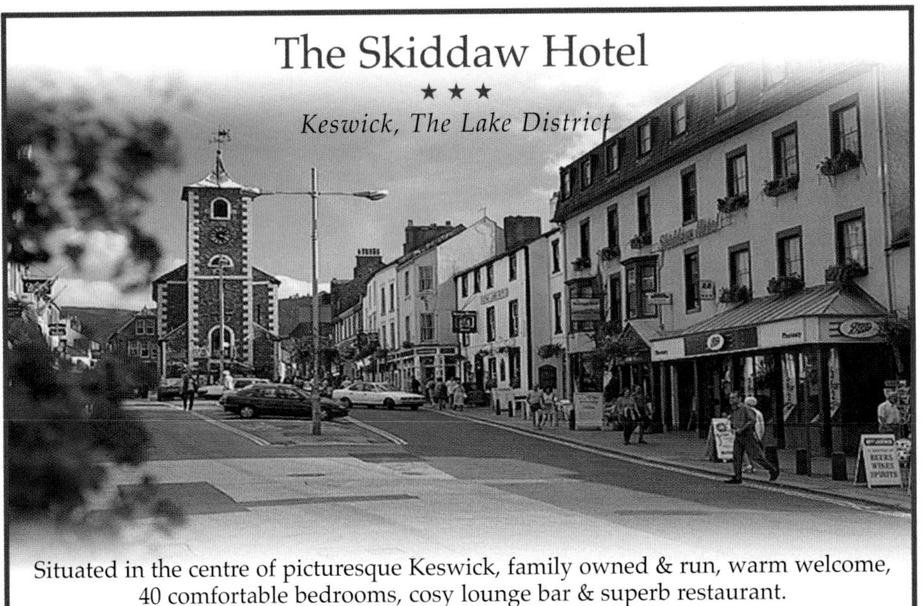

KETTERING, continued

Travel Inn
Rothwell Rd NN16 8XF
☎ 08701 977147 🖷 01536 415020
Dir: *on A14, off junct 7*
Travel Inn offers good-quality, value-for-money accommodation. Spacious, en suite rooms with bath and shower comfortably accommodate a family of up to two adults and two children (to age 15). The restaurant and bar offers a varied menu. For further details and the Travel Inn phone number, consult the Hotel Groups page.
ROOMS: 39 en suite s £44.95; d £44.95 **CONF:** Thtr 15

Travelodge
On the A14 (Westbound) NN14 1WR
☎ 08700 850 950
Travelodge offers good quality, good value, modern accommodation. Ideal for families, the spacious, en suite bedrooms include remote-control TV, tea and coffee-making facilities, luxury beds and free morning newspaper. Meals can be taken at the nearby family restaurant. For further details and the Travelodge phone number, consult the Hotel Groups page.
ROOMS: 40 en suite s fr £42.95; d fr £42.95

KEW, Greater London
See LONDON SECTION plan 1 C3

★★★66% Coach & Horses
8 Kew Green TW9 3BH
☎ 020 8940 1208 🖷 020 8948 8787
e-mail: coachandhorses@youngs.co.uk
This coaching inn on Kew Green dates back to the 17th century, now refurbished and offers smart contemporary accommodation. Bedrooms are all air conditioned, comfortable and well appointed. Public areas include a popular bar and an adjacent restaurant where freshly prepared meals can be enjoyed.
ROOMS: 31 en suite (7 GF) s £80-£108; d £85-£118 (incl. bkfst) **LB** **FACILITIES:** STV **CONF:** Thtr 60 Class 30 Board 30 **SERVICES:** Lift air con **PARKING:** 39 **NOTES:** No smoking in restaurant Civ Wed 60 **CARDS:**

KIDDERMINSTER, Worcestershire Map 10 SO87
See also Stourport-on-Severn

★★★★68% Stone Manor
Stone DY10 4PJ
☎ 01562 777555 🖷 01562 777834
e-mail: enquiries@stonemanorhotel.co.uk
Dir: *2.5 miles from Kidderminster on A448, right hand side*
This converted, much extended former manor house stands in 25 acres of impressive grounds and gardens. The well-equipped accommodation includes rooms with four-poster beds and some more recently created, luxuriously appointed annexe bedrooms. The hotel is a popular venue for wedding receptions.
ROOMS: 52 en suite 5 annexe en suite (7 GF) No smoking in 11 bedrooms s £95-£150; d £95-£150 **FACILITIES:** STV Outdoor swimming Tennis (hard) Croquet lawn Putting green Xmas **CONF:** Thtr 150 Class 48 Board 60 Del £150 **PARKING:** 400 **NOTES:** No smoking in restaurant Civ Wed 150 **CARDS:**

★★★66% Gainsborough House
Bewdley Hill DY11 6BS
☎ 01562 820041 🖷 01562 66179
e-mail: reservations@gainsboroughhotel.co.uk
Dir: *on A456. At hospital, over lights, hotel 200yds on right*
This listed Georgian property, situated on the edge of the town,
continued

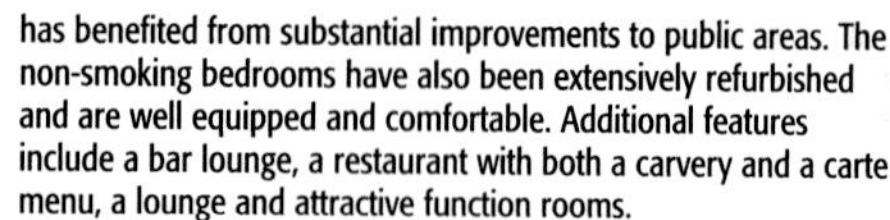

has benefited from substantial improvements to public areas. The non-smoking bedrooms have also been extensively refurbished and are well equipped and comfortable. Additional features include a bar lounge, a restaurant with both a carvery and a carte menu, a lounge and attractive function rooms.
ROOMS: 43 en suite (8 fmly) No smoking in 12 bedrooms **CONF:** Thtr 250 Class 80 Board 60 Del from £99 **PARKING:** 130 **NOTES:** No smoking in restaurant Civ Wed 250 **CARDS:**

★★★66% The Granary Hotel & Restaurant
Heath Ln, Shenstone DY10 4BS
☎ 01562 777535 🖷 01562 777722
e-mail: info@granary-hotel.co.uk
Dir: *on A450, 0.5m from junct with A448*
This modern hotel offers spacious, well-equipped accommodation with many rooms enjoying views towards Great Witley and the Amberley Hills. There is an attractive modern restaurant and a carvery is available at weekends. There are also extensive conference facilities and the hotel is popular as a wedding venue.
ROOMS: 18 en suite (1 fmly) No smoking in 9 bedrooms s £65; d £75 (incl. bkfst) **LB** **CONF:** Thtr 200 Class 80 Board 70 Del £125 **PARKING:** 96 **NOTES:** No smoking in restaurant Closed 25 Dec Civ Wed 120 **CARDS:**

KILLINGTON LAKE MOTORWAY SERVICE AREA (M6), Cumbria Map 18 SD59

Travel Inn
Killington Lake, Motorway Service Area, Killington LA8 0NW
☎ 08701 977145 🖷 01539 621660
Dir: *M6 junct 37, 1m southbound*
Travel Inn offers good-quality, value-for-money accommodation. Spacious, en suite rooms with bath and shower comfortably accommodate a family of up to two adults and two children (to age 15). The restaurant and bar offers a varied menu. For further details and the Travel Inn phone number, consult the Hotel Groups page.
ROOMS: 36 en suite s £44.95; d £44.95 **CONF:** Thtr 10

KINGHAM, Oxfordshire Map 10 SP22

★★★74% Mill House Hotel & Restaurant
OX7 6UH
☎ 01608 658188 🖷 01608 658492
e-mail: stay@millhousehotel.co.uk
Dir: *off A44 onto B4450. Hotel indicated by tourist sign*

This former Cotswold stone mill house has been carefully converted into a comfortable and attractive hotel, and is set in well-kept grounds bordered by its own trout stream. The refurbished bedrooms are comfortable and provide thoughtfully
continued

equipped accommodation. There is a peaceful lounge and bar and an atmospheric restaurant, which has a strong local following.
ROOMS: 21 en suite 2 annexe en suite (1 fmly) (7 GF) s £62.50-£85; d £135-£170 (incl. bkfst & dinner) **LB FACILITIES:** STV Fishing Croquet lawn ch fac Xmas **CONF:** BC Thtr 70 Class 24 Board 20 Del from £135 **PARKING:** 62 **NOTES:** No smoking in restaurant
CARDS:

KINGSBRIDGE, Devon Map 03 SX74

Top 200 - Hotel

★★★ ◎◎ Buckland-Tout-Saints
Goveton TQ7 2DS
☎ 01548 853055 📠 01548 856261
e-mail: buckland@tout-saints.co.uk
Dir: *off A381 Totnes/Kingsbridge road to Goveton. Left into Goveton, up hill to St Peter's Church. Hotel 2nd right after church*
It's well worth navigating the winding country lanes to find this delightful Queen Anne manor house that has been host to many famous guests over the years. Set in seven acres of gardens and grounds the hotel offers a peaceful retreat. Bedrooms are tastefully furnished and attractively decorated, most of them enjoying views of the gardens. Local produce is used with care and imagination in the restaurant. The large function room opens on to the terrace and is a popular choice for weddings.
ROOMS: 12 en suite (1 fmly) No smoking in 1 bedroom s fr £80; d £150-£340 (incl. bkfst) **LB FACILITIES:** Croquet lawn Putting green Petanque pitch Xmas **CONF:** Thtr 150 Class 100 Board 70 **PARKING:** 42 **NOTES:** No smoking in restaurant Closed 3 wks Jan Civ Wed 130 **CARDS:**

KINGSGATE, Kent Map 07 TR37

★★★70% The Fayreness
Marine Dr CT10 3LG
☎ 01843 868641 📠 01843 608750
e-mail: fayreness@thorleytaverns.com
Dir: *A28 onto B2051 which becomes B2052. Pass Holy Trinity Church on right and '19th Hole' public house. Next left, down Kingsgate Ave, hotel at end on left*
Situated on the cliff tops overlooking the English Channel, just a few steps from a sandy beach and adjacent to the North Foreland Golf Club. The spacious bedrooms are tastefully furnished with many thoughtful touches; some rooms have stunning sea views. Public rooms include a large open-plan lounge-bar, a function room, dining room and conservatory restaurant.
ROOMS: 29 en suite No smoking in 17 bedrooms s £48-£125; d £62-£135 (incl. bkfst) **LB FACILITIES:** STV **CONF:** Thtr 50 Class 28 Board 36 **NOTES:** No dogs (ex guide dogs) No smoking in restaurant Civ Wed 80 **CARDS:**

See advert on page 311

KINGS LANGLEY, Hertfordshire Map 06 TL00

Premier Lodge (Kings Langley)

Hempstead Rd WD4 8BR
☎ 0870 9906372 📠 0870 9906373
Premier Lodge offers modern, well-equipped, en suite accommodation suitable for both business and leisure travellers. Meals can be taken at the adjacent popular restaurant and bar, which is fully licensed. For further details, consult the Hotel Groups page.
ROOMS: 60 en suite s £54; d £54

KING'S LYNN, Norfolk Map 12 TF62

★★★ ◎◎ Congham Hall Country House
Lynn Rd PE32 1AH
☎ 01485 600250 📠 01485 601191
e-mail: info@conghamhallhotel.co.uk
(For full entry see Grimston)

★★★70% Knights Hill

Knights Hill Village, South Wootton PE30 3HQ
☎ 01553 675566 📠 01553 675568
e-mail: reception@knightshill.co.uk
Dir: *junct A148/A149*
Knights Hill is a hotel village complex, set around a 16th-century site, conveniently located for main road access on the outskirts of the town. Smartly decorated and well-equipped bedrooms are situated in extensions to the original hunting lodge. The main house is full of historical charm, combined with modern conference, banqueting and indoor leisure facilities. Public rooms also include a choice of dining options in the Garden Restaurant and the Farmers Arms pub.
ROOMS: 43 en suite 18 annexe en suite No smoking in 24 bedrooms s fr £88; d £98-£130 **LB FACILITIES:** STV Indoor swimming (H) Tennis (hard) Sauna Solarium Gym Croquet lawn Jacuzzi Heli-pad Xmas **CONF:** Thtr 299 Class 150 Board 30 **PARKING:** 350 **NOTES:** No smoking in restaurant Civ Wed 75
CARDS:

Late for dinner?
Quality Standards mean that last orders for dinner vary according to star rating and should be no earlier than:
★★ 7.00pm ★★★ 8.00pm ★★★★ 9.00pm
★★★★★ 10.00pm

KING'S LYNN, continued

★★★62% *The Duke's Head Hotel*
Tuesday Market Place PE30 1JS
☎ 01553 774996 🖷 01553 763556
e-mail: dukeshead@corushotels.com
Dir: *on town centre one-way system left at road split then left at traffic lights. Along St Anns St into Chapel St, hotel past car park on right*

Popular 16th-century coaching inn situated in a prominent position overlooking the Tuesday market place. Bedrooms are pleasantly furnished and equipped with a good range of useful extras. Public areas include a spacious lounge, a non-smoking lounge-bar and a public bar. Dining options include the informal Griffins Brasserie or a the more formal menu of main restaurant.
ROOMS: 71 en suite (2 fmly) No smoking in 33 bedrooms **CONF:** Thtr 240 Class 120 Board 60 **SERVICES:** Lift **PARKING:** 41 **NOTES:** No smoking in restaurant Civ Wed 100
CARDS:

★★69% Stuart House
35 Goodwins Rd PE30 5QX
☎ 01553 772169 🖷 01553 774788
e-mail: stuarthousehotel@btinternet.com
Dir: *at A47/A10/A149 rdbt take signs to King's Lynn town centre. Under Southgate Arch, right into Guanock Ter and right into Goodwins Rd*
This privately-owned hotel is situated in a peaceful residential area, yet is just a short walk from the town centre. Bedrooms come in a variety of styles and sizes; all rooms are pleasantly appointed and well equipped. A choice of dining options is available, with informal dining in the bar or a daily changing menu in the elegant restaurant.
ROOMS: 18 en suite (2 fmly) No smoking in 4 bedrooms s £58; d £78-£120 **LB** **FACILITIES:** Jacuzzi entertainment **CONF:** BC Thtr 50 Class 30 Board 20 **PARKING:** 30 **NOTES:** No dogs (ex guide dogs) No smoking in restaurant RS 25-26 Dec & 1 Jan
CARDS:

★★68% Grange
Willow Park, South Wootton Ln PE30 3BP
☎ 01553 673777 & 671222 🖷 01553 673777
e-mail: grange@btinternet.com
Dir: *A148 towards King's Lynn for 1.5m. At traffic lights left into Wootton Rd, 400yds on right South Wootton Ln. Hotel 1st on left*
Expect a warm welcome at this Edwardian house, which is situated in a quiet residential area amid its own grounds. Public rooms include an entrance hall, smart lounge bar and a cosy restaurant. The spacious bedrooms are pleasantly decorated, with some located in an adjacent wing, and are equipped with many thoughtful touches.
ROOMS: 5 en suite 4 annexe en suite (2 fmly) s £40-£60; d £56-£76 (incl. bkfst) **LB** **FACILITIES:** Xmas **CONF:** Thtr 20 Class 15 Board 12 **PARKING:** 15 **NOTES:** No smoking in restaurant
CARDS:

★★66% Russet House
53 Goodwins Rd PE30 5PE
☎ 01553 773098 🖷 01553 773098
e-mail: russethouse@freenet.co.uk
Dir: *follow town centre signs along Hardwick Rd. Right at rdbt before Southgates into Vancouver Av. Hotel on left*
A friendly and relaxed ambience exists within this detached property dating back to 1890, and situated just a short walk from the River Ouse and town centre. Public rooms offer a good choice of areas in which to relax, including a cosy bar, restaurant and a lounge with an open fire. Bedrooms are pleasantly decorated with co ordinated soft furnishings and many useful extras.
ROOMS: 13 en suite (2 fmly) No smoking in 1 bedroom **PARKING:** 20 **NOTES:** No smoking in restaurant **CARDS:**

See advert on opposite page

★★64% The Tudor Rose
St Nicholas St, Tuesday Market Place PE30 1LR THE INDEPENDENTS
☎ 01553 762824 🖷 01553 764894
e-mail: KLTudorRose@aol.com
Dir: *off Tuesday Market Place in centre of King's Lynn*
A charming Grade II listed building dating back to the 14th century, situated just off the Tuesday Market Place in the heart of town. The hotel is full of character and features open fireplaces as well as a wealth of exposed beams. Public rooms include a small reception area, a lounge and two bars, where real ales and informal fare are served.
ROOMS: 13 rms (11 en suite) s fr £45; d fr £60 (incl. bkfst) **LB**
NOTES: No smoking in restaurant Closed 25-26 Dec
CARDS:

⌂ Travel Inn
Freebridge Farm PE34 3LJ
☎ 08701 977149 🖷 01553 775827
Dir: *at junct of A47 & A17*
Travel Inn offers good-quality, value-for-money accommodation. Spacious, en suite rooms with bath and shower comfortably accommodate a family of up to two adults and two children (to age 15). The restaurant and bar offers a varied menu. For further details and the Travel Inn phone number, consult the Hotel Groups page.
ROOMS: 40 en suite s £44.95; d £44.95

KINGSTON UPON HULL, East Riding of Yorkshire
Map 17 TA02
See also Little Weighton

★★★72% ❀ Willerby Manor

Well Ln HU10 6ER
☎ 01482 652616 🖷 01482 653901
e-mail: info@willerbymanor.co.uk
(For full entry see Willerby)

★★★68% Portland
Paragon St HU1 3JP
☎ 01482 326462 🖹 01482 213460
e-mail: info@portland-hotel.co.uk
Dir: *M62 onto A63, to 1st main rdbt. Left at 2nd lights and over x-rds. Right at next junct onto Carr Ln, follow one-way system*
A modern hotel situated in the city centre providing a good range of accommodation. Most of the public rooms are on the first floor and include the Wilberforce Restaurant and the Humber Bar and Lounge. In addition the Bay Tree Café, at street level, is open during the day and evening. Staff are friendly and helpful, and car parking is taken care of by the staff.
ROOMS: 126 en suite (4 fmly) No smoking in 22 bedrooms
FACILITIES: STV Complimentary use of nearby health & fitness centre
CONF: BC Thtr 220 Class 100 Board 50 Del from £99 **SERVICES:** Lift
PARKING: 12 **CARDS:**

★★★67% Quality Hotel Hull

170 Ferensway HU1 3UF
☎ 01482 325087 🖹 01482 323172
e-mail: admin@gb611.u-net.com
Dir: *From M62 join A63 to Hull.Over flyover, left at 2nd lights signed Railway Station. Hotel on left at 2nd lights*
A former Victorian railway hotel modernised in recent years. Bedrooms are well equipped and include a number of premier rooms. A spacious lounge provides an ideal setting for light meals, drinks and relaxation. There are extensive banqueting and conference facilities, as well as an adjacent leisure club.
ROOMS: 155 en suite No smoking in 85 bedrooms s £40-£105; d £49-£115 **LB** **FACILITIES:** STV Indoor swimming (H) Sauna Solarium Gym Jacuzzi Steamroom Xmas **CONF:** Thtr 450 Class 150 Board 105 Del from £60 **SERVICES:** Lift **PARKING:** 130 **NOTES:** Civ Wed 450
CARDS:

KINGSTON UPON HULL, continued

★★★65% *Elizabeth Hotel Hull*

Ferriby High Rd HU14 3LG
☎ 01482 645212 🖷 01482 643332
(For full entry see North Ferriby)

★★68% The Rowley Manor

Rowley Rd HU20 3XR
☎ 01482 848248 🖷 01482 849900
e-mail: info@rowleymanor.com
(For full entry see Little Weighton)

★★57% Comfort Inn

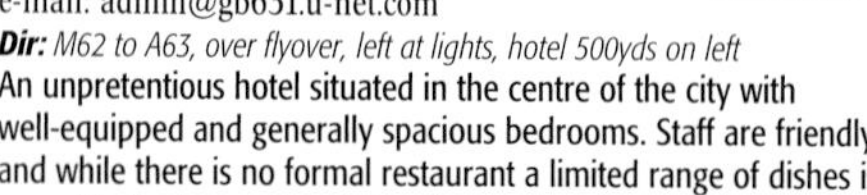

11 Anlaby Rd HU1 2PJ
☎ 01482 323299 🖷 01482 214730
e-mail: admin@gb631.u-net.com
Dir: *M62 to A63, over flyover, left at lights, hotel 500yds on left*
An unpretentious hotel situated in the centre of the city with well-equipped and generally spacious bedrooms. Staff are friendly, and while there is no formal restaurant a limited range of dishes is served in the lounge bar during the evening. Free parking is also available.
ROOMS: 59 en suite (5 fmly) No smoking in 29 bedrooms **FACILITIES:** STV leisure facilities at sister hotel **CONF:** Thtr 140 Class 80 Board 45 Del from £50 **SERVICES:** Lift **PARKING:** 100 **NOTES:** No smoking in restaurant **CARDS:**

Holiday Inn Hull Marina

The Marina, Castle St HU1 2BX
☎ 0870 400 9043 🖷 01482 213299
e-mail: hull@ichotelsgroup.com
Dir: *from M62 join A63 to Hull. Follow signs for Marina and Ice Arena. Hotel on left next to Ice Arena*
At the time of going to press, the classification for this hotel was not confirmed. Please refer to the AA internet site www.theAA.com for current information.
ROOMS: 101 en suite (12 fmly) No smoking in 66 bedrooms **FACILITIES:** STV Indoor swimming (H) Sauna Solarium Gym **CONF:** Thtr 150 Class 60 Board 50 **SERVICES:** Lift **PARKING:** 130 **NOTES:** No smoking in restaurant Civ Wed 70
CARDS:

Campanile

Beverley Rd, Freetown Way HU2 9AN
☎ 01482 325530 🖷 01482 587538
e-mail: campanile.hull@talk21.com
Dir: *From M62 join A63 to Hull, pass Humber Bridge on right. Over flyover, follow railway station signs onto A1079. Hotel at bottom of Ferensway*

This modern building offers accommodation in smart, well-equipped bedrooms, all with en suite bathrooms. Refreshments may be taken at the informal Bistro. For further details and the Campanile phone number, consult the Hotel Groups page.
ROOMS: 50 annexe en suite **CONF:** Thtr 35 Class 18 Board 20

Hotel Ibis Hull

Ferensway HU1 2NL
☎ 01482 387500 🖷 01482 385510
e-mail: h3479@accor-hotels.com
Dir: *M62/A63 straight across at rdbt, follow signs for Princes Quay onto Myton St. Hotel on corner of Osborne St & Ferensway*
Modern, budget hotel offering comfortable accommodation in bright and practical bedrooms. Breakfast is self-service and dinner is available in the restaurant. For further details, consult the Hotel Groups page.
ROOMS: 106 en suite d £39.95-£42.95

Travel Inn (Hull North)

Kingswood Park, Ennerdale HU7 4HS
☎ 08701 977137 🖷 01482 820300
Dir: *N of Hull, Ennerdale link road in Kingswood Park. A63 to city centre, then A1079 north, right onto A1033, hotel on 2nd rdbt*
Travel Inn offers good-quality, value-for-money accommodation. Spacious, en suite rooms with bath and shower comfortably accommodate a family of up to two adults and two children (to age 15). The restaurant and bar offers a varied menu. For further details and the Travel Inn phone number, consult the Hotel Groups page.
ROOMS: 42 en suite s £44.95; d £44.95

Travel Inn (Hull West)

Ferriby Rd, Hessle HU13 0JA
☎ 08701 977138 🖷 01482 645285
Dir: *From A63 take exit for A164/A15 to Humber Bridge, Beverley & Hessle Viewpoint. Travel Inn on 1st rdbt*
Travel Inn offers good-quality, value-for-money accommodation. Spacious, en suite rooms with bath and shower comfortably accommodate a family of up to two adults and two children (to age 15). The restaurant and bar offers a varied menu. For further details and the Travel Inn phone number, consult the Hotel Groups page.
ROOMS: 40 en suite s £44.95; d £44.95

Travelodge Hull

Beacon Service Area HU15 1RZ
☎ 08700 850 950 🖷 01430 424455
(For full entry see South Cave)

KINGSTON UPON THAMES, Greater London
See LONDON SECTION plan 1 C1

★★★70% Kingston Lodge

Kingston Hill KT2 7NP
☎ 0870 400 8115 🖷 020 8547 1013
e-mail: kingstonlodge@macdonald-hotels.co.uk
Dir: *A3 Robin Hood junct A308 to Kingston. Hotel 1.5m on left*
Standing on the edge of one of the capital's greatest areas of natural beauty, Richmond Park, the hotel is nevertheless only 9 miles from central London and conveniently located for access to transport links. Public rooms include a cosy bar, lounge and the

continued

Atrium Restaurant, which opens onto a paved patio area for outdoor dining in fine weather.

ROOMS: 63 en suite (20 GF) No smoking in 38 bedrooms s £69-£160; d £98-£170 (incl. bkfst) **LB** **FACILITIES:** STV **CONF:** Thtr 70 Class 30 Board 26 Del from £135 **PARKING:** 70 **NOTES:** No smoking in restaurant Civ Wed 40 **CARDS:**

⌂ Travelodge London Kingston

21-23 London Rd KT2 6ND
☎ 08700 850 950 📠 0208 546 5904
Dir: *On Queen Elizabeth Road/London Road, opposite Rotunda complex*

Travelodge offers good quality, good value, modern accommodation. Ideal for families, the spacious, en suite bedrooms include remote-control TV, tea and coffee-making facilities, luxury beds and free morning newspaper. Meals can be taken at the nearby family restaurant. For further details and the Travelodge phone number, consult the Hotel Groups page.
ROOMS: 72 en suite s fr £42.95; d fr £42.95

KINGSWINFORD, West Midlands — Map 10 SO88

⌂ Innkeeper's Lodge

Swindon Rd DY6 9XA
☎ 01384 295254 & 270066 📠 01384 287959
Dir: *A491 into Kingswinford, at x-rds lights, turn onto A4101 towards Kidderminster along 'Summerhill'. At 1st set of lights, hotel on right*
A new concept in the travel accommodation market. Smart rooms meet essential business requirements but also have home comforts. Dining options include all-day menus plus the added advantage of breakfast, which is included in the room price. For further details, consult the Hotel Groups page.
ROOMS: 22 en suite

⌂ Travel Inn (Dudley Kingswinford)

Dudley Rd DY6 8WT
☎ 08701 977303 📠 01384 402736
Dir: *A4123 to Dudley, A461 following signs for Russell's Hall Hospital. On A4101 to Kingswinford, Travel Inn opposite Pensnett Trading Estate*
Travel Inn offers good-quality, value-for-money accommodation. Spacious, en suite rooms with bath and shower comfortably accommodate a family of up to two adults and two children (to age 15). The restaurant and bar offer a varied menu. For further details and the Travel Inn phone number, consult the Hotel Groups page.
ROOMS: 43 en suite s £44.95; d £44.95 **CONF:** Thtr 30 Board 20

KINGTON, Herefordshire — Map 09 SO25

★★★65% Burton

Mill St HR5 3BQ
☎ 01544 230323 📠 01544 230323
e-mail: burton@hotelherefordshire.co.uk
Dir: *at rdbt A44/A411 junct take road signed Town Centre*
Situated in the town centre, this friendly, privately-owned hotel offers spacious, pleasantly proportioned and well equipped bedrooms. Public areas, which are maintained to a high standard, include a lounge bar, a small lounge and an attractive restaurant. There are also function and meeting facilities available in a purpose-built modern wing.
ROOMS: 16 en suite (5 fmly) No smoking in 2 bedrooms s £40-£48; d £64-£70 (incl. bkfst) **LB** **FACILITIES:** Xmas **CONF:** Thtr 150 Class 100 Board 20 Del from £65 **PARKING:** 50 **NOTES:** Civ Wed 150
CARDS:

KIRBY MUXLOE, Leicestershire — Map 11 SK50

★★64% *Castle Hotel & Restaurant*

Main St LE9 2AP
☎ 0116 239 5337 📠 0116 238 7868
e-mail: thecastle.kirbymuxloe@snr.co.uk
Dir: *M1 junct 21A northbound, follow signs for Kirby Muxloe and enter village. Hotel on main road*
This attractive creeper-clad hotel dates back to the 16th century when it started life as a farmhouse, built using stone and timbers taken from the nearby castle. The property features inglenook fireplaces and exposed timbers, and open-plan public rooms include a lounge bar and restaurant with a non-smoking area. Bedrooms vary in size and style, and all are pleasantly decorated.
ROOMS: 22 en suite (3 fmly) **CONF:** Thtr 150 Class 100 Board 100
NOTES: No dogs (ex guide dogs) Civ Wed 100
CARDS:

KIRKBURTON, West Yorkshire — Map 16 SE11

★★★69% Springfield Park

Penistone Rd HD8 0PE
☎ 01484 607788 📠 01484 607961
e-mail: quality@springfieldparkhotel.com
Dir: *3m S of Huddersfield town centre, on A629, close to M1 and M62*
This converted former Victorian textile mill lies just a few miles to the south of Huddersfield. The hotel has been completely refurbished to provide stylish, well-equipped accommodation. Thoughtfully furnished day rooms also provide contemporary venues in which guests can relax. Creative dishes are served in the open-plan brasserie.
ROOMS: 47 en suite (2 fmly) No smoking in 20 bedrooms s £72-£82; d £82-£92 (incl. bkfst) **LB** **FACILITIES:** STV **CONF:** Thtr 100 Class 45 Board 40 Del from £80 **PARKING:** 100 **NOTES:** Civ Wed 80
CARDS:

KIRKBURTON, continued

⌂ Innkeeper's Lodge Huddersfield

36a Penistone Rd HD8 0PQ
☎ 01484 602101 📠 01484 603938
Dir: *from A62 Huddersfield ring road onto A629 towards Wakefield*

A new concept in the travel accommodation market. Smart rooms meet essential business requirements but also have home comforts. Dining options include all-day menus plus the added advantage of breakfast, which is included in the room price. For further details, consult the Hotel Groups page.

ROOMS: 20 en suite 3 annexe en suite **CONF:** Thtr 30 Board 20

KIRKBY LONSDALE, Cumbria Map 18 SD67

★★67% The Whoop Hall

Burrow with Burrow LA6 2HP
☎ 015242 71284 📠 015242 72154
e-mail: info@whoophall.co.uk
Dir: *on A65 1m SE of Kirkby Lonsdale*

This popular inn combines traditional charm with modern facilities, which includes very well-equipped leisure facilities. Bedrooms, some with four-poster beds and some housed in converted barns, are attractively furnished. A fire warms the bar on cooler days and a wide variety of dishes are offered in the bar, bistro and galleried restaurant.

ROOMS: 22 en suite (3 fmly) (2 GF) No smoking in 11 bedrooms s £65; d £65-£90 (incl. bkfst) **LB FACILITIES: Spa** Indoor swimming (H) Sauna Solarium Gym Jacuzzi Children's adventure playground, Steam/Treatment room, Swimming pool supervised entertainment Xmas **CONF:** Thtr 144 Class 6040 Board 60 Del £99.50 **PARKING:** 100 **NOTES:** Civ Wed 130 **CARDS:**

★★58% *Plough Hotel*

Cow Brow LA6 1PJ
☎ 015395 67227 📠 015395 67848
Dir: *M6 junct 36, towards Skipton and Kirkby Lonsdale, 1m from M6*

This former coaching inn has been extended and modernised but retains much of its original character. Located close to the M6 and Kirkby Lonsdale, it is within easy reach of both the Lake District and the Yorkshire Dales. The oak beamed bar and restaurant offer a wide range of meals and snacks. The individually styled bedrooms are thoughtfully equipped.

ROOMS: 12 en suite (2 fmly) **FACILITIES:** Fishing **CONF:** Thtr 100 Class 100 Board 60 **PARKING:** 72 **CARDS:**

Top 200 - Hotel

★ ◎ Hipping Hall

Cowan Bridge LA6 2JJ
☎ 015242 71187 📠 015242 72452
e-mail: hippinghal@aol.com
Dir: *0.5m E of Cowan Bridge on A65*

This house dates from the 15th century and retains many original features, most notable the great hall that is now used as a spacious lounge. Bedrooms are individually styled and all are furnished with antique pieces, a real passion of the owners. The elegant dining room is the setting for carefully prepared dishes that utilise much local produce. An honesty bar is found in the courtyard conservatory.

ROOMS: 5 en suite 2 annexe en suite No smoking in 5 bedrooms s £75; d £96 **LB FACILITIES:** Croquet lawn Putting green **CONF:** Thtr 14 Class 14 Board 14 **PARKING:** 20 **NOTES:** No children 12yrs No smoking in restaurant Closed 23 Dec-10 Jan **CARDS:**

KIRKBYMOORSIDE, North Yorkshire Map 19 SE68

★★66% George & Dragon Hotel

17 Market Place YO62 6AA
☎ 01751 433334 📠 01751 432933
e-mail: georgeatkirkby@aol.com
Dir: *off A170 between Thirsk and Scarborough, in centre of market town*

Set in the market square, this coaching inn dates from the 1600s. With its blazing fire and sporting theme the pub offers a cosy, welcoming atmosphere. A wide range of hearty dishes is offered from both the menu and a blackboard. Spacious bedrooms are individually furnished and housed in two quiet buildings nearby.

ROOMS: 11 en suite 7 annexe en suite (2 fmly) (2 GF) s £49; d £79-£90 (incl. bkfst) **LB FACILITIES:** Gym Xmas **CONF:** Thtr 50 Class 20 Board 20 Del £90 **PARKING:** 20 **NOTES:** No smoking in restaurant **CARDS:**

KIRKHAM, Lancashire Map 18 SD43

⌂ Premier Lodge (Blackpool East)

Fleetwood Rd, Greenhalgh PR4 3HE
☎ 0870 9906636 📠 0870 9906637

Premier Lodge offers modern, well-equipped, en suite accommodation suitable for both business and leisure travellers. Meals can be taken at the adjacent popular restaurant and bar, which is fully licensed. For further details, consult the Hotel Groups page.

ROOMS: 28 en suite s £48; d £48

KNARESBOROUGH, North Yorkshire Map 19 SE35

★★★71% ◎◎ General Tarleton Inn

Boroughbridge Rd, Ferrensby HG5 0PZ
☎ 01423 340284 📠 01423 340288
e-mail: gti@generaltarleton.co.uk
Dir: *A1 junct 48 at Boroughbridge, take A6055 to Knaresborough. Inn 4m on right*

This popular hotel is renowned for imaginative cooking within its formal restaurant, traditional bar and bright conservatory. Recently refurbished bedrooms provide high levels of comfort and quality.

continued

Staff throughout are particularly friendly, highly skilled and keen to please.
ROOMS: 14 en suite (7 GF) No smoking in 9 bedrooms s £70-£75; d £80-£90 (incl. bkfst) **LB** **FACILITIES:** Xmas **CONF:** Thtr 40 Class 35 Board 20 Del from £130 **PARKING:** 80 **NOTES:** No smoking in restaurant Civ Wed 40 **CARDS:**

★★★70% Dower House

Bond End HG5 9AL
☎ 01423 863302 01423 867665
e-mail: enquiries@bwdowerhouse.co.uk
Dir: *A1(M) onto A59 Harrogate road. Through Knaresborough, hotel on right after traffic lights at end of high street*

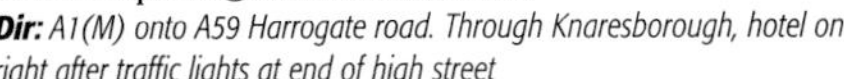

This attractive 15th-century house stands in pleasant gardens on the edge of the town. Features such as welcoming real fires enhance its charm and character. The Terrace Restaurant has a relaxed and comfortable atmosphere and overlooks the garden. There is a cosy bar and comfortable non-smoking lounge. Other facilities include two function rooms and a popular health and leisure club, which has its own lounge bar.
ROOMS: 28 en suite 3 annexe en suite (2 fmly) No smoking in 20 bedrooms s £85-£97; d £94-£115 (incl. bkfst) **LB** **FACILITIES:** Indoor swimming (H) Sauna Gym Jacuzzi Swimming pool supervised Xmas **CONF:** Thtr 65 Class 35 Board 36 Del from £99 **PARKING:** 100 **NOTES:** No smoking in restaurant **CARDS:**

Innkeeper's Lodge Harrogate East

Wetherby Rd, Plompton HG5 8LY
☎ 01423 797979 01423 887276
Dir: *turn off A658 onto A661 towards Harrogate, lodge on left*

A new concept in the travel accommodation market. Smart rooms meet essential business requirements but also have home comforts. Dining options include all-day menus plus the added advantage of breakfast, which is included in the room price. For further details, consult the Hotel Groups page.
ROOMS: 11 en suite

KNOWLE, West Midlands — Map 10 SP17

Innkeeper's Lodge Knowle

Warwick Rd, Knowle B93 0EE
☎ 01564 771177 01564 730862
Dir: *on A41*

A new concept in the travel accommodation market. Smart rooms meet essential business requirements but also have home comforts. Dining options include all-day menus plus the added advantage of breakfast, which is included in the room price. For further details, consult the Hotel Groups page.
ROOMS: 12 en suite

KNUTSFORD, Cheshire — Map 15 SJ77

★★★★71% Cottons Hotel & Spa

Manchester Rd WA16 0SU
☎ 01565 650333 01565 755351
e-mail: cottons@shirehotels.co.uk
Dir: *on A50 1m from M6 junct 19*

Super leisure facilities and a quiet location are an attraction for all types of guests at this hotel, just a short distance from Manchester Airport. Bedrooms are smartly appointed in a number of styles; executive rooms have very good working areas. The hotel has

continued on p316

KNUTSFORD, continued

invested in more spacious lounge areas and a bigger leisure centre. *Shire Hotels – AA Hotel Group of the Year 2003-2004.*

Coltons Hotel & Spa, Knutsford

ROOMS: 109 en suite (4 fmly) (38 GF) No smoking in 80 bedrooms s £85-£155; d £120-£175 (incl. bkfst) **LB** **FACILITIES: Spa** STV Indoor swimming (H) Tennis (hard) Sauna Solarium Gym Health & beauty treatment rooms, Steam room, Relaxation area Xmas **CONF:** BC Thtr 200 Class 120 Board 30 Del from £115 **SERVICES:** Lift **PARKING:** 180 **NOTES:** No dogs (ex guide dogs) No smoking in restaurant Civ Wed 120 **CARDS:**

See advert on page 313

★★★★70% Mere Court Hotel & Conference Centre

Warrington Rd, Mere WA16 0RW
☎ 01565 831000 01565 831001
e-mail: sales@merecourt.co.uk

This is a smart and attractive hotel, set in well-tended gardens. The elegant and spacious bedrooms are all individually styled and offer a host of thoughtful extras. Conference facilities are particularly impressive. Dining is available in the elegant fine dining Arboreum Restaurant or in the new modern conservatory dining area, which overlooks the lake and has a relaxed ambience.
ROOMS: 34 en suite (24 fmly) (12 GF) No smoking in 5 bedrooms s fr £130; d fr £160 **FACILITIES:** STV Croquet lawn Jacuzzi **CONF:** Thtr 100 Class 60 Board 35 Del from £149 **SERVICES:** Lift **PARKING:** 150 **NOTES:** No smoking in restaurant Civ Wed 80 **CARDS:**

See advert on page 313

★★75% The Longview Hotel & Restaurant

55 Manchester Rd WA16 0LX
☎ 01565 632119 01565 652402
e-mail: enquiries@longviewhotel.com
Dir: *M6 junct 19 take A556 W towards Chester. Left at lights onto A5033, 1.5m to rdbt then left. Hotel 200yds on right*
This friendly Victorian hotel offers high standards of hospitality and service. Attractive public areas include a cellar bar and foyer lounge area. The restaurant has a Victorian feel and offers an imaginative selection of dishes. Bedrooms are all individually styled and offer a good range of thoughtful amenities, including broadband internet access.
ROOMS: 13 en suite 13 annexe en suite (1 fmly) (4 GF) s £52.50-£115; d £72.50-£137.50 (incl. bkfst) **LB** **FACILITIES:** Free use of local fitness club **PARKING:** 20 **NOTES:** Closed 24 Dec-8 Jan
CARDS:

Premier Lodge (Knutsford North)

Bucklow Hill WA16 6RD
☎ 0870 9906428 0870 9906429
Dir: *M56 junct 7, take A556 towards Northwich and M6. Hotel 1m at lights on left*
Premier Lodge offers modern, well-equipped, en suite accommodation suitable for both business and leisure travellers. Meals can be taken at the adjacent popular restaurant and bar, which is fully licensed. For further details, consult the Hotel Groups page.
ROOMS: 66 en suite s £48; d £48 **CONF:** Thtr 60 Board 30

Premier Lodge (Knutsford North West)

Warrington Rd, Hoo Green, Mere WA16 0PZ
☎ 0870 9906482 0870 9906483
Dir: *M6 junct 19 onto A556. Left at lights onto A50. Hotel 1m on right*
Premier Lodge offers modern, well-equipped, en suite accommodation suitable for both business and leisure travellers. Meals can be taken at the adjacent popular restaurant and bar, which is fully licensed. For further details, consult the Hotel Groups page.
ROOMS: 28 en suite s £48; d £48

Travelodge

Chester Rd, Tabley WA16 0PP
☎ 08700 850 950 01565 652187
Dir: *on A556, northbound just E of junct 19 on M6*
Travelodge offers good quality, good value, modern accommodation. Ideal for families, the spacious, en suite bedrooms include remote-control TV, tea and coffee-making facilities, luxury beds and free morning newspaper. Meals can be taken at the nearby family restaurant. For further details and the Travelodge phone number, consult the Hotel Groups page.
ROOMS: 32 en suite s fr £42.95; d fr £42.95

KNUTSFORD MOTORWAY SERVICE AREA (M6), Cheshire — Map 15 SJ77

Travelodge

Granada Services, M6 junct 18/19 WA1 0TL
☎ 08700 850 950
Travelodge offers good quality, good value, modern accommodation. Ideal for families, the spacious, en suite bedrooms include remote-control TV, tea and coffee-making facilities, luxury beds and free morning newspaper. Meals can be taken at the nearby family restaurant. For further details and the Travelodge phone number, consult the Hotel Groups page.
ROOMS: 54 en suite s fr £42.95; d fr £42.95

LANCASTER, Lancashire Map 18 SD46
See also Hampson Green

★★★★69% Lancaster House

Green Ln, Ellel LA1 4GJ
☎ 01524 844822 🖷 01524 844766
e-mail: lancaster@elhmail.co.uk
Dir: *M6 junct 33 N towards Lancaster. Through Galgate and into Green Ln. Hotel before university on right*
This modern hotel enjoys a rural setting south of the city close to the university. The attractive open plan balconied reception and lounge boasts flagstone floors and a roaring log fire in season. Bedrooms are spacious and well equipped for business guests. The excellent business and leisure facilities make this hotel a popular conference venue. Staff are friendly and keen to please.
ROOMS: 80 en suite (10 fmly) (36 GF) No smoking in 60 bedrooms s £82-£129; d £82-£129 **LB** **FACILITIES:** STV Indoor swimming (H) Sauna Solarium Gym Jacuzzi entertainment Xmas **CONF:** Thtr 120 Class 50 Board 48 **PARKING:** 100 **NOTES:** No smoking in restaurant Civ Wed 100 **CARDS:**

★★★69% Menzies Royal Kings Arms

Market St LA1 1HP
☎ 01524 32451 🖷 01524 841698
e-mail: info@menzies-hotels.co.uk
Dir: *M6 to city centre, then signs for Castle and Railway Station. Turn off before traffic lights. Hotel next to Waterstones bookshop*
This period hotel occupies a prime city centre position close to both the castle and the main shopping areas. Bedrooms are smartly appointed and thoughtfully equipped, with those at the rear having a quieter aspect. Public areas have been refurbished whilst retaining many original features and include a choice of lounges and a galleried restaurant.
ROOMS: 55 en suite (2 fmly) No smoking in 15 bedrooms **FACILITIES:** STV **CONF:** Thtr 100 Class 50 Board 60 Del from £95 **SERVICES:** Lift **PARKING:** 20 **NOTES:** No smoking in restaurant Civ Wed 100 **CARDS:**

★★★61% *Thurnham Mill Hotel & Restaurant*

Thurnham Mill Ln, Conder Green LA2 0BD
☎ 01524 752852 🖷 01524 752477
e-mail: stay@thurnham-mill-hotel.fsnet.co.uk
Dir: *M6 junct 33, towards Lancaster. A6 to Galgate, turn left at traffic lights. Continue along this road for approx 1.75m. At bottom of road, turn left over bridge, then left in Thurnham Mill Lane*
This converted cloth mill dates from the 16th century and lies only a few miles from the M6 on the Lancaster canal. Spacious bedrooms are traditional in style and include a number of family rooms. Dinner can be enjoyed in the Canalside Restaurant, or on sunny days on a popular terrace.
ROOMS: 18 en suite (6 fmly) No smoking in 1 bedroom **FACILITIES:** ch fac **CONF:** Thtr 65 Class 30 Board 30 **PARKING:** 50 **NOTES:** No smoking in restaurant **CARDS:**

U *Holiday Inn Lancaster*

Waterside Park, Caton Rd LA1 3RA
☎ 0870 400 9047 🖷 01524 841265
e-mail: reservations-lancaster@ichotelsgroup.co.uk
Dir: *M6 junct 34 towards Lancaster. Hotel 1st on right*
At the time of going to press, the classification for this hotel was not confirmed. Please refer to the AA internet site www.theAA.com for current information.
ROOMS: 157 en suite (82 fmly) No smoking in 73 bedrooms **FACILITIES:** STV Indoor swimming (H) Sauna Gym Jacuzzi Health & fitness centre **CONF:** Thtr 120 Class 60 Board 60 **SERVICES:** Lift **PARKING:** 300 **CARDS:**

○ Travel Inn

Lancaster Business Park, Caton Rd
☎ 0870 238 3344 🖷 0870 241 9000
ROOMS: 60 en suite **NOTES:** Due to open Sept 2003

LANDFORD, Wiltshire Map 05 SU21

★★69% New Forest Lodge Hotel

Southampton Rd SP5 2ED
☎ 01794 390999 🖷 01794 390066
e-mail: reservations@newforestlodge.co.uk
Dir: *M27 junct 2, on A36, after 5m, hotel on left*
Set between Salisbury and Southampton, this is an ideal location for those visiting the area either for business or pleasure. Accommodation is self-contained and purpose-built, with bedrooms offering high standards of comfort and quality. Food is available in the adjacent Keepers Inn, where accomplished, contemporary cuisine is served in a convivial atmosphere.
ROOMS: 14 en suite (6 fmly) (6 GF) No smoking in all bedrooms s fr £52.50; d fr £57.50 **LB** **CONF:** Thtr 20 Board 14 **PARKING:** 36 **NOTES:** No smoking in restaurant **CARDS:**

LAND'S END, Cornwall & Isles of Scilly Map 02 SW32
See also Sennen

★★★63% The Land's End Hotel

TR19 7AA
☎ 01736 871844 🖷 01736 871599
e-mail: landsendhotel@madasafish.co.uk
Dir: *from Penzance take A30 and follow Land's End signs. After Sennen 1m to Land's End*
The famous location provides a most impressive setting for this attractive and comfortable hotel. Bedrooms, many with stunning Atlantic sea-views, are pleasantly decorated and comfortable. A comfortable lounge and attractive bar are provided and in the 'Longships' restaurant, fresh local produce and fish dishes are a speciality.
ROOMS: 33 en suite (2 fmly) s £37.50-£90; d £75-£180 (incl. bkfst) **LB** **FACILITIES:** Free entry Lands End visitor centre ch fac Xmas **CONF:** Thtr 200 Class 100 Board 50 Del from £60 **PARKING:** 1000 **NOTES:** No smoking in restaurant Civ Wed 110 **CARDS:**

LANGAR, Nottinghamshire Map 11 SK73

★★★73% ⊛⊛ Langar Hall

NG13 9HG
☎ 01949 860559 🖷 01949 861045
e-mail: langarhall-hotel@ndirect.co.uk
Dir: *via Bingham on A52 or Cropwell Bishop from A46, both signed. Hotel behind the church.*
This delightful hotel enjoys a picturesque rural location, yet is only a short drive from Nottingham. Individually styled bedrooms are furnished with fine period pieces and benefit from some thoughtful extras. There is a choice of lounges, warmed by real fires, and a snug little bar. Carefully prepared imaginative food is served in the pillared dining room.
ROOMS: 12 en suite (1 fmly) No smoking in all bedrooms s fr £90; d fr £130 (incl. bkfst) **LB** **FACILITIES:** Fishing Croquet lawn ch fac **CONF:** BC Thtr 20 Class 20 Board 20 Del from £155 **PARKING:** 20 **NOTES:** No smoking in restaurant Civ Wed 40 **CARDS:**

LANGHO, Lancashire Map 18 SD73

Restaurant with Rooms

Northcote Manor

Northcote Rd BB6 8BE
☎ 01254 240555 01254 246568
e-mail: sales@northcotemanor.com
Dir: *M6 junct 31, 9m to Northcote. Follow Clitheroe (A59) signs, hotel on left before rdbt*

Northcote Manor is a gastronomic haven where many guests return to sample the delights of its famous kitchen, which has twice in the past produced the Young Chef of the Year. Excellent cooking includes much of Lancashire's finest fare. Drinks can be enjoyed in the comfortable, elegantly furnished lounges and bar. Bedrooms have been individually furnished and thoughtfully equipped.

ROOMS: 14 en suite (4 GF) s £110-£125; d £130-£150 (incl. bkfst) **LB**
FACILITIES: STV Croquet lawn Clay and game shooting, Blackburn Rovers tickets can be purchased by the hotel Xmas **CONF:** BC Thtr 40 Class 20 Board 26 Del from £150 **PARKING:** 50 **NOTES:** No dogs (ex guide dogs) No smoking in restaurant Closed 25 Dec, 1 Jan & most BH Mondays Civ Wed 40 **CARDS:**

LANGTOFT, East Riding of Yorkshire Map 17 TA06

★★71% Old Mill Hotel & Restaurant

Mill Ln YO25 3BQ
☎ 01377 267284 01377 267383
e-mail: oldmilllangtoft@btconnect.com
Dir: *6m N of Driffield, on B1249. Through Langtoft, approx 1m N, left at hotel sign*

Standing in the open countryside of the Wolds, this modern hotel has been very well furnished throughout. Bedrooms are thoughtfully equipped, and there is a popular bar/lounge where a good range of well produced food is available. There is also a charming restaurant that is a favourite haunt for locals.

ROOMS: 9 en suite (1 fmly) s £45-£50; d £50-£65 (incl. bkfst) **LB**
CONF: BC Thtr 40 Class 20 Board 20 Del from £60 **PARKING:** 30
NOTES: No dogs (ex guide dogs) No smoking in restaurant
CARDS:

LASTINGHAM, North Yorkshire Map 19 SE79

★★★73% Lastingham Grange

YO62 6TH
☎ 01751 417345 & 417402 01751 417358
e-mail: lastinghamgrange@aol.com
Dir: *2m E on A170 to Scarborough, on to Lastingham. In village left uphill towards moors. Hotel on right*

This welcoming hotel offers warm, sincere hospitality that has been the hallmark here for over 50 years. Antique furniture abounds, and the lounge and the dining room both look out onto the terrace and sunken rose garden below. There is a large play area for older children and the moorland views are breathtaking.

ROOMS: 12 en suite (2 fmly) s £92-£95; d £175-£180 (incl. bkfst) **LB**
FACILITIES: Croquet lawn Large adventure playground ch fac
PARKING: 32 **NOTES:** No smoking in restaurant Closed Dec-Feb
CARDS:

LAUNCESTON, Cornwall & Isles of Scilly Map 03 SX38
See also Lifton

★★65% Eagle House

Castle St PL15 8BA
☎ 01566 772036 01566 772036
e-mail: eaglehousehotel@aol.com
Dir: *from Launceston on Holsworthy Rd follow brown signs for hotel*

Next to the castle, this elegant Georgian house dates back to 1767 and is within walking distance of all local amenities. Many of the bedrooms have wonderful views over the Cornish countryside. A fixed-price menu is served in the restaurant, and on Sunday evenings a more modest menu is available.

ROOMS: 14 en suite (1 fmly) s fr £34; d fr £60 (incl. bkfst) **LB**
FACILITIES: STV **CONF:** Thtr 190 Class 190 Board 190 **PARKING:** 100
NOTES: No dogs (ex guide dogs) Civ Wed 190
CARDS:

LAVENHAM, Suffolk Map 13 TL94

★★★★65% The Swan

MACDONALD HOTELS

High St CO10 9QA
☎ 0870 400 8116 01787 248286
e-mail: general.swanlavenham@macdonald-hotels.co.uk
Dir: *A12 to Colchester/Clacton, 2nd rdbt turn left onto A134 towards Sudbury. Right onto B1071*

The Swan is a collection of listed buildings dating back to the 14th century which have been lovingly restored to retain much of their original charm and character. Bedrooms are tastefully furnished and equipped with many thoughtful touches such as CD players. The elegant public rooms are full of character; they include a choice of cosy lounges as well as an intimate restaurant.

ROOMS: 51 en suite (4 fmly) (7 GF) No smoking in 4 bedrooms s £60-£159; d £120-£248 (incl. bkfst) **LB** **FACILITIES:** STV Croquet lawn Complimentary use of local leisure centre Xmas **CONF:** Thtr 40 Board 24 Del from £120 **PARKING:** 50 **NOTES:** No smoking in restaurant Civ Wed 60 **CARDS:**

★★71% Angel

Market Place CO10 9QZ
☎ 01787 247388 01787 248344
e-mail: angellav@aol.com
Dir: *from A14 take Bury East and Sudbury turn-off onto A143. After 4m take A1141 to Lavenham, Angel off High Street*

Delightful 15th-century inn situated in the heart of this historic medieval town overlooking the market place. The Angel is well known for its cuisine and offers an imaginative menu based on fresh ingredients. Bedrooms are tastefully furnished, attractively decorated and thoughtfully equipped. The spacious first-floor lounge has a magnificent ceiling.

ROOMS: 8 en suite (1 fmly) (1 GF) s fr £50; d fr £75 (incl. bkfst) **LB**
FACILITIES: Use of Lavenham Tennis Club facilities entertainment
PARKING: 5 **NOTES:** No smoking in restaurant Closed 25-26 Dec
CARDS:

LEA MARSTON, Warwickshire — Map 10 SP29

★★★★67% **Lea Marston Hotel & Leisure Complex**

Haunch Ln B76 0BY
☎ 01675 470468 Fax 01675 470871
e-mail: info@leamarstonhotel.co.uk
Dir: *M42 junct 9, take A4097 to Kingsbury. Hotel signposted 1.5m on right*

Excellent access to the motorway network and a good range of sports facilities make this hotel a popular choice for conferences and leisure breaks. Bedrooms are mostly set around an attractive quadrangle and are generously equipped. Diners can choose between the popular Sportsman's Lounge Bar and the elegant Adderley Restaurant.
ROOMS: 82 en suite (4 fmly) (46 GF) No smoking in 26 bedrooms s £65-£115; d £85-£135 (incl. bkfst) **LB FACILITIES: Spa** STV Indoor swimming (H) Golf 9 Tennis (hard) Sauna Solarium Gym Putting green Jacuzzi Golf driving range, Beauty Salon, Childrens play area, Golf simulator Xmas **CONF:** Thtr 140 Class 50 Board 30 Del from £135 **SERVICES:** Lift **PARKING:** 220 **NOTES:** No dogs (ex guide dogs) No smoking in restaurant Civ Wed 100 **CARDS:**

LEAMINGTON SPA (ROYAL), Warwickshire — Map 10 SP36

Top 200 - Hotel

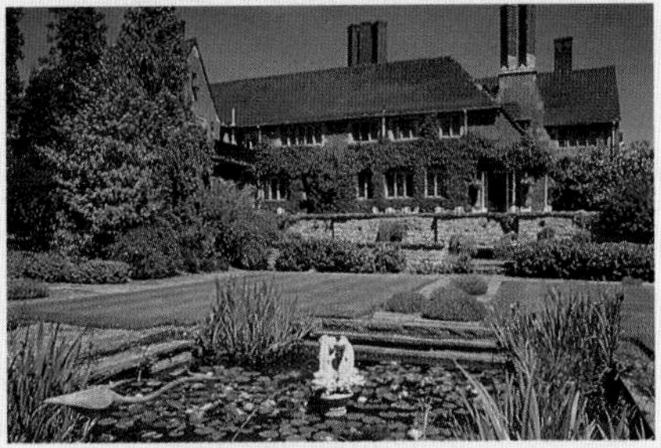

★★★ 3 Rosettes **Mallory Court**

Harbury Ln, Bishop's Tachbrook CV33 9QB
☎ 01926 330214 Fax 01926 451714
e-mail: reception@mallory.co.uk
Dir: *2m S off B4087 towards Harbury*

RELAIS & CHATEAUX

With its tranquil rural setting, this elegant Lutyens-style country house is an idyllic retreat. The hotel is set in ten acres of landscaped gardens and immaculate lawns, where guests can play croquet in fine weather. The two sumptuous lounges, drawing room, conservatory and elegant panelled restaurant provide ample opportunity for indulgence and relaxation.
continued

Bedrooms are nothing short of luxurious; each is individual in style, beautifully decorated and most have wonderful views of the gardens and surrounding countryside.
ROOMS: 18 en suite (1 fmly) s £175-£295; d £195-£350 (incl. cont bkfst) **LB FACILITIES:** STV Outdoor swimming Tennis (hard) Croquet lawn Use of nearby club facilities Xmas **CONF:** Thtr 35 Board 20 Del from £200 **PARKING:** 50 **NOTES:** No children 9yrs No smoking in restaurant Civ Wed 60
CARDS:

★★★70% ***Courtyard by Marriott Leamington Spa***

Olympus Av, Tachbrook Park CV34 6RJ
☎ 01926 425522 Fax 01926 881322
Dir: *from town centre follow signs for M40/A452 (Tachbrook Park). Over rdbt into Europa Way. Left to Olympus Ave*
Just a short distance from both Warwick and Leamington Spa, this modern hotel is conveniently situated for local businesses and tourist attractions. Bedrooms are furnished and decorated to a high standard providing a comprehensive range of extras. A friendly and helpful team efficiently delivers a professional service.
ROOMS: 91 en suite (14 fmly) No smoking in 48 bedrooms **FACILITIES:** STV Gym **CONF:** Thtr 70 Class 35 Board 30 **SERVICES:** Lift **PARKING:** 150 **CARDS:**

> Late for dinner?
> Quality Standards mean that last orders for dinner vary according to star rating and should be no earlier than:
> ★★ 7.00pm ★★★ 8.00pm ★★★★ 9.00pm
> ★★★★★ 10.00pm

LEAMINGTON SPA (ROYAL), continued

★★★67% Falstaff
16-20 Warwick New Rd CV32 5JQ
☎ 01926 312044 📠 01926 450574
e-mail: falstaff@meridianleisure.com
Dir: *M40 junct 13 or 14 follow signs for Leamington Spa. Over 4 rdbts then under bridge. Left into Princes Drive, then right at mini rdbt*

Bedrooms at this hotel come in a variety of sizes and styles and are all well equipped, with many thoughtful extras. An interesting range of dishes, both English and continental, is offered in the smartly appointed lounge bar and restaurant and 24-hour room service is available. Conference and banqueting facilities are extensive.
ROOMS: 63 en suite (2 fmly) (16 GF) No smoking in 13 bedrooms s £60-£80; d £70-£90 (incl. bkfst) **LB** **FACILITIES:** STV Arrangement with local Health Club Xmas **CONF:** Thtr 70 Class 30 Board 30 Del £110 **PARKING:** 50 **NOTES:** No smoking in restaurant Civ Wed 46
CARDS:

See advert on page 317

★★★65% The Best Western Royal Leamington Hotel
64 Upper Holly Walk CV32 4JL
☎ 01926 883777 📠 01926 330467
e-mail: royal@meridianleisure.com
Dir: *off A46 onto A412, left onto Clarendon Ave, then right into Clarendon St, then left, hotel on left*

This Victorian townhouse is situated near to the thriving shopping centre of Leamington Spa, yet retains the relaxed and peaceful feel of yesteryear. Bedrooms are individually appointed and well equipped; public areas are characterful and include a traditional residents' lounge. Guests can dine in the atmospheric brasserie, or choose from the room service menu.
ROOMS: 32 en suite (3 GF) No smoking in 10 bedrooms s £50-£80; d £60-£90 (incl. cont bkfst) **LB** **FACILITIES:** STV Xmas **CONF:** Thtr 40 Class 20 Board 20 Del from £125 **PARKING:** 20 **NOTES:** No dogs (ex guide dogs) No smoking in restaurant Civ Wed 40
CARDS:

See advert on opposite page

★★★63% Angel
143 Regent St CV32 4NZ
☎ 01926 881296 📠 01926 313853
e-mail: angelhotel143@hotmail.com
Dir: *in town centre at junct of Regent St and Holly Walk*
This centrally located hotel comes in two parts - the original inn and a more modern extension. Public rooms include a comfortable foyer lounge area, a smart restaurant and an informal bar. Bedrooms are individual in style, and, whether modern or traditional, have all the expected facilities.
ROOMS: 50 en suite (3 fmly) s £45-£65; d £60-£75 (incl. bkfst) **LB** **FACILITIES:** STV Xmas **CONF:** Thtr 70 Class 40 Board 40 Del from £85 **SERVICES:** Lift **PARKING:** 38 **NOTES:** No smoking in restaurant
CARDS:

★★★59% *Manor House*
Avenue Rd CV31 3NJ
☎ 01926 423251 📠 01926 425933
Dir: *M40/A452. At rdbt 3rd exit for Leamington. Hotel behind rail station*

This imposing building was once the headquarters of the Lawn Tennis Association and is now a characterful hotel featuring spacious and generously proportioned public areas. Bedrooms are well equipped, although some are more spacious and of a higher standard of décor than others. Plentiful car parking is available.
ROOMS: 53 en suite (2 fmly) No smoking in 19 bedrooms **FACILITIES:** Reduced price at nearby leisure club **CONF:** Thtr 200 Class 60 Board 50 **SERVICES:** Lift **PARKING:** 70 **NOTES:** No smoking in restaurant Civ Wed 96 **CARDS:**

★★73% Adams
22 Avenue Rd CV31 3PQ
☎ 01926 450742 📠 01926 313110
e-mail: bookings@adams-hotel.co.uk
Dir: *near library on A452*
This elegant Regency town house, originally built in 1827, is now a privately owned hotel offering high-quality accommodation, delicious home-cooked food and a relaxing setting. Public areas include a residents' bar with leather armchairs, and a pretty garden. Bedrooms are equipped with thoughtful extras, such as modem points and bathrobes.
ROOMS: 12 en suite (3 GF) **CONF:** Thtr 20 Class 14 Board 12 **PARKING:** 14 **NOTES:** No dogs No smoking in restaurant
CARDS:

LEATHERHEAD, Surrey
Map 06 TQ15

★★63% *Bookham Grange*
Little Bookham Common, Bookham KT23 3HS
☎ 01372 452742 📠 01372 450080
e-mail: bookhamgrange@easynet.co.uk
Dir: *off A246 at Bookham High Street onto Church Rd, 1st right after Bookham railway station*
Quietly situated in two and a half acres, this family-run hotel has

continued

the style of an English country house. As well as function and meeting rooms, there is a beamed bar, central sitting area and restaurant. The bedrooms are well equipped.
ROOMS: 27 en suite (5 fmly) **CONF:** Thtr 80 Class 24 Board 24
PARKING: 100 **NOTES:** No smoking in restaurant Civ Wed 100
CARDS:

○ Travelodge

Travelodge

The Swan Centre, High St
☎ 0870 191 1757
ROOMS: 71 en suite **NOTES:** Due to open April 2004

LEDBURY, Herefordshire

Map 10 SO73

★★★72% Feathers

High St HR8 1DS
☎ 01531 635266 01531 638955
e-mail: mary@feathers-ledbury.co.uk
Dir: *S from Worcester on A449, E from Hereford on A438, N from Gloucester on A417. Hotel in High St*

A wealth of old-fashioned charm greets the guest at this historic timber-framed hostelry, set in the High Street in the middle of town. The comfortably equipped bedrooms are authentically and tastefully decorated while well-prepared meals can be taken in Fuggles Brasserie with its adjoining bar. Facilities include a leisure centre and a function suite.
ROOMS: 19 en suite (2 fmly) No smoking in 2 bedrooms s £72.50-£90; d £99.50-£150 (incl. bkfst) **LB** **FACILITIES:** STV Indoor swimming (H) Solarium Gym Jacuzzi Steam room Xmas **CONF:** Thtr 140 Class 80 Board 40 Del £130 **PARKING:** 30 **NOTES:** Civ Wed 120
CARDS:

See advert on this page

★★68% The Verzons Country Inn & Restaurant

THE INDEPENDENTS

Hereford Rd, Trumpet HR8 2PZ
☎ 01531 670381 01531 670830
e-mail: sales@theverzons.co.uk
Dir: *2m W of Ledbury on A438*
This large country house dates back to 1790 and stands in extensive gardens with far-reaching views over the Malvern Hills. Bedrooms are well appointed and spacious, and one has a four-poster. Public areas include a characterful bar and the award-winning restaurant which are popular with locals, and a function and meeting room.
ROOMS: 8 en suite (1 fmly) s £45-£68; d £58-£98 (incl. bkfst) **LB** **FACILITIES:** STV Xmas **CONF:** Thtr 50 Class 25 Board 20 Del from £90 **PARKING:** 60 **NOTES:** No dogs (ex guide dogs)
CARDS:

AA Rosette Award for culinary excellence

LEDBURY, continued

★★ Leadon House
Ross Rd HR8 2LP
☎ 01531 631199 01531 631476
e-mail: leadon.house@amserve.net
Dir: *On A449, 500yds of by pass on right*
ROOMS: 6 en suite (2 fmly) No smoking in all bedrooms s £39-£60; d £58-£80 (incl. bkfst) **LB PARKING:** 8 **NOTES:** No dogs No smoking in restaurant **CARDS:**

LEEDS, West Yorkshire Map 19 SE23
See also Gomersal & Shipley

★★★★★66% De Vere Oulton Hall
Rothwell Ln, Oulton LS26 8HN
☎ 0113 282 1000 0113 282 8066
e-mail: oulton.hall@devere-hotels.com
Dir: *2m from M62 junct 30 on left, or 1m from M1 junct 44. Follow Castleford and Pontefract signs on A639*

Surrounded by the beautiful Yorkshire Dales, yet within 15 minutes of the city centre, this elegant 19th-century house really does offer the best of both worlds. Impressive features of the hotel include the formal gardens, which have been faithfully recreated to their original design, and the galleried Great Hall. The hotel also offers a choice of dining options and golfers can book preferential tee times at the adjacent golf club.
ROOMS: 152 en suite No smoking in 144 bedrooms s £140; d £160 (incl. bkfst) **LB FACILITIES:** STV Indoor swimming (H) Sauna Solarium Gym Croquet lawn Jacuzzi Beauty therapy Aerobics Xmas **CONF:** Thtr 350 Class 150 Board 40 Del from £125 **SERVICES:** Lift **PARKING:** 260 **NOTES:** No smoking in restaurant **CARDS:**

★★★★77% The Thorpe Park Hotel
Century Way, Thorpe Park LS15 8ZB
☎ 0113 264 1000 0113 264 1010
e-mail: thorpepark@shirehotels.co.uk
Dir: *M1 junct 46 left at top of slip road, then right at rdbt into Thorpe Park*

Conveniently close to the M1, bedrooms in this newly built property are modern in style and facilities. The terrace and courtyard offer all-day casual dining and refreshments, and the restaurant features a Mediterranean themed menu. There is also a state-of-the-art spa and leisure facility. *Shire Hotels – AA Hotel Group of the Year 2003-2004.*
ROOMS: 123 en suite (31 GF) No smoking in 80 bedrooms s £90-£140; d £130-£160 (incl. bkfst) **LB FACILITIES: Spa** STV Indoor swimming (H) Sauna Solarium Gym Steam room, Health & beauty rooms, Swimming pool supervised, Activity studio Xmas **CONF:** BC Thtr 200 Class 100 Board 50 Del from £135 **SERVICES:** Lift air con **PARKING:** 200 **NOTES:** No dogs (ex guide dogs) No smoking in restaurant Civ Wed 80 **CARDS:**

See advert on opposite page

Town House

★★★★ Radisson SAS Leeds
No 1 The Light, The Headrow LS1 8TL
☎ 0113 236 6000 0113 236 6100
e-mail: deborah.heather@radissonsas.com
Dir: *follow city centre 'loop' up Park Row, straight at lights onto Cockeridge St, hotel on left*
Situated in the new shopping complex known as 'The Light', the hotel occupies a converted building that was formerly the headquarters of the Leeds Permanent Building Society. Three styles of décor have been used in the bedrooms: Art Deco, Hi Tech and Italian. All rooms are air-conditioned, with excellent business facilities. The lobby bar area serves substantial meals and is ideal for relaxation.
ROOMS: 147 en suite No smoking in 130 bedrooms
FACILITIES: STV **CONF:** Thtr 60 Class 35 Board 16 **SERVICES:** Lift air con **PARKING:** 420 **NOTES:** No dogs (ex guide dogs)
CARDS:

Town House

★★★★ Haley's Hotel & Restaurant
Shire Oak Rd, Headingley LS6 2DE
☎ 0113 278 4446 0113 275 3342
e-mail: info@haleys.co.uk
Dir: *from city centre follow signs to University on A660. After 1.5m right in Headingley between HSBC and Starbucks*
Although only ten minutes from the city centre, this hotel has a real country feel to it. The elegant bedrooms offer tasteful décor, some with interesting period furnishings. The modern restaurant is decorated with contemporary works of art (all for sale) is the setting for imaginative meals; there is a choice of comfortable lounges.
ROOMS: 22 en suite 6 annexe en suite (3 fmly) (2 GF) No smoking in 10 bedrooms s £70-£110; d £115-£145 (incl. bkfst) **LB FACILITIES:** STV **CONF:** BC Thtr 40 Class 20 Board 25 Del from £135 **PARKING:** 29 **NOTES:** No dogs (ex guide dogs) No smoking in restaurant Closed 26-30 Dec RS Sun evening & Mon-Sat lunch Civ Wed 100 **CARDS:**

See advert on opposite page

★★★★68% Leeds Marriott Hotel
4 Trevelyan Square, Boar Ln LS1 6ET
☎ 0113 236 6366 0113 236 6367
Dir: *M621/M1 junct 3. Follow signs for city centre on A653. Stay in right lane. Energis building on left, right follow signs to hotel*
With a charming courtyard setting in the heart of the city, this modern, elegant hotel provides the perfect venue for shopping and sightseeing. Air-conditioned bedrooms are tastefully

continued

decorated and offer excellent workspace. Public areas include an informal bar, a restaurant and a smart leisure club.
ROOMS: 244 en suite No smoking in 194 bedrooms s £109-£125; d £109-£125 **LB** **FACILITIES:** STV Indoor swimming (H) Sauna Solarium Gym Jacuzzi Subsidised use of NCP car park, Swimming pool supervised **CONF:** Thtr 280 Class 120 Board 80 Del from £129 **SERVICES:** Lift air con **NOTES:** No dogs (ex guide dogs) Civ Wed 280
CARDS:

★★★★68% **The Queens**

PARAMOUNT GROUP OF HOTELS

City Square LS1 1PL
☎ 0113 243 1323 & 0870 400 8696
Fax 0113 242 5154
e-mail: queens.reservations@lemeridien.com
Dir: *Follow signs for city centre, hotel adjacent to railway station*
A legacy from the golden age of railways, this grand Victorian hotel has retained much of its original splendour and is located in the very heart of the city. Public rooms include the spacious Piano Bar, which has themed nights and special events, a range of function rooms and the restaurant.
ROOMS: 199 en suite No smoking in 72 bedrooms **FACILITIES:** STV **CONF:** Thtr 600 Class 250 Board 40 Del from £140 **SERVICES:** Lift **PARKING:** 88 **NOTES:** Civ Wed 450
CARDS:

★★★★61% **Le Meridien Metropole**

Le MERIDIEN

King St LS1 2HQ
☎ 0113 245 0841 Fax 0113 242 5156
e-mail: abrown@lemeridien.com
Dir: *from M1, M62 and M621 follow city centre signs. Take A65 into Wellington St. At 1st traffic island right into King St, hotel on right*
Said to be the best example of this type of building in the city, this splendid terracotta-fronted hotel is centrally located and convenient for the railway station. The hotel also benefits from the availability of a number of car parking spaces. Staff are genuinely cheerful and obliging, helping to cultivate a friendly and welcoming environment for guests.
ROOMS: 118 en suite No smoking in 98 bedrooms s fr £110; d fr £120 **LB** **FACILITIES:** STV **CONF:** BC Thtr 250 Class 100 Board 80 **SERVICES:** Lift **PARKING:** 40 **NOTES:** No dogs (ex guide dogs) No smoking in restaurant RS 24 Dec-1 Jan Civ Wed 200
CARDS:

★★★80% ❀❀ **Hazlewood Castle**
Paradise Ln, Hazlewood LS24 9NJ
☎ 01937 535353 Fax 01937 530630
e-mail: info@hazlewood-castle.co.uk
(For full entry see Tadcaster)

★★★75% ❀ **Malmaison Hotel**

Malmaison

Sovereign Quay LS1 1DQ
☎ 0113 398 1000 Fax 0113 398 1002
e-mail: leeds@malmaison.com
Dir: *M621/M1 junct 3, follow signs to city centre. At KPMG building, right into Sovereign St. Hotel at end of street on right.*
Close to the waterfront, this stylish property offers striking bedrooms with CD players and air conditioning. The bar leads into a brasserie, where guests can choose between a full three-course meal or a substantial snack. Service is both willing and friendly. A small fitness centre and impressive meeting rooms complete the package.
ROOMS: 100 en suite No smoking in 70 bedrooms s £125-£140; d £125-£140 **LB** **FACILITIES:** STV Gym Xmas **CONF:** Thtr 40 Class 20 Board 28 Del from £165 **SERVICES:** Lift air con **NOTES:** No dogs (ex guide dogs) **CARDS:**

GF Indicates the number of bedrooms at ground floor level.

LEEDS, continued

★★★73% ⊛ Milford
A1 Great North Rd, Peckfield LS25 5LQ
☎ 01977 681800 ▯ 01977 681245
e-mail: enquiries@mlh.co.uk
(For full entry see Garforth)

★★★70% Novotel Leeds Centre
4 Whitehall, Whitehall Quay LS1 4HR
☎ 0113 242 6446 ▯ 0113 242 6445
e-mail: H3270@accor-hotels.com

Dir: *exit M621 junct 3 follow signs to train station. Turn into Aire St and turn left at lights*
With minimilistic flair and style, this contemporary hotel provides quality, value-for-money accommodation in the city centre. Spacious bedrooms reflect the modern theme of the hotel, while public areas provide deep leather sofas and an eye-catching waterfall in reception. Light snacks are provided in the airy bar and the restaurant doubles as a bistro.
ROOMS: 195 en suite (60 fmly) No smoking in 130 bedrooms s £65-£105; d £65-£105 **LB** **FACILITIES:** STV Sauna Gym Play station computers in rooms & play area Steam room Xmas **CONF:** Thtr 80 Class 50 Board 50 Del from £120 **SERVICES:** Lift air con **PARKING:** 70
NOTES: Civ Wed **CARDS:**

★★★68% Golden Lion
2 Lower Briggate LS1 4AE
☎ 0113 243 6454 ▯ 0113 242 9327
e-mail: info@goldenlion-hotel-leeds.com
Dir: *between junct 16, junct 17*
This smartly presented hotel is set in a Victorian building on the south side of the city. The well-equipped bedrooms offer a choice of standard or executive grades. Staff are friendly and helpful, ensuring a warm and welcoming atmosphere. Free overnight parking is provided in a 24-hour car park by the hotel.
ROOMS: 89 en suite (5 fmly) No smoking in 46 bedrooms s £50-£110; d £70-£135 (incl. bkfst) **LB** **FACILITIES:** STV Xmas **CONF:** Thtr 120 Class 65 Board 45 Del from £135 **SERVICES:** Lift **PARKING:** 2
CARDS:

★★★66% The Merrion
Merrion Centre LS2 8NH
☎ 0113 243 9191 ▯ 0113 242 3527
e-mail: info@merrion-hotel-leeds.com
Dir: *from M1, M62 and A61 onto city loop road to junct 7*
This smart modern hotel benefits from a city centre location. Bedrooms are smartly appointed and thoughtfully equipped for both business and leisure guests. Public areas include a

continued

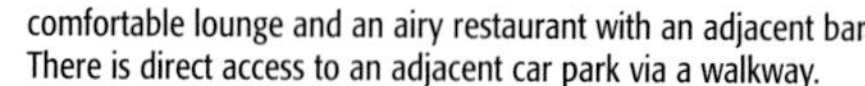
comfortable lounge and an airy restaurant with an adjacent bar. There is direct access to an adjacent car park via a walkway.
ROOMS: 109 en suite No smoking in 48 bedrooms s £90-£110; d £110-£125 **LB** **FACILITIES:** STV Discount at local leisure club Xmas **CONF:** Thtr 80 Class 25 Board 25 Del from £60 **SERVICES:** Lift
CARDS:

A ★★★ The Butlers Hotel
40 Cardigan Rd, Headingley LS6 3AG
☎ 0113 274 4755 ▯ 0113 274 4755
e-mail: info@butlershotel.co.uk
Dir: *from A660 follow signs for Headingley Stadium, then Hotel signs*
ROOMS: 15 en suite (2 GF) No smoking in all bedrooms s £44.95-£85; d £64.95-£100 (incl. bkfst) **LB** **FACILITIES:** STV **PARKING:** 12
NOTES: No smoking in restaurant **CARDS:**

★★75% Aragon
250 Stainbeck Ln LS7 2PS
☎ 0113 275 9306 ▯ 0113 275 7166
e-mail: sales@aragonhotel.co.uk
Dir: *follow A61 towards Harrogate. At 2nd rdbt left into Stainbeck Ln*
The welcoming proprietors encourage a relaxed, informal atmosphere throughout this smartly presented hotel, in a peaceful location in a leafy suburb of Leeds. Bedrooms are rich in style, comfort and facilities. There is a comfortable lounge and a small bar that overlook the gardens.
ROOMS: 12 en suite (2 fmly) (1 GF) No smoking in all bedrooms s £49.90-£56.90; d £59.90-£69.90 (incl. bkfst) **LB** **PARKING:** 20
NOTES: No dogs No smoking in restaurant Closed 25 Dec-1 Jan
CARDS:

U Park Plaza Leeds
Boar Ln LS1 5NS
☎ 0113 380 4000 ▯ 0113 380 4100
e-mail: pplinfo@parkplazahotels
Dir: *Follow signs for Leeds city centre*
At the time of going to press, the star classification for this hotel was not confirmed. Please refer to the AA internet site www.theAA.com for current information.
ROOMS: 187 en suite s £130-£225; d £130-£225 **LB** **FACILITIES:** Xmas **CONF:** Thtr 230 Class 90 Board 34 Del from £130 **SERVICES:** Lift air con **NOTES:** No smoking in restaurant
CARDS:

⌂ Express by Holiday Inn Leeds
Cavendish St LS3 1LY
☎ 0113 242 6200 ▯ 0113 242 6300
e-mail: leeds-res@khl.uk.com
Dir: *M621 junct 2, take A643 to city centre. At large rdbt 3rd exit signed A58(M). 1st left onto A65 and turn left. Hotel on right*

A modern hotel ideal for families and business travellers. Fresh and uncomplicated, the spacious bedrooms include Sky TV, power shower

continued

and tea and coffee-making facilities. Continental buffet breakfast is included in the room rate; other meals may be taken at the nearby family pub or restaurant. For further details and the Express by Holiday Inn phone number, consult the Hotel Groups pages.
ROOMS: 112 en suite (incl. cont bkfst) s £55-£68; d £55-£68
CONF: Thtr 35 Class 20 Board 25

⇧ Express by Holiday Inn Leeds East

Aberford Rd, Oulton LS26 8EJ
☎ 0113 282 6201 📠 0113 288 7210
e-mail: ebhi-leeds-east@btconnect.com
Dir: *hotel 0.5m on A642, on 1st rdbt*

A modern hotel ideal for families and business travellers. Fresh and uncomplicated, the spacious bedrooms include Sky TV, power shower and tea and coffee-making facilities. Continental buffet breakfast is included in the room rate; other meals may be taken at the nearby family pub or restaurant. For further details and the Express by Holiday Inn phone number, consult the Hotel Groups pages.
ROOMS: 77 en suite **CONF:** Thtr 30 Class 24 Board 16

⇧ Innkeeper's Lodge Leeds North

Bruntcliffe Rd, Morley LS27 0LY
☎ 0113 253 3115 📠 0113 253 9365
Dir: *M62 junct 27 take A650 towards Morley. On A650/A643 junct*

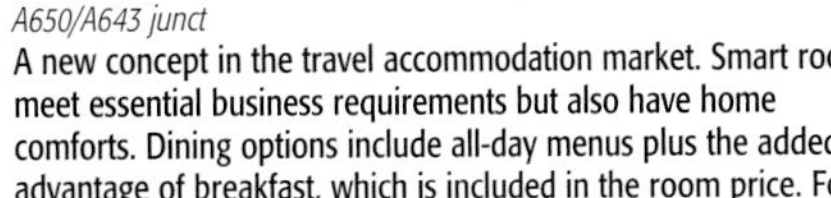

A new concept in the travel accommodation market. Smart rooms meet essential business requirements but also have home comforts. Dining options include all-day menus plus the added advantage of breakfast, which is included in the room price. For further details, consult the Hotel Groups page.
ROOMS: 32 en suite

⇧ Premier Lodge (Leeds City West)

City West One Office Park, Gelderd Rd LS12 6LX
☎ 0870 9906448 📠 0870 9906449
Premier Lodge offers modern, well-equipped, en suite accommodation suitable for both business and leisure travellers. Meals can be taken at the adjacent popular restaurant and bar, which is fully licensed. For further details, consult the Hotel Groups page.
ROOMS: 125 en suite s £48; d £48

⇧ Travel Inn (Leeds City Centre)

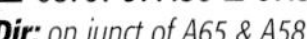

Citygate, Wellington St LS3 1LW
☎ 08701 977150 📠 0113 242 8105
Dir: *on junct of A65 & A58*

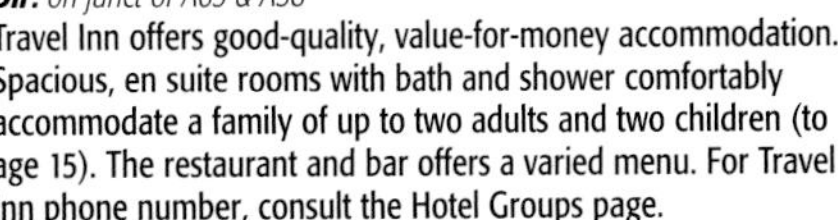

Travel Inn offers good-quality, value-for-money accommodation. Spacious, en suite rooms with bath and shower comfortably accommodate a family of up to two adults and two children (to age 15). The restaurant and bar offers a varied menu. For Travel Inn phone number, consult the Hotel Groups page.
ROOMS: 139 en suite s £49.95-£54.95; d £49.95-£54.95
CONF: Class 16 Board 16

⇧ Travel Inn Leeds (East)

Selby Rd, Whitkirk LS15 7AY
☎ 08701 977151 📠 0113 232 6195
Dir: *M1 junct 46 towards Leeds. At 2nd rdbt follow Temple Newsam signs. Inn 500mtrs on right*
Travel Inn offers good-quality, value-for-money accommodation. Spacious, en suite rooms with bath and shower comfortably accommodate a family of up to two adults and two children (to age 15). The restaurant and bar offers a varied menu. For ravel Inn phone number, consult the Hotel Groups page.
ROOMS: 87 en suite s £44.95; d £44.95

⇧ Travelodge Leeds (Central)

Blaydes Court, Blaydes Yard, off Swinegate LS1 4AD
☎ 08700 850 950

Travelodge offers good quality, good value, modern accommodation. Ideal for families, the spacious, en suite bedrooms include remote-control TV, tea and coffee-making facilities, luxury beds and free morning newspaper. Meals can be taken at the nearby family restaurant. For further details and the Travelodge phone number, consult the Hotel Groups page.
ROOMS: 100 en suite s fr £42.95; d fr £42.95

⇧ Travelodge Leeds (East)

☎ 08700 850 950
Travelodge offers good quality, good value, modern accommodation. Ideal for families, the spacious, en suite bedrooms include remote-control TV, tea and coffee-making facilities, luxury beds and free morning newspaper. Meals can be taken at the nearby family restaurant. For further details and the Travelodge phone number, consult the Hotel Groups page.
ROOMS: 60 en suite s fr £42.95; d fr £42.95

LEEDS/BRADFORD AIRPORT, West Yorkshire   Map 19 SE23

⇧ Travel Inn (Leeds Airport)

Victoria Av, Yeadon LS19 7AW
☎ 08701 977153 📠 0113 202 9383
Dir: *on A658, near Leeds/Bradford Airport*
Travel Inn offers good-quality, value-for-money accommodation. Spacious, en suite rooms with bath and shower comfortably accommodate a family of up to two adults and two children (to age 15). The restaurant and bar offers a varied menu. For Travel Inn phone number, consult the Hotel Groups page.
ROOMS: 40 en suite s £44.95; d £44.95 **CONF:** Thtr 12

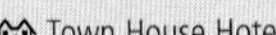

Town House Hotel
Country House Hotel
⇧ Travel Accommodation

LEEK, Staffordshire

Map 16 SJ95

★★★63% *Hotel Rudyard*

Lake Rd, Rudyard ST13 8RN
☎ 01538 306208 🖷 01538 306208

This large stone-built Victorian property is set in extensive wooded grounds in the centre of Rudyard. It provides modern and well-equipped accommodation including a four-poster bedroom. There is a function room, a large carvery restaurant and a traditional bar.

ROOMS: 15 en suite (2 fmly) No smoking in 2 bedrooms **CONF:** Thtr 80 Class 60 Board 40 **PARKING:** 100 **NOTES:** No smoking in restaurant **CARDS:**

★★70% Three Horseshoes Inn & Restaurant

Buxton Rd, Blackshaw Moor ST13 8TW
☎ 01538 300296 🖷 01538 300320
Dir: *2m N of Leek on A53*

A family owned hostelry in spacious grounds, which includes a beer garden and children's play area. The non-smoking bedrooms are tastefully appointed and furnished in keeping with the character of the hotel. The public areas include a choice of bars and eating options. The Bistro is open only for dinner.

ROOMS: 6 en suite No smoking in all bedrooms s £45-£65; d £60-£75 (incl. bkfst) **LB** **CONF:** Thtr 60 Class 50 Board 25 **PARKING:** 80 **NOTES:** No dogs (ex guide dogs) No smoking in restaurant Closed 24 Dec-1 Jan **CARDS:**

LEICESTER, Leicestershire

Map 11 SK50

See also Rothley

★★★74% Belmont House

Best Western

De Montfort St LE1 7GR
☎ 0116 254 4773 🖷 0116 247 0804
e-mail: info@belmonthotel.co.uk
Dir: *from A6, take 1st right after rail station. Hotel 200yds on left*

An attractive property situated within easy walking distance of the railway station and city centre. Extensive public rooms are smartly appointed and include a superb conservatory walkway, the informal Bowie's Bistro, formal dining within the Cherry Restaurant and a relaxed atmosphere in Jamie's Bar and Will's Lounge Bar. Bedrooms styles vary; each room is individually appointed and well equipped.

ROOMS: 77 en suite (7 fmly) No smoking in 57 bedrooms s £55-£97; d £80-£107 **LB** **FACILITIES:** Gym **CONF:** Thtr 175 Class 75 Board 65 Del from £145 **SERVICES:** Lift **PARKING:** 75 **NOTES:** No smoking in restaurant Closed 25-26 Dec Civ Wed 140 **CARDS:**

★★★68% Regency

360 London Rd LE2 2PL
☎ 0116 270 9634 🖷 0116 270 1375
e-mail: info@the-regency-hotel.com
Dir: *on A6, 1.5m from city centre*

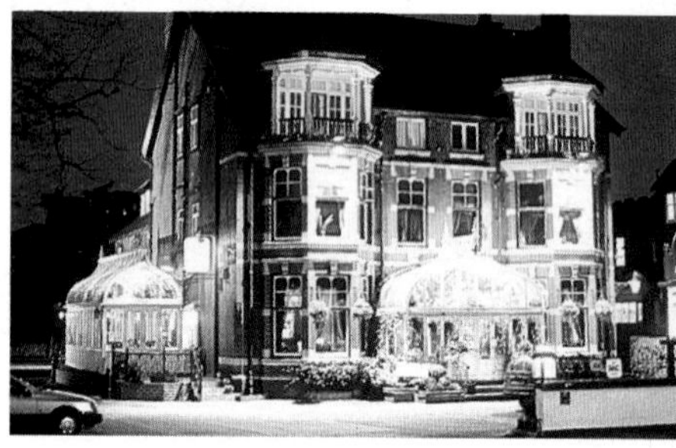

This friendly hotel is located on the edge of town and provides smart accommodation suitable for both business and leisure guests. The food options include an airy conservatory brasserie and the formal restaurant; a relaxing lounge and bar are also available, along with good conference and banqueting facilities. Bedrooms vary in size and style, and include some spacious and stylishly appointed rooms.

ROOMS: 32 en suite (4 fmly) s £38-£60; d £56-£70 (incl. bkfst) **FACILITIES:** STV entertainment Xmas **CONF:** Thtr 70 Class 50 Board 30 Del £90 **PARKING:** 40 **NOTES:** No dogs (ex guide dogs) **CARDS:**

★★★68% *Time Out Hotel*

corus hotels

Enderby Rd, Blaby LE8 4GD
☎ 0116 278 7898 🖷 0116 278 1974
e-mail: timeout@corushotels.co.uk
Dir: *M1 junct 21, A5460 to Leicester. 4th exit at 1st rdbt, ahead at 2nd, left at 3rd. Follow signs to Blaby, over 4th rdbt. Hotel on left*

Situated in a quiet location on the outskirts of the city, yet remaining convenient for the adjacent link road. Public areas include a bar brasserie, Hunters Restaurant, various meeting

continued

rooms and an extensive gym and indoor pool. Bedrooms are comfortably appointed and generally quite spacious, and many are decorated to very high standards.
ROOMS: 48 en suite (5 fmly) No smoking in 30 bedrooms
FACILITIES: Spa STV Indoor swimming (H) Sauna Solarium Gym Steam room **CONF:** Thtr 70 Class 30 Board 36 **PARKING:** 110
NOTES: Civ Wed 70 **CARDS:**

★★★66% *Leicester Stage Hotel*

Leicester Rd, Wigston LE18 1JW
☎ 0116 288 6161 📠 0116 257 3900
e-mail: reservations@stagehotel.co.uk
Dir: *M69/M1 junct 21 take ring road S to Leicester. Take Oadby and Wigston signs, right onto A5199 towards Northampton. Hotel on left*

This unusual, purpose-built, glass-fronted building is situated to the south of the city centre. Bedrooms come in a variety of styles and include executive rooms as well as four-poster bridal suites.

continued

Open-plan public areas include a lounge bar, restaurant and a further seating area in the entrance hall. Ample car parking and the swimming pool are an added bonus.
ROOMS: 75 en suite (10 fmly) No smoking in 30 bedrooms
FACILITIES: STV Indoor swimming (H) Sauna Gym Jacuzzi **CONF:** Thtr 450 Class 200 Board 100 **PARKING:** 200 **NOTES:** No dogs (ex guide dogs) Civ Wed 300 **CARDS:**

See advert under KEGWORTH and on this page

★★61% Gables

368 London Rd LE2 2PN
☎ 0116 270 6969 📠 0116 270 3988
e-mail: gableshtl@aol.com
Dir: *0.5m city side of junct of A563 SE and A6*

This privately owned friendly hotel is located south of the city centre and is conveniently placed for the university. Bedrooms are traditionally furnished and well equipped for both business and leisure guests. The public rooms include a restaurant and a cosy lounge bar; an adjoining room serves as a popular venue for business meetings and functions.
ROOMS: 30 en suite (9 fmly) (4 GF) No smoking in 5 bedrooms s £33-£40; d £46-£50 (incl. bkfst) **CONF:** Thtr 60 Class 20 Board 30 Del from £75 **PARKING:** 29 **NOTES:** No dogs (ex guide dogs) No smoking in restaurant **CARDS:**

U *Holiday Inn Leicester*

St Nicholas Circle LE1 5LX
☎ 0116 253 1161 📠 0116 251 3169
At the time of going to press, the classification for this hotel was not confirmed. Please refer to the AA internet site www.theAA.com for current information.
ROOMS: 188 en suite

LEICESTER, continued

Holiday Inn Leicester - West

Braunstone Ln East LE3 2FW
☎ 0870 400 9051 📠 0116 282 3623
e-mail: leicester@ichotelsgroup.co.uk
Dir: *M1 junct 21, at M69 junct take A5460 towards city. After 1m right at traffic lights to hotel*
At the time of going to press, the classification for this hotel was not confirmed. Please refer to the AA internet site www.theAA.com for current information.
ROOMS: 172 en suite (35 fmly) No smoking in 110 bedrooms
FACILITIES: STV **CONF:** Thtr 100 Class 54 Board 45 **SERVICES:** Lift
PARKING: 300 **NOTES:** No smoking in restaurant
CARDS:

Campanile Leicester

St Matthew's Way LE1 2BU
☎ 020 8572 3663 (CR)
e-mail: leicester@evergure.co.uk
Dir: *NE of Leicester, on inner ring road, A594*

This modern building offers accommodation in smart, well-equipped bedrooms, all with en suite bathrooms. Refreshments may be taken at the informal Bistro. For further details and the Campanile phone number, consult the Hotel Groups page.
ROOMS: 90 en suite s £48.95; d £48.95 **CONF:** Del from £21

Hotel Ibis

St Georges Way, Constitution Hill LE1 1PL
☎ 0116 248 7200 📠 0116 262 0880
e-mail: H3061@accor-hotels.com
Dir: *A5460 follow signs for railway station. Left at Mercedes garage*
Modern, budget hotel offering comfortable accommodation in bright and practical bedrooms. Breakfast is self-service and dinner is available in the restaurant. For further details, consult the Hotel Groups page.
ROOMS: 94 en suite s £43.95-£48.95; d £43.95-£48.95

Premier Lodge (Leciester West)

Leicester Rd, Glenfield LE3 8HB
☎ 0870 9906520 📠 0870 9906521
Dir: *off A50, 4m from Leicester city centre. Hotel on slip road that leads to County Hall*
Premier Lodge offers modern, well-equipped, en suite accommodation suitable for both business and leisure travellers. Meals can be taken at the adjacent popular restaurant and bar, which is fully licensed. For further details, consult the Hotel Groups page.
ROOMS: 43 en suite s £48; d £48 **CONF:** Thtr 30 Class 20 Board 20

Premier Lodge (Leicester Central)

Heathley Park, Groby Rd LE3 9QH
☎ 0870 9906398 📠 0870 9906399
Premier Lodge offers modern, well-equipped, en suite accommodation suitable for both business and leisure travellers. Meals can be taken at the adjacent popular restaurant and bar, which is fully licensed. For further details, consult the Hotel Groups page.
ROOMS: 72 en suite s £48; d £48

Premier Lodge (Leicester South)

Glen Rise, Oadby LE2 4RG
☎ 0870 9906452 📠 0870 9906453
Dir: *M1 junct 21. Follow A563 to Market Harborough & Leicester Racecourse. Then A6 through Oadby. 'Horse and Hounds' on right*
Premier Lodge offers modern, well-equipped, en suite accommodation suitable for both business and leisure travellers. Meals can be taken at the adjacent popular restaurant and bar, which is fully licensed. For further details, consult the Hotel Groups page.
ROOMS: 30 en suite s £48; d £48 **CONF:** Thtr 10 Class 8 Board 10 Del from £80

Travel Inn (Leicester South)

Hinckley Rd, Leicester Forest East LE3 3GD
☎ 08701 977155 📠 0116 239 3429
Dir: *M1 junct 21 onto A5460. At major junct (Holiday Inn on right), left Braunstone Lane. After 2m left onto A47 towards Hinkley. 400yds on left*
Travel Inn offers good-quality, value-for-money accommodation. Spacious, en suite rooms with bath and shower comfortably accommodate a family of up to two adults and two children (to age 15). The restaurant and bar offers a varied menu. For further details and the Travel Inn phone number, consult the Hotel Groups page.
ROOMS: 40 en suite s £44.95; d £44.95 **CONF:** Thtr 50 Board 25

Travel Inn Leicester (Thorpe Astley)

Meridian Business Park, Meridian Way, Braunstone LE19 1LU
☎ 08701 977154 📠 0116 282 7486
Dir: *M1 junct 21 follow signs for A563 (outer ring road) W to Thorpe Astley. Slip road past Texaco garage, Travel Inn on left.*
Travel Inn offers good-quality, value-for-money accommodation. Spacious, en suite rooms with bath and shower comfortably accommodate a family of up to two adults and two children (to age 15). The restaurant and bar offers a varied menu. For further details and the Travel Inn phone number, consult the Hotel Groups page.
ROOMS: 51 en suite s £44.95; d £44.95 **CONF:** Class 20 Board 20

LEICESTER FOREST MOTORWAY SERVICE AREA (M1), Leicestershire

Map 11 SK50

Days Inn

Leicester Forest East, Junction 21 M1 LE3 3GB
☎ 0116 239 0534 📠 0116 239 0546
e-mail: leicester.hotel@welcomebreak.co.uk
Dir: *on M1 northbound between junct 21 & 21A*
This modern building offers accommodation in smart, spacious and well-equipped bedrooms, suitable for families and business travellers, and all with en suite bathrooms. Continental breakfast is available and other refreshments may be taken at the nearby family restaurant. For further details and the Days Inn phone number, consult the Hotel Groups page.
ROOMS: 92 en suite s £45-£60; d £45-£60 **CONF:** Board 10

LEIGH DELAMERE MOTORWAY SERVICE AREA (M4), Wiltshire

Map 04 ST87

Travelodge Chippenham

Travelodge

SN14 6LB
☎ 08700 850 950 📠 01666 837112
Dir: *Between junct 17 & 18 on M4*
Travelodge offers good quality, good value, modern accommodation. Ideal for families, the spacious, en suite bedrooms include remote-control TV, tea and coffee-making facilities, luxury beds and free morning newspaper. Meals can be taken at the nearby family restaurant. For further details and the Travelodge phone number, consult the Hotel Groups page.
ROOMS: 69 en suite s fr £42.95; d fr £42.95

LENHAM, Kent

Map 07 TQ85

Top 200 - Hotel

★★★★ Chilston Park

Sandway ME17 2BE HANDPICKED
☎ 01622 859803 📠 01622 858588
e-mail: chilstonpark@handpicked.co.uk
Dir: *from A20 into Lenham village, turn right onto High St, pass rail station on right, 1st left, over crossroads, hotel 0.25 mile on left*
This elegant hotel is set in delightful meadows and parkland. The lounge displays a large collection of paintings and antiques creating a unique feel to the property. The sunken Venetian style restaurant serves contemporary quality cuisine. Bedrooms are all individual, some with four-poster beds, and many with garden views.
ROOMS: 30 en suite 23 annexe en suite s £90-£140; d £90-£140 **LB FACILITIES:** STV Tennis (hard) Fishing Croquet lawn Xmas **CONF:** Thtr 100 Class 40 Board 40 Del from £195 **SERVICES:** Lift **PARKING:** 100 **NOTES:** No smoking in restaurant Civ Wed 70 **CARDS:**

LEOMINSTER, Herefordshire

Map 10 SO45

★★★65% Talbot

Best Western

West St HR6 8EP
☎ 01568 616347 📠 01568 614880
e-mail: talbot@bestwestern.co.uk
Dir: *from A49, A44 or A4112, hotel in centre of town*
This charming former coaching inn is located in the town centre and offers an ideal base from which to explore this delightful area. Public areas boast original beams and antique furniture, and include an atmospheric bar and elegant restaurant. Bedrooms are comfortably furnished and equipped and there are also facilities available for private functions and conferences.

continued

Talbot Hotel

ROOMS: 20 en suite (3 fmly) No smoking in 6 bedrooms s £45-£50; d £64-£70 **LB FACILITIES:** Xmas **CONF:** Thtr 150 Class 25 Board 28 Del from £80 **PARKING:** 20 **NOTES:** No smoking in restaurant RS 25 Dec **CARDS:**

★★65% Royal Oak

South St HR6 8JA
☎ 01568 612610 📠 01568 612710
e-mail: reservations@royaloakhotel.net
Dir: *junct A44/A49 in town centre*
This privately owned hotel is conveniently located in the town centre. It is personally run in an informal manner and provides warm and friendly hospitality. Public areas have charm and

continued on p330

LEOMINSTER, continued

character and include a bistro style restaurant, public bar, and several function rooms.
ROOMS: 17 en suite 1 annexe en suite (2 fmly) No smoking in 2 bedrooms s fr £45; d £59-£69 (incl. bkfst) **LB CONF:** BC Thtr 200 Class 100 Board 50 Del from £72 **PARKING:** 25 **NOTES:** No smoking in restaurant **CARDS:**

See advert on page 329

LEWDOWN, Devon — Map 03 SX48

Top 200 - Hotel

★★★ Lewtrenchard Manor
EX20 4PN
☎ 01566 783256 & 783222
01566 783332
e-mail: stay@lewtrenchard.co.uk
***Dir:** A30 from Exeter to Plymouth/Tavistock road. At T-junct turn right, then left onto old A30 Lewdown road. After 6m left signed Lewtrenchard*

Lewtrenchard is surrounded by its own idyllic grounds in a quiet valley close to the northern edge of Dartmoor. This Jacobean mansion was built in the 1600s and has many interesting architectural features. Public rooms include a fine gallery, as well as magnificent carvings and oak panelling. Meals can be taken in the dining room where imaginative and carefully prepared dishes are served. Bedrooms are comfortably furnished and spacious, many have now had their bathrooms refurbished.
ROOMS: 9 en suite **FACILITIES:** Fishing Croquet lawn Clay pigeon shooting **CONF:** Thtr 50 Class 40 Board 20 Del £175 **PARKING:** 50 **NOTES:** No children 7yrs No smoking in restaurant Civ Wed 100 **CARDS:**

LEWES, East Sussex — Map 06 TQ41

★★★76% Shelleys Hotel
PEEL HOTELS
High St BN7 1XS
☎ 01273 472361 01273 483152
e-mail: info@shelleys-hotel-lewes.com
***Dir:** A23 to Brighton onto A27 to Lewes. At 1st rdbt left for town centre, after x-rds hotel on left*

This elegant hotel enjoys a central location and is steeped in history, with previous owners including the Earl of Dorset. Nowadays Shelleys boasts beautifully appointed bedrooms, furnished and decorated in traditional style. The elegant restaurant overlooks the enclosed garden and serves good food using local produce.
ROOMS: 19 en suite (2 fmly) No smoking in 4 bedrooms s £95-£140; d £120-£180 **LB FACILITIES:** STV Xmas **CONF:** Thtr 50 Class 20 Board 28 Del from £160 **PARKING:** 25 **NOTES:** No smoking in restaurant Civ Wed 50 **CARDS:**

★★★62% White Hart
55 High St BN7 1XE
☎ 01273 476694 01273 476695
e-mail: info@whitehartlewes.co.uk
***Dir:** from A27 follow signs for town centre. Hotel opposite County Court*

This historic hotel combines the old and the new. A leisure centre, patio and conservatory have been added to the Tudor bar, lounge and restaurant. Bedrooms vary between those of the character of the original inn and the more modern annexe rooms.
ROOMS: 23 en suite 29 annexe en suite (3 fmly) s fr £61; d fr £86 **LB FACILITIES: Spa** STV Indoor swimming (H) Sauna Solarium Gym Steam room, Beauty clinic, Dance studio, Swimming pool supervised entertainment ch fac Xmas **CONF:** BC Thtr 250 Class 120 Board 90 Del from £73.50 **PARKING:** 40 **CARDS:**

See advert on opposite page

LEYBOURNE, Kent — Map 06 TQ65

Travel Inn (Maidstone Leybourne)
travel inn
Castle Way ME19 5TR
☎ 08701 977170 01732 844474
***Dir:** M20 junct 4, take A228, Travel Inn on left*

Travel Inn offers good-quality, value-for-money accommodation. Spacious, en suite rooms with bath and shower comfortably accommodate a family of up to two adults and two children (to age 15). The restaurant and bar offers a varied menu. For further details and the Travel Inn phone number, consult the Hotel Groups page.
ROOMS: 40 en suite s £44.95; d £44.95

LEYBURN, North Yorkshire — Map 19 SE19

★65% Golden Lion
Market Place DL8 5AS
☎ 01969 622161 01969 623836
e-mail: AnneGoldenLion@aol.com
***Dir:** on A684 in Market Sq*

Dating back to 1765, this traditional inn overlooks the cobbled market square where weekly markets still take place. Bedrooms, including some family rooms, offer appropriate levels of comfort. The restaurant features murals of scenes from the Dales and serves a range of meals. Food can also be enjoyed in the cosy bar, a popular meeting place for local people.
ROOMS: 15 rms (14 en suite) (5 fmly) **SERVICES:** Lift **NOTES:** Closed 25 & 26 Dec **CARDS:**

LICHFIELD, Staffordshire

Map 10 SK10

★★★★78% Swinfen Hall

Swinfen WS14 9RE
☎ 01543 481494 01543 480341
e-mail: info@swinfenhallhotel.co.uk
Dir: *set back from A38 2.5m outside Lichfield, towards Birmingham*

Dating from 1757, this lavishly decorated mansion has been painstakingly restored by the present owners. Public rooms are particularly stylish, with intricately carved ceilings and impressive oil portraits. Rooms on the first floor boast period features and tall sash windows; those on the second floor (the former servants' quarters) are smaller and more contemporary.
ROOMS: 19 en suite s £110-£200; d £125-£225 (incl. cont bkfst)
FACILITIES: Tennis (hard) Fishing Croquet lawn **CONF:** Thtr 96 Class 50 Board 120 Del from £160 **PARKING:** 80 **NOTES:** No dogs (ex guide dogs) No smoking in restaurant Civ Wed 120
CARDS:

★★★68% The George

Best Western

12-14 Bird St WS13 6PR
☎ 01543 414822 01543 415817
e-mail: mail@thegeorgelichfield.co.uk
Dir: *from Bowling Green Island on A461 take Lichfield exit. Left at next island into Swan Road and where road bears left, turn right for George Hotel straight ahead*

Situated in the city centre, this privately owned hotel has been extensively refurbished by the owners, to provide good quality, well-equipped accommodation which includes a room with a four-poster bed. Facilities here include a large ballroom, plus several other rooms for meetings and functions.
ROOMS: 36 en suite (6 fmly) No smoking in 24 bedrooms s £58-£99; d £85-£111 (incl. bkfst) **LB** **CONF:** Thtr 110 Class 60 Board 40 Del from £125 **PARKING:** 45 **NOTES:** No smoking in restaurant Civ Wed 110
CARDS:

L

LICHFIELD, continued

★★★68% **Little Barrow**
62 Beacon St WS13 7AR
☎ 01543 414500 🖹 01543 415734
e-mail: reservations@tlbh.co.uk
Conveniently situated for the cathedral and the city, this friendly hotel provides well-equipped accommodation. The cosy lounge bar, popular with locals and visitors alike, has a range of real ales and a choice of bar meals. More formal dining is offered in the pleasant restaurant. Service is relaxed and attentive.
ROOMS: 24 en suite (2 fmly) s £60-£69; d £63-£80 (incl. bkfst) **LB**
FACILITIES: Xmas **CONF:** BC Thtr 100 Class 50 Board 50
PARKING: 60 **NOTES:** No dogs (ex guide dogs) No smoking in restaurant Civ Wed 100 **CARDS:**

★★63% ***Angel Croft***
Beacon St WS13 7AA
☎ 01543 258737 🖹 01543 415605
Dir: *opposite west gate entrance to Lichfield Cathedral*
This traditional, family-run, Georgian hotel is close to the cathedral and city centre. A comfortable lounge leads into a pleasantly appointed dining room; there is also a cosy bar on the lower ground floor. Bedrooms vary and most are spacious, particularly those in the adjacent Westgate House.
ROOMS: 10 rms (8 en suite) 8 annexe en suite (1 fmly) **CONF:** Thtr 30 Board 20 **PARKING:** 60 **NOTES:** No dogs (ex guide dogs) No smoking in restaurant Closed 25 & 26 Dec RS Sun evenings
CARDS:

⌂ **Express by Holiday Inn Lichfield**

Wall Island, Birmingham Rd, Shenstone WS14 0JS
☎ 01543 482700 🖹 01543 483106
e-mail: lichfield@oriel-leisure.co.uk
Dir: *M6 junct 12/A5 towards Lichfield/Tamworth, to junct with A5127. Hotel on left on Wall Island*

A modern hotel ideal for families and business travellers. Fresh and uncomplicated, the spacious bedrooms include Sky TV, power shower and tea and coffee-making facilities. Continental buffet breakfast is included in the room rate; other meals may be taken at the nearby family pub or restaurant. For further details and the Express by Holiday Inn phone number, consult the Hotel Groups pages.
ROOMS: 102 en suite s £49-£68; d £49-£68 (incl. cont bkfst)
CONF: Thtr 30 Class 30 Board 25

⌂ **Innkeeper's Lodge**
Stafford Rd WS13 8JB
☎ 01543 415789 🖹 01543 420752
Dir: *on A51, 0.75m outside city centre*
A new concept in the travel accommodation market. Smart rooms meet essential business requirements but also have home comforts. Dining options include all-day menus plus the added advantage of breakfast, which is included in the room price. For further details, consult the Hotel Groups page.
ROOMS: 10 en suite

⌂ **Premier Lodge (Lichfield)**

Rykneld St, Fradley WS13 8RD
☎ 0870 9906438 🖹 0870 9906439
Premier Lodge offers modern, well-equipped, en suite accommodation suitable for both business and leisure travellers. Meals can be taken at the adjacent popular restaurant and bar, which is fully licensed. For further details, consult the Hotel Groups page.
ROOMS: 30 en suite s £48; d £48

LIFTON, Devon Map 03 SX38

★★★74% ®®® ***Arundell Arms***
PL16 0AA
☎ 01566 784666 🖹 01566 784494
e-mail: reservations@arundellarms.com
Dir: *1m off A30 in Lifton village*

This creeperclad former coaching inn sits in the heart of a quiet Devon village. Internationally famous for its sporting facilities, the inn boasts a long history and continues to offer style, comfort and a relaxed atmosphere. Food is a major aspect here and the cuisine is a celebration of the best of Devon's produce. Angling as well as winter shooting, golf and other country pursuits are some of the Arundell Arms' facilities.
ROOMS: 22 en suite 5 annexe en suite **FACILITIES:** STV Fishing Skittle alley, 3 acre lake, Shooting in Winter **CONF:** Thtr 100 Class 30 Board 40
PARKING: 70 **NOTES:** No smoking in restaurant Closed 3 days Xmas
CARDS:

See advert on opposite page

> Popped the question?
> Hotels with Civ Wed in their entry are licensed for civil wedding ceremonies. Maximum numbers for the ceremony only are shown, e.g. Civ Wed 120

★★75% **Lifton Hall Country House**
New Rd PL16 0DR
☎ 01566 784863 & 784263 🖹 01566 784770
e-mail: mail@liftonhall.co.uk
Dir: *leave A30 at Liftondown junct, 2m E of Launceston. Right at T-junct signed Lifton, through village. Hotel on left 1m after T-junct*
This charming 350-year-old manor house is full of character. Dartmoor is on the doorstep and many of the North Cornish coastal resorts are within easy driving distance. Caring hospitality

continued

and good food are hallmarks of Lifton Hall, and the accommodation offers high levels of comfort and quality.

ROOMS: 9 en suite (2 fmly) No smoking in all bedrooms s fr £60; d fr £90 (incl. bkfst) **LB** **FACILITIES:** Xmas **CONF:** Thtr 25 Class 25 Board 16 **PARKING:** 16 **NOTES:** No dogs (ex guide dogs) No smoking in restaurant **CARDS:**

Restaurant with Rooms

Tinhay Mill Restaurant

Tinhay PL16 0AJ
☎ 01566 784201 01566 784201
e-mail: tinhay.mill@talk21.com
Dir: *A30/A388, approach Lifton, restaurant at bottom of village on right*

Converted from 15th-century mill cottages, this delightful restaurant with rooms has a character and charm all of its own. Beams and open fireplaces set the scene, with everything geared to ensure a relaxed and comfortable stay. Bedrooms are spacious and well equipped with many thoughtful extras. Cuisine is taken seriously here, with the best of local produce used to create consistently impressive dishes.

ROOMS: 3 en suite s £45-£55; d £68-£75 (incl. bkfst) **LB** **FACILITIES:** Xmas **PARKING:** 18 **NOTES:** No dogs No children 12yrs No smoking in restaurant **CARDS:**

LIMPLEY STOKE, Wiltshire — Map 04 ST76

★★★66% Limpley Stoke

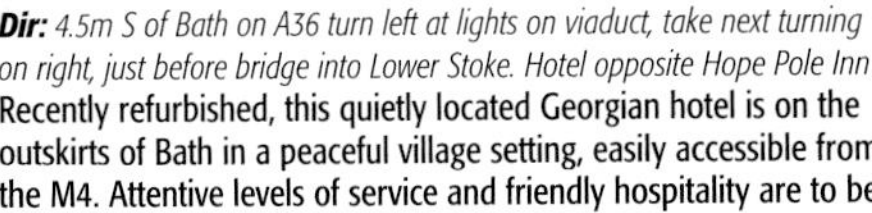

BA2 7FZ
☎ 01225 723333 01225 722406
e-mail: latonalsh@aol.com
Dir: *4.5m S of Bath on A36 turn left at lights on viaduct, take next turning on right, just before bridge into Lower Stoke. Hotel opposite Hope Pole Inn*

Recently refurbished, this quietly located Georgian hotel is on the outskirts of Bath in a peaceful village setting, easily accessible from the M4. Attentive levels of service and friendly hospitality are to be

continued

found throughout the hotel. Bedrooms come in various shapes and sizes and all are well equipped.

ROOMS: 60 en suite (8 fmly) No smoking in 10 bedrooms s £65-£75; d £85-£95 (incl. bkfst) **LB** **FACILITIES:** entertainment Xmas **CONF:** Thtr 120 Class 40 Board 30 Del from £105 **SERVICES:** Lift **PARKING:** 90 **NOTES:** No smoking in restaurant Civ Wed 80 **CARDS:**

LINCOLN, Lincolnshire — Map 17 SK97

★★★72% The Bentley Hotel & Leisure Club

Newark Rd, South Hykeham LN6 9NH
☎ 01522 878000 01522 878001
e-mail: info@thebentleyhotel.uk.com
Dir: *from A1 take A46 E towards Lincoln for 10m. Over 1st rdbt on Lincoln bypass to hotel 50yds on left*

This smart hotel offers bright, attractive accommodation. The

continued on p334

LINCOLN, continued

bedrooms are spacious and well equipped with air conditioning. There is a stylish leisure suite and a large pool with access for the less able. For the less energetic there is a beauty salon.
ROOMS: 53 en suite (3 fmly) (16 GF) No smoking in 20 bedrooms s £68-£81; d £84-£94 (incl. bkfst) **LB** **FACILITIES:** STV Indoor swimming (H) Sauna Gym Jacuzzi Beauty salon Xmas **CONF:** Thtr 300 Class 150 Board 30 **SERVICES:** Lift **PARKING:** 140 **NOTES:** No dogs (ex guide dogs) No smoking in restaurant Civ Wed 100
CARDS:

★★★70% **Washingborough Hall**
Church Hill, Washingborough LN4 1BE
☎ 01522 790340 📠 01522 792936
e-mail: washingborough.hall@btinternet.com
Dir: *on B1190 signed Bardney. Right at mini island, hotel 200yds on left*

This Georgian manor stands on the edge of the quiet village of Washingborough and sits in attractive gardens with an outdoor swimming pool. Public rooms are pleasantly furnished and comfortable, while the restaurant offers interesting menus. Bedrooms are individually designed, and most have views out over the grounds and countryside.
ROOMS: 14 en suite (1 fmly) No smoking in 2 bedrooms s £45-£65; d £90-£175 (incl. bkfst) **LB** **FACILITIES:** Outdoor swimming (H) Croquet lawn ch fac Xmas **CONF:** Thtr 50 Class 20 Board 20 Del £115 **PARKING:** 50 **NOTES:** No smoking in restaurant Civ Wed 50
CARDS:

★★★69% **Courtyard by Marriott Lincoln**
Brayford Wharf North LN1 1YW
☎ 01522 544244 📠 01522 560805
e-mail: reservations.lincoln@whitbread.co.uk
Dir: *From A46 onto A57 to Lincoln Central. Left at lights, then right, next right onto Lucy Tower St, then right onto Brayford Wharf North for hotel on right*
his smart hotel enjoys an idyllic waterfront location overlooking Brayford Pool, only minute's walk from the city centre. Bedrooms are spacious and comfortably appointed with a host of extra facilities. Public areas are focused around a galleried restaurant overlooking the spacious lounge bar.
ROOMS: 97 en suite (9 GF) No smoking in 47 bedrooms s £63-£89; d £86-£99 (incl. bkfst) **LB** **FACILITIES:** STV Fitness Room Xmas **CONF:** Thtr 30 Class 20 Board 20 Del from £100 **SERVICES:** Lift air con **PARKING:** 100 **NOTES:** No dogs (ex guide dogs) No smoking in restaurant **CARDS:**

★★★67% **The White Hart**
Bailgate LN1 3AR
☎ 0870 400 8117 📠 01522 531798
e-mail: whitehartlincoln@macdonald-hotels.co.uk
Dir: *A15 rdbt on N side of city follow Historic Lincoln signs, through Newport Arch, along Bailgate. Hotel on corner*
Lying in the shadow of Lincoln's magnificent cathedral, this hotel is perfectly positioned for exploring the shops and sights of this medieval city. The attractive bedrooms are furnished and decorated in a traditional style and many have views over the cathedral. Given the hotel's central location, car parking is a bonus.
ROOMS: 48 en suite (4 fmly) No smoking in 18 bedrooms s £70-£128; d £90-£210 **LB** **FACILITIES:** STV Xmas **CONF:** Thtr 90 Class 40 Board 30 Del from £90 **SERVICES:** Lift **PARKING:** 57 **NOTES:** No smoking in restaurant Civ Wed 120 **CARDS:**

★★★66% **Grand Hotel**
Saint Mary's St LN5 7EP
☎ 01522 524211 📠 01522 537661
e-mail: reception@thegrandhotel.uk.com
Dir: *A1 take A46, follow Lincoln Central signs and railway station signs*

This traditional family-owned hotel enjoys a central location. Bedrooms vary in style and size but include some smart spacious executive rooms and some with four-poster beds. A choice of eating options and bars are available.
ROOMS: 46 en suite (2 fmly) No smoking in 18 bedrooms s £56-£70; d £72-£82 (incl. bkfst) **LB** **FACILITIES:** STV Xmas **CONF:** Thtr 80 Class 50 Board 30 Del from £90 **PARKING:** 30 **NOTES:** No dogs (ex guide dogs) **CARDS:**

★★★65% **The Lincoln**
Eastgate LN2 1PN
☎ 0871 220 6070 📠 0871 220 6071
e-mail: sales@thelincolnhotel.com
Dir: *adjacent to cathedral*
This modern hotel enjoys a central location opposite Lincoln Cathedral, and the grounds contain ruins of the Roman wall and Eastgate. Bedrooms have modern facilities and some enjoy wonderful views of the Cathedral. Public areas include a smart airy restaurant and bar in addition to substantial conference and meeting facilities.
ROOMS: 71 en suite (7 fmly) No smoking in 46 bedrooms s £65-£85; d £65-£85 **LB** **CONF:** BC Thtr 100 Class 50 Board 40 Del from £99 **SERVICES:** Lift **PARKING:** 110 **NOTES:** No smoking in restaurant Civ Wed 50 **CARDS:**

★★73% Castle
Westgate LN1 3AS
☎ 01522 538801 🖹 01522 575457
e-mail: aa@castlehotel.net
Dir: *follow signs for Historic Lincoln. Hotel at NE corner of castle*
Located in the heart of historic Lincoln, this privately owned and run hotel has been carefully restored to offer comfortable, attractive, well-appointed accommodation. Bedrooms are all thoughtfully equipped, particularly the deluxe rooms and the spacious Lincoln suite. Specialising in fish and game, the Knights Restaurant has an interesting medieval theme.
ROOMS: 16 en suite 3 annexe en suite (5 GF) No smoking in 12 bedrooms s £62-£84; d £84-£150 (incl. bkfst) **LB FACILITIES:** Xmas **CONF:** Thtr 50 Class 18 Board 22 **PARKING:** 20 **NOTES:** No children 8yrs No smoking in restaurant **CARDS:**
See advert on this page

★★72% Hillcrest
THE CIRCLE
Selected Individual Hotels
15 Lindum Ter LN2 5RT
☎ 01522 510182 🖹 01522 510182
e-mail: reservations@hillcrest-hotel.com
Dir: *from A15 Wragby Rd and Lindum Rd, turn into Upper Lindum St at sign. Left at bottom for hotel 200mtrs on right*
The hospitality offered by Jenny Bennett and her staff is one of the strengths of Hillcrest, which sits in a quiet residential location. Thoughtfully equipped bedrooms come in a variety of sizes, all are well presented and maintained. The cosy dining room and pleasant conservatory offers a good range of freshly prepared food with views out over the adjacent park. A computer room with internet access is available for residents.
ROOMS: 14 en suite (5 fmly) (6 GF) No smoking in 6 bedrooms s £61-£70; d £81-£95 (incl. bkfst) **LB CONF:** Thtr 20 Class 16 Board 12 Del £94 **PARKING:** 8 **NOTES:** No smoking in restaurant Closed 23 Dec-3 Jan **CARDS:**
See advert on this page

★★66% Tower Hotel
38 Westgate LN1 3BD
☎ 01522 529999 🖹 01522 560596
e-mail: tower.hotel@btclick.com
Dir: *from A46 follow signs to Lincoln N then to Bailgate area. Through arch and 2nd left*

The Tower Hotel stands facing the Norman castle wall and is in a very convenient location for the city. The relaxed and friendly atmosphere is one of the strengths of this hotel. Public rooms are
continued on p336

LINCOLN, continued

now smartly appointed following a refurbishment programme which has seen the development of modern lounge bar, a separate, quieter lounge and a cosy brasserie dining area; food is also readily available in the bar.
ROOMS: 14 en suite (1 fmly) No smoking in 2 bedrooms s fr £62; d fr £80 (incl. bkfst) **LB** **CONF:** Thtr 30 Class 30 Board 30 Del from £61.95 **PARKING:** 9 **NOTES:** No smoking in restaurant Closed 24-26 Dec **CARDS:**

Hotel Ibis Lincoln

Runcorn Rd (A46), off Whisby Rd LN6 3QZ
☎ 01522 698333 📠 01522 698444
e-mail: H3161@accor-hotels.com
Dir: *off A46 ring road onto Whisby Rd. 1st turning on left*
Modern, budget hotel offering comfortable accommodation in bright and practical bedrooms. Breakfast is self-service and dinner is available in the restaurant. For further details, consult the Hotel Groups page.
ROOMS: 86 en suite s £39.95; d £39.95

Travel Inn

Lincoln Rd, Canwick Hill LN4 2RF
☎ 08701 977156 📠 01522 542521
Dir: *From Pelham Bridge through 2 sets of traffic lights continue on & up the hill. Travel Inn on the right on the junct of B1188 to Branston & B1131 to Bracebridge Heath*
Travel Inn offers good-quality, value-for-money accommodation. Spacious, en suite rooms with bath and shower comfortably accommodate a family of up to two adults and two children (to age 15). The restaurant and bar offer a varied menu. For further details and the Travel Inn phone number, consult the Hotel Groups page.
ROOMS: 40 en suite s £44.95; d £44.95

Travelodge

Thorpe on the Hill LN6 9AJ
☎ 08700 850 950
Dir: *on A46*
Travelodge offers good quality, good value, modern accommodation. Ideal for families, the spacious, en suite bedrooms include remote-control TV, tea and coffee-making facilities, luxury beds and free morning newspaper. Meals can be taken at the nearby family restaurant. For further details and the Travelodge phone number, consult the Hotel Groups page.
ROOMS: 32 en suite s fr £42.95; d fr £42.95

LIPHOOK, Hampshire — Map 05 SU83

★★★75% Old Thorns Hotel, Golf & Country Club

Griggs Green GU30 7PE
☎ 01428 724555 📠 01428 725036
e-mail: info@oldthorns.com
Dir: *A3 Guildford to Portsmouth road. Griggs Green exit S of Liphook*
This smartly presented hotel offers a range of leisure facilities, including a golf course, indoor pool, sauna, solarium and fitness room. The refurbished bedrooms are spacious and equipped with good facilities. There is a choice of eating options: the Japanese Nippon Kan Restaurant or the more informal Sands brasserie.

ROOMS: 29 en suite 4 annexe rms (3 en suite) (2 fmly) (14 GF) No smoking in 9 bedrooms s £140-£195; d £160-£195 (incl. bkfst) **LB** **FACILITIES:** STV Indoor swimming (H) Golf 18 Tennis (hard) Sauna Solarium Gym Putting green Steam room, Beauty treatment rooms Xmas **CONF:** Thtr 100 Class 50 Board 30 Del from £160 **PARKING:** 80 **NOTES:** Civ Wed 80 **CARDS:**

Travelodge

GU30 7TT
☎ 08700 850 950
Dir: *on northbound carriageway of A3, 1m from Griggs Green exit at Shell services*
Travelodge offers good quality, good value, modern accommodation. Ideal for families, the spacious, en suite bedrooms include remote-control TV, tea and coffee-making facilities, luxury beds and free morning newspaper. Meals can be taken at the nearby family restaurant. For further details and the Travelodge phone number, consult the Hotel Groups page.
ROOMS: 40 en suite s fr £42.95; d fr £42.95

LISKEARD, Cornwall & Isles of Scilly — Map 02 SX26

Top 200 - Hotel

★★ Well House

St Keyne PL14 4RN
☎ 01579 342001 📠 01579 343891
e-mail: wellhse@aol.com
Dir: *from Liskeard on A38 take B3254 to St Keyne (3 miles). At church fork left and hotel 0.5m*
Tucked away in an attractive valley and set in well-tended grounds, Well House enjoys a tranquil setting. Friendly staff provide attentive, yet relaxed service and add to the elegant atmosphere of the house. The comfortable lounge offers deep cushioned sofas and an open fire and in the intimate bar extensive choice of wines and drinks is available. The

continued

accomplished cuisine features carefully sourced ingredients from local suppliers and provides enjoyable dining.
ROOMS: 9 en suite (1 fmly) s £75-£95; d £115-£170 (incl. bkfst) **LB FACILITIES:** Outdoor swimming (H) Tennis (hard) Croquet lawn Xmas **PARKING:** 30 **NOTES:** No smoking in restaurant Closed 2 weeks in Jan **CARDS:**

★★63% Lord Eliot
Castle St PL14 3AU
☎ 01579 342717 📠 01579 347593
e-mail: information@lordeliot.co.uk
Dir: *A38 into Liskeard. Hotel 0.5m on left past St Martin's Church*
Conveniently situated on the edge of town, this popular hotel offers a warm and friendly welcome to guests. Bedrooms are comfortable and individually decorated, whilst public areas include a large function room and well patronised, convivial bar. A range of meals is offered in either the bar or the attractive dining room.
ROOMS: 15 rms (14 en suite) (1 fmly) No smoking in 2 bedrooms s fr £55; d fr £66 (incl. bkfst) **LB FACILITIES:** ch fac Xmas **CONF:** BC Thtr 180 Class 180 Board 180 **PARKING:** 60 **NOTES:** RS 25 Dec **CARDS:**

LITTLE LANGDALE, Cumbria Map 18 NY30

★★68% Three Shires Inn
LA22 9NZ
☎ 015394 37215 📠 015394 37127
e-mail: Ian@threeshiresinn.co.uk
Dir: *off A593, 2.5m from Ambleside at 2nd junct signed Langdales & Wrynose Pass. 1st left for 0.5m, then hotel 1m up lane*
Enjoying an outstanding rural location, this family-run inn was built in 1872. The brightly decorated bedrooms are individual in style and many offer panoramic views. The attractive lounge features a roaring fire in the cooler months and there is a traditional style bar with a great selection of local ales. Meals can be taken in either the bar or cosy restaurant.
ROOMS: 10 en suite (1 fmly) No smoking in all bedrooms s £42-£65; d £84-£90 (incl. bkfst) **LB PARKING:** 22 **NOTES:** No dogs No smoking in restaurant RS Dec & Jan **CARDS:**

LITTLE WEIGHTON, East Riding of Yorkshire Map 17 SE93

★★68% The Rowley Manor
Rowley Rd HU20 3XR
☎ 01482 848248 📠 01482 849900
e-mail: info@rowleymanor.com
Dir: *leave A63 at South Cave/Market Weighton exit. Into South Cave, right into Beverley Rd at clock tower, and follow signs for Rowley*
A former 17th-century vicarage, Rowley Manor is a Georgian country manor set in rural gardens and parkland. Bedrooms are traditionally decorated and furnished with period pieces, and many have panoramic views. Some rooms are particularly spacious. The public rooms feature a magnificent pine-panelled study and are of elegant design.
ROOMS: 16 en suite (2 fmly) s £60; d £80 (incl. bkfst) **LB FACILITIES:** Croquet lawn **CONF:** Thtr 110 Class 30 Board 50 Del from £100 **PARKING:** 100 **NOTES:** No smoking in restaurant Civ Wed 100 **CARDS:**

LIVERPOOL, Merseyside Map 15 SJ39

★★★★69% Liverpool Marriott Hotel City Centre
1 Queen Square L1 1RH
☎ 0151 476 8000 📠 0151 474 5000
Dir: *from city centre follow signs for Queen Sq Parking. Hotel adjacent*

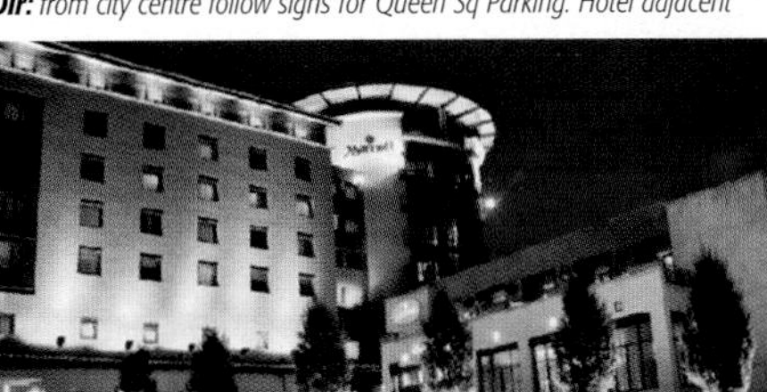

An impressive modern hotel located in the heart of the city. The elegant public rooms include a café bar, cocktail bar and Oliver's Restaurant, which provides a stylish eating option. The hotel also boasts a well-equipped health club with indoor pool. Bedrooms are stylishly appointed and benefit from a host of extra facilities.
ROOMS: 146 en suite (29 fmly) No smoking in 90 bedrooms s £115-£150; d £115-£150 **LB FACILITIES:** STV Indoor swimming (H) Sauna Solarium Gym Jacuzzi Xmas **CONF:** Thtr 300 Class 90 Board 30 Del from £156 **SERVICES:** Lift air con **PARKING:** 158 **NOTES:** No smoking in restaurant Civ Wed 250 **CARDS:**

★★★★68% Liverpool Marriott Hotel South
Speke Aerodrome L24 8QD
☎ 0870 400 7269 📠 0870 400 7369
e-mail: michelle.holden@marriotthotels.co.uk
Dir: *M62 junct 6. S onto Knowsley road to Speke. At rdbt right onto A561 to Liverpool, past Speke Hall turn and Liverpool Airport. Hotel left after Estuary Commerce Park*
Previously the North Terminal of Liverpool airport, the restoration of this hotel creates a distinctive look, reflected in art deco architecture and interior design. The spacious hotel rooms are fully air-conditioned and feature a comprehensive range of facilities. Feature rooms include the presidential suite in the base of the old control tower.
ROOMS: 164 en suite (22 fmly) (44 GF) No smoking in 120 bedrooms s £105-£185; d £105-£185 **FACILITIES: Spa** STV Indoor swimming (H) Outdoor swimming (H) Tennis (hard & grass) Squash Sauna Gym Jacuzzi Selected use of David Lloyd Leisure Centre adjacent to hotel, Pools supervised **CONF:** Thtr 300 Class 120 Board 60 Del from £130 **SERVICES:** Lift air con **PARKING:** 300 **NOTES:** No dogs (ex guide dogs) Civ Wed 200 **CARDS:**

★★★★68% ◎ Thornton Hall

Neston Rd CH63 1JF
☎ 0151 336 3938 📠 0151 336 7864
e-mail: thorntonhallhotel@btinternet.com
(For full entry see Thornton Hough)

LIVERPOOL, continued

★★★67% The Royal

Marine Ter, Waterloo L22 5PR
☎ 0151 928 2332 🖷 0151 949 0320
e-mail: enquiries@liverpool-royalhotel.co.uk
Dir: *6.5m NW of city centre, left off A565 Liverpool to Southport road at monument. Hotel at bottom of road*

On the outskirts of the city, beside the Marine Gardens, this hotel, dated 1815, has great views and modern bedrooms. Spacious public areas include a conservatory located adjacent to the brightly decorated restaurant and the comfortable, newly renovated, Seabank lounge. A wide range of interesting dishes is available.

ROOMS: 25 en suite (5 fmly) No smoking in 1 bedroom s £49.50-£69.50; d £79.50-£89.50 (incl. bkfst) **FACILITIES:** STV **CONF:** Thtr 100 Class 70 Board 40 **PARKING:** 25 **NOTES:** No dogs (ex guide dogs) **CARDS:**

★★★66% Alicia

3 Aigburth Dr, Sefton Park L17 3AA
☎ 0151 727 4411 🖷 0151 727 6752
e-mail: aliciahotel@feathers.uk.com

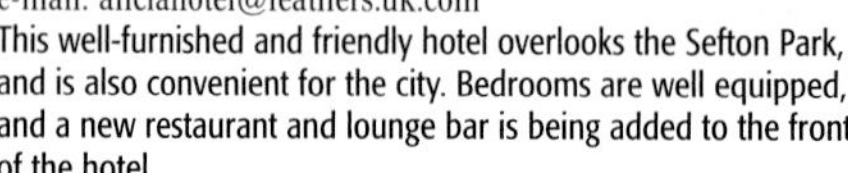

This well-furnished and friendly hotel overlooks the Sefton Park, and is also convenient for the city. Bedrooms are well equipped, and a new restaurant and lounge bar is being added to the front of the hotel.

ROOMS: 41 en suite (8 fmly) No smoking in 16 bedrooms s £40-£60; d £60-£80 (incl. bkfst) **LB** **FACILITIES:** Xmas **CONF:** Thtr 120 Class 80 Board 40 Del from £90 **SERVICES:** Lift **PARKING:** 40 **NOTES:** No dogs (ex guide dogs) No smoking in restaurant Civ Wed 110
CARDS:

⌂ *Campanile*

Chaloner St, Queens Dock L3 4AJ
☎ 0151 709 8104 🖷 0151 709 8725
Dir: *follow tourist signs marked Albert Dock. Hotel S on waterfront*

This modern building offers accommodation in smart, well-equipped bedrooms, all with en suite bathrooms. Refreshments may be taken at the informal Bistro. For further details and the Campanile phone number, consult the Hotel Groups page.

ROOMS: 102 en suite **CONF:** Thtr 25 Class 18 Board 20

⌂ Express by Holiday Inn

Ribblers Ln, Knowsley, Prescot L34 9HA
☎ 0151 549 2700 🖷 0151 549 2800
e-mail: liverpool@exhi.co.uk
Dir: *M57 junct 4, last exit off rdbt, then 1st left. Hotel on left*

A modern hotel ideal for families and business travellers. Fresh and uncomplicated, the spacious bedrooms include Sky TV, power shower and tea and coffee-making facilities. Continental buffet breakfast is included in the room rate; other meals may be taken at the nearby family pub or restaurant. For further details and the Express by Holiday Inn phone number, consult the Hotel Groups pages.

ROOMS: 86 en suite s £49.95-£65; d £49.95-£65 (incl. cont bkfst) **CONF:** BC Thtr 40 Class 20 Board 25 Del from £80

⌂ Express by Holiday Inn Liverpool Albert Dock

Brittania Pavilion, Albert Dock L3 4AD
☎ 0151 709 1133 🖷 0151 709 1144
e-mail: expressbyholidayinn@cidc.co.uk
Dir: *follow signs for Liverpool City Centre and Albert Dock*

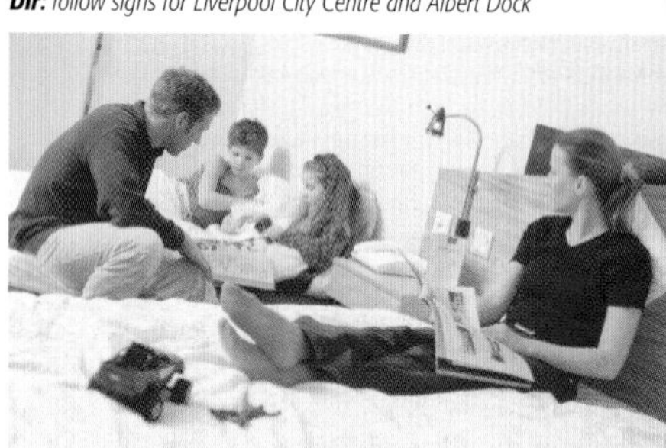

A modern hotel ideal for families and business travellers. Fresh and uncomplicated, the spacious bedrooms include Sky TV, power shower and tea and coffee-making facilities. Continental buffet breakfast is included in the room rate; other meals may be taken at the nearby family pub or restaurant. For further details and the Express by Holiday Inn phone number, consult the Hotel Groups pages.

ROOMS: 135 en suite **CONF:** Thtr 35 Class 30 Board 25 Del from £91

⌂ Hotel Ibis Liverpool

25 Wapping L1 8LY
☎ 0151 706 9800 🖷 0151 706 9810
e-mail: H3140@accor-hotels.com
Dir: *from M62 follow signs for Albert Dock. Hotel opposite entrance to Albert Dock*

Modern, budget hotel offering comfortable accommodation in bright and practical bedrooms. Breakfast is self-service and dinner is available in the restaurant. For further details, consult the Hotel Groups page.

ROOMS: 127 en suite s £45.95; d £45.95

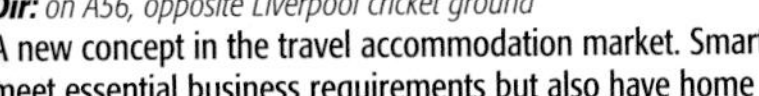

⇧ Innkeeper's Lodge
531 Aigburth Rd L19 9DN
☎ 0151 494 1032 ℻ 0151 494 3345
Dir: *on A56, opposite Liverpool cricket ground*
A new concept in the travel accommodation market. Smart rooms meet essential business requirements but also have home comforts. Dining options include all-day menus plus the added advantage of breakfast, which is included in the room price. For further details, consult the Hotel Groups page.
ROOMS: 33 en suite **CONF:** Thtr 18 Class 20 Board 12

⇧ Innkeeper's Lodge Liverpool North
502 Queen's Dr, Stoneycroft L13 0AS
☎ 0151 254 2271 ℻ 0151 254 2394
Dir: *from M62 take A5080 N towards Bootle Docks. Continue at lights at junct with A57. Hotel on left in Queens Drive*
A new concept in the travel accommodation market. Smart rooms meet essential business requirements but also have home comforts. Dining options include all-day menus plus the added advantage of breakfast, which is included in the room price. For further details, consult the Hotel Groups page.
ROOMS: 21 annexe en suite

⇧ Premier Lodge (Liverpool Albert Dock)

East Britannia Building, Albert Dock L3 4AD
☎ 0870 9906432 ℻ 0870 9906433
Premier Lodge offers modern, well-equipped, en suite accommodation suitable for both business and leisure travellers. Meals can be taken at the adjacent popular restaurant and bar, which is fully licensed. For further details, consult the Hotel Groups page.
ROOMS: 130 en suite s £50; d £50

⇧ Premier Lodge (Liverpool City Centre)

45 Victoria St L1 6JB
☎ 0870 9906584 ℻ 0870 9906585
Premier Lodge offers modern, well-equipped, en suite accommodation suitable for both business and leisure travellers. Meals can be taken at the adjacent popular restaurant and bar, which is fully licensed. For further details, consult the Hotel Groups page.
ROOMS: 39 en suite s £50; d £50

⇧ Premier Lodge (Liverpool South East)

Roby Rd, Huyton L36 4HD
☎ 0870 9906596 ℻ 0870 9906597
Dir: *M62 junct 5 onto A5080 Roby road towards Huyton town centre. Lodge 500yds on right*
Premier Lodge offers modern, well-equipped, en suite accommodation suitable for both business and leisure travellers. Meals can be taken at the adjacent popular restaurant and bar, which is fully licensed. For further details, consult the Hotel Groups page.
ROOMS: 53 en suite s £48; d £48 **CONF:** Thtr 35 Class 15 Board 22

⇧ Travel Inn Liverpool City Centre
Vernon St L2 2AY
☎ 0870 238 3323 ℻ 0870 241 9000
Dir: *from M62 follow Liverpool City Centre and then Birkenhead Tunnel signs. At rbt take 3rd exit onto Dale St then right into Vernon St. The Travel Inn is on the left*
Travel Inn offers good-quality, value-for-money accommodation. Spacious, en suite rooms with bath and shower comfortably accommodate a family of up to two adults and two children (to age 15). The restaurant and bar offers a varied menu. For further details and the Travel Inn phone number, consult the Hotel Groups page.
ROOMS: 165 en suite s £49.95; d £49.95

⇧ Travel Inn (Liverpool Aintree)
1 Ormskirk Rd, Aintree L9 5AS
☎ 08701 977157 ℻ 0151 525 8696
Dir: *M57 to end, follow A59 to Liverpool. Travel Inn is on 3rd set of traffic lights on left*
Travel Inn offers good-quality, value-for-money accommodation. Spacious, en suite rooms with bath and shower comfortably accommodate a family of up to two adults and two children (to age 15). The restaurant and bar offers a varied menu. For further details and the Travel Inn phone number, consult the Hotel Groups page.
ROOMS: 40 en suite s £44.95; d £44.95 **CONF:** Thtr 10

⇧ Travel Inn (Liverpool Tarbock)
Wilson Rd, Tarbock L36 6AD
☎ 08701 977159 ℻ 0151 480 9361
Dir: *at junct M62/M57. M62 junct 6 take A5080 Huyton then 1st right into Wilson Rd*
Travel Inn offers good-quality, value-for-money accommodation. Spacious, en suite rooms with bath and shower comfortably accommodate a family of up to two adults and two children (to age 15). The restaurant and bar offers a varied menu. For further details and the Travel Inn phone number, consult the Hotel Groups page.
ROOMS: 40 en suite s £44.95; d £44.95

⇧ Travel Inn (Liverpool West Derby)
Queens Dr, West Derby L13 0DL
☎ 08701 977160 ℻ 0151 220 7610
Dir: *on the Liverpool ring road at end of M62 turn right at 1st traffic lights onto A5058, pass Esso garage and left at next lights*
Travel Inn offers good-quality, value-for-money accommodation. Spacious, en suite rooms with bath and shower comfortably accommodate a family of up to two adults and two children (to age 15). The restaurant and bar offers a varied menu. For further details and the Travel Inn phone number, consult the Hotel Groups page.
ROOMS: 84 en suite s £44.95; d £44.95

⇧ Travelodge (Liverpool Central)
25 Haymarket L1 6ER
☎ 08700 850 950 ℻ 0151 227 5838
Dir: *Centre of Liverpool next to Birkenhead Tunnel entrance.*

Travelodge offers good quality, good value, modern accommodation. Ideal for families, the spacious, en suite bedrooms include remote-control TV, tea and coffee-making facilities, luxury beds and free morning newspaper. Meals can be taken at the nearby family restaurant. For further details and the Travelodge phone number, consult the Hotel Groups page.
ROOMS: 105 en suite s fr £42.95; d fr £42.95

L

LIVERPOOL, continued

⌂ Travelodge (Liverpool South)
Brunswick Dock, Sefton St L3 4BH
☎ 08700 850 950 🖷 0151 707 7769
Dir: *Follow signs to City Centre & Docks, Travelodge 1m after Albert Docks, next to Royal Naval headquarters*
Travelodge offers good quality, good value, modern accommodation. Ideal for families, the spacious, en suite bedrooms include remote-control TV, tea and coffee-making facilities, luxury beds and free morning newspaper. Meals can be taken at the nearby family restaurant. For further details and the Travelodge phone number, consult the Hotel Groups page.
ROOMS: 31 en suite s fr £42.95; d fr £42.95

LIZARD, THE, Cornwall & Isles of Scilly Map 02 SW71

★★★68% Housel Bay
Housel Cove TR12 7PG
☎ 01326 290417 & 290917 🖷 01326 290359
e-mail: info@houselbay.com
Dir: *A39 or A394 to Helston, then A3083. At Lizard sign left, at school left and down lane to hotel*
This long-established hotel has stunning views across the Western Approaches, equally enjoyable from the lounge and many of the bedrooms. Most bedrooms have high standards of comfort with modern facilities. Enjoyable cuisine is available in the stylish, dining room, after which a stroll to the end of the garden leads directly onto the Cornwall coastal path.
ROOMS: 20 en suite (1 fmly) No smoking in 10 bedrooms s £36-£55; d £72-£140 (incl. bkfst) **LB** **FACILITIES:** STV Xmas **CONF:** Thtr 20 Class 16 Board 12 Del from £80 **SERVICES:** Lift **PARKING:** 37
NOTES: No dogs (ex guide dogs) No smoking in restaurant RS Winter
CARDS:

★★ Tregildry
TR12 6HG
☎ 01326 231378 🖷 01326 231561
e-mail: trgildry@globalnet.co.uk
(For full entry see Gillan)

LOCKINGTON Hotels are listed under East Midlands Airport

LOLWORTH, Cambridgeshire Map 12 TL3

⌂ Travelodge
Huntingdon Rd CB3 8DR
☎ 08700 850 950 🖷 01954 781335
Dir: *on A14 northbound, 3m N of junct 14 on M11*
Travelodge offers good quality, good value, modern accommodation. Ideal for families, the spacious, en suite bedrooms include remote-control TV, tea and coffee-making facilities, luxury beds and free morning newspaper. Meals can be taken at the nearby family restaurant. For further details and the Travelodge phone number, consult the Hotel Groups page.
ROOMS: 36 en suite s fr £42.95; d fr £42.95

Early start?
Hotels at all star levels should provide in-room alarm clocks and/or alarm calls

Late for dinner?
Quality Standards mean that last orders for dinner vary according to star rating and should be no earlier than:
★★ 7.00pm ★★★ 8.00pm ★★★★ 9.00pm
★★★★★ 10.00pm

Index of London Hotels

London Plan 1
0 1 2 miles
0 1 2 3 kilometres
Central London Congestion Charging Zone
Bushey Heath
London Gateway Motorway Service Area
Totteridge
Highwood Hill
South Oxhey
Stanmore
Mill Hill
Edgware
Northwood
Hatch End
Harrow Weald
Belmont
Burnt Oak
Church End
Queensbury
Wealdstone
Pinner
Colindale
Kingsbury
Eastcote Village
Kenton
HARROW
North Harrow
Hendon
West Hendon
Brent Cross
Eastcote
Preston
Ruislip
Rayners Lane
Harrow on the Hill
Golders Green
North Wembley
Ickenham
South Harrow
South Ruislip
Neasden
WEMBLEY
Cricklewood
Sudbury
Northolt Aerodrome
North Hillingdon
Willesden
Northolt
Willesden Green
Stonebridge
Kilburn
Alperton
Harlesden
Perivale
Kensal Green
Hillingdon
Park Royal
Greenford
Hayes End
North Acton
Yeading
Wood End
North Kensington
EALING
Southall
Hanwell
East Acton
Notting Hill
Hayes
Acton
Shepherds Bush
Norwood Green
Heston Motorway Service Area
Chiswick
HAMMERSMITH
Sipson
Harlington
Heston
Kew
Osterley
Brentford
FULHAM
Cranford
KEW GARDENS
Barnes
HEATHROW AIRPORT
Mortlake
Isleworth
HOUNSLOW
East Sheen
Hatton
Putney
RICHMOND
West Bedfont
Roehampton
East Bedfont
Whitton
Twickenham
Feltham
Petersham
RICHMOND PARK
Lower Feltham
Ham
WIMBLEDON COMMON
Ashford
WIMBLEDON
Felthamhill
Hanworth
Hampton Hill
Teddington
Queen Mary Reservoir
BUSHY PARK
Hampton
Hampton Wick
Charlton
KINGSTON UPON THAMES
Sunbury
Norbiton
West Molesey
Hampton Court
HAMPTON COURT PARK
New Malden
Raynes Park
Littleton
East Molesey
Motspur Park
Shepperton
Thames Ditton
Berrylands
Walton-on-Thames
Queen Elizabeth II Reservoir
Surbiton
Old Malden
Long
A B C D
1 2 3 4 5 6

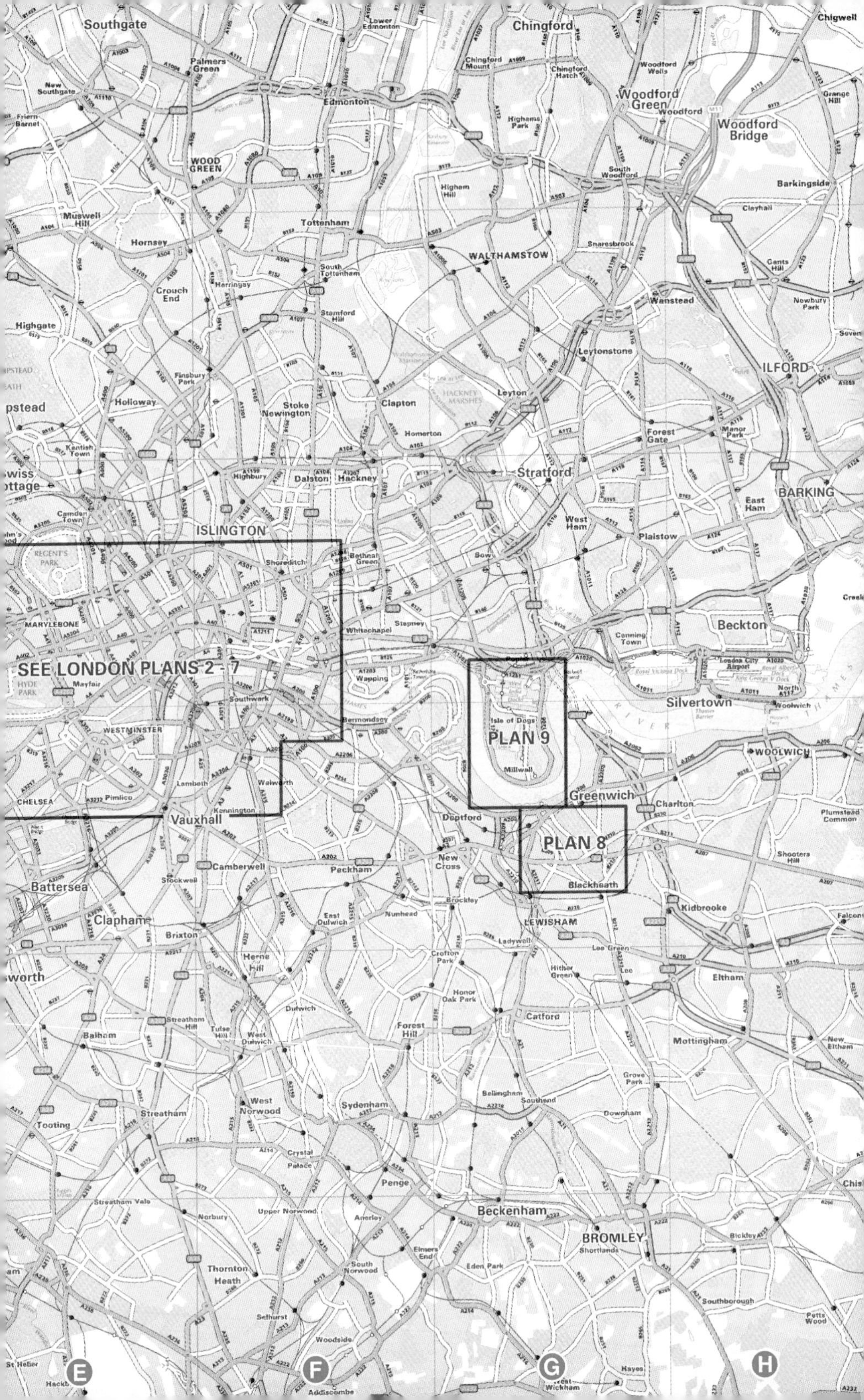

Southgate
Lower Edmonton
Chingford
Chigwell
Palmers Green
New Southgate
Friern Barnet
Edmonton
Chingford Mount
Chingford Hatch
Woodford Wells
Woodford Green
Woodford
Woodford Bridge
Grange Hill
Highams Park
WOOD GREEN
Higham Hill
South Woodford
Barkingside
Clayhall
Muswell Hill
Tottenham
Hornsey
WALTHAMSTOW
Snaresbrook
Gants Hill
Crouch End
Harringay
South Tottenham
Wanstead
Newbury Park
Highgate
Stamford Hill
Leytonstone
ILFORD
Finsbury Park
Holloway
Stoke Newington
Clapton
HACKNEY MARSHES
Leyton
Homerton
Forest Gate
Manor Park
Kentish Town
Stratford
Highbury
Dalston
Hackney
BARKING
Camden Town
East Ham
West Ham
ISLINGTON
Plaistow
REGENT'S PARK
Shoreditch
Bethnal Green
Bow
MARYLEBONE
Stepney
Whitechapel
Canning Town
Beckton
SEE LONDON PLANS 2 - 7
HYDE PARK
Mayfair
Wapping
Poplar
London City Airport
Royal Victoria Dock
Southwark
Isle of Dogs
Silvertown
RIVER THAMES
Woolwich
WESTMINSTER
Bermondsey
PLAN 9
WOOLWICH
Millwall
Lambeth
Walworth
CHELSEA
Pimlico
Kennington
Greenwich
Charlton
Vauxhall
Deptford
PLAN 8
Plumstead Common
Camberwell
New Cross
Shooters Hill
Peckham
Blackheath
Battersea
Stockwell
Brockley
Kidbrooke
Clapham
East Dulwich
Nunhead
LEWISHAM
Brixton
Ladywell
Crofton Park
Lee Green
Herne Hill
Hither Green
Lee
Eltham
Dulwich
Honor Oak Park
Streatham Hill
Tulse Hill
West Dulwich
Forest Hill
Catford
Balham
Mottingham
New Eltham
Grove Park
Bellingham
Southend
West Norwood
Sydenham
Downham
Streatham
Tooting
Crystal Palace
Penge
Streatham Vale
Norbury
Upper Norwood
Anerley
Beckenham
BROMLEY
Shortlands
Bickley
Elmers End
South Norwood
Eden Park
Thornton Heath
Southborough
Petts Wood
Selhurst
Woodside
Hayes
West Wickham
Addiscombe
E
F
G
H

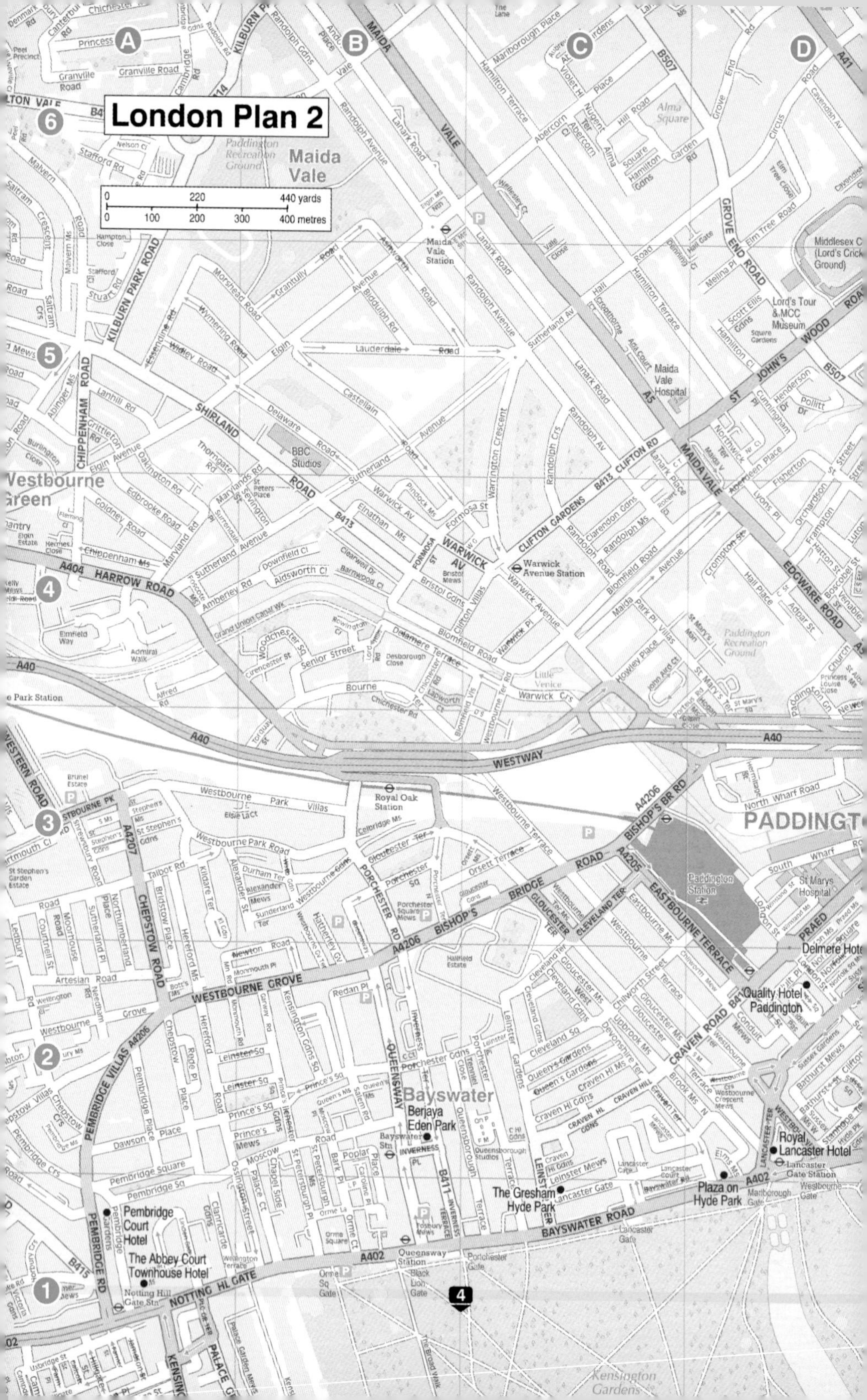
London Plan 2
220
440 yards
0
100
200
300
400 metres
A
B
C
D
1
2
3
4
5
6
Maida Vale
Paddington Recreation Ground
Maida Vale Station
Warwick Avenue Station
Royal Oak Station
BBC Studios
Westbourne Green
Little Venice
Maida Vale Hospital
Middlesex C (Lord's Crick Ground)
Lord's Tour & MCC Museum
Alma Square
PADDINGT
Paddington Station
St Marys Hospital
Delmere Hotel
Quality Hotel Paddington
Royal Lancaster Hotel
Lancaster Gate Station
Plaza on Hyde Park
The Gresham Hyde Park
Bayswater
Berjaya Eden Park
Bayswater Stn
Queensway Station
Pembridge Court Hotel
The Abbey Court Townhouse Hotel
Notting Hill Gate Stn
Kensington Gardens
Westway
A40
A404
HARROW ROAD
SHIRLAND ROAD
KILBURN PARK ROAD
CHIPPENHAM ROAD
CLIFTON GARDENS
CLIFTON RD
MAIDA VALE
EDGWARE ROAD
GROVE END ROAD
ST JOHN'S WOOD ROAD
BISHOP'S BRIDGE ROAD
EASTBOURNE TERRACE
PRAED
CRAVEN ROAD
WESTBOURNE GROVE
PORCHESTER RD
QUEENSWAY
CHEPSTOW ROAD
PEMBRIDGE VILLAS
PEMBRIDGE RD
NOTTING HL GATE
BAYSWATER ROAD
A402
4

E
F
G
H
Regent's Park
Regent's Park
London Central Mosque
Queen Mary's Garden
Inner Circle
Outer Circle
Chester Road
London Business School
Clarence Gate
York Bridge
Royal Academy of Music
Park Square
Regent's Park Stn
Great Portland Street Stn
Meliá White House Regents Park
Marylebone Station
Baker Street Stn
Madame Tussaud's
Planetarium
Lisson Grove
Regents Park Hotel
The Landmark London
Sherlock Holmes Hotel
MARYLEBONE
MARYLEBONE ROAD
PARK ROAD
BAKER STREET
GLOUCESTER PLACE
PORTLAND PL
EDGWARE ROAD
Edgware Road Stn
Jurys Clifton-Ford Hotel
The Mandeville
Grange Fitzrovia
London Marriott Hotel Marble Arch
Radisson SAS Portman Hotel
PORTMAN SQUARE
Intercontinental - The Churchill - London
Montcalm - Hotel Nikko London
Mostyn Hotel
Radisson Edwardian Sussex Hotel
Radisson Edwardian Berkshire Hotel
WIGMORE STREET
OXFORD ST
Bond Street Stn
Oxford Circus Station
Marble Arch Station
The Cumberland
London Marriott Hotel Park Lane
London Marriott Hotel, Grosvenor Square
Claridge's
The Westbury Hotel
Millennium Hotel London - Mayfair
The Connaught
Le Meridien Grosvenor House
Mayfair
Holiday Inn London - Mayfair
The Chesterfield Mayfair
The Washington Mayfair Hotel
The Dorchester
CUMBERLAND GATE
Speakers Corner
PARK LANE
NEW BOND STREET
Hyde Park
Congestion Charging Zone boundary
3
4

London Plan 3
0
220
440 yards
0
100
200
300
400 metres
A
B
C
D
Regent's Park
Somers Town
King's Cross Station
St Pancras Station
British Library
Euston Station
St Pancras
Bloomsbury
St Giles
Soho
China Town
Strand
Novotel London Euston
Hotel Ibis London Euston
Travel Inn London Euston
Meliá White House Regents Park
Radisson Edwardian Grafton Hotel
University College London
University Coll Hosp
Holiday Inn Bloomsbury
Russell Square Station
Le Meridien Russell
National Hosp for Sick Children (Great Ormond St)
Holiday Inn London Regents Park
Grange Fitzrovia
Grange Langham Court
Middlesex Hosp
Uni of London
The Montague on the Gardens
Grange Blooms Hotel
Grange Whitehall
British Museum
The Bonnington in Bloomsbury
Grange Holborn Hotel
Radisson Edwardian Kenilworth Hotel
Radisson Edwardian Marlborough Hotel
Jurys Great Russell Street
The Berners Hotel
Tottenham Court Road Stn
Holborn Station
Kingsway Hall
Oxford Circus Station
Radisson Edwardian Mountbatten Hotel
Covent Garden Station
Royal Opera House
Le Meridien Waldorf
One Aldwych
Leicester Square Stn
The Westbury Hotel
Radisson Edwardian Hampshire Hotel
Strand Palace Hotel
The Savoy
Le Meridien Piccadilly
Piccadilly Circus Stn
Raffles Brown's Hotel
Royal Academy of Arts
22 Jermyn Street Townhouse
Radisson Edwardian Pastoria Hotel
National Gallery
National Portrait Gal
Trafalgar Square
Holiday Inn Mayfair
May Fair Inter-Continental London
De Vere Cavendish St James's London
Sofitel St James London
The Ritz
Charing Cross Stn
Embankment Station
Coram's Fields Playground
Victoria Embankment Gardens
Warren Street Stn
Great Portland Street Stn
Euston Square Station
Goodge St Station
EUSTON ROAD
EUSTON ROAD
OXFORD STREET (restricted)
REGENT STREET
CHARING CROSS RD
TOTTENHAM COURT RD
SOUTHAMPTON ROW
KINGSWAY
SHAFTESBURY AV
PICCADILLY
PALL MALL
STRAND
GT PORTLAND STREET
HAMPSTEAD ROAD
UPR WOBURN PL
WOBURN PLACE
RUSSELL SQ
BLOOMSBURY WY
HIGH HOLBORN
NEW BOND STREET
CONDUIT ST
GOODGE ST
MORTIMER ST
GRAY'S INN RD
PENTONVILLE
ALDWYCH
VICTORIA
2
2
5

E
F
G
H
Congestion Charging Zone boundary
Jurys Inn London
PENTONVILLE ROAD
CITY ROAD
FINSBURY
Holiday Inn Kings Cross/ Bloomsbury
Mount Pleasant (Postal Sorting Office)
Clerkenwell
The City University
Moorfields Eye Hospital
St Luke's
OLD STREET
CLERKENWELL ROAD
GOSWELL ROAD
ROSEBERY AVENUE
FARRINGDON ROAD
FARRINGDON STREET
Farringdon Station
Barbican Station
The Barbican
Central London Mkts
St Bartholomews Hospital
Gray's Inn
Chancery Lane Stn
HIGH HOLBORN
HOLBORN VIAD
NEWGATE ST
LONDON WALL
Moorgate Stn
Guildhall
Lincoln's Inn
Public Record Office
Royal Courts of Justice
FLEET ST
STRAND
Inns of Court and Chancery
City Thameslink Station
St Paul's Station
St Paul's Cathedral
Mansion House Station
Cannon Street Stn
Blackfriars Station
Temple Stn
VICTORIA EMB
UPPER THAMES ST
CITY OF LONDON
River Thames
Millennium Bridge
Blackfriars Bridge
Southwark Bridge
Waterloo Bridge
Oxo Tower Wharf
Shakespeare's Globe Theatre
Tate Modern
The London Television Centre (LWT)
Royal National Theatre
Hotel London, The Howard
Premier Lodge (London Southwark)
Express by Holiday Inn London - Southwark
SOUTHWARK BRIDGE ROAD
1
2
3
4
5
6
7

London Plan 4
Pembridge Square
Pembridge Sq
Pembridge Court Hotel
Notting Hill Gate Stn
Notting Hill Gate
Palace Ct
Chapel Side
Ossington Street
Orme Ct
Orme Square
Orme Sq Gate
Queensway Station
Black Lion Gate
Porchester Gate
Inverness Terrace
Leinster
Leinster Mews
Lancaster Gate
Lancaster Gate Station
Westbourne Gate
Marlborough Gate
The Gresham Hyde Park
Plaza on Hyde Park
A402
B411
B415
BAYSWATER ROAD
The Broad Walk
Kensington Gardens
Round Pond
Kensington Palace
Palace Green
York House Place
Lancer Square
Royal Garden Hotel
Albert Memorial
Alexandra Gate
West Carriage Drive
Palace Gardens Mews
PALACE GDNS TER
B405
KENSINGTON CHURCH ST
Brunswick Gardens
Vicarage Gate
VICARAGE GA
A4204
Kensington Pl
Edge St
Peel St
Campden Street
Bedford Gardens
Sheffield Terrace
Campden Hill
Campden Hl
Tor Gdns
Gloucester Walk
Campden Gv
Observatory Gdns
Hornton Street
Holland St
Duchess of Bedford's Wk
Upper Phillimore Gardens
Phillimore Pl
Essex Vls
Argyll Road
Phillimore Walk
Phillimore Gardens
Kensington & Chelsea Town Hall
Drayson Ms
Milestone Hotel & Apartments Townhouse
KENSINGTON ROAD
HYDE PARK GATE
KENSINGTON GORE A315
Palace Gate
Queens Gate
Royal College of Art
Royal Geographical Soc
Royal Albert Hall
Exhibition Rd
Prince Consort Road
Princes Gate
Royal College of Music
Imperial College
Science Museum
RCA
Natural History Museum
Earth Galleries
KENSINGTON HIGH ST
A315
High Street Kensington Stn
Derry St
Young Street
Kensington House Hotel
Kensington Ct
De Vere Gdns
PALACE GA
Hyde Park Gate
Queen's Gate
Reston Pl
Canning Pl
Victoria Gv
Victoria Road
Queen's Ga Ms
Queen's Ga Terrace
Gore St
Elvaston
Copthorne Tara Hotel London Kensington
Cottesmore Gdns
Stanford Rd
Eldon Road
Kynance Ms
Launceston Pl
GLOUCESTER ROAD
KENSINGTON
St Albans Gv
Wright's La
Allen St
Abingdon Villas
Marloes
Scarsdale Villas
Earl's Wk
EARL'S COURT RD
B316
Edwardes Sq
Pembroke Square
Pembroke Rd
Stratford Rd
Lexham Gardens
Lexham Ms
Radley Ms
Cornwall Gdns
Cornwall Ms S
Queen's Gate Pl
Queen's Gate Place Mews
Queen's Gate
Gloucester Road
CROMWELL ROAD
CROMWELL ROAD A4
PEMBROKE ROAD
Cromwell Hospital
Pennant Ms
Marriott London Hotel Kensington
Holiday Inn London Kensington Forum
Gloucester Rd Stn
Radisson Edwardian Vanderbilt Hotel
Millennium Bailey's Hotel London Kensington
Millennium Gloucester Hotel London Kensington
Harrington Hall
THURLOE PL
South Kensington Station
South Kensington Station Arcade
Harrington Rd
Harrington Gdns
Stanhope Gdns
Jurys Kensington Hotel
Logan Place
Comfort Inn Kensington
CROMWELL ROAD
Cromwell Crescent
A3220
EARL'S COURT ROAD
Templeton Pl
Travel Inn London Kensington
Hogarth Rd
Kenway
Courtfield Gardens
Collingham Pl
Burns Hotel
Barkston Gdns
Earl's Ct Gdns
Bramham Gdns
Hesper Ms
Bolton Gdns
Wetherby Gdns
Gledhow Gdns
Bina Gardens
South Kensington
The Cranley Hotel
Brechin Pl
OLD BROMPTON ROAD
A3218
Onslow Gardens
Cranley Gardens
Onslow Gdns
Sumner Pl
Onslow Sq
Pelham Street
B304
Earl's Court
WARWICK ROAD
Nevern Pl
Nevern Sq
20 Nevern Square
Earl's Court Station
Philbeach Gardens
Penywern Road
Earl's Ct Sq
Earl's Court Exhibition Centre
Eardley Crs
Kempsford Gdns
OLD BROMPTON ROAD
West Brompton Station
Paragon Hotel
A3218
Redcliffe Close
Coleherne Rd
Coleherne Ms
A3220
REDCLIFFE GARDENS
Redcliffe Sq
FINBOROUGH
Westgate Ter
Redcliffe St
Harcourt Ter
The Little Boltons
The Boltons
Tregunter Road
Cathcart Rd
Redcliffe Rd
Seymour Wk
Hollywood Rd
Gilston Road
Harley Gdns
Milborne Gv
Drayton Gdns
Cresswell Place
Evelyn Gdns
Roland Gardens
Cranley Mews
Elm Park Gdns
Elm Pk Lane
Beaufort St
Callow Street
A308
FULHAM ROAD
Neville Street
Onslow Gdns
Selwood Pl
Elm Place
Old Church Street
Mulberry Walk
The Vale
Mallord St
Queen's Elm Square
South Parade
Chelsea
CH
West Bromp
Eagle Pl
Roland Wy
Drayton
Priory Wk
A
B
C
D
1
2
3
4
5
6

Mayfair
Le Meridien Grosvenor House
Millennium Hotel London - Mayfair
The Connaught
Holiday Inn London - Mayfair
The Chesterfield Mayfair
The Washington Mayfair Hotel
The Dorchester
Athenaeum Hotel & Apartments
Four Seasons Hotel London
Intercontinental London
Hyde Park
The Serpentine
Serpentine Road
Queen Mother Gate
Apsley House, The Wellington Museum
Hyde Park Corner Stn
Green Park
Knightsbridge
Mandarin Oriental Hyde Park
Sheraton Park Tower
The Berkeley
The Lanesborough
Constitution Hill
Buckingham Palace
Buckingham Palace Gardens
The Royal Mews
Basil Street Hotel
The Capital
Millennium Hotel London Knightsbridge
The Halkin Hotel
The Lowndes Hotel
Harrods Store
The Carlton Tower Hotel
Parkes Townhouse Hotel
The Beaufort
Sheraton Belgravia
No 41
The Goring
Brompton Oratory
Brompton
Rembrandt
Belgravia
Victoria Station
The Cadogan Hotel
Cliveden Townhouse
Victoria Coach Station
Sloane Sq Stn
Duke of York's HQ
Chelsea Barracks
Royal Hospital Museum
Royal Hospital Chelsea
National Army Museum
Burtons Court
Chelsea Embankment
Chelsea Bridge
Congestion Charging Zone boundary
0 220 440 yards
0 100 200 300 400 metres
E F G H

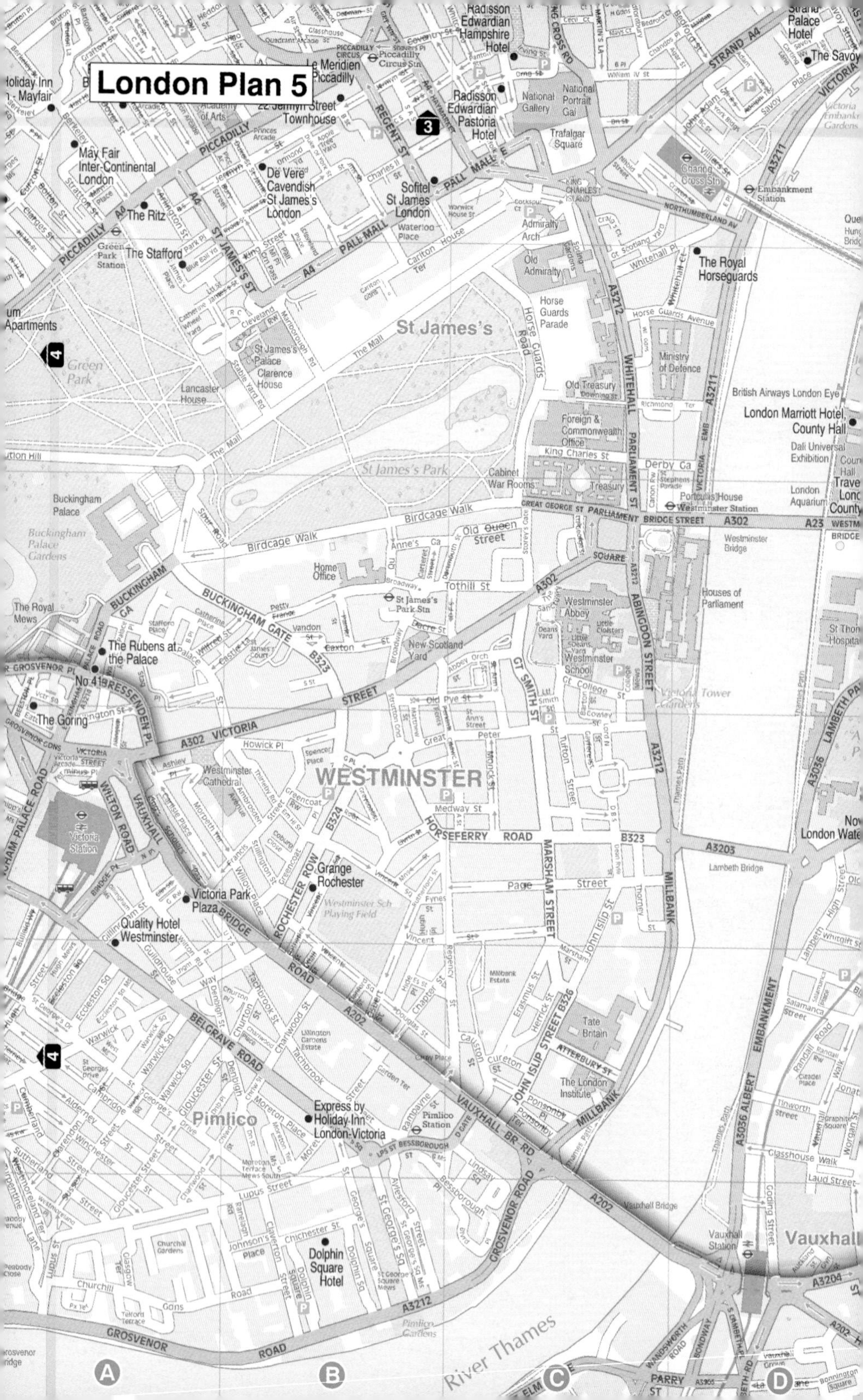

London Plan 5
Holiday Inn - Mayfair
May Fair Inter-Continental London
The Ritz
The Stafford
Green Park Station
Le Meridien Piccadilly
22 Jermyn Street Townhouse
De Vere Cavendish St James's London
Sofitel St James London
Radisson Edwardian Hampshire Hotel
Radisson Edwardian Pastoria Hotel
National Gallery
National Portrait Gal
Trafalgar Square
Strand Palace Hotel
The Savoy
Charing Cross Stn
Embankment Station
The Royal Horseguards
Admiralty Arch
Old Admiralty
Horse Guards Parade
Ministry of Defence
Old Treasury
Foreign & Commonwealth Office
Treasury
Cabinet War Rooms
Portcullis House
Westminster Station
British Airways London Eye
London Marriott Hotel, County Hall
Dali Universal Exhibition
London Aquarium
St James's
St James's Palace
Clarence House
Lancaster House
Green Park
St James's Park
Buckingham Palace
Buckingham Palace Gardens
The Royal Mews
The Rubens at the Palace
No 41
The Goring
Apartments
Home Office
St James's Park Stn
New Scotland Yard
Westminster Abbey
Westminster School
Houses of Parliament
Westminster Bridge
Victoria Tower Gardens
St Thomas' Hospital
WESTMINSTER
Westminster Cathedral
Victoria Station
Grange Rochester
Westminster Sch Playing Field
Victoria Park Plaza
Quality Hotel Westminster
Lambeth Bridge
Tate Britain
The London Institute
Millbank Estate
Pimlico
Express by Holiday Inn London Victoria
Pimlico Station
Dolphin Square Hotel
Churchill Gardens
Pimlico Gardens
Vauxhall Bridge
Vauxhall Station
Vauxhall
River Thames
PICCADILLY
REGENT ST
PALL MALL
STRAND A4
WHITEHALL
PARLIAMENT ST
ABINGDON STREET
MILLBANK
VICTORIA STREET
HORSEFERRY ROAD
MARSHAM STREET
JOHN ISLIP STREET B326
VAUXHALL BRIDGE ROAD
BELGRAVE ROAD
GROSVENOR ROAD
BUCKINGHAM GATE
ALBERT EMBANKMENT
LAMBETH PALACE ROAD
Birdcage Walk
The Mall
A B C D

LONDON
River Thames
Blackfriars Bridge
Millennium Bridge
Southwark Bridge
Thames Path
Oxo Tower Wharf
Shakespeare's Globe Theatre
Tate Modern
The London Television Centre (LWT)
Royal National Theatre
National Film Theatre
IMAX Cinema
Concert Hall
Express by Holiday Inn London - Southwark
Mercure London City Bankside
Novotel London City South
Premier Lodge (London Southwark)
Days Inn Waterloo
Southwark Cathedral
London Bridge
Waterloo East Stn
International Rail Terminal
Waterloo Station
Southwark Station
Borough Stn
Lambeth North Station
Elephant and Castle Stn
Kennington Station
ST GEORGE'S CIRCUS
South Bank University
London Coll of Printing
Imperial War Museum
Geraldine Mary Harmsworth Park
Newington Gardens
Faraday Gardens
Surrey Cricket (The Oval)
LAMBETH
Newington
The Borough
Walworth
A3200
SOUTHWARK STREET
STAMFORD ST
BLACKFRIARS ROAD
A201
UNION STREET
B300
THE CUT
WATERLOO RD
A301
BOROUGH ROAD
A3202
WESTMINSTER BR RD
LAMBETH ROAD
LONDON RD
ST GEORGE'S RD
NEW KENT ROAD
NEWINGTON BUTTS
KENNINGTON LANE
A3204
KENNINGTON PARK ROAD
KENNINGTON ROAD
A23
WALWORTH ROAD
A215
BOROUGH HIGH ST
A3
SOUTHWARK BRIDGE ROAD
GREAT DOVER ST
MARSHALSEA RD
HARPER RD
B240
NEWINGTON CSWY
Congestion Charging Zone boundary
0
220
440 yards
100
200
300
400 metres
1
2
3
4
5
6
E
F
G
H

London Plan 6
Congestion Charging Zone boundary
The Barbican
Broadgate
Liverpool Street Station
Spitalfields Market Hall
SPITAL
Great Eastern Hotel
Travelodge (London City)
International Financial Cen
Guildhall
Bank of England (& Mus)
Stock Exchange
Lloyd's
The Chamberlain Hotel
Fenchurch Street Stn
Novotel London Tower Bridge
Tower of London
Custom House
London Bridge
Millennium Bridge
Southwark Bridge
Premier Lodge (London Southwark)
London Bridge Hospital
HMS Belfast
Hays Galleria
Greater London Authority Headquarters (City Hall)
London Bridge Hotel
London Bridge Station
Guys Hospital
Novotel London City South
Mercure London City Bankside
Tower Bridge
St Katharine Docks
Travel Inn London Tower Bridge
The Borough
Borough Stn
Tabard Garden
Mansion House Station
Cannon Street Stn
Monument Stn
Bank Stn
Moorgate Stn
Aldgate Stn
Tower Gateway Stn
Tower Hill Stn
CITY ROAD
CHISWELL ST
LONDON WALL
MOORGATE
BISHOPSGATE
SHOREDITCH HIGH STREET
COMMERCIAL STREET
GRACECHURCH ST
UPPER THAMES ST
LWR THAMES ST
QUEEN ST PLACE
SOUTHWARK BRIDGE ROAD
BOROUGH HIGH ST
TOOLEY STREET
ST THOMAS ST
BERMONDSEY STREET
LONG LANE
TOWER BRIDGE ROAD
MINORIES
HOUNDSDITCH
ALDGATE HIGH ST
MANSELL ST
Cornhill
Cheapside
Leadenhall Street
Fenchurch Street
Lombard Street
Eastcheap
Threadneedle Street
0 220 440 yards
0 100 200 300 400 metres
A
B
C
D
1
2
3
4
5
6
3
5
7

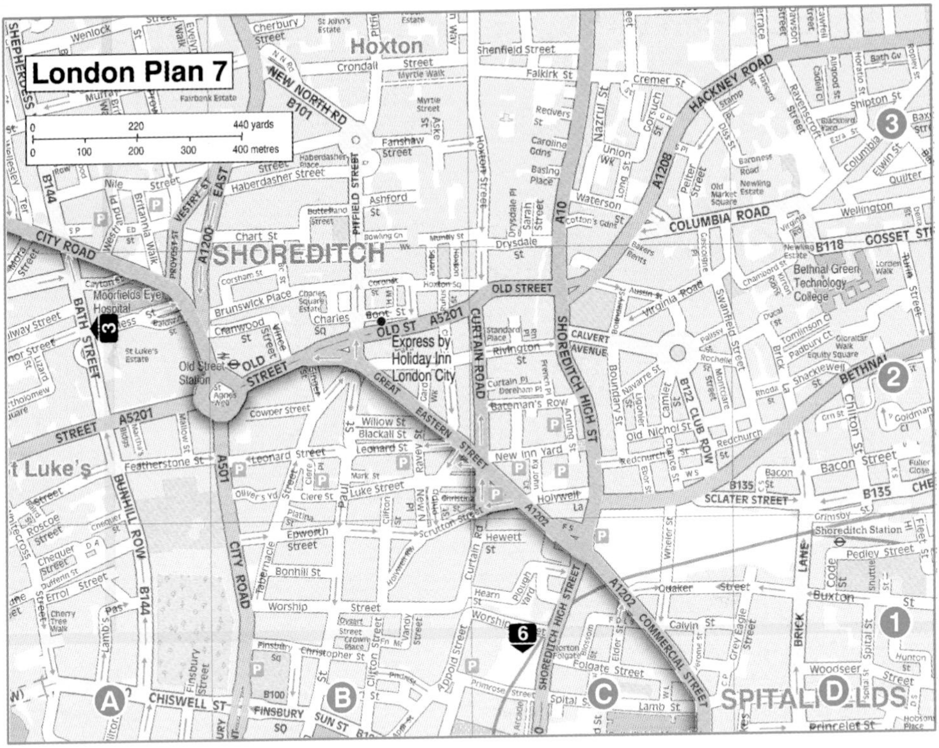

London Plan 7

London Plan 8

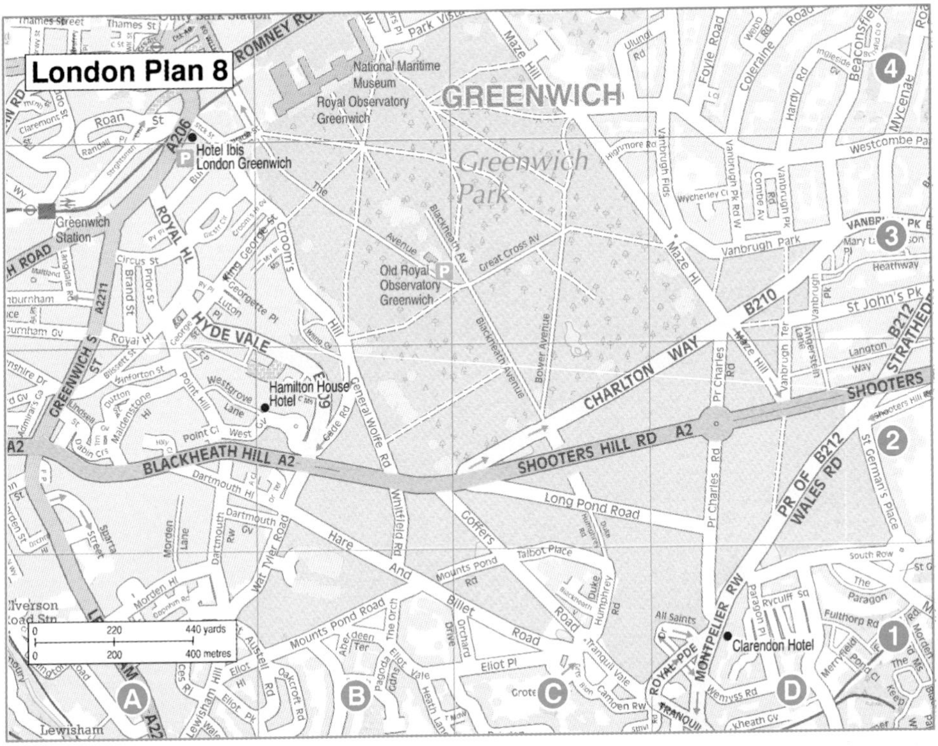

London Plan 9
POPLAR
Canary Wharf
Millwall
Cubitt Town
ISLE OF DOGS
Poplar Station
West India Quay Station
Canary Wharf Station
Heron Quays Station
South Quay Station
Crossharbour & London Arena Stn
Mudchute Station
Island Gardens Station
Blackwall Station
Museum in Docklands
Billingsgate Fish Market
Four Seasons Hotel, Canary Wharf
Hotel Ibis London Docklands
Guardian Newspapers
London Arena
Daily Telegraph
Mudchute City Farm
Community Centre (Island History Trust)
Millennium Harbour Development
ASPEN WAY
A1261
WESTFERRY ROAD
MANCHESTER ROAD
PRESTON'S ROAD
A1206
A102
River Thames
Limehouse Reach
Greenwich Reach
Greenwich Foot Tunnel
West India Docks
Millwall Docks
Blackwall Basin
Poplar Dock
Millwall Park
Island Gardens
DEPTFORD
0 220 440 yards
0 100 200 300 400 metres

LONDON Greater London Plans 1-9, pages 346-358. (Small scale map 6 at back of book.) Hotels are listed below in postal district order, commencing East, then North, South and West, with a brief indication of the area covered. Detailed plans 2-9 show the locations of AA hotels within the Central London postal districts. If you do not know the postal district of the hotel you want, please refer to the index preceding the street plans for the entry and map pages.

E1 STEPNEY AND EAST OF THE TOWER OF LONDON

⇧ Travelodge (London City)

Travelodge

1 Harrow Place E1 7DB
☎ 08700 850 950

Travelodge offers good quality, good value, modern accommodation. Ideal for families, the spacious, en suite bedrooms include remote-control TV, tea and coffee-making facilities, luxury beds and free morning newspaper. Meals can be taken at the nearby family restaurant. For further details and the Travelodge phone number, consult the Hotel Groups page.

ROOMS: 142 en suite s fr £42.95; d fr £42.95

E4 CHINGFORD
See LONDON plan 1 G6

⇧ *Express by Holiday Inn London Chingford*

Express by Holiday Inn

5 Walthamshow Ave, Chingford E4 8ST
☎ 0870 444 2789 🖷 0870 444 2790
e-mail: managerchingford@expressholidayinn.fsnet.co.uk
Dir: *on A406 (North Circular) at Crooked Billet rdbt, adjacent to A112 (Chingford-Walthamstow)*

A modern hotel ideal for families and business travellers. Fresh and uncomplicated, the spacious bedrooms include Sky TV, power shower and tea and coffee-making facilities. Continental buffet breakfast is included in the room rate; other meals may be taken at the nearby family pub or restaurant. For further details and the Express by Holiday Inn phone number, consult the Hotel Groups pages.

ROOMS: 102 en suite **CONF:** Board 12

E6 BECKTON
See LONDON plan 1 H4

⇧ Travel Inn

travel inn

1 Woolwich Manor Way, Beckton E6 4NT
☎ 08701 977029 🖷 020 7511 4214
Dir: *from A13 take A117, Woolwich Manor Way, towards City Airport, on left after 1st rdbt*

Travel Inn offers good-quality, value-for-money accommodation. Spacious, en suite rooms with bath and shower comfortably accommodate a family of up to two adults and two children (to age 15). The restaurant and bar offers a varied menu. For further details and the Travel Inn phone number, consult the Hotel Groups page.

ROOMS: 90 en suite s £49.95-£54.95; d £49.95-£54.95

○ Novotel London Excel

NOVOTEL

Western Gateway, Royal Victoria Dock E16
☎ 0207 265 6001
ROOMS: 257 en suite **NOTES:** Due to open Feb 2004

E14 CANARY WHARF & LIMEHOUSE
See LONDON plan 1 G3

Top 200 - Hotel

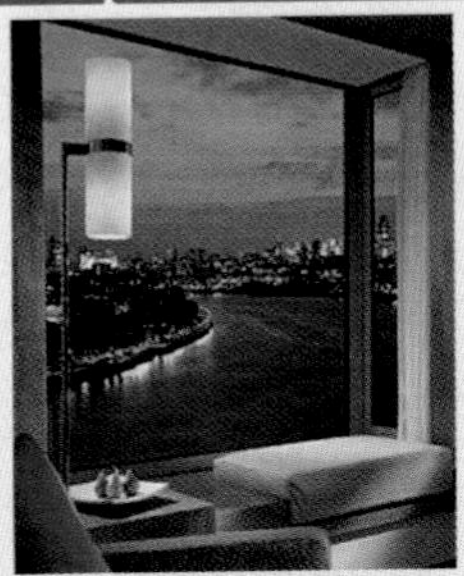

★★★★★ ◎ Four Seasons Hotel Canary Wharf

Westferry Circus, Canary Wharf E14 8RS
☎ 020 7510 1999 🖷 020 7510 1998
Dir: *from A13 follow signs to Canary Wharf, Isle of Dogs and Westferry Circus. Hotel off 3rd exit of Westferry Circus rdbt*

With superb views over the London skyline, this stylish modern hotel enjoys a delightful riverside location. Spacious contemporary bedrooms are particularly thoughtfully equipped. Public areas include the Italian Quadrato Bar and Restaurant, an impressive business centre and gymnasium. Guests also have complimentary use of the impressive Holmes Place Health Club and Spa. Welcoming staff provide exemplary levels of service and hospitality.

ROOMS: 142 en suite No smoking in 120 bedrooms s £329; d £353 **FACILITIES: Spa** STV Indoor swimming (H) Tennis (hard) Sauna Solarium Gym Jacuzzi Swimming pool supervised entertainment ch fac Xmas **CONF:** BC Thtr 200 Class 120 Board 56 **SERVICES:** Lift air con **PARKING:** 29 **NOTES:** Civ Wed 200 **CARDS:**

⇧ Hotel Ibis London Docklands

ibis ACCOR hotels

1 Baffin Way E14 9PE
☎ 020 7517 1100 🖷 020 7987 5916
e-mail: H2177@accor-hotels.com
Dir: *from Tower Bridge follow City Airport and Royal Docks signs,exit for 'Isle of Dogs'. Hotel on 1st left opposite McDonalds*

Modern, budget hotel offering comfortable accommodation in bright and practical bedrooms. Breakfast is self-service and dinner is available in the restaurant. For further details, consult the Hotel Groups page.

ROOMS: 87 en suite s £64.95-£71.95; d £64.95-£71.95

London

E14 CANARY WHARF & LIMEHOUSE, continued

⇧ Travelodge (London Dockland)

Coriander Av, East India Dock Rd E14 2AA
☎ 08700 850 950
Dir: *A13 at East India Dock Rd*

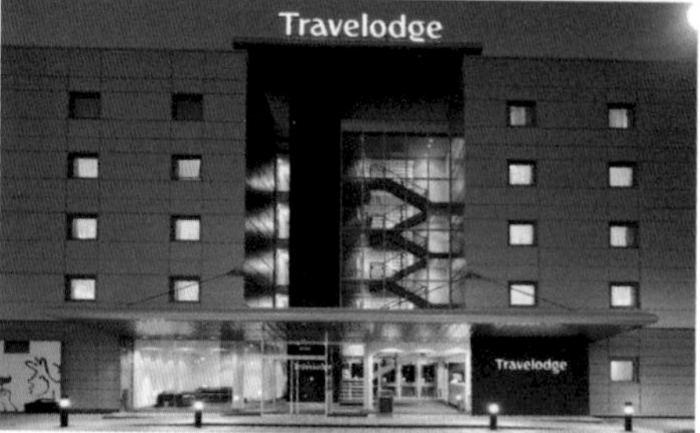

Travelodge offers good quality, good value, modern accommodation. Ideal for families, the spacious, en suite bedrooms include remote-control TV, tea and coffee-making facilities, luxury beds and free morning newspaper. Meals can be taken at the nearby family restaurant. For further details and the Travelodge phone number, consult the Hotel Groups page.
ROOMS: 232 en suite s fr £42.95; d fr £42.95

E15 STRATFORD
See LONDON plan 1 G4

⇧ Express by Holiday Inn London Stratford

196 High St, Stratford E15 2PD
☎ 0870 240 5708 📠 0870 066 0245
e-mail: stratford@londoninnhotels.com

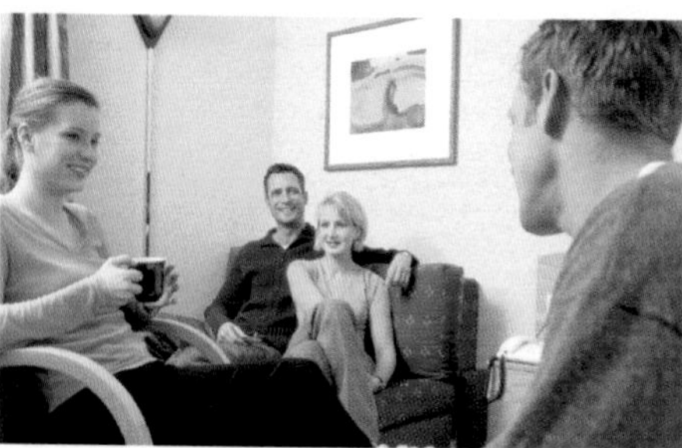

A modern hotel ideal for families and business travellers. Fresh and uncomplicated, the spacious bedrooms include Sky TV, power shower and tea and coffee-making facilities. Continental buffet breakfast is included in the room rate; other meals may be taken at the nearby family pub or restaurant. For further details and the Express by Holiday Inn phone number, consult the Hotel Groups pages.
ROOMS: 114 en suite s £59-£89; d £59-£89 (incl. cont bkfst)
CONF: Thtr 25 Class 16 Board 16 Del from £99

⇧ Hotel Ibis London Stratford

1A Romford Rd, Stratford E15 4LJ
☎ 020 8536 3700 📠 020 8519 5161
e-mail: H3099@accor-hotels.com
Modern, budget hotel offering comfortable accommodation in bright and practical bedrooms. Breakfast is self-service and dinner is available in the restaurant. For further details, consult the Hotel Groups page.
ROOMS: 108 en suite s £59.95-£64.95; d £59.95-£64.95

E16 SILVERTOWN
See LONDON plan 1 H3

⇧ Express by Holiday Inn London Royal Docks

1 Silvertown Way, Silvertown E16 1EA
☎ 020 7540 4040 📠 020 7540 4050
e-mail: info@exhi-royaldocks.co.uk
Dir: *From A13 take A1011 towards Silverton and City Airport, hotel on left*

A modern hotel ideal for families and business travellers. Fresh and uncomplicated, the spacious bedrooms include Sky TV, power shower and tea and coffee-making facilities. Continental buffet breakfast is included in the room rate; other meals may be taken at the nearby family pub or restaurant. For further details and the Express by Holiday Inn phone number, consult the Hotel Groups pages.
ROOMS: 88 en suite s £49-£99; d £49-£99 (incl. cont bkfst)
CONF: Thtr 40 Class 14 Board 22

⇧ Travel Inn London Docklands

Royal Victoria Dock E16 2AE
☎ 0870 238 3322 📠 0870 241 9000
Dir: *from A13 right A1020. At Connaught rbt take 2nd exit into Connaught Rd. Travel Inn on right*
Travel Inn offers good-quality, value-for-money accommodation. Spacious, en suite rooms with bath and shower comfortably accommodate a family of up to two adults and two children (to age 15). The restaurant and bar offers a varied menu. For further details and the Travel Inn phone number, consult the Hotel Groups page.
ROOMS: 202 en suite s £49.95-£69.95; d £49.95-£69.95

○ Premier Lodge (London City Airport)

Hatmann Rd, Silvertown Triangle E16 2DE
☎ 0870 9906384 📠 0870 9906385
ROOMS: 142 en suite
NOTES: Due to open Summer 2004

EC1 CITY OF LONDON Map 06 TQ27

⇧ Express by Holiday Inn London City

275 Old St EC1V 9LN
☎ 020 7300 4300 📠 020 7300 4400
e-mail: reservationsfc@holidayinnlondon.com
Dir: *At City Rd rdbt turn left, hotel on left, next to fire station*
A modern hotel ideal for families and business travellers. Fresh and uncomplicated, the spacious bedrooms include Sky TV, power shower and tea and coffee-making facilities. Continental buffet breakfast is included in the room rate; other meals may be taken at the nearby family pub or restaurant. For further details and the

continued

Express by Holiday Inn phone number, consult the Hotel Groups pages.

ROOMS: 224 en suite (incl. cont bkfst) s £106-£110; d £106-£110 **CONF:** Thtr 100 Class 50 Board 40 Del from £149.50

○ **Malmaison London**
18-21 Charterhouse Square EC1
☎ 01737 780 200 (reservations)
ROOMS: 96 en suite **NOTES:** Due to open Nov 2003

EC2

Top 200 - Hotel

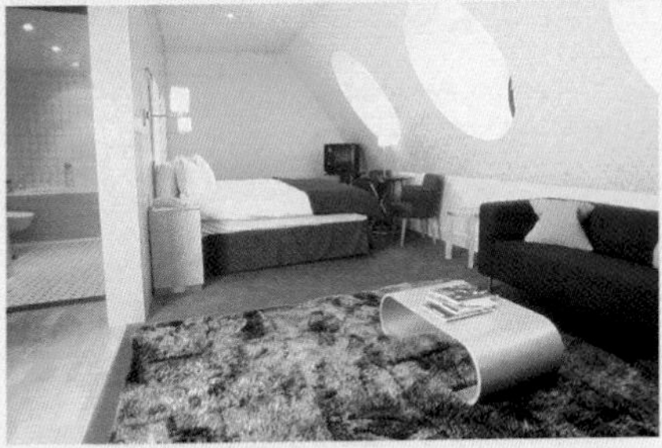

★★★★★ ◎◎◎ ***Great Eastern Hotel***
Liverpool St EC2M 7QN
☎ 020 7618 5000 📠 020 7618 5001
e-mail: sales@great-eastern-hotel.co.uk
This modern minimalist hotel enjoys a prime location in the heart of the city, adjacent to Liverpool Street station. Air-conditioned bedrooms are simple yet stylish with DVD and CD players. The impressive array of restaurants includes the elegant Aurora offering fine dining, Fish Market with its champagne bar, Terminus offering all day meals and snacks and a Japanese restaurant. There is a gym complete with treatment rooms and personal trainers.
ROOMS: 267 en suite No smoking in 74 bedrooms **FACILITIES:** STV Gym steam room **CONF:** Thtr 200 Class 120 **SERVICES:** Lift air con **NOTES:** Civ Wed **CARDS:**

Town House Hotel
Country House Hotel
Travel Accommodation

EC3 CHEAPSIDE

Town House

★★★★ **The Chamberlain**
130-135 Minories EC3N 1NU
☎ 020 7680 1500 📠 020 7702 2500
e-mail: thechamberlain@fullers.co.uk
Dir: *hotel halfway down Minories*
This newly converted hotel is ideally situated for the city, Tower Bridge and Fenchurch Street Station. Impressive bedrooms are stylish, well equipped and comfortable while the modern bathrooms are fitted with TVs to watch while you soak in the bath. Informal day rooms include a popular pub and an attractive split-level dining room.
ROOMS: 64 en suite No smoking in 30 bedrooms s £105-£185; d £105-£185 **LB FACILITIES:** STV Discounted leisure facilities for hotel guests nearby **CONF:** Thtr 50 Class 20 Board 30 **SERVICES:** Lift air con **NOTES:** No dogs (ex guide dogs) Closed 24 Dec-4 Jan **CARDS:**

★★★72% ***Novotel London Tower Bridge***
10 Pepys St EC3N 2NR
☎ 020 7265 6000 📠 020 7265 6060
e-mail: H3107@accor-hotels.com

Located near the Tower of London, this smart hotel is convenient for Docklands, the City, Heathrow and London City airports. Bedrooms are spacious, modern and offer a great range of facilities, including air conditioning. There is a smart bar and restaurant, a small gym and meeting and conference facilities. This hotel was highly commended in the AA Accessible Hotel of the Year Award 2003-2004.
ROOMS: 203 en suite (77 fmly) No smoking in 145 bedrooms **FACILITIES:** STV Sauna Gym Steam Room **CONF:** Thtr 72 Class 32 Board 28 **SERVICES:** Lift air con **CARDS:**

U The Grange City
Coopers Row EC3 2BQ
☎ 020 7863 3700 📠 020 7863 3761
e-mail: city@grangehotels.com

At the time of going to press, the star classification for this hotel was not confirmed. Please refer to the AA internet site www.theAA.com for current information.
ROOMS: 254 en suite No smoking in 120 bedrooms s £209-£1500; d £245-£1500 **FACILITIES: Spa** STV Indoor swimming (H) Sauna Gym Swimming pool supervised Xmas **CONF:** BC Thtr 800 Class 400 Board 200 Del from £302 **SERVICES:** Lift air con **NOTES:** No dogs (ex guide dogs) **CARDS:**

N1 ISLINGTON
See LONDON plan 1 F4

★★★63% **Jurys Inn London**
60 Pentonville Rd, Islington N1 9LA
☎ 020 7282 5500 📠 020 7282 5511
e-mail: london_inn@jurysdoyle.com
Dir: *from A1 right onto A501, right again onto Pentonville Rd*
This modern hotel offers spacious bedrooms with good facilities, and provides guests with a choice of comfortable public areas. There is an Irish pub serving snacks and a more formal restaurant with a daily changing menu.
ROOMS: 229 en suite (116 fmly) No smoking in 135 bedrooms s £99; d fr £99 **FACILITIES:** STV **CONF:** Thtr 50 Class 24 Board 28 Del from £180 **SERVICES:** Lift air con **NOTES:** No dogs (ex guide dogs) Closed 24-27 Dec **CARDS:**

N1 ISLINGTON, continued

◯ Premier Lodge (London Kings Cross)

York Way, Kings Cross N1 9AX
☎ 0870 9906414 🖷 0870 9906415
ROOMS: 278 en suite **NOTES:** Due to open May 2004

N14 SOUTHGATE
See LONDON SECTION plan 1 E6

⌂ Innkeeper's Lodge Southgate

22 The Green, Southgate N14 6EN
☎ 020 8447 8022 🖷 020 8447 8022
Dir: *take A111 from J24, 3m to rdbt for A1004, turn right into High Street, hotel at next rdbt*

A new concept in the travel accommodation market. Smart rooms meet essential business requirements but also have home comforts. Dining options include all-day menus plus the added advantage of breakfast, which is included in the room price. For further details, consult the Hotel Groups page.
ROOMS: 19 en suite

NW1 REGENT'S PARK

Top 200 - Hotel

★★★★★ ◎ The Landmark London

222 Marylebone Rd NW1 6JQ
☎ 020 7631 8000 🖷 020 7631 8080
e-mail: reservations@thelandmark.co.uk
Dir: *adjacent to Marylebone Station and near Paddington Station*

Said to be one of the last truly grand railway hotels. The Landmark boasts a number of stunning features, the most spectacular of which is the naturally lit central atrium which forms the focal point of the hotel. When it comes to eating and drinking there are plenty of options, among which are the Cellars for upmarket bar meals. The Winter Gardens are a beautiful venue for all day dining, set in the centre of the atrium. Air-conditioned bedrooms are spacious and have stunning marble bathrooms.
ROOMS: 299 en suite (60 fmly) No smoking in 179 bedrooms s £229-£1428; d £258-£1457 **LB** **FACILITIES: Spa** STV Indoor swimming (H) Sauna Gym Jacuzzi Beauty treatments and massages entertainment Xmas **CONF:** BC Thtr 380 Class 190 Board 50 **SERVICES:** Lift air con **PARKING:** 80 **NOTES:** No dogs (ex guide dogs) Civ Wed 300 **CARDS:**

★★★★72% Meliá White House Regents Park

Albany St, Regents Park NW1 3UP
☎ 020 7391 3000 🖷 020 7388 0091
e-mail: melia.white.house@solmelia.com
Dir: *opposite Gt Portland St underground station*

An impressive art deco building which dates back to 1936, when it was built as an apartment block. Public areas offer a high degree of comfort and include a fine dining restaurant and a more informal brasserie. Bedrooms vary in size and are elegantly styled, offer high levels of comfort, and are well equipped.
ROOMS: 582 en suite (1 fmly) No smoking in 166 bedrooms **FACILITIES:** STV Sauna Gym **CONF:** Thtr 120 Class 45 Board 40 **SERVICES:** Lift air con **PARKING:** 7 **NOTES:** No dogs (ex guide dogs) **CARDS:**

★★★★67% Novotel London Euston

100-110 Euston Rd NW1 2AJ
☎ 020 7666 9000 🖷 020 7766 9100
e-mail: H5309@accor-hotels.com
Dir: *between St Pancras & Euston stations*

Situated adjacent to the British Library and close to Euston Station, this hotel enjoys a central location. Modern and contemporary in style throughout, spacious air-conditioned bedrooms are very well equipped. Open plan public areas include a leisure suite and extensive conference facilities featuring the Shaw Theatre.
ROOMS: 312 en suite (21 fmly) No smoking in 246 bedrooms s £160; d £180 **FACILITIES:** STV Sauna Gym Xmas **CONF:** Thtr 466 Class 220 Board 80 Del £242 **SERVICES:** Lift air con **NOTES:** No dogs (ex guide dogs) **CARDS:**

★★67% Regents Park Hotel

156 Gloucester Place NW1 6DT
☎ 020 7258 1911 🖷 020 7258 0288
e-mail: rph-reservation@usa.net
Dir: *Baker St tube station. Right at Elf station, hotel on right*

This privately owned hotel is ideally located in the heart of London, close to Baker Street tube and Madame Tussaud's. Smartly appointed en suite bedrooms benefit from an excellent range of facilities. There is an attractive conservatory-style restaurant serving authentic Singaporean cuisine.
ROOMS: 17 en suite 12 annexe en suite (2 fmly) s £69-£80; d £89-£99 (incl. cont bkfst) **FACILITIES:** STV **NOTES:** No dogs (ex guide dogs) **CARDS:**

⌂ Hotel Ibis London Euston

3 Cardington St NW1 2LW
☎ 020 7388 7777 🖷 020 7388 0001
e-mail: H0921@accor-hotels.com
Dir: *from Euston Rd or station, right to Melton St leading to Cardington St*

Modern, budget hotel offering comfortable accommodation in bright and practical bedrooms. Breakfast is self-service and dinner is available in the restaurant. For further details, consult the Hotel Groups page.
ROOMS: 380 en suite s £74.95-£79.95; d £74.95-£79.95

NW2 BRENT CROSS & CRICKLEWOOD
See LONDON plan1 D5

★★68% The Garth Hotel

64-76 Hendon Way NW2 2NL
☎ 020 8209 1511 🖷 020 8455 4744
e-mail: enquiry@garth-hotel.co.uk
Dir: *S carriageway of A41 between The Vale & Cricklewood Lane*

The Garth Hotel is something of a landmark in this part of north London, just minutes away from Brent Cross Shopping Centre and

continued

the North Circular. Bedrooms are spacious and simply appointed. The Italian theme is particularly obvious in the restaurant and bar, where home-cooked Italian dishes are the highlight.
ROOMS: 37 en suite (10 fmly) No smoking in 15 bedrooms s £43-£65; d £49.95-£75 **LB** **FACILITIES:** STV Xmas **CONF:** BC Thtr 300 Class 250 Board 150 **PARKING:** 40 **NOTES:** No dogs (ex guide dogs) No smoking in restaurant **CARDS:**

U *Holiday Inn London - Brent Cross*

Tilling Rd, Brent Cross NW2 1LP
☎ 020 8455 4777 Res & 020 8201 8686
020 8455 4660
Dir: *Tilling Rd is 2nd exit off M1 rndbt. Hotel off A5 & A41 on A406*
At the time of going to press, the classification for this hotel was not confirmed. Please refer to the AA internet site www.theAA.com for current information.
ROOMS: 153 en suite **CONF:** Thtr 60 Class 30 Board 28

NW3 HAMPSTEAD AND SWISS COTTAGE
See LONDON plan 1 E5/E4

★★★★73% London Marriott Hotel Regents Park

128 King Henry's Rd NW3 3ST
☎ 0870 400 7240 0870 400 7340
Dir: *200yds off Finchley Rd on A41*
Situated in a quieter part of town and close to the tube station. It offers guests comfortably appointed, air-conditioned accommodation which meet the needs of today's business traveller. The open-plan ground floor contains all the main facilities including a well equipped leisure centre with indoor pool.
ROOMS: 303 en suite No smoking in 130 bedrooms s £116-£159; d £116-£159 **FACILITIES:** STV Indoor swimming (H) Sauna Solarium Gym Hair & Beauty salon, Steam room entertainment **CONF:** Thtr 300 Class 150 Board 150 Del from £180 **SERVICES:** Lift air con **PARKING:** 150 **NOTES:** No dogs (ex guide dogs) Civ Wed 300 **CARDS:**

U *Holiday Inn Hampstead*

215 Haverstock Hill NW3 4RB
☎ 0870 400 9037 020 7435 5586
e-mail: hampstead@ichotelsgroup.com
Dir: *A41 to Swiss Cottage. Before junct take feeder road left into Buckland Cresent onto Belsize Av and left into Haverstock Hill*
At the time of going to press, the classification for this hotel was not confirmed. Please refer to the AA internet site www.theAA.com for current information.
ROOMS: 140 en suite No smoking in 70 bedrooms **CONF:** Thtr 35 Board 20 **SERVICES:** Lift **PARKING:** 70 **NOTES:** No dogs (ex guide dogs) **CARDS:**

NW6 MAIDA VALE
See LONDON plan 1 D4

★★★★69% London Marriott Maida Vale

Plaza Pde, Maida Vale NW6 5RP
☎ 020 7543 6000 020 7543 2100
e-mail: marriottmaidavale@btinternet.com
Dir: *From M1, A406 W, A5 south, through Kilburn, hotel on left*
This smart, modern hotel enjoys a convenient location easily accessible from the M1. Bedrooms are smartly appointed and particularly well equipped. Public areas include a choice of dining options, extensive function facilities and a health and leisure centre.

ROOMS: 238 en suite (6 fmly) No smoking in 110 bedrooms s £99-£129; d £99-£129 **LB** **FACILITIES:** STV Indoor swimming (H) Sauna Solarium Gym Hair & beauty salons, Swimming pool supervised Xmas **CONF:** BC Thtr 200 Class 90 Board 40 Del from £170 **SERVICES:** Lift air con **PARKING:** 39 **NOTES:** No dogs (ex guide dogs) **CARDS:**

NW10 WEMBLEY
See LONDON plan 1 C4

⇧ Express by Holiday Inn Wembley-North Circular

Northdale House, North Circular Rd NW10 7UG
☎ 020 8965 9200 020 8965 9300
e-mail: wembleyres@khl.com
Dir: *A40, A406 N, keep left. 1st slip road on left*
A modern hotel ideal for families and business travellers. Fresh and uncomplicated, the spacious bedrooms include Sky TV, power shower and tea and coffee-making facilities. Continental buffet breakfast is included in the room rate; other meals may be taken at the nearby family pub or restaurant. For further details and Express by Holiday Inn phone number, consult Hotel Groups pages.
ROOMS: 168 en suite s £49-£74; d £49-£74 (incl. bkfst) **CONF:** Thtr 50 Class 20 Board 28 Del from £115

SE1 SOUTHWARK AND WATERLOO

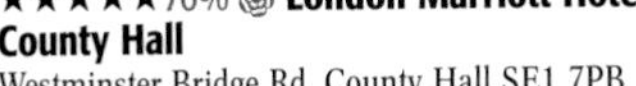

★★★★★70% ◎ London Marriott Hotel County Hall

Westminster Bridge Rd, County Hall SE1 7PB
☎ 020 7928 5200 020 7928 5300
Dir: *entrance on South Bank of Westminster Bridge, through County Hall gates into courtyard*

This magnificent hotel enjoys a prime location on the banks of the Thames and many of the smart, well-equipped bedrooms enjoy

continued on p364

London

SE1 SOUTHWARK AND WATERLOO, continued

superb views of the river, Big Ben and the London Eye. Elegant public areas include a delightful library lounge, a choice of bars and an elegant restaurant. Residents also have access to the extensive leisure and beauty facilities.
ROOMS: 200 en suite (60 fmly) No smoking in 147 bedrooms **FACILITIES:** STV Indoor swimming (H) Sauna Solarium Gym Jacuzzi entertainment **CONF:** BC Thtr 80 Class 40 Board 28 Del from £258.50 **SERVICES:** Lift air con **PARKING:** 70 **NOTES:** No dogs (ex guide dogs) Civ Wed 72 **CARDS:**

★★★★66% London Bridge Hotel

8-18 London Bridge St SE1 9SG
☎ 020 7855 2200 ⎙ 020 7855 2233
e-mail: sales@london-bridge-hotel.co.uk
Dir: *Access through London Bridge Station (bus/taxi yard), into London Bridge St (one-way). Hotel on left, 50yds from station*
This elegant independently owned hotel enjoys a prime location on the edge of the city, adjacent to London Bridge station. Smartly appointed, well-equipped bedrooms include a number of spacious deluxe rooms and suites. Compact yet sophisticated public areas include a selection of conference and meeting rooms, Georgetown Asian restaurant and a well-equipped gymnasium.
ROOMS: 138 en suite (12 fmly) No smoking in 85 bedrooms s £190; d £190 **LB** **FACILITIES:** STV Gym Arrangement with local club **CONF:** Thtr 100 Class 40 Board 40 Del £266 **SERVICES:** Lift air con **NOTES:** No dogs (ex guide dogs) **CARDS:**

★★★74% Novotel London City South

Southwark Bridge Rd SE1 9HH
☎ 020 7089 0400 ⎙ 020 7089 0410
e-mail: H3269@accor-hotels.com
Dir: *at junct with Thrale St*
The first of a new generation of Novotels, this new build hotel is contemporary in design with smart, modern bedrooms and spacious public rooms. There are a number of options for those guests wanting to unwind including treatments such as reflexology and immersion therapy, while a gymnasium is available for the more energetic.
ROOMS: 182 en suite (139 fmly) No smoking in 158 bedrooms s £140; d £160 **FACILITIES:** STV Gym **CONF:** Thtr 100 Class 40 Board 35 Del from £199 **SERVICES:** Lift air con
CARDS:

★★★72% ®
Mercure London City Bankside

71-79 Southwark St SE1 0JA
☎ 020 7902 0800 ⎙ 020 7902 0810
e-mail: H2814@accor-hotels.com
This smart, contemporary hotel forms part of the rejuvenation of the South Bank. With the City of London just over the river and a number of tourist attractions within easy reach, the hotel is well located for both business and leisure travellers. Other reasons to stay include spacious air-cooled bedrooms and modern dining in the stylish Loft Restaurant.
ROOMS: 144 en suite (24 fmly) No smoking in 88 bedrooms **FACILITIES:** STV Gym **CONF:** Thtr 60 Class 40 Board 30 **SERVICES:** Lift air con **CARDS:**

> Late for dinner?
> Quality Standards mean that last orders for dinner vary according to star rating and should be no earlier than:
> ★★ 7.00pm ★★★ 8.00pm ★★★★ 9.00pm
> ★★★★★ 10.00pm

★★★68% Novotel London Waterloo

113 Lambeth Rd SE1 7LS
☎ 020 7793 1010 ⎙ 020 7793 0202
e-mail: h1785@accor-hotels.com
Dir: *opposite Houses of Parliament on S bank of River Thames, off Lambeth Bridge, opposite Lambeth Palace*
This modern hotel is close to Waterloo Station. Bedrooms are spacious and include air conditioning. Ten rooms have facilities for less able guests. The open plan public areas include a garden brasserie, the Flag and Whistle Pub, small shop and leisure facilities. Underground parking is a real plus.
ROOMS: 187 en suite (80 fmly) No smoking in 158 bedrooms s £135; d £155 **LB** **FACILITIES:** STV Sauna Gym Steam room Fitness room **CONF:** Thtr 40 Class 24 Board 24 Del £199 **SERVICES:** Lift air con **PARKING:** 40 **CARDS:**

⌂ Days Inn Waterloo

54 Kennington Rd SE1 7BJ
☎ 020 7922 1331 ⎙ 020 7922 1441
e-mail: waterloores@khl.uk.com
This modern building offers accommodation in smart, spacious and well-equipped bedrooms, suitable for families and business travellers, and all with en suite bathrooms. Continental breakfast is available and other refreshments may be taken at the nearby family restaurant. For further details and the Days Inn phone number, consult the Hotel Groups page.
ROOMS: 162 en suite s £69-£84; d £69-£84

⌂ Express by Holiday Inn Southwark

103-109 Southwark St SE1 0JQ
☎ 020 7401 2525 ⎙ 020 7401 3322
e-mail: stay@expresssouthwark.co.uk
Dir: *A20 onto A2 to city centre towards Elephant and Castle. Right before Blackfriars Bridge at 1st large traffic lights junct*

A modern hotel ideal for families and business travellers. Fresh and uncomplicated, the spacious bedrooms include Sky TV, power shower and tea and coffee-making facilities. Continental buffet breakfast is included in the room rate; other meals may be taken at the nearby family pub or restaurant. For further details and the Express by Holiday Inn phone number, consult the Hotel Groups pages.
ROOMS: 88 en suite s £69-£98; d £69-£98 **CONF:** Board 12

⌂ Premier Lodge (London Southwark)

Anchor, Bankside, 34 Park St SE1 9EF
☎ 0870 9906402 ⎙ 0870 9906403
Premier Lodge offers modern, well-equipped, en suite accommodation suitable for both business and leisure travellers. Meals can be taken at the adjacent popular restaurant and bar, which is fully licensed. For further details, consult the Hotel Groups page.
ROOMS: s £72; d £72

⌂ Travel Inn (London County Hall)

Belvedere Rd SE1 7PB
☎ 0870 238 3300 📠 020 7902 1619
Dir: *In the County Hall, next to the London Eye*

Travel Inn offers good-quality, value-for-money accommodation. Spacious, en suite rooms with bath and shower comfortably accommodate a family of up to two adults and two children (to age 15). The restaurant and bar offers a varied menu. For further details and the Travel Inn phone number, consult the Hotel Groups page.
ROOMS: 313 en suite s £79.95-£82.95; d £79.95-£82.95

⌂ Travel Inn (London Tower Bridge)

Tower Bridge Rd SE1 3LP
☎ 0870 238 3303 📠 020 7940 3719
Dir: *South of Tower Bridge*
Travel Inn offers good-quality, value-for-money accommodation. Spacious, en suite rooms with bath and shower comfortably accommodate a family of up to two adults and two children (to age 15). The restaurant and bar offers a varied menu. For further details and the Travel Inn phone number, consult the Hotel Groups page.

Travel Inn (London Tower Bridge)

ROOMS: 195 en suite s £69.95-£74.95; d £69.95-£74.95

SE3 BLACKHEATH
See LONDON plan 1 G3

★★67% Clarendon

THE INDEPENDENTS

8-16 Montpelier Row, Blackheath SE3 0RW
☎ 020 8318 4321 📠 020 8318 4378
e-mail: relax@clarendonhotel.com
Dir: *off A2 at Blackheath junct. Hotel on left before village*
Overlooking the heath, this impressive Georgian hotel offers well-equipped attractive accommodation. A number of suites are also available. Spacious public areas include a choice of bars, a

continued on p366

London

SE3 BLACKHEATH, continued

restaurant and meeting and conference facilities. The hotel has its own car park and guests have use of local leisure facilities.

Clarendon, SE3

ROOMS: 182 en suite (3 fmly) (5 GF) No smoking in 22 bedrooms s £80-£95; d £90-£100 (incl. bkfst) **LB** **FACILITIES:** STV entertainment Xmas **CONF:** Thtr 120 Class 40 Board 50 Del from £115 **SERVICES:** Lift **PARKING:** 80 **NOTES:** Civ Wed 100
CARDS:

See advert on page 365

SE10 GREENWICH
See LONDON plan 1 G3

★★67% Hamilton House

14 West Grove, Greenwich SE10 8QT
☎ 020 8694 9899 🖷 020 8694 2370
e-mail: reception@hamiltonhousehotel.co.uk
Dir: *from Blackheath Common on A2 towards central London, 2nd right after Blackheath Tea Hut into Hyde Vale. West Grove next left*

This small Georgian hotel boasts true style and character and some impressive views of the Docklands. Bedrooms are individually appointed with some antique pieces of furniture. The restaurant is bright and offers creative cooking. The bar area opens out to an attractive garden with seating. This hotel is very popular as a wedding venue.

ROOMS: 9 en suite (8 fmly) No smoking in 4 bedrooms s £90-£100; d fr £120 (incl. bkfst) **LB** **FACILITIES:** STV Xmas **CONF:** Thtr 35 Class 22 Board 20 **PARKING:** 8 **NOTES:** No dogs (ex guide dogs) No smoking in restaurant Civ Wed 85
CARDS:

⌂ Express by Holiday Inn Greenwich

85 Bugsby's Way, Greenwich SE10 0GD
☎ 020 8269 5000 🖷 020 8269 5054
e-mail: managergreenwich@expressholidayinn.co.uk
Dir: *off A102, near Millennium Dome*

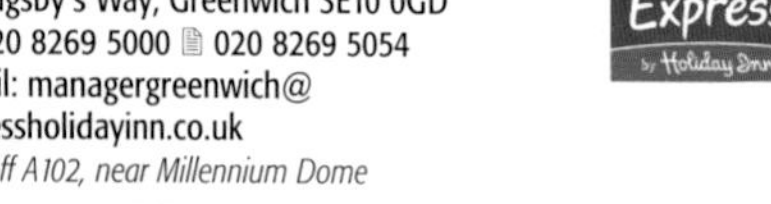

A modern hotel ideal for families and business travellers. Fresh and uncomplicated, the spacious bedrooms include Sky TV, power shower and tea and coffee-making facilities. Continental buffet breakfast is included in the room rate; other meals may be taken at the nearby family pub or restaurant. For further details and the Express by Holiday Inn phone number, consult the Hotel Groups pages.

ROOMS: 162 en suite s £99-£110; d £99-£110 (incl. cont bkfst)
CONF: Thtr 80 Class 30 Board 40

⌂ Hotel Ibis London Greenwich

30 Stockwell St, Greenwich SE10 9JN
☎ 020 8305 1177 🖷 020 8858 7139
e-mail: H0975@accor-hotels.com
Dir: *from Waterloo Bridge, Elephan & Castle, A2 to Greenwich.*

Modern, budget hotel offering comfortable accommodation in bright and practical bedrooms. Breakfast is self-service and dinner is available in the restaurant. For further details, consult the Hotel Groups page.

ROOMS: 82 en suite s £66.95-£72.95; d £66.95-£72.95

SW1 WESTMINSTER — Map 06 TQ27

Top 200 - Hotel

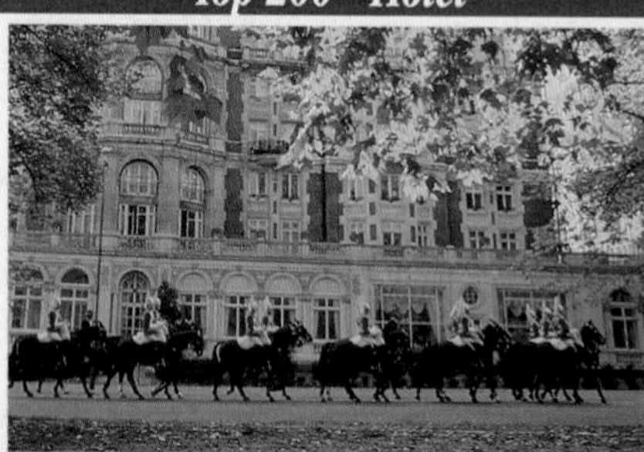

★★★★★ @@@@ Mandarin Oriental Hyde Park

66 Knightsbridge SW1X 7LA
☎ 020 7235 2000 🖷 020 7235 2001
e-mail: molon-reservations@mohg.com
Dir: *with Harrods on right, hotel 0.5m on left opp Harvey Nichols*

This elegant hotel overlooks Hyde Park and Knightsbridge. Bedrooms and suites are appointed to the highest standard, many with unrivalled views. Irish linen sheets and goose down pillows add to the luxury. There are a choice of dining options - The Park Restaurant offering light brasserie-style dishes, the sophisticated Foliage, offering a superb standard of cuisine, and the fashionable Mandarin Bar serving light snacks and cocktails. The stylish spa is a destination in its own right with booking essential.

ROOMS: 200 en suite No smoking in 72 bedrooms s fr £255; d fr £305 **LB** **FACILITIES: Spa** STV Sauna Gym Jacuzzi Fitness centre, steam room, relaxation area, sanarium entertainment Xmas **CONF:** BC Thtr 250 Class 120 Board 60 **SERVICES:** Lift air con **PARKING:** 13 **NOTES:** No dogs (ex guide dogs) Civ Wed 400
CARDS:

London

Top 200 - Hotel

★★★★★ The Goring

Beeston Place, Grosvenor Gardens SW1W 0JW
☎ 020 7396 9000 📠 020 7834 4393
e-mail: reception@goringhotel.co.uk

Dir: *off Lower Grosvenor Place, just prior to Royal Mews*

Situated in central London, the Goring is within walking distance of the Royal Parks and the principal shopping areas. The well-equipped bedrooms are furnished in a traditional style and boast high levels of comfort and quality. Stylish reception rooms include the garden bar and the drawing room, both popular for afternoon tea and cocktails. The restaurant menu has a classic repertoire but also enjoys a well-deserved reputation for its contemporary British cuisine.

ROOMS: 74 en suite s £200-£450; d £230-£450 **LB** **FACILITIES:** STV Free membership of nearby Health Club entertainment Xmas **CONF:** Thtr 60 Class 30 Board 30 **SERVICES:** Lift air con **PARKING:** 8 **NOTES:** No dogs Civ Wed 50 **CARDS:**

Top 200 - Hotel

★★★★★ *The Lanesborough*

Hyde Park Corner SW1X 7TA
☎ 020 7259 5599 📠 020 7259 5606
e-mail: info@lanesborough.co.uk

Dir: *follow signs to central London and Hyde Park Corner*

Occupying an enviable position on Hyde Park Corner, this elegant hotel has an ageless charm and engaging atmosphere, much appreciated by the loyal clientele. Quality is a hallmark here; bedrooms and public rooms reflect the highest levels of comfort. Service is equally impressive with a personal butler ensuring individual attention. The conservatory restaurant is a popular venue for accomplished international cuisine in a convivial setting.

ROOMS: 95 en suite No smoking in 24 bedrooms **FACILITIES: Spa** STV Gym Fitness studio entertainment **CONF:** Thtr 120 Class 60 Board 48 **SERVICES:** Lift air con **PARKING:** 38 **NOTES:** Civ Wed 100 **CARDS:**

Top 200 - Hotel

★★★★★ The Berkeley

Wilton Place, Knightsbridge SW1X 7RL
☎ 020 7235 6000 📠 020 7235 4330
e-mail: info@the-berkeley.co.uk

Dir: *300mtrs along Knightsbridge from Hyde Park Corner*

The Berkeley never fails to impress. Ongoing refurbishment ensures an excellent range of bedrooms, each one furnished with care and attention to detail. The striking new Blue Bar enhances the reception rooms, which are adorned with magnificent flower arrangements. The health spa offers a range of treatment rooms and includes a stunning open-air rooftop pool. This year has seen the arrival of two Gordon Ramsay restaurants at The Berkeley - the Boxwood Café and Marcus Wareing's Pétrus (formerly in St James's). At the time of going to press the rosette rating for these restaurants had not been confirmed.

ROOMS: 214 en suite No smoking in 32 bedrooms s £362-£392; d £435-£4043 **LB** **FACILITIES: Spa** STV Indoor swimming (H) Sauna Solarium Gym Beauty/therapy treatments, Swimming pool supervised **CONF:** Thtr 250 Class 80 Board 52 **SERVICES:** Lift air con **PARKING:** 50 **NOTES:** No dogs (ex guide dogs) Civ Wed 160 **CARDS:**

Top 200 - Town House

★★★★★ *No 41*

41 Buckingham Palace Rd SW1W 0PS
☎ 020 7300 0041 📠 020 7300 0141
e-mail: manager41@rchmail.com

Dir: *opp Buckingham Palace Mews entrance.*

Small, intimate and very private, this stunning town house is located opposite the Royal Mews and ideally positioned for London's theatres, shops and tourist attractions. Decorated in stylish black and white, bedrooms successfully combine comfort with state-of-the-art technology. It is the small touches that really make this town house special; rooms are crammed with thoughtful extras.

ROOMS: 18 en suite **FACILITIES:** STV use of 2 health clubs **CONF:** Board 12 **SERVICES:** Lift air con **NOTES:** No dogs (ex guide dogs) **CARDS:**

SW1 WESTMINSTER, continued

★★★★★74% The Carlton Tower
Cadogan Place SW1X 9PY
☎ 020 7235 1234 020 7235 9129
e-mail: contact@carltontower.com
Dir: A4 towards Knightsbridge, turn right onto Sloane St. Hotel on left before Cadogan Pl
In the heart of Knightsbridge but with the benefits of the park in Cadogan Place, the hotel's Grissini restaurant has super views over the gardens, while the glass-roofed pool invites guests to enjoy a swim, or use the treatment rooms and gym. Bedrooms vary in size, and the smooth, sleek lines of the new designs ensure that guest comfort is maximised. Guests may also enjoy the Rib Room and Oyster Bar, set on Sloane Street.
ROOMS: 220 en suite (60 fmly) No smoking in 116 bedrooms s £234-£382; d £234-£382 **FACILITIES: Spa** STV Indoor swimming (H) Tennis (hard) Sauna Gym Jacuzzi Massage and Spa treatments, Swimming pool supervised entertainment Xmas **CONF:** BC Thtr 400 Class 250 Board 30 **SERVICES:** Lift air con **PARKING:** 50 **NOTES:** No dogs (ex guide dogs) Civ Wed 350
CARDS:

See advert on opposite page

★★★★★71% **Sheraton Park Tower**
101 Knightsbridge SW1X 7RN
THE LUXURY COLLECTION
Starwood Hotels & Resorts
☎ 020 7235 8050 020 7235 8231
e-mail: anne.scott@luxurycollection.com
Dir: next to Harvey Nichols
This modern circular hotel is centrally located with stunning views over the city. Bedrooms combine a high degree of comfort with a contemporary edge and the new suites are particularly impressive. Other features include the intimate Knightsbridge lounge or the more formal Piano bar. The restaurant, One-O-One, is widely renowned for its cuisine, particularly for the seafood dishes.
ROOMS: 280 en suite (280 fmly) No smoking in 116 bedrooms **FACILITIES:** STV Gym Fitness room entertainment **CONF:** BC Thtr 70 Class 50 Board 26 **SERVICES:** Lift air con **PARKING:** 67 **NOTES:** No dogs (ex guide dogs) **CARDS:**

★★★★★70% **Sofitel St James London**
6 Waterloo Place SW1Y 4AN
SOFITEL
ACCOR HOTELS & RESORTS
☎ 020 7747 2222 020 7747 2210
e-mail: H3144@accor-hotels.com
Dir: On corner of Pall Mall & Waterloo Place
Located in the exclusive area of St James, this Grade II listed former bank is convenient for many of the city's attractions and businesses. The design of the hotel is a happy marriage of modern and classical, English style and the French 'Art de Vivre'. Air-conditioned bedrooms are contemporary in style and equipped with all the facilities expected in a modern five star hotel. Public areas include the Brasserie Roux, the Rose Lounge and a small fitness room.
ROOMS: 186 en suite No smoking in 97 bedrooms s £323.13; d £376 **LB FACILITIES:** STV Gym Steam rooms, Treatment rooms Xmas **CONF:** BC Thtr 180 Class 110 Board 60 **SERVICES:** Lift air con **NOTES:** Civ Wed 120 **CARDS:**

Town House

★★★★★ 22 Jermyn Street
St James's SW1Y 6HL
☎ 020 7734 2353 020 7734 0750
e-mail: office@22jermyn.com
Dir: A4 into Piccadilly, right into Duke St and left into King St. Through St James' Sq to Charles II St. Left into Regent St and left again
This attractive townhouse enjoys an enviable location close to Piccadilly, Regent Street and the fashionable St James's area. Smartly appointed accommodation comprises mainly of spacious suites with a few smaller studios. All are thoughtfully equipped with mini bar, satellite TV, video recorder and fax/modem lines. 24-hour room service is available and breakfast is served in the guests' bedrooms.
ROOMS: 18 en suite (13 fmly) s £246.75-£393.63; d £246.75-£393.63 **FACILITIES:** STV Membership of nearby Health Club **CONF:** BC Thtr 15 Class 15 Board 10 **SERVICES:** Lift air con **NOTES:** No smoking in restaurant
CARDS:

Top 200 - Hotel

★★★★ The Halkin Hotel
Halkin St, Belgravia SW1X 7DJ
☎ 020 7333 1000 020 7333 1100
e-mail: res@halkin.co.uk
Dir: hotel between Belgrave Sq & Grosvenor Place. Via Chapel St into Headfort Place and left into Halkin St
Situated in a peaceful area, yet only a short stroll from Hyde Park, this hotel has a contemporary design. Comfortable, air-conditioned bedrooms and suites, offering many thoughtful extras, are complemented by a light and airy bar lounge. A highlight of any visit must be dinner in Nahm, a memorable Thai, fine dining experience.
ROOMS: 41 en suite No smoking in 9 bedrooms s £359-£1211; d £359-£1211 **LB FACILITIES:** STV **SERVICES:** Lift air con **NOTES:** No dogs (ex guide dogs)
CARDS:

AA Rosette Award for culinary excellence

London

Top 200 - Hotel

★★★★ ◎◎ ***The Stafford***

16-18 St James's Place SW1A 1NJ

☎ 020 7493 0111 ▤ 020 7493 7121

e-mail: info@thestaffordhotel.co.uk

Dir: *off Pall Mall into St James's St. 2nd left into St James's Place*

Tucked away in a quiet corner of exclusive St James's, this lovely boutique hotel retains an air of understated luxury. The American Bar is a fabulous venue in its own right festooned with an eccentric array of celebrity photos, caps and ties. Afternoon tea is another long established tradition here. This is a traditional hotel keeping the highest standards, from the pristine, tastefully decorated and air-conditioned bedrooms, to the highly professional, yet friendly service.

ROOMS: 81 en suite **FACILITIES:** STV Membership of Fitness Club available **CONF:** Thtr 40 Board 24 **SERVICES:** Lift air con **NOTES:** No dogs No smoking in restaurant Civ Wed 80 **CARDS:**

★★★★78% ◎◎ **The Cadogan Hotel**

75 Sloane St SW1X 9SG

☎ 020 7235 7141 ▤ 020 7245 0994

e-mail: info@cadogan.com

Situated between Sloane Square and Knightsbridge, this delightful Victorian hotel lists Lillie Langtry and Oscar Wilde amongst its celebrated visitors. Comfortable, tastefully furnished bedrooms boast spacious, well-appointed bathrooms and a host of thoughtful amenities. Public rooms include an elegant drawing room, a cosy bar and a stylish restaurant.

ROOMS: 65 en suite (1 fmly) No smoking in 31 bedrooms **FACILITIES:** STV Tennis (hard) Business centre ch fac **CONF:** BC Thtr 50 Class 21 Board 30 Del from £245 **SERVICES:** Lift **PARKING:** 1 **NOTES:** RS Sat Civ Wed 50 **CARDS:**

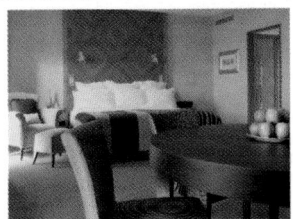

★★★★75% ◎◎

The Rubens at the Palace

Red Carnation HOTELS

39 Buckingham Palace Rd SW1W 0PS

☎ 020 7834 6600 ▤ 020 7233 6037

e-mail: bookrb@rchmail.com

Dir: *opposite Royal Mews, 100mtrs away from Buckingham Palace*

This hotel enjoys an enviable location next to Buckingham Palace. Stylish, air-conditioned bedrooms include the pinstripe-walled Saville Row rooms, which follow a tailoring theme, and the opulent Royal rooms, which are named after different monarchs. There are two choices for dining and a plush cocktail bar in which to relax. The team here pride themselves on their warmth and friendliness.

ROOMS: 173 en suite No smoking in 80 bedrooms **FACILITIES:** STV Health clubs locally entertainment **CONF:** Thtr 90 Class 40 Board 30 **SERVICES:** Lift air con **NOTES:** No smoking in restaurant **CARDS:**

London

SW1 WESTMINSTER, continued

★★★★72% ◎◎◎ *Millennium Hotel London Knightsbridge*

17 Sloane St, Knightsbridge SW1X 9NU
☎ 020 7235 4377 📠 020 7235 3705
e-mail: knightsbridge.reservations@mill.cop.com
Dir: *from Knightsbridge underground to Sloane St. Hotel 70mtrs on right*

This popular hotel continues to keep abreast of trends with a much talked about restaurant and popular lobby bar. Cuisine has more than a touch of Pacific Rim about it with a ten-course degustation menu being a popular choice. Accommodation is modern and all rooms are air-conditioned. Valet parking is available if pre-booked.
ROOMS: 222 en suite No smoking in 86 bedrooms **FACILITIES:** STV **CONF:** Thtr 120 Class 80 Board 50 **SERVICES:** Lift air con **PARKING:** 7 **NOTES:** No dogs (ex guide dogs) No smoking in restaurant
CARDS:

★★★★71% De Vere Cavendish St James's London

81 Jermyn St SW1Y 6JF
☎ 020 7930 2111 📠 020 7839 2125
e-mail: cavendish.reservations@devere-hotels.com
Dir: *from Marble Arch along Park Ln to Hyde Park Corner. Left to Piccadilly, past Ritz and right down Dukes St. Behind Fortnum and Mason*

Located a few minutes' walk from both Green Park and Piccadilly, this popular hotel has now seen an extensive refurbishment programme completed. Bedrooms and public areas have a fresh and contemporary feel. A spacious first-floor lounge is an ideal place for afternoon tea and Leyton's Brasserie service popular dishes.
ROOMS: 230 rms (229 en suite) No smoking in 36 bedrooms s fr £276; d fr £323 **LB** **FACILITIES:** STV Xmas **CONF:** BC Thtr 80 Class 50 Board 35 Del £270 **SERVICES:** Lift air con **PARKING:** 60 **NOTES:** No dogs (ex guide dogs) **CARDS:**

★★★★71% Victoria Park Plaza

239 Vauxhall Bridge Rd SW1V 1EQ
☎ 020 7769 9999 📠 020 7769 9998
e-mail: info@victoriaparkplaza.com
This smart, modern hotel is conveniently located close to Victoria station, within easy reach of all of central London's major attractions. Air-conditioned bedrooms are tastefully appointed and thoughtfully equipped for both business and leisure guests. Airy, stylish public areas include an elegant bar and restaurant, a popular coffee bar, extensive conference facilities with a business centre.
ROOMS: 299 en suite No smoking in 116 bedrooms s £179.77; d £179.7 **LB** **FACILITIES:** STV Sauna Gym entertainment **CONF:** Thtr 500 Class 240 Board 120 Del £165 **SERVICES:** Lift air con **PARKING:** 50 **NOTES:** Civ Wed 1000 **CARDS:**

★★★★69% Dolphin Square Hotel

Dolphin Square, Chichester St SW1V 3LX
☎ 020 7834 3800 📠 020 7798 8735
e-mail: reservations@dolphinsquarehotel.co.uk
Dir: *Follow signs to Central London then Earls Court, after Chelsea Bridge take 2nd left, turn right into Chichester St., hotel on right*

Conveniently located close to the Embankment and Westminster, the Dolphin Square offers accommodation predominantly in suites, which are smartly appointed and well equipped. A wealth of facilities include a swimming pool, squash courts, a fully staffed business centre and on-site shops. Guests may dine in the brasserie or the more formal restaurant.
ROOMS: 148 en suite (29 fmly) (17 GF) No smoking in 43 bedrooms s £89-£165; d £89-£195 (incl. bkfst) **FACILITIES:** STV Indoor swimming (H) Tennis (hard) Squash Sauna Gym Croquet lawn Jacuzzi Swimming pool supervised **CONF:** BC Thtr 60 Class 20 Board 20 Del £245 **SERVICES:** Lift **PARKING:** 19 **NOTES:** No dogs (ex guide dogs) Civ Wed 70 **CARDS:**

★★★★69% *The Royal Horseguards*

Whitehall Court SW1A 2EJ
☎ 020 7839 3400 📠 020 7925 2263
e-mail: royal.horseguards@thistle.co.uk
This majestic looking hotel in the heart of Whitehall sits beside the Thames. Bedrooms are all finished to a high standard, well equipped and comfortable and some provide fantastic views of the river and London's skyline. Impressive public areas and superlative meeting facilities are also available.
ROOMS: 280 en suite No smoking in 180 bedrooms **FACILITIES:** STV Gym **CONF:** Thtr 280 Class 300 **SERVICES:** Lift air con **NOTES:** No dogs (ex guide dogs) Civ Wed 200
CARDS:

★★★★68% *Sheraton Belgravia*

20 Chesham Place SW1X 8HQ
☎ 020 7235 6040 📠 020 7259 6243
e-mail: judy-kent@sheraton.com
***Dir:** A4 Brompton Rd into Central London. After Brompton Oratory right into Beauchamp Pl. Follow into Pont St, cross Sloane St & hotel on corner*
This modern hotel is situated in the heart of Belgravia, just a short walk from the shops of Knightsbridge, Kings Road and Sloane Street. Bedrooms are well equipped for business and leisure guests and public areas are elegant. Light snacks are available all day in the lounge, or Mulberry's restaurant offers a more formal option.
ROOMS: 89 en suite (16 fmly) No smoking in 37 bedrooms **FACILITIES:** STV comp membership to local health spa entertainment **CONF:** Thtr 35 Class 14 Board 20 **SERVICES:** Lift air con **NOTES:** No dogs (ex guide dogs) **CARDS:**

Town House

★★★★ *The Lowndes*
21 Lowndes St SW1X 9ES
☎ 020 7823 1234 📠 020 7235 1154
e-mail: contact@lowndeshotel.com
***Dir:** M4 onto A4 into London. Left from Brompton Rd into Sloane St. Left into Pont St and Lowndes St next left. Hotel on right*
This small hotel is located in a fashionable part of town, within walking distance of Harrods and Harvey Nicholls. Bedrooms have a modern feel with good facilities including high-tech modem points. Small public areas are attractive and include a brasserie restaurant and a meeting room.
ROOMS: 78 en suite No smoking in 31 bedrooms **FACILITIES:** STV Use of facilities at Carlton Tower Hotel **CONF:** Thtr 25 Class 25 Board 18 **SERVICES:** Lift air con **NOTES:** No dogs
CARDS:

★★★65% Grange Rochester
69 Vincent Square SW1P 2PA
☎ 020 7828 6611 📠 020 7233 6724
e-mail: rochester@grangehotels.com
Overlooking leafy Vincent Square, this boutique-style hotel is well located for access to some of the city's finest shops, theatres and tourist attractions. Attractive bedrooms are quiet and well-equipped, but do vary in size. Some have views (and balconies) overlooking the square. Public rooms are not particularly spacious, but do offer all day dining and drinking options.
ROOMS: 76 en suite (6 fmly) No smoking in 30 bedrooms s £122-£190; d £135-£210 **FACILITIES:** STV **CONF:** Thtr 45 Class 35 Board 35 Del from £207 **SERVICES:** Lift **NOTES:** No dogs (ex guide dogs)
CARDS:

★★★64% Quality Hotel Westminster
82-83 Eccleston Square SW1V 1PS
☎ 020 7834 8042 📠 020 7630 8942
e-mail: admin@gb614.u-net.com
***Dir:** from Victoria Station, turn right into Wilton Rd, take 3rd right into Gillingham St, hotel 150mtrs on left*
Situated close to Victoria, this hotel provides a good base for exploring London. Bedrooms are all en-suite but vary in size. Public areas offer a seating area, a range of conference rooms and the Connaughts Brasserie, which provides a good range of meals.
ROOMS: 107 en suite (3 fmly) No smoking in 62 bedrooms s £112; d £130 **LB FACILITIES:** STV Xmas **CONF:** Thtr 150 Class 60 Board 40 Del £165 **SERVICES:** Lift **NOTES:** No dogs (ex guide dogs) No smoking in restaurant **CARDS:**

Express by Holiday Inn London Victoria

106 - 110 Belgrave Rd, Victoria SW1V 2BJ
☎ 020 7630 8888 📠 020 7828 0441
e-mail: info@hiexpressvictoria.co.uk
***Dir:** 600mtrs from Pimlico underground*

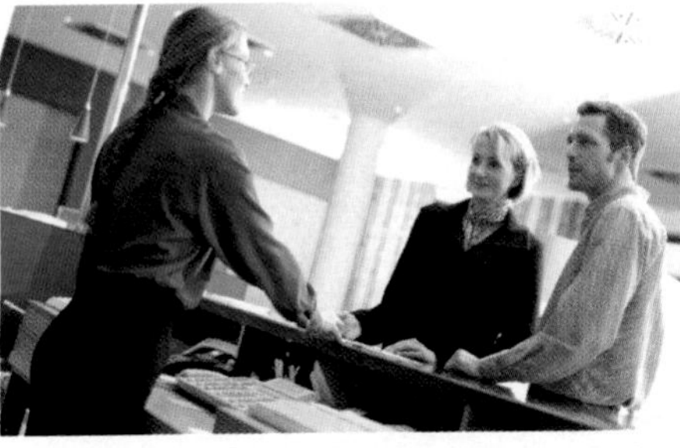

A modern hotel ideal for families and business travellers. Fresh and uncomplicated, the spacious bedrooms include Sky TV, power shower and tea and coffee-making facilities. Continental buffet breakfast is included in the room rate; other meals may be taken at the nearby family pub or restaurant. For further details and the Express by Holiday Inn phone number, consult the Hotel Groups pages.
ROOMS: 52 en suite

SW3 CHELSEA, BROMPTON

Top 200 - Town House

★★★★★ Capital
Basil St, Knightsbridge SW3 1AT
☎ 020 7589 5171 📠 020 7225 0011
e-mail: reservations@capitalhotel.co.uk
***Dir:** 20yds from Harrods*
Personal service is assured at this small, family-owned hotel set in the heart of Knightsbridge. Beautifully designed bedrooms come in a number of styles, with those in the Old Mansions furnished with Ralph Lauren fabrics. All rooms feature antique furniture and marble bathrooms. Dinner is a highlight of any visit; Eric Chavot and his committed brigade continue to cook to a consistently high standard. Cocktails are a speciality in the delightful, small bar.
ROOMS: 48 en suite No smoking in 24 bedrooms s £170-£190; d £205-£245 **LB FACILITIES:** STV **CONF:** Thtr 30 Board 12 **SERVICES:** Lift air con **PARKING:** 15
CARDS:

GF Indicates the number of bedrooms at ground floor level.

SW3 CHELSEA, continued

Town House

★★★★★ Cliveden Townhouse
26 Cadogan Gardens SW3 2RP
☎ 020 7730 6466 020 7730 0236
e-mail: reservations@clivedentownhouse.co.uk
Dir: *From Sloane Sq station towards Peter Jones, keep to left. At Kings Rd. take first right Cadogan Gdns, 2nd right, hotel on left.*
Enjoying a prime location yards from Sloane Square, this town house provides an ideal base in one of the most fashionable areas of London. Beautifully appointed bedrooms include a number of suites. All are equipped to a high standard with CD players, mini bars and satellite TV. Attractive day rooms, furnished with antique and period pieces, include a choice of lounges, one with access to a lovely sheltered garden.
ROOMS: 35 en suite (9 fmly) No smoking in 30 bedrooms s £117.50-£158.62; d £188-£340.72 **LB** **FACILITIES:** STV Beauty treatment, Massage Xmas **CONF:** Class 12 Board 12 **SERVICES:** Lift air con **CARDS:**

Town House

★★★★ The Beaufort
33 Beaufort Gardens SW3 1PP
☎ 020 7584 5252 020 7589 2834
e-mail: enquiries@beaufort.com
Dir: *100yds past Harrods on left of Brompton Rd*
This friendly attractive townhouse enjoys a peaceful location in a tree-lined cul-de-sac just minutes' walk from Knightsbridge. Air-conditioned bedrooms are delightfully furnished and particularly thoughtfully equipped with chocolates, fruit, fresh flowers, videos, CD players and free Internet and movie channel access. Guests are offered complimentary drinks and afternoon tea, served in the attractive drawing room.
ROOMS: 27 en suite (3 GF) No smoking in 6 bedrooms s £182-£364; d £229-£364 (incl. cont bkfst) **FACILITIES:** STV Complimentary entry to local health club **SERVICES:** Lift air con **NOTES:** No dogs (ex guide dogs)
CARDS:

Town House

★★★★ Parkes
41 Beaufort Gardens, Knightsbridge SW3 1PW
☎ 020 7581 9944 020 7581 1999
e-mail: reception@parkeshotel.com
Dir: *off Brompton Rd, 100yds from Harrods*
This sophisticated hotel is located in a tree-lined square in the heart of fashionable Knightsbridge. Stylish bedrooms and spacious suites with kitchens are beautifully appointed and equipped with every conceivable extra including UK/US modems and sockets, wireless ADSL and mini bars with a wide variety of spirits. Whilst there is no hotel restaurant, a wide range of dishes from local eateries can be delivered to your room.
ROOMS: 33 en suite (16 fmly) (4 GF) **FACILITIES:** STV arrangement with nearby gym **SERVICES:** Lift air con **NOTES:** No dogs (ex guide dogs) No smoking in restaurant
CARDS:

★★★73% *Basil Street*
Basil St, Knightsbridge SW3 1AH
☎ 020 7581 3311 020 7581 3693
e-mail: info@TheBasil.com
Dir: *M4 & A4 Brompton Rd, right before Harrods. Left into Basil St and hotel on left*
A traditional and friendly hotel located in the heart of this shoppers' paradise. The public rooms are full of character with antiques, parquet floors, fine paintings and tapestries, and service is professional and efficient. Bedrooms are in keeping with the original style of the property with the addition of up-to-date facilities.
ROOMS: 80 en suite (4 fmly) No smoking in 40 bedrooms **FACILITIES:** STV entertainment **CONF:** Thtr 30 Class 16 Board 20 **SERVICES:** Lift **PARKING:** 2 **NOTES:** No dogs (ex guide dogs)
CARDS:

SW4 CLAPHAM
See LONDON plan 1 E2

★★★68% The Windmill on The Common
Southside, Clapham Common SW4 9DE
☎ 020 8673 4578 020 8675 1486
e-mail: windmillhotel@youngs.co.uk
This popular hotel is located on the edge of Clapham Common and dates back 1729. The lively pub bar, with its outdoor seating, makes it a favourite venue in the summer months. The smart air-conditioned bedrooms are comfortable and well equipped for the business guest.
ROOMS: 29 en suite (12 GF) No smoking in 21 bedrooms s £85-£99; d £95-£115 (incl. bkfst) **LB** **FACILITIES:** STV entertainment **CONF:** Thtr 40 Class 25 Board 20 **SERVICES:** air con **PARKING:** 16 **NOTES:** No smoking in restaurant **CARDS:**

SW5 EARLS COURT

Map 06 TQ27

Town House

★★★★ Twenty Nevern Square
20 Nevern Square SW5 9PD
☎ 020 7565 9555 020 7565 9444
e-mail: hotel@twentynevernsquare.co.uk
Dir: *pass Earls Court Exhibition Centre on Warwick Rd, turn 2nd right into Nevern Square*
This small, smart townhouse is discreetly located in Nevern Square and is ideally situated for both Earls Court and Olympia. Bedrooms, which vary in shape and size, are appointed to a high standard and well equipped. Public areas include a delightful lounge and Café Twenty where breakfast and dinner are served.
ROOMS: 20 en suite (3 GF) No smoking in 10 bedrooms s £80-£130; d £90-£165 (incl. cont bkfst) **FACILITIES:** STV **SERVICES:** Lift **PARKING:** 4 **NOTES:** No dogs (ex guide dogs) No smoking in restaurant **CARDS:**

Town House

★★★★ The Cranley
10 Bina Gardens, South Kensington SW5 0LA
☎ 020 7373 0123 020 7373 9497
e-mail: info@thecranley.com
Dir: *down Gloucester Rd towards Old Brompton Rd. 3rd right into Hereford Sq, then 3rd left into Bina Gardens*
This elegant Victorian town house is set in a quiet residential area of South Kensington where a friendly welcome awaits guests. The bedrooms, including a number of suites, are well furnished and equipped, with many antiques and thoughtful extras. Complimentary afternoon tea is available, along with aperitifs and canapés in the evening.
ROOMS: 38 en suite (2 fmly) (4 GF) s £100-£155; d £125-£180 **LB** **FACILITIES:** STV **SERVICES:** Lift air con **NOTES:** No dogs (ex guide dogs) **CARDS:**

★★★66% *Burns*
18-26 Barkston Gardens, Kensingston SW5 0EN
Best Western
☎ 020 7373 3151 020 7370 4090
e-mail: burnshotel@vienna-group.co.uk
Dir: *Off A4, right to Earls Court Rd (A3220), 2nd left. Hotel in Barkston Gardens, 2nd left past Earls Court underground station.*
This hotel is located in a quiet residential area, not far from the Earls Court underground. Bedrooms are attractively appointed and include modern facilities. Public areas, although not extensive, are stylish.
ROOMS: 105 en suite (10 fmly) No smoking in 38 bedrooms **FACILITIES:** STV **SERVICES:** Lift **NOTES:** No dogs (ex guide dogs) No smoking in restaurant **CARDS:**

U London Marriott Kensington
Marriott HOTELS · RESORTS · SUITES
Cromwell Rd SW5 0TH
☎ 020 7973 1000
e-mail: kensington.marriott@marriotthotels.co.uk
Dir: *on A4, opposite Cromwell Rd Hospital*

At the time of going to press, the star classification for this hotel was not confirmed. Please refer to the AA internet site www.theAA.com for current information.
ROOMS: 216 en suite (39 fmly) s £140; d £140 **LB** **FACILITIES:** STV Indoor swimming (H) Sauna Gym Jacuzzi **CONF:** Thtr 200 Class 100 Board 60 Del from £195 **SERVICES:** Lift air con **PARKING:** 20 **NOTES:** No dogs (ex guide dogs) No smoking in restaurant **CARDS:**

Comfort Inn Kensington
22-32 West Cromwell Rd, Kensington SW5 9QJ
Comfort Inn
☎ 020 7373 3300 020 7835 2040
e-mail: admin@gb043.u-net.com
Dir: *on north side of West Cromwell Rd, between juncts of Cromwell Rd, Earls Court Rd & Warwick Rd*
This modern building offers accommodation in smart, spacious and well equipped bedrooms, all with en suite bathrooms. Refreshments may be taken at the nearby family restaurant. For further details and the Comfort Inn phone number, consult the Hotel Groups page under 'Choice'.
ROOMS: 125 en suite **CONF:** Thtr 70 Class 35 Board 40

Travel Inn (London Kensington)
147c Cromwell Rd, Kensington SW5 0TH
travel inn
☎ 0870 238 3304 020 7370 9292
Dir: *Just off A4 Cromwell Rd between Earls Court & Gloucester Rd underground stations*
Travel Inn offers good-quality, value-for-money accommodation. Spacious, en suite rooms with bath and shower comfortably accommodate a family of up to two adults and two children (to age 15). The restaurant and bar offers a varied menu. For further details and the Travel Inn phone number, consult the Hotel Groups page.
ROOMS: 183 en suite s £69.95-£74.95; d £69.95-£74.95

SW6 FULHAM

See LONDON plan 1 D3

★★★★71% *Chelsea Village*
Stamford Bridge, Fulham Rd SW6 1HS
☎ 020 7565 1400 020 7565 1450
e-mail: reservation@chelseavillage.co.uk
This stylish, eye-catching hotel forms a part of the ambitious development of Chelsea Football Club and is situated adjacent to the ground. Public areas are extensive and feature a wide range of facilities including two restaurants and bars; the Chelsea Club is

continued on p374

London

SW6 FULHAM, continued

one of London's premier health and beauty spas. Air-conditioned bedrooms are spacious and well equipped.
ROOMS: 291 en suite (64 fmly) No smoking in 138 bedrooms **FACILITIES:** STV **CONF:** Thtr 50 Class 25 Board 30 **SERVICES:** Lift air con **PARKING:** 250 **NOTES:** No dogs (ex guide dogs) **CARDS:**

★★★66% Paragon Hotel

47 Lillie Rd SW6 1UD
☎ 020 7610 0880 ▯ 020 7381 4450
e-mail: sales.london@paragonhotel.net
Dir: *A4 to central London. 0.5m after Hammersmith flyover turn right at traffic lights into North End Rd. After 0.5m left at mini rdbt into Lillie Rd*

Situated opposite the Earls Court Exhibition Centre, this large, modern hotel is popular with business and leisure guests. Bedrooms are comfortable and well equipped. Two restaurants offer a choice of light meals or a more formal traditional menu and carvery. There are also extensive conference facilities and an underground car park.
ROOMS: 502 en suite (20 fmly) No smoking in 240 bedrooms s £65-£140; d £65-£140 **LB** **FACILITIES:** STV Health club and gym nearby Xmas **CONF:** BC Thtr 1200 Class 700 Board 100 Del from £155 **SERVICES:** Lift **PARKING:** 130 **NOTES:** No dogs (ex guide dogs) No smoking in restaurant **CARDS:**

⌂ Travel Inn (London Putney Bridge)

travel inn

3 Putney Bridge Approach SW6 3JD
☎ 0870 238 3302 ▯ 020 7471 8315
Dir: *on north bank of River Thames by Putney Bridge*
Travel Inn offers good-quality, value-for-money accommodation. Spacious, en suite rooms with bath and shower comfortably accommodate a family of up to two adults and two children (to age 15). The restaurant and bar offers a varied menu. For further details and the Travel Inn phone number, consult the Hotel Groups page.
ROOMS: 154 en suite s £69.95-£74.95; d £69.95-£74.95

SW7 SOUTH KENSINGTON

Map 06 TQ27

★★★★75% Millennium Gloucester Hotel London Kensington

MILLENNIUM HOTELS AND RESORTS

4-18 Harrington Gardens SW7 4LH
☎ 020 7373 6030 ▯ 020 7373 0409
e-mail: sales.gloucester@mill-cop.com
Dir: *opposite Gloucester Rd underground station*
A popular choice for the international market, this hotel is located close to Gloucester Road tube station. Air-conditioned bedrooms are furnished in a variety of contemporary styles. Additional amenities are provided in club rooms, which have a dedicated lounge. There is a wide range of eating options, including Singaporean cuisine and more formal Italian food.

ROOMS: 610 en suite (6 fmly) No smoking in 439 bedrooms s £250; d £250 **LB** **FACILITIES:** STV Gym **CONF:** BC Thtr 500 Class 280 Board 40 **SERVICES:** Lift air con **PARKING:** 110 **NOTES:** Civ Wed 300 **CARDS:**

★★★★72% ⊛ Harrington Hall

5-25 Harrington Gardens SW7 4JN
☎ 020 7396 9696 ▯ 020 7396 9090
e-mail: sales@harringtonhall.co.uk
Dir: *towards Knightsbridge into Gloucester Rd. 2nd right into Harrington Gdns and hotel on left*
This classic Victorian façade conceals a modern, elegant hotel. Bedrooms are spacious, comfortable, well equipped and air-conditioned. Additional features include a multi-gym, extensive meeting rooms and the stylish restaurant which serves a quality carvery at lunch time and a creative carte menu at dinner.
ROOMS: 200 en suite No smoking in 132 bedrooms s £130-£185; d £140-£195 **LB** **FACILITIES:** STV Sauna Gym Xmas **CONF:** BC Thtr 200 Class 80 Board 25 Del from £199 **SERVICES:** Lift air con **NOTES:** No dogs (ex guide dogs) **CARDS:**

★★★★71% ⊛ Radisson Edwardian Vanderbilt

Radisson EDWARDIAN

68-86 Cromwell Rd SW7 5BT
☎ 020 7761 9000 ▯ 020 7761 9001
e-mail: resvand@radisson.com
Dir: *A4 into central London on Cromwell Rd. Hotel on left at junct of Gloucester Rd & Cromwell Rd*
This hotel is an ideal base for visitors to the capital. The interior is both cheerful and contemporary. Room facilities are superb - all have air conditioning, modems, several telephone lines, safes and mini-bars. The bar and lounge are popular places to meet, take afternoon tea and just watch the world go by.
ROOMS: 215 en suite (18 fmly) (28 GF) No smoking in 113 bedrooms s £229; d £261 **LB** **FACILITIES:** Fitness room Business centre **CONF:** BC Thtr 100 Class 56 Board 40 Del from £160 **SERVICES:** Lift air con **NOTES:** No dogs **CARDS:**

★★★★69% Jurys Kensington Hotel

JURYS DOYLE HOTELS

109-113 Queensgate, South Kensington SW7 5LR
☎ 020 7589 6300 ▯ 020 7581 1492
e-mail: Kensington@jurysdoyle.com
Dir: *From A4 take Cromwell Rd, turn right at V&A Museum onto Queensgate, hotel at end on left*
This beautiful building has been carefully refurbished and offers an excellent location for visitors to London. Smartly appointed public areas include an open plan lobby/bar, Copplestones restaurant with adjoining library lounge and the lively Kavanagh's

continued

bar. Bedrooms vary in size and are well equipped with a modern colour theme.
ROOMS: 173 annexe en suite (10 fmly) No smoking in 65 bedrooms s £137-£210; d £137-£210 **FACILITIES:** STV Health Club facilities available locally at discounted rate entertainment Xmas **CONF:** Thtr 80 Class 45 Board 35 Del from £209 **SERVICES:** Lift air con **NOTES:** No dogs (ex guide dogs) **CARDS:**

★★★★67% Millennium Baileys Hotel London Kensington

MILLENNIUM

140 Gloucester Rd SW7 4QH
☎ 020 7373 6000 📠 020 7370 3760
e-mail: baileys@mill-cop.com
Dir: *A4, turn right at Cromwell Hospital into Knaresborough Place, follow to Courtfield Rd to corner of Gloucester Rd, hotel opposite underground*

This elegant hotel has a townhouse feel to it and enjoys a prime location opposite Gloucester Road tube station. Air-conditioned bedrooms are smartly appointed and thoughtfully equipped, particularly the club rooms which have DVD players. Public areas include a stylish contemporary restaurant and bar. Guests may also use the facilities at its adjacent, larger sister hotel.
ROOMS: 212 en suite No smoking in 120 bedrooms **FACILITIES:** STV Gym **CONF:** Thtr 20 Class 18 Board 16 Del from £199 **SERVICES:** Lift air con **PARKING:** 70 **CARDS:**

★★★★62% The Rembrandt

11 Thurloe Place SW7 2RS
☎ 020 7589 8100 📠 020 7225 3363
e-mail: rembrandt@sarova.co.uk
Dir: *M4 onto A4 Cromwell Rd into Central London. Hotel opposite Victoria & Albert Museum*
This attractive, ornate hotel is conveniently situated opposite the Victoria & Albert Museum, a stone's throw from Harrods. Smart, well-appointed bedrooms are thoughtfully equipped and public areas include a carvery restaurant and an attractive bar lounge and conservatory. Guests also benefit from concessions at the adjacent Roman-styled health and leisure suite.
ROOMS: 195 en suite No smoking in 110 bedrooms s £190-£240; d £215-£240 (incl. cont bkfst) **LB** **FACILITIES: Spa** STV Indoor swimming (H) Sauna Solarium Gym Jacuzzi Aquila Health & Fitness Xmas **CONF:** BC Thtr 200 Class 84 Board 80 Del from £210 **SERVICES:** Lift **NOTES:** No dogs (ex guide dogs) Civ Wed 180 **CARDS:**

U *Holiday Inn London-Kensington Forum*

Holiday Inn HOTELS · RESORTS

97 Cromwell Rd SW7 4DN
☎ 020 7370 5757 📠 020 7373 1448
e-mail: info@hik.co.uk
Dir: *from S Circular onto N Circular at Chiswick Flyover. Join A4 Cromwell Rd as far as Gloucseter Rd*
At the time of going to press, the classification for this hotel was not confirmed. Please refer to the AA internet site www.theAA.com for current information.
ROOMS: 910 en suite (36 fmly) No smoking in 395 bedrooms **FACILITIES:** STV Fitness room entertainment **CONF:** Thtr 400 Class 200 Board 35 **SERVICES:** Lift air con **PARKING:** 75 **NOTES:** No dogs (ex guide dogs) **CARDS:**

SW10 WEST BROMPTON
See LONDON plan 1 D/E3

★★★★★66% Conrad London

Chelsea Harbour SW10 0XG
☎ 020 7823 3000 📠 020 7351 6525
e-mail: conrad-london@hilton.com
Dir: *A4 to Earls Court Rd S towards river. Right into Kings Rd, left down Lots Rd. Chelsea Harbour in front*

With the picturesque backdrop of Chelsea Harbour's small marina, this modern all suite hotel offers spacious, comfortable accommodation. Private suites, being refurbished at the time of our inspection, are superbly equipped, many enjoying splendid views, and there are also several luxurious penthouse suites. Public areas include a modern bar and restaurant, excellent leisure facilities and extensive meeting and function rooms.
ROOMS: 160 en suite (39 fmly) No smoking in 82 bedrooms s £376-£2820; d £411.25-£2820 **LB** **FACILITIES:** STV Indoor swimming (H) Sauna Solarium Gym Conrad Health Club with beauty treatments entertainment Xmas **CONF:** BC Thtr 280 Class 120 Board 50 Del from £290 **SERVICES:** Lift air con **PARKING:** 21 **NOTES:** Civ Wed 200 **CARDS:**

SW11 BATTERSEA
See LONDON plan 1 E3

⌂ Travelodge (London Battersea)

200 York Rd, Battersea SW11 3SA
☎ 08700 850 950
Dir: *from Wandsworth Bridge southern rdbt, take York Rd A3205 towards Battersea. 0.5m on left*
Travelodge offers good quality, good value, modern accommodation. Ideal for families, the spacious, en suite bedrooms include remote-control TV, tea and coffee-making facilities, luxury beds and free morning newspaper. Meals can be taken at the nearby family restaurant. For further details and the Travelodge phone number, consult the Hotel Groups page.
ROOMS: 87 en suite s fr £42.95; d fr £42.95

London

SW18 WANDSWORTH
See LONDON plan 1 D/E2

Express by Holiday Inn Wandsworth

Smugglers Way, Wandsworth SW18 1EG
☎ 020 8877 5950 📠 020 8877 0631
e-mail: wandsworth@oriel-leisure.co.uk
Dir: *from S side of Wandsworth Bridge, take A3205 W. 0.5m to Smugglers Way on right*

A modern hotel ideal for families and business travellers. Fresh and uncomplicated, the spacious bedrooms include Sky TV, power shower and tea and coffee-making facilities. Continental buffet breakfast is included in the room rate; other meals may be taken at the nearby family pub or restaurant. For further details and the Express by Holiday Inn phone number, consult the Hotel Groups pages.
ROOMS: 148 en suite s £69-£89; d £69-£89 (incl. cont bkfst)
CONF: Thtr 30 Class 30 Board 20

SW19 WIMBLEDON
See LONDON plan 1 D1

★★★★72% Cannizaro House

West Side, Wimbledon Common SW19 4UE
☎ 0870 333 9124 📠 0870 333 9224
e-mail: cannizarohouse@thistle.co.uk
Dir: *from A3 follow A219 signed Wimbledon into Parkside, past old fountain, sharp right then 2nd on right*

THISTLE HOTELS

This unique, elegant 18th-century house has a long tradition of hosting the rich and famous of London society. A few miles from the city centre, the landscaped grounds provide a peaceful escape and inside there is a country house ambience throughout with fine art, murals and stunning fireplaces. Spacious bedrooms are individually furnished and equipped to a high standard.
ROOMS: 45 en suite (4 GF) No smoking in 19 bedrooms
FACILITIES: STV Croquet lawn Massage treatments entertainment
CONF: Thtr 120 Class 50 Board 40 Del from £168 **SERVICES:** Lift
PARKING: 60 **NOTES:** No dogs (ex guide dogs) Civ Wed 60
CARDS:

Express by Holiday Inn London Wimbledon-South

200 High St, Colliers Wood, Wimbledon SW19 2BH
☎ 020 8545 7300 📠 020 8545 7301
e-mail: exhiwimbledon@ukonline.co.uk
Dir: *From M25 take A3 signed central London, then take A238, past Wimbledon, 3.2m. Hotel on left opposite large office block*

A modern hotel ideal for families and business travellers. Fresh and uncomplicated, the spacious bedrooms include Sky TV, power shower and tea and coffee-making facilities. Continental buffet breakfast is included in the room rate; other meals may be taken at the nearby family pub or restaurant. For further details and the Express by Holiday Inn phone number, consult the Hotel Groups pages.

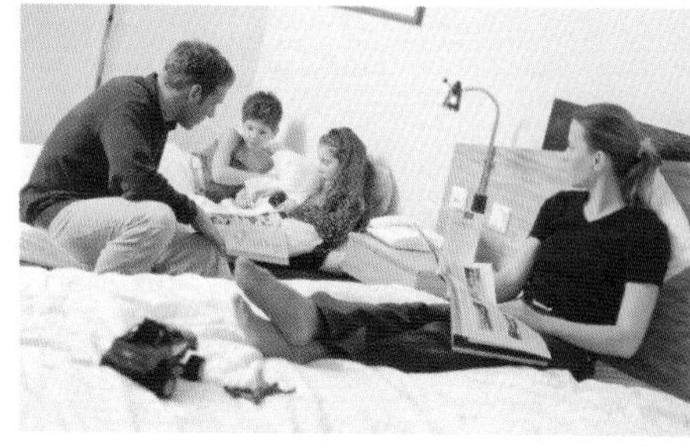

ROOMS: 83 en suite s £70-£92; d £70-£92 (incl. cont bkfst)
CONF: Thtr 40 Class 16 Board 20

○ Premier Lodge (London Merton)

Merantum Way, Merton SW19 1DD
☎ 0870 9906342 📠 0870 9906343
ROOMS: 132 en suite **NOTES:** Due to open Spring 2004

W1 WEST END

Top 200 - Hotel

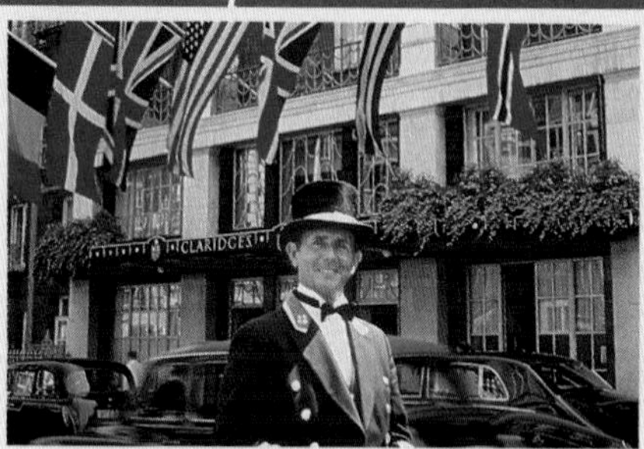

★★★★★ Claridge's

Brook St W1A 2JQ
☎ 020 7629 8860 📠 020 7499 2210
e-mail: info@claridges.co.uk
Dir: *Take 1st turn after Green Park underground station to Berkeley Sq & 4th exit into Davies St. Take 3rd turn right into Brook St*

The Savoy Group

This iconic bastion of British hospitality delivers impressive standards of luxury, style and service. The sumptuous, air-conditioned bedrooms are elegantly themed to reflect the Victorian or art deco architecture of the building. Culinary excellence is assured in Gordon Ramsay at Claridge's, where impeccable service and dishes cooked with flair set exacting standards. The sleek cocktail bar is a popular meeting place, and the stylish foyer provides an eye-catching venue in which to enjoy the popular afternoon teas.
ROOMS: 203 en suite (144 fmly) No smoking in 34 bedrooms s £210.33-£405.38; d £233.83-£4523.75 **LB** **FACILITIES:** STV Gym Beauty & health treatments. Use of sister hotel swimming pool entertainment Xmas **CONF:** Thtr 250 Class 130 Board 60 **SERVICES:** Lift air con **NOTES:** No dogs (ex guide dogs) Civ Wed 200 **CARDS:**

London

Top 200 - Hotel

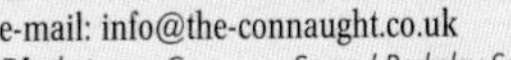

★★★★★ Connaught

Carlos Place W1K 2AL

The Savoy Group

☎ 020 7499 7070 020 7495 3262

e-mail: info@the-connaught.co.uk

Dir: *between Grosvenor Sq and Berkeley Sq in Mayfair*

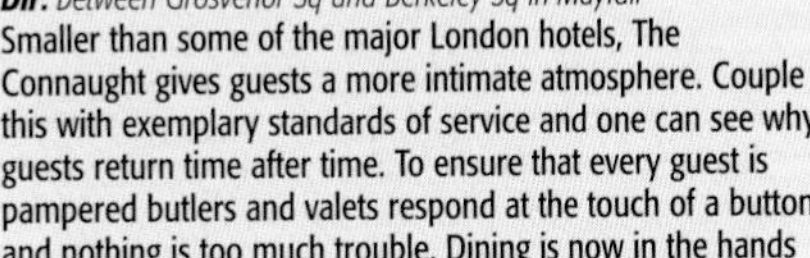

Smaller than some of the major London hotels, The Connaught gives guests a more intimate atmosphere. Couple this with exemplary standards of service and one can see why guests return time after time. To ensure that every guest is pampered butlers and valets respond at the touch of a button and nothing is too much trouble. Dining is now in the hands of Angela Hartnett, a protégé of Gordon Ramsay, and the restaurant menu has more than a hint of Italian about it.

ROOMS: 92 en suite s £280-£300; d £390-£425 **LB** **FACILITIES:** STV Gym Fitness studio, Health club facilities at sister hotels **CONF:** Board 18 **SERVICES:** Lift air con **NOTES:** No dogs **CARDS:**

Top 200 - Hotel

★★★★★ The Dorchester

Park Ln W1A 2HJ

☎ 020 7629 8888 020 7409 0114

e-mail: reservations@dorchesterhotel.com

Dir: *halfway along Park Ln between Hyde Park Corner & Marble Arch*

One of London's finest hotels, the Dorchester is sumptuously decorated. Bedrooms, which have now been refurbished, are beautifully appointed and feature huge, luxurious baths. Leading off from the foyer, The Promenade is the perfect setting for afternoon tea or drinks. In the evenings guests can relax to the sound of live jazz in the bar, and enjoy a cocktail or an Italian meal. Other dining options include the traditional Grill Restaurant and The Oriental, offering Cantonese cuisine.

ROOMS: 250 en suite No smoking in 34 bedrooms s £346.63-£370.13; d £387.75-£452.38 **LB** **FACILITIES: Spa** STV Sauna Solarium Gym Jacuzzi The Dorchester Spa Health club entertainment Xmas **CONF:** Thtr 500 Class 300 Board 42 **SERVICES:** Lift air con **PARKING:** 21 **NOTES:** No dogs (ex guide dogs) Civ Wed 500 **CARDS:**

Top 200 - Hotel

★★★★★ Four Seasons Hotel London

Hamilton Place, Park Ln W1A 1AZ

☎ 020 7499 0888 020 7493 1895

e-mail: fsh.london@fourseasons.com

Dir: *from Piccadilly into Old Park Ln then Hamilton Place*

Now long-established, The Four Seasons is discreetly located near Hyde Park Corner, in the heart of Mayfair. It successfully combines modern efficiencies with traditional luxury. Guest care is consistently of the highest order, even down to the smallest detail of the personalised wake-up call. The bedrooms are elegant and spacious, and the unique conservatory rooms are particularly special. There is ample public space on the ground and first floors, including Lanes fine-dining restaurant.

ROOMS: 220 en suite No smoking in 96 bedrooms s £364-£400; d £418-£430 **LB** **FACILITIES:** STV Gym Fitness club entertainment Xmas **CONF:** BC Thtr 400 Class 200 Board 70 **SERVICES:** Lift air con **PARKING:** 72 **NOTES:** Civ Wed 500 **CARDS:**

London

Top 200 - Hotel

★★★★★ The Ritz

150 Piccadilly W1J 9BR

☎ 020 7493 8181 020 7493 2687

e-mail: enquire@theritzlondon.com

Dir: *from Hyde Park Corner E on Piccadilly. Hotel on right*

Synonymous with style, sophistication and attention to detail, The Ritz continues its stately progress into the third millennium, having recaptured much of its former glory. All bedrooms are comfortably furnished in Louis XVI style, with fine marble bathrooms and every imaginable comfort. Elegant reception rooms include the Palm Court with its legendary afternoon teas, the beautifully refurbished Rivoli Bar and the sumptuous Ritz Restaurant, complete with gold chandeliers and extraordinary trompe-l'oeil decoration.

ROOMS: 133 en suite No smoking in 20 bedrooms s £310; d £365 **LB** **FACILITIES:** STV Gym entertainment Xmas **CONF:** Thtr 60 Class 25 Board 30 **SERVICES:** Lift air con **NOTES:** No dogs (ex guide dogs) Civ Wed 50 **CARDS:**

W1 WEST END, continued

Top 200 - Town House

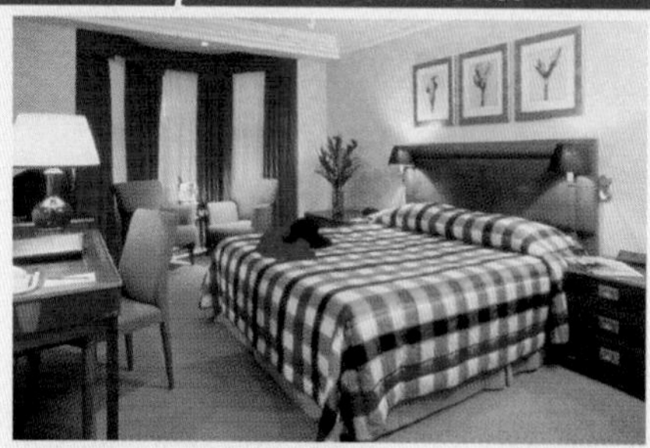

★★★★★ Athenaeum

116 Piccadilly W1J 7BJ
☎ 020 7499 3464 020 7493 1860
e-mail: info@athenaeumhotel.com
Dir: *on Piccadilly, overlooking Green Park*

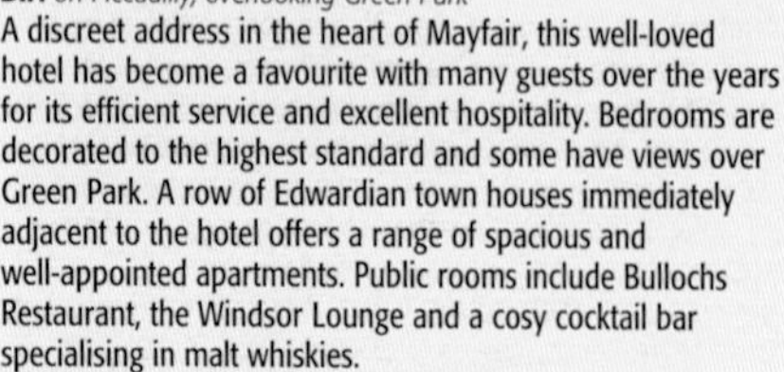

A discreet address in the heart of Mayfair, this well-loved hotel has become a favourite with many guests over the years for its efficient service and excellent hospitality. Bedrooms are decorated to the highest standard and some have views over Green Park. A row of Edwardian town houses immediately adjacent to the hotel offers a range of spacious and well-appointed apartments. Public rooms include Bullochs Restaurant, the Windsor Lounge and a cosy cocktail bar specialising in malt whiskies.
ROOMS: 157 en suite No smoking in 58 bedrooms s £265-£600; d £285-£750 **LB FACILITIES: Spa** STV Sauna Gym Jacuzzi Massage treatment, Steam rooms Xmas **CONF:** BC Thtr 55 Class 35 Board 36 **SERVICES:** Lift air con **NOTES:** No dogs (ex guide dogs) Civ Wed 55 **CARDS:**

★★★★★72% **Churchill Inter-Continental**

30 Portman Square W1A 4ZX
☎ 020 7486 5800 020 7486 1255
e-mail: churchill@interconti.com
Dir: *from Marble Arch rdbt, follow signs for Oxford Circus onto Oxford St. Left turn after 2nd traffic lights onto Portman St. Hotel on left*
This smart hotel enjoys a central location overlooking Portman Square. Excellent conference, hairdressing and beauty facilities and a fitness room make this the ideal choice for both corporate and leisure guests. Two floors of Club executive bedrooms benefit from a host of facilities and inclusive extras. The Terrace Restaurant offers a relaxed atmosphere, while the restaurant Locanda Locatelli benefits from the enormous talents of Giorgio Locatelli, offering the finest in Italian cuisine.
ROOMS: 445 en suite No smoking in 156 bedrooms s fr £320; d fr £340 **LB FACILITIES:** STV Tennis (hard) Sauna Gym entertainment Xmas **CONF:** BC Thtr 250 Class 160 Board 68 **SERVICES:** Lift air con **PARKING:** 48 **NOTES:** No dogs (ex guide dogs) Civ Wed 300 **CARDS:**

★★★★★71% **InterContinental London**

1 Hamilton Place, Hyde Park Corner W1J 7QY
☎ 020 7409 3131 020 7493 3476
e-mail: london@interconti.com
Dir: *at Hyde Park Corner, on corner of Park Ln and Piccadilly*
A well-known and well-loved landmark on Hyde Park Corner, the hotel enjoys some of the best views in London from the upper floors and lounges. Bedrooms vary from inner courtyard rooms to spacious suites. The smart marbled foyer houses the Observatory lounge for light meals and afternoon teas, and the Coffee House for breakfast and all-day dining. The jewel in the hotel's crown is Le Soufflé Restaurant.
ROOMS: 458 en suite No smoking in 312 bedrooms s fr £209; d fr £259 **FACILITIES:** STV Sauna Gym Jacuzzi Beauty treatments, Health Club, Horse riding, Crazy golf, Tennis courts nearby entertainment Xmas **CONF:** BC Thtr 750 Class 340 Board 62 **SERVICES:** Lift air con **PARKING:** 100 **NOTES:** No dogs (ex guide dogs) Civ Wed 750 **CARDS:**

★★★★★70% ***Le Meridien Grosvenor House***

Park Ln W1A 3AA
☎ 0870 400 8500 020 7493 3341
e-mail: grosvenor.enquiries@lemeridien.com
Dir: *Marble Arch, halfway down Park Ln*
Majestically positioned overlooking Hyde Park, this hotel enjoys a world wide reputation. The property is appointed to a high standard with deluxe bedrooms, Royal Club rooms and suites offering a range of facilities. The Park Room is ideal for refreshment at any time of day, and for dinner, guests can enjoy Italian cuisine in the informal La Terrazza.
ROOMS: 453 en suite (140 fmly) No smoking in 154 bedrooms **FACILITIES: Spa** STV Indoor swimming (H) Sauna Solarium Gym Jacuzzi Health & Fitness centre/Beauty salon entertainment **CONF:** Thtr 110 Class 60 Board 36 **SERVICES:** Lift air con **PARKING:** 95 **NOTES:** No dogs (ex guide dogs) Civ Wed 100 **CARDS:**

★★★★★70% ***Le Meridien Piccadilly***

21 Piccadilly W1J 0BH
☎ 0870 400 8400 020 7437 3574
e-mail: impiccres@lemeridien.com
Dir: *100mtrs from Piccadilly Circus*
This elegant hotel enjoys a prime central location on the doorstep of Piccadilly, Regent Street, Soho and theatreland. Thoughtfully equipped bedrooms vary in size and style and include some elegant refurbished rooms and stylish, spacious suites. The hotel boasts the renowned Champneys health spa, the contemporary airy Terrace Restaurant and the palatial Oak Room lounge where a pianist accompanies afternoon teas.
ROOMS: 266 en suite (19 fmly) No smoking in 91 bedrooms **FACILITIES:** STV Indoor swimming (H) Squash Sauna Solarium Gym Jacuzzi Beauty treatments Aerobics Massage **CONF:** Thtr 250 Class 160 Board 80 **SERVICES:** Lift air con **NOTES:** No dogs (ex guide dogs) Civ Wed 200 **CARDS:**

★★★★★63% ***May Fair Inter-Continental London***

Stratton St W1J 8LL
☎ 020 7629 7777 020 7629 1459
e-mail: mayfair@interconti.com
Dir: *from Hyde Park Corner or Piccadilly left onto Stratton St and hotel on left*
This well established hotel with many returning guests has an intimate atmosphere. Air-conditioned bedrooms are of varying sizes including suites and business-dedicated rooms with a useful range of amenities. The choice of eating options includes the Opus 70 restaurant, a showcase for the hotel's modern British cuisine. There is also a staffed business centre, leisure centre and a conference auditorium.
ROOMS: 289 en suite (14 fmly) No smoking in 148 bedrooms **FACILITIES:** STV Indoor swimming (H) Sauna Solarium Gym entertainment **CONF:** Thtr 292 Class 108 Board 60 **SERVICES:** Lift air con **NOTES:** No dogs (ex guide dogs) Civ Wed 250 **CARDS:**

London

★★★★78% The Montcalm-Hotel Nikko London
Great Cumberland Place W1H 7TW
020 7402 4288 020 7724 9180
e-mail: reservations@montcalm.co.uk
Dir: *2 minutes' walk north of Marble Arch station*

Ideally located on a secluded crescent close to Marble Arch, this charming Georgian property is named after the Marquis de Montcalm. Japanese-owned, the hotel offers extremely comfortable accommodation, ranging from standard to duplex 'junior' and penthouse suites. Staff are thoughtful and the stylish restaurant has a reputation for creative, modern cooking. Lunch is particularly good value for money.
ROOMS: 120 en suite No smoking in 28 bedrooms s fr £230; d £250-£600 **LB FACILITIES:** STV **CONF:** Thtr 80 Class 36 Board 36 **SERVICES:** Lift air con **PARKING:** 10 **NOTES:** No dogs (ex guide dogs)
CARDS:

★★★★76% The Westbury
Bond St W1S 2YF
020 7629 7755 020 7495 1163
e-mail: reservations@westburymayfair.com
Dir: *from Oxford Circus S down Regent St, right onto Conduit St, hotel at junct of Conduit St & Bond St*
The Westbury is located at the heart of London's finest shopping district and provides a calm atmoshpere away from London's hubbub. The standards of accommodation are high throughout, attracting an international clientele. Reception rooms offer a good choice for both relaxing and eating, including the Polo Bar for cocktails.
ROOMS: 247 en suite No smoking in 150 bedrooms s £282-£1057.50; d £282-£1057.50 **LB FACILITIES:** STV Gym Fitness centre, Steam room entertainment Xmas **CONF:** BC Thtr 120 Class 55 Board 35 Del £225 **SERVICES:** Lift air con **NOTES:** No dogs (ex guide dogs)
CARDS:

See advert on this page

★★★★75% The Chesterfield
Red Carnation HOTELS
35 Charles St, Mayfair W1J 5EB
020 7491 2622 020 7491 4793
e-mail: bookch@rchmail.com
Dir: *from Hyde Park Corner along Piccadilly, left into Half Moon St. At end left and 1st right into Queens St, then right into Charles St*
Quiet elegance and an atmosphere of exclusivity characterise this hotel, which has now completed an ambitious refurbishment programme. Bedrooms have been decorated in a variety of contemporary styles, some with fabric walls, and marble-clad bathrooms have heated floors and mirrors. Bedrooms and public areas are all air-conditioned.
ROOMS: 110 en suite (7 fmly) No smoking in 52 bedrooms **FACILITIES:** STV entertainment **CONF:** BC Thtr 120 Class 45 Board 45 Del from £199 **SERVICES:** Lift air con **NOTES:** Civ Wed 120
CARDS:

London

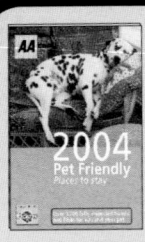

W1 WEST END, continued

★★★★75% ◎◎◎ ***Raffles Brown's***
Albemarle St, Mayfair W1S 4BP
☎ 020 7493 6020 020 7493 9381
e-mail: brownshotel@brownshotel.com
Dir: *from Green Park underground on Piccadilly, take 3rd left into Albemarle St*
Brown's is famous for its English country-house style and traditional emphasis on comfortable furnishings and quality appointments. Accommodation is of a high standard and rooms are particularly spacious. Elegant restaurant 1837, the oldest hotel restaurant in London, serves an interesting choice of menus offering mouth-watering dishes and the delightful lounges prove a popular venue for afternoon tea.
ROOMS: 118 en suite (15 fmly) **FACILITIES:** STV Gym entertainment **CONF:** Thtr 70 Class 30 Board 35 **SERVICES:** Lift air con **NOTES:** No dogs (ex guide dogs) Civ Wed 70 **CARDS:**

★★★★74% **The Washington Mayfair Hotel**
5-7 Curzon St, Mayfair W1J 5HE
☎ 020 7499 7000 020 7495 6172
e-mail: sales@washington-mayfair.co.uk
Dir: *Green Park station take Piccadilly exit and turn right. Take 4th street on right into Curzon St.*
Situated in the stylish Mayfair, this smart and modern hotel offers a very high standard of accommodation. Bedrooms are all attractively furnished and provide high levels of comfort. The hotel is also a popular venue for light refreshments, which are served in the marbled and wood-panelled public areas.
ROOMS: 171 en suite No smoking in 94 bedrooms s £188-£235; d £188-£235 **LB** **FACILITIES:** STV Gym entertainment Xmas **CONF:** BC Thtr 110 Class 40 Board 36 Del from £250 **SERVICES:** Lift air con **NOTES:** No dogs (ex guide dogs) **CARDS:**

★★★★73% ◎◎ **London Marriott Hotel Grosvenor Square**
Marriott HOTELS · RESORTS · SUITES
Grosvenor Square W1K 6JP
☎ 020 7493 1232 020 7491 3201
e-mail: businesscentre@londonmarriott.co.uk
Dir: *M4 E to Cromwell Rd through Knightsbridge to Hyde Park Corner. Park Lane right at Brook Gate onto Upper Brook St to Grosvenor Sq*
This smart hotel is situated in the heart of Mayfair and provides a high standard of accommodation and public rooms. Friendly staff remain unfailingly helpful and willing to please. Breakfasts are memorable and good food is served in the Diplomat Restaurant overlooking the gardens of Grosvenor Square.

ROOMS: 221 en suite (26 fmly) No smoking in 120 bedrooms **FACILITIES:** STV Gym Exercise & fitness centre **CONF:** BC Thtr 1000 Class 550 Board 120 Del from £200 **SERVICES:** Lift air con **PARKING:** 80 **NOTES:** No dogs (ex guide dogs) Civ Wed 400 **CARDS:**

★★★★72% ◎ **Sherlock Holmes**
Park Plaza
108 Baker St W1U 6LJ
☎ 020 7486 6161 020 7958 5211
e-mail: info@sherlockholmes.com
Dir: *from Marylebone Flyover onto Marylebone Rd and at Baker St turn right for hotel on left*
Chic and modern, this boutique style hotel is conveniently located close to a number of London underground lines and railway stations. Public rooms include a popular bar, sited just inside the main entrance, and Sherlock's Grill, where the mesquite wood burning stove is a feature of the cooking. The hotel also features an indoor health suite and a relaxing lounge.
ROOMS: 119 en suite No smoking in 59 bedrooms s £240.87-£511.12 **FACILITIES:** STV Xmas **CONF:** Thtr 50 Class 40 Board 30 Del from £230 **SERVICES:** Lift air con **NOTES:** No dogs (ex guide dogs) No smoking in restaurant **CARDS:**

★★★★71%
Radisson Edwardian Berkshire
Radisson EDWARDIAN
350 Oxford St W1N 0BY
☎ 020 7629 7474 020 7629 8156
e-mail: resberk@radisson.com
Dir: *opposite Bond St Underground*
A friendly atmosphere prevails at this elegant hotel, centrally located behind Oxford Street's major department stores. Public areas have a boutique feel and include a contemporary bar, a smart restaurant and a selection of meeting and conference rooms. Well-equipped bedrooms vary in size, and at the time of our inspection were about to undergo a stylish refurbishment.
ROOMS: 148 en suite (2 fmly) No smoking in 44 bedrooms s £115-£247 **LB** **FACILITIES:** STV **CONF:** Thtr 40 Class 16 Board 16 **SERVICES:** Lift air con **NOTES:** No dogs (ex guide dogs)
CARDS:

Late for dinner?
Quality Standards mean that last orders for dinner vary according to star rating and should be no earlier than:
★★ 7.00pm ★★★ 8.00pm ★★★★ 9.00pm
★★★★★ 10.00pm

Need a break without breaking the bank?
Latebeds offers last-minute deals with no nasty surprises at AA-approved hotels and B&Bs. Visit www.theAA.com to find out more

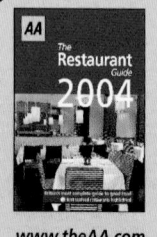

London

★★★★70% **Jurys Clifton-Ford**
47 Welbeck St W1M 8DN
☎ 020 7486 6600 📠 020 7486 7492
e-mail: cliftonford@jurysdoyle.com
Dir: *from Portland Place, turn into New Cavendish St. Welbeck St last turning on left*
This well kept and centrally located hotel is just 5 minutes' walk from Oxford Street and fashionable Bond Street. Bedrooms vary in space and style and there are even a number of penthouse apartments with balconies. Guests can take advantage of the excellent leisure facilities which includes a good-sized swimming pool, and there are extensive conference facilities.
ROOMS: 255 en suite (7 fmly) No smoking in 60 bedrooms
FACILITIES: STV Indoor swimming (H) Sauna Solarium Gym Jacuzzi Fully equipped leisure club **CONF:** Thtr 120 Class 70 Board 40 Del from £215 **SERVICES:** Lift air con **NOTES:** No dogs (ex guide dogs)
CARDS:

★★★★70% ®®
Millennium Hotel London Mayfair

Grosvenor Square W1K 2HP
☎ 020 7629 9400 📠 020 7629 7736
e-mail: sales.mayfair@mill-cop.com
Dir: *on S side of Grosvenor Square*

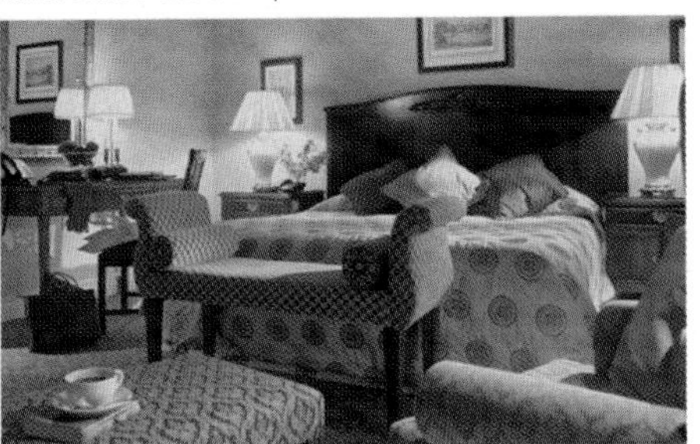

The Millennium Hotel offers a wide range of facilities including a restaurant, piano bar, fitness room and the popular Shogun restaurant. Bedrooms vary in size, and are smartly appointed and equipped. The deluxe rooms on the Club floor benefit from their own lounge and complimentary refreshments.
ROOMS: 348 en suite No smoking in 145 bedrooms s fr £223; d fr £323 **LB FACILITIES:** STV Gym entertainment Xmas **CONF:** BC Thtr 450 Class 250 Board 70 **SERVICES:** Lift air con **NOTES:** No dogs (ex guide dogs) Civ Wed 400 **CARDS:**

★★★★70%
Radisson Edwardian Grafton Hotel
130 Tottenham Court Rd W1T 5AY
☎ 020 7388 4131 📠 020 7387 7394
e-mail: resgraf@radisson.com
Dir: *Central London, along Euston Rd, onto Tottenham Court Rd. Past Warren St underground station*
Ongoing investment and a commitment to providing excellent levels of hospitality and service sees The Grafton going from strength to strength. Public areas are smart and a popular meeting venue. Bedrooms come in a variety of sizes; all have been fully refurbished to provide excellent comfort and facilities. The hotel is well placed next to Warren Street tube station.
ROOMS: 330 en suite (23 fmly) No smoking in 55 bedrooms s £125-£230; d £145-£290 **FACILITIES:** STV Gym Fitness room Xmas **CONF:** BC Thtr 100 Class 50 Board 30 Del from £160 **SERVICES:** Lift air con **NOTES:** No dogs (ex guide dogs)
CARDS:

★★★★70% **Radisson SAS Portman**
22 Portman Square W1H 7BG
☎ 020 7208 6000 📠 020 7208 6001
e-mail: sales.london@radissonsas.com
Dir: *100mtrs N of Oxford St and 500mtrs E of Edgware Rd*
Located in a quieter area of the city and just a short stroll from Oxford Street. There are five styles of bedroom, ranging from Oriental through to classical and the new Italian décor is receiving much praise. The new Talavera restaurant offers a contemporary Mediterranean menu. Parking is available.
ROOMS: 272 en suite (21 fmly) No smoking in 129 bedrooms
FACILITIES: STV Tennis (hard) Sauna Solarium Gym entertainment
CONF: Thtr 700 Class 350 Board 65 **SERVICES:** Lift air con
PARKING: 400 **NOTES:** No dogs (ex guide dogs) Civ Wed 450
CARDS:

★★★★68%
London Marriott Hotel Marble Arch
134 George St W1H 5DN
☎ 020 7723 1277 📠 020 7402 0666
e-mail: salesadmin.marblearch@marriotthotels.co.uk
Dir: *from Marble Arch turn into Edgware Rd, then 4th right into George St. Left into Forset St for entrance*

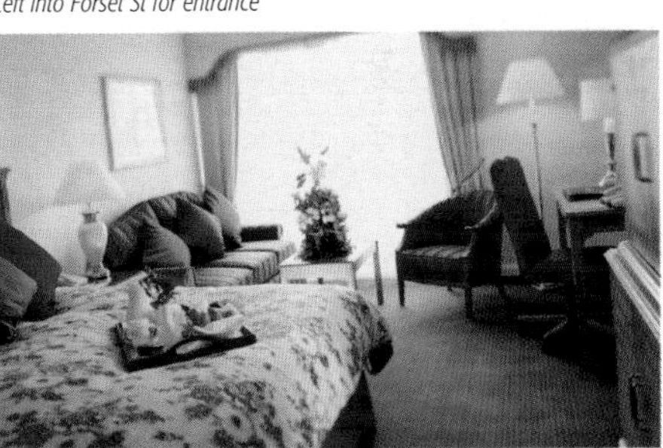

This modern hotel, conveniently situated just off the Edgware Road and close to Oxford Street shops, offers well-equipped bedrooms furnished with quality fittings. Public areas are compact, and the bar and restaurant have undergone a stylish refurbishment. Parking is also available.
ROOMS: 240 en suite (100 fmly) No smoking in 120 bedrooms s £165-£215; d £165-£215 **LB FACILITIES:** STV Indoor swimming (H) Sauna Solarium Gym Jacuzzi Xmas **CONF:** Thtr 150 Class 75 Board 80 Del from £199 **SERVICES:** Lift air con **PARKING:** 80 **NOTES:** No dogs (ex guide dogs) **CARDS:**

★★★★67% **The Berners Hotel**
Berners St W1A 3BE
☎ 020 7666 2000 📠 020 7666 2001
e-mail: berners@berners.co.uk
Ideally located in the heart of London's West End, adjacent to Oxford Street, this traditional hotel has an elegant feel with its marble-columned foyer and ornately carved ceilings. The luxurious lounge is a popular venue for afternoon tea and bedrooms are all equipped with modern facilties.
ROOMS: 216 en suite No smoking in 100 bedrooms s £190; d £215
FACILITIES: STV **CONF:** BC Thtr 160 Class 80 Board 40 Del from £195
SERVICES: Lift **NOTES:** No dogs (ex guide dogs) Civ Wed 70
CARDS:

W1 WEST END, continued

★★★★67% *The Cumberland*

Marble Arch W1A 4RF
☎ 020 7262 1234 🖷 020 7724 4621
e-mail: reservations.cumberland@lemeridien.com
Dir: *M4 to central London. At Hyde Park Corner take Park Ln to Marble Arch. Hotel above Marble Arch underground station*
This hotel is situated in an enviable location near Hyde Park. At the time of going to press, the hotel is undergoing a major refurbishment programme. Current details can be obtained by telephoning the hotel and on the AA website www.theAA.com.
ROOMS: 894 en suite (21 fmly) No smoking in 480 bedrooms **FACILITIES:** STV entertainment **CONF:** Thtr 400 Class 250 Board 55 **SERVICES:** Lift **NOTES:** No dogs (ex guide dogs) **CARDS:**

Town House

★★★★ Grange Fitzrovia

20-28 Bolsover St W1W 5NB
☎ 020 7467 7000 🖷 020 7636 5085
e-mail: fitzrovia@grangehotels.com
The Fitzrovia nestles in a quiet street south of Regents Park. Bedrooms are richly decorated and feature polished wood furnishings and marbled bathrooms. Some have air-conditioning. An atmosphere of luxury and comfort prevails in the small lobby lounge.
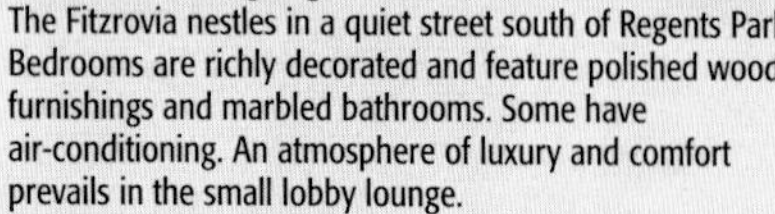
ROOMS: 88 en suite No smoking in 40 bedrooms s £155-£220; d £155-£220 **FACILITIES:** STV Xmas **CONF:** Thtr 100 Class 45 Board 40 Del from £235 **SERVICES:** Lift **NOTES:** No dogs (ex guide dogs) **CARDS:**

★★★66% Mostyn

4 Bryanston St W1H 7BY
☎ 020 7935 2361 🖷 020 7487 2759
e-mail: info@mostynhotel.co.uk
Dir: *A40(M) Marylebone Rd, close to Marble Arch and Bond St underground*

Originally built as a private residence for Lady Back, a lady in waiting to the court of George II, this hotel is set in the heart of the West End. Bedrooms feature air conditioning and public rooms include the open-plan lounge, cocktail bar, and the restaurant with magnificent ornate ceilings; a legacy from the hotel's grand origins.
ROOMS: 121 en suite (15 fmly) No smoking in 54 bedrooms **FACILITIES:** STV **CONF:** Thtr 140 Class 80 Board 60 **SERVICES:** Lift air con **NOTES:** No dogs (ex guide dogs) **CARDS:**

See advert on opposite page

★★★65% *The Mandeville*
Mandeville Place W1U 2BE
☎ 020 7935 5599 🖷 020 7935 9588
e-mail: info@mandeville.co.uk
Dir: *off Oxford Street and Wigmore St near Bond St underground station*
This elegant Edwardian building is situated only a short stroll from Oxford Street. Guests have a varied choice of eating and drinking options, and 24-hour room service is also available. The owners are currently carrying out notable refurbishment.
ROOMS: 165 en suite No smoking in 30 bedrooms **FACILITIES:** STV **CONF:** Thtr 35 Class 20 Board 20 **SERVICES:** Lift **NOTES:** No dogs (ex guide dogs) **CARDS:**

See advert on opposite page

★★★62% Grange Langham Court
31-35 Langham St W1W 6BU
☎ 020 7436 6622 🖷 020 7436 2303
e-mail: langhamcourt@grangehotels.com
Situated between Regents Park and Oxford Circus, this hotel has an elegant tiled façade, and is set in a quiet, tucked-away street. Formerly a nursing home, it now provides compact and well-equipped accommodation. Public areas include a wine bar, lounge and basement dining room.
ROOMS: 58 en suite No smoking in 20 bedrooms s £122-£210; d £133-£210 **FACILITIES:** STV Xmas **CONF:** Thtr 80 Class 35 Board 35 Del from £198 **SERVICES:** Lift **NOTES:** No dogs (ex guide dogs) **CARDS:**

U *Holiday Inn London-Mayfair*
3 Berkeley St W1X 6NE
☎ 020 7493 8282 🖷 020 7629 2827
e-mail: himres@holidayinnmayfair.co.uk
Dir: *at corner of Berkeley St and Piccadilly*
At the time of going to press, the classification for this hotel was not confirmed. Please refer to the AA internet site www.theAA.com for current information.
ROOMS: 186 en suite (64 fmly) No smoking in 101 bedrooms **FACILITIES:** STV Gym Fitness studio **CONF:** Thtr 60 Class 32 Board 32 **SERVICES:** Lift air con **PARKING:** 20 **NOTES:** No dogs (ex guide dogs) **CARDS:**

U *Holiday Inn London - Regents Park*
Carburton St, Regents Park W1W 5EE
☎ 0870 400 9111
e-mail: londonregentspark@ichotelsgroup.com
At the time of going to press, the classification for this hotel was not confirmed. Please refer to the AA internet site www.theAA.com for current information.
ROOMS: 333 en suite No smoking in 199 bedrooms **FACILITIES:** STV **CONF:** Thtr 350 Class 180 Board 50 **SERVICES:** Lift **PARKING:** 85 **NOTES:** No dogs (ex guide dogs) **CARDS:**

Bad hair day?
Hairdryers in all rooms three stars and above

U London Marriott Hotel Park Lane
140 Park Ln W1K 7AA
☎ 020 7493 7000 🖷 020 7493 8333
e-mail: mhrs.parklane@marriotthotels.com
Dir: *from Hyde Park Corner, left on Park Ln onto A4202, 0.8m. At Marble Arch onto Park Ln. Take 1st left onto North Row. Hotel on left*
At the time of going to press, the star classification for this hotel

continued

London

was not confirmed. Please refer to the AA internet site www.theAA.com for current information.

ROOMS: 157 en suite No smoking in 95 bedrooms s £205-£255; d £205-£255 **LB** **FACILITIES:** STV Indoor swimming (H) Sauna Gym Steam Room entertainment Xmas **CONF:** BC Thtr 72 Class 33 Board 42 **SERVICES:** Lift air con **NOTES:** No dogs (ex guide dogs) Civ Wed 65 **CARDS:**

U Radisson Edwardian Sussex
Granville Place W1H 0EH
☎ 020 7408 0130 020 7493 2070
Dir: off Oxford Street
At the time of going to press, the star classification for this hotel was not confirmed. Please refer to the AA internet site www.theAA.com for current information.
ROOMS: 101 en suite

W2 BAYSWATER, PADDINGTON

★★★★75% Royal Lancaster
Lancaster Ter W2 2TY
☎ 020 7262 6737 020 7724 3191
e-mail: book@royallancaster.com
Dir: above Lancaster Gate underground station
This smart hotel has an excellent range of public facilities, including impressive conference rooms, 24-hour business centre and car park. The rosette awarded Nipa Thai is among a choice of drinking and eating options; and more developments are planned. Bedrooms are modern and well equipped, with upper floors enjoying stunning views across London.
ROOMS: 416 en suite (11 fmly) No smoking in 111 bedrooms **FACILITIES:** STV entertainment **CONF:** Thtr 1500 Class 650 Board 40 **SERVICES:** Lift air con **PARKING:** 100 **NOTES:** No dogs (ex guide dogs) **CARDS:**

Town House

★★★★ The Abbey Court
20 Pembridge Gardens, Kensington W2 4DU
☎ 020 7221 7518 020 7792 0858
e-mail: info@abbeycourthotel.co.uk
Dir: 2mins from Notting Hill Gate Underground station
Situated in Notting Hill and close to Kensington, this five-storey Victorian town house stands on a quiet side road. Rooms are individually decorated and have marble bathrooms with jacuzzi-jet baths. Room service is available for light snacks and full English breakfasts can be enjoyed in the conservatory.
ROOMS: 22 en suite (1 fmly) (3 GF) No smoking in 10 bedrooms s £93-£155; d £145-£210 (incl. bkfst) **FACILITIES: Spa** STV **CONF:** BC Board 10 **NOTES:** No dogs (ex guide dogs) **CARDS:**

London

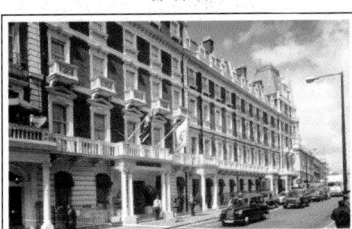

W2 BAYSWATER, PADDINGTON, continued

Town House

★★★★ Pembridge Court
34 Pembridge Gardens W2 4DX
☎ 020 7229 9977 020 7727 4982
e-mail: reservations@pemct.co.uk
Dir: *off Bayswater Rd at Notting Hill Gate by underground station*
This attractive Victorian town house is in a residential street near the Portobello Market and Notting Hill Gate tube. Bedrooms are mostly a good size, all are air conditioned. The hotel features a collection of antique clothing and fans. Two smart lounges are available for guests.
ROOMS: 20 en suite (4 fmly) (5 GF) **FACILITIES:** STV Membership of local Health Club **CONF:** BC Board 12 **SERVICES:** Lift air con **PARKING:** 2 **NOTES:** No smoking in restaurant RS 24 Dec-1 Jan **CARDS:**

★★★74% *The Gresham Hyde Park*
66 Lancaster Gate W2 3NZ
☎ 020 7262 5090 020 7723 1244
e-mail: reservations@gresham-hydeparkhotel.com

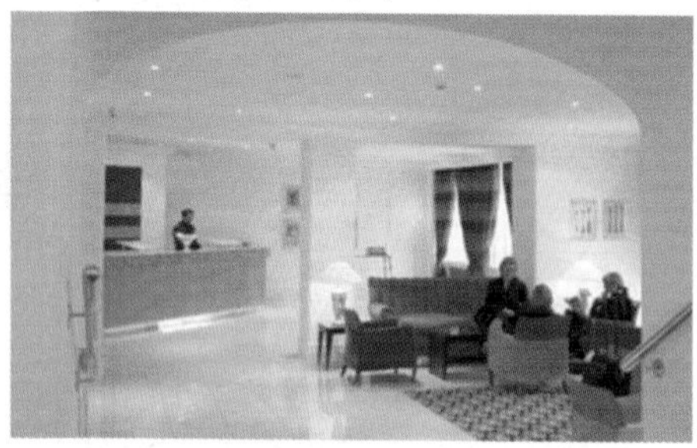

Centrally located in Lancaster Gate, this landmark building with its historic stucco façade offers modern bedrooms and attractive public rooms. Bedrooms are air conditioned, of comfortable proportions and well equipped. Room service complements the availability of full restaurant and bar services. A modern meeting room and fitness centre are also available.
ROOMS: 188 en suite (21 fmly) No smoking in 77 bedrooms **FACILITIES:** STV Gym **CONF:** Thtr 35 Class 18 Board 18 **SERVICES:** Lift air con **NOTES:** No dogs (ex guide dogs) **CARDS:**

TV dinner?
Room service at three stars and above

★★★67% *The Plaza on Hyde Park Hotel*
corus hotels
1-7 Lancaster Gate W2 3LG
☎ 020 7262 5022 020 7724 8666
e-mail: plazaonhydepark@corushotels.com
Dir: *200yds from Lancaster Gate underground. 0.25m from Paddington Station*
This hotel has undergone a massive refurbishment programme. New bedrooms have been fitted out with modern colour schemes, good lighting and attention to detail. Some have air conditioning.
continued
Public areas include the popular Olio's restaurant complete with pizza oven.

ROOMS: 401 en suite (10 fmly) No smoking in 200 bedrooms **FACILITIES:** STV **CONF:** Thtr 20 Class 12 Board 20 **SERVICES:** Lift **NOTES:** No dogs (ex guide dogs) **CARDS:**

★★★65% Berjaya Eden Park Hotel
35-39 Inverness Ter, Bayswater W2 3JS
☎ 020 7221 2220 020 7221 2286
e-mail: edenpark@dircon.co.uk
Dir: *from Marble Arch, over main rdbt onto Bayswater Rd. Right into Queensway, 1st left into Inverness Terrace*

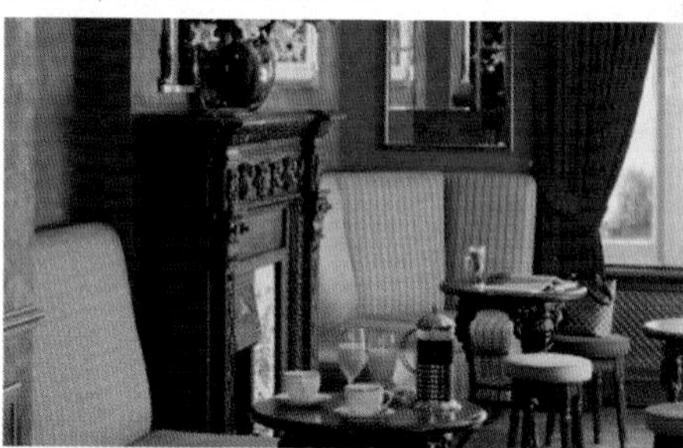

Located within easy reach of the Oxford Street shops and West End attractions and close to the Queensway underground, this is a friendly hotel. Bedrooms are attractively presented and a range of rooms is available. The public rooms feature a spacious restaurant and a cosy bar.
ROOMS: 75 en suite 61 annexe en suite (8 fmly) No smoking in 42 bedrooms s fr £82; d fr £123 **FACILITIES:** STV **CONF:** Thtr 50 Class 50 Board 25 **SERVICES:** Lift **NOTES:** No dogs (ex guide dogs) **CARDS:**

★★★64% Quality Hotel Paddington
8-14 Talbot Square W2 1TS
☎ 020 7262 6699 020 7723 3233
e-mail: quality@lth-hotels.com
Dir: *from Bayswater Rd right onto Sussex Gdns*
This well-presented hotel is ideally located close to Paddington Station. Modern bedrooms are comfortably appointed and particularly well equipped. Public areas include a compact bar and lounge, and a basement restaurant where guests can enjoy good breakfasts and evening meals.
ROOMS: 75 en suite (7 fmly) (8 GF) No smoking in 61 bedrooms s £65-£105; d £75-£125 **LB** **FACILITIES:** STV **SERVICES:** Lift **NOTES:** No smoking in restaurant **CARDS:**

London

★★70% Delmere
30 Sussex Gardens, Hyde Park W2 1UB
☎ 020 7706 3344 020 7262 1863
-mail: delmerehotel@compuserve.com
ir: *M25 take A40 to London, exit at Paddington. Along Westbourne errace and into Sussex Gdns*
)elmere Hotel is located centrally on Sussex Gardens and within easy reach of the West End. This friendly and privately owned hotel has bedrooms that make good use of space, and are well equipped. Public rooms include a jazz-theme bar and a comfortable lounge.
ROOMS: 36 en suite (6 GF) No smoking in 8 bedrooms s £77-£97; d £96-£122 (incl. cont bkfst) **LB FACILITIES:** STV **SERVICES:** Lift
PARKING: 2 **NOTES:** No dogs (ex guide dogs)
CARDS:

W3 ACTON
See LONDON plan 1 C4

Travelodge (London Park Royal)
A40 Western Ave, Acton W3 0TE
☎ 08700 850 950
Travelodge offers good quality, good value, modern accommodation. Ideal for families, the spacious, en suite bedrooms include remote-control TV, tea and coffee-making facilities, luxury beds and free morning newspaper. Meals can be taken at the nearby family restaurant. For further details and the Travelodge phone number, consult the Hotel Groups page.
ROOMS: 64 en suite s fr £42.95; d fr £42.95

W5 EALING
See LONDON plan 1 B4

Holiday Inn London-Ealing
Western Av, Hanger Ln, Ealing W5 1HG
☎ 020 8233 3200 020 8233 3201
At the time of going to press, the classification for this hotel was not confirmed. Please refer to the AA internet site www.theAA.com for current information.
ROOMS: 138 en suite
PARKING: CARDS:

W6 HAMMERSMITH
See LONDON plan 1 D3

★★★70% Novotel London West
1 Shortlands W6 8DR
☎ 020 8741 1555 020 8741 2120
e-mail: H0737@accor-hotels.com

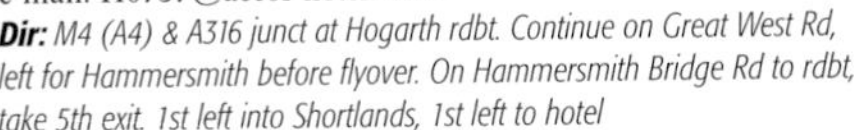

Dir: *M4 (A4) & A316 junct at Hogarth rdbt. Continue on Great West Rd, left for Hammersmith before flyover. On Hammersmith Bridge Rd to rdbt, take 5th exit. 1st left into Shortlands, 1st left to hotel*
This large and purpose-built hotel is located in the heart of Hammersmith, easily accessible from the M4. Practical and spacious bedrooms are equipped with a range of modern facilities. Refurbished public areas include a choice of restaurants and bars, a useful shop and extensive conference and banqueting facilities. Secure parking is available.
ROOMS: 629 en suite (148 fmly) No smoking in 473 bedrooms
FACILITIES: STV Snooker Gym **CONF:** BC Thtr 1000 Class 525 Board 200 Del £205 **SERVICES:** Lift air con **PARKING:** 240
NOTES: Civ Wed 1400 **CARDS:**

★★★64% Vencourt
255 King St, Hammersmith W6 9LU
☎ 020 8563 8855 020 8563 9988
e-mail: vencourt@bestwestern.co.uk
Dir: *on A4 to Hammersmith, follow A315 towards Chiswick*
Vencourt Hotel provides good value accommodation with city views from the higher floors. The hotel has open-plan public areas including a lounge bar, where snacks are served all day, and a small restaurant for more substantial meals.
ROOMS: 120 en suite (25 fmly) No smoking in 18 bedrooms
FACILITIES: STV **CONF:** BC Thtr 160 Class 100 Board 52 Del from £120
SERVICES: Lift **PARKING:** 27 **CARDS:**

Express by Holiday Inn London Hammersmith
124 King St W6 0QU
☎ 020 8746 5100 020 8746 5199
e-mail: hammersmith@expressbyholidayinn.net
Dir: *M4/A4 junct 1, continue to Hammersmith Broadway take 2nd left to A315 towards Chiswick (King St). Hotel on right*

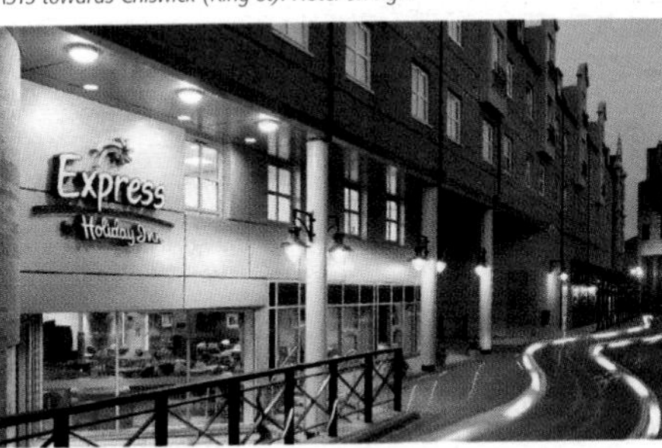

A modern hotel ideal for families and business travellers. Fresh and uncomplicated, the spacious bedrooms include Sky TV, power shower and tea and coffee-making facilities. Continental buffet breakfast is included in the room rate; other meals may be taken at the nearby family pub or restaurant. For further details and the Express by Holiday Inn phone number, consult the Hotel Groups pages.
ROOMS: 135 en suite s £99.95; d £99.95 (incl. cont bkfst)
CONF: Thtr 45 Class 25 Board 25

Late for dinner?
Quality Standards mean that last orders for dinner vary according to star rating and should be no earlier than:
★★ 7.00pm ★★★ 8.00pm ★★★★ 9.00pm
★★★★★ 10.00pm

W8 KENSINGTON

Top 200 - Hotel

★★★★★ ◎◎◎ **Royal Garden Hotel**
2-24 Kensington High St W8 4PT
☎ 020 7937 8000 ▤ 020 7361 1991
e-mail: sales@royalgardenhotel.co.uk
Dir: *next to Kensington Palace*

A well-known landmark on the edge of Hyde Park, within walking distance of the Albert Hall and Kensington's smart shops, this modern hotel provides guests with excellent levels of comfort and service, and a number of drinking and eating options. Rooms are generally spacious and overlook either Hyde Park or the Kensington rooftops. The hotel's showcase restaurant, The Tenth, is contemporary in style with great views and offers classical cooking with modern and Oriental influences.

ROOMS: 396 en suite (19 fmly) No smoking in 164 bedrooms s fr £288; d fr £358 **FACILITIES: Spa** STV Sauna Solarium Gym Health & fitness centre entertainment Xmas **CONF:** BC Thtr 550 Class 260 Board 80 **SERVICES:** Lift air con **PARKING:** 160 **NOTES:** No dogs (ex guide dogs) Civ Wed 400
CARDS:

See advert on opposite page

Top 200 - Town House

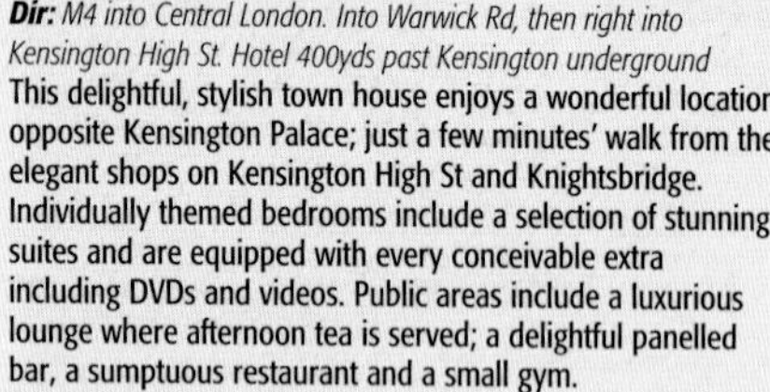

★★★★★ 🏠 **Milestone Hotel & Apartments**
1 Kensington Court W8 5DL
☎ 020 7917 1000 ▤ 020 7917 1010
e-mail: guestservicems@rchmail.com
Dir: *M4 into Central London. Into Warwick Rd, then right into Kensington High St. Hotel 400yds past Kensington underground*

Red Carnation HOTELS

This delightful, stylish town house enjoys a wonderful location opposite Kensington Palace; just a few minutes' walk from the elegant shops on Kensington High St and Knightsbridge. Individually themed bedrooms include a selection of stunning suites and are equipped with every conceivable extra including DVDs and videos. Public areas include a luxurious lounge where afternoon tea is served; a delightful panelled bar, a sumptuous restaurant and a small gym.

ROOMS: 57 en suite No smoking in 22 bedrooms s £306-£952; d £306-£952 **LB FACILITIES:** STV Sauna Gym Jacuzzi Health Club entertainment Xmas **CONF:** Thtr 28 Class 12 Board 16 **SERVICES:** Lift air con **NOTES:** Civ Wed 30
CARDS:

Town House

★★★★ 🏠 **Kensington House**
15-16 Prince of Wales Ter W8 5PQ
☎ 020 7937 2345 ▤ 020 7368 6700
e-mail: sales@kenhouse.com
Dir: *off Kensington High St, opposite Kensington Palace*

This beautiful 19th-century property has been elegantly restored to provide contemporary, well-equipped accommodation in the heart of Kensington. Tiger Bar provides an airy, informal setting for light snacks, meals and refreshments throughout the day. Bedrooms vary in size and are smartly appointed and thoughtfully equipped for both business and leisure guests.

ROOMS: 41 en suite (3 GF) No smoking in 30 bedrooms s £150; d £195 (incl. bkfst) **LB FACILITIES:** STV Arrangement with local health club **CONF:** BC **SERVICES:** Lift **NOTES:** No dogs (ex guide dogs) **CARDS:**

★★★★64% ***Copthorne Tara Hotel London Kensington***
Scarsdale Place, Wrights Ln W8 5SR
☎ 020 7937 7211 ▤ 020 7937 7100
e-mail: tara.sales@mill-cop.com
Dir: *off Kensington High St*

COPTHORNE

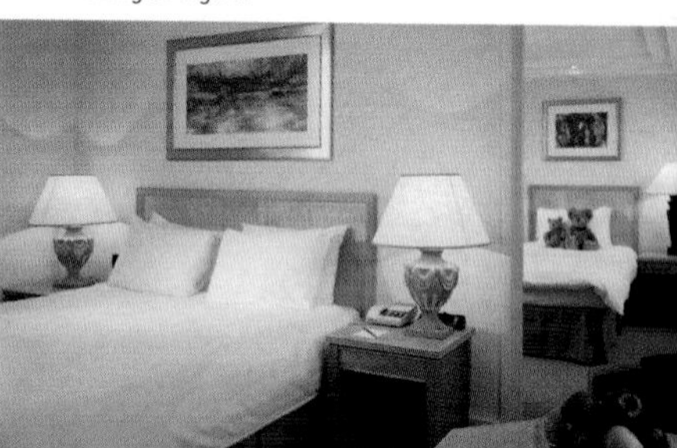

This is one of the city's larger hotels and is popular with continental tours and conferences. Smart public areas have a bustling atmosphere, and include the relaxing setting of Café Mozart and the Brasserie. Bedrooms fall into two grades, Classic and Connoisseur; there are a number of very well equipped rooms for less able guests. All bedrooms are comfort cooled.

ROOMS: 834 en suite No smoking in 265 bedrooms **FACILITIES:** STV **CONF:** Thtr 280 Class 160 Board 80 **SERVICES:** Lift air con **PARKING:** 86 **NOTES:** No dogs (ex guide dogs)
CARDS:

WC1 BLOOMSBURY, HOLBORN

★★★★★73% ◎◎ **Renaissance London Chancery Court**
252 High Holborn WC1V 7EN
☎ 020 7829 9888 ▤ 020 7829 9889
e-mail: sales.chancerycourt@renaissancehotels.com
Dir: *A4 along Piccadilly onto Shaftesbury Av. Into High Holborn, hotel on right*

RENAISSANCE

This is a grand place with splendid public areas, decorated throughout in rare marble. Craftsmen have meticulously restored the sweeping staircases, grand archways and stately rooms of the 1914 building. The result is a spacious, relaxed hotel offering everything from stylish, luxuriously appointed bedrooms to a

continued

health club and state-of-the-art meeting rooms. The Art Deco sytle QC restaurant is becoming a destination in its own right.
ROOMS: 356 en suite No smoking in 214 bedrooms s £229.12-£264.38; d £229.12-£264.38 **FACILITIES:** STV Sauna Gym Spa by ESPA Xmas **CONF:** Thtr 435 Class 264 Board 60 **SERVICES:** Lift air con **NOTES:** Civ Wed **CARDS:**

★★★★72% Jurys Great Russell Street

16-22 Great Russell St WC1B 3NN
☎ 020 7347 1000 020 7347 1001
e-mail: sales@jurysdoyle.com
Dir: *from Bedford Sq. Turn right, then first left to end of road*
On the doorstep of Covent Garden, Oxford St and the West End, this impressive building, designed by the renowned Sir Edwin Lutyens in the 1930s, retains many original features. Bedrooms are attractively appointed and benefit from an excellent range of facilities. Public areas include a grand reception lounge, an elegant bar and restaurant as well as extensive conference facilities.
ROOMS: 169 en suite No smoking in 67 bedrooms s £144-£230; d £144-£230 **LB FACILITIES:** STV Xmas **CONF:** BC Thtr 300 Class 170 Board 60 Del from £230 **SERVICES:** Lift air con **NOTES:** No dogs (ex guide dogs) **CARDS:**

★★★★71% Grange Holborn

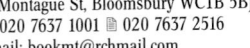

50-60 Southampton Row WC1B 4AR
☎ 020 7242 1800 020 7242 0057
e-mail: holborn@grangehotels.co.uk
This smart hotel is centrally located, close to Oxford Street and Covent Garden. Elegantly furnished, spacious bedrooms offer high levels of comfort and are equipped with every conceivable extra for both business and leisure guests. Public areas include a smart fitness centre and a choice of restaurants.
ROOMS: 200 en suite (10 fmly) No smoking in 100 bedrooms s £205-£400; d £205-£400 **FACILITIES:** STV Indoor swimming (H) Sauna Gym Swimming pool supervised Xmas **CONF:** Thtr 220 Class 120 Board 60 Del from £275 **SERVICES:** Lift air con **NOTES:** No dogs (ex guide dogs) **CARDS:**

★★★★71% Radisson Edwardian Kenilworth

Great Russell St WC1B 3LB
☎ 020 7637 3477 020 7631 3133
e-mail: resmarl@radisson.com
Dir: *past Oxford St and down New Oxford St. Turn into Bloomsbury St*
Following extensive refurbishment, the hotel has been completely transformed and now features a stylish, contemporary bar and restaurant with a theatre kitchen, as well as a range of meeting rooms and a small gym and steam room. Air-conditioned bedrooms are modern and feature a multitude of useful extras.
ROOMS: 186 en suite (15 fmly) No smoking in 139 bedrooms s £229; d £261 **LB FACILITIES:** STV Fitness room Business centre Xmas **CONF:** BC Thtr 120 Class 50 Board 40 Del from £199 **SERVICES:** Lift air con **NOTES:** No dogs (ex guide dogs)
CARDS:

★★★★70% *The Montague on the Gardens*

15 Montague St, Bloomsbury WC1B 5BJ
☎ 020 7637 1001 020 7637 2516
e-mail: bookmt@rchmail.com

Dir: *Next to British Museum*
This stylish hotel is situated right next to the British Museum. A special feature is the alfresco terrace overlooking a delightful garden. Other public rooms include the Blue Door Bistro and Chef's Table, bar, lounge and the conservatory where traditional afternoon teas are served. The air-conditioned bedrooms are

continued

beautifully appointed and range from split-level suites to more compact rooms.
ROOMS: 104 en suite No smoking in 40 bedrooms **FACILITIES:** STV Sauna Gym Jacuzzi entertainment **CONF:** Thtr 120 Class 50 Board 50 **SERVICES:** Lift air con **NOTES:** No dogs (ex guide dogs) Civ Wed 120
CARDS:

★★★★70% Radisson Edwardian Marlborough

Bloomsbury St WC1B 3QD
☎ 020 7636 5601 020 7636 0532
e-mail: resmarl@radisson.com
Dir: *past Oxford St, down New Oxford St and turn into Bloomsbury St*
Within sight of the British Museum, this smart modern hotel is ideal for cultural visits to London. The theatre district is five minutes' walk away. Bedrooms are generally spacious with plenty of comfort, and public areas feature a number of interesting works of art. There are two bars and the modern Glass Restaurant. Guests can use the fitness room at the Radisson Edwardian Kenilworth Hotel located opposite.
ROOMS: 173 en suite (3 fmly) No smoking in 82 bedrooms s £229; d £261 **LB FACILITIES:** Business centre Xmas **CONF:** BC Thtr 300 Class 150 Board 70 Del from £199 **SERVICES:** Lift **NOTES:** No dogs (ex guide dogs) **CARDS:**

Popped the question?
Hotels with Civ Wed in their entry are licensed for civil wedding ceremonies. Maximum numbers for the ceremony only are shown, e.g. Civ Wed 120

London

WC1 BLOOMSBURY, continued

★★★★65% Holiday Inn Kings Cross/Bloomsbury
1 Kings Cross Rd WC1X 9HX
☎ 020 7833 3900 020 7917 6163
e-mail: sales@holidayinnlondon.com
Dir: *0.5m from Kings Cross Station*
Conveniently located for Kings Cross station and the City, this modern hotel offers smart, spacious air conditioned accommodation with a wide range of facilities. The hotel has two restaurants, one of which is Indian, versatile meeting rooms, a bar and a well-equipped fitness centre.
ROOMS: 405 en suite (163 fmly) No smoking in 160 bedrooms s £190-£210; d £190-£210 **LB FACILITIES:** STV Indoor swimming (H) Sauna Solarium Gym Jacuzzi Swimming pool supervised **CONF:** BC Thtr 220 Class 120 Board 30 Del from £190 **SERVICES:** Lift air con **PARKING:** 12 **NOTES:** No dogs (ex guide dogs)
CARDS:

★★★★65% *Le Meridien Russell*
Russell Square WC1B 5BE
☎ 020 7837 6470 020 7837 2857
Dir: *A4 A501 towards Euston on Woburn Place to Russell Sq*
For some time now this landmark Victorian hotel has been in the process of a multi-million pound refurbishment programme which is now visible in the new state-of-the-art bedroom concept. Public areas too are being transformed. A superbly located hotel within walking distance of the theatre district.
ROOMS: 371 en suite No smoking in 80 bedrooms **FACILITIES:** STV **CONF:** Thtr 450 Class 200 Board 40 **SERVICES:** Lift air con **NOTES:** Civ Wed 600 **CARDS:**

London

Town House

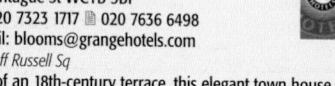

★★★★ Grange Blooms
7 Montague St WC1B 5BP
☎ 020 7323 1717 020 7636 6498
e-mail: blooms@grangehotels.com
Dir: *off Russell Sq*
Part of an 18th-century terrace, this elegant town house is near the British Museum. Bedrooms are furnished in Regency style and day rooms include the lobby lounge, garden terrace, breakfast room and cocktail bar, all featuring antique pieces and paintings. The lounge menu is also available as room service, and meals can be delivered from local restaurants.
ROOMS: 26 en suite No smoking in 12 bedrooms s £125-£220; d £155-£220 **LB FACILITIES:** STV Patio garden Xmas **CONF:** Thtr 20 Class 10 Board 18 Del from £235 **SERVICES:** Lift **NOTES:** No dogs (ex guide dogs) Civ Wed 20
CARDS:

★★★72% The Bonnington in Bloomsbury
92 Southampton Row WC1B 4BH
☎ 020 7242 2828 020 7831 9170
e-mail: sales@bonnington.com
Dir: *M40 Euston Rd. Opposite station turn S into Upper Woburn Place past Russell Sq into Southampton Row. Hotel on left*
This smart hotel is centrally located close to the city, the British Museum and Covent Garden. Spacious public areas include the Malt Bar, Waterfalls Restaurant and a comfortable lobby lounge. Bedrooms are well equipped and include superb new executive rooms and suites.
ROOMS: 215 en suite (4 fmly) No smoking in 87 bedrooms **FACILITIES:** STV **CONF:** Thtr 250 Class 80 Board 100 **SERVICES:** Lift air con **NOTES:** No dogs (ex guide dogs)
CARDS:

★★★68% Grange Whitehall
2-5 Montague St WC1B 5BP
☎ 020 7580 2224 020 7580 5554
e-mail: whitehall@grangehotel.co.uk
There is much to recommend this elegant, small hotel. It is in an excellent location, only minutes from the city's financial district and a stone's throw from the theatres of the West End. Bedrooms are furnished and decorated to a very high standard, and the landscaped gardens overlooking the British Museum are a real bonus.
ROOMS: 56 en suite (2 fmly) (3 GF) No smoking in 20 bedrooms s £155-£220; d £165-£220 **FACILITIES:** STV Xmas **CONF:** BC Thtr 90 Class 45 Board 45 Del from £235 **SERVICES:** Lift air con **NOTES:** No dogs (ex guide dogs) **CARDS:**

U *Holiday Inn Bloomsbury*
Coram St WC1N 1HT
☎ 0870 400 9222 020 7837 5374
e-mail: bloomsbury@ichotelsgroupcom
Dir: *off Upper Woburn Place near Russell Sq*
At the time of going to press, the classification for this hotel was not confirmed. Please refer to the AA internet site www.theAA.com for current information.
ROOMS: 313 en suite (29 fmly) No smoking in 211 bedrooms **FACILITIES:** STV Guests may use Health Club facilities next door **CONF:** Thtr 300 Class 180 Board 45 **SERVICES:** Lift **PARKING:** 80 **NOTES:** No dogs (ex guide dogs) **CARDS:**

Travel Inn (London Euston)
1 Dukes Rd WC1H 9PJ
☎ 0870 238 3301 020 7554 3419
Dir: *On corner of Euston Rd (south side) & Duke's Rd, between Kings Cross/St Pancras and Euston stations*
Travel Inn offers good-quality, value-for-money accommodation. Spacious, en suite rooms with bath and shower comfortably accommodate a family of up to two adults and two children (to age 15). The restaurant and bar offers a varied menu. For further details and the Travel Inn phone number, consult the Hotel Groups page.
ROOMS: 220 en suite s £74.95-£79.95; d £74.95-£79.95

○ Travelodge London Kings Cross
Willing House, Grays Inn Rd, Kings Cross WC1
☎ 0870 191 1757
ROOMS: 140 en suite **NOTES:** Due to open Jan 2004

WC2 SOHO, STRAND

Top 200 - Hotel

★★★★★ One Aldwych
1 Aldwych WC2B 4RH
☎ 020 7300 1000 020 7300 1001
e-mail: reservations@onealdwych.com
Dir: *at Aldwych & The Strand junct, near Waterloo Bridge*
Still a relatively new hotel on the London scene, One Aldwych is already well known for its chic, yet comfortable style and contemporary décor. There are a whole host of interesting features including a pool with underwater music in the health club, the dramatic "amber city" mural in the double height Axis restaurant and the contemporary lobby bar where the Martini cocktail is a speciality. Bedrooms are no less stylish

continued

and feature giant pillows, down duvets and granite surfaces in bathrooms.

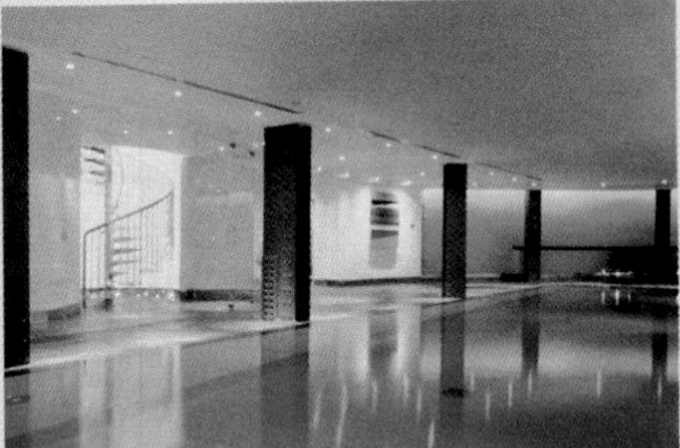

ROOMS: 105 en suite No smoking in 60 bedrooms s £195-£423; d £195-£446.50 **LB** **FACILITIES:** STV Indoor swimming (H) Sauna Gym Steam room, 2 Treatment rooms entertainment Xmas **CONF:** BC Thtr 60 Board 35 **SERVICES:** Lift air con **NOTES:** No dogs (ex guide dogs) Civ Wed 60
CARDS:

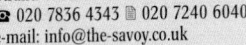

Top 200 - Hotel

★★★★★ *The Savoy*

Strand WC2R 0EU
☎ 020 7836 4343 🖷 020 7240 6040
e-mail: info@the-savoy.co.uk
The Savoy Group
Dir: *halfway along The Strand between Trafalgar Sq and Aldwych*

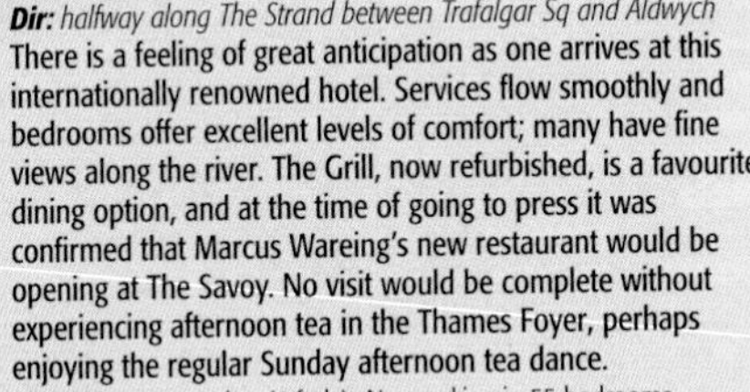

There is a feeling of great anticipation as one arrives at this internationally renowned hotel. Services flow smoothly and bedrooms offer excellent levels of comfort; many have fine views along the river. The Grill, now refurbished, is a favourite dining option, and at the time of going to press it was confirmed that Marcus Wareing's new restaurant would be opening at The Savoy. No visit would be complete without experiencing afternoon tea in the Thames Foyer, perhaps enjoying the regular Sunday afternoon tea dance.
ROOMS: 263 en suite (6 fmly) No smoking in 55 bedrooms **FACILITIES:** STV Indoor swimming (H) Sauna Gym Health & beauty treatments entertainment **CONF:** Thtr 500 Class 200 Board 32 **SERVICES:** Lift air con **PARKING:** 65 **NOTES:** No dogs (ex guide dogs) Civ Wed 300 **CARDS:**

★★★★★67% Le Meridien Waldorf

Aldwych WC2B 4DD
☎ 0870 400 8484 🖷 020 7836 7244
e-mail: reception.waldorf@lemeridien.com
Le MERIDIEN HOTELS & RESORTS
Dir: *from Trafalgar Sq, The Strand into Aldwych*
A traditional English hotel enjoying an enviable central location at the gateway to the City of London itself. The Palm Court is the
continued
heart of the hotel, a stunning venue for all day dining, including the famous afternoon tea-dances hosted here at weekends. Other public rooms include the Club Bar and the Footlights Bar, and an informal bistro. Bedrooms are decorated in an authentic Edwardian style, bathrooms are marble and generally spacious.
ROOMS: 303 en suite (6 fmly) No smoking in 150 bedrooms s £300; d £180-£300 **LB** **FACILITIES:** STV Indoor swimming (H) Sauna Solarium Gym Jacuzzi Health & Fitness Club Xmas **CONF:** BC Thtr 250 Class 120 Board 70 Del £430 **SERVICES:** Lift air con **NOTES:** No dogs (ex guide dogs) Civ Wed 410 **CARDS:**

★★★★★67% ֍ Radisson Edwardian Hampshire Hotel

Radisson EDWARDIAN
31 Leicester Square WC2H 7LH
☎ 020 7839 9399 🖷 020 7930 8122
e-mail: reshamp@radisson.com
Dir: *from Charing Cross Rd turn into Cranbourn St at Leicester Sq. Left at end, hotel at bottom of square*
Located in the very heart of London's West End, most of the capital's top entertainment venues are within easy reach. The elegant public areas include the Apex Bar and Restaurant with its beautiful wood panelling and a small, but smart gymnasium. The Crescent Bar, adjacent to the hotel, with its vaulted alcoves is an intimate venue for drinks. Air-conditioned bedrooms are smartly decorated and feature triple glazing and thoughtful extras.
ROOMS: 124 en suite (5 fmly) No smoking in 93 bedrooms s £165-£265; d £165-£385 **FACILITIES:** STV Gym Fitness room **CONF:** BC Thtr 100 Class 48 Board 35 Del from £199 **SERVICES:** Lift air con **NOTES:** No dogs (ex guide dogs)
CARDS:

★★★★★66% ֍ Swissotel London, The Howard

Temple Place WC2R 2PR
☎ 020 7836 3555 🖷 020 7379 4547
e-mail: emailus.london@swissotel.com
Dir: *opposite Temple underground station*
This smart hotel enjoys wonderful views across London's historic skyline from its riverside location. The Eurostar terminal, Covent Garden and Theatreland are all within easy reach. Air-conditioned bedrooms have been carefully refurbished and offer a host of extra facilities. The restaurant and bar open out onto a delightful garden offering alfresco dining when weather permits.
ROOMS: 189 en suite No smoking in 42 bedrooms s £295; d £295 **LB** **FACILITIES:** STV entertainment Xmas **CONF:** BC Thtr 150 Class 60 Board 60 **SERVICES:** Lift air con **PARKING:** 30 **NOTES:** No dogs (ex guide dogs) Civ Wed 100 **CARDS:**

★★★★74% ֍ Radisson Edwardian Mountbatten

Radisson EDWARDIAN
Monmouth St, Seven Dials, Covent Garden WC2H 9HD
☎ 020 7836 4300 🖷 020 7240 3540
e-mail: resmoun@radisson.com
Dir: *off Shaftesbury Av, on corner of Seven Dials rdbt*
Located in the heart of Theatreland and close to Covent Garden, this smart hotel is named after Lord Mountbatten. Air-conditioned thoughtfully equipped, stylish bedrooms include a number of spacious suites. The popular buzzing Dial restaurant and bar has a loyal following with regular guests. Attentive, friendly service is a highlight.
ROOMS: 151 en suite No smoking in 104 bedrooms s £116-£302; d £116-£335 **LB** **FACILITIES:** STV Fitness room Xmas **CONF:** BC Thtr 90 Class 45 Board 32 Del from £205 **SERVICES:** Lift air con
CARDS:

London

WC2 SOHO, continued

★★★★72% Kingsway Hall

Great Queen St, Covent Garden WC2B 5BZ
☎ 020 7309 0909 Fax 020 7309 9696
e-mail: enquiries@kingswayhall.co.uk
Dir: *from Holborn underground station follow Kingsway towards Aldwych. At 1st lights right. Hotel 50mtrs on left*

Conveniently situated close to Covent Garden, this stylish modern hotel offers very comfortable accommodation. Smart, air-conditioned bedrooms have been well designed and feature many extra facilities. The stylish compact lounge bar is available for drinks and lighter meals along with the Harlequin restaurant for more formal dining. A gym can be found in the basement.
ROOMS: 170 en suite No smoking in 125 bedrooms s £230; d £250 **FACILITIES:** STV Gym Jacuzzi Steam room **CONF:** BC Thtr 150 Class 90 Board 50 Del from £215 **SERVICES:** Lift air con **NOTES:** No dogs (ex guide dogs) **CARDS:**

See advert on this page

★★★66% Strand Palace

372 The Strand WC2R 0JJ
☎ 020 7836 8080 Fax 020 7836 2077
e-mail: reservations@strandpalacehotel.co.uk
Dir: *From Trafalgar Square, on A4 to Charing Cross, 150mtrs, hotel on left.*

At the heart of Theatreland, this vast hotel is ideal for visiting many of the capital's attractions. Bedrooms, which vary in style, include Club rooms with enhanced facilities and exclusive use of the Club lounge. The extensive public areas include four eateries and a popular cocktail bar.
ROOMS: 785 en suite No smoking in 400 bedrooms s fr £69; d fr £138 (incl. bkfst) **LB FACILITIES:** STV Pool tables Xmas **CONF:** BC Thtr 200 Class 90 Board 40 Del from £120 **SERVICES:** Lift **NOTES:** No dogs (ex guide dogs) **CARDS:**

U Radisson Edwardian Pastoria Hotel

3-6 Saint Martins St WC2H 7HL
☎ 020 7930 8641 & 020 7451 0227(res) Fax 020 7451 0191
e-mail: reshamp@radisson.com
Dir: *from Whitcomb St left to Panton St. St Martins St off Leicester Sq*

At the time of going to press, the star classification for this hotel was not confirmed. Please refer to the AA internet site www.theAA.com for current information.
ROOMS: 58 en suite No smoking in 38 bedrooms s £110-£185; d £120-£265 **FACILITIES:** STV Gym **CONF:** BC **SERVICES:** Lift **NOTES:** No dogs (ex guide dogs) **CARDS:**

LONDON AIRPORTS See under Gatwick & Heathrow

LONDON GATEWAY MOTORWAY SERVICE AREA (M1) See LONDON plan1 C6

★★★69% Days Inn

Welcome Break Service Area NW7 3HB
☎ 020 8906 7000 Fax 020 8906 7011
Dir: *on M1 between junct 2/4 northbound & southbound*

This modern hotel is the flagship of the Days Inn brand and occupies a prime location just on the outskirts of London. Bedrooms have a contemporary feel, are spacious and are well equipped. Public rooms have an airy feel and meeting rooms and convenient parking are a bonus.
ROOMS: 202 en suite (190 fmly) No smoking in 162 bedrooms d £45-£75 **LB FACILITIES:** STV **CONF:** Thtr 70 Class 30 Board 50 **SERVICES:** Lift **PARKING:** 160 **CARDS:**

LONDON COLNEY, Hertfordshire — Map 06 TL10

Innkeeper's Lodge

1 Barnet Rd AL2 1BL
☎ 01727 823698 Fax 01727 820902
Dir: *clockwise from Heathrow on M25 towards Harlow, exit at junct22 staying in left lane, at rdbt take 1st left to London Colney. Straight over rdbt The Colney Fox is 450 yds on right*

A new concept in the travel accommodation market. Smart rooms meet essential business requirements but also have home comforts. Dining options include all-day menus plus the added advantage of breakfast, which is included in the room price. For further details, consult the Hotel Groups page.
ROOMS: 14 en suite

LONG EATON, Derbyshire
Map 11 SK43

See also Sandiacre

★★★66% Novotel Nottingham/Derby
Bostock Ln NG10 4EP
☎ 0115 946 5111 📠 0115 946 5900
e-mail: H0507@accor-hotels.com
Dir: *M1 junct 25 onto B6002 to Long Eaton. Hotel 400yds on left*

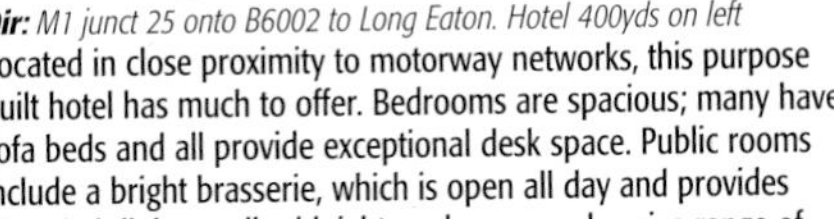

Located in close proximity to motorway networks, this purpose built hotel has much to offer. Bedrooms are spacious; many have sofa beds and all provide exceptional desk space. Public rooms include a bright brasserie, which is open all day and provides extended dining until midnight, and a comprehensive range of meeting rooms.
ROOMS: 108 en suite (40 fmly) No smoking in 66 bedrooms s £67; d £67 **LB** **FACILITIES:** STV Outdoor swimming (H) **CONF:** Thtr 220 Class 100 Board 100 Del £125 **SERVICES:** Lift **PARKING:** 220
CARDS:

★★60% *Europa*
20-22 Derby Rd NG10 1LW
☎ 0115 972 8481 📠 0115 946 0229
e-mail: k.riley3@ntlworld.com
Dir: *on A6005, in centre of Long Eaton. 1.5m from M1 junct 25 & A52*
Convenient for the town centre and the M1, this commercial hotel offers suitably furnished bedrooms. In addition to the restaurant, where mainly Chinese cooking is provided, light refreshments are available throughout the day in the conservatory.
ROOMS: 15 en suite (2 fmly) No smoking in 3 bedrooms **CONF:** Thtr 35 Class 35 Board 28 **PARKING:** 24 **NOTES:** No dogs (ex guide dogs) Closed 25-28 Dec **CARDS:**

LONGHORSLEY, Northumberland
Map 21 NZ19

★★★73% ◎◎ Linden Hall
MACDONALD HOTELS
NE65 8XF
☎ 01670 500000 📠 01670 500001
e-mail: stay@lindenhall.co.uk
Dir: *7m W on A697*
This impressive Georgian mansion lies in 400 acres of parkland and offers extensive indoor and outdoor leisure facilities including a golf course. Elegant public rooms include an imposing entrance hall, drawing room and cocktail bar. The Dobson restaurant provides a fine dining experience, or guests can dine in the more informal Linden Tree pub in the grounds.
ROOMS: 50 en suite (4 fmly) (20 GF) No smoking in 21 bedrooms s £80-£90; d £115-£135 (incl. bkfst) **LB** **FACILITIES: Spa** STV Indoor swimming (H) Golf 18 Tennis (hard) Snooker Sauna Solarium Gym Croquet lawn Putting green Jacuzzi Hairdressing Health/beauty spa steamroom Xmas **CONF:** Thtr 300 Class 100 Board 30 Del from £145 **SERVICES:** Lift **PARKING:** 260 **NOTES:** No smoking in restaurant Civ Wed 120 **CARDS:**

See advert on this page

LONG MELFORD, Suffolk
Map 13 TL84

★★★71% ◎ The Black Lion
Church Walk, The Green CO10 9DN
☎ 01787 312356 📠 01787 374557
e-mail: enquiries@blacklionhotel.net
Dir: *at junct of A134/A1092.*
This charming 15th-century hotel is situated on the edge of this bustling town overlooking the green. Bedrooms are generally spacious and each is attractively decorated, tastefully furnished and equipped with useful extras. An interesting range of food is *continued* served in the lounge bar or guests may choose to dine in the more formal restaurant.
ROOMS: 10 en suite (3 fmly) No smoking in all bedrooms s £75-£95; d £95-£130 (incl. bkfst) **LB** **FACILITIES:** Board games Xmas **CONF:** Thtr 50 Class 28 Board 28 Del from £115 **PARKING:** 10 **NOTES:** No smoking in restaurant **CARDS:**

★★★67% The Bull
OLD ENGLISH INNS
Hall St CO10 9JG
☎ 01787 378494 📠 01787 880307
e-mail: 6420@greeneking.co.uk
Dir: *3m N of Sudbury on A134*
This delightful property was built in about 1450. The public areas have a wealth of charm and character such as exposed beams, carvings, heraldic markings and huge open fireplaces. The bedrooms are pleasantly decorated, thoughtfully equipped and have many original features. Snacks or light lunches are served in the bar and the more formal restaurant offers an interesting choice of dishes.
ROOMS: 25 en suite (3 fmly) No smoking in 11 bedrooms **CONF:** Thtr 60 Class 30 Board 35 Del from £100 **PARKING:** 30 **NOTES:** No smoking in restaurant Civ Wed 70
CARDS:

LONG SUTTON, Lincolnshire
Map 12 TF42

⌂ Travelodge Kings Lynn
Travelodge
Wisbech Rd PE12 9AG
☎ 08700 850 950 📠 01406 362230
Dir: *on junct A17/A1101 rdbt*
Travelodge offers good quality, good value, modern accommodation. Ideal for families, the spacious, en suite

continued on p392

LONG SUTTON, continued

bedrooms include remote-control TV, tea and coffee-making facilities, luxury beds and free morning newspaper. Meals can be taken at the nearby family restaurant. For further details and the Travelodge phone number, consult the Hotel Groups page.
ROOMS: 40 en suite s fr £42.95; d fr £42.95

LOOE, Cornwall & Isles of Scilly Map 02 SX25

★★★64% Hannafore Point

THE INDEPENDENTS

Marine Dr, West Looe PL13 2DG
☎ 01503 263273 🖹 01503 263272
e-mail: stay@hannaforepointhotel.com
Dir: *A38, left onto A385 to Looe. Over bridge, left. Hotel 0.5m on left*
With panoramic coastal views embracing St George's Island around to Rame Head, this popular hotel provides a warm welcome. The wonderful view is also a feature of the spacious restaurant and bar, a scenic back drop for dinners and breakfasts. Additional facilities include a heated indoor pool, squash court and gymnasium.
ROOMS: 37 en suite (5 fmly) s £55-£86; d £110-£172 (incl. bkfst & dinner) **LB** **FACILITIES: Spa** Indoor swimming (H) Squash Sauna Solarium Gym Jacuzzi entertainment Xmas **CONF:** BC Thtr 120 Class 80 Board 40 Del from £65 **SERVICES:** Lift **PARKING:** 32 **NOTES:** No smoking in restaurant Civ Wed 160 **CARDS:**

See advert on opposite page

★★75% Fieldhead

Portuan Rd, Hannafore PL13 2DR
☎ 01503 262689 🖹 01503 264114
e-mail: field.head@virgin.net
Dir: *in Looe harbour road signed 'Hannafore'. Past waterside church, up hill to seafront. 1st right then right again into Portuan Rd*

Overlooking the bay from its elevated position, this engaging hotel has a relaxing atmosphere. Bedrooms are furnished with care, and many have a sea view. Smartly presented public areas include a convivial bar and restaurant, while outside a palm-filled garden with a secluded patio and swimming pool. The fixed-price menu changes daily and features quality local produce.
ROOMS: 14 en suite (2 fmly) (2 GF) s £35-£50; d £60-£90 (incl. bkfst) **LB** **FACILITIES:** Outdoor swimming (H) Swimming pool supervised **PARKING:** 15 **NOTES:** No smoking in restaurant Closed Xmas
CARDS:

See advert on opposite page

> Packed in a hurry?
> Ironing facilities should be available at all star levels, either in rooms or on request

★★63% Rivercroft Hotel

Station Rd PL13 1HL
☎ 01503 262251 🖹 01503 265494
e-mail: rivercroft.hotel@virgin.net
Dir: *from A38 take B387 to Looe. Hotel on left near bridge*

Standing high above the river, this family-run hotel is conveniently located just a short walk from the town centre and beach. Bedrooms are comfortably furnished and well equipped, and many enjoy wonderful views. An extensive menu is offered in the Croft Restaurant, or alternatively, meals can be enjoyed in the convivial atmosphere of the bar.
ROOMS: 15 en suite (8 fmly) s £25-£30; d £30-£70 (incl. bkfst) **LB** **FACILITIES:** Xmas **NOTES:** No dogs No smoking in restaurant
CARDS:

LOSTWITHIEL, Cornwall & Isles of Scilly Map 02 SX15

★★★68% Restormel Lodge

Best Western

Hillside Gardens PL22 0DD
☎ 01208 872223 🖹 01208 873568
e-mail: restlodge@aol.com
Dir: *on A390 in Lostwithiel*
Under the same family ownership for over 30 years, this hotel offers a friendly welcome to all visitors and is within a short drive of the Eden Project. The original building, housing the bar, restaurant and lounges, has kept much of its character. Bedrooms are comfortably furnished, with a number overlooking the outdoor pool.
ROOMS: 21 en suite 12 annexe en suite (2 fmly) No smoking in 24 bedrooms s £62-£70; d £90-£98 (incl. bkfst) **LB** **FACILITIES:** STV Outdoor swimming (H) Xmas **CONF:** Thtr 100 Class 80 Board 60 Del from £85 **PARKING:** 40 **NOTES:** No smoking in restaurant
CARDS:

★★★61% Lostwithiel Hotel Golf & Country Club

Lower Polscoe PL22 0HQ
☎ 01208 873550 🖹 01208 873479
e-mail: info@golf-hotel.co.uk
Dir: *off A38 at Dobwalls onto A390. In Lostwithiel right and hotel signed*
This rural hotel is based around its golf club and other leisure activities. The main building offers guests a choice of eating options, including all day snacks in the popular Sports Bar. The bedrooms are in separate buildings, attractively developed with beams and stone.
ROOMS: 22 en suite (3 fmly) No smoking in 4 bedrooms s £33-£47; d £66-£94 (incl. bkfst) **LB** **FACILITIES:** Indoor swimming (H) Golf 18 Tennis (hard) Fishing Snooker Gym Putting green Undercover floodlit driving range Xmas **CONF:** Thtr 200 Class 60 Board 40 Del from £65 **PARKING:** 120 **NOTES:** Civ Wed 120
CARDS:

LOUGHBOROUGH, Leicestershire Map 11 SK51

★★★★70% ◎◎ **Quorn Country Hotel**
Charnwood House, 66 Leicester Rd LE12 8BB
☎ 01509 415050 📠 01509 415557
e-mail: reservations@quorncountryhotel.co.uk
(For full entry see Quorn and advert on this page)

★★★65% **The Quality Hotel**

New Ashby Rd LE11 4EX
☎ 01509 211800 📠 01509 211868
e-mail: admin@gb613.u-net.com
Dir: *M1 junct 23 take A512 towards Loughborough. Hotel 1m on left*
Close to the motorway network, this popular, modern hotel offers comfortable, well-equipped accommodation. All of the bedrooms have a spacious work area, and some rooms have small lounges and kitchenettes. It is an ideal hotel for a long stay or for families. Open-plan public rooms include a lounge area, bar and carvery restaurant.
ROOMS: 94 en suite (12 fmly) No smoking in 47 bedrooms
FACILITIES: STV Indoor swimming (H) Sauna Solarium Gym Jacuzzi
CONF: Thtr 225 Class 120 Board 80 Del from £100 **PARKING:** 160
NOTES: No smoking in restaurant Civ Wed 80
CARDS:

HANNAFORE POINT HOTEL
AND LEISURE CENTRE

Marine Drive, West Looe
Cornwall PL13 2DG
Email: stay@hannaforepointhotel.com
www.hannaforepointhotel.com
Beautiful panoramic sea and coastal views

• Own car park • A la carte and table d'hôte menus, extensive wine list • Fully licensed • Ballroom, seasonal entertainment • Short breaks • All bedrooms are en-suite with Hospitality tray, Colour TV, Trouser press, Hairdryer, Direct dial telephone, Room service available, many with sea views and/or balconies • Leisure Centre has Heated indoor pool, Whirlpool, Steam Room, Sauna, Solarium, Gymnasium •

Write or telephone for further details and colour brochure – 01503 263273

L

THE QUORN COUNTRY HOTEL

AA ★★★★ ◎◎

The Luxury of Four Star

**Charnwood House, Leicester Road, Quorn
Leicestershire LE12 8BB
Telephone: 01509 415050 Fax: 01509 415557
Email: reservations@quorncountryhotel.co.uk
Web: www.quorncountryhotel.co.uk**

Set in the heart of Leicestershire amidst four acres of landscaped gardens with 30 individually designed bedrooms, the Quorn Country Hotel has held awards for its restaurants, comfort and service for ten consecutive years, as well as maintaining two AA Rosettes for fine cuisine. The hotel offers conference suites and function rooms to cater for weddings, banquets, conferences and private parties. Whether visiting the hotel for business or pleasure you will appreciate the personal friendly and professional service offered by such a highly acclaimed hotel.

FIELDHEAD HOTEL

The country house by the sea

AA ★★ **LOOE · CORNWALL** 75%

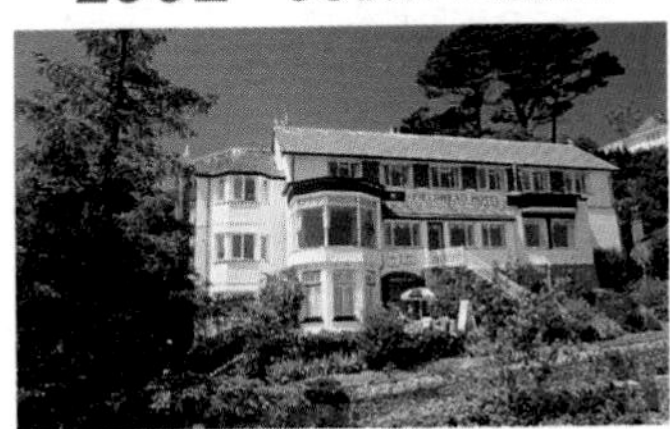

Built in 1896 as a grand private residence, the Fieldhead is now a traditional, warm and friendly country house style hotel offering a very high standard of comfort and service. Extensively refurbished within the past two years, most bedrooms have spectacular seaviews and are all ensuite with bath and shower. Elegant restaurant, with stunning views across Looe Bay, serving a wide choice of fresh dishes – including local seafood – from a daily changing menu. Relax in the lush gardens amongst palms, tree ferns, agaves and Mediterranean plants or take a dip in the heated pool set high in its own sun terrace. On site private car park, short breaks all year plus New Year programme.

**Portuan Road, Hannafore, Looe
Cornwall PL13 2DR
Tel: 01503 262689 Fax: 01503 264114
Internet: www.fieldheadhotel.co.uk
Email: enquiries@fieldheadhotel.co.uk**

LOUTH, Lincolnshire

Map 17 TF38

★★★73% *Brackenborough Arms Hotel*

Cordeaux Corner, Brackenborough LN11 0SZ
☎ 01507 609169 📠 01507 609413
e-mail: ashley@brackenborough.force9.co.uk
Dir: *off A16 2m N of Louth*

Set amid well tended gardens and patios, this hotel offers attractive bedrooms, each individually decorated with co-ordinated furnishings and many extras. Tippler's Retreat lounge bar and a quieter cocktail bar complement the informal dining option and the more formal Brackens Restaurant.

ROOMS: 24 en suite (1 fmly) No smoking in 6 bedrooms **FACILITIES:** STV ch fac **CONF:** Thtr 34 Class 24 Board 30 **PARKING:** 90 **NOTES:** No dogs (ex guide dogs) Closed 25-26 Dec Civ Wed 34 **CARDS:**

★★★70% Kenwick Park

CLASSIC BRITISH

Kenwick Park LN11 8NR
☎ 01507 608806 📠 01507 608027
e-mail: enquiries@kenwick-park.co.uk
Dir: *A16 from Grimsby, then A157 Mablethorpe/Manby Rd. Hotel 400mtrs down hill on right*

This elegant Georgian house is situated on the 500-acre Kenwick Park estate overlooking its own golf course. The bedrooms are spacious and offer a good degree of comfort as well as modern facilities. Public areas include a restaurant and a conservatory bar which overlook the grounds; there is also extensive leisure centre with a large pool.

ROOMS: 29 en suite 5 annexe en suite (10 fmly) No smoking in 11 bedrooms s £75-£89.50; d £85-£105 (incl. bkfst) **LB** **FACILITIES:** **Spa** STV Indoor swimming (H) Golf 18 Tennis (hard) Squash Sauna Solarium Gym Putting green Jacuzzi Health & Beauty Centre ch fac Xmas **CONF:** Thtr 350 Class 40 Board 60 Del from £100 **PARKING:** 50 **NOTES:** No smoking in restaurant Civ Wed 70 **CARDS:**

★★★69% Beaumont

66 Victoria Rd LN11 0BX
☎ 01507 605005 📠 01507 607768
e-mail: beaumonthotel@aol.com

This smart, family-run hotel enjoys a quiet location, within easy reach of the town centre. Bedrooms are spacious and individually designed. Public areas include a smart restaurant with a strong Italian influence and an inviting lounge bar with comfortable deep sofas and open fires. Weddings and functions are also catered for.

ROOMS: 16 en suite (2 fmly) s £48-£58; d £70-£90 (incl. bkfst) **CONF:** Thtr 70 Class 50 Board 46 **SERVICES:** Lift **PARKING:** 70 **NOTES:** RS Sun **CARDS:**

LOWER BEEDING, West Sussex

Map 06 TQ22

Top 200 - Hotel

★★★★ ❀❀❀ South Lodge

EXCLUSIVE HOTELS & GOLF CLUBS

Brighton Rd RH13 6PS
☎ 01403 891711 📠 01403 891766
e-mail: enquiries@southlodgehotel.co.uk
Dir: *on A23 left onto B2110. Turn right through Handcross to A281 junct. Turn left and hotel on right*

This delightful 19th-century lodge is an ideal retreat for guests with stunning views over the South Downs. The traditional, award-winning restaurant offers memorable seasonal dishes, and the elegant lounge is popular for afternoon teas. Bedrooms are individually designed with character and quality

continued

throughout. Leisure includes tennis, snooker and a fitness centre. The refurbished conference facilities are outstanding.

ROOMS: 39 en suite (4 fmly) (7 GF) s fr £150; d £195-£380 **LB** **FACILITIES:** STV Golf 18 Tennis (hard) Riding Snooker Gym Croquet lawn Putting green Can organise riding, shooting, fishing & quad biking entertainment Xmas **CONF:** BC Thtr 160 Class 60 Board 50 Del from £280 **SERVICES:** Lift **PARKING:** 100 **NOTES:** No dogs (ex guide dogs) No smoking in restaurant Civ Wed 120 **CARDS:**

See advert on opposite page

★★★69% ❀ Cisswood House

Sandygate Ln RH13 6NF
☎ 0871 871 3242 📠 0871 871 3243
e-mail: cisswood.house@pageant.co.uk
Dir: *Turn off A23 at Handcross, follow signs for Lower Beeding, turn right at Plough Pub. Hotel 0.5m on right*

Convenient for the M23, Cisswood House is set in beautifully maintained gardens. Bedrooms are spacious and well presented, some with whirlpool baths. Public areas include the Pageant Health Club with swimming pool, hairdresser, gym and treatment rooms. The attractive function rooms make this a popular venue for weddings and conferences.

ROOMS: 51 en suite No smoking in 6 bedrooms s fr £109; d fr £139 (incl. bkfst) **LB** **FACILITIES:** STV Indoor swimming (H) Sauna Solarium Gym Jacuzzi Health & beauty salon, Hairdressing, Swimming pool supervised Xmas **CONF:** Thtr 200 Class 70 Board 70 Del from £120 **PARKING:** 60 **NOTES:** No dogs (ex guide dogs) No smoking in restaurant Civ Wed 160 **CARDS:**

LOWER SLAUGHTER, Gloucestershire

Map 10 SP12

Top 200 - Hotel

★★★ ❀❀ *Lower Slaughter Manor*

GL54 2HP
☎ 01451 820456 📠 01451 822150
e-mail: lowsmanor@aol.com
Dir: *off A429 signed "The Slaughters". Manor 0.5m on right on entering village*

There is a timeless elegance about this wonderful manor, which dates back to the 17th century. Its imposing presence makes it very much the centrepiece of this famous Cotswold village. Once inside, the levels of comfort and quality are immediately evident, with crackling logs fires warming the many sumptuous lounges. The hotel's new dining room is an elegant creation that suitably complements the excellent

continued

cuisine on offer. Spacious and tastefully furnished bedrooms are either in the main building or in the adjacent coachhouse.

ROOMS: 11 en suite 5 annexe en suite **FACILITIES:** Indoor swimming (H) Tennis (hard) **CONF:** Thtr 36 Class 20 Board 18 **PARKING:** 30 **NOTES:** No dogs No children 12yrs No smoking in restaurant **CARDS:**

★★★75% ❀❀ ***Washbourne Court***

GL54 2HS

☎ 01451 822143 ▤ 01451 821045

e-mail: washbourne@msn.com

Dir: *off A429 at signpost 'The Slaughters', between Stow-on-the-Wold and Bourton-on-the-Water. Hotel in centre of village*

Beamed ceilings, log fires and flagstone floors are some of the attractive features of this part 17th-century hotel, set in four acres of immaculate grounds beside the River Eye. Smartly decorated bedrooms are in the main house and self-contained cottages,

continued on p396

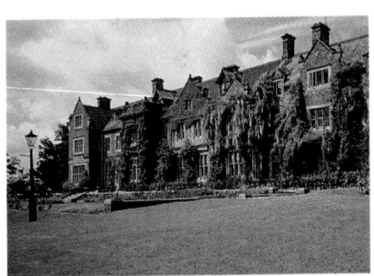

LOWER SLAUGHTER, continued

many offering lovely views. The riverside terrace is popular during summer months, whilst the elegant dining room serves an interesting menu and a comprehensive wine list.

Washbourne Court, Lower Slaughter

ROOMS: 15 en suite 13 annexe en suite **FACILITIES:** Tennis (hard) **CONF:** Thtr 30 Board 20 **PARKING:** 40 **NOTES:** No dogs (ex guide dogs) No children 7yrs **CARDS:**

See advert on page 395

LOWESTOFT, Suffolk Map 13 TM59

★★★76% Ivy House Farm Hotel

Ivy Ln, Beccles Rd, Oulton Broad NR33 8HY
☎ 01502 501353 & 588144 01502 501539
e-mail: admin@ivyhousefarm.co.uk
Dir: *on A146 SW of Oulton Broad turn into Ivy Ln beside Esso petrol station. Over railway bridge and follow private driveway*

A friendly, family-run hotel set in three acres of mature landscaped grounds just a short walk from Oulton Broad. Public rooms feature a superb 18th-century thatched barn restaurant where an interesting choice of dishes is served. The attractively decorated, thoughtfully equipped bedrooms are housed in garden wings, and many have lovely views of the garden and countryside.
ROOMS: 19 annexe en suite (1 fmly) (17 GF) No smoking in 6 bedrooms s £79-£99; d £99-£140 (incl. bkfst) **LB FACILITIES:** Reduced rates at neighbouring leisure club **CONF:** Thtr 55 Board 22 Del from £125 **PARKING:** 50 **NOTES:** No smoking in restaurant Closed 23 Dec-6 Jan **CARDS:**

See advert on opposite page

★★★69% Hotel Victoria

Kirkley Cliff NR33 0BZ
☎ 01502 574433 01502 501529
e-mail: info@hotelvictoria.freeserve.co.uk
Dir: *A12 to seafront on one-way system signed A12 Ipswich. Hotel on seafront just beyond the Thatched Cottage*
Attractive Victorian building situated at the southern end of town.

continued

Bedrooms are pleasantly decorated and thoughtfully equipped, many rooms have superb sea views. Public rooms include a choice of lounges, a comfortable bar and a restaurant, which overlooks the pretty garden. The hotel also offers conference and banqueting facilities.
ROOMS: 24 en suite (4 fmly) **FACILITIES:** STV Outdoor swimming (H) entertainment **CONF:** Thtr 200 Class 150 Board 50 Del from £95 **SERVICES:** Lift **PARKING:** 45 **NOTES:** Civ Wed 150 **CARDS:**

★★★65% Hotel Hatfield

The Esplanade NR33 0QP
☎ 01502 565337 01502 511885
e-mail: hotelhatfield@elizabethhotels.co.uk
Dir: *from town centre follow 'South Beach' signs on A12 Ipswich road. Hotel 200yds on left*

Best Western

Ideally situated overlooking the sea, this hotel is in a prominent position on the esplanade. Bedrooms are pleasantly decorated and thoughtfully equipped and some have superb sea views. The spacious public rooms include a popular lounge bar, a cocktail bar and the Chaplins restaurant offering interesting cuisine.
ROOMS: 33 en suite (1 fmly) No smoking in 7 bedrooms s £60-£70; d £70-£90 (incl. bkfst) **LB FACILITIES:** STV Xmas **CONF:** Thtr 100 Class 50 Board 40 Del from £75 **SERVICES:** Lift **PARKING:** 26 **NOTES:** Civ Wed 200 **CARDS:**

A ★★ Broadlands

58 Bridge Rd, Oulton Broad NR32 3LR
☎ 01502 516031 01502 501454
e-mail: broadlandshotel@amserve.com
ROOMS: 49 en suite (2 fmly) No smoking in 21 bedrooms s £49-£61; d £60-£71 (incl. bkfst) **LB FACILITIES: Spa** Indoor swimming (H) Snooker Sauna Beauty parlour, Games room, Swimming pool supervised entertainment Xmas **CONF:** Thtr 40 Class 60 Board 40 Del from £69 **PARKING:** 40 **CARDS:**

Travel Inn

249 Yarmouth Rd NR32 4AA
☎ 08701 977165 01502 581223
Dir: *on A12, 2m N of Lowestoft*

travel inn

Travel Inn offers good-quality, value-for-money accommodation. Spacious, en suite rooms with bath and shower comfortably accommodate a family of up to two adults and two children (to age 15). The restaurant and bar offers a varied menu. For further details and the Travel Inn phone number, consult the Hotel Groups page.
ROOMS: 40 en suite s £44.95; d £44.95

LOWESWATER, Cumbria Map 18 NY12

★★68% Grange Country House
CA13 0SU
☎ 01946 861211 & 861570
e-mail: gchloweswater@hotmail.com
Dir: *left off A5086 for Mockerkin, through village. After 2m left for Loweswater Lake. Hotel at bottom of hill on left*
This delightful country hotel sits in a quiet valley at the north-western end of Loweswater and continues to prove popular with guests seeking a 'peace-and-quiet' break. It has a friendly and relaxed atmosphere and cosy public areas. There is a small bar, a residents' lounge, and an attractive dining room. The bedrooms are well equipped and comfortable.
ROOMS: 8 en suite (2 fmly) (1 GF) s £36-£40; d £64-£70 (incl. bkfst) **FACILITIES:** National Trust boats & fishing Xmas **CONF:** Thtr 25 Class 25 Board 25 **PARKING:** 22 **NOTES:** No smoking in restaurant RS Jan-Feb

LOXTON, Somerset Map 04 ST35

U Webbington
☎ 01934 750100 ▯ 01934 750020
e-mail: webbington@latonahotels.co.uk
At the time of going to press, the star classification for this hotel was not confirmed. Please refer to the AA internet site www.theAA.com for current information.
ROOMS: 59 en suite (2 fmly) No smoking in 10 bedrooms s £65; d £75 (incl. bkfst) **LB FACILITIES:** Indoor swimming (H) Sauna Solarium Gym Beauty treatments Cardiovascular suite Steam Room Xmas **CONF:** Thtr 1000 Class 600 **PARKING:** 450 **NOTES:** No smoking in restaurant Civ Wed 500 **CARDS:**

LUDLOW, Shropshire Map 10 SO57

★★★76% ®®® Overton Grange
Old Hereford Rd SY8 4AD
☎ 01584 873500 ▯ 01584 873524
e-mail: info@overtongrangehotel.com
Dir: *off A49 at B4361 to Ludlow. Hotel 200yds on left*
Overton Grange is a traditional country house offering superb views over the Shropshire countryside, comfortable bedrooms and a dedicated customer care team. The restaurant offers an exciting cuisine of good locally sourced ingredients and demonstrates a commitment to high culinary standards. Meeting and conference facilities are available.
ROOMS: 14 en suite (3 fmly) No smoking in all bedrooms s £70-£90; d £95-£150 (incl. bkfst) **LB FACILITIES:** STV Croquet lawn Xmas **CONF:** BC Thtr 100 Class 40 Board 20 Del from £135 **PARKING:** 50 **NOTES:** No dogs (ex guide dogs) No smoking in restaurant Civ Wed 100 **CARDS:**

★★★72% ®® Dinham Hall
By the Castle SY8 1EJ
☎ 01584 876464 ▯ 01584 876019
e-mail: info@dinhamhall.co.uk
Dir: *opposite the castle*
Built in 1792, this lovely old house stands in attractive gardens immediately opposite Ludlow Castle. It has a well-deserved reputation for warm hospitality and fine cuisine. Well-equipped bedrooms include two in a converted cottage and some four-posters. The comfortable public rooms are elegantly appointed.
ROOMS: 14 en suite (3 fmly) (1 GF) s £75-£105; d £130-£180 (incl. bkfst) **LB FACILITIES:** Xmas **CONF:** Thtr 28 Class 28 Board 24 Del from £125 **PARKING:** 16 **NOTES:** No smoking in restaurant Civ Wed 100 **CARDS:**

★★★67% ® The Feathers Hotel & Ludlow Ltd
The Bull Ring SY8 1AA
☎ 01584 875261 ▯ 01584 876030
e-mail: feathers.ludlow@btconnect.com
Dir: *from A49 follow town centre signs to centre of Ludlow. Hotel on left*
Famous for the carved woodwork outside and in, this picturesque 17th-century hotel is one of the town's best-known landmarks and is in an excellent location. Bedrooms are traditional in style and décor. Public areas have retained much of the traditional charm; the first-floor lounge is particularly stunning.
ROOMS: 40 en suite (3 fmly) No smoking in 19 bedrooms s £60; d £80-£130 (incl. bkfst) **LB FACILITIES:** Xmas **CONF:** Thtr 80 Class 40 Board 40 Del from £100 **SERVICES:** Lift **PARKING:** 37 **NOTES:** No smoking in restaurant Civ Wed 80
CARDS:

★★66% Cliffe
Dinham SY8 2JE
☎ 01584 872063 ▯ 01584 873991
e-mail: cliffhotel@lineone.net
Dir: *in town centre to Castle. Left at castle gates to Dinham, follow road over bridge. Take right fork, hotel 200yds on left*
Built in the 19th century and standing in extensive grounds and gardens, this privately owned and personally run hotel is quietly located close to the castle and the river. It provides well-equipped accommodation, and facilities include a lounge bar, a pleasant restaurant and a patio overlooking the garden.
ROOMS: 9 en suite (2 fmly) No smoking in all bedrooms s £40-£50; d £60-£80 (incl. bkfst) **LB PARKING:** 22 **NOTES:** No smoking in restaurant **CARDS:**

L

LUDLOW, continued

Travelodge
Woofferton SY8 4AL
☎ 08700 850 950 ▯ 01584 711695
Dir: *on A49 at junct A456/B4362*
Travelodge offers good quality, good value, modern accommodation. Ideal for families, the spacious, en suite bedrooms include remote-control TV, tea and coffee-making facilities, luxury beds and free morning newspaper. Meals can be taken at the nearby family restaurant. For further details and the Travelodge phone number, consult the Hotel Groups page.
ROOMS: 32 en suite s fr £42.95; d fr £42.95

LULWORTH COVE See West Lulworth

LUTON, Bedfordshire
Map 06 TL02

★★★59% The Chiltern Hotel
Waller Av LU4 9RU
☎ 0870 609 6120 ▯ 01582 581859
e-mail: thechiltern@corushotels.com
Dir: *M1 junct 11 take A505 to Luton past 2 sets of lights. Over rdbt, left at lights, hotel on right*

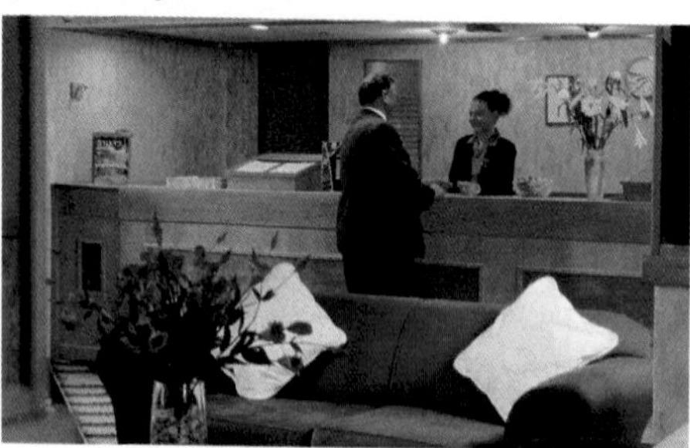

Conveniently close to the M1, this hotel is geared towards the business guest. It has a range of conference and meeting rooms. Bedrooms offer good levels of comfort. There is an air-conditioned restaurant and ample parking.
ROOMS: 91 en suite (6 fmly) No smoking in 63 bedrooms s £50-£95; d £50-£95 **LB** **FACILITIES:** STV Xmas **CONF:** Thtr 180 Class 80 Board 30 Del from £100 **SERVICES:** Lift **PARKING:** 150
CARDS:

Hotel St Lawrence
40 Guildford St LU1 2PA
☎ 01582 482119 ▯ 01582 482818
e-mail: reservations@hotelstlawrence.co.uk
Dir: *M1 junct 10a and follow signs to town centre, after university take left fork at mini rdbt. Hotel 70yds on left*
At the time of going to press, the star classification for this hotel was not confirmed. Please refer to the AA internet site www.theAA.com for current information.
ROOMS: 28 en suite s £60-£80; d £70-£80 (incl. bkfst) **LB** **FACILITIES:** STV **NOTES:** No dogs (ex guide dogs) No smoking in restaurant **CARDS:**

Travelodge
641 Dunstable Rd LU4 8RQ
☎ 08700 850 950 ▯ 01582 490065
Dir: *M1 junct 11 towards Luton, hotel 100yds on right*
Travelodge offers good quality, good value, modern accommodation. Ideal for families, the spacious, en suite bedrooms include remote-control TV, tea and coffee-making facilities, luxury beds and free morning newspaper. Meals can be taken at the nearby family restaurant. For further details and the Travelodge phone number, consult the Hotel Groups page.
ROOMS: 140 en suite (incl. bkfst) s fr £42.95; d fr £42.95 **CONF:** Thtr 80 Class 40 Board 30

LUTON AIRPORT, Bedfordshire
Map 06 TL12

Express by Holiday Inn London Luton Airport
2 Percival Way LU2 9GP
☎ 0870 444 8920 ▯ 0870 444 8930
e-mail: lutonairport@expressbyholidayinn.net
Dir: *M1 J10, follow signs for airport, turn right into Percival Way, hotel car park on right*

A modern hotel ideal for families and business travellers. Fresh and uncomplicated, the spacious bedrooms include Sky TV, power shower and tea and coffee-making facilities. Continental buffet breakfast is included in the room rate; other meals may be taken at the nearby family pub or restaurant. For further details and the Express by Holiday Inn phone number, consult the Hotel Groups pages.
ROOMS: 110 en suite s £59-£90; d £59-£90 (incl. cont bkfst)
CONF: Thtr 56 Class 26 Board 18

Hotel Ibis Luton

Spittlesea Rd LU2 9NH
☎ 01582 424488 ▯ 01582 455511
e-mail: H1040@accor-hotels.com
Dir: *M1 junct 10 follow signs to airport, hotel 1km before airport*
Modern, budget hotel offering comfortable accommodation in bright and practical bedrooms. Breakfast is self-service and dinner is available in the restaurant. For further details, consult the Hotel Groups page.
ROOMS: 98 en suite s £49.95-£62.95; d £49.95-£62.95

⌂ Travel Inn Luton Airport

Osbourne Rd LU1 3HJ
☎ 08701 977166 ▤ 01582 421900
Dir: *M1 junct 10 follow signs for Luton on A1081, at 3rd rdbt turn left onto Gypsy Lane, turn left at next rdbt*

Travel Inn offers good-quality, value-for-money accommodation. Spacious, en suite rooms with bath and shower comfortably accommodate a family of up to two adults and two children (to age 15). The restaurant and bar offers a varied menu. For further details and the Travel Inn phone number, consult the Hotel Groups page.
ROOMS: 129 en suite s £46.95-£54.95; d £46.95-£54.95
CONF: Thtr 70 Board 50

LYDFORD, Devon Map 03 SX58

★★71% *Lydford House*

EX20 4AU
☎ 01822 820347 ▤ 01822 820442
e-mail: relax@lydfordhouse.co.uk
Dir: *off A386 halfway between Okehampton and Tavistock, signed Lydford, 0.25m on right*
Set in attractive grounds in a quiet location on the edge of Dartmoor, this friendly Victorian country house offers comfortable, well-equipped and attractively decorated accommodation. Public areas are spacious and offer a range of choices. The proprietors also run a riding stables which are adjacent to the property and guests may take lessons or accompanied rides over the moors.
ROOMS: 12 rms (11 en suite) (4 fmly) **FACILITIES:** Riding **CONF:** Thtr 25 Class 25 Board 20 **PARKING:** 30 **NOTES:** No smoking in restaurant Closed 25 Dec-Jan **CARDS:**

LYME REGIS, Dorset Map 04 SY39
See also Colyford

★★★70% Ⓡ Alexandra

Pound St DT7 3HZ
☎ 01297 442010 ▤ 01297 443229
e-mail: enquiries@hotelalexandra.co.uk
Dir: *from A30, onto A35, then onto A358, A3052 to Lyme Regis*
This welcoming, family-run hotel is Grade II listed and dates back to 1735. Public areas are spacious and comfortable, with ample seating areas to relax, unwind and enjoy the magnificent views. The elegant restaurant offers imaginative, innovative dishes are served. Bedrooms vary in size and shape, having pretty chintz fabrics and attractive furniture.
ROOMS: 25 en suite 1 annexe en suite (8 fmly) (3 GF) s £50; d £90-£132 (incl. bkfst) **LB** **PARKING:** 18 **NOTES:** No smoking in restaurant Closed Xmas & Jan **CARDS:**

★★77% Ⓡ Swallows Eaves

EX24 6QJ
☎ 01297 553184 ▤ 01297 553574
e-mail: swallows.eaves@talk21.com
(For full entry see Colyford)

★★74% Ⓡ Mariners Hotel

Silver St DT7 3HS
☎ 01297 442753 ▤ 01297 442431
e-mail: marinershotel@btopenworld.com
Dir: *W of town on A3052, then right on B3070*

With period character and charm, this small friendly hotel has a relaxed atmosphere. The individually decorated bedrooms are comfortable; some rooms benefit from stunning views over the town. A beamed bar and choice of lounge is provided for guests, while in the restaurant carefully prepared meals use fresh ingredients, with local fish proving a highlight on the menus. Sunday lunches are also available.
ROOMS: 12 en suite No smoking in 8 bedrooms s £55-£66; d £75-£90 (incl. bkfst) **FACILITIES:** Xmas **PARKING:** 20 **NOTES:** No children 7yrs No smoking in restaurant Closed 27 Dec-31 Jan **CARDS:**

★★70% *Buena Vista*

Pound St DT7 3HZ
☎ 01297 442494 ▤ 01297 444670
e-mail: buenavista@amserve.net
Dir: *W on A3052 out of town*
Set in an elevated position overlooking the Cobb, harbour and Dorset coastline, this family-run hotel provides friendly service. Bedrooms are individually styled and beds are a feature, as is the collection of Victorian pictures and postcards. Guests can relax in the comfortable public areas and the award-winning gardens.
ROOMS: 18 rms (17 en suite) (1 fmly) **PARKING:** 18 **NOTES:** No smoking in restaurant Closed Dec-Jan **CARDS:**

★★68% *Bay*

Marine Pde DT7 3JQ
☎ 01297 442059 ▤ 01297 444642
Dir: *on seafront in centre of Lyme Regis*
Guests are assured of a relaxed and friendly atmosphere at this hotel set on the promenade. An interesting menu, featuring local seafood is served in the brightly decorated dining room. The terrace and spacious first-floor lounge, with its own billiard table, is the ideal spot to relax and enjoy the sight and sounds of the sea. Bedrooms are stylish and comfortable.
ROOMS: 19 en suite (3 fmly) **FACILITIES:** Snooker **CONF:** Thtr 30 Class 30 **PARKING:** 20 **NOTES:** No smoking in restaurant
CARDS:

L

LYME REGIS, continued

★★66% Royal Lion
Broad St DT7 3QF
☎ 01297 445622 📠 01297 445859
e-mail: reception@royallionhotel.fsnet.co.uk
Dir: *From W on A35, take A3052 or from E take B3165 to Lyme Regis. Hotel in centre of town, opp The Fossil Shop. Car park at rear*
This 17th-century, former coaching inn is full of character and charm, and is situated a short walk from the seafront. Bedrooms vary in size; those in the newer wing are more spacious and some have balconies, sea views or a private terrace. In addition to the elegant dining room and guest lounges, a heated pool, small gym and snooker table are available.
ROOMS: 29 en suite (11 fmly) s £37-£49; d £74-£98 (incl. bkfst) **LB** **FACILITIES: Spa** Indoor swimming (H) Snooker Sauna Gym Jacuzzi Games room Pool table Table tennis Xmas **CONF:** Thtr 50 Class 20 Board 20 **PARKING:** 30 **NOTES:** No smoking in restaurant
CARDS:

LYMINGTON, Hampshire
Map 05 SZ39

★★★75% Passford House
Mount Pleasant Ln SO41 8LS
☎ 01590 682398 📠 01590 683494
e-mail: sales@passfordhousehotel.co.uk
Dir: *from A337 at Lymington over mini rdbt. 1st right at Tollhouse pub, then after 1m right into Mount Pleasant Ln*
A peaceful hotel set in attractive grounds on the edge of the town. Bedrooms vary in size but all are comfortably furnished and well equipped. Extensive public areas include lounges, a smartly appointed restaurant and bar, and leisure facilities. A friendly and well-motivated team provides attentive service.
ROOMS: 49 en suite 2 annexe en suite (2 fmly) (10 GF) No smoking in 10 bedrooms s £65-£110; d £95-£200 (incl. bkfst) **LB** **FACILITIES: Spa** Indoor swimming (H) Outdoor swimming (H) Tennis (hard) Sauna Gym Croquet lawn Putting green Petanque Table tennis Helipad pool table Xmas **CONF:** Thtr 80 Class 30 Board 30 Del from £120 **PARKING:** 100 **NOTES:** No children 8yrs No smoking in restaurant
CARDS:

★★★73% Stanwell House
14-15 High St SO41 9AA
☎ 01590 677123 📠 01590 677756
e-mail: sales@stanwellhousehotel.co.uk
Dir: *A337 to town centre, on right of High St, before descent to quay*
Centrally situated, this stylish hotel offers friendly and attentive service. Bedrooms are comfortable and very well equipped; some rooms in the older part of the building are particularly interesting and some have four-poster beds. The award-winning cuisine provides freshly prepared and interesting dishes, available in all dining options.
ROOMS: 29 en suite (1 fmly) No smoking in 10 bedrooms **CONF:** Thtr 30 Class 20 Board 22 Del from £125 **NOTES:** No smoking in restaurant Civ Wed 50 **CARDS:**

★★★72% Elmers Court
MACDONALD HOTELS
South Baddesley Rd SO41 5ZB
☎ 01590 676011 📠 01590 679780
e-mail: elmerscourt@macdonald-hotels.co.uk
Dir: *M27 junct 1, through Lyndhurst, Brockenhurst & Lymington, hotel 200yds right after Lymington ferry terminal*
Originally known as The Elms, this Tudor-gabled manor house dates back to the 1820s. Ideally located at the edge of the New Forest and overlooking The Solent with views towards the Isle of Wight, the hotel offers suites and self-catering accommodation, along with well-appointed leisure facilities.
ROOMS: 42 annexe en suite (8 fmly) (22 GF) No smoking in 16 bedrooms s £90-£104; d £150-£178 (incl. bkfst & dinner) **LB** **FACILITIES: Spa** Indoor swimming (H) Outdoor swimming (H) Tennis (hard) Squash Sauna Solarium Gym Croquet lawn Putting green Jacuzzi Beauty treatment rooms, Outdoor pool supervised, Steam room, Aerobics classes entertainment ch fac Xmas **CONF:** Thtr 100 Class 40 Board 40 Del from £130 **PARKING:** 100 **NOTES:** No dogs (ex guide dogs) No smoking in restaurant Civ Wed 100
CARDS:

★★★66% String of Horses
Mead End Rd SO41 6EH
☎ 01590 682631 📠 01590 682911
e-mail: relax@stringofhorses.co.uk
(For full entry see Sway)

★★69% The Mill at Gordleton
Silver St, Hordle SO41 6DJ
☎ 01590 682219 📠 01590 683073
e-mail: gordletonmill@aol.com
Dir: *M27 junct 1 towards Lyndhurst to Lymington A337, turn right to Hordle at Tollhouse Inn, 1.5m to Mill*

A delightful 17th-century watermill located on the banks of the River Avon. The restaurant takes full advantage of the hotel's position and serves an extensive range of dishes at lunch and dinner. The picturesque gardens are popular for al fresco dining during the warmer months and the attractive bedrooms are equipped with whirlpool baths.
ROOMS: 9 en suite No smoking in 5 bedrooms s £75; d £110-£150 (incl. bkfst) **FACILITIES: Spa** Fishing **PARKING:** 60 **NOTES:** No dogs (ex guide dogs) RS Sun **CARDS:**

LYMM, Cheshire
Map 15 SJ68

★★★66% Lymm Hotel
MACDONALD HOTELS
Whitbarrow Rd WA13 9AQ
☎ 01925 752233 📠 01925 756035
e-mail: lymm@macdonald-hotels.co.uk
Dir: *take M6 to B5158 to Lymm. Left at junct, right at mini rdbt, left into Brookfield Rd and 3rd left into Whitbarrow Rd*
Situated in a quiet residential area, but conveniently close to several motorways, this hotel offers comfortable bedrooms equipped for both the business and leisure guest. Public areas include a modern brasserie-style bar and an elegant restaurant in which the creative dinners can be enjoyed.
ROOMS: 15 en suite 48 annexe en suite (5 fmly) No smoking in 34 bedrooms **FACILITIES:** STV **CONF:** BC Thtr 250 Class 140 Board 100 Del from £95 **PARKING:** 120 **NOTES:** No smoking in restaurant Civ Wed 120 **CARDS:**

⌂ Travelodge

Granada Services A50, Cliffe Ln WA13 0SP
☎ 08700 850 950

Travelodge offers good quality, good value, modern accommodation. Ideal for families, the spacious, en suite bedrooms include remote-control TV, tea and coffee-making facilities, luxury beds and free morning newspaper. Meals can be taken at the nearby family restaurant. For further details and the Travelodge phone number, consult the Hotel Groups page.

ROOMS: 61 en suite s fr £42.95; d fr £42.95

> Late for dinner?
> Quality Standards mean that last orders for dinner vary according to star rating and should be no earlier than:
> ★★ 7.00pm ★★★ 8.00pm ★★★★ 9.00pm
> ★★★★★ 10.00pm

LYMPSHAM, Somerset — Map 04 ST35

★★68% Batch Country Hotel

Batch Ln BS24 0EX
☎ 01934 750371 📠 01934 750501

THE CIRCLE Selected Individual Hotels GREAT BRITAIN

Dir: *exit M5 junct 22, take last exit on rdbt signed A370 to Weston-S-Mare. After 3.5m turn left into Lympsham. After 1m sign at end end of road*

Rurally situated between Weston-super-Mare and Burnham-on-Sea, this former farmhouse offers a relaxed, friendly and peaceful environment. The comfortable bedrooms have views to the Mendip and Quantock Hills. Spacious lounges overlook the

continued on p402

Le Poussin
AT PARKHILL
WHERE QUALITY IS TIMELESS
House in the country with luxury accommodation, a restaurant with stunning views, hosted by owners Alex and Caroline Aitken. Providing a menu of modern and traditional foods using wild and organic produce.
Le Poussin at Parkhill
Restaurant & Luxury Accommodation
Beaulieu Road, Lyndhurst, Hampshire
T: 023 8028 2944 F: 023 8028 3268
www.lepoussin.co.uk

LYMPSHAM, continued

extensive gardens and the function room is very popular for wedding ceremonies. Meals are served in the beamed dining room.

Batch Country Hotel, Lympsham

ROOMS: 10 en suite (6 fmly) (1 GF) No smoking in 2 bedrooms s £49-£53; d £74-£84 (incl. bkfst) **LB FACILITIES:** Fishing **CONF:** Thtr 80 Class 60 Board 100 Del from £80 **PARKING:** 80 **NOTES:** No dogs No smoking in restaurant Closed 25-26 Dec Civ Wed 120
CARDS:

See advert under WESTON-SUPER-MARE

LYNDHURST, Hampshire Map 05 SU30

Top 200 - Hotel

★★★ Le Poussin at Parkhill

Beaulieu Rd SO43 7FZ
☎ 023 8028 2944 023 8028 3268
e-mail: sales@lepoussinparkhill.co.uk
Dir: *off A35 onto B3056 towards Beaulieu, hotel 1m on left*

Set amidst unspoilt park and woodland, this Georgian country house offers elegant public rooms, with open fires during the cooler months. Bedrooms include four-poster rooms, junior suites and larger rooms with sitting areas; all are individually furnished and decorated, and most have delightful views over the forest. A meal in the renowned restaurant is the highlight of any stay, featuring local seasonal ingredients. Service is efficient and professional.

ROOMS: 15 en suite 5 annexe en suite (2 fmly) No smoking in 16 bedrooms **FACILITIES:** Outdoor swimming (H) Fishing Croquet lawn Putting green Outdoor chess **CONF:** Thtr 20 Class 20 Board 20 **PARKING:** 75 **NOTES:** No smoking in restaurant Civ Wed 60
CARDS:

See advert on page 401

★★★70% Crown

High St SO43 7NF
☎ 023 8028 2922 023 8028 2751
e-mail: reception@crownhotel-lyndhurst.co.uk
Dir: *in centre of village, opposite church*

The Crown, with its stone mullioned windows, panelled rooms and elegant period décor evokes the style of an English country house. Bedrooms are generally a good size and are undergoing further improvements. Public areas have style and comfort.

ROOMS: 39 en suite (8 fmly) s £67.50-£90; d £135-£175 (incl. bkfst) **LB FACILITIES:** STV Xmas **CONF:** Thtr 70 Class 30 Board 45 Del from £115 **SERVICES:** Lift **PARKING:** 60 **NOTES:** No smoking in restaurant Civ Wed 70 **CARDS:**

★★★67% Bell Inn

SO43 7HE
☎ 023 8081 2214 023 8081 3958
e-mail: bell@bramshaw.co.uk
(For full entry see Brook (Near Cadnam))

★★★66% Lyndhurst Park

High St SO43 7NL
☎ 023 8028 3923 023 8028 3019
e-mail: lyndhurst.park@forestdale.com
Dir: *M27 junct 1-3 to A35 to Lyndhurst. Hotel at bottom of High St*

Forestdale Hotels

Although it is only a short walk from the High Street, the hotel is offered some seclusion from the town by its five acres of mature grounds. The comfortable bedrooms have home-from-home touches such as ducks in the bath! There are two bars and an oak-panelled restaurant with a sunny conservatory.

ROOMS: 59 en suite (3 fmly) No smoking in 10 bedrooms s fr £90; d fr £110 (incl. bkfst) **LB FACILITIES:** STV Outdoor swimming (H) Tennis (hard) Snooker Sauna Table tennis Xmas **CONF:** Thtr 300 Class 120 Board 80 Del from £110 **SERVICES:** Lift **PARKING:** 100 **NOTES:** No smoking in restaurant Civ Wed 150
CARDS:

★★★65% Forest Lodge

Pikes Hill, Romsey Rd SO43 7AS
☎ 023 8028 3677 023 8028 2940
e-mail: reservations@newforesthotels.co.uk
Dir: *M27 junct 1, A337 towards Lyndhurst. In village (police station and courts on right), take 1st right into Pikes Hill*

Best Western

Situated on the edge of Lyndhurst, this hotel is set well back from the main road. Bedrooms are on different floors, and a number are suitable for family use. The indoor pool, with delightful murals, is a real bonus.

ROOMS: 28 en suite (7 fmly) (6 GF) s £72.50-£80; d £115-£130 (incl. bkfst) **LB FACILITIES:** Indoor swimming (H) Sauna Gym Xmas **CONF:** Thtr 100 Class 70 Board 50 Del from £90 **PARKING:** 50 **NOTES:** No smoking in restaurant Civ Wed 100
CARDS:

★71% Knightwood Lodge
Southampton Rd SO43 7BU
☎ 023 8028 2502 📠 023 8028 3730
e-mail: jackie4r@aol.com
Dir: *exit M27 junct 1 follow A337 to Lyndhurst. Left at traffic lights in village onto A35 towards Southampton. Hotel 0.25m on left*
This friendly, family-run hotel is situated on the outskirts of Lyndhurst. Comfortable bedrooms are modern in style and well equipped with many useful extras. The hotel offers an excellent range of facilities including a swimming pool, jacuzzi and a small gym area.
ROOMS: 15 en suite 4 annexe en suite (2 fmly) s £35-£50; d £60-£95 (incl. bkfst) **LB FACILITIES:** STV Indoor swimming (H) Sauna Solarium Gym Jacuzzi Steam room, Swimming pool supervised **PARKING:** 15 **NOTES:** No smoking in restaurant **CARDS:**

Travelodge (New Forest)
A31 Westbound SO43 7GN
☎ 08700 850 950
Travelodge offers good quality, good value, modern accommodation. Ideal for families, the spacious, en suite bedrooms include remote-control TV, tea and coffee-making facilities, luxury beds and free morning newspaper. Meals can be taken at the nearby family restaurant. For further details and the Travelodge phone number, consult the Hotel Groups page.
ROOMS: 32 en suite s fr £42.95; d fr £42.95

LYNMOUTH, Devon
Map 03 SS74
See also Lynton

★★★64% Tors
EX35 6NA
☎ 01598 753236 📠 01598 752544
e-mail: torshotel@torslynmouth.co.uk
Dir: *adjacent to A39 on Countisbury Hill just before entering Lynmouth*
In an elevated position overlooking Lynmouth Bay, this friendly hotel is set in five acres of woodland. The majority of the bedrooms benefit from the superb views, as do the public areas, which are generous and well-presented. Both fixed-price and short carte menus are offered in the restaurant.
ROOMS: 31 en suite (6 fmly) s £67-£160; d £94-£180 (incl. bkfst) **LB FACILITIES:** Outdoor swimming (H) Table tennis Pool table Xmas **CONF:** Thtr 60 Class 40 Board 25 **SERVICES:** Lift **PARKING:** 40 **NOTES:** No smoking in restaurant Closed 4-31 Jan RS Feb (wknds only) **CARDS:**

★★73% Rising Sun
Harbourside EX35 6EG
☎ 01598 753223 📠 01598 753480
e-mail: risingsunlynmouth@easynet.co.uk
Dir: *M5 junct 23 to Minehead. A39 to Lynmouth, hotel on harbourside*

This 'chocolate-box' thatched inn nestling on the harbour front was formerly a smuggler's inn. Popular with locals and hotel residents alike, guests have the option of either eating in the convivial bar or in the restaurant; a comfortable, quiet lounge is also available. Bedrooms are either in the inn or adjoining cottages, individually designed with modern facilities.
ROOMS: 11 en suite 5 annexe en suite (1 GF) No smoking in 11 bedrooms s £49-£95; d £98-£156 (incl. bkfst) **LB FACILITIES:** Xmas **CONF:** Thtr 22 Class 18 Board 14 Del from £95 **NOTES:** No dogs (ex guide dogs) No children 8yrs No smoking in restaurant
CARDS:

★★67% Bath
Sea Front EX35 6EL
☎ 01598 752238 📠 01598 752544
e-mail: bathhotel@torslynmouth.co.uk
Dir: *M5 junct 25, follow A39 to Minehead then Porlock and Lynmouth*
This well-established, friendly hotel is situated near the harbour and offers lovely views from the attractive, sea-facing bedrooms and an excellent starting point for scenic walks. There are two lounges and a sun lounge and the restaurant menu makes good use of fresh produce and local fish.
ROOMS: 22 en suite (9 fmly) s £29.50-£50; d £59-£100 (incl. bkfst) **LB PARKING:** 12 **NOTES:** No smoking in restaurant Closed Jan & Dec RS Feb-Mar and Nov **CARDS:**

LYNTON, Devon
Map 03 SS74
See also Lynmouth

★★★65% Lynton Cottage
North Walk EX35 6ED
☎ 01598 752342 📠 01598 752597
e-mail: enquiries@lynton-cottage.co.uk
Dir: *M25 junct 23 A39 to Lynmouth then Lynton, hotel 100mtrs on right*
Magnificent views can be enjoyed from this peaceful hideaway, which stands some 500 feet above the sea. Bedrooms vary size and most have scenic views, whilst public areas, such as the cosy bar, provide a relaxing environment. In the restaurant, a fixed-price menu offers a balanced selection of tempting dishes.
ROOMS: 15 en suite (2 fmly) No smoking in 3 bedrooms **CONF:** Thtr 20 Class 14 Board 12 **PARKING:** 17 **NOTES:** No smoking in restaurant Closed Dec-Jan **CARDS:**

★★65% *Sandrock*
Longmead EX35 6DH
☎ 01598 753307 📠 01598 752665
Dir: *follow signs to 'The Valley of the Rocks'*
On the edge of the village and at the head of the Valley of the Rocks, this long-established, family-run hotel offers light and airy, modern bedrooms. The public bar is popular with locals and residents alike and there is a first-floor lounge.
ROOMS: 8 en suite (3 fmly) **PARKING:** 9 **NOTES:** No smoking in restaurant Closed Nov-Jan **CARDS:**

★74% Seawood
North Walk EX35 6HJ
☎ 01598 752272 📠 01598 752272
e-mail: giinjnk@aol.com
Dir: *turn right at St. Mary's Church in Lynton High St for hotel, 2nd on left*
Tucked away in a quiet area and spectacularly situated 400 feet above the seashore, the Seawood has magnificent views over the sea. Set in delightfully planted grounds, this is a friendly place where many guests return on a regular basis. Bedrooms, many with sea views and some with four-poster beds, are comfortable and well equipped. At dinner, the daily changing menu provides freshly prepared and appetising cuisine.
ROOMS: 12 en suite s £29-£31; d £58-£66 (incl. bkfst) **PARKING:** 12 **NOTES:** No children 10yrs No smoking in restaurant Closed Nov-Etr

LYTHAM ST ANNES, Lancashire Map 18 SD32

★★★★66% Clifton Arms

West Beach, Lytham FY8 5QJ
☎ 01253 739898 01253 730657
e-mail: welcome@cliftonarms.com
Dir: *on A584 along seafront*

This well-established hotel occupies a prime position overlooking Lytham Green and the Ribble Estuary beyond. The bedrooms vary in size and style; front-facing rooms are particularly spacious and some of the side rooms are very stylish and contemporary. There is an elegant restaurant and an open-plan lounge and cocktail bar.
ROOMS: 48 en suite No smoking in 4 bedrooms s £95-£115; d £115-£140 (incl. bkfst) **LB** **FACILITIES:** STV Xmas **CONF:** Thtr 300 Class 200 Board 100 Del £155 **SERVICES:** Lift **PARKING:** 50 **NOTES:** No dogs (ex guide dogs) No smoking in restaurant Civ Wed 100
CARDS:

See advert on opposite page

★★★67% Bedford

307-311 Clifton Dr South FY8 1HN
☎ 01253 724636 01253 729244
e-mail: reservations@bedford-hotel.com
Dir: *from M55 follow signs for airport to last traffic lights. Left through 2 sets of lights. Hotel 300yds on left*

This well established, family-run hotel is close to the town centre and seafront. Bedrooms vary in size, and are attractively furnished and well equipped. They include a stylish four-poster room and some suitable for families. Public areas include a function suite, fitness facilities, the Cartland Restaurant, a popular coffee shop and Kitty's public bar offering regular entertainment.
ROOMS: 45 en suite (7 fmly) No smoking in all bedrooms s fr £45; d fr £74 (incl. bkfst) **LB** **FACILITIES:** STV Solarium Gym Jacuzzi entertainment Xmas **CONF:** Thtr 200 Class 140 Board 60 Del from £65 **SERVICES:** Lift **PARKING:** 25 **NOTES:** No dogs (ex guide dogs) No smoking in restaurant Civ Wed 180
CARDS:

★★★67% Chadwick

South Promenade FY8 1NP
THE INDEPENDENTS
☎ 01253 720061 01253 714455
e-mail: sales@thechadwickhotel.com
Dir: *M6 junct 32 take M55 to Blackpool then A5230 to South Shore. Follow signs for St Annes*

A comfortable, traditional, family-run, seafront hotel. Bedrooms vary in size and style, but all are very thoughtfully equipped; those at the front boast panoramic sea views. Public rooms are spacious and very comfortably furnished and the spacious bar comes stocked with 200 malt whiskies. The well-equipped, air-conditioned gym and indoor pool are popular facilities.
ROOMS: 75 en suite (28 fmly) (13 GF) s £46-£49; d £64-£74 (incl. bkfst) **LB** **FACILITIES: Spa** STV Indoor swimming (H) Sauna Solarium Gym Jacuzzi Turkish bath Games room Soft play adventure area entertainment Xmas **CONF:** Thtr 72 Class 24 Board 28 Del from £65 **SERVICES:** Lift **PARKING:** 40 **NOTES:** No dogs (ex guide dogs) No smoking in restaurant **CARDS:**

See advert on opposite page

★★70% Glendower

North Promenade FY8 2NQ
Best Western
☎ 01253 723241 01253 640069
e-mail: glendowerhotel@bestwestern.co.uk
Dir: *M55 follow airport signs. Left at Promenade to St Annes. Hotel, 500yds from pier*

Located on the seafront and with easy access to the town centre, this popular, friendly hotel offers comfortably furnished, well-equipped accommodation. Bedrooms vary in size and style and include four-poster rooms and very popular family suites. Public areas include a choice of smart, comfortable lounges, a bright and modern leisure club and function facilities.
ROOMS: 60 en suite (17 fmly) No smoking in 12 bedrooms s £44-£54; d £78-£98 (incl. bkfst) **LB** **FACILITIES: Spa** STV Indoor swimming (H) Snooker Sauna Solarium Gym Jacuzzi Childrens playroom Xmas **CONF:** Thtr 150 Class 120 Board 40 Del from £68 **SERVICES:** Lift **PARKING:** 45 **NOTES:** No smoking in restaurant
CARDS:

★★69% Lindum

63-67 South Promenade FY8 1LZ
☎ 01253 721534 & 722516 01253 721364
e-mail: info@lindumhotel.co.uk
Dir: *from M55 follow A5230 & signs for Blackpool Airport. After airport, left at lights to St Annes, right at lights. 1st left onto seafront. Hotel 250yds on left*

The same family has run this friendly seafront hotel for over 40 years. Bedrooms are generally spacious, comfortable and well equipped, with some enjoying superb coastal views. Constant modernisation has provided spacious lounges, a games room and

continued

a stylish and popular health suite. The open-plan restaurant offers a wide choice of well-cooked dishes.

ROOMS: 76 en suite (25 fmly) No smoking in 20 bedrooms s £32-£45; d £64-£75 (incl. bkfst) **LB FACILITIES:** Sauna Solarium Jacuzzi entertainment Xmas **CONF:** Thtr 80 Class 30 Board 25 Del from £50 **SERVICES:** Lift air con **PARKING:** 20 **NOTES:** No smoking in restaurant **CARDS:**

Premier Lodge (Lytham St Annes)

PREMIER LODGE

Church Rd FY8 5LH
☎ 0870 9906548 ▯ 0870 9906549

Premier Lodge offers modern, well-equipped, en suite accommodation suitable for both business and leisure travellers. Meals can be taken at the adjacent popular restaurant and bar, which is fully licensed. For further details, consult the Hotel Groups page.

ROOMS: 22 en suite s £48; d £48

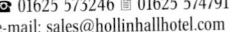

MACCLESFIELD, Cheshire

Map 16 SJ97

★★★★67% Shrigley Hall Hotel Golf & Country Club

PARAMOUNT GROUP OF HOTELS

Shrigley Park, Pott Shrigley SK10 5SB
☎ 01625 575757 ▯ 01625 573323
e-mail: shrigleyhall@paramount-hotels.co.uk
Dir: *off A523 at Legh Arms towards Pott Shrigley. Hotel 2m on left*

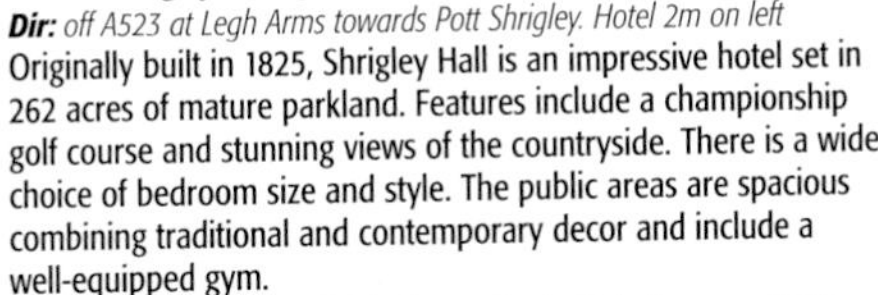

Originally built in 1825, Shrigley Hall is an impressive hotel set in 262 acres of mature parkland. Features include a championship golf course and stunning views of the countryside. There is a wide choice of bedroom size and style. The public areas are spacious combining traditional and contemporary decor and include a well-equipped gym.

ROOMS: 150 en suite (8 fmly) No smoking in 28 bedrooms s £130; d £160 (incl. bkfst) **LB FACILITIES:** STV Indoor swimming (H) Golf 18 Tennis (hard) Fishing Sauna Solarium Gym Putting green Jacuzzi Beauty salon, tydro centre, Swimming pool supervised entertainment Xmas **CONF:** Thtr 280 Class 140 Board 50 Del £175 **SERVICES:** Lift **PARKING:** 300 **NOTES:** No smoking in restaurant Civ Wed 220 **CARDS:**

★★★69% Best Western Hollin Hall

Jackson Ln, Kerridge, Bollington SK10 5BG
☎ 01625 573246 ▯ 01625 574791
e-mail: sales@hollinhallhotel.com
Dir: *off A523, 2m along B5090*

Set in the peaceful Cheshire countryside, this hotel is convenient for Manchester Airport (courtesy transport available). The main building has an impressive carved staircase, high ceilings, a

continued on p406

MACCLESFIELD, continued

restaurant and a lounge. Attractively furnished accommodation is situated in a modern extension.
ROOMS: 54 en suite (2 fmly) No smoking in 36 bedrooms d £65-£75 (incl. bkfst) **LB FACILITIES:** STV Sauna Gym Free use neighbouring Leisure Club & Golf Course **CONF:** Thtr 120 Class 50 Board 50 Del £95 **PARKING:** 200 **NOTES:** No dogs (ex guide dogs) No smoking in restaurant Civ Wed 100 **CARDS:**

Premier Lodge (Macclesfield)

Congleton Rd, Gawsworth SK11 7XD
☎ 0870 9906412 📠 0870 9906413
Premier Lodge offers modern, well-equipped, en suite accommodation suitable for both business and leisure travellers. Meals can be taken at the adjacent popular restaurant and bar, which is fully licensed. For further details, consult the Hotel Groups page.
ROOMS: 28 en suite s £48; d £48

Travel Inn

Tytherington Business Park, Springwood Way, Tytherington SK10 2XA
☎ 08701 977167 📠 01625 422874

Dir: *on A523 Tytherington Business Park*

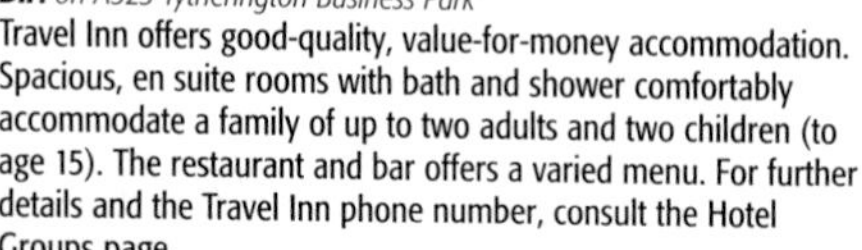

Travel Inn offers good-quality, value-for-money accommodation. Spacious, en suite rooms with bath and shower comfortably accommodate a family of up to two adults and two children (to age 15). The restaurant and bar offers a varied menu. For further details and the Travel Inn phone number, consult the Hotel Groups page.
ROOMS: 40 en suite s £44.95; d £44.95 **CONF:** Thtr 20

Travelodge Macclesfield

London Rd South SK12 4NA
☎ 08700 850 950 📠 01625 875292
Dir: *on A523*
Travelodge offers good quality, good value, modern accommodation. Ideal for families, the spacious, en suite bedrooms include remote-control TV, tea and coffee-making facilities, luxury beds and free morning newspaper. Meals can be taken at the nearby family restaurant. For further details and the Travelodge phone number, consult the Hotel Groups page.
ROOMS: 32 en suite s fr £42.95; d fr £42.95

MAIDENCOMBE See Torquay

MAIDENHEAD, Berkshire Map 06 SU88
See also Bray

Top 200 - Hotel

★★★★ Fredrick's

Shoppenhangers Rd SL6 2PZ
☎ 01628 581000 📠 01628 771054
e-mail: reservations@fredricks-hotel.co.uk
Dir: *M4 junct 8/9 onto A404(M) to Maidenhead West and Henley. 1st exit to White Waltham. Left into Shoppenhangers Rd to Maidenhead*
This delightful hotel is in a quiet location, in easy reach of the M4 and just 30 minutes from London. The spacious bedrooms are all comfortably furnished and very well equipped. An enthusiastic team of staff ensure friendly and efficient service. The highlight of any visit is a meal in the restaurant, where
continued
the focus is on high-quality ingredients. Wentworth and Sunningdale golf courses are both within 20 minutes' drive.

ROOMS: 37 en suite (11 GF) s £195-£215; d £260-£280 (incl. bkfst) **LB FACILITIES:** STV Croquet lawn **CONF:** Thtr 120 Class 80 Board 60 Del from £265 **PARKING:** 90 **NOTES:** No dogs (ex guide dogs) Closed 24 Dec-3 Jan Civ Wed 120
CARDS:

★★★65% *Thames Riviera*

At the Bridge SL6 8DW
☎ 01628 674057 📠 01628 776586
e-mail: thamesriv.sales@dial.pipex.com
Dir: *off A4 by Maidenhead Historic Bridge, hotel by bridge*
Enjoying an attractive location on the banks of the River Thames, this hotel is also well located for the motorway networks. Many of the well-equipped bedrooms have balconies and river views. A smart café bar and riverside terrace provide an ideal setting for contemporary all-day dining.
ROOMS: 34 en suite 18 annexe en suite (1 fmly) No smoking in 4 bedrooms **FACILITIES:** STV **CONF:** Thtr 50 Class 30 Board 20 **PARKING:** 60 **NOTES:** No dogs (ex guide dogs) Closed 26-30 Dec
CARDS:

★★67% Elva Lodge

Castle Hill SL6 4AD
☎ 01628 622948 📠 01628 778954
e-mail: reservations@elvalodgehotel.co.uk
Dir: *A4 Maidenhead towards Reading. Hotel at top of hill on left*

Located just minutes from the town centre, this family-run hotel offers a warm welcome and friendly service. Bedrooms are suitably appointed and well equipped. Spacious public areas include a lounge, bar and the Lion's Brasserie, which offers a wide range of popular dishes.
ROOMS: 26 rms (23 en suite) (1 fmly) (5 GF) No smoking in 6 bedrooms s £50-£98; d £65-£108 (incl. bkfst) **FACILITIES:** Reduced rates at local Leisure Centre ch fac **CONF:** Thtr 50 Class 30 Board 30 **PARKING:** 32 **NOTES:** No smoking in restaurant Closed 24-30 Dec Civ Wed 60 **CARDS:**

U *Holiday Inn Maidenhead/Windsor*
Manor Ln SL6 2RA
☎ 01628 506000 🖹 01628 506001
Dir: *From Shoppenhanger Road straight on at 2 mini-rdbts, hotel on right behind Esso Garage*
At the time of going to press, the classification for this hotel was not confirmed. Please refer to the AA internet site www.theAA.com for current information.
ROOMS: 189 en suite (20 fmly) No smoking in 80 bedrooms **FACILITIES:** STV Indoor swimming (H) Squash Sauna Solarium Gym Spirit Health Club **CONF:** Thtr 400 Class 200 Board 30 **SERVICES:** Lift **PARKING:** 250 **NOTES:** No dogs (ex guide dogs) No smoking in restaurant **CARDS:**

MAIDSTONE, Kent

Map 07 TQ75

★★★★70% ◎ Marriott Tudor Park Hotel & Country Club
Ashford Rd, Bearsted ME14 4NQ
☎ 01622 734334 🖹 01622 735360
e-mail: sharla.roy@marriott.co.uk
Dir: *M20 junct 8 to Lenham. Right at rdbt towards Bearsted and Maidstone on A20. Hotel 1m on left*

This fine country hotel provides good levels of comfort. Guests can dine in the main restaurant, Fairviews, which offers a range of modern, eclectic dishes, or in the more relaxed environment of the Long Weekend Brasserie. Take time to enjoy the excellent range of leisure options, such as golf, a workout, a swim, or be pampered in the beauty salon.
ROOMS: 120 en suite (48 fmly) (60 GF) No smoking in 65 bedrooms s fr £105; d fr £113 (incl. bkfst) **FACILITIES: Spa** STV Indoor swimming (H) Golf 18 Tennis (hard) Sauna Solarium Gym Putting green Driving range, Beauty salon, Steam room Xmas **CONF:** Thtr 250 Class 100 Board 60 Del from £140 **SERVICES:** Lift **PARKING:** 250 **NOTES:** No dogs (ex guide dogs) No smoking in restaurant Civ Wed 180
CARDS:

★★★69% Russell
136 Boxley Rd ME14 2AE
☎ 01622 692221 🖹 01622 762084
e-mail: russhotel@aol.com

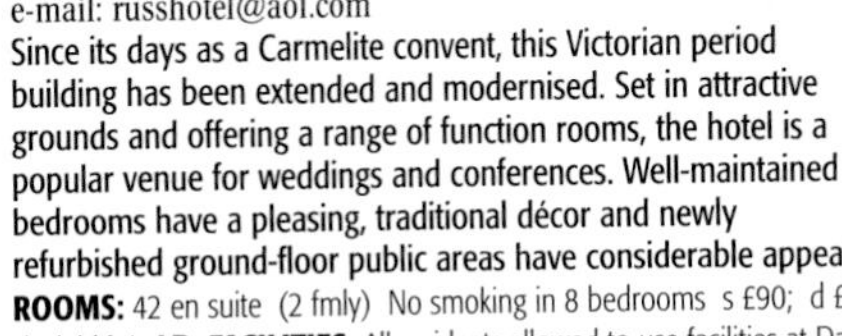

Since its days as a Carmelite convent, this Victorian period building has been extended and modernised. Set in attractive grounds and offering a range of function rooms, the hotel is a popular venue for weddings and conferences. Well-maintained bedrooms have a pleasing, traditional décor and newly refurbished ground-floor public areas have considerable appeal.
ROOMS: 42 en suite (2 fmly) No smoking in 8 bedrooms s £90; d £120 (incl. bkfst) **LB** **FACILITIES:** All residents allowed to use facilities at David Lloyd Health & Fitness Centre Xmas **CONF:** Thtr 300 Class 100 Board 70 Del £125 **PARKING:** 100 **NOTES:** No dogs (ex guide dogs) No smoking in restaurant Civ Wed 300 **CARDS:**

★★★67% *Larkfield Priory*
London Rd, Larkfield ME20 6HJ
☎ 01732 846858 🖹 01732 846786
e-mail: larkfieldpriory@corushotels.com
Dir: *M20 junct 4 take A228 to West Malling. At traffic lights left signed to Maidstone on A20, after 1m hotel on left*

Conveniently located and close to the motorway links, this hotel, which dates from the 1890s, offers comfort and services to suit either the business or touring guest. Bedrooms are bright and smart. A spacious lounge and welcoming bar are available and in the dining room, choices can be made from the table d'hôte or carte menus.
ROOMS: 52 en suite No smoking in 24 bedrooms **CONF:** Thtr 80 Class 36 Board 30 **PARKING:** 80 **NOTES:** No smoking in restaurant
CARDS:

MAIDSTONE, continued

★★69% Grange Moor
St Michael's Rd ME16 8BS
☎ 01622 677623 01622 678246
e-mail: reservations@grangemoor.co.uk
Dir: *Town centre, towards A26 Tonbridge Rd. Hotel 0.25m on left, just after Church*
Within easy walking distance of the town centre this family run hotel offers a warm welcome. Bedrooms, many of which have been recently refurbished, are comfortable and well appointed. Public areas include a popular bar, smart restaurant and a small residents' lounge.
ROOMS: 39 en suite 12 annexe en suite (6 fmly) No smoking in 21 bedrooms s £45-£49; d £54-£56 (incl. bkfst) **LB CONF:** Thtr 120 Class 60 Board 40 Del £85 **PARKING:** 60 **NOTES:** Closed 26-30 Dec Civ Wed 60 **CARDS:**

★★69% Lime Tree Restaurant and Hotel
8-9 The Limes, The Square, Lenham ME17 2PQ
☎ 01622 859509 01522 851581
e-mail: jrfinvest@aol.com
Dir: *turn off A20 onto Maidstone Rd, continue for 200yds to Square*
This charming 14th-century half timbered building is situated in the heart of the town centre, just a short drive from the M20. The public rooms are full of character and have many original features such as exposed beams and inglenook fireplaces. Bedrooms are pleasantly decorated and thoughtfully equipped, and an imaginative carte menu is offered in the popular restaurant.
ROOMS: 10 en suite (1 fmly) s £48-£65; d £65 (incl. bkfst) **LB FACILITIES:** Xmas **CONF:** Thtr 14 Class 14 Board 14 Del £125 **NOTES:** No dogs No smoking in restaurant Closed 1-14 Jan
CARDS:

Innkeeper's Lodge Maidstone
Sandling Rd ME14 2RF
☎ 01622 692212 01622 679265
Dir: *M20 junct 6, S onto A229 towards Maidstone. At 3rd rdbt, turn left and left again*
A new concept in the travel accommodation market. Smart rooms meet essential business requirements but also have home comforts. Dining options include all-day menus plus the added advantage of breakfast, which is included in the room price. For further details, consult the Hotel Groups page.
ROOMS: 12 en suite

Travel Inn (Maidstone Allington)
London Rd ME16 0HG
☎ 08701 977168 01622 672469
Dir: *M20 junct 5, 0.5m on London Rd towards Maidstone*
Travel Inn offers good-quality, value-for-money accommodation. Spacious, en suite rooms with bath and shower comfortably accommodate a family of up to two adults and two children (to age 15). The restaurant and bar offers a varied menu. For further details and the Travel Inn phone number, consult the Hotel Groups page.
ROOMS: 40 en suite s £44.95; d £44.95 **CONF:** Thtr 45 Board 30

Travel Inn (Maidstone Sandling)
Allington Lock, Sandling ME14 3AS
☎ 08701 977308 01622 715159
Dir: *M20 junct 6 follow sign for Museum of Kent Life*
Travel Inn offers good-quality, value-for-money accommodation. Spacious, en suite rooms with bath and shower comfortably accommodate a family of up to two adults and two children (to age 15). The restaurant and bar offers a varied menu. For further details and the Travel Inn phone number, consult the Hotel Groups page.
ROOMS: 40 en suite s £44.95; d £44.95

MAIDSTONE MOTORWAY SERVICE AREA (M20), Kent — Map 07 TQ75

Travel Inn (Maidstone Hollingbourne)
ME17 1SS
☎ 08701 977169 01622 739535
Dir: *M20 junct 8*
Travel Inn offers good-quality, value-for-money accommodation. Spacious, en suite rooms with bath and shower comfortably accommodate a family of up to two adults and two children (to age 15). The restaurant and bar offers a varied menu. For further details and the Travel Inn phone number, consult the Hotel Groups page.
ROOMS: 58 en suite s £44.95; d £44.95 **CONF:** Thtr 30 Board 18

MALDON See Tolleshunt Knights

MALHAM, North Yorkshire — Map 18 SD96

★★65% The Buck Inn
BD23 4DA
☎ 01729 830317 01729 830670
e-mail: thebuckinn@ukonline.co.uk
Dir: *from Skipton, take A65 to Gargrave, then 7m to Malham*
This attractive stone-built inn is located in the centre of the village. Bedrooms are comfortably furnished and include some particularly smart refurbished rooms and some with four-poster beds. Imaginative menus offer a good choice of home-made dishes. A wide range of real ales and malt whiskies are served in the two cosy bars.
ROOMS: 10 en suite (3 fmly) s £35-£47.50; d £60-£85 (incl. bkfst) **LB FACILITIES:** Riding Xmas **PARKING:** 25 **NOTES:** No dogs (ex guide dogs) No smoking in restaurant **CARDS:**

MALMESBURY, Wiltshire — Map 04 ST98

★★★75% Old Bell
Abbey Row SN16 0AG
☎ 01666 822344 01666 825145
e-mail: info@oldbellhotel.com
Dir: *off A429, in centre of Malmesbury, adjacent to the Abbey*
Reputed to be the oldest in England, this hotel has retained many original features, together with modern facilities. There is a choice of comfortable lounges in which to relax, and guests have the option of eating in the restaurant or less formally in the Great Hall. Bedrooms vary in size and style, ranging from the older antique-filled, character rooms to the newer, stylish Japanese-inspired rooms.
ROOMS: 16 en suite 15 annexe en suite (3 fmly) (6 GF) s £85-£150; d £110-£200 (incl. bkfst) **LB FACILITIES: Spa** STV Cyber room & internet access/Nintendo games Pool table Hot tub ch fac Xmas **CONF:** Thtr 45 Class 10 Board 24 Del £140 **PARKING:** 30 **NOTES:** No smoking in restaurant RS 23 Dec-2 Jan Civ Wed 80
CARDS:

★★★75% The Old Rectory Country House Hotel
SN16 9EP
☎ 01666 577194 01666 577853
e-mail: office@oldrectorycrudwell.co.uk
Dir: *M4 junct 17. Follow A429 to Cirencester, right opposite Plough pub in Crudwell. Hotel next to church*

A former rectory this beautiful house with its Victorian walled garden offers a feeling of peace and seclusion. Individually decorated bedrooms offer deep comfort coupled with a host of thoughtful touches for guests' enjoyment. The highlight is the wood-panelled restaurant where local produce forms the basis of well-prepared dishes.
ROOMS: 12 en suite No smoking in all bedrooms s £75-£105; d £98-£165 (incl. bkfst) **LB FACILITIES: Spa** Croquet lawn Xmas **CONF:** Thtr 40 Class 20 Board 20 Del £135 **PARKING:** 50 **NOTES:** No dogs (ex guide dogs) No smoking in restaurant Civ Wed 40
CARDS:

★★74% **Mayfield House**
Crudwell SN16 9EW
☎ 01666 577409 01666 577977
e-mail: reception@mayfieldhousehotel.co.uk
Dir: *3m N on A429 from Malmesbury*
Guests are assured of a warm welcome at this charming hotel, on the edge of the Cotswolds. An imaginative menu is served in the renovated restaurant, overlooking the attractive gardens. Additionally, there is a foyer lounge and a bar offering a wide range of popular dishes. The bedrooms are all equipped with modern facilities; some ground floor rooms are available.
ROOMS: 21 en suite 3 annexe en suite (2 fmly) No smoking in 6 bedrooms s £65; d £88 (incl. bkfst) **LB FACILITIES:** Xmas **CONF:** Thtr 40 Class 30 Board 25 Del £98 **PARKING:** 50 **NOTES:** No smoking in restaurant **CARDS:**
See advert on this page

MALTON, North Yorkshire Map 19 SE77

★★★72% **Burythorpe House**
Burythorpe YO17 9LB
☎ 01653 658200 01653 658204
e-mail: reception@burythorpehousehotel.com
Dir: *4m S of Malton, outside Burythorpe and 4m from A64 (York to Scarborough)*
This charming house offers spacious and individually furnished bedrooms. Five rooms are situated in a rear courtyard, two of which are equipped for less able guests, and all benefiting from small kitchen areas. Comfortable, spacious lounge areas are provided along with an impressive oak-panelled dining room
continued on p410

M

MALTON, continued

where interesting, freshly prepared meals are served. Leisure facilities are available.
ROOMS: 11 en suite 5 annexe en suite (2 fmly) (5 GF) No smoking in all bedrooms s £55; d £60-£88 (incl. bkfst) **LB** **FACILITIES:** Indoor swimming (H) Tennis (hard) Snooker Sauna Solarium Gym Xmas **PARKING:** 40 **NOTES:** No smoking in restaurant Civ Wed 55
CARDS:

★★★61% Green Man
15 Market St YO17 7LY
☎ 01653 600370 01653 696006
e-mail: greenman@englishrosehotels.co.uk
Dir: *from A64 follow signs to Malton town centre. Left into Market St, hotel on left*
This friendly hotel set in the centre of town includes an inviting reception lounge where a log fire burns in winter. There is also a cosy bar, and dining takes place in the traditional restaurant at the rear. Bedrooms vary in size and are thoughtfully equipped.
ROOMS: 24 en suite (4 fmly) s £39.50-£60; d £75-£130 (incl. bkfst) **LB** **FACILITIES:** Xmas **CONF:** Thtr 120 Class 20 Board 40 Del from £65 **PARKING:** 40 **NOTES:** No dogs (ex guide dogs) No smoking in restaurant **CARDS:**

★★67% *Talbot*
Yorkersgate YO17 7AJ
☎ 01653 694031 01653 693355
e-mail: admin@englishrosehotels.co.uk
Dir: *off A64 towards Malton. Hotel on right*
Situated close to the centre of town this long-established, creeper-covered hotel looks out towards the River Derwent and open countryside. Bedroom sizes vary, but all are comfortable. The public rooms are traditional and elegantly furnished and include a bar plus separate lounge.
ROOMS: 31 en suite (3 fmly) **CONF:** Thtr 50 Board 20 **PARKING:** 30 **NOTES:** No dogs (ex guide dogs) No smoking in restaurant
CARDS:

See advert on page 409

M

MALVERN, Worcestershire — Map 10 SO74

★★★75% Cottage in the Wood
Holywell Rd, Malvern Wells WR14 4LG
☎ 01684 575859 01684 560662
e-mail: proprietor@cottageinthewood.co.uk
Dir: *3m S of Great Malvern off A449, 500yds N of B4209 turning, on opposite side of road*

This delightful family-run hotel enjoys magnificent views across the Severn Valley. The cosy bedrooms are divided between the main house, Beech Cottage and the Coach House. All are well-equipped and have many thoughtful extras. Public rooms are elegantly appointed and feature real fires, deep-cushioned sofas and fresh flowers.
ROOMS: 8 en suite 23 annexe en suite (10 GF) No smoking in 11 bedrooms s £82-£105; d £99-£175 (incl. bkfst) **LB** **FACILITIES:** STV Direct access to Malvern Hills Xmas **CONF:** Thtr 20 Board 14 Del from £150 **PARKING:** 40 **NOTES:** No smoking in restaurant
CARDS:

See advert on opposite page

★★★73% Colwall Park
Walwyn Rd, Colwall WR13 6QG
☎ 01684 540000 01684 540847
e-mail: hotel@colwall.com
Dir: *Between Malvern & Ledbury in centre of Colwall on B4218*

Standing in extensive gardens, this hotel was purpose built in the early 20th century to serve the local racetrack. Today the proprietors and the loyal staff provide high levels of hospitality and service, and the Seasons restaurant has a well-deserved reputation for its cuisine. Bedrooms have been tastefully refurbished and public areas help to create a fine country-house atmosphere.
ROOMS: 22 en suite (1 fmly) No smoking in 6 bedrooms s £65-£80; d £110-£130 (incl. bkfst) **LB** **FACILITIES:** STV Croquet lawn Boules Xmas **CONF:** Thtr 150 Class 80 Board 50 Del £140 **PARKING:** 40 **NOTES:** No smoking in restaurant **CARDS:**

See advert on opposite page

★★★73% Foley Arms
14 Worcester Rd WR14 4QS
☎ 01684 573397 01684 569665
e-mail: reservations@foleyarmshotel.com
Dir: *M5 junct 7 N or junct 8 S or M50 junct 1 to Great Malvern on A449*

With spectacular views of the Severn Valley, this hotel provides attentive, friendly service. Reputed to be the oldest hotel in Malvern, it is situated in the heart of town. The bedrooms are comfortable and tastefully decorated with period furnishings and

continued

modern facilities. Public areas include Elgar's Restaurant, a popular bar and a choice of comfortable lounges.
ROOMS: 28 en suite (2 fmly) No smoking in 5 bedrooms s £74-£84; d £98-£135 (incl. bkfst) **LB** **FACILITIES:** STV Free use leisure centre pool, gym, solarium & sauna Xmas **CONF:** Thtr 150 Class 40 Board 45 Del from £128 **PARKING:** 64 **NOTES:** No smoking in restaurant Civ Wed 120 **CARDS:**

See advert on this page

★★★68% *Abbey*

Abbey Rd WR14 3ET
☎ 01684 892332 📠 01684 892662
e-mail: abbey@sarova.co.uk
Dir: *M5 junct 7 onto A449 to Malvern. Left by Barclays Bank into Church St. Right at traffic lights and 1st right into Abbey Rd*
This large, impressive, ivy-clad hotel stands in the centre of Great Malvern, next to the Abbey and close to the theatre. It provides well-equipped modern accommodation equally suitable for both business guests and tourists. Facilities include a good range of function rooms and the hotel is a popular venue for conferences.
ROOMS: 103 en suite (5 fmly) No smoking in 24 bedrooms **FACILITIES:** STV Free entry to Malvern Leisure Complex **CONF:** Thtr 300 Class 180 Board 65 **SERVICES:** Lift **PARKING:** 90 **NOTES:** No smoking in restaurant Civ Wed 100 **CARDS:**

★★74% Holdfast Cottage

Marlbank Rd, Little Malvern WR13 6NA
☎ 01684 310288 & 311481 📠 01684 311117
e-mail: enquiries@holdfast-cottage.co.uk
Dir: *on A4104 midway between Welland and Upper Welland*
This charming wisteria-covered hotel lies in attractive grounds at the foot of the Malvern Hills. The public areas offer all the

continued on p412

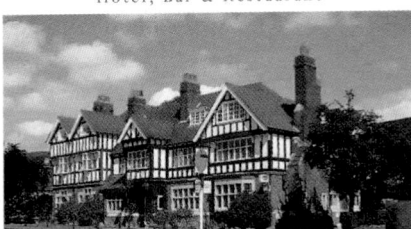

MALVERN, continued

comforts of a country retreat – log fire in the lounge, a cosy bar and an elegant dining room. The bedrooms include many thoughtful touches. A regularly changing menu features fresh local produce and ice cream and breads are made on the premises.

Holdfast Cottage, Malvern

ROOMS: 8 en suite (1 fmly) No smoking in all bedrooms s £50-£70; d £87-£99 (incl. bkfst) **LB** **FACILITIES:** Croquet lawn Walking, bird watching ch fac Xmas **CONF:** Class 30 Board 30 Del from £80 **PARKING:** 20 **NOTES:** No smoking in restaurant
CARDS:

See advert on opposite page

★★72% Cotford

51 Graham Rd WR14 2HU
☎ 01684 572427 01684 572952
e-mail: reservations@cotfordhotel.co.uk
Dir: *from Worcester follow signs to Malvern on A449. Left into Graham Rd signed town centre, hotel on right*

This delightful house, built in 1851, reputedly for the Bishop of Worcester, stands in attractive gardens with stunning views of the Malverns. Rooms have been sympathetically renovated, retaining many original features, and include all the expected comforts. Food, service and hospitality are major strengths.
ROOMS: 15 en suite (4 fmly) (1 GF) No smoking in all bedrooms s £50-£60; d £70-£80 (incl. bkfst) **LB** **FACILITIES:** STV complimentary use of leisure centre in centre of Malvern **CONF:** Thtr 26 Class 26 Del from £75 **PARKING:** 18 **NOTES:** No smoking in restaurant
CARDS:

★★68% The Malvern Hills

Wynds Point WR13 6DW
☎ 01684 540690 01684 540327
e-mail: malhilhotl@aol.com
Dir: *4m S, at junct of A449 with B4232*

This privately-owned, 19th-century hostelry is situated to the west of Malvern, opposite the British Camp, which was fortified and occupied by the Ancient Britons. Facilities include a choice of bars and a sun terrace from which customers can enjoy spectacular sunsets. The hotel is popular with walkers as well as business guests.

ROOMS: 14 en suite (2 fmly) No smoking in 4 bedrooms s £30-£50; d £70-£90 (incl. bkfst) **LB** **FACILITIES:** pool table entertainment Xmas **CONF:** Thtr 40 Class 24 Board 30 Del from £75 **PARKING:** 30 **NOTES:** No smoking in restaurant **CARDS:**

See advert on opposite page

★★67% Great Malvern

Graham Rd WR14 2HN
☎ 01684 563411 01684 560514
e-mail: sutton@great-malvern-hotel.co.uk
Dir: *from Worcester on A449, left beyond fire station into Graham Rd. Hotel at end of road on right*

This is a privately owned and personally run town-centre hotel, which is close to many cultural and scenic attractions. Popular with business people, theatregoers and leisure travellers, the hotel features well-equipped and comfortable accommodation, a busy bar, bistro and meeting room. There is also a comfortable lounge. There is now a very pleasant 1950's themed basement bar called Greatshakes.
ROOMS: 14 rms (13 en suite) (3 fmly) **CONF:** Thtr 60 Class 20 Board 30 **SERVICES:** Lift **PARKING:** 9 **NOTES:** No dogs (ex guide dogs)
CARDS:

★★67% Mount Pleasant

Belle Vue Ter WR14 4PZ
☎ 01684 561837 01684 569968
e-mail: mountpleasanthotel@btinternet.com
Dir: *on A449, in central Malvern by crossroads opposite Priory Church*
This is an attractive Georgian house in the centre of Great Malvern, that from its elevated position, overlooks the picturesque Severn Valley and Priory Church. In the last few years the owners have made many changes to both the public areas and bedrooms

continued

including the creation of the smart and attractively appointed Auberge Bar & Brasserie.

ROOMS: 14 en suite (1 fmly) s £58-£68; d £88-£98 (incl. bkfst) **LB**
FACILITIES: Xmas **CONF:** Thtr 90 Class 40 Board 50 Del from £80
PARKING: 20 **NOTES:** Closed 7-17 Jan
CARDS:

MANCHESTER, Greater Manchester — Map 16 SJ89
See also Manchester Airport & Sale

★★★★★72% **The Lowry Hotel**
50 Dearmans Place, Chapel Wharf, Salford
M3 5LH
☎ 0161 827 4000 📠 0161 827 4001
e-mail: enquiries@thelowryhotel.com

Dir: *M6 junct 19, A556 & M56 follow signs for Manchester. A5103 for 4.5m. At rdbt take A57(M) to lights & turn right onto Water St. Left to New Quay St/Trinity Way. At 1st lights turn right onto Chapel St to Hotel*

This modern hotel, set beside the River Irwell in the centre of the city, offers spacious bedrooms equipped to meet the needs of business and leisure visitors alike. Many of the rooms look out over the river, as do the sumptuous suites. The River Room restaurant, inspired by Marco Pierre White, produces good brasserie cooking. Extensive business and function facilities are available, together with a spa to provide extra pampering.
ROOMS: 165 en suite (7 fmly) No smoking in 90 bedrooms
FACILITIES: STV Sauna Gym Spa facilities & swimming available offsite entertainment **CONF:** Thtr 350 Class 250 Board 60 **SERVICES:** Lift air con **PARKING:** 100 **NOTES:** No dogs (ex guide dogs) Civ Wed 300
CARDS:

Late for dinner?
Quality Standards mean that last orders for dinner vary according to star rating and should be no earlier than:
★★ 7.00pm ★★★ 8.00pm ★★★★ 9.00pm
★★★★★ 10.00pm

M

MANCHESTER, continued

★★★★73% **Le Meridien Palace**
Oxford St M60 7HA
☎ 0161 288 1111 ▯ 0161 288 2222
e-mail: reservation.centreuk@lemeridien.com
Dir: *opposite Oxford Rd Railway Station*
This impressive neo-Gothic building occupies a central location. There is a vast lobby, spacious open-plan bar-lounge and restaurant and extensive conference and function facilities. Bedrooms vary in size and style and are all spacious and well equipped.
ROOMS: 252 en suite (59 fmly) No smoking in 30 bedrooms **FACILITIES:** STV entertainment **CONF:** Thtr 1000 Class 450 Board 100 **SERVICES:** Lift **NOTES:** No dogs (ex guide dogs) No smoking in restaurant Civ Wed 100 **CARDS:**

★★★★71% ***Marriott Worsley Park Hotel & Country Club***
Worsley Park, Worsley M28 2QT
☎ 0161 975 2000 ▯ 0161 799 6341
e-mail: salesadmin.worsleypark@marriotthotels.co.uk
Dir: *M60 junct 13, over 1st rdbt and take A575. Hotel 400yds on left*

This smart, modern hotel is set in impressive grounds that include a championship golf course. Bedrooms are comfortably appointed and well equipped for both leisure and business guests. Public areas include extensive leisure and conference facilities, an all-day bistro and an elegant restaurant offering imaginative cuisine.
ROOMS: 158 en suite (5 fmly) No smoking in 116 bedrooms **FACILITIES:** STV Indoor swimming (H) Golf 18 Sauna Solarium Gym Putting green Jacuzzi Steam room Health & Beauty salon **CONF:** Thtr 200 Class 150 Board 100 **SERVICES:** Lift **PARKING:** 400 **NOTES:** No dogs (ex guide dogs) Civ Wed 200 **CARDS:**

Town House

★★★★ **Alias Hotel Rossetti**
107 Piccadilly M1 2DB
☎ 0161 247 7744 ▯ 0161 247 7747
e-mail: info@aliashotels.com
Formerly a Victorian textile headquarters, this impressive building has been transformed to offer stylish accommodation. Bedrooms feature CD/DVD players and combine modern comfort with quirky eclectic décor. Unique 50's style diners are situated on each floor offering complimentary beverages, fresh fruit and cereals. Café Paradiso offers fresh Mediterranean food, while the basement has an exclusive club environment.
ROOMS: 61 en suite No smoking in 14 bedrooms d £95-£330 **FACILITIES:** STV entertainment Xmas **CONF:** Thtr 50 Class 20 Board 20 **SERVICES:** Lift **NOTES:** No smoking in restaurant **CARDS:**

★★★★68% **Copthorne Hotel Manchester**
Clippers Quay, Salford Quays M50 3SN
☎ 0161 873 7321 ▯ 0161 873 7318
e-mail: manchester@mill-cop.com
Dir: *from M602 follow signs for Salford Quays & Trafford Park on A5063. Hotel 0.75m on right*

This smart hotel enjoys a convenient location on the redeveloped Salford Quays close to Old Trafford, The Lowry Centre and The Imperial War Museum. Bedrooms are comfortably appointed and well equipped for both business and leisure guests. A choice of dining options includes Chandlers Restaurant serving accomplished food. Facilities include an indoor pool and gymnasium.
ROOMS: 166 en suite (6 fmly) No smoking in 118 bedrooms s £155-£180; d £155-£215 **LB** **FACILITIES:** STV **CONF:** Thtr 150 Class 70 Board 70 Del from £135 **SERVICES:** Lift **PARKING:** 120 **NOTES:** No dogs (ex guide dogs) **CARDS:**

★★★★68%
Le Meridien Victoria & Albert
Water St M3 4JQ
☎ 0870 400 8585 ▯ 0161 834 2484
e-mail: reservation.centreuk@lemeridien.com
Dir: *M602 to A57 through lights on Regent Rd. Pass Sainsbury's, left at lights onto ring road, right at lights into Water St.*
This uniquely converted warehouse is located on the banks of the River Irwell, adjacent to the famous Granada Studios. Many of the hotel's individually styled and tastefully decorated bedrooms are themed around productions from the local studios. Interior features include original exposed brick walls and iron pillars.
ROOMS: 158 en suite (2 fmly) No smoking in 90 bedrooms s £100-£200; d £100-£200 **LB** **FACILITIES:** STV Complimentary use of Livingwell Health Club **CONF:** BC Thtr 250 Class 120 Board 72 Del from £165 **SERVICES:** Lift air con **PARKING:** 120 **NOTES:** No dogs (ex guide dogs) Civ Wed 200 **CARDS:**

★★★★67% **Renaissance Manchester**
Blackfriars St M3 2EQ
☎ 0161 831 6000 ▯ 0161 835 3077
e-mail: rhi.manbr.sales@renaissancehotels.com
Dir: *Follow signs to Deansgate, turn left onto Blackfriars St at 2nd set of lights after Kendals, hotel on right*
This smart hotel enjoys a central location just off Deansgate, within easy walking distance of The Arena and the city's many shops and attractions. Stylish, well-equipped bedrooms are extremely comfortable and those on higher floors offer wonderful views. Public areas include an elegant bar and restaurant and guests have use of a secure car park.
ROOMS: 204 en suite No smoking in 153 bedrooms s £125; d £125 **FACILITIES:** STV Complimentary use of nearby leisure club **CONF:** Thtr 400 Class 300 Board 100 **SERVICES:** Lift air con **PARKING:** 80 **NOTES:** No dogs (ex guide dogs) No smoking in restaurant Civ Wed 400 **CARDS:**

★★★74% ***Malmaison***
Piccadilly M1 3AQ
☎ 0161 278 1000 ▯ 0161 278 1002
e-mail: manchester@malmaison.com
Dir: *follow city centre signs, then signs to Piccadilly station. Hotel opposite station, at bottom of station approach*
Even more chic and stylish following a substantial building programme, the Malmaison now offers extra comfort, a range of bright meeting rooms and some additional air-conditioned bedrooms. Staff demonstrate good standards of customer care throughout this well presented hotel. Good meals are served in the busy brasserie and there is a small but exclusive spa and gym.
ROOMS: 167 en suite **FACILITIES:** STV Sauna Solarium Gym Jacuzzi le petit spa treatment rooms **CONF:** Thtr 80 Class 48 Board 30 **SERVICES:** Lift air con **NOTES:** No dogs (ex guide dogs)
CARDS:

★★★70% **Novotel Manchester Centre**
21 Dickinson St M1 4LX
☎ 0161 235 2200 ▯ 0161 235 2210
e-mail: H3145@accor-hotels.com

Dir: *from Oxford St, into Portland St, left into Dickinson St. Hotel on right*
This smart property enjoys a central location convenient for theatres, shops and Manchester's business district. Spacious bedrooms are extremely well equipped and benefit from air-conditioning. Open plan, contemporary public areas include an all day restaurant and a stylish bar. Extensive conference and meeting facilities are also available.
ROOMS: 164 en suite (60 fmly) No smoking in 123 bedrooms s £99-£119; d £99-£119 **LB** **FACILITIES:** STV Sauna Gym Steam room **CONF:** Thtr 90 Class 50 Board 36 Del from £39 **SERVICES:** Lift air con
CARDS:

★★★68% ***Golden Tulip Manchester***
Waters Reach, Trafford Park M17 1WS
☎ 0161 873 8899 ▯ 0161 872 6556
e-mail: info@goldentulipmanchester.com
Dir: *from A56 turn onto Sir Matt Busby Way past Manchester United Stadium to lights. Hotel on right*
Situated opposite Old Trafford football stadium and within easy reach of the airport and motorway network, this modern establishment is the official hotel of Manchester United. The stylish rooms are spacious and comfortable and include mini-bars and CD players. Rhodes & Co Brasserie and Bar is a fashionable and popular venue in which to enjoy modern British cooking.
ROOMS: 111 en suite (22 fmly) No smoking in 70 bedrooms **FACILITIES:** STV **CONF:** Thtr 120 Class 70 Board 40 **SERVICES:** Lift **PARKING:** 160 **NOTES:** No dogs (ex guide dogs)
CARDS:

★★★68% **Willow Bank Hotel**
340-342 Wilmslow Rd, Fallowfield M14 6AF
☎ 0161 224 0461 ▯ 0161 257 2561
e-mail: willowbankhotel@feathers.uk.com
Dir: *From M60, junct 5 on to A5103, turn left on to B5093. Hotel 2.5m on left*
This popular hotel is conveniently located within three miles of the city centre and close to the universities. Bedrooms vary in style; ; some are traditionally furnished, others have been refurbished and are tastefully appointed. All are well equipped, and the newer rooms benefit from CD players and Playstations. Spacious, elegant public areas include a bar, restaurant, and meeting rooms.
ROOMS: 117 en suite (4 fmly) No smoking in 30 bedrooms s £60-£74; d £74-£109 (incl. bkfst) **LB** **FACILITIES:** STV Xmas **CONF:** Thtr 125 Class 60 Board 70 Del from £100 **PARKING:** 100 **NOTES:** No dogs (ex guide dogs) Civ Wed 125 **CARDS:**

★★★66% **Manchester Conference Centre and Hotel**
Weston Building, Sackville St M1 3BB
☎ 0161 955 8000 ▯ 0161 955 8050
e-mail: weston@umist.ac.uk
Dir: *on Sackville St between Whitworth St & Mancunian Way*
This state-of-the-art conference centre is conveniently located in the heart of the UMIST university buildings. Bedrooms are comfortable and equipped with a range of business-friendly facilities including a high-speed internet connection. Public areas comprise a stylish bar and a spacious restaurant, as well as flexible meeting room provision.
ROOMS: 117 en suite (2 fmly) No smoking in 90 bedrooms s £30-£65; d £55-£75 **CONF:** Thtr 300 Class 100 Board 40 Del £141 **SERVICES:** Lift **PARKING:** 700 **NOTES:** No dogs (ex guide dogs) No smoking in restaurant Closed 23 Dec-3 Jan **CARDS:**

★★★66% **Novotel Manchester West**
Worsley Brow M28 2YA
☎ 0161 799 3535 ▯ 0161 703 8207
e-mail: H0907@accor-hotels.com
(For full entry see Worsley)

★★★65% ***Old Rectory Hotel***
Meadow Ln, Haughton Green, Denton M34 7GD
☎ 0161 336 7516 ▯ 0161 320 3212
e-mail: reservations@oldrectoryhotelmanchester.co.uk

A former Victorian rectory with modern well-appointed bedrooms, set around an enclosed garden in a peaceful location, only a short distance from Manchester. Staff are friendly and helpful, and the attractive restaurant enjoys a good local reputation. There are conference and banqueting facilities, and weddings can also be catered for.
ROOMS: 30 en suite 6 annexe en suite (1 fmly) No smoking in 3 bedrooms **FACILITIES:** STV Gym entertainment **CONF:** Thtr 100 Class 45 Board 50 **PARKING:** 50 **NOTES:** No smoking in restaurant Civ Wed 80 **CARDS:**

★★★63% **Jury's Inn Manchester**
56 Great Bridgewater St M1 5LE
☎ 0161 953 8888 ▯ 0161 953 9090
e-mail: manchester_inn@jurysdoyle.com
Dir: *In city centre next to G-Mex centre and Bridgewater Hall*
Enjoying a prime city centre location, Jury's Inn offers good value, air-conditioned accommodation, ideal for both business travellers and families. Public areas include a smart, spacious lobby, the Inn Pub and Arches Restaurant. There are several convenient car parks with special rates available.
ROOMS: 265 en suite (70 fmly) (16 GF) No smoking in 230 bedrooms s £69; d £69 **FACILITIES:** STV **CONF:** Thtr 50 Class 25 Board 25 Del from £110 **SERVICES:** Lift air con **NOTES:** No dogs (ex guide dogs) Closed 24-26 Dec **CARDS:**

MANCHESTER, continued

★★★62% Waterside
Wilmslow Rd, Didsbury M20 5WZ
☎ 0161 445 0225 📠 0161 446 2090
e-mail: office@watersidehotel.co.uk
Dir: *M56 junct 1, right at 1st lights. Hotel 2nd right turning*
This modern hotel is conveniently located for the motorway network, city centre and the airport. Public areas are spacious and include an exceptionally well-equipped leisure centre. The brasserie and adjacent café bar, overlooking the river, offer a wide choice of meals and snacks. Staff are friendly and helpful.
ROOMS: 46 en suite (1 fmly) (18 GF) No smoking in 27 bedrooms s £55-£85; d £70-£115 (incl. bkfst) **FACILITIES:** STV Indoor swimming (H) Tennis (hard) Sauna Solarium Gym Jacuzzi Beauty salon Xmas **CONF:** Thtr 160 Class 90 Board 56 Del from £70 **PARKING:** 250 **NOTES:** No dogs (ex guide dogs) Civ Wed 150
CARDS:

★★62% Monton House
116-118 Monton Rd, Eccles M30 9HG
☎ 0161 789 7811 📠 0616 787 7609
e-mail: hotel@montonhousehotel.co.uk
Dir: *M602 junct. 2 & join A576, 2nd left onto B5229 (Half Edge Ln) right onto Monton Rd, pass garage on left, hotel 100yds on right*
This modern hotel is conveniently situated for the motorway network, just a short drive from the airport and city centre. The bedrooms are well equipped with many now having been refurbished. The Vienna Grill provides a super choice at dinner and dishes served provide excellent value for money.
ROOMS: 62 en suite (2 fmly) (1 GF) No smoking in 30 bedrooms s £39.50-£55; d £49.50-£60 (incl. bkfst) **LB** **FACILITIES:** STV **CONF:** Thtr 150 Class 50 Board 50 Del from £75 **SERVICES:** Lift **PARKING:** 80 **NOTES:** No dogs (ex guide dogs) Closed Christmas Day after 3pm Civ Wed 100 **CARDS:**

Chesters
730 Chester Rd, Old Trafford M32 0RS
☎ 0161 877 5375 📠 0161 877 5431
e-mail: info@chestershotel.co.uk
Dir: *on A56 immediately in front of Manchester United football ground*
At the time of going to press, the star classification for this hotel was not confirmed. Please refer to the AA internet site www.theAA.com for current information.
ROOMS: 21 en suite (2 fmly) s £70-£85; d £75-£95 (incl. bkfst) **LB** **FACILITIES:** STV **CONF:** Board 12 Del £115 **SERVICES:** Lift **PARKING:** 35 **NOTES:** No dogs (ex guide dogs)
CARDS:

The Mitre
Cathedral Gates M3 1SW
☎ 0161 834 4128 📠 0161 839 1646
e-mail: paul.schnepper@btopenworld.com
Dir: *next to Cathedral*
At the time of going to press, the star classification for this hotel was not confirmed. Please refer to the AA internet site www.theAA.com for current information.
ROOMS: 32 rms (26 en suite) (2 fmly) No smoking in 15 bedrooms s £45; d £70 **CONF:** Thtr 50 Class 50 Board 40 **NOTES:** No dogs (ex guide dogs) **CARDS:**

Town House Hotel
Country House Hotel
Travel Accommodation

Campanile
55 Ordsall Ln, Salford M5 4RS
☎ 0161 833 1845 📠 0161 833 1847
Dir: *M602 to Manchester, then A57. After large rdbt with Sainsbury's on left, left at next traffic lights. Hotel on right*

This modern building offers accommodation in smart, well-equipped bedrooms, all with en suite bathrooms. Refreshments may be taken at the informal Bistro. For further details and the Campanile phone number, consult the Hotel Groups page.
ROOMS: 104 en suite **CONF:** Thtr 50 Class 40 Board 30

Diamond Lodge
Hyde Rd, Belle Vue M18 7BA
☎ 0161 231 0770 📠 0161 231 0660
Dir: *On A57 Manchester E, 2.5m W of M60, junct 24, Manchester orbital*
Offering very good value for this money, this modern lodge provides comfortable accommodation near the city centre, motorway networks and football stadiums. Bright and airy, open plan day rooms include a lounge and a brasserie-style dining room where complimentary continental breakfasts are served. An evening menu is also available.
ROOMS: 85 en suite s £39.50; d £39.50 (incl. cont. bkfst)
CONF: Thtr 30 Class 15 Board 20

See advert on opposite page

Express by Holiday Inn Manchester
Waterfront Quay, Salford Quays M5 2XW
☎ 0161 868 1000 📠 0161 868 1068
e-mail: managersalfordquays@expressholidayinn.co.uk
Dir: *From M602, follow signs for A5063 Trafford Rd, turn right at lights by the Total petrol station onto The Quays, hotel over tram lines*

Express by Holiday Inn

A modern hotel ideal for families and business travellers. Fresh and uncomplicated, the spacious bedrooms include Sky TV, power shower and tea and coffee-making facilities. Continental buffet breakfast is included in the room rate; other meals may be taken

continued

at the nearby family pub or restaurant. For further details and the Express by Holiday Inn phone number, consult the Hotel Groups pages.
ROOMS: 120 en suite s £69; d £69 (incl. cont bkfst)
CONF: Thtr 25 Class 15 Board 15

⇧ Express by Holiday Inn Manchester East

Debdale Park, Hyde Rd M18 7LJ
☎ 0161 231 9900 📠 0161 220 8555
e-mail: manchestereast@oriel-leisure.co.uk
Dir: *3m from Manchester city centre on left of A57 at Debdale Park*

A modern hotel ideal for families and business travellers. Fresh and uncomplicated, the spacious bedrooms include Sky TV, power shower and tea and coffee-making facilities. Continental buffet breakfast is included in the room rate; other meals may be taken at the nearby family pub or restaurant. For further details and the Express by Holiday Inn phone number, consult the Hotel Groups pages.
ROOMS: 97 en suite s £59-£65; d £59-£65 (incl. cont bkfst)
CONF: Thtr 40 Class 30 Board 25

⇧ Hotel Ibis Manchester (Charles Street)

Charles St, Princess St M1 7DL
☎ 0161 272 5000 📠 0161 272 5010
e-mail: H3143@accor-hotels.com
Dir: *M62, towards M602 towards Manchester Centre, follow signs to UMIST(A34)*
Modern, budget hotel offering comfortable accommodation in bright and practical bedrooms. Breakfast is self-service and dinner is available in the restaurant. For further details, consult the Hotel Groups page.
ROOMS: 126 en suite s £39.95-£45.95; d £39.95-£45.95

⇧ Hotel Ibis Manchester (Portland Street)

96 Portland St M1 4GX
☎ 0161 234 0600 📠 0161 234 0610
e-mail: H3142@accor-hotels.com
Modern, budget hotel offering comfortable accommodation in bright and practical bedrooms. Breakfast is self-service and dinner is available in the restaurant. For further details, consult the Hotel Groups page.
ROOMS: 127 en suite s £41.95-£47.95; d £41.95-£47.95

⇧ Premier Lodge (City Centre GMEX 1)

Bishopsgate, 7-11 Lower Mosley St M2 3DW
☎ 0870 9906444 📠 0870 9906445
Premier Lodge offers modern, well-equipped, en suite accommodation suitable for both business and leisure travellers. Meals can be taken at the adjacent popular restaurant and bar, which is fully licensed. For further details, consult the Hotel Groups page.
ROOMS: 147 en suite s £50; d £50

⇧ Premier Lodge (City Centre GMEX 2)

Gaythorne, River St M15 5FJ
☎ 0870 9906504 📠 0870 9906505
Dir: *Adjacent to A57M (Mancunian Way) close to GMEX & Bridgewater Hall on A5103*
Premier Lodge offers modern, well-equipped, en suite accommodation suitable for both business and leisure travellers. Meals can be taken at the adjacent popular restaurant and bar, which is fully licensed. For further details, consult the Hotel Groups page.
ROOMS: 200 en suite s £50; d £50

⇧ Premier Lodge (Manchester City Centre)

North Tower, Victoria Bridge St, Salford M3 5AS
☎ 0870 9906366 📠 0870 9906367
Dir: *off Deansgate near the MEN Arena*
Premier Lodge offers modern, well-equipped, en suite accommodation suitable for both business and leisure travellers. Meals can be taken at the adjacent popular restaurant and bar, which is fully licensed. For further details, consult the Hotel Groups page.
ROOMS: 170 en suite s £50; d £50

⇧ Travel Inn (Manchester City South)

Oxford St M1 4WB
☎ 0870 238 3315 📠 01823 322054
Dir: *M6 junct 19 take 3rd exit onto A556. Join M56, exit junct 3 (A5103) to Medlock St, turn right into Whitworth St, then left into Oxford St & right into Portland St.*
Travel Inn offers good-quality, value-for-money accommodation. Spacious, en suite rooms with bath and shower comfortably

continued on p418

MANCHESTER, continued

accommodate a family of up to two adults and two children (to age 15). The restaurant and bar offers a varied menu. For further details and the Travel Inn phone number, consult the Hotel Groups page.
ROOMS: 226 en suite s £49.95; d £49.95

Travel Inn (Manchester Denton)

Manchester Rd, Denton M34 3SH
☎ 08701 977173 Fax 0161 337 9652
Dir: *M60 junct 24 onto A57 signed Denton. 1st right at traffic lights, right at next lights, Travel Inn on left*
Travel Inn offers good-quality, value-for-money accommodation. Spacious, en suite rooms with bath and shower comfortably accommodate a family of up to two adults and two children (to age 15). The restaurant and bar offers a varied menu. For further details and the Travel Inn phone number, consult the Hotel Groups page.
ROOMS: 40 en suite s £44.95; d £44.95

Travel Inn (Manchester Heaton Park)

Middleton Rd, Crumpsall M8 6NB
☎ 08701 977174 Fax 0161 740 9142
Dir: *off M60 junct 19, ring road east. Take A576 to Manchester through 2 sets of lights. Travel Inn on left*

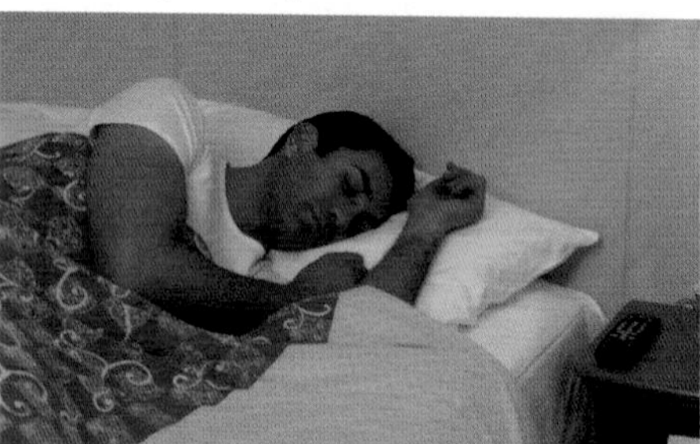

Travel Inn offers good-quality, value-for-money accommodation. Spacious, en suite rooms with bath and shower comfortably accommodate a family of up to two adults and two children (to age 15). The restaurant and bar offers a varied menu. For further details and the Travel Inn phone number, consult the Hotel Groups page.
ROOMS: 45 en suite s £44.95; d £44.95 **CONF:** Thtr 15

Travel Inn (Manchester Salford Quays)

Basin 8 The Quays, Salford Quays M5 3SQ
☎ 08701 977176 Fax 0161 876 0094
Dir: *From M602 (J3) take A5063 on Salford Quays, 1m from Manchester United's stadium.*
Travel Inn offers good-quality, value-for-money accommodation. Spacious, en suite rooms with bath and shower comfortably accommodate a family of up to two adults and two children (to age 15). The restaurant and bar offers a varied menu. For further details and the Travel Inn phone number, consult the Hotel Groups page.
ROOMS: 52 en suite s £44.95; d £44.95

Travel Inn (Manchester Trafford Centre)

Wilderspool Wood, Trafford Centre, Urmston M17 8WW
☎ 08701 977307 Fax 0161 747 4763
Dir: *M60 junct 10 on W side of Manchester*
Travel Inn offers good-quality, value-for-money accommodation. Spacious, en suite rooms with bath and shower comfortably accommodate a family of up to two adults and two children (to age 15). The restaurant and bar offers a varied menu. For further details and the Travel Inn phone number, consult the Hotel Groups page.
ROOMS: 60 en suite s £44.95; d £44.95 **CONF:** Thtr 12

Travelodge (Manchester Central)

Townbury House, Blackfriars St M3 5AB
☎ 08700 850 950
Travelodge offers good quality, good value, modern accommodation. Ideal for families, the spacious, en suite bedrooms include remote-control TV, tea and coffee-making facilities, luxury beds and free morning newspaper. Meals can be taken at the nearby family restaurant. For further details and the Travelodge phone number, consult the Hotel Groups page.
ROOMS: 181 en suite s fr £42.95; d fr £42.95

MANCHESTER AIRPORT, Greater Manchester Map 15 SJ88

See also Altrincham

★★★★70% Radisson SAS Hotel Manchester Airport

Chicago Av M90 3RA
☎ 0161 490 5000 Fax 0161 490 5095
e-mail: sales.airport.manchester@radissonsas.com
Dir: *M56 junct 5, follow signs for Terminal 2. At rdbt 2nd left and follow signs for railway station. Hotel next to station*
This modern hotel is strategically integrated into the airport's terminal system so all three terminals can be accessed quickly by covered, moving walkways. Facilities are excellent and include a well-equipped gym and indoor pool. Bedrooms are air conditioned, thoughtfully equipped and come in a variety of decorative themes: Maritime, Oriental, Scandinavian and Italian. Super views of the runway can be enjoyed in the 'Phileas Fogg' restaurant where a creative international menu is carefully prepared with flair and skill.
ROOMS: 360 en suite (27 fmly) No smoking in 280 bedrooms s £150; d £150 **LB** **FACILITIES:** STV Indoor swimming (H) Sauna Solarium Gym Swimming pool supervised, Health & beauty treatments **CONF:** BC Thtr 350 Class 180 Board 50 Del from £155 **SERVICES:** Lift air con **PARKING:** 250 **NOTES:** No dogs (ex guide dogs)
CARDS:

★★★★69% *Manchester Airport Marriott*

Hale Rd, Hale Barns WA15 8XW
☎ 0161 904 0301 Fax 0161 980 1787
e-mail: manchesterairportmarriott@whitbread.com
With good airport links and convenient access to the thriving city, this sprawling modern hotel is a popular destination. The hotel offers noteworthy leisure and business facilities, a choice of eating and drinking options and secure car parking. Bedrooms are

continued

situated around a courtyard and offer a comprehensive range of facilities.

ROOMS: 142 en suite (22 fmly) No smoking in 100 bedrooms **FACILITIES:** STV Indoor swimming (H) Sauna Gym Jacuzzi **CONF:** Thtr 170 Class 90 Board 50 **SERVICES:** Lift **PARKING:** 480 **NOTES:** No dogs (ex guide dogs) Civ Wed 100
CARDS: 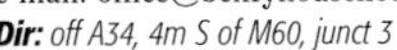

★★★★63% *Belfry House*

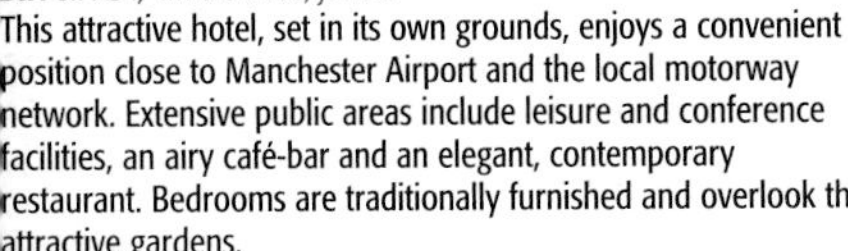

Stanley Rd SK9 3LD
☎ 0161 437 0511 📠 0161 499 0597
e-mail: office@belfryhousehotel.co.uk
Dir: *off A34, 4m S of M60, junct 3*

This attractive hotel, set in its own grounds, enjoys a convenient position close to Manchester Airport and the local motorway network. Extensive public areas include leisure and conference facilities, an airy café-bar and an elegant, contemporary restaurant. Bedrooms are traditionally furnished and overlook the attractive gardens.
ROOMS: 81 en suite (2 fmly) No smoking in 40 bedrooms **FACILITIES:** STV Indoor swimming (H) Sauna Solarium Gym Jacuzzi entertainment **CONF:** Thtr 120 Class 70 Board 50 **SERVICES:** Lift **PARKING:** 150 **NOTES:** No dogs (ex guide dogs) No smoking in restaurant **CARDS:**

★★★74% 🏵🏵 Stanneylands

Stanneylands Rd SK9 4EY
☎ 01625 525225 📠 01625 537282
e-mail: reservations@stanneylandshotel.co.uk
Dir: *from M56 for airport turn off, follow signs to Wilmslow. Left into Station Rd, onto Stanneylands Rd. Hotel on right*

This traditional hotel is being tastefully transformed, thanks to the sympathetic refurbishment of the well-equipped bedrooms and delightful, comfortable day rooms. The cuisine on offer in the restaurant is of a high standard and ranges from traditional

continued

favourites to more imaginative contemporary dishes. Staff throughout are friendly and obliging.
ROOMS: 32 en suite (2 fmly) No smoking in 10 bedrooms s £59-£96; d £82-£110 **LB** **FACILITIES:** STV **CONF:** BC Thtr 100 Class 50 Board 40 Del from £130 **PARKING:** 80 **NOTES:** No dogs (ex guide dogs) Civ Wed 100 **CARDS:**

See advert on this page

★★★72% 🏵 Etrop Grange

Thorley Ln M90 4EG
☎ 0870 609 6123 📠 0161 499 0790
e-mail: etropgrange@corushotels.com
Dir: *M56 junct 5 follow signs for Terminal 2, on slip road to rdbt, take 1st exit. Immediately left and hotel in 400yds*

This Georgian country-house style hotel is close to Terminal 2 but one would never know once inside. Stylish, comfortable bedrooms provide modern comforts and good business facilities. Comfortable, elegant day rooms include the Coach House

continued on p420

MANCHESTER AIRPORT, continued

Restaurant that serves creative, skilfully prepared dishes. A complimentary chauffeured limousine service is provided for guests wishing to connect with flights at the airport.
ROOMS: 64 en suite (10 GF) No smoking in 25 bedrooms s £79-£159; d £99-£179 **LB** **FACILITIES:** STV **CONF:** Thtr 80 Class 35 Board 35 Del from £130 **PARKING:** 80 **NOTES:** No smoking in restaurant RS 25-26 Dec Civ Wed 90 **CARDS:**

★★★66% Bewleys Hotel

Outwood Ln M90 4HL
☎ 0161 498 0333 📠 0161 498 0222
e-mail: man@bewleyshotels.com
Located adjacent to the airport this modern, stylish hotel provides an ideal stop-off for air travellers and business guests alike. All bedrooms are spacious and well equipped and include a wing of recently built superior rooms. Open-plan day rooms extend the contemporary theme.
ROOMS: 226 en suite No smoking in 158 bedrooms s £59; d £59 **FACILITIES:** STV ch fac **CONF:** Thtr 72 Class 40 Board 40 **SERVICES:** Lift **PARKING:** 120 **NOTES:** No dogs (ex guide dogs) **CARDS:**

⌂ Premier Lodge (Manchester Airport North)

PREMIER LODGE

30 Wilmslow Rd SK9 3EW
☎ 0870 9906602 📠 0870 9906603
Premier Lodge offers modern, well-equipped, en suite accommodation suitable for both business and leisure travellers. Meals can be taken at the adjacent popular restaurant and bar, which is fully licensed. For further details, consult the Hotel Groups page.
ROOMS: 35 en suite s £48; d £48

⌂ Travel Inn

travel inn

Finney Ln, Heald Green SK8 3QH
☎ 08701 977178 📠 0161 437 4910
Dir: *M56 junct 5 follow signs to Terminal 1, at rdbt take 2nd exit, at next rdbt follow signs for Cheadle. At lights turn left, then right at next lights*
Travel Inn offers good-quality, value-for-money accommodation. Spacious, en suite rooms with bath and shower comfortably accommodate a family of up to two adults and two children (to age 15). The restaurant and bar offers a varied menu. For further details and the Travel Inn phone number, consult the Hotel Groups page.
ROOMS: 66 en suite s £49.95-£54.95; d £49.95-£54.95

MANSFIELD, Nottinghamshire — Map 16 SK56

★★66% Pine Lodge

281-283 Nottingham Rd NG18 4SE
☎ 01623 622308 📠 01623 656819
e-mail: enquiries@pinelodge-hotel.co.uk
Dir: *on A60 Nottingham to Mansfield road, hotel 1m S of Mansfield*
Located on the edge of Mansfield, this hotel offers welcoming and personal service to its guests, many of whom return time and again. The public rooms include a comfortable lounge bar, a cosy restaurant and a choice of meeting and function rooms. Bedrooms are thoughtfully equipped and a suite is available.
ROOMS: 20 en suite (2 fmly) No smoking in 5 bedrooms **FACILITIES:** STV Sauna **CONF:** Thtr 50 Class 30 Board 35 Del from £88 **PARKING:** 40 **NOTES:** No dogs (ex guide dogs) No smoking in restaurant Closed 25-26 Dec **CARDS:**

★★65% Portland Hall

THE INDEPENDENTS

Carr Bank Park, Windmill Ln NG18 2AL
☎ 01623 452525 📠 01623 452550
e-mail: enquiries@portlandhallhotel.co.uk
Dir: *from town centre take A60 to Worksop for 100yds then right at pelica crossing into Nursery St, Carr Bank Park 50yds on right*
Portland Hall, a former Georgian mansion, sits on the edge of 15 acres of recently renovated parks. The house retains some fine examples of its past, with original plasterwork and friezes in the cosy lounge bar, and around the domed skylight over the spiral stairs. The attractive restaurant proves to be a popular local venue offering a flexible choice of carvery and carte options.
ROOMS: 10 en suite (1 fmly) No smoking in 5 bedrooms **FACILITIES:** STV Bowls Green **CONF:** Thtr 60 Class 30 Board 30 **PARKING:** 100 **NOTES:** No smoking in restaurant Civ Wed 70 **CARDS:**

MARAZION, Cornwall & Isles of Scilly — Map 02 SW53

★★73% ❀ *Mount Haven Hotel & St Michaels Restaurant*

Turnpike Rd TR17 0DQ
☎ 01736 710249 📠 01736 711658
e-mail: reception@mounthaven.co.uk
Dir: *from A30 towards Penzance. At rdbt take exit for Helston onto A394. Next rdbt right into Marazion, hotel on left*

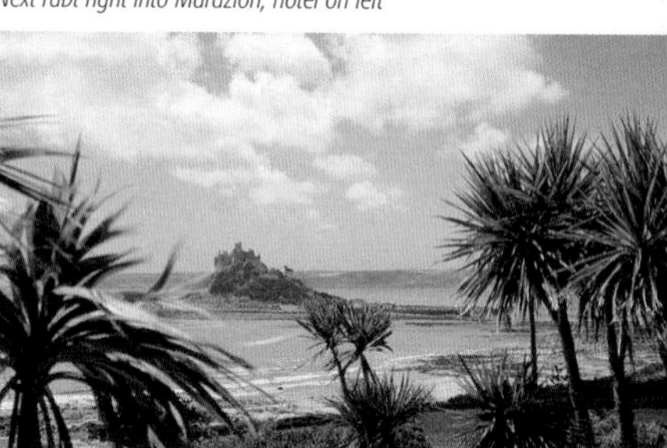

This converted coaching inn provides an enchanting environment from which to enjoy the wonderful views and unique spirituality of St Michael's Mount. Fragrant with incense, the hotel is decorated in contemporary style combined with many distinctive personal touches. Proprietor Orange Trevillion specialises in holistic therapy and the hotel has its own treatment room. There is a stunning sun deck from which to take in the mysteries of the Mount.
ROOMS: 19 en suite (4 fmly) No smoking in 7 bedrooms **FACILITIES:** Aromatherapy reflexology & reiki **CONF:** Thtr 50 Class 30 **PARKING:** 30 **NOTES:** No smoking in restaurant Closed 16 Dec-30 Dec **CARDS:**

★★69% Godolphin Arms

TR17 0EN
☎ 01736 710202 📠 01736 710171
e-mail: enquiries@godolphinarms.co.uk
Dir: *from A30 follow Marazion signs for 1m to hotel. At end of causeway to St Michael's Mount*
This 170-year-old waterside hotel is in a prime location. Stunning views of St Michael's Mount provide a backdrop for the restaurant and lounge bar. Bedrooms are colourful, comfortable and

continued

spacious. A choice of menu is offered in the main restaurant and the Gig Bar, with an emphasis on local seafood.

ROOMS: 10 en suite (2 fmly) (2 GF) s £45-£69.50; d £70-£119 (incl. bkfst) **LB** **FACILITIES:** STV Direct access to large beach **PARKING:** 48 **NOTES:** No smoking in restaurant Closed 24 & 25 Dec
CARDS:

MARCH, Cambridgeshire
Map 12 TL49

★★63% Olde Griffin
High St PE15 9JS
☎ 01354 652517 01354 650086
e-mail: grifhotel@aol.com
Dir: *on A141/142 N of Ely and off A47 E of Peterborough towards Norwich*

Overlooking the town square, this former coaching inn dates back to the 16th century, and retains many period features. Bedrooms vary in size and style and all are appropriately equipped and furnished. Meals are available in the lounge and bar areas, and there is a restaurant for more formal dining.
ROOMS: 21 rms (20 en suite) (1 fmly) s £45; d £59.50 (incl. bkfst) **CONF:** Thtr 100 Class 50 Board 36 **PARKING:** 50 **NOTES:** No smoking in restaurant **CARDS:**

MARGATE, Kent
Map 07 TR37

★★★ *Smiths Court*
Eastern Esplanade, Cliftonville CT9 2HL
☎ 01843 222310
e-mail: info@courthotels.com
ROOMS: 40 rms No smoking in 10 bedrooms **FACILITIES:** Gym entertainment **CONF:** Thtr 80 Class 50 Board 80 **SERVICES:** Lift **PARKING:** 15 **NOTES:** No smoking in restaurant
CARDS:

Travel Inn
Station Green, Marine Ter CT9 5AF
☎ 08701 977182 01843 221453
Dir: *M2 follow A299 then A28 to Margate seafront. Travel Inn adjacent to Margate station, facing sea*
Travel Inn offers good-quality, value-for-money accommodation. Spacious, en suite rooms with bath and shower comfortably accommodate a family of up to two adults and two children (to age 15). The restaurant and bar offers a varied menu. For further details and the Travel Inn phone number, consult the Hotel Groups page.
ROOMS: 44 en suite s £44.95; d £44.95

MARKET DRAYTON, Shropshire
Map 15 SJ63

★★★70% Goldstone Hall
Goldstone TF9 2NA
☎ 01630 661202 01630 661585
e-mail: enquiries@GoldstoneHall.com
Dir: *4m S of Market Drayton off A529 signed Goldstone Hall Gdns. 4m N of Newport signed from A41*

Situated in extensive grounds, this charming period property is a family-run hotel. It provides traditionally furnished, well-equipped accommodation, with some more contemporary artistic touches. Public rooms are extensive and include a choice of lounges, a snooker room and a conservatory. The hotel has a well deserved reputation for good food.
ROOMS: 11 en suite (2 GF) s £70-£95; d £95-£125 (incl. bkfst) **LB** **FACILITIES:** STV Snooker ch fac **CONF:** Thtr 50 Class 30 Board 30 Del £105 **PARKING:** 60 **NOTES:** No dogs (ex guide dogs) No smoking in restaurant Civ Wed 90 **CARDS:**

★★69% Rosehill Manor
Rosehill, Ternhill TF9 2JF
☎ 01630 638532 01630 637008
Dir: *from rdbt at Ternhill A53/41 S towards Newport or M54. Hotel 2m on right*
Parts of this charming, privately owned house, set in mature gardens, date back to the 16th century. The well-equipped accommodation includes family rooms. Public areas comprise of a pleasant restaurant serving award-winning cuisine, a bar and a comfortable lounge. There is also a conservatory, which is available for functions.
ROOMS: 9 en suite (2 fmly) s £53; d £75 (incl. bkfst) **LB** **FACILITIES:** Croquet lawn **PARKING:** 80 **NOTES:** No smoking in restaurant Civ Wed 90 **CARDS:**

MARKET HARBOROUGH, Leicestershire Map 11 SP78

See also Marston Trussell

★★★70% Three Swans

21 High St LE16 7NJ
☎ 01858 466644 🖹 01858 433101
e-mail: sales@threeswans.co.uk
Dir: *take A4304 to Market Harborough. Through town centre on A6 from Leicester, hotel on right*

Public areas in this former coaching inn include an elegant fine dining restaurant and cocktail bar, a smart foyer lounge and popular bar areas. Bedroom styles and sizes vary, all are very well appointed and equipped and the most recently created wing of bedrooms is particularly impressive, offering high quality spacious accommodation.

ROOMS: 18 en suite 43 annexe en suite (8 fmly) No smoking in 32 bedrooms s £55-£75; d £75-£135 (incl. bkfst) **LB FACILITIES:** STV Jacuzzi Xmas **CONF:** Thtr 200 Class 120 Board 120 Del from £105 **SERVICES:** Lift **PARKING:** 100 **NOTES:** No smoking in restaurant Civ Wed 160 **CARDS:**

★★★64% Menzies Angel

37 High St LE16 7NL
☎ 01858 462702 🖹 01858 410464
e-mail: info@menzies-hotels.co.uk
Dir: *M1 junct 20 and follow A427 towards the centre of town*

A former coaching inn on the town's main street, this property has been totally refurbished. Public areas include a smart cheerful brasserie, a separate comfortable lounge and a traditional bar. Bedroom sizes vary; all are furnished to a high standard and have a range of facilities to suit the regular traveller.

ROOMS: 37 en suite **FACILITIES:** Jacuzzi **CONF:** Thtr 24 Class 12 Board 14 Del from £110 **PARKING:** 30 **NOTES:** No smoking in restaurant Civ Wed 75 **CARDS:**

MARKFIELD, Leicestershire Map 11 SK40

Travelodge Leicester Markfield

Littleshaw Ln LE6 0PP
☎ 08700 850 950
Dir: *on A50 from M1, junct 22*

Travelodge offers good quality, good value, modern accommodation. Ideal for families, the spacious, en suite bedrooms include remote-control TV, tea and coffee-making facilities, luxury beds and free morning newspaper. Meals can be taken at the nearby family restaurant. For further details and the Travelodge phone number, consult the Hotel Groups page.

ROOMS: 60 en suite s fr £42.95; d fr £42.95

MARKHAM MOOR, Nottinghamshire Map 17 SK77

Travelodge Retford

DN22 0QU
☎ 08700 850 950 🖹 01777 838091
Dir: *on A1 northbound*

Travelodge offers good quality, good value, modern accommodation. Ideal for families, the spacious, en suite bedrooms include remote-control TV, tea and coffee-making facilities, luxury beds and free morning newspaper. Meals can be taken at the nearby family restaurant. For further details and the Travelodge phone number, consult the Hotel Groups page.

ROOMS: 40 en suite s fr £42.95; d fr £42.95

MARKINGTON, North Yorkshire Map 19 SE26

★★★79% Hob Green

HG3 3PJ
☎ 01423 770031 🖹 01423 771589
e-mail: info@hobgreen.com
Dir: *A61exit 4m after Harrogate. Left at Wormald Green and follow hotel signs*

This hospitable country house nestles amongst 800 acres of beautiful rolling countryside, not far from Harrogate and Ripon. Comfortable lounges boast open fires in cooler months, while the deeply comfortable bedrooms are furnished with antiques and a host of thoughtful extras. The restaurant enjoys a fine reputation and features home-grown produce from the hotel's own gardens.

ROOMS: 12 en suite (1 fmly) s £60-£85; d £100-£115 (incl. bkfst) **LB FACILITIES:** Croquet lawn ch fac Xmas **CONF:** Thtr 15 Class 10 Board 10 Del from £118 **PARKING:** 40 **NOTES:** No smoking in restaurant Civ Wed 30 **CARDS:**

See advert on opposite page

MARLBOROUGH, Wiltshire Map 05 SU16

★★★66% *The Castle & Ball*

High St SN8 1LZ
☎ 01672 515201 🖹 01672 515895
Dir: *A338 and A4 to Marlborough*

This traditional town centre coaching inn has now been upgraded. Bedrooms have been refurbished in a contemporary style and are very well equipped. Open-plan public areas include a comfortable bar/lounge area and a smartly appointed restaurant, which serves food all day.

ROOMS: 34 en suite (1 fmly) No smoking in 13 bedrooms **FACILITIES:** STV **CONF:** Thtr 45 Class 20 Board 30 **PARKING:** 48 **NOTES:** No smoking in restaurant **CARDS:**

MARLOW, Buckinghamshire Map 05 SU88

★★★★76% ◎◎ Danesfield House Hotel & Spa
Henley Rd SL7 2EY
☎ 01628 891010 🖷 01628 890408
e-mail: sales@danesfieldhouse.co.uk
Dir: *2m from Marlow on A4155 towards Henley*

Set in 65 acres of elevated grounds just 45 minutes from central London and 30 minutes from Heathrow, this hotel enjoys spectacular views across the River Thames. Impressive public rooms include the cathedral-like Great Hall, the panelled Oak Room Restaurant and The Orangery, a less formal option for dining. Some bedrooms have balconies and stunning views.
ROOMS: 87 en suite (3 fmly) (27 GF) No smoking in 5 bedrooms s £155-£270; d £185-£305 (incl. bkfst) **LB FACILITIES: Spa** STV Indoor swimming (H) Tennis (hard) Snooker Sauna Solarium Gym Croquet lawn Putting green Jogging trail, Steam room, Hydrotherapy room, Treatment rooms entertainment Xmas **CONF:** Thtr 100 Class 60 Board 50 Del from £265 **SERVICES:** Lift **PARKING:** 100 **NOTES:** No dogs (ex guide dogs) No smoking in restaurant Civ Wed 100
CARDS:

See advert on this page

★★★★67% ◎◎ The Compleat Angler
Marlow Bridge SL7 1RG
☎ 0870 400 8100 🖷 01628 486388
e-mail: compleatangler@macdonald-hotels.co.uk
Dir: *M4 J8/9, A404 to rdbt, Bisham exit, 1m to Marlow Bridge, hotel on right*

MACDONALD HOTELS

This well-established hotel enjoys a wonderful setting overlooking the River Thames and the Marlow weir. Bedrooms, varying in size and style, are all individually decorated and comfortable. Dining

continued on p424

M

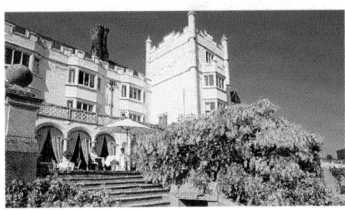

MARLOW, continued

choices include a cosy bar, informal brassiere-style restaurant and the award winning Riverside restaurant.
ROOMS: 64 en suite (6 GF) No smoking in 22 bedrooms s £228-£258; d £248-£495 **LB FACILITIES:** STV Fishing Croquet lawn Boating, Fly fishing and course fishing Xmas **CONF:** Thtr 120 Class 65 Board 36 Del £260 **SERVICES:** Lift **PARKING:** 60 **NOTES:** No smoking in restaurant Civ Wed 120 **CARDS:**

See advert on opposite page

MARSDEN, West Yorkshire Map 16 SE01

★★69% Hey Green Country House

Waters Rd HD7 6NG
☎ 01484 844235 01484 847605
e-mail: info@heygreen.com
Dir: *off A62 1m outside village, towards Manchester.*
This grand Victorian house is set in extensive landscaped gardens. Bedrooms are spacious and well equipped, public areas include many original features and a modern conservatory, and the brasserie serves a wide choice of carefully prepared dishes. The Standedge Visitor Centre and the restored Huddersfield Canal are close by.
ROOMS: 12 en suite No smoking in 6 bedrooms s £55-£60; d £90-£110 (incl. bkfst) **LB FACILITIES:** STV Xmas **CONF:** Thtr 100 Class 80 Board 50 Del £90 **PARKING:** 70 **NOTES:** No smoking in restaurant RS 2-3 Jan Civ Wed 150 **CARDS:**

MARSTON MORETAINE, Bedfordshire Map 11 SP94

Travelodge Bedford South West

Travelodge

Beancroft Rd Junction MK43 0PZ
☎ 08700 850 950 01234 766755
Dir: *on A421, northbound*
Travelodge offers good quality, good value, modern accommodation. Ideal for families, the spacious, en suite bedrooms include remote-control TV, tea and coffee-making facilities, luxury beds and free morning newspaper. Meals can be taken at the nearby family restaurant. For further details and the Travelodge phone number, consult the Hotel Groups page.
ROOMS: 54 en suite s fr £42.95; d fr £42.95

MARSTON TRUSSELL, Northamptonshire Map 11 SP68

★★71% The Sun Inn

Main St LE16 9TY
☎ 01858 465531 01858 433155
e-mail: manager@suninn.com
Dir: *M1 junct 20 take A4304. After Theddingworth, right to Marston Trussell. Hotel on right*
This pleasant inn successfully combines a mixture of modern facilities and accommodation with the classical traditions of the rural English inn. Bedrooms are comfortably furnished and tastefully appointed, offering a host of thoughtful facilities. Public areas consist of two elegant dining areas and a bar, popular with locals; service is both friendly and attentive.
ROOMS: 20 en suite (1 fmly) (10 GF) No smoking in 10 bedrooms s £69; d £69 (incl. bkfst) **FACILITIES:** Rambling trails **CONF:** Thtr 60 Class 40 Board 28 **PARKING:** 60 **NOTES:** No dogs (ex guide dogs) Closed 24 Dec-5 Jan **CARDS:**

> Popped the question?
> Hotels with Civ Wed in their entry are licensed for civil wedding ceremonies. Maximum numbers for the ceremony only are shown, e.g. Civ Wed 120

MARTINHOE, Devon Map 03 SS64

★★75% The Old Rectory Country House

EX31 4QT
☎ 01598 763368 01598 763567
e-mail: reception@oldrectoryhotel.co.uk
Dir: *M5 junct 27 onto A361, right onto A399 Blackmoor Gate and right onto A39 bypass Parracombe. 2nd left to Martinhoe and follow signs*

Originally built in the 1800s for the local rector, this peaceful hideaway is an ideal base for exploring Exmoor and is just 500 yards from the coastal footpath. In addition to the comfortable lounges, guests can relax in the vinery, overlooking the delightful gardens. Interesting menus are served in the spacious dining room. Prices include breakfast, afternoon tea and dinner. Bedrooms, two on the ground floor, are tastefully decorated and a self-catering cottage is also available.
ROOMS: 8 en suite (2 GF) No smoking in all bedrooms s £77-£97; d £124-£164 (incl. bkfst & dinner) **LB PARKING:** 8 **NOTES:** No dogs No children 14yrs No smoking in restaurant Closed Nov-Feb RS Mar **CARDS:**

MARTOCK, Somerset Map 04 ST41

★★★72% The Hollies

Bower Hinton TA12 6LG
☎ 01935 822232 01935 822249
e-mail: info@thehollieshotel.com
Dir: *on B3165 S of town centre off A303, take Bower Hinton slip road & follow hotel signs*
Within easy access of the A303, the bar and restaurant of this popular venue are housed in an attractive 17th-century farmhouse. Bar meals are available in addition to the interesting carte menu. Located at the rear of the property in a purpose-built wing, the spacious, well-equipped bedrooms include both suites and mini-suites.
ROOMS: 33 annexe en suite (2 fmly) (30 GF) No smoking in 10 bedrooms s £65-£70; d £75-£115 (incl. bkfst) **LB FACILITIES:** STV **CONF:** BC Thtr 150 Class 80 Board 60 Del £95 **PARKING:** 80 **NOTES:** No dogs (ex guide dogs) No smoking in restaurant RS Xmas & New Year **CARDS:**

MASHAM, North Yorkshire Map 19 SE28

Top 200 - Hotel

★★★★ Swinton Park

HG4 4JH
☎ 01765 680900 01765 680901
e-mail: enquiries@swintonpark.com
Dir: *A1 onto B6267 to Masham & Thirsk. Follow signs through town centre & turn right onto Swinton Terrace. 1m past GC over bridge, up hill. Hotel is on right*
Extended during the Victorian and Edwardian eras, the

continued

original part of this welcoming castle dates from the 17th century. Bedrooms are luxuriously furnished and come with a host of thoughtful extras, such as CD players. Samuel's restaurant (built by the current owner's great-great-great grandfather) features local produce, much of it from the Swinton estate.

ROOMS: 30 en suite No smoking in all bedrooms s £100-£350; d £100-£350 (incl. bkfst) **LB FACILITIES: Spa** STV Golf 9 Fishing Riding Snooker Gym Croquet lawn Putting green Jacuzzi Shooting, Falconry, Pony Trekking Xmas **CONF:** Thtr 120 Class 60 Board 40 Del £170 **SERVICES:** Lift **PARKING:** 50 **NOTES:** No smoking in restaurant Civ Wed 120 **CARDS:**

★★67% *The Kings Head*

Market Place HG4 4EF
☎ 01765 689295 01765 689070
Dir: *off A6108 Ripon to Leyburn road in centre of village*

This historic, stone-built hotel, with its uneven floors, beamed bars and attractive window boxes, looks out over the large Market Square. Bedrooms are elegantly furnished, thoughtfully equipped and continue to reflect the high standards of a refurbishment. There is a popular bar and smart restaurant.

ROOMS: 10 en suite **CONF:** Thtr 40 Class 20 Board 20 **NOTES:** No dogs (ex guide dogs) **CARDS:**

MATFEN, Northumberland — Map 21 NZ07

★★★74% Matfen Hall

NE20 0RH
☎ 01661 886500 01661 886055
e-mail: info@matfenhall.com
Dir: *off A69 to B6318. Hotel just before village*

This fine mansion house is set in landscaped parkland overlooking the golf course. Bedrooms present a variety of styles - standard, superior and luxury. There is a splendid drawing room and the Library Restaurant, both boasting carved wood fire surrounds and plaster relief ceilings. Don't leave without visiting the magnificent Great Hall. New conference and leisure facilities opening in Spring 2004.

continued

ROOMS: 31 en suite (5 fmly) No smoking in 18 bedrooms s £97.50-£137.50; d £135-£225 (incl. bkfst) **LB FACILITIES:** STV Golf 18 Putting green Xmas **CONF:** Thtr 100 Class 60 Board 40 Del from £130 **PARKING:** 150 **NOTES:** No smoking in restaurant Civ Wed 120 **CARDS:**

MATLOCK, Derbyshire — Map 16 SK35

★★★77% Riber Hall

DE4 5JU
☎ 01629 582795 01629 580475
e-mail: info@riber-hall.co.uk
Dir: *1m off A615 at Tansley*

This beautiful Elizabethan manor house enjoys an idyllic location in charming grounds overlooking Matlock. Beautifully furnished, thoughtfully equipped bedrooms, many with oak four-poster beds,

continued on p426

MATLOCK, continued

are situated round a delightful courtyard with its own fountain. Tastefully appointed public rooms are furnished with period and antique pieces and an impressive wine list complements the imaginative cuisine.
ROOMS: 3 en suite 11 annexe en suite No smoking in 4 bedrooms s £101-£116; d £136-£182 (incl. cont bkfst) **LB** **FACILITIES:** STV Tennis (hard) Croquet lawn **CONF:** Thtr 20 Class 20 Board 20 Del £148 **PARKING:** 50 **NOTES:** No children 10yrs No smoking in restaurant Civ Wed 45 **CARDS:**

See advert on opposite page

★★★69% New Bath

New Bath Rd DE4 3PX
☎ 0870 400 8119 📠 01629 580268
e-mail: general.newbath@macdonaldhotels.co.uk

MACDONALD HOTELS

Dir: *M1 junct 28 to Alfreton, follow Matlock then Matlock Bath signs. Hotel on A6 just after Matlock Bath on right*

Set in five acres of grounds in the beautiful Derwent Gorge, the hotel has indoor and outdoor pools fed by natural thermal springs, the medicinal properties of which were first recognised in Regency times. Bedrooms are tastefully furnished and decorated, two rooms have four-poster beds, and some have balconies.
ROOMS: 55 en suite (5 fmly) No smoking in 45 bedrooms s £65-£98; d £90-£123 **LB** **FACILITIES:** Indoor swimming (H) Outdoor swimming Tennis (hard) Sauna Solarium Outdoor pool supervised Xmas **CONF:** Thtr 180 Class 60 Board 50 Del from £120 **PARKING:** 200 **NOTES:** No smoking in restaurant Civ Wed 50
CARDS:

★★74% The Red House Country Hotel

Old Rd, Darley Dale DE4 2ER
☎ 01629 734854 📠 01629 734885
e-mail: enquiries@TheRedHouseCountryHotel.co.uk
Dir: *off A6 onto Old Rd signed Carriage Museum, 2.5m N of Matlock*

A peaceful country hotel with many original architectural features, set in delightful Victorian gardens just outside Matlock. Rich colour schemes are used to excellent effect throughout. Well-equipped bedrooms include three ground floor rooms in the adjacent coach house. A comfortable lounge with delightful rural views is available for refreshments and pre-dinner drinks; service is friendly and attentive.
ROOMS: 7 en suite 3 annexe en suite (1 fmly) No smoking in 8 bedrooms s £60-£65; d £90 (incl. bkfst) **LB** **CONF:** Thtr 40 Class 24 Board 24 Del £95 **PARKING:** 15 **NOTES:** No dogs (ex guide dogs) No smoking in restaurant **CARDS:**

MAWGAN PORTH, Cornwall & Isles of Scilly Map 02 SW86

★★72% Tredragon

TR8 4DQ
☎ 01637 860213 📠 01637 860269
e-mail: tredragon@btinternet.com
Dir: *From Newquay Airport follow signs to Mawgan Porth, past beach, up hill & left turn at sign*

This hotel enjoys a glorious, unspoilt location with direct footpath access to the award-winning beach just below. Its owners have made stylish improvements including the Sundowner Terrace. Both the restaurant's cuisine and views are delightful. The hotel attracts a large following of repeat custom and offers themed residential courses.
ROOMS: 26 en suite (15 fmly) s £40-£64; d £65-£98 (incl. bkfst) **LB** **FACILITIES:** Indoor swimming (H) Sauna ch fac Xmas **CONF:** Thtr 50 Class 30 Board 25 Del from £65 **PARKING:** 30 **NOTES:** No smoking in restaurant **CARDS:**

MAWNAN SMITH, Cornwall & Isles of Scilly Map 02 SW72

★★★★72% Budock Vean-The Hotel on the River

TR11 5LG
☎ 01326 252100 & 0800 833927 📠 01326 250892
e-mail: relax@budockvean.co.uk
Dir: *from A39 follow tourist signs to Trebah Gardens. Hotel 0.5m*

Set in 65 acres of attractive grounds, this peaceful hotel offers an impressive range of facilities. Convenient for visiting the Helford River Estuary and many local gardens, or simply as a tranquil base for a leisure break, This hotel offers friendly and attentive service.

continued

Bedrooms are spacious and offer a choice of styles; some overlook the grounds.
ROOMS: 57 en suite (2 fmly) No smoking in 6 bedrooms s £99-£157.50; d £132-£210 (incl. bkfst & dinner) **LB FACILITIES:** STV Indoor swimming (H) Golf 9 Tennis (hard) Fishing Snooker Putting green Natural health spa Powerboat entertainment ch fac Xmas **CONF:** Thtr 60 Class 40 Board 30 Del from £150 **SERVICES:** Lift **PARKING:** 100 **NOTES:** No smoking in restaurant Closed 3 wks Jan Civ Wed 80
CARDS:

See advert on this page

★★★78% Meudon

TR11 5HT
☎ 01326 250541 01326 250543
e-mail: wecare@meudon.co.uk
Dir: *from A39 at Hillhead rdbt, follow signs to Maenporth beach. Hotel on left 1m after beach*

This charming late Victorian mansion, with its friendly hospitality, attentive service and impressive nine acres of gardens leading

continued on p428

MAWNAN SMITH, continued

down to a private beach, provides a relaxing place to stay. Bedrooms are comfortable and spacious and cuisine features the best of local Cornish produce served in the conservatory restaurant.

ROOMS: 29 en suite (2 fmly) (15 GF) s £80-£110; d £160-£210 (incl. bkfst & dinner) **LB** **FACILITIES:** Fishing Riding Private beach, Hair salon, Yacht for skippered charter ch fac Xmas **CONF:** Thtr 30 Class 20 Board 15 Del from £80 **SERVICES:** Lift **PARKING:** 52 **NOTES:** No smoking in restaurant Closed 3-31 Jan **CARDS:**

See advert under FALMOUTH

★★★67% *Trelawne*

TR11 5HS
☎ 01326 250226 01326 250909
Dir: *A39 to Falmouth, right at Hillhead rdbt signed Maenporth. Past beach, up hill and hotel on left*

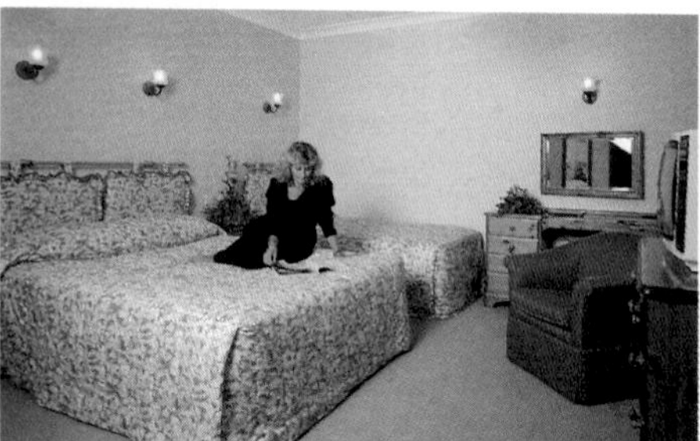

The Trelawne is surrounded by attractive lawns and gardens, and enjoys superb coastal views. An informal atmosphere prevails, and many guests return year after year. Bedrooms, many with sea views are of varying size. Dinner features quality local produce and imaginative dishes.

ROOMS: 14 en suite (2 fmly) **FACILITIES:** Indoor swimming (H) **PARKING:** 20 **NOTES:** No smoking in restaurant Closed 23 Dec-12 Feb **CARDS:**

See advert on page 427

MELKSHAM, Wiltshire — Map 04 ST96

★★70% Shaw Country

Bath Rd, Shaw SN12 8EF
☎ 01225 702836 & 790321 01225 790275
e-mail: info@shawcountryhotel.fsnet.co.uk
Dir: *1m from Melksham, 9m from Bath on A365*

Located within easy driving of both Bath and the M4, this hotel sits in wonderfully kept gardens. The house boasts some very well-appointed bedrooms, a comfortable lounge and bar and the Mulberry Restaurant, where a wide selection of well-cooked meals is available. A warm and friendly approach by the staff is offered throughout the stay.

ROOMS: 13 en suite (2 fmly) s £48-£72; d £68-£87 (incl. bkfst) **LB** **FACILITIES:** Jacuzzi ch fac **CONF:** Thtr 30 Class 20 Board 15 **PARKING:** 30 **NOTES:** No smoking in restaurant Closed 26-27 Dec & 1 Jan **CARDS:**

Restaurant with Rooms

Conigre Farm Hotel

Semington Rd SN12 6BZ
☎ 01225 702229 01225 707392
e-mail: enq@cfhotel.co.uk
Dir: *off A350 onto Semington Rd, hotel 0.5m on left after fire station*

This stone-built, 17th-century former farmhouse is a comfortable and friendly place to stay. Imaginative menus have a French influence and feature fresh and local produce, organic wherever possible. The well-furnished bedrooms are comfortable; one room boasts a four-poster bed.

ROOMS: 2 en suite 6 annexe en suite (1 fmly) No smoking in 6 bedrooms **FACILITIES:** STV **CONF:** Thtr 45 Board 25 **PARKING:** 15 **NOTES:** No smoking in restaurant Closed 26 Dec-12 Jan **CARDS:**

MELTON MOWBRAY, Leicestershire — Map 11 SK71

Top 200 - Hotel

★★★★ Stapleford Park

Stapleford LE14 2EF
☎ 01572 787522 01572 787651
e-mail: reservations@stapleford.co.uk
Dir: *1m SW of B676, 4m E of Melton Mowbray and 9m W of Colsterworth*

This stunning mansion, dating back to 14th century, sits in over 500 acres of beautiful grounds. Spacious, sumptuous public rooms include a choice of lounges and an elegant restaurant; an additional brasserie-style restaurant is located in the stunning new golf complex. In addition the hotel boasts a wonderful spa and gymnasium, a golf course, horse riding

continued

and many other country pursuits. Bedrooms are individually styled and furnished to a high standard.
ROOMS: 44 en suite 8 annexe en suite No smoking in 44 bedrooms s £205-£681.50; d £205-£681.50 (incl. bkfst) **LB FACILITIES:** STV Indoor swimming (H) Golf 18 Tennis (hard) Fishing Riding Sauna Solarium Gym Croquet lawn Putting green Jacuzzi Archery, Croquet, Falconry, Horse Riding, Petanque, Shooting entertainment ch fac Xmas **CONF:** BC Thtr 200 Class 140 Board 80 Del from £225 **SERVICES:** Lift **PARKING:** 120 **NOTES:** No smoking in restaurant Civ Wed 150 **CARDS:**

★★★72% **Sysonby Knoll**
Asfordby Rd LE13 0HP
☎ 01664 563563 📠 01664 410364
e-mail: reception@sysonby.co.uk
Dir: *0.5m from town centre beside A6006*
This well-established hotel is located towards the edge of town and is set within attractive gardens. A friendly and relaxed atmosphere prevails with the many return guests treated like old friends. Bedrooms, including superior rooms in an annexe, are generally spacious and thoughtfully equipped. Public areas include a cosy bar, choice of lounges and smart restaurant.
ROOMS: 23 en suite 7 annexe en suite (1 fmly) (6 GF) No smoking in 5 bedrooms s £57-£72; d £69-£89 (incl. bkfst) **LB FACILITIES:** STV Fishing Croquet lawn **CONF:** Thtr 30 Class 16 Board 24 Del £90 **PARKING:** 48 **NOTES:** No smoking in restaurant Closed 25 Dec-1 Jan **CARDS:**

See advert on this page

★★★65% ***Quorn Lodge***
46 Asfordby Rd LE13 0HR
☎ 01664 566660 & 562590 📠 01664 480660
e-mail: quornlodge@aol.com
Dir: *from town centre take A6006. Hotel 300yds from junct of A606/A607 on right*
Centrally located, this smart hotel offers a comfortable, welcoming atmosphere. Bedrooms are individually decorated and thoughtfully designed. The public rooms consist of a bright restaurant overlooking the garden, a cosy lounge bar and a modern function suite. High standards are maintained throughout and extensive parking is a bonus.
ROOMS: 19 en suite (2 fmly) No smoking in 13 bedrooms
FACILITIES: STV **CONF:** Thtr 90 Class 60 Board 85 **PARKING:** 33
NOTES: No dogs No smoking in restaurant
CARDS:

See advert on page 431

MEMBURY MOTORWAY SERVICE AREA (M4), Berkshire

Map 05 SU37

Days Inn
Membury Service Area RG17 7TZ
☎ 01488 72336 📠 01488 72336
e-mail: membury.hotel@welcomebreak.co.uk
Dir: *M4 between junct 14&15*
This modern building offers accommodation in smart, spacious and well-equipped bedrooms, suitable for families and business travellers, and all with en suite bathrooms. Continental breakfast is available and other refreshments may be taken at the nearby family restaurant. For further details and the Days Inn phone number, consult the Hotel Groups page.
ROOMS: 38 en suite s £49-£55; d £49-£55 **CONF:** Board 10

MERIDEN, West Midlands Map 10 SP28

★★★★72% ® Marriott Forest of Arden Hotel & Country Club

Marriott HOTELS · RESORTS · SUITES

Maxstoke Ln CV7 7HR
☎ 0870 400 7272 🖷 0870 400 7372
Dir: *M42 junct 6 onto A45 towards Coventry, over Stonebridge flyover. After 0.75m left into Shepherds Ln. Hotel 1.5m on left*
The ancient oaks, rolling hills and natural lakes of the 10,000 acre Forest of Arden estate provide an idyllic backdrop for this modern hotel and country club. The hotel boasts an excellent range of leisure facilities and is regarded as one of the finest golfing destinations in the UK. Bedrooms provide every modern convenience and a full range of facilities.
ROOMS: 214 en suite (4 fmly) (65 GF) No smoking in 135 bedrooms s £100-£172; d £130-£172 **LB FACILITIES: Spa** STV Indoor swimming (H) Golf 18 Tennis (hard) Fishing Sauna Solarium Gym Croquet lawn Putting green Jacuzzi Health & Beauty salon, Swimming pool supervised, Floodlit golf academy Xmas **CONF:** Thtr 300 Class 180 Board 40 Del from £149 **SERVICES:** Lift air con **PARKING:** 300 **NOTES:** No smoking in restaurant Civ Wed 150 **CARDS:**

★★★74% ®® Manor
Main Rd CV7 7NH
☎ 01676 522735 🖷 01676 522186
e-mail: reservations@manorhotelmeriden.co.uk
Dir: *M42 junct 6 take A45 towards Coventry then A452, signed Leamington. At rbt join B4102, signed Meriden, for hotel on left.*
A sympathetically extended Georgian manor in the heart of this sleepy village, a few minutes away from the M6, M42 and National Exhibition Centre. The Regency Restaurant offers modern dishes, while the Triumph Buttery serves lighter meals and snacks. Bedroom styles vary considerably; the Executive rooms and those in the Princess Diana wing are very smart and well equipped.
ROOMS: 110 en suite (20 GF) No smoking in 54 bedrooms s £80-£140; d £90-£175 (incl. bkfst) **LB CONF:** Thtr 250 Class 150 Board 60 Del from £110 **SERVICES:** Lift **PARKING:** 200 **NOTES:** No smoking in restaurant RS 24 Dec-2 Jan Civ Wed 150
CARDS:

M

MEVAGISSEY, Cornwall & Isles of Scilly Map 02 SX04

★★69% Tremarne
Polkirt PL26 6UL
☎ 01726 842213 🖷 01726 843420
e-mail: info@tremarne-hotel.co.uk
Dir: *from A390 at St Austell take B3273 to Mevagissey. Follow Portmellon signs through Mevagissey, at top of Polkirt Hill turn right*

This relaxing, family-run hotel is ideal for those exploring this beautiful area or visiting the nearby Eden Project. Many of the

continued

thoughtfully equipped bedrooms have views across the countryside to the sea beyond, one room has the added bonus of a balcony. The friendly team of staff make every effort to ensure a comfortable and enjoyable stay for everyone and the prevailing atmosphere is both convivial and welcoming. Public areas include a bar, well-appointed restaurant and spacious lounge.
ROOMS: 14 en suite (2 fmly) No smoking in all bedrooms s £40-£45; d £75-£85 **LB FACILITIES:** Outdoor swimming (H) Xmas **PARKING:** 1
NOTES: No dogs (ex guide dogs) No children 5yrs No smoking in restaurant Closed Nov-Feb **CARDS:**

★★65% Spa Hotel
Polkirt Hill PL26 6UY
☎ 01726 842244 🖷 01726 842244
e-mail: Alan@the-spa-hotel.fsnet.co.uk
Dir: *from St Austell follow Mevagissey then Portmellon signs. Sign for hotel on right*
Quietly situated in an elevated position, this family-run hotel offers a genuine and friendly welcome with wonderful coastal and countryside views an added bonus. A wide choice of bedrooms is available, all of which are light, airy and attractively decorated, some having patio areas leading onto well-tended gardens. A comfortable, cane-furnished lounge and a cosy bar are provided.
ROOMS: 11 en suite (5 fmly) No smoking in 7 bedrooms
FACILITIES: Putting green **PARKING:** 12 **NOTES:** No smoking in restaurant **CARDS:**

MEXBOROUGH, South Yorkshire Map 16 SE4

★★63% Pastures
Pastures Rd S64 0JJ
☎ 01709 577707 🖷 01709 577795
e-mail: sales@pastures-hotel.co.uk
Dir: *0.5m from town centre on A6023, left by ATS Tyres, signed Denaby Ings & Cadeby. Hotel on right*
This hotel has a modern, purpose built block of bedrooms and a separate lodge building where food is served. It is in a rural setting beside a working canal and convenient for the Earth Centre, Doncaster, or the Dearne Valley with its nature reserves and leisure centre. Bedrooms are quiet, comfortable and equipped with most modern facilities.
ROOMS: 29 en suite (6 fmly) (14 GF) No smoking in 21 bedrooms s fr £39.95; d fr £39.95 **FACILITIES:** STV **CONF:** Thtr 250 Class 170 Board 100 Del £99 **SERVICES:** Lift **PARKING:** 155 **NOTES:** No dogs (ex guide dogs) Civ Wed 200 **CARDS:**

MICHAEL WOOD MOTORWAY SERVICE AREA (M5), Gloucestershire Map 04 ST7

⌂ Days Inn

DAYS INN

Michaelwood Service Area, M5 Northbound, Lower Wick GL11 6DD
☎ 01454 261513 🖷 01454 269150
e-mail: michaelwood.hotel@welcomebreak.co.uk
Dir: *M5 northbound between junct 13 and 14*
This modern building offers accommodation in smart, spacious and well-equipped bedrooms, suitable for families and business travellers, and all with en suite bathrooms. Continental breakfast is available and other refreshments may be taken at the nearby family restaurant. For further details and the Days Inn phone number, consult the Hotel Groups page.
ROOMS: 38 en suite s £45-£50; d £45-£50 **CONF:** Board 10

MIDDLEHAM, North Yorkshire Map 19 SE18

★78% Waterford House
Kirkgate DL8 4PG
☎ 01969 622090 📠 01969 624020
e-mail: info@waterfordhousehotel.co.uk
Dir: *From N take A1. Turn right onto A684 to Leyburn, then take A6108 to Middleham. From S take B6267 via Masham*
This delightful establishment is located in an attractive period house, just off the village square. Furnished with antiques, china and silver, its warm, restful atmosphere is enhanced by genuinely friendly service. Individually styled bedrooms are equipped with thoughtful extras such as sherry and home-made shortbread.
ROOMS: 5 en suite (2 fmly) No smoking in all bedrooms s £50-£60; d £75-£95 (incl. bkfst) **LB** **FACILITIES:** Xmas **PARKING:** 7 **NOTES:** No dogs (ex guide dogs) No children 5 yrs No smoking in restaurant
CARDS:

MIDDLETON, Greater Manchester Map 16 SD80

Premier Lodge (Manchester North)
818 Manchester Old Rd, Rhodes M24 4RF
☎ 0870 9906406 📠 0870 9906407
PREMIER LODGE
Premier Lodge offers modern, well-equipped, en suite accommodation suitable for both business and leisure travellers. Meals can be taken at the adjacent popular restaurant and bar, which is fully licensed. For further details, consult the Hotel Groups page.
ROOMS: 42 en suite s £48; d £48

MIDDLETON STONEY, Oxfordshire Map 11 SP52

★★70% Jersey Arms
OX25 4AD
☎ 01869 343234 📠 01869 343565
Best Western
e-mail: jerseyarms@bestwestern.co.uk
Dir: *on B430 10m N of Oxford, between junct 9 & 10 of M40*
With a history dating back to the 13th century, the Jersey Arms combines old-fashioned charm with contemporary style and elegance. The individually designed bedrooms are well equipped and comfortable. The lounge has an open fire, and the spacious restaurant provides a calm atmosphere in which to enjoy the hotel's popular cuisine.
ROOMS: 6 en suite 14 annexe en suite (3 fmly) No smoking in 6 bedrooms s fr £84; d fr £96 (incl. bkfst) **LB** **FACILITIES:** Xmas **CONF:** Board 20 Del from £125 **PARKING:** 55 **NOTES:** No dogs (ex guide dogs) No smoking in restaurant
CARDS:

MIDDLE WALLOP, Hampshire Map 05 SU23

★★★70% *Fifehead Manor*
SO20 8EG
☎ 01264 781565 📠 01264 781400
e-mail: fifeheadmanorhotel@ukonline.co.uk
Dir: *M3 junct 8 onto A303 to Andover. A343 S for 6m to Middle Wallop*
This 11th-century manor house retains many of its original features. Bedrooms are comfortably furnished, well-equipped and feature many thoughtful touches. Public areas include a well-stocked bar, elegant lounge and charming restaurant, which
continued on p432

MIDDLE WALLOP, continued

offers a high standard of cuisine. Service is attentive from the friendly team of staff.
ROOMS: 8 en suite 8 annexe en suite **FACILITIES:** STV Croquet lawn ch fac **CONF:** Thtr 40 Class 20 Board 24 **PARKING:** 40 **NOTES:** No dogs (ex guide dogs) No smoking in restaurant Civ Wed 84
CARDS:

MIDDLEWICH, Cheshire

Map 15 SJ76

Travelodge

M6 Junction 18, A54 CW10 0JB
☎ 08700 850 950
Travelodge offers good quality, good value, modern accommodation. Ideal for families, the spacious, en suite bedrooms include remote-control TV, tea and coffee-making facilities, luxury beds and free morning newspaper. Meals can be taken at the nearby family restaurant. For further details and the Travelodge phone number, consult the Hotel Groups page.
ROOMS: 32 en suite s fr £42.95; d fr £42.95

MIDHURST, West Sussex

Map 06 SU82

★★★72% The Angel

North St GU29 9DN
☎ 01730 812421 01730 815928
e-mail: info@theangelmidhurst.co.uk
Dir: *on S side of A272 in centre of Midhurst*
Dating back in parts to the 15th century, this charming hotel offers a relaxed and homely atmosphere. Bedrooms are tastefully and individually presented with some, including a room suitable for less able guests, situated in an adjacent annexe. Public areas boast a cosy bar complete with log fire and an elegant brasserie, and a new bistro is planned.
ROOMS: 24 en suite 4 annexe en suite (2 GF) s £80-£115; d £110-£150 (incl. bkfst) **LB** **FACILITIES:** STV entertainment Xmas **CONF:** Thtr 70 Class 40 Board 30 Del from £125 **PARKING:** 60 **NOTES:** No smoking in restaurant Civ Wed 60 **CARDS:**

★★★68% Southdowns Country

Dumpford Ln, Trotton GU31 5JN
☎ 01730 821521 01730 821790
e-mail: reception@southdownshotel.com
Dir: *on A272, after town turn at Keepers Arms*

Ideal for a relaxing break, this private hotel enjoys a secluded location with views over the Sussex countryside. It is a popular choice for weddings, due to its setting and spacious public areas. Some of the comfortable bedrooms overlook the grounds. Meals are available in the bar and in the more formal restaurant, which focuses on local produce.
ROOMS: 22 en suite (2 fmly) (2 GF) No smoking in 12 bedrooms s £60-£100; d £80-£120 (incl. bkfst) **LB** **FACILITIES:** Indoor swimming (H) Tennis (hard) Sauna Solarium Croquet lawn Exercise equipment Xmas **CONF:** Thtr 100 Class 30 Board 30 Del from £85 **PARKING:** 70 **NOTES:** No children 10yrs No smoking in restaurant Civ Wed 100
CARDS:

See advert under PETERSFIELD

★★77% *Park House*

Bepton GU29 0JB
☎ 01730 812880 01730 815643
Dir: *from centre of Midhurst, take B2226 to Bepton. Hotel 2m on left*
Set in attractive mature grounds in peaceful rural surroundings this charming country house hotel has now been extended. Bedrooms are very comfortable and well equipped, and the smart public rooms include an elegant drawing room, honesty bar and dining room. A small team of staff provide attentive and friendly service.
ROOMS: 19 rms (17 en suite) (2 fmly) **FACILITIES:** STV Outdoor swimming (H) Golf 9 Tennis (grass) Croquet lawn Putting green **CONF:** Thtr 50 Class 50 Board 25 **PARKING:** 35
CARDS:

MIDSOMER NORTON, Somerset

Map 04 ST65

★★★71% Centurion

Charlton Ln BA3 4BD
☎ 01761 417711 01761 418357
e-mail: enquiries@centurionhotel.co.uk
Dir: *off A367, 10m S of Bath*

This family-run hotel incorporates the adjacent Fosseway Country Club with its 9-hole golf course and other extensive leisure amenities. Comfortable bedrooms are equipped and furnished to a high standard with co-ordinating fabrics. Public areas include a choice of bars, an attractive lounge and a range of meeting/function rooms.
ROOMS: 44 en suite (4 fmly) (18 GF) No smoking in all bedrooms s fr £68; d fr £90 (incl. bkfst) **LB** **FACILITIES:** **Spa** STV Indoor swimming (H) Golf 9 Sauna Gym Jacuzzi Bowling green Sports field **CONF:** Thtr 180 Class 70 Board 50 **PARKING:** 100 **NOTES:** No dogs (ex guide dogs) No smoking in restaurant Closed 24-1 Jan Civ Wed 80
CARDS:

MILDENHALL, Suffolk

Map 12 TL77

★★★76% @@ Riverside

THE CIRCLE
Selected Individual Hotels
GREAT BRITAIN

Mill St IP28 7DP
☎ 01638 717274 📠 01638 715997
e-mail: bookings@riverside-hotel.net

Dir: *from A11 at Fiveways rdbt take A1101 in Mildenhall Town. Left at mini rdbt along High St. Hotel last building on left before bridge*

An 18th-century red brick building situated in the heart of this charming town centre on the banks of the River Lark. Public rooms include a smart restaurant, which overlooks the river and the attractive gardens to the rear. The smartly decorated bedrooms have co-ordinated soft furnishings and many thoughtful touches.

ROOMS: 18 en suite 11 annexe en suite (4 fmly) **FACILITIES:** Fishing Sauna Gym Jacuzzi turkish steam room entertainment **CONF:** Thtr 150 Class 60 Board 40 **SERVICES:** Lift **PARKING:** 80 **NOTES:** Civ Wed 150 **CARDS:**

★★★66% The Smoke House

Best Western

Beck Row IP28 8DH
☎ 01638 713223 📠 01638 712202
e-mail: enquiries@smoke-house.co.uk

Dir: *A1101 into Mildenhall, follow Beck Row signs. Hotel after mini rdbt through Beck Row on right*

This extended 16th-century inn is just a short drive from the town centre and ideally placed for touring the Suffolk countryside. Public areas have been sympathetically restored to retain much of their original character and the spacious bedrooms are attractively decorated and well equipped. Facilities include a shopping mall.

ROOMS: 94 en suite 2 annexe en suite (96 GF) s £85-£125; d £110-£155 (incl. bkfst) **LB FACILITIES:** entertainment Xmas **CONF:** Thtr 120 Class 80 Board 50 Del from £85 **PARKING:** 100 **NOTES:** No dogs (ex guide dogs) No smoking in restaurant **CARDS:**

See advert on this page

MILFORD ON SEA, Hampshire

Map 05 SZ29

Top 200 - Hotel

★★★ @@ Westover Hall

Park Ln SO41 0PT
☎ 01590 643044 📠 01590 644490
e-mail: info@westoverhallhotel.com

Dir: *M3 & M27 W onto A337 to Lymington. Follow signs to Milford on Sea onto B3058. Hotel outside village centre towards cliffs*

Just a few moments' walk from the beach and boasting uninterrupted views across Christchurch Bay to the Isle of Wight in the distance, this late-Victorian mansion offers a relaxed, informal atmosphere together with friendly efficient

continued

standards of hospitality and service. Each of the bedrooms have been decorated with flair and style. Architectural delights include dramatic stained-glass windows, extensive oak panelling and a galleried entrance hall. The cuisine prepared with much care and attention to detail.

ROOMS: 12 en suite (1 fmly) No smoking in all bedrooms s £90-£120; d £145-£200 (incl. bkfst) **LB FACILITIES:** Beach Hut Xmas **CONF:** Thtr 35 Class 20 Board 20 Del £135 **PARKING:** 50 **NOTES:** No children 5 yrs No smoking in restaurant Civ Wed 50 **CARDS:**

See advert under LYMINGTON

Town House Hotel
Country House Hotel
Travel Accommodation

MILFORD ON SEA, continued

★★★73% South Lawn

Lymington Rd SO41 0RF
☎ 01590 643911 📠 01590 644820
e-mail: enquiries@southlawn.co.uk
Dir: *left off A337 at Everton onto B3058. Hotel 0.5m on right*

Peacefully located, this former dower house offers attentive and friendly service. The hotel is situated close to the sea and is set in four acres of well-tended grounds. Bedrooms are spacious, include welcome extras and are attractively decorated; many enjoy delightful views over the garden. The bright dining room serves a varied range of carefully prepared dishes using local produce.
ROOMS: 24 en suite (3 GF) No smoking in all bedrooms s £65; d £110 (incl. bkfst) **LB FACILITIES:** Xmas **PARKING:** 60 **NOTES:** No dogs No children 7yrs No smoking in restaurant Closed 30 Dec-18 Jan
CARDS:

See advert under LYMINGTON

MILTON COMMON, Oxfordshire — Map 05 SP60

★★★★76% The Oxford Belfry

OX9 2JW
☎ 01844 279381 📠 01844 279624
e-mail: oxfordbelfry@marstonhotels.com
Dir: *M40 junct 7 onto A329 to Thame. Left onto A40 by Three Pigeons pub. Hotel 300yds on right*
This modern hotel has a relatively rural location and enjoys lovely views of the countryside to the rear. The hotel is built around two very attractive courtyards and has a number of lounges and conference rooms, as well as indoor leisure facilities and outdoor tennis courts. Bedrooms are large and feature a range of extras.
ROOMS: 130 en suite (10 fmly) No smoking in 72 bedrooms s fr £108; d fr £130 **LB FACILITIES:** STV Indoor swimming (H) Tennis (hard) Sauna Solarium Gym Croquet lawn Xmas **CONF:** Thtr 300 Class 180 Board 100 Del £170 **SERVICES:** Lift **PARKING:** 250 **NOTES:** No dogs (ex guide dogs) No smoking in restaurant Civ Wed 250
CARDS:

MILTON KEYNES, Buckinghamshire — Map 11 SP83

See also Aspley Guise & Flitwick

★★★70% Courtyard by Marriott Milton Keynes

London Rd, Newport Pagnell MK16 0JA
☎ 01908 613688 📠 01908 617335
e-mail: general.miltonkeynes@whitbread.com
Dir: *M1 J14, follow signs for A509 (Newport Pagnell), hotel 0.5m on right*
This busy hotel, previously a Georgian coach house, enjoys a pleasant rural location yet is only minutes from the motorway, town centre and local attractions. Bedrooms are furnished with at least one double bed and some also have sofa beds. Public rooms include a modern bar and conservatory restaurant over looking the courtyard.

ROOMS: 50 en suite (1 fmly) (22 GF) No smoking in 26 bedrooms s £106-£112; d £106-£112 **LB FACILITIES:** STV Gym **CONF:** Thtr 200 Class 90 Board 50 Del from £128 **PARKING:** 200 **NOTES:** No dogs (ex guide dogs) No smoking in restaurant Civ Wed 100
CARDS:

★★★70% Novotel Milton Keynes

Saxon St, Layburn Court, Heelands MK13 7RA
☎ 01908 322212 📠 01908 322235
e-mail: H3272@accor-hotels.com
Dir: *M1 junct 14, follow Childsway signs towards city centre. Turn right into Saxon Way, continue straight across all rdbts to hotel on left*
Contemporary in style, this recently opened, purpose-built hotel is situated on the outskirts of town, a few minutes' drive from the centre and mainline railway station. Bedrooms provide ample workspace and a good range of facilities for the modern traveller, and public rooms include a children's play area and indoor leisure centre.
ROOMS: 124 en suite (40 fmly) (40 GF) No smoking in 105 bedrooms s £109; d £109 **LB FACILITIES:** STV Indoor swimming (H) Sauna Gym Steam bath **CONF:** Thtr 120 Class 75 Board 40 Del £149 **SERVICES:** Lift air con **PARKING:** 130 **NOTES:** Civ Wed 60
CARDS:

★★★63% Quality Hotel & Suites Milton Keynes

Monks Way, Two Mile Ash MK8 8LY
☎ 01908 561666 📠 01908 568303
e-mail: admin@gb616.u-net.com
Dir: *junct of A5/A422*
Bedrooms at this purpose-built hotel are particularly well-equipped, having extra phones and mini-bars. There are also a number of suites with fax machines and kitchenettes. Eating options include an all-day room and lounge service in addition to the restaurant.
ROOMS: 88 en suite (15 fmly) No smoking in 44 bedrooms s £28-£110; d £30-£120 **LB FACILITIES:** STV Indoor swimming (H) Sauna Solarium Gym Jacuzzi Steam room, Whirlpool spa **CONF:** Thtr 120 Class 50 Board 50 Del from £120 **PARKING:** 200 **NOTES:** No dogs (ex guide dogs) No smoking in restaurant Civ Wed 90
CARDS:

★★68% Different Drummer

94 High St, Stony Stratford MK11 1AH
☎ 01908 564733 📠 01908 260646
e-mail: info@hoteldifferentdrummer.co.uk
This attractive hotel located on the high street in historic Stony Stratford offers a genuine welcome to its guests. The oak-panelled restaurant is a popular dining venue and enjoys a good local reputation, thanks to the imaginative menus and skilful cooking.

continued

Bedrooms are generally spacious and well-equipped. The comfortable lounge incorporates a bar.

ROOMS: 15 en suite 8 annexe en suite (2 fmly) (3 GF) No smoking in 14 bedrooms s £49-£120; d £55-£120 (incl. bkfst) **NOTES:** No dogs (ex guide dogs) **CARDS:**

★★68% Swan Revived

THE INDEPENDENTS

High St, Newport Pagnell MK16 8AR
☎ 01908 610565 📠 01908 210995
e-mail: swanrevived@btinternet.com
Dir: *M1 junct 14 onto A509 B526 into Newport Pagnell. Hotel on High St*

Once a coaching inn this hotel dates from 17th century occupying a prime location in the centre of town. Well-appointed bedrooms are spacious, individually styled and have good levels of comfort. Public areas include a popular public bar and a restaurant offering a variety of freshly prepared dishes.
ROOMS: 42 en suite (2 fmly) s £50-£84; d £68-£98 (incl. bkfst) **LB**
FACILITIES: STV **CONF:** Thtr 70 Class 30 Board 28 Del £115
SERVICES: Lift **PARKING:** 18 **NOTES:** No smoking in restaurant RS 25 Dec-1 Jan Civ Wed 75 **CARDS:**

U *Holiday Inn Milton Keynes*

Holiday Inn HOTELS · RESORTS

500 Saxon Gate West MK9 2HQ
☎ 0870 400 9057 📠 01908 674714
e-mail: reservations-miltonkeynes@ichotelsgroup.com
Dir: *M1 junct 14 over 7 rdbts, right at 8th. Hotel on left*
At the time of going to press, the classification for this hotel was not confirmed. Please refer to the AA internet site www.theAA.com for current information.
ROOMS: 157 en suite No smoking in 79 bedrooms **FACILITIES:** STV Indoor swimming (H) Sauna Solarium Gym Health & fitness centre entertainment **CONF:** Thtr 150 Class 85 Board 35 **SERVICES:** Lift **PARKING:** 80 **NOTES:** No dogs (ex guide dogs)
CARDS:

> TV dinner?
> Room service at three stars and above

⌂ *Campanile*

Campanile

40 Penn Rd, Fenny Stratford, Bletchley MK2 2AU
☎ 01908 649819 📠 01908 649818
Dir: *M1 junct 14, follow A4146 to A5. Southbound on A5. 4th exit at 1st rdbt to Fenny Stratford. Hotel 500yds on left*

This modern building offers accommodation in smart, well-equipped bedrooms, all with en suite bathrooms. Refreshments may be taken at the informal Bistro. For further details and the Campanile phone number, consult the Hotel Groups page.
ROOMS: 80 en suite **CONF:** Thtr 40 Class 30 Board 25

⌂ Express by Holiday Inn

Express by Holiday Inn

Eastlake Park, Tongwell St, Fox Milne MK15 0YA
☎ 01908 681000 📠 01908 609429
e-mail: exhimiltonkeynes@aol.com
Dir: *M1 junct 14 follow sign for centre, at rdbt Northfields, straight across dual carriageway (Childs Way H6) follow signs to Fox Milne 3rd exit V11 & Northfield*

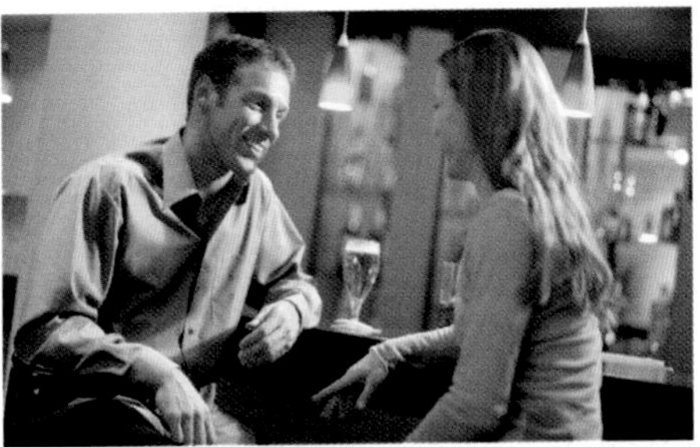

A modern hotel ideal for families and business travellers. Fresh and uncomplicated, the spacious bedrooms include Sky TV, power shower and tea and coffee-making facilities. Continental buffet breakfast is included in the room rate; other meals may be taken at the nearby family pub or restaurant. For further details and the Express by Holiday Inn phone number, consult the Hotel Groups pages.
ROOMS: 119 en suite s £50-£75; d £50-£75 (incl. cont bkfst)
CONF: Thtr 65 Class 38 Board 30 Del from £102

⌂ Premier Lodge (Central)

Shirwell Crescent, Furzton MK4 1GA
☎ 0870 9906396 📠 0870 9906397
Dir: *M1 junct 14, onto A509 to Milton Keynes. At 9th 'North Grafton' rdbt left onto V6. Right at Leadenhall rdbt onto H7. Over 'The Bowl' rdbt*
Premier Lodge offers modern, well-equipped, en suite accommodation suitable for both business and leisure travellers. Meals can be taken at the adjacent popular restaurant and bar, which is fully licensed. For further details, consult the HotelGroups page.
ROOMS: 120 en suite s £49.95-£50; d £49.95-£50

M

MILTON KEYNES, continued

⌂ Premier Lodge (Milton Keynes South)

Bletcham Way, Caldecotte MK7 8HP
☎ 0870 9906558 📠 0870 9906559
Dir: *M1 junct 14, A509 to Milton Keynes. 1st rdbt take A4146, left at 2nd rdbt, over 3rd rdbt and right at 4th. Lodge over next rdbt on right*
Premier Lodge offers modern, well-equipped, en suite accommodation suitable for both business and leisure travellers. Meals can be taken at the adjacent popular restaurant and bar, which is fully licensed. For further details, consult the Hotel Groups page.
ROOMS: 40 en suite s £50; d £50 **CONF:** Board 10

⌂ Travel Inn (Milton Keynes Central)

Secklow Gate West MK9 3BZ
☎ 08701 977184 📠 01908 607481
Dir: *from M1 junct 14 follow H6 route over 6 rdbts, at 7th (called Sth Secklow) turn right, Travel Inn on left*
Travel Inn offers good-quality, value-for-money accommodation. Spacious, en suite rooms with bath and shower comfortably accommodate a family of up to two adults and two children (to age 15). The restaurant and bar offers a varied menu. For further details and the Travel Inn phone number, consult the Hotel Groups page.
ROOMS: 38 en suite s £52.95-£54.95; d £52.95-£54.95 **CONF:** Thtr 16

⌂ Travel Inn (Milton Keynes East)

Willen Lake, Brickhill St MK15 9HQ
☎ 08701 977185 📠 01908 678561
Dir: *M1 junct 14 follow H6 Childsway. Turn right at 3rd rdbt into Brickhill St. Right at 1st mini rdbt, Travel Inn 1st left*
Travel Inn offers good-quality, value-for-money accommodation. Spacious, en suite rooms with bath and shower comfortably accommodate a family of up to two adults and two children (to age 15). The restaurant and bar offers a varied menu. For further details and the Travel Inn phone number, consult the Hotel Groups page.
ROOMS: 41 en suite s £44.95; d £44.95

⌂ Travelodge

109 Grafton Gate MK9 1AL
☎ 08700 850 950
Travelodge offers good quality, good value, modern accommodation. Ideal for families, the spacious, en suite bedrooms include remote-control TV, tea and coffee-making facilities, luxury beds and free morning newspaper. Meals can be taken at the nearby family restaurant. For further details and the Travelodge phone number, consult the Hotel Groups page.
ROOMS: 80 en suite s fr £42.95; d fr £42.95

⌂ Travelodge Milton Keynes North (Old Stratford)

Old Stratford Roundabout MK19 6AQ
☎ 08700 850 950 📠 01908 561 698
Dir: *On A5 towards Towcester, Travelodge on A508/A422 rdbt*
Travelodge offers good quality, good value, modern accommodation. Ideal for families, the spacious, en suite bedrooms include remote-control TV, tea and coffee-making facilities, luxury beds and free morning newspaper. Meals can be taken at the nearby family restaurant. For further details and the Travelodge phone number, consult the Hotel Groups page.
ROOMS: 33 en suite s fr £42.95; d fr £42.95

MINEHEAD, Somerset — Map 03 SS9

★★★67% *Northfield*

Northfield Rd TA24 5PU
☎ 01643 705155 📠 01643 707715
e-mail: reservations@northfield-hotel.co.uk
Dir: *M5 junct 23, follow A38 to Bridgwater and join A39 to Minehead*
Located conveniently close to the town centre and the seafront, this hotel is set in delightfully maintained gardens and has a loyal, regular following. A range of comfortable sitting rooms and leisure facilities, including an indoor, heated pool are provided. A fixed price menu is served every evening in the oak-panelled dining room. The attractively co-ordinated bedrooms vary in size and are equipped to a good standard.
ROOMS: 28 en suite (7 fmly) **FACILITIES:** STV Indoor swimming (H) Gym Putting green Jacuzzi Steam room **CONF:** Thtr 70 Class 45 Board 30 **SERVICES:** Lift **PARKING:** 44 **NOTES:** No smoking in restaurant
CARDS:

★★74% Alcombe House

Bircham Rd, Alcombe TA24 6BG
☎ 01643 705130 📠 01643 705130
e-mail: alcombe.house@virgin.net
Located mid way between Minehead and Dunster, this Grade II listed Georgian Hotel offers a delightful combination of efficient service delivered a friendly manner by the very welcoming resident proprietors. Public areas include a comfortable lounge and a candlelit dining room serving an enjoyable range of carefully prepared local produce.
ROOMS: 7 en suite No smoking in all bedrooms s £37; d £45 (incl. bkfst) **LB FACILITIES:** entertainment Xmas **PARKING:** 9 **NOTES:** No children 15yrs No smoking in restaurant **CARDS:**

MONK FRYSTON, North Yorkshire — Map 16 SE52

★★★70% Monk Fryston Hall

LS25 5DU
☎ 01977 682369 📠 01977 683544
e-mail: reception@monkfryston-hotel.com
Dir: *A1/A63 junct towards Selby. In centre of Monk Fryston*
This delightful 16th-century mansion house enjoys a peaceful location in 30 acres of grounds, yet is only minutes' drive from the A1. Many original features have been retained and the public rooms are furnished with antique and period pieces. Bedrooms are individually styled and thoughtfully equipped for both business and leisure guests.
ROOMS: 30 en suite (3 fmly) No smoking in 20 bedrooms s £88-£110; d £112-£160 (incl. bkfst) **LB FACILITIES:** STV Croquet lawn Xmas **CONF:** Thtr 50 Class 20 Board 20 Del £133 **PARKING:** 80 **NOTES:** No smoking in restaurant Civ Wed 58 **CARDS:**

MORCOTT, Rutland — Map 11 SK90

⌂ Travelodge Uppingham

Uppingham LE15 8SA
☎ 08700 850 950 📠 01572 747719
Dir: *on A47, eastbound*
Travelodge offers good quality, good value, modern accommodation. Ideal for families, the spacious, en suite bedrooms include remote-control TV, tea and coffee-making facilities, luxury beds and free morning newspaper. Meals can be taken at the nearby family restaurant. For further details and the Travelodge phone number, consult the Hotel Groups page.
ROOMS: 40 en suite s fr £42.95; d fr £42.95

MORDEN, Greater London
See LONDON SECTION plan 1 D1

Travelodge London Wimbledon
Epsom Rd SM4 5PH
☎ 08700 850 950 📠 020 8640 8227
Dir: *on A24*
Travelodge offers good quality, good value, modern accommodation. Ideal for families, the spacious, en suite bedrooms include remote-control TV, tea and coffee-making facilities, luxury beds and free morning newspaper. Meals can be taken at the nearby family restaurant. For further details and the Travelodge phone number, consult the Hotel Groups page.
ROOMS: 32 en suite s fr £42.95; d fr £42.95

MORECAMBE, Lancashire — Map 18 SD46

★★★66% Clarendon
76 Marine Rd West, West End Promenade LA4 4EP
☎ 01524 410180 📠 01524 421616
e-mail: clarendon@mitchellshotels.co.uk
Dir: *M6 junct 34 follow Morecambe signs. At rdbt with 'The Shrimp' on corner 1st exit to Westgate, follow to seafront. Right at traffic lights, hotel 3rd block along*
This seafront hotel was completely refurbished a few years ago. Well maintained throughout, it offers bright cheerful public areas and smartly appointed bedrooms all with fully tiled bathrooms.
ROOMS: 29 en suite (4 fmly) No smoking in 10 bedrooms s £70; d £90 (incl. bkfst) **LB FACILITIES:** Xmas **CONF:** Thtr 90 Class 40 Board 40 Del from £64 **SERVICES:** Lift **PARKING:** 22
CARDS:

★★★66% Strathmore
East Promenade LA4 5AP
☎ 01524 421234 📠 01524 414242
e-mail: info@strathmore-hotel.co.uk
Dir: *from Lancaster on A589 to Morecambe. 3rd rdbt follow Promenade signs. On coast road turn left and hotel on left*
This smart hotel enjoys a seafront location and has benefited from a total refurbishment of bedrooms and public areas. Rooms are smartly and brightly decorated and public areas, overlooking Morecambe Bay, include a bright airy restaurant and spacious lounge bar, both offering a wide selection of dishes. In addition the hotel boasts spacious function facilities.
ROOMS: 50 en suite (3 fmly) No smoking in 34 bedrooms s £50-£65; d £90-£120 (incl. bkfst) **LB FACILITIES:** STV Xmas **CONF:** Thtr 180 Class 100 Board 50 Del from £65 **SERVICES:** Lift **PARKING:** 19 **NOTES:** No smoking in restaurant Civ Wed 100
CARDS:

★★★62% *Elms*
Bare Village LA4 6DD
☎ 01524 411501 📠 01524 831979
This long-established hotel lies just off the North Promenade and is popular with business and leisure guests. Public rooms include a spacious lounge bar, a classical style restaurant, function facilities and a pub in the grounds. Many bedrooms have been upgraded.
ROOMS: 40 en suite (3 fmly) **CONF:** Thtr 200 Class 72 Board 60 **SERVICES:** Lift **PARKING:** 80 **NOTES:** No smoking in restaurant Civ Wed 100 **CARDS:**

> Popped the question?
> Hotels with Civ Wed in their entry are licensed for civil wedding ceremonies. Maximum numbers for the ceremony only are shown, e.g. Civ Wed 120

MORETON, Merseyside — Map 15 SJ28

★★★68% Leasowe Castle
Leasowe Rd CH46 3RF
☎ 0151 606 9191 📠 0151 678 5551
e-mail: reservations@leasowecastle.com
Dir: *M53 junct 1, 1st exit from rdbt, then take A551. Hotel 0.75m on right*

Partly dating back to 1592, this hotel was built to allow the owner to watch horseracing on the sands. Many impressive features remain, including ornately carved wall panels and a ceiling brought from the Palace of Westminster. Bedrooms are well equipped and comfortable. The beamed bar offers a range of meals and there is also a more formal restaurant.
ROOMS: 47 en suite (3 fmly) No smoking in 3 bedrooms s £70; d £80-£90 (incl. bkfst) **LB FACILITIES:** Water sports Sea Fishing Sailing Xmas **CONF:** Thtr 400 Class 200 Board 40 **SERVICES:** Lift **PARKING:** 200 **NOTES:** No dogs (ex guide dogs) Civ Wed 200
CARDS:

MORETONHAMPSTEAD, Devon — Map 03 SX78

★★★★70% ® Le Meridien Manor House
TQ13 8RE
☎ 01647 445000 📠 01647 440961
e-mail: reception.centreuk@lemeridien.com
Dir: *2m from Moretonhampstead towards Princetown on B3212*
Set within 270 acres of magnificent grounds and with stunning views of the surrounding Dartmoor countryside, this Jacobean-style mansion offers a range of country pursuits ranging from angling to a championship golf course. Bedrooms are particularly spacious and many enjoy superb views. The style of the house has been maintained in the comfortable lounges and public areas.
ROOMS: 61 en suite 19 annexe en suite (5 fmly) s fr £80; d fr £120 (incl. bkfst) **LB FACILITIES:** STV Golf 18 Tennis (hard) Fishing Croquet lawn Putting green clay pigeon shooting Xmas **CONF:** Thtr 100 Class 50 Board 40 Del from £125 **SERVICES:** Lift **PARKING:** 100 **NOTES:** No smoking in restaurant Civ Wed 100
CARDS:

MORETON-IN-MARSH, Gloucestershire — Map 10 SP23

★★★73% ®® Manor House
High St GL56 0LJ
☎ 01608 650501 📠 01608 651481
e-mail: bookings@cotswold-inns-hotels.co.uk
Dir: *off A429 at south end of the town*
Dating back to the 16th century, this charming Cotswold coaching inn retains much of its original character with stone walls, impressive fireplaces and a relaxed, country-house atmosphere. Bedrooms vary in size and reflect the individuality of the building,

continued on p438

MORETON-IN-MARSH, continued

all are well equipped and some are particularly opulent. Public rooms are comfortable and smartly presented with additional facilities including a heated indoor pool.
ROOMS: 35 en suite 3 annexe en suite (3 fmly) No smoking in 4 bedrooms s £119-£250; d £135-£250 (incl. bkfst) **LB FACILITIES: Spa** Indoor swimming (H) Croquet lawn Putting green Jacuzzi Xmas **CONF:** Thtr 120 Class 48 Board 56 Del from £145 **SERVICES:** Lift **PARKING:** 24 **NOTES:** No smoking in restaurant Civ Wed 120 **CARDS:**

★★★70% **Redesdale Arms**
High St GL56 0AW
☎ 01608 650308 📠 01608 651843
e-mail: info@redesdalearmsmoreton.co.uk
Dir: *on A429, 1km from train station, free shuttle bus*
This fine old inn has played a central role in this picturesque town for centuries. Extensive refurbishment has sensitively combined the traditional features with contemporary comforts and the resulting mix proves highly successful. Bedrooms are split between the main building and the former stables, all of which reflect high standards of comfort and quality. Cuisine is a focal point here and guests can choose to dine either in the stylish restaurant or in the conservatory.
ROOMS: 14 en suite No smoking in all bedrooms s £56-£65; d £65-£85 (incl. bkfst) **FACILITIES:** STV Xmas **CONF:** Thtr 50 Class 65 Board 45 **PARKING:** 14 **NOTES:** No dogs (ex guide dogs) No smoking in restaurant **CARDS:**

★★63% ***White Hart Royal***
High St GL56 0BA
☎ 01608 650731 📠 01608 650880
Dir: *on A429 in town centre*
This Cotswold coaching inn dates back to the 17th century and once provided a hiding place for Charles I. Much of the original character has been retained with flagstone floors, a cobbled entrance hall and a feature fireplace. Bedrooms are brightly decorated and comfortably appointed.
ROOMS: 19 en suite (2 fmly) **FACILITIES:** STV **CONF:** Thtr 80 **PARKING:** 20 **NOTES:** No smoking in restaurant
CARDS:

MORLEY, West Yorkshire — Map 19 SE22

★★67% **The Old Vicarage**
Bruntcliffe Rd LS27 0JZ
☎ 0113 253 2174 📠 0113 253 3549
e-mail: oldvicarage@btinternet.com
Dir: *M62 junct 27, A650 towards Wakefield. Hotel on left adjacent to St Andrews Church*
A warm welcome awaits guests at this extended Victorian vicarage. The bedrooms are split between the main house and modern extension; all offer a range of extra facilities. There is a cosy lounge with honesty bar; hearty meals are served in the pleasant dining room. Private parking is provided.
ROOMS: 21 en suite (1 fmly) No smoking in 14 bedrooms s £36-£50; d £57-£64 (incl. bkfst) **LB FACILITIES:** Access to park with football, tennis & basketball **CONF:** Board 15 Del from £65 **PARKING:** 21 **NOTES:** No dogs (ex guide dogs) No smoking in restaurant Closed 24-26 Dec RS 1 Jan **CARDS:**

MORPETH, Northumberland — Map 21 NZ1

★★★73% **Linden Hall**
NE65 8XF
☎ 01670 500000 📠 01670 500001
e-mail: stay@lindenhall.co.uk
(For full entry see Longhorsley)

MORTEHOE, Devon — Map 03 SS4

★★66% **Lundy House Hotel**
Chapel Hill EX34 7DZ
☎ 01271 870372 📠 01271 871001
e-mail: info@lundyhousehotel.co.uk
Dir: *A361 to Braunton and Ilfracombe. Woolacombe exit at rdbt. In village right along esplanade, up hill to Mortehoe, hotel on left*
Facing south across the rugged North Devon coastline to Lundy Island in the distance, this personally run hotel offers a warm, friendly welcome. In the dining room, honest home cooking is served; vegetarians are particularly well catered for. Very much a 'dog-friendly' hotel, there is direct access to the coastal path from the hotel's terraced gardens.
ROOMS: 9 en suite (4 fmly) No smoking in all bedrooms s £35; d £50 (incl. bkfst) **LB PARKING:** 9 **NOTES:** No smoking in restaurant Closed Nov-Mar **CARDS:**

MOUSEHOLE, Cornwall & Isles of Scilly — Map 02 SW42

★★70% **Old Coastguard Hotel**
The Parade TR19 6PR
☎ 01736 731222 📠 01736 731720
e-mail: bookings@oldcoastguardhotel.co.uk
Dir: *A30 to Penzance, coast road to Newlyn then Mousehole. 1st building on left on entering village*

A place to relax and unwind, whilst enjoying magnificent views and good food. The staff here are friendly and offer good service. Bedrooms, most with magnificent sea views, and some with private balconies, are bright and stylish. A meal in the restaurant, or in summer months, al fresco on the terrace, offers fresh local produce with fish fresh from the nearby Newlyn markets.
ROOMS: 14 en suite 7 annexe en suite (2 fmly) s £35-£72; d £80-£100 (incl. bkfst) **LB FACILITIES:** Sub- tropical garden **PARKING:** 12 **NOTES:** No smoking in restaurant Closed 25 Dec RS Nov-Mar **CARDS:**

Restaurant with Rooms

The Cornish Range Restaurant with Rooms
6 Chapel St TR19 6SB
☎ 01736 731488 01736 732173
e-mail: info@cornishrange.co.uk
Dir: *from Penzance, through Newlyn. In village follow road, keeping harbour on left. After S-bend, on right*

This charming restaurant-with-rooms is a memorable place to eat and stay. Comfortable, stylish rooms, with delightful Cornish handmade furnishings, and attentive, friendly service create a relaxing environment. Interesting and accurate cuisine relies heavily on local freshly landed fish and shellfish, as well as local meat and poultry and the freshest fruit and vegetables.
ROOMS: 3 en suite (1 fmly) No smoking in all bedrooms s £70-£85; d £70-£85 (incl. bkfst) **LB FACILITIES:** Xmas **NOTES:** No dogs (ex guide dogs) RS Mon & Tue during Nov-Mar
CARDS:

M

MUCH BIRCH, Herefordshire — Map 10 SO53

★★★65% Pilgrim
Ross Rd HR2 8HJ
THE INDEPENDENTS
☎ 01981 540742 01981 540620
e-mail: stay@pilgrimhotel.co.uk
Dir: *on A49 6m from Ross-on-Wye; 5m from Hereford*
This much extended former rectory is set back from the A49 and has sweeping views over the surrounding countryside. The extensive grounds contain a pitch-and-putt course. Privately owned and personally run, it provides accommodation that includes ground floor and four-poster rooms. Public areas comprise a restful lounge, a traditionally furnished restaurant and a pleasant bar.
ROOMS: 20 en suite (3 fmly) (8 GF) No smoking in 12 bedrooms s £59-£75; d £59-£130 (incl. bkfst) **LB FACILITIES:** Croquet lawn Putting green Pitch & putt Badminton Xmas **CONF:** Thtr 45 Class 45 Board 25 Del from £75 **PARKING:** 42 **NOTES:** No dogs (ex guide dogs) No smoking in restaurant **CARDS:**

See advert on this page & under HEREFORD

MUCH WENLOCK, Shropshire — Map 10 SO69

★★★72% *Raven*
Barrow St TF13 6EN
☎ 01952 727251 01952 728416
e-mail: enquiry@ravenhotel.com
Dir: *M54 junct 4 or 5, take A442 S, then A4169 to Much Wenlock*
This town centre hotel is spread across several historic buildings with a 17th-century coaching inn at its centre. Accommodation is well furnished and equipped to offer modern comfort, with some ground floor rooms. Public areas feature an interesting collection

continued

of prints and memorabilia connected with the modern-day Olympic Games, the idea for which interestingly was born in Much Wenlock.
ROOMS: 8 en suite 7 annexe en suite **FACILITIES:** STV Beauty salon **CONF:** Thtr 16 Board 16 **PARKING:** 30 **NOTES:** No dogs (ex guide dogs) No smoking in restaurant **CARDS:**

★★69% *Reynards*
46 High St TF13 6AD
☎ 01952 727292 01952 728574
e-mail: reynardshotel@aol.co.uk
Dir: *off A458 opposite Gaskell Arms. Along High St, 100yds on left*
This Grade II listed building, in part dating back to 1669, offers modern and smartly equipped accommodation. The public areas include an attractive bar/bistro, where modern furnishings have been tastefully combined with the original character of the building. The service is friendly and attentive.
ROOMS: 8 en suite (2 fmly) No smoking in 2 bedrooms
FACILITIES: entertainment **PARKING:** 20
CARDS:

★★63% Gaskell Arms
Bourton Rd TF13 6AQ
☎ 01952 727212 01952 728505
e-mail: maxine@gaskellarms.co.uk
Dir: *from M6 turn off at junct 10A onto M54. Take junct 4 off M54 follow signs for Ironbridge/Much Wenlock*
This 17th-century former coaching inn has exposed beams and log fires in the public areas. In addition to the lounge bar and restaurant, featuring a wide range of meals and snacks, there is a small bar that proves popular with locals. Well-maintained

continued on p440

MUCH WENLOCK, continued

bedrooms, which vary in size, are attractively furnished; family rooms are available.

Gaskell Arms, Much Wenlock

ROOMS: 16 rms (14 en suite) (3 fmly) (4 GF) No smoking in 5 bedrooms s £48-£50; d £70-£80 (incl. bkfst) **LB** **CONF:** BC **PARKING:** 41 **NOTES:** No dogs (ex guide dogs) **CARDS:**

MUDEFORD See Christchurch

MULLION, Cornwall & Isles of Scilly Map 02 SW61

★★★70% Polurrian

TR12 7EN

THE INDEPENDENTS

☎ 01326 240421 01326 240083

e-mail: polurotel@aol.com

Dir: *A30 onto A3076 to Truro. Follow signs for Helston on A39 then A394 to The Lizard and Mullion*

This long-established hotel is set in 12 acres of landscaped gardens, 300 feet above the sea. The spectacular views over Mullion Cove will remain long in the memory, along with the wonderful sunsets. Public areas are spacious and comfortable, and the bedrooms are individually styled. There is a well-equipped leisure centre.

ROOMS: 39 en suite (22 fmly) s £55-£85; d £110-£240 (incl. bkfst & dinner) **LB** **FACILITIES:** STV Indoor swimming (H) Outdoor swimming (H) Tennis (hard) Squash Snooker Sauna Solarium Gym Croquet lawn Putting green Jacuzzi Cricket net Whirlpool Mountain bikes Surfing Body boarding entertainment ch fac Xmas **CONF:** BC Thtr 100 Class 60 Board 30 Del from £65 **PARKING:** 80 **NOTES:** No smoking in restaurant Civ Wed 90 **CARDS:**

See advert on opposite page

★★★69% Mullion Cove Hotel

TR12 7EP

☎ 01326 240328 01326 240998

e-mail: mullion.cove@btinternet.com

Dir: *from Helston follow signs to The Lizard, right at Mullion Holiday Park. Through village, left for Cove. Then right and hotel on top of hill*

Built at the turn of the last century and set high above the working harbour of Mullion, this hotel has spectacular view and seaward facing rooms are always popular. The stylish restaurant offers some carefully prepared dishes with local produce to the fore. After dinner, why not retreat to one of the elegant lounges and relax on a deep sofa.

ROOMS: 29 en suite (9 fmly) s £45-£191.50; d £90-£210 (incl. bkfst & dinner) **LB** **FACILITIES:** Outdoor swimming (H) Sauna Solarium Beauty treatments ch fac Xmas **PARKING:** 60 **NOTES:** No smoking in restaurant **CARDS:**

MUNDESLEY, Norfolk Map 13 TG33

★★68% Manor Hotel

Beach Rd NR11 8BG

☎ 01263 720309 01263 721731

e-mail: mundesleymanor@amserve.co.uk

An imposing Victorian property situated in an elevated position with superb views of the sea. The hotel has been owned and run by the same family for over 30 years. The spacious public rooms offer a choice of bars, two lounges, a conservatory, and traditional restaurant as well as the Bar Victoriana. The comfortable bedrooms are smartly decorated; some rooms have stunning sea views.

ROOMS: 22 en suite 4 annexe en suite s £50-£55; d £74-£84 (incl. bkfst) **LB** **FACILITIES:** Outdoor swimming (H) Xmas **CONF:** Thtr 20 Class 20 Board 15 **PARKING:** 40 **NOTES:** No smoking in restaurant Closed 2-18 Jan **CARDS:**

MUNGRISDALE, Cumbria Map 18 NY33

★76% The Mill

CA11 0XR

☎ 01768 779659 01768 779155

e-mail: quinlan.themill@bushinternet.com

Dir: *M6 junct 40, 2m N of A66*

Formerly a mill cottage dating from 1651 and set in magnificent rural scenery, this charming hotel and restaurant lies beside the old millstream. Inside there are cosy lounges, low ceilings, books, antiques, paintings and period pieces. Excellent five-course dinners will satisfy the heartiest of appetites.

ROOMS: 7 rms (5 en suite) s £59-£85 (incl. bkfst & dinner) **FACILITIES:** Fishing Games room **PARKING:** 15 **NOTES:** Closed Nov-Feb

NAILSWORTH, Gloucestershire Map 04 ST89

★★70% Egypt Mill

GL6 0AE

☎ 01453 833449 01453 836098

e-mail: reception@egyptmill.co.uk

Dir: *on A46, midway between Cheltenham and Bath*

Millstones and working waterwheels have been incorporated in the innovative refurbishment of this 17th-century former corn mill. Well-equipped bedrooms are located in two adjacent buildings and are tastefully furnished and facilities include a restaurant with

continued

adjoining bar, a stylish cellar bar and popular bistro. During the summer, the riverside patios and gardens are great places to enjoy a drink.

ROOMS: 8 en suite 10 annexe en suite (2 fmly) s fr £55; d fr £75 (incl. bkfst) **LB** **FACILITIES:** STV Croquet lawn Boules pitch Xmas **CONF:** Thtr 100 Class 80 Board 80 Del from £80 **PARKING:** 120 **NOTES:** No dogs (ex guide dogs) No smoking in restaurant **CARDS:**

NANTWICH, Cheshire

Map 15 SJ65

Top 200 - Hotel

★★★ Rookery Hall

Main Rd, Worleston CW5 6DQ

HandPICKED

☎ 01270 610016 📠 01270 626027

e-mail: info@rookeryhallhotel.com

Dir: *B5074 off 4th rdbt, on Nantwich by-pass. Hotel 1.5m on right*

This fine 19th-century mansion is set in 38 acres of gardens, pasture and parkland. Bedrooms, some in an adjacent coach house, are spacious and luxuriously appointed. The public areas are particularly stylish and include a salon with enormous sofas, a cigar-friendly bar and a mahogany-panelled dining room. The staff are notable for their professionalism and hospitality.

ROOMS: 30 en suite 15 annexe en suite (6 GF) s £100-£120; d £130-£200 (incl. bkfst) **LB** **FACILITIES:** STV Tennis (hard) Fishing Croquet lawn Xmas **CONF:** Thtr 90 Class 40 Board 40 Del from £140 **SERVICES:** Lift **PARKING:** 80 **NOTES:** No smoking in restaurant Civ Wed 66 **CARDS:**

★★70% Crown

High St CW5 5AS

Best Western

☎ 01270 625283 📠 01270 628047

e-mail: info@crown-hotel.net

Dir: *A52 to Nantwich, hotel in centre of town*

Ideally set in the heart of this historic and delightful market town, The Crown has been offering hospitality for many centuries. It has

continued

an abundance of original features and the well-equipped bedrooms retain an old world charm. There is also a character bar with live entertainment throughout the week and diners can enjoy Italian food in the atmospheric brasserie.

ROOMS: 18 en suite (2 fmly) No smoking in 2 bedrooms s £59-£69; d £72-£76 (incl. bkfst) **LB** **FACILITIES:** Putting green entertainment **CONF:** Thtr 200 Class 150 Board 70 **PARKING:** 18 **NOTES:** Civ Wed 150 **CARDS:**

Premier Lodge (Nantwich)

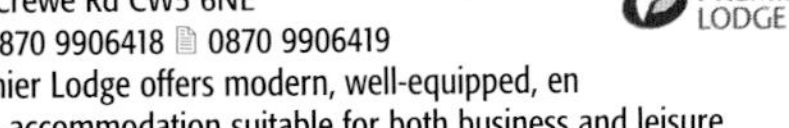

221 Crewe Rd CW5 6NE

PREMIER LODGE

☎ 0870 9906418 📠 0870 9906419

Premier Lodge offers modern, well-equipped, en suite accommodation suitable for both business and leisure travellers. Meals can be taken at the adjacent popular restaurant and bar, which is fully licensed. For further details, consult the Hotel Groups page.

ROOMS: 37 en suite s £48; d £48

NEEDHAM MARKET, Suffolk

Map 13 TM05

Travelodge Ipswich Beacon

Beacon Hill IP6 8LP

Travelodge

☎ 08700 850 950 📠 01449 721640

Dir: *A14/A140*

Travelodge offers good quality, good value, modern accommodation. Ideal for families, the spacious, en suite bedrooms include remote-control TV, tea and coffee-making facilities, luxury beds and free morning newspaper. Meals can be taken at the nearby family restaurant. For further details and the Travelodge phone number, consult the Hotel Groups page.

ROOMS: 40 en suite s fr £42.95; d fr £42.95

N

NETHER STOWEY, Somerset Map 04 ST13

★★70% Apple Tree

Keenthorne TA5 1HZ
☎ 01278 733238 01278 732693
e-mail: appletreehotel@hotmail.com
Dir: *from Bridgwater follow A39 towards Minehead, Hotel on left 2m after Cannington*

With parts of the original building dating back 350 years, this is a conveniently located and ever popular establishment. Bedrooms vary in character and style, with several in an adjoining wing, overlooking the garden. Every effort is made to ensure that guests have an enjoyable stay, with the friendly, resident owners and their small team of staff on hand. Public areas include an attractive conservatory restaurant, bar and library lounge.

ROOMS: 14 en suite (2 fmly) (5 GF) No smoking in 5 bedrooms s £52.50; d £65-£75 (incl. bkfst) **LB** **CONF:** Thtr 25 Class 12 Board 14 **PARKING:** 40 **NOTES:** No dogs (ex guide dogs) No smoking in restaurant **CARDS:**

NETHER WASDALE, Cumbria Map 18 NY10

★★75% Low Wood Hall Hotel & Restaurant

CA20 1ET
☎ 019467 26100 019467 26111
e-mail: reservations@lowwoodhall.co.uk
Dir: *off A595 at Gosforth, left for Wasdale, 3m right for Nether Wasdale*

This delightful country-house hotel is peacefully set in five acres wooded gardens overlooking the village and valley. Personal service and a warm welcome are assured. Stylish interior designs blend well with the classical architecture and two lovely lounges have lots to read and roaring fires in season. Thoughtfully equipped bedrooms vary in size and style. Carefully prepared meals are a highlight.

ROOMS: 6 rms (5 en suite) 6 annexe en suite (4 GF) No smoking in all bedrooms d £65-£130 (incl. bkfst) **CONF:** Thtr 30 Class 30 Board 20 **PARKING:** 15 **NOTES:** No dogs (ex guide dogs) No children 12yrs No smoking in restaurant Closed Xmas, New Year
CARDS:

N

NEW ALRESFORD, Hampshire Map 05 SU53

★★61% Swan

11 West St SO24 9AD
☎ 01962 732302 & 734427 01962 735274
e-mail: swanhotel@btinternet.com
Dir: *off A31 onto B3047*

This former coaching inn dates back to the 18th century and remains a busy and popular destination for travellers and locals. Bedrooms are in the main building and the more modern wing. The lounge bar and adjacent restaurant are open all day; for more traditional dining there is another restaurant which overlooks the busy village street.

ROOMS: 11 rms (10 en suite) 12 annexe en suite (3 fmly) **CONF:** Thtr 90 Class 60 Board 40 **PARKING:** 75 **NOTES:** No dogs (ex guide dogs) No smoking in restaurant RS 25-26 Dec **CARDS:**

See advert on opposite page

> Early start?
> Hotels at all star levels should provide in-room alarm clocks and/or alarm calls

NEWARK-ON-TRENT, Nottinghamshire Map 17 SK75

★★★68% The Grange Hotel

73 London Rd NG24 1RZ
☎ 01636 703399 01636 702328
e-mail: info@grangenewark.co.uk
Dir: *from A1 follow signs to town centre. At castle rdbt follow signs to Balderton. Over 2 sets of lights. Hotel 0.25m on left*

Expect a warm welcome at this family-run hotel, situated just a short walk from the town. Bedrooms are attractively decorated with co-ordinated soft furnishings and equipped with many thoughtful extras. Public rooms include the Potters bar, Cutlers restaurant and a residents' lounge; in the summer guests may enjoy the pretty terrace garden.

ROOMS: 10 en suite 9 annexe en suite (1 fmly) No smoking in 14 bedrooms s £58-£79; d £79-£92 (incl. bkfst) **LB** **PARKING:** 17 **NOTES:** No dogs (ex guide dogs) No smoking in restaurant
CARDS:

Travel Inn

travel inn

Lincoln Rd NG24 2DB
☎ 08701 977186 01636 605135
Dir: *at junct of A1/A46/A17, follow signs B6166*

Travel Inn offers good-quality, value-for-money accommodation. Spacious, en suite rooms with bath and shower comfortably accommodate a family of up to two adults and two children (to age 15). The restaurant and bar offers a varied menu. For further details and the Travel Inn phone number, consult the Hotel Groups page.

ROOMS: 40 en suite s £44.95; d £44.95

NEWBURY, Berkshire Map 05 SU46

Top 200 - Hotel

★★★★★ The Vineyard at Stockcross

RELAIS & CHÂTEAUX

Stockcross RG20 8JU
☎ 01635 528770 01635 528398
e-mail: general@the-vineyard.co.uk
Dir: *from M4 take A34 towards Newbury, exit at 3rd junct for Speen. Right at rdbt then right again at 2nd rdbt.*

A haven of style in the Berkshire countryside, this hotel prides itself on a superb art collection, which can be seen throughout the building. Bedrooms come in a variety of styles, many of which are suites. Comfortable lounges lead into the split-level restaurant, which serves imaginative and precise cooking, complemented by an equally impressive selection of wines

continued

from California and around the world. The welcome is warm and sincere; the service professional yet relaxed.
ROOMS: 31 en suite (7 GF) No smoking in 10 bedrooms s £160-£600; d £229-£600 (incl. bkfst) **LB** **FACILITIES: Spa** STV Indoor swimming (H) Sauna Gym Jacuzzi Treatment rooms entertainment Xmas **CONF:** Thtr 60 Class 50 Board 30 Del from £300 **SERVICES:** Lift air con **PARKING:** 60 **NOTES:** No dogs (ex guide dogs) Civ Wed 120 **CARDS:**

★★★★76% Donnington Valley

Old Oxford Rd, Donnington RG14 3AG
☎ 01635 551199 01635 551123
e-mail: general@donningtonvalley.co.uk
Dir: *M4 junct 13, take A34 southbound, exit at Donnington Castle. Right over bridge then left hotel 1m on right*

This friendly hotel stands on its own 18-hole golf course and provides excellent accommodation. The striking modern building houses well-equipped meeting rooms and public areas which are furnished to a high standard. The WinePress restaurant offers imaginative food and a comprehensive choice of wine in comfortable surroundings; service is attentive and friendly.
ROOMS: 58 en suite (11 fmly) (18 GF) No smoking in 30 bedrooms s £150; d £150-£220 **LB** **FACILITIES:** STV Golf 18 Putting green Leisure fac available at sister hotel entertainment Xmas **CONF:** Thtr 140 Class 60 Board 40 Del from £185 **SERVICES:** Lift **PARKING:** 160 **NOTES:** No dogs (ex guide dogs) Civ Wed 85 **CARDS:**

★★★★75% Regency Park Hotel

Bowling Green Rd, Thatcham RG18 3RP
☎ 01635 871555 01635 871571
e-mail: info@regencyparkhotel.co.uk
Dir: *from Newbury take A4 signed Thatcham and Reading. 2nd rdbt exit signed Cold Ash. Hotel 1m on left*

Peacefully situated in five acres of grounds, within easy reach of the M4, this smart hotel provides spacious, well-equipped accommodation. Public areas include a new conservatory lounge, a stylish restaurant, a modern leisure club as well as a

continued on p444

NEWBURY, continued

state-of-the-art function suite and business centre. The attractive Watermark restaurant offers Mediterranean-style cuisine.
ROOMS: 82 en suite (7 fmly) No smoking in 52 bedrooms s £145-£345; d £185-£365 **LB FACILITIES: Spa** STV Indoor swimming (H) Tennis (hard) Sauna Solarium Gym Jacuzzi 4 Health & Beauty treatment rooms Xmas **CONF:** Thtr 200 Class 80 Board 70 Del from £175 **SERVICES:** Lift **PARKING:** 160 **NOTES:** No dogs (ex guide dogs) No smoking in restaurant Civ Wed 100 **CARDS:**

See advert on page 443

★★★65% *The Chequers Hotel*

6-8 Oxford St RG14 1JB
☎ 01635 38000 01635 37170
Dir: *off A34 at Newbury follow town centre signs. 2nd mini rdbt right, hotel on right*

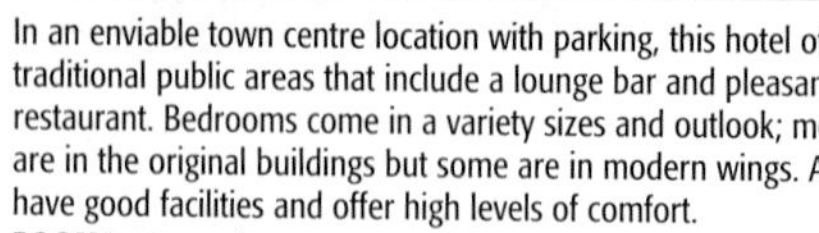

In an enviable town centre location with parking, this hotel offers traditional public areas that include a lounge bar and pleasant restaurant. Bedrooms come in a variety sizes and outlook; most are in the original buildings but some are in modern wings. All have good facilities and offer high levels of comfort.
ROOMS: 46 en suite 10 annexe en suite (3 fmly) No smoking in 41 bedrooms **FACILITIES:** STV **CONF:** Thtr 100 Class 50 Board 40 **PARKING:** 60 **NOTES:** No dogs (ex guide dogs) No smoking in restaurant Closed 24 Dec-2 Jan **CARDS:**

Premier Lodge (Newbury)

Bath Rd, Midgham RG7 5UX
☎ 0870 9906556 0870 9906557
Premier Lodge offers modern, well-equipped, en suite accommodation suitable for both business and leisure travellers. Meals can be taken at the adjacent popular restaurant and bar, which is fully licensed. For further details, consult the Hotel Groups page.
ROOMS: 49 en suite s £50; d £50

Travelodge (Newbury Chieveley)

Chieveley, Oxford Rd RG18 9XX
☎ 08700 850 950
Dir: *on A34 off junct 13 of M4*
Travelodge offers good quality, good value, modern accommodation. Ideal for families, the spacious, en suite bedrooms include remote-control TV, tea and coffee-making facilities, luxury beds and free morning newspaper. Meals can be taken at the nearby family restaurant. For further details and the Travelodge phone number, consult the Hotel Groups page.
ROOMS: 127 en suite s fr £42.95; d fr £42.95

> Destination dining!
> This symbol indicates a Restaurant with Rooms

Travelodge Newbury South

Tot Hill Services (A34), Newbury by-pass RG20 9ED
☎ 08700 850 950
Dir: *Tot Hill Services on A34*
Travelodge offers good quality, good value, modern accommodation. Ideal for families, the spacious, en suite bedrooms include remote-control TV, tea and coffee-making facilities, luxury beds and free morning newspaper. Meals can be taken at the nearby family restaurant. For further details and the Travelodge phone number, consult the Hotel Groups page.
ROOMS: 52 en suite s fr £42.95; d fr £42.95

NEWBY BRIDGE, Cumbria — Map 18 SD38

★★★★76% Lakeside

Lakeside LA12 8AT
☎ 015395 30001 015395 31699
e-mail: sales@lakesidehotel.co.uk
Dir: *M6 junct 36 join A590 to Barrow, follow signs to Newby Bridge. Right over bridge, hotel 1m on right or follow Lakeside Steamers signs from junct 36*
This impressive hotel has an enviable location on the southern edge of Lake Windermere. Bedrooms are tastefully and individually styled, many with patios and wonderful lake views. Spacious lounges and a choice of restaurants are available. The addition of a luxury spa complex completes the picture.
ROOMS: 80 en suite (7 fmly) (8 GF) No smoking in 34 bedrooms s £110-£275; d £140-£280 (incl. bkfst) **LB FACILITIES: Spa** STV Indoor swimming (H) Fishing Sauna Gym Croquet lawn Jacuzzi Private jetty Use of health club entertainment Xmas **CONF:** Thtr 100 Class 50 Board 40 Del from £164.50 **SERVICES:** Lift **PARKING:** 200 **NOTES:** No smoking in restaurant Civ Wed 80
CARDS:

★★★★71% Swan

LA12 8NB
☎ 015395 31681 015395 31917
e-mail: enquiries@swanhotel.com
Dir: *M6 junct 36 follow A590 signed Barrow for 16m. Hotel on right of old 5-arch bridge, at Newby Bridge*

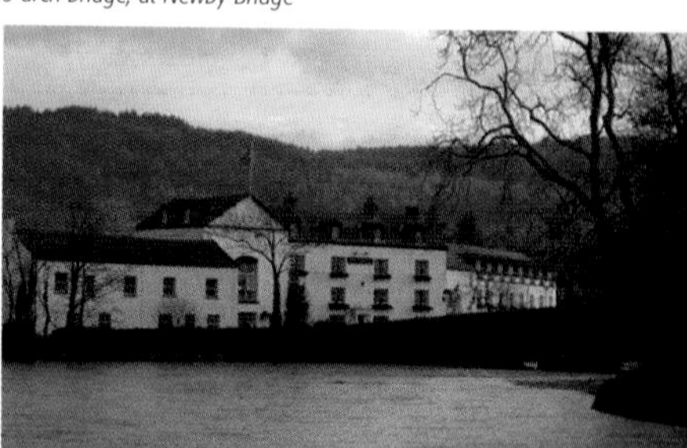

Set amongst 14 acres of gardens and lakeside pathways with mooring for 80 boats, this hotel stands on the River Leven at the south end of Lake Windermere. Bedrooms are comfortable, spacious and thoughtfully equipped. Public areas include a choice of lounges and restaurants, a traditional bar and impressive spa facilities.
ROOMS: 55 en suite (4 fmly) (14 GF) No smoking in 16 bedrooms **FACILITIES: Spa** STV Indoor swimming (H) Fishing Sauna Solarium Gym Steam Room, Indoor swimming pool supervised **CONF:** Thtr 120 Class 40 Board 40 Del from £120 **SERVICES:** Lift **PARKING:** 100 **NOTES:** No dogs (ex guide dogs) No smoking in restaurant Civ Wed 80
CARDS:

★★★66% Whitewater
The Lakeland Village LA12 8PX
☎ 015395 31133 ▯ 015395 31881
e-mail: enquiries@whitewater-hotel.co.uk
Dir: *M6 junct 36 follow signs for A590 Barrow, 1m through Newby Bridge. Right at sign for Lakeland Village, hotel on left*

This tasteful conversion of an old mill on the River Leven is close to the southern end of Lake Windermere. Bedrooms, many with lovely river views, are spacious and comfortable. Public areas include a luxurious, well-equipped spa, squash courts, mountain bikes and a choice of dining options. The Fisherman's bar hosts regular jazz nights popular with locals.
ROOMS: 35 en suite (10 fmly) (2 GF) No smoking in 10 bedrooms s £70-£90; d £120-£125 (incl. bkfst) **LB FACILITIES: Spa** STV Indoor swimming (H) Tennis (hard) Squash Sauna Solarium Gym Putting green Beauty treatment Table tennis Steam room Golf driving range Pool supervised entertainment ch fac Xmas **CONF:** Thtr 80 Class 32 Board 40 Del from £90 **SERVICES:** Lift **PARKING:** 50 **NOTES:** No dogs (ex guide dogs) No smoking in restaurant Civ Wed 100
CARDS:

NEWCASTLE-UNDER-LYME, Staffordshire — Map 10 SJ84

★★62% Comfort Inn
Liverpool Rd, Cross Heath ST5 9DX
☎ 01782 717000 ▯ 01782 713669
e-mail: admin@gb617.u-net.com
Dir: *M6 junct 16 onto A500 to Stoke-on-Trent. Take A34 to Newcastle-under-Lyme, hotel on right after 1.5m*
Some of the well-equipped bedrooms at this purpose-built hotel are in a separate block at the rear. There is a large lounge bar with a pool table and the restaurant offers a good range of food.
ROOMS: 43 en suite 24 annexe en suite (6 fmly) (23 GF) No smoking in 25 bedrooms s £40-£60; d £40-£60 **LB FACILITIES:** STV Xmas **CONF:** Thtr 150 Class 100 Board 80 Del from £79 **PARKING:** 160 **NOTES:** No smoking in restaurant **CARDS:**

Holiday Inn Stoke-on-Trent
Clayton Rd ST5 4DL
☎ 0870 400 9077 ▯ 01782 717138
Dir: *from M6 junct 15 onto A519*
At the time of going to press, the classification for this hotel was not confirmed. Please refer to the AA internet site www.theAA.com for current information.
ROOMS: 119 en suite (41 fmly) No smoking in 54 bedrooms **FACILITIES:** Indoor swimming (H) Sauna Solarium Gym Jacuzzi **CONF:** Thtr 70 Class 40 Board 34 **PARKING:** 128 **NOTES:** Civ Wed 55
CARDS:

Travel Inn
Talke Rd, Chesterton ST5 7AH
☎ 08701 977191 ▯ 01782 578901

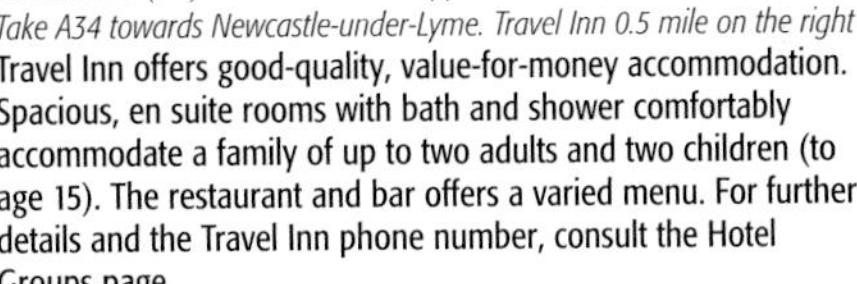

Dir: *Exit M6 (J16) - follow A500 for approx. 3.5 miles. Take A34 towards Newcastle-under-Lyme. Travel Inn 0.5 mile on the right*
Travel Inn offers good-quality, value-for-money accommodation. Spacious, en suite rooms with bath and shower comfortably accommodate a family of up to two adults and two children (to age 15). The restaurant and bar offers a varied menu. For further details and the Travel Inn phone number, consult the Hotel Groups page.
ROOMS: 58 en suite s £44.95; d £44.95

NEWCASTLE UPON TYNE, Tyne & Wear — Map 21 NZ26

See also Seaton Burn & Whickham

★★★★78% ⊛⊛ Newcastle Marriott Hotel Gosforth Park
High Gosforth Park, Gosforth NE3 5HN
☎ 0191 236 4111 ▯ 0191 236 8192

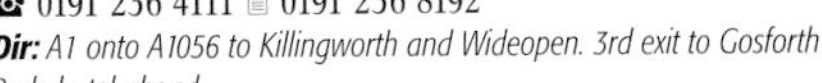

Dir: *A1 onto A1056 to Killingworth and Wideopen. 3rd exit to Gosforth Park, hotel ahead*
This hotel is set in twelve and a half acres of woodland and attractive gardens, with easy access to the A1, the racecourse and the airport. Bedrooms are tastefully decorated and fully equipped. The Park Restaurant serves classical and modern dishes, while Chats offers a less formal dining option.
ROOMS: 178 en suite (30 fmly) No smoking in 115 bedrooms s £130-£140; d £130-£150 **LB FACILITIES: Spa** STV Indoor swimming (H) Tennis (hard) Squash Sauna Solarium Gym Jacuzzi Trim & jogging trail in hotel grounds, Swimming pool supervised entertainment **CONF:** BC Thtr 750 Class 280 Board 50 Del from £120 **SERVICES:** Lift **PARKING:** 340 **NOTES:** RS Xmas & New year Civ Wed 150
CARDS:

★★★★76% ⊛⊛ Vermont
Castle Garth NE1 1RQ
☎ 0191 233 1010 ▯ 0191 233 1234
e-mail: info@vermont-hotel.co.uk
Dir: *city centre by high level bridge and Castle Keep*
In the heart of the city's buzzing quayside area and adjacent to the castle this stylish hotel enjoys super views of the Tyne Bridge. Bedrooms, including grand suites, are thoughtfully equipped and vary in style. The Bridge restaurant serves modern, simple food, while the Blue Room offers classically inspired, award-winning cuisine. The compact, yet well equipped, fitness room is the perfect place to counter the calories.
ROOMS: 101 en suite (12 fmly) No smoking in 20 bedrooms s £85-£165; d £95-£185 **LB FACILITIES:** STV Solarium Gym Xmas **CONF:** BC Thtr 200 Class 60 Board 30 Del £165 **SERVICES:** Lift **PARKING:** 100 **NOTES:** Civ Wed 200 **CARDS:**

★★★★71% Copthorne Hotel Newcastle
The Close, Quayside NE1 3RT
☎ 0191 222 0333 ▯ 0191 230 1111
e-mail: sales@newcastle.mill-cop.com
Dir: *follow signs to Newcastle city centre. Take B1600 Quayside exit, hotel on right*
Set on the banks of the River Tyne close to the city centre, this purpose-built hotel provides modern amenities that include a leisure centre and a range of conference facilities. There is also a choice of restaurants for dinner. All bedrooms overlook the river

continued on p446

NEWCASTLE UPON TYNE, continued

and there is a floor of 'Connoisseur' rooms with their own exclusive lounge and business support services.

Copthorne Hotel, Newcastle

ROOMS: 156 en suite No smoking in 85 bedrooms s £95-£190; d £95-£190 **FACILITIES: Spa** STV Indoor swimming (H) Sauna Solarium Gym Jacuzzi Steam room, Beauty treatment room, Swimming pool supervised Xmas **CONF:** Thtr 200 Class 85 Board 60 Del from £165 **SERVICES:** Lift air con **PARKING:** 180 **NOTES:** Civ Wed **CARDS:**

★★★★68% Newcastle Marriott Hotel MetroCentre

MetroCentre NE11 9XF
☎ 0191 493 2233 📠 0191 493 2030
e-mail: reservations.newcastle@marriotthotels.co.uk
(For full entry see Gateshead)

★★★★67% Menzies Silverlink Park

Silverlink, Coast Rd NE28 9HP
☎ 0191 202 9955 📠 0191 263 4172
e-mail: silverlinkpark@menzies-hotels.co.uk
Dir: *Through the Tyne Tunnel follow signs for A19 Morpeth and then signs for Silverlink*

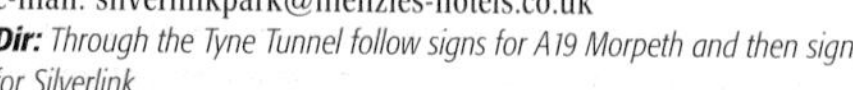

A purpose-built hotel located close to the Tyne Tunnel and major business in the area. Public areas are well proportioned and inviting, with pride of place going to the new Waves health and leisure club. Bedrooms meet the needs of the business guest, and it is worth asking for one of the larger Club rooms.
ROOMS: 122 en suite (4 fmly) No smoking in 60 bedrooms **FACILITIES:** Indoor swimming (H) Sauna Solarium Gym Jacuzzi **CONF:** Thtr 400 Class 200 Board 40 Del from £130 **SERVICES:** Lift **PARKING:** 226 **NOTES:** No smoking in restaurant **CARDS:**

★★★76% ⊛ Malmaison

Quayside NE1 3DX
☎ 0191 245 5000 📠 0191 245 4545
e-mail: newcastle@malmaison.com
Dir: *follow signs for Newcastle City Centre, then for Quayside/Law Courts. Hotel 100yds past Law Courts*

Overlooking the river and the new Millennium Bridge, the hotel has a prime position in the up and coming redeveloped quayside district. Bedrooms are spacious and contemporary in style, offering large beds and music and communications systems as standard. Public areas include a spa and gym facility, some meeting rooms and the popular riverside brasserie.
ROOMS: 116 en suite (10 fmly) s £79-£125; d £79-£125 **LB FACILITIES:** STV Sauna Gym Xmas **CONF:** Thtr 50 Class 10 Board 24 Del £155 **SERVICES:** Lift air con **PARKING:** 50 **NOTES:** No dogs (ex guide dogs) **CARDS:**

★★★67% The Caledonian Hotel, Newcastle

PEEL HOTELS

64 Osborne Rd, Jesmond NE2 2AT
☎ 0191 281 7881 📠 0191 281 6241
e-mail: info@caledonian-hotel-newcastle.com
Dir: *from A1 follow signs to Newcastle City Centre, cross Tyne Bridge to Tynemouth. Left at rdbt at Osborne Rd, hotel on right*

This modern hotel is located in the popular Jesmond area of the city, with its vibrant nightlife. Spacious bedrooms offer a bright decorative theme and are well equipped for business guests. Public rooms include the Billabong Bar and Bistro, which serves a range of meals and snacks all day, and a terrace bar where a cosmopolitan atmosphere can be enjoyed.
ROOMS: 89 en suite (6 fmly) (7 GF) No smoking in 32 bedrooms s £60-£100; d £70-£130 (incl. bkfst) **LB FACILITIES:** STV Xmas **CONF:** Thtr 100 Class 50 Board 50 Del from £95 **SERVICES:** Lift **PARKING:** 35 **NOTES:** Civ Wed 100 **CARDS:**

★★★67% Jurys Inn Newcastle

JURYS DOYLE HOTELS

St James Gate, Scotswood Rd NE2 7JH
☎ 0191 201 4400 📠 0191 201 4411
e-mail: jurysinnnewcastle@jurysdoyle.com

This modern, stylish hotel is easily accessible from major road networks and occupies a prominent location in the city. Bedrooms provide good guest comfort and in-room facilities are suited for both leisure and business markets. Public areas include a number of meeting rooms and a popular bar and restaurant.
ROOMS: 274 en suite No smoking in 186 bedrooms s £63-£67; d £63-£67 **CONF:** Thtr 100 Class 60 Board 60 Del from £110 **SERVICES:** Lift **NOTES:** No dogs (ex guide dogs) No smoking in restaurant **CARDS:**

★★★66% New Kent Hotel

127 Osborne Rd NE2 2TB
☎ 0191 281 7711 📠 0191 281 3369
e-mail: newkenthotel@hotmail.com
Dir: *beside B1600, opposite St Georges Church*

This popular business hotel offers relaxed service and typical Geordie hospitality. Bedrooms, most of which are spacious, offer bright, modern décor. The refurbished bar is an ideal meeting point and a range of generous meals are served in the restaurant, which doubles as a wedding venue.
ROOMS: 32 en suite (4 fmly) s £47.50-£69.50; d £69.50-£79.50 (incl. bkfst) **LB FACILITIES:** STV Xmas **CONF:** Thtr 60 Class 30 Board 40 Del £110 **PARKING:** 22 **NOTES:** No smoking in restaurant Civ Wed 90 **CARDS:**

★★★66% Novotel Newcastle

NOVOTEL

Ponteland Rd, Kenton NE3 3HZ
☎ 0191 214 0303 📠 0191 214 0633
e-mail: H1118@accor-hotels.com
Dir: *off A1(M) airport junct onto A696, take Kingston Park exit*

This modern well-proportioned hotel lies just off the bypass and is

continued

within easy reach of the airport and city centre. Bedrooms are spacious with a range of extras. The Garden Brasserie offers a flexible dining option and is open until late. There is also a small leisure centre for the more energetic.
ROOMS: 126 en suite (56 fmly) No smoking in 82 bedrooms s £75; d £75 **LB** **FACILITIES:** STV Indoor swimming (H) Sauna Gym **CONF:** Thtr 200 Class 90 Board 40 Del from £120 **SERVICES:** Lift **PARKING:** 260 **NOTES:** Civ Wed 200
CARDS:

★★★65% George Washington County Hotel
Stone Cellar Rd, High Usworth NE37 1PH
☎ 0870 609 6173 ⎙ 0191 415 1166
e-mail: georgewashington@corushotels.com
(For full entry see Washington)

★★★63% Quality
Newgate St NE1 5SX
☎ 0191 232 5025 ⎙ 0191 232 8428
e-mail: admin@gb077.u-net.com
Dir: *A1(M) take A184 Gateshead and Newcastle centre, follow A6082. Croos Redheugh Bridge take right lane, right at 3rd set of lights, then immediate right onto Fenkle St. Car park behind Old Assembly Rooms*
Benefiting from a convenient city centre location and with the advantage of secure car parking, this hotel is popular with business travellers. Public areas include a rooftop restaurant and bar and a number of meeting rooms. Accommodation is provided in compact yet thoughtfully equipped bedrooms.
ROOMS: 93 en suite (4 fmly) No smoking in 42 bedrooms **FACILITIES:** STV **CONF:** Thtr 100 Class 40 Board 40 Del from £80 **SERVICES:** Lift **PARKING:** 120 **NOTES:** No smoking in restaurant
CARDS:

★★76% Eslington Villa
8 Station Rd, Low Fell NE9 6DR
☎ 0191 487 6017 & 420 0666 ⎙ 0191 420 0667
e-mail: admin@eslingtonvilla.fsnet.co.uk
(For full entry see Gateshead)

★★61% Cairn
97/103 Osborne Rd, Jesmond NE2 2TJ

☎ 0191 281 1358 ⎙ 0191 281 9031
e-mail: arvanhanda@aol.com

This commercial hotel, just a short distance from the city centre, offers well-equipped bedrooms. There is a choice of dining options in either the brightly furnished dining room or the lively bar, as well as a spacious function suite.
ROOMS: 50 en suite (2 fmly) s £52-£60; d £72-£80 (incl. bkfst) **LB** **FACILITIES:** STV Xmas **CONF:** Thtr 150 Class 110 Board 100 **PARKING:** 22 **CARDS:**

★★61% *Whites Hotel*
38-42 Osborne Rd, Jesmond NE2 2AL
☎ 0191 281 5126 ⎙ 0191 281 9953
e-mail: apuri80741@aol.com
Dir: *follow A1058 signs for coast, left into Osborne Rd at 1st rdbt*
This commercial hotel in Jesmond has the benefit of a secure car park and good transport links. Service is cheery, and the public rooms have been modernised. The upgrade of bedrooms is currently in progress. There is also a restaurant which offers good value meals.
ROOMS: 39 rms (38 en suite) (3 fmly) No smoking in 3 bedrooms **FACILITIES:** STV **CONF:** Thtr 75 Class 50 Board 40 **PARKING:** 40
CARDS:

★66% Hadrian Lodge Hotel
Hadrian Rd, Wallsend NE28 6HH
☎ 0191 262 7733 & 08081 086892 ⎙ 0191 263 0714
e-mail: Claire.Stubbs@barbox.net
Dir: *from Newcastle city centre follow signs for Tyne Tunnel and Wallsend. Then follow A187 to Wallsend and Newcastle. Hotel opposite Hadrian Rd Metro station*
The hotel is situated on the main road into Newcastle and is conveniently located for easy access to the city and its nightlife, Whitley Bay and local tourist attractions. This hotel offers well-equipped accommodation; bedrooms vary in size, with the ground floor rooms tending to be larger. Home-cooked meals are served in the spacious bar or restaurant area.
ROOMS: 24 en suite (1 fmly) No smoking in 8 bedrooms s £38.50-£45; d £49.50 (incl. bkfst) **FACILITIES:** Xmas **CONF:** BC Class 15 Board 15 Del £95 **PARKING:** 60 **NOTES:** No dogs (ex guide dogs) No smoking in restaurant **CARDS:**

U *Holiday Inn Newcastle City*
New Bridge St NE1 8BS
☎ 0870 400 9058 ⎙ 0191 261 8529
e-mail: reservations-newcastlecity@ichotelsgroup.com
Dir: *follow Gateshead and Newcastle signs on A167(M), over Tyne Bridge. Take A193 to Wallsend and city centre, left to Carliol Sq, hotel on corner*
At the time of going to press, the classification for this hotel was not confirmed. Please refer to the AA internet site www.theAA.com for current information.
ROOMS: 172 en suite (2 fmly) No smoking in 108 bedrooms **FACILITIES:** Indoor swimming (H) Sauna Solarium Gym Jacuzzi adjoning leisure club **CONF:** Thtr 600 Class 350 Board 50 **SERVICES:** Lift **PARKING:** 132 **CARDS:**

⌂ Innkeeper's Lodge Newcastle
Kenton Bank NE3 3TY
☎ 0191 214 0877 ⎙ 0191 214 1922
Dir: *from A1(M), exit A696/B6918. At 1st rdbt, take B6918 (Kingston Park), 2nd rdbt turn right. Lodge on left*
A new concept in the travel accommodation market. Smart rooms meet essential business requirements but also have home comforts. Dining options include all-day menus plus the added advantage of breakfast, which is included in the room price. For further details, consult the Hotel Groups page.
ROOMS: 30 en suite **CONF:** Thtr 40 Class 25 Board 20

NEWCASTLE UPON TYNE, continued

⇧ Premier Lodge (Newcastle City Centre)
The Quayside NE1 3DW
☎ 0870 9906530 📄 0870 9906531
Dir: *A167(M) then A186 and B1600. Hotel next to Tyne Bridge*
Premier Lodge offers modern, well-equipped, en suite accommodation suitable for both business and leisure travellers. Meals can be taken at the adjacent popular restaurant and bar, which is fully licensed. For further details, consult the Hotel Groups page.
ROOMS: 150 en suite s £52; d £52 **CONF:** Thtr 50 Class 30 Board 30 Del £99

⇧ Travel Inn (City Centre)
City Rd, Quayside NE1 2AN
☎ 0870 238 3318 📄 0191 232 6557
Dir: *at corner of City Rd (A186) & Crawhall Rd*
Travel Inn offers good-quality, value-for-money accommodation. Spacious, en suite rooms with bath and shower comfortably accommodate a family of up to two adults and two children (to age 15). The restaurant and bar offers a varied menu. For further details and the Travel Inn phone number, consult the Hotel Groups page.
ROOMS: 81 en suite s £49.95-£52.95; d £49.95-£52.95
CONF: Thtr 15 Board 12

⇧ Travel Inn (Newcastle-Upon-Tyne Holystone)
Holystone Roundabout NE27 0DA
☎ 08701 977189 📄 0191 259 9509
Dir: *3m N of Tyne Tunnel, adjacent to A19. Take A191 signed Gosforth/Whitley Bay*

Travel Inn offers good-quality, value-for-money accommodation. Spacious, en suite rooms with bath and shower comfortably accommodate a family of up to two adults and two children (to age 15). The restaurant and bar offers a varied menu. For further details and the Travel Inn phone number, consult the Hotel Groups page.
ROOMS: 40 en suite s £44.95; d £44.95

⇧ Travelodge (Newcastle Central)
Forster St NE1 2NH
☎ 08700 850 950
Travelodge offers good quality, good value, modern accommodation. Ideal for families, the spacious, en suite bedrooms include remote-control TV, tea and coffee-making facilities, luxury beds and free morning newspaper. Meals can be taken at the nearby family restaurant. For further details and the Travelodge phone number, consult the Hotel Groups page.
ROOMS: 120 en suite s fr £42.95; d fr £42.95

NEWCASTLE UPON TYNE AIRPORT, Tyne & Wear — Map 21 NZ17

⇧ Premier Lodge (Newcastle Airport)
Callerton Ln Ends, Woolsington NE13 8DF
☎ 0870 9906338 📄 0870 9906339
Dir: *A1 onto A696 Jedburgh Rd to Newcastle airport. 2nd slip road signed Throckley & Woolsington. Right at top of road, over 2 rdbts and level crossing. Hotel on left*
Premier Lodge offers modern, well-equipped, en suite accommodation suitable for both business and leisure travellers. Meals can be taken at the adjacent popular restaurant and bar, which is fully licensed. For further details, consult the Hotel Groups page.
ROOMS: 42 en suite 10 annexe en suite s £48; d £48
CONF: Thtr 60 Class 20 Board 26 Del £77.50

⇧ Travel Inn
Newcastle Int. Airport, Ponteland Rd, Prestwick NE20 9DB
☎ 08701 977190 📄 01661 824940
Dir: *adjacent to airport main entrance*
Travel Inn offers good-quality, value-for-money accommodation. Spacious, en suite rooms with bath and shower comfortably accommodate a family of up to two adults and two children (to age 15). The restaurant and bar offers a varied menu. For further details and the Travel Inn phone number, consult the Hotel Groups page.
ROOMS: 86 en suite s £46.95-£49.95; d £46.95-£49.95 **CONF:** Thtr 20

NEWENT, Gloucestershire — Map 10 SO72

Restaurant with Rooms

Three Choirs Vineyards
GL18 1LS
☎ 01531 890223 📄 01531 890877
e-mail: info@threechoirs.com
Dir: *on B4215 N of Newent, follow brown tourist signs*
This thriving vineyard continues to go from strength to strength. The restaurant, which overlooks the 100-acre estate, enjoys a popular following. Spacious, high quality bedrooms are equipped with many extras and all have doors opening on to private patio areas, from which wonderful views can be enjoyed.
ROOMS: 8 annexe en suite (2 fmly) No smoking in all bedrooms s £65-£105; d £85-£105 (incl. bkfst) **LB** **FACILITIES:** Wine tasting, 75 acres of vineyards, guided & self guided tours **CONF:** Thtr 20 Class 15 Board 20 Del from £135 **PARKING:** 8 **NOTES:** No dogs (ex guide dogs) No smoking in restaurant Closed 24-26 Dec
CARDS:

NEWHAVEN, East Sussex — Map 06 TQ40

⇧ Travel Inn
The Drove, Avis Rd BN9 0AG
☎ 08701 977192 📄 01273 612359
Dir: *from A26 (New Rd) through Drove Industrial Estate, left turn after underpass. On same complex as Sainsburys, A259*
Travel Inn offers good-quality, value-for-money accommodation. Spacious, en suite rooms with bath and shower comfortably accommodate a family of up to two adults and two children (to age 15). The restaurant and bar offers a varied menu. For further details and the Travel Inn phone number, consult the Hotel Groups page.
ROOMS: 40 en suite s £44.95; d £44.95

NEWICK, East Sussex

Map 06 TQ42

Top 200 - Hotel

★★★ ®® **Newick Park Hotel & Country Estate**
BN8 4SB
☎ 01825 723633 📠 01825 723969
e-mail: bookings@newickpark.co.uk
Dir: *S off A272 in Newick between Haywards Heath and Uckfield. Pass church, left at junct and hotel 0.25m on right*

Delightful Grade II listed Georgian country house set amidst 250 acres of Sussex parkland and landscaped gardens. The spacious, individually decorated bedrooms are tastefully furnished, thoughtfully equipped and have superb views of the grounds; many rooms have huge American king-size beds. The comfortable public rooms include a study, a sitting room, lounge bar and an elegant restaurant.

ROOMS: 13 en suite 3 annexe en suite (5 fmly) (1 GF) No smoking in 12 bedrooms s £95-£120; d £165-£235 (incl. bkfst) **LB** **FACILITIES:** STV Outdoor swimming (H) Tennis (hard) Fishing Croquet lawn Badminton, Tank driving, Quad biking, Clay pigeon shooting Xmas **CONF:** Thtr 80 Class 80 Board 30 Del £185 **PARKING:** 52 **NOTES:** No smoking in restaurant Civ Wed 74
CARDS:

NEWMARKET, Suffolk

Map 12 TL66

★★★★69% ® **Bedford Lodge**
Bury Rd CB8 7BX
☎ 01638 663175 📠 01638 667391
e-mail: info@bedfordlodgehotel.co.uk

CLASSIC BRITISH

Dir: *from town centre take Bury St Edmunds road, hotel 0.5m on left*

This imposing 18th-century Georgian hunting lodge is set in three acres of secluded landscaped gardens. The public rooms have now been enhanced by the creation of a small lounge area adjacent to the lounge bar, whilst interesting cuisine continues to be offered in the elegant Orangery restaurant. The hotel also features superb leisure facilities and self-contained conference and banqueting suites. Contemporary bedrooms have a light, airy feel; each room is tastefully furnished and well equipped.

ROOMS: 55 en suite (3 fmly) No smoking in 33 bedrooms s £110; d £145 (incl. bkfst) **LB** **FACILITIES:** STV Indoor swimming (H) Sauna Solarium Gym Jacuzzi Steam room & beauty salon Xmas **CONF:** Thtr 200 Class 80 Board 60 Del £150 **SERVICES:** Lift **PARKING:** 120 **NOTES:** No dogs No smoking in restaurant
CARDS:

> Bad hair day?
> Hairdryers in all rooms three stars and above

★★★73% ® ***Swynford Paddocks Hotel***
CB8 0UE
☎ 01638 570234 📠 01638 570283
e-mail: info@swynfordpaddocks.com
(For full entry see Six Mile Bottom)

★★★68% **Heath Court**
Moulton Rd CB8 8DY
☎ 01638 667171 📠 01638 666533
e-mail: quality@heathcourt-hotel.com

Best Western

Dir: *leave A14 at Newmarket and Ely exit on A142. Follow town centre signs over mini rdbt. At clocktower left into Moulton Rd*

Close to Newmarket Heath, this modern red-brick hotel is popular for its pleasant facilities and relaxed atmosphere. Refurbished public rooms offer a choice of dining options: informal meals can be taken in the lounge bar, alternatively a modern carte/carvery is offered in the restaurant. Bedrooms are spacious and smartly presented, a number are equipped with air conditioning.

ROOMS: 41 en suite (2 fmly) No smoking in 11 bedrooms s £79-£89; d £102-£112 (incl. bkfst) **LB** **FACILITIES:** STV **CONF:** Thtr 150 Class 40 Board 40 Del £110 **SERVICES:** Lift **PARKING:** 50 **NOTES:** Civ Wed 80
CARDS:

NEW MILTON, Hampshire

Map 05 SZ29

Top 200 - Hotel

★★★★★ ®®® **Chewton Glen**
Christchurch Rd BH25 6QS
☎ 01425 275341 📠 01425 272310
e-mail: reservations@chewtonglen.com

RELAIS & CHATEAUX

Dir: *A35 from Lyndhurst for 10m, left at staggered junct. Follow tourist sign for hotel through Walkford, take 2nd left*

This outstanding hotel has been at the forefront of British hotel-keeping for many years. Once past the wrought iron entrance gates, guests are transported into a world of luxury. Log fires and afternoon tea are part of the tradition here, and lounges enjoy fine views over sweeping croquet lawns. Most bedrooms are very spacious, with private patios or balconies. Dining is a treat, and extensive wine lists are a must for the enthusiast. The spa and leisure facilities are among the best in the country.

ROOMS: 59 en suite (9 GF) s £285-£425; d £285-£425 **LB** **FACILITIES: Spa** STV Indoor swimming (H) Outdoor swimming (H) Golf 9 Tennis (hard) Snooker Sauna Gym Croquet lawn Putting green Jacuzzi Hairdresser Hydrotherapy pool Swimming pool supervised entertainment Xmas **CONF:** BC Thtr 150 Class 70 Board 40 Del from £230 **PARKING:** 100 **NOTES:** No dogs (ex guide dogs) No children 5yrs No smoking in restaurant Civ Wed 120
CARDS:

N

NEWPORT See Wight, Isle of

NEWPORT, Shropshire Map 15 SJ71

★★66% *Royal Victoria*

St Mary's St TF10 7AB
☎ 01952 820331 01952 820209
e-mail: info@royal-victoria.com.uk
Dir: *off A41 at 2nd Newport by-pass rdbt towards town centre. Right at 1st traffic lights, hotel 150mtrs on left*

This town-centre hotel stands behind St Nicholas' Church. Dating from Georgian times, it derives its name from a visit made by Princess Victoria in 1832. The hotel provides well-equipped, modern accommodation. Facilities available to guests include an attractively appointed restaurant, a choice of bars and a large function/conference suite.

ROOMS: 24 rms (2 fmly) No smoking in 6 bedrooms **CONF:** Thtr 60 Class 40 Board 30 **PARKING:** 70 **NOTES:** No smoking in restaurant **CARDS:**

NEWPORT PAGNELL MOTORWAY SERVICE AREA (M1), Buckinghamshire Map 11 SP84

Welcome Lodge

Newport Pagnell MK16 8DS
☎ 01908 610878 01908 216539
e-mail: newport.hotel@welcomebreak.co.uk
Dir: *M1 junct 14-15*

This modern building offers accommodation in smart, spacious and well-equipped bedrooms, suitable for families and business travellers, and all with en suite bathrooms. Refreshments may be taken at the nearby family restaurant. For further details and the Welcome Break phone number, consult the Hotel Groups page.

ROOMS: 90 en suite s £45-£60; d £45-£60 **CONF:** Thtr 40 Class 12 Board 16

NEWQUAY, Cornwall & Isles of Scilly Map 02 SW86

★★★★65% Headland

Fistral Beach TR7 1EW
☎ 01637 872211 01637 872212
e-mail: office@headlandhotel.co.uk
Dir: *off A30 onto A392 at Indian Queens, approaching Newquay follow signs for Fistral Beach, hotel adjacent*

This unique Victorian hotel enjoys a spectacular location surrounded by the sea on three sides. Improvements have provided comfortable and spacious bedrooms, most of which have the benefit of the sea views. Public areas, with impressive floral

continued

displays, provide a number of choices with a range of lounges, a cocktail bar and also a choice of dining options.

ROOMS: 105 en suite (44 fmly) d £115-£180 (incl. bkfst) **LB** **FACILITIES: Spa** Indoor swimming (H) Outdoor swimming (H) Golf 9 Tennis (hard) Snooker Sauna Gym Croquet lawn Putting green Jacuzzi Children's outdoor play area, Harry Potter playroom entertainment ch fac **CONF:** Thtr 250 Class 120 Board 50 Del from £140 **SERVICES:** Lift **PARKING:** 400 **NOTES:** No smoking in restaurant Closed 23-27 Dec Civ Wed 250 **CARDS:**

★★★70% Barrowfield

Hilgrove Rd TR7 2QY
☎ 01637 878878 01637 879490
e-mail: booking@barrowfield.demon.co.uk
Dir: *A3058 to Newquay towards Quintrell Downs. Right at rdbt into town, left at Texaco garage*

Offering a pleasant range of facilities and spacious public rooms, this popular hotel is ideally situated and is equally suited for all guests' needs. Bedrooms, some with sea views and balconies, are well appointed and comfortable. Public areas include an elegant restaurant, spacious foyer lounge, attractive coffee shop and an intimate piano bar.

ROOMS: 81 en suite 2 annexe en suite (18 fmly) s £50-£65; d £100-£130 (incl. bkfst & dinner) **LB** **FACILITIES:** STV Indoor swimming (H) Outdoor swimming (H) Snooker Sauna Solarium Gym Jacuzzi Table tennis, Coffee shop, pool room entertainment Xmas **CONF:** Thtr 250 Class 150 Board 90 **SERVICES:** Lift **PARKING:** 70 **NOTES:** No smoking in restaurant Civ Wed 250 **CARDS:**

★★★69% Hotel Bristol

Narrowcliff TR7 2PQ
☎ 01637 875181 01637 879347
e-mail: info@hotelbristol.co.uk
Dir: *off A30 onto A392, then A3058. Hotel 2.5m on left*

The Hotel Bristol is conveniently situated and many of the bedrooms enjoy fine sea views. Staff are friendly and provide a professional and attentive service. There is a range of comfortable lounges, ideal for relaxing prior to dining in the elegant dining room, and also leisure and conference facilities.

ROOMS: 74 en suite (23 fmly) s £51-£71; d £82-£122 **LB** **FACILITIES:** STV Indoor swimming (H) Snooker Sauna Solarium Table tennis ch fac Xmas **CONF:** Thtr 200 Class 80 Board 20 Del from £75 **SERVICES:** Lift **PARKING:** 105 **NOTES:** No smoking in restaurant **CARDS:**

See advert on opposite page

★★★69% Esplanade Hotel

Esplanade Rd, Pentire TR7 1PS
☎ 01637 873333 01637 851413
e-mail: info@newquay-hotels.co.uk
Dir: *from A30 take A392 at Indian Queens towards Newquay, follow to rdbt and take left to Pentire, then right fork to beach*

Overlooking the rolling breakers at Fistral Beach, this

continued on p452

N

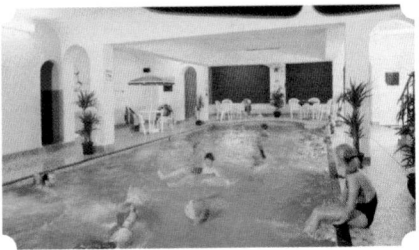

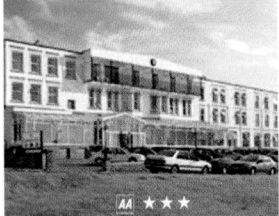

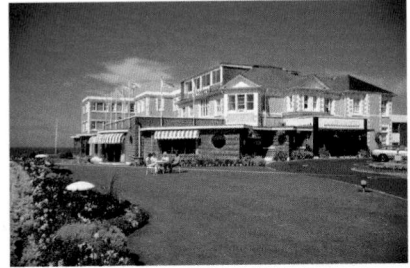

NEWQUAY, continued

family-owned hotel offers a warm welcome. There is a choice of bedroom sizes; all have modern facilities and the most popular rooms have stunning sea views. There are a number of bars, a continental-style coffee shop and the more formal Ocean View Restaurant.
ROOMS: 93 en suite (44 fmly) No smoking in 5 bedrooms s £27-£52.50; d £54-£105 (incl. bkfst & dinner) **LB** **FACILITIES: Spa** STV Indoor swimming (H) Outdoor swimming (H) Sauna Solarium Jacuzzi Table tennis entertainment ch fac Xmas **CONF:** Thtr 300 Class 180 Board 150 Del from £40 **SERVICES:** Lift **PARKING:** 40 **NOTES:** No smoking in restaurant **CARDS:**

See advert on page 451

★★★68% Trebarwith

Trebarwith Crescent TR7 1BZ
☎ 01637 872288 01637 875431
e-mail: trebahotel@aol.com
Dir: *from A3058 to Mount Wise Rd. 3rd right down Marcus Hill, across East St into Trebarwith Cres. Hotel at end*

With breathtaking views of the rugged north Cornish coastline, this friendly, family-run hotel is set in its own grounds, close to the town centre and with a path leading to the beach. The public rooms include a lounge, ballroom, restaurant and cinema. The comfortable bedrooms include four-poster and family rooms, many benefiting from the sea views.
ROOMS: 41 en suite (8 fmly) (1 GF) s £35-£71; d £70-£142 (incl. bkfst & dinner) **LB** **FACILITIES: Spa** Indoor swimming (H) Fishing Snooker Sauna Solarium Jacuzzi Video theatre Games room entertainment **CONF:** Thtr 45 Del from £59 **PARKING:** 41 **NOTES:** No dogs (ex guide dogs) No smoking in restaurant Closed Nov-5 Apr
CARDS:

See advert on page 451

★★★65% Hotel Riviera

Lusty Glaze Rd TR7 3AA
☎ 01637 874251 01637 850823
e-mail: a.newton@btinternet.com
Dir: *towards Newquay from Porth right at The Barrowfields. Hotel on right*
This popular cliff-top hotel enjoys panoramic views across the gardens to the sea beyond. Bedrooms vary in size and style, are well equipped and many have sea-views. Comfortable lounges are provided for rest and relaxation; the more energetic may wish to use the squash court or heated outdoor pool. There is also a range of conference and function facilities.
ROOMS: 48 en suite (6 fmly) s fr £55; d fr £110 (incl. bkfst) **FACILITIES:** Outdoor swimming (H) Squash Sauna Swimming Pool supervised by CCTV entertainment Xmas **CONF:** Thtr 200 Class 150 Board 50 Del from £100 **SERVICES:** Lift **PARKING:** 80 **NOTES:** No dogs (ex guide dogs) No smoking in restaurant Civ Wed 200
CARDS:

See advert on page 451

★★★60% *Kilbirnie*

Narrowcliff TR7 2RS
☎ 01637 875155 01637 850769
e-mail: enquirykilbirnie@aol.com
Dir: *on A392*
With delightful views over the Barrowfields and the sea, this family-run hotel offers a range of facilities. The recently refurbished reception rooms are spacious and comfortable, and during summer months feature a programme of entertainment. Bedrooms vary in size and style and some enjoy fine sea views. A daily changing menu is offered in the spacious dining room.
ROOMS: 66 en suite (3 fmly) **FACILITIES:** Indoor swimming (H) Outdoor swimming (H) Snooker Sauna Solarium Jacuzzi Table tennis **SERVICES:** Lift air con **PARKING:** 68 **NOTES:** No smoking in restaurant **CARDS:**

See advert on opposite page

★★71% Porth Veor Manor

Porth Way, Porth Bay TR7 3LW
☎ 01637 873274 01637 851690
e-mail: booking@porthveor.co.uk
Dir: *200yds from junct A3058/B3276, on B3276 towards Padstow*
Set in a quiet area, this pleasant hotel overlooks Porth Beach which is accessed from its two-acre grounds. A relaxed and friendly atmosphere is maintained at this family-run establishment. Bedrooms are decorated in varying styles and all are pleasantly spacious. A daily changing set price menu is served.
ROOMS: 22 en suite (7 fmly) (3 GF) No smoking in 6 bedrooms s £50-£60; d £100-£120 (incl. bkfst & dinner) **LB** **FACILITIES:** Croquet lawn Putting green Xmas **CONF:** BC Thtr 36 Class 24 Board 24 Del from £47.50 **PARKING:** 40 **NOTES:** No smoking in restaurant RS Nov-Feb **CARDS:**

★★71% Whipsiderry

Trevelgue Rd, Porth TR7 3LY
☎ 01637 874777 01637 874777
e-mail: info@whipsiderry.co.uk
Dir: *onto B3276 out of Newquay, in 0.5m right into Trevelgue Rd*
In a quiet location with views over Porth beach and the sea, the friendly Whipsiderry hotel offers bedrooms in a variety of sizes and styles, many with superb views. A daily changing menu offers interesting and well-cooked dishes with the emphasis on fresh, local produce. An outdoor pool is available, and at dusk guests can enjoy badger watching in the attractive grounds.
ROOMS: 20 rms (19 en suite) (5 fmly) No smoking in 8 bedrooms s £42-£54; d £84-£108 (incl. bkfst & dinner) **LB** **FACILITIES:** Outdoor swimming (H) Sauna American pool entertainment ch fac Xmas **PARKING:** 30 **NOTES:** No smoking in restaurant Closed Nov-Etr (ex Xmas) **CARDS:**

> Popped the question?
> Hotels with Civ Wed in their entry are licensed for civil wedding ceremonies. Maximum numbers for the ceremony only are shown, e.g. Civ Wed 120

★★67% Philema

1 Esplanade Rd, Pentire TR7 1PY
☎ 01637 872571 01637 873188
e-mail: info@philema.co.uk
Dir: *from A30 follow A392 then signs for Fistral Beach*
With excellent views over Fistral beach, the Philema provides a relaxed and friendly family environment. Extensive leisure facilities are available, including the heated indoor pool, which overlooks the garden. Many rooms have wonderful views and all are

continued

N

comfortably furnished. The attractive dining room offers a range of home-cooked dishes.
ROOMS: 32 en suite (27 fmly) s £23.50-£43; d £47-£86 (incl. bkfst & dinner) **FACILITIES: Spa** STV Indoor swimming (H) Snooker Sauna Solarium Jacuzzi Table tennis entertainment Xmas **PARKING:** 40
NOTES: No smoking in restaurant Closed 2 Jan-2 Feb
CARDS:

★★64% *Trenance Hotel*
The Crescent TR7 1DF
☎ 01637 873159 01637 850008
e-mail: reception@trenancehotel.co.uk
Set close to the town's many attractions, yet quietly located, this popular and friendly hotel overlooks the harbour and continues to be a popular venue. Bedrooms, some with large bay windows and sea views, are well equipped and comfortable. Entertainment is provided most evenings and guests can relax in the lounge, bar or games room.
ROOMS: 57 en suite (4 fmly) **FACILITIES:** pool table entertainment **SERVICES:** Lift **PARKING:** 20 **NOTES:** No dogs (ex guide dogs) No smoking in restaurant **CARDS:**

★★63% Cedars
Mount Wise TR7 2BA
☎ 01637 874225 01637 850421
e-mail: cedarshotel@btopenworld.com
Dir: *enter Newquay via Narrowcliff into Berry Rd and Mount Wise. 500yds on right from Mount Wise car park*
Remaining popular with leisure guests, this family-run hotel with friendly and enthusiastic staff has distant views of the coastline. Entertainment is provided in the spacious lounge/bar in season.
continued on p454

N

NEWQUAY, continued

Bedrooms vary in size, shape and style, and some are especially suitable for families.
ROOMS: 42 rms (31 en suite) (8 fmly) (6 GF) s £25-£35; d £50-£70 (incl. bkfst) **LB** **FACILITIES:** Outdoor swimming (H) Sauna Solarium Gym Jacuzzi entertainment Xmas **PARKING:** 42 **NOTES:** No smoking in restaurant Closed Dec-mid Mar **CARDS:**

★★63% Eliot
Edgcumbe Av TR7 2NH
☎ 01637 878177 01637 852053
e-mail: eliot.newquay@alfatravel.co.uk
Dir: *A30 onto A392 towards Quintrell Downs. Right at rdbt onto A3058. 4m to Newquay, left at amusements onto Edgcumbe Av. Hotel on left*
Located in a quiet residential area and just a short walk from the beaches and the varied attractions of the town, this long established hotel offers comfortable accommodation. Entertainment is provided most nights throughout the season and guests can relax in the spacious public areas.
ROOMS: 76 en suite (10 fmly) s £25-£30; d £42-£52 (incl. bkfst) **LB** **FACILITIES:** Outdoor swimming (H) Sauna Solarium Jacuzzi Pool table, Table tennis entertainment Xmas **SERVICES:** Lift **PARKING:** 20 **NOTES:** No dogs (ex guide dogs) No smoking in restaurant Closed Dec-Jan RS Nov & Feb-Mar **CARDS:**

Leisureplex

★★61% Tremont
Pentire Av TR7 1PB
☎ 01637 872984 01637 851984
Dir: *from A30 onto B3902 into Newquay and follow Pentire signs*
With views of Fistral beach, this popular hotel offers an impressive range of leisure facilities and, sat almost at the beach side, Tremont is within a short walk from the town. Entertainment is provided most nights in the season and public areas are spacious. Bedrooms are available in a range of sizes and all are comfortably furnished.
ROOMS: 54 en suite (26 fmly) No smoking in all bedrooms s £28-£45; d £56-£90 (incl. bkfst & dinner) **LB** **FACILITIES:** Indoor swimming (H) Tennis (hard) Sauna Solarium Gym Putting green Table tennis entertainment Xmas **SERVICES:** Lift **PARKING:** 60 **NOTES:** No smoking in restaurant **CARDS:**

NEWTON ABBOT, Devon — Map 03 SX87
See also Ilsington

★★★69% Passage House
Hackney Ln, Kingsteignton TQ12 3QH
☎ 01626 355515 01626 363336
e-mail: mail@passagehousehotel.co.uk
Dir: *from A380 onto A381 and follow racecourse signs*
With memorable views of the Teign Estuary, this popular hotel provides spacious, well-equipped bedrooms. An impressive range of leisure and meeting facilities are offered and a new conservatory provides a pleasant extension to the bar and lounge. A choice of dining is available in either the main restaurant, or the adjacent Passage House Inn for less formal dining.
ROOMS: 38 en suite (32 fmly) (6 GF) No smoking in 9 bedrooms s £69.50-£79.50; d £80-£90 (incl. bkfst) **LB** **FACILITIES: Spa** STV Indoor swimming (H) Sauna Solarium Gym Indoor swimming pool supervised **CONF:** BC Thtr 120 Class 50 Board 40 Del from £80 **SERVICES:** Lift **PARKING:** 300 **NOTES:** No dogs (ex guide dogs) No smoking in restaurant **CARDS:**

★★68% Queens
Queen St TQ12 2EZ
☎ 01626 363133 01626 354106
e-mail: queens@bestwestern.co.uk
Dir: *M5 onto A380, follow signs for railway station. Hotel opposite station*
Pleasantly and conveniently located close to the railway station and racecourse, this hotel continues to be a popular venue for business and touring guests alike. Bedrooms are pleasantly appointed and are well equipped. The lounge bar provides bar meals and specials, and a more extensive menu is available in the restaurant.
ROOMS: 20 en suite (3 fmly) No smoking in 8 bedrooms s £45-£55; d £65-£75 (incl. bkfst) **FACILITIES:** STV **CONF:** Thtr 130 Class 90 Board 40 Del £110 **PARKING:** 7 **NOTES:** No smoking in restaurant **CARDS:**

Best Western

★★67% Hazelwood Hotel
33a Torquay Rd TQ12 2LW
☎ 01626 366130 01626 365021
Dir: *A380 to Newton Abbot. At main rdbt right past McDonalds. Left through 2 sets of lights. Hotel at top of hill on right*
Conveniently located a short stroll from the town centre, this smart hotel offers a friendly environment. An ideal base for either the business or leisure guest, many regularly return to the Hazelwood. Bedrooms are smartly decorated and well equipped with thoughtful extra touches and attractive fabrics. Freshly prepared home-cooked dishes are offered in the panelled dining room.
ROOMS: 8 en suite No smoking in all bedrooms s £36-£40; d £50-£55 (incl. bkfst) **CONF:** Board 12 **PARKING:** 7 **NOTES:** No dogs (ex guide dogs) No smoking in restaurant **CARDS:**

NEWTON AYCLIFFE, Co Durham — Map 19 NZ22

⌂ Travel Inn Durham (Newton Aycliffe)
Great North Rd DL5 6JG
☎ 08701 977085 01325 324910
Dir: *on A167 E of Newton Aycliffe, 2m from A1(M)*
Travel Inn offers good-quality, value-for-money accommodation. Spacious, en suite rooms with bath and shower comfortably accommodate a family of up to two adults and two children (to age 15). The restaurant and bar offers a varied menu. For further details and the Travel Inn phone number, consult the Hotel Groups page.
ROOMS: 44 en suite s £44.95; d £44.95

travel inn

NEWTON-LE-WILLOWS, Merseyside — Map 15 SJ59

★★66% *Kirkfield Hotel*
2/4 Church St WA12 9SU
☎ 01925 228196 01925 291540
e-mail: kirkfieldhotel@netscape.net
Dir: *on A49 Newton-le-Willows opposite St Peter's Church*
A conveniently located hotel situated directly opposite the church, where car parking is also available. The hotel is family run and offers comfortable accommodation. A table d'hôte menu is available, or there are options for lighter dining in the bar area. Guests receive a friendly welcome and an informal atmosphere prevails.
ROOMS: 20 en suite (3 fmly) No smoking in 10 bedrooms **CONF:** Thtr 70 Class 60 Board 20 **PARKING:** 50 **CARDS:**

NORMAN CROSS, Cambridgeshire — Map 12 TL19

U **Holiday Inn Peterborough**

Great North Rd PE7 3TB
☎ 0870 400 9063 📠 01733 244455
Dir: *100yds from A1(M) junct 16 towards Yaxley on A15*

At the time of going to press, the classification for this hotel was not confirmed. Please refer to the AA internet site www.theAA.com for current information.

ROOMS: 96 en suite No smoking in 47 bedrooms **FACILITIES: Spa** Indoor swimming (H) Sauna Gym Steam room **CONF:** Thtr 50 Class 16 Board 24 **PARKING:** 150 **NOTES:** RS 24-27 Dec
CARDS:

NORTHALLERTON, North Yorkshire — Map 19 SE39

★★★67% **Solberge Hall**

Newby Wiske DL7 9ER
☎ 01609 779191 📠 01609 780472
e-mail: solberge@bestwestern.co.uk

Dir: *S of Northallerton on A167. Hotel on right passing through North Otterington*

This Grade II listed Georgian country house is set in 16 acres of parkland and commands panoramic views over open countryside. Spacious bedrooms, some with four-poster beds, vary in style. Public areas include a comfortable bar and an elegant drawing room. The Garden Room restaurant offers a wide range of carefully prepared dishes.

ROOMS: 24 en suite (2 fmly) No smoking in 4 bedrooms s fr £75; d fr £100 (incl. bkfst) **LB** **FACILITIES:** STV Croquet lawn Xmas **CONF:** Thtr 100 Class 50 Board 40 Del from £88.07 **PARKING:** 100 **NOTES:** No smoking in restaurant Civ Wed 100
CARDS:

See advert on this page

★★64% **The Golden Lion**

High St DL7 8PP
☎ 01609 777411 📠 01609 773250
Dir: *A684 for 5m onto A167. Through built-up area, 3rd exit at next rdbt to town centre. 3rd rdbt left into High St*

This popular hotel has a convenient location in the heart of the town centre. Bedrooms and bathrooms are spacious and offer a good range of amenities. Public areas include a choice of dining options and a lively bar.

ROOMS: 25 en suite (2 fmly) No smoking in 18 bedrooms s £45-£60; d £70-£85 (incl. bkfst) **LB** **FACILITIES:** Xmas **CONF:** Thtr 150 Class 80 Board 60 **PARKING:** 100 **NOTES:** No smoking in restaurant Civ Wed 150
CARDS:

Restaurant with Rooms

The Three Tuns

9 South End, Osmotherley DL6 3BN
☎ 01609 883301 📠 01609 883988
e-mail: claire.watson@steelriver.co.uk
Dir: *turn off A19 signed Northallerton/Osmotherley. Turn at junction signed Osmotherley at Kings Head Hotel. Into village, inn straight ahead*

Nestled in the popular village of Osmotherley, this restaurant with rooms is full of character. Bedrooms are all individual, stylish, comfortable and well equipped. The restaurant and bar retain many original features and offer an interesting imaginative menu and wine list to complement.

ROOMS: 7 en suite (1 fmly) (1 GF) No smoking in all bedrooms s £49-£65; d £65-£95 **PARKING:** 6 **NOTES:** No dogs (ex guide dogs) No smoking in restaurant **CARDS:**

NORTHAMPTON, Northamptonshire — Map 11 SP76

See also Flore

★★★★70% **Northampton Marriott Hotel**

Eagle Dr NN4 7HW
☎ 01604 768700 📠 01604 769011
e-mail: northampton@marriotthotels.co.uk
Dir: *M1 J15, follow signs to Delapre Golf Course, hotel on right*

On the outskirts of town, this modern hotel has a great deal to offer to a cross section of guests. A self-contained management centre makes this a popular conference venue; spacious and well-designed bedrooms cater especially well to business travellers, while the hotel's proximity to a number of attractions make this a good base to explore the area.

ROOMS: 120 en suite (12 fmly) No smoking in 82 bedrooms s £105-£115; d £125-£145 **LB** **FACILITIES: Spa** STV Indoor swimming (H) Sauna Solarium Gym Jacuzzi Steam room, Swimming pool supervised Xmas **CONF:** BC Thtr 220 Class 100 Board 36 Del from £135 **SERVICES:** air con **PARKING:** 187 **NOTES:** No smoking in restaurant Civ Wed 80 **CARDS:**

★★★70% **Lime Trees**

8 Langham Place, Barrack Rd NN2 6AA
☎ 01604 632188 📠 01604 233012
e-mail: info@limetrees.co.uk
Dir: *from city centre 0.5m N on A508 towards Leicester near racecourse park and cathedral*

A particularly well-presented hotel, popular with business travellers during the week and leisure guests at the weekend. Bedrooms are comfortable and in addition to all the usual facilities, many offer air conditioning. Notable features include an

continued on p456

NORTHAMPTON, continued

internal courtyard and a row of charming mews houses which have been converted into rooms.
ROOMS: 27 en suite (3 fmly) No smoking in 6 bedrooms s £45-£75; d £69-£90 (incl. bkfst) **LB CONF:** Thtr 50 Class 30 Board 30 Del from £119 **PARKING:** 24 **NOTES:** No dogs (ex guide dogs) Closed 25-26 Dec RS 27 Dec-New Year **CARDS:**

★★★68% Courtyard by Marriott Northampton

Bedford Rd NN4 7YF
☎ 0870 400 7214 ⎙ 0870 400 7314
e-mail: reservations.northamptoncourtyard@whitbread.com
Dir: *M1 junct 15 onto A508 towards Northampton. Follow A45 towards Wellingborough for 2m then A428 towards Bedford, hotel on left*
On the eastern edge of the town and easily accessible for the business traveller, this modern, purpose-built hotel offers spacious accommodation and a good range of facilities. Open-plan public areas help to create an informal atmosphere and the staff are genuinely friendly.
ROOMS: 104 en suite (50 fmly) (27 GF) No smoking in 91 bedrooms s £52-£95; d £66-£103 (incl. bkfst) **LB FACILITIES:** STV Gym Xmas **CONF:** Thtr 60 Class 40 Board 40 Del from £130 **SERVICES:** Lift air con **PARKING:** 156 **NOTES:** No dogs (ex guide dogs) No smoking in restaurant **CARDS:**

★★★64% Quality Hotel Northampton

Ashley Way, Weston Favell NN3 3EA
☎ 01604 739955 ⎙ 01604 415023
e-mail: admin@gb070.u-net.com
Dir: *leave A45 at junct with A43 towards Weston Favell. After 0.5m left to town centre. Left at top of slip road, hotel signed off A4500*

On the edge of town, this hotel offers well-equipped accommodation in an old style building and a more modern block. Public rooms are attractive and include an air-conditioned lounge area, an attractively furnished flag-stoned conservatory restaurant, and a number of versatile meeting rooms.
ROOMS: 33 en suite 38 annexe en suite (4 fmly) No smoking in 40 bedrooms s £99-£109; d £109-£125 **LB FACILITIES:** STV Xmas **CONF:** Thtr 140 Class 40 Board 50 Del from £90 **SERVICES:** Lift **PARKING:** 100 **NOTES:** No smoking in restaurant Civ Wed 150
CARDS:

⌂ Hotel Ibis Northampton

Sol Central, Marefair NN1 1SR
☎ 01604 608900 ⎙ 01604 608910
e-mail: H3657@accor-hotels.com

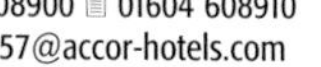

Dir: *M1 junct 15/15a towards city centre & railway station*
Modern, budget hotel offering comfortable accommodation in bright and practical bedrooms. Breakfast is self-service and dinner is available in the restaurant. For further details, consult the Hotel Groups page.
ROOMS: 151 en suite s £35.95-£42.95; d £35.95-£42.95

⌂ Innkeeper's Lodge Northampton East

Talavera Way, Round Spinney NN3 8RN
☎ 01604 494241 ⎙ 01604 673701
Dir: *M1 junct 15a, N on A43. Right at rdbt, pass 2 rdbts. At 3rd rdbt, A45 N until exit for A43, continue to Round Spinney rdbt and Talavera Way*
A new concept in the travel accommodation market. Smart rooms meet essential business requirements but also have home comforts. Dining options include all-day menus plus the added advantage of breakfast, which is included in the room price. For further details, consult the Hotel Groups page.
ROOMS: 31 en suite **CONF:** Thtr 36 Class 24 Board 28

⌂ Innkeeper's Lodge Northampton South

London Rd, Wootton NN4 0TG
☎ 01604 769676 ⎙ 01604 677981
Dir: *M1 junct 15 take A508, towards Northampton. Under flyover, exit left immediately & turn right at rdbt into London Rd. Lodge on right.*
A new concept in the travel accommodation market. Smart rooms meet essential business requirements but also have home comforts. Dining options include all-day menus plus the added advantage of breakfast, which is included in the room price. For further details, consult the Hotel Groups page.
ROOMS: 51 en suite **CONF:** Thtr 100 Board 40

⌂ Premier Lodge (Northampton East)

Crow Ln, Great Billing NN3 9DA
☎ 0870 9906510 ⎙ 0870 9906511

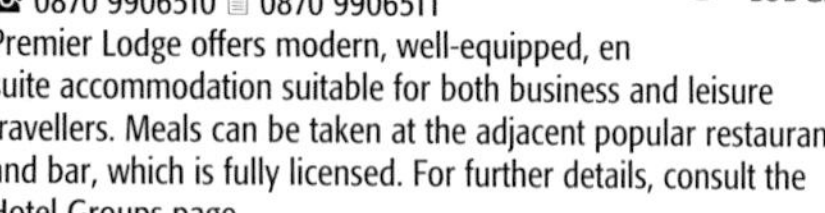

Premier Lodge offers modern, well-equipped, en suite accommodation suitable for both business and leisure travellers. Meals can be taken at the adjacent popular restaurant and bar, which is fully licensed. For further details, consult the Hotel Groups page.
ROOMS: 60 en suite s £48; d £48

⌂ Premier Lodge (Northampton South)

Newport Pagnall Road West, Wootton NN4 7JJ
☎ 0870 9906426 ⎙ 0870 9906427
Dir: *M1 junct 15 towards Northampton at A508/A45 junct. 5th exit off rdbt and lodge on right*
Premier Lodge offers modern, well-equipped, en suite accommodation suitable for both business and leisure travellers. Meals can be taken at the adjacent popular restaurant and bar, which is fully licensed. For further details, consult the Hotel Groups page.
ROOMS: 39 en suite s £48; d £48 **CONF:** Thtr 75 Class 48 Board 30 Del from £95

⌂ Travel Inn

Harpole Turn, Weedon Rd, Harpole NN7 4DD
☎ 08701 977195 ⎙ 01604 831807
Dir: *on A45, 1m from junct 16, on left.*

Travel Inn offers good-quality, value-for-money accommodation. Spacious, en suite rooms with bath and shower comfortably accommodate a family of up to two adults and two children (to age 15). The restaurant and bar offers a varied menu. For further details and the Travel Inn phone number, consult the Hotel Groups page.
ROOMS: 51 en suite s £44.95; d £44.95 **CONF:** Thtr 40 Board 30

⌂ Travel Inn

The Lakes, Bedford Rd NN4 7YD
☎ 08701 977196 ⎙ 01604 621935
Dir: *M1 junct 15 follow A508 (A45) to Northampton. A428 exit then at rbt take 4th exit (signed Bedford). Left at next rbt for Travel Inn on right*
Travel Inn offers good-quality, value-for-money accommodation. Spacious, en suite rooms with bath and shower comfortably accommodate a family of up to two adults and two children (to age 15). The restaurant and bar offers a varied menu. For further details and the Travel Inn phone number, consult the Hotel Groups page.
ROOMS: 44 en suite s £44.95; d £44.95

> Popped the question?
> Hotels with Civ Wed in their entry are licensed for civil wedding ceremonies. Maximum numbers for the ceremony only are shown, e.g. Civ Wed 120

⇧ Travelodge
Upton Way NN5 6EG
☎ 08700 850 950 📄 01604 758395
Dir: *A45, towards M1 junct 16*
Travelodge offers good quality, good value, modern accommodation. Ideal for families, the spacious, en suite bedrooms include remote-control TV, tea and coffee-making facilities, luxury beds and free morning newspaper. Meals can be taken at the nearby family restaurant. For further details and the Travelodge phone number, consult the Hotel Groups page.
ROOMS: 62 en suite s fr £42.95; d fr £42.95

○ Campanile Northampton
Off Junction 15 / M1, Grange Park
☎ 0208 572 3663
ROOMS: 80 en suite **NOTES:** Due to open Dec 2003

NORTH FERRIBY, East Riding of Yorkshire — Map 17 SE92

★★★65% *Elizabeth Hotel Hull*
Ferriby High Rd HU14 3LG
☎ 01482 645212 📄 01482 643332
Dir: *M62 onto A63 to Hull. Exit for Humber Bridge. At rdbt follow Leeds signs until signs for North Ferriby. Hotel 0.5m on left*
A modern, purpose built hotel which commands fine views of the Humber Bridge. Bedrooms are comfortable and well equipped. Public areas are functional and both the restaurant and lounge bar look out over the river. There is ample car parking and also a children's play area at the rear. 24-hour room service is available.
ROOMS: 95 en suite (3 fmly) No smoking in 66 bedrooms **FACILITIES:** STV Nearly full size pool table ch fac **CONF:** Thtr 120 Class 45 Board 45 **PARKING:** 140 **NOTES:** No smoking in restaurant Civ Wed 50 **CARDS:**

NORTH KILWORTH, Leicestershire — Map 11 SP68

★★★★72% Kilworth House
Lutterworth Rd LE17 6JE
☎ 01858 880058 📄 01858 880349
e-mail: reservations@kilworthhouse.co.uk
Dir: *A4304 toward Market Harborough, after Walcote, hotel 0.5m on right*
A newly restored Victorian country house located in thirty-eight acres of private grounds. Gracious public areas include many period pieces and original artwork. Bedrooms are very comfortable and well equipped, and the large Orangery is now used for informal dining while an opulent restaurant has a more formal air.
ROOMS: 40 en suite (2 fmly) (13 GF) s £120-£200; d £140-£220 **LB** **FACILITIES:** STV Gym Croquet lawn Beauty therapy rooms Xmas **CONF:** Thtr 100 Class 50 Board 28 Del from £165 **SERVICES:** Lift **PARKING:** 98 **NOTES:** No smoking in restaurant **CARDS:**

NORTH MUSKHAM, Nottinghamshire — Map 17 SK75

⇧ Travelodge (Newark)
NG23 6HT
☎ 08700 850 950 📄 01636 703635
Dir: *3m N, on A1 southbound*
Travelodge offers good quality, good value, modern accommodation. Ideal for families, the spacious, en suite bedrooms include remote-control TV, tea and coffee-making facilities, luxury beds and free morning newspaper. Meals can be taken at the nearby family restaurant. For further details and the Travelodge phone number, consult the Hotel Groups page.
ROOMS: 30 en suite s fr £42.95; d fr £42.95

NORTHOLT, Greater London
See LONDON SECTION plan 1 B4

⇧ Innkeeper's Lodge
Mandeville Rd UB5 4LU
☎ 020 8422 2050
Dir: *A40 at the Target rdbt*
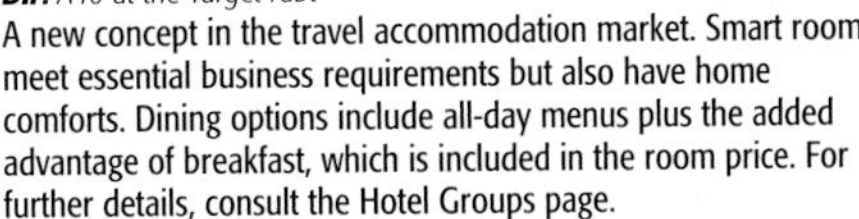
A new concept in the travel accommodation market. Smart rooms meet essential business requirements but also have home comforts. Dining options include all-day menus plus the added advantage of breakfast, which is included in the room price. For further details, consult the Hotel Groups page.
ROOMS: 21 en suite

NORTH WALSHAM, Norfolk — Map 13 TG23

Top 200 - Hotel

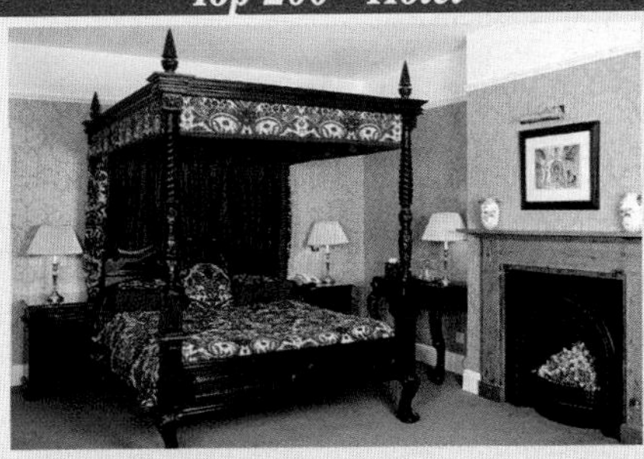

★★ Beechwood
Cromer Rd NR28 0HD
☎ 01692 403231 📄 01692 407284
e-mail: enquiries@beechwood-hotel.co.uk
Dir: *B1150 from Norwich. At North Walsham left at 1st traffic lights, then right at next*
Expect a warm welcome at this elegant 18th-century house, situated just a short walk from the town centre. The individually styled bedrooms are tastefully furnished with well-chosen antique pieces, attractive co-ordinated soft fabrics and many thoughtful touches. The spacious public areas include a lounge bar with plush furnishings, a further lounge and a smartly appointed restaurant serving award-winning food.
ROOMS: 11 en suite (2 GF) No smoking in 9 bedrooms s fr £65; d fr £90 (incl. bkfst) **LB** **PARKING:** 20 **NOTES:** No children 10yrs No smoking in restaurant **CARDS:**

NORTH WALTHAM, Hampshire — Map 05 SU54

⇧ Premier Lodge (Basingstoke)
RG25 2BB
☎ 0870 9906476 📄 0870 9906477
Dir: *on A30 1.5m from M3 junct 7. Follow signs for Basingstoke then Kings Worthy and Popham*
Premier Lodge offers modern, well-equipped, en suite accommodation suitable for both business and leisure travellers. Meals can be taken at the adjacent popular restaurant and bar, which is fully licensed. For further details, consult the Hotel Groups page.
ROOMS: 28 en suite s £48; d £48 **CONF:** Thtr 80 Class 30 Board 35 Del from £85

GF Indicates the number of bedrooms at ground floor level.

NORTHWICH, Cheshire
Map 15 SJ67

★★★65% **Quality Hotel Northwich**
London Rd CW9 5HD
☎ 01606 44443 📠 01606 42596
e-mail: admin@gb618.u-net.com
Dir: *M6 J19, follow A556 for 4 miles, take right turn & follow signs for Northwich & Town Centre*
A first in the UK - this floating hotel has been built over the river and a very successful concept has been created. The bedrooms are modern and well equipped, and there is a carvery style restaurant which overlooks the river.
ROOMS: 60 en suite (2 fmly) No smoking in 30 bedrooms s £45-£79; d £45-£89 **LB FACILITIES:** STV Xmas **CONF:** Thtr 80 Class 40 Board 30 Del from £65 **SERVICES:** Lift **PARKING:** 110 **NOTES:** No smoking in restaurant Civ Wed 80 **CARDS:**

★★62% **Hartford Hall**
School Ln, Hartford CW8 1PW
☎ 01606 780320 📠 01606 782285
Dir: *in village of Hartford, between Northwich & Chester signed off A556*
Situated in four acres of gardens and grounds, on the edge of the village of Hartford, this 17th-century manor house offers well equipped accommodation. Public areas are characteristic of the period and feature the heavily beamed Nunn's Room in which civil weddings and other functions are held.
ROOMS: 20 en suite (4 fmly) (8 GF) No smoking in 13 bedrooms s £45-£105; d £49-£105 (incl. bkfst) **LB FACILITIES:** STV Games room **CONF:** Thtr 50 Class 50 Board 50 **PARKING:** 50 **NOTES:** No smoking in restaurant RS 25 Dec Civ Wed 70 **CARDS:**

Premier Lodge (Northwich)
520 Chester Rd, Sandiway CW8 2DN
☎ 0870 9906494 📠 0870 9906495
Premier Lodge offers modern, well-equipped, en suite accommodation suitable for both business and leisure travellers. Meals can be taken at the adjacent popular restaurant and bar, which is fully licensed. For further details, consult the Hotel Groups page.
ROOMS: 54 en suite s £48; d £48

Premier Lodge (Northwich South)
London Rd, Leftwich CW9 8EG

☎ 0870 9906362 📠 0870 9906363
Premier Lodge offers modern, well-equipped, en suite accommodation suitable for both business and leisure travellers. Meals can be taken at the adjacent popular restaurant and bar, which is fully licensed. For further details, consult the Hotel Groups page.
ROOMS: 32 en suite s £48; d £48 **CONF:** Thtr 25 Class 25 Board 25

NORTHWOLD, Norfolk
Map 13 TL79

★★67% **Comfort Inn Thetford**
Thetford Rd IP26 5LQ
☎ 01366 728888 📠 01366 727121
e-mail: admin@gb632.u-net.com
Dir: *W of Mundford on A134*
This modern, purpose-built hotel is set in a rural location just off the A134. The generously proportioned bedrooms are situated in courtyard style wings adjacent to the main building; they are pleasantly decorated and equipped with a good range of facilities.
continued

Dinner and breakfast is served in the beamed Woodland Inn, which combines the roles of country pub and hotel restaurant.
ROOMS: 34 en suite (12 fmly) (18 GF) No smoking in 17 bedrooms s £45-£65; d £55-£75 **LB FACILITIES:** STV mini gym Xmas **CONF:** Th 150 Class 55 Board 60 Del from £74.50 **PARKING:** 250 **NOTES:** No smoking in restaurant Civ Wed 80
CARDS:

NORTON, Shropshire
Map 10 SJ7

★★76% **Hundred House Hotel**
Bridgnorth Rd TF11 9EE
☎ 01952 730353 📠 01952 730355
e-mail: hundredhouse@lineone.net
Dir: *midway between Telford and Bridgnorth on A442. In centre of Norto*

Primarily Georgian, but with parts dating back to the 14th century, this friendly, family-owned and run hotel offers individually styled well-equipped bedrooms which have period furniture and attractive soft furnishings. Public areas include cosy bars and intimate dining areas where memorable meals are served.
ROOMS: 10 en suite (4 fmly) s £75-£85; d £99-£125 (incl. bkfst) **LB FACILITIES:** Xmas **CONF:** Class 20 Board 15 **PARKING:** 30 **NOTES:** Closed Xmas night & Boxing Day Night RS Sunday evenings
CARDS:

NORWICH, Norfolk
Map 13 TG2

★★★★75% ***Marriott Sprowston Manor Hotel & Country Club***
Sprowston Park, Wroxham Rd, Sprowston NR7 8RP
☎ 01603 410871 📠 01603 423911
e-mail: sprowston.manor@marriotthotels.co.uk
Dir: *From A11/A47, 2m NE on A115 (Wroxham Rd). Follow signs to Sprowston Park*

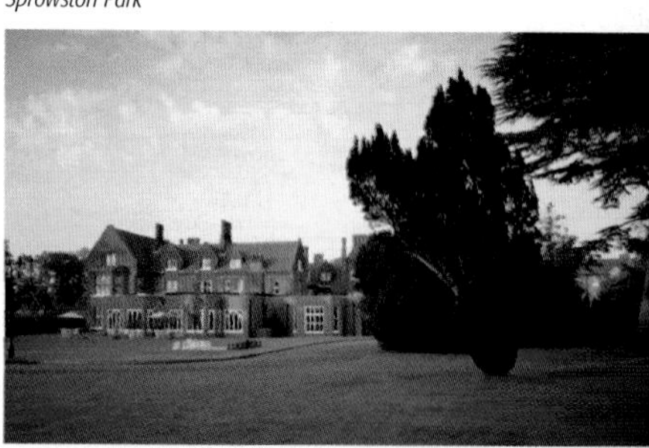

An imposing property set amidst attractive landscaped grounds and surrounded by open parkland just a short drive from the city
continued

entre. The spacious bedrooms come in a variety of styles; each ne is tastefully furnished and thoughtfully equipped. Public ooms feature an elegant restaurant where an interesting range of shes is available. The hotel has extensive conference, banqueting nd leisure facilities as well as a golf course.

OOMS: 94 en suite (3 fmly) No smoking in 65 bedrooms **ACILITIES: Spa** STV Indoor swimming (H) Golf 18 Sauna Solarium ym Putting green Jacuzzi Beauty salon Health spa Driving range **ONF:** Thtr 120 Class 50 Board 50 **SERVICES:** Lift **PARKING:** 150 **OTES:** No dogs (ex guide dogs) No smoking in restaurant Civ Wed 110 **ARDS:**

★★★★70% *De Vere Dunston Hall*

DE VERE HOTELS

pswich Rd NR14 8PQ

☎ 01508 470444 🖹 01508 471499

-mail: dhreception@devere-hotels.com

Dir: *from A47, take A140 Ipswich road, hotel off road on left after 0.25m*

mposing Grade II listed building set amidst 170 acres of andscaped grounds just a short drive from the city centre. The pacious bedrooms are smartly decorated, tastefully furnished and equipped to a high standard. The attractively appointed public ooms offer a wide choice of areas in which to relax and the hotel also boasts a superb range of leisure facilities that include an 8-hole PGA golf course, floodlit tennis courts and a football pitch.

ROOMS: 130 en suite No smoking in 58 bedrooms **FACILITIES: Spa** TV Indoor swimming (H) Golf 18 Tennis (hard) Snooker Sauna olarium Gym Putting green Jacuzzi Bowling green, Floodlit Driving ange **CONF:** Thtr 299 Class 140 Board 90 **SERVICES:** Lift **PARKING:** 500 **NOTES:** No dogs (ex guide dogs) No smoking in estaurant Civ Wed 90 **CARDS:**

★★★75% Annesley House

. Newmarket Rd NR2 2LA

☎ 01603 624553 🖹 01603 621577

-mail: annesleyhouse@bestwestern.co.uk

Dir: *on A11 0.5m before city centre*

A delightful Georgian property, situated amid three acres of andscaped gardens, and just a short walk from the city centre.

continued

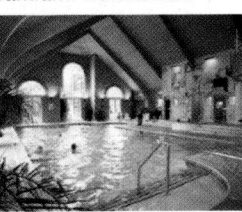

N

Bedrooms are split between three separate houses, two of which are linked by a glass walkway; they are attractively decorated, tastefully furnished and equipped with many useful extras. Public rooms feature a smart conservatory restaurant, which overlooks the gardens, and a comfortable lounge bar.

ROOMS: 18 en suite 8 annexe en suite (3 fmly) (7 GF) No smoking in 22 bedrooms s £75-£90; d £90-£105 (incl. bkfst) **LB FACILITIES:** STV **CONF:** Thtr 16 Board 16 **PARKING:** 25 **NOTES:** No dogs (ex guide dogs) No smoking in restaurant Closed 24-27 & 30-31 Dec **CARDS:**

★★★75% Barnham Broom Hotel, Golf & Country Club

NR9 4DD

☎ 01603 759393 759522 🖹 01603 758224

e-mail: enquiry@barnhambroomhotel.co.uk

(For full entry see Barnham Broom)

TV dinner?
Room service at three stars and above

★★★70% Beeches Hotel & Victorian Gardens

THE INDEPENDENTS

2-6 Earlham Rd NR2 3DB

☎ 01603 621167 🖹 01603 620150

e-mail: reception@beeches.co.uk

Dir: *W of city centre on B1108, next to Cathedral, off inner ring road*

Ideally situated just a short walk from the city centre, this charming privately-owned hotel is set in grounds with a lovely sunken Victorian garden. The bedrooms are situated in three separate buildings; each room is tastefully decorated and

continued on p460

NORWICH, continued

equipped with many thoughtful touches. Public rooms include a smart lounge bar, a bistro-style restaurant and a residents' lounge.
ROOMS: 36 en suite No smoking in all bedrooms s £64-£79; d £82-£99 (incl. bkfst) **LB** **FACILITIES:** Putting green Xmas **CONF:** BC Thtr 30 Class 20 Board 12 Del £80 **PARKING:** 50 **NOTES:** No dogs (ex guide dogs) No children 12yrs No smoking in restaurant
CARDS:

See advert on opposite page

★★★70% The Georgian House

32-34 Unthank Rd NR2 2RB
☎ 01603 615655 📠 01603 765689
e-mail: reception@georgian-hotel.co.uk
Dir: *follow Roman Catholic Cathedral signs from city centre, hotel off inner ring road*

A pair of Victorian houses have been carefully converted to create this comfortable hotel, a few minutes' walk from the city centre. Public areas include a cosy bar, a TV lounge and an elegant restaurant offering a daily changing carte menu. The smartly refurbished bedrooms are well maintained and equipped with modern facilities.
ROOMS: 28 en suite (2 fmly) (10 GF) No smoking in 20 bedrooms s £64-£67.50; d £90-£95 (incl. bkfst) **LB** **FACILITIES:** STV **CONF:** BC Thtr 25 Class 20 Board 20 Del from £27.50 **PARKING:** 40 **NOTES:** No smoking in restaurant Closed 24 Dec-2 Jan
CARDS:

See advert on opposite page

★★★68% The George Hotel

10 Arlington Ln, Newmarket Rd NR2 2DA
☎ 01603 617841 📠 01603 663708
e-mail: reservations@georgehotel.co.uk
Dir: *on A11 follow city centre signs, Newmarket Rd towards centre. Hotel on left*

Within just 10 minutes' walk of the town centre, this friendly, family-run hotel is well placed for guests wishing to explore the many sights of this historic city. The hotel occupies three adjacent buildings, the restaurant, bar and most bedrooms are located in the main building, while the adjacent cottages have been converted into comfortable and modern guest bedrooms.
ROOMS: 36 en suite 4 annexe en suite (3 fmly) No smoking in 9 bedrooms s £56-£70; d £65-£79 (incl. bkfst) **LB** **FACILITIES:** Xmas **CONF:** Thtr 70 Class 50 Board 50 Del from £88 **PARKING:** 40
CARDS:

AA Rosette Award for culinary excellence

★★★66% Quality Hotel

2 Barnard Rd, Bowthorpe NR5 9JB
☎ 01603 741161 📠 01603 741500
e-mail: admin@gb619.u-net.com
Dir: *A1074 to Norwich and Cromer. Hotel off A47 southern bypass*

This modern hotel is situated on the west side of the city, four miles from the centre. Bedrooms are spacious and well equipped and the public areas include a carvery restaurant and lounge. The hotel offers conference and banqueting facilities, as well as a leisure centre.
ROOMS: 80 en suite (13 fmly) (40 GF) No smoking in 40 bedrooms s £60-£89; d £80-£99 **LB** **FACILITIES:** STV Indoor swimming (H) Sauna Solarium Gym Jacuzzi Steamroom Xmas **CONF:** Thtr 200 Class 80 Board 60 Del from £80 **PARKING:** 200 **NOTES:** No dogs (ex guide dogs) No smoking in restaurant Civ Wed 70
CARDS:

★★★63% The Maids Head Hotel

Tombland NR3 1LB
☎ 0870 609 6110 📠 01603 613688
e-mail: maidshead@corushotels.com
Dir: *follow city centre signs past Norwich Castle. 3rd turning after castle into Upper King St, hotel opposite Norman Cathedral*

Imposing 13th-century building situated close to the impressive Norman cathedral and within easy walking distance of the city centre. The bedrooms are pleasantly decorated and thoughtfully equipped, some rooms have original oak beams. The spacious public rooms include a Jacobean bar, a range of seating areas and the Courtyard restaurant.
ROOMS: 84 en suite (7 fmly) No smoking in 30 bedrooms s £85-£95 **LB** **FACILITIES:** Xmas **CONF:** Thtr 300 Class 120 Board 40 Del from £115 **SERVICES:** Lift **PARKING:** 70 **NOTES:** No smoking in restaurant Civ Wed 100 **CARDS:**

Top 200 - Hotel

★★ The Old Rectory

103 Yarmouth Rd, Thorpe St Andrew NR7 0HF
☎ 01603 700772 📠 01603 300772
e-mail: enquiries@oldrectorynorwich.com
Dir: *from A47 southern bypass onto A1042 towards Norwich N and E. Left at mini rdbt onto A1242. 0.3m over lights, hotel 100mtrs on right*

Unwind and enjoy the relaxed atmosphere at this delightful Grade II listed, Georgian property, ideally located in a peaceful area overlooking the River Yare, just a few minutes' drive from the city centre. Spacious bedrooms are individually designed and equipped with modern facilities, and most overlook the swimming pool and landscaped gardens. An

continued

interesting daily-changing menu features local produce skilfully prepared and served in the panelled dining room.

ROOMS: 5 en suite 3 annexe en suite No smoking in all bedrooms s £68; d £88-£100 (incl. bkfst) **LB** **FACILITIES:** STV Outdoor swimming (H) **CONF:** Thtr 25 Class 18 Board 16 **PARKING:** 15 **NOTES:** No dogs (ex guide dogs) No smoking in restaurant Closed 21 Dec-4 Jan **CARDS:**

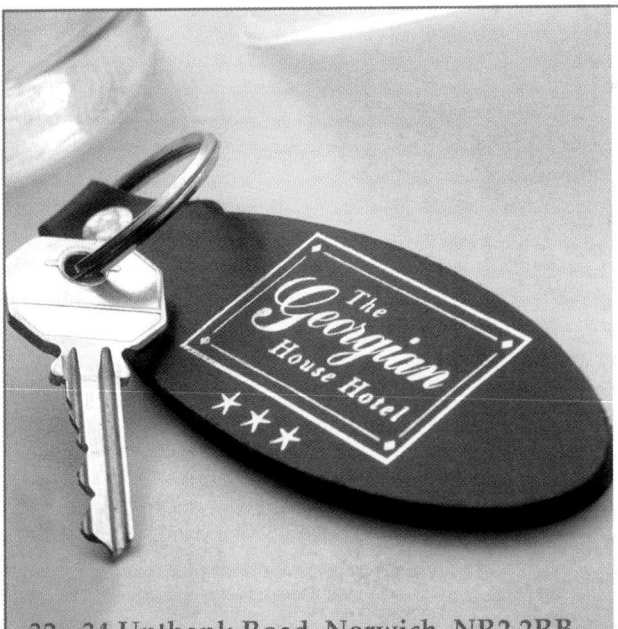

Late for dinner?
Quality Standards mean that last orders for dinner vary according to star rating and should be no earlier than:
★★ 7.00pm ★★★ 8.00pm ★★★★ 9.00pm
★★★★★ 10.00pm

NORWICH, continued

★★73% Stower Grange
School Rd, Drayton NR8 6EF
☎ 01603 860210 01603 860464
e-mail: enquiries@stowergrange.co.uk
Dir: *Norwich ring road N to Asda supermarket. Take A1067 Fakenham Rd at Drayton, right at lights into School Rd. Hotel 150yds on right*

A 17th-century ivy-clad property situated in a peaceful residential area just a short drive from the city centre and airport. The individually decorated bedrooms are generally quite spacious; each one is individually decorated, tastefully furnished and equipped with many thoughtful touches. Public rooms include a smart open-plan lounge bar and an elegant restaurant.
ROOMS: 11 en suite (1 fmly) s fr £68; d fr £88 (incl. bkfst) **FACILITIES:** Croquet lawn **CONF:** Thtr 100 Class 45 Board 30 Del from £130 **PARKING:** 40 **NOTES:** No smoking in restaurant Civ Wed 100 **CARDS:**

N

★★70% The Old Rectory
North Walsham Rd, Crostwick NR12 7BG
☎ 01603 738513 01603 738712
e-mail: info@therectoryhotel.fsnet.co.uk
Dir: *left off Norwich ring road onto B1150. Hotel 4m on left*
This attractive family-run hotel is situated on the outskirts of Norwich city centre. Public rooms feature a superb hexagonal conservatory-style dining room, which overlooks the pretty gardens, and there is a smart lounge, a cosy bar and dining room. Bedrooms are smartly decorated and well equipped.
ROOMS: 13 en suite (8 fmly) (13 GF) No smoking in 5 bedrooms s £46-£48; d £62.50-£65 (incl. bkfst) **FACILITIES:** Outdoor swimming (H) ch fac **CONF:** Thtr 110 Class 80 Board 50 **PARKING:** 100 **NOTES:** No smoking in restaurant Civ Wed 150 **CARDS:**

★★68% Cumberland
212-216 Thorpe Rd NR1 1TJ
☎ 01603 434550 01603 433355
e-mail: cumberland@paston.co.uk
Dir: *on A1242, 0.5m from railway station towards Great Yarmouth*
A family owned and run hotel situated just a short drive from the railway station and city centre. Bedrooms are pleasantly decorated and thoughtfully equipped. An interesting choice of dishes is served in the Cape Dutch restaurant and there is a smart lounge bar and cosy sitting room.
ROOMS: 21 en suite 3 annexe en suite (2 fmly) No smoking in 3 bedrooms s £39.95-£45; d £55-£69.95 (incl. bkfst) **LB** **CONF:** Thtr 90 Class 50 Board 40 Del from £89.95 **PARKING:** 40 **NOTES:** No dogs (ex guide dogs) No children 5yrs No smoking in restaurant Closed 26 Dec-2 Jan **CARDS:**

AA Rosette Award for culinary excellence

★★64% The Old Vicarage Hotel
82 Unthank Rd NR2 2RW
☎ 01603 621105 01603 667827
e-mail: info@vicaragehotel.com
Dir: *A11 onto A140, right at lights. Hotel on the right*
A former Victorian rectory dating back to 1886, set in the heart of this historic city within easy walking distance of the castle, cathedral and shops. Bedrooms vary in style and are pleasantly decorated and equipped with modern facilities. Public rooms include a cosy lounge bar, a smart restaurant and a residents' lounge.
ROOMS: 16 en suite (3 fmly) (5 GF) No smoking in all bedrooms s £52.50-£55; d £75-£85 (incl. bkfst) **LB** **CONF:** Thtr 20 Class 12 Board 12 **PARKING:** 16 **NOTES:** No smoking in restaurant Closed 25-30 Dec **CARDS:**

U *Holiday Inn Norwich*
Ipswich Rd NR4 6EP
☎ 0870 400 9060 01603 506400
e-mail: norwich@ichotelsgroup.com
Dir: *take A47 to sign for A140 and into Norwich. Hotel 0.5m on right*
At the time of going to press, the classification for this hotel was not confirmed. Please refer to the AA internet site www.theAA.com for current information.
ROOMS: 120 en suite (5 fmly) No smoking in 92 bedrooms **FACILITIES:** STV Indoor swimming (H) Sauna Gym Jacuzzi Health & fitness centre ch fac **CONF:** Thtr 150 Class 40 Board 40 **PARKING:** 200 **NOTES:** No dogs (ex guide dogs) **CARDS:**

U Wensum Valley Hotel Golf & Country Club
Beech Av, Taverham NR8 6HP
☎ 01603 261012 01603 261664
e-mail: enqs@wensumvalley.co.uk
Dir: *off A1067 at Taverham into Beech Ave. Hotel on right*
At the time of going to press, the star classification for this hotel was not confirmed. Please refer to the AA internet site www.theAA.com for current information.
ROOMS: 84 en suite (12 fmly) (32 GF) No smoking in all bedrooms s fr £54; d fr £88 (incl. bkfst) **LB** **FACILITIES:** Indoor swimming (H) Golf 36 Fishing Snooker Sauna Solarium Gym Putting green Jacuzzi Beauty therapy Golf driving range Hairdressing salon entertainment Xmas **CONF:** Thtr 200 Board 30 Del from £70 **PARKING:** 250 **NOTES:** No dogs (ex guide dogs) No smoking in restaurant Civ Wed 200 **CARDS:**

Travel Inn
Longwater Interchange, Dereham Rd, New Costessey NR5 0TL
☎ 08701 977197 01603 741219
Dir: *Follow tourist signs Royal Norfolk Showground on A47 & A1074. Inn opposite showground*
Travel Inn offers good-quality, value-for-money accommodation. Spacious, en suite rooms with bath and shower comfortably accommodate a family of up to two adults and two children (to age 15). The restaurant and bar offers a varied menu. For Travel Inn phone number, consult the Hotel Groups page.
ROOMS: 40 en suite s £44.95; d £44.95

Travel Inn Norwich Airport
Holt Rd, Norwich Airport
☎ 0870 238 3344 0870 241 9000
Travel Inn offers good-quality, value-for-money accommodation. Spacious, en suite rooms with bath and shower comfortably accommodate a family of up to two adults and two children (to age 15). The restaurant and bar offers a varied menu. For Travel Inn phone number, consult the Hotel Groups page.
ROOMS: 40 en suite

Travel Inn (Norwich East)

roadland Business Park, Old Chapel Way
R7 0WG
☎ 08701 977198 📠 01603 307617
ir: *A47 onto A1042, 3m E of city centre*
ravel Inn offers good-quality, value-for-money accommodation. pacious, en suite rooms with bath and shower comfortably ccommodate a family of up to two adults and two children (to ge 15). The restaurant and bar offers a varied menu. For further etails and the Travel Inn phone number, consult the Hotel roups page.
OOMS: 60 en suite s £44.95; d £44.95 **CONF:** Thtr 20 Board 14

Travelodge

hickthorn Service Area, Norwich Southern ypass NR9 3AU
☎ 08700 850 950 📠 01603 457549
ir: *A11 & A47*
ravelodge offers good quality, good value, modern ccommodation. Ideal for families, the spacious, en suite edrooms include remote-control TV, tea and coffee-making acilities, luxury beds and free morning newspaper. Meals can be aken at the nearby family restaurant. For further details and the ravelodge phone number, consult the Hotel Groups page.
ROOMS: 62 en suite s fr £42.95; d fr £42.95

Premier Lodge (Norwich)

16 Yarmouth Rd, Thorpe St Andrew NR7 0HE
☎ 0870 9906468 📠 0870 9906469
ROOMS: 41 en suite **NOTES:** Due to open Spring 2004

NOTTINGHAM, Nottinghamshire

Map 11 SK53

See also Langar

Town House

★★★★ ◎◎ Harts

Standard Hill, Park Row NG1 6FN
☎ 0115 988 1900 📠 0115 983 8485
e-mail: ask@hartshotel.co.uk
Dir: *Junct of Park Row & Rope Walk, close to city centre*
Standing high and proud on the site of the ramparts of the mediaeval castle, Julian Marsh's outstanding modern building looks out over the city and park towards the university. Despite being just a couple of minutes' walk from the city centre, this fine hotel has an enviably quiet location, which combined with secure car parking ensures its popularity; the private gardens for the use of residents only are an additional draw. The building is light and contemporary, with splendid views from many of the bedrooms. Rooms are particularly well appointed and stylish, while the Park Bar is the focal point of the limited public areas; service is both professional and caring, without being stuffy. Fine dining continues to be offered at Hart's Restaurant, which is located just twenty yards from the front door of the hotel.
ROOMS: 32 en suite s £112-£225; d £112-£225 **FACILITIES:** STV Gym **CONF:** Thtr 80 Class 75 Board 33 **PARKING:** 16 **NOTES:** No smoking in restaurant Civ Wed 80 **CARDS:**

Late for dinner?
Quality Standards mean that last orders for dinner vary according to star rating and should be no earlier than:
★★ 7.00pm ★★★ 8.00pm ★★★★ 9.00pm
★★★★★ 10.00pm

Town House

★★★★ ◎ Lace Market

29-31 High Pavement NG1 1HE
☎ 0115 852 3232 📠 0115 852 3223
e-mail: reservations@lacemarkethotel.co.uk
Dir: *follow tourist signs for Galleries of Justice; hotel opposite*
This smart town house, a conversion of two Georgian houses, is located in the trendy Lace Market area of the city. Public areas, including the popular Merchants Bar and Restaurant that have now been complemented by the opening of the adjacent 'Cock and Hoop', a tastefully furnished traditional pub offering real ales and fine wines. Accommodation comes in the form of stylish, contemporary bedrooms (includes a selection of spacious superior rooms and split-level suites); all are thoughtfully equipped with a host of extras including CD players and mini bars.
ROOMS: 42 en suite s £65-£89; d £105-£179 **LB FACILITIES:** STV Complimentary use of nearby health club. **CONF:** Thtr 35 Class 35 Board 20 Del from £120 **SERVICES:** Lift **NOTES:** Closed 24-26 Dec **CARDS:**

★★★★66% Park Plaza Nottingham

41 Maid Marian Way NG1 6GD
☎ 0115 947 7200 📠 0115 947 7300
e-mail: info@parkplazanottingham.com
This ultra modern hotel is located in the centre of the city within walking distance of retail, commercial and tourist attractions. Bedrooms are spacious and comfortable, with many extras including laptop safes and high-speed telephone lines, and air-conditioning. Service is discreetly attentive in the Foyer lounge and the Chino Latino restaurant where fusion cooking is a feature.
ROOMS: 178 en suite (10 fmly) No smoking in 126 bedrooms s £80-£135; d £80-£135 **FACILITIES:** STV Xmas **CONF:** Thtr 175 Class 100 Board 54 Del from £130 **SERVICES:** Lift air con
CARDS:

★★★68% The Strathdon

Derby Rd, City Centre NG1 5FT
☎ 0115 941 8501 📠 0115 948 3725
e-mail: info@strathdon-hotel-nottingham.com
Dir: *follow city centre signs. Enter one-way system down Wollaton St, keep right and next right to hotel*
This popular city centre hotel is conveniently located for the Albert Hall Conference and Exhibition Centre. The newly refurbished public rooms include the popular American Boston Bean Company Bar and Diner, the first-floor Bobbins Restaurant and a range of meeting rooms. Bedrooms are modern in style and suitably well equipped for corporate guests.
ROOMS: 68 en suite (4 fmly) No smoking in 46 bedrooms s £60-£95; d £75-£125 (incl. bkfst) **LB FACILITIES:** STV **CONF:** Thtr 150 Class 60 Board 40 Del from £75 **SERVICES:** Lift
CARDS:

N

NOTTINGHAM, continued

★★★67% Westminster Hotel

312 Mansfield Rd, Carrington NG5 2EF
☎ 0115 955 5000 🖷 0115 955 5005
e-mail: mail@westminster-hotel.co.uk
Dir: *on A60 1m N of town centre*

This smart hotel is conveniently located close to the city centre, and offers well-appointed accommodation, suitably equipped for both business and leisure guests. Spacious superior rooms are particularly impressive. Public areas include a lounge bar, restaurant and range of meeting and function rooms.
ROOMS: 73 en suite (9 GF) No smoking in 40 bedrooms s £85-£95; d £95-£110 **LB FACILITIES:** STV **CONF:** Thtr 60 Class 30 Board 30 Del from £100 **SERVICES:** Lift **PARKING:** 66 **NOTES:** No dogs (ex guide dogs) No smoking in restaurant Closed 25 Dec-2 Jan
CARDS:

See advert on opposite page

★★★66% Bestwood Lodge

Bestwood Country Park, Arnold NG5 8NE
☎ 0115 920 3011 🖷 0115 964 9678
Dir: *3m N off A60. Left at lights into Oxclose Ln, right at next lights into Queens Bower Rd. 1st right, keep right at fork in road*

A Victorian hunting lodge in 700 acres of parkland, providing modern bedrooms of varying styles and sizes. The interior architecture includes Gothic features and high vaulted ceilings in the lounge bar and the gallery. This is a popular venue for weddings and conferences.
ROOMS: 39 en suite (5 fmly) No smoking in 5 bedrooms s £38-£80; d £76-£120 (incl. bkfst) **LB FACILITIES:** Riding Guided walks Xmas **CONF:** Thtr 200 Class 65 Board 50 Del from £90 **PARKING:** 120 **NOTES:** No smoking in restaurant RS 25 Dec & 1 Jan
CARDS:

See advert on opposite page

★★★66% Nottingham Gateway

Nuthall Rd, Cinderhill NG8 6AZ
☎ 0115 979 4949 🖷 0115 979 4744
e-mail: nottingateway@btconnect.com
Dir: *M1 junct 26, take A610, follow signs to City Centre. Hotel at 2nd rdbt*

This is a modern hotel that is conveniently placed for the city and the motorway network. Public areas lead off from the glass-atriumed reception foyer, and provide a choice of bars and varied dining options. An extensive range of conference suites is popular. The inviting modern bedrooms are of comfortable proportions.
ROOMS: 108 en suite (18 fmly) No smoking in 54 bedrooms s £85; d £100 (incl. bkfst) **LB FACILITIES:** STV Discounted entrance to David Lloyd H.C Xmas **CONF:** Thtr 250 Class 150 Board 60 Del from £125 **SERVICES:** Lift **PARKING:** 250 **NOTES:** Civ Wed 250
CARDS:

See advert on opposite page

★★★65% Comfort Hotel Nottingham

Comfort Hotel BY CHOICE HOTELS

George St NG1 3BP
☎ 0115 947 5641 🖷 0115 948 3292
e-mail: enquiries@comfort-hotels-nottingham.com
Dir: *follow city centre signs. Top of hill follow road to right, left fork onto Talbot St, left lane and right to George St, hotel on left*
Situated in heart of the city, this hotel dates back to the late 17th century. Smartly appointed, compact public areas include a bar lounge, where all day snacks are served, and a brightly decorated restaurant. Parking is available at a multi-storey a short walk away. The refurbished bedrooms are comfortable and thoughtfully equipped, well suited for both business and leisure guests.
ROOMS: 70 en suite (3 fmly) No smoking in 22 bedrooms s fr £69; d fr £69 **LB FACILITIES:** STV Xmas **CONF:** Thtr 200 Class 40 Board 35 Del from £100 **SERVICES:** Lift **NOTES:** No smoking in restaurant
CARDS:

★★★65% Rutland Square Hotel

Forestdale Hotels

St James St NG1 6FJ
☎ 0115 941 1114 🖷 0115 941 0014
e-mail: rutland.square@forestdale.com
Dir: *in city follow signs to castle. Hotel on right 50yds from castle*
An enviable location in the heart of the city by the castle, makes this hotel a popular choice. Behind its Regency facade the hotel is modern and comfortable with good business facilities. The well-equipped bedrooms are tastefully decorated. Public rooms include the informal Terrace Bar & Restaurant and Woods Restaurant.
ROOMS: 105 en suite (3 fmly) No smoking in 38 bedrooms s fr £90; d fr £110 (incl. bkfst) **LB FACILITIES:** STV Discounted day passes to nearby gym Xmas **CONF:** Thtr 200 Class 70 Board 45 Del from £120 **SERVICES:** Lift **NOTES:** No smoking in restaurant
CARDS:

NOTTINGHAM, continued

★★★61% Swans Hotel & Restaurant
84-90 Radcliffe Rd, West Bridgford NG2 5HH
☎ 0115 981 4042 0115 945 5745
e-mail: enquiries@swanshotel.co.uk
Dir: *on A6011, approached from A60 or A52; close to Trent Bridge*
This privately owned hotel is located on the outskirts of the city, conveniently placed for the various sports stadia. Bedrooms, in various sizes, are equipped to meet the needs both of business and leisure visitors. An interesting range of dishes is served in either the cosy bar or, more formally, in the restaurant.
ROOMS: 30 en suite (3 fmly) (1 GF) No smoking in all bedrooms s £45-£65; d £60-£70 (incl. bkfst) **LB** **FACILITIES:** STV **CONF:** Thtr 50 Class 10 Board 24 Del £90 **SERVICES:** Lift **PARKING:** 31 **NOTES:** No dogs (ex guide dogs) No smoking in restaurant Closed 24-28 Dec
CARDS:

Top 200 – Restaurant with Rooms

Restaurant Sat Bains at Hotel des Clos
Old Lenton Ln NG7 2SA
☎ 0115 986 6566 0115 986 0343
e-mail: enquiries@hoteldesclos.com
Dir: *M1 junct 24 take A453 Nottingham S. Over R. Trent in central lane to rdbt. Left then left again towards river. Hotel on left after bend*
This small hotel, a sympathetic conversion of Victorian farm buildings, is situated on the river. The bedrooms are attractively presented with quality soft furnishings and antique/period furniture; suites and four-poster bedrooms are available. Public rooms are cosy, and the delightful restaurant complements the fine cuisine on offer.
ROOMS: 4 en suite 5 annexe en suite (1 fmly) (7 GF) No smoking in 4 bedrooms s £99.50-£139.50; d £119.50-£149.50 (incl. bkfst) **LB** **FACILITIES:** STV Fishing Jacuzzi Facilities available at nearby David Lloyd club Xmas **CONF:** Thtr 20 Class 10 Board 14 Del from £170 **PARKING:** 22 **NOTES:** No dogs (ex guide dogs) No smoking in restaurant Closed 26-30 Dec, 1-7 Jan, Sun & BH's RS Mon
CARDS:

U Holiday Inn Nottingham City
St James's St NG1 6BN
☎ 0870 400 9061 0115 948 4366
e-mail: nottinghamcity@ichotelsgroup.com
Dir: *M1 junct 24, 25 or 26 follow city centre, Nottingham Castle, Tales of Robin Hood signs, hotel next door*
At the time of going to press, the classification for this hotel was not confirmed. Please refer to the AA internet site www.theAA.com for current information.
ROOMS: 160 rms (158 en suite) (37 fmly) No smoking in 121 bedrooms **FACILITIES:** entertainment **CONF:** Thtr 550 Class 230 Board 100 **SERVICES:** Lift air con **NOTES:** No smoking in restaurant
CARDS:

Citilodge Wollaton St NG1 5FW
☎ 0115 912 8000 0115 912 8080
e-mail: mail@citilodge.co.uk ***Dir:*** *In city centre opposite Royal Centre*
This city centre lodge offers superior accommodation along with a good range of bar and food options. Conferencing at the Citilodge is also a strength, offering a comprehensive range of quality meeting rooms and unusually a 100 seater tiered lecture theatre. Bedrooms are spacious and light with warm colour schemes, offering an excellent range of facilities that business guests will appreciate; air-conditioning and ISDN connections in each room and a separate Citinet internet room is available.
ROOMS: 90 en suite s £58; d £58 **CONF:** Thtr 100 Class 25 Board 30 Del from £110

Innkeeper's Lodge Nottingham
Derby Rd, Wollaton Vale NG8 2NR
☎ 0115 922 1691 0115 951 8941
Dir: *M1 junct 25, take A52 to Notttingham. At 3rd rdbt, left into Wollaton Vale, right across central reservation into car park*
A new concept in the travel accommodation market. Smart rooms meet essential business requirements but also have home comforts. Dining options include all-day menus plus the added advantage of breakfast, which is included in the room price. For further details, consult the Hotel Groups page.
ROOMS: 34 en suite **CONF:** Thtr 105 Class 62 Board 70

Premier Lodge (Nottingham City Centre)
Island Site, London Rd NG2 4UU
☎ 0870 9906574 0870 9906575
Dir: *just off A6001, next to BBC building*
Premier Lodge offers modern, well-equipped, en suite accommodation suitable for both business and leisure travellers. Meals can be taken at the adjacent popular restaurant and bar, which is fully licensed. For further details, consult the Hotel Groups page. **ROOMS:** 87 en suite s £52; d £52

Premier Lodge (Nottingham North)
101 Mansfield Rd, Daybrook NG5 6BH
☎ 0870 9906328 0870 9906329
Dir: *M1 junct 27 onto A60. M1 junct 26 onto A610 & A6514 towards A60. Turn off A60 for Mansfield*
Premier Lodge offers modern, well-equipped, en suite accommodation suitable for both business and leisure travellers. Meals can be taken at the adjacent popular restaurant and bar, which is fully licensed. For further details, consult the Hotel Groups page. **ROOMS:** 64 en suite s £48; d £48

Premier Lodge (Nottingham South)
Loughborough Rd, Ruddington NG11 6LS
☎ 0870 9906422 0870 9906423
Premier Lodge offers modern, well-equipped, en suite accommodation suitable for both business and leisure travellers. Meals can be taken at the adjacent popular restaurant and bar, which is fully licensed. For further details, consult the Hotel Groups page. **ROOMS:** 42 en suite s £48; d £48

Travel Inn Nottingham (City Centre)
Goldsmith St NG1 5LT
☎ 0870 238 3314 0115 908 1388
Dir: *Follow A610 to City Centre. Follow signs for Nottingham Trent University into Talbot Street. Take 1st left into Clarendon Street and at lights turn right for Travel Inn on right.*

Travel Inn offers good-quality, value-for-money accommodation. Spacious, en suite rooms with bath and shower comfortably

continued

accommodate a family of up to two adults and two children (to age 15). The restaurant and bar offers a varied menu. For further details and the Travel Inn phone number, consult the Hotel Groups page. **ROOMS:** 161 en suite d £52.95

⌂ Travel Inn (Nottingham Riverside)

The Phoenix Centre, Millennium Way West
NG8 6AS
☎ 08701 977200 📠 0115 977 0113
Dir: *M1 junct 26, 1m on A610 towards Nottingham*
Travel Inn offers good-quality, value-for-money accommodation. Spacious, en suite rooms with bath and shower comfortably accommodate a family of up to two adults and two children (to age 15). The restaurant and bar offers a varied menu. For further details and the Travel Inn phone number, consult the Hotel Groups page.
ROOMS: 86 en suite s £44.95; d £44.95

⌂ Travel Inn (Nottingham South)
Castle Marina Park, Castle Bridge Rd NG7 1GX
☎ 08701 977199 📠 0115 958 2362
Dir: *0.5m from city centre, follow signs for Castle Marina*
Travel Inn offers good-quality, value-for-money accommodation. Spacious, en suite rooms with bath and shower comfortably accommodate a family of up to two adults and two children (to age 15). The restaurant and bar offers a varied menu. For further details and the Travel Inn phone number, consult the Hotel Groups page.
ROOMS: 38 en suite s £49.95-£52.95; d £49.95-£52.95

⌂ Travelodge (Nottingham Riverside)
Riverside Retail Park NG2 1RT
☎ 08700 850 950
Dir: *on Riverside Retail Park*
Travelodge offers good quality, good value, modern accommodation. Ideal for families, the spacious, en suite bedrooms include remote-control TV, tea and coffee-making facilities, luxury beds and free morning newspaper. Meals can be taken at the nearby family restaurant. For further details and the Travelodge phone number, consult the Hotel Groups page.
ROOMS: 61 en suite s fr £42.95; d fr £42.95

NUNEATON, Warwickshire — Map 11 SP39

★★★65% Weston Hall

Weston Ln, Bulkington CV12 9RU
☎ 024 7631 2989 📠 024 7664 0846
e-mail: info@westonhallhotel.co.uk
Dir: *M6 junct 2 follow B4065 through Ansty. Left in Shilton, follow Nuneaton signs out of Bulkington, turn into Weston Ln at 30mph sign*
This Grade II listed hotel, whose origins date back to the reign of Elizabeth I, sits within seven acres of peaceful grounds. The original three gabled building retains many original panelling and features, such as the carved wooden fireplace situated in the library. Service is provided in a friendly manner and bedrooms vary in size and are thoughtfully equipped.
ROOMS: 40 en suite (1 fmly) No smoking in 6 bedrooms
FACILITIES: Fishing Sauna Gym Croquet lawn Jacuzzi Steam room
CONF: BC Thtr 200 Class 100 Board 60 Del from £125 **PARKING:** 300
NOTES: No smoking in restaurant Civ Wed 190
CARDS:

See advert on this page

⌂ Travel Inn
Coventry Rd CV10 7PJ
☎ 08701 977201 📠 024 7634 3584
Dir: *M6 junct 3 follow A444 towards Nuneaton. Travel Inn on right just off Griff rdbt towards Bedworth on B4113*
Travel Inn offers good-quality, value-for-money accommodation. Spacious, en suite rooms with bath and shower comfortably accommodate a family of up to two adults and two children (to age 15). The restaurant and bar offers a varied menu. For further details, consult the Hotel Groups page.
ROOMS: 48 en suite s £44.95; d £44.95 **CONF:** Thtr 25

⌂ Travelodge
St Nicholas Park Dr CV11 6EN
☎ 08700 850 950 📠 024 7635 3885 ***Dir:*** *on A47*
Travelodge offers good quality, good value, modern accommodation. Ideal for families, the spacious, en suite bedrooms include remote-control TV, tea and coffee-making facilities, luxury beds and free morning newspaper. Meals can be taken at the nearby family restaurant. For further details and the Travelodge phone number, consult the Hotel Groups page.
ROOMS: 28 en suite s fr £42.95; d fr £42.95

⌂ Travelodge Bedworth
Bedworth CV10 7TF
☎ 08700 850 950 📠 024 7638 2541
Dir: *2m S, on A444*
Travelodge offers good quality, good value, modern accommodation. Ideal for families, the spacious, en suite bedrooms include remote-control TV, tea and coffee-making facilities, luxury beds and free morning newspaper. Meals can be taken at the nearby family restaurant. For further details and the Travelodge phone number, consult the Hotel Groups page.
ROOMS: 40 en suite s fr £42.95; d fr £42.95

NUNNEY, Somerset Map 04 ST74

★★65% *The George at Nunney*
11 Church St BA11 4LW
☎ 01373 836458 📠 01373 836565
e-mail: georgenunneyhotel@barbox.net
Dir: *0.5m N off A361 Frome to Shepton Mallet road*
Situated in the centre of Nunney, opposite the castle, The George dates back to the 17th century. Guests may choose from an extensive range of bar meals or a selection of dishes offered in the more intimate restaurant. Bedrooms vary in size, have plenty of character and a very good selection of extras.
ROOMS: 9 rms (8 en suite) (2 fmly) No smoking in 2 bedrooms
PARKING: 30 **NOTES:** No dogs **CARDS:**

OAKHAM, Rutland Map 11 SK80

Top 200 - Hotel

★★★ ⊛⊛⊛⊛ Hambleton Hall
Hambleton LE15 8TH
☎ 01572 756991 📠 01572 724721
e-mail: hotel@hambletonhall.com
Dir: *3m E off A606*
This delightful country house hotel enjoys a tranquil location amidst landscaped gardens overlooking Rutland Water. Stylish bedrooms are individually designed, tastefully decorated and thoughtfully equipped. Luxurious public areas include a cosy bar, a sumptuous drawing room and an elegant restaurant. Carefully prepared imaginative and inspired cuisine, featuring locally sourced and seasonal produce, is a highlight.
ROOMS: 15 en suite 2 annexe en suite No smoking in 1 bedroom **FACILITIES:** STV Outdoor swimming (H) Tennis (hard) Croquet lawn Outdoor pool has CCTV, private access to lake **CONF:** Thtr 40 Board 24 Del from £220 **SERVICES:** Lift **PARKING:** 40
NOTES: No smoking in restaurant Civ Wed 60
CARDS:

★★★75% ⊛ Barnsdale Lodge
The Avenue, Rutland Water, North Shore LE15 8AH
☎ 01572 724678 📠 01572 724961
e-mail: barnsdale.lodge@btconnect.com
Dir: *off A1 onto A606. Hotel 5m on right, 2m E of Oakham*
A popular and interesting hotel, converted from a farmstead, overlooking Rutland Water. A very successful food operation dominates the public areas with informal meals served in the brasserie, whilst the more formal restaurant offers a good range of appealing meals. Bedrooms are comfortably appointed with excellent beds and period furnishings, enhanced by contemporary soft furnishings and thoughtful extras.

ROOMS: 45 en suite (2 fmly) No smoking in 34 bedrooms s £75; d £95-£120 (incl. bkfst) **LB** **FACILITIES:** STV Fishing Shooting Archery Golf arranged Xmas **CONF:** BC Thtr 330 Class 120 Board 76
PARKING: 200 **NOTES:** No smoking in restaurant Civ Wed 100
CARDS:

★★★70% ⊛ Barnsdale Hall
Barnsdale LE15 8AB
☎ 01572 757901 📠 01572 756235
e-mail: reservations@barnsdalehotel.co.uk
Dir: *from A1 take A606 to Oakham, through villages of Empingham and Whitwell. After 1m hotel on left overlooking Rutland Water*

Overlooking Rutland Water, this complex is set in attractive grounds leading to the water's edge. Public rooms offer a good choice of modern dining options and extensive leisure facilities; customer care is a particular strength. Spacious modern bedrooms have been refurbished and are equipped with many thoughtful extras, most are in adjacent buildings and many have a balcony.
ROOMS: 9 en suite 56 annexe en suite (9 fmly) (17 GF) No smoking in 61 bedrooms s £73.50; d £94.50 (incl. bkfst) **LB** **FACILITIES:** STV Indoor swimming (H) Tennis (hard) Squash Snooker Sauna Solarium Gym Croquet lawn Putting green Jacuzzi Boule, Bowls, Crazy Golf, Pitch & Putt, Soccer Pitch, Swimming pool supervised Xmas **CONF:** BC Thtr 200 Class 70 Board 42 Del £129 **SERVICES:** Lift **PARKING:** 100
NOTES: No dogs (ex guide dogs) No smoking in restaurant Civ Wed 120
CARDS:

★★★68% ⊛ Whipper-in Hotel
Market Place LE15 6DT
☎ 01572 756971 📠 01572 757759
e-mail: whipper.in@lineone.net
Dir: *from A1 take B668 for Oakham then into Market Sq*
A 17th-century former coaching inn located in the market square. Hunting memorabilia, uneven sloping floors and a beamed dining room provide plenty of character. Bedrooms are attractively presented and well equipped and include four-poster and

continued

executive rooms. In the summer months, the pretty patio, festooned with hanging baskets, is perfect for pre-dinner drinks.
ROOMS: 24 en suite No smoking in 4 bedrooms s £74-£84; d £84-£104 **LB FACILITIES:** Xmas **CONF:** Thtr 60 Class 30 Board 30 Del from £99 **PARKING:** 40 **NOTES:** No smoking in restaurant
CARDS:

★★68% Admiral Hornblower

64 High St LE15 6AS
☎ 01572 723004 📠 01572 722325
e-mail: enquiries@hornblowerhotel.co.uk

This sympathetically restored 17th-century farmhouse in the heart of Oakham is now an exceedingly popular small hotel offering tastefully appointed accommodation, good food and a lively bar. Bedrooms are individually appointed, furnished in country style and retain much of their original character; four poster rooms are particularly popular. Public rooms are dominated by the three dining areas with open fires. A friendly and relaxed atmosphere is complemented by a helpful and efficient staff.
ROOMS: 5 en suite 5 annexe en suite s £60-£95; d £85-£125 (incl. bkfst) **FACILITIES:** STV **PARKING:** 6 **NOTES:** No dogs (ex guide dogs) No smoking in restaurant **CARDS:**

OCKLEY, Surrey — Map 06 TQ14

★★★64% Gatton Manor Hotel Golf & Country Club

Standon Ln RH5 5PQ
☎ 01306 627555 📠 01306 627713
e-mail: gattonmanor@enterprise.net
Dir: *off A29 at Ockley turn into Cat Hill Ln. Hotel signed 2m on right*

Gatton Manor enjoys a peaceful setting within its own grounds. This popular golf and country club, with an 18-hole professional course, offers a range of comfortable, modern bedrooms. The public areas include the main club bar, a small restaurant and an attractive drawing room.
ROOMS: 18 en suite (2 fmly) No smoking in 6 bedrooms **FACILITIES:** STV Golf 18 Tennis (grass) Fishing Sauna Solarium Gym Putting green Jacuzzi **CONF:** Thtr 50 Class 40 Board 30 Del from £120 **PARKING:** 250 **NOTES:** No dogs (ex guide dogs) No smoking in restaurant Civ Wed 50 **CARDS:**

ODIHAM, Hampshire — Map 05 SU75

★★74% George

High St RG29 1LP
☎ 01256 702081 📠 01256 704213
e-mail: reception@georgehotelodiham.com
Dir: *M3 junct 5 follow signs to Farnham and Odiham. In Odiham left at mini rdbt, hotel on left*

The George is over 450 years old and is a fine example of an old English inn. Bedrooms come in a number of styles; the older part

continued

of the property has old beams and period features, whilst new rooms have a contemporary feel. Guests can dine in the all-day café bar and bistro or the popular restaurant.

George Hotel

ROOMS: 19 en suite 9 annexe en suite (1 fmly) (6 GF) No smoking in 14 bedrooms s £80; d £90-£115 (incl. bkfst) **LB FACILITIES:** STV **CONF:** Thtr 30 Class 10 Board 26 Del from £125 **PARKING:** 20 **NOTES:** Closed 24-26 Dec **CARDS:**

OKEHAMPTON, Devon — Map 03 SX59

★★67% White Hart

Fore St EX20 1HD
☎ 01837 52730 & 54514 📠 01837 53979
e-mail: whitehart.oke@btopenworld.com
Dir: *in town centre, adjacent to lights, car park at rear of hotel*

An historic establishment dating back to the 17th century, the White Hart offers modern facilities. Bedrooms are well equipped

continued on p470

OKEHAMPTON, continued

and spacious and some rooms have four-poster beds. A choice of dining options is offered with a range of bar meals or more relaxed dining in the Courtney restaurant. Guests may choose to relax in the lounge, and there is a choice of bars as well as a traditional skittles and games room.
ROOMS: 19 en suite (2 fmly) No smoking in 8 bedrooms s £45-£55; d £70-£80 (incl. bkfst) **LB FACILITIES:** Putting green Games room Skittle alley Xmas **CONF:** Thtr 100 Class 80 Board 40 **PARKING:** 20 **NOTES:** No dogs (ex guide dogs) **CARDS:**

See advert on page 469

★★66% Ashbury Hotel

Higher Maddaford, Southcott EX20 4NL
☎ 01837 55453 📠 01837 55468
Dir: *off A30 at Sourton Cross onto A386. Left onto A3079 to Bude at Fowley Cross. After 1m right to Ashbury. Hotel 0.5m on right*
Now boasting four courses and a clubhouse with lounge, bar and dining facilitites, The Ashbury is a golfer's paradise. In addition, guests can enjoy the many on-site leisure facilities or join the activities available at the adjacent sister hotel. The majority of the well-equipped bedrooms are located in the adjacent farmhouse and courtyard-style development around the putting green.
ROOMS: 61 en suite 30 annexe en suite (54 fmly) (29 GF) s £121-£166; d £230-£316 (incl. bkfst & dinner) **LB FACILITIES:** Indoor swimming (H) Golf 63 Tennis (hard) Fishing Snooker Sauna Solarium Putting green Jacuzzi Driving range, Indoor bowls, Ten-pin bowling, table tennis,outdoor chess **PARKING:** 100 **NOTES:** No dogs (ex guide dogs) No smoking in restaurant **CARDS:**

★★66% Manor House Hotel

Fowley Cross EX20 4NA
☎ 01837 53053 📠 01837 55027
Dir: *off A30 at Sourton Cross flyover, right onto A386. Hotel 1.5m on right*
Enjoying views to Dartmoor in the distance, this hotel is set within 17 acres of grounds and is located close to the A30. An impressive range of facilities, including golf at their adjacent, sister hotel, is available at this friendly establishment which specialises in catering for short breaks. Bedrooms, many located on the ground floor, are comfortable and well equipped.
ROOMS: 180 en suite (77 fmly) (96 GF) s £131-£176; d £250-£334 (incl. bkfst & dinner) **LB FACILITIES: Spa** Indoor swimming (H) Tennis (hard) Squash Snooker Sauna Gym Croquet lawn Putting green Jacuzzi Craft centre Indoor bowls Shooting range Laser clay pigeon shooting Aerobics ch fac Xmas **PARKING:** 200 **NOTES:** No dogs (ex guide dogs) No smoking in restaurant **CARDS:**

See advert on opposite page

Travelodge (Okehampton East)

Travelodge

Whiddon Down EX20 2QT
☎ 08700 850 950 📠 01647 231626
Dir: *at Merrymeet rdbt on A30/A382*
Travelodge offers good quality, good value, modern accommodation. Ideal for families, the spacious, en suite bedrooms include remote-control TV, tea and coffee-making facilities, luxury beds and free morning newspaper. Meals can be taken at the nearby family restaurant. For further details and the Travelodge phone number, consult the Hotel Groups page.
ROOMS: 40 en suite s fr £42.95; d fr £42.95

> Popped the question?
> Hotels with Civ Wed in their entry are licensed for civil wedding ceremonies. Maximum numbers for the ceremony only are shown, e.g. Civ Wed 120

OLDBURY, West Midlands — Map 10 SO98

Express by Holiday Inn Oldbury

Express by Holiday Inn

Birchley Park B69 2BD
☎ 0121 511 0000 📠 0121 511 0051
e-mail: manageroldbury@expressholidayinn.co.uk
Dir: *off M5 junct 2, behind Total Garage on Wolverhampton Rd*

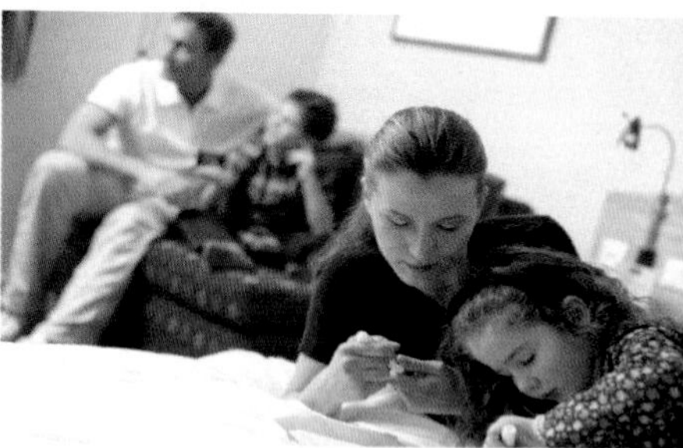

A modern hotel ideal for families and business travellers. Fresh and uncomplicated, the spacious bedrooms include Sky TV, power shower and tea and coffee-making facilities. Continental buffet breakfast is included in the room rate; other meals may be taken at the nearby family pub or restaurant. For further details and the Express by Holiday Inn phone number, consult the Hotel Groups pages.
ROOMS: 109 en suite s £45-£67; d £45-£67 (incl. cont bkfst)
CONF: Thtr 30 Class 20 Board 15

Travel Inn

travel inn

Wolverhampton Rd B69 2BH
☎ 08701 977202 📠 0121 552 1012
Dir: *M5 junct 2, take A4123 towards Wolverhampton, hotel 0.75m on left*
Travel Inn offers good-quality, value-for-money accommodation. Spacious, en suite rooms with bath and shower comfortably accommodate a family of up to two adults and two children (to age 15). The restaurant and bar offers a varied menu. For further details and the Travel Inn phone number, consult the Hotel Groups page.
ROOMS: 40 en suite s £44.95; d £44.95

Travelodge

Travelodge

Wolverhampton Rd B69 2BH
☎ 08700 850 950 📠 0121 552 2967
Dir: *on A4123, northbound off junct 2 of M5*
Travelodge offers good quality, good value, modern accommodation. Ideal for families, the spacious, en suite bedrooms include remote-control TV, tea and coffee-making facilities, luxury beds and free morning newspaper. Meals can be taken at the nearby family restaurant. For further details and the Travelodge phone number, consult the Hotel Groups page.
ROOMS: 33 en suite s fr £42.95; d fr £42.95

OLDHAM, Greater Manchester — Map 16 SD90

★★★★66% ® Menzies Avant

MENZIES HOTELS

Windsor Rd, Manchester St OL8 4AS
☎ 0161 627 5500 📠 0161 627 5896
e-mail: info@menzies-hotels.co.uk
Dir: *M60 junct 22 onto A62 into Oldham, right after Esso Garage*
The Avant is a contemporary landmark building only a few minutes from the M60 and now features a great new leisure

continued

complex which includes fitness studios, a gym and a good-sized pool. Accommodation is smart, comfortable and spacious. A covered walkway leads to the public areas, which include the brasserie and bar.
ROOMS: 103 en suite (2 fmly) No smoking in 16 bedrooms **FACILITIES:** STV Indoor swimming (H) Sauna Solarium Gym Jacuzzi **CONF:** Thtr 200 Class 100 Board 60 Del from £125 **SERVICES:** Lift **PARKING:** 120 **NOTES:** No smoking in restaurant Civ Wed 250
CARDS:

★★★73% Hotel Smokies Park

Best Western

Ashton Rd, Bardsley OL8 3HX
☎ 0161 785 5000 🖹 0161 785 5010
e-mail: sales@smokies.co.uk
Dir: *on A627 between Oldham and Ashton-under-Lyne*

This modern, stylish hotel offers smart, comfortable bedrooms and suites. A wide range of Italian and English dishes is offered in the Mediterranean-style restaurant and there is a welcoming lounge
continued

bar with live entertainment at weekends. A small but well-equipped fitness centre is available for use by residents only. There is also a nightclub on site, to which residents' gain free admission.
ROOMS: 73 en suite (2 fmly) No smoking in 36 bedrooms s £60-£140; d £60-£140 (incl. bkfst) **LB** **FACILITIES:** STV Sauna Solarium Gym Night club Cabaret lounge entertainment **CONF:** BC Thtr 200 Class 100 Board 40 Del from £115 **SERVICES:** Lift **PARKING:** 120 **NOTES:** No dogs (ex guide dogs) Civ Wed 120
CARDS:

★★★67% Bower Hotel

MACDONALD HOTELS

Hollinwood Av, Chadderton OL9 8DE
☎ 0161 682 7254 🖹 0161 683 4695
e-mail: bower@macdonald-hotels.co.uk
Dir: *A62 Oldham road from Manchester to Roxy Cinema. Left onto A6104. Under railway, past Mirror Group to lights, left to hotel*

Located just off junction 22 of the M60, this hotel provides a comfortable destination for both the business and leisure guest. Bedrooms vary in size and style and are well equipped with a host of thoughtful extras. Creative menus are served in the restaurant whilst extensive function capabilities make this hotel a popular venue for weddings and conferences.
ROOMS: 92 en suite (14 fmly) No smoking in 38 bedrooms s £92-£102; d £92-£102 **LB** **FACILITIES:** STV Xmas **CONF:** Thtr 250 Class 60 Board 60 Del from £110 **PARKING:** 140 **NOTES:** No smoking in restaurant Civ Wed 200 **CARDS:**

> Popped the question?
> Hotels with Civ Wed in their entry are licensed for civil wedding ceremonies. Maximum numbers for the ceremony only are shown, e.g. Civ Wed 120

OLDHAM, continued

★★★65% La Pergola
Rochdale Rd, Denshaw OL3 5UE
THE INDEPENDENTS
☎ 01457 871040 🖷 01457 873804
e-mail: reception@lapergola.freeserve.co.uk
Dir: *M62 junct 21, right at rdbt onto A640, under motorway, left at Wagon & Horses public house. Hotel 500yds on left*
Situated in open moorland and convenient for the M62, this friendly, family-owned and run hotel offers comfortable and well-equipped bedrooms. There is a good range of food available either in the bar or restaurant, and a comfortable lounge in which to relax.
ROOMS: 26 en suite (4 fmly) No smoking in 14 bedrooms s £43-£52.50; d £60.50-£65.50 (incl. bkfst) **LB FACILITIES: Spa** Xmas **CONF:** Thtr 150 Board 25 Del £83.50 **PARKING:** 75 **NOTES:** No smoking in restaurant Closed 26 Dec & 1 Jan Civ Wed 75
CARDS:

★★72% *Old Bell Inn*
Huddersfield Rd, Delph OL3 5EG
☎ 01457 870130 🖷 01457 876597
Dir: *on A62 Oldham-Huddersfield Rd, 100yds on left after crossroads*
Situated close to the centre of Delph, this stone-built inn dates back to the 1770s, but has been extensively renovated by the present owners to provide well equipped and tastefully appointed accommodation. The pleasant public areas are very popular, particularly with customers attracted by the wide range of food, available in either the restaurant or the bar.
ROOMS: 14 en suite (3 fmly) **CONF:** Thtr 40 Class 24 Board 30 **PARKING:** 21 **NOTES:** No dogs (ex guide dogs) No smoking in restaurant **CARDS:**

Travel Inn (Oldham Chadderton)
The Broadway OL9 8DW
travel inn
☎ 08701 977203 🖷 0161 682 7974
Dir: *M60 ringroad (anticlockwise) junct 21, signed Manchester City Centre. A663, 400yds on left*
Travel Inn offers good-quality, value-for-money accommodation. Spacious, en suite rooms with bath and shower comfortably accommodate a family of up to two adults and two children (to age 15). The restaurant and bar offers a varied menu. For further details and the Travel Inn phone number, consult the Hotel Groups page.
ROOMS: 40 en suite s £44.95; d £44.95

Travelodge
432 Broadway, Chadderton OL9 8AU
Travelodge
☎ 08700 850 950
Travelodge offers good quality, good value, modern accommodation. Ideal for families, the spacious, en suite bedrooms include remote-control TV, tea and coffee-making facilities, luxury beds and free morning newspaper. Meals can be taken at the nearby family restaurant. For further details and the Travelodge phone number, consult the Hotel Groups page.
ROOMS: 50 en suite s fr £42.95; d fr £42.95

ORFORD, Suffolk — Map 13 TM45

★★73% Crown & Castle Inn
IP12 2LJ
☎ 01394 450205
e-mail: info@crownandcastle.co.uk
Dir: *turn right from B1084 on entering village, towards castle*
Situated adjacent to the Norman castle, this delightful inn dates back to Tudor times. The contemporary-style bedrooms are split

continued

between the main house and a purpose-built wing; the latter are more spacious and have a patio with access to the gardens. The restaurant focuses on dishes using good quality local produce.
ROOMS: 7 en suite 11 annexe en suite (1 fmly) (11 GF) No smoking in all bedrooms s £60-£135; d £80-£135 (incl. bkfst) **LB**
FACILITIES: ch fac **CONF:** Thtr 14 Class 8 Board 12 Del from £110
PARKING: 25 **NOTES:** No smoking in restaurant Closed 24-27 Dec, 4-8 Jan RS Nov-Etr **CARDS:**

ORMSKIRK, Lancashire — Map 15 SD40

★★★66% Beaufort
High Ln, Burscough L40 7SN
THE INDEPENDENTS
☎ 01704 892655 🖷 01704 895135
e-mail: info@beaufort.uk.com
Dir: *M58 junct 3 follow signs for Ormskirk 7m. Hotel between Ormskirk and Burscough on A59*
This is a modern and privately owned hotel with pleasing public areas, which include an open-plan lounge, a bar and a restaurant. There is a wide choice of food available that is served throughout the day. The bedrooms are well equipped and comfortable, and conference facilities are available.
ROOMS: 20 en suite s £70-£75; d £95-£105 (incl. bkfst) **LB**
FACILITIES: STV Free use of sister Hotel's (Stutelea Hotel, Southport) facilities **CONF:** Thtr 120 Class 32 Board 30 **PARKING:** 109 **NOTES:** No dogs (ex guide dogs) No smoking in restaurant Civ Wed 120
CARDS:

OSTERLEY, Greater London
See LONDON SECTION plan 1 B3

★★★62% Osterley Four Pillars Hotel
764 Great West Rd TW7 5NA
FOUR PILLARS HOTELS
☎ 0800 374 692 🖷 020 8569 7819
e-mail: osterley@four-pillars.co.uk
Dir: *at junct of A4 and Wood Ln. 1m past Osterley underground station, eastbound on A4. 0.5m past Gillette, westbound on A4*
Situated close to Heathrow and with easy access to the city and major road networks, this hotel offers a range of bedrooms above the inn, in a purpose-built annexe and in an adjacent house. Meals can be taken in the popular bar or the restaurant, and there are conference facilities and a ballroom.
ROOMS: 61 en suite (9 fmly) No smoking in 21 bedrooms s £47-£92; d £47-£92 **LB FACILITIES:** STV entertainment **CONF:** Thtr 250 Class 126 Board 80 Del £130 **PARKING:** 98 **NOTES:** No dogs (ex guide dogs) Closed 26-27 Dec **CARDS:**

OSWESTRY, Shropshire — Map 15 SJ22

★★★77% Pen-y-Dyffryn Hall Country Hotel
Rhydycroesau SY10 7JD
☎ 01691 653700 🖷 01691 650066
e-mail: stay@peny.co.uk
Dir: *from A5 into Oswestry town centre. Follow signs to Llansilin on B4580, hotel 3m before Rhydycroesau village*
Peacefully situated in five acres of grounds, this charming old house dates back to around 1840, when it was built as a rectory. The tastefully appointed public rooms have real fires during cold weather, and accommodation includes several mini-cottages, each with their own patio. The hotel has a well-deserved reputation for its food, using local and organic ingredients.
ROOMS: 8 en suite 4 annexe en suite (1 fmly) (1 GF) No smoking in all bedrooms s fr £75; d £92-£99 (incl. bkfst) **LB FACILITIES: Spa** Jacuzzi Guided walks **PARKING:** 14 **NOTES:** No smoking in restaurant Closed 24 Dec-19 Jan **CARDS:**

★★★70% Wynnstay

Church St SY11 2SZ
☎ 01691 655261 📠 01691 670606
e-mail: info@wynnstayhotel.com

Dir: *B4083 to town, fork left at Honda Garage and right at lights. Hotel opposite church*

This Georgian property was once a posting house and surrounds a unique 200-year-old Crown Bowling Green. Public areas include a health, leisure and beauty centre. Well-equipped bedrooms are individually styled and decorated and include several suites, four-poster rooms and a self-catering apartment. There is a traditional restaurant and bar food is also on offer.
ROOMS: 29 en suite (4 fmly) No smoking in 14 bedrooms s £50-£95; d £65-£120 **LB FACILITIES: Spa** Indoor swimming (H) Sauna Solarium Gym Jacuzzi Crown green bowling Beauty suite **CONF:** Thtr 290 Class 150 Board 50 Del from £75 **PARKING:** 70 **NOTES:** No smoking in restaurant Civ Wed 90 **CARDS:**

★★73% Sebastian's Hotel & Restaurant

45 Willow St SY11 1AQ
☎ 01691 655444 📠 01691 653452
e-mail: sebastians.rest@virgin.net
Dir: *follow town centre signs. Junct with small pedestrian triangle take road towards Selattyn and Llansilin for 300yds into Willow St, hotel on left*
Parts of this privately-owned and personally-run small hotel date back to 1640. It has a wealth of charm and character, enhanced by original features such as exposed beams and oak panelling in the cosy lounge, bar and popular bistro-style restaurant. Bedrooms include four newly constructed rooms to the rear of the building.
ROOMS: 7 en suite 1 annexe en suite (4 fmly) No smoking in all bedrooms s £60; d £70 **CONF:** BC **PARKING:** 8 **NOTES:** No dogs (ex guide dogs) No smoking in restaurant Closed 25-26 Dec & 1 Jan
CARDS:

★★67% Sweeney Hall Hotel

Morda SY10 9EU
☎ 01691 652450 📠 01691 668023
e-mail: enquiries@sweeneyhall.co.uk
Dir: *from A5 on outskirts of Oswestry, take A483 towards Welshpool direction, hotel 2m on left*
Dating in part from 1640, this fine house was a refuge for Protestant Dissenters and is now a friendly family hotel. It is set in several acres of mature parkland. Bedrooms are mostly quite large, and all are well equipped. The hall has a welcoming log fire, and there are two dining rooms and meeting facilities.
ROOMS: 9 en suite (1 fmly) s £54.50-£59.50; d £69.50-£77.50 (incl. bkfst) **LB CONF:** Thtr 60 Class 40 Board 25 Del from £64.85
PARKING: 50 **NOTES:** No smoking in restaurant Civ Wed 72
CARDS:

⌂ Travelodge

Mile End Service Area SY11 4JA
☎ 08700 850 950 📠 01691 658178
Dir: *junct A5/A483*
Travelodge offers good quality, good value, modern accommodation. Ideal for families, the spacious, en suite bedrooms include remote-control TV, tea and coffee-making facilities, luxury beds and free morning newspaper. Meals can be taken at the nearby family restaurant. For further details and the Travelodge phone number, consult the Hotel Groups page.
ROOMS: 40 en suite s fr £42.95; d fr £42.95

For central reservation numbers and more information on Hotel Groups, turn to pages 33-39

OTLEY, West Yorkshire

Map 19 SE24

★★★69% Chevin Country Park Hotel

Yorkgate LS21 3NU
☎ 01943 467818 📠 01943 850335
e-mail: reception@chevinhotel.com
Dir: *From Leeds/Bradford Airport rdbt take A658 N, towards Harrogate, for 0.75m to 1st x-rds. Turn left, then 2nd left onto 'Yorkgate'. Hotel 0.5m on left*
This hotel, peacefully situated in its own woodland yet conveniently located for major road links, offers comfortable accommodation. Rooms are split between the original main log building and chalet style accommodation situated in the grounds.

continued on p474

OTLEY, continued

Public areas are spacious and well equipped. The split-level restaurant provides views over the small lake.

Chevin Country Park Hotel, Otley

ROOMS: 19 en suite 30 annexe en suite (7 fmly) (45 GF) No smoking in 10 bedrooms s £99; d £116 (incl. bkfst) **LB** **FACILITIES:** STV Indoor swimming (H) Tennis (hard) Fishing Sauna Solarium Gym Jacuzzi Mountain bikes, jogging trails, CCTV surveillance on indoor pool Xmas **CONF:** BC Thtr 120 Class 90 Board 50 Del £131 **PARKING:** 100 **NOTES:** Civ Wed 130 **CARDS:**

OTTERBURN, Northumberland Map 21 NY89

★★★64% ***The Otterburn Tower Hotel***
NE19 1NS
☎ 01830 520620 01830 521504
e-mail: reservations@otterburntower.co.uk
Dir: *on A696 Newcastle to Edinburgh road*

Originally built by the cousin of William the Conqueror in 1076, this hotel is steeped in history and Sir Walter Scott stayed here in 1812 and gathered information for his poem *Rokeby* during his visit. Bedrooms, some with huge gothic fireplaces, are individual in style and the restaurant features 16th-century oak panelling.

ROOMS: 17 en suite (2 fmly) No smoking in 10 bedrooms **FACILITIES:** STV Fishing **CONF:** Thtr 90 Class 90 Board 90 **PARKING:** 70 **NOTES:** No smoking in restaurant Civ Wed 90 **CARDS:**

★★66% **Percy Arms**
NE19 1NR
☎ 01830 520261 01830 520567
e-mail: percyarmshotel@yahoo.co.uk
Dir: *centre of Otterburn on A696*

This former coaching inn lies in the centre of the village and gives good access to the Northumberland countryside. Real fires warm welcoming public areas in season and guests can dine in either the restaurant or cosy bar/bistro. Bedrooms are cheerfully decorated and thoughtfully equipped.

ROOMS: 28 en suite (2 fmly) No smoking in 2 bedrooms **FACILITIES:** Fishing **CONF:** Thtr 70 Class 40 Board 50 **PARKING:** 74 **NOTES:** No smoking in restaurant **CARDS:**

OTTERSHAW, Surrey Map 06 TQ0

★★★★70% **Foxhills**
Stonehill Rd KT16 0EL
☎ 01932 872050 01932 874762
e-mail: reservations@foxhills.co.uk
Dir: *A320 to Woking from M25. 2nd rdbt last exit into Chobham Rd. Right into Foxhills Rd, right at T-junct, then left into Stonehill Rd*

This hotel enjoys a peaceful setting in extensive grounds, not far from the M25 and Heathrow. Spacious well-appointed bedrooms are provided in an annexe, a short walk from the main house. Golf, tennis, three pools and impressive indoor leisure facilities are on offer. Two styles of restaurant are available.

ROOMS: 38 en suite (3 fmly) (23 GF) s £170; d £170 **LB** **FACILITIES:** STV Indoor swimming (H) Outdoor swimming (H) Golf 45 Tennis (hard) Squash Snooker Sauna Solarium Gym Croquet lawn Putting green Boules, Childrens adventure playground ch fac Xmas **CONF:** Thtr 100 Class 52 Board 56 Del from £195 **PARKING:** 500 **NOTES:** No dogs (ex guide dogs) Civ Wed 60 **CARDS:**

OTTERY ST MARY, Devon Map 03 SY1

★★69% **Tumbling Weir Hotel & Restaurant**
Canaan Way EX11 1AQ
☎ 01404 812752 01404 812752
e-mail: reception@tumblingweirhotel.com
Dir: *off A30 take B3177 into Ottery St Mary, hotel signed off Mill St, access through old mill*

Quietly located between the River Otter and its millstream and set in well-tended gardens, this family-run hotel offers friendly and attentive service. Bedrooms are attractively presented and equipped with modern comforts. In the dining room, where a selection of carefully prepared dishes makes up the à la carte menu, beams and subtle lighting help to create an intimate atmosphere.

ROOMS: 10 en suite (1 fmly) No smoking in all bedrooms s £50-£52; d £75-£82 (incl. bkfst) **LB** **FACILITIES:** Croquet lawn ch fac **CONF:** Thtr 90 Class 60 Board 50 Del from £80 **PARKING:** 10 **NOTES:** No dogs (ex guide dogs) No smoking in restaurant Civ Wed 80 **CARDS:**

OXFORD, Oxfordshire Map 05 SP5
See also Milton Common

★★★★ @@@@@
Le Manoir Aux Quat' Saisons

Church Rd OX44 7PD
☎ 01844 278881 01844 278847
e-mail: lemanoir@blanc.co.uk
(For full entry see Great Milton)

Town House

★★★★ The Old Bank Hotel
92-94 High St OX1 4BN
☎ 01865 799599 01865 799598
e-mail: info@oldbank-hotel.co.uk
Dir: *city centre to Magdalen Bridge into High St, hotel 50yds on left*
This former bank has been converted into a very stylish and comfortable hotel. A wonderful collection of modern pictures and photographs livens the entire building. Bedrooms are smart and have CD players and air conditioning. Public areas are occupied mainly by the vibrant all-day Quod Bar and Restaurant, and there is a separate residents' bar. Parking and an outside courtyard are additional features.
ROOMS: 42 en suite (10 fmly) (1 GF) s £140; d £160-£320 **FACILITIES:** STV **CONF:** Thtr 20 Class 20 Board 14 **SERVICES:** Lift air con **PARKING:** 40 **NOTES:** No dogs (ex guide dogs) Closed 25-27 Dec **CARDS:**

★★★★70% The Oxford Hotel
Godstow Rd, Wolvercote Roundabout OX2 8AL
☎ 01865 489952 01865 310259
e-mail: oxford@paramount-hotels.co.uk
Dir: *adjacent to A34/A40, 2m from city centre*
Conveniently located on the northern edge of the city centre, this purpose-built hotel offers bedrooms that are bright, modern and well equipped. Guests can eat in the 'Medio' restaurant or try the Cappuccino bar menu. The hotel has undergone substantial refurbishment and now offers impressive conference, business and leisure facilities.
ROOMS: 168 en suite No smoking in 110 bedrooms **FACILITIES:** STV Indoor swimming (H) Squash Sauna Solarium Gym Steam room **CONF:** BC Thtr 300 Class 150 Board 60 Del from £160 **SERVICES:** Lift **PARKING:** 250 **NOTES:** No smoking in restaurant **CARDS:**

PARAMOUNT GROUP OF HOTELS

★★★★67% Cotswold Lodge
66a Banbury Rd OX2 6JP
☎ 01865 512121 01865 512490
e-mail: aa@cotswoldlodgehotel.co.uk
Dir: *off A40 Oxford ring road onto A4165 Banbury Rd. Signed city centre and Summertown. Hotel 2m on left*
This family-run hotel is a Victorian building close to the centre of Oxford has undergone a total refurbishment. Bedrooms are smartly presented and well equipped and the comfortable public areas have an elegant country-house charm. This hotel is popular with business guests and caters for conferences and banquets.
ROOMS: 49 en suite No smoking in 40 bedrooms s £125; d £175 (incl. bkfst) **FACILITIES:** STV Discount at local gymnasium available to residents **CONF:** Thtr 80 Class 42 Board 24 Del £150 **PARKING:** 40 **NOTES:** No dogs (ex guide dogs) No smoking in restaurant **CARDS:**

THE INDEPENDENTS

★★★★67% The Randolph
Beaumont St OX1 2LN
☎ 0870 400 8200 01865 792133
e-mail: randolph@macdonald-hotels.co.uk
Dir: *M40 J8, A40 towards Oxford in City Centre, to St Giles hotel on right*
Superbly located near the centre of town, The Randolph boasts impressive neo-Gothic architecture and tasteful décor. The restaurants with picture windows are ideal places to watch the world go by and delicious traditional teas may be enjoyed in the lounge. Refurbished bedrooms are classical in style and have a timeless elegance.
ROOMS: 111 en suite No smoking in 78 bedrooms s £120-£140; d £140-£190 **LB FACILITIES:** STV Xmas **CONF:** Thtr 300 Class 130 Board 60 Del from £150 **SERVICES:** Lift **NOTES:** No smoking in restaurant Civ Wed 120 **CARDS:**

MACDONALD HOTELS

★★★★66% Oxford Spires Four Pillars Hotel
Abingdon Rd OX1 4PS
☎ 0800 374 692 01865 324325
e-mail: spires@four-pillars.co.uk
Dir: *M40 junct 8 towards Oxford. Left at rdbt towards Cowley. Straight over next 2 rdbts. At next rdbt follow signs for City Centre. Hotel 1m on right*
This purpose built hotel is surrounded by extensive parkland, yet is only a short walk to the city centre. Bedrooms are attractively furnished, well equipped and include several apartments. Smartly appointed public areas include a spacious restaurant, open plan bar/lounge, leisure club and extensive conference facilities.
ROOMS: 115 en suite (8 fmly) No smoking in 44 bedrooms s £75-£139; d £96-£172 **LB FACILITIES:** STV Indoor swimming (H) Sauna Gym Jacuzzi Beauty, games, steam rooms entertainment Xmas **CONF:** BC Thtr 266 Class 96 Board 76 Del £169 **SERVICES:** Lift **PARKING:** 95 **NOTES:** No dogs (ex guide dogs) Civ Wed 140
CARDS:

FOUR PILLARS HOTELS

★★★★65% Oxford Thames Four Pillars Hotel
Henley Rd, Sandford-on-Thames OX4 4GX
☎ 0800 374 692 01865 334400
e-mail: thames@four-pillars.co.uk
Dir: *M40 junct 8. To Oxford follow ring road. Left at rdbt towards Cowley. At rdbt with lights take Left exit to Littlemore, the hotel approx 1m on right*

FOUR PILLARS HOTELS

The main house of this hotel is built from local, yellow stone. The spacious, traditional River Restaurant has superb views over the hotel's own boat moored on the river. The gardens can be enjoyed from the patios or balconies in the newer wings of bedrooms. Public rooms include a beamed bar and lounge area with minstrels' gallery.
ROOMS: 60 en suite (4 fmly) (24 GF) No smoking in 35 bedrooms s £75-£139; d £96-£172 **LB FACILITIES:** STV Indoor swimming (H) Tennis (hard) Sauna Gym Jacuzzi Steam room entertainment Xmas **CONF:** BC Thtr 160 Class 80 Board 60 Del £169 **PARKING:** 120 **NOTES:** No dogs (ex guide dogs) Civ Wed 120
CARDS:

O

OXFORD, continued

Town House

★★★★ Old Parsonage
1 Banbury Rd OX2 6NN
☎ 01865 310210 📠 01865 311262
e-mail: info@oldparsonage-hotel.co.uk
Dir: *from Oxford ring road to city centre via Summertown. Hotel last building on right next to St Giles Church before city centre*
Dating back in parts to the 16th century, this stylish town house hotel offers great character and charm and is conveniently located at the northern edge of the city centre. Bedrooms vary in size and are attractively furnished. The focal point is the all day bar restaurant. Two small garden areas are available for residents.
ROOMS: 30 en suite (4 fmly) s £100-£165; d £135-£195
FACILITIES: STV Putting nearby **PARKING:** 16 **NOTES:** No dogs (ex guide dogs) Closed 24-27 Dec
CARDS:

★★★75% Studley Priory
OX33 1AZ
☎ 01865 351203 & 351254 📠 01865 351613
e-mail: res@studley-priory.co.uk
(For full entry see Horton-cum-Studley)

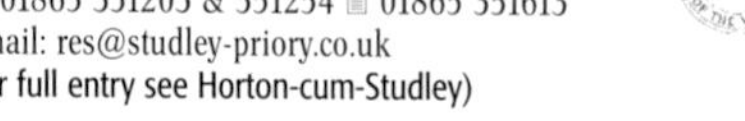

★★★70% Fallowfields Country House Hotel
Faringdon Rd, Kingston Bagpuize, Southmoor OX13 5BH
☎ 01865 820416 📠 01865 821275
e-mail: stay@fallowfields.com
Dir: *from A420, take A415 towards Abingdon for 100yds. Right at mini rdbt, through Kingston Bagpuize, Southmoor and Longworth, follow signs*

With a history stretching back over 300 years, this spacious, comfortable hotel provides friendly, old-fashioned service. The thoughtfully equipped bedrooms are very much of this century and are decorated with skill. Public areas include an elegant drawing room and a charming conservatory restaurant in which the hotel's own seasonal produce is served.
ROOMS: 10 en suite (2 fmly) No smoking in all bedrooms s £85-£115; d £120-£160 (incl. bkfst) **LB FACILITIES:** STV Tennis (hard) Croquet lawn Falconry **CONF:** Thtr 60 Board 20 **PARKING:** 21 **NOTES:** No smoking in restaurant Civ Wed 100 **CARDS:**

★★★70% Weston Manor Hotel
OX25 3QL
☎ 01869 350621 📠 01869 350901
e-mail: reception@wetonmanor.co.uk
(For full entry see Weston-on-the-Green)

★★★69% Hawkwell House
Church Way, Iffley Village OX4 4DZ
☎ 01865 749988 📠 01865 748525
e-mail: info@hawkwellhouse.co.uk
Dir: *A34 follow signs to Cowley. At Littlemore rdbt take A4158 exit onto Iffley Rd. After traffic lights left to Iffley*

Set in a peaceful residential location, Hawkwell House is just a few minutes' drive from the Oxford ring road. The spacious rooms are modern, attractively decorated and well equipped. Public areas are tastefully appointed and the conservatory style restaurant offers an interesting choice of dishes. The hotel also has a range of conference and function facilities.
ROOMS: 51 en suite (3 fmly) No smoking in 13 bedrooms s £45-£120; d fr £140 (incl. bkfst) **LB FACILITIES:** STV Croquet lawn Xmas **CONF:** Thtr 200 Class 100 Board 80 Del from £125 **SERVICES:** Lift **PARKING:** 85 **NOTES:** No dogs (ex guide dogs) No smoking in restaurant Civ Wed 200 **CARDS:**

See advert on opposite page

★★★67% Linton Lodge
11-13 Linton Rd OX2 6UJ
☎ 01865 553461 📠 01865 310365
e-mail: sales@lintonlodge.com

Dir: *to Oxford city centre along Banbury Rd. After 0.5m, right into Linton Rd. Hotel opposite St Andrews Church*
Located in a residential area, Linton Lodge is within walking distance of the town centre. Bedrooms are well equipped and comfortable and all have undergone refurbishment and decoration. There are is a wood-panelled restaurant and a bar overlooking the croquet lawn.
ROOMS: 71 en suite (2 fmly) No smoking in 40 bedrooms s £65-£115; d £65-£135 (incl. bkfst) **LB FACILITIES:** STV Croquet lawn Putting green **CONF:** Thtr 120 Class 50 Board 40 Del from £129 **SERVICES:** Lift **PARKING:** 40 **NOTES:** No smoking in restaurant Civ Wed 140
CARDS:

See advert on opposite page

★★★65% Eastgate
73 High St OX1 4BE
☎ 0870 400 8201 📠 01865 791681
e-mail: sales.eastgate@macdonald-hotels.co.uk
Dir: *A40 follow signs to Headington & Oxford city centre, over Magdalen Bridge, stay in left lane, left into Merton St, entrance to car park on left*
Just a short stroll from the city centre, this hotel, as its name suggests, occupies the site of the city's medieval East Gate. The

continued

tastefully furnished and decorated bedrooms are situated on three floors, and the public areas include the popular Merton's bistro and bar.
ROOMS: 64 en suite (3 fmly) No smoking in 30 bedrooms s £115-£130; d £125-£150 **LB** **FACILITIES:** STV **SERVICES:** Lift **PARKING:** 40
NOTES: No dogs (ex guide dogs) No smoking in restaurant
CARDS:

★★★64% Westwood Country

Hinksey Hill, Boars Hill OX1 5BG
☎ 01865 735408 📠 01865 736536
e-mail: reservations@westwoodhotel.co.uk

This Edwardian country house hotel is prominently set in terraced landscaped gardens and is within easy reach of the city centre by car. The bedrooms are very comfortable, well equipped and tastefully decorated. Public areas include a contemporary bar and a cosy lounge. Guests can choose to dine in the Oaks Restaurant or the more intimate Oriel Room.
ROOMS: 23 en suite (4 fmly) No smoking in 22 bedrooms s £75-£85; d £99-£110 (incl. bkfst) **FACILITIES:** Croquet lawn **CONF:** Thtr 60 Class 36 Board 35 Del from £110 **PARKING:** 60 **NOTES:** Civ Wed 85
CARDS:

★★67% Victoria

180 Abingdon Rd OX1 4RA
☎ 01865 724536 📠 01865 794909
e-mail: victoriahotel@aol.com
Dir: *from M40/A40 take Eastern bypass and A4144 into city*
Located within easy reach of Oxford city centre and the motorway networks, this hotel offers a warm welcome. Bedrooms are comfortable, well maintained and furnished to a high standard. A conservatory bar and large dining room are ideal places to relax.
ROOMS: 15 en suite 5 annexe en suite (1 fmly) No smoking in 15 bedrooms s £62.50-£68.50; d £78.50-£85.50 (incl. bkfst) **LB**
CONF: Board 20 Del from £125 **PARKING:** 20 **NOTES:** No smoking in restaurant **CARDS:**

★★65% The Balkan Lodge Hotel

315 Iffley Rd OX4 4AG
☎ 01865 244524 📠 01865 251090
e-mail: balkanlodge@aol.co.uk
Dir: *from M40/A40 take eastern bypass, into city on A4158*
Conveniently located for the city centre and the ring road, this family operated hotel offers a comfortable stay. Bedrooms are attractive and well equipped; one has a four-poster bed and jacuzzi. Public areas include a lounge, bar and restaurant. Private car park is located to the rear of the building.
ROOMS: 13 en suite No smoking in all bedrooms **FACILITIES:** STV
NOTES: No smoking in restaurant **CARDS:**

O

OXFORD, continued

★★64% *Manor House*

250 Iffley Rd OX4 1SE
☎ 01865 727627 🖹 01865 200478
Dir: *on A4158 1m from city centre*
This conveniently situated hotel is easily accessible to the city centre and all major road links. Private parking is an asset. Family run, this hotel provides informal but friendly and attentive service levels. Public areas are well maintained and presented. The comfortably furnished bedrooms are well equipped.
ROOMS: 8 en suite (2 fmly) No smoking in all bedrooms **PARKING:** 6
NOTES: No dogs Closed 20 Dec-20 Jan
CARDS:

Holiday Inn Oxford

Peartree Roundabout, Woodstock Rd OX2 8JD
☎ 0870 400 9086 🖹 01865 888333
e-mail: reservations-oxford@ichotelsgroup.com
At the time of going to press, the classification for this hotel was not confirmed. Please refer to the AA internet site www.theAA.com for current information.
ROOMS: 154 en suite (25 fmly) No smoking in 113 bedrooms
FACILITIES: Spa STV Indoor swimming (H) Sauna Solarium Gym
CONF: Thtr 160 Class 64 Board 65 **SERVICES:** Lift air con
PARKING: 184 **NOTES:** No dogs (ex guide dogs) No smoking in restaurant **CARDS:**

Express by Holiday Inn Oxford-Kassam Stadium

Grenoble Rd OX4 4XP
☎ 01865 780888 🖹 01865 780999
e-mail: reservations@expressoxford.com
Dir: *M40 junct 8 onto A40 for 4m. Left at Mcdonalds onto A4142. After 3.5m left onto A4074 take 1st exit signed Science Park & Kassam Stadium*

A modern hotel ideal for families and business travellers. Fresh and uncomplicated, the spacious bedrooms include Sky TV, power shower and tea and coffee-making facilities. Continental buffet breakfast is included in the room rate; other meals may be taken at the nearby family pub or restaurant. For further details and the Express by Holiday Inn phone number, consult the Hotel Groups pages.
ROOMS: 162 en suite s fr £69; d fr £69 (incl. cont bkfst)
CONF: Thtr 40 Class 20 Board 20

Travel Inn

Oxford Business Park, Garsington Rd OX4 2JZ
☎ 08701 977204 🖹 01865 775887
Dir: *Situated on the Oxford Business Park, just off the A4142 on the junction with the B480, opposite the BMW Works, 3 miles from Oxford city centre*
Travel Inn offers good-quality, value-for-money accommodation.
continued
Spacious, en suite rooms with bath and shower comfortably accommodate a family of up to two adults and two children (to age 15). The restaurant and bar offers a varied menu. For further details and the Travel Inn phone number, consult the Hotel Groups page.
ROOMS: 120 en suite s £52.95-£56.95; d £52.95-£56.95

Travelodge

Peartree Roundabout, Woodstock Rd OX2 8JZ
☎ 08700 850 950 🖹 01865 513474
Dir: *junct A34/A43*
Travelodge offers good quality, good value, modern accommodation. Ideal for families, the spacious, en suite bedrooms include remote-control TV, tea and coffee-making facilities, luxury beds and free morning newspaper. Meals can be taken at the nearby family restaurant. For further details and the Travelodge phone number, consult the Hotel Groups page.
ROOMS: 150 en suite s fr £42.95; d fr £42.95 **CONF:** Thtr 300 Class 150 Board 60

Travelodge (Oxford East)

London Rd, Wheatley OX33 1JH
☎ 08700 850 950 🖹 01865 875905
Dir: *off A40 next to The Harvester on outskirts of Wheatley*
Travelodge offers good quality, good value, modern accommodation. Ideal for families, the spacious, en suite bedrooms include remote-control TV, tea and coffee-making facilities, luxury beds and free morning newspaper. Meals can be taken at the nearby family restaurant. For further details and the Travelodge phone number, consult the Hotel Groups page.
ROOMS: 36 en suite s fr £42.95; d fr £42.95

OXFORD MOTORWAY SERVICE AREA (M40), Oxfordshire — Map 05 SP60

Days Inn

M40 junction 8A, Waterstock OX33 1LJ
☎ 01865 877000 🖹 01865 877016
e-mail: oxford.hotel@welcomebreak.co.uk
Dir: *M40 junct 8a, Welcome Break service area.*
This modern building offers accommodation in smart, spacious and well-equipped bedrooms, suitable for families and business travellers, and all with en suite bathrooms. Continental breakfast is available and other refreshments may be taken at the nearby family restaurant. For further details and the Days Inn phone number, consult the Hotel Groups page.
ROOMS: 59 en suite s £54-£60; d £54-£60

PADSTOW, Cornwall & Isles of Scilly — Map 02 SW97
See also Constantine Bay

★★★70% The Metropole

Station Rd PL28 8DB
☎ 01841 532486 🖹 01841 532867
e-mail: info@the-metropole.co.uk
Dir: *M5/A30 pass Launceston, turn off & follow signs for Wadebridge & N Cornwall. Take A39 & follow signs for Padstow*
This long established hotel first opened its doors to guests back in 1904 and there is still an air of the sophistication and elegance of a bygone age. Bedrooms are soundly appointed and equipped and dining options include the informal Met Café Bar and the main restaurant, with enjoyable cuisine and wonderful views over the Camel estuary.
ROOMS: 50 en suite (3 fmly) No smoking in 10 bedrooms
FACILITIES: Outdoor swimming (H) Swimming pool open Jul & Aug only
SERVICES: Lift **PARKING:** 36 **NOTES:** No smoking in restaurant
CARDS:

★★★65% ◎ Old Custom House Inn
South Quay PL28 8BL
☎ 01841 532359 ▯ 01841 533372
e-mail: oldcustomhouse@smallandfriendly.co.uk
Dir: *A359 from Wadebridge, take 2nd right. In Padstow follow road round bend to bottom of hill. Hotel 2nd building*
Situated by the harbour, this charming inn continues to be a popular choice for locals and visitors alike. The lively bar serves real ales and good bar meals. Pescadou's restaurant provides a stylish and convivial venue for imaginative dishes that place the emphasis on locally caught fish.
ROOMS: 24 en suite (8 fmly) No smoking in all bedrooms s fr £78; d fr £95 (incl. bkfst) **LB** **FACILITIES:** STV **CONF:** Board 85 **PARKING:** 9 **NOTES:** No smoking in restaurant Closed 25-26 Dec **CARDS:**

★★67% The Old Ship Hotel
Mill Square PL28 8AE
☎ 01841 532357 ▯ 01841 533211
e-mail: stay@oldshiphotel-padstow.co.uk
Dir: *from M5 take A30 to Bodmin then A389 to Padstow, follow brown tourist signs to car park*
Situated in the midst of the quaint and winding streets of the old town and just a short stroll from the harbourside, this attractive old inn offers comfortable and friendly accommodation. Bedrooms are pleasantly furnished and very well equipped. Freshly caught fish features prominently on both the bar and restaurant menus.
ROOMS: 14 en suite s £35-£45; d £70-£90 (incl. bkfst) **LB** **FACILITIES:** STV entertainment Xmas **CONF:** Board 20 **PARKING:** 20 **NOTES:** No smoking in restaurant **CARDS:**

★★66% *Green Waves*
West View Rd, Trevone Bay PL28 8RD
☎ 01841 520114 ▯ 01841 520568
e-mail: info@greenwaveshotel.co.uk
Dir: *off A39 to Padstow onto B3276 signed Newquay and Trevone. After 4m 1st right signed Trevone. Hotel at bottom of road after Beach Car Parks*
This ever popular, family-run hotel is just a short stroll from the beach and coastal footpaths. Bedrooms are varied in size and style, some with wonderful sea views. Public areas include a spacious lounge and a separate bar, ideal for enjoying a drink before a home-cooked dinner.
ROOMS: 15 en suite No smoking in all bedrooms **CONF:** Class 25 **PARKING:** 16 **NOTES:** No dogs (ex guide dogs) No children 4yrs No smoking in restaurant Closed end Nov-Mar **CARDS:**

See advert on this page

Restaurant with Rooms

◎◎◎ The Seafood Restaurant
Riverside PL28 8BY
☎ 01841 532700 ▯ 01841 532942
e-mail: reservations@rickstein.com
Dir: *A38 towards Newquay, then A389 towards Padstow. After 3m, R at T-junct, follow signs for Padstow town centre. Restaurant on L*
Rick Stein's Seafood Restaurant enjoys an enviable reputation for the freshness and quality of its cuisine, and it is no surprise to discover that such high standards are repeated in the accommodation here. Each of the bedrooms is spacious and comfortable, complete with fine quality fixtures and fittings. Additional rooms are housed close by in St Edmunds, where refurbishment has resulted in luxurious standards with much style.
ROOMS: 13 en suite 19 annexe en suite (7 fmly) (3 GF) d £80-£220 (incl. bkfst) **LB** **FACILITIES:** STV **PARKING:** 22 **NOTES:** Closed 1 May & 22-26 Dec **CARDS:**

PAIGNTON, Devon — Map 03 SX86

★★★71% Redcliffe
Marine Dr TQ3 2NL — THE INDEPENDENTS
☎ 01803 526397 ▯ 01803 528030
e-mail: redclfe@aol.com
Dir: *follow signs for Paignton. Hotel on seafront at Torquay end of Paignton Green*
Set on the edge of the sea in three acres of well-tended grounds, this popular hotel enjoys uninterrupted views across Tor Bay. Offering a diverse range of facilities, including leisure, business and beauty treatments, the Redcliffe is suitable for either the leisure or business guest. Bedrooms are pleasantly appointed and comfortably furnished and public areas spacious.
ROOMS: 67 en suite (8 fmly) (2 GF) s £52-£56; d £104-£112 (incl. bkfst) **FACILITIES: Spa** STV Indoor swimming (H) Outdoor swimming (H) Fishing Sauna Solarium Gym Putting green Jacuzzi Table tennis, Carpet Bowls, Indoor Pool supervised ch fac Xmas **CONF:** Thtr 150 Class 50 Board 50 Del from £59 **SERVICES:** Lift **PARKING:** 80 **NOTES:** No dogs (ex guide dogs) No smoking in restaurant Civ Wed 150 **CARDS:**

★★70% Dainton
95 Dartmouth Rd, Three Beaches, Goodrington TQ4 6NA
☎ 01803 550067 ▯ 01803 666339
e-mail: enquiries@daintonhotel.com
Dir: *on A379 at Goodrington. Pass zoo entrance, right onto Penwill Way. At bottom of road right into Dartmouth Rd. Hotel 0.25m on left*
Located in a convenient position close to the beaches and Leisure Park, the Dainton provides a friendly and welcoming place to stay. Service is attentive, particularly in the new Christie's restaurant

continued on p480

P

PAIGNTON, continued

where an extensive menu choice is offered, including vegetarian options. Bedrooms are well equipped and brightly decorated.
ROOMS: 10 en suite (3 fmly) (2 GF) No smoking in all bedrooms s £37.50; d £65 (incl. bkfst) **LB** **FACILITIES:** Xmas **PARKING:** 20
NOTES: No dogs (ex guide dogs) No smoking in restaurant
CARDS:

★★67% Sea Verge Hotel
21 Marine Dr TQ3 2NJ
☎ 01803 557795
With the added benefit of dedicated owners, this family-run hotel is conveniently situated close to the seafront and Preston Green. Several of the light and airy bedrooms have balconies, with views over Torbay. Spacious public areas include a comfortable lounge with adjacent sun-room, a cosy bar and the soundly appointed dining room.
ROOMS: 10 en suite (1 fmly) No smoking in 4 bedrooms **PARKING:** 14
NOTES: No dogs No children 9yrs Closed Dec-Feb

★★66% Torbay Holiday Motel
Totnes Rd TQ4 7PP
☎ 01803 558226 📠 01803 663375
e-mail: enquiries@thm.co.uk
Dir: *on A385 Totnes to Paignton road, 2.5m from Paignton*
Situated between Paignton and Totnes, this small complex offers purpose built, leisure facilities, self-catering apartments and motel accommodation. The spacious bedrooms are comfortable and well co-ordinated. There are two restaurants, which provide a choice of smoking or non-smoking, and traditional dining is offered throughout.
ROOMS: 16 en suite s £35-£39; d £54-£62 (incl. bkfst) **LB**
FACILITIES: STV Indoor swimming (H) Outdoor swimming (H) Sauna Solarium Gym Putting green Crazy golf, Adventure playground
PARKING: 150 **NOTES:** RS 24-31 Dec **CARDS:**
See advert on opposite page

★70% The Commodore Hotel
14 Esplanade Rd TQ4 6EB
☎ 01803 553107 📠 01803 553107
e-mail: commodoretorbay@aol.com
Dir: *follow A3022, left lane to seafront, after multiplex cinema complex, hotel on right*
Enjoying a prime seafront position, this family-run hotel benefits from the added bonus of lovely views across the bay. Public areas are spacious and well presented, with ample seating in both the lounge and bar lounge. Bedrooms are comfortable and well equipped.
ROOMS: 12 en suite (4 fmly) (3 GF) s £23-£25; d £46-£50 (incl. bkfst)
FACILITIES: Xmas **PARKING:** 10 **NOTES:** No dogs (ex guide dogs) No smoking in restaurant Closed Nov-Feb

★69% Britney
29 Esplanade Rd TQ4 6BL
☎ 01803 557820 📠 01803 551285
Dir: *on seafront by pier*
In an impressive location on the seafront, this pleasant hotel offers a convenient location and comfortable accommodation. The hotel is family run and the proprietors are friendly and attentive. Bedrooms, some of which are sea facing and some with balconies, are available in a range of sizes. A lively bar is available as well as a quieter lounge and sunroom.
ROOMS: 19 en suite (2 fmly) No smoking in 3 bedrooms s £30-£38; d £60-£76 (incl. bkfst & dinner) **LB** **FACILITIES:** Xmas **SERVICES:** Lift
PARKING: 8 **NOTES:** No smoking in restaurant **CARDS:**

PAINSWICK, Gloucestershire Map 04 SO80

★★★75% Painswick
Kemps Ln GL6 6YB
☎ 01452 812160 📠 01452 814059
e-mail: reservations@painswickhotel.com
Dir: *off A46 in centre of village by church. Hotel off 2nd road behind church off Tibbiwell Ln*

Quietly situated in the heart of an enchanting Cotswolds village, this family-run hotel was built in 1790. Elegant day rooms feature antiques and an array of interesting artwork, all contributing to a sense of timeless elegance. No two bedrooms are the same, and all reflect high standards and an abundance of character. The oak-panelled restaurant is the venue for accomplished cuisine, accompanied by carefully chosen wines.
ROOMS: 19 en suite (2 fmly) s £75-£150; d £125-£200 (incl. bkfst) **LB**
FACILITIES: Croquet lawn ch fac Xmas **CONF:** Thtr 40 Class 20 Board 20 Del £150 **PARKING:** 25 **NOTES:** No smoking in restaurant Civ Wed 100 **CARDS:**
See advert on opposite page

PANGBOURNE, Berkshire Map 05 SU67

★★★76% The Copper Inn Hotel and Restaurant
Best Western
RG8 7AR
☎ 0118 984 2244 📠 0118 984 5542
e-mail: reservations@copper-inn.co.uk
Dir: *M4 junct 12 take A4 W then A340 to Pangbourne. Hotel next to church at junct of A329 & A340*

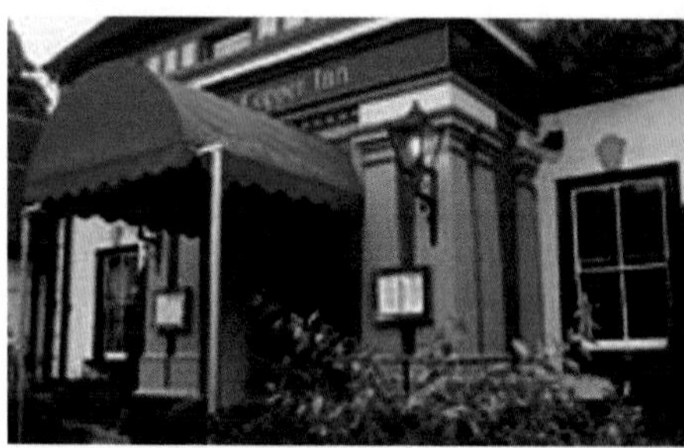

This 19th-century coaching inn is well known for its high standards of hotel keeping. Public rooms include a popular and lively bar, a quiet lounge and lovely restaurant where service is friendly and efficient. Well-equipped bedrooms, many of which overlook the
continued

secluded rear gardens, are comfortably appointed and individually decorated.
ROOMS: 14 en suite 8 annexe en suite (1 fmly) No smoking in all bedrooms s £60-£120; d £60-£120 (incl. bkfst) **LB** **FACILITIES:** STV Xmas **CONF:** BC Thtr 60 Class 24 Board 30 Del from £140
PARKING: 20 **NOTES:** No smoking in restaurant Civ Wed 80
CARDS:

★★★68% George Hotel
The Square RG8 7AJ
☎ 0118 984 2237 🖷 0118 984 4354
e-mail: info@georgehotelpangbourne.co.uk
Best Western
Dir: *M4 junct 12 towards Newbury. Right at 2nd rdbt onto A340, 3m to Pangbourne. Right at rdbt, hotel 50yds on left*
Having undergone a transformation, this former coaching inn now offers modern facilities. Bedrooms are thoughtfully appointed and comfortable, a number are specially equipped for families. The 'Kidsden' rooms have computers and playstations and considering the hotel's location just 20 minutes from Legoland, this is a popular venue for families. Dinner is available with an Italian theme in Mia Bene Restaurant.
ROOMS: 24 en suite (6 fmly) No smoking in 12 bedrooms s £55-£90; d £70-£100 (incl. cont bkfst) **FACILITIES:** STV **CONF:** Thtr 60 Class 25 Board 20 Del from £130 **PARKING:** 30
CARDS:

PARKHAM, Devon

Map 03 SS32

★★★72% ⊛ Penhaven Country House
Rectory Ln EX39 5PL
☎ 01237 451388 & 451711 🖷 01237 451878
e-mail: reservations@penhaven.co.uk
Dir: *off A39 at Horns Cross, follow signs to Parkham, 2nd left after church into Rectory Ln*
The countryside and local wildlife are very much a feature here and the loveliness of the grounds is matched by the tameness of the local badgers who frequent the lawn most evenings. The staff are friendly and with the tranquillity of the location, Penhaven provides a truly relaxing venue. Bedrooms are spacious and well equipped; some rooms are located in the cottage annexe and two are on the ground floor. Dinners feature fresh local produce and vegetarians are especially welcome.
ROOMS: 12 en suite s £80-£85; d £160-£180 (incl. bkfst & dinner) **LB** **FACILITIES:** 9 acres of woodland trail Xmas **PARKING:** 50 **NOTES:** No children 10yrs No smoking in restaurant **CARDS:**

PATTERDALE, Cumbria

Map 18 NY31

★★62% Patterdale
CA11 0NN
☎ 0845 458 4333 & 017684 82231 🖷 01253 754222
e-mail: reservations@choice-hotels.co.uk
Dir: *M6 junct 40, take A592 towards Ullswater, then 10m up Lakeside Rd to Patterdale*
Patterdale is a real tourist destination and this hotel enjoys delightful views of the valley and fells, being located at the southern end of Ullswater. Bedrooms vary in style with the refurbished ones brightly decorated with a modern feel.
ROOMS: 61 en suite (16 fmly) s £59-£159; d £59-£159 (incl. bkfst & dinner) **LB** **FACILITIES:** Tennis (hard) Fishing Croquet lawn Free bike hire entertainment Xmas **SERVICES:** Lift **PARKING:** 30 **NOTES:** No dogs (ex guide dogs) No smoking in restaurant
CARDS:

PATTINGHAM, Staffordshire Map 10 SO89

★★★68% Patshull Park Hotel Golf & Country Club

Patshull Park WV6 7HR
☎ 01902 700100 🖹 01902 700874
e-mail: sales@patshull-park.co.uk
Dir: *1.5m W of Pattingham, at Pattingham Church take Patshull Rd, hotel 1.5m on right*

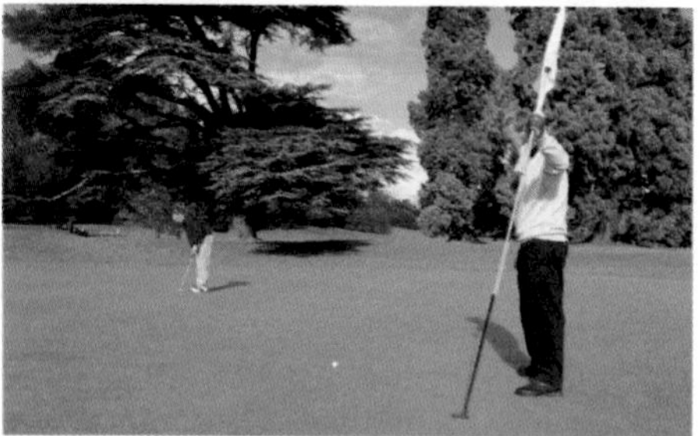

There has been a manor house here since before the Norman Conquest; the present house dates back to the 1730s and is now a comfortably appointed hotel. Sitting within 280 acres of parkland (with good golf and fishing) this hotel has a range of modern leisure and conference facilities. Public rooms include a lounge bar, coffee shop and restaurant with delightful views out over the lake. Bedrooms are well appointed and thoughtfully equipped; most have good views.
ROOMS: 49 en suite (6 fmly) (15 GF) No smoking in 40 bedrooms s £99-£109; d £109-£139 (incl. bkfst) **LB** **FACILITIES: Spa** STV Indoor swimming (H) Golf 18 Fishing Sauna Solarium Gym Putting green Jacuzzi Beauty therapist, Pool table, Cardio suite entertainment Xmas **CONF:** Thtr 160 Class 75 Board 44 Del from £95 **PARKING:** 200 **NOTES:** No dogs (ex guide dogs) No smoking in restaurant Civ Wed 100
CARDS:

See advert under WOLVERHAMPTON

PEASLAKE, Surrey Map 06 TQ04

★★★66% Hurtwood Inn Hotel

Walking Bottom GU5 9RR
☎ 01306 730851 🖹 01306 731390
e-mail: sales@hurtwoodinnhotel.com
Dir: *off A25 at Gomshall opposite Jet Filling Station towards Peaslake. After 2.5m turn right at village shop, hotel in village centre*

Situated in the peaceful village of Peaslake, this hotel offers brightly appointed bedrooms, some in an adjacent wing overlooking the hotel garden. Public areas are being altered and extended - new lounge and meeting rooms are being developed.
continued

Pre-dinner drinks can be taken in the cosy bar/lounge by a warming fire, and carefully prepared meals are served in the delightful oak-panelled 'Oscars' restaurant.
ROOMS: 16 en suite 6 annexe en suite (6 fmly) (6 GF) No smoking in 5 bedrooms s £65; d £75-£95 **CONF:** Thtr 40 Class 15 Board 20 Del £115 **PARKING:** 22 **NOTES:** No smoking in restaurant
CARDS:

PEASMARSH, East Sussex Map 07 TQ82

★★★73% Flackley Ash

TN31 6YH
☎ 01797 230651 🖹 01797 230510
e-mail: enquiries@flackleyashhotel.co.uk
Dir: *3m from Rye, beside A268*

Best Western

Five acres of beautifully kept grounds are the lovely backdrop to this elegant Georgian country house. The hotel is superbly located for exploring the many local attractions including the ancient Cinque Port of Rye. Bedrooms are individually decorated and have a homely feel, and include added extras.
ROOMS: 45 en suite (3 fmly) **FACILITIES: Spa** STV Indoor swimming (H) Sauna Gym Croquet lawn Putting green Beautician aromatherapy reflexology Xmas **CONF:** Thtr 100 Class 50 Board 40 Del £99 **PARKING:** 70 **NOTES:** No smoking in restaurant Civ Wed 100
CARDS:

PELYNT, Cornwall & Isles of Scilly Map 02 SX25

★★66% Jubilee Inn

PL13 2JZ
☎ 01503 220312 🖹 01503 220920
e-mail: rickard@jubileeinn.freeserve.co.uk
Dir: *take A390 signed St Austell at East Taphouse. Left onto B3359 signed Looe and Polperro. Hotel on left leaving Pelynt*

Situated close to Looe and within a short drive of The Eden Project, this popular 16th-century inn has abundant character with flagstone floors and beams. A choice of bars is available, and menus focus on fresh local produce. Individual in size and decor, the bedrooms are comfortable with modern facilities.
ROOMS: 11 en suite (3 fmly) s £35-£42; d £60-£70 (incl. bkfst) **LB** **FACILITIES:** Xmas **PARKING:** 80 **NOTES:** No smoking in restaurant
CARDS:

PENDLEBURY, Greater Manchester Map 15 SD70

⌂ Premier Lodge (Manchester North West)

PREMIER LODGE

219 Bolton Rd M27 8TG
☎ 0870 9906528 🖹 0870 9906529

Premier Lodge offers modern, well-equipped, en suite accommodation suitable for both business and leisure travellers. Meals can be taken at the adjacent popular restaurant and bar, which is fully licensed. For further details, consult the Hotel Groups page.
ROOMS: 31 en suite s £48; d £48

PENKRIDGE, Staffordshire Map 10 SJ91

★★★66% Quality Hotel Stafford

Pinfold Ln ST19 5QP
☎ 01785 712459 🖹 01785 715532
e-mail: admin@gb067.u-net.com
Dir: *M6 junct 12 onto A5 towards Telford. Right at 1st rdbt onto A449, 2m into Penkridge, left just beyond Ford Garage, opposite White Hart*

Just a few minutes' drive from the M6, this hotel is pleasantly located down a country lane. Bedrooms are comfortable with a
continued

good range of facilities. Public areas are neatly appointed with conference rooms and a leisure club. The Choices Restaurant serves popular meals to its guests.
ROOMS: 47 en suite (1 fmly) No smoking in 25 bedrooms
FACILITIES: STV Indoor swimming (H) Squash Sauna Solarium Gym
CONF: Thtr 300 Class 120 Board 60 Del £130 **PARKING:** 160
NOTES: No dogs (ex guide dogs) No smoking in restaurant Civ Wed 70
CARDS:

PENRITH, Cumbria

Map 18 NY53

See also Shap & Temple Sowerby

★★★★72% North Lakes Hotel & Spa

Ullswater Rd CA11 8QT
☎ 01768 868111 📠 01768 868291
e-mail: nlakes@shirehotels.co.uk
Dir: *M6 junct 40 at junct with A66*

With its great location just off the north Lake District junction of

continued on p484

PENRITH, continued

the M6, it is no wonder that this hotel enjoys a busy trade. Amenities include a good range of meeting and function rooms and excellent health and leisure facilities including full spa. Themed public areas have a contemporary Scandinavian country style and offer plenty of space and comfort. *Shire Hotels – AA Hotel Group of the Year 2003-2004.*
ROOMS: 84 en suite (6 fmly) (22 GF) No smoking in 25 bedrooms s £80-£105; d £110-£130 (incl. bkfst) **LB FACILITIES: Spa** STV Indoor swimming (H) Squash Sauna Solarium Gym Childrens pool, 5 Health & Beauty rooms, Steam room, Swimming pool supervised Xmas **CONF:** BC Thtr 200 Class 140 Board 24 Del from £142 **SERVICES:** Lift **PARKING:** 150 **NOTES:** No dogs (ex guide dogs) No smoking in restaurant Civ Wed 200 **CARDS:**

See advert on page 483

★★★75% Temple Sowerby House
CA10 1RZ
☎ 017683 61578 017683 61958
e-mail: stay@temple-sowerby.com
(For full entry see Temple Sowerby)

★★★73% Westmorland Hotel
Orton CA10 3SB
☎ 015396 24351 015396 24354
e-mail: sales@westmorlandhotel.com
(For full entry and advert see Tebay)

★★★65% The George
Devonshire St CA11 7SU
☎ 01768 862696 01768 868223
e-mail: info@georgehotelpenrith.co.uk
Dir: *M6 junct 40, 1m to town centre. From A6/A66 to Penrith*

Much of this long-established town centre hotel has now been upgraded, including most of the well-equipped bedrooms. The spacious public areas retain their old-fashioned charm and include a choice of lounge areas, which are a popular venue for morning coffees and afternoon teas.
ROOMS: 34 en suite (3 fmly) No smoking in 24 bedrooms s fr £48; d fr £80 (incl. bkfst) **LB FACILITIES:** STV Free use of local pool and gym Xmas **CONF:** Thtr 120 Class 50 Board 40 Del from £90 **PARKING:** 34 **NOTES:** No smoking in restaurant Civ Wed 120
CARDS:

See advert under KESWICK and on page 483

★★67% Brantwood Country Hotel
Stainton CA11 0EP
☎ 01768 862748 01768 890164
e-mail: brantwood2@aol.com
Dir: *M6 junct 40, A66. Left in 0.5m then right signed Stainton*
Located in a peaceful village this family-run hotel enjoys an open outlook to the rear. The traditional bedrooms are individual and cheerful in colour; five rooms are in a converted courtyard building. Meals are served in both the bar and restaurant and there is a separate conservatory-style residents' lounge.

ROOMS: 7 en suite (3 fmly) No smoking in 5 bedrooms s £40-£48; d £62 (incl. bkfst) **LB FACILITIES:** Croquet lawn Xmas **CONF:** Thtr 60 Class 30 Board 30 Del from £60 **PARKING:** 35 **NOTES:** No dogs No smoking in restaurant **CARDS:**

★★67% *Edenhall Country Hotel*
Edenhall CA11 8SX
☎ 01768 881454 01768 881266
Dir: *take A686 from Penrith to Alston. Hotel signed in 3m on right*
Located in a peaceful hamlet yet convenient for the M6, this hotel is popular with business guests and has a number of meeting rooms. The spacious bar is comfortable and has an open fire where chestnuts can be roasted on cold winter nights. Carefully prepared, tasty meals are served in the dining room that overlooks the well-tended gardens.
ROOMS: 17 en suite 8 annexe en suite (3 fmly) (7 GF) **FACILITIES:** Fishing Croquet lawn ch fac **CONF:** Thtr 50 Class 20 Board 20 Del from £70 **PARKING:** 60 **NOTES:** No smoking in restaurant
CARDS:

Travelodge
Redhills CA11 0DT
☎ 08700 850 950 01768 866958
Dir: *on A66*
Travelodge offers good quality, good value, modern accommodation. Ideal for families, the spacious, en suite bedrooms include remote-control TV, tea and coffee-making facilities, luxury beds and free morning newspaper. Meals can be taken at the nearby family restaurant. For further details and the Travelodge phone number, consult the Hotel Groups page.
ROOMS: 54 en suite s fr £42.95; d fr £42.95

PENSILVA, Cornwall & Isles of Scilly Map 03 SX27

★★65% Wheal Tor Country Hotel
Caradon Hill PL14 5PJ
☎ 01579 362281 01579 363401
e-mail: enquiries@whealtorhotel.co.uk
Reputed to be Bodmin Moor's highest inn, Wheal Tor has splendid views over the moor and is set well away of the road. The proprietors, the Lewis and Hazel families provide friendly hospitality. The hotel's 'Restaurant des Hauteurs' is proving increasingly popular with locals and offers attractive and accomplished cuisine.
ROOMS: 7 en suite (1 fmly) No smoking in all bedrooms s £45-£50; d £60-£95 (incl. bkfst) **FACILITIES:** Xmas **PARKING:** 50 **NOTES:** No smoking in restaurant **CARDS:**

PENZANCE, Cornwall & Isles of Scilly
Map 02 SW43

★★★74% Mount Prospect
Britons Hill TR18 3AE
☎ 01736 363117 01736 350970
e-mail: mtpros2000@aol.com

THE CIRCLE
Selected Individual Hotels
GREAT BRITAIN

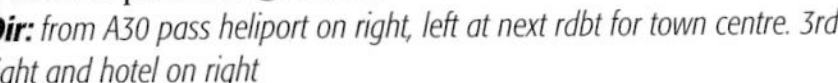

Dir: *from A30 pass heliport on right, left at next rdbt for town centre. 3rd right and hotel on right*

An Edwardian house, now tastefully designed with the contemporary Bay Restaurant as the central feature. Style is not only limited to the rooms, but is also apparent in the cuisine where fresh Cornish produce forms the basis for the dishes. Bedrooms also have been appointed to modern standards and are particularly well equipped; many rooms have views across the harbour and Mounts Bay.

ROOMS: 24 en suite (2 fmly) (2 GF) No smoking in 20 bedrooms s £40-£85; d £40-£120 (incl. bkfst) **LB FACILITIES:** STV Outdoor swimming (H) Xmas **CONF:** Thtr 80 Class 50 Board 25 Del £95 **PARKING:** 14 **NOTES:** No smoking in restaurant **CARDS:**

★★★67% Queen's
The Promenade TR18 4HG
☎ 01736 362371 01736 350033
e-mail: enquiries@queens-hotel.com

Dir: *A30 to Penzance, follow signs for seafront pass harbour and into promenade, hotel 0.5m on right*

With views across Mounts Bay and towards Newlyn, this impressive Victorian Hotel has a long and distinguished history. Comfortable public areas are filled with interesting pictures and artefacts, and in the dining room guests can choose from the daily changing menu. Bedrooms, many with sea views, are of varying style and size.

ROOMS: 70 en suite (10 fmly) s £57-£72; d £114-£144 (incl. bkfst) **LB FACILITIES:** STV Xmas **CONF:** Thtr 200 Class 100 Board 80 Del from £60 **SERVICES:** Lift **PARKING:** 50 **NOTES:** No smoking in restaurant Civ Wed 180 **CARDS:**

See advert on this page

★★67% Tarbert
11-12 Clarence St TR18 2NU
☎ 01736 363758 & 364317 01736 331336
e-mail: reception@tarbert-hotel.co.uk

Dir: *take Land's End turn at town approach. At 3rd rdbt, turn left signed to hospital, over mini rdbt. After 100yds right into Clarence St*

The proprietor and his family provide a friendly and relaxing environment at this former captain's house, which dates back to the 1830s. A range of bedrooms is available. The public rooms offer a convivial atmosphere and comfortable furnishings. The dining room, which has French doors opening on to the rear patio

continued

area, offers interesting and carefully prepared cuisine featuring fresh local produce.

Tarbert Hotel

ROOMS: 12 en suite (2 fmly) No smoking in all bedrooms s £34-£38; d £60-£68 (incl. bkfst) **LB NOTES:** No dogs (ex guide dogs) No smoking in restaurant Closed 6 Jan-14 Feb **CARDS:**

PETERBOROUGH, Cambridgeshire
Map 12 TL19

See also Wansford

★★★★67% Peterborough Marriott
Peterborough Business Park, Lynchwood
PE2 6GB
☎ 01733 371111 01733 236725
e-mail: reservations.peterborough@whitbread.com

Dir: *opposite East of England Showground. From A1 at Alwalton Showground, Chesterton. Left at T-junct, hotel on left at next rdbt*

Just a few minutes' drive from the heart of the city, this modern

continued on p486

PETERBOROUGH, continued

hotel is located in the village of Alwalton, birthplace of Sir Frederick Henry Royce and the Rolls Royce motorcar. Air-conditioned bedrooms are spacious and well designed for business use. Public rooms include the Garden Lounge, Cocktail Bar, Laurels Restaurant and leisure club.
ROOMS: 157 en suite (8 fmly) No smoking in 108 bedrooms
FACILITIES: Spa STV Indoor swimming (H) Sauna Solarium Gym Putting green Jacuzzi Beauty therapist Hairdressing Fitness classes
CONF: Thtr 300 Class 160 Board 45 **SERVICES:** air con **PARKING:** 175
NOTES: No dogs (ex guide dogs) No smoking in restaurant Civ Wed 200
CARDS:

★★★70% **Bell Inn**
Great North Rd PE7 3RA
☎ 01733 241066 01733 245173
e-mail: reception@thebellstilton.co.uk
(For full entry see Stilton)

★★★68% ***Bull***
Westgate PE1 1RB
☎ 01733 561364 01733 557304
Dir: *off A1, follow city centre signs. Hotel opp Queensgate shopping centre. Car park on Broadway next to Library*
A very pleasant city-centre hotel, offering well-equipped modern accommodation which includes a new wing of deluxe bedrooms, well suited for corporate guests. Public rooms include a popular bar and a modern restaurant, which offers a flexible range of dishes with further informal dining available in the lounge. A good range of meeting rooms and conference facilities are available.
ROOMS: 118 en suite (3 fmly) No smoking in 40 bedrooms
FACILITIES: STV **CONF:** Thtr 200 Class 80 Board 60 **PARKING:** 100
NOTES: No smoking in restaurant Civ Wed 80
CARDS:

★★★67% **Orton Hall**
Orton Longueville PE2 7DN
☎ 01733 391111 01733 231912
e-mail: reception@ortonhall.co.uk
Dir: *off A605 E opposite Orton Mere*
Set in 20 acres of woodland, this impressive country house has spacious and relaxing public areas. Original features include oak panelling in the Huntly Restaurant, in the Grand Hall, which is a popular banqueting venue, and some 16th-century terracotta floors. The Ramblewood Inn, across the courtyard from the main hotel, offers an alternative, informal dining and bar option.
ROOMS: 65 en suite (2 fmly) (15 GF) No smoking in 42 bedrooms s £80-£95; d £95-£140 **LB FACILITIES:** STV Three quarter size snooker table Xmas **CONF:** Thtr 120 Class 48 Board 42 Del from £133
PARKING: 200 **NOTES:** No smoking in restaurant Civ Wed 90
CARDS:

Express by Holiday Inn Peterborough
East of England Way, Alwalton PE2 6HE
☎ 01733 284450 01733 284451
e-mail: peterborough@oriel-leisure.co.uk
Dir: *Follow signs on A1(M) for Peterborough Showground, hotel adjacent to showground*
A modern hotel ideal for families and business travellers. Fresh and uncomplicated, the spacious bedrooms include Sky TV, power shower and tea and coffee-making facilities. Continental buffet breakfast is included in the room rate; other meals may be taken at the nearby family pub or restaurant. For further details and the Express by Holiday Inn phone number, consult the Hotel Groups pages.

ROOMS: 80 en suite s £49-£69; d £49-£69 (incl. cont bkfst)
CONF: Thtr 40 Class 30 Board 25

Sleep Inn
Peterborough Services, Great North Rd, Haddon PE7 3UQ
☎ 01733 396850 01733 396869
This modern, purpose built accommodation offers smartly appointed, well-equipped bedrooms, with good power showers. There is a choice of adjacent food outlets where guests may enjoy breakfast, snacks and meals.
ROOMS: 82 en suite

Travel Inn
Ham Ln, Orton Meadows, Nene Park PE7 8BT
☎ 08701 977206 01733 310923
Dir: *S: A1(M) J16, follow A15 through Yaxley. Inn on left at 1st rbt. N: A1(M) J17 follow A1139, 2nd exit J3 follow signs for Yaxley. Inn on right at 2nd rdbt.*
Travel Inn offers good-quality, value-for-money accommodation. Spacious, en suite rooms with bath and shower comfortably accommodate a family of up to two adults and two children (to age 15). The restaurant and bar offers a varied menu. For further details and the Travel Inn phone number, consult the Hotel Groups page.
ROOMS: 40 en suite s £44.95; d £44.95 **CONF:** Thtr 35 Board 30

Travel Inn (Peterborough Hampton)
4 Ashbourne Rd, Off London Rd, Hampton PE2 5UU
☎ 08701 977205 01733 235794
Dir: *From A1 follow signs 'Alwalton, Chesterton/ Show Ground'. Left at T-Junct, to 4th rdbt. 1st exit , 1st right. Travel Inn behind Beefeater*
Travel Inn offers good-quality, value-for-money accommodation. Spacious, en suite rooms with bath and shower comfortably accommodate a family of up to two adults and two children (to age 15). The restaurant and bar offers a varied menu. For further details and the Travel Inn phone number, consult the Hotel Groups page.
ROOMS: 80 en suite s £44.95; d £44.95 **CONF:** Thtr 35 Board 30

Travelodge Alwalton
Great North Rd, Alwalton PE7 3UR
☎ 08700 850 950 01733 231109
Dir: *on A1, southbound*
Travelodge offers good quality, good value, modern accommodation. Ideal for families, the spacious, en suite bedrooms include remote-control TV, tea and coffee-making

continued

facilities, luxury beds and free morning newspaper. Meals can be taken at the nearby family restaurant. For further details and the Travelodge phone number, consult the Hotel Groups page.
ROOMS: 32 en suite s fr £42.95; d fr £42.95

Travelodge Peterborough

Travelodge

Crowlands Rd PE6 7SZ
☎ 08700 850 950 📠 01733 223199
Dir: *at junct of A47 & A1073*
Travelodge offers good quality, good value, modern accommodation. Ideal for families, the spacious, en suite bedrooms include remote-control TV, tea and coffee-making facilities, luxury beds and free morning newspaper. Meals can be taken at the nearby family restaurant. For further details and the Travelodge phone number, consult the Hotel Groups page.
ROOMS: 42 en suite s fr £42.95; d fr £42.95

PETERLEE, Co Durham — Map 19 NZ44

★★69% *Hardwicke Hall Manor*

Hesleden TS27 4PA
☎ 01429 836326 📠 01429 837676
Dir: *NE on B1281, off A19 at sign for Durham and Blackhall*
This country mansion house nestles in pleasant gardens and is an ideal venue for secluded weddings or meetings. The comfortable bedrooms are well furnished and thoughtfully equipped, and the oak-panelled public rooms are comfortable and inviting.
ROOMS: 15 en suite (2 fmly) **CONF:** Thtr 60 Board 20 **PARKING:** 100
NOTES: No smoking in restaurant Civ Wed 110
CARDS:

PETERSFIELD, Hampshire — Map 05 SU72

★★71% ® Langrish House

Langrish GU32 1RN
☎ 01730 266941 📠 01730 260543
e-mail: frontdesk@langrishhouse.co.uk
Dir: *off A3 onto A272 towards Winchester. Hotel signed, 3m on left*

Located in a secluded spot just outside Petersfield, this family home dates back to the 17th century. Rooms offer good levels of comfort with beautiful views over the countryside. The public areas consist of a small cosy restaurant, a bar in the vaults, and conference and banqueting rooms that are popular for weddings.
ROOMS: 13 en suite (1 fmly) (3 GF) No smoking in all bedrooms
FACILITIES: Fishing Xmas **CONF:** Thtr 60 Class 18 Board 25 Del from £85 **PARKING:** 80 **NOTES:** No smoking in restaurant Civ Wed 60
CARDS:

> Destination dining!
> This symbol indicates a Restaurant with Rooms

PICKERING, North Yorkshire — Map 19 SE78

★★★72% Forest & Vale

Best Western

Malton Rd YO18 7DL
☎ 01751 472722 📠 01751 472972
e-mail: forestvale@bestwestern.co.uk
Dir: *on A169 between York and Pickering at rdbt on outskirts of Pickering*

This lovely 18th-century hotel is an excellent base from which to explore the North Yorkshire Moors, one of England's most beautiful retreats. A robust maintenance programme means that the hotel is particularly well kept, inside and out. Bedrooms vary in size and include some spacious 'superior' rooms, including one with a four-poster bed.
ROOMS: 13 en suite 5 annexe en suite (5 fmly) No smoking in 6 bedrooms s £65-£82; d £90-£120 (incl. bkfst) **LB** **CONF:** Thtr 120 Class 50 Board 50 Del £102 **PARKING:** 70 **NOTES:** No dogs (ex guide dogs) No smoking in restaurant Civ Wed 80 **CARDS:**

P

PICKERING, North Yorkshire Map 19 SE78

★★76% ⊛ White Swan
Market Place YO18 7AA
☎ 01751 472288 🖷 01751 475554
e-mail: welcome@white-swan.co.uk
Dir: *in Market Place between Church and Steam Railway Station*
This refurbished 16th-century coaching inn offers well-equipped, very comfortable bedrooms, including one suite. Service is friendly and attentive and the standard of cuisine high, in both the attractive restaurant and the cosy bars where log fires burn. A comprehensive wine list specialises in many fine vintages.
ROOMS: 12 en suite (3 fmly) No smoking in all bedrooms s £70-£105; d £110-£160 (incl. bkfst) **LB** **FACILITIES:** Ballooning, Horseriding, Bike hire, Micro-Lyte, Gliding, Paragliding, Xmas **CONF:** Thtr 20 Class 14 Board 14 Del from £100 **PARKING:** 35 **NOTES:** No smoking in restaurant **CARDS:**

Restaurant with Rooms

⊛ Fox & Hounds Country Inn
Main St, Sinnington YO62 6SQ
☎ 01751 431577 🖷 01751 432791
e-mail: foxhoundsinn@easynet.co.uk
Dir: *3m W of Pickering, off A170*
This attractive inn lies in the quiet village of Sinnington just off the main road. It offers attractive, well-equipped bedrooms together with a cosy residents' lounge. The restaurant provides a good selection of modern British dishes; there is also a good range of bar meals. Service throughout is friendly and attentive.
ROOMS: 10 en suite No smoking in all bedrooms s £44-£54; d £70-£80 (incl. bkfst) **LB** **PARKING:** 40 **NOTES:** No smoking in restaurant
CARDS:

PICKHILL, North Yorkshire Map 19 SE38

★★68% Nags Head Country Inn
YO7 4JG
☎ 01845 567391 & 567570 🖷 01845 567212
e-mail: reservations@nagsheadpickhill.freeserve.co.uk
Dir: *4m SE of Leeming Bar, 1.25m E of A1*

Convenient for the A1, this 200-year-old country inn offers superb hospitality, and an extensive range of food either in the bar or the attractive Library Restaurant. The bars offer an extensive range of wines and are full of character particularly featuring country sport memorabilia. Bedrooms are well equipped and modern, some in an adjacent building, and service is friendly.
ROOMS: 8 en suite 7 annexe en suite (1 fmly) s £45; d £70 (incl. bkfst) **LB** **FACILITIES:** Putting green Quoits pitch **CONF:** Thtr 36 Class 18 Board 24 Del from £55 **PARKING:** 50 **NOTES:** No smoking in restaurant
CARDS:

PINNER, Greater London
See LONDON SECTION plan 1 A5

★★70% Tudor Lodge
50 Field End Rd, Eastcote HA5 2QN
☎ 020 8429 0585 🖷 020 8429 0117
e-mail: tudorlodge@meridianleisure.com
Dir: *off A40 at Swakeleys rdbt to Ickenham, onto A312 to Harrow. Left at Northholt Station to Eastcote*

This friendly hotel, set in its own grounds, is convenient for Heathrow Airport and many local golf courses. Bedrooms come in a variety of styles and sizes; all are well equipped and some are suitable for families. A good range of bar snacks is offered as an alternative to the main restaurant.
ROOMS: 24 en suite 8 annexe en suite (11 fmly) s £60-£84; d £70-£89 (incl. bkfst) **LB** **FACILITIES:** Xmas **CONF:** Thtr 60 Class 20 Board 26 Del from £80 **PARKING:** 30 **NOTES:** No smoking in restaurant
CARDS:

See advert on opposite page

PLYMOUTH, Devon Map 03 SX45
See also St Mellion

★★★★63% Copthorne Hotel Plymouth
COPTHORNE
Armada Way PL1 1AR
☎ 01752 224161 🖷 01752 670688
e-mail: sales.plymouth@mill-cop.com
Dir: *from M5 follow A38 to Plymouth city centre. Follow ferryport signs over 3 rdbts. Hotel on 1st exit left before 4th rdbt*

Located right in the city centre, this hotel possesses plentiful conference facilities and parking. Suites, Connoisseur and Classic rooms are available; all are spacious and well equipped. Public areas are spread over two floors and include Bentley's brasserie and bar and a small leisure centre with a pool and gym.
ROOMS: 135 en suite (29 fmly) No smoking in 93 bedrooms s £40-£130; d £40-£150 **LB** **FACILITIES:** STV Indoor swimming (H) Gym Steam room Xmas **CONF:** Thtr 140 Class 60 Board 60 Del from £110 **SERVICES:** Lift **PARKING:** 50 **NOTES:** No dogs (ex guide dogs) Civ Wed 100 **CARDS:**

PLYMOUTH, continued

★★★★ Kitley House Hotel
Kitley Estate, Yealmpton PL8 2NW
☎ 01752 881555 📠 01752 881667
e-mail: sales@kitleyhousehotel.com
***Dir:** from Plymouth take A379 to Kingsbridge. Hotel on right after Brixton and before Yealmpton*
ROOMS: 19 en suite (9 fmly) (1 GF) No smoking in 12 bedrooms s £75-£95; d £95-£110 (incl. bkfst) **LB** **FACILITIES:** STV Fishing Croquet lawn Beauty salon Xmas **CONF:** Thtr 70 Class 40 Board 35 Del from £95 **PARKING:** 100 **NOTES:** No smoking in restaurant
CARDS:

★★★69% Elfordleigh Hotel Golf Leisure
Colebrook, Plympton PL7 5EB
☎ 01752 336428 📠 01752 344581
e-mail: reception@elfordleigh.co.uk
***Dir:** Leave A38 at Plymouth city centre exit, at Marsh Mills/Sainsburys rdbt take 3rd exit for Plympton. At 4th lights left into Larkham Ln, at end of road turn right then left into Crossway. At end left into the Moors, hotel approx 1m on right*
Located in the beautiful Plym Valley, this well-established hotel is set in attractive wooded countryside. Bedrooms, many with lovely views, offer good levels of space and comfort, and there is an excellent range of leisure facilities including an 18-hole golf course. A choice of dining options is available, including the friendly brasserie or the more formal restaurant.
ROOMS: 34 en suite (2 fmly) (7 GF) s £79.50; d £95 (incl. bkfst) **LB** **FACILITIES: Spa** Indoor swimming (H) Golf 18 Tennis (hard) Fishing Squash Sauna Solarium Gym Croquet lawn Putting green Jacuzzi Hairdresser, Beautician, Dance/Aerobics studio, 5 aside football pitch (hard) ch fac Xmas **CONF:** Thtr 200 Class 120 Board 50 Del £120 **SERVICES:** Lift **PARKING:** 200 **NOTES:** No smoking in restaurant Civ Wed 200 **CARDS:**

★★★69% New Continental
Millbay Rd PL1 3LD
☎ 01752 220782 📠 01752 227013
e-mail: newconti@aol.com
***Dir:** A38, follow city centre signs for Continental Ferryport. Hotel before ferryport & next to Plymouth Pavilions Conference Centre*
Within easy reach of the city centre and The Hoe, this privately owned hotel continues to offers high standards of service and hospitality. A variety of bedroom sizes and styles are available, all with the same levels of equipment and comfort. The hotel is a popular choice for conferences and functions.
ROOMS: 99 en suite (20 fmly) No smoking in 28 bedrooms **FACILITIES:** STV Indoor swimming (H) Sauna Solarium Gym Steam Room Beautician **CONF:** Thtr 400 Class 100 Board 70 Del from £90 **SERVICES:** Lift **PARKING:** 100 **NOTES:** Closed 24 Dec-2 Jan Civ Wed 130 **CARDS:**

See advert on page 489

★★★68% ® *Duke of Cornwall*
Millbay Rd PL1 3LG
☎ 01752 275850 📠 01752 275854
e-mail: duke@Bhere.co.uk
***Dir:** follow city centre, then Plymouth Pavilions Conference & Leisure Centre signs past hotel*
A historic landmark, this city centre hotel is conveniently located. The spacious public areas include a popular bar, comfortable lounge and multi-functional ballroom. Bedrooms, many with far reaching views, are individually styled and comfortably appointed.
continued

A range of dining options include bar meals and more formal atmosphere in the elegant dining room.
ROOMS: 71 en suite (6 fmly) No smoking in 20 bedrooms **FACILITIES:** **CONF:** Thtr 300 Class 125 Board 84 **SERVICES:** Lift **PARKING:** 50 **NOTES:** No smoking in restaurant Civ Wed 120
CARDS:

★★★65% Novotel Plymouth
Marsh Mills PL6 8NH
☎ 01752 221422 📠 01752 223922
e-mail: H0508@accor-hotels.com
***Dir:** Exit A38 at Marsh Mills, follow Plympton signs, hotel on left*
Conveniently located on the outskirts of the city, close to Marsh Mills roundabout, this modern hotel offers good value accommodation which caters for all types of guest. All rooms are spacious and designed with flexibility for family use. Public areas are open-plan with meals available throughout the day in either the Garden Brasserie, the bar, or from room service.
ROOMS: 100 en suite (18 fmly) No smoking in 72 bedrooms s £59; d £64 **LB** **FACILITIES:** STV Outdoor swimming (H) Xmas **CONF:** Thtr 300 Class 120 Board 100 Del from £87 **SERVICES:** Lift **PARKING:** 140
CARDS:

★★★64% Grand
Elliot St, The Hoe PL1 2PT
☎ 01752 661195 📠 01752 600653
e-mail: info@plymouthgrand.com

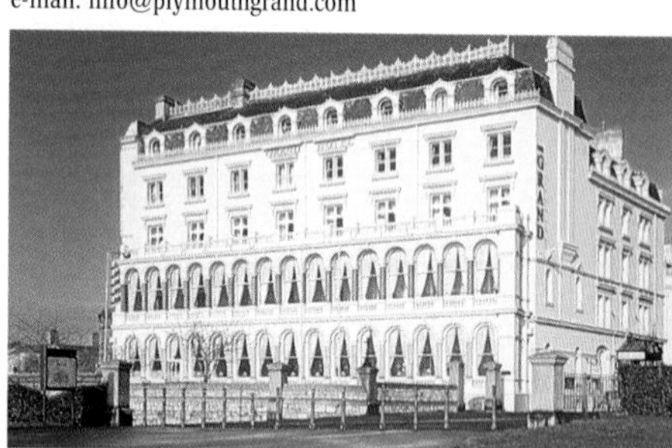

Conveniently situated on the famous Plymouth Hoe, this Grade II listed hotel is an impressive example of Victorian architecture. From its high vantage point, front-facing rooms in the hotel, including the restaurant and many of the executive bedrooms, enjoy magnificent views over the Sound.
ROOMS: 77 en suite (6 fmly) No smoking in 45 bedrooms s £95-£145; d £105-£155 (incl. bkfst) **LB** **FACILITIES:** STV for groups archery,clays,sailing,riding entertainment Xmas **CONF:** Thtr 70 Class 35 Board 30 Del from £95 **SERVICES:** Lift **PARKING:** 60 **NOTES:** No smoking in restaurant **CARDS:**

★★70% *Victoria Court*
62/64 North Rd East PL4 6AL
☎ 01752 668133 📠 01752 668133
e-mail: victoria.court@btinternet.com
***Dir:** from A38 follow city centre signs, past railway station. Follow North Road E for 200yds and hotel on left*
Situated within walking distance of the city centre and railway station, this long established, family run hotel offers impeccably presented accommodation. The public areas retain the Victorian character of the building and include a comfortable lounge, bar and dining area. The attractively decorated bedrooms are well maintained with modern facilities.
ROOMS: 13 en suite (4 fmly) **PARKING:** 6 **NOTES:** No dogs No smoking in restaurant Closed 22 Dec-1 Jan
CARDS:

★★69% *Invicta*
11-12 Osborne Place, Lockyer St, The Hoe PL1 2PU
☎ 01752 664997 📠 01752 664994
e-mail: info@invictahotel.co.uk
Dir: *A38 to Plymouth, follow city centre signs, then Hoe Park signs. Hotel opposite park entrance*
Just a short stroll from the city centre, this elegant Victorian establishment stands opposite the famous bowling green. Family owned, the atmosphere is relaxed and friendly and bedrooms are neatly presented, well-equipped and attractively decorated. Dining options include informal bar meals or the more formal setting of the dining room.
ROOMS: 23 en suite (6 fmly) No smoking in 8 bedrooms **FACILITIES: CONF:** Board 45 Del from £105 **PARKING:** 14 **NOTES:** No dogs (ex guide dogs) No smoking in restaurant **CARDS:**

★★67% Langdon Court
Down Thomas PL9 0DY
☎ 01752 862358 📠 01752 863428
e-mail: enquiries@langdoncourt.co.uk
Dir: *follow HMS Cambridge signs from Elburton and tourist signs on A379*

This magnificent Grade II listed Tudor manor is set in seven acres of lush countryside with a direct path leading to the beach at Wembury and coastal footpaths. Bedrooms all enjoy countryside views while public areas include a stylishly updated bar and brasserie restaurant where the contemporary menu incorporates local produce with excellent seafood.
ROOMS: 18 en suite (4 fmly) No smoking in 5 bedrooms **CONF:** Thtr 60 Board 20 **PARKING:** 100 **NOTES:** No smoking in restaurant Closed 25 & 26 Dec Civ Wed 75 **CARDS:**

★★63% Grosvenor
7-9 Elliot St, The Hoe PL1 2PP
☎ 01752 260411 📠 01752 668878
e-mail: enquiries@grosvenorplymouth.co.uk
Dir: *approaching city centre turn left signed Barbican, follow road to Walrus Pub and turn left. Over x-rds, hotel on left*
Convenient for the city centre, The Hoe and close to the ferry port, this small, family-run hotel provides friendly and comfortable accommodation. Converted from two Victorian houses, with much of the original character maintained, a choice of dining options is available with snacks from the bar, or the Lemon Tree restaurant which offers dishes using local produce.
ROOMS: 28 en suite (2 fmly) s £25-£35; d £35-£45 (incl. bkfst) **LB** **PARKING:** 3 **NOTES:** Closed 24 Dec-1 Jan
CARDS:

★★61% *Camelot*
5 Elliot St, The Hoe PL1 2PP
☎ 01752 221255 & 606376 📠 01752 603660
e-mail: camelot@hotelplymouth.fsnet.co.uk
Dir: *from A38 follow city centre signs, then signs to The Hoe. Citadel Rd and then onto Elliot St*
Just a short walk from The Hoe, Barbican and city centre, this is a convenient choice for visitors to this historic naval city. The friendly, small hotel provides comfortable accommodation with bedrooms varying in size and style. The convivial bar is a popular meeting point and additional facilities include a TV lounge and function room.
ROOMS: 18 en suite (5 fmly) No smoking in 3 bedrooms **CONF:** Thtr 60 Class 60 Board 40 **NOTES:** No dogs (ex guide dogs) No smoking in restaurant **CARDS:**

★67% Drake
THE CIRCLE
Selected Individual Hotels
GREAT BRITAIN

1 & 2 Windsor Villas, Lockyer St, The Hoe PL1 2QD
☎ 01752 229730 📠 01752 255092
e-mail: drakehotel@themutual.net
Dir: *follow city centre signs, left at Theatre Royal, last left and 1st right*
Handily placed for easy access to the city centre and the historic Hoe, this popular hotel was originally two adjoining Victorian houses. Bedrooms are neatly presented, whilst public areas include a lounge, bar and elegant dining room. The convenient location makes this an ideal choice for both business and leisure guests.
ROOMS: 35 rms (3 fmly) s £36-£46; d £56 (incl. bkfst) **LB** **PARKING:** 26 **NOTES:** No dogs (ex guide dogs) No smoking in restaurant Closed 24 Dec-3 Jan **CARDS:**

★61% Grosvenor Park
114-116 North Rd East PL4 6AH
☎ 01752 229312 📠 01752 252777
Dir: *150yds from rail station in city centre*
Conveniently located for the railway station and the city centre, this small hotel provides friendly and attentive service. Facilities available include a small bar and comfortable lounge. A range of popular dishes is offered at dinner, and traditional breakfasts make for a satisfying start to the day.
ROOMS: 16 rms (11 en suite) (1 fmly) No smoking in 3 bedrooms s £22-£33; d £44 (incl. bkfst) **FACILITIES:** STV **PARKING:** 6 **NOTES:** No dogs (ex guide dogs) No smoking in restaurant
CARDS:

U *Holiday Inn Plymouth*
Holiday Inn
HOTELS · RESORTS

Cliff Rd, The Hoe PL1 3DL
☎ 0870 400 9064 📠 01752 660974
e-mail: plymouthhi@ichotelsgroup.com
Dir: *off A38 at Plymouth, follow signs for city centre then signs for The Hoe. Hotel on Cliff Rd in West Hoe*
At the time of going to press, the classification for this hotel was not confirmed. Please refer to the AA internet site www.theAA.com for current information.
ROOMS: 112 en suite No smoking in 65 bedrooms **FACILITIES:** STV Childrens play area **CONF:** Thtr 90 Class 30 Board 40 **SERVICES:** Lift **PARKING:** 149 **NOTES:** No dogs (ex guide dogs) Civ Wed
CARDS:

P

PLYMOUTH, continued

The Moorland
Wotter, Shaugh Prior PL7 5HP
☎ 01752 839228 📠 01752 839153
e-mail: reservations@moorlandhotel.com
At the time of going to press, the star classification for this hotel was not confirmed. Please refer to the AA internet site www.theAA.com for current information.
ROOMS: 18 en suite (2 fmly) No smoking in 4 bedrooms s £35-£44; d £60 (incl. bkfst) **LB** **FACILITIES:** Games room **CONF:** BC Thtr 80 Class 22 Board 40 Del from £52 **PARKING:** 40 **NOTES:** No smoking in restaurant **CARDS:**

Hotel Ibis
Marsh Mills, Longbridge Rd, Forder Valley PL6 8LD
☎ 01752 601087 📠 01752 223213
e-mail: H2093@accor-hotels.com
***Dir:** A38 to Plymouth, 1st exit over flyover towards Estover, Leigham and Parkway Industrial Est. At rdbt, hotel on 4th exit*
Modern, budget hotel offering comfortable accommodation in bright and practical bedrooms. Breakfast is self-service and dinner is available in the restaurant. For further details, consult the Hotel Groups page.
ROOMS: 51 en suite s £39.95-£42.95; d £39.95-£42.95

Travel Inn (Plymouth Centre)
Lockyers Quay, Coxside PL4 0DX
☎ 08701 977207 📠 01752 663872
***Dir:** A38 Marsh Mills rdbt then A374 into Plymouth. Follow signs for Coxside & National Marine Aquarium*
Travel Inn offers good-quality, value-for-money accommodation. Spacious, en suite rooms with bath and shower comfortably accommodate a family of up to two adults and two children (to age 15). The restaurant and bar offers a varied menu. For further details and the Travel Inn phone number, consult the Hotel Groups page.
ROOMS: 60 en suite s £54.95; d £54.95 **CONF:** Thtr 25 Board 20

Travel Inn (Plymouth East)
300 Plymouth Rd, Crabtree, Marsh Mills PL3 6RW
☎ 08701 977208 📠 01752 600112
***Dir:** From E: Exit A38 Marsh Mill junction. Straight across rbt, exit slip road 100mtrs on left. From W: Plympton junction A38, at rbt exit slip road next to A38 Liskeard*
Travel Inn offers good-quality, value-for-money accommodation. Spacious, en suite rooms with bath and shower comfortably accommodate a family of up to two adults and two children (to age 15). The restaurant and bar offers a varied menu. For further details and the Travel Inn phone number, consult the Hotel Groups page.
ROOMS: 40 en suite s £44.95; d £44.95 **CONF:** Thtr 50 Board 30

GF Indicates the number of bedrooms at ground floor level.

○ Premier Lodge (Plymouth)
Sutton Rd, Shepherds Wharf PL4 0HX
☎ 0870 9906458 📠 0870 9906459
ROOMS: 107 en suite **NOTES:** Due to open Oct 2003

○ Travelodge
Derry's Cross PL1 2SW
☎ 0870 191 1752
ROOMS: 96 en suite **NOTES:** Due to open Sept 2003

POCKLINGTON, East Riding of Yorkshire — Map 17 SE84

★★65% Yorkway Motel
Hull-York Rd YO42 2NX
☎ 01759 303071 📠 01759 305215
e-mail: info@yorkway-motel.co.uk
***Dir:** between Beverley and York at A1079/B1247 junct*
This family-owned and run motel was formerly a coaching inn. Close to the old market town of Pocklington, it offers friendly service and value-for-money accommodation. Bedrooms are thoughtfully equipped and public rooms include a bar and cosy dining area, where a wide range of food is served all day.
ROOMS: 15 annexe en suite (6 fmly) (15 GF) s fr £40; d fr £45 (incl. bkfst) **LB** **CONF:** Thtr 30 Class 12 Board 16 **PARKING:** 40 **NOTES:** No dogs (ex guide dogs) No smoking in restaurant
CARDS:

★★64% Feathers
56 Market Place YO42 2AH
☎ 01759 303155 📠 01759 304382
e-mail: info@thefeathers-hotel.co.uk
***Dir:** from York, B1246 signed Pocklington. Hotel just off A1079*
This is busy, traditional inn has been sympathetically modernised to provide comfortable, well-equipped and spacious accommodation. Public areas are smartly presented and enjoyable meals are served in the bar and the conservatory restaurant. A wide choice of dishes makes excellent use of local and seasonal produce.
ROOMS: 6 en suite 6 annexe en suite (1 fmly) s £40-£44; d £46-£49.50 (incl. bkfst) **LB** **CONF:** Thtr 20 Class 8 Board 12 **PARKING:** 46 **NOTES:** No dogs (ex guide dogs) **CARDS:**

PODIMORE, Somerset — Map 04 ST52

Travelodge Yeovil
BA22 8JG
☎ 08700 850 950 📠 01935 840074
***Dir:** on A303, near junct with A37*
Travelodge offers good quality, good value, modern accommodation. Ideal for families, the spacious, en suite bedrooms include remote-control TV, tea and coffee-making facilities, luxury beds and free morning newspaper. Meals can be taken at the nearby family restaurant. For further details and the Travelodge phone number, consult the Hotel Groups page.
ROOMS: 41 en suite s fr £42.95; d fr £42.95

POLPERRO, Cornwall & Isles of Scilly Map 02 SX25

★★★75% Talland Bay

PL13 2JB
☎ 01503 272667 01503 272940
e-mail: reception@tallandbayhotel.co.uk
Dir: *signed from x-rds on A387 Looe to Polperro road*

Mid-way between Looe and Polperro, this hotel overlooks the bay and has extensive gardens. The atmosphere is warm and friendly and staff are helpful. Quality and comfort is apparent throughout bedrooms, with many different styles available, some with sea views. After a day's exploration, the kitchen can be relied upon to provide good local Cornish produce.

ROOMS: 20 en suite 3 annexe en suite (4 fmly) (6 GF) No smoking in 3 bedrooms s £45-£90; d £90-£180 (incl. bkfst) **LB** **FACILITIES:** STV Outdoor swimming (H) Croquet lawn Putting green Xmas **PARKING:** 23 **NOTES:** No smoking in restaurant **CARDS:**

PONTEFRACT, West Yorkshire Map 16 SE42

★★★65% Rogerthorpe Manor Hotel

Best Western

Thorpe Ln, Badsworth WF9 1AB
☎ 01977 643839 01977 641571
e-mail: ops@rogerthorpemanor.co.uk
Dir: *A639 from Pontefract to Badsworth. Follow B6474 through Thorpe Audlin, hotel on left at end of Thorpe Audlin village*

This Jacobean manor house is situated in extensive grounds and lovely gardens in a delightful rural setting, with easy access to road networks. Bedrooms vary between those in the old house with their inherent charm, and the more modern rooms in new extensions. The range of function rooms available are popular for parties and conferences.

ROOMS: 23 en suite (3 fmly) No smoking in 8 bedrooms s £70-£80; d £85-£95 (incl. bkfst) **FACILITIES:** STV Croquet lawn Xmas **CONF:** BC Thtr 200 Class 150 Board 50 Del from £115 **SERVICES:** air con **PARKING:** 90 **NOTES:** No dogs (ex guide dogs) No smoking in restaurant Civ Wed 300 **CARDS:**

Travel Inn

travel inn

Knottingley Rd, Knottingley WF11 0BU
☎ 08701 977209 01977 607954
Dir: *From M62 (J33) onto A1 North. Take next junction (A645) Pontefract. Follow road to T-junct, right towards Pontefract, Travel Inn on right*

Travel Inn offers good-quality, value-for-money accommodation. Spacious, en suite rooms with bath and shower comfortably accommodate a family of up to two adults and two children (to age 15). The restaurant and bar offers a varied menu. For further details and the Travel Inn phone number, consult the Hotel Groups page.

ROOMS: 40 en suite s £44.95; d £44.95

POOLE, Dorset Map 04 SZ09

★★★★74% Haven

Banks Rd, Sandbanks BH13 7QL
☎ 01202 707333 01202 708796
e-mail: reservations@havenhotel.co.uk
Dir: *B3965 towards Poole Bay, left onto the Peninsula. Hotel 1.5m on left next to Swanage Toll Ferry point*

Enjoying a water's edge location and with enviable views of Poole Bay this attractive hotel was also the site of the world's first

continued

wireless transmission. Comfortable lounge areas and a choice of restaurants complement an extensive range of indoor and outdoor leisure facilities. Bedrooms vary in size and style with some enjoying wonderful sea views and balconies.

ROOMS: 78 en suite (4 fmly) s £90-£150; d £180-£300 (incl. bkfst) **LB** **FACILITIES:** **Spa** STV Indoor swimming (H) Outdoor swimming (H) Tennis (hard) Sauna Solarium Gym Jacuzzi Steam room, Hair salon, Health & Beauty suite entertainment Xmas **CONF:** BC Thtr 160 Class 70 Board 50 Del from £155 **SERVICES:** Lift **PARKING:** 160 **NOTES:** No dogs (ex guide dogs) No smoking in restaurant Civ Wed 80 **CARDS:**

★★★★70% Harbour Heights

73 Haven Rd, Sandbanks BH13 7LW
☎ 01202 707272 01202 708594
e-mail: harbourheights@fjbhotels.co.uk
Dir: *Follow signs for Sandbanks, hotel on left after Canford Cliffs*

The unassuming appearance of this hotel belies a wealth of innovation, quality and style. Following a four million pound refit, contemporary bedrooms now combine state-of-the-art facilities with traditional comforts. Throughout the smart public areas, which include a choice of dining options, popular bars and sitting areas, picture windows accentuate panoramic views of Poole Harbour. The sun deck, elevated above terraced gardens, is the perfect setting for watching the cross channel ferries come and go.

ROOMS: 38 en suite (5 fmly) No smoking in all bedrooms s £116-£150; d £200-£340 (incl. bkfst) **FACILITIES:** STV Full use of leisure facilities at nearby hotel Xmas **SERVICES:** Lift **PARKING:** 46 **NOTES:** No dogs (ex guide dogs) No smoking in restaurant
CARDS:

Looking for a last-minute weekend away?
Check out Latebeds,
the AA's late availability booking service, at www.theAA.com

POOLE, continued

Top 200 - Hotel

★★★ Mansion House

Thames St BH15 1JN
☎ 01202 685666 01202 665709
e-mail: enquiries@themansionhouse.co.uk
Dir: A31 to Poole, follow channel ferry signs. Left at Poole bridge onto Poole Quay, 1st left into Thames St. Hotel opposite St James Church

Best Western

This sophisticated hotel offers friendly hospitality and award-winning cuisine, equalled only by its relaxing charm and elegance. The comfortably furnished bedrooms are very well equipped with many thoughtful touches. Ideal for business or pleasure, the Mansion House is tucked away off the Old Quay, with the added bonus of parking.

ROOMS: 32 en suite (2 fmly) (2 GF) No smoking in 6 bedrooms s £70-£90; d £120-£135 (incl. bkfst) **LB FACILITIES:** STV facilities available locally Watersports, use of local fitness club Xmas **CONF:** Thtr 40 Class 18 Board 20 Del from £120 **PARKING:** 46 **NOTES:** No dogs (ex guide dogs) Civ Wed 35 **CARDS:**

Bad hair day?
Hairdryers in all rooms three stars and above

★★★72% Sandbanks

15 Banks Rd, Sandbanks BH13 7PS
☎ 01202 707377 01202 708885
e-mail: reservations@sandbankshotel.co.uk
Dir: A338 from Bournemouth onto Wessex Way, to Liverpool Victoria rdbt. Left and take 2nd exit onto B3965. Hotel on left

Set on the delightful Sandbanks peninsula, this large hotel has direct access to a blue flag beach and stunning views across Poole Harbour. Most of the spacious bedrooms have sea views, and there is an extensive range of leisure facilities and family activities. In addition the Sands Brasserie serves an imaginative selection of dishes.

ROOMS: 110 en suite (31 fmly) (4 GF) No smoking in 40 bedrooms s £65-£120; d £130-£240 (incl. bkfst & dinner) **LB FACILITIES:** STV Indoor swimming (H) Sauna Solarium Gym Jacuzzi Sailing, Mntn bikes, kids play area, swimming pool supervised, massage room entertainment ch fac Xmas **CONF:** BC Thtr 150 Class 40 Board 25 Del from £110 **SERVICES:** Lift **PARKING:** 120 **NOTES:** No dogs (ex guide dogs) No smoking in restaurant **CARDS:**

★★★66% Arndale Court

62/66 Wimborne Rd BH15 2BY
☎ 01202 683746 01202 668838
e-mail: info@arndalecourthotel.com
Dir: on A349 close to town centre, opp Poole Stadium

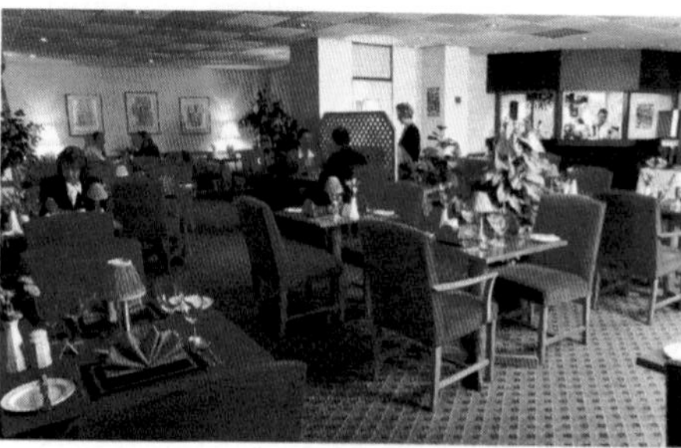

Ideally situated for the town centre and ferry terminal, this small, privately-owned hotel has now been extensively refurbished. Bedrooms are well equipped, pleasantly spacious and comfortable. Particularly suited for the business guest, the Arndale Court has a pleasant range of stylish public areas and conveniently offers good parking.

ROOMS: 39 en suite (7 fmly) (14 GF) No smoking in 12 bedrooms s £61; d £70 (incl. bkfst) **FACILITIES:** STV **CONF:** Thtr 50 Class 35 Board 35 Del £80 **PARKING:** 40 **NOTES:** No smoking in restaurant **CARDS:**

Express by Holiday Inn

Walking Field Ln BH15 1TJ
☎ 01202 649222 01202 649666
e-mail: poole@holidayinnexpress.co.uk
Dir: A350 to town centre, pass bus station. Right at next rdbt and take slip road to left. Hotel next to Dolphin Swimming Pool

Express by Holiday Inn

A modern hotel ideal for families and business travellers. Fresh and uncomplicated, the spacious bedrooms include Sky TV, power shower and tea and coffee-making facilities. Continental buffet breakfast is included in the room rate; other meals may be taken at the nearby

continued

family pub or restaurant. For further details and the Express by Holiday Inn phone number, consult the Hotel Groups pages.
ROOMS: 85 en suite s £60-£66; d £60-£66 (incl. cont bkfst)
CONF: Thtr 30 Class 15 Board 18

⇧ Premier Lodge (Poole)

Cabot Ln BH17 7BX
☎ 0870 9906332 📠 0870 6606333
Dir: *off A349*
Premier Lodge offers modern, well-equipped, en suite accommodation suitable for both business and leisure travellers. Meals can be taken at the adjacent popular restaurant and bar, which is fully licensed. For further details, consult the Hotel Groups page.
ROOMS: 126 en suite s £48; d £48

⇧ Travel Inn

Holes Bay Rd BH15 2BD
☎ 08701 977210 📠 01202 661497
Dir: *follow Poole Channel Ferry signs, hotel S of A35/A349 on A350 dual carriageway*

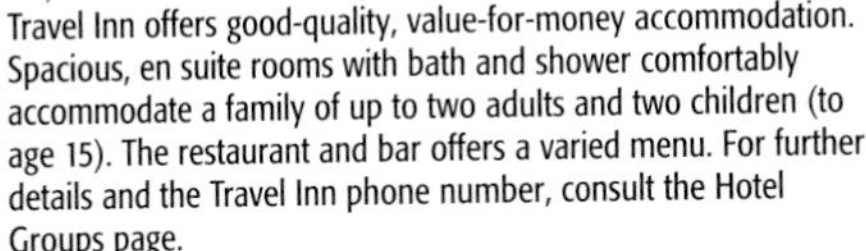

Travel Inn offers good-quality, value-for-money accommodation. Spacious, en suite rooms with bath and shower comfortably accommodate a family of up to two adults and two children (to age 15). The restaurant and bar offers a varied menu. For further details and the Travel Inn phone number, consult the Hotel Groups page.
ROOMS: 62 en suite s £52.95; d £52.95

PORLOCK, Somerset

Map 03 SS84

★★★65% Anchor Hotel & Ship Inn

Porlock Harbour TA24 8PB
☎ 01643 862753 📠 01643 862843
e-mail: anchorhotel@clara.net
Dir: *from A39 take B3225 Porlock Weir road. Hotel in 1.5m in cul-de-sac*
This long-established hotel overlooks the harbour and the Bristol Channel. Bedrooms in the original, 16th-century Ship Inn are full of traditional character, while those in the main hotel are more spacious. A relaxed atmosphere is a hallmark here, especially in the elegant drawing room. The Harbour Restaurant offers set price and carte menus; bar meals are also available.
ROOMS: 14 en suite 6 annexe en suite (2 fmly) d £79.50-£118 (incl. bkfst) **LB** **FACILITIES:** Xmas **CONF:** Thtr 20 Board 12 **PARKING:** 20
NOTES: No smoking in restaurant RS Jan
CARDS:

See advert on this page

Late for dinner?
Quality Standards mean that last orders for dinner vary according to star rating and should be no earlier than:
★★ 7.00pm ★★★ 8.00pm ★★★★ 9.00pm
★★★★★ 10.00pm

Town House Hotel
Country House Hotel
⇧ Travel Accommodation

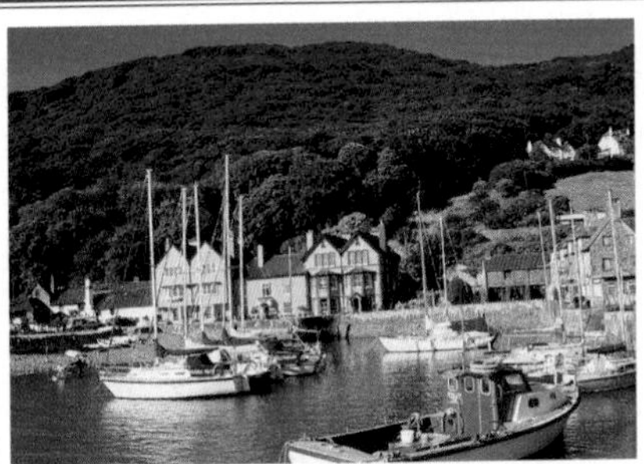

Top 200 - Hotel

★★ The Oaks

TA24 8ES
☎ 01643 862265 📠 01643 863131
e-mail: info@oakshotel.co.uk
A relaxing atmosphere can be found at this charming Edwardian house, located near to the setting of *Lorna Doone*. Quietly located and set in attractive grounds, the hotel enjoys elevated views across the village towards the sea. Bedrooms are thoughtfully furnished and comfortable, and the public rooms include a charming bar and a peaceful drawing room. In the dining room, guests can choose from the daily changing menu, which features fresh, quality local produce.

ROOMS: 8 en suite No smoking in all bedrooms s £75; d £110 (incl. bkfst) **LB** **FACILITIES:** Xmas **PARKING:** 12 **NOTES:** No children 8yrs No smoking in restaurant Closed Nov-Mar (excl. Xmas & New Year) **CARDS:**

PORLOCK, continued

Restaurant with Rooms

Andrews on the Weir

Porlock Weir TA24 8PB

☎ 01643 863300 01643 863311

e-mail: information@andrewsontheweir.co.uk

Dir: *A39 from Minehead to Porlock, through village, 1st R signed Harbour (Porlock Weir) for 1.5m*

Enjoying a delightful location overlooking Porlock Bay, Andrews on the Weir is decorated in country-house style. Bedrooms are spacious and comfortable; one has a four-poster bed. During colder months, a log fire creates a cosy atmosphere in the sitting room/bar. One of the highlights is the choice of imaginative, innovative dishes available in the restaurant - Andrew Dixon is an accomplished chef.

ROOMS: 5 en suite s £45-£80; d £65-£100 (incl. bkfst) **LB** **FACILITIES:** Xmas **PARKING:** 6 **NOTES:** No children 12yrs No smoking in restaurant Closed Jan & Mon RS Sun night

CARDS:

PORT GAVERNE, Cornwall & Isles of Scilly Map 02 SX08

★★68% Port Gaverne

PL29 3SQ

☎ 01208 880244 01208 880151

e-mail: pghotel@telinco.co.uk

Dir: *signed from B3314*

In a romantic location in a quiet seaside port half a mile from the old fishing village of Port Isaac, the Port Gaverne Hotel is also a romantic building, and retains its flagged floors, beamed ceilings and steep stairways. Bedrooms are available in a range of sizes. Local produce often features on the hotel menus, which include bar meals.

ROOMS: 16 en suite (4 fmly) s £35-£45; d £70-£90 (incl. bkfst) **LB** **PARKING:** 30 **NOTES:** No smoking in restaurant Closed 5 Jan-11 Feb

CARDS:

PORT ISAAC, Cornwall & Isles of Scilly Map 02 SW98

★★68% Castle Rock

4 New Rd PL29 3SB

☎ 01208 880300 01208 880219

e-mail: info@castlerockhotel.co.uk

Dir: *from A30 after Launceston onto A395. Left at junct with A39 then 1st right signed Port Isaac, follow signs to village*

With spectacular views of the rugged Cornish coastline, this friendly hotel is an ideal base for holidaymakers. It has comfortable and spacious accommodation, with public areas benefiting from wonderful sea views. In addition to the carte and fixed price menus, an extensive range of dishes is served in the bar or on the terrace.

ROOMS: 15 en suite 3 annexe en suite (3 fmly) s £30-£45; d £60-£80 (incl. bkfst) **LB** **PARKING:** 18 **NOTES:** No smoking in restaurant

CARDS:

PORTISHEAD, Somerset Map 04 ST47

Travel Inn

Wyndham Way BS20 7GA

☎ 08701 977212 01275 846534

travel inn

Dir: *From M5 (J19) follow A369 towards Portishead. Across 1st rdbt and Travel Inn on next rdbt*

Travel Inn offers good-quality, value-for-money accommodation. Spacious, en suite rooms with bath and shower comfortably accommodate a family of up to two adults and two children (to age 15). The restaurant and bar offers a varied menu. For further details and the Travel Inn phone number, consult the Hotel Groups page.

ROOMS: 40 en suite s £44.95; d £44.95

PORTLOE, Cornwall & Isles of Scilly Map 02 SW93

★★★70% The Lugger

TR2 5RD

☎ 01872 501322 01872 501691

e-mail: office@luggerhotel.com

Having changed ownership, this delightful hotel has reopened its doors after a smart, stylish refurbishment. The hotel enjoys a unique location adjacent to the slipway of the harbour. Bedrooms are appealing and well equipped while day rooms include a comfortable lounge and a contemporary-styled restaurant that enjoys super views. In warmer months a sun terrace overlooking the harbour proves a popular feature.

ROOMS: d £200-£280 (incl. bkfst) **LB** **FACILITIES:** STV Beauty treatments Xmas **PARKING:** 21 **NOTES:** No dogs (ex guide dogs) No children 12 yrs No smoking in restaurant

CARDS:

PORTSCATHO, Cornwall & Isles of Scilly Map 02 SW83

Top 200 - Hotel

★★★ Rosevine

TR2 5EW

☎ 01872 580206 01872 580230

e-mail: info@rosevinehotels.co.uk

Dir: *from St Austell take A390 for Truro. Left onto B3287 to Tregony. Take A3078 through Ruan High Lanes. Hotel 3rd left*

Set in secluded splendour with views over gardens towards the sea, this Georgian country house has its own beach at the

continued

P

head of the Roseland peninsula. The proprietors and staff are attentive and friendly and create a relaxed atmosphere. Bedrooms are impressively equipped, with fresh fruit, flowers and up-to-date reading in all rooms, most of which have views. Cuisine features the local harvest of fresh fish and shellfish and the best of Cornish produce.

ROOMS: 11 en suite 6 annexe en suite (7 fmly) (3 GF) s £123-£183; d £160-£220 (incl. bkfst) **LB** **FACILITIES:** Indoor swimming (H) Table tennis Childrens playroom entertainment Xmas **PARKING:** 20 **NOTES:** No smoking in restaurant Closed Dec-8 Feb (ex Xmas) **CARDS:**

★★72% Driftwood

Rosevine TR2 5EW
☎ 01872 580644 01872 580801
e-mail: info@driftwoodhotel.co.uk

Perched overlooking Gerrans Bay, Driftwood is one of the new 'chic' Cornish hotels; contemporary in design and with a comfortably, relaxed and friendly atmosphere. The kitchen is at the heart of this hotel, producing a very short, simple evening menu of well conceived dishes, and at breakfast using the very best of local produce. Bedrooms are exceptionally well equipped; for those who want to get away from it all, book the cabin - even closer to the sea!

ROOMS: 10 en suite 1 annexe en suite (3 fmly) (1 GF) No smoking in all bedrooms s £90-£127; d £152.50-£172.50 (incl. bkfst) **FACILITIES:** Private Beach ch fac **PARKING:** 20 **NOTES:** No dogs No smoking in restaurant Closed 3-31Jan **CARDS:**

PORTSMOUTH, Hampshire — Map 05 SU60

★★★★65% Portsmouth Marriott Hotel

Marriott HOTELS · RESORTS · SUITES

Southampton Rd PO6 4SH
☎ 0870 400 7285 0870 400 7385
e-mail: reservations.portsmouth@marriotthotels.com
Dir: *M27 junct 12 keep left and hotel on left*

Close to the motorway and ferry port, this hotel is well suited to business trade. The comfortable and well laid-out bedrooms provide a comprehensive range of facilities including up-to-date workstations. The leisure club offers a pool, a gym, and a health and beauty salon.

ROOMS: 174 en suite (77 fmly) No smoking in 130 bedrooms s £69-£113; d £98-£113 **FACILITIES:** STV Indoor swimming (H) Sauna Solarium Gym Jacuzzi Exercise studio, Beauty salon, Swimming pool supervised Xmas **CONF:** Thtr 350 Class 180 Board 30 Del from £135 **SERVICES:** Lift air con **PARKING:** 250 **NOTES:** No dogs (ex guide dogs) Civ Wed 100 **CARDS:**

★★★68% Queen's Hotel

Best Western

Clarence Pde, Southsea PO5 3LJ
☎ 023 9282 2466 023 9282 1901
e-mail: bestwestqueens@aol.com
Dir: *M27 junct 12 onto M275. Follow Southsea seafront signs. Hotel opposite hovercraft terminal*

This elegant Edwardian hotel has dominated the Southsea seafront for over 100 years and enjoys magnificent views. Bedrooms vary, there is a choice of room categories, from family rooms to single rooms; all are traditionally furnished and decorated. Public areas include a restaurant, garden and pool, two comfortable bars and a nightclub.

ROOMS: 73 en suite (4 fmly) No smoking in 43 bedrooms s £60-£80; d £124-£141 (incl. bkfst) **LB** **FACILITIES:** STV Outdoor swimming (H) Private garden Xmas **CONF:** Thtr 150 Class 70 Board 50 Del from £99 **SERVICES:** Lift **PARKING:** 70 **NOTES:** No dogs (ex guide dogs) **CARDS:**

★★★68% Westfield Hall

65 Festing Rd, Southsea PO4 0NQ
☎ 023 9282 6971 023 9287 0200
e-mail: enquirys@whhotel.info
Dir: *follow seafront signs, left at South Parade Pier then 3rd left*

Westfield Hall is situated in a quiet side road close to the seafront and town centre. The accommodation is split between two identical houses; all rooms are smartly appointed and well equipped. Public rooms are attractively decorated and include three lounges, a bar and a restaurant.

ROOMS: 15 en suite 11 annexe en suite (5 fmly) (6 GF) No smoking in 18 bedrooms s £53-£58; d £78-£90 (incl. bkfst) **LB** **FACILITIES:** STV **PARKING:** 18 **NOTES:** No dogs No smoking in restaurant **CARDS:**

★★73% The Beaufort

71 Festing Rd, Southsea PO4 0NQ
☎ 023 9282 3707 023 9287 0270
e-mail: enq@beauforthotel.co.uk
Dir: *follow seafront signs. Left at South Parade Pier then 4th on left*

A warm welcome is guaranteed at this intimate hotel located within easy reach of the sea front and the city centre. Ideal for accessing both local attractions and amenities. Individually decorated bedrooms are generally spacious providing good levels of comfort. Public areas include a pleasant lounge and cosy bar.

ROOMS: 19 en suite (1 fmly) (6 GF) No smoking in 10 bedrooms s £50-£55; d £60-£100 (incl. bkfst) **LB** **FACILITIES:** STV **CONF:** Class 20 **PARKING:** 10 **NOTES:** No dogs No smoking in restaurant **CARDS:**

P

PORTSMOUTH, continued

★★70% Seacrest

11/12 South Pde, Southsea PO5 2JB
☎ 023 9273 3192 023 9283 2523
e-mail: seacrest@boltblue.com
Dir: *from M27 follow signs for seafront, Pyramids and Sea Life Centre. Hotel opposite Rock Gardens and Pyramids*
In a premier seafront location, this smart hotel provides the ideal base for exploring the town. Bedrooms, many benefiting from sea views, are decorated to a high standard with good facilities. Guests can relax in either the south-facing lounge, furnished with large leather sofas, or the adjacent bar; there is also a cosy dining room.
ROOMS: 28 en suite (3 fmly) No smoking in 15 bedrooms s £45-£55; d £55-£90 (incl. bkfst) **LB** **FACILITIES:** STV Xmas **SERVICES:** Lift **PARKING:** 12 **NOTES:** No smoking in restaurant
CARDS:

U *Holiday Inn Portsmouth*

Pembroke Rd PO1 2TA
☎ 0870 400 9065 023 9275 6715
e-mail: portsmouth@ichotelsgroup.com
Dir: *from M275, follow signs for Southsea and Hovercroft for 1m. At Southsea Common hotel on right*
At the time of going to press, the classification for this hotel was not confirmed. Please refer to the AA internet site www.theAA.com for current information.
ROOMS: 167 en suite (12 fmly) No smoking in 82 bedrooms **FACILITIES:** Indoor swimming (H) Sauna Solarium Gym Jacuzzi Turkish steam room,Beauty Room, Pool room, Play room **CONF:** Thtr 220 Class 120 Board 80 **SERVICES:** Lift **PARKING:** 80 **NOTES:** No smoking in restaurant **CARDS:**

U Royal Beach

South Pde, Southsea PO4 0RN
☎ 023 9273 1281 023 9281 7572
e-mail: enquiries@royalbeachhotel.co.uk
Dir: *M27 to M275, follow signs to seafront. Hotel on seafront*
At the time of going to press, the star classification for this hotel was not confirmed. Please refer to the AA internet site www.theAA.com for current information.
ROOMS: 115 en suite (9 fmly) No smoking in 72 bedrooms s £75-£95; d £85-£105 (incl. bkfst) **LB** **FACILITIES:** STV Xmas **CONF:** Thtr 280 Class 180 Board 40 Del from £85 **SERVICES:** Lift **PARKING:** 50 **NOTES:** No dogs (ex guide dogs) No smoking in restaurant
CARDS:

⌂ Hotel Ibis

Winston Churchill Av PO1 2LX
☎ 023 9264 0000 023 9264 1000
e-mail: h1461@accor-hotels.com
Dir: *M27 junct 2 onto M275. Follow signs for city centre then Sealife Centre and then Guildhall. Right at rdbt into Winston Churchill Ave*
Modern, budget hotel offering comfortable accommodation in bright and practical bedrooms. Breakfast is self-service and dinner is available in the restaurant. For further details, consult the Hotel Groups page.
ROOMS: 144 en suite s £37.95-£42.95; d £37.95-£42.95

⌂ Innkeeper's Lodge Portsmouth

Copnor Rd, Hilsea PO3 5HS
☎ 0870 243 0500 & 023 9265 4645
Dir: *From A27 take A2030. Right at lights, over 3 rdbts, into Norway Rd. Inn on A288.*
A new concept in the travel accommodation market. Smart rooms meet essential business requirements but also have home comforts. Dining options include all-day menus plus the added advantage of breakfast, which is included in the room price. For further details, consult the Hotel Groups page.
ROOMS: 33 en suite

⌂ Travel Inn

Southampton Rd, North Harbour, Cosham PO6 4SA
☎ 08701 977213 023 9232 4895
Dir: *on A27, close to M27 junct 12*
Travel Inn offers good-quality, value-for-money accommodation. Spacious, en suite rooms with bath and shower comfortably accommodate a family of up to two adults and two children (to age 15). The restaurant and bar offers a varied menu. For further details and the Travel Inn phone number, consult the Hotel Groups page.
ROOMS: 64 en suite s £44.95; d £44.95 **CONF:** Thtr 25

⌂ Travel Inn (Southsea)

Long Curtain Rd, Clarence Pier, Southsea PO5 3XX
☎ 08701 977236 023 9273 3048
Dir: *Pier Rd leads to Clarence Pier. Travel Inn next to amusement park and Isle of Wight hovercraft*

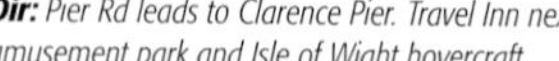

Travel Inn offers good-quality, value-for-money accommodation. Spacious, en suite rooms with bath and shower comfortably accommodate a family of up to two adults and two children (to age 15). The restaurant and bar offers a varied menu. For further details and the Travel Inn phone number, consult the Hotel Groups page.
ROOMS: 40 en suite s £44.95; d £44.95

⌂ Travelodge

Kingston Crescent, North End PO2 8AB
☎ 08700 850 950
Travelodge offers good quality, good value, modern accommodation. Ideal for families, the spacious, en suite bedrooms include remote-control TV, tea and coffee-making facilities, luxury beds and free morning newspaper. Meals can be taken at the nearby family restaurant. For further details and the Travelodge phone number, consult the Hotel Groups page.
ROOMS: 78 en suite s fr £42.95; d fr £42.95

PRESTBURY, Cheshire — Map 16 SJ87

Town House

★★★★ White House Manor

New Rd SK10 4HP
☎ 01625 829376 01625 828627
e-mail: info@thewhitehouse.uk.com
Dir: *on A538 Macclesfield road*
This elegant Georgian house, situated in attractive gardens on the edge of the village, offers charming, individually styled bedrooms, many with four-poster beds. Meals can be ordered from the room service menu and breakfast is served in the conservatory. The White House restaurant, under the same ownership, is just a short walk away but guests may be driven there if needed.
ROOMS: 11 en suite (2 GF) No smoking in all bedrooms s £75-£90; d £80-£130 **FACILITIES:** STV Jacuzzi Xmas **CONF:** Thtr 60 Class 40 Board 26 Del from £100 **PARKING:** 11 **NOTES:** No dogs (ex guide dogs) No children 10yrs Closed 24-26 Dec
CARDS:

★★★71% **Bridge**
The Village SK10 4DQ
☎ 01625 829326 01625 827557
e-mail: reception@bridge-hotel.co.uk
Dir: *off A538 through village. Hotel next to church*

Dating in part from the 17th century, this delightful hotel stands between the River Bollin and the ancient church. The cocktail bar is the ideal place to relax before enjoying a satisfying meal in the beamed restaurant. A wide range of bedrooms styles are available in the original building and in the extension.
ROOMS: 23 en suite (1 fmly) No smoking in 5 bedrooms s £50-£155; d £85-£155 **LB FACILITIES:** entertainment **CONF:** Thtr 100 Class 56 Board 48 Del from £105 **PARKING:** 52 **NOTES:** No dogs (ex guide dogs) Civ Wed 110 **CARDS:**

PRESTON, Lancashire Map 18 SD52
See also Garstang

★★★★65% **Preston Marriott Hotel**
Garstang Rd, Broughton PR3 5JB
☎ 01772 864087 01772 861728
e-mail: reservations.preston@marriotthotels.co.uk
Dir: *M6 junct 32 onto M55 junct 1, follow A6 towards Garstang. Hotel 0.5m on right*
With a country club feel, this hotel enjoys good links to both the city centre and motorway network. There are two dining options, and extensive leisure facilities ensure there is plenty to do in the hotel. The bedrooms are smartly decorated and equipped with a comprehensive range of extras.
ROOMS: 150 en suite (40 fmly) (63 GF) No smoking in 94 bedrooms s £69-£109; d £78-£119 (incl. bkfst) **LB FACILITIES: Spa** STV Indoor swimming (H) Sauna Solarium Gym Steam room, Beauty salon/hairdressing **CONF:** Thtr 220 Class 100 Board 70 Del from £135 **SERVICES:** Lift **PARKING:** 250 **NOTES:** No dogs (ex guide dogs) No smoking in restaurant Civ Wed 180
CARDS:

★★★72% **Barton Grange**
Garstang Rd PR3 5AA
☎ 01772 862551 01772 861267
e-mail: stay@bartongrangehotel.com
(For full entry see Barton)

★★★70% ***Pines***
570 Preston Rd, Clayton-Le-Woods PR6 7ED
☎ 01772 338551 01772 629002
e-mail: info@thepineshotel.co.uk
Dir: *on A6, 1m S of M6 junct 29*
This smart, friendly hotel sits in four acres of mature grounds just a short drive from the motorway network. Elegant bedrooms are individually designed and offer high levels of comfort and facilities. Day rooms include a smart bar and 'Haworths' brasserie, while

continued

extensive function rooms make this hotel a popular venue for weddings.

Pines Hotel

ROOMS: 37 en suite (12 fmly) No smoking in 21 bedrooms **FACILITIES:** STV Jacuzzi entertainment **CONF:** Thtr 300 Class 150 Board 60 **PARKING:** 120 **NOTES:** No dogs (ex guide dogs) Closed 26 Dec Civ Wed 150 **CARDS:**

★★★65% **Novotel Preston**
Reedfield Place, Walton Summit PR5 8AA
☎ 01772 313331 01772 627868
e-mail: H0838@accor-hotels.com
Dir: *M6 junct 29, M61 junct 9, then A6 Chorley Road. Hotel next to Bamber Bridge rdbt*
The hotel is ideally located just off main motorway networks. Bedrooms are spacious and feature ample desk space and additional bed space making them ideal for families or business travellers. Flexible dining is a feature with the Garden

continued on p500

PRESTON, continued

Brasserie, open throughout the day until midnight. The hotel also boasts an outdoor pool and children's play area.
ROOMS: 96 en suite (22 fmly) No smoking in 49 bedrooms s £60; d £60 **LB** **FACILITIES:** STV Outdoor swimming (H) **CONF:** Thtr 180 Class 80 Board 52 Del from £90 **SERVICES:** Lift **PARKING:** 140
CARDS:

★★★65% Tickled Trout

MACDONALD HOTELS

Preston New Rd, Samlesbury PR5 0UJ
☎ 01772 877671 📠 01772 877463
e-mail: tickledtrout@macdonald-hotels.co.uk
Dir: *close to M6 junct 31*
Set on the banks of the River Ribble, the hotel is conveniently located for the motorway, making it popular for business guests and providing leisure guests access to some beautiful countryside in four counties. Bedrooms, many of which have now been refurbished, are tastefully decorated and equipped with a range of extras.
ROOMS: 102 en suite (6 fmly) No smoking in 43 bedrooms
FACILITIES: STV Fishing Sauna Solarium entertainment **CONF:** BC Thtr 120 Class 60 Board 50 Del from £90 **SERVICES:** Lift
PARKING: 240 **NOTES:** No smoking in restaurant Civ Wed 100
CARDS:

★★66% Claremont

516 Blackpool Rd, Ashton-on-Ribble PR2 1HY
☎ 01772 729738 📠 01772 726274
Dir: *M6 junct 31 onto A59 towards Preston. Right at hilltop rdbt onto A583. Hotel on right past pub and over bridge*
This friendly, family-run hotel enjoys a convenient location for access to the town centre and the local motorway network. Bedrooms are traditionally furnished and thoughtfully equipped. Public areas include a cosy lounge, a bar lounge and adjacent restaurant that overlooks the attractive rear garden. There is also a popular self-contained function room.
ROOMS: 10 en suite **CONF:** Thtr 85 Class 45 Board 50 **PARKING:** 27
NOTES: No dogs (ex guide dogs) **CARDS:**

P

🅄 *Holiday Inn Preston*

Holiday Inn HOTELS · RESORTS

Ringway PR1 3AU
☎ 0870 400 9066 📠 01772 201923
e-mail: prestonhi@ichotelsgroup.com
Dir: *M6 junct 31, A59 signs for town centre. Right at T-junct, hotel on left*
At the time of going to press, the classification for this hotel was not confirmed. Please refer to the AA internet site www.theAA.com for current information.
ROOMS: 129 en suite (11 fmly) No smoking in 106 bedrooms
CONF: Thtr 120 Class 50 Board 40 **SERVICES:** Lift **PARKING:** 38
NOTES: No dogs (ex guide dogs) **CARDS:**

⇧ Hotel Ibis

ibis Accor hotels

Garstang Rd, Broughton PR3 5JE
☎ 01772 861800 📠 01772 861900
e-mail: H3162@accor-hotels.com
Dir: *M6 junct 32, then M55. Left lane onto A6. Left at slip road and left again at mini rdbt. 2nd turn and hotel on right past pub*
Modern, budget hotel offering comfortable accommodation in bright and practical bedrooms. Breakfast is self-service and dinner is available in the restaurant. For further details, consult the Hotel Groups page.
ROOMS: 82 en suite s £35.95-£42.95; d £35.95-£42.95

⇧ Premier Lodge (Preston)

Lostock Ln, Bamber Bridge PR5 6BA
☎ 0870 9906462 📠 0870 9906463
Dir: *M65 junct 1, 0.5m from junct 29 of M6 close to rdbt of A582 and A6*
Premier Lodge offers modern, well-equipped, en suite accommodation suitable for both business and leisure travellers. Meals can be taken at the adjacent popular restaurant and bar, which is fully licensed. For further details, consult the Hotel Groups page.
ROOMS: 40 en suite s £48; d £48 **CONF:** Thtr 30 Board 30

⇧ Travel Inn (Preston East)

travel inn

Bluebell Way, Preston East Link Rd, Fulwood PR2 5RU
☎ 08701 977215 📠 01772 651619
Dir: *M6 junct 31A left at rdbt, follow ring road under motorway & Inn on left. No junction for southbound traffic so take junct 31 & join motorway northbound, take exit off junct 31A*
Travel Inn offers good-quality, value-for-money accommodation. Spacious, en suite rooms with bath and shower comfortably accommodate a family of up to two adults and two children (to age 15). The restaurant and bar offers a varied menu. For further details and the Travel Inn phone number, consult the Hotel Groups page.
ROOMS: 65 en suite s £44.95; d £44.95 **CONF:** Thtr 20

⇧ Travel Inn (Preston South)

travel inn

Blackpool Rd, Lea PR4 0XB
☎ 08701 977214 📠 01772 729971
Dir: *Off A583, opposite Texaco garage.*
Travel Inn offers good-quality, value-for-money accommodation. Spacious, en suite rooms with bath and shower comfortably accommodate a family of up to two adults and two children (to age 15). The restaurant and bar offers a varied menu. For further details and the Travel Inn phone number, consult the Hotel Groups page.
ROOMS: 38 en suite s £44.95; d £44.95

PRESTWICH, Greater Manchester — Map 15 SD80

⇧ Travel Inn (Manchester Prestwich)

travel inn

Bury New Rd M25 3AJ
☎ 08701 977175 📠 0161 773 8099
Dir: *M60 junct 17, on A56*
Travel Inn offers good-quality, value-for-money accommodation. Spacious, en suite rooms with bath and shower comfortably accommodate a family of up to two adults and two children (to age 15). The restaurant and bar offers a varied menu. For further details and the Travel Inn phone number, consult the Hotel Groups page.
ROOMS: 60 en suite s £44.95; d £44.95

PUDDINGTON, Cheshire — Map 15 SJ37

★★★★74% Craxton Wood

MACDONALD HOTELS

Parkgate Rd, Ledsham CH66 9PB
☎ 0151 347 4000 📠 0151 347 4040
e-mail: craxtonwood@macdonald-hotels.co.uk
Dir: *from M6 take M56 towards N Wales, then A5117 then A540 to Hoylake. Hotel 200yds past lights*
This hotel has nvested in significant improvements in the form of smart new bedrooms, which are both spacious and very

continued

houghtfully equipped, as well as the addition of extensive meeting and leisure facilities. The restaurant is comfortable and offers guests the choice from a modern menu.
ROOMS: 72 en suite (8 fmly) (30 GF) No smoking in all bedrooms **FACILITIES:** STV Indoor swimming (H) Sauna Solarium Gym Beauty pa **CONF:** Thtr 400 Class 150 Board 60 **SERVICES:** Lift **PARKING:** 220 **NOTES:** No smoking in restaurant Civ Wed 400
CARDS:

Premier Lodge (Wirral South)

Parkgate Rd, Two Mills CH66 9PD
☎ 0870 9906564 📠 0870 9906565
Premier Lodge offers modern, well-equipped, en suite accommodation suitable for both business and leisure travellers. Meals can be taken at the adjacent popular restaurant and bar, which is fully licensed. For further details, consult the Hotel Groups page.
ROOMS: 31 en suite s £48; d £48

PUDSEY, West Yorkshire — Map 19 SE23

Travelodge Bradford

Mid Point, Dick Ln BD3 8QD
☎ 08700 850 950
Travelodge offers good quality, good value, modern accommodation. Ideal for families, the spacious, en suite bedrooms include remote-control TV, tea and coffee-making facilities, luxury beds and free morning newspaper. Meals can be taken at the nearby family restaurant. For further details and the Travelodge phone number, consult the Hotel Groups page.
ROOMS: 48 en suite s fr £42.95; d fr £42.95

PULBOROUGH, West Sussex — Map 06 TQ01

★★★66% Chequers

Old Rectory Ln RH20 1AD
☎ 01798 872486 📠 01798 872715
e-mail: info@thechequershotel.com
Dir: *100mtrs N of junct of A283/A29 opposite church in Pulborough*
Personally run by friendly owners, this charming Grade II listed hotel is located just north of Pulborough overlooking the South Downs. All rooms are individual in style with character and good facilities. Public areas include two cosy lounges where drinks are served and also a conservatory coffee shop. The restaurant serves carefully prepared dishes using quality fresh produce.
ROOMS: 10 en suite (3 fmly) No smoking in all bedrooms s £50-£65; d £90-£110 (incl. bkfst) **LB** **FACILITIES:** Xmas **CONF:** Thtr 20 Class 20 Board 20 **PARKING:** 20 **NOTES:** No smoking in restaurant
CARDS:

PURFLEET, Essex — Map 06 TQ57

Travel Inn

High St RM19 1QA
☎ 08701 977216 📠 01708 860852
Dir: *from Dartford Tunnel follow signs Dagenham(A13), at rdbt take 1st exit to Purfleet (A1090)*
Travel Inn offers good-quality, value-for-money accommodation. Spacious, en suite rooms with bath and shower comfortably accommodate a family of up to two adults and two children (to age 15). The restaurant and bar offers a varied menu. For further details and the Travel Inn phone number, consult the Hotel Groups page.
ROOMS: 30 en suite s £44.95; d £44.95

PURTON, Wiltshire — Map 05 SU08

★★★78% The Pear Tree at Purton

Church End SN5 4ED
☎ 01793 772100 📠 01793 772369
e-mail: stay@peartreepurton.co.uk
Dir: *M4 junct 16 follow signs to Purton, at Spar shop turn right. Hotel 0.25m on left*
Set is attractive gardens and grounds, this 15th-century, former vicarage offers a comfortable haven for guests. The resident proprietors and staff provide efficient, dedicated service and friendly hospitality. Individually styled bedrooms are spacious and feature thoughtful extra touches such as fresh flowers and sherry. Fresh ingredients feature on the menus at both lunch and dinner.
ROOMS: 17 en suite (2 fmly) (6 GF) s £120-£180; d £120-£180 (incl. bkfst) **FACILITIES: Spa** STV Croquet lawn **CONF:** BC Thtr 70 Class 30 Board 30 Del from £165 **PARKING:** 60 **NOTES:** No smoking in restaurant Closed 26-30 Dec Civ Wed 50
CARDS:

QUORN, Leicestershire — Map 11 SK51

★★★★70% Quorn Country

Charnwood House, 66 Leicester Rd LE12 8BB
☎ 01509 415050 📠 01509 415557
e-mail: reservations@quorncountryhotel.co.uk
Dir: *M1 junct 23 onto A512 into Loughborough. Follow A6 signs. At 1st rdbt towards Quorn, through lights, hotel 500yds from 2nd rdbt*

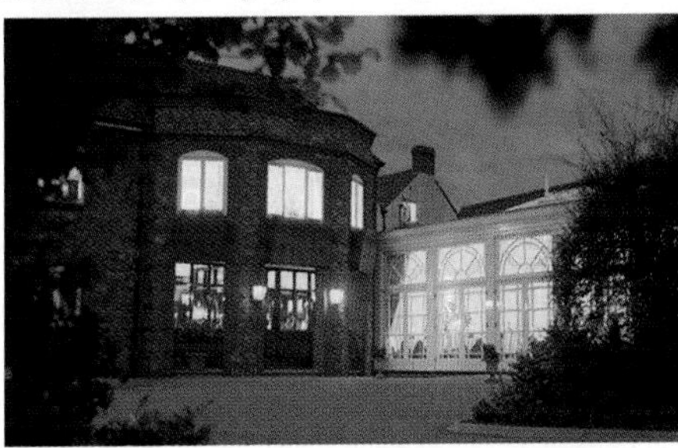

Professional service is one of the key strengths of this pleasant hotel, which sits beside the river in four acres of landscaped grounds. New this year is the creation of a smart modern conference centre and function suites. Public rooms include a comfortable lounge and bar, whilst guests have the choice from two dining options: the formal Shires restaurant and the informal conservatory-style Orangery.
ROOMS: 30 en suite (1 fmly) (9 GF) No smoking in 13 bedrooms s £82-£105; d £95-£120 **LB** **FACILITIES:** STV Fishing **CONF:** BC Thtr 300 Class 162 Board 40 Del from £140 **PARKING:** 100 **NOTES:** No dogs (ex guide dogs) Civ Wed 250
CARDS:
See advert under LOUGHBOROUGH

RADLETT, Hertfordshire — Map 06 TL10

Travel Inn (Bricketwood)

Smug Oak Ln AL2 3PN
☎ 08701 977040 📠 01727 873289
Dir: *From M10 take A5183 towards Radlett. After bridge over M25 turn right. From M25 or M1, follow signs to Bricketwood then turn into Smug Oak Lane at The Gate pub*
Travel Inn offers good-quality, value-for-money accommodation. Spacious, en suite rooms with bath and shower comfortably
continued on p502

RADLETT, continued

accommodate a family of up to two adults and two children (to age 15). The restaurant and bar offers a varied menu. For further details and the Travel Inn phone number, consult the Hotel Groups page.

Travel Inn (Bricketwood), Radlett

ROOMS: 56 en suite s £49.95-£54.95; d £49.95-£54.95

RAINHAM, Greater London — Map 06 TQ58

Travel Inn

New Rd, Wennington RM13 9ED
☎ 08701 977217 📠 01708 634821
Dir: *M25 J30/31 - follow A13 for Dagenham/Rainham, then A1306 for Wennington, Aveley, Rainham. Inn is 0.5 mile on right.*
Travel Inn offers good-quality, value-for-money accommodation. Spacious, en suite rooms with bath and shower comfortably accommodate a family of up to two adults and two children (to age 15). The restaurant and bar offers a varied menu. For further details and the Travel Inn phone number, consult the Hotel Groups page.
ROOMS: 60 en suite s £49.95-£54.95; d £49.95-£54.95

RAINHILL, Merseyside — Map 15 SJ49

Premier Lodge (Liverpool East)

804 Warrington Rd L35 6PE
☎ 0870 9906446 📠 0870 9906447
Premier Lodge offers modern, well-equipped, en suite accommodation suitable for both business and leisure travellers. Meals can be taken at the adjacent popular restaurant and bar, which is fully licensed. For further details, consult the Hotel Groups page.
ROOMS: 34 en suite s £48; d £48

RAMSBOTTOM, Greater Manchester — Map 15 SD71

★★★62% Old Mill

Springwood BL0 9DS
☎ 01706 822991 📠 01706 822291
e-mail: reservations@oldmill-uk.com
Dir: *Turn off A676 from Greenmount, 300yds turn right onto Springwood*
Extended from an original water mill, this friendly hotel enjoys fine views over the town and Rossendale Valley. In addition to a comfortable bar and beamed restaurant, a well-equipped leisure centre is available to guests during their stay. Now refurbished bedrooms have attractive floral furnishings and inter-connecting family rooms are available.
ROOMS: 28 en suite (5 fmly) s £59; d £67-£74 (incl. bkfst) **LB**
FACILITIES: Indoor swimming (H) Sauna Solarium Gym Jacuzzi Steam Room **CONF:** Thtr 70 Class 30 Board 20 Del £99 **PARKING:** 50
NOTES: No dogs (ex guide dogs) No smoking in restaurant
CARDS:

RAMSGILL, North Yorkshire — Map 19 SE1

Top 200 - Restaurant with Rooms

Yorke Arms

HG3 5RL
☎ 01423 755243 📠 01423 755330
e-mail: enquiries@yorke-arms.co.uk
Dir: *off B6265 at Pateley Bridge at Nidderdale filling station onto Low Wath road, signed to Ramsgill. Continue 4.5m*
Dominating the tiny hamlet, this ivy clad former hunting lodge overlooks the village green in picturesque Nidderdale and a warm and welcoming ambience prevails throughout. Flagstone floors lead through to a cosy bar, and beams and open fires grace the two delightful dining rooms, where excellent cuisine is matched by caring and attentive service.
ROOMS: 13 en suite 1 annexe en suite (2 fmly) (5 GF) s £95-£120; d £190-£320 (incl. bkfst & dinner) **LB**
FACILITIES: shooting,mountain biking,walking, bird watching Xmas
CONF: Class 20 Board 10 **PARKING:** 20 **NOTES:** No dogs (ex guide dogs) No smoking in restaurant RS Sun
CARDS:

RANGEWORTHY, Gloucestershire — Map 04 ST6

★★72% Rangeworthy Court

Church Ln, Wotton Rd BS37 7ND
☎ 01454 228347 📠 01454 228945
e-mail: hotel@rangeworthy.demon.co.uk
Dir: *signposted off B4058*
This welcoming manor house hotel is peacefully located within its own grounds, and is within easy reach of the motorway network. The relaxed atmosphere and characterful surroundings include a choice of comfortable lounges and well-equipped bedrooms. The candlelit restaurant offers a varied and interesting menu.
ROOMS: 13 en suite (4 fmly) No smoking in 3 bedrooms s £65-£70; d £85-£90 (incl. bkfst) **FACILITIES:** STV Outdoor swimming (H) Croquet lawn Boules Xmas **CONF:** BC Thtr 22 Class 14 Board 16 **PARKING:** 4
NOTES: No smoking in restaurant **CARDS:**

RAVENSCAR, North Yorkshire — Map 19 NZ9

★★★67% Raven Hall Country House

YO13 0ET
☎ 01723 870353 📠 01723 870072
e-mail: enquiries@ravenhall.co.uk
Dir: *from Scarborough take A171 to Whitby Rd. Through Cloughton and right to Ravenscar*
Run by the Gridley family for over 40 years this impressive cliff top mansion enjoys breathtaking views over Robin Hood's Bay. Extensive well-kept grounds include tennis courts, putting green, swimming pools and historic battlements. The spacious bedrooms

continued

ffer many thoughtful extras. Public rooms are extensive while the estaurant enjoys fine views over the bay.
OOMS: 51 en suite (22 fmly) (5 GF) No smoking in 1 bedroom £65-£95; d £70-£170 (incl. bkfst) **LB** **FACILITIES:** Indoor swimming H) Golf 9 Tennis (hard) Snooker Sauna Croquet lawn Putting green rown green bowls Giant chess Table tennis, indoor pool supervised(CCTV) ntertainment ch fac Xmas **CONF:** Thtr 160 Class 100 Board 60 Del om £85 **SERVICES:** Lift **PARKING:** 200 **NOTES:** No dogs (ex guide ogs) No smoking in restaurant Civ Wed 120
ARDS:

See advert under SCARBOROUGH

AVENSTONEDALE, Cumbria — Map 18 NY70

★★66% **The Fat Lamb**
rossbank CA17 4LL
☎ 015396 23242 📠 015396 23285
-mail: fatlamb@cumbria.com
ir: *on A683, between Kirkby Stephen and Sedbergh*
Open fires and solid stone walls are a feature of this 17th-century nn set in its own nature reserve. There is a choice of dining ptions with an extensive menu available in the traditional bar or more formal dining experience in the restaurant. Bedrooms are right and cheerful and include family rooms and easily accessible ooms for guests with limited mobility.
OOMS: 12 en suite (4 fmly) No smoking in all bedrooms s £45-£48; £70-£76 (incl. bkfst) **LB** **FACILITIES:** Fishing Private 5 acre nature eserve Xmas **PARKING:** 60 **NOTES:** No smoking in restaurant
ARDS:

AYLEIGH, Essex — Map 07 TQ89

Express by Holiday Inn asildon/Rayleigh

rterial Rd SS6 7SP
☎ 01268 775001 📠 01268 777505
-mail: ebhi-rayleigh@btconnect.com

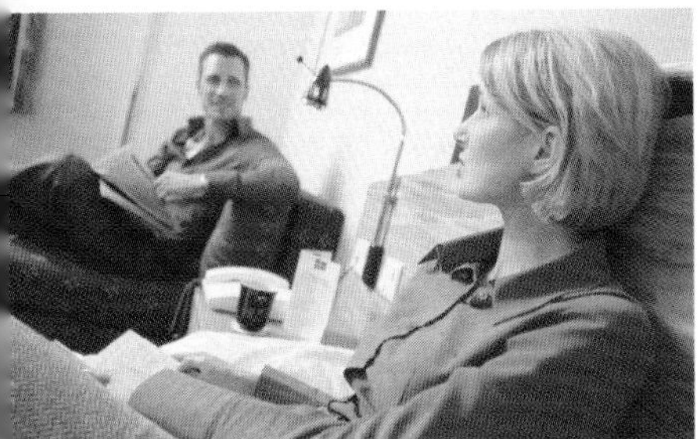

modern hotel ideal for families and business travellers. Fresh nd uncomplicated, the spacious bedrooms include Sky TV, power hower and tea and coffee-making facilities. Continental buffet reakfast is included in the room rate; other meals may be taken t the nearby family pub or restaurant. For further details and the xpress by Holiday Inn phone number, consult the Hotel roups pages.
OOMS: 49 en suite **CONF:** Thtr 30 Class 24 Board 16

READING, Berkshire — Map 05 SU77

See also Swallowfield & Wokingham

★★★★74% **Millennium Madejski Hotel Reading**
MILLENNIUM HOTELS AND RESORTS
Madejski Stadium RG2 0FL
☎ 0118 925 3500 📠 0118 925 3501
e-mail: sales.reading@mill-cop.com
Dir: *M4 junct 11 onto A33, follow signs for Madejski Complex*

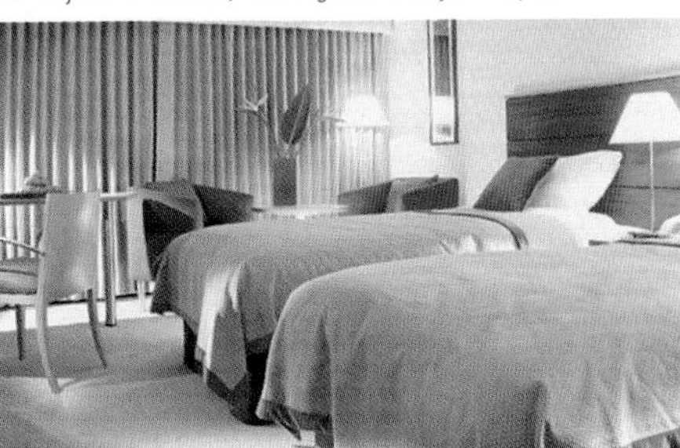

A stylish hotel, which is part of the Reading Madejski Football Stadium. Features include a fine dining restaurant, Cilantro, and an atrium lobby with specially commissioned water sculpture. Bedrooms are appointed in a similar high style with spacious workstations and plenty of amenities. A choice of suites and club floor with its own lounge give additional choice.
ROOMS: 140 en suite (4 fmly) No smoking in 92 bedrooms s £195-£265; d £195-£265 **LB** **FACILITIES: Spa** STV Indoor swimming (H) Sauna Solarium Gym Jacuzzi Swimming pool supervised
CONF: BC **SERVICES:** Lift air con **PARKING:** 150
CARDS:

★★★★69% **Renaissance Hotel Reading**
RENAISSANCE HOTELS
Oxford Rd RG1 7RH
☎ 0118 958 6222 📠 0118 959 7842
e-mail: rhi.lhrlr.gm@renaissancehotels.com
Situated in the heart of the town, this long established hotel is equally well positioned for the business traveller and the shopper. Air-conditioned bedrooms feature a host of extras and are well geared to the needs of the business traveller. Public areas include a fully equipped gymnasium, swimming pool, a variety of meeting rooms and a business centre.
ROOMS: 196 en suite (67 fmly) No smoking in 160 bedrooms s £70-£145; d £70-£145 **LB** **FACILITIES:** STV Indoor swimming (H) Sauna Solarium Gym Jacuzzi Swimming pool supervised **CONF:** BC Thtr 220 Class 130 Board 60 Del from £99 **SERVICES:** Lift air con **PARKING:** 70 **NOTES:** No dogs (ex guide dogs) Civ Wed 140
CARDS:

★★★69% **Calcot Hotel**
98 Bath Rd, Calcot RG31 7QN
☎ 0118 941 6423 📠 0118 941 1223
e-mail: enquiries@calcothotel.co.uk
Dir: *M4 junct 12 onto A4 towards Reading, hotel in 0.5m on S side of A4*
The Calcot Hotel is conveniently located for both London and the motorway. Bedrooms are well equipped and tastefully decorated; bedroom styles vary slightly, the newer bedrooms are particularly appealing. Attractive public rooms and function suites are additional features; the restaurant offers enjoyable food in welcoming surroundings.
ROOMS: 80 en suite (2 fmly) No smoking in 38 bedrooms s £45-£130 **FACILITIES:** STV entertainment **CONF:** Thtr 120 Class 35 Board 35 Del from £141 **PARKING:** 130 **NOTES:** No dogs (ex guide dogs) Closed 25-27 Dec Civ Wed 60 **CARDS:**

R

READING, continued

★★★69% Courtyard by Marriott Reading
Bath Rd, Padworth RG7 5HT
☎ 0870 400 7234 📠 0870 400 7334
Dir: *M4 junct 12 onto A4 towards Newbury. Hotel 3.5m on left, after petrol station*
This purpose-built hotel combines the benefits of a peaceful rural location with the accessibility afforded by good road links. Modern comforts include air-conditioned bedrooms and rooms with easy access for the less able guests. A feature of the hotel is its pretty courtyard garden which is overlooked from the restaurant.
ROOMS: 50 en suite (25 GF) No smoking in 45 bedrooms s £45-£118; d £58-£128 (incl. bkfst) **LB FACILITIES:** STV Gym Fitness room Xmas **CONF:** Thtr 200 Class 70 Board 80 Del from £120 **SERVICES:** air con **PARKING:** 200 **NOTES:** No smoking in restaurant Civ Wed 120 **CARDS:**

★★★68% Hanover International Hotel & Club
Pingewood RG30 3UN
☎ 0118 950 0885 📠 0118 939 1996
e-mail: reading@hanover-international.com
Dir: *A33 towards Basingstoke. At Three Mile Cross rdbt right signed Burghfield. After 300mtrs 2nd right, over M4, through lights, hotel on left*

Quietly located a short distance south of Reading, this modern hotel been built around a man-made lake which is occasionally used for water sports. Bedrooms are generally spacious with good facilities, and some have balconies overlooking the lake. Public areas include Brasserie 209 and a well-equipped leisure club with adjacent bar.
ROOMS: 81 en suite (23 fmly) No smoking in 57 bedrooms s £140-£155; d £140-£155 **LB FACILITIES:** STV Indoor swimming (H) Tennis (hard) Squash Snooker Sauna Gym Jacuzzi Watersports **CONF:** Thtr 110 Class 50 Board 45 Del £170 **SERVICES:** Lift **PARKING:** 250 **NOTES:** No dogs (ex guide dogs) No smoking in restaurant Civ Wed 70
CARDS:

★★★63% Quality Hotel Reading
648-654 Oxford Rd RG30 1EH
☎ 0118 950 0541 📠 0118 956 7220
e-mail: info@qualityreading.co.uk
Dir: *M4 J11, follow A33 bypass towards town centre, then A329 towards Pangbourne, follow signs for Oxford Rd*
Close to the city centre this modern, purpose-built hotel is a popular choice with business guests. Bedrooms are generally spacious and offer a good range of facilities. Guests have a choice of eating lighter meals and snacks in the bar lounge or a more formal menu is offered in the spacious restaurant. The hotel benefits from conference facilities and ample car parking.
ROOMS: 95 en suite (9 fmly) No smoking in 28 bedrooms s £39-£99; d £39-£99 **LB FACILITIES:** STV **CONF:** Thtr 100 Class 50 Board 40 Del from £99 **SERVICES:** Lift **PARKING:** 60 **NOTES:** No dogs (ex guide dogs) No smoking in restaurant **CARDS:**

★★70% The Mill House
Old Basingstoke Rd, Swallowfield RG7 1PY
☎ 0118 988 3124 📠 0118 988 5550
e-mail: info@themillhousehotel.co.uk
(For full entry see Swallowfield)

Holiday Inn Reading South
Basingstoke Rd RG2 0SL
☎ 0870 400 9067 📠 0118 931 1958
e-mail: reservations-reading@ichotelsgroup.com
At the time of going to press, the classification for this hotel was not confirmed. Please refer to the AA internet site www.theAA.com for current information.
ROOMS: 204 en suite (60 fmly) No smoking in 110 bedrooms **FACILITIES:** Indoor swimming (H) Sauna Solarium Gym Jacuzzi Health & fitness centre ch fac **CONF:** Thtr 100 Class 50 Board 45 **PARKING:** 450 **CARDS:**

Express by Holiday Inn
Richfield Av RG1 8EQ
☎ 0118 958 2558 📠 0118 958 2858
e-mail: ebhi-reading@btconnect.com
Dir: *Follow city centre & Caversham signs*

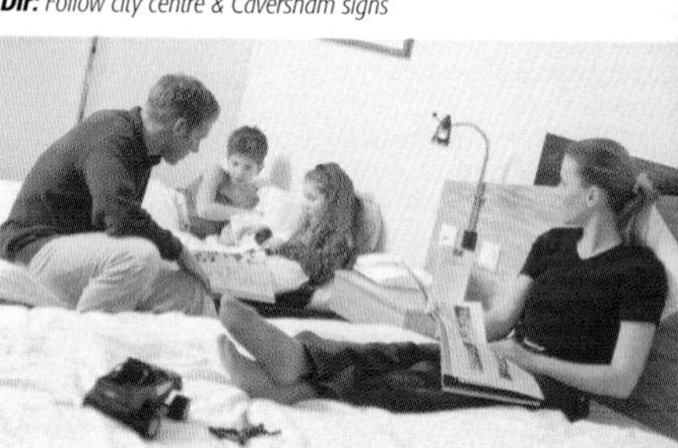

A modern hotel ideal for families and business travellers. Fresh and uncomplicated, the spacious bedrooms include Sky TV, power shower and tea and coffee-making facilities. Continental buffet breakfast is included in the room rate; other meals may be taken at the nearby family pub or restaurant. For further details and the Express by Holiday Inn phone number, consult the Hotel Groups pages.
ROOMS: 74 en suite **CONF:** Thtr 30 Class 24 Board 16

Premier Lodge
Grazeley Green Rd RG7 1LS
☎ 0870 9906454 📠 0870 9906455
Dir: *M4 junct 11 follow A33 towards Basingstoke, take Mortimer exit at 1st rdbt. 3rd right into Grazeley Rd, under railway bridge turn left. Lodge next to Old Bell Millers Kitchen*
Premier Lodge offers modern, well-equipped, en suite accommodation suitable for both business and leisure travellers. Meals can be taken at the adjacent popular restaurant and bar, which is fully licensed. For further details, consult the Hotel Groups page.
ROOMS: 32 en suite s £50; d £50

Travelodge
387 Basingstoke Rd RG2 0JE
☎ 08700 850 950
Dir: *On A33, southbound.*
Travelodge offers good quality, good value, modern accommodation. Ideal for families, the spacious, en suite bedrooms include remote-control TV, tea and coffee-making

continued

R

cilities, luxury beds and free morning newspaper. Meals can be
ıken at the nearby family restaurant. For further details and the
ravelodge phone number, consult the Hotel Groups page.
OOMS: 36 en suite s fr £42.95; d fr £42.95

Travelodge (Reading Central)

xford Rd RG1 7LT
☎ 08700 850 950
ravelodge offers good quality, good value, modern accommodation. Ideal for families, the spacious, en suite edrooms include remote-control TV, tea and coffee-making cilities, luxury beds and free morning newspaper. Meals can be ıken at the nearby family restaurant. For further details and the ravelodge phone number, consult the Hotel Groups page.
OOMS: 80 en suite s fr £42.95; d fr £42.95

Travelodge Reading M4 (Eastbound)

urghfield RG30 3UQ
☎ 08700 850 950 ▯ 0118 959 5444
ir: *M4 between junct 11 & 12*
ravelodge offers good quality, good value, modern ccommodation. Ideal for families, the spacious, en suite edrooms include remote-control TV, tea and coffee-making acilities, luxury beds and free morning newspaper. Meals can be ıken at the nearby family restaurant. For further details and the ravelodge phone number, consult the Hotel Groups page.
OOMS: 86 en suite s fr £42.95; d fr £42.95
ONF: Thtr 20 Class 20 Board 20

Travelodge Reading M4 (Westbound)

urghfield RG30 3UQ
☎ 08700 850 950
ir: *M4 between junct 11 & 12*
ravelodge offers good quality, good value, modern ccommodation. Ideal for families, the spacious, en suite edrooms include remote-control TV, tea and coffee-making acilities, luxury beds and free morning newspaper. Meals can be ıken at the nearby family restaurant. For further details and the ravelodge phone number, consult the Hotel Groups page.
OOMS: 102 en suite s fr £42.95; d fr £42.95

EDDITCH, Worcestershire — Map 10 SP06

★★★★67% The Abbey Hotel Golf & Country Club

Hither Green Ln, Dagnell End Rd, Bordesley
98 9BE
☎ 01527 406600 ▯ 01527 406514
-mail: info@theabbeyhotel.co.uk
ir: *M42 junct 2 take A441 to Redditch. End of carriageway turn left A441), Dagnell End Rd on left. Hotel 600yds on right*

ery convenient for the motorway, this modern hotel complex is popular with business and leisure guests. Accommodation is well equipped, spacious (particularly the executive corner rooms) and attractively decorated. An 18-hole golf course, pro shop, large indoor pool and extensive conference facilities are some of the added attractions.
ROOMS: 72 en suite (2 fmly) (30 GF) No smoking in 30 bedrooms s £65-£115; d £85-£135 (incl. bkfst) **LB FACILITIES:** STV Indoor swimming (H) Golf 18 Fishing Sauna Solarium Gym Putting green Jacuzzi Beauty Salon,Golf driving range ch fac Xmas **CONF:** Thtr 150 Class 60 Board 30 Del from £135 **SERVICES:** Lift **PARKING:** 170 **NOTES:** No dogs (ex guide dogs) No smoking in restaurant Civ Wed 70 **CARDS:**

★★★64% Quality Hotel

Pool Bank, Southcrest B97 4JS
☎ 01527 541511 ▯ 01527 402600
e-mail: admin@gb646.u-net.com
Dir: *follow hotel signs, 2nd on right after B&Q. Follow Redditch signs onto A441. In Redditch follow signs for all other Redditch Districts until Southcrest signed, then take signs for hotel*
Originally a manor house, this hotel enjoys a peaceful location set in extensive wooded grounds. Bedrooms vary in size and style, and are all well appointed and equipped. Both the restaurant and bar/conservatory overlook the attractive, sloping gardens, with views stretching across to the Vale of Evesham.
ROOMS: 73 en suite (20 fmly) (22 GF) No smoking in 35 bedrooms s fr £85; d fr £99 **LB FACILITIES:** STV Xmas **CONF:** Thtr 100 Class 45 Board 50 Del from £99 **PARKING:** 100 **NOTES:** No smoking in restaurant Civ Wed 100 **CARDS:**

★★63% Montville

101 Mount Pleasant, Southcrest B97 4JE
☎ 01527 544411 ▯ 01527 544341
e-mail: sales@montvillehotel.co.uk
Dir: *M42 junct 3 onto A435 following Redditch centre signs, then signs towards Southcrest on A441*
Situated less than half a mile from the town centre, this is a small, friendly, privately owned hotel, suitable for both business and leisure guests. Rooms vary in size and style, and all have the necessary comforts. A well-stocked bar, a homely lounge and an interesting dining room complete the picture.
ROOMS: 14 en suite (2 fmly) No smoking in 5 bedrooms s £40-£55; d £55-£70 (incl. bkfst) **LB FACILITIES:** Board games **CONF:** Thtr 60 Class 30 Board 24 Del £95 **PARKING:** 12 **NOTES:** No smoking in restaurant **CARDS:**

Campanile

Far Moor Ln, Winyates Green B98 0SD
☎ 01527 510710 ▯ 01527 517269
Dir: *A435 towards Redditch, then A4023 to Redditch and Bromsgrove*

This modern building offers accommodation in smart,

continued on p504

REDDITCH, continued

well-equipped bedrooms, all with en suite bathrooms. Refreshments may be taken at the informal Bistro. For further details and the Campanile phone number, consult the Hotel Groups page.
ROOMS: 46 annexe en suite **CONF:** Thtr 35 Class 18 Board 20

Premier Lodge (Redditch)

Birchfield Rd B97 6PX
☎ 0870 9906392 ▯ 0870 9906393
Dir: *A448 to Redditch & take 1st exit to Webheath, at rdbt take 3rd exit & 1st right*
Premier Lodge offers modern, well-equipped, en suite accommodation suitable for both business and leisure travellers. Meals can be taken at the adjacent popular restaurant and bar, which is fully licensed. For further details, consult the Hotel Groups page.
ROOMS: 33 en suite s £48; d £48

REDHILL, Surrey — Map 06 TQ25

★★★★74% Nutfield Priory

Nutfield RH1 4EL
☎ 01737 824400 ▯ 01737 823321
e-mail: nutfield@arcadianhotels.co.uk
Dir: *M25 junct 6, follow Redhill signs via Godstone on A25. Hotel 1m on left after Nutfield*

This Victorian country house dates back to 1872 and is set in forty acres of grounds with stunning views over the Surrey countryside. Bedrooms are individually decorated and equipped with an excellent range of facilities. Public areas include the impressive grand hall, Cloisters restaurant, the library, and a cosy lounge bar area.
ROOMS: 60 en suite (4 fmly) No smoking in 24 bedrooms s £120-£140; d £120-£320 **LB** **FACILITIES: Spa** STV Indoor swimming (H) Squash Sauna Solarium Gym Jacuzzi Steam room Beauty therapy Aerobic & Step classes Xmas **CONF:** BC Thtr 80 Class 45 Board 40 Del from £170 **SERVICES:** Lift **PARKING:** 130 **NOTES:** No smoking in restaurant Civ Wed 80 **CARDS:**

Innkeeper's Lodge Redhill

2 Redstone Hill RH1 4BL
☎ 01737 768434 ▯ 01737 770742
Dir: *M25 junct 8, follow signs for Redhill (A25). At railway station, left towards Godstone, located on right*
A new concept in the travel accommodation market. Smart rooms meet essential business requirements but also have home comforts. Dining options include all-day menus plus the added advantage of breakfast, which is included in the room price. For further details, consult the Hotel Groups page.
ROOMS: 37 en suite **CONF:** Thtr 50 Class 20 Board 24

Travel Inn

Brighton Rd, Salfords RH1 5BT
☎ 08701 977218 ▯ 01737 778099
Dir: *on A23, 2m south of Redhill and 3m north of Gatwick Airport*
Travel Inn offers good-quality, value-for-money accommodation. Spacious, en suite rooms with bath and shower comfortably accommodate a family of up to two adults and two children (to age 15). The restaurant and bar offers a varied menu. For further details and the Travel Inn phone number, consult the Hotel Groups page.
ROOMS: 48 en suite s £44.95; d £44.95 **CONF:** Thtr 35

REDRUTH, Cornwall & Isles of Scilly — Map 02 SW6

★★★65% Penventon Park

TR15 1TE
☎ 01209 203000 ▯ 01209 203001
e-mail: manager@penventon.com
Dir: *off A30 at Redruth, hotel 1m S*

Set in attractive parkland, this Georgian mansion is ideal for either the business or leisure guest. Bedrooms are well equipped and comfortable. Cuisine offers a wide choice and specialises in Italian, French, British and Cornish dishes. Leisure facilities available include a fitness suite and health spa as well as function rooms and bars.
ROOMS: 69 en suite (3 fmly) (25 GF) No smoking in 6 bedrooms s £32-£76; d £58-£112 (incl. bkfst) **LB** **FACILITIES: Spa** Indoor swimming (H) Sauna Solarium Gym Jacuzzi Leisure spa Masseuse Steam bath Pool table, beautician, indoor pool supervised entertainment ch fac Xmas **CONF:** Thtr 200 Class 100 Board 60 Del from £50 **PARKING:** 100 **NOTES:** No smoking in restaurant Civ Wed 200 **CARDS:**

★★65% Crossroads Lodge

Scorrier TR16 5BP
☎ 01872 260068 ▯ 01872 261069
e-mail: crossroads@hotelstruro.com
Dir: *turn off A30 onto A3047 towards Scorrier*
Situated on an historic stanary site and conveniently located just off the A30, the Crossroads Lodge has a smart appearance with attractive flower baskets. Bedrooms are soundly furnished and include executive and family rooms. Public areas include an attractive dining room, a quiet lounge and a lively bar. Conference, banqueting and business facilities are also available.
ROOMS: 36 en suite (2 fmly) (8 GF) No smoking in 8 bedrooms s £40-£57; d £57-£65 (incl. bkfst) **LB** **CONF:** BC Thtr 150 Class 80 Board 60 Del from £21.25 **SERVICES:** Lift **PARKING:** 140 **NOTES:** No smoking in restaurant **CARDS:**

EDWORTH, Co Durham Map 19 NZ22

★★★★73% ◎◎ *Redworth Hall Hotel*
)L5 6NL
☎ 01388 770600 🖷 01388 770654
-mail: redworthhall@paramount-hotels.co.uk
ir: from A1(M) junct 58 take A68 'Corbridge'. Follow hotel signs

PARAMOUNT GROUP OF HOTELS

his imposing Georgian building has been extensively enlarged nd includes a health club with state-of-the-art equipment. There re several spacious lounges and two restaurants, the relaxed onservatory and the intimate 1744 fine-dining option. Bedrooms re thoughtfully equipped and impressive conference facilities nake this a popular destination for business travellers.
OOMS: 100 en suite (8 fmly) No smoking in 45 bedrooms
ACILITIES: STV Indoor swimming (H) Tennis (hard) Sauna Solarium ym Croquet lawn Jacuzzi Bodysense Health & Beauty Club ntertainment **CONF:** Thtr 300 Class 150 Board 100 **SERVICES:** Lift
ARKING: 300 **NOTES:** Civ Wed 220
ARDS:

EEPHAM, Norfolk Map 13 TG12

★★68% The Old Brewery House Hotel
Market Place NR10 4JJ
☎ 01603 870881 🖷 01603 870969
-mail: enquiries@oldbreweryhousehotel.co.uk
ir: off A1067 Norwich to Fakenham. Take B1145 signed Reepham
he Old Brewery House dates back to 1729 and is situated in the orner of the market square. Bedrooms are generally quite pacious; each is pleasantly decorated and equipped with modern acilities and some rooms have four-poster beds. Public rooms nclude a popular lounge bar, conservatory restaurant, a cosy ounge and a well-equipped leisure centre.
OOMS: 23 en suite (2 fmly) No smoking in 7 bedrooms £37.50-£47.50; d £75-£85 (incl. bkfst) **LB FACILITIES:** Indoor wimming (H) Squash Sauna Solarium Gym Aerobics & Steps wimming lessons, indoor pool supervised Xmas **CONF:** Thtr 200 Class 50 Board 100 Del from £73.50 **PARKING:** 60 **NOTES:** No dogs (ex uide dogs) No smoking in restaurant Civ Wed 200
CARDS:

EIGATE, Surrey Map 06 TQ25

★★★67% Reigate Manor Hotel
Reigate Hill RH2 9PF
☎ 01737 240125 🖷 01737 223883
-mail: hotel@reigatemanor.co.uk
Dir: on A217, 1m S of junct 8 on M25

Best Western

On the slopes of Reigate Hill, the hotel is ideally located for access to the town and for motorway links. A range of public rooms is provided along with a variety of function rooms. Bedrooms styles

continued

are divided between the more traditional rooms in the old house and contemporary rooms in the newer wing.
ROOMS: 50 en suite (1 fmly) No smoking in 33 bedrooms s £80-£105; d £90-£125 **FACILITIES:** STV Sauna Solarium Gym **CONF:** Thtr 200 Class 80 Board 50 Del £145 **PARKING:** 130 **NOTES:** No dogs (ex guide dogs) No smoking in restaurant Civ Wed 210
CARDS:

★★★63% Bridge House
Reigate Hill RH2 9RP
☎ 01737 246801 & 244821 🖷 01737 223756
Dir: on A217 between M25 and Reigate
Enjoying a prime position on top of Reigate Hill, this hotel offers some impressive views. Bedrooms are spacious and most have balconies. The Mediterranean-style restaurant is well established and is the venue for entertainment evenings. Parking and conference rooms are also available.
ROOMS: 39 en suite (3 fmly) (11 GF) d £55-£65 **FACILITIES:** STV entertainment Xmas **CONF:** Thtr 100 Class 70 Board 60 Del £145.50
PARKING: 110 **NOTES:** No dogs (ex guide dogs)
CARDS:

See advert on this page

RENISHAW, Derbyshire Map 16 SK47

★★★64% Sitwell Arms
Station Rd S21 3WF
☎ 01246 435226 🖷 01246 433915
e-mail: sitwellarms@renishaw79.fsnet.co.uk
Dir: on A6135 to Sheffield, W of M1 junct 30
This stone-built hotel, parts of which date back to the 18th century, is well maintained and conveniently situated close to the M1. It

continued on p508

R

RENISHAW, continued

offers good value accommodation. Bedrooms are of a comfortable size and include the expected range of facilities and appointments. There are extensive bars and a restaurant providing a wide range of popular dishes and grills.

Sitwell Arms, Renishaw

ROOMS: 29 en suite (8 fmly) No smoking in 10 bedrooms s £38-£61; d £60-£80 (incl. bkfst) **LB** **FACILITIES:** Xmas **CONF:** Thtr 160 Class 60 Board 60 Del from £70 **PARKING:** 150 **NOTES:** No dogs (ex guide dogs) No smoking in restaurant Civ Wed 80
CARDS:

See advert on opposite page

RETFORD (EAST), Nottinghamshire — Map 08 SK78

★★★65% The West Retford Hotel

24 North Rd DN22 7XG
☎ 0870 609 6162 🖹 01777 709951
Dir: *From A1 take A620 to Ranby/Retford. Left at rdbt into North Rd (A638). Hotel on right*

Set in attractive grounds close to the town centre, this 18th-century manor house offers a good range of well-equipped meeting facilities. The spacious, well laid out bedrooms and suites are located in separate buildings; the Garden Cottage rooms are particularly pleasing.
ROOMS: 62 annexe en suite (37 fmly) (34 GF) No smoking in 36 bedrooms s £65-£99; d £77-£99 **LB** **FACILITIES:** STV Croquet lawn **CONF:** Thtr 150 Class 40 Board 43 Del from £80 **PARKING:** 100 **NOTES:** No smoking in restaurant Civ Wed 120
CARDS:

GF Indicates the number of bedrooms at ground floor level.

RICHMOND, North Yorkshire — Map 19 NZ

★★★66% King's Head

Market Place DL10 4HS
☎ 01748 850220 🖹 01748 850635
e-mail: res@kingsheadrichmond.co.uk
Dir: *leave A1 or A66 at Scotch Corner & take A6108 to Richmond. Follow signs to town centre*

Centrally located in the historic market square, this hotel is a converted former coaching inn. Bedrooms are comfortable and tastefully furnished. The lounge, furnished with deep sofas, displays an interesting collection of antique clocks. Afternoon tea is served in the lounge/bar along with light meals and the elegant restaurant offers a varied choice of more formal dining.
ROOMS: 26 en suite 4 annexe en suite (1 fmly) No smoking in 11 bedrooms s £67; d £92-£120 (incl. bkfst) **LB** **FACILITIES:** STV **CONF:** Thtr 180 Class 80 Board 50 Del from £80 **PARKING:** 25 **NOTES:** No smoking in restaurant **CARDS:**

★★65% Frenchgate

59-61 Frenchgate DL10 7AE
☎ 01748 822087 🖹 01748 823596
e-mail: info@frenchgatehotel.com
Dir: *from Scotch Corner take A6108. Through Richmond to New Queens Rd rdbt, left into Dundas St and left again into Frenchgate*

This elegant townhouse dates from the 16th and 17th centuries. Bedrooms are brightly decorated and comfortably equipped. Public areas include an upstairs lounge with a low ceiling and original wooden beams. At dinner there is a good choice of freshly prepared dishes, and bar meals are also available.
ROOMS: 10 en suite 1 annexe en suite (1 fmly) (3 GF) No smoking in all bedrooms s £42-£75; d £70-£75 (incl. bkfst) **LB** **FACILITIES:** Award winning gardens ch fac Xmas **CONF:** BC Del from £60 **PARKING:** 9 **NOTES:** No smoking in restaurant **CARDS:**

Early start?
Hotels at all star levels should provide in-room alarm clocks and/or alarm calls

ICHMOND (UPON THAMES), Greater London
ee LONDON SECTION plan 1 C2

★★★★72% ⊛⊛
he Richmond Gate Hotel
ichmond Hill TW10 6RP
☎ 020 8940 0061 📠 020 8332 0354
-mail: richmondgate@corus.co.uk
ir: *from Richmond to top of Richmond Hill, hotel on left opposite Star & arter at Richmond Gate exit*

stylish Georgian hotel, sitting at the top of Richmond Hill and pposite the gates to Richmond Park. Bedrooms are equipped to a ery high standard and include luxury doubles and spacious

continued

suites. Dinner in the Park Restaurant features bold, contemporary cooking and is the highlight of any visit.

ROOMS: 68 en suite No smoking in 35 bedrooms s £120-£150; d £150-£178 (incl. bkfst) **LB FACILITIES: Spa** STV Indoor swimming (H) Sauna Solarium Gym Jacuzzi Health & beauty suite Steam room Xmas **CONF:** Thtr 50 Class 20 Board 30 Del £210 **PARKING:** 50 **NOTES:** No dogs (ex guide dogs) No smoking in restaurant Civ Wed 70 **CARDS:**

★★★68% ***Richmond Hill***
Richmond Hill TW10 6RW
☎ 020 8940 2247 📠 020 8940 5424
e-mail: richmondhill@corushotels.co.uk
Dir: *top of Richmond Hill on B321*

This attractive Georgian Manor built on Richmond Hill enjoys elevated views of the Thames. The town and the park are within easy walking distance. Bedrooms vary in size and style, all are comfortable and of modern design. The stylish, well-designed

continued on p510

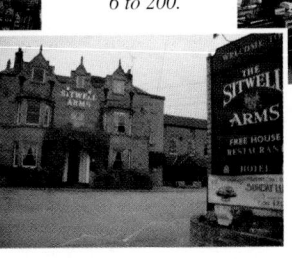

RICHMOND (UPON THAMES), continued

health club with large pool is shared with sister hotel the Richmond Gate.
ROOMS: 138 en suite (2 fmly) No smoking in 48 bedrooms **FACILITIES:** STV Indoor swimming (H) Sauna Solarium Gym Jacuzzi Steam room Health & beauty suite entertainment **CONF:** Thtr 180 Class 100 Board 50 **SERVICES:** Lift **PARKING:** 150 **NOTES:** Civ Wed 200
CARDS:

★★★62% *Bingham Hotel*

61-63 Petersham Rd TW10 6UT
☎ 020 8940 0902 020 8948 8737
e-mail: reservations@binghamhotel.co.uk
Dir: *on A307*

This period Georgian building overlooks the Thames and is within walking distance of the town centre. Bedrooms vary in size and style and comfortable public rooms enjoy views of the pretty garden and river. Diners can choose from a selection of meals from light snacks to three-course dinners.
ROOMS: 23 en suite (2 fmly) **FACILITIES:** Gym **CONF:** Thtr 60 Class 40 Board 25 **PARKING:** 12 **NOTES:** Civ Wed 40
CARDS:

RINGWOOD, Hampshire Map 05 SU10

★★★69% Tyrrells Ford Country House

Avon BH23 7BH
☎ 01425 672646 01425 672262
e-mail: tyrrellsford@aol.com
Dir: *off A31 to Ringwood. Follow B3347 and hotel 3m S on left at Avon*
Set in the New Forest, this delightful family-run hotel has much to offer. Most bedrooms have views over the open country. Diners may eat in the formal restaurant, or sample the wide range of bar meals, all prepared using fresh local produce. The Gallery lounge offers guests a peaceful area in which to relax.
ROOMS: 16 en suite s £70-£75; d £100-£130 (incl. bkfst) **LB** **FACILITIES:** Xmas **CONF:** Thtr 40 Class 20 Board 20 Del from £120 **PARKING:** 100 **NOTES:** No dogs (ex guide dogs) No smoking in restaurant Civ Wed 60 **CARDS:**

> Late for dinner?
> Quality Standards mean that last orders for dinner vary according to star rating and should be no earlier than:
> ★★ 7.00pm ★★★ 8.00pm ★★★★ 9.00pm
> ★★★★★ 10.00pm

★★72% Moortown Lodge Hotel

244 Christchurch Rd BH24 3AS
☎ 01425 471404 01425 476052
e-mail: hotel@moortownlodge.co.uk
Dir: *off A31 onto B3347. Hotel 1.5m S on right*
This charming Georgian hotel enjoys a good local reputation and attracts a healthy local dining trade, with many residents choosin to stay on a regular basis. Friendly and attentive service and comfortable bedrooms are provided. All rooms are tastefully decorated, one having a four-poster bed, and all are very well equipped with many thoughtful extras.
ROOMS: 6 rms (5 en suite) (1 fmly) No smoking in 3 bedrooms s £55-£70; d £70-£90 (incl. bkfst) **LB** **PARKING:** 8 **NOTES:** No dogs No smoking in restaurant Closed 24 Dec-mid Jan & 1 week in July
CARDS:

★★64% Candlesticks Inn

136 Christchurch Rd BH24 3AP
☎ 01425 472587 01425 471600
e-mail: info@hotelnewforest.co.uk
Dir: *from M27/A31, take B3347 to Christchurch. Hotel on right 0.5m from junct and flyover*
This attractive, thatched 15th-century inn is close to the town centre. The cottage-style bedrooms are contained in a modern adjacent lodge and include ground floor rooms together with a bedroom equipped for less able guests. Snacks can be taken in a bright conservatory bar lounge and there is also an atmospheric restaurant for more formal meals.
ROOMS: 8 en suite (1 fmly) s £49-£68; d £68 (incl. bkfst) **LB** **PARKING:** 45 **NOTES:** No dogs No children 2yrs Closed 23 Dec-9 Jan
CARDS:

Travelodge

St Leonards BH24 2NR
☎ 08700 850 950 0870 191 1736
Travelodge offers good quality, good value, modern accommodation. Ideal for families, the spacious, en suite bedrooms include remote-control TV, tea and coffee-making facilities, luxury beds and free morning newspaper. Meals can be taken at the nearby family restaurant. For further details and the Travelodge phone number, consult the Hotel Groups page.
ROOMS: s fr £42.95; d fr £42.95

RIPON, North Yorkshire Map 19 SE3

★★★69% Ripon Spa

Park St HG4 2BU
☎ 01765 602172 01765 690770
e-mail: spahotel@bronco.co.uk
Dir: *from A61 follow signs for B6265 towards Fountains Abbey. Hotel on left after hospital*
This privately owned and personally run hotel is set in extensive and attractive gardens, whilst being just a short walk from the city centre. It provides comfortable and traditional accommodation in a pleasant and relaxing environment. There are comfortable lounges, a terrace overlooking the gardens and the popular Turf Tavern. Traditional English cooking is served in the elegant main restaurant.
ROOMS: 40 en suite (5 fmly) (4 GF) No smoking in 8 bedrooms s £89-£110; d £97-£110 (incl. bkfst) **LB** **FACILITIES:** STV Croquet lawn Xmas **CONF:** Thtr 150 Class 35 Board 40 Del from £110 **SERVICES:** Lift **PARKING:** 60 **NOTES:** No smoking in restaurant Civ Wed 150
CARDS:

★★63% Unicorn
larket Place HG4 1BP
☎ 01765 602202 01765 690734
-mail: info@unicorn-hotel.co.uk
ir: on SE corner of Market Place, 4m from A1 on A61
entrally located in Ripon's ancient market place, this traditional nn dates back 500 years to when it was a coaching house. The usy pub and attractive restaurant feature a wide selection of ood value dishes. Bedrooms are of mixed styles and all offer the xpected amenities.
OOMS: 33 en suite (4 fmly) s £48; d £68 (incl. bkfst) **LB**
ACILITIES: entertainment **CONF:** Thtr 60 Class 10 Board 26 Del 94.50 **PARKING:** 20 **NOTES:** No smoking in restaurant Closed 24-25 ec **CARDS:**

ISLEY, Derbyshire — Map 11 SK43

★★★73% Risley Hall
)erby Rd DE72 3SS
☎ 0115 939 9000 0115 939 7766
-mail: enquiries@risleyhallhotel.co.uk
ir: M1 junct 25, Sandiacre exit. Left at T-junct, hotel 0.5m on left
his impressive, 11th-century manor house is set in beautiful listed ardens. Relaxing areas include a choice of bars, morning room, rivate dining rooms serving interesting menus, and a grand aronial hall. Many of the individually-styled bedrooms in the nain house boast antique furnishings, exposed beams and wall mbers, while the newly developed suites are exceptionally omfortable.
OOMS: 16 en suite 18 annexe en suite (8 fmly) **FACILITIES:** STV rchery **CONF:** Thtr 150 Class 80 Board 60 **SERVICES:** Lift **ARKING:** 120 **NOTES:** No dogs (ex guide dogs) No smoking in estaurant Civ Wed 120 **CARDS:**

See advert on this page

OCHDALE, Greater Manchester — Map 16 SD81

★★★★62% Norton Grange

Manchester Rd, Castleton OL11 2XZ
☎ 01706 630788 01706 649313
-mail: nortongrange@macdonald-hotels.co.uk
Dir: M62 junct 20, follow signs for A664, left after "All-in-One" Garden entre
tanding in nine acres of grounds and mature gardens, this /ictorian house provides comfort in elegant surroundings. The vell-equipped bedrooms have been refurbished to provide a host of extras for both the business and leisure guest. Public areas nclude the Pickwick bistro and bar and a smart restaurant, both ffering a good choice of dishes.
OOMS: 51 en suite No smoking in 40 bedrooms s £70-£99; d £80-£109 incl. bkfst) **LB** **FACILITIES:** STV Complimentary use of leisure centre mas **CONF:** Thtr 220 Class 120 Board 70 Del from £120 **ERVICES:** Lift **PARKING:** 150 **NOTES:** No smoking in restaurant Civ Wed 200 **CARDS:**

Town House Hotel
Country House Hotel
Travel Accommodation

Travel Inn
Newhey Rd, Milnrow OL16 4JF
☎ 08701 977219 01706 299074
Dir: M62 junct 21 at rdbt, right towards Shaw, under motorway bridge & take 1st left
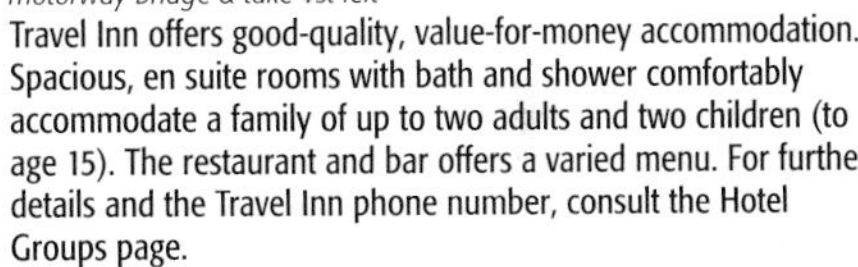
Travel Inn offers good-quality, value-for-money accommodation. Spacious, en suite rooms with bath and shower comfortably accommodate a family of up to two adults and two children (to age 15). The restaurant and bar offers a varied menu. For further details and the Travel Inn phone number, consult the Hotel Groups page.
ROOMS: 40 en suite s £44.95; d £44.95 **CONF:** Thtr 25 Board 12

ROCHESTER, Kent — Map 06 TQ76

U *Holiday Inn Rochester*
Maidstone Rd ME5 9SF
☎ 0870 400 9069 01634 684512
Dir: on A229 1m N of M2 junct 3. From A229 over rdbt. Hotel and airport signed 100yds on left
At the time of going to press, the classification for this hotel was not confirmed. Please refer to the AA internet site www.theAA.com for current information.
ROOMS: 150 en suite (45 fmly) No smoking in 93 bedrooms
FACILITIES: Indoor swimming (H) Sauna Solarium Gym Jacuzzi Steam room Beautician available at charge **CONF:** Thtr 90 Class 48 Board 40
SERVICES: Lift **PARKING:** 250 **CARDS:**

ROMALDKIRK, Co Durham
Map 19 NY92

Top 200 - Hotel

★★ Rose & Crown
DL12 9EB
☎ 01833 650213 01833 650828
e-mail: hotel@rose-and-crown.co.uk
Dir: *6m NW from Barnard Castle on B6277*

This charming country inn is located in the heart of the village, overlooking fine fell scenery. Attractively furnished bedrooms, including suites, are split between the main house and the rear courtyard. There is a cosy bar, warmed by log fires, and the welcoming restaurant, where good local produce features extensively on the menu. Service is both friendly and attentive.

ROOMS: 7 en suite 5 annexe en suite (1 fmly) No smoking in all bedrooms s £70-£80; d £98-£110 (incl. bkfst) **LB FACILITIES:** STV **PARKING:** 20 **NOTES:** No smoking in restaurant Closed 24-26 Dec **CARDS:**

ROMFORD, Greater London
Map 06 TQ58

Premier Lodge (Romford)

Whalebone Ln North, Chadwell Heath RM6 6QU
☎ 0870 9906450 0870 9906451

Premier Lodge offers modern, well-equipped, en suite accommodation suitable for both business and leisure travellers. Meals can be taken at the adjacent popular restaurant and bar, which is fully licensed. For further details, consult the Hotel Groups page.

ROOMS: 40 en suite s £56; d £56

Travel Inn

Mercury Gardens RM1 3EN
☎ 08701 977220 01708 760456
Dir: *off M25(J28), take A12 to Gallows Corner. Take A118 to next rbt and turn left*

Travel Inn offers good-quality, value-for-money accommodation. Spacious, en suite rooms with bath and shower comfortably accommodate a family of up to two adults and two children (to age 15). The restaurant and bar offers a varied menu. For further details and the Travel Inn phone number, consult the Hotel Groups page.

ROOMS: 40 en suite s £49.95-£54.95; d £49.95-£54.95

 AA Rosette Award for culinary excellence

ROMSEY, Hampshire
Map 05 SU3

★★★65% Potters Heron
Winchester Rd, Ampfield SO51 9ZF
☎ 0870 609 6155 023 8025 1359
e-mail: pottersheron@corushotels.com
Dir: *M3 junct 12 follow Chandlers Ford signs. 2nd exit at rdbt and follow signs for Ampfield, over x-rds and hotel on left after 1m*

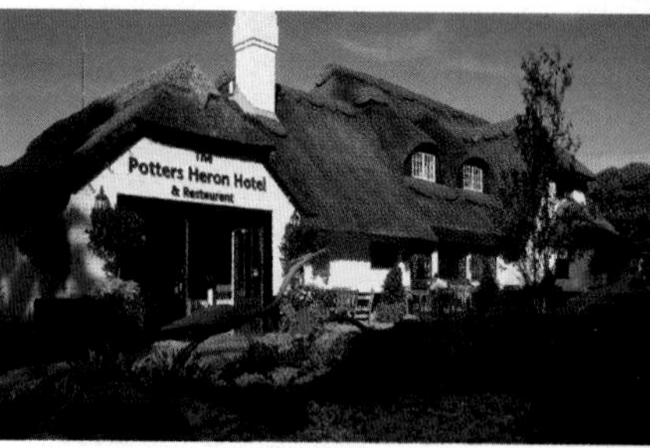

This distinctive thatched hotel retains many of its original features. Extensive refurbishment has taken place to offer modern, stylish accommodation and spacious public areas. The re-styled pub and restaurant offers an interesting range of dishes to suit a variety of tastes.

ROOMS: 54 en suite (29 GF) No smoking in 32 bedrooms s £55-£99; d £75-£109 **LB FACILITIES:** STV Sauna Xmas **CONF:** Thtr 120 Class 5 Board 45 Del £135 **SERVICES:** Lift **PARKING:** 150 **NOTES:** No smoking in restaurant Civ Wed 100 **CARDS:**

★★★62% The White Horse
Market Place SO51 8ZJ
☎ 0870 400 8123 01794 517485
e-mail: whitehorseromsey@macdonald-hotels.co.uk
Dir: *M27 junct 3, follow A3057 to Romsey, signs to town centre. Past hotel take 1st left into Latimer St, then left again into car park.*

Set in the heart of this historic town, the White Horse dates back to Elizabethan times. Bedrooms vary in size and all are well equipped. The majority of rooms have now benefited from refurbishment. The popular restaurant and the relaxing, character lounge are two particular attractions of the hotel.

ROOMS: 26 en suite 7 annexe en suite (7 fmly) (7 GF) No smoking in 10 bedrooms s £90; d £110 **LB FACILITIES:** STV Complimentary tickets for use of nearby leisure facilities Xmas **CONF:** Thtr 90 Class 60 Board 40 Del from £110 **PARKING:** 40 **NOTES:** No smoking in restaurant **CARDS:**

Premier Lodge (Southampton)
Romsey Rd, Ower SO51 6ZJ
☎ 0870 9906350 0870 9906351
Dir: *M27 junct 2, follow A36 towards Salisbury, follow brown tourist sign 'The Vine Inn'. 200yds on Romsey Rd on right*

Premier Lodge offers modern, well-equipped, en suite accommodation suitable for both business and leisure travellers. Meals can be taken at the adjacent popular restaurant and bar, which is fully licensed. For further details, consult the Hotel Groups page.

ROOMS: 50 en suite s £48; d £48 **CONF:** Thtr 150 Class 80 Board 60 Del from £85

ROSEDALE ABBEY, North Yorkshire Map 19 SE79

★★★68% Blacksmith's Country Inn

Hartoft End YO18 8EN
☎ 01751 417331 🖷 01751 417167
e-mail: blacksmiths.rosedale@virgin.net
Dir: *off A170 in village of Wrelton, N to Hartoft*

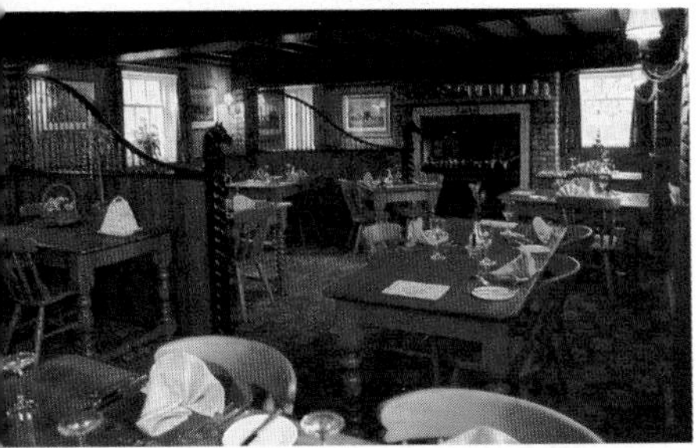

Set amongst the wooded valleys and hillsides of the Yorkshire Moors, this charming hotel offers a choice of popular bars and intimate, cosy lounges, and retains the friendly atmosphere of a country inn. Food is available either in the bars or the spacious restaurant while bedrooms vary in size and are all equipped to comfortable modern standards.

ROOMS: 19 en suite (2 fmly) No smoking in all bedrooms s £36.50; d £53-£63 (incl. bkfst) **LB FACILITIES:** Xmas **PARKING:** 50 **NOTES:** No smoking in restaurant **CARDS:**

See advert on this page

The
Blacksmith's Country Inn
ROSEDALE

Hartoft End, Rosedale Abbey
Pickering, North Yorkshire YO18 8EN
Tel: (01751) 417331 Fax: (01751) 417167

Set in the heart of the North Yorkshire Moors, this lovely 16th century hostelry has been fully refurbished to provide modern facilities yet retain all the original ambiance of years past. Cosy lounges, log fires. Enjoy superb food and wine in wonderful surroundings. Quality individual ensuite bedrooms some ground floor. Views over moors and forest. Resident owners.

★★72% *Milburn Arms*

YO18 8RA
☎ 01751 417312 🖷 01751 417541
e-mail: info@milburnarms.co.uk

This attractive inn dates back to the 16th century and enjoys an idyllic, peaceful location in this scenic village. Bedrooms, some of which are located in an adjacent stone block, are spacious, comfortable and smartly appointed. Guests can enjoy carefully prepared food either in the traditional bar or in the elegant panelled restaurant.

ROOMS: 3 en suite 8 annexe en suite (2 fmly) (4 GF) No smoking in all bedrooms **PARKING:** 10 **NOTES:** No smoking in restaurant Civ Wed 100 **CARDS:**

★★66% *White Horse Farm*

YO18 8SE
☎ 01751 417239 🖷 01751 417781
e-mail: sales@whitehorsefarmhotel.co.uk
Dir: *A170, from Pickering towards Thirsk, right to Wrelton, Cropton & Rosedale for 7m. At Rosedale take 1st left along Chimney Bark, hotel 500yds on left.*

From its elevated position above the village, this hotel enjoys

continued

magnificent views over the moors. Bedrooms, whether in the main house or an adjoining building in the gardens, are individually and attractively decorated. Meals are served in the bar or in the restaurant. There is also a cosy residents' lounge, and extensive private dog-walking areas.

ROOMS: 9 en suite 4 annexe en suite (3 fmly) No smoking in all bedrooms **PARKING:** 60 **NOTES:** No smoking in restaurant **CARDS:**

ROSSINGTON, South Yorkshire Map 16 SK69

★★★73% Mount Pleasant

Great North Rd DN11 0HW
☎ 01302 868696 & 868219 🖷 01302 865130
e-mail: reception@mountpleasant.co.uk
Dir: *on A638 Great North Rd between Bawtry and Doncaster*

Best Western

This charming house dates back to the 18th century and stands in 100 acres of wooded parkland. The spacious bedrooms have been thoughtfully equipped and pleasantly furnished, the Premier bedrooms being particularly comfortable. Public rooms have been extended to include an elegant restaurant and a very comfortable bar lounge. The hotel has good meeting facilities and a licence for civil weddings.

ROOMS: 37 en suite (12 fmly) (18 GF) No smoking in all bedrooms s £90-£160; d £105-£175 (incl. bkfst) **LB CONF:** Thtr 100 Class 60 Board 60 Del from £135 **PARKING:** 100 **NOTES:** No dogs (ex guide dogs) No smoking in restaurant Closed 25 Dec RS 24 Dec Civ Wed 150 **CARDS:**

ROSS-ON-WYE, Herefordshire

Map 10 SO52

See also Goodrich & Symonds Yat

★★★74% Pengethley Manor

Pengethley Park HR9 6LL
☎ 01989 730211 01989 730238
e-mail: reservations@pengethleymanor.co.uk
Dir: *4m N on A49 Hereford road, from Ross-On-Wye*

This fine Georgian mansion is set in extensive grounds with two vineyards and glorious views. The accommodation is tastefully appointed and there is a wide variety of bedroom styles, all similarly well equipped. The elegant public rooms are furnished in a style sympathetic to the character of the house.

ROOMS: 11 en suite 14 annexe en suite (3 fmly) (4 GF) **FACILITIES:** Outdoor swimming (H) Golf 9 Fishing Croquet lawn Golf improvement course, walks accessible from Hotel Xmas **CONF:** Thtr 70 Class 25 Board 28 **PARKING:** 70 **NOTES:** No smoking in restaurant Civ Wed 90 **CARDS:**

See advert on opposite page

★★★69% Chase

Gloucester Rd HR9 5LH
☎ 01989 763161 01989 768330
e-mail: info@chasehotel.co.uk
Dir: *M50 junct 4, 1st left exit towards rdbt, left at rdbt towards A40. Right at 2nd rdbt towards Ross-on-Wye town centre, hotel 0.5m on left*

This attractive Georgian mansion sits in its own landscaped grounds and is only a short walk from the town centre. Bedrooms, some of which have been refurbished, vary in size and character and include two four-poster rooms. There is also a light and spacious bar and an elegant restaurant together with a large function suite.

ROOMS: 36 en suite (1 fmly) No smoking in 10 bedrooms s £75-£115; d £90-£155 (incl. bkfst) **LB** **FACILITIES:** STV Gym fitness room **CONF:** Thtr 300 Class 100 Board 80 Del from £117 **PARKING:** 150 **NOTES:** No dogs (ex guide dogs) No smoking in restaurant Closed 26-30 Dec Civ Wed 300 **CARDS:**

★★★69% *Pencraig Court*

Pencraig HR9 6HR
☎ 01989 770306 01989 770040
e-mail: info@pencraig-court.co.uk
Dir: *off A40 into Pencraig, 4m S of Ross-on-Wye*

Impressive views of the River Wye and Ross-on-Wye beyond set the scene for a relaxing stay at this former Georgian mansion. The proprietors are also on hand to ensure personal attention and service whilst the bedrooms enjoy a traditional feel and include a room with a four-poster bed. The country house ambience is completed with a choice of lounges and an elegant restaurant.

ROOMS: 10 en suite (1 fmly) No smoking in 6 bedrooms **FACILITIES:** Fishing Croquet lawn **PARKING:** 20 **NOTES:** No smoking in restaurant **CARDS:**

★★★67% The Royal

Palace Pound HR9 5HZ
☎ 01989 565105 01989 768058
e-mail: 6504@greeneking.co.uk
Dir: *at end of M50 take A40 'Monmouth'. At 3rd rdbt, left to Ross, over bridge and take road signed 'The Royal Hotel' after left bend*

Close to the town centre, this imposing hotel enjoys panoramic views from its prominent hilltop position. Reputedly visited by Charles Dickens in 1867, The Royal Hotel has been sympathetically furnished to create the ambience of a bygone era with comforts of today. In addition to the lounge and elegant restaurant, there is an attractive garden and function rooms.

ROOMS: 42 en suite (1 fmly) No smoking in 18 bedrooms s £75-£95; d £95-£135 (incl. bkfst) **LB** **FACILITIES:** Xmas **CONF:** Thtr 85 Class 20 Board 28 Del from £100 **PARKING:** 44 **NOTES:** No smoking in restaurant Civ Wed 60 **CARDS:**

★★74% *Glewstone Court*

Glewstone HR9 6AW
☎ 01989 770367 01989 770282
e-mail: glewstone@aol.com
Dir: *from Ross Market Place take A40/A49 Monmouth/Hereford, over Wilton Bridge to rdbt, turn left onto A40 to Monmouth, after 1m turn right for Glewstone*

This elegant and charming hotel enjoys an elevated position with views over Ross-on-Wye, and is set in well-tended gardens. Informal service is delivered with great enthusiasm by Bill Reeve-Tucker, and the kitchen is the domain of Christine Reeve-Tucker who offers an extensive menu of well executed dishes. Bedrooms come in a variety of sizes and are tastefully furnished and well equipped.

ROOMS: 8 en suite (2 fmly) **FACILITIES:** Croquet lawn **CONF:** Thtr 35 Board 16 **PARKING:** 25 **NOTES:** Closed 25-27 Dec **CARDS:**

Early start?
Hotels at all star levels should provide in-room alarm clocks and/or alarm calls

★★74% Wilton Court Hotel

Wilton Ln HR9 6AQ
☎ 01989 562569 01989 768460
e-mail: info@wiltoncourthotel.com
Dir: *M50 junct 4 onto A40 towards Monmouth at 3rd rdbt turn left signed Ross then take 1st right, hotel on right*

Dating back to the 16th century, this engaging hotel has great charm with a wealth of character. Standing on the banks of the River Wye and just a short walk from the town centre, there is a genuinely relaxed, friendly and unhurried atmosphere here. Bedrooms are tastefully furnished and well equipped, while public

continued

reas include a comfortable lounge, traditional bar and pleasant estaurant with a conservatory extension overlooking the garden.

ROOMS: 11 en suite (1 fmly) No smoking in all bedrooms s £55-£75; d £80-£105 (incl. bkfst) **LB** **FACILITIES:** Fishing Xmas **CONF:** Thtr 40 Class 25 Board 25 Del from £107.50 **PARKING:** 24 **NOTES:** No smoking in restaurant **CARDS:**

★★71% Castle Lodge Hotel

Wilton HR9 6AD
☎ 01989 562234 📠 01989 768322
e-mail: carlos@castlelodge.co.uk
Dir: *on rdbt at junct of A40/A49, 0.5m from centre of Ross-on-Wye*

This friendly hotel dates back to the 16th century and offers a convenient base on the outskirts of the town. Bedrooms are well equipped and comfortably furnished, while diners can choose between a good selection of bar meals and a varied restaurant menu, which features a wide range of fresh seafood.

ROOMS: 10 en suite (3 fmly) s £41.95; d £49.95 **LB** **FACILITIES:** tennis courts(0.5m) **CONF:** Thtr 100 Class 80 Board 60 Del £95 **PARKING:** 40 **CARDS:**

★★67% Bridge House

Wilton HR9 6AA
☎ 01989 562655
Dir: *0.5m N of Ross-on-Wye, rdbt at junct of A40/A49, hotel 250yds from rdbt, towards Ross, at end of Wilton Bridge*

This Georgian house has a large garden extending to the banks of the River Wye. The privately-owned and personally-run hotel has a well-deserved reputation for friendliness. Modern accommodation includes several spacious rooms, including one with a four-poster bed as a feature.

ROOMS: 8 en suite (1 fmly) s £40-£45; d £68-£75 (incl. bkfst) **LB** **PARKING:** 12 **NOTES:** No dogs (ex guide dogs) No smoking in restaurant **CARDS:**

★★67% Orles Barn

THE CIRCLE
Selected Individual Hotels
GREAT BRITAIN

Wilton HR9 6AE
☎ 01989 562155 📠 01989 768470
e-mail: orles.barn@clara.net
Dir: *off junct A40/A49*

This privately-owned and personally-run hotel stands in extensive gardens. All of the bedrooms are well maintained and thoughtfully equipped. The owners' South African heritage is reflected in the restaurant menu. Extra facilities include an outdoor heated swimming pool

ROOMS: 8 en suite (1 fmly) No smoking in 2 bedrooms s £51; d £68-£78 (incl. bkfst) **LB** **FACILITIES:** Outdoor swimming (H) Fishing Xmas **CONF:** Board 16 **PARKING:** 20 **NOTES:** No dogs (ex guide dogs) No smoking in restaurant **CARDS:**

TV dinner?
Room service at three stars and above

R

ROSS-ON-WYE, continued

★★66% Chasedale
Walford Rd HR9 5PQ
☎ 01989 562423 ▯ 01989 567900
e-mail: chasedale@supanet.com
Dir: *from Ross-on-Wye town centre, S on B4234, hotel 0.5m on left*
This large mid-Victorian property is situated on the south-west outskirts of the town. Privately owned and personally run, it provides with spacious, well-proportioned public areas and extensive grounds. The accommodation is well equipped and includes ground floor and family rooms, whilst the restaurant offers a wide selection of wholesome food.
ROOMS: 10 en suite (2 fmly) (1 GF) No smoking in 1 bedroom s £35.50-£37.50; d £71-£75 (incl. bkfst) **LB** **FACILITIES:** Xmas **CONF:** Thtr 40 Class 30 Board 25 **PARKING:** 14 **NOTES:** No smoking in restaurant **CARDS:**

★★65% King's Head
8 High St HR9 5HL
THE INDEPENDENTS
☎ 01989 763174 ▯ 01989 769578
e-mail: reception@kingshead.co.uk
Dir: *in town centre*

The King's Head dates back to the 14th century and has a wealth of charm and character. Bedrooms are well equipped and include a room with a four-poster bed and family rooms. Over half are located on the ground and first floors of a purpose built annexe to the rear. The restaurant doubles as a coffee shop during the day and is popular with locals. There is also a very pleasant bar and comfortable lounge.
ROOMS: 16 en suite 9 annexe en suite s £48.50; d £90 (incl. bkfst) **LB** **FACILITIES:** Xmas **PARKING:** 24 **NOTES:** No smoking in restaurant **CARDS:**

Travel Inn
Ledbury Rd HR9 7QL
travel inn
☎ 08701 977221 ▯ 01989 566124
Dir: *1m from town centre on M50 rdbt*
Travel Inn offers good-quality, value-for-money accommodation. Spacious, en suite rooms with bath and shower comfortably accommodate a family of up to two adults and two children (to age 15). The restaurant and bar offers a varied menu. For further details and the Travel Inn phone number, consult the Hotel Groups page.
ROOMS: 43 en suite s £44.95; d £44.95

ROSTHWAITE, Cumbria — Map 18 NY2
See also Borrowdale

★★64% Scafell
CA12 5XB
☎ 017687 77208 ▯ 017687 77280
e-mail: info@scafell.ws
Dir: *6m S of Keswick on B5289*

This friendly hotel is popular with walkers and enjoys a peaceful location. Bedrooms vary in style from traditional to modern, and are all well equipped and neatly decorated. Public areas include a residents' cocktail bar, lounge and spacious restaurant as well as the popular Riverside Inn pub, offering all day dining in summer months.
ROOMS: 24 en suite (2 fmly) (8 GF) s £66.50; d £133 (incl. bkfst & dinner) **LB** **FACILITIES:** Guided walks Xmas **PARKING:** 50 **NOTES:** No smoking in restaurant Civ Wed 75 **CARDS:**

ROTHERHAM, South Yorkshire — Map 16 SK49

★★★★64% Hellaby Hall
Old Hellaby Ln, Hellaby S66 8SN
☎ 01709 702701 ▯ 01709 700979
e-mail: reservations@hellabyhallhotel.co.uk
Dir: *1m off M18 junct 1, onto A631 towards Maltby, in village of Hellaby*

This 17th-century house was built to a Flemish design with high, beamed ceilings, and staircases which lead off to the private meeting rooms and a series of oak-panelled lounges. Bedrooms are elegant and well equipped. Guests can dine in the formal Attic Restaurant, or Rizzio's informal pizzeria-restaurant/bar, and there

continued

are extensive leisure facilities, conference areas and the hotel holds a civil wedding licence.
ROOMS: 52 en suite (4 fmly) No smoking in 31 bedrooms s £45-£105; d £79-£165 (incl. bkfst) **LB** **FACILITIES: Spa** STV Indoor swimming (H) Sauna Solarium Gym Croquet lawn Putting green Indoor swimming pool supervised, Beauty room Xmas **CONF:** Thtr 140 Class 21 Board 40 Del from £100 **SERVICES:** Lift **PARKING:** 140 **NOTES:** No dogs (ex guide dogs) No smoking in restaurant Civ Wed 85
CARDS:

See advert on this page

★★★74% Consort

Brampton Rd, Thurcroft S66 9JA
☎ 01709 530022 🖹 01709 531529
e-mail: info@consorthotel.com
Dir: *M18 junct 1, right towards Bawtry on A631. 250yds to rdbt and in further 200yds turn left then 1.5m to x-rds, hotel opposite*
Bedrooms at this modern, friendly hotel are comfortable, attractive and air conditioned, and include ten superior rooms in a new wing. A wide range of dishes is served in the open-plan bar and restaurant, and there is a comfortable foyer lounge. Conference and function facilities are excellent; entertainment evenings are often hosted here.
ROOMS: 27 en suite (2 fmly) (9 GF) No smoking in 8 bedrooms s £42-£63; d £63-£84 (incl. bkfst) **LB** **FACILITIES:** STV entertainment **CONF:** Thtr 300 Class 120 Board 50 Del from £80 **SERVICES:** air con **PARKING:** 90 **NOTES:** No dogs (ex guide dogs) No smoking in restaurant Civ Wed 300 **CARDS:**

See advert on this page

★★★69% Best Western Elton

Main St, Bramley S66 2SF
☎ 01709 545681 🖹 01709 549100
e-mail: bestwestern.eltonhotel@btinternet.com
Dir: *M18 junct 1 follow A631 Rotherham, turn right to Ravenfield, hotel at end of Bramley village, follow brown signs*
Within easy reach of the M18, this welcoming, stone-built hotel has well-tended gardens. Elton Hotel offers good modern accommodation, with larger rooms in the extension, that are particularly comfortable and well equipped. A civil licence is held for wedding ceremonies and conference rooms are available.
ROOMS: 13 en suite 16 annexe en suite (4 fmly) (11 GF) No smoking in 11 bedrooms s £49-£80; d £68-£88.50 (incl. bkfst) **LB** **FACILITIES:** STV **CONF:** Thtr 55 Class 24 Board 26 Del from £90 **PARKING:** 48 **NOTES:** Civ Wed 50 **CARDS:**

★★★67% Courtyard by Marriott, Rotherham

West Bawtry Rd S60 4NA
☎ 01709 830630 🖹 01709 830549
e-mail: rotherham@courtyardhotels.co.uk
Dir: *M1 junct 33, A630 towards Rotherham, hotel 0.5m on right*
Stylish and contemporary, this modern hotel is well located just five minutes from the motorway. Bedrooms are spacious and boast an excellent range of facilities. Guests have the use of the refurbished leisure club with its extensive swimming pool, spa bath and steam room.
ROOMS: 104 en suite (10 fmly) (22 GF) No smoking in 76 bedrooms s £47-£89; d £64-£102 (incl. bkfst) **LB** **FACILITIES: Spa** STV Indoor swimming (H) Solarium Gym Jacuzzi Steam room, Childrens pool **CONF:** Thtr 300 Class 120 Board 40 Del from £110 **SERVICES:** Lift **PARKING:** 222 **NOTES:** No dogs (ex guide dogs) Civ Wed 100 **CARDS:**

R

ROTHERHAM, continued

★★★62% **Carlton Park**
102/104 Moorgate Rd S60 2BG
☎ 01709 849955 📠 01709 368960
e-mail: reservations@carltonparkhotel.com
Dir: *M1 junct 33, onto A631, then A618. Hotel 800yds past Hospital*
This modern hotel is situated in a pleasant residential area of the town, close to the District General Hospital, yet within minutes of the M1. Bedrooms and bathrooms have been totally refurbished and offer very modern comfort and facilities. Three have separate sitting rooms. The restaurant and bar provide a lively atmosphere, and are popular with locals.
ROOMS: 80 en suite (14 fmly) (16 GF) No smoking in 33 bedrooms s £35.50-£79; d £51-£89.50 (incl. bkfst) **LB FACILITIES:** STV Sauna Solarium Gym Jacuzzi entertainment Xmas **CONF:** Thtr 250 Class 160 Board 60 Del from £99 **SERVICES:** Lift **PARKING:** 120 **NOTES:** No dogs (ex guide dogs) No smoking in restaurant Civ Wed 100
CARDS:

⌂ ***Campanile***
Hellaby Industrial Estate, Lowton Way, Denby Way S66 8RY
☎ 01709 700255 📠 01709 545169
e-mail: rotherham@envergure.co.uk
Dir: *M18 junct 1. Follow signs for Maltby off rdbt. Left at lights, 2nd on left*

This modern building offers accommodation in smart, well-equipped bedrooms, all with en suite bathrooms. Refreshments may be taken at the informal Bistro. For further details and the Campanile phone number, consult the Hotel Groups page.
ROOMS: 50 en suite **CONF:** Thtr 35 Class 18 Board 20

⌂ **Hotel Ibis Rotherham**
Moorhead Way, Bramley S66 1YY
☎ 01709 730333 📠 01709 730444
e-mail: H3163@accor-hotels.com
Dir: *M18 junct 1, left at rdbt & left at 1st lights. Hotel next to supermarket*
Modern, budget hotel offering comfortable accommodation in bright and practical bedrooms. Breakfast is self-service and dinner is available in the restaurant. For further details, consult the Hotel Groups page.
ROOMS: 86 en suite s £29.95-£42.95; d £29.95-£42.95

⌂ **Travel Inn**
Bawtry Rd S65 3JB
☎ 08701 977222 📠 01709 531546
Dir: *on A631 towards Wickersley, between M18 junct 1 & M1 junct 33*
Travel Inn offers good-quality, value-for-money accommodation. Spacious, en suite rooms with bath and shower comfortably accommodate a family of up to two adults and two children (to age 15). The restaurant and bar offers a varied menu. For further details and the Travel Inn phone number, consult the Hotel Groups page.
ROOMS: 37 en suite s £44.95; d £44.95

ROTHERWICK, Hampshire Map 05 SU75

Top 200 - Hotel

★★★★ ⊛⊛ **Tylney Hall**
RG27 9AZ
☎ 01256 764881 📠 01256 768141
e-mail: sales@tylneyhall.com
Dir: *M3 junct 5, A287 to Basingstoke, over junct with A30, over railway bridge, towards Newnham. Right at Newnham Green. Hotel 1m on left*
A superb Grade II listed Victorian country house set in 66 acres of beautiful parkland. The hotel offers very high standards of comfort in relaxed yet elegant surroundings and features magnificent restored water gardens, which were originally laid out by Gertrude Jekyll. The spacious public rooms include the Wedgwood drawing room and panelled Oak Room, which are filled with fresh flowers and warmed by log fires. The spacious bedrooms are traditionally furnished and offer a high degree of comfort.
ROOMS: 35 en suite 77 annexe en suite (1 fmly) s £135-£400; d £165-£430 (incl. bkfst) **LB FACILITIES: Spa** STV Indoor swimming (H) Outdoor swimming (H) Tennis (hard) Snooker Sauna Solarium Gym Croquet lawn Clay pigeon shooting, Archery, Falconry, Balloon rides, Laser shooting entertainment Xmas
CONF: BC Thtr 120 Class 70 Board 40 Del from £190
PARKING: 120 **NOTES:** No dogs (ex guide dogs) No smoking in restaurant Civ Wed 100 **CARDS:**

ROTHLEY, Leicestershire Map 11 SK51

★★★61% ***Rothley Court***
Westfield Ln LE7 7LG
☎ 0116 237 4141 📠 0116 237 4483
Dir: *on B5328*

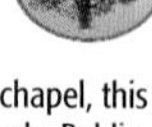

Dating back to the 1500s and complete with its own chapel, this historic property sits in six acres of well-tended grounds. Public areas retain much of their original character and include an oak-panelled restaurant and a choice of function and meeting rooms. Bedrooms, some located in an adjacent stable block, are individually styled.
ROOMS: 13 en suite 21 annexe en suite No smoking in 14 bedrooms **CONF:** Thtr 100 Class 35 Board 35 **PARKING:** 100 **NOTES:** No smoking in restaurant **CARDS:**

★★72% ***The Limes***
35 Mountsorrel Ln LE7 7PS
☎ 0116 230 2531
Dir: *turn of old A6. Hotel off village green*
A relaxed and friendly environment prevails at The Limes. Public areas include a comfortable lounge bar and a smart restaurant. The well-maintained accommodation is equipped for the needs of its predominantly business clientele, with excellent facilities and comfortable executive swivel chairs. Good secure car parking is a bonus.
ROOMS: 11 en suite **SERVICES:** air con **PARKING:** 15 **NOTES:** No dogs (ex guide dogs) No children 14yrs Closed 23 Dec-2 Jan
CARDS:

ROWLAND'S CASTLE, Hampshire Map 05 SU71

⌂ Innkeeper's Lodge Portsmouth North
Whichers Gate Rd PO9 6BB
☎ 0870 243 0500 & 02392 413761
Dir: *M3 junct 2, at rdbt, right onto B2149 (Rowlands Castle). After 2m, left onto B2148 Whichers Gate Rd, lodge on left*
A new concept in the travel accommodation market. Smart rooms meet essential business requirements but also have home comforts. Dining options include all-day menus plus the added advantage of breakfast, which is included in the room price. For further details, consult the Hotel Groups page.
ROOMS: 21 en suite

ROWNHAMS MOTORWAY SERVICE AREA (M27), Hampshire Map 05 SU31

⌂ Travel Inn (Southampton West)
Rownhams Service Area SO16 8AP
☎ 08701 977234 📠 023 8074 0204
Dir: *M27 westbound between junct 3 & 4*
Travel Inn offers good-quality, value-for-money accommodation. Spacious, en suite rooms with bath and shower comfortably accommodate a family of up to two adults and two children (to age 15). The restaurant and bar offers a varied menu. For further details and the Travel Inn phone number, consult the Hotel Groups page.
ROOMS: 39 en suite s £44.95; d £44.95

ROWSLEY, Derbyshire Map 16 SK26

★★★77% ® **East Lodge Country House**
DE4 2EF
☎ 01629 734474 📠 01629 733949
e-mail: info@eastlodge.com
Dir: *A6, 3m from Bakewell, 5m from Matlock*

This delightful country-house hotel enjoys a romantic setting in ten acres of landscaped grounds and gardens. Stylish bedrooms are thoughtfully equipped and have lovely garden views. Comfortable public areas include an elegant restaurant, popular for its imaginative cuisine, and a tastefully furnished conservatory lounge where afternoon teas and light meals are served.
ROOMS: 14 en suite (2 fmly) No smoking in all bedrooms s £80-£120; d £100-£150 (incl. bkfst) **LB FACILITIES:** Croquet lawn Xmas **CONF:** Thtr 75 Class 20 Board 22 Del £125 **PARKING:** 40 **NOTES:** No dogs No children 7yrs No smoking in restaurant Civ Wed 100
CARDS:

See advert under BAKEWELL

RUAN HIGH LANES, Cornwall & Isles of Scilly Map 02 SW93

★★74% **Hundred House**
TR2 5JR
☎ 01872 501336 📠 01872 501151
e-mail: clarke@hundredhousehotel.co.uk
Dir: *from B3287 at Tregony, left onto A3078 to St Mawes, hotel 4m on right*
Set in attractive gardens, this Edwardian house offers good access to the Roseland Peninsula, and is an ideal base for a relaxing break or for touring the area. Bedrooms are comfortable and spacious. Both dinner and breakfast offer freshly cooked and appetising dishes. Staff are friendly and attentive.
ROOMS: 10 en suite No smoking in all bedrooms s £66-£74; d £132-£148 (incl. bkfst & dinner) **LB FACILITIES:** Croquet lawn **PARKING:** 15 **NOTES:** No dogs (ex guide dogs) No children 12yrs No smoking in restaurant Closed 2 Nov-4 Mar **CARDS:**

RUGBY, Warwickshire Map 11 SP57

★★★66% **Brownsover Hall**
Brownsover Ln, Old Brownsover CV21 1HU
☎ 0870 609 6104 📠 01788 579241
e-mail: brownsoverhall@corushotels.com
Dir: *M6 junct 1, signs to Rugby A426. Dual-carriageway for 0.5m at rdbt signed "Ambulance & Brownsover Hall Hotel" turn right. Hotel 400mtrs on right*

A mock-Gothic hall designed by Sir Gilbert Scott, set in seven acres of wooded parkland. Bedrooms vary in size and style, including spacious and contemporary rooms in the converted stable block. The former chapel makes a stylish restaurant, and for a less formal meal or a relaxing drink, the rugby-themed bar is popular.
ROOMS: 27 en suite 20 annexe en suite (3 fmly) (12 GF) No smoking in 31 bedrooms s £35-£105; d £50-£112 **LB FACILITIES:** STV Free use of Esparta Gym (0.5 mile away) Xmas **CONF:** Thtr 70 Class 36 Board 35 Del from £100 **PARKING:** 100 **NOTES:** No smoking in restaurant Civ Wed 56 **CARDS:**

RUGBY, continued

★★★63% Grosvenor Hotel Rugby

81-87 Clifton Rd CV21 3QQ
☎ 01788 535686 🖷 01788 541297
e-mail: grosvenorrugby@btconnect.com
Dir: *M6 junct 1, turn right onto A426 towards Rugby centre, at 1st rdbt turn left on to T-junct and turn right onto B5414, hotel 2m on right*

Close to the town centre, this family-owned hotel is popular with both business and leisure guests. The public rooms are cosy, inviting and pleasantly furnished and service is both friendly and attentive. Bedrooms come in a variety of styles and sizes and include several newer rooms.
ROOMS: 26 en suite (3 fmly) No smoking in 21 bedrooms s £35-£78; d £89 **LB** **CONF:** Thtr 30 Class 20 Board 30 **PARKING:** 50
NOTES: No dogs (ex guide dogs) No smoking in restaurant Civ Wed 100
CARDS:

★★69% Golden Lion Inn

Easenhall CV23 0JA
☎ 01788 832265 🖷 01788 832878
e-mail: goldenlioninn@aol.com
Dir: *A426 Avon Mill rdbt turn to Newbold-upon-Avon B4112, approx 2m left at Harborough Parva sign, opposite agricultural showroom, then 1m to Easenhall*
This friendly, family-run, 16th-century inn is situated between Rugby and Coventry, near the M6. Bedrooms are all individually furnished (one with a stunning Chinese-style bed) and well equipped. There is a traditional, welcoming bar and a restaurant, both offering a wide choice of interesting dishes.
ROOMS: 12 en suite (1 fmly) No smoking in 8 bedrooms s £49; d £55-£69 (incl. bkfst) **FACILITIES:** STV Jacuzzi **CONF:** Thtr 8 Class 8 Board 8 Del £112 **PARKING:** 80 **NOTES:** No dogs (ex guide dogs) No smoking in restaurant **CARDS:**

R

★★65% *Hillmorton Manor*

78 High St, Hillmorton CV21 4EE
☎ 01788 565533 & 572403 🖷 01788 540027
Dir: *M1 junct 18, onto A428 to Rugby*
Formerly a Victorian manor house, this family-run hotel sits on the outskirts of Rugby, offering a delightful combination of home and hotel. Public rooms include an attractive airy restaurant and a comfortable bar and lounge. The bedrooms vary in style and size, and each room is comfortable and well equipped.
ROOMS: 11 en suite (1 fmly) **CONF:** Class 30 Board 65 **PARKING:** 40
NOTES: No smoking in restaurant **CARDS:**

⇧ Express by Holiday Inn Rugby

Brownsover Rd CV21 1HL
☎ 01788 550333 🖷 01788 550666
e-mail: ebhi-rugby@btconnect.com
A modern hotel ideal for families and business travellers. Fresh and uncomplicated, the spacious bedrooms include Sky TV, power shower and tea and coffee-making facilities. Continental buffet breakfast is included in the room rate; other meals may be taken at the nearby family pub or restaurant. For further details and the Express by Holiday Inn phone number, consult the Hotel Groups pages.

ROOMS: 49 en suite **CONF:** Thtr 30 Class 24 Board 16

⇧ Hotel Ibis Rugby East

Parklands NN6 7EX
☎ 01788 824331 🖷 01788 824332
e-mail: H3588@accor-hotels.com
(For full entry see Crick)

⇧ Innkeeper's Lodge Rugby

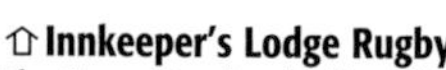

The Green, Dunchurch CV22 6NJ
☎ 01788 810305 🖷 01788 810931
Dir: *M1 junct 17/M45/A45. Follow signs for Dunchurch B4429. Lodge located in the village centre on x-rds of the A426 and B4429*
A new concept in the travel accommodation market. Smart rooms meet essential business requirements but also have home comforts. Dining options include all-day menus plus the added advantage of breakfast, which is included in the room price. For further details, consult the Hotel Groups page.
ROOMS: 16 en suite

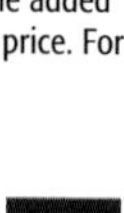

⇧ Travel Inn

Central Park Dr, Central Park CV23 0WE
☎ 08701 977223 🖷 01788 565949
Dir: *M6 junct 1, southbound onto A426. Travel Inn approx 1m on left at rdbt*
Travel Inn offers good-quality, value-for-money accommodation. Spacious, en suite rooms with bath and shower comfortably accommodate a family of up to two adults and two children (to age 15). The restaurant and bar offers a varied menu. For further details and the Travel Inn phone number, consult the Hotel Groups page.
ROOMS: 60 en suite s £44.95; d £44.95

⇧ Travel Inn Rugby

Central Park Dr, Central Park CV23 0WE
☎ 08701 977 223 🖷 01788 - 565949
Travel Inn offers good-quality, value-for-money accommodation. Spacious, en suite rooms with bath and shower comfortably accommodate a family of up to two adults and two children (to age 15). The restaurant and bar offers a varied menu. For further details and the Travel Inn phone number, consult the Hotel Groups page.
ROOMS: 60 en suite

RUGELEY, Staffordshire Map 10 SK01

⌂ Travelodge

Western Springs Rd WS15 2AS
☎ 08700 850 950 🖹 01889 570096
Dir: *on A51/B5013*
Travelodge offers good quality, good value, modern accommodation. Ideal for families, the spacious, en suite bedrooms include remote-control TV, tea and coffee-making facilities, luxury beds and free morning newspaper. Meals can be taken at the nearby family restaurant. For further details and the Travelodge phone number, consult the Hotel Groups page.
ROOMS: 32 en suite s fr £42.95; d fr £42.95

RUISLIP, Greater London
See LONDON SECTION plan 1 A5

★★★65% Barn Hotel

West End Rd HA4 6JB
☎ 01895 636057 🖹 01895 638379
e-mail: info@thebarnhotel.co.uk
Dir: *take A4180 (Polish War Memorial) exit off A40 to Ruislip, 2m to hotel entrance off a mini-rdbt before Ruislip underground station*
Once a farm, with parts dating back to the 17th century, this impressive property sits in three acres of gardens. Bedrooms vary in style, from contemporary to traditional oak-beamed varieties. All are comfortable and well appointed. The refurbished public areas provide a high level of quality and luxury.
ROOMS: 59 en suite (3 fmly) No smoking in 3 bedrooms s £70-£135; d £90-£185 (incl. bkfst) **LB FACILITIES:** STV Xmas **CONF:** Thtr 80 Class 50 Board 30 Del £140 **PARKING:** 42 **NOTES:** No dogs (ex guide dogs) No smoking in restaurant Civ Wed 70
CARDS:

See advert under UXBRIDGE

RUNCORN, Cheshire Map 15 SJ58

Holiday Inn Runcorn

Wood Ln, Beechwood WA7 3HA
☎ 0870 400 9070 🖹 01928 714611
Dir: *M56 junct 12, turn left at rdbt then 100yds on left, turn into Halton Station Rd under a railway bridge, continue into Wood Ln*
At the time of going to press, the classification for this hotel was not confirmed. Please refer to the AA internet site www.theAA.com for current information.
ROOMS: 150 en suite No smoking in 112 bedrooms **FACILITIES: Spa** STV Indoor swimming (H) Sauna Solarium Gym Jacuzzi Steam room **CONF:** Thtr 500 Class 60 Board 36 **SERVICES:** Lift **PARKING:** 210 **NOTES:** Civ Wed 200 **CARDS:**

⌂ *Campanile*

Lowlands Rd WA7 5TP
☎ 01928 581771 🖹 01928 581730
Dir: *M56 junct 12, take A557, then follow signs for Runcorn rail station*
This modern building offers accommodation in smart, well-equipped bedrooms, all with en suite bathrooms. Refreshments may be taken at the informal Bistro. For further details and the Campanile phone number, consult the Hotel Groups page.

ROOMS: 53 en suite **CONF:** Thtr 35 Class 28 Board 20

⌂ Travel Inn

Chester Rd, Preston Brook WA7 3BB
☎ 08701 977224 🖹 01928 719852
Dir: *1m from M56 junct 11, at Preston Brook*
Travel Inn offers good-quality, value-for-money accommodation. Spacious, en suite rooms with bath and shower comfortably accommodate a family of up to two adults and two children (to age 15). The restaurant and bar offers a varied menu. For further details and the Travel Inn phone number, consult the Hotel Groups page.
ROOMS: 40 en suite s £44.95; d £44.95 **CONF:** Thtr 40

RUSHDEN, Northamptonshire Map 11 SP96

⌂ Travelodge Wellingborough

Saunders Lodge NN10 9AP
☎ 08700 850 950 🖹 01933 57008
Dir: *on A45, eastbound*
Travelodge offers good quality, good value, modern accommodation. Ideal for families, the spacious, en suite bedrooms include remote-control TV, tea and coffee-making facilities, luxury beds and free morning newspaper. Meals can be taken at the nearby family restaurant. For further details and the Travelodge phone number, consult the Hotel Groups page.
ROOMS: 40 en suite s fr £42.95; d fr £42.95

RUSTINGTON, West Sussex Map 06 TQ00

⌂ Travelodge Littlehampton

Worthing Rd BN17 6LZ
☎ 08700 850 950 🖹 01903 733150
Dir: *on A259, 1m E of Littlehampton*
Travelodge offers good quality, good value, modern accommodation. Ideal for families, the spacious, en suite bedrooms include remote-control TV, tea and coffee-making facilities, luxury beds and free morning newspaper. Meals can be taken at the nearby family restaurant. For further details and the Travelodge phone number, consult the Hotel Groups page.
ROOMS: 36 en suite s fr £42.95; d fr £42.95

RYDE See Wight, Isle of

R

RYE, East Sussex Map 07 TQ92

★★★73% Flackley Ash
TN31 6YH
☎ 01797 230651 01797 230510
e-mail: enquiries@flackleyashhotel.co.uk
(For full entry see Peasmarsh and advert on opposite page)

★★★70% Mermaid Inn
Mermaid St TN31 7EY
☎ 01797 223065 & 223788 01797 225069
e-mail: mermaidinnrye@btclick.com
Dir: *A259, follow signs to town centre then into Mermaid St*

Situated near the top of a cobbled side street, this famous smugglers' inn is steeped in history. The charming interior has many architectural features such as attractive stone work. The bedrooms vary in size and style and are all tastefully furnished. Delightful public rooms include a choice of lounges, cosy bar and smart restaurant.
ROOMS: 31 en suite (5 fmly) s £75-£80; d £140-£190 (incl. bkfst) **LB** **FACILITIES:** Xmas **CONF:** Thtr 50 Class 40 Board 30 Del from £125 **PARKING:** 25 **NOTES:** No dogs (ex guide dogs) No smoking in restaurant **CARDS:**

★★★70% Rye Lodge
Hilder's Cliff TN31 7LD
☎ 01797 223838 01797 223585
e-mail: info@ryelodge.co.uk
Dir: *one-way system in Rye & signs for town centre, through Landgate arch, hotel 100yds on right*

Standing in an elevated position, Rye Lodge has panoramic views across Romney Marshes and the Rother Estuary. Bedrooms come in a variety of sizes and styles; they are attractively decorated, tastefully furnished and thoughtfully equipped. Public rooms feature The Terrace Room Restaurant, where an interesting choice of home-made dishes is available, and indoor leisure facilities.
ROOMS: 18 en suite s £60-£105; d £95-£185 (incl. bkfst) **LB** **FACILITIES: Spa** STV Indoor swimming (H) Sauna Aromatherapy Steam cabinet Xmas **PARKING:** 20 **NOTES:** No smoking in restaurant **CARDS:**

★★★63% The George
High St TN31 7JP
☎ 01797 222114 01797 224065
Situated in the centre of this popular town amidst a range of specialist shops, The George is full of character and offers comfortable public rooms including a bar, lounge and cosy restaurant which reflect the period of the building. The bedrooms have been sympathetically modernised and each one is thoughtfully equipped.
ROOMS: 22 en suite No smoking in 5 bedrooms s £60-£75; d £70-£90 (incl. bkfst) **LB** **FACILITIES:** STV entertainment Xmas **CONF:** BC Thtr 100 Class 40 Board 40 Del from £70 **PARKING:** 7 **NOTES:** No smoking in restaurant **CARDS:**

★★71% *Broomhill Lodge*
Rye Foreign TN31 7UN
☎ 01797 280421 01797 280402
Dir: *1.5m N on A268*
Built in the 1820s and set in its own grounds of three acres, this hotel is within easy reach of historic Rye, one of the Cinque Ports. Bedrooms are individually decorated, comfortably furnished and well-equipped. There are two lounges and an attractive restaurant.
ROOMS: 12 en suite **FACILITIES:** Sauna Mini gym **CONF:** Thtr 60 Class 60 Board 30 **PARKING:** 20 **NOTES:** No dogs No smoking in restaurant **CARDS:**

★★65% *The Hope Anchor*
Watchbell St TN31 7HA
☎ 01797 222216 01797 223796
e-mail: info@hotel-rye.freeserve.co.uk
This historic inn sits high above the town with enviable views out over the harbour and Romney Marsh, and is accessible from delightful cobbled streets. A relaxed and friendly atmosphere prevails and the attractively furnished bedrooms are well equipped and many enjoy good views over the marshes.
ROOMS: 12 rms (11 en suite) (1 fmly) No smoking in all bedrooms **NOTES:** No smoking in restaurant Closed 6 Jan-12 Jan **CARDS:**

SAFFRON WALDEN, Essex Map 12 TL53
See also Great Chesterford

★★69% Saffron
10-12 High St CB10 1AZ
☎ 01799 522676 01799 513979
e-mail: saffron.saffronwalden@oldenglishinns.co.uk
Dating back to the 16th century, this coaching inn retains much of its original character. The refurbished bedrooms are of a contemporary style and boast numerous facilities. There is a popular public bar and conservatory restaurant where a wide range of freshly prepared dishes is served.
ROOMS: 16 en suite (1 fmly) No smoking in all bedrooms s £70; d £90 (incl. bkfst) **LB** **FACILITIES:** Xmas **CONF:** Thtr 70 Class 50 Board 30 Del from £110 **PARKING:** 9 **NOTES:** No dogs (ex guide dogs) No smoking in restaurant **CARDS:**

ST AGNES, Cornwall & Isles of Scilly Map 02 SW75

★★71% Rosemundy House
Rosemundy Hill TR5 0UF
☎ 01872 552101 01872 554000
e-mail: info@rosemundy.co.uk
Dir: *off A30 to St Agnes continue for approx 3m. On entering village take 1st right signed Rosemundy, hotel at foot of hill*
This elegant Queen Anne house has been carefully restored and

continued

extended to provide comfortable bedrooms and spacious, inviting public areas. The hotel is set in well-maintained gardens complete with an outdoor pool for warmer months. There is a choice of relaxing lounges, two restaurants and a cosy bar.

ROOMS: 46 en suite (6 fmly) (9 GF) s £27-£47; d £54-£94 (incl. bkfst) **LB FACILITIES:** Outdoor swimming (H) Croquet lawn Putting green Xmas **CONF:** Board 80 **PARKING:** 50 **NOTES:** No dogs (ex guide dogs) No children 10 yrs No smoking in restaurant **CARDS:**

★★67% Sunholme

Goonvrea Rd TR5 0NW
☎ 01872 552318 📠 01872 552318
e-mail: jefferies@sunholme.co.uk
Dir: *on B3277, (museum on left at mini rdbt), follow brown signs*

Set in a quiet and attractive area away from the busy village, Sunholme has splendid views over the countryside towards the sea. Guests are assured of a friendly welcome, and many guests return to this relaxed, family run hotel. Bedrooms are comfortable and well equipped and many have good views.

ROOMS: 10 en suite (2 fmly) (2 GF) No smoking in all bedrooms s £26-£54; d £52-£78 (incl. bkfst) **LB PARKING:** 14 **NOTES:** No smoking in restaurant **CARDS:**

U Rose in Vale Country House

Mithian TR5 0QD
☎ 01872 552202 📠 01872 552700
e-mail: reception@rose-in-vale-hotel.co.uk
Dir: *A30 onto B3284 towards Perranporth, cross A3075, after 0.75m take 3rd left for Rose-in-Vale, hotel 0.5m on left*

At the time of going to press, the star classification for this hotel was not confirmed. Please refer to the AA internet site www.theAA.com for current information.

ROOMS: 18 en suite (3 fmly) s £62.50-£150; d £115-£185 (incl. bkfst) **LB FACILITIES:** Sauna Solarium Croquet lawn Xmas **CONF:** Thtr 75 Class 50 Board 40 Del £82 **PARKING:** 40 **NOTES:** No smoking in restaurant Closed Jan-Feb Civ Wed 75 **CARDS:**

ST ALBANS, Hertfordshire — Map 06 TL10

★★★★72% @@ Sopwell House Hotel, Country Club & Spa

Cottonmill Ln, Sopwell AL1 2HQ
☎ 01727 864477 📠 01727 844741/845636
e-mail: enquiries@sopwellhouse.co.uk
Dir: *M25 junct 22, follow A1081 St Albans. At Grill Bar lights, turn left, over mini rdbt into Cottonmill Lane*

This imposing Georgian country-house hotel retains an exclusive ambience. Bedrooms vary in style and include a number of self-contained cottages within the Sopwell Mews. Meeting and function rooms are housed in a separate section while the leisure

continued

facilities are particularly impressive. Eating options include the brasserie and the fine-dining Magnolia restaurant.

Sopwell House Hotel

ROOMS: 112 en suite 16 annexe en suite (12 fmly) s £99-£129; d £158-£169 **LB FACILITIES:** STV Indoor swimming (H) Sauna Solarium Gym Jacuzzi Health & Beauty Spa, Hairdressing salon Xmas **CONF:** BC Thtr 400 Class 220 Board 120 Del from £215 **SERVICES:** Lift **PARKING:** 350 **NOTES:** No smoking in restaurant Civ Wed 400 **CARDS:**

★★★78% @@ St Michael's Manor

Fishpool St AL3 4RY
☎ 01727 864444 📠 01727 848909
e-mail: reservations@stmichaelsmanor.com
Dir: *from St Albans Abbey follow Fishpool Street toward St Michael's village. Hotel 0.5m on left*

Adjacent to listed buildings, mills and ancient inns, this hotel is set in five acres of beautiful grounds, hidden from the street. Inside

continued on p524

S

ST ALBANS, continued

there is a real sense of luxury, encouraged by the high standard of décor and service. Award-winning food is served overlooking the immaculate gardens and the lake.

St Michael's Manor, St Albans

ROOMS: 22 en suite (1 fmly) No smoking in 3 bedrooms s £110-£140; d £130-£170 (incl. bkfst) **LB FACILITIES:** STV Croquet lawn Xmas **CONF:** Thtr 30 Class 20 Board 20 Del from £210 **PARKING:** 70 **NOTES:** No dogs (ex guide dogs) No smoking in restaurant Civ Wed 90
CARDS:

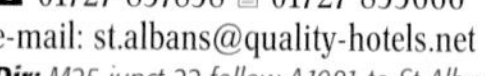

★★★61% Quality Hotel St Albans

232-236 London Rd AL1 1JQ
☎ 01727 857858 📠 01727 855666
e-mail: st.albans@quality-hotels.net
Dir: *M25 junct 22 follow A1081 to St Albans, after 2.5m hotel on left, before overhead bridge*

This hotel offers convenient access to and from the motorway network and the railway station in the town centre. The bedrooms are well equipped and there are also conference facilities. For relaxation, there is a comfortable bar which serves light snacks, and the Grapevine Restaurant serving more substantial meals.
ROOMS: 43 en suite (2 fmly) (12 GF) No smoking in 22 bedrooms s £49-£85; d £69-£110 (incl. bkfst) **FACILITIES:** STV **CONF:** Thtr 220 Class 40 Board 50 Del from £110 **PARKING:** 70 **NOTES:** No dogs (ex guide dogs) No smoking in restaurant
CARDS:

★★69% Comfort Hotel - Ryder House

Holywell Hill AL1 1HG
☎ 01727 848849 📠 01727 812210
e-mail: adin@gb055.u-net.com

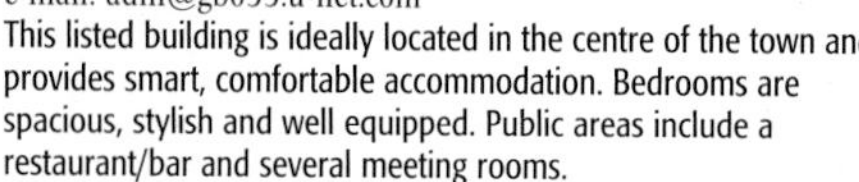

This listed building is ideally located in the centre of the town and provides smart, comfortable accommodation. Bedrooms are spacious, stylish and well equipped. Public areas include a restaurant/bar and several meeting rooms.
ROOMS: 60 en suite (18 fmly) No smoking in 40 bedrooms s £69; d £75 **FACILITIES:** STV **CONF:** Thtr 45 Class 30 Board 25 Del from £101 **SERVICES:** Lift **PARKING:** 60 **NOTES:** No smoking in restaurant
CARDS:

⇧ Express by Holiday Inn Luton-Hemel

London Rd, Flamstead AL3 8HT
☎ 01582 841332 📠 01582 842486
e-mail: ebhi-flamstead@btconnect.com

A modern hotel ideal for families and business travellers. Fresh and uncomplicated, the spacious bedrooms include Sky TV, power shower and tea and coffee-making facilities. Continental buffet breakfast is included in the room rate; other meals may be taken at the nearby family pub or restaurant. For further details and the Express by Holiday Inn phone number, consult the Hotel Groups pages.

ROOMS: 75 en suite **CONF:** Thtr 30 Class 24 Board 16

ST ANNES See Lytham St Annes

ST AUSTELL, Cornwall & Isles of Scilly

Map 02 SX05

★★★★74% ֍ Carlyon Bay

Sea Rd, Carlyon Bay PL25 3RD
☎ 01726 812304 📠 01726 814938
e-mail: reservations@carlyonbay.com
Dir: *from St Austell, follow signs for Charlestown. Carlyon Bay is signed on left, hotel at end of Sea Road*

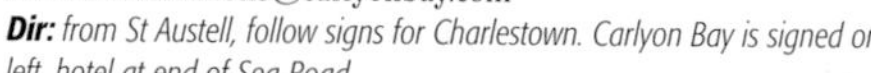

Originally built in the 1920s, this long established hotel lies on the cliff top in 250 acres of grounds, which include indoor and outdoor pools and a golf course. Facilities for families include kids' clubs and entertainment, and bedrooms are well maintained and include rooms with marvellous views of St Austell Bay. There is a good choice of comfortable lounges.
ROOMS: 87 en suite (14 fmly) s £85-£102; d £164-£258 (incl. bkfst) **LB FACILITIES: Spa** STV Indoor swimming (H) Outdoor swimming (H) Golf 18 Tennis (hard) Snooker Sauna Solarium Putting green Table tennis 9-hole approach course, Health and beauty salon entertainment ch fac Xmas **SERVICES:** Lift **PARKING:** 100 **NOTES:** No dogs (ex guide dogs) No smoking in restaurant Civ Wed 100
CARDS:

See advert on opposite page

★★★72% Porth Avallen

Sea Rd, Carlyon Bay PL25 3SG
☎ 01726 812802 📠 01726 817097
e-mail: info@porthavallen.co.uk
Dir: *A30 onto A391. Follow signs to St Austell, Charlestown and Carlyon Bay. Turn right into Sea Rd*

This traditional hotel boasts panoramic views over the rugged Cornish coastline. Refurbishment over recent years has resulted in smartly appointed public areas and well-presented bedrooms,

continued

many with sea views. The family-run hotel has a friendly atmosphere, and both the oak-panelled lounge and conservatory are ideal for relaxation. Both fixed-price and carte menus are offered in the elegant restaurant.
ROOMS: 27 en suite (2 fmly) No smoking in 16 bedrooms s £73-£128; d £112-£150 (incl. bkfst) **CONF:** Thtr 100 Class 40 Board 40 Del £93 **PARKING:** 40 **NOTES:** No dogs (ex guide dogs) No smoking in restaurant Closed 26 Dec-2 Jan **CARDS:**

See advert on this page

★★★68% Cliff Head

Sea Rd, Carlyon Bay PL25 3RB
☎ 01726 812345 📠 01726 815511
e-mail: cliffheadhotel@btconnect.com
Dir: *2m E off A390*

Set in extensive grounds and conveniently located for visiting the Eden Project, this hotel faces south and enjoys views over Carlyon Bay. A choice of lounges is provided, together with a swimming pool and solarium. 'Expressions' restaurant offers a range of menus, featuring an interesting selection of dishes.
ROOMS: 60 rms (59 en suite) (2 fmly) s £55-£60; d £110 (incl. bkfst) **LB FACILITIES:** Indoor swimming (H) Sauna Solarium Gym entertainment Xmas **CONF:** Thtr 150 Class 130 Board 170 Del from £75 **PARKING:** 60 **NOTES:** No dogs (ex guide dogs) No smoking in restaurant Civ Wed 130 **CARDS:**

★★76% *Boscundle Manor Country House*

Tregrehan PL25 3RL
☎ 01726 813557 📠 01726 814997
e-mail: stay@boscundlemanor.co.uk
Dir: *2m E on A390, 200yds on road signed Tregrehan*

Set in beautifully maintained gardens and grounds, this handsome 18th-century, stone built manor house is a short distance from the Eden Project. Quality and comfort are apparent in the public areas and spacious, well-equipped bedrooms. Equally suitable for both leisure and business travellers, Boscundle Manor boasts both indoor and outdoor pools.
ROOMS: 9 en suite 3 annexe en suite (1 fmly) **FACILITIES:** STV Indoor swimming (H) Outdoor swimming (H) Golf 2 Snooker Gym Croquet lawn Golf practice area Table Tennis Badminton **PARKING:** 15 **NOTES:** No smoking in restaurant RS Mon eve
CARDS:

★★71% Pier House

Harbour Front, Charlestown PL25 3NJ
☎ 01726 67955 📠 01726 69246
Dir: *follow A390 to St Austell, Mt Charles rdbt left down Charlestown Rd*

Formerly two farm cottages dating back to 1794, this genuinely friendly, relaxing and popular hotel boasts a wonderful harbourside location. Unspoilt over the years, this working port has been the setting for many film and television productions.

continued on p526

S

ST AUSTELL, continued

Many bedrooms have the added bonus of sea views, and the convivial public bar is popular with locals and tourists alike. Locally caught fish regularly features on the varied and interesting restaurant menu.
ROOMS: 26 en suite (4 fmly) No smoking in all bedrooms s £50-£55; d £80-£95 (incl. bkfst) **PARKING:** 56 **NOTES:** No dogs (ex guide dogs) No smoking in restaurant Closed 24-25 Dec **CARDS:**

★★69% *White Hart*
Church St PL25 4AT
☎ 01726 72100 01726 74705
Situated in the town centre, this 18th-century, stone-built inn has been completely refurbished with impressive results. Bedrooms offer high standards of comfort and public areas are stylish and contemporary. The light and airy restaurant is the venue for a modern menu that makes good use of local produce.
ROOMS: 18 en suite (1 fmly) No smoking in all bedrooms **CONF:** Thtr 50 Board 20 **PARKING:** 13 **NOTES:** Closed 25 & 26 Dec
CARDS:

★★68% Victoria Inn & Lodge
Victoria, Roche PL26 8LQ
☎ 01726 890207 01726 891233
e-mail: victoriainn@talk21.com
Dir: *6m W of Bodmin on A30. 1st left after garage, Victoria Inn approx 500yds on right*
Situated on the A30, midway between Bodmin and Newquay, this is a convenient choice for both the business and leisure traveller. Bedrooms are purpose built, lodge-style and offer spacious, comfortable and well equipped accommodation. A wide choice of meals is available in the convivial surroundings of the inn.
ROOMS: 42 en suite (11 fmly) (20 GF) No smoking in all bedrooms s £43.50; d £43.50 **LB** **FACILITIES:** STV **CONF:** Thtr 30 Class 18 Board 18 **PARKING:** 100 **NOTES:** No dogs (ex guide dogs) RS 24-26 Dec
CARDS:

ST HELENS, Merseyside — Map 15 SJ59
See also Rainhill

Premier Lodge (St Helens)

Garswood Old Rd, East Lancs Rd WA11 7LX
☎ 0870 9906374 0870 9906375
Dir: *3m from M6 junct 23, on A580 towards Liverpool*
Premier Lodge offers modern, well-equipped, en suite accommodation suitable for both business and leisure travellers. Meals can be taken at the adjacent popular restaurant and bar, which is fully licensed. For further details, consult the Hotel Groups page.
ROOMS: 43 en suite s £48; d £48 **CONF:** Thtr 85 Class 30 Board 40 Del from £80

Travel Inn

Mickle Head Green, Eurolink, Lea Green WA9 4TT
☎ 08701 977237 01744 851427
Dir: *M62 junct 7, on A570 towards St Helens*
Travel Inn offers good-quality, value-for-money accommodation. Spacious, en suite rooms with bath and shower comfortably accommodate a family of up to two adults and two children (to age 15). The restaurant and bar offers a varied menu. For further details and the Travel Inn phone number, consult the Hotel Groups page.
ROOMS: 40 en suite s £44.95; d £44.95

ST IVES, Cambridgeshire — Map 12 TL37

★★★69% Olivers Lodge
Needingworth Rd PE27 5JP
☎ 01480 463252 01480 461150
e-mail: reception@oliverslodge.co.uk
Dir: *follow A14 towards Huntingdon/Cambridge, take B1040 to St Ives. Cross 1st rdbt, left at 2nd then 1st right. Hotel 500mtrs on right*

Olivers Lodge sits in quiet residential area on the outskirts of the town. A popular and well-run hotel, the proprietors and staff providing a helpful and friendly service. Bedrooms are situated in the main house and adjoining wing, each room is well equipped with a good range of facilities. Public rooms include a conservatory dining area and a cosy lounge bar; function and meeting rooms are available.
ROOMS: 12 en suite 5 annexe en suite (3 fmly) No smoking in 16 bedrooms s £65-£75; d £75-£100 (incl. bkfst) **LB** **FACILITIES:** STV Free use of local health club entertainment **CONF:** Thtr 65 Class 35 Board 28 Del from £100 **PARKING:** 30 **NOTES:** No smoking in restaurant Civ Wed 85 **CARDS:**

★★★69% Slepe Hall
Ramsey Rd PE27 5RB
☎ 01480 463122 01480 300706
e-mail: mail@slepehall.co.uk
Dir: *from A14 on A1096 & follow by-pass signed Huntingdon towards St Ives, left into Ramsey Rd at lights by Toyota garage hotel on left*

A welcoming and friendly atmosphere exists within Slepe Hall, which is located close to the town centre. Bedroom types vary, with traditional and modern styles available. A choice of dining options are provided within the refurbished public rooms, with light meals served in the lounge and bar or more formal dining options in the restaurant.
ROOMS: 16 en suite (1 fmly) s £50-£80; d £65-£107.50 (incl. bkfst) **LB** **FACILITIES:** STV **CONF:** Thtr 200 Class 80 Board 60 Del £99 **PARKING:** 70 **NOTES:** No smoking in restaurant Closed 26-29 Dec & 1 Jan Civ Wed 60 **CARDS:**

★★★67% **Dolphin**
London Rd PE27 5EP
☎ 01480 466966 01480 495597
e-mail: enquiries@dolphinhotelcambs.co.uk
Dir: *from A14 between Huntingdon & Cambridge onto A1096 towards St Ives. Left at 1st rdbt & immediately right. Hotel on left after 0.5m*
A modern hotel located on the River Ouse, beside the bridge leading to the town centre. Open-plan public rooms include a choice of bars and a pleasant restaurant offering enjoyable cuisine and views over the river. Modern bedrooms of comfortable proportions are divided between the hotel and an adjacent wing. Conference and function suites are available.
ROOMS: 30 en suite 37 annexe en suite (4 fmly) (33 GF) No smoking in 36 bedrooms **FACILITIES:** STV Fishing Sauna Gym **CONF:** Thtr 150 Class 50 Board 50 Del from £98 **PARKING:** 400 **NOTES:** No dogs (ex guide dogs) RS 24 Dec-2 Jan Civ Wed 60
CARDS:

ST IVES, Cornwall & Isles of Scilly Map 02 SW54

★★★73% *Carbis Bay*
Carbis Bay TR26 2NP
☎ 01736 795311 01736 797677
e-mail: carbisbayhotel@talk21.com
Dir: *M5 junct 31, take A30 then A3074. After 2m through Lelant, pass garage on right. Take next right (Porthreptor Rd), continue to sea*

Set in a peaceful location with direct access to its own white-sand beach, this hotel offers comfortable accommodation. Attractive public areas feature a smart bar and lounge, and guests can relax in the sun lounge overlooking the sea. Bedrooms, many with fine views, are well equipped and spacious. Carefully prepared cuisine is offered in the spacious dining room.
ROOMS: 35 en suite (9 fmly) No smoking in 5 bedrooms
FACILITIES: Outdoor swimming (H) Fishing Snooker Private beach entertainment **CONF:** Thtr 120 Class 80 Board 100 **PARKING:** 200
NOTES: No smoking in restaurant Closed Jan Civ Wed 140
CARDS:

See advert on this page

★★★72% **Porthminster**
The Terrace TR26 2BN
☎ 01736 795221 01736 797043
e-mail: reception@porthminster-hotel.co.uk
Dir: *on A3074*
This friendly hotel has an enviable location with spectacular views of St Ives Bay. Extensive leisure facilities, a versatile function suite and a number of lounges are offered, all making for a relaxing stay. Bedrooms are comfortable and well equipped and many rooms have sea views.
ROOMS: 43 en suite (14 fmly) s £48-£65; d £96-£130 (incl. bkfst) **LB**
FACILITIES: Spa Indoor swimming (H) Outdoor swimming (H) Sauna Solarium Gym Xmas **CONF:** Thtr 130 Class 20 Board 35
SERVICES: Lift **PARKING:** 43 **NOTES:** Closed 2-15 Jan Civ Wed 130
CARDS:

★★★66% *Tregenna Castle Hotel*
TR26 2DE
☎ 01736 795254 01736 796066
e-mail: tregenna-castle@demon.co.uk
Dir: *A30 from Exeter to Penzance, at Lelant W of Hayle take A3074 to St Ives, through Carbis Bay, signed main entrance on left*
Sitting at the top of town in beautiful landscaped gardens, this popular hotel boasts spectacular views of St Ives. Many leisure facilities are available, including indoor and outdoor pools, gymnasium and sauna. Families are particularly welcome with a babysitting service and a nursery facility with qualified staff. Bedrooms are generally spacious. A carte menu or carvery buffet are offered in the restaurant. There is also an Italian bistro adjacent to the golf course.
ROOMS: 84 en suite (12 fmly) No smoking in 49 bedrooms
FACILITIES: STV Indoor swimming (H) Outdoor swimming (H) Golf 18 Tennis (hard) Squash Sauna Solarium Gym Putting green Jacuzzi Health spa Steam room **CONF:** Thtr 300 Class 150 **SERVICES:** Lift **PARKING:** 200 **NOTES:** No dogs (ex guide dogs) No smoking in restaurant Civ Wed 100 **CARDS:**

AA Rosette Award for culinary excellence

★★★65% **Garrack**
Burthallan Ln, Higher Ayr TR26 3AA
☎ 01736 796199 01736 798955
e-mail: garrack@accuk.co.uk
Dir: *turn off A30 for St Ives. Follow yellow holiday route signs on B3311. In St Ives, hotel is signed from 1st mini rdbt*
Enjoying a peaceful elevated position with splendid views across the harbour and Porthmeor beach, the Garrack sits in its own delightful grounds and gardens. Bedrooms are comfortable and

continued on p528

S

ST IVES, continued

many have sea views. Public areas include a small leisure suite, a choice of lounges and an attractive restaurant.

Garrack, St Ives

ROOMS: 16 en suite 2 annexe en suite (2 fmly) s £65.50-£68; d £114-£168 (incl. bkfst) **LB** **FACILITIES:** Indoor swimming (H) Sauna Solarium Gym Jacuzzi ch fac Xmas **CONF:** Thtr 30 Board 12 **PARKING:** 30 **NOTES:** No dogs (ex guide dogs) No smoking in restaurant **CARDS:**

★★★64% Chy-an-Albany

Albany Ter TR26 2BS
☎ 01736 796759 01736 795584
e-mail: info@chyanalbanyhotel.com
Dir: *from A30 onto A3074 signed St Ives, hotel on left just before junct*
Conveniently located, the Chy-an-Albany enjoys splendid sea views. The comfortable bedrooms, some with balconies and sea views, come in a variety of sizes. Friendly staff provide a relaxing environment, and many guests return on a regular basis. Freshly prepared and appetising cuisine is served in the dining room and a bar menu is also available.
ROOMS: 40 en suite (11 fmly) No smoking in all bedrooms s £47-£67; d £94-£134 (incl. bkfst) **LB** **FACILITIES:** STV entertainment ch fac Xmas **CONF:** Thtr 80 Class 40 Board 30 Del from £70 **SERVICES:** Lift **PARKING:** 37 **NOTES:** No dogs (ex guide dogs) No smoking in restaurant Civ Wed 80 **CARDS:**

★★72% Boskerris

Boskerris Rd, Carbis Bay TR26 2NQ
☎ 01736 795295 01736 798632
e-mail: Boskerris.Hotel@btinternet.com
Dir: *on entering Carbis Bay take 3rd right after petrol station*
The Boskerris Hotel enjoys a peaceful location and great views, particularly from the terraced area, which looks out over Carbis Bay and St Ives harbour. Service is friendly and attentive, and bedrooms are stylish and comfortable. Public areas provide a range of facilities including a swimming pool and attractive gardens.
ROOMS: 16 en suite (2 fmly) (2 GF) No smoking in 4 bedrooms d £84-£104 (incl. bkfst) **LB** **FACILITIES:** Outdoor swimming (H) Table tennis **PARKING:** 20 **NOTES:** No smoking in restaurant Closed Nov-Etr **CARDS:**

★★72% Pedn-Olva

West Porthminster Beach TR26 2EA
☎ 01736 796222 01736 797710
e-mail: pedn-olva@westcountryhotelrooms.co.uk
Dir: *A30 to Hayle, then A3074 to St Ives. In St Ives turn sharp right at bus station into railway station car park, down steps to Hotel*
Perched on the water's edge, this hotel is the closest thing to being aboard a ship, and the stylish public areas complement the unique location. Bedrooms combine comfort with quality and many have spectacular views across the bay. An imaginative, fixed-price menu is offered in the restaurant; during the summer, lighter meals are served on the terraces.
ROOMS: 30 en suite (5 fmly) No smoking in all bedrooms **FACILITIES:** STV Outdoor swimming (H) **CONF:** Thtr 20 Class 20 Board 16 Del from £85 **PARKING:** 17 **NOTES:** No dogs (ex guide dogs) No smoking in restaurant Civ Wed 60 **CARDS:**

★★67% Hotel St Eia

Trelyon Av TR26 2AA
☎ 01736 795531 01736 793591
e-mail: hotelsteia@tinyonline.co.uk
Dir: *off A30 onto A3074, follow signs to St Ives, approaching town, hotel on right*
This smart hotel is conveniently located and enjoys spectacular views over St Ives, the harbour and Porthminster Beach. The friendly proprietors provide a relaxing environment and many guests return on a regular basis. Bedrooms are comfortable and well equipped, some with sea views. The spacious lounge-bar has a well-stocked bar and views can be enjoyed from the rooftop terrace.
ROOMS: 18 en suite (3 fmly) No smoking in all bedrooms s £28.50-£38.50; d £57-£77 (incl. bkfst) **LB** **PARKING:** 16 **NOTES:** No dogs (ex guide dogs) No smoking in restaurant Closed Dec-Jan **CARDS:**

★★66% Cottage Hotel

Leisureplex

Boskerris Rd, Carbis Bay TR26 2PE
☎ 01736 795252 01736 798636
e-mail: cottage.stives@alfatravel.co.uk
Dir: *from A30 take A3074 to Carbis Bay. Right into Porthrepta Rd. Just before rail bridge left through railway car park and into hotel car park*
Set in a quiet, lush gardens, this pleasant hotel offers friendly and attentive service. Smart bedrooms are pleasantly spacious and many rooms enjoy splendid views. Public areas are varied and include a snooker room, a comfortable lounge and spacious dining room with sea views over the beach and Carbis Bay.
ROOMS: 80 en suite (7 fmly) (2 GF) s £25-£33; d £42-£58 (incl. bkfst) **LB** **FACILITIES:** Outdoor swimming (H) Squash Snooker Sauna Gym entertainment Xmas **SERVICES:** Lift **PARKING:** 10 **NOTES:** No dogs (ex guide dogs) No smoking in restaurant Closed Dec-Feb (ex Xmas) RS Nov & Mar **CARDS:**

ST LAWRENCE See Wight, Isle of

ST LEONARDS-ON-SEA See Hastings & St Leonards

ST MARTIN'S See Scilly, Isles of

ST MARY CHURCH See Torquay

ST MARY'S See Scilly, Isles of

ST MAWES, Cornwall & Isles of Scilly

Map 02 SW83

★★★77% Idle Rocks

Harbour Side TR2 5AN
☎ 01326 270771 01326 270062
e-mail: reception@idlerocks.co.uk
Dir: *off A390 onto A3078, 14m to St Mawes. Hotel on left*
Superbly situated on the waterside and overlooking the attractive fishing port, the Idle Rocks has splendid sea views. The lounge and bar also benefit from the views and in warmer months service is available on the terrace. Bedrooms are individually styled and tastefully furnished to a high standard, the rooms in nearby

continued

Bonella House and the waterside cottage are particularly spacious. The daily-changing menu features fresh local produce and imaginative cooking.
ROOMS: 23 en suite 10 annexe en suite (1 GF) s £64-£99; d £128-£250 (incl. bkfst & dinner) **LB** **FACILITIES:** Xmas **PARKING:** 5 **NOTES:** No smoking in restaurant **CARDS:**

★★73% Rising Sun
TR2 5DJ
☎ 01326 270233 01326 270198
Dir: *from A39 take A3078 signed St Mawes, hotel in village centre*
Looking out across the attractive harbour and the Fal Estuary, this smart looking hotel is a popular venue for both locals and visitors alike. Food is a key factor here and cuisine is accomplished. In the bar, which offers a large selection of ales, quality wines and malt whiskies, a range of dishes is offered. More casual dining is available in the brasserie. Bedrooms are stylish and many have sea views.
ROOMS: 8 en suite (1 fmly) s fr £50; d fr £100 (incl. bkfst) **LB** **PARKING:** 6 **NOTES:** No smoking in restaurant
CARDS:

ST MELLION, Cornwall & Isles of Scilly — Map 03 SX36

★★★68% St Mellion International
PL12 6SD
☎ 01579 351351 01579 350537
e-mail: stmellion@americangolf.uk.com
Dir: *from M5/A38 towards Plymouth & Saltash. St Mellion off A38 on A388 towards Callington & Launceston*
This purpose-built hotel, golfing and leisure complex is surrounded by 450 acres of land with two highly regarded 18-hole golf courses. The bedrooms generally have views over the courses and public areas include a choice of bars and eating options. Function suites are also available.
ROOMS: 39 annexe en suite (15 fmly) (8 GF) s £73-£93; d £96-£116 (incl. bkfst) **LB** **FACILITIES:** Indoor swimming (H) Golf 18 Tennis (hard) Squash Snooker Sauna Solarium Gym Putting green Jacuzzi Steam room Skincare Indoor Pool is supervised ch fac Xmas **CONF:** Thtr 350 Class 140 Board 80 Del £89.50 **SERVICES:** Lift **PARKING:** 400 **NOTES:** No dogs (ex guide dogs) No smoking in restaurant Civ Wed 120
CARDS:

ST NEOTS, Cambridgeshire — Map 12 TL16

★★68% Abbotsley Golf Hotel
Potton Rd, Eynesbury Hardwicke PE19 6XN
☎ 01480 474000 01480 471018
e-mail: abbotsley@americangolf.uk.com
Dir: *A1(M) onto A428 towards Cambridge*
This purpose-built hotel caters well for its many avid golfing guests, with a 250-acre estate encompassing two courses, a golf school and leisure complex. The bedrooms are generally spacious and surround a pleasing courtyard garden with a putting green. Public rooms overlook the adjacent greens.
ROOMS: 42 annexe en suite (2 fmly) No smoking in 10 bedrooms s £54; d £78 (incl. bkfst) **LB** **FACILITIES:** Golf 18 Squash Solarium Gym Putting green Holistic Health & Beauty Salon, pool tables **CONF:** Thtr 60 Class 30 Board 30 Del £90 **PARKING:** 80 **NOTES:** No smoking in restaurant **CARDS:**

⌂ Premier Lodge (Eaton Socon)

Great North Rd, Eaton Socon PE19 8EN
☎ 0870 9906314 0870 9906315
Premier Lodge offers modern, well-equipped, en suite accommodation suitable for both business and leisure travellers. Meals can be taken at the adjacent popular restaurant and bar, which is fully licensed. For further details, consult the Hotel Groups page.
ROOMS: 63 en suite s £48; d £48

⌂ Travel Inn
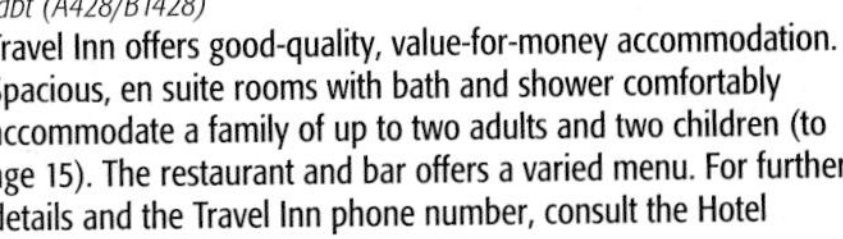
Colmworth Business Park PE19 8YH
☎ 08701 977238 01480 405541
Dir: *from A1 at southern St Neots junt. Travel Inn at 1st rdbt (A428/B1428)*
Travel Inn offers good-quality, value-for-money accommodation. Spacious, en suite rooms with bath and shower comfortably accommodate a family of up to two adults and two children (to age 15). The restaurant and bar offers a varied menu. For further details and the Travel Inn phone number, consult the Hotel Groups page.
ROOMS: 41 en suite s £44.95; d £44.95

SALCOMBE, Devon — Map 03 SX73
See also Hope Cove, Kingsbridge & Thurlestone

★★★★75% Soar Mill Cove
Soar Mill Cove, Malborough TQ7 3DS
☎ 01548 561566 01548 561223
e-mail: info@makepeacehotels.co.uk
Dir: *3m W of town off A381at Malborough. Follow 'Soar' signs*
Situated amidst spectacular scenery with dramatic sea views, this hotel provides a relaxing stay. Family-run, with a committed team, keen standards of hospitality and service are apparent. Bedrooms are well equipped, many rooms having private terraces. There are different seating areas where impressive cream teas are served, or for the more active a choice of swimming pools. In the restaurant local produce is used to good effect.
ROOMS: 22 en suite (5 fmly) (21 GF) No smoking in all bedrooms s £112-£213; d £196-£290 (incl. bkfst & dinner) **LB** **FACILITIES:** Indoor swimming (H) Outdoor swimming (H) Tennis (grass) Sauna Putting green Table tennis, Games room, 9 hole Pitch n putt, Spa treatment suite entertainment Xmas **CONF:** BC **PARKING:** 30 **NOTES:** No smoking in restaurant Closed 2 Jan-8 Feb **CARDS:**

★★★★72% *Thurlestone Hotel*
TQ7 3NN
☎ 01548 560382 01548 561069
e-mail: enquiries@thurlestone.co.uk
(For full entry see Thurlestone and advert on opposite page)

★★★★68% Menzies Marine
Cliff Rd TQ8 8JH
☎ 01548 844444 01548 843109
e-mail: info@menzies-hotels.co.uk
Dir: *from A38 towards Exeter take A384 to Totnes then follow A381 to Kingsbridge & Salcombe*
Enjoying a superb position overlooking the river and with views towards the sea, this hotel offers a range of facilities. Ideal as a base to tour the area or for the business guest. Bedrooms, many with balconies and sea views, are spacious and comfortable and most are at the front of the hotel.
ROOMS: 53 en suite (10 fmly) **FACILITIES:** STV Indoor swimming (H) Sauna Solarium Gym Jacuzzi **SERVICES:** Lift **PARKING:** 50 **NOTES:** No smoking in restaurant Civ Wed 70
CARDS:

SALCOMBE, continued

★★★ Buckland-Tout-Saints
Goveton TQ7 2DS
☎ 01548 853055 01548 856261
e-mail: buckland@tout-saints.co.uk
(For full entry see Kingsbridge)

★★★75% Tides Reach
South Sands TQ8 8LJ
☎ 01548 843466 01548 843954
e-mail: enquire@tidesreach.com
Dir: *off A38 at Buckfastleigh to Totnes. Then take A381 to Salcombe, follow signs to South Sands*

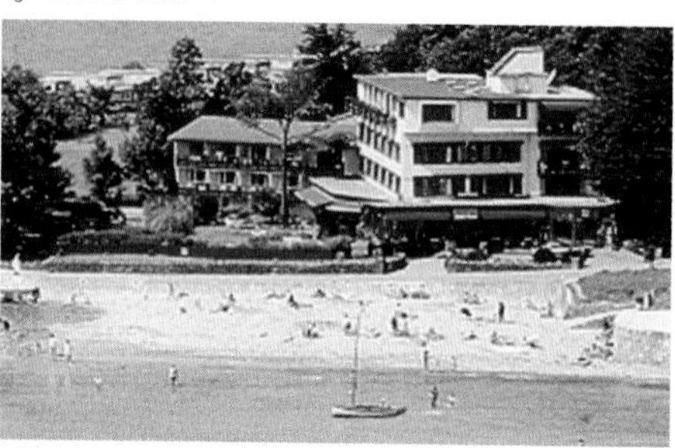

Superbly situated at the waters edge, this personally run, friendly hotel has splendid views of the estuary and beach. Bedrooms, many with balconies, are spacious and comfortable. In the bar and lounge attentive service can be enjoyed along with the view, and the Garden Room restaurant serves appetising and accomplished cuisine.
ROOMS: 35 en suite (7 fmly) No smoking in 2 bedrooms s £60-£110; d £100-£248 (incl. bkfst & dinner) **LB FACILITIES:** Indoor swimming (H) Squash Snooker Sauna Solarium Gym Jacuzzi Indoor pool supervised, windsurfing, dinghy sailing, kayaking, scuba diving entertainment **SERVICES:** Lift **PARKING:** 100 **NOTES:** No children 8yrs No smoking in restaurant Closed Dec-early Feb **CARDS:**
See advert on opposite page

SALE, Greater Manchester — Map 15 SJ79

★★★★68% *Belmore Hotel*
143 Brooklands Rd M33 3QN
☎ 0161 973 2538 0161 973 2665
e-mail: belmore_hotel@hotmail.com
Dir: *from A56 turn onto A6144. At traffic lights (Brooklands Station on right) turn right into Brooklands Rd*

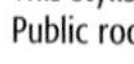

This stylish, refurbished hotel is set in a quiet residential area. Public rooms include a choice of dining options: cooking in the fine dining Classic restaurant is imaginative and prepared with skill, as is the more informal menu of the downstairs brasserie. Bedrooms are tastefully furnished, spacious, and well equipped.
ROOMS: 23 en suite (2 fmly) No smoking in 13 bedrooms **FACILITIES:** STV Free access to local Health Club **CONF:** Thtr 100 Class 50 Board 40 **PARKING:** 38 **NOTES:** No smoking in restaurant Civ Wed 60 **CARDS:**

⌂ Travel Inn (Manchester South)
Carrington Ln, Ashton-Upon-Mersey M33 5BL
☎ 08701 977179 0161 905 1742
Dir: *M60 junct 8 take A6144(M) towards Carrington. Left at 1st set of lights, Inn on left*
Travel Inn offers good-quality, value-for-money accommodation. Spacious, en suite rooms with bath and shower comfortably accommodate a family of up to two adults and two children (to age 15). The restaurant and bar offers a varied menu. For further details and the Travel Inn phone number, consult the Hotel Groups page.
ROOMS: 40 en suite s £44.95; d £44.95 **CONF:** Thtr 25

SALISBURY, Wiltshire — Map 05 SU12
See also Landford

★★★70% Milford Hall
206 Castle St SP1 3TE
☎ 01722 417411 01722 419444
e-mail: milfordhallhotel@aol.com
Dir: *a few hundred yds from junct of Castle St, A30 ring road & A345 Amesbury Rd.*
This hotel offers high standards of accommodation within easy walking distance of the city centre. There are two categories of bedroom; traditional rooms in the original Georgian house and spacious, modern rooms in a purpose built extension - all are extremely well equipped. Meals are served in the smart brasserie where a choice of dishes cater for all tastes.
ROOMS: 35 en suite (1 fmly) No smoking in 6 bedrooms s £100-£110; d £110-£130 **LB FACILITIES:** STV Free facilities at local leisure centre **CONF:** Thtr 90 Class 70 Board 40 Del from £145 **PARKING:** 60 **NOTES:** No smoking in restaurant Civ Wed 80 **CARDS:**

★★★70% The White Hart
St John St SP1 2SD
☎ 0870 400 8125 01722 412761
e-mail: whitehartsalisbury@macdonald-hotels.co.uk
Dir: *M3 junct 7/8 take A303 to A343 for Salisbury then A30. Follow signs for City Centre on ring rd into Exeter St, leading into Saint John St*
There has been a hotel on this site since the 16th century. Bedrooms vary between the contemporary-style, newly refurbished rooms and those decorated in more traditional style, all of which boast a comprehensive range of facilities. The bar and lounge areas are popular with guests and locals for morning coffees and afternoon teas.
ROOMS: 68 en suite (6 fmly) No smoking in 28 bedrooms s £80-£100; d £100-£130 (incl. bkfst) **LB FACILITIES:** STV Xmas **CONF:** Thtr 100 Class 40 Board 40 Del from £100 **PARKING:** 90 **NOTES:** No smoking in restaurant Civ Wed 96 **CARDS:**

> Popped the question?
> Hotels with Civ Wed in their entry are licensed for civil wedding ceremonies. Maximum numbers for the ceremony only are shown, e.g. Civ Wed 120

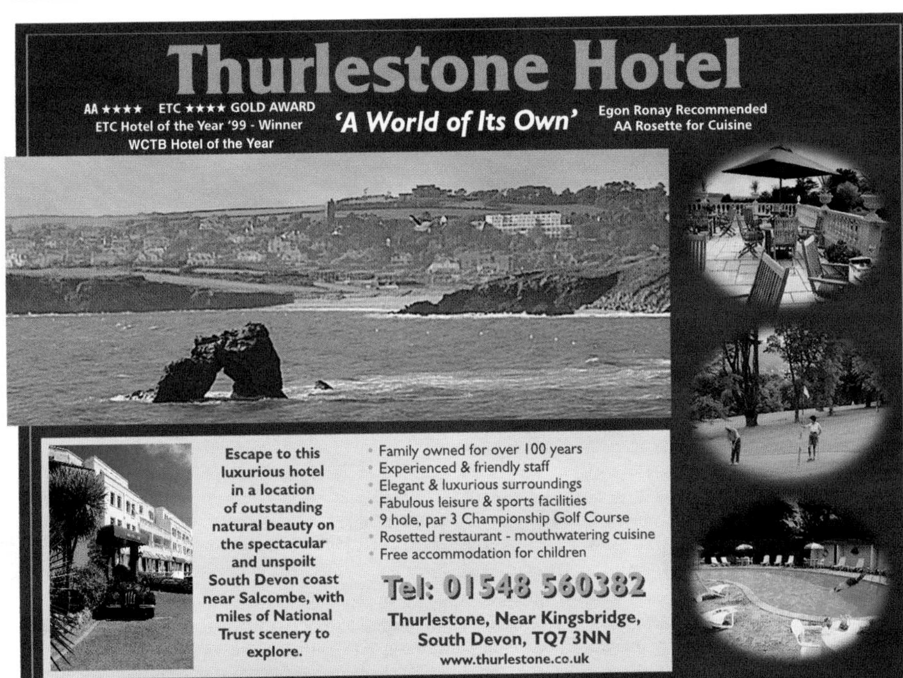
Thurlestone Hotel
AA ★★★★ ETC ★★★★ GOLD AWARD
ETC Hotel of the Year '99 - Winner
WCTB Hotel of the Year
'A World of Its Own'
Egon Ronay Recommended
AA Rosette for Cuisine
Escape to this luxurious hotel in a location of outstanding natural beauty on the spectacular and unspoilt South Devon coast near Salcombe, with miles of National Trust scenery to explore.
• Family owned for over 100 years
• Experienced & friendly staff
• Elegant & luxurious surroundings
• Fabulous leisure & sports facilities
• 9 hole, par 3 Championship Golf Course
• Rosetted restaurant - mouthwatering cuisine
• Free accommodation for children
Tel: 01548 560382
Thurlestone, Near Kingsbridge,
South Devon, TQ7 3NN
www.thurlestone.co.uk

S

SALISBURY, continued

★★★69% Red Lion
Milford St SP1 2AN
☎ 01722 323334 🖷 01722 325756
e-mail: reception@the-redlion.co.uk
Dir: *in city centre off Market Sq*

If you are looking for character, look no further than this 750 year old hotel. The individual bedrooms combine contemporary comforts with historic features, including one room with a medieval fireplace dating back to 1220. Public areas are also distinctive with a bar, lounge and the elegant Vine Restaurant.
ROOMS: 51 en suite (2 fmly) No smoking in 34 bedrooms s £87.50-£104; d £110-£130 **LB** **FACILITIES:** STV **CONF:** Thtr 100 Class 50 Board 40 Del from £110 **SERVICES:** Lift **NOTES:** No dogs (ex guide dogs) No smoking in restaurant **CARDS:**

See advert on opposite page

★★★67% *Grasmere House*
Harnhan Rd SP2 8JN
☎ 01722 338388 🖷 01722 333710
e-mail: grasmerehotel@mistral.co.uk
Dir: *on A3094 on S side of Salisbury next to All Saints Church in Harnham*

This popular hotel dates from 1896 and has gardens overlooking the water meadows and the cathedral. The attractive bedrooms vary in size; those in the original building are very appealing and some are well-suited for less able guests. There is a spacious conservatory, comfortable lounge, cosy bar and restaurant.
ROOMS: 4 en suite 16 annexe en suite (2 fmly) No smoking in 4 bedrooms **FACILITIES:** Fishing Croquet lawn Jacuzzi **CONF:** Thtr 110 Class 45 Board 45 **PARKING:** 64 **NOTES:** Civ Wed 120
CARDS:

See advert on opposite page

★★★64% The Rose & Crown Hotel
Harnham Rd, Harnham SP2 8JQ
☎ 0870 6096163 🖷 01722 339816
Dir: *M3 junct 8 to A303 then A30 to centre of Salisbury*

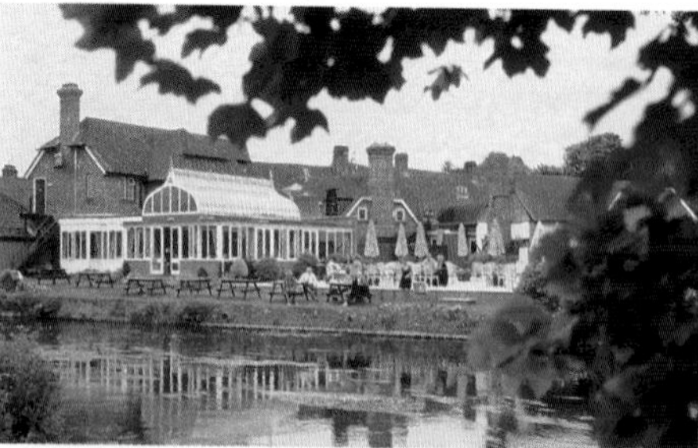

The hotel is situated on a quiet stretch of the River Avon, just five minutes from town. Most bedrooms are large and enjoy views of the cathedral and gardens, which reach down to the river. Public areas are spacious and there is plenty of parking.
ROOMS: 28 en suite (5 fmly) (3 GF) No smoking in 10 bedrooms s £85-£110; d £95-£140 **LB** **FACILITIES:** STV Fishing Xmas **CONF:** Thtr 80 Class 40 Board 40 Del from £110 **PARKING:** 42 **NOTES:** No smoking in restaurant Civ Wed 90
CARDS:

⌂ Travel Inn
Bishopdown Retail Park, Pearce Way SP1 3YU
☎ 08701 977225 🖷 01722 337889
Dir: *on main A30 NE of city centre, on rdbt*
Travel Inn offers good-quality, value-for-money accommodation. Spacious, en suite rooms with bath and shower comfortably accommodate a family of up to two adults and two children (to age 15). The restaurant and bar offers a varied menu. For further details and the Travel Inn phone number, consult the Hotel Groups page.
ROOMS: 60 en suite s £44.95; d £44.95

SALTASH, Cornwall & Isles of Scilly — Map 03 SX45

⌂ Travelodge
Callington Rd, Carkeel PL12 6LF
☎ 08700 850 950 🖷 01752 849028
Dir: *on A38 Saltash by-pass - 1m from Tamar Bridge*
Travelodge offers good quality, good value, modern accommodation. Ideal for families, the spacious, en suite bedrooms include remote-control TV, tea and coffee-making facilities, luxury beds and free morning newspaper. Meals can be taken at the nearby family restaurant. For further details and the Travelodge phone number, consult the Hotel Groups page.
ROOMS: 53 en suite s fr £42.95; d fr £42.95 **CONF:** Thtr 25 Class 15 Board 12

SALTBURN-BY-THE-SEA, North Yorkshire — Map 19 NZ62

★★★68% Rushpool Hall Hotel
Saltburn Ln TS12 1HD
☎ 01287 624111 🖷 01287 625255
A grand Victorian mansion nestling in its own grounds and woodlands. Stylish, elegant bedrooms are well equipped and spacious; many enjoy amazing sea views. The interesting public rooms are filled with charm and character, and roaring fires welcome guests in cooler months. The hotel boasts an excellent reputation as a wedding venue thanks to its super location and experienced event management.
ROOMS: 21 en suite s £50-£85; d £80-£120 (incl. bkfst) **LB** **FACILITIES:** STV Fishing Croquet lawn ch fac Xmas **CONF:** Thtr 95 Class 75 Board 60 Del from £70 **PARKING:** 120 **NOTES:** No dogs (ex guide dogs) No smoking in restaurant Civ Wed 100
CARDS:

> Packed in a hurry?
> Ironing facilities should be available at all star levels, either in rooms or on request

★★63% Hunley Hall Golf Club & Hotel
Ings Ln, Brotton TS12 2QQ
☎ 01287 676216 🖷 01287 678250
e-mail: enquiries@hunleyhall.co.uk
Dir: *A174 bypass take left at rdbt with monument at T-junct turn left pass church turn right. 50yds turn right, through housing estate, approx 0.5m*
Spectacularly situated, this hotel overlooks a 27-hole golf course

continued

S

and beyond to the surrounding coastline. The Members' Bar is licensed and serves snacks all day, and the restaurant offers a wide choice of food. Bedrooms are comfortable and well equipped.
ROOMS: 8 en suite (1 fmly) (8 GF) No smoking in all bedrooms s £35-£37.50; d £65 (incl. bkfst) **LB FACILITIES:** Golf 27 Snooker Putting green **CONF:** Thtr 70 Class 50 Board 24 Del from £44 **PARKING:** 88 **NOTES:** No dogs (ex guide dogs) No smoking in restaurant **CARDS:**

SAMPFORD PEVERELL, Devon — Map 03 ST01

★★65% Parkway House Country Hotel

EX16 7BJ
☎ 01884 820255 01884 820780
e-mail: p-way@m-way.freeserve.co.uk
Dir: *M5 junct 27, follow signs for Tiverton Parkway Station. Hotel on right, entering village*

An ideal choice for both business and leisure travellers, this hotel is located within a mile of the M5 and benefits from extensive views across the Culm Valley. The well-equipped bedrooms are neatly presented. A popular venue for conferences and day meetings.
ROOMS: 10 en suite (2 fmly) s £37.50-£45; d £55 (incl. bkfst) **LB FACILITIES:** STV Childrens Play Area **CONF:** BC Thtr 100 Class 50 Board 40 Del £65.50 **PARKING:** 100 **NOTES:** No dogs (ex guide dogs) No smoking in restaurant **CARDS:**

Travelodge Tiverton

Travelodge

Sampford Peverell Service Area EX16 7HD
☎ 08700 850 950
Dir: *M5 junct 27*

Travelodge offers good quality, good value, modern accommodation. Ideal for families, the spacious, en suite bedrooms include remote-control TV, tea and coffee-making facilities, luxury beds and free morning newspaper. Meals can be taken at the nearby family restaurant. For further details and the Travelodge phone number, consult the Hotel Groups page.
ROOMS: 40 en suite s fr £42.95; d fr £42.95

SANDBACH, Cheshire — Map 15 SJ76

★★★65% The Chimney House Hotel

corus hotels

Congleton Rd CW11 4ST
☎ 0870 609 6164 01270 768916
e-mail: chimneyhouse@corushotels.com
Dir: *on A534, 1m from M6 junct 17 towards Congleton*

This conveniently positioned Tudor-style building benefits from ease of access to major motorway networks. The hotel is ideal for business meetings and functions. Bedrooms are well planned and

continued on p534

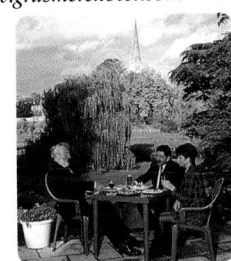

S

SANDBACH, continued

equipped. Relax in the spacious lounge areas, or enjoy a meal in the patio restaurant overlooking the hotel gardens.
ROOMS: 48 en suite (16 fmly) (18 GF) No smoking in 33 bedrooms s £56-£89; d £72-£104 **LB** **FACILITIES:** STV Sauna Putting green **CONF:** Thtr 120 Class 40 Board 40 Del from £125 **PARKING:** 110 **NOTES:** No dogs (ex guide dogs) No smoking in restaurant RS Bank Holidays Civ Wed 60 **CARDS:**

Innkeeper's Lodge Sandbach

Bereton Green CW11 1RS
☎ 01477 544732
Dir: *M6, junction 17, at roundabout bear left towards Holmes Chapel, follow road until Breton, lodge on left at Breton Green*
A new concept in the travel accommodation market. Smart rooms meet essential business requirements but also have home comforts. Dining options include all-day menus plus the added advantage of breakfast, which is included in the room price. For further details, consult the Hotel Groups page.
ROOMS: 23 en suite

SANDBANKS See Poole

SANDIACRE, Derbyshire Map 11 SK43

Holiday Inn Derby/Nottingham

Bostocks Ln NG10 5NJ
☎ 0870 400 9062 🖷 0115 949 0469
Dir: *M1 junct 25 follow exit to Sandiacre, hotel on right*
At the time of going to press, the classification for this hotel was not confirmed. Please refer to the AA internet site www.theAA.com for current information.
ROOMS: 93 en suite (6 fmly) No smoking in 50 bedrooms **FACILITIES:** Day membership to David Lloyd Leisure **CONF:** Thtr 60 Class 26 Board 28 **PARKING:** 180
CARDS:

SANDOWN See Wight, Isle of

SANDWICH, Kent Map 07 TR35

★★67% The Blazing Donkey Country Hotel & Inn

Hay Hill, Ham CT14 0ED
☎ 01304 617362 🖷 01304 615264
e-mail: info@blazingdonkey.co.uk
Dir: *off A256 at Eastry into village, right at Five Bells public house, hotel 0.75m on left*
This former labourer's cottage and barn, has been upgraded over the years and is now a distinctive inn of character. Set in the heart of peaceful Kentish farmland, the atmosphere is convivial and informal, with an open-plan bar and lounge and more formal dining area. Comfortably appointed bedrooms are spacious and arranged around a courtyard.
ROOMS: 19 en suite 3 annexe en suite (2 fmly) No smoking in 5 bedrooms s £75-£80; d £89.50-£99.50 (incl. cont bkfst) **LB** **FACILITIES:** STV Croquet lawn Putting green Xmas **CONF:** BC Thtr 200 Class 200 Board 200 Del from £125 **SERVICES:** air con **PARKING:** 108 **NOTES:** No smoking in restaurant Civ Wed 350
CARDS:

> Destination dining!
> This symbol indicates a Restaurant with Rooms

SAUNDERTON, Buckinghamshire Map 05 SP70

★★64% Rose & Crown

Wycombe Rd HP27 9NP
☎ 01844 345299 🖷 01844 343140
e-mail: info@rosecrowninn.co.uk
Dir: *2m S of Princes Risborough on A4010, on right*
The Rose and Crown may have been offering hospitality to travellers for over a century, but the focal point of this hotel, a strikingly minimalist bar and restaurant, is resolutely modern. Rooms are comfortable and offer a range of extra facilities and the attractive patio is perfect for summer drinking.
ROOMS: 15 en suite No smoking in all bedrooms s £59-£85; d £72-£95 (incl. bkfst) **LB** **FACILITIES:** STV Xmas **CONF:** Thtr 35 Class 20 Board 16 **PARKING:** 50 **NOTES:** No dogs (ex guide dogs) No smoking in restaurant **CARDS:**

SAUNTON, Devon Map 03 SS43

★★★★70% Saunton Sands

EX33 1LQ
☎ 01271 890212 🖷 01271 890145
e-mail: info@sauntonsands.com
Dir: *off A361 at Braunton, signposted Croyde B3231, hotel 2m on left*

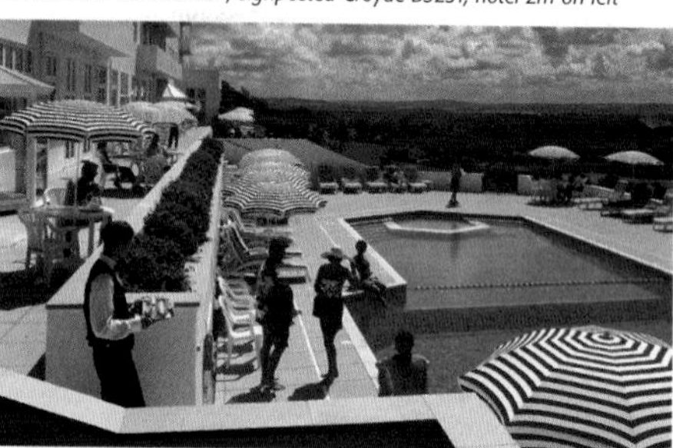

Stunning sea views and direct access to five miles of sandy beach are just two of the features of this popular hotel. The majority of sea-facing rooms benefit from balconies and splendid views are enjoyed from all of the public areas, which include comfortable lounges. The Sands café/bar is a successful innovation and provides an informal eating option.
ROOMS: 92 en suite (39 fmly) s £73-£108; d £146-£226 (incl. bkfst) **LB** **FACILITIES:** STV Indoor swimming (H) Outdoor swimming (H) Tennis (hard) Squash Snooker Sauna Solarium Gym Putting green Table tennis, Swimming pools supervised, Sun Shower, Health and beauty salon entertainment ch fac Xmas **SERVICES:** Lift **PARKING:** 142 **NOTES:** No dogs (ex guide dogs) No smoking in restaurant Civ Wed 100
CARDS:

See advert on opposite page

SAWBRIDGEWORTH, Hertfordshire Map 06 TL41

Manor of Groves Hotel, Golf & Country Club

High Wych CM21 0JU
☎ 01279 600777 🖷 01279 600374
e-mail: info@manorofgroves.co.uk
Dir: *A1184 to Sawbridgeworth left to High Wych, in High Wych at village green. Hotel 200yds left*
At the time of going to press, the star classification for this hotel

continued

was not confirmed. Please refer to the AA internet site www.theAA.com for current information.
ROOMS: 80 en suite (2 fmly) (17 GF) s fr £95; d fr £135 (incl. bkfst) **LB FACILITIES: Spa** STV Indoor swimming (H) Golf 18 Sauna Solarium Gym Putting green Jacuzzi Indoor pool supervised, dance studio, beauty salon entertainment Xmas **CONF:** BC Thtr 400 Class 250 Board 50 Del from £150 **SERVICES:** Lift **PARKING:** 200 **NOTES:** No smoking in restaurant Civ Wed 400 **CARDS:**

SCARBOROUGH, North Yorkshire

Map 17 TA08

★★★70% The Crescent

2 Belvoir Ter YO11 2PP
☎ 01723 360929 📠 01723 354126
e-mail: reception@crescent-hotel.co.uk
Dir: *towards railway station, follow signs to Brunswick Pavilion, at lights turn into Crescent*

This smart hotel is a listed building, a short distance from the town centre. The comfortable accommodation is comprehensively equipped, and there are spacious bars and lounges. There is a choice of dining areas and bars: an elegant restaurant serves a set-price menu and carte, and a separate carvery offers a less formal option. Service is caring and attentive.
ROOMS: 20 en suite No smoking in 7 bedrooms s £49; d £90-£105 (incl. bkfst) **CONF:** Thtr 30 Class 25 Board 25 **SERVICES:** Lift **NOTES:** No dogs (ex guide dogs) Closed 25-26 Dec
CARDS:

★★★69% *Beiderbecke's Hotel*

1-3 The Crescent YO11 2PW
☎ 01723 365766 📠 01723 367433
e-mail: info@beiderbeckes.com
Dir: *in town centre, 200mtrs from railway station*

Situated in a Georgian Crescent this hotel is close to all the main attractions. Bedrooms are very smart with plenty of space and comfort. Some rooms have views over the town to the sea. The restaurant has live music at weekends.
ROOMS: 27 en suite (1 fmly) No smoking in 10 bedrooms **FACILITIES:** Snooker entertainment **CONF:** Thtr 35 Class 35 Board 28 **SERVICES:** Lift **PARKING:** 18 **NOTES:** No dogs (ex guide dogs)
CARDS:

★★★69% *Crown*

Esplanade YO11 2AG
☎ 01723 357400 📠 01723 357404
e-mail: reservations@ScarboroughHotel.com
Dir: *on A64 follow town centre signs to lights opp railway station, turn right across Valley Bridge, then 1st left, right up Belmont Rd to cliff top*

Occupying a prime position on the South Cliff, this elegant hotel overlooks the sea and is only a short walk from the town centre. Several bedrooms enjoy spectacular views over Scarborough Bay.

continued on p536

S

SCARBOROUGH, continued

The hotel has comfortable lounges, extensive conference facilities, and an impressive leisure centre.
ROOMS: 83 en suite (7 fmly) No smoking in 20 bedrooms **FACILITIES: Spa** Indoor swimming (H) Snooker Sauna Solarium Gym Fitness, Aqua & Retreat suites **CONF:** Thtr 180 Class 100 Board 100 **SERVICES:** Lift **PARKING:** 30 **NOTES:** No smoking in restaurant Civ Wed 70 **CARDS:**

★★★69% Ox Pasture Hall Country Hotel

Lady Ediths Dr, Raincliffe Woods YO12 5TD
☎ 01723 365295 01723 355156
e-mail: hawksmoor@oxpasture.freeserve.co.uk
Dir: *A171 out of Scarborough, past hospital, follow sign for "Forge Valley & Raincliffe Woods" turn left, hotel 1.5m on right*
This delightful country hotel is a lovely conversion of a farmhouse, set in the quiet North Riding Forest Park. Bedrooms are split between the main house and the delightful courtyard. Public areas include a split-level bar, quiet lounge, and attractive restaurant offering interesting menus.
ROOMS: 23 en suite (4 fmly) (14 GF) No smoking in 4 bedrooms s £29.50-£47.50; d £59-£95 (incl. bkfst) **LB FACILITIES:** Fishing Croquet lawn Xmas **PARKING:** 30 **NOTES:** No smoking in restaurant
CARDS:

★★★68% Wrea Head Country Hotel

Scalby YO13 0PB
☎ 01723 378211 01723 371780
e-mail: wreahead@englishrosehotels.co.uk
Dir: *from Scarborough follow A171 to hotel sign on left, turn into Barmoor Lane, hotel drive is on left*
This elegant Victorian country house is situated in 14 acres of landscaped grounds and gardens amongst splendid scenery on the edge of the town. The comfortable bedrooms are individually furnished and decorated, many of them with fine views. Public rooms include the oak-panelled lounge with an inglenook fireplace and a beautiful library lounge, full of books and games. Staff are friendly, helpful and enthusiastic.
ROOMS: 20 en suite (2 fmly) (1 GF) s £49.50-£75; d £95-£190 (incl. bkfst) **LB FACILITIES:** STV Croquet lawn Putting green Xmas **CONF:** Thtr 30 Class 16 Board 20 Del from £80 **PARKING:** 50 **NOTES:** No dogs (ex guide dogs) No smoking in restaurant Civ Wed 60
CARDS:

See advert on opposite page

★★★66% Hotel St Nicholas

St Nicholas Cliff YO11 2EU
CRERAR HOTELS
☎ 01723 364101 01723 500538
e-mail: reservations.stnicholas@crerarhotels.com
Dir: *in town centre, railway station on right, turn right at traffic lights, left at next lights, across rdbt, next left*

This attractive Victorian hotel enjoys fine views over the South Bay and is just a short walk from the town. In recent years much of the hotel has been refurbished, and the public rooms and many of the bedrooms are now looking very smart. The hotel has a variety of seating areas, a traditional carvery restaurant and a street-side bar/bistro.
ROOMS: 139 en suite (17 fmly) No smoking in 39 bedrooms s £45-£95; d £75-£150 (incl. bkfst) **LB FACILITIES:** STV Indoor swimming (H) Sauna Solarium Gym Games room, Swimming pool supervised entertainment Xmas **CONF:** Thtr 400 Class 150 Board 50 Del from £75 **SERVICES:** Lift **PARKING:** 24 **NOTES:** No dogs (ex guide dogs) No smoking in restaurant Civ Wed 300
CARDS:

★★★65% Esplanade

Belmont Rd YO11 2AA
THE INDEPENDENTS
☎ 01723 360382 01723 376137
Dir: *from Scarborough town centre over Valley Bridge, left then immediate right onto Belmont Rd, hotel 100mtrs on right*
This large hotel enjoys a superb position overlooking South Bay and the harbour. Both the terrace, leading from the lounge bar, and the restaurant, with its striking oriel window, benefit from these magnificent views. Bedrooms are comfortably furnished to a stylish, modern standard and are well equipped.
ROOMS: 73 en suite (9 fmly) s £49; d £92-£102 (incl. bkfst) **LB FACILITIES:** Table tennis Xmas **CONF:** Thtr 140 Class 100 Board 40 **SERVICES:** Lift **PARKING:** 20 **NOTES:** No smoking in restaurant Closed 2 Jan-4 Feb **CARDS:**

★★★64% Palm Court

St Nicholas Cliff YO11 2ES
☎ 01723 368161 01723 371547
e-mail: palmcourt@scarborough.co.uk
Dir: *follow signs for Town Centre & Town Hall, hotel before Town Hall on right*

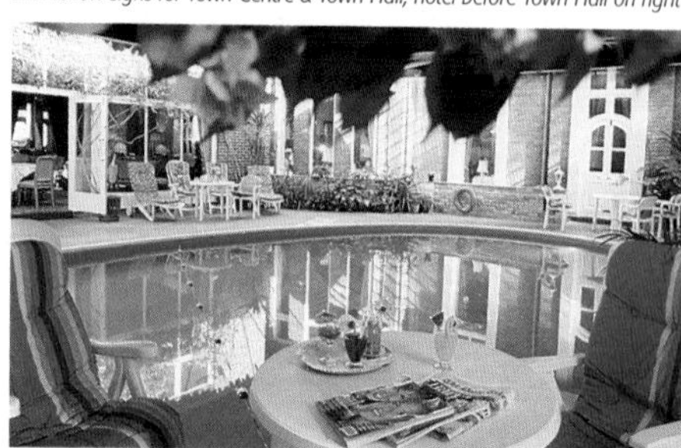

The public rooms are spacious and comfortable at this modern, town centre hotel. Traditional cooking is provided in the attractive restaurant and staff are friendly and helpful. The bedrooms are comfortable and well equipped. Extra facilities include a swimming pool and free, covered parking.
ROOMS: 44 en suite (7 fmly) s £43-£48; d £80-£90 (incl. bkfst) **LB FACILITIES:** Indoor swimming (H) entertainment Xmas **CONF:** Thtr 200 Class 100 Board 60 Del £65 **SERVICES:** Lift **PARKING:** 80 **NOTES:** No dogs (ex guide dogs) No smoking in restaurant
CARDS:

See advert on page 539

ENGLISH ROSE HOTELS

WREA HEAD
COUNTRY HOUSE HOTEL

Sample the delights of this beautifully restored Victorian Country House set in acres of glorious gardens and park lands at the edge of the North York Moors National Park. Twenty individually styled bedrooms. Award winning Four Seasons restaurant offers superb cuisine using fresh local produce. Ample free car parking. Situated three miles north of Scarborough – a perfect base for touring the heritage coast. Meeting facilities for up to 20 persons in privacy and seclusion.

For details ring 01723 378211
Barmoor Lane, Scalby
Scarborough YO13 0PB
Fax: 01723 355936

★★★

HACKNESS GRANGE COUNTRY HOTEL

North Yorkshire Moors National Park
nr Scarborough YO13 0JW

Situated on the outskirts of Scarborough, this gracious Country House is set in acres of beautiful gardens and grounds beside the River Derwent, within the North York Moors National Park. Excellent leisure choices - indoor heated swimming pool with jacuzzi, tennis court, trout fishing (in season), croquet and nine hole pitch 'n putt. 33 delightful en-suite bedrooms, many with scenic country views, and award winning restaurant renowned for good food. Some ground floor rooms available. Perfect location for Board Meetings and available for exclusive use for corporated events and activities.

See entry under Hackness

Tel: 01723 882345 Fax: 01723 882391

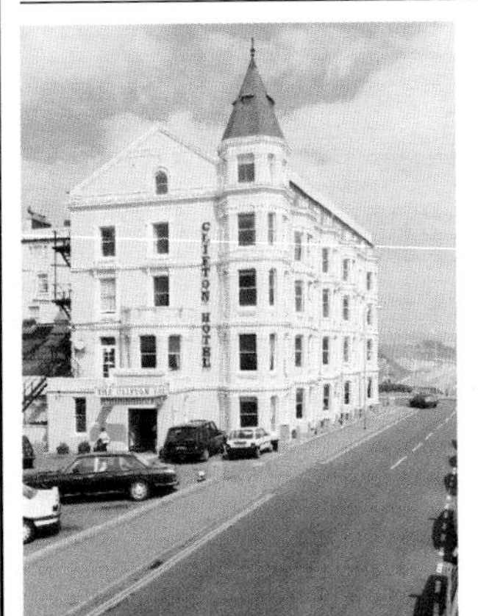

THE CLIFTON HOTEL

QUEENS PARADE, NORTH SHORE
SCARBOROUGH YO12 7HX
Tel: 01723 375691 Fax: 01723 364203

AA ★★★

The finest location on Scarborough's North Shore with many of the 71 en-suite bedrooms having panoramic sea views over the Bay and Scarborough Castle headland.
Excellent food with good old fashioned Yorkshire portions! Free private car parking.
Adjacent to Alexander Bowls Centre and Scarborough Cricket Ground.

ENGLISH ROSE HOTELS

SCARBOROUGH, continued

★★★63% *Ambassador*

Centre of the Esplanade YO11 2AY
☎ 01723 362841 🖷 01723 366166
e-mail: enquiries@scarboroughhotel.com
Dir: *A64, right at 1st small rdbt opposite B&Q, right at next small rdbt, immediate left down Avenue Victoria to Cliff Top*

Standing on the South Cliff with excellent views over the bay, this friendly hotel offers well-equipped bedrooms, some of which are executive rooms. A large indoor swimming pool, sauna and solarium are available, and residents can also use the spa facilities at the Crown Hotel just along the road. Entertainment is provided during the summer season.
ROOMS: 59 en suite (10 fmly) No smoking in 10 bedrooms **FACILITIES: Spa** STV Indoor swimming (H) Sauna Steam room entertainment **CONF:** Thtr 140 Class 90 Board 60 **SERVICES:** Lift **NOTES:** No smoking in restaurant **CARDS:**

★★★61% *Clifton*

Queens Pde, North Cliff YO12 7HX
☎ 01723 375691 🖷 01723 364203
e-mail: clifton@englishrosehotels.co.uk
Dir: *on entering town centre, follow signs for North Bay*
Standing in an impressive position commanding fine views over the bay, this large holiday hotel is convenient for Peasholm Park and other local leisure attractions. Bedrooms are pleasant and entertainment is provided in the spacious public rooms during high season.
ROOMS: 71 en suite (11 fmly) **FACILITIES:** Sauna Solarium **CONF:** Thtr 120 Class 50 Board 50 **SERVICES:** Lift **PARKING:** 45 **NOTES:** No dogs (ex guide dogs) No smoking in restaurant **CARDS:**

★★73% *The Mount*

Cliff Bridge Ter, Saint Nicholas Cliff YO11 2HA
☎ 01723 360961 🖷 01723 360961
Standing in a superb, elevated position and enjoying magnificent views of the South Bay, this elegant Regency hotel is personally owned and managed to a high standard. The richly furnished and comfortable public rooms are inviting, and the well-equipped bedrooms have been attractively decorated. The deluxe rooms are mini-suites and very comfortable.
ROOMS: 50 en suite (5 fmly) No smoking in 2 bedrooms **FACILITIES:** **SERVICES:** Lift **NOTES:** Closed Jan-mid Mar **CARDS:**

See advert on opposite page

★★68% Park Manor

Northstead Manor Dr YO12 6BB
☎ 01723 372090 🖷 01723 500480
e-mail: info@parkmanor.co.uk
Dir: *off A165, next to Peasholm Park*

Enjoying a peaceful residential setting, this smartly presented, friendly hotel provides the seaside tourist with a wide range of facilities. Bedrooms vary in size and style but all are smartly furnished and well equipped. There is a spacious lounge, smart restaurant, games room and indoor pool and steam room for relaxation.
ROOMS: 42 en suite (6 fmly) s £35.50-£40; d £71-£86 (incl. bkfst) **LB** **FACILITIES: Spa** Indoor swimming (H) Solarium Jacuzzi Pool table Steam room Table tennis Xmas **CONF:** Thtr 25 Class 20 Board 20 Del from £58 **SERVICES:** Lift **PARKING:** 20 **NOTES:** No dogs No children 3yrs **CARDS:**

★★67% Red Lea

Prince of Wales Ter YO11 2AJ
☎ 01723 362431 🖷 01723 371230
e-mail: redlea@globalnet.co.uk
Dir: *follow signs for South Cliff, Prince of Wales Terrace off esplanade opp cliff lift*

This friendly, family-run hotel is situated close to the cliff lift. Bedrooms are well equipped and comfortably furnished, and many at the front have picturesque views of the coast. There are two large lounges and a spacious dining room in which good-value, traditional food is served.
ROOMS: 67 en suite (7 fmly) (2 GF) s £34-£38; d £68-£76 (incl. bkfst) **LB** **FACILITIES:** Indoor swimming (H) Sauna Solarium Gym Xmas **CONF:** Thtr 40 Class 25 Board 25 Del £50 **SERVICES:** Lift **NOTES:** No dogs (ex guide dogs) No smoking in restaurant **CARDS:**

S

★★65% *Bradley Court Hotel*
Filey Rd, South Cliff YO11 2SE
☎ 01723 360476 🖷 01723 376661
e-mail: bradley@yorkshirecoast.co.uk
Dir: *from A64 into Scarborough; at 1st rdbt turn right signed Filey & South Cliff, at next rdbt turn left, hotel 50yds on left*
This popular hotel is only a short walk from both the town centre and the South Cliff promenade. Bedrooms are well equipped and there are spacious public rooms which include a bar lounge and a large, modern function room suitable for weddings and conferences.
ROOMS: 40 en suite (4 fmly) No smoking in 6 bedrooms **CONF:** Thtr 160 Class 100 Board 60 **SERVICES:** Lift **PARKING:** 20 **NOTES:** No dogs No smoking in restaurant **CARDS:**

★★64% The New Southlands
15 West St, South Cliff YO11 2QW
☎ 01723 361461 🖷 01723 376035
e-mail: sales@southlandshotel.co.uk
Dir: *in Scarborough, follow town centre signs, right at railway station, left at 2nd lights, car park 200yds on left*
This hotel, popular with tour groups, is situated in a quiet area close to the South Cliff. Bedrooms are spacious and the refurbished public rooms are bright and airy. Friendly and attentive service is provided by pleasant and well-managed team.
ROOMS: 58 en suite (14 fmly) No smoking in 2 bedrooms s £36-£54; d £72-£108 (incl. bkfst & dinner) **LB** **FACILITIES:** entertainment Xmas **CONF:** Thtr 120 Class 30 Board 30 **SERVICES:** Lift **PARKING:** 35 **NOTES:** No smoking in restaurant **CARDS:**

★★62% Manor Heath Hotel
67 Northstead Manor Dr YO12 6AF
☎ 01723 365720 🖷 01723 365720
e-mail: enquiries@manorheath.co.uk
Dir: *follow signs for North Bay and Peasholm Park*
A warm welcome is offered at this pleasant, traditional, private hotel. Public areas include a cosy bar, comfortable lounge and a relaxing dining room. The bedrooms vary in size and style but all are modern and bright and offer all the expected comforts. The front garden is very well cared for.
ROOMS: 14 en suite (6 fmly) s £21-£26; d £42-£52 (incl. bkfst) **LB** **PARKING:** 16 **NOTES:** No smoking in restaurant Closed Dec-1 Jan **CARDS:**

★★60% Brooklands
Esplanade Gardens, South Cliff YO11 2AW
☎ 01723 376576 🖷 01723 341093
Dir: *from A64 York, turn left at B&Q rdbt, right at next mini rdbt then 1st left onto Victoria Ave, at end turn left then 2nd left*

The Brooklands is a traditional, privately owned and run seaside hotel. It often caters for tours and offers good value for money. The hotel stands on the South Cliff overlooking Esplanade

continued on p540

S

SCARBOROUGH, continued

Gardens, and is within easy access of the sea. There are ample lounges to relax in and wholesome home cooking to enjoy.
ROOMS: 56 en suite (11 fmly) (1 GF) No smoking in 4 bedrooms s £28-£35; d £55-£70 (incl. bkfst) **LB FACILITIES:** entertainment Xmas **CONF:** Thtr 120 Class 80 Board 30 Del from £60 **SERVICES:** Lift **PARKING:** 1 **NOTES:** No smoking in restaurant Closed Jan RS Feb
CARDS:

★★57% **The Bedford**
The Crescent YO11 2PP
☎ 01723 360084 📠 01723 507374
e-mail: reception@bedfordhotel.info
The Bedford is a traditional family-owned and run seaside hotel, ideally situated on the historic Crescent. The comfortable bedrooms vary in size; some are suitable for family occupancy, several benefit from sea views. Public areas are spacious and comfortable with informal and friendly service provided.
ROOMS: 27 en suite (8 fmly) (1 GF) s £30-£40; d £50-£70 (incl. bkfst) **LB FACILITIES:** entertainment Xmas **CONF:** Thtr 60 Class 40 Board 25 Del from £25 **NOTES:** No smoking in restaurant
CARDS:

SCILLY, ISLES OF — Map 02

BRYHER — Map 02 SV81

★★★80% **Hell Bay Hotel**
TR23 0PR
☎ 01720 422947 📠 01720 423004
e-mail: contactus@hellbay.co.uk
Dir: *Island location means it is only accessible by helicopter from Penzance, ship from Penzance or plane from Bristol, Exeter, Plymouth or Land's End*

Located on the smallest of the inhabited Scilly islands, this hotel provides a really special destination. Much of the hotel has been completely refurbished and bedrooms, many with garden access and stunning sea views, are stylish and very well equipped. Cuisine features fresh local produce and is a delight.
ROOMS: 12 en suite 11 annexe en suite (4 fmly) (18 GF) No smoking in all bedrooms d £170-£360 (incl. bkfst & dinner) **LB FACILITIES: Spa** STV Outdoor swimming (H) Golf 9 Sauna Gym Croquet lawn Putting green Boules Par 3 golf **CONF:** Thtr 36 Class 36 Board 36 Del from £150 **NOTES:** No smoking in restaurant Closed Mov-Feb
CARDS:

Late for dinner?
Quality Standards mean that last orders for dinner vary according to star rating and should be no earlier than:
★★ 7.00pm ★★★ 8.00pm ★★★★ 9.00pm
★★★★★ 10.00pm

ST MARTIN'S — Map 02 SV91

Top 200 - Hotel

★★★ **St Martin's on the Isle**
Lower Town TR25 0QW
☎ 01720 422090 📠 01720 422298
e-mail: stay@stmartinshotel.co.uk
Dir: *20-minute helicopter flight to St Mary's, then 20-minute launch to St Martin's*
This attractive hotel, complete with its own sandy beach, enjoys an idyllic position on the waterfront overlooking Tresco and Tean. Bedrooms are brightly appointed, comfortably furnished and overlook the sea or the well-tended gardens. There is an elegant, award-winning restaurant and a split-level lounge bar where guests can relax and enjoy the memorable view. Locally caught fish features significantly on the daily-changing menus.
ROOMS: 30 en suite (10 fmly) (14 GF) s £115.50-£198; d £210-£360 (incl. bkfst & dinner) **LB FACILITIES:** Indoor swimming (H) Tennis (hard) Snooker Clay pigeon shooting Boating Bikes Diving Snorkelling ch fac **CONF:** Thtr 50 Class 50 Board 50 **NOTES:** No smoking in restaurant Closed Nov-Feb Civ Wed 60
CARDS:

See advert on opposite page

ST MARY'S — Map 02 SV91

★★★74% ***Tregarthens***
Hugh Town TR21 0PP
☎ 01720 422540 📠 01720 422089
e-mail: reception@tregarthens-hotel.co.uk
Dir: *100yds from quay*
Opened in 1848 by Captain Tregarthen this is now a well-established hotel. The impressively refurbished public areas provide wonderful views overlooking St Mary's harbour and some of the many islands, including Tresco and Bryher. The spacious bedrooms are well-equipped and neatly furnished. Traditional cuisine is served in the restaurant.
ROOMS: 31 en suite 1 annexe en suite (5 fmly) No smoking in 4 bedrooms **NOTES:** No dogs (ex guide dogs) No smoking in restaurant Closed late Oct-mid Mar **CARDS:**

See advert on opposite page

★★★73% ***Star Castle***
The Garrison TR21 0JA
☎ 01720 422317 & 423342 📠 01720 422343
e-mail: recep@starcastlescilly.demon.co.uk
Dir: *overlooking the harbour*
Built in 1593 as a fortress, the Star Castle maintains an imposing position overlooking St Mary's, and enjoys magnificent views of the outer islands. Bedrooms are situated in the main castle and

continued

others have been built in the garden, where many of the rooms have private balconies and sea views. There is a choice of dining options - in the conservatory or the traditional restaurant.
ROOMS: 10 en suite 23 annexe en suite (17 fmly) **FACILITIES:** Indoor swimming (H) Tennis (grass) Games room ch fac **PARKING:** 6
NOTES: No smoking in restaurant Closed end Oct-Feb
CARDS:

TRESCO Map 02 SV81

Top 200 - Hotel

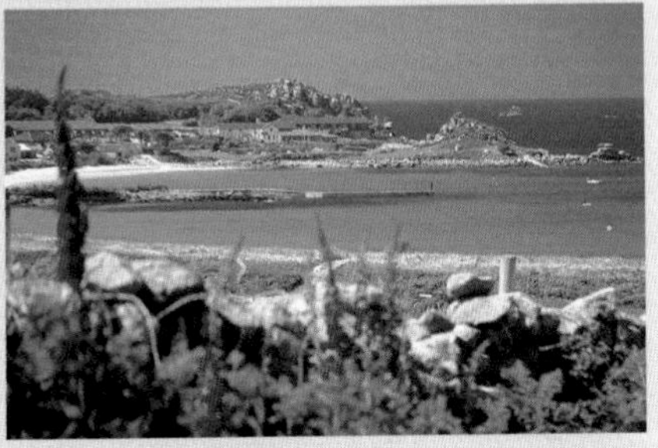

★★★ The Island
TR24 0PU
☎ 01720 422883 📠 01720 423008
e-mail: islandhotel@tresco.co.uk
Dir: *helicopter service Penzance to Tresco, hotel on NE of island*
This delightful colonial-style hotel enjoys a waterside location in its own attractive gardens. The spacious, comfortable lounges, airy restaurant and many of the bedrooms enjoy stunning sea views. All of the rooms are brightly furnished and many benefit from lounge areas, balconies or terraces. Carefully prepared, imaginative cuisine makes good use of locally caught fish.
ROOMS: 48 en suite (27 fmly) s £114-£152; d £228-£472 (incl. bkfst & dinner) **LB** **FACILITIES:** Outdoor swimming (H) Tennis (hard) Fishing Croquet lawn Boating Table tennis Bowls ch fac
CONF: Thtr 80 Class 80 Board 80 Del £165 **NOTES:** No dogs (ex guide dogs) No smoking in restaurant Closed Nov-Feb
CARDS:

★★76% New Inn
TR24 0QQ
☎ 01720 422844 📠 01720 423200
e-mail: newinn@tresco.co.uk
Dir: *by New Grimsby Quay*
This friendly, popular inn enjoys a central location and offers bright, attractive, well-equipped bedrooms, many with splendid sea views. The popular bar offering real ales, serves an interesting range of snacks and meals. In addition guests may choose to dine in the airy bistro-style Pavilion or the elegant restaurant complete with its own bar.
ROOMS: 15 en suite (1 GF) d £138-£230 (incl. bkfst & dinner) **LB**
FACILITIES: Outdoor swimming (H) Tennis (hard) Sea fishing Xmas
NOTES: No dogs No smoking in restaurant
CARDS:

Town House Hotel
Country House Hotel
Travel Accommodation

S

SCOTCH CORNER (NEAR RICHMOND), North Yorkshire — Map 19 NZ20

★★★64% Quality Hotel, Scotch Corner

DL10 6NR
☎ 01748 850900 📠 01748 825417
e-mail: admin@gb609.u-net.com
Dir: *at A1/A66 junct turn off towards Penrith*

This hotel is ideally located for access to main road networks and offers excellent parking facilities. Bedrooms are generally spacious and are equipped with thoughtful extras. A popular venue for both conference and leisure guests, there are spacious lounges, meeting rooms and a particularly well equipped leisure club.

ROOMS: 90 en suite (5 fmly) (17 GF) No smoking in 45 bedrooms s £85; d £110 **LB FACILITIES:** STV Indoor swimming (H) Sauna Solarium Gym Jacuzzi Beauty Therapist Physiotherapy Suite Dance Studio entertainment Xmas **CONF:** Thtr 280 Class 110 Board 40 Del £100 **SERVICES:** Lift **PARKING:** 200 **NOTES:** No smoking in restaurant Civ Wed 200 **CARDS:**

⌂ Travelodge

Middleton Tyas Ln DL10 6PQ
☎ 08700 850 950 📠 01325 377890
Dir: *A1/A66*

Travelodge offers good quality, good value, modern accommodation. Ideal for families, the spacious, en suite bedrooms include remote-control TV, tea and coffee-making facilities, luxury beds and free morning newspaper. Meals can be taken at the nearby family restaurant. For further details and the Travelodge phone number, consult the Hotel Groups page.

ROOMS: 50 en suite s fr £42.95; d fr £42.95

⌂ Travelodge Skeeby (Scotch Corner)

Skeeby DL10 5EQ
☎ 08700 850 950 📠 01748 823768
Dir: *0.5m S on A1*

Travelodge offers good quality, good value, modern accommodation. Ideal for families, the spacious, en suite bedrooms include remote-control TV, tea and coffee-making facilities, luxury beds and free morning newspaper. Meals can be taken at the nearby family restaurant. For further details and the Travelodge phone number, consult the Hotel Groups page.

ROOMS: 40 en suite s fr £42.95; d fr £42.95

SCUNTHORPE, Lincolnshire — Map 17 SE81

★★★★72% ® Forest Pines Hotel

Ermine St, Broughton DN20 0AQ
☎ 01652 650770 📠 01652 650495
e-mail: enquiries@forestpines.co.uk
Dir: *200yds from M180 junct 4, on Brigg-Scunthorpe rdbt*

This smart, modern hotel offers professional and friendly service and a range of facilities and leisure pursuits. Public rooms offer a choice of dining options, with fine dining available in the Beech Tree Restaurant or more informal dining within the Garden Room or Mulligans Bar. Bedrooms are mostly spacious and well equipped.

ROOMS: 114 en suite (66 fmly) (41 GF) No smoking in 77 bedrooms **FACILITIES:** STV Indoor swimming (H) Golf 27 Sauna Gym Putting green Jacuzzi Mountain bikes Jogging track, indoor pool is supervised entertainment ch fac Xmas **CONF:** Thtr 220 Class 100 Board 60 Del £140 **SERVICES:** Lift **PARKING:** 300 **NOTES:** No dogs (ex guide dogs) No smoking in restaurant Civ Wed 120
CARDS:

★★★68% Wortley House

Rowland Rd DN16 1SU
☎ 01724 842223 📠 01724 280646
e-mail: quality@wortleyhousehotel.com
Dir: *from M180 junct 3 follow signs for town centre. At lights turn right, continue over the rail bridge to the rdbt & take 1st exit. Hotel 50yds on right*

A friendly hotel with good facilities for conferences, meetings, banquets and other functions. Bedrooms offer modern comfort and facilities. Popular bar meals are served in the cocktail lounge, and more formal meals can be enjoyed in the pleasant restaurant.

ROOMS: 38 en suite (4 fmly) No smoking in 20 bedrooms s £74-£84; d £84-£94 (incl. bkfst) **FACILITIES:** STV **CONF:** Thtr 300 Class 120 Board 80 Del from £90 **PARKING:** 100 **NOTES:** Civ Wed 240
CARDS:

⌂ Travel Inn

Lakeside Retail Park, Lakeside Parkway DN16 3UA
☎ 08701 977226 📠 01724 278651
Dir: *M180 junct 4, A18 towards Scunthorpe. At Morrisons rdbt left onto Lakeside Retail Park, Inn behind Morrisons petrol station*

Travel Inn offers good-quality, value-for-money accommodation. Spacious, en suite rooms with bath and shower comfortably accommodate a family of up to two adults and two children (to age 15). The restaurant and bar offers a varied menu. For further details and the Travel Inn phone number, consult the Hotel Groups page.

ROOMS: 40 en suite s £44.95; d £44.95

SEAHAM, Co Durham — Map 19 NZ44

Hotel of the Year
Top 200 - Hotel

★★★★ ®®® Seaham Hall Hotel

Lord Byron's Walk SR7 7AG
☎ 0191 516 1400 📠 0191 516 1410
e-mail: reservations@seaham-hall.com
Dir: *from A19 take B1404 to Seaham. At lights straight over level crossing. Hotel approx 0.25m on right*

This imposing house was the setting for the wedding of Lord Byron and has been restored with an opulence he would have appreciated. Bedrooms, including some stunning suites, offer cutting edge technology, contemporary artwork and a real sense of style. Bathrooms are particularly lavish with two-person baths a feature. Public rooms are equally impressive and accomplished cooking is a hallmark. A stunning new Oriental Spa, accessed via a underground

continued

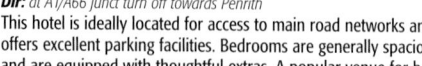

walkway, offers guests a wide range of treatments and a Thai brasserie. Seaham Hall has been awarded the AA Hotel of the Year Award for England 2003-2004.

ROOMS: 19 en suite No smoking in all bedrooms s £165; d £175 (incl. cont bkfst) **LB** **FACILITIES:** STV Oriental Spa to open 2002 Xmas **CONF:** Thtr 120 Class 40 Board 40 Del from £230 **SERVICES:** Lift air con **PARKING:** 122 **NOTES:** No dogs (ex guide dogs) No smoking in restaurant Civ Wed 120
CARDS:

SEAHOUSES, Northumberland — Map 21 NU23

★★74% Olde Ship
NE68 7RD
☎ 01665 720200 📠 01665 721383
e-mail: theoldeship@seahouses.co.uk
Dir: *lower end of main street above harbour*

The same family has run this friendly hotel since 1910. The sense of history is equally evident in the amount of nautical memorabilia on display in the public areas. Bedrooms, including two annexe rooms with stunning sea views, are thoughtfully equipped. Sir William Russell Flint resided at the Olde Ship while painting Bamburgh Castle and the Farne Islands.
ROOMS: 12 en suite 6 annexe en suite (3 GF) s £39-£46; d £78-£92 (incl. bkfst) **LB** **FACILITIES:** Putting green **PARKING:** 19 **NOTES:** No dogs No children 10yrs No smoking in restaurant Closed Dec-Jan
CARDS:

★★70% Bamburgh Castle
NE68 7SQ
☎ 01665 720283 📠 01665 720848
e-mail: bamburghcastlehotel@talk21.com
Dir: *from A1 follow signs for Seahouses, car park entrance on rbt opposite Barclays Bank, automatic barrier will rise*
Enjoying a seafront location, with views of the harbour and Farne Islands, this hotel is well situated for visiting all the tourist attractions of north Northumberland. Bedrooms vary in size and style, yet all are thoughtfully equipped and superior rooms are

continued

particularly spacious and attractively appointed. Guests have a choice of several comfortable lounges including one that is for non-smokers.

ROOMS: 20 en suite (3 fmly) (3 GF) No smoking in 5 bedrooms s £46-£52; d £80-£98 (incl. bkfst) **LB** **FACILITIES:** Putting green **CONF:** Thtr 40 Class 20 Board 25 **PARKING:** 30 **NOTES:** No smoking in restaurant Closed 24-26 Dec & 2wks mid Jan **CARDS:**

★★69% *Beach House*
Sea Front NE68 7SR
☎ 01665 720337 📠 01665 720921
e-mail: beach.house.hotel.seahouses@tinyonline.co.uk
Dir: *follow signs from A1 between Alnwick & Berwick*
Enjoying a seafront location and views of the Farne Islands, this non-smoking family-run hotel offers a relaxed and friendly atmosphere. Bedrooms, many of which have been refurbished, are bright, airy and elegantly decorated. Dinner makes use of fresh produce and breakfast features local specialities. A well-stocked bar and lounge with coal fire are also available.
ROOMS: 14 en suite (5 fmly) No smoking in all bedrooms
PARKING: 16 **NOTES:** No dogs No smoking in restaurant Closed Jan
CARDS:

SEATON, Devon — Map 04 SY29

★★70% Seaton Heights Hotel
Seaton Down Hill EX12 2TF
☎ 01297 20932 📠 01297 24839
e-mail: stay@seatonheightshotel.co.uk
Dir: *on A3052 at Tower Cross, hotel near watertower*
Conveniently located, the Seaton Heights overlooks the Axe Valley towards the sea. The restaurant and function suite have lovely views and the imaginative cuisine features freshly prepared dishes and includes a bar meal service. Bedrooms are modern in style and are well equipped.
ROOMS: 26 en suite (8 fmly) (11 GF) s £35-£63; d £70-£102 (incl. bkfst) **LB** **FACILITIES:** Outdoor swimming (H) Squash Snooker Sauna Solarium Gym Croquet lawn Badminton Basketball Table tennis Short mat bowls Aerobics Yoga entertainment Xmas **CONF:** Thtr 500 Class 300 Board 150 Del from £80 **PARKING:** 128 **NOTES:** No smoking in restaurant **CARDS:**

SEATON BURN, Tyne & Wear — Map 21 NZ27

⌂ Travelodge (Newcastle North)
Travelodge

Front St NE13 6ED
☎ 08700 850 950
Travelodge offers good quality, good value, modern accommodation. Ideal for families, the spacious, en suite bedrooms include remote-control TV, tea and coffee-making facilities, luxury beds and free morning newspaper. Meals can be taken at the nearby family restaurant. For further details and the Travelodge phone number, consult the Hotel Groups page.
ROOMS: 40 en suite s fr £42.95; d fr £42.95

S

SEAVIEW See Wight, Isle of

SEDGEFIELD, Co Durham Map 19 NZ32

★★★67% Hardwick Hall
TS21 2EH
☎ 01740 620253 📠 01740 622771
e-mail: reception@hardwickhallhotel.co.uk
Dir: *off A1M junct 60 towards Sedgefield, left at 1st rdbt, hotel 400mtrs on left*

This 18th-century house is set in extensive parkland, on an estate dating back to 1183. Additions to the hotel include impressive conference and banqueting facilities with state-of-the-art equipment, and a new wing of stunning bedrooms. The atmospheric Cellar Bar and Bistro offers a relaxed atmosphere and modern cuisine.

ROOMS: 52 en suite (6 fmly) No smoking in all bedrooms s £75-£130; d £95-£150 (incl. bkfst) **LB FACILITIES:** STV **CONF:** Thtr 700 Board 80 Del £140 **SERVICES:** Lift **PARKING:** 200 **NOTES:** No dogs (ex guide dogs) No smoking in restaurant Civ Wed 75
CARDS:

⌂ Travelodge
TS21 2JX
☎ 08700 850 950 📠 01740 623399
Dir: *on A689, 3m E of junct A1(M)*

Travelodge offers good quality, good value, modern accommodation. Ideal for families, the spacious, en suite bedrooms include remote-control TV, tea and coffee-making facilities, luxury beds and free morning newspaper. Meals can be taken at the nearby family restaurant. For further details and the Travelodge phone number, consult the Hotel Groups page.

ROOMS: 40 en suite s fr £42.95; d fr £42.95

SEDGEMOOR MOTORWAY SERVICE AREA (M5), Somerset Map 04 ST35

⌂ Welcome Lodge
M5 Northbound J22-21, Sedgemoor BS24 0JL
☎ 01934 750831 📠 01934 750808
e-mail: sedgemoor.hotel@welcomebreak.co.uk
Dir: *M5 junct 21/22*

This modern building offers accommodation in smart, spacious and well-equipped bedrooms, suitable for families and business travellers, and all with en suite bathrooms. Refreshments may be taken at the nearby family restaurant. For further details and the Welcome Break phone number, consult the Hotel Groups page.

ROOMS: 40 en suite s £45; d £45

SEDLESCOMBE, East Sussex Map 07 TQ71

★★★68% Brickwall
The Green TN33 0QA
☎ 01424 870253 📠 01424 870785
e-mail: brickwallhotel@hotmail.com
Dir: *off A21 on B2244 at top of Sedlescombe Green*

This well-maintained 15th-century Tudor house is situated in the heart of this pretty village overlooking the green. The spacious public rooms feature a lovely wood-panelled restaurant with a wealth of oak beams and a choice of lounges as well as a bar. Bedrooms are located in a modern extension adjoining the rear of the property; each is pleasantly decorated and thoughtfully equipped.

ROOMS: 26 en suite (2 fmly) (9 GF) No smoking in 9 bedrooms s £55-£60; d £80-£90 (incl. bkfst) **LB FACILITIES:** STV Outdoor swimming (H) Xmas **CONF:** Thtr 30 Class 40 Board 30 **PARKING:** 50 **NOTES:** No smoking in restaurant **CARDS:**

SENNEN, Cornwall & Isles of Scilly Map 02 SW32

★★67% *Old Success Inn*
Sennen Cove TR19 7DG
☎ 01736 871232 📠 01736 871457
e-mail: oldsuccess@hotmail.com
Dir: *turn right off A30 approx 1m before Land's End, signed Sennen Cove. Hotel on left at bottom of hill*

Romantically located at the water's edge with spectacular views of Sennen Cove, this old inn is popular with locals and visitors alike. The friendly management and staff provide a welcoming environment. A range of bar snacks is available and the restaurant features fresh local seafood and traditional dishes.

ROOMS: 12 en suite (1 fmly) **FACILITIES:** entertainment **PARKING:** 12 **NOTES:** No smoking in restaurant **CARDS:**

SEVENOAKS, Kent Map 06 TQ55

★★★70% Donnington Manor
London Rd, Dunton Green TN13 2TD
☎ 01732 462681 📠 01732 458116
e-mail: donningtonmanor@btconnect.com
Dir: *M25 junct 4, follow signs for Bromley/Orpington to rdbt. Left onto A224 (Dunton Green), left at 2nd rdbt. At Rose & Crown left, hotel 300yds on right*

This extended 15th-century manor house is situated on the outskirts of Sevenoaks. Public rooms in the original part of the building have a wealth of character; they include an attractive oak-beamed restaurant, a comfortable lounge and a cosy bar. The purpose-built bedrooms are smartly decorated and well equipped. The hotel also features a squash court, a gym and swimming pool.

ROOMS: 60 en suite (2 fmly) No smoking in 20 bedrooms s £75-£85; d £95-£110 (incl. bkfst) **LB FACILITIES:** STV Indoor swimming (H) Squash Sauna Gym Jacuzzi Indoor Swimming pool supervised Xmas **CONF:** Thtr 180 Class 60 Board 40 Del from £120 **PARKING:** 120 **NOTES:** No dogs (ex guide dogs) No smoking in restaurant Civ Wed 100 **CARDS:**

See advert on opposite page

★★★65% ⊛ Royal Oak
Upper High St TN13 1HY
☎ 01732 451109 📠 01732 740187
e-mail: info@royaloak.demon.co.uk
Dir: *on A225, through town centre on right, opposite Sevenoaks School*

Delightful 17th-century building made of Kentish ragstone situated on the main high street. The smartly appointed, well-equipped bedrooms are split between the main building and an adjacent wing. Public rooms feature the contemporary-style No. 5 Bar and brasserie where an interesting range of dishes is available.

ROOMS: 21 en suite 16 annexe en suite (2 fmly) No smoking in 19 bedrooms s £60-£90; d £70-£105 **LB FACILITIES:** STV Tennis (hard) Xmas **CONF:** Thtr 35 Class 14 Board 20 Del from £110 **PARKING:** 50 **NOTES:** No smoking in restaurant **CARDS:**

S

SEVERN VIEW MOTORWAY SERVICE AREA (M4), Gloucestershire Map 04 ST58

Travelodge

M48 Motorway, Severn Bridge BS35 4BH
☎ 08700 850 950 📠 01454 632482
Dir: *M48 junct 21*
Travelodge offers good quality, good value, modern accommodation. Ideal for families, the spacious, en suite bedrooms include remote-control TV, tea and coffee-making facilities, luxury beds and free morning newspaper. Meals can be taken at the nearby family restaurant. For further details and the Travelodge phone number, consult the Hotel Groups page.
ROOMS: 50 en suite s fr £42.95; d fr £42.95

SHAFTESBURY, Dorset Map 04 ST82

★★★68% Royal Chase

Royal Chase Roundabout SP7 8DB
☎ 01747 853355 📠 01747 851969
e-mail: royalchasehotel@btinternet.com
Dir: *A303 to A350 signed Blandford Forum. (Avoid town centre, follow road to 3rd rdbt)*
Equally suitable for both leisure and business guests, this well-known local landmark is situated close to the famous Gold Hill. Bedrooms come in 'standard' and 'crown' and both types offer good levels of comfort and quality. In addition to the fixed-price menu in the Byzant Restaurant, guests have the option of eating in the convivial bar.
ROOMS: 33 en suite (13 fmly) No smoking in 10 bedrooms s £85-£95; d £100-£115 **LB** **FACILITIES: Spa** STV Indoor swimming (H) Turkish steam bath Xmas **CONF:** Thtr 140 Class 90 Board 50 Del £107.50 **PARKING:** 100 **NOTES:** No smoking in restaurant Civ Wed 78
CARDS:

SHALDON See Teignmouth

SHANKLIN See Wight, Isle of

SHAP, Cumbria Map 18 NY51

★★★68% Shap Wells

CA10 3QU
☎ 01931 716628 📠 01931 716377
e-mail: manager@shapwells.com
Dir: *M6 junct 39, follow signs for Kendal, turn left at A6, after approx 1m turn left into drive. Hotel approx 1m*

This friendly, family-owned hotel occupies a wonderful secluded position amid trees and waterfalls. Extensive public areas include function and meeting rooms, a well-stocked bar, a choice of lounges and a spacious restaurant. Bedrooms vary in size and style and all are equipped with the expected facilities.
ROOMS: 91 en suite 7 annexe en suite (10 fmly) **FACILITIES:** Tennis (hard) Snooker Games room, walking in the 30 acre grounds **CONF:** Thtr 170 Class 80 Board 40 Del from £67.50 **SERVICES:** Lift **PARKING:** 200 **NOTES:** No smoking in restaurant Closed 23-28 Dec & 4 Jan-14 Feb Civ Wed 150 **CARDS:**

See advert under KENDAL p303

SHAPWICK, Somerset Map 04 ST43

★★74% *Shapwick House*

Monks Dr TA7 9NL
☎ 01458 210321 📠 01458 210729
e-mail: keith@shapwickhouse.free-on-line.co.uk
Dir: *M5 junct 23 towards Glastonbury. Left onto A39 (Glastonbury). After 5m hotel signed on left*
Dating back to the 15th century, this fabulous stone manor house was originally built by Glastonbury Abbey. Shapwick House is surrounded by lovely gardens and grounds and offers easy access to Junction 23 of the M5. The main hall, with its splendid fireplace is the ideal place to relax after a busy day exploring. Bedrooms are spacious and well-equipped with many thoughtful touches. The Georgian dining room offers an imaginative, fixed-price menu.
ROOMS: 12 en suite No smoking in 10 bedrooms **CONF:** Thtr 40 Class 25 Board 15 **PARKING:** 40 **NOTES:** No dogs (ex guide dogs) No children 10yrs No smoking in restaurant RS 25 Dec-31 Jan Civ Wed 100
CARDS:

SHEDFIELD, Hampshire

Map 05 SU51

★★★★67% Marriott Meon Valley Hotel & Country Club

Sandy Ln SO32 2HQ
☎ 01329 833455 01329 834411
Dir: from W, M27 junct 7 take A334 towards Wickham and Botley. Sandy Lane on left 2m from Botley

This modern, smartly appointed hotel and country club has extensive indoor and outdoor leisure facilities, including two golf courses. Bedrooms are spacious and well equipped, and guests have a choice of eating and drinking options.

ROOMS: 113 en suite No smoking in 80 bedrooms **FACILITIES:** STV Indoor swimming (H) Golf 18 Tennis (hard) Sauna Solarium Gym Putting green Jacuzzi Cardio-Vascular Aerobics Health & Beauty salon **CONF:** Thtr 90 Class 50 Board 36 **SERVICES:** Lift **PARKING:** 320 **NOTES:** No dogs (ex guide dogs) No smoking in restaurant Civ Wed 80
CARDS:

SHEFFIELD, South Yorkshire

Map 16 SK38

★★★★69% Sheffield Marriott Hotel

Kenwood Rd S7 1NQ
☎ 0114 258 3811
0114 250 0138/0114 255 4744
e-mail: sales.sheffield@marriotthotels.co.uk
Dir: follow A61 past Red Tape Studios on right , right at 2nd lights into St Marys Rd. At rdbt straight across, left into London Rd, right at lights, at top of hill straight across 1st and 2nd rdbt

Extensive refurbishment at this hotel has provided a smart, modern environment for the 21st-century traveller. The bedrooms offer quiet, spacious accommodation and an extensive range of facilities. The hotel also has an extensive range of leisure and meeting facilities. Drivers have the peace of mind of secure parking.

ROOMS: 114 en suite (33 fmly) No smoking in 89 bedrooms s £60-£119; d £70-£129 (incl. bkfst) **LB FACILITIES: Spa** STV Indoor swimming (H) Fishing Sauna Solarium Gym Croquet lawn Jacuzzi Steam room, Health & beauty treatments, Swimming pool supervised **CONF:** Thtr 250 Class 100 Board 60 Del from £135 **SERVICES:** Lift **PARKING:** 200 **NOTES:** No dogs (ex guide dogs) No smoking in restaurant Civ Wed 120
CARDS:

★★★74% Staindrop Lodge

Lane End, Chapeltown S35 3UH
☎ 0114 284 3111 0114 284 3110
e-mail: info@staindroplodge.co.uk
Dir: M1 junct 35, take A629 for 1m over 1st rdbt, right at 2nd rdbt, hotel 0.5m on right

Now fully refurbished and extended, this hotel, bar and brasserie offers smart modern public areas and accommodation. An art deco theme runs through the open plan areas and also the comfortably appointed, spacious bedrooms. Service is relaxed and friendly.

ROOMS: 31 en suite (6 fmly) No smoking in all bedrooms s £70-£100; d £90-£145 (incl. bkfst) **LB FACILITIES:** STV Xmas **CONF:** Thtr 40 Class 60 Board 40 **SERVICES:** Lift air con **PARKING:** 80 **NOTES:** No dogs (ex guide dogs) No smoking in restaurant
CARDS:

★★★72% Whitley Hall

Elliott Ln, Grenoside S35 8NR
☎ 0114 245 4444 0114 245 5414
e-mail: reservations@whitleyhall.com
Dir: A61 past football ground and 2m, right just before Norfolk Arms, left at bottom of hill. Hotel on left

This 16th-century house stands in 30 acres of well-tended, landscaped grounds and gardens. Public rooms are full of character, with an impressive gallery, and oak-panelled restaurant, bar and lounge. Bedrooms are individually furnished in a style in keeping with this country house setting; each room is equipped with a range of modern facilities and useful extras.

ROOMS: 19 en suite (1 fmly) s £65-£105; d £90-£125 (incl. bkfst) **LB FACILITIES:** Croquet lawn Putting green entertainment **CONF:** Thtr 70 Class 50 Board 40 Del from £140 **PARKING:** 100 **NOTES:** No dogs (ex guide dogs) No smoking in restaurant RS Sat Civ Wed 80
CARDS:

★★★71% The Beauchief Hotel

161 Abbeydale Rd South S7 2QW
☎ 0114 262 0500 0114 235 0197
e-mail: beauchief@corushotels.com
Dir: 2m from city centre on A621 signed Bakewell

On the southern outskirts of the city, this busy property attracts both resident and local business. The popular restaurant and Merchant's bar have an excellent reputation for good food and hospitality. Bedrooms are well proportioned with many extras such as movie channels on the TV. Ample parking is a bonus.

ROOMS: 50 en suite No smoking in 30 bedrooms **FACILITIES:** STV **CONF:** Thtr 100 Class 50 Board 50 **PARKING:** 200 **NOTES:** No smoking in restaurant Civ Wed 120
CARDS:

★★★71% Charnwood

10 Sharrow Ln S11 8AA
☎ 0114 258 9411 0114 255 5107
e-mail: reception@charnwoodhotel.co.uk
Dir: Sharrow Lane is near London Rd/Abbeydale Rd junct, on A621, 1.5m SW of city centre

The Charnwood, a Georgian mansion house once owned by a Master Cutler, is within walking distance of the city centre. The bedrooms are well equipped; lounges and bars are well furnished

continued

and comfortable. Leo's Brasserie is a modern, informal restaurant serving freshly cooked and interesting meals.
ROOMS: 22 en suite No smoking in all bedrooms s £63-£93; d £83-£110 (incl. bkfst) **LB** **FACILITIES:** STV **CONF:** Thtr 90 Class 40 Board 35 **PARKING:** 22 **NOTES:** No dogs (ex guide dogs) Civ Wed 100 **CARDS:**

★★★67% Novotel Sheffield

50 Arundel Gate S1 2PR
☎ 0114 278 1781 0114 278 7744
e-mail: h1348@accor-hotels.com
Dir: *between Registry Office and Crucible/Lyceum Theatres, follow signs to Town Hall/Theatres & Hallam University*

Located in the heart of the city centre, this modern hotel is popular with both business and leisure guests. Local theatres and shops are within easy reach, while within the hotel, facilities include an indoor heated swimming pool and a range of meeting rooms. Spacious bedrooms are suitable for family occupation but also provide an equally ideal environment for business users.
ROOMS: 144 en suite (40 fmly) No smoking in 108 bedrooms s fr £84; d fr £84 **LB** **FACILITIES:** STV Indoor swimming (H) Local gym facilities free for residents use **CONF:** Thtr 220 Class 180 Board 100 Del from £110 **SERVICES:** Lift **PARKING:** 44 **NOTES:** RS 24 Dec-2 Jan Civ Wed 200 **CARDS:**

★★★66% Mosborough Hall

High St, Mosborough S20 5EA
☎ 0114 248 4353 0114 247 9759
e-mail: hotel@mosboroughhall.co.uk
Dir: *M1 J30, take A6135 towards Sheffield, 0.5m after large set lights, on right*

This 16th-century, Grade II listed manor house, is set in gardens not far from the M1 and convenient for the city centre. Bedrooms vary from 'character' to modern, and some are very spacious. There is a galleried bar and conservatory lounge, and freshly prepared dishes are served in the brightly furnished dining room.
ROOMS: 52 en suite (1 fmly) (12 GF) No smoking in 30 bedrooms s £44-£69; d £52-£77 (incl. bkfst) **LB** **CONF:** Thtr 300 Class 125 Board 70 Del from £89 **PARKING:** 100 **NOTES:** No smoking in restaurant Civ Wed 250 **CARDS:**

★★★65% *The Garrison*

Hillsborough Barracks, Penistone Rd S6 2GB
☎ 0114 249 9555 0114 249 1900
e-mail: enquiries@garrisonhotel.com

Standing close to Hillsborough football ground, leisure centre and dry-ski slope, and with good access to the city centre, the former Hillsborough Barracks have been redeveloped into this unique hotel. The Jailhouse has become an interesting bar and restaurant serving fine meals, and the Armoury a meeting room. Bedrooms are comfortable and well equipped.
ROOMS: 43 en suite (2 fmly) No smoking in 34 bedrooms **FACILITIES:** entertainment **CONF:** Thtr 30 Class 30 Board 30 **PARKING:** 60 **NOTES:** No dogs (ex guide dogs) No smoking in restaurant **CARDS:**

★★★64% Rutland

452 Glossop Rd S10 2PY
☎ 0114 266 4411 0114 267 0348
e-mail: roomsrutland@aol.com
Dir: *M1 J33 to City Centre, follow signs Hallamshire Hospital. Hotel past hospital main entrance*

Enjoying a relatively quiet location, this hotel is well placed for the city centre and universities. Bedrooms, some of which are in a separate annexe, have modern facilities and are well equipped.

continued

The Broomfields conservatory restaurant offers a range of meals, and several meeting rooms are also available.
ROOMS: 76 en suite (10 fmly) No smoking in 41 bedrooms s £70-£80; d £85-£95 **LB** **FACILITIES:** Xmas **CONF:** Thtr 100 Class 35 Board 40 Del from £85 **SERVICES:** Lift **PARKING:** 100 **NOTES:** No smoking in restaurant Civ Wed 100 **CARDS:**

★★★63% Hotel Bristol

Blonk St S1 2AU
☎ 0114 220 4000 0114 220 3900
e-mail: Sheffield@hotel-bristol.co.uk

The outside of the hotel, a converted office building, belies the stylish interior. A smart contemporary theme runs through the thoughtfully appointed bedrooms, which are equipped with videos and trouser presses. The Picasso Restaurant overlooks the local cityscape and serves quality ingredients with a quirky, Mediterranean twist.
ROOMS: 111 en suite (70 fmly) No smoking in 90 bedrooms s £52.50-£69.50; d £57.50-£74.50 **FACILITIES:** STV **CONF:** Thtr 50 Class 50 Board 20 Del from £94.50 **SERVICES:** Lift **NOTES:** No smoking in restaurant Closed 24-26 Dec **CARDS:**

★★66% Cutlers Hotel

Theatreland George St S1 2PF
☎ 0114 273 9939 0114 276 8332
e-mail: enquiries@cutlershotel.co.uk
Dir: *city centre, 50yds from the Crucible Theatre*

Situated close to the Crucible Theatre in the city centre, this boutique hotel offers accommodation in well-equipped bedrooms that include hairdryers, trouser presses and business facilities. Public areas include a lower ground floor bistro although room service is available if required. Small meeting rooms are also available. Discounted overnight parking is provided in the nearby public car park.
ROOMS: 45 en suite (4 fmly) No smoking in 18 bedrooms s £45-£59; d £50-£69 (incl. bkfst) **LB** **FACILITIES:** Xmas **CONF:** BC Thtr 90 Class 40 Board 30 Del from £60 **SERVICES:** Lift **NOTES:** No dogs (ex guide dogs) No smoking in restaurant **CARDS:**

U Aston Hall

Worksop Rd, Aston S26 2EE
☎ 0114 287 2309 0114 287 3228
e-mail: reservations@astonhallhotel.demon.co.uk

At the time of going to press, the star classification for this hotel was not confirmed. Please refer to the AA internet site www.theAA.com for current information.
ROOMS: 20 en suite (4 fmly) No smoking in 10 bedrooms s £80-£90; d £98-£110 (incl. bkfst) **FACILITIES:** STV **CONF:** Thtr 350 Class 200 Board 35 Del from £135 **SERVICES:** air con **PARKING:** 150 **NOTES:** No dogs (ex guide dogs) Civ Wed 250
CARDS:

U *Holiday Inn Sheffield - West*

Manchester Rd, Broomhill S10 5DX
☎ 0870 400 9071 0114 268 2620
e-mail: reservations-sheffield@ichotelsgroup.com
Dir: *M1 junct 33, follow city centre signs, then A57 Glossop. Hotel 2.5m on left*

At the time of going to press, the classification for this hotel was not confirmed. Please refer to the AA internet site www.theAA.com for current information.
ROOMS: 138 en suite No smoking in 70 bedrooms **FACILITIES:** Indoor swimming (H) Sauna Solarium Gym Jacuzzi Health & fitness centre **CONF:** Thtr 300 Class 130 Board 80 **SERVICES:** Lift **PARKING:** 120 **NOTES:** No dogs (ex guide dogs) **CARDS:**

S

SHEFFIELD, continued

⌂ Hotel Ibis Sheffield City

Shude Hill S1 2AR
☎ 0114 241 9600 📠 0114 241 9610
e-mail: H2891@accor-hotels.com
Dir: *M1 junct 33, follow signs to Sheffield City Centre, 7m at rdbt take 5th exit, signed Ponds Forge*

Modern, budget hotel offering comfortable accommodation in bright and practical bedrooms. Breakfast is self-service and dinner is available in the restaurant. For further details, consult the Hotel Groups page.
ROOMS: 95 en suite s £42.95-£45.95; d £42.95-£45.95

⌂ Innkeeper's Lodge Sheffield South

Hathersage Rd, Longshaw S11 7TY
☎ 01433 630374 📠 01433 637102
Dir: *8m from Sheffield city centre on A625 junct with B6051.*
A new concept in the travel accommodation market. Smart rooms meet essential business requirements but also have home comforts. Dining options include all-day menus plus the added advantage of breakfast, which is included in the room price. For further details, consult the Hotel Groups page.
ROOMS: 10 annexe en suite

⌂ Premier Lodge (Sheffield)

Sheffield Rd, Meadowhall S9 2YL
☎ 0870 9906440 📠 0870 9906441
Dir: *1.5m from M1 junct 34 on A6178*
Premier Lodge offers modern, well-equipped, en suite accommodation suitable for both business and leisure travellers. Meals can be taken at the adjacent popular restaurant and bar, which is fully licensed. For further details, consult the Hotel Groups page.
ROOMS: 103 en suite s £48; d £48

⌂ Travel Inn (Sheffield Centre)

Attercliffe Common Rd S9 2LU
☎ 0870 238 3316 📠 0114 242 3703
Dir: *M1 junct 34, follow signs to city centre. Inn opposite Arena*
Travel Inn offers good-quality, value-for-money accommodation. Spacious, en suite rooms with bath and shower comfortably accommodate a family of up to two adults and two children (to age 15). The restaurant and bar offers a varied menu. For further details and the Travel Inn phone number, consult the Hotel Groups page.
ROOMS: 61 en suite s £44.95; d £44.95

⌂ Travel Inn Sheffield City Centre

Angel St / Bank St Corner S3 8LN
☎ 0870 238 3324 📠 0870 241 9000
Dir: *from M1 junct 33, follow Sheffield City Centre signs (A630 onto A57). At Park Square rbt 4th exit (A61 Barnsley). Left at 4th lights into Snig Hill then right at lights into Bank Street*
Travel Inn offers good-quality, value-for-money accommodation. Spacious, en suite rooms with bath and shower comfortably accommodate a family of up to two adults and two children (to age 15). The restaurant and bar offers a varied menu. For further details and the Travel Inn phone number, consult the Hotel Groups page.
ROOMS: 160 en suite s £46.95-£49.95; d £46.95-£49.95

⌂ Travelodge

340 Prince of Wales Rd S2 1FF
☎ 08700 850 950 📠 0114 253 0935
Dir: *follow A630, take turn off for ring road & services*
Travelodge offers good quality, good value, modern accommodation. Ideal for families, the spacious, en suite bedrooms include remote-control TV, tea and coffee-making facilities, luxury beds and free morning newspaper. Meals can be taken at the nearby family restaurant. For further details and the Travelodge phone number, consult the Hotel Groups page.
ROOMS: 67 en suite s fr £42.95; d fr £42.95 **CONF:** Thtr 30 Board 20

SHEPTON MALLET, Somerset Map 04 ST64

Top 200 - Hotel

★★★ ®®®

Charlton House & Mulberry Restaurant

Charlton Rd BA4 4PR
☎ 01749 342008 📠 01749 346362
e-mail: enquiry@charltonhouse.com
Dir: *on A361 towards Frome, 1m after town centre*
Charlton House is a most relaxing and elegant house, set back from the road in beautifully landscaped gardens. The house, in parts, dates back to the 1500s and new developments are currently increasing rooms, leisure and beauty treatment facilities. Dining in the Mulberry restaurant provides a memorable experience and cuisine is accomplished. Service throughout is professional and pampered. The connection with Mulberry furnishings and fabrics is clearly evident in Charlton House's unique style of comfort and quality.
ROOMS: 13 en suite 4 annexe en suite (1 fmly) (1 GF) s £112.50; d £155 (incl. bkfst) **LB FACILITIES:** STV Fishing Croquet lawn Archery Clay pigeon shooting Ballooning Xmas **CONF:** Thtr 120 Class 60 Board 40 Del £160 **PARKING:** 41 **NOTES:** No smoking in restaurant Civ Wed 120 **CARDS:**

★★71% *Shrubbery*

17 Commercial Rd BA4 5BU
☎ 01749 346671 📠 01749 346581
Dir: *off A37 at Shepton Mallet onto A371 Wells Rd, hotel 50mtrs past lights*
This small hotel is located in the town centre and offers comfortable, well-equipped bedrooms, several of which are on the ground floor. The atmosphere here is relaxed and informal, and the intimate restaurant, which overlooks a delightful award-winning garden, offers a varied choice of enjoyable and well-presented dishes.
ROOMS: 6 en suite 4 annexe en suite (3 fmly) No smoking in 4 bedrooms **PARKING:** 30 **NOTES:** No dogs (ex guide dogs) No smoking in restaurant **CARDS:**

S

SHERBORNE, Dorset Map 04 ST61

★★★71% Eastbury
Long St DT9 3BY
☎ 01935 813131 01935 817296
e-mail: enquiries@theeastburyhotel.co.uk
Dir: *From A30 westbound, left into North Rd, then St Swithins, left at bottom, hotel 800yds on right*
Much of the original Georgian charm and elegance is maintained at this smart, comfortable hotel. Just five minutes' stroll from the abbey and close to the town centre, the Eastbury's friendly and attentive staff ensure a relaxed and enjoyable stay. The award-winning cuisine is served in the attractive dining room, which overlooks the walled garden.
ROOMS: 15 en suite (1 fmly) No smoking in 3 bedrooms **FACILITIES:** STV Croquet lawn **CONF:** Thtr 80 Class 40 Board 28 Del from £105.50 **PARKING:** 30 **NOTES:** No dogs (ex guide dogs) No smoking in restaurant Civ Wed 120 **CARDS:**

SHERINGHAM, Norfolk Map 13 TG14

★★★★69% Dales Country House Hotel
Lodge Hill, Upper Sheringham NR26 8TJ
☎ 01263 824555 01263 822647
e-mail: reservations@mackenziehotels.com
Dir: *on B1157 1m S of Sheringham, from A148 take turning at entrance to Sheringham Park, 0.5m hotel on left*

Superb Grade II listed building situated in extensive landscaped grounds on the edge of Sheringham Park. The attractive public rooms are full of original charm and character; they include a choice of lounges as well as an intimate restaurant and a cosy lounge bar. The spacious bedrooms are individually decorated, with co-ordinated soft furnishings and many thoughtful touches.
ROOMS: 17 en suite (1 fmly) (2 GF) No smoking in all bedrooms s £73; d £106 (incl. bkfst) **LB** **FACILITIES:** Tennis (grass) Croquet lawn Xmas **CONF:** Thtr 40 Class 20 Board 27 Del from £75 **SERVICES:** Lift **PARKING:** 30 **NOTES:** No dogs (ex guide dogs) No children 12 No smoking in restaurant **CARDS:**

★★71% Roman Camp Inn
Holt Rd, Aylmerton NR11 8QD
☎ 01263 838291 01263 837071
e-mail: romancampinn@lineone.net
Dir: *on A148 between Sheringham and Cromer, approx 1.5m from Cromer*
Situated on the A148 and ideally placed for touring the north Norfolk coastline, this hotel provides spacious bedrooms, pleasantly decorated with a good range of useful extras. Public rooms include a smart conservatory-style restaurant, a comfortable lounge, a smart bar and a dining room.
ROOMS: 15 en suite No smoking in 2 bedrooms **CONF:** Thtr 25 Class 6 Board 12 **PARKING:** 50 **NOTES:** No dogs (ex guide dogs) No smoking in restaurant Closed 25 Dec **CARDS:**

★★70% Beaumaris
South St NR26 8LL
☎ 01263 822370 01263 821421
e-mail: beauhotel@aol.com
Dir: *turn off A148, turn left at rdbt, 1st right over railway bridge, 1st left by church, 1st left into South St*

Ideally situated in a peaceful cul-de-sac just a short walk from the beach, town centre and golf course. This friendly hotel has been owned and run by the same family for over 50 years and continues to provide comfortable, thoughtfully equipped accommodation throughout. Public rooms feature a smart dining room, a cosy bar and two quiet lounges.
ROOMS: 21 en suite (5 fmly) s £45-£50; d £90-£100 (incl. bkfst) **LB** **CONF:** Board 12 **PARKING:** 25 **NOTES:** No smoking in restaurant Closed mid Dec-1 Mar **CARDS:**

★★70% *Southlands*
South St NR26 8LL
☎ 01263 822679 01263 822679
Dir: *from A1082, turn left at rdbt. Take 1st right & then 1st left at St Peter's Church. Then 1st left again & hotel on left*
A friendly, family-run hotel situated just a short walk from the town centre and seafront. The pleasantly decorated bedrooms are well maintained and equipped with a good range of useful extras. The open-plan public rooms, including a choice of lounges, a bar and several dining areas, offer a wide choice of areas to relax in.
ROOMS: 17 en suite (3 fmly) No smoking in all bedrooms **FACILITIES:** ch fac **PARKING:** 20 **NOTES:** No smoking in restaurant Closed Oct-Etr **CARDS:**

SHIFNAL, Shropshire Map 10 SJ70

S

★★★★67% Park House
MACDONALD HOTELS
Park St TF11 9BA
☎ 01952 460128 01952 461658
e-mail: res.parkhouse@macdonald-hotels.co.uk
Dir: *M54 junct 4 follow A464 Wolverhampton road for approx 2m, under railway bridge and hotel 100yds on left*
A major programme of expansion and redesign has created a hotel from what was originally two country homes of very different architectural styles. Located on the edge of the historic market town, the hotel is situated for easy access to motorway networks. A choice of banqueting, meeting rooms and leisure facilities is available.
ROOMS: 38 en suite 16 annexe en suite (4 fmly) No smoking in 15 bedrooms s £55-£66; d £70-£92 (incl. bkfst) **LB** **FACILITIES:** STV Indoor swimming (H) Sauna Solarium Jacuzzi Xmas **CONF:** Thtr 180 Class 100 Board 40 Del from £109 **SERVICES:** Lift **PARKING:** 200 **NOTES:** No smoking in restaurant Civ Wed 130
CARDS:

SHIPHAM, Somerset Map 04 ST45

★★★72% Daneswood House
Cuck Hill BS25 1RD
☎ 01934 843145 & 843945 01934 843824
e-mail: info@daneswoodhotel.co.uk
Dir: *turn off A38 towards Cheddar, through village, hotel on left*

With wonderful views over the countryside to the Bristol Channel and Wales in the distance, this charming Edwardian hotel is set in its own carefully tended grounds. Each individually decorated bedroom is well equipped; the cottage suites have private lounges. Public rooms include a breakfast conservatory, comfortable lounge and inter-connecting dining areas.
ROOMS: 14 en suite 3 annexe en suite (3 fmly) No smoking in 4 bedrooms s £89.50-£99.50; d £105-£150 (incl. bkfst) **LB CONF:** Thtr 40 Board 24 **PARKING:** 27 **NOTES:** No dogs (ex guide dogs) No smoking in restaurant RS 24 Dec-6 Jan **CARDS:**

SHIPLEY, West Yorkshire Map 19 SE13

★★★★70% Marriott Hollins Hall Hotel & Country Club
Hollins Hill, Baildon BD17 7QW
☎ 0870 400 7227 0870 400 7327
e-mail: reservations.hollinshall@marriotthotels.co.uk
Dir: *At lights in Shipley take A6038. Hotel 3m on left*
This Elizabethan-style hotel was built during the 19th century but has undergone a stylish refurbishment in recent years. Set in over 200 acres of beautiful countryside, its extensive leisure facilities include a golf course and a well-equipped gymnasium. Guests have a choice of dining options including the lively Long Weekend Café Bar and the more formal restaurant, Heathcliff's.
ROOMS: 122 en suite (50 fmly) (25 GF) No smoking in 75 bedrooms s fr £99; d fr £99 **LB FACILITIES:** STV Indoor swimming (H) Golf 18 Sauna Solarium Gym Croquet lawn Putting green Jacuzzi Creche, Health Spa, Dance studio, Swimming lessons, Pool supervised at times Xmas **CONF:** BC Thtr 175 Class 90 Board 80 Del from £125 **SERVICES:** Lift **PARKING:** 260 **NOTES:** No dogs (ex guide dogs) No smoking in restaurant Civ Wed 150 **CARDS:**

Restaurant with Rooms

Beeties Gallery Restaurant
7 Victoria Rd, Saltaire Village BD18 3LA
☎ 01274 595988 581718 01274 582118
e-mail: jayne@beeties.co.uk
Beeties is located in the Saltaire model industrial village. The ground floor comprises a Tapas bar and bistro serving light meals and drinks at lunch and dinner, and on the first floor there is the elegant, contemporary restaurant serving imaginative, skilfully prepared dishes every evening. Bedrooms are smartly appointed and individually decorated.
ROOMS: 5 en suite (1 fmly) No smoking in all bedrooms s £35-£45; d £50-£60 (incl. bkfst) **NOTES:** No dogs (ex guide dogs) Closed 25 - 26 Dec, 1 Jan **CARDS:**

Hotel Ibis Bradford
Quayside, Salts Mill Rd BD18 3ST
☎ 01274 589333 01274 589444
e-mail: H3158@accor-hotels.com
Dir: *from Bradford follow signs for Salts Mill then A650 signs. 5m to Shipley. Hotel on Salts Mill Rd*
Modern, budget hotel offering comfortable accommodation in bright and practical bedrooms. Breakfast is self-service and dinner is available in the restaurant. For further details, consult the Hotel Groups page.
ROOMS: 78 en suite s £35.95-£45.95; d £35.95-£45.95

SHREWSBURY, Shropshire Map 15 SJ41
See also Church Stretton

★★★★68% Albrighton Hall
Albrighton SY4 3AG
☎ 01939 291000 01939 291123
e-mail: albrighton@macdonald-hotels.co.uk
Dir: *from S M6 junct 10a to M54 to end. From N M6 junct 12 to M5 then M54. Follow signs Harlescott & Ellesmere to A528*
Originally dating back to 1630, this former ancestral home is set within 15 acres of attractive gardens. Rooms are well-kept and generally spacious, with attic rooms popular for their sloping beams. Elegant public rooms have rich oak panelling and there is a modern, well-equipped health and fitness centre.
ROOMS: 29 en suite 42 annexe en suite (2 fmly) No smoking in 30 bedrooms s £112; d £123 (incl. bkfst) **LB FACILITIES: Spa** STV Indoor swimming Squash Snooker Sauna Solarium Gym Jacuzzi Beauty treatment rooms Xmas **CONF:** Thtr 400 Class 120 Board 60 Del £159 **SERVICES:** Lift **PARKING:** 200 **NOTES:** No smoking in restaurant Civ Wed 200 **CARDS:**

★★★77% Albright Hussey
Ellesmere Rd SY4 3AF
☎ 01939 290571 & 290523 01939 291143
e-mail: abhhotel@aol.com
Dir: *2.5m N of Shrewsbury on A528, follow signs for Ellesmere*
First mentioned in the Domesday Book, this enchanting medieval manor house comes complete with a moat. Bedrooms are in either the sumptuously appointed main house or in the modern wing. The intimate restaurant displays an abundance of original features and there is also a comfortable cocktail bar and lounge.
ROOMS: 26 en suite (4 fmly) No smoking in 3 bedrooms s £69-£93; d £95-£160 (incl. bkfst) **LB FACILITIES:** Croquet lawn Jacuzzi Xmas **CONF:** BC Thtr 250 Class 180 Board 80 Del from £95 **PARKING:** 85 **NOTES:** No children 3yrs No smoking in restaurant Civ Wed 200 **CARDS:**

See advert on page 552

★★★75% Rowton Castle Hotel
Halfway House SY5 9EP
☎ 01743 884044 01743 884949
e-mail: post@rowtoncastle.com
Dir: *A5 take A458 to Welshpool. Hotel 4m on right*
Standing in 17 acres of grounds on the site of a Roman fort, this hotel dates back in parts to 1696. Many original features remain, including the oak panelling in the restaurant and a magnificent carved oak fireplace. Most of the bedrooms are spacious and all

continued

have modern facilities. Rooms with four-poster beds are available. The hotel has lovely formal gardens.

ROOMS: 19 en suite (3 fmly) s £64-£69; d £84 (incl. bkfst) **LB**
FACILITIES: Croquet lawn **CONF:** Thtr 80 Class 30 Board 30 Del from £86.25 **PARKING:** 100 **NOTES:** No dogs (ex guide dogs) No smoking in restaurant Civ Wed 110 **CARDS:**

★★★71% Prince Rupert

Butcher Row SY1 1UQ
☎ 01743 499955 📠 01743 357306
e-mail: post@prince-rupert-hotel.co.uk
Dir: *follow town centre signs, into Fish St, 200yds to hotel*

Parts of this popular town centre hotel date back to medieval times and many bedrooms have exposed beams and other original features. Luxury suites, family rooms and rooms with four-poster beds are all available. As an alternative to the main Royalist Restaurant, diners can eat in the less formal and popular Chambers bar-bistro. Car parking service available.

ROOMS: 70 en suite (4 fmly) s £77; d £98-£165 **LB**
FACILITIES: Snooker Sauna Gym Jacuzzi Weight training room Beauty Salon Xmas **CONF:** Thtr 120 Class 80 Board 40 Del from £95
SERVICES: Lift **PARKING:** 70 **CARDS:**
See advert on this page

★★★66% Lord Hill

THE INDEPENDENTS

Abbey Foregate SY2 6AX
☎ 01743 232601 📠 01743 369734
e-mail: reservations@lordhill.u-net.com
Dir: *from M54 take A5, at 1st rdbt left then 2nd rdbt take 4th exit into London Rd. At next rdbt (Lord Hill Column) take 3rd exit, hotel 300yds on left*

A pleasant, attractively appointed hotel located close to the town centre. Most of the bedrooms are set in a purpose-built separate building, but those in the main building include one with a

continued on p552

SHREWSBURY, continued

four-poster and a newly created suite. There is also a conservatory restaurant and a large function suite.
ROOMS: 12 en suite 24 annexe en suite (2 fmly) (8 GF) No smoking in 12 bedrooms s £63.50-£65.50; d £82-£85 (incl. bkfst) **CONF:** Thtr 250 Class 180 Board 180 Del £95 **PARKING:** 110 **NOTES:** No smoking in restaurant Civ Wed 70 **CARDS:**

★★★63% The Lion

Wyle Cop SY1 1UY
☎ 0870 609 6167 🖷 01743 352744
e-mail: thelion@corushotels.com
Dir: *from S over English Bridge, take right fork, hotel at top of hill on left. From N to town centre, follow Castle St into Dogpole, hotel is ahead*

This 14th-century coaching inn, located in the town centre, boasts Charles Dickens amongst its earlier guests and is steeped in character. Bedrooms come in a variety of sizes, those at the rear being quieter. Public areas include the original ballroom and a bar, and restaurant with oak beams and inglenook fireplace.
ROOMS: 59 en suite (3 fmly) No smoking in 30 bedrooms s £65-£90; d £75-£120 (incl. bkfst) **LB FACILITIES:** use of local gym Xmas **CONF:** Thtr 200 Class 80 Board 60 Del from £85 **SERVICES:** Lift **PARKING:** 70 **NOTES:** No smoking in restaurant Civ Wed 200 **CARDS:**

★★66% Mytton & Mermaid

Atcham SY5 6QG
☎ 01743 761220 🖷 01743 761292
e-mail: admin@myttonandmermaid.co.uk
Dir: *from Shrewsbury over old bridge in Atcham. Hotel on River Severn opposite main entrance to Attingham Park*

Convenient for Shrewsbury, this ivy-clad former coaching inn enjoys a pleasant location beside the River Severn. Some bedrooms, including family suites, are in a converted stable block adjacent to the hotel. The large lounge bar has now been refurbished, and

continued

there is also a comfortable lounge and brasserie that is gaining a well deserved local reputation for the quality of the food.
ROOMS: 11 en suite 7 annexe en suite (1 fmly) No smoking in 11 bedrooms s £50-£80; d £70-£100 (incl. bkfst) **FACILITIES:** Fishing entertainment Xmas **CONF:** BC Thtr 70 Class 24 Board 28 Del from £90 **PARKING:** 50 **NOTES:** No smoking in restaurant Civ Wed 70
CARDS:

★★65% Lion & Pheasant
49-50 Wyle Cop SY1 1XJ
☎ 01743 236288 Fax 01743 244475
e-mail: info@lionandpheasant.co.uk
This 16th-century coaching inn is privately owned and personally run, and it is close to the town centre. The accommodation which includes no smoking rooms, is well equipped and the public areas are full of character, with exposed beams and wall timbers. An extensive choice of food is served in the bar/bistro.
ROOMS: 27 rms (25 en suite) (2 fmly) No smoking in 8 bedrooms s £35-£45; d £60 (incl. bkfst) **LB** **CONF:** Thtr 25 Class 25 Board 20 **PARKING:** 18 **NOTES:** No smoking in restaurant Closed 24-25 Dec & 1 Jan **CARDS:**

★★64% Abbots Mead
9 St Julian's Friars SY1 1XL
☎ 01743 235281 Fax 01743 369133
e-mail: res@abbotsmeadhotel.co.uk
Dir: *1st left after English Bridge, from S into Shrewsbury*
This neatly maintained Georgian town house lies in a quiet cul-de-sac, near the English Bridge and close to the river and town centre. Bedrooms are compact, neatly decorated and well equipped. The hotel also has a bright dining room, overlooking the garden, and a bar which features horse racing pictures.
ROOMS: 15 en suite (1 fmly) s £45; d £59 (incl. bkfst) **LB**
PARKING: 10 **NOTES:** No smoking in restaurant
CARDS:

⌂ Travelodge
Travelodge

Bayston Hill Services SY3 0DA
☎ 08700 850 950 Fax 01743 874256
Dir: *A5/A49 junct*
Travelodge offers good quality, good value, modern accommodation. Ideal for families, the spacious, en suite bedrooms include remote-control TV, tea and coffee-making facilities, luxury beds and free morning newspaper. Meals can be taken at the nearby family restaurant. For further details and the Travelodge phone number, consult the Hotel Groups page.
ROOMS: 40 en suite s fr £42.95; d fr £42.95

SIDMOUTH, Devon
Map 03 SY18

★★★★74% ⊛ Victoria
Brend Hotels

The Esplanade EX10 8RY
☎ 01395 512651 Fax 01395 579154
e-mail: info@victoriahotel.co.uk
Dir: *on Sidmouth seafront*
This imposing building is set within manicured gardens and occupies the prime position on The Esplanade. Wonderful sea views can be enjoyed from many of the comfortable bedrooms and elegant public areas. Carefully prepared meals are served in

continued on p554

S

SIDMOUTH, continued

the refined atmosphere of the restaurant, with staff providing a professional and friendly service.

Victoria Hotel, Sidmouth

ROOMS: 61 en suite (18 fmly) s £74-£113; d £122-£244 (incl. bkfst) **LB** **FACILITIES: Spa** STV Indoor swimming (H) Outdoor swimming (H) Tennis (hard) Snooker Sauna Solarium Gym Putting green entertainment ch fac Xmas **CONF:** Thtr 60 **SERVICES:** Lift **PARKING:** 104 **NOTES:** No dogs (ex guide dogs) No smoking in restaurant **CARDS:**

★★★★72% **Riviera**
The Esplanade EX10 8AY
☎ 01395 515201 01395 577775
e-mail: enquiries@hotelriviera.co.uk
Dir: *M5 junct 30 & follow A3052*

Overlooking the sea, the Riviera is a fine Regency building, offering high standards of both service and hospitality. Bedrooms combine comfort with quality, many also benefiting from wonderful views. The daily changing menu places an emphasis upon fresh local produce, served by friendly staff in an elegant dining room.

Riviera Hotel, Sidmouth

ROOMS: 27 en suite (6 fmly) s £100-£132; d £180-£244 (incl. bkfst & dinner) **LB** **FACILITIES:** STV entertainment Xmas **CONF:** Thtr 85 Class 60 Board 30 **SERVICES:** Lift **PARKING:** 26 **NOTES:** No smoking in restaurant **CARDS:**

See advert on page 553

★★★★71% **Belmont**
The Esplanade EX10 8RX
☎ 01395 512555 01395 579101
e-mail: reservations@belmont-hotel.co.uk
Dir: *on Sidmouth seafront*

Brend Hotels

Prominently positioned on the seafront and just a few minutes' walk from the town centre, this traditional hotel has a regular following. A choice of comfortable lounges provide ample space for relaxation, and the air-conditioned restaurant has a pianist accompanying dinner. Bedrooms are attractively furnished and many have fine views over the esplanade. Leisure facilities are available at the adjacent sister hotel, the Victoria.

ROOMS: 50 en suite (4 fmly) (2 GF) s £63-£114; d £108-£228 (incl. bkfst) **LB** **FACILITIES:** STV Putting green entertainment ch fac Xmas **CONF:** Thtr 50 **SERVICES:** Lift **PARKING:** 45 **NOTES:** No dogs (ex guide dogs) No smoking in restaurant Civ Wed 110 **CARDS:**

★★★79% **Westcliff**
Manor Rd EX10 8RU
☎ 01395 513252 01395 578203
e-mail: stay@westcliffhotel.co.uk
Dir: *A3052 to Sidmouth then Esplanade, turn right, hotel ahead*

This charming hotel, run by the same family for more than 35 years, is within walking distance of the promenade. Elegant lounges and the cocktail bar open onto a terrace, leading to the pool and croquet lawn. Bedrooms, several with balconies and glorious sea views, are spacious and comfortable, and the restaurant offers a choice of well-prepared dishes.

ROOMS: 40 en suite (4 fmly) (5 GF) No smoking in 4 bedrooms s £63-£117; d £114-£248 (incl. bkfst & dinner) **LB** **FACILITIES:** STV Outdoor swimming (H) Gym Croquet lawn Putting green Jacuzzi Mini tennis Pool table Table tennis entertainment **SERVICES:** Lift **PARKING:** 40 **NOTES:** No dogs No children 6yrs No smoking in restaurant Closed Nov-Mar **CARDS:**

See advert on opposite page

★★★69% **Salcombe Hill House**
Beatlands Rd EX10 8JQ
☎ 01395 514697 & 514398 01395 578310
e-mail: salcombehillhousehotel@eclipse.co.uk
Dir: *At Radway Cinema in town centre turn left, over bridge, turn sharp right, left into Beatlands Rd. Hotel 50yds on left*

This family-run hotel has an elevated position just a short walk from the seafront and is in a quiet location in attractive gardens. The south facing aspect means the lounge and patio get the best of the sun. Bedrooms are spacious and comfortable, and

continued

S

ppetising, freshly prepared dishes are offered on the daily-hanging menu in the dining room.
OOMS: 28 en suite (7 fmly) **FACILITIES:** Outdoor swimming (H) ennis (grass) Putting green Games room **SERVICES:** Lift **PARKING:** 39 **OTES:** No smoking in restaurant Closed Nov-Feb
ARDS:

★★★65% *Fortfield*
tation Rd EX10 8NU
☎ 01395 512403 01395 512403
-mail: reservations@fortfield-hotel.co.uk
)ffering good standards of hospitality and service, this ong-established hotel overlooks the sea and cricket ground. A hoice of comfortable lounges is available, and the 'Norske' bar is relaxing venue for a pre-dinner drink. Bedrooms are undergoing programme of extensive upgrading; a number of rooms have ne benefit of sea views.
ROOMS: 52 en suite 3 annexe en suite (7 fmly) **FACILITIES:** Indoor wimming (H) Sauna Health & beauty salon entertainment ch fac **CONF:** Thtr 70 Class 40 Board 20 **SERVICES:** Lift **PARKING:** 60 **NOTES:** No smoking in restaurant **CARDS:**

★★★65% Royal Glen
Glen Rd EX10 8RW
☎ 01395 513221 & 513456 01395 514922
e-mail: sidmouthroyalglen.hotel@virgin.net
Dir: *A175 to Sidmouth, follow seafront signs, right onto esplanade, right at end*
This historic, 19th-century hotel has been in the same family ownership for several generations. The connection is emphasised n the names of the comfortable bedrooms, which are furnished in period style. Guests have use of the well-maintained gardens and a heated indoor pool, and can enjoy well-prepared food in the dining room.

ROOMS: 32 en suite (4 fmly) s £33-£46; d £66-£92 (incl. bkfst) **LB** **FACILITIES:** Indoor swimming (H) **PARKING:** 24 **NOTES:** No smoking in restaurant RS 2-31 Jan **CARDS:**

★★75% Kingswood
The Esplanade EX10 8AX
☎ 01395 516367 01395 513185
e-mail: enquiries@kingswood-hotel.co.uk
Dir: *in centre of Esplanade*
Super standards of hospitality are only surpassed by The Kingswood's prominent position on The Esplanade. All bedrooms have modern facilities and some enjoy the stunning sea views. The two lounges offer comfort and space and the attractive dining room serves good traditional cooking.
ROOMS: 26 rms (25 en suite) (7 fmly) (2 GF) No smoking in all bedrooms s £40-£60; d £80-£120 (incl. bkfst & dinner) **LB** **FACILITIES:** Swimming vouchers given to guests to use at the local swimming pool **SERVICES:** Lift **PARKING:** 17 **NOTES:** No smoking in restaurant Closed Dec-13 Feb **CARDS:**

★★74% Royal York & Faulkner
The Esplanade EX10 8AZ
☎ 01395 513043 & 0800 220714 (Freephone) 01395 577472
e-mail: stay@royalyorkhotel.net
Dir: *from M5 take A3052, 10m to Sidmouth, hotel in centre of esplanade*
This seafront hotel, owned and run by the same family for generations, maintains its Regency charm and grandeur, and offers well-equipped and comfortable accommodation. The attractive bedrooms vary in size and many have balconies and sea views. Staff are friendly and efficient. Public rooms are spacious, and traditional dining is provided in either the dining room overlooking Lyme Bay, or in the more upbeat Tappers bar.
ROOMS: 68 en suite (8 fmly) (5 GF) s £41-£67; d £82-£134 (incl. bkfst & dinner) **LB** **FACILITIES: Spa** Snooker Sauna Solarium Gym Jacuzzi Indoor short mat bowls Free swim at local indoor pool entertainment Xmas **SERVICES:** Lift **PARKING:** 20 **NOTES:** No smoking in restaurant Closed Jan **CARDS:**

★★72% Mount Pleasant
Salcombe Rd EX10 8JA
☎ 01395 514694
Dir: *turn off A3052 at Sidford, 1.25m turn left into Salcombe Rd, hotel opposite Radway Cinema*
Quietly located within almost an acre of gardens, this sympathetically modernised Georgian hotel is just minutes from the town centre and seafront. Bedrooms and public areas offer good levels of comfort and high quality furnishings. Guests return on a regular basis especially for the friendly, relaxed atmosphere. The daily-changing menu offers a choice of imaginative, yet tradional home-cooked dishes.
ROOMS: 16 en suite (2 fmly) s £34.50-£51; d £69-£102 (incl. bkfst & dinner) **LB** **FACILITIES:** Putting green **PARKING:** 20 **NOTES:** No children 8yrs No smoking in restaurant Closed Nov-Feb

S

SIDMOUTH, continued

★★71% Devoran
Esplanade EX10 8AU
☎ 01395 513151 🖷 01395 579929
e-mail: devoran@cosmic.org.uk
Dir: *turn off B3052 at Bowd Inn follow Sidmouth sign 2m turn left onto seafront, hotel 50yds at centre of Esplanade*

Known locally as the 'pink hotel on the seafront' and situated in the centre of The Esplanade, the Devoran has comfortable and attractively decorated bedrooms, some with their own balconies and sea views. It has well-maintained public rooms include a large dining room, where guests can enjoy a five-course dinner, and a comfortable lounge and bar.
ROOMS: 24 en suite (4 fmly) No smoking in all bedrooms s £36-£46; d £37.50-£49 (incl. bkfst & dinner) **LB SERVICES:** Lift **PARKING:** 4 **NOTES:** No smoking in restaurant Closed mid Nov-mid Mar RS Dec-Mar **CARDS:**

★★70% Hunters Moon
Sid Rd EX10 9AA
☎ 01395 513380 🖷 01395 514270
e-mail: huntersmoon.hotel@virgin.net
Dir: *from A3052 to Sidford, pass Blue Ball Pub, then next right at Fortescue, hotel 1m*

Set amid three acres of attractive and well-tended grounds, this friendly, family-run hotel is peacefully located in a quiet area within walking distance of the town and esplanade. Bedrooms are comfortable and well equipped and there is a spacious lounge. Dining provides a choice of well-cooked and imaginative dishes, and tea may be taken on the lawn.
ROOMS: 21 en suite (6 fmly) (6 GF) No smoking in all bedrooms s £60-£64; d £108-£120 (incl. bkfst & dinner) **LB FACILITIES:** Putting green Xmas **PARKING:** 26 **NOTES:** No children 2yrs No smoking in restaurant Closed Jan-Feb (ex Xmas) RS Dec **CARDS:**

SILCHESTER, Hampshire Map 05 SU6

★★★73% ❀ Romans
Little London Rd RG7 2PN
☎ 0118 970 0421 🖷 0118 970 0691
e-mail: romanhotel@hotmail.com
Dir: *A340 Basingstoke to Reading, hotel is signed*

Best Western

This Lutyens-style manor house is in a tranquil and attractive location. Bedrooms are smartly presented and well equipped, some located in an adjacent wing. Dining offers interesting dishes featuring local produce. Conference and leisure facilities are also available.

ROOMS: 11 en suite 14 annexe en suite (1 fmly) (11 GF) No smoking in 5 bedrooms s £95-£110; d £105-£120 (incl. bkfst) **LB FACILITIES:** STV Outdoor swimming (H) Sauna Gym Jacuzzi Swimming pool supervised Xmas **CONF:** Thtr 60 Class 30 Board 24 Del from £110 **PARKING:** 60 **NOTES:** No smoking in restaurant Civ Wed 65
CARDS:

See advert under BASINGSTOKE

SILLOTH, Cumbria Map 18 NY15

★★★61% *The Skinburness*
CA7 4QY
☎ 016973 32332 🖷 016973 32549
Dir: *M6 junct 41, take B5305 to Wigton, then B5302 to Silloth. M6 junct 44, take A595 to Carlisle then on to Wigton, B5302 to Silloth*
Enviably located on the peaceful Solway Estuary, close to sandy beaches and coastal walks, this popular hotel provides traditionally furnished bedrooms with a host of modern facilities. There is also a leisure complex with a small pool, sauna and spa. Good meals are available in the Mediterranean-styled bar and the pleasant restaurant.
ROOMS: 33 en suite (3 fmly) No smoking in 6 bedrooms
FACILITIES: Indoor swimming (H) Fishing Sauna Solarium Gym Jacuzzi entertainment **CONF:** Thtr 120 Class 100 Board 60 **PARKING:** 120
NOTES: Closed 4-31 Jan **CARDS:**

★★64% *Golf Hotel*
Criffel St CA5 4AB
☎ 016973 31438 🖷 016973 32582
e-mail: golf.hotel@virgin.net
Dir: *off B5302, in Silloth at T-junct turn left, hotel overlooks the green*
This friendly, family-run hotel occupies a prime position in the centre of the historic market town. Bedrooms are well equipped, generally modern in style and benefit from ongoing refurbishment. Public areas include a spacious bar, restaurant, lounge and games room. The varied menus offer a wide selection of dishes.
ROOMS: 22 en suite (4 fmly) **FACILITIES:** Snooker **CONF:** Thtr 100 Class 40 Board 40 **NOTES:** Closed 25 Dec
CARDS:

S

SILVERSTONE, Northamptonshire — Map 11 SP64

⌂ Premier Lodge (Silverstone)
Brackley Hatch, Syresham NN13 5TX
☎ 0870 9906382 🖷 0870 9906383
Dir: *on A43 next to Green Man Chef & Brewer*
Premier Lodge offers modern, well-equipped, en suite accommodation suitable for both business and leisure travellers. Meals can be taken at the adjacent popular restaurant and bar, which is fully licensed. For further details, consult the Hotel Groups page.
ROOMS: 41 en suite s £48; d £48

SIMONSBATH, Somerset — Map 03 SS73

★★73% Simonsbath House
TA24 7SH
☎ 01643 831259 & 831382 🖷 01643 831557
e-mail: hotel@simonsbathhouse.co.uk
Dir: *B3223 from Exford to Lynton on right, on leaving village*

This 17th-century house boasts a stunning rural location and a relaxed and friendly atmosphere ensures a memorable stay. Bedrooms have plenty of character, are equipped with modern facilities and offer good levels of comfort. Delightful public areas include a choice of lounges with many original features.
ROOMS: 8 en suite No smoking in all bedrooms s £43-£60; d £85-£90 (incl. bkfst) **LB** **FACILITIES:** Mountain biking, Archery, Orienteering trails, Nature walks Golf Fishing Walking packages **CONF:** BC Thtr 50 Class 35 Board 20 **PARKING:** 25 **NOTES:** No children 12yrs No smoking in restaurant Closed 25-26 Dec **CARDS:**

SITTINGBOURNE, Kent — Map 07 TQ96

★★★68% Hempstead House Country Hotel
London Rd, Bapchild ME9 9PP
☎ 01795 428020 🖷 01795 436362
e-mail: info@hempsteadhouse.co.uk
Expect a warm welcome at this charming detached Victorian property which is situated in three acres of mature landscaped gardens. Bedrooms are attractively decorated with lovely fabrics, tastefully furnished and equipped with many thoughtful touches. Public rooms feature a choice of beautifully furnished lounges as well as a superb conservatory dining room.
ROOMS: 15 en suite (3 fmly) s £75; d £80-£105 (incl. bkfst) **LB** **FACILITIES:** Outdoor swimming (H) Xmas **CONF:** Thtr 150 Class 150 Board 100 Del £145 **PARKING:** 100 **NOTES:** No smoking in restaurant Civ Wed 180 **CARDS:**

⌂ Travel Inn
Bobbing Corner, Sheppy Way, Bobbing ME9 8PD
☎ 08701 977229 🖷 01795 436748

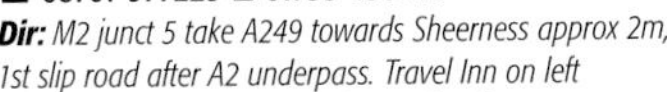

Dir: *M2 junct 5 take A249 towards Sheerness approx 2m, 1st slip road after A2 underpass. Travel Inn on left*
Travel Inn offers good-quality, value-for-money accommodation. Spacious, en suite rooms with bath and shower comfortably accommodate a family of up to two adults and two children (to age 15). The restaurant and bar offers a varied menu. For further details and the Travel Inn phone number, consult the Hotel Groups page.
ROOMS: 40 en suite s £44.95; d £44.95

SIX MILE BOTTOM, Cambridgeshire — Map 12 TL55

★★★73% ◎ *Swynford Paddocks*
CB8 0UE
☎ 01638 570234 🖷 01638 570283
e-mail: info@swynfordpaddocks.com
Dir: *M11 junct 9, take A11 towards Newmarket, onto A1304 to hotel 0.75m on left*

This smart country house is set in attractive grounds, within easy reach of Newmarket. Bedrooms are comfortably appointed, thoughtfully equipped and include some delightful four-poster rooms. Imaginative, carefully prepared food is served in the elegant restaurant and meeting and conference facilities are available. Service is friendly and attentive.
ROOMS: 15 en suite **FACILITIES:** STV Tennis (hard) Croquet lawn Putting green ch fac **CONF:** Thtr 60 Class 40 Board 40 **PARKING:** 180 **NOTES:** No smoking in restaurant Civ Wed 50
CARDS:

SKEGNESS, Lincolnshire — Map 17 TF56

★★★67% Vine
Vine Rd, Seacroft PE25 3DB
☎ 01754 763018 & 610611 🖷 01754 769845
e-mail: info@thevinehotel.com
Dir: *A52 to Skegness, S towards Gibraltar Point, hotel 1m from clocktower*

Reputedly the second oldest building in Skegness, this traditional style hotel offers two character bars that serve excellent local beers. Freshly prepared dishes are served in both the bar and the restaurant; service is both friendly and helpful. The smartly refurbished bedrooms are well equipped and comfortably appointed.
ROOMS: 24 en suite (3 fmly) No smoking in 5 bedrooms s £68-£78; d £88-£110 (incl. bkfst) **LB** **FACILITIES:** STV ch fac Xmas **CONF:** Thtr 100 Class 25 Board 30 Del from £90 **PARKING:** 50 **NOTES:** No smoking in restaurant Civ Wed 90
CARDS:

★★★64% Crown
Drummond Rd, Seacroft PE25 3AB
☎ 01754 610760 🖷 01754 610847
Dir: *take A52 to town centre, turn left onto Drummond Road, hotel 1m from clock tower*
The Crown is ideally situated just a short walk from the seafront and town centre, close to Seacroft Village golf course and bird sanctuary. Smart bedrooms are attractively decorated and thoughtfully equipped. Public areas include a spacious bar offering

continued on p558

S

SKEGNESS, continued

a wide selection of dishes, a formal restaurant, residents' TV lounge and indoor pool.
ROOMS: 30 en suite (9 fmly) s £50; d £80 (incl. bkfst) **LB** **FACILITIES:** STV Indoor swimming (H) **CONF:** Thtr 120 Class 130 Board 120 **SERVICES:** Lift **PARKING:** 90 **NOTES:** No dogs (ex guide dogs) RS 25-26 Dec Civ Wed 80 **CARDS:**

See advert on opposite page

★★66% North Shore

North Shore Rd PE25 1DN
☎ 01754 763298 🖹 01754 761902
e-mail: golf@north-shore.co.uk
Dir: *1m N of town centre on A52 Ingoldmells Rd, right opposite Fenland laundry*

This hotel enjoys an enviable position on the beach front, adjacent to its own championship golf course and only ten minutes from the town centre. Spacious public areas include a busy bar serving snacks and real ales, a formal restaurant and impressive function facilities. Bedrooms are smartly decorated and thoughtfully equipped.
ROOMS: 33 en suite 3 annexe en suite (4 fmly) s £35-£55; d £48-£75 (incl. bkfst) **LB** **FACILITIES:** Golf 18 Snooker Putting green Xmas **CONF:** Thtr 220 Class 60 Board 60 Del from £65 **PARKING:** 200 **NOTES:** No dogs (ex guide dogs) No smoking in restaurant Civ Wed 200 **CARDS:**

SKIPTON, North Yorkshire

Map 18 SD95

★★★72% The Coniston

Coniston Cold BD23 4EB
☎ 01756 748080 🖹 01756 749487
e-mail: info@theconistonhotel.com
Dir: *on A65, 6m NW of Skipton*

Situated within a 1200-acre estate, the grounds of Coniston Hall Lodge are dominated by a vast 24-acre lake. Here guests can try trout fly-fishing, or rough shooting in the adjacent woodland. The modern bedrooms are spacious and comfortable; most have king-size beds. Macleod's Bar and the Buttery offer all-day meals, and formal dining is provided from the carte menu in the restaurant.
ROOMS: 40 en suite (4 fmly) (20 GF) s £87.50-£97.50; d £120-£130 (incl. bkfst & dinner) **LB** **FACILITIES:** STV Fishing 4 wheel drive Clay pigeon shooting, Paintball, Falconry, Archery, Honda Pilots Xmas **CONF:** Thtr 150 Class 80 Board 50 Del from £130 **PARKING:** 120 **NOTES:** No smoking in restaurant Civ Wed 50
CARDS:

★★★65% Hanover International

Keighley Rd BD23 2TA
☎ 01756 700100 🖹 01756 700107
e-mail: hihskipton@totalise.co.uk
Dir: *on A629, 1m from town*

Located beside the canal just outside the town, the hotel has the advantage of plenty of parking and good amenities for the leisure guest. Bedrooms are well equipped and spacious, and have delightful views over the rolling countryside. Added attractions include the indoor pool, gym and supervised children's play areas.
ROOMS: 75 en suite (10 fmly) (12 GF) No smoking in 14 bedrooms s fr £85; d fr £90 (incl. bkfst) **LB** **FACILITIES:** STV Indoor swimming (H) Squash Sauna Solarium Gym Jacuzzi Whirlpool spa, Steam room, Swimming pool supervised Xmas **CONF:** Thtr 400 Class 180 Board 120 Del from £95 **SERVICES:** Lift **PARKING:** 150 **NOTES:** No smoking in restaurant Closed 25-27 Dec Civ Wed 200
CARDS:

★★66% Herriots Hotel, Bar & Dining Rooms

Broughton Rd BD23 1RT
☎ 01756 792781 🖹 01756 793967
e-mail: herriots@mgrleisure.com
Dir: *off A59, opposite railway station*

Close to the centre of the market town and on the doorstep of the Yorkshire Dales National Park, this friendly hotel offers brightly decorated, modern bedrooms that are well equipped. The stylish open-plan brasserie is a relaxing place in which to dine, and has a varied menu. Meals and snacks are also available in the bar.
ROOMS: 12 en suite (3 fmly) No smoking in 8 bedrooms s £41-£60; d £54-£65 (incl. bkfst) **FACILITIES:** Xmas **CONF:** Thtr 20 Class 15 Board 15 Del from £85 **PARKING:** 28 **NOTES:** No smoking in restaurant
CARDS:

⌂ Travelodge

Travelodge

Gargrave Rd BD23 1UD
☎ 08700 850 950 🖹 01756 798091
Dir: *A65/A59 rdbt*

Travelodge offers good quality, good value, modern accommodation. Ideal for families, the spacious, en suite bedrooms include remote-control TV, tea and coffee-making facilities, luxury beds and free morning newspaper. Meals can be taken at the nearby family restaurant. For further details and the Travelodge phone number, consult the Hotel Groups page.
ROOMS: 32 en suite s fr £42.95; d fr £42.95

SLEAFORD, Lincolnshire

Map 12 TF04

★★★64% The Lincolnshire Oak

East Rd NG34 7EH

THE INDEPENDENTS

☎ 01529 413807 🖷 01529 413710

e-mail: reception@lincolnshire-oak.co.uk

Dir: *From A17 (by-pass) exit on A153 into Sleaford. Hotel 0.75m on left*

This is a pleasant, hospitable Victorian house, set in well-tended grounds on the edge of town. It offers modern, well-furnished bedrooms and comfortable public rooms. There are ample function rooms and an attractive garden.

ROOMS: 17 en suite No smoking in 12 bedrooms s £58-£71; d £71-£86 (incl. bkfst) **LB FACILITIES:** STV **CONF:** Thtr 140 Class 70 Board 50 Del £80 **PARKING:** 80 **NOTES:** No dogs No smoking in restaurant Civ Wed 80 **CARDS:**

★★70% Carre Arms

1 Mareham Ln NG34 7JP

☎ 01529 303156 🖷 01529 303139

e-mail: enquiries@carrearmshotel.co.uk

Dir: *take A153 to Sleaford, hotel on right at level crossing*

This friendly, family run hotel is located close to the station and offers well-appointed, thoughtfully equipped bedrooms. Public areas include two comfortable spacious bars where are a good selection of bar meals is offered and a smart Brasserie. There is also a conservatory and an old stable housing a spacious, elegant function room.

ROOMS: 13 en suite (1 fmly) s £50; d £70 (incl. bkfst) **CONF:** Thtr 120 Class 54 Board 40 **PARKING:** 100 **NOTES:** No dogs (ex guide dogs) No smoking in restaurant **CARDS:**

⌂ Travelodge

Holdingham NG34 8PN

Travelodge

☎ 08700 850 950 🖷 01529 414752

Dir: *1m N, at A17/A15 rdbt*

Travelodge offers good quality, good value, modern accommodation. Ideal for families, the spacious, en suite bedrooms include remote-control TV, tea and coffee-making facilities, luxury beds and free morning newspaper. Meals can be taken at the nearby family restaurant. For further details and the Travelodge phone number, consult the Hotel Groups page.

ROOMS: 40 en suite s fr £42.95; d fr £42.95

S

SLOUGH, Berkshire Map 06 SU97

★★★★66% Copthorne Hotel Slough/Windsor

COPTHORNE

400 Cippenham Ln SL1 2YE
☎ 01753 516222 🖹 01753 516237
e-mail: sales.slough@mill-cop.com
Dir: *M4 junct 6, A355 to Slough at rdbt left & left again for hotel*

This is a modern property just off the M4 with views over to Heathrow and Windsor. Public areas include a good leisure centre and the Veranda restaurant. Bedrooms are spacious with excellent facilities including air conditioning. The hotel is popular for weekend breaks; special vouchers are issued offering discounts to various attractions in the area.
ROOMS: 219 en suite (47 fmly) No smoking in 148 bedrooms s £80-£180; d £80-£180 **FACILITIES:** STV Indoor swimming (H) Sauna Gym Jacuzzi Xmas **CONF:** Thtr 250 Class 160 Board 60 Del from £195 **SERVICES:** Lift air con **PARKING:** 300 **NOTES:** No dogs (ex guide dogs) No smoking in restaurant **CARDS:**

★★★69% Courtyard by Marriott Slough/Windsor

Church St SL1 2NH
☎ 0870 400 7215 🖹 0870 400 7315
Dir: *M4 junct 6, follow A355 to rdbt, turn right, hotel approx 50yds on right*
Just 30 minutes from Heathrow Airport and with local motorway networks just minutes away by car, the hotel is well located and a popular venue for smaller meetings. Spacious bedrooms feature a range of extras and public areas are lively and modern in style. There is also a small fitness room.
ROOMS: 150 en suite (64 fmly) (6 GF) No smoking in 113 bedrooms s £60-£125; d £70-£135 (incl. bkfst) **FACILITIES:** STV Xmas **CONF:** Thtr 80 Class 32 Board 40 Del from £135 **SERVICES:** Lift air con **PARKING:** 130 **NOTES:** No dogs (ex guide dogs) No smoking in restaurant **CARDS:**

★★★66% Quality Hotel Heathrow

QUALITY HOTEL

London Rd, Brands Hill SL3 8QB
☎ 01753 684001 🖹 01753 685767
e-mail: info@qualityheathrow.com
Dir: *M4 junct 5, follow signs for Colnbrook. Hotel approx 250mtrs on right*
A smart modern hotel ideally located for Heathrow Airport, and for commercial visitors to Slough. Bedrooms have good facilities and benefit from all-day room service. There is a bright and airy open-plan restaurant, bar and lounge. Transport is available to and from the airport.
ROOMS: 128 en suite (23 fmly) (5 GF) No smoking in 60 bedrooms s £49-£139; d £49-£139 **LB FACILITIES:** STV Gym **CONF:** Thtr 120 Class 50 Board 40 Del from £99 **SERVICES:** Lift **PARKING:** 100 **NOTES:** No dogs (ex guide dogs) **CARDS:**

⌂ Innkeeper's Lodge Slough/Windsor

Innkeeper's Lodge

399 London Rd, Langley SL3 8PS
☎ 01753 591212 🖹 01753 211362
Dir: *M4 junct 5 onto London Rd, 100yds on right*
A new concept in the travel accommodation market. Smart rooms meet essential business requirements but also have home comforts. Dining options include all-day menus plus the added advantage of breakfast, which is included in the room price. For further details, consult the Hotel Groups page.
ROOMS: 57 en suite **CONF:** Board 15

⌂ Premier Lodge (Slough)

PREMIER LODGE

76 Uxbridge Rd SL1 1SU
☎ 0870 9906500 🖹 0870 9906501
Dir: *2m from M4 junct 5, just off A4*
Premier Lodge offers modern, well-equipped, en suite accommodation suitable for both business and leisure travellers. Meals can be taken at the adjacent popular restaurant and bar, which is fully licensed. For further details, consult the Hotel Groups page.
ROOMS: 84 en suite s £52; d £52

⌂ Travelodge

Travelodge

Landmark Place SL1 1BZ
☎ 01753 639565 🖹 01753 - 516897

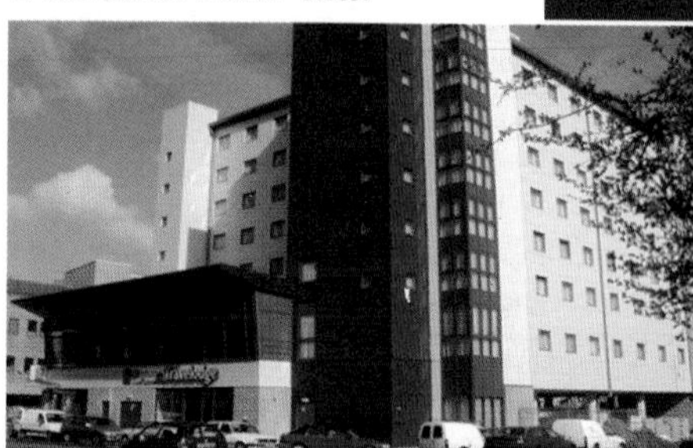

Travelodge offers good quality, good value, modern accommodation. Ideal for families, the spacious, en suite bedrooms include remote-control TV, tea and coffee-making facilities, luxury beds and free morning newspaper. Meals can be taken at the nearby family restaurant. For further details and the Travelodge phone number, consult the Hotel Groups page.
ROOMS: 157 en suite (incl. bkfst) s fr £42.95; d fr £42.95

> Early start?
> Hotels at all star levels should provide in-room alarm clocks and/or alarm calls

SNETTISHAM, Norfolk Map 12 TF63

★★70% ֍ Rose & Crown
Old Church Rd PE31 7LX
☎ 01485 541382 🖹 01485 543172
e-mail: info@roseandcrownsnettisham.co.uk
Dir: *Hotel 100yds along Old Church Rd on left*
This lovely old pub is found in the centre of the village and provides quality bedrooms, which are very well equipped and comfortable. A wide range of quality cooked food is served in the many dining areas while a good range of real ales are on offer.

continued

S

Service is friendly and a delightful atmosphere prevails. A walled garden is available on sunny days, as is a children's play area.

ROOMS: 11 en suite (3 fmly) No smoking in all bedrooms s £55-£65; d £80-£100 (incl. bkfst) **LB** **FACILITIES:** ch fac **PARKING:** 70 **CARDS:**

SOLIHULL, West Midlands Map 10 SP17
See also Dorridge

★★★★68% Renaissance Solihull

651 Warwick Rd B91 1AT
☎ 0121 711 3000
0121 705 6629/0121 711 3963
e-mail: ed.schofield@whitbread.com
Dir: *M42 junct 5, follow signs for Solihull centre. 2nd left at rdbt (Warwick Rd). Straight over 3rd lights. Straight ahead, hotel on right.*

An attractive modern hotel, convenient for the NEC and airport and with easy access to the main arterial routes. Bedrooms are comfortable, particularly those with air conditioning, and tastefully decorated. Extensive conference facilities attract a predominantly business clientele, whilst the 651 restaurant offers a contemporary brasserie menu and a resident pianist.

ROOMS: 179 en suite (6 fmly) No smoking in 87 bedrooms **FACILITIES:** STV Indoor swimming (H) Sauna Solarium Gym Jacuzzi Beauty therapist Large screen TV entertainment **CONF:** Thtr 700 Class 350 Board 60 Del from £120 **SERVICES:** Lift **PARKING:** 300 **NOTES:** Civ Wed 70 **CARDS:**

★★★64% The Regency Hotel

Stratford Rd, Shirley B90 4EB
☎ 0121 745 6119 0121 733 3801
e-mail: regency@corushotels.com
Dir: *M42 junct 4 onto A34, cross 1st 3 rdbts, double back along dual carriageway, hotel on left*

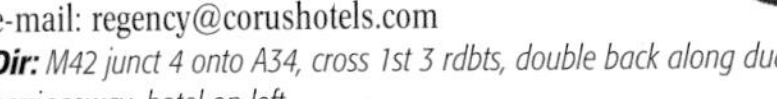

This popular business hotel offers its guests some extra facilities such as an indoor leisure club and Morrissey's Irish Bar, with

continued

occasional live music. The bedrooms are well-laid out, and some benefit from an attractive modern refurbishment.

ROOMS: 112 en suite (6 fmly) No smoking in 45 bedrooms **FACILITIES: Spa** STV Indoor swimming (H) Sauna Solarium Gym Jacuzzi Beauty health salon, Steam room **CONF:** Thtr 180 Class 80 Board 60 Del £150 **SERVICES:** Lift **PARKING:** 275 **NOTES:** No smoking in restaurant **CARDS:**

Travel Inn (Solihull North)

Stratford Rd, Shirley B90 3AG
☎ 08701 977231 0121 733 2762
Dir: *M42 junct 4 follow signs for Birmingham. Travel Inn in Shirley Town Centre, on A34*

Travel Inn offers good-quality, value-for-money accommodation. Spacious, en suite rooms with bath and shower comfortably accommodate a family of up to two adults and two children (to age 15). The restaurant and bar offers a varied menu. For further details and the Travel Inn phone number, consult the Hotel Groups page.

ROOMS: 44 en suite s £44.95; d £44.95

Travel Inn (Solihull Shirley)

Stratford Rd, Shirley B90 4EP
☎ 08701 977232 0121 733 7075
Dir: *M42 junst 4 on A34*

Travel Inn offers good-quality, value-for-money accommodation. Spacious, en suite rooms with bath and shower comfortably accommodate a family of up to two adults and two children (to age 15). The restaurant and bar offers a varied menu. For further details and the Travel Inn phone number, consult the Hotel Groups page.

ROOMS: 51 en suite s £44.95; d £44.95

SONNING, Berkshire
Map 05 SU77

★★★77% French Horn
RG4 6TN
☎ 0118 969 2204 📠 0118 944 2210
e-mail: thefrenchhorn@compuserve.com
Dir: *turn left off A4 into Sonning follow road through village over bridge, hotel on right, car park on left*

This long established Thames-side restaurant-with-rooms has a lovely village setting and retains the traditions of classic hotel-keeping. The restaurant is a particular attraction and provides attentive service. Bedrooms are spacious and comfortable, many offering stunning views over the river and include four cottage suites. A private boardroom is available for corporate guests.

ROOMS: 13 en suite 8 annexe en suite (8 GF) s £105-£160; d £130-£195 (incl. bkfst) **FACILITIES:** Fishing **CONF:** Board 16 Del £235 **PARKING:** 40 **NOTES:** No dogs (ex guide dogs) Closed 26 Dec-30 Jan RS 1st Jan **CARDS:**

★★★68% The Great House at Sonning
Thames St RG4 6UT
☎ 0118 969 2277 📠 0118 944 1296
e-mail: greathouse@btconnect.com
Dir: *exit A4 at rdbt with Texaco Garage & take B478 into Sonning (signed). Through village, over mini rdbt, down steep hill and bear right. Hotel on right, before bridge*

Enjoying a most attractive riverside setting, the Great House is a popular venue. Having a mile and a half of private moorings, a terrace and lawns that lead down to the river, this is a really beautiful location. Bedrooms, many in the main house, enjoy the great views and others situated in courtyard buildings are all attractive and comfortable. A number of function suites and conference rooms are available and is popular for weddings.

ROOMS: 12 en suite 37 annexe en suite (11 GF) s £109; d £129 (incl. bkfst) **LB** **FACILITIES:** STV Tennis (hard) **CONF:** Thtr 100 Class 50 Board 35 Del from £159 **PARKING:** 120 **NOTES:** RS 27 Dec -1 wk Jan **CARDS:**

SOURTON, Devon
Map 03 SX59

★★73% Collaven Manor
EX20 4HH
☎ 01837 861522 📠 01837 861614
e-mail: collavenmanor@supanet.com
Dir: *off A30 onto A386 to Tavistock, hotel 2m on right*

This delightful 15th-century manor house is quietly located in five acres of well-tended grounds. The friendly proprietors provide attentive service and ensure a relaxing environment. Charming public rooms have old oak beams and granite fireplaces, and provide a range of comfortable lounges and a well stocked bar. In the restaurant, a daily changing menu offers interesting dishes.

ROOMS: 9 en suite (1 fmly) s £56; d £88-£124 (incl. bkfst) **LB** **FACILITIES:** Croquet lawn Bowls Badminton **CONF:** Thtr 30 Class 20 Board 16 Del from £87 **PARKING:** 50 **NOTES:** No smoking in restaurant Civ Wed 40 **CARDS:**

SOURTON CROSS, Devon
Map 03 SX59

Travelodge Okehampton West
EX20 4LY
☎ 08700 850 950 📠 01837 52124
Dir: *4m W, at junct of A30/A386*

Travelodge offers good quality, good value, modern accommodation. Ideal for families, the spacious, en suite bedrooms include remote-control TV, tea and coffee-making facilities, luxury beds and free morning newspaper. Meals can be taken at the nearby family restaurant. For further details and the Travelodge phone number, consult the Hotel Groups page.

ROOMS: 42 en suite s fr £42.95; d fr £42.95

SOUTHAMPTON, Hampshire
Map 05 SU41

See also Landford (Wilts) & Shedfield

★★★★64% De Vere Grand Harbour
West Quay Rd SO15 1AG
☎ 023 8063 3033 📠 023 8063 3066
e-mail: grandharbour@devere-hotels.com
Dir: *M27 junct 3 follow Waterfront signs keep in left lane of dual carrriageway, then follow signs, Heritage & Waterfront to old town & waterfront onto West Quay Rd*

Enjoying views of the harbour, this hotel stands alongside the medieval town walls and close to the West Quay centre. The modern design is impressive, with leisure facilities located in the dramatic glass pyramid. The spacious and thoughtfully equipped bedrooms are currently undergoing refurbishment, with completion due May 2004. For dining, guests can choose between two bars as well as Allertons Restaurant and Brewsters Brasserie.

ROOMS: 172 en suite (22 fmly) No smoking in 120 bedrooms s £165-£195; d £185-£215 (incl. bkfst) **LB** **FACILITIES: Spa** STV Indoor swimming (H) Snooker Sauna Solarium Gym Xmas **CONF:** BC Thtr 500 Class 200 Board 150 Del from £140 **SERVICES:** Lift **PARKING:** 190 **NOTES:** No dogs (ex guide dogs) No smoking in restaurant Civ Wed 500 **CARDS:**

★★★★69% *Botleigh Grange*
Hedge End SO30 2GA
☎ 01489 787700 📠 01489 788535
e-mail: enquiries@botleighgrangehotel.co.uk
Dir: *follow A334 to Botley, hotel on left*

An upgrade of this impressive mansion ensures good quality throughout. Many of the bedrooms are newly decorated and all

continued

are spacious with a good range of facilities. Public areas include a large conference room and a pleasant terrace with views overlooking the gardens and lake. The restaurant offers interesting menus using fresh local produce.

ROOMS: 56 en suite (8 fmly) No smoking in 17 bedrooms **FACILITIES:** STV Fishing Putting green Coarse fishing **CONF:** Thtr 500 Class 175 Board 60 **SERVICES:** Lift **PARKING:** 200 **NOTES:** No dogs (ex guide dogs) No smoking in restaurant Civ Wed 200
CARDS:

See advert on this page

★★★68% The Woodlands Lodge

Bartley Rd, Woodlands SO40 7GN
☎ 023 8029 2257 📠 023 8029 3090
e-mail: woodlands@nortels.ltd.uk
Dir: *A326 towards Fawley. 2nd rdbt turn right, left after 0.25m by White Horse PH. In 1.5m cross cattle grid, hotel 70yds on left*

An 18th-century former hunting lodge, this hotel is set in four acres of impressive and well-tended grounds on the edge of the New Forest. Well equipped bedrooms come in varying sizes and styles and all bathrooms have a jacuzzi bath. Public areas provide a pleasant lounge and intimate cocktail bar. The dining room, with its hand-painted ceiling, serves delicious award-winning cuisine.
ROOMS: 16 en suite (1 fmly) (3 GF) No smoking in 2 bedrooms s £71-£92; d £99-£185 (incl. bkfst) **LB FACILITIES:** STV Jacuzzi Xmas **CONF:** Thtr 55 Class 14 Board 20 Del from £118 **PARKING:** 31 **NOTES:** No smoking in restaurant Civ Wed 60
CARDS:

★★★66% Southampton Park

Forestdale Hotels

Cumberland Place SO15 2WY
☎ 023 8034 3343 📠 023 8033 2538
e-mail: southampton.park@forestdale.com
Dir: *at north end of Inner Ring Rd opposite Watts Park & Civic Centre*

Located in the heart of the city, opposite Watts Park, this modern hotel provides well equipped, smartly appointed bedrooms with comfortable furnishings. The public areas include a good leisure centre, a spacious bar and lounge and MJ's Brasserie. Parking is available in the multi-storey car park behind the hotel.
ROOMS: 72 en suite (10 fmly) No smoking in 20 bedrooms s fr £85; d fr £110 (incl. bkfst) **LB FACILITIES: Spa** STV Indoor swimming (H) Sauna Solarium Gym Jacuzzi **CONF:** Thtr 200 Class 60 Board 70 Del from £125 **SERVICES:** Lift **NOTES:** No smoking in restaurant Closed 25 & 26 Dec nights **CARDS:**

★★★64% *Highfield House*

Highfield Ln, Portswood SO17 1AQ
☎ 023 8035 9955 📠 023 8058 3910
Dir: *M27 junct 5 take A335 to city centre, at 5th set lights follow signs for Portswood/University, hotel on right after Shaftesbury Avenue*

Close to the university and within easy reach of the motorway, this hotel remains a popular choice with all guests. The owners have initiated a major refurbishment programme and bedrooms and public areas have all been upgraded.
ROOMS: 66 en suite (6 fmly) No smoking in 30 bedrooms **FACILITIES:** STV **CONF:** Thtr 200 Class 100 Board 60 **PARKING:** 85 **NOTES:** No smoking in restaurant **CARDS:**

★★★64% *Novotel Southampton*

NOVOTEL

1 West Quay Rd SO15 1RA
☎ 023 8033 0550 📠 023 8022 2158
e-mail: H1073@accor-hotels.com

Dir: *M27 junct 3 & signs for City Centre (A33). After 1m take right lane for West Quay & Dock Gates 4-10. Hotel entrance on left. Turn at lights by McDonalds, left at rdbt, hotel straight ahead*

This modern, purpose-built hotel is conveniently located in the heart of the city centre, close to the railway station and road network. The bright, spacious bedrooms are ideal for both families and business guests; four rooms have facilities for guests with disabilities. Public areas include the Garden brasserie and bar, which is open throughout the day, and a leisure complex.
ROOMS: 121 en suite (50 fmly) No smoking in 71 bedrooms **FACILITIES:** STV Indoor swimming (H) Sauna Gym **CONF:** Thtr 500 Class 300 Board 150 **SERVICES:** Lift air con **PARKING:** 300
CARDS:

SOUTHAMPTON, continued

★★68% Elizabeth House

42-44 The Avenue SO17 1XP
☎ 023 8022 4327 🖹 023 8022 4327
e-mail: enquiries@elizabethhousehotel.com
Dir: *towards town on A33, on left (after Southampton Common, before main lights)*

The Elizabeth House is conveniently situated on The Avenue, and as such provides an ideal base for both business and leisure guests. The bedrooms are well equipped and are attractively furnished with comfort in mind. There is also a relaxing and attractive restaurant and a cosy cellar bar.

ROOMS: 21 en suite 7 annexe en suite (7 fmly) (8 GF) s fr £49.50; d fr £59.50 (incl. bkfst) **CONF:** Thtr 40 Class 24 Board 24 Del £80 **PARKING:** 30 **NOTES:** No smoking in restaurant **CARDS:**

★★64% *Busketts Lawn*

174 Woodlands Rd, Woodlands SO40 7GL
☎ 023 8029 2272 & 8029 3417 🖹 023 8029 2487
e-mail: enquiries@buskettslawnhotel.co.uk
Dir: *A35 W of city through Ashurst, over rail bridge, sharp right into Woodlands Rd*

This small, family run hotel is set in tranquil grounds on the edge of the New Forest. Bedrooms vary in size; some are on the ground floor and one has a four-poster bed, all have many thoughtful extras. A small lounge and cocktail bar is available. The hotel is a popular venue for weddings.

ROOMS: 14 en suite (3 fmly) **FACILITIES:** Outdoor swimming (H) Croquet lawn Putting green Mini Football pitch **CONF:** Thtr 100 Class 60 Board 40 **PARKING:** 50 **NOTES:** No smoking in restaurant Closed Xmas Civ Wed 70 **CARDS:**

U *Holiday Inn Southampton*

Herbert Walker Av SO15 1HJ
☎ 0870 400 9073 🖹 023 8033 2510
e-mail: southamptonhi@ichotelsgroup.com
Dir: *M27 junct3 follow signs for 'Dockgate 1-10' & Southampton Waterfront. Hotel situated next to Dock Gate 8*

At the time of going to press, the classification for this hotel was not confirmed. Please refer to the AA internet site www.theAA.com for current information.

ROOMS: 132 en suite (14 fmly) No smoking in 75 bedrooms **FACILITIES: Spa** Indoor swimming (H) Sauna Solarium Gym Jacuzzi **CONF:** Thtr 250 Class 80 Board 50 **SERVICES:** Lift **PARKING:** 250 **NOTES:** No dogs (ex guide dogs) Civ Wed 30 **CARDS:**

⇧ Express by Holiday Inn

Adanac Park, Redbridge Ln, Nursling SO16 0YP
☎ 023 8074 3100 🖹 023 8073 1827
e-mail: southampton@oriel-leisure.co.uk
Dir: *M271 from M27 junct 3, hotel on left at junct 1 (Lordshill Interchange) via Redbridge Lane*

A modern hotel ideal for families and business travellers. Fresh and uncomplicated, the spacious bedrooms include Sky TV, power shower and tea and coffee-making facilities. Continental buffet breakfast is included in the room rate; other meals may be taken at the nearby family pub or restaurant. For further details and the *continued* Express by Holiday Inn phone number, consult the Hotel Groups pages.

ROOMS: 105 en suite s £49-£65; d £49-£65 (incl. cont bkfst) **CONF:** Thtr 40 Class 30 Board 25

⇧ Express by Holiday Inn

Botley Rd, West End SO30 3XA
☎ 0870 242 1368

A modern hotel ideal for families and business travellers. Fresh and uncomplicated, the spacious bedrooms include Sky TV, power shower and tea and coffee-making facilities. Continental buffet breakfast is included in the room rate; other meals may be taken at the nearby family pub or restaurant. For further details and the Express by Holiday Inn phone number, consult the Hotel Groups pages.

ROOMS: 131 en suite

⇧ Hotel Ibis

West Quay Rd, Western Esplanade SO15 1RA
☎ 023 8063 4463 🖹 023 8022 3273
e-mail: H1039@accor-hotels.com
Dir: *M27 junct 3/M271. A35 to city centre, follow Old Town Waterfront until 4th lights, left, then left again, hotel opposite station*

Modern, budget hotel offering comfortable accommodation in bright and practical bedrooms. Breakfast is self-service and dinner is available in the restaurant. For further details, consult the Hotel Groups page.

ROOMS: 93 en suite s £49.95-£56.95; d £49.95-£56.95

⇧ Travel Inn Southampton (City Centre)

New Rd SO14 0AB
☎ 0870 238 3308 🖹 023 8033 8395
Dir: *M27 junct 5/A335 towards city centre, at Charlotte Place rdbt take 2nd left into East Park Terrace, then 1st left onto New Rd. Travel Inn on right*

Travel Inn offers good-quality, value-for-money accommodation. Spacious, en suite rooms with bath and shower comfortably accommodate a family of up to two adults and two children (to age 15). The restaurant and bar offers a varied menu. For further details and the Travel Inn phone number, consult the Hotel Groups page.

ROOMS: 172 en suite s £52.95-£54.95; d £52.95-£54.95

⌂ Travel Inn (Southampton North)
Romsey Rd, Nursling SO16 0XJ
☎ 08701 977233 📠 023 8074 0947
Dir: *M27 junct 3 take M271 towards Romsey. At next rdbt take 3rd exit towards Southampton (A3057) Travel Inn 1.5m on right*
Travel Inn offers good-quality, value-for-money accommodation. Spacious, en suite rooms with bath and shower comfortably accommodate a family of up to two adults and two children (to age 15). The restaurant and bar offers a varied menu. For further details and the Travel Inn phone number, consult the Hotel Groups page.
ROOMS: 32 en suite s £44.95; d £44.95

⌂ Travelodge
Lodge Rd SO14 6QR ☎ 08700 850 950
Travelodge offers good quality, good value, modern accommodation. Ideal for families, the spacious, en suite bedrooms include remote-control TV, tea and coffee-making facilities, luxury beds and free morning newspaper. Meals can be taken at the nearby family restaurant. For further details and the Travelodge phone number, consult the Hotel Groups page.
ROOMS: 59 en suite s fr £42.95; d fr £42.95

○ Premier Lodge (Southampton Airport)

Wide Ln SO18 2NL
☎ 0870 9906436 📠 0870 9906437
ROOMS: 121 en suite **NOTES:** Due to open Feb 2004

SOUTH CAVE, East Riding of Yorkshire — Map 17 SE93

⌂ Travelodge Hull

Beacon Service Area HU15 1RZ
☎ 08700 850 950 📠 01430 424455
Dir: *at services on A63 eastbound*
Travelodge offers good quality, good value, modern accommodation. Ideal for families, the spacious, en suite bedrooms include remote-control TV, tea and coffee-making facilities, luxury beds and free morning newspaper. Meals can be taken at the nearby family restaurant. For further details and the Travelodge phone number, consult the Hotel Groups page.
ROOMS: 40 en suite s fr £42.95; d fr £42.95

SOUTHEND-ON-SEA, Essex — Map 07 TQ88

★★★68% Roslin Hotel
Thorpe Esplanade SS1 3BG
☎ 01702 586375 📠 01702 586663 e-mail: sales@roslinhotel.com
Dir: *A127, follow signs for Southend-on-Sea. Hotel between Walton Road & Clieveden Road*

A friendly, family-run hotel situated at the quiet end of the esplanade overlooking the beach and sea. The spacious bedrooms are pleasantly decorated and thoughtfully equipped; some rooms have superb sea views. Public rooms include a large lounge bar and the attractive Mulberry restaurant, which also overlooks the sea.
ROOMS: 39 rms (35 en suite) (4 fmly) (6 GF) s £44-£72; d £77-£87 (incl. bkfst) **LB** **FACILITIES:** STV Temp membership of local sports centre **CONF:** Thtr 40 Class 30 Board 30 Del from £78.50 **PARKING:** 34 **NOTES:** RS 26 Dec **CARDS:**

★★★68% Westcliff
Westcliff Pde, Westcliff-on-Sea SS0 7QW
☎ 01702 345247 📠 01702 431814
e-mail: westcliff@zolahotels.com
Dir: *M25 junct 29, A127 towards Southend, follow signs for Cliffs Pavillion when approaching town centre*

This impressive Grade II listed Victorian building is situated in an elevated position overlooking the cliffs, gardens and sea beyond. The spacious bedrooms are tastefully decorated and thoughtfully equipped; many have lovely sea views. Public rooms include a smart conservatory-style restaurant, a spacious lounge and a range of function rooms.
ROOMS: 55 en suite (2 fmly) No smoking in 32 bedrooms s £75-£80; d £95-£100 (incl. bkfst) **LB** **FACILITIES:** STV entertainment Xmas **CONF:** Thtr 225 Class 90 Board 64 Del from £95 **SERVICES:** Lift **NOTES:** No dogs (ex guide dogs) No smoking in restaurant Civ Wed 60 **CARDS:**

★★70% Balmoral
34 Valkyrie Rd, Westcliff-on-Sea SS0 8BU
☎ 01702 342947 📠 01702 337828
e-mail: enq@balmoralsouthend.com
Dir: *off A13*
A delightful hotel ideally situated just a short walk from the main shopping centre, railway station and seafront. The attractively decorated bedrooms are tastefully furnished and equipped with many thoughtful touches. Public rooms feature a smart open plan bar/restaurant and further seating is provided in the reception area.
ROOMS: 29 en suite (4 fmly) (2 GF) s £48-£90; d £73-£110 (incl. bkfst) **LB** **FACILITIES:** STV Arrangement with nearby health club **PARKING:** 23 **NOTES:** No smoking in restaurant Closed Xmas **CARDS:**

★★70% Camelia
178 Eastern Esplanade, Thorpe Bay SS1 3AA
☎ 01702 587917 📠 01702 585704
e-mail: cameliahotel@fsbdial.co.uk
Dir: *from A13 or A127 follow signs to Southend seafront. On seafront turn left, hotel 1m east of pier*
A smartly presented, privately-owned hotel, ideally situated at the quiet end of the seafront overlooking the beach. Bedrooms are pleasantly decorated and thoughtfully equipped; many rooms

continued on p566

S

SOUTHEND-ON-SEA, continued

have superb sea views. The air-conditioned public areas include a cosy lounge bar, an informal restaurant and a coffee lounge.

Camelia Hotel, Southend-on-Sea

ROOMS: 21 en suite 8 annexe en suite (7 fmly) (8 GF) No smoking in 19 bedrooms s £46-£70; d £60-£100 (incl. bkfst) **LB** **FACILITIES:** STV Jacuzzi Cycle hire and tours arranged entertainment **PARKING:** 102 **NOTES:** No dogs (ex guide dogs) No smoking in restaurant **CARDS:**

★★66% *Erlsmere*

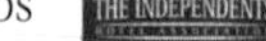

24/32 Pembury Rd, Westcliff-on-Sea SS0 8DS
☎ 01702 349025 01702 337724
e-mail: erlsmerehotel@madasafish.com
Dir: *M25 junct 29 to A127 to Southend. Pass Kent Elms Corner, at next set of lights take A1158 to Westbourne Grove signed seafront. At next junct (A13) straight on to Chalkwell Ave, under rail bridge left, 4th on right*

This hotel is situated in a peaceful side road, just a short walk from the seafront and shops. Bedrooms come in a variety of styles; each one is pleasantly decorated and well equipped. Dinner is served in the Knights Restaurant and guests may also use the Patio Bar and cosy lounge.
ROOMS: 30 en suite 2 annexe en suite (2 fmly) **CONF:** Thtr 120 Class 40 Board 60 **PARKING:** 12 **NOTES:** No dogs (ex guide dogs) **CARDS:**

⌂ Premier Lodge (Southend-on-Sea)

213 Eastern Esplanade SS1 3AD
☎ 0870 9906370 0870 9906371
Dir: *on entering Southend follow A1159/(A13)/Shoebury onto dual carriageway. At rbt follow Thorpe Bay seafront signs. At seafront turn right for hotel on right.*
Premier Lodge offers modern, well-equipped, en suite accommodation suitable for both business and leisure travellers. Meals can be taken at the adjacent popular restaurant and bar, which is fully licensed. For further details, consult the Hotel Groups page.
ROOMS: 42 en suite s £48; d £48

⌂ Travel Inn

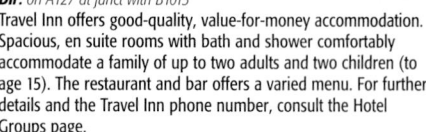

Thanet Grange SS2 6GB
☎ 08701 977235 01702 430838
Dir: *on A127 at junct with B1013*
Travel Inn offers good-quality, value-for-money accommodation. Spacious, en suite rooms with bath and shower comfortably accommodate a family of up to two adults and two children (to age 15). The restaurant and bar offers a varied menu. For further details and the Travel Inn phone number, consult the Hotel Groups page.
ROOMS: 60 en suite s £44.95; d £44.95

SOUTH MIMMS, Hertfordshire — Map 06 TL20

U *Holiday Inn South Mimms*

EN6 3NH
☎ 0870 400 9072 01707 646728
e-mail: southmimms@ichotelsgroup.com
Dir: *M25 junct 23 & A1 take services exit off main rdbt then 1st left & follow hotel signs*
At the time of going to press, the classification for this hotel was not confirmed. Please refer to the AA internet site www.theAA.com for current information.
ROOMS: 144 en suite (18 fmly) No smoking in 91 bedrooms **FACILITIES:** Outdoor childrens play area **CONF:** Thtr 110 Class 60 Board 40 **PARKING:** 200 **NOTES:** No dogs (ex guide dogs) Civ Wed 80 **CARDS:**

SOUTH MIMMS SERVICE AREA (M25), Hertfordshire — Map 06 TL20

⌂ Days Inn

Bignells Corner EN6 3QQ
☎ 01707 665440 01707 660189
e-mail: southmimmshotel@welcomebreak.co.uk
Dir: *M25 junct 23, at rdbt follow signs*
This modern building offers accommodation in smart, spacious and well-equipped bedrooms, suitable for families and business travellers, and all with en suite bathrooms. Continental breakfast is available and other refreshments may be taken at the nearby family restaurant. For further details and the Days Inn phone number, consult the Hotel Groups page.
ROOMS: 74 en suite s £59-£74; d £59-£74 **CONF:** Board 10

SOUTH MOLTON, Devon — Map 03 SS72

★★68% The George Hotel

1 Broad St EX36 3AB
☎ 01769 572514 01769 572514
e-mail: george@s-molton.freeserve.co.uk
Dir: *off A361 at road island signed South Molton, 1.5m to town centre, hotel in square*
Retaining many of its original features, this charming 17th-century hotel is situated in the centre of town. Providing comfortable accommodation, complemented by informal and friendly service, the property has now undergone extensive refurbishment. Regularly changing menus, featuring local produce, are offered in the restaurant and bar.
ROOMS: 9 en suite (2 fmly) s £45-£50; d £60-£65 (incl. bkfst) **LB** **CONF:** Thtr 100 Class 20 Board 24 **PARKING:** 12 **NOTES:** No dogs (ex guide dogs) No smoking in restaurant Closed 1st wk Jan RS Sun **CARDS:**

SOUTH NORMANTON, Derbyshire Map 16 SK45

★★★★70% Renaissance Derby/Nottingham Hotel

Carter Ln East DE55 2EH
☎ 01773 812000 📠 01773 580032
e-mail: derby@renaissancehotels.co.uk
Dir: *M1 junct 28, E on A38 to Mansfield*

This hotel provides comfortable bedrooms, stylishly furnished and decorated with a comprehensive range of extras provided. Public rooms include a smart leisure centre, conference facilities and Chatterley's Restaurant.

ROOMS: 158 en suite (7 fmly) (61 GF) No smoking in 100 bedrooms s £115-£140; d £135-£160 (incl. bkfst) **LB FACILITIES:** STV Indoor swimming (H) Sauna Solarium Gym Jacuzzi Steam room, Whirlpool, Swimming pool supervised Xmas **CONF:** Thtr 220 Class 100 Board 60 Del from £145 **PARKING:** 220 **NOTES:** No smoking in restaurant Civ Wed 180 **CARDS:**

Travel Inn (Mansfield)

Carter Ln East DE55 2EH
☎ 08701 977180 📠 01773 861155
Dir: *just off M1 junct 28, on A38 signed Mansfield. Entrance 200yds on left*

Travel Inn offers good-quality, value-for-money accommodation. Spacious, en suite rooms with bath and shower comfortably accommodate a family of up to two adults and two children (to age 15). The restaurant and bar offers a varied menu. For further details and the Travel Inn phone number, consult the Hotel Groups page.

ROOMS: 80 en suite s £44.95; d £44.95

SOUTHPORT, Merseyside Map 15 SD31
See also Formby

★★★71% Scarisbrick

Lord St PR8 1NZ
☎ 01704 543000 📠 01704 533335
e-mail: info@scarisbrickhotel.com
Dir: *from S: M6 junct 26, M58 to Ormskirk then onto Southport; from N: A59 from Preston, well signed. Also M6 junct 26, then M58 junct A570*

Centrally located on Southport's famous Lord Street, this privately owned hotel offers a high standard of attractively furnished, thoughtfully equipped accommodation. A wide range of eating options is available, from the bistro style of Maloney's Kitchen to the more formal Knightsbridge restaurant. Extensive leisure facilities are provided in a newly built extension.

ROOMS: 88 en suite (5 fmly) s £30-£65; d £60-£110 (incl. bkfst) **LB FACILITIES: Spa** STV Indoor swimming (H) Sauna Solarium Gym Jacuzzi Use of private leisure centre, Beauty & aromatherapy studio entertainment Xmas **CONF:** BC Thtr 200 Class 100 Board 80 Del from £90 **SERVICES:** Lift **PARKING:** 68 **NOTES:** No dogs (ex guide dogs) No smoking in restaurant Civ Wed 170
CARDS:

★★★69% Stutelea Hotel & Leisure Club

Alexandra Rd PR9 0NB
☎ 01704 544220 📠 01704 500232
e-mail: info@stutelea.co.uk
Dir: *off promenade near town & Hesketh Park*

This family owned and run hotel enjoys a quiet location in a residential area, a short walk from Lord Street and the Promenade. Bedrooms vary in size and style and include family suites and rooms with balconies overlooking the attractive gardens. The elegant restaurant has a cosmopolitan theme; *continued*

alternatively the Garden Bar, located in the leisure centre, offers light snacks throughout the day.

ROOMS: 20 en suite (4 fmly) s £70-£75; d £99-£104 (incl. bkfst) **LB FACILITIES:** STV Indoor swimming (H) Sauna Solarium Gym Jacuzzi Games room Keep fit classes Steam room Xmas **SERVICES:** Lift **PARKING:** 10 **NOTES:** No dogs (ex guide dogs) No smoking in restaurant **CARDS:**

★★★64% Royal Clifton

Promenade PR8 1RB
☎ 01704 533771 📠 01704 500657
e-mail: sales@royalclifton.co.uk
Dir: *hotel on Promenade adjacent to Marine Lake*

This grand, traditional hotel benefits from a prime location on the promenade. Bedrooms range in size and style, but all are comfortable and thoughtfully equipped. Public areas include the lively Bar C, the elegant Pavilion Restaurant and a modern, well-equipped leisure club. Extensive function and banqueting facilities make this hotel a popular function venue.

ROOMS: 110 en suite (22 fmly) (6 GF) No smoking in 30 bedrooms s £60-£80; d £85-£105 (incl. bkfst) **LB FACILITIES: Spa** STV Indoor swimming (H) Sauna Solarium Gym Jacuzzi Hair & beauty Steam room, Aromatherapy entertainment Xmas **CONF:** Thtr 250 Class 100 Board 65 Del from £71.68 **SERVICES:** Lift **PARKING:** 60 **NOTES:** No dogs (ex guide dogs) No smoking in restaurant Civ Wed 150
CARDS:

S

SOUTHPORT, continued

★★71% Balmoral Lodge
41 Queens Rd PR9 9EX
☎ 01704 544298 & 530751 📠 01704 501224
e-mail: balmorallg@aol.com
Dir: *edge of town on A565 Preston road*
Situated in a quiet residential area close to Lord Street, this friendly hotel is particularly popular with golfers. Smartly appointed bedrooms are well equipped and some benefit from private patios overlooking the attractive gardens. There is a cosy bar and a comfortable residents' lounge. The restaurant offers good, freshly cooked food.
ROOMS: 15 en suite (1 fmly) **FACILITIES:** STV Sauna **PARKING:** 12 **NOTES:** No dogs **CARDS:**

★★70% Bold
585 Lord St PR9 0BE
☎ 01704 532578 📠 01704 532528
e-mail: info@boldhotel.com
Dir: *M6 J26, onto M58, then take A570 towards Southport. In Southport follow signs to Lord St, hotel on corner of Seabank Rd*
Enjoying a central location, this family hotel is just a minute's walk from the promenade and local attractions. Thoughtfully equipped, spacious bedrooms are suitable for business or leisure guests as well as for families. Public areas include a spacious bar and bistro and a large carvery which is available for parties.
ROOMS: 23 en suite (4 fmly) s £40-£50; d £60-£80 (incl. bkfst) **LB** **FACILITIES:** Special rates for local squash club Xmas **CONF:** Thtr 40 Class 40 Board 11 **SERVICES:** air con **PARKING:** 15 **NOTES:** No dogs (ex guide dogs) **CARDS:**

★★63% Metropole
Portland St PR8 1LL
☎ 01704 536836 📠 01704 549041
e-mail: metropole.southport@btinternet.com
Dir: *off Lord St and behind Prince of Wales Hotel*
This family-run hotel of long standing, popular with golfers, is ideally situated just 50 yards from the famous Lord Street. Accommodation is bright and modern with family rooms available. In addition to the restaurant that offers a selection of freshly prepared dishes, there is a choice of lounges including a popular bar-lounge.
ROOMS: 23 en suite (4 fmly) No smoking in 6 bedrooms s £39.50; d £70 (incl. bkfst) **LB** **FACILITIES:** Snooker Golf can be arranged at 8 local courses Xmas **PARKING:** 12 **NOTES:** No smoking in restaurant **CARDS:**

SOUTH SHIELDS, Tyne & Wear — Map 21 NZ36

★★★65% Sea
Sea Rd NE33 2LD
☎ 0191 427 0999 📠 0191 454 0500
e-mail: sea@bestwestern.co.uk
Dir: *A1(M) past Washington Services to A194. Then take A183 through town centre along Ocean Rd. Hotel on seafront*
A relaxed and friendly atmosphere prevails at this long-established business hotel, dating from the 1930s. Bedrooms, some overlooking the boating lake and the Tyne estuary, are generally spacious. A range of generously portioned meals is served in both the bar and restaurant. The extensive function rooms enable weddings to be catered for.
ROOMS: 32 en suite (5 fmly) No smoking in 8 bedrooms s £52-£54; d £62-£64 (incl. bkfst) **FACILITIES:** STV **CONF:** Thtr 200 Class 100 Board 50 **PARKING:** 70 **CARDS:**

SOUTHWAITE MOTORWAY SERVICE AREA (M6), Cumbria — Map 18 NY44

Travelodge Carlisle (Southwaite)
Broadfield Site CA4 0NT
☎ 08700 850 950 📠 01525 878450
Dir: *M6 junct 41/42*
Travelodge offers good quality, good value, modern accommodation. Ideal for families, the spacious, en suite bedrooms include remote-control TV, tea and coffee-making facilities, luxury beds and free morning newspaper. Meals can be taken at the nearby family restaurant. For further details and the Travelodge phone number, consult the Hotel Groups page.
ROOMS: 38 en suite s fr £42.95; d fr £42.95

SOUTHWELL, Nottinghamshire — Map 17 SK65

★★★67% Saracens Head
Market Place NG25 0HE
☎ 01636 812701 📠 01636 815408
Dir: *from A1 to Newark turn off & follow B6386 for approx 7m*
This half-timbered inn, with a rich history, is set in the centre of town. There is a relaxing atmosphere within the recently refurbished public areas, which include a small bar, a comfortable lounge and a large restaurant. Bedroom styles vary; all are appealing, comfortable and well equipped following a recent refurbishment.
ROOMS: 27 en suite (2 fmly) No smoking in all bedrooms s fr £75; d fr £85 (incl. bkfst) **LB** **FACILITIES:** STV Xmas **CONF:** Thtr 80 Class 60 Board 40 Del £120 **PARKING:** 102 **NOTES:** No dogs (ex guide dogs) No smoking in restaurant Civ Wed 70 **CARDS:**

SOUTH WITHAM, Lincolnshire — Map 11 SK91

Travelodge Grantham New Fox
New Fox NG33 5LN
☎ 08700 850 950 📠 01572 767586
Dir: *on A1, northbound*
Travelodge offers good quality, good value, modern accommodation. Ideal for families, the spacious, en suite bedrooms include remote-control TV, tea and coffee-making facilities, luxury beds and free morning newspaper. Meals can be taken at the nearby family restaurant. For further details and the Travelodge phone number, consult the Hotel Groups page.
ROOMS: 32 en suite s fr £42.95; d fr £42.95

SOUTHWOLD, Suffolk — Map 13 TM57

★★★74% Swan
Market Place IP18 6EG
☎ 01502 722186 📠 01502 724800
e-mail: swan.hotel@adnams.co.uk
Dir: *take A1095 to Southwold, hotel in town centre, parking via archway to left of building*
Charming 17th-century coaching inn situated in the heart of this bustling town centre overlooking the market place. Public rooms feature an elegant restaurant, a comfortable drawing room, a cosy bar and a lounge where guests can enjoy afternoon tea. The spacious bedrooms are attractively decorated, tastefully furnished and thoughtfully equipped.
ROOMS: 25 en suite 17 annexe en suite (17 GF) s £75-£104; d £140-£170 (incl. bkfst) **LB** **FACILITIES:** Croquet lawn Xmas **CONF:** Thtr 40 Class 24 Board 12 Del from £155 **SERVICES:** Lift **PARKING:** 35 **NOTES:** No smoking in restaurant Civ Wed 40 **CARDS:**

★★75% ⚜⚜ *The Crown*
90 High St IP18 6DP
☎ 01502 722275 📠 01502 727263
e-mail: crown.hotel@adnams.co.uk
Dir: *off A12 take A1095 to Southwold, into town centre, hotel on left in High St*
Delightful old posting inn situated in the heart of the town centre. The property combines pub, wine bar, intimate restaurant with superb accommodation. The tastefully decorated bedrooms have attractive co-ordinated soft furnishings and many thoughtful touches. Public rooms feature a back room bar serving traditional Adnams ales as well as an elegant first-floor lounge.
ROOMS: 13 rms (12 en suite) (2 fmly) **PARKING:** 23 **NOTES:** No dogs (ex guide dogs) No smoking in restaurant Closed 1st or 2nd wk Jan
CARDS:

★★69% The Blyth Hotel
Station Rd IP18 6AY
☎ 01502 722632 📠 01502 724123
e-mail: accommodation@blythhotel.com
Dir: *A12 onto A1045; on entering at town mini rdbt, hotel ahead*
Expect a warm welcome at this friendly, family-run hotel, which is situated just a short walk from the centre of this delightful seaside town. Bedrooms are thoughtfully equipped and individually decorated with co-ordinated soft furnishings and fabrics. Public rooms include two different bars serving the local Adnams ales, as well as a smart restaurant.
ROOMS: 12 en suite (5 fmly) No smoking in all bedrooms s £55; d fr £75 (incl. bkfst) **LB** **FACILITIES:** Outdoor swimming Boule pitch **PARKING:** 10 **NOTES:** No smoking in restaurant
CARDS:

SOUTH ZEAL, Devon — Map 03 SX69

★★67% Oxenham Arms
EX20 2JT
☎ 01837 840244 & 840577 📠 01837 840791
e-mail: theoxenhamarms@aol.com
Dir: *off A30, 4m E of Okehampton in centre of village*
Dating back to the 12th century this attractive inn features original stonework, an ancient standing stone, aged beams, flagstone floors and interesting nooks and crannies. Now equipped with modern facilities, the bedrooms are comfortable and spacious. A welcoming fire crackles in the lounge during colder months and dining options include bar meals and meals in the relaxed dining room.
ROOMS: 8 rms (7 en suite) (3 fmly) **PARKING:** 5 **NOTES:** No smoking in restaurant **CARDS:**

SPALDING, Lincolnshire — Map 12 TF22

★★70% ⚜ Cley Hall
22 High St PE11 1TX
☎ 01775 725157 📠 01775 710785
e-mail: cleyhall@enterprise.net
Dir: *from A16/A151 rbt into Spalding, keep river on right, hotel 1.5m on left*
A Georgian house overlooking the River Welland, with landscaped gardens to the rear. Most bedrooms are in an adjacent building; all are smart and include modern amenities. There is a choice of places to eat; the informal bistro has a warm, welcoming Mediterranean feel, while the Garden Restaurant offers 'fine dining' menus. Both are popular with locals. A reception based

continued

internet/pc workstation with language translation facility is available.
ROOMS: 4 en suite 8 annexe en suite (4 fmly) (1 GF) s £55-£80; d £65-£100 (incl. bkfst) **FACILITIES:** STV competition river fishing **CONF:** Thtr 35 Class 20 Board 18 **PARKING:** 20 **NOTES:** No smoking in restaurant Civ Wed 35 **CARDS:**

SPENNYMOOR, Co Durham — Map 19 NZ23

★★★74% Whitworth Hall Country Park Hotel
Best Western
Stanners Ln DL16 7QX
☎ 01388 811772 📠 01388 818669
e-mail: enquiries@whitworthhall.co.uk
This hotel, peacefully situated in its own grounds in the centre of the Deer Park, offers comfortable accommodation. Spacious bedrooms, some with excellent views over the lake, offer stylish and elegant décor. Public areas include a choice of restaurants and bars, a bright conservatory and well-equipped function and conference rooms.
ROOMS: 29 en suite (3 fmly) No smoking in 25 bedrooms s £105; d £120 (incl. bkfst) **LB** **FACILITIES:** Fishing Xmas **CONF:** Thtr 100 Class 30 Board 30 Del £135 **PARKING:** 100 **NOTES:** No dogs (ex guide dogs) No smoking in restaurant Civ Wed 120
CARDS:

⚜ AA Rosette Award for culinary excellence

STAFFORD, Staffordshire — Map 10 SJ92

★★★★72% ⚜⚜ The Moat House
CLASSIC BRITISH
Lower Penkridge Rd, Acton Trussell ST17 0RJ
☎ 01785 712217 📠 01785 715344
e-mail: info@moathouse.co.uk
Dir: *M6 junct 13 onto A449 through village of Acton Trussell. Hotel on right*

This 17th-century, timbered building, with a peaceful canal-side setting, has been skilfully extended. Bedrooms are attractively decorated, well equipped and comfortable. The bar offers a wide range of snacks and the restaurant offers a fine dining option where chef Matthew Davies displays his excellent skills using top quality produce.
ROOMS: 32 en suite (4 fmly) No smoking in 22 bedrooms s £120; d £135 (incl. bkfst) **LB** **FACILITIES:** STV Fishing **CONF:** BC Thtr 200 Class 60 Board 50 Del £147.50 **PARKING:** 200 **NOTES:** No dogs (ex guide dogs) No smoking in restaurant Closed 25-26 Dec & 1-2 Jan Civ Wed 130 **CARDS:**

See advert on page 571

S

STAFFORD, continued

★★★69% The Swan

46 Greengate St ST16 2JA
☎ 01785 258142 📠 01785 223372
Dir: *from S on A449 (from N on A34) to town centre via Mill Street*

This former coaching inn is over 400 years old and was built on the site of monastic college buildings. The hotel has now been completely refurbished and has a modern theme throughout the comfortable public areas and the bedrooms. The brasserie offers a wide choice of dishes, and service is attentive and professional.

ROOMS: 27 en suite (2 fmly) No smoking in 25 bedrooms s £70-£85; d £80-£95 (incl. bkfst) **FACILITIES:** STV **CONF:** Thtr 40 Board 20 Del £115 **SERVICES:** Lift **PARKING:** 40 **NOTES:** No dogs (ex guide dogs) Closed 25-26 Dec, 1 Jan **CARDS:**

★★★65% *The Garth Hotel*

Wolverhampton Rd, Moss Pit ST17 9JR
☎ 01785 256124 📠 01785 255152
e-mail: reservations@corushotels.com
Dir: *M6 junct 13 take A449*

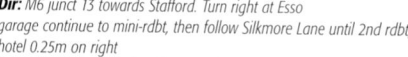

Conveniently located close to the M6, this hotel complex is set in pleasant gardens. It offers comfortable, well-equipped and attractively furnished bedrooms. Light meals and snacks are served in the popular bar along with real ales. More substantial fare can be taken in the restaurant.

ROOMS: 60 en suite (4 fmly) No smoking in 42 bedrooms **FACILITIES:** STV **CONF:** Thtr 175 Class 50 Board 50 **PARKING:** 175 **NOTES:** No smoking in restaurant RS 25-26 Dec Civ Wed 100 **CARDS:**

★★67% Abbey

65-68 Lichfield Rd ST17 4LW
☎ 01785 258531 📠 01785 246875
Dir: *M6 junct 13 towards Stafford. Turn right at Esso garage continue to mini-rdbt, then follow Silkmore Lane until 2nd rdbt, hotel 0.25m on right*

This privately owned and personally run hotel provides well-equipped accommodation and is particularly popular with commercial visitors. Family and ground floor rooms are both available. Facilities here include a choice of smoking and non-smoking lounges.

ROOMS: 17 en suite (3 fmly) s fr £45; d fr £60 (incl. bkfst) **LB PARKING:** 25 **NOTES:** No dogs (ex guide dogs) No smoking in restaurant Closed 22 Dec-7 Jan **CARDS:**

> Destination dining!
> This symbol indicates a Restaurant with Rooms

⌂ *Express by Holiday Inn Stafford*

Stafford South, Acton Gate, Acton Court ST18 9AR
☎ 01785 212244 📠 01785 212377
e-mail: express_stafford@ingramhotels.co.uk
Dir: *M6 junct 13. Hotel just off junct on A449 to Stafford*

A modern hotel ideal for families and business travellers. Fresh and uncomplicated, the spacious bedrooms include Sky TV, power shower and tea and coffee-making facilities. Continental buffet breakfast is included in the room rate; other meals may be taken at the nearby family pub or restaurant. For further details and the Express by Holiday Inn phone number, consult the Hotel Groups pages.

ROOMS: 103 en suite **CONF:** Thtr 40

⌂ Premier Lodge (Stafford)

1 Hurricane Close ST16 1GZ
☎ 0870 9906478 📠 0870 9906479
Dir: *M6 junct 14. 2.5m NW of Stafford*

Premier Lodge offers modern, well-equipped, en suite accommodation suitable for both business and leisure travellers. Meals can be taken at the adjacent popular restaurant and bar, which is fully licensed. For further details, consult the Hotel Groups page.

ROOMS: 96 en suite s £48; d £48

STAFFORD MOTORWAY SERVICE AREA (M6), Staffordshire
Map 10 SJ82

⌂ Travel Inn (Stafford Southbound)

Stafford Motorway Service Area ST15 0EY
☎ 08701 977239 📠 01785 826303
Dir: *M6 southbound 8m S of junct 15*

Travel Inn offers good-quality, value-for-money accommodation. Spacious, en suite rooms with bath and shower comfortably accommodate a family of up to two adults and two children (to age 15). The restaurant and bar offers a varied menu. For further details and the Travel Inn phone number, consult the Hotel Groups page.

ROOMS: 40 en suite s £44.95; d £44.95 **CONF:** Thtr 25 Board 15

⌂ Travelodge (Northbound only)

Moto Service Area, Eccleshall Rd ST15 0EU
☎ 08700 850 950
Dir: *between M6 juncts 14 & 15 northbound only*

Travelodge offers good quality, good value, modern accommodation. Ideal for families, the spacious, en suite bedrooms include remote-control TV, tea and coffee-making facilities, luxury beds and free morning newspaper. Meals can be taken at the nearby family restaurant. For further details and the Travelodge phone number, consult the Hotel Groups page.

ROOMS: 49 en suite s fr £42.95; d fr £42.95

STAINES, Surrey
Map 06 TQ07

★★★70% The Thames Lodge
MACDONALD HOTELS

Thames St TW18 4SF
☎ 0870 400 8121 🖷 01784 454858
e-mail: thameslodge@macdonald-hotels.co.uk
Dir: *follow signs A30/Staines town centre, bus station on right, hotel straight ahead*

Occupying a prominent position beside the river, and close to the centre of town, this hotel offers well-equipped bedrooms, many of which have been refurbished. The smart, contemporary style brasserie serves modern and imaginative food. There is a choice of function rooms.

ROOMS: 78 en suite (16 fmly) (28 GF) No smoking in 48 bedrooms s £40-£150; d £60-£170 **LB** **FACILITIES:** STV Riverside tea garden with mooring, Use of facilities at local leisure centre Xmas **CONF:** Thtr 40 Class 20 Board 20 Del from £110 **PARKING:** 40 **NOTES:** No smoking in restaurant **CARDS:**

⌂ Travelodge
Travelodge

Hale St, Two Rivers Retail Park TW18 4UW
☎ 08700 850 950 🖷 01784 491 026
Dir: *M25 junct 13, take B376 to Staines, Travelodge located in Two Water Retail Park.*

Travelodge offers good quality, good value, modern accommodation. Ideal for families, the spacious, en suite bedrooms include remote-control TV, tea and coffee-making facilities, luxury beds and free morning newspaper. Meals can be taken at the nearby family restaurant. For further details and the Travelodge phone number, consult the Hotel Groups page.

ROOMS: 65 en suite s fr £42.95; d fr £42.95

STALHAM, Norfolk
Map 13 TG32

★★66% Kingfisher
High St NR12 9AN
☎ 01692 581974 🖷 01692 582544
Dir: *from A149 between Gt Yarmouth & North Walsham into Stalham, hotel just off High St at west end*

This hotel is situated in the centre of this busy little market town, in the heart of the Norfolk Broads. The spacious bedrooms are pleasantly decorated and thoughtfully equipped with a good range of useful facilities. Public rooms include a smart lounge bar and an intimate restaurant serving carte or fixed-price menus.

ROOMS: 18 en suite (2 fmly) s £40-£50; d £55 (incl. bkfst) **LB** **FACILITIES:** Xmas **CONF:** Thtr 120 Class 50 Board 50 **PARKING:** 40 **NOTES:** No smoking in restaurant **CARDS:**

STALLINGBOROUGH, Lincolnshire
Map 17 TA11

★★★65% Stallingborough Grange Hotel
Riby Rd DN41 8BU
☎ 01469 561302 🖷 01469 561338
e-mail: grange.hot@virgin.net
Dir: *from A180 take signs for Stallingborough Ind Est and then through village, from rdbt take A1173 Caistor, hotel 1m on left just past windmill*

This 18th-century country house has been tastefully extended to provide spacious, well-equipped bedrooms. Popular with locals, this family-run hotel is just outside the village. A good range of food is offered in the Tavern, and there is also more formal dining in the restaurant: both have a friendly atmosphere.

ROOMS: 40 en suite (6 fmly) (9 GF) No smoking in all bedrooms s £80-£100; d £95-£115 (incl. bkfst) **LB** **FACILITIES:** STV Gym **CONF:** Thtr 60 Class 40 Board 28 Del £106 **PARKING:** 100 **NOTES:** No dogs (ex guide dogs) No smoking in restaurant Civ Wed 65 **CARDS:**

STAMFORD, Lincolnshire
Map 11 TF00

★★★78% ® The George of Stamford
71 St Martins PE9 2LB
☎ 01780 750750 & 750700 (Res) 🖷 01780 750701
e-mail: reservations@georgehotelofstamford.com
Dir: *turn off A1 onto B1081, 1m on left*

Steeped in hundreds of years of history, this delightful coaching inn provides spacious public areas which include a choice of dining options, inviting lounges, a business centre and a range of quality shops. A highlight is afternoon tea, taken in the colourful courtyard when weather permits. Bedrooms are stylishly appointed, ranging from traditional to contemporary in design.

ROOMS: 47 en suite (2 fmly) No smoking in 3 bedrooms s £78-£110; d £105-£220 (incl. bkfst) **LB** **FACILITIES:** STV Croquet lawn Xmas **CONF:** Thtr 50 Class 25 Board 25 Del from £135 **PARKING:** 120 **NOTES:** Civ Wed 50 **CARDS:**

S

STAMFORD, continued

★★★69% Garden House
High St, St Martin's PE9 2LP
☎ 01780 763359 📠 01780 763339
e-mail: enquiries@gardenhousehotel.com
Dir: *A1 to S Stamford, B1081. Hotel on left entering town*
Situated within a few minutes' walk of the town centre, this sympathetically transformed 18th-century town house provides pleasant accommodation. Bedrooms styles vary; all are well equipped and attractively furnished. Public rooms include a charming lounge bar, conservatory restaurant and a smart breakfast room; service is attentive and friendly throughout.
ROOMS: 20 en suite (2 fmly) (4 GF) No smoking in 12 bedrooms s £65; d £90 (incl. bkfst) **LB FACILITIES:** STV Xmas **CONF:** Thtr 40 Class 20 Board 20 **PARKING:** 22 **NOTES:** No smoking in restaurant Closed 1-9 Jan RS 10-12 Jan Civ Wed 30
CARDS:

★★69% Crown
All Saints Place PE9 2AG
☎ 01780 763136 📠 01780 756111
e-mail: thecrownhotel@excite.com
Dir: *A1 onto A43, into town to Red Lion Sq, hotel behind church*

This small, privately-owned hotel is ideally situated in the town centre. Tasty meals are served in the attractive restaurant and breakfast room, and the bar proves to be a lively and popular venue. Bedrooms are mostly spacious and well equipped, some with four-poster beds.
ROOMS: 21 rms (20 en suite) 3 annexe en suite (2 fmly) No smoking in all bedrooms s £60-£85; d £75-£125 (incl. bkfst) **LB FACILITIES:** STV Use of local health/gym club **CONF:** Thtr 50 Class 40 Board 35 Del from £105 **PARKING:** 30 **NOTES:** No dogs (ex guide dogs)
CARDS:

STANDISH, Greater Manchester — Map 15 SD51

⌂ Premier Lodge (Wigan North)
Almond Brook Rd WN6 0SS

☎ 0870 9906474 📠 0870 9906475
Premier Lodge offers modern, well-equipped, en suite accommodation suitable for both business and leisure travellers. Meals can be taken at the adjacent popular restaurant and bar, which is fully licensed. For further details, consult the Hotel Groups page.
ROOMS: 36 en suite s £48; d £48

STANSTEAD ABBOTS, Hertfordshire — Map 06 TL31

★★★63% Briggens House
Stanstead Rd SG12 8LD
☎ 01279 829955 📠 01279 793685
Dir: *M11, A414 to Hertford, after 10th rdbt follow Briggens Park sign*

Sitting in 80 acres of open countryside, this hotel was once a stately home and boasts a marvellous arboretum, 9-hole golf course, two all weather tennis courts and a heated swimming pool. Meeting and conference rooms are available, and there is comfortable lounge seating in the traditional public rooms.
ROOMS: 54 en suite (3 fmly) s £96; d £106-£125 **LB FACILITIES:** Outdoor swimming (H) Golf 9 Tennis (hard) Croquet lawn Putting green Xmas **CONF:** Thtr 100 Class 50 Board 50 Del £150 **SERVICES:** Lift **PARKING:** 100 **NOTES:** No smoking in restaurant Civ Wed 100 **CARDS:**

STANSTED AIRPORT, Essex — Map 06 TL52

★★★71% ® Whitehall
Church End CM6 2BZ
☎ 0870 873 0876 📠 0870 873 0877
e-mail: sales@whitehallhotel.co.uk
Dir: *M11 junct 8, follow signs to Stansted Airport, then hotel signs*
Very near Stansted Airport and the M25, this delightful Elizabethan manor house is set in landscaped grounds surrounded by open countryside. The attractively decorated bedrooms are tastefully furnished and thoughtfully equipped. Public rooms feature a superb timber-vaulted restaurant, a cosy lounge, a residents' bar and a range of conference and banqueting facilities.
ROOMS: 25 en suite (3 fmly) **CONF:** Thtr 120 Class 80 Board 48 **PARKING:** 35 **NOTES:** No dogs (ex guide dogs) Closed 27-30 Dec RS Sat lunch & Sun evening Civ Wed 120 **CARDS:**

★★★68% The Stansted Manor
Birchanger Ln CM23 5ST
☎ 01279 859800 📠 01279 467245
e-mail: sales@stanstedmanor-hotel.co.uk
Dir: *M11 junct 8/A120 signed Hertford, next rdbt to Birchanger, hotel on left*
A new hotel situated close to the M11 and Stansted Airport. Located at the end of a long drive and landscaped grounds. The spacious bedrooms are pleasantly decorated, tastefully furnished and equipped with a range of useful extras. Open-plan public areas include lounge/bar and conservatory restaurant.
ROOMS: 70 en suite (6 fmly) (23 GF) No smoking in 15 bedrooms s £100-£180; d £115-£180 **FACILITIES:** STV **CONF:** Thtr 100 Class 100 Board 75 Del from £150 **SERVICES:** Lift **PARKING:** 87
CARDS:

STANTON ST QUINTIN, Wiltshire
Map 04 ST97

★★★72% Stanton Manor Country House Hotel
SN14 6DQ
☎ 01666 837552 01666 837022
e-mail: reception@stantonmanor.co.uk
Dir: *M4 junct 17 onto A429 Malmesbury/Cirencester, 200yds, 1st left signed Stanton St Quintin, entrance to hotel on left just after church*

Set in seven acres of lovely grounds including a 9-hole golf course, this charming Cotswold-stone manor house has easy access to the M4. Each bedroom and the delightful public areas have been totally refurbished with comfort in mind. In the restaurant, a short carte of imaginative dishes is supported by a selection of interesting wines.
ROOMS: 24 en suite (2 fmly) (8 GF) No smoking in 8 bedrooms s £77.50-£99.50; d £99.50-£135 (incl. bkfst) **LB** **FACILITIES:** Golf 9 Croquet lawn Putting green **CONF:** BC Thtr 60 Class 50 Board 40 Del from £125 **PARKING:** 40 **NOTES:** No smoking in restaurant Closed 24-30 Dec **CARDS:**

STAVERTON, Devon
Map 03 SX76

★★67% *Sea Trout Inn*
TQ9 6PA
☎ 01803 762274 01803 762506
Dir: *turn off A38 onto A384 at Buckfastleigh, follow signs to Staverton*
Set in a delightful location in the Dart Valley, this 15th-century inn has bags of character. Ideal for a relaxing break, and particularly suitable for anglers with the River Dart almost on the doorstep. A range of dining options is available and includes bar food and the conservatory restaurant, using local and some organic produce and offering excellent choices.
ROOMS: 10 en suite (1 fmly) **CONF:** Board 30 **PARKING:** 48 **NOTES:** No smoking in restaurant **CARDS:**

STEEPLE ASTON, Oxfordshire
Map 11 SP42

★★★68% *The Holt Hotel*
The Holt Hotel, Nr Steeple Aston, Oxford Rd OX25 5QQ
☎ 01869 340259 01869 340865
e-mail: info@holthotel-oxford.co.uk
Dir: *junct of B4030/A4260*
This attractive former coaching inn has given hospitality to many over the centuries, not least Claude Duval a notorious 17th-century highwayman. Today guests are offered well-equipped, modern bedrooms and restful public areas which include a relaxing bar, attractive restaurant and a well appointed lounge. A selection of meeting rooms is also available.
ROOMS: 86 en suite (19 fmly) No smoking in 16 bedrooms **FACILITIES:** STV **CONF:** Thtr 140 Class 70 Board 44 **PARKING:** 200 **NOTES:** No smoking in restaurant Closed 24 Dec-2 Jan Civ Wed 100 **CARDS:**

STEVENAGE, Hertfordshire
Map 12 TL22

★★★66% *The Cromwell Hotel*
corus hotels
High St, Old Town SG1 3AZ
☎ 01438 779954 01438 742169
e-mail: cromwellhotel@corushotels.com
Dir: *A1(M) junct 8. Follow signs for town centre, over 2 rdbts onto one-way system. Turn off into Old Town. Hotel on left after mini rdbt*

Easily accessible from the nearby A1(M), this High Street hotel has retained much of its historic charm. The bedroom styles vary between modern and traditional; each room is well equipped and comfortably appointed. There are two bars and a smart modern business centre.
ROOMS: 76 en suite No smoking in 33 bedrooms **FACILITIES:** STV **CONF:** Thtr 200 Class 60 Board 60 **PARKING:** 70 **NOTES:** No smoking in restaurant **CARDS:**

★★★66% *Novotel Stevenage*
NOVOTEL
Knebworth Park SG1 2AX
☎ 01438 346100 01438 723872
e-mail: H0992@accor-hotels.com
Dir: *A1(M) junct 7, at entrance to Knebworth Park*
Located at the entrance to Knebworth Park and only moments from the A1(M), this modern red-brick building is a popular meeting and conference venue. The large bedrooms are well appointed for both business guests and families and an informal bar, restaurant and extensive room service menu add to the appeal.
ROOMS: 100 en suite (20 fmly) No smoking in 85 bedrooms **FACILITIES:** STV Special rates at local health club **CONF:** Thtr 150 Class 80 Board 70 **SERVICES:** Lift **PARKING:** 100 **CARDS:**

★★★66% The Roebuck Inn
Best Western
London Rd, Broadwater SG2 8DS
☎ 0870 011 9076 0870 011 9077
e-mail: hotel@roebuckinn.com
Dir: *off B197*
Suitable for both the business and leisure traveller, this hotel provides spacious contemporary accommodation in well-equipped bedrooms. The older part of the building dates back to the 15th century, this contains the restaurant and a cosy public bar with log fire and real ales.
ROOMS: 54 en suite (8 fmly) No smoking in 27 bedrooms s £69-£119; d £69-£119 **LB** **FACILITIES:** Xmas **CONF:** Thtr 50 Class 20 Board 30 **PARKING:** 70 **NOTES:** No dogs (ex guide dogs) **CARDS:**

Early start?
Hotels at all star levels should provide in-room alarm clocks and/or alarm calls

S

STEVENAGE, continued

⇧ Ibis Stevenage

Danestrete SG1 1EJ
☎ 01438 779955 📠 01438 741880
e-mail: H2794@accor-hotels.com
Dir: *in town centre adjacent to Tesco & Westgate multi-store*
Modern, budget hotel offering comfortable accommodation in bright and practical bedrooms. Breakfast is self-service and dinner is available in the restaurant. For further details, consult the Hotel Groups page.
ROOMS: 98 en suite s £29.95-£44.95; d £29.95-£44.95

⇧ Travel Inn

Corey's Mill Ln SG1 4AA
☎ 08701 977240 📠 01438 351318
Dir: *A1(M) junct 8, at junct of A602 Hitchin Rd & Corey's Mill Lane*
Travel Inn offers good-quality, value-for-money accommodation. Spacious, en suite rooms with bath and shower comfortably accommodate a family of up to two adults and two children (to age 15). The restaurant and bar offers a varied menu. For further details and the Travel Inn phone number, consult the Hotel Groups page.
ROOMS: 39 en suite s £44.95; d £44.95

STEYNING, West Sussex — Map 06 TQ11

★★★69% The Old Tollgate

The Street BN44 3WE
☎ 01903 879494 📠 01903 813399
e-mail: otr@fastnet.co.uk
Dir: *on A283 at Steyning rdbt, turn off to Bramber, hotel approx 200yds on right*
As its name suggests, this well-presented hotel is built on the site of the old tollhouse. The spacious bedrooms are smartly designed and are furnished to a high standard. Open for both lunch and dinner, the popular carvery-style restaurant offers an extensive choice of dishes. The hotel also has adaptable function rooms for weddings and conferences.
ROOMS: 11 en suite 20 annexe en suite (5 fmly) (10 GF) No smoking in 16 bedrooms s £76-£125; d £76-£125 **LB FACILITIES:** STV **CONF:** Thtr 50 Class 32 Board 26 Del from £93.95 **SERVICES:** Lift **PARKING:** 60 **NOTES:** No dogs (ex guide dogs) Civ Wed 60
CARDS:

S

Town House Hotel
Country House Hotel
⇧ Travel Accommodation

STILTON, Cambridgeshire — Map 12 TL18

★★★70% Bell Inn

Great North Rd PE7 3RA
☎ 01733 241066 📠 01733 245173
e-mail: reception@thebellstilton.co.uk
Dir: *A1(M) junct 16, follow signs for Stilton, hotel on main road in centre of village*
This delightful inn is steeped in history and retains many original features. Refreshments can be enjoyed in the attractive courtyard and rear gardens when weather permits. Stylish bedrooms are individually designed and equipped to a high standard.

continued

Imaginative food is served in both the village bar and the elegant beamed restaurant.

ROOMS: 19 en suite (1 fmly) No smoking in 17 bedrooms s £72.50-£92.50; d £96.50-£109.50 (incl. bkfst) **FACILITIES:** STV **CONF:** Thtr 100 Class 46 Board 50 Del £115 **PARKING:** 30 **NOTES:** No dogs (ex guide dogs) Closed 25 Dec RS 26 Dec Civ Wed 80
CARDS:

STOCKPORT, Greater Manchester — Map 16 SJ89

See also Manchester Airport

★★★67% Bredbury Hall Hotel & Country Club

Goyt Valley SK6 2DH
☎ 0161 430 7421 📠 0161 430 5079
e-mail: reservations@bredburyhallhotel.co.uk
Dir: *M60 junct 25 signposted Bredbury, right at traffic lights, left onto Osbourne St, hotel 500mtrs on right*
With views over open countryside, this large modern hotel is very convenient for the M60. Bedrooms offer space and comfort and the restaurant serves a very wide range of freshly prepared dishes. There is a popular night-club next door to the hotel.
ROOMS: 150 en suite (2 fmly) (50 GF) s £54.50; d £74.50 **FACILITIES:** STV Fishing Snooker Night club entertainment Xmas **CONF:** Thtr 200 Class 120 Board 60 Del £95 **PARKING:** 400 **NOTES:** No dogs (ex guide dogs) Civ Wed 150
CARDS:

★★★66% Alma Lodge Hotel

149 Buxton Rd SK2 6EL
☎ 0161 483 4431 📠 0161 483 1983
Dir: *M60 junct 1 at rdbt take 2nd exit under railway viaduct at traffic lights opp. Debenhams turn right onto A6, hotel approx 1.5m on left*
A large hotel, located on the main road close to the town, offering modern and well-equipped bedrooms. It is family owned and run and serves a good range of quality Italian cooking in Luigi's restaurant. Good function rooms are also provided.
ROOMS: 20 en suite 32 annexe en suite (2 fmly) No smoking in 22 bedrooms s £67.50; d £77.50 (incl. bkfst) **LB CONF:** Thtr 250 Class 100 Board 60 **PARKING:** 120 **NOTES:** No dogs (ex guide dogs) RS Bank Hols Civ Wed 100 **CARDS:**

★★★61% The County Hotel
Bramhall Ln South SK7 2EB
☎ 0870 609 6148 📠 0161 440 8071
(For full entry see Bramhall)

★★68% Wycliffe
74 Edgeley Rd, Edgeley SK3 9NQ
☎ 0161 477 5395 📠 0161 476 3219
e-mail: wycliffe_hotel@yahoo.co.uk
Dir: *M60 junct 2 follow A560 for Stockport, at 1st lights turn right, hotel 0.5m on left*
This welcoming family-run hotel provides immaculately maintained and well-equipped bedrooms. There is popular restaurant where the menu has an Italian bias, and a well stocked bar.
ROOMS: 20 en suite **FACILITIES:** STV **CONF:** Thtr 30 Class 20 Board 20 **PARKING:** 46 **NOTES:** No dogs (ex guide dogs) Closed 25-27 Dec RS BH's **CARDS:**

⇧ Premier Lodge (Stockport)

Churchgate SK1 1YG
☎ 0870 9906544 📠 0870 9906545
Dir: *M60 junct 27 onto A626 St Marys Way, turn right at Behhams BMW garage into Spring Gardens then 2nd right into car park*
Premier Lodge offers modern, well-equipped, en suite accommodation suitable for both business and leisure travellers. Meals can be taken at the adjacent popular restaurant and bar, which is fully licensed. For further details, consult the Hotel Groups page.
ROOMS: 46 en suite s £48; d £48 **CONF:** Thtr 20 Board 20

⇧ Travel Inn
Buxton Rd SK2 6NB
☎ 08701 977242 📠 0161 477 8320
Dir: *on A6, 1.5m from town centre*

Travel Inn offers good-quality, value-for-money accommodation. Spacious, en suite rooms with bath and shower comfortably accommodate a family of up to two adults and two children (to age 15). The restaurant and bar offers a varied menu. For further details and the Travel Inn phone number, consult the Hotel Groups page.
ROOMS: 40 en suite s £44.95; d £44.95

STOCKTON-ON-TEES, Co Durham — Map 19 NZ41

★★★71% ® Parkmore
636 Yarm Rd, Eaglescliffe TS16 0DH
☎ 01642 786815 📠 01642 790485
e-mail: enquiries@parkmorehotel.co.uk
Dir: *off A19 at Crathorne, follow A67 to Yarm. Through Yarm right onto A135 to Stockton. Hotel 1m on left*
This modern, bustling hotel has grown from its Victorian house origins to provide stylish, comfortable bedrooms, extensive fitness and swimming facilities, and opulent public rooms. The 'Reeds at Six Three Six' restaurant boasts a reputation for flair and creativity. Staff throughout are friendly and nothing is too much trouble. Spacious function suites make this a popular venue for weddings.
ROOMS: 55 en suite (8 fmly) (9 GF) No smoking in 30 bedrooms s £50-£66; d £70-£78 **LB FACILITIES:** STV Indoor swimming (H) Sauna Solarium Gym Jacuzzi Beauty salon Badminton Aerobics studio, Swimming pool supervised **CONF:** Thtr 140 Class 40 Board 40 **PARKING:** 90 **NOTES:** No smoking in restaurant Civ Wed 90 **CARDS:**

> TV dinner?
> Room service at three stars and above

★★68% Claireville
519 Yarm Rd, Eaglescliffe TS16 9BG
☎ 01642 780378 📠 01642 784109
e-mail: reception@clairevillehotel.com
Dir: *on A135 between Stockton-on-Tees & Yarm*
A family-run hotel with very comfortable bedrooms. There is a cosy bar/lounge and an attractive dining room that offers reasonably priced meals. A delightful conservatory to the rear provides a relaxing garden lounge area.
ROOMS: 18 en suite (2 fmly) No smoking in 4 bedrooms s £44-£50; d £55-£62 (incl. bkfst) **FACILITIES:** STV **CONF:** Thtr 40 Class 20 Board 25 **PARKING:** 30 **NOTES:** No smoking in restaurant RS Xmas & New Year **CARDS:**

U *Holiday Inn Middlesbrough/Teesside*
Low Ln, Stainton Village, Thornaby TS17 9LW
☎ 0870 400 9081 📠 01642 594989
e-mail: teesidehi@ichotelsgroup.com
Dir: *A174, then B1380 towards Stainton, at rdbt, hotel on right*
At the time of going to press, the classification for this hotel was not confirmed. Please refer to the AA internet site www.theAA.com for current information.
ROOMS: 136 en suite (10 fmly) No smoking in 87 bedrooms
CONF: Thtr 120 Class 60 Board 70 **PARKING:** 250
CARDS:

⇧ Express by Holiday Inn Stockton
Junction A19 & A689, Coal Ln, Wynyard Park Services, Wolviston TS22 5PZ
☎ 01740 644000 📠 01740 644111
e-mail: ebhi-stockton@btconnect.com
Dir: *A1(M) junct 60, follow signs for Hartlepool & Teeside. On A689 straight across at rdbts. Hotel on left entering Services.*

A modern hotel ideal for families and business travellers. Fresh and uncomplicated, the spacious bedrooms include Sky TV, power shower and tea and coffee-making facilities. Continental buffet breakfast is included in the room rate; other meals may be taken at the nearby family pub or restaurant. For further details & Express by Holiday Inn phone number, consult Hotel Groups pages.
ROOMS: 49 en suite **CONF:** Thtr 30 Class 24 Board 16

⇧ Travel Inn
Yarm Rd TS18 3RT
☎ 08701 977244 📠 01642 633339
Dir: *at junct A66/A135*
Travel Inn offers good-quality, value-for-money accommodation. Spacious, en suite rooms with bath and shower comfortably accommodate a family of up to two adults and two children (to age 15). The restaurant and bar offers a varied menu. For further details and the Travel Inn phone number, consult the Hotel Groups page.
ROOMS: 40 en suite s £44.95; d £44.95

S

STOCKTON-ON-TEES, continued

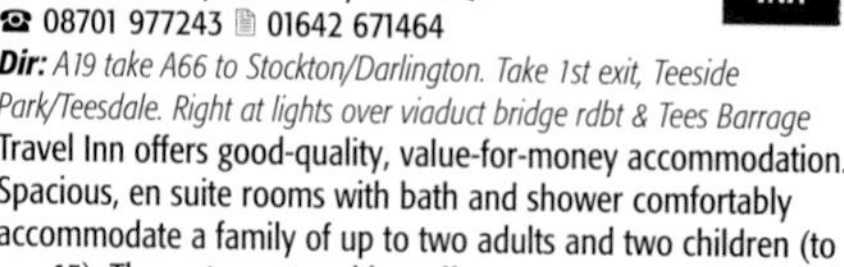

Travel Inn Stockton-on-Tees/Middlesbrough

Whitewater Way, Thornaby TS17 6QB
☎ 08701 977243 📠 01642 671464
Dir: *A19 take A66 to Stockton/Darlington. Take 1st exit, Teeside Park/Teesdale. Right at lights over viaduct bridge rdbt & Tees Barrage*
Travel Inn offers good-quality, value-for-money accommodation. Spacious, en suite rooms with bath and shower comfortably accommodate a family of up to two adults and two children (to age 15). The restaurant and bar offers a varied menu. For further details and the Travel Inn phone number, consult the Hotel Groups page.
ROOMS: 62 en suite s £44.95; d £44.95

STOKE D'ABERNON, Surrey — Map 06 TQ15

★★★★72% Woodlands Park

Woodlands Ln KT11 3QB
☎ 01372 843933 📠 01372 842704
e-mail: info@woodlandspark.co.uk
Dir: *from A3 towards London, exit at Cobham. Through town centre, left at garden centre into Woodlands Ln, hotel 0.5m on right*

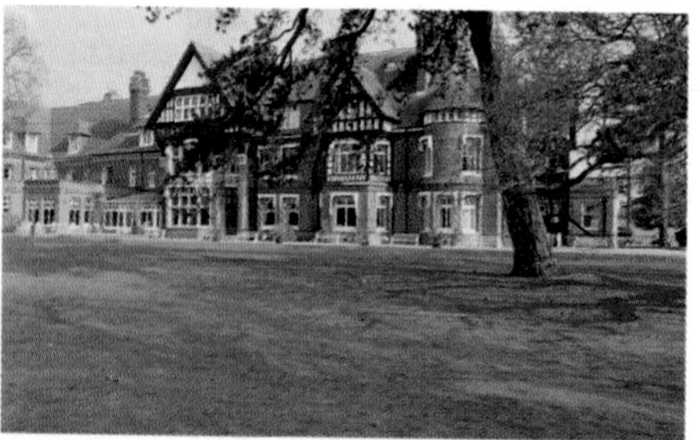

This lovely Victorian mansion was originally built for the Bryant family and enjoys an attractive parkland setting. Bedrooms have been extensively refurbished ranging from modern rooms in contemporary style ones to more traditionally furnished rooms in the main house. There is a choice of two good dining options - Quotes Bar & Brasserie, and the Oak Room Restaurant. The hotel also features an extensive range of well appointed conference rooms.
ROOMS: 59 en suite (4 fmly) No smoking in 20 bedrooms s £120-£210; d £140-£210 **LB** **FACILITIES:** STV Tennis (hard) Croquet lawn Xmas **CONF:** BC Thtr 150 Class 80 Board 50 Del from £190 **SERVICES:** Lift **PARKING:** 150 **NOTES:** No dogs (ex guide dogs) Civ Wed 150
CARDS:

STOKE GABRIEL, Devon — Map 03 SX85

★★★73% Gabriel Court

TQ9 6SF
☎ 01803 782206 📠 01803 782333
e-mail: obeacom@aol.com
Dir: *off A38 down A384 onto A385 (Paignton), turn right by Parkers Arms, follow road to Stoke Gabriel*
A relaxed charm exists at this comfortable hotel which has been family run for over 30 years and where many guests return on a regular basis. Set in Elizabethan terraced gardens, where much of the produce is used for the hotel's kitchen; Gabriel Court provides a relaxing environment. Bedrooms are individually styled and in the public areas, a choice of comfortable sitting areas are provided.
ROOMS: 19 en suite s £60; d £85 (incl. bkfst) **FACILITIES:** Outdoor swimming (H) Tennis (grass) Croquet lawn Xmas **CONF:** Thtr 20 Board 20 **PARKING:** 20 **NOTES:** No smoking in restaurant
CARDS:

STOKENCHURCH, Buckinghamshire — Map 05 SU79

★★★68% The Kings Arms

Oxford Rd HP14 3TA
☎ 01494 609090 📠 01494 484582
e-mail: kares@dhillonhotels.co.uk
Dir: *M40 junct 5, turn right over motorway bridge, hotel 600yds on left*
Located on the village green, this hotel blends traditional elegance with contemporary design. Rooms are attractively decorated and well equipped, particularly for the business guest. Public areas include a busy bar and a relaxed, informal restaurant serving a wide range of dishes throughout the day. The smart conference rooms are air conditioned.
ROOMS: 43 en suite (3 fmly) No smoking in 22 bedrooms s £89-£109; d £99-£129 (incl. bkfst) **LB** **FACILITIES:** STV Wycombe sports & leisure centre Xmas **CONF:** BC Thtr 200 Class 100 Board 70 Del from £130 **SERVICES:** Lift air con **PARKING:** 95 **NOTES:** No dogs (ex guide dogs) Civ Wed 200 **CARDS:**

STOKE-ON-TRENT, Staffordshire — Map 10 SJ84

See also Newcastle-under-Lyme

★★★69% *George*

Swan Square, Burslem ST6 2AE
☎ 01782 577544 📠 01782 837496
e-mail: georgestoke@btinternet.com
Dir: *take A53 towards Leek, turn left at 1st lights onto A50, follow road to Burslem centre, hotel on right*
This privately owned, friendly hotel stands in the centre of Burslem, close to the Royal Doulton factory. Well-equipped modern bedrooms are equally suitable for business people and tourists. Public areas include a spacious lounge bar, a comfortable lounge and a choice of function rooms. A good choice of dishes is available in the elegant restaurant.
ROOMS: 39 en suite (5 fmly) **CONF:** Thtr 180 Class 150 Board 60 **SERVICES:** Lift **PARKING:** 28 **NOTES:** No dogs (ex guide dogs) No smoking in restaurant Closed 24-27 Dec
CARDS:

★★★69% Manor House

Audley Rd ST7 2QQ
☎ 01270 884000 📠 01270 882483
e-mail: mhres@compasshotels.co.uk
(For full entry see Alsager)

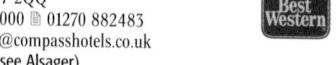

★★★66% Haydon House

Haydon St, Basford ST4 6JD
☎ 01782 711311 📠 01782 717470
Dir: *M6 junct 15, A500 to Stoke-on-Trent, turn onto A53 at rdbt take 1st exit, up hill, take 2nd left at top of hill before lights*
A Victorian property, within easy reach of Newcastle-under-Lyme. The public rooms are furnished in a style in keeping with the age and character of the house, and bedrooms have modern furnishings; several rooms in a separate house across the road. The hotel has a good reputation for its food and is popular with locals.
ROOMS: 17 en suite 6 annexe en suite (4 fmly) s £65; d £85 (incl. bkfst) **CONF:** Thtr 80 Class 30 Board 24 Del £98 **PARKING:** 52 **NOTES:** No smoking in restaurant Civ Wed 80
CARDS:

★★★65% **Quality Hotel**
66 Trinity St, Hanley ST1 5NB
☎ 01782 202361 📠 01782 286464
e-mail: info@grandhotel-stoke.co.uk
Dir: *M6 junct 15(S)/16(N) then A500 to city centre & Festival Park. A53 to Leek, keep to left lane, 3rd exit at rdbt for Hanley/city centre/Cultural Quarter. Hotel on left at top of hill*
This large town centre hotel offers well-equipped bedrooms and benefits from its own large car park. There is also a well-equipped leisure centre, together with good conference facilities.
ROOMS: 128 en suite 8 annexe en suite (54 fmly) (5 GF) No smoking in 85 bedrooms s £45-£105; d £55-£115 **LB FACILITIES: Spa** STV Indoor swimming (H) Sauna Solarium Gym Jacuzzi Xmas **CONF:** Thtr 300 Class 125 Board 60 Del from £85 **SERVICES:** Lift **PARKING:** 150 **NOTES:** No smoking in restaurant Civ Wed 300
CARDS:

⌂ **Express by Holiday Inn**
Stanley Matthews Way, Trentham Lakes ST4 4EG
☎ 01782 377000 📠 01782 377037
e-mail: manager@stokeexpress.fsnet.co.uk
Dir: *M6 junct 15, follow signs for Uttoxeter/Derby which leads to A50. Hotel by Britannia Stadium on A50*

A modern hotel ideal for families and business travellers. Fresh and uncomplicated, the spacious bedrooms include Sky TV, power shower and tea and coffee-making facilities. Continental buffet breakfast is included in the room rate; other meals may be taken at the nearby family pub or restaurant. For further details and the Express by Holiday Inn phone number, consult the Hotel Groups pages.
ROOMS: 123 en suite s £55-£67; d £55-£67 (incl. cont bkfst)
CONF: Thtr 35 Class 35 Board 35

⌂ **Innkeeper's Lodge Stoke on Trent**
Longton Rd ST4 8BU
☎ 01782 644448 📠 01782 644163
Dir: *M6 junct 15, follow A500 slip road for A34 towards Stone. At rndbt left onto A5035, lodge 0.5m on right*

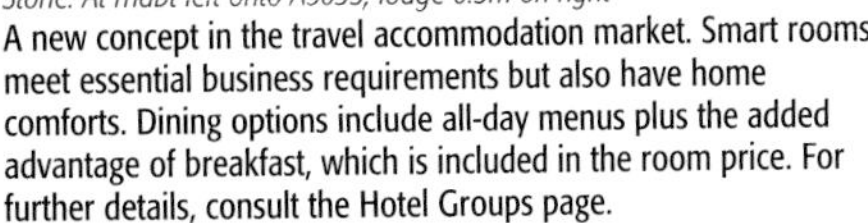

A new concept in the travel accommodation market. Smart rooms meet essential business requirements but also have home comforts. Dining options include all-day menus plus the added advantage of breakfast, which is included in the room price. For further details, consult the Hotel Groups page.
ROOMS: 30 en suite

STONE, Staffordshire

Map 10 SJ93

★★★68% **Stone House**
Stafford Rd ST15 0BQ
☎ 0870 609 6140 📠 01785 814764
Dir: *beside A34, 0.5m S of town centre*

This former country house, set in attractive grounds, is located within easy reach of the M6. Attractive comfortable bedrooms and tastefully appointed public areas complete with leisure and conference facilities make the hotel popular with both corporate and leisure guests. A light menu is offered in the bar and lounge areas or guests can choose to dine in the stylish restaurant.
ROOMS: 50 en suite (1 fmly) No smoking in 33 bedrooms
FACILITIES: STV Indoor swimming (H) Tennis (hard) Sauna Solarium Gym **CONF:** Thtr 190 Class 60 Board 50 Del from £95 **PARKING:** 120 **NOTES:** No dogs (ex guide dogs) No smoking in restaurant RS Sat Civ Wed 60 **CARDS:**

★★★66% **Crown**
38 High St ST15 8AS
☎ 01785 813535 📠 01785 815942
Dir: *M6 junct 14, A34 N to Stone. M6 junct 15, A34 S to Stone*
A traditional hotel in the centre of town with oak panelling and a glass domed restaurant offering a choice of menus. The front lounge is delightfully furnished while staff are helpful and friendly.
ROOMS: 12 en suite 16 annexe en suite (2 fmly) (8 GF) No smoking in 13 bedrooms s £55-£110; d £55-£120 **LB FACILITIES:** STV **CONF:** Thtr 150 Class 80 Board 60 **PARKING:** 100 **NOTES:** No dogs (ex guide dogs) No smoking in restaurant Civ Wed 100 **CARDS:**

Late for dinner?
Quality Standards mean that last orders for dinner vary according to star rating and should be no earlier than:
★★ 7.00pm ★★★ 8.00pm ★★★★ 9.00pm
★★★★★ 10.00pm

S

STON EASTON, Somerset Map 04 ST65

Top 200 - Hotel

★★★★ ®® **Ston Easton Park**
BA3 4DF
☎ 01761 241631 📠 01761 241377
e-mail: stoneastonpark@stoneaston.co.uk
Dir: *on A37*

This stunning Palladian mansion dates back to 1740 and enjoys a tranquil location amidst parkland and landscaped gardens. Individually styled, spacious bedrooms include three rooms located in the charming Gardener's Cottage. Delightful, inviting public rooms retain much of their original character and are adorned with beautiful antiques and fine paintings. Imaginative cooking at both dinner and breakfast is a highlight.

ROOMS: 20 en suite 3 annexe en suite (2 fmly) (2 GF) No smoking in all bedrooms s £99-£130; d £185-£345 (incl. bkfst) **LB** **FACILITIES:** Tennis (hard) Fishing Snooker Croquet lawn Xmas **CONF:** Thtr 65 Board 26 Del from £160 **PARKING:** 120 **NOTES:** No smoking in restaurant Civ Wed 70 **CARDS:**

STONEHOUSE, Gloucestershire Map 04 SO80

★★★68% ® **Stonehouse Court**
GL10 3RA
☎ 0871 871 3240 📠 0871 871 3241
e-mail: stonehouse.court@pageant.co.uk
Dir: *M5 junct 13, follow signs for Stonehouse, hotel on right 0.25m after 2nd rdbt*

Set in six acres of secluded gardens, this fine Grade II listed manor house dates back to 1601, since when it has been extended considerably. The individually decorated bedrooms offer all modern comforts, two of which have four-poster beds. Elegant public rooms provide a range of amenities, including a panelled lounge, a bar, restaurant and a gymnasium. Extensive conference facilities are also available.

ROOMS: 9 en suite 27 annexe en suite (2 fmly) (2 GF) No smoking in 6 bedrooms s £85-£135; d £95-£135 (incl. bkfst) **LB** **FACILITIES:** STV Fishing Gym Croquet lawn Xmas **CONF:** Thtr 150 Class 75 Board 50 Del £125 **PARKING:** 150 **NOTES:** No smoking in restaurant Civ Wed 85 **CARDS:**

See advert under GLOUCESTER

⇧ **Travelodge**
A 419, Easington GL10 3SQ
☎ 08700 850 950

Travelodge

Travelodge offers good quality, good value, modern accommodation. Ideal for families, the spacious, en suite bedrooms include remote-control TV, tea and coffee-making facilities, luxury beds and free morning newspaper. Meals can be taken at the nearby family restaurant. For further details and the Travelodge phone number, consult the Hotel Groups page.

ROOMS: 40 en suite s fr £42.95; d fr £42.95

STONOR, Oxfordshire Map 05 SU78

★★★77% ®® **Stonor Hotel**
RG9 6HE
☎ 01491 638866 📠 01491 638863
e-mail: info@mystonor.com
Dir: *off A4130 onto B480, hotel 3m on right in Stonor*

Set in a picturesque village close to Henley-on-Thames, this attractive establishment has undergone a refreshment of public rooms and provides a comfortable and relaxed style plus attentive service. Bedrooms are comfortably furnished and come with many thoughtful extras. Accomplished cuisine is a feature not to be missed here and the conservatory dining room overlooking the garden is extremely pleasant.

ROOMS: 11 en suite (7 GF) No smoking in 4 bedrooms s £120-£150; d £150-£185 (incl. bkfst) **FACILITIES:** STV Xmas **CONF:** Thtr 20 Board 16 Del from £150 **PARKING:** 27 **NOTES:** No smoking in restaurant Civ Wed 80 **CARDS:**

STOURPORT-ON-SEVERN, Worcestershire Map 10 SO87

★★★★71% **Menzies Stourport Manor**
Hartlebury Rd DY13 9JA
☎ 01299 289955 📠 01299 878520
e-mail: info@menzies-hotels.co.uk
Dir: *M5 junct 6, follow A449 towards Kidderminster, take B4193 towards Stourport, hotel on right*

MENZIES HOTELS

Once the home of Prime Minister Sir Stanley Baldwin, this much extended country house is set in attractive grounds. A number of bedrooms are located in the original building, although the majority are in a more modern, purpose-built section. Spacious public areas include a range of lounges, a popular brasserie, a leisure club and conference facilities.

ROOMS: 68 en suite (4 fmly) No smoking in 25 bedrooms **FACILITIES:** STV Indoor swimming (H) Tennis (hard) Squash Sauna Solarium Gym Putting green Jacuzzi **CONF:** Thtr 420 Class 120 Board 80 Del from £130 **PARKING:** 200 **NOTES:** No dogs (ex guide dogs) No smoking in restaurant Civ Wed 350 **CARDS:**

STOWMARKET, Suffolk
Map 13 TM05

★★66% Cedars
THE INDEPENDENTS HOTEL ASSOCIATION

Needham Rd IP14 2AJ
☎ 01449 612668 🖷 01449 674704
e-mail: info@cedarshotel.co.uk

Dir: *A1308, 1m outside Stowmarket towards Needham Market*

Expect a friendly welcome at this privately owned hotel, which is situated just off the A14 within easy reach of the town centre. Public rooms are full of charm and character with features such as exposed beams and open fireplaces. Bedrooms are pleasantly decorated and thoughtfully equipped.

ROOMS: 25 en suite (3 fmly) (9 GF) s fr £50; d fr £60 (incl. bkfst) **LB** **CONF:** Thtr 150 Class 60 Board 40 Del from £70 **PARKING:** 75 **NOTES:** No smoking in restaurant Closed 25 Dec-1 Jan Civ Wed 50 **CARDS:**

⌂ Travelodge Ipswich Stowmarket
Travelodge

IP14 3PY
☎ 08700 850 950 🖷 01449 615347

Dir: *on A14 westbound*

Travelodge offers good quality, good value, modern accommodation. Ideal for families, the spacious, en suite bedrooms include remote-control TV, tea and coffee-making facilities, luxury beds and free morning newspaper. Meals can be taken at the nearby family restaurant. For further details and the Travelodge phone number, consult the Hotel Groups page.

ROOMS: 40 en suite s fr £42.95; d fr £42.95

STOW-ON-THE-WOLD, Gloucestershire
Map 10 SP12

★★★★75% ®® Wyck Hill House
WREN'S HOTELS

Burford Rd GL54 1HY
☎ 01451 831936 🖷 01451 832243
e-mail: wyckhill@wrensgroup.com

Dir: *3m SE on A424 towards Burford & Swindon*

This charming 18th-century house enjoys superb views across the Windrush Valley and is ideally positioned for a relaxing weekend exploring the Cotswolds. The spacious and thoughtfully equipped bedrooms have been refurbished to a high standard and are divided between the main house and the original coach house. An open fire burns in the magnificent front hall and there is a cosy bar. The imaginative cuisine makes good use of local produce.

ROOMS: 16 en suite 16 annexe en suite (1 fmly) s £110-£165; d £170-£270 (incl. bkfst) **LB** **FACILITIES:** STV Croquet lawn Archery Clay pigeon shooting Ballooning Honda pilots Xmas **CONF:** Thtr 60 Class 20 Board 20 **SERVICES:** Lift **PARKING:** 100 **NOTES:** No smoking in restaurant Civ Wed 80 **CARDS:**

★★★73% ®®® The Royalist at Stow-on-the-Wold
Digbeth St GL54 1BN
☎ 01451 830670 🖷 01451 870048
e-mail: info@theroyalisthotel.co.uk

Dir: *M40 junct 8, A40 to Burford. A424 to Stow-on-the-Wold, right onto A436, down hill, hotel on left of green*

Recorded as the 'oldest inn in England', this super hotel has a wealth of history and character. Public areas and the charming bedrooms have benefited from a very sympathetic refurbishment to ensure guest comfort at every turn. The award-winning 947 Restaurant offers imaginative, high quality cooking, and the Eagle and Child provides a more informal alternative.

ROOMS: 8 en suite No smoking in all bedrooms s £50-£60; d £90-£130 (incl. bkfst) **LB** **FACILITIES:** Jacuzzi Discounted rates at local private gym Xmas **CONF:** Thtr 25 Class 25 Board 16 Del from £80 **PARKING:** 8 **NOTES:** No dogs (ex guide dogs) No smoking in restaurant **CARDS:**

★★★72% ® *Grapevine*
Best Western

Sheep St GL54 1AU
☎ 01451 830344 🖷 01451 832278
e-mail: enquiries@vines.co.uk

Dir: *on A436 towards Chipping Norton. 150yds on right, facing green*

This delightful 17th-century hotel is situated in the centre of town, and retains much of its original charm and character. The bedrooms vary in size, and are thoughtfully equipped with charming furnishings. Accomplished cooking is offered in the Conservatory Restaurant, with a more informal brasserie-style menu available at lunch.

ROOMS: 12 en suite 10 annexe en suite (2 fmly) (5 GF) No smoking in all bedrooms **CONF:** Thtr 70 Class 45 Board 30 **PARKING:** 25 **NOTES:** No dogs (ex guide dogs) No smoking in restaurant Civ Wed 70 **CARDS:**

★★★70% Fosse Manor
Best Western

GL54 1JX
☎ 01451 830354 🖷 01451 832486
e-mail: enquiries@fossemanor.co.uk

Dir: *1m S on A429, 300yds past junct with A424*

Deriving its name from the historic Roman Fosse Way, this popular hotel is ideally located for exploring the many delights of this picturesque area. Relaxed and friendly, the style here is contemporary country house with public areas including a comfortable lounge, elegant restaurant and convivial bar.

continued on p580

S

STOW-ON-THE-WOLD, continued

Bedrooms, located both in the main building and adjacent coach house, all offer high standards of comfort and quality.

Fosse Manor, Stow-on-the-Wold

ROOMS: 16 en suite 6 annexe en suite (3 fmly) No smoking in 5 bedrooms s fr £75; d £125-£250 (incl. bkfst) **LB** **FACILITIES:** Croquet lawn Beautician Xmas **CONF:** Thtr 40 Class 20 Board 20 Del from £100 **PARKING:** 40 **NOTES:** No smoking in restaurant Closed 1-8 Jan Civ Wed 50 **CARDS:**

★★★70% The Unicorn

Sheep St GL54 1HQ
☎ 01451 830257 01451 831090
e-mail: reception@birchhotels.co.uk
Dir: *at junct of A429 & A436*
This attractive limestone hotel dates back to the 17th century. Individually designed bedrooms are stylish and include some delightful four-poster rooms. Spacious public areas retain much character and include a choice of inviting lounges and a traditional bar offering a good selection of bar meals and ales, as well as an attractive restaurant.
ROOMS: 20 en suite No smoking in 8 bedrooms s £35-£65; d £45-£105 (incl. bkfst) **LB** **FACILITIES:** STV Xmas **CONF:** Thtr 50 Class 20 Board 28 Del from £115 **PARKING:** 40 **NOTES:** No smoking in restaurant Civ Wed 50 **CARDS:**

★★★68% Stow Lodge

The Square GL54 1AB
☎ 01451 830485 01451 831671
e-mail: enquiries@stowlodge.com
Dir: *in town centre*
Situated in smart grounds, this family-run hotel has direct access to the market square and provides an hospitable welcome to all. Bedrooms are offered both in the main building or alternatively in the converted coach house, all of which provide similar standards of homely comfort. Extensive menus and an interesting wine list make for an enjoyable dining experience.
ROOMS: 11 en suite 10 annexe en suite (1 fmly) No smoking in all bedrooms s £55-£105; d £70-£125 (incl. bkfst) **LB** **PARKING:** 30 **NOTES:** No dogs No children 5yrs No smoking in restaurant Closed Xmas-end Jan **CARDS:**

★★71% Old Stocks

THE INDEPENDENTS

The Square GL54 1AF
☎ 01451 830666 01451 870014
e-mail: theoldstocks@btinternet.com
Dir: *turn off A429 to town centre*
Overlooking the old market square, this Grade II listed hotel offers a warm welcome to those visiting this lovely Cotswold town. Built of mellow Cotswold stone, the hotel has much original charm and character, with deep stone walls and oak beams throughout. The lounge, restaurant and bar provide attractive, comfortable areas in which to relax, unwind and enjoy the genuine hospitality.
ROOMS: 15 en suite 3 annexe en suite (1 fmly) (1 GF) No smoking in 10 bedrooms s £40; d £80-£90 (incl. bkfst) **LB** **FACILITIES:** ch fac Xmas **PARKING:** 14 **NOTES:** No smoking in restaurant Closed 18-27 Dec **CARDS:**

STRATFIELD TURGIS, Hampshire — Map 05 SU65

★★★65% Wellington Arms

RG27 0AS
☎ 01256 882214 01256 882934
e-mail: Wellington.Arms@virgin.net
Dir: *A33 between Basingstoke & Reading*
Situated at one of the entrances to the ancestral home of the Duke of Wellington, the white Georgian façade is a familiar landmark on the A33. The majority of bedrooms are located in the Garden Wing and offer every modern convenience, whereas rooms in the original building are more individual and have a period feel. Public rooms include a comfortable lounge bar with log fire and formal dining within the pleasant restaurant; informal dining is available in the bar.
ROOMS: 35 en suite (2 fmly) No smoking in 3 bedrooms s £65-£130; d £75-£140 (incl. bkfst) **LB** **CONF:** Thtr 160 Class 40 Board 50 Del from £150 **PARKING:** 150 **CARDS:**

STRATFORD-UPON-AVON, Warwickshire — Map 10 SP25

★★★★72% *Welcombe Hotel & Golf Course*

Warwick Rd CV37 0NR
☎ 01789 295252 01789 414666
e-mail: sales@welcombe.co.uk
Dir: *1.5m NE of Stratford on A439*
This privately-owned, Jacobean manor house is set in 157 acres of landscaped parkland. Public rooms are impressive, especially the lounge, with its wood panelling and ornate marble fireplace, and the gentleman's club-style bar. Bedrooms in the original building are the stylish and gracefully proportioned; those in the newer garden wing are comfortable and thoughtfully equipped.
ROOMS: 64 en suite (1 fmly) No smoking in 21 bedrooms **FACILITIES:** STV Golf 18 Tennis (hard) Fishing Snooker Solarium Gym Putting green Table tennis **CONF:** Thtr 120 Class 75 Board 40 **PARKING:** 100 **NOTES:** No dogs (ex guide dogs) No smoking in restaurant Civ Wed 120 **CARDS:**

★★★★71% Billesley Manor

FURLONG

Billesley, Alcester B49 6NF
☎ 01789 279955 01789 764145
e-mail: enquiries@billesleymanor.co.uk
Dir: *A46 towards Evesham. Over 3 rdbts, right turn for Billesley after 2m*

This 16th-century manor is set in peaceful grounds and parkland with a delightful yew topiary garden. The spacious bedrooms and

continued

suites, most in traditional country house style, are thoughtfully designed and well-equipped. The new cedar barns have bedrooms with a more contemporary feel and also the conference facilities. Public areas retain many original features, such as oak panelling, fireplaces and exposed stone.
ROOMS: 42 en suite 20 annexe en suite (8 fmly) (5 GF) s £94-£115; d £130-£170 (incl. bkfst) **LB FACILITIES:** STV Indoor swimming (H) Tennis (hard) Croquet lawn Putting green Pitch and putt Xmas **CONF:** Thtr 100 Class 60 Board 50 Del from £130 **PARKING:** 100 **NOTES:** No smoking in restaurant Civ Wed 75
CARDS:

See advert on this page

★★★★70% Stratford Manor

Warwick Rd CV37 0PY
☎ 01789 731173 📠 01789 731131
e-mail: stratfordmanor@marstonhotels.com
Dir: *3m N of town centre on A439 towards Warwick, or from M40 junct 15, take A439, hotel 2m on left*

MARSTON HOTELS

Just outside Stratford, this hotel is set against a rural backdrop with lovely gardens and ample car parking. Public areas include a lounge bar and a busy split-level restaurant, while the leisure centre boasts a large indoor pool; service is both professional and helpful. Bedrooms are spacious with generously-sized beds and a range of useful facilities.
ROOMS: 104 en suite (8 fmly) No smoking in 52 bedrooms s fr £108; d fr £130 **LB FACILITIES:** STV Indoor swimming (H) Tennis (hard) Sauna Solarium Gym Beauty treatments Xmas **CONF:** Thtr 350 Class 200 Board 100 Del from £165 **SERVICES:** Lift **PARKING:** 220 **NOTES:** No dogs (ex guide dogs) No smoking in restaurant Civ Wed 300
CARDS:

★★★★69% ◎ Stratford Victoria

Arden St CV37 6QQ
☎ 01789 271000 📠 01789 271001
e-mail: stratfordvictoria@marstonhotels.com
Dir: *A439 into Stratford, then follow A3400 Birmingham, at lights left into Arden St, hotel 150yds on right*

Situated adjacent to the hospital, this eye-catching modern hotel, with its red brick façade, is within walking distance of the town centre. The open-plan public areas include a comfortable lounge, a small atmospheric bar and spacious restaurant with exposed beams and ornately carved furniture. Bedrooms are spacious and feature framed embroideries.
ROOMS: 100 en suite (35 fmly) No smoking in 40 bedrooms s fr £99; d fr £125 **LB FACILITIES:** STV Gym Jacuzzi Xmas **CONF:** Thtr 140 Class 66 Board 54 Del from £140 **SERVICES:** Lift **PARKING:** 100 **NOTES:** No dogs (ex guide dogs) No smoking in restaurant
CARDS:

★★★★64% ◎◎ The Shakespeare

Chapel St CV37 6ER
☎ 0870 400 8182 📠 01789 415411
e-mail: shakespeare@macdonald-hotels.co.uk
Dir: *M40 J15, take A46 then A439 into one-way system, left at rdbt opposite HSBC Bank, hotel on left*

MACDONALD HOTELS

Dating back to the early 17th century, The Shakespeare is one of the oldest hotels in this historic town. The hotel name also represents one of the earliest exploitations of Stratford as the birthplace of one of the world's leading poets and playwrights. With exposed beams and open fires, the public rooms retain an ambience reminiscent of this romantic era.
ROOMS: 63 en suite 11 annexe en suite (3 GF) No smoking in 16 bedrooms s £64-£83; d £128-£166 (incl. bkfst) **LB FACILITIES:** STV Xmas **SERVICES:** Lift **PARKING:** 34 **NOTES:** No smoking in restaurant Civ Wed 50 **CARDS:**

S

STRATFORD-UPON-AVON, continued

★★★★63% The Alveston Manor

Clopton Bridge CV37 7HP
☎ 0870 400 8181 🖷 01789 414095
e-mail: sales.alvestonmanor@macdonald-hotels.co.uk
Dir: *S of Clopton Bridge*

MACDONALD HOTELS

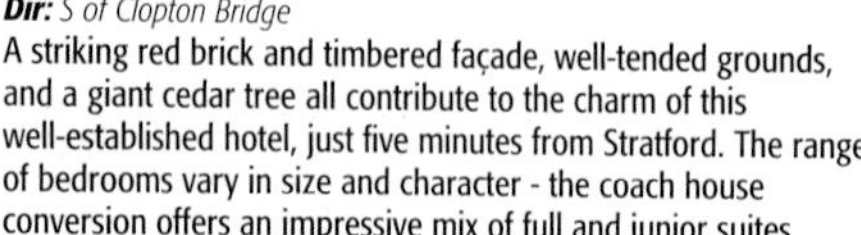

A striking red brick and timbered façade, well-tended grounds, and a giant cedar tree all contribute to the charm of this well-established hotel, just five minutes from Stratford. The range of bedrooms vary in size and character - the coach house conversion offers an impressive mix of full and junior suites.

ROOMS: 113 en suite (8 fmly) (45 GF) No smoking in 46 bedrooms s £65-£125; d £85-£145 (incl. bkfst) **FACILITIES:** STV Sauna Solarium Gym Swimming pool supervised Xmas **CONF:** Thtr 140 Class 80 Board 40 Del from £120 **PARKING:** 150 **NOTES:** No smoking in restaurant Civ Wed 110 **CARDS:**

★★★74% Salford Hall

WR11 8UT
☎ 01386 871300 🖷 01386 871301
e-mail: reception@salfordhall.co.uk
(For full entry see Abbot's Salford)

★★★67% The Swan's Nest

MACDONALD HOTELS

Bridgefoot CV37 7LT
☎ 0870 400 8183 🖷 01789 414547
e-mail: swansnest@macdonald-hotels.co.uk
Dir: *M40 junct 15, A46 for 2m, at 1st island turn left onto A439 towards Stratford. Follow one-way system, left over river bridge, hotel on right*

Enjoying a prime location on the banks of the River Avon, this hotel was one of the first brick built buildings in Stratford. Now the refurbished bedrooms, all named after birds, are stylish and comfortable.

ROOMS: 67 en suite (2 fmly) (25 GF) No smoking in 45 bedrooms **FACILITIES:** STV **CONF:** Thtr 150 Class 80 Board 40 Del from £99 **PARKING:** 80 **NOTES:** Civ Wed 150
CARDS:

★★★67% The White Swan

Rother St CV37 6NH
☎ 01789 297022 🖷 01789 268773
e-mail: whiteswan.stratforduponavon@nhguk.com
Dir: *M40 junct 15 signposted Stratford-on-Avon. Hotel in market square*

Dating from the 15th century, this former coaching inn retains many original features. Bedrooms offer a blend of tradition and comfort; some boasting beamed ceilings and larger beds. The public areas are full of character, with open log fires and oak panelling, and offer a range of snacks and meals to complement the more formal restaurant.

ROOMS: 41 en suite (3 fmly) No smoking in 16 bedrooms s £70; d £85-£95 **LB FACILITIES:** entertainment Xmas **CONF:** Thtr 30 Class 10 Board 20 Del from £115 **PARKING:** 10 **NOTES:** No dogs (ex guide dogs) No smoking in restaurant **CARDS:**

See advert on opposite page

★★★66% Grosvenor House

THE INDEPENDENTS

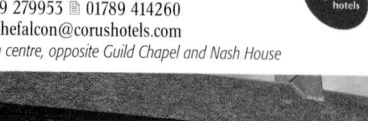

Warwick Rd CV37 6YT
☎ 01789 269213 🖷 01789 266087
e-mail: info@groshotelstratford.co.uk
Dir: *M40 junct 15, follow Stratford signs to A439 Warwick Rd, hotel 7m from junct on town centre one-way system*

Grosvenor House is a short distance from the town centre and its many of the historic attractions. Bedroom styles and sizes vary and staff are both friendly and efficient providing a useful range of services; an all-day menu of refreshments in the lounge and room service is readily available. The Garden Room restaurant offers a choice of dishes from set price and carte menus.

ROOMS: 66 en suite (1 fmly) (22 GF) No smoking in 25 bedrooms s £95-£115; d £110-£130 **LB FACILITIES:** Xmas **CONF:** Thtr 100 Class 45 Board 50 Del from £110 **PARKING:** 53 **NOTES:** No dogs (ex guide dogs) No smoking in restaurant Civ Wed 60
CARDS:

★★★64% The Falcon

Chapel St CV37 6HA
☎ 01789 279953 🖷 01789 414260
e-mail: thefalcon@corushotels.com
Dir: *town centre, opposite Guild Chapel and Nash House*

This 16th-century inn, situated in the heart of town, provides public rooms with much original character, including a choice of bars, a brasserie-style restaurant (with tables in the conservatory and garden), and a more formal dining option. Accommodation comes in a variety of styles; the older, beamed rooms in the original Tudor section retain much charm.

ROOMS: 73 en suite 11 annexe en suite (13 fmly) (3 GF) No smoking in 38 bedrooms s £52-£110; d £80-£130 **LB FACILITIES:** Xmas **CONF:** Thtr 200 Class 110 Board 40 Del from £100 **SERVICES:** Lift **PARKING:** 124 **NOTES:** No smoking in restaurant Civ Wed 160
CARDS:

★★★63% The Charlecote Pheasant Hotel

corus hotels

Charlecote CV35 9EW
☎ 01789 279954 🖷 01789 470222
e-mail: reservations@corushotels.com
Dir: *M40 junct 15, take A429 towards Cirencester through Barford, after 2m turn right into Charlecote, hotel opposite Charlecote Manor Park*

Located just outside Stratford, this hotel is set in extensive grounds and is a popular conference venue. A variety of bedroom styles is available within the annexe wings, ranging from standard to

continued

executive suites. The main building consists of the restaurant and a lounge bar area.

ROOMS: 70 en suite (2 fmly) No smoking in 26 bedrooms s £65-£75; d £100-£120 (incl. bkfst) **LB** **FACILITIES:** Outdoor swimming (H) Tennis (hard) Childrens Play area Xmas **CONF:** Thtr 160 Class 90 Board 50 Del from £100 **PARKING:** 100 **NOTES:** No smoking in restaurant Civ Wed 120 **CARDS:**

★★65% The New Inn Hotel & Restaurant
Clifford Chambers CV37 8HR
☎ 01789 293402 01789 292716
e-mail: thenewinn65@aol.com
Dir: *off A3400 onto B4632, follow signs to Shire Horse Centre, hotel 200yds on left*
This welcoming, family-run hotel is located in the pretty village of Clifford Chambers. The bar has an open log fire and, together with the restaurant, offers a choice of dining options. Bedrooms are appealing, both those in the new wing and the original six rooms

continued on p584

S

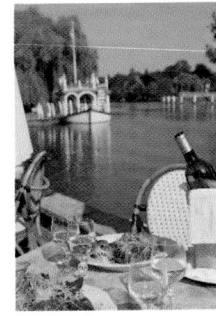

STRATFORD-UPON-AVON, continued

which have been upgraded; rooms with four-poster beds and rooms suitable for less able guests are available.
ROOMS: 12 en suite (2 fmly) (3 GF) No smoking in all bedrooms s £49-£65; d £60-£75 (incl. bkfst) **LB FACILITIES:** entertainment **CONF:** Class 30 **PARKING:** 40 **NOTES:** No dogs (ex guide dogs) No smoking in restaurant Closed 23-28 Dec **CARDS:**

STREATLEY, Berkshire — Map 05 SU58

★★★★69% The Swan at Streatley

High St, Streatley on Thames RG8 9HR
☎ 01491 878800 01491 872554
e-mail: sales@swan-at-streatley.co.uk
Dir: from S right at lights in Streatley, Swan on left before bridge
A stunning location set beside the Thames, ideal on an English summer's day. Many bedrooms enjoy the views and rooms are well appointed. The hotel offers a range of facilities for meetings and leisure, the 'Streatley Belle', is moored beside the hotel and is a perfect, yet unusual meeting venues and in the leisure club guests can also enjoy the views. Cuisine is accomplished and dining here should not be missed.
ROOMS: 46 en suite (2 fmly) (8 GF) No smoking in 15 bedrooms s £95; d £115 (incl. bkfst) **FACILITIES:** STV Indoor swimming (H) Fishing Sauna Solarium Gym Croquet lawn Jacuzzi ch fac Xmas **CONF:** BC Thtr 150 Class 50 Board 40 Del from £165 **PARKING:** 170 **NOTES:** No smoking in restaurant Civ Wed 150
CARDS:

See advert on page 583

STREET, Somerset — Map 04 ST43

★★★62% Wessex

High St BA16 0EF
☎ 01458 443383 01458 446589
e-mail: info@wessexhotel.com
Dir: from A303 onto B3151 to Somerton. 7m, past lights by Millfield School. Left at mini-rdbt
This purpose-built hotel in the centre of town has plenty of parking and is only a short walk from Clarks Village. Spacious bedrooms are equipped with modern facilities. Public areas include a range of function rooms, a cosy bar, and a comfortable restaurant offering a fixed-price menu and popular carvery.
ROOMS: 49 en suite (4 fmly) No smoking in 24 bedrooms s £50-£70; d £60-£70 **LB FACILITIES:** STV Xmas **CONF:** BC Thtr 250 Class 120 Board 50 Del from £80 **SERVICES:** Lift **PARKING:** 70 **NOTES:** No dogs (ex guide dogs) No smoking in restaurant Closed 27-29 Dec
CARDS:

STRENSHAM MOTORWAY SERVICE AREA (M5), Worcestershire — Map 10 SO84

⇧ Travel Inn (Tewkesbury)

WR8 0BZ
☎ 08701 977252 01684 273606
Dir: M5 northbound J8 M5/M50 (access available to southbound)
Travel Inn offers good-quality, value-for-money accommodation. Spacious, en suite rooms with bath and shower comfortably accommodate a family of up to two adults and two children (to age 15). The restaurant and bar offers a varied menu. For further details and the Travel Inn phone number, consult the Hotel Groups page.
ROOMS: 49 en suite s £44.95; d £44.95
CONF: Thtr 22 Class 18 Board 24

STRETTON, Rutland — Map 11 SK91

★★72% Ram Jam Inn

Great North Rd LE15 7QX
☎ 01780 410776 01780 410361
e-mail: rji@rutnet.co.uk
Dir: on N'bound carriageway of A1 past B668 junct through service station into hotel car park. S'bound take B668 - Oakham & follow signs under A1
This delightful inn has an informal but stylish ambience, much like a café-bar and bistro with rooms. Warm colour schemes work well through the main public rooms which are dominated by the popular restaurant. The spacious, high quality bedrooms have cheerful soft furnishings and most overlook the orchard.
ROOMS: 7 en suite (1 fmly) s £47; d £57 **CONF:** Thtr 60 Class 40 Board 40 Del £77.50 **PARKING:** 64 **NOTES:** No dogs (ex guide dogs) No smoking in restaurant Closed 25 Dec
CARDS:

STROUD, Gloucestershire — Map 04 SO80

★★★72% Burleigh Court

Burleigh, Minchinhampton GL5 2PF
☎ 01453 883804 01453 886870
e-mail: info@burleighcourthotel.co.uk
Dir: 0.75m off A419 E of Stroud

Dating back to the 18th century, this former gentleman's manor house is in a secluded, yet accessible, position with some wonderful views over the surrounding countryside. Public rooms are elegantly styled and include a wonderful oak-panelled bar for pre-dinner drinks beside a crackling fire. Combining comfort and quality, no two bedrooms are the same and a number of rooms are in an adjoining coach house.
ROOMS: 18 en suite (2 fmly) (3 GF) s £80-£90; d £105-£145 (incl. bkfst) **LB FACILITIES:** Outdoor swimming (H) Croquet lawn **CONF:** Thtr 50 Class 30 Board 30 Del from £130 **PARKING:** 40 **NOTES:** No smoking in restaurant Civ Wed 50
CARDS:

★★★70% The Bear of Rodborough

Rodborough Common GL5 5DE
☎ 01453 878522 01453 872523
e-mail: bookings@cotswold-inns-hotels.co.uk
Dir: 1m S on A46, turn left to Rodborough Common
This popular 17th-century coaching inn is situated high above Stroud within acres of National Trust parkland. Character abounds with the lounges, cocktail bar and elegant Mulberry restaurant epitomising the inherent charm of the building. Bedrooms offer equal measures of comfort and style with lots of extra touches.

continued

There is also a traditional and well patronised public bar. Food is taken seriously here and based, where possible, on local produce.
ROOMS: 46 en suite (2 fmly) No smoking in 13 bedrooms s £75-£95; d £120-£160 (incl. bkfst) **LB** **FACILITIES:** Croquet lawn Xmas **CONF:** Thtr 60 Class 30 Board 30 Del from £145 **PARKING:** 70 **NOTES:** No smoking in restaurant Civ Wed 100
CARDS:

★★66% The Bell

Wallbridge GL5 3J5
☎ 01453 763556 📠 01453 758611
e-mail: sarahclose@thebellhotel.demon.co.uk
Dir: *at junct of A419/A46, outside Stroud Town Centre*

This former coaching inn dates back to Victorian times and is conveniently situated close to the town centre. Small and friendly, there is an informal and relaxed atmosphere here and many guests return on a regular basis. Bedrooms are well equipped and comfortably furnished with a four-poster room available. Facilities include a meeting room, popular lounge bar and restaurant.
ROOMS: 12 en suite (2 fmly) **FACILITIES:** ch fac Xmas **CONF:** Thtr 27 Class 20 Board 16 **PARKING:** 15 **NOTES:** No smoking in restaurant
CARDS:

⌂ Premier Lodge (Stroud)

Stratford Lodge, Stratford Rd GL5 4AF
☎ 0870 9906378 📠 0870 9906379

Premier Lodge offers modern, well-equipped, en suite accommodation suitable for both business and leisure travellers. Meals can be taken at the adjacent popular restaurant and bar, which is fully licensed. For further details, consult the Hotel Groups page.
ROOMS: 32 en suite s £48; d £48

STUDLAND, Dorset — Map 05 SZ08

★★68% Manor House

BH19 3AU
☎ 01929 450288 📠 01929 450288
e-mail: themanorhousehotel@lineone.net
Dir: *A338 from Bournemouth, follow signs to Sandbanks/Sandbanks ferry, cross on ferry, then 3m to Studland*

Set in 20 acres of attractive grounds and with delightful views overlooking Studland Bay, this elegant hotel provides an impressive range of facilities. Bedrooms, many with excellent sea views, are all well equipped and many retain charming features of the original Gothic house. In the oak-panelled dining room, there is an interesting choice of dishes on the daily changing menu.
ROOMS: 20 en suite (9 fmly) (4 GF) s £85-£100; d £130-£198 (incl. bkfst & dinner) **LB** **FACILITIES:** Tennis (hard) Croquet lawn Xmas **CONF:** Class 35 Board 20 **PARKING:** 80 **NOTES:** No children 5yrs No smoking in restaurant Closed 3 wks Jan
CARDS:

STURMINSTER NEWTON, Dorset — Map 04 ST71

★★★70% ® Plumber Manor

Hazelbury Bryan Rd DT10 2AF
☎ 01258 472507 📠 01258 473370
e-mail: book@plumbermanor.com
Dir: *Off A357. Follow tourist signs to hotel*

This 17th-century manor, set in extensive, lovingly tended grounds, is full of charm and character. Bedrooms, some set apart from the main house, are pleasantly spacious and modern in style. The public areas retain much of the style of the manor and guests can relax in the bar or lounge, or stroll in the grounds. Using fresh and local produce, the restaurant is very much the focus of the hotel.

ROOMS: 6 en suite 10 annexe en suite No smoking in all bedrooms s fr £90; d £105-£165 (incl. bkfst) **LB** **FACILITIES:** Tennis (hard) Croquet lawn **CONF:** Thtr 25 Board 16 Del £145 **PARKING:** 30 **NOTES:** No smoking in restaurant Closed Feb
CARDS:

SUDBURY, Derbyshire — Map 10 SK13

★★★68% *The Boars Head*

Lichfield Rd DE6 5GX
☎ 01283 820344 📠 01283 820075
e-mail: enquiries@boars-head-hotel.co.uk
Dir: *off A50 onto A515 towards Lichfield, hotel 1m on right*

This busy hotel offers comfortable accommodation in well-equipped bedrooms. There is a relaxed atmosphere in the public rooms, which offer a choice of bars and dining options. The refurbished beamed lounge bar provides informal dining while the restaurant and cocktail bar offer a more formal environment.
ROOMS: 22 en suite 1 annexe en suite (1 fmly) **FACILITIES:** STV **CONF:** Thtr 25 Class 16 Board 16 **PARKING:** 85 **NOTES:** No smoking in restaurant **CARDS:**

See advert under BURTON UPON TRENT

SUDBURY, Suffolk — Map 13 TL84

★★★69% Mill

Walnut Tree Ln CO10 1BD
☎ 01787 375544 📠 01787 373027
Dir: *A134 to Sudbury, 2nd right after town square*

Thus impressive building is situated on the banks of the River Stour, overlooking open pastures on the edge of town. The hotel has its own mill pond and retains many charming features such as open fires, exposed beams and a working waterwheel. Bedrooms vary but are all well equipped and pleasantly furnished.
ROOMS: 52 en suite (2 fmly) s £59; d £87-£127 **LB** **FACILITIES:** STV Xmas **CONF:** Thtr 70 Class 35 Board 35 Del £79 **PARKING:** 60
CARDS:

SUNDERLAND, Tyne & Wear Map 19 NZ35

★★★★70% ⊛ *Sunderland Marriott*

Queen's Pde, Seaburn SR6 8DB
☎ 0191 529 2041 📠 0191 529 4227
e-mail: sunderland-marriott@whitbread.com
Dir: *A19, A184 (Boldon/ Sunderland North), continue for 3m. At rdbt turn left, then right. At rdbt turn left, follow to coast. Turn right, hotel on right*
Comfortable and spacious accommodation, some with fabulous views of the North Sea and vast expanses of sandy beach, is provided in this seafront hotel. Public rooms are bright and modern and a number of meeting rooms are available. The hotel is conveniently located for access to the local visitor attractions.
ROOMS: 82 en suite (20 fmly) No smoking in 60 bedrooms
FACILITIES: Spa STV Indoor swimming (H) Sauna Solarium Gym
CONF: Thtr 300 Class 150 Board 100 **SERVICES:** Lift **PARKING:** 120
NOTES: No smoking in restaurant Civ Wed 80
CARDS:

★★★68% Quality Friendly Hotel

Witney Way, Boldon NE35 9PE
☎ 0191 519 1999 📠 0191 519 0655
e-mail: admin@gb621.u-net.com
Dir: *from Tyne Tunnel (A19) 2.5m south, 1st exit to A184 rdbt*
This modern, purpose-built hotel is within easy reach of major business and tourism amenities and is well suited to the needs of both business and leisure travellers. The bedrooms are spacious and well equipped. Public areas include a leisure centre, a variety of meeting rooms and a spacious bar and restaurant.
ROOMS: 82 en suite (10 fmly) (41 GF) No smoking in 42 bedrooms s £85-£95; d £95-£105 **LB FACILITIES:** STV Indoor swimming (H) Sauna Solarium Gym Jacuzzi Swimming pool supervised Xmas
CONF: Thtr 230 Class 100 Board 75 Del from £115 **PARKING:** 150
NOTES: Civ Wed 300 **CARDS:**

⌂ Premier Lodge (Sunderland)

Timber Beach Rd, Off Wessington Way, Castletown SR5 3XG
☎ 0870 9906514 📠 0870 9906515
Dir: *A1 junct 64 onto A1231 towards Sunderland, lodge on last rdbt on right*
Premier Lodge offers modern, well-equipped, en suite accommodation suitable for both business and leisure travellers. Meals can be taken at the adjacent popular restaurant and bar, which is fully licensed. For further details, consult the Hotel Groups page.
ROOMS: 63 en suite s £48; d £48 **CONF:** Thtr 12 Class 12 Board 12 Del from £70.95

⌂ Travel Inn

Wessington Way, Castletown SR5 3HR
☎ 08701 977245 📠 0191 548 4044
Dir: *from A19 take A1231 towards Sunderland, Travel Inn 100yds from junction*
Travel Inn offers good-quality, value-for-money accommodation. Spacious, en suite rooms with bath and shower comfortably accommodate a family of up to two adults and two children (to age 15). The restaurant and bar offers a varied menu. For further details and the Travel Inn phone number, consult the Hotel Groups page.
ROOMS: 41 en suite s £44.95; d £44.95 **CONF:** Thtr 15 Board 10

⌂ Travelodge

Low Row SR1 3PT
☎ 0870 850950

Travelodge offers good quality, good value, modern accommodation. Ideal for families, the spacious, en suite bedrooms include remote-control TV, tea and coffee-making facilities, luxury beds and free morning newspaper. Meals can be taken at the nearby family restaurant. For further details and the Travelodge phone number, consult the Hotel Groups page.
ROOMS: 60 en suite s fr £42.95; d fr £42.95

SUTTON, Greater London Map 06 TQ26

★★63% *Thatched House*

135 Cheam Rd SM1 2BN
☎ 020 8642 3131 📠 020 8770 0684
Dir: *M25 junct 8, follow A217 to London, right onto A232, hotel 0.25m on right*
A large thatched hotel on the Epsom/Croydon road. Bedrooms, which vary in shape and size, are neatly decorated and well-equipped. Public rooms include a small lounge, a bar and a dining room overlooking the attractive garden.
ROOMS: 32 rms (29 en suite) **CONF:** Thtr 50 Class 30 Board 26
PARKING: 25 **NOTES:** No dogs (ex guide dogs) No smoking in restaurant **CARDS:**

U *Holiday Inn*

Gibson Rd SM1 2RF
☎ 020 8770 1311 📠 020 8770 1539
Dir: *M25 junct 8 follow A217, then B2230. Pass railway station, follow one-way system in right lane. At lights, right then immediately left, and left again into Gibson Rd*
At the time of going to press, the classification for this hotel was not confirmed. Please refer to the AA internet site www.theAA.com for current information.
ROOMS: 116 en suite No smoking in 62 bedrooms **FACILITIES:** STV Indoor swimming (H) Sauna Solarium Gym Jacuzzi Beauty treatment rooms entertainment **CONF:** Thtr 180 Class 105 Board 60
SERVICES: Lift air con **PARKING:** 116 **NOTES:** Civ Wed 50
CARDS:

SUTTON COLDFIELD, West Midlands Map 10 SP19

★★★★73% New Hall

Walmley Rd B76 1QX
☎ 0121 378 2442 📠 0121 378 4637
e-mail: new.hall@thistle.co.uk

***Dir:** follow A38 signed Lichfield until B4148 signed Walmley. in 2.5m, at 2nd rdbt turn left and then right into Walmley Road. Hotel is on left*

Set in immaculate grounds and gardens, this 12th-century hotel is reputedly the oldest moated manor house in England. Charming public rooms include an impressive panelled restaurant, which offers imaginative dishes. Divided between a purpose-built wing and the main house, the bedrooms vary in size and all are furnished and decorated to a high standard. The hotel also offers a variety of leisure facilities including a smart health club.

ROOMS: 60 en suite (24 GF) No smoking in 56 bedrooms s £166; d £196 **LB** **FACILITIES: Spa** STV Indoor swimming (H) Golf 9 Tennis (hard) Sauna Solarium Gym Croquet lawn Putting green Jacuzzi Swimming pool supervised, Woodland walks Xmas **CONF:** Thtr 60 Class 30 Board 30 Del from £178 **PARKING:** 70 **NOTES:** No dogs (ex guide dogs) No smoking in restaurant RS closed Sat lunch Civ Wed 80 **CARDS:**

★★★★68% Moor Hall

Moor Hall Dr, Four Oaks B75 6LN
☎ 0121 308 3751 📠 0121 308 8974
e-mail: mail@moorhallhotel.co.uk

***Dir:** at junct of A38/A453 take A453 towards Sutton Coldfield, at lights turn right into Weeford Rd, hotel 150yds on left*

Although only a short distance from the city centre this hotel enjoys a peaceful setting, overlooking extensive grounds and an adjacent golf course. Bedrooms are well equipped and executive rooms are particularly spacious. Public rooms include the formal Oak Room Restaurant, and the informal Country Kitchen, which offers carvery and blackboard specials.

ROOMS: 82 en suite (8 fmly) (9 GF) No smoking in 53 bedrooms s £65-£120; d £85-£140 (incl. bkfst) **LB** **FACILITIES: Spa** STV Indoor swimming (H) Sauna Gym Jacuzzi Steam room, Spa treatment rooms **CONF:** Thtr 250 Class 120 Board 45 Del £145 **SERVICES:** Lift **PARKING:** 170 **NOTES:** No dogs (ex guide dogs) Civ Wed 120 **CARDS:**

See advert under BIRMINGHAM

★★★66% *Marston Farm*

BROOK HOTELS

Bodymoor Heath B76 9JD
☎ 01827 872133 📠 01827 875043
e-mail: marstonfarm@brook-hotels.demon.co.uk

***Dir:** A4091 towards Tamworth, turn right for Bodymoor Heath. Turn right after humpback bridge*

This 17th-century farmhouse is situated close to Birmingham, the NEC and the airport. It provides attractive and well-equipped accommodation for both the leisure and business markets.

continued

Features include the courtyard restaurant, permanent marquee, conference rooms and ample car parking.

ROOMS: 37 en suite No smoking in 5 bedrooms **FACILITIES:** STV Tennis (hard) Fishing Croquet lawn BoulesMountain bikes **CONF:** Thtr 150 Class 80 Board 50 **PARKING:** 150 **NOTES:** No smoking in restaurant Civ Wed 120 **CARDS:**

★★★66% Sutton Court

60-66 Lichfield Rd B74 2NA
☎ 0121 354 4991 📠 0121 355 0083
e-mail: res@schotel.co.uk

***Dir:** M42 junct 9, then A446 to Lichfield. At rdbt take A453 (Sutton Coldfield). Hotel at 2nd lights at junct of A5127/A453*

This privately owned hotel is easy to find and close to the town centre. The newly decorated bedrooms are well equipped with good attention to detail especially for business travellers' needs. There is an extensive business centre, a conference room and Savannahs is the 'Deep South American' restaurant.

ROOMS: 54 en suite 8 annexe en suite (9 fmly) No smoking in 40 bedrooms s £35-£95; d £40-£118 **LB** **FACILITIES:** STV Free use of local leisure centre entertainment ch fac Xmas **CONF:** BC Thtr 90 Class 70 Board 50 Del from £65 **PARKING:** 90 **NOTES:** Civ Wed 130 **CARDS:**

Innkeeper's Lodge Birmingham East

Chester Rd, Streetley B73 6SP
☎ 0121 353 7785 📠 0121 352 1443

***Dir:** M6 junct 7 to A34 S & turn left onto A4041. At 4th rdbt turn right onto A452-Chester Road, lodge 1m on right.*

A new concept in the travel accommodation market. Smart rooms meet essential business requirements but also have home comforts. Dining options include all-day menus plus the added advantage of breakfast, which is included in the room price. For further details, consult the Hotel Groups page.

ROOMS: 7 en suite 59 annexe en suite **CONF:** Thtr 40 Board 20

Innkeeper's Lodge Birmingham South

2225 Coventry Rd, Sheldon B26 3EH
☎ 0121 742 6201 📠 0121 722 2703

***Dir:** M42 junct 6/A45 towards Birmingham for 2m. Lodge on left approaching overhang traffic lights*

A new concept in the travel accommodation market. Smart rooms meet essential business requirements but also have home comforts. Dining options include all-day menus plus the added advantage of breakfast, which is included in the room price. For further details, consult the Hotel Groups page.

ROOMS: 85 en suite

Premier Lodge (Birmingham North)

Whitehouse Common Rd B75 6HD
☎ 0870 9906320 📠 0870 9906321

***Dir:** 6m from M42 junct 9*

Premier Lodge offers modern, well-equipped, en suite accommodation suitable for both business and leisure travellers. Meals can be taken at the adjacent popular restaurant and bar, which is fully licensed. For further details, consult the Hotel Groups page.

ROOMS: 42 en suite s £48; d £48 **CONF:** Board 10

Travelodge

Boldmere Rd B73 5UP
☎ 08700 850 950 📠 0121 355 0017

***Dir:** 2m S, on B4142*

Travelodge offers good quality, good value, modern accommodation. Ideal for families, the spacious, en suite bedrooms include remote-control TV, tea and coffee-making

continued on p588

SUTTON COLDFIELD, continued

facilities, luxury beds and free morning newspaper. Meals can be taken at the nearby family restaurant. For further details and the Travelodge phone number, consult the Hotel Groups page.
ROOMS: 32 en suite s fr £42.95; d fr £42.95

SUTTON IN THE ELMS, Leicestershire — Map 11 SP59

★★66% *Mill On The Soar*

Coventry Rd LE9 6QD
☎ 01455 282419 01455 285937
Dir: *SE of Leicester, on B4114*
This is a popular inn which caters well for family dining. The open plan bar offers meals and snacks throughout the day, and is divided into non-smoking, family and adult-only areas. For the summer months, there is also an attractive patio. Bedrooms are situated in a lodge-style annexe.
ROOMS: 25 en suite (10 fmly) **FACILITIES:** Fishing Falconry centre **CONF:** Thtr 50 Class 20 Board 15 **PARKING:** 200 **NOTES:** No dogs (ex guide dogs) **CARDS:**

SUTTON ON SEA, Lincolnshire — Map 17 TF58

★★★68% Grange & Links

Sea Ln, Sandilands LN12 2RA
☎ 01507 441334 01507 443033
e-mail: grangelinks@ic24.net
Dir: *A1111 to Sutton-on-Sea, follow signs to Sandilands*
This friendly, family-run hotel sits in five acres of grounds, close to both the beach and its own 18-hole links golf course. Bedrooms are pleasantly appointed and are well equipped for both business and leisure guests. Public rooms include ample lounge areas, a formal restaurant and a traditional bar serving a wide range of meals and snacks.
ROOMS: 23 en suite (10 fmly) No smoking in 3 bedrooms s fr £59.50; d fr £78 (incl. bkfst) **LB FACILITIES:** Golf 18 Tennis (hard) Snooker Gym Croquet lawn Putting green Bowls Xmas **CONF:** Thtr 200 Board 100 Del from £75 **PARKING:** 60 **NOTES:** No dogs (ex guide dogs) Civ Wed 190 **CARDS:**

SUTTON SCOTNEY, Hampshire — Map 05 SU43

Travelodge Winchester

SO21 3JY
☎ 08700 850 950
Dir: *on A34 northbound*
Travelodge offers good quality, good value, modern accommodation. Ideal for families, the spacious, en suite bedrooms include remote-control TV, tea and coffee-making facilities, luxury beds and free morning newspaper. Meals can be taken at the nearby family restaurant. For further details and the Travelodge phone number, consult the Hotel Groups page.
ROOMS: 30 en suite s fr £42.95; d fr £42.95

Travelodge Winchester

SO21 3JY
☎ 08700 850 950
Dir: *on A34 southbound*
Travelodge offers good quality, good value, modern accommodation. Ideal for families, the spacious, en suite bedrooms include remote-control TV, tea and coffee-making facilities, luxury beds and free morning newspaper. Meals can be taken at the nearby family restaurant. For further details and the Travelodge phone number, consult the Hotel Groups page.
ROOMS: 40 en suite s fr £42.95; d fr £42.95

SUTTON UPON DERWENT, East Riding of Yorkshire — Map 17 SE74

★★65% Old Rectory

Sandhill Ln YO41 4BX
☎ 01904 608548 01904 608548
Dir: *off A1079 at Grimston Bar rdbt onto B1228 for Howden, through Elvington to Sutton upon Derwent, hotel on left opposite tennis courts*
Dating from 1854, this large country rectory on the outskirts of York stands in the village centre, overlooking the Derwent Valley. The hotel is handy for the Retail Outlet, the Yorkshire Air Museum and the city. Bedrooms and public areas are spacious and comfortable, and home cooking is a speciality in the dining room.
ROOMS: 6 rms (5 en suite) (2 fmly) s £35-£40; d £52-£56 (incl. bkfst) **LB PARKING:** 30 **NOTES:** No smoking in restaurant Closed 2 wks Xmas **CARDS:**

SWAFFHAM, Norfolk — Map 13 TF80

★★★67% George

Station Rd PE37 7LJ
☎ 01760 721238 01760 725333
e-mail: george@bestwestern.co.uk
Dir: *off A47 signed Swaffham, hotel opp church of St Peter & St Paul*
A popular Georgian hotel situated in the heart of this bustling market town. Bedrooms vary in size and style and all are pleasantly decorated and well equipped. Public rooms include a cosy restaurant, a lounge and a busy bar where a range of drinks and snacks are available.
ROOMS: 29 en suite (1 fmly) s £70-£80; d £80-£90 (incl. bkfst) **LB FACILITIES:** STV Xmas **CONF:** Thtr 150 Class 70 Board 70 Del from £80 **PARKING:** 100 **NOTES:** No smoking in restaurant **CARDS:**

SWALLOWFIELD, Berkshire — Map 05 SU76

★★70% The Mill House

Old Basingstoke Rd, Swallowfield RG7 1PY
☎ 0118 988 3124 0118 988 5550
e-mail: info@themillhousehotel.co.uk
Dir: *M4 junct 11, S on A33, left at 1st rdbt onto B3349. Approx 1m after sign for Three Mile Cross & Spencer's Wood, hotel on right*
This smart Georgian house hotel enjoys a tranquil setting in its own delightful gardens, making it an ideal wedding venue. Guests can enjoy fine dining in the conservatory-style restaurant or lighter meals in the cosy bar. Well-equipped bedrooms vary in size and style and include a number of spacious, well-appointed executive rooms.
ROOMS: 12 en suite (2 fmly) No smoking in 2 bedrooms s £70-£90; d £75-£100 (incl. bkfst) **LB FACILITIES:** Croquet lawn **CONF:** Thtr 250 Class 100 Board 60 Del from £105 **PARKING:** 60 **NOTES:** No smoking in restaurant Closed 24 Dec-4 Jan RS Sun evenings Civ Wed 125 **CARDS:**

SWANAGE, Dorset — Map 05 SZ07

★★★67% Grand

Burlington Rd BH19 1LU
☎ 01929 423353 01929 427068
e-mail: grandhotel@tiscali.co.uk
Dir: *via Sandbanks Toll Ferry from Bournemouth, follow signs to Swanage, at 2nd town centre sign 4th left into Burlington Rd*
Dating back to 1898, the Grand Hotel is located on the Isle of Purbeck and has spectacular views across Swanage Bay and Peveril Point. Bedrooms are individually decorated and well

continued

equipped; public rooms offer a number of choices from relaxing lounges to extensive leisure facilities. The hotel also has its own private beach.

ROOMS: 30 en suite (2 fmly) No smoking in 8 bedrooms s £61-£69; d £122-£138 (incl. bkfst & dinner) **LB** **FACILITIES:** STV Indoor swimming (H) Fishing Sauna Solarium Gym Jacuzzi Table tennis entertainment Xmas **CONF:** Thtr 120 Class 40 Board 40 Del from £83 **SERVICES:** Lift **PARKING:** 15 **NOTES:** No dogs No smoking in restaurant Closed 10 days in Jan (dates on application) Civ Wed 120 **CARDS:**

See advert on this page

Packed in a hurry?
Ironing facilities should be available at all star levels, either in rooms or on request

★★★67% The Pines
Burlington Rd BH19 1LT
☎ 01929 425211 Fax 01929 422075
e-mail: reservations@pineshotel.co.uk
Dir: *A351 to seafront, left then 2nd right. Hotel at end of road*

Enjoying a peaceful location with spectacular views over the cliffs and sea, the Pines is a pleasant place to stay. Bedrooms, many with sea views, are comfortable and some have now been refurbished. Guests can take tea in the lounge, enjoy appetising bar snacks in the attractive bar and interesting cuisine in the restaurant.

ROOMS: 49 en suite (26 fmly) (6 GF) s £52-£64; d £104-£128 (incl. bkfst) **LB** **FACILITIES:** ch fac Xmas **CONF:** Thtr 80 Class 80 Board 80 Del £81.50 **SERVICES:** Lift **PARKING:** 60 **NOTES:** No smoking in restaurant **CARDS:**

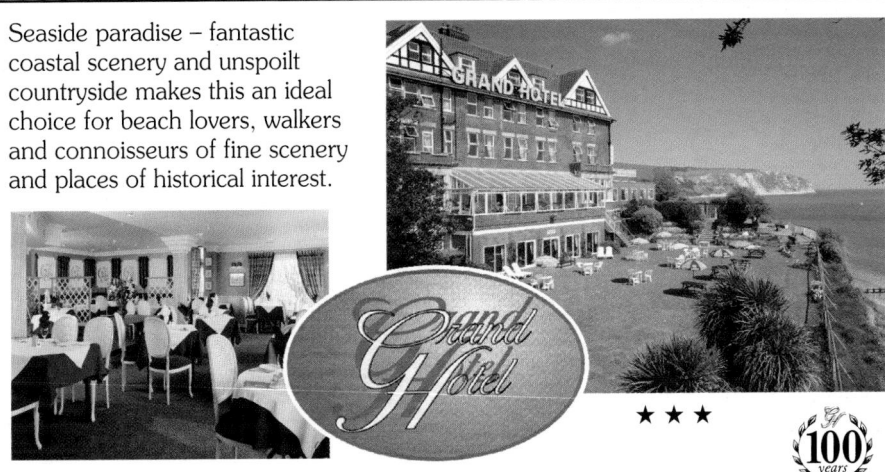

SWANAGE, continued

★★★65% Purbeck House
91 High St BH19 2LZ
☎ 01929 422872 01929 421194
e-mail: purbeckhouse@easynet.co.uk
Dir: *A351 to Swanage, right into Shore Rd, then Institute Rd, right into High St*
Located close to the town centre, this former convent is set in well-tended grounds. The bedrooms are tastefully decorated and appointed with old pine furnishings. As well as a pleasant and spacious conservatory, the smart public areas have many features, such as painted ceilings and fine tiled floors.
ROOMS: 18 en suite 20 annexe en suite (5 fmly) No smoking in 3 bedrooms s £49-£61; d £88-£112 (incl. bkfst) **LB FACILITIES:** STV Croquet lawn Xmas **CONF:** Thtr 100 Class 36 Board 25 **PARKING:** 50 **NOTES:** No dogs (ex guide dogs) No smoking in restaurant Civ Wed 100 **CARDS:** *See advert on opposite page*

★★69% Havenhurst
3 Cranborne Rd BH19 1EA
THE INDEPENDENTS
☎ 01929 424224 01929 422173
e-mail: reception@havenhursthotel.co.uk
Dir: *A351 to Swanage. At lights before beach, right towards town centre, hotel 1st right*
The Havenhurst is a friendly small hotel, quietly located close to the seafront, which offers comfortable accommodation. Cuisine is notable, especially in the enormous range of home-made desserts. Bedrooms offer a range of sizes and all are well equipped. There is a comfortable lounge, a conservatory and popular bar.
ROOMS: 17 en suite (4 fmly) **FACILITIES:** Xmas **PARKING:** 17 **NOTES:** No dogs (ex guide dogs) No smoking in restaurant **CARDS:**

SWANWICK See Alfreton

SWAVESEY, Cambridgeshire Map 12 TL36

Travelodge Cambridge (West)
Cambridge Rd CB4 5QR
Travelodge
☎ 08700 850 950 01954 789113
Dir: *on eastbound carriageway of A14*
Travelodge offers good quality, good value, modern accommodation. Ideal for families, the spacious, en suite bedrooms include remote-control TV, tea and coffee-making facilities, luxury beds and free morning newspaper. Meals can be taken at the nearby family restaurant. For further details and the Travelodge phone number, consult the Hotel Groups page.
ROOMS: 36 en suite s fr £42.95; d fr £42.95

SWAY, Hampshire Map 05 SZ29

★★★66% String of Horses
Mead End Rd SO41 6EH
☎ 01590 682631 01590 682911
e-mail: relax@stringofhorses.co.uk
Dir: *A337 to Brockenhurst, right opp Carey's Manor onto B3055. Right into Station Rd, 2nd left after rail station, 350mtrs on left*
A well-maintained hotel set in peaceful, mature grounds, adjoining the New Forest. The majority of the well-presented bedrooms are equipped with large spa baths, and all feature thoughtful extras such as dressing gowns. There is a cosy bar, separate breakfast room and comfortable lounge overlooking the pool and garden.
ROOMS: 8 en suite (6 GF) s £75-£85; d £110-£130 (incl. bkfst) **LB FACILITIES: Spa** STV Outdoor swimming (H) Sauna Croquet lawn Jacuzzi Health suite, Swimming pool supervised Xmas **CONF:** Thtr 40 Board 30 Del from £123 **PARKING:** 32 **NOTES:** No dogs No children 16yrs No smoking in restaurant **CARDS:**

★★68% Sway Manor Restaurant & Hotel
Station Rd SO41 6BA
☎ 01590 682754 01590 682955
e-mail: info@swaymanor.com
Dir: *turn off B3055 Brockenhurst/New Milton road into Sway village centre*
Built at the turn of the century, this attractive mansion is set in it own grounds, which include an outdoor swimming pool, and is also conveniently located in the centre of the village. Bedrooms are well appointed and generously equipped whilst the bar and restaurant, which both have views over the gardens, are popular with locals.
ROOMS: 15 en suite (3 fmly) No smoking in 12 bedrooms s £43-£51; d £70-£86 (incl. bkfst) **LB FACILITIES:** Outdoor swimming Xmas **SERVICES:** Lift **PARKING:** 40 **NOTES:** No smoking in restaurant Civ Wed 60 **CARDS:**

SWINDON, Wiltshire Map 05 SU18
See also Wootton Bassett

★★★★73% De Vere Swindon
Shaw Ridge Leisure Park, Whitehill Way SN5 7DW
DE VERE HOTELS
☎ 01793 878785 01793 877822
e-mail: dvs.sales@devere-hotels.com
Dir: *M4 junct 16, signs for Swindon off 1st rdbt, 2nd rdbt follow signs for Link Centre over next 2 rdbts, 2nd left at 3rd rdbt, left onto slip road*

Whether on business or pleasure, this hotel is conveniently located for easy access to the Cotswolds, motorway network and town centre. The bedrooms are modern and smartly appointed and offer a comprehensive range of in-room facilities. A comprehensive range of dishes is offered in the Park Brasserie to suit all tastes, and this menu is also available as room service.
ROOMS: 158 en suite (12 fmly) No smoking in 93 bedrooms s £125; d £125 **LB FACILITIES:** STV Indoor swimming (H) Sauna Solarium Gym Jacuzzi Health & beauty treatment rooms Xmas **CONF:** BC Thtr 300 Class 160 Board 80 Del from £130 **SERVICES:** Lift **PARKING:** 170 **NOTES:** No smoking in restaurant Civ Wed 300
CARDS:

★★★★71% Blunsdon House Hotel & Leisure Club
Blunsdon SN26 7AS
Best Western
☎ 01793 721701 01793 721056
e-mail: info@blunsdonhouse.co.uk
Dir: *200yds off A419 at Swindon, 1m N of Swindon*
With a variety of public areas including three bars, Blunsdon House is set in 30 acres of well-tended grounds with views to the Cotswold Hills. Christopher's Restaurant continues to be very popular, while the Ridge Restaurant provides an extensive selection of dishes in more formal surroundings. Bedrooms are
continued

S

comfortably furnished, and the contemporary Pavilion rooms are especially spacious.
ROOMS: 118 en suite (14 fmly) (27 GF) No smoking in 75 bedrooms s £105-£135; d £115-£145 (incl. bkfst) **LB FACILITIES:** STV Indoor swimming (H) Tennis (hard) Squash Sauna Solarium Gym Putting green Jacuzzi Beauty therapy, Woodland walk, 9 hole par 3 golf course ch fac Xmas **CONF:** Thtr 300 Class 200 Board 40 Del from £150 **SERVICES:** Lift **PARKING:** 300 **NOTES:** No dogs (ex guide dogs) No smoking in restaurant Civ Wed 100 **CARDS:**

★★★★64% Swindon Marriott Hotel

Marriott HOTELS · RESORTS · SUITES

Pipers Way SN3 1SH
☎ 0870 400 7281 📠 0870 400 7381
Dir: *M4 junct 15, follow A419, then A4259 to Coate rdbt and B4006 signed 'Old Town'*
With convenient access to the motorway, this hotel is an easily accessible venue for meetings, and an ideal base from which to explore Wiltshire and the Cotswolds. The hotel offers a good range of public rooms, including a well-equipped leisure centre, Chats café bar and the informal, brasserie-style Mediterrano restaurant.
ROOMS: 155 en suite (42 fmly) No smoking in 86 bedrooms s £127-£167; d fr £127 **LB FACILITIES: Spa** STV Indoor swimming (H) Tennis (hard) Sauna Solarium Gym Jacuzzi Steam Room, Health & Beauty, Hair salon, Sports massage therapy **CONF:** Thtr 250 Class 100 Board 40 Del from £125 **SERVICES:** Lift air con **PARKING:** 185 **NOTES:** No dogs (ex guide dogs) No smoking in restaurant Civ Wed 200 **CARDS:**

Looking for a last-minute weekend away?
Check out Latebeds,
the AA's late availability booking service, at www.theAA.com

SWINDON, continued

★★★78% The Pear Tree at Purton

Church End SN5 4ED
☎ 01793 772100 01793 772369
e-mail: stay@peartreepurton.co.uk
(For full entry see Purton)

★★★69% Chiseldon House

New Rd, Chiseldon SN4 0NE
☎ 01793 741010 01793 741059
e-mail: chishoho@hotmail.com
Dir: *M4 junct 15, onto A346 signposted Marlborough, at brow of hill turn right by Esso garage onto B4005 into New Rd, hotel 200yds on right*

Chiseldon is a traditional country house near Swindon that is ideal for a peaceful and comfortable stay. Quiet and spacious bedrooms are tastefully decorated and include a number of thoughtful extras. A varied selection of tempting dishes is offered at dinner. Guests may also enjoy the comfortable lounge, swimming pool and well-kept gardens.
ROOMS: 21 en suite (4 fmly) No smoking in 7 bedrooms s £85-£110; d £110-£140 (incl. bkfst) **FACILITIES:** STV Croquet lawn ch fac **CONF:** Thtr 50 Class 30 Board 20 Del from £115 **PARKING:** 40 **NOTES:** Civ Wed 85 **CARDS:**

★★★69% Stanton House

The Avenue, Stanton Fitzwarren SN6 7SD
☎ 01793 861777 01793 861857
e-mail: reception@stantonhouse.co.uk
Dir: *A419 onto A361 towards Highworth, pass Honda factory and left towards Stanton Fitzwarren 600yds past business park, hotel on left*
Extensive grounds and super gardens surround this Cotswold-stone manor house. Smart, well-maintained bedrooms have been equipped with modern comforts. Public areas include a games room, a lounge, a bar, conference facilities and an informal restaurant specialising in Japanese cuisine. Multi-lingual staff are friendly and a relaxed atmosphere prevails.
ROOMS: 86 en suite No smoking in 3 bedrooms s £69-£74; d £109-£125 (incl. bkfst) **LB** **FACILITIES:** STV Tennis (hard) Mah Jong **CONF:** Thtr 110 Class 70 Board 40 **SERVICES:** Lift air con **PARKING:** 110 **NOTES:** No dogs (ex guide dogs) Civ Wed 40
CARDS:

See advert on page 591

★★★67% *Landmark Hotel Swindon*

Station Rd, Chiseldon SN4 0PW
☎ 01793 740149 01793 741326
e-mail: reservations@landmarkhotel.com
Dir: *M4 junct 15/A346 signed Marlborough, at brow of hill turn right by Esso garage, take B4005 into New Rd. 2nd right signed Station Rd. Hotel at end of lane on left*
Situated in the centre of the village of Chiseldon, this modern hotel offers efficient and friendly service. The spacious bedrooms and bathrooms provide high standards of comfort; many thoughtful extras further enhance the overall experience. The cosy restaurant offers an excellent choice of fresh cuisine and in the summer months, guests can dine on the pleasant rear patio.

ROOMS: 16 en suite No smoking in 14 bedrooms **CONF:** Thtr 30 Class 12 Board 16 **SERVICES:** Lift **PARKING:** 24 **NOTES:** No smoking in restaurant Closed 23 Dec-3 Jan **CARDS:**

★★★64% The Madison Inn

Corus hotels

Oxford Rd, Stratton St Margaret SN3 4TL
☎ 0870 609 6150 01793 831401
e-mail: reservations.madisoninn@corushotels.com
Dir: *M4 junct 15, A419 to Cirencester. Over rdbt, then exit left (signed Oxford A420). Right at next 2 rdbts, hotel on left*

Conveniently located just off the M4, the hotel is ideal for touring the area. Bedrooms are large and well appointed, rooms to the rear being quieter. Facilities include four versatile conference rooms and the "Olio" bar and restaurant.
ROOMS: 94 en suite (3 fmly) (45 GF) No smoking in 47 bedrooms s £50-£90; d £75-£120 **LB** **FACILITIES:** STV Free use of nearby gym, pool and beauty parlour Xmas **CONF:** Thtr 100 Class 50 Board 40 Del from £119 **PARKING:** 150 **NOTES:** No dogs (ex guide dogs) No smoking in restaurant Civ Wed 70 **CARDS:**

★★★63% Goddard Arms

Forestdale Hotels

High St, Old Town SN1 3EG
☎ 01793 692313 01793 512984
e-mail: goddard.arms@forestdale.com
Dir: *M4 junct 15, take A4259 towards Swindon, onto B4006 to Old Town follow signs to PM Hospital/High St. Hotel next to Lloyds Bank*
Situated in the attractive Old Town area, this ivy-clad coaching inn offers bedrooms in either the main building or in a modern annexe to the rear of the property. Public areas are tastefully decorated in a traditional style; there is a lounge, Vaults bar and a

continued

S

popular restaurant. The conference rooms are extensive and the car park secure.
ROOMS: 18 en suite 47 annexe en suite (3 fmly) (24 GF) No smoking in 33 bedrooms s fr £95; d fr £115 (incl. bkfst) **LB** **FACILITIES:** STV **CONF:** Thtr 180 Class 100 Board 40 Del from £115 **PARKING:** 90 **NOTES:** No dogs (ex guide dogs) No smoking in restaurant Civ Wed 180 **CARDS:**

★★★59% Villiers Inn

Moormead Rd, Wroughton SN4 9BY
☎ 01793 814744 ▯ 01793 814119
e-mail: hotels@villiersinn.co.uk
Dir: *1m S of Swindon, on A4361*
Conveniently situated with easy access to the motorway and Swindon, this attractive period property provides well-equipped accommodation in the main building and in a purpose built extension. Public areas include a comfortable library lounge and a spacious bar, and an interesting range of dishes is offered in the restaurant. Function facilities are also available.
ROOMS: 33 en suite No smoking in 10 bedrooms s £49-£79; d £69-£89 (incl. bkfst) **LB** **FACILITIES:** STV Xmas **CONF:** Thtr 60 Class 30 Board 32 Del £125 **PARKING:** 60 **NOTES:** Civ Wed 100 **CARDS:**

See advert on this page

U *Holiday Inn Swindon*

Marlborough Rd SN3 6AQ
☎ 0870 400 9079 ▯ 01793 512887
e-mail: reservations-swindon@ichotelsgroup.com
Dir: *off A419 for Swindon at rdbt, onto A4259. 1m, hotel on right opposite Coate Water Country Park*
At the time of going to press, the classification for this hotel was not confirmed. Please refer to the AA internet site www.theAA.com for current information.
ROOMS: 100 en suite (24 fmly) No smoking in 24 bedrooms **FACILITIES:** Indoor swimming (H) Sauna Solarium Gym Jacuzzi **CONF:** Thtr 70 Class 30 Board 30 **PARKING:** 200 **NOTES:** No dogs (ex guide dogs) **CARDS:**

⇧ Express by Holiday Inn Swindon West

Frankland Rd, Blagrove SN5 8UD
☎ 01793 818800 ▯ 01793 818888
e-mail: swindon@expressbyholidayinn.net
Dir: *M4 junct 16, follow signs for Swindon (A3102),1st left after rdbt*

A modern hotel ideal for families and business travellers. Fresh and uncomplicated, the spacious bedrooms include Sky TV, power shower and tea and coffee-making facilities. Continental buffet breakfast is included in the room rate; other meals may be taken at the nearby family pub or restaurant. For further details and the Express by Holiday Inn phone number, consult the Hotel Groups pages.
ROOMS: 121 en suite s £49.95-£74.95; d £49.95-£74.95 (incl. cont bkfst) **CONF:** Thtr 50 Class 40 Board 30 Del from £106

⇧ Hotel Ibis Swindon

Delta Business Park, Great Western Way SN5 7XG
☎ 01793 514777 ▯ 01793 514570
e-mail: H1041@accor-hotels.com
Dir: *A3102 to Swindon, straight over rdbt, slip road onto Delta Business Park and turn left*
Modern, budget hotel offering comfortable accommodation in bright and practical bedrooms. Breakfast is self-service and dinner is available in the restaurant. For further details, consult the Hotel Groups page.
ROOMS: 120 en suite s £29.95-£43.95; d £29.95-£43.95

⇧ Premier Lodge (Swindon)

Ermin St, Blunsdon SN26 8DJ
☎ 0870 9906356 ▯ 0870 9906357
Premier Lodge offers modern, well-equipped, en suite accommodation suitable for both business and leisure travellers. Meals can be taken at the adjacent popular restaurant and bar, which is fully licensed. For further details, consult the Hotel Groups page.
ROOMS: 60 en suite s £48; d £48

⇧ Travel Inn

Lydiard Way, Great Western Way SN5 8UY
☎ 08701 977247 ▯ 01793 886890
Dir: *M4 junct 16, 3m SW of Swindon, left lane towards Swindon, A3102*
Travel Inn offers good-quality, value-for-money accommodation. Spacious, en suite rooms with bath and shower comfortably accommodate a family of up to two adults and two children (to age 15). The restaurant and bar offers a varied menu. For further details and the Travel Inn phone number, consult the Hotel Groups page.
ROOMS: 63 en suite s £44.95; d £44.95

S

SWINTON, Greater Manchester Map 15 SD70

⇧ Premier Lodge (Manchester West)

East Lancs Rd M27 0AA

☎ 0870 9906480 📠 0870 9906481

Premier Lodge offers modern, well-equipped, en suite accommodation suitable for both business and leisure travellers. Meals can be taken at the adjacent popular restaurant and bar, which is fully licensed. For further details, consult the Hotel Groups page.

ROOMS: 27 en suite s £48; d £48

SYMONDS YAT (EAST), Herefordshire Map 10 SO51

★★66% *Saracens Head*

HR9 6JL

☎ 01600 890435 📠 01600 890034

e-mail: bookings@saracenshead.com

Dir: *A40 Monmouth/Ross-on-Wye, turn at Little Chef, signed Goodrich & Symonds. 0.5m turn right, 1m right by River Wye to hotel*

Dating from the 16th century, this family-run hotel faces onto the River Wye and enjoys lovely views. Bedrooms are well equipped and sympathetically decorated in a cottage style. There is also a separate cosy residents' lounge, an attractive dining room and an atmospheric and popular public bar.

ROOMS: 9 en suite (1 fmly) **FACILITIES:** Fishing Canoeing Mountain bike hire Walking Climbing Horse riding **PARKING:** 15 **NOTES:** No dogs (ex guide dogs) No smoking in restaurant **CARDS:**

TADCASTER, North Yorkshire Map 16 SE44

★★★80% Hazlewood Castle

Paradise Ln, Hazlewood LS24 9NJ

☎ 01937 535353 📠 01937 530630

e-mail: info@hazlewood-castle.co.uk

Dir: *signed off A64, W of Tadcaster & before A1/M1 link road*

Mentioned in the Domesday Book, this castle is set in 77 acres of parkland. Hospitality and service are of the highest order and staff are only too happy to assist. Bedrooms, many of them with private sitting rooms, are split between the main house and other buildings in the courtyard. Dinner provides the highlight of any stay with eclectic, creative dishes.

ROOMS: 9 en suite 12 annexe en suite s £110-£195; d £130-£300 (incl. bkfst) **LB FACILITIES:** STV Croquet lawn Clay pigeon shooting Xmas **CONF:** Thtr 160 Class 60 Board 36 Del from £170 **PARKING:** 150 **NOTES:** No dogs (ex guide dogs) No smoking in restaurant Civ Wed 120 **CARDS:**

Town House Hotel
Country House Hotel
⇧ Travel Accommodation

TADWORTH, Surrey Map 06 TQ25

⇧ Premier Lodge (Epsom South)

Brighton Rd, Burgh Heath KT20 6BW

☎ 0870 9906442 📠 0870 9906443

Premier Lodge offers modern, well-equipped, en suite accommodation suitable for both business and leisure travellers. Meals can be taken at the adjacent popular restaurant and bar, which is fully licensed. For further details, consult the Hotel Groups page.

ROOMS: 78 en suite s £56; d £56

TALKE, Staffordshire Map 15 SJ85

⇧ Travelodge Stoke

Newcastle Rd ST7 1UP

☎ 08700 850 950 📠 01782 777000

Dir: *at junct of A34/A500*

Travelodge offers good quality, good value, modern accommodation. Ideal for families, the spacious, en suite bedrooms include remote-control TV, tea and coffee-making facilities, luxury beds and free morning newspaper. Meals can be taken at the nearby family restaurant. For further details and the Travelodge phone number, consult the Hotel Groups page.

ROOMS: 62 en suite s fr £42.95; d fr £42.95 **CONF:** Thtr 50 Class 25 Board 32

TAMWORTH, Staffordshire Map 10 SK20

★★74% *Drayton Court Hotel*

65 Coleshill St, Fazeley B78 3RG

☎ 01827 285805 📠 01827 284842

e-mail: draytoncthotel@yahoo.co.uk

Dir: *M42 junct 9 then A446 to Litchfield at next rdbt turn right onto A4091 after 2m Drayton Manor Park on left hotel further along on right*

Conveniently located close to the M42, this lovingly restored hotel has been considerably upgraded. The bedrooms are elegant and have been thoughtfully equipped to suit both business and leisure guests. Beds are particularly comfortable (a hand-made four poster is also available). Public areas include a panelled bar, a relaxing lounge and an attractive restaurant.

ROOMS: 19 en suite (3 fmly) **CONF:** Board 12 **PARKING:** 22 **NOTES:** No dogs (ex guide dogs) No smoking in restaurant Closed 24-27 Dec **CARDS:**

See advert under BIRMINGHAM (NATIONAL EXHIBITION CENTRE)

★★65% Globe Inn

Lower Gungate B79 7AW

☎ 01827 60455 📠 01827 63575

Dir: *follow signs Lower Gungate, car park & shops. Hotel by car park*

Located in the centre of Tamworth, this popular inn provides well-equipped and pleasantly decorated accommodation. The

continued

refurbished public areas feature a spacious lounge bar and a relaxed dining area where a varied selection of dishes is available. There is also a function room available and adjacent parking.
ROOMS: 18 en suite (2 fmly) No smoking in 2 bedrooms d £45 (incl. bkfst) **LB** **FACILITIES:** STV entertainment Xmas **CONF:** Class 90 Board 90 **NOTES:** No dogs (ex guide dogs) No smoking in restaurant
CARDS:

Travel Inn

Bonehill Rd, Bitterscote B78 3HQ
☎ 08701 977248 01827 310420
Dir: *M42 junct 10 follow A5 towards Tamworth. After 3m turn left onto A51. Straight over 1st rdbt, 3rd exit off next rdbt*
Travel Inn offers good-quality, value-for-money accommodation. Spacious, en suite rooms with bath and shower comfortably accommodate a family of up to two adults and two children (to age 15). The restaurant and bar offers a varied menu. For further details and the Travel Inn phone number, consult the Hotel Groups page.
ROOMS: 58 en suite s £44.95; d £44.95 **CONF:** Thtr 50 Board 20

Travelodge

Green Ln B77 5PS
☎ 08700 850 950 0800 850950 01525 878450
Dir: *A5/M42 junct 10*
Travelodge offers good quality, good value, modern accommodation. Ideal for families, the spacious, en suite bedrooms include remote-control TV, tea and coffee-making facilities, luxury beds and free morning newspaper. Meals can be taken at the nearby family restaurant. For further details and the Travelodge phone number, consult the Hotel Groups page.
ROOMS: 62 en suite s fr £42.95; d fr £42.95

TANKERSLEY, South Yorkshire

Map 16 SK39

★★★★71% Tankersley Manor

Church Ln S75 3DQ
☎ 01226 744700 01226 745405
e-mail: tankersley@marstonhotels.com
Dir: *M1 junct 36 take A61 Sheffield road. Hotel 0.5m on left*
High on the moors with views over the surrounding countryside, this 17th-century residence is well located for major cities, tourist attractions and motorway links. Where appropriate, bedrooms retain original features such as exposed beams or Yorkshire stone windowsills. The hotel has its own traditional country pub, complete with old beams and open fires, alongside the more formal restaurant and bar.
ROOMS: 69 en suite (2 fmly) No smoking in 63 bedrooms s fr £94; d fr £117 **LB** **FACILITIES:** STV Special rates at local gym Xmas **CONF:** Thtr 400 Class 200 Board 100 Del from £140 **PARKING:** 300 **NOTES:** No smoking in restaurant Civ Wed 120
CARDS:

Travel Inn (Sheffield Barnsley)

Maple Rd S75 3DL
☎ 08701 977228 01226 741524
Dir: *M1junct 35A (northbound exit only) follow A616 for 2m. From junct 36 take A61 towards Sheffield*
Travel Inn offers good-quality, value-for-money accommodation. Spacious, en suite rooms with bath and shower comfortably accommodate a family of up to two adults and two children (to age 15). The restaurant and bar offers a varied menu. For further details and the Travel Inn phone number, consult the Hotel Groups page.
ROOMS: 42 en suite s £44.95; d £44.95

TAPLOW, Buckinghamshire

Map 06 SU98

Top 200 - Hotel

★★★★★ Cliveden

SL6 0JF
☎ 01628 668561 01628 661837
e-mail: reservations@clivedenhouse.co.uk
Dir: *M4 junct 7, follow A4 towards Maidenhead for 1.5 miles, turn onto B476 towards Taplow, 2.5 miles, hotel on left*
This wonderful Stately Home stands at the top of a gravelled boulevard. Visitors are treated as house guests and staff recapture the tradition of fine hospitality. Bedrooms have a unique individual quality and style. Reception rooms enhance the timeless elegance of the house, and views from the Terrace Restaurant are delightful. For discreet, well-upholstered luxury, try Waldos where menus have innovation and flair. Exceptional leisure facilities include cruises along Cliveden Reach and massages in the Pavilion.
ROOMS: 39 en suite (8 GF) No smoking in 12 bedrooms s £250-£850; d £250-£850 (incl. bkfst) **LB** **FACILITIES:** STV Indoor swimming (H) Outdoor swimming (H) Tennis (hard) Squash Snooker Sauna Solarium Gym Croquet lawn Jacuzzi Full range of beauty treatments at the Pavilion Spa, 3 vintage launches entertainment ch fac Xmas **CONF:** Thtr 40 Board 24 Del from £382 **SERVICES:** Lift **PARKING:** 60 **NOTES:** No smoking in restaurant Civ Wed 60 **CARDS:**

★★★70% Taplow House Hotel

Berry Hill SL6 0DA
☎ 01628 670056 01628 773625
e-mail: taplow@wrensgroup.com
Dir: *off A4 onto Berry Hill, hotel 0.5m on right*

This elegant Georgian manor is set amid beautiful gardens and has been skilfully restored. Character public rooms are pleasing and include a number of air-conditioned conference rooms.

continued on p596

TAPLOW, continued

Comfortable bedrooms are individually decorated and furnished to a high standard.
ROOMS: 34 en suite (4 fmly) No smoking in all bedrooms **FACILITIES:** STV Croquet lawn Putting green ch fac **CONF:** Thtr 100 Class 45 Board 40 Del from £190 **SERVICES:** air con **PARKING:** 100 **NOTES:** No dogs (ex guide dogs) No smoking in restaurant Civ Wed 70 **CARDS:**

TARPORLEY, Cheshire

Map 15 SJ56

★★★70% Swan

50 High St CW6 0AG
☎ 01829 733838 01829 732932
***Dir:** M56 junct 10, follow A49 signposted Whitchurch*
Dating back to the 16th century, the Swan is situated in the heart of the village. Bedrooms, found in the main house and an adjacent converted coaching house, have been refurbished to a high standard. Public areas are full of charm and character and include a restaurant where guests can enjoy excellent cooking.
ROOMS: 10 en suite 6 annexe en suite (3 fmly) No smoking in all bedrooms s £52-£68; d £73-£100 (incl. bkfst) **FACILITIES:** Xmas **CONF:** Thtr 65 Class 40 Board 25 Del from £85 **PARKING:** 26 **NOTES:** No smoking in restaurant Closed 25 Dec evening **CARDS:**

★★★67% The Wild Boar

Whitchurch Rd, Beeston CW6 9NW
☎ 01829 260309 01829 261081
e-mail: wildboarpop@hotmail.com
***Dir:** A51 onto A49 to Whitchurch at Red Fox pub lights, hotel on left at brow of hill after about 1.5m*

This 17th-century, half timbered, hunting lodge has been extended over the years to create a smart, spacious hotel with comfortable bedrooms and stylish public areas. Guests can choose between the elegant Tower Restaurant or the more informal Stables Grill. The hotel is a popular venue for meetings, functions and weddings, boasting impressive conference facilities.
ROOMS: 37 en suite (20 fmly) No smoking in 23 bedrooms s £64.63-£88.13; d £94-£105.75 (incl. bkfst) **LB** **FACILITIES:** Golf 18 Putting green Xmas **CONF:** Thtr 100 Class 40 Board 40 Del £109 **PARKING:** 70 **NOTES:** No smoking in restaurant Civ Wed 100 **CARDS:**

★★★65% Willington Hall

Willington CW6 0NB
☎ 01829 752321 01829 752596
e-mail: enquiries@willingtonhall.co.uk
***Dir:** 3m NW off unclass road linking A51 & A54, at Clotton turn off A51 at Bulls Head, then follow signs*
Situated in 17 acres of parkland and built in 1829, this well furnished country house hotel offers spacious bedrooms, many with views over open countryside. Service is courteous and friendly and freshly prepared meals are offered in the dining room or adjacent bar and drawing room.
ROOMS: 10 en suite s fr £70; d fr £110 (incl. bkfst) **LB** **FACILITIES:** STV Fishing Riding Croquet lawn **CONF:** Thtr 160 Class 80 Board 50 Del £115 **PARKING:** 60 **NOTES:** Closed 25 & 26 Dec Civ Wed 70 **CARDS:**

TAUNTON, Somerset

Map 04 ST22

Top 200 - Hotel

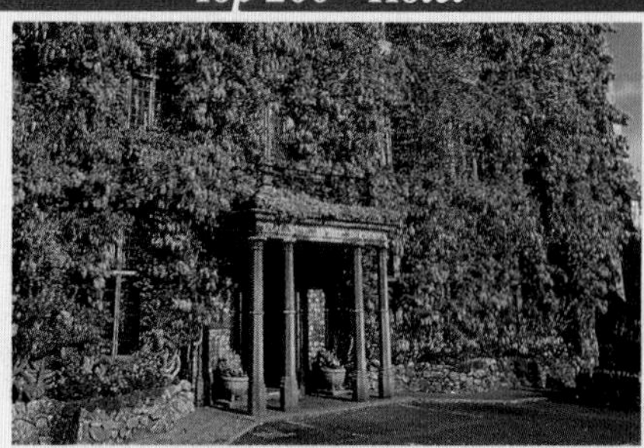

★★★ Castle

Castle Green TA1 1NF
☎ 01823 272671 01823 336066
e-mail: reception@the-castle-hotel.com
***Dir:** from M5 junct 25/26 follow town centre and hotel signs*
The wisteria covered Castle has been owned and run by the same family for over half a century and, with its Norman keep, is a landmark in the centre of the town. Much thought has gone into furnishing the bedrooms and public areas, ensuring guest comfort whilst retaining the character of the original building. Renowned for their interpretation of many classic British dishes in the restaurant, this hotel also offers a lively, modern brasserie for less formal dining.
ROOMS: 44 en suite No smoking in 4 bedrooms s £108-£175; d £165-£185 (incl. bkfst) **LB** **FACILITIES:** Xmas **CONF:** Thtr 100 Class 40 Board 40 Del from £160 **SERVICES:** Lift **PARKING:** 50 **NOTES:** No smoking in restaurant **CARDS:**

★★★73% Rumwell Manor

Best Western

Rumwell TA4 1EL
☎ 01823 461902 01823 254861
e-mail: reception@rumwellmanor.co.uk
***Dir:** M5 junct 26 follow signs to Wellington, turn right onto A38 to Taunton, hotel 3m on right*
With easy access to Taunton and the M5, Rumwell Manor is situated in the countryside. A selection of freshly prepared dishes is offered each evening in the candlelit restaurant. Bedrooms vary in size and style, with those in the main house offering greater space and character. In addition to the cosy bar and adjacent lounge, several meeting/conference rooms are available.
ROOMS: 10 en suite 10 annexe en suite (3 fmly) (6 GF) No smoking in 6 bedrooms s £63-£83; d £89-£125 **LB** **FACILITIES:** Xmas **CONF:** BC Thtr 40 Class 24 Board 26 Del from £114 **PARKING:** 40 **NOTES:** No smoking in restaurant Civ Wed 50 **CARDS:**

★★★72% ❀❀ The Mount Somerset

Lower Henlade TA3 5NB
☎ 01823 442500 📠 01823 442900
e-mail: Info@mountsomersethotel.co.uk
Dir: *M5 junct 25, take A358 towards Chard/Ilminster, at Henlade right into Stoke Rd, left at T-junct at end Stoke Rd then right into drive*

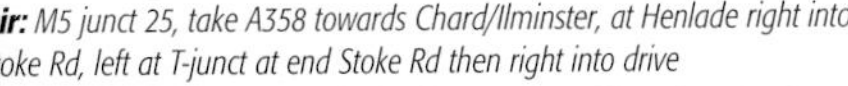

From its elevated and rural position, this impressive Regency house has wonderful views over Taunton Vale. Some of the well-appointed bedrooms have feature bathrooms and the elegant public rooms are stylish with an intimate atmosphere. In addition to the daily-changing, fixed-price menu, a carefully selected seasonal carte is also available in the restaurant.
ROOMS: 11 en suite (1 fmly) s £95-£105; d £135-£200 (incl. bkfst) **LB**
FACILITIES: Croquet lawn Arrangement with health club adjacent Xmas
CONF: Thtr 60 Class 30 Board 20 Del £155 **SERVICES:** Lift
PARKING: 100 **NOTES:** No dogs (ex guide dogs) Civ Wed 60
CARDS:

★★★70% Corner House Hotel

Park St TA1 4DQ
☎ 01823 284683 📠 01823 323464
e-mail: res@corner-house.co.uk
Dir: *0.3m from centre of Taunton (5 mins walk). Hotel on junct of Park Street & A38 Wellington Road*

The unusual Victorian façade of the Corner House, with its turrets and stained glass windows, belies a wealth of innovation, quality and style. Following a three-quarters of a million pound refit, contemporary bedrooms, equipped with state-of-the-art facilities still offer traditional comforts. Throughout the smart public areas, which include Bistro 4DQ - a relaxed place to eat good food - the combination of informality and exceptional value-for-money make this a perfect venue whether for business or leisure.
ROOMS: 28 en suite (12 fmly) (1 GF) No smoking in 20 bedrooms s £55-£63; d £55-£63 **CONF:** Thtr 60 Class 20 Board 35 Del from £99
PARKING: 40 **NOTES:** No dogs (ex guide dogs)
CARDS:

★★78% ❀ Farthings Hotel & Restaurant

Hatch Beauchamp TA3 6SG
☎ 01823 480664 📠 01823 481118
e-mail: farthing1@aol.com
Dir: *from A358, between Taunton and Ilminster turn into Hatch Beauchamp for hotel in village centre*

This delightful family run hotel, set in its own extensive gardens in a peaceful village location close to the M5, offers comfortable accommodation combined with all the character and charm of a building dating back over 200 years. The atmosphere is relaxed and friendly and innovative menus feature best quality local ingredients.
ROOMS: 10 en suite (2 fmly) (1 GF) No smoking in all bedrooms s £75-£90; d £105-£130 (incl. bkfst) **LB** **FACILITIES:** Xmas **CONF:** BC Thtr 30 Board 20 Del from £130 **PARKING:** 22 **NOTES:** No dogs (ex guide dogs) No smoking in restaurant Civ Wed 50
CARDS:

TAUNTON, continued

Holiday Inn Taunton

Deane Gate Av TA1 2UA
☎ 0870 400 9080 📠 01823 332266
Dir: adjacent to M5 junct 25
At the time of going to press, the classification for this hotel was not confirmed. Please refer to the AA internet site www.theAA.com for current information.
ROOMS: 99 en suite (68 fmly) No smoking in 55 bedrooms
FACILITIES: STV Indoor swimming (H) Sauna Solarium Gym Jacuzzi
CONF: Thtr 300 Class 110 Board 105 **SERVICES:** Lift **PARKING:** 300
NOTES: No dogs No smoking in restaurant Civ Wed
CARDS:

Express by Holiday Inn Taunton

Blackbrook Business Park, Blackbrook Park Av TA1 2PX
☎ 01823 624000 📠 01823 624024
e-mail: taunton@expressholidayinn.co.uk
Dir: M5 junct 25. Follow signs for Blackbrook Business Park. 100yds on right, just off rdbt at junct 25

A modern hotel ideal for families and business travellers. Fresh and uncomplicated, the spacious bedrooms include Sky TV, power shower and tea and coffee-making facilities. Continental buffet breakfast is included in the room rate; other meals may be taken at the nearby family pub or restaurant. For further details and the Express by Holiday Inn phone number, consult the Hotel Groups pages.
ROOMS: 92 en suite s £58-£65; d £58-£65 (incl. cont bkfst)
CONF: Thtr 35 Class 20 Board 24

Premier Lodge (Taunton)

Ilminster Rd, Ruishton TA3 5LU
☎ 0870 9906534 📠 0870 9906535
Premier Lodge offers modern, well-equipped, en suite accommodation suitable for both business and leisure travellers. Meals can be taken at the adjacent popular restaurant and bar, which is fully licensed. For further details, consult the Hotel Groups page.
ROOMS: 38 en suite s £48; d £48

Travel Inn

81 Bridgwater Rd TA1 2DU
☎ 08701 977249 📠 01823 322054
Dir: M5 junct 25 follow signs to Taunton over 1st rdbt & keep left at Creech Castle lights, Travel Inn 200yds on right
Travel Inn offers good-quality, value-for-money accommodation. Spacious, en suite rooms with bath and shower comfortably accommodate a family of up to two adults and two children (to age 15). The restaurant and bar offers a varied menu. For further details and the Travel Inn phone number, consult the Hotel Groups page.
ROOMS: 40 en suite s £44.95; d £44.95

Travelodge

Riverside Retail Park, Hankridge Farm TA1 2LR
☎ 08700 850 950
Dir: M5 junct 25
Travelodge offers good quality, good value, modern accommodation. Ideal for families, the spacious, en suite bedrooms include remote-control TV, tea and coffee-making facilities, luxury beds and free morning newspaper. Meals can be taken at the nearby family restaurant. For further details and the Travelodge phone number, consult the Hotel Groups page.
ROOMS: 48 en suite s fr £42.95; d fr £42.95

TAUNTON DEANE MOTORWAY SERVICE AREA (M5), Somerset — Map 04 ST1

Travel Inn

Trull TA3 7PF
☎ 08701 977250 📠 01823 338131
Dir: M5 southbound between junct 25 & 26
Travel Inn offers good-quality, value-for-money accommodation. Spacious, en suite rooms with bath and shower comfortably accommodate a family of up to two adults and two children (to age 15). The restaurant and bar offers a varied menu. For further details and the Travel Inn phone number, consult the Hotel Groups page.
ROOMS: 39 en suite s £44.95; d £44.95

TAVISTOCK, Devon — Map 03 SX4

★★★70% Bedford

1 Plymouth Rd PL19 8BB
☎ 01822 613221 📠 01822 618034
e-mail: jane@bedford-hotel.co.uk
Dir: M5 junct 31 - Launceston/Okehampton A30. Take A386 to Tavistock, follow town centre signs. Hotel opp church

Built on the site of a Benedictine abbey, this impressive castellated building has been welcoming visitors for over 200 years. Very much a local landmark, the hotel offers comfortable and relaxing public areas, all reflecting the charm and character which are hallmarks throughout. Bedrooms are traditionally styled with contemporary comforts, whilst the Woburn Restaurant provides a refined setting for enjoyable cuisine.
ROOMS: 30 en suite (1 fmly) No smoking in 11 bedrooms **CONF:** Thtr 70 Class 45 Board 25 **PARKING:** 45 **NOTES:** No smoking in restaurant
CARDS:

EBAY, Cumbria Map 18 NY60

★★★73% Westmorland Hotel & Bretherdale ɫestaurant

ɫrton CA10 3SB

015396 24351 015396 24354

-mail: sales@westmorlandhotel.com

***ir:** next to Westmorland's Tebay Services on M6, accessed from S'bound arriageway on road linking two service areas*

his modern, friendly hotel affords breathtaking views over the eautiful Cumbrian countryside. Spacious, open plan public areas re visually appealing and include a split-level restaurant where ɔcal produce features highly. Bedrooms, varying in style, are all omfortably appointed and particularly well equipped. Meetings nd conferences are well catered for.

ɫOOMS: 50 en suite (18 fmly) No smoking in 20 bedrooms s £51-£71; £61-£81 **LB FACILITIES:** STV Xmas **CONF:** BC Thtr 80 Class 40 oard 30 Del from £90 **SERVICES:** Lift **PARKING:** 100 **NOTES:** No moking in restaurant Civ Wed 100

ARDS:

See advert on this page

EES-SIDE AIRPORT, Co Durham Map 19 NZ31

★★★64% *The St George*

ʌiddleton St George, Darlington DL2 1RH

01325 332631 01325 333851

-mail: bookings@stgeorgehotel.net.

***ir:** turn off A67 by-pass directly into Airport grounds*

his former wartime officers' mess is conveniently situated within valking distance of the airport terminal. Bedrooms, most of which re spacious, are located in two wings. Public areas include a vell-stocked bar, with games room, and a comfortable restaurant. 'arious conference and meeting rooms are also available.

ɫOOMS: 59 en suite No smoking in 14 bedrooms **FACILITIES:** STV ɜauna Solarium **CONF:** Thtr 160 Class 60 Board 50 **PARKING:** 100 **NOTES:** Civ Wed 100 **CARDS:**

Express by Holiday Inn Middlesbrough

Express by Holiday Inn

ʌarton Rd TS4 3BS

01642 814444 01642 829999

-mail: ebhi-middlesboro@btconnect.com

***ir:** from A19 take A174 towards Whitby, then take A172 signed Middlesborough Centre. Hotel 1m on left*

A modern hotel ideal for families and business travellers. Fresh and uncomplicated, the spacious bedrooms include Sky TV, power shower and tea and coffee-making facilities. Continental buffet breakfast is included in the room rate; other meals may be taken at the nearby family pub or restaurant. For further details and the Express by Holiday Inn phone number, consult the Hotel Groups pages.

ROOMS: 74 en suite **CONF:** Thtr 30 Class 24 Board 16

TEIGNMOUTH, Devon Map 03 SX97

★★★70% Ness House

Ness Dr, Shaldon TQ14 0HP

01626 873480

e-mail: nesshouse@talk21.com

***Dir:** M5 take A380 then A381 to Teignmouth, cross bridge to Shaldon, hotel 0.5m on left on Torquay Rd*

Enjoying breathtaking views of the busy Teign Estuary, Ness House maintains much of its original charm. Friendly and attentive service is provided along with comfortable and well-equipped rooms; many boast balconies with sea views. A choice of dining in either the Terrace or Conservatory restaurants provides interesting dishes featuring fresh local produce and seafood from the Teign.

ROOMS: 7 en suite 5 annexe en suite (2 fmly) No smoking in all bedrooms s £50-£75; d £85 (incl. bkfst) **LB PARKING:** 20 **NOTES:** No smoking in restaurant Closed 24 & 25 Dec **CARDS:**

Popped the question?
Hotels with Civ Wed in their entry are licensed for civil wedding ceremonies. Maximum numbers for the ceremony only are shown, e.g. Civ Wed 120

T

TEIGNMOUTH, continued

Action for Blind People Hotel

Cliffden
Dawlish Rd TQ14 8TE
☎ 01626 770052 01626 770594
e-mail: cliffden_hotel@afbp.org
Dir: *From M5 junct 31 take A31 then A380. Then B3192 to Teignmouth. Down hill on Exeter Rd to lights, left to rdbt, left and follow Dawlish signs. Up hill and hotel next right*
This welcoming hotel is housed in a listed Victorian building set in six acres of delightful gardens overlooking a small valley. Bedrooms are comfortable, very spacious and thoughtfully equipped. The hotel caters for the specific needs of blind and partially sighted people, their friends, relatives, carers and guide dogs.
ROOMS: 48 en suite (4 fmly) (10 GF) No smoking in all bedrooms **FACILITIES:** STV Indoor swimming (H) Croquet lawn Putting green Outdoor chess, Pool table, Skittles, Indoor pool supervised entertainment Xmas **CONF:** Class 45 Board 30 **SERVICES:** Lift **PARKING:** 40 **NOTES:** No dogs (ex guide dogs) No smoking in restaurant **CARDS:**

TELFORD, Shropshire
Map 10 SJ60
See also Worfield

★★★★65% Buckatree Hall
The Wrekin, Wellington TF6 5AL
☎ 01952 641821 01952 247540
MACDONALD HOTELS
e-mail: res.buckatree@macdonald-hotels.co.uk
Dir: *M54 junct 7, turn left, at T-junct turn left, hotel 0.25m on left*
The name Buckatree means 'the well where deer drink'. Little wonder then that the hotel started life as a hunting lodge. The extensive wooded estates on the slopes of the Wrekin make for a peaceful retreat for business guests as well as a scenic wedding venue. Bedrooms are furnished and decorated in a traditional style and some have balconies.
ROOMS: 62 en suite (4 fmly) (12 GF) s £80-£99; d £110-£116 (incl. bkfst) **LB** **FACILITIES:** STV Xmas **CONF:** Thtr 200 Class 100 Board 50 Del from £95 **SERVICES:** Lift **PARKING:** 80 **NOTES:** No smoking in restaurant Civ Wed 200 **CARDS:**

★★★72% Valley
TF8 7DW
☎ 01952 432247 01952 432308
Best Western
e-mail: info@thevalleyhotel.co.uk
Dir: *M6, M54 junct 6 onto A5223 to Ironbridge*
This privately owned hotel is situated in attractive gardens, close to the famous iron bridge. It was once the home of the Maws family who manufactured ceramic tiles, and fine examples of their craft are found throughout the house. Bedrooms vary in size and are split between the main house and a mews development.
ROOMS: 35 en suite s £85-£105; d £95-£130 (incl. bkfst) **LB** **FACILITIES:** STV **CONF:** BC Thtr 200 Class 100 Board 60 Del from £120 **PARKING:** 100 **NOTES:** No dogs (ex guide dogs) No smoking in restaurant RS 24 Dec-1 Jan Civ Wed 200
CARDS:

★★★70% Clarion Hotel Madeley Court
Castlefields Way, Madeley TF7 5DW
☎ 01952 680068 01952 684275
Clarion Hotel BY CHOICE HOTELS
e-mail: admin@gb068.u-net.com
Dir: *M54 junct 4, A4169 Telford, A442 at 2nd rdbt signs for Kidderminster, continue (ignore sign to Madeley & Kidderminster), 1st left off rdbt*
This beautifully restored 16th-century manor house is set in extensive grounds and gardens. Bedrooms vary between character rooms and the newer annexe rooms. There are two wood panelled lounges and the restaurant is a mix of old stone walls with modern colour themes. Facilities include a large self-contained banqueting suite and a new conservatory.
ROOMS: 29 en suite 18 annexe en suite (1 fmly) (21 GF) No smoking in 16 bedrooms s £100-£110; d £130-£150 (incl. bkfst) **LB** **FACILITIES:** STV Archery,Horse riding arranged Xmas **CONF:** Thtr 175 Class 100 Board 45 Del from £120 **PARKING:** 180 **NOTES:** No smoking in restaurant Civ Wed 190 **CARDS:**

★★★64% *Telford Golf & Country Club*
Great Hay Dr, Sutton Heights TF7 4DT
☎ 01952 429977 01952 586602
e-mail: telfordcountryclub@corushotels.com
Dir: *M54 junct 4, A442 - Kidderminster, follow signs for Telford Golf Club*

A modern and much extended former farmhouse in an elevated situation. Comfortable bedrooms are located in several different wings, some have fine views of Ironbridge Gorge and others overlook the golf course. Guests can choose to dine in the brasserie or the more informal café. Extensive leisure facilities include the 18-hole golf course and large indoor swimming pool.
ROOMS: 96 en suite (16 fmly) No smoking in 36 bedrooms **FACILITIES: Spa** Indoor swimming (H) Golf 18 Squash Snooker Sauna Solarium Gym Putting green Jacuzzi Health & Beauty Golf driving range entertainment **CONF:** Thtr 250 Class 140 Board 60 **PARKING:** 200 **NOTES:** No smoking in restaurant Civ Wed 250
CARDS:

★★68% White House
Wellington Rd, Muxton TF2 8NG
☎ 01952 604276 & 603603 01952 670336
e-mail: james@whhotel.co.uk
Dir: *off A518 Telford-Stafford road*
The White House is a friendly, family-run hotel which provides well-equipped modern accommodation. The attractive public areas offer a choice of bars and a very pleasant restaurant, where a wide range of dishes is available. There is also a small lounge for residents, and a beer garden.
ROOMS: 31 en suite (3 fmly) s £50-£62.50; d £65-£80 (incl. bkfst) **LB** **CONF:** Board 10 **PARKING:** 100 **NOTES:** No smoking in restaurant
CARDS:

Travel Inn
Euston Way TF3 4LY
☎ 08701 977251 01952 290742
travel inn
Dir: *M54 junct 5 follow signs for central railway station (A442). Travel Inn at 2nd rdbt, 2nd exit*
Travel Inn offers good-quality, value-for-money accommodation. Spacious, en suite rooms with bath and shower comfortably accommodate a family of up to two adults and two children (to age 15). The restaurant and bar offers a varied menu. For further details and the Travel Inn phone number, consult the Hotel Groups page.
ROOMS: 60 en suite s £44.95; d £44.95 **CONF:** Thtr 30 Board 20

⌂ Travelodge

Whitchurch Dr, Shawbirch TF1 3QA
☎ 08700 850 950 ▤ 01952 251244
Dir: *1m NW, on A5223*
Travelodge offers good quality, good value, modern accommodation. Ideal for families, the spacious, en suite bedrooms include remote-control TV, tea and coffee-making facilities, luxury beds and free morning newspaper. Meals can be taken at the nearby family restaurant. For further details and the Travelodge phone number, consult the Hotel Groups page.
ROOMS: 40 en suite s fr £42.95; d fr £42.95

TELFORD SERVICE AREA (M54), Shropshire — Map 10 SJ70

⌂ Days Inn Telford

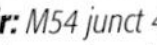

Telford Services, Priorslee Rd
☎ 01952 238400 ▤ 01952 238410
Dir: *M54 junct 4*
This modern building offers accommodation in smart, spacious and well-equipped bedrooms, suitable for families and business travellers, and all with en suite bathrooms. Continental breakfast is available and other refreshments may be taken at the nearby family restaurant. For further details and the Days Inn phone number, consult the Hotel Groups page.
ROOMS: 48 en suite d £35-£60

TEMPLE SOWERBY, Cumbria — Map 18 NY62

★★★75% Temple Sowerby House
CA10 1RZ
☎ 017683 61578 ▤ 017683 61958
e-mail: stay@temple-sowerby.com
Dir: *midway between Penrith and Appleby, 7m from M6 junct 40*
Set in the heart of the Eden Valley, this hotel is ideally placed for both the Pennines and Lake District. The original part of the building dates from the 16th century and was the principal house of the village. Stylish bedrooms are comfortable and include rooms with four-poster beds. There is a choice of lounges and a conservatory overlooking attractive landscaped gardens.
ROOMS: 9 en suite 4 annexe en suite (2 GF) No smoking in 6 bedrooms s £75; d £103-£125 (incl. bkfst) **LB FACILITIES:** Croquet lawn **CONF:** Thtr 30 Class 20 Board 20 Del from £125 **PARKING:** 15 **NOTES:** No smoking in restaurant Closed 24-27 Dec Civ Wed 40
CARDS:

TENBURY WELLS, Worcestershire — Map 10 SO56

★★67% Cadmore Lodge
Berrington Green, St Michaels WR15 8TQ
☎ 01584 810044 ▤ 01584 810044
e-mail: info@cadmorelodge.demon.co.uk
Dir: *Off A4112 for Berrington, hotel 0.75m on left*

Cadmore Lodge is situated in a secluded location on a 70-acre private estate that features a 9-hole golf course, two fishing lakes and indoor leisure facilities. The traditionally furnished bedrooms have modern amenities. A large function room with lake views is a popular venue for special occasions. The hotel is also earning itself a well-deserved reputation for its food.
ROOMS: 15 rms (14 en suite) (1 fmly) No smoking in all bedrooms s £45-£65; d £75-£115 (incl. bkfst) **LB FACILITIES:** Indoor swimming (H) Golf 9 Fishing Gym Jacuzzi Bowling green Steam room Nature reserve Xmas **CONF:** BC Thtr 100 Class 40 Board 20 Del from £76 **PARKING:** 100 **NOTES:** No dogs No smoking in restaurant Civ Wed 100
CARDS:

See advert on this page

Restaurant with Rooms

The Peacock Inn
Worcester Rd WR15 8LL
☎ 01584 810506 ▤ 01584 811236
e-mail: jvidler@rsbdial.co.uk
Dir: *on A456 from Worcester follow A443 to Tenbury Wells. Inn 1.25m E of Tenbury Wells*
A warm welcome can be expected from resident proprietors at this 14th-century roadside inn, which has a wealth of original features such as wood panelling, beams and low ceilings. The atmospheric bar and restaurant are popular locally and bedrooms are not only spacious and comfortable but are also usefully and thoughtfully equipped.
ROOMS: 3 en suite (1 GF) No smoking in all bedrooms s £55; d £70 (incl. bkfst) **LB PARKING:** 30 **NOTES:** No dogs
CARDS:

TEN

TENTERDEN, Kent Map 07 TQ83

★★★74% London Beach Hotel & Golf Club
Ashford Rd TN30 6SP
☎ 01580 766279 📠 01580 763884
e-mail: enquiries@londonbeach.com
Dir: *M20 junct 9, follow signs to Tenterden on A28, turn right after 0.5m, hotel after 1m*

Modern, purpose-built hotel situated amid mature landscaped grounds on the outskirts of Tenterden. The spacious bedrooms are smartly decorated, have co-ordinated soft furnishings and many thoughtful extras; most rooms have balconies with superb views over the golf course and putting green. The open-plan public rooms feature a brasserie style restaurant where an interesting choice of home-made dishes is served.

ROOMS: 26 en suite (16 fmly) No smoking in 22 bedrooms s £65-£105; d £95-£105 **LB** **FACILITIES:** STV Golf 9 Fishing Putting green Driving range, Pitch 'n' putt entertainment Xmas **CONF:** BC Thtr 200 Class 100 Board 40 Del from £135 **SERVICES:** Lift **PARKING:** 200 **NOTES:** No dogs No smoking in restaurant Civ Wed 200
CARDS:

TETBURY, Gloucestershire Map 04 ST89

Top 200 - Hotel

★★★ Calcot Manor
Calcot GL8 8YJ
☎ 01666 890391 📠 01666 890394
e-mail: reception@calcotmanor.co.uk
Dir: *3m W of Tetbury at junct A4135/A46*

Cistercian monks built the ancient barns and stables around this lovely English farmhouse. No two rooms are identical, and each is beautifully decorated in country-house style and equipped with the comforts of home. Sumptuous sitting rooms, with crackling log fires in the winter, look out over well-kept gardens. There are two dining options: the elegant conservatory restaurant and the informal Gumstool Inn. A superb health and leisure spa includes an indoor pool, high-tech gym, massage tables, complementary therapies and much more. For children, a crèche and 'playzone' have been provided.

ROOMS: 9 en suite 19 annexe en suite (10 fmly) s £140; d £165-£205 (incl. bkfst) **LB** **FACILITIES: Spa** Indoor swimming (H) Outdoor swimming (H) Sauna Solarium Gym Croquet lawn Jacuzzi Clay pigeon shooting ch fac Xmas **CONF:** BC Thtr 100 Class 24 Board 35 Del from £195 **PARKING:** 120 **NOTES:** No dogs (ex guide dogs) No smoking in restaurant Civ Wed 100
CARDS:

Top 200 - Hotel

★★★ *Close*
8 Long St GL8 8AQ
☎ 01666 502272 📠 01666 504401
e-mail: reception@theclosehotel.co.uk
Dir: *in the centre of Tetbury, from M4 junct 17 onto A429 to Malmesbury, for M5 junct 14 onto B4509 and follow signs to Tetbury*

The warm, country-house feel of The Close has been a favourite with many for years. Bedrooms are decorated and furnished with an air of luxury and include many thoughtful touches. The public rooms provide a range of relaxing areas with log fires in the winter. In the summer guests can enjoy the terrace in the lovely walled garden. The restaurant is the venue for some impressive and highly accomplished modern British cooking.

ROOMS: 15 en suite **FACILITIES:** STV Croquet lawn **CONF:** Thtr 50 Board 22 **PARKING:** 22 **NOTES:** No smoking in restaurant Civ Wed 50 **CARDS:**

★★★71% Snooty Fox
Market Place GL8 8DD
☎ 01666 502436 📠 01666 503479
e-mail: res@snooty-fox.co.uk
Dir: *in town centre*

The Snooty Fox is a popular venue for weekend breaks, and retains many of the historic features associated with a 16th-century coaching inn. The atmosphere is relaxed and friendly, the accommodation of a high standard, and the food, offered in both the bar and restaurant, is another reason why many guests return.

ROOMS: 12 en suite No smoking in 2 bedrooms s £73-£89; d £97-£175 (incl. bkfst) **LB** **FACILITIES:** Xmas **CONF:** Thtr 30 Board 15 Del from £112 **NOTES:** No dogs (ex guide dogs) No smoking in restaurant
CARDS:

See advert on opposite page

★★★69% Hare & Hounds
Westonbirt GL8 8QL
☎ 01666 880233 & 881000 📠 01666 880241
e-mail: hareandhoundswbt@aol.com
Dir: *2.5m SW of Tetbury on A433*

This popular hotel, in extensive grounds, is situated close to Westonbirt Arboretum and has been run by the same family for 50 years. Staff are keen to help and public areas are charming. Bedrooms are traditional in style and located in the main house and adjacent coach house.

ROOMS: 24 en suite 7 annexe en suite (3 fmly) (5 GF) No smoking in 12 bedrooms s fr £84; d fr £105 (incl. bkfst) **LB** **FACILITIES:** Tennis (hard) Squash Croquet lawn Putting green Table tennis Half size snooker table entertainment Xmas **CONF:** Thtr 120 Class 80 Board 40 Del from £115 **PARKING:** 85 **NOTES:** No smoking in restaurant Civ Wed 130
CARDS:

TEWKESBURY, Gloucestershire

Map 10 SO83

★★★69% The Tewkesbury Park Hotel Golf & Country Club

Lincoln Green Ln GL20 7DN
☎ 0870 609 6101 📠 01684 292386
e-mail: tewkesburypark@corushotels.com
Dir: *M5 junct 9/A438 through Tewkesbury, A38 (Abbey on left) right into Lincoln Green Ln before Esso Station*

Only two miles from the M5, this extended 18th-century manor house boasts wonderful views across the Malvern Hills from its hilltop position. Bedrooms offer contemporary comforts and many have the added bonus of countryside views. In addition to the well-established golf course, an indoor pool, gym, sauna, squash and tennis courts are also available.
ROOMS: 80 en suite (8 fmly) No smoking in 35 bedrooms s £145-£173; d £220-£276 (incl. bkfst & dinner) **LB FACILITIES: Spa** STV Indoor swimming (H) Golf 18 Tennis (hard) Squash Sauna Solarium Gym Putting green Activity field Xmas **CONF:** Thtr 150 Class 100 Board 50 Del £149 **PARKING:** 250 **NOTES:** No smoking in restaurant Civ Wed 100
CARDS:

★★★62% Royal Hop Pole

Church St GL20 5RT
☎ 01684 293236 📠 01684 296680
Dir: *M5 junct 9 for Tewkesbury approx 1.5m. At War Memorial rdbt, straight across, hotel on right*
This former coaching inn is within walking distance of historic Tewkesbury Abbey. As would be expected from a building with 14th-century origins, there is a wealth of original features including exposed beams and sloping floors. Bedrooms are located in the main house or the more recent garden wing and meals can be taken in the atmospheric restaurant or the locally popular bar.
ROOMS: 29 en suite (1 fmly) No smoking in 20 bedrooms s fr £94; d fr £128 (incl. bkfst & dinner) **FACILITIES:** All guests have use of facilities at Tewkesbury Park Hotel golf and country club Xmas **CONF:** Thtr 50 Board 20 Del from £125 **PARKING:** 35 **NOTES:** No dogs (ex guide dogs) No smoking in restaurant **CARDS:**

★★65% Bell

57 Church St GL20 5SA
☎ 01684 293293 📠 01684 295938
e-mail: 6408@greeneking.co.uk
Dir: *on A38 in town centre opposite Abbey*
This 14th-century, former coaching house is situated on the edge of the town, opposite the Norman Abbey. An atmospheric and friendly establishment, the bar and lounge are the focal point with a large open fire providing warmth. Bedrooms have been refurbished and offer good levels of comfort and quality with many extra facilities provided, such as CD players.
ROOMS: 24 en suite (1 fmly) No smoking in 5 bedrooms s fr £65; d fr £65 (incl. bkfst) **LB FACILITIES:** Xmas **CONF:** Thtr 50 Class 15 Board 20 Del from £80 **PARKING:** 35 **NOTES:** No dogs (ex guide dogs) No smoking in restaurant **CARDS:**

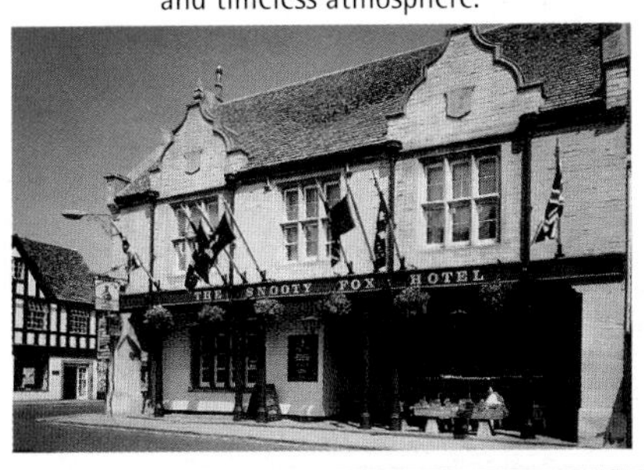

THAME, Oxfordshire

Map 05 SP70

★★★76% Spread Eagle

Cornmarket OX9 2BW
☎ 01844 213661 📠 01844 261380
e-mail: enquiries@spreadeaglehotel.fsnet.co.uk
Dir: *M40 junct 6 S, junct 8 N, town centre on A418 Oxford to Aylesbury Road*

A privately-owned former coaching inn, set on the main thoroughfare of this delightful market town. Well-equipped bedrooms vary in size and style, with some located in an extension. Public areas include a comfortable bar and the more formal Fothergills Restaurant, which is named after the diarist and raconteur who owned the hotel in the 1920s. The hotel offers an extensive range of banqueting facilities.
ROOMS: 33 en suite (1 fmly) s £100-£116.50; d £116.50-£137 (incl. bkfst) **LB FACILITIES:** Xmas **CONF:** Thtr 250 Class 100 Board 50 Del from £140 **PARKING:** 80 **NOTES:** No dogs (ex guide dogs) Civ Wed 200
CARDS:

THAME, continued

Travelodge

OX9 7XA
☎ 08700 850 950 🖷 01844 218740
Dir: *A418/B4011*
Travelodge offers good quality, good value, modern accommodation. Ideal for families, the spacious, en suite bedrooms include remote-control TV, tea and coffee-making facilities, luxury beds and free morning newspaper. Meals can be taken at the nearby family restaurant. For further details and the Travelodge phone number, consult the Hotel Groups page.
ROOMS: 31 en suite s fr £42.95; d fr £42.95

THETFORD, Norfolk — Map 13 TL88

See also Brandon (Suffolk)

★★65% The Thomas Paine Hotel

White Hart St IP24 1AA
☎ 01842 755631 🖷 01842 766505
e-mail: bookings@thomaspainehotel.com
Dir: *N on A11, at rdbt immediately before Thetford take A1075, hotel on right*
This Grade II listed building is believed to be the birthplace of Thomas Paine, who was a pioneer of democratic thinking. The property is situated close to the town centre and Thetford Forest Park is just a short drive away. Bedrooms vary in size and style and are all pleasantly decorated and thoughtfully equipped.
ROOMS: 13 en suite (1 fmly) s £50-£55; d £60-£66 (incl. bkfst) **LB** **FACILITIES:** Xmas **CONF:** Thtr 70 Class 35 Board 30 **PARKING:** 30 **NOTES:** No smoking in restaurant **CARDS:**

THIRSK, North Yorkshire — Map 19 SE48

★★72% Golden Fleece

42 Market Place YO7 1LL
☎ 01845 523108 🖷 01845 523996
e-mail: goldenfleece@bestwestern.co.uk
Dir: *off A19 at Thirsk turn off, to the town centre*
This delightful hotel began life as a coaching inn, and enjoys a central location in the market square. Bedrooms are comfortably furnished, extremely well equipped and individually styled with beautiful soft furnishings. Guests have a choice of casual dining in the attractive bar, or more formal dining in the smart restaurant.
ROOMS: 18 en suite (3 fmly) No smoking in 4 bedrooms s £58-£65; d £85-£105 (incl. bkfst) **LB** **FACILITIES:** STV Xmas **CONF:** Thtr 75 Class 20 Board 30 Del from £95 **PARKING:** 35 **NOTES:** No smoking in restaurant Civ Wed 85 **CARDS:**

THORNBURY, Gloucestershire — Map 04 ST69

Top 200 - Hotel

★★★ Thornbury Castle

Castle St BS35 1HH
☎ 01454 281182 🖷 01454 416188
e-mail: info@thornburycastle.co.uk
Dir: *from Bristol take A38 N, take 1st turn to Thornbury at end of High St left into Castle St, follow brown sign, entrance to Castle on left behind St Marys church*
Henry VIII beheaded Edward Stafford, the first owner of this castle. Guests today have the opportunity to sleep in historical surroundings with all modern amenities such as marble bathrooms and satellite TV; most rooms have four-poster or coronet beds and real fires. Tranquil lounges enjoy views over the gardens, while elegant, wood-panelled dining rooms make a memorable setting for a leisurely meal.

ROOMS: 26 en suite (3 fmly) **FACILITIES:** STV Snooker Croquet lawn Hot air ballooning Archery **CONF:** Thtr 90 Class 40 Board 30 **PARKING:** 40 **NOTES:** No smoking in restaurant Closed 4 days Jan Civ Wed 50 **CARDS:**

★★66% Thornbury Golf Lodge

Bristol Rd BS35 3XL
☎ 01454 281144 🖷 01454 281177
e-mail: info@thornburygc.co.uk
Dir: *M4/M5 junct take A38 N. At lights (Berkeley Vale Motors) take left. Entrance 1m on left*

The old farmhouse exterior of Thornbury Golf Lodge disguises a completely refurbished interior with spacious and comfortable bedrooms, all well equipped and attractively decorated. Many have pleasant views over the centre's two golf courses or towards the Severn Estuary. Meals are taken in the adjacent golf clubhouse which features a full bar and a range of food served all day.
ROOMS: 11 en suite (7 GF) s £49.50; d £57.50 **LB** **FACILITIES:** STV Golf 18 Putting green **CONF:** Thtr 100 Class 40 Board 40 **PARKING:** 150 **NOTES:** No dogs (ex guide dogs) No children 5yrs **CARDS:**

THORNE, South Yorkshire — Map 17 SE6

★★★64% Belmont

Horsefair Green DN8 5EE
☎ 01405 812320 🖷 01405 740508
e-mail: belmonthotel@aol.com
Dir: *M18 junct 6 A614 signed Thorne. Hotel on right of Market Place*
This privately owned, smartly appointed hotel enjoys a prime location in the centre of town. Bedrooms vary in size and style and are all extremely well equipped for both business and leisure guests. Public areas include the popular Belmont Bar offering a

continued

ood range of meals and snacks at both lunch and dinner, and the nore formal restaurant and cocktail bar.
OOMS: 23 en suite (3 fmly) (5 GF) No smoking in 5 bedrooms £67-£72; d £83-£105 (incl. bkfst) **LB FACILITIES:** STV Putting green ntertainment **CONF:** Thtr 60 Class 20 Board 25 Del from £56.50 **ARKING:** 30 **NOTES:** Closed 24-28 Dec, 1 Jan
ARDS:

HORNHAM, Norfolk Map 12 TF74

★★68% Lifeboat Inn
hip Ln PE36 6LT
☎ 01485 512236 01485 512323
-mail: reception@lifeboatinn.co.uk
ir: *follow coast road from Hunstanton A149 for approx 6m and take 1st eft after Thornham sign*
his 16th-century smugglers' alehouse enjoys superb views across pen meadows to Thornham Harbour. The attractive bedrooms re furnished with pine pieces and have many thoughtful touches. he public rooms have a wealth of character and feature open ireplaces and oak beams. A range of bar meals is available or uests can choose from the carte menu in the smart restaurant.
OOMS: 13 en suite (3 fmly) (1 GF) No smoking in all bedrooms £56-£70; d £72-£100 (incl. bkfst) **LB FACILITIES:** Xmas **CONF:** Thtr 0 Class 30 Board 30 **PARKING:** 120 **NOTES:** No smoking in restaurant
CARDS:

HORNTON HOUGH, Merseyside Map 15 SJ38

★★★★68% Thornton Hall

CLASSIC BRITISH

Neston Rd CH63 1JF
☎ 0151 336 3938 0151 336 7864
-mail: thorntonhallhotel@btinternet.com
Dir: *M53 junct 4 take B5151 onto B5136 to Thornton Hough*
Built in the mid 1800s for a wealthy shipping merchant, this ountry house hotel lies on the edge of the village in well-kept nature grounds. Public rooms include the Italian Restaurant with ts ornate oak carvings, leisure centre and bar area with views over the garden. Bedrooms are divided between those in the original house and the more modern extension.
ROOMS: 63 en suite (6 fmly) No smoking in 22 bedrooms s £99-£140; d £119-£160 **LB FACILITIES: Spa** STV Indoor swimming (H) Tennis (grass) Sauna Solarium Gym Croquet lawn Putting green Jacuzzi Hot ub Beauty Spa Hairdressing salon **CONF:** Thtr 200 Class 100 Board 60 **PARKING:** 250 **NOTES:** No smoking in restaurant Civ Wed 140
CARDS:

HORNTON WATLASS, North Yorkshire Map 19 SE28

★69% ***Buck Inn***
HG4 4AH
☎ 01677 422461 01677 422447
e-mail: buckwatlass@btconnect.com
Dir: *A684 towards Bedale, B6268 towards Masham, after 2m turn right at crossroads to Thornton Watlass, hotel by cricket green*
This traditional country inn is situated on the edge of the village green overlooking the cricket pitch. Cricket prints and old photographs are found throughout and an open fire in the bar adds to the warm and intimate atmosphere. Wholesome lunches and dinners are served in the bar or dining room from an extensive menu. Bedrooms are brightly decorated and well equipped.
ROOMS: 7 rms (5 en suite) (1 fmly) **FACILITIES:** Fishing Quoits Childrens play area entertainment ch fac **CONF:** Thtr 70 Class 40 Board 30 **PARKING:** 10 **NOTES:** No smoking in restaurant Closed 24 & 25 Dec for accommodation **CARDS:**

THORPE (DOVEDALE), Derbyshire Map 16 SK15

★★★75% Izaak Walton
DE6 2AY
☎ 01335 350555 01335 350539
e-mail: reception@izaakwaltonhotel.com
Dir: *A515 on B5054 to Thorpe village, over cattle grid & 2 small bridges, 1st right & sharp left*

This hotel is peacefully situated, with magnificent views over the valley of Dovedale to Thorpe Cloud. Many of the bedrooms have lovely views, and 'executive' rooms are particularly spacious. Meals are served in the bar area, with more formal dining in the Haddon restaurant. Staff are friendly and efficient. Fishing on the River Dove can be arranged.
ROOMS: 37 en suite (6 fmly) (7 GF) No smoking in 31 bedrooms **FACILITIES:** STV Fly fishing on nearby River Dove Xmas **CONF:** Thtr 50 Class 40 Board 30 Del £135 **PARKING:** 80 **NOTES:** No smoking in restaurant Civ Wed 80 **CARDS:**

See advert on this page

THORPE (DOVEDALE), continued

★★★68% The Peveril of the Peak
DE6 2AW
☎ 01335 350396 📠 01335 350507
e-mail: frontdesk@peverilofthepeak.co.uk
Dir: *M1 junct 25, A52 towards Ashbourne, A515 towards Buxton for 1m to Thorpe. From M6 junct 15/16, A50 to Stoke, A515 to Ashbourne & Thorpe*
Situated in the picturebook scenery of Dovedale, this hotel is named after one of Sir Walter Scott's heroic novels. Most of the bedrooms have doors opening on to the gardens, while the rest have individual patios. Some rooms have been adapted for less able guests. There is a cosy cocktail bar, a comfortable lounge and an attractive restaurant, which overlooks the extensive gardens. Conference and meeting rooms are also available.
ROOMS: 46 en suite (11 fmly) No smoking in 35 bedrooms s £50-£70; d £30-£40 (incl. bkfst) **LB** **FACILITIES:** STV ch fac Xmas **CONF:** Thtr 100 Class 50 Board 30 Del from £80 **PARKING:** 60 **NOTES:** No smoking in restaurant Civ Wed 110
CARDS:

THORPE-LE-SOKEN, Essex — Map 07 TM12

Restaurant with Rooms

The Olive Branch Brasserie, Bar & Rooms
High St CO16 0EA
☎ 01255 861199 📠 01255 860758
e-mail: p.wharrier@btopenworld.com
Dir: *from Colchester take A120, then A133 to Weeley, then B1033 to Thorpe-le-Soken*
This smartly maintained wine bar and brasserie is situated in the heart of the village. Contemporary-style bedrooms have light wood furniture, quality fabrics and hand-painted pictures of rural France. The open-plan Brasserie/wine bar has a convivial atmosphere with leather dining chairs, neatly clothed tables, plush sofas and modern artwork.
ROOMS: 4 en suite s fr £52.50; d fr £70 (incl. bkfst) **LB** **FACILITIES:** STV **PARKING:** 50 **NOTES:** No dogs No smoking in restaurant **CARDS:**

THORPE MARKET, Norfolk — Map 13 TG23

★★74% Elderton Lodge Hotel & Langtry Restaurant
Gunton Park NR11 8TZ
☎ 01263 833547 📠 01263 834673
e-mail: enquiries@eldertonlodge.co.uk
Dir: *at N Walsham take A149 towards Cromer, hotel 3m from North Walsham on left, just prior to entering Thorpe Market*

Ideally placed for touring the north Norfolk coastline, this delightful former shooting lodge is set amidst six acres of mature gardens adjacent to Gunton Hall estate. The individually decorated bedrooms are tastefully furnished and thoughtfully equipped. Public rooms include a smart lounge bar, an elegant restaurant and a sunny conservatory breakfast room.
ROOMS: 11 en suite (2 fmly) No smoking in all bedrooms s £60-£70; d £95-£115 (incl. bkfst) **LB** **FACILITIES:** Croquet lawn Xmas **CONF:** BC **PARKING:** 50 **NOTES:** No children 6yrs No smoking in restaurant Civ Wed 60 **CARDS:**

★★64% Green Farm Restaurant & Hotel
North Walsham Rd NR11 8TH
☎ 01263 833602 📠 01263 833163
e-mail: grfarmh@aol.com
Dir: *at Roughton turn right off A140 Norwich to Cromer road, beside fish and chip shop. 1.5m to 'Give Way' sign, turn right, hotel 200yds on left*
This attractive flint-faced, 16th-century inn has spacious bedrooms located in two courtyard-style wings adjacent to the main building each is tastefully furnished with pine pieces and has co-ordinated fabrics. Public rooms include a popular restaurant, a comfortable lounge bar, an informal dining area and a new function suite.
ROOMS: 5 en suite 9 annexe en suite (1 fmly) s £55-£60; d £70-£90 (incl. bkfst) **LB** **FACILITIES:** Xmas **CONF:** Thtr 50 Class 40 Board 100 **PARKING:** 50 **NOTES:** No smoking in restaurant
CARDS:

THRAPSTON, Northamptonshire — Map 11 SP9

Travelodge
Thrapston Bypass NN14 4UR
☎ 08700 850 950
Dir: *on A14 link road A1/M1*
Travelodge offers good quality, good value, modern accommodation. Ideal for families, the spacious, en suite bedrooms include remote-control TV, tea and coffee-making facilities, luxury beds and free morning newspaper. Meals can be taken at the nearby family restaurant. For further details and the Travelodge phone number, consult the Hotel Groups page.
ROOMS: 40 en suite s fr £42.95; d fr £42.95

THRUSSINGTON, Leicestershire — Map 11 SK6

Travelodge Leicester North
LE7 8TF
☎ 08700 850 950 📠 01664 424525
Dir: *on A46, southbound*
Travelodge offers good quality, good value, modern accommodation. Ideal for families, the spacious, en suite bedrooms include remote-control TV, tea and coffee-making facilities, luxury beds and free morning newspaper. Meals can be taken at the nearby family restaurant. For further details and the Travelodge phone number, consult the Hotel Groups page.
ROOMS: 32 en suite s fr £42.95; d fr £42.95

THURLESTONE, Devon — Map 03 SX6

★★★★72% *Thurlestone*
TQ7 3NN
☎ 01548 560382 📠 01548 561069
e-mail: enquiries@thurlestone.co.uk
Dir: *A38 take A384 into Totnes, A381 towards Kingsbridge, onto A379 towards Churchstow, onto B3197 turn into lane signed to Thurlestone*
This perennially popular hotel has been in the same family ownership since 1896. A range of indoor and outdoor leisure facilities provide something for everyone and wonderful views of the south Devon coast can be enjoyed from several vantage

continued

points, including many of the bedrooms, some of which also have balconies. Elegant public rooms are styled to ensure rest and relaxation.

ROOMS: 67 en suite (20 fmly) **FACILITIES: Spa** Indoor swimming (H) Outdoor swimming (H) Golf 9 Tennis (hard) Squash Snooker Sauna Solarium Gym Croquet lawn Putting green Jacuzzi Games rm Badminton Beauty fitness entertainment ch fac **CONF:** Thtr 140 Class 100 Board 40 **SERVICES:** Lift **PARKING:** 121 **NOTES:** No smoking in restaurant **CARDS:**

See advert under SALCOMBE

TIBSHELF MOTORWAY SERVICE AREA (M1), Derbyshire — Map 16 SK46

Travel Inn (Mansfield Tibshelf)

Tibshelf Motorway Service Area DE55 5TZ
☎ 08701 977181 ▤ 01773 876609
Dir: *M1 northbound between junct 28/29, access available southbound*

Travel Inn offers good-quality, value-for-money accommodation. Spacious, en suite rooms with bath and shower comfortably accommodate a family of up to two adults and two children (to age 15). The restaurant and bar offers a varied menu. For further details and the Travel Inn phone number, consult the Hotel Groups page.

ROOMS: 40 en suite s £44.95; d £44.95

TICEHURST, East Sussex — Map 06 TQ63

★★★★68% Dale Hill Hotel & Golf Club

TN5 7DQ
☎ 01580 200112 ▤ 01580 201249
e-mail: info@dalehill.co.uk
Dir: *M25 junct 5/A21. 5m after Lamberhurst turn right at lights onto B2087 to Flimwell. Hotel 1m on left*

Modern purpose-built hotel situated just off the A21 in the centre of the village. The extensive public rooms include a large lounge bar with plush seating, a conservatory brasserie, a formal restaurant and the Spike Bar, which is mainly frequented by golf club members and has a lively atmosphere. The hotel also has superb leisure facilities that include a swimming pool and an 18-hole golf course.

ROOMS: 35 en suite (8 fmly) (23 GF) No smoking in all bedrooms s £70-£140; d £100-£210 (incl. bkfst) **LB FACILITIES:** STV Indoor swimming (H) Golf 36 Sauna Gym Putting green Covered driving range, 2 putting greens, Pool table Xmas **CONF:** Thtr 55 Class 16 Board 25 Del from £140 **SERVICES:** Lift **PARKING:** 220 **NOTES:** No dogs (ex guide dogs) No smoking in restaurant Civ Wed 55
CARDS:

TINTAGEL, Cornwall & Isles of Scilly — Map 02 SX08

★★66% *The Wootons Country Hotel*

Fore St PL34 0DD
☎ 01840 770170 ▤ 01840 770978
Dir: *follow A30 sign for N Cornwall, then right onto A395. Right onto B3314, over x-rds onto B3263 to Tintagel*

This hotel enjoys glorious country views and offers well-equipped bedrooms. Located in the main street of this much visited village, the bar proves a popular venue for locals and visitors alike. An extensive range of bar meals is available, and a carte menu is offered in the restaurant.

ROOMS: 11 en suite **FACILITIES: Spa** Snooker ch fac **PARKING:** 35 **NOTES:** No dogs (ex guide dogs) **CARDS:**

★★65% Atlantic View

Treknow PL34 0EJ
☎ 01840 770221 ▤ 01840 770995
e-mail: atlantic-view@eclipse.co.uk
Dir: *B3263 to Tregatta, left into Treknow, hotel on road to Trebarwith Strand Beach*

Conveniently located for all the attractions of Tintagel, this family-run hotel has a wonderfully relaxed and welcoming atmosphere. Public areas include a bar, comfortable lounge, TV/games room and heated swimming pool. Bedrooms are generally spacious and some have the added advantage of distant sea views.

ROOMS: 9 en suite (1 fmly) No smoking in all bedrooms s £30-£36; d £60-£72 (incl. bkfst) **LB FACILITIES:** Indoor swimming (H) Indoor pool heated Apr-Oct **PARKING:** 10 **NOTES:** No dogs (ex guide dogs) No smoking in restaurant Closed Nov-Jan RS Feb-Mar
CARDS:

★★61% *Bossiney House*

Bossiney PL34 0AX
☎ 01840 770240 ▤ 01840 770501
e-mail: bossineyhh@eclipse.co.uk
Dir: *from A39 take B3263 into Tintagel, then Boscastle Rd, 0.5m to hotel on left*

This personally-run, friendly hotel is located on the outskirts of the picturesque coastal village. Set in the grounds, an attractive Scandinavian-style log cabin houses the majority of the leisure facilities, including a swimming pool. Public areas include a comfortable lounge and the convivial bar, which is a popular venue for pre-dinner drinks.

ROOMS: 19 en suite (1 fmly) **FACILITIES:** Indoor swimming (H) Sauna Solarium Putting green **PARKING:** 17 **NOTES:** No smoking in restaurant Closed Nov-Jan **CARDS:**

Town House Hotel
Country House Hotel
Travel Accommodation

T

TITCHWELL, Norfolk

Map 13 TF74

★★77% Titchwell Manor

PE31 8BB
☎ 01485 210221 01485 210104
e-mail: margaret@titchwellmanor.co.uk
Dir: *on A149 coast road between Brancaster and Thornham*

This delightful family-run hotel overlooks the marshes of the RSPB reserve. Ideally placed for touring the north Norfolk coastline, the hotel is a popular venue for golfers, bird watchers and walkers. Bedrooms are smartly appointed and have co-ordinated soft furnishings; some in the adjacent annexe have ground floor access. Smart public rooms include a lounge area, an informal bar and a conservatory restaurant that overlooks the walled garden. Imaginative menus feature quality local produce and fresh fish.
ROOMS: 8 en suite 7 annexe en suite (2 fmly) No smoking in 4 bedrooms s £35-£100; d £70-£110 (incl. bkfst) **LB FACILITIES:** ch fac Xmas **CONF:** Thtr 20 Class 35 Board 25 **PARKING:** 50 **NOTES:** No smoking in restaurant **CARDS:**

See advert under BURNHAM MARKET

★★72% Briarfields

Main St PE31 8BB
☎ 01485 210742 01485 210933
e-mail: briarfields@norfolk-hotels.co.uk
Dir: *A149 coastal road, hotel on left into village*

This delightful hotel is situated close to the RSPB reserve. Spacious bedrooms are attractively decorated and thoughtfully equipped; some rooms are in an adjacent building and ground floor rooms have private access. The open plan public rooms feature a range of eating areas that include a conservatory extension and a restaurant.
ROOMS: 4 en suite 17 annexe en suite (4 fmly) No smoking in 10 bedrooms s £45-£50; d £72-£90 (incl. bkfst) **LB FACILITIES:** Xmas **CONF:** Thtr 40 Class 20 Board 20 Del from £75 **PARKING:** 50 **NOTES:** No smoking in restaurant **CARDS:**

TIVERTON, Devon

Map 03 SS9

★★★67% Tiverton

Blundells Rd EX16 4DB
☎ 01884 256120 01884 258101
e-mail: sales@tivertonhotel.co.uk
Dir: *M5 junct 27, onto dual carriageway A361, Tiverton exit 7m W. Hotel next to business park*

Best Western

Conveniently situated on the outskirts of the town, with easy access to the M5, this comfortable hotel has a relaxed atmosphere. The spacious bedrooms are well equipped and decorated in a contemporary style. A formal dining option is offered in the Gallery Restaurant, while lighter snacks are served in the bar area. Room service is extensive, as is the range of conference facilities.
ROOMS: 70 en suite (10 fmly) No smoking in 54 bedrooms s £60; d £90 (incl. bkfst) **LB FACILITIES:** STV Xmas **CONF:** Thtr 300 Class 140 Board 70 Del £85 **PARKING:** 130 **NOTES:** No smoking in restaurant Civ Wed 170 **CARDS:**

TIVETSHALL ST MARY, Norfolk

Map 13 TM1

★★75% The Old Ram Coaching Inn

Ipswich Rd NR15 2DE
☎ 01379 676794 01379 608399
e-mail: theoldram@btinternet.com
Dir: *on A140 15m S of Norwich*

This busy 17th-century coaching inn was once a staging post on the Norwich to London run. The property has been sympathetically restored to retain many of its original features such as oak beams, fireplaces and exposed brickwork. The tastefully appointed bedrooms are split between the main building and a new wing; they include two split-level suites, and several modern executive rooms.
ROOMS: 11 en suite (1 fmly) s £49-£55; d £63-£73 **LB FACILITIES:** STV **CONF:** Thtr 20 Class 20 Board 20 Del £83.95 **PARKING:** 150 **NOTES:** No dogs (ex guide dogs) Closed 25 & 26 Dec **CARDS:**

> Late for dinner?
> Quality Standards mean that last orders for dinner vary according to star rating and should be no earlier than:
> ★★ 7.00pm ★★★ 8.00pm ★★★★ 9.00pm
> ★★★★★ 10.00pm

> Early start?
> Hotels at all star levels should provide in-room alarm clocks and/or alarm calls

T

TODDINGTON MOTORWAY SERVICE AREA (M1), Bedfordshire Map 11 TL02

Travelodge (Luton North)
LU5 6HR
☎ 08700 850 950 01525 878452
Dir: *M1 between juncts 11 & 12*
Travelodge offers good quality, good value, modern accommodation. Ideal for families, the spacious, en suite bedrooms include remote-control TV, tea and coffee-making facilities, luxury beds and free morning newspaper. Meals can be taken at the nearby family restaurant. For further details and the Travelodge phone number, consult the Hotel Groups page.
ROOMS: 66 en suite s fr £42.95; d fr £42.95

TOLLESHUNT KNIGHTS, Essex Map 07 TL91

★★★★73% Five Lakes Country House
Colchester Rd CM9 8HX
☎ 01621 868888 01621 869696
e-mail: enquiries@fivelakes.co.uk
Dir: *exit A12 at Great Braxted/Silver End, then follow the brown tourist board signs through Tiptree to Salcott and hotel*

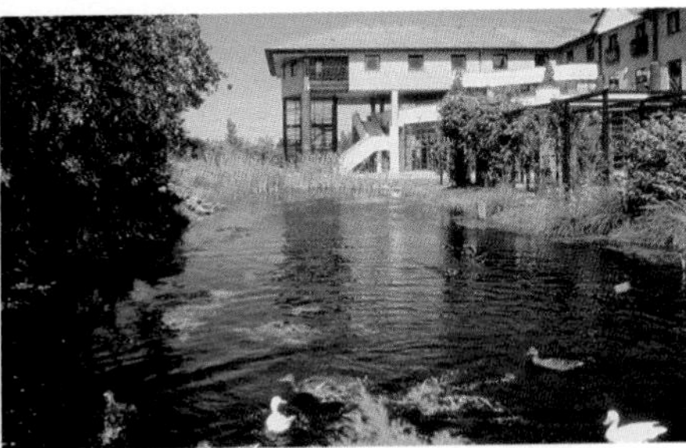

This hotel is set in 320 acres of open countryside, featuring two golf courses. The spacious bedrooms are finished to a high standard and have excellent facilities. The public rooms offer a high degree of comfort and include five bars, two restaurants and a large lounge. The property also boasts extensive leisure facilities.
ROOMS: 114 en suite 80 annexe en suite (4 fmly) (40 GF) No smoking in 14 bedrooms s £110; d £155-£225 **LB** **FACILITIES:** STV Indoor swimming (H) Golf 18 Tennis (hard) Squash Snooker Sauna Solarium Gym Putting green Jacuzzi Steam room Health & Beauty Spa Badminton Aerobics Studio Hairdresser Xmas **CONF:** Thtr 2000 Class 700 Board 50 Del £185 **SERVICES:** Lift **PARKING:** 500 **NOTES:** No smoking in restaurant Civ Wed 350 **CARDS:**

TONBRIDGE, Kent Map 06 TQ54

★★★64% Rose & Crown
125 High St TN9 1DD
☎ 01732 357966 01732 357194
e-mail: rose.crown@bestwestern.co.uk
Dir: *A21 to Hastings. Then take B245 through Hildenborough and on to Tonbridge. Right at 1st lights, over next set. Hotel on left*
Charming 15th-century coaching inn situated in the town, adjacent to the ruins of the old Norman castle. The hotel still retains much of its original character such as oak beams and Jacobean panelling.
continued

The bedrooms are tastefully decorated and well-equipped. The bar is equally popular with locals and residents.
ROOMS: 54 en suite (2 fmly) (10 GF) No smoking in 27 bedrooms s £60-£92; d £75-£124 (incl. bkfst) **LB** **FACILITIES:** STV Xmas **CONF:** Thtr 80 Class 30 Board 35 Del from £110 **PARKING:** 39 **NOTES:** No dogs (ex guide dogs) No smoking in restaurant Civ Wed 40 **CARDS:**

Premier Lodge (Tonbridge)
Pembury Rd TN11 0NA
☎ 0870 9906552 0870 9906553
Dir: *S off A21*
Premier Lodge offers modern, well-equipped, en suite accommodation suitable for both business and leisure travellers. Meals can be taken at the adjacent popular restaurant and bar, which is fully licensed. For further details, consult the Hotel Groups page.
ROOMS: 38 en suite s £50; d £50 **CONF:** Class 14 Board 14

TOPCLIFFE, North Yorkshire Map 19 SE37

★★66% The Angel Inn
Long St YO7 3RW
☎ 01845 577237 01845 578000
e-mail: mail@angelinn.co.uk
Dir: *turn off A168 (between A1(M) & A19) & Inn in town centre*

At the heart of Topcliffe, this attractive inn is very popular for its country-style cooking using high quality, local produce. Pleasant bars lead through to a fine water garden. The bedrooms are well equipped and comfortable. Staff are friendly, and wedding ceremonies can take place here.
ROOMS: 15 en suite (1 fmly) s £47.50-£52.50; d fr £65 (incl. bkfst) **LB** **FACILITIES:** STV **CONF:** Thtr 150 Class 60 Board 50 Del from £90 **PARKING:** 150 **NOTES:** No dogs (ex guide dogs) No smoking in restaurant Civ Wed 150 **CARDS:**

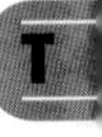

TORBAY See under Brixham, Paignton & Torquay

TORMARTON, Gloucestershire Map 04 ST77

★★70% Compass Inn
GL9 1JB
☎ 01454 218242 & 218577 01454 218741
e-mail: info@compass-inn.co.uk
Dir: *0.5m from M4 junct 18*
Dating from the 18th-century and once a coaching inn, this friendly and welcoming hostelry has grown considerably over the years. Bedrooms are spacious and well equipped, and public areas
continued on p610

TORMARTON, continued

include a choice of bars and varied dining options. A range of conference rooms also available.
ROOMS: 26 en suite (7 fmly) (12 GF) No smoking in 3 bedrooms s £79.50-£89.50; d £89.50-£99.50 **LB FACILITIES:** STV ch fac **CONF:** Thtr 100 Class 30 Board 34 Del from £99.50 **PARKING:** 160 **NOTES:** Closed 24-26 Dec Civ Wed 80
CARDS:

TORPOINT, Cornwall & Isles of Scilly Map 03 SX45

★★70% Whitsand Bay Hotel, Golf & Country Club

Portwrinkle PL11 3BU
☎ 01503 230276 01503 230329
e-mail: earlehotels@btconnect.com
Dir: *from A38 take A374 towards Torpoint. Follow signs for Crafthole then Portwinkle*

An imposing Victorian building with oak panelling, stained glass windows and a sweeping staircase. Bedrooms, many with superb sea views, include family rooms and a suite with a balcony. Facilities include an 18-hole, cliff-top golf course and indoor swimming pool. The fixed-price menu offers an interesting selection of dishes.
ROOMS: 39 rms (37 en suite) (15 fmly) s £55-£60; d £60-£120 (incl. bkfst) **LB FACILITIES:** Indoor swimming (H) Golf 18 Sauna Solarium Gym Putting green Beauty & hair salon Steam & Games room ch fac Xmas **CONF:** BC Thtr 100 Class 100 Board 40 Del from £50 **PARKING:** 60 **NOTES:** No smoking in restaurant Civ Wed 150
CARDS:

TORQUAY, Devon Map 03 SX96

★★★★★70% ® The Imperial

PARAMOUNT GROUP OF HOTELS

Park Hill Rd TQ1 2DG
☎ 01803 294301 01803 298293
e-mail: imperialtorquay@paramount-hotels.co.uk
Dir: *A380 towards seafront. Left to harbour, at clocktower turn right. Hotel 300yds on right*

This hotel has an enviable location with extensive views over the coastline. Traditional in style, public areas are elegant with choice of dining – TQ1 brasserie and the more formal Regatta Restaurant. Bedrooms are spacious, most with private balconies, and the hotel has an extensive range of indoor and outdoor leisure facilities.
ROOMS: 152 en suite (7 fmly) No smoking in 26 bedrooms s £65-£110; d £90-£210 (incl. bkfst) **LB FACILITIES:** STV Indoor swimming (H) Outdoor swimming (H) Tennis (hard) Squash Snooker Sauna Solarium Gym Jacuzzi Beauty salon Hairdresser entertainment ch fac Xmas **CONF:** BC Thtr 350 Class 200 Board 30 Del from £99 **SERVICES:** Lift **PARKING:** 140 **NOTES:** Civ Wed 200
CARDS:

★★★★71% Palace

Babbacombe Rd TQ1 3TG
☎ 01803 200200 01803 299899
e-mail: info@palacetorquay.co.uk
Dir: *towards harbour, left by clocktower into Babbacombe Rd, hotel on right after 1m*

Set in 25 acres of attractive and well-tended wooded grounds; the Palace offers a tranquil environment. Suitable for business or leisure, the hotel offers extensive facilities. Much of the original charm and grandeur has been maintained in the spacious public rooms, and particularly in the refurbished dining room. Bedrooms are smartly decorated and many have good views.
ROOMS: 141 en suite (20 fmly) No smoking in 18 bedrooms s £71-£96; d fr £142 (incl. bkfst) **LB FACILITIES:** STV Indoor swimming (H) Outdoor swimming (H) Golf 9 Tennis (hard) Squash Snooker Sauna Gym Croquet lawn Putting green Indoor pool supervised, Table tennis Xmas **CONF:** Thtr 1000 Class 800 Board 40 Del from £121 **SERVICES:** Lift **PARKING:** 180 **NOTES:** No dogs (ex guide dogs) No smoking in restaurant **CARDS:**

See advert on opposite page

★★★★66% ® The Osborne

THE INDEPENDENTS

Hesketh Crescent, Meadfoot TQ1 2LL
☎ 01803 213311 01803 296788
e-mail: enq@osborne-torquay.co.uk
Dir: *A380, then A3022 and turn left, then onto B379 to hotel*

The Osborne is almost hidden away in the tranquil Meadfoot Bay. The hotel has superb sea views and is set in five acres of grounds, which reach down to the beach; there are separate lounges and leisure facilities. Bedrooms, many with views of Tor Bay and some with balconies, are comfortably appointed. The adjacent brasserie serves food all day, while Langtry's Restaurant provides a more formal dining option.
ROOMS: 29 en suite (2 fmly) s £60-£78; d £120-£146 (incl. bkfst & dinner) **LB FACILITIES:** STV Indoor swimming (H) Outdoor swimming (H) Tennis (hard) Snooker Sauna Solarium Gym Putting green Xmas **CONF:** Thtr 80 Class 30 Board 30 Del from £91 **SERVICES:** Lift **PARKING:** 100 **NOTES:** No dogs (ex guide dogs) No smoking in restaurant Civ Wed 100 **CARDS:**

T

TORQUAY, continued

★★★★62% ® Grand Hotel
Sea Front TQ2 6NT
☎ 01803 296677 📠 01803 213462
e-mail: info@grandtorquay.co.uk
Dir: *A380 to Torquay. Right at seafront, then 1st right. Hotel on corner, entrance 1st left*

Within level walking distance of the town, this large Edwardian hotel overlooks the bay and offers modern facilities. Many of the bedrooms enjoy the best of the view and some have balconies; all are very well equipped. Boaters Bar also benefits from the hotel's stunning position and offers an informal alternative to the Gainsborough Restaurant.
ROOMS: 114 en suite (30 fmly) No smoking in 20 bedrooms s £65; d £150 (incl. bkfst) **LB** **FACILITIES:** STV Indoor swimming (H) Outdoor swimming (H) Tennis (hard) Snooker Sauna Solarium Gym Jacuzzi Hairdresser Beauty clinic entertainment ch fac Xmas **CONF:** Thtr 300 Class 130 Board 60 Del from £125 **SERVICES:** Lift **PARKING:** 25 **NOTES:** No smoking in restaurant Civ Wed 250
CARDS:

See advert on page 611

★★★81% ®® Orestone Manor Hotel & Restaurant
Rockhouse Ln, Maidencombe TQ1 4SX
☎ 01803 328098 📠 01803 328336
e-mail: enquiries@orestone.co.uk
Dir: *off A379,Torquay-Teignmouth road (formerly B3199)*

This country house hotel is located on the fringe of Torbay and is set in a spectacular location overlooking Lyme Bay. There is a colonial theme throughout the public areas, which are very charming and comfortable. Bedrooms are individually styled and all are spacious; some have balconies. The hotel's cuisine is highly-regarded and dishes are skilfully prepared.
ROOMS: 12 en suite (3 fmly) s £79-£129; d £109-£179 (incl. bkfst) **LB** **FACILITIES:** STV Outdoor swimming (H) Xmas **CONF:** Thtr 30 Class 20 Board 15 Del from £135 **PARKING:** 40 **NOTES:** No smoking in restaurant **CARDS:**

★★★73% ®® Corbyn Head Hotel & Orchid Restaurant
Torquay Rd, Sea Front, Livermead TQ2 6RH
☎ 01803 213611 📠 01803 296152
e-mail: info@corbynhead.com
Dir: *follow signs to Torquay seafront, turn right on seafront. Hotel on right*
The Corbyn Head has a prime position overlooking Tor Bay. Well-equipped bedrooms, many with sea views and some with balconies, offer a range of sizes. Staff are friendly and attentive, and a well-stocked bar and comfortable lounge are available. Guest can enjoy fine dining in the award-winning Orchid Restaurant or more traditional fare in the Harbour View restaurant.

ROOMS: 50 en suite (4 fmly) (9 GF) No smoking in 15 bedrooms s £52-£62; d £104-£124 (incl. bkfst) **LB** **FACILITIES:** Outdoor swimming Squash Snooker Sauna Solarium entertainment Xmas **CONF:** Thtr 30 Class 20 Board 20 **PARKING:** 50 **NOTES:** No smoking in restaurant
CARDS:

See advert on opposite page

★★★72% Toorak
Chestnut Av TQ2 5JS
☎ 01803 400400 📠 01803 400140
e-mail: toorak@tlh.co.uk
Dir: *opposite Riviera Conference Centre*
Forming part of a much larger complex, the Toorak Hotel offers excellent leisure facilities including indoor bowls, a cyber café and a magnificent indoor swimming pool. Bedrooms have modern facilities, and superior and standard rooms are available. There are several lounges to relax in.
ROOMS: 92 en suite (29 fmly) (20 GF) No smoking in 40 bedrooms s £49-£70; d £98-£126 (incl. bkfst) **LB** **FACILITIES:** Indoor swimming (H) Outdoor swimming (H) Tennis (hard) Snooker Sauna Solarium Croquet lawn Jacuzzi Childrens play area, Indoor Games Arena, Swimming Pool Supervised, Internet Cafe entertainment ch fac Xmas **CONF:** Thtr 220 Class 150 Board 60 Del from £65 **SERVICES:** Lift **PARKING:** 90 **NOTES:** No dogs (ex guide dogs) No smoking in restaurant
CARDS:

★★★71% Lincombe Hall
Meadfoot Rd TQ1 2JX
☎ 01803 213361 📠 01803 211485
e-mail: lincombehall@lineone.net
Dir: *along seafront past Princess Theatre towards harbour. At mini rdbt with clocktower, left, turn right at 1st lights. Hotel on left*
With views over Torquay, this hotel is conveniently close to the town centre and is set in five acres of gardens and grounds. Facilities include both indoor and outdoor swimming pools. The tastefully furnished bedrooms vary in size, and the Sutherland rooms are most spacious. There are comfortable lounges and Harleys restaurant offers a comprehensive choice of dishes.
ROOMS: 44 en suite (14 fmly) No smoking in 5 bedrooms s £60-£67; d £94-£117 (incl. bkfst & dinner) **LB** **FACILITIES:** STV Indoor swimming (H) Outdoor swimming (H) Tennis (hard) Putting green Jacuzzi Play area, Crazy golf entertainment Xmas **CONF:** Thtr 50 Class 30 Board 20 **PARKING:** 40 **NOTES:** No smoking in restaurant
CARDS:

Corbyn Head Hotel ☆☆☆

The Jewel in Torbay's Crown

- 3 STAR HOTEL & RESTAURANT WITH AA 2 ROSETTES
- SITUATED ON THE SEA FRONT
- REGENCY LOUNGE AND BAR WITH PANORAMIC SEA VIEWS
- 50 TASTEFULLY DECORATED EN SUITE ROOMS MANY WITH SEA VIEWS AND PRIVATE BALCONYS
- TEA AND COFFEE MAKING FACILITIES, TELEVISION, HAIR DRYERS, DIRECT DIAL TELEPHONES IN BEDROOMS
- OUTDOOR SWIMMING POOL AND SUN TERRACE
- SAUNA, SNOOKER TABLE AND SOLARIUM
- AMPLE FREE ON SITE PARKING

The Corbyn Head Hotel is the jewel in Torbay's crown. It has everything you could possibly wish for - the perfect hotel to compliment your holiday.

Our Gastronomic Orchid Restaurant holds a prestigious AA 2 Rosettes for culinary excellence.

This superb climate controlled restaurant is sure to leave a lasting impression providing you with a dining experience you will never forget.

Corbyn Head Hotel
Sea Front - Torquay
Devon - TQ2 6RH

TEL: 01803 213611
www.corbynhead.com
info@corbynhead.com

AA ★★★

Our Gastronomic Orchid Restaurant holds a prestigious AA 2 Rosettes

TORQUAY, continued

★★★71% Livermead Cliff

Torbay Rd TQ2 6RQ
☎ 01803 299666 📠 01803 294496
e-mail: enquiries@livermeadcliff.co.uk
Dir: *A379/A3022 to Torquay, through town centre, right towards Paignton. Hotel 600yds*

Situated at the water's edge this long-established hotel offers friendly and attentive service. The splendid views can be enjoyed from the lounge and dining room where carefully prepared dishes provide enjoyable dining. Bedrooms, many with sea views and some with balconies, are comfortable and well equipped and a range of sizes is available.

ROOMS: 67 en suite (21 fmly) s £39.50-£72.50; d £79-£145 (incl. bkfst) **LB FACILITIES:** Outdoor swimming (H) Fishing Solarium Sun terrace, Outdoor Pool supervised in summer entertainment Xmas **CONF:** Thtr 80 Class 35 Board 35 Del from £74.95 **SERVICES:** Lift **PARKING:** 92 **NOTES:** No smoking in restaurant **CARDS:**

★★★70% Livermead House

Torbay Rd TQ2 6QJ
☎ 01803 294361 📠 01803 200758
e-mail: stay@livermead.com
Dir: *from seafront follow A379 towards Paignton. Hotel opposite Institute Beach*

Having a splendid waterfront location, this hotel dates back to the 1820s and is where Charles Kingsley is said to have written *'The Water Babies'.* Bedrooms vary in size and style; excellent public rooms are popular for private parties and meetings and a range of leisure facilities is provided. Enjoyable cuisine is served in the impressively refurbished restaurant.

ROOMS: 67 en suite (6 fmly) (2 GF) No smoking in 12 bedrooms s £57-£68; d £114-£136 (incl. bkfst & dinner) **LB FACILITIES:** Outdoor swimming (H) Squash Snooker Sauna Solarium Gym entertainment Xmas **CONF:** Thtr 320 Class 175 Board 80 Del from £48 **SERVICES:** Lift **PARKING:** 131 **NOTES:** No smoking in restaurant **CARDS:**

See advert on opposite page

★★★68% Belgrave

Seafront TQ2 5HE
☎ 01803 296666 📠 01803 211308
e-mail: info@belgrave-hotel.co.uk
Dir: *A380 to Torquay, to lights with Torre Station on right. Right into Avenue Rd to Kings Drive. Left at seafront, hotel at lights*

Enjoying an impressive position overlooking Tor Bay, the Belgrave has now refurbished much of its public rooms, which include a stylish lounge and traditional dining in the restaurant. The new Dickens bar is particularly stylish, and offers an innovative menu which features local produce. Many of the bedrooms have also been refurbished, and have stunning sea views.

ROOMS: 70 en suite (18 fmly) (18 GF) No smoking in 20 bedrooms s £49-£95; d £98-£130 (incl. bkfst) **LB FACILITIES:** Outdoor swimming entertainment Xmas **CONF:** BC Thtr 200 Class 100 Board 60 Del from £62 **SERVICES:** Lift **PARKING:** 100 **NOTES:** No smoking in restaurant **CARDS:**

★★★67% The Grosvenor

Belgrave Rd TQ2 5HG
☎ 01803 294373 📠 01803 291032
e-mail: enquiries@grosvenor-torquay.co.uk
Dir: *just off main beach/seafront road*

Offering spacious and attractively furnished bedrooms, the Grosvenor Hotel is situated close to the seafront and the main attractions of the bay. Guests can choose to dine in the restaurant, coffee shop or Mima's Bistro. Many leisure facilities are available.

ROOMS: 46 en suite (8 fmly) s £48-£82; d £96-£164 (incl. bkfst) **LB FACILITIES: Spa** STV Indoor swimming (H) Outdoor swimming (H) Tennis Sauna Solarium Gym Jacuzzi Mini snooker table Library entertainment Xmas **CONF:** Thtr 150 Class 100 Board 40 Del from £60 **PARKING:** 50 **NOTES:** No dogs (ex guide dogs) No smoking in restaurant **CARDS:**

See advert on page 617

★★★61% Rainbow International

Belgrave Rd TQ2 5HJ
☎ 01803 213232 📠 01803 212925
e-mail: raven2@supanet.com
Dir: *close to harbour*

This large hotel is located within easy walking distance of the seafront. Bedrooms vary in size and shape; many family rooms are available. An all day café-bar is open to both residents and non-residents, providing an informal relaxed eating option. Entertainment is provided every evening in the nightclub.

ROOMS: 134 en suite (70 fmly) s £30-£75; d £60-£150 (incl. bkfst) **LB FACILITIES:** Indoor swimming (H) Outdoor swimming (H) Solarium Gym entertainment Xmas **CONF:** Thtr 500 Class 250 Board 80 Del from £47.50 **SERVICES:** Lift **NOTES:** No smoking in restaurant **CARDS:**

★★★59% *Kistor Hotel*

Belgrave Rd TQ2 5HF
☎ 01803 212632 📠 01803 293219
e-mail: kistorhotel@hotmail.com
Dir: *A380 to Torquay, hotel at junct of Belgrave Rd and promenade*

Within a short stroll of Torquay's many amenities and the promenade, the Kistor is conveniently located. Popular with groups, the hotel offers a relaxing and informal base for guests. Most bedrooms have sea views. In the restaurant, a fixed-price menu offers good, straightforward cooking.

ROOMS: 50 en suite (14 fmly) **FACILITIES:** Indoor swimming (H) Sauna Putting green Childrens play area entertainment **CONF:** Thtr 80 Class 30 Board 40 **SERVICES:** Lift **PARKING:** 40 **NOTES:** No smoking in restaurant **CARDS:**

★★74% Albaston House

27 St Marychurch Rd TQ1 3JF
☎ 01803 296758 📠 01803 211509

Many guests return to this friendly, family run hotel where hospitality is genuine and welcoming. Situated close to the town centre and also convenient for the more quieter attractions of Babbacombe, the Albaston also has some parking available.

continued on p616

The Country House by the Sea

The Livermead House is a hotel unlike any other. Situated directly on Torquay's beautiful sea front, this hotel will meet your every need. Our careful attention to detail and friendly atmosphere making every guest feel relaxed and longing to return to this comfortable Country House by the Sea.

The Livermead House

★★★

Highly competitive rates
•
1800sq ft conference area
•
Large meeting rooms & lounges
•
Very large car park
•
Easy access, sea front position
•
3 bars including cocktail bar
•
Deluxe bedrooms available
•
Restaurant with sea views
•
Extensive menu
•
Heated outdoor pool & sun terrace
•
67 fully en-suite rooms, many with sea views
•
All rooms with tea/coffee, radio, television, direct dial telephone & hair dryer

AA ★★★

Telephone: 01803 294361
Fax: 01803 200758

www.livermead.com - E-mail: info@livermead.com

The Livermead House Hotel - Sea Front - Torquay - Devon - TQ2 6QJ

T

TORQUAY, continued

Standards are high throughout with both public areas and bedrooms reflecting a combination of comfort and quality.
ROOMS: 13 en suite (4 fmly) s fr £36; d fr £68 (incl. bkfst) **LB** **PARKING:** 12 **NOTES:** No smoking in restaurant Closed Jan **CARDS:**

★★72% ***Bute Court***
Belgrave Rd TQ2 5HQ
☎ 01803 293771 🖷 01803 213429
e-mail: stay@butecourthotel.co.uk
Dir: *A380 to Torquay, to lights, right past police station, straight on at lights, hotel 200yds on right*
This popular hotel is only a short, level walk from the seafront. Comfortably furnished with modern facilities, the refurbished bedrooms benefit from some helpful extras. Spacious public rooms, evening entertainment and leisure facilities are all added attractions.
ROOMS: 45 en suite (10 fmly) **FACILITIES:** Outdoor swimming (H) Snooker Table tennis Darts billiards **CONF:** Class 40 **SERVICES:** Lift **PARKING:** 37 **CARDS:**

★★71% **Rawlyn House**
Rawlyn Rd, Chelston TQ2 6PL
☎ 01803 605208 🖷 01803 607040
e-mail: shirley@rawlynhousehotel.co.uk
Dir: *A380 to Torquay, follow seafront signs, right at Halfords lights to Avenue Rd, at 2nd lights right to Walnut Rd, left to Old Mill Rd, then sharp right at top of hill*
Quietly located close to Cockington village and within easy reach of the centre, this friendly, family-run hotel is set in well-tended grounds. Bedrooms are individual in style and offer all the expected facilities, with some rooms located on the ground floor. Dinner features freshly cooked dishes and residents can take a snack lunch around the pool or in the bar.
ROOMS: 12 rms (11 en suite) 2 annexe en suite (1 fmly) (2 GF) No smoking in all bedrooms s £33-£37; d £66-£74 (incl. bkfst) **LB** **FACILITIES:** Outdoor swimming (H) Badminton Table tennis **PARKING:** 16 **NOTES:** No dogs No smoking in restaurant Closed Nov-Apr **CARDS:**

★★70% **Carlton**
Falkland Rd TQ2 5JJ
☎ 01803 400300 🖷 01803 400130
e-mail: carlton@tlh.co.uk
Dir: *A380 to Torquay, follow signs to seafront. At lights on Belgrave Rd, turn right into Falkland Rd, hotel 100yds on left*
Conveniently located close to the town centre, beaches and other amenities, this smart hotel is suitable for either a leisure break or for the business guest. Providing an extensive range of business and leisure facilities, which are shared with other hotels in this small group complex, the Carlton also offers comfortable and well-equipped bedrooms, some with sea views. Regular entertainment is staged in the spacious ballroom and bar.
ROOMS: 47 en suite (26 fmly) No smoking in 18 bedrooms s £39-£87; d £78-£144 (incl. bkfst & dinner) **LB** **FACILITIES: Spa** Indoor swimming (H) Outdoor swimming (H) Tennis (hard) Snooker Sauna Solarium Croquet lawn Childrens play den Ten pin bowling Swimming pools supervised entertainment ch fac Xmas **CONF:** Thtr 120 Class 60 Board 25 Del from £60 **SERVICES:** Lift **PARKING:** 28 **NOTES:** No dogs (ex guide dogs) No smoking in restaurant **CARDS:**

★★70% **Frognel Hall**
Higher Woodfield Rd TQ1 2LD
☎ 01803 298339 🖷 01803 215115
e-mail: mail@frognel.co.uk
Dir: *follow signs to seafront, then follow esplanade to harbour, left to Babbacombe, right at lights towards Meadfoot Beach, 3rd left, hotel on left*
The friendly owners and staff at this hotel ensure a welcoming atmosphere and a pleasant stay. Enjoying fine views over Torquay, the hotel has comfortable bedrooms with modern facilities. There is a basement games room, a sauna and exercise equipment. Traditional English food is served, including vegetarian options.
ROOMS: 28 rms (27 en suite) (4 fmly) s £26-£33; d £52-£66 (incl. bkfst) **LB** **FACILITIES:** Sauna Croquet lawn Putting green Games room Exercise equipment Xmas **CONF:** Class 30 Board 15 Del from £41 **SERVICES:** Lift **PARKING:** 25 **NOTES:** No smoking in restaurant **CARDS:**

See advert on opposite page

★★70% **Torcroft**
Croft Rd TQ2 5UE
☎ 01803 298292 🖷 01803 291799
e-mail: torcroft@torquaydevon.fsnet.co.uk
Dir: *from A390 take A3022 to Avenue Rd. Follow signs to seafront then turn left, cross lights and up Shedden Hill, 1st left into Croft Rd*
This Grade II listed Victorian property is pleasantly located in a quiet area, and with well-tended gardens and a large patio, it is attractive and well maintained. The friendly proprietors are natural hosts and many guests choose to return here. Bedrooms are individually furnished, and some rooms have views. Pleasant home-cooked meals are enthusiastically offered and provide enjoyable dining.
ROOMS: 16 en suite (2 fmly) No smoking in all bedrooms s fr £25; d fr £50 (incl. bkfst) **LB** **FACILITIES:** Xmas **CONF:** Thtr 30 Class 20 Board 26 **PARKING:** 16 **NOTES:** No dogs No children 3yrs No smoking in restaurant **CARDS:**

★★69% ® **Dunstone Hall**
Lower Warberry Rd TQ1 1QS
☎ 01803 293185 🖷 01803 201180
e-mail: info@dunstonehall.com
From its elevated position, this imposing Victorian mansion has panoramic views over the town, to Torbay in the distance. Bedrooms are comfortable and equipped with modern facilities. Public areas include a choice of lounges, a magnificent wooden staircase and gallery and the Edwardian conservatory which provides an intimate restaurant where both dinner and the view may be enjoyed.
ROOMS: 13 en suite (3 fmly) s £35-£50; d £60-£100 (incl. bkfst) **LB** **FACILITIES:** Outdoor swimming (H) Arrangement with nearby Health Club ch fac Xmas **CONF:** Thtr 30 Class 30 Board 24 Del from £58 **PARKING:** 18 **NOTES:** No smoking in restaurant **CARDS:**

★★69% **Ansteys Cove**
327 Babbacombe Rd TQ1 3TB
☎ 0800 0284953
e-mail: info@ansteyscove.co.uk
Dir: *A380/A3022 left onto B379. At Babbacombe right onto Babbacombe Rd, hotel 1m on right opposite Place Hotel*
A totally no smoking hotel, located close to the beaches of both Torquay and Babbacombe. This hotel is set in a quieter location away from the town centre and hospitality is welcoming. Bedrooms are well maintained and attractively decorated.

continued

T

A pleasant bar and lounge are available and the cuisine, offering vegetarian dishes, is a feature here.
ROOMS: 9 en suite No smoking in all bedrooms s £34-£38; d £62-£80 (incl. bkfst) **FACILITIES:** STV **PARKING:** 12 **NOTES:** No dogs (ex guide dogs) No children 12 No smoking in restaurant Closed Nov-Mar
CARDS:

★★69% Ansteys Lea

Babbacombe Rd, Wellswood TQ1 2QJ
☎ 01803 294843 Fax 01803 214333
e-mail: stay@ansteys-lea.com
Dir: *from Torquay harbour take Babbacombe road, hotel approx 0.75m*
Taking its name from nearby Ansteys Cove, this friendly hotel is conveniently placed for both the town centre and seafront. The well-furnished bedrooms are comfortable and provide a good range of facilities. Public areas include an attractive lounge/TV room overlooking the garden and a heated outdoor pool. The fixed-price, 5-course dinner menu offers a choice of home-cooked dishes.
ROOMS: 24 en suite (4 fmly) No smoking in all bedrooms s £24-£30; d £48-£60 (incl. bkfst) **LB** **FACILITIES:** Outdoor swimming (H) Sauna ch fac Xmas **CONF:** Thtr 50 Class 40 Board 35 **PARKING:** 20 **NOTES:** No smoking in restaurant **CARDS:**

★★69% Hotel Balmoral

Meadfoot Sea Rd TQ1 2LQ
☎ 01803 293381 & 299224 Fax 01803 299224
e-mail: barry@hotel-balmoral.co.uk
Dir: *at Torquay harbour left at clock tower towards Babbacombe, after 100yds right at lights. Follow road to Meadfoot beach. Hotel on right*
Situated a short walk from the beach, this is a friendly, privately-owned and personally run hotel has modern, well-equipped bedrooms including family rooms and a room on ground floor level. The comfortable, spacious lounge has views over the well-tended gardens and the bar is an ideal venue for a drink before home-cooked dinners in the attractive dining room.
ROOMS: 24 en suite (7 fmly) s £27-£30; d £54-£60 (incl. bkfst) **LB** **FACILITIES:** Xmas **PARKING:** 18 **NOTES:** No smoking in restaurant
CARDS:

★★69% Elmington Hotel

St Agnes Ln, Chelston TQ2 6QE
☎ 01803 605192 Fax 01803 690488
e-mail: mail@elmington.co.uk
Dir: *to the rear of Torquay Station*
Set in sub-tropical gardens with wonderful views over the bay, this splendid Victorian villa has been lovingly restored. The comfortable bedrooms are brightly decorated and vary in size and style. There is a spacious lounge, bar and dining room. As an alternative to the menu of British dishes, diners also have the option of choosing from the oriental buffet.
ROOMS: 22 rms (19 en suite) (5 fmly) No smoking in all bedrooms s £22-£40; d £44-£38 (incl. bkfst) **LB** **FACILITIES:** STV Outdoor swimming (H) Croquet lawn Pool table ch fac Xmas **CONF:** Thtr 40 Class 40 Board 30 **PARKING:** 22 **NOTES:** No dogs (ex guide dogs) No smoking in restaurant **CARDS:**

★★69% Red House

Rousdown Rd, Chelston TQ2 6PB
☎ 01803 607811 Fax 01803 200592
e-mail: stay@redhouse-hotel.co.uk
Dir: *towards seafront/Chelston, turn into Avenue Rd, 1st lights turn right. Past shops and church, take next left. Hotel on right*
With views over Torbay, this pleasant and relaxing hotel enjoys a quiet location close to Cockington village. The comfortable bedrooms are well equipped and a good choice of bar meals are

continued on p618

T

TORQUAY, continued

available in addition to the fixed-price menu for residents. Many guests return here on a regular basis for the excellent range of leisure facilities.

Red House, Torquay

ROOMS: 10 en suite (5 fmly) s £23-£36; d £46-£72 (incl. bkfst) **FACILITIES: Spa** Indoor swimming (H) Outdoor swimming (H) Sauna Solarium Gym Games room Table tennis Beauty salon pool table Xmas **CONF:** Thtr 20 Class 20 Board 16 **PARKING:** 10 **NOTES:** No smoking in restaurant **CARDS:**

★★68% Gresham Court

Babbacombe Rd TQ1 1HG
☎ 01803 293007 01803 215951
e-mail: stay@gresham-court-hotel.co.uk

Dir: *along seafront, left at clocktower, with museum on left. Hotel immediately on left on corner*

This privately-owned and personally-run hotel is soundly maintained and provides modern accommodation, including bedrooms on the ground floor. There is a bright and pleasant dining room, a lounge bar where live entertainment is provided, a no-smoking lounge and a games room with pool table. The hotel is a popular venue for coach tour parties.

ROOMS: 30 en suite (6 fmly) (5 GF) s £36-£41; d £52-£62 (incl. bkfst) **LB FACILITIES:** Snooker entertainment Xmas **SERVICES:** Lift **PARKING:** 4 **NOTES:** No dogs (ex guide dogs) No smoking in restaurant **CARDS:**

★★68% Meadfoot Bay

Meadfoot Sea Rd TQ1 2LQ
☎ 01803 294722 01803 214473
e-mail: stay@meadfoot.com

Dir: *from harbour, follow signs to Meadfoot Beach. Turn right at lights into Meadfoot Rd, after 0.5m into Meadfoot Sea Road. Hotel on right*

Guests are assured of a warm welcome at this neatly presented Victorian villa, just a short walk from Meadfoot Beach and approximately 10 minutes from the town centre and harbour. Every effort is made to ensure guests have a relaxed and enjoyable stay. A changing daily menu is offered with an emphasis on home cooking.

ROOMS: 20 en suite (1 fmly) (3 GF) No smoking in all bedrooms s £23-£38; d £46-£76 (incl. bkfst) **FACILITIES:** Xmas **PARKING:** 16 **NOTES:** No dogs (ex guide dogs) No smoking in restaurant **CARDS:**

★★68% *Shelley Court*

29 Croft Rd TQ2 5UD
☎ 01803 295642 01803 215793
e-mail: shelleycourthotel@hotmail.com

Dir: *A380 to Torquay, approach seafront lights by footbridge, up Shedden Hill, 1st left after corner hotel car park and immediately left*

A popular family-run hotel with friendly staff, located in a pleasant and quiet area, which overlooks the town towards Tor Bay. Many guests return here; there is entertainment provided most evenings in season and fresh, local produce is used in dishes offered in the dining room. Bedrooms are in a range of sizes and there is a large and comfortable lounge bar.

ROOMS: 27 en suite (3 fmly) **FACILITIES:** entertainment **PARKING:** 20 **NOTES:** No dogs No smoking in restaurant Closed 23 Dec-1 Feb **CARDS:**

★★66% *Anchorage Hotel*

Cary Park, Aveland Rd TQ1 3NQ
☎ 01803 326175 01803 316439
e-mail: landlin@aol.com

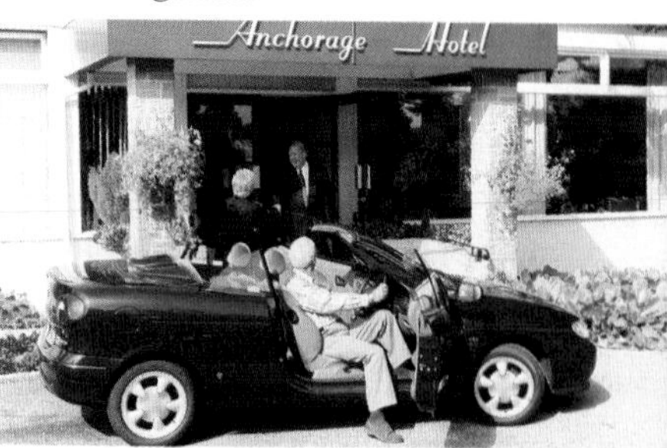

Anchorage Hotel is quietly located in a residential area and has undergone refurbishment in the bedrooms and dining room. Providing a friendly welcome, this family-run establishment attracts a strong repeat clientele. Bedrooms offer a range of sizes and all are neatly presented. Evening entertainment is provided regularly in the large comfortable lounge.

ROOMS: 53 en suite (5 fmly) No smoking in all bedrooms **FACILITIES:** Outdoor swimming (H) entertainment **SERVICES:** Lift **PARKING:** 26 **NOTES:** No smoking in restaurant **CARDS:**

★★66% Seascape

8-10 Tor Church Rd TQ2 5UT
☎ 01803 292617 01803 299260
e-mail: pj@seascapehotel

Dir: *A380 to Torquay, at Torre station turn right, left at 2nd lights. Through lights, hotel 100yds on right*

Enjoying a convenient location, just a short stroll from the town centre, this friendly, family run hotel prides itself on genuine hospitality. Bedrooms are comfortable and well equipped, some of which have the added bonus of views across the bay. Public rooms include the convivial bar with regular live entertainment, and a sauna and solarium.

ROOMS: 60 en suite (10 fmly) No smoking in 25 bedrooms s £35-£42; d £64-£80 (incl. bkfst) **FACILITIES:** Sauna Solarium entertainment Xmas **SERVICES:** Lift **PARKING:** 13 **NOTES:** No dogs No smoking in restaurant **CARDS:**

T

★★65% **Coppice**
Babbacombe Rd TQ1 2QJ
☎ 01803 297786 01803 211085
e-mail: peter@coppicehotel.demon.co.uk
Dir: *from harbour left at clocktower for hotel 1m on left*
A friendly, comfortable and well-established hotel, The Coppice is a popular choice and provides a convenient location within walking distance of the beaches and shops. In addition to the indoor and outdoor swimming pools, evening entertainment is often provided in the spacious bar. Bedrooms are bright and airy with modern amenities.
ROOMS: 39 en suite (16 fmly) (22 GF) s £26-£30; d £52-£60 (incl. bkfst) **LB FACILITIES: Spa** Indoor swimming (H) Outdoor swimming Snooker Sauna Solarium Gym Putting green **PARKING:** 36 **NOTES:** No smoking in restaurant Closed Dec-Jan
CARDS:

★★64% ***Burlington***
462-466 Babbacombe Rd TQ1 1HN
☎ 01803 210950 01803 200189
e-mail: info@burlingtontorquay.co.uk
Dir: *follow signs to seafront, left at harbour, left at clocktower rdbt, hotel 0.5m on right*

Popular with groups, this hotel is conveniently situated for the many attractions the area has to offer. A range of traditional dishes is served in the spacious dining room and public areas include a games room, entertainment room, leisure facilities and a popular bar. Bedrooms are comfortable and available in a variety of sizes.
ROOMS: 55 en suite (7 fmly) **FACILITIES: Spa** Indoor swimming (H) Sauna Solarium Jacuzzi entertainment **PARKING:** 20 **NOTES:** No smoking in restaurant **CARDS:**

★★64% ***Maycliffe***
St Lukes Rd North TQ2 5DP
☎ 01803 294964 01803 201167
Dir: *left from Kings Dr, along seafront keep in left lane, next lights (Belgrave Rd) up Shedden Hill, 2nd right into St Lukes Rd then 1st left*
Set in a quiet and elevated position which is convenient for the town centre and attractions, the Maycliffe is a popular venue for leisure breaks. Bedrooms are individually decorated and equipped with modern facilities, there are two rooms on the ground floor for less able guests. There is a quiet lounge and, in the bar, cabaret is offered on some nights during the season.
ROOMS: 28 en suite (1 fmly) No smoking in 9 bedrooms **FACILITIES:** entertainment **SERVICES:** Lift **PARKING:** 10 **NOTES:** No dogs No children 10yrs No smoking in restaurant Closed 2 Jan-12 Feb
CARDS:

★★63% **Ashley Court**
107 Abbey Rd TQ2 5NP
☎ 01803 292417 01803 215035
e-mail: reception@ashleycourt.demon.co.uk
Dir: *A380 onto seafront, left to Shedden Hill to lights, hotel opposite*

Located close to the town centre and within easy strolling distance of the seafront, the Ashley Court offers a warm welcome to guests. Bedrooms are pleasantly appointed and some have sea views. The outdoor pool and patio are popular with guests wishing to soak up some sunshine. Live entertainment is provided regularly throughout the season.
ROOMS: 53 en suite (6 fmly) (8 GF) s £29-£40; d £58-£80 (incl. bkfst & dinner) **LB FACILITIES:** Outdoor swimming (H) entertainment Xmas **SERVICES:** Lift **PARKING:** 30 **NOTES:** No smoking in restaurant Closed 3 Jan-1 Feb **CARDS:**

★★63% **Norcliffe**
7 Babbacombe Downs Rd, Babbacombe TQ1 3LF
☎ 01803 328456 01803 328023
e-mail: res@norcliffehotel.co.uk
Dir: *A380, after Sainsburys turn left at lights, across rdbt, next left at lights into Manor Rd, from Babbacombe Rd turn left*
With marvellous views across Lyme Bay, the Norcliffe is conveniently situated on the Babbacombe Downs and ideally located for visitors to St Marychurch or nearby Oddicombe Beach. Public areas are relaxing, taking advantage of the views, and include an indoor swimming pool. All bedrooms are comfortable, varying in style and size.
ROOMS: 27 en suite (3 fmly) (1 GF) s £20-£35; d £40-£70 (incl. bkfst) **LB FACILITIES:** Indoor swimming (H) Sauna Table tennis, indoor pool has CCTV Xmas **SERVICES:** Lift **PARKING:** 20 **NOTES:** No smoking in restaurant **CARDS:**

★★62% **Regina**
Victoria Pde TQ1 2BE

☎ 01803 292904 01803 290270
e-mail: regina.torquay@alfatravel.co.uk
Dir: *on entering Torquay, follow harbour signs, hotel on outer corner of harbour*
The Regina Hotel enjoys a pleasant and convenient location right on the harbour side, a short stroll from the town's attractions. Bedrooms, some with harbour views, vary in size. Entertainment is provided on most nights and there is a choice of bars.
ROOMS: 68 en suite (5 fmly) s £25-£33; d £42-£58 (incl. bkfst) **LB FACILITIES:** entertainment Xmas **SERVICES:** Lift **PARKING:** 6 **NOTES:** No dogs (ex guide dogs) No smoking in restaurant Closed Jan RS Nov-Dec (ex Xmas) & Feb-Mar **CARDS:**

T

TORQUAY, continued

★★60% Villa Marina
Cockington Ln, Livermead TQ2 6QU
☎ 01803 605440 & 606122 📠 01803 606122
e-mail: stay@villa-marina.co.uk
Dir: *from seafront towards Paignton, turn right towards Cockington. Hotel 70yds on left*
Convenient for the seafront and Cockington village, the Villa Marina provides friendly and attentive service. Bedrooms are comfortable and some rooms have balconies with splendid views over Torbay. The views can also be enjoyed from the public rooms and the terrace swimming pool. Live entertainment is provided during the high season.
ROOMS: 26 en suite (5 fmly) (8 GF) No smoking in all bedrooms s £20-£30; d £40-£60 (incl. bkfst) **LB FACILITIES:** Outdoor swimming (H) Xmas **PARKING:** 22 **NOTES:** No dogs (ex guide dogs) No smoking in restaurant Closed Jan **CARDS:**

★66% *Westwood*
111 Abbey Rd TQ2 5NP
☎ 01803 293818 📠 01803 293818
e-mail: reception@westwoodhotel.co.uk
Dir: *from A380 follow signs for seafront. At lights facing sea turn left straight through next lights up Shedden Hill. At lights at top left into Abbey Rd, hotel on right*
An enthusiastic and friendly welcome is offered at this small, family-run hotel within walking distance of the town centre. Regular guests enjoy the informal atmosphere, particularly in the comfortable bar. Bedrooms are tastefully decorated, offering many modern facilities.
ROOMS: 25 en suite (6 fmly) **FACILITIES:** entertainment **PARKING:** 12 **NOTES:** No dogs (ex guide dogs) No smoking in restaurant
CARDS:

TOTLAND BAY See Wight, Isle of

TOTNES, Devon Map 03 SX86
See also Staverton

★★65% Royal Seven Stars
The Plains TQ9 5DD
☎ 01803 862125 & 863241 📠 01803 867925
e-mail: royal7starshotel@aol.com
Dir: *A38 Devon Expressway, Buckfastleigh turn off onto A384, follow signs to Totnes town centre*
In a prominent position at the foot of the town and close to the river, this 17th-century hostelry is a popular place. Bedrooms are comfortable and well equipped, many retaining the original charm of the building. A central atrium offers a pleasant area adjacent to the busy bar, and in the restaurant a large choice of freshly prepared dishes is offered.
ROOMS: 16 rms (14 en suite) (2 fmly) **FACILITIES:** Xmas **CONF:** Thtr 70 Class 20 Board 20 **PARKING:** 20 **CARDS:**

TOWCESTER, Northamptonshire Map 11 SP64

⇧ Travelodge (Silverstone)
NN12 6TQ
☎ 08700 850 950 📠 01327 359105
Dir: *A43 East Towcester by-pass*
Travelodge offers good quality, good value, modern accommodation. Ideal for families, the spacious, en suite bedrooms include remote-control TV, tea and coffee-making facilities, luxury beds and free morning newspaper. Meals can be taken at the nearby family restaurant. For further details and the Travelodge phone number, consult the Hotel Groups page.
ROOMS: 55 en suite s fr £42.95; d fr £42.95

TRESCO See Scilly, Isles of

TRING, Hertfordshire Map 06 SP91

★★★★66% Pendley Manor
Cow Ln HP23 5QY
☎ 01442 891891 📠 01442 890687
e-mail: info@pendley-manor.co.uk
Dir: *M25 junct 20. Exit A41 for Tring. At rdbt take exit for Berkhamsted/London. Take 1st left signed Tring Station & Pendley Manor*
This impressive Victorian mansion is set in extensive and mature landscaped grounds complete with peacocks. Bedrooms, situated in the manor house or in the new wing, offer a useful range of facilities and many have four-poster beds. Public areas include a cosy bar, a conservatory lounge and a leisure centre.
ROOMS: 74 en suite (6 fmly) No smoking in 3 bedrooms s £90-£130; d £110-£160 (incl. bkfst) **LB FACILITIES: Spa** STV Indoor swimming (H) Tennis (hard) Snooker Sauna Gym Croquet lawn Jacuzzi Steam room, Dance Studio, Internet coffee shop, Indoor pool supervised Xmas **CONF:** BC Thtr 230 Class 100 Board 50 Del from £190 **SERVICES:** Lift **PARKING:** 250 **NOTES:** No smoking in restaurant Civ Wed 200
CARDS:

See advert on opposite page

★★★62% *The Rose & Crown*
High St HP23 5AH
☎ 01442 824071 📠 01442 890735
Dir: *just off A41, hotel in town centre*

This Tudor-style manor house offers a great deal of charm. Bedrooms vary in size, though all are comfortably equipped, with particularly smart bathrooms. The restaurant and bar form the centre of the hotel, popular with both local customers and residents.
ROOMS: 27 en suite (3 fmly) No smoking in 3 bedrooms **FACILITIES:** STV Full indoor leisure facilities available at sister hotel **CONF:** Thtr 80 Class 30 Board 30 **PARKING:** 60 **NOTES:** No dogs (ex guide dogs) Civ Wed 100 **CARDS:**

⇧ Travel Inn
Tring Hill HP23 4LD
☎ 08701 977254 📠 01442 890787
Dir: *M25 junct 20 take A41 towards Aylesbury, at end of Hemel Hempstead/Tring bypass go straight over rdbt, Travel Inn on the right in approx 100yds*
Travel Inn offers good-quality, value-for-money accommodation. Spacious, en suite rooms with bath and shower comfortably accommodate a family of up to two adults and two children (to age 15). The restaurant and bar offers a varied menu. For further details and the Travel Inn phone number, consult the Hotel Groups page.
ROOMS: 30 en suite s £44.95; d £44.95

TROUTBECK (NEAR WINDERMERE), Cumbria Map 18 NY40

★★69% *Mortal Man*

LA23 1PL
☎ 015394 33193 📠 015394 31261
e-mail: the-mortalman@btinternet.com
Dir: *2.5m N from junct of A591 & A592, turn left before church into village, right at T-junct, hotel 800mtrs on right*
Dating from 1689, this traditional inn enjoys a superb setting with stunning lakeland views. Public areas retain many original features and include an elegant restaurant and a comfortable lounge. A range of meals can be served in either the well-stocked bar, with real fires, or in the more formal restaurant. Bedrooms are particularly well equipped and include a four-poster room.
ROOMS: 12 en suite **FACILITIES:** Fishing,Hrse Riding,Sailing,Guided Walks, Watersports **CONF:** Thtr 30 **PARKING:** 20 **NOTES:** No smoking in restaurant **CARDS:**

TROWBRIDGE, Wiltshire Map 04 ST85

★★66% Fieldways Hotel & Health Club

Hilperton Rd BA14 7JP
☎ 01225 768336 📠 01225 753649
Dir: *last property on left when leaving Trowbridge on A361 towards Melksham/Chippenham/Devizes*
This hotel is quietly set in well-kept grounds and provides a pleasant combination of spacious, comfortably furnished bedrooms, an impressive wood-panelled dining room and a considerable range of indoor leisure facilities. 'Top to Toe' days are especially popular, incorporating the wide range of beauty treatments on offer.
ROOMS: 8 en suite 5 annexe en suite (2 fmly) (2 GF) s £60; d £75-£85 (incl. bkfst) **LB FACILITIES:** Indoor swimming (H) Sauna Solarium Gym Jacuzzi Range of beauty treatments/massage **CONF:** Thtr 50 Class 40 Board 8 **PARKING:** 70 **NOTES:** No dogs (ex guide dogs) No smoking in restaurant **CARDS:**

TROWELL MOTORWAY SERVICE AREA (M1), Nottinghamshire Map 11 SK43

Travelodge Nottingham Trowell

Travelodge

NG9 3PL
☎ 08700 850 950
Dir: *M1 junct 25/26 northbound*
Travelodge offers good quality, good value, modern accommodation. Ideal for families, the spacious, en suite bedrooms include remote-control TV, tea and coffee-making facilities, luxury beds and free morning newspaper. Meals can be taken at the nearby family restaurant. For further details and the Travelodge phone number, consult the Hotel Groups page.
ROOMS: 35 en suite s fr £42.95; d fr £42.95

TRURO, Cornwall & Isles of Scilly Map 02 SW84

★★★70% Royal

Lemon St TR1 2QB
☎ 01872 270345 📠 01872 242453
e-mail: reception@royalhotelcornwall.co.uk
Dir: *follow A30 to Carland Cross then Truro. Follow brown tourists signs to hotel in city centre. To barrier & obtain pass from reception*
This popular hotel is located in the heart of Truro and public areas offer a stylish atmosphere. The new bar and restaurant are proving popular with locals and residents alike. Bedrooms are pleasantly appointed. Cuisine offers a wide range of choices of

continued on p622

TRURO, continued

appetising dishes, which feature ethnic, classical and vegetarian choices as well as daily specials.
ROOMS: 35 en suite 9 annexe en suite (4 fmly) (3 GF) No smoking in 31 bedrooms s £59-£65; d £85-£99 (incl. cont bkfst) **LB**
FACILITIES: STV **CONF:** Thtr 25 Class 25 Board 25 **PARKING:** 44
NOTES: No dogs (ex guide dogs) Closed 25 & 26 Dec
CARDS:

★★★68% Alverton Manor
Tregolls Rd TR1 1ZQ
☎ 01872 276633 01872 222989
e-mail: reception@alvertonmanor.demon.co.uk
Dir: *from at Carland Cross take A39 to Truro*
Formerly a convent, this impressive sandstone property stands in six acres of grounds, within walking distance of the city centre. It has a wide range of smart bedrooms, combining comfort with character. Stylish public areas include the library and the former chapel, now a striking function room. An interesting range of dishes is offered in the elegant restaurant.
ROOMS: 32 en suite (3 GF) No smoking in 10 bedrooms s £75-£136; d £115-£165 (incl. cont bkfst) **LB** **FACILITIES:** STV Golf 18 Xmas
CONF: Thtr 80 Class 60 Board 40 Del from £120 **SERVICES:** Lift
PARKING: 120 **NOTES:** No smoking in restaurant Civ Wed 80
CARDS:

See advert on page 621

★★★58% Brookdale
Tregolls Rd TR1 1JZ
THE INDEPENDENTS
☎ 01872 273513 01872 272400
e-mail: brookdale@hotelstruro.com
Dir: *from A30 onto A39, at A390 junct turn right into city centre. Hotel 600mtrs down hill*
Pleasantly situated in an elevated position close to the city centre, the Brookdale provides a range of accommodation options; all rooms are pleasantly spacious and well equipped, with some located in an adjacent annexe. Meals can be served in guests' rooms, and in the dining room a pleasant selection of dishes are available.
ROOMS: 30 en suite (2 fmly) No smoking in 11 bedrooms s £55; d £79.50 (incl. bkfst) **LB** **FACILITIES:** STV Xmas **CONF:** Thtr 85 Class 65 Board 25 **PARKING:** 55 **NOTES:** No smoking in restaurant
CARDS:

★★66% Carlton
Falmouth Rd TR1 2HL
☎ 01872 272450 01872 223938
e-mail: reception@carltonhotel.co.uk
Dir: *on A39 straight across 1st & 2nd rdbts onto bypass (Morlaix Ave). At top of sweeping bend/hill turn right at mini rdbt into Falmouth Rd. Hotel 100mtrs on right*

This popular, family-run hotel is pleasantly located just a short stroll from the city centre. A friendly welcome is assured here and both business and leisure guests choose the Carlton on a regular basis. A smart, comfortable lounge is available along with leisure facilities. A wide selection of home-cooked dishes is offered in the dining room.
ROOMS: 29 en suite (4 fmly) No smoking in 15 bedrooms s £38-£43; d £55-£60 (incl. bkfst) **FACILITIES:** STV Sauna Jacuzzi **CONF:** Thtr 70 Class 24 Board 36 **PARKING:** 31 **NOTES:** Closed 23 Dec-6 Jan
CARDS:

Travel Inn
Old Carnon Hill, Carnon Downs TR3 6JT
travel inn
☎ 08701 977255 01872 865620
Dir: *on A39, 3m SW of Truro*
Travel Inn offers good-quality, value-for-money accommodation. Spacious, en suite rooms with bath and shower comfortably accommodate a family of up to two adults and two children (to age 15). The restaurant and bar offers a varied menu. For further details and the Travel Inn phone number, consult the Hotel Groups page.
ROOMS: 40 en suite s £44.95; d £44.95

TUNBRIDGE WELLS (ROYAL), Kent
Map 06 TQ53

Town House

★★★★ Hotel Du Vin & Bistro
Crescent Rd TN1 2LY
☎ 01892 526455 01892 512044
e-mail: reception@tunbridgewells.hotelduvin.com
Dir: *follow town centre to main Mount Pleasant Rd & Crescent Rd/Church Rd junct. Hotel 150yds on right just past Phillips House*
This impressive Grade II listed building dates from 1762, and as a princess Queen Victoria often stayed here. Bedrooms are spacious, beautifully and individually appointed, and equipped with a host of thoughtful extras. Public rooms include a bistro-style restaurant, two elegant lounges and a small bar. Outside, there are delightful gardens and a terrace.
ROOMS: 32 en suite 4 annexe en suite s £89-£140; d £89-£140
FACILITIES: STV Snooker Boules court in garden **CONF:** Thtr 40 Class 30 Board 25 **SERVICES:** Lift **PARKING:** 30 **NOTES:** No dogs (ex guide dogs) **CARDS:**

★★★77% The Spa
Mount Ephraim TN4 8XJ
☎ 01892 520331 01892 510575
e-mail: info@spahotel.co.uk
Dir: *off A21 to A26, follow signs to A264 East Grinstead, hotel on right*
An imposing 18th-century country house situated amidst 14 acres of attractive landscaped grounds, overlooking the town. The spacious bedrooms are individually decorated with co-ordinated fabrics, tastefully furnished and thoughtfully equipped, many rooms overlook the pretty gardens. Public rooms include a comfortable lounge, a large bar, the Chandelier restaurant and excellent leisure facilities.
ROOMS: 69 en suite (10 fmly) (2 GF) s £91-£101; d £115-£170 **LB**
FACILITIES: STV Indoor swimming (H) Tennis (hard) Riding Sauna Gym Croquet lawn Steam room Beauty Salon Jogging trail, indoor pool supervised entertainment ch fac Xmas **CONF:** BC Thtr 300 Class 93 Board 90 Del from £125 **SERVICES:** Lift **PARKING:** 120 **NOTES:** No dogs (ex guide dogs) No smoking in restaurant Civ Wed 250
CARDS:

See advert on opposite page

T

★★★72% Royal Wells Inn
Mount Ephraim TN4 8BE
☎ 01892 511188 📠 01892 511908
e-mail: info@royalwells.co.uk
Dir: *from London on A21 onto A264 to Tunbridge Wells. In town right at 1st mini rdbt. At 2nd mini rdbt, Mount Ephraim and hotel 150yds on right*

Delightful family-run hotel situated in an elevated position with stunning views of the town centre. The accommodation is being continually upgraded to provide stylish, tastefully furnished, well-equipped bedrooms throughout. There are two eating options, The Brasserie with its extensive blackboard menu, and the refurbished Conservatory with a full carte and daily menu. The dishes are interesting and carefully prepared from fresh local produce, and the wine list is well chosen and reasonably priced.
ROOMS: 18 en suite (2 fmly) **FACILITIES:** STV entertainment **CONF:** BC Thtr 80 Class 30 Board 40 **SERVICES:** Lift **PARKING:** 35 **NOTES:** Closed 25-26 Dec Civ Wed 80 **CARDS:**
See advert on this page

★★65% Russell

80 London Rd TN1 1DZ
☎ 01892 544833 📠 01892 515846
e-mail: Sales@russell-hotel.com
Dir: *at junct A26 & A264 uphill onto A26, hotel on right*
A detached Victorian property situated just a short walk from the centre of town. The generously proportioned bedrooms in the main house are pleasantly decorated and well equipped. In addition there are several smartly appointed self-contained suites in an adjacent building. The newly refurbished public rooms include a lounge, a cosy bar and a restaurant.
ROOMS: 19 en suite 5 annexe en suite (2 fmly) (1 GF) No smoking in 10 bedrooms **FACILITIES:** STV ch fac **CONF:** Board 12 **PARKING:** 15 **NOTES:** No dogs (ex guide dogs) **CARDS:**

⌂ Innkeeper's Lodge Tunbridge
21 London Rd, Southborough TN4 0RL
☎ 01892 529292 📠 01892 510620
Dir: *Off M25 onto A21, take A26 Tonbridge/Southborough turn off. Lodge in Southborough on A26, opposite cricket green.*
A new concept in the travel accommodation market. Smart rooms meet essential business requirements but also have home comforts. Dining options include all-day menus plus the added advantage of breakfast, which is included in the room price. For further details, consult the Hotel Groups page.
ROOMS: 15 en suite

Town House Hotel
Country House Hotel
Travel Accommodation

T

TURNERS HILL, West Sussex — Map 06 TQ33

Top 200 - Hotel

★★★ Alexander House Hotel

East St RH10 4QD
☎ 01342 714914 01342 717328
e-mail: info@alexanderhouse.co.uk

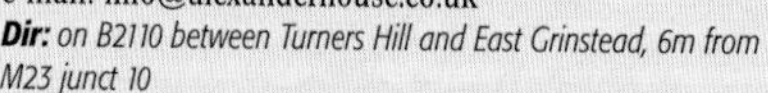

Dir: *on B2110 between Turners Hill and East Grinstead, 6m from M23 junct 10*

Set in 175 acres of parklands and landscaped gardens, this delightful country house hotel dates back to the 17th century. Comfortable, stylish bedrooms have been individually refurbished to a high standard; all are thoughtfully equipped and benefit from superbly appointed bathrooms. Spacious, elegant public areas, furnished with antique pieces and paintings, include a choice of comfortable lounges and a stylish restaurant.

ROOMS: 18 en suite (3 fmly) (1 GF) No smoking in all bedrooms s fr £145; d £185-£310 **LB** **FACILITIES:** STV Tennis (hard) Croquet lawn Clay shooting,Archery by arrangement. entertainment Xmas **CONF:** Thtr 24 Board 18 Del from £215 **SERVICES:** Lift **PARKING:** 50 **NOTES:** No dogs (ex guide dogs) No children 7yrs No smoking in restaurant Civ Wed 60 **CARDS:**

See advert under GATWICK AIRPORT (LONDON)

TWICKENHAM, Greater London
See LONDON SECTION plan 1 B2

★★★67% Popes Grotto

Cross Deep TW1 4RB
☎ 020 8892 3050 020 8892 2758
e-mail: popesgrotto@youngs.co.uk

Dir: *A316 keep left for Twickenham, from slip road take 3rd exit at rdbt & follow signs through lights & into town centre*

Taking its name from the poet Alexander Pope, this hotel sits in a prime location overlooking the River Thames. Smart accommodation is well appointed and provides good levels of comfort. The spacious public bar and restaurant will soon take on a more traditional feel, in keeping with the hotel's history.

ROOMS: 32 en suite (9 fmly) (7 GF) No smoking in 25 bedrooms s £80-£108; d £120-£136 (incl. bkfst) **LB** **FACILITIES:** STV Xmas **CONF:** Thtr 50 Class 20 Board 20 **SERVICES:** Lift air con **PARKING:** 55 **NOTES:** No dogs (ex guide dogs) **CARDS:**

Premier Lodge (Twickenham)

Chertsey Rd, Whitton TW2 6LS
☎ 0870 9906416 0870 9906417

Premier Lodge offers modern, well-equipped, en suite accommodation suitable for both business and leisure travellers. Meals can be taken at the adjacent popular restaurant and bar, which is fully licensed. For further details, consult the Hotel Groups page.

ROOMS: 31 en suite s £56; d £56

TWO BRIDGES, Devon — Map 03 SX67

Top 200 - Hotel

★★ Prince Hall

PL20 6SA
☎ 01822 890403 01822 890676
e-mail: bookings@princehall.co.uk

Dir: *on B3357 1m E of Two Bridges road junct*

A charm and peacefulness along with a relaxed informality exists at this small hotel which has a stunning location in the heart of Dartmoor. Each of the spacious bedrooms, named after Dartmoor's tors, has been equipped with thoughtful extras. The history of the house and its location are reflected throughout the public areas, which are most comfortable. Guests can expect memorable and accomplished cuisine that uses the best local produce.

ROOMS: 8 en suite (1 fmly) s £80-£115; d £82.50-£105 (incl. bkfst & dinner) **LB** **FACILITIES:** Fishing Riding Croquet lawn Guided Dartmoor Walks, Fly fishing, Garden tours **CONF:** Del from £105 **PARKING:** 13 **NOTES:** No children 10yrs No smoking in restaurant Closed Jan **CARDS:**

★★71% *Two Bridges Hotel*

PL20 6SW
☎ 01822 890581 01822 890575
e-mail: enquiries@warm-welcome-hotels.co.uk

Dir: *junct of B3212 & B3357*

This wonderfully relaxing hotel is set in the heart of the Dartmoor National Park, in a beautiful riverside location. Comfortable rooms, offering three standards, provide every modern convenience. Fine dining is available in the restaurant with menus featuring local game and seasonal produce; alternatively, traditional bar food is served in Saracen's Bar.

ROOMS: 29 en suite (2 fmly) No smoking in 21 bedrooms **FACILITIES:** STV Fishing **CONF:** Thtr 110 Class 60 Board 40 **PARKING:** 100 **NOTES:** No smoking in restaurant **CARDS:**

See advert on opposite page

TYNEMOUTH, Tyne & Wear Map 21 NZ36

★★★68% Grand

Grand Pde NE30 4ER
☎ 0191 293 6666 📠 0191 293 6665
e-mail: info@grandhotel-uk.com
Dir: *A1058 for Tynemouth, turn right at coast. Hotel on right approx 0.5m*

Completely refurbished some years ago and attracting a wide customer base, this grand Victorian building offers stunning views of the coastline. In addition to the restaurant there are two bars, and an elegant and imposing staircase is the focal point. Bedrooms come in a variety of styles and are well equipped, tastefully decorated and have impressive bathrooms.

ROOMS: 40 en suite 4 annexe en suite (15 fmly) s £50-£90; d £55-£95 (incl. bkfst) **FACILITIES:** STV entertainment Xmas **CONF:** Thtr 130 Class 40 Board 40 **SERVICES:** Lift **PARKING:** 16 **NOTES:** No dogs (ex guide dogs) RS Sun evening Civ Wed 100
CARDS:

U The Park Hotel

Grand Pde NE30 4JQ
☎ 0191 257 1406 📠 0191 257 1716
Dir: *0.5m N of Tynemouth Priory*

At the time of going to press, the star classification for this hotel was not confirmed. Please refer to the AA internet site www.theAA.com for current information.

ROOMS: 50 en suite (2 fmly) (9 GF) s £55; d £65 (incl. bkfst) **FACILITIES:** STV Sauna Gym Xmas **CONF:** Thtr 2260 Class 1600 Board 240 Del from £60 **PARKING:** 300 **NOTES:** No dogs (ex guide dogs) Civ Wed 700 **CARDS:**

TYWARDREATH, Cornwall & Isles of Scilly Map 02 SX05

★★★72% Trenython Manor

Castle Dore Rd PL24 2TS
☎ 01726 814797 📠 01726 817030
e-mail: hotel@trenython.co.uk
Dir: *A390/B3269 towards Fowey, after 2m, turn right into Castledore. Hotel 100mtrs on left*

Dating from the 1800s, there is something distinctly different about Trenython, an English manor house designed by an Italian architect. Peacefully situated in extensive grounds, public areas have grace and elegance with many original features. The splendour of the panelled restaurant is the venue for contemporary cuisine and many of the bedrooms have wonderful views; all offer high standards of comfort with a range of extras.

ROOMS: 24 en suite (2 fmly) No smoking in all bedrooms s £69-£160; d £99-£190 (incl. bkfst) **LB FACILITIES:** Indoor swimming (H) Tennis (hard) Sauna Solarium Gym Croquet lawn Jacuzzi Woodland walks, health & beauty centre ch fac Xmas **CONF:** Thtr 100 Class 60 Board 40 Del from £125 **PARKING:** 50 **NOTES:** No dogs (ex guide dogs) No smoking in restaurant Civ Wed 100 **CARDS:**

UCKFIELD, East Sussex Map 06 TQ42

★★★★74% ⊛⊛ Buxted Park Country House Hotel

HandPICKED

Buxted TN22 4AY
☎ 01825 732711 📠 01825 732770
e-mail: events.bph@arcadianhotels.co.uk
Dir: *on A272. From A22, A26, or A267 onto A27 towards Heathfield then Buxted*

An attractive Grade II listed Georgian mansion dating back to the 17th century. The property is set amidst 300 acres of beautiful

continued

countryside and landscaped gardens. The stylish, thoughtfully equipped bedrooms are split between the main house and the modern Garden Wing. An interesting choice of dishes is served in the original Victorian Orangery.

ROOMS: 44 en suite (6 fmly) (16 GF) No smoking in 16 bedrooms s £90-£190; d £130-£235 (incl. bkfst) **LB FACILITIES: Spa** STV Fishing Snooker Sauna Solarium Gym Croquet lawn Putting green Jacuzzi Beauty salon Clay pigeon shooting Archery Fly fishing entertainment Xmas **CONF:** Thtr 130 Class 70 Board 60 Del from £125 **PARKING:** 150 **NOTES:** No smoking in restaurant Civ Wed 130
CARDS:

U

UCKFIELD, continued

Top 200 - Hotel

★★★ Horsted Place
Little Horsted TN22 5TS
☎ 01825 750581 01825 750459
e-mail: hotel@horstedplace.co.uk
Dir: *2m S on A26 towards Lewes*

This 17th-century property was designed by Augustus Pugin and is one of Britain's finest examples of Gothic revivalist architecture. It is situated amid extensive landscaped grounds, with tennis court and croquet lawn, and is adjacent to the East Sussex National Golf Club. The spacious bedrooms are attractively decorated, tastefully furnished and equipped with many thoughtful touches such as flowers and books. Most rooms also have a separate sitting area.

ROOMS: 17 en suite 3 annexe en suite (5 fmly) (2 GF) s £130-£330; d £130-£330 (incl. bkfst) **LB FACILITIES:** STV Golf 36 Tennis (hard) Croquet lawn entertainment ch fac Xmas **CONF:** Thtr 80 Class 50 Board 40 Del from £160 **SERVICES:** Lift **PARKING:** 32 **NOTES:** No dogs (ex guide dogs) No children 7yrs No smoking in restaurant Civ Wed 100
CARDS:

ULLESTHORPE, Leicestershire — Map 11 SP58

★★★67% Ullesthorpe Court Hotel & Golf Club
Frolesworth Rd LE17 5BZ
☎ 01455 209023 01455 202537
e-mail: bookings@ullesthorpecourt.co.uk
Dir: *M1 junct 20 towards Lutterworth, then follow brown tourist signs*

Complete with its own golf club, this impressively equipped hotel is within easy reach of the motorway network, the NEC and Birmingham airport. Public areas include a choice of restaurants, conference and leisure facilities. Bedrooms are mostly spacious and thoughtfully equipped for both the corporate and leisure guests and a four-poster is available.

ROOMS: 38 en suite (1 fmly) No smoking in 20 bedrooms s £40-£90; d £80-£115 (incl. bkfst) **LB FACILITIES:** STV Indoor swimming (H) Golf 18 Tennis (hard) Snooker Sauna Solarium Gym Putting green Jacuzzi Beauty room, Steam Room **CONF:** Thtr 80 Class 48 Board 30 Del £110 **PARKING:** 500 **NOTES:** No smoking in restaurant RS 25 & 26 Dec
CARDS:

ULLSWATER See Glenridding, Patterdale & Watermillock

ULVERSTON, Cumbria — Map 18 SD27

★★65% Lonsdale House Hotel
11 Daltongate LA12 7BD
☎ 01229 582598 01229 581260
e-mail: info@lonsdalehousehotel.co.uk
Dir: *In Ulverston turn right at 2nd rdbt, follow one-way system to mini-rdbt. Turn left pass zebra crossing then right & 1st right*

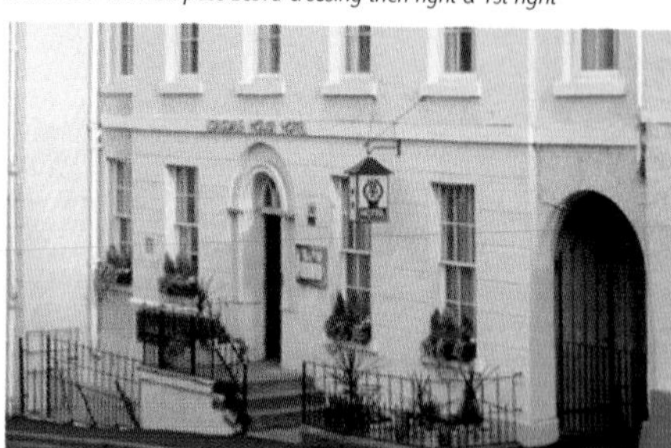

Enjoying a town centre location, this family-run hotel was once a coaching inn. Bedrooms vary in style and size but all are extremely well-equipped, and refurbished rooms benefit from stylish furniture and soft furnishings. Public areas include an attractive bar and restaurant, an inviting lounge and a delightful rear garden.

ROOMS: 20 en suite (3 fmly) No smoking in 10 bedrooms s £55-£85; d £60-£90 (incl. bkfst) **LB FACILITIES:** Xmas **NOTES:** No smoking in restaurant **CARDS:**

UMBERLEIGH, Devon — Map 03 SS62

★★69% Rising Sun Inn
EX37 9DU
☎ 01769 560447 01769 560764
e-mail: risingsuninn@btinternet.com
Dir: *on A377, Exeter/Barnstaple Rd, at junct of B3227*

Overlooking the Taw River and Valley, this 13th-century inn has retained much of its charm and character and offers comfortable modern facilities. Local musicians, fishing memorabilia and an inglenook fireplace set the style in the bar, where a good choice of interesting dishes, many featuring fresh fish, are offered.

ROOMS: 6 en suite 3 annexe en suite (1 fmly) No smoking in all bedrooms **FACILITIES:** STV Fishing entertainment **CONF:** Thtr 60 **PARKING:** 20 **NOTES:** No smoking in restaurant
CARDS:

See advert on opposite page

TV dinner?
Room service at three stars and above

UPHOLLAND, Lancashire

Map 15 SD50

★★★64% Quality Hotel Skelmersdale

Prescott Rd WN8 9PU
☎ 01695 720401 📠 01695 50953
e-mail: enquiries@hotels-skelmersdale.com
Dir: *M6 junct 26 to M58. Leave at junct 5 for 'Pimbo' & turn left at rdbt follow into Prescott Road. Hotel on right*

This friendly hotel has attractive grounds and a magnificent Great Hall, dating back to 1580, now used primarily for banquets and weddings. The modern bedrooms are well equipped, and include facilities for less able guests. The bare stone walls in the bar and restaurant give added character.

ROOMS: 55 en suite (3 fmly) (21 GF) No smoking in 35 bedrooms s fr £79; d £89-£110 **LB** **FACILITIES:** STV Xmas **CONF:** Thtr 200 Class 125 Board 70 Del £109.50 **PARKING:** 200 **NOTES:** No smoking in restaurant Civ Wed 200 **CARDS:**

U Holland Hall Country House

Lafford Ln WN8 0QZ
☎ 01695 624426 📠 01695 622433
e-mail: ronjones@freeuk.com
Dir: *M6 junct 26 follow signs for Wigan & Upholland. At lights turn left, hotel 1.5m on right*

At the time of going to press, the star classification for this hotel was not confirmed. Please refer to the AA internet site www.theAA.com for current information.

ROOMS: 25 en suite 5 annexe en suite (5 fmly) (11 GF) No smoking in 22 bedrooms s £45-£110; d £55-£110 (incl. bkfst) **LB** **CONF:** Thtr 300 Class 110 Board 60 Del from £64 **PARKING:** 120 **NOTES:** No dogs (ex guide dogs) **CARDS:**

UPPER SLAUGHTER, Gloucestershire

Map 10 SP12

Top 200 - Hotel

★★★ ◎◎◎ Lords of the Manor

GL54 2JD
☎ 01451 820243 📠 01451 820696
e-mail: lordsofthemanor@btinternet.com
Dir: *2m W of A429. Turn off A40 onto A429, follow 'The Slaughters' signs. Continue through Lower Slaughter for 1m to Upper Slaughter. Hotel on right*

This wonderfully welcoming 17th-century manor house hotel sits in eight acres of gardens and parkland surrounded by Cotswold countryside. A relaxed atmosphere underpinned by professional and attentive service are the hallmarks here with guests often reluctant to leave. The public rooms are elegant and comfortable and the restaurant is the venue for consistently impressive cuisine. Bedrooms enjoy all the character and charm of the old building, combined with the extra touches expected of a hotel of this stature.

ROOMS: 27 en suite (9 GF) s £99; d £155-£305 (incl. bkfst) **LB** **FACILITIES:** STV Fishing Croquet lawn Xmas **CONF:** Thtr 30 Class 20 Board 20 Del £170 **PARKING:** 40 **NOTES:** No dogs (ex guide dogs) No smoking in restaurant Civ Wed 50 **CARDS:**

UPPINGHAM, Rutland

Map 11 SP89

★★★67% Falcon

The Market Place LE15 9PY
☎ 01572 823535 📠 01572 821620
e-mail: sales@thefalconhotel.com
Dir: *turn off A47 onto A6003, left at lights, hotel on right*

An attractive 16th-century coaching inn situated in the heart of this bustling market town. Public areas feature a superb open-plan lounge bar, with a relaxing atmosphere and comfortable sofas. The brasserie offers a cosmopolitan-style snack menu and more formal meals are provided in the Garden Terrace Restaurant. The hotel also has conference and functions rooms.

ROOMS: 25 en suite (4 fmly) (3 GF) s £50-£60; d £80-£115 (incl. bkfst) **LB** **FACILITIES:** STV Snooker entertainment Xmas **CONF:** Thtr 60 Class 40 Board 34 Del from £98 **PARKING:** 33 **NOTES:** No smoking in restaurant Civ Wed **CARDS:**

Late for dinner?
Quality Standards mean that last orders for dinner vary according to star rating and should be no earlier than:
★★ 7.00pm ★★★ 8.00pm ★★★★ 9.00pm
★★★★★ 10.00pm

U

UPPINGHAM, continued

★★72% ✪✪ The Lake Isle Restaurant & Town House Hotel
16 High St East LE15 9PZ
☎ 01572 822951 📠 01572 824400
e-mail: info@lakeislehotel.com
Dir: *in the centre of Uppingham via Queen Street*

This attractive town house hotel centres round a delightful restaurant and small elegant bar. There is also an inviting comfortable first floor guest lounge. Bedrooms, named after wine growing regions, and some with whirlpool baths, are extremely well appointed and thoughtfully equipped and include some spacious split-level cottage suites situated in a quiet courtyard. Imaginative cooking and an extremely impressive list of wines are a highlight.
ROOMS: 10 en suite 3 annexe en suite (1 fmly) No smoking in all bedrooms s £55-£65; d £70-£100 (incl. bkfst) **LB FACILITIES:** ch fac Xmas **CONF:** Board 10 **PARKING:** 8 **NOTES:** No smoking in restaurant
CARDS:

UPTON UPON SEVERN, Worcestershire — Map 10 SO84

★★★69% ✪ *White Lion*
21 High St WR8 0HJ
☎ 01684 592551 📠 01684 593333
e-mail: reservations@whitelionhotel.biz
Dir: *A422, A38 towards Tewkesbury. In 8m take B4104, after 1m over bridge, turn left to hotel, past bend on left*

Famed for being the inn depicted in Henry Fielding's novel *Tom Jones*, this 16th-century hotel brings 'ye olde England' to the fore with exposed beams, wall timbers, traditional furniture with lace table cloths and vases of fresh flowers. The White Lion has a well-deserved reputation for the quality of its food, which is complemented by friendly, attentive service.
ROOMS: 11 en suite **CONF:** Thtr 24 Class 12 Board 12 **PARKING:** 18
NOTES: No smoking in restaurant Closed 1 Jan RS 25,26 Dec & 1 Jan
CARDS:

URMSTON, Greater Manchester — Map 15 SJ79

⌂ Premier Lodge (Manchester Trafford Centre)
PREMIER LODGE
Trafford Boulevard M41 7JE
☎ 0870 9906310 📠 0870 9906311
Premier Lodge offers modern, well-equipped, en suite accommodation suitable for both business and leisure travellers. Meals can be taken at the adjacent popular restaurant and bar, which is fully licensed. For further details, consult the Hotel Groups page.
ROOMS: 42 en suite s £48; d £48

UTTOXETER, Staffordshire — Map 10 SK03

⌂ Travel Inn
travel inn
Derby Rd, (A518/A50) ST14 5AA
☎ 08701 977256 📠 01889 561801
Dir: *Situated at junction of A50/A518, one mile north of Uttoxeter town centre*
Travel Inn offers good-quality, value-for-money accommodation. Spacious, en suite rooms with bath and shower comfortably accommodate a family of up to two adults and two children (to age 15). The restaurant and bar offers a varied menu. For further details and the Travel Inn phone number, consult the Hotel Groups page.
ROOMS: 41 en suite s £44.95; d £44.95

⌂ Travelodge
Travelodge
Ashbourne Rd ST14 5AA
☎ 08700 850 950 📠 01889 562043
Dir: *on A50/A5030*
Travelodge offers good quality, good value, modern accommodation. Ideal for families, the spacious, en suite bedrooms include remote-control TV, tea and coffee-making facilities, luxury beds and free morning newspaper. Meals can be taken at the nearby family restaurant. For further details and the Travelodge phone number, consult the Hotel Groups page.
ROOMS: 32 en suite s fr £42.95; d fr £42.95

UXBRIDGE See advert on opposite page

VENTNOR See Wight, Isle of

VERYAN, Cornwall & Isles of Scilly — Map 02 SW93

★★★★77% ✪ Nare
Carne Beach TR2 5PF
☎ 01872 501111 📠 01872 501856
e-mail: office@narehotel.co.uk
Dir: *from Tregony follow A3078 for approx 1.5m turn left at Veryan signs, through village towards sea and hotel*
This delightful property offers a relaxed, country-house atmosphere in a spectacular coastal setting. Many of the bedrooms have balconies, and fresh flowers, carefully chosen artwork and antiques all contribute to the engaging individuality. A choice of dining options is available, from light snacks to superb local seafood.
ROOMS: 38 en suite (4 fmly) **FACILITIES: Spa** STV Indoor swimming (H) Outdoor swimming (H) Tennis (hard) Snooker Sauna Gym Croquet lawn Jacuzzi Health & Beauty clinic Hotel Boat Shooting **SERVICES:** Lift **PARKING:** 80 **NOTES:** No smoking in restaurant **CARDS:**

VIRGINIA WATER, Surrey Map 06 TQ06

★★70% *The Wheatsheaf*
London Rd GU25 4QF
☎ 01344 842057 📠 01344 842932
e-mail: sales@wheatsheafhotel.com
Dir: *M25 junct 13/A30 towards Camberley, follow A30 for approx 3m. From M3 junct 3/A30 towards London, through Sunningdale, 3m, pass Wentworth Golf Course. Hotel on left at lights*

This 19th-century inn is in a prime location overlooking the lake in Great Windsor Park. Bedrooms are well proportioned and comfortable, with stylish décor and a good range of facilities. The public rooms consist of a country-style bar and restaurant which offers a substantial lunch and dinner menu. Secure car parking is provided.
ROOMS: 17 en suite (2 fmly) No smoking in 10 bedrooms
FACILITIES: STV **CONF:** Thtr 50 Class 30 Board 25 **SERVICES:** air con
PARKING: 100 **NOTES:** No dogs (ex guide dogs) Civ Wed 60
CARDS:

WADEBRIDGE, Cornwall & Isles of Scilly Map 02 SW97

★★66% Molesworth Arms
Molesworth St PL27 7DP
☎ 01208 812055 📠 01208 814254
e-mail: info@molesworthharms.co.uk
Dir: *A30 to Bodmin town centre and follow signs to Wadebridge. Over old bridge turn right and then 1st left*
Situated in a pedestrian area of the town, this 16th-century former coaching inn is a popular base for exploring the area. The comfortable bedrooms retain their original character and charm. In addition to the wide range of snacks and meals served in the lively bar, the Courtyard Restaurant offers a comprehensive carte with daily specials.
ROOMS: 16 rms (14 en suite) (2 fmly) s £42.50; d £65 (incl. bkfst) **LB**
FACILITIES: STV **CONF:** Thtr 60 Class 50 Board 40 Del £85
PARKING: 16 **NOTES:** No smoking in restaurant
CARDS:

WAKEFIELD, West Yorkshire Map 16 SE32

★★★★64% Cedar Court
Denby Dale Rd WF4 3QZ
☎ 01924 276310 📠 01924 280221
e-mail: sales@cedarcourthotels.co.uk
Dir: *adjacent to M1 junct 39*
This hotel enjoys a convenient location just off the M1. Traditionally-styled bedrooms offer a good range of facilities while open-plan public areas include a busy bar and restaurant
continued

operation. Conferences and functions are extremely well catered for and a new leisure club completes the picture.
ROOMS: 151 en suite (2 fmly) (74 GF) No smoking in 100 bedrooms s £60-£120; d £70-£130 **LB** **FACILITIES: Spa** STV Indoor swimming (H) Sauna Solarium Gym Jacuzzi Indoor pool supervised **CONF:** BC Thtr 400 Class 200 Board 80 Del from £109 **SERVICES:** Lift **PARKING:** 350
NOTES: No smoking in restaurant Civ Wed 400
CARDS:

★★★74% Waterton Park
Walton Hall, The Balk, Walton WF2 6PW
☎ 01924 257911 & 249800 📠 01924 259686
e-mail: watertonpark@bestwestern.co.uk
Dir: *3m SE off B6378 - off M1 junct 39 towards Wakefield. At rdbt right for Crofton. At 2nd set of lights turn right and follow signs*

Best Western

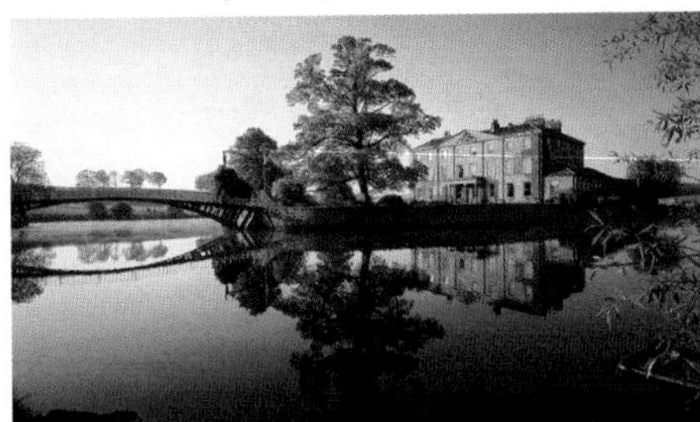

Built on an island in the centre of a lake this hotel has an idyllic setting. The Hall contains many feature bedrooms, and the new annexe houses more spacious rooms, all equally well equipped
continued on p630

W

WAKEFIELD, continued

with modern facilities. The delightful beamed restaurant, two bars and leisure centre are located in the old hall, and the hotel has a licence for civil weddings.
ROOMS: 25 en suite 35 annexe en suite No smoking in 10 bedrooms s £50-£95; d £80-£140 (incl. bkfst) **LB** **FACILITIES:** **Spa** STV Indoor swimming (H) Golf 18 Fishing Sauna Solarium Gym Jacuzzi Steam room Xmas **CONF:** Thtr 150 Class 80 Board 80 Del from £120 **PARKING:** 180 **NOTES:** No dogs (ex guide dogs) No smoking in restaurant Civ Wed 80 **CARDS:**

★★★69% Hotel St Pierre

Barnsley Rd, Newmillerdam WF2 6QG
☎ 01924 255596 01924 252746
e-mail: sales@hotelstpierre.co.uk
Dir: *M1 junct 39 take A636 to Wakefield, turn right at rdbt, into Asdale Road to lights. Turn right onto A61 towards Barnsley. Hotel just after lake*
This well-furnished hotel lies south of Wakefield close to Newmiller Dam. The interior of the modern building has comfortable and thoughtfully equipped bedrooms and smart public rooms. A good selection of conference rooms, a small gymnasium and an intimate restaurant are all provided for guests' use.
ROOMS: 54 en suite (3 fmly) No smoking in 33 bedrooms s £75; d £85 **LB** **FACILITIES:** STV Gym Xmas **CONF:** Thtr 120 Class 60 Board 60 **SERVICES:** Lift **PARKING:** 70 **NOTES:** Civ Wed 60
CARDS:

★★★64% Chasley Hotel

Queen St WF1 1JU
☎ 01924 372111 01924 383648
e-mail: anybody@chasleywakefield.supanet.com
Dir: *leave M1 junct 39 & follow signs for town centre. Queen St on left*
Situated in the centre of the city and close to the cathedral, this modern multi-storey hotel offers well-equipped and pleasantly furnished bedrooms. There is a comfortable bar lounge next to the spacious restaurant, where a set-price menu is offered. Conference facilities are also available.
ROOMS: 64 en suite (4 fmly) No smoking in 16 bedrooms s £34.95-£49.95; d £39.95-£54.95 (incl. bkfst) **FACILITIES:** Sunbeds, Fitness Room Xmas **CONF:** Thtr 250 Class 90 Board 54 Del from £65 **SERVICES:** Lift **PARKING:** 30 **NOTES:** No dogs (ex guide dogs) No smoking in restaurant Civ Wed 250 **CARDS:**

U *Holiday Inn Wakefield*

Queen's Dr, Ossett WF5 9BE
☎ 0870 400 9082 01924 276437
e-mail: reservations-wakefield@ichotelsgroup.com
Dir: *M1 junct 40 follow signs for Wakefield. Hotel on right after 200yds*
At the time of going to press, the classification for this hotel was not confirmed. Please refer to the AA internet site www.theAA.com for current information.
ROOMS: 105 en suite (5 fmly) No smoking in 71 bedrooms **FACILITIES:** **SERVICES:** Lift **PARKING:** 130 **CARDS:**

Campanile

Monckton Rd WF2 7AL
☎ 01924 201054 01924 201055
e-mail: wakefield@envergure.co.uk
Dir: *M1 junct 39, A636 1m towards Wakefield, left onto Monckton Rd, hotel on left*
This modern building offers accommodation in smart, well-equipped bedrooms, all with en suite bathrooms. Refreshments may be taken at the informal Bistro. For further details and the Campanile phone number, consult the Hotel Groups page.

ROOMS: 77 annexe en suite **CONF:** Thtr 35 Class 18 Board 20

Express By Holiday Inn

Denby Dale Rd WF4 3BB
☎ 01924 257555 01924 249888
e-mail: ebhi-wakefield@btconnect.com

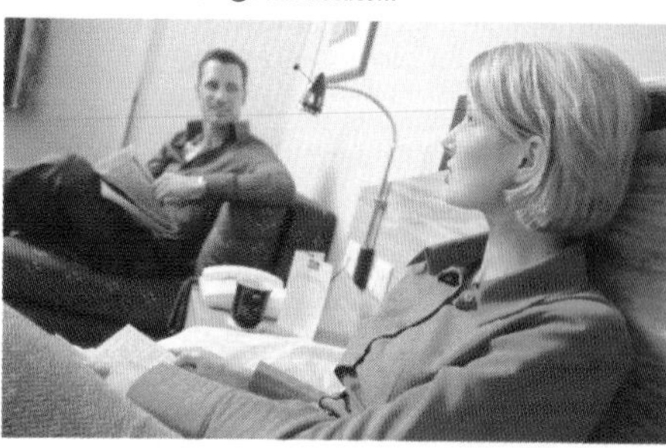

A modern hotel ideal for families and business travellers. Fresh and uncomplicated, the spacious bedrooms include Sky TV, power shower and tea and coffee-making facilities. Continental buffet breakfast is included in the room rate; other meals may be taken at the nearby family pub or restaurant. For further details and the Express by Holiday Inn phone number, consult the Hotel Groups pages.
ROOMS: 74 en suite **CONF:** Thtr 30 Class 24 Board 16

Travel Inn

Thornes Park, Denby Dale Rd WF2 8DY
☎ 08701 977257 01924 373620
Dir: *From M1 junct take A636 towards Wakefield town centre. Inn on left at 3rd rbt.*
Travel Inn offers good-quality, value-for-money accommodation. Spacious, en suite rooms with bath and shower comfortably accommodate a family of up to two adults and two children (to age 15). The restaurant and bar offers a varied menu. For further details and the Travel Inn phone number, consult the Hotel Groups page.
ROOMS: 42 en suite s £44.95; d £44.95 **CONF:** Thtr 54 Board 24

Travelodge Wakefield (Northbound)

M1 Service Area, West Bretton WF4 4LQ
☎ 08700 850 950
(For full entry see Woolley Edge)

WALLASEY, Merseyside Map 15 SJ29

★★★70% Grove House

Grove Rd CH45 3HF
☎ 0151 639 3947 & 0151 630 4558 📠 0151 639 0028
e-mail: reception@thegrovehouse.co.uk

This is an immaculately maintained, family-owned hotel. Many of the bedrooms enjoy a view over the attractive gardens to the rear of the hotel; all are comfortably furnished and particularly well-equipped. The bar lounge provides a venue to relax with a drink, before dinner in the oak-panelled restaurant.

ROOMS: 14 en suite (7 fmly) s £56.50; d £59.75 **FACILITIES:** STV Xmas **CONF:** Thtr 50 Class 30 Board 50 Del from £95 **PARKING:** 28 **NOTES:** No dogs (ex guide dogs) RS Bank holidays Civ Wed 50 **CARDS:**

WALLINGFORD, Oxfordshire Map 05 SU68

★★★72% Springs Hotel & Golf Club

Wallingford Rd, North Stoke OX10 6BE
☎ 01491 836687 📠 01491 836877
e-mail: info@thespringshotel.com
Dir: *off A4074 Oxford-Reading road onto B4009. Hotel approx 1m on right*

Set on its own golf course, this Victorian mansion has a timeless and peaceful atmosphere. Bedrooms vary in size; many are spacious, and all are generously equipped. The elegant restaurant enjoys splendid views over the spring-fed lake. There is also a comfortable lounge with original features, and a cosy bar in which to relax.

ROOMS: 31 en suite (3 fmly) (8 GF) No smoking in 6 bedrooms s £90-£140; d £105-£150 (incl. bkfst) **LB FACILITIES:** STV Outdoor swimming Golf 18 Fishing Sauna Croquet lawn Putting green Clay pigeon shooting entertainment ch fac Xmas **CONF:** BC Thtr 60 Class 16 Board 26 Del from £155 **PARKING:** 150 **NOTES:** No smoking in restaurant Civ Wed 100 **CARDS:**

★★★68% The George

PEEL HOTELS

High St OX10 0BS
☎ 01491 836665 📠 01491 825359
e-mail: info@george-hotel-wallingford.com
Dir: *E side of A329 on N entry to town*

Old World charm and modern facilities merge seamlessly in this former coaching inn. Bedrooms in the main house have charm and character in abundance. Those in the new wing have a more contemporary style, and all are well equipped and attractively decorated. Diners can choose between the restaurant and bistro, or relax in the bar.

ROOMS: 39 en suite (1 fmly) No smoking in 21 bedrooms s £110-£120; d £115-£140 **LB FACILITIES:** STV Xmas **CONF:** Thtr 120 Class 60 Board 40 Del from £135 **PARKING:** 60 **NOTES:** No dogs (ex guide dogs) No smoking in restaurant Civ Wed 100
CARDS:

★★★68% Shillingford Bridge

Forestdale Hotels

Shillingford OX10 8LZ
☎ 01865 858567 📠 01865 858636
e-mail: shillingford.bridge@forestdale.com
Dir: *M4 junct 10 follow A329 through Wallingford towards Thame, follow B4009 through Watlington turn right on A4074 at Benson, then left at Shillingford rdbt (unclass road) Wallingford Rd*

The hotel enjoys an unrivalled position right on the banks of the Thames, and benefits from private moorings and a waterside open-air swimming pool. The public areas have large picture windows making the best use of the view. Bedrooms are well equipped and furnished with comfort in mind.

ROOMS: 34 en suite 8 annexe en suite (6 fmly) No smoking in 8 bedrooms s fr £90; d fr £115 (incl. bkfst) **LB FACILITIES:** Outdoor swimming (H) Fishing Squash Swimming pool supervised entertainment Xmas **CONF:** Thtr 80 Class 36 Board 26 Del from £120 **PARKING:** 100 **NOTES:** No smoking in restaurant Civ Wed
CARDS:

WALLINGTON, Greater London Map 06 TQ26

★★★63% Dukes Head

6 Manor Rd, The Green SM6 0AA
☎ 020 8401 7410 📠 020 8401 7420
e-mail: dukeshead@youngs.co.uk

This traditional coaching inn, between Croydon and Sutton, has been modernised and restored to provide superior accommodation. Bedrooms are spacious, furnished to a high standard and well equipped. Public areas include a popular bar and a bright airy dining area where a range of freshly prepared dishes are served.

ROOMS: 24 en suite (4 fmly) (9 GF) No smoking in 15 bedrooms s £65-£99; d £75-£109 (incl. bkfst) **LB FACILITIES:** STV Xmas **CONF:** Thtr 24 Class 28 Board 24 **SERVICES:** air con **PARKING:** 35 **NOTES:** No dogs (ex guide dogs) No smoking in restaurant RS 25th and 31st Dec **CARDS:**

WALSALL, West Midlands Map 10 SP09

★★★★65% Menzies Baron's Court

MENZIES HOTELS

Walsall Rd, Walsall Wood WS9 9AH
☎ 01543 452020 📠 01543 361276
e-mail: info@menzies-hotels.co.uk
Dir: *M6 junct 7, take A34 towards Walsall, follow the A4148 ring road, at rdbt turn right onto A461 towards Lichfield, hotel 3 miles on right*

This hotel prides itself on warm hospitality and is conveniently situated for business guests to this area. The lounge, bar and restaurant are modern and thoughtfully designed following refurbishment. Additional features include a small leisure complex and conference facilities.

ROOMS: 94 en suite (2 fmly) No smoking in 19 bedrooms **FACILITIES:** STV Indoor swimming (H) Sauna Solarium Gym Jacuzzi entertainment **CONF:** Thtr 200 Class 100 Board 100 Del from £125 **SERVICES:** Lift **PARKING:** 200 **NOTES:** No smoking in restaurant Civ Wed 200 **CARDS:**

WALSALL, continued

★★★76% ◎◎ **The Fairlawns at Aldridge**

178 Little Aston Rd, Aldridge WS9 0NU
☎ 01922 455122 ▯ 01922 743210
e-mail: welcome@fairlawns.co.uk
Dir: *off A452 towards Aldridge at x-roads with A454, Hotel 600yds on right*

In a rural location, this friendly hotel offers a wide range of facilities and modern, comfortable bedrooms. Family rooms, one room with a four-poster bed, suites and even budget rooms are available. The Fairlawns Restaurant serves a wide range of delectable seasonal dishes. The leisure complex is predominantly for adult use and has restricted availability for young people.
ROOMS: 50 en suite (8 fmly) (1 GF) No smoking in 34 bedrooms s £69.50-£107.50; d £89.50-£127.50 (incl. bkfst) **LB FACILITIES: Spa** STV Indoor swimming (H) Tennis (hard) Sauna Solarium Gym Croquet lawn Jacuzzi Dance studio Beauty Salon, Indoor Pool Supervised **CONF:** Thtr 80 Class 40 Board 30 Del from £135 **PARKING:** 150 **NOTES:** No smoking in restaurant Civ Wed 100
CARDS:

★★★68% **Beverley**
58 Lichfield Rd WS4 2DJ
☎ 01922 614967 & 622999 ▯ 01922 724187
Dir: *1m N of Walsall town centre on A461 to Lichfield*
A privately-owned hotel dating back to 1880. Bedrooms are comfortably appointed and equipped with thoughtful extras. The tastefully decorated public areas include a relaxing guest lounge and a spacious bar combined with a conservatory. The Gallery Restaurant offers guests a choice of carefully prepared dishes.
ROOMS: 40 en suite (2 fmly) (4 GF) No smoking in 6 bedrooms s £55-£70; d £65-£100 (incl. bkfst) **LB FACILITIES:** Games room **CONF:** BC Thtr 60 Class 30 Board 30 Del from £100 **PARKING:** 68 **NOTES:** No dogs (ex guide dogs) No smoking in restaurant
CARDS:

★★★65% **Quality Hotel & Suites Walsall**

20 Wolverhampton Rd West, Bentley WS2 0BS
☎ 01922 724444 ▯ 01922 723148
e-mail: enquiries@hotels-walsall.com
Dir: *on rdbt at M6 junct 10*
This conveniently located hotel offers well-equipped rooms including air-conditioned suites with personal fax and a kitchen. There is an extensive all day menu plus room service. Guests can also choose to dine in the carvery restaurant.
ROOMS: 154 en suite (120 fmly) (78 GF) No smoking in 64 bedrooms s £45-£99; d £65-£135 **LB FACILITIES: Spa** STV Indoor swimming (H) Sauna Gym Jacuzzi Swimming pool supervised **CONF:** Thtr 180 Class 70 Board 80 Del from £65 **PARKING:** 160 **NOTES:** No dogs (ex guide dogs) No smoking in restaurant Civ Wed 120
CARDS:

★★★64% **Quality Hotel**
Birmingham Rd WS5 3AB
☎ 01922 633609 ▯ 01922 635727
e-mail: info@boundaryhotel.com
Dir: *M6 junct 7, A34 to Walsall. Hotel 1.5m on left*
Bedrooms at this purpose-built hotel, including some on the ground floor, are soundly furnished and well equipped. Public areas include a pleasantly appointed main restaurant (more informal meals are served in the public bar) and a cellar bar which occasionally features live music. Hotel guests also have the use of a well-maintained tennis court.
ROOMS: 94 en suite (3 fmly) (5 GF) No smoking in 24 bedrooms s £65-£95; d £75-£105 **LB FACILITIES:** STV Tennis (hard) entertainment **CONF:** Thtr 60 Class 30 Board 30 Del from £110 **SERVICES:** Lift **PARKING:** 250 **NOTES:** No smoking in restaurant Civ Wed 40
CARDS:

★★63% **Bescot**
87 Bescot Rd WS2 9DG
☎ 01922 622447 ▯ 01922 630256
e-mail: enquiries@bescothotel.com
Dir: *M6 junct 9 take A461 to Walsall. Hotel 100mtrs on right*
The Bescot is a privately owned and business-focused hotel. Public rooms are comfortable and freshly furnished, and include a large function suite and a spacious restaurant. Bedrooms have a good range of facilities and the annexe rooms are spacious, especially the two ground floor courtyard rooms. The owners have positive plans for major refurbishment.
ROOMS: 22 en suite 11 annexe en suite (4 fmly) s £40-£43.50; d £50-£53.50 (incl. bkfst) **FACILITIES:** STV Xmas **CONF:** Thtr 80 Class 50 Board 40 Del from £61.50 **PARKING:** 55 **NOTES:** No dogs (ex guide dogs) **CARDS:**

⌂ **Travel Inn**
Bentley Green, Bentley Rd North WS2 0WB
☎ 08701 977258 ▯ 01922 724098
Dir: *M6 junct 10, A454 signed Wolverhampton & then 2nd exit (Ansons junct). Left at rdbt, 1st left at next rdbt, Travel Inn on right*
Travel Inn offers good-quality, value-for-money accommodation. Spacious, en suite rooms with bath and shower comfortably accommodate a family of up to two adults and two children (to age 15). The restaurant and bar offers a varied menu. For further details and the Travel Inn phone number, consult the Hotel Groups page.
ROOMS: 40 en suite s £44.95; d £44.95

WALTERSTONE, Herefordshire Map 09 SO32

★★★68% **Allt-yr-Ynys Country House Hotel**
HR2 0DU
☎ 01873 890307 ▯ 01873 890539
e-mail: allthotel@compuserve.com
(For full entry see Abergavenny)

WALTHAM ABBEY, Essex Map 06 TL30

★★★★69% **Waltham Abbey Marriott**
Old Shire Ln EN9 3LX
☎ 01992 717170 ▯ 01992 711841
e-mail: waltham.abbey@marriotthotels.co.uk
Dir: *M25 junct 26*
This Marriott lies within easy reach of London and the major road networks. Following a substantial refurbishment programme it offers good guest bedrooms. Each room is well designed, attractively decorated and has a useful range of extras. It also
continued

boasts a range of meeting rooms, substantial car parking and a well-equipped leisure facility.

ROOMS: 162 en suite (16 fmly) No smoking in 132 bedrooms s £80-£109; d £90-£109 **LB FACILITIES:** STV Indoor swimming (H) Sauna Solarium Gym Jacuzzi Steam room, Beauty Salon entertainment Xmas **CONF:** BC Thtr 250 Class 120 Board 50 Del £185 **SERVICES:** air con **PARKING:** 240 **NOTES:** No dogs (ex guide dogs) No smoking in restaurant Civ Wed 180 **CARDS:**

Premier Lodge (Waltham Abbey)

The Grange, Sewardstone Rd EN9 3QF

☎ 0870 9906568 ▯ 0870 9906569

Dir: *1m S of town & 0.5m from M25 junct 26*

Premier Lodge offers modern, well-equipped, en suite accommodation suitable for both business and leisure travellers. Meals can be taken at the adjacent popular restaurant and bar, which is fully licensed. For further details, consult the Hotel Groups page.

ROOMS: 93 en suite s £56; d £56

WALTON-ON-THAMES, Surrey
See LONDON SECTION plan 1 A1

Innkeeper's Lodge Walton-on-Thames

Ashley Park Rd KT12 1JP

☎ 01932 220196 ▯ 01932 220660

Dir: *M25 junct 11 E towards A317 Weybridge, at B365 rdbt for Ashley Park, left then right into Station Ave, left opp station*

A new concept in the travel accommodation market. Smart rooms meet essential business requirements but also have home comforts. Dining options include all-day menus plus the added advantage of breakfast, which is included in the room price. For further details, consult the Hotel Groups page.

ROOMS: 32 en suite **CONF:** Thtr 60 Class 24 Board 24

WANSFORD, Cambridgeshire — Map 12 TL09

★★★73% *The Haycock Hotel*

PE8 6JA

☎ 01780 782223 ▯ 01780 783031

e-mail: gm.haycock@arcadianhotels.co.uk

Dir: *at junct of A47/A1, signed in village adjacent to bridge*

Charming 17th-century coaching inn set amidst attractive landscaped grounds in the heart of this peaceful village just off the A1 & A47. The pleasantly decorated bedrooms are tastefully furnished and equipped with many useful extras, some rooms have lovely views over the gardens. The hotel features a staffed business centre with a range of meeting rooms, and banqueting facilities are also available.

ROOMS: 50 en suite (3 fmly) No smoking in 6 bedrooms **FACILITIES:** STV Fishing Petanque **CONF:** Thtr 250 Class 100 Board 40 **PARKING:** 300 **NOTES:** No smoking in restaurant Civ Wed 100 **CARDS:**

WARDLEY, Tyne & Wear — Map 21 NZ36

Travelodge Newcastle East

Leam Ln, Whitemare Pool NE10 8YB

☎ 08700 850 950 ▯ 0191 438 3333

Dir: *at junc of A194M/A184*

Travelodge offers good quality, good value, modern accommodation. Ideal for families, the spacious, en suite bedrooms include remote-control TV, tea and coffee-making facilities, luxury beds and free morning newspaper. Meals can be taken at the nearby family restaurant. For further details and the Travelodge phone number, consult the Hotel Groups page.

ROOMS: 71 en suite s fr £42.95; d fr £42.95

WARE, Hertfordshire — Map 06 TL31

★★★★★74% Marriott Hanbury Manor Hotel & Country Club

SG12 0SD

☎ 01920 487722 & 0870 400 7222

▯ 01920 487692

e-mail: salesadmin.hanburymanor@marriotthotels.co.uk

Dir: *M25 junct 25, take A10 north for 12m, hotel on left*

Set in 200 acres of landscaped grounds, this impressive Jacobean style mansion boasts an enviable range of leisure facilities, including an excellent health club and championship golf course. Bedrooms are traditionally and comfortably furnished in the country-house style and have lovely marbled bathrooms. There are a number of food and drink options, including the renowned Zodiac and Oakes restaurants.

ROOMS: 134 en suite 27 annexe en suite (3 GF) No smoking in 96 bedrooms s £139-£339; d £139-£339 **LB FACILITIES: Spa** STV Indoor swimming (H) Golf 18 Tennis (hard) Snooker Sauna Solarium Gym Croquet lawn Putting green Jacuzzi Health & beauty treatments, Aerobics, Yoga Dance class, Swimming pool supervised Xmas **CONF:** BC Thtr 120 Class 76 Board 36 Del from £200 **SERVICES:** Lift **PARKING:** 200 **NOTES:** Civ Wed 120 **CARDS:**

★★★64% Roebuck

Baldock St SG12 9DR

☎ 01920 409955 ▯ 01920 468016

e-mail: roebuck@forestdale.com

Dir: *turn off A10 onto B1001, turn left at rdbt 1st left behind Fire Station*

Close to the town centre, this modern hotel is a popular choice for business guests. Bedrooms are mostly spacious and have been refurbished; a number are on the ground floor and some are suitable for less able guests. Public areas are smart and consist of a range of conference rooms, a bar and cosy lounge area.

ROOMS: 50 en suite (1 fmly) (16 GF) No smoking in 16 bedrooms s fr £95; d fr £115 (incl. bkfst) **LB FACILITIES:** STV **CONF:** Thtr 200 Class 75 Board 60 Del from £125 **SERVICES:** Lift **PARKING:** 64 **NOTES:** No smoking in restaurant **CARDS:**

WAREHAM, Dorset — Map 04 SY98

★★★68% *Springfield Country Hotel & Leisure Club*

Grange Rd BH20 5AL

☎ 01929 552177 ▯ 01929 551862

Dir: *from Wareham take Stoborough road then 1st right in village to join by-pass. Then left, and immediately right*

This attractive hotel is quietly located in the countryside and offers extensive leisure facilities along with a diverse range of conference and business facilities. Bedrooms include a choice of executive or

continued on p634

WAREHAM, continued

standard rooms and all are comfortable, well furnished and pleasantly spacious.
ROOMS: 48 en suite (7 fmly) **FACILITIES:** Indoor swimming (H) Outdoor swimming (H) Tennis (hard) Squash Snooker Sauna Gym Jacuzzi Steam room Table tennis Beauty treatment ch fac **CONF:** Thtr 200 Class 50 Board 60 **SERVICES:** Lift **PARKING:** 150 **NOTES:** No smoking in restaurant **CARDS:**

★★67% Kemps Country House

East Stoke BH20 6AL
☎ 01929 462563 01929 405287
e-mail: kemps.hotel@lineone.net
Dir: *midway between Wareham & Wool on A352*
A relaxing family-owned hotel with views to the Purbeck Hills in the distance. Bedrooms are spacious and include modern garden rooms, and there are two comfortable lounges and an adjoining bar. An extensive choice is offered from the imaginative set menu and carte; bar meals are available at lunchtime.
ROOMS: 5 rms (4 en suite) 10 annexe en suite (4 fmly) s £67-£80; d £98-£140 (incl. bkfst) **LB** **FACILITIES:** Jacuzzi Xmas **CONF:** Thtr 100 Class 50 Board 24 Del from £84.95 **PARKING:** 50 **NOTES:** No dogs (ex guide dogs) No smoking in restaurant
CARDS:

★★66% Worgret Manor

Worgret Rd BH20 6AB
☎ 01929 552957 01929 554804
e-mail: admin@worgretmanorhotel.co.uk
Dir: *on A352 from Wareham to Wool, 0.5m from Wareham rdbt*
On the edge of Wareham, with easy access to major routes, this privately owned Georgian manor house offers a friendly, cheerful atmosphere. The bedrooms come in a variety of sizes. Public rooms comprise a popular bar, a quiet lounge and a restaurant where good home-cooked meals are served.
ROOMS: 12 en suite (1 fmly) No smoking in 4 bedrooms s £55-£60; d £80-£90 (incl. bkfst) **LB** **FACILITIES:** Free use of local sports centre **CONF:** Thtr 50 **PARKING:** 25 **NOTES:** No smoking in restaurant
CARDS:

WARMINSTER, Wiltshire — Map 04 ST84

★★★★74% Bishopstrow House

BA12 9HH
☎ 01985 212312 01985 216769
e-mail: reservations@bishopstrow.co.uk
Dir: *A303, A36, B3414, premises 2m on right*
This is a fine example of a Georgian country home, situated in 27 acres of Wiltshire countryside. Public areas are traditional in style enhanced with antiques and open fires. The spa, tennis court and country walks ensure there is something for all guests. The restaurant serves quality contemporary cuisine.
ROOMS: 32 en suite (3 fmly) No smoking in 1 bedroom s £99; d £160-£375 (incl. bkfst) **LB** **FACILITIES:** STV Indoor swimming (H) Outdoor swimming (H) Tennis (hard) Fishing Sauna Gym Croquet lawn Clay pigeon shooting Archery Cycling entertainment Xmas **CONF:** Thtr 65 Class 32 Board 36 Del from £175 **PARKING:** 60 **NOTES:** No smoking in restaurant Civ Wed 70 **CARDS:**

Travelodge

Travelodge

A36 Bath Rd BA12 7RU
☎ 08700 850 950 01525 878450
Dir: *junct A350/A36*
Travelodge offers good quality, good value, modern accommodation. Ideal for families, the spacious, en suite bedrooms include remote-control TV, tea and coffee-making facilities, luxury beds and free morning newspaper. Meals can be taken at the nearby family restaurant. For further details and the Travelodge phone number, consult the Hotel Groups page.
ROOMS: 31 en suite s fr £42.95; d fr £42.95

WARRINGTON, Cheshire — Map 15 SJ68

★★★★72% Hanover International Hotel & Club

Stretton Rd, Stretton WA4 4NS
☎ 01925 730706 01925 730740
e-mail: reception@hanover-international.com
Dir: *M56 junct 10, A49 to Warrington, at lights turn right to Appleton Thorn, hotel 200yds on right*

This modern hotel enjoys a peaceful setting, yet is conveniently located just minutes from the M56. Comfortable bedrooms are smartly appointed and thoughtfully equipped. Spacious, attractive public areas include extensive conference and function facilities, and a comprehensive leisure centre complete with outdoor tennis courts and an impressive beauty centre.
ROOMS: 142 en suite (15 fmly) (31 GF) No smoking in 54 bedrooms s £115-£180; d £125-£180 **LB** **FACILITIES:** STV Indoor swimming (H) Tennis (hard) Sauna Solarium Gym Jacuzzi Retreat Beauty centre, Dance studio, Steam room Xmas **CONF:** BC Thtr 400 Class 200 Board 90 Del from £110 **SERVICES:** Lift **PARKING:** 400 **NOTES:** No dogs (ex guide dogs) No smoking in restaurant Civ Wed 400
CARDS:

★★★★71% De Vere Daresbury Park

DE VERE HOTELS

Chester Rd, Daresbury WA4 4BB
☎ 01925 267331 01925 265615
e-mail: daresburypark.salesmanager@devere-hotels.com
Dir: *hotel entrance off M56 junct 11*

Close to motorway networks and tourist attractions, this modern hotel is a very popular venue for business and leisure travellers. Public areas are themed around 'Alice in Wonderland' in tribute to

continued

local author Lewis Carroll. These include a range of eating and drinking options, leisure facilities and extensive conference facilities.
ROOMS: 181 en suite (14 fmly) (62 GF) No smoking in 114 bedrooms s £139-£224; d £149-£234 **LB** **FACILITIES: Spa** STV Indoor swimming (H) Squash Snooker Sauna Solarium Gym Jacuzzi Steam Room Xmas **CONF:** BC Thtr 300 Class 250 Board 100 Del from £145 **SERVICES:** Lift **PARKING:** 400 **NOTES:** Civ Wed 300 **CARDS:**

★★★72% Fir Grove
Knutsford Old Rd WA4 2LD
☎ 01925 267471 🖷 01925 601092
e-mail: firgrovehotel@bestwestern.co.uk
Dir: *M6 junct 20, follow signs for A50 to Warrington for 2.4m, before swing bridge over canal, turn right, and right again*
Situated in a quiet residential area, this hotel is convenient for both the town centre and the motorway network. Comfortable, smart bedrooms, including new spacious executive rooms, offer some excellent extra facilities such as playstations and CD players. Public areas include a smart lounge/bar, a neatly appointed restaurant and function and meeting facilities.
ROOMS: 52 en suite (3 fmly) (20 GF) No smoking in 20 bedrooms s £65-£85; d £79-£99 (incl. bkfst) **FACILITIES:** STV Xmas **CONF:** Thtr 200 Class 150 Board 50 Del from £99 **PARKING:** 100 **NOTES:** No smoking in restaurant Civ Wed 150 **CARDS:**

★★66% Paddington House
514 Old Manchester Rd WA1 3TZ
☎ 01925 816767 🖷 01925 816651
e-mail: hotel@paddingtonhouse.co.uk
Dir: *1m from M6 junct 21, off A57, 2m from town centre*
This busy mainly commercial hotel is conveniently situated just over a mile from the M6. The bedrooms are attractively furnished, and include four-poster and ground-floor rooms. Guests can dine in the wood-panelled Padgate restaurant or in the cosy bar.
ROOMS: 37 en suite (9 fmly) (6 GF) No smoking in 17 bedrooms s £41.50-£62; d £49.50-£85 (incl. bkfst) **LB** **CONF:** Thtr 180 Class 100 Board 40 Del from £85 **SERVICES:** Lift **PARKING:** 50 **NOTES:** No smoking in restaurant Civ Wed 150
CARDS:

U Holiday Inn Warrington/Cheshire
Woolston Grange Av, Woolston WA1 4PX
☎ 01925 838779 🖷 01925 838859
At the time of going to press, the classification for this hotel was not confirmed. Please refer to the AA internet site www.theAA.com for current information.
ROOMS: 97 en suite (41 fmly) No smoking in 75 bedrooms **FACILITIES:** STV Gym **CONF:** Thtr 25 Class 10 Board 14 **SERVICES:** Lift **PARKING:** 125 **CARDS:**

⌂ Innkeeper's Lodge Warrington
322 Newton Rd, Lowton Village WA3 1HD
☎ 0870 243 0500 & 01942 671421 🖷 01942 269692
Dir: *M56 junct 23, A580 towards Manchester, follow signs for Toby Carvery*
A new concept in the travel accommodation market. Smart rooms meet essential business requirements but also have home comforts. Dining options include all-day menus plus the added advantage of breakfast, which is included in the room price. For further details, consult the Hotel Groups page.
ROOMS: 58 en suite

Packed in a hurry?
Ironing facilities should be available at all star levels, either in rooms or on request

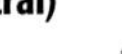

⌂ Premier Lodge (Warrington Central)
Manchester Rd, Woolston WA1 4GB
☎ 0870 9906524 🖷 0870 9906525

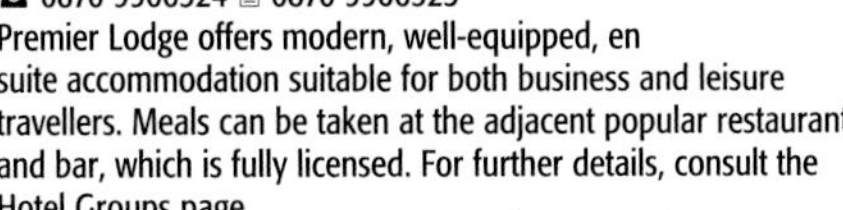

Premier Lodge offers modern, well-equipped, en suite accommodation suitable for both business and leisure travellers. Meals can be taken at the adjacent popular restaurant and bar, which is fully licensed. For further details, consult the Hotel Groups page.
ROOMS: 105 en suite s £48; d £48

⌂ Premier Lodge (Warrington North)
Golborne Rd, Winwick WA2 8LF
☎ 0870 9906600 🖷 0870 9906601
Premier Lodge offers modern, well-equipped, en suite accommodation suitable for both business and leisure travellers. Meals can be taken at the adjacent popular restaurant and bar, which is fully licensed. For further details, consult the Hotel Groups page.
ROOMS: 42 en suite s £48; d £48 **CONF:** Thtr 30 Class 20 Board 25 Del £85

⌂ Premier Lodge (Warrington South)
Tarporley Rd, Stretton WA4 4NB
☎ 0870 9906526 🖷 0870 9906527
Premier Lodge offers modern, well-equipped, en suite accommodation suitable for both business and leisure travellers. Meals can be taken at the adjacent popular restaurant and bar, which is fully licensed. For further details, consult the Hotel Groups page.
ROOMS: 29 en suite s £48; d £48

⌂ Travel Inn (Warrington East)
1430 Centre Park, Park Boulevard WA1 1QR
☎ 08701 977259 🖷 01925 244259
Dir: *at Bridgefoot junct of A49/A50/A56 in centre of Warrington*
Travel Inn offers good-quality, value-for-money accommodation. Spacious, en suite rooms with bath and shower comfortably accommodate a family of up to two adults and two children (to age 15). The restaurant and bar offers a varied menu. For further details and the Travel Inn phone number, consult the Hotel Groups page.
ROOMS: 42 en suite s £44.95; d £44.95

⌂ Travel Inn (Warrington North)
Woburn Rd WA2 8RN
☎ 08701 977260 🖷 01925 414544
Dir: *M62 junct 9 towards Warrington, 100yds from junct*
Travel Inn offers good-quality, value-for-money accommodation. Spacious, en suite rooms with bath and shower comfortably accommodate a family of up to two adults and two children (to age 15). The restaurant and bar offers a varied menu. For further details and the Travel Inn phone number, consult the Hotel Groups page.
ROOMS: 40 en suite s £44.95; d £44.95

⌂ Travelodge
Kendrick/Leigh St WA1 1UZ
☎ 08700 850 950
Dir: *M6 junct 21, follow A57 towards Liverpool & Widnes to Warrington town centre, through Asda rdbt, lodge next left at lights*
Travelodge offers good quality, good value, modern accommodation. Ideal for families, the spacious, en suite bedrooms include remote-control TV, tea and coffee-making facilities, luxury beds and free morning newspaper. Meals can be taken at the nearby family restaurant. For further details and the Travelodge phone number, consult the Hotel Groups page.
ROOMS: 63 en suite s fr £42.95; d fr £42.95

WARWICK, Warwickshire
Map 10 SP26

See also Honiley & Leamington Spa (Royal)

★★★★74% ® Ardencote Manor Hotel & Country Club
Lye Green Rd CV35 8LS
☎ 01926 843111 📠 01926 842646
e-mail: hotel@ardencote.com
(For full entry see Claverdon)

★★★64% Lord Leycester
Jury St CV34 4EJ
☎ 01926 491481 📠 01926 491561
e-mail: reception@lord-leycester.co.uk
Dir: *M40 junct 15, A429 into town centre, past West Gate onto High St & Jury St.*

This historic Grade II listed property is just a short walk from the famous castle. Upgraded bedrooms and public rooms provide comfortable accommodation. A choice of eating options is available in either the informal Squires Buttery or the Knights Restaurant.
ROOMS: 49 en suite (3 fmly) No smoking in 15 bedrooms s £59-£79; d £68-£90 (incl. bkfst) **LB** **FACILITIES:** Xmas **CONF:** Thtr 120 Class 50 Board 40 Del from £95 **SERVICES:** Lift **PARKING:** 40 **NOTES:** No smoking in restaurant **CARDS:**

★★62% Warwick Arms
17 High St CV34 4AT
☎ 01926 492759 📠 01926 410587
e-mail: warwickarms@ukonline.co.uk
Dir: *M40 junct 15, main rd into Warwick, premises 100yds past Lord Leycester Hospital*
A relaxed hotel in the heart of Warwick, close to the castle walls. Typical in an older building, bedrooms vary in size and style but have a good range of facilities. Bar meals are very popular, and thanks to the work of some local art students, the restaurant is stylishly decorated and well worth a look too.
ROOMS: 35 en suite (4 fmly) s £55; d £65 (incl. bkfst)
FACILITIES: Xmas **CONF:** Thtr 100 Class 30 Board 30 Del £95
PARKING: 21 **CARDS:**

⌂ Express by Holiday Inn Warwick
Stratford Rd CV34 6TW
☎ 01926 483000 📠 01926 483033
e-mail: warwick@expressbyholidayinn.co.uk
Dir: *M40 junct 15, follow signs A429 to Warwick. Take 1st on right*
A modern hotel ideal for families and business travellers. Fresh and uncomplicated, the spacious bedrooms include Sky TV, power shower and tea and coffee-making facilities. Continental buffet breakfast is included in the room rate; other meals may be taken at the nearby family pub or restaurant. For further details and the Express by Holiday Inn phone number, consult the Hotel Groups pages.

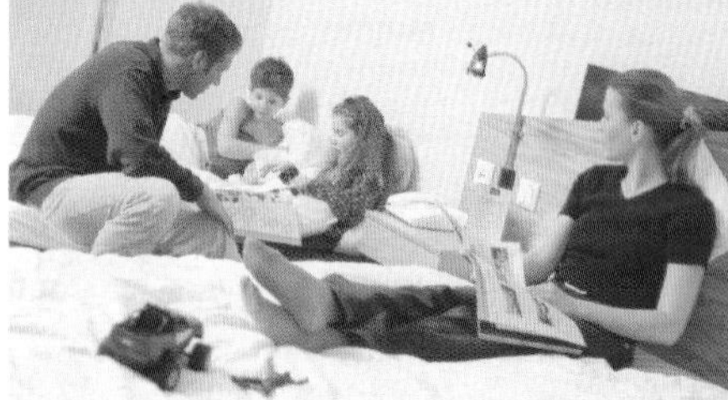

ROOMS: 117 en suite s £55-£69; d £55-£69 (incl. cont bkfst)
CONF: Thtr 30 Class 24 Board 18

WARWICK MOTORWAY SERVICE AREA (M40), Warwickshire
Map 10 SP35

⌂ Days Inn
Warwick Services, M40 Northbound junction 12-13, Banbury Rd CV35 0AA
☎ 01926 651681 📠 01926 651634
e-mail: warwick.north.hotel@welcomebreak.co.uk
Dir: *M40 northbound between junct 12 & 13*
This modern building offers accommodation in smart, spacious and well-equipped bedrooms, suitable for families and business travellers, and all with en suite bathrooms. Continental breakfast is available and other refreshments may be taken at the nearby family restaurant. For further details and the Days Inn phone number, consult the Hotel Groups page.
ROOMS: 54 en suite s £49-£65; d £49-£65 **CONF:** Board 10

⌂ Welcome Lodge
Warwick Services, M40 Southbound, Banbury Rd CV35 0AA
☎ 01926 650168 📠 01926 651601

Dir: *M40 southbound between junct 14 & 12*
This modern building offers accommodation in smart, spacious and well-equipped bedrooms, suitable for families and business travellers, and all with en suite bathrooms. Refreshments may be taken at the nearby family restaurant. For further details and the Welcome Break phone number, consult the Hotel Groups page.
ROOMS: 40 en suite s £45-£55; d £45-£55

® AA Rosette Award for culinary excellence

WASHINGTON, Tyne & Wear
Map 19 NZ35

★★★65% George Washington Golf & Country Club
Stone Cellar Rd, High Usworth NE37 1PH
☎ 0870 609 6173 📠 0191 415 1166
e-mail: georgewashington@corushotels.com
Dir: *off A1(M) junct 65 onto A194(M) take A195 signed Washington North. Take last exit from rdbt for Washington then right at mini rdbt. Hotel 0.5m on right*
Popular with both business and leisure guests, this purpose-built hotel boasts two golf courses and a driving range. Bedrooms, including a number of suites, are generally spacious and comfortably equipped. Public areas include extensive conference

continued

facilities, a business centre, a choice of restaurants and a well-stocked bar.

ROOMS: 103 en suite (9 fmly) (41 GF) No smoking in 44 bedrooms **FACILITIES: Spa** Indoor swimming (H) Golf 18 Squash Sauna Solarium Gym Putting green Jacuzzi Golf driving range, Pitch & Putt, Pool table, Swimming pool supervised **CONF:** Thtr 200 Class 100 Board 80 Del from £85 **PARKING:** 200 **NOTES:** No smoking in restaurant Civ Wed 180 **CARDS:**

U *Holiday Inn Washington*

Emerson District 5 NE37 1LB
☎ 0870 400 9084 📠 0191 415 3371
e-mail: reservations-washington@ichotelsgroup.com
Dir: *off A1(M) exit A195-take left hand sliproad signposted district 5. Turn left at rdbt and hotel is on the left*

At the time of going to press, the classification for this hotel was not confirmed. Please refer to the AA internet site www.theAA.com for current information.

ROOMS: 138 en suite (5 fmly) No smoking in 99 bedrooms **FACILITIES:** Pitch & putt **CONF:** Thtr 100 Class 40 Board 50 **SERVICES:** Lift **PARKING:** 198 **CARDS:**

⇧ *Campanile*

Emerson Rd, District 5 NE37 1LE
☎ 0191 416 5010 📠 0191 416 5023
Dir: *A1 junct 64, A195 to Washington, 1st left at rdbt into Emerson Road, Hotel 800yds on left*

This modern building offers accommodation in smart, well-equipped bedrooms, all with en suite bathrooms. Refreshments may be taken at the informal Bistro. For further details and the Campanile phone number, consult the Hotel Groups page.

ROOMS: 77 annexe en suite **CONF:** Thtr 35 Class 18 Board 20

⇧ Express by Holiday Inn

Emerson House NE37 1LA
☎ 0800 434040
e-mail: ebhi-wasington@btconnect.com

A modern hotel ideal for families and business travellers. Fresh and uncomplicated, the spacious bedrooms include Sky TV, power shower and tea and coffee-making facilities. Continental buffet breakfast is included in the room rate; other meals may be taken at the nearby family pub or restaurant. For further details and the Express by Holiday Inn phone number, consult the Hotel Groups pages.

ROOMS: 74 en suite s £42.50-£49.95; d £42.50-£49.95 (incl. cont bkfst) **CONF:** Thtr 30 Class 18 Board 16

WASHINGTON SERVICE AREA (A1(M)), Tyne & Wear — Map 19 NZ25

Travelodge (North)

Motorway Service Area, Portobello DH3 2SJ
☎ 08700 850 950
Dir: *northbound carriageway of A1(M)*
Travelodge offers good quality, good value, modern accommodation. Ideal for families, the spacious, en suite bedrooms include remote-control TV, tea and coffee-making facilities, luxury beds and free morning newspaper. Meals can be taken at the nearby family restaurant. For further details and the Travelodge phone number, consult the Hotel Groups page.
ROOMS: 31 en suite s fr £42.95; d fr £42.95

Travelodge (South)

Portobello DH3 2SJ
☎ 08700 850 950 ***Dir:*** *A1(M)*
Travelodge offers good quality, good value, modern accommodation. Ideal for families, the spacious, en suite bedrooms include remote-control TV, tea and coffee-making facilities, luxury beds and free morning newspaper. Meals can be taken at the nearby family restaurant. For further details and the Travelodge phone number, consult the Hotel Groups page.
ROOMS: 36 en suite s fr £42.95; d fr £42.95

WATERGATE BAY, Cornwall & Isles of Scilly — Map 02 SX18

★67% Tregurrian

TR8 4AB
☎ 01637 860280 🖷 01637 860540
e-mail: tregurrianhotel@virgin.net
Dir: *A30, A3059 towards airport, at rdbt, onto B3276, left to Watergate Bay*
Located almost on the beach at this increasingly popular destination, this hotel is a friendly and convenient place to stay. Bedrooms are comfortable and attractively presented, and some rooms have sea views. Both breakfast and dinner are buffet style, with hearty portions served and good use is made of fresh ingredients.
ROOMS: 27 rms (22 en suite) (8 fmly) No smoking in all bedrooms s £22-£38; d £44-£76 (incl. bkfst) **LB** **FACILITIES:** Outdoor swimming (H) Sauna Jacuzzi Games room **PARKING:** 27 **NOTES:** No dogs (ex guide dogs) No smoking in restaurant Closed Nov-Feb RS Mar
CARDS: *See advert under NEWQUAY*

WATERINGBURY, Kent — Map 06 TQ65

Premier Lodge (Maidstone)

103 Tonbridge Rd ME18 5NS
☎ 0870 9906346 🖷 0870 9906347
Premier Lodge offers modern, well-equipped, en suite accommodation suitable for both business and leisure travellers. Meals can be taken at the adjacent popular restaurant and bar, which is fully licensed. For further details, consult the Hotel Groups page.
ROOMS: 40 en suite s £50; d £50

WATERMILLOCK, Cumbria — Map 18 NY42

★★★★70% Leeming House

CA11 0JJ
☎ 0870 400 8131 🖷 017684 86443
e-mail: leeminghouse@macdonald-hotels.co.uk
Dir: *M6 junct 40, take A66 to Keswick. A592 (to Ullswater). 5m T-junct right to Hotel 3m*
This hotel enjoys a superb location - it is set in 20 acres of mature wooded gardens in the Lake District National Park, overlooking Ullswater. Many rooms offer views of the lake and the rugged fells beyond, with more than half having their own balcony. Public rooms include three sumptuous lounges, a cosy bar and library.
ROOMS: 40 en suite No smoking in 11 bedrooms s £52-£102; d £104-£164 (incl. bkfst) **LB** **FACILITIES:** STV Fishing Croquet lawn Xmas **CONF:** Thtr 35 Board 20 Del from £140 **PARKING:** 50 **NOTES:** No smoking in restaurant Civ Wed 30
CARDS:

Top 200 - Hotel

★★★ Rampsbeck Country House

CA11 0LP
☎ 017684 86442 & 86688 🖷 017684 86688
e-mail: enquiries@rampsbeck.fsnet.co.uk
Dir: *M6 junct 40, signs for A592 to Ullswater, at T-junct with lake in front, turn right, hotel 1.5m along lake's edge*
This fine country house, furnished with many period and antique pieces, lies in 18 acres of parkland on the shores of Lake Ullswater. There are three delightful lounges, an elegant restaurant and a traditional bar. Bedrooms come in three grades; the most spacious rooms overlooking the lake are spectacular. Service is attentive and the cuisine a real highlight.
ROOMS: 20 en suite No smoking in 2 bedrooms s £60-£150; d £100-£210 (incl. bkfst) **LB** **FACILITIES:** Fishing Croquet lawn Xmas **CONF:** Board 15 **PARKING:** 30 **NOTES:** No smoking in restaurant Closed early Jan-early Feb **CARDS:**

WATFORD, Hertfordshire — Map 06 TQ19

★★★65% The White House

Upton Rd WD18 0JF
☎ 01923 237316 🖷 01923 233109
e-mail: info@whitehousehotel.co.uk
Dir: *main Watford centre ring road into Exchange Rd, Upton Rd left turn off, hotel on left*

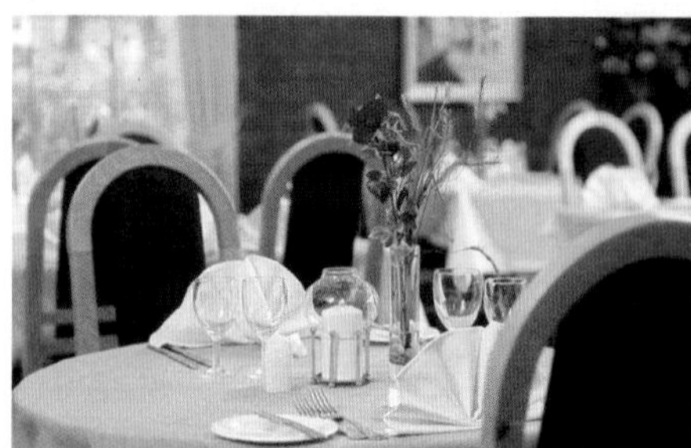

This is a well-located and popular commercial hotel. Bedrooms are practically furnished and decorated, and offer a good range of

continued

in-room facilities including interactive TV. The public areas are open plan in style and comprise a lounge/bar and an attractive conservatory restaurant. Functions suites are also available.
ROOMS: 59 en suite No smoking in 24 bedrooms s £50-£149; d £75-£164 **LB** **FACILITIES:** STV **CONF:** Thtr 200 Class 80 Board 50 Del £120 **SERVICES:** Lift **PARKING:** 40 **NOTES:** No dogs (ex guide dogs) No smoking in restaurant **CARDS:** 

See advert on this page

⌂ Premier Lodge (Watford)

Timms Meadow, Water Ln WD17 2NJ

PREMIER LODGE

☎ 0870 9906620 📠 0870 9906621

Premier Lodge offers modern, well-equipped, en suite accommodation suitable for both business and leisure travellers. Meals can be taken at the adjacent popular restaurant and bar, which is fully licensed. For further details, consult the Hotel Groups page.
ROOMS: 105 en suite s £56; d £56

⌂ Travel Inn

859 St Albans Rd, Garston WD5 0LH

travel inn

☎ 08701 977261 📠 01923 682164

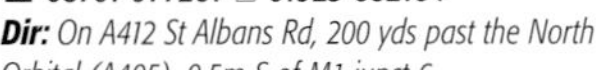

Dir: *On A412 St Albans Rd, 200 yds past the North Orbital (A405), 0.5m S of M1 junct 6*

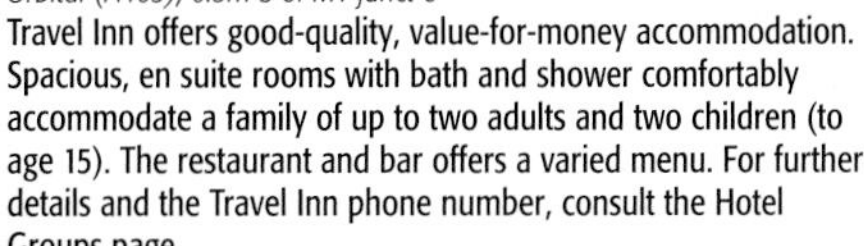

Travel Inn offers good-quality, value-for-money accommodation. Spacious, en suite rooms with bath and shower comfortably accommodate a family of up to two adults and two children (to age 15). The restaurant and bar offers a varied menu. For further details and the Travel Inn phone number, consult the Hotel Groups page.
ROOMS: 45 en suite s £49.95-£54.95; d £49.95-£54.95

WATFORD GAP MOTORWAY SERVICE AREA (M1), Northamptonshire — Map 11 SP66

⌂ Travel Inn (Daventry)

NN6 7UZ

travel inn

☎ 08701 977301 📠 01327 871333

Dir: *M1 Southbound - 1m south junct (access available from northbound)*

Travel Inn offers good-quality, value-for-money accommodation. Spacious, en suite rooms with bath and shower comfortably accommodate a family of up to two adults and two children (to age 15). The restaurant and bar offers a varied menu. For further details and the Travel Inn phone number, consult the Hotel Groups page.
ROOMS: 36 en suite s £44.95; d £44.95

WEEDON, Northamptonshire — Map 11 SP64

⌂ Premier Lodge (Daventry)

High St NN7 4PX

PREMIER LODGE

☎ 0870 9906364 📠 0870 9906365

Dir: *at A5/A45 crossroads*

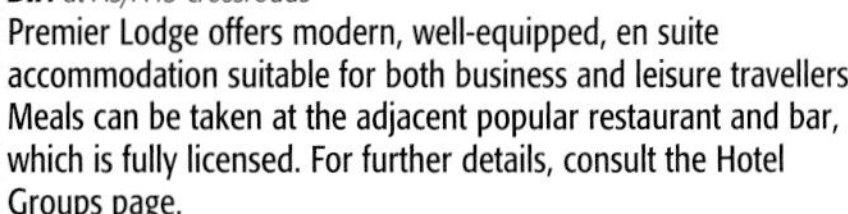

Premier Lodge offers modern, well-equipped, en suite accommodation suitable for both business and leisure travellers. Meals can be taken at the adjacent popular restaurant and bar, which is fully licensed. For further details, consult the Hotel Groups page.
ROOMS: 47 en suite s £48; d £48 **CONF:** Thtr 70 Class 25 Board 24

WEELEY, Essex — Map 07 TM12

⌂ Travel Inn (Clacton-on-Sea)

Weeley CO16 9AA

travel inn

☎ 08701 977064 📠 01255 833106

Dir: *A120 towards Harwich. After 4m, A133 to Clacton-on-Sea. Weeley rdbt*

Travel Inn offers good-quality, value-for-money accommodation. Spacious, en suite rooms with bath and shower comfortably accommodate a family of up to two adults and two children (to age 15). The restaurant and bar offers a varied menu. For further details and the Travel Inn phone number, consult the Hotel Groups page.
ROOMS: 40 en suite s £44.95; d £44.95

WELLESBOURNE, Warwickshire — Map 10 SP25

⌂ Innkeeper's Lodge Stratford-upon-Avon East

Warwick Rd CV35 9LX

Innkeeper's Lodge

☎ 01789 840206 📠 01789 472902

Dir: *M40 junct 15 S onto A429 towards Wellesbourne. Left at rdbt onto B4086 & lodge 300yds on right*

A new concept in the travel accommodation market. Smart rooms meet essential business requirements but also have home comforts. Dining options include all-day menus plus the added advantage of breakfast, which is included in the room price. For further details, consult the Hotel Groups page.
ROOMS: 9 en suite

WELLINGBOROUGH, Northamptonshire Map 11 SP86

★★★65% The Hind
Sheep St NN8 1BY
☎ 01933 222827 📠 01933 421921
Dir: *on A509 in town centre*
Dating back to Jacobean times, this centrally located hotel provides a good base for business and leisure guests visiting the town. A good choice of dishes is available in the restaurant, alternatively the all-day coffee shop offers light snacks. Bedrooms come in a variety of styles, mostly of spacious dimensions.
ROOMS: 34 en suite (2 fmly) No smoking in 10 bedrooms s £50-£75; d £65-£85 (incl. bkfst) **LB FACILITIES:** Xmas **CONF:** Thtr 70 Class 40 Board 40 **PARKING:** 17 **NOTES:** No smoking in restaurant Civ Wed 90
CARDS:

A ★★ High View
156 Midland Rd NN8 1NG
☎ 01933 278733 📠 01933 225948
e-mail: hotelhighview@hotmail.com
Dir: *turn off A45 onto B573, follow sign to rail station, at Midland road T-junct turn left towards town centre, hotel approx 100yds on left*
ROOMS: 14 en suite (2 fmly) s £30-£45; d £40-£50 (incl. bkfst)
PARKING: 8 **NOTES:** No dogs No children 3yrs No smoking in restaurant Closed 25 Dec-1 Jan **CARDS:**

⌂ Hotel Ibis Wellingborough
Enstone Court NN8 2DR
☎ 01933 228333 📠 01933 228444
e-mail: H3164@accor-hotels.com
Dir: *At junct of A45 & A509 towards Kettering SW of Wellingborough*
Modern, budget hotel offering comfortable accommodation in bright and practical bedrooms. Breakfast is self-service and dinner is available in the restaurant. For further details, consult the Hotel Groups page.
ROOMS: 78 en suite

⌂ Travel Inn
London Rd NN8 2DP
☎ 08701 977262 📠 01933 278606
Dir: *0.5m from Wellingborough town centre on A5193 near Dennington Industrial Estate*
Travel Inn offers good-quality, value-for-money accommodation. Spacious, en suite rooms with bath and shower comfortably accommodate a family of up to two adults and two children (to age 15). The restaurant and bar offers a varied menu. For further details and the Travel Inn phone number, consult the Hotel Groups page.
ROOMS: 40 en suite s £44.95; d £44.95

WELLINGTON See Telford (Shropshire)

WELLINGTON, Somerset Map 03 ST12

Top 200 - Hotel

★★★ ®® Bindon Country House Hotel & Restaurant
Langford Budville TA21 0RU
☎ 01823 400070 📠 01823 400071
e-mail: stay@bindon.com
Dir: *from Wellington B3187 to Langford Budville, through village, right towards Wiveliscombe, right at junct, pass Bindon Farm, right 450yds*
This delightful country retreat is set in seven acres of formal and woodland gardens. Mentioned in the Domesday Book, it offers peace and tranquillity, the perfect antidote to stress. Bedrooms are named after battles fought by the Duke of Wellington and each is individually decorated with sumptuous fabrics and equipped with useful extras. Elegance, style and comfort can all be found within the public rooms, and the dining room is the venue for impressive and accomplished cuisine.
ROOMS: 12 en suite (2 fmly) (1 GF) No smoking in all bedrooms s fr £95; d £115-£215 (incl. bkfst) **LB FACILITIES:** Outdoor swimming (H) Tennis (hard) Croquet lawn entertainment Xmas **CONF:** Thtr 50 Class 25 Board 25 Del from £135 **PARKING:** 30 **NOTES:** No smoking in restaurant Civ Wed 50
CARDS:

See advert under TAUNTON

★★★66% The Cleve Hotel & Country Club
Mantle St TA21 8SN
☎ 01823 662033 📠 01823 660874
e-mail: reception@clevehotel.com
Dir: *M5 junct 26 follow signs to Wellington, left before Total Petrol Station*
Offering comfortable bedrooms and public areas, The Cleve Hotel is quietly located in an elevated position above the town. The atmosphere is relaxed and guests can enjoy Mediterranean influenced cuisine in the stylish restaurant. Extensive leisure facilities are available including a heated indoor pool, well-equipped gym, sauna, solarium and snooker table.
ROOMS: 20 en suite (5 fmly) (3 GF) No smoking in all bedrooms s £65-£79.50; d £80-£95.50 (incl. bkfst) **LB FACILITIES: Spa** Indoor swimming (H) Snooker Sauna Solarium Gym Swimming pool supervised **CONF:** Thtr 300 Class 100 Board 50 Del from £75.50 **PARKING:** 60 **NOTES:** No smoking in restaurant Civ Wed 120
CARDS:

WELLS, Somerset Map 04 ST54

★★★72% Swan
Sadler St BA5 2RX
☎ 01749 836300 📠 01749 836301
e-mail: swan@bhere.co.uk
Dir: *A39, A371, opp cathedral*
A former coaching inn with a wonderful view of the west front of

continued

Wells Cathedral. The individually decorated bedrooms vary from the newer ones in an adjacent wing to the more traditionally furnished rooms many with four-poster beds. Dinner includes a varied selection of carefully prepared dishes.

ROOMS: 50 en suite (2 fmly) (5 GF) No smoking in 20 bedrooms s £85-£105; d £110-£150 **LB FACILITIES:** Xmas **CONF:** Thtr 70 Class 30 Board 35 Del £99 **PARKING:** 30 **NOTES:** No smoking in restaurant Civ Wed 70 **CARDS:**

★★71% White Hart

THE INDEPENDENTS

Sadler St BA5 2RR
☎ 01749 672056 🖹 01749 671074
e-mail: info@whitehart-wells.co.uk
Dir: *At start of one-way system opp cathedral*

A former coaching inn dating back to the 15th century. Public areas include a spacious bar-lounge, a cosy landing lounge and a beamed restaurant where there is a fixed-price and brasserie-style menu. The bedrooms, some in a nearby former stable block, offer comfortable, modern accommodation.
ROOMS: 15 en suite (3 fmly) No smoking in 5 bedrooms s £65-£70; d £86-£96 (incl. bkfst) **LB FACILITIES:** Xmas **CONF:** Thtr 150 Class 50 Board 35 Del from £99 **PARKING:** 17 **NOTES:** No smoking in restaurant Civ Wed 100 **CARDS:**

★★64% Crown at Wells

Market Place BA5 2RP
☎ 01749 673457 🖹 01749 679792
e-mail: reception@crownatwells.co.uk
Dir: *in Market Place, follow signs for Hotels/Deliveries*
Retaining its original features and period charm, this historic inn is in the heart of Wells, just a short stroll from the cathedral. Bedrooms vary and have modern facilities. Public areas focus around Anton's, the popular 'bistro', with its bold paintings and relaxed atmosphere and the Penn Bar which offers an alternative eating option.

ROOMS: 15 en suite (1 fmly) No smoking in 6 bedrooms s £45-£75; d £60-£90 (incl. bkfst) **LB PARKING:** 15 **NOTES:** No smoking in restaurant RS 25 Dec food not available in the evening
CARDS:

★70% Ancient Gate House

20 Sadler St BA5 2SE
☎ 01749 672029 🖹 01749 670319
e-mail: info@ancientgatehouse.co.uk
Dir: *1st hotel on left on Cathedral Green*
Guests are treated to good old-fashioned hospitality in a friendly informal atmosphere here. Bedrooms, many of which boast unrivalled cathedral views and four-poster beds, are furnished in keeping with the building's age. The Rugantino Restaurant remains popular, offering typically Italian specialities and traditional English dishes.
ROOMS: 9 en suite No smoking in 2 bedrooms s £63-£68; d £78-£79 (incl. bkfst) **LB FACILITIES:** ch fac **NOTES:** No smoking in restaurant Closed 25-26 Dec **CARDS:**

WELWYN, Hertfordshire — Map 06 TL21

★★★63% Quality Hotel Welwyn

The Link AL6 9XA
☎ 01438 716911 🖹 01438 714065
e-mail: admin@gb623.u-net.com
Dir: *A1(M) junct 6 A1000 Welwyn. Follow A1(M) Stevenage towards motorway again but at 3rd rdbt take first left and turn into hotel*
The hotel is well located for motorway access and offers a versatile range of conference rooms, making it popular with business guests. Bedrooms are suitably appointed and offer a useful range of facilities. Guests have the choice of two informal dining rooms and a comfortable bar.
ROOMS: 96 en suite (6 fmly) (28 GF) No smoking in 47 bedrooms s £44-£90; d £64-£99 **LB FACILITIES:** STV Gym Xmas **CONF:** Thtr 250 Class 60 Board 50 **PARKING:** 150 **NOTES:** No dogs (ex guide dogs) No smoking in restaurant Civ Wed 100 **CARDS:**

WELWYN GARDEN CITY, Hertfordshire — Map 06 TL21

★★★66% The Homestead Court Hotel

Best Western

Homestead Ln AL7 4LX
☎ 01707 324336 🖹 01707 326447
e-mail: enquiries@homesteadcourt.co.uk
Dir: *off A1000, left at Bushall Hotel. Right at rdbt into Howlands, 2nd left at Hollybush PH into Hollybush Ln. 2nd right at War Memorial*
Less than two miles from the city centre, this friendly hotel is set in a tranquil location, next to parkland. It boasts stylish, brightly-

continued on p642

WELWYN GARDEN CITY, continued

decorated public areas, comfortable bedrooms and ample parking. Conference facilities are popular with local businesses.
ROOMS: 58 en suite No smoking in 25 bedrooms s £49-£104; d £59-£115 **LB** **FACILITIES:** STV Xmas **CONF:** Thtr 80 Class 40 Board 30 Del from £126 **SERVICES:** Lift **PARKING:** 60 **NOTES:** No dogs (ex guide dogs) No smoking in restaurant Civ Wed 80
CARDS:

Travel Inn

Gosling Park AL8 6DQ
☎ 08701 977263 📠 01707 393789
Dir: *on A6129 off junct 4 A1(M)*

Travel Inn offers good-quality, value-for-money accommodation. Spacious, en suite rooms with bath and shower comfortably accommodate a family of up to two adults and two children (to age 15). The restaurant and bar offers a varied menu. For further details and the Travel Inn phone number, consult the Hotel Groups page.
ROOMS: 60 en suite s £44.95; d £44.95

WEMBLEY, Greater London
See LONDON SECTION plan 1 C5

Hotel Ibis Wembley

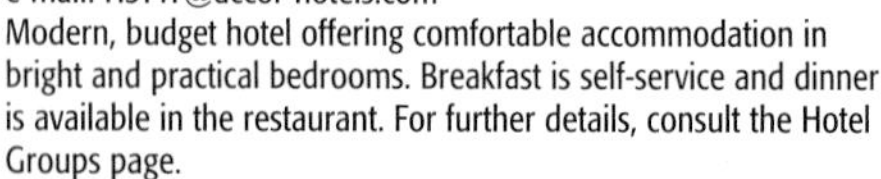

Southway HA9 6BA
☎ 0870 609 0963
e-mail: H3141@accor-hotels.com
Modern, budget hotel offering comfortable accommodation in bright and practical bedrooms. Breakfast is self-service and dinner is available in the restaurant. For further details, consult the Hotel Groups page.
ROOMS: 210 en suite s £50; d £50

Premier Lodge (London Wembley)

151 Wembley Park Dr HA9 8HQ
☎ 0870 9906484 📠 0870 9906485
Dir: *M1 junct 1 onto A406, then right onto A404, through three sets of lights. Lodge on left*
Premier Lodge offers modern, well-equipped, en suite accommodation suitable for both business and leisure travellers. Meals can be taken at the adjacent popular restaurant and bar, which is fully licensed. For further details, consult the Hotel Groups page.
ROOMS: 154 en suite s £56; d £56

WENTBRIDGE (NEAR PONTEFRACT), West Yorkshire — Map 16 SE41

★★★72% ◎ Wentbridge House

WF8 3JJ
☎ 01977 620444 📠 01977 620148
e-mail: info@wentbridgehouse.co.uk
Dir: *Wentbridge is 0.5m off A1 and 4m S of the M62/A1 junct*

This well established hotel sits in 20 acres of landscaped gardens, offering spacious, well-equipped bedrooms and a choice of dining styles. Service in the Fleur de Lys restaurant is polished and friendly, and a varied menu offers a good choice of interesting dishes. The Brasserie offers a more relaxed style of dining.
ROOMS: 14 en suite 4 annexe en suite (4 GF) s £65-£98; d £80-£120 (incl. bkfst) **CONF:** Thtr 130 Class 100 Board 60 Del from £95 **PARKING:** 100 **NOTES:** No dogs (ex guide dogs) Closed 25 Dec-evening only Civ Wed 130 **CARDS:**

WEST AUCKLAND, Co Durham — Map 19 NZ12

★★★68% The Manor House Hotel & Country Club

The Green DL14 9HW
☎ 01388 834834 📠 01388 833566
e-mail: enquiries@manorhousehotel.net
Dir: *A1(M) junct 58, then A68 to West Auckland. At T-junct turn left, hotel 150yds on right*

This historic manor house, dating back to the 14th century, is full of character. Welcoming log fires await guests on the cooler evenings. Bedrooms are all individual, each one being comfortable, tastefully furnished and well equipped. There is choice of eating options - the brasserie and Juniper's restaurant - both offering an interesting selection of freshly prepared dishes.
ROOMS: 24 en suite 11 annexe en suite (6 fmly) (2 GF) s £50-£62.50; d £80-£92.50 (incl. bkfst) **LB** **FACILITIES:** Indoor swimming (H) Sauna Solarium Gym Jacuzzi Beauty treatment Xmas **CONF:** Thtr 100 Class 80 Board 50 Del from £92 **PARKING:** 200 **NOTES:** Civ Wed 120
CARDS:

W

WEST BAY See Bridport

WEST BEXINGTON, Dorset Map 04 SY58

★★69% The Manor

Beach Rd DT2 9DF
☎ 01308 897616 & 897785 📠 01308 897035
e-mail: themanorhotel@btconnect.com
Dir: *B3157 Weymouth/Bridport coast road, turn at Swyre, towards West Bexington*

Surrounded by scenic splendour and tranquillity, this south-facing hotel enjoys sea views. Each bedroom has its own charm and a number of thoughtful extras. The Cellar Bar provides a range of meals, and an imaginative selection of dishes is offered in the recently totally refurbished, delightful restaurant.

ROOMS: 13 en suite (2 fmly) s £70-£75; d £110-£120 (incl. bkfst) **LB** **CONF:** Thtr 40 Class 20 Board 20 **PARKING:** 40 **NOTES:** No dogs (ex guide dogs) Civ Wed 60 **CARDS:**

WEST BROMWICH, West Midlands Map 10 SP09

⌂ Travel Inn

New Gas St B70 0NP
☎ 08701 977264 📠 0121 500 5670
Dir: *From M5(J1) take A41 Expressway towards Wolverhampton. At 3rd rdt, Travel Inn on right.*

Travel Inn offers good-quality, value-for-money accommodation. Spacious, en suite rooms with bath and shower comfortably accommodate a family of up to two adults and two children (to age 15). The restaurant and bar offers a varied menu. For further details and the Travel Inn phone number, consult the Hotel Groups page.

ROOMS: 40 en suite s £44.95; d £44.95

WESTBURY, Wiltshire Map 04 ST85

★★65% The Cedar

Warminster Rd BA13 3PR
☎ 01373 822753 📠 01373 858423
e-mail: cedarwestbury@aol.com
Dir: *on A350, 0.5m S of town towards Warminster*

This 18th-century hotel offers attractive accommodation in well-equipped, individually decorated bedrooms. The hotel is an ideal base for exploring Bath and the surrounding area. An interesting selection of meals is available in both the bar lounge and conservatory; the Regency restaurant is popular for more formal dining.

ROOMS: 8 en suite 8 annexe en suite (2 fmly) (8 GF) s £50-£70; d £60-£85 (incl. bkfst) **FACILITIES:** STV **CONF:** Thtr 35 Class 20 Board 20 **PARKING:** 30 **NOTES:** No smoking in restaurant RS 26 Dec-1 Jan **CARDS:**

WEST CHILTINGTON, West Sussex Map 06 TQ01

★★★69% Roundabout

Monkmead Ln RH20 2PF
☎ 01798 813838 📠 01798 812962
e-mail: roundabouthotelltd@btinternet.com
Dir: *A24 onto A283 turn right at mini rdbt in Storrington, left at hill top. Left after 1m*

Enjoying a most peaceful setting, surrounded by gardens, this well-established hotel is located deep in the Sussex countryside.

continued

Mock Tudor in style, the hotel has plenty of character. The comfortably furnished bedrooms are well-equipped, and public areas offer a spacious lounge and bar, and a neatly appointed restaurant, serving an extensive range of dishes.

Roundabout Hotel

ROOMS: 23 en suite (4 fmly) (5 GF) No smoking in 5 bedrooms s £67.95-£72.95; d £112-£125 (incl. bkfst) **LB** **FACILITIES:** STV Xmas **CONF:** Thtr 60 Class 20 Board 26 Del from £105 **PARKING:** 46 **NOTES:** No children 3yrs No smoking in restaurant Civ Wed 55 **CARDS:**

See advert on this page

WEST DRAYTON Hotels are listed under Heathrow Airport

WESTLETON, Suffolk
Map 13 TM46

★★75% @@ Westleton Crown
IP17 3AD
☎ 0800 328 6001 🖷 01728 648239
e-mail: reception@westletoncrown.com
Dir: *N on A12 turn just beyond Yoxford, northbound, and follow AA signs for 2m*

A charming coaching inn situated in a peaceful village location just a few minutes from the A12. An interesting choice of dishes is served in the smart, award-winning restaurant and guests also have the use of a comfortable lounge as well as the busy bar with its exposed beams and open fireplaces. Although the bedrooms vary in size and style they are all individually decorated and equipped with many thoughtful little extras.
ROOMS: 10 en suite 9 annexe en suite (2 fmly) No smoking in all bedrooms **CONF:** Thtr 60 Class 40 Board 30 **PARKING:** 40 **NOTES:** RS 24-26 Dec (Meals only) **CARDS:**

WEST LULWORTH, Dorset
Map 04 SY88

★★65% Cromwell House
Lulworth Cove BH20 5RJ
☎ 01929 400253 & 400332 🖷 01929 400566
e-mail: catriona@lulworthcove.co.uk
Dir: *200yds beyond end of West Lulworth village, left onto high slip road, hotel 100yds on left opposite beach car park*

Built in 1881 by the Mayor of Weymouth, specifically as a guest house, this family-run hotel now provides guests with an ideal base for touring the area and for exploring the beaches and coast. Cromwell House enjoys spectacular views across the sea and countryside. Bedrooms, many with sea views, are comfortable and some have been specifically designed for family use.
ROOMS: 17 en suite (3 fmly) (17 GF) s £30-£41.50; d £60-£83 (incl. bkfst) **LB** **FACILITIES:** Outdoor swimming (H) Access to Dorset Coastal footpath **PARKING:** 15 **NOTES:** No smoking in restaurant Closed 22 Dec-3 Jan **CARDS:**

WESTON-ON-THE-GREEN, Oxfordshire
Map 11 SP51

★★★70% @@ Weston Manor
OX25 3QL
☎ 01869 350621 🖷 01869 350901
e-mail: reception@westonmanor.co.uk
Dir: *M40 junct 9 towards Oxford (A34), leave A34 at 1st exit, turn right at rdbt (B4030), hotel 100yds on left*
Character, charm and sophistication blend effortlessly in this friendly hotel set in well-tended gardens. Bedrooms are well equipped and are located in the main house, coach house or a cottage annexe. Award-winning food can be enjoyed in the impressive vaulted restaurant, complete with original oak panelling and minstrels' gallery; other public areas include an atmospheric foyer lounge, bar and meeting facilities.
ROOMS: 15 en suite 20 annexe en suite (5 fmly) No smoking in 6 bedrooms s £99-£115; d £121-£154 (incl. bkfst) **LB**
FACILITIES: Outdoor swimming (H) Croquet lawn Xmas **CONF:** Thtr 60 Class 20 Board 25 Del from £160 **PARKING:** 100 **NOTES:** No dogs (ex guide dogs) No smoking in restaurant Civ Wed 90
CARDS:

WESTON-SUPER-MARE, Somerset
Map 04 ST36

★★★64% Beachlands
17 Uphill Rd North BS23 4NG
☎ 01934 621401 🖷 01934 621966
e-mail: info@beachlandshotel.com
Dir: *M5 junct 21, follow signs for Hospital. At Hospital rdbt follow signs for beach, hotel 300yds before beach*

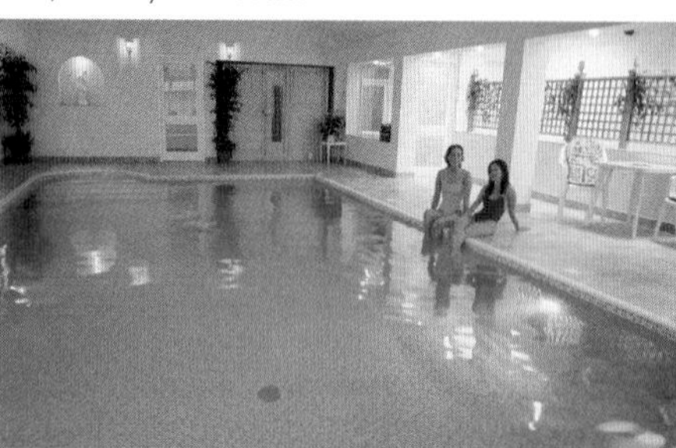

This popular hotel has the added bonus of a 10-metre indoor pool and sauna. It is very close to the 18-hole links course and a short walk from the seafront. Elegantly decorated public areas include a bar, a choice of lounges and a bright dining room. Bedrooms vary slightly in size and comfort and all are well-equipped for both the business and leisure guest.
ROOMS: 23 en suite (6 fmly) (11 GF) No smoking in all bedrooms s £47-£67.50; d £73-£94.50 (incl. bkfst) **LB** **FACILITIES:** Indoor swimming (H) Sauna **CONF:** Thtr 60 Class 20 Board 30 Del from £89.50 **PARKING:** 28 **NOTES:** No dogs (ex guide dogs) No smoking in restaurant Closed 23 Dec-2 Jan Civ Wed 85
CARDS:

★★★62% Commodore
Beach Rd, Sand Bay, Kewstoke BS22 9UZ
☎ 01934 415778 🖷 01934 750020
e-mail: latonacom@aol.com
Dir: *From Weston-Super-Mare take Kewstoke road through Weston Woods*
Located in the pleasant village of Kewstoke by unspoilt Sand Bay, there is direct access to the beach. This popular hotel attracts many guests back to enjoy its range of dining options from the relaxed carvery and two-for-one specials in the beamed bar to the

continued

W

more formal menu of Alice's Restaurant. Bedrooms vary for size and are located in the main hotel or two adjacent buildings.
ROOMS: 19 en suite No smoking in 1 bedroom s £60; d £90 (incl. bkfst) **LB FACILITIES:** Putting green Xmas **CONF:** Thtr 90 Class 50 Board 40 Del from £25 **SERVICES:** Lift **PARKING:** 70 **NOTES:** No dogs No smoking in restaurant Civ Wed 120
CARDS:

★★★61% Royal Hotel
1 South Pde BS23 1JP
☎ 01934 423100 📠 01934 415135
e-mail: royalhotel@37.com
Opening in 1810, The Royal was the first hotel in Weston and occupies a prime position on the seafront, just two minutes' walk from the town centre. Bedrooms are soundly appointed and include both four-poster and family rooms, many having the added bonus of sea views. Public areas include a choice of bars and the refurbished restaurant, offering a range of dishes to meet all tastes. Entertainment is provided during the season with a regular jazz slot on Sundays.
ROOMS: 37 en suite (5 fmly) No smoking in 9 bedrooms s £52-£58; d £76-£86 (incl. bkfst) **FACILITIES:** entertainment **CONF:** Thtr 200 Class 100 Board 80 **SERVICES:** Lift **PARKING:** 150 **NOTES:** No dogs (ex guide dogs) **CARDS:**

★★70% Madeira Cove Hotel
32-34 Birnbeck Rd BS23 2BX
☎ 01934 626707 📠 01934 624882
e-mail: madeiracove@telco4u.net
Dir: *signs to Western Seafront, pass Grand Pier, hotel on right*
Within easy walking distance of the town centre, this popular and friendly hotel enjoys an ideal location overlooking the sea. It provides comfortable and well-equipped accommodation. A good range of food is offered in the spacious restaurant and in addition to the bar, a separate upper floor lounge is available to guests.
ROOMS: 19 en suite 4 annexe en suite (2 fmly) No smoking in 3 bedrooms s £25-£30; d £60-£70 (incl. bkfst) **LB CONF:** Thtr 20 **SERVICES:** Lift **PARKING:** 10 **NOTES:** No smoking in restaurant
CARDS:

★★68% Battleborough Grange Hotel
Bristol Rd TA9 4HJ
☎ 01278 760208 📠 01278 761950
e-mail: info@battleboroughgrangehotel.co.uk
(For full entry see Brent Knoll)

★★63% Anchorhead
19 Claremont Crescent, Birnbeck Rd BS23 2EE
☎ 01934 620880 📠 01934 621767
e-mail: anchor.weston@alfatravel.co.uk

Dir: *M5 junct 21/ A370 to Weston sea front, turn right towards northern end of resort past Grand Pier towards Brimbeck Pier. Hotel at end of terrace on left.*
Enjoying a very pleasant location with views across the bay, the Anchorhead offers a varied choice of comfortable lounges and a relaxing outdoor patio area. Bedrooms and bathrooms are traditionally furnished and include several ground floor rooms. Dinner and breakfast are served in the spacious dining room that also benefits from sea views.
ROOMS: 52 en suite (1 fmly) (5 GF) s £25-£33; d £42-£58 (incl. bkfst) **LB FACILITIES:** entertainment Xmas **SERVICES:** Lift **NOTES:** No dogs (ex guide dogs) No smoking in restaurant Closed Dec-Feb RS Mar & Nov
CARDS:

W

WESTON-SUPER-MARE, continued

★★63% New Ocean
Madeira Cove BS23 2BS
☎ 01934 621839 🖷 01934 626474
e-mail: info@newoceanhotel.co.uk
Ideally positioned on the seafront, opposite the Marine Lake, several bedrooms at this family-run hotel enjoy pleasant views over Weston Bay. In the downstairs restaurant, dinner offers traditional home cooking using fresh ingredients. The smart public areas include a well-furnished bar and lounge, where entertainment is regularly provided.
ROOMS: 53 en suite (2 fmly) s £30; d £50 (incl. bkfst) **LB**
FACILITIES: entertainment Xmas **SERVICES:** Lift **PARKING:** 6
NOTES: No dogs (ex guide dogs) No smoking in restaurant RS Jan
CARDS:

★69% *Timbertop Aparthotel*
8 Victoria Park BS23 2HZ
☎ 01934 631178 🖷 01934 414716
e-mail: stay@aparthoteltimbertop.com
Dir: *follow signs to pier, then 1st right (with Winter Gardens on right), 1st left Lower Church Road. Left then turn right to hotel*

Located in a leafy cul-de-sac, close to the seafront and Winter Gardens, this homely hotel offers a warm and personal welcome. Bedrooms are bright and fresh with pine furnishings and in addition to a small bar, there is a relaxing lounge. Substantial home-cooked dinners are provided with the emphasis on fresh ingredients.
ROOMS: 8 rms (7 en suite) 4 annexe en suite (2 fmly) **CONF:** Board 20
PARKING: 15 **NOTES:** No dogs (ex guide dogs) No smoking in restaurant **CARDS:**

Action for Blind People Hotel

U Lauriston
6-12 Knightstone Rd BS23 2AN
☎ 01934 620758 🖷 01934 621154
e-mail: lauriston_hotel@afbp.org
Dir: *1st right after Winter Gardens building, Hotel entrance opposite Cabot public house*
A friendly welcome is assured at this pleasant hotel, located right on the seafront, just a few minutes' stroll from the pier. Bedrooms and bathrooms are neatly decorated and well equipped, and there is a choice of comfortable lounges in which to relax. The hotel caters for the specific needs of blind and partially sighted people, their friends, relatives, carers and guide dogs.
ROOMS: 37 en suite s £27-£37; d £54-£74 (incl. bkfst & dinner) **LB**
FACILITIES: entertainment Xmas **SERVICES:** Lift **PARKING:** 25
NOTES: No dogs (ex guide dogs) No smoking in restaurant
CARDS:

Travel Inn
Hutton Moor Rd BS22 8LY
☎ 08701 977266 🖷 01934 627401
Dir: *M5(J21) follow A370 towards Weston-Super-Mare. Right at lights into Hutton Moor Leisure Centre. Left and follow to car park*
Travel Inn offers good-quality, value-for-money accommodation. Spacious, en suite rooms with bath and shower comfortably accommodate a family of up to two adults and two children (to age 15). The restaurant and bar offers a varied menu. For further details and the Travel Inn phone number, consult the Hotel Groups page.
ROOMS: 60 en suite s £44.95; d £44.95

WEST THURROCK, Essex Map 06 TQ5

Hotel Ibis London Thurrock
Weston Av RM20 3JQ
☎ 01708 686000 🖷 01708 680525
e-mail: H2176@accor-hotels.com
Dir: *M25 junct 31 to West Thurrock Services, turn right at 1st and 2nd rdbts then left at 3rd rdbt. Hotel on right after 500yds*
Modern, budget hotel offering comfortable accommodation in bright and practical bedrooms. Breakfast is self-service and dinner is available in the restaurant. For further details, consult the Hotel Groups page.
ROOMS: 102 en suite s £35.95-£48.95; d £35.95-£48.95

Premier Lodge (Thurrock)
Stonehouse Ln RM19 1NS
☎ 0870 9906490 🖷 0870 9906491
Premier Lodge offers modern, well-equipped, en suite accommodation suitable for both business and leisure travellers. Meals can be taken at the adjacent popular restaurant and bar, which is fully licensed. For further details, consult the Hotel Groups page.
ROOMS: 161 en suite s £56; d £56

Travel Inn (Thurrock)
Fleming Rd, Unicorn Estate, Chafford Hundred RM16 6YJ
☎ 08701 977253 🖷 01375 481876
Dir: *from A13 follow signs for Lakeside Shopping Centre. Turn right at 1st rdbt, straight over next rdbt then 1st slip road. Turn left at next rdbt*
Travel Inn offers good-quality, value-for-money accommodation. Spacious, en suite rooms with bath and shower comfortably accommodate a family of up to two adults and two children (to age 15). The restaurant and bar offers a varied menu. For further details and the Travel Inn phone number, consult the Hotel Groups page.
ROOMS: 62 en suite s £49.95-£54.95; d £49.95-£54.95

Travelodge Thurrock
Arterial Rd RM16 3BG
☎ 08700 850 950 & 0800 850950
🖷 01525 878450
Dir: *off A1306*
Travelodge offers good quality, good value, modern accommodation. Ideal for families, the spacious, en suite bedrooms include remote-control TV, tea and coffee-making facilities, luxury beds and free morning newspaper. Meals can be taken at the nearby family restaurant. For further details and the Travelodge phone number, consult the Hotel Groups page.
ROOMS: 48 en suite s fr £42.95; d fr £42.95

WEST WITTON, North Yorkshire Map 19 SE08

★★71% Wensleydale Heifer Inn

DL8 4LS
☎ 01969 622322 📠 01969 624183
e-mail: info@wensleydaleheifer.co.uk
Dir: *A1 to Leeming Bar junct, A684 towards Bedale for approx 10m to Leyburn, then Hawes 3.5m to West Witton*

Originally a 17th-century coaching inn, this sympathetically restored hotel retains much of its original character. Bedrooms are all individual, comfortable and well equipped. Welcoming log fires await guests in the cooler evenings. The beamed bar serves real ales and meals can be taken in the cosy bistro or the more formal restaurant.

ROOMS: 9 en suite (2 fmly) No smoking in all bedrooms s £60; d £72-£98 (incl. bkfst) **LB** **FACILITIES:** Xmas **CONF:** Board 20 **PARKING:** 40 **NOTES:** No smoking in restaurant
CARDS:

WETHERBY, West Yorkshire Map 16 SE44

★★★74% Wood Hall

Trip Ln, Linton LS22 4JA HandPICKED
☎ 01937 587271 📠 01937 584353
e-mail: events.woodhall@arcadianhotels.co.uk
Dir: *from Wetherby take Harrogate Rd N (A661) for 0.5m, left to Sicklinghall & Linton. Cross bridge, left to Linton & Woodhall. Turn right opposite Windmill Inn, 1.25m to hotel*

A striking Georgian hall nestling in 100 acres of parkland. Spacious bedrooms are well equipped, and many have been refurbished to a high standard. Elegant public rooms include a smart drawing room and dining room, both of which enjoy the fantastic view. The hotel also features a range of meeting rooms and a small leisure club.

ROOMS: 14 en suite 30 annexe en suite (7 fmly) **FACILITIES: Spa** STV Indoor swimming (H) Fishing Gym Swimming pool supervised **CONF:** Thtr 140 Class 70 Board 40 Del from £125 **SERVICES:** Lift **PARKING:** 200 **NOTES:** No dogs (ex guide dogs) No smoking in restaurant Civ Wed 110 **CARDS:**

★★★63% The Bridge Hotel

Walshford LS22 5HS THE INDEPENDENTS
☎ 01937 580115 📠 01937 580556
e-mail: info@bridgeinn-bridgehotel.co.uk
Dir: *A1 Southbound - leave A1(M) at junct 47 (York), 1st left signed Walshford and follow the brown tourist signs*

A very conveniently located hotel close to the A1, spacious public areas and a good range of services make this an ideal venue for business or leisure. Bedrooms are comfortable and well appointed. The Bridge offers a choice of bars and a spacious

continued

open-plan restaurant. Also available are conference and banqueting suites.

ROOMS: 30 en suite (1 fmly) s £65-£75; d £85-£105 (incl. bkfst) **LB** **FACILITIES:** Mini Gym Xmas **CONF:** Thtr 150 Class 50 Board 50 **NOTES:** Civ Wed 120 **CARDS:**

WEYBRIDGE, Surrey
See LONDON SECTION plan 1 A1

★★★★68% Oatlands Park

146 Oatlands Dr KT13 9HB
☎ 01932 847242 📠 01932 842252
e-mail: info@oatlandsparkhotel.com
Dir: *through Weybridge High Street to top of Monument Hill. Hotel 0.3m on left*

Once a palace for Henry VIII, this impressive building sits in extensive grounds encompassing tennis courts and a 9-hole golf course. The spacious lounge and bar create a wonderful first impression with tall marble pillars and plush comfortable seating. Bedrooms, including some suites, are comfortable and well equipped.

ROOMS: 144 en suite (5 fmly) (31 GF) No smoking in 68 bedrooms s £139-£195; d £185-£222 **LB** **FACILITIES:** STV Golf 9 Tennis (hard) Gym Croquet lawn Putting green Jogging course Fitness suite entertainment Xmas **CONF:** BC Thtr 300 Class 150 Board 80 Del from £170 **SERVICES:** Lift **PARKING:** 140 **NOTES:** Civ Wed 200
CARDS:

★★★68% The Ship

Monument Green KT13 8BQ
☎ 01932 848364 📠 01932 857153
e-mail: info@shiphotel.co.uk
Dir: *M25 junct 11, at 3rd rdbt left into Weybridge High Street. Hotel on left approx 300yds*

This traditional coaching inn is conveniently located on the high street. Retaining much of the period charm in public areas the hotel offer comfortable contemporary accommodation. A popular public bar is on offer along with a smart restaurant serving freshly prepared dishes. Conference facilities and ample parking are also provided.

ROOMS: 39 en suite No smoking in 10 bedrooms s £130-£140; d £160-£170 **LB** **FACILITIES:** STV **CONF:** Thtr 140 Class 70 Board 60 Del from £122 **PARKING:** 65 **NOTES:** No dogs (ex guide dogs) No smoking in restaurant **CARDS:**

Innkeeper's Lodge

25 Oatlands Chase KT13 9RW Innkeeper's Lodge
☎ 01932 253277 📠 01932 252412
e-mail: badgers.rest@bass.com
Dir: *M25 junct 11, take A317 towards Weybridge, at 3rd rdbt take A3050, left, 1m. Turn into Oatlands Chase, Lodge on right*

A new concept in the travel accommodation market. Smart rooms

continued on p648

W

WEYBRIDGE, continued

meet essential business requirements but also have home comforts. Dining options include all-day menus plus the added advantage of breakfast, which is included in the room price. For further details, consult the Hotel Groups page.
ROOMS: 18 en suite

WEYMOUTH, Dorset

Map 04 SY67

★★★73% Moonfleet Manor

Fleet DT3 4ED
☎ 01305 786948 01305 774395
Dir: *A354 to Weymouth; right on B3157 to Bridport. At Chickerell left at mini rdbt to Fleet*

This enchanting hideaway, peacefully located at the end of the village of Fleet, enjoys a wonderful sea-facing position. Many of the well equipped bedrooms overlook Chesil Beach and the hotel is furnished with style and panache, particularly the sumptuous lounges. Accomplished cuisine is served in the beautiful restaurant.
ROOMS: 33 en suite 6 annexe en suite (26 fmly) **FACILITIES:** STV Indoor swimming (H) Tennis (hard) Squash Snooker Sauna Solarium Croquet lawn Childrens nursery ch fac Xmas **CONF:** Thtr 50 Class 18 Board 26 **SERVICES:** Lift **PARKING:** 50 **NOTES:** No smoking in restaurant **CARDS:**

See advert on opposite page

★★★63% Hotel Rex

29 The Esplanade DT4 8DN
☎ 01305 760400 01305 760500
e-mail: rex@kingshotels.co.uk
Dir: *on seafront opp Alexandra Gardens*

Originally built as the summer residence for the Duke of Clarence, this hotel benefits from its seafront location with stunning views across Weymouth Bay. Bedrooms include several sea-facing rooms and are all well equipped. A wide range of imaginative dishes is served in the popular vaulted restaurant.
ROOMS: 31 en suite (5 fmly) s £51-£59; d £75-£104 (incl. bkfst) **LB** **FACILITIES:** STV **CONF:** Thtr 40 Class 30 Board 25 Del £68 **SERVICES:** Lift **PARKING:** 6 **NOTES:** No dogs (ex guide dogs) Closed Xmas **CARDS:**

★★★61% Hotel Rembrandt

12-18 Dorchester Rd DT4 7JU
☎ 01305 764000 01305 764022
e-mail: reception@hotelrembrandt.co.uk
Dir: *0.75m on left after Manor rdbt on A354 from Dorchester*

Only a short distance from the seafront and town centre, this hotel is ideal for visiting local attractions. Facilities include indoor leisure, a bar and extensive meeting rooms. The hotel restaurant is open for lunch and dinner, offering an impressive carvery or carte menu.
ROOMS: 74 en suite (5 fmly) No smoking in 30 bedrooms s £65-£80; d £80-£98 (incl. bkfst) **LB** **FACILITIES:** STV Indoor swimming (H) Sauna Solarium Gym Jacuzzi Steam room Xmas **CONF:** Thtr 200 Class 100 Board 50 Del from £85 **SERVICES:** Lift **PARKING:** 80 **NOTES:** No smoking in restaurant Civ Wed 100
CARDS:

★★71% Glenburn

42 Preston Rd DT3 6PZ
☎ 01305 832353 01305 835610
e-mail: info@glenburnhotel.com
Dir: *on A353 1.5m E of town centre*

This small hotel is family run and close to the seafront. Offering good parking and attractive gardens, including a pleasant play area, the Glenburn is ideal for either business or leisure guests. Bedrooms are comfortable and well-equipped. Good use of fresh local produce is made to create the dishes on the daily changing menu.
ROOMS: 13 en suite (2 fmly) No smoking in 8 bedrooms s £33-£48; d £54-£75 (incl. bkfst) **LB** **FACILITIES:** Jacuzzi **CONF:** Thtr 20 Class 20 Board 15 **PARKING:** 15 **NOTES:** No dogs (ex guide dogs) No smoking in restaurant **CARDS:**

★★70% Acropolis

53-55 Dorchester Rd DT4 7JT
☎ 01305 784282 01305 767172
e-mail: acropolishotel@plantours.fsnet.co.uk

A friendly hotel offering comfortable, stylishly decorated and well-equipped rooms; the Acropolis has now undergone refurbishment. A pleasant lounge and bar is provided and guests can relax around the pool in warmer months where vines and olive trees provided a Mediterranean feel. Appetising authentic Greek cuisine and wines are served in the restaurant.
ROOMS: 11 en suite (4 fmly) No smoking in 6 bedrooms s £45-£55; d £70-£80 (incl. bkfst) **FACILITIES:** Outdoor swimming (H) Xmas **PARKING:** 17 **CARDS:**

★★70% Hotel Prince Regent

139 The Esplanade DT4 7NR
☎ 01305 771313 📠 01305 778100
e-mail: hprwell@aol.com

Dir: *from A354 follow seafront signs. Left at Jubilee Clock, 0.25m along seafront*

Dating back to 1855, this welcoming resort hotel boasts splendid views over Weymouth Bay from the majority of public rooms and front-facing bedrooms. Conveniently close to the town centre and harbour, and opposite the beach, the hotel has been extensively refurbished. The restaurant offers a choice of menus, and entertainment is regularly provided in the ballroom during the season.
ROOMS: 63 en suite (14 fmly) (2 GF) No smoking in 35 bedrooms s £45-£70; d £60-£115 (incl. bkfst) **LB** **FACILITIES:** Use of leisure facilities at sister hotel **CONF:** Thtr 180 Class 150 Board 150 **SERVICES:** Lift **PARKING:** 26 **NOTES:** No dogs (ex guide dogs) No smoking in restaurant **CARDS:**

★★65% Crown

51-53 St Thomas St DT4 8EQ
☎ 01305 760800 📠 01305 760300
e-mail: crown@kingshotels.co.uk
Dir: *From Dorchester, A354 to Weymouth. Follow Back Water on left & cross second bridge*

Conveniently located, this popular hotel is adjacent to the old harbour and is ideal for shopping, local attractions or transportation links including the ferry. Public areas include an extensive bar, ballroom and comfortable residents' lounge on the first floor. Themed events such as mock cruises are a speciality.
ROOMS: 86 en suite (11 fmly) s £35-£42; d £68-£76 (incl. bkfst) **LB** **FACILITIES:** STV **CONF:** Class 140 Board 80 **SERVICES:** Lift **PARKING:** 14 **NOTES:** No dogs (ex guide dogs) Closed 25-26 Dec **CARDS:**

⌂ Travel Inn

Green Hill DT4 7SX
☎ 08701 977267 📠 01305 760589
Dir: *Follow signs to Weymouth, then brown signs to Lodmoor Country Park*

Travel Inn offers good-quality, value-for-money accommodation. Spacious, en suite rooms with bath and shower comfortably accommodate a family of up to two adults and two children (to age 15). The restaurant and bar offers a varied menu. For further details and the Travel Inn phone number, consult the Hotel Groups page.
ROOMS: 40 en suite s £44.95; d £44.95

WHATTON, Nottinghamshire — Map 11 SK73

★★64% The Haven

Grantham Rd NG13 9EU
☎ 01949 850800 📠 01949 851454
Dir: *off A52, take turning to Redmile/Belvoir Castle*

This welcoming, family-run hotel has a large public bar and dining room, in which a good range of popular dishes is available. The bedrooms are spacious and have thoughtful facilities.
ROOMS: 33 en suite (5 fmly) s fr £45; d fr £65 (incl. bkfst) **FACILITIES:** STV Pool table **CONF:** Thtr 80 Class 60 Board 60 **PARKING:** 70 **NOTES:** No smoking in restaurant **CARDS:**

Destination dining!
This symbol indicates a Restaurant with Rooms

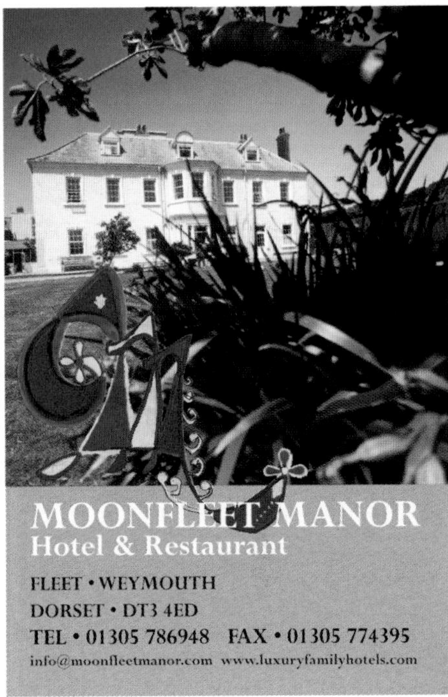

MOONFLEET MANOR
Hotel & Restaurant
FLEET • WEYMOUTH
DORSET • DT3 4ED
TEL • 01305 786948 FAX • 01305 774395
info@moonfleetmanor.com www.luxuryfamilyhotels.com

WHEDDON CROSS, Somerset — Map 03 SS93

★★72% Raleigh Manor

TA24 7BB
☎ 01643 841484 📠 01643 841484
e-mail: enquiries@raleighmanorhotel.co.uk
Dir: *at Wheddon Cross, turn right on A396 for Dunster. Private drive to Raleigh Manor on left*

Set in Exmoor National Park, this Victorian country house enjoys stunning views over Snowdrop Valley. The individually decorated bedrooms are comfortably furnished and equipped. A relaxing atmosphere can be enjoyed in the lounges, snug library and conservatory, each taking full advantage of the spectacular vista. The dining room offers a choice of carefully prepared dishes.
ROOMS: 7 en suite No smoking in all bedrooms s £35.25-£41.25; d £70.50-£82.50 (incl. bkfst) **LB** **PARKING:** 10 **NOTES:** No dogs No children 12yrs No smoking in restaurant Closed Mid Dec-Jan **CARDS:**

WHICKHAM, Tyne & Wear — Map 21 NZ26

★★★70% Gibside Arms

Front St NE16 4JG
☎ 0191 488 9292 📠 0191 488 8000
e-mail: reception@gibside-hotel.co.uk
Dir: *off A1(M) towards Whickham on B6317, onto Whickham Front Street, 2m on right*

Conveniently located in the village centre, this hotel is close to major transport links and its hilltop setting affords views over the Tyne Valley. Bedrooms are comfortable and smartly decorated.

continued on p650

WHICKHAM, continued

Public rooms include the Egyptian-themed Sphinx bar and a more formal restaurant. Secure garage parking is available.
ROOMS: 45 en suite (2 fmly) (13 GF) No smoking in 10 bedrooms s £40-£59.50; d £50-£71 **LB FACILITIES:** STV Golf Academy at The Beamish Park entertainment Xmas **CONF:** Thtr 100 Class 50 Board 50 Del from £74 **SERVICES:** Lift **PARKING:** 28
CARDS:

WHITBY, North Yorkshire Map 19 NZ81

★★★71% Dunsley Hall
Dunsley YO21 3TL
☎ 01947 893437 01947 893505
e-mail: reception@dunsleyhall.com
Dir: *3m N of Whitby, signed off A171*
Friendly hospitality and fine cooking are strong features of this country house, situated in four acres of well-tended gardens. Oak panelling, carved fireplaces and mullion windows all add to the character of the house, which offers a well-appointed restaurant and a popular bar. Spacious bedrooms are bright, comfortable and beautifully furnished, and many have sea views.
ROOMS: 18 en suite (2 fmly) (2 GF) No smoking in all bedrooms s £78-£105; d £126-£168 (incl. bkfst) **LB FACILITIES:** Indoor swimming (H) Tennis (hard) Sauna Solarium Gym Croquet lawn Putting green Xmas **CONF:** Thtr 95 Class 50 Board 40 Del from £120 **PARKING:** 60 **NOTES:** No smoking in restaurant Civ Wed 50 **CARDS:**

★★★67% Saxonville
Ladysmith Av, Argyle Rd YO21 3HX
☎ 01947 602631 01947 820523
e-mail: newtons@saxonville.co.uk
Dir: *A174 on to North Promenade. Turn inland at large four towered building visible on West Cliff into Argyle Road, then 1st turning on right*
This comfortable holiday hotel provides very well presented modern bedrooms. Public areas include a choice of lounges, a newly created and enlarged bar, and an attractive restaurant where an extensive range of carefully prepared English dishes is offered. Operated by the same family for several generations, friendly hospitality is a key feature.
ROOMS: 23 en suite (2 fmly) (1 GF) No smoking in all bedrooms s £50-£57.50; d £100-£115 (incl. bkfst) **LB FACILITIES:** STV **CONF:** Thtr 100 Class 64 Board 48 Del £80 **PARKING:** 20 **NOTES:** No dogs (ex guide dogs) No smoking in restaurant Closed Dec-Jan RS Feb-Mar & Nov
CARDS:

★★71% Stakesby Manor
Manor Close, High Stakesby YO21 1HL
☎ 01947 602773 01947 602140
e-mail: rod@stakesby-manor.co.uk
Dir: *at rdbt junct of A171/B1416 take road for West Cliff. 3rd turning on right*
Situated in a residential area, this Georgian mansion's friendly and relaxed atmosphere attracts many regulars, both business guests and tourists. Inviting public areas include a comfortable bar lounge, attractive oak-panelled dining room and lawned gardens. The bedrooms are impressively furnished and thoughtfully equipped, and the management very professional.
ROOMS: 13 en suite (2 fmly) No smoking in 6 bedrooms s £62; d £88 (incl. bkfst) **LB CONF:** Thtr 100 Class 46 Board 40 Del from £101 **PARKING:** 40 **NOTES:** No dogs (ex guide dogs) No smoking in restaurant Closed 24-30 Dec **CARDS:**

★★70% Cliffemount
Runswick Bay TS13 5HU
☎ 01947 840103 01947 841025
e-mail: cliffemount@runswickbay.fsnet.co.uk
Dir: *turn off A174 8m N of Whitby, follow road 1m to end. Hotel on clifftop*
Standing in a delightful elevated position, overlooking the pretty cliff-side village and with splendid views across the bay, a warm welcome awaits you here. The cosy bar leads to the stylish restaurant where locally caught fish features strongly on the interesting, extensive menus and special boards. The bedrooms, many with sea-view balconies, are well equipped and comfortably furnished.
ROOMS: 19 en suite (5 GF) s £31-£50; d £64-£95 (incl. bkfst) **LB PARKING:** 30 **NOTES:** Closed 25-26 Dec **CARDS:**

★★68% White House
Upgang Ln, West Cliff YO21 3JJ
☎ 01947 600469 01947 821600
Dir: *turn off A171 onto High Stakesby road, follow signs for West Cliff and Sandsend. Hotel adjacent to golf course*
This hotel is on the cliff top overlooking the golf course and Sandsend Bay. Attractively appointed bedrooms vary in size, and there is a choice of two bars where locals and visitors mingle. Both the bars and the dining room offer a varied selection of dishes including fresh local fish.
ROOMS: 10 en suite (3 fmly) **PARKING:** 30 **NOTES:** No smoking in restaurant **CARDS:**

★★64% Old West Cliff Hotel
42 Crescent Av YO21 3EQ
☎ 01947 603292 01947 821716
e-mail: oldwestcliff@telinco.co.uk
Dir: *from A171 follow signs for West Cliff, approach spa complex. Hotel 100yds from centre off Crescent Gardens*
This family owned and run hotel is close to the sea and convenient for the town centre. It provides well-equipped bedrooms, a cosy lounge and separate bar. A wide range of food is served in the cosy basement restaurant.
ROOMS: 12 en suite (6 fmly) s £49; d £58 (incl. bkfst) **NOTES:** No dogs (ex guide dogs) No smoking in restaurant Closed 24 Dec-Jan
CARDS:

WHITCHURCH, Shropshire Map 15 SJ54

★★★65% Dodington Lodge
Dodington SY13 1EN
☎ 01948 662539 01948 667992
e-mail: dodingtonlodge@aol.com
Dir: *follow town centre signs to Whitchurch (ignore by-pass)*
This family run hotel is conveniently situated close to the centre of the town, within easy reach of Chester and North Wales. Bedrooms are tastefully decorated and well equipped, while a welcoming atmosphere prevails in the lounge bar. A choice of eating options is offered, from a light snack to a full meal, and the function suite is a popular choice for wedding receptions.
ROOMS: 10 en suite (2 fmly) s £55; d £65 (incl. bkfst) **CONF:** Thtr 60 Class 24 Board 30 **PARKING:** 30 **NOTES:** No smoking in restaurant Closed 24-27 Dec **CARDS:**

 AA Rosette Award for culinary excellence

W

WHITEHAVEN, Cumbria Map 18 NX91

Travel Inn
Howgate CA28 6PL
☎ 08701 977268 01946 590106
Dir: *On outskirts of Whitehaven on A595 towards Workington*
Travel Inn offers good-quality, value-for-money accommodation. Spacious, en suite rooms with bath and shower comfortably accommodate a family of up to two adults and two children (to age 15). The restaurant and bar offers a varied menu. For further details and the Travel Inn phone number, consult the Hotel Groups page.
ROOMS: 38 en suite s £44.95; d £44.95

WHITEWELL, Lancashire Map 18 SD64

Restaurant with Rooms

The Inn at Whitewell
Forest of Bowland, Clitheroe BB7 3AT
☎ 01200 448222 01200 448298
This long established culinary destination hides away in quintessential Lancashire countryside just 20 minutes from the M6. The fine dining restaurant is complemented by two historic, cosy bars, and roaring fires, real ales and slick service provide an irresistible combination. Bedrooms are richly furnished with antiques and eye-catching bijouterie, whilst many of the bathrooms have voluminous Victorian brass showers.
ROOMS: 13 en suite 4 annexe en suite (1 fmly) s £66-£105; d £89-£133 (incl. bkfst) **FACILITIES:** STV Fishing **CONF:** Class 60 Board 35 Del from £110 **PARKING:** 60 **NOTES:** Civ Wed 60
CARDS:

WHITLEY, Wiltshire Map 04 ST86

The Pear Tree Inn
Top Ln SN12 8QX
☎ 01251 709131 01251 702276
At the time of going to press, the star classification for this hotel was not confirmed. Please refer to the AA internet site www.theAA.com for current information.
ROOMS: 4 en suite 4 annexe en suite (2 fmly) (4 GF) No smoking in all bedrooms s £60; d £85-£120 (incl. bkfst) **FACILITIES:** boules pitch **PARKING:** 60 **NOTES:** No dogs (ex guide dogs) No smoking in restaurant Closed 25-26 Dec **CARDS:**

WHITLEY BAY, Tyne & Wear Map 21 NZ37

★★★72% **Windsor**
South Pde NE26 2RF
☎ 0191 251 8888 0191 297 0272
e-mail: info@windsorhotel-uk.com
Dir: *from A19 Tyne Tunnel follow for A1058 to Tynemouth. At coast rdbt turn left to Whitley Bay. After 2m turn left at Rex Hotel, Windsor on left*
This tastefully modernised hotel is conveniently located between the town centre and the sea front, where lively bars transform Thursday to Sunday nights with a carnival atmosphere. Bedrooms are of a good standard, many with superior bathrooms with bath

continued

and separate shower cubicle. Public areas are smartly presented and include Bazil, a trendy and stylish brasserie.

ROOMS: 70 en suite (24 fmly) (4 GF) s £49-£65; d £60-£70 (incl. bkfst) **LB** **FACILITIES:** STV **CONF:** Thtr 80 Class 60 Board 40 Del from £69 **SERVICES:** Lift **PARKING:** 46 **NOTES:** No dogs (ex guide dogs)
CARDS:

WHITNEY-ON-WYE, Herefordshire Map 09 SO24

★★73% **The Rhydspence Inn**
HR3 6EU
☎ 01497 831262 01497 831751
e-mail: info@rhydspence-inn.co.uk
Dir: *1m W of Whitney-on-Wye on A438 Hereford to Brecon road*

With a history as an inn stretching back 600 years, this hotel offers the charm of yesteryear with the comforts of today. Personally run by the proprietors, guests can expect well-equipped bedrooms and public areas with exposed beams and timber framed walls. There is an extensive menu in the elegant restaurant and the atmospheric bar also ahs a blackboard menu.
ROOMS: 7 en suite s £37.50-£42.50; d £65-£75 (incl. bkfst) **LB** **PARKING:** 30 **NOTES:** No dogs (ex guide dogs) No smoking in restaurant Closed 2wks Jan **CARDS:** 

WHITSTABLE, Kent Map 07 TR16

Travel Inn
Thanet Way CT5 3DB
☎ 08701 977269 01227 263151
Dir: *2m W of town centre on B2205*
Travel Inn offers good-quality, value-for-money accommodation. Spacious, en suite rooms with bath and shower comfortably accommodate a family of up to two adults and two children (to age 15). The restaurant and bar offers a varied menu. For further details and the Travel Inn phone number, consult the Hotel Groups page.
ROOMS: 40 en suite s £44.95; d £44.95 **CONF:** Thtr 30 Board 20

WHITTINGTON, Shropshire
Map 15 SJ33

★★67% Ye Olde Boot Inn
Castle St SY11 4DF
☎ 01691 662250
Dir: *off A495, Oswestry bypass*
This old coaching inn stands opposite Whittington Castle and moat, which is home to a variety of wild fowl. It has a warm and friendly atmosphere throughout. The bars and restaurant are popular with locals and a comprehensive range of good value meals is always available. The refurbished bedrooms are attractively appointed, modern and well equipped.
ROOMS: 6 en suite (2 fmly) No smoking in all bedrooms s fr £35; d fr £48 (incl. bkfst) **PARKING:** 60 **NOTES:** No smoking in restaurant
CARDS:

WHITTLEBURY, Northamptonshire
Map 11 SP64

★★★★77% Whittlebury Hall
NN12 8QH
☎ 01327 857857 01237 857867
e-mail: sales@whittleburyhall.co.uk
Dir: *A43/A413 towards Buckingham, through Whittlebury village, turning for Whittlebury Hall on right. Signed*
A purpose-built, Georgian-style country house hotel with excellent spa and leisure facilities and pedestrian access to the Silverstone circuit. Grand public areas include F1 memorabilia and the accommodation includes some lavishly-appointed suites. Food is a strength, particularly in the lavish afternoon teas and the fine-dining Murray's Restaurant.
ROOMS: 122 en suite No smoking in 110 bedrooms s £100-£130; d £130-£160 (incl. bkfst) **LB** **FACILITIES:** STV Indoor swimming (H) Sauna Solarium Gym Putting green Jacuzzi Beauty treatments, Relaxation Room, Aerobic Studio, Hair Studio Xmas **CONF:** Thtr 350 Class 175 Board 40 Del from £150 **SERVICES:** Lift **PARKING:** 250 **NOTES:** No dogs (ex guide dogs) No smoking in restaurant Civ Wed 200
CARDS:

WICKFORD, Essex
Map 06 TQ79

Innkeeper's Lodge Basildon/Wickford
Innkeeper's Lodge
Runwell Rd SS11 7QJ
☎ 01268 769671 01268 578012
Dir: *M25 junct 29/A127 Southend, leave at Basildon/Wickford, left at rdbt towards Wickford. Straight over next 2 rdbts 3rd rdbt 2nd exit*
A new concept in the travel accommodation market. Smart rooms meet essential business requirements but also have home comforts. Dining options include all-day menus plus the added advantage of breakfast, which is included in the room price. For further details, consult the Hotel Groups page.
ROOMS: 24 en suite

WICKHAM, Hampshire
Map 05 SU51

★★70% Old House
The Square PO17 5JG
☎ 01329 833049 01329 833672
e-mail: enq@theoldhousehotel.co.uk
Dir: *M27 junct 10 N on A32 for 2m towards Alton*
This creeper-clad former Georgian residence occupies a prime position in a charming square in the centre of town. Ongoing refurbishment is resulting in smart and comfortable public areas that include a choice of eating areas and an inviting bar and lounge. Bedrooms are well equipped although some are larger than others.
ROOMS: 8 en suite No smoking in all bedrooms s £70-£85; d £75-£120 (incl. bkfst) **LB** **PARKING:** 8 **NOTES:** No dogs (ex guide dogs) No smoking in restaurant **CARDS:**

WIDNES, Cheshire
Map 15 SJ5

★★★64% *The Hillcrest Hotel*
75 Cronton Ln WA8 9AR
☎ 0151 424 1616 0151 495 1348
e-mail: thehillcrest@corushotels.com
Dir: *A5080 Cronton to lights turn right for 0.75m, right at T-junct, follow A5080 for 500yds. Hotel on right*

This modern hotel is situated within easy reach of the motorway to the northwest. All bedrooms are comfortable and well-equipped, particularly the executive rooms, and suites with four-poster or canopy beds and spa baths are also available. Public areas include extensive conference facilities, Palms restaurant and bar, as well as Nelsons public bar.
ROOMS: 50 en suite (5 fmly) No smoking in 25 bedrooms **FACILITIES:** STV entertainment ch fac **CONF:** Thtr 140 Class 80 Board 40 **SERVICES:** Lift **PARKING:** 150 **NOTES:** Civ Wed 160
CARDS:

Travelodge
Travelodge
Fiddlers Ferry Rd WA8 2NR
☎ 08700 850 950
Dir: *on A562*
Travelodge offers good quality, good value, modern accommodation. Ideal for families, the spacious, en suite bedrooms include remote-control TV, tea and coffee-making facilities, luxury beds and free morning newspaper. Meals can be taken at the nearby family restaurant. For further details and the Travelodge phone number, consult the Hotel Groups page.
ROOMS: 32 en suite s fr £42.95; d fr £42.95

WIGAN, Greater Manchester
Map 15 SD5

★★★★62% Kilhey Court
MACDONALD HOTELS
Chorley Rd, Standish WN1 2XN
☎ 01257 472100 01257 422401
e-mail: kilheycourt@macdonald-hotels.co.uk
Dir: *M6 J27, A5209 Standish/Chorley, left at T-junct, straight over the traffic lights, past church on right, left at T-junct, hotel on right 600yds*
This hotel, peacefully situated in its own grounds yet conveniently located for the motorway network, offers comfortable accommodation. Rooms are split between the original Victorian house and a modern extension. Public areas display many original

continued

features, and the split-level restaurant offers views over the Worthington lakes.
ROOMS: 62 en suite (5 fmly) (8 GF) No smoking in 33 bedrooms s £110-£170; d £110-£190 **LB** **FACILITIES:** STV Indoor swimming (H) Sauna Solarium Gym Jacuzzi Aerobics and yoga classes entertainment Xmas **CONF:** BC Thtr 400 Class 250 Board 60 Del from £135 **SERVICES:** Lift **PARKING:** 100 **NOTES:** No dogs (ex guide dogs) No smoking in restaurant Civ Wed 100
CARDS:

★★★73%
Wrightington Hotel & Country Club
Moss Ln, Wrightington WN6 9PB
☎ 01257 425803 📠 01257 425830
e-mail: 100631.3514@compuserve.com
Dir: *M6 junct 27, 0.25m W, hotel on right after church*
Situated in open countryside, this privately owned hotel offers friendly hospitality. Accommodation is well equipped and spacious. Public areas include an extensive leisure complex, Blazers Restaurant, two bars and air conditioned function and banqueting facilities. A further block of luxury bedrooms is under construction.
ROOMS: 74 en suite (4 fmly) No smoking in 24 bedrooms s £68-£95; d £78-£110 (incl. bkfst) **LB** **FACILITIES:** STV Indoor swimming (H) Squash Sauna Solarium Gym Jacuzzi Sprt Inj clinic,Hlth&Bty clinic,H'drsr **CONF:** Thtr 200 Class 120 Board 40 **PARKING:** 240 **NOTES:** Civ Wed
CARDS:

★★★66% **Quality Hotel Wigan**
Riverway WN1 3SS
☎ 01942 826888 📠 01942 825800
e-mail: admin@gb058.u-net.com
Dir: *from A49 take B5238 from rdbt, continue for 1.5m through lights, through 3 more sets of lights, right at 4th set, 1st left*
Close to the centre of the town this modern hotel offers spacious and well-equipped bedrooms. The open plan public areas include a comfortable lounge bar adjacent to the popular restaurant, which serves a good range of dishes. Secure car parking is a bonus.
ROOMS: 88 en suite (16 GF) No smoking in 35 bedrooms s £47-£89; d £50-£99 **LB** **FACILITIES:** STV **CONF:** Thtr 200 Class 90 Board 50 Del £95 **SERVICES:** Lift **PARKING:** 100 **NOTES:** No smoking in restaurant Civ Wed 60 **CARDS:**

★★65% **Bel-Air**
236 Wigan Ln WN1 2NU
☎ 01942 241410 📠 01942 243967
e-mail: belair@hotelwigan.freeserve.co.uk
Dir: *M6 junct 27, follow signs for Standish. In Standish turn right at lights towards A49. Hotel 1.5m on right towards Wigan*
This friendly, family owned and run hotel is located just to the north of town on the A49. Accommodation is modern, bright and well-equipped. An extensive range of freshly prepared dishes is offered in the restaurant.
ROOMS: 11 en suite (1 fmly) s £35-£39.50; d £45-£49.50 (incl. bkfst) **CONF:** Thtr 20 Board 8 **PARKING:** 10 **NOTES:** No dogs (ex guide dogs) No smoking in restaurant **CARDS:**

Premier Lodge (Wigan South)
53 Warrington Rd, Ashton-in-Makerfield WN4 9PJ
☎ 0870 9906582 📠 0870 9906583
Dir: *M6 junct 23, onto A49 towards Ashton. Hotel 0.5m on left*
Premier Lodge offers modern, well-equipped, en suite accommodation suitable for both business and leisure travellers. Meals can be taken at the adjacent popular restaurant and bar, which is fully licensed. For further details, consult the Hotel Groups page.
ROOMS: 28 en suite s £48; d £48

Travel Inn (Wigan South)
Warrington Rd, Marus Bridge WN3 6XB
☎ 08701 977270 📠 01942 498679
Dir: *M6 junct 25 (N'bound) slip road to rdbt turn left, Travel Inn on left*
Travel Inn offers good-quality, value-for-money accommodation. Spacious, en suite rooms with bath and shower comfortably accommodate a family of up to two adults and two children (to age 15). The restaurant and bar offers a varied menu. For further details and the Travel Inn phone number, consult the Hotel Groups page.
ROOMS: 40 en suite s £44.95; d £44.95

Travel Inn (Wigan West)
Orrell Rd, Orrell WN5 8HQ
☎ 08701 977271 📠 01942 215002
Dir: *From M6 junct 26 follow signs for Upholland and Orrell. At 1st lights turn left. Travel Inn on right behind Priory Wood Beefeater*
Travel Inn offers good-quality, value-for-money accommodation. Spacious, en suite rooms with bath and shower comfortably accommodate a family of up to two adults and two children (to age 15). The restaurant and bar offers a varied menu. For further details and the Travel Inn phone number, consult the Hotel Groups page.
ROOMS: 40 en suite s £44.95; d £44.95 **CONF:** Thtr 75 Board 40

WIGHT, ISLE OF — Map 05

BEMBRIDGE — Map 05 SZ68

★★★64% **The Windmill Inn Hotel & Restaurant**
1 Steyne Rd PO35 5UH
☎ 01983 872875 📠 01983 874760
e-mail: info@thewindmillhotel.co.uk
Dir: *0.5m from town centre, towards lifeboat station*

This newly refurbished hotel offers a range of comfortably furnished public rooms where an excellent choice of freshly prepared food is available to suit virtually all tastes. Bedrooms are generally spacious and thoughtfully equipped while service is both attentive and friendly. There is an attractive garden to the rear.
ROOMS: 15 en suite (4 fmly) No smoking in 3 bedrooms s £40-£85; d £70-£100 (incl. bkfst) **LB** **FACILITIES:** entertainment ch fac **CONF:** Thtr 100 Class 100 Board 100 **PARKING:** 50 **NOTES:** No dogs (ex guide dogs) Civ Wed 100 **CARDS:**

BONCHURCH See Ventnor

COWES

Map 05 SZ49

★★★68% *New Holmwood*

Queens Rd, Egypt Point PO31 8BW
☎ 01983 292508 01983 295020
e-mail: nholmwdh@aol.com
Dir: *from A3020 at Northwood Garage lights, left & follow road to rdbt. 1st left then sharp right into Baring Rd, 4th left into Egypt Hill. At bottom turn right, hotel on right*

Just metres from the Esplanade, this hotel has an enviable outlook. Bedrooms are comfortable and very well equipped. The glass-fronted restaurant is light and airy, and the sun terrace is ideal for relaxing in the summer months. A range of enjoyable meals is available. There is a small pool area and a conference room.
ROOMS: 26 en suite (1 fmly) No smoking in 6 bedrooms
FACILITIES: Spa STV Outdoor swimming (H) **CONF:** Thtr 150 Class 60 Board 50 **PARKING:** 20 **CARDS:**

See advert on opposite page

★63% Duke of York

Mill Hill Rd PO31 7BT
☎ 01983 295171 01983 295047
This family-run inn is in a quiet situation close to the town centre. Bedrooms are split between the main building and a nearby annexe and are neatly appointed. There is a well-stocked bar and a pleasant restaurant offering a range of popular dishes.
ROOMS: 7 en suite 5 annexe rms (1 fmly) No smoking in 4 bedrooms
PARKING: 12 **CARDS:**

FRESHWATER

Map 05 SZ38

★★★67% Farringford

Bedbury Ln PO40 9TQ
☎ 01983 752500 01983 756515
e-mail: enquiries@farringford.co.uk
Dir: *A3054, left to Norton Green down Pixlie Hill. Left to Freshwater Bay. At bay turn right into Bedbury Ln, hotel on left*

Upon seeing Farringford, Alfred Lord Tennyson is said to have remarked "we will go no further, this must be our home" and so it was for some forty years. 150 years later, the hotel provides bedrooms ranging in style and size, from large rooms in the main house to adjoining chalet-style rooms. The atmosphere is relaxed and dinner includes fresh local produce.
ROOMS: 14 en suite 4 annexe en suite (5 fmly) (4 GF) s £29-£60; d £58-£120 (incl. bkfst) **LB** **FACILITIES:** Outdoor swimming (H) Golf 9 Tennis (hard) Croquet lawn Putting green Bowling green entertainment ch fac Xmas **CONF:** BC Thtr 120 Class 50 Board 50 Del from £75
PARKING: 55 **NOTES:** Civ Wed 150 **CARDS:**

U Albion

PO40 9RA
☎ 01983 755755 01983 755295
e-mail: info@albion-hotel.net
At the time of going to press, the star classification for this hotel was not confirmed. Please refer to the AA internet site www.theAA.com for current information.
ROOMS: 42 en suite (9 fmly) (8 GF) No smoking in 21 bedrooms s £36-£64; d £72-£128 (incl. bkfst) **LB** **FACILITIES: Spa** Indoor swimming (H) Jacuzzi Xmas **CONF:** Thtr 60 Class 30 Board 40 **SERVICES:** Lift **PARKING:** 42 **NOTES:** No dogs (ex guide dogs) No smoking in restaurant **CARDS:**

NEWPORT

Map 05 SZ5

U Calverts

27 Quay St PO30 5BA
☎ 01983 525281 01983 525281
e-mail: info@calvertshotel.com
Dir: *opposite Guidlhall*
At the time of going to press, the star classification for this hotel was not confirmed. Please refer to the AA internet site www.theAA.com for current information.
ROOMS: 32 en suite (4 fmly) s £29; d £58 (incl. bkfst) **LB** **NOTES:** No dogs (ex guide dogs) No smoking in restaurant
CARDS:

Travel Inn Isle of Wight (Newport)

Seaclose, Fairlee Rd PO30 2DN
☎ 08701 977144 0870 241 9000
Dir: *From Newport town centre take A3054 sign-posted Ryde. After 0.75m at Seaclose lights, turn left. Travel Inn adjacent to council offices*

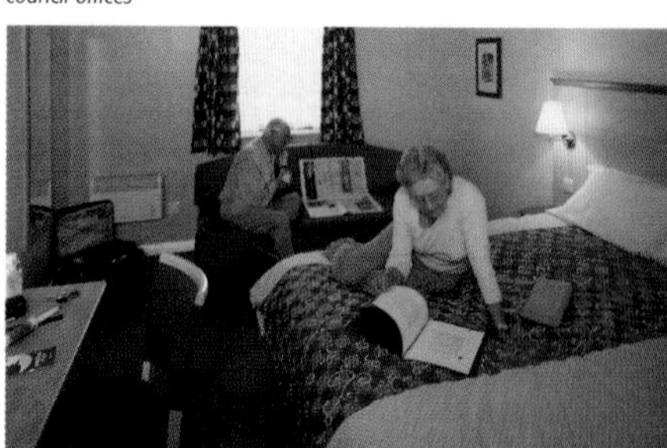

Travel Inn offers good-quality, value-for-money accommodation. Spacious, en suite rooms with bath and shower comfortably accommodate a family of up to two adults and two children (to age 15). The restaurant and bar offers a varied menu. For further details and the Travel Inn phone number, consult the Hotel Groups page.
ROOMS: 42 en suite s £44.95; d £44.95

RYDE

Map 05 SZ59

★★★64% Appley Manor

Appley Rd PO33 1PH
☎ 01983 564777 01983 564704
e-mail: appleymanor@lineone.net
Dir: *A3055 onto B3330. Hotel 0.25m on left*
Originally a Victorian manor house, Appley is located just five minutes from the town centre in very peaceful surroundings. The spacious bedrooms are well furnished, with all the expected modern facilities. There is residents' lounge and breakfast room

continued

overlooking the gardens, and the popular Manor Inn provides a wide range of well-cooked meals and real ales.
ROOMS: 12 en suite (2 fmly) No smoking in 3 bedrooms s £36; d £46 **CONF:** Thtr 40 Class 40 Board 30 **PARKING:** 60 **NOTES:** No dogs (ex guide dogs) **CARDS:**

★★64% Yelf's
Union St PO33 2LG
☎ 01983 564062 01983 563937
e-mail: manager@yelfshotel.com
Dir: *from Ryde Esplanande, turn into Union St. Hotel on right*
This former coaching inn has smart public areas including a busy bar, a separate lounge and an attractive dining room. Bedrooms are comfortably furnished and well equipped; several new bedrooms are available and a new, popular café bar offers a further dining option.
ROOMS: 30 en suite (2 fmly) No smoking in 3 bedrooms s £47-£49; d £62.50-£64 (incl. bkfst) **LB FACILITIES:** STV **CONF:** Thtr 70 Class 30 Board 50 **CARDS:**

ST LAWRENCE
Map 05 SZ57

★★69% *Rocklands*
Undercliffe Dr PO38 1XH
☎ 01983 852964 01983 856029
e-mail: rocklands@btconnect.com
Dir: *follow Undercliffe Drive from Ventor to St Lawrence. Hotel 50yds past church on right*
This elegant hotel is set in a peaceful location with attractive gardens. Bedrooms vary in size and décor, some with views of the gardens, and all are en suite with good facilities. Public areas are
continued
spacious with many original features and include a bar, games room and outdoor pool.
ROOMS: 16 en suite (5 fmly) **FACILITIES:** Outdoor swimming (H) Snooker Sauna Croquet lawn Putting green **CONF:** Thtr 30 Class 20 Board 20 **SERVICES:** Lift **PARKING:** 20 **NOTES:** No dogs (ex guide dogs) No smoking in restaurant Closed 3 Jan-Etr
CARDS:

SANDOWN
Map 05 SZ58

★★68% Riviera
2 Royal St PO36 8LP
☎ 01983 402518 01983 402518
e-mail: enquiries@rivierahotel.org.uk
Dir: *pass Heights Leisure Centre and church on left. Turn 2nd right (Melville St), then 2nd right again into Royal St*
Regular guests return year after year to this really friendly and welcoming of family-run hotels. Located near to the High Street and just a short stroll to the beach, pier and shops. Bedrooms, including several at ground floor level, are very well furnished and comfortably equipped. Enjoyable home-cooked meals are served in the spacious dining room.
ROOMS: 41 en suite (6 fmly) (10 GF) s £25-£32; d £50-£64 (incl. bkfst) **LB FACILITIES:** entertainment **PARKING:** 20 **NOTES:** No smoking in restaurant Closed Nov-Mar **CARDS:**

★★66% Cygnet Hotel
58 Carter St PO36 8DQ
☎ 01983 402930 01983 405112
e-mail: info@cygnethotel.com
Dir: *on corner of Broadway and Carter St*
Popular with tour groups, this family-run hotel offers bedrooms
continued on p656

SANDOWN, continued

that are generally spacious, comfortably furnished and well equipped. Extensive public areas include an indoor swimming pool, two lounge areas and a bar where live entertainment is regularly staged.
ROOMS: 46 rms (45 en suite) (8 fmly) (21 GF) s fr £25; d fr £50 (incl. bkfst) **LB** **FACILITIES: Spa** Indoor swimming (H) Outdoor swimming (H) Sauna Solarium Jacuzzi pool table Xmas **SERVICES:** Lift **PARKING:** 25 **NOTES:** No dogs (ex guide dogs) No smoking in restaurant Closed Jan **CARDS:**

★★62% Sandringham

Esplanade PO36 8AH
☎ 01983 406655 ▯ 01983 404395
e-mail: info@sandringhamhotel.co.uk
With a prime seafront location and splendid views, The Sandringham is one of the largest hotels on the island. Comfortable public areas include a large lounge, a newly extended dining room and a heated indoor swimming pool and jacuzzi. Bedrooms vary in size with many sea-facing rooms including a balcony. Regular entertainment is provided in the separate ballroom.
ROOMS: 110 en suite (39 fmly) (6 GF) No smoking in 3 bedrooms s £33-£49; d £66-£98 (incl. bkfst & dinner) **LB** **FACILITIES:** Indoor swimming (H) Snooker Sauna Jacuzzi entertainment Xmas **SERVICES:** Lift **PARKING:** 82 **NOTES:** No dogs (ex guide dogs) No smoking in restaurant **CARDS:**

★★61% Bayshore

Leisureplex

12 - 16 Pier St PO36 8JX
☎ 01983 403154 ▯ 01983 406574
e-mail: bayshore.sandown@alfatravel.co.uk
Dir: *from the Broadway into Melville St, signed to Tourist Information Office. Across High St and bear right opposite pier. Hotel on right.*
This large hotel is found on the sea front opposite the pier and offers extensive public rooms where live entertainment is provided in season. The bedrooms are well-equipped and staff very friendly and helpful.
ROOMS: 78 en suite (19 fmly) s £25-£33; d £42-£58 (incl. bkfst) **LB** **FACILITIES:** Sauna entertainment Xmas **SERVICES:** Lift **NOTES:** No dogs (ex guide dogs) No smoking in restaurant Closed Dec-Feb RS Mar & Nov **CARDS:**

SEAVIEW — Map 05 SZ69

★★★74% ◎ Priory Bay

Priory Dr PO34 5BU
☎ 01983 613146 ▯ 01983 616539
e-mail: enquiries@priorybay.co.uk
Dir: *B3330 towards Seaview, through Nettlestone. Do not take Seaview turning, instead continue 0.5m until sign for Hotel*

This peacefully located hotel with its own stretch of beach, has undergone extensive refurbishment. Public areas are especially comfortable, as are the well-equipped and mostly spacious bedrooms. The kitchen creates interesting and imaginative dishes, using local produce as much as possible.
ROOMS: 19 en suite 10 annexe en suite (10 fmly) s £59-£165; d £108-£198 (incl. bkfst) **LB** **FACILITIES:** Outdoor swimming Golf 9 Tennis (hard) Croquet lawn Private beach Xmas **CONF:** Thtr 80 Class 60 Board 40 Del from £75 **PARKING:** 100 **NOTES:** No smoking in restaurant Civ Wed 50 **CARDS:**

★★67% Springvale Hotel & Restaurant

Springvale PO34 5AN
☎ 01983 612533 ▯ 01983 812905
e-mail: reception@springvalehotel.com
Dir: *towards Ryde, follow A3055 onto A3330 towards Bembridge. Left at signs to Seaview, follow brown tourist signs for hotel*

A friendly hotel in a quiet beach-front location with views across the Solent. Bedrooms, varying in shape and size, are attractive and well equipped. Public areas are traditionally furnished and include a cosy bar, dining room and small separate lounge.
ROOMS: 13 en suite (2 fmly) s £35-£65; d £70-£130 (incl. bkfst) **LB** **FACILITIES:** Tennis (grass) Jacuzzi Sailing dinghy hire & tuition, Cruiser Charter entertainment ch fac Xmas **CONF:** Class 30 Board 20 Del from £80 **PARKING:** 1 **NOTES:** No smoking in restaurant **CARDS:**

SHANKLIN — Map 05 SZ58

★★★67% Keats Green

3 Queens Rd PO37 6AN
☎ 01983 862742 ▯ 01983 868572
e-mail: enquiries@keatsgreenhoteliow.co.uk
Dir: *on A3055 follow signs Old Village/Ventnor, avoiding town centre, hotel on left past St Saviors church*

This well-established hotel enjoys a super location overlooking Keats Green and Sandown Bay. Bedrooms are attractively decorated and furnished with pine. Public rooms include a comfortable bar/lounge and a smartly appointed dining room, both affording lovely sea views.
ROOMS: 33 en suite (7 fmly) s £44-£52 (incl. bkfst & dinner) **LB** **FACILITIES:** Outdoor swimming (H) ch fac Xmas **SERVICES:** Lift **PARKING:** 34 **NOTES:** No smoking in restaurant Closed Jan-Mar **CARDS:**

★★★65% **Luccombe Hall**
3 Luccombe Rd PO37 6RL
☎ 01983 869000 🖹 01983 863082
e-mail: enquiries@luccombehall.co.uk
Dir: *take A3055 to Shanklin, through old village then 1st left into Priory Rd, left into Popham Rd, 1st right into Luccombe Rd. Hotel on right*
Appropriately described as 'the view with the hotel', this property was originally built in 1870 as a summer home for the Bishop of Portsmouth. Enjoying an impressive cliff-top location, the hotel benefits from wonderful sea views, delightful gardens and direct access to the beach. Well-equipped bedrooms are comfortably furnished and there is a range of leisure facilities.
ROOMS: 30 en suite (15 fmly) (7 GF) s £35-£50; d £70-£100 (incl. bkfst) **FACILITIES:** Indoor swimming (H) Outdoor swimming (H) Squash Sauna Solarium Gym Jacuzzi Games room, Treatment room entertainment ch fac Xmas **PARKING:** 20 **NOTES:** No dogs (ex guide dogs) No smoking in restaurant **CARDS:**
See advert on this page

★★69% **Aqua**
17 The Esplanade PO37 6BN
☎ 01983 863024 🖹 01983 864841
e-mail: aa@aquahotel.co.uk
Dir: *off Arthurs Hill/North Rd at fiveways junction into Hope Rd and follow to Esplanade*
This friendly family run hotel has been in the same hands since 1980 and enjoys fine sea views. Public areas are light and airy and include a spacious lounge bar where live entertainment is available on most evenings and the attractive Boaters Restaurant. Bedrooms are well equipped, many have sea views and some have the added bonus of a balcony.
ROOMS: 22 en suite (4 fmly) No smoking in all bedrooms s £25-£60; d £50-£120 (incl. bkfst) **LB FACILITIES:** entertainment **NOTES:** No dogs No smoking in restaurant **CARDS:**

★★69% **Fernbank**
Highfield Rd PO37 6PP
☎ 01983 862790 🖹 01983 864412
e-mail: enquiries@fernbankhotel.com
Dir: *at Shanklin's old village traffic lights turn onto Victoria Ave, take 3rd left into Highfield Rd*
Fernbeck Hotel is set in a peaceful location, just minutes from the old village. Bedrooms are comfortably appointed and equipped with modern facilities, and the smart dining room overlooks the gardens and countryside beyond. Friendly hospitality throughout any stay remains a considerable strength here.
ROOMS: 19 en suite (8 fmly) s £32-£37; d £64-£74 (incl. bkfst) **LB FACILITIES:** Indoor swimming (H) Sauna Jacuzzi Xmas **CONF:** BC Thtr 120 Board 20 Del £65 **PARKING:** 19 **NOTES:** No dogs No children 5yrs No smoking in restaurant **CARDS:**

Packed in a hurry?
Ironing facilities should be available at all star levels, either in rooms or on request

★★68% **Channel View**
Hope Rd PO37 6EH
☎ 01983 862309 🖹 01983 868400
e-mail: enquiries@channelviewhotel.co.uk
Dir: *off A3055 at sign for esplanade & beach, hotel 250mtrs on left*
With an elevated cliff-top location overlooking Shanklin Bay, several rooms at this hotel enjoy pleasant views and all are very well decorated and furnished. It is a family-run hotel where guests can enjoy efficient service, regular evening entertainment, a heated indoor swimming pool and holistic therapy.

Channel View

ROOMS: 56 en suite (15 fmly) s £26-£32; d £52-£64 (incl. bkfst) **LB FACILITIES: Spa** Indoor swimming (H) Sauna Solarium entertainment **SERVICES:** Lift **PARKING:** 22 **NOTES:** No smoking in restaurant Closed Jan-Feb **CARDS:**

★★64% **Curraghmore**
22 Hope Rd PO37 6EA
☎ 01983 862605 🖹 01983 867431
e-mail: curraghmore@ukgateway.net
Dir: *from Sandown towards Shanklin, along Arthurs Hill. L before lights into Beatrice Ave, 100mtrs to hotel car park*
This hotel is pleasantly located, close to the beach and just a short stroll to the shops and the famous Shanklin village. Bedrooms include several with sea views. Entertainment is provided three
continued on p658

SHANKLIN, continued

or four nights of the week with dancing in the lounge and a separate adjoining bar.
ROOMS: 24 en suite (8 fmly) s £22-£25; d £44-£50 (incl. bkfst)
FACILITIES: entertainment **PARKING:** 20 **NOTES:** No smoking in restaurant Closed Nov-Feb

★★64% Malton House
8 Park Rd PO37 6AY
☎ 01983 865007 🖹 01983 865576
e-mail: christos@excite.co.uk
Dir: *from Hope Road lights up the hill then turn left into 3rd road*
A well kept Victorian hotel set in its own gardens in a quiet area, conveniently located for cliff-top walks and the public lift down to the promenade. The bedrooms are brightly appointed. Public rooms include a small comfortable lounge, a bar and a dining room for traditional meals.
ROOMS: 15 en suite (3 fmly) s £29-£31; d £52-£55 (incl. bkfst)
FACILITIES: Xmas **PARKING:** 12 **NOTES:** No dogs No smoking in restaurant **CARDS:**

★★64% Villa Mentone
11 Park Rd PO37 6AY
☎ 01983 862346 🖹 01983 862130
e-mail: enquiry@villa-mentone.co.uk
Built in 1860, the Villa Mentone enjoys an excellent cliff-top position close to the town centre. Bedrooms vary in size but are all well equipped, and a smart new conservatory extension offers views over Shanklin Bay. Enjoyable home cooking is served in the pleasant dining room, and entertainment is regularly provided in the bar.
ROOMS: 30 en suite (3 fmly) s £35-£48; d £50-£60 (incl. bkfst) **LB**
FACILITIES: STV entertainment Xmas **CONF:** Thtr 45 Class 25 Board 10 Del from £75 **PARKING:** 10 **NOTES:** No dogs (ex guide dogs) No smoking in restaurant **CARDS:**

★★63% *Bay House Hotel*
8 Chine Av PO37 6AG
☎ 01983 863180 🖹 01983 868934
e-mail: david@arthurshill.demon.co.uk
Dir: *Follow A3055 from Sandown to lights, take Queens Rd to end & turn left into Chine Ave*
Overlooking the sea, this friendly holiday hotel provides good all round comforts. There is an indoor pool available and good home cooking is served. The village centre is within easy walking distance.
ROOMS: 21 en suite **FACILITIES:** Indoor swimming (H) Sauna
PARKING: 15 **CARDS:**

★★62% Melbourne Ardenlea
Queen's Rd PO37 6AP
☎ 01983 862283 🖹 01983 862865
Dir: *turn left at Fiveways Crossroads, off A3055, hotel on right 150yds past the tall spired church*
This quietly located hotel is within easy walking distance of the town centre and the lift down to the promenade and successfully caters for the needs of holidaymakers. Bedrooms are traditionally furnished and guests can enjoy the various spacious public areas including a welcoming bar and a large heated indoor swimming pool.
ROOMS: 50 en suite (14 fmly) s £32-£50; d £64-£100 (incl. bkfst & dinner) **LB** **FACILITIES: Spa** Indoor swimming (H) Sauna Table tennis Pool table entertainment **SERVICES:** Lift **PARKING:** 28 **NOTES:** Closed mid Dec-mid Feb RS Nov-mid Dec & mid Feb-Mar
CARDS:

TOTLAND BAY Map 05 SZ3

★★★67% *Sentry Mead*
Madeira Rd PO39 0BJ
☎ 01983 753212 🖹 01983 753212
e-mail: julie@sentry-mead.co.uk
Dir: *off A3054 at Totland war memorial rdbt, 300yds on right*
Just two minutes' walk from the sea at Totland Bay, this well-kept Victorian villa has a comfortable lounge and separate bar, as well as a conservatory that looks out over the delightful garden. Bedrooms feature co-ordinated soft furnishings and welcome extras such as mineral water and biscuits.
ROOMS: 14 en suite (4 fmly) **PARKING:** 10 **NOTES:** No smoking in restaurant Closed 20 Dec-4 Jan **CARDS:**

VENTNOR Map 05 SZ5

★★★★71% The Royal Hotel
Belgrave Rd PO38 1JJ
☎ 01983 852186 🖹 01983 855395
e-mail: royalhotel@zetnet.co.uk
Dir: *A3055, into Ventnor follow one-way system – after lights turn left into Belgrave Road. Hotel on right*
The Royal Hotel provides good quality accommodation and the staff deliver a professional service in a friendly manner. Public areas include a sunny conservatory and restful lounge, and there is also an outdoor pool. The restaurant provides an appropriate setting for good cooking.
ROOMS: 55 en suite (7 fmly) No smoking in all bedrooms s £70-£95; d £115-£135 (incl. bkfst) **LB** **FACILITIES:** STV Outdoor swimming (H) Croquet lawn Xmas **CONF:** Thtr 100 Class 80 Board 50 **SERVICES:** Lift **PARKING:** 56 **NOTES:** No dogs (ex guide dogs) No smoking in restaurant Closed 1'st 2 wks Jan **CARDS:**
See advert on opposite page

★★★66% Burlington
Bellevue Rd PO38 1DB
☎ 01983 852113 🖹 01983 853862
e-mail: patmctoldrige@burlingtonhotel.freeserve.co.uk
Eight of the attractively decorated bedrooms benefit from balconies, and the three ground floor rooms have French doors which lead onto the garden. There is a cosy bar, a comfortable lounge and a dining room where home-made bread rolls accompany the five-course dinners. Service is friendly and attentive.
ROOMS: 24 en suite (8 fmly) **FACILITIES:** Outdoor swimming (H)
PARKING: 20 **NOTES:** No dogs No children 3yrs No smoking in restaurant Closed Nov-Etr **CARDS:**

★★★66% Eversley
Park Av PO38 1LB
☎ 01983 852244 & 852462 🖹 01983 856534
e-mail: eversleyhotel@yahoo.co.uk
Dir: *on A3055 W of Ventnor*
Located west of Ventnor, this hotel enjoys a quiet location with some rooms offering garden and pool views. The spacious and refurbished restaurant is also used for local functions and there is a newly decorated bar, a television room, a lounge area and a card room. Bedrooms are generally a good size.
ROOMS: 30 en suite (8 fmly) s £35-£50; d £59-£79 (incl. bkfst) **LB**
FACILITIES: Outdoor swimming (H) Childrens play equipment Pool table ch fac Xmas **CONF:** Class 40 Board 20 Del from £55 **PARKING:** 23
NOTES: No smoking in restaurant Closed 31 Nov-22 Dec & 2 Jan-8 Feb
CARDS:

W

★★★66% **Ventnor Towers**

Madeira Rd PO38 1QT
☎ 01983 852277 🖷 01983 855536
e-mail: reservations@ventnortowers.com
Dir: *1st left after Trinity church, follow road for 0.25m*

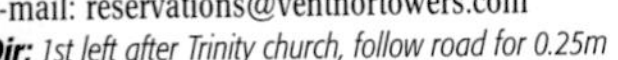

This mid-Victorian hotel set in spacious grounds - from which a path leads down to the shore - is high above the bay and enjoys splendid sea views. Many potted plants and fresh flowers grace day rooms, which include two lounges and a spacious bar. Bedrooms include two four-posters and some with their own balconies.
ROOMS: 27 en suite (4 fmly) No smoking in 14 bedrooms s fr £65; d fr £105 (incl. bkfst) **LB FACILITIES:** Outdoor swimming (H) Tennis (hard) Croquet lawn Putting green Games room with table tennis & pool table entertainment Xmas **CONF:** Thtr 80 Class 50 Board 35 Del from £76 **PARKING:** 26 **NOTES:** No smoking in restaurant Closed 21-27 Dec
CARDS:

★★68% **Hillside Hotel**
Mitchell Av PO38 1DR
☎ 01983 852271 🖷 01983 852271
e-mail: aa@hillside-hotel.co.uk
Dir: *off A3055 onto B3327. Hotel 0.5m on right behind tennis courts*

Hillside Hotel dates back to the 19th century and enjoys a superb location overlooking Ventnor and the sea beyond. Public areas consist of a traditional lounge, a cosy bar area with adjoining conservatory and light, airy dining room. Bedrooms have now been refurbished with quality fabrics. A welcoming homely atmosphere is assured.
ROOMS: 12 en suite (1 fmly) (1 GF) No smoking in all bedrooms s £25-£27; d £50-£54 (incl. bkfst) **LB FACILITIES:** Tennis (hard) **PARKING:** 12 **NOTES:** No children 5yrs No smoking in restaurant Closed Xmas **CARDS:**

★★67% ***St Maur Hotel***
Castle Rd PO38 1LG
☎ 01983 852570 & 853645 🖷 01983 852306
e-mail: sales@stmaur.co.uk
Dir: *W of Ventnor off A3055. Right at end of Park Avenue*
Guests will find a warm welcome awaits them at this hotel, which is pleasantly and quietly located overlooking the bay. The well-equipped bedrooms are traditionally decorated. In addition to a spacious lounge the hotel benefits from a cosy residents' bar. The gardens here are a delight.
ROOMS: 13 en suite (2 fmly) No smoking in all bedrooms
FACILITIES: STV **PARKING:** 12 **NOTES:** No dogs No children 5yrs No smoking in restaurant Closed Dec **CARDS:**

W

YARMOUTH

Map 05 SZ38

Top 200 - Hotel

★★★ ®®® George Hotel

Quay St PO41 0PE
☎ 01983 760331 🖷 01983 760425
e-mail: res@thegeorge.co.uk
Dir: *between the castle and the pier*

This 17th-century elegant hotel enjoys a wonderful location adjacent to the castle and the quay, overlooking the sea. Public areas include an elegant fine dining restaurant and a bright brasserie which opens onto a delightful waterside garden. In addition, guests can also relax in either the cosy bar or an inviting lounge. Individually styled bedrooms, with many thoughtful extras, are beautifully appointed and some benefit from spacious balconies. The hotel's motor yacht is available for hire by guests.

ROOMS: 17 en suite No smoking in 4 bedrooms s £125; d £175-£225 (incl. bkfst) **FACILITIES:** STV Sailing from Yarmouth Xmas **CONF:** Thtr 30 Class 10 Board 18 Del £185 **NOTES:** No children 10yrs Civ Wed 50 **CARDS:**

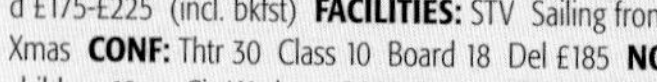

★★65% Bugle Coaching Inn

The Square PO41 0NS
☎ 01983 760272 🖷 01983 760883
Dir: *200yds from Yarmouth Wightlink Ferry Terminal, in town square*

Situated in the small, historic town of Yarmouth, this hotel takes pride of place in the market square. The 17th-century listed building offers a variety of spacious, well-furnished bedrooms in addition to a selection of bars and lounges. A varied range of delicious home-cooked meals is offered including a blackboard of specials.

ROOMS: 7 en suite (1 fmly) No smoking in all bedrooms s £42-£61; d £72-£110 (incl. bkfst) **LB** **FACILITIES:** entertainment **PARKING:** 15 **NOTES:** No dogs (ex guide dogs) No smoking in restaurant **CARDS:**

WILLERBY, East Riding of Yorkshire

Map 17 TA0

★★★72% ® Willerby Manor

Well Ln HU10 6ER
☎ 01482 652616 🖷 01482 653901
e-mail: info@willerbymanor.co.uk
Dir: *off A63, signed Humber Bridge. Follow road, right at rdbt by Safeway. At next rdbt hotel is signed*

Set in a quiet residential area, amid well tended gardens, this hotel was originally a private mansion, now thoughtfully extended to provide very comfortable bedrooms, equipped with many useful extras. The extensive public areas include a choice of eating styles including the smart Icon Restaurant. Extensive leisure facilities and a retail wine store are features of the hotel.

ROOMS: 51 en suite (16 GF) No smoking in 38 bedrooms **FACILITIES:** STV Indoor swimming (H) Sauna Solarium Gym Croquet lawn Jacuzzi Steam room Beauty therapist Aerobic classes entertainment **CONF:** Thtr 500 Class 200 Board 100 Del from £98 **PARKING:** 300 **NOTES:** No dogs (ex guide dogs) RS 24-26 Dec Civ Wed 300 **CARDS:**

⌂ Innkeeper's Lodge Hull

Beverley Rd HU10 6NT
☎ 01482 651518 🖷 01482 658380
Dir: *M62/A63, Humber Bridge exit off A63, follow signs for A164. Lodge 3m on left opp Willerby shopping centre*

A new concept in the travel accommodation market. Smart rooms meet essential business requirements but also have home comforts. Dining options include all-day menus plus the added advantage of breakfast, which is included in the room price. For further details, consult the Hotel Groups page.

ROOMS: 32 en suite

WILLITON, Somerset Map 03 ST04

★★73% @@ White House
Long St TA4 4QW
☎ 01984 632306 & 632777
Dir: *on A39 in village centre*
A relaxed and easygoing atmosphere is the hallmark of this charming little Georgian hotel. Bedrooms in the main building being more spacious, and all are well equipped with extra touches that make the White House a home-from-home. Delicious award-winning cooking and an impressive wine list can be found in the dining room.
ROOMS: 6 rms (5 en suite) 4 annexe en suite (1 fmly) s £49-£75; d £84-£120 (incl. bkfst) **LB PARKING:** 12 **NOTES:** No smoking in restaurant Closed 28 Oct -mid May

WILMSLOW, Cheshire Map 16 SJ88
See also Manchester Airport

★★★★69% @ De Vere Mottram Hall
DE VERE HOTELS
Wilmslow Rd, Mottram St Andrew, Prestbury SK10 4QT
☎ 01625 828135 🖷 01625 828950
e-mail: dmh.sales@devere-hotels.com
Dir: *M6 junct 18 from S, M6 junct 20 from N, M56 junct 6, A538 Prestbury*

Set in 272 acres of some of Cheshire's most beautiful parkland, this 18th-century Georgian House is certainly an idyllic retreat. The hotel boasts extensive leisure facilities, including a championship golf course, a swimming pool and gymnasium. Hotel bedrooms are elegantly furnished, well-equipped and include a number of four-poster rooms and suites.
ROOMS: 132 en suite (44 GF) No smoking in 64 bedrooms s £145-£230; d £170-£255 (incl. bkfst) **LB FACILITIES:** STV Indoor swimming (H) Golf 18 Tennis (hard) Squash Snooker Sauna Solarium Gym Putting green Jacuzzi Childrens play ground, Swimming pool supervised at certain times entertainment Xmas **CONF:** Thtr 275 Class 140 Board 60 Del from £120 **SERVICES:** Lift **PARKING:** 300
NOTES: No smoking in restaurant Civ Wed 160
CARDS:

Premier Lodge (Manchester Airport South)
PREMIER LODGE
Racecourse Rd SK9 5LR
☎ 0870 9906506 🖷 0870 9906507
Dir: *off A538*
Premier Lodge offers modern, well-equipped, en suite accommodation suitable for both business and leisure travellers. Meals can be taken at the adjacent popular restaurant and bar, which is fully licensed. For further details, consult the Hotel Groups page.
ROOMS: 37 en suite s £48; d £48

WIMBORNE MINSTER, Dorset Map 05 SZ09

★★77% @ Beechleas
17 Poole Rd BH21 1QA
☎ 01202 841684 🖷 01202 849344
e-mail: information@beechleas.com
Dir: *off A31 onto A349, hotel 100mtrs from mini-rdbt in town centre*

This elegant Georgian town house is located on the edge of this busy market town and set in smart grounds. Inside, the tranquil stylishness places the guest at ease in comfortable surroundings, and the proprietors and staff provide attentive service. The bedrooms are all spacious and individually styled. The bright and airy conservatory dining room offers fresh and local produce, much of which is organic.
ROOMS: 5 en suite 4 annexe en suite (2 fmly) (2 GF) No smoking in all bedrooms s £69-£99; d £79-£119 (incl. bkfst) **LB FACILITIES:** Sailing Hotel's yacht-Poole Harbour **CONF:** Thtr 24 Class 24 Board 14 Del from £129 **PARKING:** 14 **NOTES:** No smoking in restaurant Closed 25 Dec-11 Jan **CARDS:**

WINCANTON, Somerset Map 04 ST72

★★★78% @@ *Holbrook House*
Holbrook BA9 8BS
☎ 01963 32377 🖷 01963 32681
e-mail: reception@holbrookhouse.co.uk
Dir: *from A303 at Wincanton, turn left on A371 towards Castle Cary and Shepton Mallet*

This handsome country house offers a unique blend of quality and comfort combined with a friendly atmosphere. Set in peaceful gardens and wooded grounds, Holbrook House is the perfect retreat. The restaurant provides a selection of innovative dishes prepared with enthusiasm, served by a team of caring staff.
ROOMS: 16 en suite 5 annexe en suite (2 fmly) **FACILITIES:** STV Indoor swimming (H) Outdoor swimming (H) Tennis (hard & grass) Sauna Solarium Gym Croquet lawn Jacuzzi Beauty treatment ch fac **CONF:** Thtr 200 Class 50 Board 55 **PARKING:** 100 **NOTES:** No dogs (ex guide dogs) No smoking in restaurant Civ Wed 80
CARDS:

WINCHCOMBE, Gloucestershire Map 10 SP02

Restaurant with Rooms

Wesley House
High St GL54 5LJ
☎ 01242 602366 01242 609046
e-mail: enquiries@wesleyhouse.co.uk
Dir: *On High St, B4632 (between Cheltenham and Broadway)*
This engaging property dates back to the 15th century and is situated in the heart of bustling Winchcombe. There are a number of original features, such as open fires and exposed beams, combined comfort and quality, with bedrooms offering plenty of character and individuality. The elegant restaurant is the setting for accomplished cuisine served by friendly, attentive staff.
ROOMS: 6 en suite No smoking in all bedrooms s £40-£55; d £70-£80 (incl. bkfst) **LB** **NOTES:** No dogs No smoking in restaurant Closed 25-26 Dec **CARDS:**

WINCHESTER, Hampshire Map 05 SU42

Top 200 - Hotel

★★★★ **Lainston House**
Sparsholt SO21 2LT
☎ 01962 863588 01962 776672
e-mail: enquiries@lainstonhouse.com
Dir: *2m NW off B3049 towards Stockbridge*
This graceful example of a William and Mary house is set in mature gardens and grounds, amid open countryside. Staff demonstrate good levels of courtesy and care with their polished, professional service. Bedrooms are tastefully appointed and include some spectacular new rooms with stylish handmade beds and stunning bathrooms. Public rooms include a remarkable cocktail bar built entirely from a single cedar and stocked with an impressive range of rare drinks and cigars.
ROOMS: 50 en suite (6 fmly) (18 GF) s £100-£325; d £155-£325 **LB** **FACILITIES:** STV Tennis (hard) Fishing Gym Croquet lawn Putting green Archery Clay pigeon shooting entertainment Xmas **CONF:** Thtr 80 Class 50 Board 40 Del from £175 **PARKING:** 150 **NOTES:** No smoking in restaurant Civ Wed 120
CARDS:

Town House

★★★★ **Hotel du Vin & Bistro**
14 Southgate St SO23 9EF
☎ 01962 841414 01962 842458
e-mail: info@winchester.hotelduvin.com
Dir: *M3 junct 11 towards Winchester, follow signs. Hotel approx 2m on left side just past cinema*
Continuing to set high standards, this inviting hotel is best known for its high profile bistro. The individually decorated bedrooms, each sponsored by a different wine house, show considerable originality of style, and are very well equipped. The bistro serves imaginative yet simply cooked dishes from a seasonal, daily-changing menu.
ROOMS: 23 en suite (1 fmly) (4 GF) s £105-£115; d £105-£115 **FACILITIES:** STV Xmas **CONF:** Thtr 40 Class 30 Board 20 Del £150 **PARKING:** 35 **NOTES:** No dogs (ex guide dogs) Civ Wed 60
CARDS:

★★★★65% **The Wessex**
Paternoster Row SO23 9LQ
☎ 0870 400 8126 01962 841503
e-mail: wessex@macdonald-hotels.co.uk
MACDONALD HOTELS
Dir: *M3, follow signs for town centre, at rdbt by King Alfred's statue past Guildhall, take next left, hotel on right*
A modern hotel occupying an enviable location in the centre of this historic city and adjacent to the spectacular cathedral, yet quietly situated in a side street. Inside, the ambience is modern, restful and welcoming with many public areas and bedrooms enjoying unrivalled views of its ancient neighbour.
ROOMS: 94 en suite (6 fmly) No smoking in 61 bedrooms s £100-£138; d £120-£170 (incl. bkfst) **LB** **FACILITIES:** STV Solarium Gym Free use of local leisure centre. entertainment ch fac Xmas **CONF:** Thtr 200 Class 60 Board 60 Del from £150 **SERVICES:** Lift **PARKING:** 60 **NOTES:** No smoking in restaurant Civ Wed 150
CARDS:

★★★73% **Royal**
Saint Peter St SO23 8BS
☎ 01962 840840 01962 841582
e-mail: royal@marstonhotels.com
MARSTON HOTELS
Dir: *M3 junct 9 to Winnal Trading Estate. Follow road to city centre, cross river, left, 1st right. Onto one-way system and 2nd right. Hotel immediately on right*
Situated in the heart of the former capital of England, this friendly hotel dates back in parts to the 16th century. The hotel is undergoing a continual refurbishment programme and enjoys spacious public areas. There is a variety of bedrooms, split between the main house and the modern annexe, which look over the attractive gardens.
ROOMS: 75 en suite No smoking in 48 bedrooms s fr £99; d fr £110 **LB** **FACILITIES:** STV Xmas **CONF:** Thtr 120 Class 50 Board 40 Del £140 **PARKING:** 50 **NOTES:** No smoking in restaurant Civ Wed 110
CARDS:

★★★67% **Marwell**
Thompsons Ln, Colden Common, Marwell SO21 1JY
☎ 01962 777681 01962 777625
e-mail: info@marwellhotel.co.uk
FURLONG
Dir: *Follow brown signs for Marwell Zoological Park, hotel is adjacent*
Taking its theme from the adjacent zoo, this unusual hotel is based on the famous TreeTops safari lodge in Kenya. Bedrooms are being refurbished and are well appointed and equipped, while the smart public areas include an airy lobby bar and an "Out of

continued

Africa" style restaurant. There is also a selection of meeting and leisure facilities.

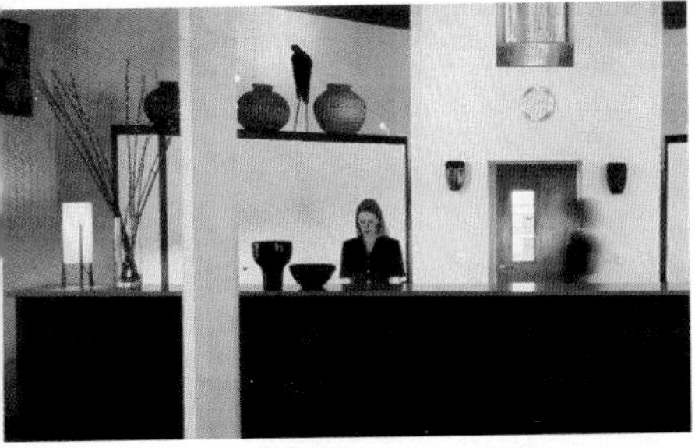

ROOMS: 68 en suite (10 fmly) No smoking in 40 bedrooms s fr £125; d fr £105 (incl. bkfst) **LB FACILITIES: Spa** STV Indoor swimming (H) Fishing Sauna Solarium Gym Xmas **CONF:** BC Thtr 150 Class 60 Board 60 Del from £140 **PARKING:** 120 **NOTES:** No smoking in restaurant Civ Wed 100 **CARDS:**

See advert on this page

WINCHESTER MOTORWAY SERVICE AREA (M3), Hampshire

Map 05 SU53

⇧ Travel Inn (Winchester)

SO5 9YX

☎ 08701 977272 🖷 01962 791137

***Dir:** M3 southbound - between J8 and J9. (Please be advised that mileage to Travel Inn from Winchester is approx 26 miles due to location on motorway)*

Travel Inn offers good-quality, value-for-money accommodation. Spacious, en suite rooms with bath and shower comfortably accommodate a family of up to two adults and two children (to age 15). The restaurant and bar offers a varied menu. For further details and the Travel Inn phone number, consult the Hotel Groups page.

ROOMS: 40 en suite s £44.95; d £44.95

WINDERMERE, Cumbria

Map 18 SD49

★★★★66% Low Wood

LA23 1LP

☎ 015394 33338 🖷 015394 34072

e-mail: lowwood@elhmail.co.uk

***Dir:** M6 junct 36, follow A590 then A591 to Windermere, then 3m towards Ambleside, hotel on right*

Benefiting from a lakeside location, this hotel offers an excellent range of leisure and conference facilities. Bedrooms, many with panoramic lake views, are attractively furnished, and include a number of larger executive rooms and suites. There is a choice of bars, a spacious restaurant and the more informal Café del Lago. The Poolside bar offers internet and e-mail access.

ROOMS: 112 en suite (13 fmly) No smoking in 40 bedrooms s £98-£103; d £146-£156 (incl. bkfst) **LB FACILITIES: Spa** STV Indoor swimming (H) Fishing Squash Snooker Sauna Solarium Gym Croquet lawn Jacuzzi Water skiing Sub aqua diving Windsurfing Canoeing Laser clay pigeon shooting entertainment Xmas **CONF:** Thtr 340 Class 180 Board 150 Del from £105 **SERVICES:** Lift **PARKING:** 200 **NOTES:** No smoking in restaurant Civ Wed 150 **CARDS:**

Popped the question?
Hotels with Civ Wed in their entry are licensed for civil wedding ceremonies. Maximum numbers for the ceremony only are shown, e.g. Civ Wed 120

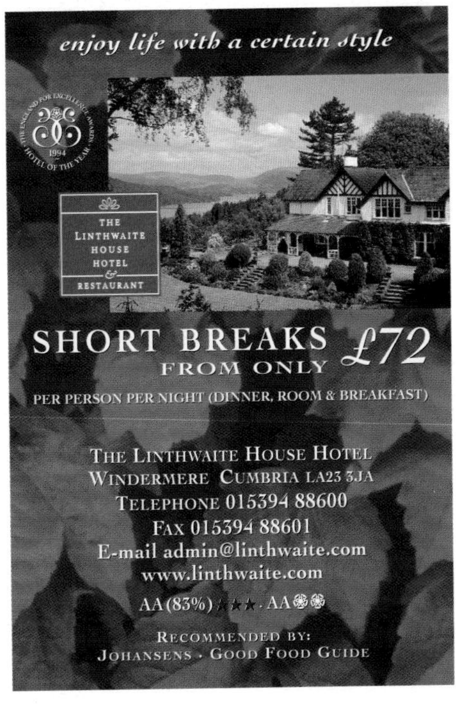

W

WINDERMERE, continued

Top 200 - Hotel

★★★ Gilpin Lodge Country House Hotel & Restaurant
Crook Rd LA23 3NE
☎ 015394 88818 015394 88058
e-mail: hotel@gilpinlodge.co.uk
Dir: *M6 junct 36, take A590/A591 to rdbt north of Kendal, take B5284, hotel 5m on right*

Set amidst delightful gardens high in the fells, this smart Victorian residence is a short drive from the lake. Bedrooms are individually styled, a number benefit from private terraces and all are spacious and thoughtfully equipped. The welcoming atmosphere is a real feature and the attractive day rooms are perfect for relaxing in front of a real fire. Vibrant, exciting cuisine is served in one of four intimate dining rooms.
ROOMS: 14 en suite No smoking in all bedrooms s £150; d £200-£270 (incl. bkfst & dinner) **LB** **FACILITIES:** Croquet lawn Free membership at local Leisure Club Xmas **PARKING:** 30 **NOTES:** No dogs No children 7yrs No smoking in restaurant **CARDS:**

Top 200 - Hotel

★★★
Holbeck Ghyll Country House
Holbeck Ln LA23 1LU
☎ 015394 32375 015394 34743
e-mail: stay@holbeckghyll.com
Dir: *3m N on A591, right into Holbeck Lane (signed Troutbeck), hotel 0.5m on left*

With a peaceful setting in extensive grounds, this beautifully maintained hotel enjoys breathtaking views over Lake Windermere and the Langdale Fells. Public rooms include luxurious, comfortable lounges and two elegant dining rooms, where memorable meals are served. Bedrooms are individually styled, beautifully furnished and many have balconies or patios. Some in an adjacent, more private lodge are less traditional in design and have superb views. The professionalism and attentiveness of the staff is exemplary.
ROOMS: 14 en suite 6 annexe en suite (1 fmly) No smoking in 6 bedrooms s £150-£300; d £200-£350 (incl. bkfst & dinner) **LB** **FACILITIES: Spa** STV Tennis (hard) Sauna Gym Croquet lawn Putting green Jacuzzi Beautician Steam room Xmas **CONF:** Thtr 45 Class 25 Board 25 Del from £100 **PARKING:** 28 **NOTES:** No smoking in restaurant Civ Wed 65 **CARDS:**

Top 200 - Hotel

★★★ The Samling
Ambleside Rd LA23 1LR
☎ 015394 31922 015394 30400
e-mail: info@thesamling.com
Dir: *turn right off A591, 300mtrs after Low Wood Hotel*

This delightful house built in the late 1700s sits in 67 acres of grounds and enjoys an elevated position overlooking Lake Windermere. Spacious, beautifully furnished bedrooms and suites, some in adjacent buildings, are thoughtfully equipped with every conceivable extra and all have superb bathrooms. Public rooms include a sumptuous drawing room, a small library and an elegant dining room where imaginative, carefully prepared food is served.
ROOMS: 5 en suite 5 annexe en suite s £145-£345; d £145-£345 (incl. bkfst) **FACILITIES:** STV Jacuzzi **CONF:** Thtr 60 Class 14 Board 14 Del £260 **PARKING:** 15 **NOTES:** No dogs No smoking in restaurant Civ Wed 100 **CARDS:**

Top 200 - Hotel

★★★ Linthwaite House Hotel
Crook Rd LA23 3JA
☎ 015394 88600 015394 88601
e-mail: admin@linthwaite.com
Dir: *A591 towards The Lakes for 8m to large rdbt, take 1st exit (B5284), 6m, hotel on left , 1m past Windermere golf club*

Linthwaite House is set in 14 acres of hilltop grounds, including its own fishing tarn, and enjoys stunning views of Lake Windermere. Public rooms include a bright, attractive conservatory benefiting from the views, a cosy lounge, a smokers' bar and a restaurant in which guests can enjoy carefully prepared meals. Bedrooms, which are individually decorated in both contemporary and traditional styles, are

continued

W

thoughtfully equipped. Service and hospitality are real strengths at this delightful hotel.

ROOMS: 26 en suite (1 fmly) (7 GF) No smoking in 19 bedrooms s £94-£127; d £99-£286 (incl. bkfst) **LB** **FACILITIES:** STV Fishing Croquet lawn Putting green Free use of nearby leisure spa, Practice golf hole Xmas **CONF:** Thtr 47 Class 19 Board 25 Del from £120 **PARKING:** 40 **NOTES:** No dogs (ex guide dogs) No smoking in restaurant Civ Wed 60 **CARDS:**

See advert on page 663

★★★81% Lindeth Howe Country House

CLASSIC BRITISH

Lindeth Dr, Longtail Hill LA23 3JF
☎ 015394 45759 🖹 015394 46368
e-mail: hotel@lindeth-howe.co.uk
Dir: *turn off A592, 1m S of Bowness onto B5284 (Longtail Hill) signed Kendal & Lancaster, hotel last driveway on right*

Old photographs commemorate the fact that this delightful house was once the family home of Beatrix Potter. Secluded in landscaped grounds, it enjoys views across the valley and Lake Windermere. Public rooms are plentiful and inviting, with the restaurant the perfect setting for modern country house cooking. Deluxe and superior bedrooms are spacious and smartly appointed.
ROOMS: 36 en suite (3 fmly) No smoking in 28 bedrooms s £40-£115; d £80-£180 (incl. bkfst) **LB** **FACILITIES:** STV Indoor swimming (H) Sauna Solarium Gym Xmas **CONF:** Thtr 30 Class 20 Board 18 Del from £112.50 **PARKING:** 50 **NOTES:** No dogs (ex guide dogs) No smoking in restaurant **CARDS:**

★★★64% *Beech Hill Hotel*

Best Western

Newby Bridge Rd LA23 3LR
☎ 015394 42137 🖹 015394 43745
e-mail: beechhill@richardsonhotels.co.uk
Dir: *A591 towards Windermere, turn onto A590 to Newby Bridge,then A592 towards Bowness, hotel on left, 4m S from Bowness*
This stylish hotel is set on high ground leading to the shore of Lake Windermere and offers a spacious open plan lounge which,

continued

like the restaurant, affords splendid views across the lake. Bedrooms offer a range of styles, some with four poster beds and are equipped to meet guests' needs. Leisure facilities and a choice of conference rooms complete the package.
ROOMS: 57 en suite (4 fmly) **FACILITIES:** Indoor swimming (H) Fishing Sauna Solarium entertainment ch fac **CONF:** Thtr 80 Class 50 Board 40 **PARKING:** 70 **NOTES:** No smoking in restaurant Civ Wed 80
CARDS:

★★★76% Storrs Hall

Storrs Park LA23 3LG
☎ 015394 47111 🖹 015394 47555
e-mail: reception@storrshall.co.uk
Dir: *on A592 2m S of Bowness on Newby Bridge road*
Set in 17 acres of landscaped grounds, this sumptuously furnished Georgian house is a delight. There are numerous lounges to relax in, furnished with fine art and antique pieces, as are the attractive bedrooms. Dinner is served in the spacious restaurant and there are fine views to be had over the lake, just across the lawn, to the Fells beyond.
ROOMS: 30 en suite No smoking in 10 bedrooms s fr £125; d fr £150 (incl. bkfst) **LB** **FACILITIES:** Fishing Sailing Water skiing Water sports Xmas **CONF:** Thtr 36 Board 24 Del from £145 **PARKING:** 50 **NOTES:** No dogs (ex guide dogs) No children 12yrs No smoking in restaurant Civ Wed 64 **CARDS:**

★★★72% Burn How Garden House Hotel

Best Western

Back Belsfield Rd, Bowness LA23 3HH
☎ 015394 46226 🖹 015394 47000
e-mail: info@burnhow.co.uk
Dir: *Exit A591 at Windermere, following signs to Bowness. Pass Lake Piers on right, take 1st left to hotel entrance*
Set in its own leafy grounds, this hotel is only minutes' walk from both the lakeside and the town centre. Attractive, spacious rooms, some with four-poster beds, are situated in either modern chalets or in an adjacent Victorian house. Many have private patios or terraces. Coffee can be enjoyed in the comfortable open-plan lounge after dinner in the formal restaurant.
ROOMS: 28 annexe en suite (10 fmly) (6 GF) No smoking in 8 bedrooms s £69-£114; d £78-£114 (incl. bkfst) **LB** **FACILITIES:** Xmas **PARKING:** 30 **NOTES:** No dogs (ex guide dogs) No smoking in restaurant **CARDS:**

★★★72% Fayrer Garden Hotel

Lyth Valley Rd, Bowness on Windermere LA23 3JP
☎ 015394 88195 🖹 015394 45986
e-mail: lakescene@fayrergarden.com
Dir: *on A5074, 1m from Bowness Bay*

Nestled in lovely landscaped gardens, this elegant hotel enjoys spectacular views over the lake. Bedrooms come in a variety of styles and sizes, some with bathrooms of a high specification, and all are comfortably appointed. There is a choice of lounges and a

continued on p666

WINDERMERE, continued

stylish, conservatory restaurant. The attentive, hospitable staff ensure a relaxing stay.
ROOMS: 18 en suite (3 fmly) No smoking in 6 bedrooms s £59-£125; d £90-£250 (incl. bkfst & dinner) **LB FACILITIES:** STV Fishing Free membership of leisure club Xmas **PARKING:** 25 **NOTES:** No dogs (ex guide dogs) No smoking in restaurant Civ Wed 40
CARDS:

★★★70% Langdale Chase

Langdale Chase LA23 1LW
☎ 015394 32201 015394 32604
e-mail: sales@langdalechase.co.uk
Dir: *2m S of Ambleside and 3m N of Windermere, on A591*

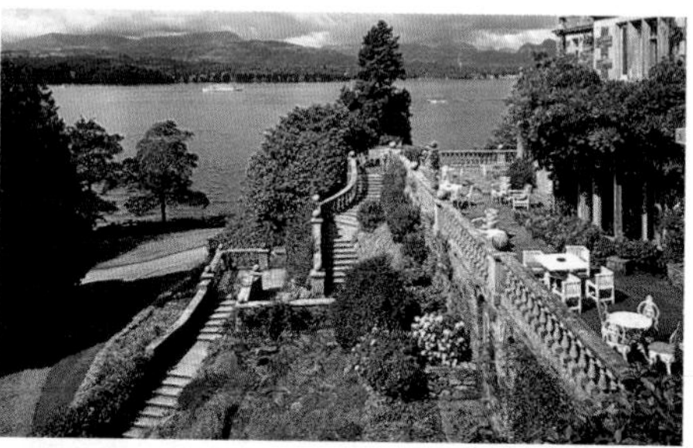

Enjoying unrivalled views of Lake Windermere, this imposing country manor has been trading as a hotel for over seventy years. Public areas feature carved fireplaces, oak panelling and a galleried staircase. Bedrooms, many refurbished, include stylish, spacious bathrooms and outstanding views.
ROOMS: 20 en suite 7 annexe en suite (2 fmly) (1 GF) s £100-£130; d £130-£190 (incl. bkfst) **LB FACILITIES:** Fishing Croquet lawn Putting green Sailing boats ch fac Xmas **CONF:** Thtr 30 Class 30 Board 28 Del from £120 **PARKING:** 50 **NOTES:** No smoking in restaurant Civ Wed 100
CARDS:

★★★69% Burnside

Kendal Rd, Bowness LA23 3EP
☎ 015394 42211 015394 43824
e-mail: stay@burnsidehotel.com
Dir: *A592 towards Bowness. Hotel 300yds past pier*
Set in terraced gardens, this hotel attracts holidaymakers, business people and tour groups. At its heart is a Victorian house, extended to include comfortable public rooms including numerous lounges, a choice of restaurants and a stylish bar.
ROOMS: 57 en suite (15 fmly) (6 GF) No smoking in 18 bedrooms s £65-£90; d £90-£235 (incl. bkfst) **LB FACILITIES:** STV Indoor swimming (H) Squash Snooker Sauna Solarium Gym Jacuzzi Badminton Beauty salon Steam room entertainment ch fac Xmas **CONF:** Thtr 100 Class 60 Board 38 Del from £122 **SERVICES:** Lift **PARKING:** 100 **NOTES:** No smoking in restaurant Civ Wed 120
CARDS:

★★★66% The Old England

MACDONALD HOTELS

Church St, Bowness LA23 3DF
☎ 0870 400 8130 015394 43432
e-mail: oldengland@macdonald-hotels.co.uk
Dir: *Through town to Bowness. Hotel behind Church*
Occupying arguably one of the best positions on Lake Windermere, this elegant Victorian mansion is tastefully furnished with period and antique pieces. Many of the stylish bedrooms have wonderful lake views, as do the restaurant, bar and lounge.

continued

The hotel benefits from an outdoor heated swimming pool and a private jetty. Stylish conference facilities are impressive.
ROOMS: 76 en suite (8 fmly) (6 GF) No smoking in 26 bedrooms s £45-£65; d £90-£130 (incl. bkfst) **LB FACILITIES:** Outdoor swimming (H) Snooker Xmas **CONF:** Thtr 100 Class 40 Board 26 Del from £85 **SERVICES:** Lift **PARKING:** 82 **NOTES:** No smoking in restaurant Civ Wed 100 **CARDS:**

★★★64% Famous Wild Boar

Best Western

Crook LA23 3NF
☎ 015394 45225 015394 42498
e-mail: wildboar@elhmail.co.uk
Dir: *2.5m S of Windermere on B5284, 3.5m, hotel on right*
This historic former coaching inn enjoys a peaceful rural location close to Windermere. Public areas include a cosy bar, with a wide range of wines served by the glass, and a welcoming lounge. Bedrooms, some with four-poster beds, vary in style and size.
ROOMS: 36 en suite (3 fmly) No smoking in 6 bedrooms s £32-£59 (incl. bkfst) **LB FACILITIES:** STV Use of leisure facilities at sister hotel whilst in residence. entertainment Xmas **CONF:** Thtr 40 Class 20 Board 26 Del from £75 **PARKING:** 60 **NOTES:** No smoking in restaurant
CARDS:

★★★63% The Belsfield Hotel

corus hotels

Kendal Rd, Bowness LA23 3EL
☎ 0870 609 6109 015394 46397
e-mail: belsfield@corushotels.com
Dir: *In Bowness take 1st left after Royal Hotel*

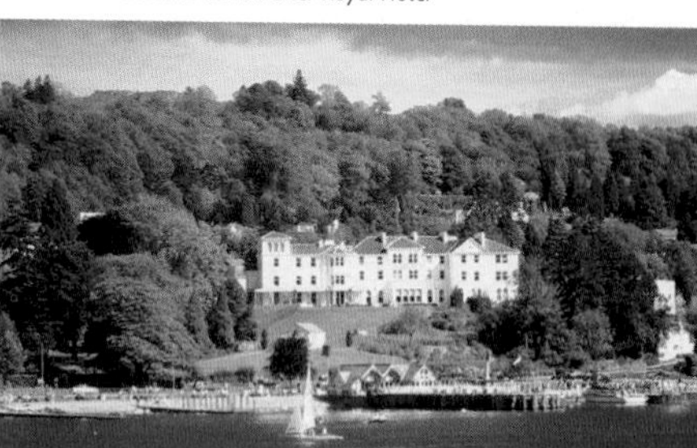

Standing in six acres of gardens, this hotel has one of the best locations in the area. Bedrooms are generally spacious and offer a variety of styles. Views from public areas are outstanding and breakfasts are taken overlooking the lake. The swimming pool has the benefit of a sliding roof.
ROOMS: 64 en suite (6 fmly) (6 GF) No smoking in 30 bedrooms s £90-£95; d £120-£130 **LB FACILITIES:** Indoor swimming (H) Snooker Sauna Putting green Mini golf - Pitch & Putt 9 holes Xmas **CONF:** Thtr 130 Class 60 Board 50 Del from £110 **SERVICES:** Lift **PARKING:** 64 **NOTES:** No dogs (ex guide dogs) No smoking in restaurant Civ Wed 100
CARDS:

★★★61% *Craig Manor*

Lake Rd LA23 2JF
☎ 015394 88877 015394 88878
e-mail: info@craigmanor.co.uk
Dir: *A590, then A591 into Windermere, left at Windermere Hotel, through village, pass Magistrates' Court, hotel on left*
There are fine views to be had across the lake towards the surrounding fells from this family-run hotel. Traditionally furnished bedrooms, including family rooms and some with four poster beds, are complemented by spacious public areas. A wide selection of dishes is served in the refurbished restaurant overlooking the lake.
ROOMS: 16 en suite **PARKING:** 70 **NOTES:** No smoking in restaurant
CARDS:

W

Top 200 - Hotel

★★ Lindeth Fell

Lyth Valley Rd, Bowness-on-Windermere LA23 3JP
☎ 015394 43286 & 44287 015394 47455
e-mail: kennedy@lindethfell.co.uk
Dir: *1m south of Bowness on A5074*
Enjoying delightful views, this smart Edwardian residence stands in seven acres of glorious, landscaped gardens. Bedrooms, which vary in size and style, are comfortably equipped. Skilfully prepared dinners are served in the spacious dining room, which also provides fine views. The resident owners and their attentive, friendly staff provide high levels of hospitality and service.
ROOMS: 14 en suite (2 fmly) s £60-£75; d £120-£150 (incl. bkfst) **LB FACILITIES:** Fishing Croquet lawn Putting green Bowling Pitch&Putt Xmas **CONF:** Board 12 Del from £120 **PARKING:** 20 **NOTES:** No dogs (ex guide dogs) No smoking in restaurant Closed 6-31 Jan **CARDS:**

Top 200 - Hotel

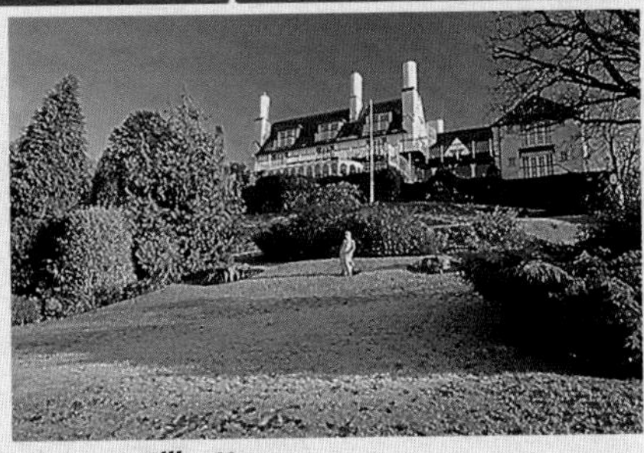

★★ *Miller Howe*

Rayrigg Rd LA23 1EY
☎ 015394 42536 015394 45664
e-mail: lakeview@millerhowe.com
Dir: *on A592 between Bowness & Windermere*
This long established hotel enjoys a lakeside setting amidst delightful landscaped gardens. Day rooms are bright and welcoming and include sumptuous lounges, a conservatory and an opulently decorated restaurant. Imaginative dinners make use of fresh, local produce where possible and there is an extensive, well-balanced wine list. Stylish bedrooms, many with fabulous lake views, include well-equipped cottage rooms.
ROOMS: 12 en suite 3 annexe en suite **FACILITIES:** entertainment **PARKING:** 40 **NOTES:** No children 8yrs No smoking in restaurant Civ Wed 60 **CARDS:**

★★70% Glenburn

New Rd LA23 2EE
☎ 015394 42649 015394 88998
e-mail: glen.burn@virgin.net
Dir: *M6 junct 36, A591, through Windermere, hotel 500yds on left*
This friendly family-run hotel enjoys a convenient location. Smartly presented and well maintained throughout, it offers stylish, well-equipped accommodation in a variety of sizes and styles. Bedrooms include both family and four-poster rooms. There is a spacious bar lounge and an attractive restaurant, where carefully prepared meals are served.
ROOMS: 16 en suite (2 fmly) No smoking in all bedrooms s £37.50-£52.50; d £55-£85 (incl. bkfst) **LB FACILITIES:** Fishing Free use of nearby country club Xmas **PARKING:** 17 **NOTES:** No dogs (ex guide dogs) No children 5yrs No smoking in restaurant Closed 20-28 Dec **CARDS:**

★★70% Hideaway

Phoenix Way LA23 1DB
☎ 015394 43070 015394 48664
e-mail: enquiries@hideaway-hotel.co.uk
Dir: *off A591 at Ravensworth Hotel. Hotel 100yds on right*

Enjoying a secluded location, yet only a few minutes from the centre of town, hospitality is a real feature at this family-run hotel. Bedrooms, some housed in a separate building across the courtyard, are smartly appointed and individually furnished. Four-poster and family rooms are available. Dinner features tasty, home-made food and breakfast are hearty.
ROOMS: 10 en suite 5 annexe en suite (3 fmly) s £55-£70; d £92-£150 (incl. bkfst) **LB FACILITIES:** Free use of nearby leisure facilities Xmas **PARKING:** 16 **NOTES:** No smoking in restaurant Closed 3-31 Jan **CARDS:**

See advert on page 669

★★67% Cranleigh

Kendal Rd, Bowness on Windermere LA23 3EW
☎ 015394 43293 015394 47283
e-mail: mike@thecranleigh.com
Dir: *off Lake Rd, opp St Martin's church and along Kendal Rd for 150mtrs*
This friendly hotel is located minutes' walk from the centre of town. Comfortable bedrooms, including a number with four-poster beds, vary in style. Guests have a choice of lounges, one with a real fire, a small bar that offers a wide range of drinks and freshly prepared meals are served in the attractive dining room.
ROOMS: 9 en suite 6 annexe en suite (3 fmly) s £40-£72; d £50-£120 (incl. bkfst) **LB FACILITIES:** Free membership of leisure club **PARKING:** 15 **NOTES:** No dogs (ex guide dogs) No smoking in restaurant **CARDS:**

WINDERMERE, continued

Action for Blind People Hotel

U Windermere Manor

Rayrigg Rd LA23 1ES
☎ 01539 445801 📠 01539 448397
e-mail: windermere@afbp.org

Dir: *A591, pass Windermere turning, towards Ambleside. At mini-rdbt, turn left, hotel driveway 1st on left*

Set above the shores of Lake Windermere, this former manor house has been restored to its original splendour. The attractive dining room has an unusual barrel-vaulted wooden roof and serves delicious home cooking. There are pleasant landscaped gardens with areas of natural woodland. The hotel caters for the specific needs of blind and partially sighted people, their friends, relatives, carers and guide dogs.

ROOMS: 18 en suite (2 fmly) (5 GF) No smoking in all bedrooms s £32-£40; d £64-£80 (incl. bkfst & dinner) **LB FACILITIES:** STV Indoor swimming (H) Sauna Solarium Gym Various activities available, indoor pool supervised entertainment Xmas **SERVICES:** Lift **PARKING:** 20 **NOTES:** No smoking in restaurant **CARDS:**

WINDSOR, Berkshire Map 06 SU97

★★★★69%

Sir Christopher Wren's House Hotel

Thames St SL4 1QB
☎ 01753 861354 📠 01753 860172
e-mail: reservations@wrensgroup.com

Dir: *M4 junct 6, 1st exit from relief road, follow signs to Windsor, 1st major exit on left, turn left at lights*

This hotel has an enviable location right on the edge of the River Thames overlooking Eton Bridge. Diners in Strokes, the award-winning restaurant, enjoy the best views. A variety of well appointed bedrooms is available, including several in adjacent annexes. There is also a luxury health and leisure spa.

ROOMS: 92 en suite (11 fmly) (3 GF) No smoking in 22 bedrooms s £150; d £200 **LB FACILITIES: Spa** STV Solarium Gym Jacuzzi Health & beauty club Xmas **CONF:** Thtr 120 Class 70 Board 50 Del from £190 **PARKING:** 15 **NOTES:** No dogs (ex guide dogs) No smoking in restaurant Civ Wed 200 **CARDS:**

★★★71%

The Castle

18 High St SL4 1LJ
☎ 0870 400 8300 📠 01753 830244
e-mail: castle@macdonald-hotels.co.uk

Dir: *M4 junct 6/M25 junct 15 - follow signs to Windsor town centre and castle. Hotel at top of hill by castle opp Guildhall*

The Castle Hotel is a fine example of Georgian architecture, but was originally a coaching inn in the 16th century. Located opposite Windsor Castle, it is an ideal base from which to explore the town. Bedrooms are traditional and include four-poster and executive rooms. Guests have a choice of formal and informal dining options and an all day lounge menu.

ROOMS: 41 en suite 70 annexe en suite (18 fmly) No smoking in 50 bedrooms s £150-£190; d £170-£290 (incl. bkfst) **LB FACILITIES:** STV Xmas **CONF:** BC Thtr 370 Class 155 Board 80 Del from £145 **SERVICES:** Lift **PARKING:** 100 **NOTES:** No smoking in restaurant Civ Wed 70 **CARDS:**

See advert on opposite page

★★★70%

Christopher Hotel

110 High St, Eton SL4 6AN
☎ 01753 852359 📠 01753 830914
e-mail: sales@christopher-hotel.co.uk

Dir: *M4 junct 5 (Slough E), Colnbrook Datchet Eton (B470). At rdbt 2nd exit for Datchet. Right at mini rdbt (Eton), left into Eton Rd (3rd rdbt). Left, hotel on right*

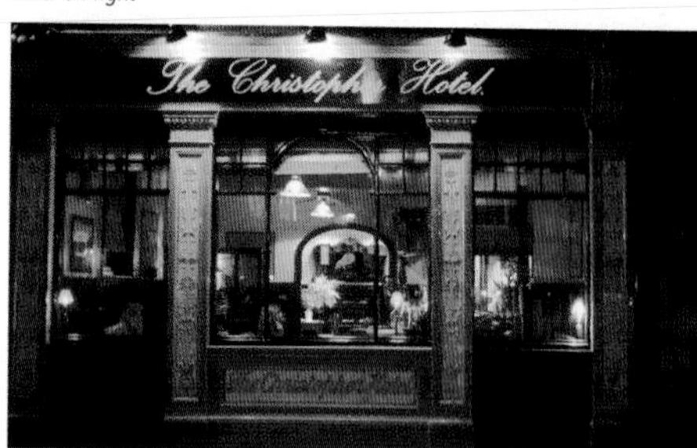

Located on Eton High Street this former coaching inn is ideal for visiting Windsor or other local attractions. Comfortable bedrooms in the main house or in a separate wing vary in size; some boasting recently refurbished stylish features. Award-winning cuisine is served in Renata's, the hotel's contemporary restaurant.

ROOMS: 11 en suite 22 annexe en suite (3 fmly) (17 GF) No smoking in 17 bedrooms s £115; d £150 **LB FACILITIES:** STV Use of Health & beauty centre at nearby sister hotel (3 mins walk) Xmas **CONF:** Thtr 40 Class 30 Board 28 Del £195 **PARKING:** 23 **NOTES:** No smoking in restaurant **CARDS:**

> Late for dinner?
> Quality Standards mean that last orders for dinner vary according to star rating and should be no earlier than:
> ★★ 7.00pm ★★★ 8.00pm ★★★★ 9.00pm
> ★★★★★ 10.00pm

THE BEST RIVERSIDE ADDRESS
IN THE THAMES VALLEY

Runnymede Hotel & Spa

★ ★ ★ ★

Windsor Road · Egham · Surrey · TW20 0AG
Tel: 01784 436171 · Fax: 01784 436340
Internet: http://www.runnymedehotel·com
Email: info@runnymedehotel.com

Privately owned hotel on the banks of the River Thames. Just seven miles from Heathrow and five miles from Royal Windsor.
Our dramatic waterfront restaurant **Left Bank** offers a Mediterranean inspired menu and **Charlie Bell's** is a popular café bar with a riverside terrace.
State of the art Health & Fitness Spa including indoor pool, tennis courts, gym, saunas and steam room. Extensive conference and banqueting facilities.

★★ Hideaway Hotel

Windermere · The Lake District

High all round standards and personal service by the proprietors Josephine and Henry Gornall and their manager/chef Alison. Our highly experienced chef John cooks fresh food to perfection and the menu is changed daily with wide ranging choice.
15 en-suite rooms, some with 4-poster bed and jacuzzi bath, all with colour TV, telephone and tea making facilities. Leisure facilities available.
A central and yet quiet location makes this one of the most sought after hotels in the area.

Please ring Windermere (015394) 43070
or visit www.hideaway-hotel.co.uk

Royal Adelaide

AA ★★★ Meridian Leisure Hotels ETC ★★★

Windsor Town Centre
46 Kings Road, Windsor, Berks SL4 2AG
Tel: 01753 863916 Fax: 01753 830682
E-mail: royaladelaide@meridianleisure.com
www.meridianleisure.com

Ideally situated in the heart of Windsor town centre and within walking distance of Windsor Castle. This beautiful Georgian property offers 42 fully refurbished en-suite bedrooms with satellite TV, courtesy tray, modem telephone, ironing board, hairdryer & bedroom safe.
A perfect venue for weddings, anniversaries & conferences for up to 140, benefiting from complimentary car parking.
Special Leisure Break & Legoland packages available.

Bed & Full English Breakfast daily from £60-£119.

The Castle Hotel

18 High Street, Windsor
Berks SL4 1LJ
Tel: 0870 400 8300 Fax: 01753 830244
Web: www.granada.co.uk
Email: heritagehotels_windsor.castle @forte-hotels.com

Built in the early 16th century as a coaching inn, the hotel is a fine example of Georgian architecture.

Located opposite the castle, the hotel is an ideal base from which to explore the town, which teems with royal history and pagentry.

Bedrooms are classical in style and room types include four poster and executive rooms.

W

WINDSOR, continued

★★★69% Royal Adelaide

46 Kings Rd SL4 2AG
☎ 01753 863916 ☐ 01753 830682
e-mail: royaladelaide@meridianleisure.com
Dir: *M4 junct 6, A322 to Windsor. 1st left off rdbt into Clarence Rd. At 4th lights right into Sheet St and into Kings Rd. Hotel on right*

This attractive Georgian-style hotel has had much renovation and enhancement in the past year. Close to the town centre and with parking, it offers tastefully furnished and well-equipped bedrooms. Public areas include a range of meeting rooms, a bar and an elegant restaurant.
ROOMS: 38 en suite 4 annexe en suite (5 fmly) No smoking in 12 bedrooms s £69-£99; d £89-£119 (incl. bkfst) **LB FACILITIES:** STV Xmas **CONF:** Thtr 120 Class 80 Board 60 Del from £130 **PARKING:** 22 **NOTES:** No smoking in restaurant Civ Wed 120
CARDS:

See advert on page 669

★★★63% *Ye Harte & Garter*

High St SL4 1PH
☎ 01753 863426 ☐ 01753 830527
Dir: *in town centre opposite front entrance to Windsor Castle*
Situated on the High Street this hotel combines traditional style with modern comforts. Bedrooms vary in size and offer a useful range of facilities, and many have exceptional views of the castle courtyards opposite. Popular public areas include a café bar, two restaurants and a traditional pub.
ROOMS: 39 en suite (4 fmly) **FACILITIES:** STV entertainment **CONF:** Thtr 300 Class 150 Board 80 **SERVICES:** Lift **NOTES:** No dogs (ex guide dogs) Civ Wed 200 **CARDS:**

See advert on opposite page

★★73% Aurora Garden

Bolton Av SL4 3JF
☎ 01753 868686 ☐ 01753 831394
e-mail: aurora@auroragarden.co.uk
Dir: *M4 junct 6 onto A332 (Windsor). At 1st rdbt, 2nd exit towards Staines. At 3rd rdbt, 3rd exit for 500yds. Hotel on right*
Located in a quiet residential area near the town centre and close to Windsor Great Park, this privately-run hotel has a relaxing environment. The restaurant overlooks the landscaped water-gardens and offers a wide choice of dishes at breakfast and dinner; service is professional and friendly. Bedrooms are individually appointed with a good range of facilities.
ROOMS: 19 en suite (7 fmly) (4 GF) s £85-£95; d £100-£115 (incl. bkfst) **LB FACILITIES:** STV **CONF:** Thtr 90 Class 30 Board 25 Del £135 **PARKING:** 25 **NOTES:** No dogs (ex guide dogs) No smoking in restaurant Closed 25 Dec Civ Wed 120
CARDS:

Innkeeper's Lodge Old Windsor

14 Straight Rd, Old Windsor SL4 2RR
☎ 01753 860769 ☐ 01753 851649
A new concept in the travel accommodation market. Smart rooms meet essential business requirements but also have home comforts. Dining options include all-day menus plus the added advantage of breakfast, which is included in the room price. For further details, consult the Hotel Groups page.
ROOMS: 15 en suite

WINSCOMBE, Somerset — Map 04 ST45

Premier Lodge (Bristol Airport)

Bridgwater Rd BS25 1NN
☎ 0870 9906302 ☐ 0870 9906303

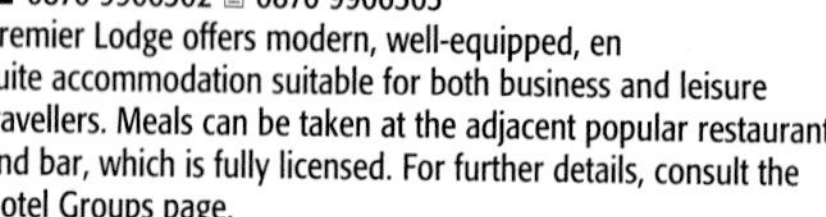

Premier Lodge offers modern, well-equipped, en suite accommodation suitable for both business and leisure travellers. Meals can be taken at the adjacent popular restaurant and bar, which is fully licensed. For further details, consult the Hotel Groups page.
ROOMS: 31 en suite s £48; d £48

WINTERINGHAM, Lincolnshire — Map 17 SE92

Top 200 – Restaurant with Rooms

Winteringham Fields

DN15 9PF
☎ 01724 733096 ☐ 01724 733898
e-mail: wintfields@aol.com
Dir: *in the centre of the village at crossroads*
Situated deep in the countryside, it is well worth the drive to find this highly regarded restaurant with rooms. Located in Winteringham village, only six miles west of the Humber Bridge, Germain Schwab has a hand in every skilfully crafted dish that leaves his kitchen. Public rooms and bedrooms, some of which are housed in renovated barns and cottages, are delightfully cosseting but it is the inspired cooking that remains the main draw.
ROOMS: 4 en suite 6 annexe en suite No smoking in all bedrooms s £85-£135; d £115-£200 (incl. cont bkfst) **PARKING:** 17 **NOTES:** No children 8yrs No smoking in restaurant Closed Sun, Mon & BH/2wks Xmas/Aug/late Mar **CARDS:**

WISBECH, Cambridgeshire — Map 12 TF40

★★★68% *Elme Hall*

Elm High Rd PE14 0DQ
☎ 01945 475566 ☐ 01945 475566
e-mail: elme@paktel.co.uk
Dir: *off A47 onto A1101 towards Wisbech. Hotel on right*
An imposing Georgian-style property situated on the outskirts of the town centre just off the A47. The spacious, individually decorated bedrooms are tastefully furnished with quality reproduction pieces and equipped to a high standard. Public rooms include a choice of attractive lounges as well as two bars, meeting rooms and a banqueting suite.
ROOMS: 7 en suite (3 fmly) No smoking in all bedrooms **CONF:** Thtr 350 Class 200 Board 20 **PARKING:** 100 **NOTES:** No smoking in restaurant Civ Wed 350 **CARDS:**

Bad hair day?
Hairdryers in all rooms three stars and above

★★★65% *White Lion*
5 South Brink PE13 1JD
☎ 01945 463060 🖷 01945 463069
e-mail: whitelion@osibhotels.co.uk
Dir: *from A47 to city centre, turn right before lights into Sommers Rd, 1st left*

A smartly appointed former coaching inn situated close to the town centre overlooking the River Nene. The spacious bedrooms are pleasantly furnished and well equipped. Public areas include a comfortable lounge bar, a stylish restaurant, a further back bar and a pretty rear garden. There is also an air-conditioned function room.
ROOMS: 14 en suite (1 fmly) No smoking in 4 bedrooms **CONF:** Thtr 80 Class 40 Board 30 **PARKING:** 70 **NOTES:** No dogs (ex guide dogs)
CARDS:

★★73% Crown Lodge
Downham Rd, Outwell PE14 8SE
☎ 01945 773391 & 772206 🖷 01945 772668
e-mail: crownlodgehotel@hotmail.com
Dir: *on A1122/A1101 approx 5m from Wisbech and 7m from Downham Market*

THE INDEPENDENTS

This friendly, privately-owned hotel enjoys a peaceful location on the banks of Well Creek in the village of Outwell, a short drive from Wisbech. The property has been carefully extended and both bedrooms and public areas are smartly appointed and well equipped. Hotel facilities include squash courts, a popular restaurant and bar.
ROOMS: 10 en suite (10 GF) No smoking in 8 bedrooms s £55; d £70 (incl. bkfst) **LB FACILITIES:** Squash Snooker Solarium **CONF:** Thtr 40 Class 30 Board 20 **PARKING:** 57 **NOTES:** No smoking in restaurant
CARDS:

WISBECH, continued

★★66% Rose & Crown Hotel
23/24 Market Place PE13 1DG
☎ 01945 589800 🖷 01945 474610
e-mail: randcwisbech@aol.com
Dir: *in centre of Wisbech, access from A47 & A1101*
This former hostelry has provided hospitality for travellers for over 500 years. The wide range of spacious public rooms includes the Tidnams Tipple Inn, an Italian restaurant and several function rooms. Bedrooms are bright and comfortable, and most have now been upgraded.
ROOMS: 29 en suite No smoking in 10 bedrooms s £60; d £75-£80 (incl. bkfst) **LB** **CONF:** Thtr 120 Class 70 Board 70 **PARKING:** 20 **NOTES:** No dogs (ex guide dogs) Civ Wed 180
CARDS:

WISHAW, Warwickshire — Map 10 SP19

★★★★75% The De Vere Belfry
B76 9PR
DE VERE HOTELS
☎ 01675 470301 🖷 01675 470178
e-mail: enquiries@thebelfry.com
Dir: *M42 junct 9, follow A446 towards Lichfield, hotel 1m on right*

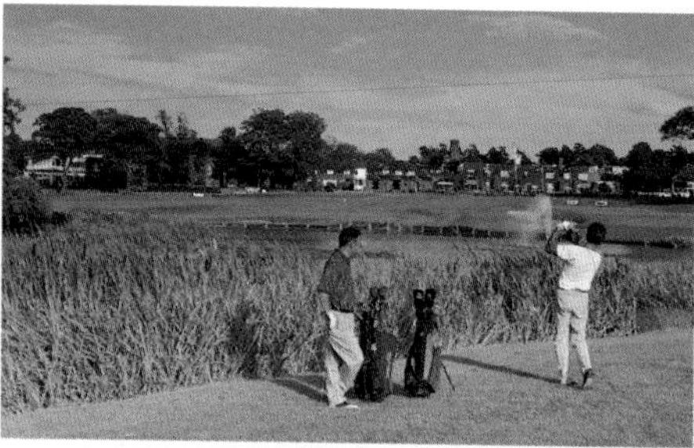

Well known as a venue for the Ryder Cup, The Belfry offers three championship golf courses along with many other leisure facilities. There is a sophisticated French restaurant and cocktail bar and the spa centre boasts an impressive range of health and beauty treatments. Bedrooms vary in size; many have spectacular views.
ROOMS: 324 en suite (109 fmly) No smoking in 187 bedrooms s £89-£169; d £99-£189 (incl. bkfst) **LB** **FACILITIES: Spa** STV Indoor swimming (H) Golf 18 Tennis (hard) Squash Snooker Sauna Solarium Gym Putting green Jacuzzi Night club in grounds, Driving range, Aquaspa, Swimming pool supervised entertainment ch fac Xmas **CONF:** Thtr 400 Class 220 Board 40 Del from £99 **SERVICES:** Lift **PARKING:** 1000 **NOTES:** No smoking in restaurant Civ Wed 200
CARDS:

W

WITHYPOOL, Somerset — Map 03 SS83

★★75% Royal Oak Inn
TA24 7QP
☎ 01643 831506 🖷 01643 831659
e-mail: enquiries@royaloakwithypool.co.uk
Dir: *7m N of Dulverton, off B3223*
For centuries this old inn has provided travellers with food, drink and shelter. Lovers of the great outdoors will find this an ideal base for exploration. Bedrooms are comfortable and each displays individuality and charm. Public areas include a choice of bars, complete with beams and crackling log fires, and the Acorn Restaurant is the venue for accomplished cuisine with an emphasis on local produce.

continued

ROOMS: 8 rms (7 en suite) s fr £60 (incl. bkfst) **FACILITIES:** Fishing Riding Shooting Safaris arranged Xmas **PARKING:** 20 **NOTES:** No smoking in restaurant **CARDS:**

WITNEY, Oxfordshire — Map 05 SP31

★★★69% Witney Four Pillars Hotel
Ducklington Ln OX28 4TJ
FOUR PILLARS HOTELS
☎ 0800 374 692 🖷 01993 703467
e-mail: witney@four-pillars.co.uk
Dir: *M40 junct 9, A34 to A40, exit A415 Witney/Abingdon. Hotel on left, 2nd exit for Witney*

This attractive modern hotel is situated close to Oxford and Burford and offers spacious, well-equipped bedrooms. The cosy Spinners Bar has comfortable seating areas and popular Weavers Restaurant offers a good range of dishes. Other facilities include a swimming pool, gym, spa, sauna and live entertainment each Saturday.
ROOMS: 83 en suite (16 fmly) No smoking in 30 bedrooms s £73-£92; d £83-£105 **LB** **FACILITIES: Spa** STV Indoor swimming (H) Sauna Gym Whirlpool spa, steam room entertainment Xmas **CONF:** Thtr 160 Class 80 Board 46 Del £140 **SERVICES:** air con **PARKING:** 170 **NOTES:** No dogs (ex guide dogs) No smoking in restaurant Closed 28-29 Dec Civ Wed 120 **CARDS:**

Restaurant with Rooms

Fleece Hotel & Brasserie
11 Church Green OX28 4AZ
☎ 01993 892270 🖷 01993 892284
e-mail: reservations@thefleecehotelandbrasserie.co.uk
Dir: *from Oxford A40 take Witney exit towards town centre. Right at lights and left at 2nd rdbt. Left again on green*
Set on the picturesque church green and close to the heart of this historic market town, the Fleece Hotel has now been fully refurbished to provide a modern and attractive environment. The

continued

stylish bedrooms are mostly located in a separate building across the courtyard and are comprehensively equipped, and the public areas include a lively brasserie and popular bar.
ROOMS: 11 rms (7 en suite) (1 fmly) (2 GF) No smoking in all bedrooms s £65; d £75 (incl. bkfst) **LB** **CONF:** Board 15 **PARKING:** 20 **NOTES:** No dogs (ex guide dogs) **CARDS:**

WOBURN, Bedfordshire Map 11 SP93

★★★70% The Inn at Woburn

George St MK17 9PX
☎ 01525 290441 01525 290432
e-mail: enquiries@theinnatwoburn.com
Dir: *M1 junct 13, left to Woburn, at Woburn left at T-junct, hotel in village*
This inn has been substantially refurbished and provides a high standard of accommodation. Bedrooms are divided between the original house and a modern extension. Public areas include the beamed, club-style Tavistock Bar, an attractive restaurant and a range of meeting rooms. Lounge service and carefully prepared bar snacks are available throughout the day.
ROOMS: 51 en suite 7 annexe en suite (4 fmly) (21 GF) No smoking in 10 bedrooms s £105-£116; d £120-£148 **LB** **FACILITIES:** STV Golf 54 Access to Woburn Safari Park and Wodburn Abbey Xmas **CONF:** Thtr 60 Class 40 Board 40 Del £135 **PARKING:** 80 **NOTES:** No children No smoking in restaurant **CARDS:**

WOKING, Surrey Map 06 TQ05

Travel Inn

Bridge Barn Ln, Horsell GU21 6NL
☎ 08701 977276 01483 771735
Travel Inn offers good-quality, value-for-money accommodation. Spacious, en suite rooms with bath and shower comfortably accommodate a family of up to two adults and two children (to age 15). The restaurant and bar offers a varied menu. For further details and the Travel Inn phone number, consult the Hotel Groups page.
ROOMS: 34 en suite s £49.95-£54.95; d £49.95-£54.95

WOKINGHAM, Berkshire Map 05 SU86

★★★65% Edward Court Hotel

Wellington Rd RG40 2AN
☎ 0118 977 5886 0118 977 2018
e-mail: edward_court@hotmail.com
Dir: *from Wokingham follow A329 towards Reading. Left at mini-rdbt signed Railway Station/Arborfield. Next left before level crossing. Hotel on right*

This modern hotel is located close to the town's station and is popular with business visitors. Most bedrooms are quite spacious and provide plenty of desk space. The bar and restaurant, with comfortable seating and a friendly atmosphere, offer a good selection of well prepared dishes.
ROOMS: 27 en suite (4 GF) No smoking in 16 bedrooms s £45-£95; d £55-£135 (incl. bkfst) **FACILITIES:** Xmas **CONF:** Thtr 55 Class 38 Board 24 Del from £140 **PARKING:** 45 **NOTES:** No dogs (ex guide dogs) No smoking in restaurant **CARDS:**

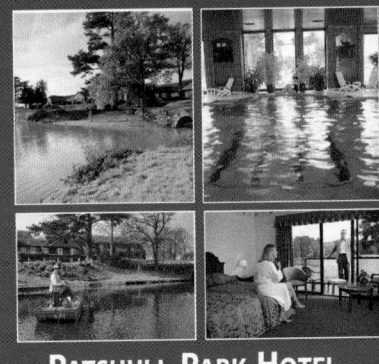

WOLVERHAMPTON, West Midlands Map 10 SO99

See also Himley & Worfield

★★★68% Ely House

53 Tettenhall Rd WV3 9NB
☎ 01902 311311 01902 421098
e-mail: mail@elyhousehotel.co.uk
Dir: *A41 towards Whitchurch from town centre ring road. 200yds on left after lights*

This delightful property dates back to 1742 and has been tastefully converted into a charming hotel. Privately owned and personally
continued on p674

WOLVERHAMPTON, continued

run in a warm and friendly manner, it provides spacious, comfortably furnished bedrooms, some of which are on ground floor level. There is also an attractive dining room and a spacious, elegant lounge containing a bar.
ROOMS: 18 en suite (1 fmly) (4 GF) No smoking in 6 bedrooms s £49-£79; d £69-£99 (incl. bkfst) **FACILITIES:** Xmas **CONF:** Thtr 20 Class 20 Board 20 Del from £175 **PARKING:** 22 **NOTES:** No dogs (ex guide dogs) No smoking in restaurant Closed 25-31 Dec
CARDS:

★★★67% **Park Hall Hotel**
Park Dr, Goldthorn Park WV4 5AJ
☎ 01902 331121 📠 01902 344760
e-mail: enquiries@parkhallhotel.co.uk
Dir: *off A4039 towards Penn and Wombourne, take 2nd left (Ednam Rd) hotel at end of road*
This 18th-century house stands in extensive grounds and gardens, a short drive from the town centre. Bedrooms vary in style, but all are well equipped. Meals can be taken in the Terrace restaurant, which offers a carvery buffet. There are conference facilities available.
ROOMS: 58 en suite (6 fmly) No smoking in 11 bedrooms s £45-£74.50; d £55-£99.50 (incl. bkfst) **LB FACILITIES:** STV Croquet lawn Xmas **CONF:** BC Thtr 450 Class 250 Board 100 Del from £90 **PARKING:** 250 **NOTES:** No smoking in restaurant Civ Wed 400
CARDS:

★★★66% **Novotel Wolverhampton**
Union St WV1 3JN
☎ 01902 871100 📠 01902 870054
e-mail: H1188@accor-hotels.com
Dir: *6m from M6 junct 10. Take A454 to Wolverhampton. Hotel on main ring road*
This large, modern, purpose-built hotel stands close to the town centre and ring road. It provides spacious, smartly presented and well-equipped bedrooms, all of which contain convertible bed settees for family occupancy. In addition to the open plan lounge and bar area, there is an attractive brasserie-style restaurant, which overlooks the small outdoor swimming pool.
ROOMS: 132 en suite (10 fmly) No smoking in 88 bedrooms s £55-£75; d £55-£75 **LB FACILITIES:** STV Outdoor swimming (H) **CONF:** Thtr 200 Class 100 Board 80 Del from £105 **SERVICES:** Lift **PARKING:** 120 **NOTES:** Civ Wed 200 **CARDS:**

★★★66% **Quality Hotel Wolverhampton**
Penn Rd WV3 0ER
☎ 01902 429216 📠 01902 710419
e-mail: admin@gb069.u-net.com
Dir: *on A449, Wolverhampton to Kidderminster, 0.25m from ring road on right, turn onto Oaklands Rd, at 1st lights*

The original Victorian house has been considerably extended to create a large, busy and popular hotel. Ornately carved woodwork and ceilings still remain in the original building. All the bedrooms are well equipped. The pleasant public areas have a lot of character and offer a choice of bars.
ROOMS: 66 en suite 26 annexe en suite (4 fmly) (17 GF) No smoking in 48 bedrooms s £47-£95; d £64-£119 (incl. bkfst) **LB FACILITIES: Spa** STV Indoor swimming (H) Sauna Gym Steam room, Playstation, Pay movies Xmas **CONF:** Thtr 140 Class 70 Board 40 Del from £75 **PARKING:** 120 **NOTES:** No smoking in restaurant Civ Wed 100
CARDS:

★★★64% **The Mount Hotel**
Mount Rd, Tettenhall Wood WV6 8HL
☎ 01902 752055 📠 01902 745263
e-mail: sales@themounthotel.com
Dir: *2.5m W off A454*
Built in the 1870s, The Mount is set in 4.5 acres of gardens and woods, yet is just 10 minutes' drive from the centre of Wolverhampton. Public areas retain many original features, including intricate ceiling designs, wood panelling and a ballroom with minstrels' gallery and balcony. The hotel has been tastefully extended to provide well-equipped accommodation.
ROOMS: 56 en suite (8 fmly) No smoking in 28 bedrooms s £80; d £90 **LB FACILITIES:** Xmas **CONF:** Thtr 200 Class 40 Del £145 **PARKING:** 250 **NOTES:** No dogs (ex guide dogs) No smoking in restaurant **CARDS:**

⌂ **Travel Inn**
Wolverhampton Business Park, Stafford Rd WV10 6TA
☎ 08701 977277 📠 01902 785260
Dir: *M54 junct 2, Travel Inn on rdbt*
Travel Inn offers good-quality, value-for-money accommodation. Spacious, en suite rooms with bath and shower comfortably accommodate a family of up to two adults and two children (to age 15). The restaurant and bar offers a varied menu. For further details and the Travel Inn phone number, consult the Hotel Groups page.
ROOMS: 54 en suite s £44.95; d £44.95 **CONF:** Thtr 20 Board 10

WOOBURN COMMON, Buckinghamshire Map 06 SU98

★★69% **Chequers Inn**
Kiln Ln, Wooburn HP10 0JQ
☎ 01628 529575 📠 01628 850124
e-mail: info@chequers-inn.com
Dir: *M40 junct 2 take A40 through Beaconsfield Old Town towards High Wycombe. 2m from town turn left into Broad Lane. Hotel 2.5m*
This 17th-century inn enjoys a peaceful, rural location beside the common. Bedrooms feature stripped-pine furniture, co-ordinated fabrics and an excellent range of extra facilities. The bar, with its massive oak post, beams and flagstone floor, and the restaurant, which overlooks a pretty patio, are very much the focal point.
ROOMS: 17 en suite (1 fmly) (8 GF) s £72.50-£99.50; d £77.50-£107.50 (incl. bkfst) **LB FACILITIES:** STV **CONF:** Thtr 50 Class 30 Board 20 Del £150 **PARKING:** 60 **NOTES:** No dogs (ex guide dogs)
CARDS:

See advert on opposite page

WOODALL MOTORWAY SERVICE AREA (M1), South Yorkshire Map 16 SK48

⌂ **Days Inn**
Woodall Service Area S26 7XR
☎ 0114 248 7992 📠 0114 248 5634
e-mail: woodall.hotel@welcomebreak.co.uk
Dir: *M1 S'bound at Woodall Services between juncts 30/31*
This modern building offers accommodation in smart, spacious and well-equipped bedrooms, suitable for families and business travellers, and all with en suite bathrooms. Continental breakfast is available and other refreshments may be taken at the nearby family restaurant. For further details and the Days Inn phone number, consult the Hotel Groups page.
ROOMS: 38 en suite s £45-£55; d £45-£55 **CONF:** Board 10

WOODBRIDGE, Suffolk
Map 13 TM24

★★★76% Seckford Hall
IP13 6NU
☎ 01394 385678 01394 380610
e-mail: reception@seckford.co.uk
Dir: *signed on A12. Do not follow signs for town centre*
This superb Tudor manor house is set amid lovely landscaped grounds just off the A12. The property is reputed to have been visited by Queen Elizabeth I, and retains much of its original charm and character. Public rooms include a superb panelled lounge, a cosy bar and an intimate restaurant. Bedrooms are spacious, attractively decorated, tastefully furnished and equipped with many thoughtful touches.
ROOMS: 22 en suite 10 annexe en suite (4 fmly) s £79-£130; d £120-£190 (incl. bkfst) **LB FACILITIES: Spa** Indoor swimming (H) Golf 18 Fishing Gym Putting green Beauty Salon **CONF:** Thtr 100 Class 46 Board 40 Del from £140 **PARKING:** 200 **NOTES:** No smoking in restaurant Closed 25 Dec Civ Wed 125
CARDS:

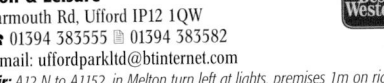

★★★72% Ufford Park Hotel Golf & Leisure
Yarmouth Rd, Ufford IP12 1QW
☎ 01394 383555 01394 383582
e-mail: uffordparkltd@btinternet.com
Dir: *A12 N to A1152, in Melton turn left at lights, premises 1m on right*

Modern, purpose-built hotel set in open countryside that boasts superb leisure facilities, including a challenging golf course. The spacious public areas provide a wide choice of areas in which to relax and include a busy lounge bar, a carvery restaurant and the Vista restaurant. Bedrooms are pleasantly decorated and thoughtfully equipped; many rooms overlook the golf course.
ROOMS: 42 en suite 8 annexe en suite (20 fmly) No smoking in 20 bedrooms s £75-£90; d £99-£129 (incl. bkfst) **LB FACILITIES: Spa** Indoor swimming (H) Golf 18 Fishing Sauna Solarium Gym Putting green Jacuzzi Steam room, Golf Academy with PGA tuition, Beauty salon, indoor pool supervised Xmas **CONF:** Thtr 200 Class 80 Board 80 Del £99 **PARKING:** 200 **NOTES:** No smoking in restaurant Civ Wed 200
CARDS:

WOODBURY, Devon
Map 03 SY08

★★★★67% Woodbury Park Hotel Golf & Country Club
Woodbury Castle EX5 1JJ
☎ 01395 233382 01395 233384
e-mail: enquiries@woodburypark.co.uk
Dir: *M5 junct 30 follow A376 then A302 towards Sidmouth, onto B3180, hotel signed*
Situated in 500 acres of beautiful and unspoilt countryside, just a short drive from the M5, this hotel offers smart, well-equipped and immaculately presented accommodation with a host of leisure, sporting and banqueting facilities. Re-live the thrills and drama of Nigel Mansell's career in "The Nigel Mansell World of Racing", enjoy a game of golf on one of the two parkland courses or be pampered in the new bodyzone beauty centre.
ROOMS: 57 en suite (4 fmly) No smoking in all bedrooms s £90-£98; d £120-£136 (incl. bkfst) **LB FACILITIES: Spa** STV Indoor swimming (H) Golf 27 Tennis (hard) Fishing Squash Snooker Sauna Gym Putting green Jacuzzi beauty salon, football pitch, driving range, 2 golf courses, hydrotherapy spa Xmas **CONF:** Thtr 250 Class 100 Board 50 Del £145 **SERVICES:** Lift **PARKING:** 400 **NOTES:** No dogs (ex guide dogs) No smoking in restaurant Civ Wed 150 **CARDS:**

WOODFORD BRIDGE, Greater London
See LONDON SECTION plan 1 H6

★★★★66% Menzies Prince Regent
Manor Rd IG8 8AE
☎ 020 8505 9966 020 8506 0807
e-mail: info@menzies-hotels.co.uk
Dir: *M25 junct 26, then to Loughton and Chigwell, hotel on Manor Rd*
Situated on the edge of Woodford Bridge and Chingford, this hotel offers easy access into London and the M11 & M25. There is a good range of spacious, well-equipped bedrooms, most with quiet aspects. The six conference and banqueting rooms have good facilities and are well suited to weddings and business events.
ROOMS: 61 en suite No smoking in 10 bedrooms **FACILITIES:** STV **CONF:** Thtr 500 Class 150 Board 120 Del from £140 **SERVICES:** Lift **PARKING:** 60 **NOTES:** No smoking in restaurant Civ Wed 300
CARDS:

WOODFORD GREEN, Greater London
See LONDON SECTION plan 1 G6

★★★59% County
30 Oak Hill IG8 9NY
☎ 0870 609 6159 020 8506 0941
e-mail: eppingcounty@compuserve.com
Dir: *A406 onto A104 towards Woodford. At rdbt right, then take 3rd exit A104. At filling station left into Oak Hill, hotel 200yds on right*
In a residential area on the edge of Epping Forest, this modern hotel is convenient for both the North Circular and M11. Bedrooms

continued on p676

WOODFORD GREEN, continued

have been decorated and equipped to a sound standard. Public areas include an informal brasserie and extensive meeting rooms.

County Hotel, Woodford Green

ROOMS: 99 en suite (16 fmly) (24 GF) No smoking in 50 bedrooms s £50-£100; d £60-£120 **LB FACILITIES:** Forest around hotel for walking Xmas **CONF:** Thtr 150 Class 80 Board 40 Del from £85 **SERVICES:** Lift **PARKING:** 100 **NOTES:** No dogs (ex guide dogs) No smoking in restaurant Civ Wed 200 **CARDS:**

WOODHALL SPA, Lincolnshire Map 17 TF16

★★★67% Petwood
Stixwould Rd LN10 6QF
☎ 01526 352411 01526 353473
e-mail: reception@petwood.co.uk
Dir: *from Sleaford take A153 (signed Skegness). At Tattershall turn left on B1192. Hotel is signed from village*

This lovely Edwardian house, set in 30 acres of gardens and woodlands, is steeped in history. Built in 1904 for Lady Weigall, the house was used by the famous 'Dambusters' as an officers' mess during World War II. Bedrooms and public areas are spacious, comfortable and retain many original period features. Weddings and conferences are well catered for.

ROOMS: 50 en suite No smoking in 9 bedrooms s £70-£85; d £126-£171 (incl. bkfst) **LB FACILITIES:** Snooker Croquet lawn Putting green Complimentary pass to leisure centre entertainment Xmas **CONF:** Thtr 160 Class 60 Board 50 Del from £95 **SERVICES:** Lift **PARKING:** 80 **NOTES:** No smoking in restaurant Civ Wed 100
CARDS:

★★★63% Golf Hotel
The Broadway LN10 6SG
☎ 01526 353535 01526 353096
e-mail: receptiongolf@lemeredienhotels.com
Dir: *from A158 Lincoln-Horncastle turn onto B1191 towards Woodhall Spa. Hotel just past Woodhall Spa Golf Club*
Located near the centre of the village, this traditional hotel is ideally situated to explore the Lincolnshire countryside and coast. The adjacent golf course makes this a popular venue for golfers and gives rise to the hotel's name and much of its decorative theme. Bedrooms vary in size and include several 'Club' style rooms.
ROOMS: 50 en suite (4 fmly) (8 GF) No smoking in 21 bedrooms s £70-£84; d £90-£118 (incl. bkfst & dinner) **LB FACILITIES:** STV Croquet lawn Guests have use of private leisure centre 1m from hotel Xmas **CONF:** Thtr 150 Class 45 Board 50 Del £85 **PARKING:** 100 **NOTES:** No smoking in restaurant Civ Wed 120
CARDS:

★★65% *Eagle Lodge*
The Broadway LN10 6ST
☎ 01526 353231 01526 352797
e-mail: user@eaglelodge.fsbusiness.co.uk
Dir: *in the centre of Woodhall Spa*
This family owned hotel is located in the centre of town, close to local shops and golf courses. Spacious bedrooms are well equipped for both business and leisure guests. Public areas include a bar and brasserie in addition to a formal restaurant offering a good range of dishes to suit all tastes. Conference and meeting facilities are also available.
ROOMS: 23 en suite (2 fmly) **FACILITIES:** STV entertainment **CONF:** Thtr 100 Class 50 Board 50 **PARKING:** 70 **NOTES:** No smoking in restaurant **CARDS:**

WOODSTOCK, Oxfordshire Map 11 SP41

★★★73% Feathers
Market St OX20 1SX
☎ 01993 812291 01993 813158
e-mail: enquiries@feathers.co.uk
Dir: *from Oxford take A44 to Woodstock, 1st left after lights. Hotel on left*

This small and individual hotel enjoys a town centre location with easy access to nearby Blenheim Palace. The public areas are elegant and full of traditional character from the cosy drawing room to the atmospheric restaurant. Bedrooms are individually appointed to a high standard and are filled with attractive period and reproduction furniture.
ROOMS: 20 en suite (4 fmly) (2 GF) s £85-£230; d £135-£230 (incl. bkfst) **LB FACILITIES:** STV 1 suite has steam room Xmas **CONF:** Thtr 25 Class 10 Board 16 Del £150 **NOTES:** No smoking in restaurant
CARDS:

★★★69% The Bear
MACDONALD HOTELS
Park St OX20 1SZ
☎ 0870 400 8202 01993 813380
e-mail: bear@macdonald-hotels.co.uk
Dir: *M40 junct 8 onto A40 to Oxford/M40 junct 9 onto A34 S to Oxford. Take A44 into Woodstock. Left to town centre hotel on left opp town hall*
With its ivy-clad façade, oak beams and open fireplaces, this

continued

13th-century coaching inn exudes charm and cosiness. The hotel boasts up-to-date bedrooms decorated in a modern style, which does not detract from their original character. Public rooms include a variety of function rooms, an intimate bar area and an attractive restaurant.
ROOMS: 40 en suite 14 annexe en suite (1 fmly) (9 GF) No smoking in 20 bedrooms s £59-£109; d £118-£178 (incl. bkfst) **LB FACILITIES:** STV Xmas **CONF:** Thtr 40 Class 12 Board 26 Del from £145 **PARKING:** 40 **NOTES:** No smoking in restaurant RS 1 Jan
CARDS:

★★★69% Kings Arms

19 Market St OX20 1SU
☎ 01993 813636 01993 813737
e-mail: enquiries@kings-woodstock.fsnet.co.uk
Dir: *on corner of Market St and A44 Oxford Rd in town centre*

This appealing and contemporary hotel is situated in the centre of town just a short walk from Blenheim Palace. Public areas include an attractive bistro-style restaurant and a smart bar. Bedrooms and bathrooms are comfortably furnished and equipped, having been totally refurbished to a high standard.
ROOMS: 15 en suite No smoking in all bedrooms s £60-£100; d £90-£150 (incl. bkfst) **NOTES:** No dogs (ex guide dogs) No smoking in restaurant **CARDS:**

WOODY BAY, Devon — Map 03 SS64

★★64% *Woody Bay Hotel*

EX31 4QX
☎ 01598 763264 & 763563
Dir: *Signed off A39 between Blackmoor Gate & Lynton*
Popular with walkers, this hotel is perfectly situated to enjoy sweeping views over Woody Bay. Bedrooms vary in style and size; the majority have stunning views. Guests have a choice of dining options, either from the imaginative fixed-price menu in the restaurant or the simple bar menu.
ROOMS: 10 rms (8 en suite) (1 fmly) **PARKING:** 10 **NOTES:** No smoking in restaurant Closed Jan RS Nov, Dec & Feb
CARDS:

WOOLACOMBE, Devon — Map 03 SS44

See also Mortehoe

★★★77% ® Watersmeet

Mortehoe EX34 7EB
☎ 01271 870333 01271 870890
e-mail: info@watersmeethotel.co.uk
Dir: *follow B3343 into Woolacombe, turn right onto esplanade, hotel 0.75m on left*
Offering attentive service, this popular hotel boasts magnificent views over the bay. Bedrooms benefit from wonderful sea views and some have the added bonus of private balconies. The public areas, now upgraded, all benefit from the hotel's stunning

continued

position, especially the attractive tiered restaurant. An imaginative and innovative range of dishes is offered each evening from a fixed-price menu.

Watersmeet

ROOMS: 22 en suite (3 fmly) s £71-£161; d £142-£262 (incl. bkfst & dinner) **LB FACILITIES:** STV Indoor swimming (H) Outdoor swimming (H) Tennis (grass) Croquet lawn Jacuzzi entertainment Xmas **PARKING:** 39 **NOTES:** No dogs (ex guide dogs) No smoking in restaurant Closed 4 Jan-10 Feb **CARDS:**

See advert on this page

WOOLACOMBE, continued

★★★74% **Woolacombe Bay**
South St EX34 7BN
☎ 01271 870388 📠 01271 870613
e-mail: woolacombe.bayhotel@btinternet.com
Dir: *from A361 take B3343 to Woolacombe. Hotel in centre on left*

This family-friendly hotel is adjacent to the beach and the village centre, and has a welcoming and friendly environment. The public areas are spacious and comfortable, and many of the well-equipped bedrooms have balconies with splendid views over the bay. In addition to the fixed-price menu served in the stylish restaurant, Maxwell's bistro offers an informal alternative.
ROOMS: 64 en suite (27 fmly) No smoking in all bedrooms s £60-£105; d £120-£210 (incl. bkfst & dinner) **LB FACILITIES: Spa** STV Indoor swimming (H) Outdoor swimming (H) Golf 9 Tennis (hard) Squash Snooker Sauna Solarium Gym Jacuzzi Beauty salon Creche Childrens club, Table Tennis entertainment ch fac Xmas **CONF:** Thtr 200 Class 150 Board 150 Del from £75 **SERVICES:** Lift **PARKING:** 150 **NOTES:** No dogs (ex guide dogs) No smoking in restaurant Closed 3 Jan-mid Feb
CARDS:

★73% **Crossways**
The Esplanade EX34 7DJ
☎ 01271 870395 📠 01271 870395
Dir: *M5 junct 27 onto A361 to Barnstaple, follow signs for Ilfracombe, then Woolacombe. At seafront turn right onto esplanade, hotel 0.5m on right*
Overlooking the picturesque Combesgate Beach, and with access to National Trust moorland at the rear, this hotel offers comfortably furnished and well-equipped bedrooms, many with dramatic sea views. The friendly proprietors are attentive and provide a welcoming environment. Guests can relax in the lounge or take a drink in the cosy bar or on the terrace.
ROOMS: 9 rms (7 en suite) (3 fmly) (1 GF) No smoking in all bedrooms s £31-£38; d £62-£76 (incl. bkfst & dinner) **LB PARKING:** 9 **NOTES:** No children 1 month No smoking in restaurant Closed last Sat in Oct-1st Sat in Mar

WOOLER, Northumberland Map 21 NT92

★★69% **Tankerville Arms**
Cottage Rd NE71 6AD
☎ 01668 281581 📠 01668 281387
e-mail: enquiries@tankervillehotel.co.uk
Dir: *on A697*
Dating from the 17th century, this popular inn is ideally placed for the many local attractions. The comfortable and thoughtfully equipped bedrooms come in a variety of styles and sizes. The traditional bar has an adjacent brasserie and there is a spacious restaurant. Wide-ranging menus provide a choice to suit all.
ROOMS: 15 en suite (2 fmly) s £47-£49; d £88-£92 (incl. bkfst) **LB CONF:** Thtr 60 Class 60 Board 30 **PARKING:** 100 **NOTES:** No smoking in restaurant Closed 22-28 Dec Civ Wed 80 **CARDS:**

WOOLLEY EDGE MOTORWAY SERVICE AREA (M1), West Yorkshire Map 16 SE31

Travelodge Wakefield (Northbound)
M1 Service Area, West Bretton WF4 4LQ
☎ 08700 850 950
Dir: *between junct 38/39, adj to service area*
Travelodge

Travelodge offers good quality, good value, modern accommodation. Ideal for families, the spacious, en suite bedrooms include remote-control TV, tea and coffee-making facilities, luxury beds and free morning newspaper. Meals can be taken at the nearby family restaurant. For further details and the Travelodge phone number, consult the Hotel Groups page.
ROOMS: 32 en suite s fr £42.95; d fr £42.95

Travelodge Wakefield (Southbound)
M1 Service Area Southbound, West Bretton WF4 4LQ
☎ 08700 850 950
Travelodge

Travelodge offers good quality, good value, modern accommodation. Ideal for families, the spacious, en suite bedrooms include remote-control TV, tea and coffee-making facilities, luxury beds and free morning newspaper. Meals can be taken at the nearby family restaurant. For further details and the Travelodge phone number, consult the Hotel Groups page.
ROOMS: 41 en suite s fr £42.95; d fr £42.95

WOOTTON BASSETT, Wiltshire Map 05 SU08

★★★71% **Marsh Farm**
Coped Hall SN4 8ER
☎ 01793 848044 📠 01793 851528
e-mail: marshfarmhotel@btconnect.com
Dir: *from M4 take A3102, straight on at 1st rdbt, at next rdbt (with garage on left) turn right. Hotel 200yds on left*
Originally a Victorian farmhouse, this hotel combines character and elegance with modern facilities. Bedrooms, including superior rooms, are decorated to a high standard; some are self contained in cottages adjacent to the main building. An enjoyable and varied selection of dishes is available at dinner offered in the new conservatory dining room.
ROOMS: 11 en suite 39 annexe en suite (1 fmly) No smoking in 23 bedrooms s £55-£110; d £70-£135 (incl. bkfst) **LB FACILITIES:** STV Putting green **CONF:** Thtr 120 Class 60 Board 50 Del from £120 **PARKING:** 150 **NOTES:** No dogs (ex guide dogs) No smoking in restaurant RS 26-30 Dec Civ Wed 100
CARDS:

See advert under SWINDON

Early start?
Hotels at all star levels should provide in-room alarm clocks and/or alarm calls

WORCESTER, Worcestershire Map 10 SO85

★★★73% **Pear Tree Inn & Country Hotel**
Smite WR3 8SY
☎ 01905 756565 📠 01905 756777
e-mail: thepeartreeuk@aol.com
Dir: *M5 junct 6 take Droitwich road after 300yds take 1st right into small country lane over canal bridge, up a hill, hotel on left*
This traditional English inn and country hotel has spacious bedrooms with attractive colour schemes and good facilities. Ground-floor bedrooms are available, as are suites. Guests can

continued

enjoy good food and a drink in warm and relaxed surroundings, with an excellent range of conference and function rooms.

ROOMS: 24 en suite (2 fmly) (12 GF) No smoking in 12 bedrooms s £57-£95; d £80-£150 (incl. bkfst) **LB FACILITIES:** STV **CONF:** Thtr 300 Class 150 Board 30 **SERVICES:** Lift air con **PARKING:** 200 **NOTES:** No dogs (ex guide dogs) No smoking in restaurant Civ Wed 120 **CARDS:**

★★★70% Bank House Hotel Golf & Country Club

Bransford WR6 5JD
☎ 01886 833551 📠 01886 832461
e-mail: info@bankhousehotel.co.uk
Dir: *M5 junct 7 follow signs to Worcester West, then Hereford on A4440 & A4103. Turn left, hotel approx 2m on left*

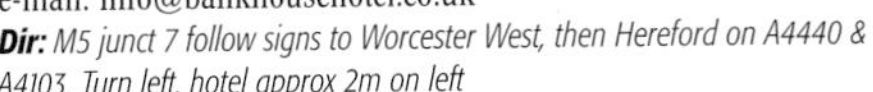

Partly dating back to the 17th century, Bank House is set in 123 acres overlooking the Malvern Hills, three miles west of Worcester. There is a good choice of function and conference suites, and the bedrooms are traditionally appointed. Facilities here include a leisure and fitness suite and an 18-hole golf course with pro shop and clubhouse.

ROOMS: 68 en suite (20 fmly) (12 GF) No smoking in 15 bedrooms s £65-£88; d £85-£111 (incl. bkfst) **LB FACILITIES: Spa** Outdoor swimming Golf 18 Sauna Solarium Gym Putting green Jacuzzi Xmas **CONF:** Thtr 400 Class 150 Board 70 Del from £120 **PARKING:** 350 **NOTES:** No smoking in restaurant Civ Wed 200 **CARDS:**

★★★58% *The Gifford*

High St WR1 2QR
☎ 01905 726262 📠 01905 723458
e-mail: events.giffard@macdonald-hotels.co.uk
Dir: *M5 junct 7 and follow signs for city centre. Hotel opp Cathedral*

This popular city centre hotel provides all the services today's traveller could need. Bedrooms all have modern facilities; some of the larger rooms are suitable for families. A choice of bars and restaurants cater for a mixture of tastes.

ROOMS: 103 en suite (3 fmly) No smoking in 50 bedrooms **CONF:** Thtr 150 Class 100 Board 40 **SERVICES:** Lift **CARDS:**

⌂ Travel Inn

Wainwright Way, Warndon WR4 9FA
☎ 08701 977278 📠 01905 756601
Dir: *M5 junct 6, at entrance of Wardon commercial development area*

Travel Inn offers good-quality, value-for-money accommodation. Spacious, en suite rooms with bath and shower comfortably accommodate a family of up to two adults and two children (to age 15). The restaurant and bar offers a varied menu. For Travel Inn phone number, consult the Hotel Groups page.

ROOMS: 60 en suite s £44.95; d £44.95 **CONF:** Thtr 8

WORFIELD, Shropshire — Map 10 SO79

Top 200 - Hotel

★★★ ◎◎◎ Old Vicarage

Worfield WV15 5JZ
☎ 01746 716497 📠 01746 716552
e-mail: admin@the-old-vicarage.demon.co.uk
Dir: *off A454 between Bridgnorth & Wolverhampton*

Located in a quiet and peaceful area of Shropshire, this delightful hotel is set in acres of farm and woodland and was originally an elegant Edwardian vicarage. The charming bedrooms are thoughtfully and luxuriously furnished and well equipped, while the lounge and conservatory are the perfect places to unwind with a pot of tea or a glass of wine. The restaurant serves award-winning, memorable, modern British cuisine.

ROOMS: 10 en suite 4 annexe en suite (1 fmly) (2 GF) No smoking in all bedrooms s £80-£110; d £120-£175 (incl. bkfst) **LB FACILITIES: Spa** Croquet lawn **CONF:** Thtr 30 Class 30 Board 20 Del £140 **PARKING:** 30 **NOTES:** No smoking in restaurant **CARDS:**

WORKINGTON, Cumbria — Map 18 NY02

★★★80% Washington Central

Washington St CA14 3AY
☎ 01900 65772 📠 01900 68770
e-mail: kawildwchotel@aol.com
Dir: *M6 junct 40 towards Keswick, follow to Workington. At lights at bottom of Ramsey Brow, turn right and follow signs for hotel*

Enjoying a prominent town centre location, this modern hotel boasts memorably hospitable staff. The well-maintained bedrooms are equipped with a range of thoughtful extras. Public areas

continued on p680

WORKINGTON, continued

include numerous lounges, a spacious bar, Caesars leisure club, a smart restaurant and a popular coffee shop. The comprehensive conference facilities are ideal for meetings and weddings.

Washington Central, Workington

ROOMS: 46 en suite (4 fmly) No smoking in 37 bedrooms s £76.95-£96.95; d £109.95-£159.95 (incl. bkfst) **LB FACILITIES:** STV Indoor swimming (H) Sauna Solarium Gym Jacuzzi Free bike hire, indoor pool supervised, Nightclub entertainment **CONF:** BC Thtr 300 Class 250 Board 150 Del from £104.95 **SERVICES:** Lift **PARKING:** 16 **NOTES:** No dogs (ex guide dogs) No smoking in restaurant RS 25 Dec Civ Wed 300 **CARDS:**

★★★67% Hunday Manor Country House

Hunday, Winscales CA14 4JF
☎ 01900 61798 📠 01900 601202
e-mail: hundaymanorhotel@lineone.net

Dir: *off A66 onto A595 towards Whitehaven, hotel is 3m on R, signed*

Delightfully situated and enjoying distant views of the Solway Firth, this charming hotel has comfortable, well-furnished rooms. The open-plan bar and foyer lounge boast welcoming open fires, and the attractive restaurant is set in the lawned, woodland gardens. The new function suite has ensured that the hotel makes an excellent wedding venue.

ROOMS: 13 en suite s £55-£69; d £69 (incl. bkfst) **LB FACILITIES:** STV Tennis (grass) Xmas **CONF:** Thtr 100 Class 100 Board 50 **PARKING:** 50 **NOTES:** No smoking in restaurant Civ Wed 150 **CARDS:**

WORKSOP, Nottinghamshire — Map 16 SK57

★★★67% Clumber Park

Clumber Park S80 3PA
☎ 01623 835333 📠 01623 835525

Dir: *M1 junct 30/31 follow signs for Worksop. A1 Fiveways rdbt onto A614, 5m NE*

Beside the A614, this hotel is situated in open countryside, edging onto Sherwood Forest and Clumber Park. Bedrooms are comfortably furnished and well-equipped and public areas include a choice of formal and informal eating options. The refurbished Dukes Tavern is lively and casual, while the restaurant offers a more traditional style of service.

ROOMS: 48 en suite (6 fmly) No smoking in 31 bedrooms **FACILITIES:** STV **CONF:** Thtr 270 Class 150 Board 90 **PARKING:** 200 **NOTES:** No smoking in restaurant Civ Wed 150 **CARDS:**

★★★67% Lion

112 Bridge St S80 1HT
☎ 01909 477925 📠 01909 479038
e-mail: enquiries@lionhotelworksop.co.uk

Dir: *A57 to town centre, turn at Walkers Garage on right and follow road to Norfolk Arms and turn left*

This former coaching inn has been extended to offer spacious and comfortable accommodation, including a number of suites. It is conveniently situated on the edge of the main shopping and business area of Worksop; many locals join visitors in enjoying the wide range of dishes offered in the bar and restaurant.

ROOMS: 45 en suite (3 fmly) (5 GF) No smoking in 7 bedrooms s £70; d £85-£95 (incl. bkfst) **LB FACILITIES:** STV Xmas **CONF:** Thtr 160 Class 80 Board 70 Del from £65 **SERVICES:** Lift **PARKING:** 50 **NOTES:** No smoking in restaurant Civ Wed 75 **CARDS:**

⌂ Travelodge

St Anne's Dr, Dukeries Dr S80 3QD
☎ 08700 850 950 📠 01909 501528

Dir: *on rdbt junct of A60/A57*

Travelodge offers good quality, good value, modern accommodation. Ideal for families, the spacious, en suite bedrooms include remote-control TV, tea and coffee-making facilities, luxury beds and free morning newspaper. Meals can be taken at the nearby family restaurant. For further details and the Travelodge phone number, consult the Hotel Groups page.

ROOMS: 40 en suite s fr £42.95; d fr £42.95

WORSLEY, Greater Manchester — Map 15 SD70

★★★66% Novotel

Worsley Brow M28 2YA
☎ 0161 799 3535 📠 0161 703 8207
e-mail: H0907@accor-hotels.com

Dir: *adjacent to M60 junct 13*

Well-placed for access to the Peak and Lake Districts, as well as the thriving City of Manchester, this modern hotel successfully caters for both families and business guests. Spacious bedrooms all have sofa beds and a large work area, and the hotel also boasts an outdoor swimming pool and children's play area.

ROOMS: 119 en suite (4 fmly) s £72; d £72 **LB FACILITIES:** STV Outdoor swimming (H) **CONF:** Thtr 230 Class 140 Board 20 Del from £99 **SERVICES:** Lift **PARKING:** 140 **NOTES:** Civ Wed 230 **CARDS:**

WORTHING, West Sussex — Map 06 TQ10

★★★72% ⊛ Ardington

Steyne Gardens BN11 3DZ
☎ 01903 230451 📠 01903 526526

Dir: *A27 to Lancing, and then to seafront. Follow signs for Worthing. Left at 1st Church into Steyne Gardens*

Overlooking the Steyne Gardens next to the seafront, this popular hotel offers well-appointed bedrooms with a good range of facilities. An elegant lounge/bar area caters for guests throughout

continued

the day and has ample seating. The restaurant has been designed in a contemporary style, and offers good standards of cuisine.

ROOMS: 45 en suite (4 fmly) No smoking in 10 bedrooms s £58-£89; d £90-£105 (incl. bkfst) **LB FACILITIES:** STV ch fac Xmas **CONF:** Thtr 140 Class 60 Board 35 Del from £80 **NOTES:** Closed 25 Dec-4 Jan **CARDS:**

★★★70% Berkeley
86-95 Marine Pde BN11 3QD
☎ 01903 820000 📠 01903 821333
e-mail: berkbn@aol.com
Dir: *follow signs to Worthing seafront, hotel 0.5m W from pier*

Best Western

This hotel occupies a prime location on the seafront just a short walk from the high street. Bedrooms are modern in style and equipped with a good range of facilities; many have superb sea views. The public areas are tastefully decorated, and include a comfortable cocktail bar and a spacious restaurant.
ROOMS: 80 en suite (3 fmly) No smoking in 29 bedrooms **FACILITIES:** STV Xmas **CONF:** Thtr 100 Class 50 Board 50 Del from £95 **SERVICES:** Lift **PARKING:** 35 **NOTES:** No dogs (ex guide dogs) Civ Wed 60 **CARDS:**

★★★69% Windsor House
14/20 Windsor Rd BN11 2LX
☎ 01903 239655 & 0800 9804442 📠 01903 210763
e-mail: reception@thewindsor.co.uk
Dir: *from A27, A259 follow Hotels signs through town centre to seafront towards Brighton. Follow signs for hotel.*

Located on a quiet road near to the seafront, this well-established hotel is popular with both business and leisure guests. Public areas include a smart lounge bar, an appealing conservatory reception and lounge area and a popular restaurant. A choice of tastefully furnished bedrooms is available, each with a good range of facilities.
ROOMS: 30 en suite (4 fmly) No smoking in 10 bedrooms s £74-£99; d £89-£119 (incl. bkfst) **LB FACILITIES:** STV **CONF:** Thtr 120 Class 48 Board 40 Del £99 **PARKING:** 18 **NOTES:** No dogs (ex guide dogs) No smoking in restaurant Closed 23-31 Dec Civ Wed 120
CARDS:

★★★68% Beach
Marine Pde BN11 3QJ
☎ 01903 234001 📠 01903 234567
e-mail: thebeachhotel@btinternet.com
Dir: *W of town centre, approx 0.3m from pier*

A well-established, popular hotel, with an impressive 1930s facade. Bedrooms, some of which have sea views and balconies, are comfortably furnished and well equipped. Public areas are spacious and comfortable, and the restaurant serves a wide choice of popular dishes. The hotel has secure parking.
ROOMS: 79 en suite (8 fmly) No smoking in 24 bedrooms s £55-£70; d £81-£100 (incl. bkfst) **LB FACILITIES:** STV Xmas **CONF:** Thtr 250 Class 60 Board 60 Del from £67 **SERVICES:** Lift **PARKING:** 55 **NOTES:** No dogs (ex guide dogs) **CARDS:**

★★★67% Kingsway
Marine Pde BN11 3QQ
☎ 01903 237542 📠 01903 204173
e-mail: thekingsway@totalise.co.uk
Dir: *A27 follow signs to Worthing, then at seafront follow signs Hotel West. Hotel 0.75m west of pier*

THE CIRCLE
Selected Individual Hotels
GREAT BRITAIN

Ideally located on the seafront and close to the town centre, the Kingsway continues to provide warm hospitality to guests. Bedrooms, which are gradually being upgraded, are comfortably furnished and equipped with modern facilities. Day rooms include two comfortable lounge areas, a bar offering a good range of meals and a well-appointed restaurant.
ROOMS: 29 en suite 7 annexe en suite (2 fmly) (3 GF) No smoking in 13 bedrooms s £74-£78; d £102-£130 (incl. bkfst) **LB FACILITIES:** STV Xmas **CONF:** Thtr 50 Class 20 Board 30 Del £96 **SERVICES:** Lift **PARKING:** 10 **NOTES:** No smoking in restaurant
CARDS:

★★64% Cavendish
115 Marine Pde BN11 3QG
☎ 01903 236767 📠 01903 823840
e-mail: cavendishworthing@btinternet.com
Dir: *on seafront 600yds W of pier*

THE INDEPENDENTS

This popular, family-run hotel enjoys a prominent seafront location. Bedrooms are well-equipped and soundly decorated. Guests have an extensive choice of meal options, with a varied bar menu, and carte and daily menus offered in the restaurant. Limited car parking is available at the rear of the hotel.
ROOMS: 17 en suite (4 fmly) No smoking in 3 bedrooms s £39.50-£45; d £65-£75 (incl. bkfst) **LB FACILITIES:** STV **CONF:** Thtr 30 Class 20 Board 16 **SERVICES:** air con **PARKING:** 5
CARDS:

WOTTON-UNDER-EDGE, Gloucestershire — Map 04 ST79

★★★★66% Tortworth Court Four Pillars
Tortworth GL12 8HH
☎ 0800 374 692 📠 01454 263001
e-mail: bristol@four-pillars.co.uk
Dir: *M5 junct 14, B4509 pass Tortworth Visitors Centre take next right, hotel 0.5m on right*

FOUR PILLARS HOTELS

Set within 30 acres of parkland, this Gothic mansion displays original features cleverly combined with contemporary additions.

continued on p682

WOTTON-UNDER-EDGE, continued

Elegant public rooms include a choice of dining options, one housed within the library, another in the atrium and the third in the orangery. Bedrooms are suitably equipped, while additional facilities include a host of conference rooms and leisure centre.
ROOMS: 189 en suite No smoking in 95 bedrooms s £75-£139; d £96-£172 **LB** **FACILITIES:** STV Indoor swimming (H) Sauna Gym Jacuzzi Beauty suite, Steam room Xmas **CONF:** BC Thtr 400 Class 200 Board 80 Del £179 **SERVICES:** Lift **PARKING:** 350 **NOTES:** No dogs (ex guide dogs) Civ Wed 180 **CARDS:**

WREA GREEN, Lancashire Map 18 SD33

★★★68% Manor House

Ribby Hall Village, Ribby Rd PR4 2PR
☎ 01772 688000 📠 01772 688036
e-mail: themanorhousehotel@ribbyhall.co.uk
Dir: *M55 junct 33 follow A585 towards Kirkham & brown tourist signs for manor house. Straight across 3 rdbts. Ribby Hall Village 200yds on left*
This newly opened hotel, located in Ribby Hall Holiday Village, overlooks an ornamental lake, complete with 50ft fountain. Accommodation is on three floors and consists of modern one and two bedroom apartments, including two opulent penthouse suites. Meals are served in the nearby restaurant. Hotel guests can make use of the extensive leisure and conference facilities.
ROOMS: 29 en suite (6 fmly) (13 GF) No smoking in all bedrooms **FACILITIES: Spa** STV Indoor swimming (H) Golf 9 Tennis (hard) Fishing Squash Riding Snooker Sauna Solarium Gym Jacuzzi Various other facilities available, Indoor Swimming pool supervised entertainment Xmas **CONF:** Thtr 350 Class 200 **SERVICES:** Lift **PARKING:** 100 **NOTES:** No dogs (ex guide dogs) No smoking in restaurant Civ Wed 350 **CARDS:**

WROTHAM, Kent Map 06 TQ65

U *Holiday Inn Maidstone*

London Rd, Wrotham Heath TN15 7RS
☎ 0870 400 9054 📠 01732 885850
e-mail: maidstonehi@ichotelsgroup.com
At the time of going to press, the classification for this hotel was not confirmed. Please refer to the AA internet site www.theAA.com for current information.
ROOMS: 106 en suite (15 fmly) No smoking in 42 bedrooms **FACILITIES:** Indoor swimming (H) Sauna Solarium Gym Jacuzzi Health & fitness centre ch fac **CONF:** Thtr 60 Class 30 Board 30 **PARKING:** 110 **CARDS:**

Travel Inn (Sevenoaks/Maidstone)

London Rd, Wrotham Heath TN15 7RX
☎ 08701 977227 📠 01732 870368
Dir: *from either M20 junct 2 or M26 junct 2a follow A20 to Wrotham Heath/West Malling. Inn after lights on right*
Travel Inn offers good-quality, value-for-money accommodation. Spacious, en suite rooms with bath and shower comfortably accommodate a family of up to two adults and two children (to age 15). The restaurant and bar offers a varied menu. For further details and the Travel Inn phone number, consult the Hotel Groups page.
ROOMS: 40 en suite s £44.95; d £44.95 **CONF:** Thtr 18

WROXHAM, Norfolk Map 13 TG31

★★66% *Hotel Wroxham*

The Bridge NR12 8AJ
☎ 01603 782061 📠 01603 784279
e-mail: hotelwroxham@barbox.net
Dir: *From Norwich, A1151 signed Wroxham & The Broads for approx 7m. Over bridge at Wroxham take 1st right, & sharp right again. Hotel car park on right*

Overlooking the Norfolk Broads in the heart of this bustling town centre. Bedrooms are pleasantly decorated and well equipped; some rooms have balconies with lovely views of the busy waterways. The open-plan public rooms include the lively riverside bar, a lounge, a large sun terrace and a smart restaurant serving an interesting choice of dishes.
ROOMS: 18 en suite **FACILITIES:** Fishing Boating facilities (by arrangement) entertainment **CONF:** Thtr 200 Class 50 Board 20 **PARKING:** 45 **NOTES:** No dogs (ex guide dogs) No smoking in restaurant **CARDS:**

★★58% *Kings Head*

Station Rd NR12 8UR
☎ 01603 782429 📠 01603 784622
Dir: *in centre of village*

In the heart of the bustling town centre and on the edge of the Norfolk Broads, this hotel has spacious public rooms leading out onto the river frontage and gardens. There is a popular carvery restaurant and a conservatory that overlooks the busy waterways. The well-equipped bedrooms are pleasantly furnished and simply decorated.
ROOMS: 8 en suite (2 fmly) No smoking in all bedrooms **FACILITIES:** Fishing **PARKING:** 45 **NOTES:** No dogs (ex guide dogs) No smoking in restaurant **CARDS:**

WYMONDHAM, Norfolk

Map 13 TG10

★★★70% Abbey

10 Church St NR18 0PH
☎ 01953 602148 🖷 01953 606247
e-mail: info@abbeyhotels.co.uk
Dir: *from A11 follow Wymondham sign. At lights left and 1st left into one-way system. Left into Church St*

Charming 16th-century hotel situated close to the abbey just off the main high street of this delightful market town. The spacious bedrooms are pleasantly decorated, tastefully furnished and thoughtfully equipped. Public rooms include a cosy lounge bar, the Benims restaurant and a further sitting room.
ROOMS: 19 en suite 1 annexe en suite (3 fmly) s £49-£60; d £65-£80 (incl. bkfst) **LB FACILITIES:** Xmas **SERVICES:** Lift **PARKING:** 3
NOTES: No dogs (ex guide dogs) No smoking in restaurant
CARDS:

See advert on this page

★★73% Wymondham Consort Hotel

28 Market St NR18 0BB
☎ 01953 606721 🖷 01953 601361
e-mail: wymondham@bestwestern.co.uk
Dir: *off A11 (M11) Thetford to Norwich road, left at lights and left again*

Privately-owned hotel situated in the centre of this bustling market town. The individually decorated bedrooms come in a variety of sizes; each one is pleasantly decorated and thoughtfully equipped. Public rooms include a cosy bar, a separate lounge, a coffee shop and an intimate restaurant, which overlooks the busy high street.
ROOMS: 20 en suite (1 fmly) (3 GF) No smoking in all bedrooms s £60-£70; d £70-£90 (incl. bkfst) **LB CONF:** Thtr 20 Board 20
PARKING: 16 **NOTES:** No smoking in restaurant
CARDS:

> Looking for a last-minute weekend away?
> Check out Latebeds,
> the AA's late availability booking service, at www.theAA.com

YARM, North Yorkshire Map 19 NZ41

Top 200 - Hotel

★★★ ⓇⓇⓇ **Judges Country House Hotel**
Kirklevington Hall TS15 9LW
☎ 01642 789000 🖹 01642 782878
e-mail: enquiries@judgeshotel.co.uk
Dir: *1.5m from A19. At A67 junct, follow Yarm road and hotel on left*
Formerly a lodging for local circuit judges, this gracious mansion lies in landscaped grounds through which a stream runs. Stylish bedrooms are individually decorated and come with one hundred and one extra services including a pet goldfish! The Conservatory restaurant serves award-winning cuisine of modern British dishes using local produce. The genuinely caring and attentive service is equally memorable.
ROOMS: 21 en suite (3 fmly) (5 GF) No smoking in 10 bedrooms s £104-£130; d £120-£170 (incl. bkfst) **LB FACILITIES:** STV Tennis Gym Croquet lawn Putting green Boating, 4x4 hire, mountain bikes, nature trails entertainment ch fac Xmas **CONF:** BC Thtr 200 Class 120 Board 80 Del from £140 **PARKING:** 102 **NOTES:** No dogs (ex guide dogs) No smoking in restaurant Civ Wed 200
CARDS:

YARMOUTH See Wight, Isle of

YATTENDON, Berkshire Map 05 SU57

★★72% ⓇⓇ ***The Royal Oak***
The Square RG18 0UG
☎ 01635 201325 🖹 01635 201926
e-mail: theroyaloakhotel@hotmail.com
Dir: *M4 junct 13, N on A34, 1st slip road right to Hermitage, left at t-junct, 2nd right signed Yattendon*

This smart country inn dates back to the 16th century and is located in a charming Berkshire village within easy access of the M4. Bedrooms are equipped to a high standard and bathrooms are well appointed. Cuisine offers interesting dishes and the menu is available in both the bar and more formal restaurant.
ROOMS: 5 en suite **CONF:** Thtr 30 Class 18 Board 22 **NOTES:** No children 6yrs No smoking in restaurant
CARDS:

YELVERTON, Devon Map 03 SX56

★★★72% **Moorland Links**
PL20 6DA
☎ 01822 852245 🖹 01822 855004
e-mail: moorland.links@forestdale.com
Dir: *A38 from Exeter to Plymouth, then A386 towards Tavistock. 5m onto open moorland, hotel 1m on left*

Forestdale Hotels

In the Dartmoor National Park, set in nine acres of well-tended grounds, Moorland Links has spectacular views from many of the rooms across open moorland and the Tamar Valley. Bedrooms are well equipped and comfortably furnished, and some rooms have open balconies. An ideal hotel for weddings and with ample, quiet meeting room facilities.
ROOMS: 45 en suite (4 fmly) (17 GF) No smoking in 2 bedrooms s fr £95; d fr £115 (incl. bkfst) **LB FACILITIES:** STV Tennis (hard) Xmas **CONF:** Thtr 120 Class 60 Board 40 Del from £120 **PARKING:** 120 **NOTES:** No smoking in restaurant Civ Wed 160
CARDS:

See advert under PLYMOUTH

YEOVIL, Somerset Map 04 ST51
See also Martock

★★★73% ⓇⓇ **Yeovil Court**
West Coker Rd BA20 2HE
☎ 01935 863746 🖹 01935 863990
e-mail: unwind@yeovilhotel.com
Dir: *2.5m W of town centre on A30*

This comfortable, family-run hotel benefits from a very relaxed and caring atmosphere. Bedrooms are well equipped and neatly presented; some are located in a new building adjacent. Public

continued

areas consist of a smart lounge, a popular bar and an attractive restaurant. An interesting selection from the menus combines lighter options with dishes more suited to special occasion dining.
ROOMS: 18 en suite 12 annexe en suite (3 fmly) (11 GF) No smoking in 8 bedrooms s £57-£74; d £85-£95 (incl. bkfst) **LB** **CONF:** Thtr 50 Class 18 Board 22 **PARKING:** 65 **NOTES:** No smoking in restaurant RS Sat lunch/Sun eve **CARDS:**

See advert on page 683

★★60% Preston

64 Preston Rd BA20 2DL
☎ 01935 474400 ▯ 01935 410142
e-mail: prestonhotelyeo@aol.co.uk
Dir: *A303 onto A3088, left at 1st rdbt, over 2nd rdbt & turn right at 3rd rdbt*
A relaxed and friendly atmosphere has been maintained at this popular hotel which has undergone a change in ownership. Well suited to both business and leisure guests, a spacious bar and cosy restaurant are available where home cooked meals satisfy the heartiest of appetites.
ROOMS: 6 en suite 7 annexe en suite (1 fmly) (7 GF) s £45; d £55 (incl. bkfst) **CONF:** BC Class 15 Board 15 **NOTES:** No dogs (ex guide dogs) No smoking in restaurant **CARDS:**

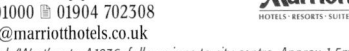

Top 200 - Hotel

★ ◎◎◎ Little Barwick House

Barwick Village BA22 9TD
☎ 01935 423902 ▯ 01935 420908
e-mail: reservations@barwick.fsnet.co.uk
Dir: *from Yeovil on A37 towards Dorchester, turn left at 1st rdbt. Through village, 1st left, and hotel 0.25m on left*
Situated in a quiet hamlet, this delightful listed Georgian dower house is an ideal retreat for those seeking peaceful surroundings and good food. Just one of the highlights of a stay here is a meal in the restaurant. Each of the bedrooms has its own character and charm and a range of thoughtful extras such as fresh flowers and magazines. At Little Barwick, the informal atmosphere of a private home coupled with the facilities and comforts of a modern hotel result in a very special combination.
ROOMS: 6 en suite s £65-£108; d £94-£108 (incl. bkfst) **LB** **PARKING:** 30 **NOTES:** No smoking in restaurant
CARDS:

YORK, North Yorkshire — Map 16 SE65

See also Aldwark, Escrick, Pocklington & Sutton upon Derwent

★★★★66% York Marriott

Tadcaster Rd YO24 1QQ
☎ 01904 701000 ▯ 01904 702308
e-mail: york@marriotthotels.co.uk
Dir: *A64 at York 'West' onto A1036, follow signs to city centre. Approx 1.5m, hotel on right after church and lights*
Overlooking the racecourse and Knavesmire Parkland, the hotel

continued

offers modern accommodation, including family rooms, all with a comfort cooling system. Within the hotel, guests benefit from the use of extensive leisure facilities including indoor pool, putting green and tennis court. For those guests wishing to explore the historic and cultural attractions of the city there is a daily courtesy mini-bus service to the city centre, less than a mile from the hotel.
ROOMS: 108 en suite (14 fmly) (16 GF) No smoking in 60 bedrooms s fr £110; d fr £120 **LB** **FACILITIES: Spa** STV Indoor swimming (H) Tennis (hard) Sauna Solarium Gym Putting green Jacuzzi Beauty treatment Xmas **CONF:** BC Thtr 170 Class 90 Board 40 Del from £145 **SERVICES:** Lift air con **PARKING:** 200 **NOTES:** No dogs (ex guide dogs) No smoking in restaurant Civ Wed 120
CARDS:

★★★★65% Le Meridien York

Station Rd YO24 2AA
☎ 01904 653681 ▯ 01904 623503
e-mail: reservation.centreuk@lemeridien.com
Dir: *adjacent to railway station*
Situated in three acres of landscaped grounds in the very heart of the city, this Victorian railway hotel has views over the city and York Minster. Contemporary bedrooms are divided between those in the main hotel and the air-conditioned garden mews. There is also a leisure complex and state-of-the-art conference centre.
ROOMS: 165 en suite (10 fmly) s £60-£145; d £80-£165 **LB** **FACILITIES:** STV Indoor swimming (H) Sauna Solarium Gym Jacuzzi Steam room, Swimming pool supervised Xmas **CONF:** BC Thtr 450 Class 250 Board 80 Del from £125 **SERVICES:** Lift **PARKING:** 80 **NOTES:** No smoking in restaurant Civ Wed 300
CARDS:

YORK, continued

Top 200 - Hotel

★★★ The Grange
1 Clifton YO30 6AA
☎ 01904 644744 01904 612453
e-mail: info@grangehotel.co.uk
Dir: *on A19 York/Thirsk road, approx 500yds from city centre*
This bustling Regency town house is just a few minutes' walk from the centre of York. A professional service is efficiently delivered by caring staff in a very friendly and helpful manner. Public rooms are comfortable and have been stylishly furnished, these include two dining options, the popular informal brasserie in the cellar, whilst The Ivy offers fine dining in a lavishly decorated environment. The individually designed bedrooms are comfortably appointed and have been thoughtfully equipped.
ROOMS: 30 en suite s £110-£180; d £130-£240 (incl. bkfst) **LB** **FACILITIES:** STV Discount at local health spa Xmas **CONF:** Thtr 50 Class 20 Board 24 Del from £150 **PARKING:** 26 **NOTES:** No smoking in restaurant Civ Wed 60
CARDS:

Top 200 - Hotel

★★★ Middlethorpe Hall
Bishopthorpe Rd, Middlethorpe YO23 2GB
☎ 01904 641241 01904 620176
e-mail: info@middlethorpe.com
Dir: *from A1036 signed York (west), follow signs to Bishopthorpe and racecourse. Hotel on right just before racecourse*
This fine Georgian house, convenient for town and the racecourse, sits in acres of beautifully landscaped gardens. The bedrooms are all comfortably furnished and are split between the main house and converted stables set around an attractive courtyard. Public areas, in keeping with the style of the house, include a stately drawing room and an oak-panelled dining room, where carefully prepared seasonal fare is served. There is also a small spa facility adjacent to the hotel.
ROOMS: 30 en suite s £109-£155; d £160-£360 **LB**
FACILITIES: Spa Indoor swimming (H) Sauna Solarium Gym Croquet lawn Jacuzzi Leisure Spa Xmas **CONF:** Thtr 56 Class 30 Board 25 Del £170.38 **SERVICES:** Lift **PARKING:** 70 **NOTES:** No dogs No children 8yrs No smoking in restaurant RS 25 & 31 Dec
CARDS:

★★★75% Dean Court

Duncombe Place YO1 7EF
☎ 01904 625082 01904 620305
e-mail: info@deancourt-york.co.uk
Dir: *city centre opposite York Minster*

This smart hotel enjoys an central location overlooking the Minster. Bedrooms are smartly appointed and thoughtfully equipped. Public areas include Terry's all-day tea lounge and an elegant, popular restaurant enjoying wonderful views of the cathedral. Service is particularly efficient and friendly, and valet parking is offered.
ROOMS: 39 en suite (4 fmly) No smoking in 14 bedrooms s £75-£100; d £110-£185 (incl. bkfst) **LB** **FACILITIES:** Xmas **CONF:** Thtr 50 Class 24 Board 32 Del from £125 **SERVICES:** Lift **PARKING:** 30 **NOTES:** No dogs (ex guide dogs) No smoking in restaurant Civ Wed 50
CARDS:

★★★73% Mount Royale
The Mount YO24 1GU
☎ 01904 628856 01904 611171
e-mail: reservations@mountroyale.co.uk
Dir: *W on A1036, 0.5m after racecourse. Hotel on right after lights*
This friendly hotel offers comfortable bedrooms in a variety of styles, several of which lead into the delightful gardens. Public rooms include a lounge, a meeting room and a cosy bar. Overlooking the gardens is a separate restaurant and cocktail lounge called Sous le Mont where all meals and drinks can be charged to the room account. A beauty therapist is also available by appointment.
ROOMS: 23 en suite (2 fmly) (6 GF) s £85-£115; d £97.50-£150 (incl. bkfst) **LB** **FACILITIES:** STV Outdoor swimming (H) Sauna Solarium Beauty treatment centre **CONF:** BC Thtr 20 Board 16 Del £120
PARKING: 18 **CARDS:**

★★★73% York Pavilion
45 Main St, Fulford YO10 4PJ
☎ 01904 622099 01904 626939
e-mail: help@yorkpavilionhotel.com
Dir: *off A64 at A19 junct towards York. Hotel 0.5m on right opposite filling station*
An attractive Georgian hotel situated in its own grounds. All the

continued

bedrooms are individually designed to a high specification; some are in the old house and some in the converted stables set around a garden terrace. There is a comfortable lounge, a conference centre and an inviting brasserie-style restaurant with a regularly changing menu.

ROOMS: 57 en suite No smoking in 23 bedrooms s £90-£100; d £120-£150 (incl. bkfst) **LB** **FACILITIES:** STV Xmas **CONF:** Thtr 150 Class 60 Board 45 Del £135 **PARKING:** 40 **NOTES:** No dogs (ex guide dogs) No smoking in restaurant Civ Wed 120
CARDS:

See advert on this page

★★★72% Parsonage Country House

York Rd YO19 6LF
☎ 01904 728111 01904 728151
e-mail: reservations@parsonagehotel.co.uk
(For full entry see Escrick)

★★★71% Kilima Hotel

129 Holgate Rd YO24 4AZ
☎ 01904 625787 01904 612083
e-mail: sales@kilima.co.uk
Dir: *on A59, on W outskirts*

Kilima is conveniently situated within easy walking distance of the city centre. There is a relaxed and friendly atmosphere in the hotel, with professional, friendly staff providing attentive service. Bedrooms are comfortable and well equipped. The hotel benefits from private parking and leisure facilities.
ROOMS: 26 en suite (2 fmly) (10 GF) No smoking in all bedrooms s £68; d £96 (incl. bkfst) **LB** **FACILITIES:** STV Indoor swimming (H) Gym Leisure complex, Steam room, Fitness Suite Xmas **CONF:** Board 14 Del £115 **PARKING:** 26 **NOTES:** No dogs (ex guide dogs) No smoking in restaurant **CARDS:**

TV dinner?
Room service at three stars and above

★★★67% Monkbar

Monkbar YO31 7JA
☎ 01904 638086 01904 629195
e-mail: sales@monkbarhotel.co.uk
Dir: *From A64 take A1079 to City, turn right at city wall, take middle lane at lights. Hotel on right*

This smart hotel enjoys a prominent position adjacent to the city walls, minutes' walk from the cathedral. Individually styled bedrooms are well equipped for both business and leisure guests. Spacious public areas include comfortable lounges, an American style bar, an airy restaurant and impressive meeting and training facilities.
ROOMS: 99 en suite (3 fmly) No smoking in 45 bedrooms s £95-£125; d £135-£175 (incl. bkfst) **LB** **FACILITIES:** STV Xmas **CONF:** Thtr 140 Class 80 Board 50 Del from £130 **SERVICES:** Lift **PARKING:** 70 **NOTES:** No smoking in restaurant Civ Wed 60
CARDS:

Y

YORK, continued

★★★66% ***The Gateway to York***
Hull Rd, Kexby YO4 5LD
☎ 01759 388223 🖷 01759 388822
e-mail: enquiry@thegatewaytoyorkhotel.co.uk
Dir: *off A64 onto A1079, 3m from York, hotel on left*

Three miles from York's Park-and-Ride, and close to the retail shopping outlet, this hotel is set in eight acres of gardens which include private fishing available for residents. Its spacious bedrooms are well equipped, and there is a pleasant bar-lounge and restaurant serving enjoyable food.
ROOMS: 30 en suite (9 fmly) No smoking in 23 bedrooms **FACILITIES:** STV Fishing **CONF:** Thtr 50 Class 30 Board 30 **PARKING:** 60 **NOTES:** No smoking in restaurant Closed Jan **CARDS:**

★★★66% **Novotel York**
Fishergate YO10 4FD
☎ 01904 611660 🖷 01904 610925
e-mail: H0949@accor-hotels.com
Dir: *A19 north to city centre, hotel set back on left*
Set just outside the ancient city walls, this modern, family-friendly hotel is conveniently located for visitors to the city. Bedroom features include bathroom with separate toilet area, excellent desk space and sofa beds. Four rooms have facilities for less able guests. Hotel facilities include indoor and outdoor children's play areas and an indoor pool.
ROOMS: 124 en suite (124 fmly) No smoking in 91 bedrooms s fr £85; d fr £90 **LB** **FACILITIES:** STV Indoor swimming (H) **CONF:** Thtr 220 Class 100 Board 120 Del from £122 **SERVICES:** Lift **PARKING:** 150 **CARDS:**

★★71% **Clifton Bridge**
Water End YO30 6LL
☎ 01904 610510 🖷 01904 640208
e-mail: enq@cliftonbridgehotel.co.uk
Dir: *turn off A1237 onto A19 towards city centre. Right at lights by church, hotel 50yds on left*
Standing between Clifton Green and the River Ouse and within walking distance of the city, this hotel offers good hospitality and attentive service. The house is well furnished and features oak panelling in the public rooms. Bedrooms are attractively decorated and thoughtfully equipped. Good home cooking is served in the cosy dining room.
ROOMS: 14 en suite (1 fmly) (3 GF) No smoking in 2 bedrooms s £45-£54; d £74-£94 (incl. bkfst) **LB** **CONF:** Board 12 Del from £50 **PARKING:** 16 **NOTES:** No smoking in restaurant Closed 24-26, 31 Dec, 1 Jan **CARDS:**

★★71% **Knavesmire Manor**
302 Tadcaster Rd YO24 1HE
☎ 01904 702941 🖷 01904 709274
e-mail: knavesmire@tiscali.co.uk
Dir: *A1036 into city centre. Hotel on right, overlooking racecourse*

THE CIRCLE
Selected Individual Hotels
GREAT BRITAIN

Commanding super views across York's famous racecourse, this former manor house offers comfortable, well-equipped bedrooms, either in the main house or the garden rooms to the rear. Comfortable day rooms are stylishly furnished whilst the heated indoor pool provides a popular addition.
ROOMS: 11 en suite 9 annexe en suite (3 fmly) s £55-£65; d £65-£90 (incl. bkfst) **LB** **FACILITIES:** Indoor swimming (H) Sauna Xmas **CONF:** Thtr 40 Class 36 Board 30 Del from £79.95 **SERVICES:** Lift **PARKING:** 28 **NOTES:** No smoking in restaurant Civ Wed 60 **CARDS:**

> Early start?
> Hotels at all star levels should provide in-room alarm clocks and/or alarm calls

★★71% **Minster**
60 Bootham YO30 7BZ
☎ 01904 621267 🖷 01904 654719
e-mail: res@minsterhotel.co.uk
Dir: *leave A1237 onto A19 towards York city centre. Hotel 2.5m on right*

Within easy walking distance of the Minster and the city centre, this careful conversion of two large Victorian houses has been refurbished to provide comfortable, well-equipped bedrooms. There is a cosy bar and a bistro serving imaginative dishes, and meeting facilities are also available.
ROOMS: 31 en suite (11 fmly) (4 GF) No smoking in 17 bedrooms s £55-£110; d £75-£150 (incl. bkfst) **LB** **FACILITIES:** STV **CONF:** Thtr 70 Class 40 Board 35 Del £120 **PARKING:** 31 **NOTES:** No dogs (ex guide dogs) No smoking in restaurant **CARDS:**

See advert on opposite page

★★70% Heworth Court
Heworth Green YO31 7TQ
☎ 01904 425156 🖷 01904 415290
e-mail: hotel@heworth.co.uk
Dir: *outer ring road towards Scarborough rdbt on NE side of York, exit onto A1036 Malton Rd, hotel on left*

Friendly and attentive service is provided at this family-owned hotel, conveniently located within walking distance of the city. Public rooms are comfortable and bedrooms are thoughtfully equipped. An extensive range of freshly prepared food is served in the Lamp Light Restaurant, and parking facilities are excellent.
ROOMS: 17 en suite 11 annexe en suite (5 fmly) (9 GF) No smoking in 16 bedrooms s £52-£88; d £66-£111 (incl. bkfst) **LB FACILITIES:** STV Whisky bar Xmas **CONF:** Thtr 50 Class 24 Board 28 **PARKING:** 29 **NOTES:** No dogs (ex guide dogs) No smoking in restaurant
CARDS:

See advert on page 691

★★69% Alhambra Court
31 St Mary's, Bootham YO30 7DD
☎ 01904 628474 🖷 01904 610690
e-mail: enq@alhambracourthotel.co.uk
Dir: *off Bootham A19*

In a quiet side road within easy walking distance of the Minster, this attractive Georgian building is pleasantly furnished and the bedrooms are well equipped. Service is cheerful and attentive, and good home cooking is a feature.
ROOMS: 24 en suite (4 fmly) (4 GF) No smoking in 14 bedrooms s £38-£53; d £55-£85 (incl. bkfst) **LB SERVICES:** Lift **PARKING:** 25 **NOTES:** No dogs (ex guide dogs) No smoking in restaurant Closed 24-31 Dec & 1-7 Jan **CARDS:**

★★69% Beechwood Close
19 Shipton Rd, Clifton YO30 5RE
☎ 01904 658378 🖷 01904 647124
e-mail: bch@selcom.co.uk
Dir: *on A19 (Thirsk Rd, between ring road and city centre) on right on entering 30mph zone*
This long established, comfortable hotel, personally managed by

continued

the owners, is situated just a mile north of the city centre. Beechwood Close Hotel offers spacious, well-equipped and well-maintained bedrooms. There is a cosy bar-lounge, and wide ranging menus in the dining room.
ROOMS: 14 en suite (2 fmly) s £45-£50; d £60-£80 (incl. bkfst) **LB FACILITIES:** STV **CONF:** Thtr 50 Class 40 Board 30 Del from £75 **PARKING:** 36 **NOTES:** No dogs Closed 25 Dec
CARDS:

★★68% The Groves
8 St Peters Grove, Clifton YO30 6AQ
☎ 01904 559777 🖷 01904 627729
e-mail: groves@ecsyork.co.uk
Dir: *off A19 at Clifton*
This hotel is peacefully situated on both sides of the quiet side road and within easy walking distance of the city and the Minster. Bedrooms offer comfortable well-equipped accommodation and are available in the main buildings or courtyard. Public areas are split between the two main buildings.
ROOMS: 17 en suite 27 annexe en suite (6 fmly) (13 GF) s £35-£50; d £70-£100 (incl. bkfst) **LB FACILITIES:** STV **CONF:** Thtr 32 Class 24 Board 26 Del from £79 **PARKING:** 39 **NOTES:** No smoking in restaurant RS 20 Dec-3 Jan **CARDS:**

★★66% Blue Bridge
Fishergate YO10 4AP
☎ 01904 621193
Convenient for the Barbican Centre and within walking distance of the city centre, this hotel provides pine-furnished bedrooms which include three spacious apartment rooms across the courtyard. Good value breakfast and dinner will satisfy the heartiest of appetites. Residents and diners have their own bar.
ROOMS: 15 rms (13 en suite) s £45-£50; d £55-£90 (incl. bkfst) **LB PARKING:** 15 **CARDS:**

YORK, continued

★★65% Jacobean Lodge

Plainville Ln, Wigginton YO32 2RG
☎ 01904 762749 📠 01904 768403
e-mail: jaco.mk1@breathemail.net
Dir: *from A19 to Skelton. Right at Blacksmith Arm, 2m to hotel*

This comfortable inn stands in extensive lawned gardens amid open farmland. The hotel is family owned and run and provides compact and well-equipped bedrooms. Excellent home-cooked meals are available in the pleasant bars or the restaurant, which are well patronised by locals.
ROOMS: 8 en suite 6 annexe en suite (2 fmly) s £40-£45; d £65 (incl. bkfst) **LB FACILITIES:** Giant chess Childrens play area entertainment **CONF:** Thtr 40 Class 30 Board 30 **PARKING:** 52 **NOTES:** No smoking in restaurant RS 25-26 Dec **CARDS:**

★★65% Lady Anne Middletons Hotel

Skeldergate YO1 6DS
☎ 01904 611570 📠 01904 613043
e-mail: bookings@ladyannes.co.uk
Dir: *from A1036 towards city centre. Right at City Walls lights, keep left, 1st left before bridge, then 1st left into Cromwell Rd. Hotel on right*
This well furnished city-centre hotel has been created from several listed buildings and is very well located in the centre of York. Among its amenities are a bar-lounge and a dining room where a satisfying range of food is served and an extensive fitness club.
ROOMS: 37 en suite 15 annexe en suite (3 fmly) No smoking in 15 bedrooms s £40-£80; d £75-£115 (incl. bkfst) **LB FACILITIES:** Indoor swimming (H) Sauna Solarium Gym No leisure facilities for under 16yrs, indoor swimming pool supervised ch fac **CONF:** Thtr 100 Class 30 Board 30 Del £105 **PARKING:** 40 **NOTES:** No dogs (ex guide dogs) No smoking in restaurant Closed 24-29 Dec Civ Wed 60
CARDS:

★★64% *Orchard Court*

4 St Peters Grove, Bootham YO30 6AQ
☎ 01904 653964 📠 01904 622656
e-mail: joancross@orchardhotel.fsnet.co.uk
Dir: *A19 N to York city centre opp School, entrance at base of footbridge*

This friendly hotel is situated in a quiet side-road, yet within easy walking distance of the city centre. Orchard Court provides modern and comfortable accommodation. A range of appetising dishes is available at dinner and staff are very polite, friendly and attentive.
ROOMS: 15 rms (13 en suite) 4 annexe en suite (5 fmly) No smoking in 4 bedrooms **FACILITIES:** ch fac **PARKING:** 24 **NOTES:** No dogs (ex guide dogs) No smoking in restaurant Closed 24-28 Dec RS Sun
CARDS:

★★61% *Cottage*

3 Clifton Green YO30 6LH
☎ 01904 643711 📠 01904 611230
Dir: *From A64/A1237 follow signs to York N, A19 until York city centre sign is visible, A19 Rawcliffe/Clifton right at rdbt, to lights at Clifton Green, straight on and hotel right of Green*
Privately operated and personally managed by the proprietor, this conveniently located, intimate hotel offers comfortable accommodation. The public areas include a cosy bar and a stylish beamed restaurant. Guests have the added bonus of secure car parking.
ROOMS: 20 en suite 5 annexe en suite (2 fmly) No smoking in 5 bedrooms **FACILITIES:** Jacuzzi **PARKING:** 10 **NOTES:** No dogs (ex guide dogs) No smoking in restaurant **CARDS:**

U *Holiday Inn York*

Holiday Inn HOTELS · RESORTS

Tadcaster Rd YO24 1QF
☎ 0870 400 9085 📠 01904 702804
e-mail: york@ichotelsgroup.com
Dir: *from A1(M) take A64 towards York. 7m, take A106 to York. Straight over at rdbt to York city centre. Hotel 0.5m on right*
At the time of going to press, the classification for this hotel was not confirmed. Please refer to the AA internet site www.theAA.com for current information.
ROOMS: 143 en suite (37 fmly) No smoking in 83 bedrooms **FACILITIES:** ch fac **CONF:** Thtr 100 Class 40 Board 40 **SERVICES:** Lift **PARKING:** 137 **NOTES:** No smoking in restaurant Civ Wed
CARDS:

⌂ Express by Holiday Inn York

Express by Holiday Inn

Malton Rd YO3 9TE
☎ 01904 438660 📠 01904 438560
e-mail: ebhi-york-east@btconnect.com
Dir: *A64 signed Scarborough & at large rdbt turn left towards York/Harrogate. 2nd small rdbt left towards York & Huntington. Hotel on left behind Stockton on The Forrest Inn*

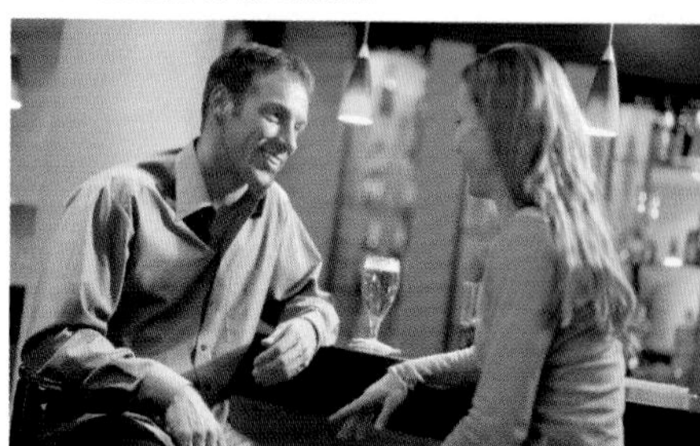

A modern hotel ideal for families and business travellers. Fresh and uncomplicated, the spacious bedrooms include Sky TV, power shower and tea and coffee-making facilities. Continental buffet breakfast is included in the room rate; other meals may be taken at the nearby family pub or restaurant. For further details and the Express by Holiday Inn phone number, consult the Hotel Groups pages.
ROOMS: 49 en suite **CONF:** Thtr 30 Class 24 Board 16

Looking for a last-minute weekend away?
Check out Latebeds,
the AA's late availability booking service, at www.theAA.com

'You deserve a break'

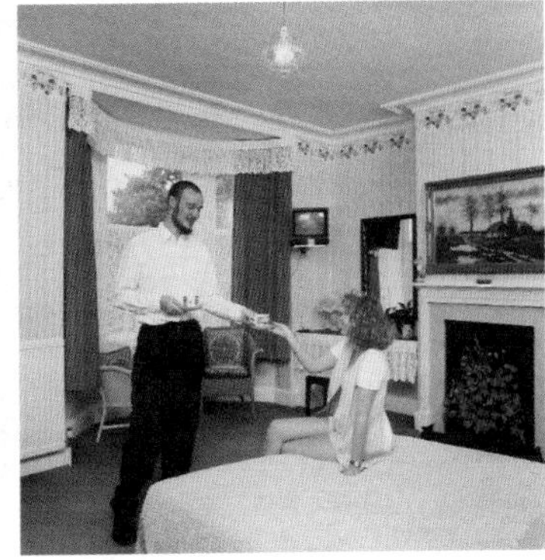

COMFORTABLE BEDROOMS

A traditional English hotel only 3/4 mile from York Minster, ideally located for exploring York on foot.

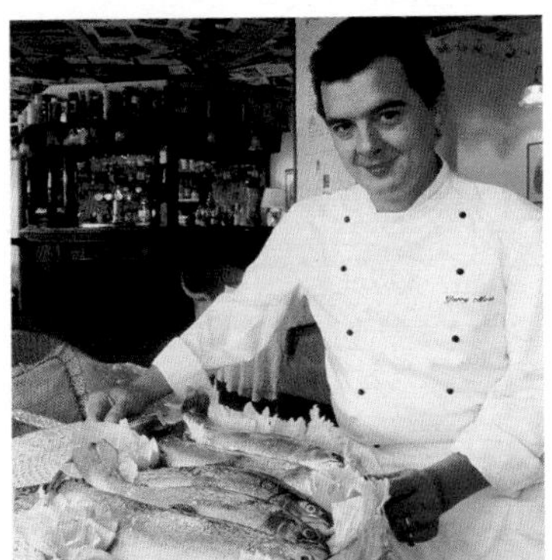

WHISKY BAR

12 minutes stroll to the Medieval Walled City of York, ample private car parking is provided at the hotel. Simply park your car and discover all the attractions "in and around" York.

HEWORTH COURT HOTEL
Lamplight RESTAURANT

All 28 en-suite bedrooms contain tv with 24hr news, direct dial telephone, voicemail, tea, coffee and modem point – luxury rooms have Chandeliers or 4-poster beds.

http://www.visityork.com
Email: hotel@heworth.co.uk

LAMPLIGHT RESTAURANT

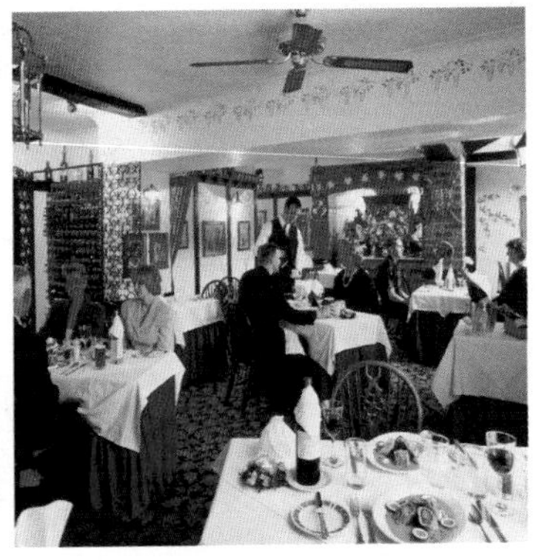

AA ★★

Relax and unwind in the hotel Whisky bar before sampling the delights of the Lamplight Restaurant.

4-POSTER ROOMS

(01904) 425156 www.visityork.com

Y

YORK, continued

⌂ Express by Holiday Inn York Clifton

Clifton Business Park, Shipton Rd YO30 5PA
☎ 01904 659992 📠 01904 659994
e-mail: ebhi-york-west@btconnect.com
Dir: *A19 from Thirsk and North - main road into York*

A modern hotel ideal for families and business travellers. Fresh and uncomplicated, the spacious bedrooms include Sky TV, power shower and tea and coffee-making facilities. Continental buffet breakfast is included in the room rate; other meals may be taken at the nearby family pub or restaurant. For further details and the Express by Holiday Inn phone number, consult the Hotel Groups pages.
ROOMS: 49 en suite **CONF:** Thtr 30 Class 24 Board 16

⌂ Premier Lodge (York City Centre)

20 Blossom St YO24 1AJ
☎ 0870 9906594 📠 0870 9906595
Premier Lodge offers modern, well-equipped, en suite accommodation suitable for both business and leisure travellers. Meals can be taken at the adjacent popular restaurant and bar, which is fully licensed. For further details, consult the Hotel Groups page.
ROOMS: 86 en suite (incl. bkfst) s £52; d £52

⌂ Travel Inn (York North West)

White Rose Close, York Business Park, Nether Poppleton YO26 6RL
☎ 08701 977280 📠 01904 787633
Dir: *on A1237 between A19 Thirsk road & A59 Harrogate road*

Travel Inn offers good-quality, value-for-money accommodation. Spacious, en suite rooms with bath and shower comfortably accommodate a family of up to two adults and two children (to age 15). The restaurant and bar offers a varied menu. For further details and the Travel Inn phone number, consult the Hotel Groups page.
ROOMS: 44 en suite s £44.95; d £44.95

⌂ Travelodge (York Central)

Travelodge

90 Piccadilly YO1 9NX
☎ 08700 850 950

Travelodge offers good quality, good value, modern accommodation. Ideal for families, the spacious, en suite bedrooms include remote-control TV, tea and coffee-making facilities, luxury beds and free morning newspaper. Meals can be taken at the nearby family restaurant. For further details and the Travelodge phone number, consult the Hotel Groups page.
ROOMS: 90 en suite s fr £42.95; d fr £42.95

YOXFORD, Suffolk

Map 13 TM36

★★75% ⊛⊛ Satis House

IP17 3EX
☎ 01728 668418 📠 01728 668640
e-mail: yblackmore@aol.com
Dir: *off A12 midway between Ipswich & Lowestoft. 9m E Alderburgh & Snape*

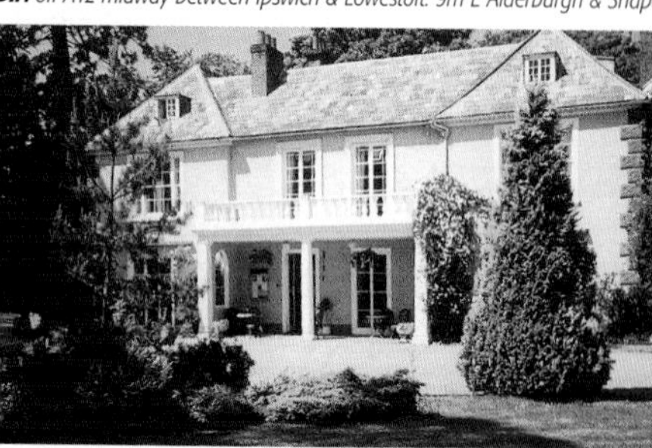

A charming, privately owned hotel set in landscaped grounds just off the A12. The property was once frequented by Charles Dickens, and the name Satis House features in *Great Expectations.* The spacious, individually decorated bedrooms are tastefully furnished and equipped with many thoughtful touches. Public areas include an elegant lounge, smart bar and a choice of dining rooms.
ROOMS: 8 en suite (1 GF) No smoking in 1 bedroom s £65-£75; d £85-£125 (incl. bkfst) **LB FACILITIES:** Tennis (hard) Sauna Jacuzzi **CONF:** Thtr 22 Class 20 Board 14 **PARKING:** 30 **NOTES:** No dogs No children 7yrs No smoking in restaurant Closed 26-27 Dec, 2 wks Jan RS 25 Dec **CARDS:**

Channel Islands

Directory of establishments in alphabetical order of location.

CHANNEL ISLANDS Map 24

GUERNSEY

CATEL Map 24

★★77% ❀ Hotel Hougue du Pommier
Hougue du Pommier Rd GY5 7FQ
☎ 01481 256531 📠 01481 256260
e-mail: hotel@houguedupommier.guernsey.net
Dir: *turn inland from Cobo Village (coast road). Turn left at first junct. Hotel 50yds on right*

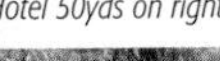

Retaining much of its original 18th-century character and charm, this hotel combines modern comforts with friendly yet efficient service. Bedrooms vary in size and standard, with exceptionally well appointed and spacious deluxe rooms. An informal eating option is available in the beamed bar and the restaurant offers a carefully cooked, fixed-price menu.
ROOMS: 37 en suite 6 annexe en suite (5 fmly) No smoking in all bedrooms s £35-£62; d £70-£104 (incl. bkfst) **LB FACILITIES:** STV Outdoor swimming (H) Golf 6 Sauna Croquet lawn Xmas
PARKING: 50 **NOTES:** No smoking in restaurant
CARDS:

See advert on this page

COBO Map 24

★★★75% ❀❀ Cobo Bay
Coast Rd GY5 7HB
☎ 01481 257102 📠 01481 254542
e-mail: reservations@cobobayhotel.com
Dir: *from airport turn right, follow road to W coast at L'Eree. Turn right onto coast road for 3m to Cobo Bay. Hotel on right*
This very popular hotel, overlooking Cobo Bay, offers modern, well-equipped and tastefully decorated accommodation. Bedrooms at the front have balconies and there is a secluded sun terrace. Guests can enjoy the candle-lit restaurant and the Chesterfield bar with its leather sofas and armchairs. The Cobo Suite is available for private parties. Hospitality is a strength here.
ROOMS: 36 en suite (4 fmly) s £44-£89; d £68-£118 (incl. bkfst) **LB FACILITIES:** STV Snooker Sauna Jacuzzi **CONF:** Thtr 50 Class 30 Board 20 Del from £77 **SERVICES:** Lift **PARKING:** 60 **NOTES:** No dogs (ex guide dogs) No smoking in restaurant Closed Jan-Feb
CARDS:

FERMAIN BAY Map 24

★★★69% *La Favorita*
GY4 6SD
☎ 01481 235666 📠 01481 235413
e-mail: admin@favorita.com
Dir: *at Fort Rd, Sausmarez Rd & Fermain Lane junct, take Fermain Lane signed to La Favorita Hotel & Fermain Bay*

Within walking distance of Fermain Bay, this charming hotel is on the side of a wooded valley, with glorious sea views in the distance. The generally spacious bedrooms are comfortably

continued on p694

FERMAIN BAY, continued

furnished. Public areas include a choice of lounges, bar restaurant and a coffee shop/brasserie, open all day. Indoor leisure facilities are also available.
ROOMS: 37 en suite (6 fmly) No smoking in all bedrooms **FACILITIES:** Indoor swimming (H) Sauna Jacuzzi ch fac **CONF:** Thtr 70 Class 30 Board 30 **SERVICES:** Lift **PARKING:** 40 **NOTES:** No dogs No smoking in restaurant Closed 20 Dec-1 Mar
CARDS:

★★★68% Le Chalet

GY4 6SD
☎ 01481 235716 01481 235718
e-mail: chalet@sarniahotels.com
Dir: *from airport left towards St Martins village. Right at filter to Sausmarez Rd, follow sign for Fermain Bay & Le Chalet Hotel*
Located in the wooded valley above Fermain Bay, this family-run hotel is popular, and many guests return on a regular basis. Bedrooms vary in size and are tastefully furnished and decorated. The public areas include a panelled lounge, bar area, restaurant and a stunning sun terrace adjoining the small indoor leisure facility.
ROOMS: 41 en suite (5 fmly) s £41-£52.50; d £64-£105 (incl. bkfst) **LB** **FACILITIES:** Indoor swimming (H) Sauna Solarium Jacuzzi **PARKING:** 35 **NOTES:** No smoking in restaurant Closed mid Oct-mid Apr **CARDS:**

FOREST — Map 24

★★71% Le Chene

Forest Rd GY8 0AH
☎ 01481 235566 01481 239456
e-mail: info@lechene.co.uk
Within easy reach of the coast, this Victorian manor house is well located for guests wishing to explore Guernsey's spectacular south coast. The building has been skilfully extended to house a range of well-equipped, modern bedrooms. There is a swimming pool, a cosy cellar bar and a varied range of enjoyable freshly cooked dishes at dinner.
ROOMS: 26 en suite (2 fmly) s £24-£33 (incl. bkfst) **LB** **FACILITIES:** Outdoor swimming (H) Xmas **PARKING:** 20 **NOTES:** No children 12yrs No smoking in restaurant **CARDS:**

PERELLE — Map 24

★★★73% ◎◎ *L'Atlantique*

Perelle Bay GY7 9NA
☎ 01481 264056 01481 263800
e-mail: enquiries@perellebay.com
Dir: *from airport, turn right and continue to sea. Turn right, follow coast road for 1.5m*
This modern seaside hotel offers spectacular views of the sea and often, memorable sunsets. Bedrooms vary, those with sea views have balconies, and there are suites suitable for families. L'Atlantique Restaurant has an enviable reputation on the island, and the Victorian bar offers a less formal dining option.
ROOMS: 23 rms (21 en suite) (4 fmly) No smoking in 12 bedrooms **FACILITIES:** STV Outdoor swimming (H) Tariff prices include car hire **PARKING:** 80 **NOTES:** No dogs (ex guide dogs) No smoking in restaurant Closed Nov-Feb **CARDS:**

Late for dinner?
Quality Standards mean that last orders for dinner vary according to star rating and should be no earlier than:
★★ 7.00pm ★★★ 8.00pm ★★★★ 9.00pm
★★★★★ 10.00pm

ST MARTIN — Map 24

★★★75% ◎ La Barbarie

Saints Rd, Saints Bay GY4 6ES
☎ 01481 235217 01481 235208
e-mail: barbarie@guernsey.net
This former priory dates back to the 17th century and retains much of its charm and style. Staff are very friendly and attentive, and together with the modern facilities guests are assured of a relaxing stay. Menus provide excellent choices, and fresh, local ingredients form the basis of the interesting dishes offered in the attractive restaurant and bar.
ROOMS: 23 en suite (4 fmly) (8 GF) No smoking in all bedrooms s £29-£57; d £58-£86 (incl. bkfst) **LB** **FACILITIES:** Outdoor swimming (H) **PARKING:** 50 **NOTES:** No dogs Closed 3 Nov- 28 Feb
CARDS:

★★★71% Bella Luce Hotel & Restaurant

La Fosse GY4 6EB
☎ 01481 238764 01481 239561
e-mail: info@bellalucehotel.guernsey.net
Dir: *from airport, turn left to St Martin. At 3rd set of lights continue 30yds, turn right, straight on to hotel*
This hotel dates back to the 12th century and much of its original charm and character remains. Located in an attractive area and set amidst well-tended gardens, this is a tranquil setting. Bedrooms are comfortable and individually styled and public rooms are bright, comfortable and tastefully decorated. Local produce features on the bar menu and also in the more formal dining room.
ROOMS: 31 en suite (5 fmly) s £35-£55; d £70-£110 (incl. bkfst) **LB** **FACILITIES:** STV Outdoor swimming (H) Sauna Solarium Gym equipment is available Xmas **PARKING:** 60 **NOTES:** No smoking in restaurant **CARDS:**

See advert on opposite page

★★★70% ◎ Hotel Jerbourg

Jerbourg Point GY4 6BJ
☎ 01481 238826 01481 238238
e-mail: hoteljerbourg@aol.com
Dir: *from airport turn left and follow road to St Martin village, right onto filter road, straight on at lights, hotel at end of road on right*
Situated at the end of a quiet lane, this hotel boasts excellent sea views, from its cliff-top location. The public areas are extensive and smartly appointed and include an extensive bar/lounge and bright conservatory-style restaurant. In addition to the fairly extensive carte, a daily changing fixed-price menu is available. Bedrooms are all well presented and comfortable, the newer luxury Bay rooms being generally more spacious.
ROOMS: 32 en suite (4 fmly) (5 GF) No smoking in all bedrooms s £35-£55; d £60-£100 (incl. bkfst) **LB** **FACILITIES:** STV Outdoor swimming (H) Xmas **PARKING:** 50 **NOTES:** No dogs (ex guide dogs)
CARDS:

★★★69% Green Acres

Les Hubits GY4 6LS
☎ 01481 235711 01481 235978
e-mail: greenacres@guernsey.net
Dir: *from airport, take road to St Martin. Turn off road leading to parish church, continue to hotel*
Quietly located in a leafy lane of St Martin, this pleasant hotel is ideal as a base for a relaxing break. Bedrooms are comfortable and well equipped, and staff are friendly and attentive. The public areas boast a stylish lounge, which opens out on to the terrace pool area. Cuisine offers a choice of menus and dining areas.
ROOMS: 43 en suite (3 fmly) **FACILITIES:** Outdoor swimming (H) **CONF:** Thtr 60 Class 35 Board 25 Del from £70 **PARKING:** 75 **NOTES:** No dogs (ex guide dogs) No smoking in restaurant
CARDS:

★★★69% Hotel Bon Port
Moulin Huet Bay GY4 6EW
☎ 01481 239249 📠 01481 239596
e-mail: mail@bonport.com
Dir: *from airport turn left into St Martins village, at final lights turn right, follow signs*
From its peaceful cliff-top location, this well maintained hotel boasts spectacular views over Saints Bay. The comfortable, well-equipped bedrooms vary in size and some have sea-facing balconies. In addition to the spacious lounge, there is a cosy bar, adjoining sun terrace and pleasant grounds with a 9-hole golf course. Courteous staff serve an imaginative range of international dishes.
ROOMS: 18 en suite (2 fmly) (1 GF) No smoking in 6 bedrooms s £45-£115; d £60-£99 (incl. bkfst) **LB** **FACILITIES:** Outdoor swimming (H) Golf 9 Sauna Gym Xmas **CONF:** Del from £60 **PARKING:** 40
NOTES: No smoking in restaurant Closed 2 Jan-13 Feb
CARDS:

★★★69% La Trelade
Forest Rd GY4 6UB
☎ 01481 235454 📠 01481 237855
e-mail: latrelade@guernsey.net
Dir: *3m from St Peter Port, 1m from airport*
Having undergone extensive refurbishment, this hotel now offers a stylish and versatile range of public areas and a very impressive leisure suite. Located close to the airport, La Trelade is an ideal base from which to explore the island, or equally suitable for business guests. Bedrooms are tastefully decorated and equipped with modern comforts.
ROOMS: 45 en suite (3 fmly) s £40-£72; d £70-£116 (incl. bkfst) **LB** **FACILITIES:** STV Indoor swimming (H) Sauna Gym **CONF:** Thtr 120 Class 48 Board 40 Del from £65 **SERVICES:** Lift **PARKING:** 80
NOTES: No smoking in restaurant **CARDS:**
See advert on this page

★★★68% La Villette
GY4 6QG
☎ 01481 235292 📠 01481 237699
e-mail: reservations@lavillettehotel.co.uk
Dir: *turn left out of airport. Follow road past La Trelade Hotel. Take next right, hotel on left*
Set in spacious grounds, this peacefully located, family-run hotel has a friendly atmosphere. The well-equipped, refurbished bedrooms are spacious and comfortable. Live music is a regular feature in the large bar, while in the separate restaurant a fixed-price menu is provided. Hotel residents have use of the excellent indoor leisure facilities.
ROOMS: 37 en suite (6 fmly) No smoking in all bedrooms s £36-£49; d £62-£86 (incl. bkfst) **LB** **FACILITIES:** Indoor swimming (H) Outdoor swimming (H) Solarium Gym Jacuzzi Steam room Petanque Leisure suite Beauty salon Xmas **PARKING:** 50 **NOTES:** No dogs No smoking in restaurant **CARDS:**

★★★67% Idlerocks
Jerbourg Point GY4 6BJ
☎ 01481 237711 📠 01481 235592
e-mail: info@idlerocks.com
Dir: *from airport, turn left at junct. Through 2 sets of lights, at filter turn right. At 3rd lights straight over, follow road for 1.5m, hotel on left*
Fine sea views of Sark and Herm Islands towards France can be enjoyed from this pleasant, family-run hotel. Bedrooms, many with sea views, are spacious and individually decorated. There are pleasant terraced gardens and a cosy lounge where guests can
continued on p696

ST MARTIN, continued

relax. A choice of dining options is provided in Admirals Restaurant or the informal Raffles Bistro.
ROOMS: 28 en suite (4 fmly) No smoking in 11 bedrooms s £33-£110; d £37-£121 (incl. bkfst) **LB** **FACILITIES:** STV Outdoor swimming (H) Covered swimming pool Xmas **CONF:** Thtr 100 Class 50 Board 30 Del from £55 **PARKING:** 100 **NOTES:** No smoking in restaurant
CARDS:

★★74% Hotel La Michele

Les Hubits GY4 6NB
☎ 01481 238065 01481 239492
e-mail: info@lamichelehotel.com
Dir: *approx 1.5m from St Peter Port*
Family run, this hotel, in a quiet country lane, provides a friendly and attentive environment and many guests return on a regular basis to enjoy this quiet and relaxing location. Bedrooms are particularly well equipped and comfortable. Public areas include a conservatory and cosy bar, and guests can relax in the well-tended gardens around the pool.
ROOMS: 16 en suite (3 fmly) (6 GF) s £38-£50; d £76-£100 (incl. bkfst & dinner) **LB** **FACILITIES:** Outdoor swimming (H) **PARKING:** 16 **NOTES:** No dogs (ex guide dogs) No children 10yrs No smoking in restaurant Closed Nov-Mar **CARDS:**

★★66% *Carlton*

Les Caches, Forest Rd GY4 6PR
☎ 01481 235678 01481 236590
e-mail: carltonguernsey@netlineuk.net
Dir: *on road from airport to St Peter Port*

Conveniently located within St Martin's Parish, this hotel is within minutes of many of the island's superb cliff walks. The public areas are smart and inviting, particularly the swimming pool and health centre. In addition to the Fox and Hounds traditional pub, there is a separate coffee lounge where snacks are available.
ROOMS: 41 en suite 2 annexe en suite (8 fmly) **FACILITIES:** Indoor swimming (H) Snooker Sauna Gym entertainment **CONF:** Thtr 150 Class 100 Board 30 **PARKING:** 40 **NOTES:** No dogs (ex guide dogs) No smoking in restaurant Closed Nov-Etr wknd RS groups only in winter
CARDS:

See advert on opposite page

ST PETER PORT

Map 24

★★★★71% Old Government House Hotel

Ann's Place GY1 4AZ
☎ 01481 724921 01481 724429
e-mail: ogh@guernsey.net
Dir: *hotel in centre of St Peter Port*
Appointed to a very high standard, the affectionately known OGH is one of the island's leading hotels. Bedrooms are comfortable and offer high quality accommodation. The restaurant overlooks the town and neighbouring islands, and offers fine dining while snacks are available in the Centenary bar. The varied leisure facilities entitled "Beauty and The East" are well worth a visit.
ROOMS: 68 en suite (3 fmly) (1 GF) No smoking in 30 bedrooms s £85-£95; d £95-£125 (incl. bkfst) **LB** **FACILITIES:** **Spa** STV Outdoor swimming (H) Sauna Solarium Gym Jacuzzi Xmas **CONF:** BC Thtr 300 Class 180 Board 90 Del from £112.50 **SERVICES:** Lift **PARKING:** 24 **NOTES:** No dogs (ex guide dogs) **CARDS:**

★★★★66% St Pierre Park

Rohais GY1 1FD
☎ 01481 728282 01481 712041
e-mail: info@stpierreparkhotel.com
Dir: *10mins from airport. From harbour straight over rdbt, up hill through 3 sets of lights. Right at filter and continue to lights. Straight ahead, hotel 100mtrs on left*

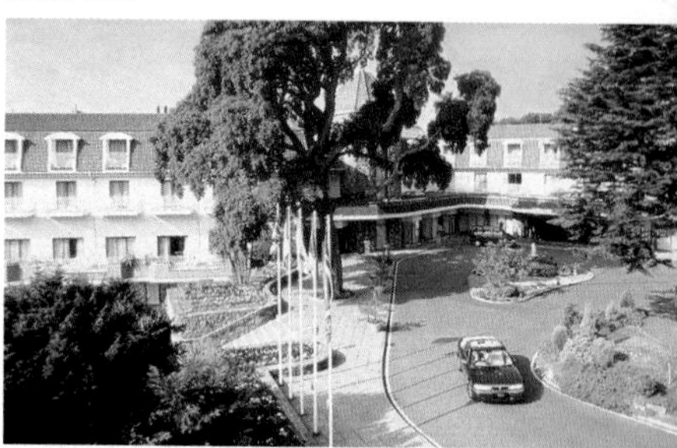

Peacefully located in 45 acres of gardens and grounds on the outskirts of St Peter Port, this attractive hotel features its own golf course. Bedrooms include many overlooking the pleasant grounds and all have either balcony or terrace. Guests have a choice of two dining options. The lounge bar opens onto a spacious terrace, which overlooks an elegant water feature.
ROOMS: 131 en suite (4 fmly) No smoking in 17 bedrooms
FACILITIES: STV Indoor swimming (H) Golf 9 Tennis (hard) Snooker Sauna Solarium Gym Croquet lawn Putting green Jacuzzi Bird watching, Childrens playground, Crazy golf Xmas **CONF:** Thtr 300 Class 120 Board 30 **SERVICES:** Lift **PARKING:** 150 **NOTES:** No dogs (ex guide dogs)
CARDS:

★★★73% La Fregate

Les Cotils GY1 1UT
☎ 01481 724624 01481 720443
e-mail: c.sharp@lafregatehotel.com
Ask for directions to this charming small hotel, which enjoys splendid views over the town and harbour from its elevated position. Bedrooms are comfortably furnished and well-equipped; many have private balconies. The restaurant is popular with both residents and locals for its carefully cooked meals and formal yet efficient service.
ROOMS: 13 en suite s £67; d £80-£165 (incl. bkfst) **LB** **CONF:** Thtr 36 Class 24 Board 18 **PARKING:** 25 **NOTES:** No dogs
CARDS:

★★★73% Hotel de Havelet

Best Western

Havelet GY1 1BA
☎ 01481 722199 01481 714057
e-mail: havelet@sarniahotels.com
Dir: *from airport follow signs for St Peter Port through St. Martins. At bottom of 'Val de Terres' hill turn left into Havelet*
This extended Georgian hotel looks over the harbour to Castle Cornet. Many of the well-equipped bedrooms are set around a

continued

pretty colonial-style courtyard. Day rooms in the original building have period elegance; the restaurant and bar are on the other side of the car park in converted stables.
ROOMS: 34 en suite (4 fmly) No smoking in 8 bedrooms s £47-£63.50; d £80-£127 (incl. bkfst) **LB FACILITIES:** STV Indoor swimming (H) Sauna Jacuzzi Xmas **CONF:** Thtr 40 Class 24 Board 26 **PARKING:** 40 **NOTES:** No dogs (ex guide dogs) **CARDS:**

★★★70% The Duke of Richmond

Cambridge Park GY1 1UY
☎ 01481 726221 01481 728945
e-mail: duke@guernsey.net
Dir: *hotel on corner of Cambridge Park Rd and L'Hyvreuse Ave, opposite leisure centre*

Peacefully located in a predominantly residential area overlooking Cambridge Park, this hotel has comfortable, well-appointed bedrooms that vary in size. Public areas include a spacious lounge, a terrace and the unique Sausmarez Bar, with its nautical theme. The smartly uniformed team of staff provide professional standards of service.
ROOMS: 75 en suite (16 fmly) No smoking in 35 bedrooms s £57.50-£140; d £70-£150 (incl. bkfst) **LB FACILITIES:** STV Outdoor swimming (H) Leisure centre close to hotel Xmas **CONF:** BC Thtr 150 Class 50 Board 36 **SERVICES:** Lift **PARKING:** 4 **CARDS:**

★★★70% Moore's

Pollet GY1 1WH
☎ 01481 724452 01481 714037
e-mail: moores@sarniahotels.com
Dir: *left at airport, follow signs to St Peter Port, Fort Road to seafront, straight on, turn right before rdbt, continue to hotel*

Located in the very heart of St Peter Port, the hotel dates back in parts from the 18th century. The comfortably appointed bedrooms vary in size and are priced accordingly. Attractive public areas include an Austrian patisserie, conservatory restaurant, library bar, health suite and carvery. Service is both attentive and friendly.
ROOMS: 46 en suite 3 annexe en suite (8 fmly) No smoking in 12 bedrooms **FACILITIES:** STV Sauna Solarium Gym Jacuzzi Xmas **CONF:** Thtr 40 Class 20 Board 18 **SERVICES:** Lift **NOTES:** No dogs (ex guide dogs) **CARDS:**

★★69% Sunnycroft

5 Constitution Steps GY1 2PN
☎ 01481 723008 01481 712225
e-mail: sunnycroft@accom.guernseyci.com
Dir: *in centre of town, past Salvation Army Building in Clifton*

This welcoming, small hotel has glorious views of the neighbouring islands of Herm, Jethou and Sark. Many of the well-equipped bedrooms have the benefit of balconies. Public
continued

rooms include a bar/lounge, a sitting room, a reading room, a pleasant garden and an attractive dining room.
ROOMS: 13 en suite (7 GF) s £30.50-£36; d £61-£72 (incl. bkfst) **FACILITIES:** STV **NOTES:** No dogs (ex guide dogs) No smoking in restaurant **CARDS:**

★★63% Duke of Normandie

Lefebvre St GY1 2JP
☎ 01481 721431 01481 711763
e-mail: dukeofnormandie@cwgsy.net
Dir: *from harbour rdbt St Julians Ave, 3rd left into Anns Place, continue to right, up hill, then left into Lefebvre St, archway entrance on right*

Dating back to the 18th century, this modernised hotel is perfectly located just a stroll from the harbour and high street. Well-equipped accommodation is set around a courtyard, which also provides guest parking. Public areas include the busy bar, now restored with beams, a varied menu and an open fireplace.
ROOMS: 20 en suite 17 annexe en suite (1 fmly) s £33-£44; d £66-£88 (incl. bkfst) **LB FACILITIES:** STV Xmas **CONF:** BC **PARKING:** 15 **NOTES:** No dogs (ex guide dogs) No smoking in restaurant **CARDS:**

VALE

Map 24

★★★63% Peninsula

Les Dicqs GY6 8JP
☎ 01481 248400 01481 248706
e-mail: peninsula@guernsey.net
Dir: *Coast Rd, Grand Havre Bay*

Adjacent to a sandy beach and set in five acres of grounds, this modern hotel provides comfortable accommodation. Bedrooms have additional sofa beds to suit families and good workspace for
continued on p698

V

VALE, continued

the business traveller. Both fixed-price and carte menus are served in the restaurant, or guests may eat more informally in the bar.
ROOMS: 99 en suite (99 fmly) No smoking in 18 bedrooms s £51-£65; d £82-£110 (incl. bkfst) **LB FACILITIES:** STV Outdoor swimming (H) Croquet lawn Putting green Petanque Playground entertainment Xmas **CONF:** Thtr 250 Class 140 Board 105 Del from £93 **SERVICES:** Lift **PARKING:** 120 **NOTES:** No smoking in restaurant
CARDS:

HERM

Map 24

★★75% White House

GY1 3HR
☎ 01481 722159 01481 710066
e-mail: hotel@herm-island.com
Dir: *close to harbour*

Enjoying a unique island setting, this attractive hotel is just a twenty minute boat trip from Guernsey. Set in well-tended gardens, the hotel offers neatly decorated bedrooms, located in either the main house or adjacent cottages; the majority of rooms benefit from sea views. Guests can relax in one of several comfortable lounges, enjoy a drink in one of two bars and choose from the imaginative and ambitious dishes served in the Conservatory Restaurant or more informally from the Captain's Table menu in the Ship Inn.
ROOMS: 17 en suite 23 annexe en suite (12 fmly) s £75-£107; d £150-£182 (incl. bkfst & dinner) **LB FACILITIES:** no TV in bdrms Outdoor swimming (H) Tennis (hard) Croquet lawn Fishing trips, Yacht & Motor boat charters ch fac **CONF:** Board 10 Del from £100 **NOTES:** No dogs (ex guide dogs) No smoking in restaurant Closed 6 Oct-3 Apr
CARDS:

JERSEY

Map 24

GOREY

Map 24

★★★68% Old Court House

JE3 9FS
☎ 01534 854444 01534 853587
e-mail: ochhotel@itl.net
Situated on the east of the island, a short walk from the beach, this long established hotel continues to have a loyal following for its relaxed atmosphere and friendly staff. Bedrooms are of similar standard throughout and some have balconies overlooking the gardens. Spacious public areas include a restaurant, a large bar with a dance floor and a comfortable, quiet lounge.
ROOMS: 58 en suite (4 fmly) (9 GF) s £48-£69; d £96-£150 (incl. bkfst & dinner) **FACILITIES:** STV Outdoor swimming (H) Sauna entertainment **SERVICES:** Lift **PARKING:** 40 **NOTES:** Closed Nov-Mar
CARDS:

★★★67% *The Moorings*

Gorey Pier JE3 6EW
☎ 01534 853633 01534 857618
e-mail: reservations@themooringshotel.com
Dir: *at foot of Mont Orgueil Castle*
Enjoying an enviable position by the harbour, the heart of this hotel is the restaurant, where a wide choice of menus is offered. Other public areas include two bars and a comfortable first-floor residents' lounge. Bedrooms at the front have a fine view of the harbour; three rooms have access to a balcony. A small sun terrace at the back of the hotel is also available for guests.
ROOMS: 15 en suite **FACILITIES:** STV **CONF:** Thtr 20 Class 20 Board 20 **CARDS:**

ROZEL

Map 2

Top 200 - Hotel

★★★ Château la Chaire

Rozel Bay JE3 6AJ
☎ 01534 863354 01534 865137
e-mail: res@chateau-la-chaire.co.uk
Dir: *from St Helier on B38 turn left in village by the Rozel Bay Inn, hotel 100yds on right*
Built as a gentleman's residence in 1843, Château La Chaire is a haven of peace and tranquillity, set within a secluded wooded valley. Picturesque Rozel harbour is within easy walking distance and the house is surrounded by terraced gardens. There is a wonderful atmosphere here and helpful staff ensure high standards of guest care. Imaginative menus, making best use of local produce, are served in the oak-panelled dining room. Bedrooms are purposely varied, with a range of differing sizes and styles available.
ROOMS: 14 en suite (1 fmly) s £143-£176; d £165-£198 (incl. bkfst) **LB FACILITIES:** STV Xmas **CONF:** Board 20 Del £145 **PARKING:** 30 **NOTES:** No dogs (ex guide dogs) No children 7yrs
CARDS:

See advert on opposite page

ST AUBIN

Map 24

★★★73% Somerville

Mont du Boulevard JE3 8AD

☎ 01534 741226 01534 746621

e-mail: somerville@dolanhotels.com

Dir: *from village, follow harbour then take Mont du Boulevard and 2nd right bend*

Enjoying spectacular views of St Aubin's Bay, this friendly, long established hotel is popular with both leisure and business guests. Bedrooms vary in style with a number of superior rooms offering higher levels of luxury and wonderful views. Public areas are smartly presented and include a spacious bar lounge and elegant dining room, both of which take full advantage of the hotel's enviable position.

ROOMS: 59 en suite (7 fmly) (4 GF) **FACILITIES:** STV Outdoor swimming (H) entertainment **CONF:** Thtr 40 Class 25 Board 30 **SERVICES:** Lift **PARKING:** 26 **NOTES:** No dogs No children 4yrs No smoking in restaurant **CARDS:**

See advert on this page

ST BRELADE Map 24

Top 200 - Hotel

★★★★ ◎◎ **The Atlantic**

Le Mont de la Pulente JE3 8HE
☎ 01534 744101 📠 01534 744102
e-mail: info@theatlantichotel.com
Dir: *Take road to Petit Port, turn right into Rue de la Sergente & right again, hotel signed*

Adjoining the manicured fairways of La Moye championship golf course, The Atlantic Hotel enjoys a peaceful setting with breathtaking views over St Ouen's Bay. Stylish bedrooms look out over golf course or sea and offer a blend of high quality and reassuring comfort. An air of understated luxury is apparent throughout, with attentive service which achieves the perfect balance of friendliness and professionalism. Lunch and drinks are available around the pool or on the terrace, whilst award-winning cuisine awaits at dinner.

ROOMS: 50 en suite (8 GF) s £140-£170; d £185-£265 (incl. bkfst) **LB FACILITIES:** STV Indoor swimming (H) Outdoor swimming (H) Tennis (hard) Sauna Solarium Gym Jacuzzi Xmas **CONF:** Thtr 60 Class 40 Board 20 Del from £175 **SERVICES:** Lift **PARKING:** 60 **NOTES:** No dogs (ex guide dogs) No smoking in restaurant Closed 5 Jan-5 Feb Civ Wed 60 **CARDS:**

★★★★73% ◎◎ **Hotel L'Horizon**

St Brelade's Bay JE3 8EF
☎ 01534 743101 📠 01534 746269
e-mail: hotellhorizon@jerseymail.co.uk
Dir: *3m from airport. 6m from harbour*

HandPICKED

The combination of a truly wonderful setting on the golden sands of St Brelade's Bay, a relaxed atmosphere and excellent facilities has to be a winning formula. The best of the bedrooms enjoy the south facing views over the bay but all have been stylishly decorated and equipped with modern comforts and many thoughtful touches. Public areas are spacious and bright and include a leisure club which has been extended and upgraded. A choice of eating options includes the more formal Grill and a smart new brasserie.

ROOMS: 107 en suite (7 fmly) (15 GF) s £65-£105; d £110-£155 (incl. bkfst) **LB FACILITIES:** STV Indoor swimming (H) Sauna Gym Jacuzzi Windsurfing Water skiing entertainment Xmas **CONF:** Thtr 250 Class 100 Board 50 Del from £115 **SERVICES:** Lift **PARKING:** 125 **NOTES:** No dogs (ex guide dogs) Civ Wed 230

CARDS:

★★★★71% ◎◎ **Hotel La Place**

Route du Coin, La Haule JE3 8BT
☎ 01534 744261 📠 01534 745164
e-mail: hotlaplace@aol.com
Dir: *off main St Helier/St Aubin coast road at La Haule Manor (B25). Up hill, 2nd left (to Redhouses), 1st right. Hotel 100mtrs on right*

Developed around a 17th-century farmhouse, this friendly hotel is well placed for exploration of the island. A range of bedroom types are provided, some with private patios and direct access to the sheltered pool area. The stylish cocktail bar is a popular venue for pre-dinner drinks and a more traditional lounge is also available. An interesting menu is offered, making good use of local produce.

ROOMS: 42 en suite (1 fmly) No smoking in 25 bedrooms s £70-£116; d £80-£180 (incl. bkfst) **LB FACILITIES:** STV Outdoor swimming (H) Sauna Discount at Les Ormes Country Club, including golf, gym & indoor tennis ch fac Xmas **CONF:** Thtr 120 Class 40 Board 40 Del from £110 **PARKING:** 100 **NOTES:** No smoking in restaurant Civ Wed 100

CARDS:

See advert on opposite page

★★★★70% **St Brelade's Bay**

JE3 8EF
☎ 01534 746141 📠 01534 747278
e-mail: info@stbreladesbayhotel.com
Dir: *SW corner of the island*

This family hotel overlooking St Brelade's Bay has many loyal guests and members of staff. The attractive gardens and grounds are ablaze with colour during summer. In addition to easy beach access, there is a choice of pools. Most bedrooms have king-size

continued

beds, and many have a children's room within the unit. Morning and afternoon tea are included in the tariff.
ROOMS: 72 en suite (50 fmly) s £70-£105; d £100-£120 (incl. bkfst) **FACILITIES:** STV Outdoor swimming (H) Tennis (hard & grass) Snooker Sauna Gym Croquet lawn Putting green Petanque, Mini-gym, Games room, Table tennis, Outdoor pool supervised entertainment **CONF:** Thtr 20 Board 12 Del from £130 **SERVICES:** Lift **PARKING:** 60 **NOTES:** No dogs (ex guide dogs) No smoking in restaurant Closed 8 Oct-27 Apr **CARDS:**

★★★70% Golden Sands

St Brelade's Bay JE3 8EF
☎ 01534 741241 01534 499366
e-mail: goldensands@dolanhotels.com
Dir: *follow signs to St Brelade's Bay. Hotel on coast side of road*

With direct access to the beach, this popular holiday hotel is centrally located overlooking the wonderful sandy expanse of St Brelade's Bay. Fortunately many of the comfortable bedrooms are seafacing with balconies, thus many hours can be spent relaxing, breathing in the fresh air and looking out across the sands to the sea beyond! Public areas include a lounge, bar and restaurant, all of which look out over the bay.
ROOMS: 62 en suite (5 fmly) s £44-£60; d £70-£136 (incl. bkfst) **FACILITIES:** STV Childrens play room entertainment ch fac **SERVICES:** Lift **NOTES:** No dogs No smoking in restaurant Closed Nov-mid Apr **CARDS:**

See advert on page 699

★★71% *Beau Rivage*

St Brelade's Bay JE3 8EF
☎ 01534 745983 01534 747127
e-mail: beaurivage@jerseyweb.demon.co.uk
Dir: *seaward side of coast rd in centre of St Brelades Bay, 1.5m S of airport*
With direct access on to one of Jersey's most popular beaches, this hotel welcomes both residents and non-residents to its bar and terrace. The majority of the well-equipped bedrooms have wonderful sea views, and some have balconies. Residents have a choice of lounges, plus a sun deck, exclusively for their use. A short, set menu featuring English and Continental cuisine is served each evening.
ROOMS: 27 en suite (9 fmly) No smoking in 1 bedroom
FACILITIES: STV Sunbathing terrace Video games entertainment ch fac
SERVICES: Lift **PARKING:** 16 **NOTES:** No dogs No smoking in restaurant Closed Nov-Mar **CARDS:**

> Late for dinner?
> Quality Standards mean that last orders for dinner vary according to star rating and should be no earlier than:
> ★★ 7.00pm ★★★ 8.00pm ★★★★ 9.00pm
> ★★★★★ 10.00pm

ST HELIER

Map 24

★★★★69% De Vere Grand Jersey

The Esplanade JE4 8WD
DE VERE HOTELS
☎ 01534 722301 01534 737815
e-mail: grand.jersey@devere-hotels.com

An imposing Victorian building with the bustling streets to the rear and pleasant views across St Aubin's Bay to the front. Guests can choose to dine in the Regency Restaurant with views of Elizabeth Castle or in the more formal, Victoria Restaurant. A full range of indoor leisure is available.
ROOMS: 118 en suite (7 GF) No smoking in 22 bedrooms s fr £135; d fr £150 (incl. bkfst) **LB FACILITIES: Spa** STV Indoor swimming (H) Snooker Sauna Solarium Gym Jacuzzi Beauty therapy, Hairdressing, Swimming pool supervised entertainment Xmas **CONF:** Thtr 250 Class 120 Board 80 Del from £140 **SERVICES:** Lift **PARKING:** 27 **NOTES:** No dogs (ex guide dogs) No smoking in restaurant Civ Wed **CARDS:**

ST HELIER, continued

★★★70% Pomme d'Or

Liberation Square JE1 3UF
☎ 01534 880110 🖹 01534 737781
e-mail: enquiries@pommedorhotel.com
Dir: *opposite harbour*

This historic hotel overlooks Liberation Square and the marina and offers comfortably furnished, well-equipped bedrooms. Popular with commercial guests, a range of conference facilities and meeting rooms are available. Dining options include the traditional fine dining of the 'Petite Pomme', the smart carvery restaurant or the informal coffee shop.
ROOMS: 142 en suite (3 fmly) No smoking in 72 bedrooms s £70-£161; d £50-£111 (incl. bkfst) **LB** **FACILITIES:** STV Use of Aquadome at Merton Hotel Xmas **CONF:** Thtr 220 Class 100 Board 50 Del from £125 **SERVICES:** Lift **NOTES:** No dogs (ex guide dogs)
CARDS:

★★★69% Royal Yacht

The Weighbridge JE2 3NF
☎ 01534 720511 🖹 01534 767729
e-mail: theroyalyacht@mail.com
Dir: *in town centre, opp the Marina and harbour, 0.5m from beach*
Overlooking the marina and steam clock, the Royal Yacht is thought to be the oldest established hotel on the island. It has had considerable investment in recent years with bedrooms offering both comfort and quality; all are soundproofed and thoughtfully equipped. There is something for everyone in the choice of dining options, with the traditional grill room, bar carvery and the first-floor restaurant which has views over the harbour.
ROOMS: 45 en suite **FACILITIES:** STV entertainment Xmas **CONF:** Thtr 20 Class 20 Board 20 **SERVICES:** Lift **NOTES:** No dogs Civ Wed
CARDS:

★★★68% The Revere Hotel & Restaurants

Kensington Place JE2 3PA
☎ 01534 611111 🖹 01534 611116
e-mail: reservations@revere.co.uk
Dir: *follow signs to St Helier, 1st left after Grand Hotel, approx 150yds up road, hotel on right*
Situated on the west side of the town and convenient for the centre and harbourside, this hotel continues to be a popular destination. Originally dating back to the 17th century, the style here is engagingly different with bedrooms all individually decorated with a choice of no less than eight four-poster rooms. A stylish bistro provides one of the three dining options.
ROOMS: 58 en suite (4 fmly) (3 GF) No smoking in 14 bedrooms s £58-£87; d £76-£124 (incl. bkfst) **LB** **FACILITIES:** STV Outdoor swimming (H) entertainment Xmas **CONF:** BC Board 8 Del from £107 **NOTES:** No dogs (ex guide dogs) Civ Wed 60
CARDS:

★★★67% Apollo

St Saviours Rd JE2 4GJ
☎ 01534 725441 🖹 01534 722120
e-mail: huggler@psilink.co.je
Dir: *on St Saviours Road at its junct with La Motte Street*

Centrally located, just five minutes' walk from the town centre this popular hotel has a relaxed, informal atmosphere. Bedrooms are comfortably furnished and include useful extras. Many guests return regularly to enjoy the variety of leisure facilities which include an outdoor pool with water slide and indoor pool with separate jacuzzi. The elegant cocktail bar is an ideal place for a pre-dinner drink.
ROOMS: 85 en suite (5 fmly) s £68-£80; d £90-£115 (incl. bkfst) **LB** **FACILITIES:** Indoor swimming (H) Outdoor swimming (H) Sauna Solarium Gym Jacuzzi Xmas **CONF:** Thtr 150 Class 100 Board 80 **SERVICES:** Lift **PARKING:** 50 **NOTES:** No dogs (ex guide dogs)
CARDS:

★★★67% Royal

David Place JE2 4TD
☎ 01534 726521 🖹 01534 811046
e-mail: royal@bestwestern.co.uk

Best Western

Dir: *follow signs for Ring Rd, pass Queen Victoria rdbt keep left, left at lights, left into Piersons Rd. Follow one-way system to Cheapside, Rouge Bouillon, at A14 turn to Midvale Rd, hotel on left*
This long established hotel is located in the centre of town and is within easy walking distance of the business district and shops. It provides comfortable bedrooms and a range of public areas. Dining choices include the No 27 Bar and Brasserie and the Henry VII restaurant. The hotel also boasts extensive conference facilities.
ROOMS: 88 en suite (39 fmly) No smoking in 16 bedrooms s £76; d £123-£140 (incl. bkfst) **LB** **FACILITIES:** entertainment Xmas **CONF:** BC Thtr 400 Class 120 Board 80 Del £125 **SERVICES:** Lift **PARKING:** 15 **CARDS:**

> Popped the question?
> Hotels with Civ Wed in their entry are licensed for civil wedding ceremonies. Maximum numbers for the ceremony only are shown, e.g. Civ Wed 120

★★★64% Beaufort

Green St JE2 4UH
☎ 01534 732471 🖹 01534 720371
e-mail: huggler@psilink.co.je
Dir: *on Green Street, 5 mins walk from main shopping centre*
Within walking distance of the main business and shopping areas, the Beaufort is ideally located for both the business and leisure traveller. All bedrooms are spacious and have excellent facilities. Refurbishment of public areas has included the creation of

continued

S

Bohemia' a stylish bar and restaurant, whilst steam and sauna rooms are now available in addition to the indoor and outdoor pools.

ROOMS: 54 en suite (4 fmly) s £71-£79; d £96-£112 (incl. bkfst) **LB** **FACILITIES: Spa** Indoor swimming (H) Outdoor swimming (H) Sauna Jacuzzi Xmas **SERVICES:** Lift **PARKING:** 20 **NOTES:** No dogs (ex guide dogs) **CARDS:**

★★69% Uplands

St John's Rd JE2 3LE
☎ 01534 730151 🖹 01534 639899
e-mail: morfarmho@itl.net
Dir: *off main esplanade (A1) onto Pierson Rd by Grand Hotel, follow ring road for 200mtrs, 3rd on left into St Johns Rd, hotel in 0.5m*

Uplands Hotel is set in twelve acres of farmland just one mile from the centre of St Helier. Bedrooms are modern, spacious and comfortable; some overlook the swimming pool while others having country views. Twelve self-catering cottages are also available. Plenty of parking and spacious public areas add to the attraction of this friendly and popular hotel.
ROOMS: 43 en suite (3 fmly) s £31-£42.50; d £31-£42.50 (incl. bkfst) **FACILITIES:** STV Outdoor swimming (H) Xmas **PARKING:** 44 **NOTES:** No dogs (ex guide dogs) No smoking in restaurant **CARDS:**

ST LAWRENCE

Map 24

★★★71% Hotel Cristina

Mont Feland JE3 1JA
☎ 01534 758024 🖹 01534 758028
e-mail: cristina@dolanhotels.com
Dir: *turn off A10 onto Mont Felard, hotel on left*

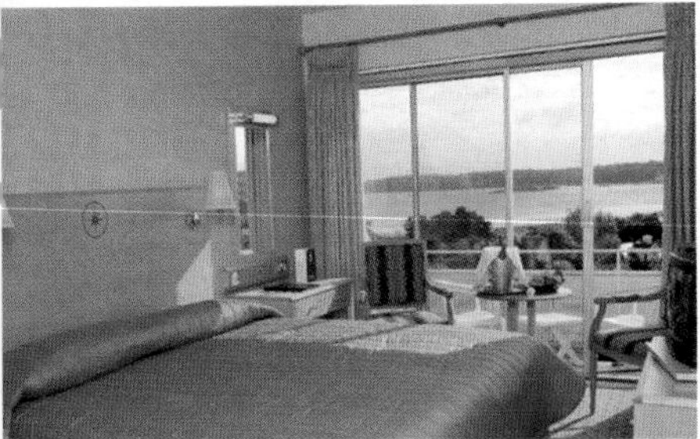

From its hillside location, this hotel has impressive views of the bay, which can be enjoyed from most of the hotel's stylish bedrooms. Public areas reflect the contemporary style which makes this a refreshingly different hotel, with the modern restaurant serving a range of fresh produce in a bistro-like atmosphere. The terrace is adorned with flowers and is a popular place to soak up the sun.
ROOMS: 62 en suite (3 fmly) s £51-£70; d £66-£136 (incl. bkfst) **LB** **FACILITIES:** STV Outdoor swimming (H) Off peak membership to Les Ormes Golf/Leisure Club entertainment **CONF:** Thtr 100 Class 70 **PARKING:** 80 **NOTES:** No dogs No children 4yrs No smoking in restaurant Closed Nov-Mar **CARDS:**

See advert on page 699

★★67% *Hotel White Heather*

Rue de Haut, Millbrook JE3 1JZ
☎ 01534 720978 🖹 01534 720968
Dir: *from A11 turn right at school, follow road, hotel on right*

Tucked away in a quiet residential area within walking distance of the beach and local amenities, this family-run hotel offers a warm and genuine welcome to all guests. Bedrooms are brightly decorated and most have the added bonus of balconies with sun beds. Public areas are similarly comfortable and well-presented.
ROOMS: 33 en suite (3 fmly) **FACILITIES:** STV Indoor swimming (H) **PARKING:** 11 **NOTES:** No dogs (ex guide dogs) No smoking in restaurant Closed Nov-Mar **CARDS:**

ST SAVIOUR

Map 24

Top 200 - Hotel

★★★★ ®®® Longueville Manor

JE2 7WF
☎ 01534 725501 🖹 01534 731613
e-mail: info@longuevillemanor.com
Dir: *A3 E from St Helier towards Gorey. Hotel 1m on left*

RELAIS & CHATEAUX

Dating back to the 13th century, there is something very special about Longueville, which explains why so many guests return here. It is set in 17 acres of grounds, including woodland walks, a spectacular rose garden and a lake. Bedrooms have great style and individuality, with fresh flowers, fine embroidered bed linen and plenty of extras. The committed team of staff create a welcoming atmosphere with every effort made to ensure a memorable stay and accomplished cuisine is a real delight.
ROOMS: 29 en suite 1 annexe en suite (7 GF) s £160-£180; d £200-£230 (incl. bkfst) **LB** **FACILITIES:** STV Outdoor swimming (H) Tennis (hard) Croquet lawn Xmas **CONF:** Thtr 45 Class 30 Board 30 Del £247 **SERVICES:** Lift **PARKING:** 40 **NOTES:** Civ Wed 30 **CARDS:**

Town House Hotel
Country House Hotel
Travel Accommodation

TRINITY

Map 24

★★★70% Water's Edge

Bouley Bay JE3 5AS
☎ 01534 862777 01534 863645
e-mail: mail@watersedgehotel.co.je

Set in the tranquil surroundings of Bouley Bay on Jersey's north coast, this hotel is exactly as the name implies and offers breathtaking views. Many of the bedrooms here have now been upgraded to offer high standards of quality and comfort. Dining options include the relaxed character of the adjoining Black Dog bar or the more formal award-winning restaurant.

ROOMS: 51 en suite (3 fmly) No smoking in 10 bedrooms s £40-£59; d £80-£118 (incl. bkfst) **LB FACILITIES:** Outdoor swimming (H) Sauna Solarium entertainment **CONF:** Thtr 30 Class 25 Board 20 Del from £86 **SERVICES:** Lift **PARKING:** 20 **NOTES:** No dogs No smoking in restaurant 17 Apr-10 Oct Civ Wed 100 **CARDS:**

★★★68% Highfield Country

Best Western

Route d'Ebenezer JE3 5DT
☎ 01534 862194 01534 865342
e-mail: reservations@highfieldjersey.com
Dir: *on A8 next to Ebenezer Chapel*

Located in the countryside in landscaped gardens, this family-friendly hotel offers comfortable bedrooms and a relaxed atmosphere. Public areas are light and attractively styled, with the conservatory a popular venue for pre-dinner drinks. Leisure facilities include an indoor pool and sauna, and an outdoor pool with waterslide. A varied menu is provided at dinner, and breakfast is a self-service buffet.

ROOMS: 38 en suite (32 fmly) (1 GF) s £52-£61; d £90-£108 (incl. bkfst) **FACILITIES:** Indoor swimming (H) Outdoor swimming Sauna Gym Petanque **SERVICES:** Lift **PARKING:** 41 **NOTES:** No dogs No smoking in restaurant Closed Dec-Mar
CARDS:

SARK

★★70% Dixcart Bay

Dixcart Valley GY9 0SD
☎ 01481 832015 01481 832164
e-mail: dixcart@itl.net
Dir: *10mins S of village, following signed footpath*

Offering a warm welcome, the Dixcart provides all the comforts o home. Bedrooms come in a variety of shapes and sizes; all are well equipped. Log fires burn, even in summer, two cosy lounges offer seclusion and the gardens beckon on a sunny day. Two eating options are available.

ROOMS: 15 en suite (5 fmly) (5 GF) s £37.50-£55; d £75-£110 (incl. bkfst) **FACILITIES:** Horse-drawn carriage tours available **CONF:** Board 2(**NOTES:** No smoking in restaurant Closed mid Oct-Etr
CARDS:

T

Isle of Man

Directory of establishments in alphabetical order of location.

AN, ISLE OF

Map 24

ASTLETOWN

Map 24 SC26

★★68% Castletown Golf Links

Best Western

rt Island IM9 1UA

01624 822201 01624 824633

mail: golflinks@manx.net

r: A1 S of airport, turn left then left again

ith the sea on three sides and adjoining a championship golf urse, this hotel has much to offer those who look for traditional, endly service in a relaxing environment. Bedrooms are modern d well equipped; ground-floor rooms and suites are available. onference facilities and proximity to the airport make it a popular usiness venue.

OOMS: 50 en suite (3 fmly) (8 GF) s £62.50-£70; d £92.50-£95 (incl. fst) **LB FACILITIES:** STV Indoor swimming (H) Golf 18 Snooker una Solarium Putting green Xmas **CONF:** Thtr 250 Class 50 Board 20 **RKING:** 200 **NOTES:** No smoking in restaurant **RDS:**

OUGLAS

Map 24 SC37

★★★72% Sefton

arris Promenade IM1 2RW

01624 645500 01624 676004

mail: info@seftonhotel.co.im

ir: 500yds from Ferry Dock on Douglas promenade

nis Victorian hotel has been sympathetically extended and pgraded over recent years. Many of the spacious and omfortably furnished bedrooms have balconies overlooking the trium water garden, whilst other boast sweeping views across the ay. A choice of comfortable lounges is available and freshly repared dishes are served in the informal Gallery restaurant.

OOMS: 100 en suite (2 fmly) No smoking in 36 bedrooms s £72-£87; £82-£94 (incl. bkfst) **LB FACILITIES:** STV Indoor swimming (H) auna Solarium Gym Jacuzzi Cycle hire, Steam room, Atrium water arden **CONF:** BC Thtr 120 Class 40 Board 20 **SERVICES:** Lift **ARKING:** 44 **NOTES:** No dogs (ex guide dogs) **ARDS:**

★★★★70% Mount Murray

Santon IM4 2HT

☎ 01624 661111 01624 611116

e-mail: hotel@mountmurray.com

***Dir:** 4m from Douglas towards airport, Hotel signposted at Santon*

This large, modern hotel and country club offers a wide range of sporting and leisure facilities, and a health and beauty salon. The attractively appointed public areas give a choice of bars and eating options. The spacious bedrooms are well equipped and many enjoy fine views over the 200-acre grounds and golf course. There is a very large function suite.

ROOMS: 90 en suite (4 fmly) No smoking in 12 bedrooms s £55-£110; d £75-£180 (incl. bkfst) **FACILITIES: Spa** STV Indoor swimming (H) Golf 18 Tennis (hard) Squash Sauna Solarium Gym Putting green Jacuzzi Bowling green, Driving range, Sports hall, Squash courts Xmas **CONF:** Thtr 300 Class 260 Board 100 Del from £114 **SERVICES:** Lift **PARKING:** 400 **NOTES:** No dogs (ex guide dogs) No smoking in restaurant **CARDS:**

★★★69% Welbeck Hotel

13/15 Mona Dr IM2 4LF

☎ 01624 675663 01624 661545

e-mail: mail@welbeck.com

***Dir:** at crossroads of Mona & Empress Drive off Central Promenade*

The Welbeck is a privately owned and personally run hotel. It offers guests a friendly welcome and a choice of attractive accommodation, ranging from well-equipped bedrooms to six newly constructed luxury apartments, each with its own lounge and small kitchen. Other facilities include two rooms for meetings and functions, plus a mini-gym and steam room. The hotel is located within easy reach of the seafront.

ROOMS: 27 en suite (7 fmly) s £48-£65 (incl. bkfst) **FACILITIES:** STV Gym Steam room **CONF:** Thtr 50 Class 30 Board 30 Del from £45 **SERVICES:** Lift **NOTES:** No dogs (ex guide dogs) Closed 19 Dec-5 Jan **CARDS:**

★★★68% *Empress*

Central Promenade IM2 4RA

☎ 01624 661155 01624 673554

e-mail: empresshotel@manx.net

The Empress Hotel is a large Victorian building on the central promenade, overlooking Douglas Bay. Well-equipped, modern bedrooms include suites, and rooms with sea views. A pianist entertains in the lounge bar most evenings. Other facilities

continued on p706

DOUGLAS, continued

available to guests include a lounge, a sun lounge and a brasserie-style restaurant.

Empress Hotel, Douglas

ROOMS: 102 en suite No smoking in 6 bedrooms **FACILITIES:** STV Indoor swimming (H) Sauna Solarium Gym Jacuzzi entertainment **CONF:** Thtr 200 Class 150 Board 50 **SERVICES:** Lift **NOTES:** No dogs (ex guide dogs) **CARDS:**

See advert on this page

★★★66% *Claremont*

18-19 Loch Promenade IM1 2LX
☎ 01624 698800 01624 698899
e-mail: claremont@sleepwellhotels.com

Standing in good position overlooking the bay and close to the ferry terminal, this modern well-furnished hotel offers very well equipped bedrooms. Some have large screen televisions and separate lounge areas. The public rooms are modern in style and service is attentive.

ROOMS: 28 en suite (15 fmly) **FACILITIES:** STV **CONF:** Thtr 80 Class 60 Board 30 **SERVICES:** Lift **NOTES:** No dogs (ex guide dogs) **CARDS:**

★★64% *Chesterhouse*

37-42 Loch Promenade IM1 2LY
☎ 01624 675511 01624 670966
e-mail: chesterhouse@sleepwellhotels.com

This large seafront hotel appeals to coach parties and individuals alike and provides practical accommodation, the larger executive rooms offering greater comfort as well as splendid views across the bay. The Old Bailey bar has plenty of interest for visitors and substantial meals are served in the airy restaurant.

ROOMS: 67 en suite (20 fmly) **CONF:** Thtr 120 Class 80 Board 40 **SERVICES:** Lift **NOTES:** No dogs (ex guide dogs) **CARDS:**

PEEL

Map 24 SC28

★★70% Ballacallin House

THE INDEPENDENTS

Dalby Village, Patrick IM5 3BT
☎ 01624 841100 01624 845055
e-mail: ballacallin@advsys.co.uk

Dir: *A27 Peel to Port Erin Rd at S end of Dalby Village*

This small, privately owned hotel situated in Dalby Village is personally run and offers well-equipped, modern accommodation of a very good standard. Bedrooms with four-posters and a two-bedroom suite are available. Some bedrooms enjoy sea views, as do the bright restaurant and the spacious lounge bar.

ROOMS: 10 en suite (1 fmly) No smoking in all bedrooms s £40-£50; d £70 (incl. bkfst) **LB** **FACILITIES:** Xmas **CONF:** Thtr 30 Class 24 Board 24 Del from £79.95 **PARKING:** 70 **NOTES:** No smoking in restaurant Closed 5-25 Jan **CARDS:**

PORT ERIN

Map 24 SC

★★★67% Ocean Castle

The Promenade IM9 6LH
☎ 01624 836399 01624 836537
e-mail: oceancastle@btinternet.com

The Ocean Castle is set overlooking the harbour, with spacious bedrooms enjoying views over the bay. The hotel offers a choice of restaurants at weekends, with a combination of local menus with a French twist. A large function room is ideal for conference guests as well those enjoying a family party.

ROOMS: 40 en suite (2 fmly) **FACILITIES:** STV Ballroom entertainmen **CONF:** Thtr 200 Class 150 Board 100 **SERVICES:** Lift **NOTES:** No smoking in restaurant Closed Nov - before Easter **CARDS:**

★★65% Falcon's Nest

The Promenade IM9 6AF
☎ 01624 834077 01624 835370
e-mail: falconsnest@enterprise.net

Dir: *follow coastal road, S from airport or ferry. Hotel on seafront, immediately after steam railway station*

Situated overlooking the bay and harbour, this Victorian hotel offers generally spacious bedrooms. There is a choice of bars, one of which attracts many locals, and of dining options also. Meals can be taken in the lounge bar or in the attractively decorated main restaurant.

ROOMS: 37 en suite (10 fmly) No smoking in 3 bedrooms s £25-£39.50 d £25-£39.50 (incl. bkfst) **LB** **FACILITIES:** STV **CONF:** Thtr 70 Class 70 Board 70 Del from £50 **PARKING:** 40 **CARDS:**

Hotel of the Year, Scotland

Lochgreen House
Troon, South Ayrshire

ABERDEEN, Aberdeen City Map 23 NJ90
See also Aberdeen Airport

A

★★★★78% The Marcliffe at Pitfodels
North Deeside Rd AB15 9YA
☎ 01224 861000 01224 868860
e-mail: enquiries@marcliffe.com
Dir: *turn off A90 onto A93 signed Braemar. 1m on right after turn at lights*

Set in attractive landscaped grounds west of the city, this impressive hotel presents a blend of styles backed by caring and attentive service. A split-level conservatory restaurant, terraces and courtyards all give a sense of the Mediterranean, whilst the elegant and sophisticated cocktail lounge is classical in style. Bedrooms are well-proportioned and thoughtfully equipped.
ROOMS: 40 en suite (2 fmly) (12 GF) No smoking in 12 bedrooms s £115-£175; d £130-£195 (incl. bkfst) **LB FACILITIES:** STV Snooker Croquet lawn Putting green Xmas **CONF:** BC Thtr 500 Class 300 Board 84 Del from £185 **SERVICES:** Lift **PARKING:** 220 **NOTES:** Civ Wed 400 **CARDS:**

★★★★74% Ardoe House
South Deeside Rd, Blairs AB12 5YP
☎ 01224 860600 01224 861283
e-mail: ardoe@macdonald-hotels.co.uk
Dir: *4m W of city off B9077*

MACDONALD HOTELS

From its elevated position on the banks of the River Dee, this baronial-style mansion commands excellent countryside views. Tastefully decorated bedrooms are located in the main house, or more modern extension. Public rooms include an impressive leisure club, cosy lounge and cocktail bar with no less than 180 different malt whiskies.
ROOMS: 117 en suite (4 fmly) No smoking in 86 bedrooms s £99-£160; d £109-£180 **LB FACILITIES:** STV Indoor swimming (H) Tennis (hard) Sauna Solarium Gym Jacuzzi Petanque, Swimming pool supervised Xmas **CONF:** Thtr 500 Class 200 Board 150 Del from £140 **SERVICES:** Lift **PARKING:** 250 **NOTES:** No smoking in restaurant Civ Wed 60 **CARDS:**

★★★★67% Aberdeen Patio
Beach Boulevard AB24 5EF
☎ 01224 633339 & 380000 01224 638833
e-mail: patioab@globalnet.co.uk
Dir: *from A90 follow signs for city centre, then for sea. On Beach Blvd, turn left at lights, hotel on right*

Popular with both business and leisure guests, this modern, purpose-built hotel is close to the seafront and its many attractions. Bedrooms come in two different styles with the spacious Premier Club rooms particularly appealing. The conservatory-style restaurant holds regular themed dining nights and there is also a striking Atrium bar.
ROOMS: 124 en suite (8 fmly) (10 GF) No smoking in 93 bedrooms s £43.50-£185; d £57-£185 (incl. bkfst) **LB FACILITIES:** STV Indoor swimming (H) Sauna Solarium Gym Jacuzzi Steam room, Treatment Room, Swimming pool supervised Xmas **CONF:** Thtr 150 Class 80 Boa 50 Del from £75 **SERVICES:** Lift **PARKING:** 196 **NOTES:** No smoking in restaurant **CARDS:**

★★★★67%
Copthorne Hotel Aberdeen
122 Huntly St AB10 1SU
☎ 01224 630404 01224 640573
e-mail: reservations.aberdeen@mill-cop.com
Dir: *W of city centre, off Union Street, up Rose Street, hotel 0.25m on rig on corner with Huntly Street*

COPTHORN

Set just away from the city centre this hotel offers friendly, attentive service. The smart bedrooms are well proportioned and guests will appreciate the added quality of the Connoisseur room Mac's bar provides a relaxed atmosphere in which to enjoy a dri or to dine informally, whilst Poachers Restaurant offers a comfortable fine dining experience.
ROOMS: 89 en suite (15 fmly) No smoking in 37 bedrooms **FACILITIES:** STV **CONF:** Thtr 200 Class 100 Board 70 Del from £146 **SERVICES:** Lift **PARKING:** 20 **NOTES:** RS 25-26 Dec Civ Wed 80 **CARDS:**

★★74% Atholl
 Kings Gate AB15 4YN
 01224 323505 🖹 01224 321555
mail: info@atholl-aberdeen.co.uk
r: in West End 400yds from Anderson Drive, the main ring road

high level of hospitality and guest care are features of this hotel, t in the suburbs within easy reach of central amenities and the ng road. The smart modern bedrooms include ADSL Internet ccess. Guests can choose between the restaurant or bar to enjoy e dinner menu.
OOMS: 35 en suite (1 fmly) No smoking in all bedrooms s fr £75; fr £100 (incl. bkfst) **LB** **FACILITIES:** STV free membership to local ealth club **CONF:** Thtr 60 Class 25 Board 25 **PARKING:** 60 **OTES:** No dogs (ex guide dogs) No smoking in restaurant Closed 1 Jan **ARDS:**

★★71% Norwood Hall
arthdee Rd, Cults AB15 9FX
 01224 868951 🖹 01224 869868
mail: info@norwood-hall.co.uk
ir: off A90, at 1st rdbt cross Bridge of Dee and turn left at rdbt onto arthdee Rd (B&Q and Sainsbury on left) continue until hotel sign

his imposing Victorian mansion has retained many of its features, ost notably the fine oak staircase, stained glass and ornately ecorated walls and ceilings. Accommodation comes in different tyles with a major bedroom extension being undertaken. The xtensive grounds ensure the hotel is a popular wedding venue.
OOMS: 37 en suite (3 fmly) No smoking in 15 bedrooms s £75-£135; £95-£155 (incl. bkfst) **LB** **FACILITIES:** STV Xmas **CONF:** Thtr 200 lass 100 Board 70 Del from £145 **SERVICES:** Lift **PARKING:** 100 **IOTES:** No dogs (ex guide dogs) No smoking in restaurant Civ Wed 100 **ARDS:**

★★★70% The Craighaar
Waterton Rd, Bucksburn AB21 9HS
☎ 01224 712275 🖹 01224 716362
e-mail: info@craighaar.co.uk
***Dir:** turn off A96 (Airport/Inverness) onto A947, hotel signed*
Conveniently located for the airport, this welcoming hotel is a popular base for business people. Guests can make use of a quiet library/lounge, and enjoy meals in the bar or restaurant. Bedrooms are well equipped and a wing of galleried suites offer a lounge with bedroom upstairs.
ROOMS: 55 en suite (6 fmly) s £45-£105; d £55-£115 (incl. bkfst) **LB** **FACILITIES:** STV **CONF:** BC Thtr 90 Class 33 Board 30 Del from £110 **PARKING:** 80 **NOTES:** No dogs (ex guide dogs) Closed 26 Dec & 1-2 Jan Civ Wed 40 **CARDS:**

★★★70% Queens Hotel
51-53 Queens Rd AB15 4YP
☎ 01224 209999 🖹 01224 209009
e-mail: thequeens@vagabond-hotels.com

This well-established hotel is located a short drive from the city centre and is popular with both business travellers and for functions. Public areas include a welcoming lounge and a traditionally-styled bar, where guests can dine from the same menu as served in the restaurant. Bedrooms, many of which are spacious, are housed in both the original house and a more recently extended wing.
ROOMS: 27 en suite (3 fmly) No smoking in 4 bedrooms s £35-£90; d £50-£100 (incl. bkfst) **FACILITIES:** STV **CONF:** Thtr 400 Class 150 Board 60 Del from £97.50 **PARKING:** 80 **NOTES:** No dogs (ex guide dogs) No smoking in restaurant Closed 25-26 Dec & 1-2 Jan
CARDS:

★★★69% Westhill
Westhill AB32 6TT
☎ 01224 740388 🖹 01224 744354
e-mail: info@westhillhotel.co.uk
***Dir:** follow A944 W of city towards Alford. Hotel 6m on right*

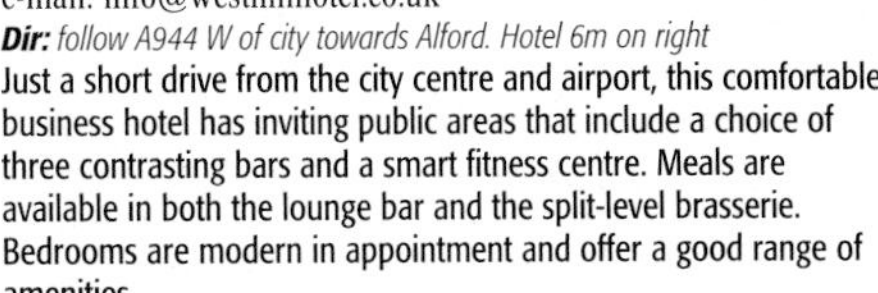

Just a short drive from the city centre and airport, this comfortable business hotel has inviting public areas that include a choice of three contrasting bars and a smart fitness centre. Meals are available in both the lounge bar and the split-level brasserie. Bedrooms are modern in appointment and offer a good range of amenities.
ROOMS: 38 en suite (2 fmly) No smoking in 8 bedrooms s £40-£75; d £50-£95 (incl. bkfst) **LB** **FACILITIES:** STV Sauna Solarium Gym entertainment Xmas **CONF:** Thtr 300 Class 200 Board 200 Del from £85 **SERVICES:** Lift **PARKING:** 150 **NOTES:** No smoking in restaurant Civ Wed 150 **CARDS:**

ABERDEEN, continued

A

★★★67% Maryculter House Hotel
South Deeside Rd, Maryculter AB12 5GB
☎ 01224 732124 01224 733510
e-mail: info@maryculterhousehotel.com
Dir: *off A90 on S side of Aberdeen, onto B9077. Hotel 8m on right. (0.5m beyond Lower Deeside Caravan Park)*

Set in grounds on the banks of the River Dee, this mansion dates back to medieval times and is now a popular wedding and conference venue. Exposed stonework and open fires feature in the oldest parts, which house the cocktail bar and Priory Restaurant. Lunch and breakfast are taken overlooking the river and bedrooms are equipped with business travellers in mind.
ROOMS: 23 en suite (1 fmly) (12 GF) No smoking in 17 bedrooms s £45-£75; d £70-£110 (incl. bkfst) **LB** **FACILITIES:** STV Fishing Clay pigeon shooting, Archery Xmas **CONF:** BC Thtr 220 Class 100 Board 50 Del from £120 **PARKING:** 150 **NOTES:** No smoking in restaurant Civ Wed 200 **CARDS:**

★★★65% Grampian
Stirling St AB11 6JU
☎ 01224 589101 01224 574288
e-mail: gm.grampian@countrytown-hotels.co.uk
Dir: *From S follow signs to Centre, continue along riverside, left at rdbt onto South Market St, through 1st lights, left at next set then left onto Guild St and 1st right onto Stirling St, hotel on left*

The Grampian Hotel is set in the heart of the city, located close to the railway station. This hotel provides modern accommodation, a library style lounge and a bar and brasserie.
ROOMS: 49 en suite (3 fmly) s £45-£85; d £55-£98 **LB**
FACILITIES: Xmas **CONF:** Thtr 120 Class 60 Board 40 Del from £105
SERVICES: Lift **NOTES:** No smoking in restaurant RS 25 Dec-3 Jan
CARDS:

★★★65% Mariner
349 Great Western Rd AB10 6NW
☎ 01224 588901 01224 571621
e-mail: enquiries@vagabond-hotels.com
Dir: *E off Anderson Drive at Great Western Road. Hotel on right on the corner of Gray Street*
A good range of tasty meals is served in both the conservatory restaurant and lounge bar of this friendly family-run hotel, located near the town centre and airport. Smart modern bedrooms are well equipped, and there are four apartment style rooms complete with kitchenettes, ideal for the long-stay guest.
ROOMS: 14 en suite 11 annexe en suite s £80; d £100 (incl. bkfst)
FACILITIES: STV Xmas **PARKING:** 51 **NOTES:** No dogs (ex guide dogs)
CARDS:

★★69% *Dunavon House*
60 Victoria St, Dyce AB21 7EE
☎ 01224 722483 & 772496 01224 772721
e-mail: info@dunavon-hotel.com
Dir: *from A96 follow A947 into Victoria St, Dyce. Hotel 500yds on right*
Within easy reach of the airport, this hotel is housed in a sympathetically converted Victorian villa. Bedrooms, many of which have now been refurbished, are generally spacious and well laid out. An extensive range of meals is served in both the lounge bar and the restaurant.
ROOMS: 17 en suite No smoking in 5 bedrooms **FACILITIES:** STV
PARKING: 23 **NOTES:** No dogs (ex guide dogs) No smoking in restaurant Closed 25 Dec-4 Jan **CARDS:**

THE INDEPENDENT

U *Holiday Inn Aberdeen*
Claymore Dr, Bridge of Don AB23 8BL
☎ 0870 400 9046 01224 823923
e-mail: reservations-aberdeen@ichotelsgroup.com
Dir: *follow signs for Peterhead and Aberdeen Exhibition Conference Centre hotel adjacent to AECC*
At the time of going to press, the classification for this hotel was not confirmed. Please refer to the AA internet site www.theAA.com for current information.
ROOMS: 123 en suite (23 fmly) No smoking in 49 bedrooms
FACILITIES: STV **SERVICES:** Lift **PARKING:** 200
CARDS:

Holiday Inn HOTELS · RESORTS

Express by Holiday Inn Aberdeen City Centre
Chapel St AB10 1SQ
☎ 01224 623500 01224 623523
e-mail: info@express-aberdeencc.co.uk

Express by Holiday Inn

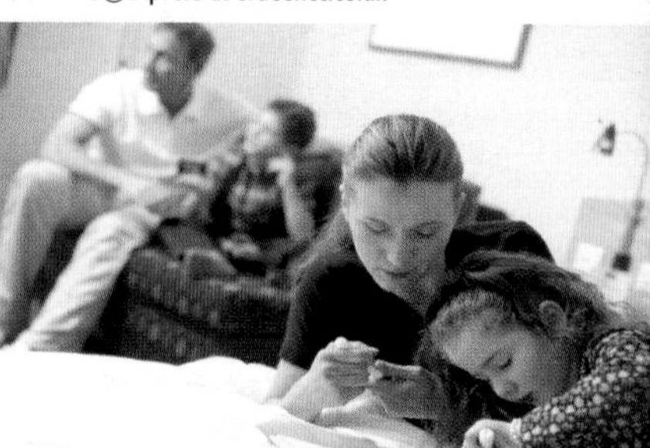

A modern hotel ideal for families and business travellers. Fresh and uncomplicated, the spacious bedrooms include Sky TV, power

continued

ıower and tea and coffee-making facilities. Continental buffet ɾeakfast is included in the room rate; other meals may be taken t the nearby family pub or restaurant. For further details and the ϰpress by Holiday Inn phone number, consult the Hotel roups pages.

OOMS: 155 en suite s £59.95; d £59.95 (incl. cont bkfst)

ONF: Thtr 40 Class 16 Board 20

Premier Lodge (Aberdeen City Centre)

ıverlair House, West North St AB24 5AR
☎ 0870 9906300 📠 0870 9906301
ʼremier Lodge offers modern, well-equipped, en ɿite accommodation suitable for both business and leisure ɾavellers. Meals can be taken at the adjacent popular restaurant nd bar, which is fully licensed. For further details, consult the łotel Groups page.

ROOMS: 162 en suite s £52; d £52

Premier Lodge (Aberdeen South West)

PREMIER LODGE

ƚtraik Rd, Westhill AB32 6HF
☎ 0870 9906348 📠 0870 9906349
Dir: *off A944 next to Shepherds Rest Chef & Brewer*
ʼremier Lodge offers modern, well-equipped, en suite ɪccommodation suitable for both business and leisure travellers. Meals can be taken at the adjacent popular restaurant and bar, which is fully licensed. For further details, consult the Hotel Groups page.

ROOMS: 61 en suite s £44; d £44

Premier Lodge (Aberdeen West)

North Anderson Dr AB15 6DW
☎ 0870 9906430 📠 0870 9906431
Dir: *adjacent to Fire Station*
Premier Lodge offers modern, well-equipped, en suite accommodation suitable for both business and leisure travellers. Meals can be taken at the adjacent popular restaurant and bar, which is fully licensed. For further details, consult the Hotel Groups page.

ROOMS: 60 en suite s £44; d £44

Travel Inn (Aberdeen North)

Murcar, Bridge of Don AB23 8BP
☎ 08701 977012 📠 01224 706869
Dir: *on A90 Ellon Road N of city centre, 1m past Aberdeen Exhibition Centre on left side of rdbt. Entrance from B999*
Travel Inn offers good-quality, value-for-money accommodation. Spacious, en suite rooms with bath and shower comfortably accommodate a family of up to two adults and two children (to age 15). The restaurant and bar offers a varied menu. For further details and the Travel Inn phone number, consult the Hotel Groups page.

ROOMS: 40 en suite s £44.95; d £44.95

Travel Inn (Aberdeen South West)

travel inn

Mains of Balquharn, Portlethen AB12 4QS
☎ 08701 977013 📠 01224 783836
Dir: *on A90, exit signed Portlethen Shopping Centre & Badentoy Industrial Estate*
Travel Inn offers good-quality, value-for-money accommodation. Spacious, en suite rooms with bath and shower comfortably accommodate a family of up to two adults and two children (to age 15). The restaurant and bar offers a varied menu. For further details and the Travel Inn phone number, consult the Hotel Groups page.

ROOMS: 40 en suite s £44.95; d £44.95

Travelodge

Travelodge

9 Bridge St AB11 6JL
☎ 08700 850 950 📠 01224 584587
Travelodge offers good quality, good value, modern accommodation. Ideal for families, the spacious, en suite bedrooms include remote-control TV, tea and coffee-making facilities, luxury beds and free morning newspaper. Meals can be taken at the nearby family restaurant. For further details and the Travelodge phone number, consult the Hotel Groups page.

ROOMS: 97 en suite s fr £42.95; d fr £42.95

Travelodge (Aberdeen West)

Travelodge

Inverurie Rd, Bucksburn AB21 9BB
☎ 08700 850 950
Travelodge offers good quality, good value, modern accommodation. Ideal for families, the spacious, en suite bedrooms include remote-control TV, tea and coffee-making facilities, luxury beds and free morning newspaper. Meals can be taken at the nearby family restaurant. For further details and the Travelodge phone number, consult the Hotel Groups page.

ROOMS: 48 en suite s fr £42.95; d fr £42.95

ABERDEEN AIRPORT, Aberdeen City — Map 23 NJ81

★★★★66% Aberdeen Marriott Hotel

Marriott HOTELS · RESORTS · SUITES

Overton Circle, Dyce AB21 7AZ
☎ 01224 770011 📠 01224 722347
e-mail: reservations.aberdeen@marriotthotels.co.uk
Dir: *follow A96 to Bucksburn village, turn right at rdbt onto A947. Hotel 2m at 2nd rdbt*
Close to the airport and conveniently located for the business

continued on p712

ABERDEEN AIRPORT, continued

A

district, this purpose-built hotel is a popular conference venue. The well-proportioned bedrooms come with many thoughtful extras. Public areas include an informal bar and lounge, a split-level restaurant and a leisure centre that can be accessed directly from a number of bedrooms.
ROOMS: 155 en suite (68 fmly) No smoking in 88 bedrooms s £55-£150; d £70-£150 (incl. bkfst) **LB FACILITIES: Spa** STV Indoor swimming (H) Sauna Solarium Gym Jacuzzi Xmas **CONF:** Thtr 400 Class 200 Board 60 Del from £120 **SERVICES:** air con **PARKING:** 180 **NOTES:** No dogs (ex guide dogs) Civ Wed 320
CARDS:

⌂ Travel Inn (Aberdeen Dyce)

Burnside Dr, off Riverside Dr, Dyce AB21 0HW
☎ 08701 977304 01224 772968
Dir: *from Aberdeen A96 towards Inverness, turn right at rdbt onto A947, at 2nd rdbt turn right then 2nd on right*

travel inn

Travel Inn offers good-quality, value-for-money accommodation. Spacious, en suite rooms with bath and shower comfortably accommodate a family of up to two adults and two children (to age 15). The restaurant and bar offers a varied menu. For further details and the Travel Inn phone number, consult the Hotel Groups page.
ROOMS: 40 en suite s £44.95; d £44.95

ABERDOUR, Fife — Map 21 NT18

★★★65% Woodside

High St KY3 0SW
☎ 01383 860328 01383 860920
e-mail: reception@thewoodsidehotel.co.uk
Dir: *M90 junct 1, E on A291 for 5m, hotel on left on entering village*

This well-established hotel is popular with business travellers and enjoys a convenient location in the centre of the village. Bedrooms, all named after Scottish clans, vary in size and style.
continued

Enjoyable meals are served in either the formal restaurant or the atmospheric bar, decorated with wood taken from an old cruise liner.
ROOMS: 20 en suite (1 fmly) s £55-£65; d £70-£80 (incl. bkfst) **LB FACILITIES:** Xmas **CONF:** Thtr 80 Class 40 Board 40 Del from £99 **PARKING:** 40 **NOTES:** No smoking in restaurant
CARDS:

See advert on opposite pag

★★64% The Aberdour Hotel

38 High St KY3 0SW
☎ 01383 860325 01383 860808
e-mail: reception@aberdourhotel.co.uk
Dir: *M90 junct 1, E on A921 for 5m. Hotel in centre of village opp post offic*

THE CIRCLE
Selected Individual Hotel
GREAT BRITAIN

This small hotel has a relaxed and welcoming atmosphere. Real ales are featured in the cosy bar and good value home-cooked meals are available there as well as in the beamed dining room. Though all are well equipped, bedrooms vary in size and style, with those in the stable block being particularly comfortable.
ROOMS: 12 en suite 4 annexe en suite (4 fmly) (2 GF) s £40-£48; d £50-£65 (incl. bkfst) **LB FACILITIES:** STV **PARKING:** 8
CARDS:

ABERFELDY, Perth & Kinross — Map 23 NN8

★★★63% Moness House Hotel & Country Club

Crieff Rd PH15 2DY
☎ 0870 443 1460 0870 443 1461
e-mail: info@moness.com
Part of a holiday ownership resort, this small hotel is set in extensive grounds. Accommodation is provided in generally spacious bedrooms a short walk away from the public rooms and leisure facilities. There is a choice of bars where meals are served in addition to the restaurant.
ROOMS: 12 en suite (1 fmly) s £36.40-£70; d £52-£100 (incl. bkfst) **LB FACILITIES:** Indoor swimming (H) Squash Snooker Solarium Putting green Jacuzzi Badminton Indoor Bowls Pool Table Tennis entertainment ch fac Xmas **CONF:** Thtr 120 Class 120 Board 50 Del from £100 **PARKING:** 12 **NOTES:** No dogs No smoking in restaurant Closed 5-12 Dec Civ Wed 140 **CARDS:**

ABERFOYLE, Stirling — Map 20 NN5C

★★★★65% Forest Hills

Kinlochard FK8 3TL
☎ 01877 387277 01877 387307
e-mail: forest_hills@macdonald-hotels.co.uk
Dir: *3m W on B829*

MACDONALD HOTELS

Situated in the heart of The Trossachs with wonderful views of Loch Ard, this popular hotel forms part of a resort complex offering a range of indoor and outdoor facilities. The main hotel has relaxing lounges and a restaurant which overlook landscaped gardens. A separate building houses the leisure centre, lounge bar and bistro.
ROOMS: 54 en suite (16 fmly) (12 GF) No smoking in 26 bedrooms
FACILITIES: Indoor swimming (H) Tennis (hard) Fishing Snooker Sauna Solarium Gym Putting green Jacuzzi Quad biking, Sailing, Canoeing, Abseiling, Archery, Mountain bikes, Guided walks entertainment
CONF: Thtr 150 Class 60 Board 45 Del from £125 **SERVICES:** Lift **PARKING:** 80 **NOTES:** No dogs (ex guide dogs) No smoking in restaurant Civ Wed 80 **CARDS:**

ABERLOUR See Archiestown

BINGTON, South Lanarkshire
Map 21 NS92

★66% Abington Hotel
bington By Biggar ML12 6SD
THE INDEPENDENTS
☎ 01864 502467 🖷 01864 502223
mail: info@ab-hotel.com
ir: *M74 junct 13 & follow signs into village or A702 S of Edinburgh at nct for M74 follow signs into Abington*

his family-run hotel is situated in the quiet village of Abington, lose to Biggar and just off the M74 motorway. It makes a onvenient stop-off and its central position makes it ideal for small neetings. Guests will find friendly attention, good comfortable ccommodation, and wholesome meals at affordable prices.
OOMS: 28 en suite (6 fmly) No smoking in 19 bedrooms s £45-£55; £65-£78 (incl. bkfst) **LB** **FACILITIES:** entertainment Xmas **CONF:** Thtr 0 Class 50 Board 50 Del from £35 **PARKING:** 30 **NOTES:** No dogs ex guide dogs) No smoking in restaurant
ARDS:

BINGTON MOTORWAY SERVICE AREA (M74), South Lanarkshire
Map 21 NS92

⌂ Days Inn
ML12 6RG
DAYS INN
☎ 01864 502782 🖷 01864 502759
-mail: abington.hotel@welcomebreak.co.uk
ir: *M74 junct 13, accessible from N'bound and S'bound carriageways*
his modern building offers accommodation in smart, spacious nd well-equipped bedrooms, suitable for families and business ravellers, and all with en suite bathrooms. Continental breakfast is vailable and other refreshments may be taken at the nearby amily restaurant. For further details and the Days Inn phone umber, consult the Hotel Groups page.
ROOMS: 52 en suite s £45-£55; d £45-£55 **CONF:** Board 10

ALLOWAY, South Ayrshire
Map 20 NS31

★★★76% ⊛⊛ Ivy House
KA7 4NL
☎ 01292 442336 🖷 01292 445572
e-mail: enquiries@theivyhouse.uk.com
Dir: *M74 junct 8, A71/A77 S, for approx 2m & follow signs for Burns National Heritage Park. Right along Doonholm Rd to t-junct. Right past Burns Cottage, hotel 300mtrs on left*
Situated almost next door to Burns' Cottage and overlooking the Bellisle Golf Course, this small boutique style hotel provides friendly, personal service. A series of conservatories and lounge areas plus a patio give a feel of the Mediterranean and this

 AA Rosette Award for culinary excellence

influence extends to the food. Bedrooms are all individual and well equipped to include music centres.

Ivy House

ROOMS: 5 en suite No smoking in all bedrooms s fr £95; d fr £120 (incl. bkfst) **FACILITIES:** STV entertainment Xmas **CONF:** Thtr 50 Class 30 Board 24 **PARKING:** 48 **NOTES:** No dogs (ex guide dogs) No smoking in restaurant Civ Wed **CARDS:**

ANNANDALE WATER MOTORWAY SERVICE AREA (M74), Dumfries & Galloway
Map 21 NY19

⌂ Travel Inn (Lockerbie Annandale Water)
Johnstonbridge DG11 1HD
travel inn
☎ 08701 977163 🖷 01576 470644
Dir: *A74(M) junct 16*
Travel Inn offers good-quality, value-for-money accommodation.

continued on p714

ANNANDALE WATER, continued

Spacious, en suite rooms with bath and shower comfortably accommodate a family of up to two adults and two children (to age 15). The restaurant and bar offers a varied menu. For further details and the Travel Inn phone number, consult the Hotel Groups page.
ROOMS: 42 en suite s £44.95; d £44.95

ANSTRUTHER, Fife Map 21 NO50

★★65% **Smugglers Inn**
High St East KY10 3DQ
☎ 01333 310506 01333 312706
e-mail: smuggs106@aol.com
Dir: *on High Street East A719 after bridge*
Fine views across the river towards the harbour contrast with this friendly inn's main street façade. A wide selection of hearty, good value dishes is served in both bars and dining room. Bedrooms boast co-ordinated fabrics, attractive colour schemes and comfortable furnishings.
ROOMS: 9 en suite (1 fmly) s £30-£37; d £49-£62 (incl. bkfst) **LB FACILITIES:** Darts, Pool **PARKING:** 14 **NOTES:** No dogs (ex guide dogs) Closed 25 Dec **CARDS:**

ARBROATH, Angus Map 21 NO64

★★65% ***Hotel Seaforth***
Dundee Rd DD11 1QF
☎ 01241 872232 01241 877473
e-mail: hotelseaforth@ukonline.co.uk
Dir: *on southern outskirts, on A92*

Behind this long-established commercial hotel's rather plain facade lies a welcoming environment which includes an attractive restaurant serving good value meals (try the Friday/Saturday night sizzle menu) and comfortable well-equipped bedrooms, all of which have been attractively refurbished and include smart bathrooms. The leisure centre is a bonus.
ROOMS: 19 en suite (4 fmly) **FACILITIES:** Indoor swimming (H) Snooker Sauna Gym Jacuzzi Steam room ch fac **CONF:** Thtr 120 Class 60 Board 40 **PARKING:** 60 **NOTES:** No smoking in restaurant Civ Wed 120 **CARDS:**

ARCHIESTOWN, Moray Map 23 NJ24

★★75% Archiestown
AB38 7QL
☎ 01340 810218 01340 810239
e-mail: rml@archiestownhotel.co.uk
Dir: *from A95 Grantown to Elgin road, at Craigellachie onto B9102. Archiestown is 4m from main road, hotel in village square*
This is a small village hotel in the heart of Speyside. Always popular with anglers, the owners are now promoting its charm and character to a broader market, especially on the food side.

ROOMS: 11 en suite s fr £44; d £60-£88 (incl. bkfst) **LB PARKING:** 1[illegible]
NOTES: No smoking in restaurant Closed 24-27 Dec, 3 wks in Jan
CARDS:

ARDUAINE, Argyll & Bute Map 20 NM[illegible]

★★★76% **Loch Melfort**
PA34 4XG
☎ 01852 200233 01852 200214
e-mail: reception@lochmelfort.co.uk
Dir: *on A816, midway between Oban and Lochgilphead*

Scotland's Hotels of Distinction

Enjoying one of the finest locations on the West Coast, this popular, family-run hotel has outstanding views across Asknish Bay towards the Islands of Jura, Scarba and Shuna. Accommodation is provided in either the balconied rooms of the Cedar wing or the more traditional rooms in the main hotel. Dinner can be enjoyed in both the informal Skerry Bistro and the restaurant.
ROOMS: 7 en suite 20 annexe en suite (2 fmly) s £49-£79; d £78-£158 (incl. bkfst) **LB FACILITIES:** Xmas **CONF:** Thtr 50 Class 35 Board 24 Del from £80 **PARKING:** 65 **NOTES:** No smoking in restaurant
CARDS:

ARDVASAR See Skye, Isle of

ARISAIG, Highland Map 22 NM6[illegible]

★★72% **Arisaig**
PH39 4NH
☎ 01687 450210 01687 450310
e-mail: arisaighotel@dial.pipex.com
Dir: *on A830 opposite the harbour*
This inviting roadside hotel offers fine sea views towards the islands of Rhum, Eigg, Muck and Skye. Bedrooms are smartly appointed and thoughtfully equipped; front-facing ones look out across the bay. The comfortable public areas include a children's

continued

layroom. A good range of freshly prepared dishes is on offer in oth bars and the restaurant.

OOMS: 13 en suite (2 fmly) No smoking in all bedrooms s £35-£40; £70-£80 (incl. bkfst) **LB** **PARKING:** 30 **NOTES:** No smoking in estaurant Closed 24-26 Dec **CARDS:**

ARRAN, ISLE OF, North Ayrshire — Map 20

BLACKWATERFOOT — Map 20 NR92

★★★67% Kinloch
KA27 8ET
☎ 01770 860444 📠 01770 860447
e-mail: kinloch@cqm.co.uk
Dir: *Ferry from Ardrossan to Brodick, follow signs for Blackwaterfoot, hotel in centre of village*

Best Western

This family-run hotel overlooks the Mull of Kintyre. Spacious public areas include a choice of lounges, bars and good leisure facilities. Bedrooms offer mixed modern appointments and are gradually being upgraded. The main dining room offers a well-prepared and innovative 4-course dinner menu in addition to meals served in the bars.
ROOMS: 43 en suite (7 fmly) (7 GF) s £39-£49; d £78-£98 (incl. bkfst) **LB** **FACILITIES:** STV Indoor swimming (H) Squash Snooker Sauna Solarium Gym entertainment Xmas **CONF:** Thtr 120 Class 20 Board 40 Del £85 **SERVICES:** Lift **PARKING:** 2 **NOTES:** No smoking in restaurant Civ Wed 100 **CARDS:**

BRODICK — Map 20 NS03

★★★76% Auchrannie Country House
KA27 8BZ
☎ 01770 302234 📠 01770 302812
e-mail: info@auchrannie.co.uk
Dir: *turn right from Brodick Ferry terminal, through Brodick village, 2nd left after Brodick Golf Course clubhouse, 300yds to hotel*
This Victorian mansion lies in landscaped grounds and provides well-equipped bedrooms, those in the newer wing being particularly spacious. The Garden Restaurant will be joined by a more informal bistro during 2003. Residents have their own leisure facilities but will be attracted to a superb spa set in the grounds and which also has excellent family accommodation.
ROOMS: 28 en suite (3 fmly) (4 GF) s £51-£78; d £72-£126 (incl. bkfst) **LB** **FACILITIES: Spa** STV Indoor swimming (H) Tennis (hard) Snooker Sauna Solarium Gym Hair salon Aromatherapy Shiatsu Hockey Badminton Swimming pool supervised ch fac Xmas **CONF:** Thtr 120 Class 80 Board 50 Del from £105 **PARKING:** 50 **NOTES:** No dogs (ex guide dogs) No smoking in restaurant Civ Wed 120
CARDS:

Top 200 - Hotel

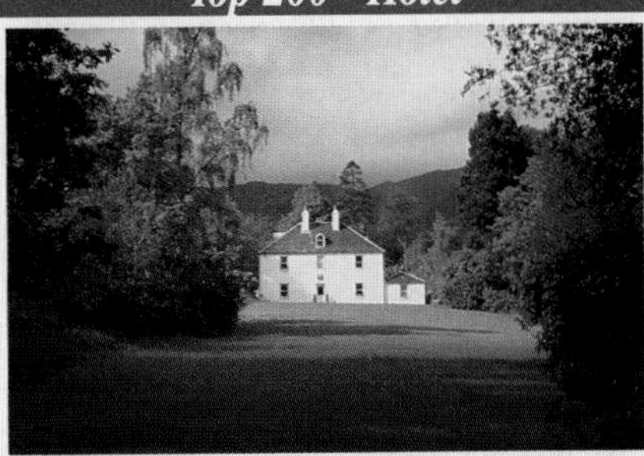

★★ Kilmichael Country House
Glen Cloy KA27 8BY
☎ 01770 302219 📠 01770 302068
e-mail: enquiries@kilmichael.com
Dir: *from Brodick ferry terminal follow N'bound (Lochranza) road for 1m. Left at golf course, inland between sports field & church, follow signs*
This lovely house, reputed to be the oldest on the island, lies in attractive gardens in a quiet glen less than five minutes drive from the ferry terminal. It has been lovingly restored to create a stylish, elegant little gem of country-house hotel, adorned with furnishings and ornaments from around the world. There are two inviting drawing rooms and a bright colourful dining room serving award-winning contemporary cuisine. The delightful bedrooms are furnished in classical style; some contained in a pretty courtyard conversion.
ROOMS: 4 en suite 3 annexe en suite (6 GF) No smoking in all bedrooms s £95; d £150-£195 (incl. bkfst) **LB** **FACILITIES:** STV Jacuzzi **PARKING:** 12 **NOTES:** No children 12yrs No smoking in restaurant Closed Nov-Feb (ex for prior bookings)
CARDS:

AUCHENCAIRN, Dumfries & Galloway — Map 21 NX75

★★★72% Balcary Bay
DG7 1QZ
☎ 01556 640217 & 640311 📠 01556 640272
e-mail: reservations@balcary-bay-hotel.co.uk
Dir: *on the A711 between Dalbeattie and Kirkcudbright, hotel on Shore road, 2m from village*

Scotland's Hotels of Distinction

Overlooking Balcary Bay, this comfortable 17th-century hotel has lawns running down to the shore. The larger bedrooms enjoy stunning views over the bay, whilst others have garden views.

continued on p716

A

AUCHENCAIRN, continued

Imaginative dishes feature at dinner, accompanied by a good wine list.

Balcary Bay Hotel, Auchencairn

ROOMS: 20 en suite (1 fmly) (3 GF) s £62; d £112-£134 (incl. bkfst) **LB PARKING:** 50 **NOTES:** No smoking in restaurant Closed Dec-Feb **CARDS:**

AUCHTERARDER, Perth & Kinross — Map 21 NN91

Top 200 - Hotel

★★★★★ The Gleneagles Hotel

PH3 1NF

☎ 01764 662231 🖹 01764 662134

e-mail: resort.sales@gleneagles.com

Dir: *on A823*

With its international reputation for high standards, this grand hotel provides something for everyone. Set in a delightful location, Gleneagles offers a peaceful retreat, as well as many sporting activities, including the famous championship golf courses. Afternoon tea is a feature, and cocktails are prepared with flair and skill at the bar. Amongst the dining options is Strathearn with two AA rosettes, and some inspired cooking at Andrew Fairlie at Gleneagles, a restaurant with three rosettes. Service is always professional, staff are friendly and nothing is too much trouble.

ROOMS: 275 en suite (116 fmly) (22 GF) No smoking in 149 bedrooms s £215; d £320-£445 (incl. bkfst) **LB FACILITIES: Spa** STV Indoor swimming (H) Outdoor swimming (H) Golf 18 Tennis (hard & grass) Fishing Squash Riding Snooker Sauna Solarium Gym Croquet lawn Putting green Jacuzzi Falconry, Equestrian, Off road driving, Golf range, Archery, Pool supervised entertainment ch fac Xmas **CONF:** BC Thtr 360 Class 240 Board 60 Del from £516 **SERVICES:** Lift **PARKING:** 200 **NOTES:** Civ Wed **CARDS:**

★★77% Cairn Lodge

Orchil Rd PH3 1LX

☎ 01764 662634 & 662431 🖹 01764 664866

e-mail: email@cairnlodge.co.uk

Dir: *from A9 take A824 into Auchterarder then A823 signed Crieff & Gleneagles approx 200yds, hotel at junct*

This charming hotel stands in wooded grounds on the edge of the town and the friendly staff provide good levels of service. The smart public rooms offer a choice of lounges, one with a bistro menu, and the Capercaillie Restaurant. Bedrooms are individual, with four luxury rooms providing extra quality and comfort.

ROOMS: 11 en suite (6 fmly) (2 GF) No smoking in 4 bedrooms s £65-£130; d £120-£200 (incl. bkfst) **LB FACILITIES:** Putting green Xmas **CONF:** Thtr 20 Class 20 Board 20 Del from £130 **PARKING:** 40 **NOTES:** No dogs No smoking in restaurant Civ Wed 60 **CARDS:**

AVIEMORE, Highland — Map 23 NH8

★★★62% *Aviemore Highlands*

Aviemore Mountain Resort PH22 1PJ

☎ 01479 810771 🖹 01479 811473

e-mail: sales@aviehighlands.demon.co.uk

Dir: *off A9 signed Aviemore B9152, turn left opp railway station on ring road. Hotel 2nd on left.*

Popular with tour groups, this purpose-built hotel enjoys a central position within the village resort. The restaurant and bar boast super views of the Cairngorms as do many of the spacious bedrooms. Useful conference and function facilities make this a popular venue for weddings and meetings.

ROOMS: 103 en suite (37 fmly) **FACILITIES:** ch fac **CONF:** Thtr 140 Class 80 Board 60 **SERVICES:** Lift **PARKING:** 140 **NOTES:** No smoking in restaurant **CARDS:**

AYR, South Ayrshire — Map 20 NS3

★★★★71% Fairfield House

12 Fairfield Rd KA7 2AR

☎ 01292 267461 🖹 01292 261456

e-mail: reservations@fairfieldhotel.co.uk

Dir: *from A77 for Ayr South (A30). Follow signs for town centre, down Miller Road and turn left then right into Fairfield Road*

This hotel is situated close to both the town centre and the esplanade and enjoys views of the Isle of Arran from the public areas. Bedrooms come in a variety of styles, those in the main house are spacious and traditional while those in the extended section are more modern in style, but equally well equipped. Enjoyable, well-constructed meals are served in either the brasserie or more formal restaurant.

ROOMS: 40 en suite 4 annexe en suite (3 fmly) No smoking in 7 bedrooms s £95-£135; d £125-£180 (incl. cont bkfst) **LB FACILITIES:** STV Indoor swimming (H) Sauna Solarium Gym Jacuzzi Swimming pool supervised Xmas **CONF:** Thtr 150 Class 60 Board 60 Del from £135 **SERVICES:** Lift **PARKING:** 52 **NOTES:** No dogs (ex guide dogs) No smoking in restaurant Civ Wed 110 **CARDS:**

★★★74% Enterkine House

Annbank KA6 5AL

☎ 01292 521608 🖹 01292 521582

e-mail: mail@enterkine.com

This imposing building dates from the 1930s and retains many original features, notably the luxurious bathroom suites. Genuine hospitality and a guest-focussed approach to service is a real feature. Bedrooms are spacious and fitted out to a high specification. Douglas Smith's menus feature seasonal, local

continued

B

produce that is simply treated and a private dining room is also available.
ROOMS: 6 en suite s £80-£110; d £150-£200 (incl. bkfst) **LB**
FACILITIES: STV Fishing Sauna Croquet lawn Xmas **CONF:** Thtr 40 Class 40 Board 14 Del from £110 **SERVICES:** Lift **PARKING:** 20
NOTES: No dogs (ex guide dogs) No children 14 yrs No smoking in restaurant Civ Wed 100 **CARDS:**

★★★72% **Savoy Park**
16 Racecourse Rd KA7 2UT
THE INDEPENDENTS
☎ 01292 266112 🖹 01292 611488
e-mail: mail@savoypark.com
Dir: *from A77 follow Holmston Road(A70) for 2m, through Parkhouse Street, turn left into Beresford Terrace, 1st right into Bellevue Rd*

This well-established hotel retains many of its traditional values. Public rooms feature impressive panelled walls, ornate ceilings and open fires. The restaurant is reminiscent of a Highland shooting lodge and offers a good value menu to suit all tastes. The large superior bedrooms retain a classical elegance while others are smart and modern; all have good bathrooms.
ROOMS: 15 en suite (3 fmly) No smoking in all bedrooms
FACILITIES: STV ch fac **CONF:** Thtr 50 Class 40 Board 30
PARKING: 60 **NOTES:** No smoking in restaurant Civ Wed 80
CARDS:

See advert on this page

★★ **Ladyburn**
KA19 7SG
☎ 01655 740585 🖹 01655 740580
e-mail: jh@ladyburn.co.uk
(For full entry see Maybole)

Travel Inn
Kilmarnock Rd, Monkton KA9 2RJ
☎ 08701 977020 🖹 01292 678248
Dir: *on A77/A78 rdbt at Monkton, approx 2m from Prestwick Airport*

Travel Inn offers good-quality, value-for-money accommodation. Spacious, en suite rooms with bath and shower comfortably accommodate a family of up to two adults and two children (to age 15). The restaurant and bar offers a varied menu. For further details and the Travel Inn phone number, consult the Hotel Groups page.
ROOMS: 40 en suite s £44.95; d £44.95 **CONF:** Thtr 50 Board 20

> Late for dinner?
> Quality Standards mean that last orders for dinner vary according to star rating and should be no earlier than:
> ★★ 7.00pm ★★★ 8.00pm ★★★★ 9.00pm
> ★★★★★ 10.00pm

BALLACHULISH, Highland Map 22 NN05

★★★69% **Ballachulish Hotel**
PH49 4JY
☎ 0871 222 3415 🖹 0871 222 3416
e-mail: reservations@freedomglen.co.uk
Dir: *on A828, Fort William-Oban road, 3m N of Glencoe*

A relaxed and welcoming atmosphere prevails at this long-established holiday hotel which overlooks Loch Linnhe. Inviting public areas include a spacious and comfortable lounge, the informal Ferry Bar and a cocktail bar adjacent to the bold and attractive restaurant. Bedrooms vary in size and in style and all are comfortably appointed.
ROOMS: 54 en suite (4 fmly) s £70-£90; d £140-£240 (incl. bkfst & dinner) **LB** **FACILITIES:** Complimentary Membership of Leisure Club at nearby sister hotel entertainment Xmas **CONF:** Thtr 100 Class 50 Board 30 **PARKING:** 50 **NOTES:** No smoking in restaurant Closed 9-23 Dec & 5-27 Jan **CARDS:**

B

BALLANTRAE, South Ayrshire

Map 20 NX08

Top 200 - Hotel

★★★ ◎◎ Glenapp Castle

KA26 0NZ

☎ 01465 831212 🖷 01465 831000

e-mail: enquiries@glenappcastle.com

RELAIS & CHATEAUX

Dir: *1m from A77 near Ballantrae village*

Impressively restored over a six-year period, this magnificent castle sits in smart grounds and gardens just south of the village, and provides stunning views towards Ailsa Craig and Arran. The all-inclusive price covers a skilfully prepared five-course dinner with carefully selected wines, afternoon tea, and aperitifs and liqueurs. Impeccably furnished bedrooms are graced with antiques and period pieces and there are a number of spacious, luxurious suites. Service is both attentive and welcoming.

ROOMS: 17 en suite (2 fmly) (7 GF) No smoking in all bedrooms s £315-£415; d £440-£550 (incl. bkfst & dinner) **FACILITIES:** Tennis (hard) Croquet lawn 30 acres of beautifully tended gardens **CONF:** Thtr 17 Class 12 Board 17 Del from £315 **SERVICES:** Lift **PARKING:** 20 **NOTES:** No smoking in restaurant Closed Nov-Mar Civ Wed 34 **CARDS:**

BALLATER, Aberdeenshire

Map 23 NO39

Top 200 - Hotel

★★★ ◎◎◎ Darroch Learg

Braemar Rd AB35 5UX

☎ 013397 55443 🖷 013397 55252

e-mail: nigel@darrochlearg.co.uk

Dir: *on A93, at western side of Ballater*

Set high above the road in large wooded grounds, this character hotel enjoys fine views of Royal Deeside. Bedrooms, some with four-poster beds, are individually styled, bright and spacious. Food is a highlight of any visit, whether it is a freshly

continued

prepared breakfast, a light lunch or the award-winning Scottish cuisine served in the delightful conservatory restaurant.

ROOMS: 13 en suite 5 annexe en suite (1 GF) No smoking in all bedrooms s £93-£113; d £185-£215 (incl. bkfst & dinner) **LB** **FACILITIES:** Xmas **CONF:** Thtr 25 Board 12 Del from £99 **PARKING:** 25 **NOTES:** No smoking in restaurant Closed Xmas & Jan (ex New Year) **CARDS:**

Top 200 - Hotel

★★ ◎◎ Balgonie Country House

Braemar Place AB35 5NQ

☎ 013397 55482 🖷 013397 55482

e-mail: balgoniech@aol.com

SCOTLAND'S HOTELS OF DISTINCTION

Dir: *off A93 [Aberdeen - Perth] on western outskirts of village of Ballater, hotel is signposted*

Genuinely warm hospitality is a feature of this delightful Edwardian house, set in well-tended gardens adjacent to the river and golf course. Accommodation is provided in thoughtfully equipped, immaculately maintained bedrooms. The cosy bar offers a wide selection of malt whisky and there is a comfortable sitting room. Carefully prepared meals are served in the attractive dining room.

ROOMS: 9 en suite s £70-£75; d £120-£130 (incl. bkfst) **LB** **FACILITIES:** Croquet lawn Xmas **PARKING:** 12 **NOTES:** No dogs (ex guide dogs) No smoking in restaurant Closed 6 Jan-Feb **CARDS:**

★★72% ◎ Loch Kinord

Ballater Rd, Dinnet AB34 5JY

☎ 013398 85229 🖷 013398 87007

e-mail: ask@kinord.com

THE CIRCLE
Selected Individual Hotels
GREAT BRITAIN

Dir: *on A93, in village of Dinnet*

Family-run, this roadside hotel lies between Aboyne and Ballater and is well located for leisure and sporting pursuits. It has lots of character and a friendly atmosphere. There are two bars, one

continued

outside and a cosy one inside, plus a dining room in bold, stylish colour schemes. Food is well promoted throughout the hotel.
ROOMS: 17 rms (15 en suite) (3 fmly) s £35-£65; d £60-£80 (incl. bkfst) **LB** **FACILITIES:** Sauna Jacuzzi ch fac Xmas **CONF:** Thtr 40 Class 30 Board 30 Del from £75 **PARKING:** 20 **NOTES:** No smoking in restaurant **CARDS:**

Auld Kirk
Braemar Rd AB35 5RQ
☎ 013397 55762 013397 55707
e-mail: info@auldkirkhotel.com
Dir: *on A93 Aberdeen/Braemar Road, 600mtrs W of village centre at junct. with Invercauld Road*
ROOMS: 7 en suite (2 fmly) No smoking in 4 bedrooms s £40-£45; d £60-£70 (incl. bkfst) **LB** **PARKING:** 7 **NOTES:** ★★★ No smoking in restaurant Closed 24-27 Dec & 1-4 Jan **CARDS:**

Cambus O'May
AB35 5SE
☎ 013397 55428 013397 55428
e-mail: mckechnie@cambusomay.freeserve.co.uk
Dir: *From Ballater follow A93 for 4m towards Aberdeen, hotel on left*
ROOMS: 12 en suite (1 fmly) s £30-£35; d £60-£70 (incl. bkfst) **LB** **PARKING:** 12 **NOTES:** ★★★ No smoking in restaurant

BALLOCH, West Dunbartonshire Map 20 NS38

★★★★★64%
De Vere Cameron House
DE VERE HOTELS
G83 8QZ
☎ 01389 755565 01389 759522
e-mail: reservations@cameronhouse.co.uk
Dir: *M8 (W) junct 30 for Erskine Bridge. Then A82 for Crainlarich. After 14m, at rdbt signed Luss straight on towards Luss, hotel on right*
This imposing hotel, once the home of a wealthy merchant, benefits from a picturesque location on the shores of Loch Lomond. A popular conference and leisure destination, it has been restored to provide an extensive range of facilities. Public rooms are spacious and there is a choice of eating options to suit all tastes; dinner in the award-winning Georgian room is a highlight of any stay.
ROOMS: 96 en suite (9 fmly) No smoking in all bedrooms s £110-£175; d £150-£242 (incl. bkfst) **LB** **FACILITIES: Spa** STV Indoor swimming (H) Golf 9 Tennis (hard) Fishing Squash Snooker Sauna Solarium Gym Croquet lawn Jacuzzi Whole range of outdoor sports, Motor boat on Loch Lomond, Hair dressers ch fac Xmas **CONF:** Thtr 300 Class 80 Board 80 Del from £170 **SERVICES:** Lift **PARKING:** 200 **NOTES:** No dogs (ex guide dogs) Civ Wed 180
CARDS:

See advert on this page

Innkeeper's Lodge Loch Lomond
Balloch Rd G83 8LQ
☎ 0870 243 0500
Dir: *M8 junct 30 onto M898. Left at Duntocher rdbt onto A82, right at rdbt (A811) left into Daluart Rd, lodge opposite*
A new concept in the travel accommodation market. Smart rooms

continued on p720

BALLOCH, continued

meet essential business requirements but also have home comforts. Dining options include all-day menus plus the added advantage of breakfast, which is included in the room price. For further details, consult the Hotel Groups page.
ROOMS: 12 en suite

BALQUHIDDER, Stirling — Map 20 NN52

★★74% Monachyle Mhor

FK19 8PQ
☎ 01877 384622 01877 384305
e-mail: info@monachylemhor.com
Dir: *11m N of Callander on A84, turn right at Kingshouse Hotel and under the A84 towards Balquhidder, hotel 6m on right*

A warm welcome and delicious food are assured at this country hotel, set amid a 2000-acre estate and reached by a single-track road alongside Loch Voil. Bedrooms, including those in the rear courtyard, combine traditional furnishings with 'cutting-edge' fixtures and fittings. The conservatory-style restaurant gives fine views across the glen, an ideal setting for the imaginative fixed-price menu.
ROOMS: 5 en suite 5 annexe en suite (3 GF) No smoking in all bedrooms s £60-£140; d £85-£150 (incl. bkfst) **FACILITIES:** Fishing Grouse shooting, Hill walking, Deer Stalking Xmas **CONF:** Board 10 Del from £160 **PARKING:** 20 **NOTES:** No dogs (ex guide dogs) No children 12yrs No smoking in restaurant Closed January **CARDS:**

BANCHORY, Aberdeenshire — Map 23 NO69

★★★78% Raemoir House

Raemoir AB31 4ED
☎ 01330 824884 01330 822171
e-mail: relax@raemoir.com
Dir: *A93 to Banchory right onto A980, to Torphins, 2m at T-junct*

A fine country mansion set in parkland which is part of a 3,500-acre estate. Gracious public rooms include a choice of sitting rooms, a cocktail bar and a Georgian dining room. These rooms have tapestry-covered walls, open fires, and fine antiques, all reflecting the elegance of yesteryear. The bedrooms are individual in style and size.
ROOMS: 14 en suite 6 annexe en suite (1 fmly) s £60-£80; d £100-£130 (incl. bkfst) **LB** **FACILITIES:** Golf 9 Tennis (hard) Croquet lawn Putting green Shooting Stalking **CONF:** Thtr 40 Class 50 Board 30 **PARKING:** 100 **NOTES:** No smoking in restaurant Civ Wed 50
CARDS:

★★★78% Tor-na-Coille

AB31 4AB
☎ 01330 822242 01330 824012
e-mail: tornacoille@btinternet.com
Dir: *on the main A93 Aberdeen/Braemar road, opposite golf course.*

This fine granite-built house sits in tree-studded grounds on the west side of the town. Inviting public areas include a lovely sitting room and an elegant restaurant. Bedrooms come in a variety of styles and sizes, many mirroring the period charm of the house.
ROOMS: 22 en suite (4 fmly) No smoking in 17 bedrooms
FACILITIES: Squash Croquet lawn entertainment ch fac **CONF:** BC Thtr 90 Class 60 Board 30 Del from £95 **SERVICES:** Lift **PARKING:** 130 **NOTES:** No smoking in restaurant Closed 25-28 Dec Civ Wed 95
CARDS:

GF Indicates the number of bedrooms at ground floor level.

★★★75% Banchory Lodge

AB31 5HS
☎ 01330 822625 01330 825019
e-mail: enquiries@banchorylodge.co.uk
Dir: *off A93, 13m W of Aberdeen, hotel is off Dee St*

Long-established, this hotel enjoys a picture postcard setting in grounds by the River Dee. Inviting public areas include two lounges, a cosy bar and a restaurant giving views of the Dee and

continued

...eugh. There is a choice of bedroom styles; the individual rooms in the original house, or huge rooms in a modern wing.
ROOMS: 22 en suite (11 fmly) No smoking in 10 bedrooms s £70-£80; d £90-£130 (incl. bkfst) **LB FACILITIES:** Fishing Pool room Xmas
CONF: Thtr 30 Class 30 Board 28 Del from £105 **PARKING:** 50
NOTES: No smoking in restaurant Civ Wed 70
CARDS:

★★70% ***Burnett Arms***
25 High St AB31 5TD
☎ 01330 824944 01330 825553
e-mail: theburnett@totalise.co.uk
Dir: *town centre on N side of A93, 18m from centre of Aberdeen*

This popular, town centre hotel offers comfortably modern and well-equipped bedrooms. A variety of meals can be enjoyed not only in the dining room but in the bar and foyer lounge.
ROOMS: 16 en suite No smoking in 5 bedrooms **FACILITIES:** STV
CONF: Thtr 100 Class 50 Board 50 **PARKING:** 40 **NOTES:** No smoking in restaurant **CARDS:**

See advert under ABERDEEN

BANFF, Aberdeenshire — Map 23 NJ66

★★★68% **Banff Springs**
Golden Knowes Rd AB45 2JE
☎ 01261 812881 01261 815546
e-mail: info@banffspringshotel.co.uk
Dir: *western outskirts of town on A98 Banff to Inverness road*
Attentive service by cheerful staff is a feature of this comfortable business and tourist hotel, which enjoys lovely sea views. Public areas include a smart foyer lounge and a popular bar/bistro, which provides an informal dining alternative to the restaurant. The bedrooms are spacious and comfortable.
ROOMS: 31 en suite s £49.50-£60.50; d £70-£90 (incl. bkfst) **LB**
FACILITIES: STV Gym Xmas **CONF:** Thtr 400 Class 100 Board 40
PARKING: 200 **NOTES:** No smoking in restaurant Closed 25 Dec
CARDS:

BARRA, ISLE OF, Western Isles — Map 22

TANGASDALE — Map 22 NF60

★★68% **Isle of Barra**
Tangasdale Beach HS9 5XW
☎ 01871 810383 01871 810385
e-mail: barrahotel@aol.com
Dir: *left after leaving ferry terminal onto A888, hotel 2m on left*
Overlooking the white sands of Halaman Bay and the Atlantic Ocean beyond, this modern hotel enjoys a stunning location. Public areas, including a comfortable lounge and light and airy restaurant, make the most of the views, as do most of the bedrooms. The restaurant features superb local shellfish. Service is both friendly and attentive.
ROOMS: 30 en suite (2 fmly) (7 GF) s £55-£65; d £100-£118 (incl. bkfst & dinner) **LB FACILITIES:** STV Beach **CONF:** BC Thtr 70 Class 70 Board 60 Del from £56 **PARKING:** 50 **NOTES:** No smoking in restaurant Closed mid Oct-Mar **CARDS:**

BATHGATE, West Lothian — Map 21 NS96

Express by Holiday Inn Livingston
Starlaw Rd EH48 1LQ
☎ 01506 650650 01506 650651
e-mail: ebhi-livingston@btconnect.com
Dir: *M8 junct 3A. Follow slip road to 1st rdbt, take 1st exit (Bathgate). Over bridge and at 2nd rdbt take 1st exit for hotel 200yds on left*

A modern hotel ideal for families and business travellers. Fresh and uncomplicated, the spacious bedrooms include Sky TV, power shower and tea and coffee-making facilities. Continental buffet breakfast is included in the room rate; other meals may be taken at the nearby family pub or restaurant. For further details and the Express by Holiday Inn phone number, consult the Hotel Groups pages.
ROOMS: 74 en suite **CONF:** Thtr 30 Class 24 Board 16

BEARSDEN, East Dunbartonshire — Map 20 NS57

Premier Lodge (Glasgow North)
Milngavie Rd G61 3TA
☎ 0870 9906532 0870 9906533
Premier Lodge offers modern, well-equipped, en suite accommodation suitable for both business and leisure travellers. Meals can be taken at the adjacent popular restaurant and bar, which is fully licensed. For further details, consult the Hotel Groups page.
ROOMS: 162 en suite s £44; d £44

BEAULY, Highland — Map 23 NH54

★★★72% **Priory**
The Square IV4 7BX
☎ 01463 782309 01463 782531
e-mail: reservations@priory-hotel.com
Dir: *signed from A832, into Beauly, hotel in square on left*
This popular hotel occupies an enviable location in the town square. There are two standards of accommodation offered, with the executive rooms providing very high standards of comfort and facilities. A wide range of meals is served throughout the day in the open plan public areas.
ROOMS: 34 en suite (3 fmly) No smoking in 9 bedrooms
FACILITIES: STV Snooker **CONF:** BC Thtr 40 Class 40 Board 30 Del from £59.50 **SERVICES:** Lift **PARKING:** 20 **NOTES:** No smoking in restaurant Civ Wed 100 **CARDS:**

BENBECULA, Western Isles Map 22 NF74

A Dark Island Hotel
Liniclate HS7 5PJ
☎ 01870 603030 📠 01870 602347
e-mail: reception@darkislandhotel.co.uk
ROOMS: 42 en suite (1 fmly) s £69-£85; d £97-£112 (incl. bkfst) **LB** **FACILITIES:** Fishing entertainment **CONF:** Thtr 100 Class 70 Board 50 **PARKING:** 100 **NOTES:** ★★★ Closed 26 Dec, 1-2 Jan **CARDS:**

BIGGAR, South Lanarkshire Map 21 NT03

★★★73% Shieldhill Castle
Quothquan ML12 6NA
☎ 01899 220035 📠 01899 221092
e-mail: enquiries@shieldhill.co.uk
Dir: *off A702 onto B7016 Biggar to Carnwath Rd, after 2m turn left into Shieldhill Rd. Hotel 1.5m on right*

This imposing castle is set in rolling countryside and parts are over 800 years old. Public areas are atmospheric and include the high ceilinged Chancellor's restaurant and oak-panelled lounge. Bedrooms, many with oversized baths, are spacious. A friendly welcome is assured from both the enthusiastic staff and even the proprietor's dogs! Food is a highlight of any stay and uses local produce where possible.
ROOMS: 16 en suite No smoking in all bedrooms s £95-£248; d £140-£248 (incl. bkfst) **LB** **FACILITIES:** Croquet lawn Jacuzzi Cycling, Clay shoot, Hot air ballooning Xmas **CONF:** Thtr 500 Class 200 Board 250 Del from £175 **PARKING:** 50 **NOTES:** No smoking in restaurant Civ Wed 250 **CARDS:**

BLACKWATERFOOT See Arran, Isle of

BLAIR ATHOLL, Perth & Kinross Map 23 NN86

★★71% Atholl Arms
Old North Rd PH18 5SG
☎ 01796 481205 📠 01796 481550
e-mail: hotel@athollarms.u-net.com
Dir: *off A9 to B8079, 1m into Blair Atholl, hotel near entrance to Blair Castle*
Set close to Blair Castle, this hotel has welcoming public rooms that include a choice of bars, with the Bothy offering an extensive menu as an alternative to dinner in the splendid baronial-style dining room. Bedrooms come in mixed sizes, all have a good range of amenities.
ROOMS: 30 en suite (3 fmly) **FACILITIES:** Fishing Rough shooting **CONF:** Thtr 140 Class 80 Board 60 **PARKING:** 130 **NOTES:** No smoking in restaurant **CARDS:**

★★62% Bridge of Tilt
Bridge of Tilt PH18 5SU
☎ 01796 481333 📠 01796 481335
e-mail: hotels@theholidaygroup.com
Dir: *turn off A9 onto B8079, hotel 0.75m on left (with wishing well in front)*
Frequented by tour groups, this friendly hotel is situated close to Blair Castle. Bedrooms come in a variety of styles, with the chalet rooms being particularly popular. Public areas include a lounge, dining areas and a bar which offers live entertainment three times a week in season.
ROOMS: 20 en suite 7 annexe en suite (7 fmly) (7 GF) s £31-£43; d £62-£86 (incl. bkfst) **LB** **FACILITIES:** Jacuzzi entertainment Xmas **PARKING:** 40 **NOTES:** No smoking in restaurant Closed Jan-Feb **CARDS:**

BLAIRGOWRIE, Perth & Kinross Map 21 NO14

Top 200 - Hotel

★★★ Kinloch House
PH10 6SG
☎ 01250 884237 📠 01250 884303
e-mail: reception@kinlochhouse.com
Dir: *3m W on A923*
Significant investment has taken place at this delightful country hotel under new owners the Allen family (formerly of Airds Hotel). Accommodation is provided in elegantly furnished, spacious rooms, many featuring opulent bathrooms. Public areas are welcoming and comfortable and include a conservatory and bar with an impressive range of malt whiskies. Carefully prepared meals feature high quality, local produce. The beauty and fitness centre is run exclusively for hotel guests.
ROOMS: 18 en suite (1 fmly) (4 GF) s fr £105; d fr £290 (incl. bkfst) **LB** **FACILITIES:** Indoor swimming (H) Fishing Sauna Gym Croquet lawn Xmas **CONF:** Thtr 16 Class 14 Board 20 **PARKING:** 36 **NOTES:** No smoking in restaurant Closed 18 -29 Dec **CARDS:**

★★★62% Angus
46 Wellmeadow PH10 6NQ
☎ 01250 872455 📠 01250 875615
e-mail: reception@theangushotel.com
Dir: *on A93 Perth/Blairgowrie Rd overlooking Wellmeadow in town centre*
Inside this traditional town centre building is an attractive modern hotel which is popular with visiting tour groups. Bedrooms are smartly furnished and come in a variety of sizes. There is a spacious bar lounge and a restaurant offering good value meals.
ROOMS: 81 en suite (4 fmly) No smoking in 13 bedrooms s £35-£45; d £70-£90 (incl. bkfst) **LB** **FACILITIES:** Indoor swimming (H) Sauna Solarium Jacuzzi entertainment Xmas **CONF:** Thtr 200 Class 100 Board 50 **SERVICES:** Lift **PARKING:** 62 **NOTES:** No smoking in restaurant Civ Wed 150 **CARDS:**

BOAT OF GARTEN, Highland Map 23 NH91

★★★72% Boat

PH24 3BH

☎ 01479 831258 01479 831414

e-mail: holidays@boathotel.co.uk

Dir: *off A9 N of Aviemore onto A95, follow signs to Boat of Garten*

In the heart of the Spey Valley, this Victorian station hotel is adjacent to the Strathspey Steam Railway. Bedrooms, all individually decorated, have been tastefully upgraded and comfortably appointed. The Capercaille restaurant offers classic cuisine with a Scottish twist, while the warm cocktail bar has a selection of meals and specialises in a wide range of malt whiskies.

ROOMS: 30 en suite (2 fmly) No smoking in 22 bedrooms s £53-£58; d £105-£115 (incl. bkfst) **LB** **FACILITIES:** Snooker Golf course adjacent Xmas **CONF:** Thtr 50 Class 35 Board 25 Del from £85 **PARKING:** 36 **NOTES:** No smoking in restaurant RS 3 wks Jan Civ Wed 60

CARDS:

BOTHWELL, South Lanarkshire Map 20 NS75

★★★67% Bothwell Bridge

89 Main St G71 8EU

☎ 01698 852246 01698 854686

e-mail: enquiries@bothwellbridge-hotel.com

Dir: *M74 junct 5 & follow signs to Uddingston, right at mini-rdbt. Hotel just past shops on left*

This red-sandstone mansion house is a popular business, function and conference hotel conveniently placed for the motorway. The bedrooms are mostly spacious and all are well equipped. The conservatory bar focuses on food in an informal setting and there is also a comfortable seating area. The main restaurant has a strong Italian influence.

ROOMS: 90 en suite (14 fmly) No smoking in 27 bedrooms s £60-£68; d £70-£80 (incl. bkfst) **LB** **FACILITIES:** STV entertainment Xmas **CONF:** BC Thtr 200 Class 80 Board 50 Del from £99.50 **SERVICES:** Lift **PARKING:** 125 **NOTES:** No dogs (ex guide dogs) Civ Wed 180

CARDS:

See advert on this page

BOWMORE See Islay, Isle of

BRAE See Shetland

BRAEMAR, Aberdeenshire Map 23 NO19

★★70% ***Braemar Lodge***

Glenshee Rd AB35 5YQ

☎ 013397 41627 013397 41627

Dir: *on A93 S approach to Braemar*

This welcoming small hotel stands in its own garden on the north side of the village. Log fires warm the cosy bar and adjacent lounge in cold weather. Dinner offers an interesting selection of dishes, served in the attractive dining room. Period and antique furniture adorns most of the bedrooms.

ROOMS: 7 rms (6 en suite) (2 fmly) No smoking in all bedrooms **PARKING:** 16 **NOTES:** No smoking in restaurant

CARDS:

BRIDGEND See Islay, Isle of

BRIDGEND OF LINTRATHEN, Angus — Map 23 NO25

Restaurant with Rooms

Lochside Lodge & Roundhouse Restaurant
DD8 5JJ
☎ 01575 560340 01575 560202
e-mail: enquiries@lochsidelodge.com
Dir: *B951 from Kirriemuir Howards Glenisla for 7m & take left turn to Lintrathen. Follow road over top of loch & into village. Hotel on left*
This converted farmstead enjoys a rural location in the heart of Angus. The comfortable bedrooms are in the former hayloft and the original windows have been retained. Accomplished modern cuisine is served in the atmospheric Roundhouse restaurant. A spacious bar bedecked with agricultural implements and church pews features a wide range of drinks including local beers.
ROOMS: 4 en suite (1 fmly) **CONF:** Class 20 Board 25 Del from £95 **PARKING:** 40 **NOTES:** No smoking in restaurant Closed Mon (Oct - Etr) & Sun eve (all year) **CARDS:**

BRIDGE OF ALLAN, Stirling — Map 21 NS79

★★★71% **Royal**
Henderson St FK9 4HG
☎ 01786 832284 01786 834377
e-mail: stay@royal-stirling.co.uk
Dir: *M9 junct 11, turn right at rdbt for Bridge of Allan. Hotel in centre*

Best Western

This impressive Victorian building is a smart hotel offering a welcoming atmosphere and a fine dining experience. The bedrooms are comfortably modern in style and offer a good range of amenities. Public areas include an elegant restaurant serving innovative dishes and a bar providing a good range of bar meals.
ROOMS: 32 en suite (4 fmly) No smoking in 10 bedrooms s £60-£85; d £100-£130 (incl. bkfst) **LB** **FACILITIES:** STV Xmas **CONF:** Thtr 150 Class 60 Board 50 Del from £105 **SERVICES:** Lift **PARKING:** 40 **NOTES:** No dogs (ex guide dogs) No smoking in restaurant Civ Wed 130 **CARDS:**

BRODICK See Arran, Isle of

BRORA, Highland — Map 23 NC90

★★★72% ***Royal Marine***
Golf Rd KW9 6QS
☎ 01408 621252 01408 621181
e-mail: info@highlandescape.com
Dir: *off A9 in village toward beach and golf course*

Scotland's Hotels of Distinction

A distinctive Edwardian residence sympathetically extended, the Royal Marine attracts a mixed market. Its leisure centre is popular, and the restaurant, Hunters Lounge and café bar offer three contrasting eating options. A modern bedroom wing complements the original bedrooms, which retain their period style.
ROOMS: 22 en suite (1 fmly) **FACILITIES:** Indoor swimming (H) Golf 18 Tennis (hard) Fishing Snooker Sauna Solarium Gym Croquet lawn Putting green Jacuzzi Ice curling rink in season **CONF:** Thtr 70 Class 40 Board 40 **PARKING:** 40 **NOTES:** No smoking in restaurant RS Dec-Jan **CARDS:**

BROUGHTY FERRY, Dundee City — Map 21 NO43

Premier Lodge (Dundee East)
115-117 Lawers Dr, Panmurefield Village DD5 3TS
☎ 0870 9906324 0870 9906325

PREMIER LODGE

Premier Lodge offers modern, well-equipped, en suite accommodation suitable for both business and leisure travellers. Meals can be taken at the adjacent popular restaurant and bar, which is fully licensed. For further details, consult the Hotel Groups page.
ROOMS: 60 en suite s £44; d £44

BURNTISLAND, Fife — Map 21 NT28

★★★61% **Kingswood**
Kinghorn Rd KY3 9LL
☎ 01592 872329 01592 873123
e-mail: rankin@kingswoodhotel.co.uk
Dir: *A921 coastal road at Burntisland, right at rdbt, left at T-junct, at bottom of hill to Kingshorn road, hotel 0.5m on left*

Lying in sheltered grounds east of the town, this hotel has views across the Firth of Forth to Edinburgh. There is a lounge bar furnished with comfortable sofas and a restaurant providing a wide range of good value dishes. Bedrooms are contained in a modern extension.
ROOMS: 9 en suite (1 fmly) No smoking in 2 bedrooms s £52; d £76.50-£85 (incl. bkfst) **LB** **FACILITIES:** ch fac **CONF:** Thtr 150 Class 20 Board 40 Del from £80 **PARKING:** 50 **NOTES:** Closed 26 Dec & 1 Jan **CARDS:**

★★68% **Inchview Hotel**
69 Kinghorn Rd KY3 9EB
☎ 01592 872239 01592 874866
e-mail: reception@inchview.co.uk
Dir: *on A921, in Burntisland towards town centre*
A welcoming atmosphere prevails at this family-run hotel, a listed Georgian terraced house, which looks out over the links to the Firth of Forth. Comfortable public areas include an inviting lounge, a bar and an elegant restaurant, both of which offer a wide selection of tasty dishes. Bedrooms are well equipped and come in a range of sizes.
ROOMS: 12 en suite (1 fmly) No smoking in 4 bedrooms s £40-£53; d £70-£75 (incl. bkfst) **LB** **FACILITIES:** Xmas **CONF:** Thtr 60 Class 20 Board 20 **PARKING:** 15 **CARDS:**

CAIRNDOW, Argyll & Bute
Map 20 NN11

★★65% Cairndow Stagecoach Inn

PA26 8BN
☎ 01499 600286 & 600252 🖷 01499 600220
e-mail: cairndowinn@aol.com
Dir: *from Tarbet take A83 pass Dunoon Junction to Cairndow*

A relaxed, friendly atmosphere prevails at this 18th-century inn, overlooking the beautiful Loch Fyne. Traditional public areas include a comfortable beamed lounge, a well-stocked bar where food is served throughout the day, and a spacious restaurant with conservatory extension. Bedrooms are individually furnished and well equipped.
ROOMS: 13 en suite (2 fmly) No smoking in 3 bedrooms s £30-£50; d £50-£70 (incl. bkfst) **LB FACILITIES:** Sauna Solarium Gym Xmas **PARKING:** 32 **CARDS:**

CALLANDER, Stirling
Map 20 NN60

Top 200 - Hotel

★★★ ◎◎◎ Roman Camp Country House

FK17 8BG
☎ 01877 330003 🖷 01877 331533
e-mail: mail@roman-camp-hotel.co.uk
Dir: *N on A84, turn left at east end of Callander High Street, down a 300yd driveway into the hotel grounds*
Sitting in 20 acres of woodland gardens and grounds beside the River Teith, this long established country house is just a short walk from from the town centre and key attractions. Individually furnished bedrooms, varying in size and aspect, are complemented by a choice of lounges, including an atmospheric candle-lit library and a welcoming drawing room. Highly accomplished cooking, drawing on excellent Scottish produce, is served in the light and airy restaurant.
ROOMS: 14 en suite (3 fmly) **FACILITIES:** Fishing **CONF:** Thtr 100 Class 40 Board 20 **PARKING:** 80 **NOTES:** No smoking in restaurant **CARDS:**

CAMPBELTOWN, Argyll & Bute
Map 20 NR72

★★68% Seafield

Kilkerran Rd PA28 6JL
☎ 01586 554385 🖷 01586 552741
Dir: *300yds from ferry terminal, overlooking loch*
This comfortable, privately-owned hotel enjoys lovely views of the bay. Bedrooms, some in the garden annexe, come in various sizes and offer modern appointments and amenities. There is a bright and comfortable open-plan foyer lounge and bar and an extensive range of home-cooked dishes is available in the attractive restaurant.
ROOMS: 3 en suite 6 annexe en suite (6 GF) **PARKING:** 9 **NOTES:** No children 5yrs No smoking in restaurant **CARDS:**

CANONBIE, Dumfries & Galloway
Map 21 NY37

★★65% Cross Keys

DG14 0SY
☎ 013873 71205 🖷 013873 71878
e-mail: sg.laverack@ukonline.co.uk
Located in the quiet village of Canonbie, this former 17th-century coaching inn is full of character. The hotel is family run, and guests will experience a welcoming and friendly atmosphere. Bedrooms are all individually appointed, comfortable and well equipped. The restaurant and public bar retain many original features and offer an interesting selection of freshly prepared dishes.
ROOMS: 10 rms (9 en suite) (1 GF) s £30-£35; d £55-£58 (incl. bkfst) **FACILITIES:** STV **PARKING:** 30 **NOTES:** No smoking in restaurant **CARDS:**

CARNOUSTIE, Angus
Map 21 NO53

★★68% Carlogie House Hotel

Carlogie Rd DD7 6LD
☎ 01241 853185 🖷 01241 856528
e-mail: enquiries@carlogie-house-hotel.com
Dir: *A92 (Dundee to Arbroath), right at Pambride/West Haven. Sharp right at junct with A930. Hotel 300yds on right*
This comfortable hotel lies in open countryside north of the town. Bedrooms are well equipped, modern in style and benefit from individual touches and colourful fabrics. The adjacent, former stable block has been converted to provide accommodation for less able guests. Golfers and pet owners will also find this hotel is a suitable choice.
ROOMS: 12 en suite 4 annexe en suite (2 fmly) No smoking in 8 bedrooms s £45-£65; d £70-£100 (incl. bkfst) **LB FACILITIES:** Putting green **CONF:** Thtr 25 Class 25 Board 25 **PARKING:** 40 **NOTES:** No smoking in restaurant Civ Wed 25 **CARDS:**

A Kinloch Arms

27-29 High St DD7 6AN
☎ 01241 853127 🖷 01241 855183
Dir: *A92 towards Arbroath, take 1st sign for Carnoustie to main street. Hotel next to library*
ROOMS: 7 en suite (1 fmly) s £25-£35; d £45-£59 (incl. bkfst) **LB FACILITIES:** STV Tennis (hard) Putting green **PARKING:** 28 **NOTES:** ★★ **CARDS:**

C

CARRADALE, Argyll & Bute Map 20 NR83

★★68% Carradale
PA28 6RY
☎ 01583 431223 01583 431223
e-mail: carradaleh@aol.com
Dir: *off A82, 5m S of Tarbert, signed*
This well established holiday hotel, set in its own grounds overlooking Kilbrannan Sound, is next door to the local golf course. Public areas and bedrooms are sympathetic to the style of the house and include a comfortable lounge and a spacious formal dining room serving well prepared dinners. Bar meals are available in both the public and lounge bars.
ROOMS: 9 en suite s £30-£40; d £60-£72 (incl. bkfst) **LB** **FACILITIES:** Fishing Riding Sauna **PARKING:** 20 **NOTES:** No smoking in restaurant RS Oct-Feb **CARDS:**

CARRBRIDGE, Highland Map 23 NH92

★★★68% Dalrachney Lodge
PH23 3AT
☎ 01479 841252 01479 841383
e-mail: stay@dalrachney.co.uk
Dir: *follow Carrbridge signs off A9. At north end of village on A938*
A traditional Highland lodge, Dalrachney lies in grounds by the River Dulnain on the edge of the village. Spotlessly maintained public areas include a comfortable and relaxing sitting room and a cosy well-stocked bar, which has a popular menu providing an alternative to the dining room. Bedrooms are generally spacious and furnished in period style.
ROOMS: 11 en suite (3 fmly) No smoking in 7 bedrooms s £45-£75; d £66-£130 (incl. bkfst) **LB** **FACILITIES:** STV Fishing Xmas **PARKING:** 40 **NOTES:** No smoking in restaurant
CARDS:

A Fairwinds
PH23 3AA
☎ 01479 841240 01479 841240
e-mail: enquiries@fairwindshotel.com
Dir: *S from Inverness A938, N of Aviemore, onto B9153, hotel on left at side of village hall*
ROOMS: 5 en suite (1 GF) No smoking in all bedrooms s £30-£35; d £58-£70 (incl. bkfst) **LB** **PARKING:** 8 **NOTES:** ★★★★ No dogs (ex guide dogs) No children 3yrs No smoking in restaurant Closed 11 Nov-4 Dec & 24-26 Dec **CARDS:**

> Late for dinner?
> Quality Standards mean that last orders for dinner vary according to star rating and should be no earlier than:
> ★★ 7.00pm ★★★ 8.00pm ★★★★ 9.00pm
> ★★★★★ 10.00pm

CARRUTHERSTOWN, Dumfries & Galloway Map 21 NY17

★★★68% Hetland Hall
Best Western
DG1 4JX
☎ 01387 840201 01387 840211
e-mail: info@hetlandhallhotel.co.uk
Dir: *midway between Annan & Dumfries on A75*
This well-established hotel is set in extensive parkland and is conveniently located just off the A75. Hetland Hall appeals to a wide market, including weddings and conferences. It offers well-equipped bedrooms in a variety of styles and sizes, all enhanced by attractive fabrics and furnishings.

ROOMS: 14 en suite 15 annexe en suite (5 fmly) (1 GF) No smoking in 5 bedrooms s fr £70; d fr £80 (incl. bkfst) **LB** **FACILITIES:** STV Indoor swimming (H) Sauna Solarium Gym Putting green Pitch & putt, Toning tables/sun beds Xmas **CONF:** Thtr 200 Class 100 Board 100 Del from £85 **PARKING:** 60 **NOTES:** No dogs (ex guide dogs) No smoking in restaurant Civ Wed 80 **CARDS:**

CASTLECARY, Falkirk Map 21 NS77

★★66% Castlecary House
Castlecary Rd G68 0HD
☎ 01324 840233 01324 841608
e-mail: enquiries@castlecaryhotel.com
Dir: *off A80 onto B816 between Glasgow and Stirling*
Close to the Forth Clyde canal and convenient for the M80, this popular hotel provides a versatile range of accommodation, within purpose built units in the grounds and in an extension to the original house. The attractive and spacious restaurant serves a short carte menu and enjoyable meals are also served in the busy bars.
ROOMS: 60 rms (55 en suite) (2 fmly) s £60-£75; d £60-£75 (incl. bkfst) **CONF:** BC Thtr 60 Class 30 Board 24 **SERVICES:** Lift **PARKING:** 100 **NOTES:** Civ Wed 40 **CARDS:**

CASTLE DOUGLAS, Dumfries & Galloway Map 21 NX76

★★67% Imperial
35 King St DG7 1AA
☎ 01556 502086 01556 503009
e-mail: david@thegolfhotel.co.uk
Dir: *off A75 at sign for Castle Douglas, on main street, hotel opp the town library.*
Situated in the main street, this former coaching inn, popular with many golfers, offers guests well-equipped and cheerfully decorated bedrooms. There is a choice of bars for guests to relax in, and good value meals are served either in the foyer bar or the upstairs dining room.
ROOMS: 12 en suite (1 fmly) No smoking in 6 bedrooms s fr £39; d fr £60 (incl. bkfst) **LB** **FACILITIES:** local pool and sauna/gym 75 yds away ch fac **CONF:** Thtr 40 Class 20 Board 20 Del from £85 **PARKING:** 29 **NOTES:** No smoking in restaurant Closed 23-26 Dec & 1-3 Jan **CARDS:**

★★65% King's Arms
St Andrew's St DG7 1EL
☎ 01556 502626 01556 502097
e-mail: david@galloway-golf.co.uk
Dir: *through main street, left at town clock, hotel on corner*
The historic King's Arms Hotel is a former coaching inn and boasts a traditional and comfortable interior. Cosy day rooms include a

continued

choice of bar areas and a restaurant overlooking an ivy-clad courtyard. Creative menus are offered in both the bar and the restaurant.
ROOMS: 10 rms (9 en suite) (2 fmly) No smoking in 3 bedrooms s £39-£47; d £60 (incl. bkfst) **LB** **CONF:** Thtr 35 Class 20 Board 25 **PARKING:** 15 **NOTES:** No smoking in restaurant Closed 25-26 Dec & 1-2 Jan **CARDS:**

CASTLE KENNEDY, Dumfries & Galloway Map 20 NX15

★★65% **The Plantings Inn**
DG9 8SQ
☎ 01581 400633 🖷 01581 400637
Convenient for Stranraer and the Irish ferries, this small hotel focuses on an pleasantly informal eating operation with a wide-ranging menu that offers hearty good-value dishes. Bedrooms are smartly furnished.
ROOMS: 7 en suite No smoking in all bedrooms s £32-£40; d £60-£70 (incl. bkfst) **LB** **FACILITIES:** Xmas **CONF:** Thtr 30 Class 16 Board 16 Del from £45 **PARKING:** 30 **CARDS:**

CHIRNSIDE, Scottish Borders Map 21 NT85

★★★68% **Chirnside Hall**
TD11 3LD
☎ 01890 818219 🖷 01890 818231
e-mail: chirnsidehall@globalnet.co.uk
Dir: *on A6105 Berwick on Tweed/Duns road approx 3m after village Foulden hotel sign on right*
At the end of a tree-lined drive, this hotel is ideal for guests wishing to get away from the hustle and bustle of city life. Bedrooms are spacious, many with views of the rolling Borders' countryside. Real fires warm the elegantly styled lounges and fresh local produce features on the restaurant menus.
ROOMS: 10 en suite (2 fmly) s £75-£130; d £130-£140 (incl. bkfst) **LB** **FACILITIES:** Fishing Snooker Gym Croquet lawn Putting green Shooting Xmas **CONF:** Board 16 Del from £50 **PARKING:** 20 **NOTES:** No smoking in restaurant **CARDS:**

CLACHAN-SEIL, Argyll & Bute Map 20 NM71

★★76% **Willowburn**
PA34 4TJ
☎ 01852 300276 🖷 01852 300597
e-mail: willowburn.hotel@virgin.net
Dir: *0.5m from Atlantic Bridge, on left*
This welcoming country-cottage hotel, 12 miles south of Oban, enjoys a peaceful outlook over Clachan Sound. Friendly, attentive service and fine food are the keys to the hotel's success. There is a cosy bar with an attractive veranda, a formal dining room and a comfortable, inviting lounge. Most of the pleasant, thoughtfully equipped bedrooms are furnished in pine.
ROOMS: 7 en suite (1 GF) No smoking in all bedrooms s fr £68; d fr £136 (incl. bkfst & dinner) **LB** **PARKING:** 20 **NOTES:** No smoking in restaurant Closed Dec-Feb **CARDS:**

CLUANIE INN, Highland Map 22 NH01

★★63% **Cluanie Inn**
Glenmoriston IV63 7YW
☎ 01320 340238 🖷 01320 340293
e-mail: cluanie@ecosse.net
Dir: *On A87 mid-way between Loch Ness & Isle of Skye*
THE CIRCLE Selected Individual Hotels GREAT BRITAIN
Set in splendid isolation at the western end of Loch Cluanie and surrounded by mountains, this roadside inn is a haven for climbers and a welcoming stop for travellers to and from Skye.
continued
The bedrooms are smartly pine-furnished. There is no TV or radio reception here, but each room has a VCR.
ROOMS: 15 en suite (4 fmly) (10 GF) s £40-£45; d £44-£55 (incl. bkfst) **LB** **FACILITIES:** Fishing Sauna Xmas **PARKING:** 20 **NOTES:** No smoking in restaurant **CARDS:**

CLYDEBANK, West Dunbartonshire Map 20 NS47

★★★★71% **Beardmore**
Beardmore St G81 4SA
☎ 0141 951 6000 🖷 0141 951 6018
e-mail: beardmore.hotel@hci.co.uk
Best Western
Dir: *M8 junct 19/A814 towards Dumbarton then follow tourist signs. Turn left onto Beardmore St & follow signs*
Attracting business and conference custom, this impressive modern hotel lies beside the River Clyde and shares a building with a hospital (but the latter does not intrude). Spacious and imposing public areas include a stylish restaurant providing innovative contemporary cooking. The café bar offers a more extensive choice of equally tempting dishes.
ROOMS: 168 en suite No smoking in 92 bedrooms **FACILITIES:** **Spa** STV Indoor swimming (H) Sauna Solarium Gym Swimming pool supervised, Selection of complimentary therapies **CONF:** Thtr 170 Class 24 Board 26 **SERVICES:** Lift air con **PARKING:** 147 **NOTES:** No dogs (ex guide dogs) **CARDS:**

★★★65% **Patio**
1 South Av, Clydebank Business Park G81 2RW
☎ 0141 951 1133 🖷 0141 952 3713
e-mail: patiocly@globalnet.co.uk
Dir: *M8 J19, follow signs for Clydebank, turn right at lights into Kilbowie Rd, hotel on left over hill*
Situated in the local business park, this modern hotel is a popular conference and function venue. Public areas are contemporary in style and the restaurant offers a range of menus at lunch and dinner. Bedrooms have interesting lacquer and marble effect furniture. Several look inwards as part of an atrium.
ROOMS: 82 en suite (8 GF) No smoking in 16 bedrooms s £50-£69; d £50-£79 **LB** **FACILITIES:** STV Xmas **CONF:** BC Thtr 150 Class 30 Board 30 Del from £75 **SERVICES:** Lift **PARKING:** 120 **NOTES:** No smoking in restaurant **CARDS:**

COATBRIDGE, North Lanarkshire Map 20 NS76

A **Georgian Hotel**
26 Lefroy St ML5 1LZ
☎ 01236 421888 🖷 01236 421173
Dir: *Follow brown tourist signs for Time Capsule, hotel signed on A89*
ROOMS: 8 rms (6 en suite) s £25-£40; d £40-£60 (incl. bkfst) **CONF:** Thtr 120 Class 70 Board 60 Del from £50 **PARKING:** 16 **NOTES:** ★★ No dogs (ex guide dogs) Closed 26 Dec & 1 Jan **CARDS:**

COLBOST See Skye, Isle of

COLVEND, Dumfries & Galloway Map 21 NX85

★★69% **Clonyard House**
DG5 4QW
☎ 01556 630372 🖷 01556 630422
e-mail: nickthompson@clara.net
Dir: *through Dalbeattie, left onto A710 for about 4m, hotel on left*
This family-run hotel is set in seven acres of grounds, that include a children's play area and an 'enchanted tree'. Most of the

continued on p728

COLVEND, continued

spacious, comfortable bedrooms are housed in a purpose-built extension. Meals are served in the bar lounge or in the restaurant. **ROOMS:** 15 en suite (3 fmly) (12 GF) s £35-£40; d £55-£65 (incl. bkfst) **LB CONF:** Class 35 Board 20 Del £55 **PARKING:** 40 **CARDS:**

C

COMRIE, Perth & Kinross Map 21 NN72

★★★73% **Royal**
Melville Square PH6 2DN
☎ 01764 679200 01764 679219
e-mail: reception@royalhotel.co.uk
Dir: *situated on main square*

A traditional façade gives little indication of the total refurbishment that has brought much style and elegance to this long-established hotel in the village centre. Public areas include a bar and library, a bright modern restaurant and a conservatory-style brasserie. Bedrooms are tastefully appointed and furnished with smart reproduction antiques.
ROOMS: 11 en suite s £70-£90; d £110-£150 (incl. bkfst) **LB FACILITIES:** STV Fishing Pool table, Fishing/shooting arranged Xmas **CONF:** Thtr 20 Class 10 Board 20 Del from £110 **PARKING:** 22 **NOTES:** No smoking in restaurant **CARDS:**

CONNEL, Argyll & Bute Map 20 NM93

★★72% **Falls of Lora**
PA37 1PB
☎ 01631 710483 01631 710694
Dir: *hotel is set back from A85 from Glasgow, 0.5m past Connel sign*

Personally run and welcoming, this long-established holiday hotel enjoys fine views over Loch Etive. The pleasant public areas include a comfortable, traditional lounge and a well-stocked bar with a popular bistro and there is a separate breakfast room.

continued

Bedrooms come in a variety of styles, ranging from the standard cabin rooms to high quality, luxury rooms.
ROOMS: 30 en suite (4 fmly) (4 GF) s £35-£53; d £43-£111 (incl. bkfst) **LB CONF:** Thtr 45 Class 20 Board 15 **PARKING:** 40 **NOTES:** Closed mid Dec & Jan **CARDS:**

See advert on opposite page

CONTIN, Highland Map 23 NH45

★★★74% **Coul House**
IV14 9ES
☎ 01997 421487 01997 421945
e-mail: coulhouse@bestwestern.co.uk
Dir: *from S bypass Inverness on A9 over Moray Firth bridge, after 5m, A835 (2nd exit at rdbt, follow to Contin)*
Set in its own secluded grounds with glimpses of distant mountains, this fine country mansion provides a friendly and relaxed atmosphere. Public rooms are inviting and comfortable, as are the individual bedrooms. Crisp linen and crystal feature in the dining room, and a cosy bistro provides a more informal setting.
ROOMS: 20 en suite (3 fmly) (4 GF) No smoking in 4 bedrooms s £56-£94; d £82-£118 (incl. bkfst) **LB FACILITIES:** STV Putting green 9 hole pitch & putt, Pool table ch fac Xmas **CONF:** Thtr 50 Class 30 Board 30 Del from £64.50 **PARKING:** 40 **NOTES:** No smoking in restaurant **CARDS:**

★★74% **Achilty**
IV14 9EG
☎ 01997 421355 01997 421923
Dir: *A9 over Kessock bridge then 2nd road on left at Tor rbt onto A835, hotel on right through Contin*
Friendly owners contribute to great hospitality and a relaxed atmosphere at this roadside hotel. Public areas are full of interest; the lounges have books and games and the breakfast room has a musical theme. The Steading bar features exposed stone walls and offers a good selection of tasty home-cooked meals. Bedrooms are smartly furnished and well equipped.
ROOMS: 9 en suite 2 annexe en suite (3 GF) No smoking in all bedrooms s £39-£63; d £60-£92 (incl. bkfst) **LB FACILITIES:** Xmas **CONF:** Thtr 50 Class 50 Board 20 **PARKING:** 100 **NOTES:** No dogs (ex guide dogs) **CARDS:**

CRAIGELLACHIE, Moray Map 23 NJ24

★★★78% **Craigellachie**
AB38 9SR
☎ 01340 881204 01340 881253
e-mail: sales@craigellachie.com
Dir: *on A95 in Craigellachie, 300yds from A95/A941 junct*
This impressive hotel is located in the heart of Speyside, so it is no surprise that malt whisky is a real feature. The Quaich bar boasts one of the largest collections of malts in the world and the enthusiasm for them is infectious! Bedrooms come in a various sizes, all are tastefully decorated and bathrooms are of a high specification.
ROOMS: 25 en suite s £100-£135; d £120-£155 (incl. bkfst) **LB FACILITIES:** STV Gym Xmas **CONF:** Thtr 60 Class 36 Board 26 Del from £140 **PARKING:** 50 **NOTES:** No smoking in restaurant Civ Wed 30 **CARDS:**

CRAIGNURE See Mull, Isle of

Bad hair day?
Hairdryers in all rooms three stars and above

CRAIL, Fife Map 21 NO60

★★65% Balcomie Links
Balcomie Rd KY10 3TN
☎ 01333 450237 🖷 01333 450540
e-mail: mikekadir@balcomie.fsnet.co.uk
Dir: *In Crail follow road to village shops, at junct of High St & Market Gate turn right. This road becomes Balcomie Rd, hotel on left*
Especially popular with visiting golfers, this family-run hotel on the east side of the village represents good value for money together with relaxing atmosphere. Bedrooms come in a variety of sizes and styles and offer all the expected amenities. Food is served from midday in the attractive lounge bar and in the evening also in the bright cheerful dining room.
ROOMS: 15 rms (13 en suite) (2 fmly) No smoking in 3 bedrooms s £35; d £75-£95 (incl. bkfst) **LB** **FACILITIES:** STV Games room entertainment ch fac Xmas **PARKING:** 25 **NOTES:** No smoking in restaurant Civ Wed 80 **CARDS:**

CRIEFF, Perth & Kinross Map 21 NN82

★★★72% Crieff Hydro

Ferntower Rd PH7 3LQ
☎ 01764 655555 🖷 01764 653087
e-mail: enquiries@crieffhydro.com
Dir: *A85 from Perth, 1st right up Connaught Terrace, 1st right again*
Commanding a panoramic setting high above the town and the focus of a 900-acre estate, the Hydro is the ultimate leisure break hotel appealing to all age groups, especially families. It offers an unrivalled range of leisure and sporting facilities, both inside and out. There is a choice of bars and restaurants, plus a shop and cinema. Spacious bedrooms range from standard to executive.
ROOMS: 203 en suite 6 annexe en suite (67 fmly) **FACILITIES:** Indoor swimming (H) Golf 18 Tennis (hard) Fishing Squash Riding Snooker Sauna Solarium Gym Croquet lawn Putting green Jacuzzi Bowling Football Water ski-ing Cinema entertainment ch fac **CONF:** Thtr 335 Class 125 Board 68 **SERVICES:** Lift **PARKING:** 205 **NOTES:** No dogs (ex guide dogs) No smoking in restaurant Civ Wed 150
CARDS:

CROCKETFORD, Dumfries & Galloway Map 21 NX87

🅰 Galloway Arms
DG2 8RA
☎ 01556 690248 🖷 01556 690266
e-mail: info@gallowayarmshotel.co.uk
ROOMS: 12 rms (8 en suite) s £35; d £55 (incl. bkfst) **LB**
FACILITIES: Xmas **CONF:** Del from £55 **PARKING:** 20 **NOTES:** ★★ No smoking in restaurant **CARDS:**

CRUDEN BAY, Aberdeenshire Map 23 NK03

★★70% Red House
Aulton Rd AB42 0NJ
☎ 01779 812215 🖷 01779 812320
e-mail: ian@redhousehotel7.freeserve.co.uk
Dir: *off A952 Aberdeen/Peterhead road at Little Chef onto A975 (Cruden Bay), hotel opposite golf course*
Naturally popular with golfers, this welcoming small hotel overlooks the golf course and the sea beyond. Bedrooms are comfortably modern in style and well equipped to include hair dryers, trousers presses and safes. Guests can dine in the attractive dining room or choice of bars, from an extensive menu selection.
ROOMS: 6 rms (5 en suite) (1 fmly) **FACILITIES:** Pool tables ch fac **CONF:** Board 180 **PARKING:** 40 **CARDS:**

CULLEN, Moray Map 23 NJ56

★★★64% The Seafield Hotel
Seafield St AB56 4SG
☎ 01542 840791 🖷 01542 840736
e-mail: accom@theseafieldhotel.com
Dir: *in centre of town on A950*

Originally built by the Earl of Seafield as a coaching inn, this hotel was modernised in the early 1970s to provide individually designed, comfortable bedrooms and is now gradually being refurbished. One of the features here is a lovely carved wooden fireplace in the spacious lounge bar. Service is friendly and attentive with good value and enjoyable meals being served in the restaurant.
ROOMS: 19 en suite (2 fmly) s £48-£58; d £75-£100 (incl. bkfst) **LB**
FACILITIES: STV Tennis (hard) Snooker Clay pigeon shooting, Cycling, Quads, 4x4 driving Xmas **CONF:** Thtr 140 Class 90 Board 30 Del from £95 **PARKING:** 28 **NOTES:** No smoking in restaurant
CARDS:

C

CUMBERNAULD, North Lanarkshire

Map 21 NS77

★★★★69% Westerwood Hotel Golf & Country Club

1 St Andrews Dr, Westerwood G68 0EW
☎ 01236 457171 🖹 01236 738478
e-mail: westerwood@morton-hotels.com
Dir: *A80 exit after passing Oki factory signed Wardpark/Castlecary, 2nd left at Old Inns rdbt and right at mini rdbt*

This stylish, contemporary hotel enjoys an elevated position within 400 acres at the foot of the Campsie Hills. Bedrooms are spacious, well equipped and comfortable, and day rooms include sumptuous lounges and extensive golf, fitness and conference facilities.
ROOMS: 100 en suite (13 fmly) No smoking in 51 bedrooms s £95-£118; d £95-£132 (incl. bkfst) **LB FACILITIES: Spa** STV Indoor swimming (H) Golf 18 Tennis (hard) Sauna Solarium Gym Putting green Jacuzzi Beauty salon Hairdresser Xmas **CONF:** Thtr 200 Class 120 Board 60 Del £130 **SERVICES:** Lift air con **PARKING:** 204 **NOTES:** No smoking in restaurant Civ Wed 120 **CARDS:**

⌂ Travel Inn Glasgow (Cumbernauld)

travel inn

4 South Muirhead Rd G67 1AX
☎ 08701 977108 🖹 01236 736380
Dir: *From A80, A8011 following signs to Cumbernauld and town centre. Travel Inn opposite Asda/McDonalds. Turn at rdbt towards Esso garage. Turn right at mini-rdbt*
Travel Inn offers good-quality, value-for-money accommodation. Spacious, en suite rooms with bath and shower comfortably accommodate a family of up to two adults and two children (to age 15). The restaurant and bar offers a varied menu. For further details and the Travel Inn phone number, consult the Hotel Groups page.
ROOMS: 37 en suite s £44.95; d £44.95

CUPAR, Fife

Map 21 NO31

★★★75% ®® *Craigsanquhar House*

KY15 4PZ
☎ 01334 653426 🖹 01334 653457
e-mail: info@craigsanquhar.com
Set amidst farmland this imposing country mansion is a haven of calm and relaxation. Attentive and friendly staff provide high levels of customer care and the cuisine displays an innovative and adventurous style. Elegant public rooms and master bedrooms are graced with rich fabrics and period pieces. The second floor rooms vary in size but all have character.
ROOMS: 13 en suite No smoking in all bedrooms **FACILITIES:** STV **CONF:** Thtr 200 Class 80 **PARKING:** 50 **NOTES:** No dogs (ex guide dogs) **CARDS:**

★★62% Eden House

2 Pitscottie Rd KY15 4HF
☎ 01334 652510 🖹 01334 652277
e-mail: hotel@eden.group.com
Dir: *on A91 on eastern side of Cupar, opposite Haugh Park*

This small hotel enjoys a location convenient for the many attractions and golf courses in Fife and Perthshire. The comfortably appointed bedrooms are thoughtfully equipped and include rooms in an adjacent cottage. Dinner can be enjoyed in either the stylish conservatory restaurant or the cosy bar.
ROOMS: 9 en suite 2 annexe en suite (2 GF) s £50; d £75 (incl. bkfst) **LB FACILITIES:** STV **PARKING:** 20 **NOTES:** No smoking in restaurant **CARDS:**

DERVAIG See Mull, Isle of

DIRLETON, East Lothian

Map 21 NT58

★★★71% ® The Open Arms

EH39 5EG
☎ 01620 850241 🖹 01620 850570
e-mail: openarms@clara.co.uk
Dir: *from A1 follow signs for North Berwick, through Gullane, 2m on left*

This long-established hotel sits by the village green and looks across to Dirleton Castle. It has the ambience of a country house, with friendly service to match. Public areas include an inviting lounge and a cosy bar. There are two restaurants; the bright cheerful Deaveau's Brasserie and the intimate Library for that special occasion. Bedrooms come in a variety of sizes.
ROOMS: 10 en suite (1 fmly) s £75-£95; d £100-£190 (incl. bkfst) **LB FACILITIES:** Xmas **CONF:** Thtr 200 Class 150 Board 100 **PARKING:** 30 **NOTES:** No smoking in restaurant Closed 4-15 Jan
CARDS:

DOLLAR, Clackmannanshire Map 21 NS99

★★70% **Castle Campbell Hotel**
11 Bridge St FK14 7DE
☎ 01259 742519 📠 01259 743742
e-mail: bookings@castle-campbell.co.uk
Dir: *on A91 Stirling to St Andrews Rd, in the centre of Dollar, by bridge overlooking Dollar Burn & Clock Tower*
This welcoming country town hotel is blossoming under new owners. Attractive and inviting public areas feature a delightful lounge with lots to read and a real fire in season. Tasty meals are served in both the comfortable bar and cosy restaurant.
ROOMS: 8 en suite (2 fmly) No smoking in all bedrooms s fr £48; d fr £70 (incl. bkfst) **FACILITIES:** Xmas **CONF:** Thtr 80 Class 60 Board 40 Del from £80 **PARKING:** 8 **NOTES:** No smoking in restaurant **CARDS:**

DORNOCH, Highland Map 23 NH78

★★★71% ***Royal Golf Hotel***
The 1st Tee IV25 3LG
☎ 01862 810283 📠 01862 810923
e-mail: royalgolf@morton-hotels.com
Dir: *from A9, turn to Dornoch and continue through main street. Straight ahead at crossroads, hotel is 200yds on right*

This stylish, refurbished hotel enjoys a super location adjacent to the Royal Dornoch Golf Club, and has glorious views over the Dornoch Firth. A split-level conservatory restaurant gives sweeping views of the golf course and there is also a smart cocktail lounge. Main house bedrooms are modern and stylish.
ROOMS: 25 en suite (2 fmly) **PARKING:** 20 **NOTES:** No smoking in restaurant **CARDS:**

★★68% **Burghfield House**
IV25 3HN
☎ 01862 810212 📠 01862 810404
e-mail: burghfield@cali.co.uk
Dir: *off A9 at Evelix junct, 1m into Dornoch. Just before War Memorial turn left and follow road up hill to tower in the trees*
Set in gardens above the town this extended Victorian mansion provides a friendly and relaxing atmosphere. Public areas, including a delightful lounge, are enhanced with antiques, fresh flowers and real fires. The freshly decorated bedrooms are generally well proportioned and split between the main house and an annexe building.
ROOMS: 13 en suite 15 annexe en suite s £60-£75; d £90-£120 (incl. bkfst) **LB** **FACILITIES:** Sauna Putting green ch fac Xmas **CONF:** Thtr 100 Board 80 **PARKING:** 62 **NOTES:** No smoking in restaurant Closed Jan - Feb Civ Wed 50 **CARDS:**

DRUMNADROCHIT, Highland Map 23 NH53

★★★67% **Polmaily House Hotel**
IV63 6XT
☎ 01456 450343 📠 01456 450813
e-mail: polmaily@btinternet.com
Dir: *in Drumnadrochit, next to the monster exhibition, turn onto A831(signed Cannich), hotel 2m on right. 1.5m from Loch Ness*
Run by a family, this relaxing country house is geared for children, with a pets' corner and well-stocked play areas. The 18 acres of lawns and woods also include good leisure facilities, such as a swimming pool, horse riding and tennis. Good home-cooked dinners are also on offer.
ROOMS: 10 en suite (6 fmly) No smoking in 5 bedrooms s £33-£72; d £66-£144 (incl. bkfst) **LB** **FACILITIES:** Indoor swimming (H) Tennis (hard) Fishing Riding Solarium Croquet lawn Indoor/outdoor childs play area, Boating, Pony rides, Beauty massage, bicycles ch fac Xmas **CONF:** BC Thtr 25 Class 8 Board 14 Del from £80 **PARKING:** 20 **NOTES:** No smoking in restaurant Civ Wed 50 **CARDS:**

A Loch Ness Lodge
IV63 6TU
☎ 01456 450342 📠 01456 450429
e-mail: info@lochness-hotel.com
Dir: *off A82 onto A831 Cannich Rd, hotel above junction*
ROOMS: 7 en suite 20 annexe en suite No smoking in 10 bedrooms s £60-£65; d £80-£100 (incl. bkfst) **CONF:** Thtr 50 Class 40 Board 40 Del from £80 **PARKING:** 80 **NOTES:** ★★★ No dogs (ex guide dogs) Closed Oct-Apr **CARDS:**

DRYMEN, Stirling Map 20 NS48

★★★65% **Winnock**
Best Western
The Square G63 0BL
☎ 01360 660245 📠 01360 660267
e-mail: info@winnockhotel.com
Dir: *from S follow M74 onto M8 through Glasgow. Exit junct 16B, follow A809 to Aberfoyle*

Occupying a prominent position overlooking the village green, this is a popular hotel offering well-equipped bedrooms of various sizes and styles. The public rooms consist of a comfortable foyer lounge with open fire, a popular lounge bar, and a cosy and attractive restaurant, as well as several other versatile rooms.
ROOMS: 48 en suite (12 fmly) No smoking in 17 bedrooms s £60-£69; d £82-£92 (incl. bkfst) **LB** **FACILITIES:** Petanque entertainment Xmas **CONF:** Thtr 140 Class 60 Board 70 Del from £50 **PARKING:** 60 **NOTES:** No dogs (ex guide dogs) No smoking in restaurant Civ Wed 120 **CARDS:**

DUISDALEMORE See Skye, Isle of

DUMBARTON, West Dunbartonshire — Map 20 NS37

⌂ Travelodge
Milton G82 2TZ
☎ 08700 850 950 📠 01389 765202
Dir: *1m E, on A82 westbound*
Travelodge offers good quality, good value, modern accommodation. Ideal for families, the spacious, en suite bedrooms include remote-control TV, tea and coffee-making facilities, luxury beds and free morning newspaper. Meals can be taken at the nearby family restaurant. For further details and the Travelodge phone number, consult the Hotel Groups page.
ROOMS: 32 en suite s fr £42.95; d fr £42.95

DUMFRIES, Dumfries & Galloway — Map 21 NX97
See also Carrutherstown

★★★69% Cairndale Hotel & Leisure Club
English St DG1 2DF
☎ 01387 254111 📠 01387 250555
e-mail: sales@cairndale.fsnet.co.uk
Dir: *from S turn off M6 onto A75 to Dumfries, left at 1st rdbt, cross railway bridge, continue to traffic lights, hotel 1st building on left*

Within walking distance of the town centre, this hotel provides a wide range of amenities, including extensive leisure facilities and an impressive conference and entertainment centre. Bedrooms range from stylish new suites to cosy singles. Restaurants and a coffee shop offer everything from a full dinner to a quick snack.
ROOMS: 91 en suite (22 fmly) (5 GF) No smoking in 45 bedrooms s fr £89; d £109-£149 (incl. bkfst) **LB FACILITIES: Spa** STV Indoor swimming (H) Sauna Solarium Gym Jacuzzi Steam room entertainment Xmas **CONF:** Thtr 300 Class 150 Board 50 Del £145 **SERVICES:** Lift **PARKING:** 120 **NOTES:** No smoking in restaurant Civ Wed 300 **CARDS:**

★★★69% *Station*
49 Lovers Walk DG1 1LT
☎ 01387 254316 📠 01387 250388
e-mail: info@stationhotel.co.uk
Dir: *A75, follow signs to Dumfries town centre, hotel opp railway station*

This hotel, sympathetically modernised to blend with its fine Victorian characteristics, offers well-equipped bedrooms. The Courtyard Bistro serves an extensive menu in an informal

continued

atmosphere during the evening, and good value meals can also b served in the lounge bar and conservatory.

ROOMS: 32 en suite (2 fmly) No smoking in 12 bedrooms **FACILITIES: Spa** STV **CONF:** Thtr 60 Class 20 Board 30 **SERVICES:** Li **PARKING:** 40 **NOTES:** Civ Wed 60 **CARDS:**

⌂ Travel Inn
Annan Rd, Collin DG1 3JX
☎ 08701 977078 📠 01387 266475
Dir: *on main rdbt junct of the Euroroute bypass (A75)*
Travel Inn offers good-quality, value-for-money accommodation. Spacious, en suite rooms with bath and shower comfortably accommodate a family of up to two adults and two children (to age 15). The restaurant and bar offers a varied menu. For further details and the Travel Inn phone number, consult the Hotel Groups page.
ROOMS: 40 en suite s £44.95; d £44.95

⌂ Travelodge
Annan Rd, Collin DG1 3SE
☎ 08700 850 950 📠 01387 750658
Dir: *on A75*
Travelodge offers good quality, good value, modern accommodation. Ideal for families, the spacious, en suite bedrooms include remote-control TV, tea and coffee-making facilities, luxury beds and free morning newspaper. Meals can be taken at the nearby family restaurant. For further details and the Travelodge phone number, consult the Hotel Groups page.
ROOMS: 40 en suite s fr £42.95; d fr £42.95

DUNBLANE, Stirling — Map 21 NN7

Top 200 - Hotel

★★★ Cromlix House
Kinbuck FK15 9JT
☎ 01786 822125 📠 01786 825450
e-mail: reservations@cromlixhouse.com
Dir: *off A9 N of Dunblane. Exit B8033 to Kinbuck Village then after village cross narrow bridge drive 200yds on left*
Sitting in sweeping gardens and surrounded by a 2000-acre estate, Cromlix House is an imposing Victorian mansion, boasting gracious and inviting public areas. The two dining rooms provide delightful settings for the creative and skilled

continued

output from the kitchen. Bedrooms are individual, classically styled and many have a private sitting room.

ROOMS: 14 en suite s £125-£200; d £225-£380 (incl. bkfst) **LB** **FACILITIES:** Tennis (hard) Fishing Croquet lawn Clay pigeon shooting Falconry Archery Xmas **CONF:** Thtr 40 Class 24 Board 24 Del from £200 **PARKING:** 51 **NOTES:** No smoking in restaurant Closed 2-29 Jan RS Oct-Apr Civ Wed 55
CARDS:

DUNDEE, Dundee City

Map 21 NO43

★★★★74% Apex City Quay Hotel & Spa

1 West Victoria Dock Rd DD1 3JP
☎ 01382 202404 & 0845 608 3456 Fax 01382 201401
e-mail: cityquay@apexhotels.co.uk

This stylish, purpose built, modern hotel occupies an enviable position in the heart of the regenerated centre of Dundee. Bedrooms, including a number of smart suites, feature the very latest in design. Warm hospitality and professional service are an integral part of the appeal. Open plan public areas with panoramic windows and contemporary food options complete the package.

ROOMS: 153 en suite (16 fmly) No smoking in 122 bedrooms s fr £120; d fr £120 **LB** **FACILITIES: Spa** STV Indoor swimming (H) Sauna Gym Jacuzzi Swimming pool supervised Xmas **CONF:** BC Thtr 450 Class 320 Board 80 Del from £109 **SERVICES:** Lift **PARKING:** 150 **NOTES:** No dogs (ex guide dogs) No smoking in restaurant Civ Wed 300
CARDS:

★★★68% Sandford Country House Hotel

Newton Hill, Wormit DD6 8RG
☎ 01382 541802 Fax 01382 542136
e-mail: sandford.hotel@btinternet.com

Dir: *off A92 at junct B946, hotel entrance 100yds from junct on left*

Built around the turn of the last century, this hotel lies in wooded grounds well off the main road. Set around a small terraced courtyard, it is a popular venue for meals, which are served in the bar or restaurant. Bedrooms come in a variety of sizes and have been refurbished in a smart modern style.

ROOMS: 16 en suite (2 fmly) No smoking in 15 bedrooms s £30-£60; d £60-£120 (incl. bkfst) **LB** **FACILITIES:** STV Adj to sports club, Cycle hire Xmas **CONF:** Thtr 45 Class 25 Board 25 Del from £95 **PARKING:** 30 **NOTES:** No smoking in restaurant Civ Wed 55
CARDS:

★★73% The Shaftesbury

THE CIRCLE
Selected Individual Hotels
GREAT BRITAIN

1 Hyndford St DD2 1HQ
☎ 01382 669216 Fax 01382 641598
e-mail: reservations@shaftesbury-hotel.co.uk

Dir: *from Perth signed to Airport, take 1st left at circle, turn right, follow Perth Rd, turn right*

A comfortable, welcoming hotel situated in the west end where the owners and their staff are friendly and willing to please. Spotlessly maintained, this impressive Victorian house has been sympathetically converted, offering inviting public areas including a cosy lounge, bar and restaurant. Bedrooms are individually decorated.

ROOMS: 12 en suite (2 fmly) s £51; d £68-£80 (incl. bkfst) **LB** **NOTES:** No smoking in restaurant **CARDS:**

⌂ Premier Lodge (Dundee North)

PREMIER LODGE

Dayton Dr, Camberdown Leisure Park, Kingsway DD2 3SQ
☎ 0870 9906420 Fax 0870 9906421

Dir: *off A90 into Coupar Angus Rd, hotel visible from dual-carriageway, exit by slip road for Camperdown Leisure Park*

Premier Lodge offers modern, well-equipped, en suite accommodation suitable for both business and leisure travellers. Meals can be taken at the adjacent popular restaurant and bar, which is fully licensed. For further details, consult the Hotel Groups page.

ROOMS: 78 en suite s £44; d £44

⌂ Travel Inn (Dundee Discovery Quay)

travel inn

Discovery Quay, Riverside Dr DD1 4XA
☎ 08701 977079 Fax 01382 203237

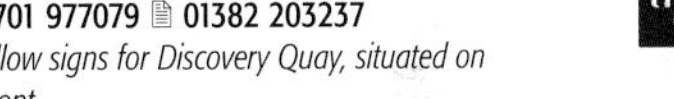

Dir: *follow signs for Discovery Quay, situated on waterfront*

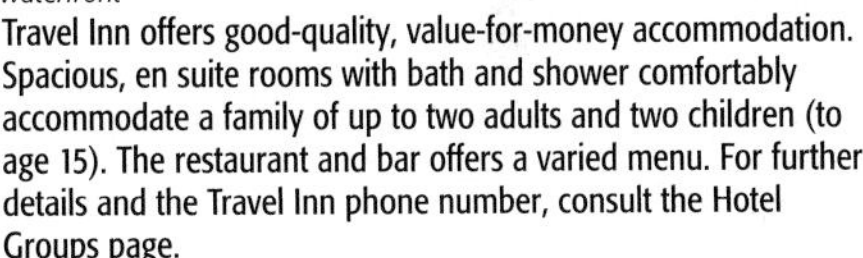

Travel Inn offers good-quality, value-for-money accommodation. Spacious, en suite rooms with bath and shower comfortably accommodate a family of up to two adults and two children (to age 15). The restaurant and bar offers a varied menu. For further details and the Travel Inn phone number, consult the Hotel Groups page.

ROOMS: 40 en suite s £49.95; d £49.95

⌂ Travel Inn (Dundee East)

travel inn

Arbroath Rd, Monifieth DD5 4HB
☎ 08701 977080 Fax 01382 530468

Dir: *From A90 Kingsway Road follow signs for Carnoustie/Arbroath (A92)*

Travel Inn offers good-quality, value-for-money accommodation. Spacious, en suite rooms with bath and shower comfortably accommodate a family of up to two adults and two children (to age 15). The restaurant and bar offers a varied menu. For further details and the Travel Inn phone number, consult the Hotel Groups page.

ROOMS: 40 en suite s £44.95; d £44.95 **CONF:** Board 8

⌂ Travel Inn (Dundee West)

travel inn

Kingsway West, Invergowrie DD2 5JU
☎ 08701 977081 Fax 01382 568431

Dir: *approaching Swallow rdbt next to Technology Park rdbt take A90 towards Aberdeen, Travel Inn on left after 250yds*

Travel Inn offers good-quality, value-for-money accommodation. Spacious, en suite rooms with bath and shower comfortably accommodate a family of up to two adults and two children (to age 15). The restaurant and bar offers a varied menu. For further details and the Travel Inn phone number, consult the Hotel Groups page.

ROOMS: 64 en suite s £44.95; d £44.95

> Late for dinner?
> Quality Standards mean that last orders for dinner vary according to star rating and should be no earlier than:
> ★★ 7.00pm ★★★ 8.00pm ★★★★ 9.00pm
> ★★★★★ 10.00pm

DUNDEE, continued

⌂ Travelodge

A90 Kingsway DD2 4TD
☎ 08700 850 950
Dir: *on A90*

Travelodge

Travelodge offers good quality, good value, modern accommodation. Ideal for families, the spacious, en suite bedrooms include remote-control TV, tea and coffee-making facilities, luxury beds and free morning newspaper. Meals can be taken at the nearby family restaurant. For further details and the Travelodge phone number, consult the Hotel Groups page.
ROOMS: 32 en suite s fr £42.95; d fr £42.95

D

DUNDONNELL, Highland Map 22 NH08

★★★74% Dundonnell

Little Loch Broom IV23 2QR
☎ 01854 633204 01854 633366
e-mail: selbie@dundonnellhotel.co.uk
Dir: *off A835 at Braemore junct on to A832*

Scotland's Hotels of Distinction

A beautiful but isolated location at the head of Little Loch Broom is an unlikely spot for such a smart and extensively developed hotel. A haven of relaxation and good food, it offers a range of attractive and comfortable public areas and a choice of eating options and bars. Many of the bedrooms enjoy fine views.
ROOMS: 28 en suite (2 fmly) s £60-£75; d £120 (incl. bkfst) **LB** **FACILITIES:** Xmas **CONF:** Thtr 70 Class 50 Board 40 Del from £80 **PARKING:** 60 **NOTES:** No smoking in restaurant Closed 22 Nov-Feb (ex Xmas/New Year) **CARDS:**

DUNFERMLINE, Fife Map 21 NT08

★★★74% Keavil House

Crossford KY12 8QW
☎ 01383 736258 01383 621600
e-mail: sales@keavilhouse.co.uk
Dir: *2m W of Dunfermline on A994*

Best Western

This former manor house dates from the 16th century and is set in extensive gardens and woodland. Bedrooms vary in size and style, and include a number in the original part of the house. Spacious public areas include a number of lounges, a well-equipped leisure club and a stylish conservatory restaurant.
ROOMS: 47 en suite (6 fmly) (16 GF) No smoking in 28 bedrooms s £95-£110; d £120-£180 (incl. bkfst) **LB** **FACILITIES:** **Spa** STV Indoor swimming (H) Sauna Solarium Gym Jacuzzi Aerobics studio, Steam room, Swimming pool supervised, Beautician Xmas **CONF:** Thtr 200 Class 60 Board 50 Del from £125 **PARKING:** 150 **NOTES:** No dogs (ex guide dogs) No smoking in restaurant Civ Wed 150
CARDS:

★★★73% Garvock House Hotel

St John's Dr, Transy KY12 7TU
☎ 01383 621067 01383 621168
e-mail: sales@garvock.co.uk
Dir: *M90 junct 3/A907 (Dunfermline). Left after football stadium (Garvock Hill), 1st right (St John's Drive), hotel on right*

A welcoming atmosphere prevails at this handsome Georgian house which stands in its own grounds on the east side of town. Smartly appointed throughout, it offers spacious and comfortable bedrooms plus elegant public areas with a restaurant offering modern cuisine.

ROOMS: 12 en suite (1 fmly) No smoking in all bedrooms s £65-£80; d £85-£120 (incl. bkfst) **LB** **FACILITIES:** Xmas **CONF:** Thtr 70 Class 50 Board 30 Del from £104 **PARKING:** 70 **NOTES:** No smoking in restaurant Civ Wed **CARDS:**

★★★69% Pitbauchlie House

Aberdour Rd KY11 4PB
☎ 01383 722282 01383 620738
e-mail: info@pitbauchlie.com
Dir: *M90 junct 2, onto A823, then B916. Hotel 0.5m on right*

This family hotel sits in wooded, landscaped gardens just a mile from the town centre. Comfortable day rooms include a foyer lounge, an attractive restaurant overlooking the garden, and a smart, stylish bistro. Bedrooms vary in size and style with executive rooms offering CD players and videos. Extensive event facilities make this a popular venue for weddings.
ROOMS: 50 en suite (2 fmly) (19 GF) No smoking in 19 bedrooms s £82-£92; d £100-£110 (incl. bkfst) **LB** **FACILITIES:** STV Gym **CONF:** BC Thtr 150 Class 80 Board 60 Del from £109.50 **PARKING:** 80 **NOTES:** No smoking in restaurant Civ Wed 120
CARDS:

★★★63% *King Malcolm*

Queensferry Rd KY11 8DS
☎ 01383 722611 01383 730865
e-mail: info@kingmalcolm-hotel-dunfermline.com
Dir: *on A823, S of town*

PEEL HOTELS

This purpose-built business hotel is located south of the town. Public rooms include a smart foyer lounge and a conservatory bar, as well as a restaurant. Bedrooms are not large but well laid out and equipped.
ROOMS: 48 en suite (2 fmly) No smoking in 24 bedrooms **FACILITIES:** STV entertainment **CONF:** Thtr 150 Class 60 Board 50 **PARKING:** 60 **NOTES:** Civ Wed 70
CARDS:

★★★62% **Pitfirrane Hotel & Restaurant**
Main St, Crossford KY12 8NJ
☎ 01383 736132 🖷 01383 621760
e-mail: info@scothotels.com
Dir: *from Kincardine, follow A985, at large rdbt take A994 to Dunfermline, hotel on right in Crossford*
A relaxed atmosphere prevails at this long-established family-run hotel, situated in the village of Crossford, west of the town. Bedrooms are compact and practical in appointment and have benefited from refurbishment. Cosy public areas include a restaurant and a choice of bars.
ROOMS: 40 en suite (1 fmly) s £33-£59; d £53-£72 (incl. bkfst) **LB** **FACILITIES:** STV Xmas **CONF:** Thtr 90 Class 60 Board 40 **PARKING:** 72 **NOTES:** No smoking in restaurant **CARDS:**

DUNKELD, Perth & Kinross — Map 21 NO04

Top 200 - Hotel

★★★ ◎◎◎ **Kinnaird**
Kinnaird Estate PH8 0LB
☎ 01796 482440 🖷 01796 482289
e-mail: enquiry@kinnairdestate.com
Dir: *from Perth, A9 towards Inverness towards Dunkeld (but do not enter town), continue N for 2m then B898 on left*
Set in 9,000 acres of beautiful countryside, this Edwardian mansion enjoys views of the River Tay. Public rooms are furnished with rare antique pieces and beautiful paintings. Sitting rooms are warm and inviting with deep-cushioned sofas and open fires. Bedrooms are furnished with rich, soft, luxurious fabrics, and have marble bathrooms. Food is a highlight of any stay; cooking is creative and imaginative with abundant local produce featuring on all menus.
ROOMS: 9 en suite (1 GF) s £225-£475; d £325-£525 (incl. bkfst & dinner) **LB** **FACILITIES:** STV Tennis (hard) Fishing Snooker Croquet lawn Shooting **CONF:** Thtr 25 Class 10 Board 15 **SERVICES:** Lift **PARKING:** 22 **NOTES:** No dogs No children 12yrs No smoking in restaurant RS Jan-Feb (closed Mon-Wed) **CARDS:**

★★66% **Atholl Arms**
Bridgehead PH8 0AQ
☎ 01350 727219 🖷 01350 727991
e-mail: enquiries@athollarmshotel.com
Dir: *15m N of Perth, turn off A9, cross bridge into Dunkeld*
Enjoying a location close to both the banks of the River Tay and the picturesque town centre, this long established hotel is a former coaching inn. Bedrooms, with the expected amenities, are modern in style and some overlook the river. Public areas include a popular local bar and enjoyable food is offered in the formal dining room or the comfortable foyer lounge.
ROOMS: 16 en suite (1 fmly) No smoking in all bedrooms s £45-£53; d £64-£75 (incl. bkfst) **LB** **FACILITIES:** entertainment Xmas **CONF:** Thtr 30 Class 20 Board 20 Del from £85 **PARKING:** 12 **NOTES:** No smoking in restaurant **CARDS:**

DUNOON, Argyll & Bute — Map 20 NS17

★★78% ◎ **Enmore**
Marine Pde, Hunters Quay PA23 8HH
☎ 01369 702230 🖷 01369 702148
e-mail: enmorehotel@btinternet.com
Dir: *on coastal route between two ferries, 1m N of Dunoon*
This delightful seafront hotel enjoys panoramic views over the Firth of Clyde. Stylish day rooms, enhanced by fresh floral displays, include a comfortable and relaxing lounge and an elegant dining room where carefully prepared dishes are cooked with skill from quality local ingredients. Some of the attractive bedrooms have four-poster beds and feature baths.
ROOMS: 9 en suite (1 fmly) No smoking in all bedrooms s £59-£89; d £79-£130 (incl. bkfst) **LB** **FACILITIES:** Squash Jacuzzi **CONF:** Thtr 25 Class 20 Board 12 Del from £99 **PARKING:** 10 **NOTES:** No smoking in restaurant Closed 12 Dec-12 Feb RS Nov-Mar Civ Wed 50 **CARDS:**

★★70% **Royal Marine**
Hunters Quay PA23 8HJ
☎ 01369 705810 🖷 01369 702329
e-mail: rmhotel@sol.co.uk
Dir: *on A815 opposite Western Ferries terminal*

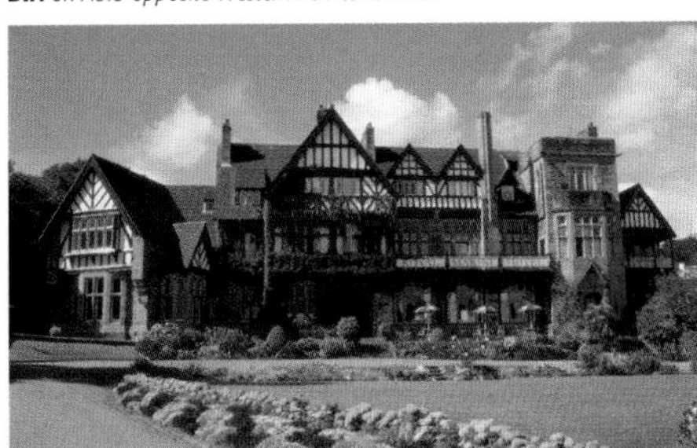

This welcoming family-run hotel commands impressive views over the Firth of Clyde. The variable sized bedrooms are modern in appointment and offer a good range of amenities. Public areas include a formal dining room where a fixed-price menu is available, a well-stocked bar and the popular Ghillies café-bar with its attractive garden area.
ROOMS: 31 en suite 10 annexe en suite (3 fmly) (5 GF) s £42-£49; d £72-£99 (incl. bkfst) **LB** **FACILITIES:** entertainment Xmas **CONF:** Thtr 90 Class 40 Board 30 Del from £55 **PARKING:** 40 **NOTES:** No dogs (ex guide dogs) No smoking in restaurant **CARDS:**

★★67% ***Esplanade Hotel***
West Bay PA23 7HU
☎ 01369 704070 🖷 01369 702129
e-mail: relax@ehd.co.uk
Dir: *in town centre pass main pier and continue up hill, then 1st left and left again at the bottom of the Avenue*
A warm welcome is assured at this family-run holiday hotel which enjoys glorious views. Relaxing public areas include comfortable lounges at ground and first-floor levels and a large split-level

continued on p736

DUNOON, continued

dining room. Bedrooms range from superior and premier rooms to smaller standard rooms, all of which are modern in style.
ROOMS: 60 en suite 5 annexe en suite (5 fmly) (17 GF) No smoking in 30 bedrooms **FACILITIES:** STV Croquet lawn Putting green entertainment **CONF:** Thtr 50 Class 50 Board 40 Del from £30 **SERVICES:** Lift **PARKING:** 23 **NOTES:** No dogs (ex guide dogs) No smoking in restaurant Closed 2 Jan-9 Apr **CARDS:**

★★62% Selborne
Clyde St, West Bay PA23 7HU

☎ 01369 702761 📠 01369 704032
e-mail: selborne.dunoon@alfatravel.co.uk
Dir: *from Caledonian Macbrayne pier. Follow road past castle, left into Jane St and then right into Clyde St*
This holiday hotel is situated overlooking the West Bay and provides unrestricted views of the Clyde Estuary towards the Isles of Cumbrae. Tour groups are especially well catered for in this good-value establishment which offers entertainment most nights. Bedrooms offer the good facilities, many having sea views.
ROOMS: 98 en suite (14 GF) s £25-£33; d £42-£58 (incl. bkfst) **LB** **FACILITIES:** Pool table, Table tennis entertainment Xmas **SERVICES:** Lift **PARKING:** 30 **NOTES:** No dogs (ex guide dogs) No smoking in restaurant Closed Dec-Feb ex Xmas RS Nov & Mar **CARDS:**

EAST KILBRIDE, South Lanarkshire — Map 20 NS65

★★★★72% ®
Crutherland Country House Hotel
MACDONALD HOTELS
Strathaven Rd G75 0QZ
☎ 01355 577000 📠 01355 220855
e-mail: crutherland@macdonald-hotels.co.uk
Dir: *Follow A726 signed Strathaven, straight over Torrance Rdbt, hotel on left after 250yds*

Extensively renovated, this mansion is set in 37 acres of landscaped grounds two miles from the town centre. Behind its Georgian façade is a very relaxing hotel with elegant public areas plus extensive banqueting and leisure facilities. The bedrooms are spacious and comfortable. Staff provide good levels of attention and enjoyable meals are served in the restaurant.
ROOMS: 75 en suite (16 fmly) (16 GF) No smoking in 65 bedrooms s £70-£110; d £110-£160 **FACILITIES:** STV Indoor swimming (H) Sauna Solarium Gym Xmas **CONF:** Thtr 500 Class 100 Board 50 Del from £135 **SERVICES:** Lift **PARKING:** 200 **NOTES:** No dogs (ex guide dogs) No children 15yrs No smoking in restaurant Civ Wed 250
CARDS:

> Popped the question?
> Hotels with Civ Wed in their entry are licensed for civil wedding ceremonies. Maximum numbers for the ceremony only are shown, e.g. Civ Wed 120

★★★65% Bruce Hotel
Cornwall St G74 1AF
☎ 01355 229771 📠 01355 242216
e-mail: enquiries@thebrucehotel.com
Dir: *M74 junct 5, onto A725, follow to East Kilbride town centre, turn right (Cornwall St), hotel 200yds on left*
Purpose-built in the 1960s, this hotel is centrally located and forms part of the main shopping centre. A smart and comfortable cocktail lounge is a feature of the public areas and secure underground car parking is available.
ROOMS: 65 en suite (5 fmly) No smoking in 5 bedrooms s £59; d £75-£95 (incl. bkfst) **FACILITIES:** STV entertainment Xmas **CONF:** BC Thtr 300 Class 100 Board 50 Del from £95 **SERVICES:** Lift **PARKING:** 30 **NOTES:** No dogs (ex guide dogs) No smoking in restaurant Civ Wed 150 **CARDS:**

Premier Lodge (East Kilbride)
PREMIER LODGE
Eaglesham Rd G75 8LW
☎ 0870 9906542 📠 0870 9906543
Dir: *8m from M74 junct 5, on A726 at rdbt of B764*
Premier Lodge offers modern, well-equipped, en suite accommodation suitable for both business and leisure travellers. Meals can be taken at the adjacent popular restaurant and bar, which is fully licensed. For further details, consult the Hotel Groups page.
ROOMS: 40 en suite s £46; d £46

Travel Inn (Glasgow East Kilbride)
travel inn
Brunel Way, The Murray G75 0JY
☎ 08701 977110 📠 01355 230517
Dir: *M74 junct 5, follow signs for East Kilbride A725, then signs Paisley A726, turn left at Murray rdbt and left into Brunel Way*
Travel Inn offers good-quality, value-for-money accommodation. Spacious, en suite rooms with bath and shower comfortably accommodate a family of up to two adults and two children (to age 15). The restaurant and bar offers a varied menu. For further details and the Travel Inn phone number, consult the Hotel Groups page.
ROOMS: 40 en suite s £44.95; d £44.95

EDINBURGH, City of Edinburgh — Map 21 NT27

Top 200 - Town House

★★★★★ ®® The Scotsman
20 North Bridge EH1 1YT
☎ 0131 556 5565 📠 0131 652 3652
e-mail: reservations@thescotsmanhotelgroup.co.uk
Dir: *A8 to city centre, left onto Charlotte St. Right into Queen St, right at rdbt onto Leith Street. Straight on, left onto North Bridge, hotel on right*
Situated in the city centre and enjoying commanding views, this boutique hotel occupies a magnificent Victorian building formerly the headquarters of The Scotsman newspaper from

continued

which it takes its name. The classical elegance of public areas blends seamlessly with the contemporary bedrooms and their state-of-the-art technology. The galleried Brasserie/bar is where to be seen, whilst the Vermilion Restaurant offers fine dining in a more intimate atmosphere. The subterranean 'Escape' leisure club is worth a visit.
ROOMS: 68 en suite No smoking in 25 bedrooms s £180-£265; d £180-£265 **FACILITIES: Spa** STV Indoor swimming (H) Sauna Solarium Gym Jacuzzi Beauty treatments, Swimming pool supervised **CONF:** Thtr 100 Class 50 Board 40 **SERVICES:** Lift **NOTES:** Civ Wed 100 **CARDS:**

★★★★★71% @@
Sheraton Grand Hotel & Spa
1 Festival Square EH3 9SR
☎ 0131 229 9131 📠 0131 228 4510
e-mail: grandedinburgh.sheraton@sheraton.com
Dir: *follow City Centre signs(A8). Through Shandwick, right at lights into Lothian Rd. Right at next lights. Hotel on left at next lights*

Sheraton HOTELS & RESORTS

This modern hotel has one of the best leisure centre and spas in the city; the pool is well worth a look. Bedrooms are spacious and are available in a variety of types – the suites are very popular. There are a range of eating options, The Terrace, Santini's and the Grillroom which have a popular local following.
ROOMS: 260 en suite (25 fmly) No smoking in 204 bedrooms s £105-£230; d £140-£270 **LB** **FACILITIES: Spa** STV Indoor swimming (H) Outdoor swimming (H) Sauna Gym Jacuzzi Indoor/Outdoor hydropool entertainment Xmas **CONF:** BC Thtr 485 Class 350 Board 120 **SERVICES:** Lift air con **PARKING:** 150 **NOTES:** No dogs (ex guide dogs) Civ Wed 480 **CARDS:**

★★★★★69% @@ **Balmoral**
1 Princes St EH2 2EQ
☎ 0131 556 2414 📠 0131 557 8740
e-mail: reservations@thebalmoralhotel.com
Dir: *The east end of Princes Street, corner of North Bridge, adjacent to main railway station*

ROCCO FORTE HOTELS

Built in the tradition of the great Victorian transport hotels, this grand city centre hotel first opened its doors in 1902. Even today, the clock in the tower is kept two minutes fast so that people don't miss their trains. Many of the elegantly furnished bedrooms enjoy fine views of the city and the castle. Indulge yourself with treatments at the Roman-style health spa or cream teas in the Palm Court bar; and choose from two very different dining options - Number One offers fine dining, while Hadrians is a bustling, informal brasserie.
ROOMS: 188 en suite (23 fmly) No smoking in 82 bedrooms s £190-£230; d £220-£280 **LB** **FACILITIES: Spa** STV Indoor swimming (H) Sauna Solarium Gym Swimming pool supervised Fitness abd treatment rooms entertainment Xmas **CONF:** BC Thtr 350 Class 180 Board 60 Del from £195 **SERVICES:** Lift air con **PARKING:** 100 **NOTES:** No dogs (ex guide dogs) **CARDS:**

Top 200 - Town House

★★★★ @@ **The Bonham**
35 Drumsheugh Gardens EH3 7RN
☎ 0131 623 6060 & 226 6050 📠 0131 226 6080
e-mail: reserve@thebonham.com
Dir: *located close to West End & Princes St*

This award-winning hotel sets high standards of style and luxury. Comfortable day rooms and bedrooms combine Victorian architecture with 21st-century technology, and there is a refreshing contemporary atmosphere throughout. Imaginative dinners highlight the chef's commitment to accuracy and good use is made of local fresh produce. The skilled, friendly staff work with initiative and guests are very well looked after.
ROOMS: 48 en suite (1 GF) No smoking in 24 bedrooms s £108-£165; d £127-£330 (incl. bkfst) **LB** **FACILITIES:** STV **CONF:** Thtr 50 Board 26 Del £185 **SERVICES:** Lift **PARKING:** 20 **NOTES:** No dogs (ex guide dogs) **CARDS:**

Top 200 - Town House

★★★★ **The Howard**
34 Great King St EH3 6QH
☎ 0131 315 2220 & 557 3500 📠 0131 557 6515
e-mail: reserve@thehoward.com
Dir: *travelling E on Queen St, take 2nd left, Dundas St. Continue through 3 sets of lights, turn right & hotel on left*

Quietly elegant, The Howard is made up of three linked Georgian houses and is situated just a short walk from Princes Street. There are some splendid suites and well-proportioned rooms, with equally impressive bathrooms featuring claw-foot baths and individual power showers. Ornate chandeliers and lavish drapes adorn the drawing room, while the Atholl Dining Room contains some unique hand-painted murals dating from the 1800s. Room service provides an extensive choice.
ROOMS: 18 en suite s £108-£210; d £206-£475 (incl. bkfst) **LB** **FACILITIES:** STV Xmas **CONF:** Thtr 16 Board 14 **SERVICES:** Lift **PARKING:** 10 **NOTES:** No dogs (ex guide dogs) No smoking in restaurant **CARDS:**

E

EDINBURGH, continued

★★★★74% Norton House
Ingliston EH28 8LX

☎ 0131 333 1275 0131 333 5305
e-mail: res.nhh@arcadianhotels.co.uk
Dir: *off A8, 5m W of city centre*

Situated close to the airport on the western outskirts of the city, this extended Victorian mansion lies in 55 acres of parkland. Public rooms adopt a mainly contemporary style with a conservatory bar lounge, adjoining brasserie and intimate fine dining restaurant. Bedrooms offer a choice of the elegant rooms in the main house and those in the wing have a trendy boutique style.
ROOMS: 47 en suite (2 fmly) (10 GF) No smoking in 27 bedrooms s £110-£180; d £135-£200 **LB FACILITIES:** STV Archery, Laser, Clay pigeon shooting, Quad biking Xmas **CONF:** Thtr 300 Class 100 Board 60 Del from £145 **PARKING:** 200 **NOTES:** No smoking in restaurant Civ Wed 160 **CARDS:**

Town House

★★★★ Channings
15 South Learmonth Gardens EH4 1EZ
☎ 0131 332 3232 & 315 2226
0131 332 9631
e-mail: reserve@channings.co.uk
Dir: *from A90 and Forth Road Bridge, follow signs for city centre*

CLASSIC BRITISH

Classical elegance and contemporary style define this town house occupying five Edwardian terraced houses. Sumptuous day rooms have a club-like feel to them, whilst Channings Restaurant provides dishes cooked with flair and accomplished technique. The individually styled bedrooms vary in size but all are well equipped and furnished with style.
ROOMS: 46 en suite (4 GF) No smoking in 30 bedrooms s £105-£140; d £138-£185 (incl. bkfst) **LB FACILITIES:** STV **CONF:** Thtr 35 Board 18 Del £185 **SERVICES:** Lift **NOTES:** No dogs (ex guide dogs) No smoking in restaurant Civ Wed 80
CARDS:

★★★★72% Holyrood Hotel
Holyrood Rd EH8 8AU
☎ 0131 550 4500 0131 550 4545
e-mail: holyrood@macdonald-hotels.co.uk
Dir: *parallel to Royal Mile, near Holyrood Palace & Dynamic Earth*

MACDONALD HOTELS

Situated just a short walk from Holyrood Palace, this impressive hotel lies next to the new Scottish Parliament building. Air-conditioned bedrooms are comfortably furnished, whilst the Club floor boasts a private lounge. Full business services complement the extensive conference suites and the spa provides an opportunity for relaxation.
ROOMS: 157 en suite (10 fmly) No smoking in 140 bedrooms s £69-£210; d £69-£210 **LB FACILITIES:** STV Indoor swimming (H) Sauna Solarium Gym Beauty treatment rooms Xmas **CONF:** BC Thtr 300 Class 80 Board 80 Del from £89 **SERVICES:** Lift air con **PARKING:** 70 **NOTES:** No dogs (ex guide dogs) Civ Wed 60
CARDS:

★★★★72% Roxburghe
38 Charlotte Square EH2 4HG
☎ 0131 240 5500 0131 240 5555
e-mail: roxburghe@csmm.co.uk
Dir: *on corner of Charlotte St & George St*

MACDONALD HOTELS

This long-established hotel lies in the heart of the city overlooking Charlotte Square Gardens. Public areas are inviting and include relaxing lounges, a choice of bars (in the evening) and an inner concourse that looks onto a small lawn area. Smart bedrooms come in classic or contemporary style. There is a secure underground car park.
ROOMS: 197 en suite (4 fmly) No smoking in 167 bedrooms s £85-£210; d £130-£230 **LB FACILITIES:** STV Indoor swimming (H) Sauna Solarium Gym Dance studio, Spa treatment rooms entertainment Xmas **CONF:** Thtr 300 Class 120 Board 80 Del from £130 **SERVICES:** Lift **NOTES:** No smoking in restaurant Civ Wed 120
CARDS:

★★★★71% Marriott Dalmahoy Hotel & Country Club
Kirknewton EH27 8EB
☎ 0131 333 1845 0131 333 1433
Dir: *Edinburgh City Bypass (A720) turn onto A71, hotel 3m on left*

Marriott HOTELS · RESORTS · SUITES

The rolling Pentland hills and beautifully kept parkland provide a stunning backdrop for this imposing Georgian mansion. With two championship golf courses and a health and beauty club, there is plenty here to occupy guests. Bedrooms are spacious and most have fine views, while public rooms offer a choice of formal and informal drinking and dining options.
ROOMS: 43 en suite 172 annexe en suite (59 fmly) No smoking in 136 bedrooms s £110-£135; d £135-£175 (incl. bkfst) **LB FACILITIES:** STV Indoor swimming (H) Golf 18 Tennis (hard) Sauna Solarium Gym Putting green Jacuzzi Health & beauty treatments, Steam room, Dance studio, Driving range, Hair salon Xmas **CONF:** BC Thtr 350 Class 150 Board 90 Del from £135 **SERVICES:** Lift **PARKING:** 350 **NOTES:** No dogs (ex guide dogs) No smoking in restaurant Civ Wed
CARDS:

Destination dining!
This symbol indicates a Restaurant with Rooms

★★★★70% Carlton
North Bridge EH1 1SD
☎ 0131 472 3000 📠 0131 556 2691
e-mail: carlton@paramount-hotels.co.uk
Dir: *on North Bridge which links Princes St to the Royal Mile*
Located on North Bridge the hotel is just off the Royal Mile. The Carlton has been extensively upgraded in a modern and stylish design. Public areas include an impressive open-plan reception/lobby, modern first floor bar and restaurant and basement leisure club. Air-conditioned bedrooms are generally spacious with an excellent range of facilities.
ROOMS: 189 en suite (20 fmly) No smoking in 140 bedrooms **FACILITIES: Spa** STV Indoor swimming (H) Squash Sauna Solarium Gym Jacuzzi Table tennis, Dance studio, Creche, Exercise classes entertainment ch fac **CONF:** BC Thtr 240 Class 100 Board 60 Del from £135 **SERVICES:** Lift **NOTES:** No dogs (ex guide dogs) No smoking in restaurant Civ Wed 180 **CARDS:**

★★★★70% Menzies Belford
69 Belford Rd EH4 3DG
☎ 0131 332 2545 📠 0131 332 3805
e-mail: belford@menzies-hotels.co.uk
Dir: *in Belford Rd off Queensferry Rd, close to the city centre*
This purpose-built hotel enjoys a quiet location by the Water of Leith. Bright airy public areas include a comfortable reception lounge and spacious open-plan bar and restaurant overlooking the river, as does the separate Granary bar which focuses on pub food. Conference areas have their own manned business centre. The majority of bedrooms have been stylishly refurbished.
ROOMS: 146 en suite (1 fmly) No smoking in 56 bedrooms **CONF:** Thtr 120 Class 50 Board 45 Del from £145 **SERVICES:** Lift **PARKING:** 57 **NOTES:** No smoking in restaurant **CARDS:**

★★★★68% *Apex International*
31/35 Grassmarket EH1 2HS
☎ 0131 300 3456 & 0845 608 3456 📠 0131 220 5345
e-mail: international@apexhotels.co.uk
Dir: *into Lothian Rd at West End of Princes Street, turn 1st left along King Stables Rd. This leads into the Grassmarket*
This modern hotel enjoys a superb city centre location, lying in a historic square in the shadow of Edinburgh Castle. It has a versatile business and conference centre, and the bedrooms are contemporary in style and well equipped. The fifth-floor restaurant boasts stunning views of the castle with a good value, short, innovative menu.
ROOMS: 175 en suite (99 fmly) No smoking in 100 bedrooms **FACILITIES:** STV **CONF:** Thtr 200 Class 120 Board 50 **SERVICES:** Lift **PARKING:** 60 **NOTES:** No dogs (ex guide dogs) Civ Wed 180 **CARDS:**

★★★★68% Edinburgh Marriott Hotel
111 Glasgow Rd EH12 8NF
☎ 0131 334 9191 📠 0131 316 4507
e-mail: edinburgh@marriotthotels.co.uk
Dir: *M8 junct 1 for Gogar, at rdbt turn right for city centre, hotel on right*
From its position on the city's western fringe, close to the bypass and convenient for the airport, showground and business park, this purpose-built hotel attracts an international clientele. Public areas radiate from the attractive marbled foyer and include two

continued

bars, a restaurant providing a choice of modern dishes, and an inviting carvery.

ROOMS: 245 en suite (131 fmly) (64 GF) No smoking in 89 bedrooms s £70-£150; d £70-£150 **LB FACILITIES:** STV Indoor swimming (H) Sauna Solarium Gym Jacuzzi Steam room, Massage and beauty treatment room, Swimming pool supervised Xmas **CONF:** BC Thtr 300 Class 120 Board 45 Del from £135 **SERVICES:** Lift air con **PARKING:** 300 **NOTES:** No dogs (ex guide dogs) Civ Wed 80 **CARDS:**

★★★★68% *George Inter-Continental*
19-21 George St EH2 2PB
☎ 0131 225 1251 📠 0131 226 5644
e-mail: edinburgh@interconti.com
Dir: *Charlotte Sq, follow signs to Leith, along Queen St. Take 2nd turning on right, Hanover St, to rdbt. Left onto George St, hotel 50mtrs on right*
This hotel enjoys an enviable location in the city. The splendid public areas consist of many original features, such as intricate plasterwork, marble-floored foyer and chandeliers. Bedrooms vary in size and are comfortable, some offer city views. There are two restaurants, the formal, elegant Chambertin or the more informal Carvers.
ROOMS: 195 en suite No smoking in 73 bedrooms **FACILITIES:** STV Complimentary fitness club nearby entertainment **CONF:** Thtr 200 Class 80 Board 80 **SERVICES:** Lift **PARKING:** 20 **NOTES:** No dogs (ex guide dogs) Civ Wed 100 **CARDS:**

★★★★64% *Apex City*
61 Grassmarket EH1 2JF
☎ 0131 243 3456 & 0845 608 3456 📠 0131 225 6346
e-mail: city@apexhotels.co.uk
Dir: *turn into Lothian Rd at the west end of Princes Street, then turn 1st left along King Stables Rd. This leads into the Grassmarket*
This modern, stylish hotel is located in the heart of the city, within easy walking distance of many of Edinburgh's attractions. The spacious, design-led bedrooms are fresh and contemporary and all come with artwork by Richard Dimarco. Aqua bar and restaurant is a smart open-plan area in dark wood and chrome that serves a range of meals and cocktails.
ROOMS: 119 en suite **CONF:** Thtr 100 Class 50 Board 40 **SERVICES:** Lift **PARKING:** 10 **NOTES:** No dogs (ex guide dogs) No smoking in restaurant **CARDS:**

★★★★60% *Le Meridien Edinburgh*
18 Royal Ter EH7 5AQ
☎ 0131 557 3222 📠 0131 557 5334
Dir: *from A1 - follow sign into city centre, turn left at end of London Rd into Bleinheim Place continuing onto Royal Terrace*
With the atmosphere of a town house, this hotel forms part of a quiet Georgian terrace. Bedrooms are in a variety of styles, some lofty and spacious with four-poster beds, others more compact.

continued on p740

EDINBURGH, continued

The upper rooms look out either over the city to the north, or onto terraced gardens at the rear.
ROOMS: 108 en suite (19 fmly) **FACILITIES:** STV Indoor swimming (H) Sauna Solarium Gym Jacuzzi Giant Chess **CONF:** Thtr 100 Class 36 Board 40 **SERVICES:** Lift **NOTES:** No dogs (ex guide dogs) No smoking in restaurant Civ Wed 70 **CARDS:**

★★★77% ®®
Dalhousie Castle Hotel & Spa
Bonnyrigg EH19 3JB
☎ 01875 820153 📠 01875 821936
e-mail: enquiries@dalhousiecastle.co.uk
Dir: *A7 S from Edinburgh through Lasswade/Newtongrange, right at Shell Garage (B704), hotel 0.5m from junct*

Set amid manicured lawns and parkland this historic castle dates from the 13th Century. Bedrooms, which vary in size, include opulently decorated themed rooms and suites named after various historical figures (Edward I stayed here before being defeated at Bannockburn). Accomplished food is served in the impressive Dungeon restaurant, open for dinner, and the less formal Orangery is open all day.
ROOMS: 27 en suite 5 annexe en suite (3 fmly) No smoking in all bedrooms s fr £95; d fr £125 (incl. bkfst) **LB FACILITIES: Spa** STV Fishing Sauna Solarium Jacuzzi Clay pigeon shooting, Archery, Falconry, Loch fishing Xmas **CONF:** Thtr 120 Class 60 Board 40 Del from £175 **PARKING:** 110 **NOTES:** No smoking in restaurant RS 5-22 Jan Civ Wed 100 **CARDS:**

★★★75% ® **Best Western Bruntsfield**

69/74 Bruntsfield Place EH10 4HH
☎ 0131 229 1393 📠 0131 229 5634
e-mail: sales@thebruntsfield.co.uk
Dir: *from S into Edinburgh on A702. Hotel 1m S of the W end of Princes Street*

Overlooking Bruntsfield Links, this smart hotel has stylish public rooms including relaxing lounge areas and a lively pub.

continued

Imaginative dinner menus and hearty Scottish breakfasts are served in the bright 'Potting Shed' conservatory restaurant. Bedrooms come in a variety of sizes and styles and are well equipped. Smart staff provide good levels of service and attention.
ROOMS: 75 en suite (5 fmly) No smoking in 49 bedrooms s £75-£150; d £125-£275 (incl. bkfst) **LB FACILITIES:** STV Xmas **CONF:** Thtr 75 Class 30 Board 30 Del from £130 **SERVICES:** Lift **PARKING:** 25 **NOTES:** No smoking in restaurant Civ Wed 70
CARDS:

★★★73% ® **Malmaison**
One Tower Place EH6 7DB
☎ 0131 468 5000 📠 0131 468 5002
e-mail: edinburgh@malmaison.com
Dir: *A900 from city centre towards Leith, at end of Leith Walk continue over lights through 2 more sets of lights, left into Tower St, hotel on right at the end of road*
Overlooking the port of Leith, this former seaman's mission is now home to the stylish Malmaison. Bedrooms have striking décor, CD players, mini-bars and a number of individual, welcoming touches. Food and drink are equally important here, with brasserie-style dining and a café bar, both of which are popular with the local clientele.
ROOMS: 101 en suite (18 fmly) No smoking in 12 bedrooms **FACILITIES:** STV Gym **CONF:** Thtr 55 Class 30 Board 26 Del £146 **SERVICES:** Lift **PARKING:** 50 **CARDS:**

★★★71% **Best Western Edinburgh City**
79 Laurieston Place EH3 9HZ
☎ 0131 622 7979 📠 0131 622 7900
e-mail: reservations@bestwesternedinburghcity.co.uk
Dir: *follow signs for city centre A8. Onto A702, 3rd exit on left, hotel on right*
Formerly named Simpsons Hotel after the old maternity hospital that once occupied the site, this tasteful conversion is located close to the city centre. The spacious bedrooms are smartly modern in style and well equipped to include fridges. Meals can be enjoyed in the contemporary restaurant, and guests can relax in the bar and reception lounge. Staff are helpful and willing to please.
ROOMS: 52 en suite (12 fmly) (5 GF) No smoking in 37 bedrooms s £70-£120; d £80-£165 (incl. bkfst) **LB FACILITIES:** STV **SERVICES:** Lift **NOTES:** No dogs (ex guide dogs) No smoking in restaurant **CARDS:**

★★★70% ***Braid Hills***

134 Braid Rd EH10 6JD
☎ 0131 447 8888 📠 0131 452 8477
e-mail: bookings@braidhillshotel.co.uk
Dir: *2.5m S A702, opposite Braid Burn Park*

From its elevated position on the south side, this long-established hotel enjoys splendid panoramic views of the city and castle. Bedrooms are smart, stylish and well equipped. The public areas

continued

are comfortable and inviting, and guests can dine in either the restaurant or popular bistro/bar.
ROOMS: 67 en suite (6 fmly) No smoking in 8 bedrooms
FACILITIES: STV **CONF:** Thtr 100 Class 50 Board 30 **PARKING:** 38
NOTES: No dogs (ex guide dogs) No smoking in restaurant Civ Wed 170
CARDS:

See advert on this page

★★★67% *Apex European*

90 Haymarket Ter EH12 5LQ
☎ 0131 474 3456 & 0845 608 3456 📠 0131 474 3400
e-mail: european@apexhotels.co.uk
Dir: *A8 to city centre, hotel at Haymarket (just after Donaldsons School for Deaf)*

This modern, purpose-built hotel is ideally located for Haymarket Station and the conference centre. It offers contemporary, cutting-edge bedrooms which are equipped with full valet facilities, plus a safe and fridge. Public areas include Metro, a stylish bistro.
ROOMS: 67 en suite No smoking in 51 bedrooms **FACILITIES:** STV **CONF:** Thtr 100 Class 60 Board 40 **SERVICES:** Lift **PARKING:** 17 **NOTES:** No dogs (ex guide dogs) Closed 24-27 Dec Civ Wed 100 **CARDS:**

★★★67% Kings Manor

100 Milton Rd East EH15 2NP
☎ 0131 669 0444 📠 0131 669 6650
e-mail: info@kingsmanor.com
Dir: *A720 E until Old Craighall Junct, left into city, turn right at A1/A199 junct, hotel 200mtrs on right*

Lying on the eastern side of the city and convenient for the by-pass, this hotel is popular with business guests for conferences and tour groups. It boasts a fine leisure complex and a bright modern bistro, which complements the more traditional restaurant.
ROOMS: 67 en suite (2 fmly) (5 GF) No smoking in 31 bedrooms s £75-£95; d £120-£135 (incl. cont bkfst) **LB** **FACILITIES:** STV Indoor swimming (H) Tennis (hard) Sauna Solarium Gym Jacuzzi Health & beauty salon, Swimming pool supervised Xmas **CONF:** BC Thtr 140 Class 70 Board 50 Del from £120 **SERVICES:** Lift **PARKING:** 100 **NOTES:** Civ Wed 120 **CARDS:**

★★★65% Greens Hotel

CRERAR HOTELS

24 Eglinton Crescent, Haymarket EH12 5BY
☎ 0131 337 1565 📠 0131 346 2990
e-mail: greens@crerarhotels.com
Dir: *Close to Haymarket Station in west of city, at head of Coates Gardens off Haymarket Terrace*

Four Georgian houses have been converted to create this friendly hotel in the West End. Bedrooms are well equipped and superior rooms are particularly spacious. Public rooms include a cosy panelled bar adjacent to the Club Room, where rugby buffs can

continued

savour a host of international team photographs. Here, a bistro style menu offers an alternative to the Garden Restaurant.

Greens Hotel

ROOMS: 55 en suite (6 fmly) No smoking in 20 bedrooms s £85; d £140 (incl. bkfst) **LB** **FACILITIES:** Xmas **CONF:** Thtr 50 Class 24 Board 30 Del from £70 **SERVICES:** Lift **NOTES:** No smoking in restaurant Civ Wed 35 **CARDS:**

★★★63% Jurys Inn Edinburgh

JURYS DOYLE HOTELS

43 Jeffrey St EH1 1DH
☎ 0131 200 3300 📠 0131 200 0400
e-mail: jurysinnedinburgh@jurysdoyle.com
Dir: *A8/M8 onto Princes Street - 1m right at Waverley Station, next left. Hotel on right*

This modern hotel is located in the heart of the city, close to Waverley Station and the Royal Mile. Bedrooms are spacious and those at the front of the building enjoy fine views of Calton Hill.

continued on p742

EDINBURGH, continued

There is an informal restaurant serving a wide range of dishes and a busy pub. Breakfast is served canteen style.
ROOMS: 186 en suite (68 fmly) No smoking in 121 bedrooms s £72-£110; d £72-£110 **FACILITIES:** STV entertainment **CONF:** Thtr 50 Class 35 Board 30 Del from £125 **SERVICES:** Lift **NOTES:** No dogs (ex guide dogs) Closed 24-25 Dec **CARDS:**

★★★63% *Quality Hotel*

Edinburgh Airport, Ingliston EH28 8NF
☎ 0131 333 4331 📠 0131 333 4124
Dir: *from M8 take turn for airport. At rdbt before airport terminal turn left, then 2nd left then 1st right*
Located adjacent to the Royal Highland Showground at Ingliston, this modern hotel is also convenient for the airport. The spacious executive bedrooms are the pick of the accommodation, and there is a café restaurant offering a range of contemporary dishes.
ROOMS: 95 en suite No smoking in 64 bedrooms **FACILITIES:** STV **CONF:** Thtr 70 Class 24 Board 24 **SERVICES:** Lift **PARKING:** 100 **NOTES:** No smoking in restaurant **CARDS:**

E

★★★62% Old Waverley

PARAMOUNT GROUP OF HOTELS

43 Princes St EH2 2BY
☎ 0131 556 4648 📠 0131 557 6316
e-mail: oldwaverleyreservation@paramount-hotels.co.uk
Dir: *in city centre, opposite Scott Monument, Waverley Station & Jenners*
Enjoying a prime location on Princes Street, right in the heart of the city, this long-established hotel enjoys stunning views that include the Scott Monument and historic castle. The front-facing bedrooms and the public areas, all on the first floor, enjoy these views.
ROOMS: 66 en suite (3 fmly) No smoking in 54 bedrooms s £99-£129; d £129-£169 **LB** **FACILITIES:** STV leisure facilities at sister hotel **CONF:** Thtr 70 Class 30 Board 26 Del from £95 **SERVICES:** Lift **NOTES:** No dogs (ex guide dogs) No smoking in restaurant **CARDS:**

★★70% *Allison House*

15/17 Mayfield Gardens EH9 2AX
☎ 0131 667 8049 📠 0131 667 5001
e-mail: david@allisonhousehotel.com
Dir: *1m S of city centre on A701*
Set in a Georgian terrace on the south side of the city, this well-maintained, family-run hotel continues to set high standards of quality and comfort. Delightful public rooms include a relaxing lounge complete with 'honesty' bar, and Murray's Restaurant where bold and creative dishes match the stylish décor. Well worth considering dining in.
ROOMS: 23 rms (21 en suite) (1 fmly) **CONF:** Thtr 25 Class 12 Board 16 **PARKING:** 12 **NOTES:** No smoking in restaurant **CARDS:**

★★67% *Orwell Lodge*

29 Polwarth Ter EH11 1NH
☎ 0131 229 1044 📠 0131 228 9492
Dir: *from A702, into Gilmore Place (opposite King's theatre) hotel 1m on left*
Set in one of the city's leafy residential areas, this converted Victorian mansion offers modern facilities in comfortable surroundings. The spacious bar is popular with locals and visitors alike, whilst the extensive dinner menu is available either here or in the first-floor dining room.
ROOMS: 10 en suite No smoking in all bedrooms **FACILITIES:** entertainment **CONF:** Thtr 250 Class 120 Board 80 **PARKING:** 40 **NOTES:** No dogs (ex guide dogs) No smoking in restaurant Closed 25 Dec Civ Wed 200 **CARDS:**

★★66% Thrums Private Hotel

14 Minto St EH9 1RQ
☎ 0131 667 5545 & 667 8545 📠 0131 667 8707
Dir: *off A701 follow city bypass - Edinburgh South - Newington/A7 - A701*
A relaxed atmosphere prevails at this personally run hotel on the south side. Public areas include a lounge with a residents' bar, while the dining room has a conservatory extension looking out onto the attractive garden. Main house bedrooms are cheerfully decorated, whilst large family rooms are contained in a substantial building next door.
ROOMS: 6 en suite 8 annexe en suite (5 fmly) s £30-£50; d £50-£85 (incl. bkfst) **LB** **PARKING:** 10 **NOTES:** Closed Xmas **CARDS:**

Restaurant with Rooms

The Witchery by the Castle

352 Castlehill, Royal Mile EH1 2NF
☎ 0131 225 5613 📠 0131 220 4392
e-mail: mail@thewitchery.com
Dir: *near Edinburgh Castle gate*

Dating back to the 16th century, two original suites in this hotel are located above the restaurant, which lies close to Edinburgh Castle. The newly opened suites are in another old building across the road - all are lavishly furnished in a gothic style. Dinner, modern Scottish in style, is served in the candlelit and equally theatrical Secret Garden restaurant.
ROOMS: 2 en suite 5 annexe en suite (1 GF) d fr £225 (incl. cont bkfst) **FACILITIES:** STV **NOTES:** No dogs (ex guide dogs) No children 10yrs **CARDS:**

U Christopher North House

6 Gloucester Place EH3 6EF
☎ 0131 225 2720 📠 0131 220 4706
e-mail: reservations@christophernorth.co.uk
At the time of going to press, the star classification for this hotel was not confirmed. Please refer to the AA internet site www.theAA.com for current information.
ROOMS: 15 en suite (5 fmly) No smoking in 10 bedrooms s £68-£98; d £98-£130 (incl. bkfst) **LB** **FACILITIES:** STV Guests may use leisure facilities at the Caledonian Hotel **CARDS:**

U *Holiday Inn Edinburgh*

Holiday Inn HOTELS · RESORTS

Corstorphine Rd EH12 6UA
☎ 0870 400 9026 📠 0131 334 9237
e-mail: edinburghhi@ichotelsgroup.com
Dir: *adjacent to Edinburgh Zoo*
At the time of going to press, the classification for this hotel was not confirmed. Please refer to the AA internet site www.theAA.com for current information.
ROOMS: 303 en suite (35 fmly) No smoking in 176 bedrooms **FACILITIES: Spa** Indoor swimming (H) Solarium Gym Jacuzzi **CONF:** Thtr 110 Class 70 Board 50 **SERVICES:** Lift **PARKING:** 100 **NOTES:** No smoking in restaurant **CARDS:**

Holiday Inn Edinburgh North
107 Queensferry Rd EH4 3HL
☎ 0131 332 2442 0131 332 3408
e-mail: reservations-edinburgh@
ichotelsgroup.com
Dir: *on A90 approx 1m from city centre*
At the time of going to press, the classification for this hotel was not confirmed. Please refer to the AA internet site www.theAA.com for current information.
ROOMS: 102 en suite **FACILITIES:** Gym **PARKING:** 80 **NOTES:** No smoking in restaurant **CARDS:**

Express by Holiday Inn Edinburgh Leith
Britannia Way, Ocean Dr, Leith EH6 6JJ
☎ 0131 555 4422 0131 555 4646
e-mail: info@hiex-edinburgh.com
Dir: *follow signs for Royal Yacht Britannia. Hotel just before Britannia on right*

A modern hotel ideal for families and business travellers. Fresh and uncomplicated, the spacious bedrooms include Sky TV, power shower and tea and coffee-making facilities. Continental buffet breakfast is included in the room rate; other meals may be taken at the nearby family pub or restaurant. For further details and the Express by Holiday Inn phone number, consult the Hotel Groups pages.
ROOMS: 105 en suite s £61-£85; d £61-£85 (incl. cont bkfst)
CONF: Thtr 35 Class 16 Board 16

Hotel Ibis
6 Hunter Square, (off The Royal Mile) EH1 1QW
☎ 0131 240 7000 0131 240 7007
e-mail: H2039@accor-hotels.com
Dir: *from Queen St (M8/M9) or Waterloo Place (A1) over North Bridge (A7) & High St, take 1st right off South Bridge, into Hunter Sq*
Modern, budget hotel offering comfortable accommodation in bright and practical bedrooms. Breakfast is self-service and dinner is available in the restaurant. For further details, consult the Hotel Groups page.
ROOMS: 99 en suite s £49.95; d £49.95

Innkeeper's Lodge Edinburgh West
114-116 St John's Rd, Corstophine EH12 8AX
☎ 0131 334 8235 0131 316 5012
Dir: *M8 junct 1, N on A720. At Gogar rdbt, right onto A8, straight over next rdbt, hotel on left just past church at St John's Rd*
A new concept in the travel accommodation market. Smart rooms meet essential business requirements but also have home comforts. Dining options include all-day menus plus the added advantage of breakfast, which is included in the room price. For further details, consult the Hotel Groups page.
ROOMS: 28 en suite

Premier Lodge (Edinburgh City Centre)
94-96 Grassmarket EH1 2JR
☎ 0870 9906400 0870 9906401
Premier Lodge offers modern, well-equipped, en suite accommodation suitable for both business and leisure travellers. Meals can be taken at the adjacent popular restaurant and bar, which is fully licensed. For further details, consult the Hotel Groups page.
ROOMS: 45 en suite s £50; d £50

Premier Lodge (Edinburgh City Centre South)
Lauriston Place, Lady Lawson St EH3 9HZ
☎ 0870 9906610 0870 9906611
Premier Lodge offers modern, well-equipped, en suite accommodation suitable for both business and leisure travellers. Meals can be taken at the adjacent popular restaurant and bar, which is fully licensed. For further details, consult the Hotel Groups page.
ROOMS: 112 en suite s £52; d £52

Premier Lodge (Edinburgh East)
91 Newcraighall Rd, Newcraighall EH21 8RX
☎ 0870 9906336 0870 9906337
Premier Lodge offers modern, well-equipped, en suite accommodation suitable for both business and leisure travellers. Meals can be taken at the adjacent popular restaurant and bar, which is fully licensed. For further details, consult the Hotel Groups page.
ROOMS: 42 en suite s £48; d £48

Travel Inn (Edinburgh City Centre)

1 Morrison Link EH3 8DN
☎ 0870 238 3319 0131 228 9836
Dir: *next to Edinburgh International Conference Centre*

Travel Inn offers good-quality, value-for-money accommodation. Spacious, en suite rooms with bath and shower comfortably accommodate a family of up to two adults and two children (to age 15). The restaurant and bar offers a varied menu. For further details and the Travel Inn phone number, consult the Hotel Groups page.
ROOMS: 281 en suite s £49.95; d £49.95

Travel Inn (Edinburgh East)
228 Willowbrae Rd EH8 7NG
☎ 08701 977091 0131 652 2789
Dir: *2m from city (east), just before Esso garage*
Travel Inn offers good-quality, value-for-money accommodation. Spacious, en suite rooms with bath and shower comfortably accommodate a family of up to two adults and two children (to age 15). The restaurant and bar offers a varied menu. For further details and the Travel Inn phone number, consult the Hotel Groups page.
ROOMS: 39 en suite s £44.95; d £44.95

E

E

EDINBURGH, continued

⌂ Travel Inn (Edinburgh Inveresk)

Carberry Rd, Inveresk, Musselburgh EH21 8PT
☎ 08701 977092 Fax 0131 653 2270
Dir: *from A1, take exit signed Dalkeith(A6094). Follow signs until rdbt, turn right, Travel Inn 300yds on right*
Travel Inn offers good-quality, value-for-money accommodation. Spacious, en suite rooms with bath and shower comfortably accommodate a family of up to two adults and two children (to age 15). The restaurant and bar offers a varied menu. For further details and the Travel Inn phone number, consult the Hotel Groups page.
ROOMS: 40 en suite s £44.95; d £44.95 **CONF:** Thtr 80

⌂ Travel Inn (Edinburgh Leith)
Pier Place, Newhaven Dicks EH6 4LX
☎ 08701 977093 Fax 0131 554 5994
Dir: *From A1 follow coast road through Leith. Pass Ocean Terminal, straight ahead at mini-rndbt, take 2nd exit marked Harry Ramsden's car park*
Travel Inn offers good-quality, value-for-money accommodation. Spacious, en suite rooms with bath and shower comfortably accommodate a family of up to two adults and two children (to age 15). The restaurant and bar offers a varied menu. For further details and the Travel Inn phone number, consult the Hotel Groups page.
ROOMS: 60 en suite s £44.95; d £44.95 **CONF:** Thtr 35 Board 25

⌂ Travelodge (Edinburgh Central)
33 Saint Marys St EH1 1TA
☎ 08700 850 950

Travelodge offers good quality, good value, modern accommodation. Ideal for families, the spacious, en suite bedrooms include remote-control TV, tea and coffee-making facilities, luxury beds and free morning newspaper. Meals can be taken at the nearby family restaurant. For further details and the Travelodge phone number, consult the Hotel Groups page.
ROOMS: 193 en suite s fr £42.95; d fr £42.95

⌂ Travelodge (Edinburgh East)
Old Craighall EH21 8RE
☎ 08700 850 950
Dir: *off A1, 2m from E outskirts*
Travelodge offers good quality, good value, modern accommodation. Ideal for families, the spacious, en suite bedrooms include remote-control TV, tea and coffee-making facilities, luxury beds and free morning newspaper. Meals can be taken at the nearby family restaurant. For further details and the Travelodge phone number, consult the Hotel Groups page.
ROOMS: 45 en suite s fr £42.95; d fr £42.95

⌂ Travelodge (Edinburgh South)
46 Dreghorn Link EH13 9QR
☎ 08700 850 950 Fax 0131 441 4296
Dir: *6m S, A720 Ring Rd S*
Travelodge offers good quality, good value, modern accommodation. Ideal for families, the spacious, en suite bedrooms include remote-control TV, tea and coffee-making facilities, luxury beds and free morning newspaper. Meals can be taken at the nearby family restaurant. For further details and the Travelodge phone number, consult the Hotel Groups page.
ROOMS: 72 en suite s fr £42.95; d fr £42.95

○ Novotel Edinburgh Centre
Lauriston Place, Lady Lawson St EH3
☎ 0208 237 7497
ROOMS: 180 en suite **NOTES:** Due to open Nov 2003

EDZELL, Angus
Map 23 NO66

★★★65% Glenesk
High St DD9 7TF
☎ 01356 648319 Fax 01356 647333
e-mail: gleneskhotel@btconnect.com
Dir: *off A90 just after Brechin Bypass*
This long established family-run hotel lies at the south end of the village beside the golf course. Comfortable public areas include a choice of lounges, a spacious dining room overlooking the garden, and a well-equipped leisure centre.
ROOMS: 24 en suite (5 fmly) **FACILITIES:** Indoor swimming (H) Snooker Sauna Solarium Gym Croquet lawn Jacuzzi **CONF:** Thtr 120 Class 60 Board 30 **PARKING:** 81 **NOTES:** No smoking in restaurant Civ Wed 60 **CARDS:**

ELGIN, Moray
Map 23 NJ26

★★★74% ⊛ Mansion House
The Haugh IV30 1AW
☎ 01343 548811 Fax 01343 547916
e-mail: reception@mhelgin.co.uk
Dir: *turn off A96 into Haugh Rd, and then 1st left*
This baronial-style mansion is quietly situated by the River Lossie, yet close to the town centre. Facilities include a comfortable lounge, cosy bar, leisure centre and a bistro which is an informal alternative to the elegant restaurant. Many bedrooms are spacious and feature four-poster beds.
ROOMS: 23 en suite (5 GF) s £85-£98; d £135-£165 (incl. bkfst) **LB** **FACILITIES: Spa** STV Indoor swimming (H) Fishing Snooker Sauna Solarium Gym Jacuzzi Swimming pool supervised **CONF:** BC Thtr 200 Class 100 **PARKING:** 50 **NOTES:** No dogs (ex guide dogs) No smoking in restaurant Civ Wed 180 **CARDS:**

See advert on opposite page

TV dinner?
Room service at three stars and above

★★★69% Laichmoray
Maisondieu Rd IV30 1QR
☎ 01343 540045 Fax 01343 540055
e-mail: enquiries@laichmorayhotel.co.uk
Dir: *opposite the railway station*
Convenient for the railway station, this family-run hotel has a great reputation for its range of menus, from high teas to à la carte dinners, served in the bar, conservatory and restaurant. The

continued

former features an impressive range of malt whiskies. Service throughout the hotel is friendly and obliging.

ROOMS: 35 rms (34 en suite) (4 fmly) No smoking in 8 bedrooms s £40-£55; d £68-£80 (incl. bkfst) **LB** **FACILITIES:** Pool **CONF:** Thtr 200 Class 160 Board 40 Del from £84.50 **PARKING:** 60 **NOTES:** Closed 24-26 Dec & 31 Dec - 3 Jan Civ Wed 120
CARDS:

Travel Inn
1 Linkwood Way IV30 1HY
☎ 08701 977095 📠 01343 540635

Dir: *on A96, 1.5m E of city centre*
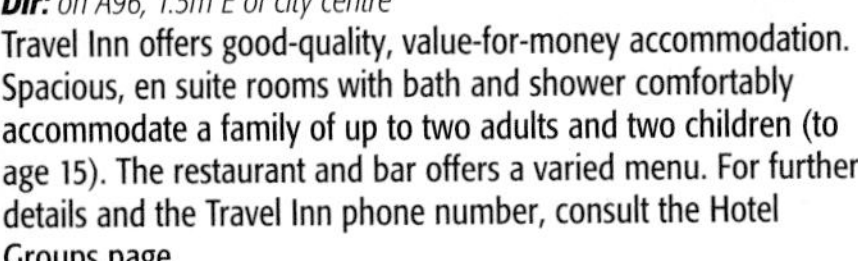
Travel Inn offers good-quality, value-for-money accommodation. Spacious, en suite rooms with bath and shower comfortably accommodate a family of up to two adults and two children (to age 15). The restaurant and bar offers a varied menu. For further details and the Travel Inn phone number, consult the Hotel Groups page.
ROOMS: 40 en suite s £44.95; d £44.95 **CONF:** Thtr 24

ERISKA, Argyll & Bute
Map 20 NM94

Top 200 - Hotel

★★★★ **Isle of Eriska**
Eriska, Ledaig PA37 1SD
☎ 01631 720371 📠 01631 720531
e-mail: office@eriska-hotel.co.uk
Dir: *leave A85 at Connel, onto A828, follow for 4m, then follow signs from N of Benderloch*
Situated on its own private island with delightful beaches and walking trails, this hotel offers a tranquil, private setting for total relaxation. Spacious bedrooms are comfortable and boast some fine antique pieces. Local seafood, meats and game feature prominently on the award-winning menu, as do vegetables and herbs grown in the hotel's kitchen garden. An *continued* indoor swimming pool and spa treatment rooms are available to residents.
ROOMS: 17 en suite s £135-£190; d £240-£290 (incl. bkfst) **LB** **FACILITIES:** Indoor swimming (H) Golf 6 Tennis (hard) Fishing Sauna Gym Croquet lawn Putting green Jacuzzi Steam room, Skeet shooting, Nature trails, Swimming pool supervised Xmas **CONF:** Thtr 30 Class 30 Board 30 **PARKING:** 40 **NOTES:** No smoking in restaurant Closed Jan Civ Wed 40
CARDS:

ERSKINE, Renfrewshire
Map 20 NS47

★★★68% ***The Erskine Bridge Hotel***
North Barr PA8 6AN
☎ 0141 812 0123 📠 0141 812 7642
e-mail: erskineres@cosmopolitan-hotels.com
Dir: *M8 junct 30, A726 to Erskine. At 1st rdbt turn right, 2nd straight on, 3rd turn left*
Enjoying elevated views over the River Clyde and within sight of Erskine Bridge, this bright, purpose-built hotel offers well-equipped bedrooms. Function facilities are extensive and there is a good leisure centre.
ROOMS: 177 en suite (26 fmly) No smoking in 88 bedrooms **FACILITIES:** Indoor swimming (H) Sauna Solarium Gym Jacuzzi **CONF:** Thtr 600 Class 400 Board 50 **SERVICES:** Lift **PARKING:** 350 **NOTES:** Civ Wed 200 **CARDS:**

Popped the question?
Hotels with Civ Wed in their entry are licensed for civil wedding ceremonies. Maximum numbers for the ceremony only are shown, e.g. Civ Wed 120

FALKIRK, Falkirk
Map 21 NS88

★★★72% Radisson SAS Airth Castle & Hotel
FK2 8JF
☎ 01324 831411 01324 831184/831419
e-mail: reservations.stirlingshire@radissonsas.com
Dir: *M9 junct 7, M876 take 1st left A905 towards Airth. Hotel 0.5m on left*
Accommodation is provided in spacious rooms, housed in two separate buildings, one of which is an imposing castle. A popular choice for weddings, this hotel boasts excellent conference and leisure facilities. A choice of restaurants is provided with a fine dining restaurant in the castle and a bistro-style eatery in the main building.
ROOMS: 99 en suite 23 annexe en suite (36 fmly) No smoking in 65 bedrooms s £70-£130; d £80-£140 (incl. bkfst) **FACILITIES:** STV Indoor swimming (H) Sauna Solarium Gym Jacuzzi Steam room Xmas **CONF:** Thtr 300 Class 180 Board 80 Del from £100 **SERVICES:** Lift **PARKING:** 150 **NOTES:** No dogs (ex guide dogs) No smoking in restaurant Civ Wed 120 **CARDS:**

★★★66% Park
Camelon Rd FK1 5RY
☎ 01324 628331 01324 611593
e-mail: enquiries@parkhotelfalkirk.co.uk
Dir: *from M8 take A803 into Falkirk, hotel 1m beyond Mariner Leisure Centre, opposite Dollar Park. From M9, A803 through Falkirk follow signs for Dollar Park*
This purpose-built, well-established hotel is popular with business travellers and easily accessible from all major transport routes. Public areas have undergone a transformation and include a spacious lounge, restaurant and bar, all with understated modern décor.
ROOMS: 55 en suite (3 fmly) No smoking in 32 bedrooms s £45-£75; d £60-£85 (incl. bkfst) **LB** **FACILITIES:** STV **CONF:** BC Thtr 300 Class 140 Board 80 Del from £85 **SERVICES:** Lift **PARKING:** 160 **NOTES:** Civ Wed 80 **CARDS:**

⇧ Premier Lodge (Falkirk)

Glenbervie Business Park, Bellsdyke Rd, Larbert FK5 4EG
☎ 0870 9906550 0870 9906551
Premier Lodge offers modern, well-equipped, en suite accommodation suitable for both business and leisure travellers. Meals can be taken at the adjacent popular restaurant and bar, which is fully licensed. For further details, consult the Hotel Groups page.
ROOMS: 60 en suite s £46; d £46

FORRES, Moray
Map 23 NJ05

★★★67% *Ramnee*
Victoria Rd IV36 3BN
☎ 01309 672410 01309 673392
e-mail: ramneehotel@btconnect.com
Dir: *off A96 at rdbt on E side of Forres, hotel 200yds on right*
Set in well-tended gardens on the eastern side of town, this long-established hotel offers a very high level of hospitality and comfortable accommodation. It is popular with guests and locals for its hearty bar meals, which supplement the imaginative cooking in the restaurant.

ROOMS: 20 en suite (4 fmly) **FACILITIES:** STV use of leisure facilities at sister hotel ch fac **CONF:** Thtr 100 Class 30 Board 45 **PARKING:** 50 **NOTES:** No smoking in restaurant Closed 25 Dec & 1-3 Jan Civ Wed 100 **CARDS:**

See advert under FORT WILLIAM

FORT WILLIAM, Highland
Map 22 NN17

Top 200 - Hotel

★★★★ ⚘⚘⚘ Inverlochy Castle
Torlundy PH33 6SN
☎ 01397 702177 01397 702953
e-mail: info@inverlochy.co.uk
Dir: *accessible from either A82 Glasgow-Fort William or A9 Edinburgh-Dalwhinnie. Hotel 3m N of Fort William on A82, in Torlundy*
With a backdrop of Ben Nevis, this imposing and gracious castle sits amidst extensive grounds and gardens overlooking the hotel's own loch to the valley of the Lochy. Lavishly appointed in classic country-house style, bedrooms are well proportioned and extremely comfortable. Imposing public rooms include the main hall and lounge, both inviting quiet relaxation. Meals are taken in one of three dining rooms where service is quietly attentive. A snooker room and a private video library are available if the weather is inclement.
ROOMS: 17 en suite s £205-£290; d £290-£395 (incl. bkfst) **LB** **FACILITIES:** STV Tennis (hard) Fishing Snooker Croquet lawn entertainment Xmas **CONF:** Thtr 50 Class 20 Board 20 **PARKING:** 18 **NOTES:** No smoking in restaurant Closed 6 Jan-12 Feb Civ Wed 50 **CARDS:**

★★★74% Moorings

Banavie PH33 7LY

☎ 01397 772797 01397 772441

e-mail: reservations@moorings-fortwilliam.co.uk

Dir: *3m N, off A830. Take A830 for 1m, cross the Caledonian Canal, 1st right*

This modern hotel is beside 'Neptune's Staircase' on the Caledonian Canal with views of Ben Nevis. Interesting meals are available in the Jacobean-style dining room and bar food is available in the Upper Deck lounge bar or popular Mariners Bar. Bedrooms have fresh decor and good facilities, and a new wing of well-appointed bedrooms have great views.

ROOMS: 28 en suite (1 fmly) (1 GF) No smoking in 9 bedrooms s £38-£64; d £76-£128 (incl. bkfst) **LB FACILITIES:** STV Xmas **CONF:** Thtr 120 Class 40 Board 40 Del from £75 **PARKING:** 60 **NOTES:** No smoking in restaurant Civ Wed 120 **CARDS:**

See advert on this page

FORT WILLIAM, continued

★★★66% Grand
Gordon Square PH33 6DX
☎ 01397 702928 🖷 01397 702928
e-mail: enquiries@grandhotel-scotland.co.uk
Dir: *on A82 at W end of High St*
A relaxed and welcoming atmosphere is provided at this long-established, family-run hotel, at the south end of the high street. The bedrooms are smart and modern, and there is a choice of lounges. A good range of innovative dishes is served in both the restaurant and bar.
ROOMS: 30 en suite (4 fmly) No smoking in 15 bedrooms s £38-£48; d £55-£75 (incl. bkfst) **LB FACILITIES:** ch fac **CONF:** Thtr 110 Class 60 Board 20 **PARKING:** 20 **NOTES:** No dogs (ex guide dogs) No smoking in restaurant Closed 31 Dec-6 Feb Civ Wed 80
CARDS:

★★71% Imperial
Fraser's Square PH33 6DW
☎ 01397 702040 & 703921 🖷 01397 706277
e-mail: imperial@bestwestern.co.uk
Dir: *from town centre along Middle St, approx 400mtrs from junct with A82*

Many improvements have taken place at this popular tourist and business hotel including a transformation of the public areas to provide a smart foyer lounge, a cosy library bar and a stylish modern restaurant. In addition to standard accommodation, good quality executive rooms are now on offer.
ROOMS: 35 rms (34 en suite) (2 fmly) No smoking in 6 bedrooms s £38-£90; d £65-£100 (incl. bkfst) **LB FACILITIES:** Xmas **CONF:** Thtr 60 Class 12 Board 16 Del from £95 **PARKING:** 15 **NOTES:** No smoking in restaurant **CARDS:**

★★71% Nevis Bank
Belford Rd PH33 6BY
☎ 01397 705721 🖷 01397 706275
e-mail: info@nevisbankhotel.co.uk
Dir: *on A82, at junct to Glen Nevis*
A relaxed and welcoming atmosphere is provided at this long-established Highland hotel, which stands close to the access road to Glen Nevis and the Highland Way start/finish. Public areas include a choice of contrasting bars, a lounge and an attractive dining room. Bedrooms vary in size and offer modern appointments along with a good range of facilities.
ROOMS: 31 en suite 8 annexe en suite (3 fmly) (2 GF) s £35-£49; d £65-£95 (incl. bkfst) **LB FACILITIES:** Xmas **CONF:** BC Thtr 50 Class 30 Board 25 Del from £55 **PARKING:** 50 **NOTES:** No smoking in restaurant **CARDS:**

See advert on opposite page

★★63% Croit Anna
Achaintore Rd, Drimarben PH33 6RR
☎ 01397 702268 🖷 01397 704099
e-mail: croitanna.fortwilliam@alfatravel.co.uk

Located on the edge of Loch Linnhe, just two miles out of town, this hotel offers some spacious bedrooms, many of which have fine views over the loch. There is a choice of two lounges and a large airy restaurant. The hotel appeals to coach parties and individual visitors alike.
ROOMS: 89 rms (79 en suite) s £28-£37; d £48-£66 (incl. bkfst) **LB FACILITIES:** entertainment **PARKING:** 25 **NOTES:** No dogs (ex guide dogs) No smoking in restaurant Closed Dec-Jan **CARDS:**

⌂ Travel Inn
Loch Iall, An Aird PH33 6AN
☎ 08701 977104 🖷 01397 703618
Dir: *N end of Fort William Shopping Centre, just off A82 ring road*
Travel Inn offers good-quality, value-for-money accommodation. Spacious, en suite rooms with bath and shower comfortably accommodate a family of up to two adults and two children (to age 15). The restaurant and bar offers a varied menu. For further details and the Travel Inn phone number, consult the Hotel Groups page.
ROOMS: 40 en suite s £44.95; d £44.95

FREUCHIE, Fife — Map 21 NO20

★★67% Lomond Hills
Parliament Square KY15 7EY
☎ 01337 857329 & 857498 🖷 01337 858180
e-mail: reception@lomondhillshotel.net
Dir: *in centre of village off A92, 2m N of Glenrothes*
This long-established former coaching inn has been extended to create a welcoming tourist and business hotel, in the centre of the village. Bedrooms come in varying sizes and styles, all offering a good range of facilities. Public areas include a cosy bar, a range of dining areas providing good value meals and a small leisure centre.
ROOMS: 24 en suite (3 fmly) No smoking in 3 bedrooms s £40-£54; d £65-£85 (incl. bkfst) **LB FACILITIES:** STV Indoor swimming (H) Sauna Solarium Gym Jacuzzi Xmas **CONF:** Thtr 200 Class 100 Board 80 **PARKING:** 21 **NOTES:** No smoking in restaurant Civ Wed 100
CARDS:

GAIRLOCH, Highland — Map 22 NG87

★★72% *Myrtle Bank*
Low Rd IV21 2BS
☎ 01445 712004 🖷 01445 712214
e-mail: myrtlebank@msn.com
Dir: *off B8012 Melvaig road*
An attractive and friendly family-run hotel set right by the seashore with a smart conservatory lounge. All of the bedrooms are comfortably furnished and well-proportioned, front facing rooms enjoy fine views across to Skye.
ROOMS: 12 en suite (2 fmly) **PARKING:** 20 **NOTES:** No smoking in restaurant **CARDS:**

GALASHIELS, Scottish Borders — Map 21 NT43

★★★67% Woodlands House Hotel & Restaurants
Windyknowe Rd TD1 1RG
☎ 01896 754722 🖷 01896 754892
e-mail: woodlands.uk@virgin.net
Dir: *A7 into Galashiels*
Quietly situated in two acres of grounds, this fine Victorian Gothic mansion is sited high above the town centre. Bedrooms come in a variety of sizes; some are very spacious, with many having views over the gardens. Both the bar and restaurant feature fine period architecture. Meals offered in both are well worth trying.
ROOMS: 10 en suite (1 fmly) s £50-£55; d £72-£96 (incl. bkfst) **LB FACILITIES:** Xmas **CONF:** Thtr 40 Class 40 Board 20 Del from £35.50 **PARKING:** 35 **NOTES:** No smoking in restaurant Civ Wed 50
CARDS:

NEVIS BANK HOTEL

Belford Road PH33 6BY
Tel: 01397 705721 Fax: 01397 706275
e-mail: info@nevisbankhotel.co.uk
web: www.nevisbankhotel.co.uk

Ideally situated close to the centre of Fort William, this privately owned hotel offers the very best in Highland hospitality, with the welcoming staff being both attentive and friendly. Bedrooms are equipped with all modern amenities, and the hotel's two bars and "Lower Falls" restaurant offer the very best in food, drink and atmosphere, capturing the true spirit of the Highlands.

Cally Palace

AA Rosette for Food

Gatehouse of Fleet *Tel: 01557 814341*

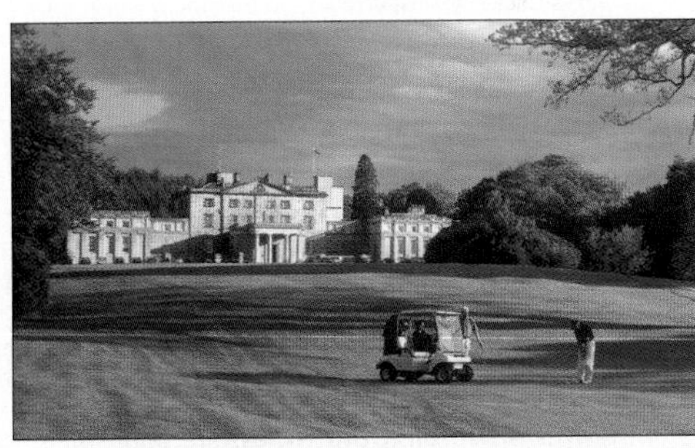

Set in over 150 acres of its own grounds, Cally Palace is the ideal relaxing hideaway. Landscaped gardens overlook the hotel's private Par 70, 18 hole golf course. A hearty Scottish welcome is assured in this opulent hotel which dates back to 1763. Mouth-watering cuisine from Chef Jamie Muirhead is guaranteed.

Other outstanding McMillan Hotels in South West Scotland...

North West Castle	***Kirroughtree House***	***Fernhill Hotel***
★★★★	★★★	★★★
Stranraer	*Newton Stewart*	*Portpatrick*
01776 704413	*01671 402141*	*01776 810220*

www.mcmillanhotels.com

GALASHIELS, continued

★★★65% Kingsknowes
Selkirk Rd TD1 3HY
☎ 01896 758375 🖹 01896 750377
e-mail: sylvia@kingsknowes.co.uk
Dir: *off A7 at Galashiels/Selkirk rdbt*
Friendly service is the trademark of this family run hotel, set in attractive gardens overlooking the River Tweed on the outskirts of town. A fine turreted mansion, it boasts elegant public areas and many spacious bedrooms, some with excellent views. There is a choice of bars, one with a popular menu to supplement the restaurant.
ROOMS: 11 en suite (3 fmly) s £54; d £80 (incl. bkfst) **LB** **FACILITIES:** STV Xmas **CONF:** BC Thtr 65 Class 45 Board 30 **PARKING:** 72 **NOTES:** No smoking in restaurant Civ Wed 100 **CARDS:**

G

★★65% King's
56 Market St TD1 3AN
☎ 01896 755497 🖹 01896 755497
e-mail: kingshotel@talk21.com
Dir: *adjacent to southbound A7 in town centre*
A welcoming atmosphere prevails at this family-run hotel, located close to the town centre. The bedrooms are smartly decorated and equipped with a good range of amenities. Freshly prepared meals are provided in the dining room and bar, and home baking accompanies the morning coffees and afternoon teas.
ROOMS: 7 en suite (2 fmly) No smoking in all bedrooms s £38-£46; d £65-£72 (incl. bkfst) **LB** **CONF:** Thtr 80 Class 30 Board 40 **PARKING:** 6 **NOTES:** No dogs (ex guide dogs) No smoking in restaurant Closed 1-3 Jan Civ Wed 70 **CARDS:**

★★63% *Abbotsford Arms*
63 Stirling St TD1 1BY
☎ 01896 752517 🖹 01896 750744
e-mail: roberts750@aol.com
Dir: *off A7 down Ladhope Vale, turn left opposite bus station*
A friendly and informal hotel conveniently located within walking distance of the town centre. Food is served throughout the day and guests can enjoy a range of generous dishes in the lounge bar and Beef Tub Restaurant. Bedrooms are cheerfully decorated and well equipped and golf is available nearby.
ROOMS: 14 en suite (3 fmly) **FACILITIES:** STV **CONF:** Thtr 100 Class 25 Board 40 **NOTES:** No dogs (ex guide dogs) Closed 25-26 Dec & 2 Jan RS New Years day Civ Wed 40 **CARDS:**

GATEHOUSE OF FLEET, Dumfries & Galloway Map 20 NX55

★★★★70% Cally Palace
DG7 2DL
☎ 01557 814341 🖹 01557 814522
e-mail: info@callypalace.co.uk
Dir: *M6 & A74, signed A75 Dumfries then Stranraer. At Gatehouse-of-Fleet turn right onto B727, left at Cally*
This grand, 18th-century building is set in 500 acres of forest and parkland, which includes a private golf course. Bedrooms are spacious and well equipped, and some of the wing rooms have been attractively upgraded. The short dinner menu focuses on freshly prepared dishes (jacket and tie are requested to be worn in the evening). There are extensive leisure facilities.
ROOMS: 55 en suite (7 fmly) s £97-£107; d £148-£160 (incl. bkfst & dinner) **LB** **FACILITIES:** STV Indoor swimming (H) Golf 18 Tennis (hard) Fishing Snooker Sauna Solarium Croquet lawn Putting green Jacuzzi Table tennis Practice fairway Xmas **CONF:** Thtr 40 Class 40 Board 25 Del £136 **SERVICES:** Lift **PARKING:** 100 **NOTES:** No smoking in restaurant Closed Jan-early Feb **CARDS:**

See advert on page 749

★★★66% Murray Arms
DG7 2HY
☎ 01557 814207 🖹 01557 814370
e-mail: murrayarmshotel@ukonline.co.uk
Dir: *off A75, hotel at edge of town, near clock tower*
A relaxed and welcoming atmosphere prevails at this family-run hotel, a former coaching inn at the north end of the main street. Public areas retain a comfortable, traditional feel and include a choice of lounges, a snug bar and the popular Lunky Hole restaurant where food is available all day.
ROOMS: 12 en suite (3 fmly) s £50-£60; d £90-£110 (incl. bkfst) **LB** **FACILITIES:** Tennis (hard) Croquet lawn Xmas **CONF:** Thtr 120 Class 50 Board 30 Del from £55 **PARKING:** 50 **CARDS:**

GLAMIS, Angus Map 21 NO34

Top 200 - Hotel

★★★ Castleton House
Castleton of Eassie DD8 1SJ
☎ 01307 840340 🖹 01307 840506
e-mail: hotel@castletonglamis.co.uk
Dir: *on A94 midway between Forfar/Cupar Angus, 3m W of Glamis*
Exemplary levels of guest care by enthusiastic owners and their young team, are features of this delightful Victorian house set in its own grounds. Bedrooms are all individually furnished and noted for their comfortable beds. Both lunch and dinner attract a strong local following and are served in the conservatory dining room, and the inviting lounge is ideal for relaxing after dinner.
ROOMS: 6 en suite (2 fmly) No smoking in 1 bedroom s fr £90; d fr £120 (incl. bkfst) **LB** **FACILITIES:** Croquet lawn Putting green Xmas **CONF:** Thtr 30 Class 20 Board 20 Del from £115 **PARKING:** 50 **NOTES:** Civ Wed 50 **CARDS:**

GLASGOW, City of Glasgow Map 20 NS56
See also Clydebank & Uplawmoor

Top 200 - Town House

★★★★ One Devonshire Gardens
1 Devonshire Gardens G12 0UX
☎ 0141 339 2001 🖹 0141 337 1663
e-mail: reservations@onedevonshiregardens.com
Dir: *M8 junct 17, follow signs for A82, after 1.5m turn left into Hyndland Rd, 1st right, right at mini rdbt, right at end to end*
This renowned town house hotel occupies four houses of a Victorian terrace in a residential area. Revitalised under new

continued

ownership it offers the best of personal attention in a discrete and intimate environment. Bedrooms are mainly classical in style, individually designed and thoughtfully equipped to a high standard. Suites and four-posters are available. There is a choice of drawing rooms and two restaurants, Amaryllis and House Five, both with an AA rosette award.
ROOMS: 38 en suite (4 GF) s £125-£475; d £125-£475 **FACILITIES:** STV Gym Tennis facilities at nearby club **CONF:** BC Thtr 40 Class 30 Board 30 Del from £225 **NOTES:** No smoking in restaurant Civ Wed 50 **CARDS:**

★★★★73%
Millennium Hotel Glasgow

MILLENNIUM HOTELS AND RESORTS

George Square G2 1DS
☎ 0141 332 6711 0141 332 4264
e-mail: reservations.glasgow@mill-cop.com
Dir: *M8 junct 15 follow road through 4 sets of lights, at 5th set turn left into Hanover Street. George Square directly ahead, hotel right*

Right in the heart of the city, the Millennium has pride of place overlooking George Square. Inside, the property has a contemporary air, with a spacious reception concourse and a glass veranda overlooking the square. There is a stylish brasserie and separate wine bar, and bedrooms come in a variety of sizes.
ROOMS: 117 en suite No smoking in 54 bedrooms s £55-£250; d £80-£265.50 (incl. bkfst) **FACILITIES:** STV Xmas **CONF:** Thtr 40 Class 24 Board 32 Del £150 **SERVICES:** Lift air con **NOTES:** No dogs (ex guide dogs) **CARDS:**

★★★★73% Radisson SAS Glasgow

Radisson SAS HOTELS & RESORTS

301 Argyle St G2 8DL
☎ 0141 204 3333 0141 204 3344
e-mail: reservations.glasgow@radissonsas.com
Dir: *M8 junct 19 take 1st right, continue to Argyle St. 1st left and hotel on left opposite central station*
This hotel offers contemporary design as well as comfort and style. The huge glass and wood atrium forms the central core of the hotel leading to the lobby, both restaurants, the leisure centre and bars. Bedrooms feature the best in design with the focus on comfort - reflected in the choice of fabrics and ease of use of the furnishings and fittings.
ROOMS: 247 en suite No smoking in 200 bedrooms s £70-£140; d £90-£150 (incl. bkfst) **FACILITIES:** STV Indoor swimming (H) Sauna Solarium Gym Jacuzzi Indoor pool supervised **CONF:** BC Thtr 800 Class 360 Del from £120 **SERVICES:** Lift air con **NOTES:** No dogs (ex guide dogs) **CARDS:**

★★★★71% Beardmore

Beardmore St G81 4SA
☎ 0141 951 6000 0141 951 6018
e-mail: beardmore.hotel@hci.co.uk
(For full entry see Clydebank)

★★★★69% Milton Hotel & Lesiure Club

CLASSIC BRITISH

27 Washington St G3 8AZ
☎ 0141 222 2929 0141 222 2626
e-mail: sales@miltonhotels.com
Dir: *M8 junct 19 for SECC & follow signs for Broomielaw. Turn left at lights*
Centrally located, this modern hotel is a short drive from the airport and an even shorter walk from the centre of the city. Hotel bedrooms are generally spacious and boast a range of facilities, including high speed internet access. Public rooms include the Tuscan-themed Medici Grill and an impressive indoor leisure facility.
ROOMS: 139 en suite (49 fmly) No smoking in 121 bedrooms s £79-£159; d £79-£159 **LB FACILITIES:** STV Indoor swimming (H) Sauna Solarium Gym Jacuzzi Xmas **CONF:** Thtr 150 Class 50 Board 50 Del £159 **SERVICES:** Lift air con **PARKING:** 50 **NOTES:** No smoking in restaurant Civ Wed 120 **CARDS:**

★★★★68% Glasgow Moat House

Congress Rd G3 8QT
☎ 0141 306 9988 0141 221 2022
Dir: *M8, junct 19 follow signs for SECC. Hotel adjacent to centre*
This modern building, instantly recognisable from its mirrored glass exterior, has a convenient location alongside the River Clyde. A feature of the public rooms is a huge wall mural, depicting the city's history, which looks down over the informal No 1 Dockhouse restaurant and the stylish Mariners Restaurant. Bedrooms are comfortable and well appointed and most enjoy splendid panoramic views.
ROOMS: 283 en suite (10 fmly) No smoking in 171 bedrooms s £70-£159; d £80-£179 **LB FACILITIES:** STV Indoor swimming (H) Sauna Solarium Gym **CONF:** Thtr 800 Class 462 Board 68 Del from £99 **SERVICES:** Lift air con **PARKING:** 300 **NOTES:** Civ Wed 261 **CARDS:**

★★★★68% Langs Hotel

2 Port Dundas Place G2 3LD
☎ 0141 333 1500 & 352 2452 0141 333 5700
e-mail: genman@langshotel.fsnet.co.uk
Dir: *in front of Royal Concert Hall*
The contemporary style of this exciting city centre hotel more than meets expectations. The spacious bedrooms, which include duplex suites, invite relaxation with Sony Play Stations and CD players and also cater well for business travellers. There is a choice of restaurants and an efficient health and beauty salon.
ROOMS: 100 en suite No smoking in 60 bedrooms s £110-£140; d £110-£140 **FACILITIES:** STV Sauna Gym Spa & treatment rooms **CONF:** Thtr 60 Class 10 Board 12 Del £145 **SERVICES:** Lift **NOTES:** No dogs (ex guide dogs) No smoking in restaurant Civ Wed **CARDS:**

GLASGOW, continued

★★★★67% *Glasgow Marriott Hotel*

500 Argyle St, Anderston G3 8RR
☎ 0141 226 5577 📠 0141 221 7676
Dir: *M8 junct 19, turn left at lights, then left into hotel*
The Glasgow Marriott is a well-established and conveniently located hotel with a smart open plan lounge, informal café bar and bright fashionable restaurant. The leisure club has been upgraded and includes a gym and pool. High quality, well-equipped bedrooms benefit from air conditioning and generously sized beds; the suites are particularly comfortable.
ROOMS: 300 en suite (89 fmly) No smoking in 212 bedrooms **FACILITIES:** STV Indoor swimming (H) Sauna Solarium Gym Heated whirlpool Beautician **CONF:** Thtr 700 Class 300 Board 50 **SERVICES:** Lift air con **PARKING:** 180 **NOTES:** No dogs (ex guide dogs) Civ Wed 450 **CARDS:**

G

★★★75% *Malmaison*

278 West George St G2 4LL
☎ 0141 572 1000 📠 0141 572 1002
e-mail: glasgow@malmaison.com
Dir: *from S & E - M8 junct 18 (Charing Cross), from W & N - M8 City Centre Glasgow*
The Malmaison is built around a former church in the historic Charing Cross district. Bedrooms are spacious and feature a host of modern facilities such as CD players and mini bars. There is also a range of split-level suites. Dining is a treat with European brasserie-style cuisine served in the original crypt. There is a small gym where guests can work off the extra calories.
ROOMS: 72 en suite (4 fmly) No smoking in 20 bedrooms **FACILITIES:** STV Gym Cardiovascular gym **CONF:** Thtr 35 Class 20 Board 20 **SERVICES:** Lift **NOTES:** No dogs (ex guide dogs) **CARDS:**

★★★70% *Novotel Glasgow Centre*

181 Pitt St G2 4DT
☎ 0141 222 2775 📠 0141 204 5438
e-mail: H3136@accor-hotels.com
Dir: *next to Strathclyde Police HQ. Close to the SECC, just off Sauchiehall St*
Friendly staff, competitive rates and a limited amount of free parking ensure guests return to this hotel. Bedrooms are bright and functional with good working areas and there are a number of larger family rooms. The all-day brasserie and bar menus provide good value and are also available on room service.
ROOMS: 139 en suite (139 fmly) No smoking in 90 bedrooms **FACILITIES:** STV Sauna Gym **CONF:** Thtr 40 Class 20 Board 20 **SERVICES:** Lift air con **PARKING:** 19 **CARDS:**

★★★67% Corus hotel Glasgow

377 Argyle St G2 8LL
☎ 0870 609 6166 📠 0141 221 1014
Dir: *from S, M8 junct 19, at pedestrian lights turn left onto Argyle St. Hotel 200yds on right*
At the west end of one of the city's best-known streets, this refurbished hotel is ideal for business guests. The compact and well-equipped bedrooms are contemporary in style and have all the essential facilities. There is a bright restaurant, lounge bar and a number of meeting rooms, and free overnight parking is available nearby.

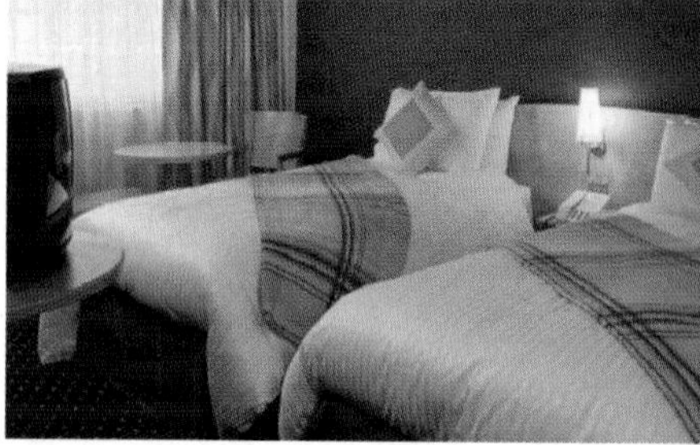

ROOMS: 121 en suite No smoking in 79 bedrooms s £95-£100; d £95-£100 **LB** **FACILITIES:** STV Xmas **CONF:** Thtr 40 Class 15 Board 20 Del from £95 **SERVICES:** Lift **NOTES:** No dogs (ex guide dogs) No smoking in restaurant **CARDS:**

★★★66% Ewington

Balmoral Ter, 132 Queens Dr, Queens Park G42 8QW
☎ 0141 423 1152 📠 0141 422 2030
e-mail: ewington.info@countryhotels.net
Dir: *M8 junct 20, A77, through 8 sets of lights, left (Allison St), right (Victoria Rd) to Park Gates. Turn right, hotel 500yds on right*

Quietly located on the south side of the city, this town house style hotel forms part of a Victorian terrace opposite Queens Park. Public areas include a foyer lounge, restaurant and comfortable cocktail lounge. It's worth asking for one of the larger bedrooms that overlook the park.
ROOMS: 43 en suite (5 fmly) No smoking in 6 bedrooms s £49-£89; d £59-£119 **LB** **FACILITIES:** STV Xmas **CONF:** Thtr 70 Class 20 Board 30 Del from £100 **SERVICES:** Lift **PARKING:** 10 **NOTES:** No smoking in restaurant Civ Wed 60 **CARDS:**

★★★64% Jurys Glasgow

Great Western Rd G12 0XP
☎ 0141 334 8161 📠 0141 334 3846
e-mail: glasgow_hotel@jurys.com
Dir: *M8 junct 17, A82, onto Gt Western Rd. Through 2 sets of lights, left by Gartnavel Hospital & just before Safeway. Sharp right into Shelley Rd*
This purpose-built hotel is situated on the west side of the city. Most single occupancy bedrooms provide a double bed and sofa, whilst others cater for the family/leisure market. Public areas include an Irish bar, an attractive split-level restaurant, a

continued

well-equipped leisure club and conference and banqueting facilities.
ROOMS: 137 en suite (12 fmly) No smoking in 100 bedrooms s £39-£120; d £39-£120 **LB** **FACILITIES:** STV Indoor swimming (H) Sauna Solarium Gym Jacuzzi Swimming pool supervised Xmas **CONF:** Thtr 140 Class 80 Board 40 Del from £90 **SERVICES:** Lift **PARKING:** 300 **NOTES:** No smoking in restaurant Civ Wed 120 **CARDS:**

★★★63% Bewley's

110 Bath St G2 2EN
☎ 0141 353 0800 0141 353 0900
e-mail: gla@bewleyshotels.com
Dir: *M8 junct 18, left to Sauchiehall St & right to Birthwood St then left to West Regent St & left into Bath St.*

In the heart of the city this modern hotel is ideally suited for both business and leisure breaks. Bedrooms are comfortable and well equipped, with several enjoying impressive views over the Glasgow skyline. Loop restaurant and bar serves cosmopolitan food all day in a relaxed informal setting.
ROOMS: 103 en suite (47 fmly) No smoking in 64 bedrooms s £59; d £59 **FACILITIES:** STV **SERVICES:** Lift **NOTES:** No dogs (ex guide dogs) Closed 24-26 Dec **CARDS:**

★★★60% The Kelvin Park Lorne Hotel

923 Sauchiehall St G3 7TE
☎ 0141 314 9955 0141 337 1659
e-mail: kelvinparklorne@corushotels.com
Dir: *M8 (E) junct 18 towards city centre, left at lights, left again at 2nd set. Continue turning right into Elderslie Street & left into Sauchiehall St*

This popular hotel is five minutes' walk from the S.E.C.C. and the Art Galleries. It offers mixed styles of smart attractive accommodation, and staff are helpful and friendly. Guests can eat informally in the bar, from the room service menu or in the smart restaurant. There are conference facilities in a separate wing.
ROOMS: 100 en suite (5 fmly) No smoking in 30 bedrooms s £45-£85; d £55-£95 (incl. bkfst) **LB** **FACILITIES:** STV Xmas **CONF:** Thtr 300 Class 120 Board 80 Del from £90 **SERVICES:** Lift **PARKING:** 27 **NOTES:** No smoking in restaurant Civ Wed 200 **CARDS:**

★★★60% Quality Hotel Glasgow

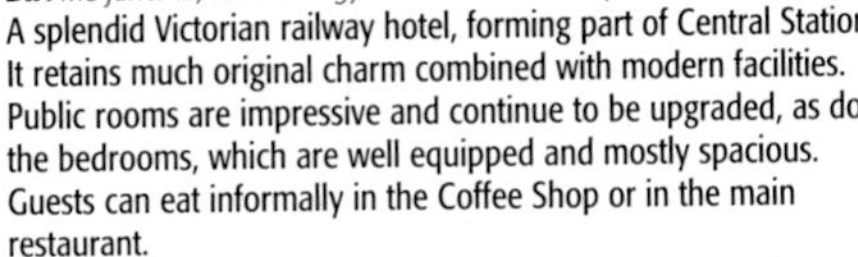

99 Gordon St G1 3SF
☎ 0141 221 9680 0141 226 3948
e-mail: enquiries@quality-hotels-glasgow.com
Dir: *M8 junct 19, left into Argyle St and left into Hope St*
A splendid Victorian railway hotel, forming part of Central Station. It retains much original charm combined with modern facilities. Public rooms are impressive and continue to be upgraded, as do the bedrooms, which are well equipped and mostly spacious. Guests can eat informally in the Coffee Shop or in the main restaurant.
ROOMS: 222 en suite (8 fmly) No smoking in 70 bedrooms s fr £95; d fr £105 **LB** **FACILITIES: Spa** STV Indoor swimming (H) Sauna Solarium Gym Jacuzzi Hair & beauty salon, Steam room, Sports therapist Xmas **CONF:** Thtr 600 Class 160 Board 40 Del from £85 **SERVICES:** Lift **NOTES:** No smoking in restaurant Civ Wed 250
CARDS:

★★75% Uplawmoor

Neilston Rd G78 4AF
☎ 01505 850565 01505 850689
e-mail: enquiries@uplawmoor.co.uk
(For full entry see Uplawmoor)

Holiday Inn Glasgow City - West

Bothwell St G2 7EN
☎ 0870 400 9032 0141 221 8986
At the time of going to press, the classification for this hotel was not confirmed. Please refer to the AA internet site www.theAA.com for current information.
ROOMS: 247 en suite **CONF:** Thtr 850 Class 450 Board 100

Campanile Glasgow

Tunnel St G3 8HL
☎ 020 7515 5045
e-mail: glasgow@evergure.co.uk

This modern building offers accommodation in smart, well-equipped bedrooms, all with en suite bathrooms. Refreshments may be taken at the informal Bistro. For further details and the Campanile phone number, consult the Hotel Groups page.
ROOMS: 106 en suite s £48.95; d £48.95

Express by Holiday Inn Glasgow City Centre

Express by Holiday Inn

122 Stockwell St G1 4LT
☎ 0141 548 5000 0141 548 5048
e-mail: managerglasgow@expressholidayinn.co.uk
Dir: *From M8 east and south take junct 19 signed SECC, left at end, follow river past casino and under Central Station bridge to Stockwell St*
A modern hotel ideal for families and business travellers. Fresh

continued on p754

GLASGOW, continued

and uncomplicated, the spacious bedrooms include Sky TV, power shower and tea and coffee-making facilities. Continental buffet breakfast is included in the room rate; other meals may be taken at the nearby family pub or restaurant. For further details and the Express by Holiday Inn phone number, consult the Hotel Groups pages.

Express by Holiday Inn, Glasgow City Centre

ROOMS: 128 en suite s £58-£70; d £58-£70 (incl. cont bkfst)
CONF: Thtr 30 Class 15 Board 16

⇧ Express by Holiday Inn Theatreland

165 West Nile St G1 2RL
☎ 0141 331 6800 ▯ 0141 331 6828
e-mail: express@higlasgow.com
Dir: *follow signs to Royal Concert Hall*

A modern hotel ideal for families and business travellers. Fresh and uncomplicated, the spacious bedrooms include Sky TV, power shower and tea and coffee-making facilities. Continental buffet breakfast is included in the room rate; other meals may be taken at the nearby family pub or restaurant. For further details and the Express by Holiday Inn phone number, consult the Hotel Groups pages.
ROOMS: 88 en suite s £59-£69; d £59-£69 (incl. cont bkfst)
CONF: Thtr 20 Board 12

⇧ Hotel Ibis Glasgow City Centre

220 West Regent St G2 4DQ
☎ 0141 225 6000 ▯ 0141 225 6010
e-mail: H3139@accor-hotels.com
Modern, budget hotel offering comfortable accommodation in bright and practical bedrooms. Breakfast is self-service and dinner is available in the restaurant. For further details, consult the Hotel Groups page.
ROOMS: 141 en suite s £42.95; d £42.95

⇧ Premier Lodge (Glasgow City Centre)

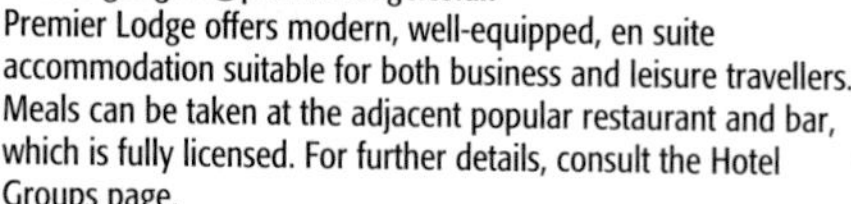

10 Elmbank Gardens G2 4PP
☎ 0870 9906312 ▯ 0870 9906313
e-mail: glasgow@premierlodge.co.uk
Premier Lodge offers modern, well-equipped, en suite accommodation suitable for both business and leisure travellers. Meals can be taken at the adjacent popular restaurant and bar, which is fully licensed. For further details, consult the Hotel Groups page.
ROOMS: 278 en suite s £50; d £50 **CONF:** Thtr 60 Class 25 Board 20 Del from £60

⇧ Premier Lodge (Glasgow North East)

Cumbernauld Rd, Muirhead, Chryston G69 9BS
☎ 0870 9906508 ▯ 0870 9906509
Dir: *M8 junct 13 on A80 Glasgow to Stirling road. 400 yds from Stepps Bypass).*
Premier Lodge offers modern, well-equipped, en suite accommodation suitable for both business and leisure travellers. Meals can be taken at the adjacent popular restaurant and bar, which is fully licensed. For further details, consult the Hotel Groups page.
ROOMS: 38 en suite s £44; d £44 **CONF:** Thtr 85 Class 25 Board 30

⇧ Travel Inn (Glasgow Cambuslang)

Cambuslang G32 8EY
☎ 08701 977306 ▯ 0141 778 1703
Dir: *on the rdbt at end of the M74, turn right at rdbt, at traffic lights turn right & Travel Inn on right*
Travel Inn offers good-quality, value-for-money accommodation. Spacious, en suite rooms with bath and shower comfortably accommodate a family of up to two adults and two children (to age 15). The restaurant and bar offers a varied menu. For further details and the Travel Inn phone number, consult the Hotel Groups page.
ROOMS: 40 en suite s £44.95; d £44.95

⇧ Travel Inn (Glasgow City Centre)

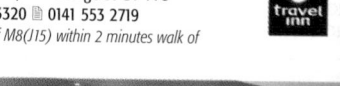

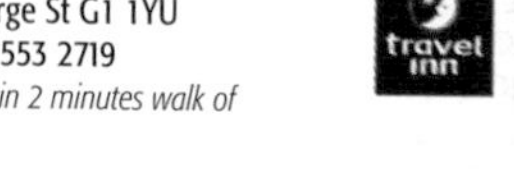

Montrose House, 187 George St G1 1YU
☎ 0870 238 3320 ▯ 0141 553 2719
Dir: *Located off M8(J15) within 2 minutes walk of George Square*

Travel Inn offers good-quality, value-for-money accommodation. Spacious, en suite rooms with bath and shower comfortably accommodate a family of up to two adults and two children (to age 15). The restaurant and bar offers a varied menu. For further details and the Travel Inn phone number, consult the Hotel Groups page.
ROOMS: 254 en suite s £49.95; d £49.95 **CONF:** Thtr 20 Board 10

Travel Inn (Glasgow East)
Hamilton Rd G71 7SA
☎ 08701 977109 🖹 0141 773 8554
Dir: *at entrance to Glasgow Zoo by M73 & M74 junct 4*
Travel Inn offers good-quality, value-for-money accommodation. Spacious, en suite rooms with bath and shower comfortably accommodate a family of up to two adults and two children (to age 15). The restaurant and bar offers a varied menu. For further details and the Travel Inn phone number, consult the Hotel Groups page.
ROOMS: 66 en suite s £44.95; d £44.95

Travelodge (Glasgow Central)
Hill St G3 6PR
☎ 08700 850 950
Travelodge offers good quality, good value, modern accommodation. Ideal for families, the spacious, en suite bedrooms include remote-control TV, tea and coffee-making facilities, luxury beds and free morning newspaper. Meals can be taken at the nearby family restaurant. For further details and the Travelodge phone number, consult the Hotel Groups page.
ROOMS: 95 en suite s fr £42.95; d fr £42.95

Travelodge Glagow Paisley Road
251 Paisley Rd G5 8RA
☎ 08700 850 950
Dir: *0.5m from city centre just off M8 junct 20 from S, M8 junct 21 from N. Behind Harry Ramsden's*
Travelodge offers good quality, good value, modern accommodation. Ideal for families, the spacious, en suite bedrooms include remote-control TV, tea and coffee-making facilities, luxury beds and free morning newspaper. Meals can be taken at the nearby family restaurant. For further details and the Travelodge phone number, consult the Hotel Groups page.
ROOMS: 75 en suite s fr £42.95; d fr £42.95

○ Jurys Inn Glasgow
30 Jamacia St G1 4QE
☎ 0870 907 2222
ROOMS: 321 en suite
NOTES: Due to open Autumn 2003

GLASGOW AIRPORT, Renfrewshire — Map 20 NS46

★★★70% Glynhill Hotel & Leisure Club
Paisley Rd PA4 8XB
☎ 0141 886 5555 & 885 1111 🖹 0141 885 2838
e-mail: glynhillleisurehotel@msn.com
Dir: *M8 junct 27, take A741 towards Renfrew cross, small rdbt - approx 300yds from motorway exit, hotel on right*
A smart and welcoming hotel with bedrooms that range from spacious executive rooms to smaller standard rooms; all are tastefully appointed with a good range of amenities. The hotel boasts a luxurious leisure complex and extensive conference facilities; the choice of contrasting bars and restaurants should suit most tastes and budgets.
ROOMS: 125 en suite (25 fmly) No smoking in 51 bedrooms s £64-£89; d £74-£109 (incl. bkfst) **LB** **FACILITIES:** STV Indoor swimming (H) Sauna Solarium Gym Jacuzzi Beauty room entertainment Xmas **CONF:** Thtr 450 Class 240 Del from £95 **PARKING:** 230 **NOTES:** No dogs (ex guide dogs) Civ Wed 450 **CARDS:**

★★★69% Lynnhurst
Park Rd PA5 8LS
☎ 01505 324331 & 324600 🖹 01505 324219
e-mail: enquiries@lynnhurst.co.uk
Dir: *past airport, take slip road (A737). Continue 2m & take B789. At slip rd left into Johnstone. 1st main lights right, then 1st left and 2nd right*
Genuine hospitality together with high standards of guest care are the hallmarks of this family run hotel, set in a quiet residential area. Two Victorian houses are connected by a purpose built extension giving contrasting styles, reflected in both bedrooms and public areas.
ROOMS: 21 en suite (2 fmly) s £40-£55; d £70-£80 (incl. bkfst) **LB** **FACILITIES:** STV Arrangement with local leisure centre Xmas **CONF:** Thtr 160 Class 160 Board 20 Del from £70 **PARKING:** 100 **NOTES:** No dogs (ex guide dogs) Closed 1-3 Jan **CARDS:**

★★★64% Dean Park
91 Glasgow Rd PA4 8YB
☎ 0141 886 3771 🖹 0141 885 0681
e-mail: deanparkres@cosmopolitan-hotels.com
Dir: *off M8 junct 26 onto A8 for Renfrew, follow road for 600yds, hotel on left*
Situated close to the airport, this modern purpose-built and refurbished hotel attracts both the business and leisure guests and is also a popular venue for local functions. Although not expansive, bedrooms are comfortable and well equipped.
ROOMS: 118 en suite (6 fmly) (50 GF) s £69-£84; d £74-£89 **LB** **FACILITIES:** STV Snooker Beautician & arrangement with leisure club Xmas **CONF:** BC Thtr 350 Class 150 Board 100 Del from £85 **PARKING:** 200 **NOTES:** Civ Wed 200
CARDS:

U *Holiday Inn Glasgow Airport*

Abbotsinch PA3 2TR
☎ 0870 400 9031 🖹 0141 887 3738
e-mail: glasgowairport@ichotelsgroup.com
Dir: *from E M8 junct 28 follow signs for hotel; from W M8 junct 29, airport slip road to hotel*
At the time of going to press, the classification for this hotel was not confirmed. Please refer to the AA internet site www.theAA.com for current information.
ROOMS: 298 en suite (9 fmly) No smoking in 158 bedrooms
FACILITIES: Solarium **CONF:** Thtr 250 Class 120 Board 20
SERVICES: Lift air con **PARKING:** 73 **CARDS:**

Express by Holiday Inn
St Andrews Dr PA3 2TJ
☎ 0141 842 1100 🖹 0141 842 1122
e-mail: info@hiex-glasgow.com
Dir: *M8 junct 28, at 1st rdbt turn right, hotel on right*

A modern hotel ideal for families and business travellers. Fresh
continued on p756

GLASGOW AIRPORT, continued

and uncomplicated, the spacious bedrooms include Sky TV, power shower and tea and coffee-making facilities. Continental buffet breakfast is included in the room rate; other meals may be taken at the nearby family pub or restaurant. For further details and the Express by Holiday Inn phone number, consult the Hotel Groups pages.
ROOMS: 143 en suite (incl. cont bkfst) s £69; d £69 **CONF:** Thtr 75 Class 30 Board 30

Travel Inn Glasgow Airport

Whitecart Rd PA3 2TH
☎ 0870 238 3321 📠 0141 842 1570
Dir: *close to airport terminal, follow signs*
Travel Inn offers good-quality, value-for-money accommodation. Spacious, en suite rooms with bath and shower comfortably accommodate a family of up to two adults and two children (to age 15). The restaurant and bar offers a varied menu. For further details and the Travel Inn phone number, consult the Hotel Groups page.
ROOMS: 104 en suite s £44.95; d £44.95 **CONF:** Thtr 30

Travel Inn (Glasgow Paisley)

Phoenix Retail Park PA1 2BH
☎ 08701 977113 📠 0141 887 2799
Dir: *M8 junct 28A St James Interchange follow A737 signed Irvine, take 1st exit signed Linwood & turn left at 1st rdbt to Phoenix Park*

Travel Inn offers good-quality, value-for-money accommodation. Spacious, en suite rooms with bath and shower comfortably accommodate a family of up to two adults and two children (to age 15). The restaurant and bar offers a varied menu. For further details and the Travel Inn phone number, consult the Hotel Groups page.
ROOMS: 40 en suite s £44.95; d £44.95 **CONF:** Thtr 20 Board 15

Travelodge (Glasgow Airport)

Marchburn Dr, Glasgow Airport Business Park, Paisley PA3 2AR
☎ 08700 850 950 📠 0141 889 0583
Travelodge offers good quality, good value, modern accommodation. Ideal for families, the spacious, en suite bedrooms include remote-control TV, tea and coffee-making facilities, luxury beds and free morning newspaper. Meals can be taken at the nearby family restaurant. For further details and the Travelodge phone number, consult the Hotel Groups page.
ROOMS: 98 en suite s fr £42.95; d fr £42.95

GF Indicates the number of bedrooms at ground floor level.

GLENEAGLES See Auchterarder

GLENFINNAN, Highland — Map 22 NM9

★★72% The Prince's House

PH37 4LT
☎ 01397 722246 📠 01397 722323
e-mail: princeshouse@glenfinnan.co.uk
Dir: *On A830, 0.5m on right past Glenfinnan Monument*
A welcoming atmosphere is provided at this delightful hotel which is close to the site where Bonnie Prince Charlie raised the Jacobite standard. Comfortably appointed bedrooms offer pleasing décor and bathrooms have now been upgraded. Meals can be taken in either Flora's restaurant or the spacious bar.
ROOMS: 9 en suite (1 fmly) No smoking in all bedrooms s £40-£45; d £65-£95 (incl. bkfst) **LB FACILITIES:** Fishing **CONF:** Thtr 40 Class 20 **PARKING:** 18 **NOTES:** No smoking in restaurant Closed Jan-early Feb
CARDS:

GLENLUCE, Dumfries & Galloway — Map 20 NX1

★★67% Kelvin House Hotel

53 Main St DG8 0PP
☎ 01581 300303 📠 01581 300303
e-mail: kelvinhouse@lineone.net
Dir: *midway between Newton Stewart & Stranraer, just off A75*
This small, privately run hotel is in the centre of a village in unspoilt countryside. The bedrooms are bright and spacious and there is a comfortable residents' lounge. Wholesome, good value meals are served either in the popular bar or separate restaurant overlooking the garden. Special golf packages are worth enquiring about.
ROOMS: 6 rms (5 en suite) (3 fmly) No smoking in 3 bedrooms s £25-£30; d £53 (incl. bkfst) **LB FACILITIES:** Xmas **CONF:** Thtr 50 Class 20 Board 20 **CARDS:**

GLENROTHES, Fife — Map 21 NO2

★★77% Rescobie House Hotel & Restaurant

6 Valley Dr, Leslie KY6 3BQ
☎ 01592 749555 📠 01592 620231
e-mail: rescobiehotel@compuserve.com
Dir: *off A92 at Glenrothes onto A911, through Leslie. End of High St follow straight ahead. Left at AM Design hairdressing salon. Hotel 1st left*
This country house, which lies secluded in gardens on the fringe of the town, as been transformed. Victorian architecture is stylishly enhanced by a combination of contemporary and Art Deco styling, a theme carried through to the bright airy bedrooms. Cooking is imaginative, whilst the friendly service leaves a lasting impression.
ROOMS: 10 en suite No smoking in 8 bedrooms s £55-£75; d £70-£110 (incl. bkfst) **LB PARKING:** 12 **NOTES:** No dogs (ex guide dogs) No children 12yrs No smoking in restaurant Closed 24 Dec-3 Jan
CARDS:

Express by Holiday Inn Glenrothes

Leslie Roundabout, Leslie Rd KY7 6XX
☎ 01592 745509 📠 01592 743377
e-mail: ebhi-glenrothes@bt.connect.com
Dir: *off A92 onto A911. Straight over 4 rdbts. Hotel on left*
A modern hotel ideal for families and business travellers. Fresh and uncomplicated, the spacious bedrooms include Sky TV, power shower and tea and coffee-making facilities. Continental buffet breakfast is included in the room rate; other meals may be taken at the nearby family pub or restaurant. For further details and the

continued

Express by Holiday Inn phone number, consult the Hotel Groups pages.

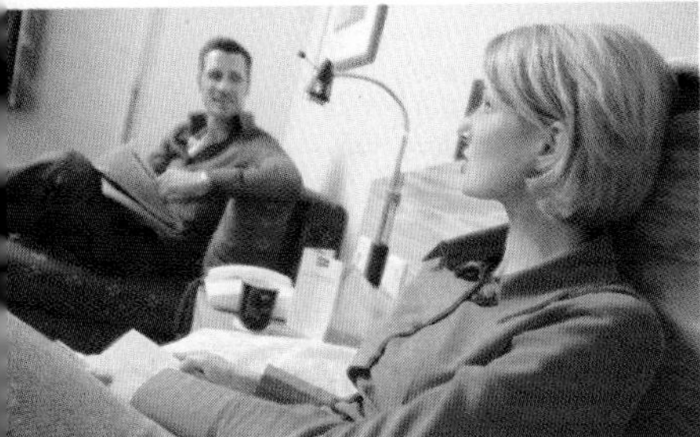

ROOMS: 49 en suite **CONF:** Thtr 30 Class 24 Board 16

Travel Inn
Beaufort Dr KY7 4UJ
☎ 08701 977114 01592 773453
Dir: *From M90 junct 2A, north, take A92 to Glenrothes. Travel Inn on 3rd exit of 1st rbt (Bankhead), in Glenrothes*
Travel Inn offers good-quality, value-for-money accommodation. Spacious, en suite rooms with bath and shower comfortably accommodate a family of up to two adults and two children (to age 15). The restaurant and bar offers a varied menu. For further details and the Travel Inn phone number, consult the Hotel Groups page.
ROOMS: 40 en suite s £44.95; d £44.95

GLENSHEE (SPITTAL OF), Perth & Kinross — Map 23 NO17

★★72% Dalmunzie House
PH10 7QG
☎ 01250 885224 01250 885225
e-mail: dalmunzie@aol.com
Dir: *on A93 at Spittal of Glenshee, follow signs to hotel*

This turreted mansion house enjoys a remote setting in the heart of a 6,500 acre estate, yet is within easy reach of the ski slopes of Glenshee. Accommodation ranges in style from large rooms with period furnishings to more compact rooms with modern décor. Public areas include a traditional bar, a spacious restaurant and a choice of lounges.
ROOMS: 18 rms (16 en suite) s £43-£65; d £66-£120 (incl. bkfst) **LB**
FACILITIES: Golf 9 Tennis (hard) Fishing Croquet lawn Clay pigeon shooting, Mountain bikes, Estate tours, Grouse shooting, Stalking Xmas
CONF: Thtr 20 Class 20 Board 20 Del from £76 **SERVICES:** Lift
PARKING: 32 **NOTES:** No smoking in restaurant Closed end Nov-28 Dec
CARDS:

GRANGEMOUTH, Falkirk — Map 21 NS98

★★★74% The Grange Manor
Glensburgh FK3 8XJ
☎ 01324 474836 01324 665861
e-mail: info@grangemanor.co.uk
Dir: *E off M9 junct 6, hotel 200mtrs right. W off M9 junct 5, A905 for 2m*
Located south of town close to the M9 this stylish hotel, popular with business and corporate clientele, benefits from hands-on family ownership. It offers high quality spacious accommodation with superb bathrooms. Public areas include a comfortable foyer area, lounge bar and smart restaurant. There is also a bar/bistro in the grounds. Staff throughout are especially friendly.
ROOMS: 6 en suite 30 annexe en suite (6 fmly) No smoking in 22 bedrooms s £65-£85; d £80-£120 (incl. bkfst) **LB** **FACILITIES:** STV Xmas **CONF:** Thtr 190 Class 68 Board 40 Del from £130 **SERVICES:** Lift
PARKING: 154 **NOTES:** No dogs (ex guide dogs) Civ Wed 170
CARDS:

G

GRANTOWN-ON-SPEY, Highland — Map 23 NJ02

★★★71% Muckrach Lodge
Dulnain Bridge PH26 3LY
☎ 01479 851257 01479 851325
e-mail: info@muckrach.co.uk
Dir: *from A95 Dulnain Bridge exit follow A938 towards Carrbridge. Hotel 500mtrs on right*

This former sporting lodge is set in 10 acres of landscaped grounds, at the foot of the Cairngorm Mountains. Bedrooms come in a variety of sizes and styles; the larger ones are particularly well appointed. The cosy bar is popular with the sporting clientele and features a roaring log fire. Dinner can be taken in either the bistro or award-winning Finlarig restaurant.
ROOMS: 9 en suite 4 annexe en suite (3 fmly) No smoking in all bedrooms s £60-£110; d £120-£140 (incl. bkfst) **LB**
FACILITIES: Croquet lawn Beauty & aroma therapy Xmas **CONF:** Thtr 30 Class 20 Board 16 Del from £125 **PARKING:** 53 **NOTES:** No smoking in restaurant Closed 5-20 Jan RS Nov-Mar Civ Wed 50
CARDS:

★★77% *Culdearn House*
Woodlands Ter PH26 3JU
☎ 01479 872106 01479 873641
e-mail: enquiries@culdearn.com
Dir: *enter Grantown on A95 from SW and turn left at 30mph sign*
Immaculately maintained both outside and in, this small hotel sits in gardens on the edge of town. Cheerful proprietors and their

continued on p758

GRANTOWN-ON-SPEY, continued

staff provide excellent hospitality and keep everyone smiling. The hotel has the atmosphere of a relaxed country house.

Culdearn House, Grantown-on-Spey

ROOMS: 7 en suite (1 GF) No smoking in 9 bedrooms **PARKING:** 12 **NOTES:** No dogs (ex guide dogs) No children 10yrs No smoking in restaurant Closed Dec-Jan **CARDS:**

GREENOCK, Inverclyde — Map 20 NS27

Express by Holiday Inn

Cartsburn PA15 4RT
☎ 01475 786666 01475 786777
e-mail: greenock@expressbyholidayinn.net
Dir: *M8 junct 31, A8 till Greenock, right at 4th rdbt, hotel on right*

A modern hotel ideal for families and business travellers. Fresh and uncomplicated, the spacious bedrooms include Sky TV, power shower and tea and coffee-making facilities. Continental buffet breakfast is included in the room rate; other meals may be taken at the nearby family pub or restaurant. For further details and the Express by Holiday Inn phone number, consult the Hotel Groups pages.
ROOMS: 71 en suite s £43-£55; d £43-£55 (incl. cont bkfst) **CONF:** Thtr 40 Class 16 Board 22 Del £85

Travel Inn

1-3 James Watt Way PA15 2AJ
☎ 08701 977120 01475 730890
Dir: *Follow M8 until it becomes A8 at Langbank, straight ahead through rdbt to Greenock, turn right off A8 at 3rd rdbt, next to McDonalds*

Travel Inn offers good-quality, value-for-money accommodation. Spacious, en suite rooms with bath and shower comfortably accommodate a family of up to two adults and two children (to age 15). The restaurant and bar offers a varied menu. For further details and the Travel Inn phone number, consult the Hotel Groups page.
ROOMS: 40 en suite s £44.95; d £44.95

GRETNA (WITH GRETNA GREEN), Dumfries & Galloway — Map 21 NY3

★★★67% *Garden House*

Sarkfoot Rd DG16 5EP
☎ 01461 337621 01461 337692
e-mail: info@gardenhouse.co.uk
Dir: *just off M6 junct 45 at Gretna*

This purpose-built modern hotel lies on the edge of the village. With a focus on weddings its landscaped gardens are a feature, whilst inside, corridor walls are adorned with photographs portraying 'that special day'. Accommodation is well presented and there is a new wing of massive bedrooms.
ROOMS: 38 en suite (10 fmly) **FACILITIES: Spa** STV Indoor swimming (H) Sauna Jacuzzi entertainment **CONF:** Thtr 100 Class 80 Board 40 **PARKING:** 105 **NOTES:** No dogs (ex guide dogs) **CARDS:**

See advert on opposite page

★★★67% Gretna Chase

DG16 5JB
☎ 01461 337517 01461 337766
e-mail: enquiries@gretnachase.co.uk
Dir: *off A74 onto B7076, left at top of slip road, hotel 400yds on right*

THE INDEPENDENTS

With its colourful landscaped gardens, this hotel is a favourite venue for wedding parties. The well-equipped bedrooms are split between the older Victorian style building and the modern extension; all are comfortable and full of character. There is a foyer lounge, a spacious dining room that can accommodate functions, and a popular cosy lounge bar.
ROOMS: 19 en suite (9 fmly) No smoking in 6 bedrooms s £65-£85; d £79-£155 (incl. bkfst) **LB** **FACILITIES:** Jacuzzi **CONF:** Thtr 50 Class 30 Board 20 Del from £75 **PARKING:** 40 **NOTES:** No dogs (ex guide dogs) Closed First 2 wks of Jan **CARDS:**

GRETNA SERVICE AREA (A74(M)), Dumfries & Galloway — Map 21 NY36

Welcome Lodge

Welcome Break Service Area DG16 5HQ
☎ 01461 337566 01461 337823
e-mail: gretna.hotel@welcomebreak.co.uk
Dir: *between junct 21 & 22 on M74*

This modern building offers accommodation in smart, spacious and well-equipped bedrooms, suitable for families and business travellers, and all with en suite bathrooms. Refreshments may be taken at the nearby family restaurant. For further details and the Welcome Break phone number, consult the Hotel Groups page.
ROOMS: 64 en suite s £45-£50; d £45-£50 **CONF:** Thtr 40 Board 20

GULLANE, East Lothian Map 21 NT48

Top 200 - Hotel

★★★ **Greywalls**
Muirfield EH31 2EG
☎ 01620 842144 01620 842241
e-mail: hotel@greywalls.co.uk
Dir: *A198, hotel signed at E end of village*
A dignified but relaxing Edwardian country house designed by Sir Edwin Lutyens; Greywalls overlooks the famous Muirfield Golf Course and is ideally placed just a half hours drive from Edinburgh. Delightful public rooms look onto beautiful gardens and freshly prepared cuisine may be enjoyed in the restaurant. Bedrooms, whether cosy singles or spacious master rooms, are mostly furnished in period style and many command views of the course. A gatehouse lodge is ideal for golfing parties.
ROOMS: 17 en suite 5 annexe en suite (5 GF) s fr £120; d fr £240 (incl. bkfst) **LB FACILITIES:** STV Tennis (hard & grass) Croquet lawn Putting green **CONF:** Thtr 30 Class 20 Board 20 Del from £200 **PARKING:** 40 **NOTES:** No smoking in restaurant Closed Nov-Mar **CARDS:**

HADDINGTON, East Lothian Map 21 NT57

★★★60% **Maitlandfield House**
24 Sidegate EH41 4BZ
☎ 01620 826513 01620 826713
e-mail: reception@maitlandfieldhouse.co.uk
Dir: *on reaching Haddington follow signs to St Mary's church/Lennoxlove Hotel on B6369 (road to Gifford)*
This popular hotel is just outside of the town centre and has an attractive outlook across pretty gardens to the historic St Mary's church. Public areas include a comfortable lounge leading to the conservatory brasserie which serves a range of Portuguese, Italian and Scottish cuisine. Bedrooms, whilst mostly compact, have good facilities.
ROOMS: 25 en suite (3 GF) No smoking in all bedrooms s £60-£98; d £98-£200 (incl. bkfst) **LB FACILITIES:** Xmas **CONF:** Thtr 180 Class 100 Board 98 Del from £95 **PARKING:** 80 **NOTES:** No children 12yrs No smoking in restaurant Civ Wed 180 **CARDS:**

HALKIRK, Highland Map 23 ND15

★★63% ***Ulbster Arms***
Bridge St KW12 6XY
☎ 01847 831206 & 831641 01847 831206
e-mail: ulbster-arms@ecosse.net
Dir: *A9 to Thurso from Perth, 3m after village of Spittal turn left*
This long-established hotel sits close to the River Thurso and

continued

attracts a mainly sporting clientele. It offer friendly service and good food, and bedrooms vary in size and style.
ROOMS: 10 en suite 16 annexe en suite **FACILITIES:** Fishing Shooting entertainment **CONF:** Thtr 30 Class 25 Board 20 **PARKING:** 36 **NOTES:** No smoking in restaurant **CARDS:**

HAMILTON, South Lanarkshire Map 20 NS75
See also Bothwell

Express by Holiday Inn Strathclyde

Hamilton Rd ML1 3RB
☎ 01698 858585 01698 852375
Dir: *M74 junct 5 follow signs for Strathclyde Country Park*

A modern hotel ideal for families and business travellers. Fresh and uncomplicated, the spacious bedrooms include Sky TV, power shower and tea and coffee-making facilities. Continental buffet breakfast is included in the room rate; other meals may be taken

continued on p760

HAMILTON, continued

at the nearby family pub or restaurant. For further details and the Express by Holiday Inn phone number, consult the Hotel Groups pages.
ROOMS: 120 en suite **CONF:** Thtr 30 Class 10 Board 15

HAMILTON MOTORWAY SERVICE AREA (M74), South Lanarkshire — Map 20 NS75

Travel Inn
Hamilton Motorway Service Area ML3 6JW
☎ 08701 977124 01698 891682
Dir: *M74 northbound, 1m N of junct 6. For southbound access exit junct 6 onto A723, double back at rdbt & join M74 Glasgow exit*
Travel Inn offers good-quality, value-for-money accommodation. Spacious, en suite rooms with bath and shower comfortably accommodate a family of up to two adults and two children (to age 15). The restaurant and bar offers a varied menu. For further details and the Travel Inn phone number, consult the Hotel Groups page.
ROOMS: 36 en suite s £44.95; d £44.95 **CONF:** Thtr 30 Board 20

HARRIS, ISLE OF, Western Isles — Map 22

SCARISTA — Map 22 NG09

Restaurant with Rooms

Scarista House
HS3 3HX
☎ 01859 550238 01859 550277
e-mail: timandpatricia@scaristahouse.com
Dir: *on A859, 15 miles south of Tarbert*

A former manse, Scarista lies in an idyllic position with a panoramic view of the Atlantic and just a short walk to miles of sandy beach. The house is run in a relaxed country house manner by the friendly hosts. Expect wellies in the hall and masses of books and CDs in one of two lounges. Bedrooms are cosy and delicious set dinners and memorable breakfasts are provided.
ROOMS: 3 en suite 2 annexe en suite (2 GF) No smoking in all bedrooms s £70-£85; d £125-£140 (incl. bkfst) **LB FACILITIES:** no TV in bdrms ch fac **CONF:** Thtr 20 Class 16 Board 16 **PARKING:** 12
NOTES: No smoking in restaurant Closed Xmas RS Nov-Mar
CARDS:

HELENSBURGH, Argyll & Bute — Map 20 NS2

★★★55% ***Rosslea Hall Country House***
Ferry Rd G84 8NF
☎ 01436 439955 01436 820897
e-mail: rosslea.info@countryhotels.net
Dir: *on A814, opposite church*
This early Victorian mansion stands in grounds by the shore of Gare Loch. There are two eating options; the main restaurant provides an attractive and formal dining environment, whilst the bar provides an informal eating alternative. The bedrooms are well equipped, each having been upgraded.
ROOMS: 29 en suite 5 annexe en suite (2 fmly) No smoking in 5 bedrooms **FACILITIES:** STV **CONF:** Thtr 120 Class 120 Board 60
PARKING: 60 **NOTES:** No smoking in restaurant
CARDS:

HUNTLY, Aberdeenshire — Map 23 NJ53

★★63% ***Gordon Arms Hotel***
The Square AB54 8AF
☎ 01466 792288 01466 794556
e-mail: reception@gordonarms.demon.co.uk
This friendly family-run hotel is centrally located in the town square and offers a good selection of tasty well-portioned dishes served in either the bar or restaurant. Bedrooms come in a variety of sizes, all being cheerfully decorated. There is a lounge in which guests can relax, and a function room is available.
ROOMS: 13 en suite (3 fmly) **FACILITIES:** entertainment **CONF:** Thtr 160 Class 80 Board 40 **CARDS:**

INVERARAY, Argyll & Bute — Map 20 NN00

★★★68% **The Argyll**
Front St PA32 8XB
☎ 01499 302466 01499 302389
e-mail: reception@the-argyll-hotel.co.uk
Dir: *A82 Glasgow - Tarbet A83 to Inveraray. Hotel is 1st building facing the loch on entering town*
Located beside The Arch and enjoying views of Loch Fyne, this hotel offers smartly refurbished bedrooms which are comfortable and well-equipped. Four executive bedrooms are available and facilities include a choice of bars, foyer lounge and conservatory. The attractive restaurant features carefully prepared fare based on quality Scottish ingredients.
ROOMS: 35 en suite (7 fmly) No smoking in 4 bedrooms
FACILITIES: ch fac **CONF:** Thtr 150 Class 80 Board 70 **PARKING:** 50
NOTES: No dogs (ex guide dogs) No smoking in restaurant Closed 25-26 Dec Civ Wed 120 **CARDS:**

★★★68% **Loch Fyne Hotel & Leisure Club**
PA32 8XT
☎ 01499 302148 01499 302348
e-mail: lochfyne@crerarhotels.com
Dir: *From A83 Loch Lomond, through centre of Inveraray on A80 to Lochgilphead. 0.5m from town centre*
This popular holiday hotel overlooks Loch Fyne. Bedrooms are mainly spacious and offer comfortable modern appointments. Guests can relax in the well-stocked bar and enjoy views over the

continued

Loch, or enjoy a meal in the contemporary-style bistro or more formal restaurant. There is also a well-equipped leisure centre.

ROOMS: 80 en suite s £75; d £125 (incl. bkfst) **LB** **FACILITIES:** **Spa** Indoor swimming (H) Sauna Jacuzzi Steam Room, Swimming pool supervised entertainment Xmas **CONF:** Thtr 50 Class 30 Board 20 Del from £75 **SERVICES:** Lift **PARKING:** 50 **NOTES:** No smoking in restaurant **CARDS:**

INVERGARRY, Highland

Map 22 NH30

★★★74% Glengarry Castle

PH35 4HW
☎ 01809 501254 01809 501207
e-mail: castle@glengarry.net
Dir: *on A82 beside Loch Oich, 0.5m from A82/A87 junct*

This charming country-house hotel is set in 50 acres of grounds on the shores of Loch Oich. Inviting public areas include a choice of comfortable sitting rooms with lots to read, and the classical dining room has an innovative menu. Bedrooms are mainly well proportioned; some have four-poster or half-tester beds.
ROOMS: 26 en suite (2 fmly) No smoking in 8 bedrooms s £55-£80; d £86-£150 (incl. bkfst) **FACILITIES:** Tennis (hard) Fishing **PARKING:** 32 **NOTES:** No smoking in restaurant Closed early Nov-mid Mar **CARDS:**

See advert on this page

INVERKEITHING, Fife

Map 21 NT18

★★★65% Queensferry Lodge

corus hotels

St Margaret's Head, North Queensferry
KY11 1HP
☎ 01383 410000 0870 609 6160
01383 419708
e-mail: queensferry@corushotels.com
Dir: *from N take exit after M90 junct 1 signed Park & Ride, follow signs for Deep Sea World, hotel on left. From S cross Forth Road Bridge, take 1st exit then 1st left, hotel 0.5m on left*

From its position on the north side of the river this smart modern

continued

hotel enjoys fine views of famous road and rail bridges. Bright modern public areas include a comfortable foyer lounge and bar, a smart restaurant, and a good range of banqueting facilities. Bedrooms are comfortable and offer a good range of amenities.
ROOMS: 77 en suite (4 fmly) (15 GF) No smoking in 46 bedrooms s fr £90; d fr £100 **LB** **FACILITIES:** STV Xmas **CONF:** Thtr 150 Class 60 Board 45 Del from £99 **SERVICES:** Lift **PARKING:** 165 **NOTES:** Civ Wed 120 **CARDS:**

INVERMORISTON, Highland

Map 23 NH41

★★77% Glenmoriston Arms Hotel & Restaurant

IV63 7YA
☎ 01320 351206 01320 351308
e-mail: scott@lochness-glenmoriston.co.uk
Dir: *at junct of A82/A877*

Close to Loch Ness, and at the start of the Glen from which it takes it name, this charming, beautifully maintained, small hotel offers a warm welcome. Inviting public areas include a cosy bar and attractive formal restaurant where fine dinners, prepared and cooked with care and dedication, are served. An alternative is offered by the Tavern bar/bistro in the grounds. The well-equipped bedrooms reflect the individuality of the house.
ROOMS: 8 en suite (1 fmly) s £60-£80; d £90-£120 (incl. bkfst) **LB** **FACILITIES:** Fishing Xmas **CONF:** Board 8 **PARKING:** 24 **NOTES:** No dogs No smoking in restaurant Closed early Jan-end Feb
CARDS:

I

INVERNESS, Highland Map 23 NH64
See also Kirkhill

★★★★71% Culloden House
Culloden IV2 7BZ
☎ 01463 790461 01463 792181
e-mail: reserv@cullodenhouse.co.uk
Dir: *from town take A96 and turn right for Culloden. After 1m, turn left at White Church after 2nd traffic lights*
This imposing Georgian mansion is set in 40 acres of grounds. Its character has been retained, with day rooms boasting a grand drawing room, clubby bar and elegant Adam dining room. Bedrooms come in a range of styles and sizes; a number of suites are in a separate mansion house in the grounds.
ROOMS: 23 en suite 5 annexe en suite (1 fmly) No smoking in 8 bedrooms s £85-£155; d £135-£279 (incl. bkfst) **LB FACILITIES:** STV Tennis (hard) Sauna Croquet lawn Boules, Badminton entertainment Xmas **CONF:** Thtr 60 Class 40 Board 30 **PARKING:** 50 **NOTES:** No smoking in restaurant Civ Wed 60
CARDS:

★★★★71% Inverness Marriott Hotel
Culcabock Rd IV2 3LP
☎ 01463 237166 01463 225208
e-mail: events@marriotthotels.co.uk
Dir: *from A9 S, exit Culduthel/Kingsmills 5th exit at rdbt, 0.5m, over mini-rdbt past golf club, hotel on left after lights*
Set in four acres of gardens on the south side of town, this long-established hotel provides a smart, modern environment within the carefully extended original house. Well-proportioned public rooms include a choice of relaxing lounges and a conservatory overlooking the garden. The bedrooms are spacious and very comfortable.
ROOMS: 76 en suite 6 annexe en suite (11 fmly) (26 GF) No smoking in 29 bedrooms **FACILITIES: Spa** STV Indoor swimming (H) Sauna Solarium Gym Putting green Hair & beauty salon Steam room **CONF:** Thtr 100 Class 35 Board 36 **SERVICES:** Lift **PARKING:** 120 **NOTES:** No smoking in restaurant **CARDS:**

Marriott HOTELS · RESORTS · SUITES

Courtesy & Care Award

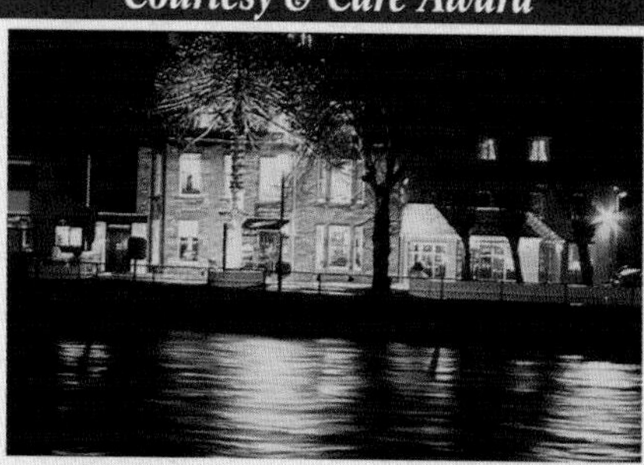

★★★79% Glenmoriston Town House Hotel
20 Ness Bank IV2 4SF
☎ 01463 223777 01463 712378
e-mail: glenmoriston@cali.co.uk
Dir: *on river opposite theatre, 5 mins from town centre*
Bold contemporary designs blend seamlessly with the classical architecture of this stylish hotel, situated on the banks of the River Ness. Delightful day rooms include a cosy cocktail bar and a sophisticated restaurant offering a tempting range of Mediterranean influenced dishes. The smart modern

continued

bedrooms have every facility, including CD players. Service is very friendly and attentive. Glenmoriston Town House Hotel has been awarded the AA Couresty & Care Award for Scotland & Northern Ireland 2003-2004.
ROOMS: 15 en suite (1 fmly) s £85-£105; d £115-£140 (incl. bkfst) **LB FACILITIES:** STV Xmas **CONF:** Thtr 100 Class 50 Board 30 Del from £135 **PARKING:** 40 **NOTES:** No dogs (ex guide dogs)
CARDS:

★★★76% Bunchrew House
Bunchrew IV3 8TA
☎ 01463 234917 01463 710620
e-mail: welcome@bunchrew-inverness.co.uk
Dir: *W on A862 along shore. Hotel on right 2m after crossing canal*

Friendly service and good food are all part of the appeal of this 17th-century mansion house, which is set in wooded grounds on the shores of the Beauly Firth. The inviting public rooms reflect the period style of the building and include a relaxing drawing room, separate bar and well-proportioned restaurant with views across the Firth. The bedrooms are individual in design.
ROOMS: 14 en suite (2 fmly) No smoking in 4 bedrooms s £89-£145; d £125-£205 (incl. bkfst) **LB FACILITIES:** Fishing **CONF:** Thtr 80 Class 30 Board 30 Del from £140 **PARKING:** 40 **NOTES:** No smoking in restaurant Civ Wed 120 **CARDS:**

★★★76% Craigmonie
9 Annfield Rd IV2 3HX
☎ 01463 231649 01463 233720
e-mail: info@craigmonie.com
Dir: *off A9/A96 follow signs Hilton, Culcabock pass golf course to lights, then 1st right*
A long-established, family-run hotel set in a residential area. Inviting public areas include a quiet lounge and wood-panelled bar. Meals can be enjoyed in the conservatory and in the restaurant. Guests can choose between standard and superior bedrooms, as well as attractive poolside suites with spa baths and balconies.
ROOMS: 35 en suite s £79-£90; d £100-£120 (incl. bkfst) **LB FACILITIES: Spa** Indoor swimming (H) Sauna Gym Jacuzzi **CONF:** Thtr 170 Class 70 Board 50 Del £120 **SERVICES:** Lift **PARKING:** 60 **NOTES:** No dogs (ex guide dogs) No smoking in restaurant
CARDS:

★★★67% Royal Highland
Station Square, Academy St IV1 1LG
☎ 01463 231926 01463 710705
e-mail: info@royalhighlandhotel.co.uk
Adjacent to the railway station, this hotel was built in 1858 and has the typically grand foyer of the Victorian era. The generally spacious bedrooms are comfortably equipped for the business

continued

traveller. A choice of bars is available and imaginative meals are served in the restaurant.
ROOMS: 70 en suite (12 fmly) No smoking in 40 bedrooms s £30-£69; d £60-£110 (incl. bkfst) **LB** **FACILITIES:** STV Croquet lawn Putting green Jacuzzi Xmas **CONF:** Thtr 200 Class 80 Board 80 Del from £105 **SERVICES:** Lift **PARKING:** 8 **NOTES:** No dogs (ex guide dogs) **CARDS:**

★★★66% Lochardil House

Stratherrick Rd IV2 4LF
☎ 01463 235995 🖹 01463 713394
e-mail: lochardil@ukonline.co.uk
Dir: *follow Island Bank Road for 1m, fork left into Drummond Crescent, into Stratherrick Road, 0.5m hotel on left*
A fine Victorian mansion set in extensive gardens in a residential area south of the city centre. Though not large, bedrooms are smartly furnished and boast attractive bathrooms. Meals in the conservatory restaurant will satisfy the heartiest of appetites.
ROOMS: 12 en suite No smoking in 3 bedrooms s fr £78; d fr £112 (incl. bkfst) **LB** **FACILITIES:** STV **CONF:** Thtr 200 Class 100 Board 60 Del from £105 **PARKING:** 123 **NOTES:** No dogs (ex guide dogs) Civ Wed **CARDS:**

★★★66% Loch Ness House

Glenurquhart Rd IV3 8JL
☎ 01463 231248 🖹 01463 239327
e-mail: lnhhchris@aol.com
Dir: *1.5m from town centre, overlooking Tomnahurich Bridge on canal. From A9, left at Longman rdbt, follow signs for A82 for 2.5m*
This is a family-run hotel, lying close to the canal, which offers friendly and attentive service. Tasty meals can be chosen from a good range of dishes, which are available in both the restaurant and the bar.
ROOMS: 21 en suite (3 fmly) No smoking in 6 bedrooms s £50-£67.50; d £110 (incl. bkfst) **LB** **FACILITIES:** STV Xmas **CONF:** Thtr 150 Class 60 Board 40 Del from £85 **PARKING:** 60 **NOTES:** No smoking in restaurant Civ Wed 100 **CARDS:**

★★70% The Maple Court

12 Ness Walk IV3 5SQ
☎ 01463 230330 🖹 01463 237700
e-mail: maplecourt@macleodhotels.co.uk
Set in gardens on the banks of the River Ness and close to the Eden Court Theatre, this hotel is within a short stroll of the city centre. It has been substantially upgraded and provides smart ground-floor bedrooms and a restaurant providing good value meals. The friendliness of staff leaves a lasting impression.
ROOMS: 9 en suite (2 fmly) (9 GF) No smoking in 5 bedrooms s £45-£80; d £50-£85 (incl. bkfst) **LB** **FACILITIES:** Xmas **CONF:** BC Thtr 80 Class 30 Board 30 Del from £50 **PARKING:** 32 **NOTES:** No smoking in restaurant Civ Wed 70 **CARDS:**

⌂ Express by Holiday Inn

Stoneyfield IV2 7PA
☎ 01463 732700 🖹 01463 732732
e-mail: inverness@expressholidayinn.co.uk
Dir: *from A9 follow signs for A96 and Inverness Airport, hotel on right*
A modern hotel ideal for families and business travellers. Fresh and uncomplicated, the spacious bedrooms include Sky TV, power shower and tea and coffee-making facilities. Continental buffet breakfast is included in the room rate; other meals may be taken at the nearby family pub or restaurant. For further details and the Express by Holiday Inn phone number, consult the Hotel Groups pages.

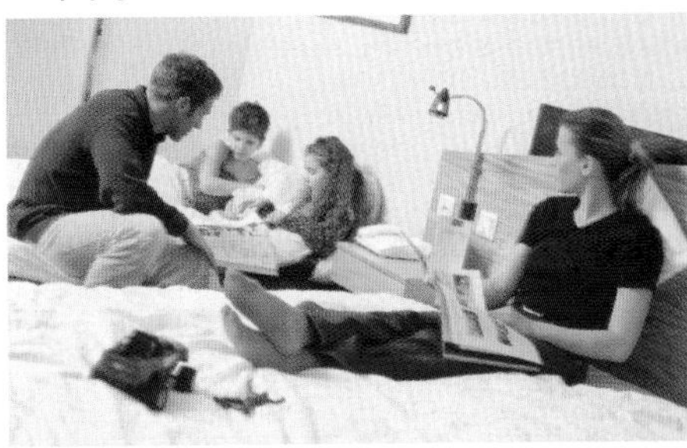

ROOMS: 94 en suite s £50-£65; d £50-£65 (incl. cont bkfst)
CONF: Thtr 35 Class 12 Board 16

⌂ Travel Inn

Millburn Rd IV2 3QX
☎ 08701 977141 🖹 01463 717826
Dir: *on A9 junct with A96 (Raigmore, signed Airport/Aberdeen), follow B865 towards town centre, hotel 100yds past next rdbt*
Travel Inn offers good-quality, value-for-money accommodation. Spacious, en suite rooms with bath and shower comfortably accommodate a family of up to two adults and two children (to age 15). The restaurant and bar offers a varied menu. For further details and the Travel Inn phone number, consult the Hotel Groups page.
ROOMS: 39 en suite s £49.95; d £49.95

⌂ Travel Inn (Inverness East)

Beechwood Business Park IV2 3BW
☎ 08701 977142 🖹 01463 225233
Dir: *on A9, turn left signed Raigmore Hospital, Police HQ & Inshes Retail Park*
Travel Inn offers good-quality, value-for-money accommodation. Spacious, en suite rooms with bath and shower comfortably accommodate a family of up to two adults and two children (to age 15). The restaurant and bar offers a varied menu. For further details and the Travel Inn phone number, consult the Hotel Groups page.
ROOMS: 60 en suite s £44.95; d £44.95

⌂ Travelodge

Stoneyfield, A96 Inverness Rd IV2 7PA
☎ 08700 850 950
Dir: *Junction of A9 & A96*
Travelodge offers good quality, good value, modern accommodation. Ideal for families, the spacious, en suite bedrooms include remote-control TV, tea and coffee-making facilities, luxury beds and free morning newspaper. Meals can be taken at the nearby family restaurant. For further details and the Travelodge phone number, consult the Hotel Groups page.
ROOMS: s fr £42.95; d fr £42.95

Popped the question?
Hotels with Civ Wed in their entry are licensed for civil wedding ceremonies. Maximum numbers for the ceremony only are shown, e.g. Civ Wed 120

INVERURIE, Aberdeenshire
Map 23 NJ72

★★★★63% Thainstone House
AB51 5NT
☎ 01467 621643 01467 625084
e-mail: thainstone@macdonald-hotels.co.uk

Dir: *A96 from Aberdeen. Entrance to hotels at 1st rdbt (Thainstone Rndbt). Take 1st left then sharp right to hotel*

Popular for conference and banqueting events, this attractive mansion house, set within 40 acres of mature grounds, combines the best of rural calm and easy access from the main road between Aberdeen and Inverurie. Public rooms include a galleried reception area, a refurbished leisure club and an elegant bar and drawing room.

ROOMS: 48 en suite (3 fmly) (12 GF) No smoking in 32 bedrooms s £95-£111; d £110-£140 (incl. bkfst) **LB FACILITIES:** STV Indoor swimming (H) Snooker Sauna Solarium Gym Jacuzzi Archery Shooting, Grass Karts, Quad Bikes Xmas **CONF:** BC Thtr 400 Class 100 Board 40 Del from £120 **SERVICES:** Lift **PARKING:** 100 **NOTES:** No smoking in restaurant Civ Wed 130 **CARDS:**

★★★68% Strathburn
Burghmuir Dr AB51 4GY
☎ 01467 624422 01467 625133
e-mail: strathburn@btconnect.com

Dir: *at Blackhall rbt into Blackhall Rd for 100yds then into Burghmuir Drive*

Maintained in pristine condition, this friendly purpose-built hotel is situated on the western side of town. The attractive public areas include a split-level foyer lounge, a comfortable bar and a tastefully appointed restaurant. The well-equipped bedrooms come in a variety of sizes.

ROOMS: 25 en suite (2 fmly) No smoking in 20 bedrooms s £55-£85; d £80-£120 (incl. bkfst) **LB FACILITIES:** STV **CONF:** Thtr 30 Class 24 Board 18 Del from £95 **PARKING:** 40 **NOTES:** No dogs (ex guide dogs) No smoking in restaurant Closed 25-26 Dec & 1-2 Jan
CARDS:

★★★67% Pittodrie House
Chapel of Garioch, Pitcaple AB51 5HS
☎ 01467 681444 01467 681648
e-mail: pittodrie@macdonald-hotels.co.uk

Dir: *from A96, take turn for Chapel of Garioch*

This historic house dates from the 15th century and retains many original features. Bedrooms come in two distinct styles, those in the original house are full of character and the newer wing has been refurbished. Public areas include a striking drawing room, restaurant and a cosy bar.

ROOMS: 27 en suite (6 fmly) No smoking in 13 bedrooms s £95-£160; d £105-£180 (incl. bkfst) **LB FACILITIES:** STV Squash Snooker Croquet lawn Clay pigeon shooting Quad biking Archery etc on estate Xmas **CONF:** Thtr 100 Class 70 Board 40 Del from £130 **PARKING:** 150 **NOTES:** No smoking in restaurant Civ Wed 120
CARDS:

IRVINE, North Ayrshire
Map 20 NS33

⇧ Gailes Lodge Restaurant and Inn
Marine Dr, Gailes KA11 5AE
☎ 01294 204040 01294 204047
e-mail: info@gaileslodge.com

With several golf courses on its doorstep and within easy reach of Prestwick Airport, Gailes Lodge offers comfortable bedrooms furnished in contemporary style. A bright attractive café bar/restaurant provides food throughout the day until late.

ROOMS: 41 en suite s £49; d £49 **CONF:** Thtr 400 Class 100 Board 80

ISLE OF
Placenames incorporating the words 'Isle' or 'Isle of' will be found under the actual name, eg Isle of Arran is under Arran, Isle of.

ISLAY, ISLE OF, Argyll & Bute
Map 20

BOWMORE
Map 20 NR35

★★60% *Lochside*
19 Shore St PA43 7LB
☎ 01496 810244 01496 810390
e-mail: ask@lochsidehotel.co.uk

Dir: *on A846, 100yds from main village square on shore side of road*

Many of the fairly compact bedrooms benefit from fine views across Loch Indaal at this traditional island hotel. The cosy dining room features mainly local produce, which is true also of the hotel bar, which offers guests a choice of 400 single malt whiskies – that was at the last count!

ROOMS: 8 en suite (1 fmly) **CONF:** Class 20 Board 12 **NOTES:** No smoking in restaurant **CARDS:**

BRIDGEND
Map 20 NR36

★★68% *Bridgend*
PA44 7PQ
☎ 01496 810212 01496 810960

Centrally situated for ease of access to all parts of the island, this small hotel offers comfortably furnished bedrooms of various sizes. Meals are served in either of the bars, popular also with locals, or a fuller menu is available in the bright and spacious restaurant. Service is friendly and attentive.

ROOMS: 10 rms (9 en suite) (3 fmly) **FACILITIES:** Fishing Bowls **PARKING:** 30 **NOTES:** No smoking in restaurant
CARDS:

PORT ASKAIG
Map 20 NR46

★★63% *Port Askaig*
PA46 7RD
☎ 01496 840245 01496 840295
e-mail: hotel@portaskaig.co.uk

Dir: *at Ferry Terminal*

This family-run hotel, set in an 18th-century building, offers comfortable bedrooms. The lounge provides fine views over to nearby Jura and there is a choice of bars, popular with locals. Traditional dinners are served in the bright restaurant and a full range of bar snacks and meals is also available.

ROOMS: 8 rms (6 en suite) (1 fmly) **PARKING:** 21 **NOTES:** No children 5yrs No smoking in restaurant **CARDS:**

ISLE ORNSAY See Skye, Isle of

JEDBURGH, Scottish Borders
Map 21 NT62

★★★77% Jedforest Hotel
Camptown TD8 6PJ
☎ 01835 840222 01835 840226
e-mail: mail@jedforesthotel.freeserve.co.uk

Dir: *3m S of Jedburgh off A68*

The phrase 'small is beautiful' is no more aptly applied than to this immaculately maintained, family-run country hotel. The bedrooms are very smart, and the larger ones are particularly impressive. It

continued

is the food that attracts custom, with a choice of smart brasserie or intimate restaurant, the latter gaining our Rosette award.

ROOMS: 8 en suite (1 fmly) No smoking in all bedrooms s £65-£85; d £90-£120 (incl. bkfst) **LB FACILITIES:** Fishing Xmas **PARKING:** 20 **NOTES:** No dogs (ex guide dogs) No smoking in restaurant **CARDS:**

KELSO, Scottish Borders Map 21 NT73

★★★76% The Roxburghe Hotel & Golf Course

Heiton TD5 8JZ
☎ 01573 450331 01573 450611
e-mail: hotel@roxburghe.net
Dir: *from A68 Jedburgh join A698 to Heiton, 3m SW of Kelso*

Set in 500 acres of mature wood and parkland, this impressive Jacobean mansion is owned by the Duke of Roxburghe. Sporting pursuits are popular with many guests enjoying the shooting, fishing and golf. Bedrooms are individually designed and a number have real fires. Comfortably furnished lounges are a perfect setting for lavish afternoon teas, whilst the restaurant serves carefully prepared meals.

ROOMS: 16 en suite 6 annexe en suite (3 fmly) No smoking in 1 bedroom s £120; d £125-£265 (incl. bkfst) **LB FACILITIES:** STV Golf 18 Tennis (hard) Fishing Croquet lawn Putting green Clay shooting Health & Beauty Salon Mountain bike hire Xmas **CONF:** Thtr 50 Class 20 Board 20 Del from £99 **PARKING:** 150 **NOTES:** No smoking in restaurant Civ Wed 50 **CARDS:**

★★★71% Ednam House

Bridge St TD5 7HT
☎ 01573 224168 01573 226319
e-mail: contact@ednamhouse.com
Dir: *50mtrs from Town Square on Bridge Street leading to Abbey and Kelso Old Bridge*

This fine Georgian mansion overlooks the River Tweed and is popular with a regular sporting clientele. Accommodation styles range from standard to grand, with a house in the grounds converted to an impressive two-bedroom apartment. Public areas

continued

display the character of the house with a choice of lounges and an elegant dining room overlooking the gardens. Service is helpful and attentive.

ROOMS: 30 en suite (4 fmly) No smoking in 3 bedrooms s £85-£99; d £129-£163 (incl. bkfst & dinner) **LB FACILITIES:** Croquet lawn Free access to Abbey Fitness Centre **CONF:** Thtr 250 Board 200 **PARKING:** 60 **NOTES:** Closed 24 Dec-06 Jan Civ Wed 80 **CARDS:**

★★★63% Cross Keys

36-37 The Square TD5 7HL
☎ 01573 223303 01573 225792
e-mail: cross-keys-hotel@easynet.co.uk
Dir: *into Kelso, follow town centre signs. Hotel in main square*

Originally a coaching inn, but now tastefully modernised, this family-run hotel overlooks Kelso's fine cobbled square. Bedrooms are either superior or standard level, and the spacious lounge bar and restaurant are supplemented by the Oak Room bar/bistro.

ROOMS: 27 en suite (5 fmly) No smoking in 12 bedrooms s £49-£62; d £51-£85 (incl. bkfst) **LB FACILITIES:** STV Xmas **CONF:** BC Thtr 220 Class 160 Board 60 Del from £89 **SERVICES:** Lift air con **NOTES:** Civ Wed 100 **CARDS:**

KENMORE, Perth & Kinross Map 21 NN74

★★★64% Kenmore Hotel

The Square PH15 2NU
☎ 01887 830205 01887 830262
e-mail: reception@kenmorehotel.co.uk
Dir: *A9 at Ballinluig onto A827 through Aberfeldy to Kenmore. Hotel in village centre*

Dating back to 1572, this riverside hotel is Scotland's oldest inn and has a rich and interesting history. Bedrooms have been tastefully upgraded and modernised, with stylish decor and spaciousness. Dinner can be enjoyed in the restaurant with its panoramic views of the River Tay. There is a choice of bars including one with real fires.

ROOMS: 27 en suite 13 annexe en suite (4 fmly) (4 GF) s £54-£59; d £88-£98 (incl. bkfst) **LB FACILITIES:** STV Tennis (hard) Fishing Jacuzzi Discounted salmon fishing on River Tay Xmas **CONF:** Thtr 80 Class 60 Board 50 Del from £82 **SERVICES:** Lift **PARKING:** 30 **NOTES:** No smoking in restaurant **CARDS:**

KILCHRENAN, Argyll & Bute Map 20 NN02

★★★76% Taychreggan

PA35 1HQ
☎ 01866 833211 & 833366 01866 833244
e-mail: info@taychregganhotel.co.uk
Dir: *W from Glasgow A82 to Crianlarich, onto A85 to Taynuilt. S for 7m on B845 to Kilchrenan*

Scotland's Hotels of Distinction

This friendly hotel is peacefully located on the banks of Loch Awe.

continued on p766

KILCHRENAN, continued

Bedrooms are smartly appointed, with the larger individually styled rooms located in the original part of the house and new extensions. There is a choice of lounges, a well-stocked bar adjoined by the new Orangery where lunches are served and carefully prepared dinners are served in the elegant dining room.

Taychreggan Hotel, Kilchrenan

ROOMS: 19 en suite No smoking in 3 bedrooms s £99-£117; d £127-£250 (incl. bkfst) **LB FACILITIES:** no TV in bdrms Fishing Snooker Jacuzzi **CONF:** Class 15 Board 20 **PARKING:** 40 **NOTES:** No children 14yrs No smoking in restaurant Civ Wed 70 **CARDS:**

★★★70% The Ardanaiseig

by Loch Awe PA35 1HE
☎ 01866 833333 01866 833222
e-mail: ardanaiseig@clara.net
Dir: *turn S off A85 at Taynuilt onto B845 to Kilchrenan. Left in front of pub, road very small and signed Ardanaiseig Hotel and No Through Road*

Set amid lovely gardens and breathtaking scenery beside the shore of Loch Awe, this peaceful country house hotel was built in the Scottish baronial style in 1834. Many fine pieces of furniture are evident in the bedrooms and charming day rooms, which include a drawing room, a library bar, and an elegant dining room.

ROOMS: 16 en suite (4 fmly) **FACILITIES:** Tennis (hard) Fishing Snooker Croquet lawn Boating, Clay pigeon shooting, Bikes for hire **PARKING:** 20 **NOTES:** No smoking in restaurant Closed 2 Jan-14 Feb Civ Wed 60 **CARDS:**

KILLIECRANKIE, Perth & Kinross — Map 23 NN96

★★77% Killiecrankie House

PH16 5LG
☎ 01796 473220 01796 472451
e-mail: enquiries@killiecrankiehotel.co.uk
Dir: *off A9 at Killiecrankie, hotel 3m on B8079 on right*

A long-established hotel set in mature grounds close to the historic Pass of Killiecrankie. The owners Tim and Maillie Waters and their charming staff provide friendly and attentive service. Inviting public areas include an attractive restaurant looking onto the gardens. The cosy bar and adjacent sun lounge are popular, or residents can always choose the quiet lounge full of books and board games.

ROOMS: 10 en suite (2 fmly) (2 GF) No smoking in all bedrooms s £79-£99; d £158-£198 (incl. bkfst & dinner) **LB FACILITIES:** Croquet lawn Putting green Xmas **PARKING:** 20 **NOTES:** No smoking in restaurant Closed 3 Jan - 14 Feb **CARDS:**

KILLIN, Stirling — Map 20 NN53

★★★68% *Dall Lodge Country House*

Main St FK21 8TN
☎ 01567 820217 01567 820726
e-mail: wilson@dalllodgehotel.co.uk
Dir: *from M9 at Stirling turn left A84-Crianlarich, 3m after Lochearnhead turn right onto A827 to Killin*

This fine Victorian mansion has been a local landmark for over 100 years and provides friendly and attentive service. Smartly maintained bedrooms are comfortably modern; some have lounge areas. Public areas include an inviting conservatory lounge, whilst Scottish cooking is provided in the attractive restaurant, which has views of Ben Lawers.

ROOMS: 10 en suite (2 fmly) **FACILITIES:** Tennis (grass) **CONF:** Thtr 20 Class 16 Board 12 **PARKING:** 20 **NOTES:** No smoking in restaurant Closed Nov-Feb **CARDS:**

KILMARNOCK, East Ayrshire — Map 20 NS43

★★★68% Fenwick

Best Western

Ayr Rd, Fenwick KA3 6AU
☎ 01560 600478 01560 600334
e-mail: fenwick@bestwestern.co.uk
Dir: *approx 4m N of Kilmarnock, adjacent to A77 & B751*

This stylish, comfortable hotel is conveniently situated between Glasgow and the Ayrshire coast. Stylish public rooms include a cosy fireside lounge, a bright restaurant and informal bar. The hotel enjoys a fine reputation for food with creative menus forming the basis for its own dining club. Bedrooms are soundly equipped and suited to the business traveller.

ROOMS: 31 en suite (2 fmly) (10 GF) No smoking in 4 bedrooms s £55-£72; d £75-£102 (incl. bkfst) **LB FACILITIES:** STV Clay pigeon Quad bike ch fac Xmas **CONF:** Thtr 160 Class 60 Board 50 Del from £82 **PARKING:** 80 **NOTES:** No smoking in restaurant Civ Wed 100 **CARDS:**

Travel Inn

travel inn

Annadale KA1 2RS
☎ 08701 977148 01563 570536
Dir: *from A71, follow signs for Crosshouse Hospital, Travel Inn on right off Moorfield rdbt*

Travel Inn offers good-quality, value-for-money accommodation. Spacious, en suite rooms with bath and shower comfortably accommodate a family of up to two adults and two children (to age 15). The restaurant and bar offers a varied menu. For further details and the Travel Inn phone number, consult the Hotel Groups page.

ROOMS: 40 en suite s £44.95; d £44.95

Town House Hotel
Country House Hotel
Travel Accommodation

⇧ Travelodge
Kilmarnock By Pass KA1 5LQ
☎ 08700 850 950 📠 01563 573810
Dir: *at Bellfield junct just off A77*
Travelodge offers good quality, good value, modern accommodation. Ideal for families, the spacious, en suite bedrooms include remote-control TV, tea and coffee-making facilities, luxury beds and free morning newspaper. Meals can be taken at the nearby family restaurant. For further details and the Travelodge phone number, consult the Hotel Groups page.
ROOMS: 40 en suite s fr £42.95; d fr £42.95

KILWINNING, North Ayrshire — Map 20 NS34

★★★75% *Montgreenan Mansion House*
Montgreenan Estate KA13 7QZ
☎ 01294 557733 📠 01294 850397
e-mail: info@montgreenanhotel.co.uk
Dir: *4m north of Irvine on A736*
Set in 48 acres of parkland and woods, this 19th-century mansion offers a peaceful atmosphere. Gracious public areas retain many original features such as ornate ceilings and marble fireplaces, and include a splendid drawing room, a library, a club-style bar and a restaurant. Bedrooms are well equipped and come in a variety of sizes.
ROOMS: 21 en suite **FACILITIES:** STV Golf 5 Tennis (hard) Snooker Croquet lawn Putting green Jacuzzi Clay pigeon shooting Quad Biking **CONF:** Thtr 110 Class 60 Board 60 **SERVICES:** Lift **PARKING:** 50 **NOTES:** No smoking in restaurant Civ Wed 110
CARDS:

KINCARDINE, Fife — Map 21 NS98

⇧ Travel Inn (Falkirk North)
Bowtrees Farm FK2 8PJ
☎ 08701 977099 📠 01324 831934
Dir: *From north M9 junct 7 towards Kincardine Bridge, from south M876 for Kincardine Bridge. On rdbt at end of slip road*
Travel Inn offers good-quality, value-for-money accommodation. Spacious, en suite rooms with bath and shower comfortably accommodate a family of up to two adults and two children (to age 15). The restaurant and bar offers a varied menu. For further details and the Travel Inn phone number, consult the Hotel Groups page.
ROOMS: 40 en suite s £44.95; d £44.95

KINCLAVEN, Perth & Kinross — Map 21 NO13

Top 200 - Hotel

★★★ ◎◎ Ballathie House
PH1 4QN
☎ 01250 883268 📠 01250 883396
e-mail: email@ballathiehousehotel.com
Dir: *from A9 2m N of Perth, B9099 through Stanley & signed or off A93 at Beech Hedge, follow signs for Ballathie 2.5m*
Set in delightful grounds, this splendid Scottish mansion house combines classical grandeur with modern comfort. Bedrooms range from well-proportioned master rooms to modern standard rooms and many boast antique furniture and Art Deco bathrooms. For the ultimate in quality, request one of the Riverside Rooms, a purpose-built development right on the banks of the river, complete with balconies and terraces. The elegant restaurant has views over the River Tay.

ROOMS: 26 en suite 16 annexe en suite (2 fmly) s £75-£85; d £150-£210 (incl. bkfst) **LB** **FACILITIES:** STV Fishing Croquet lawn Putting green Xmas **CONF:** Thtr 50 Class 20 Board 30 Del from £150 **SERVICES:** Lift **PARKING:** 50 **NOTES:** No smoking in restaurant Civ Wed 90 **CARDS:**

KINGUSSIE, Highland — Map 23 NH70

★★74% *The Scot House*
Newtonmore Rd PH21 1HE
☎ 01540 661351 📠 01540 661111
e-mail: enquiries@scothouse.com
Dir: *A9, take Kingussie exit, hotel approx 0.5m at S end of village*
This former manse has been tastefully converted and offers comfortable accommodation in thoughtfully equipped bedrooms. Public areas include a cosy bar, popular with locals, and a restaurant providing wholesome home-cooked food. A friendly atmosphere is guaranteed with the warmth of hospitality a real feature.
ROOMS: 9 en suite (1 fmly) No smoking in all bedrooms **PARKING:** 30 **NOTES:** No smoking in restaurant Closed 7 Jan-15 Feb
CARDS:

Top 200 – Restaurant with Rooms

◎◎ The Cross
Tweed Mill Brae, Ardbroilach Rd PH21 1LB
☎ 01540 661166 📠 01540 661080
e-mail: relax@thecross.co.uk
Dir: *from lights in centre of Kingussie, along Ardbroilach Rd for 300mtrs, left into Tweed Mill Brae*
This converted tweed mill in a wooded riverside setting offers comfortable bedrooms in a mix of traditional and quality pine styles. Lounges are also inviting, but it is the light and airy restaurant that forms the highlight of any visit. Refreshingly and deceptively simple in concept, dinner displays fine local ingredients sympathetically cooked to draw out the natural flavours. Service is attentive, backed up by a genuine feeling that guests are very welcome indeed.
ROOMS: 8 en suite (1 fmly) No smoking in all bedrooms s £135-£140; d £210-£220 (incl. bkfst & dinner) **LB** **CONF:** Thtr 20 Class 20 Board 20 Del from £145 **PARKING:** 12 **NOTES:** No dogs (ex guide dogs) No smoking in restaurant Closed Xmas, New Year & Jan RS Sun & Mon **CARDS:**

KINNESSWOOD, Perth & Kinross Map 21 NO10

★★68% Lomond Country Inn

Main St KY13 9HN
☎ 01592 840253 01592 840693
e-mail: lomondcountryinn@aol.com

THE CIRCLE
Selected Individual Hotels

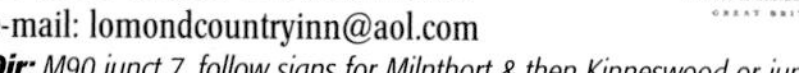

Dir: *M90 junct 7, follow signs for Milnthort & then Kinneswood or junct 5 follow signs for Glenrothes & Scotlandwell then Kinneswood*

Keen proprietors provide a welcoming atmosphere at this village inn. There is a cosy bar with real ales, a small sitting room, and a dining room with fine views towards Loch Leven. Innovative bar meals and restaurant dinners are available, and bedrooms come in various sizes, with some contained in a separate building.
ROOMS: 4 en suite 8 annexe en suite (3 fmly) No smoking in 4 bedrooms **FACILITIES:** ch fac **CONF:** Thtr 60 Class 40 Board 40 **PARKING:** 50 **NOTES:** No smoking in restaurant Civ Wed 60 **CARDS:**

KINROSS, Perth & Kinross Map 21 NO10

★★★73% Green

2 The Muirs KY13 8AS
☎ 01577 863467 01577 863180
e-mail: reservations@green-hotel.com
Dir: *M90 junct 6 follow signs for Kinross, turn onto A922, hotel on this road*

A unique conversion of the old High School, centred on a courtyard overlooking the town and close to the castle. Public rooms are set in the original classrooms and studies, while by contrast the bedrooms feature modern décor and furnishings.
ROOMS: 46 en suite (4 fmly) (14 GF) No smoking in 12 bedrooms s £85-£100; d £150 (incl. bkfst) **LB** **FACILITIES:** STV Indoor swimming (H) Golf 18 Fishing Squash Sauna Gym Croquet lawn Putting green Curling in season, Swimming pool supervised entertainment ch fac Xmas **CONF:** BC Thtr 130 Class 75 Board 60 Del from £95 **PARKING:** 60 **NOTES:** No smoking in restaurant Closed 21-28 Dec excluding Xmas day RS 25 Dec **CARDS:**

See advert on opposite page

★★★69% Windlestrae Hotel and Leisure Club

The Muirs KY13 8AS
☎ 0870 609 6153 01577 864733
e-mail: windlestrae@corushotels.com
Dir: *M90 junct 6 turn E into Kinross, 2nd mini rdbt turn left approx 350yds, hotel on right*

Situated off the main road in nicely landscaped gardens, this hotel combines a welcoming atmosphere with impressive leisure and conference facilities. Both bedrooms and public areas are comfortable and well proportioned.
ROOMS: 45 en suite (5 fmly) (14 GF) No smoking in 15 bedrooms s £70-£75; d £80-£85 **LB** **FACILITIES:** STV Indoor swimming (H) Snooker Sauna Solarium Gym Jacuzzi Beautician, Steam room, Toning tables Xmas **CONF:** Thtr 250 Class 100 Board 80 Del £110 **SERVICES:** air con **PARKING:** 80 **NOTES:** No smoking in restaurant Civ Wed 100 **CARDS:**

Travelodge

Travelodge

Kincardine Rd KY13 7NQ
☎ 08700 850 950 01577 864108
Dir: *on A977, M90 junct 6 Turthills Tourist Centre*
Travelodge offers good quality, good value, modern accommodation. Ideal for families, the spacious, en suite bedrooms include remote-control TV, tea and coffee-making facilities, luxury beds and free morning newspaper. Meals can be taken at the nearby family restaurant. For further details and the Travelodge phone number, consult the Hotel Groups page.
ROOMS: 35 en suite s fr £42.95; d fr £42.95

KINTORE, Aberdeenshire Map 23 NJ71

★★67% Torryburn

School Rd AB51 0XP
☎ 01467 632269 01467 632271
e-mail: vel@torryburnhotel.co.uk
Dir: *N from Aberdeen leave dual carriageway for Kintore. Hotel on corner of Dunecht Rd*
This welcoming family-run hotel has attractive public areas which feature a choice of comfortable bars, and a bright conservatory that operates as a tea room during the day and as an extension to the supper room in the evening. Bedrooms come in a variety of sizes, are tastefully decorated and offer a good range of amenities.
ROOMS: 10 en suite (2 fmly) No smoking in all bedrooms **FACILITIES:** STV Tennis (hard) Fishing Snooker Shooting ch fac **CONF:** Thtr 50 Class 50 Board 40 **PARKING:** 30 **NOTES:** Closed 1 Jan **CARDS:**

Packed in a hurry?
Ironing facilities should be available at all star levels, either in rooms or on request

KIRKBEAN, Dumfries & Galloway
Map 21 NX95

★★77% Cavens
DG2 8AA
☎ 01387 880234 Fax 01387 880467
e-mail: enquiries@cavens.com
Dir: *on entering Kirkbean on A710, hotel signed*

Set in parkland gardens, Cavens encapsulates all the virtues of an intimate country house hotel. Quality is the keynote, and Angus and Jane Fordyce have spared no effort in completing a fine renovation of the house. Bedrooms - some with their own sun lounge - are delightfully individual, whilst lounges invite peaceful relaxation. A set dinner offers the best of local produce.
ROOMS: 7 en suite No smoking in all bedrooms s £65-£75; d £90-£125 (incl. bkfst) **LB** **FACILITIES:** Croquet lawn Shooting, Fishing, Horse Riding Xmas **CONF:** Thtr 20 Class 20 Board 20 Del from £140 **PARKING:** 12 **NOTES:** No dogs (ex guide dogs) No smoking in restaurant
CARDS:

KIRKCALDY, Fife
Map 21 NT29

★★★68% Dean Park
Chapel Level KY2 6QW
☎ 01592 261635 Fax 01592 261371
e-mail: reception@deanparkhotel.co.uk
Dir: *signed from A92, Kirkcaldy West junct*
This hotel has particular appeal for the business traveller and its impressive conference centre is also popular for weddings. Bedrooms are comfortable and smartly appointed with good bathrooms. There are chalet-style houses in the grounds of a similar standard but to which room service is not available. Public areas include a choice of bars and a restaurant.
ROOMS: 34 en suite 12 annexe en suite (2 fmly) (5 GF) No smoking in 10 bedrooms s £50-£69; d £78-£89 (incl. bkfst) **FACILITIES:** STV **CONF:** Thtr 250 Class 125 Board 54 **SERVICES:** Lift **PARKING:** 250 **NOTES:** No dogs (ex guide dogs) Civ Wed 250
CARDS:

★★★64% Dunnikier House Hotel
Dunnikier Park KY1 3LP
☎ 01592 268393 Fax 01592 642340
e-mail: recp@dunnikier-house-hotel.co.uk
Dir: *off A92 at Kirkcaldy West, then 3rd exit on rdbt signed 'Hospital/Crematorium'. 1st left past school*
This privately owned hotel is a mansion house dating from the 18th century and set in parkland beside Dunnikier Golf Course. Original features have been retained in the public areas. Views over the parkland can be enjoyed from the lounge, and the bar offers a wide selection of whiskies. The Oswald restaurant provides fine meals which feature carefully prepared fresh, local produce.
ROOMS: 15 en suite s £60-£68; d £80-£90 (incl. bkfst) **FACILITIES:** Pay and play golf course adjacent Xmas **CONF:** Thtr 70 Class 30 Board 40 Del from £105 **PARKING:** 100 **NOTES:** No smoking in restaurant Civ Wed 30 **CARDS:**

★★68% The Belvedere
Coxstool, West Wemyss KY1 4SL
☎ 01592 654167 Fax 01592 655279
e-mail: info@thebelvederehotel.com
Dir: *A92 from M90 junct 2A, at Kirkcaldy East take A915, 1m NE turn right to Coaltown, at T-junct turn right then left, hotel 1st building in village*
This welcoming hotel enjoys a lovely location in the small village of Coxstool and has scenic views over the Firth of Forth. The bright airy bedrooms are attractively decorated and offer comfortable modern furnishings. Public areas include a small character bar and a stylish restaurant.
ROOMS: 5 en suite 15 annexe en suite (2 fmly) s £50-£63; d £60-£70 (incl. bkfst) **LB** **FACILITIES:** STV **CONF:** Thtr 40 Class 12 Board 20 **PARKING:** 50 **NOTES:** No smoking in restaurant Civ Wed 40
CARDS:

KIRKCUDBRIGHT, Dumfries & Galloway
Map 20 NX65

★★★71% Selkirk Arms
Old High St DG6 4JG
☎ 01557 330402 Fax 01557 331639
e-mail: reception@selkirkarmshotel.co.uk
Dir: *off A75 5m W of Castle Douglas onto A711, 5m to Kirkcudbright in centre of town*
Originally a hostelry frequented by Robert Burns (he wrote the Selkirk Grace here) the Selkirk Arms is now a smart hotel with well-equipped bedrooms. Service is friendly and attentive and guests can eat well in either the attractive restaurant or in the bistro and lounge bar.
ROOMS: 13 en suite 3 annexe en suite (2 fmly) (1 GF) No smoking in 8 bedrooms s £67-£75; d £99-£115 (incl. bkfst) **LB** **FACILITIES:** STV Xmas **CONF:** Thtr 70 Class 60 Board 40 Del from £85 **PARKING:** 9 **NOTES:** No smoking in restaurant Closed Xmas Civ Wed 70
CARDS:

K

KIRKCUDBRIGHT, continued

★★65% Arden House Hotel
Tongland Rd DG6 4UU
☎ 01557 330544 🖷 01557 330742
Dir: *off A57 Euro route (Stranraer), 4m W of Castle Douglas onto A711. Signed for Kirkcudbright, cross Telford Bridge. Hotel 400mtrs on left*
Set well back from the main road in extensive grounds on the north east side of town, this well-maintained hotel offers attractive bedrooms, a lounge bar and adjoining conservatory serving a range of popular dishes, which are also available in the dining room. It boasts an impressive function suite in its grounds.
ROOMS: 9 rms (8 en suite) (7 fmly) s £35; d £60 (incl. bkfst)
CONF: Thtr 175 Class 175 **PARKING:** 70

★★61% Royal
St Cuthbert St DG6 4DY
THE INDEPENDENTS
☎ 01557 331213 🖷 01557 331513
e-mail: reception@theroyalhotel.net
Dir: *off A75 onto A711. Hotel in centre of town, on corner at crossroads*
Refurbishment has enhanced the accommodation at this town centre hotel, which offers brightly decorated bedrooms with good facilities. There is a comfortable first floor lounge, a coffee lounge and lounge bar. Good value meals are provided in the dining room.
ROOMS: 17 en suite (7 fmly) s £28-£34; d fr £49 (incl. bkfst) **LB**
FACILITIES: entertainment **CONF:** Thtr 120 Class 60 Board 60
NOTES: No smoking in restaurant Civ Wed 100 **CARDS:**

K

KIRKHILL, Highland Map 23 NH54

★★64% Bogroy Inn
IV5 7PX
☎ 01463 831296 🖷 01463 831296
Dir: *at junct of A862 & B9164*
This small and friendly, roadside inn has a rich history and was closely associated with whisky smuggling in the 16th century. There is a choice of bars and meals can be taken in both the lounge bar and dining room. Bedrooms offer a practical standard of accommodation.
ROOMS: 7 en suite (3 fmly) **PARKING:** 40 **NOTES:** No dogs (ex guide dogs) **CARDS:**

KIRRIEMUIR, Angus Map 23 NO35

Airlie Arms
4 St Malcolms Wynd DD8 4HB
☎ 01575 572847 🖷 01575 573055
e-mail: info@airliearms-hotel.co.uk
ROOMS: 10 en suite (2 fmly) (5 GF) No smoking in 2 bedrooms s £40-£45; d £68-£80 (incl. bkfst) **LB** **FACILITIES:** STV Xmas
CONF: Thtr 90 Class 70 Board 50 Del from £60 **PARKING:** 5
NOTES: ★★ **CARDS:**

KYLE OF LOCHALSH, Highland Map 22 NG72

★★★62% *Lochalsh*
Ferry Rd IV40 8AF
☎ 01599 534202 🖷 01599 534881
e-mail: mdmacrae@lochalsh-hotel.demon.co.uk
Dir: *turn off A82 onto A87*
Benefiting from lovely views over to the Isle of Skye, this hotel is set in the heart of the town close to the old ferry slip. Many of the bedrooms overlook the harbour and the contrasting aspect of the modern Skye Bridge. Meals can be enjoyed in either the relaxed atmosphere of the lounge and bar or the spacious restaurant.
ROOMS: 38 en suite (8 fmly) **FACILITIES:** STV **CONF:** Thtr 20 Class 20 Board 20 **SERVICES:** Lift **PARKING:** 50 **NOTES:** No smoking in restaurant **CARDS:**

See advert on opposite page

LADYBANK, Fife Map 21 NO30

★★★65% Fernie Castle
Letham KY15 7RU
☎ 01337 810381 🖷 01337 810422
e-mail: mail@ferniecastle.demon.co.uk
Dir: *M90 junct 6 take A91E (Tay Bridge/St Andrews) to Melville Lodges rdbt. Left onto A92 signed Tay Bridge. Hotel 1.2m on right*

This turreted castle is set amid 17 acres of wooded grounds in the heart of Fife. Bedrooms range from King and Queen rooms, to the more standard sized Squire and Lady rooms. The elegant Auld Alliance Restaurant presents a formal setting, whilst guests can also dine in the keep bar with its impressive vaulted stone walls and ceiling.
ROOMS: 20 en suite (2 fmly) No smoking in 15 bedrooms s £67-£85; d £135-£198 (incl. bkfst & dinner) **LB** **FACILITIES:** Croquet lawn Xmas
CONF: Thtr 180 Class 120 Board 25 Del from £140 **PARKING:** 80
NOTES: No smoking in restaurant Civ Wed 180
CARDS:

LAIRG, Highland Map 23 NC50

★★68% Overscaig
Loch Shin IV27 4NY
☎ 01549 431203
Dir: *on A838*
Popular with fishermen and birdwatchers, this Highland hotel enjoys a lochside location amid unspoilt scenery. The dining room overlooks Loch Shin and there is a choice of bars plus a coffee lounge. Bedrooms are modern in style and comfortably appointed. Fishing excursions can be arranged.
ROOMS: 9 en suite (2 fmly) s £27-£35; d £54-£70 (incl. bkfst)
FACILITIES: Fishing Cycle hire service **PARKING:** 30 **NOTES:** No dogs (ex guide dogs) No smoking in restaurant

LANARK, South Lanarkshire Map 21 NS84
See also Biggar

★★★67% *Cartland Bridge*
Glasgow Rd ML11 9UF
☎ 01555 664426 🖷 01555 663773
e-mail: sales@cartlandbridge.co.uk
Dir: *follow A73 through Lanark towards Carluke. Hotel 1.25m on right*
Sitting in delightful grounds on the edge of the town, this Grade I listed mansion continues to be popular with both the business and

continued

leisure guest. Public areas feature splendid wood panelling and a gallery staircase. In addition to the restaurant, food is also available in the bar, and there is a small cocktail lounge and a bright conservatory. The well-equipped bedrooms vary in size and style.
ROOMS: 20 rms (18 en suite) (2 fmly) No smoking in 9 bedrooms
FACILITIES: STV ch fac **CONF:** Thtr 250 Class 180 Board 30
PARKING: 120 **NOTES:** No smoking in restaurant Civ Wed 70
CARDS:

LANGBANK, Renfrewshire — Map 20 NS37

★★★★68% Gleddoch House
PA14 6YE
☎ 01475 540711 📠 01475 540201
e-mail: info@gleddochhouse.com
Dir: *signed from B789 at Langbank rdbt*
Set above Langbank, this well-established hotel enjoys spectacular views over the River Clyde. The elegant restaurant is the setting for innovative dining and attentive service, and bedrooms come in a range of styles, including traditional in the main house and modern in the wings. There is a new link between the hotel and the golf club as well as a modern gymnasium.
ROOMS: 39 en suite (8 fmly) (5 GF) No smoking in 6 bedrooms s fr £99; d fr £150 (incl. bkfst) **LB** **FACILITIES:** STV Indoor swimming (H) Golf 18 Fishing Riding Sauna Gym Putting green Clay pigeon shooting, Offroad driving, Swimming pool supervised Xmas **CONF:** Thtr 150 Class 60 Board 52 Del from £105 **PARKING:** 200
CARDS:

LARGS, North Ayrshire — Map 20 NS25

★★69% Willowbank
96 Greenock Rd KA30 8PG
☎ 01475 672311 & 675435 📠 01475 689027
e-mail: iain@willowbankhotellargs.freeserve.co.uk
Dir: *on A78*
A relaxed, friendly atmosphere prevails at this well-maintained hotel. The well decorated bedrooms tend to be spacious and offer comfortable modern appointments, while public areas include a large, well-stocked bar, a lounge and a dining room. Attractive floral baskets hanging outside are a feature in the summer.
ROOMS: 30 en suite (4 fmly) s £50-£70; d £80-£100 (incl. bkfst) **LB** **FACILITIES:** entertainment Xmas **CONF:** Thtr 200 Class 100 Board 40 **PARKING:** 40 **NOTES:** No smoking in restaurant
CARDS:

LAUDER, Scottish Borders — Map 21 NT54

★★66% *Lauderdale*
1 Edinburgh Rd TD2 6TW
☎ 01578 722231 📠 01578 718642
e-mail: enquiries@lauderdale-hotel.co.uk
Dir: *on A68 from S, through centre of Lauder, hotel on right. From Edinburgh, hotel on left at 1st bend after passing sign for Lauder*
This friendly, family run hotel is located close to the centre of this charming border town. Bedrooms are spacious, comfortable and thoughtfully equipped. An extensive range of meals is served in both the informal bar and the restaurant, which is also the setting for breakfast. The landscaped gardens and function room make this a popular wedding venue.
ROOMS: 10 en suite (1 fmly) No smoking in all bedrooms
FACILITIES: STV ch fac **PARKING:** 200 **NOTES:** No dogs (ex guide dogs) No smoking in restaurant **CARDS:**

LERWICK See Shetland

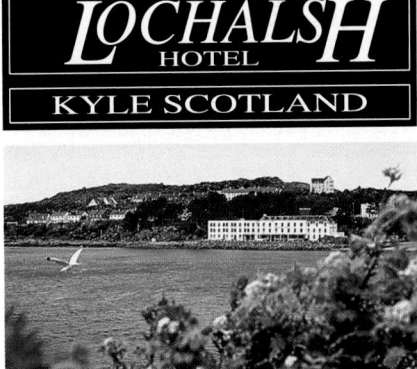

LETTERFINLAY, Highland — Map 22 NN29

★★67% Letterfinlay Lodge
PH34 4DZ
☎ 01397 712622
e-mail: forsyth@letterfinlay.fsnet.co.uk
Dir: *7m N of Spean Bridge, on A82 beside Loch Lochy*
This comfortable, family-run hotel stands in grounds beside the A82, overlooking Loch Lochy. There is a cosy bar, a choice of lounges - one of which has stunning lochside views and is popular for its bar food - and an attractive dining room. Bedrooms come in a variety of sizes, some being particularly spacious.
ROOMS: 13 rms (11 en suite) (5 fmly) s £28-£40; d £56-£80 (incl. bkfst) **LB** **FACILITIES:** Fishing **PARKING:** 100 **NOTES:** No smoking in restaurant Closed Nov-Feb **CARDS:**

LIVINGSTON, West Lothian — Map 21 NT06

Travel Inn (Livingston Nr Edinburgh)
Deer Park Av, Knightsridge EH54 8AD
☎ 08701 977161 📠 01506 438912
Dir: *on M8 junct 3 between Edinburgh and Glasgow. Adjacent to petrol station*
Travel Inn offers good-quality, value-for-money accommodation. Spacious, en suite rooms with bath and shower comfortably accommodate a family of up to two adults and two children (to age 15). The restaurant and bar offers a varied menu. For further details and the Travel Inn phone number, consult the Hotel Groups page.
ROOMS: 83 en suite s £44.95; d £44.95

LOCHEARNHEAD, Stirling Map 20 NN52

★★67% *Lochearnhead*
Lochside FK19 8PU
☎ 01567 830229 01567 830364
Dir: *from A84 follow signs Crianlarich/Callander for Lochearnhead turn right at T-junct, hotel is 500mtrs ahead*
This friendly hotel overlooks Loch Earn, a popular resort for visitors attracted by the extensive range of water pursuits. Lovely views can be enjoyed from all the public rooms and lochside bedrooms. The varied menus offer a good range of tasty home-cooked dishes in both the bar and restaurant.
ROOMS: 10 en suite (1 fmly) No smoking in 12 bedrooms
FACILITIES: STV Fishing Water, skiing. Windsurfing, Sailing, Cycling ch fac **PARKING:** 20 **NOTES:** No smoking in restaurant Closed Dec-Mar
CARDS:

LOCHGILPHEAD, Argyll & Bute Map 20 NR88

★★★72% *Cairnbaan*
Crinan Canal, Cairnbaan PA31 8SJ
☎ 01546 603668 01546 606045
e-mail: cairnbaanhotel@virgin.net
Dir: *2m N, A816 from Lochgilphead, hotel off B841*
Located on the Crinan Canal, this small hotel offers relaxed hospitality in a delightful setting. Bedrooms are thoughtfully equipped, generally spacious and benefit from bright décor. Fresh seafood is a real feature in both the formal restaurant and the comfortable bar area. Al fresco dining is popular in the warmer months.
ROOMS: 12 en suite No smoking in all bedrooms **CONF:** Thtr 160 Class 100 Board 80 **PARKING:** 53 **NOTES:** No smoking in restaurant Civ Wed 120 **CARDS:**

L

★★62% Stag Hotel & Restaurant
Argyll St PA31 8NE
☎ 01546 602496 01546 603549
e-mail: staghotel@ukhotels.com
Dir: *on entering Lochgilphead take main mini rbt into Argyll Street for hotel at junct of Lorne Street & Argyll Street*
This long-established hotel benefits from a central location in this popular tourist destination. The refurbished restaurant offers a range of popular dishes at reasonable prices. The thoughtfully equipped bedrooms offer good value accommodation.
ROOMS: 18 en suite (2 fmly) No smoking in 1 bedroom s £35-£40; d £40-£55 **LB** **FACILITIES:** STV pool table and walking guides Xmas **CONF:** Thtr 50 Class 16 Board 20 Del from £65.45 **NOTES:** No dogs (ex guide dogs) RS Winter **CARDS:**

LOCHINVER, Highland Map 22 NC02

Top 200 - Hotel

★★★ Inver Lodge
CLASSIC BRITISH

IV27 4LU
☎ 01571 844496 01571 844395
e-mail: stay@inverlodge.com
Dir: *A835 to Lochinver continue through village and turn left after village hall, follow private road for 0.5m*
This well-run, comfortable modern hotel is set on a hillside above the village with a backdrop of unspoilt wilderness and mountain scenery, and spectacular views of the harbour and bay. There is a choice of lounges and a restaurant where local ingredients are prepared with ingenuity. Bedrooms are stylish and all have ocean views. The staff here are friendly and obliging.

ROOMS: 20 en suite d fr £140 (incl. bkfst) **LB** **FACILITIES:** STV Fishing Snooker Sauna Solarium **CONF:** Thtr 30 Board 20 **PARKING:** 30 **NOTES:** No smoking in restaurant Closed Nov-Etr
CARDS:

LOCH LOMOND See Balloch & Luss

LOCKERBIE, Dumfries & Galloway Map 21 NY18

★★★79% Dryfesdale
Dryfebridge DG11 2SF
☎ 01576 202427 01576 204187
e-mail: reception@dryfesdalehotel.co.uk
Dir: *from M74 take 'Lockerbie North' junct 17, 3rd left at 1st rdbt, 1st exit left at 2nd rdbt, hotel 200yds on left*
Conveniently situated for the M74, yet suitably screened from it, this hotel features upgraded public areas. Bedrooms, some with access to patio areas, vary in size and all are discerningly decorated. Dinner makes good use of local produce and is served in the airy restaurant overlooking the gardens. A warm welcome is offered by the enthusiastic young staff.
ROOMS: 16 en suite (2 fmly) (7 GF) No smoking in 4 bedrooms s £65-£75; d £85-£95 (incl. bkfst) **LB** **FACILITIES:** STV Golf 9 Fishing Croquet lawn Putting green Clay pigeon shooting,Fishing entertainment Xmas **CONF:** BC Thtr 100 Class 80 Board 45 Del from £100
PARKING: 40 **NOTES:** No smoking in restaurant Civ Wed 100
CARDS:

★★73% *Somerton House*
35 Carlisle Rd DG11 2DR
☎ 01576 202583 & 202384 01576 204218
Dir: *off A74*
This delightful, family run Victorian mansion has been well preserved and features beautiful woodwork, particularly in the restaurant. An attractive conservatory adds a new dimension and is equally popular for bar meals. The bedrooms, many of which have been refurbished, are particularly stylish and come equipped with modern, well-equipped bathrooms.
ROOMS: 7 en suite 4 annexe en suite (2 fmly) No smoking in 4 bedrooms **CONF:** Thtr 25 Class 15 Board 15 **PARKING:** 100
NOTES: No smoking in restaurant **CARDS:**

★★66% Kings Arms Hotel
High St DG11 2JL
☎ 01576 202410 01576 202410
e-mail: reception@kingsarmshotel.co.uk
Dir: *A74(M), 0.5m into town centre, hotel is opposite Town Hall*
Located centrally within the town, this traditional inn provides extensive function facilities, an all-day menu served in the cosy

continued

bars, and well-equipped accommodation. A smart restaurant sets a comfortable scene for the popular, creative dinner menus.
ROOMS: 13 en suite (2 fmly) s £38; d £65 (incl. bkfst) **FACILITIES:** Xmas **CONF:** Thtr 80 Class 40 Board 30 Del from £52.50 **PARKING:** 8 **NOTES:** No smoking in restaurant **CARDS:**

★★65% Ravenshill House

12 Dumfries Rd DG11 2EF
☎ 01576 202882 📠 01576 202882
e-mail: aaenquiries@ravenshillhotellockerbie.co.uk
Dir: *on A709 signed from A74(M) Lockerbie junct, W of town centre. Hotel 0.5m on right*

This friendly, family-run hotel is located close to the town and is set in its own tidy gardens. Ravenshill House boasts cheerful service and features good value, home-cooked meals. The bright bedrooms are very well equipped and comfortable.
ROOMS: 8 rms (7 en suite) (2 fmly) No smoking in 5 bedrooms s £38-£56; d £56-£66 (incl. bkfst) **LB** **FACILITIES:** ch fac **CONF:** Thtr 30 Class 20 Board 12 **PARKING:** 35 **NOTES:** No smoking in restaurant **CARDS:**

LUNDIN LINKS, Fife
Map 21 NO40

★★★77% ®® Old Manor

Leven Rd KY8 6AJ
☎ 01333 320368 📠 01333 320911
e-mail: enquiries@oldmanorhotel.co.uk
Dir: *1m E of Leven on A915 Kirkaldy-St Andrews road, for hotel on right*

Scotland's Hotels of Distinction

This long-established hotel lies on the edge of the village and overlooks the golf course to the Firth of Forth. Enthusiastically run, it provides high standards throughout. Bedrooms come in a variety of styles and there are two restaurants, the elegant Aithernie and the Coachman's Bistro in the grounds.
ROOMS: 24 en suite (2 fmly) No smoking in 4 bedrooms s £60-£90; d £60-£200 (incl. bkfst) **LB** **FACILITIES:** Complimentary membership of Lundin Sports Club Xmas **CONF:** Thtr 140 Class 70 Board 50 Del from £90 **PARKING:** 100 **NOTES:** No smoking in restaurant Civ Wed 100 **CARDS:**

LUSS, Argyll & Bute
Map 20 NS39

★★★71% ® *The Lodge on Loch Lomond*

G83 8PA
☎ 01436 860201 📠 01436 860203
e-mail: lusslomond@aol.com
Dir: *off A82, follow sign for hotel*

This purpose-built hotel has an idyllic setting right on the shores of Loch Lomond. Public areas consist of an open-plan, split-level bar and restaurant overlooking the loch. The pine finished bedrooms also enjoy the views. Comfortable and spacious, they are well equipped, some with DVDs/internet access and all with saunas.
ROOMS: 29 en suite (20 fmly) **FACILITIES:** STV Sauna fishing, boating **CONF:** Thtr 35 Class 18 Board 25 **PARKING:** 82 **CARDS:**

MALLAIG, Highland
Map 22 NM69

★★67% West Highland

PH41 4QZ
☎ 01687 462210 📠 01687 462130
e-mail: westhighland.hotel@virgin.net
Dir: *from Fort William turn right at rdbt then 1st right up hill, from ferry left at rdbt then 1st right up hill*

This well-proportioned, family-run holiday hotel sits on a hill above the town, and enjoys lovely views towards the Isle of Skye. The bedrooms come in a variety of sizes, but all are smartly furnished. There are attractive and comfortable public areas in which guests can relax.
ROOMS: 34 en suite (6 fmly) No smoking in 6 bedrooms s £36-£40; d £70-£74 (incl. bkfst) **LB** **FACILITIES:** entertainment **CONF:** Thtr 100 Class 80 Board 100 **PARKING:** 40 **NOTES:** No smoking in restaurant Closed 16 Oct-15 Mar RS 16 Mar-1 Apr **CARDS:**

★★65% *Marine*

PH41 4PY
☎ 01687 462217 📠 01687 462821
e-mail: marinehotel@btinternet.com
Dir: *1st hotel on right on entering Mallaig, off A830*

This town centre family-run hotel sits beside the railway station and close to the ferry terminal and harbour. All amenities are found upstairs from street level, where a bright spacious lounge bar and attractive restaurant feature seafood on their menus. The comfortable bedrooms are smartly appointed.
ROOMS: 19 rms (18 en suite) (2 fmly) (4 GF) No smoking in 5 bedrooms **FACILITIES:** **PARKING:** 6 **CARDS:**

MARKINCH, Fife
Map 21 NO20

Top 200 - Hotel

★★★★ ®® Balbirnie House

Balbirnie Park KY7 6NE
☎ 01592 610066 📠 01592 610529
e-mail: info@balbirnie.co.uk
Dir: *off A92 onto B9130, entrance 0.5m on left*

SLH Small Luxury Hotels of the World

Set in the midst of the scenic Balbirnie Park, this listed Georgian building overlooks the challenging golf course. Bedrooms, many of which are spacious, offer tasteful décor and high quality furnishings. There are a number of comfortable lounges of which the Long Gallery is the most striking. A visit to the award-winning Orangery restaurant is a highlight of any visit.
ROOMS: 30 en suite (9 fmly) (7 GF) s £130-£160; d £190-£250 (incl. bkfst) **LB** **FACILITIES:** STV Golf 18 Croquet lawn Putting green Woodland walks Jogging trails Xmas **CONF:** Thtr 220 Class 100 Board 60 Del from £162 **PARKING:** 120 **NOTES:** No smoking in restaurant Civ Wed 200 **CARDS:**

MAYBOLE, South Ayrshire

Map 20 NS20

Top 200 - Hotel

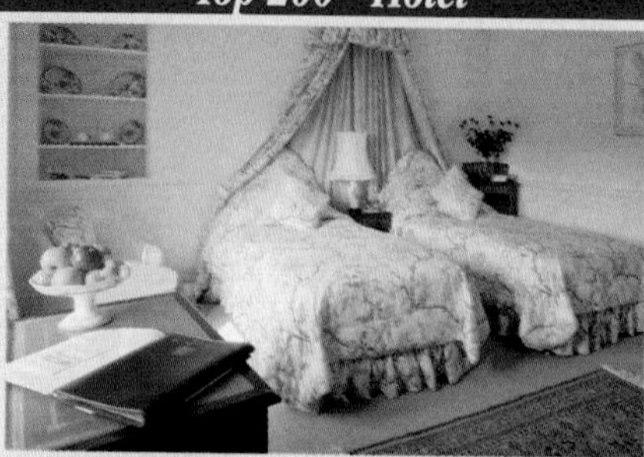

★★ Ladyburn

KA19 7SG

☎ 01655 740585 01655 740580

e-mail: jh@ladyburn.co.uk

Dir: *A77 (Glasgow/Stranraer) at Maybole turn to B7023 to Crosshill, turn right at War Memorial, 2m turn left. Ladyburn approx 1m on right*

This delightful country house is the elegant home of the Hepburn family. It sits in open countryside and attractive gardens. Classically styled bedrooms, two with four-poster beds, offer every comfort and are complemented by the library and the drawing room. Dinner comprises a carefully cooked three course set menu, discussed beforehand, and is served in a gracious candlelit setting. The genuine hospitality and care is a particular hallmark at this hotel.

ROOMS: 5 en suite No smoking in all bedrooms s £50-£80; d £100-£160 (incl. bkfst) **LB** **FACILITIES:** Croquet lawn Boules **PARKING:** 12 **NOTES:** No dogs (ex guide dogs) No children 16yrs No smoking in restaurant RS 2 wks Nov-Dec, 4 wks Jan/Mar Civ Wed 250 **CARDS:**

MELROSE, Scottish Borders

Map 21 NT53

★★★69% Burt's

Market Square TD6 9PL

☎ 01896 822285 01896 822870

e-mail: burtshotel@aol.com

Dir: *A6091, 2m from A68 3m S of Earlston*

Under the same family's ownership for over 30 years, this eye-catching hotel makes a colourful feature in the market square and provides good levels of hospitality and guest care. There is a popular lounge bar serving tasty lunches and suppers, and for memorable meals in elegant and relaxed surroundings the restaurant is a must.

ROOMS: 20 en suite No smoking in all bedrooms **FACILITIES:** Shooting Salmon Fishing **CONF:** Thtr 38 Class 20 Board 20 Del from £88 **PARKING:** 40 **NOTES:** No smoking in restaurant Closed 24-26 Dec **CARDS:**

MILNGAVIE, East Dunbartonshire

Map 20 NS57

Travel Inn (Glasgow North)

103 Main St G62 6JJ

☎ 08701 977112 0141 9567839

Dir: *on A81 6m N of Glasgow city centre. Close to Loch Mond*

Travel Inn offers good-quality, value-for-money accommodation. Spacious, en suite rooms with bath and shower comfortably accommodate a family of up to two adults and two children (to age 15). The restaurant and bar offers a varied menu. For further details and the Travel Inn phone number, consult the Hotel Groups page.

ROOMS: 60 en suite s £44.95; d £44.95 **CONF:** Class 16 Board 16

MOFFAT, Dumfries & Galloway

Map 21 NT00

★★★73% Moffat House

High St DG10 9HL

☎ 01683 220039 01683 221288

e-mail: moffat@talk21.com

Dir: *M74 junct 15, Beattock, take A701 in 1m hotel at end of High St*

Positioned in the centre of this picturesque farming town Moffat House has a good level of trade from both visitors and locals. The spacious bar lounge serves a variety of lunches and dinners; the restaurant offers a more formal environment. Bedrooms are generally spacious and quiet. Many have now been refurbished to provide high levels of comfort.

ROOMS: 21 en suite (2 fmly) No smoking in 6 bedrooms **FACILITIES:** **CONF:** Thtr 70 Class 50 Board 40 **PARKING:** 61 **NOTES:** Civ Wed 110 **CARDS:**

★★★70% Auchen Castle

Beattock DG10 9SH

☎ 01683 300407 01683 300667

e-mail: reception@auchencastle.com

Dir: *M74 junct 15, 1 mile on B7076 Abington road*

Though sharing a valley with the motorway, extensive grounds, terraced gardens and a lake separate this imposing mansion from it. Public rooms include a comfortable drawing room an elegant restaurant overlooking the valley. Bedrooms are classical in style,

continued

M

come in a variety of sizes and include some superior four-poster rooms with DVDs and mini bars.

ROOMS: 15 en suite 10 annexe en suite (12 fmly) No smoking in 10 bedrooms s £48-£75; d £55-£95 (incl. bkfst) **LB** **FACILITIES:** STV Fishing Xmas **CONF:** Thtr 40 Board 20 Del from £65 **PARKING:** 50 **NOTES:** No dogs (ex guide dogs) No smoking in restaurant Civ Wed 95 **CARDS:**

★★77% Beechwood Country House

Harthope Place DG10 9HX
☎ 01683 220210 01683 220889
e-mail: enquiries@beechwoodcountryhousehotel.co.uk
Dir: *at north end of town turn right at St Marys Church into Harthope Place and follow sign to hotel*

This delightful country house is set in its own attractive gardens, just a short walk from the town centre. The smart bedrooms have all benefited from refurbishment. There are two comfortable lounges, one of which has its own small bar. The kitchen continues to delight guests with imaginative cooking.

ROOMS: 7 en suite (1 fmly) No smoking in all bedrooms s £50-£62; d £76-£90 (incl. bkfst) **LB** **FACILITIES:** Croquet lawn Childrens' swings **CONF:** Class 20 Board 20 **PARKING:** 15 **NOTES:** No smoking in restaurant Closed Jan-mid Feb Civ Wed 25 **CARDS:**

See advert on this page

★★66% The Star

44 High St DG10 9EF
☎ 01683 220156 01683 221524
e-mail: tim@famousstarhotel.com
Dir: *M74 junct 15 signed Moffat, hotel 2m. 1st hotel on right in High Street*

Smart, modern and well-equipped bedrooms plus enjoyable food, served either in the bar or the restaurant, are just some of the virtues of this friendly hotel. Its claim to be the world's narrowest hotel is a novel talking point.

ROOMS: 8 en suite (1 fmly) s £40-£45; d £56-£65 (incl. bkfst) **LB** **FACILITIES:** STV Large screen in bar for sport **NOTES:** No dogs (ex guide dogs) No smoking in restaurant **CARDS:**

Top 200 - Hotel

★ Well View

Ballplay Rd DG10 9JU
☎ 01683 220184 01683 220088
e-mail: info@wellview.co.uk

THE CIRCLE
Selected Individual Hotels

Dir: *on A708 from Moffat, pass fire station & 1st left*

Well View is situated on a quiet road within walking distance of the small town of Moffat. The hotel retains many original Victorian features. Individually furnished bedrooms are comfortable and thoughtfully equipped. Dinner is certainly the highlight of a stay in this small family-run hotel; the six-course tasting menu emphasises fine ingredients which are locally sourced whenever possible.

ROOMS: 6 en suite No smoking in all bedrooms s £60-£70; d £80-£150 (incl. bkfst) **LB** **FACILITIES:** Xmas **CONF:** Thtr 12 Board 8 Del from £110 **PARKING:** 8 **NOTES:** No smoking in restaurant Closed 2wks Feb & 2wks Oct **CARDS:**

MONTROSE, Angus
Map 23 NO75

★★★73% Links Hotel
Mid Links DD10 8RL
☎ 01674 671000 01674 672698
e-mail: reception@linkshotel.com
Dir: *off A90 at Brechin, take A935 to Montrose, 10m turn right at Lochside junct, left at swimming pool, right by tennis courts, hotel 200yds*

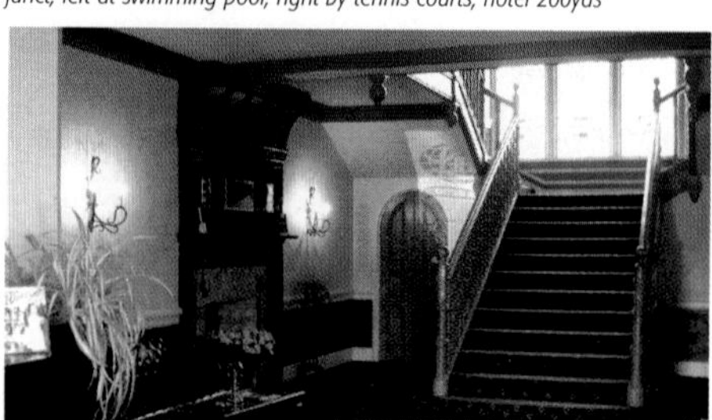

This former Edwardian town house has been fully refurbished and restored. Bedrooms offer a choice of attractively modern styles and are extremely well equipped to cater for business guests. Public areas include a bar, a restaurant, and a popular coffee shop where food is available all day.
ROOMS: 25 en suite (1 GF) No smoking in 15 bedrooms s £49-£79; d £59-£89 (incl. bkfst) **LB FACILITIES:** STV entertainment Xmas **CONF:** Thtr 220 Class 70 Board 70 Del from £99 **PARKING:** 45 **NOTES:** No smoking in restaurant Civ Wed 350 **CARDS:**

★★★66% Montrose Park
61 John St DD10 8RJ
☎ 01674 663400 01674 677091
e-mail: recep@montrosepark.co.uk
Dir: *from A90 off at A935 to A92, turn off Montrose High St into John St*
A welcoming hotel which focuses on business and oil-industry personnel during the week. Bedrooms are mostly spacious and well equipped. The same menu can be enjoyed in the bar while watching TV, or in the restaurant.
ROOMS: 52 en suite 5 annexe en suite (2 fmly) No smoking in 19 bedrooms s £40-£72; d £58-£90 (incl. bkfst) **LB FACILITIES:** STV Pool table Xmas **CONF:** Thtr 200 Class 80 Board 80 **PARKING:** 50 **NOTES:** No smoking in restaurant Civ Wed 220 **CARDS:**

MORAR, Highland
Map 22 NM69

★★65% Morar
PH40 4PA
☎ 01687 462346 01687 462212
e-mail: agmacleod@morarhotel.freeserve.co.uk
Dir: *in village on A830 "Road to the Isles"*
This long-established hotel lies in the centre of the village close to where the West Highland Railway once crossed the road. Bedrooms are furnished in modern style and those in the extension, along with the dining room, enjoy delightful views across Morar Bay to the silver sands, with the mountains of Skye in the distance.
ROOMS: 27 en suite No smoking in 3 bedrooms **FACILITIES:** Fishing entertainment **PARKING:** 50 **NOTES:** No smoking in restaurant Closed 22 Oct-Mar **CARDS:**

MOTHERWELL, North Lanarkshire
Map 21 NS75

Travel Inn (Glasgow Bellshill)
Belziehill Farm ML4 3HH
☎ 08701 977106 01698 845969
Dir: *M74 junct 5 follow signs towards Coatbridge & Bellshill on the A725. At the 2nd exit off the A725 Travel Inn on left of rdbt*
Travel Inn offers good-quality, value-for-money accommodation. Spacious, en suite rooms with bath and shower comfortably accommodate a family of up to two adults and two children (to age 15). The restaurant and bar offers a varied menu. For further details and the Travel Inn phone number, consult the Hotel Groups page.
ROOMS: 40 en suite s £44.95; d £44.95

Travel Inn Glasgow (Nr Motherwell)
Edinburgh Rd, Newhouse ML1 5SY
☎ 08701 977164 01698 861353
Dir: *From south M74 junct 5 onto A725 towards Coatbridge. Take A8 towards Edinburgh & leave at junct 6, follow signs for Lanark. Travel Inn 400yds on right*
Travel Inn offers good-quality, value-for-money accommodation. Spacious, en suite rooms with bath and shower comfortably accommodate a family of up to two adults and two children (to age 15). The restaurant and bar offers a varied menu. For further details and the Travel Inn phone number, consult the Hotel Groups page.
ROOMS: 40 en suite s £44.95; d £44.95 **CONF:** Thtr 40

MUIR OF ORD, Highland
Map 23 NH55

★★67% Ord House
IV6 7UH
☎ 01463 870492 01463 870492
e-mail: eliza@ord-house.com
Dir: *off A9 at Tore rdbt onto A832. Follow for 5m into Muir of Ord. Turn left to Ullapool remaining on A832. Hotel 0.5m on left*
Dating back to 1637, this country-house hotel sits peacefully in wooded grounds and offers brightly furnished and well-proportioned accommodation. Comfortable day rooms reflect the character and charm of the house, with inviting lounges, a cosy snug bar and an elegant dining room where wide-ranging, creative menus are served.
ROOMS: 11 en suite (2 GF) s £40-£65; d £90-£100 (incl. bkfst) **FACILITIES:** no TV in bdrms Croquet lawn Putting green Clay pigeon shooting ch fac **PARKING:** 30 **NOTES:** No smoking in restaurant Closed Nov-Feb **CARDS:**

Top 200 - Hotel

★ The Dower House
Highfield IV6 7XN
☎ 01463 870090 01463 870090
e-mail: aa@thedowerhouse.co.uk
Dir: *on A862 Dingwall rd, 1m from town on left*
This lovely house enjoys a secluded location on the northern edge of the village. The relaxed, friendly atmosphere and attentive service are key features of the hotel and guests are made to feel that this is a home-from-home. The cosy sitting room is full of books, whilst the dining room has quiet

continued

elegance and antique furniture. The charming bedrooms come in various sizes; one has its own sitting room.

ROOMS: 5 en suite 2 annexe en suite (1 fmly) (5 GF) No smoking in all bedrooms s £55-£85; d £110-£150 (incl. bkfst) **LB** **FACILITIES:** Croquet lawn Bird watching **PARKING:** 20 **NOTES:** No smoking in restaurant Closed 25 Dec & 2wks Nov Civ Wed 15 **CARDS:**

MULL, ISLE OF, Argyll & Bute — Map 20

CRAIGNURE — Map 20 NM73

U Isle Of Mull Hotel

PA65 5BN
☎ 01680 812351 📠 01680 812462
e-mail: isleofmull@british-trust-hotels.com

At the time of going to press, the star classification for this hotel was not confirmed. Please refer to the AA internet site www.theAA.com for current information.
ROOMS: 85 en suite (6 fmly) No smoking in 55 bedrooms s £29-£55; d £49-£99 (incl. bkfst) **LB** **FACILITIES:** STV entertainment Xmas **CONF:** Thtr 150 Class 85 Board 60 Del from £35.50 **PARKING:** 36 **NOTES:** No smoking in restaurant **CARDS:**

DERVAIG — Map 22 NM45

★★78% Druimard Country House
PA75 6QW
☎ 01688 400345 & 400291 📠 01688 400345
e-mail: druimard.hotel@virgin.net
Dir: *from Craignure ferry terminal right towards Tobermory, through Salen Village, 1.5m left to Dervaig, hotel on right*
A charming Victorian country house, on the edge of the village beside the Mull Little Theatre. Attractive colour schemes feature in the bedrooms, which are comfortably furnished and thoughtfully equipped. Two new rooms, one suitable for less mobile guests, have been added this year. There is a relaxing lounge and conservatory bar, but the focal point is the dining room, where tempting five-course dinners attract high praise.
ROOMS: 5 en suite 2 annexe en suite (2 fmly) (2 GF) s £88-£90; d £125-£170 (incl. bkfst & dinner) **LB** **FACILITIES:** Mull Little Theatre within grounds **PARKING:** 20 **NOTES:** No smoking in restaurant Closed Nov-Mar **CARDS:**

TOBERMORY — Map 22 NM55

★★★73% Western Isles
PA75 6PR
☎ 01688 302012 📠 01688 302297
e-mail: wihotel@aol.com
Dir: *After leaving ferry follow signs to Tobermory. Straight over 1st mini-rdbt & over small bridge. Take immediate right & follow road to T-junct, right again then keep left & take 1st left. Hotel at top of hill on right*
Built in 1883 this hotel enjoys spectacular views over Tobermory harbour and the Sound of Mull. During World War II it was used as an officers' mess for the numerous troops being trained on the island. Day rooms, warmed by roaring fires, are spacious and elegantly decorated. Rooms come in a variety of styles and include a suite complete with piano.
ROOMS: 28 en suite s £47-£113; d £99-£120 (incl. bkfst) **LB** **FACILITIES:** Xmas **CONF:** Thtr 35 Class 20 Board 20 Del £83 **PARKING:** 28 **NOTES:** No smoking in restaurant Closed 17-27 Dec Civ Wed 70 **CARDS:**

Top 200 - Hotel

★★ Highland Cottage
Breadalbane St PA75 6PD
☎ 01688 302030
e-mail: davidandjo@highlandcottage.co.uk
Dir: *A848 Craignure/Fishnish ferry terminal, pass Tobermory signs, ahead at mini rdbt across narrow bridge, turn right. Hotel on right*
Visitors are assured of a warm personal welcome at this charming cottage-style hotel. Bedrooms, with an island theme, are appointed to a high standard and feature antique beds and a range of thoughtful extras. Public areas include a relaxing first-floor lounge, an honesty bar, a smart conservatory and an elegant dining room.
ROOMS: 6 en suite (1 GF) No smoking in all bedrooms s £75-£95; d £99-£120 (incl. bkfst) **LB** **FACILITIES:** STV **PARKING:** 6 **NOTES:** No children 8yrs No smoking in restaurant Closed 4 wks mid Oct/mid Nov RS 6 Jan - Feb **CARDS:**

★★69% Tobermory
53 Main St PA75 6NT
☎ 01688 302091 📠 01688 302254
e-mail: tobhotel@tinyworld.co.uk
Dir: *on waterfront, overlooking Tobermory Bay*
This friendly hotel, with its pretty pink frontage, sits on the

continued on p778

M

TOBERMORY, continued

seafront amidst the other brightly coloured former fishing cottages. Enjoyable dinners feature mainly seafood dishes from a short daily-changing menu. Bedrooms, many brightly decorated, vary in size, and a number have views of the harbour.
ROOMS: 16 rms (15 en suite) (3 fmly) No smoking in all bedrooms s £30-£38; d £60-£76 (incl. bkfst) **LB** **FACILITIES:** ch fac **NOTES:** No smoking in restaurant Closed Xmas **CARDS:**

NAIRN, Highland Map 23 NH85

★★★★70% Newton

Inverness Rd IV12 4RX
☎ 01667 453144 01667 454026
e-mail: info@morton-hotels.com
Dir: *15m from Inverness on A96, turn left into tree lined driveway*

This baronial mansion lies secluded in extensive grounds looking towards the Moray Firth. An impressive extension houses an excellent conference centre and 22 superb bedrooms that provide a contrast to those in the original building. Residents can use the leisure centre at sister hotel The Golf View.
ROOMS: 56 en suite (2 fmly) No smoking in 15 bedrooms s £107-£190; d £114-£198 (incl. bkfst) **LB** **FACILITIES:** STV Tennis (hard) Fishing Use of leisure club at sister hotel Xmas **CONF:** BC Thtr 400 Class 150 Board 50 Del from £139.50 **SERVICES:** Lift **PARKING:** 200 **NOTES:** No smoking in restaurant Closed 23-27 Dec
CARDS:

★★★★68% Golf View

The Seafront IV12 4HD
☎ 01667 452301 01667 455267
e-mail: golfview@morton-hotels.com
Dir: *off A96 into Seabank Rd, follow road to end, hotel on right*

Set in grounds leading down to the beach, this hotel offers friendly and attentive service. Its leisure centre is a major attraction and guests have a choice of eating options in the conservatory and the main restaurant. Accommodation includes very impressive master bedrooms with DVD players.
ROOMS: 42 en suite (7 fmly) No smoking in 7 bedrooms
FACILITIES: STV Indoor swimming (H) Tennis (hard) Sauna Solarium Gym Putting green Jacuzzi Cycle hire, Swimming pool supervised
CONF: Thtr 120 Class 80 Board 55 Del from £139 **SERVICES:** Lift
PARKING: 65 **NOTES:** No smoking in restaurant Civ Wed 120
CARDS:

Top 200 - Hotel

★★ Boath House

Auldearn IV12 5TE
☎ 01667 454896 01667 455469
e-mail: wendy@boath-house.demon.co.uk
Dir: *2m past Nairn on A96 E towards Forres, signed on main road*
Standing in its own grounds, this splendid Georgian mansion has been lovingly restored. Hospitality is first class. Owners Don and Wendy Matheson are passionate about what they do, and have an ability to establish a special relationship with their guests that will be particularly remembered. The food is also memorable at Boath House; the five-course dinners are a culinary adventure, matched only by the excellence of breakfasts. The house itself is delightful, with inviting lounges and a dining room overlooking a trout loch. Bedrooms are striking, comfortable and include many fine antique pieces.
ROOMS: 5 en suite 1 annexe en suite (1 fmly) No smoking in all bedrooms s £95; d £150-£200 (incl. bkfst) **LB** **FACILITIES:** STV Fishing Sauna Gym Croquet lawn Jacuzzi Beauty salon
CONF: Board 10 **PARKING:** 30 **NOTES:** No smoking in restaurant Closed Xmas **CARDS:**

★★64% Alton Burn

Alton Burn Rd IV12 5ND
☎ 01667 452051 & 453325 01667 456697
e-mail: enquiries@altonburn.co.uk
Dir: *follow signs from A96 at western boundary of Nairn*
This long-established, family-run hotel is located on the western edge of town with views over the Moray Firth. The friendly relaxed atmosphere is a major strength here, and bedrooms are simple in style and practical. There is a cosy bar, and spacious lounges and a dining room.
ROOMS: 23 en suite (7 GF) s fr £38; d fr £65 (incl. bkfst) **LB**
FACILITIES: Outdoor swimming (H) Tennis (hard) Putting green Table tennis ch fac **CONF:** Thtr 100 Class 50 Board 40 Del from £76.50
PARKING: 40 **NOTES:** Closed Nov-Mar **CARDS:**

NETHY BRIDGE, Highland
Map 23 NJ02

★★71% ® The Mountview Hotel
Grantown Rd PH25 3EB
☎ 01479 821248 ▤ 01479 821515
e-mail: mviewhotel@aol.com
Dir: *from Aviemore follow signs through Boat of Garten to Nethy Bridge, through village, hotel on right, 100mtrs beyond Nethy Bridge Hotel.*
Aptly named, this country-house hotel enjoys stunning panoramic views from its elevated position on the edge of the village. It specialises in guided holidays and is a favoured base for birdwatching and walking groups. Public rooms include inviting lounges, while imaginative well-prepared dinners are served in a bright, modern restaurant extension.
ROOMS: 12 rms (11 en suite) (1 GF) s fr £38; d fr £70 (incl. bkfst) **FACILITIES:** Xmas **PARKING:** 16 **NOTES:** No dogs No smoking in restaurant **CARDS:**

NEW ABBEY, Dumfries & Galloway
Map 21 NX96
See also Carrutherstown

A Abbey Arms
1 The Square DG2 8BX
☎ 01387 850489 ▤ 01387 850501
e-mail: enquiries@abbeyarms.netlineuk.net
Dir: *centre of village square*
ROOMS: 7 en suite (2 fmly) No smoking in all bedrooms s £26; d £52 (incl. bkfst) **LB PARKING:** 4 **NOTES:** ★★ No smoking in restaurant **CARDS:**

NEWBURGH, Aberdeenshire
Map 23 NJ92

★★72% ® *Udny Arms*
Main St AB41 6BL
☎ 01358 789444 ▤ 01358 789012
e-mail: enquiry@udny.demon.co.uk
Dir: *off A92 at Newburgh sign, hotel 2m, in village centre on right*
This comfortable family-run hotel stands in the centre of the village overlooking the golf course on the Ythan estuary. Inviting public areas display lots of historical artefacts. There is a lovely lounge, and guests can eat well in both the rustic country bars and smart split-level bistro restaurant. The individual bedrooms are traditionally furnished but well equipped for the modern traveller.
ROOMS: 26 en suite (1 fmly) No smoking in all bedrooms **FACILITIES:** Fishing Petanque **CONF:** Thtr 100 Class 30 Board 30 **PARKING:** 100 **NOTES:** No smoking in restaurant **CARDS:**

NEW LANARK, South Lanarkshire
Map 21 NS84

★★★71% New Lanark Mill Hotel
Mill One, New Lanark Mills ML11 9DB
☎ 01555 667200 ▤ 01555 667222
e-mail: hotel@newlanark.org
Dir: *signposted from all major roads, M74 junct 7 also signed from M8*
This hotel occupies an impressively restored 18th-century cotton mill and is part of the heritage of the village. Inside, a bright modern style is balanced with features from the original mill. There is a comfortable foyer lounge with a galleried restaurant above and views of the valley from the upper floors are wonderful.

ROOMS: 38 en suite (2 fmly) No smoking in 28 bedrooms s fr £65; d fr £99 (incl. bkfst) **LB FACILITIES:** Fishing Xmas **CONF:** Thtr 180 Class 60 Board 40 Del from £95 **SERVICES:** Lift **PARKING:** 75 **NOTES:** No smoking in restaurant Civ Wed 140 **CARDS:**

NEWTON STEWART, Dumfries & Galloway
Map 20 NX46

Top 200 - Hotel

★★★ ®® Kirroughtree House
Minnigaff DG8 6AN
☎ 01671 402141 ▤ 01671 402425
e-mail: info@kirroughtreehouse.co.uk
Dir: *from A75 take A712, New Galloway road, entrance to hotel 300yds on left*
This imposing mansion enjoys a peaceful location in eight acres of landscaped gardens near Galloway Forest Park. Inviting day rooms offer a choice of lounges and two elegant dining rooms. Well-proportioned, individually styled bedrooms include some suites and mini suites and many rooms enjoy fine views. Service is very friendly and attentive.
ROOMS: 17 en suite s £70-£120; d £120-£216 (incl. bkfst & dinner) **LB FACILITIES:** STV Tennis (grass) Croquet lawn 9 hole pitch and putt Xmas **CONF:** Thtr 30 Class 20 Board 20 Del from £110 **PARKING:** 50 **NOTES:** No children 10yrs No smoking in restaurant Closed 4 Jan-16 Feb **CARDS:**

★★★67% ® Creebridge House
DG8 6NP
☎ 01671 402121 ▤ 01671 403258
e-mail: info@creebridge.co.uk
Dir: *off A75, at Newton Stewart sign, approx 0.75m to hotel sign*
This former shooting lodge lies secluded in attractive gardens close to the river and town centre. Public areas have been refurbished to provide a comfortable drawing room and a

continued on p780

NEWTON STEWART, continued

contemporary restaurant, as well as a lively bar/bistro offering an interesting and wide selection of dishes. The smart bedrooms come in a variety of styles and include some family suites.

Creebridge House, Newton Stewart

ROOMS: 19 en suite (2 fmly) s £64-£74; d £108-£128 (incl. bkfst) **LB FACILITIES:** STV Fishing shooting& fishing packages Xmas **CONF:** Thtr 70 Class 70 Board 35 Del from £76 **PARKING:** 30 **NOTES:** No smoking in restaurant **CARDS:**

★★★66% ***Bruce***
88 Queen St DG8 6JL
☎ 01671 402294 📠 01671 402294
e-mail: brucehotel@totalise.co.uk
Dir: *leave A75 at Newton Stewart rdbt, hotel 600mtrs on right past filling station, at junct*
Named after the Scottish historic patriot Robert the Bruce, this welcoming family-run hotel is just a short distance from the A75. One of the well-appointed bedrooms features a four-poster bed and popular family suites contain separate spacious bedrooms for children. Public areas include a traditional lounge, a formal restaurant and a lounge bar, both offering a choice of dishes.
ROOMS: 18 en suite (3 fmly) No smoking in 6 bedrooms **FACILITIES:** ch fac **CONF:** Thtr 60 Class 70 Board 60 **PARKING:** 20 **NOTES:** No smoking in restaurant **CARDS:**

N

NORTH BERWICK, East Lothian — Map 21 NT58

★★★67% **The Marine**
Cromwell Rd EH39 4LZ
☎ 0870 400 8129 📠 01620 894480
e-mail: marine@macdonald-hotels.co.uk
Dir: *from A198 turn into Hamilton Rd at lights then take 2nd right*
This imposing leisure, conference and golfing hotel commands stunning views across the golf course to the Firth of Forth. A good range of leisure facilities accompanies well-proportioned public areas. Bedrooms come in a variety of sizes, some being impressively large. The hotel awaits the start of an extensive upgrading.
ROOMS: 83 en suite (4 fmly) (4 GF) No smoking in 20 bedrooms s £35-£110; d £70-£220 (incl. bkfst) **LB FACILITIES:** STV Outdoor swimming (H) Tennis (hard) Snooker Sauna Solarium Putting green Childrens playground Xmas **CONF:** Thtr 300 Class 150 Board 100 Del from £85 **SERVICES:** Lift **PARKING:** 50 **NOTES:** No smoking in restaurant Civ Wed 200 **CARDS:**

Town House Hotel
Country House Hotel
Travel Accommodation

★★64% **Nether Abbey**
20 Dirleton Av EH39 4BQ
☎ 01620 892802 📠 01620 895298
e-mail: bookings@netherabbey.co.uk
Dir: *leave A1 at junct with A198, and continue S to rdbt, take B6371 to N Berwick, hotel 2nd on left on entering town*
Popular with golfers this hotel boasts stylish well-equipped bedrooms, the two junior suites having CD/video players. Downstairs the focus is on a lively bar/bistro where tasty home cooked dishes are on offer.
ROOMS: 14 en suite (4 fmly) (1 GF) s £35-£65; d £70-£97 (incl. bkfst) **LB FACILITIES:** Xmas **CONF:** Thtr 80 Class 50 Board 30 **PARKING:** 40 **NOTES:** Civ Wed 50 **CARDS:**

OBAN, Argyll & Bute — Map 20 NM82

★★★74% **The Oban Caledonian Hotel & Spa**
Station Square PA34 5RT
☎ 01855 821582 📠 01855 821463
e-mail: reservations@freedomglen.co.uk
Dir: *at head of main pier, close to rail terminal*

This Victorian hotel, overlooking the bay, has undergone a transformation. Public areas are modern and stylish and include a smart restaurant, spacious lounges and an informal dining option in Café Caledonian. Bedrooms come in a number of different styles and grades, some with feature bathrooms and fine sea views. Valet parking is available.
ROOMS: 59 en suite (4 fmly) No smoking in 10 bedrooms s £80-£100; d £160-£300 (incl. bkfst & dinner) **LB FACILITIES:** Discounted entry to local leisure centre entertainment Xmas **CONF:** Del from £59.50 **SERVICES:** Lift **PARKING:** 6 **NOTES:** No smoking in restaurant **CARDS:**

★★★72% ® **Manor House**
Gallanach Rd PA34 4LS
☎ 01631 562087 📠 01631 563053
e-mail: manorhouse@aol.com
Dir: *follow signs MacBrayne Ferries and pass ferry entrance for hotel on right*

An elegant Georgian residence, this historic building was built for

continued

the Duke of Argyll and enjoys fine views over the harbour. Bedrooms, many of which have now been upgraded, offer stylish design. Public rooms include a well-stocked bar, a choice of lounges and a smart restaurant where carefully prepared dinners are served.
ROOMS: 11 en suite No smoking in all bedrooms s £80-£110; d £120-£170 (incl. bkfst & dinner) **LB** **FACILITIES:** STV **PARKING:** 20 **NOTES:** No children 12yrs No smoking in restaurant Closed 25-26 Dec **CARDS:**

★★76% Willowburn
PA34 4TJ
☎ 01852 300276 01852 300597
e-mail: willowburn.hotel@virgin.net
(For full entry see Clachan-Seil)

★★72% Falls of Lora
PA37 1PB
☎ 01631 710483 01631 710694
(For full entry see Connel)

★★61% Lancaster
Corran Esplanade PA34 5AD
☎ 01631 562587 01631 562587
e-mail: john@lancasteroban.com
Dir: *on seafront next to St Columba's Cathedral*
Lovely views over the bay towards the Isle of Mull can be enjoyed from this welcoming family-run hotel on the Esplanade. Comfortable bedrooms vary in size and style and offer a good range of amenities. Public areas include a choice of contrasting lounges and bars.
ROOMS: 27 rms (24 en suite) (3 fmly) s £28-£33; d £60-£64 (incl. bkfst) **LB** **FACILITIES:** STV Indoor swimming (H) Sauna Jacuzzi Steam room **CONF:** Thtr 30 Class 20 Board 12 **PARKING:** 20 **CARDS:**

OLDMELDRUM, Aberdeenshire Map 23 NJ82

★★65% Meldrum Arms
The Square AB51 0DS
☎ 01651 872238 01651 872238
Dir: *off the B947, in centre of village*
Located in the centre of the village, the Meldrum Arms Hotel combines a cosy and welcoming atmosphere with a good range of tasty dishes available in both the bar and comfortable restaurant. Try their popular high tea that consists of a main course, tea and toast plus scones and cakes.
ROOMS: 7 en suite (1 fmly) s £38; d £58 (incl. bkfst) **CONF:** Thtr 80 Board 40 **PARKING:** 25 **NOTES:** No smoking in restaurant **CARDS:**

AA Rosette Award for culinary excellence

ONICH, Highland Map 22 NN06

★★★74% Onich
PH33 6RY
☎ 01855 821214 01855 821484
e-mail: enquiries@onich-fortwilliam.co.uk
Dir: *beside A82, 2m N of Ballachulish Bridge*
Genuine hospitality is part of the appeal of this hotel, which has gardens extending to the shore of picturesque Loch Linnhe. Nicely presented public areas include a choice of inviting lounges and contrasting bars, and views of the loch can be enjoyed from the *continued* attractive restaurant. Bedrooms, with pleasing colour schemes, are comfortably modern in appointment.

ROOMS: 25 en suite (6 fmly) No smoking in 6 bedrooms s £36-£55; d £115-£144 (incl. bkfst) **LB** **FACILITIES:** STV Jacuzzi Games room Xmas **CONF:** Thtr 30 Class 20 Board 20 **PARKING:** 50 **NOTES:** No smoking in restaurant **CARDS:**
See advert under FORT WILLIAM

★★★70% Lodge on the Loch
PH33 6RY
☎ 0871 222 3462 0871 222 3416
e-mail: reservations@freedomglen.co.uk
Dir: *beside A82 in Onich - 5m N of Glencoe, 10m S of Fort William*

Guests return regularly to this comfortable holiday hotel, with its spectacular outlook over Loch Linnhe. Inviting public areas include a relaxing foyer lounge, a cosy bar with fabric draped ceiling, and a spacious restaurant offering modern Scottish cuisine. Many superior bedrooms have luxury bathrooms and views of the loch.
ROOMS: 16 en suite (1 GF) No smoking in all bedrooms d £180-£260 (incl. bkfst & dinner) **LB** **FACILITIES:** Free use of leisure facilities at sister hotel Xmas **CONF:** Thtr 40 Class 30 Board 30 **PARKING:** 25 **NOTES:** No children 16yrs No smoking in restaurant Closed Jan-14 Feb & Nov-23 Dec RS 14 Feb - 4 April **CARDS:**

★★★69% Allt-nan-Ros
PH33 6RY
☎ 01855 821210 01855 821462
e-mail: AA@allt-nan-ros.co.uk
Dir: *1.5m N of Ballachulish Bridge on A82*

THE CIRCLE
Selected Individual Hotels
GREAT BRITAIN

Highland hospitality and good food are just part of the appeal of this comfortable hotel set in attractive gardens overlooking Loch Linnhe. Bedrooms are variable in size and modern in style. Inviting public areas include a pleasant lounge and a bright spacious dining room, both enjoying splendid views.
ROOMS: 20 en suite (2 fmly) s £76-£88; d £152-£175 (incl. bkfst & dinner) **LB** **FACILITIES:** Xmas **PARKING:** 30 **NOTES:** No smoking in restaurant Civ Wed 75 **CARDS:**
See advert under FORT WILLIAM

O

PAISLEY Hotels are listed under Glasgow Airport.

PEAT INN, Fife — Map 21 NO40

Top 200 - Hotel

★★ ❀❀❀ **Peat Inn**
KY15 5LH
☎ 01334 840206 📠 01334 840530
e-mail: reception@thepeatinn.co.uk
Dir: *6m SW of St Andrews at B940/B941 junct*

This former coaching inn is set in peaceful countryside just six miles from St Andrews. Accommodation, luxuriously appointed, is provided in an adjacent building and comprises split-level suites with a comfortable upstairs lounge. In the main building, a cosy lounge leads through into the restaurant where quality local ingredients are used to produce memorable meals.
ROOMS: 8 en suite (2 fmly) s £75-£95; d £145-£155 (incl. bkfst) **LB PARKING:** 24 **NOTES:** No smoking in restaurant Closed Sun, Mon, 25 Dec & 1 Jan **CARDS:**

PEEBLES, Scottish Borders — Map 21 NT24

★★★★69% **Peebles Hotel Hydro**
EH45 8LX
☎ 01721 720602 📠 01721 722999
e-mail: info@peebleshydro.com
Dir: *on A702, one third mile out of town*

This privately owned resort hotel benefits from an elevated location with striking views across the valley. Accommodation comes in a range of styles and includes a number of family rooms. A super range of leisure activities is available and the hotel is popular with both families and conference delegates.
ROOMS: 129 en suite (25 fmly) (15 GF) s £107-£120; d £176-£240 (incl. bkfst & dinner) **LB FACILITIES: Spa** STV Indoor swimming (H) Tennis (hard) Riding Snooker Sauna Solarium Gym Croquet lawn Putting green Badminton, Beautician, Hairdressing, Swimming pool supervised entertainment ch fac Xmas **CONF:** Thtr 450 Class 200 Board 74 Del from £110 **SERVICES:** Lift **PARKING:** 200 **NOTES:** No dogs (ex guide dogs) Civ Wed 200 **CARDS:**

★★★76% ❀❀ **Cringletie House**
EH45 8PL
☎ 01721 730233 📠 01721 730244
e-mail: enquiries@cringletie.com
Dir: *2m N on A703*

This long-established hotel is a fine baronial mansion set in 28 acres of gardens and woodland two miles north of Peebles. Delightful public rooms include a cocktail lounge with adjoining conservatory, whilst the first-floor restaurant is graced by a magnificent hand-painted ceiling. Bedrooms come in a variety of sizes and are being upgraded.
ROOMS: 14 en suite (2 fmly) s fr £95; d £115-£180 (incl. bkfst) **FACILITIES:** Tennis (hard) Fishing Croquet lawn Putting green Xmas **CONF:** Thtr 45 Class 20 Board 20 Del from £130 **PARKING:** 25 **NOTES:** No smoking in restaurant Civ Wed 50 **CARDS:**

★★★73% ❀❀ **Castle Venlaw**
Edinburgh Rd EH45 8QG
☎ 01721 720384 📠 01721 724066
e-mail: enquiries@venlaw.co.uk
Dir: *off A703 Peebles/Edinburgh road, 0.75m from Peebles*

Scotland's Hotels of Distinction

This 18th-century castle is set in four acres of landscaped gardens, set high above the town. Bedrooms, many with delightful views, are named after malt whiskies and include three with adjoining turrets. Well-prepared meals are served in the formal restaurant, while light meals are served in the wood-panelled library bar.
ROOMS: 12 en suite (3 fmly) No smoking in all bedrooms s £75-£90; d £120-£170 (incl. bkfst) **LB FACILITIES:** STV Croquet lawn Xmas **CONF:** BC Thtr 30 Class 20 Board 20 Del from £120 **PARKING:** 30 **NOTES:** No smoking in restaurant Civ Wed 35 **CARDS:**

★★★68% **Park**
Innerleithen Rd EH45 8BA
☎ 01721 720451 📠 01721 723510
e-mail: reserve@parkpeebles.co.uk
Dir: *in centre of Peebles opposite filling station*

Best Western

The Park Hotel offers pleasant, well-equipped bedrooms, which vary in size; those in the original house are particularly spacious. Public areas enjoy views of the gardens and include a tartan-clad bar, a relaxing lounge and a spacious wood-panelled restaurant. Guests can use the extensive leisure facilities on offer at the sister hotel, The Hydro.
ROOMS: 24 en suite No smoking in 6 bedrooms s £72-£99; d £131-£174 (incl. bkfst & dinner) **LB FACILITIES:** Putting green Use of facilities of Peebles Hotel Hydro entertainment Xmas **SERVICES:** Lift **PARKING:** 50 **CARDS:**

★★70% ***Kingsmuir***
Springhill Rd EH45 9EP
☎ 01721 720151 📠 01721 721795
e-mail: enquiries@kingsmuir.com
Dir: *from High St cross Tweed Bridge, then straight ahead up Springhill Rd, hotel 300yds on right*

The Independents

A warm welcome is assured at this friendly hotel located in a residential area on the south side of the River Tweed. There is a choice of lounges and good value, home-cooked meals are available in both the dining room and bar.
ROOMS: 10 en suite (2 fmly) No smoking in 5 bedrooms **CONF:** Thtr 40 Class 20 Board 20 **PARKING:** 35 **NOTES:** No dogs (ex guide dogs) No smoking in restaurant **CARDS:**

U Cardrona Hotel Golf & Country Club
Cardrona Mains EH45 6LZ
☎ 01896 831144 01896 831166
e-mail: cardrona@macdonald-hotels.co.uk

MACDONALD HOTELS

At the time of going to press, the star classification for this hotel was not confirmed. Please refer to the AA internet site www.theAA.com for current information.
ROOMS: 100 en suite s £85-£125; d £110-£170 (incl. bkfst) **LB** **FACILITIES:** STV Indoor swimming (H) Golf 18 Fishing Sauna Solarium Gym Quad biking, Kayaking, Shooting, Archery, Horse riding, Tank driving, **CONF:** Thtr 200 Class 140 Board 100 Del from £125 **SERVICES:** Lift **PARKING:** 150 **NOTES:** No smoking in restaurant Civ Wed 200
CARDS:

PERTH, Perth & Kinross

Map 21 NO12

Top 200 - Hotel

★★★ Kinfauns Castle
Kinfauns PH2 7JZ
☎ 01738 620777 01738 620778
e-mail: email@kinfaunscastle.co.uk
Dir: *2m beyond Perth on A90 Perth/Dundee road*
This impressive castle dates from 1827 and sits high above the road in a secluded setting. Day rooms offer opulent levels of comfort and ornately decorated ceilings and large marble fireplaces are a feature. The bar is made from a striking oriental dragon boat. Bedrooms are spacious and offer individual décor and high-quality furnishings. The panelled restaurant is the setting for carefully prepared, award-winning cuisine.
ROOMS: 16 en suite s £130-£190; d £200-£320 (incl. bkfst) **FACILITIES:** STV Fishing Croquet lawn Clay pigeon shooting, Archery, Falconry available with prior notice Xmas **CONF:** Thtr 50 Class 40 Board 26 Del from £165 **PARKING:** 40 **NOTES:** No children 8yrs No smoking in restaurant Closed 4-24 Jan
CARDS:

★★★74% Huntingtower
Crieff Rd PH1 3JT
☎ 01738 583771 01738 583777
e-mail: reservations@huntingtowerhotel.co.uk
Dir: *3m W off A85*
Enjoying an idyllic country setting, this Edwardian house has been extended to offer smart, comfortable public areas and a high standard of accommodation. Comfortable lounges lead to a conservatory where lunches are served, whilst the elegant restaurant offers skilfully prepared dinners. Bedrooms are generally spacious and provide a host of modern facilities.
ROOMS: 31 en suite 3 annexe en suite (2 fmly) (8 GF) s £75-£85; d £90-£110 (incl. bkfst) **LB** **FACILITIES:** STV Xmas **CONF:** BC Thtr 200 Class 140 Board 30 Del from £110 **SERVICES:** Lift **PARKING:** 150 **NOTES:** No smoking in restaurant Civ Wed 100
CARDS:

★★★74% Murrayshall Country House Hotel & Golf Course
New Scone PH2 7PH
☎ 01738 551171 01738 552595
e-mail: lin.murrayshall@virgin.net
Dir: *from Perth take A94 (Coupar Angus), 1m from Perth, right to Murrayshall just before New Scone*
This imposing country house is set in 350 acres of grounds, which include two golf courses, one of which is of championship standard. Bedrooms come in two distinct styles; modern suites in a purpose-built building contrast with more traditional rooms in the main building. The Clubhouse bar serves a range of meals all day, while more accomplished cooking can be enjoyed in the Old Masters Restaurant.
ROOMS: 27 en suite 14 annexe en suite (17 fmly) (4 GF) No smoking in 1 bedroom s £90-£100; d £130-£180 (incl. bkfst) **LB** **FACILITIES: Spa** STV Golf 36 Tennis (hard) Sauna Gym Putting green Jacuzzi Driving range Xmas **CONF:** Thtr 180 Class 60 Board 30 Del from £100 **PARKING:** 80 **NOTES:** No smoking in restaurant Civ Wed 100
CARDS:

★★★71% Parklands
St Leonards Bank PH2 8EB
☎ 01738 622451 01738 622046
e-mail: parklands.perth@virgin.net
Dir: *exit M90 junct 10, after 1m turn left at end of park area at lights, hotel on left*
Originally two separate houses, one of which was the home of the Lord Provost of Perth; the buildings have been sensitively converted to create a stylish and individual hotel. Well-equipped bedrooms are tastefully furnished with many overlooking the colourful, flower-filled expanse of South Inch Park. Similar shades are reflected in The Colourist's Bistro, or for a more formal meal, the Acanthus Restaurant will certainly please.
ROOMS: 14 en suite (1 fmly) (4 GF) No smoking in 4 bedrooms s £59-£89; d £79-£115 (incl. bkfst) **LB** **FACILITIES:** STV **CONF:** Thtr 25 Board 16 Del £105 **PARKING:** 25 **NOTES:** No smoking in restaurant Closed 26-27 Dec & 1-7 Jan **CARDS:**

P

★★★68% Lovat
90 Glasgow Rd PH2 0LT
☎ 01738 636555 01738 643123
e-mail: e-mail@lovat.co.uk

Best Western

Dir: *from M90 follow signs for Stirling to rdbt, then turn right into Glasgow Rd, hotel 1.5m on right*
This popular, long established hotel on the Glasgow road offers excellent function facilities and largely attracts a business clientele. Public areas include a conservatory lounge and a well stocked bar where the Bistro menu provides an informal eating alternative to the restaurant. Bedrooms are smartly appointed and thoughtfully equipped.
ROOMS: 30 en suite (1 fmly) (9 GF) No smoking in 12 bedrooms s £75; d £110 (incl. bkfst) **LB** **FACILITIES:** STV Use of facilities at nearby sister hotel (indoor pool, gym, steam room, jacuzzi) Xmas **CONF:** Thtr 200 Class 70 Board 70 Del from £72 **PARKING:** 40 **NOTES:** No dogs (ex guide dogs) No smoking in restaurant
CARDS:

Late for dinner?
Quality Standards mean that last orders for dinner vary according to star rating and should be no earlier than:
★★ 7.00pm ★★★ 8.00pm ★★★★ 9.00pm
★★★★★ 10.00pm

PERTH, continued

★★★65% Queens Hotel

Leonard St PH2 8HB
☎ 01738 442222 01738 638496
e-mail: email@queensperth.co.uk

Conveniently situated for both the bus and the railway stations this hotel provides well-equipped bedrooms in various sizes. Public areas include a smart leisure centre and there is a selection of meeting and conference rooms.

ROOMS: 50 en suite (7 fmly) No smoking in 20 bedrooms s £50-£80; d £60-£110 (incl. bkfst) **LB** **FACILITIES: Spa** STV Indoor swimming (H) Sauna Gym Jacuzzi Steam room Xmas **CONF:** Thtr 200 Class 120 Board 70 Del from £70 **SERVICES:** Lift **PARKING:** 50 **NOTES:** No dogs (ex guide dogs) No smoking in restaurant Civ Wed 140
CARDS:

★68% Woodlea

23 York Place PH2 8EP
☎ 01738 621744 01738 621744
e-mail: info@woodleaperthuk.co.uk
Dir: *take A9/A93 into Perth, hotel on left after lights*

A relaxed and friendly atmosphere prevails at this small family-run hotel close to the town centre. The bedrooms are bright and airy and offer modern facilities. Public areas include a cosy lounge and the high tea menu is popular in the attractive dining room.

ROOMS: 12 rms (11 en suite) (2 fmly) (5 GF) No smoking in 5 bedrooms s £31-£41; d £46-£50 (incl. bkfst) **LB** **PARKING:** 4 **NOTES:** No dogs (ex guide dogs) No smoking in restaurant

⌂ Express by Holiday Inn

200 Dunkeld Rd, Inveralmond PH1 3AQ
☎ 01738 636666 01738 633363
e-mail: info@hiexpressperth.co.uk
Dir: *off A9 onto A912 signed Perth. Right at 1st rdbt follow hotel signs*

A modern hotel ideal for families and business travellers. Fresh and uncomplicated, the spacious bedrooms include Sky TV, power shower and tea and coffee-making facilities. Continental buffet breakfast is included in the room rate; other meals may be taken at the nearby family pub or restaurant. For further details and Express by Holiday Inn phone number, consult Hotel Groups pages.

ROOMS: 81 en suite s £50-£62; d £50-£62 (incl. cont bkfst)
CONF: Thtr 40 Class 20 Board 22

⌂ Travelodge

☎ 0870 191 1751

Travelodge offers good quality, good value, modern accommodation. Ideal for families, the spacious, en suite bedrooms include remote-control TV, tea and coffee-making facilities, luxury beds and free morning newspaper. Meals can be taken at the nearby family restaurant. For further details and the Travelodge phone number, consult the Hotel Groups page.

ROOMS: s fr £42.95; d fr £42.95

○ Premier Lodge (Perth)

Huntingtower PR1 3JW
☎ 0870 9906486 0870 9906487
ROOMS: 64 en suite **NOTES:** Due to open March 2004

PETERHEAD, Aberdeenshire — Map 23 NK14

★★★★64% Waterside Inn

Fraserburgh Rd AB42 3BN
☎ 01779 471121 01779 470670
e-mail: waterside@macdonald-hotels.co.uk
Dir: *from Aberdeen A90, 1st rdbt turn left signed Fraserburgh, cross small rdbt, hotel at end of road*

Attracting a mixed market, this popular hotel is located to the north of the town and lies on the banks of the River Ugie. The hotel offers a wide range of child friendly leisure facilities making this a popular destination for families. Bedrooms, the majority of which are contained in two separate blocks, offer a variety of styles and standards.

ROOMS: 67 en suite 40 annexe en suite (10 fmly) (50 GF) No smoking in 55 bedrooms s £75-£85; d £85-£95 (incl. bkfst) **LB** **FACILITIES:** STV Indoor swimming (H) Snooker Sauna Solarium Gym Jacuzzi Beauty treatment rooms, Pool table, Bouncy castle, Swimming pool supervised entertainment ch fac Xmas **CONF:** Thtr 250 Class 100 Board 30 Del from £115 **PARKING:** 200 **NOTES:** No smoking in restaurant Civ Wed 250 **CARDS:**

★★★66% *Palace*

Prince St AB42 1PL
☎ 01779 474821 01779 476119
e-mail: info@palacehotel.co.uk
Dir: *from Aberdeen, take A90 and follow signs to Peterhead, entering town, turn into Prince Street, then right into main car park*

This popular business and function hotel close to the town centre has two eating options. There is a split-level Brasserie Restaurant and a diner set above a theme bar and reached by spiral staircase. Bedrooms range from the spacious executive to the smaller standard ones.

ROOMS: 66 en suite (2 fmly) No smoking in 24 bedrooms **FACILITIES:** STV Snooker pool table, snooker room & liveentertainment entertainment **CONF:** Thtr 250 Class 120 Board 250 **SERVICES:** Lift **PARKING:** 90 **NOTES:** Civ Wed 150 **CARDS:**

PITLOCHRY, Perth & Kinross — Map 23 NN95

★★★74% Green Park

Clunie Bridge Rd PH16 5JY
☎ 01796 473248 01796 473520
e-mail: bookings@thegreenpark.co.uk
Dir: *turn off A9 at Pitlochry, follow signs 0.25m through town*

This family-run hotel benefits from an outstanding location on the banks of Loch Faskally. Enjoy a complimentary pre-dinner sherry

continued

in the relaxing lounge, which along with the restaurant enjoys fine views of the gardens. Bedrooms are split between the main house and a modern extension.

ROOMS: 39 en suite (10 GF) No smoking in all bedrooms s £49-£71; d £98-£142 (incl. bkfst & dinner) **LB** **FACILITIES:** Putting green Xmas **PARKING:** 45 **NOTES:** No smoking in restaurant **CARDS:**

See advert on this page

★★★72% Pine Trees

Strathview Ter PH16 5QR
☎ 01796 472121 Fax 01796 472460
e-mail: info@pinetreeshotel.co.uk
Dir: *along main street, turn into Larchwood Road, follow signs for hotel*

Set in 10 acres of tree-studded grounds high above the town, this fine Victorian mansion retains many fine features including wood panelling, ornate ceilings and a wonderful marble staircase. The atmosphere is refined and relaxing, with public rooms looking onto the lawns. Bedrooms come in a variety of sizes and many are well proportioned.

ROOMS: 20 en suite (1 fmly) No smoking in all bedrooms s £60-£84; d £104-£148 (incl. bkfst & dinner) **LB** **FACILITIES:** entertainment Xmas **PARKING:** 20 **NOTES:** No smoking in restaurant Civ Wed 70 **CARDS:**

★★★71% Dundarach

Perth Rd PH16 5DJ
☎ 01796 472862 Fax 01796 473024
e-mail: mail@pitlochryhotel.co.uk
Dir: *S of town centre on main route*

This welcoming family-run hotel stands in mature grounds at the south end of the town. Well-proportioned public areas feature inviting lounges and a conservatory restaurant giving fine views of the Tummel Valley. Bedrooms offer a variety of styles, including a block of large purpose-built rooms that will appeal to business guests.

ROOMS: 20 en suite 19 annexe en suite (7 fmly) No smoking in 11 bedrooms **FACILITIES:** STV Sauna **CONF:** Thtr 60 Class 40 Board 40 **PARKING:** 39 **NOTES:** No dogs (ex guide dogs) No smoking in restaurant Closed Jan RS Dec-early Feb **CARDS:**

★★★66% Scotland's

Best Western

40 Bonnethill Rd PH16 5BT
☎ 01796 472292 Fax 01796 473284
e-mail: stay@scotlandshotel.co.uk
Dir: *follow A924 Perth road into town until War Memorial then take next right for hotel 200mtrs on right*

Enjoying a convenient town-centre location, this long established hotel is a popular base for tourists. Bedrooms, including a number that have been refurbished, vary in size and style. A choice of restaurants and bars are offered and guests can relax in the comfortable lounges.

ROOMS: 57 en suite 15 annexe en suite (21 fmly) s £50-£75; d £100-£140 (incl. bkfst) **LB** **FACILITIES:** Indoor swimming (H) Sauna Solarium Gym Jacuzzi Therapy treatments entertainment Xmas **CONF:** Thtr 200 Class 75 Board 30 Del from £90 **SERVICES:** Lift **PARKING:** 100 **NOTES:** No dogs (ex guide dogs) No smoking in restaurant **CARDS:**

★★77% Knockendarroch House

Higher Oakfield PH16 5HT
☎ 01796 473473 Fax 01796 474068
e-mail: info@knockendarroch.co.uk
Dir: *off A9 at Pitlochry sign. After railway bridge, take 1st right, then 2nd left*

An immaculate Victorian mansion overlooking the town and Tummel Valley. There is no bar, but guests can enjoy a drink in the delightful lounge while studying the daily menu of freshly

continued on p786

PITLOCHRY, continued

prepared and enjoyable dishes. Bedrooms are tastefully furnished, comfortable and well equipped. Those on the top floor are smaller but are not without character and appeal.
ROOMS: 12 en suite No smoking in all bedrooms s £71-£89; d £96-£136 (incl. bkfst & dinner) **LB** **FACILITIES:** Leisure facilities at nearby hotel **PARKING:** 30 **NOTES:** No dogs (ex guide dogs) No children 10yrs No smoking in restaurant Closed 2nd wk Nov-mid Feb
CARDS:

★★71% *Birchwood*
2 East Moulin Rd PH16 5DW
☎ 01796 472477 01796 473951
e-mail: viv@birchwoodhotel.co.uk
Dir: *signed from Atholl Rd on S side of town*

THE CIRCLE *Selected Individual Hotels* GREAT BRITAIN

This Victorian house is peacefully situated at the southern side of town and is within walking distance of the towns many attractions. The refurbished bedrooms blend contemporary style with traditional architecture to provide comfortable, well-equipped accommodation. Day rooms are elegantly furnished and creative dinners can be enjoyed in the dining room. The hotel operates a no-smoking policy.
ROOMS: 12 en suite No smoking in all bedrooms **PARKING:** 25 **NOTES:** No dogs (ex guide dogs) No smoking in restaurant Closed Dec-mid Mar **CARDS:**

★★71% Moulin Hotel
11-13 Kirkmichael Rd, Moulin PH16 5EW
☎ 01796 472196 01796 474098
e-mail: hotel@moulin.u-net.com
Dir: *off A9 into Pitlochry in centre of town take A924 signed Braemar. Moulin village 0.75m outside Pitlochry*

Steeped in history, original parts of this friendly hotel date back to 1695. The Moulin bar, serves an excellent choice of bar meals as well as real ales from the hotel's own microbrewery. Alternatively, guests can choose the comfortable restaurant that overlooks the Moulin Burn. Bedrooms are well equipped with many having been refurbished.
ROOMS: 15 en suite (3 fmly) s £40-£70; d £50-£80 (incl. bkfst) **LB** **FACILITIES:** Xmas **CONF:** Thtr 15 Class 12 Board 10 **PARKING:** 30 **NOTES:** No smoking in restaurant **CARDS:**

★★70% Balrobin
Higher Oakfield PH16 5HT
☎ 01796 472901 01796 474200
e-mail: info@balrobin.co.uk
Dir: *leave A9 at Pitlochry junct, continue to town centre and follow brown tourists signs to hotel*

THE CIRCLE *Selected Individual Hotels* GREAT BRITAIN

A welcoming atmosphere prevails at this family-run hotel which, from its position above the town, enjoys delightful countryside views. Public rooms include a relaxing lounge, a well-stocked bar and an attractive restaurant offering traditional home-cooked fare. The bedrooms are comfortable and many enjoy the fine views.
ROOMS: 15 en suite (2 fmly) No smoking in all bedrooms s £42-£50; d £64-£84 (incl. bkfst) **LB** **PARKING:** 15 **NOTES:** No children 5yrs No smoking in restaurant Closed Nov-Feb **CARDS:**

★★70% Craigvrack
West Moulin Rd PH16 5EQ
☎ 01796 472399 01796 473990
e-mail: info@craigvrack-hotel.demon.co.uk
Dir: *from Main St, turn into West Moulin Rd (hotel has large flagpoles on lawn and is illuminated at night)*

Situated above the town, this comfortable hotel has well-presented public areas which include an attractive restaurant and comfortable bar serving a varied menu. The bedrooms come in a variety of sizes and are smartly furnished, with several enjoying fine views of the countryside.
ROOMS: 16 en suite (2 fmly) (3 GF) No smoking in 7 bedrooms s £54-£64; d £88-£104 (incl. bkfst & dinner) **LB** **FACILITIES:** Xmas **CONF:** Thtr 30 Class 32 Board 16 Del from £64.95 **PARKING:** 26 **NOTES:** No smoking in restaurant **CARDS:**

★★69% Donavourd House
PH16 5JS
☎ 01796 472100 01796 474455
e-mail: reservations@donavourd.co.uk
Dir: *From A9 take immediate right under railway, continue 0.5m, then left up hill. At junct take left. Hotel 0.5m on left*
This attractive country house sits in its own gardens in a quiet, elevated location overlooking Strathtummel. Bedrooms are mostly spacious, and well appointed, and the public areas reflect a period style. The short table d'hôte dinner menu demonstrates sound cooking skills by chef patron Nicole McKechnie.
ROOMS: 9 en suite (1 fmly) (1 GF) s £35-£45; d £50-£70 (incl. bkfst) **LB** **FACILITIES:** Xmas **PARKING:** 15 **NOTES:** No smoking in restaurant Closed 25 Dec, 5 Jan-Feb **CARDS:**

PLOCKTON, Highland Map 22 NG83

★★75% Haven
Innes St IV52 8TW
☎ 01599 544334 & 544223 01599 544467
e-mail: thehavenhotel@aol.com
Dir: *off A87 just before Kyle of Lochalsh, after Balmacara signed to Plockton, hotel on main road just before lochside*
A delightful hotel in the picturesque west Highland village of Plockton that indeed lives up to its name. Comfortable public areas include a choice of lounges, a snug bar for residents and diners only, and an attractive restaurant which offers an

continued

P

imaginative dinner menu. Smart modern bedrooms include two delightful and very spacious suites.

ROOMS: 15 en suite s £43-£46; d £86-£118 (incl. bkfst) **LB** **PARKING:** 7 **NOTES:** No children 7yrs No smoking in restaurant Closed 20 Dec-1 Feb **CARDS:**

★★71% The Plockton

41 Harbour St IV52 8TN
☎ 01599 544274 🖹 01599 544475
e-mail: info@plocktonhotel.co.uk
Dir: *6m from Kyle of Lochalsh and 6m from Balmacara*

This small hotel occupies an idyllic position on the waterfront of Loch Carron. Bedrooms offer individual, pleasing décor and many have spacious balconies or panoramic views. There is a choice of three dining areas offering different atmospheres in which seafood is very much a speciality. The staff and owners provide a relaxed and informal style of attentive service.

ROOMS: 11 en suite 4 annexe en suite (1 fmly) (1 GF) No smoking in 11 bedrooms s £40-£50; d £60-£80 (incl. bkfst) **LB** **FACILITIES:** STV Pool table Xmas **NOTES:** No dogs (ex guide dogs) No smoking in restaurant **CARDS:**

POLMONT, Falkirk — Map 21 NS97

★★★★69% The Inchyra

Grange Rd FK2 0YB
☎ 01324 711911 🖹 01324 716134
e-mail: inchyra@macdonald-hotels.co.uk
Dir: *just beyond BP Social Club*

Well positioned for the M9 and Grangemouth terminal, this former manor house has been tastefully extended. It provides extensive conference facilities and a choice of eating options within the leisure club or in the Priory Restaurant , which provides a more formal dining experience. Bedrooms are mostly spacious and comfortable.

ROOMS: 109 en suite (5 fmly) No smoking in 57 bedrooms s £45-£85; d £70-£180 (incl. bkfst) **LB** **FACILITIES:** STV Indoor swimming (H) Tennis (hard) Sauna Solarium Gym Jacuzzi Steam room, Beauty therapy salons, Aromatherapist ch fac Xmas **CONF:** Thtr 700 Class 250 Board 80 Del from £99 **SERVICES:** Lift **PARKING:** 400 **NOTES:** No smoking in restaurant Civ Wed 500 **CARDS:**

⌂ Travel Inn (Falkirk East)

travel inn

Beancross Rd FK2 0YS
☎ 08701 977098 🖹 01324 720777
Dir: *M9 junct 5 at rdbt take exit signed Polmont A9. Travel Inn on left*

Travel Inn offers good-quality, value-for-money accommodation. Spacious, en suite rooms with bath and shower comfortably accommodate a family of up to two adults and two children (to age 15). The restaurant and bar offers a varied menu. For further details and the Travel Inn phone number, consult the Hotel Groups page.

ROOMS: 40 en suite s £44.95; d £44.95

POOLEWE, Highland — Map 22 NG88

Top 200 - Hotel

★★★ 🏵🏵 *Pool House Hotel*

Scotland's Hotels of Distinction

IV22 2LD
☎ 01445 781272 🖹 01445 781403
e-mail: enquiries@poolhousehotel.com
Dir: *6m N of Gairloch on A832. In village centre*

Set only a few yards from the shores of Loch Ewe, there are fine views towards the famed Inverewe Gardens. The spacious suites have been individually designed and furnished and all are named after World War II ships, reflecting the buildings former use as a military base. The striking dining room follows a nautical theme and local seafood features extensively on the menus.

ROOMS: 5 en suite (1 fmly) No smoking in all bedrooms **FACILITIES:** Snooker Sea fishing from jetty in front of hotel **PARKING:** 20 **NOTES:** No dogs (ex guide dogs) No children 8yrs No smoking in restaurant Closed Jan-Feb RS Nov & Dec **CARDS:**

P

PORT APPIN, Argyll & Bute

Map 20 NM94

Top 200 - Hotel

★★★ ®®® Airds

PA38 4DF
☎ 01631 730236 🖷 01631 730535
e-mail: airds@airds-hotel.com

Dir: *N on A828, left at Appin signed Port Appin and Lismore Ferry. Hotel 2.5m on left*

Stunning views are a real feature at this delightful small hotel on the shores of Loch Linnhe. The panoramic dining room is the setting for carefully prepared meals that utilise first rate ingredients including shellfish from the loch. Bedrooms offer pleasing, tasteful décor and bathrooms of a high specification. An extensive range of walks can be recommended by the helpful staff.

ROOMS: 12 en suite (1 fmly) No smoking in all bedrooms d £230-£360 (incl. bkfst & dinner) **LB PARKING:** 21 **NOTES:** No smoking in restaurant Closed 23-27 Dec & 6-22 Jan RS late-Jan - Feb **CARDS:**

PORT ASKAIG See Islay, Isle of

PORT OF MENTEITH, Stirling

Map 20 NN50

★★76% ®® Lake of Menteith

FK8 3RA
☎ 01877 385258 🖷 01877 385671
e-mail: enquiries@lake-of-menteith-hotel.com

Dir: *just off A81, beside village church 200yds on right*

This charming hotel combines the ambience of a country house with authentic Art Deco styling. It enjoys a superb setting right on the lakeside and the views from the conservatory restaurant are second to none. Bedrooms offer a range of sizes and all are comprehensively equipped.

ROOMS: 16 en suite No smoking in all bedrooms s £40-£85; d £80-£176 (incl. bkfst) **LB FACILITIES:** Xmas **CONF:** Thtr 30 Board 20 **PARKING:** 35 **NOTES:** No children 8yrs No smoking in restaurant Closed 2-21 Jan RS Nov-Feb Civ Wed 40 **CARDS:**

PORTPATRICK, Dumfries & Galloway

Map 20 NW95

★★★73% ® Fernhill

Heugh Rd DG9 8TD
☎ 01776 810220 🖷 01776 810596
e-mail: info@fernhillhotel.co.uk

Dir: *from Stranraer A77 to Portpatrick, 100yds past Portpatrick village sign, turn right before war memorial. Hotel is 1st on left*

Commanding panoramic views over the harbour and the Irish Sea, this friendly hotel is ideally situated for access to the many activities in the area. Bedrooms are comfortable, some with balconies overlooking the harbour. The conservatory restaurant is an ideal location for a relaxing breakfast or dinner.

ROOMS: 25 en suite 9 annexe en suite (3 fmly) s £55-£65; d £110-£130 (incl. bkfst & dinner) **LB FACILITIES:** STV Leisure facilities available at sister hotel in Stranraer Xmas **CONF:** Thtr 24 Class 12 Board 12 **PARKING:** 45 **NOTES:** Closed mid-Jan - mid-Feb Civ Wed 45 **CARDS:**

★★69% Downshire Arms

10-14 Main St DG9 8JJ
☎ 01776 810300 🖷 01776 810620
e-mail: downshirearmshotel@mail.com

Dir: *Follow A77/A75 to Stranraer turn off at sign for Portpatrick. Hotel on left*

Set in the centre of the village, this family-run hotel provides several styles of rooms, with refurbishment on going. There is a choice of bars, with real ales, and a restaurant that offers a good range of well prepared dishes. Service is friendly and efficient, with good value being given.

ROOMS: 13 en suite (2 fmly) No smoking in 3 bedrooms s £26-£32; d £52-£60 (incl. bkfst) **LB FACILITIES:** Xmas **CONF:** Thtr 60 Class 30 Board 40 **NOTES:** No smoking in restaurant **CARDS:**

PORTREE See Skye, Isle of

PRESTWICK, South Ayrshire

Map 20 NS32

★★★69% ® Parkstone

Esplanade KA9 1QN
☎ 01292 477286 🖷 01292 477671
e-mail: info@parkstonehotel.co.uk

Dir: *from Prestwick A79 turn W to seafront - hotel 600yds*

Situated on the seafront in a quiet residential area, this family-run hotel caters for business visitors as well as golfers. Bedrooms come in a variety of sizes, all being furnished in a smart

continued

contemporary style. The attractive, modern look of the bar and restaurant is matched by an equally up-to-date menu.
ROOMS: 22 en suite (2 fmly) No smoking in all bedrooms s £42-£52; d £69-£79 (incl. bkfst) **LB** **CONF:** Thtr 100 **PARKING:** 34 **NOTES:** No dogs No smoking in restaurant Civ Wed 100
CARDS:

RENFREW For hotels see Glasgow Airport

ROSEBANK, South Lanarkshire Map 21 NS84

★★★71% Popinjay
Lanark Rd ML8 5QB
☎ 01555 860441 01555 860204
e-mail: popinjayhotel@attglobal.net
Dir: *on A72 between Hamilton & Lanark*
This attractive Tudor-style hotel is set in landscaped grounds leading down to the River Clyde. The panelled bar is complemented by a light and airy restaurant where a wide choice of dishes is offered. Well-equipped bedrooms come in a variety of sizes, all featuring smart, modern en suites. Stylish function suites attract weddings and conferences.
ROOMS: 38 en suite (2 fmly) No smoking in 19 bedrooms s £63-£150; d £75-£150 (incl. bkfst) **LB** **FACILITIES:** STV Fishing Xmas **CONF:** Thtr 250 Class 120 Board 60 Del from £99 **PARKING:** 300 **NOTES:** No smoking in restaurant Civ Wed 160 **CARDS:**

See advert on this page

ROSYTH, Fife Map 21 NT18

★★64% *Gladyer Inn*
Heath Rd, Ridley Dr KY11 2BT
☎ 01383 419977 01383 411728
e-mail: gladyer@aol.com
Dir: *M90 junct 1, along Admiralty Road, past rdbt then 1st road on left*
This purpose-built hotel is ideally placed for access to the new ferry terminal and popular with commercial travellers. Bedrooms, though compact, are comfortably equipped. Hearty, good value meals are served in both the restaurant and bar. There is also a spacious function suite available.
ROOMS: 21 en suite (3 fmly) **FACILITIES:** STV entertainment **CONF:** Thtr 100 Class 70 Board 80 **PARKING:** 81 **NOTES:** No dogs (ex guide dogs) **CARDS:**

ROWARDENNAN, Stirlingshire Map 20 NS39

★★67% Rowardennan
G63 0AR
☎ 01360 870273 01360 870251
e-mail: rowardennanhotel@btinternet.com
Dir: *access via B837*
Located beside the West Highland Way on the eastern shore of Loch Lomond, this small hotel, which has been refurbished, is surrounded by stunning rugged scenery. Popular and generously portioned meals are served in the bar at lunchtime and evening as well as dinner in the restaurant. Bedrooms are well appointed and freshly decorated.
ROOMS: 13 en suite s £60; d £85-£100 (incl. bkfst) **FACILITIES:** Fishing Boat jetty, Private beach, Ferry service from Rowardennan to Inverbeg Xmas **PARKING:** 80 **NOTES:** No smoking in restaurant
CARDS:

R

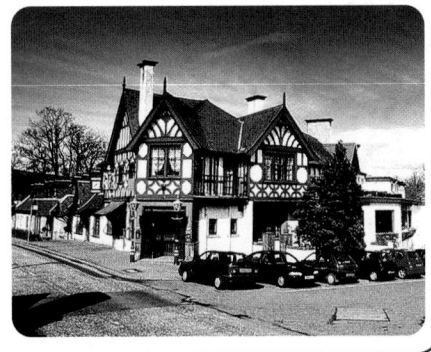

ROY BRIDGE, Highland Map 22 NN28

★★★70% Glenspean Lodge Hotel
PH31 4AW
☎ 01397 712223 01397 712660
e-mail: reservations@glenspeanlodge.co.uk
Dir: *2m E of Roy Bridge, right off A82 at Spean Bridge onto A86*

Originally a Victorian hunting lodge, this hotel has been impressively extended and enjoys stunning views from its elevated position in the Spean Valley. These are particularly memorable from the restaurant, which seems to suspend itself out over the valley. Substantial bar meals are also available, and service is provided efficiently and with a smile.
ROOMS: 15 en suite No smoking in 10 bedrooms **FACILITIES:** Sauna Gym Jacuzzi **CONF:** Thtr 50 Class 25 Board 25 **PARKING:** 50 **NOTES:** No smoking in restaurant Civ Wed 65
CARDS:

★★66% The Stronlossit Inn
PH31 4AG
☎ 01397 712253 & 0800 015 5321 01397 712641
e-mail: stay@stronlossit.co.uk
Dir: *off A82 at Spean Bridge onto A86, signed Roy Bridge. Hotel on left at E end of village*
A relaxed, informal atmosphere prevails at this family-run holiday hotel. The spacious bar is the focal point and a favourite with both resident and non-resident diners. Alternatively one can eat in the attractive restaurant. Bedrooms come in a mix of sizes and styles, most being smartly modern.
ROOMS: 10 en suite (5 GF) No smoking in all bedrooms s £35-£45; d £56-£75 (incl. bkfst) **LB FACILITIES:** Pool table, Internet Cafe Xmas **CONF:** Thtr 30 Class 18 Board 12 **PARKING:** 30 **NOTES:** No dogs (ex guide dogs) No children No smoking in restaurant Closed 10 Nov-10 Dec & 6-31 Jan Civ Wed 30 **CARDS:**

R

ST ANDREWS, Fife Map 21 NO51

Top 200 - Hotel

★★★★★ The Old Course Hotel
KY16 9SP
☎ 01334 474371 01334 477668
e-mail: reservations@oldcoursehotel.co.uk
Dir: *close to A91 on outskirts of the city*
A haven for golfers, this internationally renowned hotel sits adjacent to the 17th hole of the championship course. Bedrooms vary in size and range from the traditional to the contemporary and stylish Fairway rooms complete with course facing balconies. Day rooms include intimate lounges, a bright conservatory, a well equipped spa and a range of golf shops. Dining venues include the fine dining 'Grill', the seafood bar 'Sands' or the informal Stringers pub.
ROOMS: 146 en suite (6 fmly) No smoking in 118 bedrooms **FACILITIES:** STV Indoor swimming (H) Golf 18 Sauna Solarium Gym Jacuzzi Health spa Steam room **CONF:** Thtr 300 Class 150 Board 60 **SERVICES:** Lift **PARKING:** 150 **NOTES:** Closed 24-28 Dec Civ Wed 150 **CARDS:**

★★★★74% *Rusacks*
Pilmour Links KY16 9JQ
☎ 0870 400 8128 01334 477896
e-mail: rusacks@macdonald-hotels.co.uk
Dir: *from A91 past golf course, hotel 200mtrs on left*

In a superb location looking out across the famous golf course towards St Andrews Bay, this longstanding and well-managed hotel is naturally a mecca for golfers, as well as other guests. Bedrooms come in a variety of sizes and include some fine course-facing rooms. Public rooms also enjoy the views.
ROOMS: 68 en suite **FACILITIES:** STV Sauna Golf Mgr to organise golf **CONF:** Thtr 90 Class 40 Board 20 **SERVICES:** Lift **PARKING:** 21 **NOTES:** No smoking in restaurant Civ Wed 60
CARDS:

Top 200 - Hotel

★★★ Rufflets Country House
Strathkinness Low Rd KY16 9TX
☎ 01334 472594 01334 478703
e-mail: reservations@rufflets.co.uk
Dir: *1.5m W on B939*

Owned and run by the same family for over 50 years, this imposing country mansion is set in extensive, award winning gardens. The committed, friendly team ensures a memorable stay with seamless service. The individually decorated bedrooms are bright and airy and many come with impressive bathrooms. The Garden Room is a delightful setting in which to enjoy carefully prepared meals that utilise produce from the hotel's own gardens where possible.

ROOMS: 19 en suite 3 annexe en suite (1 fmly) No smoking in 13 bedrooms **FACILITIES: Spa** STV Putting green Golf driving net **CONF:** Thtr 50 Class 30 Board 25 **PARKING:** 52 **NOTES:** No dogs (ex guide dogs) No smoking in restaurant
CARDS:

Top 200 - Hotel

★★★ St Andrews Golf
40 The Scores KY16 9AS
☎ 01334 472611 01334 472188
e-mail: reception@standrews-golf.co.uk
Dir: *follow signs 'Golf Course' into Golf Place and in 200yds turn right into The Scores*

Friendly attentive service is a particular feature of this hotel, which overlooks the bay and enjoys fine views of the coastline and Links. The thoughtfully equipped bedrooms are currently undergoing refurbishment which is introducing a crisp, clean, contemporary design. Public rooms remain traditional, with comfortable and relaxing lounge areas, a choice of bars and a wood panelled restaurant.

ROOMS: 21 en suite (9 fmly) s £80-£180; d £160-£200 (incl. bkfst) **LB FACILITIES:** STV Xmas **CONF:** Thtr 200 Class 80 Board 20 **SERVICES:** Lift **PARKING:** 6 **NOTES:** No smoking in restaurant
CARDS:

★★★66% Scores
76 The Scores KY16 9BB
☎ 01334 472451 01334 473947
e-mail: office@scoreshotel.co.uk
Dir: *into St Andrews follow signs to West Sands/Sea Life Centre, hotel opposite Royal & Ancient Clubhouse*

Best Western

This elegant hotel enjoys views over St Andrews Bay and is situated only a few yards from the first tee of the famous Old Course. Public areas include a choice of bars, an all day coffee shop, and an attractive restaurant. Bedrooms are well equipped and come in various sizes, many quite spacious.

ROOMS: 30 en suite (1 fmly) No smoking in 9 bedrooms s £75-£96; d £90-£162 (incl. bkfst) **LB FACILITIES:** STV Xmas **CONF:** Thtr 150 Class 60 Board 40 Del from £110 **SERVICES:** Lift **PARKING:** 10 **NOTES:** No dogs (ex guide dogs) No smoking in restaurant
CARDS:

★★73% The Inn at Lathones
Largoward KY9 1JE
☎ 01334 840494 01334 840694
e-mail: lathones@theinn.co.uk
Dir: *5m S of St Andrews on A915, 0.5m before village of Largoward on left just after hidden dip*

THE INDEPENDENTS

A lovely little country inn, full of character and individuality, parts of which date back 400 years. The friendly staff help to create a relaxed atmosphere. The colourful, cosy restaurant is the main focus, the menu adding a modern style to Scottish and European dishes. Bedrooms are in two separate wings, both accessed from outside.

ROOMS: 14 annexe en suite (2 fmly) **CONF:** Thtr 30 Class 10 Board 20 Del from £125 **PARKING:** 35 **NOTES:** No smoking in restaurant Closed 25-26 Dec & 3-23 Jan RS 24 Dec Civ Wed 40
CARDS:

Popped the question?
Hotels with Civ Wed in their entry are licensed for civil wedding ceremonies. Maximum numbers for the ceremony only are shown, e.g. Civ Wed 120

S

ST ANDREWS, continued

★★70% ® *Russell Hotel*
26 The Scores KY16 9AS
☎ 01334 473447 01334 478279
e-mail: russellhotel@talk21.com
Dir: *A91, into Golf Place, right into The Scores, hotel 300yds*

This family-run hotel enjoys lovely views over the east bay, especially from its upper sea-facing bedrooms. The town centre and famous Old Course are nearby and well appointed bedrooms come in a variety of sizes. A good range of dishes is available in the bar, but for that added experience its worth taking dinner in the cosy little restaurant.
ROOMS: 10 en suite (3 fmly) **FACILITIES:** STV **NOTES:** No dogs (ex guide dogs) No smoking in restaurant Civ Wed 40
CARDS:

ST BOSWELLS, Scottish Borders Map 21 NT53

★★★76% ® *Dryburgh Abbey*
TD6 0RQ
☎ 01835 822261 01835 823945
e-mail: enquiries@dryburgh.co.uk
Dir: *A68 onto B6404 then B6356, hotel 1.8m*
An imposing red sandstone mansion in an attractive riverside setting next to the Abbey. There is a choice of lounges and the elegant first-floor dining room overlooks the river. Bedrooms are spacious and include suites.
ROOMS: 37 en suite 1 annexe en suite (5 fmly) **FACILITIES:** Indoor swimming (H) Fishing Croquet lawn Putting green ch fac **CONF:** Thtr 150 Class 90 Board 70 **SERVICES:** Lift **PARKING:** 103 **NOTES:** No smoking in restaurant **CARDS:**

★★71% Buccleuch Arms
The Green TD6 0EW
☎ 01835 822243 01835 823965
e-mail: bucchotel@aol.com
Dir: *on A68, 8m N of Jedburgh*
Formerly a coaching inn, this long established hotel stands opposite the village green. The lounge bar is a popular eating venue and complements the restaurant. Morning coffees and afternoon teas are served in the attractive lounge with its open fire. The well-equipped bedrooms come in a variety of sizes.
ROOMS: 19 en suite (2 fmly) No smoking in all bedrooms s fr £45; d fr £75 (incl. bkfst) **LB** **FACILITIES:** Putting green Xmas **CONF:** Thtr 100 Class 40 Board 30 Del from £55 **PARKING:** 50 **NOTES:** No smoking in restaurant **CARDS:**

GF Indicates the number of bedrooms at ground floor level.

ST FILLANS, Perth & Kinross Map 20 NN62

★★★70% ®® The Four Seasons Hotel
Loch Earn PH6 2NF
☎ 01764 685333 01764 685444
e-mail: info@thefourseasonshotel.co.uk
Dir: *on A85, towards W of village facing Loch*

Set on the edge of Loch Earn, there are fine views to be enjoyed from the public rooms and many of the bedrooms at this welcoming hotel. There is a choice of lounges, including a library, warmed by log fires during the cooler months. Local produce is used to good effect in both the Meall Reamhar restaurant and the more informal Tarken Room.
ROOMS: 12 en suite 6 annexe en suite (7 fmly) No smoking in 3 bedrooms s £35-£74; d £70-£98 (incl. bkfst) **LB** **FACILITIES:** STV Xmas **CONF:** Thtr 95 Class 45 Board 38 **PARKING:** 40 **NOTES:** No smoking in restaurant Closed 5 Jan-end of Feb RS Nov, Dec, Mar Civ Wed 80
CARDS:

★★72% Achray House
Loch Earn PH6 2NF
☎ 01764 685231 01764 685320
e-mail: achrayhotelsltd@btinternet.com
Dir: *on A85, 12m from Crieff*
A friendly holiday hotel set in gardens overlooking picturesque Loch Earn, Achray House offers smart attractive bedrooms, including a self contained lodge with fine views. A good range of dishes, often featuring fresh fish, is served in both the conservatory and residents' dining room.
ROOMS: 9 rms (8 en suite) 1 annexe en suite (2 fmly) No smoking in 3 bedrooms s fr £49; d fr £73 (incl. bkfst) **LB** **FACILITIES:** Xmas **CONF:** Class 20 Board 20 **PARKING:** 30 **NOTES:** No dogs (ex guide dogs) No smoking in restaurant **CARDS:**

SANQUHAR, Dumfries & Galloway Map 21 NS70

★★65% Blackaddie House
Blackaddie Rd DG4 6JJ
☎ 01659 50270 01659 50900
e-mail: enquiries@blackaddiehousehotel.co.uk
Dir: *off A76 at Service Station. Private road hotel 300mtrs*
This charming house, a former rectory, is quietly situated on the edge of the village, beside the river. As well as an inviting lounge, public areas include a cosy bar, adorned with angling memorabilia, and a conservatory restaurant giving a very fine view over the neat garden to the River Nith.
ROOMS: 9 en suite (2 fmly) s fr £40; d fr £70 (incl. bkfst) **FACILITIES:** Riding **CONF:** Thtr 50 Class 20 Board 20 **PARKING:** 25 **NOTES:** No smoking in restaurant **CARDS:**

SCARISTA See Harris, Isle of

S

SCOURIE, Highland Map 22 NC14

★★72% Eddrachilles
Badcall Bay IV27 4TH
☎ 01971 502080 01971 502477
e-mail: enq@eddrachilles.com
Dir: *2m S on A894, 7m N of Kylesku Bridge*
This appealing holiday hotel is in an idyllic woodland setting beside the Badcall Bay and enjoys stunning sea and island views. There are inviting lounges and a popular conservatory overlooking the bay. The dining room offers both fixed-price and carte menus and the well-equipped bedrooms are pleasantly decorated and furnished.
ROOMS: 11 en suite (1 fmly) (4 GF) s £39-£55; d £68-£97 (incl. bkfst) **LB FACILITIES:** Fishing Boats for hire **PARKING:** 25 **NOTES:** No dogs (ex guide dogs) No children 3yrs No smoking in restaurant Closed Nov-Feb **CARDS:**

★★70% Scourie
IV27 4SX
☎ 01971 502396 01971 502423
e-mail: patrick@scourie-hotel.co.uk
Dir: *on A894 in village*
This well-established hotel is an angler's paradise with extensive fishing rights available on a 25,000-acre estate. Public areas include a choice of comfortable lounges, a cosy bar and a smart dining room offering wholesome fare. The bedrooms are comfortable and generally spacious and the resident proprietors and their staff create a relaxed and friendly atmosphere.
ROOMS: 18 rms (17 en suite) 2 annexe en suite (2 fmly) (5 GF) s £35-£46; d £60-£80 (incl. bkfst) **LB FACILITIES:** no TV in bdrms Fishing Trout and Salmon fishing, Hill walking, Sea fishing **PARKING:** 30 **NOTES:** No smoking in restaurant Closed mid Oct-end Mar
CARDS:

SHETLAND Map 24

BRAE Map 24 HU36

★★★69% Busta House
ZE2 9QN
☎ 01806 522506 01806 522588
e-mail: reservations@bustahouse.com
Dir: *after Brae follow road north, bearing left around Busta Voe, within 1m hotel signed Muckle Roe*

THE CIRCLE
Selected Individual Hotels
GREAT BRITAIN

Dating back to 1724, this popular hotel boasts the reputation of being Britain's most northerly country-house hotel. Bedrooms vary in size and style but are well equipped, comfortable, and many boast excellent sea views. Day rooms include the comfortable 'long room' lounge; and wide-ranging menus are to be found in the Pitcairn restaurant and popular, traditional bar. All the staff are friendly and keen to please.
ROOMS: 20 en suite (1 fmly) s £70-£75; d £100-£140 (incl. bkfst) **LB CONF:** Thtr 44 **PARKING:** 40 **NOTES:** No smoking in restaurant Closed 23 Dec-5 Jan Civ Wed 59 **CARDS:**

LERWICK Map 24 HU44

★★★69% Shetland
Holmsgarth Rd ZE1 0PW
☎ 01595 695515 01595 695828
e-mail: reception@shetlandhotel.co.uk
Dir: *opposite ferry terminal, on main route N from town centre*
This modern hotel, situated opposite the main ferry terminal, offers spacious and comfortable bedrooms on three floors. Two *continued* dining options are available, including the informal Oasis bistro and Ninians Restaurant. Service is prompt and willing.
ROOMS: 64 en suite (4 fmly) No smoking in 14 bedrooms s £69; d £90 (incl. bkfst) **LB FACILITIES:** STV **CONF:** Thtr 300 Class 75 Board 50 **SERVICES:** Lift **PARKING:** 150 **NOTES:** No dogs (ex guide dogs) Civ Wed 200 **CARDS:**

★★★68% Lerwick
15 South Rd ZE1 0RB
☎ 01595 692166 01595 694419
e-mail: reception@lerwickhotel.co.uk
Dir: *near town centre, on main road south from airport. 25m from main airport, in central Lerwick*
Enjoying fine views across Breiwick Bay from the restaurant and some of the bedrooms, this purpose-built hotel appeals to tourists and business guests alike. Bedrooms, varying in size and aspect, are attractively furnished and family accommodation is available. The Breiwick restaurant has fine sea views, and there is also a more informal brasserie.
ROOMS: 34 en suite (3 fmly) s £72; d £90 (incl. bkfst) **LB FACILITIES:** STV **CONF:** BC Thtr 100 Class 40 Board 26 **PARKING:** 50 **NOTES:** No dogs (ex guide dogs) Civ Wed 100
CARDS:

UNST Map 24 HP60

★★64% The Baltasound
ZE2 9DS
☎ 01957 711334 01957 711358
e-mail: balta.hotel@zetnet.co.uk
Dir: *from ferry in Lerwick, follow main road N. Hotel in Baltasound close to pier.*
Set amid the sea lochs of the most northerly inhabited island in the British Isles, this welcoming hotel offers a variety of accommodation styles. Most rooms are located in log cabins in the grounds. The comfortable lounge leads into an open-plan bar and dining area, with a separate bright and airy room used for breakfast.
ROOMS: 8 rms (6 en suite) 17 annexe en suite (17 fmly) No smoking in 17 bedrooms s £44-£49; d £68-£74 (incl. bkfst) **FACILITIES:** Pool table **CONF:** Board 20 **PARKING:** 20 **NOTES:** No smoking in restaurant
CARDS:

SHIELDAIG, Highland Map 22 NG85

★77% *Tigh an Eilean*
IV54 8XN
☎ 01520 755251 01520 755321
e-mail: tighaneileanhotel@shieldaig.fsnet.co.uk
Dir: *off A896 onto village road signed Shieldaig. Hotel in centre of village*

This delightful hotel is continues to build a well-earned reputation. It enjoys an idyllic situation, looking out over the bay and
continued on p794

S

SHIELDAIG, continued

surrounded by traditional whitewashed crofts and fishermen's cottages. There are three comfortable lounges and an honesty bar. The dinner menu features seafood and quality local produce, with lighter snacks served in the bar at lunchtime.
ROOMS: 11 en suite (1 fmly) **FACILITIES:** no TV in bdrms **PARKING:** 15 **NOTES:** No smoking in restaurant Closed late Oct-end Mar **CARDS:**

SKEABOST BRIDGE, Highland

Map 22 NG44

★★★68% Skeabost Country House

IV51 9NP
☎ 01470 532202 01470 532454
e-mail: reception@skeabostcountryhouse.com
Dir: *from Portree after 3m onto A850, hotel 3m after junction*

This lovely 19th-century house is peacefully set amid 12 acres of secluded woodland and gardens, beside the picturesque shore of Loch Snizort. Comfortable public areas include a choice of inviting lounges warmed by roaring log fires. The modern conservatory offers a more informal food option to the main dining room. Facilities include the hotels own nine hole golf course. Dinner provides a sense of occasion; the daily-changing fixed-price menu features tempting, carefully prepared dishes, mostly locally sourced.
ROOMS: 15 en suite 4 annexe en suite (1 fmly) No smoking in 6 bedrooms s £49-£54; d £85-£95 (incl. bkfst) **LB FACILITIES:** Golf 9 Fishing Snooker Xmas **CONF:** Class 50 Board 50 **PARKING:** 100 **NOTES:** No smoking in restaurant **CARDS:**

SKYE, ISLE OF, Highland

Map 22

ARDVASAR

Map 22 NG60

★★67% *Ardvasar Hotel*

Sleat IV45 8RS
☎ 01471 844223 01471 844495
e-mail: richard@ardvasar-hotel.demon.co.uk
Dir: *leave ferry, drive 500mtrs & turn left*

Less than five minutes' drive from the Mallaig ferry, this well maintained hotel is the hub of the community. Bedrooms are smartly furnished and well equipped and public areas include a cosy lounge for residents. Seafood is prominent on menus, and meals can be enjoyed in either the popular bar or the attractive dining room.
ROOMS: 10 en suite (4 fmly) No smoking in 6 bedrooms **CONF:** Thtr 50 Board 24 **PARKING:** 30 **NOTES:** No smoking in restaurant **CARDS:**

COLBOST

Map 22 NG2

Top 200 – Restaurant with Rooms

Three Chimneys Restaurant & House Over-By

IV55 8ZT
☎ 01470 511258 01470 511358
e-mail: eatandstay@threechimneys.co.uk
Dir: *4m W of Dunvegan village on B884 signed Glendale*

A trip to Skye is not complete withouta visit to this popular hotel. Each bedroom in the 'House Over-By' boasts stunning views across Loch Dunvegan and seals can often be seen playing on nearby rocks. The recently built bedrooms are particularly spacious and furnished in contemporary interior designs. Dinner provides the highlight of any stay and quality local ingredients are handled with great skill. Breakfasts also impress and an array of locally smoked fish and meats provide one of many reasons to return.
ROOMS: 6 en suite (1 fmly) (6 GF) No smoking in all bedrooms s £155; d £190 (incl. bkfst) **LB FACILITIES:** Xmas **CONF:** Thtr 30 Class 12 Board 12 **PARKING:** 8 **NOTES:** No dogs (ex guide dogs) No smoking in restaurant Closed 5-30 Jan RS Sun & Nov-Mar **CARDS:**

ISLE ORNSAY

Map 22 NG71

★★★72% Duisdale Country House

IV43 8QW
☎ 01471 833202 01471 833404
e-mail: marie@duisdalehotel.demon.co.uk
Dir: *on A851 Armadale to Broadford road, just N of village*

The Campbell family delights in welcoming guests to their charming country house. Standing in wooded grounds and gardens, the hotel enjoys superb views over the Sound of Sleat to the mainland hills beyond. There is a cosy library bar with a good range of malts and well-filled bookshelves. The restaurant is the main focal point with the innovative culinary skills attracting much praise.
ROOMS: 17 en suite 2 annexe en suite (3 fmly) No smoking in all bedrooms s £65-£80; d £80-£140 (incl. bkfst) **LB FACILITIES:** no TV in bdrms Fishing Croquet lawn Putting green Sea Fishing,Cycling Hill walking Rock climbing **CONF:** Thtr 40 Class 40 Board 40 **PARKING:** 20 **NOTES:** No dogs No smoking in restaurant Closed Nov-Feb (prebooking possible) Civ Wed 40 **CARDS:**

★★74% ❀❀ Hotel Eilean Iarmain

IV43 8QR
☎ 01471 833332 🖷 01471 833275
e-mail: hotel@eilean-iarmain.co.uk
Dir: *A851, A852, right to Isle Ornsay Harbour front*

A hotel of charm and character, this 19th-century former inn lies by the pier and enjoys fine views across the sea loch. Bedrooms are individual and retain a traditional style (not all have TV), and a stable block has been converted into four delightful suites. Public rooms are cosy and inviting, and the dining room has an attractive extension.

ROOMS: 6 en suite 10 annexe en suite (6 fmly) No smoking in 10 bedrooms s fr £90; d fr £135 (incl. bkfst) **LB FACILITIES:** Fishing Shooting Exibitions Whisky tasting entertainment Xmas **CONF:** Thtr 50 Class 30 Board 25 **PARKING:** 35 **NOTES:** No smoking in restaurant **CARDS:**

See advert on this page

PORTREE Map 22 NG44

★★★74% ❀ Cuillin Hills

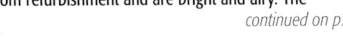

IV51 9QU
☎ 01478 612003 🖷 01478 613092
e-mail: office@cuillinhills.demon.co.uk
Dir: *turn right 0.25m N of Portree off A855 and follow signs for hotel*

Built in 1870 as a hunting lodge for Lord MacDonald with unrivalled views over Portree Bay to the Cuillin Hills, this hotel enjoys a fabulous setting. Bedrooms, which vary in size, have benefited from refurbishment and are bright and airy. The

continued on p796

PORTREE, continued

smart restaurant offers an interesting range of freshly prepared dishes with food in the bar a less formal option.

Cuillin Hills, Portree

ROOMS: 20 en suite 8 annexe en suite (2 fmly) (5 GF) No smoking in 14 bedrooms s £60-£200; d £100-£210 (incl. bkfst) **LB** **FACILITIES:** STV Xmas **CONF:** Thtr 100 Class 60 Board 30 **PARKING:** 56 **NOTES:** No smoking in restaurant Civ Wed **CARDS:**

See advert on page 795

★★73% Rosedale

Beaumont Crescent IV51 9DB
☎ 01478 613131 01478 612531
e-mail: rosedalehotelsky@aol.com
Dir: *follow directions to village centre & harbour, hotel on waterfront*

The atmosphere is wonderfully warm at this delightful family-run waterfront hotel. A labyrinth of stairs and corridors connect the comfortable lounge, well-stocked bar, coffee shop and wine bar. The charming restaurant serves a daily-changing set menu of carefully prepared specialities and modern bedrooms offer a good range of amenities.

ROOMS: 18 en suite (1 fmly) No smoking in all bedrooms s £35-£48; d £70-£104 (incl. bkfst) **LB** **PARKING:** 2 **NOTES:** No smoking in restaurant Closed mid Nov-mid Mar **CARDS:**

★★72% Bosville

Bosville Ter IV51 9DG
☎ 01478 612846 01478 613434
e-mail: bosville@macleodhotels.co.uk
Dir: *A87 signed Portree, then A855 into town for hotel*

The MacLeod family delight in welcoming guests to their comfortable, stylish island hotel. The bedrooms are smartly modern and offer a good range of amenities whilst the popular Chandlery Restaurant provides a relaxed venue in where excellent seafood and game can be sampled.

ROOMS: 25 en suite (2 fmly) No smoking in 10 bedrooms s £55-£75; d £76-£100 (incl. bkfst) **LB** **FACILITIES:** Use of nearby leisure club Xmas **CONF:** BC Thtr 20 Class 20 Board 20 Del from £50 **PARKING:** 10 **NOTES:** No smoking in restaurant **CARDS:**

SOUTH QUEENSFERRY, City of Edinburgh Map 21 NT17

Innkeeper's Lodge South Queensferry

7 Newhalls Rd EH30 9TA
☎ 0131 331 1990 0131 331 3168
Dir: *M8 junct 2 onto M9/A8000. At rdbt take B907 junct with B249. Right and lodge in Newhalls Rd*

A new concept in the travel accommodation market. Smart rooms meet essential business requirements but also have home comforts. Dining options include all-day menus plus the added advantage of breakfast, which is included in the room price. For further details, consult the Hotel Groups page.

ROOMS: 10 en suite 4 annexe en suite s £57.50; d £57.50 (incl. cont bkfst) **CONF:** Class 18 Board 18 Del £70

Travel Inn (Edinburgh Queensferry)

Builyeon Rd EH30 3YJ
☎ 08701 977094 0131 319 1156
Dir: *M8 junct 2 follow signs M9 Stirling, exit at junct 1A take A8000 towards Forth Road Bridge, at 3rd rdbt take 2nd exit into Builyeon Road (do not go onto Forth Road Bridge)*

Travel Inn offers good-quality, value-for-money accommodation. Spacious, en suite rooms with bath and shower comfortably accommodate a family of up to two adults and two children (to age 15). The restaurant and bar offers a varied menu. For further details and the Travel Inn phone number, consult the Hotel Groups page.

ROOMS: 46 en suite s £44.95; d £44.95

STEPPS, North Lanarkshire Map 20 NS66

★★★68% Garfield House Hotel

Cumbernauld Rd G33 6HW
☎ 0141 779 2111 0141 779 9799
e-mail: rooms@garfieldhotel.co.uk
Dir: *M8 J11 exit at Stepps/Queenslie, follow signs Stepps/A80*

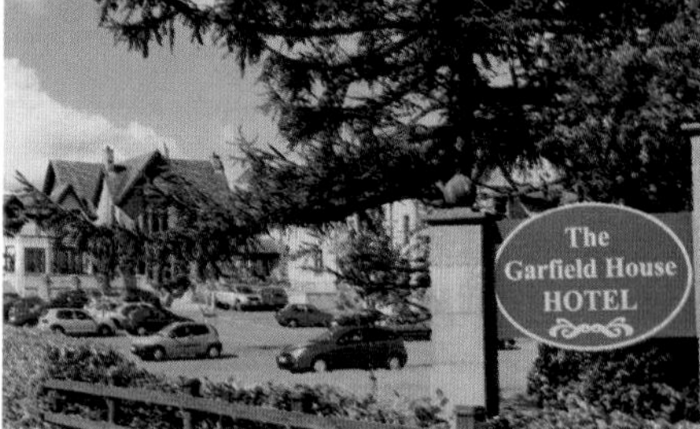

Situated close to the A80, this considerably extended business hotel is a popular venue for local conferences and functions. Public areas include a welcoming reception lounge and the popular Distillery Bar/Restaurant, an all-day eatery providing good value meals in an informal setting. Smart, well-presented bedrooms come in a range of sizes.

ROOMS: 45 en suite (10 fmly) (8 GF) No smoking in 31 bedrooms s £75-£90; d £75-£113 (incl. bkfst) **LB** **CONF:** Thtr 150 Class 40 Board 36 Del from £110 **PARKING:** 90 **NOTES:** Closed 1-2 Jan

CARDS:

⌂ Travel Inn Glasgow (North East)

Crowood Roundabout, Cumbernauld Rd G33 6LE
☎ 08701 977111 🖷 0141 779 8060
Dir: *M8 junct 13 signed M80. Exit M80 at Crowwood rdbt, take 3rd exit signed A80 west. Travel Inn 1st left*
Travel Inn offers good-quality, value-for-money accommodation. Spacious, en suite rooms with bath and shower comfortably accommodate a family of up to two adults and two children (to age 15). The restaurant and bar offers a varied menu. For further details and the Travel Inn phone number, consult the Hotel Groups page.
ROOMS: 80 en suite s £44.95; d £44.95

STIRLING, Stirling — Map 21 NS79

★★★★66% ® *Stirling Highland*

Spittal St FK8 1DU
☎ 01786 272727 🖷 01786 272829
e-mail: stirling@paramount-hotels.co.uk
Dir: *take A84 into Stirling and follow Stirling Castle signs to the Albert Hall. Turn left and left again, following signs to Castle*
Enjoying a location close to the castle and historic old town, this atmospheric hotel was previously the High School. Public rooms have been converted from the original classrooms and retain many interesting features. Bedrooms are more modern in style and comfortably equipped.
ROOMS: 96 en suite (4 fmly) No smoking in 67 bedrooms **FACILITIES:** STV Indoor swimming (H) Squash Sauna Solarium Gym Jacuzzi Steam room Dance Studio Beauty therapist **CONF:** Thtr 100 Class 80 Board 45 **SERVICES:** Lift **PARKING:** 96 **NOTES:** No smoking in restaurant Civ Wed 100 **CARDS:**

★★65% Terraces

4 Melville Ter FK8 2ND
☎ 01786 472268 🖷 01786 450314
e-mail: sales@terraceshotel.com
Dir: *A872 1st left at 2nd rdbt, at lights onto Melville Terrace (inside lane) parallel to main road on left. Hotel at bottom*
Popular with both business and leisure guests, this hotel has an excellent location close to the town centre and its attractions. The comfortable bedrooms are modern in style and thoughtfully equipped. Public areas include a bar, a recently refurbished steakhouse and a good-sized function suite.
ROOMS: 17 en suite (3 fmly) No smoking in 2 bedrooms s £57-£71.50; d fr £90 (incl. bkfst) **FACILITIES:** STV Xmas **CONF:** Thtr 100 Class 35 Board 38 Del from £27.50 **PARKING:** 23 **NOTES:** No smoking in restaurant **CARDS:**

⌂ Express by Holiday Inn Stirling

Springkerse Business Park FK7 7XH
☎ 01786 449922 🖷 01786 449932
e-mail: info@hiex-stirling.com
Dir: *M9/M80 junct 9/A91 Stirling/St Andrews exit. Follow road for 2.8m and at 4th rdbt, take 2nd exit to sports stadium & then 3rd to hotel*
A modern hotel ideal for families and business travellers. Fresh and uncomplicated, the spacious bedrooms include Sky TV, power shower and tea and coffee-making facilities. Continental buffet breakfast is included in the room rate; other meals may be taken at the nearby family pub or restaurant. For further details and the Express by Holiday Inn phone number, consult the Hotel Groups pages.

ROOMS: 78 en suite s £56-£65; d £56-£65 (incl. cont bkfst)
CONF: Thtr 30 Class 18 Board 16

⌂ Travel Inn

Whins of Milton, Glasgow Rd FK7 8EX
☎ 08701 977241 🖷 01786 816415
Dir: *on A872, 0.25m from M9/M80 junct 9 junct*
Travel Inn offers good-quality, value-for-money accommodation. Spacious, en suite rooms with bath and shower comfortably accommodate a family of up to two adults and two children (to age 15). The restaurant and bar offers a varied menu. For further details and the Travel Inn phone number, consult the Hotel Groups page.
ROOMS: 60 en suite s £44.95; d £44.95

⌂ Travelodge

Pirnhall Roundabout, Snabhead FK7 8EU
☎ 08700 850 950 🖷 01525 878450
Dir: *junct M9/M80*
Travelodge offers good quality, good value, modern accommodation. Ideal for families, the spacious, en suite bedrooms include remote-control TV, tea and coffee-making facilities, luxury beds and free morning newspaper. Meals can be taken at the nearby family restaurant. For further details and the Travelodge phone number, consult the Hotel Groups page.
ROOMS: 37 en suite s fr £42.95; d fr £42.95

STONEHAVEN, Aberdeenshire — Map 23 NO88

★★66% County Hotel & Squash Club

Arduthie Rd AB39 2EH
☎ 01569 764386 🖷 01569 762214
Dir: *off A90, opposite railway station*
This family-run hotel lies on the outskirts of town, close to the railway station. It is popular for its good-value meals featuring a wide-ranging selection, served in a choice of dining rooms. The breakfast room displays a fascinating collection of photographs and posters of old theatre, music hall and Hollywood stars.
ROOMS: 14 en suite (1 fmly) s £42-£46; d £50-£60 (incl. bkfst) **LB** **FACILITIES:** Squash Sauna Gym Table tennis **CONF:** Thtr 150 Class 60 Board 32 **PARKING:** 40 **NOTES:** No dogs (ex guide dogs) Civ Wed 180 **CARDS:**

STRACHUR, Argyll & Bute
Map 20 NN00

★★★67% Creggans Inn
PA27 8BX
☎ 01369 860279 01369 860637
e-mail: info@creggans-inn.co.uk
Dir: *follow A82/A83 Loch Lomond road to Arrochar. Continue on A83 then take A815 Strachur*
Benefiting from a super location on the shores of Loch Fyne, this well-established hotel is well placed for both tourists and business travellers. Many of the bedrooms have fine views and a number have high quality bathrooms. There is a choice of spacious lounges and freshly prepared meals can be enjoyed in either the popular bar or stylish restaurant.
ROOMS: 14 en suite s £55-£85; d £95-£130 (incl. bkfst) **LB** **FACILITIES:** Fishing **CONF:** Thtr 25 Class 25 Board 25 Del from £120 **PARKING:** 50 **NOTES:** No dogs (ex guide dogs) No smoking in restaurant **CARDS:**

STRANRAER, Dumfries & Galloway
Map 20 NX06
See also Castle Kennedy

★★★★68% North West Castle
DG9 8EH
☎ 01776 704413 01776 702646
e-mail: info@northwestcastle.co.uk
Dir: *on seafront, close to Stena ferry terminal*

This is long-established hotel, overlooks the bay and the ferry terminal which will eventually be relocated to Cairn Ryan. The public areas include a classical dining room where a pianist plays during dinner and an adjoining lounge with large leather armchairs and blazing fire in season. There is a shop, leisure centre, and a curling rink which is the focus in winter. Bedrooms are comfortable and spacious.
ROOMS: 70 en suite 2 annexe en suite (22 fmly) No smoking in 26 bedrooms s £61-£81; d £92-£122 (incl. bkfst) **LB** **FACILITIES:** STV Indoor swimming (H) Snooker Sauna Solarium Gym Jacuzzi Curling (Oct-Apr) Games room, Swimming pool supervised Xmas **CONF:** Thtr 150 Class 60 Board 40 Del from £65 **SERVICES:** Lift **PARKING:** 100 **NOTES:** No smoking in restaurant Civ Wed 120
CARDS:

★★★69% Corsewall Lighthouse Hotel
Corsewall Point, Kirkcolm DG9 0QG
☎ 01776 853220 01776 854231
e-mail: lighthousehotel@btopenworld.com
Dir: *B718 from Stranraer to Kirkcolm (approx 8m) then follow signs to Hotel, 4m*
This listed 19th-century lighthouse is situated at the northern tip of the Rhinns of Galloway. There are a variety of styles of attractively furnished and well-equipped bedrooms, with some cottage suites within the 20 acres of grounds. Public areas are cosy and atmospheric, and the dining room serves local produce.

ROOMS: 6 en suite 3 annexe en suite (2 fmly) (5 GF) No smoking in 6 bedrooms s £90-£220; d £110-£270 (incl. bkfst & dinner) **LB** **CONF:** Thtr 20 **PARKING:** 20 **NOTES:** No smoking in restaurant Civ Wed 28 **CARDS:**

STRATHAVEN, South Lanarkshire
Map 20 NS74

★★★72% Strathaven
Hamilton Rd ML10 6SZ
☎ 01357 521778 01357 520789
e-mail: info@strathavenhotel.com
Best Western
This Robert Adam designed mansion house on the outskirts of town is a popular venue for functions. A wing of modern, stylish bedrooms have been added, and all are well equipped. Public areas include a comfortable lounge, Lauders restaurant and an attractive bar/lounge.
ROOMS: 22 en suite No smoking in 12 bedrooms s £55-£72; d £80-£90 (incl. bkfst) **LB** **FACILITIES:** STV **CONF:** Thtr 180 Class 120 Board 40 Del from £80 **PARKING:** 80 **NOTES:** No dogs (ex guide dogs) No smoking in restaurant Civ Wed 110 **CARDS:**

STRATHBLANE, Stirling
Map 20 NS57

★★★69% *Strathblane Country House Hotel*
Milngavie Rd G63 9EH
☎ 01360 770491 01360 770345
e-mail: martin.hollis@countryhotels.net
Dir: *From Glasgow city centre take Bearsden road or Maryhill road to Canniesburn toll, then A81 Milneavie road to Strathblane, hotel 0.75m past Mugdock Country Park on right.*
Set in 15 acres of grounds, this Victorian country house provides a relaxing retreat for business guests and is also a popular wedding and function venue. Public areas, which include two lounges and a brasserie restaurant, mix classical and contemporary styles. The individually styled bedrooms vary in size.
ROOMS: 10 en suite (3 fmly) **FACILITIES:** Use of private leisure complex nearby **CONF:** Thtr 100 Class 50 Board 25 **PARKING:** 100 **NOTES:** No smoking in restaurant **CARDS:**

STRATHDON, Aberdeenshire
Map 23 NJ31

A The Colquhonnie
AB36 8UN
☎ 01975 651210 019756 51398
e-mail: mail@colquhonnie.co.uk
Dir: *on A944 Alford to Tomintoul Rd, 1m E of Bellabeg shop and post office*
ROOMS: 9 rms (7 en suite) (1 fmly) No smoking in 8 bedrooms s £20-£35; d £50-£60 (incl. bkfst) **LB** **FACILITIES:** Fishing ch fac Xmas **CONF:** Class 60 Board 20 **PARKING:** 12 **NOTES:** ★★ No dogs (ex guide dogs) No smoking in restaurant Closed 25-26 Dec
CARDS:

STRATHYRE, Stirling Map 20 NN51

Top 200 - Hotel

★ Creagan House
FK18 8ND
☎ 01877 384638 01877 384319
e-mail: eatandstay@creaganhouse.co.uk
Dir: *0.25m N of Strathyre on A84*

This restored 17th-century farmhouse is now a friendly, cosy hotel backed by forest walks in the Queen Elizabeth Park. The attractive bedrooms are thoughtfully equipped, with excellent CD/radio sets, and TV available on request. The little lounge is inviting and refreshments are served here before and after an enjoyable meal in the impressive baronial-style dining room. Cuisine is bold and imaginative.

ROOMS: 5 en suite (1 fmly) (1 GF) No smoking in all bedrooms s £58; d £95 (incl. bkfst) **LB FACILITIES:** Xmas **CONF:** Thtr 35 Class 12 Board 35 **PARKING:** 26 **NOTES:** No smoking in restaurant Closed 25 Jan - 5 Mar **CARDS:**

STRONTIAN, Highland Map 22 NM86

Top 200 - Hotel

★★ Kilcamb Lodge
PH36 4HY
☎ 01967 402257 01967 402041
e-mail: enquiries@kilcamblodge.com
Dir: *off A861, 200yds on left after crossing bridge in village*

This sympathetically modernised former hunting lodge has fine loch views, with open fires, deep cushioned sofas, flowers, books and magazines in the elegant public rooms. The delightfully furnished bedrooms are thoughtfully equipped and attractively decorated. The short choice of well-prepared dishes is complemented by a carefully selected wine list, which adds to the fine dining experience.

ROOMS: 11 en suite (3 fmly) No smoking in all bedrooms s £70; d £95-£155 (incl. bkfst) **LB FACILITIES: Spa** Xmas **CONF:** BC Del from £110 **PARKING:** 20 **NOTES:** No smoking in restaurant Civ Wed 45 **CARDS:**

SWINTON, Scottish Borders Map 21 NT84

Restaurant with Rooms

The Wheatsheaf
TD11 3JJ
☎ 01890 860257 01890 860688
e-mail: reception@wheatsheaf-swinton.co.uk
Dir: *6m N of Duns on A6112*

Overlooking the village green, The Wheatsheaf combines smart bedrooms with a country pub atmosphere. The food that is the main focus however, served in a bright pine-furnished sun lounge, or when times are busy also in the more traditional dining room. Bedrooms offer a mix of sizes, and all are well equipped; the larger ones have luxury bathrooms.

ROOMS: 7 en suite 1 annexe en suite (1 fmly) No smoking in all bedrooms s £58-£78; d £90-£110 (incl. bkfst) **LB PARKING:** 6 **NOTES:** No smoking in restaurant Closed 1-14 Jan RS Mon & Sun Eve **CARDS:**

TAIN, Highland Map 23 NH78

★★★74% Morangie House
Morangie Rd IV19 1PY
☎ 01862 892281 01862 892872
e-mail: wynne@morangiehotel.com
Dir: *turn right off A9 northwards*

This welcoming family-run hotel has fine views of the Dornoch Firth. Spacious bedrooms in the newer wing are comfortable and modern, and those in the main house are more traditional; all are well equipped with useful accessories. A wide range of dishes is available in the smart Garden Restaurant.

ROOMS: 26 en suite (1 fmly) (6 GF) No smoking in 6 bedrooms s £65-£75; d £120-£130 (incl. bkfst) **LB FACILITIES:** STV **CONF:** Thtr 40 Class 40 Board 24 Del from £90 **PARKING:** 40 **CARDS:**

T

TAIN, continued

Top 200 - Hotel

★★ ◎◎

Glenmorangie Highland Home at Cadboll

Cadboll, Fearn IV20 1XP
☎ 01862 871671 ▯ 01862 871625
e-mail: relax@glenmorangieplc.co.uk
Dir: *from A9 turn onto B9175 towards Nigg and follow tourist signs*
A warm welcome is assured at this historic house that has been converted into a very individual hotel by the famous whisky distillers. Stylish accommodation is provided in both the main house and in a row of converted cottages. A relaxed atmosphere prevails with dinner taken house-party style in the impressive dining room. Enjoy a walk on the nearby beach before tucking in to a hearty local breakfast.
ROOMS: 6 en suite 3 annexe en suite (4 fmly) (3 GF) No smoking in all bedrooms s £120-£185; d £240-£370 (incl. bkfst & dinner) **LB** **FACILITIES:** Fishing Croquet lawn Putting green Falconry, Clay pigeon shooting, Beauty treatments, Husky Sledding, Archery entertainment Xmas **CONF:** Thtr 12 Class 12 Board 12 Del from £135 **PARKING:** 20 **NOTES:** No smoking in restaurant Closed 3-31 Jan Civ Wed 24 **CARDS:**

TANGASDALE See Barra, Isle of

TARBERT LOCH FYNE, Argyll & Bute Map 20 NN30

★★69% *The Columba Hotel*

East Pier Rd PA29 6UF
☎ 01880 820808 ▯ 01880 820808
e-mail: info@columbahotel.com
Dir: *off A82 into village, hotel 0.25m on right*
Overlooking the approach to the busy harbour, this Victorian hotel is a short walk from the village centre. Accommodation, including upgraded rooms, is generally spacious and offers appropriate levels of comfort. Meals can be taken in either the atmospheric bar or the restaurant with its fine views.
ROOMS: 10 en suite (2 fmly) **CONF:** Thtr 30 Class 30 Board 18 **PARKING:** 11 **NOTES:** No smoking in restaurant
CARDS:

TAYNUILT, Argyll & Bute Map 20 NN03

★★63% Taynuilt

PA35 1JN
☎ 01866 822437 ▯ 01866 822105
e-mail: taynuilthotel@barbox.net
This well-established roadside hotel has undergone considerable refurbishment and upgrading under enthusiastic ownership. Most bedrooms are spacious and comfortably furnished. The bar and lounge are bright and restful, with a good range of cask ales normally on tap. The dining room is most attractive and excellent steaks and seafood are regular features on the extensive menu.
ROOMS: 12 rms (10 en suite) (2 fmly) No smoking in all bedrooms s £25-£35; d £50-£70 (incl. bkfst) **LB** **FACILITIES:** Tennis (hard) entertainment **PARKING:** 27 **NOTES:** No dogs (ex guide dogs) No smoking in restaurant **CARDS:**

★★60% Polfearn

PA35 1JQ
☎ 01866 822251 ▯ 01866 822251
Dir: *turn N off A85, continue 1.5m through village down to Loch Shore*
A relaxed and friendly atmosphere prevails at this homely family-run hotel which overlooks Loch Etive. Public areas include a well-stocked bar with open fire and separate dining room. A good range of home cooked food is available in both areas. Bedrooms vary in size and in style.
ROOMS: 14 en suite (2 fmly) s £25-£35; d £50-£70 (incl. bkfst) **LB** **FACILITIES:** Fishing, Boating, Walking Xmas **PARKING:** 21 **NOTES:** No smoking in restaurant Closed 26 Dec RS Nov-Apr **CARDS:**

THORNHILL, Dumfries & Galloway Map 21 NX8

★★74% Trigony House

Closeburn DG3 5EZ
☎ 01848 331211 ▯ 01848 331303
e-mail: info@trigonyhotel.co.uk
Dir: *off A76 between Thornhill & Closeburn on left, clearly signed*

A friendly and relaxed atmosphere prevails at this family run Edwardian hunting lodge, set in four acres of gardens and grounds south of the village. Food, either in the cosy bar or formal dining room, is refreshingly simple and honest and features all fresh produce, organically grown when available. Bedrooms come in a variety of sizes, some are quite spacious.
ROOMS: 8 en suite s fr £58; d fr £115 (incl. bkfst & dinner) **LB** **FACILITIES:** Fishing Croquet lawn Bicycle loan free of charge **CONF:** Thtr 30 Class 30 Board 30 **PARKING:** 20 **NOTES:** No smoking in restaurant **CARDS:**

THURSO, Highland Map 23 ND16
See also Halkirk

★★★60% Royal

BRITISH TRUST HOTELS

Traill St KW14 8EH
☎ 01847 893191 ▯ 01847 895338
e-mail: royal@british-trust-hotels.com
Dir: *A9 to Thurso, cross Thurso Bridge and at 1st lights turn right. Hotel on right*
Set in the town centre, this traditional hotel attracts a mixed market including tour groups. The Royal Hotel has been completely refurbished inside and it offers public rooms such as

continued

comfortable lounges and a trendy bar which appeals to business guests.

ROOMS: 102 en suite (4 fmly) s £39-£49; d £78-£88 (incl. bkfst) **LB** **FACILITIES:** entertainment **SERVICES:** Lift **NOTES:** No dogs (ex guide dogs) No smoking in restaurant **CARDS:**

★★63% *Ulbster Arms*
Bridge St KW12 6XY
☎ 01847 831206 & 831641 01847 831206
e-mail: ulbster-arms@ecosse.net
(For full entry see Halkirk)

TIGHNABRUAICH, Argyll & Bute Map 20 NR97

★★77% Royal Hotel
Shore Rd PA21 2BE
☎ 01700 811239 01700 811300
e-mail: info@royalhotel.org.uk
Dir: *from Stachur on A886 turn right onto A8003 to Tighnabruaich. Hotel on right at bottom of hill, at T-junct*
This outstanding family-run hotel continues to go from strength to strength. Set back just yards from the loch shore, stunning views are guaranteed from many rooms, including the elegant restaurant and informal brasserie bar in which fresh seafood and game are served. The comfortable bedrooms vary in size and style.
ROOMS: 11 en suite (2 fmly) No smoking in all bedrooms s £77-£117; d £94-£174 (incl. bkfst) **LB** **FACILITIES:** sailing, fishing, windsurfing, riding, walking, bird watching **CONF:** Class 20 Board 10 Del from £90 **PARKING:** 20 **NOTES:** No smoking in restaurant Closed 25-26 Dec **CARDS:**

TOBERMORY See Mull, Isle of

TONGUE, Highland Map 23 NC55

★★71% Ben Loyal
Main St IV27 4XE
☎ 01847 611216 01847 611336
e-mail: benloyalhotel@btinternet.com
Dir: *A838 or A836. Hotel in centre of village by Royal Bank of Scotland*
This welcoming and informal hotel enjoys dramatic views of the Kyle of Tongue. The well-equipped bedrooms are smartly furnished, and both the comfortable lounge and adjoining dining room take full advantage of the views. Five-course dinners are available in the restaurant and a wide-ranging menu is provided in the bar.
ROOMS: 11 en suite No smoking in all bedrooms s £32; d £50-£64 (incl. bkfst) **LB** **FACILITIES:** Fishing Fly fishing tuition and equipment **PARKING:** 20 **NOTES:** No smoking in restaurant RS Nov-Mar **CARDS:**

TORRIDON, Highland Map 22 NG95

Top 200 - Hotel

★★★ Loch Torridon Country House Hotel
IV22 2EY
☎ 01445 791242 01445 791296
e-mail: stay@lochtorridonhotel.com
Dir: *from A832 at Kinlochewe, take A896 towards Torridon, do not turn into village, 1m, hotel on right*
Delightfully set amidst inspiring loch and mountain scenery, this elegant Victorian shooting lodge has been beautifully restored to make the most of its many original features. The attractive bedrooms are all individually furnished and most enjoy stunning Highland views. Comfortable day rooms feature fine wood panelling and roaring fires in cooler months. The whisky bar is aptly named, boasting over 300 malts and in-depth tasting notes. Outdoor activities include shooting, cycling and walking.
ROOMS: 19 en suite (1 fmly) No smoking in all bedrooms s £60-£104; d £97-£145 (incl. bkfst) **LB** **FACILITIES:** STV Fishing Croquet lawn Pony trekking, Mountain biking, Archery, Clay pigeon shooting, Falconry Xmas **CONF:** Board 16 Del from £145 **SERVICES:** Lift **PARKING:** 20 **NOTES:** No smoking in restaurant Closed 2-31 Jan **CARDS:**

TROON, South Ayrshire Map 20 NS33

★★★★64% Marine
PARAMOUNT GROUP OF HOTELS
Crosbie Rd KA10 6HE
☎ 01292 314444 01292 316922
e-mail: marine@paramount-hotels.co.uk
Dir: *from A77 to A78, then A79 onto B749. Hotel on left beyond Golf Course*
A favourite with conference and leisure guests, this hotel overlooks Royal Troon's 18th fairway. The cocktail lounge and split-level restaurant enjoy panoramic views of the Firth of Clyde across to the Isle of Arran. Bedrooms are undergoing an impressive upgrade, which is due for completion by May 2004.
ROOMS: 90 en suite (6 fmly) No smoking in 58 bedrooms s £58-£110; d £116-£160 (incl. bkfst) **LB** **FACILITIES:** STV Indoor swimming (H) Tennis (hard) Squash Sauna Solarium Gym Putting green Jacuzzi Steam room, Beauty room, Swimming pool supervised Xmas **CONF:** BC Thtr 220 Class 120 Board 60 Del from £99 **SERVICES:** Lift **PARKING:** 200 **NOTES:** No smoking in restaurant **CARDS:**

TROON, continued

Hotel of the Year
Top 200 - Hotel

★★★ ⊛⊛⊛ Lochgreen House
Monktonhill Rd, Southwood KA10 7EN
☎ 01292 313343 01292 318661
e-mail: lochgreen@costley-hotels.co.uk
Dir: *from A77 follow signs for Prestwick airport, 0.5m before airport take B749 to Troon. Hotel 1m on left*

This extended hotel offers spacious, comfortable and stylishly furnished bedrooms and is peacefully situated in 30 acres of immaculately maintained grounds. There is a choice of lounges, warmed by open fires in the cooler months, and the brasserie menu includes interesting options for a light lunch. The restaurant provides the main dining experience and quality produce is carefully prepared with imagination to delight diners. Lochgreen House has been awarded the AA Hotel of the Year for Scotland 2003-2004.

ROOMS: 32 en suite 8 annexe en suite (18 GF) s £99-£125; d £160-£195 (incl. bkfst & dinner) **FACILITIES:** Tennis (hard) Xmas **CONF:** BC Thtr 100 Class 50 Board 50 Del from £125 **SERVICES:** Lift **PARKING:** 50 **NOTES:** No dogs (ex guide dogs) No smoking in restaurant Civ Wed 100 **CARDS:**

★★★74% Piersland House
Craigend Rd KA10 6HD
☎ 01292 314747 01292 315613
e-mail: reservations@piersland.co.uk
Dir: *just off A77 on B749 opposite Royal Troon Golf Club*

A Grade I listed building, this well presented hotel is located opposite to the famous championship golf course. Public areas retain delightful oak panelling. Bedrooms are thoughtfully equipped and include a row of 15 'cottages' each with a lounge and its own entrance, ideal for golfers. The hotel is popular both for its bar and for the good food in the restaurant.

ROOMS: 15 en suite 15 annexe en suite (2 fmly) s £68-£90; d £124-£170 (incl. bkfst) **LB** **FACILITIES:** STV Xmas **CONF:** Thtr 100 Class 60 Board 30 Del £90 **PARKING:** 150 **NOTES:** No smoking in restaurant Civ Wed 80 **CARDS:**

See advert on opposite page

TURNBERRY, South Ayrshire Map 20 NS2(

Top 200 - Hotel

★★★★★ ⊛ Westin Turnberry Resort
KA26 9LT
☎ 01655 331000 01655 331706
e-mail: turnberry@westin.com

Dir: *from Glasgow take A77/M77 S towards Stranraer, 2m past Kirkoswald, follow signs for A719 Turnberry Village, hotel 500mtrs*

This famous hotel enjoys magnificent views over to Arran, Ailsa Craig and the Mull of Kintyre. Facilities include a world-renowned golf course, the excellent Colin Montgomerie Golf Academy, a luxurious spa and a host of outdoor and country pursuits. Elegant bedrooms and suites are located in the main hotel, whilst the adjacent lodges provide spacious, well-equipped accommodation. As well as the elegant main restaurant for dining, there is a Mediterranean Terrace Brasserie, or the relaxed Clubhouse.

ROOMS: 132 en suite 89 annexe en suite (9 fmly) No smoking in 28 bedrooms s £115-£715; d £144-£770 (incl. bkfst) **LB** **FACILITIES:** STV Indoor swimming (H) Golf 18 Tennis (hard) Fishing Squash Riding Snooker Sauna Gym Putting green Jacuzzi Health Spa & Leisure Club, Outdoor activity centre, Colin Montgomerie Golf Academy Entertainment **CONF:** BC Thtr 275 Class 145 Board 100 **SERVICES:** Lift **PARKING:** 200 **NOTES:** No smoking in restaurant **CARDS:**

★★★76% ֍֍ **Malin Court**
KA26 9PB
☎ 01655 331457 ▤ 01655 331072
e-mail: info@malincourt.co.uk
dir: *on A74 take Ayr exit. Then A719 to Turnberry and Maidens*

This comfortable hotel enjoys delightful views over the Firth of Clyde and Turnberry golf courses. Attractive public areas are plentiful, some boast views over the links. The restaurant serves light lunches and more formal dinners. Standard and executive rooms are available; all of them are well equipped.
ROOMS: 18 en suite (9 fmly) s £72-£82; d £104-£124 (incl. bkfst) **LB**
FACILITIES: STV Tennis (grass) Putting green Pitch & putt Xmas
CONF: Thtr 200 Class 60 Board 30 **SERVICES:** Lift **PARKING:** 110
NOTES: No dogs (ex guide dogs) No smoking in restaurant RS Oct - Mar Civ Wed 120 **CARDS:**

See advert on this page

UNST See Shetland

U

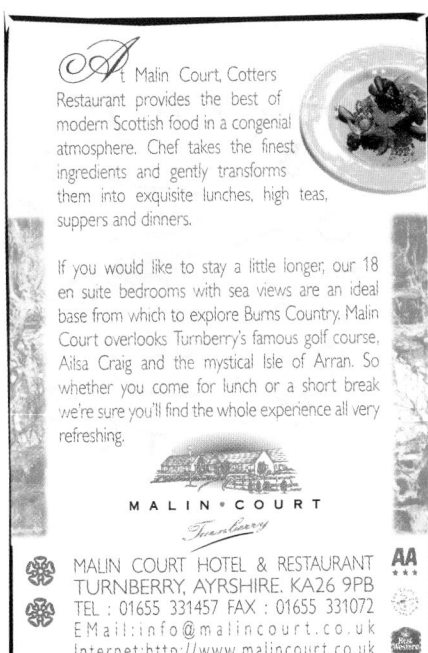

UPHALL, West Lothian Map 21 NT07

★★★★67% Houstoun House
EH52 6JS
☎ 01506 853831 01506 854220
e-mail: houstoun@macdonald-hotels.co.uk
Dir: *M8 junct 3 follow signs for Broxburn, straight over rdbt then at mini-rdbt turn right towards Uphall, hotel 1m on right*

This historic 17th-century tower house lies in landscaped grounds and features a leisure club, steak house restaurant and impressive executive rooms in a courtyard setting. In the original house, a stone staircase leads from the vaulted cocktail bar to three elegant dining areas and to bedrooms above.
ROOMS: 24 en suite 47 annexe en suite (30 fmly) No smoking in 63 bedrooms s fr £90; d fr £130 **LB FACILITIES:** STV Indoor swimming (H) Sauna Solarium Gym Croquet lawn Steam room, Dance studio, Beauty therapy room Xmas **CONF:** Thtr 350 Class 120 Board 70 Del from £135 **PARKING:** 200 **NOTES:** No dogs (ex guide dogs) No smoking in restaurant Civ Wed 80 **CARDS:**

UPLAWMOOR, East Renfrewshire Map 20 NS45

★★75% Uplawmoor Hotel
Neilston Rd G78 4AF
☎ 01505 850565 01505 850689
e-mail: enquiries@uplawmoor.co.uk
Dir: *M77 junct 2, take A736 towards Barrhead and Irvine. Hotel 4m beyond Barrhead*

THE CIRCLE
Selected Individual Hotels
GREAT BRITAIN

Originally an old coaching inn, this friendly hotel is set in a village off the Glasgow to Irvine road. The comfortable restaurant (with

continued

cocktail lounge adjacent) features imaginative dishes, whilst the separate lounge bar is popular for freshly prepared bar meals. The modern bedrooms are both comfortable and well equipped.
ROOMS: 14 en suite (1 fmly) No smoking in 4 bedrooms s £39-£49; d £59-£79 (incl. bkfst) **FACILITIES:** STV **CONF:** BC Thtr 40 Class 12 Board 12 Del from £65 **PARKING:** 40 **NOTES:** No dogs No smoking in restaurant **CARDS:**

See advert on page 80

WHITBURN, West Lothian Map 21 NS9

★★★66% The Hilcroft
East Main St EH47 0JU
☎ 01501 740818 01501 744013
e-mail: hilcroft@bestwestern.co.uk
Dir: *M8 junct 4 follow signs for Whitburn, hotel 0.5m on left from junct*

Best Western

This modern hotel offers well-equipped bedrooms which vary in size and style; the executive rooms offer particularly good levels of space and comfort. The split-level bar and restaurant offers an extensive menu throughout the day.
ROOMS: 31 en suite (7 fmly) (5 GF) No smoking in 17 bedrooms s £60-£66; d £72-£80 (incl. bkfst) **LB FACILITIES:** STV Free use of Balbardie Sports Centre Xmas **CONF:** Thtr 200 Class 50 Board 30 Del from £85 **PARKING:** 80 **NOTES:** No dogs (ex guide dogs) Civ Wed 200 **CARDS:**

WHITEBRIDGE, Highland Map 23 NH4

★★66% Whitebridge
IV2 6UN
☎ 01456 486226 & 486272 01456 486413
e-mail: info@whitebridgehotel.co.uk
Dir: *off A9 onto B851, follow signs to Fort Augustus*
Set amid mountain and moorland, this friendly roadside hotel attracts tourists and those keen on fishing in the area. There is a cosy, snug public bar, which is the focal point for chat with the locals. Bedrooms are modestly furnished, and a programme of stylish upgrading is underway.
ROOMS: 12 rms (11 en suite) (3 fmly) **FACILITIES:** Fishing **CONF:** Class 30 Board 25 **PARKING:** 32 **NOTES:** No smoking in restaurant Closed 2 Dec-Feb **CARDS:**

WICK, Highland Map 23 ND35

★★69% Mackay's
Union St KW1 5ED
☎ 01955 602323 01955 605930
e-mail: res@mackayshotel.co.uk
Dir: *opposite Caithness General Hospital*
This well-established hotel is situated just off the town centre and overlooks the River Wick. Mackays's provides first class accommodation especially suited to the business traveller. Also on offer is an attractive restaurant and a choice of bars that also offer food.
ROOMS: 27 rms (19 en suite) (4 fmly) **FACILITIES:** STV entertainment **CONF:** Thtr 100 Class 100 Board 60 **SERVICES:** Lift **NOTES:** No smoking in restaurant Closed 1-2 Jan **CARDS:**

U

Hotel of the Year, Wales

Morgans Hotel
Swansea

A

ABERDYFI, Gwynedd

Map 14 SN69

★★★74% Trefeddian

LL35 0SB
☎ 01654 767213 🖷 01654 767777
e-mail: enquiries@trefwales.com
Dir: *0.5m N of Aberdyfi off A493*

This privately owned hotel overlooks the golf course and is surrounded by grounds and gardens. It provides sound modern accommodation with well-equipped bedrooms and bathrooms, plus some luxury rooms with balconies and sea views. Public areas include elegantly furnished lounges, a beauty salon and indoor swimming pool. Children are welcome and recreation areas are provided.
ROOMS: 59 en suite (13 fmly) No smoking in all bedrooms s £56-£83; d £98-£166 (incl. bkfst & dinner) **LB FACILITIES:** Indoor swimming (H) Tennis (hard) Snooker Solarium Putting green Table tennis, Play area, Beauty salon ch fac Xmas **CONF:** Class 25 **SERVICES:** Lift **PARKING:** 68 **NOTES:** No smoking in restaurant
CARDS:

See advert on opposite page

★★74% Penhelig Arms Hotel & Restaurant

LL35 0LT
☎ 01654 767215 🖷 01654 767690
e-mail: info@penheligarms.com
Dir: *take A493 coastal road, hotel opposite harbour*
Situated opposite the old harbour, this delightful 18th-century hotel overlooks the Dyfi Estuary. The well-maintained bedrooms have good quality furnishings and modern facilities. The public bar retains its original character and is much loved by locals who enjoy the bar food, particularly the seafood, and the range of real ale on offer.
ROOMS: 10 en suite 4 annexe en suite (4 fmly) No smoking in all bedrooms s £35-£45; d £75-£90 (incl. bkfst) **LB PARKING:** 14 **NOTES:** No smoking in restaurant Closed 25 & 26 Dec
CARDS:

★★66% *Dovey Inn*

Seaview Ter LL35 0EF
☎ 01654 767332 🖷 01654 767996
e-mail: info@doveyinn.com
Dir: *In centre of village on north bank of River Dovey, on A493, 9m to Machynlleth*
In the heart of Aberdyfi, this inn offers attractive refurbished rooms which are comfortable and very well equipped; most have sea views. Downstairs there are four bars where a wide range of dishes, featuring local produce, is available. Breakfast is served in a separate upstairs dining room.

ROOMS: 8 en suite (2 fmly) No smoking in all bedrooms
FACILITIES: STV Guest may use facilities at Plas Talgarth Country Club
NOTES: No dogs (ex guide dogs) No smoking in restaurant
CARDS:

ABERGAVENNY, Monmouthshire

Map 09 SO21

★★★68% Allt-yr-Ynys Country House Hotel

HR2 0DU
☎ 01873 890307 🖷 01873 890539
e-mail: allthotel@compuserve.com
Dir: *take A465 N of Abergavenny. After 5m turn left at Old Pandy Inn in Pandy. After 300yds turn right, hotel on right*

Set in rolling countryside, the main house of this charming hotel dates back to 1550 and Elizabeth I is reputed to have stayed here. The bedrooms are mostly contained in comfortable, purpose-built stone chalets. Homely lounges, a bar with a cider mill as a feature and an adjoining swimming pool complete the experience, together with the atmospheric restaurant.
ROOMS: 3 en suite 18 annexe en suite (2 fmly) (18 GF) No smoking in 6 bedrooms s £58-£95; d £75-£120 (incl. bkfst) **LB FACILITIES: Spa** Indoor swimming (H) Fishing Sauna Clay pigeon range Xmas **CONF:** BC Thtr 100 Class 30 Board 40 Del from £100 **PARKING:** 100 **NOTES:** No smoking in restaurant Civ Wed 80 **CARDS:**

★★★65% Llansantffraed Court

Llanvihangel Gobion NP7 9BA
☎ 01873 840678 🖷 01873 840674
e-mail: reception@llch.co.uk
Dir: *at A465/A40 Abergavenny junct take B4598 signed to Usk (do not join A40). Continue towards Raglan and hotel on left after 4.5m*
In a commanding position and in its own grounds this red brick country hotel has enviable views of the Brecon Beacons. Extensive

continued

public areas are complemented by a spacious restaurant. Bedrooms are comfortably furnished with modern facilities.

ROOMS: 21 en suite (3 fmly) No smoking in 7 bedrooms s fr £76; d fr £94 (incl. bkfst) **LB** **FACILITIES:** STV Tennis (grass) Fishing Croquet lawn Putting green Ornamental trout lake, Salmon fishing on River Usk **CONF:** BC Thtr 220 Class 120 Board 100 Del from £135 **SERVICES:** Lift **PARKING:** 250 **NOTES:** No smoking in restaurant Civ Wed 150 **CARDS:**

★★70% **Pantrhiwgoch Hotel & Riverside Restaurant**
Brecon Rd NP8 1EP
☎ 01873 810550 01873 811880
e-mail: info@pantrhiwgoch.co.uk
Dir: *on A40 midway between Abergavenny & Crickhowell beside River Usk*
Dating from the 16th century and set in magnificent scenery, this delightful hotel offers guests the chance to relax and unwind in style. Bedrooms are in a detached wing, with most enjoying views

continued

over the river and beyond. Many have private balconies. The airy conservatory lounge and restaurant also have lovely views.
ROOMS: 18 en suite (2 fmly) (8 GF) No smoking in 2 bedrooms s £63; d £73 (incl. bkfst) **LB** **FACILITIES:** Fishing Reflexology, Yoga, Massage, Reiki **CONF:** Thtr 20 Class 20 Board 20 **PARKING:** 40 **NOTES:** No dogs (ex guide dogs) No smoking in restaurant Civ Wed 60
CARDS:

ABERGELE, Conwy

Map 14 SH97

★★★65% **Kinmel Manor**
St George's Rd LL22 9AS
☎ 01745 832014 01745 832014
e-mail: kinmelmanor@virgin.net
Dir: *exit A55 at junct 24, hotel entrance on rdbt*
Parts of this predominantly modern hotel complex date back to the 16th century and some original features are still in evidence. Set in extensive grounds, it provides well-equipped rooms and extensive leisure facilities.
ROOMS: 51 en suite (3 fmly) No smoking in 12 bedrooms s £55-£65; d £75-£85 (incl. bkfst) **LB** **FACILITIES: Spa** STV Indoor swimming (H) Sauna Solarium Gym Steam room Xmas **CONF:** Thtr 250 Class 100 Board 100 Del from £75 **PARKING:** 120 **NOTES:** Civ Wed 250
CARDS:

Late for dinner?
Quality Standards mean that last orders for dinner vary according to star rating and should be no earlier than:
★★ 7.00pm ★★★ 8.00pm ★★★★ 9.00pm
★★★★★ 10.00pm

A

ABERPORTH, Ceredigion Map 08 SN25

★★★70% Hotel Penrallt
SA43 2BS
☎ 01239 810227 01239 811375
e-mail: info@hotelpenrallt.co.uk
Dir: *take B4333 signed Aberporth. Hotel 1m on right*
Privately owned and personally run, this attractive Edwardian mansion is set in extensive, grounds and offers spacious accommodation. The well-maintained public areas retain original features such as carved ceiling beams and an eye catching large stained glass window, and guests can enjoy the relaxing atmosphere in the comfortable lounge, the popular bar and elegant restaurant.
ROOMS: 16 en suite (2 fmly) s £68; d £110 (incl. bkfst) **LB**
FACILITIES: Indoor swimming (H) Outdoor swimming (H) Tennis (hard) Sauna Solarium Gym Putting green Jacuzzi Pool table, Swimming pool supervised during peak periods **CONF:** Class 60 Board 30
PARKING: 100 **NOTES:** No smoking in restaurant Closed 25-31 Dec
CARDS:

★★73% Penbontbren Farm
Glynarthen, Llandysul SA44 6PE
☎ 01239 810248 01239 811129
e-mail: welcome@penbontbren.com
Dir: *N on A487, 2nd right after Tan-y-Groes, signed*

Set in rolling countryside this hotel has been sympathetically converted from farm buildings. Bedrooms are furnished in a cottage style, are thoughtfully and extensively equipped and include some that are suitable for use by less able guests. There is an atmospheric restaurant, with an adjoining bar and a comfortable lounge.
ROOMS: 10 annexe en suite (6 GF) s £58-£63; d £96 (incl. bkfst) **LB**
FACILITIES: Museum of farming tools **CONF:** Thtr 25 Class 25 Board 25
PARKING: 50 **NOTES:** No smoking in restaurant Closed Xmas
CARDS:

★★61% Highcliffe
SA43 2DA
☎ 01239 810534 01239 810534
Dir: *(off B4333) 7m NE of Cardigan, 30m S of Aberystwyth*
A hotel on the coast above Cardigan Bay, with sandy beaches close by. Service is relaxed and informal. Reasonably priced meals are offered in the bar and restaurant. Bedrooms are comfortable with modern facilities.
ROOMS: 9 rms (8 en suite) 6 annexe en suite (4 fmly) s £34-£40; d £50-£60 (incl. bkfst) **LB** **FACILITIES:** ch fac Xmas **PARKING:** 18
NOTES: No smoking in restaurant **CARDS:**

ABERSOCH, Gwynedd Map 14 SH32

★★★75% Porth Tocyn
Bwlch Tocyn LL53 7BU
☎ 01758 713303 01758 713538
e-mail: porthtocyn.hotel@virgin.net
Dir: *2.5m S follow 'Porth Tocyn' signs, after hamlet of Sarnbach*
Located above Cardigan Bay with fine views over the area, Porth Tocyn is set in attractive gardens. Several elegantly furnished sitting rooms are provided and bedrooms are comfortably furnished. Children are especially welcome and have a play room. Award-winning food is served in the restaurant.
ROOMS: 17 en suite (1 fmly) (3 GF) No smoking in all bedrooms s £59-£77; d £78-£143 (incl. cont bkfst) **LB** **FACILITIES:** Outdoor swimming (H) Tennis (hard) **PARKING:** 50 **NOTES:** No smoking in restaurant Closed mid Nov-wk before Etr **CARDS:**

See advert on opposite page

★★77% Neigwl
Lon Sarn Bach LL53 7DY
☎ 01758 712363 01758 712544
e-mail: relax@neigwl.com
Dir: *on A499, through Abersoch, hotel on left*
This delightful, small, family-run hotel is conveniently located for access to the town, harbour and beach. It has a well-deserved high reputation for its food and warm hospitality. Both the attractive restaurant and very pleasant lounge bar overlook sea views, as do several of the tastefully appointed bedrooms.
ROOMS: 7 en suite 2 annexe en suite (3 fmly) s £55-£92; d £100-£160 (incl. bkfst & dinner) **LB** **FACILITIES:** ch fac **PARKING:** 30 **NOTES:** No dogs (ex guide dogs) Closed January
CARDS:

★★66% Deucoch
LL53 7LD
☎ 01758 712680 01758 712670
e-mail: deucoch@supanet.com
Dir: *through Abersoch to Sarn Bach. At crossroads in Sarn Bach (approx 1m from village centre) turn right, hotel on top of hill on left*
This hotel sits in an elevated position above the village and enjoys lovely views. There is a choice of bars and food options; the regular carvery is excellent value and has a large following, so booking is essential. Pretty bedrooms are equipped with modern amenities and the hotel specialises in golfing packages.
ROOMS: 10 rms (9 en suite) (2 fmly) s £35-£39; d £70-£78 (incl. bkfst) **LB** **FACILITIES:** Xmas **PARKING:** 30 **NOTES:** No smoking in restaurant
CARDS:

ABERYSTWYTH, Ceredigion Map 08 SN58

★★★75% Conrah
Ffosrhydygaled, Chancery SY23 4DF
☎ 01970 617941 01970 624546
e-mail: enquiries@conrah.co.uk
Dir: *on A487, 3.5m S of Aberystwyth*
This privately owned and personally run country-house hotel stands in 22 acres of mature grounds. The elegant public rooms include a choice of comfortable lounges with welcoming open fires. Bedrooms are located in both the main house and a nearby wing. The cuisine, which is French with modern influences,

continued

achieves very high standards. Conference and leisure facilities are available.

ROOMS: 11 en suite 6 annexe en suite (1 fmly) (3 GF) s £75-£85; d £115-£145 (incl. bkfst) **LB** **FACILITIES:** Indoor swimming (H) Sauna Croquet lawn Table tennis, Swimming pool supervised **CONF:** Thtr 40 Class 20 Board 20 Del £125 **SERVICES:** Lift **PARKING:** 50 **NOTES:** No dogs No children 5yrs No smoking in restaurant Closed 22-30 Dec Civ Wed 60 **CARDS:**

★★★66% **_Belle Vue Royal_**
Marine Ter SY23 2BA
☎ 01970 617558 🖹 01970 612190
e-mail: reception@bellevueroyalhotel.co.uk
Dir: *on seafront, 200yds from pier*

Dating back more than 170 years, this family owned hotel stands on the promenade, a short walk from the shops. Family and sea-view rooms are available, all are well equipped. Public areas include extensive function rooms and a choice of bars, and for dining there are bar meals or a more formal restaurant.
ROOMS: 37 rms (34 en suite) (6 fmly) (1 GF) No smoking in 10 bedrooms **FACILITIES:** STV **CONF:** Thtr 100 Class 30 Board 30 Del £95 **PARKING:** 14 **NOTES:** No dogs **CARDS:**

See advert on this page

★★68% **Four Seasons**
50-54 Portland St SY23 2DX
☎ 01970 612120 🖹 01970 627458
e-mail: reservations@fourseasonshotel.demon.co.uk
Dir: *From railway station, turn left onto Terrace Rd by lights, into North Pde & left onto Queens Rd & 2nd left into Portland St. Hotel on right*
This privately owned hotel is well-maintained and friendly. Bedrooms are well equipped. A cosy lounge is provided, plus a separate bar. A wide choice of food is available.
ROOMS: 16 rms (15 en suite) (2 fmly) No smoking in 8 bedrooms s £45-£55; d £55-£70 (incl. bkfst) **LB** **FACILITIES:** ch fac **CONF:** Thtr 15 Class 15 Board 12 **PARKING:** 8 **NOTES:** No dogs (ex guide dogs) No smoking in restaurant **CARDS:**

ABERYSTWYTH, continued

★★68% *Richmond*
44-45 Marine Ter SY23 2BX
☎ 01970 612201 🖷 01970 626706
e-mail: reservations@richmondhotel.uk.com
Dir: *on entering town follow signs for Promenade*

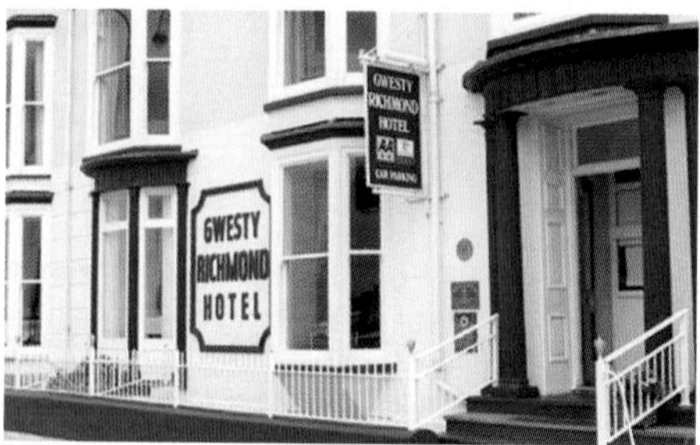

This hotel has good sea views from its day rooms and many of the bedrooms. The public areas and bedrooms are comfortably furnished. An attractive dining room and a comfortable lounge and bar are provided.
ROOMS: 15 en suite (6 fmly) **FACILITIES:** STV **CONF:** Thtr 60 Class 22 Board 28 **PARKING:** 24 **NOTES:** No dogs (ex guide dogs) No smoking in restaurant Closed 20 Dec-3 Jan **CARDS:**

★★65% Harry's
40-46 North Pde SY23 2NF
☎ 01970 612647 🖷 01970 627068
e-mail: info@harrysaberystwyth.com
Dir: *N on A487, in town centre*
Conveniently located for the shopping area and seafront, this is a friendly and popular hotel. The main attraction is the popular Harry's restaurant with its wide selection of dishes and specialising in local produce. Bedrooms are well equipped with modern facilities.
ROOMS: 24 en suite (2 fmly) No smoking in 6 bedrooms s £25-£45; d £50-£80 (incl. bkfst) **LB** **CONF:** Thtr 24 Class 24 Board 40 **PARKING:** 6 **NOTES:** Closed 25-26 Dec **CARDS:**

★★63% Marine Hotel
The Promenade SY23 2BX
☎ 01970 612444 🖷 01970 617435
e-mail: marinehotel1@btconnect.com
Dir: *from W on A44. From N or S Wales on A487. On seafront west of pier*
The Marine is a privately owned hotel situated on the promenade overlooking Cardigan Bay. Bedrooms have been tastefully decorated, some have four-poster beds and many have sea views. The refurbished reception rooms are comfortable and relaxing, and meals are served in the elegant dining room or the bar.
ROOMS: 44 rms (43 en suite) (7 fmly) No smoking in 1 bedroom s £40-£50; d £65-£85 (incl. bkfst) **LB** **FACILITIES: Spa** Sauna Solarium Gym Jacuzzi Xmas **CONF:** BC Thtr 220 Class 150 Board 60 Del from £85 **SERVICES:** Lift **PARKING:** 15 **NOTES:** No smoking in restaurant Civ Wed 220 **CARDS:**

AMLWCH See Anglesey, Isle of

AMMANFORD, Carmarthenshire — Map 08 SN61

★★67% *Mill at Glynhir*
Glynhir Rd, Llandybie SA18 2TE
☎ 01269 850672 🖷 01269 850672
e-mail: millatglynhir@aol.com
Dir: *Turn off A483 Llandybie signposted Golf Course*
This former flour mill is set peacefully on the side of a hill complete with a river at the end of the garden. For the energetic there is an indoor swimming pool or a golf practice range in the grounds. The bedrooms are all of a good size, are well equipped and most have private balconies, whilst public areas consist of a comfortable lounge bar and a cheerful dining room.
ROOMS: 7 en suite 3 annexe en suite **FACILITIES:** Indoor swimming (H) Golf 18 Jacuzzi **PARKING:** 15 **NOTES:** No children 11yrs No smoking in restaurant RS 23-29 Dec **CARDS:**

ANGLESEY, ISLE OF, Isle of Anglesey — Map 14

AMLWCH — Map 14 SH49

★★69% Lastra Farm
Penrhyd LL68 9TF
☎ 01407 830906 🖷 01407 832522
e-mail: booking@lastra-hotel.com
Dir: *after 'Welcome to Amlwch' sign turn left. Straight across main road, left at T-junct on to Rhosgoch Rd*
This 17th-century farmhouse offers pine-furnished, colourfully decorated bedrooms. There is also a comfortable lounge and a cosy bar. A wide range of good-value food is available either in the restaurant or Granary's Bistro. The hotel can cater for functions in a separate purpose built suite.
ROOMS: 5 en suite 3 annexe en suite (1 fmly) s £35; d £58 (incl. bkfst) **LB** **FACILITIES:** ch fac **CONF:** Thtr 100 Class 80 Board 30 **PARKING:** 40 **NOTES:** No smoking in restaurant Civ Wed 100 **CARDS:**

★★67% Trecastell
Bull Bay LL68 9SA
☎ 01407 830651 🖷 01407 832114
e-mail: trecastellhotel@aol.com
Dir: *1m N on A5025, adjacent to Bull Bay Golf Club*
Situated near to the local golf course, this traditional hotel overlooks Bull Bay. There is a popular bar, which serves a range of food and formal dining is available in the attractive restaurant. Refurbished bedrooms are well equipped and family and sea view rooms are available.
ROOMS: 16 en suite (4 fmly) (1 GF) s £40; d £60 (incl. bkfst) **LB** **FACILITIES:** entertainment Xmas **CONF:** Thtr 30 Class 30 Board 30 **PARKING:** 60 **NOTES:** No dogs (ex guide dogs) No smoking in restaurant **CARDS:**

BEAUMARIS — Map 14 SH67

★★★62% The Bulkeley Hotel
Best Western
Castle St LL58 8AW
☎ 01248 810415 🖷 01248 810146
e-mail: bulkeley@bestwestern.co.uk
Dir: *from M56 & M6 take A5 trunk road or A55 coast road*
A Grade I listed hotel built in 1831, the Bulkeley has fine views from many rooms. Well-equipped bedrooms are generally spacious, with pretty fabrics and wallpapers. There is a choice of bars, an all-day coffee lounge and a health club. Regular jazz

continued

evenings, a resident pianist and a friendly staff create a relaxed atmosphere.
ROOMS: 43 en suite (6 fmly) No smoking in 10 bedrooms
FACILITIES: Spa Sauna Solarium Gym Jacuzzi Hair & Beauty Salon
CONF: Thtr 180 Class 120 Board 36 **SERVICES:** Lift **PARKING:** 30
NOTES: No smoking in restaurant Civ Wed 160
CARDS:

★★75% Ye Olde Bulls Head Inn

Castle St LL58 8AP
☎ 01248 810329 🖷 01248 811294
e-mail: info@bullsheadinn.co.uk
Dir: *from Britannia road bridge follow A545, Inn in town centre*
Charles Dickens and Samuel Johnson were regular visitors to this inn where features include exposed beams, fireplaces and antique weaponry. Richly decorated bedrooms are well equipped and there is a spacious lounge. Meetings and small functions are catered for and food continues to attract praise in the restaurant and brasserie.
ROOMS: 12 en suite 1 annexe en suite No smoking in all bedrooms s £65-£67; d £92-£140 (incl. bkfst) **LB** **FACILITIES:** Leisure centre nearby **CONF:** Thtr 25 Board 16 **PARKING:** 10 **NOTES:** No dogs (ex guide dogs) No smoking in restaurant Closed 25-26 Dec & 1 Jan
CARDS:

★★73% Bishopsgate House

54 Castle St LL58 8BB
☎ 01248 810302 🖷 01248 810166
e-mail: hazel@johnson-ollier.freeserve.co.uk
Dir: *turn off in Menai Bridge onto A545. Follow only road into Beaumaris, hotel on left in main street*
This immaculately maintained, privately owned and personally run small hotel dates back to 1760. It features fine examples of wood panelling and a Chinese Chippendale staircase. Well-equipped bedrooms are attractively decorated and two have four-poster beds.
ROOMS: 9 en suite s £45; d fr £73 (incl. bkfst) **LB** **PARKING:** 8
NOTES: No smoking in restaurant **CARDS:**

HOLYHEAD — Map 14 SH28

★★65% Boathouse

Newry Promenade, Newry Beach LL65 1YF
☎ 01407 762094 🖷 01407 764898
e-mail: sasha.howard@care4free.net
Dir: *follow expressway into Holyhead, follow signs for Marina. From ferry terminal, right at 1st lights, right at 2nd set, follow signs for Marina. Hotel at bottom of hill on seafront*
Situated in a prominent position overlooking the harbour, the hotel makes an ideal stop for ferry travellers. Bedrooms are attractively decorated to a high standard and are well-equipped. Downstairs the attractive lounge bar offers a wide range of home cooked food and there is a separate dining room.
ROOMS: 17 en suite (1 fmly) (5 GF) No smoking in 15 bedrooms s £40-£45; d £65-£75 (incl. bkfst) **LB** **FACILITIES:** Painting & sketching guidance available **CONF:** Thtr 40 Class 30 Board 30 **PARKING:** 40
NOTES: No smoking in restaurant **CARDS:**

LLANFAIRPWLLGWYNGYLL — Map 14 SH57

★★60% Carreg Bran Country Hotel

Church Ln LL61 5YH
☎ 01248 714224 🖷 01248 716516
e-mail: info@carregbran.uk.com
Dir: *from Holyhead 1st junct for Llanfairpwll. Through village then 1st right before dual carriageway and bridge*
This privately owned and personally run hotel is situated close to the banks of the Menai Strait. Rooms are spacious and well-equipped. The restaurant is attractive and the food is locally inspired. There is a choice of bars and a large function room, popular for weddings and business meetings.
ROOMS: 20 en suite (2 fmly) No smoking in 5 bedrooms s £49; d £69 (incl. bkfst) **CONF:** Thtr 120 Class 60 Board 30 **PARKING:** 150
NOTES: No smoking in restaurant Civ Wed 100
CARDS:

LLANGEFNI — Map 14 SH47

★★★76% Tre-Ysgawen Hall

Capel Coch LL77 7UR
☎ 01248 750750 🖷 01248 750035
e-mail: enquiries@treysgawen-hall.co.uk
Dir: *take B5111 from Llangefni for Amlwch/Llanerchymedd. After Rhosmeich, turn right to Capel Coch. Hotel 1m on left at end of long drive*
Quietly located in extensive wooded grounds, this charming mansion was built in 1882 and has been extended over time. It offers a range of delightful bedrooms, thoughtfully equipped with many personal touches. Public areas are elegant, spacious and comfortable. The restaurant offers an interesting choice of dishes and there is a bar/bistro and coffee shop.
ROOMS: 19 en suite 10 annexe en suite (2 fmly) (8 GF) No smoking in 15 bedrooms s £90-£190; d £140-£190 (incl. bkfst & dinner)
FACILITIES: Indoor swimming (H) Sauna Solarium Gym Jacuzzi
CONF: Thtr 200 Class 70 Board 50 **PARKING:** 60 **NOTES:** No dogs (ex guide dogs) No smoking in restaurant Closed 25 Dec-2 Jan Civ Wed 120
CARDS:

★★66% Bull Hotel

Bulkley Square LL77 7LR
☎ 01248 722119 🖷 01248 750488
e-mail: bull@welsh-historic-inns.com
Dir: *leave A55 at Llangefni follow signs for town centre, hotel on right on entering town through one-way system*

This town centre hostelry was built in 1817. Now refurbished, it provides well-equipped, tastefully furnished accommodation, including a room with a four-poster bed and a family room. Public areas offer a choice of bars, a spacious and traditionally appointed restaurant and a comfortable lounge where residents may relax.
ROOMS: 13 en suite (2 fmly) No smoking in all bedrooms s £55-£85; d £60-£85 (incl. bkfst) **FACILITIES:** STV Xmas **PARKING:** 18
NOTES: No dogs (ex guide dogs) **CARDS:**

> Late for dinner?
> Quality Standards mean that last orders for dinner vary according to star rating and should be no earlier than:
> ★★ 7.00pm ★★★ 8.00pm ★★★★ 9.00pm
> ★★★★★ 10.00pm

A

MENAI BRIDGE Map 14 SH57

★★66% **Anglesey Arms**
LL59 5EA
☎ 01248 712305 01248 712076
e-mail: bookings@theangleseyarmshotel.co.uk
Dir: *1st slip road off Britannia Bridge, follow signs to Menai Bridge, hotel on rdbt at end of Menai Bridge*
This popular hotel sits next to the Menai Suspension Bridge and lies in well-maintained gardens. The hotel provides smart, well-equipped accommodation. Bedrooms are attractively furnished in pine and equipped with thoughtful extras. There is a choice of bars and an excellent selection of meals.
ROOMS: 16 en suite (2 fmly) s £40; d £40 **FACILITIES:** Xmas **CONF:** Thtr 60 Class 40 Board 40 Del £58.75 **PARKING:** 60 **NOTES:** Civ Wed 60 **CARDS:**

★★63% **Victoria Hotel**
Telford Rd LL59 5DR
☎ 01248 712309 01248 716774
e-mail: vicmenai@barbox.net
Dir: *Over Menai Suspension Bridge, take 2nd exit from rdbt, continue 100yds, hotel on right*
This family-run hotel is situated in Menai Bridge and has panoramic views of the Menai Straits and Britannia Bridge. Many bedrooms have their own balconies. There are two character bars where meals are available, and also a more formal conservatory dining room.
ROOMS: 14 en suite 3 annexe en suite (4 fmly) s £35; d £46 (incl. bkfst) **LB** **FACILITIES:** Childrens playground Xmas **CONF:** Thtr 80 Class 80 Board 50 **PARKING:** 40 **NOTES:** No smoking in restaurant Civ Wed 80 **CARDS:**

TREARDDUR BAY Map 14 SH27

★★★72% ***Trearddur Bay***
LL65 2UN
☎ 01407 860301 01407 861181
e-mail: enquiries@trearddurbayhotel.co.uk
Dir: *leave A55 at junct to Caergeiliog. Then A5. Left at lights onto B4545 towards Trearddur Bay, with Power garage on right, left, hotel on right*
Facilities at this fine modern hotel include extensive function and conference rooms, an indoor swimming pool and a games room. Bedrooms are well-equipped, many have sea views and suites are available. An all-day bar serves a wide range of snacks and lighter meals, supplemented by a cocktail bar and the more formal hotel restaurant.
ROOMS: 36 en suite (7 fmly) No smoking in 1 bedroom **FACILITIES:** STV Indoor swimming (H) Sailing, Shooting, Horse riding, Fishing, Diving, Golf packages entertainment ch fac **CONF:** Thtr 120 Class 60 Board 40 **PARKING:** 300 **NOTES:** No dogs (ex guide dogs) No smoking in restaurant Civ Wed 120
CARDS:

BALA, Gwynedd Map 14 SH93

★★★78% ®® **Palé Hall Country House**
Palé Estate, Llandderfel LL23 7PS
☎ 01678 530285 01678 530220
e-mail: enquiries@palehall.co.uk
Dir: *off B4401 Corwen/Bala road, 4m from Llandrillo*
This enchanting mansion was built in 1870 and overlooks extensive grounds and beautiful woodland. The fine entrance hall, with its stained glass lantern ceiling and galleried oak staircase, leads off to the library bar, two elegant lounges and the smart dining room. The standard of cooking remains high and is complemented by fine wines. The spacious bedrooms are furnished to the highest standards with many thoughtful extras.
ROOMS: 17 en suite (1 fmly) No smoking in 10 bedrooms s £80-£125; d £100-£185 (incl. bkfst) **LB** **FACILITIES:** Fishing Croquet lawn Clay pigeon/Game shooting Xmas **CONF:** Board 22 Del from £125 **PARKING:** 40 **NOTES:** No dogs No children No smoking in restaurant Civ Wed 40 **CARDS:**

See advert on opposite page

★★65% **Plas Coch**
High St LL23 7AB
☎ 01678 520309 01678 521135
e-mail: info@plascoch.com
Dir: *on A494, located in centre of Bala*
A focal point in this bustling town, this 18th-century former coaching inn is popular with locals and resident guests alike. The public areas are very attractive and bedrooms are spacious. No-smoking bedrooms are available, but public areas do not include a no-smoking zone.
ROOMS: 10 en suite (4 fmly) No smoking in all bedrooms s £39-£45; d £65 (incl. bkfst) **LB** **FACILITIES:** Windsurfing, Canoeing, Sailing, Whitewater Rafting, **PARKING:** 12 **NOTES:** No dogs (ex guide dogs)
CARDS:

BANGOR, Gwynedd Map 14 SH57

★★66% **Garden Hotel**
1 High St LL57 1DQ
☎ 01248 362189 01248 371328
e-mail: reception@gardenhotelbangor.co.uk
Dir: *Before railway station take 1st turning left, past Plaza cinema, car park on right*
A city hotel located close to the university, hospital and railway station and a good base for touring Snowdonia and North Wales. The newly completed bedrooms are spacious and very well equipped, and the hotel also has a renowned Cantonese restaurant. A function suite is also available.
ROOMS: 11 rms (10 en suite) (1 fmly) No smoking in all bedrooms s fr £42; d fr £70 (incl. bkfst) **FACILITIES:** STV Xmas **PARKING:** 6 **NOTES:** No dogs No children 10yrs
CARDS:

Travel Inn
Menai Business Park LL57 4FA
☎ 08701 977023 01248 679214
Dir: *From A55 take 3rd Bangor turn off signed Caernarfon A487, Bangor & hospital. Take 3rd exit at 1st rdbt*
Travel Inn offers good-quality, value-for-money accommodation. Spacious, en suite rooms with bath and shower comfortably accommodate a family of up to two adults and two children (to age 15). The restaurant and bar offers a varied menu. For further details and the Travel Inn phone number, consult the Hotel Groups page.
ROOMS: 40 en suite s £44.95; d £44.95

Travelodge
Llys-y-Gwynt LL57 4BG
☎ 08700 850 950 01248 370345
Dir: *junct A5/A55*
Travelodge offers good quality, good value, modern accommodation. Ideal for families, the spacious, en suite bedrooms include remote-control TV, tea and coffee-making facilities, luxury beds and free morning newspaper. Meals can be taken at the nearby family restaurant. For further details and the Travelodge phone number, consult the Hotel Groups page.
ROOMS: 62 en suite s fr £42.95; d fr £42.95

BARMOUTH, Gwynedd Map 14 SH61

★★★68% Bae Abermaw

Panorama Hill LL42 1DQ
☎ 01341 280550 🖷 01341 280346
e-mail: enquiries@baeabermaw.com

This large stone-built Victorian house, now a privately owned and personally run hotel, stands in its own wooded grounds, on a hillside from where it overlooks stunning views across the Mawddach estuary. It is decorated and furnished throughout in a striking contemporary style and provides spacious, well equipped accommodation. Facilities here include a room for conferences and other functions.

ROOMS: 14 en suite (4 fmly) No smoking in all bedrooms s £65-£88; d £95-£140 (incl. bkfst) **LB FACILITIES:** Xmas **CONF:** Thtr 100 Class 40 Board 40 **PARKING:** 40 **NOTES:** No dogs (ex guide dogs) No smoking in restaurant Civ Wed 80 **CARDS:**

★★70% ® Ty'r Graig Castle Hotel

Llanaber Rd LL42 1YN
☎ 01341 280470 🖷 01341 281260
e-mail: reservations@tyr-graig-castle.co.uk

Dir: *0.75m from Barmouth on Harlech road, seaward side*

This impressive and unusual house was designed and built by the famous Birmingham gun maker WW Greener. Victorian and gothic charm are combined and original features include some magnificent stained glass windows and wood panelling. Bedrooms are well equipped and many overlook Cardigan Bay. Dishes range from the truly Welsh to eclectic choices.

ROOMS: 11 en suite No smoking in all bedrooms s £51; d £84 (incl. bkfst) **LB PARKING:** 15 **NOTES:** No smoking in restaurant Closed 25 Dec-1 Feb **CARDS:**

★★70% *Wavecrest Hotel*

8 Marine Pde LL42 1NA
☎ 01341 280330 🖷 01341 280330
e-mail: thewavecrest@talk21.com

Dir: *left over level-crossing, then immediately right onto Marine Parade*

There are superb views over Cardigan Bay towards the Cader Idris Mountains from many of the attractive rooms at this delightful hotel on the promenade. There is an open-plan bar and restaurant serving excellent cuisine using local produce, complemented by an impressive wine list and extensive collection of malt whiskies.

ROOMS: 9 en suite (3 fmly) No smoking in all bedrooms **NOTES:** No smoking in restaurant Closed Nov-Mar **CARDS:**

★★68% Bryn Melyn

Panorama Rd LL42 1DQ
☎ 01341 280556 🖷 01341 280342
e-mail: bryn.melyn@virgin.net

Dir: *off A496 from Dolgellau, right up hill for drive on left*

This privately-owned hotel has superb views over the Mawddach Estuary to the Cader Idris Mountains. Bedrooms are decorated with pretty wallpapers and fabrics and equipped with modern facilities. Public areas include a comfortable lounge and a cane-furnished conservatory. Good home cooking is on offer and vegetarians are well looked after.

ROOMS: 9 rms (8 en suite) (1 fmly) s £35-£41; d £56-£68 (incl. bkfst) **LB PARKING:** 10 **NOTES:** No smoking in restaurant **CARDS:**

BARRY, Vale of Glamorgan Map 09 ST16

★★★73% ® *Egerton Grey Country House*

Porthkerry CF62 3BZ
☎ 01446 711666 🖷 01446 711690
e-mail: info@egertongrey.co.uk

Dir: *M4 junct 33 follow signs for airport, left at rdbt for Porthkerry, after 500yds turn left down lane between thatched cottages*

This former rectory enjoys a peaceful setting and views over delightful countryside with distant glimpses of the sea. Public areas offer charm and elegance, and include an airy lounge and restaurant, which has been sympathetically converted from the billiards room. Bedrooms are spacious and individually furnished.

ROOMS: 10 en suite (4 fmly) **FACILITIES:** STV Croquet lawn 9 hole golf course 200 yds away. **CONF:** Thtr 30 Class 30 Board 22 **PARKING:** 41 **NOTES:** No smoking in restaurant Civ Wed 120 **CARDS:**

★★★67% Mount Sorrel

Best Western

Porthkerry Rd CF62 7XY
☎ 01446 740069 🖷 01446 746600
e-mail: reservations@mountsorrel.co.uk

Dir: *M4 J33 on A4232. Follow signs for A4050 through Barry. At mini rdbt with church opposite turn left, hotel 300mtrs*

Situated in an elevated position above the town centre, this extended Victorian property is ideally situated for exploring the nearby coast and Cardiff, and offers comfortable accommodation.

continued on p814

BARRY, continued

The public areas include a choice of conference rooms, a restaurant and a bar, together with leisure facilities.
ROOMS: 42 en suite (3 fmly) (5 GF) No smoking in 8 bedrooms s £65-£90; d £120 (incl. bkfst) **LB FACILITIES:** STV Indoor swimming (H) Sauna Gym Swimming pool supervised Xmas **CONF:** Thtr 150 Class 100 Board 50 Del from £100 **PARKING:** 17 **NOTES:** No smoking in restaurant Civ Wed 150 **CARDS:**

BEAUMARIS See Anglesey, Isle of

BEDDGELERT, Gwynedd Map 14 SH54

★★★67% Royal Goat
LL55 4YE
☎ 01766 890224 📠 01766 890422

e-mail: info@royalgoathotel.co.uk
Dir: *From Caernarfon take A4085 to Beddgelert 14m. From Porthmadog take A498 to Beddgelert 7m*
An impressive building steeped in history, the Royal Goat provides well-equipped accommodation and public areas include a choice of bars and restaurants, a residents' lounge and function rooms.
ROOMS: 32 en suite (3 fmly) No smoking in 10 bedrooms s £47-£64; d £82-£116 (incl. bkfst) **LB FACILITIES:** STV Fishing Xmas **CONF:** Thtr 80 Class 70 Board 70 **SERVICES:** Lift **PARKING:** 100 **NOTES:** No smoking in restaurant Closed 6 Nov-28 Feb
CARDS:

★★71% Tanronnen Inn
LL55 4YB
☎ 01766 890347 📠 01766 890606
Dir: *in the centre of village*
This delightful small hotel offers comfortable, well equipped and attractively appointed accommodation, including a family room. There is also a selection of pleasant and relaxing public areas. The wide range of bar food is popular with tourists, and more formal meals are served in the restaurant.
ROOMS: 7 en suite (3 fmly) s £48; d £85 (incl. bkfst) **LB FACILITIES:** STV Xmas **PARKING:** 15 **NOTES:** No dogs
CARDS:

BETWS-Y-COED, Conwy Map 14 SH75
See also Llanrwst

★★★71% ◎ Royal Oak
Holyhead Rd LL24 0AY
☎ 01690 710219 📠 01690 710603
e-mail: royaloakmail@btopenworld.com
Dir: *on A5 in centre of town, next to St Mary's Church*
This fine, privately owned hotel started life as a coaching inn and now provides smart bedrooms and a wide range of public areas. The choice of eating options includes the Grill Bar and the main dining room, which provides a more formal dinner option from Wednesdays to Saturdays.
ROOMS: 27 en suite (3 fmly) No smoking in 6 bedrooms s £56-£60; d £70 (incl. bkfst) **LB FACILITIES:** STV entertainment **CONF:** BC Thtr 20 Class 20 Board 20 **PARKING:** 90 **NOTES:** No dogs (ex guide dogs) No smoking in restaurant Closed 25-26 Dec Civ Wed 85
CARDS:

See advert on opposite page

Packed in a hurry?
Ironing facilities should be available at all star levels, either in rooms or on request

★★★68% Best Western Waterloo
LL24 0AR
☎ 01690 710411 📠 01690 710666
e-mail: reservations@waterloo-hotel.info
Dir: *on A5 near Waterloo Bridge*

This long-established hotel, named after the nearby Waterloo Bridge, is ideally located for Snowdonia. Accommodation is split between rooms in the main hotel and modern, cottage-style rooms located in buildings to the rear. The attractive Garden Room Restaurant serves traditional Welsh specialities, and the Wellington Bar offers light meals and snacks.
ROOMS: 10 en suite 30 annexe en suite (2 fmly) (30 GF) No smoking in 14 bedrooms s £55-£63; d £90-£105 (incl. bkfst) **LB FACILITIES: Spa** Indoor swimming (H) Sauna Solarium Gym Jacuzzi Steam room, Swimming pool supervised Xmas **CONF:** Thtr 50 Class 16 Board 20 Del from £65 **PARKING:** 200 **NOTES:** No smoking in restaurant
CARDS:

★★★65% Craig-y-Dderwen Riverside Hotel
THE INDEPENDENTS
LL24 0AS
☎ 01690 710293 📠 01690 710362
e-mail: craig-y-dderwen@betws-y-coed.co.uk
Dir: *A5 to town, cross Waterloo Bridge and take 1st left*
This Victorian country-house hotel is set in well-maintained grounds alongside the River Conwy, at the end of a tree-lined drive. Very pleasant views can be enjoyed from many rooms, and two of the bedrooms have four-poster beds. There are comfortable lounges and the atmosphere is tranquil and relaxing.
ROOMS: 16 en suite (2 fmly) (1 GF) s £60-£100; d £70-£110 (incl. bkfst) **LB FACILITIES: Spa** Croquet lawn Badminton, Volleyball **CONF:** Thtr 50 Class 25 Board 20 **PARKING:** 50 **NOTES:** No smoking in restaurant Closed 23-26 Dec & 30 Dec-1 Feb
CARDS:

See advert on opposite page

Top 200 - Hotel

★★ ◎◎◎ Tan-y-Foel Country House
Capel Garmon LL26 0RE
☎ 01690 710507 📠 01690 710681
e-mail: enquiries@tyfhotel.co.uk
Dir: *off A5 at Betws-y-Coed onto A470, 2m N follow sign for Capel Garmon, 1.5m, hotel sign on left*
In an idyllic hillside location with stunning views of Conwy Valley, this stylish, sophisticated hotel is a must for travellers seeking a modern, eclectic hotel. The traditional exterior portrays its 16th-century origins, whilst inside the hotel the furnishings are of a cutting edge design. Dinner, using local organic produce whenever possible, is a highlight of any stay.
continued

Individually furnished bedrooms, including imaginative use of an old hayloft, are designed for comfort and relaxation.

ROOMS: 4 en suite 2 annexe en suite (1 GF) No smoking in all bedrooms s £99-£120; d £120-£170 (incl. bkfst) **LB** **PARKING:** 16 **NOTES:** No dogs (ex guide dogs) No children 7yrs No smoking in restaurant Closed Jan **CARDS:**

★★68% **Fairy Glen**
LL24 0SH
☎ 01690 710269
e-mail: fairyglenhotel@amserve.net
Dir: *off A5 onto A470 southbound (Dolwyddelan Road). Hotel 0.5m on left by Beaver Bridge*

This privately owned and personally run former coaching inn is over 300 years old. It is located near the Fairy Glen beauty spot, south of Betws-y-Coed. The modern accommodation is well equipped and service is willing, friendly and attentive. Facilities include a cosy bar and a separate comfortable lounge.
ROOMS: 8 rms (6 en suite) (2 fmly) s £23-£35; d £46-£50 (incl. bkfst) **LB** **PARKING:** 10 **NOTES:** No dogs (ex guide dogs) No smoking in restaurant Closed Nov-Jan RS Feb **CARDS:**

★★68% **Park Hill**
Llanrwst Rd LL24 0HD
☎ 01690 710540 📠 01690 710540
e-mail: welcome@park-hill-hotel.co.uk
Dir: *0.5m N of Betws-y-Coed on A470 Llanrwst road*
This friendly hotel benefits from a peaceful location overlooking the village. Comfortable bedrooms come in a wide range of sizes and are well equipped. A four-poster room and family rooms are available. There is a choice of lounges, a heated swimming pool, sauna and whirlpool bath for residents.
ROOMS: 9 en suite (2 fmly) s £50; d £55-£78 (incl. bkfst) **LB** **FACILITIES:** Indoor swimming (H) Sauna Jacuzzi Xmas **PARKING:** 11 **NOTES:** No dogs (ex guide dogs) No children 6yrs No smoking in restaurant **CARDS:**

B

BLACKWOOD, Caerphilly
Map 09 ST19

★★★67% *Maes Manor*
NP12 0AG
☎ 01495 224551 & 220011 ▣ 01495 228217
Dir: *A4048 to Tredega. At Pontllanfraith left at rdbt, through Blackwood High St. After 1.25m left at Rack Inn. Hotel 400yds on left*

Standing high above the town, this 19th-century manor house is set in nine acres of gardens and woodland. Bedrooms are attractively decorated with co-ordinated furnishings. As well as the restaurant, public rooms include a choice of bars, a lounge/lobby area and a large function room.
ROOMS: 8 en suite 14 annexe en suite (2 fmly) **PARKING:** 100
CARDS:

See advert on opposite page

BLAENAU FFESTINIOG, Gwynedd
Map 14 SH74

★★69% Queens Hotel
1 High St LL41 3ES
☎ 01766 830055 ▣ 01766 830046
e-mail: cathy@queensffestiniog.freeserve.co.uk
Dir: *on A470 adjacent to Ffestiniog railway, between Betws-y-Coed & Dolgellau*
This flourishing hotel has an all-day bistro serving meals and snacks. Bedrooms are well-equipped and attractive. The hotel lies at the northern end of the famous Ffestiniog railway, and the bedrooms are named after locomotives which have operated on the line.
ROOMS: 12 en suite (4 fmly) s £40-£60; d £55-£80 (incl. bkfst) **LB** **FACILITIES:** STV **CONF:** Thtr 80 Class 30 Board 30 **NOTES:** No dogs (ex guide dogs) No smoking in restaurant Closed 25 Dec
CARDS:

BONTDDU, Gwynedd
Map 14 SH61

★★★70% ֍֍ *Bontddu Hall*
LL40 2UF
☎ 01341 430661 ▣ 01341 430284
e-mail: reservations@bontdduhall.co.uk
Dir: *A470 N of Dolgellau towards Barmouth. Halfway between Dolgellau & Barmouth on A496*
Overlooking the beautiful Mawddach Estuary, this 19th-century house was once the country retreat of the Lord Mayor of Birmingham and is surrounded by 14 acres of landscaped gardens and wooded grounds. Bedrooms are spacious and well-equipped, some are located in purpose-built buildings in the grounds. Elegant public areas include lounges and a conservatory-style restaurant.
ROOMS: 15 en suite 5 annexe en suite (6 fmly) **CONF:** Thtr 100 Class 100 Board 50 **PARKING:** 50 **NOTES:** No children 3yrs Civ Wed 50
CARDS:

BRECON, Powys
Map 09 SO02

★★★76% ֍ Nant Ddu Lodge, Bistro & Spa
Cwm Taf, Nant Ddu CF48 2HY
☎ 01685 379111 ▣ 01685 377088
e-mail: enquiries@nant-ddu-lodge.co.uk
(For full entry see Nant-Ddu and advert opposite and p.849)

★★★73% Peterstone Court
Llanhamlach LD3 7YB
☎ 01874 665387 ▣ 01874 665376
e-mail: enquiries@Peterstone-Court.com
Dir: *A40 towards Abergavenny, hotel approx 4m, on right*
This impressive 18th-century house is the ideal base for exploring this remote and beautiful corner of Wales. It offers spacious bedrooms furnished with antiques, comfortable armchairs and thoughtful extras. There is an elegant drawing room displaying some fine paintings, and a library.
ROOMS: 8 en suite 4 annexe en suite (2 fmly) s fr £98; d fr £150 (incl. bkfst) **LB** **FACILITIES:** Outdoor swimming (H) Sauna Solarium Gym Jacuzzi ch fac Xmas **CONF:** Thtr 130 Class 50 Board 30 Del from £120.75 **PARKING:** 45 **NOTES:** No dogs (ex guide dogs) No smoking in restaurant Civ Wed 100 **CARDS:**

★★70% Lansdowne Hotel & Restaurant
The Watton LD3 7EG
☎ 01874 623321 ▣ 01874 610438
e-mail: reception@lansdownehotel.co.uk
Dir: *off A40/A470 onto B4601, hotel in town centre*
Now a privately owned and personally-run hotel, this Georgian house is conveniently located close to the town centre. The accommodation is well equipped and includes family rooms and a bedroom on ground floor level. There is a comfortable lounge and an attractive split-level dining room containing a bar.
ROOMS: 9 en suite (2 fmly) (1 GF) s £28; d £49 (incl. bkfst) **LB** **NOTES:** No children 5yrs **CARDS:**

★★67% The Castle of Brecon
Castle Square LD3 9DB
☎ 01874 624611 ▣ 01874 623737
e-mail: hotel@breconcastle.co.uk
Dir: *A40 to Brecon, follow town centre for 2kms, left at lights, right towards Cradoc, right into Castle Sq*

This former coaching inn occupies an elevated position overlooking the town and River Usk. This view is shared by the restaurant and some of the bedrooms, and the remaining public areas are roomy and relaxed. Function and meeting rooms are available and incorporate one of the castle walls.
ROOMS: 31 en suite 12 annexe en suite (8 fmly) (2 GF) No smoking in 12 bedrooms s £49-£59; d £64-£79 (incl. bkfst) **LB** **FACILITIES:** STV Xmas **CONF:** Thtr 160 Class 60 Board 80 Del from £74 **PARKING:** 30 **NOTES:** No smoking in restaurant Civ Wed 120
CARDS:

BRIDGEND, Bridgend Map 09 SS97
See also Porthcawl

★★★★76% Coed-y-Mwstwr
Coychurch CF35 6AF
☎ 01656 860621 01656 863122
e-mail: anything@coed-y-mwstwr.com
Dir: *leave A473 at Coychurch right at petrol station. Follow signs at top of hill*

This former Victorian mansion, set in 17 acres of grounds a few miles from Bridgend, is an inviting retreat for both business people and leisure guests. An original oak-panelled billiards room houses the elegant restaurant. Bedrooms have been refurbished in individual styles with a good range of facilities, and include two full suites. A gymnasium and other fitness facilities including an outdoor swimming pool are available.
ROOMS: 28 en suite (2 fmly) No smoking in 20 bedrooms s £85-£95; d £115-£135 (incl. bkfst) **LB FACILITIES:** STV Outdoor swimming (H) Golf 12 Tennis (hard) Sauna Solarium Gym Croquet lawn Xmas **CONF:** Thtr 180 Class 120 Board 50 Del from £105 **SERVICES:** Lift **PARKING:** 100 **NOTES:** No dogs (ex guide dogs) No smoking in restaurant Civ Wed 170 **CARDS:**

★★★77% The Great House Restaurant & Hotel
Laleston CF32 0HP
☎ 01656 657644 01656 668892
e-mail: enquiries@great-house-laleston.co.uk
Dir: *at side of A473, 400yds from its junct with A48*
A delightful Grade II listed building, dating back to 1550. Mullioned windows, flagstone floors, oak beams, inglenook fireplaces and the great stone arch over the fireplace in the bar add character. Leicester's restaurant offers a wide range of freshly prepared dishes; lighter snacks can be taken in the more informal bistro. The stylish, well-equipped bedrooms are located in the original building and a purpose-built wing.
ROOMS: 8 en suite 8 annexe en suite (8 GF) No smoking in 4 bedrooms s fr £85; d £120-£140 (incl. bkfst) **LB FACILITIES:** STV Sauna Gym Croquet lawn Jacuzzi Health suite with sauna **CONF:** Thtr 40 Class 25 Board 20 Del from £110 **PARKING:** 40 **NOTES:** No dogs (ex guide dogs) No smoking in restaurant Closed 25 Dec-2 Jan Civ Wed 50 **CARDS:**

★★★69% Heronston
Best Western
Ewenny Rd CF35 5AW
☎ 01656 668811 01656 767391
e-mail: reservations@heronston-hotel.demon.co.uk
Dir: *M4 junct 35, follow signs for Porthcawl, at 4th rdbt turn left towards Ogmore-by-Sea (B4265) hotel, 200yds on left*
Situated within easy reach of the town centre and the M4, this large modern hotel offers spacious well-equipped

continued on p818

B

BRIDGEND, continued

accommodation, including no-smoking bedrooms and ground floor rooms. Public areas include an open plan lounge/bar, attractive restaurant and a smart leisure & fitness club. The hotel also has a choice of function/conference rooms.
ROOMS: 69 en suite 6 annexe en suite (4 fmly) (37 GF) No smoking in 21 bedrooms s £55-£95; d £65-£130 (incl. bkfst) **LB** **FACILITIES:** STV Indoor swimming (H) Outdoor swimming (H) Sauna Solarium Gym Jacuzzi Steamroom **CONF:** Thtr 200 Class 80 Board 60 Del from £85 **SERVICES:** Lift **PARKING:** 250 **NOTES:** No smoking in restaurant RS 26-31 Dec Civ Wed 250 **CARDS:**

Express by Holiday Inn

The Derwyn CF32 9SH
☎ 01656 646200 01656 663929
e-mail: ebhi-bridgend@btconnect.com

A modern hotel ideal for families and business travellers. Fresh and uncomplicated, the spacious bedrooms include Sky TV, power shower and tea and coffee-making facilities. Continental buffet breakfast is included in the room rate; other meals may be taken at the nearby family pub or restaurant. For further details and the Express by Holiday Inn phone number, consult the Hotel Groups pages.
ROOMS: 68 en suite **CONF:** Thtr 30 Class 24 Board 16

BUILTH WELLS, Powys — Map 09 SO05

★★★70% Caer Beris Manor

LD2 3NP

THE INDEPENDENTS

☎ 01982 552601 01982 552586
e-mail: caerberismanor@btinternet.com
Dir: *SW on A483*

With extensive landscaped grounds, guests can expect a relaxing stay at this friendly and privately owned hotel. Bedrooms are individually decorated and furnished and retain a feel of a bygone era. A spacious and comfortable lounge and a bar enhance this atmosphere together with the elegant restaurant, complete with its 16th-century panelling.
ROOMS: 23 en suite (1 fmly) (3 GF) s £60-£70; d £89-£109 (incl. bkfst) **LB** **FACILITIES:** STV Fishing Riding Sauna Gym Clay pigeon shooting ch fac Xmas **CONF:** Thtr 100 Class 75 Board 50 Del from £59.95 **PARKING:** 32 **NOTES:** No smoking in restaurant Civ Wed 100 **CARDS:**

CAERNARFON, Gwynedd — Map 14 SH46

Top 200 - Hotel

★★★ Seiont Manor

Llanrug LL55 2AQ

HandPICKED

☎ 01286 673366 01286 672840
e-mail: seiontmanor@arcadianhotels.co.uk
Dir: *E on A4086, 2.5m from Caernarfon*

A splendid hotel created from authentic rural buildings, set in tranquil countryside near Snowdonia. Bedrooms are individually decorated and well equipped, with luxurious extra touches. Public rooms are cosy and comfortable and furnished in country-house style. The kitchen team use the best of local produce to provide exciting interpretations of traditional dishes.
ROOMS: 28 en suite (10 fmly) (14 GF) No smoking in 8 bedrooms s £70-£100; d £70-£200 (incl. bkfst) **LB** **FACILITIES: Spa** STV Indoor swimming (H) Fishing Sauna Solarium Gym Xmas **CONF:** Thtr 100 Class 40 Board 40 Del from £135 **PARKING:** 100 **NOTES:** No smoking in restaurant Civ Wed 100 **CARDS:**

★★★71% Celtic Royal Hotel

Bangor St LL55 1AY
☎ 01286 674477 01286 674139
e-mail: admin@celtic-royal.co.uk
Dir: *7m off A55 Expressway at Bangor. Follow A487 towards Caernarfon*

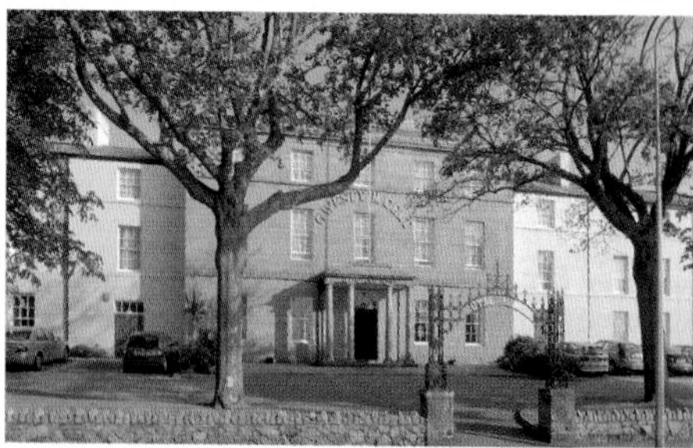

This impressive, privately owned hotel is situated in the town centre. It provides attractively appointed accommodation, which includes no smoking rooms, bedrooms for less able guests and family rooms. The spacious public areas include a bar, a choice of lounges and a pleasant split-level restaurant. Guests also have the use of the excellent health club.
ROOMS: 110 en suite s £60-£65; d £90-£100 (incl. bkfst) **LB** **FACILITIES:** STV Indoor swimming (H) Sauna Solarium Gym Jacuzzi Sun shower Xmas **CONF:** Thtr 300 Class 170 Board 125 **SERVICES:** Lift **PARKING:** 180 **NOTES:** No dogs (ex guide dogs) No smoking in restaurant Civ Wed 120 **CARDS:**

★★75% Ty'n Rhos Country Hotel & Restaurant
Llanddeiniolen LL55 3AE
☎ 01248 670489 01248 670079
e-mail: enquiries@tynrhos.co.uk
Dir: *situated in the hamlet of Seion between B4366 and B4547*
Ty'n Rhos is a peaceful converted farmhouse, set in lovely countryside between Snowdon and the Menai Straits. The lounge, with its slate inglenook fireplace, is elegantly furnished and there is a small bar for pre-dinner drinks. The conservatory offers a comfortable vantage point from which to admire the views and the gardens. The bedrooms are well-equipped and have modern facilities. There is now a self contained conference centre.
ROOMS: 11 en suite 3 annexe en suite No smoking in all bedrooms s £50-£75; d £70-£90 (incl. bkfst) **LB FACILITIES:** Croquet lawn **CONF:** Thtr 40 Class 30 Board 20 Del from £68.50 **PARKING:** 20 **NOTES:** No dogs (ex guide dogs) No children 6yrs No smoking in restaurant Closed 22-30 Dec RS Sun evening (rest closed to non-res)
CARDS:

★★67% *Stables*
Llanwnda LL54 5SD
☎ 01286 830711 01286 830413
Dir: *3m S of Caernarfon, on A499*
This privately owned and personally run hotel is set in 15 acres of its own land, south of Caernarfon. The bar and restaurant are located in converted stables. The bedrooms are all situated in two purpose built, motel-style wings.
ROOMS: 22 annexe en suite (8 fmly) **FACILITIES:** Guests may bring own horse to stables **CONF:** Thtr 50 Class 30 Board 30 **PARKING:** 40
CARDS:

CAERPHILLY, Caerphilly Map 09 ST18

Premier Lodge (Caerphilly)
Corbetts Ln CF83 3HX
☎ 0870 9906368 0870 9906369
Premier Lodge offers modern, well-equipped, en suite accommodation suitable for both business and leisure travellers. Meals can be taken at the adjacent popular restaurant and bar, which is fully licensed. For further details, consult the Hotel Groups page.
ROOMS: 40 en suite s £48; d £48

Travel Inn
Crossways Business Park, Pontypandy CF8 3NL
☎ 08701 977046 029 2086 5546
Dir: *M4 junct 32 take A470 towards Merthyr Tydfil or junct 4 take A458 to Caerphilly. On ring rd to Crossways Business Park. Travel Inn on right at McDonald's rdbt.*
Travel Inn offers good-quality, value-for-money accommodation. Spacious, en suite rooms with bath and shower comfortably accommodate a family of up to two adults and two children (to age 15). The restaurant and bar offers a varied menu. For further details and the Travel Inn phone number, consult the Hotel Groups page.
ROOMS: 40 en suite s £44.95; d £44.95 **CONF:** Class 30

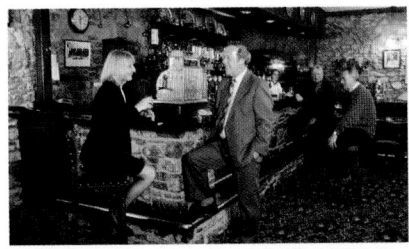

Packed in a hurry?
Ironing facilities should be available at all star levels, either in rooms or on request

C

CAPEL CURIG, Conwy

Map 14 SH75

★★66% Cobdens
LL24 0EE
☎ 01690 720243 📠 01690 720354
e-mail: info@cobdens.co.uk
Dir: *on A5, 4m N of Betws-y-Coed*
In the heart of Snowdonia, this hotel has been a centre for mountaineering and other outdoor pursuits for 200 years. The bedrooms are modern and well-equipped, and many enjoy lovely views. There is a bar and a wide range of meals using local produce are served in the restaurant. A small conference room is also available.
ROOMS: 16 en suite (3 fmly) s £30-£34; d £59-£68 (incl. bkfst) **FACILITIES:** Fishing **CONF:** Thtr 50 Del £70 **PARKING:** 40 **NOTES:** No smoking in restaurant Closed Jan RS 25 & 31 Dec
CARDS:

CARDIFF, Cardiff

Map 09 ST17

See also Barry

★★★★★72% ®® St David's Hotel & Spa

ROCCO FORTE HOTELS

Havannah St CF10 5SD
☎ 029 2045 4045 📠 029 2048 7056
e-mail: reservations@thestdavidshotel.com
Dir: *M4 junct 33/A4232 for 9m, for Techniquest, at top exit slip road, 1st left at rdbt, 1st right*

This imposing contemporary building sits in a prime position on Cardiff Bay. A seven storey atrium provides a dramatic first impression on entering and leading off from this are the practically laid out and comfortable bedrooms. Tides restaurant, adjacent to the stylish cocktail bar, offers views across the water to Penarth, whilst there is a quiet lounge on the first floor for guests seeking a peaceful environment. A well-equipped spa and extensive business areas complete the package.
ROOMS: 132 en suite (6 fmly) No smoking in 108 bedrooms s £200; d £200 **LB FACILITIES: Spa** STV Indoor swimming (H) Sauna Gym Jacuzzi Fitness studio, 14 treatment rooms entertainment Xmas **CONF:** BC Thtr 270 Class 110 Board 60 Del from £195 **SERVICES:** Lift air con **PARKING:** 80 **NOTES:** No dogs (ex guide dogs) No smoking in restaurant Civ Wed 180 **CARDS:**

★★★★69% ® Copthorne Hotel Cardiff-Caerdydd

COPTHORNE

Copthorne Way, Culverhouse Cross CF5 6DH
☎ 029 2059 9100 📠 029 2059 9080
e-mail: sales.cardiff@mill-cop.com
Dir: *M4 junct 33, take A4232 for 2.5m towards Cardiff West then A48*
A comfortable, popular and modern hotel, conveniently located for the airport and city. Bedrooms are a good size and some have a private lounge. Public areas are smartly presented with features including a gym, pool, meeting rooms and a restaurant which overlooks the lake.

ROOMS: 135 en suite (14 fmly) (27 GF) No smoking in 79 bedrooms s £150-£225; d £170-£225 **LB FACILITIES:** STV Indoor swimming (H) Sauna Gym Jacuzzi Steam room Xmas **CONF:** Thtr 300 Class 140 Board 80 Del from £160 **SERVICES:** Lift **PARKING:** 225 **NOTES:** Civ Wed 180 **CARDS:**

★★★★67% Cardiff Marriott Hotel

Marriott HOTELS · RESORTS · SUITES

Mill Ln CF10 1EZ
☎ 029 2039 9944 📠 029 2039 5578
e-mail: sara.nurse@marriotthotels.co.uk
Dir: *M4 junct 29 follow City Centre signs. Turn left into High Street opposite Castle, then 2nd left, at bottom of High St into Mill Lane*

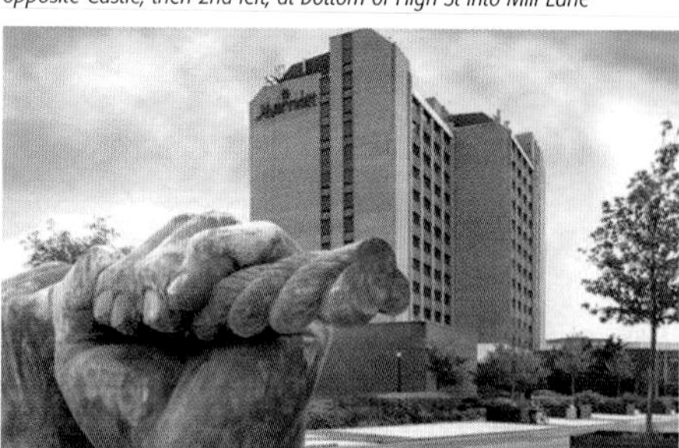

A centrally located modern hotel, with spacious public areas and a good range of services is ideal for business or leisure. Eating options include the informal Chats café bar and the contemporary Mediterrano restaurant. Well-equipped bedrooms are comfortable and air conditioned.
ROOMS: 182 en suite (58 fmly) No smoking in 127 bedrooms s £75-£200; d £85-£275 **LB FACILITIES:** STV Indoor swimming (H) Sauna Solarium Gym Jacuzzi Steam room Xmas **CONF:** Thtr 400 Class 200 Board 100 Del from £135 **SERVICES:** Lift air con **PARKING:** 110 **NOTES:** No dogs (ex guide dogs) No smoking in restaurant Civ Wed 150 **CARDS:**

★★★★66% Angel Hotel

PARAMOUNT GROUP OF HOTELS

Castle St CF10 1SZ
☎ 029 2064 9200 📠 029 2039 6212
e-mail: angelreservations@paramount-hotels.co.uk
Dir: *opposite Cardiff Castle*
This well-established hotel is in the heart of the city overlooking the castle. All bedrooms offer air conditioning and are decorated and furnished to a high standard. Public areas include an

continued

impressive lobby, a modern restaurant and a selection of conference rooms. There is limited parking at the rear of the hotel.
ROOMS: 102 en suite (4 fmly) No smoking in 62 bedrooms s £85-£200; d £95-£240 **LB** **FACILITIES:** Xmas **CONF:** Thtr 300 Class 180 Board 80 Del from £110 **SERVICES:** Lift air con **PARKING:** 60 **NOTES:** No smoking in restaurant Civ Wed 200
CARDS:

★★★★64% ***Jurys Cardiff***
JURYS DOYLE HOTELS
Mary Ann St CF10 2JH
☎ 029 2034 1441 🖹 029 2022 3742
e-mail: info@jurysdoyle.com
Dir: *next to Ice Rink, opposite Cardiff International Arena*
This modern hotel is situated opposite the Cardiff International Arena. Bedrooms are largely set around an impressive atrium which houses the reception and offers access to Dylan's restaurant and Kavanagh's Irish bar, whilst those rooms on the executive floor are particularly well appointed. Conference and function facilities are offered, together with a business centre.
ROOMS: 146 en suite (6 fmly) No smoking in 24 bedrooms
FACILITIES: STV **CONF:** Thtr 300 Class 120 Board 50 **SERVICES:** Lift
PARKING: 55 **NOTES:** No dogs (ex guide dogs) Civ Wed 250
CARDS:

★★★★61%
Hanover International Hotel & Club
Hanover International Hotels & Clubs
Schooner Way, Atlantic Wharf CF10 4RT
☎ 029 2047 5000 🖹 029 2048 1491
Dir: *M4 junct 33/A4232 follow Cardiff Bay signs, to Atlantic Wharf & Hotel*

Situated in the heart of the city's new development area, this hotel is equally convenient for the centre and Cardiff Bay. Bedrooms vary between standard rooms in the original wing and deluxe rooms in the more modern extension. The hotel offers good seating space in public rooms, a galleried bar and a popular leisure club.
ROOMS: 156 en suite (6 fmly) No smoking in 50 bedrooms
FACILITIES: STV Indoor swimming (H) Snooker Sauna Solarium Gym Jacuzzi **CONF:** Thtr 250 Class 90 Board 40 **SERVICES:** Lift
PARKING: 150 **NOTES:** No dogs (ex guide dogs) No smoking in restaurant Civ Wed 180 **CARDS:**

★★★75% ◎ **Manor Parc Country Hotel & Restaurant**
Thornhill Rd, Thornhill CF14 9UA
☎ 029 2069 3723 🖹 029 2061 4624
Dir: *on A469*
Set in open countryside on the outskirts of Cardiff, this delightful hotel retains traditional values of hospitality and service. Bedrooms, including a suite, are spacious and attractive, and

continued on p822

CARDIFF, continued

public areas comprise a comfortable lounge and a restaurant with a magnificent lantern ceiling overlooking the well-tended grounds.
ROOMS: 12 en suite (2 fmly) s £65-£75; d £95-£130 (incl. bkfst) **LB** **FACILITIES:** STV Tennis (hard) **CONF:** Thtr 120 Class 80 Board 50 **PARKING:** 70 **NOTES:** No dogs (ex guide dogs) No smoking in restaurant Closed 24-26 Dec & 1 Jan Civ Wed 120
CARDS:

★★★72% St Mellons Hotel & Country Club

Castleton CF3 2XR
☎ 01633 680355 🖷 01633 680399
e-mail: stmellons@bestwestern.co.uk
Dir: *M4 junct 28 follow signs into Castleton. Through village, then sharp left at brow of hill following hotel sign into driveway*
This former Regency mansion has been tastefully converted into an elegant hotel and has an adjoining leisure complex with a strong local following. Bedrooms are spacious and smart; some are in purpose-built wings. The public areas retain their pleasing former proportions and include relaxing lounges and a restaurant.
ROOMS: 21 en suite 20 annexe en suite (9 fmly) No smoking in 18 bedrooms s £100-£110; d £110-£120 (incl. bkfst) **LB** **FACILITIES:** STV Indoor swimming (H) Tennis (hard) Squash Sauna Solarium Gym Jacuzzi Beauty salon Xmas **CONF:** Thtr 220 Class 70 Board 40 Del from £130 **PARKING:** 90 **NOTES:** No smoking in restaurant Civ Wed 160
CARDS:

★★★71% New House Country Hotel

Thornhill CF14 9UA
☎ 029 2052 0280 🖷 029 2052 0324
e-mail: enquiries@newhousehotel.com
Dir: *M4 junct 32, A470 towards Cardiff, then A469 to Caerphilly, past Thornhill Crematorium, 1 mile on left*
Enjoying a hilltop position, the New House enjoys unrivalled views of the city. The public areas consist of a lounge and bar, an elegant restaurant and various function suites. Accommodation is spacious and comfortable, in attractive, well-equipped rooms, many having their own balcony or terrace.
ROOMS: 36 en suite (5 fmly) (10 GF) No smoking in 7 bedrooms s £65-£93; d £85-£145 (incl. bkfst) **LB** **FACILITIES:** STV Gym Xmas **CONF:** BC Thtr 200 Class 150 Board 200 Del from £115 **PARKING:** 100 **NOTES:** No dogs (ex guide dogs) No smoking in restaurant Civ Wed 200
CARDS:

★★★69% Quality

Merthyr Rd, Tongwynlais CF15 7LD
☎ 029 2052 9988 🖷 029 2052 9977
e-mail: admin@gb629.u-net.com
Dir: *M4 junct 32, take exit for Tongwynlais A4054 off large rdbt, hotel on right*
This modern hotel is conveniently located off the M4 with easy access to Cardiff. Guests can enjoy the spacious open plan public areas and impressive leisure facilities and relax in the well-proportioned and equipped bedrooms, which include some suites. A good range of meeting rooms make it a popular conference venue.
ROOMS: 95 en suite (12 fmly) No smoking in 47 bedrooms s £36.50-£98; d £72-£105 **LB** **FACILITIES:** STV Indoor swimming (H) Sauna Solarium Gym Jacuzzi Xmas **CONF:** Thtr 180 Class 80 Board 80 Del from £70 **SERVICES:** Lift **PARKING:** 150 **NOTES:** No smoking in restaurant Civ Wed 180 **CARDS:**

★★66% Sandringham

21 St Mary St CF10 1PL
☎ 029 2023 2161 🖷 029 2038 3998
e-mail: hotel@sandringham21.fsnet.co.uk
Dir: *M4 junct 29 follow 'City Centre' signs. Opposite the castle turn into High Street which leads to Saint Mary St*
This friendly hotel is near to the Millennium Stadium and offers a convenient base for access to the city centre. Bedrooms are well and usefully equipped, and diners can relax in Café Jazz, the hotel's adjoining restaurant, where live music is provided most nights of the week. There is also a separate lounge bar and an airy breakfast room.
ROOMS: 28 en suite (1 fmly) No smoking in 14 bedrooms s £35-£100; d £40-£120 (incl. bkfst) **LB** **FACILITIES:** entertainment **CONF:** Thtr 100 Class 70 Board 60 Del from £65 **PARKING:** 10 **NOTES:** No dogs (ex guide dogs) **CARDS:**

Holiday Inn Cardiff City

Castle St CF10 1XB
☎ 0870 400 8140 🖷 029 2023 1482
e-mail: cardiff@ichotelsgroup.com
Dir: *M4 junct 29E/A48(M) city centre signs, onto A470 then left to hotel*
At the time of going to press, the classification for this hotel was not confirmed. Please refer to the AA internet site www.theAA.com for current information.
ROOMS: 155 en suite No smoking in 102 bedrooms **FACILITIES:** STV **CONF:** Thtr 150 Class 65 Board 50 **SERVICES:** Lift **PARKING:** 90
CARDS:

Holiday Inn Cardiff North

Pentwyn Rd, Pentwyn CF23 7XA
☎ 0870 400 8141 🖷 029 2054 9147
e-mail: cardiffm4@ichotelsgroup.com
Dir: *M4 junct 29/A48(M), 2nd exit (Pentwyn), 3rd exit off rdbt. Hotel on right, past Mercedes garage.*
At the time of going to press, the classification for this hotel was not confirmed. Please refer to the AA internet site www.theAA.com for current information.
ROOMS: 142 en suite (50 fmly) No smoking in 55 bedrooms **FACILITIES:** Indoor swimming (H) Sauna Solarium Gym Jacuzzi Childrens play area ch fac **CONF:** Thtr 140 Class 70 Board 40 **SERVICES:** Lift **PARKING:** 300 **NOTES:** No smoking in restaurant
CARDS:

Campanile

Caxton Place, Pentwyn CF2 7HA
☎ 029 2054 9044 🖷 029 2054 9900
Dir: *take Pentwyn exit from A48, follow signs for Pentwyn Industrial Estate*
This modern building offers accommodation in smart, well-equipped bedrooms, all with en suite bathrooms. Refreshments may be taken at the informal Bistro. For further details and the Campanile phone number, consult the Hotel Groups page.
ROOMS: 50 annexe en suite **CONF:** Thtr 35 Class 18 Board 20

Express by Holiday Inn Cardiff Bay

Longueil Close, Schooner Way, Atlantic Wharf CF10 4EE
☎ 029 2044 9000 🖷 029 2048 8922
e-mail: silke@firstinn.co.uk
Dir: *M4 junct 33, take A4232 & follow road to end. Left at 1st rdbt & left again past the Country Hall on right. Take 1st right, hotel on right*
A modern hotel ideal for families and business travellers. Fresh and uncomplicated, the spacious bedrooms include Sky TV, power

continued

shower and tea and coffee-making facilities. Continental buffet breakfast is included in the room rate; other meals may be taken at the nearby family pub or restaurant. For further details and the Express by Holiday Inn phone number, consult the Hotel Groups pages.

ROOMS: 87 en suite s £67; d £67 (incl. cont bkfst)
CONF: Thtr 35 Class 20 Board 20 Del £92.50

⇧ Hotel Ibis Cardiff

Churchill Way CF10 2HA
☎ 029 2064 9260 🖹 029 2920 9260
e-mail: H2936@accor-hotels.com
Modern, budget hotel offering comfortable accommodation in bright and practical bedrooms. Breakfast is self-service and dinner is available in the restaurant. For further details, consult the Hotel Groups page.
ROOMS: 102 en suite s £43.95; d £43.95

⇧ Hotel Ibis Cardiff Gate

Malthouse Av, Cardiff Gate Business Park, Pontprennau CF23 8RA
☎ 029 2073 3222 🖹 029 2073 4222
e-mail: H3159@accor-hotels.com
Dir: *M4 junct 30, take slip rd signed Cardiff Service Station. Hotel on left.*
Modern, budget hotel offering comfortable accommodation in bright and practical bedrooms. Breakfast is self-service and dinner is available in the restaurant. For further details, consult the Hotel Groups page.
ROOMS: 78 en suite s £39.95-£41.95; d £39.95-£41.95

⇧ Innkeeper's Lodge Cardiff

Tyn-y-Parc Rd, Whitchurch CF14 6BG
☎ 029 2069 2554 🖹 029 2052 7052
Dir: *M4 junct 32, southbound on A470. At 3rd set of lights turn left , hotel opposite Safeway supermarket*
A new concept in the travel accommodation market. Smart rooms meet essential business requirements but also have home comforts. Dining options include all-day menus plus the added advantage of breakfast, which is included in the room price. For further details, consult the Hotel Groups page.
ROOMS: 52 en suite **CONF:** Thtr 40 Class 40 Board 20

⇧ Travel Inn (Cardiff Bay)

Keen Rd CF24 5JT
☎ 08701 977050 🖹 029 2049 0403
Dir: *Cardiff Docks & Bay signs from A48(M), over flyover & next 4 rdbts. At 5th rdbt, take 3rd exit. Travel Inn 1st right & 1st right again*
Travel Inn offers good-quality, value-for-money accommodation. Spacious, en suite rooms with bath and shower comfortably accommodate a family of up to two adults and two children (to age 15). The restaurant and bar offers a varied menu. For further details and the Travel Inn phone number, consult the Hotel Groups page.
ROOMS: 73 en suite s £44.95; d £44.95 **CONF:** Thtr 15

⇧ Travel Inn (Cardiff North East)

David Lloyd Club, Ipswich Rd, Roath CF23 7AQ
☎ 08701 977049 🖹 029 2046 2482
Dir: *M4 junct 29/A48(M). Leave at Cardiff East stay in left lane. Follow city centre signs. 1st lights turn right, take right after Sainsbury's into Ipswich Rd*
Travel Inn offers good-quality, value-for-money accommodation. Spacious, en suite rooms with bath and shower comfortably accommodate a family of up to two adults and two children (to age 15). The restaurant and bar offers a varied menu. For further details and the Travel Inn phone number, consult the Hotel Groups page.
ROOMS: 70 en suite s £44.95; d £44.95 **CONF:** Thtr 300

⇧ Travel Inn (Cardiff West)

The Walston Castle, Port Road, Nantisaf, Wenvoe CF5 6DD
☎ 08701 977052 🖹 029 2059 1436
Dir: *From M4 (J33) south on A4232. Take 1st exit (signed Airport), take 3rd exit at Culverhouse Cross rdbt for Travel Inn 0.5m on Barry Rd (A4050)*
Travel Inn offers good-quality, value-for-money accommodation. Spacious, en suite rooms with bath and shower comfortably accommodate a family of up to two adults and two children (to age 15). The restaurant and bar offers a varied menu. For further details and the Travel Inn phone number, consult the Hotel Groups page.
ROOMS: 39 en suite s £44.95; d £44.95 **CONF:** Thtr 12

⇧ Travelodge (Cardiff Central)

Imperial Gate, Saint Marys St CF10 1FA
☎ 08700 850 950

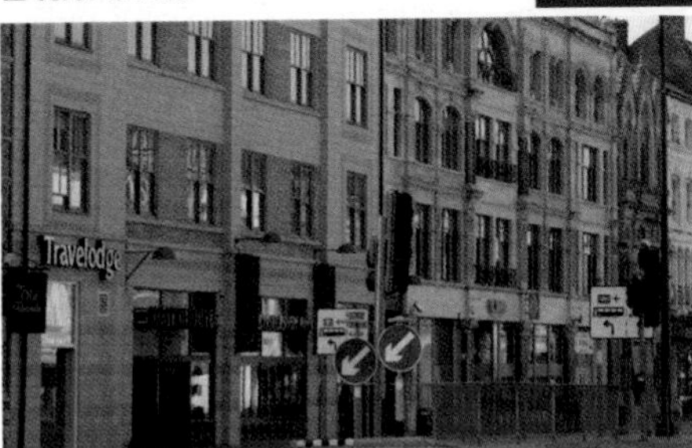

Travelodge offers good quality, good value, modern accommodation. Ideal for families, the spacious, en suite bedrooms include remote-control TV, tea and coffee-making facilities, luxury beds and free morning newspaper. Meals can be taken at the nearby family restaurant. For further details and the Travelodge phone number, consult the Hotel Groups page.
ROOMS: 100 en suite s fr £42.95; d fr £42.95

⇧ Travelodge (Cardiff East)

Circle Way East, Llanedeyrn CF23 9PD
☎ 08700 850 950 🖹 029 2054 9564
Dir: *M4 junct 30, take A4232 to North Pentwyn junct. A48 & signs for Cardiff East & Docks. 3rd exit at Llanedeyrn junct, follow Circle Way East*
Travelodge offers good quality, good value, modern accommodation. Ideal for families, the spacious, en suite bedrooms include remote-control TV, tea and coffee-making facilities, luxury beds and free morning newspaper. Meals can be taken at the nearby family restaurant. For further details and the Travelodge phone number, consult the Hotel Groups page.
ROOMS: 32 en suite s fr £42.95; d fr £42.95

CARDIFF, continued

Travelodge (Cardiff West)
Granada Service Area M4, Pontyclun CF72 8SA
☎ 08700 850 950 029 2089 2497
Dir: *M4, junct 33/A4232*
Travelodge offers good quality, good value, modern accommodation. Ideal for families, the spacious, en suite bedrooms include remote-control TV, tea and coffee-making facilities, luxury beds and free morning newspaper. Meals can be taken at the nearby family restaurant. For further details and the Travelodge phone number, consult the Hotel Groups page.
ROOMS: 50 en suite s fr £42.95; d fr £42.95 **CONF:** Thtr 45 Board 34

CARDIGAN See Gwbert-on-Sea

CARMARTHEN, Carmarthenshire Map 08 SN42

★★70% *Falcon*
Lammas St SA31 3AP
☎ 01267 234959 & 237152 01267 221277
e-mail: reception@falconcarmarthen.co.uk
Dir: *in town centre pass bus station turn left, hotel 200yds on left*

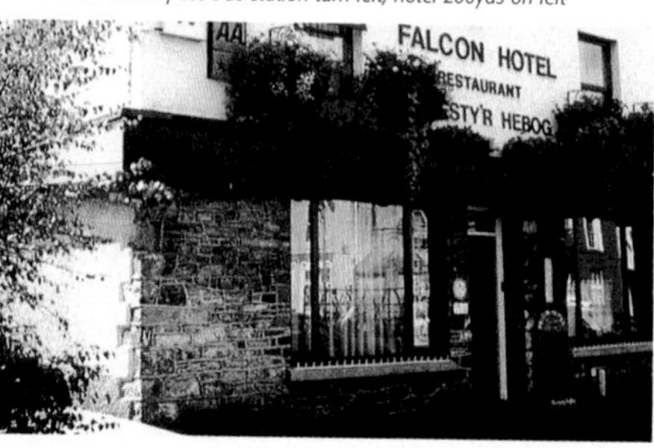

This friendly hotel has been owned by the Exton family for 45 years. Personally run, it is well placed in the centre of the town. Bedrooms, some with four-poster beds, are tastefully decorated with good facilities. There is an comfortable lounge with adjacent bar and the restaurant, open for lunch and dinner, has a varied selection of dishes on the carte menu.
ROOMS: 14 en suite (1 fmly) **CONF:** Thtr 80 Class 50 Board 40 **PARKING:** 38 **NOTES:** Closed 25-26 Dec RS Sun
CARDS:

Restaurant with Rooms

Four Seasons Restaurant with Rooms
Cwmtwrch Farm, Nantgaredig SA32 7NY
☎ 01267 290238 01267 290808
e-mail: bill@btconnect.com
Dir: *from A40 5m E of Carmarthen, take B4310 towards Brechfa at crossroads in Nantgaredig, 0.25m on right*
Peacefully located amidst grounds that include a self-contained leisure complex, this owner-managed hotel has been sympathetically renovated from a fine old farmhouse and associated buildings. Warm hospitality and imaginative food feature in the award-winning Four Seasons Restaurant.
ROOMS: 6 en suite (2 fmly) s fr £50; d fr £75 (incl. bkfst) **FACILITIES:** Indoor swimming (H) Gym Jacuzzi Steam room Swimming pool supervised ch fac **PARKING:** 20 **NOTES:** No smoking in restaurant Closed 23-28 Dec **CARDS:**

TV dinner?
Room service at three stars and above

CASTLETON, Newport Map 09 ST28

Travel Inn (Cardiff East)
Newport Rd CF3 2UQ
☎ 08701 977051 01633 681143
Dir: *M4 junct 8, at rdbt take 2nd exit A48 Castleton and follow for 3m, Travel Inn on right*
Travel Inn offers good-quality, value-for-money accommodation. Spacious, en suite rooms with bath and shower comfortably accommodate a family of up to two adults and two children (to age 15). The restaurant and bar offers a varied menu. For further details and the Travel Inn phone number, consult the Hotel Groups page.
ROOMS: 49 en suite s £44.95; d £44.95

CHEPSTOW, Monmouthshire Map 04 ST59

★★★★71% Marriott St Pierre Hotel & Country Club
St Pierre Park NP16 6YA
☎ 01291 625261 01291 629975
Dir: *M48 junct 2. At rdbt on slip road take A466 Chepstow. At next rdbt take 1st exit Caerwent A48. Hotel approx 2m on left*
This 14th-century hotel offers an extensive range of leisure and conference facilities. Bedrooms are comfortable and are located in adjacent wings or in a lakeside cottage complex. The main bar, popular with golfers, overlooks the 18th green, and diners can choose between a traditional elegant restaurant and modern brasserie.
ROOMS: 148 en suite No smoking in 74 bedrooms s £108-£134; d £130-£156 (incl. bkfst) **LB FACILITIES:** STV Indoor swimming (H) Golf 18 Tennis (hard) Fishing Sauna Solarium Gym Croquet lawn Putting green Jacuzzi Health spa, Floodlit driving range, Chipping green, Short game area Xmas **CONF:** BC Thtr 240 Class 120 Board 90 Del from £145 **PARKING:** 430 **NOTES:** No dogs (ex guide dogs) No smoking in restaurant Civ Wed 200
CARDS:

★★★66% Chepstow
Newport Rd NP16 5PR
☎ 01291 626261 01291 626263
e-mail: info@chepstowhotel.com
Dir: *M48 junct 2, follow signs to Chepstow, A466 & A48 into town, hotel on left*
This privately owned hotel is conveniently situated on the main road into town with easy access for the M4 and M48. Bedrooms vary in size and style, but all have modern equipment and facilities. The majority have been refurbished, as have the pleasant and attractively appointed public areas. Facilities here include an air-conditioned conference room and a large ballroom.
ROOMS: 31 en suite (4 fmly) No smoking in 6 bedrooms s £50-£60; d £60 **LB FACILITIES:** Xmas **CONF:** Thtr 200 Class 70 Board 50 Del from £92.50 **SERVICES:** Lift **PARKING:** 180 **NOTES:** No smoking in restaurant **CARDS:**

See advert on opposite page

★★66% *Beaufort*
Beaufort Square NP6 5EP
☎ 01291 622497 01291 627389
e-mail: info@thebeauforthotel.co.uk
Dir: *off A48, at St Mary's church turn left, left again at end of public car park (Nelson St). Hotel car park 100yds on right*
Privately owned and personally run, this 16th-century coaching inn is centrally located in town. The bedrooms vary in style and size and include two rooms on ground floor level with direct access to the car park. The inviting and popular public areas have plenty of charm and character. They include a friendly bar and a pleasant

continued

restaurant where well-prepared meals are served. There is also a large meeting and function room available.
ROOMS: 22 en suite (2 fmly) **FACILITIES:** STV **CONF:** Thtr 140 Class 70 Board 40 **PARKING:** 14 **CARDS:**

★★66% ***Castle View***
16 Bridge St NP6 5EZ
☎ 01291 620349 📠 01291 627397
e-mail: dave@castview.demon.co.uk
Dir: *M48 junct 2 for Wye Valley on A466, at 1st rdbt turn right onto A48 towards Gloucester. Follow 2nd sign to town centre & Chepstow Castle, hotel directly opposite*
This privately owned inn is situated opposite the Norman castle. Bedrooms vary in size, and all are similarly furnished and well equipped. Several family bedded rooms are available and some rooms are situated in separate buildings. Public areas include a comfortable lounge, a pleasant lounge bar and a cosy restaurant offering freshly prepared cuisine.
ROOMS: 9 en suite 4 annexe en suite (7 fmly) **FACILITIES:** STV
CARDS:

See advert on this page

CHIRK, Wrexham Map 15 SJ23

★★★66% **Moreton Park Lodge**
Moreton Park, Gledrid LL14 5DG
☎ 01691 776666 📠 01691 776655
e-mail: reservations@moretonpark.com
Dir: *200yds from A5 and B5070 rdbt*
This privately-owned and purpose-built modern hotel is on the outskirts of Chirk. It offers well-equipped accommodation, which includes bedrooms suitable for guests with disabilities, and some with separate lounge areas. Meals are available in the Lord Moreton pub/restaurant, and there is an indoor play area for children.
ROOMS: 46 en suite (20 fmly) No smoking in 26 bedrooms s £40-£70; d £40-£70 **LB FACILITIES:** STV Xmas **PARKING:** 400 **NOTES:** No dogs (ex guide dogs) **CARDS:**

See advert under OSWESTRY

COLWYN BAY, Conwy Map 14 SH87

★★★66% ***Hopeside***
63-67 Prince's Dr, West End LL29 8PW
☎ 01492 533244 📠 01492 532850
e-mail: hopesidejd@aol.com
Dir: *off A55 at Rhos-on-Sea exit, turn left at lights, hotel 50yds on right*
The promenade and town centre are within easy walking distance of this friendly hotel. The restaurant offers a good choice, and bar food and blackboard specials are also available. The bedrooms are mostly pine-furnished and all are attractively decorated. The hotel also holds a licence for civil marriage ceremonies.
ROOMS: 18 en suite (2 fmly) No smoking in 9 bedrooms
FACILITIES: STV Sauna Gym **CONF:** Thtr 50 Class 50 Board 34
PARKING: 14 **NOTES:** No smoking in restaurant **CARDS:**

★★★65% ***Norfolk House***
39 Princes Dr LL29 8PF
☎ 01492 531757 📠 01492 533781
e-mail: bookings@norfolkhousehotel.fsnet.co.uk
Dir: *A55 at Colwyn Bay, into right lane of slip rd, right at lights, pass station, hotel almost opp filling station*
Norfolk House is a privately owned and personally run hotel with a warm, friendly atmosphere. It is within easy walking distance of the seafront, town centre and railway station. The accommodation is well-equipped, comfortable and relaxing. Bedrooms are prettily

continued on p826

COLWYN BAY, continued

decorated with family suites available. There are several lounges, a popular bar and conference facilities.
ROOMS: 21 en suite (4 fmly) No smoking in 2 bedrooms
FACILITIES: STV **CONF:** Thtr 35 Class 30 Board 20 **SERVICES:** Lift
PARKING: 30 **NOTES:** No smoking in restaurant Closed 3 wks Xmas
CARDS:

★★64% Lyndale

410 Abergele Rd, Old Colwyn LL29 9AB
☎ 01492 515429 📠 01492 518805
e-mail: lyndale@tinyworld.co.uk
Dir: *exit at A55 junct 22 Old Colwyn, turn left. 1m on A547*

THE INDEPENDENTS

A range of accommodation is available at this friendly, family-run hotel, including suites that are suitable for family use and a four-poster bedroom. There is a cosy bar and a comfortable foyer lounge, and weddings and other functions can be catered for.
ROOMS: 14 en suite (3 fmly) No smoking in 3 bedrooms s £25-£39; d £45-£59 (incl. bkfst) **LB** **CONF:** Thtr 40 Class 20 Board 20
PARKING: 20 **CARDS:**

★★64% Marine

West Promenade LL28 4BP
☎ 01492 530295 📠 0870 168 9400
e-mail: reservations@marinehotel.co.uk
Dir: *exit A55 junct 22 Old Colwyn to seafront. Turn left, after pier left before lights, car park on corner*

This privately owned and personally run hotel stands on the promenade, overlooking the sea. The accommodation is soundly maintained and equipped to suit both commercial visitors and holidaymakers. Facilities include a small bar and a lounge.
ROOMS: 14 rms (12 en suite) (4 fmly) No smoking in 9 bedrooms s £25-£30; d £50-£52 (incl. bkfst) **LB** **PARKING:** 11 **NOTES:** No smoking in restaurant Closed mid Oct-Apr
CARDS:

CONWY, Conwy

Map 14 SH77

★★★73% Groes Inn

Tyn-y-Groes LL32 8TN
☎ 01492 650545 📠 01492 650855
Dir: *from A55, cross Old Conwy Bridge, 1st left through Castle Walls on B5106 (Trefriw road), hotel 2m on right.*

This inn dates back in part to the 16th century and has charming features. It offers a choice of bars and has a beautifully appointed restaurant, with a conservatory extension opening onto the lovely rear garden. The comfortable, well-equipped bedrooms are contained in a separate building; some have balconies or terraces.
ROOMS: 14 en suite (1 fmly) (4 GF) No smoking in 6 bedrooms s £75-£110; d £90-£135 (incl. bkfst) **LB** **CONF:** Thtr 22 Class 20 Board 20 **PARKING:** 100 **NOTES:** No smoking in restaurant Closed Xmas
CARDS:

★★★66% Castle Hotel Conwy

High St LL32 8DB
☎ 01492 582800 📠 01492 582300
e-mail: mail@castlewales.co.uk
Dir: *A55 junct 18, cross estuary. Right then left at mini rdbts onto one way system. Right at Town Wall Gate, right onto Berry St then High St on left*

This personally-run 16th-century hotel is one of Conwy's most distinguished buildings and offers a hospitable atmosphere. Bedrooms have modern facilities, and fresh flowers and paintings by a local artist feature in the traditional public rooms. A good selection of enjoyable dishes is available in the award-winning restaurant and the popular bar also serves meals.
ROOMS: 29 en suite (2 fmly) No smoking in 14 bedrooms s £60-£70; d £75-£95 (incl. bkfst) **LB** **FACILITIES:** Xmas **CONF:** Thtr 30 Class 20 Board 20 Del from £89 **PARKING:** 34 **NOTES:** No smoking in restaurant
CARDS:

See advert on opposite page

Top 200 - Hotel

★★ The Old Rectory Country House

Llanrwst Rd, Llansanffraid Glan Conwy LL28 5LF
☎ 01492 580611 📠 01492 584555
e-mail: info@oldrectorycountryhouse.co.uk
Dir: *0.5m S from A470/A55 junct on left by 30mph sign*

This friendly and welcoming hotel enjoys elevated views of the Conwy estuary and Snowdonia. Traditionally styled day rooms ooze luxury and elegance and home-baked afternoon teas can be taken in the elegant lounge. Dinner is the highlight of any stay and the daily changing, set menu makes excellent use of fresh, local, seasonal produce. Bedrooms make the most of the views and are furnished with thought and care. Super hospitality sustains a real 'home-from-home' ambience.
ROOMS: 4 en suite 2 annexe en suite No smoking in all bedrooms s £99-£139; d £129-£169 (incl. bkfst) **LB** **PARKING:** 10
NOTES: No children 5yrs No smoking in restaurant Closed Dec-Jan
CARDS:

★★71% Lodge
LL32 8YX
☎ 01492 660766 📠 01492 660534
e-mail: bbaldon@lodgehotel.co.uk
(For full entry see Tal-y-Bont)

★★69% Tir-y-Coed Country House
Rowen LL32 8TP
☎ 01492 650219 📠 01492 650219
e-mail: info@tirycoedhotel.co.uk
Dir: *off B5106 onto unclassified road signed Rowen, hotel 60mtrs N of Post Office*

This small hotel is a haven of peace and relaxation. Standing in its own extensive and delightful garden, the house is located in the picturesque Conwy Valley. It is convenient for access to Snowdonia and the coast. The accommodation is well maintained and equipped, and the hospitality warm and friendly.
ROOMS: 7 en suite 1 annexe en suite (1 fmly) s £30-£34; d £56-£63 (incl. bkfst) **LB** **FACILITIES:** ch fac **PARKING:** 8 **NOTES:** No smoking in restaurant Closed Xmas & New Year RS Nov-Feb **CARDS:**

CRICCIETH, Gwynedd

Map 14 SH43

★★★75% Bron Eifion Country House
LL52 0SA
☎ 01766 522385 📠 01766 522003
e-mail: stay@broneifion.co.uk
Dir: *0.5m outside Criccieth on A497 towards Pwllheli*

This delightful country house is set in extensive grounds to the west of Criccieth. Most of the tasteful bedrooms have period and antique furniture, and some have four-poster beds or attractive canopies. The central hall features a minstrels' gallery, and there is a choice of comfortable lounges.
ROOMS: 19 en suite (1 fmly) (1 GF) No smoking in 4 bedrooms s £67-£92; d £104-£141 (incl. bkfst) **LB** **CONF:** Thtr 30 Class 25 Board 25 **PARKING:** 80 **NOTES:** No smoking in restaurant
CARDS:

★★70% *Caerwylan*
LL52 0HW
☎ 01766 522547
Dir: *Hotel near lifeboat station*
Privately owned and personally run, this long established holiday hotel commands panoramic sea views of Cardigan Bay and the castle. Comfortably furnished lounges are available for residents and the five-course menu changes daily. Bedrooms, including family rooms, are smart and modern, and several have their own private sitting areas. The friendly atmosphere ensures that many guests return year after year.
ROOMS: 25 en suite (3 fmly) **SERVICES:** Lift **PARKING:** 9 **NOTES:** No smoking in restaurant Closed Nov-Etr **CARDS:**

★★67% Gwyndy
Llanystumdwy LL52 0SP
☎ 01766 522720 📠 01766 522720
e-mail: gwyndy@lineone.net
Dir: *A497 into Llanystumdwy follow road for 0.25m, hotel by church*
This a popular hotel comprises a 17th-century cottage and a nearby purpose-built bedroom complex. The original cottage contains the lounge, bar and restaurant, which are all comfortably furnished. Exposed timbers and several stone fireplaces are lovely features and bedrooms are spacious and relaxing.
ROOMS: 10 annexe en suite (5 fmly) (6 GF) s £25-£30; d £50 (incl. bkfst) **FACILITIES:** Fishing Xmas **PARKING:** 20 **NOTES:** No smoking in restaurant Closed Nov-Mar **CARDS:**

CRICCIETH, continued

★★66% Lion
Y Maes LL52 0AA
☎ 01766 522460 01766 523075
e-mail: info@lionhotelcriccieth.co.uk
Dir: *A497 centre of Criccieth, hotel on green*
This hotel lies just a short walk from Criccieth castle and seafront, with fine views from many rooms. The bars enjoy a good local following and staff are friendly and welcoming. Bedrooms are well decorated and furnished, divided between the main building and a nearby annexe. Regular live entertainment is provided during the summer.
ROOMS: 34 en suite 12 annexe en suite (8 fmly) s £35-£39; d £59-£66 (incl. bkfst) **LB** **FACILITIES:** STV entertainment Xmas **SERVICES:** Lift **PARKING:** 30 **NOTES:** No smoking in restaurant
CARDS:

CRICKHOWELL, Powys Map 09 SO21

★★★71% Gliffaes Country House Hotel
NP8 1RH
☎ 01874 730371 & 0800 146719 (Freephone) 01874 730463
e-mail: calls@gliffaeshotel.com
Dir: *2.5m W of Crickhowell, 1m off A40*
This impressive Victorian mansion, standing in 33 acres of its own gardens and wooded grounds by the River Usk, is a privately-owned and personally-run hotel. Public rooms retain elegance and generous proportions and include a balcony and conservatory from which to enjoy the views. Bedrooms are furnished to a high standard and offer high levels of comfort.
ROOMS: 19 en suite 3 annexe en suite (3 fmly) No smoking in all bedrooms s £62-£165; d £72-£180 (incl. bkfst) **LB** **FACILITIES:** Tennis (hard) Fishing Snooker Croquet lawn Putting green Cycling, Birdwatching, Walking, Fishing, Falconry ch fac **CONF:** Thtr 40 Class 16 Board 16 Del from £140 **PARKING:** 34 **NOTES:** No dogs (ex guide dogs) No smoking in restaurant Civ Wed 30
CARDS:

★★★70% Bear
NP8 1BW
☎ 01873 810408 01873 811696
e-mail: bearhotel@aol.com
Dir: *on A40 between Abergavenny and Brecon*
A favourite with locals as well as visitors, the character and friendliness of this 15th-century coaching inn are renowned. The bar and restaurant areas are furnished in keeping with the building and provide a comfortable area in which to enjoy some of the finest locally sourced ingredients.
ROOMS: 13 en suite 13 annexe en suite (6 fmly) **CONF:** Thtr 60 Class 30 Board 20 **PARKING:** 38 **CARDS:**
See advert on opposite page

Popped the question?
Hotels with Civ Wed in their entry are licensed for civil wedding ceremonies. Maximum numbers for the ceremony only are shown, e.g. Civ Wed 120

★★★68% Manor
Brecon Rd NP8 1SE
☎ 01873 810212 01873 811938
e-mail: info@manorhotel.co.uk
Dir: *on A40, Crickhowell/Brecon, 0.5m from Crickhowell*
This impressive manor house set in a stunning location was the birthplace of Sir George Everest. The bedrooms and public areas are elegant, and there are extensive leisure facilities. The restaurant has panoramic views and is the setting for exciting modern cooking. Guests can also dine informally at the nearby Nantyffin Cider Mill, a sister operation of this hotel.

ROOMS: 22 en suite (1 fmly) No smoking in 8 bedrooms **FACILITIES:** STV Indoor swimming (H) Sauna Solarium Gym Jacuzzi Fitness assessment Sunbed **CONF:** Thtr 400 Class 300 Board 300 **PARKING:** 200 **NOTES:** Civ Wed 180
CARDS:
See advert on opposite page

★★74% Ty Croeso
The Dardy, Llangattock NP8 1PU
THE INDEPENDENTS
☎ 01873 810573 01873 810573
e-mail: tycroeso@ty-croeso-hotel.freeserve.co.uk
Dir: *from A40 at Shell garage take road opposite, down hill over river bridge. Turn right, after 0.5m turn left, up hill over canal, hotel signed*
Ty Croeso, meaning 'House of Welcome', lives up to its name. The restaurant has an interesting carte and set-price menu. Glamorgan Sausages and laverbread are available at breakfast. Public areas are comfortable and feature log fires. Bedrooms are decorated with pretty fabrics and all have good facilities.
ROOMS: 8 en suite (1 fmly) s £35-£45; d £60-£75 (incl. bkfst) **LB** **PARKING:** 20 **NOTES:** No smoking in restaurant RS 24-26 Dec
CARDS:

CROSS HANDS, Carmarthenshire Map 08 SN51

Travelodge Llanelli
Travelodge
SA14 6NW
☎ 08700 850 950 01269 845700
Dir: *on A48, westbound*
Travelodge offers good quality, good value, modern accommodation. Ideal for families, the spacious, en suite bedrooms include remote-control TV, tea and coffee-making facilities, luxury beds and free morning newspaper. Meals can be taken at the nearby family restaurant. For further details and the Travelodge phone number, consult the Hotel Groups page.
ROOMS: 32 en suite s fr £42.95; d fr £42.95

CWMBRAN, Torfaen Map 09 ST29

★★★★65% Parkway
Best Western
Cwmbran Dr NP44 3UW
☎ 01633 871199 01633 869160
e-mail: enquiries@parkwayhotel.co.uk
Dir: *M4 junct 25A/26/A4051 follow signs Cwmbran-Llantarnam Park. Turn right at rdbt then right for hotel*
This hotel is purpose built and offers comfortable bedrooms and public areas for a wide range of guests. There is a sports centre and a range of conference and meeting facilities. The coffee shop
continued

offers an informal eating option during the day and there is fine dining in Ravello's Restaurant.
ROOMS: 70 en suite (4 fmly) (34 GF) No smoking in 24 bedrooms s £70-£104; d £90-£116 (incl. bkfst) **LB** **FACILITIES:** STV Indoor swimming (H) Sauna Solarium Gym Jacuzzi Steam room, Private sun bathing terrace, Sports shop entertainment Xmas **CONF:** Thtr 500 Class 240 Board 100 Del £121 **PARKING:** 300 **NOTES:** Civ Wed 90
CARDS:

DEVIL'S BRIDGE, Ceredigion

Map 09 SN77

★★66% *Hafod Arms*

SY23 3JL
☎ 01970 890232 🖷 01970 890394
e-mail: enquiries@hafodarms.co.uk
Dir: *Leave A44 at Ponterwyd. Hotel 5m along A4120, 11m E of Aberystwyth*

This former hunting lodge, in six acres of grounds, dates back to the 17th century and is now a family owned and run hotel providing accommodation suitable for both business people and tourists. Family rooms and a four-poster room are available, plus a lounge and dining area.
ROOMS: 15 rms (11 en suite) (1 fmly) **CONF:** Board 25 **PARKING:** 70 **NOTES:** No children 12yrs No smoking in restaurant Closed 15 Dec-Jan
CARDS:

Late for dinner?
Quality Standards mean that last orders for dinner vary according to star rating and should be no earlier than:
★★ 7.00pm ★★★ 8.00pm ★★★★ 9.00pm
★★★★★ 10.00pm

DOLGELLAU, Gwynedd

Map 14 SH71

★★★80% Penmaenuchaf Hall

Penmaenpool LL40 1YB
☎ 01341 422129 01341 422787
e-mail: relax@penhall.co.uk
Dir: *off A470 onto A493 to Tywyn. Hotel approx 1m on left*

Built in 1860, this impressive hall stands in 20 acres of formal gardens, grounds and woodland and enjoys magnificent views across the River Mawddach. Careful restoration by the present owners has created a comfortable and welcoming hotel. Fresh produce cooked in modern British style is served in the panelled restaurant.
ROOMS: 14 en suite (2 fmly) No smoking in 5 bedrooms s £75-£115; d £116-£176 (incl. bkfst) **LB FACILITIES:** Fishing Snooker Croquet lawn Xmas **CONF:** BC Thtr 50 Class 30 Board 22 Del from £139 **PARKING:** 30 **NOTES:** No children 6yrs No smoking in restaurant Civ Wed 50 **CARDS:**

★★★72% Dolserau Hall

LL40 2AG
☎ 01341 422522 01341 422400
e-mail: aa@dhh.co.uk
Dir: *1.5m from town between A494 to Bala & A470 to Dinas Mawddwy*

This privately owned, friendly hotel lies in attractive grounds extending to the river, and is surrounded by green fields. Several comfortable lounges are provided and welcoming log fires are lit during cold weather. The smart bedrooms are well equipped and comfortable. A varied menu offers very competently prepared dishes.
ROOMS: 15 en suite (3 fmly) s £40-£65; d £80-£130 (incl. bkfst & dinner) **LB FACILITIES:** STV Xmas **SERVICES:** Lift **PARKING:** 40 **NOTES:** No children 6yrs No smoking in restaurant Closed mid Nov-Jan (ex Xmas & New Year) **CARDS:**

See advert on opposite page

★★★72% Plas Dolmelynllyn

Ganllwyd LL40 2HP
☎ 01341 440273 01341 440640
e-mail: info@dolly-hotel.co.uk
Dir: *5m N of Dolgellau on A470*
Surrounded by three acres of gardens and National Trust land, this fine house dates back to the 16th century. Spacious bedrooms are attractive and offer many thoughtful extras. Dinner is served in the comfortable dining room, adjacent to the conservatory bar.
ROOMS: 10 en suite No smoking in all bedrooms s £55-£60; d £88-£98 (incl. bkfst) **LB FACILITIES:** STV Fishing Mountain walking Mountain Bike riding **CONF:** Thtr 20 Class 20 Board 20 **PARKING:** 20 **NOTES:** No smoking in restaurant Closed Dec-Feb **CARDS:**

★★72% *George III Hotel*

Penmaenpool LL40 1YD
☎ 01341 422525 01341 423565
e-mail: reception@george-3rd.co.uk
Dir: *2m from Dolgellau on A493*

On the banks of the Mawddach Estuary, this delightful small hotel started life as an inn and chandlers to the local boatyard. A nearby building, now housing several bedrooms, was the local railway station. Bedrooms are well equipped and many enjoy river views. There is a choice of bars and a formal restaurant, all providing a wide range of food.
ROOMS: 6 en suite 5 annexe en suite **FACILITIES:** Fishing **CONF:** Class 32 **PARKING:** 30 **NOTES:** No smoking in restaurant Closed Christmas Day **CARDS:**

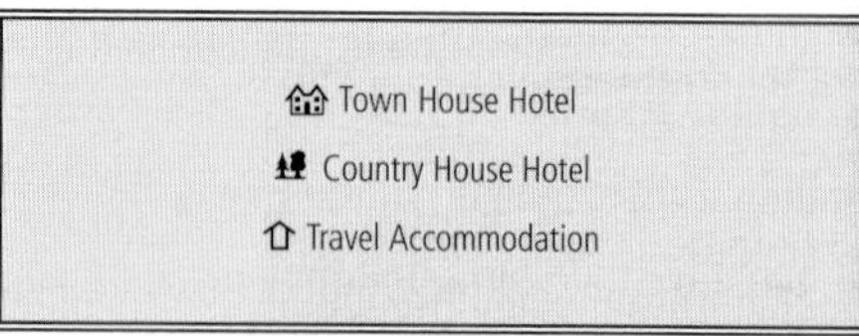

Town House Hotel
Country House Hotel
Travel Accommodation

★★67% *Fronoleu Country Hotel*

Tabor LL40 2PS
☎ 01341 422361 & 422197 01341 422023
e-mail: fronleu@fronleu0.fsnet.co.uk
Dir: *A487/A470 junct, towards Tabor opposite Cross Foxes & continue for 1.25m. From Dolgellau take road for hospital & continue 1.25m up the hill*
This 16th-century farmhouse lies in the shadow of Cader Idris. Carefully extended, it retains many original features. The bar and lounge are located in the old building where there are exposed

continued

timbers and open fires. Most of the bedrooms are in a modern extension. The restaurant attracts a large local following.

ROOMS: 11 en suite (3 fmly) No smoking in 6 bedrooms **FACILITIES:** Fishing entertainment ch fac **CONF:** Thtr 150 Class 80 Board 80 **PARKING:** 60 **NOTES:** No smoking in restaurant **CARDS:**

★★67% Royal Ship

Queens Square LL40 1AR
☎ 01341 422209 📠 01341 421027
Dir: *in town centre*
The Royal Ship dates from 1813 when it was a coaching inn. There are three bars and several lounges, all most comfortably furnished and appointed. It is very much the centre of local activities and a wide range of food is available. Bedrooms are tastefully decorated.
ROOMS: 24 en suite (4 fmly) s £45-£48; d £68-£85 (incl. bkfst) **LB** **FACILITIES:** Fishing arrangements available Xmas **CONF:** Thtr 80 Class 60 Board 60 **PARKING:** 12 **NOTES:** No dogs (ex guide dogs) No smoking in restaurant **CARDS:**

See advert on this page

DOLWYDDELAN, Conwy — Map 14 SH75

★★64% Elen's Castle

LL25 0EJ
☎ 01690 750207 📠 01690 750207
e-mail: info@elenscastlehotel.co.uk
Dir: *on A470, 5m S of Betws-y-Coed*
This small hotel is very friendly and was operated as a beer house in the 18th century. The original bar, complete with a slab floor and potbelly stove, remains, and there are two cosy sitting rooms with open fires and exposed timbers. Two of the bedrooms have four-poster beds and families can be accommodated. A good range of bar and restaurant food is provided.
ROOMS: 9 rms (8 en suite) (2 fmly) No smoking in 2 bedrooms s £30-£40; d £50-£60 (incl. bkfst) **LB** **FACILITIES:** Coarse & fly fishing ch fac Xmas **CONF:** Thtr 30 Class 20 Board 15 **PARKING:** 40 **NOTES:** No smoking in restaurant **CARDS:**

EGLWYSFACH, Ceredigion

Map 14 SN69

Top 200 - Hotel

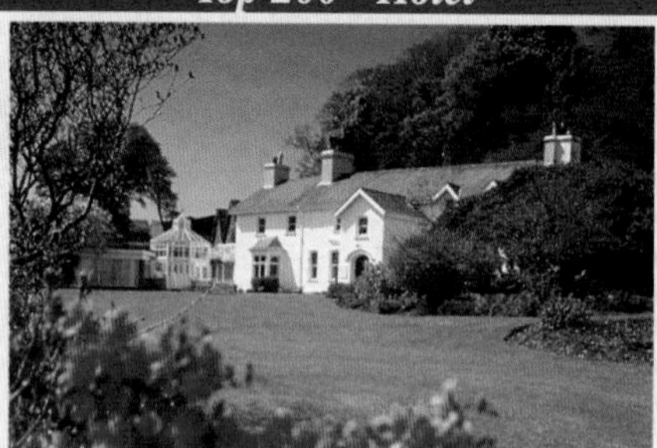

★★★ ◎◎◎ **Ynyshir Hall**
SY20 8TA
☎ 01654 781209 📠 01654 781366
e-mail: info@ynyshir-hall.co.uk
Dir: *off A487, 5.5m S of Machynlleth, signposted from the main road*

RELAIS & CHATEAUX

Ynyshir Hall dates back to the 16th century and was once a retreat for Queen Victoria. Lavishly styled bedrooms offer real luxury and deep comfort whilst refurbished marble bathrooms have stylish facilities. Day rooms also balance the classical with the modern and deep sofas and roaring fires welcome guests in the cooler months. Hospitality is attentive and staff are keen to please. Expertly crafted dinners are served in the stylish dining room that also doubles as an art gallery.

ROOMS: 7 en suite 2 annexe en suite No smoking in all bedrooms s £95-£180; d £160-£315 (incl. bkfst) **LB** **FACILITIES:** Croquet lawn Xmas **CONF:** Thtr 25 Class 20 Board 18 Del from £190 **PARKING:** 20 **NOTES:** No children 9yrs No smoking in restaurant Closed 5-23 Jan Civ Wed 40 **CARDS:**

EWLOE, Flintshire

Map 15 SJ36

★★★★70% **De Vere St David's Park**
St Davids Park CH5 3YB
☎ 01244 520800 📠 01244 520930
e-mail: reservations.stdavids@devere-hotels.com
Dir: *A494 Queensferry to Mold for 4m, then left slip road B5127 signed Buckley, hotel can be seen at rdbt*

DE VERE HOTELS

This modern hotel is conveniently situated and offers a range of room types including four-poster suites and family rooms. Public areas include leisure and spa facilities, an all-day café, and,

continued

nearby, the hotel's own golf course. Younger guests are not forgotten either and can have fun in the Dai the Dove Club.

ROOMS: 145 en suite (27 fmly) (43 GF) No smoking in 54 bedrooms **FACILITIES:** STV Indoor swimming (H) Golf 18 Tennis (hard) Snooker Sauna Solarium Gym Putting green Jacuzzi Steam bath, Beauty Therapist, Playroom, Swimming pool supervised ch fac **CONF:** BC Thtr 300 Class 150 Board 40 Del from £100 **SERVICES:** Lift **PARKING:** 240 **NOTES:** No smoking in restaurant Civ Wed 100
CARDS:

FISHGUARD, Pembrokeshire

Map 08 SM93

★★69% **Cartref**
15-19 High St SA65 9AW
☎ 01348 872430 📠 01348 873664
e-mail: cartref@themail.co.uk
Dir: *on A40 in town centre*

Personally run by the proprietor, this friendly hotel offers convenient access to the town centre and ferry terminal. Bedrooms are well maintained and include some family bedded rooms. There is also a cosy lounge bar and a welcoming restaurant which looks out over the High Street.

ROOMS: 10 en suite (2 fmly) s £30-£38; d £52-£57 (incl. bkfst) **LB** **PARKING:** 4 **NOTES:** No smoking in restaurant
CARDS:

FLINT, Flintshire

Map 15 SJ27

★★★59% ***Mountain Park Hotel***
Northop Rd, Flint Mountain CH6 5QG
☎ 01352 736000 & 730972 📠 01352 736010
Dir: *Turn off A55 for Flint onto A5119, hotel 1 mile on left*

This former farmhouse has modern, well-equipped bedrooms and is conveniently situated close to the motorway. Facilities include the Sevens Brasserie Restaurant serving modern cuisine; a comfortable lounge bar offering a range of bar meals; and an attractively designed function/conference room. There is also a 9-hole golf course.

ROOMS: 21 annexe en suite (1 fmly) No smoking in 11 bedrooms **FACILITIES:** Golf 9 Jacuzzi ch fac **CONF:** Thtr 80 Class 80 Board 60 **SERVICES:** air con **PARKING:** 94 **NOTES:** No dogs (ex guide dogs) No smoking in restaurant **CARDS:**

GLYN CEIRIOG, Wrexham

Map 15 SJ23

★★★66% **Golden Pheasant**
LL20 7BB
☎ 01691 718281 📠 01691 718479
e-mail: goldenpheasant@micro-plus-web.net
Dir: *A5/B4500 at Chirk, continue for 5m, to Pontfadog & follow signs for hotel, 1st left after Cheshire Home, follow road to top of small hill & hotel*

This 18th-century hostelry is quietly situated in open countryside surrounded by rolling hills. There is a choice of bars, as well as a lounge and a restaurant. To the rear is a courtyard with shrubs and flowerbeds and an aviary with exotic birds. The bedrooms include four-poster and family rooms.

ROOMS: 19 en suite (5 fmly) s £40-£60; d £75-£80 (incl. bkfst) **LB** **FACILITIES:** Xmas **CONF:** Thtr 60 Board 10 **PARKING:** 45 **NOTES:** No smoking in restaurant **CARDS:**

GWBERT-ON-SEA, Ceredigion — Map 08 SN15

★★★67% Cliff
SA43 1PP
☎ 01239 613241 📠 01239 615391
e-mail: cliffhotel@btopenworld.com
Dir: *off A487 into Cardigan, follow signs to Gwbert, in 3m straight to hotel*
Set in 30 acres of grounds and enjoying a cliff-top location overlooking Cardigan Bay, it is not surprising that this hotel offers superb sea views. Bedrooms come in a variety of sizes, some looking over the bay. Public areas are spacious and there is a range of leisure amenities.
ROOMS: 72 en suite (5 fmly) No smoking in 10 bedrooms s £50-£70; d £70-£90 (incl. bkfst) **LB FACILITIES:** STV Outdoor swimming (H) Golf 9 Fishing Snooker Sauna Putting green entertainment Xmas **CONF:** BC Thtr 350 Class 100 Board 70 Del from £85 **SERVICES:** Lift **PARKING:** 95 **NOTES:** No smoking in restaurant Civ Wed 200
CARDS:

See advert on this page

HALKYN, Flintshire — Map 15 SJ27

Travelodge
CH8 8RF
☎ 08700 850 950 📠 01352 780952
Dir: *on A55, westbound*
Travelodge offers good quality, good value, modern accommodation. Ideal for families, the spacious, en suite bedrooms include remote-control TV, tea and coffee-making facilities, luxury beds and free morning newspaper. Meals can be taken at the nearby family restaurant. For further details and the Travelodge phone number, consult the Hotel Groups page.
ROOMS: 31 en suite s fr £42.95; d fr £42.95

HANMER, Wrexham — Map 15 SJ43

★★64% Hanmer
SY13 3DE
☎ 01948 830532 📠 01948 830740
e-mail: enquiry@hanmerhotel.co.uk
Dir: *from Whitchurch bypass (A41/A49) take A525 and after 4m turn left onto A539 Overton/Ruabon road. In 1.5m turn left into village, hotel 1st on right*
A friendly, country-style hotel set close to the town of Whitchurch and an excellent base whether touring or on business. The accommodation includes annexe rooms and is well equipped. There is a comfortable friendly bar and a choice of eating options including a carvery. Conference and wedding facilities are also available.
ROOMS: 3 en suite 22 annexe en suite s £52-£55; d £45-£80 (incl. bkfst) **LB FACILITIES:** STV Gym Use of Crown Green bowling lawn can be arranged Xmas **CONF:** Thtr 60 Class 45 Board 45 Del from £83.25 **PARKING:** 80 **NOTES:** No smoking in restaurant Civ Wed 75
CARDS:

HARLECH, Gwynedd — Map 14 SH53
See also Talsarnau

The Castle
Castle Square LL46 2YH
☎ 01766 780529 📠 01766 780499
Dir: *directly opposite the entrance to Harlech Castle*
ROOMS: 7 en suite (1 fmly) s £20-£30; d £40-£60 **PARKING:** 30 **NOTES:** ★★ No dogs (ex guide dogs) No smoking in restaurant
CARDS:

HAVERFORDWEST, Pembrokeshire

Map 08 SM91

★★68% *Hotel Mariners*

Mariners Square SA61 2DU

THE INDEPENDENTS

☎ 01437 763353 🖷 01437 764258

Dir: *follow town centre signs, over bridge, up High St, 1st turning on right (Dark St) hotel at the end*

Located just out of the town centre, this privately owned and friendly hotel is reputed to date back to 1625. The bedrooms are equipped with modern facilities and are soundly maintained. The popular bar is a focus for the town and offers a good range of food in addition to that available in the more formal restaurant. Facilities here include a choice of meeting rooms.

ROOMS: 28 en suite (5 fmly) No smoking in 11 bedrooms **FACILITIES:** STV Short mat bowls **CONF:** Thtr 50 Class 20 Board 20 **PARKING:** 50 **NOTES:** Closed 25-27 Dec & 1 Jan **CARDS:**

★★67% *Wilton House*

6 Quay St SA61 1BG

☎ 01437 760033 🖷 01437 760297

e-mail: phil@wiltonhousehotel.co.uk

Dir: *M4 junct 49/A48 to Carmarthen & A40 to Haverfordwest. Follow signs into town centre & take 1st left into Quay St. Hotel 50mtrs on left*

Formerly a saddlery, this family owned and run hotel is situated in a quiet side street close to the town centre and the River Cleddau. The well-proportioned bedrooms are tastefully decorated and well equipped, whilst public areas consist of a lounge and a bistro-style restaurant serving home-made food.

ROOMS: 9 en suite (3 fmly) **FACILITIES:** Outdoor swimming (H) Solarium **PARKING:** 6 **NOTES:** No dogs (ex guide dogs) No smoking in restaurant **CARDS:**

★★61% *Castle Hotel*

Castle Square SA61 2AA

☎ 01437 769322 🖷 01437 769253

Dir: *from the main rdbt into Haverfordwest follow town centre signs, follow the road for approx 200yds, hotel on right*

This 19th-century inn is centrally located off the High Street of this bustling town. Bedrooms are tastefully decorated and thoughtfully equipped and the spacious bar, which fronts Castle Square, is popular with locals for its evening entertainment. Relaxed dining is offered in Turrets Restaurant where enjoyable home-cooked meals can be enjoyed.

ROOMS: 9 en suite (1 fmly) **NOTES:** No dogs (ex guide dogs) Closed 24-25 & 31 Dec **CARDS:**

HAY-ON-WYE, Powys

Map 09 SO24

★★★66% The Swan-at-Hay

Church St HR3 5DQ

☎ 01497 821188 🖷 01497 821424

e-mail: info@swanathay.co.uk

Dir: *Hay-on-Wye on B4350 from Brecon, hotel on left. From any other route follow signs for Brecon & just before leaving town hotel on right*

This former coaching inn dates back to the 1800s and is only a short walk from the town centre. Bedrooms are well equipped and some are located in converted cottages across the courtyard. The public areas are spacious and relaxing and include a comfortable lounge, a choice of bars and a more formal restaurant. There is also a large function room and a smaller meeting room.

ROOMS: 15 en suite 4 annexe en suite (1 fmly) s £55-£115; d £80-£125 (incl. bkfst) **LB FACILITIES:** Fishing Xmas **CONF:** Thtr 140 Class 60 Board 50 Del from £95 **PARKING:** 18 **NOTES:** No smoking in restaurant Civ Wed 90 **CARDS:**

★★69% Baskerville Arms

Clyro HR3 5RZ

☎ 01497 820670 🖷 01497 821609

e-mail: arms@baskerville.com

Dir: *from Hereford follow Brecon A438 into Clyro. Hotel signed*

Situated near to Hay-on-Wye in the peaceful village of Clyro, this former Georgian coaching inn is personally run by its friendly and enthusiastic owners. Bedrooms are well equipped with comfort in mind, whilst public areas include a bar with a village inn atmosphere, a separate restaurant and a comfortable residents' lounge. There is also a large function room, plus a meeting room.

ROOMS: 10 en suite (1 fmly) No smoking in 3 bedrooms **FACILITIES:** Fishing Games room **CONF:** Thtr 65 Class 40 Board 36 **PARKING:** 12 **NOTES:** No dogs (ex guide dogs) No smoking in restaurant **CARDS:**

★★69% ® Old Black Lion

26 Lion St HR3 5AD

☎ 01497 820841 🖷 01497 820841

e-mail: info@oldblacklion.co.uk

Dir: *Tourist Information car park turn right along Oxford Rd, pass Nat West bank, next left (Lion St), hotel 20yds on right*

This fine old coaching inn, with a history stretching back several centuries, has a wealth of charm and character. It was occupied by Oliver Cromwell during the siege of Hay Castle. Privately owned and personally run, it provides cosy and well-equipped bedrooms, some of which are located in an adjacent building. A wide range of competently prepared food is provided and service is friendly.

ROOMS: 6 rms (5 en suite) 4 annexe en suite (2 GF) No smoking in all bedrooms s £43-£50; d £80-£110 (incl. bkfst) **LB FACILITIES:** Xmas **PARKING:** 16 **NOTES:** No dogs (ex guide dogs) No children 5yrs No smoking in restaurant **CARDS:**

HENSOL, Vale of Glamorgan

Map 09 ST07

★★★★71% Vale Hotel Golf & Country Club

Hensol Park CF72 8JY

☎ 01443 667800 🖷 01443 665850

e-mail: reservations@vale-hotel.com

Dir: *M4 junct 34, towards Pendoylan, hotel is signed, approx 3 mins drive from junct.*

A wealth of leisure facilities are offered at this large resort, including two golf courses and a driving range, extensive health spa, gym, swimming pool and squash courts. Public areas are spacious and attractive, whilst bedrooms, many of which have balconies, are well appointed. Meeting and conference facilities are also available.

ROOMS: 29 en suite 114 annexe en suite (17 fmly) (36 GF) No smoking in 71 bedrooms s £85-£130; d £130-£140 (incl. bkfst) **LB FACILITIES: Spa** STV Indoor swimming (H) Golf 18 Tennis (hard) Fishing Squash Riding Sauna Solarium Gym Putting green Jacuzzi Beauty treatments, Hydrotherapy treatments, Childrens club ch fac **CONF:** Thtr 300 Class 180 Board 60 Del from £145 **SERVICES:** Lift air con **PARKING:** 300 **NOTES:** No smoking in restaurant Civ Wed 300 **CARDS:**

See advert under CARDIFF

HIRWAUN, Rhondda Cynon Taff

Map 09 SN90

★★★64% *Ty Newydd Country Hotel*

Penderyn Rd CF44 9SX

☎ 01685 813433 🖷 01685 813139

Dir: *off A4059, close to A465*

Set in over two acres of woodland, this country mansion has been carefully restored and extended. The older bedrooms have antique furnishings and most rooms are spacious, well equipped

continued

and comfortable. There is a pleasant panelled bar, an attractive restaurant and comfortable lounges, where welcoming log fires are lit in cold weather.
ROOMS: 27 en suite (2 fmly) **CONF:** Thtr 300 Class 100 Board 40 **PARKING:** 100 **NOTES:** No dogs No smoking in restaurant Civ Wed 160 **CARDS:**

HOLYHEAD See Anglesey, Isle of

HOLYWELL, Flintshire Map 15 SJ17

★★68% Stamford Gate

Halkyn Rd CH8 7SJ
☎ 01352 712942 01352 713309
e-mail: hotel@stamfordgate.freeserve.co.uk
Dir: *take Holywell turn off A55 on to A5026, hotel 1m on right*
This busy, friendly hotel has impressive views across the Dee Estuary from its elevated position. It provides well-equipped accommodation, including bedrooms on ground floor level. Public areas include a choice of restaurants and a refurbished and spacious bar.
ROOMS: 12 en suite (6 GF) **FACILITIES:** STV entertainment **CONF:** Thtr 100 Class 50 Board 30 **PARKING:** 100 **NOTES:** No dogs (ex guide dogs) **CARDS:**

ISLE OF Placenames incorporating the words 'Isle' or 'Isle of' will be found under the actual name, eg Isle of Anglesey is under Anglesey, Isle of.

KNIGHTON, Powys Map 09 SO27

★★★63% *The Knighton Hotel*

Broad St LD7 1BL
☎ 01547 520530 01547 520529
e-mail: knightonhotel@freeuk.com
The impressive free-standing staircase at the centre of this market town hotel is reputedly the only example in Europe. The hotel is an amalgamation of a 16th-century coaching inn and a 19th-century manor house. The public areas comprise a bar, an attractive and spacious restaurant and a coffee shop.
ROOMS: 15 en suite **CONF:** Thtr 200 Class 100 Board 95 **SERVICES:** Lift **PARKING:** 15 **NOTES:** No children 12yrs No smoking in restaurant Civ Wed 120 **CARDS:**

★★78% Milebrook House

Milebrook LD7 1LT
☎ 01547 528632 01547 520509
e-mail: hotel@milebrook.kc3ltd.co.uk
Dir: *2m E of Knighton, on A4113*
Set in three acres of grounds in the Teme Valley, this charming house dates back to 1760. Since it was converted into a hotel in 1987, it has acquired a well-deserved reputation for its warm hospitality, comfortable accommodation and the quality of its food. As much use as possible is made of local produce and practically all vegetables are home grown.
ROOMS: 10 en suite (2 fmly) (2 GF) No smoking in all bedrooms s £56-£60; d £86-£92 (incl. bkfst) **LB** **FACILITIES:** Croquet lawn Badminton,Trout Fly Fishing Xmas **CONF:** Class 30 **PARKING:** 21 **NOTES:** No dogs No children 8yrs No smoking in restaurant RS Mon **CARDS:**

Popped the question?
Hotels with Civ Wed in their entry are licensed for civil wedding ceremonies. Maximum numbers for the ceremony only are shown, e.g. Civ Wed 120

LAMPETER, Ceredigion Map 08 SN54

★★★71% Falcondale Mansion

Best Western

SA48 7RX
☎ 01570 422910 01570 423559
e-mail: info@falcondalehotel.com
Dir: *800yds W of Lampeter High St, A475 or 1.5m NW of Lampeter A482*
Built in the Italianate style, this charming Victorian property is set in extensive grounds and beautiful parkland. Bedrooms are generally spacious, well equipped and following a refurbishment programme are individually and tastefully decorated. Bars and lounges are similarly well appointed with additional facilities including a conservatory and function room.
ROOMS: 20 en suite (2 fmly) No smoking in 8 bedrooms s £70-£100; d £110-£140 (incl. bkfst) **LB** **FACILITIES:** Tennis (hard) Croquet lawn Xmas **CONF:** Thtr 60 Class 30 Board 25 Del from £85 **SERVICES:** Lift **PARKING:** 60 **NOTES:** No smoking in restaurant Civ Wed 60 **CARDS:**

LAMPHEY See Pembroke

LANGLAND BAY, Swansea Map 08 SS68

★★67% Wittemberg

2 Rotherslade Rd SA3 4QN
☎ 01792 369696 01792 366995
e-mail: enquiries@wittemberghotel.co.uk
Dir: *from A4067 in centre of Mumbles, right at rdbt into Newton Rd. Take 4th left into Langland Rd, at traffic islands 2nd left into Rotherslade Rd. Hotel on right*
This privately owned and personally run, friendly hotel is conveniently situated near to the beaches and coastal walks that

continued on p836

LANGLAND BAY, continued

make this area so popular. The no smoking bedrooms are decorated and furnished to a high standard and are well equipped. Family rooms are available. Guests can also relax in the bar or television lounge and enjoy wholesome home cooking in the attractive dining room.
ROOMS: 11 en suite (3 fmly) s £37-£48; d £60-£80 (incl. bkfst) **LB** **FACILITIES:** Jacuzzi **PARKING:** 8 **NOTES:** No dogs (ex guide dogs) No smoking in restaurant **CARDS:**

LLANARMON DYFFRYN CEIRIOG, Wrexham Map 15 SJ13

Courtesy & Care Award

★★74% West Arms
LL20 7LD
☎ 01691 600665 & 600612 01691 600622
e-mail: gowestarms@aol.com
Dir: *off A483/A5 at Chirk, in Chirk take B4500 to Ceiriog Valley, Llanarmon is 11m at end of B4500*
Set in the beautiful Ceiriog Valley, this delightful hotel has a wealth of charm and character. There is a comfortable lounge, a room for private dining and two bars, as well as a pleasant restaurant offering a fixed-price menu of freshly cooked dishes. The attractive bedrooms have a mixture of modern and period furnishings. The team at West Arms has been awarded the AA Courtesy & Care Award for Wales 2003-2004.
ROOMS: 15 en suite (2 fmly) (3 GF) s £48-£74; d fr £99 (incl. bkfst) **LB** **FACILITIES:** Fishing Xmas **CONF:** Thtr 60 Class 50 Board 50 **PARKING:** 22 **NOTES:** No smoking in restaurant Civ Wed 80 **CARDS:**

LLANBEDR, Gwynedd Map 14 SH52

★★68% Cae Nest Hall Country House
LL45 2NL
☎ 01341 241349 01341 241349
e-mail: cae-nest@orbix.uk.net
Dir: *off A496 at Victoria Pub, turn left at the War Memorial (100yds from pub) then straight ahead to hotel approx 300yds*
This delightful, small 15th-century country house lies in pleasant grounds. Original features include flagstone floors in the bar and an old black stove in the dining room. The use of many Japanese features creates a special character. Bedrooms are modern and there is a choice of smoking or no-smoking lounges. Guests can choose from either British or Japanese menus.
ROOMS: 10 en suite (3 fmly) No smoking in all bedrooms s £42-£52; d £64-£79 (incl. bkfst) **LB** **PARKING:** 10 **NOTES:** No dogs No smoking in restaurant

★★64% Ty Mawr
LL45 2NH
☎ 01341 241440 01341 241440
e-mail: tymawrhotel@onetel.com
Dir: *from Barmouth A496 Harlech road and at Llanbedr turn right after bridge in the village, hotel 50yds on left, brown tourist signs on junct*

Located in a picturesque village, this family-run hotel has a relaxed, friendly atmosphere. The pleasant grounds opposite the River Artro became a popular beer garden during fine weather. The attractive, cane-furnished bar offers a blackboard selection and a good choice of real ales. A more formal menu is available in the restaurant. Bedrooms are smart and brightly decorated.
ROOMS: 10 en suite (2 fmly) No smoking in 5 bedrooms s £30-£40; d £60-£70 (incl. bkfst) **LB** **FACILITIES:** STV **CONF:** Class 25 **PARKING:** 30 **NOTES:** No smoking in restaurant Closed 24-26 Dec **CARDS:**

LLANBERIS, Gwynedd Map 14 SH56

★★★68% Royal Victoria
LL55 4TY
THE INDEPENDENTS
☎ 01286 870253 01286 870149
e-mail: info@royalvictoria.fsnet.co.uk
Dir: *on A4086 Caernarfon to Llanberis road, directly opposite Snowdon Mountain railway*
This well-established hotel sits near the foot of Snowdon, between the Peris and Padarn Lakes. Pretty gardens and grounds make an attractive backdrop for the many weddings held here. Bedrooms have been refurbished and are well equipped. There are spacious lounges and bars, and a large dining room with conservatory overlooks the lakes.
ROOMS: 106 en suite (7 fmly) s £50-£55; d £100-£110 (incl. bkfst) **LB** **FACILITIES:** STV Mountaineering, Cycling, Walking entertainment Xmas **CONF:** Thtr 100 Class 60 Board 50 Del from £58.75 **SERVICES:** Lift **PARKING:** 300 **NOTES:** No smoking in restaurant RS 24-28 Dec Civ Wed 100 **CARDS:**

See advert on opposite page

Lake View Hotel & Restaurant
Tan-y-Pant LL55 4EL
☎ 01286 870422 01286 872591
e-mail: reception@lakeviewhotel.co.uk
Dir: *1m from Llanberis on A4086 towards Caernarfon*
ROOMS: 10 rms (9 en suite) (2 fmly) No smoking in all bedrooms s £30-£35; d £50-£62 (incl. bkfst) **LB** **FACILITIES:** 2 footpaths adjacent to hotel **PARKING:** 20 **NOTES:** ★★ No dogs No smoking in restaurant **CARDS:**

LANDEGLA, Denbighshire
Map 15 SJ25

★★★72% ◎◎ Bodidris Hall
L11 3AL
☎ 0870 7292292 ▤ 01978 790335
-mail: ceri@bodidrishall.com
ir: in village take A5104 towards Chester. Hotel 2m on left, signposted
his impressive manor house is in a quiet location surrounded by rnamental gardens and mature woodlands. It has an interesting istory and a wealth of charm and character, with original features uch as oak beams and inglenook fireplaces. Bedrooms are urnished with antique pieces and some have four-poster beds. ining here is an enjoyable experience; the food is cooked with air and is stylishly presented.
OOMS: 9 en suite No smoking in 3 bedrooms d £99-£199 (incl. bkfst) **B FACILITIES:** Fishing Shooting Xmas **CONF:** Thtr 65 Class 20 Board 0 Del from £129.95 **PARKING:** 60 **NOTES:** No dogs No smoking in estaurant Civ Wed 65 **CARDS:**

LANDEILO, Carmarthenshire
Map 08 SN62

★★★70% The Plough Inn
Rhosmaen SA19 6NP
☎ 01558 823431 ▤ 01558 823969
-mail: enquiries@ploughrhosmaen.co.uk
Dir: 1m N, on A40

This privately owned hotel has memorable views over the Towy Valley and the Black Mountains. Bedrooms, situated in a separate wing, are tastefully furnished, spacious and comfortable. The public lounge bar is popular with locals, as is the spacious restaurant where freshly prepared food can be enjoyed. Additional facilities include a sauna, gym and conference facilities.
ROOMS: 12 en suite s £50; d £65-£70 (incl. bkfst) **FACILITIES:** STV Sauna Gym **CONF:** Thtr 45 Class 24 Board 24 **PARKING:** 70 **NOTES:** No dogs (ex guide dogs) No smoking in restaurant Closed 25 Dec RS Sun (restaurant closed) Civ Wed 60
CARDS:

See advert on this page

★★67% White Hart Inn
36 Carmarthen Rd SA19 6RS
☎ 01558 823419 ▤ 01558 823089
e-mail: therese@whitehartinn.fsnet.co.uk
Dir: off A40 onto A483, hotel 200yds on left
Dating back to the 19th century, this privately owned roadside hostelry is situated on the outskirts of town. The modern bedrooms are well equipped and tastefully furnished. Family rooms are available. Public areas offer a choice of bars and there are both smoking and non-smoking dining areas, where a wide range of grill dishes are available. Other facilities include a choice of function rooms including a large self-contained suite.
ROOMS: 11 en suite (2 fmly) s fr £36; d fr £54 (incl. bkfst) **FACILITIES:** STV **PARKING:** 50 **NOTES:** No dogs (ex guide dogs) Civ Wed 80 **CARDS:**

L

LLANDOVERY, Carmarthenshire Map 09 SN73

★★★64% **Castle**
King's Rd SA20 0AP
☎ 01550 720343 📠 01550 720673
e-mail: castlehotl@aol.com
Dir: *on A40 in town centre, between Brecon and Carmarthen*

Overlooked by the original Norman keep, the Castle Hotel is in the heart of this market town. There is a warm atmosphere about the place, heightened by roaring log fires in the winter. Many of the bedrooms have benefited from refurbishment, including rooms once occupied by George Borrow and Lord Nelson.

ROOMS: 23 en suite (4 fmly) No smoking in 21 bedrooms s £39.50; d £60 (incl. bkfst) **FACILITIES:** STV ch fac Xmas **CONF:** Class 150 Board 100 **PARKING:** 30 **NOTES:** No dogs (ex guide dogs) No smoking in restaurant **CARDS:**

LLANDRILLO, Denbighshire Map 15 SJ03

Top 200 – Restaurant with Rooms

Tyddyn Llan
LL21 0ST
☎ 01490 440264 📠 01490 440414
e-mail: tyddynllanhotel@compuserve.com
Dir: *take B4401 from Corwen to Llandrillo. Tyddyn Llan on right leaving the village*

It is difficult not to relax at this charming Georgian house, set in its own grounds amidst beautiful countryside. Guests have a choice of comfortable lounges in which to enjoy a real log fire and consider the menu, whilst mouth-watering dishes are served in the peaceful and elegant restaurant. Bedrooms are thoughtfully equipped and sympathetically styled and many have glorious views.

ROOMS: 12 en suite s £65-£110; d £90-£180 (incl. bkfst) **LB** **FACILITIES:** Fishing Croquet lawn ch fac Xmas **CONF:** Thtr 30 Class 10 Board 20 Del from £110 **PARKING:** 20 **NOTES:** No smoking in restaurant Closed 18 Jan-4 Feb Civ Wed 35
CARDS:

LLANDRINDOD WELLS, Powys Map 09 SO06

★★★71% **Hotel Metropole**
Temple St LD1 5DY
☎ 01597 823700 📠 01597 824828
e-mail: info@metropole.co.uk
Dir: *on A483 in centre of town*

The centre of this famous spa town is dominated by this Victorian hotel, which has been personally run by the same family for over 100 years. The lobby leads to a choice of bars and an elegant lounge. Bedrooms, the majority of which are non-smoking, vary in style and all are quite spacious and well-equipped. Facilities here include conference and function rooms as well as a leisure centre.

ROOMS: 120 en suite (7 fmly) No smoking in 57 bedrooms s £75; d £98 (incl. bkfst) **LB** **FACILITIES:** Indoor swimming (H) Sauna Solarium Gym Jacuzzi Beauty salon, Rowing & Cycling machines, Holistic treatments Xmas **CONF:** Thtr 300 Class 200 Board 80 Del from £102 **SERVICES:** Lift **PARKING:** 150 **NOTES:** No smoking in restaurant Civ Wed 250 **CARDS:**

See advert on opposite page

LLANDUDNO, Conwy Map 14 SH78

Top 200 - Hotel

★★★★ **Bodysgallen Hall**
LL30 1RS
☎ 01492 584466 📠 01492 582519
e-mail: info@bodysgallen.com
Dir: *A55 junct 19, then follow A470 towards Llandudno. Hotel 1m on right*

RELAIS & CHATEAUX

Set in 200 acres of parkland and formal gardens, this 17th-century house is in an elevated position, allowing views towards Snowdonia and across to Conwy Castle. Bedrooms, some of which are in converted cottages in the grounds, are comfortably furnished, and public areas include a choice of lounges displaying fine antiques and great character. Friendly and attentive service is discreetly offered, whilst the restaurant features fine local produce, carefully prepared.

ROOMS: 19 en suite 16 annexe en suite (3 fmly) No smoking in 19 bedrooms s £120-£220; d £165-£280 **LB** **FACILITIES:** Indoor swimming (H) Tennis (hard) Sauna Solarium Gym Croquet lawn Jacuzzi Beauty salons Steam room Club room entertainment Xmas **CONF:** Thtr 50 Class 30 Board 24 Del from £145 **PARKING:** 50 **NOTES:** No dogs (ex guide dogs) No children 8yrs No smoking in restaurant **CARDS:**

Top 200 - Town House

★★★★ **Osborne House**
17 North House LL30 2LP
☎ 01492 860330 📠 01492 860791
e-mail: sales@osbornehouse.com
Dir: *exit A55 junct 19. Follow signs for Llandudno then Promenade. Continue until junction, turn right. Osborne House on left opposite pier entrance*

A number of years have been spent converting this Victorian house into a luxurious hotel and that effort has certainly paid off. Spacious suites offer unrivalled comfort and luxury, tastefully combining antique furnishings with state-of-the-art technology and facilities. Each suite provides super views over the pier and bay. Creative menus are presented in the candlit

continued

restaurant whilst the bar blends historic elegance with plasma screens, dazzling chandeliers and guilt edged mirrors.

ROOMS: 6 en suite s £130-£200; d £130-£200 (incl. cont bkfst) **FACILITIES:** STV use of swimming pool/sauna/jacuzzi at Empire Hotel (100 yds) **SERVICES:** air con **PARKING:** 6 **NOTES:** No dogs (ex guide dogs) No children 11yrs Closed 21-30 Dec
CARDS:

★★★74% **Empire**
Church Walks LL30 2HE
☎ 01492 860555 01492 860791
e-mail: reservations@empirehotel.co.uk
Dir: *from Chester A55 - leave at junct 19 for Llandudno. Follow signs for town centre - hotel is at end & facing main street*

Run by the same family for over 50 years, the Empire offers luxuriously appointed bedrooms with every modern facility. The 'Number 72' rooms are particularly sumptuous. The indoor pool is overlooked by an all-day restaurant, and there is also an outdoor pool and roof garden. The Watkins restaurant offers an interesting fixed-price menu.

ROOMS: 51 en suite 8 annexe en suite (3 fmly) s £60-£75; d £90-£110 (incl. bkfst) **LB** **FACILITIES: Spa** STV Indoor swimming (H) Outdoor swimming (H) Sauna Full range of beauty treatments **CONF:** Thtr 36 Class 20 Board 20 Del from £85 **SERVICES:** Lift **PARKING:** 40 **NOTES:** No dogs (ex guide dogs) Closed 10 days Xmas
CARDS:

See advert on this page

★★★73% **Imperial**
The Promenade LL30 1AP
☎ 01492 877466 01492 878043
e-mail: imphotel@btinternet.com
Dir: *A470 to Llandudno*

The Imperial is a large and impressive hotel, situated on the promenade, within easy reach of the town centre and other amenities. Many of the bedrooms have views over the bay and there are also several suites available. The elegant Chantrey

continued on p840

L

LLANDUDNO, continued

restaurant offers a fixed-price menu which changes monthly and dishes take full advantage of local produce. There is a fully equipped leisure club and extensive conference and banqueting facilities.
ROOMS: 100 en suite (10 fmly) s fr £70; d fr £100 (incl. bkfst) **LB** **FACILITIES:** STV Indoor swimming (H) Sauna Solarium Gym Jacuzzi Beauty therapist Hairdressing entertainment Xmas **CONF:** Thtr 150 Class 50 Board 50 Del from £110 **SERVICES:** Lift **PARKING:** 25 **NOTES:** No dogs (ex guide dogs) No smoking in restaurant Civ Wed 150
CARDS:

See advert on opposite page

★★★68% Dunoon
Gloddaeth St LL30 2DW
☎ 01492 860787 📠 01492 860031
e-mail: reservations@dunoonhotel.co.uk
Dir: *exit Promenade at War Memorial by pier onto wide avenue. 200yds from Promenade on right*

The Dunoon Hotel is centrally located in the town. The Chadderton family have run this comfortable, smart hotel for many years and have built up an impressive number of repeat guests. The restaurant offers freshly prepared tasty meals, whilst lighter snacks or afternoon tea may be taken in one of the lounges or bar.
ROOMS: 50 en suite 3 annexe en suite (10 fmly) (1 GF) s £52-£57; d £80-£114 (incl. bkfst & dinner) **LB** **FACILITIES:** STV entertainment ch fac Xmas **CONF:** BC **SERVICES:** Lift **PARKING:** 24 **NOTES:** No dogs (ex guide dogs) No smoking in restaurant Closed 28 Dec - mid-Mar
CARDS:

★★★64% St George's
The Promenade LL30 2LG
☎ 01492 877544 📠 01492 877788
e-mail: stgeorges@macdonald-hotels.co.uk
Dir: *A55-A470, follow road to the promenade, 0.25m, hotel on corner*

MACDONALD HOTELS

This popular and friendly seafront hotel was the first to be built in the town. Its many Victorian features include the splendid, ornate

continued

Wedgwood Room. The main lounges overlook the bay and incorporate a coffee shop serving hot and cold snacks. Several bedrooms have views over the sea and some have balconies.
ROOMS: 86 en suite (6 fmly) No smoking in 12 bedrooms s £52-£108; d £84-£190 (incl. bkfst) **LB** **FACILITIES:** STV Sauna Solarium Jacuzzi Hairdressing Health & beauty salon Xmas **CONF:** Thtr 250 Class 200 Board 45 Del from £83 **SERVICES:** Lift **PARKING:** 50 **NOTES:** No smoking in restaurant Civ Wed 200
CARDS:

★★★63% *Chatsworth House*
Central Promenade LL30 2XS
☎ 01492 860788 📠 01492 871417
e-mail: manager@chatsworth-hotel.co.uk
This traditional family-run Victorian hotel occupies a central position on the promenade and caters for many families and groups. There is an indoor swimming pool, a sauna and a solarium. Well-maintained public areas complement modern bedrooms, some of them quite spacious.
ROOMS: 72 en suite (19 fmly) **FACILITIES:** Indoor swimming (H) Sauna Jacuzzi **SERVICES:** Lift **PARKING:** 9 **CARDS:**

★★★63% Risboro
Clement Av LL30 2ED
☎ 01492 876343 📠 01492 879881
e-mail: risborohotel@ukonline.co.uk
Dir: *A55 to Llandudno, follow A470 into town centre, left at large rdbt, then take 3rd right*

Situated close to the foot of the Great Orme and convenient for the seafront and town centre, this popular family hotel provides agreeable bedrooms. Amongst the extensive public areas there is a comfortable lounge with a small terrace and a large restaurant overlooking the pool.
ROOMS: 65 en suite (7 fmly) s £35-£45; d £70-£90 (incl. bkfst) **LB** **FACILITIES: Spa** Indoor swimming (H) Sauna Solarium Gym Jacuzzi Swimming pool supervised entertainment Xmas **CONF:** BC Thtr 150 Class 100 Board 80 Del from £55 **SERVICES:** Lift **PARKING:** 40 **NOTES:** No smoking in restaurant **CARDS:**

Top 200 - Hotel

★★ ®®® St Tudno Hotel and Restaurant
The Promenade LL30 2LP
☎ 01492 874411 📠 01492 860407
e-mail: sttudnohotel@btinternet.com
Dir: *on reaching Promenade drive towards the pier, hotel opposite pier entrance & gardens*
A high quality family owned hotel, which enjoys fine sea views from some of the bedrooms and also from the comfortable lounges. Public rooms include a no-smoking lounge, a welcoming bar-lounge together with a small indoor

continued

pool. The air-conditioned Garden Room Restaurant is the focal point for enjoying excellent cuisine using the finest of local produce. Expect to be well cared for by a warm and friendly staff.

ROOMS: 19 en suite (4 fmly) No smoking in 3 bedrooms s £70-£80; d £88-£200 (incl. bkfst) **LB FACILITIES:** STV Indoor swimming (H) Swimming pool supervised entertainment Xmas **CONF:** Thtr 40 Class 25 Board 20 Del from £140 **SERVICES:** Lift **PARKING:** 12 **NOTES:** No smoking in restaurant **CARDS:**

★★73% **Epperstone**
15 Abbey Rd LL30 2EE
☎ 01492 878746 01492 871223
e-mail: epperstonehotel@btconnect.com
Dir: *A55-A470 to Mostyn Street. Left at rdbt, 4th right into York Rd. Hotel on junct of York Rd & Abbey Rd*
This delightful hotel is located in wonderful gardens in a residential part of town, within easy walking distance of the seafront and shopping area. Bedrooms are attractively decorated and thoughtfully equipped. Two lounges, a comfortable no-smoking room and a Victorian-style conservatory are available. A daily changing menu is offered in the bright dining room.
ROOMS: 8 en suite (5 fmly) (1 GF) No smoking in all bedrooms s £23-£33; d £46-£66 (incl. bkfst) **LB FACILITIES:** STV Xmas **PARKING:** 8 **NOTES:** No smoking in restaurant **CARDS:**

★★72% **Sunnymede**
West Pde LL30 2BD
☎ 01492 877130 01492 871824
Dir: *from A55 follow signs for Llandudno & Deganwy. At 1st rdbt after Deganwy take 1st exit towards sea. At corner turn hotel 400yds*
Sunnymede is a friendly family-run hotel located on Llandudno's West Shore. Many rooms have views over the Conwy Estuary and Snowdonia. Modern bedrooms are attractively decorated and well equipped. Bar and lounge areas are particularly comfortable and attractive. All areas of the hotel have benefited from a refurbishment.
ROOMS: 15 en suite (3 fmly) (4 GF) No smoking in all bedrooms s £41-£82; d £41-£90 (incl. bkfst & dinner) **LB FACILITIES:** Xmas **PARKING:** 18 **NOTES:** No children 3yrs No smoking in restaurant Closed Jan-Feb & Nov RS Xmas period **CARDS:**

★★72% **TanLan**
Great Orme's Rd, West Shore LL30 2AR
☎ 01492 860221 01492 870219
e-mail: info@tanlanhotel.co.uk
Dir: *off A55 junct 18 onto A546 signposted Deganwy. Approx 3m from A55, straight over mini-rndbt and hotel 50mtrs on left*
Warm and friendly hospitality is one of the many strengths at this well-maintained, small, privately owned and personally run hotel. It is located on Llandudno's West Shore, close to the Great Orme. The refurbished bedrooms are modern and well-equipped. No-smoking rooms and bedrooms on ground floor level are both available. Facilities here include a pleasant dining room, lounge and bar.
ROOMS: 17 en suite (3 fmly) (6 GF) No smoking in all bedrooms s £30-£39; d £50-£58 (incl. bkfst) **LB PARKING:** 12 **NOTES:** No dogs (ex guide dogs) No smoking in restaurant Closed Nov - early Mar **CARDS:**

★★72% **Tynedale**
Central Promenade LL30 2XS
☎ 01492 877426 01492 871213
e-mail: enquiries@tynedalehotel.co.uk
Dir: *on promenade opposite bandstand*
Tour groups are well catered for at this privately owned and personally run hotel, and regular live entertainment is a feature. Public areas include good lounge facilities and an attractive patio overlooking the bay. The well maintained, no-smoking bedrooms are fresh and well equipped. Many have good views over the seafront and the Great Orme.
ROOMS: 54 en suite (4 fmly) No smoking in all bedrooms s £25-£35; d £50-£70 (incl. bkfst) **LB FACILITIES:** entertainment Xmas **SERVICES:** Lift **PARKING:** 30 **NOTES:** No dogs (ex guide dogs) No smoking in restaurant **CARDS:**

L

LLANDUDNO, continued

★★67% Bedford
Promenade LL30 1BN
☎ 01492 876647 🖹 01492 860185
e-mail: enquiries@thebedford.com
Dir: *at junct of A55/A470, take exit for Llandudno (A470) and continue until 4th rdbt. Take exit for Craig-y-Don (B115) and turn right*
This hotel is located on the eastern approach to Llandudno at Craig-y-Don. Many of the well-equipped bedrooms are suitable for families and enjoy fine views over the bay towards both the Great Orme and Little Orme. The hotel's Italian restaurant and pizzeria is popular with locals. Facilities include a choice of lounges and a function/meeting room.
ROOMS: 27 en suite (2 fmly) No smoking in 3 bedrooms s £35; d £50-£65 (incl. bkfst) **LB FACILITIES:** Xmas **CONF:** Thtr 30 Class 20 Board 20 Del from £50 **SERVICES:** Lift **PARKING:** 21
CARDS:

★★67% Ravenhurst
West Pde LL30 2BB
☎ 01492 875525 🖹 01248 681143
e-mail: ravenhursthotel@aol.co.uk
Dir: *on West Shore, opposite boating pool*
This privately owned, comfortable hotel lies on the quieter West Shore of the town and enjoys lovely views over the Conwy Estuary towards Snowdonia. The traditionally-styled accommodation includes bedrooms on ground floor level. There is a choice of lounges and a bar, and a daily changing fixed-price menu is provided in the dining room.
ROOMS: 25 en suite (3 fmly) (6 GF) s £28-£32; d £56-£64 (incl. bkfst) **LB FACILITIES:** Xmas **PARKING:** 15 **NOTES:** No smoking in restaurant Closed Dec-Feb **CARDS:**

★★67% Somerset
St Georges Crescent, Promenade LL30 2LF
☎ 01492 876540 🖹 01492 863700
e-mail: somerset@favroy.freeserve.co.uk
Dir: *on the Promenade*
With its sister hotel, The Wavecrest, this cheerful holiday hotel occupies an ideal location on the central promenade and affords superb views over the bay from many rooms. Regular entertainment is provided as well as a range of bar and lounge areas. Bedrooms are well decorated and modern facilities are provided.
ROOMS: 37 en suite (4 fmly) s £45-£55; d £90-£110 (incl. bkfst & dinner) **LB FACILITIES:** Games room entertainment Xmas **CONF:** Thtr 70 Class 70 Board 30 **SERVICES:** Lift **PARKING:** 20 **NOTES:** No smoking in restaurant Closed Jan-Feb **CARDS:**

★★67% Wavecrest
St Georges Crescent, Central Promenade LL30 2LF
☎ 01492 860615 🖹 01492 863700
e-mail: somerset@favroy.freeserve.co.uk
Dir: *on promenade behind Marks & Spencer*
The Wavecrest is the sister hotel of the adjoining Somerset, and public areas are shared. It lies on the central promenade and most bedrooms have lovely sea views. Lounge and bar areas are comfortably furnished and a games room is available. Staff are friendly and regular entertainment is staged.
ROOMS: 41 en suite (7 fmly) s £45-£55; d £90-£110 (incl. bkfst & dinner) **LB FACILITIES:** Games room, Patio garden entertainment Xmas **CONF:** Class 70 **SERVICES:** Lift **PARKING:** 12 **NOTES:** No smoking in restaurant Closed Jan-Feb **CARDS:**

★★66% Esplanade
Glan-y-Mor Pde, Promenade LL30 2LL
☎ 0800 318688 (freephone) & 01492 860300 🖹 01492 860418
e-mail: info@esplanadehotel.co.uk
Dir: *off A55 at Llandudno junct, onto A470, follow signs to promenade, turn left towards Great Orme. Hotel 500yds left*
This family owned and run hotel stands on the promenade, conveniently close to the town centre and with views of the bay. Bedrooms vary in size and style, but all have modern equipment and facilities. Public areas are bright and attractively appointed, and include a room for functions and conferences.
ROOMS: 59 en suite (17 fmly) s £15-£68; d £30-£96 (incl. bkfst) **LB FACILITIES:** entertainment Xmas **CONF:** Thtr 80 Class 40 Board 40 Del from £37.50 **SERVICES:** Lift **PARKING:** 30 **NOTES:** No dogs (ex guide dogs) No smoking in restaurant Closed 3 Jan-1 Feb
CARDS:

★★66% Hydro Hotel
Neville Crescent LL30 1AT
☎ 01492 870101 🖹 01492 870992
Leisureplex
e-mail: hydro.llandudno@alfatravel.co.uk
Dir: *follow signs for theatre to seafront, then towards pier. Hotel short distance after theatre on left facing North Bay*
This large hotel is situated on the promenade, overlooking the sea and offers very good value-for-money, modern accommodation. Public areas are quite extensive and include a choice of lounges, a games/snooker room and a ballroom, where entertainment is provided every night. The hotel is a popular venue for coach tour parties.
ROOMS: 112 en suite (4 fmly) (8 GF) s £25-£33; d £42-£58 (incl. bkfst) **LB FACILITIES:** Snooker Sauna Gym Table tennis entertainment Xmas **CONF:** Thtr 260 Class 40 **SERVICES:** Lift **PARKING:** 10 **NOTES:** No dogs (ex guide dogs) No smoking in restaurant Closed Jan-mid Feb RS Nov -Dec & mid Feb-Mar **CARDS:**

★★66% Oak Alyn
2 Deganwy Av LL30 2YB
☎ 01492 860320
Dir: *in centre of Llandudno, 200yds from Town Hall, opposite Catholic Church*
This private hotel has been much improved by the present owners since they took over in 1998. It is close to the town centre and within a few minutes' walk of the promenade. Bedrooms have modern facilities. There is a bright and pleasant dining room with a conservatory extension, and a lounge bar.
ROOMS: 12 en suite (2 fmly) s £22-£24; d £44-£48 (incl. bkfst) **LB CONF:** Thtr 26 Class 30 **PARKING:** 16 **NOTES:** No dogs (ex guide dogs) No smoking in restaurant Closed 22-31 Dec **CARDS:**

★★66% Stratford
8 Craig-y-Don Pde, Promenade LL30 1BG
☎ 01492 877962 🖹 01492 877962
e-mail: stratfordhotel@aol.com
Dir: *from A55 take A470 to Llandudno, take Craig-y-Don sign from A470 to Promenade turn right*
A pleasant holiday hotel on the Craig-y-Don promenade. The conference centre and theatre are nearby, and local shops are only a short walk. Many of the comfortable bedrooms have canopied beds. A daily changing menu provides good home cooking and there is a comfortable lounge, bar and inviting patio overlooking the sea.
ROOMS: 10 en suite (4 fmly) (2 GF) s £27-£31; d £44-£56 (incl. bkfst) **LB FACILITIES: Spa NOTES:** No smoking in restaurant RS Nov - Mar
CARDS:

★★65% **Ambassador Hotel**
Grand Promenade LL30 2NR
☎ 01492 876886 🖷 01492 876347
e-mail: reception@ambasshotel.demon.co.uk
Dir: off A55 onto A470. Take turn to Promenade, then left towards pier
This friendly, family run hotel is on the seafront, close to the town centre. Bedrooms are tasteful and many have sea views. There is a choice of lounges, a patisserie, bar and restaurant.
ROOMS: 57 en suite (8 fmly) s £38-£51; d £70-£120 (incl. bkfst & dinner) **LB FACILITIES:** entertainment Xmas **CONF:** Thtr 45 Class 14 Board 20 Del from £57 **SERVICES:** Lift **PARKING:** 11 **NOTES:** No dogs (ex guide dogs) No smoking in restaurant **CARDS:**

★★65% **Evans**
Charlton St LL30 2AA
☎ 01492 860784 🖷 01492 860784
Dir: from A470 to Llandudno pass Asda, stay in left lane, turn left, hotel on 1st right corner
This is a privately owned and friendly hotel, which provides well-maintained accommodation, including family bedrooms. The spacious public areas include a well-equipped games room and a comfortable lounge bar, where regular live evening entertainment is held. The hotel is particularly popular with coach tour groups.
ROOMS: 50 en suite (4 fmly) s £45-£47; d £80-£84 (incl. bkfst & dinner) **LB FACILITIES:** STV Snooker Solarium entertainment Xmas **SERVICES:** Lift **NOTES:** No dogs (ex guide dogs) No smoking in restaurant Closed Jan

★★65% **Headlands**
Hill Ter LL30 1NT
☎ 01492 877485 🖷 01492 874867
e-mail: enquiries@headlands-hotel.com
Dir: off A55 onto A470. Continue along Mostyn St, at T-junct turn right then immediately left. After 70yds, right onto Hill Terrace
This personally run hotel stands high on the side of the Great Orme and enjoys panoramic views of the seafront, beach and bay. Bedrooms vary in size and style. All are well equipped and equally suitable for business and leisure guests. Family rooms and rooms with four-poster beds are available.
ROOMS: 15 en suite (4 fmly) No smoking in all bedrooms s fr £33; d fr £66 (incl. bkfst) **LB FACILITIES:** Xmas **PARKING:** 7 **NOTES:** No children 5yrs No smoking in restaurant Closed Jan-20 Feb
CARDS:

★★65% **Ormescliffe**
East Pde LL30 1BE
☎ 01492 877191 🖷 01492 860311
e-mail: ormescliffe@clara.net
Dir: M6, M56, A55 exit Llandudno. A470 promenade near theatre and conference centre
A family-run hotel at the eastern end of the promenade. Bedrooms are modern and well equipped; most have superb views over the seafront and Great Orme. Comfortable bars and lounges are provided and there is a ballroom with regular entertainment.
ROOMS: 61 en suite (7 fmly) No smoking in 6 bedrooms **FACILITIES:** Snooker Table tennis **CONF:** Thtr 120 Class 120 Board 80 **SERVICES:** Lift **PARKING:** 15 **NOTES:** No smoking in restaurant Closed 2 Jan-2 Feb **CARDS:**

★★62% **Branksome**
Lloyd St LL30 2YP
☎ 01492 875989 🖷 01429 875989
This family owned and run hotel lies between the town's two shores and is a short walk from the main shopping area. Modern furnished and equipped bedrooms include family and ground floor rooms. Public rooms are spacious and comfortable, and regular live entertainment is provided. The hotel is popular with coach tour groups.
ROOMS: 52 en suite (5 fmly) (9 GF) s £24-£28; d £68-£80 (incl. bkfst) **LB FACILITIES:** entertainment Xmas **PARKING:** 25 **NOTES:** No smoking in restaurant **CARDS:**

★★62% ***Royal***
Church Walks LL30 2HW
☎ 01492 876476 🖷 01492 870210
e-mail: royallllandudno@aol.com
Dir: exit A55 for A470 to Llandudno. Follow through town to T-junct, then left into Church Walks. Hotel 200yds on left, almost opposite Great Orme tram station
Reputed to be the first hotel in Llandudno, the Royal is located on the eastern side of the Great Orme, close to the town centre and seafront. The well-equipped accommodation is particularly popular with golfers and coach tour groups.
ROOMS: 38 rms (36 en suite) (7 fmly) **FACILITIES:** Putting green **CONF: SERVICES:** Lift **PARKING:** 20 **NOTES:** No dogs (ex guide dogs) No smoking in restaurant **CARDS:**

★63% ***Min-y-Don***
North Pde LL30 2LP
☎ 01492 876511 🖷 01492 878169
Dir: leave A55 Expressway Llandudno junct onto A470. Through Martyn St, turn right at rdbt then left North Parade
This cheerful family-run hotel is located under the Great Orme, opposite the pier. Bedrooms include several suitable for families and many have lovely views over the bay. Regular entertainment is held and there are comfortable lounge and bar areas.
ROOMS: 28 rms (19 en suite) (12 fmly) **FACILITIES: SERVICES:** air con **PARKING:** 7 **NOTES:** No dogs No smoking in restaurant Closed Jan-Feb
CARDS:

LLANDUDNO JUNCTION, Conwy — Map 14 SH77

Travel Inn
Afon Conway, Llandudno Junction LL28 5LB
☎ 08701 977162 🖷 01492 583614
Dir: at A55 junct 19. Exit rdbt at A470 Betws-y-Coed. The Travel Inn on left, opposite petrol station
Travel Inn offers good-quality, value-for-money accommodation. Spacious, en suite rooms with bath and shower comfortably accommodate a family of up to two adults and two children (to age 15). The restaurant and bar offers a varied menu. For further details and the Travel Inn phone number, consult the Hotel Groups page.
ROOMS: 40 en suite s £44.95; d £44.95

Early start?
Hotels at all star levels should provide in-room alarm clocks and/or alarm calls

LLANELLI, Carmarthenshire — Map 08 SN50

★★★67% **Diplomat Hotel**
Felinfoel SA15 3PJ
☎ 01554 756156 🖷 01554 751649
e-mail: enquiries@diplomat-hotel-wales.com
Dir: M4 junct 48 onto A4138 then B4303 hotel in 0.75m on right
This former Victorian mansion, set in mature grounds, has been extended over the years to provide a comfortable and relaxing hotel. Public areas include Trubshaw's restaurant, a large function suite and a modern and leisure centre. The well-appointed

continued on p844

LLANELLI, continued

bedrooms are located in the main house and the nearby coach house.
ROOMS: 23 en suite 8 annexe en suite (2 fmly) No smoking in 6 bedrooms s £65-£70; d £85-£90 (incl. bkfst) **LB** **FACILITIES: Spa** Indoor swimming (H) Sauna Solarium Gym Jacuzzi Swimming pool supervised entertainment Xmas **CONF:** Thtr 450 Class 150 Board 100 Del from £86 **SERVICES:** Lift **PARKING:** 250 **NOTES:** Civ Wed 400 **CARDS:**

★★★67% **Stradey Park**
Furnace SA15 4HA
☎ 01554 758171 🖷 01564 777974
e-mail: reservations@stradey-park-hotel.fsnet.co.uk
Dir: *M4 junct 48/A484 to B4309*
The present owners have extensively upgraded this large, modern complex. It provides a good range of accommodation, including full suites, no-smoking bedrooms and bedrooms on ground floor level. The spacious and attractively appointed public areas include a choice of comfortable lounges, a pleasant lounge bar and a bright brasserie-style restaurant.
ROOMS: 84 en suite (3 fmly) (19 GF) No smoking in 40 bedrooms s £59.50-£95; d £85-£140 (incl. bkfst) **LB** **FACILITIES:** Xmas **CONF:** Thtr 300 Class 300 Board 240 Del from £79.90 **SERVICES:** Lift **PARKING:** 100 **NOTES:** No dogs (ex guide dogs) No smoking in restaurant Civ Wed 200 **CARDS:**

L

★★69% ***Ashburnham***
Ashburnham Rd, Pembrey SA16 0TH
☎ 01554 834343 & 834455 🖷 01554 834483
e-mail: post@epco.demon.co.uk
Dir: *M4 junct 48, A4138 to Llanelli, A484 West to Pembrey, road sign on entering village*
Amelia Earhart stayed at this friendly hotel after finishing her historic transatlantic flight of 1928. Public areas include a bright bar and restaurant offering a good choice of menus, extensive function facilities and a children's outdoor play area. Bedrooms have modern furnishings and facilities.
ROOMS: 12 en suite (2 fmly) **FACILITIES:** various within 1 mile of hotel ch fac **CONF:** Thtr 150 Class 150 Board 80 **PARKING:** 100 **NOTES:** No smoking in restaurant RS 25 Dec Civ Wed 120
CARDS:

★★64% **Miramar**
158 Station Rd SA15 1YU
☎ 01554 754726 🖷 01554 772454
e-mail: hotelmiramar1@aol.com
Dir: *M4 junct 48. Follow road to Llanelli. In Llanelli follow railway station signs. Hotel is adjacent to the station*
This family-run hotel is conveniently located near to the railway station and is within walking of the town centre. Bedrooms are well maintained and generously equipped, whilst public areas include a cheerful bar providing a good range of bar meals and a pleasantly appointed restaurant where Portuguese dishes are a speciality.
ROOMS: 12 en suite (2 fmly) (2 GF) s £27-£29; d £45-£48 (incl. bkfst) **FACILITIES:** Golf course and racing course nearby **CONF:** Del from £30 **PARKING:** 10 **NOTES:** No dogs (ex guide dogs) No smoking in restaurant **CARDS:**

LLANFAIRPWLLGWYNGYLL See Anglesey, Isle of

LLANFYLLIN, Powys — Map 15 SJ

★★67% **Cain Valley**
High St SY22 5AQ
☎ 01691 648366 🖷 01691 648307
e-mail: info@cainvalleyhotel.co.uk
Dir: *at end of A490 - Llanfyllin, 12m from Welshpool. Hotel in centre of town on square, car park at rear*
An unpretentious, privately-owned, Grade II listed coaching inn with exposed beams and a Jacobean staircase. The comfortable accommodation includes family rooms and food is available in a choice of bars (the public bar is popular with locals) or in the restaurant, which has a well-deserved reputation for its locally-sourced steaks.
ROOMS: 13 en suite (3 fmly) s £38-£42; d £62-£69 (incl. bkfst) **LB** **PARKING:** 12 **NOTES:** No smoking in restaurant RS 24-25 Dec **CARDS:**

LLANGAMMARCH WELLS, Powys — Map 09 SN9

Top 200 - Hotel

★★★ **Lake Country House**
LD4 4BS
☎ 01591 620202 & 620474 🖷 01591 620457
e-mail: info@lakecountryhouse.co.uk
Dir: *from Builth Wells W on A483 to Garth (6m approx) turn left for Llangammarch Wells follow signs for hotel*
Expect good old fashioned values of service and hospitality at this Victorian country house hotel which comes complete with a 9-hole, par three golf course, fifty acres of wooded grounds and a river. Bedrooms, many of which are suites, are individually decorated and have many extra comforts as standard. Traditional afternoon teas are served in the lounge in front of a log fire and award-winning cuisine in the spacious and elegant restaurant.
ROOMS: 19 en suite (1 fmly) (2 GF) No smoking in 6 bedrooms s £95-£155; d £160-£275 (incl. bkfst & dinner) **LB** **FACILITIES:** Golf 9 Tennis (hard) Fishing Snooker Croquet lawn Putting green Clay pigeon shooting, horse riding, mountain biking, quad biking, archery ch fac Xmas **CONF:** Thtr 80 Class 30 Board 25 Del from £115 **PARKING:** 72 **NOTES:** No smoking in restaurant Civ Wed 90 **CARDS:**

LLANGEFNI See Anglesey, Isle of

LLANGOLLEN, Denbighshire Map 15 SJ24
See also Glyn Ceiriog

★★★74% The Wild Pheasant Hotel & Restaurant
Berwyn Rd LL20 8AD
☎ 01978 860629 01978 861837
e-mail: wild.pheasant@talk21.com
Dir: *hotel 0.5m from town centre on left side of A5 towards Betws-y-Coed/Holyhead*

This professionally run hotel provides friendly hospitality and smart accommodation, including ground floor, four-poster and no-smoking rooms. The reception area, resembling an old village square, has comfortable seating. There is a choice of bars and a range of eating options. Facilities include a large function suite.
ROOMS: 46 en suite (4 fmly) (12 GF) No smoking in 9 bedrooms s £70-£115; d £104-£230 (incl. bkfst) **LB FACILITIES: Spa** Jacuzzi Xmas **CONF:** BC Thtr 200 Class 70 Board 50 Del £95 **SERVICES:** Lift **PARKING:** 100 **NOTES:** No dogs (ex guide dogs) Civ Wed 140
CARDS:

★★★70% Bryn Howel
LL20 7UW
☎ 01978 860331 01978 860119
e-mail: hotel@brynhowel.co.uk
Dir: *Llangollen signs on A539. Pass through Acrefair & Trevor, continue for 2m, hotel on left*

Best Western

The Bryn Howel occupies an enviable position in the Vale of Llangollen, with views directly over the canal, formal gardens and mountains. Bedrooms vary in size and style between the original main house rooms and the newer room, all are comfortable with good seating and desk space. Dinner is a must with dishes demonstrating much skill and featuring lots of local produce.
ROOMS: 36 en suite s £48-£72; d £95-£108 (incl. bkfst) **LB FACILITIES:** STV Fishing Sauna Solarium Croquet lawn Xmas **CONF:** Thtr 250 Class 60 Board 50 Del £99.70 **SERVICES:** Lift **PARKING:** 200 **NOTES:** No dogs (ex guide dogs) No smoking in restaurant Civ Wed 300 **CARDS:**

★★67% Chain Bridge Hotel
Berwyn LL20 8BS
☎ 01978 860215 01978 861841
e-mail: chainbridgehotel@aol.com
Dir: *1.5m A539 W of Llangollen (signed Horseshoe Pass), left to B5103 500yds signed entrance (over narrow bridge, along towpath to hotel)*
Chain Bridge is situated in an idyllic location between the River Dee and the Shropshire Union Canal. It takes its name from the footbridge, which spans the river at this point. Several of the comfortably furnished bedrooms have balconies and some are suitable for families. The restaurant overlooks the river and meals are also available in the Tudor bar.

ROOMS: 29 en suite 4 annexe en suite (2 fmly) No smoking in 5 bedrooms s £32-£40; d £64-£80 (incl. bkfst) **LB FACILITIES:** STV Fishing entertainment Xmas **CONF:** Thtr 80 Class 80 Board 50 **PARKING:** 40 **NOTES:** No smoking in restaurant Civ Wed 120
CARDS:

★★63% *Abbey Grange Hotel*
LL20 8DD
☎ 01978 860753 01978 869070
e-mail: enquiries@abbey-grange-hotel.co.uk
Dir: *A542 signed Ruthin Abbey Grange. Hotel approx 2m on left*

This hotel, situated close to Llangollen, is a good base for exploring Offa's Dyke and the surrounding countryside. Rooms are spacious and well-equipped, and some are suitable for families. Guests can dine in the restaurant or the bar, and outside are a sun patio and a large children's play area.
ROOMS: 8 en suite (3 fmly) **PARKING:** 40
CARDS:

GF Indicates the number of bedrooms at ground floor level.

LLANRHIDIAN, Swansea Map 08 SS49

★★64% North Gower
SA3 1EE
☎ 01792 390042 01792 391401
e-mail: gbanchor@aol.com
Dir: *on B4295, turn left at Llanrhidian Esso Service Station*
Situated on the Gower Peninsula with delightful views over the sea, this family owned hotel offers guests a relaxing and comfortable stay. Bedrooms are spacious and airy whilst public

continued on p846

LLANRHIDIAN, continued

areas consist of a character bar, a pleasant restaurant and a choice of meeting and function rooms.

North Gower, Llanrhidian

ROOMS: 18 en suite (10 fmly) (7 GF) No smoking in 8 bedrooms s fr £45; d fr £60 (incl. bkfst) **LB FACILITIES:** Xmas **CONF:** BC Thtr 250 Class 170 Board 60 Del from £72 **PARKING:** 100 **NOTES:** No smoking in restaurant **CARDS:**

See advert under SWANSEA

LLANRWST, Conwy Map 14 SH86
See also Betws-y-Coed

L

★★★66% **Maenan Abbey**
Maenan LL26 0UL
☎ 01492 660247 01492 660734
e-mail: reservations@manab.co.uk
Dir: *3m N on A470*

This personally run private hotel was built as an abbey in 1850 on the site of a 13th-century monastery. It is now a popular venue for weddings as the grounds and magnificent galleried staircase make an ideal backdrop for photographs. Bedrooms include a large suite and are equipped with modern facilities. Meals are served in the bar and restaurant.

ROOMS: 14 en suite (2 fmly) s £40-£50; d £60-£70 (incl. bkfst) **LB FACILITIES:** Fishing guided mountain walks Xmas **CONF:** BC Thtr 50 Class 30 Board 30 Del £75 **PARKING:** 60 **NOTES:** No smoking in restaurant Civ Wed 90 **CARDS:**

LLANWDDYN, Powys Map 15 SJ01

★★★73% **Lake Vyrnwy**
Lake Vyrnwy SY10 0LY
☎ 01691 870692 01691 870259
e-mail: res@lakevyrnwy.com
Dir: *on A4393, 200yds past dam*

This fine country house hotel lies in 26,000 acres of woodland above Lake Vyrnwy. It provides a wide range of bedrooms, most with superb views and many with four-poster beds and balconies. The extensive public rooms are elegantly furnished and include a terrace, a choice of bars serving meals and the more formal dining in the restaurant.

ROOMS: 35 en suite (4 fmly) **FACILITIES:** STV Tennis (hard) Fishing Riding Game/Clay shooting, Sailing, Cycling, Archery, Quad trekking, Fly fishing **CONF:** Thtr 120 Class 60 Board 45 **PARKING:** 70 **NOTES:** No smoking in restaurant Civ Wed 120
CARDS:

LLANWRTYD WELLS, Powys Map 09 SN84

★★69% **Lasswade Country House Hotel**
Station Rd LD5 4RW
☎ 01591 610515 01591 610611
e-mail: rstevens@messages.co.uk
Dir: *off A483 into Ifron Terrace, right into Station Rd, hotel 350yds on right*

This friendly hotel set on the edge of the town has impressive views over the surrounding countryside. Bedrooms are comfortably furnished and well equipped, while the public areas consist of a tastefully decorated lounge, an elegant restaurant and an airy conservatory which looks out onto the neighbouring hills. The hotel is non-smoking throughout.

ROOMS: 8 en suite No smoking in all bedrooms s fr £45; d fr £68 (incl. bkfst) **LB FACILITIES:** Sauna **CONF:** Thtr 16 Class 16 Board 16 Del from £78 **PARKING:** 8 **NOTES:** No dogs (ex guide dogs) No smoking in restaurant **CARDS:**

Restaurant with Rooms

Carlton House
Dolycoed Rd LD5 4RA
☎ 01591 610248 01591 610242
e-mail: info@carltonrestaurant.co.uk
Dir: *centre of town*

Guests are made to feel like one of the family here. Carlton House is set in reputedly the smallest rural town in Britain which is surrounded by stunning countryside. It offers award-winning cuisine, complemented by a well chosen wine list, that is served in the atmospheric restaurant. The themed bedrooms, like the public areas, have period furniture and are decorated in warm colours.

ROOMS: 6 rms (5 en suite) (2 fmly) s £45; d £65-£80 (incl. bkfst) **LB FACILITIES:** Pony trekking Mountain biking **NOTES:** No smoking in restaurant Closed 15-30 Dec RS All year **CARDS:**

LLYSWEN, Powys Map 09 SO13

★★★★73% **Llangoed Hall**
LD3 0YP
☎ 01874 754525 01874 754545
e-mail: llangoed_hall_co_wales_uk@compuserve.com
Dir: *A470 through village for 2m. Hotel drive on right*

This imposing Edwardian house stands amidst glorious countryside, with views across the Wye Valley to the Black Mountains beyond. The interior is no less impressive, the superb art collection complementing the many antiques featured in day rooms and bedrooms. Look out particularly for the drawings in the appropriately named Whistler Room. Comfortable and spacious bedrooms and suites are matched by the equally inviting lounges.

ROOMS: 23 en suite s £120-£160; d £220-£260 (incl. bkfst) **LB FACILITIES:** STV Tennis (hard) Fishing Snooker Croquet lawn Maze, Clay pigeon shooting Xmas **CONF:** Thtr 60 Class 30 Board 28 Del from £187 **PARKING:** 80 **NOTES:** No dogs (ex guide dogs) No children 8yrs No smoking in restaurant Civ Wed 50
CARDS:

MACHYNLLETH, Powys
Map 14 SH70

See also Eglwysfach

★★69% Penmaendyfi
Cwrt, Pennal SY20 9LD
☎ 01654 791246 📠 01654 791616
e-mail: farmcott@aol.com
Dir: *at Cwrt onto A493 from Machynlleth to Aberdyfi. Hotel 0.5m on left.*

Overlooking the Dyfi Estuary, this hotel is surrounded by its own farm which supplies meat and produce for the restaurant, where a wide selection of dishes are available. It provides luxurious and well-equipped rooms, as well as a comfortable bar and extensive grounds with a heated swimming pool.
ROOMS: 6 en suite 1 annexe en suite No smoking in all bedrooms s £40-£45; d £90-£110 (incl. bkfst) **LB FACILITIES:** Outdoor swimming (H) Tennis (hard) Xmas **PARKING:** 40 **NOTES:** No dogs (ex guide dogs) No smoking in restaurant Civ Wed 100
CARDS:

★★66% Wynnstay
Maengwyn St SY20 8AE
☎ 01654 702941 📠 01654 703884
e-mail: info@wynnstay-hotel.com
Dir: *at junct of A487/A489, in the town centre, 25yds from the clock tower*
Long established, this former posting house lies in the centre of historic Machynlleth. Bedrooms, which include no-smoking rooms and family bedded rooms, have modern facilities. The bars are popular with locals and a good range of food is available. The restaurant offers more formal dining and guests can choose from a fixed-price menu.
ROOMS: 23 en suite (3 fmly) No smoking in 7 bedrooms s £50-£65; d £80-£100 (incl. bkfst) **LB FACILITIES:** Fishing Clay shooting, Game shooting, Mountain biking Xmas **CONF:** Thtr 40 Class 12 Board 16 Del from £83.45 **PARKING:** 30 **NOTES:** No smoking in restaurant RS New Years Day **CARDS:**

See advert on this page

MAGOR SERVICE AREA (M4), Monmouthshire
Map 09 ST48

Travelodge
Magor Service Area NP26 3YL
☎ 08700 850 950
Dir: *M4 junct 23A*
Travelodge offers good quality, good value, modern accommodation. Ideal for families, the spacious, en suite bedrooms include remote-control TV, tea and coffee-making facilities, luxury beds and free morning newspaper. Meals can be taken at the nearby family restaurant. For further details and the Travelodge phone number, consult the Hotel Groups page.
ROOMS: 43 en suite s fr £42.95; d fr £42.95

MANORBIER, Pembrokeshire
Map 08 SS09

★★66% Castle Mead
THE CIRCLE Selected Individual Hotels GREAT BRITAIN

SA70 7TA
☎ 01834 871358 📠 01834 871358
e-mail: castlemeadhotel@aol.com
Dir: *A4139 towards Pembroke, turn onto B4585 into village & follow signs to beach & castle. Hotel on left above beach*
Benefiting from a superb location with spectacular views of the bay, the Norman church and Manorbier Castle, this family-run establishment is friendly and welcoming. Public areas include a sea view restaurant, bar and residents' lounge and an extensive garden. Bedrooms are generally quite spacious and offer modern facilities throughout.
ROOMS: 5 en suite 3 annexe en suite (2 fmly) (3 GF) No smoking in 2 bedrooms s fr £40; d fr £75 (incl. bkfst) **LB PARKING:** 20
NOTES: Closed Jan-Feb **CARDS:**

MENAI BRIDGE See Anglesey, Isle of

MERTHYR TYDFIL, Merthyr Tydfil
Map 09 SO00

See also Nant-Ddu

★★★67% Tregenna
Park Ter CF47 8RF
☎ 01685 723627 & 382055 📠 01685 721951
e-mail: reception@tregennahotel.co.uk
Set in quiet suburbs just north of the town centre, this friendly, family-run hotel offers guests an oasis of peace in which to enjoy their stay. Bedrooms are light, maintained to a high standard and

continued on p848

MERTHYR TYDFIL, continued

some are located in a purpose-built annexe. Meals can be taken in the inviting restaurant or the comfortable, less formal bar.
ROOMS: 14 en suite 7 annexe en suite (6 fmly) No smoking in 4 bedrooms s £45-£48; d £55-£60 (incl. bkfst) **LB FACILITIES:** STV **CONF:** Thtr 50 Class 40 Board 20 **PARKING:** 10 **CARDS:**

Travel Inn

Pentrebach CF48 4BD
☎ 08701 977183 01443 699171
Dir: *M4 junct 32 follow A470 to Merthyr Tydfil. At 2nd rdbt turn right to Pentrebach, follow signs to Ind Estate*
Travel Inn offers good-quality, value-for-money accommodation. Spacious, en suite rooms with bath and shower comfortably accommodate a family of up to two adults and two children (to age 15). The restaurant and bar offers a varied menu. For further details and the Travel Inn phone number, consult the Hotel Groups page.
ROOMS: 40 en suite s £44.95; d £44.95 **CONF:** Thtr 65 Board 30

MISKIN, Rhondda Cynon Taff — Map 09 ST08

★★★★69% Miskin Manor Hotel & Health Club

Groes Faen, Pontyclun CF72 8ND
☎ 01443 224204 01443 237606
e-mail: info@miskin-manor.co.uk
Dir: *M4 junct 34, exit onto A4119, signed Llantrisant, hotel is 300yds on left*
This manor house is set in 20 acres of grounds, only minutes away from the M4. Public areas are spacious and comfortable and include a variety of function rooms. Bedrooms are furnished to a high standard and include some located in converted stables and cottages. Frederick's health club has leisure facilities and a bar/bistro.
ROOMS: 33 en suite 9 annexe en suite (3 GF) No smoking in 8 bedrooms s £94-£126; d £126-£175 (incl. bkfst) **LB FACILITIES:** STV Indoor swimming (H) Squash Sauna Solarium Gym Croquet lawn Jacuzzi Swimming pool supervised ch fac Xmas **CONF:** Thtr 160 Class 80 Board 65 Del from £120 **PARKING:** 200 **NOTES:** No smoking in restaurant Civ Wed 200 **CARDS:**

See advert under CARDIFF

MOLD, Flintshire — Map 15 SJ26

See also Northop Hall

★★★67% Beaufort Park Hotel

Alltami Rd, New Brighton CH7 6RQ
☎ 01352 758646 01352 757132
e-mail: bph@beaufortparkhotel.co.uk
Dir: *A55/A494. Through Alltami lights, over mini rdbt by petrol station towards Mold, A5119. Hotel 100yds on right*
This large, modern hotel is conveniently located a short drive from the North Wales Expressway and offers various styles of spacious accommodation. There are extensive public areas, and several meeting and function rooms are available. There is a wide choice of meals in the formal restaurant and in the popular Arches bar.
ROOMS: 106 en suite (4 fmly) (33 GF) No smoking in 25 bedrooms s £95; d £110 (incl. bkfst) **LB FACILITIES:** Squash Jacuzzi Games Room,Darts entertainment ch fac Xmas **CONF:** Thtr 250 Class 120 Board 50 Del from £110 **PARKING:** 200 **NOTES:** Civ Wed 80 **CARDS:**

★★66% *Bryn Awel*

Denbigh Rd CH7 1BL
☎ 01352 758622 01352 758625
e-mail: bryn@awel.fsbusiness.co.uk
Dir: *NW edge of town, on A541*
Located on the edge of the town centre, this privately operated hotel provides well-equipped modern accommodation, some of it located in a purpose-built annexe. Public rooms include a small but well equipped function room, a lounge bar offering an extensive selection of bar meals and an attractive bistro-style restaurant.
ROOMS: 8 en suite 10 annexe en suite No smoking in 11 bedrooms **CONF:** Thtr 30 Class 15 Board 20 **PARKING:** 45 **NOTES:** No smoking in restaurant **CARDS:**

MONMOUTH, Monmouthshire — Map 10 SO5

See also Whitebrook

★★63% Riverside

Cinderhill St NP25 5EY
☎ 01600 715577 & 713236 01600 712668
e-mail: riverside@compass-rose.org.uk
Dir: *leave A40 signposted Rockfield & Monmouth hotel on left beyond garage & before rdbt*
Just a short walk from the famous 13th-century bridge, this privately owned hotel offers accommodation in a relaxed and informal atmosphere. Bedrooms are well equipped and soundly decorated. Public areas include a separate restaurant, a popular bar and a conservatory lounge at the rear of the property.
ROOMS: 17 en suite (2 fmly) No smoking in 2 bedrooms s £40-£56; d £50-£68 (incl. bkfst) **LB FACILITIES:** Xmas **CONF:** Thtr 150 Class 60 Board 40 Del from £59.50 **PARKING:** 30 **NOTES:** No smoking in restaurant **CARDS:**

MONTGOMERY, Powys — Map 15 SO2

★★71% Dragon

SY15 6PA
☎ 01686 668359 01686 668287
e-mail: reception@dragonhotel.com
Dir: *behind the Town Hall*
This fine 17th-century coaching inn stands in the centre of Montgomery. Beams and timbers from the nearby castle, which was destroyed by Cromwell, are visible in the lounge and bar. A wide choice of soundly prepared, wholesome food is available in both the restaurant and bar. Bedrooms are well-equipped and family rooms are available.
ROOMS: 20 en suite (6 fmly) No smoking in 16 bedrooms s £47-£57; d £80-£90 (incl. bkfst) **LB FACILITIES:** Indoor swimming (H) Sauna entertainment Xmas **CONF:** Thtr 40 Class 30 Board 25 **PARKING:** 21 **NOTES:** No smoking in restaurant **CARDS:**

MUMBLES (NEAR SWANSEA), Swansea — Map 08 SS6

★★★65% St Anne's

Western Ln SA3 4EY
☎ 01792 369147 01792 360537
e-mail: info@stanneshotel-mumbles.com
Dir: *A483/A4067 along coastal road to Mumbles, at village straight over mini rdbt, Western Ln is 3rd right*
This privately owned hotel stands on a steep hillside close to the town centre, and enjoys some superb views over the Swansea Bay. The accommodation is modern and the bedrooms are well equipped. No smoking bedrooms, family rooms, interconnecting

continued

rooms and bedrooms on ground floor level are all available. The bright and pleasant public areas include a spacious lounge.

ROOMS: 33 en suite (3 fmly) No smoking in 7 bedrooms s £55-£60; d £63-£70 (incl. bkfst) **LB** **FACILITIES:** STV Xmas **CONF:** Thtr 100 Class 50 Board 50 Del £65 **PARKING:** 50 **NOTES:** No smoking in restaurant **CARDS:**

See advert on this page

NANT-DDU (NEAR MERTHYR TYDFIL), Powys Map 09 SO01

★★★76% Nant Ddu Lodge

Cwm Taf, Nant Ddu CF48 2HY
☎ 01685 379111 01685 377088
e-mail: enquiries@nant-ddu-lodge.co.uk

Dir: *6m N of Merthyr Tydfil & 12m S of Brecon on A470 between Merthyr and Brecon*

Close to the Brecon Beacons and with origins stretching back 200 years, this delightful hotel has seen many improvements in the caring hands of the present owners. Decor throughout is contemporary and the bedrooms are thoughtfully furnished and well equipped. Meals can be taken in the modern bistro and there is a bar with a more traditional 'village inn' atmosphere. There is also a well-equipped health, beauty, leisure and fitness centre and spa.

ROOMS: 12 en suite 16 annexe en suite (3 fmly) No smoking in 6 bedrooms s £65-£75; d £80-£100 (incl. bkfst) **FACILITIES: Spa** STV Indoor swimming (H) Sauna Solarium Gym Jacuzzi Swimming pool supervised **CONF:** BC Thtr 30 Class 20 Board 20 Del from £100 **PARKING:** 60 **NOTES:** No smoking in restaurant RS 24-26 Dec **CARDS:**

See advert on this page and under BRECON

NEATH, Neath Port Talbot Map 09 SS79

★★65% Castle Hotel

The Parade SA11 1RB
☎ 01639 641119 & 643581 01639 641624
e-mail: info@castlehotelneath.co.uk

Dir: *M4 junct 43, follow signs for Neath, 500yds past railway station, hotel on right. Car park 50yds further on left*

Lord Nelson is reputed to have stayed at this former Georgian coaching inn, where Welsh Rugby Union was founded over a century ago. The bedrooms are thoughtfully equipped and comfortable while the character bar and restaurant have a local following.

ROOMS: 29 en suite (3 fmly) No smoking in 4 bedrooms s £55-£65; d £65-£75 (incl. bkfst) **LB** **FACILITIES:** STV **CONF:** Thtr 160 Class 75 Board 50 Del from £80 **PARKING:** 26 **NOTES:** No dogs (ex guide dogs) **CARDS:**

AA Rosette Award for culinary excellence

NEVERN, Pembrokeshire
Map 08 SN04

★★68% Trewern Arms
SA42 0NB
☎ 01239 820395 🖷 01239 820173
e-mail: trevor.wood4@virgin.net
Dir: *off A487 coast road - midway between Cardigan and Fishguard*
Set in a peaceful and picturesque village, this charming 16th-century inn is well positioned to offer a relaxing stay. There are many original features to be seen in the two character bars and attractive restaurant whilst the spacious bedrooms are appointed to a high standard and include some family rooms.
ROOMS: 10 en suite (4 fmly) s £35; d £50-£60 (incl. bkfst) **FACILITIES:** Fishing Riding Xmas **PARKING:** 100 **NOTES:** No dogs **CARDS:**

NEWPORT, Newport
Map 09 ST38

★★★★★72% The Celtic Manor Resort
Coldra Woods NP18 1HQ
☎ 01633 413000 🖷 01633 412910
e-mail: postbox@celtic-manor.com
Dir: *M4 junct 24, take A48 towards Newport. Hotel 1st right past Alcatel*
This luxurious resort offers a whole host of facilities to suit any guest, whether they be conference delegates, business users or leisure guests. Three golf courses are complemented by superb leisure facilities, whilst the convention centre can accommodate 1500 delegates. There is also a wide choice of dining options to tempt guests out of the deeply comfortable bedrooms and suites, some of which are located in the original Grade II listed manor house.
ROOMS: 400 en suite (28 fmly) No smoking in 167 bedrooms s £130-£194; d £130-£194 **LB FACILITIES: Spa** STV Indoor swimming (H) Golf 18 Tennis (hard) Snooker Sauna Solarium Gym Putting green Jacuzzi Golf school, Spa with beauty treatments, Swimming pool supervised entertainment ch fac Xmas **CONF:** BC Thtr 1500 Class 300 Board 50 Del from £170 **SERVICES:** Lift air con **PARKING:** 1300 **NOTES:** No dogs (ex guide dogs) Civ Wed 100
CARDS:

★★★67% Newport Lodge
THE INDEPENDENTS
Bryn Bevan, Brynglas Rd NP20 5QN
☎ 01633 821818 🖷 01633 856360
e-mail: info@newportlodgehotel.co.uk
Dir: *M4 junct 26 follow signs Newport. Turn left after 0.5m onto Malpal Rd, up hill for 0.5m to hotel*
On the edge of the town centre and convenient for the M4, this purpose-built, friendly hotel provides comfortable and well-maintained bedrooms, with modern facilities. A room with a four-poster bed is available. The bistro-style restaurant offers a wide range of freshly prepared dishes, often using local ingredients.
ROOMS: 27 en suite No smoking in 8 bedrooms s £80-£100; d £90-£125 (incl. bkfst) **LB CONF:** Thtr 25 Class 20 Board 20 **PARKING:** 63 **NOTES:** No children 14yrs No smoking in restaurant
CARDS:

★★★65% *Kings*
High St NP20 1QU
☎ 01633 842020 🖷 01633 244667
e-mail: kingshotels.wales@netscapeonline.co.uk
Dir: *from town centre, take left road (not flyover) right lane to next rdbt, 3rd exit off across front of hotel then left for car park*
This large, imposing property is situated right in the town centre. Privately owned, it offers comfortable bedrooms including no smoking and family rooms, and bright spacious public areas. Facilities include a choice of function rooms and a large ballroom.
ROOMS: 61 en suite (15 fmly) No smoking in 20 bedrooms **FACILITIES:** STV entertainment **CONF:** Thtr 150 Class 70 Board 50 **SERVICES:** Lift **PARKING:** 50 **NOTES:** No dogs (ex guide dogs) Closed 26 Dec-4 Jan Civ Wed **CARDS:**

See advert on opposite page

Travel Inn
Coldra Junction, Chepstow Rd NP18 2NX
☎ 08701 977193 🖷 01633 411376
Dir: *Just off junct 24 of M4. Take A48 to Langstone, at next rdbt return towards junct 24. Travel Inn 50 metres on left, only 20 minute drive from the Millennium Stadium.*
Travel Inn offers good-quality, value-for-money accommodation. Spacious, en suite rooms with bath and shower comfortably accommodate a family of up to two adults and two children (to age 15). The restaurant and bar offers a varied menu. For further details and the Travel Inn phone number, consult the Hotel Groups page.
ROOMS: 63 en suite s £44.95; d £44.95

NEWTOWN, Powys
Map 15 SO19

U Elephant & Castle
Broad St SY16 2BQ
☎ 01686 626271 🖷 01686 622123
e-mail: enquire@elephanthotelfsnet.co.uk
Dir: *A483 to town on t-junct of town centre*
At the time of going to press, the star classification for this hotel was not confirmed. Please refer to the AA internet site www.theAA.com for current information.
ROOMS: 24 en suite 11 annexe en suite (3 fmly) (4 GF) No smoking in all bedrooms s fr £39; d fr £58 (incl. bkfst) **LB FACILITIES: Spa** STV Fishing entertainment **CONF:** Thtr 250 Class 175 Board 175 Del from £60 **PARKING:** 60 **NOTES:** No dogs (ex guide dogs) No smoking in restaurant Civ Wed 40 **CARDS:**

NORTHOP, Flintshire
Map 15 SJ26

★★★75% Soughton Hall
CH7 6AB
☎ 01352 840811 🖷 01352 840382
e-mail: info@soughtonhall.co.uk
Dir: *A55/B5126, after 500mtrs turn left for Northop, left at traffic lights (A5119-Mold). After 0.5m follow signs*
Built as a bishop's palace in 1714, this elegant country house has magnificent grounds. Bedrooms are individually decorated and furnished with fine antiques and rich fabrics. There are several spacious day rooms furnished in keeping with the style of the house. The trendy bar and restaurant offer a good range of dishes at both lunch and dinner.
ROOMS: 14 en suite (2 fmly) (2 GF) No smoking in all bedrooms s £100-£120; d £120-£170 (incl. bkfst) **LB FACILITIES: Spa** Tennis (hard) Riding Croquet lawn Jacuzzi Riding stables nearby Xmas **CONF:** BC Thtr 40 Class 40 Board 20 Del £135 **PARKING:** 100 **NOTES:** No smoking in restaurant Civ Wed 120 **CARDS:**

NORTHOP HALL, Flintshire

Map 15 SJ26

A ★★★ Northop Hall Country House
Chester Rd CH7 6HJ
☎ 01244 816181 ▤ 01244 814661
e-mail: northop@hotel-chester.com
Dir: *M56/A5117/A494. Exit Buckley/St David's Park. At rdbt, 3rd exit then 1st right to Northop Hall. After 2m, bear left at mini rdbt. Hotel entrance 200yds on left*
ROOMS: 39 en suite (16 fmly) No smoking in 12 bedrooms s £60-£70; d £70-£105 **LB FACILITIES:** ch fac Xmas **CONF:** Thtr 120 Class 80 Board 70 Del from £89.50 **PARKING:** 100 **NOTES:** No dogs (ex guide dogs) No smoking in restaurant **CARDS:**

THE INDEPENDENTS

⌂ Travelodge
CH7 6HB
☎ 08700 850 950 ▤ 01244 816473
Dir: *on A55, eastbound*
Travelodge offers good quality, good value, modern accommodation. Ideal for families, the spacious, en suite bedrooms include remote-control TV, tea and coffee-making facilities, luxury beds and free morning newspaper. Meals can be taken at the nearby family restaurant. For further details and the Travelodge phone number, consult the Hotel Groups page.
ROOMS: 40 en suite s fr £42.95; d fr £42.95

Travelodge

PEMBROKE, Pembrokeshire

Map 08 SM90

★★★74% Lamphey Court
Lamphey SA71 5NT
☎ 01646 672273 ▤ 01646 672480
e-mail: info@lampheycourt.co.uk
Dir: *A477 to Pembroke. Turn left at Village Milton. In Lamphey hotel on right*

Best Western

This former Georgian mansion is set in attractive countryside and within a short walk of the village of Lamphey. Bedrooms are well appointed and some are situated in a tastefully converted coach house in the grounds. The elegant public areas include a choice of formal and informal dining rooms and a relaxing lounge.
ROOMS: 26 en suite 11 annexe en suite (15 fmly) s £72-£84; d £100-£140 (incl. bkfst) **LB FACILITIES:** STV Indoor swimming (H) Tennis (hard) Sauna Solarium Gym Jacuzzi Yacht charter Xmas **CONF:** Thtr 60 Class 40 Board 30 Del from £98 **PARKING:** 50 **NOTES:** No dogs (ex guide dogs) No smoking in restaurant Civ Wed 60 **CARDS:**

See advert on this page

> Late for dinner?
> Quality Standards mean that last orders for dinner vary according to star rating and should be no earlier than:
> ★★ 7.00pm ★★★ 8.00pm ★★★★ 9.00pm
> ★★★★★ 10.00pm

P

PEMBROKE, continued

★★67% Beggars Reach
SA73 1PD
☎ 01646 600700 📠 01646 600560
e-mail: stay@beggars-reach.com
Dir: *8m S of Haverfordwest, 6m N of Pembroke, off A477*
This privately owned and personally run hotel was once a Georgian rectory. It stands in four acres of grounds and is peacefully located close to the village of Burton. Milford Haven and the ferry terminal at Pembroke Dock are both within easy reach. It provides modern equipped accommodation and two of the bedrooms are located in former stables, which date back to the 14th century.

ROOMS: 15 en suite 2 annexe en suite (4 fmly) (2 GF) No smoking in 3 bedrooms s £45-£65; d £65-£85 (incl. bkfst) **LB** **FACILITIES:** STV **CONF:** Thtr 100 Class 60 Board 60 Del from £75 **PARKING:** 50 **NOTES:** No smoking in restaurant **CARDS:**

See advert under HAVERFORDWEST

★★66% Highgate Inn
Hundleton SA71 5RD
☎ 01646 685904 📠 01646 681888
e-mail: windy.gail@virgin.net
Dir: *B4320 signed Angle, follow signs to Highgate in Hundleton, hotel opposite playing fields*
The hotel is a popular village meeting place, with the bar and games room offering interesting views of the Pembroke Docks and surrounding countryside. Staff are friendly in the restaurant at dinner, or over a Welsh breakfast. Bedrooms are comfortable and equipped with lots of useful extras.
ROOMS: 6 rms (5 en suite) (2 fmly) No smoking in all bedrooms s £60-£65; d £100-£120 (incl. bkfst) **LB** **FACILITIES:** Tennis (hard) Riding Pool table & games bar Xmas **CONF:** BC Thtr 30 Class 30 Board 30 **PARKING:** 65 **NOTES:** No dogs (ex guide dogs) No smoking in restaurant **CARDS:**

★★64% Old Kings Arms
Main St SA71 4JS
☎ 01646 683611 📠 01646 682335
e-mail: reception@oldkingsarmshotel.freeserve.co.uk
Dir: *M4/A477 to Pembroke. Turn left for Pembroke, at rdbt follow town centre sign. Turn right onto the parade, car park is signed*
At the centre of the bustling town, this former coaching inn is very much at the heart of local activities and is a favourite with locals. The restaurant and bar have traditional stone walls, flagstone floors and roaring log fires. Both areas offer good, wholesome food.
ROOMS: 18 en suite s £35-£45; d £55 (incl. bkfst) **FACILITIES:** STV **PARKING:** 21 **NOTES:** Closed 25-26 Dec & 1 Jan
CARDS:

PEMBROKE DOCK, Pembrokeshire Map 08 SM9

★★★69% Cleddau Bridge
Essex Rd SA72 6EG
☎ 01646 685961 & 0800 279 4055 📠 01646 685746
e-mail: information@cleddaubridgehotel.co.uk
Dir: *M4/A40 to St Clears A477 to Pembroke Dock at rdbt 2nd exit for Haverfordwest via toll bridge, take left before the toll bridge*
A purpose-built hotel adjacent to the Cleddau Bridge and with far reaching views of the estuary. The well-equipped bedrooms are all on the ground floor, while the comfortable public areas consist of an attractive bar and restaurant, both with impressive views.
ROOMS: 24 en suite (2 fmly) No smoking in 12 bedrooms s £55-£60; d £70-£75 (incl. bkfst) **LB** **FACILITIES:** STV Xmas **CONF:** Thtr 160 Class 60 Board 60 **PARKING:** 140 **NOTES:** No smoking in restaurant Closed 25-26 Dec RS Xmas Eve and New Years Day Civ Wed 140
CARDS:

PENCOED, Bridgend Map 09 SS98

★★★73% St Mary's Hotel & Country Club
Best Western
St Marys Golf Club CF35 5EA
☎ 01656 861100 & 860280 📠 01656 863400
e-mail: stmaryshotel@hotmail.com
Dir: *M4 junct 35, on A473*

This charming 16th-century farmhouse has been converted and extended into a modern and restful hotel, surrounded by its own two golf courses. Guests are offered a choice of bars, which are popular with club members, and may dine in the Rafters Restaurant. Bedrooms are generously appointed, well equipped and most feature whirlpool baths.
ROOMS: 24 en suite (19 fmly) s £60-£70; d £75-£90 (incl. bkfst) **LB** **FACILITIES:** STV Golf 18 Tennis (hard) Putting green Floodlit driving range Xmas **CONF:** Thtr 120 Class 60 Board 40 **PARKING:** 140 **NOTES:** No dogs (ex guide dogs) Civ Wed 100
CARDS:

See advert under BRIDGEND

Travel Inn (Bridgend)
travel inn
Pantruthyn Farm, Pencoed CF35 5HY
☎ 08701 977041 📠 01656 864792
Dir: *at J35 of M4, behind petrol station and McDonalds.*
Travel Inn offers good-quality, value-for-money accommodation. Spacious, en suite rooms with bath and shower comfortably accommodate a family of up to two adults and two children (to age 15). The restaurant and bar offers a varied menu. For further details and the Travel Inn phone number, consult the Hotel Groups page.
ROOMS: 40 en suite s £44.95; d £44.95

⌂ Travelodge

Old Mill, Felindre Rd CF3 5HU
☎ 08700 850 950 🖷 01656 864404
Dir: *on A473*
Travelodge offers good quality, good value, modern accommodation. Ideal for families, the spacious, en suite bedrooms include remote-control TV, tea and coffee-making facilities, luxury beds and free morning newspaper. Meals can be taken at the nearby family restaurant. For further details and the Travelodge phone number, consult the Hotel Groups page.
ROOMS: 39 en suite s fr £42.95; d fr £42.95

PONTERWYD, Ceredigion — Map 09 SN78

★★65% The George Borrow Hotel

SY23 3AD
☎ 01970 890230 🖷 01970 890587
e-mail: georgeborrow@lycos.co.uk
Dir: *on A44 Aberystwyth-Llangurig road. Aberystwyth side of village*

This friendly hotel sits in the foothills of the Cambrian Mountains, about 12 miles from the university town of Aberystwyth. The hotel provides an ideal base for walking, fishing and bird watching (look out for red kites). Bedrooms are comfortable and there are two character bars and a restaurant.
ROOMS: 9 en suite (2 fmly) s £30; d £60 (incl. bkfst) **LB CONF:** Thtr 40 Class 30 Board 30 **PARKING:** 30 **NOTES:** No dogs (ex guide dogs) No smoking in restaurant **CARDS:**

PONTYPOOL, Torfaen — Map 09 SO20

⌂ Express by Holiday Inn

New Mill Roundabout NP4 0RH
☎ 01495 755266 🖷 01495 755331
e-mail: exhi-pontypool@btconnect.com
Dir: *at junct of A4042/A472, adjacent to the Harvester Restaurant*

A modern hotel ideal for families and business travellers. Fresh and uncomplicated, the spacious bedrooms include Sky TV, power shower and tea and coffee-making facilities. Continental buffet breakfast is included in the room rate; other meals may be taken at the nearby family pub or restaurant. For further details and the Express by Holiday Inn phone number, consult the Hotel Groups pages.
ROOMS: 49 en suite **CONF:** Thtr 30 Class 24 Board 16

PONTYPRIDD, Rhondda Cynon Taff — Map 09 ST08

★★★70% Llechwen Hall

Llanfabon CF37 4HP
☎ 01443 742050 & 743020 🖷 01443 742189
e-mail: llechwen@aol.com
Dir: *A470 N towards Merthyr Tydfil, then A472, then onto A4054 for Cilfynydd. After 0.25m, turn left at hotel sign & follow to top of hill*

Set on top of a hill with a stunning approach, this hotel has served a variety of uses in its 200 year history, including a private school and a magistrates' court. Bedrooms are individually decorated and well equipped and some are situated in the comfortable coach house nearby. Meals can be chosen from an extensive menu in the split-level restaurant.
ROOMS: 12 en suite 8 annexe en suite (11 fmly) (4 GF) No smoking in 8 bedrooms s £49-£65; d £65-£107 (incl. bkfst) **LB FACILITIES:** Xmas **CONF:** Thtr 80 Class 30 Board 30 Del from £80 **PARKING:** 100 **NOTES:** No smoking in restaurant Closed 25-28 Dec Civ Wed 80 **CARDS:**

★★★67% Heritage Park

Coed Cae Rd, Trehafod CF37 2NP
☎ 01443 687057 🖷 01443 687060
e-mail: heritageparkhotel@talk21.com
Dir: *off A4058, follow signs to the Rhondda Heritage Park*
This privately-owned, modern hotel is suitable for all types of guest. The spacious bedrooms include ground floor and interconnecting rooms, and a room equipped for less mobile guests. Meals can be taken in the attractive, wood-beamed Loft Restaurant. Facilities include a large function suite, a choice of meeting rooms and a leisure/fitness centre.
ROOMS: 44 en suite (4 fmly) No smoking in 19 bedrooms s £61-£70; d £80-£90 (incl. bkfst) **LB FACILITIES:** STV Indoor swimming (H) Sauna Solarium Gym Jacuzzi Xmas **CONF:** Thtr 220 Class 40 Board 30 Del from £95 **PARKING:** 150 **NOTES:** No smoking in restaurant Civ Wed 90 **CARDS:**

PORTHCAWL, Bridgend — Map 09 SS87

★★★68% Atlantic

West Dr CF36 3LT
☎ 01656 785011 🖷 01656 771877
e-mail: enquiries@atlantichotelporthcawl.co.uk
Dir: *M4 junct 35/37, follow Porthcawl signs, then signs for Seafront/Promenade*
This friendly hotel is privately owned and located on the seafront,

continued on p854

P

PORTHCAWL, continued

a short walk from the town centre. Guests can enjoy sea views from the sun terrace, bright conservatory and some of the bedrooms, which are well equipped and maintained, and tastefully decorated.
ROOMS: 18 en suite (2 fmly) s £50-£69; d £80-£95 (incl. bkfst) **LB** **FACILITIES:** STV Xmas **CONF:** Thtr 50 Class 50 Board 25 **SERVICES:** Lift **PARKING:** 20 **NOTES:** No dogs (ex guide dogs) **CARDS:**

★★★65% **Seabank**
The Promenade CF36 3LU
☎ 01656 782261 01656 785363
e-mail: info@seabankhotel.co.uk
Dir: *M4 junct 37, follow A4229 to seafront, hotel on the promenade*
This large, privately owned hotel stands on the promenade overlooking the Severn Estuary. The well-equipped accommodation includes rooms with four-poster beds, and most enjoy panoramic sea views. There is a spacious restaurant, a lounge bar and a choice of lounges. This hotel is also a popular venue for weddings and conferences.
ROOMS: 67 en suite (2 fmly) No smoking in 14 bedrooms s £39-£65; d £58-£85 (incl. bkfst) **LB** **FACILITIES: Spa** STV Sauna Gym Jacuzzi entertainment Xmas **CONF:** Thtr 250 Class 150 Board 70 Del £85 **SERVICES:** Lift **PARKING:** 140 **NOTES:** No dogs (ex guide dogs) Civ Wed 100 **CARDS:**

PORTHMADOG, Gwynedd — Map 14 SH53

★★76% **Royal Sportsman**
131 High St LL49 9HB
☎ 01766 512015 01766 512490
e-mail: enquiries@royalsportsman.co.uk
Ideally located in the centre of Porthmadog, this former Victorian coaching inn dates from 1862 and has been restored into a friendly, family-run hotel. Rooms are tastefully decorated and well equipped and some are in an annexe close to the hotel. There is a large comfortable lounge and a wide range meals are served both in the bar or restaurant.
ROOMS: 19 en suite 9 annexe en suite (7 fmly) (9 GF) No smoking in all bedrooms **FACILITIES:** entertainment Xmas **CONF:** Thtr 50 Class 50 Board 30 **PARKING:** 18 **NOTES:** No smoking in restaurant **CARDS:**

PORTMEIRION, Gwynedd — Map 14 SH53

Top 200 - Hotel

★★★ **Castell Deudraeth**
LL48 6EN
☎ 01766 772400 01766 771771
e-mail: castell@portmeirion-village.com
Dir: *A4212 for Trawsfynydd/Porthmadog. 1.5m beyond Penrhyndeudraeth, hotel on right*
This recently refurbished castellated mansion overlooks Snowdonia and the famous Italianate village featured in the 1960s cult series *The Prisoner.* An original concept, Castell Deudraeth combines traditional materials, such as oak and slate, with state-of-the-art technology and design. Dynamically styled bedrooms boast underfloor heating, real-flame gas fires and wide-screen TVs with DVDs and cinema surround sound. The brasserie themed dining room provides an informal option at dinner.

ROOMS: 11 en suite (5 fmly) **FACILITIES: Spa** STV entertainment **CONF:** Thtr 30 Class 18 Board 25 **SERVICES:** Lift air con **PARKING:** 30 **NOTES:** No dogs (ex guide dogs) Civ Wed 30 **CARDS:**

★★★77% **The Hotel Portmeirion**
LL48 6ET
☎ 01766 770000 01766 771331
e-mail: hotel@portmeirion-village.com
Dir: *2m W, Portmeirion village is S off A487*
Saved from dereliction in the 1920s by Clough Williams-Ellis, the elegant Hotel Portmeirion enjoys one of the finest settings in Wales, nestling beneath the wooded slopes of the village, overlooking the sandy estuary towards Snowdonia. Many rooms have private sitting rooms and balconies with spectacular views. The mostly Welsh-speaking staff offer warm hospitality.
ROOMS: 25 en suite 26 annexe en suite (4 fmly) **FACILITIES:** STV Outdoor swimming (H) Tennis (hard) Beauty Salon **CONF:** Thtr 100 **PARKING:** 40 **NOTES:** No dogs No smoking in restaurant Civ Wed 100 **CARDS:**

PORT TALBOT, Neath Port Talbot — Map 09 SS78

★★★68% **Aberavon Beach**
SA12 6QP
☎ 01639 884949 01639 897885
e-mail: sales@aberavonbeach.com
Best Western
Dir: *M4 junct 41/A48 & follow signs for Aberavon Beach & Hollywood Park*
This friendly and purpose-built hotel enjoys a prominent position on the seafront overlooking Swansea Bay. Bedrooms, many of which have sea views, are comfortably appointed and thoughtfully equipped. Public areas include a leisure suite, open-plan bar and restaurant and a selection of function rooms.
ROOMS: 52 en suite (6 fmly) No smoking in 26 bedrooms s £72-£74; d £82-£84 (incl. bkfst) **LB** **FACILITIES:** Indoor swimming (H) Sauna Jacuzzi All weather leisure centre entertainment Xmas **CONF:** Thtr 300 Class 200 Board 100 Del from £95 **SERVICES:** Lift **PARKING:** 150 **NOTES:** No smoking in restaurant Civ Wed 300 **CARDS:**

See advert under SWANSEA

Travel Inn
Baglan Rd, Baglan SA12 8ES
☎ 08701 977211 01639 823096
travel inn
Dir: *Leave M4 (junct 41 westbound). Follow road to rdbt. Travel Inn just off 4th exit. junct 42 eastbound, left turn for Port Talbot. 2nd exit off 2nd rbt.*
Travel Inn offers good-quality, value-for-money accommodation. Spacious, en suite rooms with bath and shower comfortably

continued

accommodate a family of up to two adults and two children (to age 15). The restaurant and bar offers a varied menu. For further details and the Travel Inn phone number, consult the Hotel Groups page.
ROOMS: 42 en suite s £44.95; d £44.95

PRESTATYN, Denbighshire — Map 15 SJ08

★★67% Traeth Ganol Hotel

41 Beach Rd West LL19 7LL
☎ 01745 853594 🖹 01745 886687
e-mail: info@hotel-prestatyn.co.uk
Dir: *A55 follow to Nova Centre & beaches. Hotel beyond Nova, 4th property from end of cul-de-sac*

This small, friendly, family-run hotel is close to the seafront, the championship golf course and the Nova leisure complex. The no-smoking bedrooms are comfortable, freshly decorated and well equipped. Facilities include a comfortable lounge, a small bar and a bright dining room, which overlooks the garden.
ROOMS: 9 en suite (6 fmly) (3 GF) No smoking in all bedrooms s £40-£56; d £60-£70 (incl. bkfst) **LB** **PARKING:** 12 **NOTES:** No dogs (ex guide dogs) No smoking in restaurant
CARDS:

RAGLAN, Monmouthshire — Map 09 SO40

U The Beaufort Arms Coaching Inn & Restaurant

High St NP15 2DY
☎ 01291 690412 🖹 01291 690935
e-mail: thebeauforthotel@hotmail.com

At the time of going to press, the star classification for this hotel was not confirmed. Please refer to the AA internet site www.theAA.com for current information.
ROOMS: 15 en suite (1 fmly) (5 GF) No smoking in 6 bedrooms s £45; d £55 (incl. bkfst) **FACILITIES:** Xmas **CONF:** Thtr 120 Class 60 Board 30 Del from £40 **PARKING:** 30 **NOTES:** No smoking in restaurant Closed 31 Dec-1 Jan **CARDS:**

Travelodge Monmouth

Travelodge

Granada Services A40, Nr Monmouth NP5 4BG
☎ 08700 850 950
Dir: *on A40 near junct with A449*

Travelodge offers good quality, good value, modern accommodation. Ideal for families, the spacious, en suite bedrooms include remote-control TV, tea and coffee-making facilities, luxury beds and free morning newspaper. Meals can be taken at the nearby family restaurant. For further details and the Travelodge phone number, consult the Hotel Groups page.
ROOMS: 43 en suite s fr £42.95; d fr £42.95

REYNOLDSTON, Swansea — Map 08 SS48

Top 200 - Hotel

★★ @@@ Fairyhill

SA3 1BS
☎ 01792 390139 🖹 01792 391358
e-mail: postbox@fairyhill.net
Dir: *just outside Reynoldston off A4118*

Peace and tranquillity are to be found at this charming Georgian mansion set in the heart of the beautiful Gower peninsula. Bedrooms are furnished with care individuality and are filled with many thoughtful extras. There are also a range of comfortable seating areas with crackling log fires to choose from and a smartly appointed restaurant featuring local
continued
produce and specialities. If exercise should be needed there is a selection of woodland walks in the 24 acres of grounds.

ROOMS: 8 en suite s £120-£225; d £140-£245 (incl. bkfst) **LB** **FACILITIES:** Croquet lawn mountain bikes available **CONF:** Thtr 40 Class 20 Board 26 Del from £62.50 **PARKING:** 50 **NOTES:** No dogs (ex guide dogs) No children 8yrs No smoking in restaurant Closed 24-26 Dec & 1-16 Jan **CARDS:**

RHAYADER, Powys — Map 09 SN96

★★68% Brynafon Country House

South St LD6 5BL
☎ 01597 810735 🖹 01597 810111
e-mail: info@brynafon.co.uk
Dir: *0.5m from Rhayader on A470*

This imposing stone-built, former workhouse dates back to 1878 and stands in its own pleasant gardens, half a mile south of the town. Now a privately owned and personally run hotel, it provides well-equipped accommodation including four-poster beds and no smoking bedrooms. Public areas have lots of charm and character and include a no smoking lounge and a choice of conference rooms.
ROOMS: 20 en suite (2 fmly) No smoking in 15 bedrooms s £35-£50; d £55-£80 (incl. bkfst) **LB** **CONF:** Thtr 30 Class 30 Board 20 Del from £90 **PARKING:** 40 **NOTES:** No dogs (ex guide dogs) No smoking in restaurant Closed 18-27 Dec **CARDS:**

ROSSETT, Wrexham — Map 15 SJ35

★★★71% Llyndir Hall

Llyndir Ln LL12 0AY
☎ 01244 571648 🖹 01244 571258
e-mail: llyndir.hall@pageant.co.uk
Dir: *5m S of Chester on B5445 follow Pulford signs. Hotel is set back off road*

Located on the English/Welsh border within easy reach of Chester and Wrexham, this charming manor house lies in several acres of mature grounds. The well-equipped accommodation is popular
continued on p856

R

ROSSETT, continued

with leisure and business guests. Facilities include conference rooms, the Business Training Centre, an impressive leisure centre, a choice of comfortable lounges and a brasserie-style restaurant.
ROOMS: 48 en suite (3 fmly) No smoking in 12 bedrooms s £60-£85; d £70-£95 (incl. bkfst) **LB FACILITIES:** STV Indoor swimming (H) Solarium Gym Croquet lawn Jacuzzi Steam room ch fac Xmas **CONF:** Thtr 140 Class 60 Board 40 Del £110 **PARKING:** 80 **NOTES:** No smoking in restaurant Civ Wed 120 **CARDS:**

RUTHIN, Denbighshire Map 15 SJ15

★★★68% Ruthin Castle
LL15 2NU
☎ 01824 702664 01824 705978
e-mail: reservations@ruthincastle.co.uk
Dir: *A550 to Mold, A494 to Ruthin, hotel at end of Castle St just off Town Square*
The main part of this impressive castle was built in the early 19th century, but many ruins in the impressive grounds date back much further. The elegantly panelled public areas include a restaurant and bar along with a medieval banqueting hall and there is also a tea shop. Many of the modern-equipped bedrooms are spacious and furnished with fine period pieces.
ROOMS: 58 en suite (6 fmly) No smoking in 10 bedrooms s £59-£79; d £109-£150 (incl. bkfst) **LB FACILITIES:** Fishing Snooker entertainment **CONF:** Thtr 150 Class 100 Board 80 Del from £101 **SERVICES:** Lift **PARKING:** 200 **NOTES:** No dogs (ex guide dogs) Civ Wed 150 **CARDS:**

ST ASAPH, Denbighshire Map 15 SJ07

★★★70% Oriel House
Upper Denbigh Rd LL17 0LW
☎ 01745 582716 01745 585208
e-mail: bookings@orielhousehotel
Dir: *A55/A525, left at cathedral, 1m along A525 on right*
Set in several acres of mature grounds south of St Asaph, Oriel House offers generally spacious bedrooms, many of which have been refurbished. Staff are friendly and hospitable. The Terrace restaurant serves imaginative food specialising in local produce. Extensive function facilities cater for business meetings and weddings and the extensive leisure club is available to guests.
ROOMS: 31 en suite (3 fmly) (9 GF) No smoking in 26 bedrooms s £42-£80; d £75-£110 (incl. bkfst) **LB FACILITIES:** STV Indoor swimming (H) Fishing Sauna Solarium Gym Swimming pool supervised Xmas **CONF:** Thtr 250 Class 100 Board 50 Del from £99 **PARKING:** 200 **NOTES:** No dogs (ex guide dogs) No smoking in restaurant Civ Wed 240 **CARDS:**

★★67% Plas Elwy Hotel & Restaurant
The Roe LL17 0LT
☎ 01745 582263 & 582089 01745 583864
e-mail: plaselwy@gtleisure.co.uk
Dir: *off A55 junct 27, A525 signposted Rhyl/St Asaph. On left opposite petrol station*
This hotel, which dates back to 1850, has retained much of its original character. Bedrooms in the purpose-built extension are spacious - one has a four-poster bed - and those in the main building are equally well equipped. Public rooms are smart and comfortably furnished and a range of food options is provided in the attractive restaurant.
ROOMS: 7 en suite 6 annexe en suite (3 fmly) (2 GF) No smoking in 6 bedrooms s £40-£48; d £58-£70 (incl. bkfst) **PARKING:** 25 **NOTES:** No dogs (ex guide dogs) No smoking in restaurant Closed 25 Dec - 5 Jan **CARDS:**

ST CLEARS, Carmarthenshire Map 08 SN21

Travelodge (Carmarthen)
Tenby Rd SA33 4JN
☎ 08700 850 950
Travelodge offers good quality, good value, modern accommodation. Ideal for families, the spacious, en suite bedrooms include remote-control TV, tea and coffee-making facilities, luxury beds and free morning newspaper. Meals can be taken at the nearby family restaurant. For further details and the Travelodge phone number, consult the Hotel Groups page.
ROOMS: 32 en suite (incl. bkfst) s fr £42.95; d fr £42.95

ST DAVID'S, Pembrokeshire Map 08 SM72

★★★77% Warpool Court
SA62 6BN
☎ 01437 720300 01437 720676
e-mail: warpool@enterprise.net
Dir: *At Cross Square left beside Cartref Restaurant (Goat St). Pass Farmers Arms, after 400mtrs take left follow hotel signs, entrance on right*

Originally the cathedral choir school, Warpool Court Hotel is set in landscaped gardens looking out to sea and is within easy walking distance of the Pembrokeshire coastal path. The lounges are spacious and comfortable and bedrooms are well furnished and equipped with modern facilities. The restaurant offers delightful cuisine.
ROOMS: 25 en suite (3 fmly) s £77-£99; d £125-£230 (incl. bkfst) **LB FACILITIES:** Indoor swimming (H) Tennis (hard) Sauna Gym Croquet lawn Xmas **CONF:** Thtr 40 Class 25 Board 25 Del from £99 **PARKING:** 100 **NOTES:** No smoking in restaurant Closed Jan Civ Wed 100 **CARDS:**

★★70% *Old Cross*
Cross Square SA62 6SP
☎ 01437 720387 01437 720394
e-mail: enquiries@oldcrosshotel.co.uk
Dir: *in centre of St David's facing Cross Square*
This friendly and comfortable hotel is situated in the centre of the town, just a short walk from the famous cathedral. Bedrooms are generally spacious and have a good range of facilities with some being suitable for families. Public areas include comfortable lounges, a popular bar and an airy restaurant where good wholesome food is offered.
ROOMS: 16 en suite (1 fmly) No smoking in 5 bedrooms **FACILITIES:** ch fac **PARKING:** 18 **NOTES:** Closed Xmas-1 Feb **CARDS:**

SARN PARK MOTORWAY SERVICE AREA (M4), Bridgend Map 09 SS98

Welcome Lodge

Sarn Park Services CF32 9RW
☎ 01656 659218 📠 01656 768665
e-mail: sarnpark.hotel@welcomebreak.co.uk
Dir: *M4 junct 36*

This modern building offers accommodation in smart, spacious and well-equipped bedrooms, suitable for families and business travellers, and all with en suite bathrooms. Refreshments may be taken at the nearby family restaurant. For further details and the Welcome Break phone number, consult the Hotel Groups page.

ROOMS: 40 en suite s £30-£40; d £30-£40

SAUNDERSFOOT, Pembrokeshire Map 08 SN10

★★★67% St Brides

St Brides Hill SA69 9NH
☎ 01834 812304 📠 01834 811766
e-mail: reservations@stbrideshotel.com
Dir: *on Tenby Rd, overlooking the harbour*

This privately owned hotel is situated above the village and has stunning views of the harbour and coastline. The refurbished public areas are spacious and tastefully decorated, and feature exhibitions of Welsh artists' work. Bedrooms, many of which have sea views, vary in size and style.

ROOMS: 43 en suite (2 fmly) No smoking in 6 bedrooms s fr £59; d fr £110 (incl. bkfst) **LB** **FACILITIES:** Xmas **CONF:** Thtr 150 Class 80 Board 60 Del from £95 **PARKING:** 70 **NOTES:** No smoking in restaurant Civ Wed 175 **CARDS:**

★★69% Rhodewood House

St Brides Hill SA69 9NU
☎ 01834 812200 📠 01834 815005
e-mail: relax@rhodewood.co.uk
Dir: *from St Clears, take A477 to Kilgetty, then A478 to Tenby, turn left onto B4316 signposted Saundersfoot*

Personally run by the owners, this busy hotel is situated on the outskirts of the village and is popular with coach tour groups. Live entertainment is a regular feature and the public areas include two restaurants, a comfortable bar and a reception lounge. The bedrooms are well equipped and some are on the ground floor.

ROOMS: 45 en suite (14 fmly) No smoking in 6 bedrooms s £38-£45; d £56-£70 (incl. bkfst) **LB** **FACILITIES:** STV entertainment ch fac Xmas **CONF:** Thtr 100 Board 100 **PARKING:** 70 **NOTES:** No dogs (ex guide dogs) Closed 3 Jan-1Feb **CARDS:**

★★64% Merlewood

St Brides Hill SA69 9NP
☎ 01834 812421 & 813295 📠 01834 814886
e-mail: merlewood@saundersfoot.freeserve.co.uk
Dir: *A477/A4316, hotel on other side of village on St Brides Hill*

Possessing delightful views over the village and bay and with regular live entertainment, this hotel is a popular destination for coach parties. Bedrooms include ground floor and family rooms and there is a comfortable dining room and a large lounge bar. A pleasant outdoor swimming pool is also available for guests' use.

ROOMS: 29 en suite (8 fmly) s £33-£37; d £56-£64 (incl. bkfst) **LB** **FACILITIES:** Outdoor swimming (H) Putting green Children's swings & slide, Table tennis entertainment ch fac Xmas **CONF:** Thtr 60 Class 100 Board 40 **PARKING:** 34 **NOTES:** No dogs (ex guide dogs) No smoking in restaurant Closed Nov-Mar RS Xmas & New Year
CARDS:

Bad hair day?
Hairdryers in all rooms three stars and above

SKENFRITH, Monmouthshire Map 09 SO42

Restaurant with Rooms

The Bell at Skenfrith

NP7 8UH
☎ 01600 750235 📠 01600 750525
e-mail: enquiries@skenfrith.com
Dir: *A466 Monmouth towards Hereford. 4m left onto B4521, hotel 2m*

The Bell is a beautifully restored, 17th-century former coaching inn which still retains much of its charm and character. Natural materials have been used throughout while the bedrooms, which include full suites and rooms with four-poster beds, are stylish, luxurious and equipped with DVDs.

ROOMS: 8 en suite No smoking in all bedrooms s £65-£110; d £85-£150 (incl. bkfst) **LB** **FACILITIES:** Pool table Xmas **CONF:** Thtr 20 Board 16 Del from £140 **PARKING:** 36 **NOTES:** No smoking in restaurant RS end Oct-Etr **CARDS:**

SWANSEA, Swansea Map 09 SS69
See also Port Talbot

Hotel of the Year
Top 200 - Hotel

★★★★ Morgans

Somerset Place SA1 1RR
☎ 01792 484848 📠 01792 484849
e-mail: info@morganshotel.co.uk

This new and stunning hotel has been imaginatively developed from the Port's Authority building near the harbour side. The bedrooms are modern in design without neglecting guest comfort. Features include big beds, best linen, large screen TV, high ceilings, and DVDs. Public areas enjoy wonderful period elements and guests have a choice of eating and drinking options. Morgans Hotel has been awarded the AA Hotel of the Year for Wales 2003-2004.

ROOMS: 20 en suite (4 fmly) No smoking in all bedrooms s £100-£250 (incl. bkfst) **FACILITIES:** STV **SERVICES:** Lift air con **PARKING:** 27 **NOTES:** No dogs (ex guide dogs) No smoking in restaurant **CARDS:**

S

SWANSEA, continued

★★★★68% Swansea Marriott Hotel
The Maritime Quarter SA1 3SS
☎ 01792 642020 🖷 01792 650345
Dir: *M4 junct 42, A483 to city centre past Leisure Centre, then follow signs to Maritime Quarter*
Just opposite the City Hall, this busy hotel enjoys fantastic views over the bay and marina. Bedrooms are spacious and equipped with a range of extras. Public rooms include a popular leisure club and Abernethy's restaurant, which overlooks the marina. It is worth noting however that lounge seating is limited.
ROOMS: 117 en suite (49 fmly) No smoking in 85 bedrooms s fr £109; d fr £109 **LB** **FACILITIES:** STV Indoor swimming (H) Sauna Gym Jacuzzi **CONF:** Thtr 250 Class 120 Board 30 Del from £105 **SERVICES:** Lift air con **PARKING:** 122 **NOTES:** No dogs (ex guide dogs) No smoking in restaurant Civ Wed 250
CARDS:

★★ ◎◎◎ Fairyhill
SA3 1BS
☎ 01792 390139 🖷 01792 391358
e-mail: postbox@fairyhill.net
(For full entry see Reynoldston)

★★72% Beaumont
72-73 Walter Rd SA1 4QA
☎ 01792 643956 🖷 01792 643044
e-mail: info@beaumonthotel.co.uk
Dir: *M4, towards city centre. Follow Uplands & Sketty signs. 0.5m from centre along Walter Rd, hotel on left opposite St James Church*

Situated within walking distance of the city centre, this family owned hotel offers a high level of comfort and stylish décor. Bedrooms are well equipped and thoughtfully furnished. There is a relaxing lounge bar in which to enjoy a drink before sampling good home cooking in the Conservatory Restaurant. Guests have the reassurance of a secure car park.
ROOMS: 16 en suite (3 fmly) s £45-£75; d £60-£90 (incl. bkfst) **LB** **CONF:** BC Class 50 Board 30 **PARKING:** 12 **NOTES:** No smoking in restaurant Closed 25-26 Dec & 31 Dec-1 Jan
CARDS:

See advert on opposite page

★★71% ◎ *Windsor Lodge*
Mount Pleasant SA1 6EG
☎ 01792 642158 & 652744 🖷 01792 648996
Dir: *M4 junct 42, A483, right at lights past Sainsburys, left at station, right immediately after 2nd set of lights*
This privately owned and personally run hotel is just a short walk from the city centre. Bedrooms vary in size, but all are similarly well equipped. There is a choice of lounge areas and a deservedly popular restaurant.
ROOMS: 18 en suite (2 fmly) **CONF:** Thtr 30 Class 15 Board 24 **PARKING:** 26 **NOTES:** No smoking in restaurant Closed 25-26 Dec
CARDS:

U *Holiday Inn Swansea*
The Kingsway Circle SA1 5LS
☎ 0870 400 9078 🖷 01792 456044
e-mail: swansea@ichotelsgroup.com
Dir: *M4 junct 42/A483 Swansea exit. Signs for city centre W. At lights after Sainsbury's, right along Wind St then left at lights, hotel ahead at rdbt*
At the time of going to press, the star classification for this hotel was not confirmed. Please refer to the AA internet site www.theAA.com for current information.
ROOMS: 106 en suite (12 fmly) No smoking in 66 bedrooms **FACILITIES:** Indoor swimming (H) Sauna Solarium Gym **CONF:** Thtr 230 Class 120 Board 60 **SERVICES:** Lift **PARKING:** 42
CARDS:

⌂ Travel Inn
Upper Fforest Way, Morriston SA6 8WB
☎ 08701 977246 🖷 01792 311929
Dir: *M4 junct 45/A4067 towards Swansea. At 2nd exit, after 0.5m, turn left onto Clase Rd. Travel Inn 400yds on left*
Travel Inn offers good-quality, value-for-money accommodation. Spacious, en suite rooms with bath and shower comfortably accommodate a family of up to two adults and two children (to age 15). The restaurant and bar offers a varied menu. For further details and the Travel Inn phone number, consult the Hotel Groups page.
ROOMS: 40 en suite s £44.95; d £44.95

⌂ Travelodge
Penllergaer SA4 1GT
☎ 08700 850 950 🖷 01792 898806
Dir: *M4 junct 47*
Travelodge offers good quality, good value, modern accommodation. Ideal for families, the spacious, en suite bedrooms include remote-control TV, tea and coffee-making facilities, luxury beds and free morning newspaper. Meals can be taken at the nearby family restaurant. For further details and the Travelodge phone number, consult the Hotel Groups page.
ROOMS: 50 en suite s fr £42.95; d fr £42.95 **CONF:** Thtr 25 Class 32 Board 20

TALSARNAU, Gwynedd — Map 14 SH63

Top 200 - Hotel

★★ ◎◎ Maes y Neuadd Country House
LL47 6YA
☎ 01766 780200 🖷 01766 780211
e-mail: maes@neuadd.com
Dir: *3m NE of Harlech, signposted on an unclassed road off B4573*
This 14th-century hotel enjoys fine views over the mountains and across the bay to the Lleyn Peninsula. The team here are committed to highlighting and restoring some of the hidden features of the house. Bedrooms, some in an adjacent coach house, are individually furnished and many boast fine antique pieces. Public areas display a similar welcoming charm,

continued

including the restaurant which serves locally sourced and many home grown ingredients.

ROOMS: 16 en suite (3 GF) s £73-£95; d £141-£255 (incl. bkfst & dinner) **LB** **FACILITIES:** Croquet lawn clay pigeon,cooking tuition Xmas **CONF:** Thtr 20 Class 10 Board 12 **PARKING:** 50 **NOTES:** No smoking in restaurant Civ Wed 65

CARDS:

★★67% Estuary Motel

Stryd Fawr LL47 6TA

☎ 01766 771155 📠 01766 771393

e-mail: enquiries@the-estuary.fsnet.co.uk

Dir: *from Barmouth take A496 to Portamdog. Talsarnau is approximately 4m N of Harlech. Motel on right*

This single storey, purpose built, small hotel is conveniently located for visiting Snowdonia, Harlech Castle and the many coastal attractions of the area. Privately owned and personally run,

continued on p960

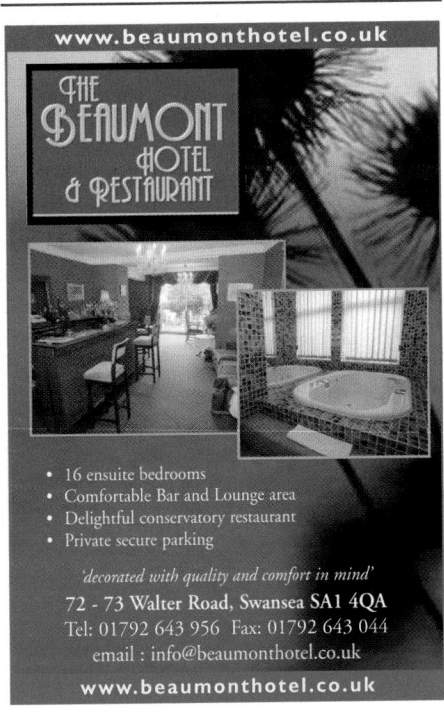

TALSARNAU, continued

it provides friendly hospitality and well equipped, motel style accommodation.
ROOMS: 10 annexe en suite (3 fmly) (10 GF) No smoking in 8 bedrooms s £34-£39; d £48-£58 (incl. bkfst) **LB** **PARKING:** 20 **NOTES:** No smoking in restaurant **CARDS:**

★★66% *Tregwylan*
LL47 6YG
☎ 01766 770424 01766 771317
Dir: *off A496, 0.5m N of Talsarnau and 4m N of Harlech*
Set in mature grounds and with superb views of the Snowdonia Range and Lleyn Peninsula, this family-run hotel has been under the same ownership for 30 years. It offers genuine Welsh hospitality and provides attractively decorated, well-equipped bedrooms. There is a pleasant restaurant, a cosy bar and a newly created lounge overlooking the garden.
ROOMS: 10 en suite (3 fmly) **PARKING:** 20 **NOTES:** No dogs (ex guide dogs) No smoking in restaurant Closed Jan-mid Feb
CARDS:

TAL-Y-BONT (NEAR CONWY), Gwynedd Map 14 SH76

★★71% Lodge
LL32 8YX
☎ 01492 660766 01492 660534
e-mail: bbaldon@lodgehotel.co.uk

THE CIRCLE
Selected Individual Hotels
GREAT BRITAIN

Dir: *on B5106, hotel on right when entering village*
Situated in a beautiful part of the Conwy Valleys, the Lodge Hotel has modern bedrooms, some of which are suitable for families. A log fire burns during the winter months to welcome guests back from exploring the local area. Much of the produce on the daily changing menu comes from the hotel's gardens and home-cooked meals are served in generous portions.
ROOMS: 14 annexe en suite (4 fmly) No smoking in 6 bedrooms s £44-£54; d £72-£100 (incl. bkfst) **LB** **FACILITIES:** Free hard court tennis at local playing fields Xmas **PARKING:** 50 **NOTES:** No smoking in restaurant RS Winter **CARDS:**

TENBY, Pembrokeshire Map 08 SN10

★★★75% Atlantic
The Esplanade SA70 7DU
☎ 01834 842881 & 844176 01834 842881 ex 256
e-mail: enquiries@atlantic-hotel.uk.com
Dir: *A478 into Tenby & follow town centre signs, keep town walls on left then turn right at Esplanade, hotel half way along on right*
This privately owned and personally run, friendly hotel has an enviable position looking out over South Beach towards Caldy Island. Bedrooms vary in size and style, and are well equipped and tastefully appointed. The comfortable public areas include a choice of restaurants and in fine weather guests can also enjoy the cliff-top gardens.
ROOMS: 42 en suite (11 fmly) No smoking in 3 bedrooms s £66-£70; d £92-£140 (incl. bkfst) **FACILITIES:** **Spa** STV Indoor swimming (H) Solarium Steam room **CONF:** Board 10 **SERVICES:** Lift **PARKING:** 28 **NOTES:** Closed 21-29 Dec **CARDS:**

★★★75% ® *Penally Abbey Country House*
Penally SA70 7PY
☎ 01834 843033 01834 844714
e-mail: penally.abbey@btinternet.com
Dir: *1.5m from Tenby, off A4139, close to Penally*
With monastic origins, this delightful country house stands in five acres of grounds with views over Carmarthen Bay. The drawing room, bar and restaurant are tastefully decorated and attractively furnished and set the scene for a relaxing stay. The bedrooms are similarly appointed; some are situated in the stylish coach house annexe.

ROOMS: 8 en suite 4 annexe en suite (3 fmly) **FACILITIES:** Indoor swimming (H) Snooker **CONF:** Board 14 **PARKING:** 14 **NOTES:** No dogs (ex guide dogs) No smoking in restaurant Civ Wed 50
CARDS:

★★★69% Fourcroft
North Beach SA70 8AP
☎ 01834 842886 01834 842888
e-mail: hospitality@fourcroft-hotel.co.uk
Dir: *A478, after 'Welcome to Tenby' sign left towards North Beach & walled town. At seafront turn sharp left. Hotel on left*
This friendly, family-run hotel offers a beach-front location, together with a number of extra facilities that make it particularly suitable for families with children. Guests have direct access to the beach through the hotel's cliff-top gardens. Bedrooms are of a good size, with modern facilities.
ROOMS: 40 en suite (12 fmly) No smoking in 10 bedrooms s £37-£56; d £74-£112 (incl. bkfst) **LB** **FACILITIES:** STV Outdoor swimming (H) Sauna Jacuzzi Table tennis Giant chess Human Gyroscope Snooker Pool Xmas **CONF:** BC Thtr 90 Class 40 Board 50 Del from £95 **SERVICES:** Lift **PARKING:** 12 **NOTES:** No smoking in restaurant Civ Wed 100 **CARDS:**

★★★69% Heywood Mount
Heywood Ln SA70 8DA
☎ 01834 842087 01834 842087
e-mail: reception@heywoodmount.co.uk
Dir: *A478 into Tenby, follow Heywood Mount signs then right into Serpentine Rd, turn right at T-junct into Heywood Lane, 3rd hotel on left*
This privately-owned hotel is situated in a peaceful residential area, close to Tenby's beaches and town centre. The well-maintained house is surrounded by extensive gardens and public areas include a comfortable lounge, bar, restaurant and health & fitness spa. Several of the well-appointed and equipped bedrooms are on ground floor level.
ROOMS: 17 en suite (3 fmly) (4 GF) No smoking in all bedrooms s £40-£45; d £80-£90 (incl. bkfst) **LB** **FACILITIES:** Indoor swimming (H) Sauna Solarium Gym Jacuzzi entertainment Xmas **CONF:** Thtr 50 Class 50 Board 30 Del from £35 **PARKING:** 25 **NOTES:** No dogs No smoking in restaurant Civ Wed 80 **CARDS:**

★★72% ® *Panorama Hotel & Restaurant*
The Esplanade SA70 7DU
☎ 01834 844976 01834 844976
e-mail: mail@panoramahotel.f9.co.uk
Dir: *A478 follow 'South Beach' & 'Town Centre' signs. Sharp left under railway arches, up Greenhill Rd, onto South Pde then Esplanade*
This charming little hotel is part of a Victorian terrace, overlooking the South Beach and Caldy Island. It provides a variety of

continued

no-smoking bedrooms, all of which are well-equipped. Facilities include a cosy bar and an elegant restaurant, where a good choice of skilfully prepared dishes is available.
ROOMS: 7 en suite (2 fmly) No smoking in all bedrooms **NOTES:** No dogs (ex guide dogs) No children 5yrs No smoking in restaurant
CARDS:

★★67% *Tenby House Hotel*

Tudor Square SA70 7AJ
☎ 01834 842000 🖹 01834 844647
e-mail: tenbyhouse@virgin.net
Dir: *in town centre pass St Mary's Church on right into Tudor Square. Hotel on right at end of Square*
This privately owned and personally run hotel is conveniently located in the town centre, just a few minutes' walk from the harbour, beach and other amenities. The accommodation has been upgraded to a good standard and is well-equipped. Facilities include a pleasant bar with tremendous character and a separate bistro-style restaurant. Garage parking is available nearby.
ROOMS: 18 en suite No smoking in all bedrooms **FACILITIES:** Games room entertainment **PARKING:** 14 **NOTES:** No dogs (ex guide dogs)
CARDS:

★★66% Hammonds Park

Narberth Rd SA70 8HT
☎ 01834 842696 🖹 01834 844295
e-mail: info@hoteltenby.com
Dir: *left off A478 into Narberth Rd, hotel 200yds on left*
This friendly and privately owned hotel is situated within walking distance of North Beach and the town centre. There are some four-poster and ground floor rooms and all are thoughtfully equipped. Homely and wholesome cooking can be enjoyed in the bright conservatory restaurant and there is also a cosy lounge in which to relax.
ROOMS: 13 en suite (6 fmly) (5 GF) No smoking in all bedrooms s £30-£36; d £46-£58 (incl. bkfst) **LB** **FACILITIES:** Gym **PARKING:** 15 **NOTES:** No dogs (ex guide dogs) No smoking in restaurant
CARDS:

THREE COCKS, Powys — Map 09 SO13

★★73% Three Cocks

LD3 0SL
☎ 01497 847215 🖹 01497 847339
Dir: *on A438, between Brecon & Hereford*
This inn has welcomed guests for over 500 years and is set in the glorious countryside of the Brecon Beacons National Park. There are a wealth of original features and wooden beams in the comfortable lounges, whilst the elegant restaurant overlooks the garden. Bedrooms are tastefully decorated and a television lounge is available to guests.
ROOMS: 7 rms (6 en suite) (2 fmly) s £45-£70; d £70 (incl. bkfst) **LB** **FACILITIES:** no TV in bdrms ch fac **PARKING:** 40 **NOTES:** No dogs (ex guide dogs) Closed Dec & Jan RS Tue **CARDS:**

TINTERN PARVA, Monmouthshire — Map 04 SO50

★★★69% The Abbey Hotel

THE INDEPENDENTS

NP16 6SF
☎ 01291 689777 🖹 01291 689727
e-mail: info@theabbeyhoteltintern.com
Dir: *M48 junct 2/A466, hotel opposite the abbey ruins*
Now refurbished to a high standard and possessing stunning views of nearby Tintern Abbey, this friendly hotel provides modern bedrooms, including a family suite. Diners are almost spoilt for choice between the brasserie with its daytime carvery and more formal carte service for dinner, and the pleasant hotel bar where lighter meal options are on offer.

ROOMS: 23 en suite No smoking in 7 bedrooms s £60-£80; d £90-£99 (incl. bkfst) **LB** **FACILITIES: Spa** STV Fishing Jacuzzi entertainment ch fac Xmas **CONF:** Thtr 150 Class 60 Board 30 Del from £89 **PARKING:** 60 **NOTES:** No smoking in restaurant Civ Wed 120
CARDS:

★★★66% *Royal George*

Best Western

NP16 6SF
☎ 01291 689205 🖹 01291 689448
e-mail: royalgeorgetintern@hotmail.com
Dir: *off M48/A466, 4m along this rd into Tintern 2nd on left*
This delightful hotel provides comfortable, spacious accommodation, including bedrooms with balconies overlooking the well-tended garden. There are some ground floor rooms. The public areas include a choice of bars, and a large function room.
ROOMS: 2 en suite 14 annexe en suite (13 fmly) No smoking in 9 bedrooms **FACILITIES:** entertainment **CONF:** Thtr 120 Class 40 Board 50 **PARKING:** 50 **NOTES:** No smoking in restaurant Civ Wed 60
CARDS:

★★73% Parva Farmhouse Hotel & Restaurant

THE CIRCLE *Selected Individual Hotels* GREAT BRITAIN

NP16 6SQ
☎ 01291 689411 & 689511 🖹 01291 689557
e-mail: parva_hotelintern@hotmail.com
Dir: *From S leave M48 junct 2, N edge of village on A466. From N, 10m S of Monmouth town & M50*
This relaxed and friendly hotel is situated on a sweep of the River Wye with far reaching views of the valley. Originally a farmhouse and dating from the 17th century, many of the original features have been retained to provide a character lounge, with a fire in colder months, and an atmospheric restaurant with a popular local following. Bedrooms are tastefully decorated and thoughtfully equipped.
ROOMS: 9 en suite (3 fmly) (1 GF) s fr £55 (incl. bkfst) **LB** **FACILITIES:** Cycle hire **CONF:** Thtr 12 Board 12 **PARKING:** 10 **NOTES:** No smoking in restaurant **CARDS:**

TREARDDUR BAY See Anglesey, Isle of

TREFRIW, Conwy — Map 14 SH76

★★71% Princes Arms

LL27 0JP
☎ 01492 640592 🖹 01492 640559
e-mail: enquiries@princes-arms.co.uk
Dir: *A470 to Llanrwst left onto B5106 over bridge & follow to Trefriw, hotel just through village on left*
Located in the Conwy Valley, this privately-owned and personally-run hotel offers superb views from many bedrooms.
continued on p862

T

TREFRIW, continued

The two-bedroomed apartments are ideal for families. Excellent food can be enjoyed in the attractive restaurant, and there is also a comfortable brasserie with log fires.

Princes Arms, Trefriw

ROOMS: 14 en suite (5 fmly) s fr £40; d fr £52 (incl. bkfst & dinner) **LB FACILITIES:** STV Xmas **CONF:** Thtr 80 Class 40 Board 20 **PARKING:** 40 **NOTES:** No dogs (ex guide dogs) No smoking in restaurant **CARDS:**

★★71% *Hafod Country Hotel*

LL27 0RQ
☎ 01492 640029 📠 01492 641351
e-mail: hafod@breathemail.net
Dir: *on B5106 between A5 at Betws-y-Coed & A55 at Conwy. 2nd entrance on right entering Trefriw village from S.*

This former farmhouse is a personally run and friendly hotel with a wealth of charm and character. The tasteful bedrooms feature period furnishings and thoughtful extras such as fresh fruit. There is a comfortable sitting room and a cosy bar. The fixed-price menu is imaginative and makes good use of fresh, local produce.
ROOMS: 6 en suite No smoking in all bedrooms **PARKING:** 14 **NOTES:** No children 11yrs No smoking in restaurant Closed early Jan-mid Feb **CARDS:**

TYWYN, Gwynedd

Map 14 SH50

★61% Greenfield

High St LL36 9AD
☎ 01654 710354
e-mail: greentywyn@aol.com
Dir: *on A493, opposite leisure centre*

In the middle of a small seaside town, this family-run hotel also has a busy restaurant offering a good range of inexpensive meals. Bedrooms are simply furnished but all are fresh and bright. Each has modern facilities and several are suitable for families.
ROOMS: 8 rms (6 en suite) (2 fmly) s £17-£20; d £34-£39 (incl. bkfst) **NOTES:** No dogs (ex guide dogs) No smoking in restaurant Closed Jan-Feb RS Nov-Mar **CARDS:**

USK, Monmouthshire

Map 09 SO3(

★★★70% *Glen-yr-Afon House*

Pontypool Rd NP15 1SY
☎ 01291 672302 & 673202 📠 01291 672597
e-mail: enquiries@glen-yr-afon.co.uk
Dir: *A472 through Usk High St, over river bridge following main road around to right hotel 200yds on left*

In the same private ownership for nearly 30 years, this friendly hotel bears the hallmarks of the proprietors' care and taste throughout. The elegant and well-proportioned public areas consist of a restful lounge, bar and wood-panelled restaurant. Bedrooms, which are situated in both the original building and a new wing, are well equipped and individually furnished.
ROOMS: 28 en suite (2 fmly) No smoking in 14 bedrooms **FACILITIES:** STV Croquet lawn **CONF:** Thtr 100 Class 200 Board 30 **SERVICES:** Lift **PARKING:** 101 **NOTES:** No smoking in restaurant Civ Wed 200 **CARDS:**

★★★70% ◎ Three Salmons

Porthycarne St NP15 1RY
☎ 01291 672133 📠 01291 673979
e-mail: threesalmons.hotel@talk21.com
Dir: *off A449, 1m into Usk, hotel on corner of Porthycarne St, B4598*

This 17th-century coaching inn in the heart of Usk offers spacious bedrooms that are comfortably furnished and well-maintained. Both the restaurant and bar offer a wide range of carefully prepared dishes. The function room and meeting room overlook the pretty garden and courtyard to the rear.
ROOMS: 10 en suite 14 annexe en suite (1 fmly) s fr £65; d fr £95 (incl. bkfst) **LB FACILITIES:** STV Xmas **CONF:** Thtr 100 Class 40 Board 50 Del from £100 **PARKING:** 38 **NOTES:** No dogs (ex guide dogs) No smoking in restaurant Civ Wed 100 **CARDS:**

See advert on opposite page

Restaurant with Rooms

◎◎ The Newbridge

Tredunnock NP15 1LY
☎ 01633 451000 📠 01633 451001
e-mail: thenewbridge@tinyonline.co.uk
Dir: *Turn off B4236 between Usk & Caerleon at Tredunnock sign*

This 200-year-old inn stands alongside the River Usk at Tredunnock, some four miles south of Usk. It has been renovated and converted into a spacious, traditionally furnished restaurant occupying the ground and first floor levels. Six spacious, smart, modern and well equipped bedrooms are contained within a stone-clad, purpose-built unit across the car park.
ROOMS: 6 en suite (2 fmly) (4 GF) No smoking in 2 bedrooms s £90-£105; d £105-£125 (incl. bkfst) **FACILITIES:** STV Fishing **CONF:** Thtr 20 Class 10 Board 14 **PARKING:** 65 **NOTES:** No dogs (ex guide dogs) Civ Wed 60 **CARDS:**

WELSHPOOL, Powys

Map 15 SJ20

★★★68% *Royal Oak*

The Cross SY21 7DG
☎ 01938 552217 🖹 01938 556652
e-mail: oakwpool@aol.com
Dir: *by traffic lights at junct of A483/A458*

This traditional market town hotel dates back over 350 years. It provides well-equipped bedrooms, a choice of bars and extensive function and conference facilities. The attractively appointed restaurant is a popular venue for dining out and there is also a busy coffee shop operation throughout the day.

ROOMS: 24 en suite (2 fmly) No smoking in 10 bedrooms **FACILITIES:** STV **CONF:** Thtr 150 Class 60 Board 80 **PARKING:** 40 **NOTES:** Civ Wed 30 **CARDS:**

★★66% *Golfa Hall*

Llanfair Rd SY21 9AF
☎ 01938 553399 🖹 01938 554777
e-mail: golfahall@welshpool.sagehost.co.uk
Dir: *1.5m W of Welshpool on A458 to Dolgellau*

Set on the Powys Castle estate, this privately owned and personally run hotel was originally a Georgian farmhouse. Some of the well-equipped bedrooms are contained in a separate stone built cottage. Elegant public rooms include a meeting room and a comfortable non-smoking lounge.

ROOMS: 10 en suite 4 annexe en suite (4 fmly) **CONF:** Thtr 120 Class 16 Board 16 **PARKING:** 26 **NOTES:** No dogs (ex guide dogs) No smoking in restaurant Civ Wed 50 **CARDS:**

WHITEBROOK, Monmouthshire

Map 04 SO50

Restaurant with Rooms

Crown at Whitebrook

NP25 4TX
☎ 01600 860254 🖹 01600 860607
e-mail: crown@whitebrook.demon.co.uk
Dir: *turn W off A466, 50yds S of Bigsweir Bridge*

Set in a delightful wooded valley, this former drovers' inn dates back to the 17th century. The lounge bar and restaurant are furnished with relaxation and comfort in mind and make an ideal setting for the cuisine, which uses quality local ingredients skilfully prepared. The bedrooms are well equipped and tastefully appointed.

ROOMS: 10 en suite s £55; d £90-£95 (incl. bkfst) **LB** **FACILITIES:** Fishing Jacuzzi **CONF:** Board 10 **PARKING:** 40 **NOTES:** No children 12yrs No smoking in restaurant Closed 2 wks Xmas/New Year **CARDS:**

GF Indicates the number of bedrooms at ground floor level.

WOLF'S CASTLE, Pembrokeshire

Map 08 SM92

★★73% Wolfscastle Country Hotel

SA62 5LZ
☎ 01437 741688 & 741225 🖹 01437 741383
e-mail: enquiries@wolfscastle.com
Dir: *on A40 in the village of Wolf's Castle, at top of hill on left, 6m N of Haverfordwest*

This large stone house dates back to the mid 19th century and has stunning views of the village. Now a friendly privately-owned and personally-run hotel, it provides modern, well-maintained and equipped bedrooms. There is a pleasant bar and an attractive restaurant.

ROOMS: 20 en suite 1 annexe en suite (2 fmly) No smoking in all bedrooms s £55-£65; d £79-£93 (incl. bkfst) **LB** **FACILITIES:** STV **CONF:** Thtr 100 Class 100 Board 30 Del from £80 **PARKING:** 60 **NOTES:** No smoking in restaurant Closed 24-26 Dec RS Sun nights Civ Wed 60 **CARDS:**

W

WREXHAM, Wrexham Map 15 SJ35

★★★68% Cross Lanes Hotel & Restaurant

Cross Lanes, Bangor Rd, Marchwiel LL13 0TF
☎ 01978 780555 01978 780568
e-mail: guestservices@crosslanes.co.uk
Dir: *3m SE of Wrexham, on A525, between the villages of Marchwiel and Bangor-on-Dee*

This hotel was built as a private house in 1890 and stands in over six acres of beautiful grounds. Bedrooms are well equipped and meet the needs of today's traveller, and include two that have four-poster beds. A fine selection of well produced food is available in Kagan's Brasserie.

ROOMS: 16 en suite (1 fmly) s £70-£80; d £84-£88 **LB**
FACILITIES: Croquet lawn Putting green Fishing rights Xmas **CONF:** Thtr 120 Class 60 Board 40 **PARKING:** 80 **NOTES:** No dogs (ex guide dogs) No smoking in restaurant Closed 25 Dec (night) & 26 Dec Civ Wed 120
CARDS:

See advert under CHESTER

★★★66% Llwyn Onn Hall

Cefn Rd LL13 0NY
☎ 01978 261225 01978 363233
e-mail: llwynonnhallhotel@breathemail.net
Dir: *between A525 & A534. Easy access Wrexham Ind Estate, 2m off A483*

Surrounded by open countryside, this fine 17th-century manor house is set in several acres of mature grounds. Exposed timbers remain and the original oak staircase is still in use. Bedrooms are equipped with modern facilities and one room has a four-poster bed which Bonnie Prince Charlie is reputed to have slept in.

ROOMS: 13 en suite (1 fmly) No smoking in 7 bedrooms **CONF:** Thtr 60 Class 40 Board 12 Del from £90 **PARKING:** 40 **NOTES:** No dogs (ex guide dogs) No smoking in restaurant Civ Wed 60
CARDS:

Travel Inn

Chester Rd, Gresford LL12 8PW
☎ 08701 977279 01978 856838
Dir: *on B5445 just off A483 dual carriageway near village of Gresford*

Travel Inn offers good-quality, value-for-money accommodation. Spacious, en suite rooms with bath and shower comfortably accommodate a family of up to two adults and two children (to age 15). The restaurant and bar offers a varied menu. For further details and the Travel Inn phone number, consult the Hotel Groups page.

ROOMS: 36 en suite s £44.95; d £44.95

Travelodge

Wrexham By Pass, Rhostyllen LL14 4EJ
☎ 08700 850 950 01978 365705
Dir: *2m S, A483/A5152 rdbt*

Travelodge offers good quality, good value, modern accommodation. Ideal for families, the spacious, en suite bedrooms include remote-control TV, tea and coffee-making facilities, luxury beds and free morning newspaper. Meals can be taken at the nearby family restaurant. For further details and the Travelodge phone number, consult the Hotel Groups page.

ROOMS: 32 en suite s fr £42.95; d fr £42.95

Hotel of the Year, Ireland

Hayfield Manor Hotel
Cork, Co. Cork

A

ABBEYLEIX, Co Laois Map 01 C3

★★★61% **Abbeyleix Manor Hotel**
☎ 0502 30111 ▤ 0502 30220
e-mail: info@abbeyleixmanorhotel.com
Dir: *on N8 (Dublin-Cork road) just S of Abbeyleix*

This modern hotel is situated on the outskirts of Abbeyliex, and is ideal for those travelling on the National Route. Bedrooms are spacious and well appointed to a high standard. Public areas are comfortable with a cosy lobby and conservatory and a themed bar where food is served all day.
ROOMS: 23 en suite (2 fmly) **SERVICES:** air con **PARKING:** 270 **NOTES:** No dogs (ex guide dogs) No smoking in restaurant Closed 25-26 Dec **CARDS:**

ACHILL ISLAND, Co Mayo Map 01 A4

★★★60% **Achill Cliff House**
Keel
☎ 098 43400 ▤ 098 43007
e-mail: info@achillcliff.com

A comfortable, family run hotel in the old fishing village of Keel. The bedrooms are spacious with large bathrooms and the restaurant specialises in serving locally caught seafood.
ROOMS: 10 en suite (4 fmly) (2 GF) No smoking in all bedrooms s €40-€100; d €70-€140 (incl. bkfst) **LB** **FACILITIES:** Sauna photography, painting, walking trails **PARKING:** 20 **NOTES:** No dogs No children 10yrs No smoking in restaurant Closed 23-26 Dec **CARDS:**

ADARE, Co Limerick Map 01 B3

★★★★70% ◎◎ ***Dunraven Arms***
☎ 061 396633 ▤ 061 396541
e-mail: dunraven@iol.ie

MANOR HOUSE HOTELS

This charming hotel was established in 1792 in the heart of one of Ireland's prettiest villages. It is a traditional country Inn both in style and atmosphere. Comfortable lounges and bedrooms, attractive gardens, leisure and beauty facilities and good cuisine all add to the enjoyment of a visit to the hotel. Golf and equestrian activities are a specialty in Adare.
ROOMS: 75 en suite (1 fmly) **FACILITIES:** STV Indoor swimming (H) Fishing Riding Sauna Gym Jacuzzi Beauty salon entertainment **CONF:** Thtr 180 Class 60 **SERVICES:** Lift **PARKING:** 90
CARDS:

★★★63%
Fitzgeralds Woodlands House Hotel
Knockanes

IRISH COUNTRY HOTELS

☎ 061 605100 ▤ 061 396073
e-mail: reception@woodlands-hotel.ie
Dir: *left at Lantern Lodge rdbt on N21 S of Limerick. Hotel 0.5m on right*
Set in 44 acres of woodland on the outskirts of Adare, this family-run hotel is friendly and welcoming. Comfortable bedrooms are all well-appointed and are available in three styles, the newest featuring extras such as jacuzzis. The hotel specialises in golf break holidays.
ROOMS: 92 en suite (36 fmly) **FACILITIES:** STV Indoor swimming (H) Sauna Solarium Gym Jacuzzi Health & beauty salon Thermal spa entertainment ch fac **CONF:** Thtr 400 Class 200 Board 50 **SERVICES:** air con **PARKING:** 290 **NOTES:** No dogs (ex guide dogs) Closed 24-25 Dec **CARDS:**

AGHADOWEY, Co Londonderry Map 01 C6

★★71% **Brown Trout Golf & Country Inn**
209 Agivey Rd BT51 4AD
☎ 028 7086 8209 ▤ 028 7086 8878
e-mail: bill@browntroutinn.com
Dir: *on junct of A54/B66 on road to Coleraine*
Set alongside the Agivey River and featuring its own 9-hole golf course, this welcoming inn offers a choice of accommodation. Spacious and attractively furnished bedrooms are situated around a courtyard area whilst the cottage suites also have comfortable lounge areas. Home-cooked meals are served in the restaurant; lighter fare is available in the character lounge bar.
ROOMS: 15 en suite (11 fmly) s £50-£60; d £65-£85 (incl. bkfst) **LB** **FACILITIES:** Golf 9 Fishing Gym Putting green Game fishing entertainment Xmas **CONF:** Thtr 40 Class 24 Board 28 Del from £65 **PARKING:** 80 **NOTES:** No smoking in restaurant
CARDS:

AHERLOW, Co Tipperary Map 01 B3

★★★62% **Aherlow House**
☎ 062 56153 ▤ 062 56212
e-mail: aherlow@iol.ie
Dir: *6km from Tipperary, from Limerick, right at lights, follow signs for hotel*
Located in a coniferous forest with superb views of the Galtee Mountains, this Tudor-style house offers comfortable public rooms, including a relaxing drawing room, a spacious lounge bar and a restaurant. Accommodation is well equipped and an additional wing has been added. The attentive staff create a warm and friendly atmosphere.
ROOMS: 29 en suite (23 fmly) s €98; d €165 (incl. bkfst) **LB** **FACILITIES:** STV Guided walks Xmas **CONF:** Thtr 400 Class 200 Board 50 **PARKING:** 200 **NOTES:** No dogs (ex guide dogs) RS Nov - Apr Civ Wed 300 **CARDS:**

Late for dinner?
Quality Standards mean that last orders for dinner vary according to star rating and should be no earlier than:
★★ 7.00pm ★★★ 8.00pm ★★★★ 9.00pm
★★★★★ 10.00pm

ARDMORE, Co Waterford

Map 01 C2

★62% *Round Tower*

☎ 024 94494 & 94382 🖹 024 94254
e-mail: rth@eircom.net
Dir: *N25 Rosslare-Cork route, onto R673. Hotel in centre of village*

A large country house set in its own grounds in a pretty fishing village, boasting a blue flag beach, lovely marked cliff walks and much of early monastic interest. The atmosphere is friendly and there is a comfortable lounge, panelled bar and a conservatory, where bar food is served. A carte menu is available in the restaurant, featuring 'catch of the day' seafood.

ROOMS: 12 en suite (4 fmly) **CONF:** Thtr 50 Class 25 Board 30 **PARKING:** 40 **NOTES:** RS Oct-Apr **CARDS:**

ARKLOW, Co Wicklow

Map 01 D3

★★★67% ❀ Arklow Bay

Ferrybank
☎ 0402 32309 🖹 0402 32300
e-mail: arklowbay@eircom.net
Dir: *off N11 at by-pass for Arklow. After 1m turn left, 200yds on left*

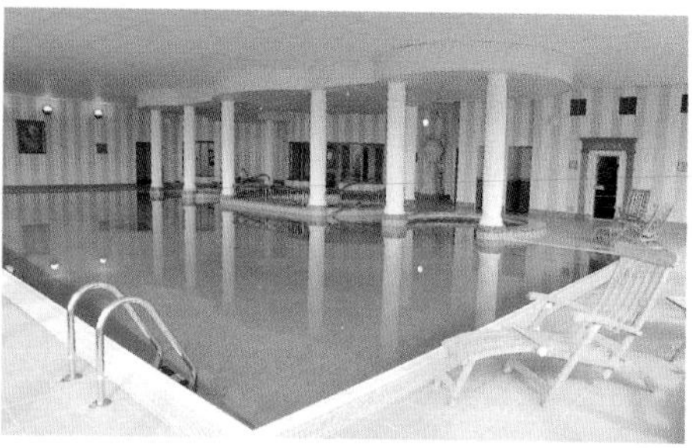

This hotel enjoys panoramic views of Arklow Bay and many of the well-appointed bedrooms take full advantage of this. The public areas are decorated in a contemporary style, and include a spacious lobby lounge and a comfortable bar where casual dining is available. For more formal dining, Howard's restaurant opens for dinner.

ROOMS: 92 en suite (3 fmly) (27 GF) No smoking in 20 bedrooms s €85-€120; d €120-€150 (incl. bkfst) **LB** **FACILITIES:** STV Indoor swimming (H) Sauna Solarium Gym Jacuzzi Swimming pool supervised entertainment Xmas **CONF:** Thtr 500 Class 200 Board 60 Del from €145 **SERVICES:** Lift **PARKING:** 100 **NOTES:** No dogs (ex guide dogs) **CARDS:**

ARMAGH, Co Armagh

Map 01 C5

★★★61% Charlemont Arms

57/65 English St BT61 7LB
☎ 028 3752 2028 🖹 028 3752 6979
e-mail: info@charlemontarmshotel.com

Centrally located for all of this historic city's principal attractions, this hotel has been under the same family ownership for almost 70 years and offers a choice of dining styles and bars. The mostly spacious bedrooms have all been refurbished in a contemporary style and provide all of the expected facilities.

ROOMS: 30 en suite (2 fmly) No smoking in all bedrooms s £45 (incl. bkfst) **LB** **FACILITIES:** entertainment Xmas **CONF:** Thtr 150 Class 100 Board 80 **SERVICES:** Lift **PARKING:** 30 **NOTES:** No dogs (ex guide dogs) Closed 25 Dec **CARDS:**

GF Indicates the number of bedrooms at ground floor level.

ATHLONE, Co Westmeath

Map 01 C4

★★★70% ❀ Hodson Bay

Hodson Bay
☎ 090 648 0500 🖹 090 648 0520
e-mail: info@hodsonbayhotel.com
Dir: *from N6 take N61 to Roscommon. Turn right - hotel situated 1km on Lough Ree*

Close to the River Shannon and right on the shore of Lough Rea, this historic hotel has been reconstructed and extended to provide comfortable accommodation. With a golf course to the rear and a marina to the front, most of the rooms have excellent views. Public areas include a sun lounge, bar, two restaurants and extensive conference and banqueting facilities.

ROOMS: 133 en suite (23 fmly) No smoking in 3 bedrooms s €95-€137; d €150-€220 (incl. bkfst) **LB** **FACILITIES:** STV Indoor swimming (H) Golf 18 Fishing Sauna Solarium Gym Steam room, play room, beauty salon, Swimming pool supervised entertainment Xmas **CONF:** Thtr 1000 Class 400 Board 300 **SERVICES:** Lift **PARKING:** 300 **NOTES:** No dogs (ex guide dogs) No smoking in restaurant **CARDS:**

See advert on opposite page

★★68% *Royal Hoey*

Mardyke St
☎ 090 647 2924 & 647 5395 🖹 090 647 5194

Upholding a tradition of warm hospitality is the priority at this family-run hotel. Located in the centre of town, it has a comfortable foyer lounge bar and restaurant and the coffee shop serves snacks all day. Bedrooms are carefully maintained and well appointed.

ROOMS: 38 en suite (8 fmly) No smoking in 10 bedrooms **FACILITIES:** STV entertainment **CONF:** Thtr 250 Class 130 Board 40 **SERVICES:** Lift air con **PARKING:** 50 **NOTES:** No dogs (ex guide dogs) Closed 25-27 Dec **CARDS:**

Restaurant with Rooms

❀ Wineport Lodge

Glasson
☎ 090 643 9010 🖹 090 648 5471
e-mail: lodge@wineport.ie
Dir: *Take Longford/Cavan exit (N55 North) off Dublin/Galway Rd (N6) at Athlone. Fork left at Dog and Duck Pub, Lodge 1 mile on left*

In an enviable location, on the shores of the inner lakes of Lough Rea on the Shannon. Customers can arrive by road or water, and dine on the deck or in the attractive dining room. The cuisine is both wholesome and innovative, using the best of local produce. There are also ten luxurious lake shore bedrooms with balconies - the perfect setting for breakfast.

ROOMS: 10 en suite s €175-€300; d €200-€300 (incl. bkfst) **FACILITIES:** STV **CONF:** Thtr 50 Class 30 Board 20 Del from €100 **SERVICES:** air con **PARKING:** 40 **NOTES:** No dogs (ex guide dogs) No smoking in restaurant Closed 24-26 Dec **CARDS:**

Glasson Golf Hotel & Country Club
Glasson
☎ 09 6485120 📠 09 6485120
e-mail: info@glassongolf.ie
Dir: *6m N of Athlone on N55*
At the time of going to press, the star classification for this hotel was not confirmed. Please refer to the AA internet site www.theAA.com for current information.
ROOMS: 29 en suite (13 fmly) s €75-€150; d €130-€190 (incl. bkfst) **FACILITIES:** STV Golf 21 Putting green **CONF:** Thtr 120 Class 50 Board 30 Del from €140 **SERVICES:** Lift **PARKING:** 150 **NOTES:** No dogs (ex guide dogs) **CARDS:**

BALLINASLOE, Co Galway — Map 01 B4

★★★64% *Haydens Gateway Hotel*
☎ 065 6823000 📠 065 6823759
e-mail: cro@lynchotels.com
Dir: *on Dublin/Galway road N6*
Built around 1803, this fine hotel offers excellent service and can provide family rooms and newly refurbished executive rooms. Meals are served throughout the day, either in the Garbally Restaurant, with its extensive carte menu, or in the coffee shop, which serves full meals, snacks and home-baking.
ROOMS: 48 en suite (8 fmly) **FACILITIES:** STV entertainment **CONF:** Thtr 300 Class 160 Board 50 **SERVICES:** Lift **PARKING:** 100 **NOTES:** No dogs (ex guide dogs) Civ Wed 300
CARDS:

BALLINLOUGH, Co Roscommon — Map 01 B4

★★★70% *Whitehouse Hotel*
☎ 0907 40112 📠 0907 40993
e-mail: thewhitehousehotel@eircom.net
Dir: *between Castlerea and Ballyhaunis*
The staff are friendly at this comfortable hotel with appealing decor and spacious bedrooms. Facilities include a TV lounge, restaurant, comfortable bars and a well-equipped conference/banqueting suite. The hotel is convenient for Lake O'Flynn and Knock Airport.
ROOMS: 19 en suite (5 fmly) No smoking in all bedrooms **FACILITIES:** STV entertainment **CONF:** Thtr 250 Class 200 Board 50 **SERVICES:** Lift air con **NOTES:** No dogs (ex guide dogs) Closed 25 Dec
CARDS:

BALLYBOFEY, Co Donegal — Map 01 C5

★★★70% Kee's
Stranorlar
☎ 074 913 1018 📠 074 913 1917
e-mail: info@keeshotel.ie
Dir: *2km NE on N15, in Stranorlar village*
This long established hotel is now in the fourth generation of the Kee family. Warm hospitality is one of the many features of the establishment, which enjoys a steady local custom at the Gallery Bistro, while award-winning fine dining is available in the Looking Glass restaurant at weekends and during the holiday season.
ROOMS: 53 en suite (10 fmly) s €93-€105; d €152-€176 (incl. bkfst) LB **FACILITIES: Spa** STV Indoor swimming (H) Sauna Solarium Gym Jacuzzi Swimming pool supervised entertainment **CONF:** Thtr 250 Class 100 Board 30 **SERVICES:** Lift **PARKING:** 90 **NOTES:** No dogs (ex guide dogs) **CARDS:**

BALLYCONNELL, Co Cavan — Map 01 C4

★★★★69% Slieve Russell Hotel Golf & Country Club
☎ 049 9526444 📠 049 9526474
e-mail: slieve-russell@quinn-hotels.com
Dir: *N3 towards Cavan. At rdbt before Cavan follow Enniskillen sign to Belturbet, then towards Ballyconnell, hotel approx 6m on left.*
This imposing hotel and country club stands in 300 acres accommodating an 18-hole PGA championship golf course and 9-hole par 3 course. Public areas include a range of lounges, choice of restaurants and an extensive leisure and banqueting centre. Bedrooms are tastefully furnished and equipped to a high standard.
ROOMS: 157 en suite (87 fmly) s €130; d €230 (incl. bkfst) **LB** **FACILITIES:** STV Indoor swimming (H) Golf 18 Tennis (hard) Snooker Sauna Solarium Gym Putting green Jacuzzi Hair & Beauty salon, Floodlit driving range, Swimming pool supervised entertainment Xmas **CONF:** BC Thtr 800 Class 400 Board 40 Del €178 **SERVICES:** Lift **PARKING:** 600 **NOTES:** No dogs (ex guide dogs) **CARDS:**

Late for dinner?
Quality Standards mean that last orders for dinner vary according to star rating and should be no earlier than:
★★ 7.00pm ★★★ 8.00pm ★★★★ 9.00pm
★★★★★ 10.00pm

BALLYCOTTON, Co Cork
Map 01 C2

★★★73% Bay View
☎ 021 4646746 021 4646075
e-mail: bayhotel@iol.ie
Dir: *off N25 at Castlemartyr and follow Ballycotton sign*
Situated in a fishing village overlooking Ballycotton Bay, the Bay View has a particularly pleasant atmosphere. The comfortable public areas and bedrooms enjoy abeautiful location. Sit on the patio or terraced gardens, or dine in the award-winning restaurant.
ROOMS: 35 en suite (5 GF) s €121-€139; d €178-€214 (incl. bkfst) **LB** **FACILITIES:** STV Horse riding, Fishing, Pitch and putt, Sea angling **CONF:** Thtr 60 Class 30 Board 24 **SERVICES:** Lift air con **PARKING:** 40 **NOTES:** No dogs (ex guide dogs) Closed Nov-Apr
CARDS:

BALLYGALLEY, Co Antrim
Map 01 D5

★★★67% Ballygally Castle
Coast Rd BT40 2QZ
☎ 028 2858 1066 028 2858 3681
e-mail: res@bgc.hastingshotels.com
Dir: *4m N of Larne on Antrim coast road*
This stylish, welcoming hotel, occupying a 17th-century castle, offers panoramic sea views from the lounge and many bedrooms. Most bedrooms are in a more recently added wing, but all are comfortable and very well equipped. The lounges are spacious and comfortable and roaring fires are lit in cooler months. Diners in the Garden Restaurant can select from creative menus.
ROOMS: 44 en suite (6 fmly) No smoking in 5 bedrooms s £75; d £95 (incl. bkfst) **LB** **FACILITIES:** STV Xmas **CONF:** Thtr 200 Class 50 Board 30 Del £95 **SERVICES:** Lift **PARKING:** 50 **NOTES:** No dogs (ex guide dogs) **CARDS:**

BALLYHEIGE, Co Kerry
Map 01 A2

★★★66% *The White Sands*
☎ 066 7133102 066 7133357
e-mail: whitesands@eircom.net
Dir: *18km from Tralee on coast road*
Friendly staff welcome guests to this family run hotel, situated beside the beach and close to golf clubs. Attractively decorated throughout, facilities include a lounge bar, traditional pub, good restaurant and comfortable bedrooms.
ROOMS: 81 en suite **FACILITIES:** STV entertainment **SERVICES:** Lift air con **PARKING:** 40 **NOTES:** Closed Nov-Feb RS Mar-Apr & Oct
CARDS:

BALLYLICKEY, Co Cork
Map 01 B2

Top 200 - Hotel

★★★ Sea View House Hotel
☎ 027 50073 & 50462 027 51555
e-mail: info@seaviewhousehotel.com
Dir: *5km from Bantry, 11km from Glengarriff on N71*
This delightful country house is framed by colourful gardens and wonderful glimpses of the sea at Bantry Bay can be seen through the mature trees. Personally run by owner, Kathleen O'Sullivan whose team of staff are exceptionally pleasant. Comfort and good cuisine are the top priorities. Bedrooms are spacious and individually styled, some are on the ground floor and fitted to facilitate less able guests.

ROOMS: 25 en suite (3 fmly) (5 GF) s €90-€100; d €160-€180 (incl. bkfst) **LB** **FACILITIES:** STV **PARKING:** 32 **NOTES:** No smoking in restaurant Closed mid Nov-mid Mar
CARDS:

BALLYMENA, Co Antrim
Map 01 D5

★★★★66% Galgorm Manor
BT42 1EA
☎ 028 2588 1001 028 2588 0080
e-mail: mail@galgorm.com
Dir: *1m outside Ballymena on A42, between Galgorm & Cullybackey*
Standing in 85 acres of private woodland and sweeping lawns beside the River Maine, this 19th-century mansion offers spacious comfortable bedrooms. Public areas include a welcoming cocktail bar and elegant restaurant, as well as Gillies, a lively and atmospheric locals' bar. Also on the estate are an equestrian centre and a grand conference hall. This hotel is a popular venue for weddings.
ROOMS: 24 en suite (6 fmly) s £89-£99; d £109-£119 (incl. bkfst) **LB** **FACILITIES:** STV Fishing Riding Clay pigeon shooting,Archery,Waterskiing entertainment Xmas **CONF:** Thtr 500 Class 200 Board 12 Del from £90 **PARKING:** 170 **NOTES:** No dogs (ex guide dogs) RS 25-26 Dec Civ Wed 200 **CARDS:**

BALLYVAUGHAN, Co Clare
Map 01 B3

Top 200 - Hotel

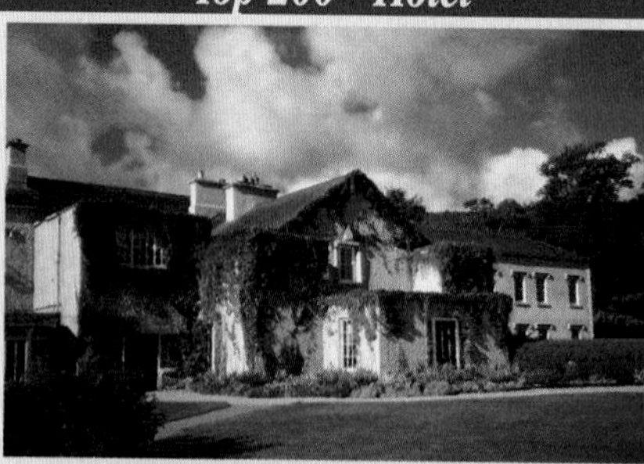

★★★ *Gregans Castle*
☎ 065 7077005 065 7077111
e-mail: res@gregans.ie
Dir: *3.5m S Ballyvaughan on N67*
Situated at the foot of Corkscrew Hill in the heart of the Burren, Gregans Castle Hotel enjoys splendid views towards

continued

Galway Bay. The area is rich in archaeological, geological and botanical interest. The Hayden family and welcoming staff offer a high level of personal service, where hospitality, good food and relaxation are high on the agenda. Bedrooms have every comfort and are individually decorated. The superior rooms and suites are particularly comfortable, some of these are at ground floor level.
ROOMS: 22 en suite **FACILITIES:** no TV in bdrms Croquet lawn **CONF:** Thtr 25 Class 25 Board 25 **PARKING:** 25 **NOTES:** No dogs No smoking in restaurant Closed 23 Dec-14 Feb
CARDS:

★★★63% ***Hylands Burren***
☎ 065 7077037 📠 065 7077131
e-mail: hylandsburren@eircom.net
This charming village hotel was built in the 18th century. The picturesque village of Ballyvaughan is in the heart of the unique Burren landscape and is ideally located for touring County Clare. Open turf fires burn in the traditional bar and lounge and local seafood is a speciality in the restaurant. Bedrooms are comfortable and well appointed.
ROOMS: 29 en suite (2 fmly) No smoking in 6 bedrooms **FACILITIES:** STV entertainment **PARKING:** 30 **NOTES:** No dogs (ex guide dogs) No smoking in restaurant Closed 22-25 Dec
CARDS:

BALTIMORE, Co Cork

Map 01 B1

★★★64% ◎
Baltimore Harbour Resort Hotel & Leisure Centre
☎ 028 20361 📠 028 20466
e-mail: info@bhrhotel.ie
Dir: *S from Cork on N71 to Skibbereen, then R595, 13km to Baltimore*

This smart, friendly hotel is set in a delightful position, overlooking the harbour. It has spacious, linked public areas. The restful lounge has deep sofas and a turf fire, and the bar and garden room open out onto the patio and gardens. Fresh local ingredients are served in the dining room. Bedrooms are well appointed, all have sea views.
ROOMS: 64 en suite (30 fmly) s €78-€109; d €116-€168 (incl. bkfst) **LB FACILITIES:** Indoor swimming (H) Sauna Gym Croquet lawn Jacuzzi Table Tennis, In-house video channel, Indoor bowls, Swimming pool supervised entertainment ch fac **CONF:** Thtr 120 Class 100 Board 30 **SERVICES:** Lift **PARKING:** 80 **NOTES:** No dogs (ex guide dogs) No smoking in restaurant Closed Jan RS Nov-Dec & Feb-mid Mar
CARDS:

★★★61% ◎ **Casey's of Baltimore**

☎ 028 20197 📠 028 20509
e-mail: caseys@eircom.net
Dir: *take N71 from Cork to Skibbereen, then R595*
Set in an elevated position overlooking the harbour, this warm and friendly hotel offers attractive, comfortable bedrooms. Both the lounge and the restaurant enjoy superb views. The restaurant features seafood dishes and there is a traditional pub. Ferry trips to the nearby islands are popular.
ROOMS: 14 en suite (1 fmly) s €89-€103; d €129-€155 (incl. bkfst) **LB FACILITIES:** STV entertainment **PARKING:** 50 **NOTES:** No dogs Closed 21-27 Dec **CARDS:**

BANGOR, Co Down

Map 01 D5

★★★78% ◎◎ **Old Inn**
15 Main St BT19 1JH
☎ 028 9185 3255 📠 028 9185 2775
e-mail: info@theoldinn.com
Dir: *A2, passing Belfast Airport and Holywood, 3m past Holywood sign for The Old Inn, 100yds turn left at lights, follow road to village, hotel on left*
This delightful hotel enjoys a peaceful rural setting just a short drive from Belfast. Dating from 1614, many of the day rooms exude charm and character. Individually styled bedrooms, many with feature beds, offer comfort and modern facilities. The popular bar and intimate restaurant offer a variety of creative menus and staff throughout are keen to please.
ROOMS: 31 en suite 1 annexe en suite (7 fmly) (7 GF) No smoking in 6 bedrooms s fr £70; d fr £90 (incl. bkfst) **LB FACILITIES:** STV entertainment Xmas **CONF:** Thtr 120 Class 27 Board 40 Del from £106 **PARKING:** 105 **NOTES:** No dogs (ex guide dogs) No smoking in restaurant RS 25 Dec Civ Wed 80 **CARDS:**

★★★76% **Clandeboye Lodge**
10 Estate Rd, Clandeboye BT19 1UR
☎ 028 9185 2500 📠 028 9185 2772
e-mail: info@clandeboyelodge.com
Dir: *from Belfast on A2 turn right at sign for Blackwood Golf Centre & Lodge. 500yds down Ballysallagh Road turn left and take Crawfordsburn road. Hotel 200yds on left*

Located three miles west of Bangor, Clandeboye Lodge sits in delightful landscaped and wooded grounds. The hotel provides high quality accommodation as well as extensive conference, banqueting and wedding facilities. Public areas also include a bright open-plan foyer bar and attractive lounge.
ROOMS: 43 en suite (2 fmly) No smoking in 13 bedrooms s £70-£80; d £80-£90 (incl. bkfst) **LB FACILITIES:** STV **CONF:** Thtr 350 Class 110 Board 50 Del from £66.50 **SERVICES:** Lift **PARKING:** 250 **NOTES:** No dogs (ex guide dogs) Closed 24-26 Dec
CARDS:

B

BANGOR, continued

★★★69% Marine Court
The Marina BT20 5ED
☎ 028 9145 1100 028 9145 1200
e-mail: admin@marinecourt.fsnet.co.uk
Dir: *pass Belfast city airport, follow A2 through Holywood to Bangor, down main street follow road to left for seafront*
Enjoying a delightful location overlooking the marina, the Marine Court offers a good range of conference and leisure facilities suited to both the business and leisure guest. Extensive public areas include the first-floor restaurant and cocktail bar. Alternatively, the popular Lord Nelson's Bistro/Bar is more relaxed and there is also the lively restyled Bar Mocha.
ROOMS: 52 en suite (11 fmly) No smoking in 16 bedrooms s £65-£90; d £75-£10 (incl. bkfst) **LB FACILITIES: Spa** STV Indoor swimming (H) Solarium Gym Steam room, Swimming pool supervised entertainment Xmas **CONF:** Thtr 350 Class 150 Del from £90 **SERVICES:** Lift **PARKING:** 30 **NOTES:** No dogs (ex guide dogs) Closed 25 Dec Civ Wed 200 **CARDS:**

★★★62% Royal
Seafront BT20 5ED
☎ 028 9127 1866 028 9146 7810
e-mail: royalhotelbangor@aol.com
Dir: *take A2 from Belfast. Through Bangor town centre to seafront. Turn right. Hotel 300yds overlooking Marina*
This substantial Victorian hotel enjoys a delightful seafront location and overlooks the marina. Bedrooms are comfortable and practical in style. Public areas are traditional and include a choice of contrasting bars and a popular brasserie.
ROOMS: 50 en suite (5 fmly) s £50-£60; d £70-£80 (incl. bkfst) **LB FACILITIES:** STV **CONF:** Thtr 80 Class 60 Board 40 **SERVICES:** Lift **NOTES:** No dogs (ex guide dogs) Closed 25 Dec
CARDS:

BANTRY, Co Cork — Map 01 B2

★★★64% Westlodge
☎ 027 50360 027 50438
e-mail: reservations@westlodgehotel.ie
Dir: *N71 to West Cork*
A superb leisure centre and good children's facilities makes this hotel very popular with families. The situation on the outskirts of the town also makes it an ideal base for touring west Cork and south Kerry. All the staff are friendly and hospitable.
ROOMS: 90 en suite (20 fmly) (20 GF) No smoking in 15 bedrooms s €60-€90; d €120-€170 (incl. bkfst) **LB FACILITIES:** STV Indoor swimming (H) Tennis (hard) Squash Snooker Sauna Solarium Gym Putting green Jacuzzi Pitch & Putt, wooded walks entertainment ch fac **CONF:** Thtr 400 Class 200 Board 24 **SERVICES:** Lift air con **PARKING:** 400 **NOTES:** No dogs (ex guide dogs) Closed 23-27 Dec
CARDS:

BELFAST — Map 01 D5

★★★★67% Ramada Belfast
117 Milltown Rd, Shaws Bridge BT8 7XP
☎ 028 9092 3500 028 9092 3600
e-mail: mail@ramadabelfast.com
Dir: *S from city centre, follow Malone Rd to rdbt and signs for Barnett Demense. Left into Milltown Rd, hotel on left, 400mtrs from rdbt*
Set within the Laggan Valley Regional Park, this modern conference and leisure hotel caters well for all markets. Bedrooms are stylish and furnished in eye-catching designs. The LA Fitness Club is very well equipped, and the Grand Ballroom attracts many top events. The Belfast Bar and Grill serves innovative Irish cuisine, whilst the trendy Suburbia bar offers a lighter alternative.
ROOMS: 120 en suite (43 GF) No smoking in 88 bedrooms s £70-£110; d £80-£110 (incl. bkfst) **FACILITIES: Spa** STV Indoor swimming (H) Sauna Solarium Gym Jacuzzi Swimming pool supervised Xmas **CONF:** Thtr 900 Class 450 Board 40 Del from £135.50 **SERVICES:** Lift air con **PARKING:** 150 **NOTES:** No dogs (ex guide dogs)
CARDS:

★★★71% Malone Lodge
60 Eglantine Av BT9 6DY
☎ 028 9038 8000 028 9038 8088
e-mail: info@malonelodgehotel.com
Dir: *at hospital rdbt exit towards Bouchar Rd, left at 1st rdbt, right at lights at top, 1st left is Eglantine Ave*
Situated in the leafy suburbs of the university area of south Belfast, this stylish hotel forms the centrepiece of an attractive row of Victorian terraced properties. The unassuming exterior belies an attractive and spacious interior with a smart lounge, popular bar and stylish Green Door restaurant. The hotel also has a small, well-equipped fitness room.
ROOMS: 51 en suite (5 fmly) (1 GF) s £59-£85; d £79-£99 (incl. bkfst) **LB FACILITIES:** STV Sauna Gym **CONF:** BC Thtr 150 Class 90 Board 40 Del from £95 **SERVICES:** Lift **PARKING:** 35 **NOTES:** No dogs (ex guide dogs) **CARDS:**

★★★70% The Crescent Townhouse
13 Lower Crescent BT7 1NR
☎ 028 9032 3349 028 9032 0646
e-mail: info@crescenttownhouse.com
Dir: *S towards Queens University, hotel on Botanic Avenue opposite Botanic Train Station*

This stylish, smartly presented Regency town house enjoys a central location close to the botanic gardens and railway station. The popular Bar Twelve and Metro Brasserie are found on the ground floor whilst the reception and well-equipped bedrooms are situated on the upper floors.
ROOMS: 11 en suite No smoking in 2 bedrooms s £50-£80; d £65-£90 (incl. bkfst) **FACILITIES:** entertainment **NOTES:** No dogs (ex guide dogs) Closed 25-27 Dec & part of Jul **CARDS:**

★★★63% Balmoral
Blacks Rd BT10 0NF
☎ 028 9030 1234 028 9060 1455
e-mail: info@balmoralhotelbelfast.co.uk
Dir: *take M1, 3m exit at Suffolk slip road, turn right and hotel approx 300yards*
This modern, refurbished hotel lies just south of the city in the village of Dunmurry. Bedrooms vary in size and offer practical furnishings and amenities. There is a choice of contrasting bars,

continued

one of which provides an informal alternative to the main restaurant.
ROOMS: 43 en suite (2 fmly) No smoking in 4 bedrooms s £35-£60; d £50-£85 (incl. bkfst) **LB** **FACILITIES:** STV Xmas **CONF:** Thtr 400 Class 200 Board 80 Del from £90 **PARKING:** 300 **NOTES:** No dogs (ex guide dogs) Closed 25 Dec **CARDS:**

★★★61% Jurys Belfast Inn

JURYS DOYLE HOTELS

Fisherwick Place, Great Victoria St BT2 7AP
☎ 028 9053 3500 📠 028 9053 3511
e-mail: info@jurys.com
Dir: *at junct of Grosvenor Rd & Great Victoria St, by Opera House*
Enjoying a central location, this modern hotel is well equipped for business guests. Public areas are contemporary in style and include a foyer lounge, a bar and a smart restaurant. Spacious bedrooms provide modern facilities.
ROOMS: 190 en suite No smoking in 76 bedrooms s fr £73; d fr £73 **FACILITIES:** STV entertainment **CONF:** Thtr 30 Class 16 Board 16 **SERVICES:** Lift **NOTES:** No dogs (ex guide dogs) Closed 24-26 Dec **CARDS:**

U *Holiday Inn Belfast*

Holiday Inn HOTELS · RESORTS

22 Ormeau Av BT2 8HS
☎ 0870 400 9005 📠 028 9062 6546
e-mail: reservation-belfast@ichotelsgroup.com
Dir: *M1/M2 onto West Link at Grosvenor Rd rdbt, follow city centre sign. Take 1st right then 2nd left into Hope St, at 2nd lights turn left into Bedford St at next lights turn right into Ormeau Ave, hotel on right*
At the time of going to press, the classification for this hotel was not confirmed. Please refer to the AA internet site www.theAA.com for current information.
ROOMS: 170 en suite (73 fmly) No smoking in 108 bedrooms **FACILITIES: Spa** STV Indoor swimming (H) Sauna Solarium Gym Jacuzzi Beauty treatments Steam room Workout studio entertainment **CONF:** Thtr 120 Class 58 Board 30 **SERVICES:** Lift air con **PARKING:** 40 **NOTES:** No dogs RS 24 Dec-3 Jan **CARDS:**

⌂ *Express by Holiday Inn*

Express by Holiday Inn

106a University St BT7 1HP
☎ 028 9031 1909 📠 028 9031 1910
e-mail: mail@exhi-belfast.com
Dir: *behind Queens University. Turn left at lights on Botanic Ave onto University St. 500yds on left*

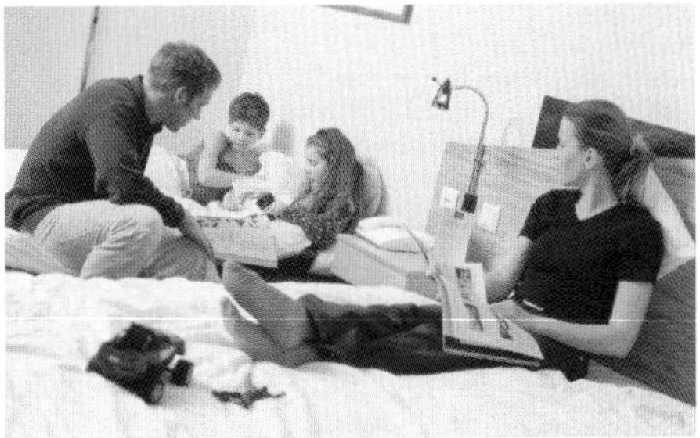

A modern hotel ideal for families and business travellers. Fresh and uncomplicated, the spacious bedrooms include Sky TV, power shower and tea and coffee-making facilities. Continental buffet breakfast is included in the room rate; other meals may be taken at the nearby family pub or restaurant. For further details and the Express by Holiday Inn phone number, consult the Hotel Groups pages.
ROOMS: 114 en suite **CONF:** Thtr 60 Class 40 Board 30

⌂ Travelodge

Travelodge

15 Brunswick St BT2 7GE
☎ 08700 850 950 📠 028 9023 2999
Dir: *from M2 follow city centre signs to Oxford St turn right to May St, Brunswick St is 4th on left*
Travelodge offers good quality, good value, modern accommodation. Ideal for families, the spacious, en suite bedrooms include remote-control TV, tea and coffee-making facilities, luxury beds and free morning newspaper. Meals can be taken at the nearby family restaurant. For further details and the Travelodge phone number, consult the Hotel Groups page.
ROOMS: 90 en suite s fr £42.95; d fr £42.95 **CONF:** Thtr 65 Class 50 Board 34

BETTYSTOWN, Co Meath — Map 01 D4

★★★★59% *Neptune Beach Hotel & Leisure Club*

☎ 041 9827107 📠 041 9827412
e-mail: info@neptunebeach.ie
Dir: *just off main Dublin/Belfast road N1*
This hotel, overlooking the sea, has access to a sandy beach. Public areas include an inviting lounge and an attractive Winter Garden. Many bedrooms enjoy sea views.
ROOMS: 38 en suite No smoking in 14 bedrooms **FACILITIES:** STV Indoor swimming (H) Sauna Solarium Gym Jacuzzi Steam room Kiddies pool entertainment **CONF:** Thtr 250 Class 150 **SERVICES:** Lift **PARKING:** 60 **NOTES:** No dogs (ex guide dogs) No smoking in restaurant **CARDS:**

BIRR, Co Offaly — Map 01 C3

★★★61% County Arms

☎ 0509 20791 📠 0509 21234
e-mail: countyarmshotel@eircom.net
Dir: *take N7 from Dublin to Roscrea, N62 to Birr, hotel on right before the church*
This fine Georgian house has comfortable bedrooms, all furnished and decorated to a very high standard. The rooms overlook the meticulously kept Victorian walled gardens which supply the fruit, vegetables and herbs to the hotel kitchens. There is a choice of two restaurants, a bar and a comfortable lounge.
ROOMS: 24 en suite (4 fmly) No smoking in 2 bedrooms **FACILITIES:** STV Gym entertainment **CONF:** Thtr 250 Class 250 Board 25 **PARKING:** 150 **NOTES:** No dogs (ex guide dogs) RS 25 Dec **CARDS:**

BLESSINGTON, Co Wicklow — Map 01 D3

★★★66% ❀ *Downshire House*

☎ 045 865199 📠 045 865335
e-mail: info@downshirehouse.com
Dir: *on N81*
This family-run Georgian house is renowned for its friendly atmosphere. Bedrooms are comfortable and come in a variety of sizes, while the public areas are relaxing and inviting. Cooking is in traditional country-house style. The hotel is on the main street in the village, near to the Wicklow Hills, amid some lovely scenery.
ROOMS: 14 en suite 11 annexe en suite **FACILITIES:** Tennis (hard) Croquet lawn Table tennis **CONF:** Thtr 40 Class 20 Board 20 **PARKING:** 30 **NOTES:** No dogs (ex guide dogs) Closed 22 Dec-6 Jan **CARDS:**

> € Don't forget, the Euro is now the unit of currency in the Republic of Ireland

B

BRAY, Co Wicklow

Map 01 D4

★★★63% Woodland Court

Southern Cross
☎ 01 2760258 📠 01 2760298
e-mail: info@woodlandscourthotel.ie
Dir: *3rd exit off N11 after Loughlinstown rdbt, Bray/Greystones turn off*
In a beautiful setting opposite Kilruddery House and famous French-style gardens, this hotel is comfortable and attractively decorated throughout. Bedrooms are spacious and well appointed with modern facilities. There is an open-plan lobby lounge with bar, a cosy restaurant and corporate facilities. An ideal venue for touring Dublin and Wicklow.
ROOMS: 65 en suite (4 fmly) (20 GF) **FACILITIES:** STV **CONF:** BC Thtr 60 Class 30 Board 20 Del from €120 **SERVICES:** Lift **PARKING:** 70 **NOTES:** No dogs (ex guide dogs) No smoking in restaurant Closed 23-27 Dec **CARDS:**

★★★62% *Royal*

Main St
☎ 01 2862935 📠 01 2867373
e-mail: royal@regencyhotels.com
Dir: *from N11, 1st exit for Bray, 2nd exit from rdbt, through 2 sets of lights across bridge, hotel on left*
The Royal Hotel stands on the main street, near to the seafront, just a few miles from the Dun Laoghaire ferryport. The hotel has a well-equipped leisure centre.
ROOMS: 91 en suite (10 fmly) No smoking in 14 bedrooms **FACILITIES:** Indoor swimming (H) Sauna Solarium Gym Jacuzzi Massage and beauty clinic Therapy room Whirlpool spa,madhatters creche entertainment ch fac **CONF:** Thtr 300 Class 200 Board 100 **SERVICES:** Lift **PARKING:** 60 **NOTES:** No dogs (ex guide dogs) Civ Wed 225 **CARDS:**

BUNRATTY, Co Clare

Map 01 B3

★★★69% ® *Fitzpatrick Bunratty*

☎ 061 361177 📠 061 471252
e-mail: reservations@bunratty.fitzpatricks.com
Dir: *take Bunratty by-pass, exit off Limerick/Shannon dual carriageway*
Situated in the picturesque village of Bunratty, and in the shadow of the famous Bunratty Medieval Castle, this modern hotel is surrounded by well-maintained lawns and colourful flowerbeds. Bedrooms and public areas are spacious comfortable and there are extensive indoor leisure facilities and an impressive conference and banqueting centre.
ROOMS: 115 en suite 4 annexe en suite (12 fmly) No smoking in 10 bedrooms **FACILITIES:** STV Indoor swimming (H) Sauna Solarium Gym Jacuzzi entertainment **CONF:** Thtr 1000 Class 650 Board 300 **PARKING:** 300 **NOTES:** No dogs (ex guide dogs) Closed 24-26 Dec **CARDS:**

> € Don't forget, the Euro is now the unit of currency in the Republic of Ireland

CAHERDANIEL, Co Kerry

Map 01 A2

★★★65% Derrynane

Best Western

☎ 066 9475136 📠 066 9475160
e-mail: info@derrynane.com
Dir: *hotel just off main road*
Halfway around the famous Ring of Kerry, this modern hotel, overlooking the sea, offers a relaxed and friendly atmosphere. The gardens and some of the bedrooms take advantage of the spectacular sea views. The area is ideal for touring and enjoying the scenery and there are plenty of quiet beaches.

ROOMS: 73 en suite (30 fmly) s €80-€100; d €120-€160 (incl. bkfst) **LB** **FACILITIES:** STV Outdoor swimming (H) Tennis (hard) Sauna Solarium Gym Steam room, Swimming pool supervised entertainment **SERVICES:** air con **PARKING:** 60 **NOTES:** No dogs No smoking in restaurant Closed 4 Oct-15 Apr **CARDS:**

CAHIR, Co Tipperary

Map 01 C3

★★★64% Cahir House

The Square
☎ 052 42727 📠 052 42728
e-mail: cahirhousehotel@eircom.net
Dir: *S on N8 turn off at Cahir by-pass follow N24 to town, hotel on square in centre of town, car park at rear*
In the centre of Cahir, this hotel has been extending hospitality to visitors since the days of the famous Bianconi horse-drawn coaches. It offers modern comforts in well-equipped and tastefully furnished rooms and maintains traditional standards of welcome and cuisine. The hotel is an ideal base from which to explore.
ROOMS: 41 en suite (3 fmly) No smoking in 17 bedrooms s €80-€100; d €100-€120 (incl. bkfst) **LB** **FACILITIES:** STV entertainment **CONF:** Thtr 400 Class 200 Board 50 Del from €90 **PARKING:** 80 **NOTES:** No dogs (ex guide dogs) Closed 25 Dec RS 24-26 Dec & Good Fri **CARDS:**

CARLOW, Co Carlow

Map 01 C3

★★★70% Seven Oaks

Athy Rd
☎ 059 913 1308 📠 059 913 2155
e-mail: info@sevenoakshotel.com
Staff are friendly and helpful at this hotel, where extensive refurbishment has considerably enhanced facilities. These include a spacious lounge, comfortable new bedrooms and a leisure club. The popular restaurant is also being extended and there is a relaxing bar.
ROOMS: 59 en suite (5 fmly) s €76-€85; d €115-€140 (incl. bkfst) **LB** **FACILITIES:** STV Indoor swimming (H) Sauna Gym Jacuzzi Aerobic studio, Steam room entertainment **CONF:** Thtr 400 Class 150 Board 80 **SERVICES:** Lift air con **PARKING:** 200 **NOTES:** No dogs (ex guide dogs) Closed 25-26 Dec RS Good Friday **CARDS:**

★★★68% *Dolmen*

Kilkenny Rd
☎ 059 914 2002 📠 059 914 2375
e-mail: reservations@dolmenhotel.ie
Dir: *approx 1m outside Carlow on Kilkenny-Waterford road. Approx 0.5m on right past The Institute of Technology*
In 20 acres of landscaped grounds, this hotel nestles in a peaceful riverside location. Guests can relax in the grounds or take advantage of the free coarse fishing. There is a spacious reception

continued

and foyer, a large bar and restaurant, and a luxurious boardroom, which doubles as an additional lounge, overlooking the river. Bedrooms are all well-equipped and comfortable.
ROOMS: 40 en suite 12 annexe en suite (1 fmly) **FACILITIES:** STV Fishing **CONF:** Thtr 1000 Class 300 Board 50 **SERVICES:** air con **PARKING:** 300 **NOTES:** No dogs (ex guide dogs)
CARDS:

CARNA, Co Galway — Map 01 A4

★★★62% Carna Bay Hotel

☎ 095 32255 📠 095 32530
e-mail: carnaby@iol.ie
Dir: *from Galway take N59 to Recess, then left onto R340 for 8-10m*

IRISH COUNTRY HOTELS

This family-run hotel overlooks Carna Bay on the Connemara coast and has a relaxed and friendly atmosphere. Public areas are comfortable and spacious. Food is available all day in the bar, where traditional music and dancing take place on weekend nights. Most of the comfortable bedrooms enjoy sea views.
ROOMS: 26 en suite (1 fmly) (11 GF) No smoking in 10 bedrooms s €73-€109; d €117-€190 (incl. bkfst) **LB** **PARKING:** 60 **NOTES:** No smoking in restaurant Closed 23-26 Dec **CARDS:**

CARNLOUGH, Co Antrim — Map 01 D6

★★★69% *Londonderry Arms*

20 Harbour Rd BT44 0EU
☎ 028 2888 5255 📠 028 2888 5263
e-mail: lda@glensofantrim.com
Dir: *14m N from Larne on the coast road, A2*

Originally built in the mid-19th century as a coaching inn by Lady Londonderry, the building was owned at one time by her grandson, Winston Churchill. Today the hotel's Georgian architecture and rooms are still evident. The hotel enjoys a prime location in this pretty fishing village overlooking the Antrim coast.
ROOMS: 35 en suite (5 fmly) **FACILITIES:** Fishing entertainment **CONF:** Thtr 120 Class 60 Board 40 **SERVICES:** Lift **PARKING:** 50 **NOTES:** No dogs Closed Xmas **CARDS:**

CARRICKFERGUS, Co Antrim — Map 01 D5

★★67% Dobbins Inn

6-8 High St BT38 7AP
☎ 028 9335 1905 📠 028 9335 1905
e-mail: info@dobbinsinnhotel.co.uk
Dir: *at Belfast take M2, keep right at rdbt, follow A2 to Carrickfergus, turn left opposite castle*

Colourful window boxes adorn the front of this popular inn, near the ancient castle and seafront. Public areas are furnished to a modern standard without compromising the inn's interesting, historical character. Bedrooms vary in size and style and all provide modern comforts. Staff throughout are very friendly.
ROOMS: 15 en suite (2 fmly) s £46; d £65 (incl. bkfst) **LB** **FACILITIES:** entertainment **CONF:** **NOTES:** Closed 25-26 Dec & 1 Jan RS Good Fri **CARDS:**

CARRICKMACROSS, Co Monaghan — Map 01 C4

★★★★75% Nuremore

☎ 042 9661438 📠 042 9661853
e-mail: nuremore@eircom.net
Dir: *3km S of Carrickmacross, on main N2 Dublin/Derry road*

Overlooking the golf course and lakes, the Nuremore is a quiet retreat with excellent facilities. There are spacious public areas and a wide variety of indoor and outdoor leisure and sporting facilities.

continued

Ray McArdle's food in the restaurant continues to impress with an imaginative range of dishes.
ROOMS: 72 en suite No smoking in 21 bedrooms s €150-€200; d €210-€300 (incl. bkfst) **LB** **FACILITIES: Spa** STV Indoor swimming (H) Golf 18 Tennis (grass) Fishing Snooker Sauna Solarium Gym Putting green Beauty treatments, Aromatherapy, Massage entertainment Xmas **CONF:** BC Thtr 250 Class 100 Board 30 Del from €180 **SERVICES:** Lift **PARKING:** 200 **NOTES:** No dogs (ex guide dogs)
CARDS:

C

CARRICK-ON-SHANNON, Co Leitrim — Map 01 C4

★★★★60% The Landmark

☎ 071 962 2222 📠 071 962 2233
e-mail: landmarkhotel@eircom.net
Dir: *N4 approaching Carrick-on-Shannon from Dublin, take first exit off roundabout, hotel on right*

Overlooking the River Shannon, close to the Marina, this hotel offers luxurious public areas including a choice of bars and restaurants, lounges, a fitness club and ballroom. Pleasant staff will be pleased to arrange cruising, horse riding, golf and angling.
ROOMS: 50 en suite (4 fmly) s €116-€131; d €180-€210 (incl. bkfst) **LB** **FACILITIES:** STV Gym entertainment **CONF:** Thtr 500 Class 170 **SERVICES:** Lift **PARKING:** 60 **NOTES:** No dogs Closed 24-25 Dec RS 26 Dec **CARDS:**

CASHEL, Co Galway — Map 01 A4

Courtesy & Care Award
Top 200 - Hotel

★★★ Cashel House

☎ 095 31001 📠 095 31077
e-mail: info@cashel-house-hotel.com
Dir: *turn S off N59, 1.5km W of Recess, well signposted*

RELAIS & CHATEAUX.

Cashel House is a mid-19th century house, standing at the head of Cashel Bay, in the heart of Connemara, quietly secluded in award-winning gardens with woodland walks. Attentive service comes with the perfect balance of friendliness and professionalis from McEvilly family and their staff. The comfortable lounges have turf fires and antique furnishings. The restaurant offers local produce such as the famous Connemara Lamb and fish from the local waters. Cashel House has been awarded the AA Courtesy & Care Award for the Republic of Ireland 2003-2004.
ROOMS: 32 en suite (4 fmly) (6 GF) No smoking in 10 bedrooms s €90-€315; d €180-€338 (incl. bkfst) **LB** **FACILITIES:** Tennis (hard) Fishing Riding Xmas **PARKING:** 40 **NOTES:** No children 5yrs No smoking in restaurant Closed 4 Jan-4 Feb
CARDS:

★★★77% *Zetland Country House*

Cashel Bay
☎ 095 31111 📠 095 31117
e-mail: zetland@iol.ie
Dir: *N59 from Galway towards Clifden, right after Recess onto R340, left after 4m (R341), hotel 1m on right*

MANOR HOUSE

Set in very attractive gardens featuring unusual rock formations, flowers, shrubs and woodland, this peaceful country house overlooks Cashel Bay. Public areas include a fine lounge and reading room as well as a smart cocktail bar. Many of the bedrooms have sea or garden views. Warm hospitality is matched by good food and service.
ROOMS: 19 en suite (10 fmly) **FACILITIES:** STV Tennis (hard) Snooker Croquet lawn **CONF:** Board 20 **PARKING:** 32 **NOTES:** No smoking in restaurant Closed Nov-9 Apr **CARDS:**

CASHEL, Co Tipperary Map 01 C3

★★★★66% Cashel Palace Hotel
062 62707 062 61521
e-mail: reception@cashel-palace.ie
Dir: *On N8 through centre of Cashel, hotel on main street near traffic lights*
The Rock of Cashel, floodlit at night, forms a dramatic backdrop to this 18th-century former bishop's palace. An elegant drawing room has garden access and luxurious bedrooms in the main house are most comfortable. Those in the adjacent mews are ideal for families or groups.
ROOMS: 13 en suite 10 annexe en suite (8 fmly) No smoking in 5 bedrooms s €152-€171; d €216-€254 (incl. bkfst) **LB FACILITIES:** STV Fishing Private path walk to the Rock of Cashel entertainment **CONF:** Thtr 80 Class 45 Board 40 **SERVICES:** Lift **PARKING:** 35 **NOTES:** No dogs (ex guide dogs) Closed 2 weeks in Xmas - Jan **CARDS:**

Restaurant with Rooms

Legends Townhouse & Restaurant
The Kiln
062 61292
e-mail: info@legendsguesthouse.com
Dir: *turn off N8 onto R660 towards Thurles, establishment 30yds on left, signed*
Sitting underneath the Rock of Cashel this distinctive house has been purpose built to blend in with the dramatic location. An interesting menu featuring local produce and skillful cooking by Chef/Proprietor Michael O'Neill is served in the restaurant that enjoys mystical views, and diners will experience an atmosphere of almost eerie magic in the evenings. A cosy guest lounge and very comfortable bedrooms complete the picture.
ROOMS: 7 en suite (2 fmly) No smoking in all bedrooms **FACILITIES:** STV **PARKING:** 7 **NOTES:** No dogs No smoking in restaurant Closed 23-26 Dec & 16 Feb-9 Mar **CARDS:**

See advert on opposite page

CASTLEBAR, Co Mayo Map 01 B4

★★64% *Welcome Inn*
094 902 2288 & 902 2054 094 902 1766
e-mail: cb.welcome@mayo-ireland.ie
Dir: *take N5 to Castlebar, hotel near town centre via ring road & rdbts past the Church of the Holy Rosary*
This town centre hotel offers a range of modern facilities behind its Tudor frontage, including a banqueting/conference centre. Bedrooms are well-equipped and there is a night club with disco on some evenings, as well as traditional music nights in the summer.
ROOMS: 40 en suite (5 fmly) **FACILITIES:** STV entertainment **CONF:** Thtr 500 Class 350 **SERVICES:** Lift **PARKING:** 100 **NOTES:** No dogs (ex guide dogs) Closed 23-25 Dec **CARDS:**

CASTLECONNELL, Co Limerick Map 01 B3

★★★66% Castle Oaks House
061 377666 061 377717
e-mail: info@castleoaks.ie
Dir: *off N7 8km outside Limerick for Castleconnell, hotel on left on entering village*
A fine old Georgian house with grounds reaching down to the River Shannon, set in the tiny village of Castleconnell. The hotel has been upgraded and guests can enjoy first class comfort in well-equipped modern bedrooms. Facilities include river walks, good fishing and free use of a leisure centre.
ROOMS: 20 en suite 44 annexe en suite (9 fmly) No smoking in 1 bedroom s €100-€110; d €140-€160 (incl. bkfst) **LB FACILITIES:** STV Indoor swimming (H) Tennis (hard) Fishing Sauna Solarium Gym Jacuzzi Swimming pool supervised Xmas **CONF:** Thtr 200 Class 150 Board 80 Del from €145 **PARKING:** 200 **NOTES:** No dogs (ex guide dogs) Closed 24-26 Dec **CARDS:**

CAVAN, Co Cavan Map 01 C4

★★★65% Kilmore
Dublin Rd
049 4332288 049 4332458
e-mail: kilmore@quinn-hotels.com
Dir: *approx 3km from Cavan on N3*
Set on a hillside on the outskirts of Cavan, easily accessible from the main N3 route, this comfortable hotel features spacious public areas. Good food is served in the Annalee Restaurant, which is always appreciated by guests returning from fishing, golf, windsurfing or boating, which are all available nearby.
ROOMS: 39 en suite (17 fmly) (19 GF) s €58-€75; d €98-€120 (incl. bkfst) **LB FACILITIES:** STV entertainment ch fac Xmas **CONF:** Thtr 300 Class 200 Board 60 Del €117 **SERVICES:** air con **PARKING:** 450 **NOTES:** No dogs (ex guide dogs) **CARDS:**

CLIFDEN, Co Galway Map 01 A4

★★★76% Abbeyglen Castle
MANOR HOUSE
Sky Rd
095 21201 095 21797
e-mail: info@abbeyglen.ie
Dir: *take N59 from Galway to Clifden. Hotel 1km from Clifden on Sky Rd*
In a tranquil setting overlooking Clifden, the charming atmosphere at Abbeyglen owes much to the dedication of father and son team, Paul and Brian Hughes, and their attentive staff. Some fine new bedrooms have been added, and there is a lovely restaurant and a bar, where musical evenings often develop. Golf tours can be arranged.
ROOMS: 38 en suite (9 GF) No smoking in 10 bedrooms s €121-€139; d €179-€215 (incl. bkfst) **LB FACILITIES:** STV Outdoor swimming (H) Tennis (hard) Snooker Sauna Putting green Jacuzzi entertainment Xmas **CONF:** Thtr 100 Class 50 Board 40 Del from €213 **SERVICES:** Lift **PARKING:** 40 **NOTES:** No dogs No children Closed 5 Jan-1 Feb **CARDS:**

★★★76% Rock Glen Country House Hotel
MANOR HOUSE
095 21035 & 21393 095 21737
e-mail: rockglen@iol.ie
Dir: *N6 from Dublin to Galway, then N57 to Clifden. Hotel 1.5m from Clifden*
The charming clematis and creeper-framed façade of this house is but an introduction to the comfort that lies inside. The hospitality of the Roche family and their staff makes a visit to this hotel relaxing and very pleasant. Many of the well-appointed bedrooms have views of the gardens and bay.
ROOMS: 26 en suite (2 fmly) (18 GF) s €128-€152; d €177-€214 (incl. bkfst) **LB FACILITIES:** Tennis (hard) Snooker Croquet lawn Putting green entertainment **PARKING:** 50 **NOTES:** No smoking in restaurant Closed mid Nov-mid Feb (ex New Year) **CARDS:**

★★★71% ◎◎◎ Ardagh
Ballyconneely Rd
☎ 095 21384 🖷 095 21314
e-mail: ardaghhotel@eircom.net
Dir: *N59 Galway to Clifden, signposted to Ballyconneely*

IRISH COUNTRY HOTELS

Situated at the head of Ardbear Bay, this family-run hotel makes full use of the spectacular views. The restaurant is renowned for its cuisine, which is complemented by friendly and knowledgeable service. Rooms are individually decorated and show great attention to detail.
ROOMS: 19 en suite (2 fmly) No smoking in all bedrooms s €108-€120; d €165-€185 (incl. bkfst) **LB FACILITIES:** Pool room **PARKING:** 35 **NOTES:** No dogs (ex guide dogs) No smoking in restaurant Closed Nov-Mar **CARDS:**

★★★64% ◎ *Alcock & Brown Hotel*
☎ 095 21206 & 21086 🖷 095 21842
e-mail: alcockandbrown@eircom.net
Dir: *take N59 from Galway via Oughterard, hotel in centre of town*
A comfortable family run town centre hotel. The bar and lounge are inviting with open fires and the restaurant is bright and visually appealing. The menu offers a wide range of good food with many fish specialities. The friendly and attentive staff offer good service.
ROOMS: 19 annexe en suite No smoking in 4 bedrooms **FACILITIES:** STV entertainment **NOTES:** No dogs (ex guide dogs) Closed 23-25 Dec **CARDS:**

CLONAKILTY, Co Cork
Map 01 B2

★★★★74% The Lodge & Spa at Inchydoney Island
☎ 023 33143 🖷 023 35229
e-mail: reservations@inchydoneyisland.com
Dir: *follow N71 West Cork road to Clonakilty, at entry rdbt in Clonakilty take 2nd exit and follow signs to Lodge*
This modern hotel is stunningly located on the coastline with steps down to two long sandy beaches. Bedrooms are decorated in warm colours and are well appointed. Diners have a choice of the third-floor Gulfstream restaurant or the more casual Dunes bar and bistro.
ROOMS: 67 en suite (24 fmly) No smoking in 17 bedrooms s €154-€182; d €260-€310 (incl. bkfst) **LB FACILITIES: Spa** STV Indoor swimming (H) Fishing Riding Snooker Sauna Gym Jacuzzi Thalassotherapy spa, Swimming pool supervised entertainment **CONF:** Thtr 300 Class 150 Board 100 Del from €210 **SERVICES:** Lift **PARKING:** 200 **NOTES:** No dogs (ex guide dogs) No smoking in restaurant Closed 25-26 Dec **CARDS:**

CLONMEL, Co Tipperary
Map 01 C2

★★★74% ◎ *Minella*
☎ 052 22388 🖷 052 24381
e-mail: hotelminella@eircom.net
This family-run hotel, set in nine acres of well kept grounds on the banks of the River Suir, offers comfort and courteous service. Facilities include a cocktail bar and lounge overlooking the gardens and a leisure centre and putting greens. Bedrooms are all tastefully decorated and well-equipped, some have jacuzzis.
ROOMS: 70 en suite (8 fmly) No smoking in 16 bedrooms **FACILITIES:** STV Indoor swimming (H) Tennis (hard) Fishing Sauna Gym Croquet lawn Jacuzzi Aerobics room **CONF:** Thtr 500 Class 300 Board 20 **PARKING:** 100 **NOTES:** No dogs No smoking in restaurant Closed 24-28 Dec **CARDS:**

COBH, Co Cork
Map 01 B2

★★★70% ◎ Waters Edge
Yacht Club Quay
☎ 021 4815566 🖷 021 4812011
e-mail: info@watersedgehotel.ie
Dir: *follow road signs for Cobh Heritage Centre & Fota Golf Club*
This delightful hotel is situated on the waterfront beside the Heritage Centre and railway station. Spectacular views of Cork Harbour can be enjoyed while dining in Jacob's Ladder Restaurant. The spacious bedrooms are furnished to a high standard, most rooms are on the waterfront and the ground floors rooms have private balconies. Secure underground parking is available.
ROOMS: 19 en suite (5 fmly) (5 GF) No smoking in 6 bedrooms s €75-€100; d €110-€200 (incl. bkfst) **LB PARKING:** 25 **NOTES:** Closed 23-28 Dec & 1-4 Jan No dogs (ex guide dogs) **CARDS:**

Town House Hotel
Country House Hotel
Travel Accommodation

€ Don't forget, the Euro is now the unit of currency in the Republic of Ireland

C

CORK, Co Cork Map 01 B2

Hotel of the Year
Top 200 - Hotel

★★★★ Hayfield Manor
Perrott Av, College Rd
☎ 021 4845900 021 4316839
e-mail: enquiries@hayfieldmanor.ie
Dir: *1m W of Cork city centre take N22 to Killarney, turn left at University Gates off Western Rd. Turn right into College Rd, left into Perrott Ave*

Hayfield Manor offers privacy and seclusion. Part of a grand two-acre estate with loverly gardens, this fine hotel has every modern comfort and maintains an atmosphere of tranquillity. Bedrooms are spacious and offer high levels of comfort with many thoughtful extras. Public rooms feature elegant architecture, carefully combined with fine furnishings and real fires to create an atmosphere of intimacy. Hayfield Manor has been chosen as AA Hotel of the Year for Ireland 2003-2004.

ROOMS: 88 en suite No smoking in 25 bedrooms s €345; d €345 **LB FACILITIES:** STV Indoor swimming (H) Gym Jacuzzi Steam room entertainment Xmas **CONF:** Thtr 100 Class 60 Board 40 Del €315 **SERVICES:** Lift air con **PARKING:** 100 **NOTES:** No dogs (ex guide dogs) No smoking in restaurant **CARDS:**

★★★★76% The Kingsley Hotel
Victoria Cross
☎ 021 4800500 021 4800527
e-mail: resv@kingsleyhotel.com
Dir: *off N22 opposite the Cork County Hall, beside River Lee*

Situated on the banks of the River Lee, the Kingsley is a luxurious hotel with good facilities. Bedrooms are excellent and feature thoughtful extra touches. Guests have use of a comfortable lounge and library. The bar and restaurant are contemporary and informal.

ROOMS: 69 en suite (4 fmly) No smoking in 36 bedrooms s fr €150; d fr €175 (incl. bkfst) **LB FACILITIES:** STV Indoor swimming (H) Fishing Sauna Solarium Gym Jacuzzi Treatment rooms & Beautician Swimming pool supervised Xmas **CONF:** Thtr 95 Class 50 Board 32 **SERVICES:** Lift air con **PARKING:** 250 **NOTES:** No dogs (ex guide dogs)
CARDS:

★★★★72% Rochestown Park Hotel
Rochestown Rd, Douglas
☎ 021 4890800 021 4892178
e-mail: info@rochestownpark.com
Dir: *from Lee Tunnel, 2nd exit left off dual carriageway. Continue for 400mtrs, then 1st left and right at small rdbt. Hotel 600mtrs on right*

Peacefully set amongst chestnut trees in mature gardens off the N25 ring road, this hotel has much to offer, including leisure and Thalasso Therapy Centre and extensive conference and exhibition facilities. Staff are pleasant and professional, and a variety of room styles is available including suites. Convenient for both the airport and the ferries.

ROOMS: 160 en suite (17 fmly) (23 GF) s €95-€320; d €140-€320 (incl. bkfst) **LB FACILITIES:** STV Indoor swimming (H) Sauna Solarium Gym Jacuzzi Thalasso therapy & beauty centre, Swimming pool supervised ch fac Xmas **CONF:** BC Thtr 800 Class 360 Board 100 **SERVICES:** Lift **PARKING:** 300 **NOTES:** No dogs Closed 25-26 Dec
CARDS:

★★★★69% Jurys
Western Rd
JURYS DOYLE HOTELS
☎ 021 4276622 & 4252700 021 4274477
e-mail: info@jurysdoyle.com
Dir: *close to city centre, on main Killarney from Cork, past court house on right, hotel 500yds on left*

This hotel enjoys a riverside setting near to the university and within walking distance of the city centre. The public areas have a fresh outlook, with a comfortable library lounge, in addition to leisure and conference facilities. Bedrooms are well-equipped.

ROOMS: 185 en suite (23 fmly) (83 GF) No smoking in 48 bedrooms s fr €120; d fr €160 (incl. bkfst) **LB FACILITIES:** STV Indoor swimming (H) Outdoor swimming (H) Squash Sauna Gym Jacuzzi entertainment **CONF:** Thtr 700 Class 400 Board 150 Del €160 **SERVICES:** Lift **PARKING:** 231 **NOTES:** No dogs (ex guide dogs) Closed 25-26 Dec
CARDS:

★★★★68% Maryborough House
Maryborough Hill
☎ 021 4365555 021 4365662
e-mail: maryboro@indigo.ie
Dir: *From Jack Lynch Tunnel take 2nd exit & slip road, signed Douglas. Turn right at 1st rdbt & follow Rochestown Rd until next "fingerpost" rdbt. Turn left, hotel on left 0.5m up hill*

Dating from 1715, Maryborough House has been renovated and extended to a fine hotel set in beautifully landscaped grounds. The suites in the main house, and the bedrooms in the new modern wing are well appointed and comfortable. The extensive lounge is very popular with Corkonians for the range of food served throughout the day.

ROOMS: 79 en suite (6 fmly) No smoking in 23 bedrooms s €145-€190; d €198-€260 (incl. bkfst) **LB FACILITIES:** STV Indoor swimming (H) Snooker Sauna Gym Jacuzzi Aromatherapy Beauty therapy Massage Reiki entertainment **CONF:** Thtr 500 Class 250 Board 60 Del from €223 **SERVICES:** Lift **PARKING:** 300 **NOTES:** No dogs (ex guide dogs)
CARDS:

★★★★65% Silver Springs Moran
Tivoli
☎ 021 4507533 🖹 021 4507641
e-mail: silversprings@morangroup.ie
Dir: *N8 south Silver Springs exit. Right across overpass - hotel on right*
Under new ownership, this hotel offers a choice of bedrooms including the refurbished Tower Rooms and the larger Club Rooms. There is a spacious lounge, a bar and restaurant, excellent conference facilities and a helipad. Guests have use of a nearby leisure centre and there is a 9-hole golf course within the grounds.
ROOMS: 109 en suite (29 fmly) No smoking in 17 bedrooms s €120-€200; d €140-€250 (incl. bkfst) **LB FACILITIES:** STV Indoor swimming (H) Tennis (hard) Squash Snooker Sauna Gym Jacuzzi Aerobics classes, Swimming pool supervised entertainment Xmas **CONF:** Thtr 700 Class 400 Board 30 **SERVICES:** Lift **PARKING:** 325 **NOTES:** No dogs (ex guide dogs) Closed 24-26 Dec
CARDS:

★★★69% Ambassador
Military Hill, St Lukes
☎ 021 4551996 🖹 021 4551997
e-mail: reservations@ambassadorhotel.ie
Dir: *city centre, just off Wellington Rd*
Many pleasing features distinguish this sandstone and granite building which dates from the 19th century and has commanding views over the city. There is a feeling of space and comfort throughout the public areas which include a cocktail lounge, bar and restaurant. There are balconies attached to some bedrooms; all are very well appointed.
ROOMS: 60 en suite (8 fmly) No smoking in 8 bedrooms s fr €110; d fr €140 (incl. bkfst) **LB FACILITIES:** STV entertainment Xmas **CONF:** Thtr 80 Class 40 Board 35 Del from €126 **SERVICES:** Lift **PARKING:** 60 **NOTES:** No dogs (ex guide dogs) Closed 24-26 Dec
CARDS:

★★★69% *Imperial Hotel*
South Mall
☎ 021 4274040 🖹 021 4275375
e-mail: imperialhotelcork.ie
This fine hotel has a hospitable and welcoming atmosphere. The reception rooms are on a grand scale, particularly the foyer, with its beautiful crystal chandelier and paintings. Bedrooms are of a high standard and Clouds Restaurant is earning a reputation for good food.
ROOMS: 90 en suite (4 fmly) No smoking in 10 bedrooms **FACILITIES:** STV entertainment **CONF:** Thtr 400 Class 200 Board 60 **NOTES:** No dogs (ex guide dogs) Closed 25 **CARDS:**

> Packed in a hurry?
> Ironing facilities should be available at all star levels, either in rooms or on request

★★★67% *Gresham Metropole*
GRESHAM HOTELS
MacCurtain St
☎ 021 4508122 🖹 021 4506450
e-mail: info@gresham-metropolehotel.com
Dir: *in city centre on MacCurtain St - leading to N25*
This city centre hotel has now been refurbished, and some good conference facilities have been added with full air conditioning and natural daylight. Bedrooms vary in size and are well-equipped

continued

and comfortable. There is a leisure centre, waterside restaurant, and a café. Ask at reception for car park information.

ROOMS: 113 en suite (3 fmly) No smoking in 26 bedrooms **FACILITIES:** STV Indoor swimming (H) Snooker Sauna Solarium Gym Jacuzzi Aerobic studio & Steam room entertainment **CONF:** Thtr 500 Class 180 Board 60 **SERVICES:** Lift **PARKING:** 240 **NOTES:** No dogs (ex guide dogs) **CARDS:**

★★★59% Jurys Inn
JURYS DOYLE HOTELS
Anderson's Quay
☎ 021 4276444 🖹 021 4276144
e-mail: enquiry@jurys.com
Dir: *in city centre, on river beside eastern approach to the city from Dublin and south link road to airport*
This hotel overlooks the River Lee and is just a short walk from the main street and shopping area. Attractively decorated in a modern style. Rooms are spacious and can accommodate families. The restaurant is informal and there is also a lively pub.
ROOMS: 133 en suite No smoking in 32 bedrooms s €76-€130; d €76-€130 **FACILITIES:** STV entertainment **CONF:** Thtr 35 Class 20 Board 20 **SERVICES:** Lift **PARKING:** 22 **NOTES:** No dogs (ex guide dogs) Closed 24-26 Dec **CARDS:**

⇧ Travelodge
Travelodge
Blackash
☎ 08700 850 950 🖹 01 21310707
Dir: *at rdbt junct of South Ring Road/Kinsale Rd R600*
Travelodge offers good quality, good value, modern accommodation. Ideal for families, the spacious, en suite bedrooms include remote-control TV, tea and coffee-making facilities, luxury beds and free morning newspaper. Meals can be taken at the nearby family restaurant. For further details and the Travelodge phone number, consult the Hotel Groups page.
ROOMS: 60 en suite s fr €65; d fr €65

COURTOWN HARBOUR, Co Wexford — Map 01 D3

★★★60% *Bay View*
☎ 055 25307 🖹 055 25576
e-mail: bayview@iol.ie
Dir: *clearly signposted to Courtown, turn left before Gorey off N11, hotel in main square*
This comfortable, refurbished seafront hotel overlooks the marina. The lounge enjoys a sea view and there is a restaurant, bar and tennis court. The McGarry family are attentive hosts, and visitors will enjoy good cuisine.
ROOMS: 17 en suite (12 fmly) **FACILITIES:** Tennis (hard) Squash **PARKING:** 30 **NOTES:** No dogs (ex guide dogs) No smoking in restaurant Closed 30 Nov-14 Mar **CARDS:**

C

COURTOWN HARBOUR, continued

★★★60% **Courtown**
☎ 055 25210 & 25108 📠 055 25304
e-mail: info@courtownhotel.com
Dir: *Turn left as you approach Gorey, 5km on the left*
Situated in the town centre, near to the beach and an 18-hole golf course, this refurbished hotel offers relaxing public areas including a comfortable lounge and spacious bar on two levels. Facilities include a restaurant and an indoor swimming pool.
ROOMS: 21 en suite (4 fmly) s €75-€85; d €100-€120 (incl. bkfst) **LB** **FACILITIES:** Indoor swimming (H) Tennis (hard & grass) Squash Sauna Solarium Gym Jacuzzi Steam room, Massage, Crazy golf, Swimming pool supervised entertainment **PARKING:** 10 **NOTES:** No dogs (ex guide dogs) Closed mid Nov - early Mar **CARDS:**

DELGANY, Co Wicklow — Map 01 D3

★★★★62% **Glenview**
Glen O' the Downs
☎ 01 2873399 📠 01 2877511
e-mail: glenview@iol.ie
Dir: *from Dublin city centre follow signs for N11, past Bray on N11 S'bound*
In a lovely hillside location overlooking terraced gardens, extensive refurbishment has resulted in luxurious lounges, a restaurant and conservatory bar with delightful views. Bedrooms are well equipped and there are extensive leisure facilites in the hotel, championship golf, horse riding and other tourist amenites are available nearby.
ROOMS: 70 en suite (11 fmly) (16 GF) No smoking in 11 bedrooms s €95-€153; d €120-€230 (incl. bkfst) **FACILITIES: Spa** STV Indoor swimming (H) Snooker Sauna Solarium Gym Croquet lawn Jacuzzi Swimming pool supervised, Aerobics studio, Massage, Beauty treatment room entertainment ch fac Xmas **CONF:** Thtr 220 Class 120 Board 50 **SERVICES:** Lift **PARKING:** 200 **NOTES:** No dogs (ex guide dogs) No smoking in restaurant **CARDS:**

See advert on opposite page

DONEGAL, Co Donegal — Map 01 B5

★★★75% ®® ***Harvey's Point Country***
Lough Eske
☎ 074 972 2208 📠 074 972 2352
e-mail: reservations@harveyspoint.com
Dir: *from Donegal, take N56 then 1st right (Loch Eske/Harvey's Point). Hotel is approx 10 mins' drive*
Situated in a clearing beside the lake shore is this distinctive hotel where comfort, quality, good cuisine and attentive customer care are top priorities. It's a magical location, where only the wildlife disturbs the tranquillity. Comfortable bedrooms are nearby in the adjacent Swiss-style building. Junior suites are available.
ROOMS: 20 en suite **FACILITIES:** STV Tennis (hard) entertainment **CONF:** Thtr 200 Class 200 Board 50 **PARKING:** 300 **NOTES:** No children 10yrs No smoking in restaurant **CARDS:**

DOOLIN, Co Clare — Map 01 B3

★★★64% ***Aran View House***
Coast Rd
☎ 065 7074061 & 7074420 📠 065 7074540
e-mail: bookings@aranview.com
Situated in 100 acres of rolling farmland and commanding panoramic views of the Aran Islands, this hotel offers attractive and comfortably furnished accommodation. Staff are welcoming, the atmosphere is convivial, and there is traditional music and song in the bar three times a week.
ROOMS: 13 en suite 6 annexe en suite (1 fmly)
FACILITIES: entertainment **PARKING:** 40 **NOTES:** Closed Nov-1 Apr
CARDS:

See advert on opposite page

DROGHEDA, Co Louth — Map 01 D4

★★★59% **Boyne Valley Hotel & Country Club**
Stameen, Dublin Rd
☎ 041 9837737 📠 041 9839188
e-mail: reservations@boynevalleyhotel.ie
Dir: *M1 towards Belfast, N of Dublin Airport on right - up Avenue before Drogheda*
This historic mansion stands in 16 acres of gardens and woodlands on the outskirts of Drogheda. Much emphasis is placed here on good food and attentive service. All the accommodation is well furnished and provides high standards of comfort. There are extensive amenities including a leisure centre.
ROOMS: 73 en suite (4 fmly) (26 GF) No smoking in 35 bedrooms s €79-€85; d €145-€160 (incl. bkfst) **LB** **FACILITIES:** STV Indoor swimming (H) Tennis (hard) Sauna Solarium Gym Jacuzzi Swimming pool supervised entertainment Xmas **CONF:** BC Thtr 500 Class 350 Board 25 Del from €120 **SERVICES:** Lift **PARKING:** 200 **NOTES:** No dogs (ex guide dogs) **CARDS:**

DUBLIN, Co Dublin — Map 01 D4
See also Portmarnock

Top 200 - Hotel

★★★★★ ®®®® **The Merrion Hotel**
Upper Merrion St
☎ 01 6030600 📠 01 6030700
e-mail: info@merrionhotel.com
Dir: *at top of Upper Merrion St on left, beyond Government buildings on right*
This terrace of gracious Georgian buildings, reputed to have been the birthplace of the Duke of Wellington, embraces the character of many changes of use through over 200 years. Bedrooms are spacious, offering deep comfort and a wide range of extra facilities. The lounges retain the charm and opulence of days gone by while the Cellar bar area is ideal for a relaxing drink. There is also a choice of dining options; Irish favourites are based on fresh and simply prepared ingredients in the Cellar Restaurant and, for that very special occasion, award-winning Restaurant Patrick Guilbaud, is Dublin's finest.
ROOMS: 145 en suite No smoking in 65 bedrooms
FACILITIES: STV Indoor swimming (H) Gym Steam room entertainment **CONF:** BC Thtr 60 Class 25 Board 25 Del from €370 **SERVICES:** Lift air con **PARKING:** 60 **NOTES:** No dogs (ex guide dogs) **CARDS:**

★★★★★69% Radisson SAS St Helen's Hotel

Stillorgan Rd
☎ 01 2186000 🖷 01 2186010
e-mail: info.dublin@radissonsas.com
Dir: *from centre take N11 S, hotel 4km on left of dual carriageway*

This 18th-century mansion has been developed into a fine hotel offering the modern facilities expected by today's traveller. Many of the original features have been retained in the public rooms of the main house, and the comfortably appointed bedrooms and suites are situated in a purpose-built block. Diners can choose from the informal Orangerie bar, the Italian Talavera trattoria or, the Le Panto fine dining restaurant.

ROOMS: 151 en suite (23 fmly) No smoking in 75 bedrooms s €199; d €285 **FACILITIES:** STV Snooker Gym Croquet lawn Beauty salon entertainment Xmas **CONF:** BC Thtr 350 Class 150 Board 70 Del from €260 **SERVICES:** Lift air con **PARKING:** 300 **NOTES:** No dogs (ex guide dogs) **CARDS:**

★★★★★65% Berkeley Court

Lansdowne Rd
☎ 01 665 3200 🖷 01 6617238
e-mail: berkeley_court@jurysdoyle.com
Dir: *from N11 turn right at Donnybrook Church, 1st left over bridge, turn right immediately then take 1st left, hotel is 1st on left*

Situated in the leafy suburb of Ballsbridge, near the Lansdowne Road Stadium, this modern hotel is well positioned for business and leisure visitors alike. A refurbishment programme has been completed, and each of the guest rooms and suites is comfortably appointed with all the expected facilities.

ROOMS: 188 en suite No smoking in 50 bedrooms s €313; d €333 **LB** **FACILITIES:** STV Hair & Beauty salon, Weirs Boutique entertainment Xmas **CONF:** BC Thtr 450 Class 210 Board 50 Del from €254 **SERVICES:** Lift **PARKING:** 130 **NOTES:** No dogs (ex guide dogs) **CARDS:**

Top 200 - Hotel

★★★★ ◎◎ *The Clarence*

6-8 Wellington Quay D2
☎ 01 4070800 🖷 01 4070820
e-mail: reservations@theclarence.ie
Dir: *from O'Connell Bridge, W along quays, through 1st set of lights (at the Ha'penny Bridge) hotel 500mtrs further on*

The Clarence is situated in the centre of Dublin City, on the banks of the River Liffey, within walking distance of the shopping areas, museums and galleries. This is a very individual hotel, where contemporary design is tastefully incorporated into the original features of the 1850 building. The unobtrusive professional staff all have a keen interest in guest care.

ROOMS: 50 en suite No smoking in 4 bedrooms **FACILITIES:** STV Beauty therapy room **CONF:** Thtr 50 Class 24 Board 30 **SERVICES:** Lift **PARKING:** 15 **NOTES:** No dogs (ex guide dogs) Closed 24-27 Dec **CARDS:**

D

DUBLIN, continued

★★★★77% The Herbert Park Hotel
Ballsbridge
☎ 01 6672200 01 6672595
e-mail: reservations@herbertparkhotel.ie
Dir: *2m from city centre along Nassau St, Mount St over canal bridge along Northumberland Rd. Cross bridge in Ballsbridge, 1st right*
In an enviable location adjoining the lovely park of the same name and close to the US Embassy, RDS and convenient to the city centre. Herbert Park Hotel has spacious, light-filled and very comfortable public areas. Staff are professional and very friendly. Views of the park from the Pavilion restaurant and many of the contemporary-style bedrooms are delightful in any season. Secure underground car parking is available.
ROOMS: 153 en suite (4 fmly) No smoking in 60 bedrooms s fr €230; d fr €275 **LB FACILITIES:** STV Tennis (hard) Gym Croquet lawn entertainment **CONF:** BC Thtr 120 Class 55 Board 50 Del from €260 **SERVICES:** Lift air con **PARKING:** 80 **NOTES:** No dogs (ex guide dogs) No smoking in restaurant **CARDS:**

★★★★76% The Fitzwilliam
St Stephen's Green
☎ 01 4787000 01 4787878
e-mail: enq@fitzwilliamhotel.com
Dir: *adjacent to top of Grafton Street*
In a central position on St Stephen's Green, this friendly hotel is a pleasing blend of contemporary style with all the traditions of good hotel keeping. Bedrooms, many of which overlook an internal rooftop garden, have been equipped with a wide range of thoughtful extras. There is plenty to tempt the palate; Citron offering an informal eating option and Thornton's a fine dining alternative.
ROOMS: 130 en suite No smoking in 90 bedrooms **FACILITIES:** STV **CONF:** Thtr 80 Class 50 Board 35 Del from €355 **SERVICES:** Lift **PARKING:** 85 **NOTES:** No dogs (ex guide dogs)
CARDS:

★★★★73% Le Meridien Shelbourne
27 St Stephen's Green
Le Meridien Hotels & Resorts
☎ 01 6634500 01 6616006
e-mail: shelbourneinfo@lemeridien.com
Dir: *M1 to city centre, along Parnell St to O'Connell St towards Trinity College, take 3rd right along Kildare St, hotel on left*
A Dublin landmark since 1824 the rare and timeless elegance of this Georgian hotel has strong literary and historical links, and boast gracious reception rooms, a choice of restaurants, a leisure center and popular bars. Bedrooms are smart, well appointed and comfortable, many offer truly beautiful views of the gardens of St. Stephen's Green.
ROOMS: 190 en suite (5 GF) No smoking in 110 bedrooms s €225-€351; d €225-€391 **LB FACILITIES: Spa** STV Indoor swimming (H) Sauna Gym Croquet lawn Jacuzzi Beauty salon, Hairdresser, Barber shop Xmas **CONF:** BC Thtr 380 Class 180 Board 60 Del from €350 **SERVICES:** Lift **PARKING:** 45 **CARDS:**

★★★★70% *Clarion I.F.S.C*
I.F.S.C
☎ 01 4338800 01 4338801
e-mail: info@clarionhotelifsc.com
Dir: *N1 to city centre, at Dorset St turn left onto Parnell Square East to O'Connell St then left onto Eden Quay. Follow quay for 1m, hotel on left*
Good design and stylish décor give the edge to this hotel where the themes of work, dining and rest are brought together with a well-managed clarity of purpose. Pleasant, attentive staff and comfortable well-appointed bedrooms are sure to please. A very well-equipped leisure facility is available to hotel guests.
ROOMS: 147 en suite (5 fmly) No smoking in 58 bedrooms **FACILITIES:** STV Indoor swimming (H) Sauna Solarium Gym Spinning room, treatment room, aerobics area. **CONF:** Thtr 100 Class 50 Board 35 **SERVICES:** Lift air con **NOTES:** No dogs (ex guide dogs) Closed 24-28 Dec **CARDS:**

★★★★70% Gresham
O'Connell St
Gresham Hotels
☎ 01 8746881 01 8787175
e-mail: info@thegresham.com
Dir: *on O'Connell St, just off M1 close to the GPO*

Friendly staff have always been a strength here. Refurbishment has meant a smart new look for the popular lounge, and a new brasserie with an emphasis on quality seasonal produce. A variety of bedroom options is available, and there are extensive corporate facilities.
ROOMS: 288 en suite (4 fmly) No smoking in 26 bedrooms s €150-€300; d €150-€300 **LB FACILITIES:** STV Gym Xmas **CONF:** Thtr 350 Class 200 Board 100 **SERVICES:** Lift air con **PARKING:** 150 **NOTES:** No dogs (ex guide dogs) **CARDS:**

★★★★70% Jurys Hotel Dublin
Pembroke Rd, Ballsbridge
Jurys Doyle Hotels
☎ 01 660 5000 01 667 5276
e-mail: ballsbridge@jurysdoyle.com
Dir: *from Dun Laoghaire, follow signs for city to Merrion Rd, Ballsbridge & Pembroke Rd, hotel at junct of Pembroke Rd and Northumberland Rd*
This establishment has two identities: Jurys Hotel and The Towers at Jurys. The first is large and popular, boasting several restaurants and bars, as well as good conference and leisure facilities. The Towers specialises in discreet luxury, with spacious bedrooms and private suites. The complex is the flagship of the Jurys chain.
ROOMS: 403 en suite (13 fmly) No smoking in 140 bedrooms s €126-€320; d €126-€320 (incl. cont bkfst) **LB FACILITIES:** Indoor swimming (H) Outdoor swimming (H) Sauna Gym Jacuzzi Hairdresser, Beauty Salon with Masseuse Xmas **CONF:** Thtr 850 Class 450 Board 40 **SERVICES:** Lift **PARKING:** 200 **NOTES:** No dogs (ex guide dogs) **CARDS:**

★★★★70% *The Morrison*
Lower Ormond Quay
☎ 01 8872400 01 8783185
e-mail: info@morrisonhotel.ie
This newly built hotel was designed by the renowned John Rocha and inside wood, stone and natural fabrics are combined with vibrant colours to create a relaxing environment. There is a lobby lounge, café bar and the Atrium Halo Restaurant. Bedrooms and

continued

suites have a contemporary style and a dedicated, hospitable team ensure a pleasant stay.
ROOMS: 94 en suite No smoking in 40 bedrooms **FACILITIES:** STV entertainment **CONF:** Thtr 90 Class 10 **SERVICES:** Lift air con **NOTES:** No dogs (ex guide dogs) Closed Xmas
CARDS:

★★★★66% *Burlington*
Upper Leeson St
☎ 01 6605222 📠 01 6603172
Close to the city, this comfortable hotel features well-appointed bedrooms, with some superior executive rooms available. Public areas include the smart Diplomat restaurant and a residents' bar, in addition to the popular Buck Mulligan's Dublin pub.
ROOMS: 506 en suite No smoking in 76 bedrooms **FACILITIES:** STV Gym Use of facilities at fitness club **CONF:** Thtr 1500 Class 650 Board 40 **SERVICES:** Lift **PARKING:** 700 **NOTES:** No dogs (ex guide dogs)
CARDS:

★★★★66% Stillorgan Park
Stillorgan Rd
☎ 01 2881621 📠 01 2831610
e-mail: sales@stillorganpark.com
Dir: *from main dual carriageway (N11) follow signs for Wexford, pass RTE studios on left, through next 5 sets of lights, hotel on left*

Attractive décor and striking design are features of this hotel situated on the southern outskirts of the city. Comfortable public areas include a contemporary restaurant and inviting bar. A new air-conditioned banqueting and conference centre has all the latest communication technology. Bedrooms are modern and smartly appointed. The hotel benefits from a good-sized car park.
ROOMS: 125 en suite (12 fmly) No smoking in 25 bedrooms s €125-€145; d €145-€170 (incl. bkfst) **LB** **FACILITIES:** STV Special rates for residents at Westwood Leisure Centre entertainment Xmas **CONF:** BC Thtr 500 Class 220 Board 130 Del fr €175 **SERVICES:** Lift air con **PARKING:** 350 **NOTES:** No dogs (ex guide dogs)
CARDS:

> **GF** Indicates the number of bedrooms at ground floor level.

★★★★64% ⊛ Red Cow Morans
Red Cow Complex, Naas Rd
☎ 01 4593650 📠 01 4591588
e-mail: reservations@morangroup.ie
Dir: *at junct of M50 & N7 Naas road on the city side of the motorway*
This smart hotel complex centres on the original Red Cow Inn, while its purpose-built extensions provide excellent conference facilities. Public areas are well furnished and strikingly decorated. Bedrooms are spacious, smartly presented and well equipped.

ROOMS: 123 en suite (21 fmly) No smoking in 44 bedrooms s €125-€190; d €190-€250 (incl. bkfst) **LB** **FACILITIES:** STV entertainment Xmas **CONF:** Thtr 700 Class 350 Board 150 Del from €190 **SERVICES:** Lift air con **PARKING:** 700 **NOTES:** No dogs (ex guide dogs) Closed 24-26 Dec **CARDS:**

★★★★62% The Plaza Hotel
Belgard Rd, Tallaght
☎ 01 4624200 📠 01 4624600
e-mail: reservations@plazahotel.ie
Dir: *6m from city centre, at S end of M50*
A contemporary hotel beside the Tallagh complex, with spacious public areas, good corporate facilities, and secure underground car park. The Vista Café and Olive Tree Restaurant are on the first floor mezzanine and enjoy views of the Dublin Mountains. Informal dining is available in the traditional Grumpy McClaffertys bar. Comfortable bedrooms are well equipped.
ROOMS: 122 en suite (2 fmly) No smoking in 61 bedrooms s €105-€175; d €105-€175 **LB** **FACILITIES:** STV entertainment **CONF:** BC Thtr 200 Class 150 Board 50 **SERVICES:** Lift air con **PARKING:** 520 **NOTES:** No dogs (ex guide dogs) Closed 24-30 Dec Civ Wed 220 **CARDS:**

★★★70% ⊛ *Finnstown Country House Hotel & Golf Course*
Newcastle Rd
☎ 01 6010700 📠 01 6281088
e-mail: manager@finnstown-hotel.ie
Dir: *from M1 take 1st exit onto M50 S/bound. 1st exit after Toll Bridge. At rdbt take 3rd left (N4 W). Left at lights. Over next 2 rdbts. Hotel on right*

Set in 45 acres of wooded grounds, Finnstown is a calm and peaceful country house. There is a wide choice of bedroom styles

continued on p884

DUBLIN, continued

and the garden suites are particularly good. Reception rooms are inviting and furnished in period style.
ROOMS: 25 en suite 28 annexe en suite No smoking in 27 bedrooms **FACILITIES:** STV Indoor swimming (H) Tennis (hard & grass) Solarium Gym Croquet lawn Putting green Turkish bath, Table tennis, Massage, Pool Table, Games Room **CONF:** Thtr 200 Class 60 Board 40 **PARKING:** 90 **CARDS:**

D

★★★70% Marine
Sutton Cross
☎ 01 8390000 01 8390442
e-mail: sales@marinehotel.ie
Dir: *from M1 towards Dublin city centre, take 2nd exit for Coolock, to T-junct and turn left, after 1m hotel on right*
On the north shore of Dublin Bay, this hotel is situated in attractive gardens. The restaurant specialises in seafood. Bedrooms are attractively decorated and well equipped, and there is also a business centre. Public areas are very comfortable.
ROOMS: 48 en suite (5 fmly) No smoking in 7 bedrooms s €115-€150; d €165-€235 (incl. bkfst) **LB** **FACILITIES:** STV Indoor swimming (H) Sauna Steam Room **CONF:** Thtr 220 Class 140 Board 40 Del from €170 **SERVICES:** Lift **PARKING:** 150 **NOTES:** No dogs (ex guide dogs) No smoking in restaurant Closed 25-27 Dec **CARDS:**

★★★68% *Jurys Green Isle*
Naas Rd
☎ 01 4593406 01 4592178
Dir: *on N7, 10km SW of the city centre*
The Green Isle Hotel lies on the southern outskirts of Dublin just off the M50. Both standard and executive bedrooms are generously proportioned and stylishly furnished. Public areas include Sorrells Restaurant, a spacious lobby, Rosie O'Gradys Bar and extensive banqueting and conference facilities.
ROOMS: 90 en suite **FACILITIES:** STV **CONF:** Thtr 300 Class 100 Board 100 **SERVICES:** Lift **PARKING:** 250 **NOTES:** No dogs (ex guide dogs) **CARDS:**

★★★67% Buswells
23-25 Molesworth St
☎ 01 6146500 01 6762090
e-mail: buswells@quinn-hotels.com
Dir: *on corner of Molesworth St & Kildare St, opposite Dail Eireann (Government Buildings)*
One of Dublin's 18th-century Georgian townhouses, Buswells is a popular rendezvous, convenient for main shopping and cultural attractions. Bedrooms are well equipped and attractively decorated. Public areas include an elegant lobby lounge, restaurant and the club-style bar is a favourite meeting place in the city centre.
ROOMS: 69 en suite (17 fmly) No smoking in 18 bedrooms s €146; d €220 **LB** **FACILITIES:** Gym Leisure suite **CONF:** BC Thtr 85 Class 30 Board 24 **SERVICES:** Lift **NOTES:** No dogs (ex guide dogs) Closed 25 & 26 Dec RS 24 Dec **CARDS:**

★★★67% The Carnegie Court
North St, Swords Village, Swords
☎ 01 8404384 01 8404505
e-mail: info@carnegiecourt.com
This modern hotel has been tastefully built and is conveniently located close to Dublin Airport just off the N1 in Swords Village. The air-conditioned bedrooms are well appointed, many are spacious. Public areas include a select residents' lounge, contemporary Courtyard Restaurant, a dramatically designed Harp Bar and modern conference and banqueting facilites. Extensive car parking facilities are provided.
ROOMS: 36 en suite (4 fmly) (1 GF) No smoking in 7 bedrooms s €99-€109; d €140-€155 (incl. bkfst) **LB** **FACILITIES:** STV entertainment **CONF:** Thtr 280 Class 50 Board 40 **SERVICES:** Lift air con **PARKING:** 150 **NOTES:** No dogs 25-26 Dec **CARDS:**

★★★67% Longfield's Hotel
MANOR HOUSE
Fitzwilliam St Lower
☎ 01 6761367 01 6761542
e-mail: info@longfields.ie
Dir: *from St Stephens Green take Shelbourne Hotel exit, continue down Baggot St for 400mtrs, turn left at Fitzwilliam St junct and hotel is on left*

Longfields has a very warm, hospitable feel to it. Staff are all focused towards guest care in an informal yet professional manner. Rooms vary in size but are well appointed and comfortable. A serious attitude to food is evident in Kevin Arundel's cookery in No 10, the hotel's restaurant.
ROOMS: 26 en suite s €150-€190; d €215-€255 (incl. bkfst) **LB** **FACILITIES:** STV **CONF:** Thtr 20 Board 20 **SERVICES:** Lift **NOTES:** No dogs (ex guide dogs) No smoking in restaurant RS 23-27 Dec **CARDS:**

★★★66% Bewley's Hotel Ballsbridge
Merrion Rd, Ballsbridge
☎ 01 6681111 01 6681999
e-mail: bb@bewleyshotels.com

This comfortable hotel is conveniently situated near the RDS Showgrounds. It offers good value accommodation with a casual restaurant serving interesting dishes. The very spacious lounges on the lower floor are a popular meeting place. Some car parking is available at a nominal fee, which should be requested on making reservation.
ROOMS: 220 en suite (25 fmly) No smoking in 140 bedrooms s €99; d €99 **FACILITIES:** STV **CONF:** Class 30 Board 14 **SERVICES:** Lift **PARKING:** 240 **NOTES:** No dogs Closed 24-26 Dec **CARDS:**

★★★66% *Camden Court*
'amden St
☎ 01 4759666 📠 01 4759677
-mail: reservations@camdencourthotel.ie
ir: *off Camden St close to St Stephens Green & Grafton St*
his hotel has a number of fine features in addition to its onvenient location. These include spacious public areas, a leisure entre, well-equipped bedrooms, a summer beer garden and the onus of a car park in the city centre.
OOMS: 246 en suite (33 fmly) No smoking in 13 bedrooms **ACILITIES:** Indoor swimming (H) Sauna Solarium Gym Jacuzzi **ONF:** Thtr 40 Class 40 Board 20 **SERVICES:** Lift **PARKING:** 96 **OTES:** No dogs Closed Xmas/New Year **CARDS:**

★★★66% *Jurys Montrose*
tillorgan Rd
☎ 01 2693311 📠 01 2691164
-mail: montrose@jurysdoyle.com
ir: *From city centre follow signs for N11 motorway*
'lose to the campus of University College, this hotel offers smartly ecorated, comfortable bedrooms. The public areas include good ounge space, a carvery bar and a more formal restaurant. The otel is situated in a quiet suburb, a short distance from the city entre.
OOMS: 178 en suite No smoking in 30 bedrooms **FACILITIES:** STV **ONF:** Thtr 80 Class 30 Board 30 **SERVICES:** Lift **PARKING:** 100 **OTES:** No dogs (ex guide dogs) **CARDS:**

★★★65% Bewley's Hotel Newlands Cross
Newlands Cross, Naas Rd
☎ 01 4640140 📠 01 4640900
-mail: res@bewleyshotels.com
Dir: *M50 junct 9 take N7 Naas road, hotel is short distance from junct of N7 with Belgard Rd at Newlands Cross*

This hotel, on the outskirts of Dublin, has a bright and airy atmosphere. There is a restaurant serving snacks during the day and more formal evening meals. Bedrooms are competitively priced and are furnished to a high standard.
ROOMS: 260 en suite (260 fmly) No smoking in 165 bedrooms s €79; d €79 **FACILITIES:** STV **CONF:** Board 12 **SERVICES:** Lift **PARKING:** 200 **NOTES:** No dogs (ex guide dogs) Closed 24-26 Dec **CARDS:**

★★★65% *Jurys Tara Hotel*
Merrion Rd
☎ 01 2694666 📠 01 2691027
e-mail: tara@jurysdoyle.com
Dir: *N11/University College towards Montrose Hotel & take 1st left before hotel. Along Woodbine Rd & take left at traffic lights*
The well-equipped bedrooms of this hotel enjoy spectacular views of Dublin Bay and Howth Head. Attractively decorated public areas

continued

include a comfortable and relaxing foyer lounge, PJ Branagans Pub and a split-level conservatory restaurant.
ROOMS: 113 en suite (2 fmly) No smoking in 20 bedrooms **FACILITIES:** STV **CONF:** Thtr 300 Class 100 Board 40 **SERVICES:** Lift **PARKING:** 100 **NOTES:** No dogs (ex guide dogs) **CARDS:**

★★★65% Temple Bar
Fleet St, Temple Bar
☎ 01 6773333 📠 01 6773088
e-mail: reservations@tbh.ie
Dir: *from Trinity College, towards O'Connell Bridge & take 1st left onto Fleet St, hotel on right*
This stylish hotel lies in the heart of old Dublin and is ideally situated for experiencing the cultural life of the city. Comfortable, well-equipped bedrooms are competitively priced, and good food is served throughout the day.
ROOMS: 129 en suite (6 fmly) No smoking in 10 bedrooms s fr €145; d fr €190 (incl. bkfst) **LB** **FACILITIES:** STV Guest reduced rates at nearby leisure facilities **CONF:** Thtr 80 Class 40 Board 40 **SERVICES:** Lift **NOTES:** No dogs (ex guide dogs) Closed 24 & 25 Dec **CARDS:**

★★★64% Cassidys
Cavendish Row, O'Connell St Upper
☎ 01 8780555 📠 01 8780687
e-mail: stay@cassidyshotel.com
This family run hotel is located at the top of O'Connell Street, on a terrace of redbrick Georgian townhouses. There is a warm and welcoming atmosphere to Grooms Bar, a traditional air in Cassidy's and Restaurant 6 is contemporary and stylish. The modern bedrooms are well appointed. Limited parking for guests and conference facilities available.
ROOMS: 88 en suite (3 fmly) No smoking in 23 bedrooms s €85-€140; d €115-€200 (incl. bkfst) **CONF:** Thtr 80 Class 45 Board 45 Del from €115 **SERVICES:** Lift **PARKING:** 15 **NOTES:** No dogs (ex guide dogs) Closed 24-26 Dec **CARDS:**

★★★63% Abberley Court
Belgard Rd, Tallaght
☎ 01 4596000 📠 01 4621000
e-mail: abberley@iol.ie
Dir: *opposite The Square at the junct of Belgard Rd and Tallaght by-pass (N81)*
Located beside an excellent complex of shops, restaurants and a cinema, this hotel is very smartly furnished. Public areas include a lounge bar that serves food all day and the first-floor Court Restaurant. There are sports facilities available nearby.
ROOMS: 40 en suite (34 fmly) No smoking in 8 bedrooms s €75-€100; d €118-€124 **CONF:** Thtr 40 Class 25 Board 20 **SERVICES:** Lift **PARKING:** 450 **NOTES:** No dogs (ex guide dogs) Closed 25 Dec **CARDS:**

★★★63% Mount Herbert Hotel
Herbert Rd, Lansdowne Rd
☎ 01 6684321 📠 01 6607077
e-mail: info@mountherberthotel.ie
Dir: *close to Lansdowne Road Rugby Stadium, 200mtrs from Dart Rail Station*
Located near to local places of interest, this hotel offers comfortable public rooms, well equipped bedrooms and a friendly atmosphere. There is a spacious lounge, a TV room, a cocktail bar and a lovely restaurant, overlooking the floodit gardens, which serves good value cuisine. There is also a children's playground.
ROOMS: 185 en suite (15 fmly) s €95-€198; d €133-€200 (incl. bkfst) **FACILITIES:** STV Sauna Childrens playground, Badminton court **CONF:** Thtr 80 Class 60 Board 40 **SERVICES:** Lift **PARKING:** 90 **NOTES:** No dogs (ex guide dogs) Closed 21-27 Dec **CARDS:**

DUBLIN, continued

★★★62% *McEniff Skylon*
Drumcondra Rd
☎ 01 8379121 🖹 01 8372778
e-mail: skylon_hotel@jurysdoyle.com
Dir: *from Airport take M1 towards city centre. Hotel 3m on right*
In a convenient location, with easy access to the city centre and the airport, this hotel offers very well appointed bedrooms. There is a spacious lobby lounge, attractive restaurant and a comfortable bar where food is available all day.
ROOMS: 88 en suite (8 fmly) No smoking in 22 bedrooms
FACILITIES: STV **CONF:** Thtr 35 Class 20 Board 20 **SERVICES:** Lift
NOTES: No dogs **CARDS:**

★★★62% The Mercer Hotel
Mercer St Lower
☎ 01 4782179 🖹 01 4780328
e-mail: stay@mercerhotel.ie
Dir: *St Stephens Green at the shopping centre turn left down King St, then left at end of road, hotel on left*
A team of friendly staff create a pleasant atmosphere at this city centre hotel. Bedrooms are attractively decorated and well equipped, with fridges and CD players, as well as the usual amenities. Public areas include an inviting lounge with cocktail bar and a restaurant.
ROOMS: 41 en suite No smoking in 4 bedrooms s €115-€170; d €145-€210 (incl. cont bkfst) **LB** **FACILITIES:** STV **CONF:** Thtr 100 Class 80 Board 60 Del from €200 **SERVICES:** Lift air con **PARKING:** 41
NOTES: No dogs Closed 24-26 Dec Civ Wed 60 **CARDS:**

★★★59% Jurys Christchurch Inn
JURYS DOYLE HOTELS
Christchurch Place
☎ 01 4540000 🖹 01 4540012
e-mail: info@jurysdoyle.com
Dir: *N7 onto Naas Rd, follow signs for city centre to O'Connell St, past Trinity College turn right onto Dame St to Lord Edward St, hotel on left*
Centrally located opposite the 12th-century Christchurch Cathedral, this hotel is close to the Temple Bar and all the city amenities. The foyer lounge and pub are popular meeting places and there is also an informal restaurant. The bedrooms are well appointed and can accommodate families. The adjoining car park is a bonus in the city centre.
ROOMS: 182 en suite No smoking in 74 bedrooms s €108-€210; d €108-€210 **SERVICES:** Lift **NOTES:** No dogs (ex guide dogs) Closed 24-26 Dec **CARDS:**

★★★59% Jurys Custom House Inn
JURYS DOYLE HOTELS
Custom House Quay
☎ 01 6075000 🖹 01 8290400
Overlooking the River Liffey, this hotel is situated less than ten minutes' walk away from the city's main shopping and tourist areas. Family rooms offer good value for money and facilities for business guests are excellent.
ROOMS: 239 en suite No smoking in 140 bedrooms s €197; d €197
FACILITIES: STV **CONF:** BC Thtr 80 Class 30 Board 30 Del €200
SERVICES: Lift **NOTES:** No dogs (ex guide dogs) Closed 25-26 Dec
CARDS:

★★★58% *The Ormond Quay*
7-11 Upper Ormond Quay
☎ 01 8721811 🖹 01 8721362
e-mail: ormondqh@indigo.ie.
Conveniently located across the river from Temple Bar, this hotel has been refurbished throughout. There is a bar and restaurant, as well as conference rooms, and the friendly staff are attentive.
ROOMS: 62 en suite (12 fmly) No smoking in 10 bedrooms
FACILITIES: STV entertainment ch fac **CONF:** Thtr 120 Class 60 Board 40 **SERVICES:** Lift **NOTES:** No dogs (ex guide dogs) Closed 24-25 Dec
CARDS:

★★★58% The Parliament Hotel
Lord Edward St
☎ 01 6708777 🖹 01 6708787
e-mail: parl@regencyhotels.com
Dir: *adjacent to Dublin Castle in the Temple Bar area*
An attractive hotel, near to the Temple Bar area and Dublin Castle, offering a friendly welcome to all its guests. It provides well-furnished bedrooms, decorated in a modern style. There is also a popular bar and a separate restaurant.
ROOMS: 63 en suite (8 fmly) No smoking in 22 bedrooms s €120-€180 d €240 (incl. bkfst) **LB** **FACILITIES:** STV **CONF:** Thtr 20 Board 10
SERVICES: Lift **NOTES:** No dogs (ex guide dogs) No smoking in restaurant **CARDS:**

★★62% Harding
Copper Alley, Fishamble St, Christchurch
☎ 01 6796500 🖹 01 6796504
e-mail: harding.hotel@usitworld.com
Dir: *at top of Dame St beside Christchurch Cathedral*
At the heart of the fascinating Temple Bar area of Dublin, this purpose-built hotel has a friendly atmosphere and offers good-value accommodation. Its Peruvian-style bar and Fitzers Restaurant are popular meeting places. There are plenty of shops, bars and restaurants in the area.
ROOMS: 53 en suite (14 fmly) s €60; d €89-€96 **FACILITIES:** STV entertainment **SERVICES:** Lift **NOTES:** No dogs (ex guide dogs) Closed 23-26 Dec **CARDS:**

U *Holiday Inn Dublin Airport*
Holiday Inn HOTELS · RESORTS
Dublin Airport
☎ 01 8080500 🖹 01 8446002
e-mail: gm1767@ichotelsgroup.com
Dir: *Hotel entrance 1000yds from main road entrance to Dublin airport, on right*
At the time of going to press, the classification for this hotel was not confirmed. Please refer to the AA internet site www.theAA.com for current information.
ROOMS: 249 en suite (3 fmly) No smoking in 100 bedrooms
FACILITIES: STV Free swim gym use at ALSAA club other facilities at small suppl charge entertainment **CONF:** Thtr 130 Class 130 Board 50
PARKING: 250 **NOTES:** No dogs (ex guide dogs) Closed 24-25 Dec RS 31 Dec **CARDS:**

Travelodge Dublin Airport
Travelodge
Swords By Pass
☎ 08700 850 950 🖹 01 8409257
Dir: *on N1 Dublin/Belfast road*
Travelodge offers good quality, good value, modern accommodation. Ideal for families, the spacious, en suite bedrooms include remote-control TV, tea and coffee-making facilities, luxury beds and free morning newspaper. Meals can be taken at the nearby family restaurant. For further details and the Travelodge phone number, consult the Hotel Groups page.
ROOMS: 100 en suite s fr €75; d fr €75

Travelodge Dublin (Navan Road)
Auburn Av Roundabout, Navan Rd
☎ 08700 850 950
Travelodge offers good quality, good value, modern accommodation. Ideal for families, the spacious, en suite bedrooms include remote-control TV, tea and coffee-making facilities, luxury beds and free morning newspaper. Meals can be taken at the nearby family restaurant. For further details and the Travelodge phone number, consult the Hotel Groups page.
ROOMS: 100 en suite (incl. bkfst) s fr €75; d fr €75

DUNDALK, Co Louth
Map 01 D4

★★★73% Ballymascanlon House
☎ 042 9358200 042 9371598
e-mail: info@ballymascanlon.com
Dir: *N of Dundalk take T62 to Carlingford. Hotel 1km*
This Victorian mansion is set in 130 acres of woodland grounds, surrounded by an 18-hole golf course. Comfortable public areas include an elegant restaurant, spacious lounge and bar, and a well-equipped leisure club. Inviting bedrooms have been refurbished and a there is a new wing of spacious rooms.
ROOMS: 90 en suite (11 fmly) (5 GF) No smoking in 28 bedrooms s €105; d €150 (incl. bkfst) **LB FACILITIES:** STV Indoor swimming (H) Golf 18 Tennis (hard) Sauna Gym Putting green Jacuzzi Swimming pool supervised entertainment Xmas **CONF:** Thtr 300 Class 160 Board 75 **SERVICES:** Lift **PARKING:** 250 **NOTES:** No dogs (ex guide dogs) **CARDS:**

★★★63% Fairways Hotel
Dublin Rd
☎ 042 9321500 042 9321511
e-mail: info@fairways.ie
Dir: *on N1 3km S of Dundalk*
Situated south of Dundalk on the Castlebellingham road, this modern hotel has been refurbished to a high standard. A wide range of food is available all day and golf can be arranged by the hotel on a choice of nearby courses.
ROOMS: 102 en suite (2 fmly) No smoking in 20 bedrooms s €85-€105; d €140-€180 (incl. bkfst) **LB FACILITIES:** STV Tennis (hard) entertainment **CONF:** BC Thtr 1000 Class 500 Del from €150 **PARKING:** 300 **NOTES:** No dogs (ex guide dogs) Closed 25 Dec **CARDS:**

★★60% Imperial
Park St
☎ 042 9332241 042 9337909
e-mail: info@imperialhoteldundalk.com
Dir: *past Heinz Factory 2nd lights turn left. Follow signs to town centre*
This hotel in the centre of the town enjoys a very strong local business following. Many of the rooms have been refurbished and its worth asking for them on reservation. Music is a nightly feature of the bar, and Sgt Peppers, the hotel nightclub, operates at weekends.
ROOMS: 47 en suite (47 fmly) s €75-€90; d €110-€130 (incl. bkfst) **LB FACILITIES:** STV Free use of facilities at sister hotel 3m away entertainment **CONF:** Thtr 400 Class 125 Board 50 **SERVICES:** Lift **PARKING:** 75 **NOTES:** Closed 25 Dec **CARDS:**

Town House Hotel
Country House Hotel
Travel Accommodation

DUNFANAGHY, Co Donegal
Map 01 C6

★★★65% Arnold's
☎ 074 913 6208 074 913 6352
e-mail: arnoldshotel@eircom.net
Dir: *on N56 from Letterkenny, hotel on left entering the village*
On the coast, with miles of sandy beaches close at hand. Public areas offer comfortable seating, and facilities include two restaurants and two bars. There is a choice of bedrooms, from well-equipped standard rooms to larger ones with sofas.
ROOMS: 30 en suite (10 fmly) s €95-€120; d €130-€180 (incl. bkfst) **LB FACILITIES:** STV Fishing Riding Croquet lawn Putting green entertainment **PARKING:** 60 **NOTES:** No dogs (ex guide dogs) No smoking in restaurant Closed Nov - mid March **CARDS:**

DUNGANNON, Co Tyrone
Map 01 C5

Cohannon Inn
212 Ballynakilly Rd BT71 6HJ
☎ 028 8772 4488 028 8775 2217
e-mail: enquiries@cohannon-inn.com
Dir: *400yds from M1 junct 14*
Handy for the M1, The Cohannon Inn offers competitive prices and well-maintained bedrooms, located behind the inn complex in a smart purpose-built wing. Public areas are smartly furnished and wide-ranging menus are served throughout the day.
ROOMS: 42 en suite s £40; d £40 **CONF:** Thtr 100 Class 50 Board 50

DUNGARVAN, Co Waterford
Map 01 C2

★★★61% *Lawlors*
☎ 058 41122 & 41056 058 41000
e-mail: info@lawlors-hotel.ie
Dir: *off N25*
This town centre hotel enjoys facilities including a comfortable lounge and bar where food is served all day, a restaurant, and conference and meeting rooms. Bedrooms are all well-equipped.
ROOMS: 89 en suite (8 fmly) **FACILITIES:** entertainment **CONF:** Thtr 420 Class 215 Board 420 **SERVICES:** Lift **NOTES:** Closed 25 Dec **CARDS:**

DUN LAOGHAIRE, Co Dublin
Map 01 D4

★★★68% *Gresham Royal Marine*
GRESHAM HOTELS
Marine Rd
☎ 01 2801911 01 2801089
e-mail: royalmarine@eircom.net
Dir: *follow signs for 'Car Ferry'*

Set in four acres overlooking Dun Laoghaire harbour, the Gresham Royal Marine is a local landmark. It combines Victorian character with the comfort and amenities of a modern hotel, as in

continued on p888

DUN LAOGHAIRE, continued

the gracious Bay Lounge and Restaurant and contemporary Toddy's Bar and Carvery. Most of the comfortable bedrooms enjoy the breathtaking views of the harbour and attractive gardens.
ROOMS: 103 en suite No smoking in 10 bedrooms **FACILITIES:** STV entertainment **CONF:** Thtr 450 Class 300 **SERVICES:** Lift **PARKING:** 300 **NOTES:** No dogs (ex guide dogs) **CARDS:**

D

ENFIELD, Co Meath Map 01 C4

★★★★69% Johnstown House

☎ 046 9540000 ▤ 9540001
e-mail: info@johnstownhouse.com
Dir: *on N4, in outskirts of village*
Built around a Georgian listed mansion on 80 acres of parkland and landscaped gardens, this fine hotel offers hi-tech conference facilities, comfortable new bedrooms and suites, two restaurants and bars. The reception hall and library reflect the elegance of 18th-century design.
ROOMS: 82 en suite (4 fmly) (1 GF) No smoking in 40 bedrooms s €140-€200; d €170-€235 (incl. bkfst) **LB** **FACILITIES:** STV Fishing Leisure centre & spa due to open mid 2004 entertainment Xmas **CONF:** Thtr 900 Class 900 Board 16 **PARKING:** 350 **NOTES:** No dogs (ex guide dogs) Closed 24-25 Dec **CARDS:**

ENNIS, Co Clare Map 01 B3

★★★★67% Woodstock

Shanaway Rd
☎ 065 684 6600 ▤ 065 684 6611
e-mail: info@woodstockhotel.com
Dir: *From Ennis continue on N18 until rdbt, take N85 to Lahinch, after 1km turn left for Woodstock & continue for 1km*
This newly built hotel overlooks Woodstock 18-hole, parkland Golf Course and offers privacy and seclusion. Pubic areas include an impressive lobby with comfortable lounges, which are complemented by welcoming log fires. Contemporary Irish dishes are served in Spikes Brassiere which enjoys spectacular views. The spacious bedrooms offer comfort and individuality in décor and furnishings. There are extensive health and leisure facilities and a choice of conference rooms.
ROOMS: 67 en suite (20 GF) No smoking in 47 bedrooms s €200-€230; d €200-€230 (incl. bkfst) **LB** **FACILITIES:** STV Indoor swimming (H) Golf 18 Sauna Gym Jacuzzi Steam room, Swimming pool supervised entertainment Xmas **CONF:** BC Thtr 200 Class 160 Board 50 Del from €210 **SERVICES:** Lift air con **NOTES:** No dogs (ex guide dogs) Closed 25-26 Dec **CARDS:**

★★★65% Temple Gate

The Square
☎ 065 682 3300 ▤ 065 682 3322
e-mail: info@templegatehotel.com
Dir: *On Limerick side of Ennis, turn off N18 and continue on Tulla Rd for 0.25 mile, hotel on left*
A smart hotel in the centre of Ennis. Incorporating a 19th-century gothic style building, public areas are carefully planned and include a comfortable lounge library, Preachers Pub and Le Bistro Restaurant. Bedrooms are well-equipped and attractive.
ROOMS: 70 en suite (3 fmly) (25 GF) No smoking in 11 bedrooms s €100-€115; d €130-€160 (incl. bkfst) **LB** **FACILITIES:** STV entertainment **CONF:** Thtr 220 Class 100 Board 80 Del from €97 **SERVICES:** Lift **PARKING:** 52 **NOTES:** No dogs (ex guide dogs) Closed 25 Dec RS 26 Dec Civ Wed 150 **CARDS:**

★★65% Magowna House

Inch
☎ 065 6839009 ▤ 065 6839258
e-mail: info@magowna.com
Dir: *on R474 off N18 pass Ennis golf course, and after approx 5km, hotel is signposted off to right, 300mtrs from junct*
This small family-run hotel stands in 14 acres of grounds just off the road to Ennis Golf Club and Kilmaley at Inch. The hotel provides a good standard of comfort and enjoyable meals. Good local fishing, boats for hire and a golf practice area are among the activities in the neighbourhood.
ROOMS: 10 en suite (3 fmly) No smoking in 4 bedrooms s €55-€61; d €88-€100 (incl. bkfst) **LB** **FACILITIES:** 3 Boats for hire, Golf driving net entertainment **CONF:** Thtr 350 Class 200 Board 20 Del from €105 **PARKING:** 60 **NOTES:** Closed 24-26 Dec **CARDS:**

ENNISCORTHY, Co Wexford Map 01 D3

★★★69% Riverside Park Hotel

The Promenade
☎ 054 37800 ▤ 054 37900
e-mail: riversideparkhotel@eircom.net
Dir: *0.5km from New Bridge, centre of Enniscorthy, N11 Dublin/Rosslare Road*

Situated in a picturesque position beside the River Slaney, this hotel is easily distinguished by its terracotta and blue colour scheme. The foyer is equally dramatic and the public areas all take full advantage of the riverside views, including the Mill House pub. The spacious, attractively decorated bedrooms have every modern comfort.
ROOMS: 60 en suite (50 fmly) No smoking in 6 bedrooms s €89-€99; d €160-€170 (incl. bkfst) **LB** **FACILITIES:** STV ch fac Xmas **CONF:** Thtr 800 Class 500 Board 100 Del from €87 **SERVICES:** Lift **PARKING:** 250 **NOTES:** No dogs (ex guide dogs) **CARDS:**

★★★62% Treacys

Templeshannon
☎ 054 37798 ▤ 054 37733
e-mail: info@treacyshotel.com
Dir: *Follow N11 into Enniscorthy, over bridge in left lane, hotel on right*
This modern hotel is family run and conveniently located in the town centre. Public areas are attractively decorated and include the Begenal Harvey Restaurant, the Temple Bar with informal dining and the Benedicts Superpub, open at weekends. Bedrooms are comfortable and well appointed, and parking is available at the leisure complex opposite.
ROOMS: 59 rms (2 fmly) No smoking in 11 bedrooms s €60-€80; d €100-€150 (incl. bkfst) **LB** **FACILITIES:** STV Discount at adjacent leisure complex entertainment **SERVICES:** Lift **NOTES:** No dogs (ex guide dogs) Closed 23 - 25 Dec **CARDS:**

ENNISKILLEN, Co Fermanagh Map 01 C5

★★★★69% Killyhevlin

BT74 6RW
☎ 028 6632 3481 📠 028 6632 4726
e-mail: info@killyhevlin.com
Dir: 2m S, off A4
A modern, stylish hotel situated on the shores of Lough Erne, just south of the town. Bedrooms are particularly spacious, well equipped, and many enjoy fine views. An open-plan restaurant and informal bar complement the comfortable lounges. Staff throughout are friendly and helpful.
ROOMS: 43 en suite (32 fmly) (9 GF) No smoking in 12 bedrooms s £65-£78; d £90-£115 (incl. bkfst) **LB FACILITIES:** STV Fishing entertainment Xmas **CONF:** BC Thtr 600 Class 350 Board 150 Del from £97.50 **PARKING:** 500 **NOTES:** No dogs (ex guide dogs) Closed 25 Dec
CARDS:

FERMOY, Co Cork Map 01 B2

★★★71% *Castlehyde Hotel*

Castlehyde
☎ 025 31865 📠 025 31485
e-mail: cashyde@iol.ie
Dir: off N8 just outside Fermoy onto N72 Fermoy-Mallow. Hotel in 2m
Carefully restored 18th-century courtyard buildings, where old meets new sympathetically. Individual, attractive bedrooms include five cottage suites. The welcoming lobby lounge features an open fire and there is a stylish restaurant overlooking the gardens and woodland.
ROOMS: 24 en suite (5 fmly) No smoking in 10 bedrooms
FACILITIES: STV Outdoor swimming (H) entertainment **CONF:** Thtr 30 Class 18 Board 14 **PARKING:** 35 **NOTES:** No dogs (ex guide dogs) No smoking in restaurant RS Feb **CARDS:**

FOXFORD, Co Mayo Map 01 B4

★★63% Healys Restaurant & Country House Hotel

Pontoon
☎ 094 9256443 📠 094 9256572
e-mail: info@healyspontoon.com
Set in a lovely location on the shores of Lough Conn, in this famous salmon and trout fishing region near the River Moy. Originally a 19th-century shooting lodge, Healys is family run and offers friendly staff, good cuisine, comfortable bars and a choice of standard and lake view bedrooms. Ghillies, fishing licences etc. are available.
ROOMS: 14 en suite (1 fmly) s €59-€75; d €98-€130 (incl. bkfst)
FACILITIES: Fishing entertainment ch fac **PARKING:** 300 **NOTES:** No dogs No smoking in restaurant Closed 25 Dec
CARDS:

GALWAY, Co Galway Map 01 B3

★★★★77% *Glenlo Abbey*

Bushypark
☎ 091 526666 📠 091 527800
e-mail: glenlo@iol.ie
Dir: 4km from Galway city centre on N59
This cut-stone Abbey was built in 1740 and lovingly restored to its original glory with sculpted cornices, fine antique furniture and includes an elegant drawing room, cocktail bar, library, delightful oval River Room restaurant and cellar bar. There is a second dining option in the unique Orient Express Pullman Restaurant. The bedrooms are in the modern wing and are spacious and well appointed with spectacular views of the 138-acre lakeside golf course.
ROOMS: 46 en suite No smoking in 10 bedrooms **FACILITIES:** STV Golf 18 Fishing Putting green Boating, Clay pigeon shooting, Archery entertainment ch fac **CONF:** Thtr 220 Class 100 Board 50
SERVICES: Lift **PARKING:** 150 **NOTES:** No dogs (ex guide dogs) No smoking in restaurant **CARDS:**

★★★★72% Radisson SAS Hotel

Lough Atalia Rd
☎ 091 538300 📠 091 538380
e-mail: sales.galway@radissonsas.com
Dir: take N6 into Galway City. At Hunstman Inn rdbt turn 1st left. At next lights take left side of fork. Continue for 0.5m, hotel at next right junct
In a prime position on the waterfront at Lough Atalia, striking interior design and excellent levels of comfort and quality are the keynotes of this new hotel. Bedrooms are well-equipped, there are spacious lounges, a bar, and a restaurant which features local seafood specialities. The corporate and leisure facilities are very good.
ROOMS: 217 en suite (7 fmly) No smoking in 132 bedrooms s €172-€189; d €172-€189 **FACILITIES: Spa** STV Indoor swimming (H) Sauna Solarium Gym Putting green Jacuzzi Swimming pool supervised Xmas **CONF:** BC Thtr 750 Class 540 Board 40 Del €190
SERVICES: Lift air con **PARKING:** 260 **NOTES:** No dogs (ex guide dogs) **CARDS:**

★★★★68% Ardilaun Conference & Leisure Centre

Taylor's Hill
☎ 091 521433 📠 091 521546
e-mail: info@ardilaunhousehotel.ie
Dir: Take N6 to Galway City West, then follow signs for N59 Clifden and then N6 for Salthill, Taylor's Hill
Located on in five acres of private grounds and landscaped gardens, the original Ardilaun House was built in 1840 and converted to a hotel in 1962. Public areas include comfortable lounges, Blazers Bar and a restaurant overlooking the garden. Bedrooms are mostly spacious and will benefit from the proposed refit before the end of this year.
ROOMS: 89 en suite (7 fmly) No smoking in 20 bedrooms
FACILITIES: STV Indoor swimming (H) Snooker Sauna Solarium Gym Jacuzzi Treatment & Analysis Rooms, Swimming pool supervised
CONF: Thtr 400 Class 200 Board 60 Del from €165 **SERVICES:** Lift
PARKING: 220 **NOTES:** No smoking in restaurant Closed 23-28 Dec
CARDS:

Late for dinner?
Quality Standards mean that last orders for dinner vary according to star rating and should be no earlier than:
★★ 7.00pm ★★★ 8.00pm ★★★★ 9.00pm
★★★★★ 10.00pm

continued

G

GALWAY, continued

★★★★67% *Galway Bay Hotel Conference & Leisure Centre*

The Promenade, Salthill
☎ 091 520520 🖷 091 520530
e-mail: info@galwaybayhotel.net
Dir: *on the promenade in Salthill on the coast road to Connemara. Follow signs to Salthill from all major routes*

This hotel enjoys a most spectacular location overlooking Galway Bay and most bedrooms, lounges and the restaurant enjoy these views. Dining options include fine dining in the Lobster Pot and the less formal Café Lido and conference/banqueting and leisure facilities are impressive.
ROOMS: 153 en suite (10 fmly) No smoking in 24 bedrooms **FACILITIES:** STV Indoor swimming (H) Sauna Gym Steam room entertainment **CONF:** Thtr 1100 Class 325 **SERVICES:** Lift **PARKING:** 300 **NOTES:** No dogs (ex guide dogs) **CARDS:**

See advert on opposite page

★★★★65% Park House Hotel & Park Room Restaurant

Forster St, Eyre Square
☎ 091 564924 🖷 091 569219
e-mail: parkhousehotel@eircom.net
Dir: *in city centre*
This centre city property offers well decorated and comfortable bedrooms which vary in size. The spacious restaurant has been a popular spot for the people of Galway for many years.
ROOMS: 57 en suite s €95-€275; d €125-€275 (incl. bkfst) **FACILITIES:** STV entertainment **CONF:** Thtr 50 Class 30 Board 30 **SERVICES:** Lift **PARKING:** 26 **NOTES:** No dogs (ex guide dogs) Closed 24-26 Dec **CARDS:**

★★★★65% Westwood House Hotel

Dangan, Upper Newcastle
☎ 091 521442 🖷 091 521400
e-mail: reservations@westwoodhousehotel.com
Dir: *on N6 follow signs for Clifden (N59). In Clifden Rd hotel on left*
Close to the university, this hotel is luxuriously appointed. The public rooms include a themed bar, a restaurant and lounges. Bedrooms are comfortable and well equipped.
ROOMS: 58 en suite (44 fmly) No smoking in 17 bedrooms s €99-€250; d €99-€250 (incl. bkfst) **LB FACILITIES:** STV Arrangement with local health and leisure club **CONF:** Thtr 350 Class 200 Board 70 **SERVICES:** Lift air con **PARKING:** 130 **NOTES:** No dogs (ex guide dogs) Closed 24-25 Dec Civ Wed 275 **CARDS:**

★★★66% Galway Ryan

Dublin Rd
☎ 091 753181 🖷 091 753187
e-mail: ryan@indigo.ie
Dir: *follow signs to Galway City East off N6, N18, N17, past Galway Crystal factory on left, hotel 1m on right*

A modern hotel, on the outskirts of the city, with comfortable, well equipped accommodation and extensive leisure facilities. All-day food is available in Toddys Bar and a carvery lunch is served daily.
ROOMS: 96 en suite (96 fmly) (32 GF) No smoking in 20 bedrooms **FACILITIES:** STV Indoor swimming (H) Tennis (hard) Sauna Solarium Gym Jacuzzi Sports hall, Steam room, Aerobic studio, Swimming pool supervised, Beauty Suite entertainment **CONF:** Thtr 35 Class 20 Board 16 **SERVICES:** Lift **PARKING:** 100 **NOTES:** No dogs (ex guide dogs) **CARDS:**

★★★66% The Harbour

The Harbour
☎ 091 569466 🖷 091 569455
e-mail: stay@harbour.ie
Dir: *follow signs for Galway City East, at rdbt take 1st exit to Galway City, follow signs to docks, hotel approx 1m from rdbt on left*
This hotel is situated on the newly developed Galway Harbour in the heart of the city. Contemporary in style, with a large lobby lounge with generous seating and open fires. Krusoes café bar and restaurant offers modern cuisine. Bedrooms are smartly furnished, comfortable and well equipped. Guests have the benefit of complimentary secure car parking at the rear.
ROOMS: 96 en suite No smoking in 34 bedrooms s €99-€250; d €118-€300 (incl. bkfst) **LB FACILITIES:** STV entertainment Xmas **CONF:** Thtr 80 Class 35 Board 25 **SERVICES:** Lift **PARKING:** 64 **NOTES:** No dogs (ex guide dogs) **CARDS:**

★★★65% Oranmore Lodge

Oranmore
☎ 091 794400 🖷 091 790227
e-mail: orlodge@eircom.net
This long-established hotel is well positioned for travellers on business in the greater Galway City area. Staff provide a warm welcome, and the bar and restaurant are popular with the local population. The bedrooms, which have been refurbished, are well appointed, and guests resident in the hotel are able to use the adjoining leisure centre.
ROOMS: 56 en suite (50 fmly) s €60-€160; d €120-€240 (incl. bkfst) **LB FACILITIES: Spa** STV Indoor swimming (H) Sauna Solarium Gym Jacuzzi entertainment **CONF:** Thtr 200 Class 100 Board 50 **PARKING:** 150 **NOTES:** No dogs (ex guide dogs) Closed 22-27 Dec **CARDS:**

★★★63% Menlo Park Hotel

erryland
☎ 091 761122 📠 091 761222
-mail: menlopkh@iol.ie
ir: *at Terryland rdbt off N6 and N84 (Castlebar Rd)*
ıajor routes are within easy reach, and the town's commercial rea is close by. Bedrooms are comfortable and offer a choice of tandard and executive rooms, the latter having sofas and fax ıachines. There is a contemporary restaurant and bar.
OOMS: 64 en suite (6 fmly) No smoking in 10 bedrooms s €75-€190; €95-€220 (incl. bkfst) **LB** **FACILITIES:** STV entertainment **CONF:** Thtr 50 Class 190 Board 40 Del from €140 **SERVICES:** Lift air con **ARKING:** 100 **NOTES:** No dogs (ex guide dogs) Closed 24-25 Dec **ARDS:**

★★★60% Brennans Yard

ower Merchants Rd
☎ 091 568166 📠 091 568262
-mail: info@brennansyardhotel.com
friendly hotel in the heart of the city, near the shops and usiness districts. All the bedrooms are individually furnished, and erry's Restaurant offers an Irish cuisine.
OOMS: 45 en suite s €78-€130; d €99-€180 (incl. bkfst) **LB** **ACILITIES:** STV entertainment **SERVICES:** Lift **NOTES:** No dogs (ex uide dogs) Closed 21-28 Dec **CARDS:**

See advert on this page

★★★60% Lochlurgain

22 Monksfield, Upper Salthill
☎ 091 529595 📠 091 522399
-mail: lochlurgain@eircom.net
Dir: *off R336 behind Bank of Ireland beside RC church*
This small family-run hotel stands in a quiet street beside the Roman Catholic church. Service is of a very good standard and the bedrooms are comfortable, extras include electric blankets in season. Public rooms are attractively decorated.
ROOMS: 13 en suite (3 fmly) s €45-€85; d €90-€185 (incl. bkfst) **LB** **FACILITIES:** STV **PARKING:** 8 **NOTES:** No dogs (ex guide dogs) No smoking in restaurant Closed 26 Oct-13 Mar **CARDS:**

★★★59% *Jurys Galway Inn*

JURYS DOYLE HOTELS

Quay St
☎ 091 566444 📠 091 568415
e-mail: enquiry@jurys.com
Dir: *N6 follow signs for Docks. Then take Salthill Rd*
This modern hotel stands at the heart of the city opposite the famous Spanish Arch. The hotel has an attractive patio and a garden bounded by the river. The 'one price' room rate and comfortable bedrooms ensure its popularity.
ROOMS: 128 en suite (6 fmly) No smoking in 39 bedrooms **FACILITIES:** STV entertainment **CONF:** Thtr 40 Class 40 Board 40 **SERVICES:** Lift **NOTES:** No dogs (ex guide dogs) Closed 24-26 Dec **CARDS:**

★★★58% Victoria

Victoria Place, Eyre Square
☎ 091 567433 📠 091 565880
e-mail: bookings@victoriahotel.ie
Dir: *off Eyre Sq on Victoria Place, beside the rail station*
This city-centre hotel lies off Eyre Square. Bedrooms are well equipped and other facilities include 24-hour room service, a good bar and a pleasant restaurant. The atmosphere is relaxing and staff are friendly and attentive.
ROOMS: 57 en suite (20 fmly) No smoking in 1 bedroom **FACILITIES:** STV **CONF:** Thtr 50 Class 30 Board 25 **SERVICES:** Lift **NOTES:** No dogs (ex guide dogs) Closed 25 Dec **CARDS:**

G

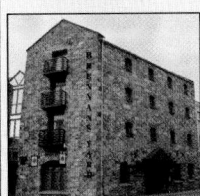

GALWAY, continued

⇧ Travelodge
Tuam Rd
☎ 0870 191 1747
Travelodge offers good quality, good value, modern accommodation. Ideal for families, the spacious, en suite bedrooms include remote-control TV, tea and coffee-making facilities, luxury beds and free morning newspaper. Meals can be taken at the nearby family restaurant. For further details and the Travelodge phone number, consult the Hotel Groups page.
ROOMS: (incl. bkfst) s fr €60; d fr €60

GARRYVOE, Co Cork — Map 01 C2

★★67% Garryvoe
☎ 021 4646718 021 4646824
e-mail: garryvoehotel@eircom.net
Dir: *off N25 onto L72 at Castlemartyr between Midleton and Youghal and continue for 6km*
A comfortable, family-run hotel with caring staff, the Garryvoe has been upgraded. It stands in a delightful position facing a sandy beach and the first-floor lounge overlooks the sea. There is a hotel bar and also a public bar.
ROOMS: 19 en suite (2 fmly) s €82-€93; d €114-€136 (incl. bkfst) **LB** **FACILITIES:** Tennis (hard) Putting green entertainment **CONF:** Thtr 400 Class 250 **PARKING:** 25 **NOTES:** No dogs (ex guide dogs) Closed 25 Dec **CARDS:**

GLENDALOUGH, Co Wicklow — Map 01 D3

★★★61% *The Glendalough*
☎ 0404 45135 0404 45142
e-mail: info@glendaloughhotel.ie
Dir: *N11 to Kilmacongue, right onto R755, straight on at Caragh then right onto R756*
Forest and mountains provide the setting for this long-established hotel, beside the famous monastic site. The hotel has been refurbished and additional bedrooms, many with lovely views, are now available. Bar food is available and the charming restaurant overlooks the river and forest. The whole area is ideal for walking, golf and trout fishing.
ROOMS: 44 en suite (3 fmly) **FACILITIES:** STV Fishing entertainment **CONF:** Thtr 200 Class 150 Board 50 **SERVICES:** Lift **PARKING:** 100 **NOTES:** No dogs (ex guide dogs) Closed Dec-Jan
CARDS:

GOREY, Co Wexford — Map 01 D3

★★★★63% Ashdown Park Hotel
The Coach Rd
☎ 055 80500 055 80777
e-mail: info@ashdownparkhotel.com
Dir: *from N11 towards Gorey, 1st left before rail bridge, hotel on left*
Situated on an elevated position overlooking the town of Gorey this modern hotel has excellent health and leisure facilities, comfortable lounges and bars and a very attractive first-floor restaurant. Bedrooms are spacious and well equipped. Close to golf, beach and hill walking.
ROOMS: 60 en suite (12 fmly) (20 GF) s €75-€95; d €150-€190 (incl. bkfst) **LB** **FACILITIES:** Indoor swimming (H) Sauna Solarium Gym Jacuzzi Steam & Therapy rooms, Beauty salon, Swimming pool supervised entertainment **CONF:** Thtr 800 Class 315 Board 100 Del from €150 **SERVICES:** Lift **PARKING:** 150 **NOTES:** No dogs (ex guide dogs) Closed 24-25 Dec **CARDS:**

Top 200 - Hotel

★★★ Marlfield House
☎ 055 21124 055 21572
e-mail: info@marlfieldhouse.ie
Dir: *1.5 hours south of Dublin off N11, 1m outside Gorey on Courtown road*
This distinctive Regency house was once the residence of the Earl of Courtown. The current hotel retains an atmosphere of elegance and luxury throughout. Public areas include a library, drawing room and dining room leading into a conservatory which overlooks the grounds, and a wildlife reserve. Bedrooms are in keeping with the style of the downstairs rooms and there are some superb suites. Druids Glen and several other golf courses are nearby.
ROOMS: 20 en suite (3 fmly) (6 GF) No smoking in all bedrooms s €140-€250; d €250-€280 (incl. bkfst) **LB** **FACILITIES:** STV Tennis (hard) Sauna Croquet lawn **CONF:** Thtr 60 Board 20 Del from €250 **PARKING:** 50 **NOTES:** No smoking in restaurant Closed 15 Dec-30 Jan **CARDS:**

GOUGANE BARRA, Co Cork — Map 01 B2

★★66% *Gougane Barra*
☎ 026 47069 026 47226
e-mail: gouganbarrahotel@tinet.ie
Dir: *off N22*
Right on the shore of the lake, the Gougane Barra Hotel is very popular. Refurbishments have improved the restaurant, bedrooms and bathrooms, all of which have lovely views. Guests can be met from their train, boat or plane by prior arrangement.
ROOMS: 27 en suite **FACILITIES:** STV Fishing **PARKING:** 25 **NOTES:** No dogs (ex guide dogs) No smoking in restaurant Closed 13 Oct-13 Apr **CARDS:**

HILLSBOROUGH, Co Down — Map 01 D5

★★★66% *White Gables*
14 Dromore Rd BT26 6HS
☎ 028 9268 2755 028 9268 9532
e-mail: enquiries@whitegableshotel.co.uk
Dir: *join M2 (Belfast) then M1 west, join A1 at junct 7 to Dublin. Take Hillsborough turn, through village, hotel on right*
Situated on the outskirts of town, this modern hotel is popular with business guests. Double-glazing and a fairly quiet location ensures quiet bedrooms and the marbled lobby area helps create a very positive first impression. Other public rooms include a smart, split-level restaurant and a popular all day coffee shop.
ROOMS: 31 en suite No smoking in 8 bedrooms **FACILITIES:** STV **CONF:** Thtr 120 Class 40 Board 25 **PARKING:** 120 **NOTES:** No dogs (ex guide dogs) Closed 24-25 Dec RS Sun (residents only before 7pm)
CARDS:

HOWTH, Co Dublin Map 01 D4

★★★64% Deer Park Hotel & Golf Courses

IRISH COUNTRY HOTELS

☎ 01 8322624 📠 01 8392405
e-mail: sales@deerpark.iol.ie

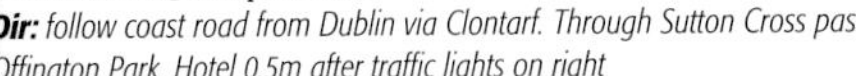

Dir: *follow coast road from Dublin via Clontarf. Through Sutton Cross pass Offington Park. Hotel 0.5m after traffic lights on right*

This modern hotel is situated overlooking Dublin Bay and Ireland's Eye in its own parkland golf courses. The spacious well-equipped bedrooms have spectacular views. The Four Earls Restaurant is famous for fresh fish from Howth Harbour, and there is a lively bar and bistro. There is a leisure centre, all-weather tennis courts and a choice of four golf courses nearby. Convenient for Dublin Airport, the ferry port and the DART service to the centre of Dublin.

ROOMS: 80 en suite (4 fmly) (36 GF) s €103-€112; d €154-€170 (incl. bkfst) **LB FACILITIES: Spa** Indoor swimming (H) Golf 18 Tennis (hard) Sauna Putting green Swimming pool supervised **CONF:** Thtr 95 Class 60 Board 25 Del from €160 **PARKING:** 200 **NOTES:** No dogs (ex guide dogs) Closed 23-26 Dec **CARDS:**

INNISHANNON, Co Cork Map 01 B2

★★★66% Innishannon House

MANOR HOUSE HOTELS

☎ 021 4775121 📠 021 4775609
e-mail: info@innishannon-hotel.ie

Dir: *off N71 at eastern end of village, left onto Kinsale road, hotel about 1m*

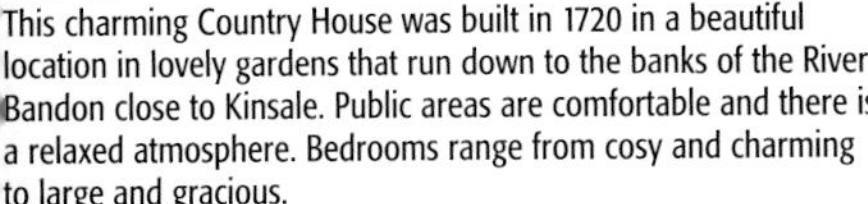

This charming Country House was built in 1720 in a beautiful location in lovely gardens that run down to the banks of the River Bandon close to Kinsale. Public areas are comfortable and there is a relaxed atmosphere. Bedrooms range from cosy and charming to large and gracious.

ROOMS: 12 en suite (4 fmly) s €115-€135; d €200-€270 (incl. bkfst) **LB FACILITIES:** STV Fishing **CONF:** BC Thtr 200 Class 80 Board 50 Del from €110 **PARKING:** 100 **NOTES:** No dogs (ex guide dogs) No smoking in restaurant Closed 22-26 Dec **CARDS:**

IRVINESTOWN, Co Fermanagh Map 01 C5

★★63% Mahons

Mill St BT94 1GS
☎ 028 6862 1656 📠 028 6862 8344
e-mail: info@mahonshotel.co.uk

Dir: *on A32 midway between Enniskillen and Omagh - beside town clock in centre of town*

This family-run hotel has been in the same ownership and offering friendly hospitality for well over 100 years. Public areas, especially the bar, have a wealth of charm and character. In the restaurant, the extensive menu offers a wide range of dishes. The prettily decorated bedrooms come in a variety of sizes.

ROOMS: 18 en suite (4 fmly) s £28-£32; d £55-£60 (incl. bkfst) **LB FACILITIES:** STV Tennis (hard) Riding Solarium entertainment **CONF:** Thtr 400 Class 250 Board 100 Del from £35 **PARKING:** 40 **NOTES:** Closed 25 Dec **CARDS:**

KENMARE, Co Kerry Map 01 B2

Top 200 - Hotel

★★★★ Park Hotel Kenmare

SMALL LUXURY HOTELS OF THE WORLD

☎ 064 41200 📠 064 41402
e-mail: info@parkkenmare.com

Dir: *on R569 beside golf course*

The Park Hotel Kenmare is a luxurious house on the famed Ring of Kerry that has been welcoming guests for over 100 years. Warm hospitality and professional service come naturally to all the team, who endeavour to make you feel pampered. The suites and bedrooms are all spacious and very well appointed, and many of them have sea views. The elegant Restaurant serves fine wines and really good food, much of which is locally sourced. A treatment spa is due to open early 2004.

ROOMS: 49 en suite (2 fmly) No smoking in 5 bedrooms s €206-€233; d €366-€726 (incl. bkfst) **LB FACILITIES: Spa** STV Golf 18 Tennis (hard) Snooker Gym Croquet lawn Putting green Beauty Suite, Tai Chi Pavilion entertainment Xmas **CONF:** Thtr 60 Class 40 Board 28 **SERVICES:** Lift **PARKING:** 60 **NOTES:** No dogs (ex guide dogs) No smoking in restaurant Closed 1-23 Dec & 2 Jan-14 Feb Civ Wed 120 **CARDS:**

K

Top 200 - Hotel

★★★★ Sheen Falls Lodge

☎ 064 41600 📠 064 41386
e-mail: info@sheenfallslodge.ie

Dir: *from Kenmare take N71 to Glengarriff over suspension bridge, take 1st turn left*

This former fishing lodge has been developed into a beautiful hotel on the banks of the Sheen River. The cascading Sheen Falls are floodlit at night, forming a romantic backdrop to the enjoyment of award-winning cuisine in the La Cascade restaurant. Bedrooms are very comfortably appointed, many of the suites being particularly spacious. The leisure centre and beauty therapy facilities are very relaxing.

ROOMS: 66 en suite (14 fmly) (14 GF) No smoking in 10 bedrooms s €260-€395; d €260-€395 **LB FACILITIES:** STV Indoor swimming (H) Tennis (hard) Fishing Riding Snooker Sauna Solarium Gym Croquet lawn Jacuzzi Table tennis, Steam room, Clay pigeon shooting, Cycling, Vintage car rides entertainment ch fac Xmas **CONF:** BC Thtr 120 Class 65 Board 50 **SERVICES:** Lift **PARKING:** 76 **NOTES:** No dogs (ex guide dogs) No smoking in restaurant Closed 2 Jan-1 Feb RS December **CARDS:**

KILKEE, Co Clare
Map 01 B3

★★64% Halpin's
Erin St
☎ 065 9056032 ▤ 065 9056317
e-mail: halpinstownhouse@iol.ie
Dir: *in centre of town*
The finest tradition of hotel service is offered at this family-run hotel which has a commanding view over the old Victorian town. The attractive bedrooms are comfortable.
ROOMS: 12 en suite (6 fmly) No smoking in 4 bedrooms s €55-€75; d €89-€109 (incl. bkfst) **FACILITIES:** STV **CONF:** Thtr 60 Class 36 Board 30 Del from €140 **SERVICES:** air con **PARKING:** 3 **NOTES:** No dogs (ex guide dogs) Closed 16 Nov-14 Mar **CARDS:**

KILKENNY, Co Kilkenny
Map 01 C3

★★★★68% ⚘ Kilkenny River Court Hotel
The Bridge, John St
☎ 056 772 3388 ▤ 056 772 3389
e-mail: reservations@kilrivercourt.com
Dir: *at bridge in town centre, just opposite Kilkenny Castle, on River Nore side of castle*
Once into the private courtyard, the superb location is a revelation. The Riverside restaurant and bar enjoy lovely views, with Kilkenny Castle in the background and attentive staff ensure good service. Friendliness, good corporate and leisure facilities and comfortable bedrooms all contribute to the experience of staying here.
ROOMS: 90 en suite (4 fmly) No smoking in 20 bedrooms s €130-€320; d €120-€400 (incl. bkfst) **LB** **FACILITIES:** STV Indoor swimming (H) Sauna Gym Jacuzzi Beauty Salon, Swimming pool supervised Xmas **CONF:** Thtr 260 Class 110 Board 45 Del from €150 **SERVICES:** Lift **PARKING:** 84 **NOTES:** No dogs (ex guide dogs) No smoking in restaurant Closed 24-26 Dec **CARDS:**

★★★73% Newpark
☎ 056 776 0500 ▤ 056 776 0555
e-mail: info@newparkhotel.com
A friendly hotel with an impressive foyer lounge, a bar/bistro and conference suites. A purpose-built bedroom wing offers a choice of rooms, decorated and equipped to a high standard.
ROOMS: 111 en suite (42 fmly) No smoking in 8 bedrooms s €120-€160; d €145-€185 **LB** **FACILITIES:** STV Indoor swimming (H) Sauna Solarium Gym Jacuzzi Plunge pool entertainment Xmas **CONF:** Thtr 600 Class 300 Board 50 **PARKING:** 350 **NOTES:** No dogs (ex guide dogs) No smoking in restaurant **CARDS:**

★★★64% Langton House
69 John St
☎ 056 776 5133 ▤ 056 776 3693
e-mail: langtons@oceanfree.net
Dir: *take N9 & N10 from Dublin follow signs for city centre at outskirts of Kilkenny turn to left Langtons. 500mtrs on left after 1st set of lights*
Langton's has a long and well founded reputation as an entertainment venue and bar. These facilities are now complemented by a range of accommodation, all very comfortably designed and well appointed. The busy restaurant is popular with visitors and locals alike.
ROOMS: 14 en suite 16 annexe en suite (4 fmly) (8 GF) s €65-€180; d €100-€220 (incl. bkfst) **LB** **FACILITIES:** STV entertainment **CONF:** Thtr 600 Class 300 Board 50 **PARKING:** 60 **NOTES:** No dogs (ex guide dogs) Closed Good Fri, 25 Dec **CARDS:**

⚘ AA Rosette Award for culinary excellence

KILL, Co Kildare
Map 01 D4

★★★59% *Ambassador*
☎ 045 877064 ▤ 045 877515
e-mail: ambassador-sales@quinn-hotels.com
Dir: *close to Dublin centre on N7*
Immediately south of Kill, close to Goffs sales complex, racecourse and Mondello Park. There is an all day lounge carvery. The restaurant is closed on Monday and Tuesday, so dinner is served in the bar.
ROOMS: 36 en suite (36 fmly) **FACILITIES:** STV entertainment **CONF:** Thtr 260 Class 140 Board 60 **PARKING:** 150 **NOTES:** No dogs (ex guide dogs) **CARDS:**

KILLALOE, Co Clare
Map 01 B3

★★★65% Watermans Lodge Country House
Ballina
☎ 061 376333 ▤ 061 375445
e-mail: info@watermanslodge.ie
Dir: *hotel on left just outside village*
On a hillside overlooking the River Shannon and marina, Waterman's is surrounded by attractive gardens. An intimate country house offering a peaceful retreat, with comfortable lounges, individually styled bedrooms and a spacious bar.
ROOMS: 10 en suite (2 fmly) (10 GF) No smoking in all bedrooms s €80-€100; d €120-€176 (incl. bkfst) **FACILITIES:** STV Riding **CONF:** BC Thtr 30 Class 20 Board 20 Del from €140 **PARKING:** 50 **NOTES:** No dogs (ex guide dogs) Closed 21-26 Dec **CARDS:**

KILLARNEY, Co Kerry
Map 01 B2

Top 200 - Hotel

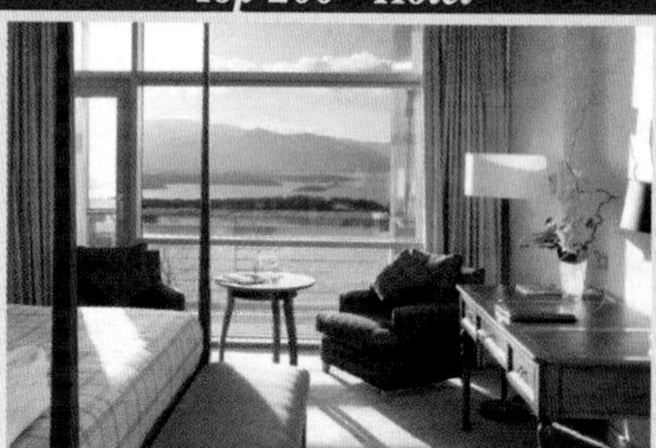

★★★★ ⚘⚘⚘ Aghadoe Heights
☎ 064 31766 ▤ 064 31345
e-mail: info@aghadoeheights.com
Dir: *5km N of Killarney. Signed off N22 Tralee road*
Superbly located overlooking Loch Lein, this hotel has been extensively refurbished to a very high standard. On the first floor the award-winning restaurant enjoys panoramic views of mountains and lakes, also shared by the stylish bedrooms, some of which have their own sun decks. There is a spacious lounge, a cocktail bar and a banqueting/conference suite. The staff are extremely friendly and welcoming.
ROOMS: 56 en suite (6 fmly) No smoking in 10 bedrooms s €250-€789; d €310-€786 (incl. bkfst) **LB** **FACILITIES:** STV Indoor swimming (H) Tennis (hard) Fishing Sauna Solarium Gym Jacuzzi Plunge pool, Beauty Treatment rooms entertainment Xmas **CONF:** BC Thtr 120 Class 60 Board 40 Del from €235 **SERVICES:** Lift **PARKING:** 120 **NOTES:** No dogs (ex guide dogs) No smoking in restaurant Closed Jan-1 Mar
CARDS:

Top 200 - Hotel

★★★★ Killarney Park

Kenmare Place
☎ 064 35555 064 35266
e-mail: info@killarneyparkhotel.ie
Dir: *N22 from Cork to Killarney. At 1st rdbt take 1st exit to town centre at 2nd rdbt take 2nd exit, 3rd rdbt take 1st exit. Hotel 2nd left*
On the edge of the town, this charming hotel combines elegance with comfort. It has a warm atmosphere with open fires, restful colours and friendly, caring staff who ensure a stay with them is an enjoyable one. A health spa has opened to further enhance the leisure facilities.
ROOMS: 75 en suite (4 fmly) No smoking in 35 bedrooms **FACILITIES:** STV Indoor swimming (H) Snooker Sauna Gym Jacuzzi Outdoor Canadian hot-tub Plunge pool **CONF:** Thtr 150 Class 70 Board 35 **SERVICES:** Lift air con **PARKING:** 70 **NOTES:** No dogs (ex guide dogs) Closed 24-26 Dec
CARDS:

★★★★67% Muckross Park Hotel

Muckross Village
☎ 064 31938 064 31965
e-mail: muckrossparkhotel@eircom.net
Dir: *from Killarney to Kenmare, hotel 4km on left*
An 18th century hotel set in the heart of the Killarney National Park. Relaxing lounge areas feature comfortable furniture, warm colour schemes and chandeliers. Bedrooms are attractively decorated and well equipped. Good food is served in the Bluepool restaurant, as well as the adjacent thatched pub, Molly Darcys.
ROOMS: 27 en suite (2 fmly) No smoking in 2 bedrooms s fr €100; d fr €200 (incl. bkfst) **LB** **FACILITIES:** STV **CONF:** Thtr 200 Class 80 Board 40 Del from €185 **PARKING:** 250 **NOTES:** No dogs (ex guide dogs) No smoking in restaurant Closed Dec-Feb **CARDS:**

★★★★66% Cahernane

MANOR HOUSE HOTELS

Muckross Rd
☎ 064 31895 064 34340
e-mail: cahernane@tinet.ie
This fine country mansion, former home of the Earls of Pembroke, has a magnificent mountain backdrop and panoramic views from its lakeside setting. Elegant period furniture is complemented by more modern pieces to create a hotel offering a warm atmosphere with friendly staff.
ROOMS: 12 en suite 26 annexe en suite **FACILITIES:** Tennis (hard) Fishing Croquet lawn entertainment **SERVICES:** Lift air con **PARKING:** 50 **NOTES:** No dogs (ex guide dogs) No smoking in restaurant Closed 2 Nov-Mar **CARDS:**

★★★★65% Randles Court

Muckross Rd
☎ 064 35333 064 35206
e-mail: info@randlescourt.com
Dir: *N22 towards Muckross, turn tight at t-junct on right. From N72 take 3rd exit on 1st rdbt into town & follow signs for Muckross, hotel on left*
Conveniently situated close to all the town's attractions, this is a family-run hotel with an emphasis on friendliness and good customer care. Facilities include a chic bistro and a leisure centre and conference/banqueting suite. Bedrooms are comfortable, and pet facilities are available by arrangement.
ROOMS: 52 en suite **FACILITIES:** STV Indoor swimming (H) Sauna Gym Putting green **CONF:** Thtr 80 Class 60 Board 40 **SERVICES:** Lift **PARKING:** 39 **NOTES:** Closed 23-27 Dec
CARDS:

★★★69% Gleneagle

☎ 064 36000 064 32646
e-mail: info@gleneaglehotel.com
Dir: *1m outside Killarney town on Kenmare Road - N71*

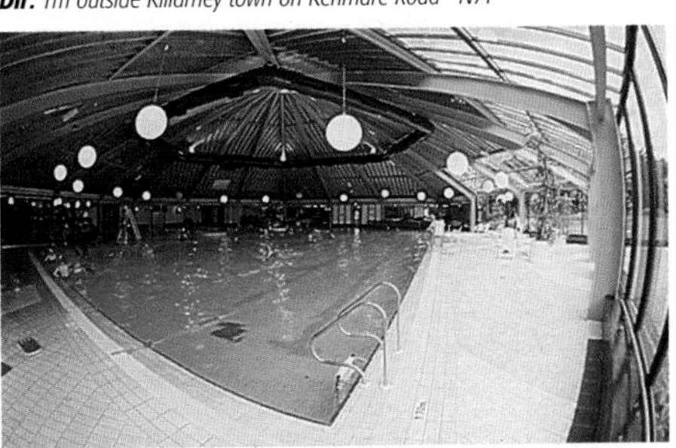

Excellent facilities for both leisure and corporate guests are on offer in this family run hotel. Comfortable bedrooms, many for families, are well equipped. The impressive new National Events Centre is one of the largest in the country. The dedicated owners personally oversee the day-to-day running of the hotel.
ROOMS: 250 en suite (57 fmly) No smoking in 20 bedrooms **FACILITIES:** STV Indoor swimming (H) Tennis (hard) Squash Snooker Sauna Gym Jacuzzi Pitch & Putt Table tennis Steam room entertainment **CONF:** Thtr 2500 Class 1000 Board 50 **SERVICES:** Lift **PARKING:** 500
CARDS:

★★★69% Lake

Muckross Rd
☎ 064 31035 064 31902
e-mail: lakehotel@eircom.net
Dir: *on Kenmare road out of Killarney*
Approached by a wooded drive, this former mansion stands in lovely countryside with lake and mountain views. Some bedrooms have balconies and four-poster beds. Public rooms are spacious and the lounge retains an atmosphere of traditional comfort.
ROOMS: 65 en suite (6 fmly) **FACILITIES:** STV Tennis (hard) Fishing Sauna Gym Putting green out door hot tub entertainment **CONF:** Thtr 80 Class 60 Board 40 **SERVICES:** Lift air con **PARKING:** 140 **NOTES:** No dogs (ex guide dogs) No smoking in restaurant Closed 18 Dec-10 Feb **CARDS:**

AA Rosette Award for culinary excellence

K

KILLARNEY, continued

★★★67% *Castlerosse*

☎ 064 31144 📠 064 31031
e-mail: castler@iol.ie
Dir: *from Killarney town take R562 for Killorglin and The Ring of Kerry, hotel 1.5km from town on left*

A lovely location on 6,000 acres of land overlooking Lough Leane, between the Castleross golf course, the National Park and the adjoining championship golf course. Bedrooms are comfortable and well appointed. The spacious lounges, restaurant and bar have panoramic views over the lakes and mountains.

ROOMS: 121 en suite (27 fmly) No smoking in 4 bedrooms **FACILITIES:** Indoor swimming (H) Golf 9 Tennis (hard) Snooker Sauna Gym Jacuzzi Golfing & riding arranged entertainment **CONF:** Thtr 200 Class 100 Board 40 **SERVICES:** Lift **PARKING:** 100 **NOTES:** No dogs (ex guide dogs) Closed Dec-Feb **CARDS:**

★★★66% *Killarney Ryan*

Cork Rd
☎ 064 31555 📠 064 32438
e-mail: info@killarneyryan.com

On the outskirts of Killarney, this hotel offers good standards of comfort. Public rooms include a large lounge, a restaurant and lounge bar opening on to the gardens. Many of the bedrooms can accommodate families, and the Ryan Group offer an all-inclusive summer holiday rate which can be good value.

ROOMS: 168 en suite (164 fmly) No smoking in 60 bedrooms **FACILITIES:** Indoor swimming (H) Tennis (hard) Snooker Sauna Jacuzzi Steam room Crazy golf Games room entertainment **SERVICES:** Lift **NOTES:** No dogs (ex guide dogs) Closed Dec & Jan **CARDS:**

★★★65% International

Best Western

Kenmare Pl
☎ 064 31816 📠 064 31837
e-mail: inter@iol.ie
Dir: *take N21 from Limerick to Farranfore. Then N22 to Killarney, turn right at 1st rdbt on entering Killarney follow town bypass road*

This hotel offers quality bedrooms with modern comforts. Hannigan's Bar and the lounge are popular and bar snacks are available. There is a more intimate dining room, where soft candlelight glows against mahogany panelling. There is a library, snooker room and a keen interest is taken in golfing guests - tee times can be arranged at any of the many courses in the area.

ROOMS: 80 en suite (6 fmly) No smoking in 30 bedrooms s €65-€100; d €90-€170 (incl. bkfst) **LB FACILITIES:** STV Billiards entertainment **CONF:** Thtr 200 Class 100 Board 25 **SERVICES:** Lift **NOTES:** No dogs (ex guide dogs) No smoking in restaurant Closed 23-27 Dec **CARDS:**

★★★64% *Arbutus*

College St
☎ 064 31037 📠 064 34033
e-mail: arbutushotel@eircom.net

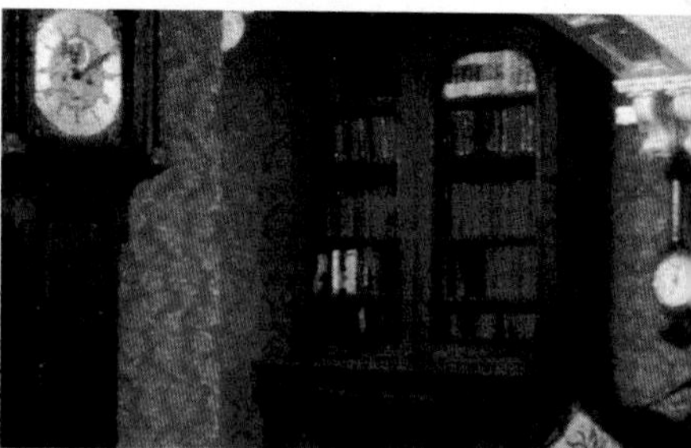

Situated in the centre of the town of Killarney, the Buckley family have run this smart hotel since 1926. Public areas include a comfortable foyer lounge, guest sitting room, traditional-style bar and restaurant. Staff are friendly and helpful.

ROOMS: 35 en suite (4 fmly) **FACILITIES:** STV **NOTES:** No dogs (ex guide dogs) Closed 12 Dec-30 Jan **CARDS:**

See advert on opposite page

★★★63% *White Gates*

IRISH COUNTRY HOTELS

Muckross Rd
☎ 064 31164 📠 064 34850
Dir: *1km from Killarney town on Muckross road on left*

Distinctive blue and ochre paintwork draws the eye to this hotel. The same flair for colour combinations is evident throughout the interior and bedrooms are particularly attractive. The natural harmony of wood and stone is a feature of the well-designed lounge bar and the restaurant, with its conservatory front that is filled with light. There is also a very comfortable lounge.

ROOMS: 27 en suite **FACILITIES:** STV entertainment **CONF:** Class 50 **PARKING:** 50 **NOTES:** No dogs (ex guide dogs) Closed 21-29 Dec **CARDS:**

★★★61% Darby O'Gills

Lissivigeen, Mallow Rd
☎ 064 34168 & 34919 📠 064 36794
e-mail: darbyogill@eircom.net
Dir: *turn off N22 (Cork road) to N72(Mallow)*

Darby O'Gills is a modern country house, offering smart, spacious and well-equipped bedrooms. Dinner is served in the restaurant, and bar food in the comfortable lounge bar. There is also a traditional Irish pub.

ROOMS: 25 en suite (7 fmly) s €40-€80; d €80-€120 (incl. bkfst) **LB FACILITIES:** STV entertainment Xmas **CONF:** Thtr 250 Class 150 Board 60 **SERVICES:** air con **PARKING:** 150 **NOTES:** No dogs (ex guide dogs) **CARDS:**

★★★59% ***Scotts Garden Hotel***
College St
☎ 064 31060 ▤ 064 36656
e-mail: scottskill@eircom.net
Dir: *N20/N22 to town, left at Friary. Entrance to car park 500mtrs on East Avenue Rd*

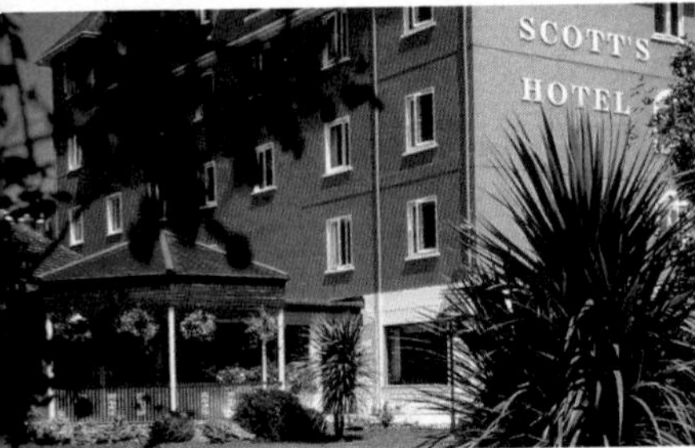

Located in the town centre, this hotel offers pleasant bedrooms, a bar and a patio garden. Special concessions are available at the sister Gleneagles Hotel's leisure facilities.
ROOMS: 52 en suite (4 fmly) **FACILITIES:** entertainment **SERVICES:** Lift **PARKING:** 60 **NOTES:** No dogs (ex guide dogs) No smoking in restaurant Closed 24-25 Dec **CARDS:**

KILLINEY, Co Dublin Map 01 D4

★★★★65% **Fitzpatrick Castle**
☎ 01 2305400 ▤ 01 2305430
e-mail: reservations@fitzpatricks.com
Dir: *leaving Dun Laoghaire port turn left, on coast road, right at lights, left at next lights to Dalkey, right at McDonaghs pub, immediate left, up hill, hotel at top*
Situated in large grounds this 18th-century castle boasts stunning views over Dublin Bay and has extensively refurbished. Facilities include an elegant lounge, PJ's Restaurant and Club Bar and leisure and conference facilities. The comfortable bedrooms include an executive floor with its own lounge. There is a helipad, and a courtesy coach available for transfers to and from the airport.
ROOMS: 113 en suite (42 fmly) No smoking in 50 bedrooms s €170-€195; d €210-€235 **LB FACILITIES:** STV Indoor swimming (H) Sauna Solarium Gym Jacuzzi Beauty/hairdressing salon, Steam room, Swimming pool supervised entertainment **CONF:** BC Thtr 400 Class 250 Board 80 **SERVICES:** Lift **PARKING:** 300 **NOTES:** No dogs (ex guide dogs) RS 24-27 Dec **CARDS:**

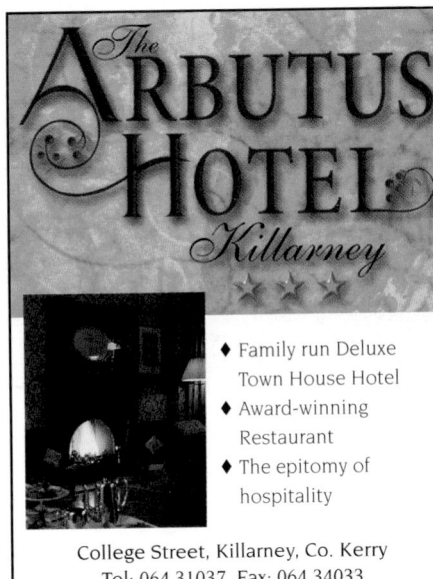

KILMESSAN, Co Meath Map 01 C/D4

★★★65% **The Station House Hotel**
☎ 046 25239 ▤ 046 25588
e-mail: info@thestationhousehotel.com
Dir: *M50, N3 towards Navan, at Dunshaughlin turn left at end of village, follow signposts*
The Station House saw its last train in 1963, and is now a comfortable, family-run hotel with a popular restaurant. The Carriage House has been refurbished and new bedrooms added; the Signal Box houses a suite. There is a sun terrace and conference/banqueting suite.
ROOMS: 6 en suite 14 annexe en suite (3 fmly) (5 GF) No smoking in 15 bedrooms s €85-€115; d €130-€180 (incl. bkfst) **LB FACILITIES:** entertainment Xmas **CONF:** BC Thtr 400 Class 300 Board 100 Del from €180 **PARKING:** 200 **NOTES:** No dogs (ex guide dogs) **CARDS:**

KINSALE, Co Cork Map 01 B2

★★★73% ❀ **Actons**
Pier Rd
☎ 021 4772135 ▤ 021 4772231
e-mail: info@actonshotelkinsale.com
Dir: *located in Town Centre area facing Kinsale Harbour, 500yds from Yacht Club Marina*
The location of this hotel, set in gardens overlooking the waterfront and marina, is ideal. The hotel has a bar and bistro and the Captain's Table restaurant, which continues to offer enjoyable food. The luxurious lounge is comfortable and bedrooms are all of

continued on p898

K

KINSALE, continued

a good standard. Friendly and attentive staff contribute greatly towards the enjoyment of a visit.

Actons Hotel, Kinsale

ROOMS: 76 en suite (20 fmly) s €100-€150; d €170-€225 (incl. bkfst) **LB** **FACILITIES:** **Spa** STV Indoor swimming (H) Sauna Solarium Gym Jacuzzi Swimming pool supervised, Aerobics studio entertainment **CONF:** Thtr 350 Class 200 Board 100 Del from €130 **SERVICES:** Lift **PARKING:** 70 **NOTES:** No dogs (ex guide dogs) Closed 24-27 Dec **CARDS:**

K

★★★69% **Trident**
Worlds End
☎ 021 4772301 021 4774173
e-mail: info@tridenthotel.com
Dir: *take R600 from Cork city to Kinsale, along the Kinsale waterfront, hotel just beyond the pier*
Located at the harbour's edge, the Trident Hotel has its own marina with boats for hire. Many of the bedrooms have superb views and two have balconies. The restaurant and lounge both overlook the harbour and pleasant staff provide hospitable service.
ROOMS: 58 en suite (2 fmly) s €98-€128; d €130-€190 (incl. bkfst) **LB** **FACILITIES:** Sauna Gym Jacuzzi Steam room, Deep sea angling **CONF:** Thtr 220 Class 130 Board 40 Del from €140 **SERVICES:** Lift **PARKING:** 60 **NOTES:** No dogs (ex guide dogs) Closed 24-26 Dec **CARDS:**

★★★63% ***Blue Haven Hotel & Restaurant***
3 Pearse St
☎ 021 4772209 021 4774268
e-mail: bluehaven@iol.ie
Situated on the site of the old fish market in the centre of Kinsale - Ireland's gourmet capital. Public areas are very comfortable, and include a wine bar, and bedrooms are individually decorated and well appointed. The Fish Market Tavern offers bar food, and fine dining is available in the conservatory restaurant.
ROOMS: 17 en suite (1 fmly) **FACILITIES:** entertainment ch fac **CONF:** Thtr 50 Class 35 Board 25 **NOTES:** No dogs (ex guide dogs) **CARDS:**

KNOCK, Co Mayo — Map 01 B4

★★★66% **Knock House**
Ballyhaunis Rd
☎ 094 938 8088 094 938 8044
e-mail: info@knockhousehotel.ie
Dir: *hotel on Ballyhaunis Road, 0.5km from Knock*
Adjacent to the Marian Shrine and Basilica, this creatively designed limestone-clad building is surrounded by landscaped gardens. Facilities include comfortable lounges and bedrooms, a dispense bar, conference rooms and a restaurant. Six bedrooms are adapted for wheelchairs, which are also available to guests.
ROOMS: 68 en suite (12 fmly) s €67-€85; d €98-€130 (incl. bkfst) **LB** **FACILITIES:** Xmas **CONF:** Thtr 150 Class 90 Board 45 **SERVICES:** Lift **PARKING:** 150 **NOTES:** No dogs (ex guide dogs) **CARDS:**

★★★61% **Belmont**
☎ 094 938 8122 094 938 8532
e-mail: reception@belmonthotel.ie
Dir: *on N17, Galway side of Knock. Turn right at Burke's supermarket & Pub. Hotel 150yds on right*
Refurbishment has enhanced this hotel's facilities, which include new bedrooms, a lift and a function room/restaurant. There is a pleasant bar with all-day carvery service, and a health and fitness club. Bedrooms vary; rooms in the old wing tend to be more compact. There are specially adapted rooms for guests with disabilities. The hotel is close to the Marian Shrine and Basilica.
ROOMS: 63 en suite (6 fmly) No smoking in 3 bedrooms s €65-€75; d €100-€120 (incl. bkfst) **LB** **FACILITIES:** Solarium Gym Jacuzzi Steamroom Natural health therapies entertainment **CONF:** Thtr 500 Class 100 Board 20 **SERVICES:** Lift air con **PARKING:** 110 **NOTES:** No dogs (ex guide dogs) No smoking in restaurant Closed 25 & 26 Dec **CARDS:**

LEIXLIP, Co Kildare — Map 01 D4

★★★75% ***Leixlip House***
Captains Hill
☎ 01 6242268 01 6244177
e-mail: info@leixliphouse.com
Dir: *from Leixlip motorway junct into village. Turn right at lights and continue up hill*
This Georgian house dates back to 1772 and retains many of its original features. Overlooking Leixlip, the hotel is just eight miles from Dublin city centre. Bedrooms and public areas are furnished and decorated to a high standard. The Bradaun Restaurant offers a wide range of interesting dishes.
ROOMS: 19 en suite (2 fmly) **FACILITIES:** STV **CONF:** Thtr 130 Class 60 Board 40 **PARKING:** 64 **NOTES:** No dogs **CARDS:**

LETTERKENNY, Co Donegal — Map 01 C5

★★★67% ***Castle Grove Country House***
Castlegrove, Ballymaleel
☎ 074 915 1118 074 915 1384
e-mail: enquiries@castlegrove.com

This elegant Georgian house, set in a sheltered position and reached by a long avenue through parkland, enjoys spectacular views of Lough Swilly. Family-owned and friendly, true Irish hospitality is offered. The dining room serves dishes using local produce. Bedrooms are spacious, equipped with modern

continued

ecessities and furnished with fine antique pieces. Ideal for touring
ıe North West.
OOMS: 15 en suite No smoking in 3 bedrooms **CONF:** Thtr 28 Class
2 Board 16 **PARKING:** 400 **NOTES:** No dogs (ex guide dogs) No
ıildren 14yrs No smoking in restaurant Closed Xmas/New Year RS
ın-May (closed Sun) **CARDS:**

IMAVADY, Co Londonderry — Map 01 C6

★★★★67%
ładisson SAS Row Park Resort
ıT49 9LB
☎ 028 7772 2222 ▯ 028 7772 2313
-mail: reservations@radissonroepark.com
Dir: *on A2 Londonderry/Limavady road, 16m from Londonderry, 1m from ımavady*
'his impressive hotel sits centrally within its own modern golf esort. The spacious, modern bedrooms are well equipped and nany have excellent views of the fairways. The 'Greens ₹estaurant' provides a refreshing dining experience and the Coach ɫouse brasserie offers a lighter menu. Leisure options are ·xtensive.
ROOMS: 118 en suite (15 fmly) No smoking in 76 bedrooms s £70-£95; ɫ £80-£110 (incl. bkfst) **LB FACILITIES:** STV Indoor swimming (H) Golf 8 Fishing Sauna Solarium Gym Croquet lawn Putting green Jacuzzi loodlit driving range Outside tees Golf training academy Bicycle hire ⅹmas **CONF:** Thtr 450 Class 190 Board 140 Del £95 **SERVICES:** Lift **PARKING:** 300 **NOTES:** No dogs (ex guide dogs)
CARDS:

LIMERICK, Co Limerick — Map 01 B3

★★★★72% **Radisson**
Ennis Rd
☎ 061 326666 ▯ 327418
e-mail: emma.murray.@radisson.com
Dir: *on the Ennis Road N18, 5 mins from city centre*
This modern hotel has recently undergone a major renovation programme, resulting in a property well suited to business and leisure use alike. Well appointed bedrooms are decorated in strong colours, with very easy-to-use facilities. Diners may opt for the formal restaurant or the more casual Herons pub.
ROOMS: 154 en suite (9 fmly) No smoking in 70 bedrooms s €69-€110; d €69-€135 (incl. bkfst) **FACILITIES: Spa** STV Indoor swimming (H) Tennis (hard) Sauna Solarium entertainment Xmas **CONF:** Thtr 500 Class 500 Board 30 **SERVICES:** Lift air con **PARKING:** 300 **NOTES:** No dogs (ex guide dogs) **CARDS:**

★★★★70% **Castletroy Park**
Dublin Rd
☎ 061 335566 ▯ 061 331117
e-mail: sales@castletroy-park.ie
Dir: *on N7, 3m from Limerick city, 25mins from Shannon International Airport*
Close to the University of Limerick, this hotel combines modern comforts with attractive décor. Public areas are light and airy and include the Merry Pedlar Irish traditional pub and the fine dining McLaughlins Restaurant with splendid views of the gardens and Clare Hills. Bedrooms are very well equipped to suite the comforts of both the leisure and business guest. There are extensive leisure and banqueting facilities and large landscaped gardens.
ROOMS: 107 en suite (78 fmly) No smoking in 79 bedrooms s €135-€205; d €135-€230 (incl. bkfst) **LB FACILITIES:** STV Indoor swimming (H) Sauna Gym Jacuzzi Running track Steam room Swimming pool supervised entertainment **CONF:** BC Thtr 450 Class 270 Board 100 **SERVICES:** Lift **PARKING:** 160 **NOTES:** No dogs (ex guide dogs)
CARDS:

★★★73% ***Jurys***
Ennis Rd
☎ 061 327777 ▯ 061 326400
e-mail: bookings@jurys.com
Dir: *at junct of Ennis Rd, O'Callaghan Strand and Sarsfield Bridge*
This hotel, standing in four acres of riverside grounds, offers excellent corporate and leisure facilities, including an indoor swimming pool. Bedrooms come in two styles, executive or standard, and there is also a bar and restaurant.
ROOMS: 95 en suite (22 fmly) No smoking in 16 bedrooms **FACILITIES:** STV Indoor swimming (H) Tennis (hard) Sauna Gym Jacuzzi Steam room Plunge pool entertainment **CONF:** Thtr 200 Class 90 Board 45 **PARKING:** 200 **NOTES:** No dogs (ex guide dogs) Closed 24-27 Dec **CARDS:**

★★★68% ***Gresham Ardhu***
Ennis Rd
☎ 061 453922 ▯ 061 326333
e-mail: info@gresham-ardhuhotel.com
Dir: *on N18, Ennis road*

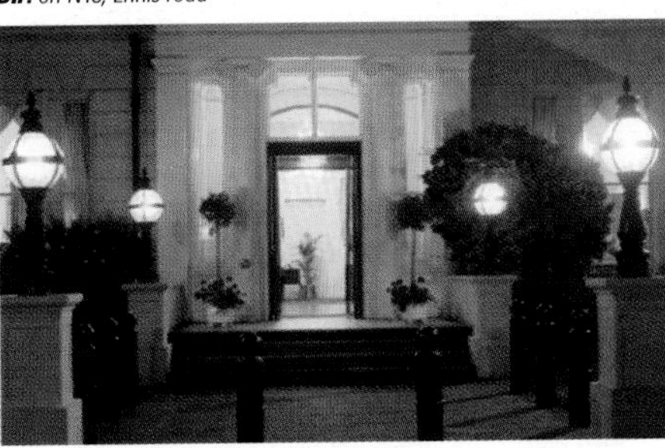

Close to the city, in its own grounds, the Gresham Ardhu has smart public areas located in the original part of this classic house including lounges and restaurants, a cocktail bar with a fire, sofas and a pianist. The well-equipped bedrooms are located in a modern extension with 24-hour room service. Other facilities include conference suites, a business centre and patio gardens.
ROOMS: 181 en suite (181 fmly) No smoking in 50 bedrooms **FACILITIES:** STV Gym entertainment **CONF:** Thtr 130 Class 60 Board 40 **SERVICES:** Lift **PARKING:** 180 **NOTES:** No dogs (ex guide dogs)
CARDS:

★★★64% ***Hotel Greenhills***
Caherdavin
☎ 061 453033 ▯ 061 453307
e-mail: info@greenhillgroup.com
Dir: *on N18, approx 2m from city centre*
Set in 3.5 acres of lovely landscaped gardens, the hotel has a fine leisure centre and good conference facilities. Bedrooms have been refurbished and are attractive and comfortable. Food is served all day in the Carvery bar, and there is a large car park.
ROOMS: 18 rms (13 en suite) (4 fmly) **FACILITIES:** STV Indoor swimming (H) Tennis (hard) Sauna Solarium Gym Jacuzzi Beauty parlour Massage entertainment **CONF:** Thtr 500 Class 200 Board 50 **PARKING:** 150 **NOTES:** No dogs **CARDS:**

★★★63% **Woodfield House**
Ennis Rd
☎ 061 453022 ▯ 061 326755
e-mail: woodfieldhousehotel@eircom.net
Dir: *on outskirts of city on main Shannon road*
This intimate hotel stands is situated on the N18 a short distance from the city centre. The smart bedrooms are comfortable and

continued on p900

L

LIMERICK, continued

well appointed. Public areas include a traditional style bar where food is served all day, a patio beer garden and an attractive Bistro.
ROOMS: 26 en suite (3 fmly) (5 GF) s €69-€90; d €110-€150 (incl. bkfst) **LB** **FACILITIES:** STV Tennis (hard) **CONF:** BC Thtr 130 Class 60 Board 60 **SERVICES:** air con **PARKING:** 80 **NOTES:** No dogs (ex guide dogs) Closed 24-25 Dec Civ Wed 100 **CARDS:**

★★★60% *Jurys Inn Limerick*

JURYS DOYLE HOTELS

Lower Mallow St
☎ 061 207000 061 400966
e-mail: info@jurysdoyle.com
Dir: *from N7 follow signs for city centre into O'Connell St, turn off at N18 (Shannon/Galway), hotel off O'Connell St*
A smartly decorated new hotel on the city side of the river, convenient for the shopping and business areas. Facilities include a spacious foyer, bar and restaurant, a boardroom for meetings and an elevator to all floors. Bedrooms are well equipped and offer good value, especially the family rooms. Staff are friendly and enthusiastic.
ROOMS: 151 en suite (108 fmly) No smoking in 56 bedrooms **FACILITIES:** STV entertainment **CONF:** Thtr 50 Class 25 Board 18 **SERVICES:** Lift **NOTES:** No dogs (ex guide dogs) Closed 24-26 Dec **CARDS:**

LISDOONVARNA, Co Clare

L

Restaurant with Rooms

Kincora Country House & Gallery Restaurant

☎ 065 7074300 065 7074490
e-mail: kincorahotel@eircom.net
Dir: *from town centre take Doolin Rd. House on 1st T-junct 200mtrs from town*
Family owned and run Kincora House has very comfortable bedrooms all with views of the garden or countryside beyond. The restaurant (which is also an art gallery) offers fine Irish cuisine using the best local ingredients.
ROOMS: 14 en suite (3 GF) No smoking in all bedrooms s €50-€120; d €80-€130 (incl. bkfst) **LB** **FACILITIES:** STV Art gallery **PARKING:** 15 **NOTES:** No dogs No children 10yrs No smoking in restaurant Closed Nov-Feb **CARDS:**

LISMORE, Co Waterford

Map 01 C2

★★66% *Ballyrafter House*

☎ 058 54002 058 53050
Dir: *1km from Lismore opposite Lismore Castle*

A welcoming country house, set in its own grounds opposite Lismore Castle. Inside, most of the bedrooms are pleasantly furnished in pine. The bar and conservatory are where guests, anglers and locals meet to discuss the day's events. The hotel has its own salmon fishing on the River Blackwater.
ROOMS: 10 en suite (1 fmly) **FACILITIES:** Fishing Riding Putting green **PARKING:** 20 **NOTES:** No dogs (ex guide dogs) Closed Nov-Feb **CARDS:**

LONDONDERRY, Co Londonderry

Map 01 C

★★★★70% Tower Hotel Derry

Off the Diamond BT48 6HL
☎ 028 7137 1000 028 7137 1234
e-mail: info@thd.ie
Dir: *From Craigavon Bridge into centre into Carlisle Rd. Hotel ahead*
This brand new, stylish hotel is proving to be a big hit with tourist and corporate guests alike. Modern bedrooms are furnished with flair and style and those on the upper floors enjoy super views of the city. Minimalistic day rooms include a popular bistro and staff in the contemporary bar provide true Irish hospitality.
ROOMS: 93 en suite (26 fmly) No smoking in 12 bedrooms s £55-£89; d £60-£110 (incl. bkfst) **LB** **FACILITIES:** STV Sauna Gym entertainmen **CONF:** BC Thtr 250 Class 150 Board 50 Del from £40 **SERVICES:** Lift **PARKING:** 25 **NOTES:** No dogs (ex guide dogs) Closed 24-27 Dec **CARDS:**

★★★★64% City Hotel

Queens Quay BT48 7AS
☎ 028 7136 5800
e-mail: res@derry-gsh.com
Dir: *Follow city centre signs. Hotel on waterfront adjacent to the Guildhall*
Occupying a central position overlooking the River Foyle, this contemporary hotel will appeal to business and leisure guests. The executive bedrooms are ideal for working and as with all rooms there are good facilities, including internet access. The open plan ground floor encourages relaxation, with the restaurant providing modern styled food.
ROOMS: 145 en suite (16 fmly) No smoking in 66 bedrooms s fr £65; d fr £85 (incl. bkfst) **LB** **FACILITIES:** Indoor swimming (H) Gym Jacuzz entertainment Xmas **CONF:** BC Thtr 350 Class 150 Board 80 Del from £80 **SERVICES:** Lift air con **PARKING:** 45 **NOTES:** No dogs Closed 24-27 Dec **CARDS:**

★★★★60% Everglades

Prehen Rd BT47 2NH
☎ 028 7132 1066 028 7134 9200
e-mail: res@egh.hastingshotels.com
Dir: *on A5, Omagh to Londonderry road, 1m from city*
This purpose built hotel, situated on the edge of the city, offers comfortable bedrooms, with family and inter-connecting rooms also available. Stylish open plan day rooms include a comfortable lounge and Library bar leading into the bright Satchmo restaurant.
ROOMS: 64 en suite (10 fmly) (20 GF) No smoking in 20 bedrooms s £55-£85; d £79-£110 (incl. bkfst) **FACILITIES:** STV Putting green **CONF:** Thtr 400 Class 150 Board 80 Del from £97 **SERVICES:** Lift air con **PARKING:** 200 **NOTES:** No dogs (ex guide dogs) RS 24-26 Dec **CARDS:**

★★★72% Beech Hill Country House Hotel

MANOR HOUSE

32 Ardmore Rd BT47 3QP
☎ 028 7134 9279 028 7134 5366
e-mail: info@beech-hill.com
Dir: *from A6 Londonderry-Belfast take Faughan Bridge turning and continue 1m to hotel opposite Ardmore Chapel*
Dating back to 1729, Beech Hill is an impressive mansion, standing in 32 acres of glorious woodlands and gardens. Traditionally styled

continued

day rooms provide deep comfort and ambitious cooking is served in the attractively extended dining room. The splendid bedroom wing provides spacious, well-equipped rooms, in addition to the more classically designed bedrooms in the main house.
ROOMS: 17 en suite 10 annexe en suite (4 fmly) s £70-£80; d £95-£120 (incl. bkfst) **LB FACILITIES:** Tennis (hard) Sauna Gym Jacuzzi Country walks **CONF:** Thtr 100 Class 50 Board 30 Del from £90 **SERVICES:** Lift **PARKING:** 75 **NOTES:** No dogs (ex guide dogs) No smoking in restaurant Closed 24-25 Dec **CARDS:**

★★★70% Quality Hotel Davincis

15 Culmore Rd BT48 8JB
☎ 028 7127 9111 📠 028 7127 9222
e-mail: info@davincishotel.com
Dir: *1m from city centre along Strand Rd, onto Culmore Rd, hotel on right*
Conveniently located just a mile north of the city centre, this stylish new hotel provides well-designed, spacious and well-equipped bedrooms, all with two double beds. The public areas include the popular Da Vinci's bar and restaurant offering light snacks and also innovative meals from a carte menu.
ROOMS: 67 en suite (4 fmly) (13 GF) No smoking in 26 bedrooms s £49.95-£80; d £49.95-£80 **LB FACILITIES:** STV entertainment **CONF:** Thtr 30 Class 30 Board 30 **SERVICES:** Lift **PARKING:** 100 **NOTES:** No dogs (ex guide dogs) Closed 25 Dec **CARDS:**

★★★66% White Horse

68 Clooney Rd, Campsie BT47 3PA
☎ 028 7186 0606 📠 028 7186 0371
e-mail: info@whitehorsehotel.biz
Dir: *on A2 5km from city centre & 1km from Derry City Airport*

The bedrooms at this privately-owned hotel and conference and leisure complex include full suites, family rooms and interconnecting rooms. All are spacious, modern and well equipped. They are complemented by bright, modern and spacious public areas. The extensive conference and function facilities and leisure & fitness centre are impressive.
ROOMS: 57 en suite (10 fmly) No smoking in 14 bedrooms s £60-£70; d £60-£80 (incl. bkfst) **LB FACILITIES:** STV Indoor swimming (H) Fishing Snooker Sauna Solarium Gym Jacuzzi Full health & leisure centre with beauty salon entertainment Xmas **CONF:** BC Thtr 500 Class 290 Board 120 Del from £70.30 **PARKING:** 200 **NOTES:** No dogs (ex guide dogs) **CARDS:**

⌂ Travelodge

Travelodge

22-24 Strand Rd BT47 2AB
☎ 08700 850 950 📠 01287 127 1277
e-mail: ifo@thetrinityhotel.com
Dir: *approx 0.5m from Guildhall adjacent to shopping centre/cinema*
Travelodge offers good quality, good value, modern accommodation. Ideal for families, the spacious, en suite bedrooms include remote-control TV, tea and coffee-making
continued

facilities, luxury beds and free morning newspaper. Meals can be taken at the nearby family restaurant. For further details and the Travelodge phone number, consult the Hotel Groups page.
ROOMS: 39 en suite (incl. bkfst) s fr £42.95; d fr £42.95 **CONF:** Thtr 70 Class 30 Board 25

LUCAN, Co Dublin — Map 01 D4

See also Dublin

★★★64% Lucan Spa

☎ 01 6280494 📠 01 6280841
e-mail: info@lucanspahotel.ie
Dir: *on N4, approx 11km from city centre, 20mins from Dublin airport*

Set in its own grounds, the Lucan Spa is a fine Georgian house. Guests have complimentary use of Lucan Golf Course, adjacent to the hotel. A conference centre is also available.
ROOMS: 71 rms (61 en suite) (15 fmly) No smoking in 21 bedrooms s €70-€90; d €120-€140 (incl. bkfst) **LB FACILITIES:** STV entertainment **CONF:** Thtr 600 Class 250 Board 80 **SERVICES:** Lift air con **PARKING:** 90 **NOTES:** No dogs (ex guide dogs) Closed 25-26 Dec **CARDS:**

MACREDDIN, Co Wicklow — Map 01 D3

★★★★74% ®® *Brooklodge at MacCreddin*

☎ 0402 36444 📠 0402 36580
e-mail: brooklodge@macreddin.ie
Dir: *N11 to Rathnew, R752 to Rathdrum, R753 to Aughrim follow signs to Macreddin*
Near the village of Aughrim, Brooklodge is a real find, where comfort predominates among restful lounges and well appointed bedrooms. The award-winning restaurant, The Strawberry Tree, is a truly romantic setting, specialising in organic and wild ingredients. The hotel also has its own microbrewery, smoke house and shop in the grounds.
ROOMS: 40 en suite (27 fmly) **FACILITIES:** STV Riding Snooker Archery Clay pigeon shooting Falconry Shiatsu Massage entertainment **CONF:** Thtr 260 Class 90 Board 40 **SERVICES:** Lift **PARKING:** 190 **CARDS:**

MACROOM, Co Cork — Map 01 B2

★★★67% ® Castle

IRISH COUNTRY HOTELS

Main St
☎ 026 41074 📠 026 41505
e-mail: castlehotel@eircom.net
Dir: *on N22 midway between Cork & Killarney*
The Castle Hotel contains a new leisure centre and some fine bedrooms. The hotel service is excellent and guests feel very much at home. There is a pleasant lounge and a function room, while
continued on p902

M

MACROOM, continued

the food in the restaurant and the bar is well-cooked and imaginatively presented.

Castle Hotel, Macroom

ROOMS: 60 en suite (6 fmly) s €89-€103; d €129-€155 (incl. bkfst) **LB** **FACILITIES: Spa** STV Indoor swimming (H) Gym Jacuzzi Steam Room, Swimming pool supervised entertainment **CONF:** Thtr 200 Class 80 Board 60 Del from €130 **SERVICES:** Lift air con **PARKING:** 30 **NOTES:** No dogs No smoking in restaurant Closed 24-28 Dec **CARDS:**

MAGHERA, Co Londonderry Map 01 C5

★★79% Ardtara Country House
8 Gorteade Rd, Upperlands BT46 5SA
☎ 028 7964 4490 028 7964 5080
e-mail: valerie@ardtara.fsbusiness.co.uk
Dir: *from Maghera take A29 towards Coleraine, in 2m take B75 for Kilrea through Upperlands, pass Wm Clark & Sons sign then next left*
Ardtara is a charming Victorian country house with extensive mature grounds. The stylish public rooms include a choice of lounges and a conservatory. The elegant dining room has period furnishings and is a perfect setting in which to enjoy the skilfully prepared cuisine. Bedrooms vary in style and size; all have been tastefully appointed.
ROOMS: 8 en suite (1 fmly) s £70-£90; d £100-£150 (incl. bkfst) **LB** **FACILITIES:** Tennis (hard) **CONF:** Thtr 45 Board 45 Del from £60 **PARKING:** 40 **NOTES:** No dogs (ex guide dogs) No smoking in restaurant Closed 25-26 Dec **CARDS:**

MALLOW, Co Cork Map 01 B2

Top 200 - Hotel

★★★ Longueville House
☎ 022 47156 & 47306 022 47459
e-mail: info@longuevillehouse.ie
RELAIS & CHATEAUX
Dir: *3m W of Mallow via N72 road to Killarney, right turn at Ballyclough junct, hotel entrance 200yds left*
This 18th-century Georgian mansion is set in a wooded estate on a 500-acre farm. The beautifully appointed bedrooms overlook the Backwater Valley. Two elegantly furnished sitting rooms feature fine examples of Italian plasterwork. William O'Callaghan's cuisine is served in the Presidents' Restaurant and newly restored Victorian Turner Conservatory, most ingredients are raised or grown on the farm, with fish from the river that runs through the estate.

ROOMS: 20 en suite (5 fmly) No smoking in 5 bedrooms d €170-€340 (incl. bkfst) **LB** **FACILITIES:** STV Fishing Croquet lawn **CONF:** Thtr 50 Class 30 Board 30 Del from €240 **PARKING:** 30 **NOTES:** No dogs (ex guide dogs) No smoking in restaurant Closed Xmas RS Nov - Feb **CARDS:**

★★★63% Springfort Hall Hotel
☎ 022 21278 022 21557
e-mail: stay@springfort-hall.com
Dir: *on Mallow/Limerick road N20, right turn off at 2 Pot House R581, hotel 500mtrs on right, sign over gate*
This 18th-century country manor is tucked away amid tranquil woodlands. There is an attractive oval dining room, as well as a drawing room and lounge bar. The spacious, comfortable bedrooms are mainly in the new wing and have superb country views.
ROOMS: 50 en suite (4 fmly) s €89-€102; d €140-€153 (incl. bkfst) **LB** **FACILITIES:** STV entertainment **CONF:** Thtr 300 Class 200 Board 50 Del from €130 **PARKING:** 200 **NOTES:** No dogs (ex guide dogs) Closed 23 Dec-2 Jan Civ Wed 250 **CARDS:**

MAYNOOTH, Co Kildare Map 01 C4

★★★75% Moyglare Manor
Moyglare
IRELAND'S BLUE BOOK
☎ 01 6286351 01 6285405
e-mail: info@moyglaremanor.ie
Dir: *turn off N4 at Maynooth/Naas, then right to Maynooth, left at T-junct. Keep right at St Marys Church and continue 2m then left at x-roads*
This elegant 18th-century house is a haven of calm, set in its own grounds in rich pasture land. Guests arrive along an imposing avenue and are greeted with genuine hospitality. Bedrooms are beautifully furnished in keeping with the Georgian style of the house, and there are several peaceful lounges and a convivial bar. The hotel cuisine has a justified high reputation.
ROOMS: 17 en suite (1 fmly) (2 GF) No smoking in 5 bedrooms s €140-€180; d fr €230 (incl. bkfst) **FACILITIES:** STV Tennis entertainment Xmas **CONF:** Thtr 30 Board 20 Del from €200 **PARKING:** 120 **NOTES:** No dogs (ex guide dogs) No children 12yrs No smoking in restaurant Closed 24-26 Dec **CARDS:**

MIDLETON, Co Cork Map 01 C2

★★★68% *Midleton Park*
☎ 021 4631767 021 4631605
e-mail: info@midletonparkhotel.ie
Dir: *from Cork, turn off N25 hotel on right. From Waterford, turn off N25, over bridge until T-junct, turn right, hotel on right*
This refurbished, purpose-built hotel is situated just off the N25

continued

Cork/Rosslare route, ten miles from Cork and convenient for golf courses and other attractions. The hotel features fine, spacious and well appointed bedrooms, and the comfortable restaurant offers good food and attentive service. Conference and banqueting facilities are available, and there is a health club offering alternative treatments and therapies.
ROOMS: 40 en suite (12 fmly) No smoking in 6 bedrooms
FACILITIES: STV **CONF:** Thtr 400 Class 200 Board 40 **SERVICES:** air con **PARKING:** 500 **NOTES:** No dogs (ex guide dogs) Closed 25 Dec
CARDS:

MONAGHAN, Co Monaghan Map 01 C5

★★★★61% **Hillgrove**
Old Armagh Rd
☎ 047 81288 📠 047 84951
e-mail: hillgrovegm@quinn-hotels.com
Dir: *turn off N2 at Cathedral, 400mtrs, on left*
This modern hotel on the outskirts of the town offers spacious bedrooms that comfortable and well equipped. A number of dining options is available, together with a popular bar. A night-club operates at week-ends.
ROOMS: 44 en suite (3 fmly) (9 GF) No smoking in 7 bedrooms s €77-€85; d €150-€190 (incl. bkfst) **LB FACILITIES:** STV Jacuzzi entertainment Xmas **CONF:** Thtr 1200 Class 600 Board 200 Del from €110 **SERVICES:** Lift air con **PARKING:** 430 **NOTES:** No dogs (ex guide dogs) Closed 25 Dec **CARDS:**

MULLINGAR, Co Westmeath Map 01 C4

Restaurant with Rooms

Crookedwood House
Crookedwood ROI
☎ 044 72165 📠 044 72166
e-mail: info@crookedwoodhouse.com
Dir: *From Dublin take exit off Mullingar Bypass, continue to Crookedwood, at Wood Pub turn right and continue for 2km*
As charming as its name, this beautifully restored old rectory overlooks Lake Derravaragh and offers exceptionally comfortable bedrooms. There is also an inviting lounge where tea is served and a bar for drinks before dinner. The evening meals are the highlight of a stay here and have earned much praise for chef/patron Niall Kenny.
ROOMS: 8 en suite s €70-€82; d €120-€150 (incl. bkfst) **LB FACILITIES:** STV Tennis (hard) Croquet lawn Basketball **SERVICES:** air con **PARKING:** 10 **NOTES:** No smoking in restaurant Closed Xmas
CARDS:

NAAS, Co Kildare Map 01 D3

★★★★69% ***Killashee House***
☎ 045 879277 📠 045 887490
e-mail: reservations@killasheehouse.com
Dir: *N7, then straight through town on Old Kilcullen Rd(R448), hotel on left, 1.5m from centre of Naas*
This Victorian manor house set in 80 acres of woodland and landscaped gardens, has been very sucessfully converted to a hotel, with excellent conference facilities, which do not impinge on the comfort of individual travellers. A Country Club is also available to residents.
ROOMS: 84 en suite (6 fmly) No smoking in 16 bedrooms
FACILITIES: STV Indoor swimming (H) Sauna Solarium Gym Croquet lawn Jacuzzi Archery Biking Clay pigeon shooting entertainment
CONF: Thtr 1600 Class 144 Board 84 **SERVICES:** Lift **PARKING:** 500
NOTES: No dogs (ex guide dogs) Closed 25-26 Dec
CARDS:

NAVAN, Co Meath Map 01 C4

★★★64% ***Ardboyne Hotel***
Dublin Rd
☎ 046 902 3119 📠 046 902 2355
e-mail: ardboyne@quinn-hotels.com
Dir: *from Dublin-N3 N through Blanchards Town to Navan, hotel on left*
This welcoming hotel is situated on the edge of Navan. Bedrooms are comfortably furnished and freshly decorated, and overlook pretty gardens. Public areas are smartly furnished and include an inviting lounge warmed by an open fire, a well-appointed dining room and a saloon style bar. Conference suites are available.
ROOMS: 29 en suite (25 fmly) No smoking in 10 bedrooms
FACILITIES: STV Leisure centre due for completion during 2003 entertainment **CONF:** Thtr 400 Class 200 Board 150 **PARKING:** 186
NOTES: No dogs (ex guide dogs) Closed 24-26 Dec
CARDS:

NENAGH, Co Tipperary Map 01 B3

★★★72% ***Abbey Court Hotel, Conference & Leisure Club***
Dublin Rd
☎ 067 41111 📠 067 41022
e-mail: info@abbeycourt.ie
Dir: *near O'Connor's Shopping Centre on Dublin side of town bypass from Dublin & Limerick*

This handsome hotel, constructed from mellow brick with a cut stone entrance, has been extensively developed in recent years to include smart bedrooms, a restaurant and a well-designed leisure centre. Other public areas include a bar, lounge, and conference and banqueting suites.
ROOMS: 82 en suite (3 fmly) No smoking in 10 bedrooms
FACILITIES: Spa STV Indoor swimming (H) Sauna Gym entertainment ch fac **CONF:** Thtr 600 Class 150 Board 60 **SERVICES:** Lift air con
PARKING: 200 **NOTES:** No dogs (ex guide dogs)
CARDS:

NEWBRIDGE, Co Kildare Map 01 C3

★★★74% ***Keadeen***
☎ 045 431666 📠 045 434402
e-mail: keadeen@iol.ie
Dir: *M7 junct 10, (Newbridge, Curragh) at rdbt follow to right towards Newbridge, hotel on left 1km from rdbt*
This family-owned hotel is set in eight acres of landscaped gardens. Comfortable public areas include a spacious drawing room, reception foyer and two bars. The hotel is well placed for Dublin Airport and the Mondello racing circuit.
ROOMS: 73 en suite (4 fmly) No smoking in 5 bedrooms
FACILITIES: STV Indoor swimming (H) Sauna Solarium Gym Jacuzzi Aerobics studio Treatment room Massage entertainment **CONF:** Thtr 800 Class 300 Board 40 **PARKING:** 200 **NOTES:** No dogs (ex guide dogs) Closed 24 Dec-2 Jan RS low season **CARDS:**

N

NEWCASTLE, Co Down

Map 01 D5

★★★★61% Slieve Donard

Downs Rd BT33 0AH
☎ 028 4372 1066 028 4372 4830
e-mail: res@sdh.hastingshotels.com
Dir: *take A2 from Belfast N & join A55 then onto A24. At Clough road take A2 follow to Newcastle. In town centre bear left onto Downs Road*

Situated at the foot of the Mourne Mountains in six acres of gardens, many rooms in this grand Victorian hotel enjoy splendid views. The bedrooms are comfortable and public areas include a choice of lounges. In addition to the wood-panelled Oak Room Restaurant, there is a grill and a bar for informal dining.

ROOMS: 126 en suite (45 fmly) (3 GF) No smoking in 20 bedrooms s £120-£140; d £175-£210 (incl. bkfst) **LB** **FACILITIES:** STV Indoor swimming (H) Sauna Solarium Gym Croquet lawn Putting green Jacuzzi Swimming pool supervised entertainment Xmas **CONF:** BC Thtr 825 Class 250 Board 70 Del £150 **SERVICES:** Lift **PARKING:** 1000 **NOTES:** No dogs (ex guide dogs) **CARDS:**

★★67% *Enniskeen House*

98 Bryansford Rd BT33 0LF
☎ 028 4372 2392 028 4372 4084
e-mail: info@enniskeen-hotel.demon.co.uk
Dir: *from town centre follow signs for Tollymore Forest Park, hotel 1m on left*

Set in ten acres of grounds and delightful gardens, the atmosphere at this hotel is enhanced by its thoughtful staff. Bedrooms vary but all are well equipped. Many enjoy super views of the surrounding mountains and countryside. The formal dining room serves traditional cuisine and the first-floor lounge makes the most of the coastal views.

ROOMS: 12 en suite (1 fmly) No smoking in 3 bedrooms **CONF:** Thtr 60 Class 24 **SERVICES:** Lift **PARKING:** 45 **NOTES:** No dogs No smoking in restaurant Closed 12 Nov-14 Mar
CARDS:

NEWMARKET-ON-FERGUS, Co Clare

Map 01 B3

Top 200 - Hotel

★★★★★ Dromoland Castle

☎ 061 368144 061 363355
e-mail: sales@dromoland.ie
Dir: *from Shannon take N18 towards Galway, take left signed 'Dromdand Interchange'*

Described as a 'very large, early 18th-century, gothic revival, castellated, irregular, multi-towered ashlar castle'. Dromoland stands on a 375-acre estate and offers extensive indoor leisure and outdoor pursuits. The spacious, thoughtfully equipped and richly decorated bedrooms provide excellent levels of comfort. Magnificent public areas, warmed by log fires, are no less impressive. The hotel has two restaurants, the elegant fine dining Earl of Thomond, and less formal Fig Tree.

ROOMS: 100 en suite (20 fmly) s €204-€370; d €204-€370 **LB** **FACILITIES:** STV Indoor swimming (H) Golf 18 Tennis (hard) Fishing Snooker Sauna Solarium Gym Putting green Jacuzzi Beauty clinic, archery, clay shooting, mountain bikes, row boats swimming pool supervised entertainment Xmas **CONF:** BC Thtr 450 Class 220 Board 80 **PARKING:** 120 **NOTES:** No dogs (ex guide dogs) No smoking in restaurant **CARDS:**

NEW ROSS, Co Wexford

Map 01 C3

★★★67% The Cedar Lodge Hotel & Restaurant

Carrigbyrne, Newbawn
☎ 051 428386 051 428222
e-mail: cedarlodge@eircom.net
Dir: *On N25*

Cedar Lodge sits in a tranquil setting beneath the slopes of Carrigbyrne Forest, just a 30-minute drive from Rosslare Port. The Martin family extend warm hospitality and provide good food in the charming conservatory restaurant with its central log fire. There are comfortable lounges and bedrooms are spacious, thoughtfully appointed and decorated, and all overlook the attractive landscaped gardens.

ROOMS: 28 en suite (2 fmly) (12 GF) s €110-€130; d €200-€210 (incl. bkfst) **LB** **FACILITIES:** entertainment **CONF:** Thtr 100 Class 60 Board 60 Del from €100 **PARKING:** 100 **NOTES:** No dogs (ex guide dogs) No smoking in restaurant Closed 21 Dec-1 Jan **CARDS:**

NEWTOWNMOUNTKENNEDY, Co Wicklow

Map 01 D3

U Druids Glen Marriott Hotel & Country Club

☎ 01 2870800 2870801
e-mail: reservations.druids@marriotthotels.com
Dir: *From Dublin take N11/H11, through Kilmacanoque to junct for Newtownmountkennedy, left and follow signs for hotel*

At the time of going to press, the star classification for this hotel was not confirmed. Please refer to the AA internet site www.theAA.com for current information.

ROOMS: 148 en suite (80 fmly) No smoking in 111 bedrooms s €125-€185; d €150-€210 (incl. bkfst) **LB** **FACILITIES:** Indoor swimming (H) Outdoor swimming (H) Golf 36 Sauna Solarium Gym Putting green Jacuzzi entertainment Xmas **CONF:** Thtr 300 Class 220 Board 54 Del from €265 **SERVICES:** Lift air con **PARKING:** 350 **NOTES:** No dogs (ex guide dogs) **CARDS:**

PARKNASILLA, Co Kerry

Map 01 A2

★★★★75% Great Southern

☎ 064 45122 064 45323
e-mail: res@parknasilla-gsh.com
Dir: *on Kenmare road 3km from Sneem*

This delightful hotel which has been in business for over a hundred years, is a popular haven of relaxation and rejuvenation for generations of Irish families. There are many spacious lounges, that together with the restaurant and many of the bedrooms, have

continued

wonderful sea views. Service is warm and friendly, underpinned by smooth professionalism.

ROOMS: 24 en suite 59 annexe en suite (6 fmly) No smoking in 11 bedrooms s €230-€250; d €230-€250 **LB** **FACILITIES: Spa** STV Indoor swimming (H) Golf 12 Tennis (hard) Fishing Riding Snooker Sauna Croquet lawn Putting green Jacuzzi Bike hire, Windsurfing, Clay pigeon shooting, Archery, Swimming pool supervised entertainment Xmas **CONF:** BC Thtr 100 Class 80 Board 20 **SERVICES:** Lift **PARKING:** 60 **NOTES:** No dogs (ex guide dogs) **CARDS:**

See advert on opposite page

PORTAFERRY, Co Down — Map 01 D5

★★★69% *Portaferry*

10 The Strand BT22 1PE
☎ 028 4272 8231 028 4272 8999
e-mail: info@portaferryhotel.com
Dir: *opposite ferry terminal*

This smartly presented, popular hotel enjoys a central location on the quayside and boasts a superb panorama of Strangford Lough. Bedrooms vary in size and style and are particularly well equipped. Day rooms include a cosy lounge and split level dining room, whilst snacks can be enjoyed in the informal bar. Hospitality here is especially warm and staff are keen to please.

ROOMS: 14 en suite **FACILITIES:** STV **CONF:** Board 14 **PARKING:** 6 **NOTES:** No dogs (ex guide dogs) Closed 24-25 Dec **CARDS:**

PORTBALLINTRAE, Co Antrim — Map 01 C6

★★★68% Bayview

2 Bayhead Rd BT57 8RZ
☎ 028 2073 4100 028 2073 4330
e-mail: info@bayviewhotelni.com
Dir: *M2 then A26 to Ballymena, onto B62 to Portrush, after approx 7m turn right onto B17 to Bushmills. Turn left then immediate right to Portballintrae*

This modern, purpose-built hotel commands excellent views of the bay, beach and harbour. Bedrooms are thoughtfully appointed and well equipped. They include rooms for less able guests, family rooms, interconnecting rooms and no smoking rooms. Public areas are bright and pleasant and the hotel has rooms for conferences and meetings.

ROOMS: 25 en suite (12 fmly) No smoking in 2 bedrooms s £50-£89; d £50-£95 (incl. bkfst) **LB** **FACILITIES:** entertainment **CONF:** Thtr 40 Class 30 Board 20 Del from £65 **SERVICES:** Lift **PARKING:** 25 **NOTES:** No dogs (ex guide dogs) **CARDS:**

P

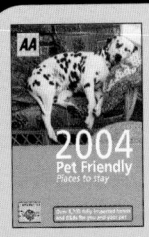

PORTMARNOCK, Co Dublin Map 01 D4

Top 200 - Hotel

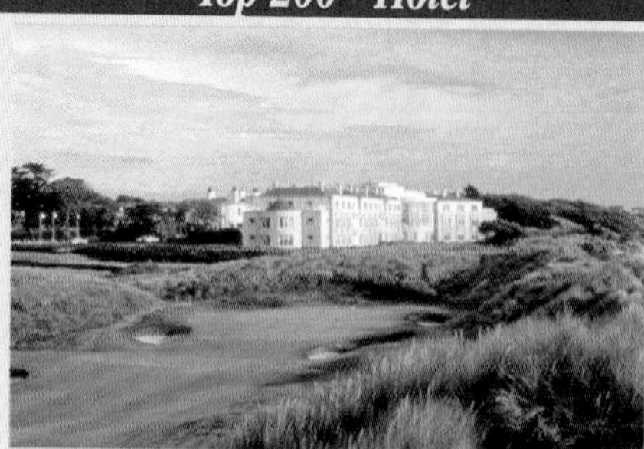

★★★★ ◎◎◎ **Portmarnock Hotel & Golf Links**
Strand Rd
☎ 01 8460611 📠 01 8462442
e-mail: sales@portmarnock.com
Dir: *Dublin Airport-N1, rdbt 1st exit, 2nd rdbt 2nd exit, next rdbt 3rd exit, T-junct turn left, over crossroads and continue, hotel is left past the Strand*

This 19th-century former home of the Jameson whiskey family is now a well run and smartly presented hotel, enjoys a superb location overlooking the sea and the PGA Championship Golf Links. Bedrooms are modern and equipped to high standard, public areas are spacious and very comfortable. The Osborne Restaurant comes highly recommended and a team of friendly staff goes out of their way to welcome guests.

ROOMS: 99 en suite No smoking in 5 bedrooms s fr €220; d fr €295 (incl. bkfst) **LB FACILITIES: Spa** STV Golf 18 Sauna Gym Putting green Beauty therapist Xmas **CONF:** BC Thtr 300 Class 110 Board 80 Del from €195 **SERVICES:** Lift **PARKING:** 200 **NOTES:** No dogs (ex guide dogs) **CARDS:**

PORTRUSH, Co Antrim Map 01 C6

★★★70% **The Royal Court**
233 Ballybogey Rd BT56 8NF
☎ 028 7082 2236 📠 028 7082 3176
e-mail: royalcourthotel@aol.com
Dir: *from Ballymena N on M2 to Ballymoney rdbt. Take 3rd exit to Portrush on B62. Hotel at end of road*

Located to the east of the town, this modern, comfortable hotel enjoys panoramic, coastal views of the East Strand beach, Donegal and the Scottish Islands. Bedrooms are spacious, and many have balconies offering superb views. Extensive menus served in the restaurant and informal bar make good use of creative, wholesome cooking.

ROOMS: 18 en suite (10 fmly) s £45-£90; d £70-£90 (incl. bkfst) **LB FACILITIES:** STV Xmas **CONF:** Thtr 300 Class 150 Board 50 Del from £72 **PARKING:** 200 **NOTES:** No dogs (ex guide dogs) Closed 26 Dec **CARDS:**

€ Don't forget, the Euro is now the unit of currency in the Republic of Ireland

PORTUMNA, Co Galway Map 01 B

★★★66% ***Shannon Oaks Hotel & Country Club***
St Joseph Rd
☎ 090 974 1777 📠 090 974 1357
e-mail: sales@shannonoaks.ie

THE INDEPENDENTS

Situated in eight acres of grounds on the edge of Portumna National Forest, this newy rebuilt hotel has a comfortable lounge, restaurant and bar where live entertainment takes place regularly. Spacious bedrooms are air conditioned and well equipped. There is an indoor pool, fitness centre, and conference and banqueting facilities.

ROOMS: 63 en suite **FACILITIES:** STV Indoor swimming (H) Tennis (hard) Sauna Solarium Gym Jacuzzi entertainment **CONF:** Thtr 600 Class 320 Board 280 **SERVICES:** Lift air con **PARKING:** 360 **NOTES:** No dogs (ex guide dogs) **CARDS:**

RATHMULLAN, Co Donegal Map 01 C6

★★★75% ◎◎ **Fort Royal**
Fort Royal
☎ 074 915 8100 📠 074 915 8103
e-mail: fortroyal@eircom.net
Dir: *take R245 from Letterkenny, through Rathmullan, hotel is signposted*

MANOR HOUSE

On the shores of Lough Swilly, this period house stands in 18 acres of grounds and has private access to a secluded beach. The sitting room is a restful place overlooking the sea. Enjoyable meals are served in the restaurant, and the bar is inviting. Bedrooms are attractively decorated.

ROOMS: 11 en suite 4 annexe en suite (3 fmly) s €102-€115; d €144-€170 (incl. bkfst) **LB FACILITIES:** Golf 9 Tennis (hard) Croquet lawn **PARKING:** 40 **NOTES:** No smoking in restaurant Closed Nov-Etr **CARDS:**

RATHNEW, Co Wicklow

Map 01 D3

★★★★69%

Tinakilly Country House & Restaurant

☎ 0404 69274 🖷 0404 67806

e-mail: reservations@tinakilly.ie

Dir: *follow the N11/M11 to Rathnew onto R750 towards Wicklow. Entrance to hotel approx 500mtrs from the village on left*

This fine hospitable hotel is situated on an elevated site up a tree lined avenue, with fine views of the Irish Sea and Broadlaugh bird sanctuary. It is full of Victorian charm, but with all the modern facilities expected of a four-star hotel today. The food served is described as country-house style, with a strong emphasis on seasonality.

ROOMS: 51 en suite s €102-€315; d €204-€630 (incl. bkfst) **LB** **FACILITIES:** STV Tennis (hard) Gym Croquet lawn 7 acres of gardens mapped for walking **CONF:** Thtr 65 Class 48 Board 41 **SERVICES:** Lift **PARKING:** 60 **NOTES:** No dogs (ex guide dogs) No smoking in restaurant Closed 24-26 Dec **CARDS:**

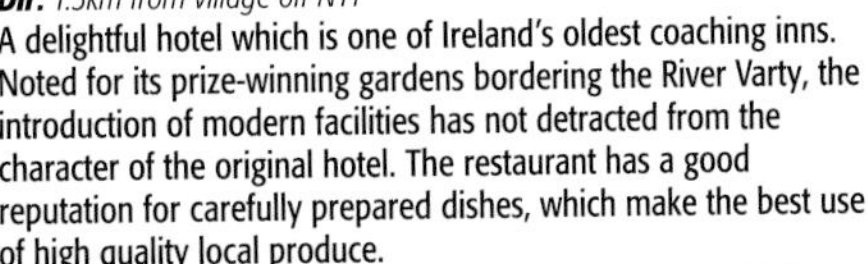

★★★67%

Hunter's

☎ 0404 40106 🖷 0404 40338

e-mail: reception@hunters.ie

Dir: *1.5km from village off N11*

A delightful hotel which is one of Ireland's oldest coaching inns. Noted for its prize-winning gardens bordering the River Varty, the introduction of modern facilities has not detracted from the character of the original hotel. The restaurant has a good reputation for carefully prepared dishes, which make the best use of high quality local produce.

ROOMS: 16 en suite (2 fmly) (2 GF) s fr €95; d fr €190 (incl. bkfst) **CONF:** Thtr 40 Class 40 Board 16 Del from €150 **PARKING:** 50 **NOTES:** No dogs (ex guide dogs) No smoking in restaurant Closed 24-26 Dec **CARDS:**

RECESS, Co Galway

Map 01 A4

★★★★74%

Ballynahinch Castle

☎ 095 31006 🖷 095 31085

e-mail: bhinch@iol.ie

Dir: *W from Galway on N59 towards Clifden. After Recess take Roundstone turn to left, 4km from turn off*

Open log fires and friendly professional service are just some of the delights of staying at this castle property that originates from the 16th century. Set among 350 acres of woodland, rivers and lakes, many of the suites and rooms have stunning views, as does the award-winning restaurant.

ROOMS: 40 en suite No smoking in 4 bedrooms **FACILITIES:** STV Tennis (hard) Fishing Croquet lawn River & Lakeside walks entertainment **CONF:** Thtr 30 Class 20 Board 20 **PARKING:** 55 **NOTES:** No dogs (ex guide dogs) Closed Feb & 20-26 Dec **CARDS:**

★★★77%

Lough Inagh Lodge

Inagh Valley

☎ 095 34706 & 34694 🖷 095 34708

e-mail: inagh@iol.ie

Dir: *after Recess take R344 towards Kylemore through Inagh valley, hotel in middle of valley*

This 19th-century former hunting lodge is now a luxurious hotel in the centre of Inagh Valley. Its setting, fronted by a good fishing lake, includes lovely mountain views. Large lounges and an oak-lined bar provide warmth and comfort, and the spacious bedrooms are beautifully furnished. The food is a highlight of any stay here.

ROOMS: 12 en suite (4 GF) s €110-€129; d €178-€213 (incl. bkfst) **LB** **FACILITIES:** STV Fishing Hill walking, Fly fishing, Cycling **CONF:** Thtr 20 Class 20 Board 20 **SERVICES:** air con **PARKING:** 16 **NOTES:** No smoking in restaurant Closed mid Dec - mid Mar **CARDS:**

RENVYLE, Co Galway

Map 01 A4

★★★66%

Renvyle House Hotel

☎ 095 43511 🖷 095 43515

e-mail: renvyle@iol.ie

Dir: *N59 W of Galway towards Clifden Pass through Oughterard & Maam Cross, at Recess turn right, Kylemore turn left, Letterfrack turn right, hotel 5m*

This historic country house sits between the mountains and the ocean on the unspoilt coast of Connemara. Spacious comfortable lounges and turf fires combined with friendly staff make a stay here relaxing and memorable. Bedrooms vary in size and are well equipped with spectacular views. Good leisure facilities include hard tennis courts, a snooker room, an outdoor pool, and a 9-hole golf course.

ROOMS: 68 en suite (8 fmly) No smoking in 5 bedrooms s €30-€115; d €60-€230 (incl. bkfst) **LB** **FACILITIES:** STV Outdoor swimming (H) Golf 9 Tennis (hard) Fishing Riding Snooker Croquet lawn Putting green Archery, Clay pigeon shooting entertainment ch fac Xmas **CONF:** Thtr 200 Class 80 Board 80 Del from €80 **PARKING:** 60 **NOTES:** No smoking in restaurant Closed 6 Jan-14 Feb **CARDS:**

ROSCOMMON, Co Roscommon

Map 01 B4

★★★65%

Abbey

Galway Rd

☎ 090 662 6240 🖷 090 662 6021

e-mail: sales@abbeyhotel.ie

Dir: *in Roscommon town, follow Galway Road, hotel first left after library*

Set in its own grounds just outside Roscommon, this fine manor house dates back over 100 years. The bedrooms are well-decorated, with a choice of period style rooms in the original

continued on p908

R

ROSCOMMON, continued

part of the house, or more contemporary rooms in the newer wing. Service is attentive and the hotel has a friendly atmosphere.
ROOMS: 50 en suite (4 fmly) (10 GF) No smoking in 35 bedrooms s €75-€85; d €140-€150 (incl. bkfst) **LB** **FACILITIES:** Indoor swimming (H) Sauna Solarium Gym Jacuzzi Swimming pool supervised Xmas **CONF:** Thtr 250 Class 160 Board 60 **SERVICES:** Lift **PARKING:** 150 **NOTES:** No dogs (ex guide dogs) Closed 25-26 Dec
CARDS:

ROSSCARBERY, Co Cork Map 01 B2

★★★69% Celtic Ross

☎ 023 48722 🖷 023 48723
e-mail: info@celticrosshotel.com
Dir: *take N71 out of Cork city, through Bandon towards Clonakilty. Follow signs for Skibbereen, hotel on main road*

Overlooking a lagoon, on the edge of a peaceful village, this hotel is a striking landmark on the West Cork coastline. The spacious public areas are luxuriously appointed with rich fabrics and polished Irish elm, yew bog oakwood and cherrywood. There is a cocktail bar and an Irish pub where a lunchtime carvery is on offer.
ROOMS: 66 en suite (30 fmly) No smoking in 10 bedrooms s €97-€122; d €140-€190 (incl. bkfst) **FACILITIES:** STV Indoor swimming (H) Sauna Gym Steam room, bubble pool, video rentals, Swimming pool supervised entertainment **CONF:** Thtr 300 Class 80 Board 40 Del from €125 **SERVICES:** Lift air con **PARKING:** 200 **NOTES:** No dogs (ex guide dogs) No smoking in restaurant Closed mid Jan - mid Feb
CARDS:

ROSSLARE, Co Wexford Map 01 D2

Top 200 - Hotel

★★★★ ◎◎ *Kelly's Resort*

☎ 053 32114 🖷 053 32222
e-mail: kellyhot@iol.ie
Dir: *10m from Wexford town, turn off N25 on the Rosslare/Wexford road*
The Kelly's have run this truly fine resort hotel since 1895. Family-friendly it is adjacent to the beach and the village center. Bedrooms are thoughtfully equipped and comfortably furnished. Extensive public areas include both indoor and outdoor leisure facilities, inviting lounges, a smart leisure club, health treatments, tennis, children's crèche and spacious gardens. La Marine Bistro is the setting for good modern
continued
cuisine while the newly refurbished Beeches restaurant serves award-winning food.

ROOMS: 99 annexe en suite (15 fmly) **FACILITIES:** STV Indoor swimming (H) Tennis (hard) Squash Snooker Sauna Solarium Gym Croquet lawn Jacuzzi Bowls Plunge pool Badminton Crazy golf Outdoor Canadian hot tub entertainment ch fac **CONF:** Thtr 30 Class 30 Board 20 **SERVICES:** Lift **PARKING:** 99 **NOTES:** No dogs Closed mid Dec-late Feb **CARDS:**

★★★64% Crosbie Cedars

☎ 053 32124 🖷 053 32243
e-mail: info@crosbiecedars.iol.ie
Dir: *turn off N25 at Ashfield crossroads. Follow brown signs at cross for Rosslare village. Take 1st left, hotel on right*

This hotel is within walking distance of miles of safe, sandy beach, championship golf links and many other activities. The attractive foyer features a white baby grand piano, and there is a choice of bars - the relaxing Tavern Bar and Library, and Bunkers which provides entertainment at weekends. Bedrooms are well equipped, bright and spacious.
ROOMS: 34 en suite (28 fmly) (10 GF) s €62-€85; d €90-€136 (incl. bkfst) **LB** **FACILITIES:** STV Tennis entertainment **CONF:** Thtr 250 Class 70 Board 70 Del from €109 **SERVICES:** Lift **PARKING:** 157 **NOTES:** No dogs (ex guide dogs) Closed 24-25 Dec RS January
CARDS:

ROSSNOWLAGH, Co Donegal Map 01 B5

★★★78% ◎◎ Sand House

MANOR HOUSE

☎ 071 985 1777 🖷 071 985 2100
e-mail: info@sandhouse-hotel.ie
Dir: *on coast road from Donegal to Ballyshannon in the centre of Donegal Bay*
Set in a crescent of golden sands five miles north of Ballyshannon, this hotel is well known for its hospitality, good cuisine and
continued

R

service. Many rooms have sea views and a conservatory lounge provides a relaxing retreat.

ROOMS: 55 en suite (6 fmly) No smoking in 15 bedrooms s €80-€120; d €160-€280 (incl. bkfst) **LB FACILITIES: Spa** STV Tennis (hard) Sauna Solarium Croquet lawn Putting green Jacuzzi Mini-golf Surfing Canoeing Sailing entertainment **CONF:** Thtr 60 Class 40 Board 30 **SERVICES:** Lift **PARKING:** 42 **NOTES:** No smoking in restaurant Closed Dec & Jan **CARDS:**

ROUNDSTONE, Co Galway

Map 01 A4

★★70% *Eldons*

☎ 095 35933 & 35942 095 35871
e-mail: eldonshotel@eircom.net
Dir: *off N59 through Toombedla then left to village*

This distinctive building stands on the main street of a picturesque fishing village. Guests are assured a warm welcome at this hotel, along with good service. The seafood restaurant, Bedla, serves a good choice of dishes.

ROOMS: 13 en suite 6 annexe en suite (2 fmly) **FACILITIES:** entertainment **SERVICES:** Lift **NOTES:** No dogs Closed 4 Nov-16 Mar **CARDS:**

SALTHILL See Galway

SHANNON, Co Clare

Map 01 B3

★★★60% Comfort Inn Shannon

Ballycasey
☎ 061 364588 061 364045
e-mail: info@shannon.comfortinns.ie
Dir: *3m from Shannon International Airport*

This friendly hotel conveniently situated just three miles from Shannon Airport and is close to Bunratty Castle. It offers contemporary styled bedrooms, the Old Lodge bar and themed restaurant and meeting rooms.

ROOMS: 54 en suite (3 fmly) No smoking in 10 bedrooms s €59-€99; d €59-€129 **LB FACILITIES:** STV entertainment **CONF:** Thtr 20 Class 12 Board 12 **SERVICES:** Lift **PARKING:** 130 **NOTES:** No dogs (ex guide dogs) Closed 24-26 Dec **CARDS:**

SKERRIES, Co Dublin

Map 01 D4

Restaurant with Rooms

Redbank House & Restaurant

THE INDEPENDENTS

5-7 Church St ROI
☎ 01 8491005 8490439 01 8491598
e-mail: redbank@eircom.net
Dir: *N1 north past the airport & bypass Swords. 3m N at the end of dual carriageway at Esso station right towards Rush, Lusk & Skerries*

Adjacent to the well-known restaurant of the same name, this comfortable double fronted period town house has two reception rooms, en suite bedrooms and a secluded garden. The restaurant is the setting for quality local produce used with an emphasis on fresh fish in imaginative cooking, served by friendly and attentive staff.

ROOMS: 7 en suite 5 annexe en suite (12 fmly) **FACILITIES:** STV **PARKING:** 4 **NOTES:** No dogs (ex guide dogs) Closed 24-28 Dec **CARDS:**

SKIBBEREEN, Co Cork

Map 01 B2

★★65% Eldon

Bridge St
☎ 028 22000 028 22191
e-mail: welcome@eldon-hotel.ie
Dir: *On N71 W to Skibbereen, follow one-way system, turn right at end of Townsend St. Hotel 100yds on right*

Good food, good drink and good company can all be found here. The atmosphere at this family run hotel is friendly, there is a comfortable bar with patio gardens, and car parking to the rear of the hotel.

ROOMS: 19 en suite No smoking in 4 bedrooms s €55-€110; d €110-€220 (incl. bkfst) **LB FACILITIES:** use of local leisure centre entertainment **PARKING:** 40 **NOTES:** Closed 24-27 Dec **CARDS:**

SLANE, Co Meath

Map 01 D4

★★★61% *Conyngham Arms*

IRISH COUNTRY HOTELS

☎ 041 9884444 041 9824205
Dir: *from N2 turn onto N51, hotel is 20mtrs on the left*

Situated in a picturesque village near the famous prehistoric tombs of New Grange, this hotel has very comfortable public rooms including the unique Estate Agent's Restaurant. There are attractive gardens and this is an ideal location from which to explore the historic area including Tara and the Boyne Valley. Bedrooms are well presented.

ROOMS: 16 en suite (4 fmly) **FACILITIES:** STV **CONF:** Thtr 150 Class 120 **PARKING:** 12 **NOTES:** No dogs (ex guide dogs) **CARDS:**

AA Rosette Award for culinary excellence

SLIGO, Co Sligo

Map 01 B5

★★★71% Sligo Park

Pearse Rd
☎ 071 916 0291 071 916 9556
e-mail: sligopk@leehotels.com
Dir: *on N4 1m from Sligo on Dublin Road*

Set in seven acres on the southern side of the town, this hotel is well positioned for touring the many attractions of the north-west and Yeates' country. Modern facilities are found in comfortable bedrooms which have been under refurbishment in recent years.

continued on p910

S

SLIGO, continued

A good leisure centre is also available to guests. A new banqueting centre is due to open by the end of 2003.
ROOMS: 110 en suite No smoking in 4 bedrooms s €85-€101; d €138-€170 **LB** **FACILITIES:** Indoor swimming (H) Tennis (hard) Snooker Sauna Solarium Gym Jacuzzi Steam room Plunge pool Swimming pool supervised entertainment Xmas **CONF:** Thtr 520 Class 350 Board 50 Del from €120 **PARKING:** 200 **NOTES:** No dogs (ex guide dogs) No smoking in restaurant RS 24-26 & 31 Dec **CARDS:**

★★★64% *Tower*

Quay St
☎ 071 914 4000 📠 071 914 6888
e-mail: towersl@iol.ie
Dir: *in the centre of Sligo*

Pleasantly located beside the quay, this attractively furnished hotel is right in the town centre. There is a smart foyer lounge, a pleasant restaurant and bar; the bedrooms are comfortable and well equipped. Guests have access to the local leisure and fitness centre at reduced rates.
ROOMS: 58 en suite No smoking in 12 bedrooms **CONF:** Thtr 200 Class 60 Board 50 **SERVICES:** Lift air con **PARKING:** 20 **NOTES:** No dogs (ex guide dogs) No smoking in restaurant Closed 24-28 Dec
CARDS:

SPANISH POINT, Co Clare — Map 01 B3

★★★64% Burkes Armada

☎ 065 7084110 📠 065 7084632
e-mail: info@burkesarmadahotel.com
Dir: *N18 from Ennis take N85 Inagh, then R460 to Miltown Malbay. Follow signs for Spanish Point*
Situated on the edge of the coast overlooking the breaking waves and golden sands, this hotel is in a natural, unspoiled environment. Public areas benefit from the stunning location, especially the contemporary restaurant and patio. Bedrooms are spacious and attractively decorated, most rooms are sea-facing. Fishing and pitch-and-putt are available nearby, and there are two championship golf courses within half an hour's drive.
ROOMS: 61 en suite (53 fmly) s €55-€90; d €80-€150 (incl. bkfst) **LB** **FACILITIES:** STV Gym Xmas **CONF:** Thtr 600 Class 400 Board 60 Del from €100 **SERVICES:** Lift **PARKING:** 175 **NOTES:** No dogs (ex guide dogs) **CARDS:**

Town House Hotel
Country House Hotel
Travel Accommodation

STRAFFAN, Co Kildare — Map 01 D4

Top 200 - Hotel

★★★★★ ⊛⊛⊛ *The Kildare Hotel & Golf Club*

☎ 01 6017200 📠 01 6017299
e-mail: resontsales@kclub.ie
Dir: *from Dublin take N4, onto R406, hotel entrance on right Straffan*
The luxurious Kildare Hotel and Country Club is set in 330 acres of park and woodland. The hotel boasts a golf course designed by Arnold Palmer - that will be the venue for the 2005 Ryder Cup. Opulent reception rooms include the Chinese Drawing Room, which overlooks the gardens and the River Liffey. Richly furnished bedrooms are very comfortable and extremely well equipped. Staff are very attentive, and there are extensive leisure and conference facilities.
ROOMS: 69 en suite 10 annexe en suite (10 fmly) **FACILITIES:** STV Indoor swimming (H) Golf 18 Tennis (hard) Fishing Squash Snooker Sauna Solarium Gym Croquet lawn Putting green Jacuzzi Beauty salon Driving range Golf tuition Fishing tuition Horse riding nearby entertainment ch fac **CONF:** Thtr 160 Class 60 Board 40 **SERVICES:** Lift **PARKING:** 205 **NOTES:** No dogs
CARDS:

★★★76% ⊛⊛ *Barberstown Castle*

☎ 01 6288157 📠 01 6277027
e-mail: castleir@iol.ie

Dating from the 13th century, this castle is now a hotel that provides the highest standards of comfort. Inviting public rooms range from the original castle keep, now housing one of the two restaurants, to the soft warmth of the drawing room and cocktail bar. Bedrooms are elegantly appointed and named after the people, some being extraordinary characters, who have lived within its walls.
ROOMS: 22 en suite **FACILITIES:** STV entertainment **CONF:** Thtr 50 Class 40 Board 30 **PARKING:** 200 **NOTES:** No dogs No children 12yrs No smoking in restaurant Closed 24-26 Dec & 1st 2wks Jan
CARDS:

THOMASTOWN, Co Kilkenny

Top 200 - Hotel

★★★★ Mount Juliet Conrad

☎ 056 777 3000 📠 056 777 3019
e-mail: info@mountjuliet.ie
Dir: *take M7 from Dublin, N9 towards Waterford then to Mount Juliet on N9 via Carlow and Gowran*

Mount Juliet Conrad is set in 1,500 acres of parkland with a Jack Nicklaus designed golf course. The elegant and spacious public areas retain much of the original architectural features including ornate plasterwork and Adam fireplaces. Bedrooms both in the main house and Hunters Yard annexe are comfortable and well appointed.

ROOMS: 32 en suite 27 annexe en suite No smoking in 1 bedroom **FACILITIES: Spa** STV Indoor swimming (H) Golf 18 Tennis (hard) Fishing Riding Snooker Sauna Gym Croquet lawn Putting green The Spa Archery Cycling Clay pigeon shooting Golf tuition **CONF:** Thtr 75 Class 40 Board 20 **PARKING:** 200 **NOTES:** No dogs (ex guide dogs) No smoking in restaurant **CARDS:**

TRALEE, Co Kerry — Map 01 A2

★★★69% Meadowlands Hotel

Oakpark
☎ 066 7180444 📠 066 7180964
e-mail: info@meadowlands-hotel.com
Dir: *1km from Tralee town centre on N69*

This smart hotel has been built to a high standard and is within walking distance of the town centre. There is stylish use of colour, tile and timber throughout, and the tastefully decorated bedrooms are comfortable and fitted with locally crafted pine furniture.

ROOMS: 58 en suite (1 fmly) (5 GF) No smoking in 17 bedrooms s €65-€120; d €65-€250 (incl. bkfst) **LB FACILITIES:** STV entertainment **CONF:** Thtr 250 Class 110 Board 30 **SERVICES:** Lift air con **PARKING:** 200 **NOTES:** No dogs (ex guide dogs) Closed 24-26 Dec **CARDS:**

★★★64% Abbey Gate

Maine St
☎ 066 7129888 📠 066 7129821
e-mail: info@abbeygate-hotel.com
Dir: *in town centre*

The Abbey Gate is a smart town centre hotel. The well-equipped bedrooms include some suitable for those with mobility problems. There is a spacious foyer and lounge area with attractive decor, a traditional pub, 'The Old Market Place' where carvery lunches are served, a cocktail bar and the Vineyard Restaurant.

ROOMS: 100 en suite (4 fmly) s €63-€140; d €110-€358 (incl. bkfst) **LB FACILITIES:** STV entertainment Xmas **CONF:** Thtr 450 Class 250 Board 40 **SERVICES:** Lift **PARKING:** 40 **NOTES:** No dogs (ex guide dogs) RS 24-26 Dec **CARDS:**

TRAMORE, Co Waterford — Map 01 C2

★★★64% Majestic

☎ 051 381761 📠 051 381766
e-mail: info@majestic-hotel.ie
Dir: *turn off N25 through Waterford onto R675 to Tramore*

A warm welcome awaits at this hotel, overlooking Tramore Bay and just 10km from Waterford City. All bedrooms are well equipped. The restaurant specialises in local fresh seafood and steak dishes. Full leisure facilities are available to residents at Splashworld Health & Fitness Club across the road from the hotel.

ROOMS: 60 en suite (4 fmly) No smoking in 5 bedrooms **FACILITIES:** STV Outdoor swimming (H) **SERVICES:** Lift **PARKING:** 10 **NOTES:** No dogs (ex guide dogs) **CARDS:**

VIRGINIA, Co Cavan — Map 01 C4

★★65% The Park

Virginia Park
☎ 049 8546100 📠 049 8547203
e-mail: virginiapark@eircom.net
Dir: *turn off N3 in Virginia onto R194. Hotel 500yds on left*

A charming hotel built in 1750 as the summer retreat of the Marquis of Headford. Situated at the end of a beech avenue on a 100-acre estate, it has a 9-hole golf course and lovely mature gardens. Dinner is served in the Marquis dining room, overlooking Lough Ramor.

ROOMS: 26 en suite (1 fmly) (8 GF) s €75-€80; d €130-€150 (incl. bkfst) **LB FACILITIES:** Golf 9 Fishing Sauna Xmas **CONF:** Thtr 70 Class 40 Board 40 Del from €130 **PARKING:** 50 **NOTES:** No dogs (ex guide dogs) No smoking in restaurant **CARDS:**

Late for dinner?
Quality Standards mean that last orders for dinner vary according to star rating and should be no earlier than:
★★ 7.00pm ★★★ 8.00pm ★★★★ 9.00pm
★★★★★ 10.00pm

V

WATERFORD, Co Waterford

Map 01 C2

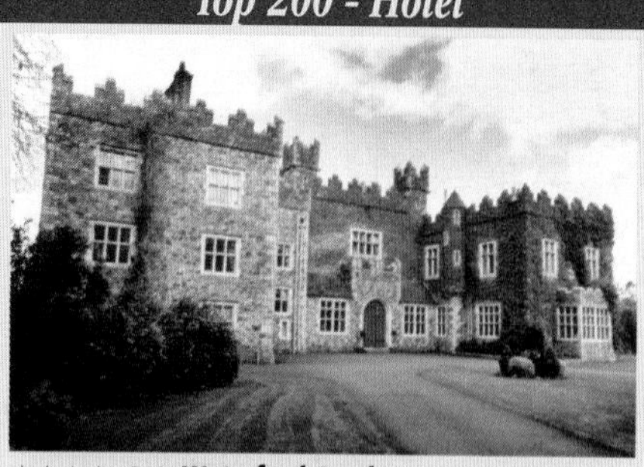

★★★★ Waterford Castle

The Island
☎ 051 878203 051 879316
e-mail: info@waterfordcastle.com
Dir: *from city centre, turn onto Dunmore East Rd, continue for 1.5m, pass hospital, 0.5m left after lights, ferry to island at end of road*

This enchanting and picturesque castle, located on a 320 acre island five minutes from the mainland, is reached by a chain-link ferry, which heightens the charm of the property. Dating from Norman times, the grand entrance hall boasts a welcoming wood fire in a cavernous fireplace. Enjoyable cuisine is served in the oak-panelled Munster Room where fixed-price and a la carte menus are complemented by a good wine list.

ROOMS: 19 en suite (2 fmly) **FACILITIES:** STV Golf 18 Tennis (hard) Croquet lawn Putting green Clay pigeon shooting, archery (group) entertainment **CONF:** Thtr 30 Board 15 **SERVICES:** Lift **PARKING:** 50 **NOTES:** No dogs (ex guide dogs) No smoking in restaurant **CARDS:**

★★★71% Granville

Best Western

The Quay
☎ 051 305555 051 305566
e-mail: stay@granville-hotel.ie
Dir: *take N25 to waterfront, city centre, opposite Clock Tower*

Centrally situated on the quayside, this long established hotel has been extensively refurbished to a very high standard, while still keeping its true character. The bedrooms come in a choice of standard and executive and are all well equipped and very comfortable. Hospitality and friendliness are hallmarks of a stay here.

ROOMS: 100 en suite (5 fmly) No smoking in 20 bedrooms s €110-€135; d €150-€190 (incl. bkfst) **LB** **FACILITIES:** STV entertainment Xmas **CONF:** Thtr 200 Class 150 Board 30 **SERVICES:** Lift **PARKING:** 300 **NOTES:** No dogs (ex guide dogs) Closed 25-26 Dec **CARDS:**

★★★68% Tower

The Mall
☎ 051 875801 051 870129
e-mail: towerw@iol.ie
Dir: *opposite Reginald's Tower in centre of town, hotel at end of quay on N25 Cork Road*

Extensive refurbishment has given the hotel a new look including two smart new restaurants, a carvery and a bistro, a new conference venue and upgraded bedrooms. A comfortable riverside lounge bar, a leisure centre and rear car park are also provided.

ROOMS: 139 en suite (20 fmly) **FACILITIES:** Indoor swimming (H) Sauna Solarium Gym Jacuzzi Swimming pool supervised entertainment **CONF:** BC Thtr 500 Class 250 Board 80 **SERVICES:** Lift **PARKING:** 90 **NOTES:** No dogs (ex guide dogs) Closed 24-28 Dec
CARDS:

★★★66% Dooley's

30 The Quay
☎ 051 873531 051 870262
e-mail: hotel@dooleys-hotel.ie
Dir: *on N25*

Situated in the heart of Waterford overlooking the quayside, Dooley's is a comfortable family-run hotel. The smart public areas and bedrooms offer comfortable and stylish accommodation, and there is an elevator to all floors. Guests are very well cared for in a warm and friendly atmosphere.

ROOMS: 113 en suite (3 fmly) No smoking in 17 bedrooms
FACILITIES: STV Land & water based activities entertainment **CONF:** Thtr 240 Class 150 Board 100 **SERVICES:** Lift **NOTES:** No dogs (ex guide dogs) Closed 25-27 Dec **CARDS:**

★★★65% Waterford Manor

Killotteran, Butlerstown
☎ 051 377814 051 354545
Dir: *N25 from Waterford to Cork, right 2m after Waterford Crystal, left at end of road, hotel on right*

Set in 20 acres of mature grounds, this period residence is situated on the outskirts of Waterford. Refurbishment has taken place, and facilities now include lounges, a restaurant and a new bar bistro which overlooks the gardens. There is also a business centre and exhibition hall.

ROOMS: 10 en suite (3 fmly) No smoking in 6 bedrooms
FACILITIES: STV Tennis (hard) ch fac **CONF:** Thtr 600 Class 300 Board 40 **PARKING:** 400 **NOTES:** No dogs (ex guide dogs) No smoking in restaurant RS 25 Dec **CARDS:**

★★★63% Bridge Hotel
1 The Quay
☎ 051 877222 📠 051 877229
e-mail: info@bridgehotelwaterford.com
Dir: *opposite City Bridge on N25*
This busy hotel stands near the City Bridge, convenient for the shops and local amenities. The bedrooms are well-furnished and really comfortable. Public areas include a country-style bistro, a restaurant, a traditional Irish pub and a relaxing lounge bar.
ROOMS: 100 en suite (20 fmly) No smoking in 4 bedrooms s €60-€85; d €104-€138 (incl. bkfst) **LB FACILITIES:** STV Sauna Gym entertainment **CONF:** Thtr 400 Class 300 Board 70 Del from €125 **SERVICES:** Lift air con **PARKING:** 200 **NOTES:** No dogs Closed Xmas & 1st 2 wks Jan **CARDS:**

★★★62% Ivory's Hotel
Tramore Rd
☎ 051 358888 📠 051 358899
e-mail: info@ivoryshotel.ie
Dir: *from city centre take N25 towards Cork. After 600yds take exit to Tramore R675. Hotel on right*
This modern family owned is near the famous Waterford Crystal factory. The bedrooms are well appointed and comfortable with family rooms available. An outdoor children's play area is also provided. The popular bar serves food throughout the day with a carvery lunch.
ROOMS: 40 en suite (20 fmly) (20 GF) No smoking in 20 bedrooms s €75-€110; d €100-€166 (incl. bkfst) **LB FACILITIES:** STV Xmas **PARKING:** 120 **NOTES:** No smoking in restaurant **CARDS:**

★★★61% *McEniff Ard Ri Hotel*
Ferrybank
☎ 051 832111 📠 051 832863
e-mail: stan_power@jurysdoyle.com
Dir: *on N25 1km from city centre*
In an elevated setting in 38 acres of parkland, this modern hotel enjoys spectacular views overlooking the city and harbour. Public areas are comfortable and bedrooms are spacious and well-equipped. Guests can enjoy the many activities available in the extensive leisure centre.
ROOMS: 98 en suite (20 fmly) No smoking in 4 bedrooms **FACILITIES:** Indoor swimming (H) Tennis (hard) Sauna Solarium Gym Jacuzzi Steam room Plunge pool entertainment **CONF:** Thtr 700 Class 400 Board 100 **SERVICES:** Lift **PARKING:** 300 **NOTES:** No dogs (ex guide dogs) Closed 24-27 Dec **CARDS:**

Restaurant with Rooms

O'Grady's
Cork Rd
☎ 051 378851 📠 051 374062
e-mail: info@ogradyshotel.com
Dir: *N25 Cork Road, between crystal factory and city centre*
Midway between the city centre and the famed Crystal factory, O'Grady's is an old Gothic styled gatehouse. Bedrooms vary in size, with singles available. Excellent food served in attractive surroundings, with an interesting wine list.
ROOMS: 9 en suite (1 fmly) (4 GF) No smoking in all bedrooms s €40-€50; d €80-€100 (incl. bkfst) **LB FACILITIES:** Tennis (hard) **PARKING:** 30 **NOTES:** No dogs Closed Xmas & New Year **CARDS:**

Travelodge
Cork Rd
☎ 08700 850 950 📠 051 358890
Dir: *on N25, 1km from Waterford Glass Visitors Centre*
Travelodge offers good quality, good value, modern accommodation. Ideal for families, the spacious, en suite bedrooms include remote-control TV, tea and coffee-making facilities, luxury beds and free morning newspaper. Meals can be taken at the nearby family restaurant. For further details and the Travelodge phone number, consult the Hotel Groups page.
ROOMS: 32 en suite s fr €60; d fr €60

WATERVILLE, Co Kerry — Map 01 A2

★★★75% Butler Arms
☎ 066 9474144 📠 066 9474520
e-mail: reservations@butlerarms.com
Dir: *centre of Waterville on seafront. N70 Ring of Kerry*
Standing on the Ring of Kerry overlooking the ocean, the Butler Arms offers traditional high standards of service. Most of the bedrooms have marble bathrooms and enjoy sea views, whilst public areas include spacious lounges and a billiards room. An 18-hole championship golf course is situated opposite.
ROOMS: 40 en suite (1 fmly) No smoking in 12 bedrooms s €134-€154; d €178-€214 (incl. bkfst) **LB FACILITIES:** STV Tennis (hard) Fishing Snooker Billiards room **SERVICES:** Lift **PARKING:** 50 **NOTES:** No dogs (ex guide dogs) No smoking in restaurant Closed Nov-Apr **CARDS:**

WESTPORT, Co Mayo — Map 01 D3

★★★73% *Hotel Westport Conference & Leisure Centre*
Newport Rd
☎ 098 25122 📠 098 26739
e-mail: reservations@hotelwestport.ie
Dir: *N5 to Westport, at end of Castlebar St turn right, 1st right, 1st left, follow road to end*
Opposite the grounds of Westport House, this hotel offers welcoming accommodation comprising a new reception foyer, lounge, spacious restaurant and comfortable bedrooms including six suites. The hotel has much to offer both leisure and business guests, with a swimming pool, sauna and gym, and conference and syndicate rooms.
ROOMS: 129 en suite (36 fmly) **FACILITIES:** STV Indoor swimming (H) Sauna Solarium Gym Jacuzzi Children's pool Jet stream Lounger pool Steam room entertainment ch fac **CONF:** Thtr 500 Class 150 Board 60 **SERVICES:** Lift **PARKING:** 220 **NOTES:** No dogs (ex guide dogs) No smoking in restaurant **CARDS:**

★★★70% Ardmore Country House
The Quay
☎ 098 25994 📠 098 27795
e-mail: ardmorehotel@eircom.net
Dir: *1.5km from town centre on coast road*
A charming country house hotel, elevated over the quay, within walking distance of the town centre. The attractive restaurant and relaxing lounges overlook Clew Bay, with Croagh Patrick in the background. Individually styled bedrooms are spacious and comfortable, most have spectacular sea views.
ROOMS: 13 en suite (2 GF) No smoking in all bedrooms s €125-€150; d €170-€250 (incl. bkfst) **LB PARKING:** 40 **NOTES:** No dogs No children 12yrs No smoking in restaurant Closed Jan & Feb **CARDS:**

W

WESTPORT, continued

★★★68% ◎◎ The Atlantic Coast Hotel
The Quay
☎ 098 29000 ▯ 098 29111
e-mail: achotel@iol.ie
Dir: *N5 follow signs into Westport then Louisburgh on R335, 1m*
This distinctive hotel is in a former mill and has been renovated to a good contemporary standard with all modern facilities. Many of the rooms have sea views, as has the award-winning restaurant on the fourth floor. The ground floor has comfortable lounge areas and a lively bar.
ROOMS: 85 en suite (3 fmly) s €65-€155; d €103-€270 (incl. bkfst) **LB FACILITIES:** STV Indoor swimming (H) Sauna Solarium Gym Treatment rooms/Hydrotherapy Swimming pool supervised entertainment ch fac **CONF:** BC Thtr 180 Class 140 Board 70 Del from €70 **SERVICES:** Lift **PARKING:** 60 **NOTES:** No dogs (ex guide dogs) No smoking in restaurant Closed 23-27 Dec **CARDS:**

★★72% ◎ The Olde Railway
The Mall
☎ 098 25166 & 25605 ▯ 098 25090
e-mail: railway@anu.ie
Dir: *overlooking the Carrowbeg River in the town centre*

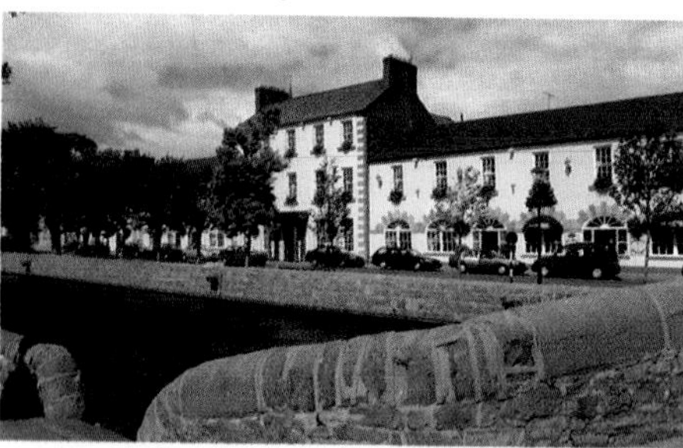

Set on a tree-lined mall overlooking the river, this classic coaching inn offers a welcoming atmosphere with blazing turf fires. There is a variety of bedroom sizes, including some very spacious rooms; all are well-equipped. Communal areas include an attractively furnished bar, a comfortable lounge and a conservatory restaurant with access to the patio and barbecue area.
ROOMS: 24 en suite (2 fmly) s €75-€125; d €100-€180 (incl. bkfst) **LB FACILITIES:** Fishing & Shooting arranged entertainment **CONF:** Thtr 75 Class 100 **PARKING:** 34 **NOTES:** No dogs (ex guide dogs) No smoking in restaurant **CARDS:**

WEXFORD, Co Wexford Map 01 D3

W

★★★★69% ◎◎ Ferrycarrig
Ferrycarrig Bridge
☎ 053 20999 ▯ 053 20982
e-mail: ferrycarrig@griffingroup.ie
Dir: *on N11 by Slaney Estuary, beside Ferrycarrig Castle*
This fine hotel has sweeping views from almost every angle of the Slaney estuary, while the restaurants and bar are almost at the water's edge. Bedrooms are very comfortable and well appointed, and many of them with french windows leading to a balcony.
continued

A particularly well-equipped leisure centre is also available together with a beauty salon.
ROOMS: 102 en suite (10 fmly) No smoking in 50 bedrooms s €80-€450; d €140-€450 (incl. bkfst) **LB FACILITIES:** STV Indoor swimming (H) Sauna Solarium Gym Jacuzzi Aerobics Beauty treatments on request Hairdresser entertainment Xmas **CONF:** Thtr 400 Class 250 Board 60 **SERVICES:** Lift **PARKING:** 235 **NOTES:** No dogs (ex guide dogs) **CARDS:**

★★★73% *Talbot*
Trinity St
☎ 053 22566 ▯ 053 23377
e-mail: sales@talbothotel.ie
Dir: *from Rosslare, take N11 & follow signs for Wexford, hotel on right of the Quays - 12m*
Centrally situated on the quayside, this hotel has been extensively refurbished. All the well-equipped bedrooms have custom-made oak furniture and attractive decor. Day rooms include a spacious foyer, comfortable lounge, and a bar with an open fireplace. The attractive restaurant serves interesting food, and there are good leisure facilities.
ROOMS: 98 en suite (12 fmly) No smoking in 10 bedrooms **FACILITIES:** STV Indoor swimming (H) Sauna Solarium Gym Jacuzzi Childrens room Beauty Salon entertainment **CONF:** Thtr 450 Class 250 Board 110 **SERVICES:** Lift **PARKING:** 160 **NOTES:** No dogs (ex guide dogs) Closed 24-25 Dec **CARDS:**
See advert on opposite page

★★★70% ◎ Whitford House Hotel Health & Leisure Club
New Line Rd
☎ 053 43444 & 43845 ▯ 053 46399
e-mail: info@whitford.ie
Dir: *from Rosslare follow N25 at Duncannon Road rndbt, turn right onto R733, hotel immediately left*

This is a friendly, family run hotel situated on the outskirts of Wexford within easy reach of Rosslare Ferry Port. There is a choice of lounges, a spacious, atmospheric bar and beer garden. Footprints Restaurant offers a variety of menus including local seafood. Comfortable bedrooms range from standard to superior deluxe; they are spacious, luxuriously furnished and decorated. An extensive leisure centre has been completed.
ROOMS: 36 en suite (28 fmly) (18 GF) s €80-€101; d €120-€152 (incl. bkfst) **LB FACILITIES: Spa** STV Indoor swimming (H) Sauna Solarium Gym Jacuzzi Childrens playground Beer garden Adult reading room, Swimming pool supervised entertainment **CONF:** Thtr 50 Class 45 Board 25 **PARKING:** 200 **NOTES:** No dogs RS 23 Dec-2 Jan
CARDS:

★★★63% River Bank House Hotel
☎ 053 23611 Fax 053 23342
e-mail: river@indigo.ie
Dir: *beside Wexford Bridge on R741*
This hotel overlooks the River Slaney at the foot of Wexford Bridge, a short distance from the town centre. The Victorian-style bar and restaurant have stunning views of the harbour, while bedrooms are attractively decorated and well equipped. There are impressive banqueting and conference facilities.
ROOMS: 23 en suite (6 fmly) (7 GF) s €80-€105; d €120-€170 (incl. bkfst) **LB FACILITIES:** STV entertainment **CONF:** Thtr 350 Class 180 Board 48 **SERVICES:** Lift **PARKING:** 25 **NOTES:** No dogs (ex guide dogs) Closed 24-25 Dec **CARDS:**

★★★60% White's Hotel
George St
☎ 053 22311 Fax 053 45000
e-mail: info@whiteshotel.iol.ie
Dir: *on entering Wexford from N11 or N25 follow signs for hotel*
This historic former coaching inn provides comfortable modern facilities while retaining much of its charm. The entrance is through a modern extension, and entertainment is provided in the converted saddlery and forge.
ROOMS: 76 en suite 6 annexe en suite (1 fmly) No smoking in 16 bedrooms s €73-€133; d €106-€210 (incl. bkfst) **LB FACILITIES:** STV Sauna Gym Jacuzzi Disco Bar entertainment Xmas **CONF:** Thtr 400 Class 250 Board 100 **SERVICES:** Lift **PARKING:** 100 **NOTES:** No dogs (ex guide dogs) **CARDS:**

WICKLOW See Rathnew

WOODENBRIDGE, Co Wicklow Map 01 D3

★★★64% Woodenbridge
☎ 0402 35146 Fax 0402 35573
e-mail: wbhotel@iol.ie
Dir: *between Avoca & Arklow*
This comfortable hotel in the Vale of Avoca, under an hour's drive from the ferry ports of Dun Laoghaire and Rosslare, and close to the N11, continues to thrive. With new bedrooms and a modern conference and banqueting suite the hotel facilities are excellent. Hospitality and good food is assured. Golf and fishing are on the doorstep.
ROOMS: 23 en suite (13 fmly) s €45-€80; d €90-€140 (incl. bkfst) **LB FACILITIES:** STV Xmas **CONF:** Thtr 200 Class 200 Board 200 **PARKING:** 100 **NOTES:** No dogs No smoking in restaurant **CARDS:**

YOUGHAL, Co Cork Map 01 C2

★★60% *Devonshire Arms*
Pearse Square
☎ 024 92827 Fax 024 92900
e-mail: reservations@dev.arms.ie
This 19th-century building is centrally situated with good parking to the rear. The ground floor facilities include comfortable lounges and two cosy bar areas where good food is served throughout the day.
ROOMS: 10 en suite **CONF:** Class 150 **PARKING:** 20 **NOTES:** No dogs (ex guide dogs) Closed 24-31 Dec **CARDS:**

Restaurant with Rooms

Ahernes
163 North Main St
☎ 024 92424 Fax 024 93633
e-mail: ahernes@eircom.net
Dir: *At rdbt on edge of town, N25. Follow signs for town centre*
In the same family since 1923, Ahernes offers a warm welcome, with turf fires and a traditional atmosphere. Spacious bedrooms are furnished to the highest standard and include antiques and modern facilities. The restaurant is well known for its daily-changing menu of the freshest seafood specialities. Guests can use the cosy drawing room.
ROOMS: 13 en suite (2 fmly) s €105-€110; d €140-€180 (incl. bkfst) **LB CONF:** Thtr 25 Class 15 Board 15 **SERVICES:** Lift **PARKING:** 20 **NOTES:** Closed Xmas **CARDS:**

Need a break without breaking the bank?
Latebeds offers last-minute deals with no nasty surprises at AA-approved hotels and B&Bs. Visit www.theAA.com to find out more

€ Don't forget, the Euro is now the unit of currency in the Republic of Ireland

KEY TO ATLAS

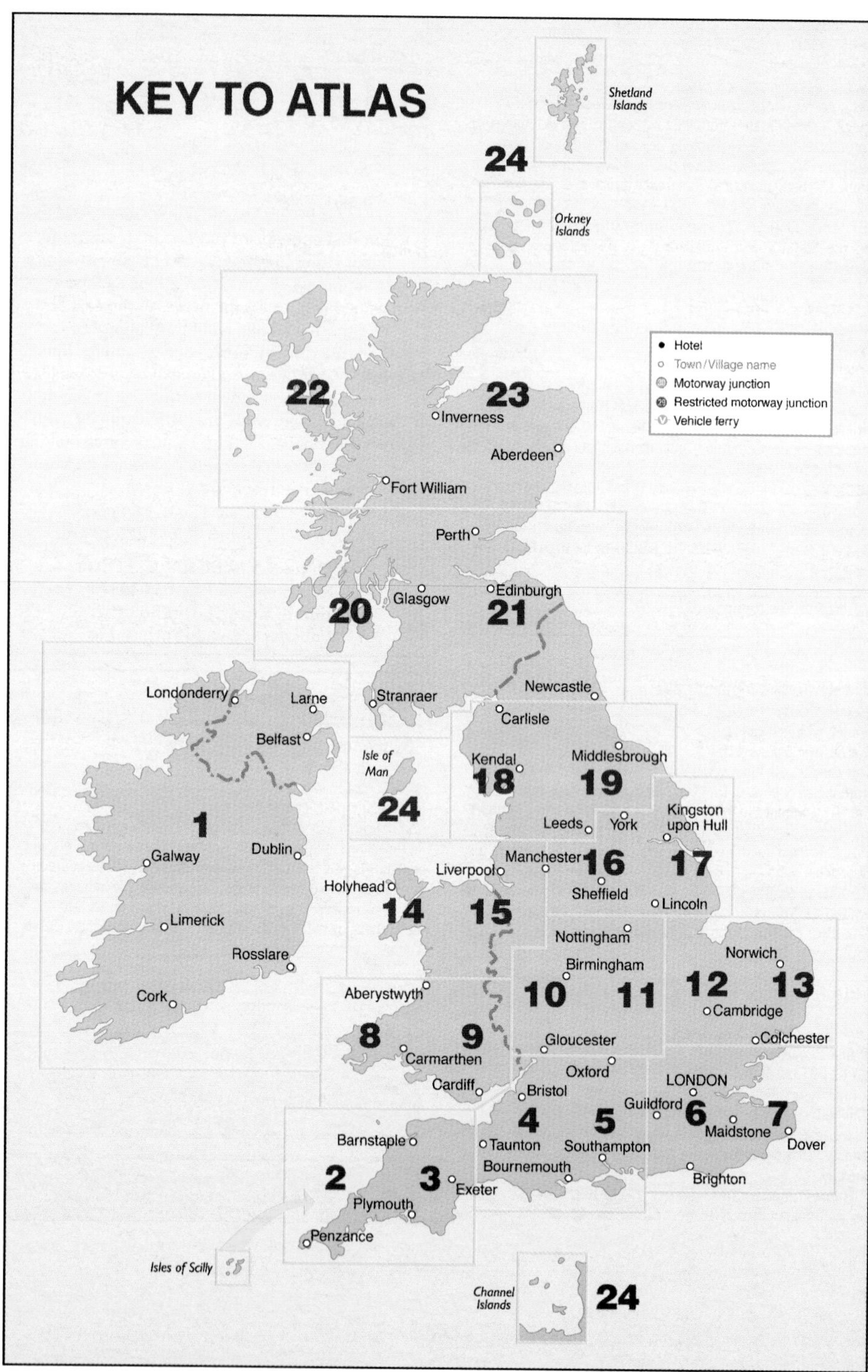

Shetland Islands
24
Orkney Islands
Hotel
Town/Village name
Motorway junction
Restricted motorway junction
Vehicle ferry
22
23
Inverness
Aberdeen
Fort William
Perth
Glasgow
Edinburgh
20
21
Londonderry
Larne
Belfast
Stranraer
Newcastle
Carlisle
Isle of Man
24
Kendal
18
Middlesbrough
19
1
Leeds
York
Kingston upon Hull
Galway
Dublin
Manchester
16
17
Liverpool
Holyhead
Sheffield
Lincoln
14
15
Limerick
Nottingham
Rosslare
Birmingham
Norwich
Cork
Aberystwyth
10
11
12
13
Cambridge
8
9
Gloucester
Colchester
Carmarthen
Oxford
LONDON
Cardiff
Bristol
Guildford
4
5
6
7
Maidstone
Dover
Barnstaple
Taunton
Southampton
Bournemouth
Brighton
2
3
Exeter
Plymouth
Penzance
Isles of Scilly
Channel Islands
24

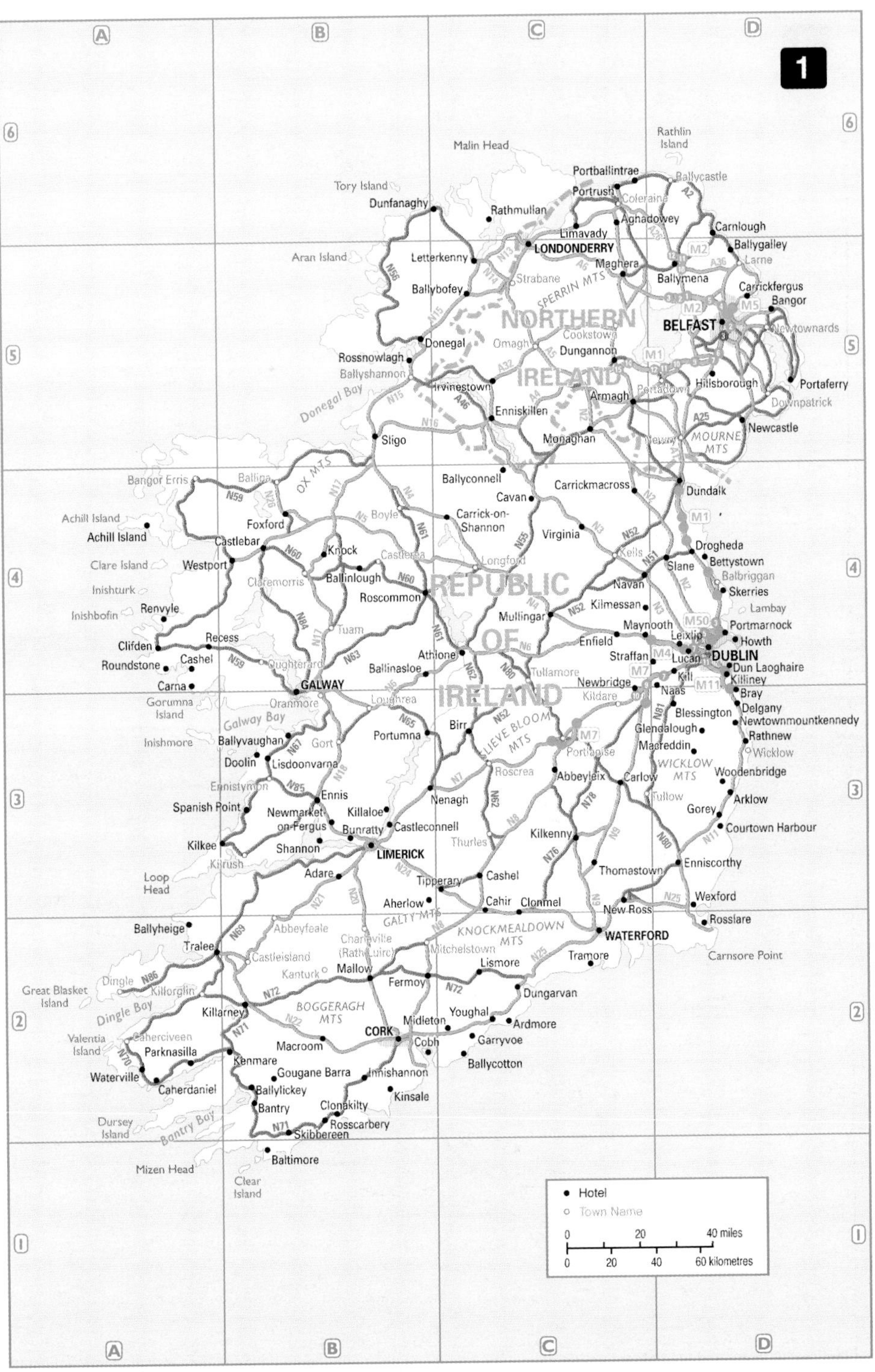

A
B
C
D
1
6
Malin Head
Rathlin Island
Portballintrae
Ballycastle
Tory Island
Portrush
Coleraine
Dunfanaghy
Rathmullan
Aghadowey
Limavady
Carnlough
Aran Island
LONDONDERRY
Ballygalley
Letterkenny
Maghera
Larne
Strabane
Ballymena
SPERRIN MTS
Carrickfergus
Ballybofey
Bangor
NORTHERN IRELAND
BELFAST
Cookstown
Newtownards
Donegal
Omagh
Dungannon
5
Rossnowlagh
Ballyshannon
Hillsborough
Irvinestown
Armagh
Portadown
Portaferry
Donegal Bay
Downpatrick
Enniskillen
Newcastle
MOURNE MTS
Monaghan
Newry
Sligo
Bangor Erris
Ballina
OX MTS
Ballyconnell
Carrickmacross
Dundalk
Cavan
Achill Island
Foxford
Boyle
Carrick-on-Shannon
Virginia
Castlebar
Drogheda
Knock
Castlerea
Longford
Bettystown
Clare Island
Westport
Slane
4
Claremorris
Ballinlough
REPUBLIC OF IRELAND
Navan
Balbriggan
Inishturk
Skerries
Roscommon
Kilmessan
Lambay
Renvyle
Inishbofin
Mullingar
Portmarnock
Tuam
Maynooth
Recess
Howth
Leixlip
Clifden
Enfield
Athlone
Cashel
DUBLIN
Roundstone
Straffan
Lucan
Oughterard
Ballinasloe
Dun Laoghaire
Tullamore
Kill
Killiney
Carna
Newbridge
GALWAY
Naas
Bray
Kildare
Gorumna Island
Oranmore
Loughrea
Blessington
Delgany
Galway Bay
Birr
Newtownmountkennedy
SLIEVE BLOOM MTS
Glendalough
Portumna
Ballyvaughan
Rathnew
Inishmore
Gort
Macreddin
Portlaoise
Doolin
Wicklow
Lisdoonvarna
WICKLOW MTS
Roscrea
Woodenbridge
Abbeyleix
Carlow
Ennistymon
3
Tullow
Ennis
Nenagh
Arklow
Spanish Point
Gorey
Killaloe
Newmarket-on-Fergus
Castleconnell
Courtown Harbour
Bunratty
Thurles
Kilkenny
Kilkee
Shannon
LIMERICK
Kilrush
Enniscorthy
Thomastown
Loop Head
Adare
Cashel
Tipperary
Wexford
Aherlow
Cahir
Clonmel
New Ross
GALTY MTS
Rosslare
Ballyheige
Abbeyfeale
KNOCKMEALDOWN MTS
WATERFORD
Charleville (Rath Luirc)
Tralee
Mitchelstown
Carnsore Point
Castleisland
Tramore
Lismore
Kanturk
Dingle
Mallow
Great Blasket Island
Killorglin
Fermoy
Dungarvan
BOGGERAGH MTS
Dingle Bay
2
Killarney
Youghal
Ardmore
Midleton
Valentia Island
Cahersiveen
Macroom
CORK
Garryvoe
Cobh
Parknasilla
Kenmare
Ballycotton
Waterville
Gougane Barra
Innishannon
Caherdaniel
Ballylickey
Kinsale
Bantry
Clonakilty
Dursey Island
Bantry Bay
Rosscarbery
Skibbereen
Baltimore
Mizen Head
Clear Island
Hotel
Town Name
0 20 40 miles
0 20 40 60 kilometres
N56
N13
N14
N15
A6
A2
A26
M2
A36
M5
M1
A32
A5
A4
A46
N16
N2
A25
A1
N59
N26
N17
N4
N5
N61
N55
N3
N52
N60
N51
N84
N63
N6
N62
N80
M50
M4
M7
M11
N81
N65
N67
N18
N85
N7
N78
N8
N9
N24
N76
N11
N21
N20
N69
N86
N72
N22
N71
N70
N25

For continuation pages refer to numbered arrows

3
9
4
SS
ST
SY
SX
DEVON
EXMOOR FOREST
DARTMOOR FOREST
QUANTOCK HILLS
Bridgwater Bay
Tor Bay
Start Bay
Bigbury Bay
Ilfracombe
Martinhoe
Lynton
Lynmouth
Woody Bay
Porlock Weir
Porlock
Minehead
Dunster
Blue Anchor
Watchet
Kilve
Stogursey
Holford
Nether Stowey
Cannington
Bridgwater
Burnham-on-Sea
Brent Knoll
West Huntspill
Mortehoe
Lee
Combe Martin
Woolacombe
Parracombe
Brendon
Challacombe
Wootton Courtenay
Carhampton
Williton
Sampford Brett
Crowcombe
Elworthy
Georgeham
Croyde
Saunton
Braunton
Muddiford
Bratton Fleming
Simonsbath
Exford
Wheddon Cross
Withypool
Winsford
Brompton Regis
Brayford
Barnstaple
Appledore
Instow
Westward Ho!
Northam
Bideford
Horns Cross
Parkham
Monkleigh
Great Torrington
Little Torrington
South Molton
North Molton
Dulverton
Exebridge
Wiveliscombe
Fitzhead
Milverton
Petton
Bampton
Taunton
North Petherton
Goathurst
Wellington
Taunton Deane Services
Sampford Arundel
Sampford Peverell
Umberleigh
Chittlehamholt
Rackenford
Burrington
Beaford
Witheridge
Chulmleigh
Chawleigh
Tiverton
Halberton
Uffculme
Willand
Culmstock
Hemyock
Upottery
Cullompton
Bickleigh
Silverton
Bradworthy
Stibb Cross
Merton
Dolton
Milton Damerel
Shebbear
Meeth
Winkleigh
Eggesford
Lapford
Black Torrington
Sheepwash
Morchard Bishop
Cheriton Fitzpaine
Highampton
Hatherleigh
Copplestone
Halwill Junction
Beaworthy
Crediton
Stoke Canon
Broadclyst
Whimple
Fenny Bridges
Honiton
Wilmington
Axminster
Shute
Colyton
Colyford
Uplyme
Lyme Regis
Axmouth
Seaton
Beer
Branscombe
Sidmouth
Ottery St Mary
Yarcombe
Tytherleigh
Ashwater
Okehampton
Tedburn St Mary
Newton St Cyres
EXETER
South Zeal
Bratton Clovelly
Sourton Cross
Sourton
Whiddon Down
Crockernwell
Dunsford
Clyst St Mary
Topsham
Exminster
Woodbury
Otterton
Budleigh Salterton
Exmouth
Kenton
Kennford
Lewdown
Lifton
Bridestowe
Lydford
Chagford
Moretonhampstead
Milton Abbot
Lamerton
Mary Tavy
Postbridge
Widecombe in the Moor
Haytor Vale
Bovey Tracey
Chudleigh
Chudleigh Knighton
Ideford
Dawlish
Tavistock
Two Bridges
Princetown
Ilsington
Bishopsteignton
Teignmouth
Shaldon
Gunnislake
Gulworthy
Callington
Hexworthy
Kingsteignton
Newton Abbot
Horrabridge
Dousland
Bere Alston
Yelverton
Ashburton
Holne
Kingskerswell
Maidencombe
St Mellion
Buckfastleigh
Ipplepen
Staverton
TORQUAY
Pillaton
Bere Ferrers
Shaugh Prior
Dartington
Landrake
Saltash
Cornwood
South Brent
Totnes
Paignton
Wrangaton
Stoke Gabriel
Churston Ferrers
Plympton
Ivybridge
Harbertonford
Dittisham
Brixham
Torpoint
PLYMOUTH
Ermington
Ugborough
Halwell
Kingswear
Crafthole
Millbrook
Heybrook Bay
Brixton
Yealmpton
Modbury
Dartmouth
Cawsand
Holbeton
Aveton Gifford
Stoke Fleming
Wembury
Newton Ferrers
Slapton
Strete
Bigbury-on-Sea
Kingsbridge
Chillington
Thurlestone
Torcross
Hope
Hope Cove
Malborough
Salcombe
Hallsands
Start Point
East Prawle
• Hotel
○ Town/Village name
0
10 miles
0
10
20 kilometres

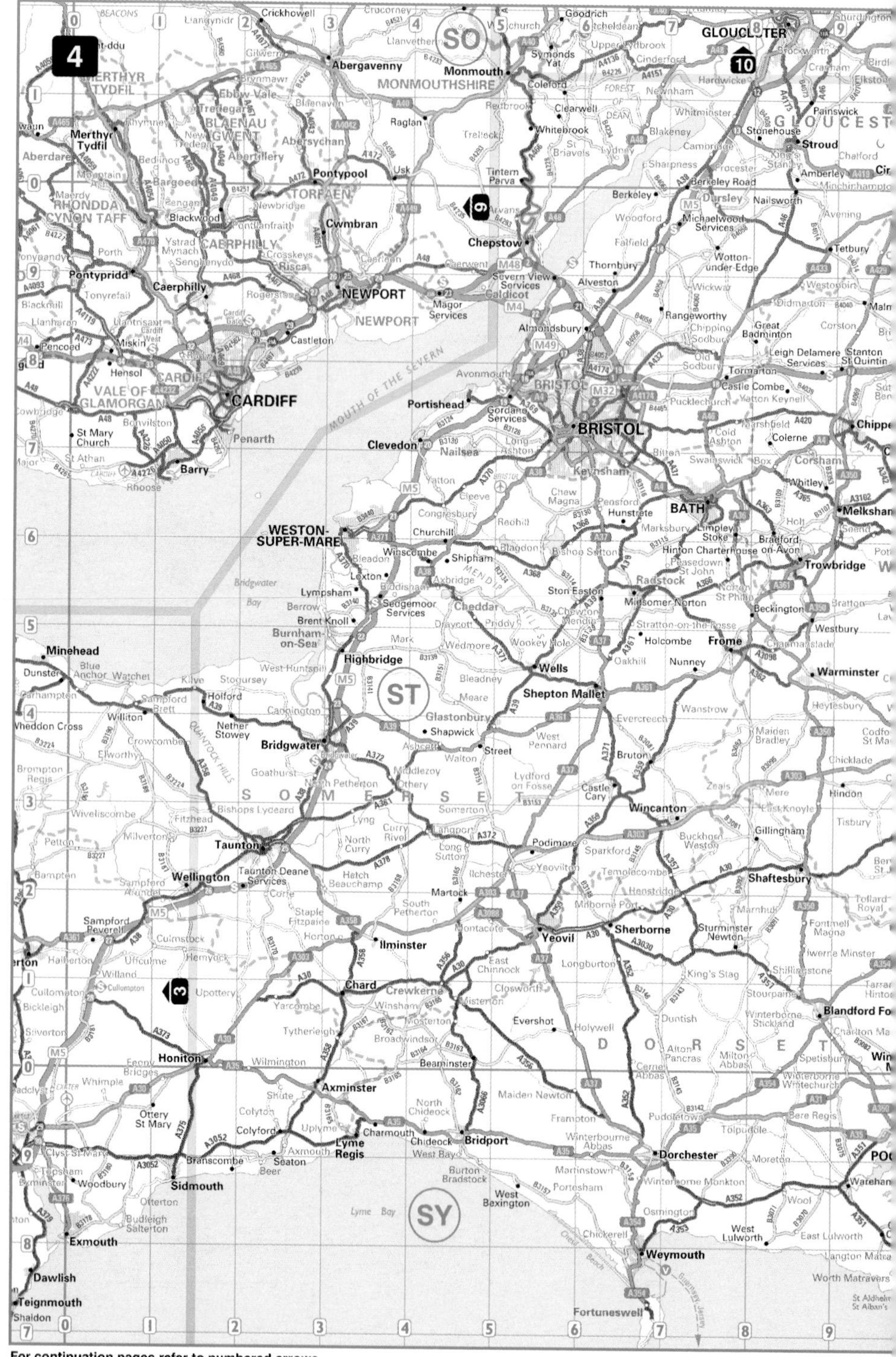

For continuation pages refer to numbered arrows

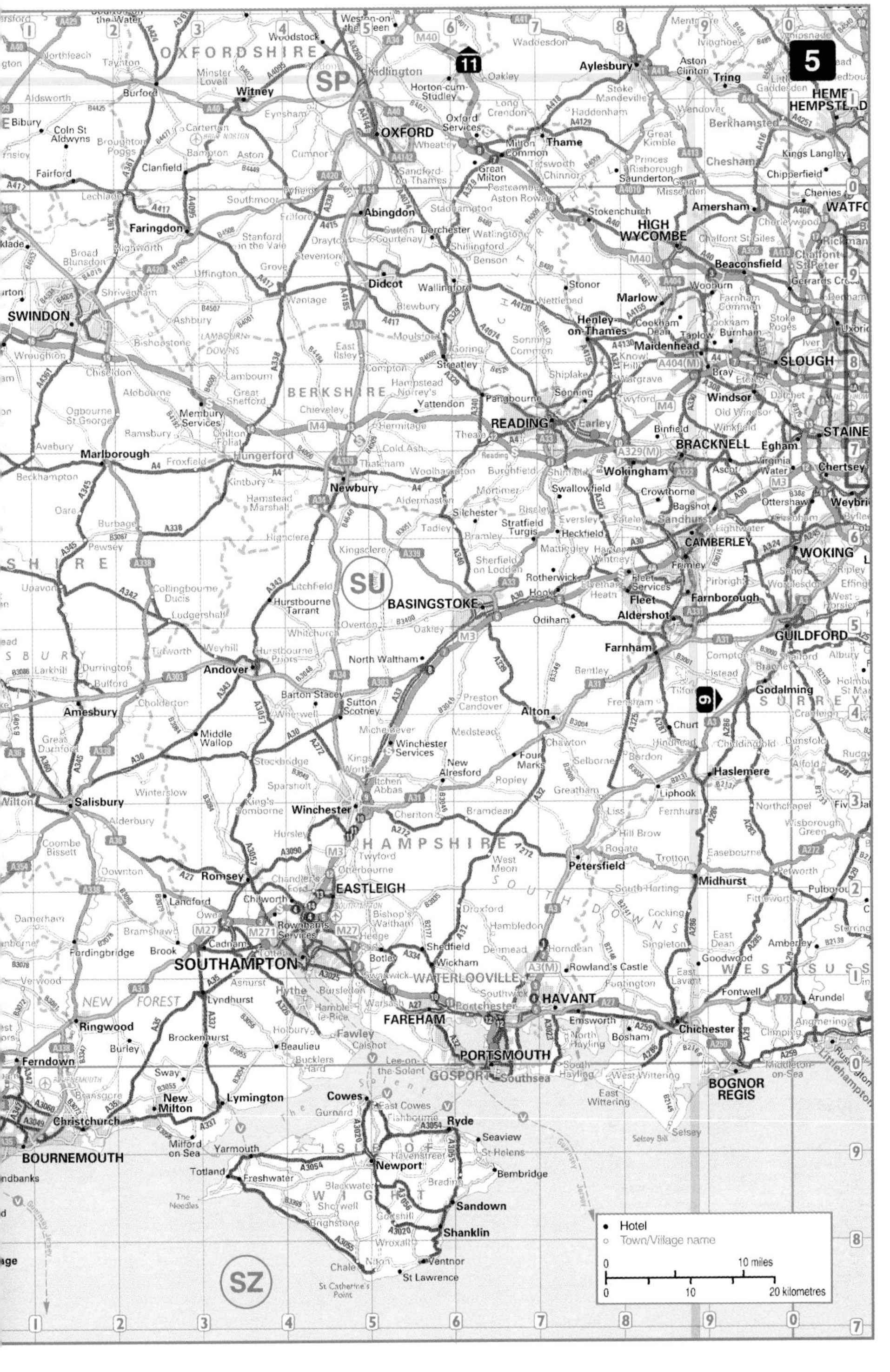
5
OXFORDSHIRE
SP
SU
SZ
Woodstock
Witney
Burford
Kidlington
OXFORD
Oakley
Aylesbury
Tring
Aston Clinton
Thame
Wheatley
Abingdon
Faringdon
Didcot
Wallingford
SWINDON
Marlborough
Hungerford
Newbury
READING
Henley-on-Thames
Marlow
HIGH WYCOMBE
Beaconsfield
Maidenhead
SLOUGH
Windsor
Egham
BRACKNELL
Wokingham
Chertsey
WOKING
CAMBERLEY
Farnborough
Fleet
Aldershot
GUILDFORD
Farnham
Godalming
Haslemere
BASINGSTOKE
Andover
Amesbury
Salisbury
Winchester
Alton
Petersfield
Midhurst
Romsey
EASTLEIGH
SOUTHAMPTON
WATERLOOVILLE
HAVANT
FAREHAM
PORTSMOUTH
GOSPORT
Chichester
BOGNOR REGIS
Ringwood
Ferndown
Christchurch
BOURNEMOUTH
New Milton
Lymington
Cowes
Ryde
Newport
Sandown
Shanklin
Ventnor
BERKSHIRE
HAMPSHIRE
SURREY
WEST SUSSEX
ISLE OF WIGHT
NEW FOREST
SOUTH DOWNS
Hotel
Town/Village name
0
10 miles
0
10
20 kilometres

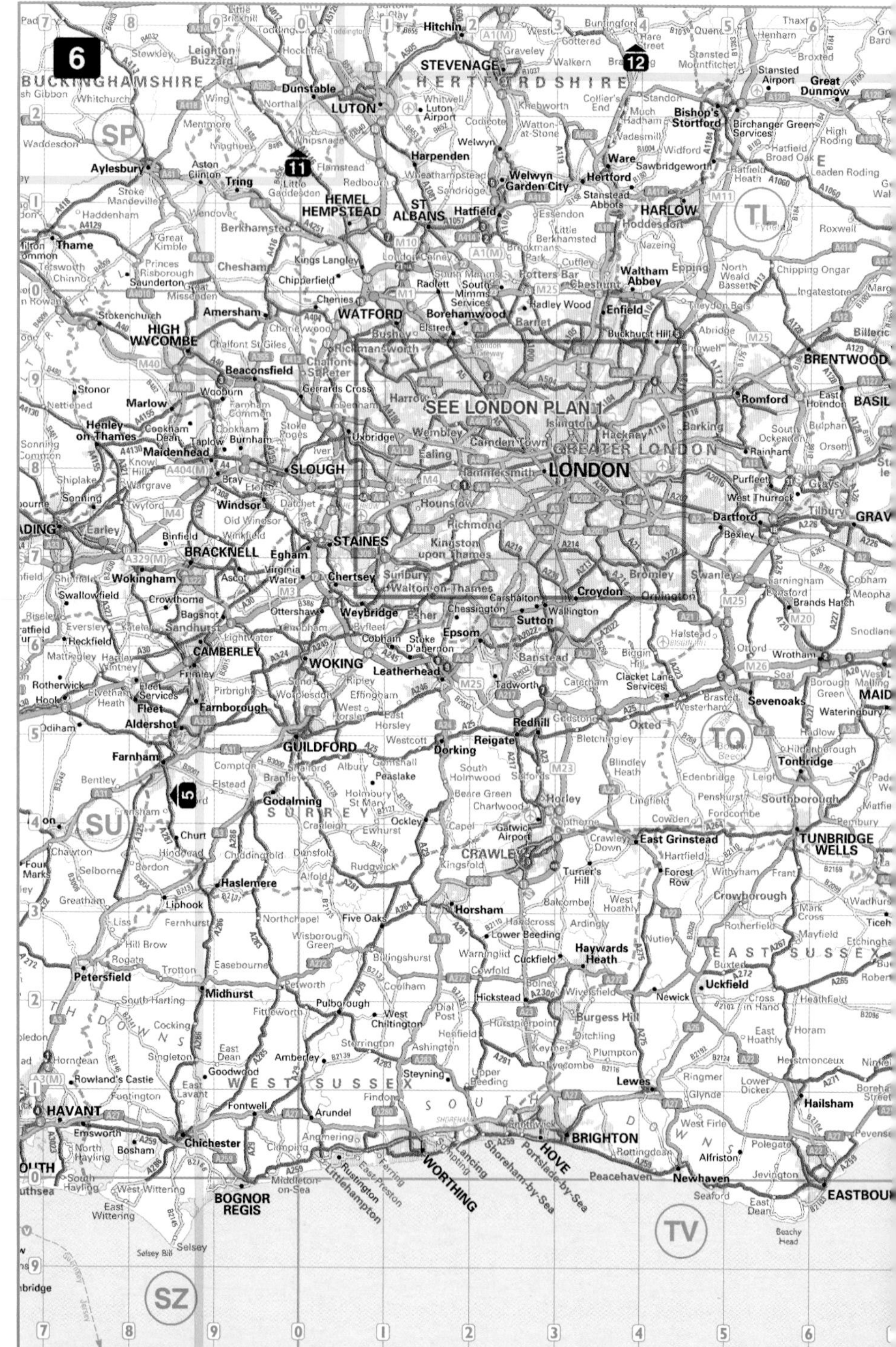

For continuation pages refer to numbered arrows

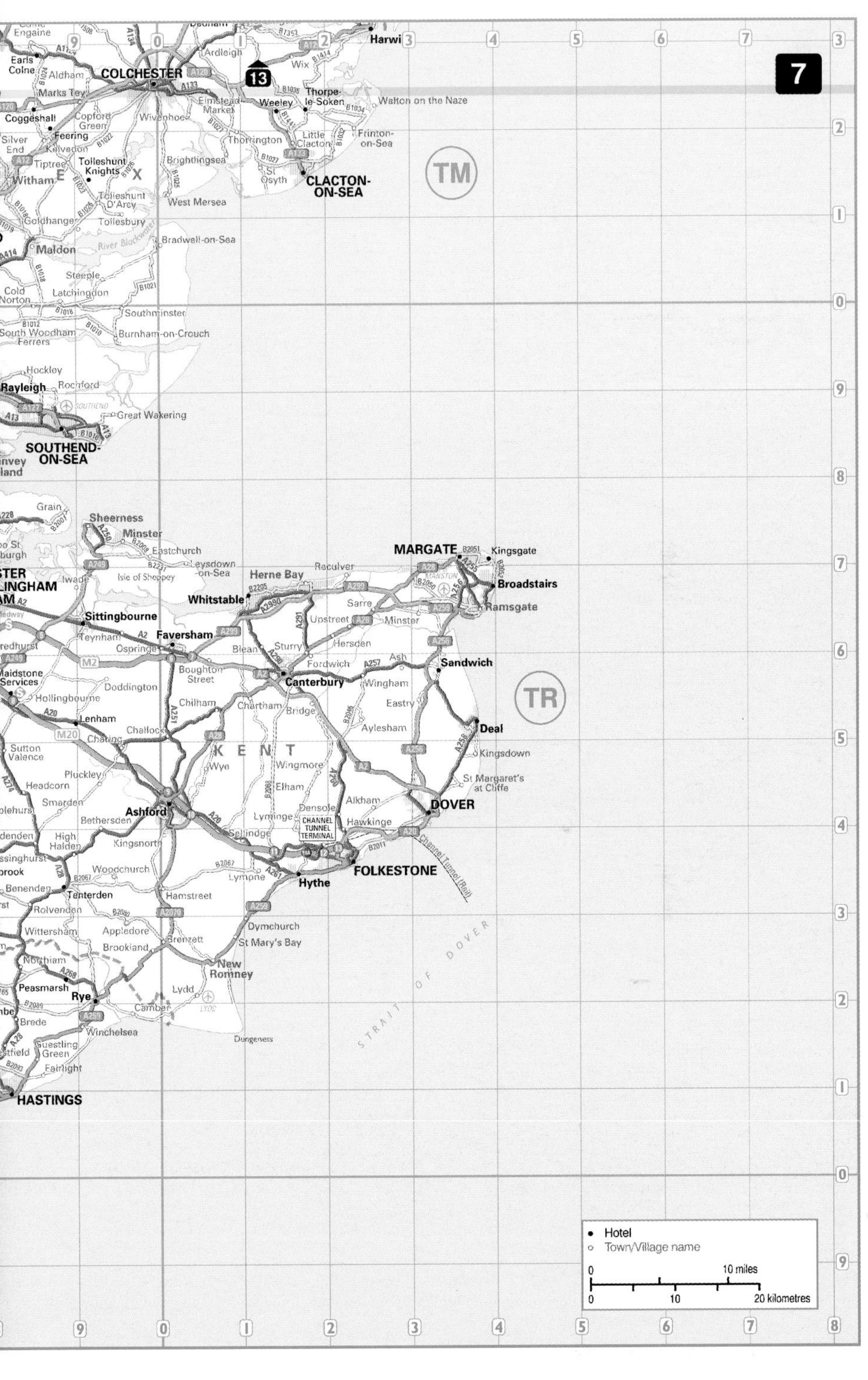
COLCHESTER
Harwich
Walton on the Naze
Frinton-on-Sea
CLACTON-ON-SEA
Brightlingsea
West Mersea
Maldon
Bradwell-on-Sea
Burnham-on-Crouch
Southminster
Rayleigh
Rochford
SOUTHEND-ON-SEA
Great Wakering
Sheerness
Minster
Eastchurch
Leysdown-on-Sea
Isle of Sheppey
Whitstable
Herne Bay
MARGATE
Kingsgate
Broadstairs
Ramsgate
Sittingbourne
Faversham
Canterbury
Sandwich
Deal
Kingsdown
St Margaret's at Cliffe
DOVER
KENT
Ashford
CHANNEL TUNNEL TERMINAL
FOLKESTONE
Hythe
Tenterden
Dymchurch
St Mary's Bay
New Romney
Lydd
Dungeness
Rye
Camber
Winchelsea
HASTINGS
STRAIT OF DOVER
Channel Tunnel (Rail)
TM
TR
13
Hotel
Town/Village name
0
10 miles
0
10
20 kilometres

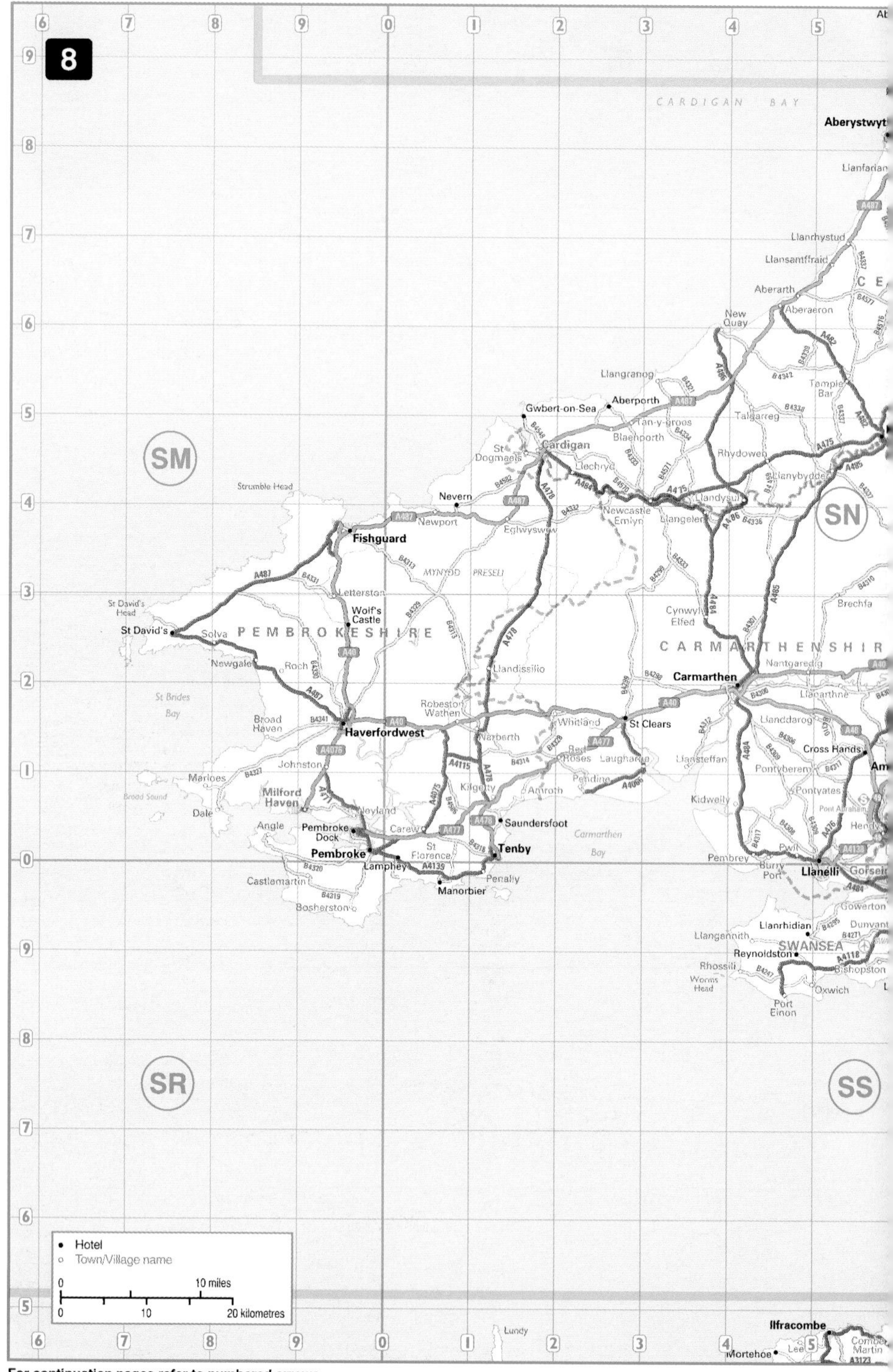

For continuation pages refer to numbered arrows

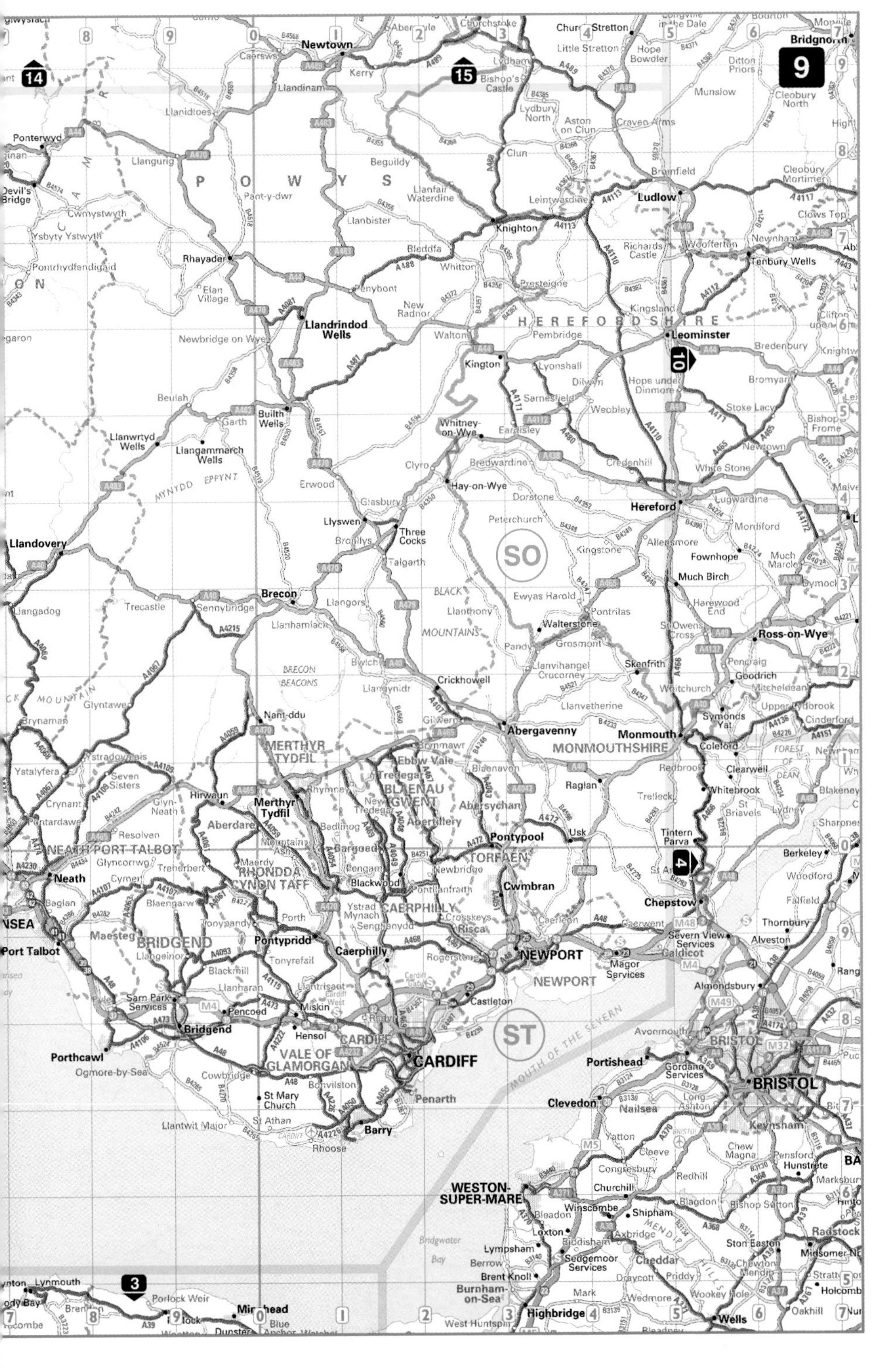

9
14
15
10
4
3
Newtown
Llandinam
Llanidloes
Ponterwyd
Llangurig
Devil's Bridge
Cwmystwyth
Ysbyty Ystwyth
Pontrhydfendigaid
Rhayader
Elan Village
P O W Y S
Pant-y-dwr
Llanbister
Llanfair Waterdine
Beguildy
Knighton
Bleddfa
Whitton
Penybont
Llandrindod Wells
Newbridge on Wye
New Radnor
Walton
Presteigne
Kington
Lyonshall
Pembridge
Dilwyn
Weobley
Sarnesfield
Eardisley
Whitney-on-Wye
Clyro
Hay-on-Wye
Bredwardine
Dorstone
Peterchurch
Beulah
Builth Wells
Garth
Llanwrtyd Wells
Llangammarch Wells
MYNYDD EPPYNT
Erwood
Glasbury
Llyswen
Three Cocks
Bronllys
Talgarth
Llandovery
Llangadog
Trecastle
Sennybridge
Brecon
Llanhamlach
Llangors
Llanthony
BLACK MOUNTAINS
BRECON BEACONS
Bwlch
Crickhowell
Llangynidr
Gilwern
Abergavenny
Nant-ddu
MERTHYR TYDFIL
Merthyr Tydfil
Brynmawr
Ebbw Vale
Tredegar
BLAENAU GWENT
Abertillery
Blaenavon
Abersychan
Pontypool
TORFAEN
Cwmbran
Newbridge
Rhymney
Bargoed
Blackwood
CAERPHILLY
Caerphilly
Risca
Crosskeys
Ystrad Mynach
Glyntawe
Brynaman
Ystradgynlais
Ystalyfera
Seven Sisters
Glyn-Neath
Hirwaun
Aberdare
Mountain Ash
RHONDDA CYNON TAFF
Crynant
Pontardawe
Resolven
NEATH PORT TALBOT
Neath
Glyncorrwg
Cymer
Treherbert
Maerdy
Baglan
Blaengarw
Tonypandy
Porth
Pontypridd
Maesteg
BRIDGEND
Llangeinor
Tonyrefail
Blackmill
Llanharan
Llantrisant
Pencoed
Miskin
Sarn Park Services
Bridgend
Pyle
Porthcawl
Ogmore-by-Sea
Hensol
VALE OF GLAMORGAN
Cowbridge
St Mary Church
Bonvilston
Llantwit Major
St Athan
Rhoose
Barry
Penarth
CARDIFF
Castleton
Rogerstone
NEWPORT
Caerleon
Magor Services
Port Talbot
Ludlow
Leintwardine
Bromfield
Craven Arms
Aston on Clun
Clun
Lydbury North
Bishop's Castle
Lydham
Churchstoke
Church Stretton
Little Stretton
Hope Bowdler
Munslow
Ditton Priors
Bridgnorth
Cleobury North
Cleobury Mortimer
Clows Top
Newnham
Tenbury Wells
Woofferton
Richards Castle
Kingsland
HEREFORDSHIRE
Leominster
Bredenbury
Bromyard
Hope under Dinmore
Stoke Lacy
Bishop's Frome
Newtown
White Stone
Credenhill
Hereford
Lugwardine
Mordiford
Allensmore
Kingstone
Fownhope
Much Marcle
Much Birch
Harewood End
Ewyas Harold
Pontrilas
Walterstone
Pandy
Grosmont
St Owens Cross
Ross-on-Wye
Skenfrith
Llanvihangel Crucorney
Pencraig
Goodrich
Whitchurch
Mitcheldean
Llanvetherine
Symonds Yat
Cinderford
Monmouth
MONMOUTHSHIRE
Coleford
Redbrook
Clearwell
FOREST OF DEAN
Raglan
Trelleck
Whitebrook
St Briavels
Lydney
Blakeney
Usk
Tintern Parva
Chepstow
Berkeley
Woodford
Falfield
Thornbury
Alveston
Severn View Services
Caldicot
Almondsbury
NEWPORT
SO
ST
MOUTH OF THE SEVERN
Avonmouth
Portishead
Gordano Services
BRISTOL
Long Ashton
Nailsea
Clevedon
Keynsham
Yatton
Claeve
Congresbury
Chew Magna
Pensford
Hunstrete
Redhill
Churchill
WESTON-SUPER-MARE
Winscombe
Shipham
Blagdon
Bishop Sutton
Bleadon
Loxton
Axbridge
MENDIP HILLS
Lympsham
Biddisham
Sedgemoor Services
Cheddar
Berrow
Brent Knoll
Draycott
Priddy
Chewton Mendip
Ston Easton
Midsomer Norton
Radstock
Burnham-on-Sea
Mark
Wedmore
Wookey Hole
Wells
Highbridge
Oakhill
Holcombe
Bridgwater Bay
Lynmouth
Porlock Weir
Porlock
Minehead
Dunster
Blue Anchor
West Huntspill
Marksbury

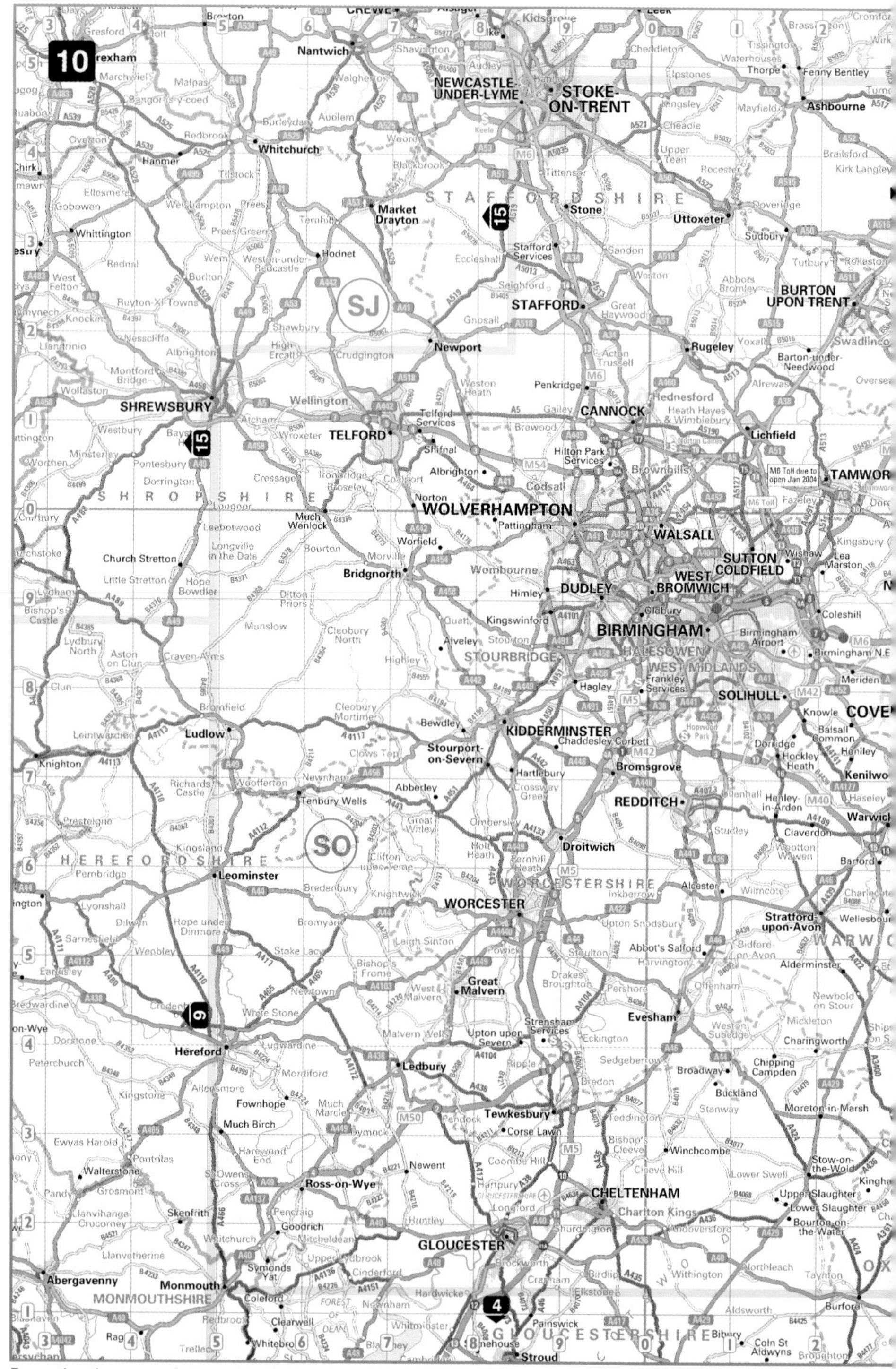

For continuation pages refer to numbered arrows

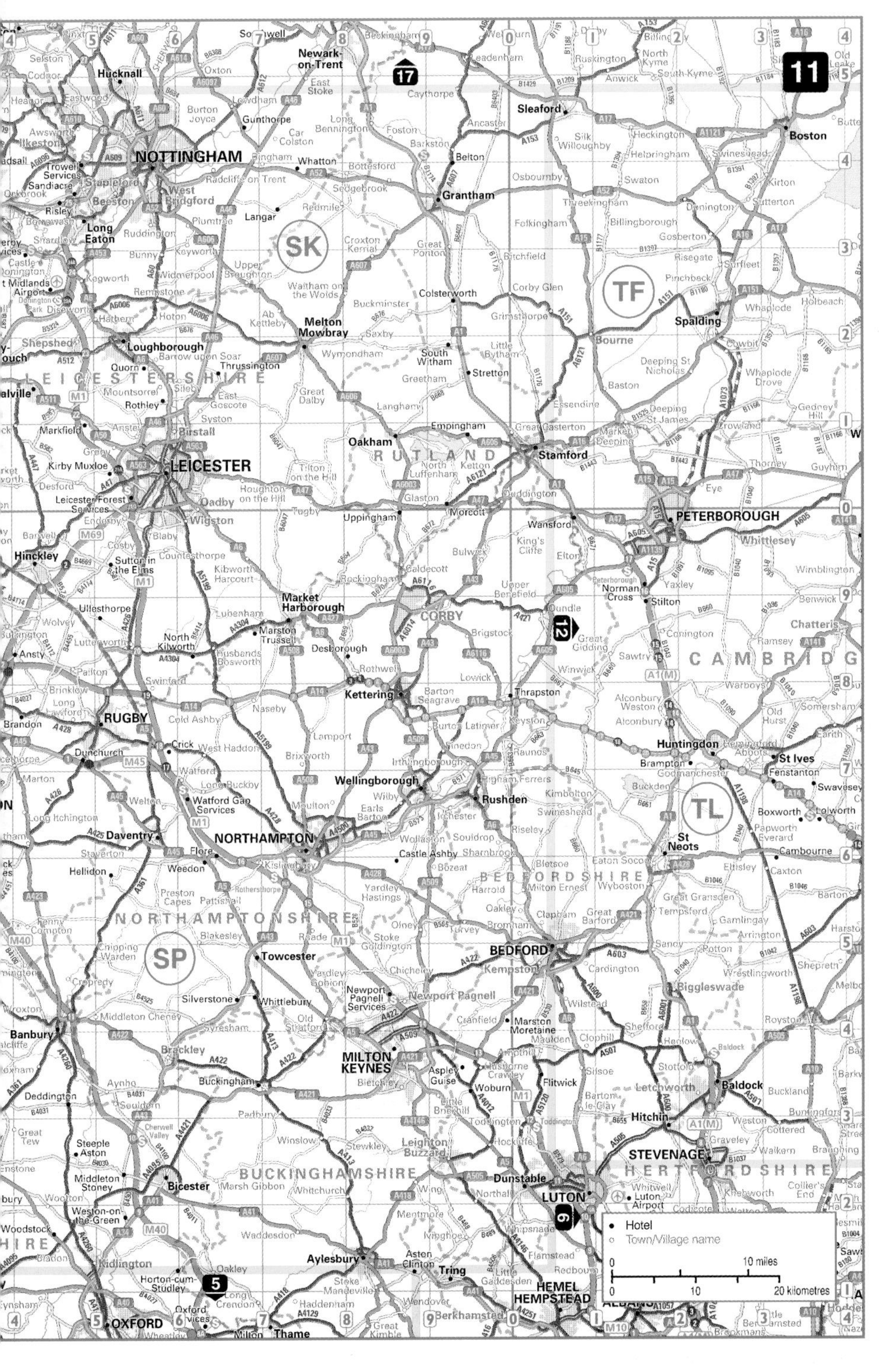

11
17
12
6
5
SK
TF
SP
TL
Newark-on-Trent
Hucknall
NOTTINGHAM
West Bridgford
Long Eaton
Beeston
Stapleford
Sleaford
Boston
Grantham
Belton
Melton Mowbray
Loughborough
Shepshed
Quorn
Rothley
LEICESTER
Oadby
Wigston
Hinckley
Oakham
Uppingham
Stamford
Spalding
Bourne
PETERBOROUGH
Whittlesey
Market Harborough
CORBY
Kettering
RUGBY
Daventry
NORTHAMPTON
Wellingborough
Rushden
Huntingdon
St Ives
St Neots
BEDFORD
Kempston
Biggleswade
Towcester
MILTON KEYNES
Newport Pagnell
Banbury
Brackley
Buckingham
Bicester
Aylesbury
Leighton Buzzard
Dunstable
LUTON
Luton Airport
Hitchin
Letchworth
Baldock
STEVENAGE
Tring
HEMEL HEMPSTEAD
Berkhamsted
OXFORD
Thame
Kidlington
Woodstock
LEICESTERSHIRE
RUTLAND
NORTHAMPTONSHIRE
BEDFORDSHIRE
BUCKINGHAMSHIRE
HERTFORDSHIRE
CAMBRIDG
Hotel
Town/Village name
0
10 miles
0
10
20 kilometres

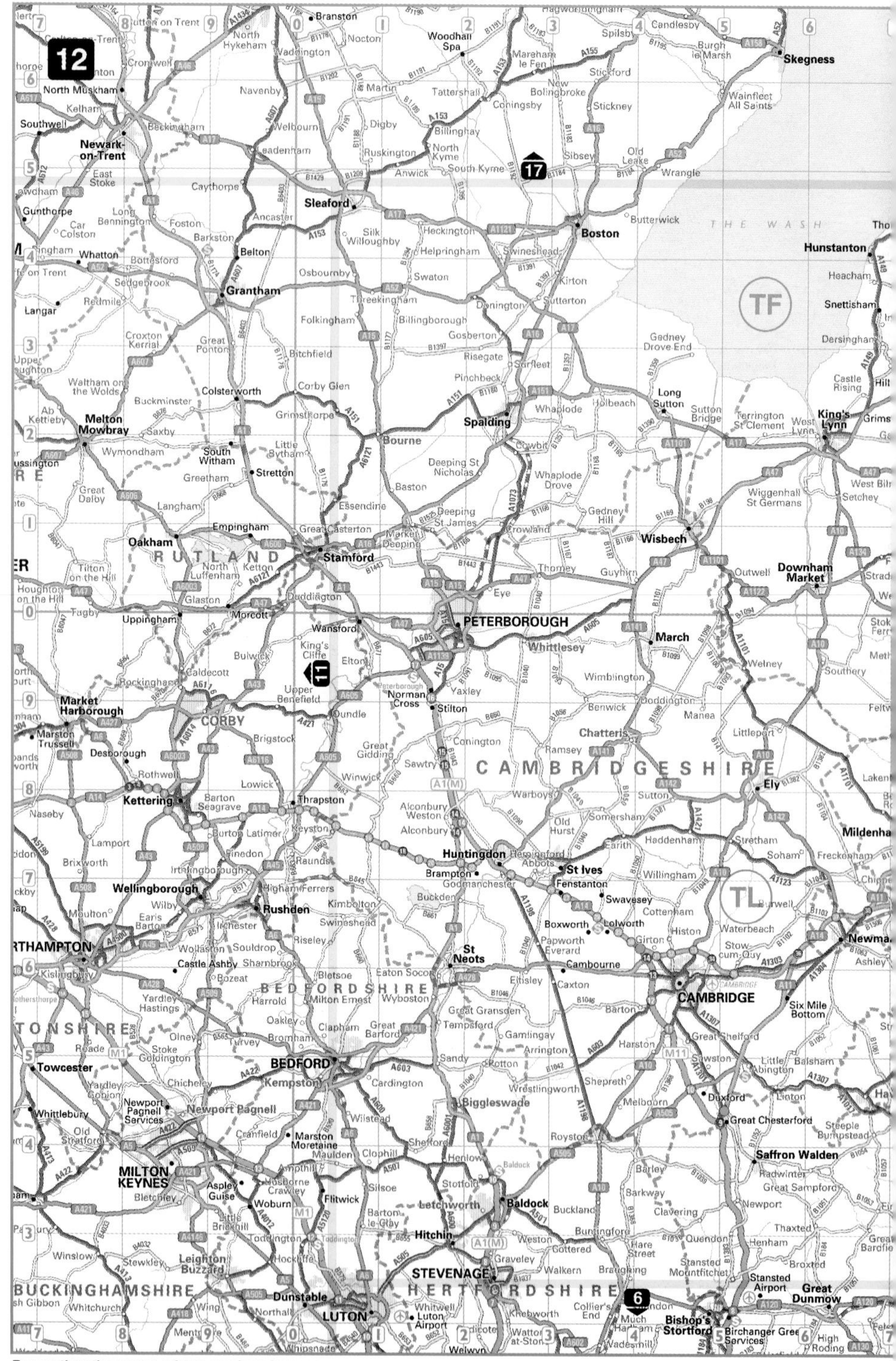

For continuation pages refer to numbered arrows

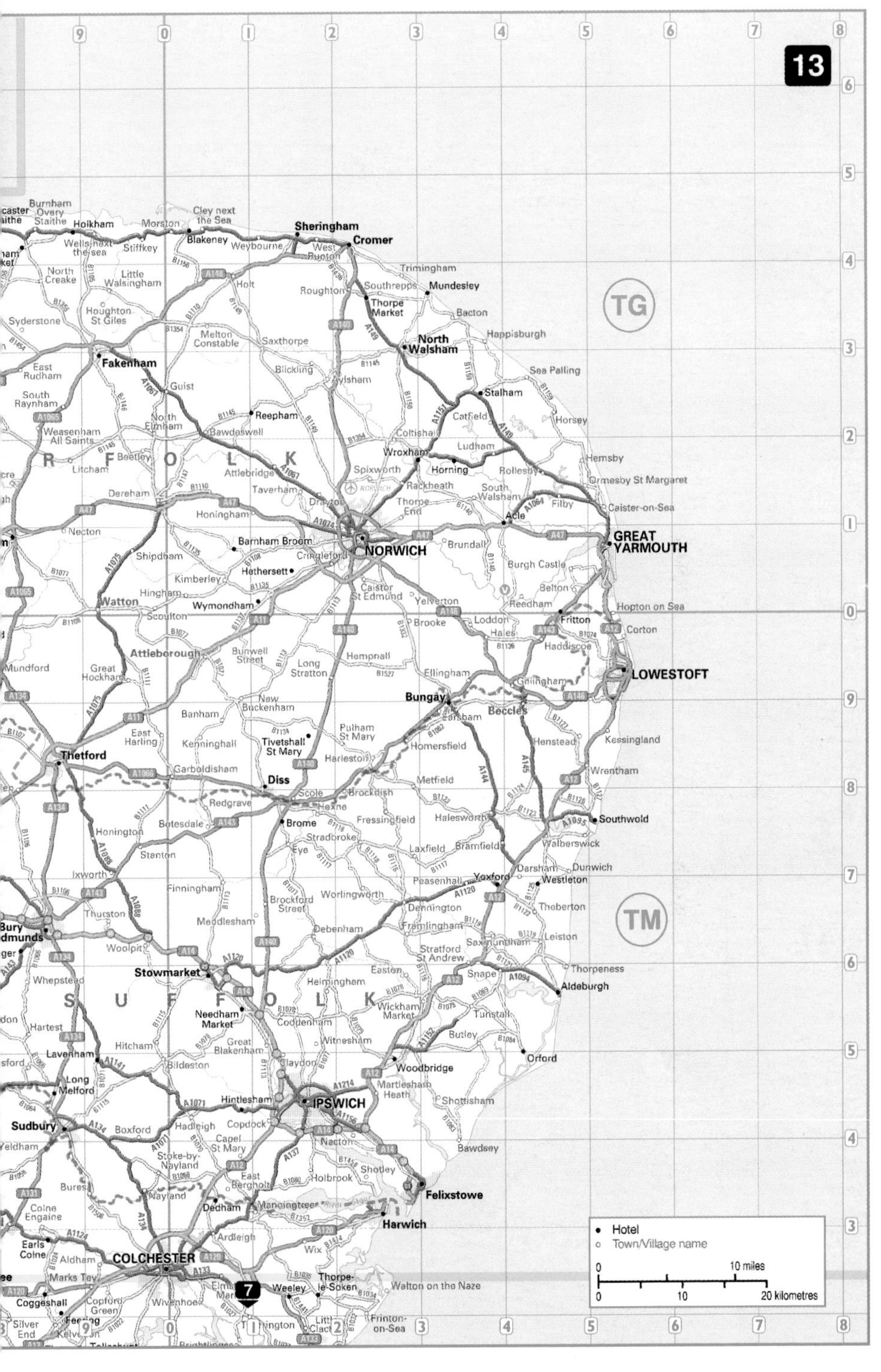
13
TG
TM
Burnham Overy Staithe
Holkham
Morston
Cley next the Sea
Sheringham
Cromer
Blakeney
Weybourne
West Runton
Wells-next-the-sea
Stiffkey
North Creake
Little Walsingham
Holt
Trimingham
Roughton
Southrepps
Mundesley
Thorpe Market
Bacton
Syderstone
Houghton St Giles
Melton Constable
Saxthorpe
Happisburgh
North Walsham
Fakenham
East Rudham
Blickling
Aylsham
Sea Palling
Guist
Stalham
South Raynham
North Elmham
Reepham
Catfield
Horsey
Weasenham All Saints
Bawdeswell
Coltishall
Ludham
Hemsby
Beetley
Litcham
Attlebridge
Wroxham
Horning
Rollesby
Spixworth
Ormesby St Margaret
Taverham
Rackheath
South Walsham
Dereham
Drayton
Thorpe End
Filby
Caister-on-Sea
Honingham
Acle
Necton
GREAT YARMOUTH
Barnham Broom
NORWICH
Brundall
Shipdham
Cringleford
Burgh Castle
Hethersett
Kimberley
Caistor St Edmund
Belton
Hingham
Yelverton
Reedham
Watton
Wymondham
Hopton on Sea
Scoulton
Brooke
Loddon
Fritton
Corton
Hales
Haddiscoe
Attleborough
Bunwell Street
Hempnall
Mundford
Great Hockham
Long Stratton
LOWESTOFT
Ellingham
Gillingham
Bungay
Beccles
New Buckenham
Earsham
Banham
Pulham St Mary
East Harling
Kenninghall
Tivetshall St Mary
Homersfield
Henstead
Kessingland
Thetford
Harleston
Garboldisham
Wrentham
Metfield
Diss
Scole
Brockdish
Redgrave
Hoxne
Southwold
Fressingfield
Botesdale
Halesworth
Brome
Honington
Stradbroke
Walberswick
Eye
Laxfield
Bramfield
Stanton
Dunwich
Darsham
Ixworth
Peasenhall
Yoxford
Westleton
Finningham
Worlingworth
Theberton
Thurston
Brockford Street
Dennington
Bury St Edmunds
Mendlesham
Framlingham
Debenham
Leiston
Woolpit
Saxmundham
Stratford St Andrew
Stowmarket
Easton
Thorpeness
Snape
Whepstead
Helmingham
Aldeburgh
Needham Market
Wickham Market
Hartest
Coddenham
Tunstall
Witnesham
Great Blakenham
Butley
Hitcham
Lavenham
Orford
Claydon
Woodbridge
Bildeston
Long Melford
Martlesham Heath
Hintlesham
IPSWICH
Shottisham
Sudbury
Boxford
Hadleigh
Copdock
Nacton
Capel St Mary
Stoke-by-Nayland
Bawdsey
East Bergholt
Holbrook
Shotley
Bures
Nayland
Felixstowe
Dedham
Manningtree
Colne Engaine
Harwich
Ardleigh
Earls Colne
Aldham
Wix
COLCHESTER
Marks Tey
Thorpe-le-Soken
Walton on the Naze
Coggeshall
Copford Green
Wivenhoe
Weeley
Feering
Kelvedon
Silver End
Frinton-on-Sea
A148
A140
A149
A1067
A1065
A47
A1074
A146
A143
A11
A1075
A134
A1066
A144
A145
A12
A1095
A1120
A1088
A14
A1094
A1152
A1214
A1156
A1071
A137
A133
A120
A1124
A131
7
Hotel
Town/Village name
0
10 miles
10
20 kilometres

For continuation pages refer to numbered arrows

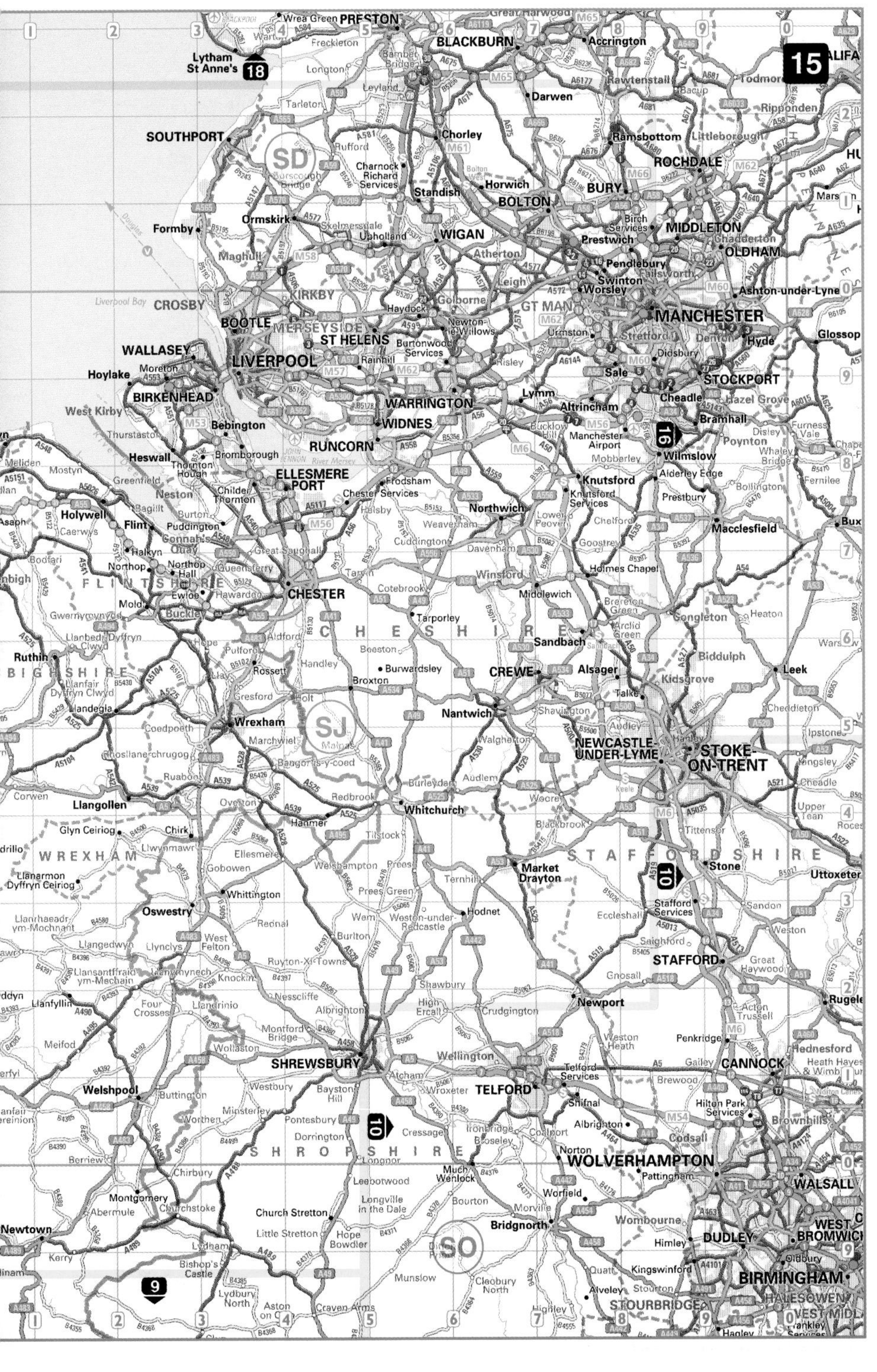

15
18
16
10
9
SD
SJ
SO
PRESTON
BLACKBURN
Accrington
Lytham St Anne's
Wrea Green
Freckleton
Longton
Leyland
Darwen
Rawtenstall
Todmorden
Bacup
Ripponden
Tarleton
SOUTHPORT
Rufford
Chorley
Ramsbottom
Littleborough
ROCHDALE
Burscough Bridge
Charnock Richard Services
Horwich
BURY
Standish
BOLTON
Formby
Ormskirk
Skelmersdale
Upholland
WIGAN
Birch Services
MIDDLETON
Prestwich
Chadderton
OLDHAM
Maghull
Atherton
Pendlebury
Failsworth
Swinton
Worsley
Leigh
Ashton-under-Lyne
Liverpool Bay
CROSBY
KIRKBY
Haydock
Golborne
GT MAN
MANCHESTER
BOOTLE
MERSEYSIDE
ST HELENS
Newton-le-Willows
Urmston
Stretford
Denton
Hyde
Glossop
WALLASEY
Burtonwood Services
Didsbury
Hoylake
Moreton
LIVERPOOL
Rainhill
Risley
Sale
STOCKPORT
BIRKENHEAD
Lymm
Cheadle
Hazel Grove
West Kirby
WARRINGTON
Altrincham
Bramhall
Bebington
WIDNES
Bucklow Hill
Manchester Airport
Poynton
Thurstaston
RUNCORN
Disley
Furness Vale
Heswall
Bromborough
Mobberley
Wilmslow
Whaley Bridge
Thornton Hough
Alderley Edge
Mostyn
ELLESMERE PORT
Frodsham
Knutsford
Knutsford Services
Fernilee
Greenfield
Neston
Childer Thornton
Chester Services
Prestbury
Bollington
Holywell
Bagillt
Burton
Helsby
Northwich
Lower Peover
Chelford
Macclesfield
Flint
Puddington
Weaverham
Caerwys
Connah's Quay
Cuddington
Davenham
Goostrey
Bodfari
Halkyn
Great Saughall
Northop
Northop Hall
Queensferry
Tarvin
Winsford
Holmes Chapel
FLINTSHIRE
Ewloe
Hawarden
CHESTER
Cotebrook
Middlewich
Mold
Buckley
Brereton Green
Gwernymynydd
Tarporley
CHESHIRE
Heaton
Congleton
Llanbedr-Dyffryn-Clwyd
Aldford
Arclid Green
Sandbach
Ruthin
Hope
Pulford
Beeston
Biddulph
Rossett
Handley
Burwardsley
CREWE
Alsager
Leek
Llanfair Dyffryn Clwyd
Broxton
Kidsgrove
Gresford
Holt
Talke
Llandegla
Wrexham
Nantwich
Shavington
Cheddleton
Coedpoeth
Audley
Marchwiel
Malpas
Walgherton
NEWCASTLE-UNDER-LYME
Hanley
STOKE-ON-TRENT
Ipstones
Rhosllanerchrugog
Bangor-is-y-coed
Kingsley
Ruabon
Burleydam
Audlem
Cheadle
Corwen
Llangollen
Overton
Redbrook
Whitchurch
Keele
Woore
Upper Tean
Hanmer
Blackbrook
Tittensor
Glyn Ceiriog
Chirk
Tilstock
Llwynmawr
Ellesmere
WREXHAM
STAFFORDSHIRE
Gobowen
Welshampton
Prees
Market Drayton
Stone
Uttoxeter
Llanarmon Dyffryn Ceiriog
Ternhill
Prees Green
Whittington
Oswestry
Hodnet
Stafford Services
Sandon
Llanrhaeadr-ym-Mochnant
Rednal
Wem
Weston-under-Redcastle
Eccleshall
Llangedwyn
Llynclys
West Felton
Weston
Burlton
Saighton
Ruyton-XI-Towns
STAFFORD
Great Haywood
Llansantffraid-ym-Mechain
Llanymynech
Knockin
Gnosall
Shawbury
Llanfyllin
Nesscliffe
Newport
Four Crosses
Llandrinio
High Ercall
Crudgington
Acton Trussell
Albrighton
Rugeley
Meifod
Montford Bridge
Weston Heath
Penkridge
Wollaston
Hednesford
Wellington
SHREWSBURY
Gailey
CANNOCK
Telford Services
Heath Hayes & Wimblebury
Atcham
Brewood
Welshpool
Bayston Hill
Wroxeter
TELFORD
Westbury
Hilton Park Services
Buttington
Shifnal
Minsterley
Pontesbury
Brownhills
Worthen
Albrighton
Dorrington
Cressage
Ironbridge
Coalport
Codsall
Broseley
SHROPSHIRE
Norton
Berriew
WOLVERHAMPTON
Longnor
Chirbury
Pattingham
WALSALL
Much Wenlock
Leebotwood
Worfield
Montgomery
Longville in the Dale
Bourton
Abermule
Churchstoke
Morville
Church Stretton
Wombourne
WEST BROMWICH
Newtown
Bridgnorth
Little Stretton
Hope Bowdler
Himley
DUDLEY
Lydham
Kerry
Oldbury
Bishop's Castle
Quatt
Kingswinford
Munslow
BIRMINGHAM
Cleobury North
Lydbury North
Alveley
Stourton
HALESOWEN
Aston on Clun
Craven Arms
Highley
STOURBRIDGE
Hagley
Frankley Services

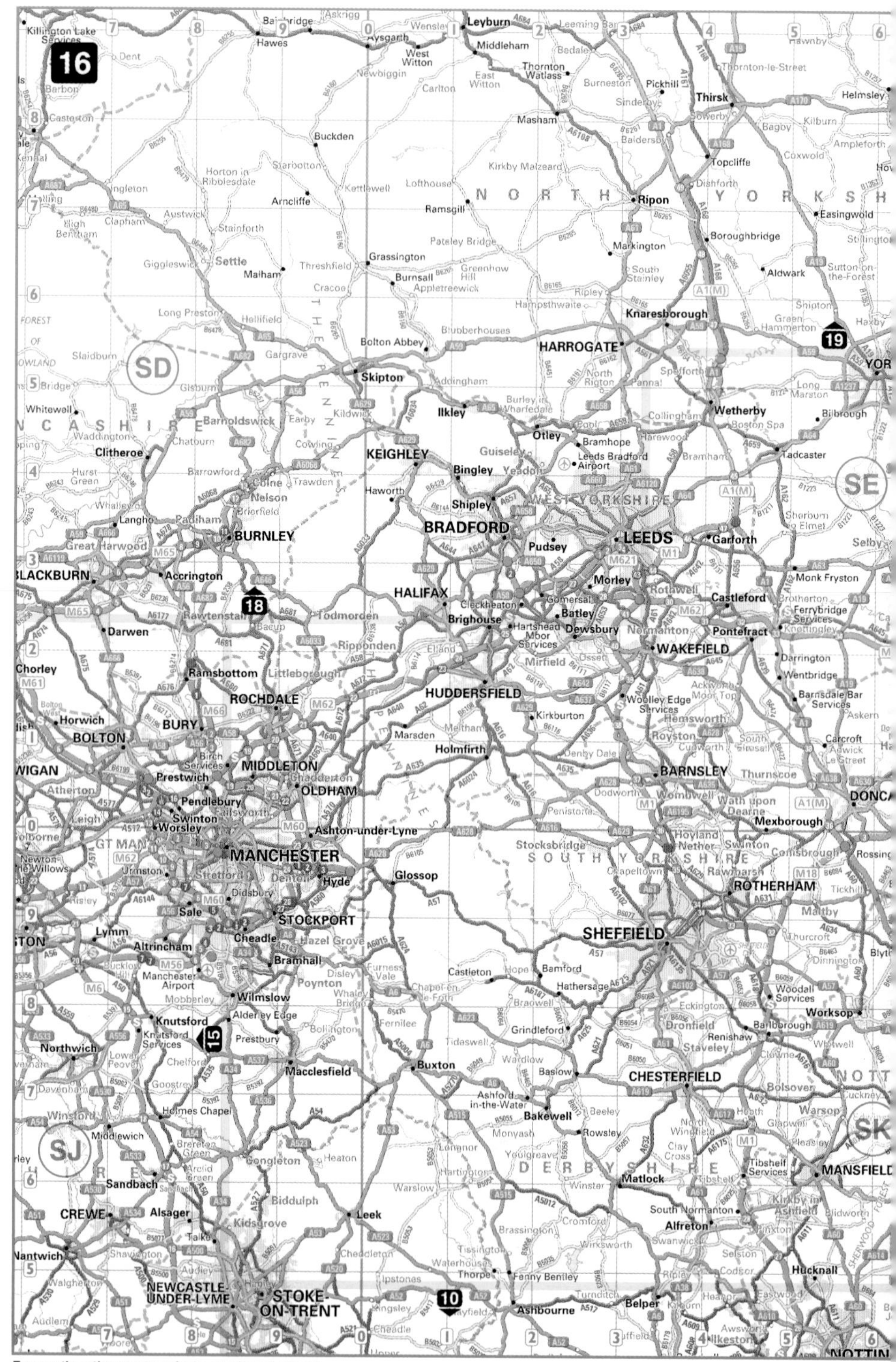

For continuation pages refer to numbered arrows

17
Hotel
Town/Village name
0
10 miles
0
10
20 kilometres
TA
TF
Scarborough
Filey
Bridlington
Driffield
Beverley
KINGSTON UPON HULL
Goole
SCUNTHORPE
GRIMSBY
Cleethorpes
Brigg
Louth
Mablethorpe
LINCOLN
Horncastle
Skegness
Boston
Sleaford
Hunstanton
EAST RIDING OF YORKSHIRE
LINCOLNSHIRE
THE WASH

For continuation pages refer to numbered arrows

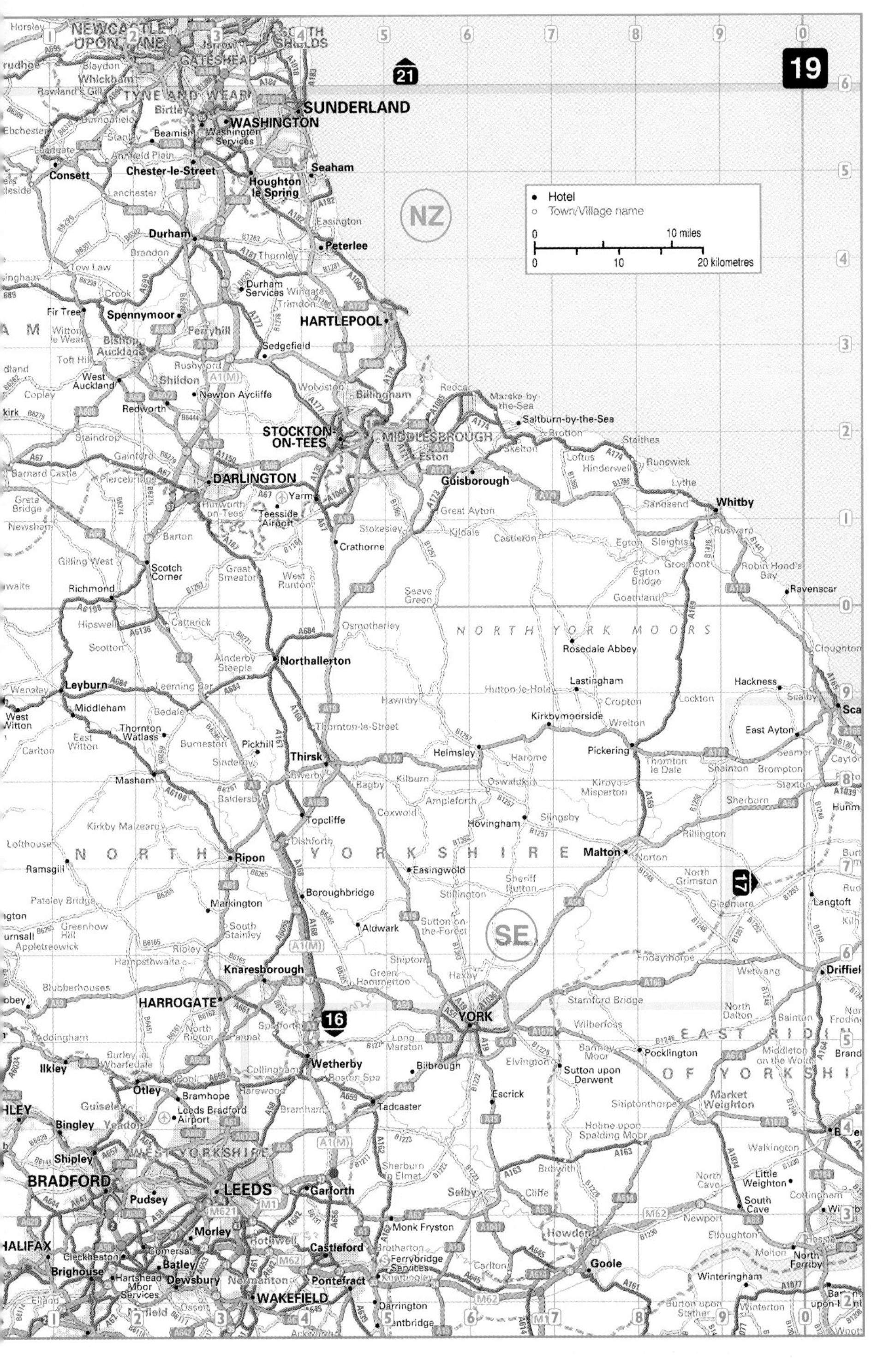
19
21
16
17
NZ
SE
Hotel
Town/Village name
0
10 miles
0
10
20 kilometres
NEWCASTLE UPON TYNE
GATESHEAD
Jarrow
SOUTH SHIELDS
TYNE AND WEAR
SUNDERLAND
WASHINGTON
Washington Services
Whickham
Blaydon
Birtley
Beamish
Stanley
Annfield Plain
Consett
Chester-le-Street
Houghton le Spring
Seaham
Lanchester
Easington
Durham
Peterlee
Brandon
Thornley
Tow Law
Crook
Durham Services
Wingate
Trimdon
Fir Tree
Spennymoor
HARTLEPOOL
Ferryhill
Bishop Auckland
Sedgefield
Toft Hill
West Auckland
Shildon
Rushyford
Wolviston
Billingham
Redcar
Marske-by-the-Sea
Saltburn-by-the-Sea
Newton Aycliffe
Copley
Redworth
STOCKTON-ON-TEES
MIDDLESBROUGH
Brotton
Skelton
Staithes
Loftus
Hinderwell
Runswick
Eston
Staindrop
Gainford
Barnard Castle
Piercebridge
DARLINGTON
Guisborough
Lythe
Sandsend
Whitby
Greta Bridge
Hurworth-on-Tees
Yarm
Teesside Airport
Great Ayton
Newsham
Barton
Stokesley
Kildale
Castleton
Egton
Sleights
Ruswarp
Crathorne
Gilling West
Scotch Corner
Great Smeaton
West Rounton
Egton Bridge
Grosmont
Robin Hood's Bay
Richmond
Seave Green
Goathland
Ravenscar
Hipswell
Catterick
Osmotherley
NORTH YORK MOORS
Scotton
Rosedale Abbey
Cloughton
Ainderby Steeple
Northallerton
Wensley
Leyburn
Leeming Bar
Hutton-le-Hole
Lastingham
Hackness
Scalby
Middleham
Bedale
Hawnby
Cropton
Lockton
West Witton
Thornton Watlass
Thornton-le-Street
Kirkbymoorside
Wrelton
East Ayton
East Witton
Carlton
Burneston
Pickhill
Thirsk
Helmsley
Harome
Pickering
Thornton le Dale
Snainton
Brompton
Seamer
Sinderby
Sowerby
Kilburn
Oswaldkirk
Kirby Misperton
Staxton
Masham
Baldersby
Bagby
Ampleforth
Sherburn
Coxwold
Slingsby
Kirkby Malzeard
Topcliffe
Hovingham
Rillington
Lofthouse
Dishforth
NORTH YORKSHIRE
Ripon
Malton
Norton
Ramsgill
Easingwold
North Grimston
Sheriff Hutton
Stillington
Pateley Bridge
Markington
Boroughbridge
Sledmere
Langtoft
Greenhow Hill
South Stainley
Aldwark
Sutton-on-the-Forest
Appletreewick
Ripley
Shipton
Fridaythorpe
Hampsthwaite
Haxby
Driffield
Knaresborough
Green Hammerton
Wetwang
Blubberhouses
HARROGATE
Stamford Bridge
North Rigton
Spofforth
YORK
North Dalton
Bainton
Addingham
Pannal
Wilberfoss
EAST RIDING OF YORKSHIRE
Long Marston
Barmby Moor
Pocklington
Burley in Wharfedale
Ilkley
Collingham
Wetherby
Boston Spa
Bilbrough
Elvington
Sutton upon Derwent
Middleton on the Wolds
Otley
Bramhope
Harewood
Escrick
Guiseley
Leeds Bradford Airport
Bramham
Tadcaster
Shiptonthorpe
Market Weighton
Bingley
Yeadon
Holme upon Spalding Moor
WEST YORKSHIRE
Walkington
Shipley
Sherburn in Elmet
Bubwith
Little Weighton
BRADFORD
LEEDS
Garforth
Selby
Cliffe
North Cave
Cottingham
Pudsey
South Cave
Monk Fryston
Newport
Morley
Rothwell
Howden
Ellough ton
HALIFAX
Cleckheaton
Gomersal
Castleford
Brotherton
Ferrybridge Services
Knottingley
Carlton
Goole
Melton
North Ferriby
Brighouse
Batley
Hartshead Moor Services
Dewsbury
Normanton
Pontefract
Winteringham
WAKEFIELD
Darrington
Burton upon Stather
Winterton
Ackworth
A1(M)
M1
M62
M621
M18

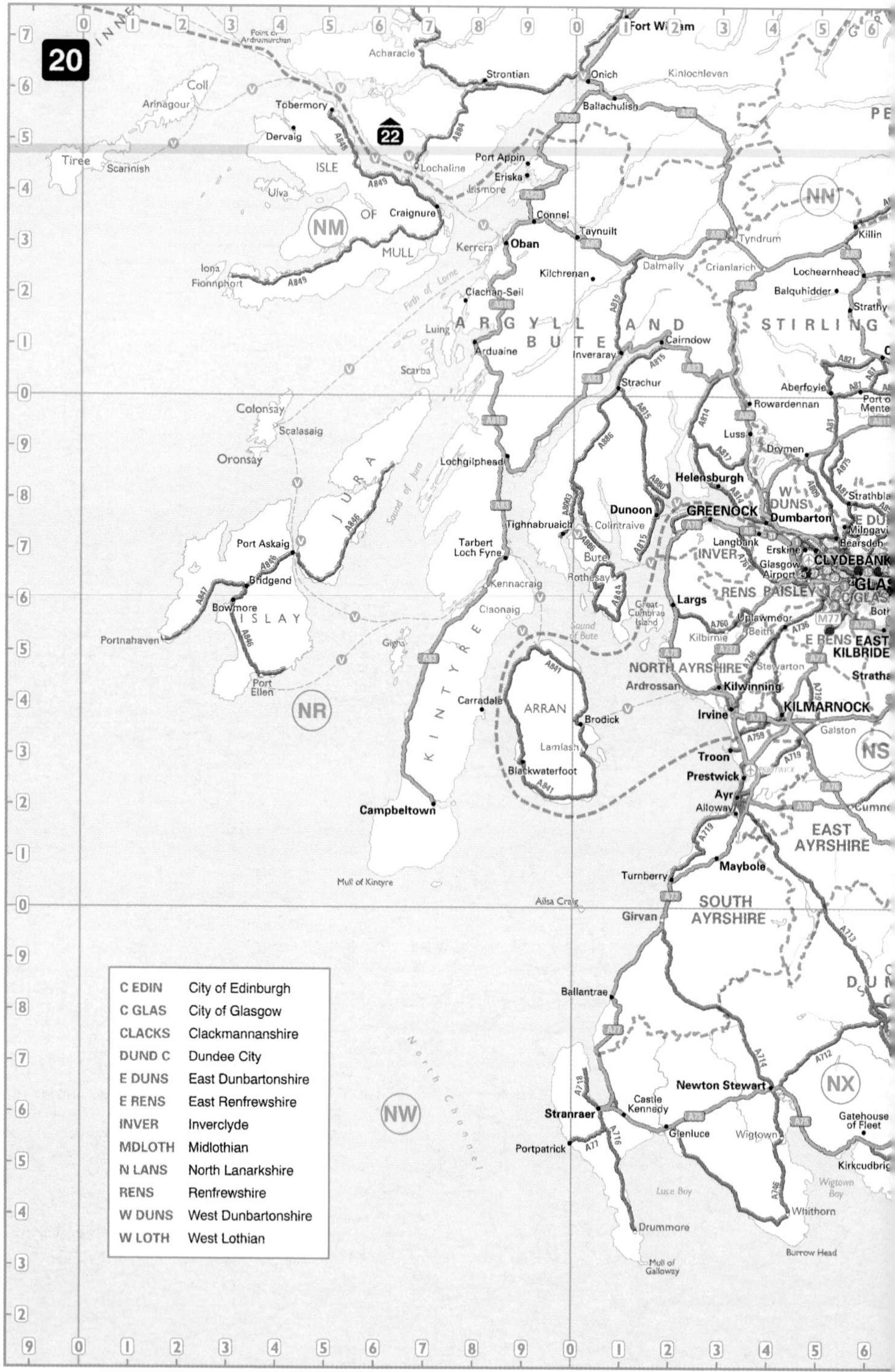

For continuation pages refer to numbered arrows

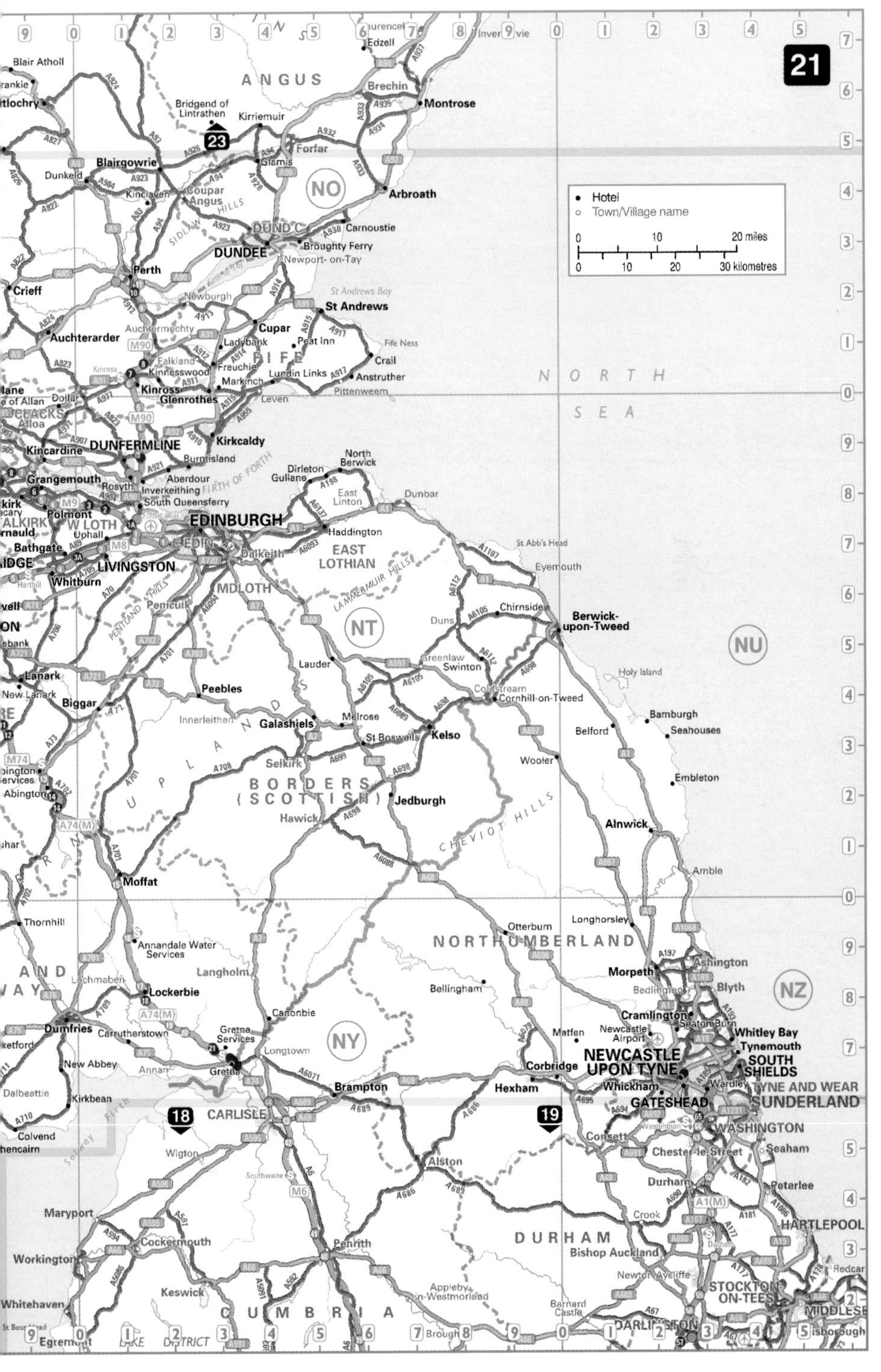

21
Hotel
Town/Village name
0
10
20 miles
0
10
20
30 kilometres
ANGUS
Blair Atholl
Bridgend of Lintrathen
23
Kirriemuir
Edzell
Brechin
Montrose
Forfar
Blairgowrie
Dunkeld
Glamis
Kinclaven
Coupar Angus
NO
Arbroath
SIDLAW HILLS
Carnoustie
DUNDEE
Broughty Ferry
Newport-on-Tay
Perth
Crieff
Newburgh
St Andrews Bay
St Andrews
Auchterarder
Auchtermuchty
Cupar
Peat Inn
Fife Ness
Ladybank
FIFE
Crail
Falkland
Kinnesswood
Freuchie
Lundin Links
Anstruther
Markinch
Pittenweem
Kinross
Glenrothes
Leven
Dollar
NORTH
SEA
Alloa
Kirkcaldy
Kincardine
DUNFERMLINE
Burntisland
North Berwick
Dirleton
Gullane
Aberdour
FIRTH OF FORTH
Grangemouth
Rosyth
Inverkeithing
East Linton
Dunbar
South Queensferry
Polmont
EDINBURGH
Haddington
Uphall
Bathgate
Dalkeith
EAST LOTHIAN
St Abb's Head
Eyemouth
LIVINGSTON
Whitburn
MIDLOTHIAN
LAMMERMUIR HILLS
Penicuik
PENTLAND HILLS
Chirnside
Berwick-upon-Tweed
NT
Duns
NU
Lauder
Greenlaw
Swinton
Holy Island
Lanark
Coldstream
New Lanark
Peebles
Cornhill-on-Tweed
Biggar
Bamburgh
Innerleithen
Galashiels
Melrose
Belford
Seahouses
St Boswells
Kelso
Selkirk
Wooler
Abington
BORDERS (SCOTTISH)
Embleton
Jedburgh
UPLANDS
Hawick
Alnwick
CHEVIOT HILLS
Amble
Moffat
Thornhill
Otterburn
Longhorsley
NORTHUMBERLAND
Annandale Water Services
Langholm
Ashington
Morpeth
Lochmaben
Bellingham
Bedlington
Blyth
NZ
Lockerbie
Canonbie
Cramlington
Seaton Burn
Dumfries
Carrutherstown
Gretna Services
Newcastle Airport
Matfen
Whitley Bay
NY
Tynemouth
Longtown
New Abbey
Annan
Gretna
NEWCASTLE UPON TYNE
Corbridge
SOUTH SHIELDS
Whickham
Brampton
Hexham
Wardley
TYNE AND WEAR
Dalbeattie
Kirkbean
GATESHEAD
SUNDERLAND
18
CARLISLE
19
Colvend
Consett
WASHINGTON
Wigton
Chester-le-Street
Seaham
Alston
Durham
Peterlee
Maryport
Crook
HARTLEPOOL
Cockermouth
Penrith
DURHAM
Workington
Bishop Auckland
Redcar
Newton Aycliffe
Keswick
Appleby-in-Westmorland
STOCKTON-ON-TEES
Whitehaven
CUMBRIA
Barnard Castle
DARLINGTON
Egremont
LAKE DISTRICT
Brough

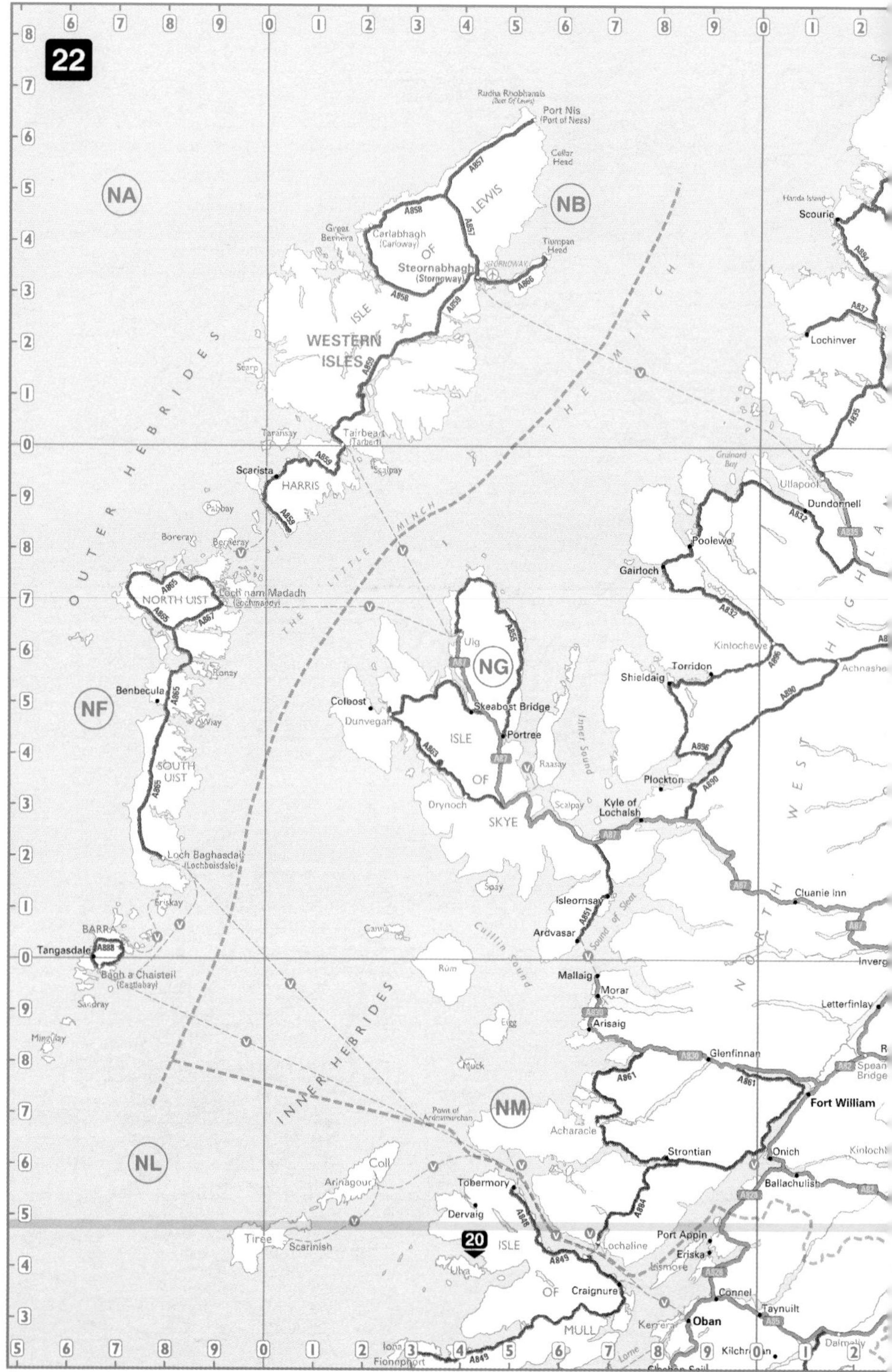

For continuation pages refer to numbered arrows

23
Hotel
Town/Village name
0
10
20 miles
0
10
20
30 kilometres
PENTLAND FIRTH
Dunnet Head
Duncansby Head
John o'Groats
Scrabster
Thurso
Strathy Point
Melvich
Bettyhill
Tongue
Halkirk
Wick
ND
NC
Lybster
Dunbeath
Helmsdale
Lairg
Golspie
Brora
Bonar Bridge
Dornoch
Tain
HIGHLAND
NH
Alness
Invergordon
Cromarty
MORAY FIRTH
Fortrose
Nairn
Forres
Lossiemouth
Elgin
Buckie
Cullen
Portsoy
Banff
Fraserburgh
NJ
MORAY
Rothes
Keith
Aberchirder
Turriff
Peterhead
Archiestown
Craigellachie
Aberlour
Dufftown
Huntly
Cruden Bay
Kirkhill
Inverness
Ellon
Oldmeldrum
Newburgh
Grantown-on-Spey
Carrbridge
Nethy Bridge
Tomintoul
Boat of Garten
Inverurie
Kintore
Aberdeen Airport
Dyce
NK
Whitebridge
Aviemore
Monadhliath Mountains
Strathdon
Alford
ABERDEEN CITY
ABERDEEN
ABERDEENSHIRE
Kingussie
Newtonmore
CAIRNGORM MOUNTAINS
Ballater
Aboyne
Banchory
Braemar
Stonehaven
GRAMPIAN MOUNTAINS
Laurencekirk
Inverbervie
Spittal of Glenshee
Edzell
NO
Blair Atholl
Killiecrankie
Pitlochry
ANGUS
Brechin
Montrose
NN
PERTH AND KINROSS
Bridgend of Lintrathen
Kirriemuir
Aberfeldy
Forfar
Blairgowrie
Glamis
21
Kenmore
Dunkeld
Kinclaven
Coupar Angus
Arbroath
SIDLAW HILLS
Killin
Carnoustie
DUNDEE
Broughty Ferry
Newport-on-Tay
St Fillans
Perth
Crieff
Comrie

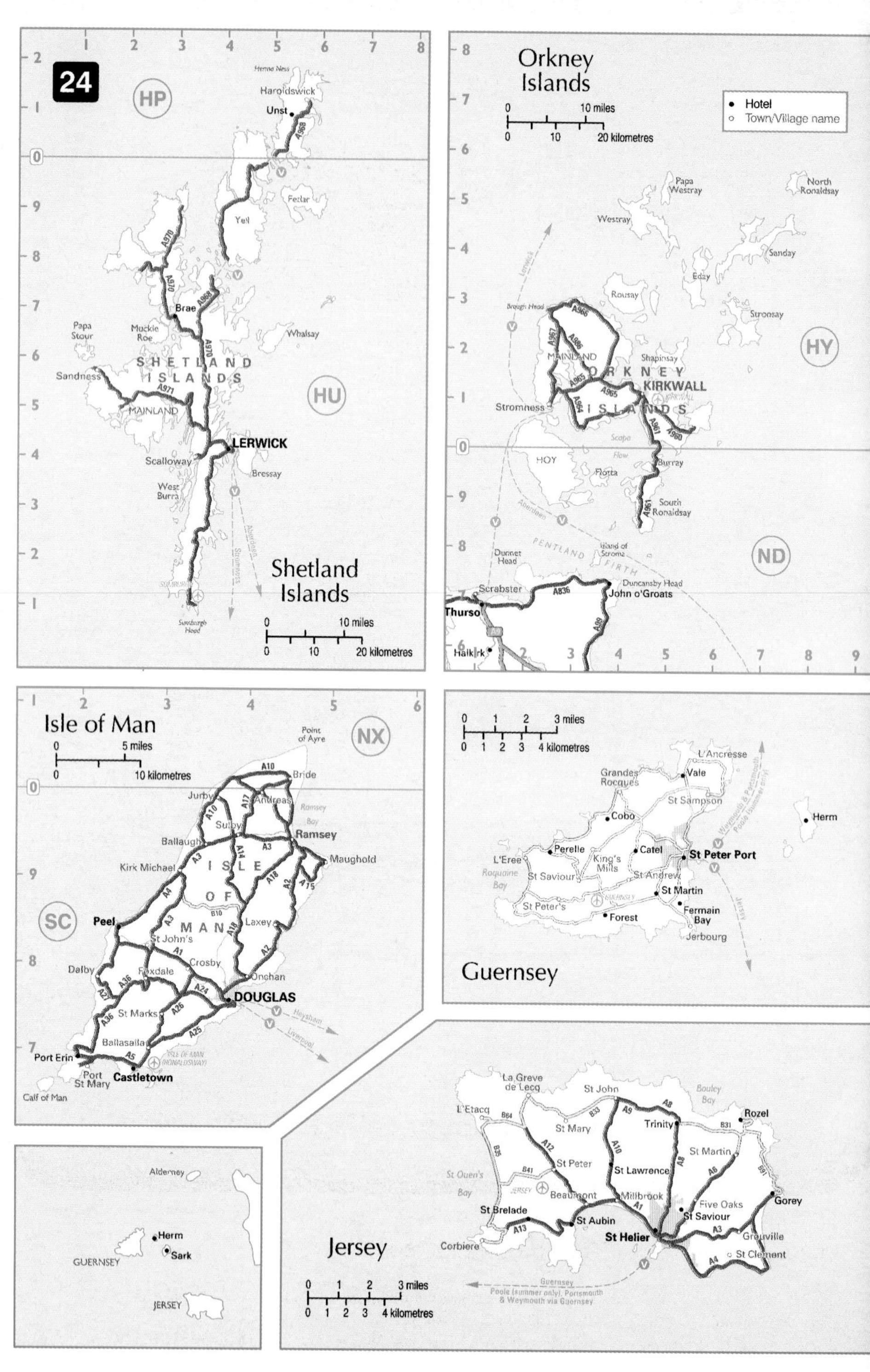
Shetland Islands
0 10 miles
0 10 20 kilometres
HP
HU
Herma Ness
Haroldswick
Unst
Fetlar
Yell
Brae
Papa Stour
Muckle Roe
Whalsay
SHETLAND ISLANDS
Sandness
MAINLAND
LERWICK
Scalloway
Bressay
West Burra
Aberdeen
Stromness
Sumburgh Head
Orkney Islands
0 10 miles
0 10 20 kilometres
Hotel
Town/Village name
Papa Westray
North Ronaldsay
Westray
Sanday
Eday
Rousay
Stronsay
Brough Head
Shapinsay
HY
MAINLAND
ORKNEY ISLANDS
KIRKWALL
Stromness
Scapa Flow
HOY
Burray
Flotta
South Ronaldsay
Aberdeen
PENTLAND FIRTH
Island of Stroma
Dunnet Head
ND
Scrabster
Duncansby Head
John o'Groats
Thurso
Halkirk
Isle of Man
0 5 miles
0 10 kilometres
Point of Ayre
NX
Bride
Jurby
Andreas
Ramsey Bay
Sulby
Ballaugh
Ramsey
Maughold
Kirk Michael
ISLE OF MAN
SC
Peel
Laxey
St John's
Crosby
Dalby
Foxdale
Onchan
DOUGLAS
St Marks
Heysham
Liverpool
Ballasalla
Port Erin
Port St Mary
Castletown
Calf of Man
0 1 2 3 miles
0 1 2 3 4 kilometres
L'Ancresse
Grandes Rocques
Vale
St Sampson
Cobo
Herm
Weymouth & Portsmouth
Poole (summer only)
L'Eree
Perelle
King's Mills
Catel
St Peter Port
Rocquaine Bay
St Saviour
St Andrew
St Martin
St Peter's
Fermain Bay
Forest
Jerbourg
Jersey
Guernsey
Alderney
Herm
Sark
GUERNSEY
JERSEY
La Greve de Lecq
St John
Bouley Bay
L'Etacq
Rozel
St Mary
Trinity
St Martin
St Peter
St Ouen's Bay
St Lawrence
Beaumont
Millbrook
Five Oaks
Gorey
St Brelade
St Aubin
St Saviour
Corbiere
St Helier
Grouville
St Clement
Jersey
0 1 2 3 miles
0 1 2 3 4 kilometres
Guernsey
Poole (summer only), Portsmouth & Weymouth via Guernsey

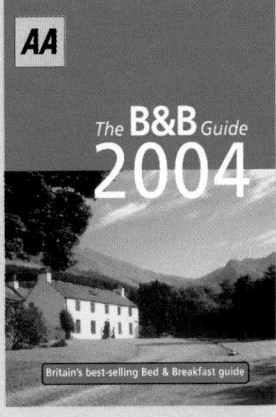

Acknowledgements - The Hotel Guide 2004

Permission for the use of photographs in the preliminary pages of this guide was kindly given by the following:
Hotel du Vin Limited 4, 5, 6, 9, 11, 19, 21, 22, 24, 26, 45, 46; Von Essen Hotels 9, 31, 43, 45, 46;
Fawsley Hall Hotel 15, 41, 43; Millienium Madjeski 15; Kings Head Masham 1, 2; Nova Developments 3, 4, 9, 13, 16, 17, 23, 26, 27;
The remaining picture is from the Association's own Library (AA PHOTO LIBRARY) and were taken by: Steve Day 29.

Readers' Report form

Please send this form to:
Editor, The Hotel Guide,
Lifestyle Guides,
The Automobile Association,
Fanum House,
Basingstoke RG21 4EA

or fax: 01256 491647
or e-mail: lifestyleguides@theAA.com

Please use this form to recommend any hotel you have visited, whether it is in the guide or not currently listed. Feedback from readers helps us to keep our guide accurate and up to date. Please note, however, that if you have a complaint to make during a visit, we strongly recommend that you discuss the matter with the establishment management there and then so that they have a chance to put things right before your visit is spoilt. The AA does not undertake to arbitrate between you and the hotel management, or to obtain compensation or engage in correspondence.

Date:

Your name (block capitals)

Your address (block capitals)

....

....

....

.... e-mail address:

Comments (please include the name & address of the establishment)

....

....

....

....

....

....

....

....

(please attach a separate sheet if necessary)

Please tick here if you DO NOT wish to receive details of AA offers or products ☐

PTO

Readers' Report Form

	YES	NO
Have you bought this guide before?	☐	☐

Have you bought any other accommodation, restaurant, pub, or food guides recently? If yes, which ones?

....

....

Why did you buy this guide? (circle all that apply)

holiday　　short break　　business travel　　special occasion

overnight stop　　find a venue for another event e.g. conference

other..

How often do you stay in hotels? (circle one choice)

more than once a month　　once a month　　once in 2-3 months

once in six months　　once a year　　less than once a year

Please answer these questions to help us make improvements to the guide:

Which of these factors are most important when choosing a hotel?

Price　　Location　　Awards/ratings　　Service

Decor/surroundings　　Previous experience　　Recommendation

Other (please state):..

Do you read the editorial features in the guide? ....

Do you use the location atlas?..

Which elements of the guide do you find the most useful when choosing somewhere to stay?

Description　　Photo　　Advertisement　　Star rating

Can you suggest any improvements to the guide?

....

....

....

....